Milestones in Abnormal Psychology

Stone Age — Mental disorders treated by trephination. p. 7

430–377 B.C. — Hippocrates cites brain as source of mental disorders. p. 8

500–1450 — Middle Ages adopts demonological explanations and treatments. p. 8

1547 — Bethlehem Hospital in London converted into asylum. p. 10

1693 — Witch-hunting trials peak in Salem, Massachusetts. p. 9

1773 — First American hospital exclusively for mental patients opens in Williamsburg, Virginia. p. 10

1793 — Philippe Pinel frees asylum patients at La Bicêtre in Paris. pp. 10, 449

1812 — Benjamin Rush writes first American textbook on psychiatry. p. 10

1842 — Dorothea Dix begins campaign to reform mental hospitals in the United States. p. 10

1865 — Gregor Mendel publishes theories of genetics. p. 49

1879 — Wilhelm Wundt establishes first laboratory for experimental study of psychology. p. 24

1883 — Emil Kraepelin publishes textbook on psychiatry, likening mental disorders to physical diseases. pp. 11, 100

1892 — American Psychological Association founded. p. 18

1893 — Sigmund Freud, with Josef Breuer, publishes first chapters of *On the Psychical Mechanisms of Hysterical Phenomena*, launching psychoanalysis. pp. 13, 292

1896 — Lightner Witmer establishes first psychological clinic in the U.S. at University of Pennsylvania. p. 12

1897 — General paresis linked to physical cause, syphilis. p. 11

1900 — Freud publishes *The Interpretation of Dreams*. p. 57

1900 — Morton Prince uses hypnosis to treat multiple personality disorder. p. 183

1901 — Ivan Pavlov demonstrates classical conditioning. pp. 60, 127

1905 — First intelligence test published. p. 97

1907 — Alzheimer's disease identified by Dr. Alois Alzheimer. p. 564

1908 — Clifford Beers writes autobiography, *A Mind That Found Itself*, launching Mental Hygiene Movement in the United States. pp. 448, 453

1909 — Freud makes his only visit to America and lectures at Clark University. pp. 13, 53

1913 — Behaviorist John Watson argues that psychology should abandon study of consciousness. p. 59

1917 — The U.S. Congress declares all nonmedical opioids illegal. p. 350

1921 — Rorschach test published. p. 90

1923 — Freud publishes *The Ego and the Id*. pp. 53–54

1929 — EEG developed. p. 96

1935 — Alcoholics Anonymous founded. p. 376

1935 — First use of lobotomy for mental disorders. p. 450

1937 — Marijuana made illegal in the United States. pp. 362, 363

1938 — Electroconvulsive therapy introduced in Rome. p. 236

1938 — B. F. Skinner proposes operant conditioning. p. 60

1939 — The Wechsler-Bellevue Intelligence Scale published. p. 97

1943 — LSD's hallucinogenic effects discovered. p. 358

1943 — Minnesota Multiphasic Personality Inventory (MMPI) published. p. 92

1943 — Jean-Paul Sartre's existential book *Being and Nothingness* published. p. 70

1949 — Lithium salts first used for bipolar disorder. p. 242

1951 — Chlorpromazine, first antipsychotic drug, tested. p. 455

1951 — Carl Rogers publishes *Client-Centered Therapy*. pp. 67, 118

1952 — First edition of DSM published by the American Psychiatric Association. pp. 100, 105

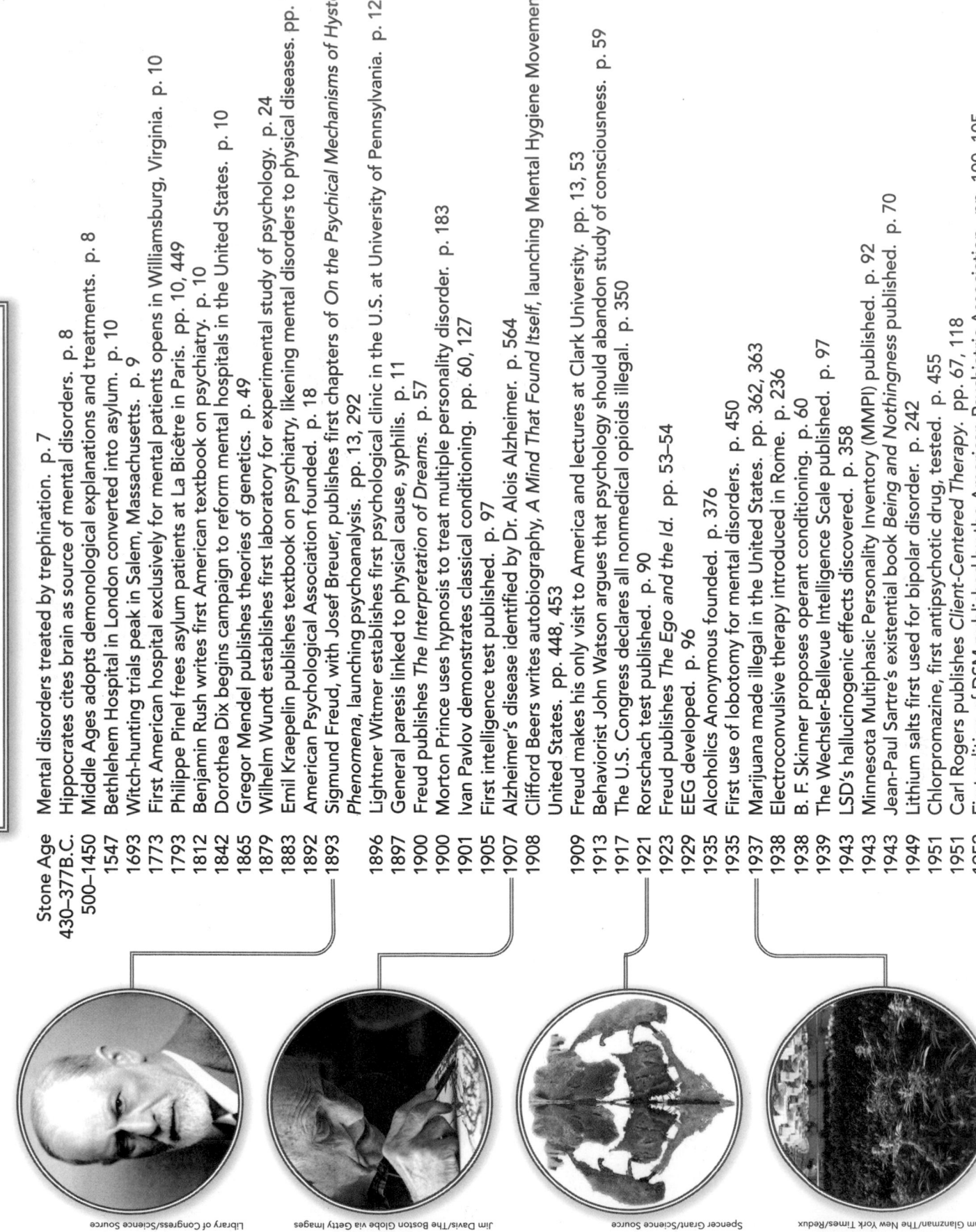

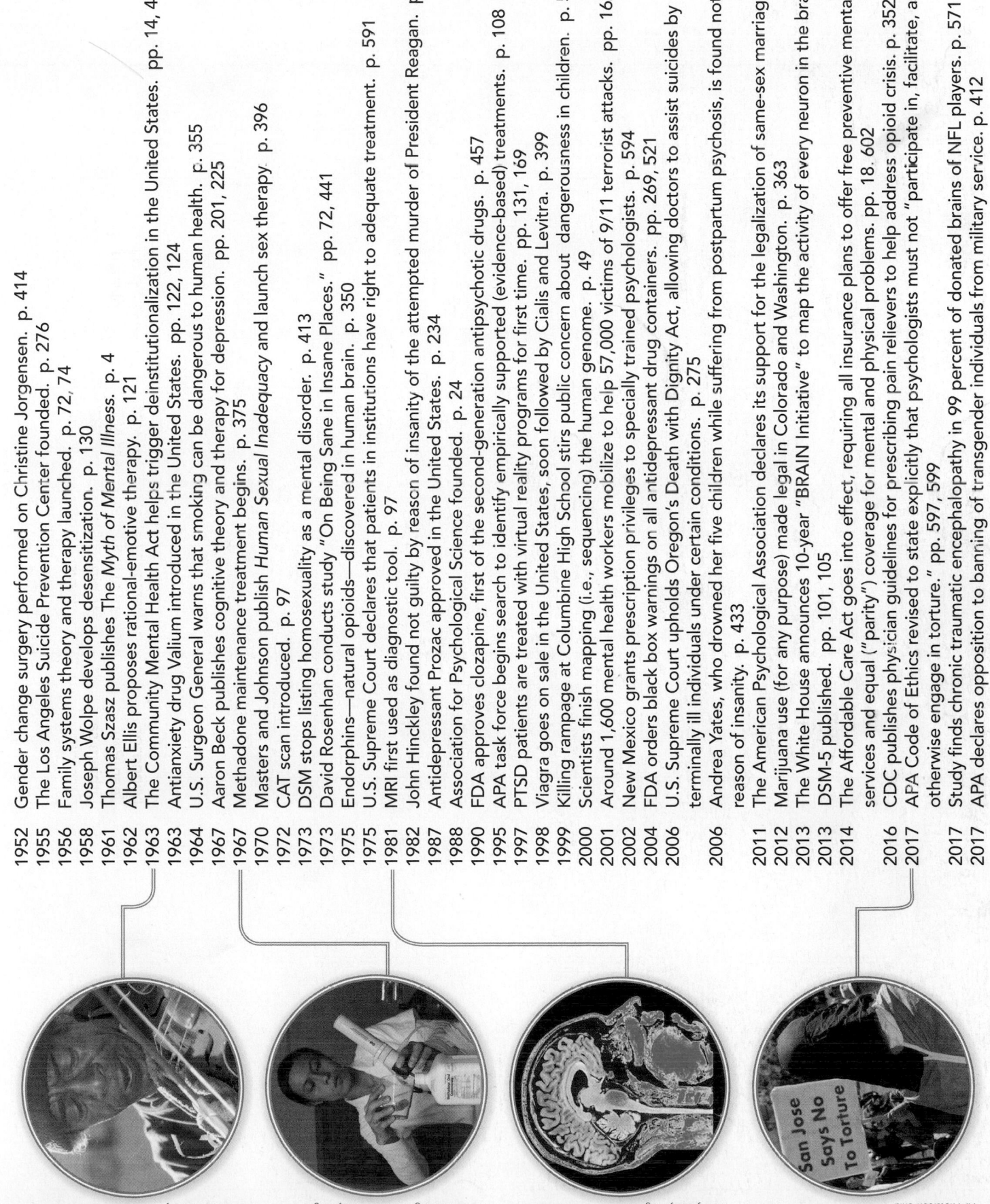

1952	Gender change surgery performed on Christine Jorgensen. p. 414
1955	The Los Angeles Suicide Prevention Center founded. p. 276
1956	Family systems theory and therapy launched. p. 72, 74
1958	Joseph Wolpe develops desensitization. p. 130
1961	Thomas Szasz publishes The Myth of Mental Illness. p. 4
1962	Albert Ellis proposes rational-emotive therapy. p. 121
1963	The Community Mental Health Act helps trigger deinstitutionalization in the United States. pp. 14, 464
1963	Antianxiety drug Valium introduced in the United States. pp. 122, 124
1964	U.S. Surgeon General warns that smoking can be dangerous to human health. p. 355
1967	Aaron Beck publishes cognitive theory and therapy for depression. pp. 201, 225
1967	Methadone maintenance treatment begins. p. 375
1970	Masters and Johnson publish Human Sexual Inadequacy and launch sex therapy. p. 396
1972	CAT scan introduced. p. 97
1973	DSM stops listing homosexuality as a mental disorder. p. 413
1973	David Rosenhan conducts study "On Being Sane in Insane Places." pp. 72, 441
1975	Endorphins—natural opioids—discovered in human brain. p. 350
1975	U.S. Supreme Court declares that patients in institutions have right to adequate treatment. p. 591
1981	MRI first used as diagnostic tool. p. 97
1982	John Hinckley found not guilty by reason of insanity of the attempted murder of President Reagan. p. 581
1987	Antidepressant Prozac approved in the United States. p. 234
1988	Association for Psychological Science founded. p. 24
1990	FDA approves clozapine, first of the second-generation antipsychotic drugs. p. 457
1995	APA task force begins search to identify empirically supported (evidence-based) treatments. p. 108
1997	PTSD patients are treated with virtual reality programs for first time. pp. 131, 169
1998	Viagra goes on sale in the United States, soon followed by Cialis and Levitra. p. 399
1999	Killing rampage at Columbine High School stirs public concern about dangerousness in children. p. 589
2000	Scientists finish mapping (i.e., sequencing) the human genome. p. 49
2001	Around 1,600 mental health workers mobilize to help 57,000 victims of 9/11 terrorist attacks. pp. 162, 171
2002	New Mexico grants prescription privileges to specially trained psychologists. p. 594
2004	FDA orders black box warnings on all antidepressant drug containers. pp. 269, 521
2006	U.S. Supreme Court upholds Oregon's Death with Dignity Act, allowing doctors to assist suicides by terminally ill individuals under certain conditions. p. 275
2006	Andrea Yates, who drowned her five children while suffering from postpartum psychosis, is found not guilty by reason of insanity. p. 433
2011	The American Psychological Association declares its support for the legalization of same-sex marriages. p. 404
2012	Marijuana use (for any purpose) made legal in Colorado and Washington. p. 363
2013	The White House announces 10-year "BRAIN Initiative" to map the activity of every neuron in the brain. p. 47
2013	DSM-5 published. pp. 101, 105
2014	The Affordable Care Act goes into effect, requiring all insurance plans to offer free preventive mental health services and equal ("parity") coverage for mental and physical problems. pp. 18, 602
2016	CDC publishes physician guidelines for prescribing pain relievers to help address opioid crisis. p. 352
2017	APA Code of Ethics revised to state explicitly that psychologists must not "participate in, facilitate, assist, or otherwise engage in torture." pp. 597, 599
2017	Study finds chronic traumatic encephalopathy in 99 percent of donated brains of NFL players. p. 571
2017	APA declares opposition to banning of transgender individuals from military service. p. 412

Abnormal Psychology

RONALD J. COMER | JONATHAN S. COMER

tenth edition

Princeton University

Florida International University

worth publishers
Macmillan Learning
New York

Vice President, Social Sciences: Charles Linsmeier
Director of Content and Assessment, Social Sciences: Shani Fisher
Executive Program Manager: Matt Wright
Senior Development Editor: Mimi Melek
Editorial Assistant: Un Hye Kim
Senior Marketing Manager: Lindsay Johnson
Marketing Assistant: Chelsea Simens
Director of Media Editorial, Social Sciences: Noel Hohnstine
Media Editor: Stefani Wallace
Media Project Manager: Elizabeth Dowden
Director, Content Management Enhancement: Tracey Kuehn
Managing Editor: Lisa Kinne
Senior Content Project Manager: Kerry O'Shaughnessy
Senior Workflow Project Supervisor: Susan Wein
Photo Editor: Jennifer Atkins
Permissions Manager: Jennifer MacMillan
Permissions Associate: Michael McCarty
Director of Design, Content Management: Diana Blume
Senior Design Manager: Blake Logan
Cover Design: Blake Logan
Text Design and Infographics: Charles Yuen
Layout Designer: Paul Lacy
Art Manager: Matthew McAdams
Composition: Lumina Datamatics, Inc.
Printing and Binding: LSC Communications
Cover: Lucille Clerc/Illustration (USA) Inc.

Library of Congress Control Number: 2017957229

ISBN-13: 978-1-319-06694-9
ISBN-10: 1-319-06694-1

Printed in the United States of America

First Printing

Worth Publishers
One New York Plaza
Suite 4500
New York, NY 10004-1562
www.macmillanlearning.com

With boundless love and appreciation,
to Marlene Comer and Jami Furr,
who fill our lives with love and joy.

♀...About the Authors

RONALD J. COMER has been a professor in Princeton University's Department of Psychology for the past 43 years, serving also as director of Clinical Psychology Studies and as chair of the university's Institutional Review Board. He has recently transitioned to emeritus status at the university. He has received the President's Award for Distinguished Teaching at Princeton, where his various courses in abnormal psychology have been among the university's most popular.

Professor Comer is also Clinical Associate Professor of Family Medicine and Community Health at Rutgers Robert Wood Johnson Medical School. He is a practicing clinical psychologist and a consultant to Eden Autism Services and to hospitals and family practice residency programs throughout New Jersey.

In addition to writing the textbooks *Abnormal Psychology* (tenth edition), *Fundamentals of Abnormal Psychology* (eighth edition), *Psychology Around Us* (second edition), and *Case Studies in Abnormal Psychology* (second edition), Professor Comer has published a range of journal articles and produced numerous widely used educational video programs, including *The Higher Education Video Library Series*, *The Video Anthology for Abnormal Psychology*, *Video Segments in Neuroscience*, *Introduction to Psychology Video Clipboard*, and *Developmental Psychology Video Clipboard*.

Professor Comer was an undergraduate at the University of Pennsylvania and a graduate student at Clark University. He currently lives in Lawrenceville, New Jersey, with his wife, Marlene. From there he can keep a close eye on the often-frustrating Philadelphia sports teams with whom he grew up.

JONATHAN S. COMER is a professor of psychology at Florida International University, where he also directs the Mental Health Interventions and Technology (MINT) Program. He is President-Elect of the Society of Clinical Psychology (Division 12 of the American Psychological Association) and a leader in the field of clinical child and adolescent psychology. The author of 130 scientific papers and chapters, he has received career awards from the American Psychological Association, the Association for Psychological Science, and the Association for Behavioral and Cognitive Therapies for his research on innovative treatment methods, childhood anxiety and disruptive behaviors, and the impact of traumatic stress, disasters, and terrorism on children. His current work also focuses on ties between psychopathology, neurocircuitry, and the intergenerational transmission of psychological problems.

In addition to *Abnormal Psychology* (tenth edition), Professor Comer has authored *Childhood Disorders* (second edition) and edited *The Oxford Handbook of Research Strategies for Clinical Psychology*, among other books. He serves as Associate Editor of the journal *Behavior Therapy* and is on the Board of Directors of the Society of Clinical Child and Adolescent Psychology. He is a Fellow of the American Psychological Association, the Society of Clinical Psychology, and the Society for Child and Family Policy and Practice. He is also a practicing clinical psychologist.

Professor Comer was an undergraduate at the University of Rochester and a graduate student at Temple University. He currently lives in South Florida, with his wife, Jami, and their children Delia and Emmett. He loves music—both playing and listening—and enjoys keeping an eye on the often-frustrating Philadelphia sports teams that his father taught him to love/hate.

♀...Brief Contents

Abnormal Psychology in Science and Clinical Practice

Problems of Anxiety and Mood

Problems of the Mind and Body

Problems of Psychosis and the Cognitive Function

Life-Span Problems

Conclusion

♀...Contents

CHAPTER **6**

Disorders of Trauma and Stress............... 153

CHAPTER **7**

Depressive and Bipolar Disorders............ 189

CHAPTER 13

Sexual Disorders and Gender Variations

CHAPTER 14

Schizophrenia and Related Disorders

CHAPTER 15

Treatments for Schizophrenia and Other Severe Mental Disorders

CHAPTER **19**

Law, Society, and the Mental Health Profession

♥...Preface

Ron Comer   I thought it was cute when my 13-year-old son Jon sometimes sat in on my 400-student Abnormal Psychology lectures at Princeton, interesting when he took his first psychology course at the University of Rochester, amusing when his undergraduate abnormal psychology course used my textbook, troubling when he autographed copies of the book for his classmates, surprising when he decided to major in psychology, and very satisfying when he entered the clinical psychology graduate program at Temple University. However, what Jon has accomplished professionally from that point forward has been nothing short of mind-boggling to me, and I am not easily mind-boggled.

He has become one of today's most productive and influential researchers, a leader in the clinical field, a magnificent teacher, and a deeply caring and wise clinician. Little of this has to do with me and everything to do with his intellectual gifts and remarkable work ethic and the giants in the field who have mentored him over the years—particularly, Dave Barlow, Phil Kendall, Dante Cicchetti, Bill Pelham, Anne Marie Albano, and Mark Olfson. Nevertheless, I'll take it.

At some point during Jon's flourishing career at Boston University and now Florida International University, an unstated question began to emerge: should he join me as co-author on my abnormal psychology textbooks *Abnormal Psychology* and *Fundamentals of Abnormal Psychology*? I had never entertained the possibility of having a co-author during my 35 years of writing these textbooks; and anyway, I believed Jon was too busy making his mark on the field and society, receiving multiple career awards from the American Psychological Association and other esteemed organizations, being elected President of the APA's Society of Clinical Psychology, writing over 130 scientific papers, and the like. But, as the saying goes, "If you want to make God laugh, tell Him your future plans." Lo and behold, beginning with this edition, Jon and I are co-authors of these books.

Ultimately, the decision for Jon to join me in this endeavor was a natural one. As textbook authors grow older, publishers seek out possible co-authors (for reasons that shall go unstated in order to protect my fragile ego and growing sense of mortality). It was clear to me that the ideal co-author would have to be a highly accomplished researcher and writer who would complement my particular areas of expertise and bring special knowledge in such areas as the developmental psychopathology perspective, technology-driven and novel treatment interventions, cognitive-behavioral approaches, brain circuitry, and more. And it became obvious that Jon was truly that person. Moreover, Jon was receiving a growing number of offers from various publishing companies to author their abnormal psychology textbooks, and the notion of having a Comer textbook competing with another Comer textbook was simply too much for me to bear (did I mention my fragile ego?). And, of course, personally, the thought of collaborating with someone whom I respect and love so much was too alluring to pass up. Thus, with this edition, Jon and I begin a new journey, from which, we hope and believe, readers will learn much and profit greatly.

Jon Comer   Roughly two decades ago, I entered the University of Rochester with the intention of studying music. But I soon realized that, despite my continuing love of music, the study of clinical psychology fascinated me most. Two pivotal undergraduate experiences brought the clinical field to life for me and prompted me to realize that work in this area should eventually be at the center of my professional life.

The first experience was taking a psychology course with (and later working in the laboratory of) Dante Cicchetti, the highly accomplished researcher and contagiously passionate professor who introduced me to developmental psychopathology—his "neurons-to-neighborhoods" perspective that focuses on how dynamic interactions among psychological, biological, and sociocultural factors unfold across time to produce both normal and abnormal human functioning. I was excited by the power of this comprehensive perspective to explain individual differences, embrace interacting causal factors, and meaningfully inform prevention and treatment interventions. To this day, the developmental psychopathology perspective explicitly guides much of my research and thinking.

The second influential undergraduate experience was the power of a unique textbook. In the fall of my sophomore year, I enrolled in an abnormal psychology course and found a familiar name on the syllabus: "Comer"... as in "the required text for this course is Ronald Comer's *Abnormal Psychology (Second Edition)*." Like most college students, at the time I did not have a particularly deep understanding of my father's work. I knew he worked very hard writing this book and that a great many colleges and universities had adopted it, but I had never sat down to read more than a few paragraphs here or there. But now, his book, cover-to-cover, was on my list of required readings.

As I read through the chapters for class, I became captivated by the book's engaging writing style, empathic and respectful descriptions of people with psychological disorders, blend of clinical research and practice, and strategic incorporation of current events and popular culture. I was also struck by how the book translated complex ideas into highly readable and easy to digest material. The book managed to present clinical psychology as a vibrant and evolving science, with many of the biggest answers still ahead. I was hooked; this was the field for me.

I recognize that it may seem like I was biased to be so favorably disposed toward this particular textbook, given the family connection. However, I would actually suggest the opposite—I was in my late teens at the time, and I must confess that I was not exactly looking to give my father copious credit for much during those years.

Over the past twenty years, from my time as a young undergraduate to my current academic and professional roles, I have been continually reminded that I am far from alone in my experiences with this extraordinary text. Countless individuals, from college freshmen to many of the field's senior leaders, have approached me to tell me what a special experience they have had with my father's textbook—whether as a student, as an instructor, or (like myself) as both.

When the opportunity arose to join *Abnormal Psychology* and *Fundamentals of Abnormal Psychology* as a co-author, it was a no-brainer for me. It has been a privilege to bring my particular background and areas of expertise to help expand an already outstanding book. For example, together my father and I have worked to incorporate the increasingly influential developmental psychopathology perspective throughout, along with a contemporary emphasis on biopsychosocial accounts of abnormality. As an instructor in psychology, I have always taken seriously my role as an ambassador for this field, someone who can introduce a captivating field to students, excite them about it, and provide them with insights that can influence their continued intellectual and professional development. Co-authoring this new edition of *Abnormal Psychology* has provided me with a special opportunity to expand this ambassadorship and to reach a greater number of students than I could have previously imagined. I am very appreciative.

On a more personal note, the greatest joy of undertaking this project has been to do so under the mentorship of my father, Ronald Comer—a peerless educator and writer who has helped teach and cultivate so many individuals over the years. Working with him has given me a coveted front row seat to learn from the "master" about how to best communicate the complexities of the field and how to respectfully portray mental dysfunction and human suffering, all with his unique blend of empathy, dignity, and humor. He has mentored me on this project—as he has throughout so many experiences of my life—with great wisdom, common sense, patience, selflessness, and love. This field has no shortage of individuals who feel fortunate to have been touched by his inimitable gifts. But no one more so than me.

Ron and Jon Comer

Between *Abnormal Psychology* and *Fundamentals of Abnormal Psychology*, the current textbook represents the eighteenth edition of one or the other of the books. This textbook journey has been a labor of love, but also one in which each edition is accompanied by an enormous amount of work and ridiculous pressure, not to mention countless sleepless nights. We mention these labors not only because we are world-class whiners but also to emphasize that we approach each edition as a totally new undertaking rather than as a superficial update of past editions. Our goal is to make each edition fresh by approaching our content coverage and pedagogical offerings as if we were writing a completely new book. As a result, each edition includes cutting-edge content reflecting new developments in the field, as well as in the world around us, delivered to readers via innovative and enlightening pedagogical techniques.

With this in mind, and with the addition of Jon's areas of expertise, we have added a considerable amount of new material and many exciting new features for this edition of *Abnormal Psychology*—while at the same time retaining the successful themes, material, and techniques that have been embraced enthusiastically by past students and instructors. The result is, we believe, a book that will excite readers and speak to them and their times. We have tried to convey our passion for the field of abnormal psychology, and we have built on the generous feedback of our colleagues in this undertaking—the students and professors who have used this textbook over the years.

New and Expanded Features

This edition of *Abnormal Psychology* reflects the many changes that have occurred over the past several years in the fields of abnormal psychology, education, and publishing, and in the world. Accordingly, we have introduced a number of new features and changes to the current edition.

•NEW• Developmental Psychopathology Perspective The *developmental psychopathology perspective* is introduced and applied throughout the book (for example, pages 80, 149, 166, and 369). This cutting-edge perspective helps integrate the explanations and treatments offered by the various models of psychopathology. The developmental psychopathology perspective—the clinical field's leading integrative perspective—brings the models together within a developmental framework, explaining how biological, psychological, and sociocultural factors may intersect and interact at key points throughout the lifespan to help produce both normal and abnormal functioning. Over the course of our discussions, readers will also come to appreciate this perspective's principles of *prevention, resilience, equifinality*, and *multifinality*.

•NEW• Brain Circuitry *Brain circuits* are now at the center of the textbook's biological discussions of anxiety, posttraumatic stress, depressive, personality, and other disorders (for example, pages 48, 123, 164, and 197). The biological model—particularly the role of genes, neurotransmitters, brain anatomy, and immune functioning—has always been an important part of our past editions, but, over the past decade, researchers have made striking discoveries about brain circuits—networks of brain structures whose interconnectivity produces distinct behaviors, cognitions, and emotions. Consistent with the growing belief that particular kinds of brain circuit dysfunction contribute to particular psychological disorders, we give special prominence to such circuits. At the same time, we discuss how genetic factors, neurotransmitter activity, brain anatomy, and immune functioning interface with the operation of the brain circuits and, in turn, with psychological dysfunction.

•NEW• The Cognitive-Behavioral Model: Merging the Behavioral and Cognitive Perspectives We now merge behavioral and cognitive explanations and treatments into a coherent and nuanced *cognitive-behavioral model*, consistent with today's most prominent point of view. Previous editions presented behavioral and cognitive discussions separately to help readers understand the important distinctions between behavior-focused and cognition-focused principles and research. However, such presentations also made it difficult for students to fully appreciate why and how today's cognitive-behavioral theorists and practitioners include both behavioral and cognitive principles in their work. This edition's presentation of the cognitive-behavioral model throughout the book enables readers to appreciate the complementary and inter-active nature of behavioral and cognitive principles while, at the same time, identifying the distinctions between such principles.

•NEW• "Trending" Boxes Throughout this edition, we present *Trending* boxes in addition to the *PsychWatch* boxes and *MindTech* boxes featured in previous editions. Whereas *PsychWatch* boxes explore important topics in the field and *MindTech* boxes give special attention to provocative technological issues, the *Trending* boxes focus on particularly hot topics that are trending, or current, in abnormal psychology. New *Trending* boxes include the following:

- TV Drug Ads Come Under Attack (Chapter 3)
- The Truth, the Whole Truth, and Nothing But the Truth (Chapter 4)
- Separation Anxiety Disorder, Not Just For Kids Anymore (Chapter 5)
- How Effective Are Antidepressant Drugs, Really? (Chapter 8)
- Internet Horrors (Chapter 9)
- Shame on Body Shamers (Chapter 11)
- The Opioid Crisis (Chapter 12)
- Mass Murders: Where Does Such Violence Come From? (Chapter 16)
- Damaging The Brain (Chapter 18)
- Doctor Do No Harm (Chapter 19)

•NEW• Additional InfoCentrals Our previous edition introduced a feature called **InfoCentrals**—numerous lively infographics on important topics in the field. These full-page infographics provide stimulating visual representations of data related to key topics and concepts in abnormal psychology. Given the very positive reader response to the InfoCentrals, we have included them again in this edition—updating all of them, substantially changing some, and adding a number of totally new ones. Brand new InfoCentrals include the following:

- Researching Research (Chapter 2, page 34)
- DSM: The Bigger Picture (Chapter 4, page 105)
- Fear (Chapter 5, page 126)
- Sadness (Chapter 7, page 218)
- Exercise and Dietary Supplements (Chapter 8, page 233)
- The Dark Triad (Chapter 16, page 507)

•NEW• Additional and Expanded Topic Coverage Over the past several years, a number of topics in abnormal psychology have received special attention. In this edition, we have provided new or expanded sections on these topics, including *the impact of changing health care laws* (pages 18, 110, 602); *transgender issues* (pages 413–415); *social media–based research* (page 41); *new patterns in drug therapy* (pages 124–125, 235, 518); *mass murders* (page 484); *terrorism and mental health* (pages 162–163, 599); *cognitive processing therapy* (page 168); *prolonged exposure therapy* (pages 169–170); *social media and sadness* (page 218); *exercise and mental health* (page 233); *the interpersonal theory of suicide* (pages 264–265); *the implicit association test for suicidal risk* (page 280); *teenage eating habits* (page 328); *body shaming* (page 338); *motivational interviewing* (pages 332, 370); *the opioid crisis* (page 352); *addiction to prescription pain relievers* (pages 351–352); *community naloxone treatments for drug overdoses* (pages 374–375); *recreational cannabis laws* (pages 362–363); *contingency management treatment* (page 372); *erotomanic delusions* (page 439); *disorders among the offspring of older fathers* (pages 215, 435); *cognitive remediation for schizophrenia* (page 460); *mental health courts* (pages 470, 588, 591); *mentalization* (pages 491–492); *selective mutism* (pages 517–518); *parent management training* (pages 525–526); *joint attention* (page 537); *biomarkers for Alzheimer's disease* (pages 568–569); *chronic traumatic encephalopathy* (page 571); *outpatient civil commitment* (pages 583, 588, 589); and *psychologists and enhanced interrogations* (page 599).

•NEW• Additional Focus on Technology In this edition we expand the previous edition's focus on the psychological impact of technology and the use of new technology in treatment. Throughout the book—in text discussions, *MindTech* boxes, photographs, and figures—we examine many additional technology topics such as telemental health (pages 20, 65, 603), Internet research (pages 35, 41), social media and sadness (pages 41, 135), and live streaming of suicides (page 254).

•NEW• Case Material Over the years, one of the hallmarks of *Abnormal Psychology* has been the inclusion of numerous and culturally diverse clinical examples that bring theoretical and clinical issues to life. In our continuing quest for relevance to the reader and to today's world, we have replaced or revised many of the clinical examples in this edition (for example, pages 285, 404, 487, 501, 513).

•NEW• Additional Critical Thought Questions *Critical thought questions* have long been a stimulating feature of *Abnormal Psychology*. These questions pop up within the text narrative, asking students to pause at precisely the right moment and think critically about the material they have just read. We have added a number of new such questions throughout this edition.

•NEW• Additional "Hashtags" This edition retains a fun and thought-provoking feature that has been very popular among students and professors over the years—reader-friendly *Hashtags* (#), previously called *Between the Lines*, consisting of surprising facts, current events, historical notes, interesting trends, lists, and quotes that are strategically placed in the book's margins. Numerous new *Hashtags* have been added to this edition.

•NEW• Thorough Update In this edition we present the most current theories, research, and events, and include more than 2,000 new references from the years 2016–2018, as well as numerous new photos, tables, and figures.

•EXPANDED COVERAGE• Prevention and Mental Health Promotion In accord with the clinical field's growing emphasis on prevention, positive psychology, and psychological wellness, we have increased the textbook's attention to these important approaches (for example, pages 15–16, 276–280, 339–340).

•EXPANDED COVERAGE• Multicultural Issues Consistent with the field's continuing appreciation of the impact of ethnicity, race, gender, gender identity, and other cultural factors on psychological functioning, this edition further expands its coverage of the *multicultural perspective* and includes additional multicultural material and research throughout the text (see, for example, pages 115–117, 274, 329–330, 413–415). Even a quick look through the pages of this textbook will reveal that it truly reflects the diversity of our society and of the field of abnormal psychology.

•EXPANDED COVERAGE• "New Wave" Cognitive-Behavioral Theories and Treatments Consistent with the increasing impact of the "new wave" cognitive-behavioral theories and therapies, including *mindfulness-based cognitive therapy* and *Acceptance and Commitment Therapy* (ACT), the current edition of *Abnormal Psychology* further expands the coverage of techniques, theories, and research in this realm (for example, pages 65–66, 119–122, 227, 373, 492–493).

Continuing Strengths

As we noted earlier, in this edition we have also retained the themes, material, and techniques that have worked successfully for and been embraced enthusiastically by past readers.

Breadth and Balance The field's many theories, studies, disorders, and treatments are presented completely and accurately. All major models—psychological, biological, and sociocultural—receive objective, balanced, up-to-date coverage, without bias toward any single approach.

Integration of Models Discussions throughout the text help students better understand where and how the various models work together and how they differ.

Empathy The subject of abnormal psychology is people—very often people in great pain. We have tried therefore to write always with empathy and to impart this awareness to students.

Integrated Coverage of Treatment Discussions of treatment are presented throughout the book. In addition to a complete overview of treatment in the opening chapters, each of the pathology chapters includes a full discussion of relevant treatment approaches.

Rich Case Material As we mentioned earlier, the textbook features hundreds of culturally diverse clinical examples to bring theoretical and clinical issues to life.

DSM-5 This edition continues to include discussions of DSM-5 throughout the book, highlighting the classification system's flaws as well as its utility. In addition to weaving DSM-5 categories, criteria, and information into the narrative of each chapter, we regularly provide a reader-friendly pedagogical feature called Dx Checklist to help students fully grasp DSM-5 and related diagnostic tools (for example, pages 114, 193, 285, 386).

Margin Glossary Hundreds of key words are defined in the margins of pages on which the words appear. In addition, a traditional glossary is featured at the back of the book.

Focus on Critical Thinking The textbook provides various tools for thinking critically about abnormal psychology. As we mentioned earlier, for example, "critical thought" questions appear at carefully selected locations within the text discussion, asking readers to stop and think critically about the material they have just read.

Striking Photos and Stimulating Illustrations Concepts, disorders, treatments, and applications are brought to life for the reader with stunning photographs, diagrams, graphs, and anatomical figures. All of the figures, graphs, and tables, many new to this edition, reflect the most up-to-date data available. The photos range from historical to today's world to pop culture. They do more than just illustrate topics: they touch and move readers.

Adaptability Chapters are self-contained, so they can be assigned in any order that makes sense to the professor.

Supplements

We are delighted by the enthusiastic responses of both professors and students to the supplements that have accompanied *Abnormal Psychology* over the years. This edition offers those supplements once again, revised and enhanced.

For Professors

Worth Video Collection for *Abnormal Psychology* *Produced and edited by Ronald J. Comer, Princeton University, and Gregory P. Comer, Princeton Academic Resources. Faculty Guide included.* This incomparable video series offers more than 125 clips—that depict disorders, show historical footage, and illustrate clinical topics, pathologies, treatments, experiments, and dilemmas. Videos are available on the *Video Collection for Abnormal Psychology* flash drive. The series is accompanied by a guide that fully describes and discusses each video clip, so that professors can make informed decisions about the use of the segments in lectures. Visit the LaunchPad for new videos.

Instructor's Resource Manual *by Jeffrey B. Henriques, University of Wisconsin–Madison and Laurie A. Frost.* This comprehensive guide, revised by an experienced instructor and a clinician, ties together the ancillary package for professors and teaching assistants. The manual includes detailed chapter outlines, lists of principal learning objectives, ideas for lectures, discussion launchers, classroom activities, extra credit projects, and DSM criteria for each of the disorders discussed in the text. It also offers strategies for using the accompanying media, including the video collection. Finally, it includes a comprehensive set of valuable materials that can be obtained from outside sources—items such as relevant feature films, documentaries, teaching references, and Internet sites related to abnormal psychology.

Lecture Slides These slides focus on key concepts and themes from the text and can be used as is or customized to fit a professor's needs.

iClicker Classroom Response System This is a versatile polling system developed by educators for educators that makes class time more efficient and interactive. iClicker allows you to ask questions and instantly record your students' responses, take attendance, and gauge students' understanding and opinions. A set of Clicker Questions for each chapter is available online and in LaunchPad.

Image Slides and Tables These slides, featuring all chapter photos, illustrations, and tables, can be used as is or customized to fit a professor's needs.

Chapter Figures and Photos This collection gives professors access to all of the photographs, illustrations, and alt text from *Abnormal Psychology*, Tenth Edition.

Assessment Tools

Computerized Test Bank powered by Diploma, includes a full assortment of test items. Each chapter features over 200 questions to test students at several levels of Bloom's taxonomy. All the questions are tagged to the outcomes recommended in the 2013 *APA Guidelines for the Undergraduate Psychology Major*, Bloom's level, the book page, the chapter section, and the learning objective from the Instructor's Resource Manual. The Diploma Test Bank files also provide tools for converting the Test Bank into a variety of useful formats as well as Blackboard- and WebCT-formatted versions of the Test Bank for *Abnormal Psychology*, Tenth Edition.

For Students

***Case Studies In Abnormal Psychology*, Second Edition,** by Ethan E. Gorenstein, Behavioral Medicine Program, New York–Presbyterian Columbia Hospital, and Ronald J. Comer, Princeton University.* This edition of our popular case study book provides 20 case histories, each going beyond diagnoses to describe the individual's history and symptoms, a theoretical discussion of treatment, a specific treatment plan, and the actual treatment conducted. The casebook also provides three cases without diagnoses or treatment so that students can identify disorders and suggest appropriate therapies. Wonderful case material for somatic symptom disorder, hoarding disorder, and gender dysphoria has been added by Danae Hudson and Brooke Whisenhunt, professors at Missouri State University.

LaunchPad macmillan learning **with LearningCurve Quizzing—*Multimedia to Support Teaching and Learning*** *Available at www.launchpadworks.com*

A comprehensive Web resource for teaching and learning psychology, LaunchPad combines Worth Publishers' award-winning media with an innovative platform for easy navigation. For students, it is the ultimate online study guide, with rich interactive tutorials, videos, an e-Book, and the LearningCurve adaptive quizzing system. For instructors, LaunchPad is a full-course space where class documents can be posted, quizzes can be easily assigned and graded, and students' progress can be assessed and recorded. Whether you are looking for the most effective study tools or a robust platform for an online course, LaunchPad is a powerful way to enhance your class.

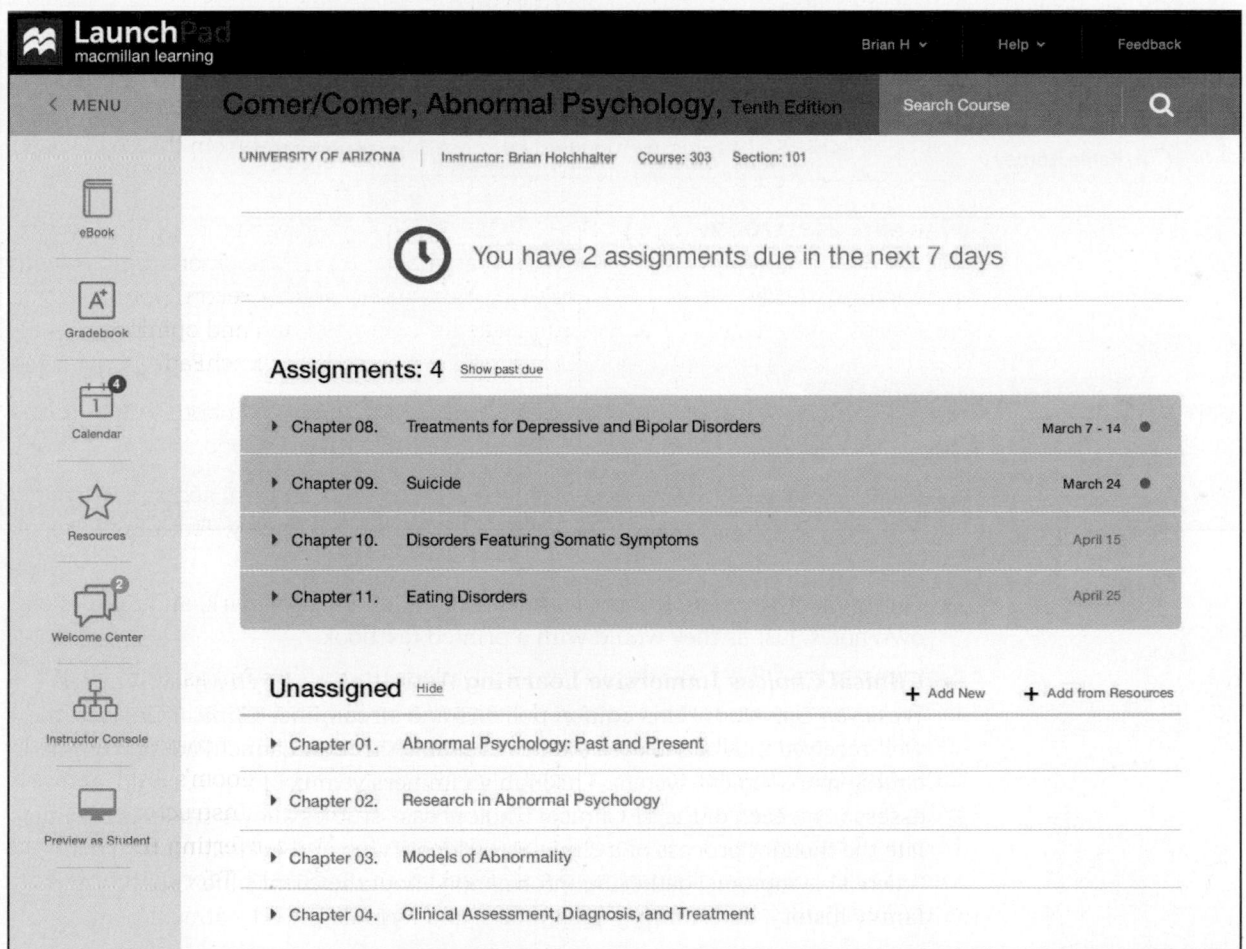

LaunchPad to Accompany *Abnormal Psychology,* Tenth Edition, can be previewed at www.launchpadworks.com. *Abnormal Psychology,* Tenth Edition, and LaunchPad can be ordered together with:

ISBN-10: 1-319-17054-4
ISBN-13: 978-1-319-17054-7

LaunchPad for *Abnormal Psychology*, Tenth Edition, includes the following resources:

- The **LearningCurve** quizzing system was designed based on the latest findings from learning and memory research. It combines adaptive question selection, immediate and valuable feedback, and a game-like interface to engage students in a learning experience that is unique to each student. Each LearningCurve quiz is fully integrated with other resources in LaunchPad through the Personalized Study Plan, so students will be able to review the material with Worth's extensive library of videos and activities. And state-of-the-art question-analysis reports allow instructors to track the progress of individual students as well as that of their class as a whole.

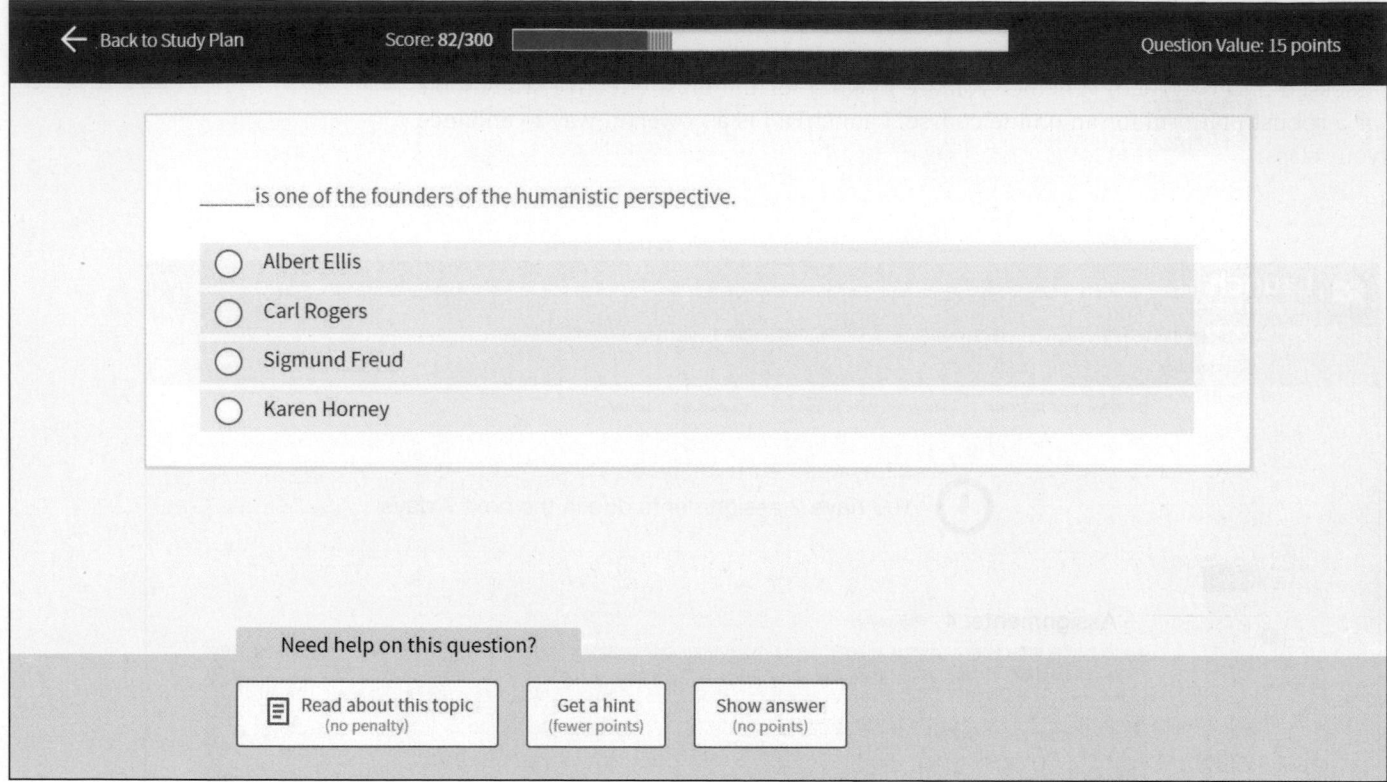

- An **interactive e-Book** allows students to highlight, bookmark, and make their own notes, just as they would with a printed textbook.

- ***Clinical Choices* Immersive Learning Activities** by *Taryn Myers, Virginia Wesleyan University*. This edition polishes and streamlines Clinical Choices, the well-received interactive case studies available through LaunchPad, our online course-management system. Through an immersive mix of video, audio, and assessment, each of the 11 Clinical Choices case studies allows students to simulate the thought process of a clinician by identifying and evaluating a virtual "client's" symptoms, gathering information about the client's life situation and family history, determining a diagnosis, and formulating a treatment plan.

- **Abnormal Psychology Video Activities**, *produced and edited by Ronald J. Comer, Princeton University, and Gregory P. Comer, Princeton Academic Resources*. These intriguing video cases run 3 to 7 minutes each and focus on people affected by disorders discussed in the text. Students first view a video case and then answer a series of thought-provoking questions.

- **Research Exercises** in each chapter help stimulate critical thinking skills. Students are asked to consider real research, make connections among ideas, and analyze arguments and the evidence on which they are based.

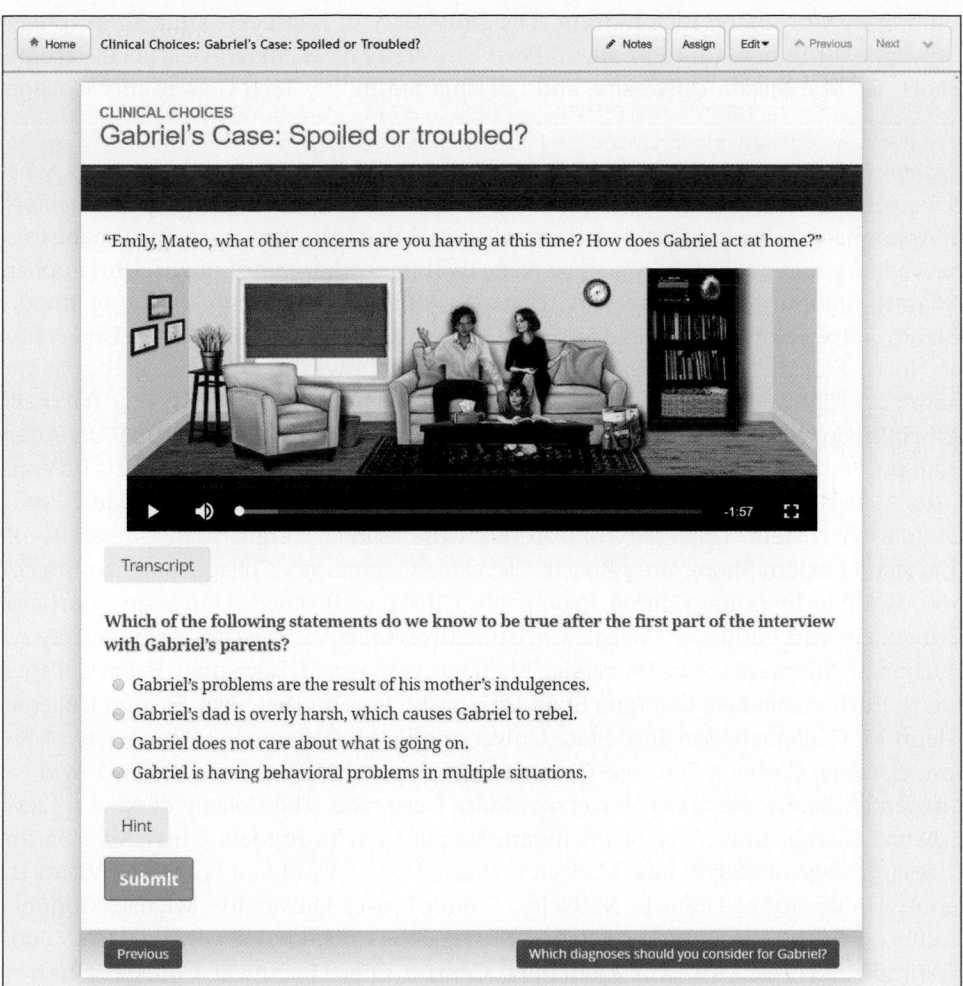

- **Deep integration** is available between LaunchPad products and Blackboard, Brightspace by Desire2Learn, Canvas, and Moodle. These deep integrations offer educators single sign-on and Gradebook sync, now with auto-refresh. Also, these best-in-class integrations offer deep linking to all Macmillan digital content at the chapter and asset level, giving professors ultimate flexibility and customization capability within their learning management system.

Acknowledgments

We are very grateful to the many people who have contributed to writing and producing this book. We particularly thank Gregory Comer for his outstanding work on a range of text and digital materials. In addition, we are indebted to Marlene Glissmann and Anthony Calcara for their fast, furious, and fantastic work on the references.

We are indebted greatly to those outstanding academicians and clinicians who have provided feedback on this new edition of *Abnormal Psychology*, along with that of its partner, *Fundamentals of Abnormal Psychology*, and have commented with great insight and wisdom on its clarity, accuracy, and completeness. Their collective knowledge has in large part shaped the current edition: Seth A Brown, University of Northern Iowa; Andrea Cartwright, Jefferson Community & Technical College; Lauren Dattilo, University of South Carolina; Andrea Glenn, University of Alabama; Amanda Haliburton, Virginia Polytechnic Institute and State University; Jacqueline Heath,

Ohio State University; Rick Ingram, The University of Kentucky; Julia Kim-Cohen, University of Illinois-Chicago; Justin Peer, University of Michigan-Dearborn; Jerome Short, George Mason University; and LaTishia Smith, Ivy Tech Community College of Indiana.

Earlier we also received valuable feedback from academicians and clinicians who reviewed portions of the previous editions of *Abnormal Psychology* and *Fundamentals of Abnormal Psychology*. Certainly their collective knowledge has also helped shape this new edition, and we gratefully acknowledge their important contributions: Christopher Adams, Fitchburg State University; Dave W. Alfano, Community College of Rhode Island; Jeffrey Armstrong, Northampton Community College; Alisa Aston, University of North Florida; Kent G. Bailey, Virginia Commonwealth University; Stephanie Baralecki, Chestnut Hill College; Sonja Barcus, Rochester College; Wendy Bartkus, Albright College; Marna S. Barnett, Indiana University of Pennsylvania; Jennifer Bennett, University of New Mexico; Jillian Bennett, University of Massachusetts Boston; Otto A. Berliner, Alfred State College; Allan Berman, University of Rhode Island; Douglas Bernstein, University of Toronto, Mississauga; Sarah Bing, University of Maryland Eastern Shore; Greg Bolich, Cleveland Community College; Stephen Brasel, Moody Bible Institute; Conrad Brombach, Christian Brothers University; Barbara Brown, Georgia Perimeter College; Christine Browning, Victory University; Jeffrey A. Buchanan, Minnesota State University, Mankato; Gregory M. Buchanan, Beloit College; Laura Burlingame-Lee, Colorado State University; Loretta Butehorn, Boston College; Glenn M. Callaghan, San José State University; E. Allen Campbell, University of St. Francis; Julie Carboni, San Jose Christian College and National University; David N. Carpenter, Southwest Texas University; Marc Celentana, The College of New Jersey; Edward Chang, University of Michigan; Daniel Chazin, Rutgers University; Sarah Cirese, College of Marin; June Madsen Clausen, University of San Francisco; Victor B. Cline, University of Utah; E. M. Coles, Simon Fraser University; Michael Connor, California State University, Long Beach; Frederick L. Coolidge, University of Colorado, Colorado Springs; Patrick J. Courtney, Central Ohio Technical College; Charles Cummings, Asheville Buncombe Technical Community College; Dennis Curtis, Metropolitan Community College; Timothy K. Daugherty, Missouri State University; Megan Davies, NOVA, Woodbridge Campus; Lauren Doninger, Gateway Community College; Pernella Deams, Grambling State University; Mary Dosier, University of Delaware; S. Wayne Duncan, University of Washington, Seattle; Anne Duran, California State University, Bakersfield; Morris N. Eagle, York University; Miriam Ehrenberg, John Jay College of Criminal Justice; Jon Elhai, University of Toledo; Frederick Ernst, University of Texas, Pan American; Daniella K. C. Errett, Pennsylvania Highlands Community College; Carlos A. Escoto, Eastern Connecticut State University; William Everist, Pima Community College; Jennifer Fiebig, Loyola University Chicago; David M. Fresco, Kent State University; Anne Fisher, University of Southern Florida; William E. Flack Jr., Bucknell University; John Forsyth, State University of New York, Albany; Alan Fridlund, University of California, Santa Barbara; Stan Friedman, Southwest Texas State University; Dale Fryxell, Chaminade University; Lawrence L. Galant, Gaston College; Kathryn E. Gallagher, Georgia State University; Rosemarie B. Gilbert, Brevard Community College; Karla Gingerich, Colorado State University; Jessica Goodwin Jolly, Gloucester County College; Nicholas Greco, College of Lake County; Jane Halonen, James Madison University; James Hansell, University of Michigan; Hansjörg Neth, Rensselaer Polytechnic Institute; David Harder, Tufts University; Morton G. Harmatz, University of Massachusetts; Jinni A. Harrigan, California State University, Fullerton; Jumi Hayaki, College of the Holy Cross; RaNae Healy, GateWay Community College; Anthony Hermann, Kalamazoo College; Paul Hewitt, University of British Columbia; Abby Hill, Trinity International University; David A. Hoffinan, University of California, Santa Cruz; Tony Hoffman, University of California, Santa Cruz; Art Hohmuth, The College of New Jersey; Art Houser, Fort Scott Community College; Danae Hudson,

Missouri State University; William G. Iacono, University of Minnesota; Ashleigh E. Jones, University of Illinois at Urbana-Champaign; Ricki E. Kantrowitz, Westfield State University; Barbara Kennedy, Brevard Community College; Lynn M. Kernen, Hunter College; Audrey Kim, University of California, Santa Cruz; Guadalupe Vasquez King, Milwaukee Area Technical College; Tricia Z. King, Georgia State University; Bernard Kleinman, University of Missouri, Kansas City; Futoshi Kobayashi, Northern State University; Alan G. Krasnoff, University of Missouri, St. Louis; Robert D. Langston, University of Texas, Austin; Kimberlyn Leary, University of Michigan; Craig Knapp, College of St. Joseph; Sally Kuhlenschmidt, Western Kentucky University; Harvey R. Lerner, Kaiser-Permanente Medical Group; Arnold D. LeUnes, Texas A&M University; Michael P. Levin, Kenyon College; Barbara Lewis, University of West Florida; Paul Lewis, Bethel College; Mary Margaret Livingston, Louisiana Technical University; Karsten Look, Columbus State Community College; Joseph LoPiccolo, University of Missouri, Columbia; L. E. Lowenstein, Southern England Psychological Services; Gregory Mallis, University of Indianapolis; Jerald J. Marshall, University of Central Florida; Toby Marx, Union County College; Janet R. Matthews, Loyola University; Robert J. McCaffrey, State University of New York, Albany; Rosemary McCullough, Ave Maria University; F. Dudley McGlynn, Auburn University; Tara McKee, Hamilton College; Lily D. McNair, University of Georgia; Mary W. Meagher, Texas A&M University; Dorothy Mercer, Eastern Kentucky University; Michele Metcalf, Coconino Community College; Joni L. Mihura, University of Toledo; Andrea Miller, Georgia Southwestern State University; Antoinette Miller, Clayton State University; Regina Miranda, Hunter College; John Mitchell, Lycoming College; Robin Mogul, Queens University; Linda M. Montgomery, University of Texas, Permian Basin; Jeri Morris, Roosevelt University; Karen Mottarella, University of Central Florida; Maria Moya, College of Southern Nevada; Karla Klein Murdock, University of Massachusetts, Boston; Taryn Myers, Virginia Wesleyan University; Sandy Naumann, Delaware Technical Community College; David Nelson, Sam Houston State University; Paul Neunuebel, Sam Houston State University; Ryan Newell, Oklahoma Christian University; Katherine M. Nicolai, Rockhurst University; Susan A. Nolan, Seton Hall University; Fabian Novello, Purdue University; Edward O'Brien, Marywood University; Ryan O'Loughlin, Nazareth College; Mary Ann M. Pagaduan, American Osteopathic Association; Crystal Park, University of Connecticut; Dominic J. Parrott, Georgia State University; Daniel Paulson, Carthage College; Paul A. Payne, University of Cincinnati; Mary Pelton-Cooper, Northern Michigan University; David V. Perkins, Ball State University; Julie C. Piercy, Central Virginia Community College; Lloyd R. Pilkington, Midlands Technical College; Harold A. Pincus, chair, DSM-IV, University of Pittsburgh, Western Psychiatric Institute and Clinic; Chris Piotrowski, University of West Florida; Debbie Podwika, Kankakee Community College; Ginger Pope, South Piedmont Community College; Norman Poppel, Middlesex County College; David E. Powley, University of Mobile; Laura A. Rabin, Brooklyn College; Max W. Rardin, University of Wyoming, Laramie; Lynn P. Rehm, University of Houston; Leslie A. Rescorla, Bryn Mawr College; R. W. Rieber, John Jay College, CUNY; Lisa Riley, Southwest Wisconsin Technical College; Esther Rothblum, University of Vermont; Vic Ryan, University of Colorado, Boulder; Randall Salekin, Florida International University; Edie Sample, Metropolitan Community College; Jackie Sample, Central Ohio Technical College; A. A. Sappington, University of Alabama, Birmingham; Martha Sauter, McLennan Community College; Laura Scaletta, Niagara County Community College; Ty Schepis, Texas State University; Elizabeth Seebach, Saint Mary's University of Minnesota; George W. Shardlow, City College of San Francisco; Shalini Sharma, Manchester Community College; Roberta S. Sherman, Bloomington Center for Counseling and Human Development; Wendy E. Shields, University of Montana; Sandra T. Sigmon, University of Maine, Orono; Susan J. Simonian, College of Charleston; Janet A. Simons, Central Iowa Psychological Services; Jay R. Skidmore, Utah State University; Rachel Sligar, James Madison University; Katrina Smith, Polk Community College; Robert Sommer, University of California, Davis; Jason S. Spiegelman, Community College of Baltimore

County; John M. Spores, Purdue University, South Central; Caroline Stanley, Wilmington College; Wayne Stein, Brevard Community College; Arnit Steinberg, Tel Aviv University; David Steitz, Nazareth College; B. D. Stillion, Clayton College & State University; Deborah Stipp, Ivy Tech Community College; Joanne H. Stohs, California State University, Fullerton; Jaine Strauss, Macalester College; Mitchell Sudolsky, University of Texas, Austin; John Suler, Rider University; Sandra Todaro, Bossier Parish Community College; Terry Trepper, Purdue University Calumet; Thomas A. Tutko, San José State University; Arthur D. VanDeventer, Thomas Nelson Community College; Maggie VandeVelde, Grand Rapids Community College; Jennifer Vaughn, Metropolitan Community College; Norris D. Vestre, Arizona State University; Jamie Walter, Roosevelt University; Steve Wampler, Southwestern Community College; Eleanor M. Webber, Johnson State College; Lance L. Weinmann, Canyon College; Doug Wessel, Black Hills State University; Laura Westen, Emory University; Brook Whisenhunt, Missouri State University; Joseph L. White, University of California, Irvine; Justin Williams, Georgia State University; Amy C. Willis, Veterans Administration Medical Center, Washington, DC; James M. Wood, University of Texas, El Paso; Lisa Wood, University of Puget Sound; Lucinda E. Woodward, Indiana University Southeast; Kim Wright, Trine University; David Yells, Utah Valley State College; Jessica Yokely, University of Pittsburgh; Carlos Zalaquett, University of South Florida; and Anthony M. Zoccolillo, Rutgers University.

We would also like to thank a group of talented professors who provided valuable feedback that shaped the development of our exciting immersive learning activities, Clinical Choices: David Berg, Community College of Philadelphia; Seth Brown, University of Northern Iowa; Julia Buckner, Louisiana State University; Robin Campbell, Eastern Florida State University; Christopher J. Dyszelski, Madison Area Technical College; Paul Deal, Missouri State University; Urminda Firlan, Kalamazoo Valley Community College; Roy Fish, Zane State College; Julie Hanauer, Suffolk County Community College; Stephanie Brooke Hindman, Greenville Technical College; Sally Kuhlenschmidt, Western Kentucky University; Alejandro Morales, California State Polytechnic University, Pomona; Erica Musser, Florida International University; Garth Neufeld, Highline Community College; Kruti Patel, Ohio University; and Jeremy Pettit, Florida International University.

A special thank you to the authors of the book's supplements package for doing splendid jobs with their respective supplements: Jeffrey B. Henriques, University of Wisconsin-Madison and Laurie A. Frost (*Instructor's Resource Manual*); Taryn Myers, Virginia Wesleyan University (*Clinical Choices*); Joy Crawford, Green River Community College (*Chapter Quizzes*). And thank you to the contributors from previous editions: Ann Brandt-Williams, Glendale Community College; Elaine Cassel, Marymount University and Lord Fairfax Community College; Danae L. Hudson, Missouri State University; John Schulte, Cape Fear Community College and University of North Carolina; and Brooke L. Whisenhunt, Missouri State University (additional Web site materials).

We also extend our deep appreciation to the core team of professionals at Worth Publishers and W. H. Freeman and Company who have worked with us almost every day for the past year to produce this edition: Mimi Melek, the book's senior development editor; Kerry O'Shaughnessy, senior content project manager; Paul Lacy, layout designer; and Jennifer Atkins, photo editor. It is accurate to say that these members of the core team were our co-authors and co-teachers in this enterprise, and we are in their debt.

We also thank the following individuals, each of whom made significant contributions to the writing and production of this textbook: Chuck Linsmeier, vice president, social sciences; Matt Wright and Dan McDonough, executive program managers; Un Hye Kim, editorial assistant; Jennifer MacMillan, permissions manager; Susan Wein, senior workflow project supervisor; Shani Fisher, director of content and assessment, social sciences; Tracey Kuehn, director of content management enhancement; Diana Blume, director of design; Blake Logan, senior design manager; Natasha Wolfe, design services manager; Matthew McAdams, art manager; Chuck Yuen, book and InfoCentral designer; Lucille Clerc, cover and chapter-opener artist; Stefani Wallace, media editor; Noel Hohnstine, director of media editorial, social sciences; Michael McCarty, text permissions associate; Arthur Johnson, text permissions researcher; Lisa Kinne, managing editor; Tina Hastings, copyeditor; Jean Erler, proofreader; and Sherri Dietrich, indexer.

And, of course, not to be overlooked are the superb professionals at Worth Publishers who continuously work with great passion, skill, and judgment to bring our books to the attention of professors across the world: Kate Nurre, executive marketing manager; Lindsay Johnson, senior marketing manager; Chelsea Simens, marketing assistant; Greg David, vice president, academic sales; and the company's wonderful sales representatives. Thank you so much.

Two remaining notes. First, as you can imagine, we have found it more than a little exciting to work together on this monumental project. But beyond our personal delight, we believe that our co-authorship brings a valuable blend to the textbook that makes it particularly informative, wide-ranging, and clinically sensitive. More than father and son, we are psychology professors and clinicians at very different points in our lives and careers, with different areas of expertise and accomplishment, and, at times, different sensibilities. Bridging such differences in the writing of this book has enabled us to grow enormously—both professionally and personally. We hope that our collaboration has, likewise, resulted in a special textbook for our readers.

Finally, both in terms of our textbooks and, more generally, with regard to our personal and professional lives, we are both very aware of just how fortunate we are. We feel profoundly privileged to be able to work with so many interesting and stimulating students during this important and exciting stage of their lives. Similarly, we are grateful beyond words for our dear friends and for our extraordinary family, particularly our magnificent wives Marlene and Jami (Marlene is also Jon's mom); our wonderful son/brother, Greg, and daughter-/sister-in-law, Emily; Jon's loving parents-in-law, Jim and Mindy Furr; and the lights of our lives, Delia (age 6) and Emmett (age 4).

Ronald J. Comer   Jonathan S. Comer

January, 2018

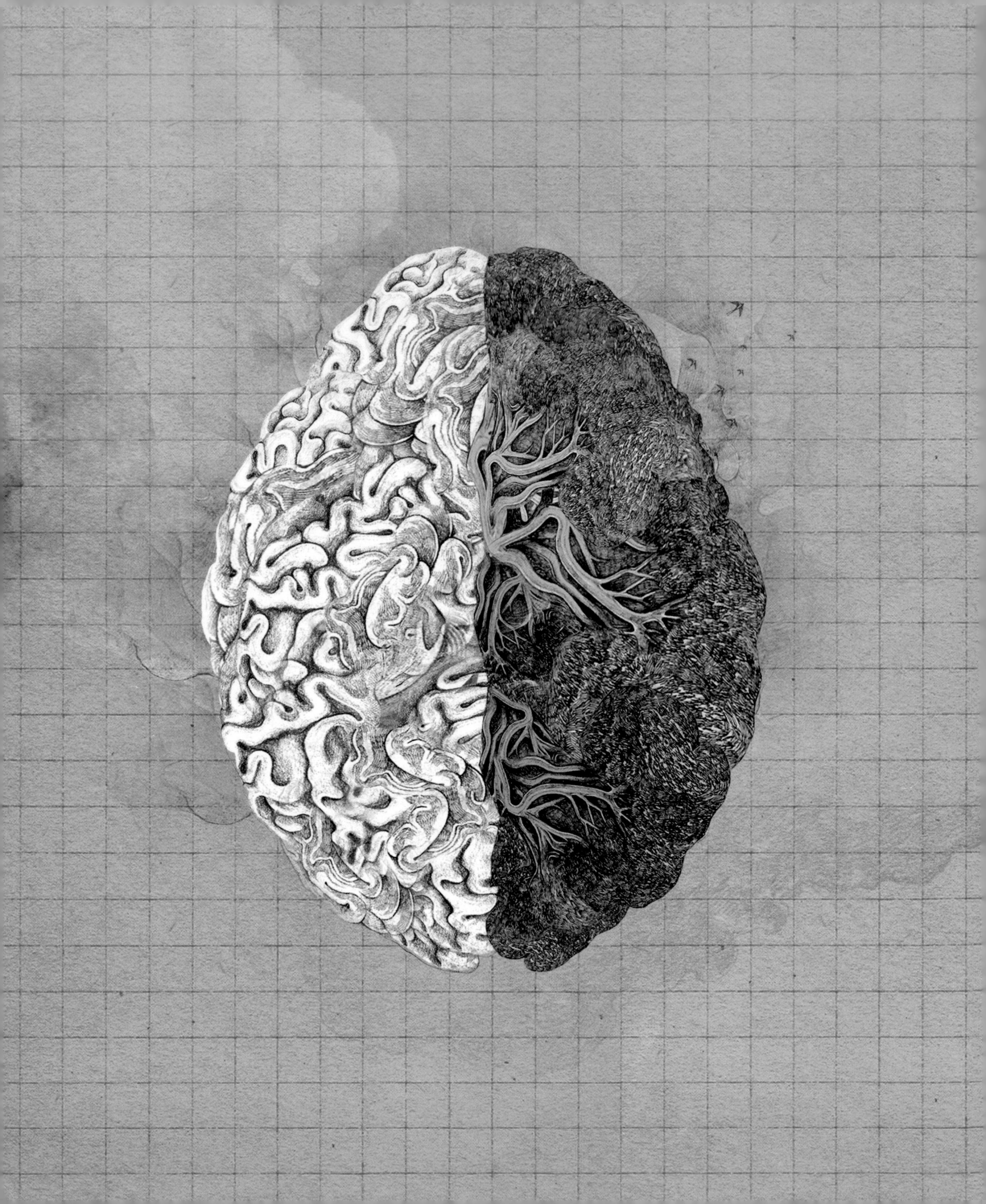

♀...Abnormal Psychology: Past and Present

Johanne cries herself to sleep every night. She is certain that the future holds nothing but misery. Indeed, this is the only thing she does feel certain about. "I'm going to suffer and suffer and suffer, and my daughters will suffer as well. We're doomed. The world is ugly. I hate every moment of my life." She has great trouble sleeping. She is afraid to close her eyes. When she does, the hopelessness of her life—and the ugly future that awaits her daughters—becomes all the clearer to her. When she drifts off to sleep, her dreams are nightmares filled with terrible images—bodies, decay, death, destruction.

Some mornings Johanne even has trouble getting out of bed. The thought of facing another day overwhelms her. She wishes that she and her daughters were dead. "Get it over with. We'd all be better off." She feels paralyzed by her depression and anxiety, overwhelmed by her sense of hopelessness, and filled with fears of becoming ill, too tired to move, too negative to try anymore. On such mornings, she huddles her daughters close to her and remains all day in the cramped tent she shares with her daughters. She feels she has been deserted by the world and left to rot. She is both furious at life and afraid of it at the same time.

During the past year Alberto has been hearing mysterious voices that tell him to quit his job, leave his family, and prepare for the coming invasion. These voices have brought tremendous confusion and emotional turmoil to Alberto's life. He believes that they come from beings in distant parts of the universe who are somehow wired to him. Although it gives him a sense of purpose and specialness to be the chosen target of their communications, the voices also make him tense and anxious. He does all he can to warn others of the coming apocalypse. In accordance with instructions from the voices, he identifies online articles that seem to be filled with foreboding signs, and he posts comments that plead with other readers to recognize the articles' underlying messages. Similarly, he posts long, rambling YouTube videos that describe the invasion to come. The online comments and feedback that he receives typically ridicule and mock him. If he rejects the voices' instructions and stops his online commentary and videos, then the voices insult and threaten him and turn his days into a waking nightmare.

Alberto has put himself on a sparse diet as protection against the possibility that his enemies may be contaminating his food. He has found a quiet apartment far from his old haunts, where he has laid in a good stock of arms and ammunition. After witnessing the abrupt and troubling changes in his behavior and watching his ranting and rambling videos, his family and friends have tried to reach out to Alberto, to understand his problems, and to dissuade him from the disturbing course he is taking. Every day, however, he retreats further into his world of mysterious voices and imagined dangers.

Most of us would probably consider Johanne's and Alberto's emotions, thoughts, and behaviors psychologically abnormal. They are the result of a state sometimes called *psychopathology, maladjustment, emotional disturbance,* or *mental illness* (see **PsychWatch** on the next page). These terms have been applied to the many problems that seem closely tied to the human brain or mind. Psychological abnormality affects the famous and the unknown, the rich and the poor. Celebrities, writers, politicians, and other public figures of the present and the past have struggled with it. Psychological problems can bring great suffering, but they can also be the source of inspiration and energy.

PSYCH**WATCH**

Verbal Debuts

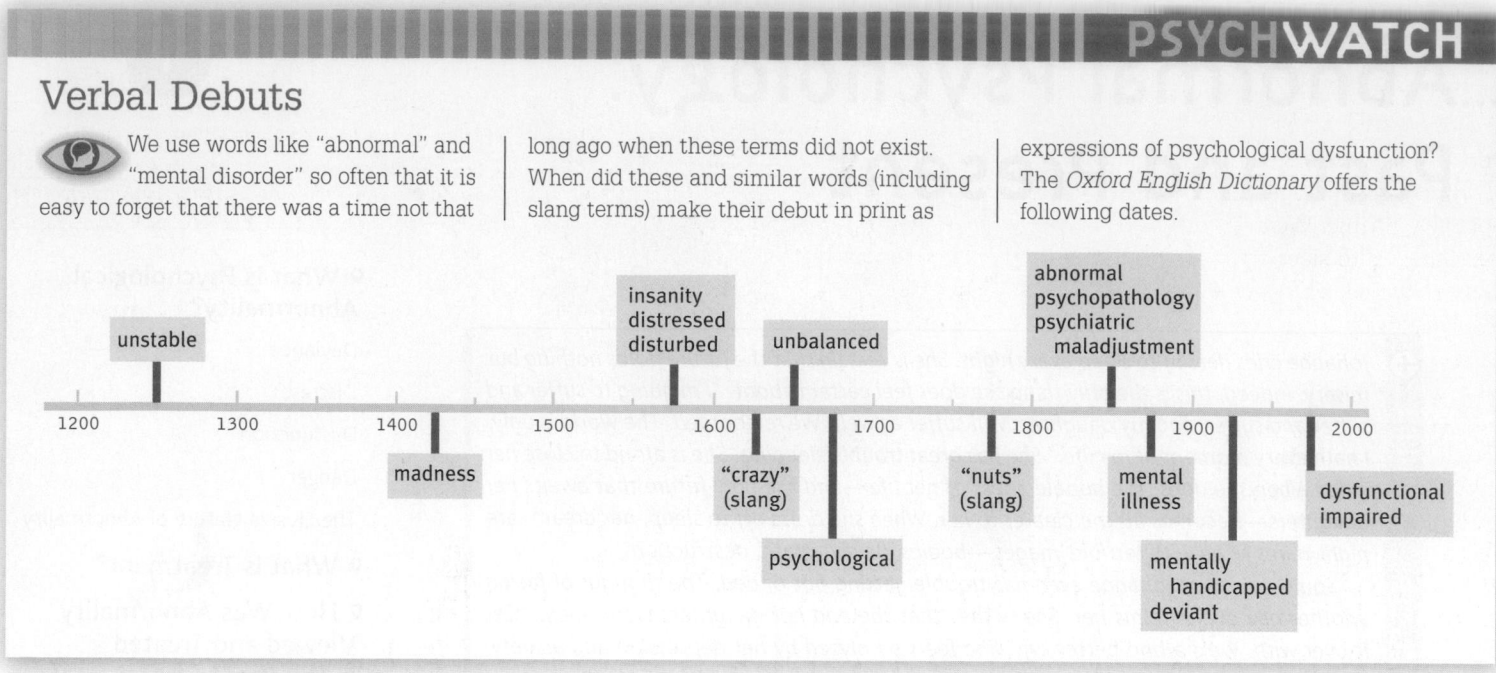

We use words like "abnormal" and "mental disorder" so often that it is easy to forget that there was a time not that long ago when these terms did not exist. When did these and similar words (including slang terms) make their debut in print as expressions of psychological dysfunction? The *Oxford English Dictionary* offers the following dates.

Because they are so common and so personal, these problems capture the interest of us all. Hundreds of novels, plays, films, and television programs have explored what many people see as the dark side of human nature, and self-help books flood the market. Mental health experts are popular guests on both television and radio, and some even have their own shows, Web sites, and blogs.

The field devoted to the scientific study of the problems we find so fascinating is usually called **abnormal psychology**. As in any science, workers in this field, called *clinical scientists,* gather information systematically so that they can describe, predict, and explain the phenomena they study. The knowledge that they acquire is then used by *clinical practitioners,* whose role is to detect, assess, and treat abnormal patterns of functioning. ∎

> Why do actors who portray characters with psychological disorders tend to receive more awards for their performances?

What Is Psychological Abnormality?

ALTHOUGH THEIR GENERAL GOALS are similar to those of other scientific professionals, clinical scientists and practitioners face problems that make their work especially difficult. One of the most troubling is that psychological abnormality is very hard to define. Consider once again Johanne and Alberto. Why are we so ready to call their responses abnormal?

While many definitions of abnormality have been proposed over the years, none has won total acceptance (Bergner & Bunford, 2014). Still, most of the definitions have certain features in common, often called "the four Ds": deviance, distress, dysfunction, and danger. That is, patterns of psychological abnormality are typically *deviant* (different, extreme, unusual, perhaps even bizarre), *distressing* (unpleasant and upsetting to the person), *dysfunctional* (interfering with the person's ability to conduct daily activities in a constructive way), and possibly *dangerous*. This definition offers a useful starting point from which to explore the phenomena of psychological abnormality. As you will see, however, it has key limitations.

abnormal psychology The scientific study of abnormal behavior undertaken to describe, predict, explain, and change abnormal patterns of functioning.

norms A society's stated and unstated rules for proper conduct.

culture A people's common history, values, institutions, habits, skills, technology, and arts.

Deviance

Abnormal psychological functioning is *deviant*, but deviant from what? Johanne's and Alberto's behaviors, thoughts, and emotions are different from those that are considered normal in our place and time. We do not expect people to cry themselves to sleep each night, hate the world, wish themselves dead, or obey voices that no one else hears.

In short, abnormal behavior, thoughts, and emotions are those that differ markedly from a society's ideas about proper functioning. Each society establishes **norms**—stated and unstated rules for proper conduct. Behavior that breaks legal norms is considered to be criminal. Behavior, thoughts, and emotions that break norms of psychological functioning are called abnormal.

Deviance and abnormality This woman, like many others from certain tribes in Myanmar (Burma), has permanently tattooed her entire face with an elaborate pattern of black lines, a tradition that began centuries ago to repel invaders and discourage kidnappings. In Western society, even with the enormous popularity of body ink, total facial disfigurement of this kind would break behavioral norms and might well be considered abnormal.

Judgments about what constitutes abnormality vary from society to society. A society's norms grow from its particular **culture**—its history, values, institutions, habits, skills, technology, and arts. A society that values competition and assertiveness may accept aggressive behavior, whereas one that emphasizes cooperation and gentleness may consider aggressive behavior unacceptable and even abnormal. A society's values may also change over time, causing its views of what is psychologically abnormal to change as well. In Western society, for example, a woman seeking the power of running a major corporation or indeed of leading the country would have been considered inappropriate and even delusional a hundred years ago. Today the same behavior is valued.

Judgments about what constitutes abnormality depend on *specific circumstances* as well as on cultural norms. What if, for example, we were to learn that Johanne is a citizen of Haiti and that her desperate unhappiness began in the days, weeks, and months following the massive earthquake that struck her country, already the poorest country in the Western hemisphere, on January 12, 2010? The quake, one of the worst natural disasters in history, killed 250,000 Haitians, left 1.5 million homeless, and destroyed most of the country's business establishments and educational institutions. Half of Haiti's homes and buildings were immediately turned into rubble, and its electricity and other forms of power disappeared. Tent cities replaced homes for most people (Ahmed, 2016; Granitz, 2014).

In the weeks and months that followed the earthquake, Johanne came to accept that she wouldn't get all of the help she needed and that she might never again see the friends and neighbors who had once given her life so much meaning. As she and her daughters moved from one temporary tent or hut to another throughout the country, always at risk of developing serious diseases, she gradually gave up all hope that her life would ever return to normal. In this light, Johanne's reactions do not seem quite so inappropriate. If anything is abnormal here, it is her situation. Many human experiences produce intense reactions—financial ruin, large-scale catastrophes and disasters, rape, child abuse, war, terminal illness, chronic pain (Wynn, 2017; Simon, Feiring, & Cleland, 2016). Is there an "appropriate" way to react to such things? Should we ever call reactions to such experiences abnormal.

Context is key A couple dressed as Supergirl and Superman stop and point upward as they cross a street in New York City. Their appearance and behavior might suggest psychological dysfunction were it not for the fact that they are attendees at a 2016 Comic-Con, one of the many popular conventions held across the country to showcase comic books, graphic novels, and the like.

Distress

Even functioning that is considered unusual does not necessarily qualify as abnormal. According to many clinical theorists, behavior, ideas, or emotions usually have to cause *distress* before they can be labeled abnormal. Consider the Ice Breakers, a group of people in Michigan who go swimming in lakes throughout the state every weekend from November through February. The colder the weather, the better they like it. One man, a member of the group for 17 years, says he loves the challenge of human against nature. A 37-year-old lawyer believes that the weekly shock is good for her health. "It cleanses me," she says. "It perks me up and gives me strength." Certainly these people are different from most of us, but is their behavior abnormal? Far from experiencing distress, they feel energized and challenged. Their positive feelings must cause us to hesitate before we decide that they are functioning abnormally.

Should we conclude, then, that feelings of distress must always be present before a person's functioning can be considered abnormal? Not necessarily. Some people who function abnormally maintain a positive frame of mind. Consider once again Alberto, the young man who hears mysterious voices. What if he enjoyed listening to the voices, felt honored to be chosen, loved sending out warnings on the Internet, and looked forward to saving the world? Shouldn't we still regard his functioning as abnormal?

Dysfunction

Abnormal behavior tends to be *dysfunctional;* that is, it interferes with daily functioning. It so upsets, distracts, or confuses people that they cannot care for themselves properly, participate in ordinary social interactions, or work productively. Alberto, for example, has quit his job, left his family, and prepared to withdraw from the productive life he once led. Because our society holds that it is important to carry out daily activities in an effective manner, Alberto's behavior is likely to be regarded as abnormal and undesirable. In contrast, the Ice Breakers, who continue to perform well in their jobs and enjoy fulfilling relationships, would probably be considered simply unusual.

Danger

Perhaps the ultimate psychological dysfunction is behavior that becomes *dangerous* to oneself or others. Individuals whose behavior is consistently careless, hostile, or confused may be placing themselves or those around them at risk. Alberto, for example, seems to be endangering both himself, with his diet, and others, with his buildup of arms and ammunition.

Although danger is often cited as a feature of abnormal psychological functioning, research suggests that it is actually the exception rather than the rule (Bonnet et al., 2016). Most people struggling with anxiety, depression, and even bizarre thinking pose no immediate danger to themselves or to anyone else.

The Elusive Nature of Abnormality

Efforts to define psychological abnormality typically raise as many questions as they answer. Ultimately, a society selects general criteria for defining abnormality and then uses those criteria to judge particular cases. One clinical theorist, Thomas Szasz (1920–2012), placed such emphasis on society's role that he found the whole concept of mental illness to be invalid, a *myth* of sorts (Szasz, 2011, 1963, 1960). According to Szasz, the deviations that society calls abnormal are simply "problems in living," not signs of something wrong within the person.

Changing times Just decades ago, a woman's love for race car driving would have been considered strange, perhaps even abnormal. Today, Danica Patrick (right) is one of America's finest race car drivers. The size difference between her first-place trophy at the Indy Japan 300 auto race and that of second-place male driver Hélio Castroneves symbolizes just how far women have come in this sport.

AP Photo/Katsumi Kasahara

Even if we assume that psychological abnormality is a valid concept and that it can indeed be defined, we may be unable to apply our definition consistently. If a behavior—excessive use of alcohol among college students, say—is familiar enough, the society may fail to recognize that it is deviant, distressful, dysfunctional, and dangerous. Thousands of college students throughout the United States are so dependent on alcohol that it interferes with their personal and academic lives, causes them great discomfort, jeopardizes their health, and often endangers them and the people around them (Patrick & Terry-McElrath, 2017; Testa & Cleveland, 2017). Yet their problem often goes unnoticed and undiagnosed. Alcohol is so much a part of the college subculture that it is easy to overlook drinking behavior that has become abnormal.

> **What behaviors fit the criteria of deviant, distressful, dysfunctional, or dangerous but would not be considered abnormal by most people?**

Conversely, a society may have trouble separating an abnormality that requires intervention from an *eccentricity,* an unusual pattern with which others have no right to interfere. From time to time we see or hear about people who behave in ways we consider strange, such as a man who lives alone with two dozen cats and rarely talks to other people. The behavior of such people is deviant, and it may well be distressful and dysfunctional, yet many professionals think of it as eccentric rather than abnormal (see *PsychWatch*).

PSYCH**WATCH**

Marching to a Different Drummer: Eccentrics

- Writer **James Joyce** always carried a tiny pair of lady's bloomers, which he waved in the air to show approval.
- **Benjamin Franklin** took "air baths" for his health, sitting naked in front of an open window.
- **Alexander Graham Bell** covered the windows of his house to keep out the rays of the full moon. He also tried to teach his dog how to talk.
- Writer **D. H. Lawrence** enjoyed removing his clothes and climbing mulberry trees.

These famous persons have been called eccentrics. The dictionary defines an *eccentric* as a person who deviates from common behavior patterns or displays odd or whimsical behavior. But how can we separate a psychologically healthy person who has unusual habits from a person whose oddness is a symptom of psychopathology? Little research has been done on eccentrics, but a few studies offer some insights (Weeks, 2015; Neuman, 2013; Weeks & James, 1995).

Researcher David Weeks (2015) studied 1,000 eccentrics and estimated that as many as 1 in 5,000 persons may be "classic, full-time eccentrics." Weeks pinpointed 15 characteristics common to the eccentrics in his study: *nonconformity, creativity, strong curiosity, idealism, extreme interests and hobbies, lifelong awareness of being different, high intelligence, outspokenness, noncompetitiveness, unusual eating and living habits, disinterest in others' opinions or company, mischievous sense of humor, nonmarriage, eldest or only child,* and *poor spelling skills*

Weeks suggests that eccentrics do not typically suffer from mental disorders. Whereas the unusual behavior of persons with mental disorders is thrust upon them and usually causes them suffering, eccentricity is chosen freely and provides pleasure. In short, "Eccentrics know they're different and glory in it" (Weeks & James, 1995, p. 14). Similarly, the thought processes of eccentrics are not severely disrupted and do not leave these persons dysfunctional. In fact, Weeks found that eccentrics in his study actually had fewer emotional problems than individuals in the general population. Perhaps being an "original" is good for mental health.

AP Photo/Thanh Nien

Eccentric, but not abnormal Tran Van Hay holds his hair—more than 20 feet in length—around his body, as if it were a cobra. By the time of his death in 2010, he had not had a haircut for 50 years and had washed his hair only a few times. The married Vietnamese man otherwise lived and worked as a highly respected and productive herbalist who successfully cared for many people in need. He just liked his hair on the long side—longer than any other person on earth.

Therapy . . . not A woman writes down her feelings on a sticky note and attaches it to a wall at the Union Square subway station in New York City. It's part of a project named "Subway Therapy," started the day after the emotion-arousing U.S. presidential election of 2016. Expressing feelings, concerns, and/or hopes in this way may indeed be therapeutic for many people, but it is not therapy. It lacks, for example, a "trained healer" and a series of systematic contacts between healer and sufferer.

Andrew Lichtenstein/Getty Images

In short, while we may agree to define psychological abnormalities as patterns of functioning that are deviant, distressful, dysfunctional, and sometimes dangerous, we should be clear that these criteria are often vague and subjective. In turn, few of the current categories of abnormality that you will meet in this book are as clear-cut as they may seem, and most continue to be debated by clinicians.

What Is Treatment?

ONCE CLINICIANS DECIDE that a person is indeed suffering from some form of psychological abnormality, they seek to treat it. **Treatment,** or **therapy,** is a procedure designed to change abnormal behavior into more normal behavior; it, too, requires careful definition. For clinical scientists, the problem is closely related to defining abnormality. Consider the case of Bill:

February: *He cannot leave the house; Bill knows that for a fact. Home is the only place where he feels safe—safe from humiliation, danger, even ruin. If he were to go to work, his coworkers would somehow reveal their contempt for him. A pointed remark, a quizzical look—that's all it would take for him to get the message. If he were to go shopping at the store, before long everyone would be staring at him. Surely others would see his dark mood and thoughts; he wouldn't be able to hide them. He dare not even go for a walk alone in the woods—his heart would probably start racing again, bringing him to his knees and leaving him breathless, incoherent, and unable to get home. No, he's much better off staying in his room, trying to get through another evening of this curse called life. Thank goodness for the Internet. Were it not for his reading of news sites and blog posts and online forums, he would, he knows, be cut off from the world altogether.*

July: *Bill's life revolves around his circle of friends: Bob and Jack, whom he knows from the office, where he was recently promoted to director of customer relations, and Frank and Tim, his weekend tennis partners. The gang meets for dinner every week at someone's house, and they chat about life, politics, and their jobs. Particularly special in Bill's life is Janice. They go to movies, restaurants, and shows together. She thinks Bill's just terrific, and Bill finds himself beaming whenever she's around. Bill looks forward to work each day and to his one-on-one dealings with customers. He is taking part in many activities and relationships and more fully enjoying life.*

(Frank, 1973, pp. 2–3)

Bill's thoughts, feelings, and behavior interfered with all aspects of his life in February. Yet most of his symptoms had disappeared by July. All sorts of factors may have contributed to Bill's improvement—advice from friends and family members, a new job or vacation, perhaps a big change in his diet or exercise regimen. Any or all of these things may have been useful to Bill, but they could not be considered treatment or therapy. Those terms are usually reserved for special, systematic procedures for helping people overcome their psychological difficulties. According to a pioneering clinical theorist, Jerome Frank, all forms of therapy have three essential features:

1. A *sufferer* who seeks relief from the healer.

2. A trained, socially accepted *healer,* whose expertise is accepted by the sufferer and his or her social group.

3. A *series of contacts* between the healer and the sufferer, through which the healer . . . tries to produce certain changes in the sufferer's emotional state, attitudes, and behavior.

Despite this seemingly straightforward definition, clinical treatment is surrounded by conflict and, at times, confusion. Some clinicians view abnormality as an illness and so consider therapy a procedure that helps *cure* the illness. Others see abnormality as a problem in living and therapists as *teachers* of more functional behavior and thought. Clinicians even differ on what to call the person who receives therapy: those who see abnormality as an illness speak of the "patient," while those who view it as a problem in living refer to the "client." Because both terms are so common, this book will use them interchangeably.

Despite their differences, most clinicians do agree that large numbers of people need therapy of one kind or another. Later you will encounter evidence that therapy is indeed often helpful.

treatment A systematic procedure designed to change abnormal behavior into more normal behavior. Also called *therapy*.

trephination An ancient operation in which a stone instrument was used to cut away a circular section of the skull to treat abnormal behavior.

How Was Abnormality Viewed and Treated in the Past?

IN ANY GIVEN YEAR, as many as 30 percent of the adults and 19 percent of the children and adolescents in the United States display serious psychological disturbances and are in need of clinical treatment (Walker & Druss, 2016; Kessler et al., 2015, 2012, 2009; Merikangas et al., 2013). The rates in other countries are similarly high. It is tempting to conclude that something about the modern world is responsible for these many emotional problems—perhaps rapid technological change, resultant losses of employment, the threat of terrorism, or a decline in religious, family, or other support systems (Elhai et al., 2017; Paslakis et al., 2015). But, as we shall see in the following sections, every society, past and present, has witnessed psychological abnormality.

Ancient Views and Treatments

Historians who have examined the unearthed bones, artwork, and other remnants of ancient societies have concluded that these societies probably regarded abnormal behavior as the work of evil spirits. People in prehistoric societies apparently believed that all events around and within them resulted from the actions of magical, sometimes sinister, beings who controlled the world. In particular, they viewed the human body and mind as a battleground between external forces of good and evil. Abnormal behavior was typically interpreted as a victory by evil spirits, and the cure for such behavior was to force the demons from a victim's body.

This supernatural view of abnormality may have begun as far back as the Stone Age, a half-million years ago. Some skulls from that period recovered in Europe and South America show evidence of an operation called **trephination,** in which a stone instrument, or *trephine,* was used to cut away a circular section of the skull (Lee, 2015). Some historians have concluded that this early operation was performed as a treatment for severe abnormal behavior—either hallucinations, in which people saw or heard things not actually present, or melancholia, characterized by extreme sadness and immobility. The purpose of opening the skull was to release the evil spirits that were supposedly causing the problem (Selling, 1940).

Later societies also explained abnormal behavior by pointing to possession by demons. Egyptian, Chinese, and Hebrew writings all account for psychological deviance this way, and the Bible describes how an evil spirit from the Lord affected King Saul and how David feigned madness to convince his enemies that he was visited by divine forces.

The treatment for abnormality in these early societies was often *exorcism.* The idea was to coax the evil spirits to leave or to make the person's body an

Professor John Verano

Expelling evil spirits The two holes in this skull recovered from ancient times indicate that the person underwent trephination, possibly for the purpose of releasing evil spirits and curing mental dysfunction.

> What demonological explanations or treatments, besides exorcism, are still around today, and why do they persist?

humors According to the Greeks and Romans, bodily chemicals that influence mental and physical functioning.

uncomfortable place in which to live. A *shaman,* or priest, might recite prayers, plead with the evil spirits, insult the spirits, perform magic, make loud noises, or have the person drink bitter potions. If these techniques failed, the shaman performed a more extreme form of exorcism, such as whipping or starving the person.

Greek and Roman Views and Treatments

In the years from roughly 500 B.C. to 500 A.D., when the Greek and Roman civilizations thrived, philosophers and physicians often offered different explanations and treatments for abnormal behaviors. Hippocrates (460–377 B.C.), often called the father of modern medicine, taught that illnesses had *natural* causes. He saw abnormal behavior as a disease arising from internal physical problems. Specifically, he believed that some form of brain pathology was the culprit and that it resulted—like all other forms of disease, in his view—from an imbalance of four fluids, or **humors,** that flowed through the body: *yellow bile, black bile, blood,* and *phlegm* (Smith & Smith, 2016). An excess of yellow bile, for example, caused *mania,* a state of frenzied activity; an excess of black bile was the source of *melancholia,* a condition marked by unshakable sadness.

Humors in action Hippocrates believed that imbalances of the four humors affected personality. In these depictions of two of the humors, yellow bile (left) drives a husband to beat his wife, and black bile (right) leaves a man melancholic and sends him to bed.

To treat psychological dysfunction, Hippocrates sought to correct the underlying physical pathology. He believed, for instance, that the excess of black bile underlying melancholia could be reduced by a quiet life, a diet of vegetables, temperance, exercise, celibacy, and even bleeding. Hippocrates' focus on internal causes for abnormal behavior was shared by the great Greek philosophers Plato (427–347 B.C.) and Aristotle (384–322 B.C.) and by influential Greek and Roman physicians.

Europe in the Middle Ages: Demonology Returns

The enlightened views of Greek and Roman physicians and scholars were not enough to shake ordinary people's belief in demons. And with the decline of Rome, demonological views and practices became popular once again. A growing distrust of science spread throughout Europe.

From 500 to 1350 A.D., the period known as the Middle Ages, the power of the clergy increased greatly throughout Europe. In those days the church rejected scientific forms of investigation, and it controlled all education. Religious beliefs, which were highly superstitious and demonological, came to dominate all aspects of life. Deviant behavior, particularly psychological abnormality, was seen as evidence of Satan's influence.

The Middle Ages were a time of great stress and anxiety—of war, urban uprisings, and plagues. People blamed the devil for these troubles and feared being possessed by him (Sluhovsky, 2011). Abnormal behavior apparently increased greatly during this period. In addition, there were outbreaks of *mass madness*, in which large numbers of people apparently shared *delusions* (absurd false beliefs) and *hallucinations* (imagined sights or sounds). In one such disorder, *tarantism* (also known as *Saint Vitus' dance*), groups of people would suddenly start to jump, dance, and go into convulsions (Corral-Corral & Corral-Corral, 2016; Sigerist, 1943). All were convinced that they had been bitten and possessed by a wolf spider, now called a tarantula, and

> How might Twitter, text messaging, Instagram, Facebook, the Internet, or other technologies facilitate current forms of mass madness?

they sought to cure their disorder by performing a dance called a tarantella. In another form of mass madness, *lycanthropy*, people thought they were possessed by wolves or other animals. They acted wolflike and imagined that fur was growing all over their bodies.

Not surprisingly, some of the earlier demonological treatments for psychological abnormality reemerged during the Middle Ages. Once again the key to the cure was to rid the person's body of the devil that possessed it. Exorcisms were revived, and clergymen, who generally were in charge of treatment during this period, would plead, chant, or pray to the devil or evil spirit (Harris, 2014; Sluhovsky, 2011, 2007). If these techniques did not work, they had others to try, some amounting to torture.

It was not until the Middle Ages drew to a close that demonology and its methods began to lose favor. Towns throughout Europe grew into cities, and government officials gained more power and took over nonreligious activities. Among their other responsibilities, they began to run hospitals and direct the care of people suffering from mental disorders. Medical views of abnormality gained favor once again, and many people with psychological disturbances received treatment in medical hospitals, such as the Trinity Hospital in England (Allderidge, 1979).

Bewitched or bewildered? A great fear of witchcraft swept Europe beginning in the 1300s and extending through the "enlightened" Renaissance. Tens of thousands of people, mostly women, were thought to have made a pact with the devil. Some appear to have had mental disorders, which caused them to act strangely (Zilboorg & Henry, 1941). This woman is being "dunked" repeatedly until she confesses to witchery.

The Renaissance and the Rise of Asylums

During the early part of the Renaissance, a period of flourishing cultural and scientific activity from about 1400 to 1700, demonological views of abnormality continued to decline. German physician Johann Weyer (1515–1588), the first physician to specialize in mental illness, believed that the mind was as susceptible to sickness as the body was. He is now considered the founder of the modern study of psychopathology.

The care of people with mental disorders continued to improve in this atmosphere. In England, such individuals might be kept at home while their families were aided financially by the local parish. Across Europe, religious shrines were devoted to the humane and loving treatment of people with mental disorders. Perhaps the best known of these shrines was at Gheel in Belgium. Beginning in the fifteenth century, people came to Gheel from all over the world for psychic healing. Local residents welcomed these pilgrims into their homes, and many stayed on to form the world's first "colony" of mental patients. Gheel was the forerunner of today's *community mental health programs*, and it continues to demonstrate that people with psychological disorders can respond to loving care and respectful treatment (Guarnieri, 2009; Aring, 1975, 1974). Many patients still live in foster homes there, interacting with other residents, until they recover.

The "crib" Outrageous devices and techniques, such as the "crib," were used in asylums, and some continued to be used even during the reforms of the nineteenth century.

THE CRIB

"Just tell me about the new continent. I don't give a damn what you've discovered about yourself."

Unfortunately, these improvements in care began to fade by the mid-sixteenth century. Government officials discovered that private homes and community residences could house only a small percentage of those with severe mental disorders and that medical hospitals were too few and too small. More and more, they converted hospitals and monasteries into **asylums,** institutions whose primary purpose was to care for people with mental illness. These institutions were begun with the intention that they would provide good care (Philo & Andrews, 2016; Kazano, 2012). Once the asylums started to overflow, however, they became virtual prisons where patients were held in filthy conditions and treated with unspeakable cruelty.

In 1547, for example, Bethlehem Hospital was given to the city of London by Henry VIII for the sole purpose of confining the mentally ill. In this asylum, patients bound in chains cried out for all to hear. The hospital even became a popular tourist attraction; people were eager to pay to look at the howling and gibbering inmates. The hospital's name, pronounced "Bedlam" by the local people, has come to mean a chaotic uproar (Arie, 2016; Selling, 1940).

The Nineteenth Century: Reform and Moral Treatment

As 1800 approached, the treatment of people with mental disorders began to improve once again. Historians usually point to La Bicêtre, an asylum in Paris for male patients, as the first site of asylum reform. In 1793, during the French Revolution, Philippe Pinel (1745–1826) was named the chief physician there. He argued that the patients were sick people whose illnesses should be treated with sympathy and kindness rather than chains and beatings (Pelletier & Davidson, 2015). He unchained the patients and allowed them to move freely about the hospital grounds; replaced the dark dungeons with sunny, well-ventilated rooms; and offered support and advice. Pinel's approach proved remarkably successful. Many patients who had been shut away for decades improved greatly over a short period of time and were released. Pinel later brought similar reforms to a mental hospital in Paris for female patients, La Salpetrière.

Meanwhile, an English Quaker named William Tuke (1732–1819) was bringing similar reforms to northern England. In 1796 he founded the York Retreat, a rural estate where about 30 mental patients lived as guests in quiet country houses and were treated with a combination of rest, talk, prayer, and manual work (Kibria & Metcalfe, 2016).

The Spread of Moral Treatment The methods of Pinel and Tuke, called **moral treatment** because they emphasized moral guidance and humane and respectful techniques, caught on throughout Europe and the United States. Patients with psychological problems were increasingly perceived as potentially productive human beings who deserve individual care, including discussions of their problems, useful activities, work, companionship, and quiet.

The person most responsible for the early spread of moral treatment in the United States was Benjamin Rush (1745–1813), an eminent physician at Pennsylvania Hospital who is now considered the father of American psychiatry. Limiting his practice to mental illness, Rush developed humane approaches to treatment (Hopkins, 2014; Grossman, 2013). For example, he required that the hospital hire intelligent and sensitive attendants to work closely with patients, reading and talking to them and taking them on regular walks. He also suggested that it would be therapeutic for doctors to give small gifts to their patients now and then.

Rush's work was influential, but it was a Boston schoolteacher named Dorothea Dix (1802–1887) who made humane care a public and political concern in the United States. From 1841 to 1881, Dix went from state legislature to state legislature and to Congress speaking of the horrors she had observed at asylums and calling for reform. Dix's campaign led to new laws and greater government funding to improve the treatment

asylum A type of institution that first became popular in the sixteenth century to provide care for persons with mental disorders. Most asylums became virtual prisons.

moral treatment A nineteenth-century approach to treating people with mental dysfunction that emphasized moral guidance and humane and respectful treatment.

state hospitals State-run public mental institutions in the United States.

somatogenic perspective The view that abnormal functioning has physical causes.

psychogenic perspective The view that the chief causes of abnormal functioning are psychological.

of people with mental disorders (Kazano, 2012; Davidson et al., 2010). Each state was made responsible for developing effective public mental hospitals, or **state hospitals,** all of which were intended to offer moral treatment. Similar hospitals were established throughout Europe.

The Decline of Moral Treatment By the 1850s, a number of mental hospitals throughout Europe and America reported success using moral approaches. By the end of that century, however, several factors led to a reversal of the moral treatment movement (Shepherd, 2016). One factor was the speed with which the movement had spread. As mental hospitals multiplied, severe money and staffing shortages developed, recovery rates declined, and overcrowding in the hospitals became a major problem. Another factor was the assumption behind moral treatment that all patients could be cured if treated with humanity and dignity. For some, this was indeed sufficient. Others, however, needed more effective treatments than any that had yet been developed. An additional factor contributing to the decline of moral treatment was the emergence of a new wave of prejudice against people with mental disorders. The public came to view them as strange and dangerous. Moreover, many of the patients entering public mental hospitals in the United States in the late nineteenth century were poor foreign immigrants, whom the public had little interest in helping.

By the early years of the twentieth century, the moral treatment movement had ground to a halt in both the United States and Europe. Public mental hospitals were providing only custodial care and ineffective medical treatments and were becoming more overcrowded every year. Long-term hospitalization became the rule once again.

Dance in a Madhouse, 1917 (litho)/Bellows, George Wesley (1882–1925)/ San Diego Museum of Art, USA/Bridgeman Images

Dance in a madhouse A popular feature of moral treatment was the "lunatic ball." Hospital officials would bring patients together to dance and enjoy themselves. One such ball is shown in this painting, *Dance in a Madhouse,* by George Bellows.

The Early Twentieth Century: The Somatogenic and Psychogenic Perspectives

As the moral movement was declining in the late 1800s, two opposing perspectives emerged and began to compete for the attention of clinicians: the **somatogenic perspective,** the view that abnormal psychological functioning has physical causes, and the **psychogenic perspective,** the view that the chief causes of abnormal functioning are psychological. These perspectives came into full bloom during the twentieth century.

The Somatogenic Perspective The somatogenic perspective has at least a 2,400-year history—remember Hippocrates' view that abnormal behavior resulted from brain disease and an imbalance of humors? Not until the late nineteenth century, however, did this perspective make a triumphant return and begin to gain wide acceptance.

Two factors were responsible for this rebirth. One was the work of a distinguished German researcher, Emil Kraepelin (1856–1926). In 1883, Kraepelin published an influential textbook arguing that physical factors, such as fatigue, are responsible for mental dysfunction. In addition, as you will see in Chapter 4, he developed the first modern system for classifying abnormal behavior, listing their physical causes and discussing their expected course (Kendler & Engstrom, 2016; Hoff, 2015).

New biological discoveries also triggered the rise of the somatogenic perspective. One of the most important discoveries was that an organic disease, *syphilis,* led to *general paresis,* an irreversible disorder with both mental symptoms such as delusions of grandeur and physical ones like paralysis (Hogebrug et al., 2013). In 1897, the German neurologist Richard von Krafft-Ebing (1840–1902) injected matter from syphilis sores

#MythBuster

Although it is popularly believed that a full moon is regularly accompanied by significant increases in crime, strange and abnormal behaviors, and admissions to mental hospitals, decades of research have failed to support this notion.

(Chaput et al., 2016; Bakalar, 2013; McLay et al., 2006)

The more things change . . . Two patients lie on a table in their cage-like ward at a modern-day mental hospital in Bekasi, Indonesia, while other patients live with a similar lack of privacy, activity, and sanitation in the wire-walled units behind them. Despite the passage of Indonesia's Mental Health Law in 2014, many patients still wind up living under conditions reminiscent of those that existed in some state hospitals throughout the United States well into the twentieth century.

into patients suffering from general paresis and found that none of the patients developed symptoms of syphilis. Their immunity could have been caused only by an earlier case of syphilis. Since all of his patients with general paresis were now immune to syphilis, Krafft-Ebing theorized that syphilis had been the cause of their general paresis. The work of Kraepelin and the new understanding of general paresis led many researchers and practitioners to suspect that physical factors were responsible for many mental disorders, perhaps all of them.

Despite the general optimism, biological approaches yielded mostly disappointing results throughout the first half of the twentieth century. Although many medical treatments were developed for patients in mental hospitals during that time, most of the techniques failed to work. Physicians tried tooth extraction, tonsillectomy, hydrotherapy (alternating hot and cold baths), and lobotomy, a surgical cutting of certain nerve fibers in the brain. Even worse, biological views and claims led, in some circles, to proposals for immoral solutions such as *eugenic sterilization,* the elimination (through medical or other means) of individuals' ability to reproduce (see **Table 1-1**). Not until the 1950s, when a number of effective medications were finally discovered, did the somatogenic perspective truly begin to pay off for patients.

The Psychogenic Perspective The late 1800s also saw the emergence of the psychogenic perspective, the view that the chief causes of abnormal functioning are often psychological. This view, too, had a long history, but it did not gain much of a following until studies of *hypnotism* demonstrated its potential.

Hypnotism is a procedure in which a person is placed in a trancelike mental state during which he or she becomes extremely suggestible. It was used to help treat psychological disorders as far back as 1778, when an Austrian physician named Friedrich Anton Mesmer (1734–1815) established a clinic in Paris. His patients suf-

| TABLE: 1-1 |

Eugenics and Mental Disorders

Year	Event
1896	Connecticut became the first state in the United States to prohibit persons with mental disorders from marrying.
1896–1933	Every state in the United States passed a law prohibiting marriage by persons with mental disorders.
1907	Indiana became the first state to pass a bill calling for people with mental disorders, as well as criminals and other "defectives," to undergo sterilization.
1927	The U.S. Supreme Court ruled that eugenic sterilization was constitutional.
1907–1945	Approximately 45,000 Americans were sterilized under eugenic sterilization laws; 21,000 of them were patients in state mental hospitals.
1929–1932	Denmark, Norway, Sweden, Finland, and Iceland passed eugenic sterilization laws.
1933	Germany passed a eugenic sterilization law, under which 375,000 people were sterilized by 1940.
1940	Nazi Germany began to use "proper gases" to kill people with mental disorders; 70,000 or more people were killed in less than two years.

Information from: Kosters et al., 2015; Fischer, 2012; Whitaker, 2002.

fered from *hysterical disorders,* mysterious bodily ailments that had no apparent physical basis. Mesmer had his patients sit in a darkened room filled with music; then he appeared, dressed in a colorful costume, and touched the troubled area of each patient's body with a special rod. A surprising number of patients seemed to be helped by this treatment, called *mesmerism* (Deeley, 2017; Ellis, 2015). Their pain, numbness, or paralysis disappeared. Several scientists believed that Mesmer was inducing a trancelike state in his patients and that this state was causing their symptoms to disappear. The treatment was so controversial, however, that eventually Mesmer was banished from Paris.

It was not until years after Mesmer died that many researchers had the courage to investigate his procedure, later called *hypnotism* (from *hypnos,* the Greek word for "sleep"), and its effects on hysterical disorders. The experiments of two physicians practicing in the city of Nancy in France, Hippolyte-Marie Bernheim (1840–1919) and Ambroise-Auguste Liébault (1823–1904), showed that hysterical disorders could actually be induced in otherwise normal people while they were under the influence of hypnosis. That is, the physicians could make normal people experience deafness, paralysis, blindness, or numbness by means of hypnotic suggestion—and they could remove these artificial symptoms by the same means. Thus they established that a *mental* process—hypnotic suggestion—could both cause and cure even a physical dysfunction. Leading scientists concluded that hysterical disorders were largely psychological in origin, and the psychogenic perspective rose in popularity.

Among those who studied the effects of hypnotism on hysterical disorders was Josef Breuer (1842–1925) of Vienna. Breuer, a physician, discovered that his patients sometimes awoke free of hysterical symptoms after speaking candidly under hypnosis about past upsetting events. During the 1890s, Breuer was joined in his work by another Viennese physician, Sigmund Freud (1856–1939). As you will see in Chapter 3, Freud's work eventually led him to develop the theory of **psychoanalysis,** which holds that many forms of abnormal and normal psychological functioning are psychogenic (Nicholson et al., 2016). In particular, Freud believed that *unconscious* psychological processes are at the root of such functioning.

Hypnotism update Hypnotism, the procedure that opened the door for the psychogenic perspective, continues to influence many areas of modern life, including psychotherapy, entertainment, and law enforcement. Here, a forensic clinician uses hypnosis to help a witness recall the details of a crime. Recent research has clarified, however, that hypnotic procedures are as capable of creating false memories as they are of uncovering real memories.

Freud also developed the *technique* of psychoanalysis, a form of discussion in which clinicians help troubled people gain insight into their unconscious psychological processes. He believed that such insight, even without hypnotic procedures, would help the patients overcome their psychological problems. Freud and his followers offered psychoanalytic treatment to patients in their offices for sessions of approximately an hour—a format of treatment now known as *outpatient therapy.* By the early twentieth century, psychoanalytic theory and treatment were widely accepted throughout the Western world.

Recent Decades and Current Trends

IT WOULD HARDLY BE ACCURATE to say that we now live in a period of great enlightenment about or dependable treatment of mental disorders. In fact, surveys have found that 43 percent of respondents believe that people bring mental disorders on themselves, 31 percent consider such disorders to be a sign of personal weakness, and 35 percent believe the disorders are caused by sinful behavior (Roper, 2017; Stuber et al., 2014; NMHA, 1999). Nevertheless, there have been major changes over the past 60 years in the ways clinicians understand and treat abnormal functioning. There are more theories and types of treatment, more research studies, more information, and—perhaps because of those increases—more disagreements about abnormal functioning today than at any time in the past.

psychoanalysis Either the theory or the treatment of abnormal mental functioning that emphasizes unconscious psychological forces as the cause of psychopathology.

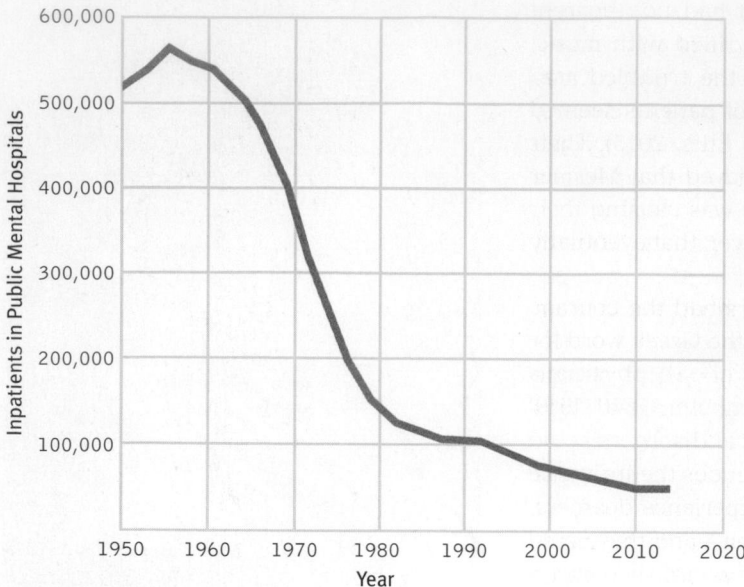

FIGURE 1-1

The Impact of Deinstitutionalization

The number of patients (around 42,000) now hospitalized in public mental hospitals in the United States is a small fraction of the number hospitalized in 1955. (Information from: Smith & Milazzo-Sayre, 2014; Torrey, 2001; Lang, 1999.)

psychotropic medications Drugs that mainly affect the brain and reduce many symptoms of mental dysfunction.

deinstitutionalization The practice, begun in the 1960s, of releasing hundreds of thousands of patients from public mental hospitals.

private psychotherapy An arrangement in which a person directly pays a therapist for counseling services.

prevention Interventions aimed at deterring mental disorders before they can develop.

positive psychology The study and enhancement of positive feelings, traits, and abilities.

How Are People with Severe Disturbances Cared For?

In the 1950s, researchers discovered a number of new **psychotropic medications**—drugs that primarily affect the brain and reduce many symptoms of mental dysfunction. They included the first *antipsychotic drugs,* which correct extremely confused and distorted thinking; *antidepressant drugs,* which lift the mood of depressed people; and *antianxiety drugs,* which reduce tension and worry.

When given these drugs, many patients who had spent years in mental hospitals began to show signs of improvement. Hospital administrators, encouraged by these results and pressured by a growing public outcry over the terrible conditions in public mental hospitals, began to discharge patients almost immediately.

Since the discovery of these medications, mental health professionals in most of the developed nations of the world have followed a policy of **deinstitutionalization,** releasing hundreds of thousands of patients from public mental hospitals. On any given day in 1955, close to 600,000 people were confined in public mental institutions across the United States (see **Figure 1-1**). Today the daily patient population in the same kinds of hospitals is around 42,000 (Smith & Milazzo-Sayre, 2014). In addition, some 58,000 people receive treatment in *private* psychiatric hospitals, care that is paid for by the patients themselves and/or their insurance companies. On average, the private facilities offer more pleasant surroundings and more favorable staff–patient ratios than the public ones.

Without question, outpatient care has now become the primary mode of treatment for people with severe psychological disturbances as well as for those with more moderate problems. When severely disturbed people do need institutionalization these days, they are usually hospitalized for a short period of time. Ideally, they are then provided with outpatient psychotherapy and medication in community programs and residences (Stein et al., 2015).

Chapters 3 and 15 will look more closely at this recent emphasis on community care for people with severe psychological disturbances—a philosophy called the *community mental health approach*. The approach has been helpful for many patients, but too few community programs are available to address current needs in the United States (Dixon & Schwarz, 2014). As a result, hundreds of thousands of persons with severe disturbances fail to make lasting recoveries, and they shuttle back and forth between the mental hospital and the community. After release from the hospital, they at best receive minimal care and often wind up living in decrepit rooming houses or on the streets. At least 100,000 people with such disturbances are homeless on any given day; another 440,000 are inmates of jails and prisons (Allison et al., 2017; NAMI, 2016). Their abandonment is truly a national disgrace.

How Are People with Less Severe Disturbances Treated?

The treatment picture for people with moderate psychological disturbances has been more positive than that for people with severe disorders. Since the 1950s, outpatient care has continued to be the preferred mode of treatment for them, and the number and types of facilities that offer such care have expanded to meet the need.

Before the 1950s, almost all outpatient care took the form of **private psychotherapy,** in which individuals meet with a self-employed therapist for counseling services.

Since the 1950s, most health insurance plans have expanded coverage to include private psychotherapy, so that it is now also widely available to people of all incomes. Today, outpatient therapy is also offered in a number of less expensive settings, such as community mental health centers, crisis intervention centers, family service centers, and other social service agencies. Surveys suggest that around 60 percent of people with psychological disorders in the United States receive treatment in the course of a year (APA, 2016).

Outpatient treatments are also becoming available for more and more kinds of problems. When Freud and his colleagues first began to practice, most of their patients suffered from anxiety or depression. Almost half of today's clients suffer from those same problems, but people with other kinds of disorders are also receiving therapy. In addition, at least 20 percent of clients enter therapy because of milder problems in living—problems with marital, family, job, peer, school, or community relationships (Ten Have et al., 2013).

Yet another change in outpatient care since the 1950s has been the development of programs devoted exclusively to specific psychological problems. We now have, for example, suicide prevention centers, substance abuse programs, eating disorder programs, phobia clinics, and sexual dysfunction programs. Clinicians in these programs have the kind of expertise that can be acquired only by concentration in a single area.

A Growing Emphasis on Preventing Disorders and Promoting Mental Health

Although the community mental health approach has often failed to address the needs of people with severe disorders, it has given rise to an important principle of mental health care—**prevention** (Costello, 2016). Rather than wait for psychological disorders to occur, many of today's community programs try to correct the social conditions that underlie psychological problems (poverty or violence in the community, for example) and to help individuals who are at risk for developing emotional problems (for example, teenage mothers or the children of people with severe psychological disorders). As you will see later, community prevention programs are not always successful, but they have grown in number, offering great promise as the ultimate form of intervention.

Prevention programs have been further energized in the past few decades by the field of psychology's ever-growing interest in **positive psychology** (Gander, Proyer, &

LHB Photo / Alamy

From Juilliard to the streets Nathaniel Ayers, subject of the book and movie *The Soloist*, plays his violin on the streets of Los Angeles while living as a homeless person in 2005. Once a promising musical student at the Juilliard School in New York, Ayers developed schizophrenia and eventually found himself without treatment and without a home. Tens of thousands of people with severe mental disorders are currently homeless.

Landon Nordeman/Redux

Green spaces and mental health A family hangs out on the grass at High Line Park, an area built several years ago on an unused elevated train track in New York City. Positive psychology research has found that people who live in urban areas feel less distress and report higher life satisfaction if they reside in greener areas of their cities (White et al., 2013). Small wonder then that New Yorkers, Londoners, and other city residents with easy access to parks and green spaces say that they have a better quality of life than those living without them.

Ruch, 2016; Seligman & Fowler, 2011). Positive psychology is the study and enhancement of positive feelings such as optimism and happiness, positive traits like hard work and wisdom, positive abilities such as social skills and other talents, and group-directed virtues, including altruism and tolerance (see *InfoCentral* on the next page).

> Why do you think it has taken psychologists so long to start studying positive behaviors?

While researchers study and learn more about positive psychology in the laboratory, clinical practitioners with this orientation are teaching people coping skills that may help to protect them from stress and adversity and encouraging them to become more involved in personally meaningful activities and relationships—thus helping to prevent mental disorders (Sergeant & Mongrain, 2014).

Multicultural Psychology

We are, without question, a society of multiple cultures, races, and languages. Members of racial and ethnic minority groups in the United States collectively make up 39 percent of the population, a percentage that is expected to grow to more than 50 percent by the year 2044 (KFF, 2016; U.S. Census Bureau, 2015). This change is due in part to shifts in immigration trends and also to higher birth rates among minority groups in the United States (NVSR, 2016, 2010).

In response to this growing diversity, an area of study called **multicultural psychology** has emerged. Multicultural psychologists seek to understand how culture, race, ethnicity, gender, and similar factors affect behavior and thought and how people of different cultures, races, and genders may differ psychologically (Alegría et al., 2016, 2013, 2010). As you will see throughout this book, the field of multicultural psychology has begun to have a powerful effect on our understanding and treatment of abnormal behavior.

The Increasing Influence of Insurance Coverage

According to the Census Bureau, 65 percent of Americans have *private* health insurance, purchased directly or through an employer, while the remainder are either uninsured or enrolled in a *public* insurance program such as Medicare, Medicaid, or military insurance. So many people now seek mental health services that most private and public insurance programs have changed their coverage for these patients in recent decades (Inglehart, 2016). The dominant form of insurance now consists of **managed care programs**—programs in which the insurance company determines such key issues as which therapists its clients may choose, the cost of sessions, and the number of sessions for which a client may be reimbursed (Bowers, Owen, & Heller, 2016).

Managed care coverage for mental health treatment follows the same basic principles as coverage for medical treatment, including a limited pool of practitioners from which patients can choose, preapproval of treatment by the insurance company, strict standards for judging whether problems and treatments qualify for reimbursement, and ongoing reviews. In the mental health realm, both therapists and clients typically dislike managed care programs (Decker, 2016; Lustig et al., 2013). They fear that the programs inevitably shorten therapy (often for the worse), unfairly favor treatments whose results are not always lasting (for example, drug therapy), pose a special hardship for those with severe mental disorders, and result in treatments determined by insurance companies rather than by therapists (Bowers et al., 2016).

A key problem with insurance coverage—both managed care and other kinds of insurance programs—is that reimbursements for mental disorders tend to be lower than those for physical disorders. This places persons with psychological difficulties at a distinct disadvantage (McGuire, 2016; Sipe et al., 2015). Thus, in 2008, the U.S. Congress passed a federal *parity* law that directed insurance companies to provide equal coverage for mental and physical problems, and in 2014 the mental health provisions

Positive psychology in action Often, positive psychology and multicultural psychology work together. Here, for example, two young girls come together as one at the end of a "slave reconciliation" walk by 400 people in Maryland. The walk was intended to promote racial understanding and to help Americans overcome the lasting psychological effects of slavery.

multicultural psychology The field that examines the impact of culture, race, ethnicity, and gender on behaviors and thoughts, and focuses on how such factors may influence the origin, nature, and treatment of abnormal behavior.

managed care program Health care coverage in which the insurance company largely controls the nature, scope, and cost of medical or psychological services.

HAPPINESS

Positive psychology is the study of positive feelings, traits, and abilities. A better understanding of constructive functioning enables clinicians to better promote psychological wellness. **Happiness** is the positive psychology topic currently receiving the most attention. Many, but far from all, people are happy. In fact, only **one-third** of adults declare themselves "very happy." Let's take a look at some of today's leading facts, figures, and notions about happiness.

WHO Is "Very Happy?"

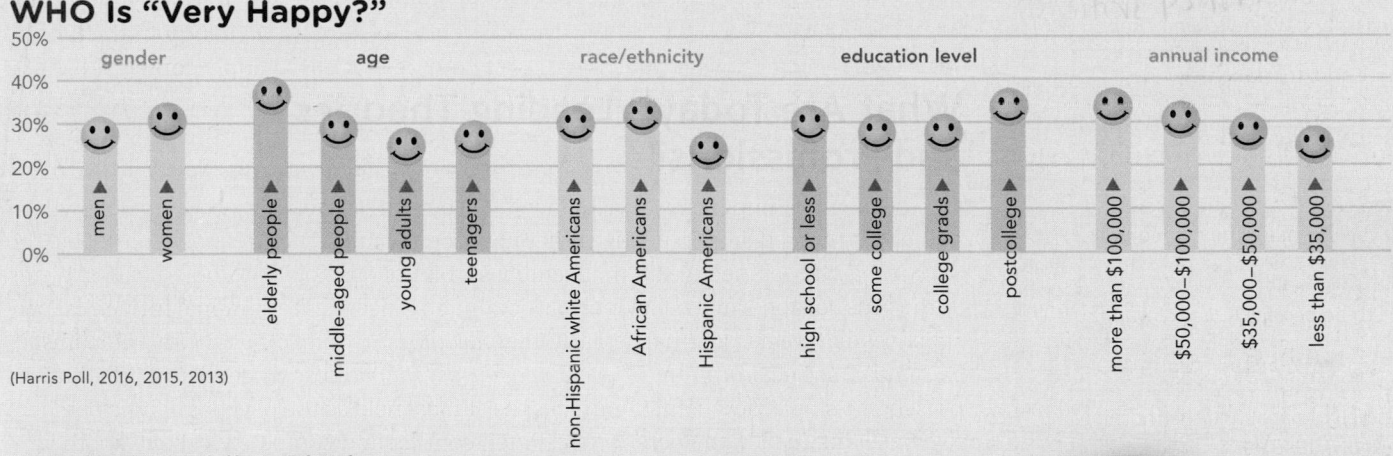

gender — age — race/ethnicity — education level — annual income

men, women, elderly people, middle-aged people, young adults, teenagers, non-Hispanic white Americans, African Americans, Hispanic Americans, high school or less, some college, college grads, postcollege, more than $100,000, $50,000–$100,000, $35,000–$50,000, less than $35,000

(Harris Poll, 2016, 2015, 2013)

Happiness Building Blocks

Are people born with a happy disposition? Or do their surroundings and life circumstances make them more or less happy? Researchers of this **nature-versus-nurture** question have learned that both sets of factors **interact** to determine one's degree of happiness. But the factors have different degrees of impact.

Life events **40%**

Values (family, friends, community, work) **12%**
(Joseph, 2015; Brooks, 2013)

Genes **48%**

Who Tends to Be *Happier*?

Unashamed people	Guilt-ridden people
Peaceful people	Angry people
Extroverts	Introverts
Regular church attenders	Church nonattenders

(Harris Poll, 2016, 2015; Brooks, 2013; DePaulo, 2013; *The Economist*, 2010)

The Pursuit of Happiness

People tend to pursue a happy life. For some, that means pursuit of a **pleasant life**—filled with as many pleasures as possible. Others pursue an **engaging life**, characterized by satisfaction in work, parenting, love, and leisure. Still others pursue a **meaningful life**—recognizing and using their strengths in the service of others. (Seligman, 2012, 2002)

WHAT Do Happy People Do?

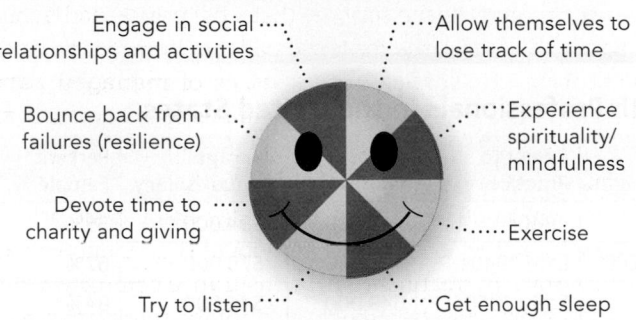

- Engage in social relationships and activities
- Allow themselves to lose track of time
- Bounce back from failures (resilience)
- Experience spirituality/mindfulness
- Devote time to charity and giving
- Exercise
- Try to listen
- Get enough sleep

(Harris Poll, 2016, 2015; Bratskeir, 2013)

Non-online Social Contact and Happiness

The more social contact, the happier we are—up to a point!

People Who Are Happy

| 0 hrs | 1 hr | 3 hrs | 6 hrs | 9 hrs |
| 30% | 34% | 43% | 53% | 43% |

Daily Social Contact (face-to-face)
(Rahim, 2017; Crabtree, 2011)

Work and Happiness

Certain jobs have a higher percentage of happy people than others.

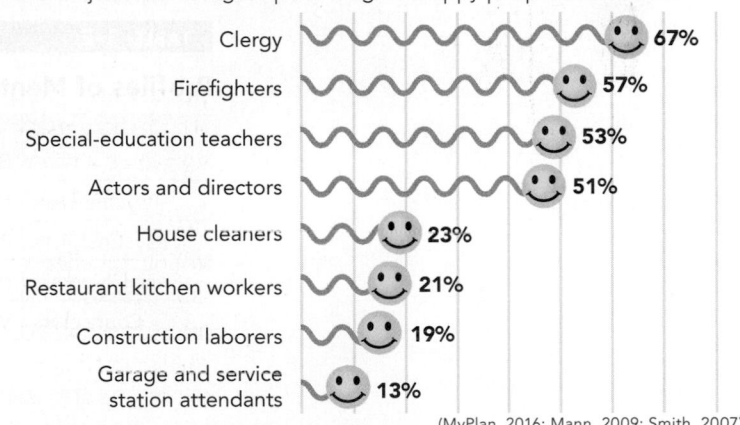

Clergy	67%
Firefighters	57%
Special-education teachers	53%
Actors and directors	51%
House cleaners	23%
Restaurant kitchen workers	21%
Construction laborers	19%
Garage and service station attendants	13%

(MyPlan, 2016; Mann, 2009; Smith, 2007)

Marriage and Happiness

Married people are, on average, a bit happier than people with a different marital status.

| Currently married **3.4** | Always single **3.2** | Currently divorced **2.9** | Currently widowed **2.9** |

(De Neve & Ward, 2017; Harris Poll, 2016: DePaulo, 2013)

of the Affordable Care Act (the ACA)—referred to colloquially as "Obamacare"—went into effect and extended the reach of the earlier law. The ACA designated mental health care as 1 of 10 types of "essential health benefits" that *must* be provided by all insurers. The changes in federal leadership brought about by the election of 2016 are expected to lead to many changes in or even the repeal of the ACA. Currently, it is not clear how such changes will affect the decade-long efforts to achieve mental health insurance parity.

What Are Today's Leading Theories and Professions?

One of the most important developments in the clinical field has been the growth of numerous theoretical perspectives that now coexist in the field. Before the 1950s, the *psychoanalytic* perspective, with its emphasis on unconscious psychological problems as the cause of abnormal behavior, was dominant. Since then, additional influential perspectives have emerged, particularly the *biological, cognitive-behavioral, humanistic-existential, sociocultural,* and *developmental psychopathology* schools of thought. At present, no single viewpoint dominates the clinical field as the psychoanalytic perspective once did. In fact, the perspectives often conflict and compete with one another.

In addition, a variety of professionals now offer help to people with psychological problems. Before the 1950s, psychotherapy was offered only by *psychiatrists,* physicians who complete three to four additional years of training after medical school (a *residency*) in the treatment of abnormal mental functioning. After World War II, however, with millions of soldiers returning home to countries throughout North America and Europe, the demand for mental health services expanded so rapidly that other professional groups had to step in to fill the need.

Among those other groups are *clinical psychologists*—professionals who earn a doctorate in clinical psychology by completing four to five years of graduate training in abnormal functioning and its treatment as well as a one-year internship in a mental health setting. Psychotherapy and related services are also provided by *counseling psychologists, educational and school psychologists, psychiatric nurses, marriage therapists, family therapists,* and—the largest group—*clinical social workers* (see **Table 1-2**).

TABLE: 1-2

Profiles of Mental Health Professionals in the United States

	Degree	Began to Practice	Current Number	Average Annual Salary	Percent Female
Psychiatrists	MD, DO	1840s	49,000	$194,000	35%
Psychologists	PhD, PsyD, EdD	Late 1940s	188,000	$73,000	67%
Social Workers	MSW, DSW	Early 1950s	649,000	$46,000	84%
Counselors	Various	Early 1950s	570,000	$45,000	71%

Information from: BLS, 2016; DPE, 2016; Salary.com, 2016; APA, 2015; Block, 2015; Pallardy, 2015.

Each of these specialties has its own graduate training program. Theoretically, each conducts therapy in a distinctive way, but in reality clinicians from the various specialties often use similar techniques.

A related development in the study and treatment of mental disorders since World War II has been the growth of effective research. *Clinical researchers* have worked to determine which concepts best explain and predict abnormal behavior, which treatments are most effective, and what kinds of changes may be required. Well-trained

Preventing an even worse outcome Children attend activities at this psychological support and education center in Damascus, Syria, in 2016. The center was set up, on the advice of mental health, medical, and education advisers, to help prevent or at least minimize the psychological and physical problems being experienced by millions of Syrian children caught up in the ongoing horrors of the country's civil war.

clinical researchers conduct studies in universities, medical schools, laboratories, mental hospitals, mental health centers, and other clinical settings throughout the world. Their work has produced important discoveries and has changed many of our ideas about abnormal psychological functioning.

Technology and Mental Health

The breathtaking rate of technological change that characterizes today's world has begun to have significant effects—both positive and negative—on the mental health field, and it will undoubtedly affect the field even more in the coming years.

Our digital world provides new triggers for abnormal behavior (Cottle, 2016; Turkle, 2015). As you'll see in Chapter 12, for example, many individuals who grapple with gambling disorder have found the ready availability of Internet gambling to be all too inviting. Similarly, the Internet, texting, and social media have become convenient tools for those who wish to stalk or bully others, express sexual exhibitionism, or pursue pedophilic desires. Likewise, some clinicians believe that violent video games may contribute to the development of antisocial behavior. And, in the opinion of many clinicians, constant texting, tweeting, and Internet browsing may become an addictive behavior or may help lead to shorter attention spans.

A number of clinicians also worry that social networking can contribute to psychological dysfunction in certain cases. On the positive side, research indicates that, on average, social media users are particularly likely to maintain close relationships, receive social support, be trusting, and lead active lives (ACOG, 2016; Rainie et al., 2011). But, on the negative side, there is research suggesting that social networking sites may increase peer pressure and social anxiety in some adolescents (Houston, 2016; Nesi & Prinstein, 2015). The sites may, for example, cause some people to develop fears that others in their network will exclude them socially. Similarly, such sites may facilitate shy or socially anxious people's withdrawal from valuable face-to-face relationships.

#CheckingIn

11 Percentage of people who check their smartphones every few minutes.

41 Percentage who check their smartphones a few times each hour.

20 Percentage who check their smartphones once an hour.

4 Percentage who check their smartphones once a day at most.

(Gallup, 2015)

"Looks like another case of someone over forty trying to understand Snapchat."

In addition, the face of clinical treatment is constantly changing in our fast-moving digital world. For example, **telemental health**, the use of various technologies to deliver mental health services without the therapist being physically present, is growing by leaps and bounds (Comer et al., 2017; Maheu, Drude, & Wright, 2017). As you'll see in Chapter 3, telemental health takes such forms as long-distance therapy between clients and therapists using videoconferencing, therapy offered by computer programs, and Internet-based support groups. And literally thousands of smartphone apps are devoted to relaxing people, cheering them up, giving them feel-good advice, helping them track their shifting moods and thoughts, or otherwise improving their psychological states.

> What kinds of problems might result from the growing availability and use of mental health apps in today's world?

Similarly, countless Web sites offer mental health information. Unfortunately, along with this wealth of online information comes an enormous amount of misinformation and so-called fake news about psychological problems and their treatments, offered by persons and sites that are far from knowledgeable. And there are numerous antitreatment Web sites that try to guide people away from seeking help for their psychological problems. In later chapters, for example, you will read about pro-anorexia and pro-suicide Web sites and their dangerous influences. Clearly, the impact of technological change presents formidable challenges for clinicians and researchers alike.

Moving Forward

By **examining the responses** of past societies to abnormal behavior, we can better understand the roots of our present views and treatments and the impressive progress that the clinical field has made. At the same time, we must recognize the many problems in the field today. Without question, our current understanding of abnormal behavior represents a work in progress. The clinical field's most important insights, investigations, and changes are yet to come.

How, then, should you proceed in your study of abnormal psychology? To begin with, you need to learn about the basic tools and perspectives used by today's scientists and practitioners. This is the task we turn to in the next several chapters. Later chapters will then help you to appreciate in depth the major categories of psychological abnormality as well as the leading explanations and treatments for each of them. In the final chapter, you will see how the science of abnormal psychology and its professionals interact with legal, social, and other institutions in our world.

telemental health The use of digital technologies to deliver mental health services without the therapist being physically present.

♀... SUMMING UP

» **What Is Psychological Abnormality?** Abnormal functioning is generally considered to be *deviant, distressful, dysfunctional,* and *dangerous.* Behavior must also be considered in the context in which it occurs, however, and the concept of abnormality depends on the *norms* and *values* of the society in question. *pp. 2–6*

» **What Is Treatment?** *Therapy* is a systematic process for helping people overcome their psychological difficulties. It typically requires a *patient,* a *therapist,* and a *series of therapeutic contacts. pp. 6–7*

» **How Was Abnormality Viewed and Treated in the Past?** The history of psychological disorders stretches back to ancient times. Prehistoric societies apparently viewed abnormal behavior as the work of evil spirits. There is evidence that Stone Age cultures used *trephination,* a primitive form of brain surgery, to treat abnormal behavior. People of early societies also sought to drive out evil spirits by *exorcism. pp. 7–8*

GREEKS AND ROMANS Physicians of the Greek and Roman empires offered more enlightened explanations of mental disorders. Hippocrates believed that abnormal behavior was caused by an imbalance of the four bodily fluids, or *humors*. *p. 8*

THE MIDDLE AGES In the Middle Ages, Europeans returned to demonological explanations of abnormal behavior. The clergy was very influential and held that mental disorders were the work of the devil. As the Middle Ages drew to a close, such explanations and treatments began to decline, and people with mental disorders were increasingly treated in hospitals instead of by the clergy. *pp. 8–9*

THE RENAISSANCE Care of people with mental disorders continued to improve during the early part of the Renaissance. Certain religious shrines became dedicated to the humane treatment of such individuals. By the middle of the sixteenth century, however, persons with mental disorders were being warehoused in *asylums*. *pp. 9–10*

THE NINETEENTH CENTURY Care of those with mental disorders started to improve again in the nineteenth century. In Paris, Philippe Pinel started the movement toward *moral treatment*. In the United States, Dorothea Dix spearheaded a movement to ensure legal rights and protection for people with mental disorders and to establish state hospitals for their care. Unfortunately, the moral treatment movement disintegrated by the late nineteenth century, and mental hospitals again became warehouses where inmates received minimal care. *pp. 10–11*

THE EARLY TWENTIETH CENTURY The turn of the twentieth century saw the return of the *somatogenic perspective*, the view that abnormal psychological functioning is caused primarily by physical factors. The same period saw the rise of the *psychogenic perspective*, the view that the chief causes of abnormal functioning are psychological. Sigmund Freud's psychogenic approach, *psychoanalysis*, eventually gained wide acceptance and influenced future generations of clinicians. *pp. 11–13*

» Recent Decades and Current Trends There have been major changes over the past 50 years in the understanding and treatment of abnormal functioning. In the 1950s, researchers discovered a number of new *psychotropic medications*, drugs that mainly affect the brain and reduce many symptoms of mental dysfunction. Their success contributed to a policy of *deinstitutionalization*, under which hundreds of thousands of patients were released from public mental hospitals. In addition, *outpatient treatment* has become the primary approach for most people with mental disorders, both mild and severe; *prevention programs* are growing in number and influence; the field of *multicultural psychology* has begun to influence how clinicians view and treat abnormality; and *insurance coverage* is having a significant impact on the way treatment is conducted.

It is also the case that a variety of *perspectives* and *professionals* have come to operate in the field of abnormal psychology, and many well-trained *clinical researchers* now investigate the field's theories and treatments. And finally, the remarkable *technological advances* of recent times have affected the mental health field. *pp. 13–20*

Visit *LaunchPad*
to access the e-Book, Clinical Choices, videos, activities, and LearningCurve, as well as study aids including flashcards, FAQs, and research exercises.

LaunchPad
macmillan learning

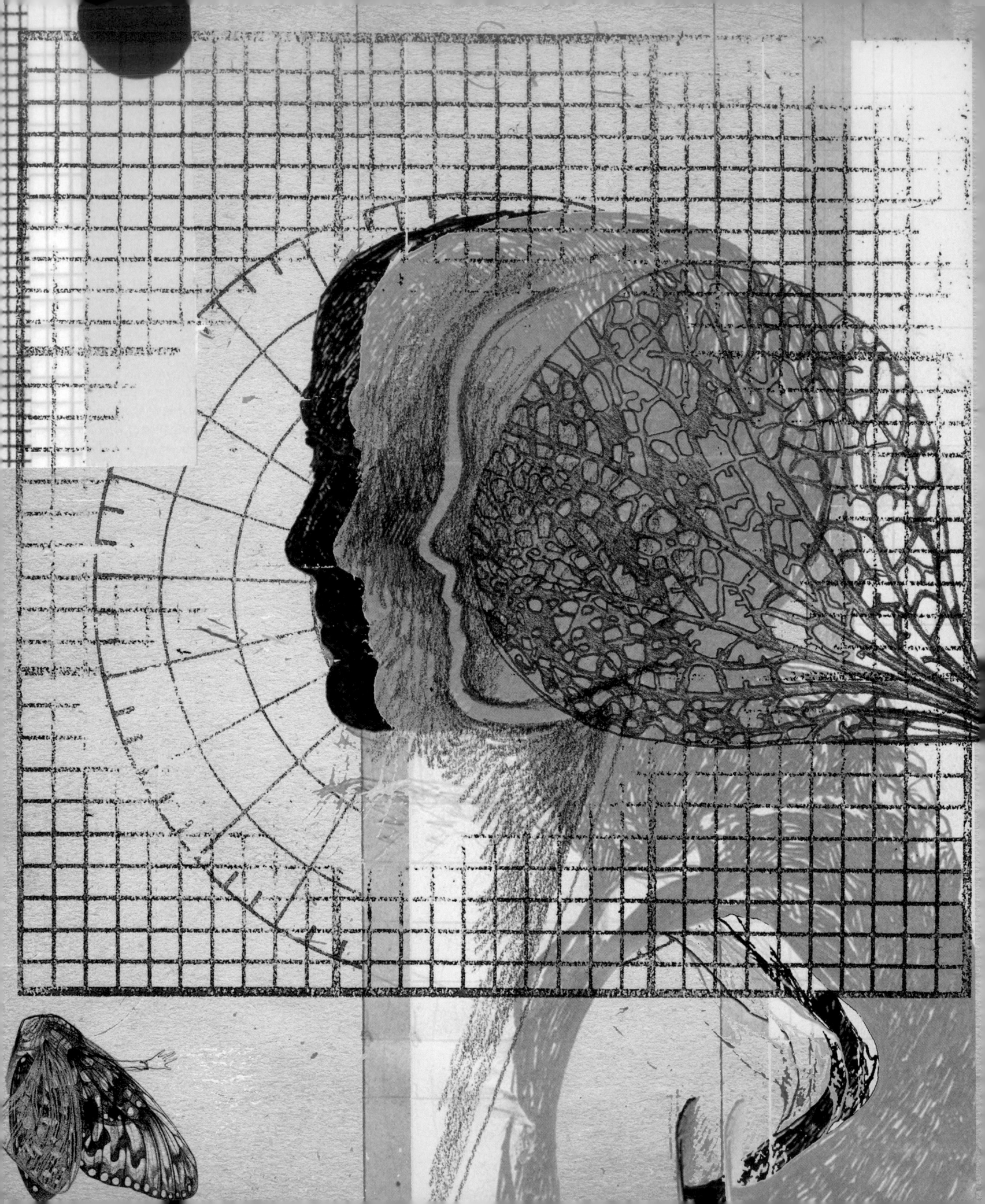

♀...Research in Abnormal Psychology

"Woman may be said to be an inferior man."
— Aristotle, 350 BC

"The 'telephone' has too many shortcomings to be seriously considered as a means of communication."
— Western Union, 1876

"The horse is here to stay but the automobile is only a novelty—a fad."
— Horace Rackham, Michigan Savings Bank, 1903

"Guitar music is on the way out."
— Decca Recording Company, 1962

"There is no reason for any individual to have a computer in their home."
— Ken Olsen, Digital Equipment Corp., 1977

"The cloning of mammals . . . is biologically impossible."
— James McGrath and Davor Solter, genetic researchers, 1984

"The Internet will soon . . . catastrophically collapse."
— Robert Metcalfe, inventor of Ethernet, 1995

"Websites will never replace newspapers."
— *Newsweek*, 1995

Each of these statements was once accepted as gospel. Had their accuracy not been tested, had they been judged on the basis of conventional wisdom alone, had new ideas not been proposed and investigated, human knowledge and progress would have been severely limited. What enabled thinkers to move beyond such misperceptions? The answer, quite simply, is research, the systematic search for facts through the use of careful observations and investigations.

Research is the key to accuracy in all fields of study; it is particularly important in abnormal psychology because a wrong belief in this field can lead to great suffering. Consider, for example, schizophrenia and the treatment procedure known as the lobotomy. Schizophrenia is a severe disorder that causes people to lose contact with reality. Their thoughts, perceptions, and emotions become distorted and disorganized, and their behavior may be bizarre and withdrawn. For the first half of the twentieth century, this condition was attributed to schizophrenogenic ("schizophrenia-causing") mothers—women described as cold, domineering, and unresponsive to their children's needs. As you will see in Chapter 14, this widely held belief turned out to be wrong (Isaac, 2016; Singh et al., 2014).

During the same era, practitioners developed a surgical procedure that supposedly cured schizophrenia. In this procedure, called a lobotomy, a pointed instrument was inserted into the frontal lobe of the brain and rotated, destroying much brain tissue (Neumaier et al., 2016). Early clinical reports described lobotomized patients as showing near-miraculous improvement. This impression, too, turned out to be wrong, although the mistake wasn't discovered until tens of thousands of people had been

nomothetic understanding A general understanding of the nature, causes, and treatments of abnormal functioning, in the form of laws or principles.

scientific method The process of systematically gathering and evaluating information, through careful observations, to understand a phenomenon.

hypothesis A hunch or prediction that certain variables are related in certain ways.

lobotomized. Far from curing schizophrenia, lobotomies caused irreversible brain damage that left many patients withdrawn and even stuporous.

These errors underscore the importance of scientific research in abnormal psychology. Only by fully testing a theory or technique on representative groups of individuals can clinicians evaluate the accuracy, effectiveness, and safety of their ideas and techniques. Until clinical researchers conducted properly designed studies, millions of parents, already heartbroken by their children's schizophrenia, were additionally labeled as the primary cause of the disorder, and countless people with schizophrenia, already debilitated by their symptoms, were made permanently apathetic and spiritless by a lobotomy. ■

> Can you think of beliefs that were once accepted as gospel but, as a result of scientific research, eventually were proven to be false?

What Do Clinical Researchers Do?

CLINICAL RESEARCHERS, ALSO CALLED clinical scientists, try to discover universal laws, or principles, of abnormal psychological functioning. They search for a general, or **nomothetic,** understanding of the nature, causes, and treatments of abnormality. They do not typically assess, diagnose, or treat individual clients; that is the job of clinical practitioners, who seek an *idiographic,* or individualistic, understanding of abnormal behavior. You will read about the work of practitioners in later chapters.

To gain nomothetic insights, clinical researchers, like scientists in other fields, use the **scientific method**—that is, they collect and evaluate information through careful observations. These observations in turn enable them to pinpoint and explain relationships between *variables*. Simply stated, a variable is any characteristic or event that can vary, whether from time to time, from place to place, or from person to person. Age, sex, and race are human variables. So are eye color, occupation, and social status. Clinical researchers are interested in variables such as childhood upsets, present life experiences, moods, social functioning, and responses to treatment. They try to determine whether two or more such variables change together and whether a change in one variable causes a change in another. Will the death of a parent cause a child to become depressed? If so, will a given treatment reduce that depression?

Flawed study, gigantic impact Outside a court hearing in Beijing on *conversion*, or *reparative*, *therapy*, an LGBTQ activist protests by pretending to inject a patient with a giant syringe. Conversion therapy, a now widely discredited psychological treatment to help gay persons change their sexual orientation, was positively received in a number of clinical circles after its development in the late 1990s. However, in 2012, Robert Spitzer, one of the world's most respected psychiatric researchers, offered a public apology to the gay community for an influential and seemingly supportive study that he had published in 2003. Spitzer called his earlier study on conversion therapy both fatally flawed and morally wrong.

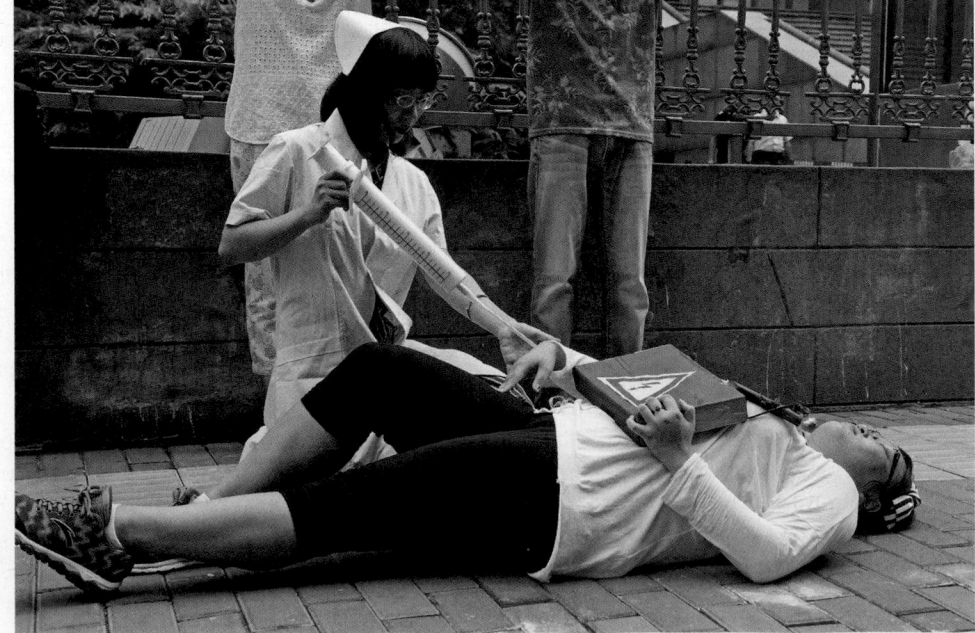

Greg Baker/Getty Images

Such questions cannot be answered by logic alone because scientists, like all human beings, frequently make errors in thinking. Thus, clinical researchers depend mainly on three methods of investigation: the *case study,* which typically is focused on one individual, and the *correlational method* and *experimental method,* approaches that are usually used to gather information about many individuals. Each is best suited to certain kinds of circumstances and questions. As a group, these methods enable scientists to form and test **hypotheses,** or hunches, that certain variables are related in certain ways—and to draw broad conclusions as to why. More properly, a hypothesis is a tentative explanation offered to provide a basis for an investigation.

As you read about the methods used by clinical researchers, it is important to keep in mind that these scientists face certain challenges that make their work particularly difficult. They must, for example, figure out how to measure such elusive concepts as unconscious motives, private thoughts, mood changes, and human potential. They must consider the different cultural backgrounds, races, and genders of the people they choose to study. And, as we are reminded in *PsychWatch*, they must always ensure that the rights of their research participants, both human and animal, are not violated (Leavy, 2017; Nobis, 2016).

PSYCH**WATCH**

Animals Have Rights

For years, researchers have learned much about human functioning, including abnormal human functioning, from experiments with animals. It is estimated that between 11 and 25 million animals are used as subjects in research studies in the United States each year (SR, 2016). Around 500,000 of them are guinea pigs, rabbits, monkeys, dogs, and cats (USDA, 2016). Most of the remainder are mice and rats.

Animals have been shocked, prematurely separated from their parents, and starved (Engel & Comstock, 2016). They have had their brains surgically changed and have even been killed, or "sacrificed," so that researchers could autopsy them. It is estimated that medical animal research (for example, cardiovascular research) has helped increase the life expectancy of humans by almost 24 years. Similarly, animal research has been key to the development of many medications, leading to a savings of hundreds of billions of dollars every year in the United States alone (Henderson et al., 2013; Shields, 2010; Lasker Foundation, 2000). Nevertheless, concerns remain: Are such actions always ethically acceptable?

Animal rights activists say no (Engel & Comstock, 2016; Grimm, 2013). They have called such undertakings cruel and unnecessary and have fought many forms of animal research with legal protests and demonstrations. Some have even harassed scientists and vandalized their labs (Nobis, 2016). In turn, some researchers have accused activists of caring more about animals than about human beings. In response to this controversy, a number of state courts, government agencies, and the American Psychological Association have issued rules and guidelines for animal research (Vogt et al., 2016). Still, the battle goes on.

Where does the public stand on this issue? In surveys, most respondents say that they dislike and are concerned about animal research (Joffe et al., 2016; Gallup, 2015). At the same time, around two-thirds of respondents say they can "accept" it as long as it is for scientific purposes, avoids inflicting unnecessary suffering on animals, and is the only way of gathering medical or other needed knowledge (Clemence & Leaman, 2016). People in such surveys approve of experiments that use mice or rats much more than those using monkeys, dogs, cats, or other kinds of animals.

Raveendran/AFP/Getty Images

Making a point With his body painted as a monkey, an activist from the organization PETA (People for the Ethical Treatment of Animals) sits in a cage to protest the use of animals in research at a medical science institute in India.

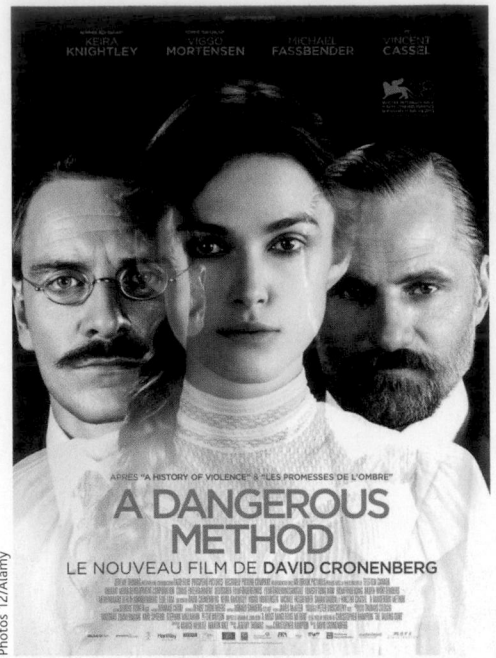

Photos 12/Alamy

Case studies go to the movies Case studies often find their way into the arts or media and capture the public's attention. One such study is that of Sabina Spierein, a young woman suffering from severe tics, grimaces, uncontrollable laughing and crying, and other symptoms of hysteria in the early 1900s. Spierein's case study was written by the pioneering psychoanalytic therapist and theorist Carl Jung, Sigmund Freud's most famous colleague. Her symptoms and successful treatment by Jung, later romance with Jung, possible role in the eventual split between Jung and Freud, and emergence as an important psychoanalyst in her own right were all chronicled in the 2011 film *A Dangerous Method*.

The Case Study

A CASE STUDY IS a detailed description of a person's life and psychological problems. It describes the person's history, present circumstances, and symptoms. It may also include speculation about why the problems developed, and it may describe the person's treatment (Tight, 2017).

In his famous case study of Little Hans (1909), Sigmund Freud discusses a 4-year-old boy who developed a fear of horses. Freud gathered his material from detailed letters sent to him by Hans's father, a physician who had attended lectures on psychoanalysis, and from his own limited interviews with the child. Freud's case study runs 140 pages in his *Collected Papers*, so only a few excerpts are presented here.

> *One day while Hans was in the street he was seized with an attack of morbid anxiety. . . . On the way back from Schönbrunn he said to his mother, . . . 'I was afraid a horse would bite me.'*
>
> *But the beginnings of this psychological situation go back [to] a period when he was not quite three years old. At that time, by means of various remarks and questions, he was showing a quite peculiarly lively interest in that portion of his body which he used to describe as his "widdler" [his word for penis].*
>
> *When he was three and a half his mother found him with his hand to his penis. She threatened him in these words: "If you do that, I shall send for Dr. A. to cut off your widdler. And then what'll you widdle with?" . . . This was the occasion of his acquiring [a] "castration complex." . . .*
>
> *[At the age of four, Hans entered] a state of intensified sexual excitement, the object of which was his mother. [For example, one] morning Hans was given his usual daily bath by his mother and afterwards dried and powdered. As his mother was powdering round his penis and taking care not to touch it, Hans said: 'Why don't you put your finger there?' . . . "*
>
> *. . . The father and son visited me during my consulting hours. [They revealed that Hans] was particularly bothered by what horses wear in front of their eyes and by the black round their mouths . . . [I asked Hans] whether his father wore eyeglasses [and] whether by "the black round the mouth" he meant a moustache [like his father's]; and I then disclosed to him that he was afraid of his father, precisely because he was so fond of his mother. It must be, I told him, that he thought his father was angry with him on that account; but this was not so, his father was fond of him in spite of it . . .*
>
> *By enlightening Hans on this subject I had cleared away his most powerful resistance. . . . It was at this stage of the analysis that he recalled the event . . . which [had] immediately preceded the outbreak of the illness . . . . He went for a walk with his mother, and saw a bus-horse fall down and kick about with its feet. This made a great impression on him. He was terrified, and thought the horse was dead; and from that time on he thought that all horses would fall down. [In our session, his] father pointed out to him that when he saw the horse fall down he must have thought of him, his father, and have wished that he might fall down in the same way and be dead. Hans did not dispute this interpretation. . . .*
>
> *It is especially interesting . . . to observe the way in which the transformation of Hans's libido into anxiety was projected on to the principal object of his phobia, on to horses. Horses interested him the most of all the large animals; playing at horses was his favorite game with the older children. I had a suspicion—and this was confirmed by Hans's father when I asked him—that the first person who had served Hans as a horse must have been his father. . . . When repression [of his desire for his mother and his fear of retribution by his father] had set in and brought a revulsion of feeling along with it, horses, which had till then been associated with so much pleasure, were necessarily turned into objects of fear. . . . With this [and subsequent insights] the analysis came to an appropriate end.*
>
> *(Freud, 1909)*

Most clinicians take notes and keep records in the course of treating their patients, and some, like Freud, further organize such notes into a formal case study to be shared with other professionals. The clues offered by a case study may help a clinician better understand or treat the person under discussion. In addition, case studies may play nomothetic roles that go far beyond the individual clinical case.

How Are Case Studies Helpful?

Case studies are useful to researchers in many ways (Gerring, 2017; Tight, 2017). They can, for example, be a source of *new ideas* about behavior and "open the way for discoveries" (Bolgar, 1965). Freud's theory of psychoanalysis was based mainly on the patients he saw in private practice. He poured over their case studies, such as the one he wrote about Little Hans, to find what he believed to be broad psychological processes and principles of development. In addition, a case study may offer *tentative support* for a theory. Freud used case studies in this way as well, regarding them as evidence for the accuracy of his ideas. Conversely, case studies may serve to *challenge a theory's assumptions*.

Case studies may also show the value of *new therapeutic techniques*. For example, Freud believed that the case study of Little Hans demonstrated the therapeutic potential of a verbal approach for children as well as for adults.

Finally, case studies may offer opportunities to study *unusual problems* that do not occur often enough to permit a large number of observations. For years, information about *dissociative identity disorder* (previously called multiple personality disorder) was based almost entirely on case studies, such as a famous case popularly referred to as *The Three Faces of Eve*, a clinical account of a woman who displayed three alternating personalities, each having a separate set of memories, preferences, and personal habits.

Does psychological abnormality run in families? One of the most celebrated case studies in abnormal psychology is a study of identical quadruplets dubbed the "Genain" sisters by researchers (after the Greek term for "dire birth"). All of the sisters developed schizophrenia in their twenties.

What Are the Limitations of Case Studies?

Case studies also have limitations (Gerring, 2017; Tight, 2017). First, they are reported by *biased observers*, that is, by therapists who have a personal stake in seeing their treatments succeed. These therapists must choose what to include in a case study, and their choices may at times be self-serving. Second, case studies rely on *subjective evidence*. Is a client's problem really caused by the events that the therapist or client says are responsible? After all, those are only a fraction of the events that may be contributing to the situation. When investigators are able to rule out all possible causes except one, a study is said to have internal accuracy, or **internal validity**. Obviously, case studies rate low on that score.

Another problem with case studies is that they provide *little basis for generalization*. Even if we agree that Little Hans developed a dread of horses because he was terrified of castration and feared his father, how can we be confident that other people's phobias are rooted in the same kinds of causes? Events or treatments that seem important in one case may be of no help at all in efforts to understand or treat others. When the findings of an investigation can be generalized beyond the immediate study, the investigation is said to have external accuracy, or **external validity**. Case studies rate low on external validity, too.

> Why do case studies and other anecdotal offerings influence people so much, often more than systematic research does?

The limitations of the case study are largely addressed by two other methods of investigation: the *correlational method* and the *experimental method*. These methods do not offer the rich detail that makes case studies so interesting, but they do help investigators draw broad conclusions about abnormality in the population at large. Thus most clinical investigators prefer these methods over the case study.

Three features of the correlational and experimental methods enable clinical investigators to gain general, or nomothetic, insights: (1) The researchers typically observe many individuals. (2) The researchers apply procedures uniformly. Other researchers

case study A detailed account of a person's life and psychological problems.

internal validity The accuracy with which a study can pinpoint one factor as the cause of a phenomenon.

external validity The degree to which the results of a study may be generalized beyond that study.

correlation The degree to which events or characteristics vary along with each other.

correlational method A research procedure used to determine how much events or characteristics vary along with each other.

can thus repeat, or *replicate,* a particular study to see whether it consistently gives the same findings. (3) The researchers use *statistical tests* to analyze the results of a study and determine whether broad conclusions are justified.

The Correlational Method

CORRELATION IS THE DEGREE to which events or characteristics vary with each other. The **correlational method** is a research procedure used to determine this "co-relationship" between variables (Salkind, 2017). This method can be used, for example, to answer the question, "Is there a correlation between the amount of stress in people's lives and the degree of depression they experience?" That is, as people keep experiencing stressful events, are they increasingly likely to become depressed?

To test this question, researchers have collected life stress scores (for example, the number of threatening events experienced during a certain period of time) and depression scores (for example, scores on a depression survey) from individuals and have correlated these scores. The people who are chosen for a study are its subjects, or *participants,* the term preferred by today's investigators. The participants in a given study are collectively called its *sample.* A sample must be representative of the larger population that the researchers wish to understand. Otherwise the relationship found in the study may not apply elsewhere in the real world—it may not have external validity. If researchers were to find a correlation between life stress and depression in a sample consisting entirely of children, for example, they could not draw clear conclusions about what, if any, correlation exists among adults.

Describing a Correlation

Suppose you were to use the correlational method to conduct a study of depression. You would collect life stress scores and depression scores for 10 people and plot the scores on a graph, as shown in **Figure 2-1**. As you can see, the participant named Jim has a recent life stress score of 7, meaning seven threatening events over the past 3

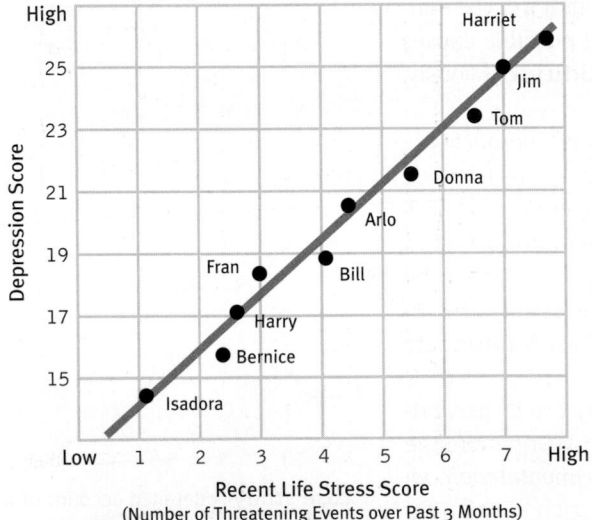

FIGURE 2-1

Positive Correlation

The relationship between amount of recent stress and feelings of depression shown by this hypothetical sample of 10 participants is a near-perfect "positive" correlation.

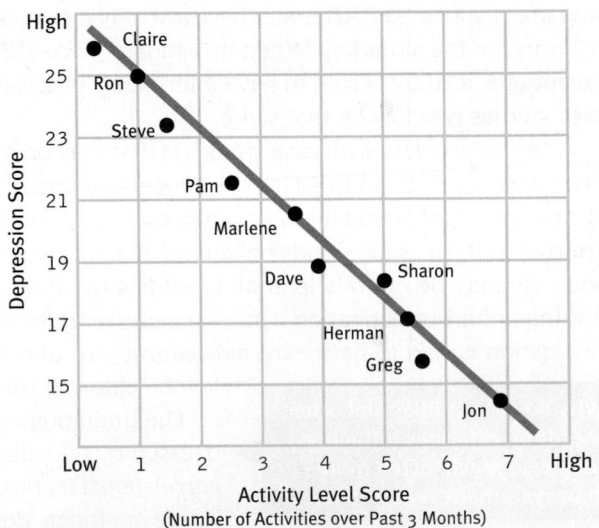

FIGURE 2-2

Negative Correlation

The relationship between number of activities and feelings of depression shown by this hypothetical sample is a near-perfect "negative" correlation.

months; he also has a depression score of 25. Thus he is "located" at the point on the graph where these two scores meet. The graph provides a visual representation of your data. Here, notice that the data points all fall roughly along a straight line that slopes upward. You would draw the line so that the data points are as close to it as possible. This line is called the *line of best fit*.

The line of best fit in Figure 2-1 slopes upward and to the right, indicating that the variables under examination are increasing or decreasing together. That is, the greater someone's life stress score, the higher his or her score on the depression scale. When variables change the same way, their correlation is said to have a positive *direction* and is referred to as a *positive correlation*. Most studies of life stress and depression have indeed found a positive correlation between those two variables (Yang et al., 2017; Hammen, 2016).

Correlations can have a negative rather than a positive direction. In a *negative correlation*, the value of one variable increases as the value of the other variable decreases. Researchers have found, for example, a negative correlation between depression and activity level. The greater one's depression, the lower the number of one's activities. When the scores of a negative correlation are plotted, they produce a downward-sloping graph, like the one shown in **Figure 2-2.**

There is yet a third possible outcome for a correlational study. The variables under study may be *unrelated,* meaning that there is no consistent relationship between them. As the measures of one variable increase, those of the other variable sometimes increase and sometimes decrease. The graph of this outcome looks like **Figure 2-3**. Here the line of best fit is horizontal, with no slope at all. Studies have found that depression and intelligence are unrelated, for example.

In addition to knowing the direction of a correlation, researchers need to know its *magnitude,* or strength (see **Figure 2-4**). That is, how closely do the two variables correspond? Does one *always* vary along with the other, or is their relationship less exact? When two variables are found to vary together very closely in person after person, the correlation is said to be high, or strong.

Look again at Figure 2-1. In this graph of a positive correlation between depression and life stress, the data points all fall very close to the line of best fit. Researchers can

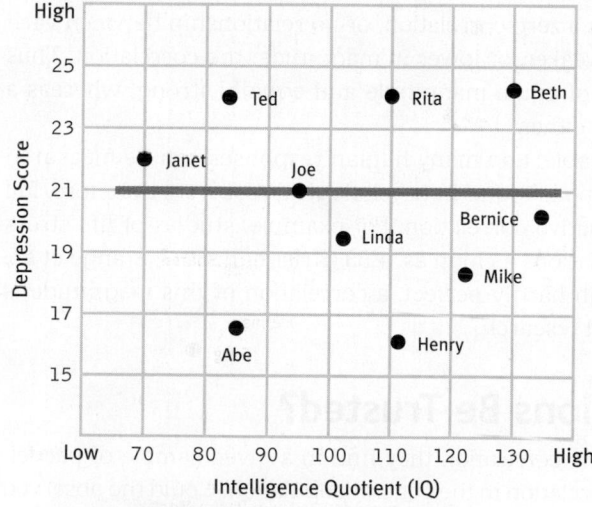

FIGURE 2-3

No Correlation

The relationship between intelligence and feelings of depression shown by this hypothetical sample is a "near-zero" correlation.

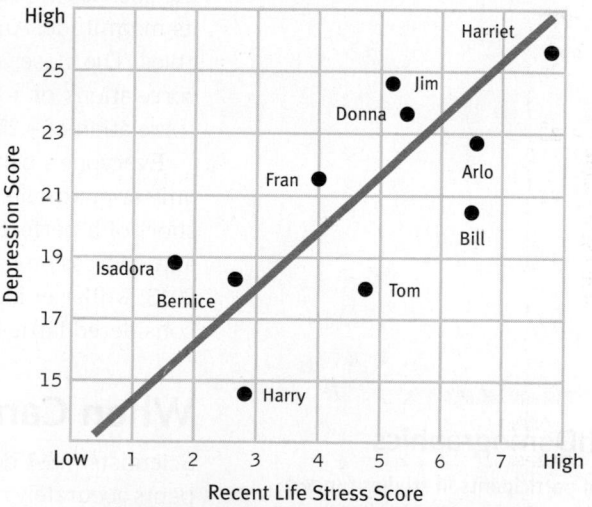

FIGURE 2-4

Magnitude of Correlation

The relationship between amount of recent stress and feelings of depression shown by this hypothetical sample is a "moderately positive" correlation.

Stress and depression A woman attends a 2016 prayer service in Flint, Michigan, holding a sign that conveys the desperate predicament faced by her and thousands of other victims in the wake of the city's water contamination crisis. Studies find that the stress produced by this and similar community catastrophes has been accompanied by depression and other psychological symptoms in many residents (Goodnough & Atkinson, 2016).

Bill Pugliano/Getty Images

predict each person's score on one variable with a high degree of confidence if they know his or her score on the other. But what if the graph of the correlation between depression and life stress looked more like Figure 2-4? In this figure the data points are loosely scattered around the line of best fit rather than hugging it closely. In this case, researchers could not predict with as much accuracy an individual's score on one variable from his or her score on the other variable. The correlation in Figure 2-1 is stronger, or greater in magnitude, than that in Figure 2-4.

The direction and magnitude of a correlation are often calculated numerically and expressed by a statistical term called the *correlation coefficient*. The correlation coefficient can vary from +1.00, which indicates a perfect positive correlation between two variables, down to –1.00, which represents a perfect negative correlation. The *sign* of the coefficient (+ or –) signifies the direction of the correlation; the *number* represents its magnitude. An *r* of .00 reflects a zero correlation, or no relationship between variables. The closer *r* is to .00, the weaker, or lower in magnitude, the correlation. Thus correlations of +.75 and –.75 are of equal magnitude and equally strong, whereas a correlation of +.25 is weaker than either.

Everyone's behavior is changeable, and many human responses can be measured only approximately. Most correlations found in psychological research, therefore, fall short of a perfect positive or negative correlation. For example, studies of life stress and depression have found correlations as high as +.53 (Krishnan, 2017; Stange et al., 2013; Miller et al., 1976). Although hardly perfect, a correlation of this magnitude is considered large in psychological research.

#ResearchDemographics

Around 63% of participants in studies funded by the National Institutes of Health (NIH) are female, and 37% are male.

Around 64% of the participants in NIH studies are non-Hispanic white Americans, and 36% are members of racial/ethnic minority groups.

(Information from: CISCRP, 2016)

When Can Correlations Be Trusted?

Scientists must decide whether the correlation they find in a given sample of participants accurately reflects a real correlation in the general population. Could the observed correlation have occurred by mere chance? Scientists can never know for certain, but they can test their conclusions with a *statistical analysis* of their data, using principles of probability (Salkind, 2017; Privitera, 2016). In essence, they ask how likely it is that the study's particular findings have occurred by chance. If the statistical analysis indicates that chance is unlikely to account for the correlation they found, researchers may conclude that their findings reflect a real correlation in the general population.

A cutoff point helps researchers make this decision. By convention, if there is less than a 5 percent probability that a study's findings are due to chance (signified as $p < .05$), the findings are said to be *statistically significant* and are thought to reflect the larger population. In one of the life stress and depression studies described earlier, a statistical analysis indicated a probability of less than 5 percent that the +.53 correlation found in its sample was due to chance. Therefore, the researchers concluded with some confidence that among adults in general, depression does tend to rise along with the amount of recent stress in a person's life. Generally, a researcher's confidence increases with the magnitude of the correlation and the size of the sample. The larger they each are, the more likely it is that a correlation will be statistically significant.

What Are the Merits of the Correlational Method?

The correlational method has certain advantages over the case study (see **Table 2-1**). First, it possesses high *external validity*. Because researchers measure their variables, observe large samples, and apply statistical analyses, they are in a better position to generalize their correlations to people beyond the ones they have studied. Furthermore, researchers can easily repeat correlational studies using new samples of participants to check the results of earlier studies.

On the other hand, correlational studies, like case studies, lack *internal validity*. Although correlations allow researchers to describe the relationship between two variables, they do not *explain* the relationship. When we look at the positive correlation found in many life stress studies, we may be tempted to conclude that increases in recent life stress cause people to feel more depressed. In fact, however, the two variables may be correlated for any one of three reasons: (1) Life stress may cause depression. (2) Depression may cause people to experience more life stress (for example, a depressive approach to life may cause people to perform poorly at work or may interfere with social relationships). (3) Depression and life stress may each be caused by a third variable, such as financial problems.

> Can you think of other correlations in life that are interpreted mistakenly as causal?

Although correlations say nothing about causation, they can still be of great use to clinicians. Clinicians know, for example, that suicide attempts increase as people become more depressed. Thus, when they work with severely depressed clients, they stay on the lookout for signs of suicidal thinking. Perhaps depression directly causes suicidal behavior, or perhaps a third variable, such as a sense of hopelessness, causes both depression and suicidal thoughts. Whatever the cause, just knowing that there is a correlation may enable clinicians to take measures (such as hospitalization) to help save lives.

Of course, in other instances, clinicians do need to know whether one variable causes another. Do parents' marital conflicts cause their children to be more anxious?

Table: 2-1

Relative Strengths and Weaknesses of Research Methods

	Provides Individual Information	Provides General Information (External Validity)	Provides Causal Information (Internal Validity)	Statistical Analysis Possible	Replicable
Case Study	Yes	No	No	No	No
Correlational method	No	Yes	No	Yes	Yes
Experimental method	No	Yes	Yes	Yes	Yes

Does job dissatisfaction lead to feelings of depression? Will a given treatment help people to cope more effectively in life? Questions about causality call for the experimental method.

The Experimental Method

AN EXPERIMENT IS A RESEARCH procedure in which a variable is manipulated and the manipulation's effect on another variable is observed (Leavy, 2017; Bryman, 2016). In fact, most of us perform experiments throughout our lives without knowing that we are behaving so scientifically. Suppose that you go to a party on campus to celebrate the end of midterm exams. As you mix with people at the party, you begin to notice many of them becoming quiet and depressed. It seems the more you talk, the more subdued the other guests become. As the party falls apart before your eyes, you decide you have to do something, but what? Before you can eliminate the problem, you need to know what's causing it.

Your first hunch may be that something you're doing is responsible. Perhaps your remarks about academic pressures have been upsetting everyone. You decide to change the topic to skiing in the mountains of Colorado and to watch for signs of depression in the next round of conversations. The problem seems to clear up; most people now smile and laugh as they chat with you. As a final check of your suspicions, you could go back to talking about school with the next several people you meet. Their dark and dismal reaction would probably convince you that your tendency to talk about school was indeed the cause of the problem.

You have just performed an experiment, testing your hypothesis about a causal relationship between your topic of conversation and the depressed mood of the people around you. You manipulated the variable that you suspected to be the cause (the topic) and then observed the effect of that manipulation on the other variable (the mood of the people around you). In scientific experiments, the manipulated variable is called the **independent variable** and the variable being observed is called the **dependent variable.**

To examine the experimental method more fully, let's consider a question that is often asked by clinicians (Priday et al., 2017; Norton & Paulus, 2016): "Does a particular therapy relieve the symptoms of a particular disorder?" Because this question is about a causal relationship, researchers may use an experiment to answer it (see **Table 2-2**). They may give the therapy in question to people who are suffering from a disorder and then observe whether they improve. In this experiment, the therapy is the independent variable, and psychological improvement is the dependent variable.

Table: 2-2

Most Investigated Questions in Clinical Research

Most Common *Correlational* Questions	Most Common *Causal* Questions
Are stress and onset of mental disorders related?	Does factor X cause a disorder?
Is culture (or gender or race) generally linked to mental disorders?	Is cause A more influential than cause B?
Are income and mental disorders related?	How does family communication and structure affect family members?
Are social skills tied to mental disorders?	How does a disorder affect the quality of a person's life?
Are family conflict and mental disorders related?	Does treatment X alleviate a disorder?
Is treatment responsiveness tied to culture?	Is treatment X more helpful than no treatment at all?
Which symptoms of a disorder appear together?	Is treatment A more helpful than treatment B?
How common is a disorder in a particular population?	Why does treatment X work?
	Can an intervention prevent abnormal functioning?

If the true cause of changes in the dependent variable cannot be separated from other possible causes, then an experiment gives very little information (see *InfoCentral* on the next page). Thus, experimenters must try to eliminate all **confounds** from their studies—variables other than the independent variable that may also be affecting the dependent variable. When there are confounds in an experiment, they, rather than the independent variable, may be causing the observed changes.

For example, situational variables, such as the location of the therapy office (say, a quiet country setting) or soothing background music in the office, may have a therapeutic effect on participants in a therapy study. Or perhaps the participants are unusually motivated or have high expectations that the therapy will work, factors that thus account for their improvement. To guard against confounds, researchers should include three important features in their experiments—a *control group, random assignment,* and a *masked design* (Comer & Bry, 2017).

The Control Group

A **control group** is a group of research participants who are not exposed to the independent variable under investigation but whose experience is similar to that of the **experimental group,** the participants who are exposed to the independent variable. By comparing the two groups, an experimenter can better determine the effect of the independent variable.

To study the effectiveness of a particular therapy, for example, experimenters typically divide participants into two groups after obtaining their consent to participate in the study. The experimental group may come into an office and receive the therapy for an hour, while the control group may simply come into the office for an hour. If the experimenters find later that the people in the experimental group improve more than the people in the control group, they may conclude that the therapy was effective, above and beyond the effects of time, the office setting, and any other confounds. To guard against confounds, experimenters try to provide all participants, both control and experimental, with experiences that are identical in every way—except for the independent variable.

Of course, it is possible that the differences observed between an experimental group and control group have occurred simply by chance. Thus, as with correlational studies, investigators who conduct experiments must do a statistical analysis on their data and find out how likely it is that the observed differences are due to chance (Salkind, 2017; Jacobsen, 2016). If the likelihood is very low—less than 5 percent ($p < .05$)—the differences between the two groups are considered to be statistically

experiment A research procedure in which a variable is manipulated and the effect of the manipulation on another variable is observed.

independent variable The variable in an experiment that is manipulated to determine whether it has an effect on another variable.

dependent variable The variable in an experiment expected to change as the independent variable is manipulated.

confound In an experiment, a variable other than the independent variable that is also acting on the dependent variable.

control group In an experiment, a group of participants who are not exposed to the independent variable.

experimental group In an experiment, the participants who are exposed to the independent variable under investigation.

#TheirWords

"The temptation to form premature theories upon insufficient data is the bane of our profession."

Sherlock Holmes in *The Valley of Fear*, 1914

Peter Mueller The New Yorker Collection/The Cartoon Bank

CONTROL GROUP   OUT OF CONTROL GROUP.

RESEARCHING RESEARCH

Clinical researchers have conducted an enormous number of studies and investigated behavior, thinking, and feeling from every angle. But one thing they have not studied much is the process of research itself. That has begun to change in recent years, as investigators have looked increasingly at the participants, scientists, and behind-the-scene factors that comprise the research enterprise.

"WEIRD" Participants

Nearly 70 percent of psychology studies use college students as participants. These research participants are frequently described by the acronym WEIRD, because they are overwhelmingly from societies that are:

W Western **E** Educated **I** Industrialized **R** Rich **D** Democratic

It turns out that WEIRD participants are actually a distinct breed, raising doubts about how generalizable WEIRD-related findings are. Compared to participants from other populations, WEIRD individuals are:

More educated
individualistic
narcissistic
self-satisfied
happiness-driven
reward-focused
concerned about personal choice

Younger

Less cooperative
conforming

Greater risk-takers

(Robson, 2017; Dance, 2015; Brookshire, 2013; Henrich et al., 2010)

Online ≠ In-Person

More and more researchers are conducting their studies on the Internet, where participants are so plentiful. But, online research participants are downright different from in-person participants.

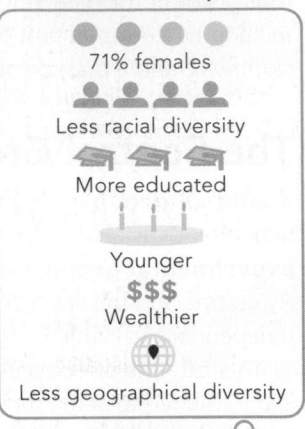

Online Participants
57% females
More racial diversity
Less educated
Older
$
Poorer
More geographical diversity

In-Person Participants
71% females
Less racial diversity
More educated
Younger
$$$
Wealthier
Less geographical diversity

(Dance, 2015; Gosling et al., 2004)

Sharing Is Important

The American Psychological Association requires authors of articles accepted for journal publication to share their data with peers for reanalysis or **replication**. However, one study found that almost 75% of such authors refused requests for their data.

(Naik, 2017; Wicherts et al., 2011, 2006).

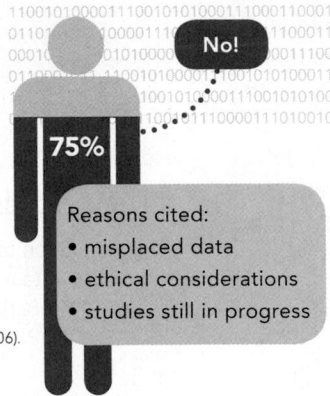

No!
75%

Reasons cited:
• misplaced data
• ethical considerations
• studies still in progress

Over-Accentuating the Positive?

Scientific journals are more likely to publish "positive" studies that **support** the tested hypothesis than "negative" (unsupportive) studies. The proportion of published studies that are positive has increased from 70% to 85% over the past 25 years.

Published Studies That Are Positive

	1990	2007	2014
	70%	86%	85%

(Fanelli et al., 2017; Franko et al., 2014; Fanelli, 2011, 2010)

Potential Conflict of Interest?

More than 2/3 of drug efficacy studies are conducted by private researchers who are paid directly by pharmaceutical companies. **80%** of published pharmaceutical company studies report favorable outcomes. In contrast, **only 50%** of the published studies sponsored by nonpharmaceutical companies report favorable outcomes.

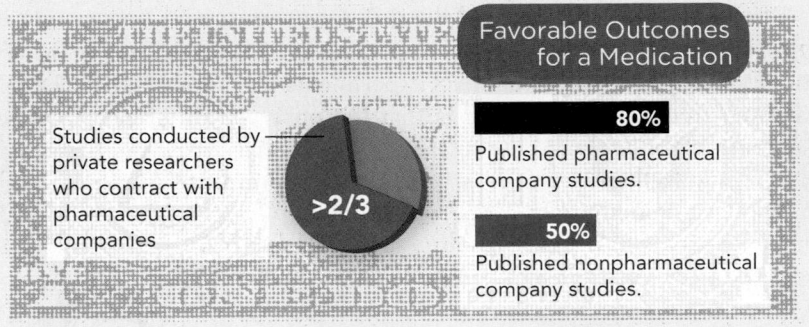

Studies conducted by private researchers who contract with pharmaceutical companies
>2/3

Favorable Outcomes for a Medication
80% Published pharmaceutical company studies.
50% Published nonpharmaceutical company studies.

(Ahn et al, 2017; Pigott et al., 2010)

Replication Is Important

Replication is the repetition of studies with different investigators, participants, and situations. Replicated studies help determine the accuracy and generalizability of the original studies. Unfortunately, today's replication undertakings are raising questions about some of psychology's research findings.

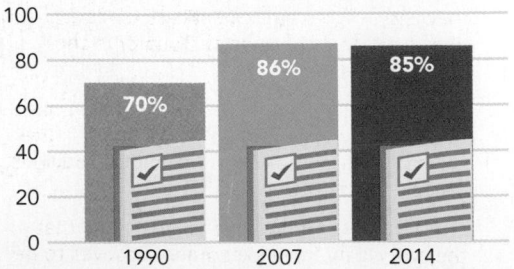
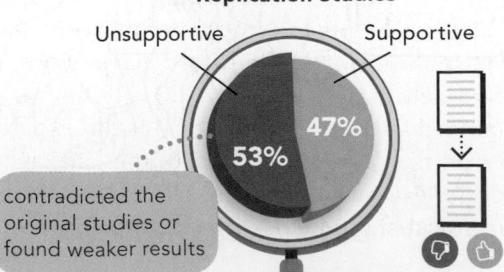

Replication Studies
Unsupportive — Supportive
53% 47%

contradicted the original studies or found weaker results

• Fewer and fewer replication studies are being conducted in psychology.
• Contradictory replicated studies are rarely published.
• Once an initial study's findings are accepted, contradictory replication findings rarely change public or scientific opinions.

(Gilbert et al., 2016; Nosek et al., 2015; John et al., 2012; Yong, 2012)

significant, and the experimenter may conclude with some confidence that they are due to the independent variable. As a general rule, if the sample of participants in an experiment is large, if the difference observed between groups is great, and if the range of scores within each group is small, the findings of the study are likely to be statistically significant.

An additional point is worth noting with regard to clinical treatment experiments. It is always important to distinguish between *statistical significance* and a notion called *clinical significance*. As you have just read, *statistical significance* indicates whether a participant's improvement in functioning—large or small—occurred because of treatment. *Clinical significance* indicates whether the amount of improvement is meaningful in the individual's life. Even if the moods of depressed participants improve because of treatment, the individuals may still be too unhappy to enjoy life.

Is animal companionship a form of therapy? A ring-tailed lemur sits on the shoulder of an individual at Serengeti Park near Hodenhagen, Germany. It's part of a monthly program called "Psychiatric Animal Days" based on the premise that animals—even lemurs—have a calming effect on people. More than 400 kinds of intervention are currently used for psychological problems. An experimental design is needed to determine whether this or any other form of treatment causes clients to improve.

Random Assignment

Researchers must also watch out for differences in the *makeup* of the experimental and control groups since those differences may also confound a study's results. In a therapy study, for example, the experimenter may unintentionally put wealthier participants in the experimental group and poorer ones in the control group. This difference, rather than their therapy, may be the cause of the greater improvement later found among the experimental participants. To reduce the effects of preexisting differences, experimenters typically use **random assignment.** This is the general term for any selection procedure that ensures that every participant in the experiment is as likely to be placed in one group as the other (Comer & Bry, 2017). Researchers might, for example, select people by flipping a coin or picking names out of a hat.

Masked Design

A final confound problem is *bias*. Participants may bias an experiment's results by trying to please or help the experimenter. In a therapy experiment, for example, if those participants who receive the treatment know the purpose of the study and which group they are in, they might actually work harder to feel better or to fulfill the experimenter's expectations. If so, *subject,* or *participant, bias* rather than therapy could be causing their improvement.

To avoid this bias, experimenters can prevent participants from finding out which group they are in (Jacobsen, 2016). This experimental strategy is called a **masked design** (previously termed a *blind design*) because the individuals are kept unaware of their assigned group. In a therapy study, for example, control participants could be given a *placebo* (Latin for "I shall please"), something that looks or tastes like real therapy but has none of its key ingredients. This "imitation" therapy is called **placebo therapy.** If the experimental (true therapy) participants then improve more than the control (placebo therapy) participants, experimenters have more confidence that the true therapy has caused their improvement.

> Why might sugar pills or other kinds of placebo treatments help some people feel better?

An experiment may also be confounded by *experimenter bias*—that is, experimenters may have expectations that they unintentionally transmit to the participants in their studies. In a drug therapy study, for example, the experimenter might smile and act confident while providing real medications to the experimental participants but

random assignment A selection procedure that ensures that participants are randomly placed either in the control group or in the experimental group.

masked design An experiment in which participants do not know whether they are in the experimental or the control condition. Previously called a *blind design*.

placebo therapy A pretend treatment that the participant in an experiment believes to be genuine.

quasi-experimental design A research design that fails to include key elements of a "pure" experiment and/or intermixes elements of both experimental and correlational studies. Also called a *mixed design*.

matched design A research design that matches the experimental participants with control participants who are similar on key characteristics.

natural experiment An experiment in which nature, rather than an experimenter, manipulates an independent variable.

frown and appear hesitant while offering placebo drugs to the control participants. This kind of bias is sometimes referred to as the *Rosenthal effect,* after the psychologist who first identified it (Rosenthal, 1966). Experimenters can eliminate their own bias by arranging to be unaware themselves. In a drug therapy study, for example, an aide could make sure that the real medication and the placebo drug look identical. The experimenter could then administer treatment without knowing which participants were receiving true medications and which were receiving false medications.

While either the participants or the experimenter may be kept unaware in an experiment, it is best that both be unaware—a research strategy called a *double-masked design*. In fact, most medication experiments now use double-masked designs to test promising drugs (Kim et al., 2017; Thase et al., 2016). Many experimenters also arrange for judges to assess and statistically analyze the patients' improvement independently, and the judges too are kept unaware of the group assignments. This strategy is called a *triple-masked design*.

Alternative Research Designs

IT IS NOT ALWAYS EASY to devise an experiment that is fully controlled and that randomly assigns participants to groups. Prevention of every possible confound is rarely achievable. Moreover, because psychological experiments typically use living beings, ethical and practical considerations limit the kinds of manipulations one can do. Thus clinical scientists must often settle for research designs that are less than ideal. These alternative designs are often called **quasi-experimental designs,** or **mixed designs**—designs that fail to include key elements of a "pure" experiment and/or intermix elements of both experimental and correlational studies (Leavy, 2017; Salkind, 2017). Such variations include the *matched design, natural experiment, analogue experiment, single-subject experiment, longitudinal study,* and *epidemiological study.*

Matched Designs

In many studies, investigators must make use of groups that already exist in the world at large. Consider, for example, research into the effects of child abuse. Because it would be unethical for investigators of this issue to create an experimental group by actually abusing a randomly chosen group of children, they must instead compare children who already have a history of abuse with children who do not. Though necessary, this strategy violates the rule of random assignment and so introduces possible confounds into the study. Children who receive excessive physical punishment, for example, usually come from poorer and larger families than children who are punished verbally. Any differences found later in the moods or self-concepts of the two groups of children may be the result of differences in wealth or family size rather than abuse.

Child-abuse researchers often try to minimize such confound problems by using a **matched design** (Jacobsen, 2016). They match the experimental participants with control participants who are similar in age, sex, race, number of children in the family, socioeconomic status, type of neighborhood, or other characteristics. When the data from studies using this kind of design show that abused children are typically sadder and have lower self-esteem than matched control participants who have not been abused, the investigators can conclude with some confidence that abuse is causing the differences (Greger et al., 2016; Jaschek et al., 2016).

Natural Experiments

In **natural experiments,** nature itself manipulates the independent variable, while the experimenter observes the effects. Natural experiments must be used for studying

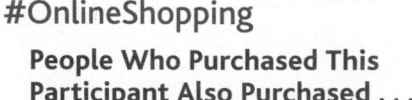

#OnlineShopping

People Who Purchased This Participant Also Purchased . . .

Leave it to Amazon. Many researchers are now finding study participants on a digital platform called *Amazon Mechanical Turk* (Pew Research Center, 2016). The researchers (known as *Requesters*) post their studies (online surveys and the like) on this Internet marketplace, and participants (called *Providers* or *Turkers*) choose which studies they want to sign up for. Participants receive payment (usually a small amount) via an Amazon.com gift certificate, and Amazon receives 10 percent of the participant's reimbursement.

Imaginechina via AP Images

Twins, correlation, and inheritance These healthy twin sisters are participating in a twin cultural festival at Honglingjin Park in Beijing, China. Correlational studies of many pairs of twins have suggested a link between genetic factors and certain psychological disorders. Identical twins (who have identical genes) display a higher correlation for some disorders than do fraternal twins (whose genetic makeup is not identical).

the psychological effects of unusual and unpredictable events, such as floods, earthquakes, plane crashes, and fires. Because the participants in these studies are selected by an accident of fate rather than by the investigators' design, natural experiments are in fact quasi-experiments.

On December 26, 2004, an earthquake occurred beneath the Indian Ocean off the coast of Sumatra, Indonesia. The earthquake triggered a series of massive tsunamis that flooded the ocean's coastal communities, killed more than 225,000 people, and injured and left millions of survivors homeless, particularly in Indonesia, Sri Lanka, India, and Thailand. Within months of this disaster, researchers conducted natural experiments in which they collected data from hundreds of survivors and from control groups of people who lived in areas not directly affected by the tsunamis. The disaster survivors scored significantly higher on anxiety and depression measures (dependent variables) than the controls did. The survivors also experienced more sleep problems, feelings of detachment, arousal, difficulties concentrating, startle responses, and guilt feelings than the controls did (Hussain et al., 2016; Nygaard et al., 2016). Over the past several years, other natural experiments have focused on survivors of the 2010 Haitian earthquake, Japan's massive earthquake in 2011, the Northeast's Superstorm Sandy in 2012, the Oklahoma tornados in 2013, and the raging wildfires that swept through Gatlinburg, Tennessee and surrounding areas in 2016. These studies have also revealed lingering psychological symptoms among survivors of those disasters (Wynn, 2017; Usami et al., 2016; Schwartz et al., 2015).

Because each natural event is unique in certain ways, broad generalizations drawn from a single study could be incorrect. Nevertheless, catastrophes have provided opportunities for hundreds of natural experiments over the years, enabling clinical scientists to identify patterns of reactions that people often have across such situations. You will read about these patterns—acute stress disorders and posttraumatic stress disorders—in Chapter 6.

Analogue Experiments

There is one way in which investigators can manipulate independent variables relatively freely while avoiding many of the ethical and practical limitations of clinical research. They can induce laboratory participants to behave in ways that seem to resemble real-life abnormal behavior and then conduct experiments on the participants

#LimitedProtection

The Animal Welfare Act, passed back in 1966, is the *only* federal law in the United States that regulates the humane care of animals in research, exhibition, transportation, or commerce. That act covers dogs, cats, and monkeys, but not birds, fish, mice, or rats. Guidelines for research on the latter animals are set by states, agencies, and scientific associations (Vogt et al., 2016).

Mikel Roberts/Getty Images

Similar enough? Celebrity chimpanzee Cheetah, age 59, does some painting along with her friend and trainer. Chimps and human beings share more than 90 percent of their genetic material, but their brains and bodies are very different, as are their perceptions and experiences. Thus, abnormal-like behavior produced in animal analogue experiments may differ from the human abnormality under investigation.

in the hope of shedding light on the real-life abnormality. This is called an **analogue experiment.**

Analogue studies often use animals as participants. While the needs and rights of animal subjects must be considered, most experimenters believe that the insights gained from such experimentation outweigh the discomfort of the animals, as long as their distress is not excessive or unnecessary (Nobis, 2016; Vogt et al., 2016). In addition, experimenters can, and often do, use human participants in analogue experiments.

As you'll see in Chapter 7, investigator Martin Seligman, in a classic body of work, has used analogue studies with great success to investigate the causes of human depression. Seligman has produced depression-like symptoms in laboratory participants—both animals and humans—by repeatedly exposing them to negative events (shocks, loud noises, task failures) over which they have no control. In these "learned helplessness" analogue studies, the participants seem to give up, lose their initiative, and become sad—suggesting to some clinicians that human depression itself may indeed be caused by loss of control over the events in one's life.

Of course, the laboratory-induced learned helplessness produced in Seligman's analogue experiments is not known with certainty to be analogous to human depression. If this laboratory phenomenon is actually only superficially similar to depression, then the clinical inferences drawn from such experiments may be misleading. This, in fact, is the major limitation of all analogue research: researchers can never be certain that the phenomena they see in the laboratory are the same as the psychological disorders they are investigating.

> Do outside restrictions on research—either animal or human studies—interfere with necessary investigations and thus limit potential gains for human beings?

Single-Subject Experiments

Sometimes scientists do not have the luxury of experimenting on many participants. They may, for example, be investigating a disorder so rare that few participants are available. Research is still possible, however, with a **single-subject experimental design** (Comer & Bry, 2017; Lane et al., 2017). Here a single participant is observed both before and after the manipulation of an independent variable. Single-subject experiments rely first on baseline data—information gathered prior to any manipulations. These data set a standard with which later changes may be compared. The experimenter next introduces the independent variable and again observes the participant's behavior. Any changes in behavior are attributed to the effects of the independent variable.

For example, using a particular kind of single-subject design, called an *ABAB*, or *reversal, design,* one researcher sought to determine whether the systematic use of rewards would reduce a teenage boy's habit of disrupting his special education class with loud talk (Deitz, 1977). He rewarded the boy, who suffered from intellectual disability (previously called mental retardation), with extra teacher time whenever he went 55 minutes without interrupting the class more than three times. In condition A, the student was observed prior to receiving any reward, and he was found to disrupt the class frequently with loud talk. In condition B, the boy was given a series of teacher reward sessions (introduction of the independent variable); as expected, his loud talk decreased dramatically. Next, the rewards from the teacher were stopped (condition A again), and the student's loud talk increased once again. Apparently the independent variable had indeed been the cause of the improvement. To be still more confident about this conclusion, the researcher had the teacher apply reward sessions yet again (condition B again). Once again the student's behavior improved.

Obviously, single-subject experiments are similar to individual case studies in their focus on one participant. In single-subject experiments, however, the independent variable is manipulated systematically so that the investigator can, with some degree of confidence, draw conclusions about the cause of an observed effect. At the same time, because only one person is studied in a single-subject experiment, the researcher cannot be sure that the participant's reaction to the independent variable is typical of people in general.

Longitudinal Studies

In **longitudinal studies** (also called *high-risk* or *developmental studies*), researchers observe the same individuals on many occasions over a long period of time (Bryman, 2016). In several such studies, investigators have observed the progress over the years of normally functioning children whose mothers or fathers suffered from schizophrenia (Hameed & Lewis, 2016; Rasic et al., 2014). The researchers have found, among other things, that the children of the parents with the most severe cases of schizophrenia were particularly likely to develop a psychological disorder and to commit crimes at later points in their development.

As with some of the other quasi-experiments, researchers cannot directly manipulate the independent variable or randomly assign participants to conditions in a longitudinal study, and so they cannot definitively pinpoint causes. However, because longitudinal studies report the order of events, they do provide compelling clues about which events are more likely to be causes and which are more likely to be consequences. Certainly, for example, the children's problems did not cause their parents' schizophrenia.

Epidemiological Studies

Epidemiological studies reveal how often a problem, such as a particular psychological disorder, occurs in a particular population. More specifically, they determine the incidence and prevalence of the problem (Jacobsen, 2016). **Incidence** is the number of new cases that emerge in a population during a given period of time. **Prevalence** is the total number of cases in the population during a given period; prevalence includes both existing and new cases.

Over the past 45 years, clinical researchers throughout the United States have worked on one of the largest epidemiological studies of mental disorders ever conducted, called the Epidemiologic Catchment Area Study (Cottler et al., 2016; Ramsey et al., 2013). They have interviewed more than 20,000 people in five cities to determine the prevalence of many psychological disorders in the United States and the treatment programs used. Two other large-scale epidemiological studies in the United States, the

analogue experiment A research method in which the experimenter produces abnormal-like behavior in laboratory participants and then conducts experiments on the participants.

single-subject experimental design A research method in which a single participant is observed and measured both before and after the manipulation of an independent variable.

longitudinal study A study that observes the same participants on many occasions over a long period of time.

epidemiological study A study that measures the incidence and prevalence of a problem, such as a disorder, in a given population.

incidence The number of new cases of a disorder occurring in a population over a specific period of time.

prevalence The total number of cases of a disorder occurring in a population over a specific period of time.

Yuri_Arcurs/Getty Images

Life is a longitudinal study Photos of this same individual at different points in his life underscore the logic behind longitudinal studies. Just as this person's eyes, nose, and overall smile at the age of 5 seem to predict similar facial features at the ages of 35 and 55, so too might an individual's early temperament, sociability, or other psychological features sometimes predict adult characteristics. In some longitudinal studies, clinical researchers have found that a number of children who seem to be at particular risk for psychological disorders do indeed develop such disorders at later stages of their lives.

#TroubledStudies

Ethically Challenged Research Designs

Placebo Studies When a new drug is being tested, control participants—often people with severe disorders—may receive only a placebo drug.

Symptom-Exacerbation Studies In some studies, patients are given drugs to intensify their symptoms so that researchers may learn more about the biology of their disorder.

Medication-Withdrawal Studies In some studies, researchers prematurely stop medications for patients who have been symptom-free for a while, hoping to learn more about when patients can be taken off particular medications.

National Comorbidity Survey and the National Comorbidity Survey Replication, have questioned almost 15,000 individuals (Kelly & Mezuk, 2017; Kessler et al., 2014, 2012; Martin et al., 2013). All these broad-population studies have been further compared with epidemiological studies of specific populations, such as Hispanic Americans and Asian Americans, or with epidemiological studies conducted in other countries, to see how rates of mental disorders and treatment programs vary from population to population and from country to country (Nobles et al., 2016).

Such epidemiological studies have helped researchers identify groups at risk for particular disorders. Women, it turns out, have a higher rate of anxiety disorders and depression than men, while men have a higher rate of alcoholism than women. Elderly people have a higher rate of suicide than young people. Hispanic Americans experience posttraumatic stress disorder more than other racial and ethnic groups in the United States. And persons in some countries have higher rates of certain mental disorders than those in other countries. Eating disorders such as anorexia nervosa, for example, appear to be more common in Western countries than in non-Western ones. These trends may lead researchers to suspect that something unique about certain populations or settings is helping to cause particular disorders. Declining health in elderly people, for example, may make them more likely to commit suicide. Similarly, the pressures or attitudes common in one country may be responsible for a rate of mental dysfunction that differs from the rate found in another. Yet, epidemiological studies alone cannot confirm such suspicions of causation.

Protecting Human Participants

LIKE THE ANIMAL SUBJECTS that you read about earlier, human research participants have needs and rights that must be respected (see *MindTech*). In fact, researchers' primary obligation is to avoid harming the human participants in their studies—physically or psychologically.

The vast majority of researchers are conscientious about fulfilling this obligation. They try to conduct studies that test their hypotheses and further scientific knowledge in a safe and respectful way (Leavy, 2017; Salkind, 2017). But there have been some notable exceptions to this over the years, particularly three infamous studies conducted in the mid-twentieth century. Partly because of such exceptions, the government and the institutions in which research is conducted now take careful measures to ensure that the safety and rights of human research participants are properly protected.

A national disgrace In a 1997 White House ceremony, President Bill Clinton offers an official apology to 94-year-old Herman Shaw and other African American men whose syphilis went untreated by government doctors and researchers in the Tuskegee Syphilis Study, a research undertaking conducted from 1932 to 1972, prior to the emergence of Institutional Review Boards. In this infamous study, 399 participants were not informed that they had the disease, and they continued to go untreated even after it was discovered that penicillin is an effective intervention for syphilis.

Stephen Jaffe/AFP/Getty Images

Who, beyond researchers themselves, might directly watch over the rights and safety of human participants? For the past few decades, that responsibility has been given to **Institutional Review Boards, or IRBs.** Each research facility has an IRB—a committee of five or more members who review and monitor every study conducted at that institution, starting when the studies are first proposed (Parker, 2016). The institution may be a university, medical school, psychiatric or medical hospital, private research facility, mental health center, or the like. If research is conducted there, the institution

MINDTECH

The Use and Misuse of Social Media

Over the past several years, more and more researchers have been turning to social networks for their studies (Flick, 2016). Given the sites' billions of monthly visitors, they certainly provide an enormous pool of potential research participants and data (Pew Research, 2016; eBizMBA, 2015).

One recent study demonstrates the power and potential of using social media data (Kosinski, Stillwell, & Graepel, 2013). In this investigation, 58,000 Facebook subscribers allowed the researchers access to their list of "likes," and the subscribers further filled out online personality tests. The study found that information about a participant's likes could predict with considerable accuracy his or her personality traits, level of happiness, use of addictive substances, and level of intelligence, among other variables. Similarly, other social media site studies have tested psychological theories about relationships, self-esteem, popularity, and the like.

What a great resource, right? Not so fast. The studies above did indeed ask subscribers whether they were willing to participate. However, in a number of other such studies, social media users do *not* know that their posted data is being examined and tested. Here, the researchers assert that because posted information is already publicly available, users need not be informed that their data is under examination—an assertion that has generated enormous debate.

Dominic Lipinski/Press Association via AP Images

An area that has raised additional ethical concerns involves the direct and secret *manipulation* of social media users by researchers—an approach illustrated in a recent study conducted by a team of researchers from both Facebook and academia (Kramer, Guillory, & Hancock, 2014). The investigators wanted to determine whether the content of news feeds on Facebook influences the moods of its users. Without the users knowing it, the researchers reduced the number of positive news feed posts seen by around 350,000 users and reduced the number of negative posts seen by another 350,000 users over a one-week period. As a result, the moods of the former users became slightly (but significantly) more negative than those of the latter users, as measured by the number of negative and positive words posted by the users themselves in their Facebook status updates over the course of that same week.

Immediately upon the publication of this study, a flood of criticism emerged—from researchers, clinicians, and the public alike (Flick, 2016; Dewey, 2014). One concern was that the users in the study were unaware of and did not give consent for their participation, breaking with a leading ethical principle of all Institutional Review Boards. Critics holding this view were unimpressed with the claim that signing on to Facebook's lengthy and small-print user agreement constitutes a sufficient form of informed consent for this or similar social media studies. Another concern was that, by inducing more negative moods, the researchers in this study might have been feeding into the clinical depressions of some negative news feed users.

A core problem for all social media studies is that most social media sites do not really have policies prohibiting researchers from studying subscribers or subscriber profiles without clear permission (Flick, 2016).

> Can an argument be made that ethical standards regarding Internet use should be different from those applied in other areas of life?

While the technology-driven questions of what's public and what's private, what's ethical and what's unethical, are under debate, it is probably best that posters follow a new version of that most sacred rule of consumerism—"poster beware."

---

must have an IRB, and that IRB has the responsibility and power to require changes in a proposed study as a condition of approval. If acceptable changes are not made by the researcher, then the IRB can disapprove the study altogether. Similarly, if over the course of the study, the safety or rights of the participants are placed in jeopardy, the IRB must intervene and can even stop the study if necessary. These powers are granted to IRBs (or similar ethics committees) by nations around the world. In the United States, for example, IRBs are empowered by two agencies of the federal government—the Office for Human Research Protections and the Food and Drug Administration.

It turns out that protecting the rights and safety of human research participants is a complex undertaking. Thus, IRBs often are forced to conduct a kind of risk-benefit analysis in their reviews. They may, for example, approve a study that poses minimal or slight risks to participants if that "acceptable" level of risk is offset by the study's

Institutional Review Board (IRB) An ethics committee in a research facility that is empowered to protect the rights and safety of human research participants.

"I'm a social scientist, Michael. That means I can't explain electricity or anything like that, but if you ever want to know about people I'm your man."

potential benefits to society. In general, IRBs try to ensure that each study grants the following rights to its participants:

- The participants enlist voluntarily.
- Before enlisting, the participants are adequately informed about what the study entails ("informed consent").
- The participants can end their participation in the study at any time.
- The benefits of the study outweigh its costs/risks.
- The participants are protected from physical and psychological harm.
- The participants have access to information about the study.
- The participants' privacy is protected by principles such as confidentiality or anonymity.

Unfortunately, even with IRBs on the job, these rights can be in jeopardy. Consider, for example, the right of informed consent. To help ensure that participants understand what they are getting into when they enlist for a study, IRBs typically require that the individuals read and sign an "informed consent form" that spells out everything they need to know. But how clear are such forms? Not very, according to some investigations (Perrault & Nazione, 2016; Albala et al., 2010; Mathew & McGrath, 2002).

It turns out that most such forms—the very forms deemed acceptable by IRBs—are too long and/or are written at an advanced college level, making them incomprehensible to a large percentage of participants. In fact, fewer than half of all participants may fully understand the informed consent forms they are signing. Still other investigations indicate that only around 10 percent of human participants carefully read the informed consent forms before signing them, and only 30 percent ask questions of the researchers during the informed consent phase of their studies (CISCRP, 2013).

In short, the IRB system is flawed, much like the research undertakings it oversees. One reason for this is that ethical principles are subtle notions that do not always translate into simple guidelines. Another reason is that ethical decisions—whether by IRB members or by researchers—are subject to differences in perspective, interpretation, decision-making style, and the like. Despite such problems, most observers agree that the creation and work of IRBs have helped improve the rights and safety of human research participants over the years.

#TheirWords

"If we knew what it was we were doing, it would not be called research, would it?"

Albert Einstein

Keeping an Eye on Research Methods

EACH METHOD OF INVESTIGATION covered in this chapter addresses some of the obstacles involved in studying human behavior, but no one approach overcomes them all. Case studies allow investigators to consider a broader range of causes, but experiments pinpoint causes more precisely. Similarly, correlational studies allow broad generalizations, but case studies are richer in detail. Thus, as you read through this textbook, it is best that you view each research method as part of a team of approaches that together may shed light on abnormal human functioning. When more than one method has been used to investigate a disorder, you should ask whether all the results seem to point in the same direction. If they do, clinical scientists are probably making progress toward understanding and treating that disorder. Conversely, if the various methods seem to produce conflicting results, knowledge in that particular area is still limited.

Moreover, before accepting research findings, scientists, practitioners, and students alike must review the details of clinical studies with a very critical eye. Were the variables properly controlled? Was the choice of participants representative, was the sample large enough to be meaningful, and has bias been eliminated? Are the investigator's conclusions justified? And did the study meet ethical standards? Only after asking these questions can we conclude that a truly informative and appropriate investigation has taken place.

♀... SUMMING UP

» What Do Clinical Researchers Do?
Researchers use the *scientific method* to uncover *nomothetic* principles of abnormal psychological functioning. They attempt to identify and examine relationships between variables and depend primarily on three methods of investigation: the case study, the correlational method, and the experimental method. *pp. 24–25*

» The Case Study
A *case study* is a detailed account of a person's life and psychological problems. It can serve as a source of ideas about behavior, provide support for theories, challenge theories, clarify new treatment techniques, or offer an opportunity to study an unusual problem. However, case studies tend to have low *internal validity* and low *external validity*. *pp. 26–28*

» The Correlational Method
Correlational studies are used to systematically observe the degree to which events or characteristics vary together. This method allows researchers to draw broad conclusions about abnormality in the population at large.

A *correlation* may have a *positive* or *negative direction* and may be high or low in *magnitude*. Researchers perform a *statistical analysis* to determine whether the correlation found in a study is truly characteristic of the larger population or due to chance. Correlational studies generally have high external validity but lack internal validity. *pp. 28–31*

» The Experimental Method
In *experiments*, researchers manipulate suspected causes to see whether expected effects will result. The variable that is manipulated is called the *independent variable*, and the variable that is expected to change as a result is called the *dependent variable*. Experimental studies generally have high external validity and, because they enable researchers to determine causation, high internal validity as well.

To minimize the possible influence of *confounds*, experimenters use *control groups*, *random assignment*, and *masked designs*. The findings of experiments, like those of correlational studies, must be analyzed statistically. *pp. 31–36*

» Alternative Research Designs
Clinical scientists must often settle for alternative research designs that are less than ideal, called *quasi-experimental designs*, or *mixed designs*. These include the *matched design*, *natural experiment*, *analogue experiment*, *single-subject experiment*, *longitudinal study*, and *epidemiological study*. *pp. 36–40*

» Protecting Human Participants
Each research facility has an *Institutional Review Board (IRB)* that has the power and responsibility to protect the rights and safety of human participants in all studies conducted at that facility. Members of the IRB review each study during the planning stages and can require changes in the proposed study before granting approval for the undertaking. Among the important participant rights that the IRB protects is the right of *informed consent*, an *acceptable risk/benefit balance*, and *privacy* (confidentiality or anonymity). *pp. 40–42*

» Keeping an Eye on Research Methods
To help address the many practical, logistical, and ethical factors that often make properly designed research difficult to do, clinical investigators must use multiple research approaches. *p. 42*

Visit *LaunchPad*
to access the e-Book, Clinical Choices, videos, activities, and LearningCurve, as well as study aids including flashcards, FAQs, and research exercises.

LaunchPad macmillan learning

⚲...Models of Abnormality

Philip Berman, a 25-year-old single unemployed former copy editor for a large publishing house . . . had been hospitalized after a suicide attempt in which he deeply gashed his wrist with a razor blade. He described [to the therapist] how he had sat on the bathroom floor and watched the blood drip into the bathtub for some time before he [contacted] his father at work for help. He and his father went to the hospital emergency room to have the gash stitched, but he convinced himself and the hospital physician that he did not need hospitalization. The next day when his father suggested he needed help, he knocked his dinner to the floor and angrily stormed to his room. When he was calm again, he allowed his father to take him back to the hospital.

The immediate precipitant for his suicide attempt was that he had run into one of his former girl-friends with her new boyfriend. The patient stated that they had a drink together, but all the while he was with them he could not help thinking that "they were dying to run off and jump in bed." He experienced jealous rage, got up from the table, and walked out of the restaurant. He began to think about how he could "pay her back."

Mr. Berman had felt frequently depressed for brief periods during the previous several years. He was especially critical of himself for his limited social life and his inability to have managed to have sexual intercourse with a woman even once in his life. As he related this to the therapist, he lifted his eyes from the floor and with a sarcastic smirk said, "I'm a 25-year-old virgin. Go ahead, you can laugh now." He has had several girlfriends to date, whom he described as very attractive, but who he said had lost interest in him. On further questioning, however, it became apparent that Mr. Berman soon became very critical of them and demanded that they always meet his every need, often to their own detriment. The women then found the relationship very unrewarding and would soon find someone else.

During the past two years Mr. Berman had seen three psychiatrists briefly, one of whom had given him a drug, the name of which he could not remember, but that had precipitated some sort of unusual reaction for which he had to stay in a hospital overnight. . . . Concerning his hospitalization, the patient said that "It was a dump," that the staff refused to listen to what he had to say or to respond to his needs, and that they, in fact, treated all the patients "sadistically." The referring doctor corroborated that Mr. Berman was a difficult patient who demanded that he be treated as special, and yet was hostile to most staff members throughout his stay. After one angry exchange with an aide, he left the hospital without [permission], and subsequently signed out against medical advice.

Mr. Berman is one of two children of a middle-class family. His father is 55 years old and employed in a managerial position for an insurance company. He perceives his father as weak and ineffectual, completely dominated by the patient's overbearing and cruel mother. He states that he hates his mother with "a passion I can barely control." He claims that his mother used to call him names like "pervert" . . . when he was growing up, and that in an argument she once "kicked me in the balls." Together, he sees his parents as rich, powerful, and selfish, and, in turn, thinks that they see him as lazy, irresponsible, and a behavior problem. When his parents called the therapist to discuss their son's treatment, they stated that his problem began with the birth of his younger brother, Arnold, when Philip was 10 years old. After Arnold's birth Philip apparently became [a disagreeable] child who cursed a lot and was difficult to discipline. Philip recalls this period only vaguely. He reports that his mother once was hospitalized for depression, but that now "she doesn't believe in psychiatry."

model A set of assumptions and concepts that help scientists explain and interpret observations. Also called a *paradigm*.

neuron A nerve cell.

> *Mr. Berman had graduated from college with average grades. Since graduating he had worked at three different publishing houses, but at none of them for more than one year. He always found some justification for quitting. He usually sat around his house doing very little for two or three months after quitting a job, until his parents prodded him into getting a new one. He described innumerable interactions in his life with teachers, friends, and employers in which he felt offended or unfairly treated . . . and frequent arguments that left him feeling bitter . . . and [he] spent most of his time alone, "bored." He was unable to commit himself to any person, he held no strong convictions, and he felt no allegiance to any group. The patient appeared as a very thin, bearded . . . young man with pale skin who maintained little eye contact with the therapist and who had an air of angry bitterness about him. Although he complained of depression, he denied other symptoms of the depressive syndrome. He seemed preoccupied with his rage at his parents, and seemed particularly invested in conveying a despicable image of himself. . . .*
>
> *Spitzer et al., 1983, pp. 59–61*

Philip Berman is clearly a troubled person, but how did he come to be that way? How do we explain and correct his many problems? To answer these questions, we must first look at the wide range of complaints we are trying to understand: Philip's depression and anger, his social failures, his lack of employment, his distrust of those around him, and the problems within his family. Then we must sort through all kinds of potential causes—internal and external, biological and interpersonal, past and present.

Although we may not realize it, we all use theoretical frameworks as we read about Philip. Over the course of our lives, each of us has developed a perspective that helps us make sense of the things other people say and do. In science, the perspectives used to explain events are known as **models**, or **paradigms**. Each model spells out the scientist's basic assumptions, gives order to the field under study, and sets guidelines for its investigation (Kuhn, 1962). It influences what the investigators observe as well as the questions they ask, the information they seek, and how they interpret this information. To understand how a clinician explains or treats a specific set of symptoms, such as Philip's, we must know his or her preferred model of abnormal functioning.

Until relatively recently, clinical scientists of a given place and time tended to agree on a single model of abnormality—a model greatly influenced by the beliefs of their culture. The *demonological model* that was used to explain abnormal functioning during the Middle Ages, for example, borrowed heavily from medieval society's concerns with religion, superstition, and warfare. Medieval practitioners would have seen the devil's guiding hand in Philip Berman's efforts to commit suicide and his feelings of depression, rage, jealousy, and hatred. Similarly, their treatments for him—from prayers to whippings—would have sought to drive foreign spirits from his body.

Today several models are used to explain and treat abnormal functioning. This variety has resulted both from shifts in values and beliefs over the past half-century and from improvements in clinical research. At one end of the spectrum is the *biological model*, which sees physical processes as key to human behavior. In the middle are three models that focus on more psychological and personal aspects of human functioning: The *psychodynamic model* looks at people's unconscious internal processes and conflicts; the *cognitive-behavioral model* emphasizes behavior, the ways in which it is learned, and the thinking that underlies behavior; and the *humanistic-existential model* stresses the role of values and choices. At the far end of the spectrum is the *sociocultural model*, which looks to social and cultural forces as the keys to human functioning. This model includes the *family-social perspective*, which focuses on an individual's family and social interactions, and the *multicultural perspective*, which emphasizes an individual's culture and the shared beliefs, values, and history of that culture.

#BigDates

FDA Approval of Pioneering Drugs

1954	Thorazine (antipsychotic drug)
1955	Ritalin (ADHD drug)
1958	MAO inhibitors (antidepressant drugs)
1960	Librium (antianxiety drug)
1961	Elavil (antidepressant drug)
1963	Valium (antianxiety drug)
1970	Lithium (mood stabilizer/antibipolar drug)
1987	Prozac (antidepressant drug)
1998	Viagra (erectile disorder drug)

Given their different assumptions and principles, the models are sometimes in conflict. Those who exclusively follow one perspective often scoff at the "naïve" interpretations, investigations, and treatment efforts of the others. Yet none of the models is complete in itself. Each focuses mainly on one aspect of human functioning, and none can explain all aspects of abnormality. ■

The Biological Model

PHILIP BERMAN IS A BIOLOGICAL being. His thoughts and feelings are the results of biochemical and bioelectrical processes throughout his brain and body. Proponents of the *biological model* believe that a full understanding of Philip's thoughts, emotions, and behavior must therefore include an understanding of their biological basis. Not surprisingly, then, they believe that the most effective treatments for Philip's problems will be biological ones.

How Do Biological Theorists Explain Abnormal Behavior?

Adopting a medical perspective, biological theorists view abnormal behavior as an illness brought about by malfunctioning parts of the organism. Typically, they point to problems in brain anatomy, brain chemistry, and/or brain circuitry as the cause of such behavior.

Brain Anatomy and Abnormal Behavior The brain is made up of approximately 86 billion nerve cells, called **neurons,** and thousands of billions of support cells, called *glia* (from the Greek word for "glue") (Herculano-Houzel, 2016). Within the brain large groups of neurons form distinct regions, or *brain structures.* Toward the top of the brain, for example, is a cluster of structures, collectively referred to as the *cerebrum,* which includes the *cortex, corpus callosum, basal ganglia, hippocampus,* and *amygdala* (see **Figure 3-1**). The neurons in each of these brain structures control important functions. The cortex is the outer layer of the brain, the corpus callosum connects the brain's two cerebral hemispheres, the basal ganglia plays a crucial role in planning and producing movement, the hippocampus helps regulate emotions and memory, and the amygdala plays a key role in emotional memory. Clinical researchers have sometimes discovered connections between particular psychological disorders and problems in specific structures of the brain. One such disorder is *Huntington's disease,* a disorder marked by violent emotional outbursts, memory loss, suicidal thinking, involuntary body movements, and absurd beliefs. This disease has been linked in part to a loss of cells in the basal ganglia and cortex.

Brain Chemistry and Abnormal Behavior Biological researchers have also learned that psychological disorders can be related to problems in the transmission of messages from neuron to neuron. Information is communicated throughout the brain in the form of electrical impulses that travel from one neuron to one or more others. An impulse is first received by a neuron's *dendrites,* antenna-like extensions located at one end of the neuron. From there it travels down the neuron's *axon,* a long fiber extending from the neuron's body. Finally, it is transmitted through the *nerve ending* at the end of the axon to the dendrites of other neurons (see **Figure 3-2**). Each neuron has multiple dendrites and a single axon. But that axon can be very long indeed, often extending all the way from one structure of the brain to another.

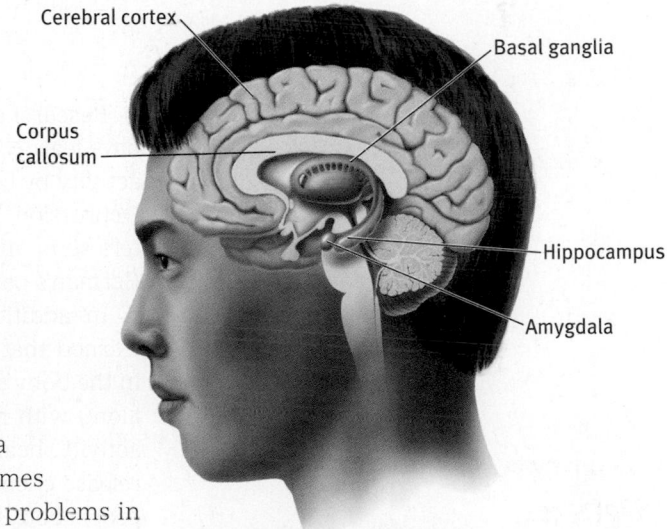

Cerebral cortex

Basal ganglia

Corpus callosum

Hippocampus

Amygdala

FIGURE 3-1

The Cerebrum

Some psychological disorders can be traced to abnormal functioning of neurons in the cerebrum, which includes brain structures such as the cerebral cortex, corpus callosum, basal ganglia, hippocampus, and amygdala.

How do messages get from the nerve ending of one neuron to the dendrites of another? After all, the neurons do not actually touch each other. A tiny space, called the **synapse,** separates one neuron from the next, and the message must somehow move across that space. When an electrical impulse reaches a neuron's ending, the nerve ending is stimulated to release a chemical, called a **neurotransmitter,** that travels across the synaptic space to **receptors** on the dendrites of the neighboring neurons. After binding to the receiving neuron's receptors, some neurotransmitters give a message to receiving neurons to "fire," that is, to trigger their own electrical impulse. Other neurotransmitters carry an inhibitory message; they tell receiving neurons to stop all firing. As you can see, neurotransmitters play a key role in moving information through the brain.

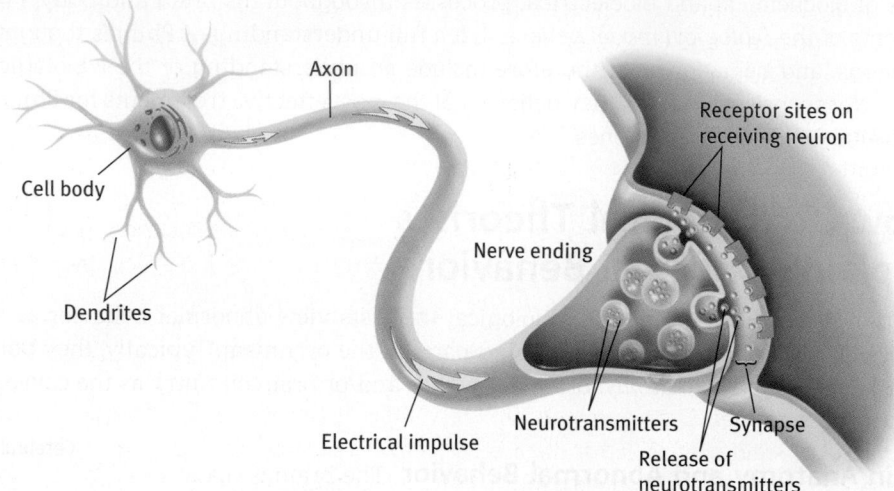

FIGURE 3-2

A Neuron Communicating Information

A message in the form of an electrical impulse travels down the sending neuron's axon to its nerve ending, where neurotransmitters are released and carry the message across the synaptic space to the dendrites of a receiving neuron.

Researchers have identified dozens of neurotransmitters in the brain, and they have learned that each neuron uses only certain kinds. Studies indicate that abnormal activity by certain neurotransmitters is sometimes associated with mental disorders. Depression, for example, has been linked in part to low activity of the neurotransmitters *serotonin* and *norepinephrine*. Perhaps low serotonin activity is at play in Philip Berman's pattern of depression and rage.

In addition to focusing on neurons and neurotransmitters, researchers have learned that mental disorders are sometimes related to abnormal chemical activity in the body's *endocrine system*. Endocrine glands, located throughout the body, work along with neurons to control such vital activities as growth, reproduction, sexual activity, heart rate, body temperature, energy, and responses to stress. The glands release chemicals called **hormones** into the bloodstream, and these chemicals then propel body organs into action. During times of stress, for example, the *adrenal glands,* located on top of the kidneys, secrete the hormone *cortisol* to help the body deal with the stress. Abnormal secretions of this chemical have been tied to anxiety and mood disorders.

Brain Circuitry and Abnormal Behavior Over the past decade, researchers have increasingly focused on **brain circuits** as the key to psychological disorders rather than on dysfunction within a single brain region or by a single brain chemical. A brain circuit is a network of particular brain structures that work together, triggering each other into action to produce a distinct behavioral, cognitive, or emotional reaction. How do the structures of a given circuit work together? The answer, as you might anticipate by now, is through their neurons. The long axons of the neurons from one structure bundle together and extend across the brain to communicate with the neurons of another structure, setting up a visible fiber pathway between the structures. The structures that comprise a given brain circuit are, of course, important, as are the neurotransmitters that enable the neurons of those structures to communicate

synapse The tiny space between the nerve ending of one neuron and the dendrite of another.

neurotransmitter A chemical that, released by one neuron, crosses the synaptic space to be received at receptors on the dendrites of neighboring neurons.

receptor A site on a neuron that receives a neurotransmitter.

hormones The chemicals released by endocrine glands into the bloodstream.

brain circuit A network of particular brain structures that work together, triggering each other into action to produce a distinct kind of behavioral, cognitive, or emotional reaction.

gene Chromosome segments that control the characteristics and traits we inherit.

with each other. But many of today's researchers are finding it most informative to look at the operation of the entire circuit, including its interconnecting fiber pathways, to fully understand human functioning—both normal and abnormal.

An example of such brain circuits is the "fear circuit." As you will see in Chapter 5, researchers have tied everyday fear reactions to a brain circuit consisting of particular structures (including the amygdala, prefrontal cortex, insula, and anterior cingulate cortex) whose neurons extend to each other though fiber pathways, enabling the structures to trigger each other into action. The neurons in this circuit further use particular neurotransmitters (including GABA, serotonin, norepinephrine, and dopamine) to communicate with each other. Studies suggest that this circuit often functions improperly in people suffering from anxiety disorders (Williams, 2017). Perhaps dysfunction by Philip Berman's fear circuit is contributing to his repeated concerns that things will go badly and that other people will have low opinions and negative motives toward him, concerns that keep triggering his depression and anger.

Sources of Biological Abnormalities Why might the brain structures, neurotransmitters, or brain circuits of some people function differently from the norm? As you will see throughout the textbook, a wide range of factors can play a role—from prenatal events to brain injuries, viral infections, environmental experiences, and stress. Two factors that have received particular attention in the biological model are *genetics* and *evolution*.

GENETICS AND ABNORMAL BEHAVIOR Each cell in the human brain and body contains 23 pairs of *chromosomes*, with each chromosome in a pair inherited from one of the person's parents. Every chromosome contains numerous **genes**—segments that control the characteristics and traits a person inherits. Altogether, each cell contains around 20,000 genes (Moraes & Goes, 2016). Scientists have known for years that genes help determine such physical characteristics as hair color, height, and eyesight. Genes can make people more prone to heart disease, cancer, or diabetes, and perhaps to possessing artistic or musical skill. Studies suggest that inheritance also can play a part in certain mental disorders.

In most instances, several or more genes combine to help produce our actions and reactions, both functional and dysfunctional. The precise contributions of various genes or gene combinations to mental disorders have become clearer in recent years, thanks in part to the completion of the *Human Genome Project* in 2000, a major

Etienne Oliveau/Getty Images

More than coincidence? Identical twins Mike and Bob Bryan, shown here returning a shot during a semifinal tennis match at the 2016 China Open, have had storied careers. Ranked as the world's top doubles tennis players, they have won multiple Olympic medals representing the United States. Studies of twins suggest that some aspects of behavior and personality are influenced by genetic factors. Many identical twins, like the Bryans, have similar tastes, behave similarly, and make similar life choices. Some even develop similar abnormal behaviors.

psychotropic medications Drugs that primarily affect the brain and reduce many symptoms of mental dysfunction.

undertaking in which scientists used the tools of molecular biology to *map,* or *sequence,* all of the genes in the human body.

EVOLUTION AND ABNORMAL BEHAVIOR Genes that contribute to mental disorders are typically viewed as unfortunate occurrences—almost mistakes of inheritance. The responsible gene may be a *mutation,* an abnormal form of the appropriate gene that emerges by accident. Or the problematic gene may be inherited by an individual after it has initially entered his or her family line as a mutation. According to some theorists, however, many of the genes that contribute to abnormal functioning are actually the result of normal *evolutionary* principles (Durisko et al., 2016; Fábrega, 2010).

In general, evolutionary theorists argue that human reactions and the genes responsible for them have survived over the course of time because they have helped individuals to thrive and adapt. Ancestors who had the ability to run fast, for example, or the craftiness to hide were most able to escape their enemies and to reproduce. Thus, the genes responsible for effective walking, running, or problem solving were particularly likely to be passed on from generation to generation to the present day.

Similarly, say evolutionary theorists, the capacity to experience fear was, and in many instances still is, adaptive. Fear alerted our ancestors to dangers, threats, and losses, so that persons could avoid or escape potential problems. People who were particularly sensitive to danger—those with greater fear responses—were more likely to survive catastrophes, battles, and the like and to reproduce and pass on their fear genes. Of course, in today's world, pressures are more numerous and often more subtle than they were in the past, condemning many individuals with such genes to a near-endless stream of fear and arousal. That is, the very genes that helped their ancestors to survive and reproduce might now leave these individuals particularly prone to fear reactions, anxiety disorders, or related psychological patterns.

The evolutionary perspective is controversial in the clinical field and has been rejected by many theorists. Imprecise and at times impossible to research, scientists often find such explanations unacceptable.

#TheirWords

"Mental illness is so much more complicated than any pill that any mortal could invent."
Elizabeth Wurtzel, *Prozac Nation*

Biological Treatments

Biological practitioners look for certain kinds of clues when they treat people who are behaving abnormally. Does the person's family have a history of that behavior, and hence a possible genetic predisposition to it? (Philip Berman's case history mentions that his mother was once hospitalized for depression.) Is the behavior produced by events that could have had a physiological effect? (Philip was having a drink when he flew into a jealous rage at the restaurant.) Once the clinicians have pinpointed physical sources of dysfunction, they are in a better position to choose a biological course of treatment. The three leading kinds of biological treatments used today are *drug therapy, brain stimulation*, and *psychosurgery*. Drug therapy is by far the most common of these approaches.

In the 1950s, researchers discovered several effective **psychotropic medications,** drugs that mainly affect emotions and thought processes. These drugs have greatly changed the outlook for a number of mental disorders and today are used widely, either alone or with other forms of therapy (see *Trending*). However, the psychotropic drug revolution has also produced some major problems. Many people believe, for example, that the drugs are overused (Maughan & James, 2017). Moreover, while drugs are effective in many cases, they do not help everyone.

> What might the popularity of psychotropic drugs suggest about coping styles and problem-solving skills in our society?

Four major psychotropic drug groups are used in therapy. *Antianxiety drugs,* also called *minor tranquilizers* or *anxiolytics,* help reduce tension and anxiety. *Antidepressant drugs* help improve the functioning of people with depression and certain other disorders. *Antibipolar drugs,* also called *mood stabilizers,* help steady the moods of those with a bipolar disorder, a condition marked by mood

TV Drug Ads Come Under Attack

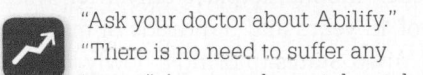

"Ask your doctor about Abilify." "There is no need to suffer any longer." Anyone who watches television or browses the Internet is familiar with phrases such as these. They are at the heart of *direct-to-consumer (DTC)* drug advertising—advertisements in which pharmaceutical companies appeal directly to consumers, coaxing them to ask their physicians to prescribe particular drugs for them. The United States and New Zealand are the only developed countries in the world that allow such advertising. Around 80 percent of American adults have seen these ads, and at least 30 percent ask their doctors about the specific medications they see advertised (ProCon, 2016; Hausman, 2008).

Nowhere is the prominence of the biological model in the mental health field more visible than in the proliferation of these ads (Brown, 2017). Half of today's leading DTC-advertised medications are *psychotropic* drugs such as antibipolar and antipsychotic drugs (Bulik, 2017; Sukel, 2016).

DTC ads have flooded the airwaves since 1997 when the U.S. Food and Drug Administration (FDA) relaxed its restrictions for drug advertising on television, ruling that DTC ads must simply recommend that consumers speak with a doctor about the drug, mention the drug's important risks, and indicate where consumers can get further information about it—often a Web site or phone number (Chesnes & Jin, 2016; FDA, 2016, 2015). Such ads have received relatively little criticism over the past two decades, but this climate of tolerance is now changing. A number of consumer groups and even the American Medical Association (AMA) are now calling for a ban on such advertising, saying that the ads often contribute to economic hardships, patient misinformation, and less-than-optimal treatment (Nelson, 2016; AMA, 2015).

First, the economic concerns. Altogether, pharmaceutical companies spend $5.2 billion a year on American television and some online advertising, an amount that keeps growing by leaps and bounds (Campbell, 2016; AMA, 2015). This leads to higher drug prices, at a time when prescription drug costs and insurance premiums are already

depression **hurts**

skyrocketing, increasing by close to 5 percent each year. Moreover, the DTC ads typically promote newer and more expensive drugs, inflating the demand for such drugs even when older, generic, and cheaper drugs might be equally or more appropriate (Campbell, 2016; AMA, 2015).

DTC ads also may adversely affect patient awareness and clinical treatment. Three-quarters of surveyed doctors believe that most of the ads overemphasize a drug's benefits while leaving out key negative information (ProCon, 2016). Similarly, 80 percent of doctors believe DTC ads help patients better understand the benefits of a drug, but only 40 percent of them believe that patients understand the possible risks of a drug after seeing the ad (FDA, 2016, 2015). Small wonder that many patients believe their mental or physical health will be put in jeopardy if they do not take advertised drugs (Campbell, 2016).

Despite these problems, doctors often feel pressured to prescribe DTC-advertised drugs, even in cases where the drugs are not appropriate for patients (ProCon, 2016; FDA, 2015). Over half of patient requests for such drugs are granted by doctors. This has apparently contributed to an overuse of psychotropic and other drugs.

So why do DTC ads continue to rise in number? One reason is that this form of advertising has its supporters. The FDA, for example, believes that the ads may indeed serve a public service, protecting consumers—although imperfectly—by directly educating them about drugs that are available in the marketplace (FDA, 2016, 2015). Many doctors also believe that DTC ads make patients more involved in their mental and physical health care, and a number report that they now have better discussions with their patients about treatment options as a result of DTC advertising.

> **Are DTC ads useful, harmful, or irrelevant for persons in your age group and life situation?**

Finally, not to be overlooked are the profits that DTC advertising helps generate for pharmaceutical companies. The average number of prescriptions written for DTC-advertised new drugs are nine times greater than those written for new drugs that do not have DTC ads (ProCon, 2016).

The current debate between consumer groups, the AMA, the FDA, and the pharmaceutical industry will have to play out some more before we know what the future holds for DTC drug ads. Fortunately, to help sort out this issue, a growing body of research is now examining the drawbacks and possible merits of these ads (Brown, 2017). In the meantime, as with ads of any kind, consumers must rely on their own good judgment about whether and how to use this particular form of advertising.

AP Photo/Bloomington Herald-Times, Jeremy Hogan

A fascinating subject The human brain increasingly has captured the attention not only of neuroscientists but also the public at large. Here an eighth-grade student holds and examines a brain ever so carefully during a visit to the psychology department at Indiana University.

brain stimulation Interventions that directly or indirectly stimulate the brain in order to bring about psychological improvement.

electroconvulsive therapy (ECT) A biological treatment in which a brain seizure is triggered as an electric current passes through electrodes attached to the patient's forehead.

psychosurgery Brain surgery for mental disorders.

id According to Freud, the psychological force that produces instinctual needs, drives, and impulses.

swings from mania to depression. And *antipsychotic drugs* help reduce the confusion, hallucinations, and delusions that often accompany *psychosis*, a loss of contact with reality found in schizophrenia and other disorders.

Psychotropic drugs, like all medications, reach the marketplace only after systematic research and review. It takes an average of 12 years and hundreds of millions of dollars for a pharmaceutical company in the United States to bring a newly identified chemical compound to market. Along the way, the drug is vigorously tested in study after study—first on animals and then on humans—to determine its efficacy, safety, dosage, and side effects, until finally it receives approval by the U.S. Food and Drug Administration. Only 3 percent of newly discovered chemical compounds make it to animal testing, only 2 percent of animal-tested compounds reach human testing, and only 21 percent of human-tested drugs are eventually approved (FDA, 2016, 2014).

As the name implies, a second form of biological treatment, **brain stimulation**, refers to interventions that directly or indirectly stimulate certain areas of the brain. The oldest (and most controversial) such approach, used primarily on severely depressed people, is **electroconvulsive therapy (ECT).** Two electrodes are attached to a patient's forehead, and an electrical current of 65 to 140 volts is passed briefly through the brain. The current causes a brain seizure that lasts up to a few minutes. After seven to nine ECT sessions, spaced two or three days apart, many patients feel considerably less depressed. This treatment is used on tens of thousands of persons annually, particularly those whose depression fails to respond to other treatments (Kolar, 2017; Dukart et al., 2014).

As you will see in Chapter 8, several other brain stimulation techniques have increasingly been used over the past decade, particularly in cases of depression. In one, *transcranial magnetic stimulation (TMS)*, an electromagnetic coil is placed on or above a person's head, sending a current into certain areas of his or her brain. In another such technique, *vagus nerve stimulation (VNS)*, a pulse generator is implanted in a person's neck, helping to stimulate his or her vagus nerve, a long nerve that extends from the brain down through the neck and on to the abdomen. The stimulated vagus nerve then delivers electrical signals to the brain. In a third technique, called *deep brain stimulation*, electrodes are implanted in specific areas of a person's brain and connected to a battery ("pacemaker") in his or her chest. The pacemaker proceeds to power the electrodes, sending a steady stream of low-voltage electricity to the targeted brain areas. As with ECT, research suggests that each of these newer brain stimulation techniques is able to improve the psychological functioning of many people whose depressive or related disorders have been unresponsive to other forms of treatment (Luber et al., 2017; Narang et al., 2016; Yuan et al., 2016).

A third kind of biological treatment is **psychosurgery**, brain surgery for mental disorders. It has roots as far back as trephining, the prehistoric practice of chipping a hole in the skull of a person who behaved strangely. Modern procedures are derived from a notorious technique developed in the late 1930s by a Portuguese neuropsychiatrist, António Egas Moniz. In that procedure, known as a *lobotomy*, a surgeon would cut the connections between the brain's frontal lobes and the lower regions of the brain. Today's psychosurgery procedures are much more precise than the lobotomies of the past (Neumaier et al., 2016). Even so, they are typically used only after certain severe disorders have continued for years without responding to any other treatment. It is worth noting that deep brain stimulation, one of the interventions described above, is also a psychosurgery procedure inasmuch as it involves making small incisions in a person's skull in order to implant electrodes in a targeted brain area.

Assessing the Biological Model

Today the biological model enjoys considerable respect. Biological research constantly produces valuable new information, and biological treatments often bring great relief when other approaches have failed. At the same time, this model has its shortcomings.

Some of its proponents seem to expect that all human behavior can be explained in biological terms and treated with biological methods. This view can limit rather than enhance our understanding of abnormal functioning. Our mental life is an interplay of biological and nonbiological factors, and it is important to understand that interplay rather than to focus on biological variables alone.

Another shortcoming is that several of today's biological treatments are capable of producing significant undesirable effects. Certain antipsychotic drugs, for example, may produce movement problems such as severe shaking, bizarre-looking contractions of the face and body, and extreme restlessness. Clearly such costs must be addressed and weighed against the drug's benefits.

The Psychodynamic Model

THE PSYCHODYNAMIC MODEL IS the oldest and most famous of the modern psychological models. Psychodynamic theorists believe that a person's behavior, whether normal or abnormal, is determined largely by underlying psychological forces of which he or she is not consciously aware. These internal forces are described as *dynamic*—that is, they interact with one another—and their interaction gives rise to behavior, thoughts, and emotions. Abnormal symptoms are viewed as the result of conflicts between these forces.

Psychodynamic theorists would view Philip Berman as a person in conflict. They would want to explore his past experiences because, in their view, psychological conflicts are tied to early relationships and to traumatic experiences that occurred during childhood. Psychodynamic theories rest on the *deterministic* assumption that no symptom or behavior is "accidental": all behavior is determined by past experiences. Thus Philip's hatred for his mother, his memories of her as cruel and overbearing, the weakness of his father, and the birth of a younger brother when Philip was 10 may all be important to the understanding of his current problems.

The psychodynamic model was first formulated by Viennese neurologist Sigmund Freud (1856–1939) at the turn of the twentieth century. After studying hypnosis, Freud developed the theory of *psychoanalysis* to explain both normal and abnormal psychological functioning as well as a corresponding method of treatment, a conversational approach also called psychoanalysis. During the early 1900s, Freud and several of his colleagues in the Vienna Psychoanalytic Society—including Carl Gustav Jung (1875–1961)—became the most influential clinical theorists in the Western world.

Freud takes a closer look at Freud Sigmund Freud, founder of psychoanalytic theory and therapy, contemplates a sculptured bust of himself in 1931 at his village home in Potzlein, near Vienna. As Freud and the bust go eyeball to eyeball, one can only imagine what conclusions each is drawing about the other.

How Did Freud Explain Normal and Abnormal Functioning?

Freud believed that three central forces shape the personality—instinctual needs, rational thinking, and moral standards. All of these forces, he believed, operate at the *unconscious level,* unavailable to immediate awareness; he further believed these forces to be dynamic, or interactive. Freud called the forces the *id,* the *ego,* and the *superego.*

The Id Freud used the term **id** to denote instinctual needs, drives, and impulses. The id operates in accordance with the *pleasure principle;* that is, it always seeks gratification. Freud also believed that all id instincts tend to be sexual, noting that from the

"I'm doing a lot better now that I'm back in denial."

very earliest stages of life a child's pleasure is obtained from nursing, defecating, masturbating, or engaging in other activities that he considered to have sexual ties. He further suggested that a person's *libido,* or sexual energy, fuels the id.

The Ego During our early years we come to recognize that our environment will not meet every instinctual need. Our mother, for example, is not always available to do our bidding. A part of the id separates off and becomes the **ego.** Like the id, the ego unconsciously seeks gratification, but it does so in accordance with the *reality principle,* the knowledge we acquire through experience that it can be unacceptable to express our id impulses outright. The ego, employing reason, guides us to know when we can and cannot express those impulses.

The ego develops basic strategies, called **ego defense mechanisms,** to control unacceptable id impulses and avoid or reduce the anxiety they arouse. The most basic defense mechanism, *repression,* prevents unacceptable impulses from ever reaching consciousness. There are many other ego defense mechanisms, and each of us tends to favor some over others (see **Table 3-1**).

The Superego The **superego** grows from the ego, just as the ego grows out of the id. This personality force operates by the *morality principle,* a sense of what is right and what is wrong. As we learn from our parents that many of our id impulses are unacceptable, we unconsciously adopt our parents' values. Judging ourselves by their standards, we feel good when we uphold their values; conversely, when we go against them, we feel guilty. In short, we develop a *conscience.*

According to Freud, these three parts of the personality—the id, the ego, and the superego—are often in some degree of conflict. A healthy personality is one in which an effective working relationship, an acceptable compromise, has formed among the three forces. If the id, ego, and superego are in excessive conflict, the person's behavior may show signs of dysfunction.

TABLE: 3-1

The Defense Never Rests

Defense Mechanism	Operation	Example
Repression	Person avoids anxiety by simply not allowing painful or dangerous thoughts to become conscious.	An executive's desire to run amok and attack his boss and colleagues at a board meeting is denied access to his awareness.
Denial	Person simply refuses to acknowledge the existence of an external source of anxiety.	You are not prepared for tomorrow's final exam, but you tell yourself that it's not actually an important exam and that there's no good reason not to go to a movie tonight.
Projection	Person attributes his or her own unacceptable impulses, motives, or desires to other individuals.	The executive who repressed his destructive desires may project his anger onto his boss and claim that it is actually the boss who is hostile.
Rationalization	Person creates a socially acceptable reason for an action that actually reflects unacceptable motives.	A student explains away poor grades by citing the importance of the "total experience" of going to college and claiming that too much emphasis on grades would actually interfere with a well-rounded education.
Displacement	Person displaces hostility away from a dangerous object and onto a safer substitute.	After a perfect parking spot is taken by a person who cuts in front of your car, you release your pent-up anger by starting an argument with your roommate.
Intellectualization	Person represses emotional reactions in favor of overly logical response to a problem.	A woman who has been beaten and raped gives a detached, methodical description of the effects that such attacks may have on victims.
Regression	Person retreats from an upsetting conflict to an early developmental stage in which no one is expected to behave maturely or responsibly.	A boy who cannot cope with the anger he feels toward his rejecting mother regresses to infantile behavior, soiling his clothes and no longer taking care of his basic needs.

"Luke . . . I am your father." This lightsaber fight between Luke Skywalker and Darth Vader highlights the most famous, and contentious, father–son relationship in movie history. According to Sigmund Freud, however, all fathers and sons have significant tensions and conflicts that they must work through, even in the absence of the special pressures faced by Luke and his father in the *Star Wars* series.

Freudians would therefore view Philip Berman as someone whose personality forces have a poor working relationship. His ego and superego are unable to control his id impulses, which lead him repeatedly to act in impulsive and often dangerous ways—suicide gestures, jealous rages, job resignations, outbursts of temper, frequent arguments.

Developmental Stages Freud proposed that at each stage of development, from infancy to maturity, new events challenge individuals and require adjustments in their id, ego, and superego. If the adjustments are successful, they lead to personal growth. If not, the person may become **fixated,** or stuck, at an early stage of development. Then all subsequent development suffers, and the individual may well be headed for abnormal functioning in the future. Because parents are the key figures during the early years of life, they are often seen as the cause of improper development.

Freud named each stage of development after the body area that he considered most important to the child at that time. For example, he referred to the first 18 months of life as the *oral stage*. During this stage, children fear that the mother who feeds and comforts them will disappear. Children whose mothers consistently fail to gratify their oral needs may become fixated at the oral stage and display an "oral character" throughout their lives, one marked by extreme dependence or extreme mistrust. Such persons are particularly prone to develop depression. As you will see in later chapters, Freud linked fixations at the other stages of development—*anal* (18 months to 3 years of age), *phallic* (3 to 5 years), *latency* (5 to 12 years), and *genital* (12 years to adulthood)—to yet other kinds of psychological dysfunction.

How Do Other Psychodynamic Explanations Differ from Freud's?

Personal and professional differences between Freud and his colleagues led to a split in the Vienna Psychoanalytic Society early in the twentieth century. Carl Jung and others developed new theories. Although the new theories departed from Freud's ideas in important ways, each held on to Freud's belief that human functioning is shaped by dynamic (interacting) psychological forces. Thus all such theories, including Freud's, are referred to as *psychodynamic*.

Two of today's most influential psychodynamic theories are self theory and object relations theory. **Self theorists** emphasize the role of the *self*—the unified personality. They believe that the basic human motive is to strengthen the wholeness of the self

ego According to Freud, the psychological force that employs reason and operates in accordance with the reality principle.

ego defense mechanisms According to psychoanalytic theory, strategies developed by the ego to control unacceptable id impulses and to avoid or reduce the anxiety they arouse.

superego According to Freud, the psychological force that represents a person's values and ideals.

fixation According to Freud, a condition in which the id, ego, or superego do not mature properly and are frozen at an early stage of development.

self theory The psychodynamic theory that emphasizes the role of the self—our unified personality.

object relations theory The psychodynamic theory that views the desire for relationships as the key motivating force in human behavior.

free association A psychodynamic technique in which the patient describes any thought, feeling, or image that comes to mind, even if it seems unimportant.

resistance An unconscious refusal to participate fully in therapy.

transference According to psychodynamic theorists, the redirection toward the psychotherapist of feelings associated with important figures in a patient's life, now or in the past.

dream A series of ideas and images that form during sleep.

catharsis The reliving of past repressed feelings in order to settle internal conflicts and overcome problems.

working through The psychoanalytic process of facing conflicts, reinterpreting feelings, and overcoming one's problems.

(Corey, 2017; Kohut, 2001, 1977). **Object relations theorists,** on the other hand, propose that people are motivated mainly by a need to have relationships with others and that severe problems in the relationships between children and their caregivers may lead to abnormal development (D'Antonio, 2016; Kernberg, 2005, 2001, 1997).

Psychodynamic Therapies

Psychodynamic therapies range from Freudian psychoanalysis to modern therapies based on self theory or object relations theory. Psychodynamic therapists seek to uncover past traumas and the inner conflicts that have resulted from them. They try to help clients resolve, or settle, those conflicts and to resume personal development.

According to most psychodynamic therapists, therapists must subtly guide therapy discussions so that the patients discover their underlying problems for themselves. To aid in the process, the therapists rely on such techniques as *free association, therapist interpretation, catharsis,* and *working through.*

Free Association In psychodynamic therapies, the patient is responsible for starting and leading each discussion. The therapist tells the patient to describe any thought, feeling, or image that comes to mind, even if it seems unimportant. This practice is known as **free association.** The therapist expects that the patient's associations will eventually uncover unconscious events. In the following excerpts from a famous psychodynamic case, notice how free association helps a woman to discover threatening impulses and conflicts within herself:

Patient: *So I started walking, and walking, and decided to go behind the museum and walk through [New York's] Central Park. . . . I saw a park bench next to a clump of bushes and sat down. There was a rustle behind me and I got frightened. I thought of men concealing themselves in the bushes. I thought of the sex perverts I read about in Central Park. I wondered if there was someone behind me exposing himself. The idea is repulsive, but exciting too. I think of father now and feel excited. . . . . There is something about this pushing in my mind. I don't know what it is, like on the border of my memory.* (Pause)

Therapist: *Mm-hmm.* (Pause) *On the border of your memory?*

Patient: (The patient breathes rapidly and seems to be under great tension.) *As a little girl, I slept with my father. I get a funny feeling. I get a funny feeling over my skin, tingly-like. It's a strange feeling, like a blindness, like not seeing something. My mind blurs and spreads over anything I look at. I've had this feeling off and on since I walked in the park.*

(Wolberg, 2005, 1967, p. 662)

Therapist Interpretation Psychodynamic therapists listen carefully as patients talk, looking for clues, drawing tentative conclusions, and sharing interpretations when they think the patient is ready to hear them. Interpretations of three phenomena are particularly important—*resistance, transference,* and *dreams.*

Patients are showing **resistance,** an unconscious refusal to participate fully in therapy, when they suddenly cannot free associate or when they change a subject to avoid a painful discussion. They demonstrate **transference** when they act and feel toward the therapist as they did or do toward important persons in their lives, especially their parents, siblings, and spouses. Consider again the woman who walked in Central Park. As she continues talking, the therapist helps her to explore her transference:

Patient: *I get so excited by what is happening here. I feel I'm being held back by needing to be nice. I'd like to blast loose sometimes, but I don't dare.*

Therapist: *Because you fear my reaction?*

Patient: *The worst thing would be that you wouldn't like me. You wouldn't speak to me friendly. . . you'd feel you can't treat me and discharge me from treatment. . . .*

Therapist: *Where do you think these attitudes come from?*

Patient: *When I was nine years old, I read a lot about great men in history. I'd quote them and be dramatic. I'd want a sword at my side; I'd dress like an Indian. Mother would scold me. Don't frown, don't talk so much. Sit on your hands, over and over again. I did all kinds of things. I was a naughty child. She told me I'd be hurt. Then at fourteen I fell off a horse and broke my back. I had to be in bed. Mother told me on the day I went riding not to . . . I went against her will and suffered an accident that changed my life, a fractured back. Her attitude was, "I told you so." I was put in a cast and kept in bed for months.*

(Wolberg, 2005, 1967, p. 662)

Finally, many psychodynamic therapists try to help patients interpret their **dreams** (Levy & Finnegan, 2016) (see **Table 3-2**). Freud (1924) called dreams the "royal road to the unconscious." He believed that repression and other defense mechanisms operate less completely during sleep and that dreams, if correctly interpreted, can reveal unconscious instincts, needs, and wishes. Freud identified two kinds of dream content—manifest and latent. *Manifest content* is the consciously remembered dream; *latent content* is its symbolic meaning. To interpret a dream, therapists must translate its manifest content into its latent content.

> Why do you think most people try to interpret and make sense of their own dreams? Are such interpretations of value?

Catharsis Insight must be an emotional as well as an intellectual process. Psychodynamic therapists believe that patients must experience **catharsis,** a reliving of past repressed feelings, if they are to settle internal conflicts and overcome their problems.

Working Through A single episode of interpretation and catharsis will not change the way a person functions. The patient and therapist must examine the same issues over and over in the course of many sessions, each time with greater clarity. This process, called **working through,** usually takes a long time, often years.

Current Trends in Psychodynamic Therapy The past 40 years have witnessed significant changes in the way many psychodynamic therapists conduct sessions. An

#FreudFacts

Freud's fee for one session of therapy was $20.

For almost 40 years, Freud treated patients 10 hours per day, 5 or 6 days per week.

Freud was nominated for the Nobel Prize in 12 different years, but never won.

(Grohol, 2015; Hess, 2009; Gay, 2006, 1999; Jacobs, 2003)

TABLE: 3-2

Percent of Research Participants Who Have Had Common Dreams

	Men	Women
Being chased or pursued, not injured	78%	83%
Sexual experiences	85	73
Falling	73	74
Schools, teachers, studying	57	71
Arriving too late, e.g., for a train	55	62
Trying to do something repeatedly	55	53
Flying or soaring through the air	58	44
Failing an examination	37	48
Being physically attacked	40	44
Being frozen with fright	32	44

Information from: Robert & Zadra, 2014; Copley, 2008; Kantrowitz & Springen, 2004.

increased demand for focused, time-limited psychotherapies has resulted in efforts to make psychodynamic therapy more efficient and affordable. Two current psychodynamic approaches that illustrate this trend are *short-term psychodynamic therapies* and *relational psychoanalytic therapy.*

SHORT-TERM PSYCHODYNAMIC THERAPIES In several short versions of psychodynamic therapy, patients choose a single problem—a *dynamic focus*—to work on, such as difficulty getting along with other people (Betan & Binder, 2016; Frederickson, 2013). The therapist and patient focus on this problem throughout the treatment and work only on the psychodynamic issues that relate to it (such as unresolved oral needs). Only a limited number of studies have tested the effectiveness of these short-term psychodynamic therapies, but their findings do suggest that the approaches are sometimes quite helpful to patients (Parikh et al., 2017; Town et al., 2017).

RELATIONAL PSYCHOANALYTIC THERAPY Whereas Freud believed that psychodynamic therapists should take on the role of a neutral, distant expert during a treatment session, a contemporary school of psychodynamic therapy referred to as *relational psychoanalytic therapy* argues that therapists are key figures in the lives of patients—figures whose reactions and beliefs should be included in the therapy process (Corey, 2017; Laidlaw & Howcroft, 2015). Thus, a key principle of relational therapy is that therapists should also disclose things about themselves, particularly their own reactions to patients, and try to establish more equal relationships with patients. Consistent with their relational approach in therapy, these clinicians draw heavily from object relations theory (and its emphasis on interpersonal relations) in their understanding of psychological problems.

"Look! I'm having enough trouble right now without your bringing up the past."

Frank Model/The New Yorker Collection/The Cartoon Bank

Assessing the Psychodynamic Model

Freud and his followers have helped change the way abnormal functioning is understood. Largely because of their work, a wide range of theorists today look for answers outside of biological processes. Psychodynamic theorists have also helped us to understand that abnormal functioning may be rooted in the same processes as normal functioning. Psychological conflict is a common experience; it leads to abnormal functioning only if the conflict becomes excessive.

> What are some of the ways that Freud's theories have affected literature, film and television, philosophy, child rearing, and education in Western society?

Freud and his many followers have also had a monumental impact on treatment. They were the first to apply theory systematically to treatment. They were also the first to demonstrate the potential of psychological, as opposed to biological, treatment, and their ideas have served as starting points for many other psychological treatments.

At the same time, the psychodynamic model has its shortcomings. Its concepts are hard to research (Golland, 2016; Levy et al., 2011). Because processes such as id drives, ego defenses, and fixation are abstract and supposedly operate at an unconscious level, there is no way of knowing for certain if they are occurring. Not surprisingly, then, psychodynamic explanations and treatments have received relatively limited research support over the years, and psychodynamic theorists rely largely on evidence from individual case studies. Nevertheless, recent research evidence suggests that long-term psychodynamic therapy may be helpful for many persons with long-term complex disorders (Lorentzen et al., 2015; Kunst, 2014), and 18 percent of today's clinical psychologists identify themselves as psychodynamic therapists (Prochaska & Norcross, 2013, 2010).

The Cognitive-Behavioral Model

THE COGNITIVE-BEHAVIORAL MODEL of abnormality focuses on the behaviors people display and the thoughts they have. The model is also interested in the interplay between behaviors and thoughts—how behavior affects thinking and how thinking affects behavior. In addition, the model is concerned with the impact the behavior–cognition interplay often has on feelings and emotions.

Whereas the psychodynamic model had its beginnings in the clinical work of physicians, the cognitive-behavioral model began in laboratories where psychology researchers had been studying *behaviors*, the responses an organism makes to its environment, since the late 1800s. Such researchers believed that behaviors can be external (going to work, say) or internal (having a feeling), and they ran experiments on **conditioning**, simple forms of learning, in order to better understand how behaviors are acquired. In these experiments, researchers would manipulate *stimuli* and *rewards*, then observe how such manipulations affect the behaviors of animal and human subjects.

During the 1950s, a number of clinicians, frustrated with what they viewed as the vagueness and slowness of the psychodynamic model, began to explain and treat psychological abnormality by applying principles derived from those laboratory conditioning studies. Consistent with the laboratory studies, the clinicians viewed severe human anxiety, depression, and the like as maladaptive behaviors, and they focused their work on how such behaviors might be learned and changed.

A decade or so later, yet other clinicians came to believe that a focus on behaviors alone, while moving in the right direction, was too simplistic, that behavioral conditioning principles failed to account fully for the complexity of human functioning and dysfunction. They recognized that human beings also engage in *cognitive processes*, such as anticipating or interpreting—ways of thinking that until then had been largely ignored in the behavior-focused explanations and therapies. These clinicians developed cognitive-behavioral theories of abnormality that took both behaviors and cognitive processes into account and cognitive-behavioral therapies that sought to change both counterproductive behaviors and dysfunctional ways of thinking (Craske, 2017; Ost et al., 2016, 2015).

conditioning A simple form of learning.

#TheirWords

"We cannot solve our problems with the same thinking we used when we created them."

Albert Einstein

Conditioning for entertainment and profit Animals can be taught a wide assortment of tricks by using the principles of conditioning—but at what cost? Here an Asian elephant performs one called "the living statue" as she acknowledges the crowd at a circus in Virginia. In recent years the public has become alarmed at the training procedures used on circus animals, leading some circuses to remove elephants from their shows. This in turn has led to declining ticket sales and contributed to the closing of several circuses, including the famous Ringling Brothers and Barnum & Bailey Circus.

The Washington Post/Getty Images

classical conditioning A process of learning by temporal association in which two events that repeatedly occur close together in time become fused in a person's mind and produce the same response.

modeling A process of learning in which an individual acquires responses by observing and imitating others.

operant conditioning A process of learning in which individuals come to behave in certain ways as a result of experiencing consequences of one kind or another whenever they perform the behavior.

Some of today's theorists and therapists still focus exclusively on the behavioral aspects of abnormal functioning, while others focus only on cognitive processes. However, most clinicians with such orientations include *both* behavioral and cognitive principles in their work. Thus what used to be considered two separate clinical models—the behavioral model and the cognitive model—have come together in the cognitive-behavioral model. The behavioral and cognitive perspectives share key principles and values that have paved the way for their merger into a single model. For example, in contrast to the psychodynamic emphasis on unconscious processes, both behavioral and cognitive theories give prominence to elements of human functioning that are readily accessible—behaviors that are observable or conscious thoughts that are reportable. Correspondingly, both behavioral and cognitive researchers favor empirical studies conducted in the laboratory or field over case studies, and both behavioral and cognitive therapists tend to be action-oriented, instructional, present-focused, directive, and structured (that is, the therapist sets the agenda for each session).

To best appreciate the cognitive-behavioral model, let us look first at its behavioral dimension and then its cognitive dimension.

The Behavioral Dimension

Many learned behaviors help people to cope with daily challenges and to lead happy, productive lives. However, abnormal behaviors also can be learned. Philip Berman, for example, might be viewed as a man who has received improper training: he has learned behaviors that offend others and get him into various kinds of trouble.

Theorists have identified several forms of conditioning, and each may produce abnormal behavior as well as normal behavior. In **classical conditioning**, for example, people learn to respond to one stimulus the same way they respond to another as a result of the two stimuli repeatedly occurring together close in time. If, say, a physician wears a white lab coat whenever she gives painful allergy shots to a little boy, the child may learn to fear not only injection needles, but also white lab coats. Many phobias are acquired by classical conditioning, as you will see in Chapter 5. In **modeling**, another form of conditioning, individuals learn responses simply by observing other individuals and then repeating their behaviors. Phobias can also be acquired by modeling. If a little girl observes her father become frightened whenever a dog crosses his path, she herself may develop a phobic fear of dogs.

In a third form of conditioning, **operant conditioning**, individuals learn to behave in certain ways as a result of experiencing consequences of one kind or another whenever they do so (Skinner, 1958, 1957). If the consequences of a behavior are satisfying, they are called *reinforcers*, and they serve to increase the likelihood of the person repeating the behavior in the future, A consequence is reinforcing when it is pleasant (a reward) or when it removes an aversive state such as pain or fear. If, on the other hand, the consequences of a behavior are unsatisfying, they are called *punishments*, and they serve to decrease the likelihood of the person repeating the behavior in the

See and do Modeling may account for some forms of abnormal behavior. A well-known study by Albert Bandura and his colleagues (1963) demonstrated that children learned to abuse a doll by observing an adult hit it. Children who had not been exposed to the adult model did not mistreat the doll.

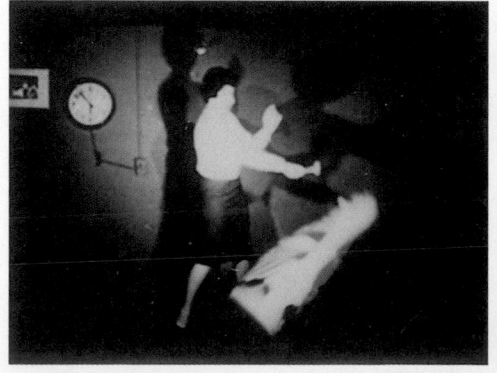

A. Bandura, Stanford University

future. A consequence is punishing when it is unpleasant or when it takes away something pleasant.

Research suggests that a number of abnormal behaviors may be acquired by operant conditioning (Calarco, 2016; Levine, 2016). Some children, for example, learn to display extremely aggressive behaviors when their parents or peers consistently surrender to their threats or demands or shower them with extra attention when they act out. A number of people learn to abuse alcohol because initially such behaviors bring feelings of calm, comfort, or pleasure. And still others may develop disordered eating patterns partly because of the praise they receive for a thinner appearance.

In treatment, behavior-focused therapists seek to replace a person's problematic behaviors with more appropriate ones, applying the principles of operant conditioning, classical conditioning, or modeling (Newman, 2016; Newman et al., 2016). When treating extremely aggressive children, for example, the therapists may guide parents to change the reinforcers they have been unintentionally providing for their children's behaviors. The parents may be taught to systematically reinforce polite and appropriate behaviors by the children with displays of extra attention, special privileges, and the like. In addition, they may be taught to systematically punish highly aggressive behaviors by withdrawing attention and withholding privileges in the aftermath of such behaviors. Studies suggest that treatment programs for highly aggressive children often work best when they include behavioral components like this (Cornacchio et al., 2017; Elkins et al., 2017).

The Cognitive Dimension

Philip Berman, like the rest of us, has *cognitive* abilities—special intellectual capacities to think, remember, and anticipate. These abilities can help him accomplish a great deal in life. Yet they can also work against him. As he thinks about his experiences, Philip may misinterpret them in ways that lead to poor decisions, maladaptive responses, and painful emotions.

In the 1960s two clinicians, Albert Ellis (1962) and Aaron Beck (1967), proposed that we can best explain and treat abnormal functioning, not only by looking at behaviors, but also by focusing on cognitions. Ellis and Beck claimed that clinicians must ask questions about the assumptions and attitudes that color a client's perceptions, the thoughts running through that person's mind, and the conclusions to which they are leading.

According to these and other cognition-focused theorists, abnormal functioning can result from several kinds of cognitive problems. Some people may make *assumptions* and adopt *attitudes* that are disturbing and inaccurate (Beck, 2016; Ellis, 2016). Philip Berman, for example, often seems to assume that his past history has locked him in his present situation. He believes that he was victimized by his parents and that he is now forever doomed by his past. He approaches all new experiences and relationships with expectations of failure and disaster.

"Don't take that tone of thought with me."

Bruce Eric Kaplan/The New Yorker Collection/The Cartoon Bank

Illogical thinking processes are another source of abnormal functioning, according to cognition-focused theorists. Beck has found that depressed people consistently think in illogical ways and keep arriving at self-defeating conclusions (Beck & Weishaar, 2014). They may, for example, *overgeneralize*—draw broad negative conclusions on the basis of single insignificant events. One depressed student couldn't remember the date of Columbus' third voyage to America during a history class. Overgeneralizing, she spent the rest of the day in despair over her wide-ranging ignorance.

In treatment, cognition-focused therapists use several strategies to help people with psychological disorders adopt new, more functional ways of thinking. In an influential approach developed by Beck, the therapists guide depressed clients to identify and challenge any negative thoughts, biased interpretations, and errors in logic that dominate their thinking and contribute to their disorder. The therapists also guide the clients to try out new ways of thinking in their daily lives. As you will see in Chapter 8, depressed people treated with Beck's approach improve much more than those who receive no treatment (Beck, 2016; Beck & Weishaar, 2014).

> Have you had problems where you felt it was most useful to address only the behavioral or only the cognitive realm?

In the excerpt that follows, a Beck-like therapist guides a depressed 26-year-old graduate student to see the link between her interpretations and her feelings and to begin questioning the accuracy of those interpretations:

> **Therapist:** *How do you understand it?*
> **Patient:** *I get depressed when things go wrong. Like when I fail a test.*
> **Therapist:** *How can failing a test make you depressed?*
> **Patient:** *Well, if I fail I'll never get into law school.*
> **Therapist:** *So failing the test means a lot to you. But if failing a test could drive people into clinical depression, wouldn't you expect everyone who failed the test to have a depression? . . . Did everyone who failed get depressed enough to require treatment?*
> **Patient:** *No, but it depends on how important the test was to the person.*
> **Therapist:** *Right, and who decides the importance?*
> **Patient:** *I do.*
> **Therapist:** *And so, what we have to examine is your way of viewing the test (or the way that you think about the test) and how it affects your chances of getting into law school. Do you agree?*
> **Patient:** *Right. . . .*
> **Therapist:** *Now what did failing mean?*
> **Patient:** *(Tearful) That I couldn't get into law school.*
> **Therapist:** *And what does that mean to you?*
> **Patient:** *That I'm just not smart enough.*
> **Therapist:** *Anything else?*
> **Patient:** *That I can never be happy.*
> **Therapist:** *And how do these thoughts make you feel?*
> **Patient:** *Very unhappy.*
> **Therapist:** *So it is the meaning of failing a test that makes you very unhappy. In fact, believing that you can never be happy is a powerful factor in producing unhappiness. So, you get yourself into a trap—by definition, failure to get into law school equals "I can never be happy."*
>
> (Beck et al., 1979, pp. 145–146)

The Cognitive-Behavioral Interplay

As you read earlier, most of today's cognitive-behavioral theorists and therapists interweave both behavioral and cognitive elements in their explanations and treatments for psychological disorders. Let's look, for example, at the cognitive-behavioral approach to social anxiety disorder, a problem that you will be reading more about in Chapter 5.

People with **social anxiety disorder** have severe anxiety about social situations in which they may face scrutiny by other people (APA, 2013). They worry that they will function poorly in front of others and will wind up feeling humiliated. Thus they may avoid speaking in public, reject social opportunities, and limit their lives in numerous ways.

social anxiety disorder A psychological disorder in which people fear social situations.

exposure therapy A behavior-focused intervention in which fearful people are repeatedly exposed to the objects or situations they dread.

Cognitive-behavioral theorists contend that people with this disorder hold a group of social beliefs and expectations that consistently work against them (Thurston et al., 2017; Heimberg et al., 2010). These include:

- Holding unrealistically high social standards and so believing that they must perform perfectly in social situations.
- Viewing themselves as unattractive social beings.
- Viewing themselves as socially unskilled and inadequate.
- Believing they are always in danger of behaving incompetently in social situations.
- Believing that inept behaviors in social situations will inevitably lead to terrible consequences.

Beset by such beliefs and expectations, people with social anxiety disorder find that their anxiety levels increase as soon as they enter into a social situation. In turn, say cognitive-behavioral theorists, the individuals learn to regularly perform "avoidance" and "safety" behaviors (Mesri et al., 2017; Moscovitch et al., 2013). Avoidance behaviors include, for example, talking only to people they already know well at gatherings or parties, or avoiding social gatherings altogether. Safety behaviors include wearing makeup to cover up blushing. Such behaviors are reinforced by eliminating or reducing the individuals' feelings of anxiety and the number of unpleasant events they encounter.

To undo this cycle of problematic beliefs and behaviors, cognitive-behavioral therapists combine several techniques, including **exposure therapy**, a behavior-focused intervention in which fearful people are repeatedly exposed to the objects or situations they dread (Thurston et al., 2017; Heimberg & Magee, 2014). In cases of social anxiety disorder, the therapists encourage clients to immerse themselves in various dreaded social situations and to remain there until their fears subside. Usually the exposure is gradual, and it often includes homework assignments that are carried out in the social situations. Then, back in therapy, the clinicians and clients re-examine and challenge the individuals' maladaptive beliefs and expectations, in light of the recent social encounters.

In the following discussion, a cognitive-behavioral therapist works with a socially anxious client who fears he will be rejected if he speaks up at gatherings. The therapy discussion is taking place after the man has done a homework assignment in which he was asked to identify his negative social expectations and force himself to say anything he had on his mind in social situations, no matter how stupid it might seem to him:

#BeingSocial

For most people, silence becomes awkward after about four seconds.

The maximum number of in-person relationships/friendships one can maintain is between 50 and 150.

(Pear, 2013)

After two weeks of this assignment, the patient came into his next session of therapy and reported: "I did what you told me to do. . . . [Every] time, just as you said, I found myself retreating from people, I said to myself: 'Now, even though you can't see it, there must be some sentences. What are they?' And I finally found them. And there were many of them! And they all seemed to say the same thing."

"What thing?"

"That I, uh, was going to be rejected. . . . [If] I related to them I was going to be rejected. And wouldn't that be perfectly awful if I was to be rejected. And there was no reason for me, uh, to take that, uh, sort of thing, and be rejected in that awful manner." . . .

"And did you do the second part of the homework assignment?"

"The forcing myself to speak up and express myself?"

"Yes, that part."

"That was worse. That was really hard. Much harder than I thought it would be. But I did it."

(continued on the next page)

"And?"

"Oh, not bad at all. I spoke up several times; more than I've ever done before. Some people were very surprised. Phyllis was very surprised, too. But I spoke up." . . .

"And how did you feel after expressing yourself like that?"

"Remarkable! I don't remember when I last felt this way. I felt, uh, just remarkable— good, that is. It was really something to feel! But it was so hard. I almost didn't make it. And a couple of other times during the week I had to force myself again. But I did. And I was glad!"

(Ellis, 1962, pp. 202–203)

#TheirWords

"The greatest discovery of my generation is that human beings can alter their lives by altering their attitudes of mind."

William James (1842–1910)

In cognitive-behavioral approaches of this kind, clients come to adopt more accurate social beliefs, engage in more and more social situations, and experience less fear during, and in anticipation of, social encounters. Avoidance and safety behaviors drop away while social approach behaviors are reinforced by opening the door to the joy and enrichment of social encounters. Studies show that such approaches do indeed help many individuals to overcome social anxiety disorder (Gregory & Peters, 2017; Heimberg & Magee, 2014).

Assessing the Cognitive-Behavioral Model

The cognitive-behavioral model has become a powerful force in the clinical field. Various cognitive and behavioral theories have been proposed over the years, and many treatment techniques have been developed. As you can see in **Figure 3-3**, nearly half of today's clinical psychologists report that their approach is cognitive and/or behavioral (Prochaska & Norcross, 2013).

One reason for the appeal of the cognitive-behavioral model is that it can be tested in the laboratory, whereas psychodynamic theories generally cannot. Many of the model's basic concepts—stimulus, response, reward, attitude, and interpretation—can be observed or, at least, measured. Experimenters have, in fact, successfully manipulated the behaviors and cognitions of laboratory participants to create clinical-like symptoms, suggesting that psychological disorders may indeed develop in the same way (Zvolensky, Forsyth, & Johnson, 2014). Similarly, investigators have found that people with psychological disorders often display the kinds of reactions, assumptions, and errors in thinking that cognitive-behavioral theorists would predict (Newman et al., 2016; Ingram et al., 2007).

Yet another reason for the popularity of this model is the impressive research performance of cognitive-behavioral therapies. Both in the laboratory and real life, they have proved very helpful to many people with anxiety disorders, depression, sexual

FIGURE 3-3

Theoretical Orientations of Today's Clinical Psychologists

In one survey, 22 percent of clinical psychologists labeled their approach as "eclectic," 46 percent considered their model "cognitive" and/or "behavioral," and 18 percent called their orientation "psychodynamic." (Information from: Prochaska & Norcross, 2013.)

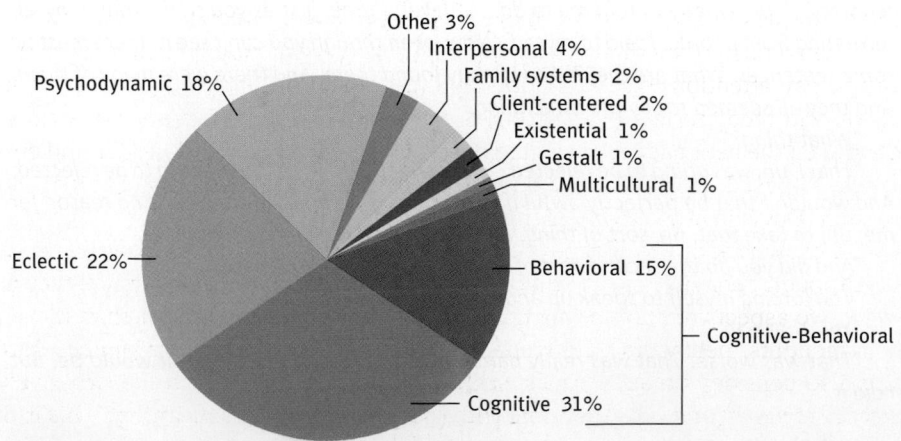

Helen H. R.chardson/Getty Images

Meeting at your place . . . and mine
Colorado psychiatrist Robert Chalfant and his office administrator demonstrate the simple digital setup that enables him to conduct treatment with distant clients each week. Such telemental health techniques make psychotherapy available to thousands of individuals who would otherwise not receive treatment, including physically disabled people and those living in isolated rural areas.

dysfunction, intellectual disability, and yet other problems (Craske, 2017; Dobson & Dobson, 2017).

At the same time, the cognitive behavioral model has drawbacks. First, although maladaptive behaviors and disturbed cognitive processes are found in many forms of abnormality, their precise role has yet to be determined. The problematic behaviors and cognitions seen in psychologically troubled people could well be a result rather than a cause of their difficulties. Second, although cognitive-behavioral therapies are clearly of help to many people, they do not help everyone. Research indicates, in fact, that it is not always possible for clients to rid themselves fully of their negative thoughts and biased interpretations (Sharf, 2015).

In response to such limitations, a new group of therapies, sometimes called the *new wave of cognitive-behavioral therapies*, has emerged in recent years. These new approaches, including the increasingly used *acceptance and commitment therapy (ACT),* help clients to *accept* many of their problematic thoughts rather than judge them, act on them, or try fruitlessly to change them (Hayes, 2016; Levin et al., 2015). The hope is that by recognizing such thoughts for what they are—just thoughts—clients will eventually be able to let them pass through their awareness without being particularly troubled by them.

As you will see in Chapter 5, ACT and similar therapies often employ *mindfulness-based* techniques to help clients achieve such acceptance. These techniques borrow heavily from a form of meditation called *mindfulness meditation,* which teaches individuals to pay attention to the thoughts and feelings that are flowing through their minds during meditation and to accept such thoughts in a nonjudgmental way (see *InfoCentral* on the next page). A growing body of research suggests that ACT and other mindfulness-based approaches are often quite helpful in the treatment of anxiety and depression (Davison et al., 2016; Eilenberger, 2016)

A final drawback of the cognitive-behavioral model is that it is narrow in certain ways. Although behavior and cognition obviously are key dimensions in life, they are still only two aspects of human functioning. Aren't human beings more than the sum of their thoughts, behaviors, and emotions? Shouldn't explanations of human functioning also consider broader issues, such as how people approach life, what value they extract from it, and how they deal with the question of life's meaning? This is the position of the humanistic-existential model.

#

#WanderingThoughts

Your mind wanders almost one-half of the time on average (Killingsworth, 2013; Killingsworth & Gilbert, 2010).

MINDFULNESS

Over the past decade, **mindfulness** has become one of the most common terms in psychology. Mindfulness involves being in the present moment, intentionally and nonjudgmentally. **Mindfulness** **training programs** use mindfulness **meditation** techniques to help treat people suffering from pain, anxiety disorders, and depressive disorders, as well as a variety of other psychological disorders.

MINDFULNESS TRAINING PROGRAMS

• Have the goal of achieving a state of intentional, non-judgmental attention on the present.

attention to body sensations

attention to **breathing** sensations

attention to **wandering** and busy thoughts

8 weeks of instruction

simple **yoga**

homework **assignments** (practice and **journal** keeping)

(Ackerman, 2017; Creswell, 2017; Winston, 2016; Noonan, 2014; Russell, 2014)

• Help treat other disorders, including:

pain conditions

PTSD and other stress disorders

depressive disorders

asthma

substance use disorders

borderline personality disorder

(Creswell, 2017; Schmidtman et al., 2017; Barnes et al., 2016; Soler et al., 2016; Wieczner, 2016)

Number of mindfulness apps **1,000**

Number of medical schools in North America that teach mindfulness **>120**

• Help reduce the anxiety found in . . .

generalized **anxiety** disorder

social **anxiety** disorder

panic disorder

test **anxiety**

illness anxiety

depressive disorder with **anxious** distress

(Creswell, 2017; Hoge et al., 2017; Dundas et al., 2016; Kim et al., 2016; Surawy et al., 2015)

Why Do People Seek Out Mindfulness?

"Cell phones, texting, social networking, e-mailing, etc., easily distract me from what I'm doing."

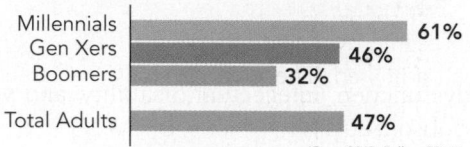

Millennials	61%
Gen Xers	46%
Boomers	32%
Total Adults	47%

(Gray, 2017; Palley, 2014)

Percentage of the U.S. population that practice mindfulness meditation techniques **10%**

(NIH, 2016; Weiczner, 2016; Brewer, 2014; Marchand, 2014; Noonan, 2014; Pickert, 2014)

Percentage of employers who offer mindfulness training **33%**

Estimated amount that U.S. adults spend on mindfulness programs each year **as much as $8 billion**

RESEARCH-SUPPORTED EFFECTS OF MINDFULNESS

Mindfulness appears to

• improve control over anxiety and related emotions

• promote more peaceful sleep

• improve functioning of the autonomic nervous system

• decrease rumination and other negative thinking

• improve occupational functioning

• lower stress

MINDFUL LIFE STRATEGIES

(Ackerman, 2017; Noonan, 2014; Russell, 2014)

Employ conscious awareness each morning—notice how you feel before starting the day.

Practice mindful breathing for 5 to 30 minutes throughout the day.

Take regular breaks from sitting at your desk.

Choose an object in your environment and observe it carefully for 60 seconds.

Unplug from technology periodically throughout the day.

Take a slow 10-minute walk, synchronizing your breathing with your steps.

Eat lunch slowly, savoring every bite and body sensation.

At the end of the day, reflect about the day, without judgment.

Do nothing for at least 5 minutes each day.

Inhale deeply and exhale deeply and focus on your breath.

Slow yourself down throughout the day.

Inhale and exhale periodically before important tasks.

• improve decision-making under stress

• heighten attention

• improve working memory and verbal reasoning

• improve functioning of the immune system

• increase enjoyment and experience of music

• decrease feelings of loneliness among elderly people

(Creswell, 2017; Hoge et al., 2017; Tang & Bruya, 2017; Schmidtman et al., 2017; Noonan, 2014)

The Humanistic-Existential Model

PHILIP BERMAN IS MORE than the sum of his psychological conflicts, learned behaviors, or cognitions. Being human, he also has the ability to pursue philosophical goals such as self-awareness, strong values, a sense of meaning in life, and freedom of choice. According to humanistic and existential theorists, Philip's problems can be understood only in the light of such complex goals. Humanistic and existential theorists are often grouped together—in an approach known as the *humanistic-existential model*—because of their common focus on these broader dimensions of human existence. At the same time, there are important differences between them.

Humanists, the more optimistic of the two groups, believe that human beings are born with a natural tendency to be friendly, cooperative, and constructive. People, these theorists propose, are driven to **self-actualize**—that is, to fulfill their potential for goodness and growth. They can do so, however, only if they honestly recognize and accept their weaknesses as well as their strengths and establish satisfying personal values to live by. Humanists further suggest that self-actualization leads naturally to a concern for the welfare of others and to behavior that is loving, courageous, spontaneous, and independent (Maslow, 1970).

Existentialists agree that human beings must have an accurate awareness of themselves and live meaningful—they say "authentic"—lives in order to be psychologically well adjusted. These theorists do not believe, however, that people are naturally inclined to live positively. They believe that from birth we have total freedom, either to face up to our existence and give meaning to our lives or to shrink from that responsibility. Those who choose to "hide" from responsibility and choice will view themselves as helpless and may live empty, inauthentic, and dysfunctional lives as a result.

The humanistic and existential views of abnormality both date back to the 1940s. At that time Carl Rogers (1902–1987), often considered the pioneer of the humanistic perspective, developed **client-centered therapy,** a warm and supportive approach that contrasted sharply with the psychodynamic techniques of the day. He also proposed a theory of personality that paid little attention to irrational instincts and conflicts.

The existential view of personality and abnormality appeared during this same period. Many of its principles came from the ideas of nineteenth-century European existential philosophers who held that human beings are constantly defining and so giving meaning to their existence through their actions (Cooper, 2016; Krug, 2016).

The humanistic and existential theories, and their uplifting implications, were extremely popular during the 1960s and 1970s, years of considerable soul-searching and social upheaval in Western society. They have since lost some of their popularity, but they continue to influence the ideas and work of many clinicians. In particular, humanistic principles are apparent throughout positive psychology (the study and enhancement of positive feelings, traits, abilities, and selfless virtues), an area of psychology that, as you read in Chapter 1, has gained much momentum in recent years (see pages 15–16).

Rogers' Humanistic Theory and Therapy

According to Carl Rogers, the road to dysfunction begins in infancy (Hazler, 2016; Rogers, 1987, 1951). We all have a basic need to receive *positive regard* from the important people in our lives (primarily our parents). Those who receive *unconditional* (nonjudgmental) *positive regard* early in life are likely to develop *unconditional self-regard*. That is, they come to recognize their worth as persons, even while recognizing that they are not perfect. Such people are in a good position to actualize their positive potential.

Unfortunately, some children repeatedly are made to feel that they are not worthy of positive regard. As a result, they acquire *conditions of worth*, standards that tell

self-actualization The humanistic process by which people fulfill their potential for goodness and growth.

client-centered therapy The humanistic therapy developed by Carl Rogers in which clinicians try to help clients by conveying acceptance, accurate empathy, and genuineness.

#CharitableActs

Self-Actualization and Caring for Others

83%	Percentage of adult Americans who make charitable contributions each year
32%	Percentage of charitable donations contributed to religious organizations
68%	Percentage of donations directed to education, human services, health, and the arts
27%	Percentage of adult Americans who do volunteer work each year

(Information from: NPT, 2017; Gallup, 2013)

Anadolu Agency/Getty Images

Unconditional positive regard Carl Rogers argued that clients must receive unconditional positive regard in order to overcome their problems. In this spirit, a number of organizations now arrange for individuals to have close relationships with gentle and nonjudgmental dogs, often called "emotional support dogs." Here a child in Moscow embraces a dog as part of a treatment program for children with psychological disabilities.

them they are lovable and acceptable only when they conform to certain guidelines. To maintain positive self-regard, these people have to look at themselves very selectively, denying or distorting thoughts and actions that do not measure up to their conditions of worth. They thus acquire a distorted view of themselves and their experiences. They do not know what they are truly feeling, what they genuinely need, or what values and goals would be meaningful for them. Problems in functioning are then inevitable.

Rogers might view Philip Berman as a man who has gone astray. Rather than striving to fulfill his positive human potential, he drifts from job to job and relationship to relationship. In every interaction he is defending himself, trying to interpret events in ways he can live with, usually blaming his problems on other people. Nevertheless, his basic negative self-image continually reveals itself. Rogers would probably link this problem to the critical ways Philip was treated by his mother throughout his childhood.

Clinicians who practice Rogers' client-centered therapy try to create a supportive climate in which clients feel able to look at themselves honestly and acceptingly (Hazler, 2016; Bohart, 2015). The therapist must display three important qualities throughout the therapy—*unconditional positive regard* (full and warm acceptance for the client), *accurate empathy* (skillful listening and restating), and *genuineness* (sincere communication). In the following classic case, the therapist uses all these qualities to move the client toward greater self-awareness:

> **Client:** *Yes, I know I shouldn't worry about it, but I do. Lots of things—money, people, clothes. In classes I feel that everyone's just waiting for a chance to jump on me. . . . When I meet somebody I wonder what he's actually thinking of me. Then later on I wonder how I match up to what he's come to think of me.*
>
> **Therapist:** *You feel that you're pretty responsive to the opinions of other people.*
>
> **Client:** *Yes, but it's things that shouldn't worry me.*
>
> **Therapist:** *You feel that it's the sort of thing that shouldn't be upsetting, but they do get you pretty much worried anyway.*
>
> **Client:** *Just some of them. Most of those things do worry me because they're true. The ones I told you, that is. But there are lots of little things that aren't true. . . . Things just seem to be piling up, piling up inside of me. . . . It's a feeling that things were crowding up and they were going to burst.*
>
> **Therapist:** *You feel that it's a sort of oppression with some frustration and that things are just unmanageable.*
>
> **Client:** *In a way, but some things just seem illogical. I'm afraid I'm not very clear here but that's the way it comes.*
>
> **Therapist:** *That's all right. You say just what you think.*
>
> (Snyder, 1947, pp. 2–24)

In such an atmosphere, clients are expected to feel accepted by their therapists. They then may be able to look at themselves with honesty and acceptance. They begin to value their own emotions, thoughts, and behaviors, and so they are freed from the insecurities and doubts that prevent self-actualization.

Client-centered therapy has not fared very well in research (Prochaska & Norcross, 2013). Although some studies show that participants who receive this therapy improve more than control participants, many other studies have failed to find any such advantage. All the same, Rogers' therapy has had a positive influence on clinical practice

(Hazler, 2016; Raskin et al., 2014). It was one of the first major alternatives to psychodynamic therapy, and it helped open up the clinical field to new approaches. Rogers also helped pave the way for *psychologists* to practice psychotherapy, which had previously been considered the exclusive territory of psychiatrists. And his commitment to clinical research helped promote the systematic study of treatment. Approximately 2 percent of today's clinical psychologists, 1 percent of social workers, and 3 percent of counseling psychologists report that they employ the client-centered approach (Prochaska & Norcross, 2013).

Gestalt Theory and Therapy

Gestalt therapy, another humanistic approach, was developed in the 1950s by a charismatic clinician named Frederick (Fritz) Perls (1893–1970). Gestalt therapists, like client-centered therapists, guide their clients toward self-recognition and self-acceptance (Haley et al., 2016; Yontef & Jacobs, 2014). But unlike client-centered therapists, they try to achieve this goal in more experiential ways by challenging and frustrating the clients, demanding that they stay in the *here and now* during therapy discussions, and pushing them to embrace their real emotions.

For example, gestalt therapists often use the technique of *role playing*, instructing clients to act out various roles. A person may be told to be another person, an object, an alternative self, or even a part of the body. The Gestalt version of role playing can become intense, as individuals are encouraged to express emotions fully. Many cry out, scream, kick, or pound. Through this experience they may come to "own" (accept) feelings that previously made them uncomfortable.

Approximately 1 percent of clinical psychologists and other kinds of clinicians describe themselves as gestalt therapists (Prochaska & Norcross, 2013). Because they believe that subjective experiences and self-awareness cannot be measured objectively, proponents of gestalt therapy have not often performed controlled research on this approach (Haley et al., 2016; Leung, Leung, & Ng, 2013).

Spiritual Views and Interventions

For most of the twentieth century, clinical scientists viewed religion as a negative—or at best neutral—factor in mental health. In the early 1900s, for example, Freud argued that religious beliefs were defense mechanisms, "born from man's need to make his helplessness tolerable" (1961, p. 23). This negative view of religion now seems to be ending, however. During the past decade, many articles and books linking spiritual issues to clinical treatment have been published, and the ethical codes of psychologists, psychiatrists, and counselors have each concluded that religion is a type of diversity that mental health professionals must respect (APA, 2017, 2010; Peteet, Lu, & Narrow, 2011).

Researchers have learned that spirituality does, in fact, often correlate with psychological health. In particular, studies have examined the mental health of people who are devout and who view God as warm, caring, helpful, and dependable. Repeatedly, these individuals are found to be less lonely, pessimistic, depressed, or anxious than people without any religious beliefs or those who view God as cold and unresponsive (Pirutinsky, Carp, & Rosmarin, 2016; Steffen, Masters, & Baldwin, 2016). Such people also seem to cope better with major life stressors—from illness to war—and to attempt suicide less often. In addition, they are less likely to abuse drugs.

> What various explanations might account for the correlation between spirituality and mental health?

Do such correlations indicate that spirituality helps *produce* greater mental health? Not necessarily. As you'll recall from Chapter 2, correlations do not indicate causation. It may be, for example, that a sense of optimism leads to more spirituality, and that, independently, optimism contributes to greater mental health. Whatever the proper interpretation, many therapists now make a point of including spiritual issues when

AP Photo/The Daily Telegram, Lad Strayer

Beating the blues Gestalt therapists often guide clients to express their needs and feelings in their full intensity by banging on pillows, crying out, kicking, or pounding things. Building on these techniques, a new approach, *drum therapy*, teaches clients, such as this woman, how to beat drums in order to help release traumatic memories, change beliefs, and feel more liberated.

gestalt therapy The humanistic therapy developed by Fritz Perls in which clinicians actively move clients toward self-recognition and self-acceptance by using techniques such as role playing and self-discovery exercises.

Spirituality and science A few years ago, Tibetan spiritual leader the Dalai Lama (right) met with professor of psychiatry Zindel Segal (left) and other mental health researchers at a conference examining possible ties between science, mental health, and spirituality.

they treat religious clients, and some further encourage clients to use their spiritual resources to help them cope with current stressors (McClintock, Lau, & Miller, 2016; Koenig, 2015). Similarly, a number of religious institutions offer counseling services to their members.

Existential Theories and Therapy

Like humanists, existentialists believe that psychological dysfunction is caused by self-deception; existentialists, however, are talking about a kind of self-deception in which people hide from life's responsibilities and fail to recognize that it is up to them to give meaning to their lives. According to existentialists, many people become overwhelmed by the pressures of present-day society and so look to others for explanations, guidance, and authority. They overlook their personal freedom of choice and avoid responsibility for their lives and decisions (Cooper, 2016; Yalom, 2014). Such people are left with empty, inauthentic lives. Their dominant emotions are anxiety, frustration, boredom, alienation, and depression.

Existentialists might view Philip Berman as a man who feels overwhelmed by the forces of society. He sees his parents as "rich, powerful, and selfish," and he perceives teachers, acquaintances, and employers as being oppressive. He fails to appreciate his choices in life and his capacity for finding meaning and direction. Quitting becomes a habit with him—he leaves job after job, ends every romantic relationship, and flees difficult situations.

In **existential therapy,** people are encouraged to accept responsibility for their lives and for their problems. Therapists try to help clients recognize their freedom so that they may choose a different course and live with greater meaning (Cooper, 2016; Yalom, 2014). The precise techniques used in existential therapy vary from clinician to clinician. At the same time, most existential therapists place great emphasis on the *relationship* between therapist and client and try to create an atmosphere of honesty, hard work, and shared learning and growth.

	Patient:	*I don't know why I keep coming here. All I do is tell you the same thing over and over. I'm not getting anywhere.*
	Doctor:	*I'm getting tired of hearing the same thing over and over, too.*
	Patient:	*Maybe I'll stop coming.*
	Doctor:	*It's certainly your choice.*
	Patient:	*What do you think I should do?*
	Doctor:	*What do you want to do?*
	Patient:	*I want to get better.*
	Doctor:	*I don't blame you.*
	Patient:	*If you think I should stay, ok, I will.*
	Doctor:	*You want me to tell you to stay?*
	Patient:	*You know what's best; you're the doctor.*
	Doctor:	*Do I act like a doctor?*

(Keen, 1970, p. 200)

existential therapy A therapy that encourages clients to accept responsibility for their lives and to live with greater meaning and value.

Existential therapists do not believe that experimental methods can adequately test the effectiveness of their treatments. To them, research dehumanizes individuals by reducing them to test measures. Not surprisingly, then, very little controlled research has been devoted to the effectiveness of this approach (Vos et al., 2015; Schneider & Krug, 2010). Nevertheless, around 1 percent of today's clinical psychologists use an approach that is primarily existential (Prochaska & Norcross, 2013).

Assessing the Humanistic-Existential Model

The humanistic-existential model appeals to many people in and out of the clinical field. In recognizing the special challenges of human existence, humanistic and existential theorists tap into an aspect of psychological life that typically is missing from the other models (Krug, 2016). Moreover, the factors that they say are essential to effective functioning—self-acceptance, personal values, personal meaning, and personal choice—are certainly lacking in many people with psychological disturbances.

The optimistic tone of the humanistic-existential model is also an attraction. Such optimism meshes quite well with the goals and principles of *positive psychology* (see pages 15–16) (Gander, Proyer, & Ruch, 2016). Theorists who follow the principles of the humanistic-existential model offer great hope when they assert that, despite past and present events, we can make our own choices, determine our own destiny, and accomplish much. Still another attractive feature of the model is its emphasis on health. Unlike clinicians from some of the other models who see individuals as patients with psychological illnesses, humanists and existentialists view them simply as people who have yet to fulfill their potential.

At the same time, the humanistic-existential focus on abstract issues of human fulfillment gives rise to a major problem from a scientific point of view: These issues are difficult to research. In fact, with the notable exception of Rogers, who tried to investigate his clinical methods carefully, humanists and existentialists have traditionally rejected the use of empirical research. This antiresearch position is now beginning to change among some humanistic and existential researchers—a change that may lead to important insights about the merits of this model in the coming years (Krug, 2016; Schneider & Krug, 2010; Strümpfel, 2006).

Actualizing the self Humanists suggest that self-actualized people show concern for others, among other positive qualities. Many work as volunteers. For example, as part of the Free Hugs Project, a worldwide campaign, volunteers offer hugs to passersby who look like they could use a quick dose of comfort.

Rick Eglinton/Getty Images

The Sociocultural Model: Family-Social and Multicultural Perspectives

PHILIP BERMAN IS ALSO A social and cultural being. He is surrounded by people and by institutions, he is a member of a family and a cultural group, he participates in social relationships, and he holds cultural values. Such forces are always operating upon Philip, setting rules and expectations that guide or pressure him, helping to shape his behaviors, thoughts, and emotions.

According to the *sociocultural model*, abnormal behavior is best understood in light of the broad forces that influence an individual. What are the norms of the individual's society and culture? What roles does the person play in the social environment? What kind of family structure or cultural background is the person a part of? And how do other people view and react to him or her? In fact, the sociocultural model is composed of two major perspectives—the *family-social perspective* and the *multicultural perspective*.

#SocialDisruptions

61%	Percentage of people who read text messages during social gatherings
52%	Percentage of people who send text messages during social gatherings
62%	Percentage of people who answer cell calls during social gatherings
61%	Percentage of people who check for cell alerts during social gatherings

(Information from: Pew Research Center, 2015)

How Do Family-Social Theorists Explain Abnormal Functioning?

Proponents of the family-social perspective argue that clinical theorists should concentrate on those broad forces that operate *directly* on an individual as he or she moves through life—that is, family relationships, social interactions, and community events. They believe that such forces help account for both normal and abnormal behavior,

family systems theory A theory that views the family as a system of interacting parts whose interactions exhibit consistent patterns and unstated rules.

group therapy A therapy format in which a group of people with similar problems meet together with a therapist to work on those problems.

and they pay particular attention to three kinds of factors: *social labels and roles, social networks,* and *family structure and communication.*

Social Labels and Roles Abnormal functioning can be influenced greatly by the labels and roles assigned to troubled people (Ruscio, 2015; Rüsch et al., 2014). When people stray from the norms of their society, the society calls them deviant and, in many cases, "mentally ill." Such labels tend to stick. Moreover, when people are viewed in particular ways, reacted to as "crazy," and perhaps even encouraged to act sick, they gradually learn to accept and play the assigned social role. Ultimately the label seems appropriate.

A famous study called "On Being Sane in Insane Places" by clinical investigator David Rosenhan (1973) supports this position. Eight normal people, actually colleagues of Rosenhan, presented themselves at various mental hospitals, falsely complaining that they had been hearing voices say the words "empty," "hollow," and "thud." On the basis of this complaint alone, each was diagnosed as having schizophrenia and admitted.

Moreover, the pseudopatients had a hard time convincing others that they were well once they had been given the diagnostic label. Their hospitalizations ranged from 7 to 52 days, even though they behaved normally and stopped reporting symptoms as soon as they were admitted. In addition, the label "schizophrenia" kept influencing the way the staff viewed and dealt with them. For example, one pseudopatient who paced the corridor out of boredom was, in clinical notes, described as "nervous." Overall, the pseudopatients came to feel powerless, invisible, and bored.

Social Connections and Supports Family-social theorists are also concerned with the social environments in which people operate, including their social and professional relationships. How well do they communicate with others? What kind of signals do they send to or receive from others? Researchers have often found ties between deficient social connections and psychological dysfunction (Brinker & Cheruvu, 2016; Fu et al., 2016; Portugal et al., 2016). They have observed, for example, that people who are isolated and lack social support or intimacy in their lives are more likely to become depressed when under stress and to remain depressed longer than are people with supportive spouses or warm friendships.

Some clinical theorists believe that people who are unwilling or unable to communicate and develop relationships in their everyday lives will, alternatively, find adequate social contacts online, using social networking platforms like Facebook or Instagram. Although this may be true for some such individuals, research suggests that people's online relationships tend to parallel their offline relationships. Several studies of college students, for example, have found that students who are self-disclosing and have many friends on Facebook also are particularly social offline, while those who reveal less about themselves and initiate fewer relationships on Facebook are less willing to communicate with other people offline (Dunbar, 2016; Tsay-Vogel, Shanahan, & Signorielli, 2016; Sheldon, 2008).

#ShiftingValues

59%	Percentage of adults who say their families have fewer family dinners than when they were growing up
10	Average number of weekly hours today's fathers spend doing housework, compared with 4 hours a half century ago
18	Average number of weekly hours today's mothers spend doing housework, compared with 32 hours a half century ago

(Information from: Pew Research Center, 2015, 2013; Harris Interactive, 2013)

Family Structure and Communication Of course, one of the important social networks for an individual is his or her family. According to **family systems theory,** the family is a system of interacting parts—the family members—who interact with one another in consistent ways and follow rules unique to each family (Goldenberg, Stanton, & Goldenberg, 2016). Family systems theorists believe that the *structure* and *communication* patterns of some families actually force individual members to behave in a way that otherwise seems abnormal. If the members were to behave normally, they would severely strain the family's usual manner of operation and would actually increase their own and their family's turmoil.

Family systems theory holds that certain family systems are particularly likely to produce abnormal functioning in individual members (Corey, 2017: Lindblom et al.,

Today's TV families Unlike television viewers during the twentieth century, when problem-free families ruled the airwaves, today's viewers prefer more complex and occasionally dysfunctional families, like the Johnsons, whose trials and tribulations, including dealing with racial-cultural dilemmas, are on display in ABC's popular series *Black-ish*.

2016). Some families, for example, have an *enmeshed* structure in which the members are grossly overinvolved in one another's activities, thoughts, and feelings. Children from this kind of family may have great difficulty becoming independent in life. Some families display *disengagement,* which is marked by very rigid boundaries between the members. Children from these families may find it hard to function in a group or to give or request support.

> How might family theorists react to writer Leo Tolstoy's famous claim that "every unhappy family is unhappy in its own fashion"?

Philip Berman's angry and impulsive personal style might be seen as the product of a disturbed family structure. According to family systems theorists, the whole family—Philip's mother, father, and brother, and Philip himself—relate in such a way as to maintain Philip's behavior. Family theorists might be particularly interested in the conflict between Philip's mother and father and the imbalance between their parental roles. They might see Philip's behavior as both a reaction to and stimulus for his parents' behaviors. With Philip acting out the role of the misbehaving child, or scapegoat, his parents may have little need or time to question their own relationship.

Family systems theorists would also seek to clarify the precise nature of Philip's relationship with each parent. Is he enmeshed with his mother and/or disengaged from his father? They would look too at the rules governing the sibling relationship in the family, the relationship between Philip's parents and brother, and the nature of parent–child relationships in previous generations of the family.

Family-Social Treatments

The family-social perspective has helped spur the growth of several treatment approaches, including *group, family,* and *couple therapy,* and *community treatment.* Therapists of any orientation may work with clients in these various formats, applying the techniques and principles of their preferred models (see *MindTech* on page 75). However, more and more of the clinicians who use these formats believe that psychological problems emerge in family and social settings and are best treated in such settings, and they include special sociocultural strategies in their work.

Group Therapy Thousands of therapists specialize in **group therapy,** a format in which a therapist meets with a group of clients who have similar problems. Typically,

---

#

#FamilyRestructuring

9% Percentage of U.S. children living with only one parent in 1960

27% Percentage of U.S. children living with only one parent today

(U.S. Census Bureau, 2016)

Kasia Wandycz/Paris Match via Getty Images

Creative group work *Psychodrama,* developed by psychiatrist Jacob Moreno in 1921, is one of the oldest forms of group treatment. Its group members act out their emotions, past or present situations, social interactions, and the like—often in creative ways and sometimes on a stage. Although not as widely conducted as conventional group therapy, this format continues to have many proponents and is offered in many locations, such as this psychodrama group in Pignan, France.

members of a therapy group meet together with a therapist and discuss the problems of one or more of the people in the group. Together they develop important insights, build social skills, strengthen feelings of self-worth, and share useful information or advice (Rutan & Shay, 2016). Many groups are created with particular client populations in mind; for example, there are groups for people with alcoholism, for those who are physically handicapped, and for people who are divorced, abused, or bereaved.

Research suggests that group therapy is of help to many clients, often as helpful as individual therapy (Law et al., 2016; Burlingame & Baldwin, 2011). The group format also has been used for purposes that are educational rather than therapeutic, such as "consciousness raising" and spiritual inspiration.

A format similar to group therapy is the **self-help group** (or **mutual-help group**). Here people who have similar problems (for example, bereavement, substance abuse, illness, unemployment, or divorce) come together to help and support one another without the direct leadership of a professional clinician (Markowitz, 2015; Lake, 2014). According to estimates, there are now between 500,000 and 3 million such groups in the United States alone, attended each year by as many as 3 to 4 percent of the population. In addition, an ever-growing number of self-help chat groups have emerged on the Internet in recent years.

> Why might group therapy actually be more helpful to some people with psychological problems than individual therapy?

Family Therapy **Family therapy** was first introduced in the 1950s. A therapist meets with all members of a family, points out problem behaviors and interactions, and helps the whole family to change its ways (Goldenberg et al., 2016). Here, the entire family is viewed as the unit under treatment, even if only one of the members receives a clinical diagnosis. The following is a typical interaction between family members and a therapist:

self-help group A group made up of people with similar problems who help and support one another without the direct leadership of a clinician. Also called a *mutual help group.*

family therapy A therapy format in which the therapist meets with all members of a family and helps them to change in therapeutic ways.

Tommy sat motionless in a chair gazing out the window. He was fourteen and a bit small for his age. . . . Sissy was eleven. She was sitting on the couch between her Mom and Dad with a smile on her face. Across from them sat Ms. Fargo, the family therapist.

Ms. Fargo spoke. "Could you be a little more specific about the changes you have seen in Tommy and when they came about?"

Mrs. Davis answered first. "Well, I guess it was about two years ago. Tommy started getting in fights at school. When we talked to him at home he said it was none of our business. He became moody and disobedient. He wouldn't do anything that we wanted him to. He began to act mean to his sister and even hit her."

"What about the fights at school?" Ms. Fargo asked.

This time it was Mr. Davis who spoke first. "Ginny was more worried about them than I was. I used to fight a lot when I was in school and I think it is normal. . . . But I was very respectful to my parents, especially my Dad. If I ever got out of line he would smack me one."

"Have you ever had to hit Tommy?" Ms. Fargo inquired softly.

"Sure, a couple of times, but it didn't seem to do any good."

All at once Tommy seemed to be paying attention, his eyes riveted on his father. "Yeah, he hit me a lot, for no reason at all!"

"Now, that's not true, Thomas." Mrs. Davis has a scolding expression on her face. "If you behaved yourself a little better you wouldn't get hit. Ms. Fargo, I can't say that I am in favor of the hitting, but I understand sometimes how frustrating it may be for Bob."

MINDTECH

Have Your Avatar Call My Avatar

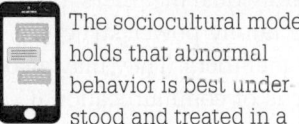

The sociocultural model holds that abnormal behavior is best understood and treated in a social context. Thus, as part of the movement toward technology-enhanced interventions, a growing number of clinicians are particularly interested in using *avatars*—three-dimensional graphical representations of the clients and/or other key persons in their lives—in their treatment programs (Craig, Ward, & Rus-Calafell, 2016; Rehm et al., 2016).

Guia Besana/Anzenberger/Redux

As you will see in Chapters 5 and 6, the use of 3D computer graphics to simulate real-world objects and situations, called *virtual reality therapy*, has become a popular technique for treating people with phobias, traumatic memories, and other disorders. In such cases, the technique enables clients to be exposed—through computer simulation—to the objects and memories they dread, thus helping them to confront their fears head-on.

On the other hand, avatar therapy, one version of virtual reality therapy, seeks primarily to immerse clients in digitalized social situations—situations in which they interact with avatars as a bridge toward social improvement.

In one form of avatar-centered therapy, users are guided by computer software programs to interact with on-screen virtual

therapist figures who ask questions such as "What kinds of things do you dislike about yourself?" The virtual therapist may also nod sympathetically when the users offer self-criticisms and may reinforce certain user statements with smiles or encouraging words (Rehm et al., 2016; Reamer, 2013).

In another use of avatars, clients are guided by their real-life therapists to enter virtual environments on their computers, acquire virtual bodies, and interact with animated figures who resemble their parents, bosses, friends, or enemies—in situations that feel very real (Myers et al., 2016). Theoretically, experiences in virtual worlds of this kind help clients change their reactions in the real social world (Rehm et al., 2016; Rus-Calafell et al, 2015; Reamer, 2013). In one highly publicized case, for example, a woman with social anxiety and

agoraphobia—a fear of leaving the house—was guided by her therapist to adopt an avatar and enter into a virtual world of other avatars, a journey that eventually enabled her to venture outside into the real world and into relationships with other persons (Smith, 2008).

Not surprisingly, given its social focus, avatar therapy is currently being used to help individuals suffering from problems such as social anxiety, loneliness, and hallucinations that hinder normal interactions. These applications are often quite helpful according to research (Rehm et al., 2016; Leff et al., 2014, 2013; Kedmey, 2013). Several explanations have been offered for this success, including the ultra-flexibility that avatar programs give therapists to manipulate treatment

> **Clients know they are entering a make-believe world when they receive avatar therapy, so why do so many apparently make real-life progress?**

stimuli, the comfortable (and sometimes anonymous) settings the programs afford persons who are too anxious or confused to partake in traditional therapist relationships, and the appeal they have for individuals who find high tech formats less intimidating than real-life interactions. 💬

"You don't know how frustrating it is for me, honey." Bob seemed upset. . . . Ginny gave him a hard stare. . . "I could use some support from you [too]. You think . . . I will do everything . . . . Well, I am not about to do that anymore." . . . [She] began to cry. "I just don't know what to do anymore. Things just seem so hopeless. Why can't people be nice in this family anymore? I don't think I am asking too much, am I?"

Ms. Fargo . . . looked at each person briefly and was sure to make eye contact. "There seems to be a lot going on . . . I think we are going to need to understand a lot of things to see why this is happening."

(Sheras & Worchel, 1979, pp. 108–110)

Family therapists may follow any of the major theoretical models, but many of them adopt the principles of *family systems theory* (Slesnick & Zhang, 2016). Today 2 percent of all clinical psychologists, 5 percent of counseling psychologists, and 14 percent of

couple therapy A therapy format in which the therapist works with two people who share a long-term relationship. Also called *marital therapy.*

community mental health treatment A treatment approach that emphasizes community care.

multicultural perspective The view that each culture within a larger society has a particular set of values and beliefs, as well as special external pressures, that help account for the behavior and functioning of its members. Also called *culturally diverse perspective.*

social workers identify themselves mainly as *family systems therapists* (Prochaska & Norcross, 2013).

As you read earlier, family systems theory holds that each family has its own rules, structure, and communication patterns that shape the individual members' behavior. Thus family systems therapists often try to change the family power structure, the roles each person plays, and the relationships between members. They may also try to help members recognize and change harmful patterns of communication (Corey, 2017; Minuchin, 2007, 1987, 1974).

Family therapy is often helpful to individuals, although research has not yet clarified how helpful (Goldenberg et al., 2016; Nichols, 2013). Some studies have found that as many as 65 percent of individuals treated with family approaches improve, while other studies suggest much lower success rates. Nor has any one type of family therapy emerged as consistently more helpful than the others (Bitter, 2013; Alexander et al., 2002).

Couple Therapy
In **couple therapy,** or **marital therapy**, the therapist works with two individuals who are in a long-term relationship. Often they are husband and wife, but the couple need not be married or even living together. Like family therapy, couple therapy often focuses on the structure and communication patterns in the relationship (Baucom et al., 2015, 2010; Gurman, Lebow, & Snyder, 2015). A couple approach may also be used when a child's psychological problems are traced to problems in the parents' relationship.

Although some degree of conflict exists in any long-term relationship, many couples in our society have serious marital discord. The divorce rate in Canada, the United States, and Europe is now close to 50 percent of the marriage rate. Many couples who live together without marrying apparently have similar levels of difficulty (Martins et al., 2014).

Couple therapy, like family and group therapy, may follow the principles of any of the major therapy orientations. *Cognitive-behavioral couple therapy,* for example, uses many techniques from the cognitive and behavioral perspectives (Fischer, Baucom, & Cohen, 2016). Therapists help spouses recognize and change problem behaviors largely by teaching specific problem-solving and communication skills. A broader, more sociocultural version, called *integrative behavioral couple therapy,* further helps partners accept behaviors that they cannot change and embrace the whole relationship nevertheless (Christensen & Doss, 2017). Partners are asked to see such behaviors as an understandable result of basic differences between them.

Couples treated by couple therapy seem to show greater improvement in their relationships than couples with similar problems who do not receive treatment, but no one form of couple therapy stands out as superior to others (Christensen et al., 2016, 2014, 2010). Although marital functioning improved in two-thirds of treated couples by the end of therapy, fewer than half of those who are treated achieve "distress-free" or "happy" relationships. One-fourth of all treated couples eventually separate or divorce.

Community Treatment
Community mental health treatment programs allow clients, particularly those with severe psychological difficulties, to receive treatment in familiar social surroundings as they try to recover. Such community-based treatments, including *community day programs* and *residential services,* seem to be of special value to people with severe mental disorders (Clausen et al., 2016; Linz & Sturm, 2016; Stein et al., 2015). A number of other countries have launched similar community movements over the past several decades.

David Sipress/The New Yorker Collection/The Cartoon Bank

"We broke up, Stuart—don't you read your e-mail?"

As you read in Chapter 1, a key principle of community treatment is *prevention*. This involves clinicians actively reaching out to clients rather than waiting for them to seek treatment. Research suggests that such efforts are often very successful (Brown et al., 2016; Costello, 2016; Membride, 2016). Community workers recognize three types of prevention, which they call *primary, secondary,* and *tertiary. Primary prevention* consists of efforts to improve community attitudes and policies. Its goal is to prevent psychological disorders altogether. Community workers may, for example, consult with a local school board, offer public workshops on stress reduction, or construct Web sites on how to cope effectively.

Secondary prevention consists of identifying and treating psychological disorders in the early stages, before they become serious. Community workers may work with teachers, ministers, or police to help them recognize the early signs of psychological dysfunction and teach them how to help people find treatment. Similarly, hundreds of mental health Web sites provide this same kind of information to family members, teachers, and the like.

The goal of *tertiary prevention* is to provide effective treatment as soon as it is needed so that moderate or severe disorders do not become long-term problems. Community agencies across the United States successfully offer tertiary care for millions of people with moderate psychological problems but, as you read in Chapter 1, they often fail to provide the services needed by hundreds of thousands with severe disturbances (NAMI, 2016; Dixon & Schwarz, 2014). One of the reasons for this failure is lack of funding, an issue that you will read about in later chapters.

How Do Multicultural Theorists Explain Abnormal Functioning?

Culture refers to the set of values, attitudes, beliefs, history, and behaviors shared by a group of people and communicated from one generation to the next (Matsumoto & Juang, 2016). We are, without question, a society of multiple cultures. Indeed, by the year 2044, members of racial and ethnic minority groups in the United States will collectively outnumber white Americans (KFF, 2016; U.S. Census Bureau, 2015).

Partly in response to this growing diversity, the **multicultural,** or **culturally diverse, perspective** has emerged (Hall, Yip, & Zarate, 2016). Multicultural psychologists seek to understand how culture, race, ethnicity, gender, and similar factors affect behavior and thought and how people of different cultures, races, and genders differ psychologically (Alegría et al., 2016, 2014, 2013). Today's multicultural view is different from past—less enlightened—cultural perspectives: it does not imply that members of racial, ethnic, and other minority groups are in some way inferior or culturally deprived in comparison with a majority population. Rather, the model holds that an individual's behavior, whether normal or abnormal, is best understood when examined in the light of that individual's unique cultural context, from the values of that culture to the special external pressures faced by members of the culture.

The groups in the United States that have received the most attention from multicultural researchers are ethnic and racial minority groups (African American, Hispanic American, American Indian, and Asian American groups) and groups such as economically disadvantaged persons, LGBTQ individuals, and women (although women are not a minority group numbers-wise). Each of these groups is subjected to special pressures in American society that may contribute to feelings of stress

NYPD ✓
November 27, 2012 · 🌐

Jennifer Foster of Florence, AZ was visiting Times Square with her husband Nov. 14 when they saw a shoeless man asking for change… See More

Reaching out On a freezing night in 2012, New York City police officer Lawrence DiPrimo bought a pair of socks and shoes for a homeless man he had come across, then knelt down and gently put them on the man's feet. Unbeknownst to the officer, his humane act was photographed by a passer-by and was viewed online by millions of people. Although DiPrimo's behavior came from the heart, it reflected the key principles of community mental health, including reaching out to the needy in the community with kindness and understanding, which may help prevent mental health problems.

#ExperiencingDiscrimination

71% Percentage of African Americans who report being regularly or occasionally treated unfairly because of their race

52% Percentage of Hispanic Americans who report being regularly or occasionally treated unfairly because of their race

(Information from: Pew Research Center, 2016)

and, in some cases, to abnormal functioning. Researchers have learned, for example, that psychological abnormality, especially severe psychological abnormality, is indeed more common among poorer people than among wealthier people (Lepiecé et al., 2015; Sareen et al., 2011) (see **Figure 3-4**). Perhaps the pressures of poverty explain this relationship.

Of course, membership in these various groups overlaps. Many members of minority groups, for example, also live in poverty. The higher rates of crime, unemployment, overcrowding, and homelessness; the inferior medical care; and the limited educational opportunities typically available to poor people may place great stress on many members of such minority groups (Acri et al., 2016; Joshi et al., 2016).

Multicultural researchers have also noted that the prejudice and discrimination faced by many minority groups may contribute to various forms of abnormal functioning (Elias & Paradies, 2016). Women in Western society receive diagnoses of anxiety disorders and of depression at least twice as often as men (NIMH, 2015). Similarly, African Americans, Hispanic Americans, and American Indians are more likely than non-Hispanic white Americans to experience serious psychological distress (CDC, 2016; HHS, 2009). American Indians also have exceptionally high alcoholism and suicide rates (Maza, 2015; Horwitz, 2014). Although many factors may combine to produce these differences, prejudice based on race and sexual orientation, and the problems such prejudice poses, may contribute to abnormal patterns of tension, unhappiness, and low self-esteem (Bhui, 2016; Held & Lee, 2016).

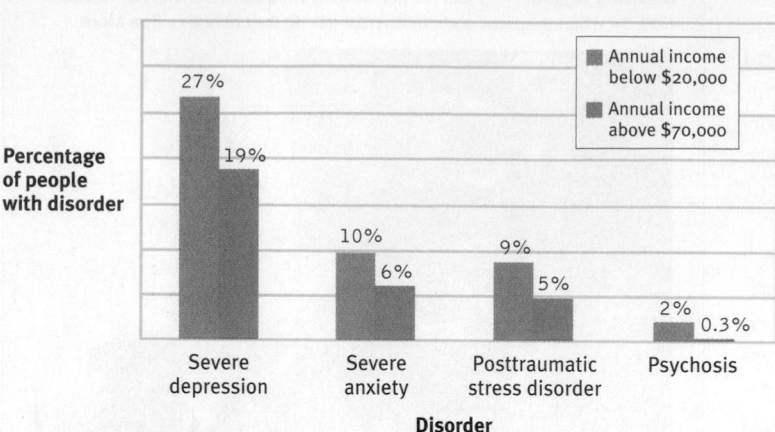

FIGURE 3-4

Poverty and Mental Health

Surveys in the United States find that people with low annual incomes (below $20,000) have a greater risk of experiencing mental disorders than do those with higher incomes (above $70,000). For example, 10 percent of low-income people have persistent symptoms of anxiety, compared with 6 percent of higher-income people. (Information from: CDC, 2015; Sareen et al., 2011.)

Multicultural Treatments

Studies conducted throughout the world have found that members of ethnic and racial minority groups tend to show less improvement in clinical treatment, make less use of mental health services, and stop therapy sooner than members of majority groups (De Luca et al., 2016; Cook et al., 2014).

A number of studies suggest that two features of treatment can increase a therapist's effectiveness with minority clients: (1) greater sensitivity to cultural issues and (2) inclusion of cultural morals and models in treatment, especially in therapies for children and adolescents (Chu et al, 2016; Gainsbury, 2016; Comas-Diaz, 2014, 2012, 2011). Given such findings, some clinicians have developed **culture-sensitive therapies,** approaches that are designed to help address the unique issues faced by members of cultural minority groups. Therapies geared to the pressures of being female, called **gender-sensitive,** or **feminist, therapies,** follow similar principles groups (Corey, 2017; Vasquez &Vasquez, 2016).

Culture-sensitive approaches typically include the following elements (Baruth & Manning, 2016; Chu et al., 2016; Wyatt & Parham, 2007):

1. Special cultural instruction for therapists in their graduate training program

2. The therapist's awareness of a client's cultural values

3. The therapist's awareness of the stress, prejudices, and stereotypes to which minority clients are exposed

4. The therapist's awareness of the hardships faced by the children of immigrants

5. Helping clients recognize the impact of both their own culture and the dominant culture on their self-views and behaviors

culture-sensitive therapies Approaches that are designed to help address the unique issues faced by members of cultural minority groups.

gender-sensitive therapies Approaches geared to the pressures of being a woman in Western society. Also called *feminist therapies.*

6. Helping clients identify and express suppressed anger and pain

7. Helping clients achieve a bicultural balance that feels right for them

8. Helping clients raise their self-esteem—a sense of self-worth that has often been damaged by generations of negative messages

Assessing the Sociocultural Model

The family-social and multicultural perspectives have added greatly to the understanding and treatment of abnormal functioning. Today most clinicians take family, cultural, social, and societal issues into account, factors that were overlooked just 35 years ago. In addition, clinicians have become more aware of the impact of clinical and social roles. Finally, the treatment formats offered by the sociocultural model sometimes succeed where traditional approaches have failed.

At the same time, the sociocultural model has certain problems. To begin with, sociocultural research findings are often difficult to interpret. Indeed, research may reveal a relationship between certain family or cultural factors and a particular disorder yet fail to establish that they are its *cause*. Studies show a link between family conflict and schizophrenia, for example, but that finding does not necessarily mean that family dysfunction causes schizophrenia. It is equally possible that family functioning is disrupted by the tension and conflict created by the psychotic behavior of a family member.

Another limitation of the sociocultural model is its inability to predict abnormality in specific individuals. If, for example, social conditions such as prejudice and discrimination are key causes of anxiety and depression, why do only some of the people subjected to such forces experience psychological disorders? Are still other factors necessary for the development of the disorders?

Given these limitations, most clinicians view the family-social and multicultural explanations as operating in conjunction with the biological or psychological explanations. They agree that family, social, and cultural factors may create a climate favorable to the development of certain disorders. They believe, however, that biological or psychological conditions—or both—must also be present for the disorders to evolve.

An unacceptable difference Dressed in traditional American Indian clothing, a high school student from the Mescalero Apache Reservation in New Mexico testifies before Congress on "The Preventable Epidemic: Youth Suicides and the Urgent Need for Mental Health Care Resources in Indian Country."

Community mental health; Argentine style Staff members and patients from Borda Neuropsychiatric Hospital in Buenos Aires set up a laptop and begin broadcasting on the popular radio station Radio La Colifata (*colifa* is slang for "crazy one"). The station was started more than 20 years ago to help patients pursue therapeutic activities and reach out to the community.

biopsychosocial theories Explanations that attribute the cause of abnormality to an interaction of genetic, biological, emotional, behavioral, cognitive, social, and societal influences.

developmental psychopathology A perspective that uses a developmental framework to understand how variables and principles from the various models may collectively account for human functioning.

equifinality The principle that a number of different developmental pathways can lead to the same psychological disorder.

multifinality The principle that persons with a similar developmental history may nevertheless react to similar current situations in very different ways.

Integrating the Models: The Developmental Psychopathology Perspective

TODAY'S LEADING MODELS vary widely (see **Table 3-3**), and none of the models has proved consistently superior. Each helps us appreciate a key aspect of human functioning, and each has important strengths as well as serious limitations.

Despite all their differences, the conclusions and techniques of the various models are often compatible. Certainly our understanding of abnormal behavior is more complete if we appreciate the biological, psychological, *and* sociocultural aspects of a person's problem rather than only one such aspect. Not surprisingly, then, many clinicians now favor explanations of abnormal behavior that consider more than one kind of cause at a time. These explanations, sometimes called **biopsychosocial theories,** state that abnormality results from the interaction of genetic, biological, emotional, behavioral, cognitive, social, cultural, and societal influences (Calkins & Dollar, 2014). In a similar quest for integration, many therapists now combine treatment techniques from several models (Beutler et al., 2016; Norcross, Goldfried, & Zimmerman, 2016). In fact, 22 percent of today's clinical psychologists, 34 percent of counseling psychologists, and 26 percent of social workers describe their approach as "eclectic" or "integrative" (Prochaska & Norcross, 2013). Studies confirm that clinical problems often respond better to combined approaches than to any one therapy alone.

One of today's most influential integrative views is the **developmental psychopathology** perspective. As its name implies, this perspective uses a *developmental* framework to understand how variables and principles from the various models may collectively account for human functioning—both adaptive and maladaptive functioning (Cicchetti, 2016; Leve & Cicchetti, 2016; Suor et al., 2016). As such, the perspective pays particular attention to the *timing* of influential variables. The emergence of particular events, experiences, or biological factors—from neurons to neighborhoods—can continue to have enormous impact on later functioning if they occur at vulnerable points in a person's life. This perspective also focuses on the *intersection* and *context*

TABLE: 3-3

Comparing the Models

	Biological	Psychodynamic	Cognitive-Behavioral	Humanistic	Existential	Family-Social	Multicultural
Cause of dysfunction	Biological malfunction	Underlying conflicts	Maladaptive thinking and learning	Self-deceit	Avoidance of responsibility	Family or social stress	External pressures or cultural conflicts
Research support	Strong	Modest	Strong	Weak	Weak	Moderate	Moderate
Consumer designation	Patient	Patient	Client	Patient or client	Patient or client	Client	Client
Therapist role	Doctor	Interpreter	Collaborator/teacher	Observer	Collaborator	Family/social facilitator	Cultural advocate/teacher
Key therapy technique	Biological intervention	Free association and interpretation	Reasoning and conditioning	Reflection	Varied	Family/social intervention	Culture-sensitive intervention
Therapy goal	Biological repair	Broad psychological change	Functional thoughts and behaviors	Self-actualization	Authentic life	Effective family or social system	Cultural awareness and comfort

of such variables throughout the lifespan. The critical question for developmental psychopathologists is not *which* single factor is the cause of an individual's current psychological problems, but rather when, how, in what context, and to what degree the multiple factors in his or her life (internal and external, historical and current) interact with one another. In Philip Berman's case, for example, when did his brother's birth occur, what was going on in Philip's life at that point in time, how did his mother's depression affect her parenting skills, did his childhood experiences teach him how to cope effectively with stress, and were his social systems during childhood, college, and adulthood supportive or did they intensify his difficulties?

What are the factors that developmental psychopathologists look at collectively when seeking to understand a person's abnormal functioning? As noted above, they draw from each of the clinical field's major models. They draw from the biological model, for example, by determining how certain genetic and brain factors have set the stage for the individual's important environmental experiences (Grigorenko et al., 2016; Monahan et al., 2016). They extract from the psychodynamic model, particularly object relations theory, by considering how the person's earlier events—including parent–child relationships—have constrained subsequent development (Fearon et al., 2016). They employ principles from the cognitive-behavioral model by determining how the individual's maladaptive behaviors have been reinforced over the years and how he or she has interpreted and processed life experiences (Hankin et al., 2016). In addition, developmental psychopathologists draw from the humanistic-existential model by considering the person's competencies, uniqueness, and resilience, even in the face of overwhelming life stress (Burt et al., 2016; Masten & Cicchetti, 2016). And finally, they embrace the sociocultural model's emphasis on the influence of social context and culture—both present and past—on the individual's functioning (Chen & Liu, 2016; Pianta, 2016; Tolan, 2016).

The developmental psychopathology perspective gives special attention to individual differences, not just differences in clinical diagnoses and outcomes, but in the developmental routes, or *pathways*, that lead to dysfunction. In fact, two key principles—*equifinality* and *multifinality*—are at the center of the perspective. According to the principle of **equifinality**, a number of different developmental pathways can lead to the same psychological disorder. Consider, for example, two teenage boys with conduct disorder, a disorder that you'll be reading about in Chapter 17. Both boys may display the characteristic symptoms of this disorder, such as stealing, skipping school, lying, and breaking into cars. However, for one of the boys, factors such as unfavorable genes, poor parenting, and a limited cognitive capacity for empathy may have interacted to foster the development of conduct disorder. In contrast, the other boy with the disorder may not have any genetic vulnerabilities, may have been raised by highly attentive parents, and may actually demonstrate a high capacity for empathy. His serious conduct problems may have resulted instead from the interaction of long-term feelings of depression, low self-esteem, strong needs for peer approval, and affiliations with peers who typically engage in delinquent activities.

According to the principle of **multifinality** (the flipside of equifinality), persons who have experienced a number of similar developmental variables (for example, comparable biological predispositions, family structures, schools, and neighborhoods) may nevertheless react to comparable current situations in very different ways or have different clinical outcomes. Consider two women who lose their jobs suddenly. Despite their similar developmental variables, one woman may react to this loss with

RETWEETS 23,207   LIKES 27,141

High-flying equifinality The principle of *equifinality*—the notion that people can arrive at the same end point through different developmental pathways—has been observed in the physical realm as well as the psychological realm. Consider Neil Douglas and Robert Stirling, two men born to different parents, inheriting different genes, experiencing different childhoods, and raised in different cities. When the two strangers took a plane flight in 2015, they each were flabbergasted to see that the passenger seated next to them was their "spitting image"—same red hair and beard, head shape, eyes, teeth, smile, and more. They immediately took this selfie, and the photo went viral.

devastation and spiral toward depression, while the other may view the job loss as an opportunity for reinvention and enthusiastically seek out a wide range of new employment opportunities. Why this enormous difference in the reactions of the two individuals? Perhaps their developmental histories or current circumstances do in fact differ in undetected ways. The latter woman may, for example, have experienced uniquely challenging events while growing up that fostered a strong sense of resilience, or she may currently have greater financial savings to help her weather a period of unemployment.

Given their emphasis on timing and development when explaining psychological disorders, it is not surprising that developmental psychopathologists focus more on the timing of treatment than on specific treatment techniques. For example, they tend to prioritize prevention and early intervention for vulnerable persons over treatment for individuals who have already developed severe disorders (Toth et al., 2016). Further, consistent with the perspective's special emphasis on context and sociocultural influences, developmental psychopathologists echo the call of community mental health advocates for community-wide interventions, commonly targeting entire schools or neighborhoods, as opposed to individual treatment formats. Indeed, developmental psychopathologists often play prominent roles in advocacy and social policy, seeking changes in societal factors that negatively influence development, such as poverty, community violence, and social inequalities.

In light of the recent rise of integrative perspectives and combination treatments, our examinations of abnormal behavior throughout this book will take two directions. As various disorders are presented, we will look at how today's models explain each disorder, how clinicians who endorse each model treat people with the disorder, and how well these explanations and treatments are supported by research. Just as important, however, we will also be observing how the explanations and treatments may build upon and strengthen one another, and we will examine current efforts toward integration of the models.

⚲... SUMMING UP

»Models of Abnormality Scientists and clinicians use *models*, or *paradigms*, to understand and treat abnormal behavior. The principles and techniques of treatment used by clinical practitioners correspond to their preferred models. *pp. 45–47*

»The Biological Model Biological theorists look at the biological processes of human functioning to explain abnormal behavior, pointing to *anatomical* or *biochemical* problems in the brain and body. Such abnormalities are sometimes the result of *genetic inheritance of abnormalities* or *normal evolution*. Biological therapists use physical and chemical methods to help people overcome their psychological problems. The leading methods are *drug therapy*, *brain stimulation*, and *psychosurgery*. *pp. 47–53*

»The Psychodynamic Model Psychodynamic theorists believe that an individual's behavior, whether normal or abnormal, is determined by underlying psychological forces. They consider psychological conflicts to be rooted in early parent–child relationships and traumatic experiences. The psychodynamic model was formulated by Sigmund Freud, who said that three dynamic forces—the *id*, *ego*, and *superego*—interact to produce thought, feeling, and behavior. Other psychodynamic theories are *self theory* and *object relations theory*.

Psychodynamic therapists help people uncover past traumas and the inner conflicts that have resulted from them. They use a number of techniques, including *free association* and interpretations of psychological phenomena such as *resistance*, *transference*, and *dreams*. The leading contemporary psychodynamic approaches include *short-term psychodynamic therapies* and *relational psychoanalytic therapy*. *pp. 53–58*

»The Cognitive-Behavioral Model Proponents of the cognitive-behavioral model focus on *maladaptive behaviors and cognitions* to explain and treat psychological disorders. Most such proponents now include both the behavioral and cognitive dimensions in their work rather than just one or the other.

On the behavioral dimension, the theorists hold that three types of conditioning—*classical conditioning*, *modeling*, and *operant conditioning*—account for behavior, whether normal or dysfunctional. Therapists try to replace problematic behaviors with more appropriate ones, using techniques based on one or more of the principles of learning.

On the cognitive dimension, theorists such as Aaron Beck further point to cognitive problems, like *maladaptive assumptions* and *illogical thinking processes,* to help explain a person's abnormal functioning. In treatment, therapists may try to help clients recognize, challenge, and change their problematic ways of thinking.

In addition to the traditional cognitive-behavioral approaches, a *new wave of cognitive-behavioral therapies,* such as *acceptance and commitment therapy,* try to teach clients to be *mindful of* and *accept* many of their problematic thoughts. *pp. 59–66*

» The Humanistic-Existential Model

The humanistic-existential model focuses on the human need to successfully deal with philosophical issues such as self-awareness, values, meaning, and choice.

Humanists believe that people are driven to *self-actualize.* When this drive is interfered with, abnormal behavior may result. One group of humanistic therapists, *client-centered therapists,* tries to create a very supportive therapy climate in which people can look at themselves honestly and acceptingly, thus opening the door to self-actualization. Another group, *gestalt therapists,* uses more active techniques to help people recognize and accept their needs. Recently the role of *religion* as an important factor in mental health and in psychotherapy has caught the attention of researchers and clinicians.

According to existentialists, abnormal behavior results from hiding from life's responsibilities. Existential therapists encourage people to accept *responsibility* for their lives, recognize their *freedom to choose* a different course, and choose to live with greater meaning. *pp. 67–71*

» The Sociocultural Model

One sociocultural perspective, the *family-social* perspective looks outward to three kinds of factors: *social labels and roles, social connections and supports,* and the *family system.* Practitioners from the family-social model may practice *group, family,* or *couple therapy,* or *community treatment.*

The *multicultural* perspective, another sociocultural perspective, holds that an individual's behavior, whether normal or abnormal, is best understood when examined in the light of his or her unique cultural context, including the values of that culture and the special external pressures faced by members of that culture. Practitioners of this perspective may practice *culture-sensitive therapies. pp. 71–79*

» Integrating the Models

Many theorists now favor explanations for abnormal behavior that consider more than one kind of cause at a time, and many therapists combine treatment techniques from several models. An influential integrative view, the *developmental psychopathology* perspective, uses a developmental framework to understand how variables and principles from the various models may collectively account for human functioning—both adaptive and maladaptive functioning. Two principles at the center of this perspective are *equifinality* and *multifinality. pp. 80–82*

Visit *LaunchPad*
to access the e-Book, Clinical Choices, videos, activities, and LearningCurve, as well as study aids including flashcards, FAQs, and research exercises.

LaunchPad
macmillan learning

♀...Clinical Assessment, Diagnosis, and Treatment

Franco started seeing a therapist at the urging of his friend Jesse. It had been almost four months since Franco broke up with his girlfriend, and he still seemed unable to pull himself together. He had totally stopped playing sports and attending concerts, things he normally did on a regular basis. When he finally returned Jesse's calls, he mentioned several serious and avoidable mistakes that he had made at work recently, but he barely seemed to care. He also confided to his friend that he felt very tired and was unable to touch his food. Jesse suspected that Franco was clinically depressed, but, then again, he was not a therapist.

Feelings of despondency led Franco to make an appointment with a therapist at a local counseling center. His clinician's first step was to learn as much as possible about Franco and his disturbance: Who is he, what is his life like, and what are his symptoms? The answers might help to reveal the causes and probable course of his present dysfunction and suggest what kinds of strategies would be most likely to help him. Treatment could then be tailored to Franco's needs and particular pattern of abnormal functioning.

In Chapters 2 and 3 you read about how researchers in abnormal psychology build a general understanding of abnormal functioning. Clinical practitioners apply this broad information in their work, but their main focus when faced with new clients is to gather **idiographic,** or individual, information about them (Beltz et al., 2016). To help a client overcome problems, clinicians must fully understand the client and his or her particular difficulties. To gather such individual information, clinicians use the procedures of *assessment* and *diagnosis*. Then they are in a position to offer *treatment.* ∎

Clinical Assessment: How and Why Does the Client Behave Abnormally?

ASSESSMENT IS SIMPLY THE COLLECTING of relevant information in an effort to reach a conclusion. It goes on in every realm of life. We make assessments when we decide what cereal to buy or which presidential candidate to vote for. College admissions officers, who have to select the "best" of the students applying to their college, depend on academic records, recommendations, achievement test scores, interviews, and application forms to help them decide. Employers, who have to predict which applicants are most likely to be effective workers, collect information from résumés, interviews, references, and perhaps on-the-job observations.

Clinical assessment is used to determine whether, how, and why a person is behaving abnormally and how that person may be helped. It also enables clinicians to evaluate people's progress after they have been in treatment for a while and decide whether the treatment should be changed. The specific tools that are used to do an assessment depend on the clinician's theoretical orientation. Psychodynamic clinicians, for example, use methods that assess a client's personality and probe for unconscious conflicts

idiographic understanding An understanding of a particular individual.

assessment The process of collecting and interpreting relevant information about a client or research participant.

standardization The process in which a test is administered to a large group of people whose performance then serves as a standard or norm against which any individual's score can be measured.

reliability A measure of the consistency of test or research results.

validity A measure of the accuracy of a test's or study's results.

he or she may be experiencing (Yalof, 2015). This enables them to piece together a clinical picture in accord with the principles of their model. Cognitive-behavioral clinicians are more likely to use assessment methods that reveal specific dysfunctional behaviors and cognitions (Groth-Marnat & Wright, 2016; Hales et al., 2015).

The hundreds of clinical assessment techniques and tools that have been developed fall into three categories: *clinical interviews, tests,* and *observations*. To be useful, these tools must be *standardized* and must have clear *reliability* and *validity*.

Characteristics of Assessment Tools

All clinicians must follow the same procedures when they use a particular type of assessment tool. To **standardize** such a tool is to set up common steps to be followed whenever it is administered. Similarly, clinicians must standardize the way they interpret the results of an assessment tool in order to be able to understand what a particular score means. They may standardize the scores of a test, for example, by first administering it to a group of research participants whose performance will then serve as a common standard, or norm, against which later individual scores can be measured. The group that initially takes the test must be typical of the larger population for whom the test is intended. If an aggressiveness test meant for the public at large were standardized on a group of Marines, for example, the resulting "norm" might turn out to be misleadingly high.

Reliability refers to the *consistency* of assessment measures. A good assessment tool will always yield similar results in the same situation (Blanchard et al., 2017). An assessment tool has high *test–retest reliability,* one kind of reliability, if it yields similar results every time it is given to the same people. If a woman's responses on a particular test indicate that she is generally a heavy drinker, the test should produce a similar result when she takes it again a week later. To measure test–retest reliability, participants are tested on two occasions and the two scores are correlated (Tenke et al., 2017). The higher the correlation (see Chapter 2), the greater the test's reliability.

> How reliable and valid are the tests you take in school? What about the tests you see online?

An assessment tool shows high *interrater* (or *interjudge*) *reliability,* another kind of reliability, if different judges independently agree on how to score and interpret it (Axelsson et al., 2016). True–false and multiple-choice tests yield consistent scores no matter who evaluates them, but other tests require that the evaluator make a judgment. Consider a test that requires the person to draw a copy of a picture, which a judge then rates for accuracy. Different judges may give different ratings to the same drawing.

Reliable assessment? Former National Basketball Association stars Magic Johnson, Shaquille O'Neal, Tracy McGrady, Dikembe Mutombo, and George Gervin served as judges at the 2016 All-Star slam dunk contest. Assigning a relatively wide range of scores after each dunk, they displayed low interrater reliability.

Finally, an assessment tool must have **validity:** it must *accurately* measure what it is supposed to measure. Suppose a weight scale reads 12 pounds every time a 10-pound bag of sugar is placed on it. Although the scale is reliable because its readings are consistent, those readings are not valid, or accurate.

A given assessment tool may appear to be valid simply because it makes sense and seems reasonable. However, this sort of validity, called *face validity,* does not by itself mean that the instrument is trustworthy. A test for depression, for example, might include questions about how often a person cries. Because it makes sense that depressed people would cry, these test questions have face validity. It turns out, however, that many people cry a great deal for reasons other than depression, and some extremely depressed people do not cry at all. Thus an assessment tool should not be used unless it has high *predictive validity* or *concurrent validity* (Conway et al., 2016; Miller & Hilsenroth, 2016).

Predictive validity is a tool's ability to predict future characteristics or behavior. Let's say that a test has been developed to identify elementary schoolchildren who are likely to take up cigarette smoking in high school. The test gathers information about the children's parents— their personal characteristics, smoking habits, and attitudes toward smoking—and on that basis identifies high-risk children. To establish the test's predictive validity, investigators could administer it to a group of elementary school students, wait until they were in high school, and then check to see which children actually did become smokers.

Concurrent validity is the degree to which the measures gathered from one tool agree with the measures gathered from other assessment techniques. Participants' scores on a new test designed to measure anxiety, for example, should correlate highly with their scores on other anxiety tests or with their behavior during clinical interviews.

Seeking the right stuff During China's annual military recruitment period, young men sit in front of computers to undergo a series of psychological tests. The tests are used by the country's armed forces to help assess the psychological stability, coping skills, intellect, and leadership potential of each enlistee.

Before any assessment technique can be fully useful, it must meet the requirements of standardization, reliability, and validity. No matter how insightful or clever a technique may be, clinicians cannot profitably use its results if they are uninterpretable, inconsistent, or inaccurate. Unfortunately, more than a few clinical assessment tools fall short, suggesting that at least some clinical assessments too miss their mark.

Clinical Interviews

Most of us feel instinctively that the best way to get to know people is to meet with them face-to-face. Under these circumstances, we can see them react to what we do and say, observe as well as listen as they answer, and generally get a sense of who they are. A *clinical interview* is just such a face-to-face encounter (Sommers-Flanagan & Sommers-Flanagan, 2017; Axelsson et al., 2016). If during a clinical interview a man looks as happy as can be while describing his sadness over the recent death of his mother, the clinician may suspect that the man actually has conflicting emotions about this loss.

Conducting the Interview The interview is often the first contact between client and clinician. Clinicians use it to collect detailed information about the person's problems and feelings, lifestyle and relationships, and other personal history. They may also ask about the person's expectations of therapy and motives for seeking it. The clinician who worked with Franco began with a face-to-face interview:

Franco arrived for his appointment in gray sweatpants and a T-shirt. His stubble suggested that he had not shaved, and the many food stains on his shirt indicated he had not washed it for quite some time. Franco spoke without emotion. He slouched into the chair, sending signals that he did not want to be there.

(continued on the next page)

mental status exam A set of interview questions and observations designed to reveal the degree and nature of a client's abnormal functioning.

clinical test A device for gathering information about a few aspects of a person's psychological functioning from which broader information about the person can be inferred.

projective test A test consisting of ambiguous material that people interpret or respond to.

When pressed, he talked about his two-year relationship with Maria, who, at 25, was 13 years younger than he was. Franco had believed that he had met his future wife, but Maria's domineering mother was unhappy about the age difference and kept telling her daughter that she could find someone better. Franco wanted Maria to stand up to her mother and to move in with him, but this was not easy for her to do. Believing that Maria's mother had too much influence over her and frustrated that she would not commit to him, he had broken up with Maria during a fight. He soon realized that he had acted impulsively, but Maria refused to take him back.

When asked about his childhood, Franco described his father's death in a gruesome car crash on his way to pick up 12-year-old Franco from soccer practice. Initially, his father had told Franco that he could not come get him from practice, but Franco "threw a tantrum" and his father agreed to rearrange his schedule. Franco believed himself responsible for his father's death.

Franco stated that, over the years, his mother had encouraged this feeling of self-blame by complaining that she had been forced to "give up her life" to raise Franco alone. She was always nasty to Franco and nasty to every woman he later dated. She even predicted that Franco would "die alone."

Franco described being very unhappy throughout his school years. He hated school and felt less smart than the other kids. On occasion, a teacher's critique—meant as encouragement—left him unable to do his homework for days, and his grades suffered. He truly believed he was stupid. Similarly, later in life, he interpreted his rise to a position as bank manager as due entirely to hard work. "I know I'm not as smart as the others there."

Franco explained that since the breakup with Maria, he had experienced more unhappiness than ever before. He often spent all night watching television. At the same time, he could barely pay attention to what was happening on the screen. He said that some days he actually forgot to eat. He had no wish to see his friends. At work, the days blurred into one another, distinguished only by a growing number of reprimands from his bank supervisors. He attributed these work problems to his basic lack of ability. His supervisors had simply figured out that he had not been good enough for the job all along.

Beyond gathering basic background data of this kind, clinical interviewers give special attention to those topics they consider most important (Miller, 2015; Stanicke et al., 2015). Psychodynamic interviewers try to learn about the person's needs and memories of past events and relationships. Cognitive-behavioral interviewers try to identify information about the stimuli that trigger responses, consequences of the responses, and/or assumptions and interpretations that influence the person. Humanistic clinicians ask about the person's self-evaluation, self-concept, and values. Biological clinicians look for signs of biochemical or brain dysfunction. And sociocultural interviewers ask about the family, social, and cultural environments.

Interviews can be either unstructured or structured. In an *unstructured interview,* the clinician asks mostly open-ended questions, perhaps as simple as "Would you tell me about yourself?" The lack of structure allows the interviewer to follow leads and explore relevant topics that could not be anticipated before the interview.

In a *structured interview,* clinicians ask prepared—mostly specific—questions. Sometimes they use a published *interview schedule*—a standard set of questions designed for all interviews. Many structured interviews include a **mental status exam,** a set of questions and observations that systematically evaluate the client's awareness, orientation with regard to time and place, attention span, memory, judgment and insight, thought content and processes, mood, and appearance (Brannon, 2016). A structured format ensures that clinicians will cover the same kinds of important issues in all of their interviews and enables them to compare the responses of different individuals.

Although most clinical interviews have both unstructured and structured portions (Lee et al., 2017), many clinicians favor one kind over the other. Unstructured interviews typically appeal to psychodynamic and humanistic clinicians, while structured

#StigmaContinues

33% Americans who would not seek counseling for fear of being labeled "mentally ill"

51% Americans who would hesitate to see a psychotherapist if a diagnosis were required

(Roper, 2017; Opinion Research Corporation, 2011, 2004)

formats are widely used by cognitive-behavioral clinicians, who need to pinpoint behaviors or thinking processes that may underlie abnormal function.

What Are the Limitations of Clinical Interviews? Although interviews often produce valuable information about people, there are limits to what they can accomplish. One problem is that they sometimes lack validity, or accuracy (Sommers-Flanagan & Sommers-Flanagan, 2017; Ventura et al., 2016). Individuals may intentionally mislead in order to present themselves in a positive light or to avoid discussing embarrassing topics (Gold & Castillo, 2010). Or people may be unable to give an accurate report in their interviews. Individuals who suffer from depression, for example, take a negative view of themselves and may describe themselves as poor workers or inadequate parents when that isn't the case at all.

Interviewers too may make mistakes in judgments that slant the information they gather (Groth-Marnat & Wright, 2016; Clinton, Fernandez, & Alicea, 2010). They usually rely too heavily on first impressions, for example, and give too much weight to unfavorable information about a client. Interviewer biases, including gender, race, and age biases, may also influence the interviewers' interpretations of what a client says (Ungar et al., 2006).

Interviews, particularly unstructured ones, may also lack reliability (Gorlin et al., 2016; Young, Bell, & Fristad, 2016). People respond differently to different interviewers, providing, for example, less information to a cold interviewer than to a warm and supportive one (Quas et al., 2007). Similarly, a clinician's race, gender, age, and appearance may influence a client's responses (Davis et al., 2010; Springman, Wherry, & Notaro, 2006).

Because different clinicians can obtain different answers and draw different conclusions even when they ask the same questions of the same person, some researchers believe that interviewing should be discarded as a tool of clinical assessment. As you'll see, however, the two other kinds of clinical assessment methods also have serious limitations.

Clinical Tests

Clinical tests are devices for gathering information about a few aspects of a person's psychological functioning, from which broader information about the person can be inferred. On the surface, it may look easy to design an effective test. Web sites, for example, regularly present new tests that supposedly tell us about our personalities, relationships, sex lives, reactions to stress, or ability to succeed. Such tests might sound convincing, but most of them lack reliability, validity, and standardization. That is, they do not yield consistent, accurate information or reveal where we stand in comparison with others.

More than 1,000 clinical tests are currently in use around the world (Anderson et al., 2016). Clinicians use six kinds most often: *projective tests, personality inventories, response inventories, psychophysiological tests, neurological and neuropsychological tests,* and *intelligence tests.*

Projective Tests. **Projective tests** require that clients interpret vague stimuli, such as inkblots or ambiguous pictures, or follow open-ended instructions such as "Draw a person." Theoretically, when clues and instructions are so general, people will "project" aspects of their personality into the task. Projective tests are used primarily

The art of assessment Clinicians often view works of art as informal projective tests in which artists reveal their conflicts and mental stability. The sometimes bizarre cat portraits by early-twentieth-century artist Louis Wain, for example, have been interpreted as reflections of the psychosis with which he struggled for many years.

D. Bayes/Lebrecht Music & Arts/Alamy

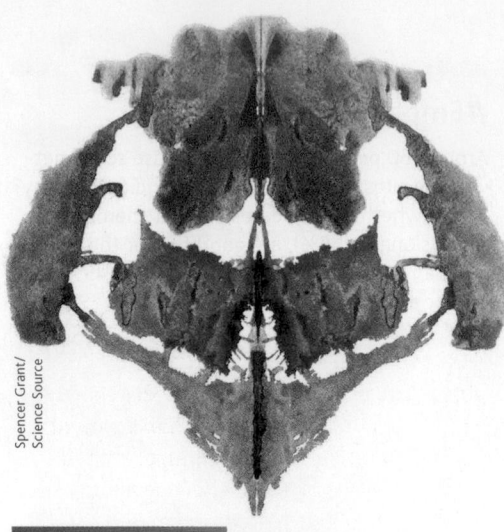

Spencer Grant/ Science Source

FIGURE 4-1

An Inkblot Similar to Those Used in the Rorschach Test

by psychodynamic clinicians to help assess the unconscious drives and conflicts they believe to be at the root of abnormal functioning (Baer & Blais, 2010). The most widely used projective tests are the *Rorschach test,* the *Thematic Apperception Test, sentence-completion tests,* and *drawings.*

RORSCHACH TEST In 1911 Hermann Rorschach, a Swiss psychiatrist, experimented with the use of inkblots in his clinical work. He made thousands of blots by dropping ink on paper and then folding the paper in half to create a symmetrical but wholly accidental design, such as the one shown in **Figure 4-1**. Rorschach found that everyone saw images in these blots. In addition, the images a viewer saw seemed to correspond in important ways with his or her psychological condition. People diagnosed with schizophrenia, for example, tended to see images that differed from those described by people experiencing depression.

Rorschach selected 10 inkblots and published them in 1921 with instructions for their use in assessment (see **MindTech**). This set was called the *Rorschach Psychodynamic Inkblot Test.* Rorschach died just 8 months later, at the age of 37, but his work was continued by others, and his inkblots took their place among the most widely used projective tests of the twentieth century.

> Despite its limitations, just about everyone has heard of the Rorschach. Why do you think it is so famous and popular?

Clinicians administer the "Rorschach," as it is commonly called, by presenting one inkblot card at a time and asking respondents what they see, what the inkblot seems to be, or what it reminds them of. In the early years, Rorschach testers paid special attention to the themes and images that the inkblots brought to mind (Groth-Marnat & Wright, 2016; Butcher, 2010). Testers now also pay attention to the style of the responses: Do the clients view the design as a whole or see specific details? Do they focus on the blots or on the white spaces between them?

THEMATIC APPERCEPTION TEST The Thematic Apperception Test (TAT) is a pictorial projective test (Cramer, 2017; Morgan & Murray, 1935). People who take the TAT are commonly shown 30 cards with black-and-white pictures of individuals in vague situations and are asked to make up a dramatic story about each card. They must tell what is happening in the picture, what led up to it, what the characters are feeling and thinking, and what the outcome of the situation will be.

Clinicians who use the TAT believe that people always identify with one of the characters on each card. The stories are thought to reflect the individuals' own circumstances, needs, and emotions. For example, a female client seems to be revealing her own feelings when telling this story about a TAT picture similar to the image shown in **Figure 4-2**:

> ⊕ *This is a woman who has been quite troubled by memories of a mother she was resentful toward. She has feelings of sorrow for the way she treated her mother, her memories of her mother plague her. These feelings seem to be increasing as she grows older and sees her children treating her the same way that she treated her mother.*
>
> (Aiken, 1985, p. 372)

carterdayne/Getty Images

FIGURE 4-2

A Picture Similar to One Used in the Thematic Apperception Test

SENTENCE-COMPLETION TEST In the sentence-completion test, first developed in the 1920s (Payne, 1928), the test-taker completes a series of unfinished sentences, such as "I wish . . ." or "My father. . . ." The test is considered a good springboard for discussion and a quick and easy way to pinpoint topics to explore (Martin et al., 2016).

Psychology's WikiLeaks?

In 2009, an emergency room physician posted the images of all 10 Rorschach cards, along with common responses to each card, on *Wikipedia*, the online encyclopedia. The publisher of the test, Hogrefe Publishing, immediately threatened to take *Wikipedia* to court, saying that the encyclopedia's willingness to post the images was "unbelievably reckless" (Cohen, 2009). However, no legal actions took place, and to this day, the 10 cards remain on *Wikipedia* for the entire world to see.

Since the initial Wikipedia posting, many psychologists have criticized the site's actions, arguing that the Rorschach test responses of patients who have previously seen the test on *Wikipedia* cannot be trusted. In support of their concerns, one study found that reading the *Wikipedia* Rorschach test article did indeed help many individuals perform more positively on the test itself (Schultz & Brabender, 2012). These clinical concerns are consistent with the long-standing positions of the British, Canadian, and American Psychological Associations, who hold that nonprofessional

Will & Deni McIntyre /Getty Images

publications of psychological test answers are wrong and potentially harmful to patients (Adamowicz, 2016).

Still other critics point out that the free online publication of the Rorschach cards jeopardizes the usefulness of thousands of published studies—studies that have tried to link patients' Rorschach responses to particular psychological disorders (Plante, 2016; Cohen, 2009). These studies were conducted on first-time inkblot observers, not on people who had already viewed the cards online.

Despite these criticisms, the number of online sites posting images of the Rorschach cards has increased steadily since the first Wikipedia presentation (Plante, 2016). Why? One reason is that the whole controversy brought to light a fact that relatively few had been aware of previously: The copyright for the test actually ran out in the 1990s in a number of countries, including Switzerland and the United States (Adamowicz, 2016; ICLG, 2016). According to copyright laws, because more than 70 years have passed since the author's death and/or because the test was first published before 1923, the Rorschach images are in the *public domain*. This

> Is the free online availability of Rorschach images a good thing, a bad thing, or both?

means that legally anyone can use or publicly display the cards. Of course, this legal distinction does not put to rest the important ethical and professional concerns that surround this controversy. 💬

DRAWINGS On the assumption that a drawing tells us something about its creator, clinicians often ask clients to draw human figures and talk about them (Scimeca et al., 2016). Evaluations of these drawings are based on the details and shape of the drawing, the solidity of the pencil line, the location of the drawing on the paper, the size of the figures, the features of the figures, the use of background, and comments made by the respondent during the drawing task. In the *Draw-a-Person (DAP) test*, the most popular of the drawing tests, individuals are first told to draw "a person" and then are instructed to draw a person of the other sex.

WHAT ARE THE MERITS OF PROJECTIVE TESTS? Until the 1950s, projective tests were the most commonly used method for assessing personality. In recent years, however, clinicians and researchers have relied on them largely to gain "supplementary" insights (McGrath & Carroll, 2012). One reason for this shift is that practitioners who follow the newer models have less use for the tests than psychodynamic clinicians do. Even more important, the tests have not consistently shown much reliability or validity (Mihura et al., 2016).

In reliability studies, different clinicians have tended to score the same person's projective test quite differently. Similarly, in validity studies, when clinicians try to describe a client's personality and feelings on the basis of responses to projective tests, their conclusions often fail to match the self-report of the client, the view of the psychotherapist, or the picture gathered from an extensive case history (Bornstein, 2007).

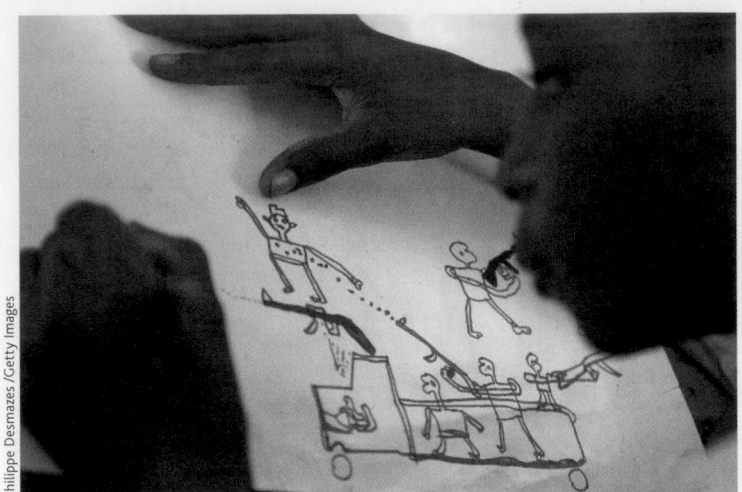

Drawing test Drawing tests are commonly used to assess the psychological functioning of children. As part of a therapy program administered by UNICEF, this young Nigerian refugee draws an attack scene. The program is provided in Baga Sola, a town in western Chad that welcomes people who have fled extremist groups in northeastern Nigeria.

Another validity problem is that projective tests are sometimes biased against minority ethnic groups (Costantino, Dana, & Malgady, 2007) (see **Table 4-1**). For example, people are supposed to identify with the characters in the TAT when they make up stories about them, yet no members of minority groups are represented in the TAT pictures. In response to this problem, some clinicians have developed other TAT-like tests with African American or Hispanic figures (Costantino et al., 2007, 1992).

Personality Inventories An alternative way to collect information about individuals is to ask them to assess themselves. Respondents to a **personality inventory** answer a wide range of questions about their behavior, beliefs, and feelings. In the typical personality inventory, individuals indicate whether each of a long list of statements applies to them. Clinicians then use the responses to draw conclusions about the person's personality and psychological functioning (Handel, 2016; Thimm, Jordon, & Bach, 2016).

By far the most widely used personality inventory is the *Minnesota Multiphasic Personality Inventory (MMPI)*. Two adult versions are available—the original test, published in 1945, and the *MMPI-2,* a 1989 revision which was itself revised in 2001. There is also an alternative and streamlined version of the inventory called the *MMPI-2-Restructured Form* and a special version of the test for adolescents, the *MMPI-A* (Handel, 2016; Moultrie & Engel, 2016).

The MMPI consists of more than 500 self-statements, to be labeled "true," "false," or "cannot say." The statements cover issues ranging from physical concerns to mood, sexual behaviors, and social activities. Altogether the statements make up 10 clinical scales, on each of which an individual can score from 0 to 120. When people score above 70 on a scale, their functioning on that scale is considered deviant. When the 10 scale scores are considered side by side, a pattern called a *profile* takes shape, indicating the person's general personality. The 10 scales on the MMPI measure the following:

Hypochondriasis Items showing abnormal concern with bodily functions ("I have chest pains several times a week.")

Depression Items showing extreme pessimism and hopelessness ("I often feel hopeless about the future.")

Hysteria Items suggesting that the person may use physical or mental symptoms as a way of unconsciously avoiding conflicts and responsibilities ("My heart frequently pounds so hard I can feel it.")

Psychopathic deviate Items showing a repeated and gross disregard for social customs and an emotional shallowness ("My activities and interests are often criticized by others.")

Masculinity–femininity Items that are thought to separate male and female respondents ("I like to arrange flowers.")

Paranoia Items that show abnormal suspiciousness and delusions of grandeur or persecution ("There are evil people trying to influence my mind.")

Psychasthenia Items that show obsessions, compulsions, abnormal fears, and guilt and indecisiveness ("I save nearly everything I buy, even after I have no use for it.")

Schizophrenia Items that show bizarre or unusual thoughts or behavior ("Things around me do not seem real.")

Hypomania Items that show emotional excitement, overactivity, and flight of ideas ("At times I feel very 'high' or very 'low' for no apparent reason.")

Social introversion Items that show shyness, little interest in people, and insecurity ("I am easily embarrassed.")

personality inventory A test, designed to measure broad personality characteristics, consisting of statements about behaviors, beliefs, and feelings that people evaluate as either characteristic or uncharacteristic of them.

The MMPI and other personality inventories have several advantages over projective tests (Cherry, 2015; Hogan, 2014). Because they are computerized or paper-and-pencil tests, they do not take much time to administer, and they are objectively scored. Most of them are standardized, so one person's scores can be compared with those of many others. Moreover, they often display greater test–retest reliability than projective tests (Thimm et al., 2016). For example, people who take the MMPI a second time after a period of less than 2 weeks receive approximately the same scores (Graham, 2014, 2006).

Personality inventories also appear to have more validity, or accuracy, than projective tests (Moultrie & Engel, 2016; Butcher, 2011, 2010). However, they can hardly be considered *highly* valid. When clinicians have used these tests alone, they have not regularly been able to judge a respondent's personality accurately (Braxton et al., 2007). One problem is that the personality traits that the tests seek to measure cannot be examined directly. How can we fully know a person's character, emotions, and needs from self-reports alone?

Another problem is that despite the use of more diverse standardization groups by the MMPI-2 designers, this and other personality tests continue to have certain cultural limitations. Responses that indicate a psychological disorder in one culture may be normal responses in another (Butcher, 2010; Dana, 2005, 2000). In Puerto Rico, for

"You tested positive for being negative."

Bruce Eric Kaplan/The New Yorker Collection/The Cartoon Bank

TABLE: 4-1

Multicultural Hot Spots in Assessment and Diagnosis

Cultural Hot Spot	Effect on Assessment or Diagnosis
Immigrant Client	**Dominant-Culture Assessor**
Homeland culture may differ from current country's dominant culture	May misread culture-bound reactions as pathology
May have left homeland to escape war or oppression	May overlook client's vulnerability to posttraumatic stress
May have weak support systems in this country	May overlook client's heightened vulnerability to stressors
Lifestyle (wealth and occupation) in this country may fall below lifestyle in homeland	May overlook client's sense of loss and frustrations
May refuse or be unable to learn dominant language	May misunderstand client's assessment responses, or may overlook or misdiagnose client's symptoms
Ethnic-Minority Client	**Dominant-Culture Assessor**
May reject or distrust members of dominant culture, including assessor	May experience little rapport with client, or may misinterpret client's distrust as pathology
May be uncomfortable with dominant culture's values (e.g., assertiveness, confrontation) and so find it difficult to apply clinician's recommendations	May view client as unmotivated
May manifest stress in culture-bound ways (e.g., somatic symptoms such as stomachaches)	May misinterpret symptom patterns
May hold cultural beliefs that seem strange to dominant culture (e.g., belief in communication with the dead)	May misinterpret cultural responses as pathology (e.g., a delusion)
May be uncomfortable during assessment	May overlook and feed into client's discomfort
Dominant-Culture Assessor	**Ethnic-Minority Client**
May be unknowledgeable or biased about ethnic-minority culture	Cultural differences may be pathologized, or symptoms may be overlooked
May nonverbally convey own discomfort to ethnic-minority client.	May become tense and anxious.

Information from: Borden, 2017; Franklin, 2017; Dana, 2015; Rose et al., 2011; Bhattacharya et al., 2010; Westermeyer, 2004, 2001, 1993; López & Guarnaccia, 2005, 2000; Kirmayer, 2003, 2002, 2001

response inventories Tests designed to measure a person's responses in one specific area of functioning, such as affect, social skills, or cognitive processes.

psychophysiological test A test that measures physical responses (such as heart rate and muscle tension) as possible indicators of psychological problems.

example, where it is common to practice spiritualism, it would be normal to answer "true" to the MMPI item "Evil spirits possess me at times." In other populations, that response could indicate psychopathology (Rogler, Malgady, & Rodriguez, 1989).

Despite such limits in validity, personality inventories continue to be popular. Research indicates that they can help clinicians learn about people's personal styles and disorders as long as they are used in combination with interviews or other assessment tools.

Response Inventories Like personality inventories, **response inventories** ask people to provide detailed information about themselves, but these tests focus on one specific area of functioning (Jackson-Koku, 2016; Wang & Gorenstein, 2013; Vaz et al., 2013). For example, one such test may measure affect (emotion), another social skills, and still another cognitive processes. Clinicians can use the inventories to determine the role such factors play in a person's disorder.

Affective inventories measure the severity of such emotions as anxiety, depression, and anger. In one of the most widely used affective inventories, the Beck Depression Inventory—an excerpt of which is shown in **Table 4-2**—people rate their level of sadness and its effect on their functioning. For *social skills inventories,* used particularly by behavioral and family-social clinicians, respondents indicate how they would react in a variety of social situations. *Cognitive inventories* reveal a person's typical thoughts and assumptions and can help uncover counterproductive patterns of thinking.

Both the number of response inventories and the number of clinicians who use them have increased steadily in the past 30 years. At the same time, however, these inventories have major limitations. With the notable exceptions of the Beck Depression Inventory and a few others, many of the tests have not been subjected to careful standardization, reliability, and validity procedures (Englbrecht et al., 2017; Jackson-Koku, 2016). Often they are created as a need arises, without being tested for accuracy and consistency.

Psychophysiological Tests Clinicians may also use **psychophysiological tests**, which measure physiological responses as possible indicators of psychological problems (Vicianova, 2015; Daly et al., 2014). This practice began three decades ago, after several studies suggested that states of anxiety are regularly accompanied by physiological changes, particularly increases in heart rate, body temperature, blood pressure, skin reactions (*galvanic skin response*), and muscle contractions. The measuring of physiological changes has since played a key role in the assessment of certain psychological disorders.

One psychophysiological test is the *polygraph*, popularly known as a *lie detector* (Rosky, 2016, 2015, 2013). Electrodes attached to various parts of a person's body detect changes in breathing, perspiration, and heart rate while the person answers questions. The clinician observes these functions while the person answers "yes" to *control questions*—questions whose answers are known to be yes, such as "Are both your parents alive?" Then the clinician observes the same physiological functions while the person answers *test questions,* such as "Did you commit this robbery?" If breathing, perspiration, and heart rate suddenly increase, the person is suspected of lying.

Like other kinds of clinical tests, psychophysiological tests have their drawbacks (Elliott & Völlm, 2016; Rusconi & Mitchener-Nissen, 2013). Many require expensive equipment that must be carefully tuned and maintained. In addition, psychophysiological measurements can be inaccurate and unreliable (see *Trending*). The laboratory

TABLE: 4-2

Sample Items from the Beck Depression Inventory

Items	Inventory	
Suicidal ideas	0	I don't have any thoughts of killing myself.
	1	I have thoughts of killing myself but I would not carry them out.
	2	I would like to kill myself.
	3	I would kill myself if I had the chance.
Work inhibition	0	I can work about as well as before.
	1	It takes extra effort to get started at doing something.
	2	I have to push myself very hard to do anything.
	3	I can't do any work at all.
Loss of libido	0	I have not noticed any recent change in my interest in sex.
	1	I am less interested in sex than I used to be.
	2	I am much less interested in sex now.
	3	I have lost interest in sex completely.

equipment itself—elaborate and sometimes frightening—may arouse a participant's nervous system and thus change his or her physical responses. Physiological responses may also change when they are measured repeatedly in a single session. Galvanic skin responses, for example, often decrease during repeated testing.

...TRENDING

The Truth, the Whole Truth, and Nothing but the Truth

In movies, criminals being grilled by the police reveal their guilt by sweating, shaking, cursing, or twitching. When they are hooked up to a *polygraph* (a lie detector), the needles bounce all over the paper. This image has been with us since World War I, when some clinicians developed the theory that people who are telling lies display systemic changes in their breathing, perspiration, and heart rate (Marston, 1917).

The danger of relying on polygraph tests is that they do not work as well as we would like (Vogel & Baran, 2016; Rosky, 2015, 2013). Research indicates that at least 1 out of 10 truths, or as many as 1 out of 4 truths, are, on average, called lies in polygraph testing (Wen, 2016; Grubin, 2010; MacLaren, 2001). Imagine how many innocent people might be convicted of crimes if polygraph findings were taken as valid evidence in criminal trials.

Given such findings, polygraphs are less trusted and less popular today than they once were. For example, few courts now admit results from such tests as evidence of criminal guilt (Vogel & Baran, 2016; Grubin, 2010). Nevertheless, the FBI and other law enforcement agencies use them extensively in criminal investigations; parole boards and probation offices routinely administer them to help decide whether to release convicted offenders; and their use may actually be on the increase in public-sector hiring, such as for police officers (Vicianova, 2015; Meijer & Verschuere, 2010).

Given the polygraph's flawed performance, researchers have been looking for other ways to detect lies over the past 15 years. The most promising alternative seems to be brain scanning. Some MRI studies have found that when participants deny clear truths, certain parts of their brain—particularly regions within the *prefrontal, anterior cingulate,* and *parietal cortex*—become more active than when they are confirming such truths (Wood,

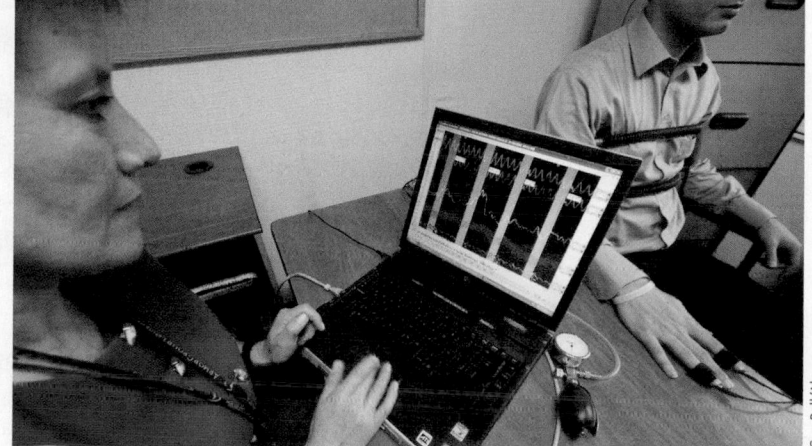

All the rage A security administrator conducts a polygraph exam in Bogota, Colombia. Despite evidence that these tests are often invalid, they are widely used by businesses in Colombia, where deception by employees has become a major problem.

2016; Langleben & Moriarty, 2013; Simpson, 2008). The interpretation of this finding is that lying involves two tasks, *recognizing and suppressing* the truth, thus making these brain areas work harder.

In general, MRI studies have yielded better lie-detection rates than have polygraph studies, but the procedures and degree of accuracy have varied from study to study. Moreover, like polygraph testing, scanning procedures can produce *false positives*. That is, the brain regions under study may also become more active when an individual is experiencing intense anxiety or related emotions. Thus some anxious truth-tellers may be viewed as lying in the MRI procedures.

These questions and limitations were partly addressed in a recent study at the University of Pennsylvania, the first investigation to directly compare the performances of polygraph and scanning procedures on the same people (Langleben et al., 2016). Participants were instructed to secretly write down one of six numbers and to then deny, while being evaluated by a polygraph and later by an MRI, the correctness of each number. That is, in each session, they were lying about their

selected number and telling the truth about the other five numbers.

Although both tools were far from perfect in detecting the particular number that each participant was lying about, the MRI conclusions were 24 percent more accurate than the polygraph conclusions. Moreover,

> **Why might an innocent person "fail" a lie detector test? How might a guilty person manage to "pass" the test?**

the accuracy of lie detection rose to 100 percent in cases where the MRI and polygraph agreed on which number was being concealed, suggesting to some theorists that the two techniques should be used jointly in real-life applications. The lies in this study were much simpler, clearer, and more contrived than those found in the real world, and so we will not know for some time whether MRI testing or combined MRI-polygraph testing will eventually gain traction in the judicial, law enforcement, security, or employment realms. But the implications of the study already have some researchers quite excited—and some ethicists very worried.

Variations in scanning A doctor prepares a patient for an MRI procedure (a). Today's most widely used neuroimaging techniques each produce pictures of the living brain. Here, an MRI scan (b) shows the image of a normal functioning brain; a CAT scan (c) reveals a mass of blood within the brain; and a PET scan (d) shows which areas of the brain are active (those colored in red, orange, and yellow) when an individual is being stimulated.

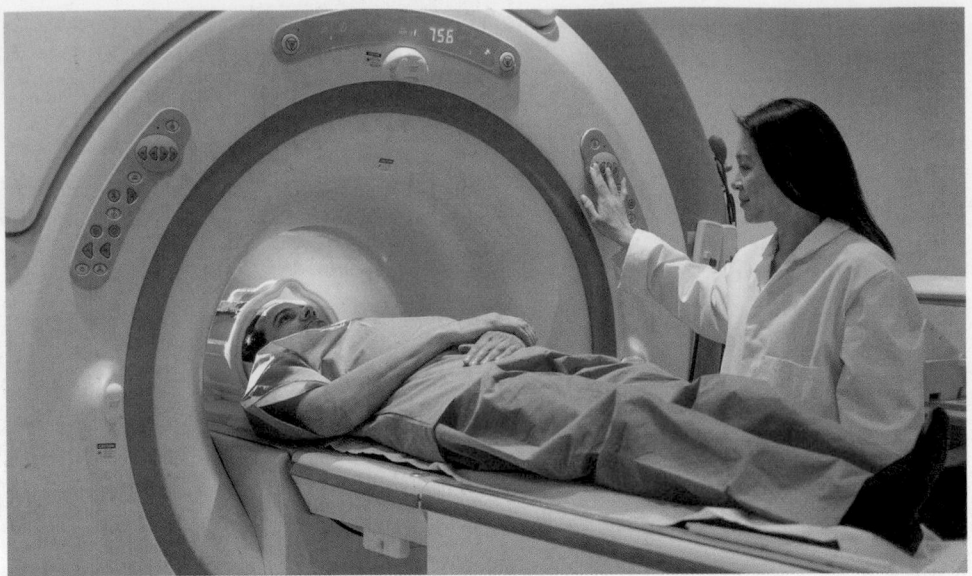

(a) MRI

Neurological and Neuropsychological Tests Some problems in personality or behavior are caused primarily by damage to the brain or by changes in brain activity. Head injuries, brain tumors, brain malfunctions, alcoholism, infections, and other disorders can all cause such impairment. If a psychological dysfunction is to be treated effectively, it is important to know whether its primary cause is a physical abnormality in the brain.

A number of techniques may help pinpoint brain abnormalities. Some procedures, such as brain surgery, biopsy, and X ray, have been used for many years. More recently, scientists have developed a number of **neurological tests,** which are designed to measure brain structure and activity directly. One neurological test is the *electroencephalogram* (*EEG*), which records *brain waves,* the electrical activity that takes place within the brain as a result of neurons firing. In an EEG, electrodes placed on the scalp send brain-wave impulses to a machine that records them.

Other neurological tests actually take "pictures" of brain structure or brain activity. These tests, called **neuroimaging,** or **brain scanning, techniques,** include

Family EEG As part of a study conducted at York University in Toronto, a mother and her 5-year-old autistic child play, socialize, and share tasks while wearing nets containing EEG sensors. The electrodes attached to their scalps help measure their brain waves, and these measurements are later compared to those derived from other mothers and their non-autistic children during similar interactions.

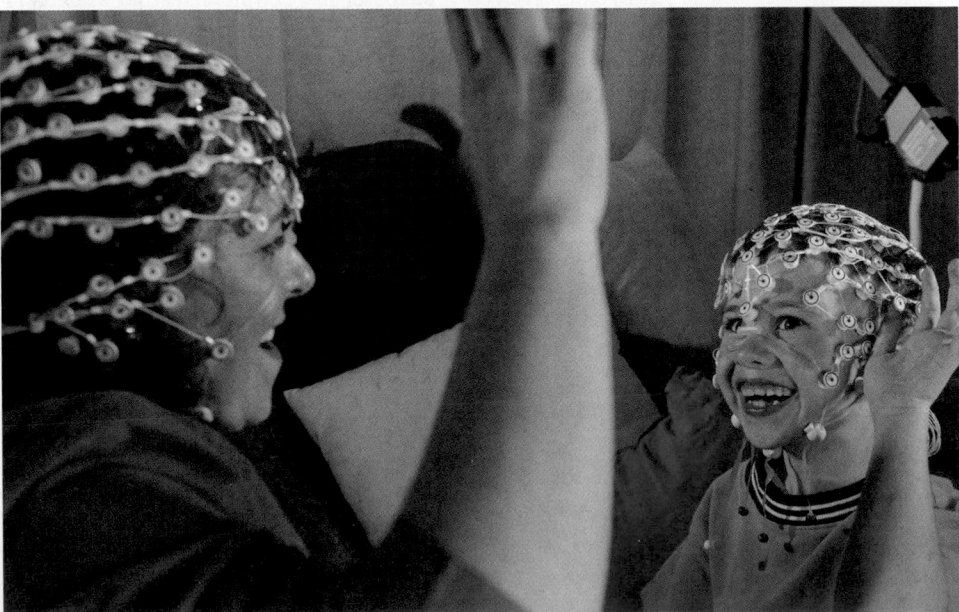

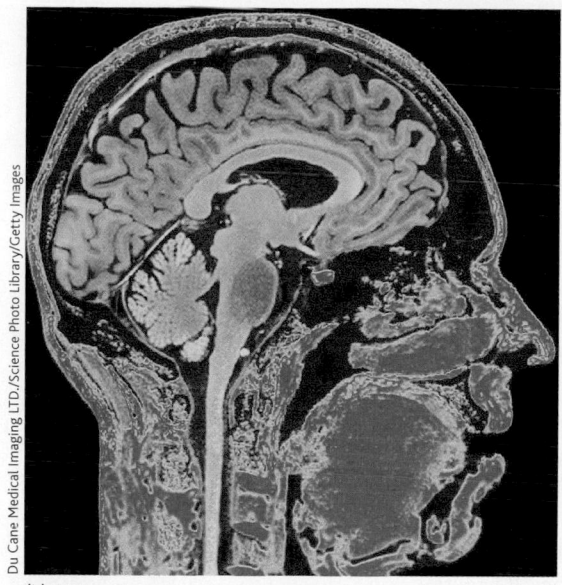

(b) MRI scan

Du Cane Medical Imaging LTD./Science Photo Library/Getty Images

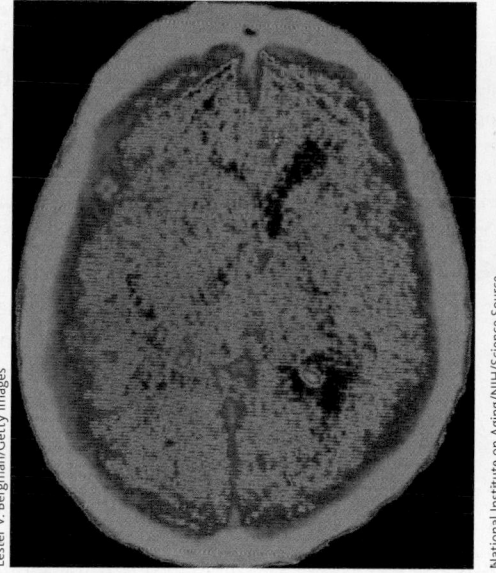

(c) CAT scan

Lester V. Bergman/Getty Images

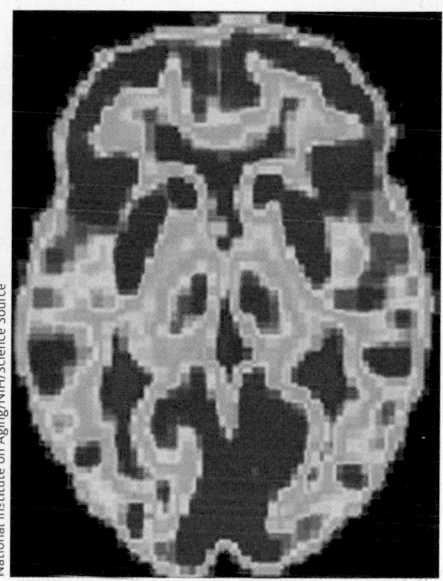

(d) PET scan

National Institute on Aging/NIH/Science Source

computerized axial tomography (*CT scan* or *CAT scan*), in which X rays of the brain's structure are taken at different angles and combined; *positron emission tomography* (*PET scan*), a computer-produced motion picture of chemical activity throughout the brain; and *magnetic resonance imaging* (*MRI*), a procedure that uses the magnetic property of certain hydrogen atoms in the brain to create a detailed picture of the brain's structure.

One version of the MRI, *functional magnetic resonance imaging* (*fMRI*), converts MRI pictures of brain structures into detailed pictures of neuron activity, thus offering a picture of the *functioning* brain. In this procedure, an MRI scanner detects rapid changes in the flow or volume of blood in the brain and interprets these changes as indications of neuron activity, thus yielding computer-generated images of the brain in action. Partly because fMRI-produced images of brain functioning are so much clearer than PET scan images, the fMRI has generated enormous enthusiasm among brain researchers since it was first developed in 1990.

Though widely used, these techniques are sometimes unable to detect subtle brain abnormalities. Clinicians have therefore developed less direct but sometimes more revealing **neuropsychological tests** that measure cognitive, perceptual, and motor performances on certain tasks; clinicians interpret abnormal performances as an indicator of underlying brain problems (Daugherty et al., 2017; John et al., 2016). Brain damage is especially likely to affect visual perception, memory, and visual-motor coordination, so neuropsychological tests focus particularly on these areas. The famous *Bender Visual-Motor Gestalt Test,* for example, consists of nine cards, each displaying a simple geometrical design (Groth-Marnat & Wright, 2016). Patients look at the designs one at a time and copy each one onto a piece of paper. Later they try to redraw the designs from memory. Notable errors in accuracy by individuals older than 12 are thought to reflect organic brain impairment. Clinicians often use a *battery,* or series, of neuropsychological tests, each targeting a specific skill area (John et al., 2016; Reitan & Wolfson, 2005, 1996).

Intelligence Tests An early definition of intelligence described it as "the capacity to judge well, to reason well, and to comprehend well" (Binet & Simon, 1916, p. 192). Because intelligence is an *inferred* quality rather than a specific physical process, it can be measured only indirectly. In 1905, French psychologist Alfred Binet and his associate Théodore Simon produced an **intelligence test** consisting of a series of tasks requiring people to use various verbal and nonverbal skills. The general score derived from this and later intelligence tests is termed an **intelligence quotient (IQ).**

neurological test A test that directly measures brain structure or activity.

neuroimaging techniques Neurological tests that provide images of brain structure or activity, such as CT scans, PET scans, and MRIs. Also called *brain scanning.*

neuropsychological test A test that detects brain impairment by measuring a person's cognitive, perceptual, and motor performances.

intelligence test A test designed to measure a person's intellectual ability.

intelligence quotient (IQ) An overall score derived from intelligence tests.

"We're going to run some tests: blood work, a cat-scan, and the S.A.T.'s."

There are now more than 100 intelligence tests available. As you will see in Chapter 17, intelligence tests play a key role in the diagnosis of intellectual disability (Karam et al., 2016), and they can also help clinicians identify other problems (Bram, 2016).

Intelligence tests are among the most carefully produced of all clinical tests (Bowden et al., 2011). Because they have been standardized on large groups of people, clinicians have a good idea how each individual's score compares with the performance of the population at large. These tests have also shown very high reliability: people who repeat the same IQ test years later receive approximately the same score. Finally, the major IQ tests appear to have fairly high validity: children's IQ scores often correlate with their performance in school, for example.

Nevertheless, intelligence tests have some key shortcomings. Factors that have nothing to do with intelligence, such as low motivation or high anxiety, can greatly influence test performance (Groth-Marnat & Wright, 2016; Chaudhry & Ready, 2012). In addition, IQ tests may contain cultural biases in their language or tasks that place people of one background at an advantage over those of another (Shuttleworth-Edwards, 2016). Similarly, members of some minority groups may have little experience with this kind of test, or they may be uncomfortable with test examiners of a majority ethnic background. Either way, their performances may suffer.

> How might IQ scores be misused by school officials, parents, or other individuals? Why is society preoccupied with these scores?

Clinical Observations

In addition to interviewing and testing people, clinicians may systematically observe their behavior. In one technique, called *naturalistic observation,* clinicians observe clients in their everyday environments. In another, *analog observation,* they observe them in an artificial setting, such as a clinical office or laboratory. Finally, in *self-monitoring,* clients are instructed to observe themselves.

Naturalistic and Analog Observations Naturalistic clinical observations usually take place in homes, schools, institutions such as hospitals and prisons, or community settings. Most of them focus on parent–child, sibling–sibling, or teacher–child interactions and on fearful, aggressive, or disruptive behavior (Alisic et al., 2016; Wang & Repetti, 2016). Often such observations are made by *participant observers*—key people in the client's environment—and reported to the clinician.

When naturalistic observations are not practical, clinicians may resort to analog observations, often aided by special equipment such as a video camera or one-way mirror. Analog observations often have focused on children interacting with their parents, married couples attempting to settle a disagreement, speech-anxious people giving a speech, and phobic people approaching an object they find frightening.

Although much can be learned from actually witnessing behavior, clinical observations have certain disadvantages. For one thing, they are not always reliable. It is possible for various clinicians who observe the same person to focus on different aspects of behavior, assess the person differently, and arrive at different conclusions (Meersand, 2011). Careful training of observers and the use of observer checklists can help reduce this problem.

Similarly, observers may make errors that affect the validity, or accuracy, of their observations (Wilson et al., 2010). The observer may suffer from *overload* and be unable to see or record all of the important behaviors and events. Or the observer may experience *observer drift,* a steady decline in accuracy as a result of fatigue

#TheirWords

"You can observe a lot just by watching."
Yogi Berra, baseball great

or of a gradual unintentional change in the standards used when an observation continues for a long period of time. Another possible problem is *observer bias*—the observer's judgments may be influenced by information and expectations he or she already has about the person (Hróbjartsson et al., 2014).

A client's *reactivity* may also limit the validity of clinical observations; that is, his or her behavior may be affected by the very presence of the observer (Antal et al., 2015). If schoolchildren are aware that someone special is watching them, for example, they may change their usual classroom behavior, perhaps in the hope of creating a good impression.

Finally, clinical observations may lack *cross-situational validity*. A child who behaves aggressively in school is not necessarily aggressive at home or with friends after school. Because behavior is often specific to particular situations, observations in one setting cannot always be applied to other settings (Kagan, 2007).

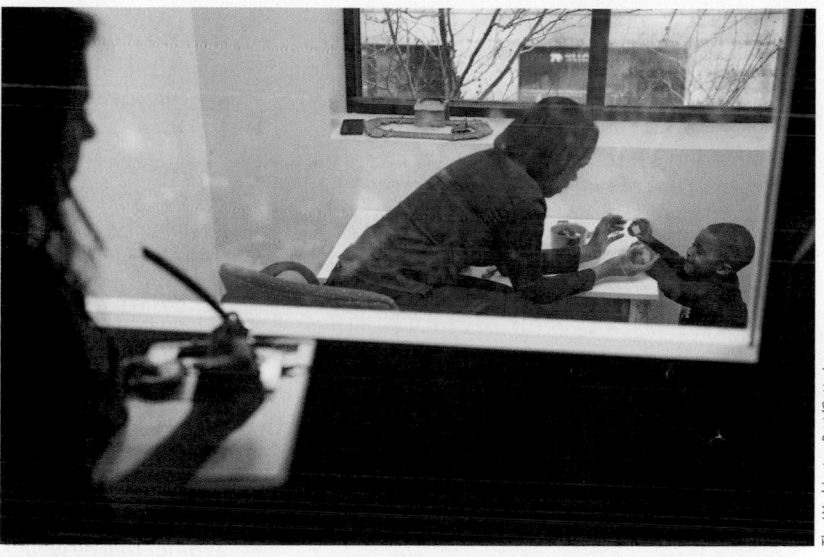

The Washington Post/Getty Images

Observation plus Using a one-way mirror, a clinical observer views a client interacting with her child during a play session. In addition, with the aid of a microphone and ear bug device, the clinician can coach the client and offer real-time parenting suggestions, a procedure commonly known as parent–child interaction therapy (PCIT).

Self-Monitoring As you saw earlier, personality and response inventories are tests in which individuals report their own behaviors, feelings, or cognitions. In a related assessment procedure, *self-monitoring,* people observe themselves and carefully record the frequency of certain behaviors, feelings, or thoughts as they occur over time. How frequently, for instance, does a drug user have an urge for drugs or a headache sufferer have a headache? Self-monitoring is especially useful in assessing behavior that occurs so infrequently that it is unlikely to be seen during other kinds of observations. It is also useful for behaviors that occur so frequently that any other method of observing them in detail would be impossible—for example, smoking, drinking, or other drug use. Finally, self-monitoring may be the only way to observe and measure private thoughts or perceptions. Increasingly, people in treatment are recording such private experiences on smartphone apps as they are occurring—observations that can be sent immediately to their therapists or collectively reported in their treatment sessions (Rickard et al., 2016; Tsanas et al., 2016).

Like all other clinical assessment procedures, however, self-monitoring has drawbacks (Huh et al., 2013). Here too validity is often a problem. People do not always manage or try to record their observations accurately. Furthermore, when people monitor themselves, they may change their behaviors unintentionally. Smokers, for example, often smoke fewer cigarettes than usual when they are monitoring themselves, and teachers give more positive and fewer negative comments to their students.

Diagnosis: Does the Client's Syndrome Match a Known Disorder?

CLINICIANS USE THE INFORMATION from interviews, tests, and observations to construct an integrated picture of the factors that are causing and maintaining a client's disturbance, a construction sometimes known as a *clinical picture* (Sommers-Flanagan & Sommers-Flanagan, 2017; Groth-Marnat & Wright, 2016). Clinical pictures also may be influenced to a degree by the clinician's theoretical orientation (Garb, 2010, 2006). The psychologist who worked with Franco held a cognitive-behavioral view of abnormality and so produced a picture that emphasized modeling and reinforcement principles and Franco's expectations, assumptions, and interpretations:

#

#EarlyBeginnings

Because of his love for sketching inkblots all the time, Hermann Rorschach's young schoolmates gave him the nickname Klex, a variant of the German *Klecks*, which means "inkblot" (Cacioppo & Freberg, 2016; Schwartz, 1993).

diagnosis A determination that a person's problems reflect a particular disorder.

syndrome A cluster of symptoms that usually occur together.

classification system A list of disorders, along with descriptions of symptoms and guidelines for making appropriate diagnoses.

Franco's mother had reinforced his feelings of insecurity and his belief that he was unintelligent and inferior. When teachers tried to encourage and push Franco, his mother actually called him "an idiot." Although he was the only one in his family to attend college and did well there, she told him he was too inadequate to succeed in the world. When he received a B in a college algebra course, his mother told him, "You'll never have money." She once told him, "You're just like your father, dumb as a post," and railed against, "the dumb men I got stuck with."

As a child Franco had watched his parents argue. Between his mother's self-serving complaints and his father's rants about his backbreaking work to provide for his family, Franco had decided that life would be unpleasant. He believed it was natural for couples to argue and blame each other. Using his parents as models, Franco believed that when he was displeased with a girlfriend—Maria or a prior girlfriend—he should yell at her. At the same time, he was confused that several of his girlfriends had complained about his temper.

He took the termination of his relationship with Maria as proof that he was "stupid." He felt foolish to have broken up with her. He interpreted his behavior and the break-up as proof that he would never be loved and that he would never find happiness. In his mind, all he had to look forward to from here on out was a lifetime of problematic relationships, fights, and getting fired from lesser and lesser jobs. This hopelessness fed his feelings of depression and also made it hard for him to try to make himself feel better.

With the assessment data and clinical picture in hand, clinicians are ready to make a **diagnosis** (from the Greek word for "a discrimination")—that is, a determination that a person's psychological problems constitute a particular disorder. When clinicians decide, through diagnosis, that a client's pattern of dysfunction reflects a particular disorder, they are saying that the pattern is basically the same as one that has been displayed by many other people, has been investigated in a variety of studies, and perhaps has responded to particular forms of treatment. They can then apply what is generally known about the disorder to the particular individual they are trying to help. They can, for example, better predict the future course of the person's problem and the treatments that are likely to be helpful.

Classification Systems

The principle behind diagnosis is straightforward. When certain symptoms occur together regularly—a cluster of symptoms is called a **syndrome**—and follow a particular course, clinicians agree that those symptoms make up a particular mental disorder. If people display this particular pattern of symptoms, diagnosticians assign them to that diagnostic category. A list of such categories, or disorders, with descriptions of the symptoms and guidelines for assigning individuals to the categories, is known as a **classification system.**

In 1883, Emil Kraepelin developed the first modern classification system for abnormal behavior (see Chapter 1). His categories formed the foundation for the *Diagnostic and Statistical Manual of Mental Disorders* (*DSM*), the classification system currently written by the American Psychiatric Association (APA, 2013). The DSM is the most widely used classification system in North America. The content of the DSM has been changed significantly over time. The current edition, called DSM-5, was published in 2013. It features a number of changes from the previous editions. Most other countries rely primarily on a system called the *International Classification of Diseases* (*ICD*), developed by the World Health Organization, which lists both medical and psychological disorders. The current edition of this system is called ICD-10.

> Why do you think many clinicians prefer the label "person with schizophrenia" over "schizophrenic person"?

The power of labeling When looking at this late-nineteenth-century photograph of a baseball team at the State Homeopathic Asylum for the Insane in Middletown, New York, most observers assume that the players are patients. As a result, they tend to "see" depression or confusion in the players' faces and posture. In fact, the players are members of the asylum staff, some of whom even sought their jobs for the express purpose of playing for the hospital team.

Although there are some differences between the disorders listed in the DSM and ICD and in their descriptions of criteria for various disorders (the DSM's descriptions are more detailed), the federal government has recently ordered that the numerical codes used by DSM-5 for all disorders must match those used by the ICD-10—a matching that is expected to produce more uniformity when clinicians fill out insurance reimbursement forms.

DSM-5

DSM-5 lists more than 500 mental disorders (see **Figure 4-3**). Each entry describes the criteria for diagnosing the disorder and the key clinical features of the disorder. The system also describes features that are often but not always related to the disorder. The classification system is further accompanied by background information such as research findings; age, culture, or gender trends; and each disorder's prevalence, risk, course, complications, predisposing factors, and family patterns.

DSM-5 requires clinicians to provide both categorical and dimensional information as part of a proper diagnosis. *Categorical information* refers to the name of the distinct category (disorder) indicated by the client's symptoms. *Dimensional information* is a rating of how severe a client's symptoms are and how dysfunctional the client is across various dimensions of personality and behavior.

Categorical Information First, the clinician must decide whether the person is displaying one of the hundreds of psychological disorders listed in the manual. Some of the most frequently diagnosed disorders are the anxiety disorders and depressive disorders.

ANXIETY DISORDERS People with anxiety disorders may experience general feelings of anxiety and worry (*generalized anxiety disorder*); fears of specific situations, objects, or activities (*phobias*); anxiety about social situations (*social anxiety*

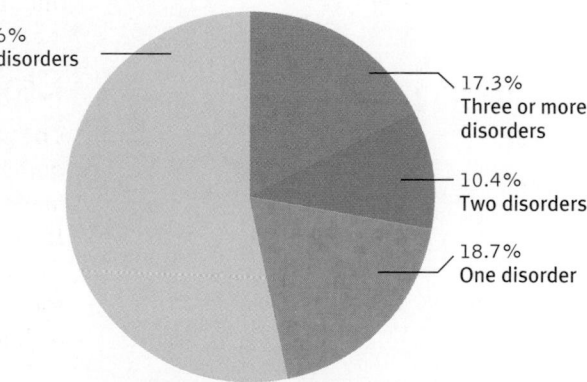

53.6%
No disorders

17.3%
Three or more disorders

10.4%
Two disorders

18.7%
One disorder

FIGURE 4-3

How Many People in the United States Qualify for a DSM Diagnosis During Their Lives?

Almost half, according to some surveys. Some people even experience two or more different disorders, which is known as comorbidity. (Information from: APA, 2017; Greenberg, 2011; Kessler et al., 2005.)

Fighting the stigma of labeling A clothing line called "Wear Your Label" offers an array of garments designed to challenge the stigma of psychiatric labeling by sparking conversations about mental health. The "Sad But Rad" T-shirt is one of the line's big sellers. (A heads-up for people over 30: "rad" is a slang term for radical, cool, and/or wonderful.)

disorder); repeated outbreaks of panic (*panic disorder*); or anxiety about being separated from one's parents or from other key individuals (*separation anxiety disorder*).

DEPRESSIVE DISORDERS People with depressive disorders may experience an episode of extreme sadness and related symptoms (*major depressive disorder*), persistent and chronic sadness (*persistent depressive disorder*), or severe premenstrual sadness and related symptoms (*premenstrual dysphoric disorder*).

Although people may receive just one diagnosis from the DSM-5 list, they often receive more than one. Franco would likely receive a diagnosis of *major depressive disorder*. In addition, let's suppose the clinician judged that Franco's worries about his teachers' opinions of him and his later concerns that supervisors at work would discover his inadequate skills were really but two examples of a much broader, persistent pattern of excessive worry, concern, and avoidance. He might then receive an additional diagnosis of *generalized anxiety disorder*. Alternatively, if Franco's anxiety symptoms did not rise to the level of generalized anxiety disorder, his diagnosis of major depressive disorder might simply specify that he is experiencing some features of anxiety (*major depressive disorder with anxious distress*).

Dimensional Information In addition to deciding what disorder a client is displaying, diagnosticians assess the current severity of the client's disorder—that is, how much the symptoms impair the client. For each disorder, the framers of DSM-5 have suggested various rating scales that may prove useful for evaluating the severity of the particular disorder (APA, 2013). In cases of major depressive disorder, for example, two scales are suggested by DSM-5: the *Cross-Cutting Symptom Measure* and the *Emotional Distress–Depression Scale*. The former scale indicates the current frequency of various problematic feelings and behaviors (for example, "I do not know who I really am or what I want out of life") and the latter indicates the frequency of general negative feelings and behaviors (for example, "I feel worthless"). Using scores from these scales, the diagnostician then rates the client's level of depression as "mild," moderate," or "severe." Based on his clinical interview, tests, and observations,

"Correct me if I'm wrong, but hasn't the fine line between sanity and madness gotten finer?"

Franco might warrant a rating of *moderate* depression from his therapist. DSM-5 is the first edition of the DSM to consistently seek both categorical and dimensional information as equally important parts of the diagnosis, rather than categorical information alone.

Additional Information Clinicians also may include other useful information when making a diagnosis. They may, for example, indicate special psychosocial problems the client has. Franco's recent breakup with his girlfriend might be noted as *relationship distress*. Altogether, Franco might receive the following diagnosis:

> **Diagnosis: Major depressive disorder with anxious distress**
>
> *Severity:* Moderate
>
> *Additional information:* Relationship distress

Each diagnostic category also has a numerical code that clinicians must state—a code listed in ICD-10, the current edition of the international classification system mentioned earlier. Thus if Franco were assigned the DSM-5 diagnosis indicated above, his clinician would also state a numerical code of *F32.1*—the code corresponding to *major depressive disorder, moderate severity.*

Is DSM-5 an Effective Classification System?

A classification system, like an assessment method, is judged by its reliability and validity. Here *reliability* means that different clinicians are likely to agree on the diagnosis when they use the system to diagnose the same client. Early versions of the DSM were at best moderately reliable (Regier et al., 2011). In the early 1960s, for example, four clinicians, each relying on DSM-I, the first edition of the DSM, independently interviewed 153 patients (Beck et al., 1962). Only 54 percent of their diagnoses were in agreement. Because all four clinicians were experienced diagnosticians, their failure to agree suggested deficiencies in the classification system.

The framers of DSM-5 followed certain procedures in their development of the new manual to help ensure that DSM-5 would have greater reliability than the previous DSMs (APA, 2013). For example, they conducted extensive reviews of research to pinpoint which categories in past DSMs had been too vague and unreliable. In addition, they gathered input from a wide range of experienced clinicians and researchers. They then developed a number of new diagnostic criteria and categories, expecting that the new criteria and categories would be reliable. Although some studies have indeed found enhanced reliability in DSM-5 (Stinchfield et al., 2016; Denis et al., 2015), others have not (Chmielewski et al., 2015; Wakefield, 2015).

Why are the reliability findings less than stellar? Critics point to faulty procedures used in the development of DSM-5. They note, for example, that the framers failed to run a sufficient number of their own studies—in particular, *field studies* that test the merits of the new criteria and categories. In turn, DSM-5 may have retained several of the reliability problems found in past editions of the DSM. It may be, for example, that, as diagnosticians use DSM-5 over the coming years, some will have difficulty distinguishing one kind of DSM-5 anxiety disorder from another. The disorder of a particular client may be classified as generalized anxiety disorder by one clinician, agoraphobia (fear of traveling outside of one's home) by another, and social anxiety disorder (fear of social situations) by yet another.

The *validity* of a classification system is the accuracy of the information that its diagnostic categories provide. Categories are of most use to clinicians when they demonstrate *predictive validity*—that is, when they help predict future symptoms or events. A common symptom of major depressive disorder is either insomnia or excessive sleep. When clinicians give Franco a diagnosis of major depressive disorder, they expect that he may eventually develop sleep problems even if none are present now. In addition, they expect him to respond to treatments that are effective for other

#CommonTerm

What Is a Nervous Breakdown?

The term "nervous breakdown" is used by laypersons, not clinicians. Most people use it to refer to a *sudden* psychological disturbance that incapacitates a person, perhaps requiring hospitalization. Some people use the term simply to connote the onset of any psychological disorder (Hall-Flavin, 2016; Padwa, 1996).

#ModernBranding

New Pop Psychology Labels

"Online disinhibition effect" The tendency of people to show less restraint when on the Internet (Suler, 2016, 2004; Sitt, 2013).

"Drunkorexia" A diet fad, particularly among young women, in which the person restricts food intake during the day so that she can drink heavily at night without gaining weight from the alcohol (Rinker, 2016; Archer, 2013).

depressed persons. The more often such predictions are accurate, the greater a category's predictive validity.

DSM-5's framers tried to also ensure the validity of this new edition by conducting extensive reviews of research and consulting with numerous clinical advisors. As a result, its criteria and categories may have stronger validity than those of the earlier versions of the DSM. Initial research seems to suggest several areas of improved validity (Gaspersz et al., 2016; Stinchfield et al., 2016). But, again, critics worry that at least some of the criteria and categories in DSM-5 are based on weak field research and that others may reflect gender or racial bias (Frances, 2016, 2015, 2013; Rhebergen & Graham, 2014).

Actually, one important organization has already concluded that the validity of DSM-5 is sorely lacking and is acting accordingly (Klein, 2016; Insel & Lieberman, 2013). The National Institute of Mental Health (NIMH), the world's largest funding agency for mental health research, no longer gives financial support to clinical studies that rely exclusively on DSM-5 criteria. And, more generally, the agency has developed its own neuroscience-focused classification tool, called the *Research Domain Criteria* (*RDoC*), that it expects will eventually be the primary classification guide used by researchers. While the NIMH decision is certainly a blow to the prestige of DSM-5, it is worth noting that the RDoC is itself receiving considerable criticism from many clinical theorists. The critics believe that the final version of this new tool, which is based on the premise that mental disorders are best viewed and studied as biological disorders, may minimize environmental and psychological factors in its classifications, while focusing excessively on genetics, brain scans, cognitive neuroscience, and other such areas of study (Frances, 2016; Maj, 2016; Lane, 2013).

Call for Change

The effort to produce DSM-5 took more than a decade. After years of preliminary work, a DSM-5 task force and numerous work groups were formed in 2006, with the goal of developing a DSM that addressed the limitations of previous DSM editions. Finally, in May 2013 DSM-5, the new diagnostic and classification system was published. The categories and criteria of DSM-5 are featured throughout this textbook (APA, 2013).

The new DSM has raised concerns among many clinical practitioners and researchers (see *InfoCentral* on the next page). In addition to the possible reliability and validity limitations described above, critics worry that some of its changes in criteria and categories are ill-advised and will lead to problems of various kinds for clients. The DSM-5 changes that have raised the most concern include the following:

- It calls for a diagnosis of "major depressive disorder" for some recently bereaved people (see Chapter 7).

- It adds a new category, "premenstrual dysphoric disorder" (see Chapter 7).

- It adds a new category, "somatic symptom disorder," that can be assigned to people who are overly anxious about serious medical problems (see Chapter 10).

- It combines the patterns of substance dependence and substance abuse (patterns that may each require different treatments) into a single category, "substance use disorder" (see Chapter 12).

- It groups the category "gambling disorder" as an addictive disorder alongside the substance use disorders (see Chapter 12).

- It combines all forms of autism into a single category, "autism spectrum disorder," thus eliminating the past category of "Asperger's syndrome" (see Chapter 17).

- It adds a new category, "mild neurocognitive disorder," that could be misapplied to normal age-related forgetfulness. (see Chapter 18).

DSM: THE BIGGER PICTURE

The Diagnostic and Statistical Manual of Mental Disorders (DSM) is the most widely used classification system in North America. It is actually a work in progress. DSM-5, the 947-page current edition, is but the latest version of this system, which has undergone many changes over the past seven decades. The DSM also faces competition from other diagnostic systems around the world.

🌐 Competitors

Both within North America and around the world, the **DSM** faces competition from two other diagnostic systems—the **International Classification of Disorders (ICD)** and **Research Domain Criteria (RDoC)**.

	DSM	ICD	RDoC
Producer	APA	WHO*	NIMH**
Disorders	Psychological	Psychological/ medical	Psychological
Criteria	Detailed	Brief	Neuro/ biological
Application	Practice/research	Practice/research	Research
Area of use	North America	Worldwide	United States

* World Health Organization   ** National Institute of Mental Health

↺ Just a Generation Ago . . .

Many of the disorders listed in the DSM are very familiar, giving the impression that they have been recognized forever. But many of the disorders and/or their labels are relatively new.

Just a generation ago, the DSM did not include:

- Bulimia nervosa
- Autistic disorder
- PTSD
- Panic disorder
- Narcissistic personality disorder
- Borderline personality disorder

Just a generation ago, the DSM had different names for certain disorders:

Past	Present
Mental retardation	Intellectual disability (page 541)
Manic-depressive disorder	Bipolar disorder (page 211)
Multiple personality disorder	Dissociative identity disorder (page 176)
Dementia	Neurocognitive disorder (page 562)
Hypochondriasis	Illness anxiety disorder (page 295)

⬆ Top DSM-5 Concerns

Many of the DSM-5 changes have raised concerns. Several have been particularly controversial in some clinical circles.

People with a **serious medical disease**, such as cancer, may also receive a psychiatric diagnosis if they are "excessively" distressed.

People experiencing **normal grief reactions** may receive a psychiatric diagnosis of depression if they are "excessively" distressed.

Many **behaviors pursued excessively**, such as sex, Internet use, and shopping, may eventually be considered behavioral addictions.

People with **normal age-related forgetfulness** may receive a psychiatric diagnosis of mild neurocognitive disorder.

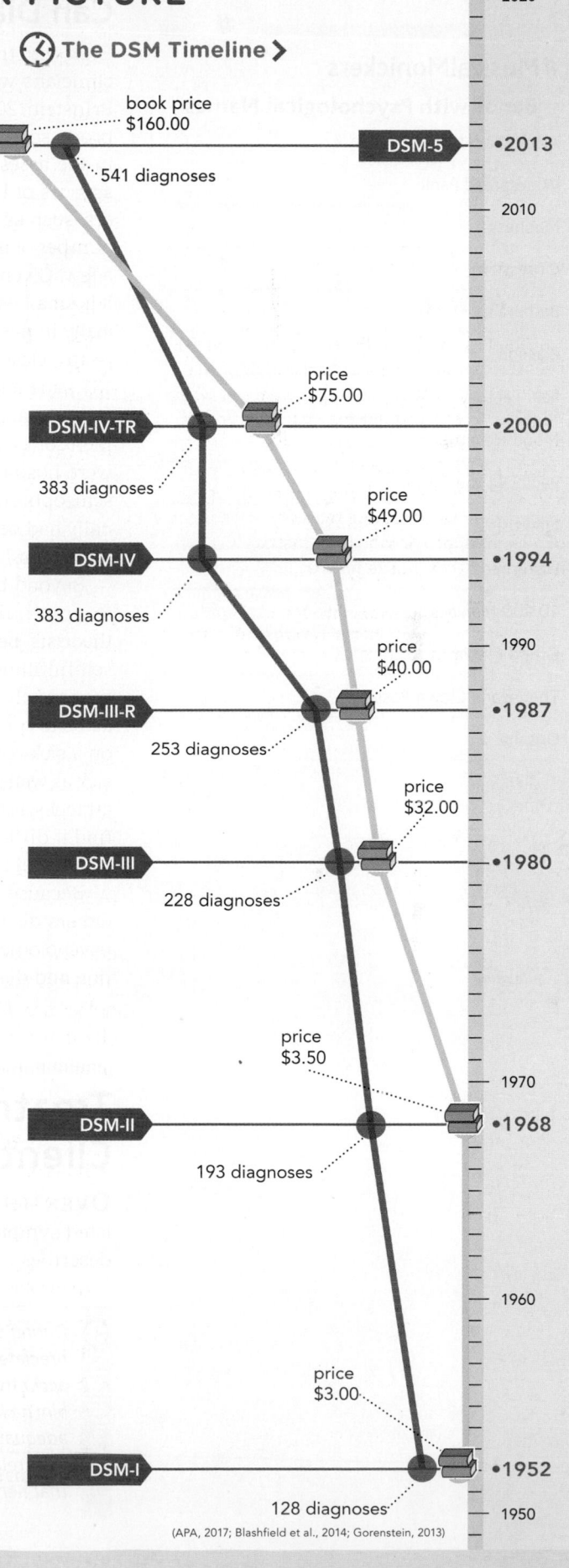

🕐 **The DSM Timeline ❯**

book price $160.00
DSM-5 • 2013
541 diagnoses

price $75.00
DSM-IV-TR • 2000
383 diagnoses

price $49.00
DSM-IV • 1994
383 diagnoses

price $40.00
DSM-III-R • 1987
253 diagnoses

price $32.00
DSM-III • 1980
228 diagnoses

price $3.50
DSM-II • 1968
193 diagnoses

price $3.00
DSM-I • 1952
128 diagnoses

2020
2010
2000
1994
1990
1987
1980
1970
1968
1960
1950

(APA, 2017; Blashfield et al., 2014; Gorenstein, 2013)

Can Diagnosis and Labeling Cause Harm?

Even with trustworthy assessment data and reliable and valid classification categories, clinicians will sometimes arrive at a wrong conclusion (Norman et al., 2017; Trull & Prinstein, 2012; Mcehl, 1996, 1960). Like all human beings, they are flawed information processors. Studies show that they are overly influenced by information gathered early in the assessment process. In addition, they may pay too much attention to certain sources of information, such as a parent's report about a child, and too little to others, such as the child's point of view. Finally, their judgments can be distorted by any number of personal biases—gender, age, race, and socioeconomic status, to name just a few. Given the limitations of assessment tools, assessors, and classification systems, it is small wonder that studies sometimes uncover shocking errors in diagnosis, especially in hospitals (Liese & Reis, 2016; Vickrey, Samuels, & Ropper, 2010).

In a classic study, for example, a clinical team was asked to reevaluate the records of 131 patients at a mental hospital in New York, conduct interviews with many of these persons, and arrive at a diagnosis for each one (Lipton & Simon, 1985). The researchers then compared the team's diagnoses with the original diagnoses for which the patients were hospitalized. Although 89 of the patients had originally received a diagnosis of schizophrenia, only 16 received it upon reevaluation. And whereas 15 patients originally had been given a diagnosis of a mood disorder, 50 received it now. It is obviously important for clinicians to be aware that such huge disagreements can occur.

Beyond the potential for misdiagnosis, the very act of classifying people can lead to unintended results. As you read in Chapter 3, for example, many family-social theorists believe that diagnostic labels can become self-fulfilling prophecies. When people are diagnosed as mentally disturbed, they may be perceived and reacted to correspondingly. If others expect them to take on a sick role, they may begin to consider themselves sick as well and act that way. Furthermore, our society attaches a stigma to abnormality (Corrigan et al., 2017). People labeled mentally ill may find it difficult to get a job, especially a position of responsibility, or to be welcomed into social relationships. Once a label has been applied, it may stick for a long time.

> Why are medical diagnoses usually valued, while the use of psychological diagnoses is often criticized?

Because of these problems, some clinicians would like to do away with diagnoses. Others disagree. They believe we must simply work to increase what is known about psychological disorders and improve diagnostic techniques. They hold that classification and diagnosis are critical to understanding and treating people in distress.

Treatment: How Might the Client Be Helped?

OVER THE COURSE OF 10 months, Franco was treated for depression and related symptoms. He improved considerably during that time, as the following report describes:

During therapy, Franco's debilitating depression relented. Increasingly, he came to appreciate that his mother's accusations against him—and his self-accusations—were not accurate. He also started to consider the possibility that Maria's reluctance to commit to him had been more about where she was in her life than a sign that he was a terrible or inadequate person. Eventually, Maria and Franco talked again, although they did not renew their relationship. Franco felt better realizing that she did not hate him. She even told him that her mother had said some kind things about him after their breakup.

> *Franco also managed to straighten out his problems at work. He explained his recent difficulties to his immediate supervisor at the bank and committed himself to improving his recent performance. His supervisor, with whom he had been friendly before his recent struggles, said she was glad that he was communicating openly, and emphasized that he would be given the opportunity to improve his performance. He was surprised to hear how highly he had been regarded over the years, although as she put it, "Why would you have been promoted otherwise?"*
>
> *Over the course of therapy, Franco also forced himself to spend more time having fun with his friends. He found his mood on the upswing as a result of these re-established relationships. In addition, he began dating a woman he met through Jesse. He often considered the lessons he learned in treatment, trying to handle this new relationship in ways different from the destructive patterns of his past.*

Clearly, treatment helped Franco, and by its conclusion he was a happier, more functional person than the man who had first sought help 10 months earlier. But how did his therapist decide on the treatment program that proved to be so helpful?

Treatment Decisions

Franco's therapist began, like all therapists, with assessment information and diagnostic decisions. Knowing the specific details and background of Franco's problem (*idiographic data*) and combining this individual information with broad information about the nature and treatment of depression (*nomothetic data*), the clinician arrived at a treatment plan for him.

Yet therapists may be influenced by additional factors when they make treatment decisions. Their treatment plans typically reflect their theoretical orientations and how they have learned to conduct therapy (Sharf, 2015). As therapists apply a favored model in case after case, they become more and more familiar with its principles and treatment techniques and tend to use them in work with still other clients.

Current research may also play a role. Most clinicians say that they value research as a guide to practice (Gyani et al., 2015; Beutler et al., 1995). However, not all of them actually read research articles, so they cannot be directly influenced by them (Holt et al., 2015; Stewart & Chambless, 2007). In fact, according to surveys, therapists gather much of their information about the latest developments in the field from colleagues, professional newsletters, workshops, conferences, Web sites, books, and the

#ContradictoryTrends

Since 1998, the number of patients receiving psychotherapy alone has fallen by 34 percent. The number receiving medication alone has increased by 23 percent.

However, today's patients express a three-times-greater preference for psychotherapy over medications

(Gaudiano, 2013).

Raising public awareness Believing that more public awareness about stress and psychological disorders will lead to better assessment and treatment, Boston's Logan International Airport displays an art exhibit of enormous-sized posters, featuring dozens of people—from ordinary to famous—who have experienced such disorders.

like (Simon, 2011; Corrie & Callanan, 2001). Unfortunately, the accuracy and usefulness of these sources vary widely.

To help clinicians become more familiar with and apply research findings, there is an ever-growing movement in North America, the United Kingdom, and elsewhere toward **empirically supported**, or **evidence-based, treatment** (Norcross et al., 2016; Pilecki & McKay, 2016). Proponents of this movement have formed task forces that seek to identify which therapies have received clear research support for each disorder, to propose corresponding treatment guidelines, and to spread such information to clinicians. Critics of the movement worry that such efforts have thus far been simplistic, biased, and at times misleading (Shean, 2016; Jager & Leek, 2013). However, the empirically supported treatment movement has been gaining considerable momentum over the past decade.

The Effectiveness of Treatment

Altogether, more than 400 forms of therapy are currently practiced in the clinical field (Zarbo et al., 2015). Naturally, the most important question to ask about each of them is whether it does what it is supposed to do. Does a particular treatment really help people overcome their psychological problems? On the surface, the question may seem simple. In fact, it is one of the most difficult questions for clinical researchers to answer.

The first problem is how to *define* "success." If, as Franco's therapist implies, he still has much progress to make at the conclusion of therapy, should his recovery be considered successful? The second problem is how to *measure* improvement (Lambert, 2015, 2010; Hunsley & Lee, 2014). Should researchers give equal weight to the reports of clients, friends, relatives, therapists, and teachers? Should they use rating scales, inventories, therapy insights, observations, or some other measure?

Perhaps the biggest problem in determining the effectiveness of treatment is the *variety* and *complexity* of the treatments currently in use. People differ in their problems, personal styles, and motivations for therapy. Therapists differ in skill, experience, orientation, and personality. And therapies differ in theory, format, and setting. Because an individual's progress is influenced by all these factors and more, the findings of a particular study will not always apply to other clients and therapists (see **Figure 4-4**).

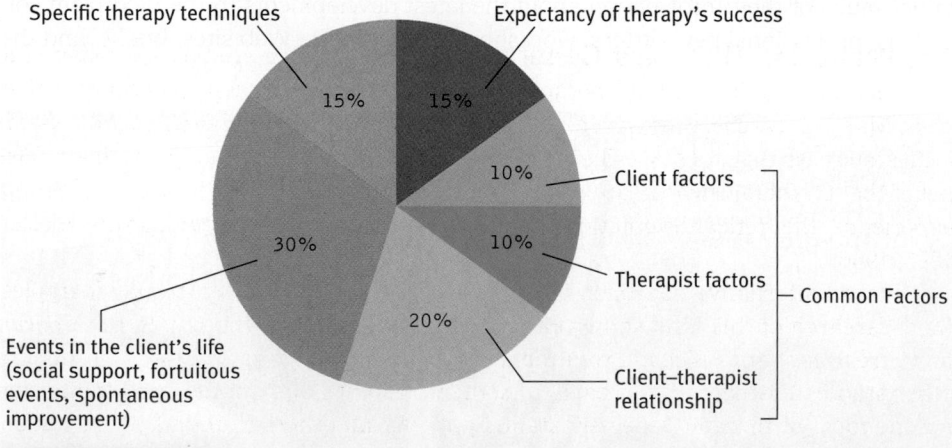

FIGURE 4-4

What Factors Contribute to Therapy Outcomes?

According to research, a client's progress in therapy relates only partly to the specific strategies used by his or her therapist. In fact, factors such as the client's expectations, the client–therapist relationship, and concurrent events in the client's life may collectively have the most influence on the outcome of treatment. (Information from: De Nadai et al., 2017; McClintock et al., 2017; Davidson & Chan, 2014; Norcross & Lambert, 2011; Cooper, 2008.)

Proper research procedures address some of these problems. By using control groups, random assignment, matched research participants, and the like, clinicians can draw certain conclusions about various therapies. Even in studies that are well designed, however, the variety and complexity of treatment limit the conclusions that can be reached (Kazdin, 2017, 2015).

Despite these issues and difficulties, the job of evaluating therapies must be done, and clinical researchers have plowed ahead with it. Investigators have, in fact, conducted thousands of *therapy outcome studies,* studies that measure and compare the effects of various treatments. The studies typically ask one of three questions: (1) Is therapy *in general* effective? (2) Are *particular* therapies generally effective? (3) Are *particular* therapies effective for *particular* problems?

Is Therapy Generally Effective? Studies suggest that therapy often is more helpful than no treatment or than placebos. A pioneering review examined 375 controlled studies, covering a total of almost 25,000 people seen in a wide assortment of therapies (Smith, Glass, & Miller, 1980; Smith & Glass, 1977).

> How can people make wise decisions about therapists and treatment approaches when they are seeking treatment?

The reviewers combined the findings of these studies by using a special statistical technique called *meta-analysis.* According to this analysis, the average person who received treatment was better off than 75 percent of the untreated persons. Other meta-analyses have found similar relationships between treatment and improvement (Sharf, 2015).

Some clinicians have concerned themselves with an important related question: Can therapy be harmful? A number of studies suggest that 5 to 10 percent of patients actually seem to get worse because of therapy (Lambert, 2015, 2010; Lambert et al., 1986). Their symptoms may become more intense, or they may develop new ones, such as a sense of failure, guilt, reduced self-concept, or hopelessness, because of their inability to profit from therapy.

Are Particular Therapies Generally Effective? The studies you have read about so far have lumped all therapies together to consider their general effectiveness. Many researchers, however, consider it wrong to treat all therapies alike. Some critics suggest that these studies are operating under a *uniformity myth*—a false belief that all therapies are equivalent despite differences in the therapists' training, experience, theoretical orientations, and personalities (Heppner et al., 2016; Kiesler, 1995, 1966).

Thus, an alternative approach examines the effectiveness of *particular* therapies. Most research of this kind shows each of the major forms of therapy to be superior to no treatment or to placebo treatment (Prochaska & Norcross, 2010). A number of other studies have compared particular therapies with one another and found that no one form of therapy generally stands out over all others (Luborsky et al., 2006, 2002, 1975).

If different kinds of therapy have similar successes, might they have something in common? People in the **rapprochement movement** have tried to identify a set of *common factors,* or *common strategies,* that may run through all effective therapies, regardless of the clinicians' particular orientations (Yang & Zhang, 2017; Wampold, 2015). Surveys of highly successful therapists suggest, for example, that most give feedback to clients, help clients focus on their own thoughts and behavior, pay attention

"Batman is getting more press than me."

Harley L. Schwadron/The New Yorker Collection/The Cartoon Bank

empirically supported treatment Therapy that has received clear research support for a particular disorder and has corresponding treatment guidelines. Also known as *evidence-based treatment.*

rapprochement movement A movement to identify a set of common factors, or common strategies, that run through all successful therapies.

psychopharmacologist A psychiatrist who primarily prescribes medications.

to the way they and their clients are interacting, and try to promote self-mastery in their clients. In short, effective therapists of any type may practice more similarly than they preach.

Are Particular Therapies Effective for Particular Problems? People with different disorders may respond differently to the various forms of therapy (Norcross et al., 2016; Norcross & Beutler, 2014). In an oft-quoted statement, influential clinical theorist Gordon Paul said a half century ago that the most appropriate question regarding the effectiveness of therapy may be "*What* specific treatment, by *whom*, is most effective for *this* individual with *that* specific problem, and under *which* set of circumstances?" (Paul, 1967, p. 111). Researchers have investigated how effective particular therapies are at treating particular disorders, and they often have found sizable differences among the various therapies. Cognitive-behavioral therapies, for example, appear to be the most effective of all in treating phobias (Grohol, 2016; Antony, 2014), whereas drug therapy seems to be the single most effective treatment for schizophrenia (Andrade, 2016).

As you read previously, studies also show that some clinical problems may respond better to *combined* approaches (Kamenov et al., 2017; Norcross & Beutler, 2014). Drug therapy is sometimes combined with certain forms of psychotherapy, for example, to treat depression. In fact, it is now common for clients to be seen by two therapists—one of them a **psychopharmacologist,** a psychiatrist who primarily prescribes medications, and the other a psychologist, social worker, or other therapist who conducts psychotherapy. Obviously, knowledge of how particular therapies fare with particular disorders can help therapists and clients alike make better decisions about treatment. We will keep returning to this issue as we examine the various disorders throughout the book.

What Lies Ahead for Clinical Assessment?

IT IS CLEAR FROM THIS chapter that proper diagnoses and effective treatments rest on the shoulders of accurate clinical assessment. Correspondingly, before the 1950s, assessment tools were a highly regarded part of clinical practice. However, as research in the 1960s and 1970s began to reveal that a number of the tools were inaccurate or inconsistent, many clinicians abandoned systematic assessment. Today, respect for assessment is on the rise once again. One reason for this renewal of interest is the drive by researchers for more rigorous tests to help them select appropriate participants for clinical studies. Still another factor is the growing belief in the field that brain-scanning techniques may soon offer assessment information about a wide range of psychological disorders. Along with heightened respect for assessment has come increased research in this area.

Ironically, just as clinicians and researchers are rediscovering systematic assessment, rising costs and economic factors may be conspiring to discourage the use of assessment tools. As you read in Chapter 1, insurance parity and treatment coverage, including assessment coverage, for people with psychological problems had been improving during the twenty-first century as a result of federal parity laws and the Affordable Care Act (see page 18). However, with new federal leadership and different health care priorities now in place, many experts fear that clinical assessment will receive only limited insurance support in the future. Which forces will ultimately have a stronger influence on clinical assessment—promising research or economic pressure? Only time will tell.

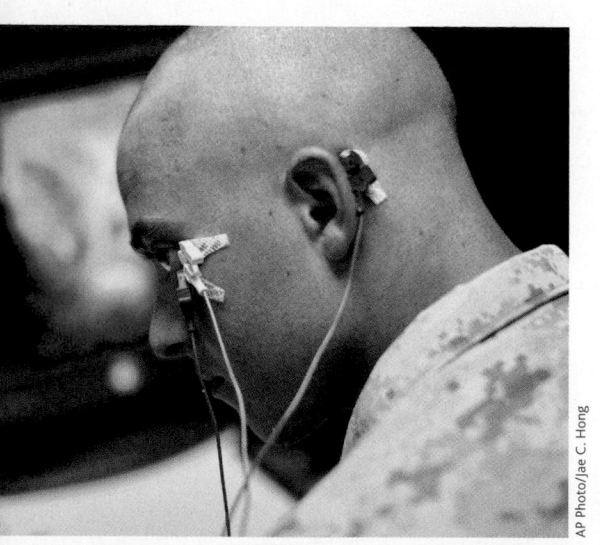

AP Photo/Jae C. Hong

Blink of the eye Before entering combat duty, this Marine takes an eyeblink test—a psychophysiological test in which sensors are attached to the eyelid and other parts of the face. The test tries to detect physical indicators of tension and anxiety and to predict which Marines might be particularly susceptible to posttraumatic stress disorder.

♥... SUMMING UP

» The Practitioner's Task Clinical practitioners are interested primarily in gathering *idiographic* information about their clients. They seek an understanding of the specific nature and origins of a client's problems through *clinical assessment* and *diagnosis*. p. 85

» Clinical Assessment To be useful, assessment tools must be *standardized, reliable,* and *valid.* Most clinical assessment methods fall into three general categories: *clinical interviews, tests,* and *observations.* A clinical interview may be either *unstructured* or *structured.* Types of clinical tests include *projective, personality, response, psychophysiological, neurological, neuropsychological,* and *intelligence* tests. Types of observation include *naturalistic observation, analog observation,* or *self-monitoring.* pp. 85–99

» Diagnosis After collecting assessment information, clinicians form a *clinical picture* and decide on a *diagnosis.* The diagnosis is chosen from a *classification system.* The system used most widely in North America is the *Diagnostic and Statistical Manual of Mental Disorders* (*DSM*). Most other countries rely primarily on a system called the *International Classification of Diseases* (*ICD*), which lists both medical and psychological disorders. pp. 99–101

» DSM-5 The most recent version of the DSM, known as *DSM-5,* lists more than 500 disorders. DSM-5 contains numerous additions and changes to the diagnostic categories, criteria, and organization found in past editions of the DSM. The reliability and validity of this revised diagnostic and classification system are currently receiving clinical review and, in some circles, criticism. pp. 101–105

» Dangers of Diagnosis and Labeling Even with trustworthy assessment data and reliable and valid classification categories, clinicians will not always arrive at the correct conclusion. They are human and so fall prey to various biases, misconceptions, and expectations. Another problem related to diagnosis is the prejudice that labels arouse, which may be damaging to the person who is diagnosed. p. 106

» Treatment The *treatment decisions* of therapists may be influenced by assessment information, the diagnosis, the clinician's theoretical orientation and familiarity with research, and the state of knowledge in the field. Determining the *effectiveness of treatment* is difficult. Nevertheless, *therapy outcome studies* have led to three general conclusions: (1) people in therapy are usually better off than people with similar problems who receive no treatment; (2) the various therapies do not appear to differ dramatically in their general effectiveness; and (3) certain therapies or combinations of therapies do appear to be more effective than others for certain disorders. Some therapists currently advocate *empirically supported treatment*—the active identification, promotion, and teaching of those interventions that have received clear research support. pp. 106–110

Visit *LaunchPad*
to access the e-Book, Clinical Choices, videos, activities, and LearningCurve, as well as study aids including flashcards, FAQs, and research exercises.

LaunchPad
macmillan learning

...Anxiety, Obsessive-Compulsive, and Related Disorders

Tomas, a 25-year-old Web designer, was afraid that he was "losing his mind." He had always been a worrier. He worried about his health, his girlfriend, his work, his social life, his future, his finances, and so on. Would his best friend get angry at him? Was his girlfriend tiring of him? Was he investing his money wisely? Were his clients pleased with his work? But, lately, those worries had increased to an unbearable level. He was becoming consumed with the notion that something terrible was about to happen to him. Within an hour's time, he might have intense concerns about going broke, developing cancer, losing one of his parents, offending his friends, and more. He was certain that disaster awaited him at every turn. No amount of reassurance, from himself or from others, brought relief for very long.

He started therapy with Dr. Adena Morven, a clinical psychologist. Dr. Morven immediately noticed how disturbed Tomas appeared. He looked tense and frightened and could not sit comfortably in his chair; he kept tapping his feet and jumped when he heard traffic noise from outside the office building. He kept sighing throughout the visit, fidgeting and shifting his position, and he appeared breathless while telling Dr. Morven about his difficulties.

Tomas described his frequent inability to concentrate to the therapist. When designing client Web sites, he would lose his train of thought. Less than 5 minutes into a project, he'd forget much of his overall strategy. During conversations, he would begin a sentence and then forget the point he was about to make. TV watching had become impossible. He found it difficult to concentrate on anything for more than 5 minutes; his mind kept drifting away from the task at hand.

To say the least, he was worried about all of this. "I'm worried about being so worried," he told Dr. Morven, almost laughing at his own remark. At this point, Tomas expected the worst whenever he began a conversation, task, plan, or outing. If an event or interaction did in fact start to go awry, he would find himself overwhelmed with uncomfortable feelings—his heart would beat faster, his breathing would increase, and he'd sweat profusely. On some occasions, he thought he was actually having a heart attack—at the ripe old age of 25.

Typically, such physical reactions lasted but a matter of seconds. However, those few seconds felt like an eternity to Tomas. He acknowledged coming back down to earth after those feelings subsided—but, for him, "back down to earth" meant back to worrying and then worrying some more.

Dr. Morven empathized with Tomas about how upsetting this all must be. She asked him why he had decided to come into therapy now—as opposed to last year, last month, or last week. Tomas was able to pinpoint several things. First, all the worrying and anxiety seemed to be on the increase. Second, he was finding it hard to sleep. His nights were filled by tossing and turning—and, of course, more worrying. Third, he suspected that all of his worrying, physical symptoms, and lack of sleep were bad for his health. Wouldn't they eventually lead to a major medical problem of some kind? And finally, his constant anxiety had begun to interfere with his life. Although his girlfriend and other acquaintances did not seem to realize how much he was suffering, he was growing weary of covering it all up. He found himself turning down social invitations and work opportunities more and more. He had even quit his once-beloved weekly poker game. Not that staying home helped in any real way. He wondered how much longer he could go on this way.

fear The central nervous system's physiological and emotional response to a serious threat to one's well-being.

anxiety The central nervous system's physiological and emotional response to a vague sense of threat or danger.

generalized anxiety disorder A disorder marked by persistent and excessive feelings of anxiety and worry about numerous events and activities.

> If fear is so unpleasant, why do many people seek out the feelings of fear brought about by amusement park rides, scary movies, bungee jumping, and the like?

You don't need to be as troubled as Tomas to experience fear and anxiety. Think about a time when your breathing quickened, your muscles tensed, and your heart pounded with a sudden sense of dread. Was it when your car almost skidded off the road in the rain? When your professor announced a pop quiz? What about when the person you were in love with went out with someone else, or your boss suggested that your job performance ought to improve? Any time you face what seems to be a serious threat to your well-being, you may react with the state of immediate alarm known as **fear.** Sometimes you cannot pinpoint a specific cause for your alarm, but still you feel tense and edgy, as if you expect something unpleasant to happen. The vague sense of being in danger is usually called **anxiety,** and it has the same features—the same increases in breathing, muscular tension, perspiration, and so forth—as fear.

Although everyday experiences of fear and anxiety are not pleasant, they often are useful. They prepare us for action—for "fight or flight"—when danger threatens. They may lead us to drive more cautiously in a storm, keep up with our reading assignments, treat our friends more sensitively, and work harder at our jobs. Unfortunately, some people suffer such disabling fear and anxiety that they cannot lead normal lives. Their discomfort is too severe or too frequent, lasts too long, or is triggered too easily. These people are said to have an *anxiety disorder* or a related kind of disorder.

Anxiety disorders are the most common mental disorders in the United States. In any given year around 18 percent of the adult population suffer from one or another of the anxiety disorders identified by DSM-5, while close to 29 percent of all people develop one of the disorders at some point in their lives (Remes et al., 2016; Kessler et al., 2012, 2010, 2009). Around 37 percent of these individuals receive treatment (NIMH, 2017; Wang et al., 2005). Surveys suggest that non-Hispanic white Americans are more likely than African, Hispanic, or Asian Americans to develop an anxiety disorder during their lifetime (NIMH, 2017; Hofmann & Hinton, 2014). The cause of this racial-ethnic difference is not well understood.

People with *generalized anxiety disorder* experience general and persistent feelings of worry and anxiety. People with *specific phobias* have a persistent and irrational fear of a particular object, activity, or situation. People with *agoraphobia* fear traveling to public places such as stores or movie theaters. Those with *social anxiety disorder* are intensely afraid of social or performance situations in which they may become embarrassed. And people with *panic disorder* have recurrent attacks of terror. Most individuals with one anxiety disorder suffer from a second one as well (Bandelow & Michaelis, 2015; Merikangas & Swanson, 2010). Tomas, for example, has the excessive worry found in generalized anxiety disorder and the repeated attacks of terror that mark panic disorder. In addition, many of those with an anxiety disorder also experience depression (Naragon-Gainey et al., 2016; Wolk et al., 2016).

Anxiety also plays a major role in a different group of problems, called *obsessive-compulsive and related disorders*. People with these disorders feel overrun by recurrent thoughts that cause anxiety or by the need to perform certain repetitive actions to reduce anxiety. Because anxiety is so prominent in these disorders, they will be examined in this chapter along with the anxiety disorders. ∎

TABLE: 5-1

Dx Checklist

Generalized Anxiety Disorder

1. For 6 months or more, person experiences disproportionate, uncontrollable, and ongoing anxiety and worry about multiple matters.

2. The symptoms include at least three of the following: edginess, fatigue, poor concentration, irritability, muscle tension, sleep problems.

3. Significant distress of impairment.

Information from: APA, 2013

Generalized Anxiety Disorder

PEOPLE WITH GENERALIZED ANXIETY DISORDER experience excessive anxiety under most circumstances and worry about practically anything. In fact, their problem is sometimes described as *free-floating anxiety*. Like the young Web designer Tomas, they typically feel restless, keyed up, or on edge; tire easily; have difficulty concentrating; suffer from muscle tension; and have sleep problems (see **Table 5-1**).

The symptoms last at least 6 months (APA, 2013) and lead to a reduced quality of life (Comer, Pincus, & Hofmann, 2012) Nevertheless, many people with the disorder are able, although with some difficulty, to carry on social relationships and job activities.

Generalized anxiety disorder is common in Western society. Surveys suggest that as many as 4 percent of the U.S. population have the symptoms of this disorder in any given year, a rate that holds across Canada, Britain, and other Western countries (NIMH, 2017; Watterson et al., 2017; Kessler et al., 2012, 2010). Altogether, around 6 percent of all people develop generalized anxiety disorder sometime during their lives. It may emerge at any age (see *Trending* on the next page). Women diagnosed with this disorder outnumber men 2 to 1. Non-Hispanic white Americans are more likely than members of minority groups to develop the disorder (Hofmann & Hinton, 2014). Around 43 percent of people who have generalized anxiety disorder receive treatment for it (NIMH, 2017; Wang et al., 2005).

A variety of explanations and treatments have been proposed for this disorder. Let's look at the views and approaches offered by the sociocultural, psychodynamic, humanistic, cognitive-behavioral, and biological models.

The Sociocultural Perspective: Societal and Multicultural Factors

According to sociocultural theorists, generalized anxiety disorder is most likely to develop in people who are faced with ongoing societal conditions that are dangerous. Studies have found that people in highly threatening environments are indeed more likely to develop the general feelings of tension, anxiety, and fatigue and the sleep disturbances found in this disorder (Comer et al., 2016). For example, there are higher rates of generalized anxiety disorder and similar syndromes among people who live in crime-ridden or hostile neighborhoods and among people living near nuclear power plants, especially ones that that have had radiation accidents in the past (Cerdá et al., 2017; Rubens et al., 2016; Yoshida et al., 2016).

One of the most powerful forms of societal stress is poverty. People without financial means are likely to live in rundown communities with high crime rates, have fewer educational and job opportunities, and run a greater risk for health problems (Friedman, Grawert, & Cullen, 2016; West, 2016). As sociocultural theorists would predict, such people also have a higher rate of generalized anxiety disorder (Delgadillo et al., 2016). Across North America, the rate is almost twice as high among people with low incomes as among those with higher incomes (Watterson et al., 2017; Sareen et al., 2011). As wages decrease, the rate of generalized anxiety disorder steadily increases (see **Table 5-2**).

It appears that race and ethnicity can affect the precise picture of generalized anxiety disorder (NIMH, 2017; Baruth & Manning, 2016). For example, researchers have noted that the disorder often takes on a pattern called *nervios* ("nerves") , or *ataques de nervios*, for Hispanic individuals in both the United States and Latin America (Vazquez et al., 2017; López et al., 2011). People with *nervios* experience enormous emotional distress, so-called brain aches marked by poor concentration and nervousness, reactions like irritability and tearfulness, and physical symptoms such as headaches, stomachaches, trembling, and heat in the chest rising into the head.

Although poverty and various societal pressures may help create a climate in which generalized anxiety disorder is more likely to develop, sociocultural variables are not the only factors at work. After

The role of society Bishop Richard Garcia hugs the father of a 6-year-old child who was killed by a stray bullet fired by gang members outside his house. People who live in dangerous environments experience greater anxiety and have a higher rate of generalized anxiety disorder than those who live in other settings.

AP Photo/The Monterey County Herald, Orville Myers

TABLE: 5-2

Looking at Demographics

Prevalence of Anxiety Disorders and Obsessive-Compulsive Disorder (Compared with Rate in Total Population)			
	Female	Low-Income	Elderly
Generalized anxiety disorder	Higher	Higher	Higher
Specific phobias	Higher	Higher	Lower
Agoraphobia	Higher	Higher	Higher
Social anxiety disorder	Higher	Higher	Lower
Panic disorder	Higher	Higher	Lower
Obsessive-compulsive disorder	Same	Higher	Lower

Information from: Watterson et al., 2017; de Jong et al., 2016; Remes et al., 2016; Polo et al., 2011; Sareen et al., 2011; Hopko et al., 2008; Schultz et al., 2008.

Separation Anxiety Disorder, Not Just For Kids Anymore

Individuals with *separation anxiety disorder* feel extreme anxiety, often panic, whenever they are separated from home or from key people in their lives. Jonah's symptoms began when he was 4 years old:

Jonah, age 4, began crying as soon as his parents tried to place him in the car for the 30-minute trip to his grandparents' house for an overnight weekend there. He screamed, "I only want to be here with you! If you make me go, I'll never see you again! What if you like it better without me? What if you die?" He cried all the way to his grandparents' house. At their door, Jonah hugged his mother as though he would never let her go.

Two hours later, his parents, Mia and Brandon, received a phone call from Mia's mother. An inconsolable Jonah had been crying nonstop since his parents had left. Reluctantly, they agreed to pick him up. That night, Jonah refused to sleep in his own room, insisting on sleeping between his parents, an arrangement that became a regular thing from that point forward. During the next several months, Jonah became hysterical every time Mia or Brandon tried to get him to leave the house for a play date or journey elsewhere.

Five months later, Jonah began kindergarten. That first day lasted all of two hours. The principal called, asking Mia to come get Jonah. Though sympathetic, the principal explained that Jonah's non-stop crying was affecting all the other children. "Perhaps tomorrow Jonah will have a better day," he said. But the next day, Jonah's reaction was the same. And the next day. And the next day.

Like Jonah, children with separation anxiety disorder have great trouble traveling away from their family, and they often refuse to visit friends' houses, go on errands, or attend camp or school. Many cannot stay alone in a room and cling to their parents around the house. Some also have temper tantrums, cry, or plead to keep their parents from leaving them. The children may fear

Steve Stoner/ Fort Morgan Times/ AP Photo

Oh, that first day! The first day of kindergarten is overwhelming for this child and perhaps also for his mother. Such reactions to the beginning of school are common. But for some individuals, separations from attachment figures repeatedly bring on severe and disabling anxiety reactions that may impair their lives.

that they will get lost when separated from their parents or that the parents will meet with an accident or illness. As long as the children are near their parents, they may function quite normally. At the first hint of separation, however, the dramatic pattern of symptoms may be set in motion.

Separation anxiety disorder is one of the most common psychological disorders among the young. In fact, for years, clinicians believed that the disorder is developed *only* by children or adolescents. Then in 2013, based on many clinical reports and some persuasive research, DSM-5 determined that the disorder can also develop in adulthood, particularly after adults have experienced traumas such as the death of a spouse or child, a relationship break-up, separation caused by military service, or the like (Gesi et al., 2017; APA, 2013). Such individuals may become consumed with concern about the health, safety, or well-being of a significant other—their spouse, a surviving child, or another important person in their life. They may constantly and excessively try to be with the other individual, check on the other's whereabouts, protect the other person, and restrict the person's activities and travels. Their extreme anxiety and invasive demands cause them severe distress and can greatly damage their social and occupational lives (Gesi et al., 2017; Baldwin et al., 2016).

Given this new perspective, DSM-5 has departed from previous editions of the diagnostic and classification system and now categorizes separation anxiety disorder as one kind of anxiety disorder rather than as a unique childhood disorder (APA, 2013). It states that symptoms must persist for at least 6 months for adults to receive a diagnosis, compared to 4 weeks for children. Applying DSM-5's criteria, studies find that as many as 2 percent of all adults have the disorder in addition to 4 percent of all children (Baldwin et al., 2016).

This new categorization is controversial (Gesi et al., 2017). Although most clinicians agree that certain adults do indeed manifest the loss-triggered symptoms described above, many of them believe that the adult syndrome may be qualitatively different from the one displayed by Jonah and other such children. These critics believe that adults who now receive a diagnosis of separation anxiety disorder may actually be suffering from one of the other anxiety disorders, posttraumatic stress disorder (see Chapter 6), an extended case of bereavement (see Chapter 7), or a personality disorder (see Chapter 16). Researchers are currently trying to sort out this controversy (Baldwin et al., 2016), but in the meantime the term "for children only" cannot be applied to this debilitating pattern.

all, most people in poor or dangerous environments do not develop this disorder. Even if sociocultural factors play a broad role, theorists still must explain why some people develop the disorder and others do not. The psychodynamic, humanistic-existential, cognitive-behavioral, and biological schools of thought have all tried to explain why and have offered corresponding treatments.

The Psychodynamic Perspective

Sigmund Freud (1933, 1917) believed that all children experience some degree of anxiety as part of growing up and that all use ego defense mechanisms to help control such anxiety (see pages 53–55). However, some children have particularly high levels of anxiety, or their defense mechanisms are particularly inadequate, and these individuals may develop generalized anxiety disorder.

Psychodynamic Explanations: When Childhood Anxiety Goes Unresolved

According to Freud, early developmental experiences may produce an unusually high level of anxiety in certain children. Say that a boy is spanked every time he cries for milk as an infant, messes his pants as a 2-year-old, and explores his genitals as a toddler. He may eventually come to believe that his various id impulses are very dangerous, and he may feel overwhelming anxiety whenever he has such impulses, setting the stage for generalized anxiety disorder.

Alternatively, a child's ego defense mechanisms may be too weak to cope with even normal levels of anxiety. Overprotected children, shielded by their parents from all frustrations and threats, have little opportunity to develop effective defense mechanisms. When they face the pressures of adult life, their defense mechanisms may be too weak to cope with the resulting anxieties.

Today's psychodynamic theorists often disagree with specific aspects of Freud's explanation for generalized anxiety disorder. Most continue to believe, however, that the disorder can be traced to inadequacies in the early relationships between children and their parents (Sharf, 2015). Researchers have tested the psychodynamic explanations in various ways. In one strategy, they have tried to show that people with generalized anxiety disorder are particularly likely to use defense mechanisms. For example, a classic investigation examined the early therapy transcripts of patients with this diagnosis and found that the patients often reacted defensively. When asked by therapists to discuss upsetting experiences, they would quickly forget (*repress*) what they had just been talking about, change the direction of the discussion, or deny having negative feelings (Luborsky, 1973).

In another line of research, investigators have studied people who as children suffered extreme punishment for id impulses. As psychodynamic theorists would predict, these people have higher levels of anxiety later in life (Wang, Wang, & Liu, 2016; Busch, Milrod, & Shear, 2010). In addition, several studies have supported the psychodynamic position that extreme protectiveness by parents may often lead to high levels of anxiety in their children (Howard et al., 2016; Manfredi et al., 2011).

Although these studies are consistent with psychodynamic explanations, some scientists question whether they show what they claim to show. When people have difficulty talking about upsetting events early in therapy, for example, they are not necessarily repressing those events. They may be focusing purposely on the positive aspects of their lives, or they may be too embarrassed to share personal negative events until they develop trust in the therapist.

#InsecureAdults?

Children may cling to blankets or cuddly toys to feel more secure. Adults, too, may hug a beloved object in order to relax: 1 in 5 women and 1 in 20 men admit to sleeping with a stuffed animal on a regular basis (Kanner, 1995).

"Since my mother was rarely home, I guess I blame my nanny."

Alex Gregory/The New Yorker Collection/The Cartoon Bank

Animated anxiety In the animated film *Inside Out*, a young girl's five basic emotions (Fear, Joy, Sadness, Disgust, and Anger) come to life and guide her every behavior. More than a few clinicians note that the emotional figure named Fear (left) personifies the core symptoms of generalized anxiety disorder. Like people with this disorder, he is always looking for potential catastrophes and evaluating possible dangers—a mindset that leads to continuous worrying and tension.

Psychodynamic Therapies Psychodynamic therapists use the same general techniques to treat all psychological problems: *free association* and the therapist's interpretations of *transference, resistance,* and *dreams. Freudian psychodynamic therapists* use these methods to help clients with generalized anxiety disorder become less afraid of their id impulses and more successful in controlling them. Other psychodynamic therapists, particularly *object relations therapists,* use them to help anxious patients identify and settle the childhood relationship problems that continue to produce anxiety in adulthood (Blass, 2014; Lucas, 2006).

Controlled studies have typically found psychodynamic treatments to be of only modest help to persons with generalized anxiety disorder (Craske, 2016; Dorsey et al., 2016). An exception to this trend is *short-term psychodynamic therapy* (see Chapter 3), which has in some cases significantly reduced the levels of anxiety, worry, and social difficulty of patients with this disorder (Fonagy, 2015; Bressi et al., 2014).

The Humanistic Perspective

Humanistic theorists propose that generalized anxiety disorder, like other psychological disorders, arises when people stop looking at themselves honestly and acceptingly. Repeated denials of their true thoughts, emotions, and behavior make these people extremely anxious and unable to fulfill their potential as human beings.

The humanistic view of why people develop this disorder is best illustrated by Carl Rogers' explanation. As you saw in Chapter 3, Rogers believed that children who fail to receive *unconditional positive regard* from others may become overly critical of themselves and develop harsh self-standards, what Rogers called *conditions of worth.* They try to meet these standards by repeatedly distorting and denying their true thoughts and experiences. Despite such efforts, however, threatening self-judgments keep breaking through and causing them intense anxiety. This onslaught of anxiety sets the stage for generalized anxiety disorder or some other form of psychological dysfunction.

Practitioners of Rogers' treatment approach, **client-centered therapy** (also called *person-centered therapy*), try to show unconditional positive regard for their clients and to empathize with them. The therapists hope that an atmosphere of genuine acceptance and caring will help clients feel secure enough to recognize their true needs, thoughts, and emotions. When clients eventually are honest and comfortable with themselves, their anxiety or other symptoms will subside. In the following excerpt, Rogers describes the progress made by a client with anxiety and related symptoms:

client-centered therapy The humanistic therapy developed by Carl Rogers in which clinicians try to help clients by being accepting, empathizing accurately, and conveying genuineness. Also known as *person-centered therapy*.

basic irrational assumptions The inaccurate and inappropriate beliefs held by people with various psychological problems, according to Albert Ellis.

Therapy was an experiencing of her self, in all its aspects, in a safe relationship . . . the experiencing of self as having a capacity for wholeness . . . a self that cared about others. This last followed . . . the realization that the therapist cared, that it really mattered to him how therapy turned out for her, that he really valued her. . . . She gradually became aware of the fact that . . . there was nothing fundamentally bad, but rather, at heart she was positive and sound.

(Rogers, 1954, pp. 261–264)

Despite such optimistic case reports, controlled studies have failed to offer strong support for this approach. Although research does suggest that client-centered therapy is usually more helpful to anxious clients than no treatment, the approach is only sometimes superior to placebo therapy (Prochaska & Norcross, 2013, 2006, 2003). In addition, researchers have found, at best, only limited support for Rogers' explanation of generalized anxiety disorder and other forms of abnormal behavior. Nor have other humanistic theories and treatment received much research support.

The Cognitive-Behavioral Perspective

As you read in Chapter 3, followers of the cognitive-behavioral model suggest that psychological disorders are often caused by problematic behaviors and dysfunctional ways of thinking. Thus their explanations and treatments focus on the nature of such behaviors and thoughts, how they are acquired, and how they influence feelings and emotions. Although cognitive-behavioral explanations and treatments center most often on *both* behavioral and cognitive dimensions of a given disorder, sometimes they focus primarily on one of these dimensions—such is the case with regard to generalized anxiety disorder, where many proponents of this model concentrate largely on the cognitive dimension of the disorder.

Maladaptive Assumptions Initially, cognitive-behavioral theorists suggested that generalized anxiety disorder is primarily caused by *maladaptive assumptions,* a notion that continues to be influential. Albert Ellis, for example, proposed that many people are guided by irrational beliefs that lead them to act and react in inappropriate ways (Ellis, 2016, 2014, 1962). Ellis called these **basic irrational assumptions,** and he claimed that people with generalized anxiety disorder often hold the following ones:

"It is a dire necessity for an adult human being to be loved or approved of by virtually every significant other person in his community."

"It is awful and catastrophic when things are not the way one would very much like them to be."

"If something is or may be dangerous or fearsome, one should be terribly concerned about it and should keep dwelling on the possibility of its occurring."

"One should be thoroughly competent, adequate, and achieving in all possible respects if one is to consider oneself worthwhile."

(Ellis, 1962)

When people who make these assumptions are faced with a stressful event, such as an exam or a first date, they are likely to interpret it as dangerous, to overreact, and to feel fear. As they apply the assumptions to more and more events, they may begin to develop generalized anxiety disorder.

Similarly, theorist Aaron Beck argued that people with generalized anxiety disorder constantly hold silent assumptions (for example, "A situation or a person is unsafe until proven to be safe" or "It is always best to assume the worst") that imply they are in imminent danger (Clark & Beck, 2012, 2010; Beck & Emery, 1985). Since the time of Ellis' and Beck's initial proposals, researchers have repeatedly found that people with generalized anxiety disorder do indeed hold maladaptive assumptions, particularly about dangerousness, and are, in turn, overattentive to potentially threatening stimuli (Craske, 2016).

Newer Cognitive-Behavioral Explanations In recent years, several additional cognitive-behavioral explanations for generalized anxiety disorder have emerged. Each of them builds on the work of Ellis and Beck and their emphasis on danger.

The *metacognitive theory,* developed by the researcher Adrian Wells suggests that people with generalized anxiety disorder implicitly hold both positive and negative beliefs about worrying (Knowles et al., 2016; Wells, 2014, 2011, 2005). On the positive side, they believe that worrying is a useful way of appraising and coping with threats in life. And so they look for and examine all possible signs of danger—that is, they worry constantly (see **Figure 5-1**).

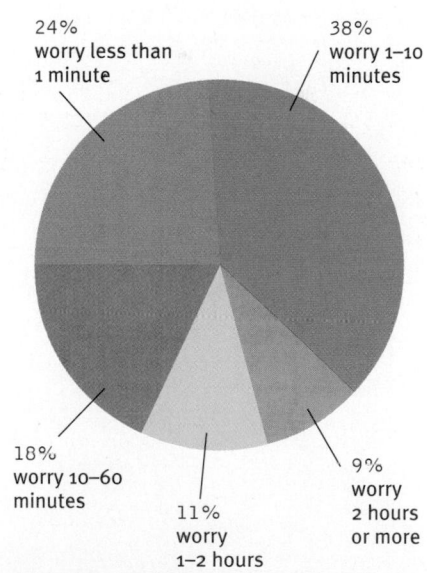

24% worry less than 1 minute

38% worry 1–10 minutes

18% worry 10–60 minutes

11% worry 1–2 hours

9% worry 2 hours or more

FIGURE 5-1

How Long Do Your Worries Last?

In one survey, 62 percent of college students said they spend less than 10 minutes at a time worrying about something. In contrast, 20 percent worry for more than an hour. (Information from: Tallis, 2015, 2014; Tallis et al., 1994.)

TABLE: 5-3

Worrying About Worrying: Items from the Meta-Worry Questionnaire

I am going crazy with worry.
My worrying will escalate and I'll cease to function.
I'm making myself ill with worry.
I'm abnormal for worrying.
My mind can't take the worrying.
I'm losing out in life because of worrying.
My body can't take the worrying.

Information from: Hagen et al., 2017; Wells, 2011, 2010, 2005.

At the same time, Wells argues, people with generalized anxiety disorder also hold negative beliefs about worrying, and these negative attitudes are the ones that open the door to the disorder. Because society teaches them that worrying is a bad thing, they come to believe that their repeated worrying is in fact harmful (mentally and physically) and uncontrollable. Now they further worry about the fact that they always seem to be worrying (so-called *meta-worries*) (see **Table 5-3**). Their meta-worries may include concerns that they are "going crazy" with worry or losing out in life because of worrying. The net effect of all this worrying: generalized anxiety disorder.

> Why might many people believe, at least implicitly, that worrying is useful—even necessary—for problems to work out?

This explanation has received considerable research support. Studies indicate, for example, that people who generally hold both positive and negative beliefs about worrying are particularly prone to developing generalized anxiety disorder and that repeated metaworrying is a powerful predictor of developing the disorder (Craske, 2016; Wells, 2014, 2011, 2005).

According to another more recent explanation for generalized anxiety disorder, the *intolerance of uncertainty theory,* certain individuals cannot tolerate the knowledge that negative events *may* occur, even if the possibility of occurrence is very small. Inasmuch as life is filled with uncertain events, these individuals worry constantly that such events are about to occur. Such intolerance and worrying leave them highly vulnerable to the development of generalized anxiety disorder (Koerner, Mejia, & Kusec, 2017; Dugas et al., 2012, 2010, 2004). Think of when you meet someone you're attracted to and how you then feel prior to texting or calling this person for the first time—or how you feel while you're waiting for the individual to contact you for the first time. The worry that you experience in such instances—the sense of unbearable uncertainty over the possibility of an unacceptable negative outcome—is, according to this theory, how people with generalized anxiety disorder feel all the time.

Proponents of this theory believe people with generalized anxiety disorder keep worrying and worrying in their efforts to find "correct" solutions for various situations in their lives and to restore certainty to the situations. However, because they can never really be sure that a given solution is a correct one, they are always left to grapple with intolerable levels of uncertainty, triggering new rounds of worrying and new efforts to find correct solutions. Like the metacognitive theory of worry, considerable research supports this theory. Studies have found, for example, that people with generalized anxiety disorder display higher levels of intolerance of uncertainty than people with normal degrees of anxiety (Koerner et al., 2017; Dugas et al., 2012, 2004). Research also suggests that intolerance of uncertainty develops in early childhood

Fearful delights Many people enjoy the feeling of fear as long as it occurs under controlled circumstances, as when they are safely watching the tension grow in the hugely popular series of *Paranormal Activity* movies. These six films are among the most profitable ever made. In this scene from the first film, the lead character Katie tries to escape a supernatural presence in her house.

Productions/REX/Shutterstock

(Osmanağaoğlu et al., 2018; Sanchez et al., 2017) and can be passed on from parents to children (Sanchez, Kendall, & Comer, 2016).

Finally, a third relatively recent explanation for generalized anxiety disorder, the *avoidance theory*, developed by researcher Thomas Borkovec, suggests that people with this disorder have greater bodily arousal (higher heart rate, perspiration, respiration) than other people and that worrying actually serves to *reduce* this arousal, perhaps by distracting the individuals from their unpleasant physical feelings (Craske, 2016; Borkovec, Alcaine, & Behar, 2004). In short, the avoidance theory holds that people with generalized anxiety disorder worry repeatedly in order to reduce or avoid uncomfortable states of bodily arousal. When, for example, they find themselves in an uncomfortable job situation or social relationship, they implicitly choose to worry about losing their job or losing a friend rather than having to stew in a state of intense negative arousal.

Borkovec's explanation has also been supported by numerous studies. Research reveals that people with generalized anxiety disorder experience particularly fast and intense bodily reactions, find such reactions overwhelming, worry more than other people upon becoming aroused, and successfully reduce their arousal whenever they worry (Liera & Newman, 2014; Hirsch et al., 2012).

Cognitive-Behavioral Therapies Two kinds of cognitive-behavioral approaches are used in cases of generalized anxiety disorder. In one, based on the pioneering work of Ellis and Beck, therapists help clients change the maladaptive assumptions that characterize their disorder (Meichenbaum, 2017). In the other, "new-wave" cognitive-behavioral therapists (see page 65) help clients to understand the special role that worrying may play in their disorder, modify their views about worrying, and change their behavioral reactions to such unnerving concerns.

CHANGING MALADAPTIVE ASSUMPTIONS In Ellis' technique of **rational-emotive therapy,** therapists point out the irrational assumptions held by clients, suggest more appropriate assumptions, and assign homework that gives the clients practice at challenging old assumptions and applying new ones (Ellis, 2016, 2014). Studies suggest that this and similar approaches bring at least modest relief to those suffering from generalized anxiety (Kishita & Laidlaw, 2017; Clark & Beck, 2012, 2010). Ellis' approach is illustrated in the following discussion between him and an anxious client who fears failure and disapproval at work, especially over a testing procedure that she has developed for her company:

Client: *I'm so distraught these days that I can hardly concentrate on anything for more than a minute or two at a time. My mind just keeps wandering to that damn testing procedure I devised, and that they've put so much money into; and whether it's going to work well or be just a waste of all that time and money. . . .*

Ellis: *Point one is that you must admit that you are telling yourself something to start your worrying going, and you must begin to look, and I mean really look, for the specific nonsense with which you keep reindoctrinating yourself. . . . The false statement is: "If, because my testing procedure doesn't work and I am functioning inefficiently on my job, my co-workers do not want me or approve of me, then I shall be a worthless person." . . .*

Client: *But if I want to do what my firm also wants me to do, and I am useless to them, aren't I also useless to me?*

Ellis: *No—not unless you think you are. You are frustrated, of course, if you want to set up a good testing procedure and you can't. But need you be desperately unhappy because you are frustrated? And need you deem yourself completely unworthwhile because you can't do one of the main things you want to do in life?*

(Ellis, 1962, pp. 160–165)

#FearfulFilms

Top Grossing Horror Movie Series

1. *Alien* (7 films)

2. *Saw* (7 films)

3. *Jaws* (4 films)

4. *Paranormal Activity* (6 films)

5. *Friday the 13th* (12 films)

6. *A Nightmare on Elm Street* (9 films)

7. *Scream* (4 films)

8. *The Conjuring* (3 films)

9. *Halloween* (10 films)

10. *The Exorcist* (5 films)

11. *Final Destination* (5 films)

Information from: Thompson, 2016.

rational-emotive therapy A cognitive therapy developed by Albert Ellis that helps clients identify and change the irrational assumptions and thinking that help cause their psychological disorder.

family pedigree study A research design in which investigators determine how many and which relatives of a person with a disorder have the same disorder.

benzodiazepines The most common group of antianxiety drugs, which includes Valium and Xanax.

gamma-aminobutyric acid (GABA) A neurotransmitter whose low activity in the brain's fear circuit has been linked to anxiety.

brain circuits Networks of brain structures that work together, triggering each other into action.

BREAKING DOWN WORRYING Alternatively, some of today's new-wave cognitive-behavioral therapists specifically guide clients with generalized anxiety disorder to recognize and change their dysfunctional use of worrying (Topper et al., 2017; Craske, 2016; Wells, 2014, 2010). They begin by educating the clients about the role of worrying in their disorder and have them observe their bodily arousal and cognitive responses across various life situations. In turn, the clients come to appreciate the triggers of their worrying, their misconceptions about worrying, and their misguided efforts to control their lives by worrying. As their insights grow, clients are expected to see the world as less threatening (and so less arousing), try out more constructive ways of dealing with arousal, and worry less about the fact that they worry so much. Research indicates that a concentrated focus on worrying is indeed a helpful addition to the traditional cognitive-behavioral treatment for generalized anxiety disorder (Topper et al., 2017; Craske, 2016).

Treating individuals with generalized anxiety disorder by helping them to recognize their inclination to worry is similar to another cognitive-behavioral approach that has gained popularity in recent years. The approach, *mindfulness-based cognitive-behavioral therapy,* which you read about in Chapter 3, was brought into the mainstream by psychologist Steven Hayes and his colleagues as part of their broader treatment approach called *acceptance and commitment therapy* (Hayes, 2016). Here therapists help clients to become aware of their streams of thoughts, including their worries, as they are occurring and to *accept* such thoughts as mere events of the mind. By accepting their worries rather than trying to eliminate them, the clients are expected to be less upset by them and less influenced by them in their behaviors and life decisions. This is indeed what happens for many clients with generalized anxiety disorder when they receive this and related forms of treatment (Hoge et al., 2018; Kishita & Laidlaw, 2017; Eustis et al., 2016).

Mindfulness-based therapy has also been applied to a range of other psychological problems, such as depression, posttraumatic stress disorder, personality disorders, and substance use disorders, often with promising results (Segal, 2017; Hayes, 2016; Levin et al., 2015). As we observed in Chapter 3, this cognitive-behavioral approach borrows heavily from a form of meditation called *mindfulness meditation,* which teaches people to pay attention to the thoughts and feelings that flow through their mind during meditation and to accept such thoughts in a nonjudgmental way.

The Biological Perspective

Biological theorists believe that generalized anxiety disorder is caused chiefly by biological factors. For years this claim was supported primarily by **family pedigree studies,** in which researchers determine how many and which relatives of a person with a disorder have the same disorder. If biological tendencies toward generalized anxiety disorder are inherited, people who are biologically related should have similar probabilities of developing this disorder. Studies have in fact found that biological relatives of persons with generalized anxiety disorder are more likely than nonrelatives to have the disorder also (Havinga et al., 2017; Schienle et al., 2011). Approximately 15 percent of the relatives of people with the disorder display it themselves—a much higher prevalence rate than that found in the general population. And the closer the relative (an identical twin, for example), the greater the likelihood that he or she will also have the disorder.

Biological Explanations In recent decades, important discoveries by brain researchers have offered clearer evidence that generalized anxiety disorder is related to biological factors (Shinba, 2017). One of the first such discoveries was made in the 1950s, when investigators determined that **benzodiazepines,** the family of drugs that includes *alprazolam* (Xanax), *lorazepam* (Ativan), and *diazepam* (Valium), provide relief from anxiety. At first, no one understood why

Do monkeys experience anxiety? Clinical researchers must be careful in interpreting the reactions of animal subjects. This infant monkey was considered "fearful" after being separated from its mother. But perhaps it was feeling depressed or experiencing arousal that does not correspond to either fear or depression.

University of Wisconsin Primate Library, Madison

benzodiazepines reduce anxiety. Eventually, however, researchers were able to pinpoint the exact neurons in the brain to which benzodiazepines travel (Mohler & Okada, 1977). Apparently certain neurons have receptors that receive the benzodiazepines, just as a lock receives a key.

Investigators then discovered that these benzodiazepine receptors ordinarily receive **gamma-aminobutyric acid (GABA),** a common neurotransmitter in the brain (Muller et al., 2017). As you read in Chapter 3, neurotransmitters are chemicals that carry messages from one neuron to another. GABA carries *inhibitory* messages: when GABA is received at a receptor, it causes the neuron to stop firing.

On the basis of these and related findings, biological researchers reasoned that GABA must play a key role in the reduction of normal, everyday fear reactions. They concluded that when people become fearful, key neurons throughout the brain fire more rapidly, creating a general state of excitability throughout the brain, and bodily reactions such as perspiration, breathing, and muscle tension increase. To counteract this state of fear, some neurons throughout the brain release the neurotransmitter GABA, which then binds to GABA receptors on certain neurons and instructs those neurons to stop firing. The state of excitability ceases, and the experience of fear or anxiety subsides (Dubrovina, 2016; Costa, 1985, 1983).

Initially, researchers believed that GABA activity throughout the brain must be deficient in people with generalized anxiety disorder. Perhaps such individuals generally produce too little GABA, have too few GABA receptors, or have faulty GABA receptors—causing an experience of unchecked anxiety much of the time (Salari et al., 2015; Bremner & Charney, 2010). This GABA-focused explanation for generalized anxiety disorder carried the day throughout the 1980s and 1990s. However, research conducted in this century indicates that the biological basis of generalized anxiety disorder is more complicated than the disturbed activity of a single neurotransmitter.

Investigators now know that fear reactions—like most other emotional, behavioral, and cognitive reactions—are tied to **brain circuits**, networks of brain structures that work together, triggering each other into action. As you read in Chapter 3, in a given brain circuit, the long axons of the neurons from one structure bundle together, extend across the brain, and use neurotransmitters to communicate with the neurons of another structure—thus setting up visible fiber pathways between the regions (see pages 48–49). The particular circuit that produces and manages fear reactions, often called the "fear circuit," includes such brain structures as the *prefrontal cortex, anterior cingulate cortex, insula,* and *amygdala,* a small almond-shaped brain structure that usually starts the emotional ball rolling (see **Figure 5-2**).

Studies reveal that the fear circuit is excessively active (that is, *hyperactive*) in people with generalized anxiety disorder, producing experiences of fear and worry that are excessive in number and duration (Williams, 2017; Makovac et al., 2016; Lang et al., 2014). Thus many theorists believe that improper functioning by this circuit is responsible for the development of generalized anxiety disorder (Duval et al., 2015). GABA is one of the important neurotransmitters at work in this circuit (particularly in the amygdala), so low GABA activity could indeed help produce circuit hyperactivity and, as initially suggested, lead to the development of generalized anxiety disorder (Delli Pizzi et al., 2016; Nuss, 2015). At the same time, however, studies suggest that improper functioning by various neurons, structures, interconnections, or other neurotransmitters throughout the fear circuit can also lead to broad circuit hyperactivity. In turn, these other sources of dysfunction could be contributing factors in the development of generalized anxiety disorder (Makovac et al., 2016).

It is important to note that although most biological researchers now believe that dysfunction of the fear circuit underlies

#DelayedDiagnosis

It is estimated that 45 percent of clients in treatment for generalized anxiety disorder had suffered from its symptoms for 2 or more years before being diagnosed correctly (Bandelow & Michaelis, 2015).

FIGURE 5-2

The Biology of Anxiety

The circuit in the brain that helps produce anxiety reactions includes structures such as the amygdala, prefrontal cortex, anterior cingulate cortex, and insula (not visible from this view of the brain).

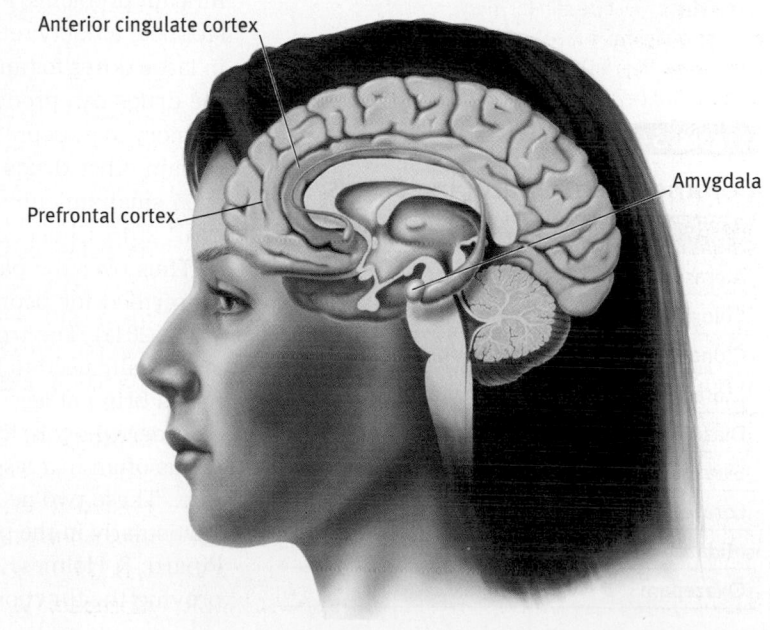

Anterior cingulate cortex

Amygdala

Prefrontal cortex

sedative-hypnotic drugs Drugs that calm people at lower doses and help them to fall asleep at higher doses.

phobia A persistent and unreasonable fear of a particular object, activity, or situation.

specific phobia A severe and persistent fear of a specific object or situation.

generalized anxiety disorder, they do not yet fully understand the fear circuit itself. They are, for example, still in the process of identifying all parts of the fear circuit (Lebow & Chen, 2016; LeDoux & Pine, 2016). Indeed, only in recent years, have they come to appreciate that a previously neglected brain structure in the fear circuit, *the bed nucleus of the stria terminalis (BNST)*, may play as large a role (or larger) in fear reactions as the four regions mentioned above.

Similarly, researchers are not yet certain that the fear circuit is in fact a *single* circuit. Pioneering neuroscientist Joseph Ledoux, the individual who first coined the term "fear circuit," now believes that it is more accurate to view it as two separate circuits—one, a circuit that produces the physical and behavioral reactions associated with fear, such as breathing faster or reflexively running away from danger, and the other, a circuit that produces the cognitive processes that often accompany fear, such as appraisal of threat, remembering, anticipation, and worry. According to LeDoux, dysfunction of the latter circuit (which includes the prefrontal cortex, insula, and BNST) may be more responsible for the development of generalized anxiety disorder than dysfunction of the former circuit (which features the amygdala and other brain structures) (LeDoux & Pine, 2016).

Drug Therapies After their discovery in the 1950s, benzodiazepines were marketed as **sedative-hypnotic drugs**—drugs that calm people in low doses and help them fall asleep in higher doses. The benzodiazepines seemed less addictive than previous sedative-hypnotic medications, such as *barbiturates,* and they appeared to produce less tiredness. Thus, these newly discovered drugs were quickly embraced by both doctors and patients, and many new ones were developed to help alleviate anxiety (see **Table 5-4**).

> Why are antianxiety drugs so popular in today's world? Does their popularity say something about our society?

As you have read, researchers eventually learned that benzodiazepines reduce anxiety by traveling to receptor sites in the brain circuit—particularly in the amygdala—that ordinarily receive the neurotransmitter GABA. Apparently, when benzodiazepines bind to these neuron receptor sites, they increase the ability of GABA itself to bind to the sites and to stop neurons from firing, thus helping to improve the overall functioning of the fear circuit and, in turn, reducing an individual's excessive levels of anxiety (Muller et al., 2017; Griebel & Holmes, 2013).

Studies indicate that as many as 60 percent of people with generalized anxiety disorder experience at least some improvement when they take benzodiazepines, compared to 40 percent of similar individuals who take placebo drugs (Bystritsky, 2016; Islam et al., 2014). However, clinicians have come to realize that these drugs pose significant problems. First, the effects of the medications are short-lived. When they are stopped, anxiety returns as strong as ever. Second, people who take benzodiazepines in large doses for an extended time can become physically dependent on them. Third, the drugs can produce undesirable effects such as drowsiness, lack of coordination, memory loss, depression, and aggressive behavior. Finally, the drugs mix badly with certain other drugs or substances. If, for example, people on benzodiazepines drink even small amounts of alcohol, their breathing can slow down dangerously (Gudin et al., 2016; Chollet et al., 2013).

Thus over the past two decades, other kinds of drugs have become more widely prescribed for people with generalized anxiety disorder (Perna et al., 2016; Comer et al., 2011). The treatment of choice is now *antidepressant* medications, drugs that are usually used to lift the moods of depressed persons. Like benzodiazepines, these drugs bring at least some relief to 60 percent of the people with generalized anxiety disorder who take them (Bystritsky, 2016). As you will see in Chapter 8, antidepressant drugs often increase the activity of the neurotransmitters *serotonin* and *norepinephrine*. These two neurotransmitters are prominent in certain parts of the fear circuit, particularly in the prefrontal cortex and the amygdala (LeDoux & Pine, 2016; Bukalo, Pinard, & Holmes, 2014). The antidepressant drugs may help relieve anxiety by improving the functioning of the fear circuit in these areas.

TABLE: 5-4

Common Benzodiazepine Drugs

Generic Name	Trade Name(s)
Alprazolam	Xanax
Chlordiazepoxide	Librium
Clonazepam	Klonopin
Clorazepate	Tranxene
Diazepam	Valium
Estazolam	ProSom
Lorazepam	Ativan
Midazolam	Versed
Oxazepam	Serax

Finally, *antipsychotic* medications, drugs commonly given to people with schizophrenia and other forms of psychosis, are also helpful to some individuals with generalized anxiety disorder (Bystritsky, 2016). These drugs may help relieve anxiety by altering the activity of *dopamine,* yet another neurotransmitter of importance in certain parts of the fear circuit (Bukalo et al., 2014). At the same time, antipsychotic medications can produce serious side effects of their own, as you will see in Chapter 15, raising concerns about their growing use for anxiety symptoms (Weber et al., 2016).

Phobias

A PHOBIA IS A PERSISTENT and unreasonable fear of a particular object, activity, or situation. People with a phobia (from the Greek word for "fear") become fearful if they even think about the object or situation they dread, but they usually remain comfortable as long as they avoid it or thoughts about it.

We all have our areas of special fear, and it is normal for some things to upset us more than other things (see *InfoCentral* on the next page). How do such common fears differ from phobias? DSM-5 indicates that a phobia is more intense and persistent and the desire to avoid the object or situation is stronger (APA, 2013). People with phobias often feel so much distress that their fears may interfere dramatically with their lives.

Most phobias technically fall under the category of *specific phobias,* DSM-5's label for an intense and persistent fear of a specific object or situation. In addition, there is a broader kind of phobia called *agoraphobia,* a fear of venturing into public places or situations where escape might be difficult if one were to become panicky or incapacitated.

Specific Phobias

A **specific phobia** is a persistent fear of a specific object or situation (see **Table 5-5**). When sufferers are exposed to the object or situation, they typically experience immediate fear. Common specific phobias are intense fears of specific animals or insects, heights, enclosed spaces, thunderstorms, and blood. Here Andrew talks about his phobic fear of flying:

> *We got on board, and then there was the take-off. There it was again, that horrible feeling as we gathered speed. It was creeping over me again, that old feeling of panic. I kept seeing everyone as puppets, all strapped to their seats with no control over their destinies, me included. Every time the plane did a variation of speed or route, my heart would leap and I would hurriedly ask what was happening. When the plane started to lose height, I was terrified that we were about to crash.*
>
> (Melville, 1978, p. 59)

Each year as many as 10 percent of all people in the United States have the symptoms of a specific phobia (McCabe, 2017; Bandelow & Michaelis, 2015; Kessler et al., 2012). Almost 14 percent of individuals develop such phobias at some point during their lives, and many people have more than one at a time. Women with the disorder outnumber men by at least 2 to 1. The impact of a specific phobia on a person's life depends on what arouses the fear (McCabe, 2017; Costa et al., 2014). People whose phobias center on dogs, insects, or water will keep encountering the objects they dread. Their efforts to avoid them must be elaborate and may greatly restrict their activities. Urban residents with snake phobias have a much easier time. At most, 32 percent of people with a specific phobia seek treatment (NIMH, 2017; McCabe, 2017; Bandelow & Michaelis, 2015). Most individuals with the disorder try instead to avoid the objects they fear.

#ImproperSuffix?

In 2012, the Associated Press banned its reporters from using the increasingly popular suffix "-phobia" when describing people who are intolerant of particular groups of individuals. The news organization's reason was that such uses of the suffix—for example, "homophobia," "xenophobia," "Islamophobia," and "transphobia")—inaccurately ascribes a mental disability to prejudiced people, suggesting a knowledge the reporters (and society) do not have (Hess, 2016).

TABLE: 5-5

Dx Checklist

Specific Phobia

1. Marked, persistent, and disproportionate fear of a particular object or situation; usually lasting at least 6 months

2. Exposure to the object produces immediate fear

3. Avoidance of the feared situation

4. Significant distress or impairment

Information from: APA 2013.

FEAR

Fear is a normal part of life. Like all emotions, it can be good or bad. On the positive side, fear can alert us to danger, help us behave constructively, and guide us to make wise decisions. Up to a point it can be stimulating and even fun. On the negative side, fear can be excessive and inappropriate and contribute to phobias and other anxiety disorders.

CROSSING THE LINE

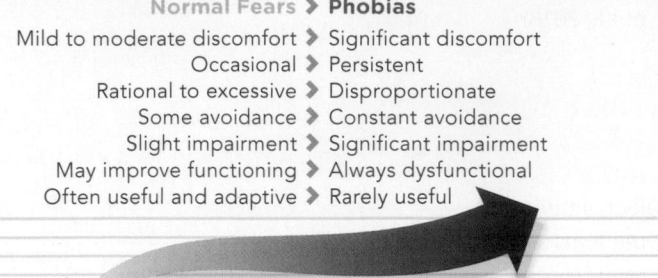

Normal Fears	❯	Phobias
Mild to moderate discomfort	❯	Significant discomfort
Occasional	❯	Persistent
Rational to excessive	❯	Disproportionate
Some avoidance	❯	Constant avoidance
Slight impairment	❯	Significant impairment
May improve functioning	❯	Always dysfunctional
Often useful and adaptive	❯	Rarely useful

FEARS HELP US TO:

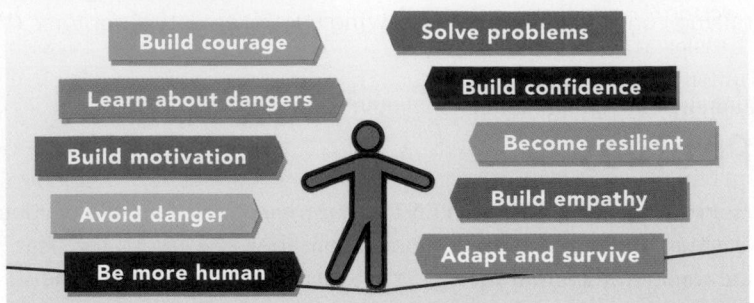

Build courage
Solve problems
Learn about dangers
Build confidence
Build motivation
Become resilient
Avoid danger
Build empathy
Be more human
Adapt and survive

(Sam, 2016)

HOW TO CONQUER OUR FEARS

Clinicians have developed special techniques — such as exposure-based treatments — to help people overcome pathological fear. However, there are a number of things people can do on their own to help reduce their problematic everyday fears. Some of these things are but minor-league versions of exposure therapy and other clinical treatments.

Perform increasingly frightening acts | Employ simple deep breathing | Exercise | Participate in relaxing activities (e.g., listen to music) | Challenge scary thoughts with evidence | Gradually and repeatedly face the fear | Recall past fears you have resolved | Don't let unreasonable fears guide your decisions or behaviors

(Smith et al., 2017)

BIGGEST FEARS IN TODAY'S WORLD

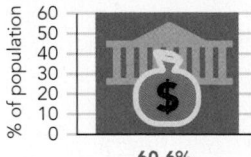

% of population (0–60)

60.6%	41%	39.9%	38.5%	38.1%	37.5%	37.1%	35.9%
Corruption of government officials	Terrorist attacks	Not having enough money for the future	Government regulations of firearms and ammunition	Death of loved ones	Economic or financial collapse	Identity theft	Serious illness of loved ones

(Bowerman, 2016)

BIGGEST EXISTENTIAL FEARS

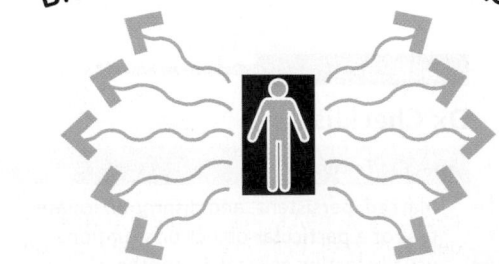

- Failure
- Death
- Rejection
- Ridicule
- Misery
- Disappointment
- Pain
- The unknown
- Loss of freedom
- Inadequacy
- Being judged
- Change
- Loneliness
- Uncertainty
- Separation
- Being unimportant
- Deprivation

(McGauran, 2016; Wisehart, 2015)

THE ODDS ARE IN YOUR FAVOR!

While we all worry about possible calamities, we typically forget that they are unlikely — sometimes very unlikely — to happen. What is the probability that what we fear will actually happen?

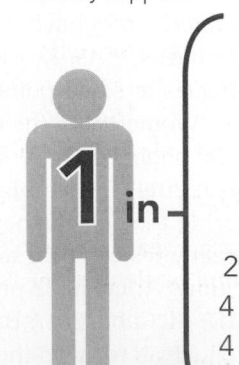

1 in

200	Your house/apartment will have a fire this year
322	You will be a victim of a violent crime
885	You will be a victim of robbery this year
8,000	You will receive a diagnosis of cancer this year
20,000	You will be murdered this year
42,000	You will be hit by a baseball at a major-league game
286,000	You will contract AIDS from a blood transfusion
4 million	You will be attacked by a shark
4 million	You will be killed on your next automobile outing
10 million	You will die from a lightning strike

(FBI, 2017, 2014; Glovin, 2014; CDC, 2013; Quillian & Pager, 2010; Britt, 2005)

Agoraphobia

People with **agoraphobia** are afraid of being in public places or situations where escape might be difficult or help unavailable, should they experience panic or become incapacitated (APA, 2013) (see **Table 5-6**). This is a pervasive and complex phobia. Around 1.7 percent of the population experience agoraphobia in any given year; around 2.6 percent display it at some point in their lives (Bandelow & Michaelis, 2015; Kessler et al., 2012). The disorder also is twice as common among women as men and among poor people as wealthy people (Bandelow & Michaelis, 2015; Sareen et al., 2011). Around 46 percent of those with agoraphobia receive treatment for it (NIMH, 2017).

It is typical of people with agoraphobia to avoid entering crowded streets or stores, driving in parking lots or on bridges, and traveling on public transportation or in airplanes. If they venture out of the house at all, it is usually only in the company of close relatives or friends. Some insist that family members or friends stay with them at home, but even at home and in the company of others they may continue to feel anxious.

In many cases the intensity of the agoraphobia fluctuates. In severe cases, people become virtual prisoners in their own homes. Their social life dwindles and they cannot hold a job. People with agoraphobia may also become depressed, sometimes as a result of the severe limitations that their disorder places on their lives (McCabe, 2016).

Many people with agoraphobia do, in fact, have extreme and sudden explosions of fear, called *panic attacks,* when they enter public places, a problem that may have first set the stage for their development of agoraphobia. Such individuals may receive two diagnoses—agoraphobia and *panic disorder,* an anxiety disorder that you will read about later in this chapter—because their difficulties extend considerably beyond an excessive fear of venturing away from home into public places (APA, 2013).

What Causes Phobias?

Each of the models offers explanations for phobias. Those offered by *cognitive-behavioral* theorists have received the most research support. Focusing primarily on the behavioral dimension of this disorder, they believe that people with phobias first learn to fear certain objects, situations, or events through conditioning (McCabe, 2017; Field & Purkis, 2012). Once the fears are acquired, the individuals avoid the dreaded object or situation, permitting the fears to become all the more entrenched.

How Are Fears Learned? Many cognitive-behavioral theorists propose **classical conditioning** as a common way of acquiring phobic reactions. Here, two events that occur close together in time become strongly associated in a person's mind, and the person then reacts similarly to both of them. If one event triggers a fear response, the other may also.

In the 1920s, a clinician described the case of a young woman who apparently acquired a specific phobia of running water through classical conditioning (Bagby, 1922). When she was 7 years old she went on a picnic with her mother and aunt and ran off by herself into the woods after lunch. While she was climbing over some large rocks, her feet became caught between two of them. The harder she tried to free herself, the more trapped she became. No one heard her screams, and she grew more and more terrified. In the language of behaviorists, the entrapment was eliciting a fear response.

Entrapment → Fear response

As she struggled to free her feet, the girl heard a waterfall nearby. The sound of the running water became linked in her mind to her terrifying battle with the rocks, and she developed a fear of running water as well.

Running water → Fear response

TABLE: 5-6

Dx Checklist

Agoraphobia

1. Pronounced, disproportionate, or repeated fear about being in at least two of the following situations:
   - Public transportation (e.g., auto or plane travel)
   - Parking lots, bridges, or other open spaces
   - Shops, theaters, or other confined places
   - Lines or crowds
   - Away from home unaccompanied

2. Fear of such agoraphobic situations derives from a concern that it would be hard to escape or get help if panic, embarrassment, or disabling symptoms were to occur

3. Avoidance of the agoraphobic situations

4. Symptoms usually continue for at least 6 months

5. Significant distress or impairment

Information from: APA, 2013.

agoraphobia An anxiety disorder in which a person is afraid to be in public situations from which escape might be difficult or help unavailable if panic-like or embarrassing symptoms were to occur.

classical conditioning A process of learning in which two events that repeatedly occur close together in time become tied together in a person's mind and so produce the same response.

Barcroft Media/Getty Images

Phobias, not Although these young women cling tightly to each other, frozen with fear as they try to walk across a bridge, they are not displaying abnormal fear or a phobia. A closer look reveals that the bridge, which stands 600 feet high and spans 1000 feet, has a glass floor, the first of its kind in China. Almost all visitors to this new tourist destination initially experience the same emotional reaction—overwhelming and near-paralyzing fear.

Eventually the aunt found the screaming child, freed her from the rocks, and comforted her, but the psychological damage had been done. From that day forward, the girl was terrified of running water. For years family members had to hold her down to bathe her. When she traveled on a train, friends had to cover the windows so that she would not have to look at any streams. The young woman had apparently acquired a specific phobia through classical conditioning.

In conditioning terms, the entrapment was an *unconditioned stimulus* (*US*) that understandably elicited an *unconditioned response* (*UR*) of fear. The running water represented a *conditioned stimulus* (*CS*), a formerly neutral stimulus that became associated with entrapment in the child's mind and came also to elicit a fear reaction. The newly acquired fear was a *conditioned response* (*CR*).

US: Entrapment → UR: Fear

CS: Running water → CR: Fear

Another way of acquiring a fear reaction is through **modeling,** that is, through observation and imitation (Bandura & Rosenthal, 1966). A person may observe that others are afraid of certain objects or events and develop fears of the same things. Consider a young boy whose mother is afraid of illnesses, doctors, and hospitals. If she frequently expresses those fears, before long the boy himself may fear illnesses, doctors, and hospitals.

Why should one or a few upsetting experiences or observations develop into a long-term phobia? Shouldn't the trapped girl see later that running water will bring her no harm? Shouldn't the boy see later that illnesses are temporary and doctors and hospitals helpful? Cognitive-behavioral theorists believe that after acquiring a fear response, people try to *avoid* what they fear. They do not get close to the dreaded objects often enough to learn that the objects are really quite harmless.

How Have Cognitive-Behavioral Explanations Fared in Research? Some laboratory studies have found that animals and humans can indeed be taught to fear objects through classical conditioning (Miller, 1948; Mowrer, 1947, 1939). In one famous report, psychologists John B. Watson and Rosalie Rayner (1920) described how they taught a baby boy called Little Albert to fear white rats. For weeks Albert was allowed to play with a white rat and appeared to enjoy doing so. One time when Albert reached

modeling A process of learning in which a person observes and then imitates others. Also, a therapy approach based on the same principle.

preparedness A predisposition to develop certain fears.

What concerns might today's human-participant research review boards raise about the study on Little Albert?

for the rat, however, the experimenter struck a steel bar with a hammer, making a very loud noise that frightened Albert. The next several times that Albert reached for the rat, the experimenter again made the loud noise. Albert acquired a fear and avoidance response to the rat.

Research has also supported the cognitive-behavioral position that fears can be acquired through modeling. In a pioneering study, for example, psychologists Albert Bandura and Theodore Rosenthal (1966), had human research participants observe a person apparently being shocked by electricity whenever a buzzer sounded. The victim was actually the experimenter's accomplice—in research terminology, a *confederate*—who pretended to feel pain by twitching and yelling whenever the buzzer was turned on. After the unsuspecting participants had observed several such episodes, they themselves had a fear reaction whenever they heard the buzzer. Similarly, some studies on children with real-life fears and phobias have found that modeling played a key role in the acquisition of such problems (Reynolds et al., 2017; Askew et al., 2016).

Although these studies support cognitive-behavioral explanations of phobias, other research has called those explanations into question (McCabe, 2017; Gamble et al., 2010). Several laboratory studies with children and adults have failed to condition fear reactions. In addition, although many case studies have traced phobias to incidents of classical conditioning or modeling, quite a few fail to do so. So, although it appears that a phobia *can* be acquired by classical conditioning or modeling, researchers have not established that the disorder is *ordinarily* acquired in this way.

A Behavioral-Evolutionary Explanation Some phobias are much more common than others. Phobic reactions to animals, heights, and darkness are more common than phobic reactions to meat, grass, and houses. Theorists often account for these differences by proposing that human beings, as a species, have a predisposition to develop certain fears (McCabe, 2017; McNally, 2016; Seligman, 1971). This idea is referred to as **preparedness** because human beings, theoretically, are "prepared" to acquire some phobias and not others. The following case makes the point:

> *A four-year-old girl was playing in the park. Thinking that she saw a snake, she ran to her parents' car and jumped inside, slamming the door behind her. Unfortunately, the girl's hand was caught by the closing car door, the results of which were severe pain and several visits to the doctor. Before this, she may have been afraid of snakes, but not phobic. After this experience, a phobia developed, not of cars or car doors, but of snakes. The snake phobia persisted into adulthood, at which time she sought treatment from me.*
>
> (Marks, 1977, p. 192)

Where might such predispositions to fear come from? According to some theorists, the predispositions have been transmitted genetically through an evolutionary process. Among our ancestors, the ones who more readily acquired fears of animals, darkness, heights, and the like were more likely to survive long enough to reproduce and to pass on their fear inclinations to their offspring (McNally, 2016; Ohman & Mineka, 2003).

How Are Phobias Treated?

Every theoretical model has its own approach to treating phobias, but the cognitive-behavioral approach is more widely used and, according to research, more successful than the rest, particularly for specific phobias. Here again, practitioners of the model focus primarily on the behavioral dimension of phobias.

New best friends? Is a mouse's fear of cats a conditioned reaction or genetically hardwired? Scientists at Tokyo University used genetic engineering to switch off this rodent's instinct to cower at the smell or presence of cats. But mouse beware! The cat has not been genetically engineered correspondingly.

AP Photo/Ko and Reiko Kobayakawa, Tokyo University, Department of Biophysics and Biochemistry, Graduate School of Science

Treatments for Specific Phobias Specific phobias were among the first anxiety disorders to be treated successfully. The major cognitive-behavioral approach to treating them is **exposure treatment**, an approach in which people are exposed to the objects or situations they dread (Choy, 2016). There are actually a number of different exposure techniques. Three of the oldest, and most famous, are *systematic desensitization, flooding,* and *modeling.*

People treated by **systematic desensitization,** an exposure technique developed by Joseph Wolpe (1987, 1969), learn to relax while gradually facing the objects or situations they fear. Since relaxation and fear are incompatible, the new relaxation response is thought to substitute for the fear response. Desensitization therapists first offer *relaxation training* to clients, teaching them how to bring on a state of deep muscle relaxation at will. In addition, the therapists help clients create a *fear hierarchy,* a list of feared objects or situations, ordered from mildly to extremely upsetting.

Then clients learn how to pair relaxation with the objects or situations they fear. While the client is in a state of relaxation, the therapist has the client face the event at the bottom of his or her hierarchy. This may be an actual confrontation, a process called *in vivo desensitization.* A person who fears heights, for example, may stand on a chair or climb a stepladder. Or the confrontation may be imagined, a process called *covert desensitization.* In this case, the person imagines the frightening event while the therapist describes it. The client moves through the entire list, pairing his or her relaxation responses with each feared item. Because the first item is only mildly frightening, it is usually only a short while before the person is able to relax totally in its presence. Over the course of several sessions, clients move up the ladder of their fears until they reach and overcome the one that frightens them most of all.

Another exposure treatment for specific phobias is **flooding.** Therapists who use flooding believe that people will stop fearing things when they are exposed to them repeatedly and made to see that they are actually quite harmless. Clients are forced to face their feared objects or situations without relaxation training and without a gradual buildup. The flooding procedure, like desensitization, can be either in vivo or covert.

When flooding therapists guide clients in imagining feared objects or situations, they often exaggerate the description so that the clients experience intense emotional arousal. In the case of a woman with a snake phobia, the therapist had her imagine the following scene, among others:

> *Close your eyes again. Picture the snake out in front of you, now make yourself pick it up. Reach down, pick it up, put it in your lap, feel it wiggling around in your lap, leave your hand on it, put your hand out and feel it wiggling around. Kind of explore its body with your fingers and hand. You don't like to do it, make yourself do it. Make yourself do it. Really grab onto the snake. Squeeze it a little bit, feel it. Feel it kind of start to wind around your hand. Let it. Leave your hand there, feel it touching your hand and winding around it, curling around your wrist.*
>
> (Hogan, 1968, p. 423)

In another exposure technique, *modeling,* it is the therapist who confronts the feared object or situation while the fearful person observes (Bandura, 2011, 1977, 1971; Bandura et al., 1977). The therapist acts as a model to demonstrate that the person's fear is groundless. After several sessions many clients are able to approach the objects or situations calmly. In one version of modeling, *participant modeling,* the client is actively encouraged to join in with the therapist.

Clinical researchers have repeatedly found that these and other exposure treatments help people with specific phobias. Around 70 percent of phobic patients show significant improvement after receiving exposure treatment (Ryan et al., 2017; Choy,

Fearless Flying An individual sits in the cockpit of an airplane as part of a "Fear of Flying" course. This program for fearful flyers includes relaxation and stress management training, cognitive-behavioral therapy, education about the mechanics of flying, interviews with pilots, and multiple experiences in a flight simulator. As many as 6.5 percent of all people have aviophobia, a severe fear of flying, and another 25 percent feel very nervous about airplane travel.

exposure treatments Treatments in which persons are exposed to the objects or situations they dread.

systematic desensitization An exposure treatment that uses relaxation training and a fear hierarchy to help clients with phobias react calmly to the objects or situations they dread.

flooding An exposure treatment for phobias in which clients are exposed repeatedly and intensively to a feared object and made to see that it is actually harmless.

2016; McCabe & Swinson, 2015). The key to greater success in all forms of exposure treatment appears to be *actual* contact with the feared object or situation. That is, in vivo exposure tends to be more effective than covert exposure. It is also worth noting that a growing number of cognitive-behavioral therapists are using *virtual reality*—3D computer graphics that simulate real-world objects and situations—as an exposure tool, and are having considerable success with this approach (Botella et al., 2016; Dunsmoor et al., 2014). As you'll see in Chapter 6, the exposures provided by this computer tool are so intense that they often are as powerful as real-life exposures.

Boris Horvat/Getty Images

The world of exposure At a treatment program in France, this man undergoes exposure therapy to help him overcome acrophobia, a severe fear of heights. Wearing a virtual reality headset, he feels as if he is approaching a vast, deep canyon. Virtual reality techniques have greatly expanded the kinds of exposure available to clients receiving treatment for various anxiety disorders or OCD..

Treatments for Agoraphobia For years clinicians made little impact on agoraphobia, the fear of leaving one's home and entering public places. However, approaches have now been developed that enable many people with agoraphobia to venture out with less anxiety. These new approaches do not always bring as much relief to sufferers as the highly successful treatments for specific phobias, but they do offer considerable relief to many people.

Cognitive-behavioral therapists have again led the way, this time by developing a variety of exposure approaches for agoraphobia (Klan, Jasper, & Hiller, 2017; Gloster et al., 2015, 2014, 2011). The therapists typically help clients to venture farther and farther from their homes and to gradually enter outside places, one step at a time. Sometimes the clinicians use support, reasoning, and coaxing to get clients to confront the outside world. They also use more precise exposure methods, such as those described in the following case study:

[Lenita] was a young woman who, shortly after she married, found herself unable to leave home. Even walking a few yards from her front door terrified her. . . .

It is not surprising . . . that this young woman found herself unable to function independently after leaving home to marry. Her inability to leave her new home was reinforced by an increasing dependence on her husband and by the solicitous overconcern of her mother, who was more and more frequently called in to stay with her. . . . Since she was cut off from her friends and from so much enjoyment in the outside world, depression added to her misery. . . .

[After several years of worsening symptoms, Lenita was admitted to our psychiatric hospital.] To measure [her] improvement, we laid out a mile-long course from the hospital to downtown, marked at about 25-yard intervals. Before beginning [treatment], we asked the patient to walk as far as she could along the course. Each time she balked at the front door of the hospital. Then the first phase of [treatment] began: we held two sessions each day in which the patient was praised for staying out of the hospital for a longer and longer time. The reinforcement schedule was simple. If the patient stayed outside for 20 seconds on one trial and then on the next attempt stayed out for 30 seconds, she was praised enthusiastically. Now, however, the criterion for praise was raised—without the patient's knowledge—to 25 seconds. If she met the criterion she was again praised, and the time was increased again. If she did not stay out long enough, the therapist simply ignored her performance. To gain the therapist's attention, which she valued, she had to stay out longer each time.

This she did, until she was able to stay out for almost half an hour. But was she walking farther each time? Not at all. She was simply circling around in the front drive of the hospital, keeping the "safe place" in sight at all times. We therefore changed the reinforcement to reflect the distance walked. Now she began to walk farther and farther each time. Supported by this simple therapeutic procedure, the patient was progressively able to increase her self-confidence. . . .

(continued on the next page)

> *Praise was then thinned out, but slowly, and the patient was encouraged to walk anywhere she pleased. Five years later, she [is] still perfectly well. We might assume that the benefits of being more independent maintained the gains and compensated for the loss of praise from the therapist.*
>
> *(Agras, 1985, pp. 77–80)*

Exposure therapy for people with agoraphobia often includes additional features—particularly the use of support groups and home-based self-help programs—to motivate clients to work hard at their treatment. In the *support group* approach, a small number of people with agoraphobia go out together for exposure sessions that last for several hours. The group members support and encourage one another, and eventually coax one another to move away from the safety of the group and perform exposure tasks on their own. In the *home-based self-help programs,* clinicians give clients and their families detailed instructions for carrying out exposure treatments themselves.

Around 70 percent of agoraphobic clients who receive exposure treatment find it easier to enter public places, and the improvement persists for years (Gloster et al., 2015, 2014, 2011; Craske & Barlow, 2014). Unfortunately, these improvements are often partial rather than complete, and as many as half of successfully treated clients have relapses, although these people readily recapture previous gains if they are treated again. Those whose agoraphobia is accompanied by a panic disorder seem to benefit less than others from exposure therapy alone (Craske, 2015). We shall take a closer look at this group when we investigate treatments for panic disorder.

Ocean/Corbis

Recovering lost revenues Several amusement parks offer behavioral programs to help prospective customers overcome their fears of roller coasters and other horror rides. After "treatment," some clients are able to ride the rails with the best of them. For others, it's back to the relative calm of the Ferris wheel.

Social Anxiety Disorder

MANY PEOPLE ARE UNCOMFORTABLE when interacting with others or talking or performing in front of others. A number of entertainers and sports figures, from the singer Adele to baseball pitcher Zack Greinke, have described episodes of significant anxiety before performing. Social fears of this kind certainly are unpleasant, but usually the people who have them manage to function adequately.

People with **social anxiety disorder,** by contrast, have severe, persistent, and irrational anxiety about social or performance situations in which they may face scrutiny by others and possibly feel embarrassment (APA, 2013) (see **Table 5-7**). The social anxiety may be narrow, such as a fear of talking in public or eating in front of others, or it may be broad, such as a general fear of functioning poorly in front of others. In both forms, people repeatedly judge themselves as performing less competently than they actually do (see *MindTech* on page 135). It is because of its wide-ranging scope that this disorder is now called social anxiety disorder rather than *social phobia,* the label it had in past editions of the DSM.

> Why do so many professional performers seem prone to performance anxiety? Might their repeated exposure to audiences have a therapeutic effect?

Social anxiety disorder can interfere greatly with one's life (Schneier, 2016). A person who cannot interact with others or speak in public may fail to carry out important responsibilities. One who cannot eat in public may reject meal invitations and other social offerings. Since many people with this disorder keep their fears secret, their social reluctance is often misinterpreted as snobbery, lack of interest, or hostility.

social anxiety disorder A severe and persistent fear of social or performance situations in which embarrassment may occur.

Surveys reveal that 8 percent of people in the United States and other Western countries (around 60 percent of them female) experience social anxiety disorder in any given year (see Table 5-8). Around 13 percent develop this disorder at some point in their lives (Bandelow & Michaelis, 2015; Kessler et al., 2012). Poor people are 50 percent more likely than wealthier people to have social anxiety disorder (Sareen et al., 2011). Non-Hispanic white Americans are more likely to experience this problem than African, Hispanic, or Asian Americans (Hofmann & Hinton, 2014). It tends to begin in late childhood or adolescence and may continue into adulthood (Schneier, 2016; Detweiler et al., 2014). Around 40 percent of individuals with social anxiety disorder are currently in treatment (NIMH, 2017).

What Causes Social Anxiety Disorder?

The leading explanation for social anxiety disorder has been proposed by cognitive-behavioral theorists (Thurston et al., 2017; Heimberg et al, 2010). The explanation features an interplay of both cognitive and behavioral factors. As you read in Chapter 3, cognitive-behavioral theorists start with the contention that people with this disorder hold a group of dysfunctional beliefs and expectations regarding the social realm. These can include:

- Holding unrealistically high social standards and so believing that they must perform perfectly in social situations.
- Believing they are unattractive social beings.
- Believing they are socially unskilled and inadequate.
- Believing they are always in danger of behaving incompetently in social situations.
- Believing that inept behaviors in social situations will inevitably lead to terrible consequences.
- Believing they have no control over feelings of anxiety that emerge in social situations.

Cognitive-behavioral theorists hold that, because of these beliefs, people with social anxiety disorder keep anticipating that social disasters will occur, overestimate how poorly things go in their social interactions, and dread most social situations (Gavric et al., 2017). Moreover, they learn to perform "avoidance" and "safety" behaviors to

TABLE: 5-7

Dx Checklist

Social Anxiety Disorder

1. Pronounced, disproportionate, and repeated anxiety about social situation(s) in which the individual could be exposed to possible scrutiny by others; typically lasting 6 months or more

2. Fear of being negatively evaluated by or offensive to others

3. Exposure to the social situation almost always produces anxiety

4. Avoidance of feared situations

5. Significant distress or impairment

Information from: APA, 2013.

TABLE: 5-8

Profile of Anxiety Disorders and Obsessive-Compulsive Disorder

	One-Year Prevalence	Female to Male Ratio	Typical Age at Onset	Prevalence Among Close Relatives	Percentage Receiving Clinical Treatment Currently
Generalized anxiety disorder	4.0%	2:1	0–35 years	Elevated	43%
Specific phobia	10.0%	2:1	Variable	Elevated	32%
Agoraphobia	1.7%	2:1	15–35 years	Elevated	46%
Social anxiety disorder	8.0%	3:2	10–20 years	Elevated	40%
Panic disorder	3.1%	5:2	15–35 years	Elevated	59%
Obsessive-compulsive disorder	1.0%–2.0%	1:1	4–25 years	Elevated	40%

Information from: McCabe, 2017; NIMH, 2017; Watterson et al., 2017; Remes et al., 2016; Roy-Byrne, 2016; Simpson, 2016; Bandelow & Michaelis, 2015; Phillips, 2015; Kessler et al., 2010, 2005, 1999, 1994; Ritter et al., 2010; Wang et al., 2005.

Graham Denholm/Getty Images

Much harder than it looks World-renowned singer Adele performs in front of 60,000 people at a stadium in Melbourne, Australia, during her "Adele Live 2017" concert tour. When the gifted artist mesmerizes her fans in such venues, it is hard to believe that she has struggled for years with severe performance anxiety and related panic attacks, particularly when singing before large crowds.

#

#TheirWords

"There are two types of speakers. Those who get nervous and those who are liars."

Mark Twain

help prevent or reduce such disasters (Mesri et al., 2017; Piccirillo, Taylor Dryman, & Heimberg, 2016). Avoidance behaviors include, for example, avoiding parties or avoiding interactions with new coworkers or acquaintances. Safety behaviors include wearing makeup to cover up blushing or gloves to hide shaking hands. Behaviors of this kind are reinforced by reducing feelings of anxiety and the number of awkward encounters.

Researchers have found that people with social anxiety disorder do indeed manifest the beliefs, expectations, interpretations, feelings, and behaviors listed above (Parsons et al., 2017; Thurston et al., 2017; Moscovitch et al., 2013). These dysfunctional cognitions and behaviors have been tied to factors such as genetic predispositions, trait tendencies, biological abnormalities, traumatic childhood experiences, and overprotective parent-child interactions (Rodebaugh et al., 2017; Schneier, 2016).

Treatments for Social Anxiety Disorder

Only in recent decades have clinicians been able to treat social anxiety disorder successfully. Their success is due in part to the growing recognition that the disorder has two distinct features that may feed upon each other: (1) sufferers have overwhelming social fears, and (2) they often lack skill at starting conversations, communicating their needs, or meeting the needs of others. Armed with this insight, clinicians now treat social anxiety disorder by trying to reduce social fears, by providing training in social skills, or both.

How Can Social Fears Be Reduced?
Medication often helps alleviate social fears (Curtiss et al., 2017). Such fears are reduced to some degree in 55 percent of patients who take either benzodiazepines or antidepressant drugs, compared to 24 percent of similar patients who take placebo drugs (Stein, 2016). It appears that these medications bring about relief by improving functioning in the brain's fear circuit, which tends to be hyperactive for people with social anxiety disorder, just as it is in cases of generalized anxiety disorder (Brühl et al., 2014).

At the same time, cognitive-behavioral therapy has proved to be at least as effective as medication at reducing social fears, and people helped by this approach seem less likely to relapse than those treated with medications alone (Gregory & Peters, 2017; Thurston et al., 2017; Heimberg & Magee, 2014). This finding suggests to some clinicians that this form of therapy should always be featured in the treatment of social fears, either alone or in combination with medication.

To undo the cycle of problematic social beliefs and behaviors described earlier, cognitive-behavioral therapists combine both behavioral and cognitive techniques. On the behavioral side, they conduct *exposure therapy,* the intervention so effective with phobias. The therapists encourage clients to expose themselves to their dreaded social situations and to remain in these situations as their fears subside. Usually the exposure is gradual, and it often includes homework assignments. On the cognitive side, the clinicians and clients have systematic therapy discussions in which the clients are guided to re-examine and challenge their maladaptive beliefs and expectations, given the less-than-dire outcomes of their social exposures.

How Can Social Skills Be Improved?
In **social skills training,** also conducted by cognitive-behavioral therapists, several techniques are combined. The therapists usually *model* appropriate social behaviors for clients and encourage the individuals to try them out. The clients then *role-play* with the therapists, *rehearsing* their new behaviors until they become more effective. Throughout the process, therapists provide frank *feedback* and *reinforce* (praise) the clients for effective performances.

Reinforcement from other people with similar social difficulties is often more powerful than reinforcement from a therapist alone. Thus in *social skills training groups* and *assertiveness training groups,* members try out and rehearse new social behaviors

MINDTECH

Social Media Jitters

Cultura RM/Alamy

In recent years, researchers have learned that the use of computers and mobile devices can unintentionally produce various forms of anxiety, including social and generalized anxiety (Gao et al., 2018; Golbeck, 2016; Lepp et al., 2014).

The biggest culprit here seems to be spending too much time on social media such as Facebook, Instagram, or Snapchat. Although frequenting social network sites helps many people feel supported and included (Hu et al., 2017; ACOG, 2016), for others, the visits seem to produce significant insecurities and fears (Houston, 2016). Surveys suggest, for example, that more than one-third of social networkers develop a fear that others will post or use information or photos of them without their permission (Smith, 2014; Szalavitz, 2013). In addition, a fourth of all users feel a constant pressure to disclose too much personal information on their social networks, and a number feel intense pressure to post material that will be popular and get numerous comments and "likes." More than a few users also worry that they will discover posts about social activities from which they were excluded.

One study found that a third of users feel distinctly worse after visiting their social network—more anxious, more envious, and more dissatisfied with their lives (Krasnova et al., 2013). These feelings are particularly triggered when users observe vacation photos of other users, read birthday greetings received by other users, and see how many "likes" or comments others receive for their postings or photos. Such experiences seem to lead some users to worry that they are less desirable, less interesting, or less capable than most other social media users (Eckler, Kalyango, & Paasch, 2017; Hanna et al., 2017).

Can you think of other negative feelings that might be triggered by social networking?

Of course, as noted earlier, many of today's users do feel more positive about their social network visits. But even these people may have some social network–induced anxiety and tension. Around two-thirds, for example, are truly afraid that they will miss something if they don't check their social networks constantly—a phenomenon known as FOMO ("fear of missing out") (Thompson, 2016; Cool Infographics, 2013).

Social networking is not the only digital source of anxiety. Recent studies show that excessive cell phone use often results in high levels of anxiety and tension (Lepp et al., 2014). Why? Some theorists speculate that frequent phone users feel obligated to stay in touch with friends, another version of FOMO. Others believe that the rise in anxiety among heavy cell phone users is really the result of other cell phone effects, such as poorer performance in school or a reduction in positive time spent alone and self-reflecting (Archer, 2013). Whatever the explanation, two-thirds of cell phone users report feeling "panicked" when they misplace or lose their phones, even for a few minutes. Many experience "nomophobia" (no-mobile-phone-phobia), a pop term for the rush of fear that people have when they realize that they are disconnected from the world, friends, and family (Prizant-Passal et al., 2016; Archer, 2013).

---

with other group members. Such groups also provide guidance on what is socially appropriate. According to research, social skills training, both individual and group formats, has helped many people perform better in social situations (Beidel et al., 2014).

Panic Disorder

SOMETIMES AN ANXIETY REACTION takes the form of a smothering, nightmarish panic in which people lose control of their behavior and, in fact, are practically unaware of what they are doing. Anyone can react with panic when a real threat looms up suddenly. Some people, however, experience **panic attacks**—periodic, short bouts of panic that occur suddenly, reach a peak within minutes, and gradually pass (APA, 2013).

The attacks feature at least four of the following symptoms of panic: palpitations of the heart, tingling in the hands or feet, shortness of breath, sweating, hot and cold

social skills training A therapy approach that helps people learn or improve social skills and assertiveness through role playing and rehearsing of desirable behaviors.

panic attacks Periodic, short bouts of panic that occur suddenly, reach a peak within minutes, and gradually pass.

panic disorder An anxiety disorder marked by recurrent and unpredictable panic attacks.

locus coeruleus A small area of the brain that seems to be active in the regulation of emotions. Many of its neurons use norepinephrine.

flashes, trembling, chest pains, choking sensations, faintness, dizziness, and a feeling of unreality (APA, 2013). Small wonder that during a panic attack many people fear they will die, go crazy, or lose control.

 My first panic attack happened when I was traveling for spring break with my mom. . . . [W]hile I was driving . . . , a random thought entered my head, . . . and BOOM—it was like my body . . . had been waiting for an invitation and jumped me right in to a full-blown panic attack. I felt huge waves of warm adrenaline surging across my chest and back, my hands were shaking, and I felt scared that I was losing control—whatever that meant. "I've got to pull over," I said. . . . Catching my breath, a part of me knew I had experienced a panic attack, but was still utterly bewildered at why it happened and how quickly it came on, taking over body and mind. . . . If you've never had a panic attack before, it feels as scary as if someone jumped out from a dark alley and put a gun to your head, leaving you pleading for your life. You would do whatever it took to get away and fast. . . . It's so intense that in the height of panic, the survival instinct kicks in and it seems like a toss-up whether you'll make it out alive or with your mental faculties in place. . . .

(LeCroy & Holschuh, 2012)

Approximately one-third of all people have one or more panic attacks at some point in their lives (de Jonge et al., 2016; Roy-Byrne, 2016). Some people, however, have panic attacks repeatedly and unexpectedly and without apparent reason. They may be suffering from **panic disorder.** In addition to the panic attacks, people who are diagnosed with panic disorder experience dysfunctional changes in their thinking or behavior as a result of the attacks (see **Table 5-9**). They may, for example, worry persistently about having additional attacks, have concerns about what such attacks mean ("Am I losing my mind?"), or plan their lives around the possibility of future attacks (APA, 2013).

Around 3.1 percent of all people in the United States suffer from panic disorder in a given year; more than 5 percent develop it at some point in their lives (Bandelow & Michaelis, 2015; Kessler et al., 2012). The disorder tends to develop in late adolescence or early adulthood and is at least twice as common among women as among men. Poor people are 50 percent more likely than wealthier people to experience panic disorder (de Jonge et al., 2016). Surveys indicate that 59 percent of those with this disorder in the United States are currently in treatment (NIMH, 2017; Wang et al., 2005).

The prevalence of panic disorder is higher among non-Hispanic white Americans than among racial-ethnic minority groups in the United States (Hofmann & Hinton, 2014). The actual features of panic attacks may also differ among these groups (Barrera et al., 2010). For example, Asian Americans appear more likely than non-Hispanic white Americans to experience dizziness, unsteadiness, and choking, while African Americans seem less likely to have those particular symptoms.

As you read earlier, panic disorder is often accompanied by agoraphobia, the broad phobia in which people are afraid to travel to public places where escape might be difficult should they have panic symptoms or become incapacitated. In such cases, the panic disorder typically sets the stage for the development of agoraphobia. That is, after experiencing multiple unpredictable panic attacks, a person becomes increasingly fearful of having new attacks in public places.

The Biological Perspective

Over the past half-century, researchers have learned that panic disorder has biological underpinnings and can respond to biological treatments. Their journey began in the 1960s, when they discovered that the symptoms of this disorder were sometimes alleviated by *antidepressant drugs,* specifically those antidepressant drugs that increase the activity of the neurotransmitter *norepinephrine* throughout the brain (Klein, 1964; Klein & Fink, 1962).

TABLE: 5-9

Dx Checklist

Panic Disorder

1. Unforeseen panic attacks occur repeatedly.

2. One or more of the attacks precedes either of the following symptoms:

   (a) At least a month of continual concern about having additional attacks

   (b) At least a month of dysfunctional behavior changes associated with the attacks (for example, avoiding new experiences)

Information from: APA, 2013.

What Biological Factors Contribute to Panic Disorder?

To understand the biology of panic disorder, researchers worked backward from their understanding of the antidepressant drugs that seemed to reduce its symptoms. Given that the drugs were so helpful in eliminating panic attacks, the researchers began to suspect that panic disorder might be caused in the first place by abnormal norepinephrine activity.

Several studies produced evidence that norepinephrine activity is indeed irregular in people who suffer from panic attacks. For example, the **locus coeruleus** is a brain area rich in neurons that use norepinephrine, and serves as a kind of "on-off" switch for many norepinephrine-using neurons throughout the brain (Hedaya, 2011). When this area is electrically stimulated in monkeys, the monkeys have a panic-like reaction, suggesting that panic reactions may be related to irregularities in norepinephrine activity in the locus coeruleus (Redmond, 1981, 1979, 1977). Similarly, in another line of research, scientists were able to produce panic attacks in human beings by injecting them with chemicals known to disturb the activity of norepinephrine (Bourin et al., 1995; Charney et al., 1990, 1987).

Based on these findings, biological theorists initially reasoned that panic attacks might be caused by abnormal activity of norepinephrine in the locus coeruleus. However, once again, more recent research suggests that the root of panic attacks is more complicated than a single neurotransmitter or a single brain structure. It turns out that panic reactions are produced by a brain circuit consisting of structures such as the *amygdala, hippocampus, ventromedial nucleus of the hypothalamus, central gray matter,* and *locus coeruleus* (Roy-Byrne, 2016; Henn, 2013; Etkin, 2010) (see **Figure 5-3**). When a person confronts a frightening object or situation, the amygdala is stimulated. In turn, the amygdala stimulates the other brain structures in the circuit, temporarily setting into motion an "alarm and escape" response (increased heart rate, respiration, blood pressure, and the like) that is very similar to a panic reaction (Gray & McNaughton, 1996). Most of today's researchers believe that this circuit—often called the "panic circuit"—tends to be hyperactive in people who suffer from panic disorder (Roy-Byrne, 2016).

Sam Greenwood/Getty Images

At any time The golfing world was shocked when professional golfer Charlie Beljan—usually a cool customer during competitions—had to sit down and wait for a panic attack to pass on the 18th fairway during a tournament in Lake Buena Vista, Florida, in 2012. Beljan successfully completed the competition and has since received great praise for his public candor about his problem.

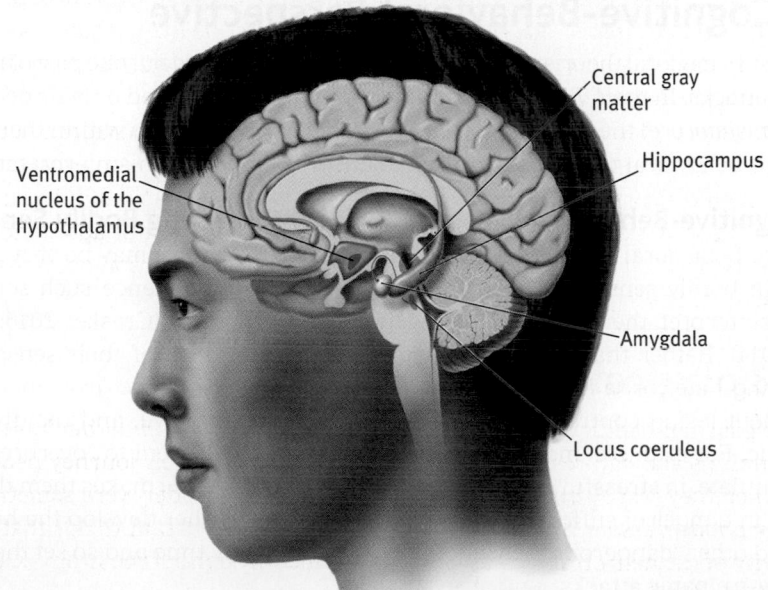

Central gray matter

Hippocampus

Ventromedial nucleus of the hypothalamus

Amygdala

Locus coeruleus

FIGURE 5-3

The Biology of Panic

The circuit in the brain that helps produce panic reactions includes structures such as the amygdala, hippocampus, ventromedial nucleus of the hypothalamus, central gray matter, and locus coeruleus.

Marcelo Sayao/EPA/Newscom

Panic's aftermath Flowers and photos are placed in front of the Kiss nightclub in Santa Maria, Brazil, on January 29, 2013, to pay tribute to the victims of a horrific fire at the club a few days earlier. A total of 242 clubbers were killed and 112 injured in the fire, many as a result of crowd panic, stampeding, and crushing. Catastrophes such as this remind us that people with panic disorder are not the only ones to experience panic.

Some of the brain structures and neurotransmitters in the panic circuit overlap with those in the fear circuit discussed earlier; for example, the amygdala is a part of each circuit. However, the panic circuit seems to be more extensive than the fear circuit, suggesting to some researchers that panic responses are more complex reactions than fear responses (Roy-Byrne, 2016).

Why might some people have hyperactive panic circuits and be prone to the development of panic disorder? One possibility is that a predisposition to develop such abnormalities is inherited (Otowa et al., 2016; Gloster et al., 2015). Once again, if a genetic factor is at work, close relatives should have higher rates of panic disorder than more distant relatives. Studies do find that among identical twins (twins who share all of their genes), if one twin has panic disorder, the other twin has the same disorder in 31 percent of cases (Roy-Byrne, 2016; Tsuang et al., 2004; Kendler et al., 1995, 1993). Among fraternal twins (who share only some of their genes), if one twin has panic disorder, the other twin has the same disorder in, at most, only 11 percent of cases.

Drug Therapies Ever since researchers discovered in 1962 that certain antidepressant drugs could prevent or reduce panic attacks, studies across the world have repeatedly confirmed this initial observation (Bighelli et al., 2016). Various antidepressant drugs bring at least some improvement to more than two-thirds of patients who have panic disorder, and the improvement can last indefinitely, as long as the drugs are continued (Roy-Byrne, 2016; Cuijpers et al., 2014). These antidepressant drugs appear to prevent or reduce panic attacks by increasing the activity of the neurotransmitters *serotonin* and *norepinephrine* in the locus coeruleus and other parts of the panic circuit, thus helping to correct the circuit's tendency to be hyperactive (Gerez et al., 2016; Duval et al., 2015). Researchers have also discovered that *alprazolam* (Xanax) and other powerful benzodiazepine drugs can be effective in many cases of panic disorder, although they are used less often than antidepressants because of their potential for producing physical dependence and other risks. These various antidepressant drugs and benzodiazepines also seem to be helpful in cases of panic disorder accompanied by agoraphobia.

The Cognitive-Behavioral Perspective

Cognitive-behavioral theorists argue that biological factors are but one part of the cause of panic attacks. In their view, full panic reactions are experienced only by people who further *misinterpret* the physiological events that are taking place within their bodies. Cognitive-behavioral treatments are aimed at correcting such misinterpretations.

The Cognitive-Behavioral Explanation: Misinterpreting Bodily Sensations

Cognitive-behavioral theorists believe that panic-prone people may be very sensitive to certain bodily sensations; when they unexpectedly experience such sensations, they misinterpret them as signs of a medical catastrophe (Craske, 2015; Gloster et al., 2014). Rather than understanding the probable cause of their sensations as "something I ate" or "a fight with the boss," those prone to panic grow increasingly upset about losing control, fear the worst, lose all perspective, and rapidly plunge into panic. For example, many people with panic disorder seem to "overbreathe," or hyperventilate, in stressful situations. The abnormal breathing makes them think that they are in danger of suffocation, so they panic. They further develop the belief that these and other "dangerous" sensations may return at any time and so set themselves up for future panic attacks.

biological challenge test A procedure used to produce panic in participants or clients by having them exercise vigorously or perform some other potentially panic-inducing task in the presence of a researcher or therapist.

anxiety sensitivity A tendency to focus on one's bodily sensations, assess them illogically, and interpret them as harmful.

In **biological challenge tests**, researchers produce hyperventilation or other biological sensations by administering drugs or by instructing clinical research participants to breathe, exercise, or simply think in certain ways. As you might expect, participants with panic disorder experience greater upset during these tests than participants without the disorder, particularly when they believe that their bodily sensations are dangerous or out of control (Leibold et al., 2017; Bunaciu et al., 2012).

Why might some people be prone to such misinterpretations? One possibility is that panic-prone individuals actually experience more frequent or intense bodily sensations than other people do. Indeed, the kinds of sensations that are most often misinterpreted in panic disorders seem to be carbon dioxide increases in the blood, shifts in blood pressure, and rises in heart rate, bodily events that are controlled in part by the brain's panic circuit—and, as you'll recall, the panic circuit is overactive in people with panic disorder (Lieberman et al., 2017). Another possibility, supported by some research, is that panic-prone people have had more trauma-filled events over the course of their lives than other persons, leading to higher expectations of catastrophe (Asselmann et al., 2018; De Cort et al., 2017; Nillni et al., 2012). Whatever the precise cause of such misinterpretations may be, once they take hold, they increasingly guide behaviors and choices in life. Panic-prone individuals may, for example, learn to display avoidance and safety behaviors that help control their bodily sensations. They may repeatedly hold onto people or objects to avoid feeling faint, or they may move slowly or sit still much of the time to avoid upsetting increases in heart rate (Craske, 2015).

Given such misinterpretations, it is not surprising that panic-prone individuals generally have a high degree of what is called **anxiety sensitivity;** that is, they focus on their bodily sensations much of the time, are unable to assess them logically, and interpret them as potentially harmful. Studies have found that people who scored high on anxiety-sensitivity surveys are up to five times more likely than other people to develop panic disorder (Hawks et al., 2011; Maller & Reiss, 1992). Other studies have found that individuals with panic disorder typically earn higher anxiety-sensitivity scores than other persons do (Kim et al., 2017; Roy-Byrne, 2016).

Cognitive-Behavioral Therapy Cognitive-behavioral therapists use a combination of techniques to correct people's misinterpretations of their bodily sensations (Craske, 2015; Craske & Barlow, 2014). First, they educate clients about the general nature of panic attacks, the actual causes of bodily sensations, and the tendency of the clients to misinterpret their sensations. Next, they teach the clients to apply more accurate interpretations during stressful situations, thus short-circuiting the panic sequence at an early point. The therapists may also teach the clients ways to cope better with anxiety—for example, by using relaxation and breathing techniques—and to distract themselves from their sensations, perhaps by striking up a conversation with someone.

In addition, cognitive-behavioral therapists often use biological challenge procedures to induce panic sensations, so that clients can apply their new interpretations and skills under watchful supervision (Gloster et al., 2014). Individuals whose attacks typically are triggered by a rapid heart rate, for example, may be instructed to jump up and down for several minutes or to run up a flight of stairs. They can then practice interpreting the resulting sensations appropriately, without dwelling on them.

According to research, cognitive-behavioral treatment often helps people with panic disorder (Allen et al., 2016; Cuijpers et al., 2016; Craske, 2015). In studies across

#

#TheirWords

"Neither a man nor a crowd nor a nation can be trusted to act humanely or to think sanely under the influence of a great fear."

Bertrand Russell

Bruce Eric Kaplan/The New Yorker Collection/The Cartoon Bank

"Weekends I like to be able to panic without having all the distractions."

the world, at least two-thirds of participants who receive this treatment have become free of panic, compared with only 13 percent of control participants. Cognitive-behavioral therapy has proved to be at least as helpful as antidepressant drugs or benzodiazepines in the treatment of panic disorder, sometimes even more so (Roy-Byrne, 2016; Bandelow et al., 2015). In view of the effectiveness of both cognitive-behavioral and drug treatments, many clinicians have tried, with some success, to combine them (Choi, Lee, & Cho, 2017; Cuijpers et al., 2014). Similarly, research suggests that cognitive-behavioral therapy, drug therapy, or a combination of these approaches are helpful to those individuals who display both panic disorder and agoraphobia (Hoffart et al., 2016; Weck et al., 2016).

Obsessive-Compulsive Disorder

OBSESSIONS ARE PERSISTENT thoughts, ideas, impulses, or images that seem to invade a person's consciousness. **Compulsions** are repetitive and rigid behaviors or mental acts that people feel they must perform in order to prevent or reduce anxiety. As **Figure 5-4** indicates, minor obsessions and compulsions are familiar to almost everyone. You may find yourself filled with thoughts about an upcoming performance or exam or keep wondering whether you forgot to turn off the stove or lock the door. You may feel better when you avoid stepping on cracks, turn away from black cats, or arrange your closet in a particular manner. Repetitive thoughts or behaviors of this kind, however, are hardly a reflection of abnormality.

According to DSM-5, a diagnosis of **obsessive-compulsive disorder** is called for when obsessions or compulsions feel excessive or unreasonable, cause great distress, take up much time, and interfere with daily functions (see **Table 5-10**). Although obsessive-compulsive disorder is not classified as an anxiety disorder in DSM-5, anxiety does play a major role in this pattern. The obsessions cause intense anxiety, while the compulsions are aimed at preventing or reducing anxiety. In addition, anxiety rises if a person tries to resist his or her obsessions or compulsions.

An individual with this disorder observed: "I can't get to sleep unless I am sure everything in the house is in its proper place so that when I get up in the morning, the house is organized. I work like mad to set everything straight before I go to bed, but, when I get up in the morning, I can think of a thousand things that I ought to do. . . . I can't stand to know something needs doing and I haven't done it" (McNeil, 1967, pp. 26–28). Research indicates that several additional disorders are closely related to obsessive-compulsive disorder in their features, causes, and treatment responsiveness, and so, as you will soon see, DSM-5 has grouped them together with obsessive-compulsive disorder.

Between 1 and 2 percent of the people in the United States and other countries throughout the world suffer from obsessive-compulsive disorder in any given year (Simpson, 2016; Kessler et al., 2012). As many as 3 percent develop the disorder at some point during their lives. It is equally common in men and women and among people of different races and ethnic groups. The disorder usually begins by childhood or young adulthood (Chou et al., 2017) and typically persists for many years, although its symptoms and their severity may fluctuate over time. It is estimated that 40 percent of people with obsessive-compulsive disorder seek treatment, many for an extended period (Phillips, 2015; Patel et al., 2014).

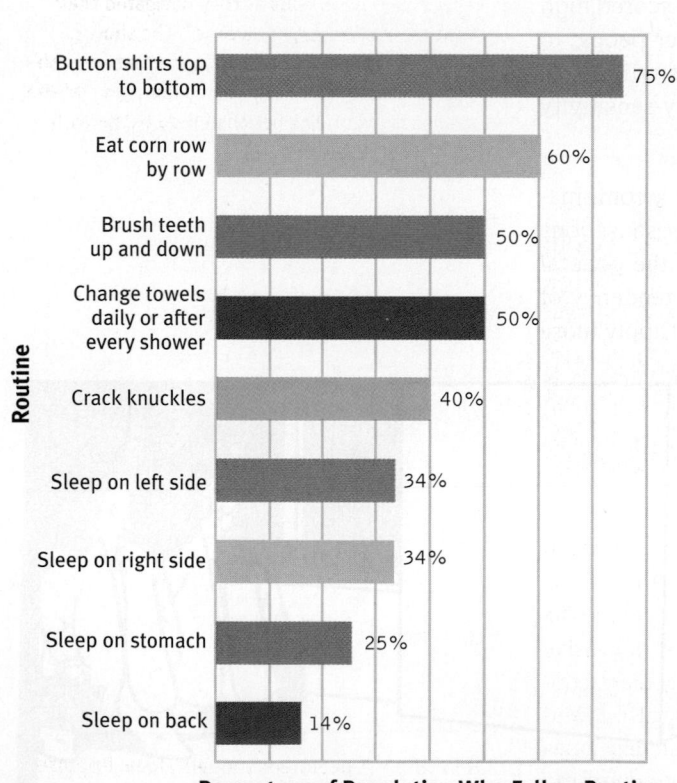

Percentage of Population Who Follow Routine

(bar chart, y-axis labeled "Routine")

- Button shirts top to bottom — 75%
- Eat corn row by row — 60%
- Brush teeth up and down — 50%
- Change towels daily or after every shower — 50%
- Crack knuckles — 40%
- Sleep on left side — 34%
- Sleep on right side — 34%
- Sleep on stomach — 25%
- Sleep on back — 14%

FIGURE 5-4

Normal Routines

Most people find it comforting to follow set routines when they carry out everyday activities, and, in fact, 40 percent become irritated if they must depart from their routines. (Information from: Kanner, 2005, 1998, 1995.)

What Are the Features of Obsessions and Compulsions?

Obsessive thoughts feel both intrusive and foreign to the people who experience them. Attempts to ignore or resist these thoughts may arouse even more anxiety, and before long they come back more strongly than ever. People with obsessions typically are quite aware that their thoughts are excessive.

Certain basic themes run through the thoughts of most people troubled by obsessive thinking (Schwartzman et al., 2017; Simpson, 2016). The most common theme appears to be dirt or contamination (Bennett, 2015; Torres et al., 2013). Other common ones are violence and aggression, orderliness, religion, and sexuality (Schwartzman et al., 2017). The prevalence of such themes may vary from culture to culture (McIngvale et al., 2017; Matsunaga & Seedat, 2011). Religious obsessions, for example, seem to be more common in cultures or countries with strict moral codes and religious values.

Compulsions are similar to obsessions in many ways. For example, although compulsive behaviors are technically under voluntary control, the people who feel they must do them have little sense of choice in the matter. Most of these individuals recognize that their behavior is unreasonable, but they believe at the same time something terrible will happen if they don't perform the compulsions. After performing a compulsive act, they usually feel less anxious for a short while. For some people the compulsive acts develop into detailed *rituals*. They must go through the ritual in exactly the same way every time, according to certain rules.

Like obsessions, compulsions take various forms. *Cleaning compulsions* are very common. People with these compulsions feel compelled to keep cleaning themselves, their clothing, or their homes. The cleaning may follow ritualistic rules and be repeated dozens or hundreds of times a day. People with *checking compulsions* check the same items over and over—door locks, gas taps, important papers—to make sure that all is as it should be. Another common compulsion is the constant effort to seek *order* or *balance*. People with this compulsion keep placing certain items (clothing, books, foods) in perfect order in accordance with strict rules. *Touching, verbal,* and *counting* compulsions are also common.

Jim Spellman/Getty Images

Although some people with obsessive-compulsive disorder experience obsessions only or compulsions only, most experience both. In fact, compulsive acts are often a response to obsessive thoughts. One study found that in most cases, compulsions seemed to represent a *yielding* to obsessive doubts, ideas, or urges (Akhtar et al., 1975). A woman who keeps doubting that her house is secure may yield to that obsessive doubt by repeatedly checking locks and gas jets, or a man who obsessively fears contamination may yield to that fear by performing cleaning rituals. The study also found that compulsions sometimes serve to help *control* obsessions. A teenager describes how she tried to control her obsessive fears of contamination by performing counting and verbal rituals:

Patient: *If I heard the word, like, something that had to do with germs or disease, it would be considered something bad, and so I had things that would go through my mind that were sort of like "cross that out and it'll make it okay" to hear that word.*

(continued on the next page)

TABLE: 5-10

Dx Checklist

Obsessive-Compulsive Disorder

1. Occurrence of repeated obsessions, compulsions, or both

2. The obsessions or compulsions take up considerable time.

3. Significant distress or impairment

Information from: APA, 2013.

Personal knowledge The recently-ended HBO hit series *Girls* followed the struggles of Hannah Horvath and her friends as they navigated their twenties, "one mistake at a time." The show's creator and star, Lena Dunham, says that Hannah's difficulties often were inspired by her own real-life experiences, including her childhood battle with OCD and anxiety.

obsession A persistent thought, idea, impulse, or image that is experienced repeatedly, feels intrusive, and causes anxiety.

compulsion A repetitive and rigid behavior or mental act that a person feels driven to perform in order to prevent or reduce anxiety.

obsessive-compulsive disorder A disorder in which a person has recurrent obsessions, compulsions, or both.

> Interviewer: *What sort of things?*
> Patient: *Like numbers or words that seemed to be sort of like a protector.*
> Interviewer: *What numbers and what words were they?*
> Patient: *It started out to be the number 3 and multiples of 3 and then words like "soap and water," something like that; and then the multiples of 3 got really high, and they'd end up to be 124 or something like that. It got real bad then.*
>
> (Spitzer et al., 1981, p. 137)

Obsessive-compulsive disorder was once among the least understood of the psychological disorders. In recent decades, however, researchers have begun to learn more about it. The most influential explanations and treatments come from the psychodynamic, cognitive-behavioral, and biological models.

The Psychodynamic Perspective

As you have seen, psychodynamic theorists believe that an anxiety disorder develops when children come to fear their own id impulses and use ego defense mechanisms to lessen the resulting anxiety. What distinguishes obsessive-compulsive disorder from other anxiety disorders, in their view, is that here the battle between anxiety-provoking id impulses and anxiety-reducing defense mechanisms is not buried in the unconscious but is played out in overt thoughts and actions. The id impulses usually take the form of obsessive thoughts, and the ego defenses appear as counterthoughts or compulsive actions. A woman who keeps imagining her mother lying broken and bleeding, for example, may counter those thoughts with repeated safety checks throughout the house.

Sigmund Freud traced obsessive-compulsive disorder to the *anal stage* of development (occurring at about 2 years of age). He proposed that during this stage some children experience intense rage and shame as a result of negative toilet-training experiences. Other psychodynamic theorists have argued instead that such early rage reactions are rooted in feelings of insecurity (Erikson, 1963; Sullivan, 1953; Horney, 1937). Either way, these children repeatedly feel the need to express their strong aggressive id impulses while at the same time knowing they should try to restrain and control the impulses. If this conflict between the id and ego continues, it may eventually blossom into obsessive-compulsive disorder. Overall, research has not clearly supported the psychodynamic explanation (Goodman, 2016; Busch et al., 2010).

When treating patients with obsessive-compulsive disorder, psychodynamic therapists try to help the individuals uncover and overcome their underlying conflicts and defenses, using the customary techniques of free association and therapist interpretation. Research has offered little evidence, however, that a traditional psychodynamic approach is of much help (Goodman, 2016; Fonagy, 2015). Thus some psychodynamic therapists now prefer to treat these patients with short-term psychodynamic therapies, which, as you saw in Chapter 3, are more direct and action-oriented than the classical techniques.

The Cognitive-Behavioral Perspective

Cognitive-behavioral theorists begin their explanation of obsessive-compulsive disorder by pointing out that everyone has repetitive, unwanted, and intrusive thoughts. Anyone might have thoughts of harming others or being contaminated by germs, for example, but

"Gretel, I don't like living in this culture of fear."

most people dismiss or ignore them with ease. Those who develop this disorder, however, typically blame themselves for such thoughts and expect that somehow terrible things will happen (Simpson, 2016; Salkovskis, 1999, 1985). To avoid such negative outcomes, they try to **neutralize** the thoughts—thinking or behaving in ways meant to put matters right or to make amends (Jacob, Larson, & Storch, 2014; Salkovskis et al., 2003).

Neutralizing acts might include requesting special reassurance from others, deliberately thinking "good" thoughts, washing one's hands, or checking for possible sources of danger. When a neutralizing effort brings about a temporary reduction in discomfort, it is reinforced and will likely be repeated (Goodman, 2016; Grayson, 2014). Eventually the neutralizing thought or act is used so often that it becomes, by definition, an obsession or compulsion. At the same time, the individual becomes more and more convinced that his or her unpleasant intrusive thoughts are dangerous. As the person's fear of such thoughts increases, the thoughts begin to occur more frequently and they, too, become obsessions.

In support of this explanation, studies have found that people with obsessive-compulsive disorder have intrusive thoughts more often than other people, resort to more elaborate neutralizing strategies, and experience reductions in anxiety after using neutralizing techniques (Jacob et al, 2014; Salkovskis et al., 2003).

Although everyone sometimes has undesired thoughts, only some people develop obsessive-compulsive disorder. Why do these individuals find such normal thoughts so disturbing to begin with? Researchers have found that this population tends (1) to have exceptionally high standards of conduct and morality; (2) to believe that intrusive negative thoughts are equivalent to actions and capable of causing harm, a point of view called *thought-action fusion*; and (3) to believe that they should have perfect control over all of their thoughts and behaviors in life (Schwartzman et al., 2017; Simpson, 2016; Whitton, Henry, & Grisham, 2014).

Cognitive-behavioral therapists use a combination of techniques to treat clients with obsessive-compulsive disorder. They begin by educating the clients, pointing out how misinterpretations of unwanted thoughts, an excessive sense of responsibility, and neutralizing acts have helped to produce and maintain their symptoms. The therapists then guide the clients to identify and challenge their distorted cognitions. Increasingly, the clients come to appreciate that their obsessive thoughts are inaccurate occurrences rather than valid and dangerous cognitions for which they are responsible. Correspondingly, they recognize their compulsive acts as unnecessary.

With such gains in hand, the clients become willing to subject themselves to the rigors of a distinctly behavioral technique called **exposure and response prevention** (or **exposure and ritual prevention**). In this technique, first developed by psychiatrist Victor Meyer (1966), the clients are repeatedly exposed to objects or situations that produce anxiety, obsessive fears, and compulsive behaviors, but they are told to *resist* performing the behaviors they usually feel so bound to perform. Because people find it very difficult to resist such behaviors, the therapists may set an example first.

> Have you ever tried an informal version of exposure and response prevention in order to stop behaving in certain ways?

In recent years, therapists who conduct exposure and response prevention have often used videoconferencing to go beyond the office and deliver specific instructions to clients directly in their home settings where compulsions cause the most problems (Comer et al., 2017). At the very least, a number of therapists compose exposure-and-response-prevention exercises that clients must carry out in the form of homework

neutralizing A person's attempt to eliminate unwanted thoughts by thinking or behaving in ways that put matters right internally, making up for the unacceptable thoughts.

exposure and response prevention
A cognitive-behavioral technique used to treat obsessive-compulsive disorder that exposes a client to anxiety-arousing thoughts or situations and then prevents the client from performing his or her compulsive acts. Also called *exposure and ritual prevention*.

Bill Pugliano/Getty Images

Getting down and dirty In one *exposure and response prevention* assignment, clients with cleaning compulsions might be instructed to do heavy-duty gardening and then resist washing their hands or taking a shower. They may never go so far as to participate in and enjoy mud wrestling, like these delightfully filthy individuals at the annual Mud Day event in Westland, Michigan, but you get the point.

Kazuhiro Nogi/AFP/Getty Images

Cultural rituals Rituals do not necessarily reflect compulsions. Indeed, cultural and religious rituals often give meaning and comfort to their practitioners. Here Buddhist monks splash water over themselves during their annual winter prayers at a temple in Tokyo. This cleansing ritual is performed to pray for good luck.

(Gellatly et al., 2017; Franklin & Foa, 2014), such as these assignments given to a woman with a cleaning compulsion:

- Do not mop the floor of your bathroom for a week. After this, clean it within three minutes, using an ordinary mop. Use this mop for other chores as well without cleaning it.

- Buy a fluffy mohair sweater and wear it for a week. When taking it off at night do not remove the bits of fluff. Do not clean your house for a week.

- You have to keep shoes on. Do not clean the house for a week.

- Drop a cookie on the contaminated floor, pick the cookie up and eat it.

- Leave the sheets and blankets on the floor and then put them on the beds. Do not change these for a week.

(Emmelkamp, 1982, pp. 299–300)

Eventually this woman was able to set up a reasonable routine for cleaning herself and her house.

Techniques of this kind often help reduce the number and impact of obsessions and compulsions (Lenhard et al., 2017; Liu et al., 2017; Grayson, 2014). Overall, between 50 and 70 percent of clients with obsessive-compulsive disorder have been found to improve considerably with cognitive-behavioral therapy, improvements that often continue indefinitely (Abramowitz, 2016). The effectiveness of this approach suggests that people with the disorder are like the superstitious man in the old joke who keeps snapping his fingers to keep elephants away. When someone points out, "But there aren't any elephants around here," the man replies, "See? It works!" One review concludes, "With hindsight, it is possible to see that the [obsessive-compulsive] individual has been snapping his fingers, and unless he stops (response prevention) and takes a look around at the same time (exposure), he isn't going to learn much of value about elephants" (Berk & Efran, 1983, p. 546).

The Biological Perspective

Family pedigree studies provided the earliest clues that obsessive-compulsive disorder may be linked in part to biological factors (Simpson, 2016; Lambert & Kinsley,

#BeneficialObsession

The experiments that led Louis Pasteur to the pasteurization process may have been driven in part by his obsession with contamination and infection. Apparently he would not shake hands and regularly wiped his glass and plate before dining (Geison, 2008; Asimov, 1997).

2010). Studies of twins found that if one identical twin has this disorder, the other twin also develops it in 53 percent of cases. In contrast, among fraternal twins (twins who share some rather than all of their genes), both twins display the disorder in only 23 percent of the cases. In short, the more similar the gene composition of two individuals, the more likely both are to experience obsessive-compulsive disorder, if indeed one of them displays the disorder.

In recent years, researchers have uncovered more direct evidence that biological factors play a key role in obsessive-compulsive disorder. For example, some genetic studies have identified clusters of gene abnormalities that characterize individuals with this disorder (Mattheisen et al., 2015; Samuels et al., 2011; Liang et al., 2008). In addition, using brain scan procedures, researchers have identified a brain circuit that helps regulate our primitive impulses such as sexual desires, aggressive instincts, and needs to excrete (Parmar & Sarkar, 2016; Tang et al., 2016). The circuit, which brings these impulses to our attention and leads us to act on or disregard them, features such brain structures as the *orbitofrontal cortex* (just above each eye), *cingulate cortex*, *striatum* (including the *caudate nucleus* and *putamen*, two other structures at the back of the striatum), and *thalamus*. Normally, a person's primitive impulses arise in the orbitofrontal cortex, are filtered in the cingulate cortex and striatum, and (if they are powerful enough) move on to the *thalamus* (see **Figure 5-5**). If the impulses reach the thalamus, the person is driven to think further about them and perhaps to act. Among the most important neurotransmitters at work in this circuit are *serotonin, glutamate,* and *dopamine* (Gerez et al., 2016; Bokor & Anderson, 2014).

Studies indicate that this circuit, called the *cortico-striato-thalamo-cortical* circuit, is hyperactive in people with obsessive-compulsive disorder, making it difficult for them to turn off or dismiss their various impulses, needs, and related thoughts (Frydman et al., 2016; Tang et al., 2016). After most people use the bathroom, for example, they have concerns about contamination and they act accordingly by washing their hands. Upon performing this behavior, their contamination concerns and cleanliness needs subside in their brain circuit. In contrast, because the cortico-striato-thalamo-cortical circuit of people with obsessive-compulsive disorder is hyperactive, these individuals may continue to experience such concerns and impulses and to perform cleaning actions—again and again and again. Some research further suggests that the brain circuit abnormalities that characterize obsessive-compulsive disorder are at least partly the result of genetic inheritance (den Braber et al., 2016; Nicolini et al., 2011).

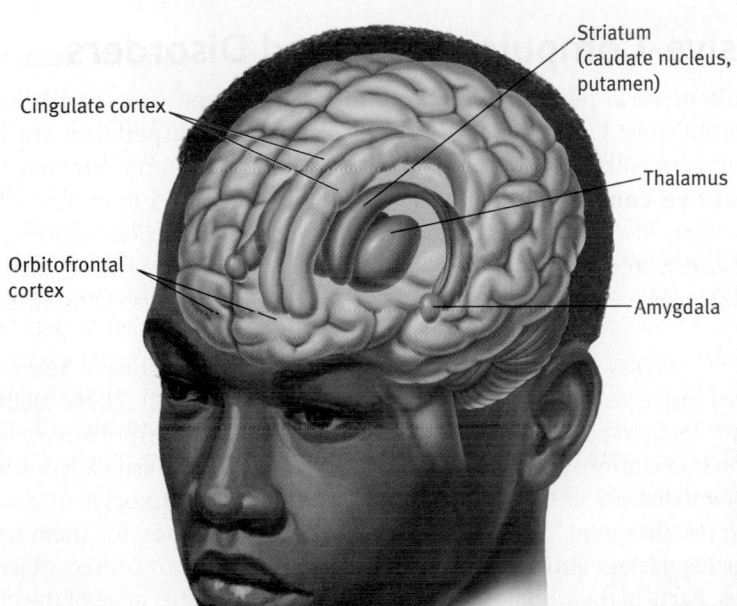

Cingulate cortex

Striatum (caudate nucleus, putamen)

Thalamus

Orbitofrontal cortex

Amygdala

FIGURE 5-5

The Biology of Obsessive-Compulsive Disorder

The brain circuit that has been linked to obsessive-compulsive disorder includes structures such as the orbitofrontal cortex, cingulate cortex, striatum, thalamus, and amygdala.

As you just read, brain scan studies have provided the most direct evidence that the cortico-striato-thalamo-cortical circuit is hyperactive in people with obsessive-compulsive disorder. In addition, medical scientists have observed for years that obsessive-compulsive symptoms often arise or subside after the orbitofrontal cortex, striatum, or other structures in the circuit are damaged by accident, illness, or surgical procedures (Hofer et al., 2013).

By far, the most widely used biological treatment for obsessive-compulsive disorder is *antidepressant drugs*, particularly ones that specifically increase activity of the neurotransmitter serotonin. The effectiveness of these drugs was first discovered in the 1970s when an antidepressant named clomipramine (trade name Anafranil) brought significant improvement to many patients with the disorder (Bokor & Anderson, 2014). Since then, numerous studies have found that this and similar antidepressant drugs bring improvement to between 50 and 60 percent of those with obsessive-compulsive disorder. Their obsessions and compulsions do not usually disappear totally, but on average they are cut almost in half (Simpson, 2015; Bareggi et al., 2004; DeVeaugh-Geiss et al., 1992).

Given the effectiveness of serotonin-enhancing drugs in treating obsessive-compulsive disorder, theorists initially reasoned that the disorder must be caused primarily by low serotonin activity throughout the brain. However, this interpretation has not received clear support over the past few decades, leading most of today's researchers to conclude instead that the drugs bring improvement by increasing the activity of serotonin within the cortico-striato-thalamo-cortical circuit, thus helping to correct the circuit's tendency to be hyperactive. Consistent with this notion, studies have found that the structures in the circuit do indeed seem to interconnect more appropriately after individuals with obsessive-compulsive disorder respond successfully to antidepressant treatment (Tang et al., 2016).

As we observed above, antidepressant drugs commonly bring only partial improvement to people with obsessive-compulsive disorder. Moreover, they must be continued indefinitely to prevent relapse. Thus more and more individuals with obsessive-compulsive disorder are now being treated by a combination of cognitive-behavioral and drug therapies. According to research, such combinations often yield higher levels of symptom reduction and bring relief to more clients than do each of the approaches alone—improvements that may continue for years (Abramowitz, 2016; Romanelli et al., 2014).

Obsessive-Compulsive-Related Disorders

Some people perform particular patterns of repetitive and excessive behavior that greatly disrupt their lives. Among the most common such patterns are hoarding, hair-pulling, skin-picking, and appearance-checking. DSM-5 has created the group name **obsessive-compulsive-related disorders** and these four patterns to that group: *hoarding disorder, trichotillomania (hair-pulling disorder), excoriation (skin-picking) disorder,* and *body dysmorphic disorder.* Collectively, these disorders are displayed by at least 5 percent of all people (Mataix-Cols & de la Cruz, 2016; Phillips, 2016).

People who display **hoarding disorder** feel that they must save items, and they become very distressed if they try to discard them (APA, 2013). These feelings make it difficult for them to part with possessions, resulting in an extraordinary accumulation of items that clutters their lives and living areas. This pattern causes the individuals significant distress and may greatly impair their personal, social, or occupational functioning (Mathes et al., 2017; Ong et al., 2015). It is common for them to wind up with numerous useless and valueless items, from junk mail to broken objects to unused clothes. Parts of their homes may become inaccessible because of the clutter. For example, sofas, kitchen appliances, or beds may be unusable. In addition, the pattern often results in fire hazards, unhealthful sanitation conditions, or other dangers.

#RepetitiousBehaviors

According to surveys, almost half of adults double back after leaving home to make sure they have turned off an appliance.

More than half of all people who use an alarm clock check it repeatedly to be sure they've set it.

(Kanner, 1995)

obsessive-compulsive-related disorders
Disorders in which obsessive-like concerns drive people to repeatedly and excessively perform certain abnormal patterns of behavior.

hoarding disorder A disorder in which individuals feel compelled to save items and become very distressed if they try to discard them, resulting in an excessive accumulation of items.

trichotillomania A disorder in which people repeatedly pull out hair from their scalp, eyebrows, eyelashes, or other parts of the body. Also called *hair-pulling disorder.*

excoriation disorder A disorder in which people repeatedly pick at their skin, resulting in significant sores or wounds. Also called *skin-picking disorder.*

body dysmorphic disorder A disorder in which individuals become preoccupied with the belief that they have certain defects or flaws in their physical appearance. Such defects or flaws are imagined or greatly exaggerated.

A messy aftermath This man prepares to clean out his mother's home after her death. This is not an easy task—emotionally or physically—under the best of circumstances, but it is particularly difficult in this instance: his mother had suffered from hoarding disorder.

People with **trichotillomania,** also known as **hair-pulling disorder**, repeatedly pull out hair from their scalp, eyebrows, eyelashes, or other parts of the body (APA, 2013). The disorder usually centers on just one or two of these body sites, most often the scalp. Typically, those with the disorder pull one hair at a time. It is common for anxiety or stress to trigger or accompany the hair-pulling behavior (Grant et al., 2017). Some sufferers follow specific rituals as they pull their hair, including pulling until the hair feels "just right" and selecting certain types of hairs for pulling (Starcevic, 2015; Keuthen et al., 2012). Because of the distress, impairment, or embarrassment caused by this behavior, the individuals often try to reduce or stop the hair-pulling. The term "trichotillomania" is derived from the Greek for "frenzied hair-pulling."

People with **excoriation (skin-picking) disorder** keep picking at their skin, resulting in significant sores or wounds (APA, 2013). Like those with hair-pulling disorder, they often try to reduce or stop the behavior. Most sufferers pick with their fingers and center their picking on one area, most often the face (Grant et al., 2015, 2012). Other common areas of focus include the arms, legs, lips, scalp, chest, and extremities such as fingernails and cuticles. The behavior is typically triggered or accompanied by anxiety or stress (Torales, Barrios, & Villalba, 2017).

People with **body dysmorphic disorder** become preoccupied with the belief that they have a particular defect or flaw in their physical appearance. Actually, the perceived defect or flaw is imagined or greatly exaggerated in the person's mind (APA, 2013). Such beliefs drive the individuals to repeatedly check themselves in the mirror, groom themselves, pick at the perceived flaw, compare themselves with others, seek reassurance, or perform other, similar behaviors. Here too, those with the problem experience significant distress or impairment.

Body dysmorphic disorder is the obsessive-compulsive-related disorder that has received the most study to date. Researchers have found that, most often, individuals with this problem focus on wrinkles; spots on the skin; excessive facial hair; swelling of the face; or a misshapen nose, mouth, jaw, or eyebrow (Phillips, 2016; Veale & Bewley, 2015). Some

Worldwide influence A lingerie ad in a subway station in Shanghai, China, displays a woman in a push-up bra. As West meets East, Asian women have been bombarded by ads encouraging them to make Western-like changes to their various body parts. Perhaps not so coincidentally, cases of body dysmorphic disorder among Asians are becoming more and more similar to those among Westerners.

worry about the appearance of their feet, hands, breasts, penis, or other body parts. Still others, like the woman described here, are concerned about bad odors coming from sweat, breath, genitals, or the rectum.

> *A woman of 35 had for 16 years been worried that her sweat smelled terrible. . . . For fear that she smelled, for 5 years she had not gone out anywhere except when accompanied by her husband or mother. She had not spoken to her neighbors for 3 years. . . . She avoided cinemas, dances, shops, cafes, and private homes. . . . Her husband was not allowed to invite any friends home; she constantly sought reassurance from him about her smell. . . . Her husband bought all her new clothes as she was afraid to try on clothes in front of shop assistants. She used vast quantities of deodorant and always bathed and changed her clothes before going out, up to 4 times daily.*
>
> *(Marks, 1987, p. 371)*

Of course, it is common in our society to worry about appearance (see **Figure 5-6**). Many teenagers and young adults worry about acne, for instance. The concerns of people with body dysmorphic disorder, however, are extreme. Sufferers may severely limit contact with other people, be unable to look others in the eye, or go to great lengths to conceal their "defects"—say, always wearing sunglasses to cover their supposedly misshapen eyes. As many as half of people with the disorder seek plastic surgery or dermatology treatment, and often they feel worse rather than better afterward (Bouman et al., 2017; Phillips, 2017). A large number are housebound, 80 percent have suicidal thoughts, and as many as 25 percent may attempt suicide at some point in their lives (Phillips, 2016).

As with the other obsessive-compulsive-related disorders, theorists typically account for body dysmorphic disorder by using the same kinds of explanations, both psychological and biological, that have been applied to obsessive-compulsive disorder. Similarly, clinicians typically treat clients with this disorder by applying the kinds of treatment used with obsessive-compulsive disorder, particularly antidepressant drugs and cognitive-behavioral therapy (Krebs et al., 2017; Phillips, 2017, 2016; Harrison et al., 2016).

In an early study, for example, 17 clients with this disorder were treated with exposure and response prevention. Over the course of 4 weeks, the clients were repeatedly reminded of their perceived physical defects and, at the same time, prevented from

---

#LookingGood

42 percent of facial plastic surgeons report that many of their patients seek cosmetic procedures in order to look better in selfies, Instagram, Snapchat, and Facebook Live, and other social media (AAFPRS, 2017).

FIGURE 5-6

"Mirror, Mirror, on the Wall . . ."

People with body dysmorphic disorder are not the only ones who have concerns about their appearance. Surveys find that in our appearance-conscious society, large percentages of people regularly think about and try to change the way they look. (Information from: ASPS, 2017; Samorodnitzky-Naveh et al., 2007; Noonan, 2003; Kimball, 1993; Poretz & Sinrod, 1991; Weiss, 1991; Simmon, 1990.)

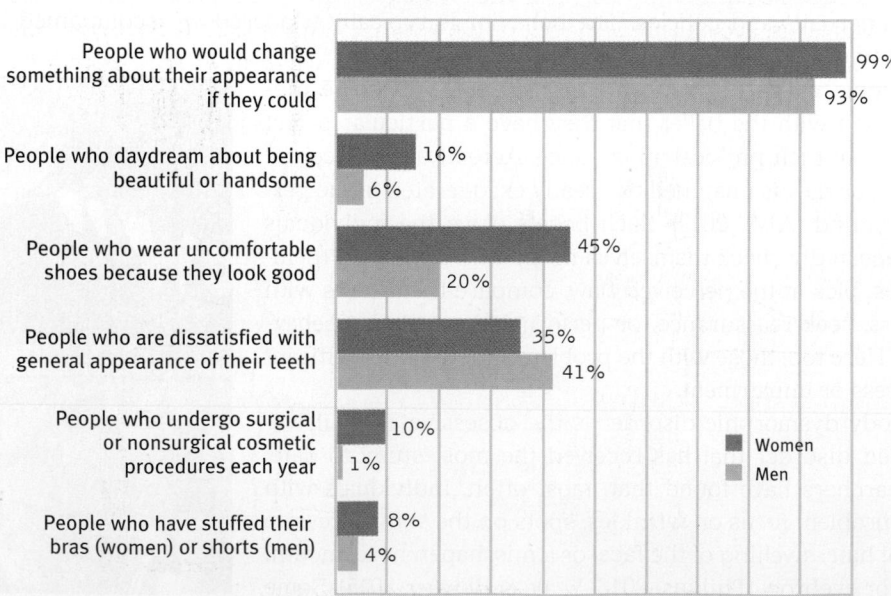

- People who would change something about their appearance if they could — 99% Women, 93% Men
- People who daydream about being beautiful or handsome — 16% Women, 6% Men
- People who wear uncomfortable shoes because they look good — 45% Women, 20% Men
- People who are dissatisfied with general appearance of their teeth — 35% Women, 41% Men
- People who undergo surgical or nonsurgical cosmetic procedures each year — 10% Women, 1% Men
- People who have stuffed their bras (women) or shorts (men) — 8% Women, 4% Men

doing anything to help reduce their discomfort (such as checking their appearance) (Neziroglu et al., 2004, 1996). By the end of treatment, these individuals were less concerned with their "defects" and spent less time checking their body parts and avoiding social interactions.

Integrating the Models: The Developmental Psychopathology Perspective

WHILE READING THROUGH THIS chapter, you may have noticed that certain findings and principles from each of the models seem compatible, and you may have wondered whether the explanations offered by the models could sometimes be combined to provide a fuller understanding of the various anxiety, obsessive-compulsive, and obsessive-compulsive-related disorders. A number of clinical theorists have asked the same question and have looked for ways to integrate the variables cited by the models. As you read in Chapter 3, one of today's most influential integrative views is the *developmental psychopathology* perspective. This perspective focuses on the *intersection* and *context* of important factors at key points of *time* throughout an individual's lifespan (Cicchetti, 2016; Leve & Cicchetti, 2016; Suor et al., 2016).

What are the factors that developmental psychopathologists look at when seeking to understand the development of anxiety-related disorders? Drawing from the biological model, they have been interested in the growing number of studies that link particular genetic variations to hyperactive fear circuits and, in turn, to inhibited— that is, fearful—temperaments in certain infants and toddlers (Johnson et al., 2016; Fox et al., 2015). From the earliest days of life, such children show a withdrawn, isolated, and cautious pattern known as *behavioral inhibition*. They are wary of new objects, people, and environments, and always seem on guard against potential threats (Fox & Pine, 2012). Research indicates that this inhibited temperament often endures throughout a person's life and places some individuals at heightened risk for the development of anxiety-related disorders (Abulizi et al., 2017; Baker et al., 2012)

Drawing from the cognitive-behavioral and psychodynamic models, developmental psychopathologists have also been interested in research findings that highlight the role of *parenting styles* in determining whether a child's early temperament will actually become a lifelong posture of worrying, fearful misinterpretations, excessive social concerns, avoidance behaviors, or the like (Hankin et al., 2016; Stifter & Dollar, 2016; Tone et al., 2016). Investigations indicate that as children grow, *overprotective*

#HealthSearch
Most Googled Health Symptoms

1. Infection symptoms

2. Measles symptoms

3. Gastritis symptoms

4. **Anxiety symptoms**

5. Heat stroke symptoms

(Drain, 2016)

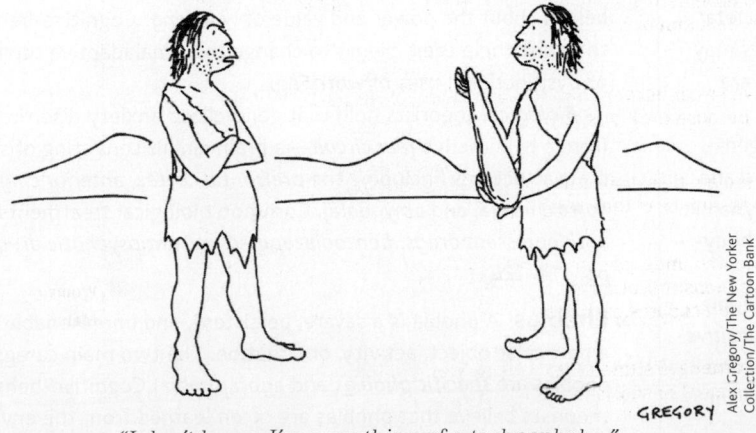

"I don't know. I'm something of a technophobe."

Alex Gregory/The New Yorker
Collection/The Cartoon Bank

GREGORY

parenting—in which parents rush in too quickly to prevent or rescue their children from experiencing distress—denies them opportunities to learn how to manage distress by themselves and to build a strong sense of self-confidence. In *parental accommodations* of child anxiety, a common form of overprotective parenting, parents repeatedly allow their anxious children to avoid social engagements, answer questions on their behalf, let them stay home from school when they feel nervous, and/or provide them with excessive reassurances (Thompson-Hollands et al., 2014). If children already have a biological vulnerability and an inhibited temperament, exposure to overprotective parenting can help promote repeated eruptions of anxiety, setting the stage for lifelong anxiety.

Finally, drawing from the sociocultural model, developmental psychopathologists have also been interested in research showing that life stress, poverty, school difficulties, family disharmony, peer pressure, and community danger can heighten the likelihood of developing anxiety-related disorders. Indeed, a growing number of studies suggest that, in many cases, some such factors must be present for these disorders to emerge, in addition to any unfavorable biological factors, temperament, or parenting experiences the individual may have (Chen & Liu, 2016; Pianta, 2016; Wadsworth et al., 2016).

While the developmental psychopathology perspective helps us appreciate that the principles of the various models may often be combined to better account for anxiety-related disorders, it also highlights that the models, operating in relative isolation, have not addressed important questions about the *development* of these disorders. Precisely *how* and *when*, for example, do the variables from each of the models interact to produce the disorders? Increasingly, research is revealing that the relationships between these variables are two-directional: the impact of biological factors, for example, can often be affected *by* parenting, life events, newly acquired behaviors, and particular ways of thinking, just as biology may have great influence *on* such variables (Cicchetti, 2016; Leve & Cicchetti, 2016). Similarly, a growing body of research suggests that the various factors may have greater or lesser impact at different points of development. The early settling in of a fearful temperament, for example, may place a lid on the later impact of positive life events. Conversely, effective parenting may reduce the impact of an unfavorable biological predisposition or of later negative life events. Clearly, in order for anxiety-related disorders to be more fully understood and effectively treated, these important developmental issues need to be clarified.

CLINICAL CHOICES

Now that you've read about anxiety, obsessive-compulsive, and related disorders, try the interactive case study for this chapter. See if you are able to identify Priya's symptoms and suggest a diagnosis based on her symptoms. What kind of treatment would be most effective for Priya? Go to **Launch**Pad to access *Clinical Choices*.

♥... SUMMING UP

» Generalized Anxiety Disorder People with *generalized anxiety disorder* experience excessive anxiety and worry about a wide range of events and activities. According to the *sociocultural* view, *societal dangers*, *economic stress*, or related *racial and cultural pressures* may create a climate in which cases of generalized anxiety disorder are more likely to develop.

In the original *psychodynamic* explanation, Freud said that generalized anxiety disorder may develop when anxiety is excessive and defense mechanisms break down and function poorly. Psychodynamic therapists use free association, interpretation, and related psychodynamic techniques to help people overcome this problem.

Carl Rogers, the leading *humanistic* theorist, believed that people with generalized anxiety disorder fail to receive *unconditional positive regard* from significant others during their childhood and so become overly critical of themselves. He treated such individuals with *client-centered therapy*.

Cognitive-behavioral theorists believe that generalized anxiety disorder is caused by various *maladaptive assumptions* and/or inaccurate beliefs about the power and value of *worrying*. Cognitive-behavioral therapists help their clients to change their maladaptive thinking and/or dysfunctional uses of worrying.

Biological theorists hold that generalized anxiety disorder results from a hyperactive *fear circuit*—a brain circuit consisting of several brain structures (including the *prefrontal cortex*, *anterior cingulate cortex*, *insula*, and *amygdala*). Common biological treatments are *antidepressant drugs*, *benzodiazepines*, and *antipsychotic drugs*. pp. 114–125

» Phobias A phobia is a severe, persistent, and unreasonable fear of a particular object, activity, or situation. The two main categories of phobias are *specific phobias* and *agoraphobia*. Cognitive-behavioral theorists believe that phobias are often learned from the environment through *classical conditioning* or *modeling* and maintained by *avoidance behaviors*.

Specific phobias have been treated most successfully with *exposure techniques*, cognitive-behavioral approaches in which people confront the objects they fear. The exposures may be gradual and relaxed (*desensitization*), intense (*flooding*), or observed (*modeling*). Agoraphobia is also treated effectively by exposure therapy. *pp. 125–132*

» Social Anxiety Disorder
People with social anxiety disorder experience severe and persistent anxiety about social or performance situations in which they may be scrutinized by others or be embarrassed. Cognitive-behavioral theorists believe that the disorder is particularly likely to develop among people who hold certain dysfunctional social beliefs and expectations and learn to perform corresponding avoidance and safety behaviors.

Therapists who treat social anxiety disorder typically distinguish two components of this disorder: *social fears* and *poor social skills*. They try to reduce social fears by *drug therapy* and/or *cognitive-behavioral therapy (including exposure techniques)*. They may try to improve social skills by *social skills training*. *pp. 132–135*

» Panic Disorder
Panic attacks are periodic, discrete bouts of panic that occur suddenly. Sufferers of *panic disorder* experience panic attacks repeatedly and unexpectedly and without apparent reason. Panic disorder may be accompanied by *agoraphobia* in some cases, leading to two diagnoses.

Many biological theorists believe that panic disorder is caused by a hyperactive *panic circuit*, a brain circuit that includes structures such as the *amygdala, hippocampus, ventromedial nucleus of the hypothalamus, central gray matter,* and *locus coeruleus*. Biological therapists use certain *antidepressant drugs* or *benzodiazepines* to treat people with this disorder.

Cognitive-behavioral theorists suggest that panic-prone people become preoccupied with some of their bodily sensations, misinterpret them as signs of medical catastrophe, have panic attacks, learn to display avoidance and safety behaviors that help control their bodily sensations, and in some cases develop panic disorder. Cognitive-behavioral therapists teach clients to interpret their physical sensations more accurately and to cope better with anxiety. *pp. 135–140*

» Obsessive-Compulsive Disorder
People with *obsessive-compulsive disorder* are beset by *obsessions*, perform *compulsions*, or both. Compulsions are often a response to a person's obsessive thoughts.

According to the psychodynamic view, obsessive-compulsive disorder arises out of a battle between id impulses and ego defense mechanisms. In contrast, cognitive-behavioral theorists believe that the disorder grows from a normal human tendency to have *unwanted and unpleasant thoughts*. The efforts of some people to understand, eliminate, or avoid such thoughts actually lead to obsessions and compulsions. Cognitive-behavioral therapists educate clients and help them correct their misinterpretations of the unwanted thoughts. With such gains in hand, the therapists then conduct *exposure and response prevention*.

Biological researchers have tied obsessive-compulsive disorder to a hyperactive brain circuit featuring such brain structures as the *orbitofrontal cortex, cingulate cortex, striatum,* and *thalamus*. Antidepressant drugs that raise serotonin activity are a widely used and useful form of treatment.

In addition to obsessive-compulsive disorder, DSM-5 lists a group of *obsessive-compulsive-related disorders*, disorders in which obsessive-like concerns drive individuals to repeatedly and excessively perform specific patterns of behavior that greatly disrupt their lives. This group consists of *hoarding disorder, trichotillomania, excoriation (skin-picking) disorder,* and *body dysmorphic disorder*. *pp. 140–149*

» Integrating the Models
To explain anxiety, obsessive-compulsive, and related disorders, proponents of the *developmental psychopathology* perspective examine how key factors emerge and intersect at points throughout an individual's lifespan. The factors of interest to them include genetic factors, a hyperactive fear circuit in the brain, an inhibited temperament, parenting style, maladaptive thinking, avoidance behaviors, life stress, and negative social factors. *pp. 149-150*

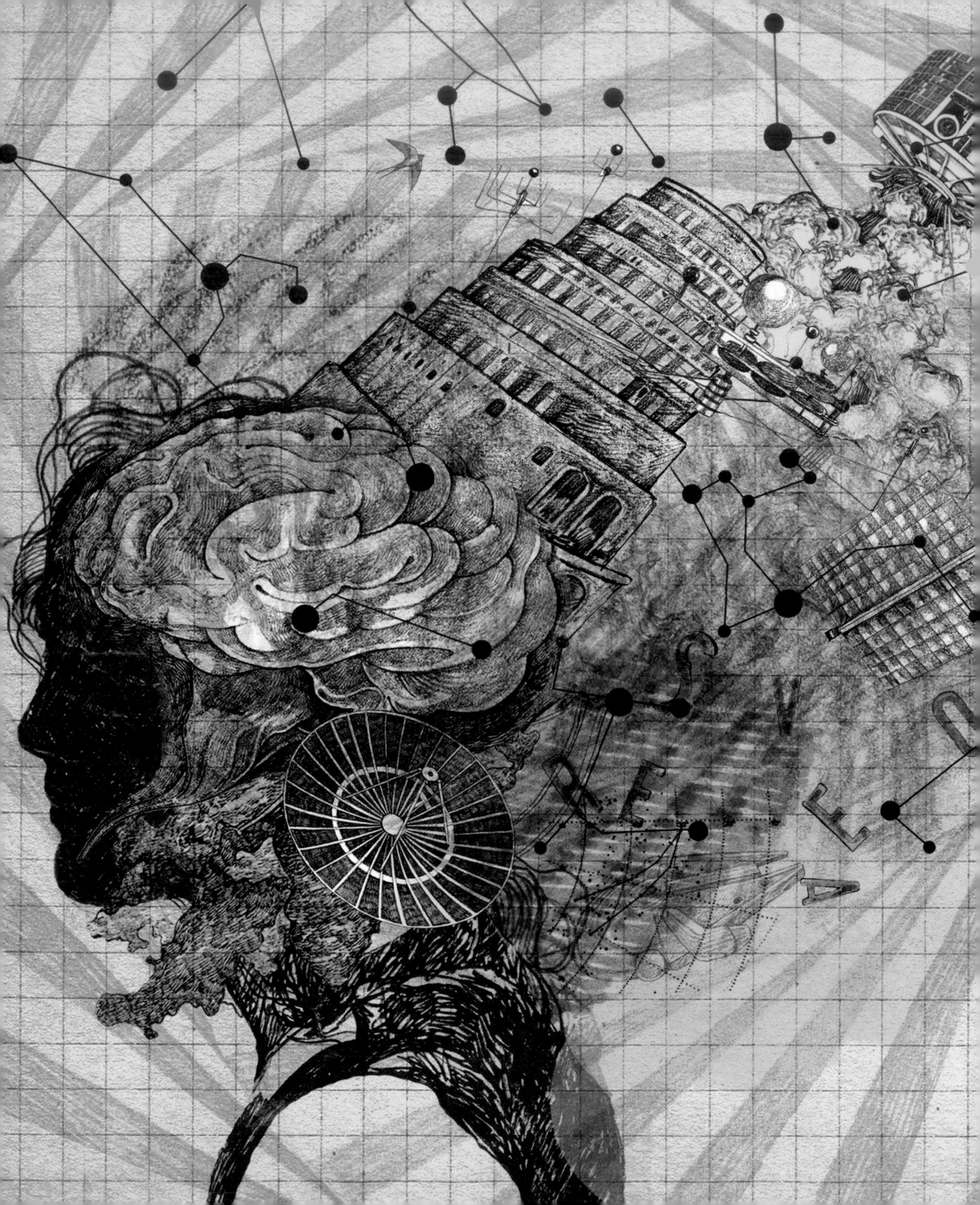

⚲...Disorders of Trauma and Stress

Specialist Latrell Robinson, a 25-year-old single African American man, was an activated National Guardsman [serving in the Iraq war]. He [had been] a full-time college student and competitive athlete raised by a single mother in public housing. . . . Initially trained in transportation, he was called to active duty and retrained as a military policeman to serve with his unit in Baghdad. He described enjoying the high intensity of his deployment and [became] recognized by others as an informal leader because of his aggressiveness and self-confidence. He [had] numerous [combat] exposures while performing convoy escort and security details [and he came] under small arms fire on several occasions, witnessing dead and injured civilians and Iraqi soldiers and on occasion feeling powerless when forced to detour or take evasive action. He began to develop increasing mistrust of the [Iraq] environment as the situation "on the street" seemed to deteriorate. He often felt that he and his fellow soldiers were placed in harm's way needlessly.

On a routine convoy mission [in 2003], serving as driver for the lead HUMVEE, his vehicle was struck by an Improvised Explosive Device showering him with shrapnel in his neck, arm, and leg. Another member of his vehicle was even more seriously injured. . . . He was evacuated to the Combat Support Hospital (CSH) where he was treated and returned to duty . . . after several days despite requiring crutches and suffering chronic pain from retained shrapnel in his neck. He began to become angry at his command and doctors for keeping him in [Iraq] while he was unable to perform his duties effectively. He began to develop insomnia, hypervigilance, and a startle response. His initial dreams of the event became more intense and frequent and he suffered intrusive thoughts and flashbacks of the attack. He began to withdraw from his friends and suffered anhedonia, feeling detached from others, and he feared his future would be cut short. He was referred to a psychiatrist at the CSH. . . .

After two months of unsuccessful rehabilitation for his battle injuries and worsening depressive and anxiety symptoms, he was evacuated to a . . . military medical center [in the United States]. . . . He was screened for psychiatric symptoms and was referred for outpatient evaluation and management. He met . . . criteria for acute PTSD and was offered medication management, supportive therapy, and group therapy. . . . He was ambivalent about taking passes or convalescent leave to his home because of fears of being "different, irritated, or aggressive" around his family or girlfriend. After three months at the military service center, he was [deactivated from service and] referred to his local VA Hospital to receive follow-up care.

(National Center for PTSD, 2008)

During the horror of combat, soldiers often become highly anxious and depressed, confused and disoriented, even physically ill. Moreover, for many, like Latrell, these and related reactions to extraordinary stress or trauma continue well beyond the combat experience itself.

Of course, it is not just combat soldiers who are affected by stress. Nor does stress have to rise to the level of combat trauma to have a profound effect on psychological and physical functioning. Stress comes in all sizes and shapes, and we are all greatly affected by it.

We feel some degree of stress whenever we are faced with demands or opportunities that require us to change in some manner. The state of stress has two components:

Peio Hernandez/EPA/Newscom

Jon Dimis/AP Photo

Different strokes for different folks
Some people are exhilarated by the opportunity to chase bulls through the streets of Pamplona, Spain, during the annual "running of the bulls" (left). Others are terrified by such a prospect and prefer instead to engage tamer animals, such as ostriches, during the "running of the ostriches" fiesta in Irurzun, Spain (right).

a *stressor,* the event that creates the demands, and a *stress response,* the person's reactions to the demands. The stressors of life may include annoying everyday hassles, such as rush-hour traffic; turning-point events, such as college graduation or marriage; long-term problems, such as poverty or poor health; or traumatic events, such as major accidents, assaults, tornadoes, or military combat. Our response to such stressors is influenced by the way we *judge* both the events and our capacity to react to them in an effective way (Biron & Link, 2014; Lazarus & Folkman, 1984). People who sense that they have the ability and the resources to cope are more likely to take stressors in stride and to respond well.

When we view a stressor as threatening, a natural reaction is arousal and a sense of fear—a response frequently discussed in Chapter 5. As you saw in that chapter, fear is actually a package of responses that are *physical, emotional,* and *cognitive.* Physically, we perspire, our breathing quickens, our muscles tense, and our heart beats faster. Turning pale, developing goose bumps, and feeling nauseated are other physical reactions. Emotional responses to extreme threats include horror, dread, and even panic, while in the cognitive realm fear can disturb our ability to concentrate and remember and may distort our view of the world. We may, for example, remember things incorrectly or exaggerate the harm that actually threatens us.

Stress reactions, and the sense of fear they produce, are often at play in psychological disorders. People who experience a large number of stressful events are particularly vulnerable to the onset of the anxiety disorders that you read about in Chapter 5 (Furr et al., 2018). Similarly, increases in stress have been linked to the onset of depression, schizophrenia, sexual dysfunctions, and other psychological problems.

Extraordinary stress and trauma play an even more central role in certain psychological disorders. In these disorders, the reactions to stress become severe and debilitating, linger for a long period of time, and may make it impossible for the individual to live a normal life. Under the heading "Trauma- and Stressor-Related Disorders," DSM-5 lists several disorders in which trauma and extraordinary stress trigger a range of significant stress symptoms, including heightened arousal, anxiety and mood problems, memory and orientation difficulties, and behavioral disturbances. Two of these disorders, *acute stress disorder* and *posttraumatic stress disorder,* are discussed in this chapter. In addition, DSM-5 lists the "dissociative disorders," a group of disorders also triggered by traumatic events, in which the primary symptoms are severe memory and orientation problems. These disorders are also examined in this chapter.

To fully understand these various stress-related disorders, it is important to appreciate the precise nature of stress and how the brain and body typically react to stress. Thus let's first discuss stress and arousal, then move on to discussions of acute and posttraumatic stress disorders and the dissociative disorders. ■

Stress and Arousal: The Fight-or-Flight Response

THE FEATURES OF AROUSAL are set in motion by the brain structure called the *hypothalamus*. When our brain interprets a situation as dangerous, neurotransmitters in the hypothalamus are released, triggering the firing of neurons throughout the brain and the release of chemicals throughout the body. Actually, the hypothalamus activates two important systems—the *autonomic nervous system* and the *endocrine system* (Biran et al., 2015). The **autonomic nervous system (ANS)** is the extensive network of nerve fibers that connect the *central nervous system* (the brain and spinal cord) to all the other organs of the body. These fibers help control the *involuntary* activities of the organs—breathing, heartbeat, blood pressure, perspiration, and the like (see **Figure 6-1**). The **endocrine system** is the network of *glands* located throughout the

autonomic nervous system (ANS) The network of nerve fibers that connect the central nervous system to all the other organs of the body.

endocrine system The system of glands located throughout the body that help control important activities such as growth and sexual activity.

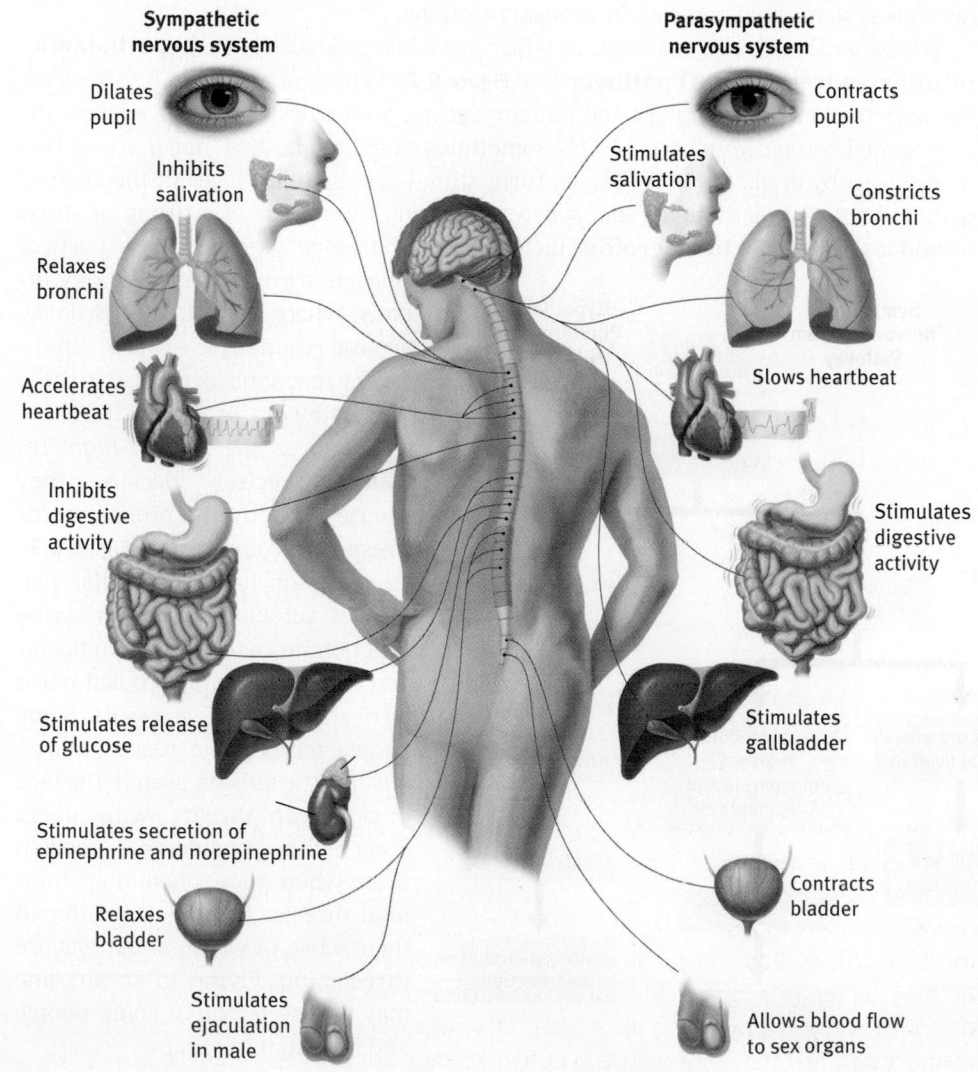

Sympathetic nervous system

- Dilates pupil
- Inhibits salivation
- Relaxes bronchi
- Accelerates heartbeat
- Inhibits digestive activity
- Stimulates release of glucose
- Stimulates secretion of epinephrine and norepinephrine
- Relaxes bladder
- Stimulates ejaculation in male

Parasympathetic nervous system

- Contracts pupil
- Stimulates salivation
- Constricts bronchi
- Slows heartbeat
- Stimulates digestive activity
- Stimulates gallbladder
- Contracts bladder
- Allows blood flow to sex organs

FIGURE 6-1

The Autonomic Nervous System (ANS)

When the sympathetic division of the ANS is activated, it stimulates some organs and inhibits others. The result is a state of general arousal. In contrast, activation of the parasympathetic division leads to an overall calming effect.

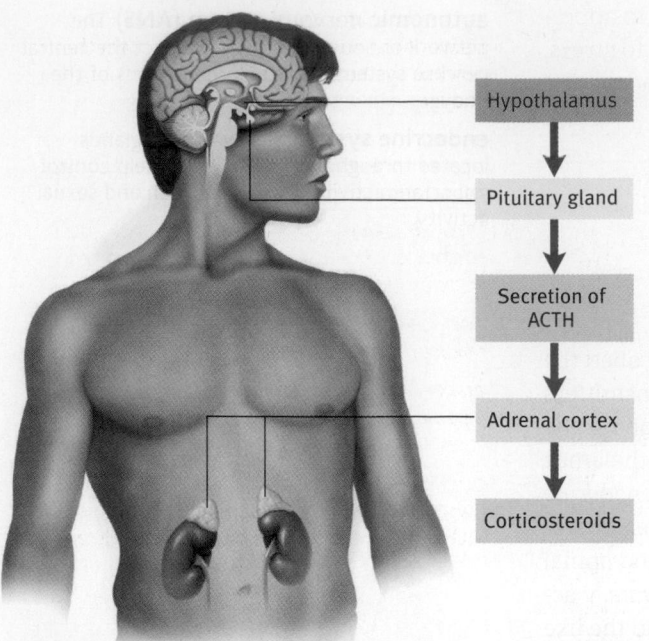

FIGURE 6-2

The Endocrine System: The HPA Pathway

When a person perceives a stressor, the hypothalamus activates the pituitary gland to secrete the adrenocorticotropic hormone, or ACTH, which stimulates the adrenal cortex. The adrenal cortex releases stress hormones called corticosteroids that act on other body organs to trigger arousal and fear reactions.

FIGURE 6-3

Pathways of Arousal and Fear

When we are confronted by a stressor, our bodies produce arousal through two pathways. In one, the hypothalamus sends a message to the sympathetic nervous system, which then activates key body organs, either directly or by causing the adrenal medulla to release epinephrine and norepinephrine into the bloodstream. In the other pathway, the hypothalamus sends a message to the pituitary gland, which then signals the adrenal cortex to release corticosteroids—the stress hormones—into the bloodstream.

body. (As you read in Chapter 3, glands release *hormones* into the bloodstream and on to the various body organs.) The ANS and the endocrine system often overlap in their responsibilities. There are two brain–body pathways, or routes, by which these systems produce arousal—the *sympathetic nervous system* pathway and the *hypothalamic-pituitary-adrenal* pathway.

When we face a dangerous situation, the hypothalamus first excites the **sympathetic nervous system,** a group of ANS fibers that work to quicken our heartbeat and produce the other changes that we come to experience as fear or anxiety. These nerves may stimulate the organs of the body directly—for example, they may directly stimulate the heart and increase heart rate. The nerves may also influence the organs indirectly, by stimulating the *adrenal glands* (glands located on top of the kidneys), particularly an area of these glands called the *adrenal medulla.* When the adrenal medulla is stimulated, the chemicals *epinephrine* (*adrenaline*) and *norepinephrine* (*noradrenaline*) are released. You have already seen that these chemicals are important neurotransmitters when they operate in the brain (see page 48). When released from the adrenal medulla, however, they act as hormones and travel through the bloodstream to various organs and muscles, further producing arousal.

When the perceived danger passes, a second group of autonomic nervous system fibers, called the **parasympathetic nervous system,** helps return our heartbeat and other body processes to normal. Together the sympathetic and parasympathetic nervous systems help control our arousal reactions.

The second brain–body pathway by which arousal is produced is the **hypothalamic-pituitary-adrenal (HPA) pathway** (see **Figure 6-2**). When we are faced by stressors, the hypothalamus also signals the *pituitary gland,* which lies nearby, to secrete the *adrenocorticotropic hormone* (*ACTH*), sometimes called the body's "major stress hormone" (Jacoby et al., 2016). ACTH, in turn, stimulates the outer layer of the adrenal glands, an area called the *adrenal cortex,* triggering the release of a group of stress hormones called **corticosteroids,** including the hormone *cortisol.* These corticosteroids travel to various body organs, where they further produce arousal reactions (Seaward, 2013).

The reactions on display in these two pathways are collectively referred to as the *fight-or-flight* response, precisely because they arouse our body and prepare us for a response to danger (see **Figure 6-3**). Each person has a particular pattern of autonomic and endocrine functioning and so a particular way of experiencing arousal when he or she confronts stressors. Some people, for example, react with relatively little tension even in the face of significant threats, while others react with considerable tension even when they encounter minimal threats. People also differ in their sense of which situations are threatening. Flying in an airplane may arouse terror in some people and boredom in others.

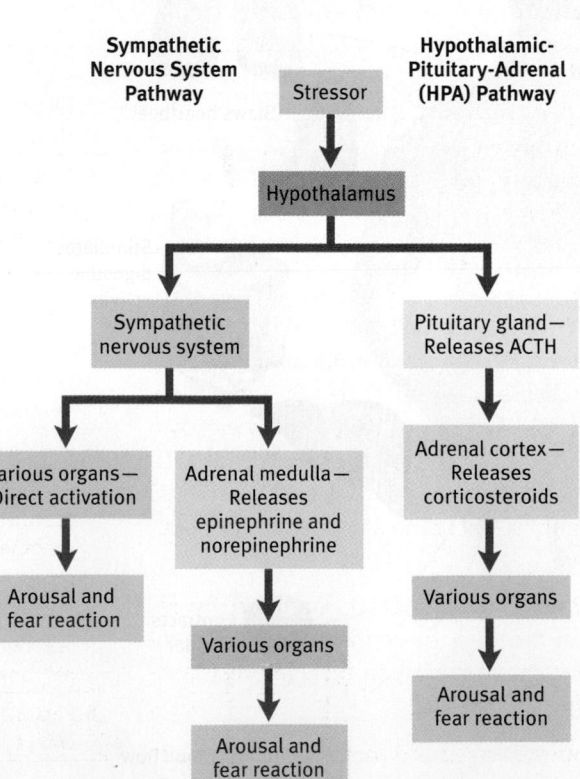

Acute and Posttraumatic Stress Disorders

OF COURSE WHEN WE ACTUALLY confront stressful situations, we do not think to ourselves, "Oh, there goes my autonomic nervous system," or "My fight-or-flight response seems to be kicking in." We just feel aroused psychologically and physically and experience a growing sense of fear. If the stressful situation is perceived as extraordinary and/or unusually dangerous, we may temporarily experience levels of arousal, fear, and depression that are beyond anything we have ever known.

For most people, such reactions subside soon after the danger passes. For others, however, the symptoms of arousal, anxiety, and depression, as well as other kinds of symptoms, persist well after the upsetting situation is over. These people may be suffering from *acute stress disorder* or *posttraumatic stress disorder*, patterns that arise in reaction to a psychologically traumatic event. A traumatic event is one in which a person is exposed to actual or threatened death, serious injury, or sexual violation (APA, 2013). Unlike the anxiety disorders that you read about in Chapter 5, which typically are triggered by situations that most people would not find threatening, the situations that cause acute stress disorder or posttraumatic stress disorder—combat, rape, an earthquake, an airplane crash—would be traumatic for almost anyone (Chou et al., 2017).

If the symptoms begin within 4 weeks of the traumatic event and last for less than a month, DSM-5 assigns a diagnosis of **acute stress disorder** (APA, 2013). If the symptoms continue longer than a month, a diagnosis of **posttraumatic stress disorder (PTSD)** is given. The symptoms of PTSD may begin either shortly after the traumatic event or months or years afterward (see **Table 6-1**). In fact, 25 percent of people with PTSD do not develop a full clinical syndrome until 6 months or more after their trauma (Sareen, 2015).

Studies indicate that at least half of all cases of acute stress disorder develop into posttraumatic stress disorder (Bryant et al., 2015, 2005). Think back to Latrell, the soldier in Iraq whose case opened this chapter. As you'll recall, Latrell became overrun by arousal, anxiety, insomnia, worry, anger, depression, irritability, intrusive thoughts, flashback memories, and social detachment within days of the attack on his convoy mission—thus qualifying him for a diagnosis of acute stress disorder. As his symptoms worsened and continued beyond one month—even long after his return to the United States—this diagnosis became PTSD. Aside from the differences in onset and duration, the symptoms of acute stress disorder and PTSD are almost identical (APA, 2013):

INCREASED AROUSAL, NEGATIVE EMOTIONS, AND GUILT People may feel excessively alert (hyperalertness), be easily startled, have trouble concentrating, and develop sleep problems. They may display anxiety, anger, or depression, and these emotions may fluctuate markedly—a pattern called *emotional dysregulation* or *labile mood* (McLean & Foa, 2017; Nicholson et al., 2017). In addition, many individuals feel extreme guilt because they survived the traumatic event while others did not (Worthen et al., 2014). Some also feel guilty about what they may have had to do to survive.

REEXPERIENCING THE TRAUMATIC EVENT People may be battered by recurring thoughts, memories, dreams, or nightmares connected to the event (Shipherd et al., 2016). A few relive the event so vividly in their minds (flashbacks) that they think it is actually happening again.

AVOIDANCE People usually avoid activities that remind them of the traumatic event and try to avoid related thoughts, feelings, or conversations.

sympathetic nervous system The nerve fibers of the autonomic nervous system that quicken the heartbeat and produce other changes experienced as arousal.

parasympathetic nervous system The nerve fibers of the autonomic nervous system that help return bodily processes to normal.

hypothalamic-pituitary-adrenal (HPA) pathway One route by which the brain and body produce arousal.

corticosteroids Hormones, including cortisol, released by the adrenal glands at times of stress.

acute stress disorder A disorder in which a person experiences fear and related symptoms soon after a trauma but for less than a month.

posttraumatic stress disorder (PTSD) A disorder in which a person experiences fear and related symptoms long after a traumatic event.

TABLE: 6-1

Dx Checklist

Posttraumatic Stress Disorder

1. Person is exposed to a traumatic event—death or threatened death, severe injury, or sexual violation.

2. Person experiences at least one of the following intrusive symptoms:
   - Repeated, uncontrolled, and distressing memories
   - Repeated and upsetting trauma-linked dreams
   - Dissociative experiences such as flashbacks
   - Significant upset when exposed to trauma-linked cues
   - Pronounced physical reactions when reminded of the event(s)

3. Person continually avoids trauma-linked stimuli.

4. Person experiences negative changes in trauma-linked cognitions and moods, such as being unable to remember key features of the event(s) or experiencing repeated negative emotions.

5. Person displays conspicuous changes in arousal or reactivity, such as excessive alertness, extreme startle responses, or sleep disturbances.

6. Person experiences significant distress or impairment, with symptoms lasting more than a month.

Information from: APA, 2013.

REDUCED RESPONSIVENESS AND DISSOCIATION People with these disorders may feel detached from other people, be unresponsive to external stimuli, and lose interest in activities that once brought enjoyment. Many endure symptoms of *dissociation,* or psychological separation: that is, they feel dazed, have trouble remembering things, experience *depersonalization* (feeling that their conscious state or body is unreal), or have a sense of *derealization* (feeling that the environment is unreal or strange).

You can see these symptoms in the recollections of a Vietnam combat veteran years after he returned home:

> *I can't get the memories out of my mind! The images come flooding back in vivid detail, triggered by the most inconsequential things, like a door slamming or the smell of stir-fried pork. Last night I went to bed, was having a good sleep for a change. Then in the early morning a storm-front passed through and there was a bolt of crackling thunder. I awoke instantly, frozen in fear. I am right back in Vietnam, in the middle of the monsoon season at my guard post. I am sure I'll get hit in the next volley and convinced I will die. My hands are freezing, yet sweat pours from my entire body. I feel each hair on the back of my neck standing on end. I can't catch my breath and my heart is pounding. I smell a damp sulfur smell.*
>
> *(Davis, 1992)*

Clinicians have come to appreciate that people who experience symptoms of dissociation and unresponsiveness as part of their stress syndrome tend to be more impaired and distressed than other sufferers (Hansen, Ross, & Armour, 2017; Lanius, Frewen, & Brand, 2016). Thus DSM-5 singles out *PTSD with dissociative symptoms* as a special subtype of the disorder that clinicians should make mention of in their diagnosis. This pattern is particularly common among PTSD victims whose traumas involved military combat, sexual abuse, or other forms of physical abuse, especially repeated abuse or childhood abuse. As many as 30 percent of all people with PTSD have dissociative symptoms.

An acute or posttraumatic stress disorder can occur at any age, even in childhood (Furr et al., 2017), and can affect one's personal, family, social, or occupational life (Alisic et al., 2014). Surveys indicate that 3.5 to 6 percent of people in North America have one of the stress disorders in any given year; 7 to 12 percent suffer from one of them during their lifetimes (Sareen, 2015; Kessler et al., 2012). Around half of these individuals seek treatment, but relatively few do so when they first develop the disorder (NIMH, 2017; Wang et al., 2005). Approximately 20 percent attempt suicide (Lanius et al., 2016). People with stress disorders often develop other psychological disorders as well, such as depressive, anxiety, or substance use disorders (Dworkin et al., 2018). They also have an increased risk of developing physical ailments such as bronchitis, asthma, heart disease, and liver disease (La Greca, Comer, & Lai, 2016; Sareen, 2015).

People with low incomes are twice as likely as people with higher incomes to experience stress disorders (Sareen, 2015; Sareen et al., 2011). Women are more likely than men to develop one of these disorders: around 20 percent of women who are exposed to a severe trauma may develop one, compared with 8 percent of men (Perrin et al., 2014; Russo & Tartaro, 2008). Similarly, Hispanic Americans, African Americans, and American Indians are more likely than non-Hispanic white Americans to develop a stress disorder after confronting a severe trauma (Tull, 2017; Loo, 2016; Ghafoori et al., 2013). The reason for this racial-ethnic difference is not clear. Some theorists believe that it is tied to the poorer financial status of many minority group members, which may limit their access to mental health care in the aftermath of traumas. Others point to specific cultural beliefs, such as the view in several racial-ethnic minority groups that traumatic events are inevitable and unchangeable, a belief that may heighten a person's risk for developing a stress disorder.

Lingering impact More than four decades after the Vietnam War, over a quarter million veterans of that war are still suffering from PTSD. Until his death in 2016, one such veteran was King Charsa Bakari Kamau, He is seen here playing the piano at a mall in Denver, Colorado, an avocation that he considered to be his best therapy.

Craig F. Walker/Getty Images

Helpers at risk Emergency rescue workers and volunteers frantically carry a victim from the ruins of an earthquake in Kathmandu, Nepal. Studies reveal that those who are called on to help people during disasters, accidents, and other life-and-death situations may themselves be at high risk for developing acute and/or posttraumatic stress disorders (Luftman et al., 2017).

What Triggers Acute and Posttraumatic Stress Disorders?

Any traumatic event can trigger a stress disorder; however, some are particularly likely to do so (Sareen, 2015). Among the most common are combat, disasters, and abuse and victimization.

Combat For years clinicians have recognized that many soldiers develop symptoms of severe anxiety and depression *during* combat. It was called "shell shock" during World War I and "combat fatigue" during World War II and the Korean War (Figley, 1978). Not until after the Vietnam War, however, did clinicians learn that a great many soldiers also experience serious psychological symptoms *after* combat (Ruzek et al., 2011).

By the late 1970s, it became apparent that many Vietnam combat veterans were still experiencing war-related psychological difficulties (Roy-Byrne et al., 2004). We now know that as many as 29 percent of all Vietnam veterans, male and female, suffered an acute or posttraumatic stress disorder, while another 22 percent have had at least some stress symptoms (Hermes, Hoff, & Rosenheck, 2014; Krippner & Paulson, 2006). In fact, 10 percent of the veterans of that war still deal with posttraumatic stress symptoms, including flashbacks, night terrors, nightmares, and persistent images and thoughts (Marmar et al., 2015).

A similar pattern has unfolded among the nearly 2.7 million veterans of the wars in Afghanistan and Iraq (Vasterling et al., 2016; Zoroya, 2013; Ruzek et al., 2011). Around 20 percent of the Americans deployed to those wars have so far reported symptoms of PTSD. Among those directly exposed to prolonged periods of combat-related stress, the percentage with PTSD is higher still.

Disasters and Accidents Acute and posttraumatic stress disorders may also follow natural and accidental disasters such as earthquakes, floods, tornadoes, fires, airplane crashes, and serious car accidents (see **Table 6-2**). Researchers have found, for example, unusually high rates of PTSD among the survivors of 2005's Hurricane Katrina, 2010's BP Gulf Coast oil spill,

TABLE: 6-2

Worst Natural Disasters of the Past 100 Years

Disaster	Year	Location	Number Killed
Flood	1931	Huang River, China	3,700,000
Tsunami	2004	South Asia	280,000
Earthquake	1976	Tangshan, China	255,000
Heat wave	2003	Europe	35,000
Volcano	1985	Nevado del Ruiz, Colombia	23,000
Hurricane	1998	(Mitch) Central America	18,277
Landslide	1970	Yungay, Peru	17,500
Avalanche	1916	Italian Alps	10,000
Blizzard	1972	Iran	4,000
Tornado	1989	Saturia, Bangladesh	1,300

Information from: Infogalactic, 2016; USGS, 2011; CBC, 2008; Ash, 2001.

rape Forced sexual intercourse or another sexual act committed against a nonconsenting person or intercourse between an adult and an underage person.

and the devastating tornado that struck Moore, Oklahoma, in 2013 (Brown et al., 2016; Pearson, 2013; Furr et al., 2010). In fact, because they occur more often, civilian traumas have been the trigger of stress disorders at least 10 times as often as combat traumas (Bremner, 2002). Studies have found that between 12 and 40 percent of people involved in traffic accidents—adult or child—may develop PTSD within a year of the accident (Sareen, 2015; Noll-Hussong et al., 2013; Hickling & Blanchard, 2007).

Victimization People who have been abused or victimized often have stress symptoms that linger. Research suggests that over one-third of all victims of physical or sexual assault develop PTSD (Sareen, 2015; Walsh et al., 2014; Koss et al., 2011). As many as half of all people directly exposed to terrorism or torture may develop the disorder (Comer et al., 2018; Basoglu et al., 2001).

SEXUAL ASSAULT A common form of victimization in our society today is sexual assault (see *InfoCentral* on the next page). **Rape** is forced sexual intercourse or another sexual act committed against a nonconsenting person or intercourse between an adult and an underage person. In the United States, approximately 91,000 cases of rape or attempted rape are reported to the police each year (FBI, 2016). Most experts believe that these are but a fraction of the actual number of rapes and rape attempts, given the reluctance of many victims to report their sexual assaults. Most rapists are men, and most victims are women. Around one in six women is raped at some time during her life. Approximately 71 percent of the victims are raped by acquaintances, intimates, or relatives (BJS, 2016, 2013).

The rates of rape differ among racial-ethnic groups. Around 27 percent of American Indian women and 22 percent of African American women have been raped at some point in their lives, compared with 19 percent of non-Hispanic white American women, 15 percent of Hispanic American women, and 12 percent of Asian American women (BJS, 2017; Black et al., 2011).

> How might physicians, police, the courts, and other agents better meet the psychological needs of rape victims?

The psychological impact of rape on a victim is immediate and may last a long time (WCSAP, 2016; Koss et al., 2015, 2011, 2008; Koss, 2005, 1993). Rape victims typically experience enormous distress during the week after the assault. Stress continues to rise for the next 3 weeks, maintains a peak level for another month or so, and then starts to improve. In one study, 94 percent of rape victims fully qualified for a clinical diagnosis of acute stress disorder when they were observed around

Raising awareness Demonstrators participate in a "SlutWalk" through downtown Chicago, declaring that survivors of sexual assault are superheroes, fighting to overcome their traumatic ordeal. Countless SlutWalks have taken place around the world since the movement began in 2011. During these marches, participants may wear revealing attire to protest a culture of victim blaming, such as the still common myth that rapes can be explained or excused if the victims were wearing skimpy outfits.

Scott Olson/Getty Images

SEXUAL ASSAULT

People who are **sexually assaulted** have been forced to engage in a sexual act against their will. According to most definitions, people who are **raped** have been forced into sexual intercourse or other forms of sexual penetration. Rape victims often experience **rape trauma syndrome (RTS),** a pattern of problematic physical and psychological symptoms. RTS is actually a form of PTSD. Approximately **one-third** of rape victims develop PTSD.

THE PSYCHOLOGICAL EFFECTS OF RAPE

suicidal thoughts
attempted **suicide**
vulnerability to develop **psychological disorders**
feelings of self-blame and **betrayal**
flashbacks
panic attacks
sleep problems
memory problems

Rape victims are more likely to:

3 X suffer from depression

4 X contemplate suicide

6 X suffer from PTSD

13 X abuse alcohol

26 X abuse drugs

(CMSAC, 2017; RAINN, 2016, 2009; Adams, 2013)

WHO ARE THE VICTIMS?

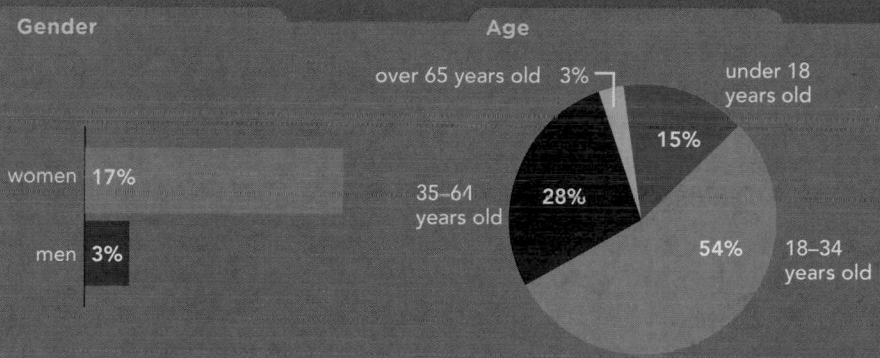

Gender

women 17%

men 3%

Age

over 65 years old 3%

under 18 years old 15%

35–64 years old 28%

54% 18–34 years old

(RAINN, 2016, 2009)

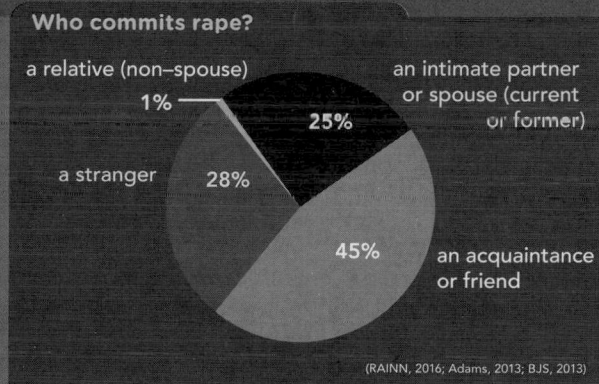

Who commits rape?

a relative (non–spouse) 1%

an intimate partner or spouse (current or former) 25%

a stranger 28%

45% an acquaintance or friend

(RAINN, 2016; Adams, 2013; BJS, 2013)

SEXUAL ASSAULT ON COLLEGE CAMPUSES

In 2014, the White House pressured colleges to develop better guidelines to address the problem of sexual assaults on campus. It also encouraged all students and university staff to sign the **"It's On Us"** pledge, which makes everyone on campus responsible for preventing and intervening in sexual assaults. That initiative has now grown into a nationwide campaign, called "It's On Us," that uses social media platforms to increase awareness about sexual assault on campus.

(itsonus.org, 2017; Reid, 2017; White House, 2017; Anderson, 2014)

IT'S ON **US**

I pledge:

To **RECOGNIZE** that non-consensual sex is sexual assault.

To **IDENTIFY** situations in which sexual assault may occur.

To **INTERVENE** in situations where consent has not or cannot be given.

To **CREATE** an environment in which sexual assault is unacceptable and survivors are supported.

Crisis on College Campuses

(RAINN, 2016, 2009; CRCC, 2014; Weiner, 2014; Adams, 2013)

23% women sexually assaulted in college

80% college rapes estimated to be unreported

47% college rape victims sustain bodily injuries

91,000 rapes are reported to police per year, but the number of rapes per year is estimated to be *at least* 432,000

(Statista, 2017; BJS, 2016)

Factors Aiding Recovery

Positive self-esteem
Social support
Previous success in coping with stress
Economic security
Accurate information about rape and rape trauma syndrome
Constructive decision-making

(NCVS, 2017, 2014)

Factors Delaying Recovery

Prior victimization
Chronic life stressors
Lack of social support
Low self-esteem
Degree of violence during attack

(NCVS, 2017, 2014)

#GenderDifference

Many researchers believe that women's higher rates of posttraumatic stress disorder are tied to the types of violent traumas they experience—namely, interpersonal assaults such as rape or sexual abuse (USDVA, 2015; Street et al., 2011).

12 days after the assault (Rothbaum et al., 1992). Although some rape victims improve psychologically within three or four months, for many others, the profound effects of their assault persist for up to 18 months or longer. Victims typically continue to have higher-than-average levels of anxiety, suspiciousness, depression, self-esteem problems, self-blame, flashbacks, sleep problems, and sexual dysfunction (Remes et al., 2016; Pietrzak et al., 2014; Au et al., 2013).

Female victims of rape and other crimes also are much more likely than other women to suffer serious long-term health problems (Morgan, Brittain, & Welch, 2015; Koss & Heslet, 1992). Interviews with 390 women revealed that such victims had poorer physical well-being for at least five years after the crime and made twice as many visits to physicians.

Ongoing victimization and abuse in the family—specifically child and spouse abuse—may also lead to psychological stress disorders (Cicchetti & Toth, 2016). Because these forms of abuse may occur over the long term and violate family trust, many victims develop other symptoms and disorders as well (Koss et al., 2015, 2011).

TERRORISM People who are victims of terrorism or who live under the threat of terrorism often experience posttraumatic stress symptoms (Comer et al., 2016; Stene et al., 2016). Unfortunately, this source of traumatic stress is on the rise in our society. "The terrorist events of September 11, 2001, have left a lasting mark on the United States and the rest of the world. Hijacked airplanes crashed into and brought down the World Trade Center in New York City and partially destroyed the Pentagon in Washington, DC, killing thousands of victims and rescue workers and forcing thousands more to desperately run, crawl, and even dig their way to safety. A number of studies have indicated that in the aftermath of that fateful day, many individuals developed immediate and long-term psychological effects, ranging from brief stress reactions, such as shock, fear, and anger, to enduring psychological disorders, such as PTSD (Comer et al., 2018; Ruggero et al., 2013; Galea et al., 2007).

Follow-up studies suggest that many such individuals continue to struggle with terrorism-related stress reactions (Shengchao et al., 2016; Adams & Boscarino, 2005). Indeed, even years after the attacks, 42 percent of all adults in the United States and 70 percent of all New York adults report high terrorism fears; 23 percent of all adults in the United States report feeling less safe in their homes; 15 percent of all U.S. adults report drinking more alcohol than they did prior to the attacks; and 9 percent

Je suis Charlie In 2015, terrorists conducted a three-day killing spree in Paris, including the murder of 12 employees of the weekly satirical newspaper *Charlie Hebdo*. Using the slogan *Je suis Charlie* ("I am Charlie"), close to 4 million people joined rallies around France, voicing their support for free speech and their resolve against terrorism. This terrorist attack, like others, led to a significant rise in the rate of PTSD across France (Ben-Ezra et al., 2015)).

of New York adults display PTSD, compared with the national annual prevalence of 3.5 percent. Studies of subsequent acts of terrorism, such as the 2004 commuter train bombings in Madrid, the 2005 London subway and bus bombings, the 2013 Boston Marathon bombing, and the 2016 Bastille Day truck attack in Nice, France, tell a similar story (Goodwin et al., 2017; Comer et al., 2014; Chacón & Vecina, 2007).

TORTURE **Torture** refers to the use of "brutal, degrading, and disorienting strategies in order to reduce victims to a state of utter helplessness" (Okawa & Hauss, 2007). Often, it is done on the orders of a government or another authority to force persons to yield information or make a confession (Dando, 2017). As you will see in Chapter 19, the question of the morality of torturing prisoners who are considered suspects in the "war on terror" has been the subject of much discussion over the past decade (Kaslow, 2014).

People from all walks of life are subjected to torture worldwide—from suspected terrorists to student activists and members of religious, ethnic, and cultural minority groups. The techniques used on them may include *physical torture* (beatings, waterboarding, electrocution), *psychological torture* (threats of death, mock executions, verbal abuse, degradation), *sexual torture* (rape, violence to the genitals, sexual humiliation), or *torture through deprivation* (sleep, sensory, social, nutritional, medical, or hygiene deprivation). Torture victims often experience physical ailments as a result of their ordeal, from scarring and fractures to neurological problems and chronic pain. It also appears that between 30 and 50 percent of torture victims develop PTSD (Ibrahim & Hassan, 2017; Taylor et al., 2013).

Why Do People Develop Acute and Posttraumatic Stress Disorders?

Clearly, extraordinary trauma can cause a stress disorder. The stressful event alone, however, may not be the entire explanation. Anyone who experiences an unusual trauma will be affected by it, but only some people develop a stress disorder. To understand the development of these disorders more fully, researchers have looked at *biological factors, childhood experiences, personal styles, social support systems,* and the *severity and nature of the traumas.* Our discussions in this section will center on PTSD because that is the stress disorder that is most researched.

Biological Factors Investigators have linked posttraumatic stress disorder to several biological factors (Suo et al., 2017). The ones that have received the most attention are the brain–body *stress pathways*, the brain's *stress circuit*, and *inherited predispositions*.

THE BRAIN–BODY STRESS PATHWAYS As you'll recall, when we are stressed, the brain's hypothalamus activates two stress pathways throughout the brain and body— the sympathetic nervous system pathway and the hypothalamic-pituitary-adrenal (HPA) pathway (see page 156). These pathways react to stress by producing a general state of arousal, the former through nerve cell firing and the latter through releasing hormones into the bloodstream.

While everyone reacts to traumatic events with increased arousal throughout these two pathways, research suggests that people who develop PTSD react with especially heightened arousal in the pathways (Dayan, Rauchs, & Guillery-Girard, 2017; Ross et al., 2017). There is evidence that, even prior to confronting a severe trauma, such individuals' pathways are overly reactive to modest stressors, thus setting up a predisposition to develop PTSD. There is also evidence that *after* confrontation with a severe trauma, those brain–body pathways become even more overly reactive (Yehuda et al., 2015, 1993; Rasmusson & Shalev, 2014). Small wonder that researchers have found abnormal activity of the hormone *cortisol* and the neurotransmitter/hormone *norepinephrine*—major players in the two pathways—in the urine, blood, and saliva of

torture The use of brutal, degrading, and disorienting strategies to reduce victims to a state of utter helplessness.

#CommonEvent

More than 60% of adults have experienced a traumatic event at least once in their lives (NCPTSD, 2016; Sidan, 2016).

Candidates for dysfunction A stock trader reacts with exhaustion, worry, and disbelief after a particularly bad—stock-plummeting—day. Business difficulties, such as the trader's, are among the most common triggers of *adjustment disorder*, a DSM-5 disorder characterized by excessive and extended feelings of anxiety, depressed mood, or antisocial behavior in response to life stressors. The symptoms of an adjustment disorder are not as severe as those in PTSD or in anxiety disorders, but they do cause individuals considerable stress and may interfere with their job, schoolwork, or social life.

combat soldiers, rape victims, concentration camp survivors, and survivors of other severe stresses (Gola et al., 2012; Gerardi et al., 2010). In short, once PTSD sets in, an individual's brain–body pathways are characterized by still greater overreactivity in the face of stress, and this persistent overreactivity may lock in brain and body dysfunction and the continuing symptoms of PTSD (Yehuda et al., 2015; Lee et al., 2014).

THE BRAIN'S STRESS CIRCUIT Researchers believe that the chronic overreactivity of the two stress pathways may help bring about dysfunction in a distinct brain circuit, sometimes called the brain's *stress circuit*. As you have seen in earlier chapters, emotional, behavioral, and cognitive reactions of various kinds are tied to brain circuits—networks of brain structures that communicate and trigger each other into action. Dysfunction in one such circuit, the stress circuit, apparently contributes to the symptoms of PTSD. The brain's stress circuit includes such structures as the *amygdala, prefrontal cortex, anterior cingulate cortex, insula,* and *hippocampus,* among others (Jacoby et al., 2016; Pedersen, 2016; Li et al., 2014). Given the close relationship between arousal, fear, and anxiety, it is not surprising that several of the structures in this circuit are also parts of the brain's fear and panic circuits that help produce anxiety disorders. But in the case of PTSD, the problematic activity and interconnections of these structures differ from those found in anxiety disorders.

Researchers have found that dysfunctions within and between three structures in this circuit—the amygdala, prefrontal cortex, and hippocampus—play particularly key roles in posttraumatic stress disorder (Young, 2017). As you read in Chapter 5, the amygdala is at the center of emotional reactions, including fear and panic reactions. In a properly functioning stress circuit, the amygdala springs into action when the person confronts a stressor, it communicates that message to the prefrontal cortex (among other structures), and the prefrontal cortex evaluates the message and sends signals back to the amygdala to slow down—thus helping to keep the person calm (Tone, Garn, & Pine, 2016). However, researchers have found that in people with PTSD, the interconnection between the amygdala and prefrontal cortex is flawed—activity by the former is too high and activity by the latter is too low. The net effect of this flawed interconnection is that the individuals persistently experience symptoms of arousal, such as intense startle reactions and increased heart rate (Ross et al, 2017; Shou et al., 2017; Campese et al., 2016).

The hippocampus, another structure in this circuit, also seems to be important in the onset and maintenance of PTSD. This structure plays a major role in forming memories and regulating the body's stress hormones. Moreover, it communicates with the amygdala to produce the emotional components of memory. Research suggests that dysfunctions in the hippocampus and in its connection to the amygdala may result in the unchecked emotional memories and persistent arousal symptoms that characterize PTSD, as well as the dissociations found in many cases (Ross et al., 2017; Sareen, 2015; Bremner et al., 2004).

INHERITED PREDISPOSITION Researchers also believe that certain individuals inherit a tendency for overly reactive brain–body stress pathways and a dysfunctional brain stress circuit. In turn, such individuals may have a susceptibility to PTSD. Genetic studies have located several genes that might be involved in this inherited susceptibility (Sheerin et al., 2017; Young, 2017). Similarly, family pedigree research supports the notion of an inherited susceptibility. Studies conducted on thousands of pairs of twins who have served in the military find that if one twin develops posttraumatic stress symptoms after combat, an identical twin is more likely than a fraternal twin to develop the same problem (Koenen et al., 2003; True & Lyons, 1999).

In related work, researchers have found that people suffering from PTSD are more likely to transmit relevant biological abnormalities to their children (Cook et al., 2018; Yehuda et al., 2015). In one study, for example, investigators examined the cortisol levels of women who had been pregnant during the September 11, 2001 terrorist attack and had developed PTSD in its aftermath (Yehuda & Bierer, 2007). Not only did these women have higher-than-average cortisol levels, but their babies born after the attacks also displayed higher cortisol levels, suggesting that the babies inherited a predisposition to develop PTSD.

Childhood Experiences   Other researchers agree that certain individuals have overly reactive stress pathways and a dysfunctional stress circuit that predispose them to develop PTSD. However, they believe that such a predisposition may be acquired during childhood rather than inherited at birth (Ross et al., 2017). In support of this notion, a number of studies have found that young children who are chronically neglected or abused or otherwise traumatized develop overly reactive stress pathways and a dysfunctional brain stress circuit that carry into later life (Anacker et al., 2014; Zannas & West, 2014). Apparently, their unfortunate childhood experiences actually play a role in reprogramming their brain and body stress responses.

> Do the vivid images children see regularly on the Web, on TV, and in video games make them more vulnerable to later developing psychological stress disorders or less vulnerable?

Consistent with these findings, researchers have also found that certain childhood experiences increase a person's risk for later PTSD (Pedersen, 2016). People whose childhoods were marked by poverty appear more likely to develop the disorder in the face of later trauma (Wadsworth et al., 2016). So do people whose childhoods included an assault, abuse, or a catastrophe; multiple traumas; parental separation or divorce; or living with family members suffering from psychological disorders (Carroll et al., 2017; Hyland et al., 2017; Ogle et al., 2014).

Personal Styles   Research suggests that people with certain personalities, attitudes, and coping styles are particularly likely to develop posttraumatic stress disorder (DiGangi et al., 2013). For example, a classic study conducted after the monster 1989 storm, Hurricane Hugo, revealed that children who had been highly anxious before the storm were more likely than other children to develop severe stress reactions (Hardin et al., 2002). Research has also found that people who generally view life's negative events as beyond their control tend to develop more severe stress symptoms after sexual abuse or other kinds of traumatic events than people who feel that they have more control over their lives (Catanesi et al., 2013; Bremner, 2002). Similarly, people who generally find it difficult to derive anything positive from unpleasant situations adjust more poorly after traumatic events than other people (Kunst, 2011).

#StressfulOutcome

20   Percentage of people who report they have no one to support them during stress

29   Percentage of people who report feeling more stress this year than last year

41   Percentage of married people who say stress has caused them to yell at their spouse during the past month

(Information from: APA, 2015)

AP Photo/Ahn Young-joon

Building resiliency   Noting that a resilient, or "hardy," personality style may help protect people from developing stress disorders, many programs now claim to build resiliency. Here young South Korean schoolchildren fall on a mud flat at a five-day winter military camp designed to strengthen them mentally and physically.

Conversely, it has been found that people with a *resilient* style of personality are *less* likely than other individuals to develop PTSD after encountering traumatic events (Thompson et al., 2018; Ross et al., 2017). The term *resilience* has been applied to people who adapt well and cope effectively in the face of life adversity (Masten & Cicchetti, 2016). Although there is evidence that genetic factors may help determine one's level of resilience, studies also find that young children who are regularly exposed to *manageable* stress often develop heightened resilience, a gain that may continue throughout childhood and adulthood. Not surprisingly, studies also find that the brain–body stress pathways and brain stress circuits of resilient persons tend to operate better than those of other people (Meng et al., 2018; Southwick & Charney, 2012).

Social Support Systems People whose social and family support systems are weak are also more likely to develop posttraumatic stress disorder after a traumatic event (Sareen, 2015). Rape victims who feel loved, cared for, valued, and accepted by their friends and relatives recover from their ordeal more successfully (Street et al., 2011). So do those treated with dignity and respect by the criminal justice system (Patterson, 2011). In contrast, clinical reports have suggested that poor social support contributes to the development of PTSD in some combat veterans (Schumm et al., 2014).

The Severity and Nature of the Trauma As you might expect, the severity and nature of the traumatic event a person encounters help determine whether the individual will develop a stress disorder. Some events may override a favorable biological foundation, nurturing childhood, positive attitudes, and/or social support (Ogle, Rubin, & Siegler, 2014). One early study examined 253 Vietnam War prisoners five years after their release. Some 23 percent qualified for a clinical diagnosis of PTSD, though all had been evaluated as well adjusted before their imprisonment (Ursano et al., 1981).

Generally, the more severe or prolonged the trauma and the more direct one's exposure to it, the greater the likelihood of developing a stress disorder (Hyland et al., 2017). Mutilation, severe physical injury, or sexual assault in particular seem to increase the risk of stress disorders, as does witnessing the injury or death of other people (Perrin et al., 2014; Ursano et al., 2003). In addition, people who experience intentionally inflicted traumas are more likely to develop a stress disorder than persons who encounter unintentional traumas (Sareen, 2015).

There is also growing evidence that encounters with multiple or recurring traumas can lead to a particularly severe pattern called *complex PTSD* (Hyland et al., 2017; Jakob et al., 2017). Persons with complex PTSD experience virtually all of the symptoms mentioned throughout this chapter along with profound disturbances in their emotional control, self-concept, and relationships.

Putting the Factors Together Most of today's stress theorists believe that the various factors we have been looking at work together to help produce posttraumatic stress disorder (Ross et al., 2017). The *developmental psychopathology* perspective, which has received considerable research support in the realm of PTSD, provides one of the most influential explanations of how this might occur (Bremner, 2016; Cicchetti, 2016).

As you'll recall from Chapters 3 and 5, theorists from this perspective focus on the *intersection* and *context* of important variables at key *points of time* throughout an individual's lifespan. In the case of PTSD, they suggest that certain people have a biological predisposition—either inherited or acquired—for overreactivity in their brain–body stress pathways (that is, the sympathetic nervous system pathway and the hypothalamic-pituitary-adrenal pathway) and for dysfunction in their brain's stress circuit. This predisposition sets the stage for, but does not guarantee, the later development of PTSD. If, however, these individuals encounter extreme stressors throughout their childhood, their stress pathways may become still more overreactive and their brain's stress circuit may become more dysfunctional, and their risk of later develop-

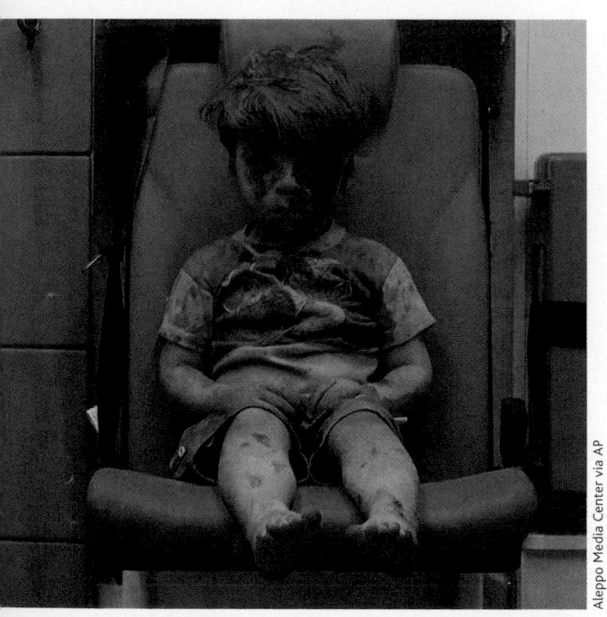

Children too In this famous and heart-wrenching photo, a bloodied and disoriented 5-year-old child named Omran Daqneesh sits in an ambulance covered with dirt and dust after being pulled from the rubble of a building destroyed by an airstrike in Aleppo, Syria. After confronting horrific traumas, especially repeated ones, children too may develop PTSD, leading clinicians to worry greatly about the mental health of children caught in the middle of Syria's civil war.

Aleppo Media Center via AP

ing PTSD may continue to grow. This risk may increase still further if, over the course of their lives, the individuals acquire poor coping mechanisms, develop problematic personal styles, and/or have weak social supports. When they confront an extraordinary trauma or series of traumas in life, such individuals will be particularly vulnerable to the development of PTSD (Ross et al., 2017; Bremner, 2016; Cicchetti, 2016).

It is important to note that in the developmental psychopathology perspective, the relationship between the contributing factors is often a two-way street. For example, while overreactive stress pathways can contribute to poor coping during childhood and beyond, it is also the case that a childhood filled with experiences of *manageable* stress can, as we saw earlier, improve the functioning of the stress pathways, facilitate better coping skills, and help build a resilient personal style, thus reducing the risk of later developing PTSD (Southwick & Charney, 2012).

According to developmental psychopathologists, the *timing* of stressors and traumas over the course of development has a profound influence on whether an individual will develop PTSD (Bremner, 2016). The developing brain is always interacting with stressful experiences. Extreme stressors in childhood disrupt and alter newly developing brain–body stress pathways and brain stress circuits, increasing the likelihood that those pathways and circuits will operate poorly over the course of life. In contrast, when extreme stressors are encountered in adulthood, they are less likely to alter the stress pathways and stress circuits, because those pathways and circuits are more deeply rooted by then. Thus experiences of intense stress early in life are particularly likely to set the stage for PTSD should an individual eventually confront an extraordinary trauma or series of traumas. At the same time, each stage of development ushers in new psychological and biological challenges, so extreme stressors at any point across the life span can increase a person's vulnerability to PTSD.

The consequence of all this, according to the developmental psychopathology perspective, is that one person born with, say, overreactive stress pathways may eventually develop PTSD when confronted by an extraordinary trauma, whereas another person born with similar predisposing stress pathways may not develop PTSD in the face of such trauma. It all depends on the presence, timing, and intersections of the various factors we have been discussing. As you'll recall from Chapter 3, this is the principle of *multifinality*, the notion that persons with similar beginnings may wind up at very different end points (Bremner, 2016; Cicchetti, 2016). Conversely, two persons—one born with overreactive stress pathways and the other with pathways

#SmellingStress

Stress is odorless. The bacteria that feed off of our sweat are what give our bodies odor during very stressful events.

End of a journey? Not necessarily, at least in the psychological realm. This small boat filled with migrants comes ashore at Lesbos, a pastoral Greek island through which a half million refugees— mostly from Syria—have passed on their way to countries throughout Europe. The rate of PTSD among refugees can be as high as 56 percent in some areas of the world, particularly for those who were tortured in their homeland or whose travels were perilous. Thus a small team of clinicians in Lesbos work full-time to help reduce the stress-related symptoms of refugees during their short stay on the island (Yaser et al., 2016).

Sergey Ponomarev/The New York Times/Redux

that react to stressors more appropriately—may both develop PTSD when eventually confronted by an extraordinary trauma. In such cases, the person born with favorable stress pathways might nonetheless come to develop overreactive pathways as a result of aversive childhood experiences, inadequate social supports, and other such factors. This principle is known as *equifinality*, the notion that different developmental pathways may lead to the same end point (Bremner, 2016; Cicchetti, 2016).

Standing down To help prevent, reduce, or treat combat-related PTSD, the U.S. military and other organizations now offer stress- and trauma-release exercises for soldiers and ex-soldiers to perform. Here relaxation training and yoga are taught to veterans during the 2013 Veteran Stand Down hosted by Goodwill Southern California.

ZUMA Press, Inc./Alamy

How Do Clinicians Treat Acute and Posttraumatic Stress Disorders?

Treatment can be very important for people who have been overwhelmed by traumatic events (Brown et al., 2016). Overall, one-third of all cases of posttraumatic stress disorder improve within 12 months. The remainder of cases may persist for years, and, indeed, one-third of people with PTSD do not achieve normal functioning even after many years (Sareen, 2015; Byers et al., 2014).

Today's treatment procedures for troubled survivors often vary from trauma to trauma. Was it combat, an act of terrorism, sexual molestation, or a major accident? Yet all the programs share basic goals: they try to help survivors put an end to their stress reactions, gain perspective on their painful experiences, and return to constructive living (Brown et al., 2016). Programs for combat veterans who suffer from PTSD illustrate how these issues may be addressed.

Treatment for Combat Veterans Therapists have used a variety of techniques to help reduce veterans' posttraumatic symptoms. Among the most common are *antidepressant drug therapy, cognitive-behavioral therapy, couple or family therapy,* and *group therapy*. Commonly, the approaches are combined, as no one of them successfully reduces all the symptoms (Mott et al., 2014; Rothbaum et al., 2014).

ANTIDEPRESSANT DRUGS Antidepressant drugs are widely used for veterans with PTSD (Stein, 2017). Typically, these medications are more helpful for the PTSD symptoms of increased arousal and negative emotions, and less helpful for the recurrent negative memories, dissociations, and avoidance behaviors that also characterize the disorder. Around half of PTSD patients who take antidepressant drugs experience some symptom reductions. Other psychotropic drugs do not fare as well in PTSD research and are prescribed less often (Stein, 2017).

COGNITIVE-BEHAVIORAL THERAPY Cognitive-behavioral therapy has proved to be of considerable help to many veterans with PTSD, bringing significant overall improvement to half or more of those who receive such treatment (Rothbaum, 2017; Shou et al., 2017). On the cognitive side, the therapists guide the veterans to examine and change the dysfunctional attitudes and styles of interpretation they have developed as a result of their traumatic experiences. Over the course of such examinations and efforts, often called *cognitive processing therapy* when applied in cases of PTSD, the veterans learn to deal with difficult memories and feelings, come to accept what they have done and experienced, become less judgmental of themselves, and begin to trust other people once again (Holliday et al., 2017; Turner et al., 2005). Increasingly, a number of cognitive-behavioral therapists are adding mindfulness-based techniques (see page 65) to further help the clients become more accepting and less judgmental of their recurring thoughts, feelings, and memories. Research indicates that such mindfulness techniques produce modest additional improvements (Rothbaum, 2017).

On the behavioral side, cognitive-behavioral therapists typically apply exposure techniques when treating veterans with PTSD. These techniques have been quite successful at reducing specific symptoms and, in turn, bringing about improvements in overall adjustment (Cooper et al., 2017; Korte et al., 2017). In fact, some studies indicate that exposure is the single most helpful intervention for people with PTSD, leading many clinical theorists to conclude that exposure techniques of one kind or another should always be part of the treatment picture (Haagen et al., 2015).

During exposure therapy, veterans with PTSD are guided to confront trauma-related—usually combat-related—objects, events, and situations that continue to cause them extreme upset and anxiety. Their exposures may be imagined or in vivo. Of course, it is technically impossible, not to mention unethical, to expose veterans with PTSD to actual combat experiences, so many of today's exposure treatments rely on the vivid, multisensory images produced by virtual reality procedures (Maples-Keller et al., 2017) (see **MindTech**).

Perhaps the most widely applied exposure technique in cases of PTSD is **prolonged exposure** (Acierno et al., 2017; Foa, 2011). Here therapists direct clients to confront not only trauma-related objects and situations, but also their painful memories of traumatic experiences—memories they have been actively avoiding. The clients repeatedly recall and describe the memories in great detail for extended periods of time, holding on to them until becoming less aroused, anxious, and upset by them.

prolonged exposure A treatment approach in which clients confront not only trauma-related objects and situations, but also their painful memories of traumatic experiences.

MINDTECH

Virtual Reality Therapy: Better than the Real Thing?

As you have read, exposure-based treatment may be the single most helpful intervention for people with PTSD (Cooper et al., 2017; Haagen et al., 2015). However, *in vivo* (actual) exposure to upsetting stimuli is more effective in treating PTSD than covert (imaginary) exposure. For years, this meant that treatment for PTSD for combat veterans was less than optimal. Unable to revisit real-life battle settings, veterans had to imagine rifle fire, bomb explosions, dead bodies, and/or other traumatic stimuli for their treatment.

All that changed a decade ago, when "virtual" exposure to combat conditions became available for veterans with PTSD. The Office of Naval Research funded the development of "Virtual Iraq," a war simulation treatment game (McIlvaine, 2011). This game was able to produce sights and sounds that seemed every bit as real and produced as much—or more—alarm as real battle conditions. The use of virtual reality as an exposure technique has since become a standard in PTSD treatment.

In *virtual reality therapy*, PTSD clients use wraparound goggles and joysticks to navigate their way through a computer-generated military convoy, battle, or bomb attack in a landscape that looks like Iraq, Afghanistan, or other war zones. The therapist controls the intensity of the horrifying sights, terrifying sounds, and awful smells of combat, triggering very real feelings of fear or panic in the client. Exposure therapy proceeds with the therapist applying the exposures to these stimuli in either *gradual steps* or abruptly.

> **Can you design a virtual reality exposure treatment program for people with social anxiety disorder?**

Study after study has suggested that virtual reality therapy is extremely helpful for combat veterans with PTSD, more so than covert exposure therapy (Maples-Keller et al., 2017; Nauert, 2014; McLay, 2013). In addition, the improvements produced by this intervention appear to last for extended periods, perhaps indefinitely. Small wonder that virtual reality therapy is now also becoming common in the treatment of other anxiety disorders and phobias, including social anxiety disorder and fears of heights, flying, and closed spaces (Bouchard et al., 2017).

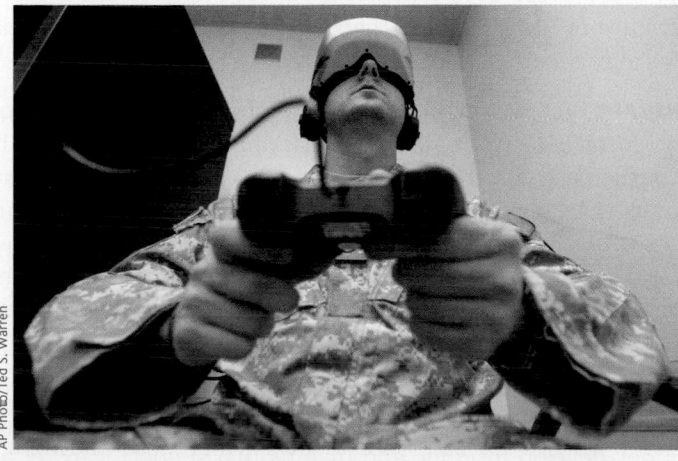

"Virtual" exposure
An ex-soldier's headset and video game–type controller take him back to a battle scene in Iraq.

AP Photo/Ted S. Warren

eye movement desensitization and reprocessing (EMDR) An exposure treatment in which clients move their eyes in a rhythmic manner from side to side while flooding their minds with images of objects and situations they ordinarily avoid.

psychological debriefing A form of crisis intervention in which victims are helped to talk about their feelings and reactions to traumatic incidents. Also called *critical incident stress debriefing*.

In the early sessions of prolonged exposure, clients are directed to describe, again and again, everything they can remember about the *entire* event that triggered their stress disorder. A combat veteran of the war in Iraq, for example, might describe the four-hour ordeal during which his Humvee was blasted by an IED (improvised explosive device). During the later sessions, clients are instructed to focus their recollections on particular "hot spots," pieces of the traumatic event that are especially dreadful. For example, the veteran whose Humvee encountered an IED might be directed to recall in great detail the deafening explosion, the shock wave produced by the IED, his body flying through the cabin, the smell of burning flesh, the sight of blood splattered throughout the cabin, the moans and screams of others in the Humvee, the dead bodies of his driver and gunner, and/or the loss of his leg and hand.

The therapist conducting prolonged exposure typically offers the following instructions during the hot spot phase of therapy:

 Up to this point . . . you have been making great progress and have been experiencing the decrease in anxiety that we expect to see. Today we are going to do the exposure a little differently . . . . I will ask you to tell me . . . what the most distressing or upsetting parts of this memory are for you now. And then today, rather than going through the entire memory from beginning to end, I will ask you to focus the revisiting and recounting on each of these "hot spots," one at a time. We will pick one to begin with and you will repeat that one part of the memory over and over just by itself, focusing in closely and describing what happened in great detail, as if in slow motion, including what you felt, saw, heard, and thought. We will repeat it as many times as necessary to "wear it out" or bring about a big decrease in your [discomfort] level. When that part seems to have been sufficiently processed, we will move to the next one.

(Foa et al., 2007, pp. 100–101)

Over the course of prolonged exposure, the client is expected to remember more and more details of each hotspot, experience less distress during such memories, become less fearful of the memories, and indeed display fewer symptoms of PTSD. Research suggests that for clients who can stay with such intense memory exercises (many cannot), prolonged exposure is even more helpful than more gradual exposure interventions (Foa & McLean, 2016; Eftekhari et al., 2013).

Another popular form of exposure therapy is **eye movement desensitization and reprocessing (EMDR),** in which clients move their eyes in a rhythmic manner from side to side while flooding their minds with images of the objects and situations they ordinarily try to avoid. Although this approach has a number of skeptics, case studies and some controlled studies suggest that the treatment can sometimes be helpful to people with PTSD (Shapiro & Forrest, 2016; Chen et al., 2015). Many theorists argue that it is the exposure feature of EMDR, rather than the eye movement per se, that accounts for its success as a treatment (Lamprecht et al., 2004).

COUPLE AND FAMILY THERAPY Veterans with PTSD may be further helped in couple therapy or family therapy formats (Vogt et al., 2017, 2011; Shnaider et al., 2014). The symptoms of PTSD are particularly apparent to spouses and other family members, who may be directly affected by the client's anxieties, depressed mood, or angry outbursts (Freytes et al., 2017; Owens et al., 2014). With the help and support of their family members, they may come to examine their impact on others, learn to communicate better, improve their problem-solving skills, and reestablish feelings of closeness (Sareen, 2015).

GROUP THERAPY In group therapy sessions, called *rap groups* when initiated during the 1980s, veterans meet with others like themselves to share experiences and feelings (particularly guilt and rage), develop insights, and give mutual support (Levi et al., 2017; Ellis et al., 2014). Today hundreds of small *Veterans Outreach Centers* across

 #

#GenderImpact

51 Percentage of U.S. women who say they often lie awake at night due to stress

32 Percentage of U.S. men who often lie awake at night due to stress

(Information from: APA, 2015)

John Moore/Getty Images

Working together A therapist counsels a couple during a group marital therapy session at a retreat for military families. Research indicates that couple therapy is often an essential part of helping combat veterans and their families to deal with and overcome the symptoms of PTSD.

the country, as well as treatment programs in Veterans Administration hospitals and mental health clinics, provide group treatment (Finley et al., 2017; Schumm et al., 2015; Ruzek & Batten, 2011). These agencies also offer individual therapy, counseling for spouses and children, family therapy, and aid in seeking jobs, education, and benefits (Mott et al., 2014). Clinical reports suggest that such programs offer a necessary, sometimes life-saving, treatment opportunity.

Psychological Debriefing People who are traumatized by disasters, victimization, or accidents profit from many of the same treatments that are used to help survivors of combat (Brown et al., 2016; Monson et al., 2014). In addition, because their traumas occur in their own community, where mental health resources are close at hand, they may, according to many clinicians, further benefit from immediate community interventions.

One of the leading such approaches is called **psychological debriefing,** or **critical incident stress debriefing,** an intervention applied widely over the past 30 years. Psychological debriefing is a form of crisis intervention that has victims of trauma talk extensively about their feelings and reactions within days of the critical incident (Tuckey & Scott, 2014; Mitchell, 2003, 1983). The clinicians then clarify to the victims that their reactions are normal responses to a terrible event, offer stress management tips, and in some cases, refer the victims to professionals for long-term counseling. Based on the assumption that such sessions prevent or reduce stress reactions, they are often provided to trauma victims who have not yet displayed any symptoms at all, as well as to those who have.

This intense approach has been applied in the aftermath of countless traumatic events (Pfefferbaum, Newman, & Nelson, 2014; Wei et al., 2010). Indeed, when a traumatic incident affects numerous individuals, debriefing-trained counselors may come from far and wide to conduct debriefing sessions with the victims. Large mobilizations of this kind have offered free emergency mental health services at the sites of disasters such as the 2001 World Trade Center attack, the floods caused by Hurricane Katrina in 2005, and the mass killing of 49 persons at Pulse, a gay nightclub in Orlando, Florida, in 2016.

Over the years, personal testimonials for rapid mobilization programs have often been favorable (Healy & Tyrrell, 2013; Watson & Shalev, 2005). However, research conducted over the past decade has called into question the effectiveness of this kind of intervention (USDVA, 2016; Tuckey & Scott, 2014). In fact, some clinicians believe that the early intervention programs may encourage victims to dwell too long on the traumatic events they have experienced. And a number worry that early disaster

\#

#TopStressors

1. Personal finances

2. Job pressure

3. The economy

4. Relationships

5. Health

(Information from: APA, 2015)

dissociative disorders Disorders marked by major changes in memory that do not have clear physical causes.

memory The faculty for recalling past events and past learning.

dissociative amnesia A disorder marked by an inability to recall important personal events and information.

counseling may unintentionally "suggest" problems to certain victims, thus helping to produce stress disorders (USDVA, 2016; McNally, 2004).

Many mental health professionals continue to believe in psychological debriefing programs. However, given the unsupportive research findings of recent years, the current clinical climate is moving away from the ready application of this approach. A growing number of clinicians believe that certain *high-risk* individuals may profit from debriefing programs and that those people should receive debriefing techniques immediately after a traumatic event, but that other trauma victims should not necessarily receive such interventions (Tarquinio et al., 2016; USDVA, 2016; North & Pfefferbaum, 2013).

Dissociative Disorders

AS YOU HAVE JUST READ, a number of people with acute and posttraumatic stress disorders have symptoms of dissociation along with their other symptoms. They may, for example, feel dazed, have trouble remembering things, or have a sense of depersonalization or derealization. Symptoms of this kind are also on display in **dissociative disorders,** another group of disorders triggered by traumatic events. The memory difficulties and other dissociative symptoms found in these disorders are particularly intense, extensive, and disruptive. Moreover, in such disorders, dissociative reactions are the main or only symptoms. People with dissociative disorders do not typically have the significant arousal, negative emotions, sleep difficulties, and other problems that characterize acute and posttraumatic stress disorders. Nor are there clear physical factors at work in dissociative disorders.

Most of us experience a sense of wholeness and continuity as we interact with the world. We perceive ourselves as being more than a collection of isolated sensory experiences, feelings, and behaviors. In other words, we have an *identity,* a sense of who we are and where we fit in our environment. **Memory** is a key to this sense of identity, the link between our past, present, and future. Without a memory, we would always be starting over; with it, our life and our identity move forward. In dissociative disorders, one part of a person's memory or identity becomes *dissociated,* or separated, from other parts of his or her memory or identity.

There are several kinds of dissociative disorders. People with *dissociative amnesia* are unable to recall important personal events and information. People with *dissociative identity disorder,* once known as *multiple personality disorder,* have two or more separate identities that may not always be aware of each other's memories, thoughts, feelings, and behavior. And people with *depersonalization-derealization disorder* feel as though they have become detached from their own mental processes or bodies or are observing themselves from the outside.

Several famous books and movies have portrayed dissociative disorders. Two classics are *The Three Faces of Eve* and *Sybil,* each about a woman who developed multiple personalities after having been subject to traumatic events in childhood. The topic is so fascinating that most television drama series seem to include at least one case of dissociation every season, creating the impression that the disorders are very common. Many clinicians, however, believe that they are rare.

Dissociative Amnesia

People with **dissociative amnesia** are unable to recall important information, usually of a stressful nature, about their lives (APA, 2013). The loss of memory is much more extensive than normal forgetting and is not caused by physical factors such as a blow to the head (see **Table 6-3**). Typically, an episode of amnesia is directly triggered by a traumatic or upsetting event (Odagaki, 2017; Loewenstein, 2014).

Barcroft/Getty Images

Managing without memory Andy Wray developed dissociative amnesia after witnessing several horrific deaths in his work as a policeman. His disorder is marked by *continuous forgetting*. Every few days, many of his new memories disappear, leaving him unable to recognize friends, relatives, and events in any detail. To help him get on with his life, he uses countless notebooks and reminder cards like the ones he is looking at here.

Dissociative amnesia may be *localized, selective, generalized,* or *continuous.* In *localized amnesia,* the most common type of dissociative amnesia, a person loses all memory of events that took place within a limited period of time, almost always beginning with some very disturbing occurrence.

> **Why do many people question the authenticity of people who seem to lose their memories at times of severe stress?**

A soldier, for example, may awaken a week after a horrific combat battle and be unable to recall the battle or any of the events surrounding it. She may remember everything that happened up to the battle, and may recall everything that has occurred over the past several days, but the events in between remain a total blank. The forgotten period is called the *amnestic episode.* During an amnestic episode, people may appear confused; in some cases they wander about aimlessly. They are already experiencing memory difficulties but seem unaware of them.

People with *selective amnesia,* the second most common form of dissociative amnesia, remember some, but not all, events that took place during a period of time. If the combat soldier mentioned in the previous paragraph had selective amnesia, she might remember certain interactions or conversations that occurred during the battle, but not more disturbing events such as the death of a friend or the screams of enemy soldiers.

In some cases the loss of memory extends back to times long before the upsetting period. In addition to forgetting battle-linked events, the soldier may not remember events that occurred earlier in her life. In this case, she would have what is called *generalized amnesia.* In extreme cases, she might not even recognize relatives and friends.

In the forms of dissociative amnesia just discussed, the period affected by the amnesia has an end. In *continuous amnesia,* however, forgetting continues into the present. The soldier might forget new and ongoing experiences as well as what happened before and during the battle.

These various forms of dissociative amnesia are similar in that the amnesia interferes mostly with a person's memory of personal material. Memory for abstract or encyclopedic information usually remains. People with dissociative amnesia are as likely as anyone else to know the name of the president of the United States and how to read or drive a car.

TABLE: 6-3

Dx Checklist

Dissociative Amnesia

1. Person cannot recall important life-related information, typically traumatic or stressful information. The memory problem is more than simple forgetting.

2. Significant distress or impairment

3. The symptoms are not caused by a substance or medical condition.

Dissociative Identity Disorder

1. Person experiences a disruption to his or her identity, as reflected by at least two separate personality states or experiences of possession.

2. Person repeatedly experiences memory gaps regarding daily events, key personal information, or traumatic events, beyond ordinary forgetting.

3. Significant distress or impairment

4. The symptoms are not caused by a substance or medical condition.

Information from: APA, 2013.

David Becker/Getty Images

An additional risk Three concertgoers desperately run for cover during the 2017 mass shooting at an outdoor country music festival in Las Vegas, Nevada, a horrific incident that left 58 people dead and 546 injured. People who experience severe threats to their health and safety—as in natural and human-produced disasters—are particularly vulnerable to amnesia and other dissociative reactions. In the aftermath of mass shootings, for example, survivors may forget specific details of their ordeal, personal information, or even their identities.

Studies suggest that at least 2 percent of all adults experience dissociative amnesia in a given year (Loewenstein, 2014). Many cases seem to begin during serious threats to health and safety, as in wartime and natural disasters. Like the soldier in the earlier examples, combat veterans often report memory gaps of hours or days, and some forget personal information, such as their name and address (Bremner, 2016, 2002).

Childhood abuse, particularly child sexual abuse, can also trigger dissociative amnesia (Hébert et al., 2018); indeed, in the 1990s there were many reports in which adults claimed to recall long-forgotten experiences of childhood abuse (see *PsychWatch*). In addition, dissociative amnesia may occur under more ordinary circumstances, such as the sudden loss of a loved one through rejection or death, or extreme guilt over certain actions (for example, an extramarital affair) (Koh et al., 2000).

The personal impact of dissociative amnesia depends on how much is forgotten. Obviously, an amnestic episode of two years is more of a problem than one of two hours. Similarly, an amnestic episode during which a person's life changes in major ways causes more difficulties than one that is quiet.

An extreme version of dissociative amnesia is called **dissociative fugue.** Here persons not only forget their personal identities and details of their past lives but also flee to an entirely different location. Some people travel a short distance and make few social contacts in the new setting (APA, 2013). Their fugue may be brief—a matter of hours or days—and end suddenly. In other cases, however, the person may travel far from home, take a new name, and establish a new identity, new relationships, and even a new line of work. Such people may also display new personality characteristics; often they are more outgoing. This pattern is seen in the century-old case of the Reverend Ansel Bourne, whose last name was the inspiration for Jason Bourne, the memory-deprived secret agent in the modern-day Bourne books and movies.

Lost and found Cheryl Ann Barnes is helped off a plane by her grandmother and stepmother upon arrival in Florida in 1996. The 17-year-old high school honor student had disappeared from her Florida home and was found one month later in a New York City hospital listed as Jane Doe, apparently suffering from a dissociative fugue.

 On January 17, 1887, [the Reverend Ansel Bourne, of Greene, R.I.] drew 551 dollars from a bank in Providence with which to pay for a certain lot of land in Greene, paid certain bills, and got into a Pawtucket horsecar. This is the last incident which he remembers. He did not return home that day, and nothing was heard of him for two months. He was published in the papers as missing, and foul play being suspected, the police sought in vain his whereabouts. On the morning of March 14th, however, at Norristown, Pennsylvania, a man calling himself A. I. Brown who had rented a small shop six weeks previously, stocked it with stationery, confectionery, fruit and small articles, and carried on his quiet trade without seeming to any one unnatural or eccentric, woke up in a fright and called in the people of the house to tell him where he was. He said that his name was Ansel Bourne, that he was entirely ignorant of Norristown, that he knew nothing of shop keeping, and that the last thing he remembered—it seemed only yesterday—was drawing the money from the bank, etc. in Providence. . . . He was very weak, having lost apparently over twenty pounds of flesh during his escapade, and had such a horror of the idea of the candy-store that he refused to set foot in it again.

(James, 1890, pp. 391–393)

Fugues tend to end abruptly. In some cases, as with Reverend Bourne, the person "awakens" in a strange place, surrounded by unfamiliar faces, and wonders how he or she got there. In other cases, the lack of personal history may arouse suspicion. Perhaps a traffic accident or legal problem leads police to discover the false identity; at other times friends search for and find the missing person. When people are found before their state of fugue has ended, therapists may find it necessary to ask them

dissociative fugue A form of dissociative amnesia in which a person travels to a new location and may assume a new identity, simultaneously forgetting his or her past.

Repressed Childhood Memories or False Memory Syndrome?

Throughout the 1990s, reports of repressed childhood memory of abuse attracted much public attention. Adults with this type of dissociative amnesia seemed to recover buried memories of sexual and physical abuse from their childhood. A woman might claim, for example, that her father had sexually molested her repeatedly between the ages of 5 and 7. Or a young man might remember that a family friend had made sexual advances on several occasions when he was very young. Often the repressed memories surfaced during therapy for another problem.

Although the number of such claims has declined dramatically in recent years, clinicians remain divided on this issue (Andrews & Brewin, 2017; McNally, 2017; Brewin & Andrews, 2016). Some believe that recovered memories are just what they appear to be—horrible memories of abuse that have been buried for years in the person's mind

(MacIntosh, Fletcher, & Collin-Vézina, 2016). Other clinicians—the majority—believe that the memories are actually illusions, false images created by a mind that is confused. Opponents of the repressed memory concept hold that the details of childhood sexual abuse are often remembered all too well, not completely wiped from memory (Loftus & Cahill, 2007). They also point out that memory in general is often flawed. Moreover, false memories of various kinds can be created in the laboratory by tapping into research participants' imaginations (McNally, 2017; Volz et al., 2017).

If the alleged recovery of childhood memories is not what it appears to be, what is it? According to opponents of the concept, it may be a powerful case of suggestibility (McNally, 2017; Loftus, 2003, 2001). These theorists hold that the attention paid to the phenomenon by both clinicians and the public leads some therapists to make the diagnosis without sufficient evidence (Haaken & Reavey, 2010). Moreover, certain therapists use special memory recovery techniques, including hypnosis

and regression therapy. Perhaps some clients respond to the techniques by unknowingly forming false memories of abuse (McNally, 2017; McNally & Garaerts, 2009)

Of course, repressed memories of childhood sexual abuse do not emerge only in clinical settings. Some individuals come forward on their own (MacIntosh et al., 2016). Opponents of the repressed memory concept explain these cases by pointing to various books, Web sites, and television shows that seem to validate the phenomenon of repressed memories of childhood abuse (Haaken & Reavey, 2010; Loftus, 1993). Still other opponents believe that, for biological or other reasons, some individuals are more prone than others to experience false memories—either of childhood abuse or of other kinds of events (McNally, 2017; McNally et al., 2005).

It is important to recognize that the theorists who question the recovery of repressed childhood memories do not in any way deny the problem of child sexual abuse. In fact, proponents and opponents alike are greatly concerned that the public may take this debate to mean that clinicians have doubts about the scope of the problem of child sexual abuse. Unfortunately, that problem is all too real and all too common.

Bettmann/Getty Images

Early recall These siblings, all born on the same day in different years, have very different reactions to their cakes at a 1958 birthday party. But how do they each remember that party today? Research suggests that our memories of early childhood may be influenced by the reminiscences of family members, our dreams, television and movie plots, and our present self-image.

many questions about the details of their lives, repeatedly remind them who they are, and even begin psychotherapy before they recover their memories (Igwe, 2013; Mamarde et al., 2013). As these people recover their past, some forget the events of the fugue period.

The majority of people who go through a dissociative fugue regain most or all of their memories and never have a recurrence. Since fugues are usually brief and totally reversible, those who have experienced them tend to have few aftereffects. People who have been away for months or years, however, often do have trouble adjusting to the changes that took place during their flight. In addition, some people commit illegal or violent acts in their fugue state and later must face the consequences.

dissociative identity disorder A dissociative disorder in which a person develops two or more distinct personalities. Also known as *multiple personality disorder.*

subpersonalities The two or more distinct personalities found in individuals suffering with dissociative identity disorder. Also known as *alternate personalities.*

Dissociative Identity Disorder

Dissociative identity disorder is both dramatic and disabling, as we see in the case of Luisa:

Luisa was first brought in for treatment after she was found walking in circles by the side of the road in a suburban neighborhood near Denver. Agitated, malnourished, and dirty, this 30-year-old woman told police that her name was Franny and that she was a 15-year-old who was running away from her home in Telluride. At first, the police officers suspected she was giving a false identity to avoid prosecution for prostitution or drug possession, but there really was no evidence for either crime when she was found.

Once it became apparent that she fully believed what she was saying, the woman, who carried no identification of any kind, was transferred to a psychiatric hospital for observation. By the time she met with a therapist, she was no longer a young child speaking rapidly about a terrible family situation. She was now calling herself Luisa, and she spoke in slow, measured, and sad tones—eloquent but often confused.

Luisa described how she had been sexually abused for years by her stepfather, starting when she was six. She said she had run away from home at the age of 15 and had not spoken since to either her mother or stepfather. She claimed that, although she had spent considerable time living on the streets over the years, she was currently living with her boyfriend, Tim, in a small apartment. However, when pressed, she was unable to say what Tim did for a living, nor could she provide his address or last name. Thus she remained in treatment.

Over the course of treatment, as her therapist continued to probe for details of her unhappy childhood and sexual abuse, Luisa became more and more agitated, until finally, she actually transformed back into 15-year-old Franny during one session. Her therapist wrote in his notes, "Her entire physical presence transformed itself suddenly and almost violently. Her face, previously relaxed and even flat, became tense and scrunched up, and her entire body hunched over. She moved her chair back almost two feet and repeatedly flinched from me if I even gestured in her direction. Her voice became high-pitched, clipped, and fast, spitting out words, and her vocabulary became limited, to that which a child would display. She seemed to be a different person in every way possible."

Over the following several sessions, Luisa's therapist wound up meeting still other personalities. One was Miss Johnson, a strict school principal who claimed to have taught Luisa when she was younger. Another was Roger—homeless, tough, and threatening— who made it clear that he was in charge of Luisa and the other personalities. In addition there was Sarah, aged 55 and divorced, and Lilly, aged 24, a math genius and accountant who seemed to appear whenever Luisa needed to deal with money or complex mathematical issues.

#AssessmentDelay

People with dissociative identity disorder do not receive that diagnosis until they have been in therapy for an average of seven years (Foote, 2016).

A person with **dissociative identity disorder,** known in the past as *multiple personality disorder,* develops two or more distinct personalities, often called **subpersonalities,** or **alternate personalities**, each with a unique set of memories, behaviors, thoughts, and emotions (see again Table 6-3). At any given time, one of the subpersonalities takes center stage and dominates the person's functioning. Usually one subpersonality, called the *primary,* or *host,* personality, appears more often than the others.

The transition from one subpersonality to another, called *switching,* is usually sudden and may be dramatic (Barlow & Chu, 2014). Luisa, for example, twisted her face and hunched her shoulders and body forward violently. Switching is usually triggered by a stressful event, although clinicians can also bring about the change with hypnotic suggestion.

Cases of dissociative identity disorder were first reported almost three centuries ago (Rieber, 2006, 2002). Many clinicians consider the disorder to be rare, but some reports suggest that it may be more common than was once thought (Dorahy et al., 2014). Most cases are first diagnosed in late adolescence or early adulthood, but more often than not, the symptoms actually began in early childhood after episodes of trauma or abuse (often sexual abuse) (Reinders et al., 2016; Vissia et al., 2016). Women receive this diagnosis at least three times as often as men.

> Why might women be more likely than men to receive a diagnosis of dissociative identity disorder?

How Do Subpersonalities Interact? How subpersonalities relate to or recall one another varies from case to case (Barlow & Chu, 2014; Ellenberger, 1970). Generally, however, there are three kinds of relationships. In *mutually amnesic relationships,* the subpersonalities have no awareness of one another. Conversely, in *mutually cognizant patterns,* each subpersonality is well aware of the rest. They may hear one another's voices and even talk among themselves. Some are on good terms, while others do not get along at all.

In *one-way amnesic relationships,* the most common relationship pattern, some subpersonalities are aware of others, but the awareness is not mutual. Those who are aware, called *coconscious subpersonalities,* are "quiet observers" who watch the actions and thoughts of the other subpersonalities but do not interact with them. Sometimes while another subpersonality is present, the coconscious personality makes itself known through indirect means, such as auditory hallucinations (perhaps a voice giving commands) or "automatic writing" (the current personality may find itself writing down words over which it has no control).

Investigators used to believe that most cases of dissociative identity disorder involved two or three subpersonalities. Studies now suggest, however, that the average number of subpersonalities per patient is much higher—15 for women and 8 for men (APA, 2000). In fact, there have been cases in which 100 or more subpersonalities were observed. Often the subpersonalities emerge in groups of 2 or 3 at a time.

In the case of "Eve White," made famous in the book and movie *The Three Faces of Eve,* a woman had three subpersonalities— Eve White, Eve Black, and Jane (Thigpen & Cleckley, 1957). Eve White, the primary personality, was quiet and serious; Eve Black was carefree and mischievous; and Jane was mature and intelligent. According to the book, these three subpersonalities eventually merged into Evelyn, a stable personality who was really an integration of the other three.

The book was mistaken, however; this was not to be the end of Eve's dissociation. In an autobiography 20 years later, she revealed that altogether 22 subpersonalities had come forth during her life, including 9 subpersonalities after Evelyn. Usually they appeared in groups of three, and so the authors of *The Three Faces of Eve* apparently never knew about her previous or subsequent subpersonalities. She later overcame her disorder, achieving a single, stable identity, and was known as Chris Sizemore for four decades until her death in 2016 (Weber, 2016; Sizemore, 1991).

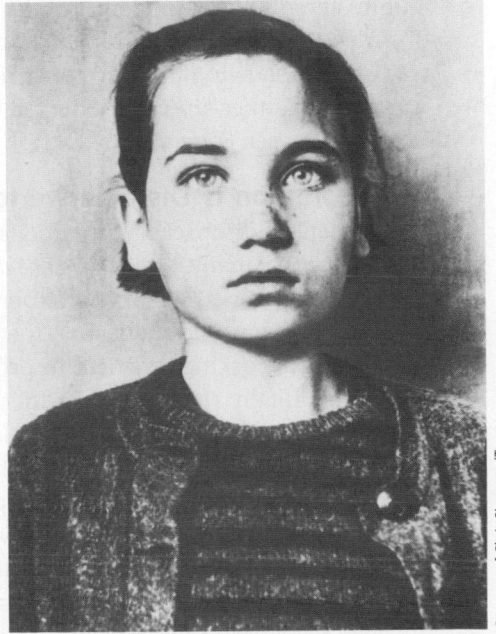

Courtesy of Chris Sizemore/Towers Productions/The Everett Collection

Early beginnings The dissociative identity disorder of Chris Sizemore (*The Three Faces of Eve*) developed long before this photograph of her was taken at age 10. It emerged during her preschool years after she experienced several traumas (witnessing two deaths and a horrifying accident) within a three-month period.

How Do Subpersonalities Differ? As in Chris Sizemore's case, subpersonalities often exhibit dramatically different characteristics. They may also have their own names and different *identifying features, abilities and preferences,* and even *physiological responses.*

IDENTIFYING FEATURES The subpersonalities may differ in features as basic as age, gender, race, and family history, as in the case of Sybil Dorsett, whose disorder is

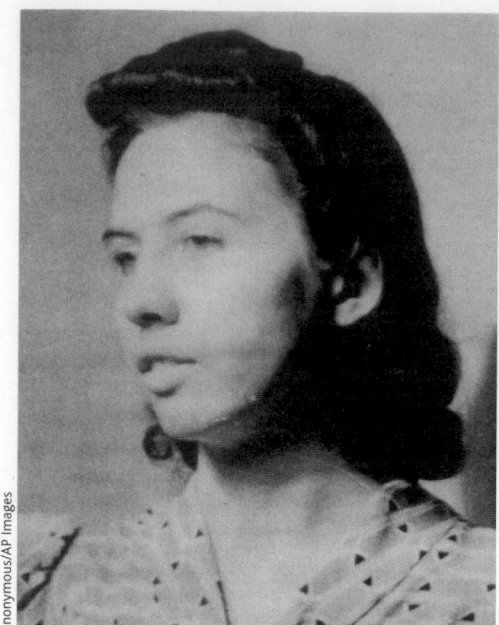

Anonymous/AP Images

The real Sybil Clinical historians have identified painter Shirley A. Mason (shown here) as the real-life person on whom the famous work of fiction *Sybil* was based.

described in the famous novel *Sybil* (Schreiber, 1973). According to the novel, Sybil displayed 17 subpersonalities, all with different identifying features. They included adults, a teenager, and even a baby. One subpersonality, Vicky, saw herself as attractive and blonde, while another, Peggy Lou, believed herself to be "a pixie with a pug nose." Yet another, Mary, was plump with dark hair, and Vanessa was a tall, thin redhead. (It is worth noting that the accuracy of the real-life case on which this novel was based has been challenged in recent years.)

ABILITIES AND PREFERENCES Although memories of abstract or encyclopedic information are not usually affected in dissociative amnesia, they are often disturbed in dissociative identity disorder. It is not uncommon for the different subpersonalities to have different abilities: one may be able to drive, speak a foreign language, or play a musical instrument, while the others cannot (Coons & Bowman, 2001). Their handwriting can also differ. In addition, the subpersonalities usually have different tastes in food, friends, music, and literature. Chris Sizemore ("Eve") later pointed out, "If I had learned to sew as one personality and then tried to sew as another, I couldn't do it. Driving a car was the same. Some of my personalities couldn't drive" (Sizemore & Pitillo, 1977, p. 4).

PHYSIOLOGICAL RESPONSES Researchers have discovered that subpersonalities may have physiological differences, such as differences in blood pressure levels and allergies (Spiegel, 2009; Putnam et al., 1990). A pioneering study looked at the brain activities of different subpersonalities by measuring their *evoked potentials*—that is, brain-response patterns recorded on an electroencephalograph (Putnam, 1984). The brain pattern a person produces in response to a specific stimulus (such as a flashing light) is usually unique and consistent. However, when an evoked potential test was administered to four subpersonalities of each of 10 people with dissociative identity disorder, the results were dramatic. The brain-activity pattern of each subpersonality was unique, showing the kinds of variations usually found in totally different people. A number of other studies conducted over the past two decades have yielded similar findings (Boysen & VanBergen, 2014).

How Common Is Dissociative Identity Disorder?

As you have seen, dissociative identity disorder has traditionally been thought of as rare. Some researchers even argue that many or all cases are *iatrogenic*—that is, unintentionally produced by practitioners (Foote, 2016; Lynn & Deming, 2010). They believe that therapists create this disorder by subtly suggesting the existence of other personalities during therapy or by explicitly asking a patient to produce different personalities while under hypnosis. In addition, they believe, a therapist who is looking for multiple personalities may reinforce these patterns by displaying greater interest when a patient displays symptoms of dissociation.

These arguments seem to be supported by the fact that many cases of dissociative identity disorder first come to attention while the person is already in treatment for a less serious problem. But such is not true of all cases; many people seek treatment because they have noticed time lapses throughout their lives or because relatives and friends have observed their subpersonalities (Putnam, 2006, 2000).

> What verdict is appropriate for accused criminals who experience dissociative identity disorder and whose crimes are committed by one of their subpersonalities?

The number of people diagnosed with dissociative identity disorder increased dramatically in the 1980s and 1990s, only to decrease again in the twenty-first century (Foote, 2016; Paris, 2012). Notwithstanding this decline, thousands of cases have now been diagnosed in the United States and Canada alone and some clinical theorists estimate that around 1 percent of the population in the United States and other Western countries displays the disorder (Foote, 2016). On the other side of the coin, many clinicians continue to question the legitimacy of this category.

#CulturalTies

Some clinical theorists argue that dissociative identity disorder is culture-bound (Boysen & VanBergen, 2013; Chaturvedi et al., 2010; Escobar, 2004). While the prevalence of this disorder has grown in North America, it is rare or nonexistent in Great Britain, Sweden, Russia, India, and Southeast Asia. Moreover, within the United States the prevalence is particularly low among Hispanic Americans and Asian Americans.

How Do Theorists Explain Dissociative Amnesia and Dissociative Identity Disorder?

A variety of theories have been proposed to explain dissociative amnesia and dissociative identity disorder. Older explanations, such as that offered by psychodynamic theorists, have not received much investigation (Merenda, 2008). However, newer viewpoints, which highlight such factors as *state-dependent learning* and *self-hypnosis,* have captured the interest of clinical scientists.

The Psychodynamic View Psychodynamic theorists believe that these dissociative disorders are caused by *repression,* the most basic ego defense mechanism: people fight off anxiety by unconsciously preventing painful memories, thoughts, or impulses from reaching awareness. Everyone uses repression to a degree (see **PsychWatch** on the next page), but people with dissociative amnesia and dissociative identity disorder are thought to repress their memories excessively (Blass, 2015; Henderson, 2010).

In the psychodynamic view, dissociative amnesia is a *single episode* of massive repression. A person unconsciously blocks the memory of an extremely upsetting event to avoid the pain of facing it (Foote, 2016; Kikuchi et al., 2010). Repressing may be his or her only protection from overwhelming anxiety.

In contrast, dissociative identity disorder is thought to result from a *lifetime* of excessive repression (Howell, 2011; Wang & Jiang, 2007). Psychodynamic theorists believe that this continuous use of repression is motivated by traumatic childhood events, particularly abusive parenting (Blass, 2015; Baker, 2010). Children who experience such traumas may come to fear the dangerous world they live in and take flight from it by pretending to be another person who is looking on safely from afar. Abused children may also come to fear the impulses that they believe are the reasons for their excessive punishments. Whenever they experience "bad" thoughts or impulses, they unconsciously try to disown and deny them by assigning them to other personalities.

Support for the psychodynamic explanation of dissociative identity disorder comes from a variety of studies, largely case studies, which report such brutal childhood experiences as beatings, cuttings, burnings with cigarettes, imprisonment in closets,

#EverydayForgetting

Online passwords

Where cell phone was left

Where keys were left

Where remote control was left

Phone numbers

Names

Dream content

Birthdays/anniversaries

Michael Maslin/The New Yorker Collection/The Cartoon Bank

"Would it surprise you to learn, Felix, that we're already married?"

Peculiarities of Memory

Usually memory problems must interfere greatly with a person's functioning before they are considered a sign of a disorder. Peculiarities of memory, on the other hand, fill our daily lives. Memory investigators have identified a number of these peculiarities—some familiar, some useful, some problematic, but none abnormal.

- **Absentmindedness** Often we fail to register information because our thoughts are focusing on other things. If we haven't absorbed the information in the first place, it is no surprise that later we can't recall it.

- **Déjà vu** Almost all of us have at some time had the strange sensation of recognizing a scene that we happen upon for the first time. We feel sure we have been there before.

- **Jamais vu** Sometimes we have the opposite experience: a situation or scene that is part of our daily life seems suddenly unfamiliar. "I knew it was my car, but I felt as if I'd never seen it before."

- **The tip-of-the-tongue phenomenon** To have something on the tip of the tongue is an acute "feeling of knowing": we are unable to recall some piece of information, but we know that we know it.

- **Eidetic images** Some people have such vivid visual afterimages that they can describe a picture in detail after looking at it just once. The images may be memories of pictures, events, fantasies, or dreams.

Barcroft/Getty Images

Memory for music Eight-year-old blind pianist Ying-Shan Tseng performs at a concert in South Africa. The young artist can breeze through complex concertos by Tchaikovsky, Mozart, and others from memory—a skill beyond the reach of most accomplished pianists.

- **Memory while under anesthesia** As many as 2 of every 1,000 anesthetized patients process enough of what is said in their presence during surgery to affect their recovery. In many such cases, the ability to understand language has continued under anesthesia, even though the patient cannot explicitly recall it.

- **Memory for music** Even as a small child, Mozart could memorize and reproduce a piece of music after having heard it only once. While no one yet has matched the genius of Mozart, many musicians can mentally hear whole pieces of music, so that they can rehearse anywhere, far from their instruments.

- **Visual memory** Most people recall visual information better than other kinds of information: they easily can bring to their mind the appearance of places, objects, faces, or the pages of a book. They almost never forget a face, yet they may well forget the name attached to it. Other people have stronger verbal memories: they remember sounds or words particularly well, and the memories that come to their minds are often puns or rhymes.

---

rape, and extensive verbal abuse (Foote, 2016; Ross & Ness, 2010). Yet some individuals with this disorder do not seem to have experiences of abuse in their background (Ross & Ness, 2010). For example, Chris Sizemore, the subject of *The Three Faces of Eve,* reported that her disorder first emerged during her preschool years after she witnessed two deaths and a horrifying accident within a three-month period.

State-Dependent Learning: A Cognitive-Behavioral View
If people learn something when they are in a particular situation or state of mind, they are likely to remember it best when they are again in that same condition. If they are given a learning task while under the influence of alcohol, for example, their later recall of the information may be strongest under the influence of alcohol. Similarly, if they smoke cigarettes while learning, they may later have better recall when they are again smoking.

state-dependent learning Learning that becomes associated with the conditions under which it occurred, so that it is best remembered under the same conditions.

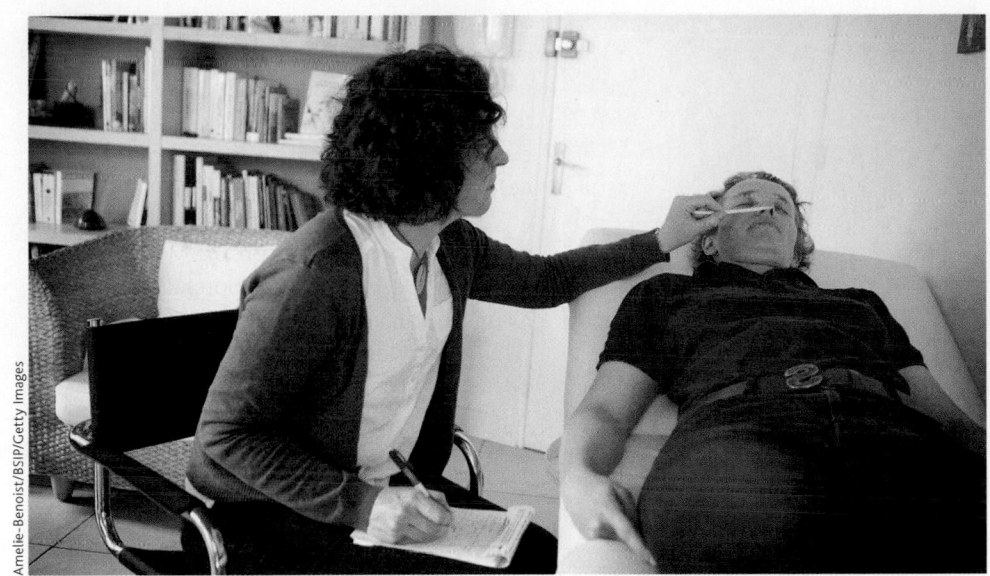

Sensory memories Sensory stimuli often trigger important memories. Thus some clinicians practice *olfactotherapy,* a method that uses the smells and vibrations of essential oils to help elicit memories from clients.

This link between state and recall is called **state-dependent learning.** It was initially observed in animals who learned things during experiments while under the influence of certain drugs (Radulovic et al., 2017; Overton, 1966, 1964). Research with human participants later showed that state-dependent learning can be associated with mood states as well: material learned during a happy mood is recalled best when the participant is again happy, and sad-state learning is recalled best during sad states (de l'Etoile, 2002; Bower, 1981) (see **Figure 6-4**).

> Might it be possible to use the principles of state-dependent learning to produce better results in school or at work?

What causes state-dependent learning? One possibility is that *arousal* levels are an important part of learning and memory. That is, a particular level of arousal will have a set of remembered events, thoughts, and skills attached to it. When a situation produces that particular level of arousal, the person is more likely to recall the memories linked to it.

Although people remember certain events better in some arousal states than in others, most can recall events under a variety of states. However, some theorists suggest, people who are prone to develop dissociative disorders have state-to-memory links that are unusually rigid and narrow (Miller, 2017; Dorahy & Huntjens, 2007). Each of their thoughts, memories, and skills may be tied *exclusively* to a particular state of arousal, so that they recall a given event only when they experience an arousal state almost identical to the state in which the memory was first acquired. When such people are calm, for example, they may forget what happened during stressful times, thus laying the groundwork for dissociative amnesia. Similarly, in dissociative identity disorder, different arousal levels may produce entirely different groups of memories, thoughts, and abilities—that is, different subpersonalities. This could explain why personality transitions in dissociative identity disorder tend to be sudden and stress-related.

Self-Hypnosis

As you first saw in Chapter 1, people who are *hypnotized* enter a sleeplike state in which they become very suggestible. While in this state, they can behave, perceive, and think in ways that would ordinarily seem impossible. They may, for example, become temporarily blind, deaf, or insensitive to pain. Hypnosis can also

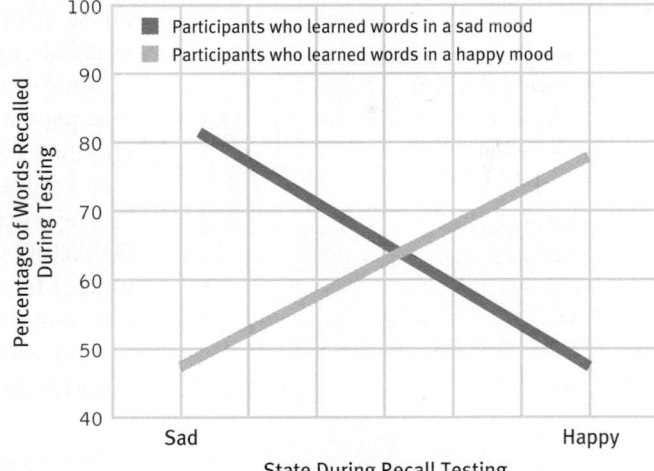

FIGURE 6-4

State-Dependent Learning

In one study, participants who learned a list of words while in a hypnotically induced happy state remembered the words better if they were in a happy mood when tested later than if they were in a sad mood. Conversely, participants who learned the words when in a sad mood recalled them better if they were sad during testing than if they were happy. (Information from Bower, 1981.)

Erin Painter/Midland Daily News/AP Photo

Hypnotic recall Northwood University students react while under hypnosis to the suggestion of being on a beach in Hawaii and needing suntan lotion. Many clinicians use hypnotic procedures to help clients recall past events, but research reveals that such procedures often create false memories.

help people remember events that occurred and were forgotten years ago, a capability used by many psychotherapists. Conversely, it can make people forget facts, events, and even their personal identities—an effect called *hypnotic amnesia.*

The parallels between hypnotic amnesia and the dissociative disorders we have been examining are striking (Foote, 2016; van der Kruijs et al., 2014). Both are conditions in which people forget certain material for a period of time yet later remember it. And in both, the people forget without any insight into why they are forgetting or any awareness that something is being forgotten. These parallels have led some theorists to conclude that dissociative disorders may be a form of **self-hypnosis** in which people hypnotize themselves to forget unpleasant events (Dell, 2010). Dissociative amnesia may develop, for example, in people who, consciously or unconsciously, hypnotize themselves into forgetting horrifying experiences that have recently taken place in their lives. If the self-induced amnesia covers all memories of a person's past and identity, that person may undergo a dissociative fugue.

The self-hypnosis theory might also be used to explain dissociative identity disorder (Vissia et al., 2016; Wood, 2016). On the basis of several investigations, some theorists believe that this disorder often begins between the ages of 4 and 6, a time when children are generally very suggestible and excellent hypnotic subjects (Lyons & Yapko, 2015; Kohen & Olness, 2011). These theorists argue that some children who experience abuse or other horrifying events manage to escape their threatening world by self-hypnosis, mentally separating themselves from their bodies and fulfilling their wish to become some other person or persons (Foote, 2016; Giesbrecht & Merckelbach, 2009). One patient with multiple personalities observed, "I was in a trance often [during my childhood]. There was a little place where I could sit, close my eyes and imagine, until I felt very relaxed just like hypnosis" (Bliss, 1980, p. 1392).

There are different schools of thought about the nature of hypnosis (Kauders, 2017; Dell, 2010). Some theorists see hypnosis as a *special process,* an out-of-the-ordinary kind of functioning. Accordingly, these theorists contend that people with dissociative amnesia and dissociative identity disorder place themselves in internal trances during which their brain and conscious functioning is significantly altered. Other theorists believe that hypnotic behaviors, and hypnotic amnesia in particular, are

"I think I accidentally repressed my good memories."

Pete Holmes/The New Yorker Collection/The Cartoon Bank

produced by *common social and cognitive processes,* such as high motivation, focused attention, role enactment, and self-fulfilling expectations. According to this point of view, hypnotized people are simply highly motivated individuals performing tasks that are asked of them, while believing all along that the hypnotic state is doing the work for them. Common-process theorists hold that people with dissociative amnesia and dissociative identity disorder provide themselves (or are provided by others) with powerful suggestions to forget and that social and cognitive mechanisms then put the suggestions into practice. Whether hypnosis consists of special or common processes, hypnosis research effectively demonstrates the power of our normal thought processes, and so renders the notion of dissociative disorders somewhat less remarkable.

How Are Dissociative Amnesia and Dissociative Identity Disorder Treated?

As you have seen, people with dissociative amnesia often recover on their own. Only sometimes do their memory problems linger and require treatment. In contrast, people with dissociative identity disorder usually require treatment to regain their lost memories and develop an integrated personality. Treatments for dissociative amnesia tend to be more successful than those for dissociative identity disorder, probably because the former pattern is less complex.

How Do Therapists Help People with Dissociative Amnesia?
The leading treatments for dissociative amnesia are *psychodynamic therapy, hypnotic therapy,* and *drug therapy,* although support for these interventions comes largely from case studies rather than controlled investigations (Gentile, Dillon, & Gillig, 2013). Psychodynamic therapists guide patients to search their unconscious in the hope of bringing forgotten experiences back to consciousness (Howell, 2011). The focus of psychodynamic therapy seems particularly well suited to the needs of people with dissociative amnesia. After all, the patients need to recover lost memories, and the general approach of psychodynamic therapists is to try to uncover memories—as well as other psychological processes—that have been repressed. Thus many theorists, including some who do not ordinarily favor psychodynamic approaches, believe that psychodynamic therapy may be the most appropriate treatment for dissociative amnesia.

Another common treatment for dissociative amnesia is **hypnotic therapy,** or **hypnotherapy**. Therapists hypnotize patients and then guide them to recall their forgotten events (Rathbone et al., 2014). Given the possibility that dissociative amnesia may be a form of self-hypnosis, hypnotherapy may be a particularly useful intervention. It has been applied both alone and in combination with other approaches (Colletti et al., 2010).

Sometimes injections of barbiturates such as *sodium amobarbital* (Amytal) or *sodium pentobarbital* (Pentothal) have been used to help patients with dissociative amnesia regain their lost memories. These drugs are often called "truth serums," but actually their effect is to calm people and free their inhibitions, thus helping them to recall anxiety-producing events (Ahern et al., 2000). These drugs do not always work, however, and if used at all, they are likely to be combined with other treatment approaches.

How Do Therapists Help People with Dissociative Identity Disorder?
Unlike victims of dissociative amnesia, people with dissociative identity disorder do not typically recover without treatment. Treatment for this pattern is complex and difficult, much like the disorder itself. Therapists usually try to help the clients (1) recognize fully the nature of their disorder, (2) recover the gaps in their memory, and (3) integrate their subpersonalities into one functional personality (Gentile et al., 2014, 2013; Howell, 2011).

self-hypnosis The process of hypnotizing oneself, sometimes for the purpose of forgetting unpleasant events.

hypnotic therapy A treatment in which the patient undergoes hypnosis and is then guided to recall forgotten events or perform other therapeutic activities. Also known as *hypnotherapy.*

#MovieMemories

Films About Memory Disturbances

Finding Dory (2016)

Split (2016)

The Bourne series (2012, 2007, 2004, 2002)

Total Recall (2012, 1990)

Black Swan (2010)

Shutter Island (2010)

The Hangover (2009)

Spider-Man 3 (2007)

Eternal Sunshine of the Spotless Mind (2004)

The Manchurian Candidate (2004, 1962)

Finding Nemo (2003)

Memento (2000)

fusion The final merging of two or more subpersonalities in dissociative identity disorder.

depersonalization-derealization disorder A dissociative disorder marked by the presence of persistent and recurrent episodes of depersonalization, derealization, or both.

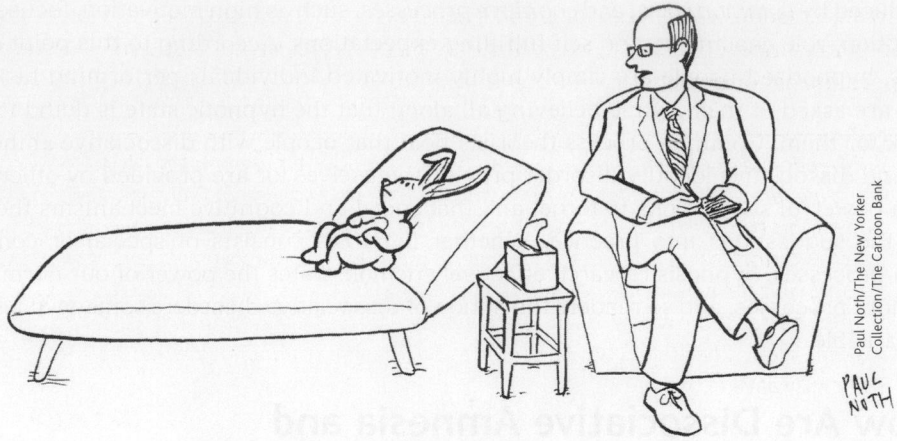

"I'm more interested in hearing about the eggs you're hiding from yourself."

Paul Noth/The New Yorker Collection/The Cartoon Bank

RECOGNIZING THE DISORDER Once a diagnosis of dissociative identity disorder is made, therapists typically try to bond with the primary personality and with each of the subpersonalities (Howell, 2011). As bonds are formed, therapists try to educate patients and help them to recognize fully the nature of their disorder. Some therapists actually introduce the subpersonalities to one another, by hypnosis, for example, or by having patients look at videos of their other personalities (Howell, 2011; Ross & Gahan, 1988). A number of therapists have also found that group therapy helps to educate patients (Fine & Madden, 2000). In addition, family therapy may be used to help educate spouses and children about the disorder and to gather helpful information about the patient (Kluft, 2001, 2000).

RECOVERING MEMORIES To help patients recover the missing pieces of their past, therapists typically use the same approaches applied in dissociative amnesia, including psychodynamic therapy, hypnotherapy, and drug treatment (Brand et al., 2014; Kluft, 2001, 1991, 1985). These techniques work slowly for patients with dissociative identity disorder, however, as some subpersonalities may keep denying experiences that the others recall. One of the subpersonalities may even assume a "protector" role to prevent the primary personality from suffering the pain of recollecting traumatic experiences.

INTEGRATING THE SUBPERSONALITIES The final goal of therapy is to merge the different subpersonalities into a single, integrated identity. Integration is a continuous process that occurs throughout treatment until patients "own" all of their behaviors, emotions, sensations, and knowledge. **Fusion** is the final merging of two or more subpersonalities. Many patients distrust this final treatment goal, and their subpersonalities may see integration as a form of death (Howell, 2011; Kluft, 2001, 1991). Therapists have used a range of approaches to help merge subpersonalities, including psychodynamic, supportive, cognitive, and drug therapies (Cronin et al., 2014; Baker, 2010).

Once the subpersonalities are integrated, further therapy is typically needed to maintain the complete personality and to teach social and coping skills that may help prevent later dissociations. In case reports, some therapists note high success rates (Brand et al., 2014; Dorahy et al., 2014), but others find that patients continue to resist full integration. A few therapists have in fact questioned the need for full integration.

#TreatingSybil

More to the Story?

Recent reports, including claims by several colleagues who worked closely with the author of *Sybil* and with Sybil's real-life therapist, suggest that Shirley Mason (the person on whom Sybil was based) was highly hypnotizable, extremely suggestible, and anxious to please her therapist, and that her disorder was in fact induced largely by hypnosis, sodium pentothal, and therapist suggestion (Nathan, 2011; Rieber, 2002, 1999; Miller & Kantrowitz, 1999).

Depersonalization-Derealization Disorder

As you read earlier, DSM-5 categorizes **depersonalization-derealization disorder** as a dissociative disorder, even though it is not characterized by the memory difficulties found in the other dissociative disorders. Its central symptoms are persistent and recurrent episodes of *depersonalization* (the sense that one's own mental functioning or body are unreal or detached) and/or *derealization* (the sense that one's surroundings are unreal or detached).

> A 24-year-old graduate student . . . had begun to doubt his own reality. He felt he was living in a dream in which he saw himself from without, and did not feel connected to his body or his thoughts. When he saw himself through his own eyes, he perceived his body parts as distorted—his hands and feet seemed quite large. As he walked across campus, he often felt the people he saw might be robots. . . .
>
> [By] his second session, he . . . had begun to perceive [his girlfriend] in a distorted manner. He . . . hesitated before returning, because he wondered whether his therapist was really alive.
>
> (Kluft, 1988, p. 580)

Like this graduate student, people experiencing depersonalization feel as though they have become separated from their body and are observing themselves from outside. Occasionally their mind seems to be floating a few feet above them—a sensation known as *doubling*. Their body parts feel foreign to them, their hands and feet smaller or bigger than usual. Many sufferers describe their emotional state as "mechanical," "dreamlike," or "dizzy." Throughout the whole experience, however, they are aware that their perceptions are distorted, and in that sense they remain in contact with reality. In some cases this sense of unreality also extends to other sensory experiences and behavior. People may, for example, have distortions in their sense of touch or smell or their judgments of time or space, or they may feel that they have lost control over their speech or actions.

In contrast to depersonalization, derealization is characterized by feeling that the external world is unreal and strange. Objects may seem to change shape or size; other people may seem removed, mechanical, or even dead. The graduate student, for example, saw other people as robots, perceived his girlfriend in a distorted manner, and hesitated to return for a second session of therapy because he wondered whether his therapist was really alive.

Depersonalization and derealization experiences by themselves do not indicate a depersonalization-derealization disorder. Transient depersonalization or derealization

#TheirWords

"I was trying to daydream, but my mind kept wandering."

Steven Wright, comedian

Daniel Morel/Reuters/Alamy

Religious dissociations As part of religious or cultural practices, many people voluntarily enter into trances that are similar to the symptoms found in dissociative identity disorder and depersonalization-derealization disorder. Here, voodoo followers sing and flail about in trances inside a sacred pool at a temple in Souvenance, Haiti.

reactions are fairly common (Simeon, 2017, 2015; Michal, 2011). One-third of all people say that on occasion they have felt as though they were watching themselves in a movie. Similarly, one-third of individuals who confront a life-threatening danger experience feelings of depersonalization or derealization (van Duijl et al., 2010). People sometimes have feelings of depersonalization after practicing meditation or after traveling to new places. Young children may also experience depersonalization from time to time as they are developing their capacity for self-awareness. In most such cases, the affected people are able to compensate for the distortion and continue to function with reasonable effectiveness until the temporary episode eventually ends.

> If you have ever experienced feelings of depersonalization or derealization, how did you explain them at the time?

The symptoms of depersonalization-derealization disorder, in contrast, are persistent or recurrent, cause considerable distress, and may impair social relationships and job performance (Simeon, 2017, 2015; Gentile et al., 2014). The disorder is experienced by around 2 percent of the population, most often adolescents and young adults, hardly ever in people over 40. It usually comes on suddenly and may be triggered by extreme fatigue, physical pain, intense stress, or recovery from substance abuse. Survivors of traumatic experiences or people caught in life-threatening situations, such as hostages or kidnap victims, seem to be particularly vulnerable to this disorder. The disorder tends to be long-lasting; the symptoms may improve and even disappear for a time, only to return or intensify during times of severe stress. Like the graduate student in our case discussion, many sufferers fear that they are losing their minds and become preoccupied with worry about their symptoms. Few theories have been offered to explain depersonalization-derealization disorder. Several different forms of psychotherapy have been applied in cases of this disorder, but there have been almost no studies that test the efficacy of these approaches (Simeon, 2017, 2015).

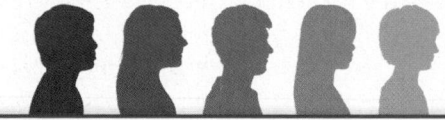

Getting a Handle on Trauma and Stress

THE CONCEPTS OF TRAUMA AND STRESS have been prominent in the field of abnormal psychology since its early days when, for example, Sigmund Freud proposed that most forms of psychopathology begin with traumatic losses or events. But why and how do trauma and stress translate into psychopathology? That question has, in fact, eluded clinical theorists and researchers—until recent times. In part because of the identification and study of acute and posttraumatic stress disorders, researchers now better understand the relationship between trauma, stress, and psychological dysfunction—viewing it as a complex and unfolding interaction of many variables, including biological factors, childhood experiences, personal styles, and social supports. Similarly, clinicians are now developing more effective treatment programs for people with acute and posttraumatic stress disorders—programs that *combine* biological, cognitive-behavioral, family, and group interventions.

> ### CLINICAL CHOICES
>
> Now that you've read about disorders of trauma and stress, try the interactive case study for this chapter. See if you are able to identify Michelle's symptoms and suggest a diagnosis based on her symptoms. What kind of treatment would be most effective for Michelle? Go to **Launch**Pad to access *Clinical Choices*.

Insights and treatments for the dissociative disorders, the other group of trauma-triggered disorders discussed in this chapter, have not moved as quickly. However, the field's focus on these disorders has surged during the past two decades—partly because of intense clinical interest in posttraumatic stress reactions and partly because of the growing effort to understand physically rooted memory disorders such as Alzheimer's disease.

Amidst the rapid developments in the realms of trauma and stress lies a cautionary tale. When problems are studied heavily, it is common for the public, as well as some researchers and clinicians, to draw conclusions that may be too bold. For example, many people—perhaps too many—are now receiving diagnoses of posttraumatic stress disorder, partly because the symptoms of PTSD are many and because PTSD has received so much attention. Similarly, some of today's clinicians worry that the resurging interest in dissociative disorders may be creating a false impression of their prevalence. We shall see such potential problems again when we look at other forms of pathology that are currently receiving great focus, such as bipolar disorder among children and attention-deficit/hyperactivity disorder. The line between enlightenment and overenthusiasm is often thin.

♀... SUMMING UP

» Effects of Stress When we appraise a *stressor* as threatening, we often experience a *stress response* consisting of arousal and a sense of fear. The features of arousal are set in motion by the *hypothalamus*, a brain structure that activates two different pathways—the *sympathetic nervous system* pathway and the *hypothalamic-pituitary-adrenal* pathway. *pp. 153–156*

» Acute and Posttraumatic Stress Disorders People with *acute stress disorder* or *posttraumatic stress disorder* react with arousal, anxiety, and other stress symptoms after a traumatic event, including reexperiencing the traumatic event, avoiding related events, being markedly less responsive than normal, and feeling guilt. Traumatic events may include *combat experiences, disasters,* or episodes of *victimization.*

In attempting to explain why some people develop a psychological stress disorder and others do not, researchers have focused on *biological factors* (particularly, *overly reactive brain–body stress pathways, a dysfunctional brain stress circuit,* and an *inherited predisposition*), *childhood experiences, personal styles, social support systems,* and the *severity and nature of traumatic events,* as well as on how these factors may work together to produce such a disorder. Techniques used to treat the stress disorders include antidepressant drugs, cognitive-behavioral therapy (including *exposure* techniques), family therapy, and group therapy. Rapidly mobilized community interventions often follow the principles of *critical incident stress debriefing.* Such approaches initially appeared helpful after large-scale disasters; however, recent studies have raised questions about their usefulness. *pp. 157–172*

» Dissociative Disorders People with *dissociative disorders* experience major changes in *memory* and *identity* that are not caused by clear physical factors—changes that often emerge after a traumatic

event. Typically, one part of the memory or identity is *dissociated,* or *separated,* from the other parts. People with *dissociative amnesia* are unable to recall important personal information or past events in their lives. Those with *dissociative fugue,* an extreme form of dissociative amnesia, not only fail to remember personal information, but also flee to a different location and may establish a new identity. In another dissociative disorder, *dissociative identity disorder,* a person develops two or more distinct subpersonalities. *pp. 172–178*

» Explanations and Treatments for Dissociative Amnesia and Dissociative Identity Disorder Dissociative amnesia and dissociative identity disorder are not well understood. Among the processes that have been cited to explain them are extreme *repression, state-dependent learning,* and *self-hypnosis.*

Dissociative amnesia may end on its own or may require treatment. Dissociative identity disorder typically requires treatment. Approaches commonly used to help people with dissociative amnesia recover their lost memories are *psychodynamic therapy, hypnotic therapy,* and *sodium amobarbital* or *sodium pentobarbital.* Therapists who treat people with dissociative identity disorder use the same approaches and also try to help the clients *recognize the nature and scope of their disorder, recover the gaps in their memory,* and *integrate their subpersonalities into one functional personality. pp. 179–184*

» Depersonalization-Derealization Disorder People with yet another kind of dissociative disorder, *depersonalization-derealization disorder,* feel as though they are detached from their own mental processes or body and are observing themselves from the outside, or feel as though the people or objects around them are unreal or detached. Transient depersonalization and derealization experiences seem to be relatively common, while depersonalization-derealization disorder is not. *pp. 184–186*

Visit *LaunchPad*
to access the e-Book, Clinical Choices, videos, activities, and LearningCurve, as well as study aids including flashcards, FAQs, and research exercises.

LaunchPad
macmillan learning

♀...Depressive and Bipolar Disorders

The first conscious thought that all was not well with me came . . . when I was twenty-two. I had been living in Los Angeles for two years, working various temp jobs while trying to establish myself as a writer and performance artist. Out of nowhere and for no apparent reason—or so it seemed—I started feeling strong sensations of grief. I don't remember the step-by-step progression of the illness. What I can recall is that my life disintegrated; first, into a strange and terrifying space of sadness and then, into a cob-web of fatigue. I gradually lost my ability to function. It would take me hours to get up out of bed, get bathed, put clothes on. By the time I was fully dressed, it was well into the afternoon. . . .

After a while I stopped showing up at my temp job, stopped going out altogether, and locked myself in my home. It was over three weeks before I felt well enough to leave. During that time, I cut myself off from everything and everyone. Days would go by be-fore I bathed. I did not have enough energy to clean up myself or my home. There was a trail of undergarments and other articles of clothing that ran from the living room to the bedroom to the bathroom of my tiny apartment. Dishes with decaying food covered every counter and tabletop in the place. Even watching TV or talking on the phone required too much concentration. . . . All I could do was take to my pallet of blankets and coats positioned on the living room floor and wait for whatever I was going through to pass. And it did. Slowly. . . .

. . . Deep down, I knew that something had gone wrong with me, in me. But what could I do? Stunned and defenseless, the only thing I felt I could do was move on. I assured myself that my mind and the behaviors it provoked were well within my control. In the future I would just have to be extremely aware. I would make sure that what happened did not happen again. But it did. Again and again, no matter how aware, responsible, or in control I tried to be. . . .

Each wave of the depression cost me something dear. I lost my job because the temp agencies where I was registered could no longer tolerate my lengthy absences. Unable to pay rent, I lost my apartment and ended up having to rent a small room in a boarding house. I lost my friends. Most of them found it too troublesome to deal with my sudden moodiness and passivity so they stopped calling and coming around.

(Danquah, 1998)

Most people's moods come and go. Their feelings of elation or sadness are understandable reactions to daily events and do not affect their lives greatly. However, the moods of certain people last a long time. As in the case of Meri Nana-Ama Danquah, a performance artist and poet who described her disorder above, their moods color all of their interactions with the world and even interfere with normal functioning. Such people struggle in particular with depression, mania, or both. **Depression** is a low, sad state in which life seems dark and its challenges overwhelming. **Mania**, the opposite of depression, is a state of breathless euphoria, or at least frenzied energy, in which people may have an exaggerated belief that the world is theirs for the taking.

depression A low, sad state marked by significant levels of sadness, lack of energy, low self-worth, guilt, or related symptoms.

mania A state or episode of euphoria or frenzied activity in which people may have an exaggerated belief that the world is theirs for the taking.

depressive disorders The group of disorders marked by unipolar depression.

unipolar depression Depression without a history of mania.

bipolar disorder A disorder marked by alternating or intermixed periods of mania and depression.

Mood problems of these kinds are at the center of two groups of disorders—depressive disorders and bipolar disorders (APA, 2013). These groups are examined in this chapter. People with **depressive disorders** suffer only from depression, a pattern called **unipolar depression**. They have no history of mania and return to a normal or nearly normal mood when their depression lifts. In contrast, those with **bipolar disorders** have periods of mania that alternate with periods of depression. You might logically expect some people to display a third pattern of mood difficulty, *unipolar mania*, in which they suffer from mania only, but this pattern is uncommon.

Mood problems have always captured people's interest, in part because so many famous people have suffered from them. The Bible speaks of the severe depressions of Nebuchadnezzar, Saul, and Moses. Queen Victoria of England and Abraham Lincoln seem to have experienced recurring depressions. Mood difficulties also have plagued writers Ernest Hemingway and Sylvia Plath, comedian Jim Carrey, and musical performers Bruce Springsteen and Beyoncé. Their problems have been shared by millions. ∎

‖‖

Unipolar Depression: The Depressive Disorders

WHENEVER WE FEEL particularly unhappy, we are likely to describe ourselves as "depressed." In all likelihood, we are merely responding to sad events, fatigue, or unhappy thoughts. This loose use of the term confuses a perfectly normal mood swing with a clinical syndrome. All of us experience dejection from time to time, but only some experience a depressive disorder. Depressive disorders bring severe and long-lasting psychological pain that may intensify

> Almost every day we have ups and downs in mood. How can we distinguish the everyday blues from clinical depression?

as time goes by. Those who suffer from such disorders may lose their will to carry out the simplest of life's activities; some even lose their will to live.

How Common Is Unipolar Depression?

Around 8 percent of adults in the United States suffer from a severe unipolar pattern of depression in any given year, while as many as 5 percent suffer from mild forms (Krishnan, 2017; Kessler et al., 2012, 2010). Around 20 percent of all adults experience an episode of severe unipolar depression at some point in their lives. These prevalence rates are similar in Canada, England, France, and many other countries (see **Table 7-1**). Moreover, the rate of depression—mild or severe—is higher among poor people than wealthier people (Thomas & Haushofer, 2015; Sareen et al., 2011).

Women are at least twice as likely as men to have episodes of severe unipolar depression (WHO, 2017). As many as 26 percent of women have an episode at some time in their lives, compared with 12 percent of men. As you will see in Chapter 17, among children the prevalence of unipolar depression is similar for girls and boys.

An episode of severe depression can occur at any point throughout the lifespan. The average age of onset is 19 years, with the peak age being late adolescence or early adulthood (Weissman et al., 2016). In any given year, the rate of severe depression is twice as high among adults under 65 years of age as among those 65 years and older (Krishnan, 2017). This age difference may be tied to the relationship between severe depression and health. As you will see later in the chapter, people who are depressed have more medical problems and a higher mortality rate than other people (Headrick et al., 2017; Coryell, 2016). They may, in turn, be less likely to live to an old age, thus

TABLE: 7-1

Countries Most Burdened By Major Depressive Disorder

Impact on National Disability and Mortality Rates
#1 India
#2 China
#3 United States
#4 Indonesia
#5 Brazil
#6 Russia
#7 Pakistan
#8 Bangladesh
#9 Nigeria
#10 Iran

Information from: McPhillips, 2016; WHO, 2016.

reducing the prevalence of depression among the elderly. Moreover, among elderly people, those with significant or chronic medical problems have a higher rate of depression than those in relatively good health (Krishnan, 2017).

Approximately 85 percent of people with unipolar depression, including severe depression, recover within 6 months, some without treatment. More than half of those who recover from severe depression have at least one other episode later in their lives (Simon & Ciechanowski, 2017; Coryell, 2016).

What Are the Symptoms of Depression?

The picture of depression may vary from person to person. Earlier you saw how Meri's profound sadness, fatigue, and cognitive deterioration brought her job and social life to a standstill. Some depressed people have symptoms that are less severe. They manage to function, although their depression typically robs them of much effectiveness or pleasure.

LOW SELF-ESTEEM

Mike Twohy/The New Yorker Collection/The Cartoon Bank

As the case of Meri indicates, depression has many symptoms other than sadness. The symptoms, which often exacerbate one another, span five areas of functioning: emotional, motivational, behavioral, cognitive, and physical.

Emotional Symptoms Most people who are depressed feel sad and dejected. They describe themselves as feeling "miserable," "empty," and "humiliated." They tend to lose their sense of humor, report getting little pleasure from anything, and in some cases display *anhedonia*, an inability to experience any pleasure at all. A number also experience anxiety, anger, or agitation. Terrie Williams, author of *Black Pain*, a book about depression in African Americans, describes the agony she went through each morning as her depression was unfolding:

> *Nights I could handle. I fell asleep easily, and sleep allowed me to forget. But my mornings were unmanageable. To wake up each morning was to remember once again that the world by which I defined myself was no more. Soon after opening my eyes, the crying bouts would start and I'd sit alone for hours, weeping and mourning my losses.*
>
> *(Williams, 2008, p. 9)*

Motivational Symptoms Depressed people typically lose the desire to pursue their usual activities. Almost all report a lack of drive, initiative, and spontaneity. They may have to force themselves to go to work, talk with friends, eat meals, or have sex. Terrie describes her social withdrawal during a depressive episode:

> *I woke up one morning with a knot of fear in my stomach so crippling that I couldn't face light, much less day, and so intense that I stayed in bed for three days with the shades drawn and the lights out.*
> *Three days. Three days not answering the phone. Three days not checking my e-mail. I was disconnected completely from the outside world, and I didn't care.*
>
> *(Williams, 2008, p. xxiv)*

Suicide represents the ultimate escape from life's challenges. As you will see in Chapter 9, many depressed people become uninterested in life or wish to die; others wish they could kill themselves, and some actually do. It has been estimated that

#WorldCount

More than 300 million people suffer from depression worldwide (WHO, 2017).

Roberto Panucci/Getty Images

Born to run "The Boss," Bruce Springsteen, performs at a sold-out concert while his image is projected on a mega-screen behind him. In his 2016 memoir, *Born to Run*, Springsteen detailed his long history of depression. He described one depressive episode, "I nose-dived like the diving horse of the old Atlantic City steel pier into a sloshing tub of grief. . . . I can be good at hiding the severity of my feelings from most of the folks around me . . . except for one strange thing: TEARS! Buckets of 'em, oceans of 'em, cold, black tears pouring down my face . . . during any and all hours of the day. . . ."

between 6 and 15 percent of people who suffer from severe depression die by suicide (MHF, 2014; Alridge, 2012).

Behavioral Symptoms Depressed people are usually less active and less productive. They spend more time alone and may stay in bed for long periods. One man recalls, "My eyes would open at the crack of dawn, but getting out of bed was impossible. I just stayed there, and stayed there, and stayed there some more, virtually paralyzed, knowing that a day filled with misery awaited me." Depressed people may also move and even speak more slowly.

Cognitive Symptoms Depressed people hold extremely negative views of themselves. They consider themselves inadequate, undesirable, inferior, perhaps even evil (Lyness, 2016). They also blame themselves for nearly every unfortunate event, even things that have nothing to do with them, and they rarely credit themselves for positive achievements.

Another cognitive symptom of depression is pessimism. Sufferers are usually convinced that nothing will ever improve, and they feel helpless to change any aspect of their lives. Because they expect the worst, they are likely to procrastinate. Their sense of hopelessness and helplessness makes them especially vulnerable to suicidal thinking (Lyness, 2016; Shiratori et al., 2014).

People with depression frequently complain that their intellectual ability is very poor (Beblo et al., 2017). They feel confused, unable to remember things, easily distracted, and unable to solve even the smallest problems. In laboratory studies, depressed people do perform somewhat, but not extremely, more poorly than nondepressed people on tasks of memory, attention, and reasoning (Baune et al., 2018; Bowler, et al., 2018). It may be, however, that these difficulties sometimes reflect motivational problems rather than cognitive ones.

Physical Symptoms People who are depressed frequently have such physical ailments as headaches, indigestion, constipation, dizzy spells, and general pain (Lyness, 2016). In fact, many depressions are misdiagnosed as medical problems at first (Williams & Nieuwsma, 2016). Disturbances in appetite and sleep are particularly common (Chang et al., 2017; Baxter, 2016). Most depressed people eat less, sleep less, and feel more fatigued than they did prior to the disorder. Some, however, eat and sleep excessively. Terrie Williams describes the changes in the pattern of her sleep:

 I always hated waking up, but slowly it was turning into something deeper; it was less like I didn't want to wake up, and more like I couldn't. I didn't feel tired, but I had no energy. . . I had the sensation of a huge weight, invisible but gigantic, pressing down on me, almost crushing me into the bed and pinning me there.

(Williams, 2008, p. xxii)

Diagnosing Unipolar Depression

According to DSM-5, a *major depressive episode* is a period of two or more weeks marked by at least five symptoms of depression, including sad mood and/or loss of pleasure (see **Table 7-2**). In extreme cases, the episode may include psychotic symptoms, ones marked by a loss of contact with reality, such as *delusions*—bizarre ideas without foundation—or *hallucinations*—perceptions of things that are not actually present. A depressed man with psychotic symptoms may imagine that he cannot eat "because my intestines are deteriorating and will soon stop working," or he may believe that he sees his dead wife.

DSM-5 lists several types of depressive disorders. People who go through a major depressive episode without having any history of mania receive a diagnosis of **major depressive disorder** (APA, 2013) (see Table 7-2 again). The disorder may be additionally further described as *seasonal* if it changes with the seasons (for example, if the depression recurs each winter), *catatonic* if it is marked by either immobility or excessive activity, *peripartum* if it occurs during pregnancy or within four weeks of giving birth (see **PsychWatch** on the next page), or *melancholic* if the person is almost totally unaffected by pleasurable events. It sometimes turns out that an apparent case of major depressive disorder is, in fact, a depressive episode occurring within a larger pattern of bipolar disorder—a pattern in which the person's manic episode has not yet appeared. When the person has a manic episode at a later time, the diagnosis is changed to bipolar disorder (Coryell, 2016).

People whose unipolar depression is chronic receive a diagnosis of **persistent depressive disorder** (see Table 7-2 again). Some people with this chronic disorder have repeated major depressive episodes, a pattern technically called *persistent depressive disorder with major depressive episodes*. Others have less severe and less disabling symptoms, a pattern technically called *persistent depressive disorder with dysthymic syndrome*.

A third type of depressive disorder is **premenstrual dysphoric disorder**, a diagnosis given to certain women who repeatedly have clinically significant depressive and related symptoms during the week before menstruation. The inclusion of this pattern in DSM-5 is controversial, as you will see later (see page 209).

major depressive disorder A severe pattern of depression that is disabling and is not caused by such factors as drugs or a general medical condition.

persistent depressive disorder A chronic form of unipolar depression marked by ongoing and repeated symptoms of either major or mild depression.

premenstrual dysphoric disorder A disorder marked by repeated episodes of significant depression and related symptoms during the week before menstruation.

TABLE: 7-2

Dx Checklist

Major Depressive Episode

1. For a 2-week period, person displays an increase in depressed mood for the majority of each day and/or a decrease in enjoyment or interest across most activities for the majority of each day.

2. For the same 2 weeks, person also experiences at least 3 or 4 of the following symptoms:
   • Considerable weight change or appetite change
   • Daily insomnia or hypersomnia
   • Daily agitation or decrease in motor activity
   • Daily fatigue or lethargy
   • Daily feelings of worthlessness or excessive guilt
   • Daily reduction in concentration or decisiveness
   • Repeated focus on death or suicide, a suicide plan, or a suicide attempt.

3. Significant distress or impairment.

Major Depressive Disorder

1. Presence of a major depressive episode

2. No pattern of mania or hypomania

Persistent Depressive Disorder

1. Person experiences the symptoms of major or mild depression for at least 2 years.

2. During the 2-year period, symptoms not absent for more than 2 months at a time.

3. No history of mania or hypomania.

4. Significant distress or impairment.

Information from: APA, 2013.

Yet another kind of depressive disorder, *disruptive mood dysregulation disorder,* is characterized by a combination of persistent depressive symptoms and recurrent outbursts of severe temper. This disorder emerges during mid-childhood or adolescence and so is discussed in Chapter 17, "Disorders Common Among Children and Adolescents."

PSYCHWATCH

Sadness at the Happiest of Times

Women usually expect the birth of a child to be a happy experience. But for at least 10 percent of new mothers, the weeks and months after childbirth bring clinical depression (Kendig et al., 2017; Ko et al., 2017; Viguera, 2016). *Peripartum depression,* popularly called *postpartum depression,* typically begins within four weeks after the birth of a child; many cases actually begin during pregnancy (APA, 2013). This disorder is far more severe than simple "baby blues." It is also different from other postpartum syndromes such as *postpartum psychosis,* a problem that is examined in Chapter 14.

The "baby blues" are so common—as many as 80 percent of women experience them—that most researchers consider them normal. As new mothers try to cope with the wakeful nights, rattled emotions, and other stresses that accompany the arrival of a new baby, they may have crying spells, fatigue, anxiety, insomnia, and sadness (Enatescu et al., 2014). These symptoms usually disappear within days or weeks (Viguera, 2016; Kendall-Tackett, 2010).

In postpartum depression, however, depressive symptoms continue and may last up to a year or more (Viguera, 2016). The symptoms include extreme sadness, despair, tearfulness, insomnia, anxiety, intrusive thoughts, compulsions, panic attacks, feelings of inability to cope, and suicidal thoughts. The mother–infant relationship and the psychological and physical health of the child may suffer as a result (Viguera, 2016; Kendall-Tacket, 2010; Monti et al., 2004). Women who have an episode of postpartum depression have a 25 to 50 percent chance of developing it again with a subsequent birth (Kendig et al., 2017; Viguera, 2016).

Fending off postpartum depression Spin instructor Anouk Malavoy works out at a quads gym with her baby. Malavoy has written columns for the *Toronto Star* about the role exercise can play in helping some women prevent or combat postpartum depression.

Many clinicians believe that the hormonal changes accompanying childbirth trigger postpartum depression. All women go through a kind of hormone "withdrawal" after delivery, as estrogen and progesterone levels, which rise as much as 50 times above normal during pregnancy, now drop sharply to levels far below normal (Horowitz et al., 2005, 1995). Perhaps some women are particularly influenced by these dramatic hormone changes (Viguera, 2016; Mehta et al., 2014). Other theorists suggest that some women may have a genetic predisposition to postpartum depression (Viguera, 2016; Guintivano et al., 2014). A woman with a family history of mood disorders appears to be at high risk, even if she herself has not previously had a mood disorder (Kendig et al., 2017; Viguera, 2016).

At the same time, psychological and sociocultural factors may play important roles in the disorder (Mauthner, 2010). The birth of a baby brings enormous psychological and social change. A woman typically faces changes in her marital relationship, daily routines, and social roles. Sleep and relaxation are likely to decrease, and financial pressures may increase. Perhaps she feels the added stress of giving up a career or of trying to maintain one. This pileup of stress may heighten the risk of depression (Viguera, 2016; Kendall-Tackett, 2010). Mothers whose infants are sick or temperamentally "difficult" may be under yet additional pressure (Viguera, 2016).

Fortunately, treatment can make a big difference for most women with postpartum depression. Self-help support groups have proved extremely helpful for many women who have or who are at risk for postpartum depression (Viguera, 2017; Dennis, 2014; Evans et al., 2012). In addition, many respond well to the same approaches that are applied to other forms of depression—antidepressant medications, cognitive-behavioral therapy, interpersonal psychotherapy, or a combination of these approaches (Viguera, 2017; Hou et al., 2014; Kim et al., 2014).

However, many women who would benefit from treatment do not seek help because they feel ashamed about being sad at a time that is supposed to be joyous and are concerned about being judged harshly (Kendig et al., 2017; Bina, 2014; Mauthner, 2010). For them, and for the spouses and family members close to them, a large dose of education is in order. Even positive events, such as the birth of a child, can be stressful if they also bring major change to one's life. Recognizing and addressing such feelings are in everyone's best interest.

What Causes Unipolar Depression?

EPISODES OF UNIPOLAR DEPRESSION often seem to be triggered by stressful events in an individual's life (Krishnan, 2017; Shin et al., 2017). In fact, researchers have found that 80 percent of all severe episodes occur within a month or two of a significant negative event (Hammen, 2016). Stressful life events also precede other psychological disorders, but depressed people report more such events than anybody else.

Some clinicians consider it important to distinguish a *reactive* (*exogenous*) *depression*, which follows clear-cut stressful events, from an *endogenous depression*, which seems to be a response to internal factors. But can one ever know for certain whether a depression is reactive or not? Even if stressful events occurred before the onset of depression, that depression may not be reactive. The events could actually be a coincidence. Thus, today's clinicians usually concentrate on recognizing both the situational and the internal aspects of any given case of unipolar depression.

> Why do you think stressful events or periods in life might trigger depressed feelings and other negative emotions?

The current explanations of unipolar depression point to biological, psychological, and sociocultural factors. Just as clinicians now recognize both internal and situational features in each case of depression, many believe that the various explanations should be viewed collectively for unipolar depression to be understood fully.

The Biological View

Medical researchers have been aware for years that certain diseases and drugs produce mood changes. Could unipolar depression itself have biological causes? Studies of genetic factors, biochemical factors, brain circuits, and the immune system suggest that often it does.

Genetic Factors Three kinds of research—family pedigree, twin, and gene studies—suggest that some people inherit a predisposition to unipolar depression (Guffanti et al., 2016). *Family pedigree studies* select people with unipolar depression as *probands* (the proband is the person who is the focus of such a study), examine their relatives, and see whether depression also afflicts other members of the family. If a predisposition to unipolar depression is inherited, a proband's relatives should have a higher rate of depression than the population at large. Researchers have in fact found that as many as 30 percent of those relatives are depressed (see **Table 7-3**), compared with fewer than 10 percent of the general population (Levinson & Nichols, 2014).

TABLE: 7-3

Comparing Depressive and Bipolar Disorders

	One-Year Prevalence (Percent)	Female-to-Male Ratio	Typical Age at Onset (Years)	Prevalence Among First-Degree Relatives	Percentage Receiving Treatment Currently
Major depressive disorder	8.0	2:1	18–29	Elevated	50
Persistent depressive disorder (with dysthymic syndrome)	1.5–5.0	Between 3:2 and 2:1	10–25	Elevated	62
Bipolar I disorder	1.6	1:1	15–44	Elevated	49
Bipolar II disorder	1.0	1:1	15–44	Elevated	49
Cyclothymic disorder	0.4	1:1	15–25	Elevated	Unknown

Information from: Krishnan, 2017; NIMH, 2017; WHO, 2017; Stovall, 2016; Weissman et al., 2016; Kessler et al., 2012, 2010; González et al., 2010; Taube-Schiff & Lau, 2008; Wang et al., 2005.

norepinephrine A neurotransmitter whose abnormal activity is linked to depression and panic disorder.

serotonin A neurotransmitter whose abnormal activity is linked to depression, obsessive-compulsive disorder, and eating disorders.

If a predisposition to unipolar depression is inherited, you might also expect to find a particularly large number of cases among the close relatives of a proband. *Twin studies* have supported this expectation. When an identical twin has unipolar depression, there is a 38 percent chance that the other twin has already had or will eventually have the same disorder. In contrast, when a fraternal twin has unipolar depression, the other twin has only a 20 percent chance of having the disorder (Krishnan, 2017; McGuffin et al., 1996).

Finally, today's scientists have at their disposal techniques from the field of molecular biology to help them directly identify genes and determine whether certain gene abnormalities are related to depression. Using such techniques, researchers have found evidence that unipolar depression may be tied to genes on chromosomes 1, 3, 4, 6, 9, 10, 11, 12, 13, 14, 17, 18, 20, 21, 22, and X (Naoi et al., 2018; Wang et al., 2018; Mullins et al., 2016; Jansen et al., 2015). For example, a number of researchers have found that people who are depressed often have an abnormality of their *5-HTT* gene, a gene located on chromosome 17 that is responsible for the activity of the neurotransmitter serotonin. As you will read in the next section, low activity of serotonin in certain regions of the brain is closely tied to depression.

Biochemical Factors Low activity of two neurotransmitter chemicals, **norepinephrine** and **serotonin**, has been strongly linked to unipolar depression. In the 1950s, several pieces of evidence began to point to this relationship. First, medical researchers discovered that certain medications for high blood pressure often caused depression (Ayd, 1956). As it turned out, some of these medications lowered norepinephrine activity and others lowered serotonin. A second piece of evidence was the discovery of the first truly effective antidepressant drugs. Although these drugs were discovered by accident, researchers soon learned that while the drugs were relieving depression, they also were bringing about increases in norepinephrine and/or serotonin activity.

For years it was thought that low activity of *either* norepinephrine or serotonin directly produce depression, but theorists now believe that their relationship to depression is more complicated (Krishnan, 2017; Ding et al., 2014). Research indicates that interactions between serotonin and norepinephrine activity, or between these and other kinds of neurotransmitters in the brain, are more influential than the operation of any one neurotransmitter alone. In addition, as you will read shortly, a number of studies suggest that the activity of these neurotransmitters may either reflect or help produce dysfunction of a depression-related circuit in the brain, dysfunction that may itself be a key to the development of depression.

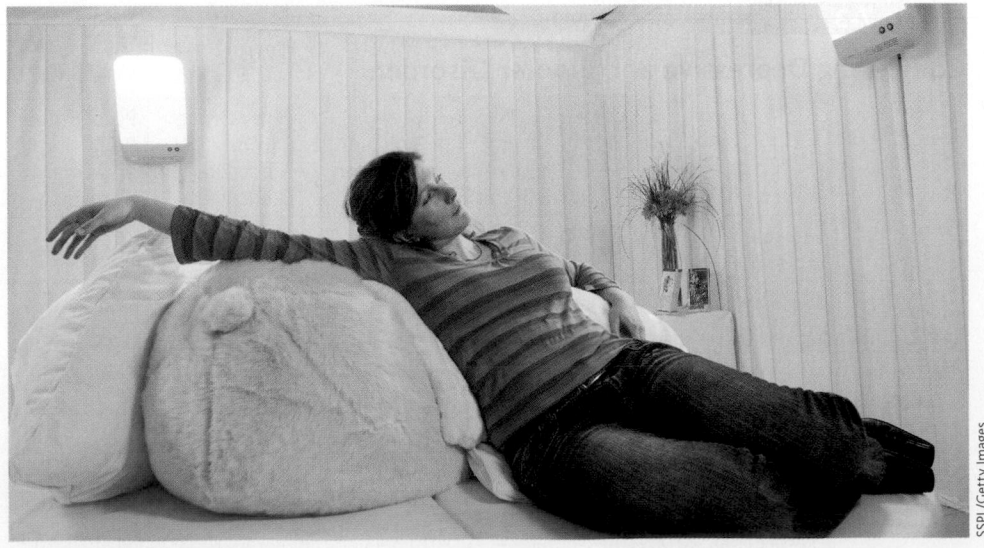

Lighting up depression This visitor to the Science Museum in London makes herself comfortable in the Light Lounge, a white enclosure containing four light boxes, where people can relax on a sofa and experience "light therapy" to help beat the winter blues and prevent seasonal recurrences of depression. Winter depression has been linked to a decrease in the amount of light people are exposed to at that time of year and to an accompanying shift in secretions of the hormone *melatonin*.

Biological researchers have also learned that another group of chemicals—the body's *hormones*—are linked to depression. As you read in Chapter 6, whenever we confront stressors in life, our brain triggers two stress pathways of the brain and body into action. One of those pathways, the *hypothalamic-pituitary-adrenal (HPA)* pathway, ultimately brings about the release of hormones at various locations throughout the body, and those hormones spur assorted body organs into action, causing us to temporarily experience a heightened state of arousal (see page 156). You may recall that the HPA pathway of people with posttraumatic stress disorder and certain anxiety disorders consistently *overreacts* when those individuals confront stressors. Research indicates that the HPA pathway of people with depression (particularly those whose depression includes feelings of anxiety) is also overly reactive in the face of stress, causing excessive and enduring releases of *cortisol* and related hormones at times of stress (Geerlings & Gerritsen, 2017; Hayden et al., 2014). This relationship is not all that surprising, given that stressful events so often seem to trigger depression. Once again, it is possible that the HPA overreactivity and heightened hormone activity found in depressed people either reflects or helps produce dysfunction in the depression-related circuit in the brain, the biological focus that we turn to next.

Brain Circuits As you have read in previous chapters, biological researchers have determined that emotional reactions of various kinds are tied to brain *circuits*—networks of brain structures that work together, triggering each other into action and producing a particular kind of emotional or behavioral reaction. Although research is far from complete, a brain circuit whose dysfunction contributes to unipolar depression has begun to emerge (Newman et al., 2017). An array of brain-imaging studies point to several brain structures that are likely members of this circuit, including the *prefrontal cortex, hippocampus, amygdala*, and *subgenual cingulate* (also called *Brodmann Area 25*), among other structures (see **Figure 7-1**). You may notice that several of the structures in this circuit are also members of the brain circuits that contribute to certain anxiety disorders and PTSD. However, the subgenual cingulate, a subregion of the brain's anterior cingulate cortex, is distinctly part of the depression-related circuit.

#DraculaHormone

#DraculaHormone

Another hormone tied to depression is *melatonin*, sometimes called the "Dracula hormone" because it is released only in the dark. People who experience a recurrence of depression each winter (a pattern called *seasonal affective disorder*) apparently secrete more melatonin during the winter's long nights than other individuals do.

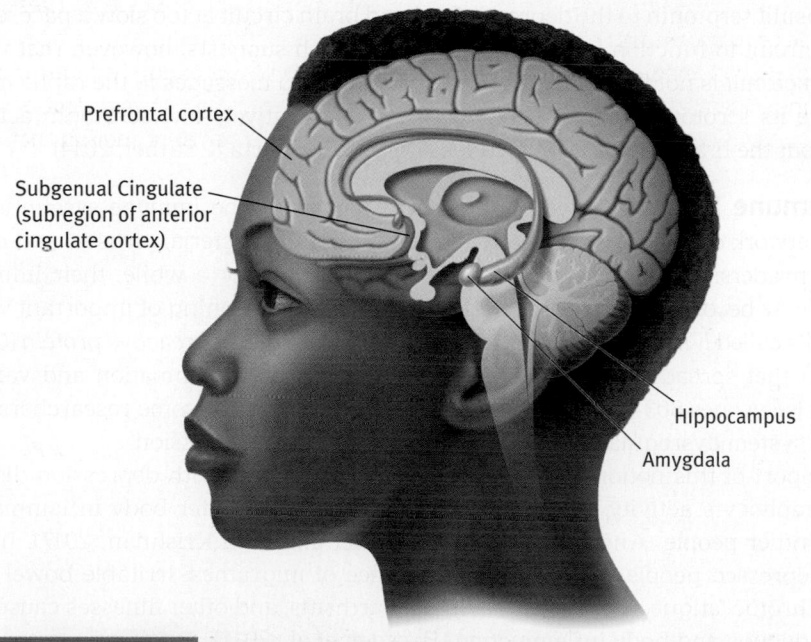

Prefrontal cortex

Subgenual Cingulate (subregion of anterior cingulate cortex)

Hippocampus

Amygdala

FIGURE 7-1

The Biology of Depression

Researchers believe that the brain circuit involved in unipolar depression includes the prefrontal cortex, hippocampus, amygdala, and subgenual cingulate, among other structures.

#DangerousPastime

Football Injuries and Depression

According to a study of 2,500 retired National Football League players, those who suffer three concussions during their careers are three times more likely later to develop a depressive disorder than those who had no concussions.

Players who experience one or two concussions are 1.5 times more likely than other players to develop a depressive disorder.

Around 26 percent of all former professional football players have suffered three or more concussions.

(Didehbani et al., 2013; Hart et al., 2013; Schwarz, 2010; McConnaughey, 2007)

#MedicalBonding

50% Stroke victims who experience clinical depression

30% Cancer patients who experience depression

20% Heart attack victims who become depressed

18% People with diabetes who are depressed

(Williams & Nieuwsma, 2016; Udesky, 2014; Jiang et al., 2011; Kerber et al., 2011; NIMH, 2004)

This structure has received enormous attention over the past 20 years (Newman et al., 2017; Eggers, 2014; Mayberg et al., 2005, 2000, 1997). Indeed, some theorists believe that dysfunction by this structure may be the single most important contributor to depression.

Unlike some of the other brain circuits we have discussed, dysfunctions of this depression-related circuit cannot be characterized in general terms, as, for example, a "hyperactive" or "underactive" circuit. But there are many indications that the circuit does indeed operate abnormally in persons with depression. Research suggests, for example, that among depressed people, activity and blood flow are unusually low in certain parts and unusually high in other parts of the prefrontal cortex; the hippocampus is undersized and its production of new neurons is low; activity and blood flow are elevated in the amygdala; the subgenual cingulate is particularly small and active; and communication between these various structures, called *interconnectivity*, is often problematic (Geerlings & Gerritsen, 2017; Newman et al., 2017; Pizzagalli, 2017; Philippi et al., 2015).

Studies indicate that under usual circumstances the neurotransmitters serotonin and norepinephrine are both plentiful and active in this brain circuit. For example, the circuit contains numerous *serotonin transporters,* or *5-HTTs* – proteins that help serotonin carry messages from one neuron to another. It appears, however, that, among depressed people, the activity of serotonin and norepinephrine in this circuit is distinctly lower than among other people (Avraham et al., 2017; James et al., 2017; Albert et al., 2014). This is not surprising, considering all the research that we observed earlier linking depression to generally low activity by these neurotransmitters.

The abnormal activity of these neurotransmitters in this brain circuit might be the result of dysfunction within or between the circuit's various structures, *or*, alternatively, the cause of such circuit dysfunction. At this point researchers do not know which is the case. Consider, for example, the neurotransmitter serotonin. In general, most brain serotonin is released from a location called the *raphe nuclei,* a cluster of neurons at the base of the brain. The neurons of the raphe nuclei extend to the depression-related circuit (as well as other areas of the brain) and release serotonin throughout the circuit. Some studies indicate that the raphe nuclei of depressed people may transmit serotonin to the depression-related brain circuit at too slow a pace, causing the circuit to function improperly. Other research suggests, however, that when the brain circuit is not functioning properly, it may send messages *to* the raphe nuclei to reduce its serotonin activity, leading in turn to relatively low serotonin activity throughout the brain (Rolls, 2017; Geddes et al., 2016; Sparta & Stuber, 2014).

The Immune System As you will see in Chapter 10, the *immune system* is the body's network of activities and body cells that fight off bacteria, viruses, and other foreign invaders. When people are under intense stress for a while, their immune systems may become dysregulated, leading to slower functioning of important white blood cells called *lymphocytes* and to increased production of *C-reactive protein* (*CRP*), a protein that spreads throughout the body and causes inflammation and various illnesses (see pages 303–304). There is a growing belief among some researchers that immune system dysregulation of this kind helps produce depression.

In support of this notion, studies have found that people with depression display lower lymphocyte activity, higher CRP production, and greater body inflammation than do other people (Anderson, 2018; Faugere et al., 2018; Krishnan, 2017). In addition, depressed people have a higher incidence of migraines, irritable bowel syndrome, chronic fatigue syndrome, rheumatoid arthritis, and other illnesses caused by CRP production and body inflammation (Euesden et al., 2017).

It is not yet clear how to interpret the relationship between depression and immune system dysregulation. While such dysregulation and chronic inflammation may help cause depression, it may be, conversely, that depression acts as a severe stressor that leads to immune system problems.

Psychological Views

The psychological models that have been most widely applied to unipolar depression are the psychodynamic and cognitive-behavioral models. The psychodynamic explanation has not been strongly supported by research, but the cognitive-behavioral explanations have received considerable support and have gained a large following.

The Psychodynamic View Sigmund Freud (1917) and his student Karl Abraham (1916, 1911) developed the first psychodynamic explanation of depression. They began by noting the similarity between clinical depression and grief in people who lose loved ones: constant weeping, loss of appetite, difficulty sleeping, loss of pleasure in life, and general withdrawal. According to the theorists, a series of unconscious processes is set in motion when a loved one dies. Unable to accept the loss, mourners at first regress to the *oral stage* of development, the period of total dependency when infants cannot distinguish themselves from their parents. By regressing to this stage, the mourners merge their own identity with that of the person they have lost, and so symbolically regain the lost person. In this process, called *introjection*, they direct all their feelings for the loved one, including sadness and anger, toward themselves. For most mourners, introjection is temporary. However, for some—particularly those whose various dependency needs were improperly met during infancy and early childhood—grief worsens over time, and they develop clinical depression (Busch et al., 2004; Bemporad, 1992).

Of course, many people become depressed without losing a loved one. To explain why, Freud proposed the concept of **symbolic**, or **imagined**, **loss**, in which a person equates other kinds of events with the loss of a loved one. A college student may, for example, experience failure in a calculus course as the loss of her parents, believing that they love her only when she excels academically.

Although many psychodynamic theorists have parted company with Freud and Abraham's theory of depression, it continues to influence current psychodynamic thinking (Gabbard & DeJean, 2016; Negele et al., 2015; Desmet, 2013). For example, *object relations theorists* (the psychodynamic theorists who emphasize relationships) propose that depression results when people's relationships—especially their early relationships—leave them feeling unsafe, insecure, and dependent on others.

The following description by the therapist of a depressed middle-aged woman illustrates the psychodynamic concepts of dependence, loss of a loved one, symbolic loss, and introjection:

Early loss The young daughter of a female police officer killed during the September 11, 2001, terrorist attack on the World Trade Center in New York City, stands onstage holding her father's hand while the names of attack victims are read during ceremonies at Ground Zero marking the fifth anniversary of the event. Research has found that people who lose their parents as children have an increased likelihood of experiencing depression as adults.

Spencer Platt/Getty Images

> *Marie Carls . . . had always felt very attached to her mother. . . . She always tried to placate her volcanic [emotions], to please her in every possible way. . . .*
>
> *After marriage [to Julius], she continued her pattern of submission and compliance. Before her marriage she had difficulty in complying with a volcanic mother, and after her marriage she almost automatically assumed a submissive role. . . .*
>
> *[W]hen she was thirty years old . . . [Marie] and her husband invited Ignatius, who was single, to come and live with them. Ignatius and [Marie] soon discovered that they had an attraction for each other. They both tried to fight that feeling; but when Julius had to go to another city for a few days, the so-called infatuation became much more than that. There were a few physical contacts. . . . There was an intense spiritual affinity. . . . A few months later everybody had to leave the city. . . . Nothing was done to maintain contact. Two years later . . . Marie heard that Ignatius had married. She felt terribly alone and despondent. . . .*
>
> *Her suffering had become more acute as she [came to believe] that old age was approaching and she had lost all her chances. Ignatius remained as the memory of lost*

symbolic loss According to Freudian theory, the loss of a valued object (for example, a loss of employment) that is unconsciously interpreted as the loss of a loved one. Also called *imagined loss.*

(continued on the next page)

opportunities. . . . Her life of compliance and obedience had not permitted her to reach her goal. . . . When she became aware of these ideas, she felt even more depressed. . . . She felt that everything she had built in her life was false or based on a false premise.

(Arieti & Bemporad, 1978, pp. 275–284)

Studies have offered general support for the psychodynamic idea that major losses, especially ones suffered early in life, may set the stage for later depression (Krishnan, 2017; Gilman, 2013; Gutman & Nemeroff, 2011). When, for example, a diagnostic survey was administered to thousands of adults in one study, the individuals whose fathers had died during their childhood scored higher on depression (Jacobs & Bovasso, 2009).

Related research supports the psychodynamic idea that people whose childhood needs were poorly met are particularly likely to become depressed after experiencing loss (Conradi et al., 2018; Paterniti et al., 2017). In some studies, depressed patients have filled out a scale called the Parental Bonding Instrument, which indicates how much care and protection people feel they received as children. Many have identified their parents' child-rearing style as "affectionless control," consisting of a mixture of low care and high protection (Karim & Begum, 2017; Otani et al., 2016).

At the same time, research does not indicate that loss or problematic early relationships are always at the core of depression. In fact, it is estimated that less than 10 percent of all people who have major losses in life actually become depressed (Hammen, 2016; Sandler et al., 2008). Moreover, research into the loss-depression link has yielded inconsistent findings. Though some studies find evidence of a relationship between childhood loss and later depression, others do not.

When the applause stops According to cognitive-behavioral theorists, the reduction in rewards brought about by retirement places athletes and other high achievers at risk for depression unless they develop a healthy perspective and find new sources of gratification. Standing in front of photos highlighting his great moments as an NFL quarterback, Terry Bradshaw waves to a crowd of 71,000 fans at Super Bowl 50 in 2016. Bradshaw, now a successful football analyst on FOX NFL Sunday, has struggled with depression throughout much of his adult life, but he went through particularly intense episodes in the years following his 1984 retirement from the game.

Patrick Smith/Getty Images

The Cognitive-Behavioral View As with other kinds of psychological disorders, cognitive-behavioral theories contend that unipolar depression results from a combination of problematic behaviors and dysfunctional ways of thinking. These theories fall into three groups: explanations that focus mostly on the behavioral realm, those that give primary attention to negative thinking, and ones that feature a complex interplay between cognitive and behavioral factors.

THE BEHAVIORAL DIMENSION Clinical researcher Peter Lewinsohn was one of the first theorists to link depression to significant changes in the number of rewards and punishments people receive in their lives (Lewinsohn et al., 1990, 1984). He suggested that the positive rewards in life dwindle for some people, leading them to perform fewer and fewer constructive behaviors. The rewards of campus life, for example, disappear when a young woman graduates from college and takes a job; and an aging baseball player loses the rewards of high salary and adulation when his skills deteriorate. Although many people manage to fill their lives with other forms of gratification, some become particularly disheartened. The positive features of their lives decrease even more, and the decline in rewards leads them to perform still fewer constructive behaviors. In this manner, they spiral toward depression.

In a number of studies, researchers have found that the number of rewards people receive in life is indeed related to the presence or absence of depression. Not only do depressed participants typically report fewer positive rewards than nondepressed participants, but when their rewards begin to increase, their mood improved as well (Chan et al., 2017; Nyström et al., 2017). Similarly, other investigations have found a strong relationship between positive life events and feelings of life satisfaction and happiness (Sotgiu, 2016).

Lewinsohn and other theorists have further proposed that *social* rewards are particularly important in the downward spiral of depression (Martell et al., 2013). This claim has been supported by research showing that depressed persons receive fewer social rewards than nondepressed persons and that as their mood improves, their social rewards increase (see **MindTech**). Although depressed people are sometimes the victims of social circumstances, it may also be that their dark mood and flat behaviors help produce a decline in social rewards (Hodgetts et al., 2017; Hammen, 2016; Coyne, 2001).

NEGATIVE THINKING Aaron Beck believes that negative thinking, rather than underlying conflicts or a reduction in positive rewards, lies at the heart of depression (Beck, 2016, 2002, 1967; Beck & Weishaar, 2014). According to Beck, *maladaptive attitudes,* a *cognitive triad, errors in thinking,* and *automatic thoughts* combine to produce unipolar depression.

MINDTECH

Texting: A Relationship Buster?

Texting has now become the leading way that most people communicate with others (Burke, 2016; Pew Research Center, 2015). The average 18- to 24-year-old, for example, sends and receives a total of 128 texts each day. In fact, surveys suggest that people often fail to fully attend to their current activities in order to juggle their text conversations. Some clinicians worry that excessive texting may damage our relationships—relationships with the people we are texting and relationships with those we are ignoring while texting.

Based on her studies, MIT professor Sherry Turkle (2015, 2013, 2012) has concluded that communicating primarily via text does indeed affect relationships negatively. Many of her participants reported, "I'd rather text than talk." Turkle concludes from her research that people often use texting as a crutch to avoid direct communication and possible confrontations. Her participants said that texting saves valuable time over face-to-face conversations, but, Turkle concludes, "People who feel they are too busy to have conversations in person are not making the important emotional connections they otherwise would."

In related work, researcher Karla Klein Murdock (2013) interviewed 83 college freshmen about their daily texting habits, along with their levels of social and personal stress, sleep patterns, and happiness. She found that hastily written texts (which is to say, most texts) often lend themselves to

Luis Acosta/Getty Images

misunderstandings between senders and receivers—misunderstandings that can quickly spin out of control. Murdock also noted that many participants in her study felt the need to constantly keep up with ongoing text conversations, interrupting their in-person conversations—thus inviting damage to those relationships as well. Small wonder that the participants who averaged the most daily texts were more likely than other participants to report more stress, unhappiness, anxiety, and sleeping problems. Murdock believes that in many such cases, the negative effects of texting on the participants' personal relationships are leading to broader feelings of stress and unhappiness.

None of this suggests that texting per se is a detriment to social or personal happiness. Rather, it seems to be the exclusive and excessive use of it that is the problem. Although half of all young adults say that text conversations are just as meaningful as other avenues of communication (Burke, 2016), it just may be that truly important discussions are better served by in-person, or at least phone, conversations. 💬

> **Can you think of ways in which texting might sometimes be helpful to relationships and communications?**

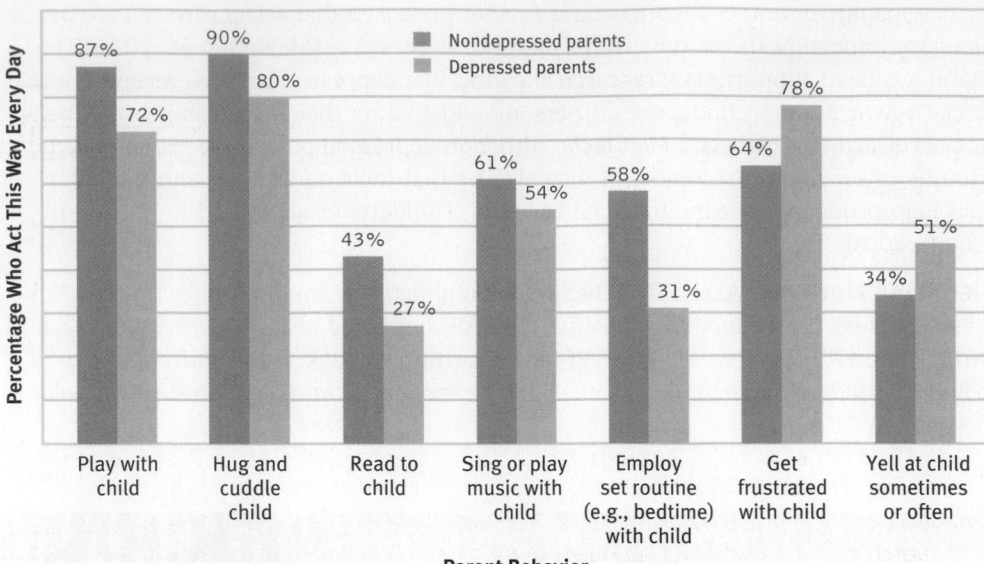

FIGURE 7-2

How Depressed Parents and Their Children Interact

Depressed parents are less likely than nondepressed parents to play with, hug, read to, or sing to their young children each day or to employ the same routine each day. They are also more likely to get frustrated with their children on a daily basis. Such problematic interactions may help explain the repeated research finding that children of depressed parents are more likely than other children to have emotional, cognitive, or behavioral difficulties. (Information from: Weissman et al., 2016; Princeton Survey Research Associates, 1996.)

#SeriousOversight

Family physicians, internists, and pediatricians fail to detect depression in at least 50 percent of their depressed patients (Lyness, 2017; Mitchell et al., 2011).

Beck believes that some people develop *maladaptive attitudes* as children, such as "My general worth is tied to every task I perform" or "If I fail, others will feel repelled by me." The attitudes result from their own experiences and the judgments of the people around them (see **Figure 7-2**). Many failures are inevitable in a full, active life, so such attitudes are inaccurate and set the stage for all kinds of negative thoughts and reactions. Beck suggests that later in these people's lives, upsetting situations may trigger an extended round of negative thinking. That thinking typically takes three forms, which he calls the **cognitive triad**: the individuals repeatedly interpret (1) their *experiences,* (2) *themselves,* and (3) their *futures* in negative ways that lead them to feel depressed. The cognitive triad is at work in the thinking of this depressed person:

> One-third of people who felt unhappy as children continue to feel unhappy as adults. Why might this be so?

> *I can't bear it. I can't stand the humiliating fact that I'm the only woman in the world who can't take care of her family, take her place as a real wife and mother, and be respected in her community. When I speak to my young son Billy, I know I can't let him down, but I feel so ill-equipped to take care of him; that's what frightens me. I don't know what to do or where to turn; the whole thing is too overwhelming. . . . I must be a laughing stock. It's more than I can do to go out and meet people and have the fact pointed out to me so clearly.*
>
> *(Fieve, 1975)*

According to Beck, depressed people also make errors in their thinking. In one common error of logic, they draw arbitrary inferences—negative conclusions based on little evidence. A man walking through the park, for example, passes a woman who is looking at nearby flowers and concludes, "She's avoiding looking at me." Similarly, depressed people often minimize the significance of positive experiences or magnify that of negative ones. A college student receives an A on a difficult English exam, for example, but concludes that the grade reflects the professor's generosity rather than her own ability (minimization). Later in the week the same student must miss an English class and is convinced that she will be unable to keep up the rest of the semester (magnification).

Finally, depressed people have **automatic thoughts**, a steady train of unpleasant thoughts that keep suggesting to them that they are inadequate and that their situation is hopeless. Beck labels these thoughts "automatic" because they seem to just happen, as if by reflex. In the course of only a few hours, depressed people may be visited by hundreds of such thoughts: "I'm worthless. . . . I'll never amount to anything . . . I let everyone down. . . . Everyone hates me. . . . My responsibilities are overwhelming. . . . I've failed as a parent . . . I'm stupid. . . . Everything is difficult for me. . . . Things will never change." One therapist said of a depressed client, "By the end of the day, she is worn out, she has lived a thousand painful accidents, participated in a thousand deaths, mourned a thousand mistakes" (Mendels, 1970).

"Really, only you can tell yourself to giddyup."

Many studies have produced evidence in support of Beck's explanation (Krishnan, 2017). Several of them confirm that depressed people hold maladaptive attitudes and that the more of these maladaptive attitudes they hold, the more depressed they tend to be (Beck, 2016; Thomas & Altareb, 2012). Still other research has found the cognitive triad at work in depressed people (Oltean et al., 2017; Lai et al., 2014). In various studies, depressed people seem to recall unpleasant experiences more readily than positive ones, rate their performances on laboratory tasks lower than nondepressed people do, and select pessimistic statements in storytelling tests (for example, "I expect my plans will fail").

Beck's claims about errors in logic have also received research support (Özdel et al., 2014; Hammen & Krantz, 1976). In one study, female participants—some depressed, some not—were asked to read and interpret paragraphs about women in difficult situations. Depressed participants made more errors in logic (such as arbitrary inference) in their interpretations than nondepressed women did.

Finally, research has supported Beck's claim that automatic thoughts are tied to depression (Wang et al., 2016; Bates et al., 1999; Strickland et al., 1975). In several classic studies, for example, nondepressed participants who were tricked into reading negative automatic-thought-like statements about themselves became increasingly depressed. In a related line of research, it has been found that people who generally make *ruminative responses* during their depressed moods—that is, repeatedly dwell mentally on their mood without acting to change it—feel dejection longer and are more likely to develop clinical depression later in life than people who avoid such ruminations (Liu et al., 2017; Watkins & Nolen-Hoeksema, 2014).

This body of research shows that negative thinking is indeed linked to depression, but it fails to show that such patterns of thought are the cause and core of unipolar depression. It could be that a central mood problem leads to thinking difficulties that then take a further toll on mood, behavior, and physiology.

LEARNED HELPLESSNESS: A COGNITIVE-BEHAVIORAL INTERPLAY According to psychologist Martin Seligman (1975), feelings of helplessness are at the center of depression. Since the mid-1960s Seligman has been developing the **learned helplessness** theory of depression (Maier & Seligman, 2016). It holds that people become depressed when

cognitive triad The three forms of negative thinking that Aaron Beck theorizes lead people to feel depressed. The triad consists of a negative view of one's experiences, oneself, and the future.

automatic thoughts Numerous unpleasant thoughts that help to cause or maintain depression, anxiety, or other forms of psychological dysfunction.

learned helplessness The perception, based on past experiences, that one has no control over the reinforcements in one's life.

they think (1) that they no longer have control over the reinforcements (the rewards and punishments) in their lives, and (2) that they themselves are responsible for this helpless state. Feelings of helplessness fill this account of a young woman's depression:

Mary was 25 years old and had just begun her senior year in college. . . . Asked to recount how her life had been going recently, Mary began to weep. Sobbing, she said that for the last year or so she felt she was losing control of her life and that recent stresses (starting school again, friction with her boyfriend) had left her feeling worthless and frightened. Because of a gradual deterioration in her vision, she was now forced to wear glasses all day. "The glasses make me look terrible," she said, and "I don't look people in the eye much any more." Also, to her dismay, Mary had gained 20 pounds in the past year. She viewed herself as overweight and unattractive. At times she was convinced that with enough money to buy contact lenses and enough time to exercise she could cast off her depression; at other times she believed nothing would help. . . . Mary saw her life deteriorating in other spheres, as well. She felt overwhelmed by schoolwork and, for the first time in her life, was on academic probation. . . . In addition to her dissatisfaction with her appearance and her fears about her academic future, Mary complained of a lack of friends. Her social network consisted solely of her boyfriend, with whom she was living. Although there were times she experienced this relationship as almost unbearably frustrating, she felt helpless to change it and was pessimistic about its permanence.

(Spitzer et al., 1983, pp. 122–123)

Seligman's theory first began to take shape when he was working with laboratory dogs. In one procedure, he strapped dogs into an apparatus called a hammock, in which they received shocks periodically no matter what they did. The next day each dog was placed in a *shuttle box*, a box divided in half by a barrier over which the animal could jump to reach the other side (see **Figure 7-3**). Seligman applied shocks to the dogs in the box, expecting that they, like other dogs in this situation, would soon learn to escape by jumping over the barrier. However, most of these dogs failed to learn anything in the shuttle box. After a flurry of activity, they simply "lay down and quietly whined" and accepted the shock.

Seligman decided that while receiving inescapable shocks in the hammock the day before, the dogs had learned that they had no control over unpleasant events (shocks) in their lives. That is, they had learned that they were helpless to do anything to change negative situations. Thus, when later they were placed in a new situation (the shuttle box) where they could in fact control their fate, they continued to believe that they were generally helpless. Seligman noted that the effects of learned helplessness greatly resemble the symptoms of human depression, and he proposed that people in fact become depressed after developing a general belief that they have no control over reinforcements in their lives.

In numerous human and animal studies, participants who undergo helplessness training have displayed reactions similar to depressive symptoms. When, for example, human participants are exposed to uncontrollable negative events, they later score higher than other individuals on a depressive mood scale. Similarly, helplessness-trained animal subjects lose interest in sexual and social activities—a common symptom of human depression. Such animals also come to display low serotonin and norepinephrine activity in their raphe nuclei and other key brain structures, similar to the reductions that characterize depressed people (Smith et al., 2017; Zhou et al., 2017; Maier & Seligman, 2016).

The learned helplessness explanation of depression has been revised somewhat over the past several decades. According to one modified version of the theory, the *attribution-helplessness theory*, when people view events as beyond their control, they ask themselves why this is so (Rubenstein et al., 2016; Abramson et al., 2002, 1989,

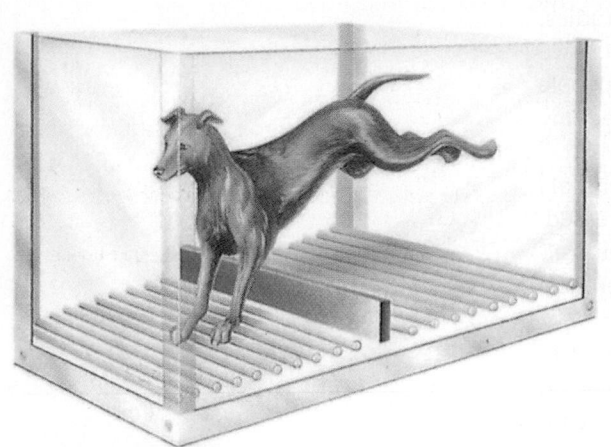

FIGURE 7-3

Jumping to Safety

Experimental animals learn to escape or avoid shocks that are administered on one side of a shuttle box by jumping to the other (safe) side.

Xinhua/eyevine/Redux

Victimization and learned helplessness
Hundreds of women's shoes cover the steps of the Vancouver Art Gallery during Canada's annual Day of Mourning for women who have suffered violent deaths, including ones caused by spouse abuse. Research suggests that many women who are abused by their spouses develop feelings of helplessness, thus helping to explain their "decision" to stay in such a dangerous relationship (Salcioglu et al., 2017). They may come to believe that nothing they can do will stop the repeated episodes of violence, and, in turn, they may develop feelings of depression, low self-esteem, and self-blame.

1978) (see **Table 7-4**). If they attribute their present lack of control to some *internal* cause that is both *global* and *stable* ("I am inadequate at everything and I always will be"), they may well feel helpless to prevent future negative outcomes and they may experience depression. If they make other kinds of attributions, they are unlikely to have this reaction.

Consider a college student whose girlfriend breaks up with him. If he attributes this loss of control to an internal cause that is both global and stable—"It's my fault [internal], I ruin everything I touch [global], and I always will [stable]"—he then has reason to expect similar losses of control in the future and may generally experience a sense of helplessness. According to the learned helplessness view, he is a prime candidate for depression. If the student had instead attributed the breakup to causes that were more *specific* ("The way I've behaved the past couple of weeks blew this relationship"), *unstable* ("I don't know what got into me—I don't usually act like that"), or *external* ("She never did know what she wanted"), he might not expect to lose control again and

#TheirWords

"No one can make you feel inferior without your consent."

Eleanor Roosevelt

TABLE: 7-4

Internal and External Attributions
Event: "I failed my psych test today."

	Internal		External	
	Stable	**Unstable**	**Stable**	**Unstable**
Global	"I have a problem with test anxiety."	"Getting into an argument with my roommate threw my whole day off."	"Written tests are an unfair way to assess knowledge"	"No one does well on tests that are given the day after vacation."
Specific	"I just have no grasp of psychology."	"I got upset and froze when I couldn't answer the first two questions."	"Everyone knows that this professor enjoys giving unfair tests."	"This professor didn't put much thought into the test because of the pressure of her book deadline."

#FathersToo

Paternal Postpartum Depression

At least 8% of new fathers may also experience some degree of postpartum depression (Cameron et al., 2017). Research indicates that, as in cases of a mother's postpartum depression, this syndrome can affect a child's psychological development (Gentile & Fusco, 2017; Koh et al., 2014).

Everyone has social needs Researchers have found that macaque monkeys—like many other animals—are greatly affected by friends and relatives (Waller, Whitehouse, & Micheletta, 2016; Waller & Micheletta, 2013). Moreover, the facial expressions of macaques show emotions ranging from anger to fear to sadness—expressions that influence each others' social judgments, behaviors, and moods.

Niall Carson/Press Association via AP Images

would probably not experience helplessness and depression. Hundreds of studies have supported the relationship between styles of attribution, helplessness, and depression (Rubenstein et al., 2016; Rotenberg et al., 2012).

Some theorists have refined the helplessness model yet again in recent years. They suggest that attributions are likely to cause depression only when they further produce a sense of *hopelessness* in a person (Liu et al., 2015; Abramson et al., 2002, 1989). By taking this factor into consideration, clinicians are often able to predict depression with still greater precision.

Although the learned helplessness theory of unipolar depression has been very influential, it too has imperfections. For example, much of the learned helplessness research relies on animal subjects. It is impossible to know whether the animals' symptoms do in fact reflect the clinical depression found in humans (Kim et al., 2017; Czéh et al., 2016). In addition, the attributional feature of the theory raises difficult questions. What about the dogs and rats who learn helplessness? Can animals make attributions, even implicitly?

Sociocultural Views

Sociocultural theorists propose that unipolar depression is strongly influenced by the social context that surrounds people. Their belief is supported by the finding, discussed earlier, that depression is often triggered by outside stressors (Krishnan, 2017; Hammen, 2016). Once again, there are two kinds of sociocultural views—the *family-social perspective* and the *multicultural perspective*.

The Family-Social Perspective Earlier you read that some cognitive-behavioral theorists believe that a decline in social rewards is particularly important in the development of depression. This view is also consistent with the family-social perspective.

The connection between declining social rewards and depression is a two-way street (Hammen, 2016; Nardi et al., 2013; Joiner, 2002). On the one hand, researchers have found that depressed people often display weak social skills and communicate poorly. They typically speak more slowly and quietly and in more of a monotone than nondepressed people, pause longer between words and sentences, and take longer to respond to others. They also seek repeated reassurances from others. Such social deficits make other people uncomfortable and may cause them to avoid the depressed individuals. As a result, the social contacts and rewards of depressed people decrease, and, as they participate in fewer and fewer social interactions, their social skills deteriorate still further.

Consistent with these findings, depression has been tied repeatedly to the unavailability of social support such as that found in a happy marriage (Cao et al., 2017; Krishnan, 2017). Generally, there is a high correlation between level of marital conflict and degree of sadness: .37 for men and .42 for women (Whisman & Baucom, 2012; Whisman, 2001). Among those who are clinically depressed, the correlation rises to .66. Research indicates that people in troubled marriages are 25 times more likely to have a depressive disorder than people in untroubled marriages (Keitner, 2017). In some cases, the spouse's depression may contribute to marital discord or divorce, but often the interpersonal conflicts and low social support found in troubled relationships seem to lead to depression (Williams & Nieuwsma, 2016).

Researchers have also found that people whose lives are characterized by weak social supports, isolation, and

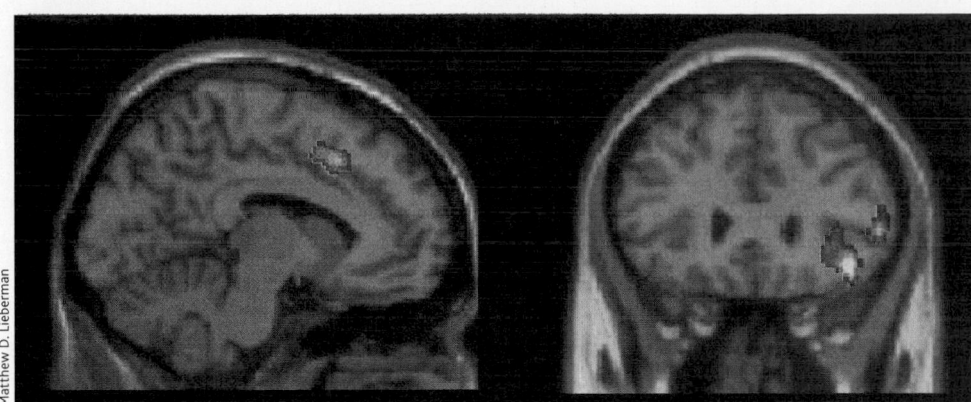

Anterior cingulate cortex   Prefrontal cortex

Matthew D. Lieberman

Social exclusion, depression, and the brain In a widely used research design called *cyberball*, a participant lies in an fMRI scanner and is told (falsely) that he or she is playing a game of cyber catch with two players in other rooms. As the other players increasingly exclude the participant from the three-way catch, the fMRI records what parts of his or her brain are being affected. As shown in these brain scans, subregions of the anterior cingulate cortex (left) and the prefrontal cortex (right), key structures in the depression-related brain circuit, become active during this lab-induced social exclusion, just as they do in cases of clinical depression.

> **Why might problems in the social arena—for example, social loss, social ties, and social rewards—be particularly tied to depression?**

lack of intimacy are particularly likely to become depressed and to remain depressed longer than other people (Krishnan, 2017; Swartz, 2016). For example, some highly publicized studies conducted in England several decades ago showed that women who had three or more young children, lacked a close confidante, and had no outside employment were more likely than other women to become depressed after going through stressful events (Brown, 2002; Brown & Harris, 1978).

The Multicultural Perspective Two kinds of relationships have captured the interest of multicultural theorists: (1) links between *gender and depression*, and (2) ties between *cultural and ethnic background and depression*. In the case of gender, a strong relationship has been found, but a clear explanation for that relationship has yet to emerge. The clinical field is still sorting out whether and what ties exist between cultural factors and depression.

GENDER AND DEPRESSION As you have read, there is a strong link between gender and depression. Women in places as far apart as France, Sweden, Lebanon, New Zealand, and the United States are at least twice as likely as men to receive a diagnosis of unipolar depression. Why the huge difference between the sexes? A variety of theories have been offered and studied (Mayo Clinic, 2016; Hammen, 2016; Rosch, 2016; Nolen-Hoeksema, 2012, 2002, 1990).

The *artifact theory* holds that women and men are equally prone to depression but that clinicians often fail to detect depression in men. Perhaps depressed women display more emotional symptoms, such as sadness and crying, which are easily diagnosed, while depressed men mask their depression behind traditionally "masculine" symptoms such as anger. Although this is a popular explanation, research indicates that women are actually no more willing or able than men to identify their depressive symptoms and to seek treatment.

The *hormone explanation* holds that hormone changes trigger depression in many women, particularly during puberty, pregnancy, and menopause. Research suggests, however, that the social and life events that accompany these developmental milestones are also profound and may account for experiences of depression as well as, or better than, hormone shifts. Hormone explanations have also been criticized as sexist, since they imply that a woman's normal biology is flawed (see **PsychWatch** on page 209).

The *life stress theory* suggests that women in our society are subject to more stress than men. On average they face more poverty, more menial jobs, less adequate housing, and more discrimination than men—all factors that have been linked to

#WaningConfidants

Intimate social contact has been declining over the past 30 years. When research participants were asked in 1985 how many confidants they turned to for discussion of important matters, most answered 3. Today, the most common response to the same question is 2 or less (GSS, 2016; Bryner, 2011; McPherson et al., 2006).

ullstein bild/Getty Images

A dance metaphor Many theorists believe that the reason for the large gender difference in depression rates is that, on average, women face more stressors, discrimination, unattainable body ideals, and victimization than men. A popular description for this gender disadvantage is that women must "dance backwards and in high heels"—a term that has its origins in the dance team of Ginger Rogers and Fred Astaire, iconic partners in 10 popular movies in the 1930s. Although they were both remarkably talented, Astaire's acclaim and professional success ultimately exceeded that of Rogers, who had, after all, done everything Astaire did, but "backwards and in high heels."

depression. And in many homes, women bear a disproportionate share of responsibility for child care and housework.

The *body dissatisfaction explanation* states that females in Western society are taught, almost from birth, but particularly during adolescence, to seek a low body weight and slender body shape—goals that are unreasonable, unhealthy, and often unattainable. As you'll read in Chapter 11, research finds that, as adolescence unfolds, girls do become more and more dissatisfied with their weight and body and, on average, display an increased rate of depression. However, it is not clear that eating and weight concerns actually cause depression; they may instead be the result of depression.

The *lack-of-control theory* draws on the learned helplessness research and proposes that women may be more prone to depression because they feel less control than men over their lives. It has been found that victimization of any kind, from discrimination to burglary to rape, often produces a sense of helplessness and increases the symptoms of depression—and women in our society are, on average, more likely than men to be victims across various domains (BJS, 2016).

A final explanation for the gender differences found in depression is the *rumination theory*. As you read earlier, rumination is related to depression. Research reveals that women are more likely than men to ruminate when their mood darkens, perhaps making them more vulnerable to the onset of clinical depression.

Each of these explanations for the gender difference in unipolar depression offers food for thought. Each has gathered just enough supporting evidence to make it interesting and just enough evidence to the contrary to raise questions about its usefulness. Thus, at present, the gender difference in depression remains one of the most talked-about but least understood phenomena in the clinical field.

CULTURAL BACKGROUND AND DEPRESSION Depression is a worldwide phenomenon, and certain symptoms of this disorder seem to be constant across all countries.

David South/Alamy

Non-Western depression Depressed people in non-Western countries tend to have fewer cognitive symptoms, such as self-blame, and more physical symptoms, such as fatigue, weakness, and sleep disturbances.

A landmark study of four countries—Canada, Switzerland, Iran, and Japan—found that the great majority of depressed people in these very different countries reported symptoms of sadness, joylessness, tension, lack of energy, loss of interest, loss of ability to concentrate, ideas of insufficiency, and thoughts of suicide (Matsumoto & Juang, 2016). Beyond such core symptoms, however, research suggests that the precise picture of depression varies from country to country (Shafi & Shafi, 2014; Kok et al., 2012; Kleinman, 2004). Depressed people in non-Western countries—China and Nigeria, for example—are more likely to be troubled by physical symptoms such as fatigue, weakness, sleep disturbances,

Premenstrual Dysphoric Disorder: Déja Vu All Over Again

Back in the early 1990s, one of the biggest controversies in the development of DSM-IV centered on the category *premenstrual dysphoric disorder (PMDD)*. The DSM-IV work group recommended that PMDD be formally listed as a new kind of depressive disorder. The category was to be applied when a woman was regularly impaired by at least 5 of 11 symptoms during the week before menstruation: depressed or hopeless feelings; tense or anxious feelings; marked mood changes; frequent irritability or anger and increased interpersonal conflicts; decreased interest in her usual activities; poor concentration; lack of energy; changes in appetite; insomnia or sleepiness; a sense of being overwhelmed or out of control; and physical symptoms such as swollen breasts, headaches, muscle pain, a "bloated" sensation, or weight gain.

This recommendation set off an uproar. Many clinicians (including some dissenting members of the work group), several national organizations, interest groups, and the media warned that this diagnostic category would "pathologize" severe cases of *premenstrual syndrome,* or *PMS,* the premenstrual discomforts that are common and normal, and might cause women's behavior in general to be attributed largely to "raging hormones" (a stereotype that society was finally rejecting). They argued that data were lacking to include the new category (Chase, 1993; DeAngelis, 1993).

The solution? A compromise. PMDD was not listed as a formal category in DSM-IV, but the pattern was listed in the DSM-IV appendix, with the suggestion that it be studied more thoroughly. Critics hoped that PMDD would die a quiet death there. However, two decades later the category gained new life. When, in 2011, the DSM-5 task force published a list of changes being considered for the new edition of the DSM, premenstrual dysphoric disorder was included as one of the depressive disorders. The reaction? As you might expect, another uproar among many clinicians and interest groups, an outcry that continues to the present day (Fauber, Fiore, & Wynn, 2017). This time, however, the proponents prevailed, citing several studies conducted over the past few decades. PMDD is now an official category in DSM-5 (APA, 2013).

David Cheskin/PA Wire via AP Images

and weight loss. Depression in those countries is less often marked by cognitive symptoms such as self-blame, low self-esteem, and guilt.

Within the United States, researchers have found few differences in the symptoms of depression among members of different ethnic or racial groups. Nor have they found significant differences in the *overall* rates of depression between such minority groups. On the other hand, research reveals that there are often striking differences between ethnic/racial groups in the *recurrence* of depression. Hispanic Americans and African Americans are 50 percent more likely than non-Hispanic white Americans to have recurrent episodes of depression (Krishnan, 2017). Why this difference? Around 54 percent of depressed non-Hispanic white Americans receive treatment for their disorders (medication and/or psychotherapy), compared with 34 percent of depressed Hispanic Americans and 40 percent of depressed African Americans (González et al., 2010). It may be that minority groups in the United States are more vulnerable to repeated experiences of depression partly because many of their members have more limited treatment opportunities when they are depressed.

Research has also revealed that depression is distributed unevenly within some minority groups. This is not totally surprising, given that each minority group itself consists of people of varied backgrounds and cultural values. For example, depression is more common among Hispanic and African Americans born in the United States than among Hispanic and African American immigrants (González et al., 2010; Miranda et al., 2005). Moreover, within the Hispanic American population, Puerto Ricans have a higher rate of depression than do Mexican Americans or Cuban Americans.

> How would you explain the relatively low rate of depression found among immigrants in the United States? Why do their depression rates eventually rise?

Integrating the Models: The Developmental Psychopathology Perspective

As with their explanations of other psychological disorders, proponents of the developmental psychopathology perspective contend that unipolar depression is caused by a combination of the factors we have been examining throughout this chapter. Moreover, they believe that the factors unfold and intersect in a developmental sequence, with early negative factors generally setting the stage for later negative factors and ultimately for depression, but with later positive factors sometimes able to offset the lingering impact of early negative factors. Developmental psychopathology explanations of unipolar depression have, in fact, received considerable research support (Calkins & Perry, 2016; Cicchetti, 2016; Lieberman & Chu, 2016).

Consistent with biological findings, developmental psychopathologists believe that the road to unipolar depression often begins with a genetically inherited predisposition—a predisposition that is characterized by low activity of key neurotransmitters (serotonin and norepinephrine) in key brain structures, an overly reactive HPA stress pathway (see page 197), and a dysfunctional depression-related brain circuit (Newman et al., 2017; Bagot et al., 2016; Guffanti et al., 2016). Researchers from this perspective have found that such biological predispositions will most likely result in later depression if the individual is *also* subjected to significant traumas early in life (particularly interpersonal losses) and/or inadequate parenting, such as parenting that is disrupted, depressive in style, inconsistent, or rejecting (Dittrich et al., 2018; Wang et al., 2018; Hammens, 2016). And still other studies indicate that this combination of biological and childhood factors often leads to a low self-concept, a temperament marked by feelings such as guilt (called "negative affectivity"), a negative style of thinking, general feelings of helplessness, and/or interpersonal dependence—variables that are themselves each linked to depression (Reinfjell et al., 2016; Lau et al., 2014; Morris et al., 2014). According to developmental psychopathologists, individuals who travel through this unfavorable developmental sequence are particularly likely to become depressed when they experience stress in adult life, especially interpersonal stress (Hammen, 2016; Morris et al., 2014).

> Why do you think so many comedians and other entertainers report that they have grappled with depression earlier in their lives?

However, this precise sequence of intersecting factors is not the only avenue to later depression. Developmental psychopathology research has clarified that some of the negative factors may, depending on their magnitude and timing, override positive developmental factors. Studies indicate, for example, that individuals who experience severe childhood traumas or inadequate parenting often develop depression when they later encounter life stress, even if they have no genetic predisposition for the disorder (Mullins et al., 2016; Oldehinkel et al., 2014). Such findings are apparently related to the two-way relationship that exists between many of these factors. Research has found, for example, that exposure to severe or repeated traumas at key points early in life may adversely affect an individual's HPA stress pathway and depression-related brain circuit, even if the pathway and circuit had previously been functioning properly (Hammen, 2016; Starr et al., 2014; Onoue et al., 2013). One study even found that the adoption of a negative attribution style and related forms of negative thinking by child

#ControversialChange

Does Bereavement Equal Depression?

In past editions of the DSM, people who lose a loved one were excluded from receiving a diagnosis of *major depressive disorder* during the first 2 months of their bereavement. However, according to DSM-5, newly bereaved people can qualify for this diagnosis if their depressive symptoms are severe enough. Critics fear that many people undergoing a normal grief reaction may now receive an incorrect diagnosis of major depressive disorder.

Across the species Back in the 1950s and 1960s, researcher Harry Harlow found that infant monkeys reacted with apparent despair to separation from their mothers. Even monkeys raised with surrogate mothers—wire cylinders wrapped with foam rubber and covered with terry cloth—formed an attachment to them and mourned their absence.

participants adversely affected the ongoing operation of their HPA stress pathway (Hayden et al., 2014).

At the same time, the developmental psychopathology perspective is not all gloom and doom. The presence of negative developmental factors does not inevitably produce a march toward depression, according to this perspective. Studies have found, for example, that individuals who experience *moderate* and *manageable* adversities throughout their childhood often develop resilience and become better able to withstand the depressive effects of life stress in adulthood (Oldehinkel et al., 2014). One study even found that participants who had repeatedly experienced moderate adversities throughout their lives were less likely to become depressed in the face of significant life stress than were participants who had faced little or no adversity in their lives (Seery et al., 2010). Correspondingly, research has revealed that the HPA stress pathway of children exposed to manageable adversities typically operates more properly than the HPA pathway of children exposed to few adversities (Gunnar et al., 2009).

Bipolar Disorders

PEOPLE WITH A BIPOLAR DISORDER experience both the lows of depression and the highs of mania. Many describe their lives as an emotional roller coaster, as they shift back and forth between extreme moods. A number of sufferers become suicidal. Approximately 10 to 15 percent of them eventually end their own lives, usually out of a sense of hopelessness (Suppes & Cosgrove, 2016). Their roller coaster ride also has a dramatic impact on relatives and friends (Sharif et al., 2016).

What Are the Symptoms of Mania?

Unlike people sunk in the gloom of depression, those in a state of mania typically experience dramatic and inappropriate rises in mood. The symptoms of mania span the same areas of functioning—*emotional, motivational, behavioral, cognitive,* and *physical*—as those of depression, but mania affects those areas in an opposite way.

A person in the throes of mania has active, powerful emotions in search of an outlet. The mood of euphoric joy and well-being is out of all proportion to the actual happenings in the person's life. One person with mania explained, "I feel no sense of restriction or censorship whatsoever. I am afraid of nothing and no one" (Fieve, 1975, p. 68). Not every person with mania is a picture of happiness, however. Some instead become very irritable and angry, especially when others get in the way of their exaggerated ambitions.

In the motivational realm, people with mania seem to want constant excitement, involvement, and companionship. They enthusiastically seek out new friends and old, new interests and old, and have little awareness that their social style is overwhelming, domineering, and excessive.

The behavior of people with mania is usually very active. They move quickly, as though there were not enough time to

Kevin Mazur/Getty Images

"Bi-Winning" In spring 2011, actor Charlie Sheen went on an extended and often bizarre tirade against his CBS employers, and other forces in society, that had many friends questioning his state of mind. Appearing here in New York City during his 2011 "Violent Torpedo of Truth/Defeat Is Not An Option" tour, Sheen was often greeted with boos and walkouts. Back then, he proclaimed, "I'm not bipolar, I'm bi-winning." More recently, with his functioning improved, he acknowledges that he has received a diagnosis of bipolar disorder over the years, although he sometimes questions the accuracy of that label.

#IrresistableWriting

Hypergraphia is a compulsive need to write. People with this rare problem write constantly, not only filling up notebooks or computer screens but also feverishly finding unusual writing surfaces, including their own skin. The problem has been linked to bipolar disorders, temporal lobe epilepsy, and schizophrenia. Some famous writers and artists may have displayed hypergraphia, such as prolific author Fyodor Dostoyevski and painter Vincent van Gogh, who produced an endless stream of paintings and letters.

do everything they want to do. They may talk rapidly and loudly, their conversations filled with jokes and efforts to be clever or, conversely, with complaints and verbal outbursts. Flamboyance is not uncommon: dressing in flashy clothes, giving large sums of money to strangers, or even getting involved in dangerous activities.

In the cognitive realm, people with mania usually show poor judgment and planning, as if they feel too good or move too fast to consider possible pitfalls. Filled with optimism, they rarely listen when others try to slow them down, interrupt their buying sprees, or prevent them from investing money unwisely. They may also hold an inflated opinion of themselves, and sometimes their self-esteem approaches grandiosity. During severe episodes of mania, some have trouble remaining coherent or in touch with reality.

Finally, in the physical realm, people with mania feel remarkably energetic. They typically get little sleep yet feel and act wide awake (Suppes & Cosgrove, 2016). Even if they miss a night or two of sleep, their energy level may remain high.

Diagnosing Bipolar Disorders

People are considered to be in a full *manic episode* when for at least one week they display an abnormally high or irritable mood, increased activity or energy, and at least three other symptoms of mania (see **Table 7-5**). The episode may even include psychotic features such as delusions or hallucinations. When the symptoms of mania are less severe (causing little impairment), the person is said to be having a *hypomanic episode* (APA, 2013).

DSM-5 distinguishes two kinds of bipolar disorders—bipolar I and bipolar II. People with **bipolar I disorder** have full manic and major depressive episodes. Most of them experience an *alternation* of the episodes; for example, weeks of mania followed by a period of wellness, followed in turn by an episode of depression. Some, however,

---

TABLE: 7-5

Dx Checklist

Manic Episode

1. For 1 week or more, person displays a continually abnormal, inflated, unrestrained, or irritable mood as well as continually heightened energy or activity, for most of every day.

2. Person also experiences at least three of the following symptoms:
   - Grandiosity or overblown self-esteem
   - Reduced sleep need
   - Increased talkativeness, or drive to continue talking
   - Rapidly shifting ideas or the sense that one's thoughts are moving very fast
   - Attention pulled in many directions
   - Heightened activity or agitated movements
   - Excessive pursuit of risky and potentially problematic activities.

3. Significant distress or impairment.

Bipolar I Disorder

1. Occurrence of a manic episode.

2. Hypomanic or major depressive episodes may precede or follow the manic episode.

Bipolar II Disorder

1. Presence or history of major depressive episode(s).

2. Presence or history of hypomanic episode(s).

3. No history of a manic episode.

Information from: APA, 2013.

"He's bipolar."

have *mixed* features, in which they display both manic and depressive symptoms within the same episode—for example, having racing thoughts amidst feelings of extreme sadness. In **bipolar II disorder**, hypomanic—that is, mildly manic—episodes alternate with major depressive episodes over the course of time. Some people with this pattern accomplish huge amounts of work during their mild manic periods.

Without treatment, the mood episodes tend to recur for people with either type of bipolar disorder. If a person has four or more episodes within a one-year period, his or her disorder is considered to be *rapid cycling*. A woman describes her rapid cycling in the following excerpt, taken from a journal article she wrote anonymously several years ago.

#FrenziedMasterpiece

George Frideric Handel wrote his *Messiah* in less than a month during a manic episode (Roesch, 1991).

My mood may swing from one part of the day to another. I may wake up low at 10 am, but be high and excitable by 3 pm. I may not sleep for more than 2 hours one night, being full of creative energy, but by midday be so fatigued it is an effort to breathe.

If my elevated states last more than a few days, my spending can become uncontrollable . . . I will sometimes drive faster than usual, need less sleep and can concentrate well, making quick and accurate decisions. At these times I can also be sociable, talkative and fun, focused at times, distracted at others. If this state of elevation continues I often find that feelings of violence and irritability towards those I love will start to creep in. . . .

My thoughts speed up. . . . I frequently want to be able to achieve several tasks at the same moment. . . . Physically my energy levels can seem limitless. The body moves smoothly, there is little or no fatigue. I can go mountain biking all day when I feel like this and if my mood stays elevated not a muscle is sore or stiff the next day. But it doesn't last, my elevated phases are short . . . [T]he shift into severe depression or a mixed mood state occurs sometimes within minutes or hours, often within days and will last weeks often without a period of normality. . . .

Initially my thoughts become disjointed and start slithering all over the place. . . . I start to believe that others are commenting adversely on my appearance or behaviour. . . . My sleep will be poor and interrupted by bad dreams. . . . The world appears bleak . . . I become repelled by the proximity of people . . . I will be overwhelmed by the slightest tasks, even imagined tasks. . . . Physically there is immense fatigue: my muscles scream with pain. . . Food becomes totally uninteresting. . . .

I start to feel trapped, that the only escape is death. . . . I become passionate about one subject only at these times of deep and intense fear, despair and rage: suicide. . . . I have made close attempts on my life . . . over the last few years. . . .

bipolar I disorder A type of bipolar disorder marked by full manic and major depressive episodes.

bipolar II disorder A type of bipolar disorder marked by mildly manic (hypomanic) episodes and major depressive episodes.

(continued on the next page)

cyclothymic disorder A disorder marked by numerous periods of hypomanic symptoms and mild depressive symptoms.

> *Then inexplicably, my mood will shift again. The fatigue drops from my limbs like shedding a dead weight, my thinking returns to normal, the light takes on an intense clarity, flowers smell sweet and my mouth curves to smile at my children, my husband and I are laughing again. Sometimes it's for only a day but I am myself again, the person that I was a frightening memory. I have survived another bout of this dreaded disorder. . . .*
>
> *(Anonymous, 2006)*

Regardless of their particular pattern, people with a bipolar disorder tend to experience depression more than mania over the years. In most cases, the initial mood episode is depression, the depressive episodes occur three times as often as manic ones, and the depressive episodes last longer (Suppes & Cosgrove, 2016).

Surveys from around the world indicate that between 1 and 2.6 percent of all adults are suffering from a bipolar disorder at any given time (NIMH, 2017; Kessler et al., 2012). As many as 4 percent experience one of the bipolar disorders at some time in their life. The bipolar disorders are equally common in women and men, but they are more common among people with low incomes than those with higher incomes (Sareen et al., 2011). Onset usually occurs between the ages of 15 and 44 years (NIMH, 2017; Stovall, 2016). In most untreated cases, the manic and depressive episodes eventually subside, only to recur at a later time.

Some people have numerous periods of hypomanic symptoms and *mild* depressive symptoms, a pattern that is called **cyclothymic disorder** in DSM-5. The symptoms of this milder form of bipolar disorder continue for two or more years, interrupted occasionally by normal moods that may last for only days or weeks. This disorder, like bipolar I and bipolar II disorders, usually begins in adolescence or early adulthood and is equally common among women and men. At least 0.4 percent of the population develops cyclothymic disorder. In some cases, the milder symptoms eventually blossom into a bipolar I or II disorder (Zeschel et al., 2015).

What Causes Bipolar Disorders?

Throughout the first half of the twentieth century, the search for the cause of bipolar disorders made little progress. More recently, biological research has produced some promising clues. The biological insights have come from research into *neurotransmitter activity, ion activity, brain structure,* and *genetic factors.*

Powerful plot device In *General Hospital,* one of television's most popular soap operas, actor Maurice Bernard plays Sonny Corinthos (left), a mob kingpin who is mercurial, impulsive, and unpredictable, to the delight of viewers. One of the show's key features is the character's bipolar disorder, which greatly affects his behaviors, decisions, and relationships. Interestingly, Bernard himself has bipolar disorder, a diagnosis he first received at the age of 22 in 1983. Today he is an ardent spokesperson for the proper diagnosis and treatment of this disorder.

Rick Rowell/ABC via Getty Images

Alexander Joe /Getty Images

While the world observed In this 2013 photo, then-President Barack Obama delivers a speech next to a sign language interpreter (right) at a memorial service for the late Nelson Mandela, former president of South Africa. However, the interpreter's signs were gibberish and unintelligible, alarming and confusing people around the world. The interpreter later explained that he had been hearing voices and seeing angels during the speech, symptoms caused by his struggle with bipolar disorder and/or schizophrenia.

Neurotransmitters Could *overactivity* of norepinephrine be related to mania? This was the expectation of clinicians back in the 1960s after investigators first found a relationship between low norepinephrine activity and unipolar depression (Schildkraut, 1965). And indeed, some studies did find the norepinephrine activity of people with mania to be higher than that of depressed or control participants (Post et al., 1980, 1978).

Because serotonin activity often parallels norepinephrine activity in unipolar depression, theorists at first expected that mania would also be related to high serotonin activity, but no such relationship has been found. Instead, research suggests that mania, like depression, may be linked to *low* serotonin activity (Hsu et al., 2014; Nugent et al., 2013). Perhaps low activity of serotonin opens the door to a mood disorder and *permits* the activity of norepinephrine (or perhaps other neurotransmitters) to define the particular form the disorder will take. That is, low serotonin activity accompanied by low norepinephrine activity may lead to depression; low serotonin activity accompanied by high norepinephrine activity may lead to mania. In recent years, researchers have also found ties between bipolar disorder and abnormal activity of other neurotransmitters, such as GABA, the brain chemical you read about in Chapter 5 (Volk et al., 2016; Benes, 2011).

Ion Activity While neurotransmitters play a significant role in the communication *between* neurons, ions seem to play a critical role in relaying messages *within* a neuron. That is, ions help transmit messages down the neuron's axon to the nerve endings. Positively charged *sodium ions* (Na^+) sit on both sides of a neuron's cell membrane. When the neuron is at *rest*, more sodium ions sit outside the membrane. When the neuron receives an incoming message at its receptor sites, pores in the cell membrane open, allowing the sodium ions to flow to the inside of the membrane, thus increasing the positive charge inside the neuron. This starts a wave of electrical activity that travels down the length of the neuron and results in its "firing." After the neuron "fires," *potassium ions* (K^+) flow from the inside of the neuron across the cell membrane to the outside, helping to return the neuron to its original resting state (see **Figure 7-4**).

If messages are to be relayed effectively down the axon, the ions must be able to travel easily between the outside and the inside of the neural membrane. Some studies suggest that, among bipolar individuals, irregularities in the transport of these ions may cause neurons to fire too easily (resulting in mania) or to stubbornly resist firing (resulting in depression) (Gottschalk et al., 2017; Li & El-Mallakh, 2004).

#HigherRisk

"The risk of developing bipolar disorder is 6 times higher for children of older men (over 45 years when their children were born) than children of young men (20–24 years). Why? One theory is that, as men age, they produce increased genetic mutations during the manufacture of sperm cells (Stovall, 2016; Chudal et al., 2014).

Brain Structure Brain imaging and postmortem studies have identified a number of abnormal brain structures in people with bipolar disorders (Eker et al., 2014; Chen et al., 2011; Savitz & Drevets, 2011). For example, the hippocampus, basal ganglia, and cerebellum of these people tend to be smaller than those of other people; they have lower amounts of gray matter in the brain; and their raphe nuclei, striatum, amygdala, and prefrontal cortex have some structural abnormalities (Sun et al., 2018; Janicak, 2017). It is not clear what role such abnormalities play in bipolar disorders. Some researchers believe that they collectively reflect dysfunction throughout a bipolar-related brain circuit. It may also be that they are related to the brain's depression-related circuit that you read about earlier (see pages 197–198).

Genetic Factors Many theorists believe that people inherit a biological predisposition to develop bipolar disorders (Charney et al., 2017; Wiste et al., 2014). Family pedigree studies support this idea. Identical twins of those with a bipolar disorder have a 40 to 70 percent likelihood of developing the same disorder, and fraternal twins, siblings, and other close relatives of such persons have a 5 to 10 percent likelihood, compared with the 1 to 2.6 percent prevalence rate in the general population (Stovall, 2016).

#DarkestColor

In Western society, *black* is often the color of choice in describing depression. British prime minister Winston Churchill called his recurrent episodes a "black dog always waiting to bare its teeth." American novelist Ernest Hemingway referred to his bouts as "black-assed" days. And the Rolling Stones sing about depressive thinking: "I see a red door and I want to paint it black."

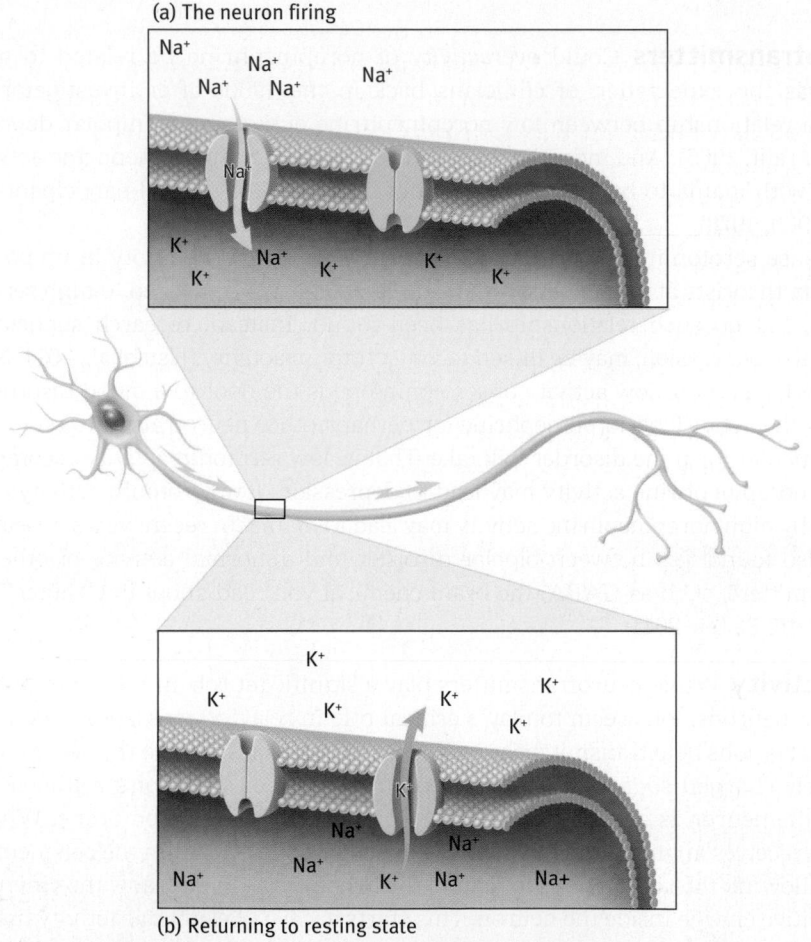

(a) The neuron firing

(b) Returning to resting state

FIGURE 7-4

Ions and the Firing of Neurons

Neurons relay messages in the form of electrical impulses that travel down the axon toward the nerve endings. As an impulse travels along the axon, sodium ions (Na⁺), on the outside of the neuron's membrane, flow inside, propelling the impulse down the axon. Once sodium ions flow in, potassium ions (K⁺) flow out, returning the membrane's electrical balance to its resting state, ready for the arrival of a new impulse.

Researchers have also used techniques from *molecular biology* to more directly examine possible genetic factors in large families. Their work has linked bipolar disorders to genes on chromosomes 1, 4, 6, 10, 11, 12, 13, 15, 18, 20, 21, and 22 (Charney et al., 2017; Bigdeli et al., 2013). Such wide-ranging findings suggest that a number of genetic abnormalities probably combine to help bring about bipolar disorders.

Depressive and Bipolar Disorders: Making Sense of All That Is Known

WITH MOOD PROBLEMS SO prevalent in all societies, it is no wonder that moods have been the focus of so much research. Great quantities of data have been gathered about moods—from normal mood states like happiness and sadness (see *InfoCentral* on the next page) to disorders of mood. Still, clinicians have yet to understand fully all that they know.

> Research participants often prefer listening to sad songs over happy songs, even though they make them depressed. Why?

Several factors have been tied closely to unipolar depression, including biological abnormalities, a reduction in positive reinforcements, negative ways of thinking, a perception of helplessness, and life stress and other sociocultural influences. Indeed, more contributing factors have been associated with unipolar depression than with most other psychological disorders. Developmental psychopathology theorists and researchers have done an admirable and promising job of trying to put these various factors together; however it is still not entirely clear how all of these factors relate to unipolar depression.

As with unipolar depression, clinicians and researchers have learned much about bipolar disorders during the past 50 years. But bipolar disorders appear to be best explained by a focus on *one* kind of variable—biological factors. The evidence suggests that biological abnormalities, perhaps inherited and perhaps triggered by life stress, cause bipolar disorders. Whatever roles other factors may play, the primary one appears to lie in this realm.

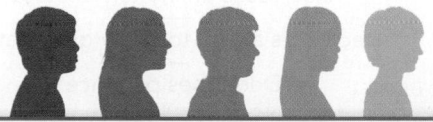

CLINICAL CHOICES

Now that you've read about disorders of mood, try the interactive case study for this chapter. See if you are able to identify John's symptoms and suggest a diagnosis based on his symptoms. What kind of treatment would be most effective for John? Go to **Launch**Pad to access *Clinical Choices*.

Maren Klemp/REX/Shutterstock

Artistic expression What is it like to experience bipolar disorder? Given that words cannot fully capture the emotional pain and turmoil produced by the symptoms, several artists have sought to describe the experience through other means. Since being diagnosed with bipolar disorder in 2013, Maren Klemp, a fine arts photographer in Oslo, Norway, has created numerous evocative images, like this photograph, that represent the experience of living with bipolar and other severe psychological disorders.

SADNESS

Depression, a clinical disorder that causes considerable distress and impairment, features a range of symptoms, including emotional, motivational, behavioral, cognitive, and physical symptoms. **Sadness** is often one of the symptoms found in depression, but most often it is a perfectly normal negative emotion triggered by a loss or other painful circumstance.

SADNESS DIFFERS FROM CLINICAL DEPRESSION

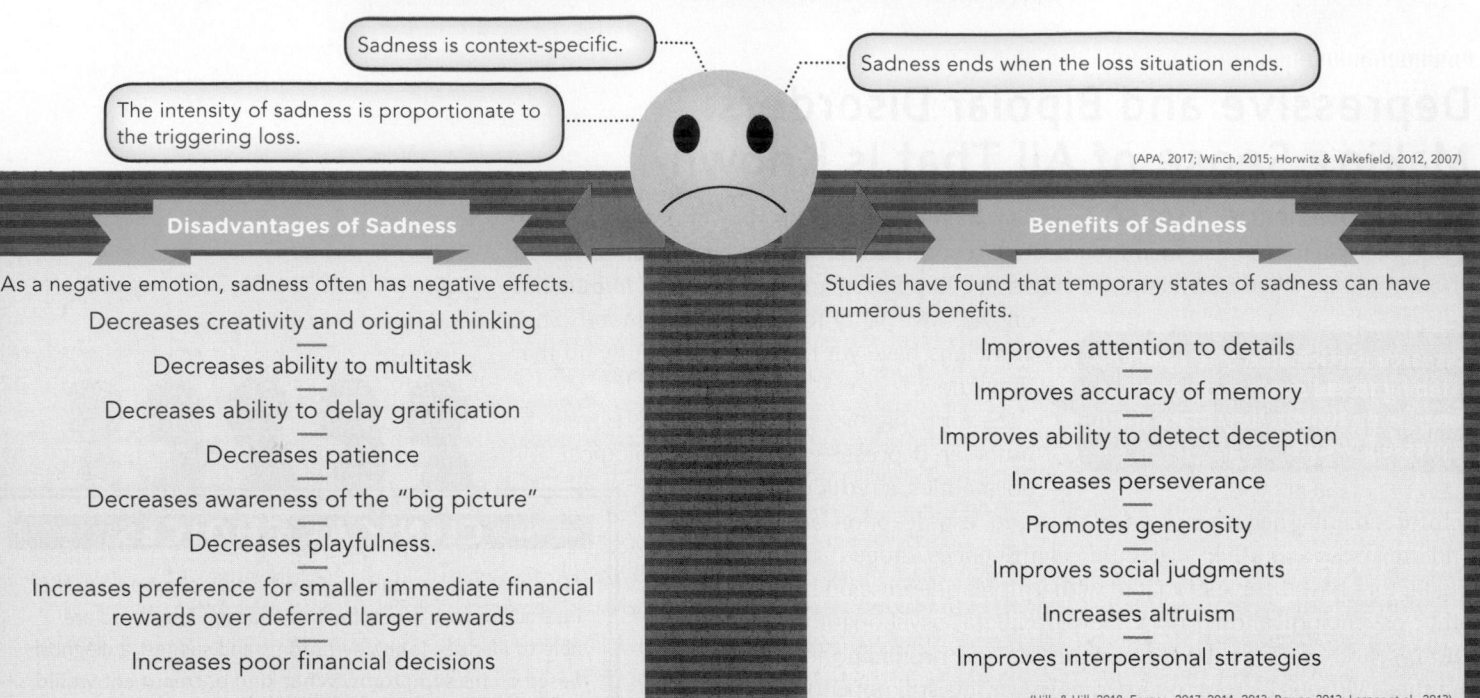

Sadness is context-specific.

Sadness ends when the loss situation ends.

The intensity of sadness is proportionate to the triggering loss.

(APA, 2017; Winch, 2015; Horwitz & Wakefield, 2012, 2007)

Disadvantages of Sadness

As a negative emotion, sadness often has negative effects.

Decreases creativity and original thinking
—
Decreases ability to multitask
—
Decreases ability to delay gratification
—
Decreases patience
—
Decreases awareness of the "big picture"
—
Decreases playfulness.
—
Increases preference for smaller immediate financial rewards over deferred larger rewards
—
Increases poor financial decisions

(Forgas, 2017, 2014, 2013; Bower, 2013; Lerner et al., 2013; Schwartz, 2011)

Benefits of Sadness

Studies have found that temporary states of sadness can have numerous benefits.

Improves attention to details
—
Improves accuracy of memory
—
Improves ability to detect deception
—
Increases perseverance
—
Promotes generosity
—
Improves social judgments
—
Increases altruism
—
Improves interpersonal strategies

(Hills & Hill, 2018; Forgas, 2017, 2014, 2013; Bower, 2013; Lerner et al., 2013)

SOCIAL MEDIA AND SADNESS

Research finds that young adults who browse and post on social media most frequently are actually more likely to feel sad (Lin et al., 2016).

Odds of Feeling Sad

More daily use vs. less daily use
2:1

More weekly visits vs. fewer weekly visits
3:1

Greater overall use vs. lower overall use
3:1

Daily Social Media Users

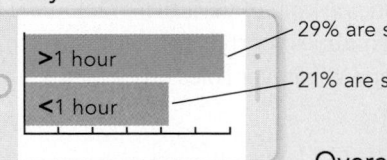

>1 hour — 29% are sad
<1 hour — 21% are sad

Weekly Social Media Visitors

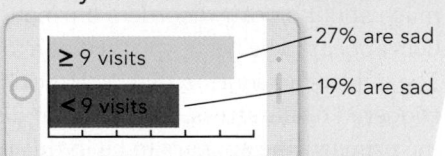

≥ 9 visits — 27% are sad
< 9 visits — 19% are sad

Overall Social Media Users

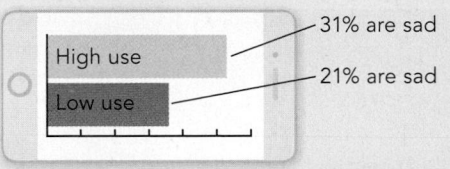

High use — 31% are sad
Low use — 21% are sad

(Lin et al., 2016)

SADNESS BUSTERS

Lifestyle Factors
• Physical exercise
• Active involvement
• Spending time in natural light
• Getting organized
• Spending time with a pet
• Getting enough sleep
• Eating healthily

Social Factors
• Social support
• Professional support

Cognitive Factors
• Positive thinking
• Creativity
• Accepting sadness with an understanding it may take a while to get over
• Challenging negative thoughts
• Scheduling positive events

(Lee et al., 2017; Molina, 2017; Holmes, 2014; MHFA, 2014; Sifferlin, 2013)

THE HOLIDAY BLUES

Many people become especially happy as holidays approach and during the holidays themselves. Others, however, become sad and anxious at holiday time—a reaction called "the holiday blues."

What causes the holiday blues?
◊ Stress and fatigue
◊ Unrealistic expectations
◊ Excessive responsibility
◊ Overcommercialization
◊ Overactivity and/or overspending
◊ Being without family and friends
◊ Reminders of sorrowful events

(Purcell, 2017; Stoppler, 2014; Sifferlin, 2013)

There is no question that investigations into the symptoms and causes of depressive and bipolar disorders have been fruitful and enlightening. And it is more than reasonable to expect that important research findings will continue to unfold in the years ahead. Now that clinical researchers have gathered so many important pieces of the puzzle, they must put the pieces together into a still more meaningful picture that will suggest even better ways to predict, prevent, and treat these disorders.

♀... SUMMING UP

» Depressive Versus Bipolar Disorders People with *depressive disorders* grapple with *depression* only, called *unipolar depression*. Those with bipolar disorders contend with both depression and *mania*. *pp. 189–190*

» Unipolar Depression: The Depressive Disorders People with *unipolar depression*, the most common pattern of mood difficulty, suffer exclusively from depression. The symptoms of depression span five areas of functioning: emotional, motivational, behavioral, cognitive, and physical. Depressed people are also at higher risk for suicidal thinking and behavior. Women are at least twice as likely as men to experience severe unipolar depression. *pp. 190–194*

» Explanations of Unipolar Depression Each of the leading models has offered explanations for unipolar depression. According to the *biological view,* low activity of two neurotransmitters, *norepinephrine* and *serotonin*, are linked to depression. *Hormonal factors,* the result of an HPA stress pathway that is overly reactive to stress, may also be at work. Research has also tied depression to abnormalities in a circuit of brain structures, including the *prefrontal cortex, hippocampus, amygdala,* and *subgenual cingulate. Immune system dysregulation* has also been linked to depression. All such biological problems may be linked to *genetic factors.*

According to the *psychodynamic view,* certain people who experience *real or imagined losses* may *regress* to an earlier stage of development, *introject* feelings for the lost object, and eventually become depressed.

The *cognitive-behavioral view* features explanations of depression that are primarily behavioral, primarily cognitive, or a combination of behavioral and cognitive principles. On the behavioral side, the model says that when people experience a large reduction in their positive rewards in life, they may display fewer and fewer positive behaviors.

This response leads to a still lower rate of positive rewards and eventually to depression.

On the cognitive side, Beck's theory of negative thinking holds that *maladaptive attitudes,* the *cognitive triad, errors in thinking,* and *automatic thoughts* help produce unipolar depression. Also, according to Seligman's *learned helplessness* theory, people become depressed when they believe that they have lost control over the reinforcements in their lives and when they attribute this loss to causes that are *internal, global,* and *stable*.

Sociocultural theorists propose that unipolar depression is influenced by social and cultural factors. *Family-social* theorists point out that a low level of social support is often linked to unipolar depression. And *multicultural* theorists have noted that the character and prevalence of depression often vary by gender and sometimes by culture.

The *developmental psychopathology* perspective contends that unipolar depression is caused by a combination of the factors cited by the various models and that these factors unfold and intersect in a developmental sequence. *pp. 195–211*

» Bipolar Disorders In *bipolar disorders*, episodes of mania alternate or intermix with episodes of depression. These disorders are much less common than unipolar depression. They may take the form of *bipolar I, bipolar II,* or *cyclothymic disorder. pp. 211–214*

» Explanations of Bipolar Disorders Mania may be related to *high norepinephrine activity along with a low level of serotonin activity.* Some researchers have also linked bipolar disorders to *improper transport of ions* back and forth between the outside and the inside of a neuron's membrane. Still others have uncovered abnormalities in key brain structures. Genetic studies suggest that people may *inherit* a predisposition to these biological abnormalities. *pp. 214–217*

Visit *LaunchPad*
to access the e-Book, Clinical Choices, videos, activities, and LearningCurve, as well as study aids including flashcards, FAQs, and research exercises.

LaunchPad
macmillan learning

Treatments for Depressive and Bipolar Disorders

> *Mid-twenties life circumstances were poor and I really plummeted. . . . The thing that made me go for help . . . was probably my daughter . . . I thought, this isn't right, this can't be right, she cannot grow up with me in this state. . . . I got counseling . . . [The therapist] absolutely saved me.*
>
> *J. K. Rowling, author of the "Harry Potter" books (in Amini, 2008)*
>
> *When you're clinically depressed the serotonin in your brain is out of balance and probably always will be out of balance. So I take medication to get that proper balance back. I'll probably have to be on it the rest of my life.*
>
> *Terry Bradshaw, Super Bowl quarterback and sports analyst (in Morgan & Shoop, 2004)*
>
> *[A holistic healer] introduced me to this new way of kind of treating depression, which is without the uptake inhibitors, to slowly get off the uptake inhibitors with the help of a doctor . . . Supplements. . . It is vitamins. . . It's a wonderful thing.*
>
> *Jim Carrey, comedy actor (Carrey, 2013, 2008)*
>
> *[My psychotherapist] and I would fight many demons together . . . his knowledge, along with his compassionate heart, guided me to the strength and freedom I needed . . . [In addition,] I've been on antidepressants for the last twelve to fifteen years of my life, and . . . they have given me a life I would not have been able to maintain without them. They work. I return to Earth, home and my family.*
>
> *Bruce Springsteen, singer and songwriter (in Springsteen, 2016)*
>
> *In my case, ECT [electroconvulsive therapy] was miraculous. My wife was dubious, but when she came into my room afterward, I sat up and said "Look who's back among the living." It was like a magic wand.*
>
> *Dick Cavett, talk show host (Cavett, 1992)*

Each of these people suffered from and overcame a depressive disorder. And, clearly, all believe that the treatment they received was a key to their improvement—a key that opened the door to a more normal, stable, and productive life. Yet the treatments that seemed to help them differed greatly. Psychotherapy helped bring meaning back to the life of J. K. Rowling. Antidepressant drugs were the key for Terry Bradshaw, vitamins for Jim Carrey, and a combination of psychotherapy and medications for Bruce Springsteen. Electroconvulsive therapy lifted Dick Cavett from the black hole of his unipolar depression.

How could such diverse therapies be so helpful to people suffering from the same or similar disorders? As this chapter will show, disorders that feature severe changes in mood—as painful and disabling as they tend to be—respond more successfully to more kinds of treatment than do most other forms of psychological dysfunction (Haggerty, 2016). This range of treatment options has been a source of reassurance and hope for the millions of people who desire desperately to regain some measure of control over their moods. ■

Treatments for Unipolar Depression

IN THE UNITED STATES, AROUND half of those with unipolar depression receive treatment from a mental health professional each year (NIMH, 2017). Access to such treatment differs among ethnic and racial groups. Only 36 percent of depressed Hispanic Americans and 41 percent of depressed African Americans receive treatment, compared with 60 percent of depressed non-Hispanic white Americans (Kalibatseva & Leong, 2014).

In addition, many people in therapy experience depressed feelings as part of another disorder, such as an eating disorder, or in association with changes or general problems that they are encountering in life. Thus much of the therapy being done today includes a focus on unipolar depression.

A variety of treatment approaches are currently in widespread use for unipolar depression (see **Figure 8-1**). In this chapter, we first look at the psychological approaches, focusing on the psychodynamic and cognitive-behavioral therapies. We then explore the sociocultural approaches, including a highly regarded intervention called *interpersonal psychotherapy*. Next, we look at effective biological approaches, including antidepressant drugs and brain stimulation interventions.

Psychological Approaches

The psychological treatments used most often to combat unipolar depression come from the psychodynamic, behavioral, and cognitive schools of thought. Psychodynamic therapy, the oldest of all modern psychotherapies, continues to be used widely for depression even though research has not offered strong evidence of its effectiveness. Cognitive-behavioral therapies have performed well in research and have a large following among clinicians.

Psychodynamic Therapy Believing that unipolar depression results from unconscious grief over real or imagined losses, compounded by excessive dependence on other people, psychodynamic therapists seek to help clients bring these underlying issues to consciousness and work them through (Gabbard & DeJean, 2016; Busch et al., 2004). Using the arsenal of basic psychodynamic procedures, they encourage the depressed client to associate freely during therapy; suggest interpretations of the client's associations, dreams, and displays of resistance and transference; and help the person review past events and

> What kinds of transference issues might psychodynamic therapists expect to see in treatment with depressed clients?

#NumberTwo

Antidepressant medications are the second most commonly prescribed class of drugs, just behind medications for high cholesterol (Stone, 2016).

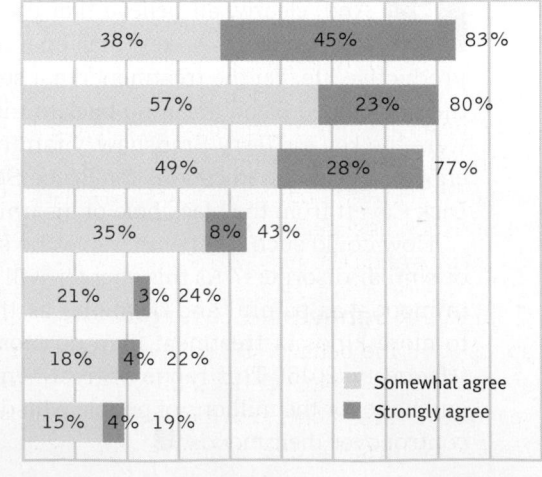

FIGURE 8-1

How Do People Feel About Depression and Treatment?

According to one survey, more than 80 percent of Americans believe that depression is a serious condition that requires treatment. Nineteen percent consider depression to be a sign of personal weakness. (Information from: NAMI (2009). Depression Survey Initiative, November 9.)

"Depression is a serious medical condition that requires treatment." — 38% / 45% / 83%

"A combination of medication and psychotherapy is often the most effective treatment for depression." — 57% / 23% / 80%

"Untreated or under-treated depression can result in long-term disability." — 49% / 28% / 77%

"Persistent depression, with recurring episodes, is a normal reaction to sadness/loss." — 35% / 8% / 43%

"Depression is a normal part of growing older." — 21% / 3% / 24%

"People diagnosed with depression would recover if they could just 'snap out of it.'" — 18% / 4% / 22%

"Depression is a sign of personal weakness." — 15% / 4% / 19%

Somewhat agree
Strongly agree

feelings. Free association, for example, helped one man recall the early experiences of loss that, according to his therapist, had set the stage for his depression:

Among his earliest memories, possibly the earliest of all, was the recollection of being wheeled in his baby cart under the elevated train structure and left there alone. Another memory that recurred vividly during the analysis was of an operation around the age of five. He was anesthetized and his mother left him with the doctor. He recalled how he had kicked and screamed, raging at her for leaving him.

(Lorand, 1968, pp. 325–326)

Psychodynamic therapists expect that in the course of treatment depressed clients will eventually gain awareness of the losses in their lives, become less dependent on others, cope with losses more effectively, and make corresponding changes in their functioning. The transition of a therapeutic insight into a real-life change is seen in the case of a middle-aged executive:

The patient's father was still living and in a nursing home, where the patient visited him regularly. On one occasion, he went to see his father full of high expectations, as he had concluded a very successful business transaction. As he began to describe his accomplishments to his father, however, the latter completely ignored his son's remarks and viciously berated him for wearing a pink shirt, which he considered unprofessional. Such a response from the father was not unusual, but this time, as a result of the work that had been accomplished in therapy, the patient could objectively analyze his initial sense of disappointment and deep feeling of failure for not pleasing the older man. Although this experience led to a transient state of depression, it also revealed to the patient his whole dependent lifestyle—his use of others to supply him with a feeling of worth. This experience added a dimension of immediate reality to the insights that had been achieved in therapy and gave the patient the motivation to change radically his childhood system of perceiving himself in relation to paternal transference figures.

(Bemporad, 1992, p. 291)

Despite successful case reports such as this, researchers have found that long-term psychodynamic therapy is only occasionally helpful in cases of unipolar depression (Prochaska & Norcross, 2013). Two features of the approach may help limit its effectiveness. First, depressed clients may be too passive and feel too weary to join fully in the subtle therapy discussions. And second, they may become discouraged and end treatment too early when this long-term approach is unable to provide the quick relief that they desperately seek. Generally, psychodynamic therapy seems to help most in cases of depression that are modest or moderate in severity and that involve a clear history of childhood loss or trauma, a long-standing sense of emptiness, feelings of perfectionism, and extreme self-criticism (Gabbard & DeJean, 2016; Blatt, 1999, 1995). Short-term psychodynamic therapies have performed better than the longer-term approaches, especially when they are combined with psychotropic medications (Fonagy, 2015).

Cognitive-Behavioral Therapy Cognitive-behavioral therapists combine behavioral and cognitive techniques to help clients suffering from depression. On the behavioral side, they seek to get the clients moving again—to engage in and enjoy more activities. On the cognitive side, they guide the clients

"After all these years, you still feel guilt? You should be ashamed of yourself."

J.B. Handelsman/The New Yorker Collection/The Cartoon Bank

behavioral activation A therapy for depression in which the therapist works systematically to increase the number of constructive and pleasurable activities and events in a client's life.

cognitive therapy A therapy developed by Aaron Beck that helps people identify and change the maladaptive assumptions and ways of thinking that help cause their psychological disorders.

to think in more adaptive, less negative ways. A variety of approaches have been developed to help bring about these changes. Two of the leading ones are *behavioral activation* and *Beck's cognitive therapy*.

BEHAVIORAL ACTIVATION In **behavioral activation**, therapists work systematically to increase the number of constructive and pleasurable activities and events in a client's life. The approach builds on the work of Peter Lewinsohn, the theorist who, as you'll recall from Chapter 7, ties mood to the rewards one experiences in life (see pages 200–201). There are three key components to the approach. The therapists (1) reintroduce depressed clients to pleasurable events and activities, (2) consistently reward nondepressive behaviors and withhold rewards for depressive behaviors, and (3) help clients improve their social skills (Farmer & Chapman, 2015; Dimidjian et al., 2014).

First, the therapist selects activities that the client considers pleasurable, such as going shopping or taking photos, and encourages the person to set up a weekly schedule for engaging in them. Studies have shown that adding positive activities to a person's life can indeed lead to a better mood (Dimidjian et al, 2014; Martell et al., 2010). In the following case description, a therapist describes this process:

> [Alicia] had never noticed a connection between her activities and her mood before. The depression had just felt like something that loomed over her, coloring everything. . . . She now recognized that there were many subtle shifts in her mood, including some moments in which she experienced relief from the depression. . . . [For example,] she felt content when she worked in her garden. . . . As Alicia reviewed these activities with [her therapist], she also began to identify activities that she could increase during the upcoming week . . . [She decided] that getting in touch with more friends [and working in her garden] could be helpful for her mood. . . . She agreed that she would report back to [the therapist] about how she felt during these activities in the next session.
>
> *(Martell et al., 2010)*

While reintroducing pleasurable events into a client's life, the therapist makes sure that the person's various behaviors are reinforced correctly. Behavioral activation theorists argue that when people become depressed, their negative behaviors—crying, ruminating, complaining, or self-depreciation—keep others at a distance, reducing chances for rewarding experiences and interactions (Hammen, 2016). To change this

Reintroducing pleasure Following the principles of *behavioral activation*, depressed patients at the Zhongshan Mental Hospital in China are encouraged to weed a garden. Behavioral activation therapists systematically guide clients to increase the number of pleasurable activities in their lives, particularly activities that brought them joy (in this case, gardening) prior to their disorders.

China Photos/Getty Images

China Photos/Getty Images

Stretching one's emotions Research shows that regular exercise can help prevent or reduce feelings of depression and other psychological symptoms. Thus, as part of the treatment program at the Zhongshan Mental Hospital, patients also are led through exercise and dance programs by nurses on the hospital ward.

pattern, therapists guide clients to monitor their negative behaviors and to try new, more positive ones (Dimidjian et al, 2014; Martell et al., 2010). Dozens of smartphone apps are now available to help clients accurately record the negative and positive activities they perform in life and the mood changes that result, making behavioral activation a more precise approach than it once was (Huguet et al., 2016). In addition, the therapist may use a *contingency management* approach, systematically ignoring a client's depressive behaviors while praising or otherwise rewarding constructive statements and behavior, such as going to work. Sometimes family members and friends are recruited to help with this feature of treatment.

> **Can you think of other uses, advantages, and disadvantages that might result from the growing use of mood-tracking apps?**

Finally, therapists train clients in effective social skills (Farmer & Chapman, 2015; Thase, 2012). In group therapy programs, for example, members may work together to improve eye contact, facial expression, posture, and other behaviors that send social messages.

Behavioral activation techniques seem to be of only limited help when they are the sole feature of treatment, particularly if the severity of depression is more than modest (Chan et al., 2017; Dimidjian et al., 2014). But when they are combined with cognitive techniques, they are, as you'll see next, often quite helpful. In fact, it is worth noting that even Lewinsohn, the theorist who first proposed this approach, now combines behavioral activation with cognitive strategies.

BECK'S COGNITIVE THERAPY In Chapter 7 you saw that Aaron Beck views unipolar depression as resulting from a pattern of negative thinking that may be triggered by current upsetting situations. *Maladaptive attitudes* lead people repeatedly to view themselves, their world, and their future in negative ways—the so-called *cognitive triad*. Such biased views combine with *illogical thinking* to produce *automatic thoughts,* unrelentingly negative thoughts that flood the mind and produce the symptoms of depression.

To help clients overcome this negative thinking, Beck has developed a treatment approach that he calls **cognitive therapy.** He uses this label because the approach focuses largely on guiding clients to recognize and change negative cognitive processes (Beck, 2016; Beck & Weishaar, 2014). However, as you will see, the approach also includes several behavioral techniques such as those we have just examined. Beck's

#GroupStandards

In 1991 the Gloucester branch of Depressives Anonymous ejected several members because they were too cheerful. Said the group chairperson, "Those with sensitive tender feelings have been put off by more robust members who have not always been depressives" (Shaw, 2004).

TABLE: 8-1

Treatments for Depressive and Bipolar Disorders

Disorder	Treatment	Average Duration of Treatment	Percent Improved by Treatment
Major depressive disorder	Cognitive-behavioral therapy	20 sessions	50–60
	Interpersonal psychotherapy	20 sessions	50–60
	Antidepressant drugs	Indefinite	50–60
	ECT	9 sessions	50–80
	Vagus nerve stimulation	1 session (plus follow-up)	50–60
	Transcranial magnetic stimulation	25 sessions	50–60
Bipolar disorder	Psychotropic drugs: Mood stabilizers, antipsychotics, and antidepressants	Indefinite	60

	Monday	Tuesday	Wednesday	Thursday
9–10		Go to grocery store	Go to museum	Get ready to go out
10–11		Go to grocery store	Go to museum	Drive to doctor's appointment
11–12	Doctor's appointment	Call friend	Go to museum	Doctor's appointment
12–1	Lunch	Lunch	Lunch at museum	
1–2	Drive home	Clean front room	Drive home	
2–3	Read novel	Clean front room	Washing	
3–4	Clean bedroom	Read novel	Washing	
4–5	Watch TV	Watch TV	Watch TV	
5–6	Fix dinner	Fix dinner	Fix dinner	
6–7	Eat with family	Eat with family	Eat with family	
7–8	Clean kitchen	Clean kitchen	Clean kitchen	
8–12	Watch TV, read novel, sleep	Call sister, watch TV, read novel, sleep	Work on rug, read novel, sleep	

FIGURE 8-2

Increasing Activity

In the early stages of cognitive therapy for depression, the client and therapist prepare an activity schedule such as this. Activities as simple as watching television and calling a friend are specified. (Republished with permission of Guilford Press from *Cognitive therapy of depression*, Beck, A. T., Rush, A. J., Shaw, B. F., & Emery, G. (1979); permission conveyed through Copyright Clearance Center, Inc.)

approach is similar to Albert Ellis' *rational-emotive therapy*, which was discussed in Chapters 3 and 5 (see **Table 8-1**). However, Beck's approach is tailored to the specific cognitive errors and behaviors found in depression. The approach follows four phases and usually requires fewer than 20 sessions.

PHASE 1: INCREASING ACTIVITIES AND ELEVATING MOOD Using behavioral techniques to set the stage for the cognitive dimensions of treatment, therapists first encourage clients to become more active and confident. Clients spend time during each session preparing a detailed schedule of hourly activities for the coming week (see **Figure 8-2**). As they become more active from week to week, their mood is expected to improve.

PHASE 2: CHALLENGING AUTOMATIC THOUGHTS Once people are more active and feeling some emotional relief, therapists begin to educate them about their negative automatic thoughts. The individuals are instructed to recognize and record automatic thoughts as they occur and to bring their lists to each session. Here again, clients may use smartphone apps to accurately identify and document such thoughts as they arise in their daily lives (Huguet et al., 2016). The therapist and client then test the reality behind the thoughts, often concluding that they are groundless.

PHASE 3: IDENTIFYING NEGATIVE THINKING AND BIASES As people begin to recognize the flaws in their automatic thoughts, the therapists show them how illogical thinking processes are contributing to these thoughts. The therapists also guide clients to recognize that almost all their interpretations of events have a negative bias and to change that style of interpretation.

PHASE 4: CHANGING PRIMARY ATTITUDES Therapists help clients change the maladaptive attitudes that set the stage for their depression in the first place. As part of the process, therapists often encourage clients to test their attitudes, as in the following therapy discussion:

Therapist: *On what do you base this belief that you can't be happy without a man?*
Patient: *I was really depressed for a year and a half when I didn't have a man.*
Therapist: *Is there another reason why you were depressed?*
Patient: *As we discussed, I was looking at everything in a distorted way. But I still don't know if I could be happy if no one was interested in me.*

> Therapist: *I don't know either. Is there a way we could find out?*
>
> Patient: *Well, as an experiment, I could not go out on dates for a while and see how I feel.*
>
> Therapist: *I think that's a good idea. Although it has its flaws, the experimental method is still the best way currently available to discover the facts. You're fortunate in being able to run this type of experiment. Now, for the first time in your adult life you aren't attached to a man. If you find you can be happy without a man, this will greatly strengthen you and also make your future relationships all the better.*
>
> *(Beck et al., 1979, pp. 253–254)*

Over the past several decades, numerous studies have shown that cognitive-behavioral approaches help with unipolar depression. Depressed adults who receive these therapies improve much more than those who receive placebos or no treatment at all (Lutz et al., 2016; Cuijpers et al., 2014; Young et al., 2014). Around 50 to 60 percent show significant improvement in or elimination of their symptoms.

NEW-WAVE COGNITIVE-BEHAVIORAL THERAPY It is worth noting that a growing number of today's cognitive-behavioral therapists do not agree with Beck's proposition that individuals must fully discard their negative cognitions in order to overcome depression. These therapists, the new-wave cognitive-behavioral therapists about whom you read in Chapters 3 and 5, including those who practice *acceptance and commitment therapy* (ACT), use mindfulness training and other cognitive-behavioral techniques to help depressed clients recognize and accept their negative cognitions simply as streams of thinking that flow through their minds, rather than as valuable guides for behavior and decisions (Segal, 2017; Kaipainen, Välkkynen, & Kilkku, 2016). As clients increasingly accept their negative thoughts for what they are, they may better work around the thoughts as they navigate their way through life. Research suggests that approaches of this kind are particularly useful as ongoing procedures that help prevent recurrences of depression once individuals recover from an episode (Segal, 2017).

#TheirWords

"Start every day off with a smile; get it over with."
W. C. Fields (1879–1946)

Ward Sutton, The New Yorker Collection/The Cartoon Bank

"Let's try focussing on your posts that do receive comments"

interpersonal psychotherapy (IPT) A treatment for unipolar depression that is based on the belief that clarifying and changing one's interpersonal problems helps lead to recovery.

Sociocultural Approaches

As you read in Chapter 7, sociocultural theorists trace the causes of unipolar depression to the broader social structure in which people live and the roles they are required to play (Keitner, 2017). Two groups of sociocultural treatments are now widely applied in cases of unipolar depression—*multicultural approaches* and *family-social approaches*.

Multicultural Treatments In Chapter 3, you read that *culture-sensitive therapies* are designed to address the unique issues faced by members of cultural minority groups (Chu et al., 2016; Hays, 2016). For such approaches, therapists typically have special cultural training and a heightened awareness of their clients' cultural values and the culture-related stressors, prejudices, and stereotypes that their clients face. They make an effort to help clients develop a comfortable (for them) bicultural balance and to recognize the impact of their own culture and the dominant culture on their views of themselves and on their behaviors.

In the treatment of unipolar depression, culture-sensitive approaches increasingly are being combined with traditional forms of psychotherapy to help minority clients overcome their disorders (Aguilera et al., 2017, 2010; Chu et al., 2016). A number of today's therapists, for example, offer cognitive-behavioral therapy for depressed minority clients while also focusing on the clients' economic pressures, minority identity, and related cultural issues. A range of studies indicate that Hispanic American, African American, American Indian, and Asian American clients are more likely to overcome their depressive disorders when a culture-sensitive focus is added to the form of psychotherapy that they are otherwise receiving (Aguilera et al., 2017, 2010; Chowdhary et al., 2014; Comas-Díaz, 2014).

> Do you think culture-sensitive therapies might be more useful for some kinds of disorders than for others? Why or why not?

Family-Social Treatments Therapists who use family and social approaches to treat depression help clients change how they deal with the close relationships in their lives. The most effective family-social approaches are *interpersonal psychotherapy* and *couple therapy*.

INTERPERSONAL PSYCHOTHERAPY Developed by clinical researchers Gerald Klerman and Myrna Weissman, **interpersonal psychotherapy (IPT)** holds that any of four

Is laughter the best medicine? A man laughs during a session of laughter therapy in a public plaza in South America. He is one of many who attended this open session of laughter therapy, a relatively new group treatment being offered around the world, based on the belief that laughing at least 15 minutes each day drives away depression and other ills.

AP Photo/Ariana Cubillos

interpersonal problem areas may lead to depression and must be addressed: interpersonal loss, interpersonal role dispute, interpersonal role transition, and interpersonal deficits (Swartz, 2016, 2015). Over the course of around 20 sessions, IPT therapists address these areas.

First, depressed people may, as psychodynamic theorists suggest, be having a grief reaction over an important *interpersonal loss,* the loss of a loved one. In such cases, IPT therapists encourage clients to explore their relationship with the lost person and express any feelings of anger they may discover. Eventually clients develop new ways of remembering the lost person and also look for new relationships.

Second, depressed people may find themselves in the midst of an *interpersonal role dispute.* Role disputes occur when two people have different expectations of their relationship and of the role each should play. IPT therapists help clients examine whatever role disputes they may be involved in and then develop ways of resolving them.

Depressed people may also be going through an *interpersonal role transition,* brought about by major life changes such as divorce or the birth of a child. They may feel overwhelmed by the role changes that accompany the life change. In such cases, IPT therapists help them develop the social supports and skills the new roles require.

Finally, some depressed people display *interpersonal deficits,* such as extreme shyness or social awkwardness, that prevent them from having intimate relationships. IPT therapists may help such clients recognize their deficits and teach them social skills and assertiveness in order to improve their social effectiveness. In the following discussion, the therapist encourages a depressed man to recognize the effect his behavior has on others:

Client: *(After a long pause with eyes downcast, a sad facial expression, and slumped posture) People always make fun of me. I guess I'm just the type of guy who really was meant to be a loner, damn it. (Deep sigh)*

Therapist: *Could you do that again for me?*

Client: *What?*

Therapist: *The sigh, only a bit deeper.*

Client: *Why? (Pause) Okay, but I don't see what . . . okay. (Client sighs again and smiles)*

Therapist: *Well, that time you smiled, but mostly when you sigh and look so sad I get the feeling that I better leave you alone in your misery, that I should walk on eggshells and not get too chummy or I might hurt you even more.*

Client: *(A bit of anger in his voice) Well, excuse me! I was only trying to tell you how I felt.*

Therapist: *I know you felt miserable, but I also got the message that you wanted to keep me at a distance, that I had no way to reach you.*

Client: *(Slowly) I feel like a loner, I feel that even you don't care about me—making fun of me.*

Therapist: *I wonder if other folks need to pass this test, too?*

(Beier & Young, 1984, p. 270)

Role transition Major life changes such as marriage, the birth of a child, or divorce can create difficulties in role transition, one of the interpersonal problem areas addressed by IPT therapists in their work with depressed clients.

Studies suggest that IPT and related interpersonal treatments for depression have a success rate similar to that of cognitive-behavioral therapy (Swartz, 2016, 2015; Bleiberg & Markowitz, 2014). That is, symptoms almost totally disappear in 50 to 60 percent of clients who receive treatment. After IPT, not only are their depressive symptoms reduced, but clients also function more effectively in their social and family interactions. Not surprisingly, IPT is considered especially useful for depressed people who are struggling with social conflicts or undergoing changes in their careers or social roles (Ravitz, Watson, & Grigoriadis, 2013).

COUPLE THERAPY As you have read, depression can result from marital discord, and recovery from depression is often slower for people who do not receive support from

laflor/Getty Images

Treating the relationship In cases in which depression is closely tied to marital difficulties, couple therapy is often as helpful or more helpful than individual therapy.

their spouse (Keitner, 2017; Whisman & Beach, 2012). In fact, as many as half of all depressed clients may be in a dysfunctional relationship. Thus it is not surprising that many cases of depression have been treated by **couple therapy,** the approach in which a therapist works with two people who share a long-term relationship (Keitner, 2017; Cohen et al., 2014).

Therapists who offer *integrative behavioral couples therapy* combine cognitive-behavioral and sociocultural techniques to teach couples specific communication and problem-solving skills, guide them to recognize that their problematic interactions often reflect basic differences between them, and steer them to become more accepting and supportive of each other (see Chapter 3). When the depressed person's spousal relationship is filled with conflict, this approach and similar ones may be as effective as—or even more effective than—individual cognitive-behavioral therapy, interpersonal psychotherapy, or drug therapy in helping to reduce depression (Keitner, 2017; Lebow et al., 2012; Lebow & Uliaszek, 2010). In addition, depressed clients who receive couple therapy are more likely than those in individual therapy to be more satisfied with their marriage after treatment.

Biological Approaches

Like several of the psychological and sociocultural therapies, biological treatments can bring significant relief to people with unipolar depression. Usually biological treatment means *antidepressant drugs* or popular alternatives such as herbal supplements (see *InfoCentral* on page 233), but for people whose depression does not respond to medications, psychotherapy, or the like, it sometimes means *brain stimulation*.

Antidepressant Drugs Two kinds of drugs discovered in the 1950s reduce the symptoms of depression: *monoamine oxidase (MAO) inhibitors* and *tricyclics*. Over the years, these drugs have been joined by a third group, the *second-generation antidepressants* (see **Table 8-2**).

MAO INHIBITORS The effectiveness of **MAO inhibitors** as a treatment for unipolar depression was discovered accidentally. Physicians noted that *iproniazid,* a drug being tested on patients with tuberculosis, had an interesting effect: it seemed to make the

TABLE: 8-2

Some Drugs That Reduce Unipolar Depression

Monoamine Oxidase Inhibitors		Tricyclics		Second-Generation Antidepressants	
Generic Name	Trade Name	Generic Name	Trade Name	Generic Name	Trade Name
Iscarboxazid	Marplan	Imipramine	Tofranil	Trazodone	Desyrel
Phenelzine	Nardil	Amitriptyline	Elavil	Fluoxetine	Prozac
Tranylcypromine	Parnate	Doxepin	Sinequan; Silenor	Sertraline	Zoloft
Selegiline	Eldepryl	Trimipramine	Surmontil	Paroxetine	Paxil
		Desipramine	Norpramin	Venlafaxine	Effexor
		Nortriptyline	Aventil; Pamelor	Bupropion	Wellbutrin
		Protriptyline	Vivactil	Citalopram	Celexa
		Clomipramine	Anafranil	Escitalopram	Lexapro
		Amoxapine	Asendin	Duloxetine	Cymbalta
		Mirtazapine	Remeron	Desvenlafaxine	Pristiq
				Atomoxetine	Strattera

patients happier (Sandler, 1990). It was found to have the same effect on depressed patients (Kline, 1958; Loomer, Saunders, & Kline, 1957). What this and several related drugs had in common biochemically was that they slowed the body's production of the enzyme *monoamine oxidase* (*MAO*). Thus they were called MAO inhibitors.

Normally, brain supplies of the enzyme MAO break down, or degrade, the neurotransmitters serotonin and norepinephrine. MAO inhibitors block MAO from carrying out this activity and thereby stop the destruction of serotonin and norepinephrine (Naoi et al., 2018). The result is a rise in the activity levels of these neurotransmitters, and, in turn, a reduction of depressive symptoms. Approximately half of depressed patients who take MAO inhibitors are helped by them (Finberg & Rabey, 2016; Ciraulo et al., 2011; Thase et al., 1995). There is, however, a potential danger with regard to these drugs. When people who take MAO inhibitors eat foods containing the chemical *tyramine*—including such common foods as cheeses, bananas, and certain wines—their blood pressure rises dangerously (David & Gourion, 2016). Thus people on these drugs must stick to a rigid diet.

TRICYCLICS The discovery of **tricyclics** in the 1950s was also accidental. Researchers who were looking for a new drug to combat schizophrenia ran some tests on a drug called *imipramine* (Kuhn, 1958). They discovered that imipramine was of no help in cases of schizophrenia, but it did relieve unipolar depression in many people. The new drug (trade name Tofranil) and related ones became known as tricyclic antidepressants because they all share a three-ring molecular structure.

In hundreds of studies, depressed patients taking tricyclics have improved significantly more than similar patients taking placebos, although the drugs must be taken for at least 10 days before such improvements take hold (David & Gourion, 2016). Around 50 to 60 percent of patients who take tricyclics are helped by them (Simon & Ciechanowski, 2017; FDA, 2014). If, however, recovered individuals stop taking the drugs immediately after obtaining relief, they run a high risk of relapsing. As many as half of recovered patients who discontinue the drugs in this way relapse within a year (Jarrett & Vittengl, 2016). As a result, most clinicians now keep patients on antidepressant drugs for at least five months after being free of depressive symptoms, an extension called "continuation therapy" or "maintenance therapy." Research indicates that this approach decreases their chances of relapse (Jarrett & Vittengl, 2016; FDA, 2014).

Most researchers have concluded that one of the ways in which tricyclics are able to reduce depression is by acting on the *neurotransmitter "reuptake" mechanisms* of key

couple therapy A therapy format in which the therapist works with two people who share a long-term relationship.

MAO inhibitor An antidepressant drug that prevents the action of the enzyme monoamine oxidase.

tricyclic An antidepressant drug such as imipramine that has three rings in its molecular structure.

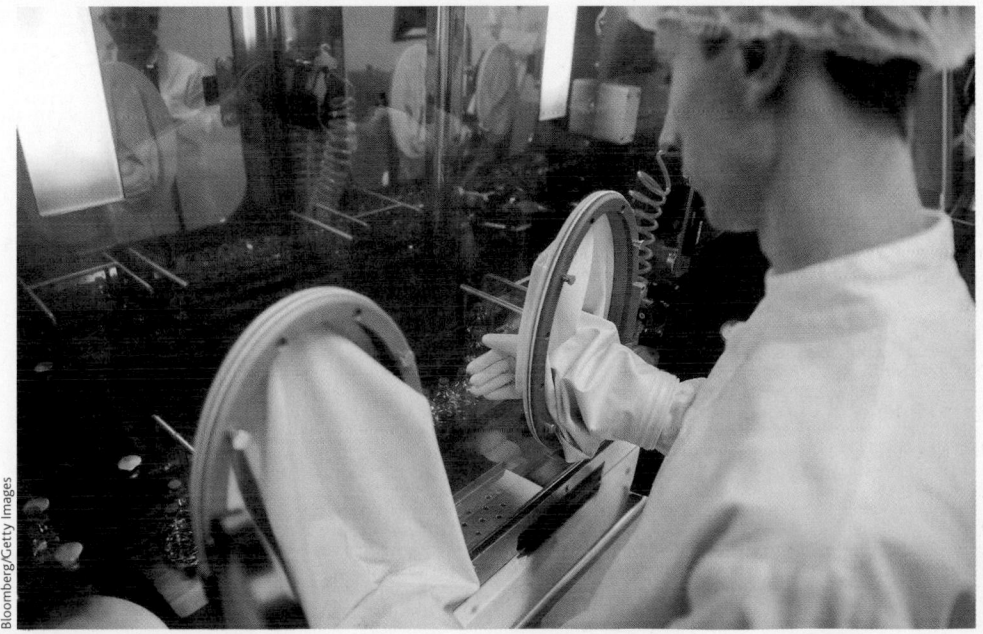

The antidepressant revolution This worker at a pharmaceutical company operates sterile equipment during the manufacture of antidepressant drugs. Global sales of antidepressants now total over $15 billion each year (MRS, 2016).

Bloomberg/Getty Images

Topham/The Image Works

Flower power *Hypericum perforatum*, known as *Saint-John's-wort*, is a low, wild-growing shrub, not an antidepressant drug. It is currently among the hottest-selling products in health stores, with studies indicating that it can be quite helpful in cases of mild or moderate depression.

neurons (Hirsch & Birnbaum, 2016; Ciraulo et al., 2011). Remember from Chapter 3 that brain messages are carried from a "sending" neuron across the synaptic space to a receiving neuron by a neurotransmitter, the chemical released from the end of the sending neuron. However, there is a complication in this process. While the sending neuron releases the neurotransmitter, a pumplike mechanism in the neuron's ending immediately starts to reabsorb it in a process called *reuptake*. The purpose of this reuptake process is to limit how long the neurotransmitter remains in the synaptic space and to prevent it from overstimulating the receiving neuron. Unfortunately, reuptake does not always progress properly. In particular, the reuptake mechanisms for depressed people are *too vigorous* in neurons that use either serotonin or norepinephrine—cutting off the activity of those neurotransmitters in their synaptic spaces too soon, preventing messages from reaching the receiving neurons, and helping to produce the symptoms of their disorder. Tricyclics inhibit (that is, *block*) this overly vigorous reuptake process, allowing serotonin and norepinephrine to remain in their synapses longer, thus increasing their stimulation of receiving neurons (see **Figure 8-3**).

Recent studies suggest that, for many depressed people, once these reuptake processes are corrected, serotonin and norepinephrine activity becomes smoother and more appropriate throughout their depression-related brain circuit, the circuit you read about in Chapter 7 (James et al., 2017; Rolls, 2017). Correspondingly, the structures and interconnections across that circuit become much more functional. For example, its hippocampus becomes more active, its subgenual cingulate becomes less active, and the interconnections between its prefrontal cortex and other structures in the circuit become more orderly—all corrections of circuit abnormalities that were described in Chapter 7 (James et al., 2017; Cullen et al., 2016). With such biological corrections in place, depression subsides for many patients.

> If antidepressant drugs are effective, why do many people seek out herbal supplements, such as Saint-John's-wort or melatonin, for depression?

Soon after tricyclics were discovered, they started being prescribed more often than MAO inhibitors. Tricyclics did not require dietary restrictions as MAO inhibitors did, although they can produce significant side effects such as very dry mouth, constipation, and blurred vision (Hirsch & Birnbaum, 2016). Also on the positive side, people taking them typically showed higher rates of improvement than those taking MAO inhibitors. On the other hand, some people respond better to MAO inhibitors than to either tricyclics or the antidepressants that will be discussed in the next section, and such people continue to be given MAO inhibitors (Hirsch & Birnbaum, 2016).

FIGURE 8-3

Reuptake and Antidepressants

(Left) Soon after a neuron releases neurotransmitters such as norepinephrine or serotonin into its synaptic space, it activates a pumplike reuptake mechanism to reabsorb excess neurotransmitters. In depression, however, this reuptake process is too active, removing too many neurotransmitters before they can bind to a receiving neuron. (Right) Tricyclic and most second-generation antidepressant drugs block the reuptake process, enabling norepinephrine or serotonin to remain in the synapse longer and bind to the receiving neuron.

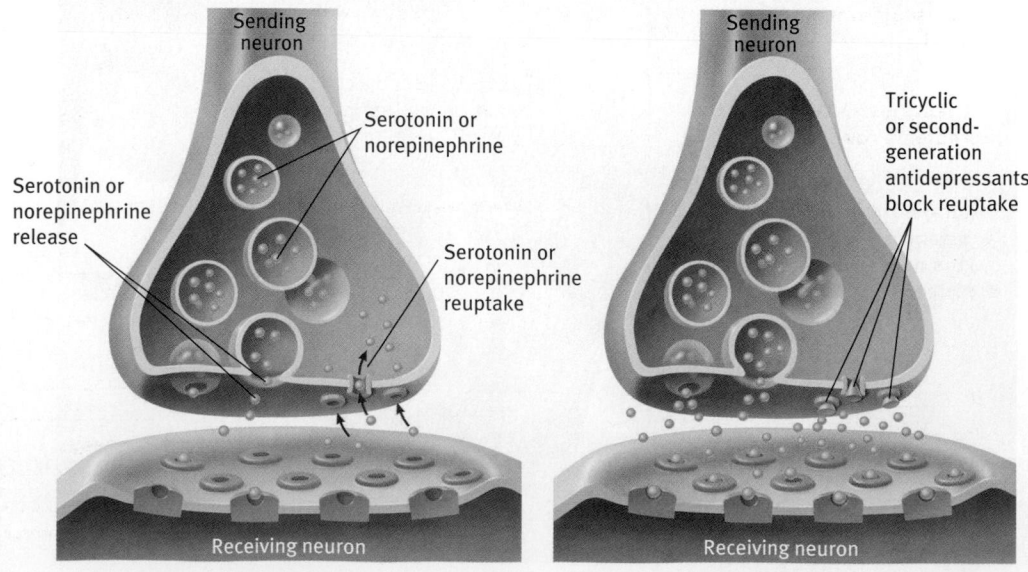

EXERCISE AND DIETARY SUPPLEMENTS

"Complementary and Alternative Medicine (CAM)" is the popular term for interventions that fall outside of conventional Western treatments. Two of the most common CAM interventions are **physical exercise** and **dietary supplements** (also known as **nutraceuticals).** Depression is the psychological problem for which these approaches are used most often, and research indicates that each can indeed help improve the moods of modestly or moderately depressed people, particularly when integrated with psychotherapy or medication, rather than applied alone (Jabr, 2017; Remick et al., 2017; Schuch et al., 2017).

EXERCISE ALLEVIATES DEPRESSION BY. . .

- Triggering positive changes in depression-related brain circuits, brain–body stress pathways, and neurotransmitter activity
- Improving immune functioning
- Raising self-confidence
- Producing social interactions
- Improving cognitive functioning
- Improving sleep
- Distracting from unhappy thoughts
- Increasing self-esteem

(Busch et al., 2017; Davenport, 2017; Hallgren et al., 2017; Jabr, 2017; Levine, 2017; Sadeghi et al., 2017; Sharma et al., 2006)

TOP EXERCISES FOR DEPRESSION

The most commonly recommended exercises for depression are *aerobic* — exercises that increase oxygen intake and raise heart rate. All aerobic exercises are equally helpful for depression (Jabr, 2017; Levine, 2017).

CYCLING · DANCING · GARDENING · SOME YOGA POSITIONS · SYSTEMATIC DEEP BREATHING · SWIMMING · JOGGING · WALKING

(Busch et al., 2017; Levine, 2017; Overdorf et al., 2016; Sharma et al., 2005)

EXERCISE VS. LEADING TREATMENTS

least effective → most effective

| No treatment or exercise | Exercise alone | Antidepressants alone **or** Psychotherapy alone | Antidepressants + exercise **or** Psychotherapy + exercise |

(Netz, 2017; Meyer et al., 2016; Sadeghi et al., 2016)

FOR BEST RESULTS, DEPRESSED PEOPLE SHOULD EXERCISE . . .

- At least 5 days per week
- At least 30 minutes per day
- With moderate or high intensity
- With a buddy or group
- Guided by a trainer
- In collaboration with their clinician

(Hallgren et al., 2017; Jain, 2017; Levine, 2017; Remick et al., 2017; Thompson, 2017; Overdorf et al., 2016; Stubbs et al., 2016)

WHY DEPRESSED PEOPLE DON'T EXERCISE

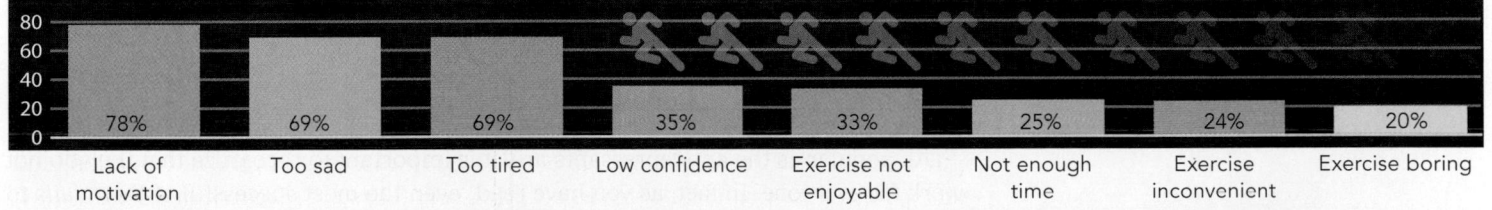

Lack of motivation	Too sad	Too tired	Low confidence	Exercise not enjoyable	Not enough time	Exercise inconvenient	Exercise boring
78%	69%	69%	35%	33%	25%	24%	20%

(Busch et al., 2017)

POPULAR NUTRACEUTICALS FOR DEPRESSION

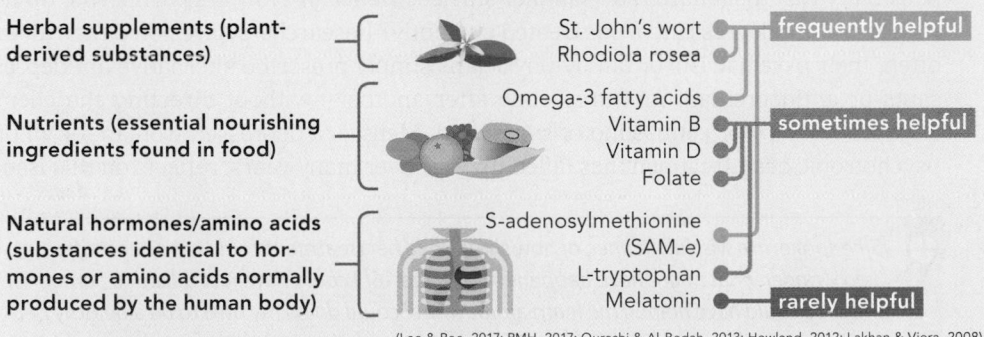

Herbal supplements (plant-derived substances)
- St. John's wort — frequently helpful
- Rhodiola rosea

Nutrients (essential nourishing ingredients found in food)
- Omega-3 fatty acids
- Vitamin B — sometimes helpful
- Vitamin D
- Folate

Natural hormones/amino acids (substances identical to hormones or amino acids normally produced by the human body)
- S-adenosylmethionine (SAM-e)
- L-tryptophan
- Melatonin — rarely helpful

(Lee & Bae, 2017; PMH, 2017; Qureshi & Al-Bedah, 2013; Howland, 2012; Lakhan & Viera, 2008)

Depressed people take nutraceuticals because . . .

- They are not helped by conventional treatments
- They developed major side effects to antidepressant drugs
- They cannot afford conventional treatments
- They dislike modern medications
- They prefer more natural treatments

(Jain, 2017; Qureshi & Al-Bedah, 2013)

NUTRACEUTICAL USE IS. . .

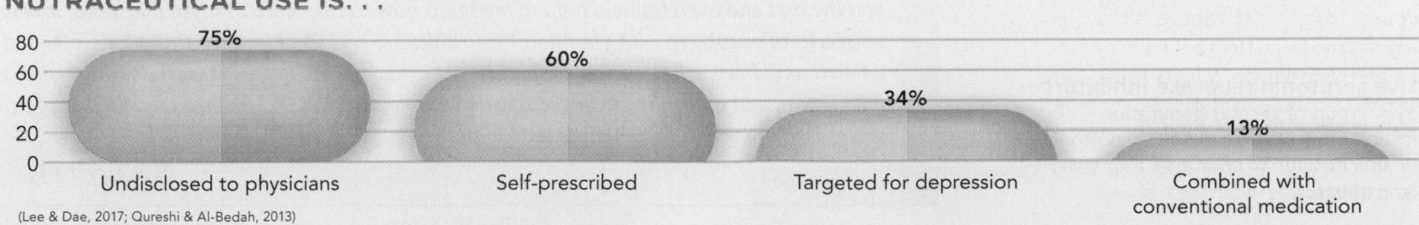

Undisclosed to physicians	Self-prescribed	Targeted for depression	Combined with conventional medication
75%	60%	34%	13%

(Lee & Dae, 2017; Qureshi & Al-Bedah, 2013)

David Sipress The New Yorker Collection/The Cartoon Bank

"This next one is a sad little blues tune about love and pain that I wrote before I started taking Celexa."

SECOND-GENERATION ANTIDEPRESSANTS A third group of effective antidepressant drugs, structurally different from the MAO inhibitors and tricyclics, has been developed during the past three decades. Most of these second-generation antidepressants are called **selective serotonin reuptake inhibitors (SSRIs)** because they increase serotonin activity specifically, without affecting norepinephrine or other neurotransmitters. The SSRIs include *fluoxetine* (trade name Prozac), *sertraline* (Zoloft), and *escitalopram* (Lexapro). Other second-generation antidepressants are *selective norepinephrine reuptake inhibitors* (such as *atomoxetine*, or Strattera), which increase norepinephrine activity only, and *serotonin-norepinephrine reuptake inhibitors* (such as *venlafaxine*, or Effexor), which increase both serotonin and norepinephrine activity.

In effectiveness and speed of action, the second-generation antidepressant drugs are about on a par with the tricyclics, yet their sales have skyrocketed (Hirsch & Birnbaum, 2016). Because they primarily affect one or at most two neurotransmitters, they do not produce as many undesired effects as MAO inhibitors or tricyclics. At the same time, these relatively newer antidepressants can produce significant side effects of their own. Some people gain weight, feel drowsy, or have a reduced sex drive, for example (Simon & Ciechanowski, 2017; David & Gourion, 2016; Stahl, 2014).

People who have been helped by the antidepressants readily sing their praises. Consider, for example, the following comments, offered in one survey of antidepressant users:

"Going on Prozac was literally going from black and white to color."
"Within a couple weeks I felt like I was me again."
"Life was still filled with problems. But suddenly . . .they were [just] problems, not this overbearing force."
"I felt like a human being again."

(Sharpe, 2012)

As popular as the antidepressants are, it is important to recognize that they do not work for everyone. In fact, as you have read, even the most successful of them *fails* to help at least 40 percent of clients with depression. In fact, some reviews have raised the possibility that the failure rate is higher still (see **Trending**). How are clients who do not respond to antidepressant drugs treated currently? Researchers have noted that, all too often, their psychiatrists or family physicians simply prescribe alternative antidepressants or antidepressant mixtures—one after another—without directing the clients to psychotherapy or counseling of some kind. Melissa, a depressed woman for whom psychotropic drug treatment has failed to work over many years, reflects on this issue:

[S]he spoke, in a wistful manner, of how she wished her treatment could have been different. "I do wonder what might have happened if [at age 16] I could have just talked to someone, and they could have helped me learn about what I could do on my own to be a healthy person. I never had a role model for that. They could have helped me with my eating problems, and my diet and exercise, and helped me learn how to take care of myself. Instead, it was you have this problem with your neurotransmitters, and so here, take this pill Zoloft, and when that didn't work, it was take this pill Prozac, and when that didn't work, it was take this pill Effexor, and then when I started having trouble sleeping, it was take this sleeping pill," she says, her voice sounding more wistful than ever. "I am so tired of the pills."

(Whitaker, 2010)

selective serotonin reuptake inhibitors (SSRIs) A group of second-generation antidepressant drugs that increase serotonin activity specifically, without affecting other neurotransmitters.

How Effective Are Antidepressant Drugs, Really?

One of the most talked-about issues in the clinical field today is the possibility that antidepressant drugs may not be as effective as previously thought. For years, clinical researchers believed that tricyclic and second-generation antidepressants help around 65 percent of people suffering from depression, an effectiveness rate that is much higher than the 30 to 35 percent of depressed people who seem to improve in response to placebo drugs. This rate of 65 percent is correct with regard to *published* studies. But, apparently, the story is different when unpublished studies are considered.

This issue actually had its beginnings a decade ago when two teams of researchers—one led by Erick Turner and the other by Irving Kirsch—each decided to examine the possible impact of *publication bias* on the reported effectiveness rates of antidepressant drugs (Kirsch, 2014; Turner et al., 2008) Publication bias refers to the tendency of professional journals to accept for publication mainly those studies that have positive findings. For example, they may primarily publish antidepressant drug studies that find antidepressants to be significantly more effective than placebo drugs. Researchers themselves might also contribute to publication bias by submitting studies for journal consideration only if they have positive findings.

The two research teams conducted similar kinds of reviews and reached similar conclusions. Turner and his colleagues, for example, reviewed 74 antidepressant drug studies registered with the U.S. Food and Drug Administration (FDA) (Turner et al., 2008). When a pharmaceutical company financially supports a drug study, it or the study's researcher must register the undertaking with the FDA, so that information is available to the public through the Freedom of Information Act, regardless of whether the study winds up being published. The Turner team found a troubling pattern in their review. Only 38 of the 74 registered studies yielded positive findings (that is, the drug was clearly effective), and all but one of these studies were published. In contrast, the other 36 studies yielded findings that were negative or questionable

(the drug was not particularly effective), and 22 of them were *not* published. When the reviewers combined the findings from all the registered studies—both published and unpublished—the percentage of people helped by antidepressant drugs turned out to be lower than the percentage yielded in published studies alone.

Using this larger pool of studies, the reviews by the two teams suggested that antidepressants help improve the symptoms of approximately *50* percent of depressed people, as opposed to 65 percent. Moreover, across all of the reviewed studies, the placebo drugs that were given to control group participants, who were equally depressed,

Jochen Tack/Getty Images

continued to bring improvement to approximately 30 to 35 percent of depressed people. In short, antidepressant drugs may not be as superior to placebo drugs as previously believed.

In recent years, other reviews have also examined the performance of antidepressant drugs, again combining findings from published and unpublished studies. These recent reviews have uncovered the same story: antidepressant drugs help around half of depressed people, compared to the 30 to 35 percent helped by placebo drugs (Deacon & Spielmans, 2017; Bschor & Kilarski, 2016;

Driessen et al., 2015). As a result of these various reviews, some clinicians now believe that antidepressant drugs are of limited help to depressed people. Other clinical theorists, however, believe that it is unwise to treat unpublished data so respectfully and unwise to combine data from very different studies as these reviews have done (Karlsson, 2017; Hieronymus et al., 2016). These latter theorists worry that clinicians and clients alike may, incorrectly, lose confidence in antidepressant drugs.

A final note, just to muddy the waters a bit more. In light of these reviews, a number of clinicians have concluded that *psychotherapy* must, in fact, be *more* effective than antidepressant drugs, not equally effective as previously believed. However, it turns out that studies of psychotherapy for depression may be subject to the same kinds of publication bias as antidepressant drug studies. One carefully conducted review looked at findings from both published and unpublished psychotherapy studies and discovered the same trends as those found in antidepressant drug studies (Driesson et al., 2015). That is, studies of psychotherapy for depression are more likely to be accepted for publication by professional journals if they have positive rather than negative results. And, when both published and unpublished psychotherapy studies are combined, psychotherapy significantly helps around 50 percent of depressed people rather than 65 percent, its previously believed effectiveness rate.

These are very serious matters to be sure. Obviously, when making decisions about treatment, clinicians must know how likely it is that depressed clients will be helped by the various available interventions. Thus the clinical field is working hard to sort out these issues. In the meantime, it may be most prudent to conclude that antidepressant drugs and psychotherapies for depression (cognitive-behavioral and interpersonal psychotherapy) are indeed helpful to many depressed people, although perhaps not as helpful nor as superior (to placebo treatments) as once believed. Hopefully, a less tentative and more precise conclusion is on the horizon.

brain stimulation Biological treatments that directly or indirectly stimulate certain areas of the brain.

electroconvulsive therapy (ECT) A treatment for depression in which electrodes attached to a patient's head send an electrical current through the brain, causing a convulsion.

Brain Stimulation

As you read in Chapter 3, a second form of biological treatment, **brain stimulation**, refers to interventions that directly or indirectly stimulate certain areas of the brain. The oldest—and most controversial—such approach is *electroconvulsive therapy (ECT)*. It is used primarily on severely depressed people. In recent years, three additional kinds of brain stimulation have been developed for the treatment of depressive disorders—*vagus nerve stimulation, transcranial magnetic stimulation,* and *deep brain stimulation.*

ELECTROCONVULSIVE THERAPY Clinicians and patients alike vary greatly in their opinions of **electroconvulsive therapy (ECT).** Some consider it a safe biological approach with minimal risks; others believe it to be an extreme measure that can cause troublesome memory loss and even neurological damage. Despite the heat of this controversy, ECT is used frequently, largely because it can be a very effective and fast-acting intervention for unipolar depression.

THE ECT PROCEDURE In an ECT procedure, two electrodes are attached to the patient's head, and 65 to 140 volts of electricity are passed through the brain for half a second or less. This results in a *brain seizure* that lasts from 15 to 70 seconds (Kellner, 2017). After 6 to 12 such treatments, spaced over 2 to 4 weeks, most patients feel less depressed (Fink, 2014, 2007). In *bilateral ECT,* one electrode is applied to each side of the forehead, and a current passes through both sides of the brain. In *unilateral ECT,* the electrodes are placed so that the current passes through only one side (Kellner, 2017).

THE ORIGINS OF ECT The discovery that electric shock can be therapeutic was made by accident. In the 1930s, clinical researchers mistakenly came to believe that brain seizures, or the *convulsions* (severe body spasms) that accompany them, could cure schizophrenia and other psychotic disorders. They observed that people with psychosis rarely suffered from *epilepsy* (*brain seizure disorder*) and that people with epilepsy rarely were psychotic, and so concluded that brain seizures or convulsions somehow prevented psychosis. We now know that the observed correlation between seizures and lack of psychotic symptoms does not necessarily imply that one causes the other. Nevertheless, swayed by faulty logic, clinicians in the 1930s searched for ways to induce seizures as a treatment for patients with psychosis.

A Hungarian physician named Joseph von Meduna gave the drug *metrazol* to patients suffering from psychosis, and a Viennese physician named Manfred Sakel gave them large doses of insulin (*insulin coma therapy*). These procedures produced the desired brain seizures, but each was quite dangerous and sometimes even caused death. Finally, an Italian psychiatrist named Ugo Cerletti discovered that he could produce seizures more safely by applying electric currents to a patient's head, and he and his colleague Lucio Bini soon developed ECT as a treatment for psychosis (Cerletti & Bini, 1938). As you might expect, much uncertainty and confusion accompanied their first clinical application of ECT. Did experimenters have the right to impose such an untested treatment against a patient's will?

#InspiringVisit

Prior to developing ECT, Ugo Cerletti visited a slaughterhouse. He observed that before slaughtering hogs with a knife, butchers clamped the animals' heads with metallic tongs and applied an electric current. The hogs fell unconscious and had convulsions, but they did not die from the current itself. Said Cerletti: "At this point I felt we could venture to experiment on man."

> *The schizophrenic arrived by train from Milan without a ticket or any means of identification. Physically healthy, he was bedraggled and alternately was mute or expressed himself in incomprehensible gibberish made up of odd neologisms. The patient was brought in but despite their vast animal experience there was great apprehension and fear that the patient might be damaged, and so the shock was cautiously set at 70 volts for one-tenth of a second. The low dosage predictably produced only a minor spasm, after which the patient burst into song. Cerletti suggested another shock at a higher voltage, and an excited and voluble discussion broke out among the spectators. . . . All of the staff objected to a further shock, protesting that the patient would probably die. Cerletti was familiar with committees and knew that postponement would inevitably mean prolonged and possibly permanent procrastination, and so he decided to proceed at 110 volts for*

one-half second. However, before he could do so, the patient who had heard but so far not participated in the discussion sat up and pontifically proclaimed in clear Italian without hint of jargon, "Non una seconda! Mortifera!" (Not again! It will kill me!). Professor Bini hesitated but gave the order to proceed. After recovery, Bini asked the patient "What has been happening to you?" and the man replied "I don't know; perhaps I've been asleep." He remained jargon-free and gave a complete account of himself, and was discharged completely recovered after 11 complete and 3 incomplete treatments over a course of 2 months.

(Brandon, 1981, pp. 8–9)

ECT soon became popular and was tried out on a wide range of psychological problems, as new techniques so often are. Its effectiveness with severe depression in particular became apparent. Ironically, however, doubts were soon raised concerning its usefulness for psychosis, and many researchers have since judged it ineffective for psychotic disorders, except for cases that also include severe depressive symptoms (Rothschild, 2017, 2016; Freudenreich & Goff, 2011).

CHANGES IN ECT PROCEDURES Although Cerletti gained international fame for his procedure, eventually he abandoned ECT and spent his later years seeking other treatments for mental disorders (Karon, 1985). The reason: he abhorred the broken bones and dislocations of the jaw or shoulders that sometimes resulted from ECT's severe convulsions, as well as the memory loss, confusion, and brain damage that the seizures could cause. Other clinicians have stayed with the procedure, however, and have changed it over the years to reduce its undesirable consequences (Kellner, 2017). Today's practitioners give patients strong *muscle relaxants* to minimize convulsions, thus eliminating the danger of fractures or dislocations. They also use *anesthetics* (*barbiturates*) to put patients to sleep during the procedure, reducing their terror. With these precautions, ECT is medically more complex than it used to be, but also less dangerous and somewhat less disturbing.

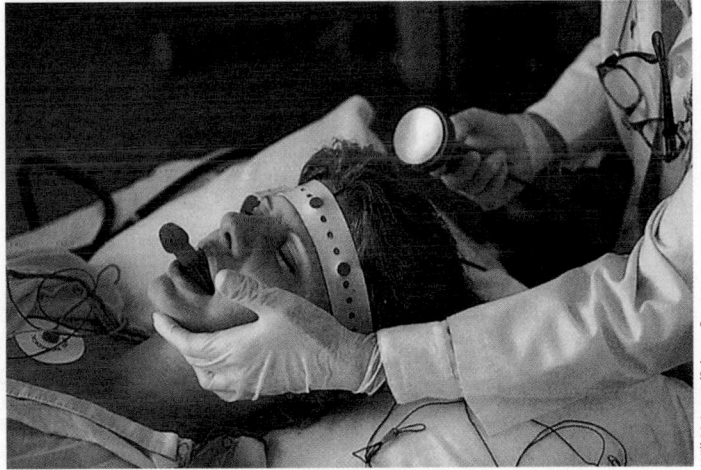

ECT today The techniques for administering ECT have changed significantly since the treatment's early days. Today, patients are given drugs to help them sleep, muscle relaxants to prevent severe jerks of the body and broken bones, and oxygen to guard against brain damage.

Will McIntyre/Science Source

Patients who receive ECT, particularly bilateral ECT, typically have difficulty remembering some events, most often events that took place immediately before and after their treatments (Kellner, 2017; Martin et al., 2015). In most cases, this memory loss clears up within a few months (Bodnar et al., 2016), but some patients are left with gaps in more distant memory, and this form of amnesia can be permanent (Hanna et al., 2009; Wang, 2007).

EFFECTIVENESS OF ECT ECT is clearly effective in treating unipolar depression. Studies find that between 50 and 80 percent of ECT patients improve (Kellner, 2017; Perugi et al., 2011). The approach is particularly effective when patients follow up the initial cluster of sessions with continuation, or maintenance, therapy—either ongoing antidepressant medications or periodic ECT sessions (Jarrett & Vittengl, 2016; Fink et al., 2014). ECT also seems to be quite effective in severe cases of depression that include delusions (Rothschild, 2017, 2016). It has been difficult, however, to determine why ECT works so well (Wang et al., 2018; Baldinger et al., 2014). After all, this procedure delivers a broad insult to the brain that activates a number of brain areas, causes neurons all over the brain to fire, affects communications between multiple brain structures, and leads to the release of all kinds of neurotransmitters, and it affects many other systems throughout the body as well.

Although ECT is effective and ECT techniques have improved, its use has generally declined since the 1950s. Two reasons for this decline are the memory loss caused by ECT and the frightening nature of the procedure (Fink, Kellner, & McCall, 2014). Another, of course, is the emergence of effective antidepressant drugs.

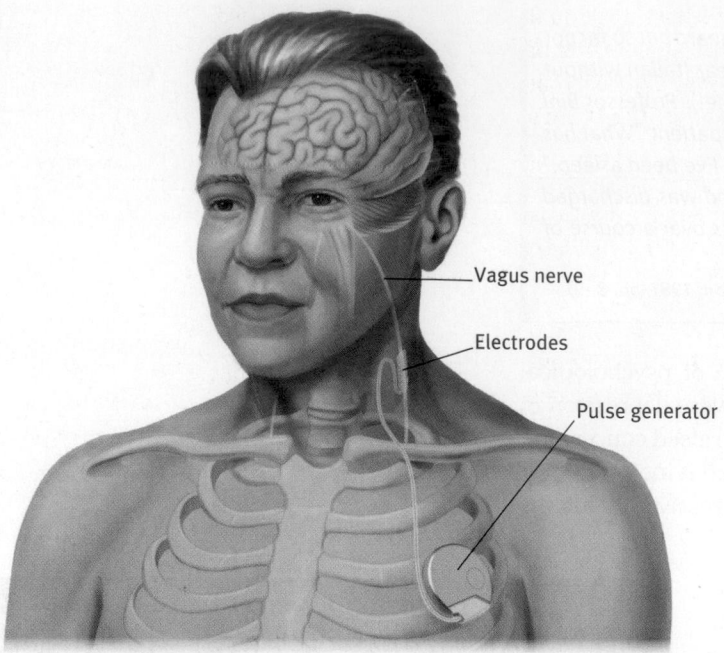

FIGURE 8-4

Vagus Nerve Stimulation

In the procedure called vagus nerve stimulation, an implanted pulse generator sends electrical signals to the vagus nerve, which then delivers electrical signals to the brain. This stimulation of the brain helps reduce depression in many patients.

Vagus nerve

Electrodes

Pulse generator

VAGUS NERVE STIMULATION The vagus nerve, the longest nerve in the human body, runs from the brain stem through the neck down the chest and on to the abdomen, serving as a primary channel of communication between the brain and major organs such as the heart, lungs, and intestines.

A number of years ago, a group of depression researchers suspected that they might be able to stimulate the brain by electrically stimulating the vagus nerve. They were hoping to mimic the positive effects of ECT without producing the undesired effects or trauma associated with ECT. Their efforts gave birth to a new treatment for depression—**vagus nerve stimulation.**

As you read in Chapter 3, in this procedure a surgeon implants a small device called a *pulse generator* under the skin of the chest. The surgeon then guides a wire, which extends from the pulse generator, up to the neck and attaches it to the vagus nerve (see **Figure 8-4**). Electrical signals travel from the pulse generator through the wire to the vagus nerve. The stimulated vagus nerve then delivers electrical signals to the brain. The pulse generator, which runs on battery power, is typically programmed to provide 30 seconds of stimulation to the vagus nerve (and, in turn, the brain) every five minutes.

In 2005, the U.S. Food and Drug Administration (FDA) approved vagus nerve stimulation as a treatment for depression. Ever since the procedure was first tried on depressed human beings in the 1990s, research has found that it can bring significant relief (Aaronson et al., 2017). In fact, studies find that a substantial number of severely depressed people who have not responded to any other form of treatment may improve significantly when treated with vagus nerve stimulation (Howland, 2014; Berry et al., 2013).

TRANSCRANIAL MAGNETIC STIMULATION Transcranial magnetic stimulation (TMS) is another technique that is being used to try to stimulate the brain without subjecting depressed patients to the undesired effects or trauma of ECT. In this procedure, first developed in 1985, the clinician places an electromagnetic coil on or

Stimulating the brain In this version of transcranial magnetic stimulation, a woman wears headgear that contains an electromagnetic coil. The coil sends currents into and stimulates her brain.

above the patient's head. The coil sends a current into the prefrontal cortex. As you'll remember from the previous chapter, at least some parts of the prefrontal cortex of depressed people are underactive. TMS appears to increase neuron activity in that structure, and, in turn, may improve functioning throughout the rest of the brain's depression-related circuit (Holtzheimer, 2017, 2015).

TMS has been tested by researchers on a range of disorders, including depression. A number of studies have found that the procedure reduces depression when it is administered daily for 4 to 6 weeks (van den Noort, 2018; Holtzheimer, 2017, 2015). In 2008 TMS was approved by the FDA as a treatment for depression.

DEEP BRAIN STIMULATION As you have read, around a decade ago, researchers linked depression to high activity in the subgenual cingulate, a key member of the depression-related brain circuit. This finding led neurologist Helen Mayberg and her colleagues (2005) to administer an experimental treatment called **deep brain stimulation (DBS)** to six severely depressed patients who had previously been unresponsive to all other forms of treatment.

Mayberg's approach was modeled after deep brain stimulation techniques that had been used successfully in cases of brain seizure disorder and Parkinson's disease, both of which are related to overly active brain structures. For depression, the Mayberg team drilled two tiny holes into the patient's skull and implanted electrodes in the subgenual cingulate. The electrodes were connected to a battery, or "pacemaker," that was implanted in the patient's chest (for men) or stomach (for women). The pacemaker powered the electrodes, sending a steady stream of low-voltage electricity to the brain structure. Mayberg's expectation was that this repeated stimulation would reduce activity in the structure to a normal level and help "recalibrate" the depression-related brain circuit.

In the initial study of DBS, four of the six severely depressed patients became almost depression-free within a matter of months (Mayberg et al., 2005). Subsequent research with other severely depressed individuals has also yielded promising findings (Riva-Posse et al., 2018; Berlim et al., 2014). Understandably, this work has produced considerable enthusiasm in the clinical field, but it is important to recognize that research on DBS is in its early stages.

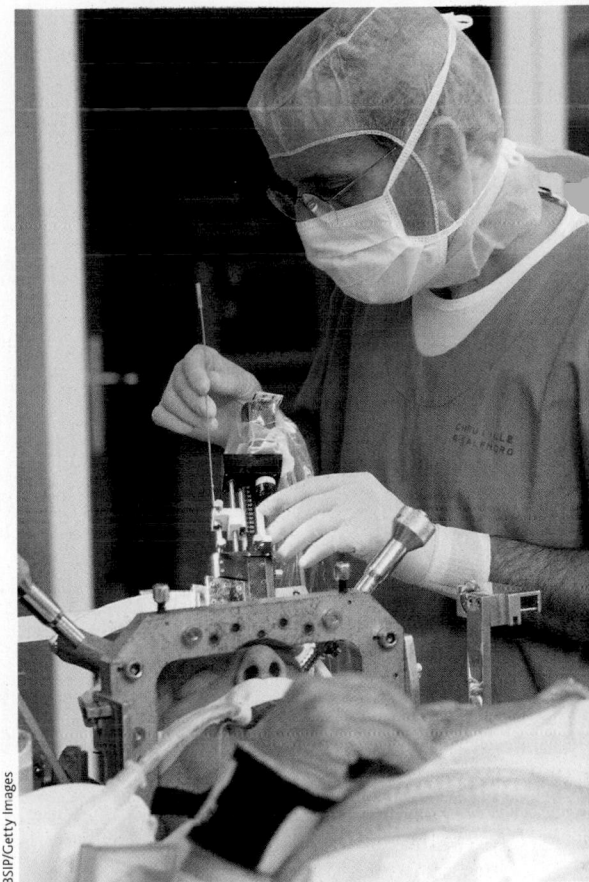

Entering the brain A neurosurgeon performs *deep brain stimulation* on a depressed patient, planting electrodes in his subgenual cingulate, a key structure in the depression-related brain circuit.

How Do the Treatments for Unipolar Depression Compare?

For most kinds of psychological disorders, no more than one or two treatments or combinations of treatments, if any, emerge as highly successful. Unipolar depression seems to be an exception. One of the most treatable of all abnormal patterns, it may respond to any of several approaches. During the past 20 years, researchers have conducted a number of treatment outcome studies, which have revealed some important trends:

1. Cognitive-behavioral, interpersonal, and biological therapies are all effective treatments for unipolar depression, from mild to severe (Hirsch & Birnbaum, 2016; Lutz et al., 2016; Swartz, 2016). In most head-to-head comparisons, they seem to be equally effective at reducing depressive symptoms; however, there are indications that some populations of depressed patients respond better to one therapy than to another.

   In a pioneering 6-year study of this issue, experimenters separated 239 moderately and severely depressed people into four treatment groups (Elkin, 1994; Elkin et al., 1989, 1985). One group was treated with 16 weeks of Beck's cognitive therapy, another with 16 weeks of interpersonal psychotherapy, and a third with the tricyclic drug *imipramine*. The fourth group received a placebo. A total of 28 therapists conducted these treatments.

vagus nerve stimulation A treatment for depression in which an implanted pulse generator sends regular electrical signals to a person's vagus nerve; the nerve then stimulates the brain.

transcranial magnetic stimulation (TMS) A treatment in which an electromagnetic coil, which is placed on or above a patient's head, sends a current into the individual's brain.

deep brain stimulation (DBS) A treatment for depression in which a pacemaker powers electrodes that have been implanted in subgenual cingulate, thus stimulating that brain area.

"Idk what peace feels like" A few months after this 2016 concert performance in New Orleans, the hugely successful rap artist and actor Kid Cudi revealed on his Facebook page that he had entered an inpatient program to receive treatment for depression and suicidal urges. He wrote to his fans, "My anxiety and depression have ruled my life for as long as I can remember . . . Idk what peace feels like." He returned to performing a month later.

Using a depression assessment instrument called the *Hamilton Rating Scale for Depression,* the investigators found that each of the three therapies almost completely eliminated depressive symptoms in 50 to 60 percent of the participants who completed treatment. Only 30 to 35 percent of those who received the placebo showed such improvement. This trend also held, although somewhat less powerfully, when other assessment measures were used. These findings are consistent with those of other comparative outcome studies.

The study found that drug therapy reduced depressive symptoms more quickly than the cognitive-behavioral and interpersonal therapies did, but these psychotherapies had matched the drugs in effectiveness by the final 4 weeks of treatment. In addition, more recent studies suggest that cognitive-behavioral therapy may be more effective than drug therapy at preventing recurrences of depression except when drug therapy is continued for an extended period of time (Jarrett & Vittengl, 2016; AIPC, 2015). Despite the comparable or even superior showing of cognitive-behavioral therapies, in the past several decades there has been a significant increase in the number of prescriptions written for antidepressant drugs: from 2.5 million in 1980 to 4.7 million in 1990 to more than 340 million today (Hrenchir, 2015; Koerner, 2007).

> Why might depression treated by cognitive-behavioral therapy be less likely to recur than depression treated by antidepressant drugs?

2. Although the cognitive-behavioral and interpersonal therapies may lower the likelihood of relapse, they are hardly relapse-proof. Some studies suggest that a number of the depressed patients who respond to these approaches may, in fact, relapse within a few years after the completion of treatment (Jarrett & Vittengl, 2016). In an effort to head off relapse, many of today's cognitive-behavioral and interpersonal therapists continue treatment, perhaps on a less frequent basis and sometimes in group or classroom formats, after the depression lifts—an approach similar to the "continuation" or "maintenance" approaches used with antidepressant drugs and brain stimulation treatments. It appears that extensions of this kind do in fact reduce the rate of relapse among successfully treated patients. In fact, research suggests that people who have recovered from depression are less likely to relapse if they receive continuation or maintenance therapy in either drug or psychotherapy form, regardless of which kind of therapy they originally received (Jarrett & Vittengl, 2016).

"Katia, I know that with the right combination of therapy and medication I could have a committed relationship with you."

Improvement through gaming A game artist works on SPARX, a popular video game that teaches users how to deal with depression. In SPARX (which stands for "Smart, Positive, Active, Realistic, X-factor thoughts"), users journey through seven different provinces in which their avatar must overcome challenges such as GNATS ("Gloomy Negative Automatic Thoughts"). According to some studies, the game, which follows the principles of cognitive-behavioral therapy, is helpful to teenagers grappling with mild depression (Poppelaars et al., 2016; Cheek et al., 2014).

3. When people with unipolar depression have significant discord in their marital relationships, couple therapy tends to be as helpful as cognitive-behavioral, interpersonal, or drug therapy (Keitner, 2017; Lebow et al., 2012).

4. Most studies suggest that traditional psychodynamic therapies are less effective than these other therapies in treating all levels of unipolar depression (Hollon & Ponniah, 2010; Svartberg & Stiles, 1991). Many psychodynamic clinicians argue, however, that this system of therapy simply does not lend itself to empirical research, and its effectiveness should be judged more by therapists' reports of individual recovery and progress (Busch et al., 2004).

5. Studies have found that a combination of psychotherapy (usually cognitive-behavioral or interpersonal) and drug therapy is often more helpful to depressed people than either treatment alone, particularly in cases of severe depression (Swartz, 2016; Rehm, 2010).

6. As you will see in Chapter 17, these various trends do not always carry over to the treatment of depressed children and adolescents. For example, a broad 6-year project called the *Treatment for Adolescents with Depression Study* (*TADS*) indicates that a combination of cognitive-behavioral and drug therapy may be *considerably* more helpful to depressed teenagers than either treatment alone (Strawn et al., 2017; NIMH, 2010; TADS, 2007).

7. Among biological treatments, ECT appears to be more effective than other brain stimulation approaches or antidepressant drugs for reducing depression. ECT also acts more quickly. Half of patients treated by any of these interventions, however, relapse within a year unless the initial treatment is followed up by continuing treatment, such as drug treatment or psychotherapy (Jarrett & Vittengl, 2016; Fink, 2014, 2007, 2001).

8. When clinicians today choose a biological treatment for mild to severe unipolar depression, they most often prescribe one of the antidepressant drugs (Simon & Ciechanowski, 2017). They are not likely to refer patients for brain stimulation unless the depression has been unresponsive to drug therapy and psychotherapy (Kellner, 2017, 2016; Thase & Connolly, 2016). ECT, the most effective of the brain stimulation techniques, also appears to be the most helpful treatment for severely depressed patients who do not respond to other interventions (Song et al., 2015; Perugi et al., 2011). If a depressed person seems to be at high

#NameDropping

One study found that 55 percent of people who posed as patients with a few depressive symptoms were given prescriptions for the antidepressant Paxil when they told their doctor that they had seen it advertised, compared with only 10 percent of pseudopatients who did not mention an ad (Kravitz et al., 2005).

risk for suicide, the person's clinician may make the referral for ECT treatment more readily (Kellner, 2017, 2016; Fink et al., 2014). Although ECT clearly has a beneficial effect on suicidal behavior in the short run, studies do not clearly indicate that it has a long-term effect on suicide rates.

Treatments for Bipolar Disorders

UNTIL THE LATTER PART OF THE twentieth century, people with bipolar disorders were destined to spend their lives on an emotional roller coaster. Psychotherapists reported almost no success, and early antidepressant drugs were of limited help. In fact, the drugs sometimes triggered a manic episode (Stovall, 2017; Bobo & Shelton, 2016). Moreover, past versions of ECT only sometimes relieved either the depressive or the manic episodes of bipolar disorders (Kellner, 2016).

This gloomy picture changed dramatically in 1970 when the FDA approved the use of **lithium,** a silvery-white element found in various simple mineral salts throughout the natural world, as a treatment for bipolar disorder. Additional **mood stabilizing,** or **antibipolar, drugs** have since been developed, and several of them are now used more widely than lithium, either because they produce fewer undesired effects or because they are even more effective than lithium.

Nevertheless, it was lithium that first brought hope to those suffering from bipolar disorder. In her widely read memoir, *An Unquiet Mind*, psychiatric researcher Kay Redfield Jamison describes how lithium, combined with psychotherapy, enabled her to overcome bipolar disorder:

> I took [lithium] faithfully and found that life was a much stabler and more predictable place than I had ever reckoned. My moods were still intense and my temperament rather quick to the boil, but I could make plans with far more certainty and the periods of absolute blackness were fewer and less extreme. . . .
>
> At this point in my existence, I cannot imagine leading a normal life without both taking lithium and having had the benefits of psychotherapy. Lithium prevents my seductive but disastrous highs, diminishes my depressions, clears out the wool and webbing from my disordered thinking, slows me down, gentles me out, keeps me from ruining my career and relationships, keeps me out of a hospital, alive, and makes psychotherapy possible. [At the same time], ineffably, psychotherapy heals. It makes some sense of the confusion, reins in the terrifying thoughts and feelings, returns some control and hope and possibility of learning from it all. Pills cannot, do not, ease one back into reality; they only bring one back headlong, careening, and faster than can be endured at times. Psychotherapy is a sanctuary; it is a battleground; . . . it is where I have believed—or have learned to believe—that I might someday be able to contend with all of this. No pill can help me deal with the problem of not wanting to take pills; likewise, no amount of psychotherapy alone can prevent my manias and depressions. I need both. . . .
>
> (Jamison, 1995)

Lithium and Other Mood Stabilizers

The discovery that lithium effectively reduces bipolar symptoms was, like so many other medical discoveries, quite accidental. In 1949 an Australian psychiatrist, John Cade, hypothesized that manic behavior is caused by a toxic level of uric acid in the body. He set out to test this theory by injecting guinea pigs with uric acid, but first he combined it with lithium to increase its solubility.

To Cade's surprise, the guinea pigs became not manic but quite lethargic after their injections. Cade suspected that the lithium had produced this effect. When he later administered lithium to 10 human beings who had mania, he discovered that it calmed

---

lithium A metallic element that occurs in nature as a mineral salt and is an effective treatment for bipolar disorders.

mood stabilizing drugs Psychotropic drugs that help stabilize the moods of people suffering from bipolar disorder. Also known as *antibipolar drugs*.

and normalized their mood. Many countries began using lithium for bipolar disorders soon after, but as noted earlier, it was not until 1970 that the FDA approved it.

Determining the correct lithium dosage for a given patient is a delicate process requiring careful adjustments in dose, regular analyses of blood, and urine samples and other laboratory tests (Janicak, 2016). Too low a dose will have little or no effect on the bipolar mood swings, but too high a dose can result in lithium intoxication (literally, poisoning), which can feature vomiting, diarrhea, sluggishness, tremors, seizures, kidney dysfunction, cardiac irregularities, and even death (Perrone & Chatterjee, 2016). With the correct dose, however, lithium often produces a noticeable change (Geddes & Miklowitz, 2013; Grof, 2010). Some patients respond better to the other mood stabilizing drugs, such as the antiseizure drugs *carbamazepine* (Tegretol) or *valproate* (Depakote), or to a combination of such drugs (Selle et al., 2014). And still others respond best to a combination of mood stabilizers and atypical antipsychotic drugs, medications that you will read about in Chapter 15 (Janicak, 2016; Stovall, 2016). Around 49 percent of all persons with a bipolar disorder now receive treatment in any given year (NIMH, 2017, 2014; Wang et al., 2005).

"More lithium."

Tom Cheney/The New Yorker Collection/The Cartoon Bank

Effectiveness of Lithium and Other Mood Stabilizers

All manner of research has attested to the effectiveness of lithium and other mood stabilizers in treating *manic* episodes (Stovall, 2016; Galling et al., 2015). More than 60 percent of patients with mania improve on these medications. In addition, most such patients have fewer new episodes as long as they continue taking the medications (Malhi et al., 2013). One study found that the risk of relapse is 28 times higher if patients stop taking a mood stabilizer (Suppes et al., 1991). These findings suggest that the mood stabilizers are also prophylactic drugs, ones that actually help prevent symptoms from developing. Thus, today's clinicians usually continue patients on some level of a mood stabilizing drug even after their manic episodes subside (Post, 2017).

In the limited body of research that has been done on this subject, the mood stabilizers also seem to help those with bipolar disorder overcome their *depressive*

Scott S. Hamrick/KRT/Newscom

"Sometimes Mommy cries" Lawyer and social worker Loran Kundra reads and laughs with her daughters at their home in Pennsylvania. Kundra, who has bipolar disorder, is co-founder of a program called *Child and Family Connections*, which helps parents with psychological disorders effectively discuss their disorders with their children. During a depressive episode, Kundra found herself explaining to her daughter, "Sometimes Mommy cries and gets upset just the way that you cry and get upset"—an exchange that spurred her to reach out to other persons with similar parenting issues.

Shaul Schwarz, Verbatim/Getty Images

Musical prescription During a rehearsal, musical director Ronald Braunstein conducts the Me2/Orchestra, a 50-member group that performs in concert venues around the United States. The ensemble is a key piece of *Me2/* ("me, too"), a classical music organization created exclusively for people with mental disorders. Braunstein, who himself has a diagnosis of bipolar disorder, co-founded Me2/ and the Me2/Orchestra with his wife to raise awareness about mental health issues and reduce stigma.

second messengers Chemical changes within a neuron just after the neuron receives a neurotransmitter message and just before it responds.

episodes, though to a lesser degree than they help with their manic episodes (Stovall, 2017; Malhi et al., 2013). In addition, continued doses of mood stabilizers may help reduce the risk of future depressive episodes and future suicide attempts, just as they seem to prevent the return of manic episodes (Janicak, 2016; Gao et al., 2010). Given the drugs' less powerful impact on depressive episodes, many clinicians use a combination of mood stabilizers and antidepressant drugs to treat bipolar depression, although research suggests that antidepressants may trigger manic episodes in some patients (Stovall, 2017; Bobo & Shelton, 2016).

Mode of Operation of Mood Stabilizers Researchers do not fully understand how mood stabilizing drugs reduce the symptoms of bipolar disorder (Janicak, 2016). One possibility is that the drugs change synaptic activity in neurons, but in a way different from that of antidepressant drugs. The firing of a neuron actually consists of several phases that ensue at lightning speed. When the neurotransmitter binds to a receptor on the receiving neuron, a series of changes occur *within* the receiving neuron to set the stage for firing. The substances in the neuron that carry out those changes are often called **second messengers** because they relay the original message from the receptor site to the firing mechanism of the neuron. (The neurotransmitter itself is considered the *first messenger.*) Whereas antidepressant drugs affect a neuron's initial reception of neurotransmitters, mood stabilizers appear to affect a neuron's second messengers. Different second-messenger systems are at work in different neurons, and neurons using certain kinds of second messengers have been implicated in bipolar disorder. It may be that mood stabilizers affect the messengers in those particular neurons and in so doing correct the biological abnormalities contributing to bipolar disorders (Janicak, 2016).

In a similar vein, it has been found that lithium and other mood stabilizing drugs also increase the production of a protein called *brain-derived neurotrophic factor (BDNF)* and other proteins within certain neurons whose job is to prevent cell death. The drugs may increase the health and functioning of those cells and thus reduce bipolar symptoms (Malhi et al., 2013; Gray et al., 2003).

Finally, it may be that lithium and other mood stabilizers reduce bipolar symptoms by improving the functioning of or communications between key structures in the brain (Altinay et al., 2018). In support of this possibility, it has been found that lithium actually increases the size of the hippocampus and the amount of gray matter in bipolar patients (Sun et al., 2018; Janicak, 2016). Recall from the previous chapter that bipolar individuals have a smaller hippocampus and lower amount of gray matter than other people, among other abnormalities (see page 216).

Adjunctive Psychotherapy

As Jamison stated in her memoir, psychotherapy alone is rarely helpful for persons with bipolar disorders. At the same time, clinicians have learned that mood stabilizing drugs alone are not always sufficient either. Thirty percent or more of patients with these disorders may not respond to lithium or a related drug, may not receive the proper dose, or may relapse while taking it. In addition, individuals stop taking mood stabilizers on their own because they are bothered by the drugs' unwanted effects, feel too well to recognize the need for the drugs, miss the euphoria felt during manic episodes, or worry about becoming less productive when they take the drugs (Vieta & Colom, 2017) (see *PsychWatch*).

Abnormality and Creativity: A Delicate Balance

The ancient Greeks believed that various forms of "divine madness" inspired creative acts, from poetry to performance (Ludwig, 1995). Even today many people expect "creative geniuses" to be psychologically disturbed. A popular image of the artist includes a glass of liquor, a cigarette, and a tormented expression. Classic examples include writer William Faulkner, who suffered from alcoholism and received electroconvulsive therapy for depression; poet Sylvia Plath, who was depressed for most of her life and eventually died by suicide at age 31; and dancer Vaslav Nijinsky, who suffered from schizophrenia and spent many years in institutions. In fact, a number of studies indicate that artists and writers are somewhat more likely than others to suffer from certain mental disorders, particularly bipolar disorders (Collingwood, 2016; Kyaga et al., 2013, 2011; Galvez et al., 2011).

Why might creative people be prone to such psychological disorders? Some may be predisposed to such disorders long before they begin their artistic careers (Simonton, 2010; Ludwig, 1995). Indeed, creative people often have a family history of psychological problems (Kyaga et al., 2013, 2011). A number also have experienced intense psychological trauma during childhood. English writer Virginia Woolf, for example, endured sexual abuse as a child.

A second explanation for the link between creativity and psychological disorders

AP Photo/Akira Suemori

is that the creative professions offer a welcome climate for those with psychological disturbances. In the worlds of poetry, painting, and acting, for example, emotional expression, unusual thinking, and/or personal turmoil are valued as sources of inspiration and success (Collingwood, 2016; Galvez et al., 2011).

Much remains to be learned about the relationship between emotional turmoil and creativity, but work in this area has already clarified two important points.

The price of creativity? Like a number of other writers and artists, author J. K. Rowling has had periods of depression and even suicidal feelings at certain times in her life. Here, the *Harry Potter* author looks at the laptop of a child while launching her Web project, Pottermore, at a London museum in 2011.

First, psychological disturbance is hardly a requirement for creativity. Most "creative geniuses" are, in fact, psychologically stable and happy throughout their entire lives (Rothenberg, 2015; Kaufman, 2013). Second, mild psychological disturbances relate to creative achievement much more strongly than severe disturbances do (Collingwood, 2016; Galvez et al., 2011). For example, nineteenth-century composer Robert Schumann produced 27 works during one hypomanic year but next to nothing during years when he was severely depressed and suicidal (Jamison, 1995).

Some artists worry that their creativity would disappear if their psychological suffering were to stop. In fact, however, research suggests that successful treatment for severe psychological disorders more often than not improves the creative process (Rothenberg, 2015; Jamison, 1995; Ludwig, 1995). Romantic notions aside, severe mental dysfunction has little redeeming value, in the arts or anywhere else.

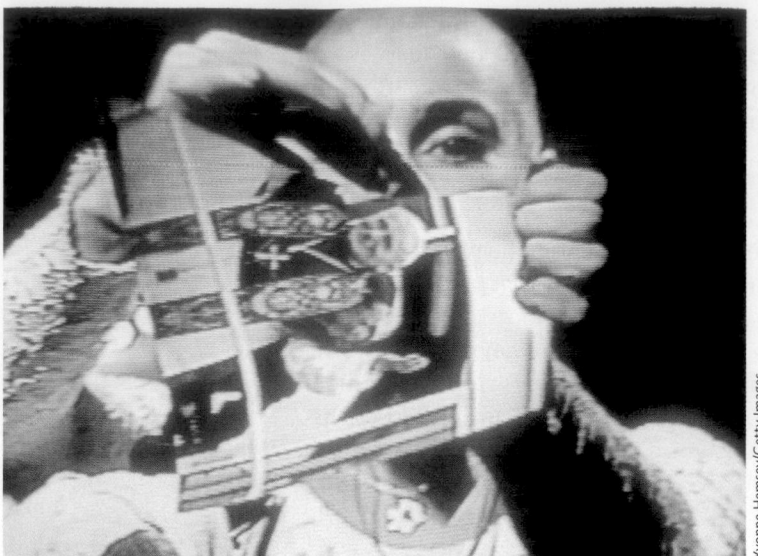
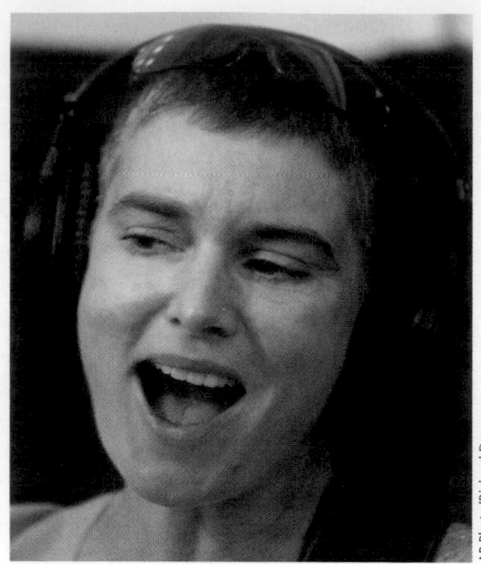

Yvonne Hemsey/Getty Images

AP Photo/Richard Drew

Seeking a correct diagnosis Throughout the 1990s, Grammy-winning Irish singer Sinead O'Connor was known for her shaved head, edgy songs, and rebelliousness. In a 1992 appearance on the TV show *Saturday Night Live*, for example, she ripped up a picture of Pope John Paul II (left) to help bring attention to the problem of sex abuse in the Catholic church. She subsequently received a diagnosis of bipolar disorder and took mood stabilizer drugs for eight years. In more recent times (right), O'Connor has learned that the bipolar diagnosis and treatment were incorrect and that she actually had been suffering from PTSD. She now speaks out about the importance of getting a proper diagnosis and obtaining opinions from multiple clinicians (Rouse, 2017; Cole, 2013).

In view of these problems, many clinicians now use individual, group, or family therapy as an *adjunct* to mood stabilizing drugs (Chu et al., 2018; Post, 2017). Most often, therapists use these formats to emphasize the importance of continuing to take medications; to improve social skills and relationships that may be affected by bipolar episodes; to educate patients and families about bipolar disorders; to help patients solve the family, school, and occupational problems caused by their disorder; and to help prevent patients from attempting suicide. Studies have found that such adjunctive therapy at least doubles the likelihood that bipolar individuals will continue to take their medications properly, and it helps reduce hospitalizations, improve social functioning, and increase patients' ability to obtain and hold a job (Vieta & Colom, 2017; Culver & Pratchett, 2010). Psychotherapy plays a more central role in the treatment of cyclothymic disorder, the mild bipolar pattern that you read about in Chapter 7. In fact, patients with cyclothymic disorder typically receive psychotherapy, alone or in combination with mood stabilizers.

With Success Come New Questions

Depressive and bipolar disorders are among the most treatable of all psychological disorders. The choice of treatment for bipolar disorders is narrow and simple: drug therapy, perhaps accompanied by psychotherapy, is the single most successful approach. The picture for unipolar depression is more varied and complex, although no less promising. Cognitive-behavioral, interpersonal, couple, drug, and brain stimulation treatments can each be helpful.

Why are several very different approaches each highly effective in the treatment of unipolar depression? It may be that since interacting factors contribute to unipolar depression, correcting dysfunction in one area helps to improve other areas of functioning as well. In fact, studies have sometimes found that when one kind of therapy is effective, clients tend to function better in all spheres. When certain antidepressant drugs are effective, for instance, clients make the same improvements in their thinking and social functioning that cognitive-behavioral or interpersonal therapy would bring about.

Whatever the ultimate explanation, the treatment picture is promising both for people with unipolar depression and for those with bipolar disorders. The odds are that one or a combination of available interventions will help relieve their symptoms. Yet the sobering fact remains that at least 40 percent of people with a mood disorder do not improve under treatment and must suffer their mania or depression until it has run its course.

♥... SUMMING UP

» **Treatments for Depressive and Bipolar Disorders** Studies suggest that many people with depressive and bipolar disorders can be helped by treatment. *p. 221*

» **Treatments for Unipolar Depression** Various treatments have been used with unipolar depression. *Psychodynamic therapists* try to help depressed clients become aware of and work through their real or imagined losses and their excessive dependence on others. *Cognitive-behavioral therapists* reintroduce clients to events and activities that they once found pleasurable, reinforce nondepressive behaviors, teach interpersonal skills, and further help the clients identify and change their dysfunctional cognitions. *Interpersonal psychotherapists* help depressed individuals develop insight into their interpersonal problems, make useful changes in the interpersonal realm, and learn skills to protect themselves in the future. Another approach, *couple therapy,* can be helpful when depressed people are in a dysfunctional relationship.

Most *biological treatments* for unipolar depression consist of antidepressant drugs, but *brain stimulation* techniques are also used for a number of depressed people, especially for those who have been unresponsive to all other forms of treatment. *Antidepressant drugs* include three classes: *MAO inhibitors, tricyclics,* and *second-generation antidepressants.* The second-generation antidepressants include *selective serotonin reuptake inhibitors,* or *SSRIs,* drugs that selectively increase the activity of serotonin. Brain stimulation techniques include *ECT, vagus nerve stimulation, transcranial magnetic stimulation,* and *deep brain stimulation.* ECT remains the most controversial procedure for unipolar depression, although it is a fast-acting intervention that is particularly effective when depression is severe, unresponsive to other kinds of treatment, or characterized by delusions. *pp. 222–239*

» **Comparing Treatments for Unipolar Depression** The cognitive-behavioral, interpersonal, and biological therapies appear to be the most effective for mild to severe depression. Combinations of psychotherapy and drug therapy are often more helpful than any one approach on its own. *pp. 239–242*

» **Treatments for Bipolar Disorders** *Lithium* and other *mood stabilizing drugs* have proved to be effective in the treatment of bipolar disorders, particularly in the reduction and prevention of manic episodes. In some cases, these drugs are combined with antidepressant drugs or certain antipsychotic drugs.

Clinicians have learned that patients with bipolar disorders may fare better when mood stabilizers are supplemented by *adjunctive psychotherapy.* The issues most often addressed by psychotherapists are medication management; social skills and relationships; education of patients; and solving the family, school, and occupational problems caused by bipolar episodes. *pp. 242–246*

Visit *LaunchPad*
to access the e-Book, Clinical Choices, videos, activities, and LearningCurve, as well as study aids including flashcards, FAQs, and research exercises.

LaunchPad
macmillan learning

♀...Suicide

The war in Iraq never ended for Jonathan Michael Boucher. Not when he flew home from Baghdad, not when he moved to Saratoga Springs for a fresh start and, especially, not when nighttime arrived.

Tortured by what he saw as an 18-year-old Army private during the 2003 invasion and occupation, Boucher was diagnosed with post-traumatic stress disorder (PTSD) and honorably discharged from the military less than two years later.

On May 15, three days before his 24th birthday, the young veteran [died by] suicide in his apartment's bathroom, stunning friends and family. . . . There was no note. . . .

Johnny Boucher joined the Army right after graduating from East Lyme High School in Connecticut in 2002 because he was emotionally moved by the Sept. 11, 2001, terrorist attacks. "He felt it was his duty to do what he could for America," his father, Steven Boucher, 50, said.

Shortly after enlisting, the 6-foot-2-inch soldier deployed with the "Wolf Pack"—1st Battalion, 41st Field Artillery—and fought his way north in Iraq. He landed with his unit at Baghdad International Airport and was responsible for helping guard it. The battalion earned a Presidential Unit Citation for "exceptional bravery and heroism in the liberation of Baghdad."

But it was during those early months of the war that Johnny Boucher had the evils of combat etched into his mind. The soldier was devastated by seeing a young Iraqi boy holding his dead father, who had been shot in the head. Later, near the airport, the soldier saw four good friends in his artillery battery killed in a vehicle accident minutes after one of them relieved him from duty, his father said.

Boucher tried to rescue the soldiers. Their deaths and other things his son saw deeply impacted his soul after he returned because he was sensitive about family and very patriotic, Steven Boucher said. . . .

But when the sun set, memories of combat and lost friends rose to the top, causing the former artilleryman severe nightmares. Sometimes he would curl up in a ball and weep, causing his parents to try to comfort him. . . . "At nighttime, he was just haunted," Steven Boucher said. . . . "Haunted, I think, by war." Bitterness about the war had crept in, and the troubled former soldier started drinking to calm himself. . . .

Supported by a huge family he adored . . . Johnny Boucher recently got his own apartment on Franklin Street and appeared to be getting back on track. He seemed to be calm and enjoying life. But it was difficult to tell, and he was still fearful of sleep, his father said. They had plans for a hike, a birthday party and attending his brother Jeffrey's graduation. . . . Then, without warning, Johnny Boucher was gone. He hanged himself next to a Bible, his Army uniform and a garden statue of an angel, said his mother, who discovered him after he failed to show up to work for two days. . . .

Yusko, 2008

Salmon spawn and then die, after an exhausting upstream swim to their breeding ground. Lemmings rush to the sea and drown. But only humans knowingly take their own lives. The actions of salmon and lemmings are instinctual responses that may even help their species survive in the long run. Only in the human act of suicide do beings act for the specific purpose of putting an end to their lives.

TABLE: 9-1

Most Common Causes of Death in the United States

Rank	Cause	Deaths per Year
1	Heart disease	614,348
2	Cancer	591,699
3	Chronic respiratory diseases	147,101
4	Accidents	136,053
5	Stroke	133,103
6	Alzheimer's	93,541
7	Diabetes	76,488
8	Pneumonia and influenza	55,227
9	Kidney disease	48,146
10	Suicide	42,773

Information from: CDC, 2017

Suicide has been recorded throughout history. The Old Testament described King Saul's suicide: "There Saul took a sword and fell on it." The ancient Chinese, Greeks, and Romans also provided examples. In more recent times, suicides by such celebrated individuals as writer Ernest Hemingway, actress Marilyn Monroe, rock star Kurt Cobain, and comedian Robin Williams both shocked and fascinated the public.

Today suicide is one of the leading causes of death in the world. By the time you finish reading this page and the next, someone in the United States will have killed himself or herself. In fact, at least 100 Americans will have taken their own lives by this time tomorrow.

It has been estimated that 1 million people die by suicide each year, more than 42,000 in the United States alone (CDC, 2017; Heron, 2016; Schreiber & Culpepper, 2016) (see **Table 9-1**). Around 25 million other people throughout the world — 650,000 in the United States—make unsuccessful attempts to kill themselves; such attempts are called **parasuicides.** Actually, it is difficult to obtain accurate figures on suicide, and many investigators believe that estimates are often low. For one thing, suicide can be difficult to distinguish from unintentional drug overdoses, automobile crashes, drownings, and other accidents. Many apparent "accidents" are probably intentional. For another, since suicide is frowned on in our society, relatives and friends often refuse to acknowledge that loved ones have taken their own lives.

Suicide is not officially classified as a mental disorder, although DSM-5's framers have proposed that a category called *suicidal behavior disorder* be studied for possible inclusion in future revisions of DSM-5. Regardless of whether suicidal acts themselves represent a distinct disorder, psychological dysfunction—a breakdown of coping skills, emotional turmoil, a distorted view of life—usually plays a role in such acts. For example, the young combat veteran about whom you read at the beginning of this chapter, had intense feelings of depression, developed a severe drinking problem, and displayed posttraumatic stress disorder. ■

||||||||||||||||||||||||||||||||||||||||||||||||||||||||||||||||||||||||||||||||||||||||||||||||||||||

What Is Suicide?

NOT EVERY SELF-INFLICTED DEATH is a suicide. A man who crashes his car into a tree after falling asleep at the steering wheel is not trying to kill himself. Thus Edwin Shneidman (2005, 1993, 1963), a pioneer in this field, defined **suicide** as an intentioned death—a self-inflicted death in which one makes an intentional, direct, and conscious effort to end one's life.

Intentioned deaths may take various forms. Consider the following examples. All three of these people intended to die, but their motives, concerns, and actions differed greatly:

Dave *was a successful man. By the age of 50 he had risen to the vice presidency of a small but profitable investment firm. He had a caring wife and two teenage sons who respected him. They lived in an upper-middle-class neighborhood, had a spacious house, and enjoyed a life of comfort.*

In August of his fiftieth year, everything changed. Dave was fired. Just like that. The economy had gone bad once again, the firm's profits were down, and the president wanted to try new, fresher investment strategies and marketing approaches. Dave had been "old school." He didn't fully understand today's investors—didn't know how to reach out to them with Web-based advertising, engage them online in the investment process, or give his firm a high-tech look. Dave's boss wanted to try a younger person.

The experience of failure, loss, and emptiness was overwhelming for Dave. He looked for another position, but found only low-paying jobs for which he was overqualified. Each day as he looked for work Dave became more depressed, anxious, and desperate. He thought of trying to start his own investment company or to be a consultant of some

parasuicide A suicide attempt that does not result in death.

suicide A self-inflicted death in which the person acts intentionally, directly, and consciously.

kind, but in the cold of night, he knew he was just fooling himself with such notions. He kept sinking, withdrew from others, and felt increasingly hopeless.

Six months after losing his job, Dave began to consider ending his life. The pain was too great, the humiliation unending. He hated the present and dreaded the future. Throughout February he went back and forth. On some days he was sure he wanted to die. On other days, an enjoyable evening or uplifting conversation might change his mind temporarily. On a Monday late in February he heard about a job possibility, and the anticipation of the next day's interview seemed to lift his spirits. But Tuesday's interview did not go well. He knew there'd be no job offer. He went home, took a recently purchased gun from his locked desk drawer, and shot himself.

Demaine never truly recovered from his mother's death. He was only seven years old and unprepared for such a loss. His father sent him to live with his grandparents for a time, to a new school with new kids and a new way of life. In Demaine's mind, all these changes were for the worse. He missed the joy and laughter of the past. He missed his home, his father, and his friends. Most of all he missed his mother.

He did not really understand her death. His father said that she was in heaven now, at peace, happy. Demaine's unhappiness and loneliness continued day after day and he began to put things together in his own way. He believed he would be happy again if he could join his mother. He felt she was waiting for him, waiting for him to come to her. The thoughts seemed so right to him; they brought him comfort and hope. One evening, shortly after saying good night to his grandparents, Demaine climbed out of bed, went up the stairs to the roof of their apartment house, and jumped to his death. In his mind he was joining his mother in heaven.

Tya and Noah had met on a speed date. On a lark, Tya and a friend had registered at the speed date event, figuring, "What's the worst thing that can happen?" On the night of the big event, Tya talked to dozens of guys, none of whom appealed to her—except for Noah! He was quirky. He was witty. And he seemed as turned off by the whole speed date thing as she was. His was the only name that she put on her list. As it turned out, he also put her name down on his list, and a week later each of them received an email with contact information about the other. A flurry of email exchanges followed, and before long, they were going together. She marveled at her luck. She had beaten the odds. She had had a successful speed date experience.

It was Tya's first serious relationship; it became her whole life. Thus she was truly shocked and devastated when, on the one-year anniversary of their speed date, Noah told her that he no longer loved her and was leaving her for someone else.

As the weeks went by, Tya was filled with two competing feelings—depression and anger. Several times she texted or called Noah, begged him to reconsider, and pleaded for a chance to win him back. At the same time, she hated him for putting her through such misery.

Tya's friends became more and more worried about her. At first they sympathized with her pain, assuming it would soon lift. But as time went on, her depression and anger worsened, and Tya began to act strangely. Always a bit of a drinker, she started to drink heavily and to mix her drinks with various kinds of drugs.

One night Tya went into her bathroom, reached for a bottle of sleeping pills, and swallowed a handful of them. She wanted to make her pain go away, and she wanted Noah to know just how much pain he had caused her. She continued swallowing pill after pill, crying and swearing as she gulped them down. When she began to feel drowsy, she decided to call her close friend Dedra. She was not sure why she was calling, perhaps to say good-bye, to explain her actions, or to make sure that Noah was told; or perhaps to be talked out of it. Dedra pleaded and reasoned with her and tried to motivate her to live. Tya was trying to listen, but she became less and less coherent. Dedra hung up the phone and quickly called Tya's neighbor and the police. When reached by her neighbor, Tya was already in a coma. Seven hours later, while her friends and family waited for news in the hospital lounge, Tya died.

#StunningComparison1

More people die by suicide (42,773) than by motor vehicle crashes (33,736) in the United States each year (CDC, 2017; Heron, 2016).

#StunningComparison2

More people die by suicide (42,773) than by homicide (15,809) in the United States each year (CDC, 2017; Heron, 2016).

While Tya seemed to have mixed feelings about her death, Dave was clear in his wish to die. Whereas Demaine viewed death as a trip to heaven, Dave saw it as an end to his existence. Such differences can be important in efforts to understand and treat suicidal persons. Accordingly, Shneidman distinguished four kinds of people who intentionally end their lives: the *death seeker, death initiator, death ignorer,* and *death darer.*

Death seekers clearly intend to end their lives at the time they attempt suicide. This singleness of purpose may last only a short time. It can change to confusion the very next hour or day, and then return again in short order. Dave, the middle-aged investment counselor, was a death seeker. He had many misgivings about suicide and was ambivalent about it for weeks, but on Tuesday night he was a death seeker—clear in his desire to die and acting in a manner that virtually guaranteed a fatal outcome.

Death initiators also clearly intend to end their lives, but they act out of a belief that the process of death is already under way and that they are simply hastening the process. Some expect that they will die in a matter of days or weeks. Many suicides among the elderly and very sick fall into this category. Robust novelist Ernest Hemingway was profoundly concerned about his failing body as he approached his sixty-second birthday—a concern that some observers believe was at the center of his suicide.

> How should clinicians decide whether to hospitalize a person who is considering suicide or even one who has made an attempt?

Death ignorers do not believe that their self-inflicted death will mean the end of their existence. They believe they are trading their present lives for a better or happier existence. Many child suicides, like Demaine's, fall into this category, as do those of adult believers in a hereafter who kill themselves to reach another form of life. In 1997, for example, the world was shocked to learn that 39 members of an unusual cult named Heaven's Gate had died by suicide at an expensive house outside San Diego. It turned out that these members had acted out of the belief that their deaths would free their spirits and enable them to ascend to a "higher kingdom."

Death darers experience mixed feelings, or ambivalence, about their intent to die, even at the moment of their attempt, and they show this ambivalence in the act itself. Although to some degree they wish to die, and they often do die, their risk-taking behavior does not guarantee death. The person who plays Russian roulette—that is, pulls the trigger of a revolver randomly loaded with one bullet—is a death darer. Tya might be considered a death darer. Although her unhappiness and anger were great, she was not sure that she wanted to die. Even while taking pills, she called her friend, reported her actions, and listened to her friend's pleas.

Death darers? A teenager jumps from one high rooftop to another, performing flips and other creative moves along the way, all part of the extremely dangerous "sport" called Parkour, or Freerunning. Are practitioners of this increasingly popular activity searching for new challenges or highs, as many of them claim, or are some actually death darers?

NurPhoto/NurPhoto via Getty Images

When people play *indirect, covert, partial,* or *unconscious* roles in their own deaths, Shneidman (2001, 1993, 1981) classified them in a suicide-like category called **subintentional deaths.** Traditionally, clinicians have cited drug, alcohol, or tobacco use, recurrent physical fighting, and medication mismanagement as behaviors that may contribute to subintentional deaths. Obviously, these kinds of behaviors are dangerous in their own right. Moreover, researchers have found a correlation between regularly engaging in such behaviors and later attempts at suicide (Ammerman et al., 2016; Juan et al., 2011).

In recent years, another behavioral pattern, *self-injury* or *self-mutilation,* has been added to this list—for example, cutting or burning oneself or banging one's head. Although this pattern is not officially classified as a mental disorder, the framers of DSM-5 have proposed that a category called *nonsuicidal self-injury* be studied for possible inclusion in future revisions of DSM-5.

Self-injurious behavior is more common than previously recognized, particularly among teenagers and young adults, and it may be on the increase (Plener et al., 2016; Rodav et al., 2014). Studies suggest that 17 percent of all adolescents try to injure themselves at least once (Brown & Plener, 2017). It appears that the behavior becomes addictive in nature. The pain brought on by self-injury seems to offer some relief from tension or other kinds of emotional suffering, the behavior serves as a temporary distraction from problems, and the scars that result may document the person's distress (Skodol, 2017). More generally, self-injury may help a person deal with chronic feelings of emptiness, boredom, and identity confusion. Although self-injury and the other risky behaviors mentioned earlier may indeed represent an indirect attempt at suicide (Victor & Klonsky, 2014), the true intent behind them is unclear, so, for the most part, these behaviors are not included in the discussions of this chapter.

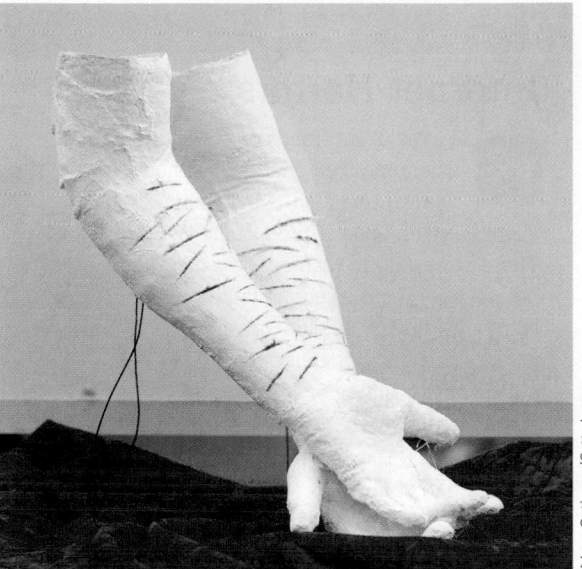

Creative expression At least 17 percent of teenagers and young adults purposely injure themselves, particularly by skin cutting (MHA, 2017). Thus, Olivia Stewart, a high school student in Colorado, chose mental illness as the topic for her senior project and produced this remarkable sculpture on self-mutilation. Stewart, whose project also featured art representations of other psychological disorders, hopes that her work will help increase education and public awareness regarding mental disorders.

How Is Suicide Studied?

Suicide researchers face a major obstacle: the people they study are no longer alive. How can investigators draw accurate conclusions about the intentions, feelings, and circumstances of those who can no longer explain their actions? Two research methods attempt to deal with this problem, each with only partial success.

One strategy is **retrospective analysis,** a kind of psychological autopsy in which clinicians and researchers piece together data from the suicide victim's past (Lin et al., 2016). Relatives, friends, therapists, or physicians may remember past statements, conversations, and behaviors that shed light on a suicide. Retrospective information may also be provided by the suicide notes that some victims leave behind. However, such sources of information are not always available or reliable (Stack & Rockett, 2016). Many suicide victims do not leave notes. Moreover, a grieving, perhaps guilt-ridden relative or a distraught therapist may be incapable of objective recollections or simply reluctant to discuss an act that is so stigmatizing in our society (Fouet, 2017).

Because of these limitations, many researchers also use a second strategy—*studying people who survive their suicide attempts.* It is estimated that there are 12 nonfatal suicide attempts for every fatal suicide (AFSP, 2017). However, it may be that people who survive suicide attempts differ in important ways from those who do not. Many of them may not really have wanted to die, for example. Nevertheless, suicide researchers have found it useful to study survivors of suicide attempts, and this chapter shall consider those who attempt suicide and those who complete suicide as more or less alike.

Patterns and Statistics

Suicide happens within a larger social setting (see *Trending*), and researchers have gathered many statistics regarding the social contexts in which such deaths take place. They have found, for example, that suicide rates vary from country to country

death seeker A person who clearly intends to end his or her life while attempting suicide.

death initiator A person who attempts suicide believing that the process of death is already under way and that he or she is simply hastening the process.

death ignorer A person who attempts suicide without recognizing the finality of death.

death darer A person who is ambivalent about the wish to die even while attempting suicide.

subintentional death A death in which the victim plays an indirect, hidden, partial, or unconscious role.

retrospective analysis A psychological autopsy in which clinicians piece together information about a person's suicide from the person's past.

Internet Horrors

Two current trends on the Internet have produced enormous concern.

One trend is the increasing availability and use of *pro-suicide Web sites*. These sites vary in their specific messages, but many of them celebrate former users who have died by suicide, others help set up appointments for joint or partner suicides, and several offer specific instructions about suicide methods, prospective suicide locations, and the writing of suicide notes (Minkkinen et al., 2017, 2016; Thornton et al., 2017; De Rosa et al., 2011).

The sites have spread across the Internet—on Web forums and chat groups; on social networks such as Facebook, Instagram, Tumblr, and Live Journal; and on video platforms such as YouTube and Vimeo (Miguel et al., 2017). Clinicians are greatly concerned that they seem to be growing in number and negative influence, especially among teenagers and young adults (Minkkinen et al., 2017). By some estimates, these sites may have tripled over the past seven years (Morris, 2017). According to one study, 7.5 percent of teenagers seek out information about suicide on the Internet (Mars et al., 2015). While most such individuals access sites offering help, constructive advice, or support, more than a third of them further access sites that provide information on how to hurt or kill oneself.

Many social networks are trying to detect and delete pro-suicide material and groups. However, as with the pro-anorexia Web sites that you'll be reading about in Chapter 11, the pro-suicide sites keep resurfacing and even multiplying under new hashtags that disguise their intent. In addition, many pro-suicide online communities readily adapt to efforts at regulation by using intentional misspellings and ambiguous headers and search terms.

A second trend of great concern is the live-streaming of suicides. On January 22, 2017, a 14-year-old girl named Nakia Venant hanged herself in her Florida bathroom while live-streaming the act on Facebook (see photo). Nakia had a long history of significant behavioral problems, as well as a background of being physically abused and

SAT AT 10:28 PM

Would Uu Like Me More Dead?? 😔😔

no df Neva say that

I Dont Wanna Live No More😔😔😔

wat happen

Im Just Tired My Life Pointless I Don't Wanna Do This AnyMore

tell me wat happen fr

A tragic end On January 22, 2017, 14-year-old Nakia Venant broadcast her suicide on Facebook while sending and receiving texts—one of at least three suicides that were live streamed in the United States that same month.

rejected. She had been in and out of numerous foster care homes for the previous eight years (Barnes, 2017; Miller & Burch, 2017). Just months before her suicide, the teen had texted her biological mother seeking to return home, but such a return never took place.

Although precise numbers are not yet available, live streaming of suicides is clearly on the rise (Reidenberg, 2017). Indeed, Nakia was the third person in the United States to broadcast her suicide on social media that same month (Bever, 2017). Public suicides are not new, but they have never before been able to reach so many viewers. Clinicians do not really know why certain people attempt suicide online. Some propose that, in addition to being in great psychological pain, the individuals may be trying to display their pain to others, memorialize their death, or solicit interventions by others (Bever, 2017).

Worried about the increase in broadcast suicides and the possible risk of copycat deaths, Facebook has recently taken steps to help prevent both live-streamed and other forms of suicides. First, it has updated tools to make it easier for users to alert Facebook about suicide and self-harm postings that may come their way (O'Brien, 2017; Schuster, 2016). Upon receiving such alerts, Facebook offers immediate guidance and resources to the concerned friends or acquaintances, for example, providing them with tips on how to talk with a suicidal friend or

how to contact a mental health professional through a lifeline. In cases of live streaming, Facebook also tries to help the streamers more directly (Harris, 2017). The screens of the streamers are partially blocked by a message that says, "Someone thinks you might need extra support right now and asked us to help." In turn, the streamer can contact a suicide helpline, view tips from Facebook, and/or text a friend directly from their window (Harris, 2017).

Facebook also now makes it possible for troubled individuals to immediately chat with a trained counselor from the National Suicide Prevention Lifeline, Crisis Text Line, and other crisis support organizations through its *Facebook Messenger* platform (Guynn, 2017). In addition, the social networking service is currently testing the use of pattern recognition software to help identify self-harm and suicide warning signals in user posts and comments. The network's community monitor team then acts proactively by reaching out to the posters and beyond (Harris, 2017).

The sincere and concentrated efforts of social networking services regarding both live-streamed and other forms of suicide are very welcome indeed. Rather than passively observing as the power of the Internet contributes to suicidal acts or other mental health problems, these networks are now trying to use their extraordinary influence to save lives and identify people at risk.

(WHO, 2017). Sri Lanka, Guyana, South Korea, Lithuania, and Angola have very high rates—more than 20 suicides annually per 100,000 persons; conversely, Egypt, Mexico, Greece, and Indonesia have relatively low rates, fewer than 5 per 100,000. Falling in between are England (7.4), China (8.5), Germany (9.1), Canada (10.4), the United States (12.6), and Russia (17.9).

Religious affiliation and beliefs may help account for these national differences (Foo et al., 2014). For example, countries that are largely Catholic, Jewish, or Muslim tend to have low suicide rates. Perhaps in these countries, strict prohibitions against suicide or a strong religious tradition deter many people from attempting suicide. Yet there are exceptions to this tentative rule. Poland, a largely Roman Catholic country, has a suicide rate of 18.5 suicides per 100,000 persons, one of the higher suicide rates in the world (WHO, 2017).

> **What factors besides religious affiliation and beliefs might help account for national variations in suicide rates?**

Research is beginning to suggest that religious doctrine may not help prevent suicide as much as the degree of an individual's *devoutness*. Regardless of their particular persuasion, very religious people seem less likely to die by suicide (Kralovec et al., 2018; Cook, 2014).

The suicide rates of men and women also differ. Three times as many women *attempt* suicide as men, yet men die from their attempts at more than three times the rate of women (AFSP, 2017; CDC, 2013). Although various explanations have been proposed for this gender difference, a popular one points to the different methods used by men and women (Anestis & Houtsma, 2018; Anestis et al., 2017). Men tend to use more violent methods, such as shooting, stabbing, or hanging themselves, whereas women use less violent methods, such as drug overdose. Guns are used in 62 percent of the male suicides in the United States, compared with 37 percent of the female suicides (Schreiber & Culpepper, 2016; CDC, 2014).

Suicide is also related to social environment and marital status. Studies suggest that at least half of individuals who carry out suicide are socially isolated and have few or no close personal friends, although they may be active on social network sites (Berman, 2018; Maris, 2001). In a related vein, research has revealed that never-married and divorced persons have a higher suicide rate than married or cohabiting individuals (Schreiber & Culpepper, 2016).

Finally, in the United States at least, suicide rates seem to vary according to race and ethnicity (see **Figure 9-1**). The overall suicide rate of non-Hispanic white Americans is more than twice as high as that of African Americans, Hispanic Americans, and Asian Americans (AFSP, 2017; CDC, 2016). A major exception to this pattern is the suicide rate of American Indians, which is higher than that of non-Hispanic white Americans. Although the extreme poverty of many American Indians may partly explain their high suicide rate, studies show that factors such as alcohol use, modeling, and the availability of guns may also play a role (Dillard et al., 2017; Lanier, 2010). In addition to differences across racial groups, researchers have found that suicide rates sometimes differ within groups. Among Hispanic Americans, for example, Puerto Ricans are significantly more likely to attempt suicide than any other Hispanic American group (Baca-Garcia et al., 2011).

Some of these statistics on suicide have been questioned. Analyses suggest, for example, that the actual rate of suicide may be 15 percent higher for African Americans and 6 percent higher for women than usually reported (Barnes, 2010; Phillips & Ruth, 1993). People in these groups are more likely than others to use methods of suicide that can be mistaken for causes of accidental death, such as poisoning, drug overdose, single-car crashes, and pedestrian accidents.

#MaritalImpact

Statistically, never-married people have the highest risk of suicide, followed in descending order by previously married people (widowed, separated, divorced), married persons without children, and married persons with children (Schreiber & Culpepper, 2016).

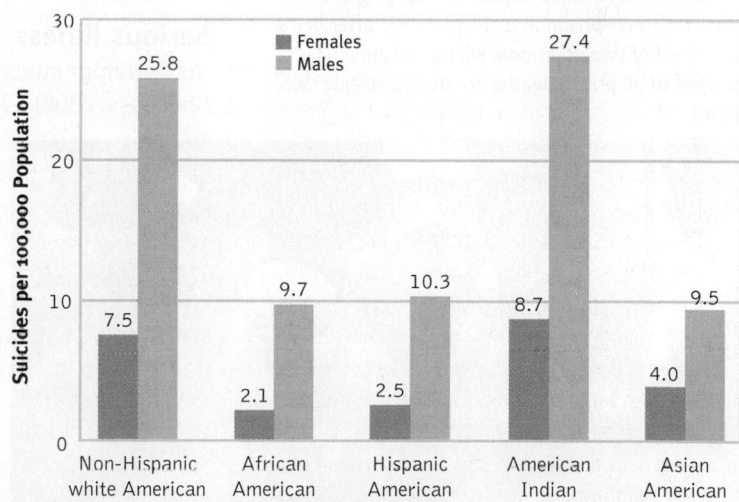

FIGURE 9-1

Suicide, Race, and Gender

In the United States, American Indians have the highest suicide rates among both males and females. (Information from: AFSP, 2017; CDC, 2016, 2014, 2010; SPRC, 2013.)

What Triggers a Suicide?

SUICIDAL ACTS MAY BE CONNECTED TO recent events or current conditions in a person's life. Although such factors may not be the basic motivation for the suicide, they can precipitate it. Common triggering factors include *stressful events, mood and thought changes, alcohol and other drug use, mental disorders,* and *modeling*.

Stressful Events and Situations

Researchers have counted more stressful events in the recent lives of suicide attempters than in the lives of nonattempters (McFeeters et al., 2015; Pompili et al., 2011). One stressor that has been consistently linked to suicide is combat stress. Research indicates that combat veterans from various wars are more than twice as likely to die by suicide as nonveterans (Nock et al., 2017, 2014, 2013). At the beginning of this chapter, for example, you read about a young man who killed himself upon returning to civilian life, after experiencing the enormous stressors of combat in Iraq.

The stressors that help lead to suicide do not need to be as horrific as those tied to combat. Common forms of *immediate stress* seen in cases of suicide are the loss of a loved one through death, divorce, or rejection (Roskar et al., 2011); loss of a job (Milner el al., 2014); significant financial loss (Houle & Light, 2014); and stress caused by hurricanes, earthquakes, or other natural disasters, even among very young children (Fujiwara et al., 2017). People may also attempt suicide in response to *long-term* rather than recent stress. Four such stressors are particularly common—social isolation, serious illness, an abusive environment, and occupational stress.

Social Isolation As you saw in the cases of Dave, Demaine, and Tya, people from loving families or supportive social systems may carry out suicide. However, those without such social supports are particularly vulnerable to suicidal thinking and actions. Researchers have found a heightened risk for suicidal behavior among those who feel little sense of "belongingness," believe that they have limited or no social support, live alone, and have ongoing conflicts with other people (Schreiber & Culpepper, 2016; You et al., 2011).

Serious Illness People whose illnesses cause them great pain or severe disability may attempt suicide, believing that death is unavoidable and imminent (Schneider & Shenassa, 2008). They may also believe that the suffering and problems caused by their illnesses are more than they can endure. Studies suggest that as many as one-third of those who die by suicide have been in poor physical health during the months prior to their suicidal acts (Schreiber & Culpepper, 2016). Illnesses that have been linked to higher suicide rates include cancer, heart disease, chronic lung disease, stroke, and diabetes mellitus (Bartoli et al., 2017; Conti et al., 2017; Zhang et al., 2017).

Abusive or Repressive Environment Victims of an abusive or repressive environment from which they have little or no hope of escape sometimes pursue suicide. For example, some prisoners of war, inmates of concentration camps, abused spouses, abused children, and prison inmates try to end their lives (Vadini et al., 2018; Ayhan et al, 2017). Like those who have serious illnesses, these people may feel that they can endure no more suffering and believe that there is no hope for improvement in their condition.

Occupational Stress Some jobs create feelings of tension or dissatisfaction that may trigger suicide attempts. Studies have

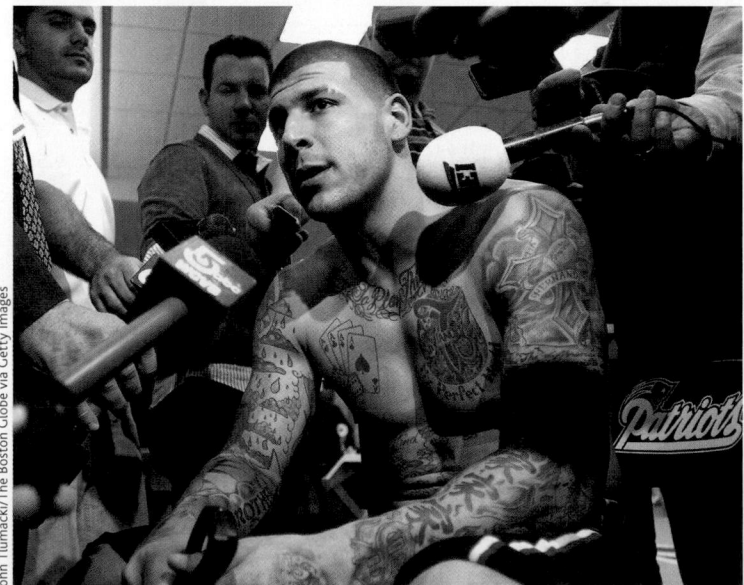

Famous prison suicide In 2015, Aaron Hernandez, a star tight end in the National Football League, was convicted of first-degree murder and sentenced to life in prison without parole for the 2013 killing of an acquaintance. Hernandez, shown here at a locker room press interview during his playing days, killed himself by hanging at a Massachusetts prison in 2017, just days after being acquitted of two additional killings. Around 11 percent of all prison deaths are due to suicide (BJS, 2016).

John Tlumacki/The Boston Globe via Getty Images

revealed higher suicide rates among people working in unskilled occupations. For persons in skilled occupations, research has found relatively high rates for psychiatrists and psychologists, physicians, nurses, dentists, lawyers, police officers, fire fighters, emergency workers, and farmers (Mckew, 2017; Witt et al., 2017; Milner et al., 2013). Of course, such correlations do not necessarily mean that occupational pressures directly cause suicidal actions. Perhaps unskilled workers are responding to financial insecurity rather than job stress when they attempt suicide. Similarly, rather than reacting to the emotional strain of their work, suicidal psychiatrists and psychologists may have long-standing emotional problems that stimulated their career interest in the first place.

Mood and Thought Changes

Many suicide attempts are preceded by a change in mood. The change may not be severe enough to warrant a diagnosis of a mental disorder, but it does represent a significant shift from the person's past mood. The most common change is an increase in sadness (Kim et al., 2015). Also common are increases in feelings of anxiety, tension, frustration, anger, or shame (Reisch et al., 2010). In fact, Shneidman (2005, 2001) believed that the key to suicide is "psychache," a feeling of psychological pain that seems intolerable to the person. A study of 88 patients found that those who scored higher on a measure called the Psychological Pain Assessment Scale were indeed more likely than others to carry out suicide (Pompili et al., 2008).

Suicide attempts may also be preceded by shifts in patterns of thinking. People may become preoccupied with their problems, lose perspective, and see suicide as the only effective solution to their difficulties (Schreiber & Culpepper, 2016; Shneidman, 2005, 2001). They often develop a sense of **hopelessness**—a pessimistic belief that their present circumstances, problems, or mood will not change (Sun et al., 2018). In fact, one study found that people who generally expressed feelings of hopelessness were 11 times more likely to die by suicide over a 13-year follow-up period than people who did not feel hopeless (Kuo et al., 2004). Thus, some clinicians believe that a feeling of hopelessness is the single most likely indicator of suicidal intent, and they take special care to look for signs of hopelessness when they assess the risk of suicide (Rosellini & Bagge, 2014).

Many people who attempt suicide fall victim to **dichotomous thinking,** viewing problems and solutions in rigid either/or terms (Shneidman, 2005, 2001, 1993). Indeed, Shneidman said that the "four-letter word" in suicide is "only," as in "suicide was the *only* thing I could do" (Maris, 2001). In the following statement a woman who survived her leap from a building describes her dichotomous thinking at the time. She saw death as the only alternative to her pain:

> *I was so desperate. I felt, my God, I couldn't face this thing. Everything was like a terrible whirlpool of confusion. And I thought to myself: There's only one thing to do. I just have to lose consciousness. That's the only way to get away from it. The only way to lose consciousness, I thought, was to jump off something good and high. . . .*
>
> (Shneidman, 1987, p. 56)

Alcohol and Other Drug Use

Studies indicate that as many as 70 percent of the people who attempt suicide drink alcohol just before they do so (Crosby et al., 2009; McCloud et al., 2004). Autopsies reveal that about one-quarter of these people are legally intoxicated (Schreiber & Culpepper,

Acting happy Fans of megastar, comedian, and actor Robin Williams were shocked when he killed himself by hanging in 2014. Close friends reported that Williams had been battling depression and the early stages of Parkinson's disease for some time—a painful emotional state that he managed to conceal from the public with his joyful performances. Williams' autopsy also revealed a type of neurocognitive disorder called Lewy body disease.

Kevin Winter/Getty Images

hopelessness A pessimistic belief that one's present circumstances, problems, or mood will not change.

dichotomous thinking Viewing problems and solutions in rigid either/or terms.

TABLE: 9-2

Common Predictors of Suicide

1. Depressive disorder and certain other mental disorders
2. Alcoholism and other forms of substance abuse
3. Suicidal ideation, talk, preparation; certain religious ideas
4. Prior suicide attempts
5. Availability of lethal weapons
6. Social withdrawal, isolation, living alone, loss of support
7. Hopelessness, feeling trapped, cognition rigidity
8. Impulsivity and risk-taking behavior
9. Being an older white American male
10. Modeling, suicide in the family, genetics
11. Economic or work problems; certain occupations
12. Martital problems, family pathology
13. Dramatic changes in mood
14. Anxiety
15. Stress and stressful events
16. Anger, aggression, irritability
17. Psychosis
18. Physical illness
19. Sleep problems.

Information from: Kennebeck & Bonin, 2017, 2016; Schreiber & Culpepper, 2016; Crump et al., 2014; Ferrari et al., 2014; Rudd et al., 2006; Papolos et al., 2005.

2016; Flavin et al., 1990). Moreover, the more intoxicated suicide attempters are, the more lethal their chosen suicide method (Park et al., 2017). It may be that the use of alcohol lowers a person's inhibitions, reduces his or her fears of suicide, releases underlying aggressive feelings, or impairs judgment and problem-solving ability. Research shows that the use of other kinds of drugs may have a similar tie to suicide, particularly in teenagers and young adults (Darke et al., 2005).

Mental Disorders

Although people who attempt suicide may be troubled or anxious, they do not necessarily have a psychological disorder. Nevertheless, the vast majority of all suicide attempters do have such a disorder (Schreiber & Culpepper, 2016; Nock et al., 2013). Research suggests that as many as 70 percent of all suicide attempters had been experiencing severe *depression* (unipolar or bipolar), 20 percent *chronic alcoholism,* and 10 percent *schizophrenia* (see **Table 9-2**). Correspondingly, as many as 25 percent of people with each of these disorders try to kill themselves. People who are both depressed and substance-dependent seem particularly prone to suicidal impulses (Harford et al., 2018; Bohnert et al., 2017). Certain anxiety disorders, including posttraumatic stress disorder and panic disorder, have also been linked to suicide (Rappaport et al., 2014), but in most cases of suicide these disorders occur in conjunction with a depressive disorder, a substance use disorder, or schizophrenia (Ishii et al., 2014; Bryan & Corso, 2011). It is also the case that many people with borderline personality disorder, a broad pattern that you will read about in Chapter 16, try to harm themselves or make suicidal gestures as part of their disorder (Soloff & Chiappetta, 2018; Skodol, 2017).

As you saw in Chapter 7, people with major depressive disorder often have suicidal thoughts. Indeed, one review in the United States found that treatments for depression consistently reduce the rate of suicidal thinking, attempts, and completions among patients (Sakinofsky, 2011). Even when depressed people are showing improvements in mood, they may remain at high risk for suicide. In fact, among those who are severely depressed, the risk of suicide may actually increase as their mood improves and they have more energy to act on their suicidal wishes.

Death of a "gentle giant" A popular finalist on the television show *MasterChef,* Josh Marks is seen working here on one of his culinary masterpieces. In 2013, just a short time after leaving the show, Marks shot himself to death. Affectionately known to viewers as the "gentle giant" because of his 7-foot-2 frame mixed with a mild manner, Marks suffered from both bipolar disorder and schizophrenia—a pair of disorders that contributed to his act of self-destruction.

Greg Gayne/© Fox/Courtesy: Everett Collection

Parallel journeys In 1994 rock star Kurt Cobain *(left)*, leader of the grunge band Nirvana, shot himself to death at age 27, shaking millions of young fans to their core. In 2017, rock star Chris Cornell *(right)*, a contemporary of Cobain's and lead singer in the grunge band Soundgarden, hanged himself at age 52. Cornell's suicide, occurring 23 years after Cobain's, stunned and disheartened many of the same (now middle-aged) fans.

Recall, for example, the combat veteran whose case opened this chapter. Just before he ended his life, he had seemed to be calm and enjoying life again, according to family members and friends.

Severe depression also may play a key role in suicide attempts made by those with serious physical illnesses (Werth, 2004; Brown et al., 1986). A study of 44 patients with terminal illnesses revealed that fewer than one-quarter of them had thoughts of suicide or wished for an early death and that those who did were all suffering from major depressive disorder.

A number of the people who drink alcohol or use drugs just before a suicide attempt actually have a long history of abusing such substances (Agrawal et al., 2017; Mukamal, 2016; Kim et al., 2015). The basis for the link between substance use disorders and suicide is not clear. Perhaps the tragic lifestyle of many persons with these disorders or their sense of being hopelessly trapped by a substance leads to suicidal thinking. Alternatively, a third factor—psychological pain, for instance, or desperation—may cause both substance abuse and suicidal thinking. Such people may be caught in a downward spiral: they are driven toward substance use by psychological pain or loss, only to find themselves caught in a pattern of substance abuse that aggravates rather than solves their problems.

People with schizophrenia, as you will see in Chapter 14, may hear voices that are not actually present (hallucinations) or hold beliefs that are clearly false and perhaps bizarre (delusions). The popular notion is that when such people kill themselves, they must be responding to an imagined voice commanding them to do so or to a delusion that suicide is a grand and noble gesture. Research indicates, however, that suicides by people with schizophrenia and other disorders featuring psychosis more often reflect feelings of demoralization, a sense of being entrapped by their disorder, and fears of further mental deterioration (Owen et al., 2018; Meltzer, 2011). Many young and unemployed people with schizophrenia who have had relapses over several years come to believe that the disorder will forever disrupt their lives. Still others seem to be disheartened by their substandard living conditions. Suicide is the leading cause of premature death among people with schizophrenia.

Modeling: The Contagion of Suicide

It is not unusual for people, particularly teenagers, to attempt suicide after observing or reading about someone else who has done so (Vitelli, 2016; Hagihara et al., 2014). Perhaps they have been struggling with major problems and the other person's suicide

#EconomicImpact

The annual cost of suicide deaths in the United States is $51 billion (lost wages and work productivity) (AFSP, 2017).

seems to reveal a possible solution, or perhaps they have been thinking about suicide and the other person's suicide seems to give them permission or finally persuades them to act. Either way, one suicidal act apparently serves as a *model* for another. Suicides by family members and friends, those by celebrities, other highly publicized suicides, and those by coworkers or colleagues are particularly common triggers.

Family Members and Friends A recent suicide by a family member or friend increases the likelihood that a person will attempt suicide (Ali et al., 2011). Of course, the death of a family member or friend, especially when self-inflicted, is a life-changing event, and suicidal thoughts or attempts may be tied largely to that trauma or sense of loss. Indeed, such losses typically have a lifelong impact on surviving relatives and friends, including a heightened risk of suicide that can continue for years (Schreiber & Culpepper, 2016; Roy, 2011). However, even when researchers factor out these issues, they find increases in the risk of suicide among the relatives and friends of people who recently committed suicide (Ali et al., 2011). This additional risk factor is often called the *social contagion effect*.

Celebrities Research suggests that suicides by entertainers, political figures, and other well-known people are regularly followed by unusual increases in the number of suicides across the nation (Sanger-Katz, 2014; Queinec et al., 2011). A classic study on this issue found, for example, that the national suicide rate rose 12 percent during the week after the suicide of actress Marilyn Monroe in 1963 (Phillips, 1974).

Other Highly Publicized Cases Suicides with bizarre or unusual aspects often receive intense coverage by the news media. Such highly publicized accounts may lead to similar suicides (Vitelli, 2016; Hagihara et al., 2014). During the year after a widely publicized, politically motivated suicide by self-burning in England, for example, 82 other people set themselves on fire, with equally fatal results (Ashton & Donnan, 1981). Inquest reports revealed that most of those people had histories of emotional problems and that none of the suicides had the political motivation of the publicized suicide. The imitators seemed to be responding to their own problems in a manner triggered by the suicide they had observed or read about.

Some clinicians argue that more responsible reporting could reduce this frightening impact of highly publicized suicides (Sullivan et al., 2015). A careful approach to reporting was seen in the media's coverage of the suicide of Kurt Cobain. MTV's repeated theme on the evening of the suicide was "Don't do it!" In fact, thousands of young people called MTV and other radio and television stations in the hours after Cobain's death, upset, frightened, and in some cases suicidal. Some of the stations responded by posting the phone numbers of suicide prevention centers, presenting interviews with suicide experts, and offering counseling services and advice directly to callers. Perhaps because of such efforts, the usual rate of suicide both in Seattle, where Cobain lived, and elsewhere held steady during the weeks that followed (Colburn, 1996).

Eye of the storm In a celebrated case, the British press blamed the music of the former emo group My Chemical Romance for the suicide of a 13-year-old girl in 2008. For years, the lyrics and melodies of various songs have been pointed to as negative influences, particularly on teenagers, that can contribute to suicide attempts. However, little research has been conducted on this issue and lawsuits making such claims have typically been dismissed.

Tim Mosenfelder/Getty Images

Coworkers and Colleagues The word-of-mouth publicity that attends suicides in a school, workplace, or small community may trigger suicide attempts. The suicide of a recruit at a U.S. Navy training school, for example, was followed within 2 weeks by another and also by an attempted suicide at the school. To head off what threatened to become a suicide epidemic, the school began a program of staff education on suicide and group therapy sessions for recruits who had been close to the suicide victims

Not just another bridge This man, one of only 26 people to survive jumping off the Golden Gate Bridge, returns to the site of his suicide attempt—made at the age of 19. The bridge is believed to be the site of more jumping suicides than any other location in the world—with an estimated 1,500 suicides since the bridge opened in 1937.

(Grigg, 1988). Today, a number of schools, for individuals of all ages, put into action programs of this kind after a student dies by suicide (Joshi et al., 2015). Such postsuicide programs are often referred to by clinicians as *postvention*.

What Are the Underlying Causes of Suicide?

MOST PEOPLE FACED WITH DIFFICULT situations never try to kill themselves. In an effort to understand why some people are more prone to suicide than others, theorists have proposed more fundamental explanations for self-destructive actions than the immediate triggers considered in the previous section. The leading theories come from the psychodynamic, sociocultural, and biological models. Some of these hypotheses have, however, received limited research support and fail to address the full range of suicidal acts. Thus the clinical field currently lacks a satisfactory understanding of suicide.

The Psychodynamic View

Many psychodynamic theorists believe that suicide results from depression and from anger at others that is redirected toward oneself. This theory was first stated by Wilhelm Stekel at a meeting in Vienna in 1910, when he proclaimed that "no one kills himself who has not wanted to kill another or at least wished the death of another" (Shneidman, 1979). Some years later Sigmund Freud (1920) wrote, "No neurotic harbors thoughts of suicide which he has not turned back upon himself from murderous impulses against others." Agreeing with this notion, the influential psychiatrist Karl Menninger called suicide "murder in the 180th degree."

As you read in Chapter 7, Freud (1917) and Abraham (1916, 1911) proposed that when people experience the real or symbolic loss of a loved one, they come to "introject" the lost person; that is, they unconsciously incorporate the person into their own identity and feel toward themselves as they had felt toward the other. For a short while, negative feelings toward the lost loved one are experienced as self-hatred. Anger toward the loved one may turn into intense anger against oneself and finally into depression. Suicide is thought to be an extreme expression of this self-hatred and self-punishment

#LegallyCulpable

In 2017, a Massachusetts judge found a young woman guilty of involuntary manslaughter in the suicide death of her boyfriend. She had sent the boyfriend numerous text messages urging him to kill himself prior and right up to his death.

(Campbell, 2010). The following description of a suicidal patient demonstrates how such forces may operate:

> *A 27-year-old conscientious and responsible woman took a knife to her wrists to punish herself for being tyrannical, unreliable, self-centered, and abusive. She was perplexed and frightened by this uncharacteristic self-destructive episode and was enormously relieved when her therapist pointed out that her invective described her recently deceased father much better than it did herself.*
>
> *(Gill, 1982, p. 15)*

#DestructiveChords

Suicides by Rock Musicians During the Past Decade

Vince Welnick, keyboardist (2006)

Brad Delp, singer (2007)

Johnny Lee Jackson, rapper (2008)

Vic Chesnutt, singer/songwriter (2009)

Mark Linkous, singer/songwriter/musician (2010)

Ronnie Montrose, guitarist (2012)

Bob Welch, guitarist/singer/songwriter (2012)

Chris Cornell, singer/songwriter/musician (2017)

Chester Bennington, singer/songwriter (2017)

In support of Freud's view, researchers have often found a relationship between childhood losses—real or symbolic—and later suicidal behaviors (Alonzo et al., 2014). A classic study of 200 family histories, for example, found that early parental loss was much more common among suicide attempters (48 percent) than among nonsuicidal individuals (24 percent) (Adam, Bouckoms, & Streiner, 1982). Common forms of loss were death of the father and divorce or separation of the parents. Similarly, a study of 343 depressed individuals found that those who had felt rejected or neglected as children by their parents were more likely than other people to attempt suicide as adults (Ehnvall et al., 2008).

Late in his career, Freud proposed that human beings have a basic "death instinct." He called this instinct *Thanatos* and said that it opposes the "life instinct." According to Freud, while most people learn to redirect their death instinct by aiming it toward others, suicidal people, caught in a web of self-anger, direct it squarely toward themselves.

Sociological findings are consistent with this explanation of suicide. National suicide rates have been found to drop in times of war (Thomas & Gunnell, 2010; Maris, 2001), when, one could argue, people are encouraged to direct their self-destructive energy against "the enemy." In addition, in many parts of the world, societies with high rates of homicide tend to have low rates of suicide, and vice versa (Bills & Li, 2005). However, research has failed to establish that suicidal people are in fact dominated by intense feelings of anger. Although hostility is an important element in some suicides, several studies find that other emotional states are even more prevalent (Conner & Weisman, 2011).

By the end of his career, Freud himself expressed dissatisfaction with his theory of suicide. Other psychodynamic theorists have also challenged his ideas over the years, yet themes of loss and self-directed aggression generally remain at the center of most psychodynamic explanations (King, 2003).

Durkheim's Sociocultural View

Toward the end of the nineteenth century, Emile Durkheim (1897), a sociologist, developed a broad theory of suicidal behavior. Today this theory continues to be influential and is often supported by research (Fernquist, 2007). According to Durkheim, the probability of suicide is determined by how attached a person is to such social groups as the family, religious institutions, and community. The more thoroughly a person belongs, the lower the risk of suicide. Conversely, people who have poor relationships with their society are at higher risk of killing themselves. He defined several categories of suicide, including *egoistic, altruistic,* and *anomic* suicide.

> **Why might towns and countries in past times have been inclined to punish both those who attempted suicide and their relatives?**

Egoistic suicides are carried out by people over whom society has little or no control. These people are not concerned with the norms or rules of society, nor are they integrated into the social fabric. According to Durkheim, this kind of suicide is more

In the service of others According to Emile Durkheim, people who intentionally sacrifice their lives for others are committing altruistic suicide. In the 2016 movie *Rogue One*, renegade Jyn Erso leads a small band of Rebel volunteers on a "suicide mission" to capture the schematic diagram of the Death Star, a powerful superweapon capable of destroying planets. Jyn and her group successfully capture and transmit the diagram back to the Rebel command ship, setting in motion the destruction of the Death Star and the saving of the galaxy, but all of them die in the process—as they knew they would.

likely in people who are isolated, alienated, and nonreligious. The larger the number of such people living in a society, the higher that society's suicide rate.

Altruistic suicides, in contrast, are undertaken by people who are so well integrated into the social structure that they intentionally sacrifice their lives for its well-being. Soldiers who threw themselves on top of a live grenade to save others, Japanese kamikaze pilots who crashed their planes into enemy ships during World War II, and Buddhist monks and nuns who protested the Vietnam War by setting themselves on fire may have been undertaking altruistic suicide (Leenaars, 2004; Stack, 2004). According to Durkheim, societies that encourage people to sacrifice themselves for others and to preserve their own honor (as East Asian societies do) are likely to have higher suicide rates.

Anomic suicides, another category proposed by Durkheim, are those pursued by people whose social environment fails to provide stable structures, such as family and religion, to support and give meaning to life. Such a societal condition, called *anomie* (literally, "without law"), leaves people without a sense of belonging. Unlike egoistic suicide, which is the act of a person who rejects the structures of a society, anomic suicide is the act of a person who has been let down by a disorganized, inadequate, often decaying society.

Durkheim argued that when societies go through periods of anomie, their suicide rates increase. Historical trends support this claim. Periods of economic depression may bring about some degree of anomie in a country, and national suicide rates tend to rise during such times (Noh, 2009; Maris, 2001). Periods of population change and increased immigration, too, tend to bring about a state of anomie, and again suicide rates rise (Kposowa et al., 2008).

A major change in a person's immediate surroundings, rather than general societal problems, can also lead to anomic suicide. People who suddenly inherit a great deal of money, for example, may go through a period of anomie as their relationships with social, economic, and occupational structures are changed. Thus Durkheim predicted that societies with more opportunities for changes in individual wealth or status would have higher suicide rates; this prediction is also supported by research (Cutright & Fernquist, 2001; Lester, 2000, 1985). Conversely, people who are removed from society and sent to a prison environment may experience anomie. As you read earlier, research confirms that such people have a heightened suicide rate (Fazel et al., 2011).

#AdditionalPunishment

Up through the nineteenth century, the bodies of suicide victims in France and England were sometimes dragged through the streets on a frame, head downward, the way criminals were dragged to their executions (Wertheimer, 2001; Fay, 1995).

Despite the considerable influence of Durkheim's theory, it cannot by itself explain why some people who face particular societal pressures attempt suicide while the majority do not. Durkheim himself concluded that the final explanation probably lies in the interaction between societal and individual factors. Although today's sociocultural theorists do not always embrace Durkheim's particular ideas, most agree that interpersonal variables, social structure, and cultural stress often play major roles in suicide. The recent work of researcher Thomas Joiner, which is discussed in the following section, is a case in point.

The Interpersonal View

For more than a decade, clinical researcher Thomas Joiner and his colleagues have been developing the **interpersonal theory of suicide** (Joiner et al., 2017; Joiner, 2009, 2005). This view, also called the *interpersonal-psychological theory*, asserts that people will be inclined to pursue suicide if they hold two key interpersonal beliefs—*perceived burdensomeness* and *thwarted belongingness*—and, at the same time, have a psychological *capability* to carry out suicide, a capability that they have acquired from life experiences. The theory does not dismiss the importance of the other factors you have been reading about throughout this chapter. However, says the Joiner research team, without the further presence of perceived burdensomeness, thwarted belongingness, and acquired capability, those factors are not likely to result in self-inflicted death (Rogers et al., 2017).

According to this theory, people with perceived burdensomeness believe that their existence places a heavy and permanent burden on their family, friends, and even society. This belief is typically inaccurate, but held dearly, and often leads to self-hatred (Joiner et al., 2017; Silva et al., 2017). It may also produce the notion that "my death would be worth more than my life to my family and friends" (Joiner, 2009).

People with thwarted belongingness feel isolated and alienated from others—not an integral part of a family or social network (Joiner et al., 2017). Their sense of social disconnect may be overstated or it may be accurate, but, either way, it feels enduring, unchangeable, and confining.

A large body of research indicates that people who experience *both* of these interpersonal perceptions are inclined to develop a *desire* for suicide (Buckner et al., 2017; Ma et al., 2017). However, a number of studies also indicate that such individuals are unlikely to attempt suicide unless they further possess the third variable cited by the theory—the psychological capability to inflict lethal harm on themselves (Ribeiro & Joiner, 2009).

According to Joiner, we all have a basic motive to live and preserve ourselves—a motive that weakens for certain people as a result of their repeated exposure to painful or frightening life experiences, like abuse, trauma, severe illness, or the like. Given such recurrent experiences, these individuals may develop a heightened tolerance for pain and a fearlessness about death (Rogers et al., 2017; Joiner, 2009). In Joiner's terms, they acquire a psychological capability for suicidal acts.

Studies conducted across a range of populations—from adolescents to the elderly—reveal that people with a combination of perceived burdensomeness, thwarted belongingness, and acquired suicide capability are significantly more likely to attempt suicide than people without these characteristics (Rogers et al., 2017; Horton et al., 2016; Ribeiro & Joiner, 2009).

Although this trio of factors has certainly been linked to civilian suicides, the theory's ability to help account for military suicides has stirred particular interest among clinical researchers (Monteith et al., 2018; Silva et al., 2017). Studies have revealed that many soldiers and veterans, perhaps due in part to the nature and impact of military training and combat, eventually develop feelings that they are a hardship on their families (perceived burdensomeness), have difficulty integrating into civilian

Altruistic suicide? A clay sculpture of a suicide bomber is displayed at a Baghdad art gallery. Some sociologists believe that the acts of such bombers fit Durkheim's definition of altruistic suicide, arguing that the bombers believe they are sacrificing their lives for the well-being of their society. Other theorists, however, point out that many such bombers seem indifferent to the innocent lives they are destroying and categorize the bombers instead as mass murderers motivated by hatred rather than by feelings of altruism (Lankford, 2013; Humphrey, 2006).

Thaier Al-Sudani/Reuters

Legitimate protest or attempted suicide? From the years 2000 to 2016, civil rights activist Irom Sharmila, seen here at a press conference in New Delhi, carried out a hunger strike to protest an Indian law that suspends many human rights protections. A form of attempted suicide? Not in Sharmila's mind, but, throughout the 16 year protest, the Indian government repeatedly charged her with attempted suicide and mandated that she be force-fed through a tube.

life (thwarted belongingness), and grow accustomed to violence (acquired suicide capability) (Lusk et al., 2015). Correspondingly, studies have found that such individuals often develop suicidal thoughts (Silva et al., 2017). If, in fact, military service and combat are capable of producing the characteristics cited by the interpersonal theory of suicide, it may not be so surprising that the rate of military suicides is more than twice as high as that of civilian suicides (Nock et al., 2017).

This promising and well-researched theory has not only uncovered some key variables in acts of suicide; it has underscored the importance of looking at those variables collectively, rather than individually. At the same time, it is reasonable to expect that future research will better clarify why and how these particular variables combine to help produce self-destructive behavior.

The Biological View

For years, biological researchers relied largely on family pedigree studies to support their position that biological factors contribute to suicidal behavior. They repeatedly found higher rates of suicide among the parents and close relatives of suicidal people than among those of nonsuicidal people (Petersen et al., 2014; Roy, 2011). Such findings may suggest that genetic, and so biological, factors are at work.

Studies of twins also supported this view of suicide. In a famous study, researchers who studied twins born in Denmark between 1870 and 1920 located 19 identical pairs and 58 fraternal pairs in which at least one twin had died by suicide (Juel-Nielsen & Videbech, 1970). In 4 of the identical pairs the other twin also died by suicide (21 percent), while none of the other twins among the fraternal pairs had done so.

> **Suicide sometimes runs in families. How might clinicians and researchers explain such family patterns?**

Over the past three decades, laboratory studies have offered more direct support for a biological view of suicide. One promising line of research focuses on *serotonin*. The activity level of this neurotransmitter has often been found to be low in people who complete suicide (Kennebeck & Bonin, 2016; Di Narzo et al., 2014). An early hint of this relationship came from a study by psychiatric researcher Marie Asberg and her colleagues (1976). They studied 68 depressed patients and found that 20 of the patients had particularly low levels of serotonin activity. It turned out that 40 percent of the research participants with such serotonin

interpersonal theory of suicide A theory that asserts that people with perceived burdensomeness, thwarted belongingness, and a psychological capability to carry out suicide are the most likely to attempt suicide. Also called *interpersonal-psychological theory*.

levels attempted suicide, compared with 15 percent of those with higher serotonin levels. The researchers interpreted this to mean that low serotonin activity may be "a predictor of suicidal acts." Later studies found that suicide attempters with low serotonin activity are 10 times more likely to make a repeat attempt and succeed than are suicide attempters with relatively higher serotonin activity (Roy, 1992).

In more recent years, brain scan studies have revealed that the low serotonin activity of suicidal persons corresponds to dysfunction throughout their depression-related brain circuit (see pages 197–198). That is, the activity of their prefrontal cortex, hippocampus, amygdala, and subgenual cingulate is abnormal, and the interconnectivity between these structures is atypical as well—the same kinds of abnormalities at work in depressed persons (Du et al., 2017; Kang et al., 2017; Mann & Currier, 2007). The low serotonin activity of suicidal persons may reflect such circuit abnormalities or they may help cause them.

At first glance, these studies may seem to tell us only that depressed people often attempt suicide. After all, depression is itself related to low serotonin activity and brain-circuit dysfunction. On the other hand, there is evidence of low serotonin activity and brain-circuit dysfunction even among suicidal people who have no history of depression (Mann & Currier, 2007). That is, low serotonin activity and brain-circuit dysfunction also seem to play a role in suicide separate from depression.

Is aggression the key? Biological theorists believe that heightened feelings of aggression and impulsivity, produced by low serotonin activity and poor brain-circuit functioning, are key factors in suicide. In 2007, professional wrestling champion Chris Benoit (right) killed his wife and son and then hanged himself, a tragedy that seemed consistent with this theory. In addition, toxicology reports found steroids, drugs known to help cause aggression and impulsivity, in Benoit's body.

How might such serotonin and circuit abnormalities directly increase the likelihood of suicidal behavior? One possibility is that they contribute to aggressive and impulsive behaviors (Huang et al., 2017; Rizzi & Marras, 2017; Preti, 2011). It has been found, for example, that aggressive and impulsive men (including those who commit arson and murder) display lower serotonin activity and poorer brain-circuit functioning than do other men (Mann & Currier, 2007; Oquendo et al., 2006, 2004). Moreover, studies have found that depressed patients with particularly low serotonin activity and poor brain-circuit functioning attempt suicide more often, use more lethal methods, and score higher in hostility and impulsivity on personality inventories than do depressed patients with relatively higher serotonin activity and better functioning circuits (Kennebeck & Bonin, 2016; Moberg et al., 2011).

Collectively these findings suggest that low serotonin activity and poor functioning of the depression-related brain circuit help produce aggressive feelings and impulsive behavior. In people who are clinically depressed, these biological abnormalities may lead to aggressive tendencies that cause them to be particularly vulnerable to suicidal thoughts and acts. Even in the absence of a depressive disorder, however, people with low serotonin activity and a dysfunctional brain circuit may develop such aggressive feelings that they, too, are dangerous to themselves or to others. Still other research indicates that these biological abnormalities combined with key psychosocial factors (such as childhood traumas) may be the strongest suicide predictor of all (Moberg et al., 2011).

Is Suicide Linked to Age?

ALTHOUGH PEOPLE OF ALL AGES may try to kill themselves, the likelihood of dying by suicide steadily increases with age up through middle age, then decreases during the early stages of old age, and then increases again beginning at age 75 (see **Figure 9-2**). Currently, 2 of every 100,000 people under 15 years of age in the United States kills himself or herself each year, compared with 11 of every 100,000 people between 15 and 24 years old, 16 of every 100,000 people between 25 and 44 years old, 20 of every 100,000 between 45 and 64 years old, 16 of every 100,000 between 65 and 74, and 21 of every 100,000 people over age 75 (CDC, 2016). The exceptional rate of suicide among those who are middle-aged is a relatively recent phenomenon and is not fully understood (Schreiber & Culpepper, 2016). Up until 2006, that rate had been considerably lower than the current rate and always lower than that of elderly people.

Clinicians have paid particular attention to self-destructive behavior in three age groups: *children, adolescents,* and the *elderly.* Although the features and theories of suicide discussed throughout this chapter apply to all age groups, each group faces unique problems that may play key roles in the suicidal acts of its members.

Children

> Tommy [age 7] and his younger brother were playing together, and an altercation arose that was settled by the mother, who then left the room. The mother recalled nothing to distinguish this incident from innumerable similar ones. Several minutes after she left, she considered Tommy strangely quiet and returned to find him crimson-faced and struggling for air, having knotted a jumping rope around his neck and jerked it tight.
>
> *(French & Berlin, 1979, p. 144)*

> Dear Mom and Dad,
> I love you. Please tell my teacher that I cannot take it anymore. I quit. Please don't take me to school anymore. Please help me. I will run away so don't stop me. I will kill myself. So don't look for me because I will be dead. I love you. I will always love you. Remember me.
> Help me.
> Love Justin [age 10]
>
> *(Pfeffer, 1986, p. 273)*

Suicide is infrequent among children, although it has been increasing over the past several decades (Schreiber & Culpepper, 2016). For children under 11 years of age, one out of every million individuals kill themselves. That rate rises to two per 100,000 among children aged 11 to 14 years and, as you will see shortly, 8 per 100,000 among teens aged 15 to 19 years (CDC, 2016; Kennebeck & Bonin, 2016). In addition, it has been estimated that 1 of every 100 children tries to harm himself or herself, and many thousands of children are hospitalized each year for deliberately self-destructive acts, such as stabbing, cutting, burning, or shooting themselves; overdosing; or jumping from high places (Fortune & Hawton, 2007).

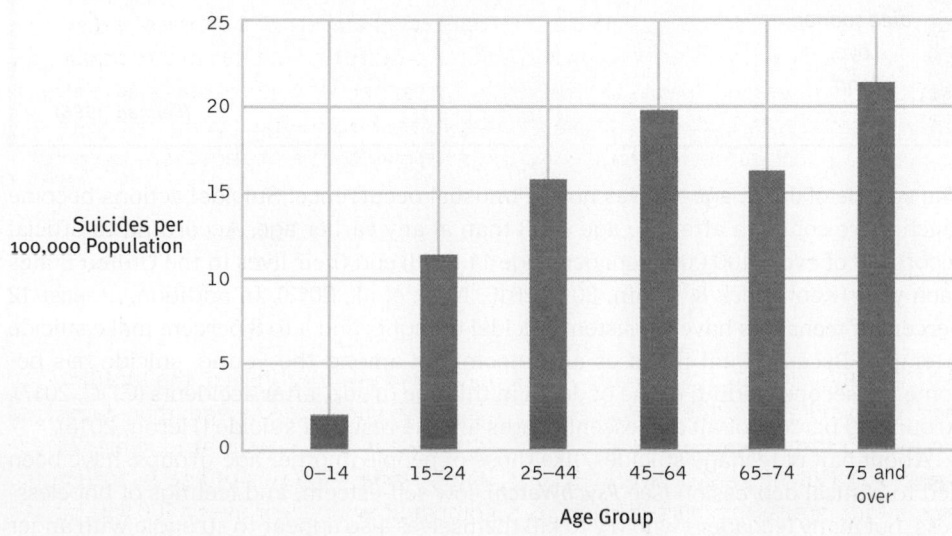

#SteadyRise

The rate of suicide in the United States has gone up year by year throughout the twenty-first century. Today's rate is 28 percent higher than the rate in the year 2000 (CDC, 2017).

FIGURE 9-2

Suicide and Age

In the United States, suicide rates keep rising through middle age, then fall during the first decade of old age, then rise again among people over the age of 74. (Information from: AFSP, 2017; CDC, 2016.)

Kaku Kurita/Getty Images

Student stress The intense training and testing that characterize Japan's educational system produce high levels of stress in many students. This child, wearing a headband that translates to "Struggle to Pass," participates in summer *juku*, a camp where children receive special academic training, extra lessons, and exam practice 11 hours a day.

Researchers have found that suicide attempts by the very young are commonly preceded by such behavioral patterns as running away from home; accident-proneness; aggressive acting out; temper tantrums; self-criticism; social withdrawal and loneliness; extreme sensitivity to criticism by others; low tolerance of frustration; sleep problems; dark fantasies, daydreams, or hallucinations; marked personality change; and overwhelming interest in death and suicide (Soole et al., 2015; Wong et al., 2011). Studies further have linked child suicides to the recent or anticipated loss of a loved one, family stress and a parent's unemployment, abuse by parents, victimization by peers (for example, bullying), and a clinical level of depression (Kennebeck & Bonin, 2016; van Geel, Vedder, & Tanilon, 2014; Renaud et al., 2008).

Most people find it hard to believe that children fully comprehend the meaning of a suicidal act. They argue that because a child's thinking is so limited, children who attempt suicide fall into Shneidman's category of "death ignorers," like Demaine, who sought to join his mother in heaven (Kennebeck & Bonin, 2016). Many child suicides, however, appear to be based on a clear understanding of death and on a clear wish to die (Pfeffer, 2003). In addition, suicidal thinking among even normal children is apparently more common than most people once believed. Clinical interviews with school-children have revealed that between 6 and 33 percent have thought about suicide (Riesch et al., 2008; Culp, Clyman, & Culp, 1995). Small wonder that many of today's elementary schools have tried to develop tools and procedures for better identifying and assessing suicide risk among their students (Miller, 2011; Whitney et al., 2011).

Adolescents

Dear Mom, Dad, and everyone else,
    I'm sorry for what I've done, but I loved you all and I always will, for eternity. Please, please, please don't blame it on yourselves. It was all my fault and not yours or anyone else's. If I didn't do this now, I would have done it later anyway. We all die some day, I just died sooner.
    Love,
    John

(Berman, 1986)

The suicide of John, age 17, was not an unusual occurrence. Suicidal actions become much more common after the age of 13 than at any earlier age. According to official records, 8 of every 100,000 teenagers (age 14 to 18) end their lives in the United States each year (Kennebeck & Bonin, 2017, 2016; Nock et al., 2013). In addition, at least 12 percent of teenagers have persistent suicidal thoughts and 4 to 8 percent make suicide attempts. Because fatal illnesses are uncommon among the young, suicide has become the second leading cause of death in this age group, after accidents (CDC, 2017). Around 19 percent of all adolescent deaths are the result of suicide (Heron, 2016).

About half of teenage suicides, like those of people in other age groups, have been tied to clinical depression (see **PsychWatch**), low self-esteem, and feelings of hopelessness, but many teenagers who try to kill themselves also appear to struggle with anger

#

#DealBreaker

If clients state an intention to kill themselves, therapists may break the doctor–patient confidentiality agreement that usually governs treatment discussions (Middleman & Olson, 2017).

The Black Box Controversy: Do Antidepressants Cause Suicide?

A major controversy in the clinical field is whether antidepressant drugs are highly dangerous for depressed children and teenagers (Pozzi et al., 2016). Throughout the 1990s, most psychiatrists believed that antidepressants—particularly the second-generation antidepressants—were safe and effective for children and adolescents, just as they seemed to be for adults, and they prescribed those medications readily (Cooper et al., 2014). However, after reviewing a large number of clinical reports and studying 3,300 patients on antidepressants, the U.S. Food and Drug Administration (FDA) concluded in 2004 that the drugs produce a real, though small, increase in the risk of suicidal behavior for certain children and adolescents, especially during the first few months of treatment, and it ordered that all antidepressant containers carry "black box" warnings stating that the drugs "increase the risk of suicidal thinking and behavior in children" (Moreland & Bonin, 2016). In 2007 the FDA expanded this warning to include young adults.

Although many clinicians have been pleased by the FDA order, others worry that it may be ill-advised (Pozzi et al., 2016; Isacsson & Rich, 2014). The latter argue that while the drugs may indeed increase the risk of suicidal thoughts and attempts in as many as 2 percent of young patients, the risk of suicide is actually reduced in the vast majority of children and teenagers who take the drugs (Christiansen et al., 2016; Mulder, 2010). To support this argument, they point out that the overall rate of teenage suicides decreased by 30 percent in the decade leading up to 2004, as the number of antidepressant prescriptions provided to children and teenagers were soaring (Isacsson & Rich, 2014; Isacsson et al., 2010).

Alias/Photo:Wolfram Steinberg/dpa /AP Images

The critics of the black box warnings also point to the initial impact that the warnings had on prescription patterns and teenage suicide rates in the United States and other countries. Some studies suggest that during the first two years following the institution of the black box warnings, the number of antidepressant prescriptions fell 22 percent in the United States and the Netherlands, while the rate of teenage suicides rose 14 percent in the United States, the largest suicide rate increase since 1979 (Fawcett, 2007). A comparable regulatory warning by Canada's health board, made at the same approximate time as the FDA's black box order, apparently resulted in nearly identical trends (Moreland & Bonin, 2016; Katz et al., 2008). Although other studies challenge these numbers (Wheeler et al., 2008), it is certainly possible that black box warnings were indirectly depriving many young patients of a medication that they truly needed to help fight depression and

head off suicide. Research indicates that antidepressant prescriptions for depressed teenagers started rising again in 2006, a trend that has continued to the present day (Bachmann et al., 2016). The effect of this trend reversal on teenage suicide rates is not yet clear.

A major outgrowth and benefit of the black box controversy is that the FDA recently has also expanded its interest in suicidal side effects to drugs other than antidepressants. It now requires pharmaceutical companies to test for suicidal side effects in certain newly developed drugs, such as those for obesity and epilepsy, before such drugs receive FDA approval (FDA, 2012). In the past, lethal effects of this kind never came to light until well after a drug had been approved and used by millions of patients.

and impulsiveness or to have serious alcohol or drug problems (Kennebeck & Bonin, 2016; Schreiber & Culpepper, 2016; Orri et al., 2014). Some also have deficiencies in their ability to sort out and solve problems.

Teenagers who consider or attempt suicide are often under great stress (Stewart et al., 2017; Kennebeck & Bonin, 2016; Orri et al., 2014). They may be dealing with long-term pressures such as poor (or missing) relationships with parents, family conflict,

#LimitedHelp

More than 55 percent of teens who attempt suicide received some form of therapy before the onset of their suicidal behavior, but it failed to prevent their later actions (Nock et al., 2013).

inadequate peer relationships, social isolation, or repeated bullying. Indeed, suicide attempts are at least twice as common among teenage victims of bullying as among other teenagers. Alternatively, their actions also may be triggered by more immediate stress, such as a parent's unemployment or medical illness, financial setbacks for the family, or a social loss such as a breakup with a boyfriend or girlfriend. Stress at school seems to be a particularly common problem for teenagers who attempt suicide. Some have trouble keeping up at school, while others may be high achievers who feel pressured to be perfect and to stay at the top of the class.

One group under particular stress are LGBTQ teenagers (lesbian, gay, bisexual, transgender, and questioning). In addition to possible sexual or gender doubts and concerns, they often experience abuse, prejudice, stigmatization, and victimization by peers, including bullying, in their lives. Studies indicate that they are 3 times more likely than other teenagers to have suicidal thoughts and to attempt suicide (Forcier & Olson-Kennedy, 2017).

Some theorists believe that the period of adolescence itself produces a stressful climate in which suicidal actions are more likely. Adolescence is a period of rapid growth that is often marked by conflicts, depressed feelings, tensions, and difficulties at home and school. Adolescents tend to react to events more sensitively, angrily, dramatically, and impulsively than individuals in other age groups; thus the likelihood of their engaging in suicidal acts during times of stress is higher (Greening et al., 2008). Finally, the suggestibility of adolescents and their eagerness to imitate others, including others who attempt suicide, may set the stage for suicidal action (Kennebeck & Bonin, 2016; Apter & Wasserman, 2007). One study found that adolescents exposed to suicide by an acquaintance or relative within the past year were more likely to attempt suicide than adolescents without a personal exposure of this kind (Swanson & Colman, 2013). It is believed that recent suicides by individuals on social networking sites—including individuals never met in person—may also raise the likelihood of attempted suicide by many young users (Briggs, Slater, & Bowley, 2017).

Teen Suicides: Attempts Versus Completions Far more teenagers attempt suicide than actually kill themselves—most experts believe that the ratio is at least 100 to 1, and in fact estimates range as high as 200 to 1 (Kennebeck & Bonin, 2016; Schreiber & Culpepper, 2016). In contrast, the ratio is thought to be 4 to 1 among the elderly

13 Reasons Why Few TV series have produced the stir caused by *13 Reasons Why*, a Netflix drama wildly popular among teenagers. The show depicts young Hannah Baker who fatally cuts her wrists after experiencing a number of traumatic events, each brought on by a different classmate. After Hannah's suicide, those classmates receive a package of tapes from her—an audio diary—describing the 13 reasons she killed herself. On the plus side, the show has raised awareness about teenage suicide and helped generate peer-to-peer and parent–child discussions about this topic. On the negative side, many clinicians and educators worry that the show depicts suicide too graphically, inadvertently normalizes it, and may trigger acts of self-destruction and self-harm by some viewers.

Beth Dubber/©Netflix/courtesy Everett Collection

(AFSP, 2017). The unusually large number of unsuccessful teenage suicides may mean that adolescents are less certain than middle-age and elderly people who make such attempts. While some do indeed wish to die, many may simply want to make others understand how desperate they are, or they may want to get help or teach others a lesson (Apter & Wasserman, 2007). Up to half of teenagers who make a suicide attempt try again in the future, and as many as 14 percent eventually die by suicide (Horwitz, Czyz, & King, 2014; Wong et al., 2008).

Why is the rate of suicide attempts so high among teenagers (as well as among young adults)? Several explanations, most pointing to societal factors, have been proposed. First, as the number and proportion of teenagers and young adults in the general population have risen, the competition for jobs, college positions, and academic and athletic honors has intensified for them, leading increasingly to shattered dreams and ambitions (Kim & Cho, 2017; Holinger & Offer, 1993, 1991, 1982). Other explanations point to weakening ties in the family (which may produce feelings of alienation and rejection in many of today's young people) and to the easy availability of alcohol and other drugs and the pressure to use them among teenagers and young adults (Kennebeck & Bonin, 2016; Brent, 2001; Cutler et al., 2001).

The mass media coverage of suicides by teenagers and young adults may also contribute to the high rate of suicide attempts among the young (Shain & AAP Committee on Adolescence, 2016). The detailed descriptions of teenage suicide that the media and the arts often offer may serve as models for young people who are contemplating suicide (Gould et al., 2014; Cheng et al., 2007). In one of the most famous examples of this phenomenon, just days after the highly publicized suicides of four adolescents in a New Jersey town in 1987, dozens of teenagers across the United States took similar actions (at least 12 of them fatal)—two in the same garage just one week later.

Teen Suicides: Multicultural Issues

Teenage suicide rates vary by race and ethnicity in the United States. Around 9 of every 100,000 non-Hispanic white American teenagers die by suicide each year, compared with 5 of every 100,000 African American teens and 5 of every 100,000 Hispanic American teens (CDC, 2016; Goldston et al., 2008). Although these numbers certainly indicate that non-Hispanic white American teens are more prone to suicide, the rates of the three groups are in fact becoming closer (Schreiber & Culpepper, 2016; Baca-Garcia et al., 2011). This closing trend may reflect increasingly similar pressures on young African, Hispanic, and non-Hispanic white Americans—competition for grades and college opportunities, for example, is now intense for all three groups (Barnes, 2010). The growing suicide rates for young African and Hispanic Americans may also be linked to their rising unemployment, the many anxieties and economic pressures of inner-city life, and the indignation many feel over racial inequities and discrimination in our society (Kennebeck & Bonin, 2016; Baca-Garcia et al., 2011; Barnes, 2010). Studies further indicate that 5.7 of every 100,000 Asian American teens now end their lives each year.

The highest teenage suicide rate of all is displayed by American Indians. Currently, around 18 of every 100,000 American Indian teenagers die by suicide each year, double the rate of non-Hispanic white American teenagers and triple that of other minority teenagers (CDC, 2016). Clinical theorists attribute this extraordinarily high rate to factors such as the extreme poverty faced by most American Indian teens, their limited educational and employment opportunities, their particularly high rate of alcohol abuse, and the geographical isolation of those who live on reservations (Dillard et al.,

MR1805/Getty Images

Far from a game The *Blue Whale Game*, or *Blue Whale Challenge*, is an Internet "game" that is currently stirring great public concern. The challenge is comprised of daily tasks that participants are assigned by administrators, culminating, on the 50th day, with an instruction to kill oneself. It is estimated that dozens of teenagers across the world have died by suicide playing the game, whose name is derived from the behavior of whales that strand themselves on beaches and die.

#BufferZone

Hispanic and African Americans have certain beliefs that may make them less likely to attempt suicide. Both groups hold stronger moral objections to suicide than other groups do. In addition, Hispanic Americans have particularly firm beliefs about the need to cope and survive and responsibility to one's families (Oquendo et al., 2005). And African Americans have higher degrees of orthodox religious belief and personal devotion and express more concern about giving others the power to end one's life (Krause & Hayward, 2015; Goff et al., 2014; Clark, 2013).

Continuing trend The rate of suicide among American Indians is much higher than the national average. Here a memorial is held for a young suicide victim at a middle school on the Fort Peck Indian Reservation in Poplar, Montana.

AP Photo/Michael Albans

2017; Alcántara & Gone, 2008; Goldston et al., 2008). In addition, it appears that certain American Indian reservations have extreme suicide rates—called *cluster suicides*—and that teenagers who live in such communities are unusually likely to be exposed to suicide, to have their lives disrupted, to observe suicidal models, and to be at risk for suicide contagion (Bender, 2006; Chekki, 2004).

The Elderly

Rose Ashby walks to the dry cleaner's to pick up her old but finest dinner dress. Although shaken at the cost of having it cleaned, Rose tells the sympathetic girl behind the counter, "Don't worry. It doesn't matter. I won't be needing the money any more."

Walking through the streets of St. Petersburg, Florida, she still wishes it had been Miami. The west coast of the fountain-of-youth peninsula is not as warm as the east. If only Chet had left more insurance money, Rose could have afforded Miami. In St. Petersburg, Rose failed to unearth de León's promised fount.

Last week, she told the doctor she felt lonely and depressed. He said she should perk up. She had everything to live for. What does he know? Has he lost a husband like Chet and his left breast to cancer all in one year? Has he suffered arthritis all his life? Were his ovaries so bad he had to undergo a hysterectomy? Did he have to suffer through menopause just to end up alone without family or friends? Does he have to live in a dungeon? Is his furniture worn, his carpet threadbare? What does he know? Might his every day be the last one for him?

As Rose turns into the walk to her white cinderblock apartment building, fat Mrs. Green asks if she is coming to the community center that evening. Who needs it? The social worker did say Rose should come. Since Rose was in such good health, she could help those not so well as she.

Help them do what? Finger-paint like little children? Make baskets like insane people? Sew? Who can see to sew? Besides, who would appreciate it? Who would thank her? Who could she tell about her troubles? Who cares?

When she told the doctor she couldn't sleep, he gave her the prescription but said that all elderly people have trouble sleeping. What does he know? Does he have a middle-aged daughter who can only think about her latest divorce, or grandchildren who only acknowledge her birthday check by the endorsement on the back? Are all his friends dead and gone? Is all the money from her dead husband's insurance used up? What does he know? Who could sleep in this dungeon?

Back in her apartment, Rose washes and sets her hair. It's good she has to do it herself. Look at this hair. So thin, so sparse, so frowsy. What would a hairdresser think?

Then make-up. Base. Rouge. Lipstick. Bright red. Perfume? No! No cheap perfume for Rose today. Remember the bottles of Joy Chet would buy for her? He always wanted her to have the best. He would boast that she had everything, and that she never had to work a day in her life for it.

"She doesn't have to lift her little finger," Chet would say, puffing on his cigar. Where is the Joy now? Dead and gone. With Chet. Rose manages a wry laugh at the play on words.

Slipping into her dinner dress, she looks into the dresser mirror. "It's good you can't see this face now, Chet. How old and ugly it looks."

Taking some lavender notepaper from the drawer, she stands at the dresser to write. Why didn't anyone warn her that growing old was like this? It is so unfair. But they don't care. People don't care about anyone except themselves.

Leaving the note on the dresser, she suddenly feels excited. Breathing hard now, she rushes to the sink—who could call a sink in the counter in the living room a kitchen?—and gets a glass of water.

Trying to relax, Rose arranges the folds in her skirt as she settles down on the chaise. Carefully sipping the water as she takes all the capsules so as to not smear her lipstick, Rose quietly begins to sob. After a lifetime of tears, these will be her last. Her note on the dresser is short, written to no one and to everyone.

You don't know what it is like to have to grow old and die

(Gernsbacher, 1985, pp. 227–228)

More than 16 of every 100,000 people between the ages of 65 and 74 years in the United States kill themselves, a rate that rises to 21.4 per 100,000 among people over the age of 74 years, as you read earlier (CDC, 2016). Elderly people account for over 18 percent of all suicides in the United States, yet they comprise only 15 percent of the total population (NVSR, 2016; U.S. Census Bureau, 2016).

Many factors contribute to this high suicide rate. As people grow older, all too often they become ill, lose close friends and relatives, lose control over their lives, and lose status in our society (Draper, 2014; O'Riley et al., 2014). Such experiences may result in feelings of hopelessness, loneliness, depression, "burdensomeness," or inevitability among aged persons and so increase the likelihood that they will attempt suicide (Kim et al., 2014; Cukrowicz et al., 2011). One study found that two-thirds of particularly elderly individuals (those over 80 years old) who died by suicide had been hospitalized for medical reasons within 2 years preceding the suicide (Erlangsen et al., 2005), and another found a heightened rate of vascular or respiratory illnesses among elderly people who attempted suicide (Levy et al., 2011). Still other research has shown that the suicide rate of elderly people who have recently lost a spouse is particularly high (Schreiber & Culpepper, 2016; Ajdacic-Gross et al., 2008). The risk is greatest during the first weeks of bereavement, but it remains high in later months and years as well.

> **Why do people often view the suicides of elderly or chronically sick people as less tragic than that of young or healthy people?**

Elderly people are typically more determined than younger people in their decision to die and give fewer warnings, so their success rate is much higher (Dennis & Brown, 2011). As you read earlier, an estimated one of every four elderly persons who attempts suicide succeeds (AFSP, 2014). Given the determination of aged persons and their physical decline, some people argue that older persons who want to die are clear in their thinking and should be allowed to carry out their wishes (Emanuel, 2017) (see *InfoCentral* on page 275). However, clinical depression appears to play an important role in as many as 60 percent of suicides by the elderly, suggesting that more elderly people who are suicidal should be receiving treatment for their depressive disorders (Kiosses et al., 2017; Levy et al., 2011). In fact, research suggests that treating depression in older persons helps reduce their risk of suicide markedly (Draper, 2014).

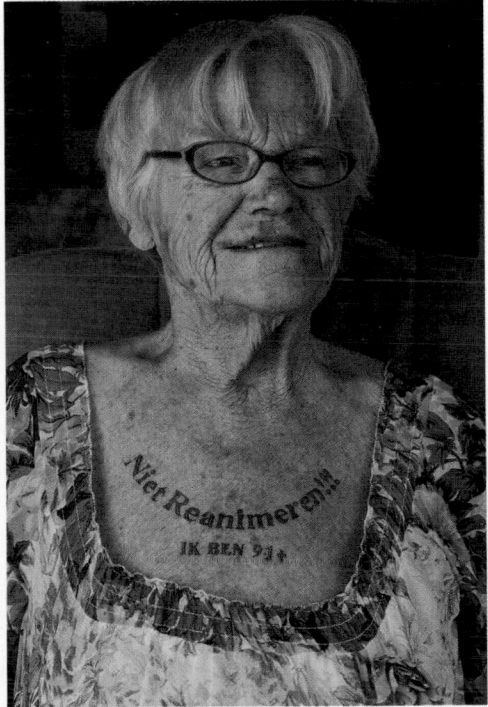

A right to die? Although she has not tried to end her life, Nel Bolten, a resident of the Netherlands, recently brought attention to the right-to-die debate when she had her chest tattooed with these words (which mean "Do not resuscitate. I am 91 plus"). The Dutch health minister has confirmed that the tattoo is a legally binding declaration in that country, where euthanasia and physician-assisted suicide are permitted.

Michel Porro/Getty Images

Lawrence Migdale/Pix

The power of respect Elderly people are held in high esteem in many traditional societies because of the store of knowledge they have accumulated. Perhaps not so coincidentally, suicides among the elderly seem to be less common in these cultures than in those of many industrialized nations.

The suicide rate among the elderly in the United States is lower in some minority groups (Heron, 2016). Although American Indians have the highest overall suicide rate, for example, the rate among elderly American Indians is relatively low. The aged are held in high esteem by American Indians and are looked to for the wisdom and experience they have acquired over the years, and this may help account for their low suicide rate. Such high regard is in sharp contrast to the loss of status often experienced by elderly non-Hispanic white Americans.

Similarly, the suicide rate is only one-quarter as high among elderly African Americans as among elderly non-Hispanic white Americans (CDC, 2016; Joe et al., 2014). One reason for this low suicide rate may be the pressures faced by African Americans, of whom it is sometimes said: "only the strongest survive" (Seiden, 1981). Those who reach an advanced age often have overcome significant adversity, and many feel proud of what they have accomplished. Because reaching old age is not in itself a form of success for non-Hispanic white Americans, their attitude toward aging may be more negative. Another possible explanation is that aged African Americans have managed to overcome or reduce the feelings of indignation that prompt many suicides in younger African Americans.

Treatment and Suicide

TREATMENT OF SUICIDAL PEOPLE falls into two major categories: *treatment after suicide has been attempted* and *suicide prevention*. Treatment may also be beneficial to relatives and friends of those who complete or attempt suicide. Indeed, their feelings of loss, guilt, and anger after a suicide fatality or attempt can be intense (Fouet, 2017; Feigelman & Feigelman, 2011). However, the discussion here is limited to the treatment afforded suicidal people themselves.

What Treatments Are Used After Suicide Attempts?

After a suicide attempt, most victims need medical care. Close to one-half million people in the United States are admitted to a hospital each year for injuries resulting from efforts to harm themselves (AFSP, 2014). Some are left with severe injuries, brain

#HospitalAlert

Suicidal behavior or thinking is the most common reason for admission to a mental hospital. Around two-thirds of patients who are admitted have aroused concern that they will harm themselves (Miret et al., 2011; Jacobson, 1999).

THE RIGHT TO DIE BY SUICIDE

In ancient Greece, citizens with a grave illness or mental anguish could obtain official permission from the Senate to take their own lives. In contrast, most Western countries have traditionally discouraged suicide, based on their belief in the "sanctity of life." Today, however, a person's "**right to die by suicide**" is receiving more and more support from the public, particularly in connection with ending great pain and terminal illness (Braverman et al., 2017; Quill & Battin, 2017; Karsoho et al., 2016).

WHO SUPPORTS THE RIGHT OF TERMINALLY ILL PATIENTS TO DIE BY SUICIDE?

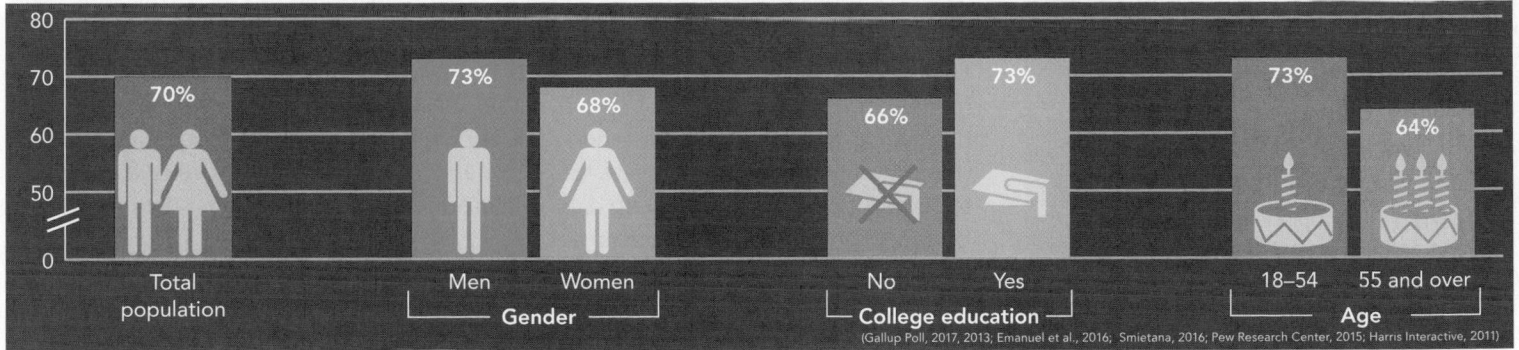

(Gallup Poll, 2017, 2013; Emanuel et al., 2016; Smietana, 2016; Pew Research Center, 2015; Harris Interactive, 2011)

EUTHANASIA AND PHYSICIAN-ASSISTED SUICIDE

Euthanasia, also called "mercy killing," is the practice of killing someone who is terminally sick or badly injured to stop the suffering. Euthanasia is not necessarily initiated by the patient. **Physician-assisted suicide** is a particular form of euthanasia, in which a physician helps a patient to end his or her life in response to the patient's request.

Should physicians provide indirect or direct assistance?

Physicians may *advise* patients about how to end their life (indirect assistance) or may *actually end* a patient's life (direct assistance). Many people who support physician-assisted suicide remain uncomfortable with the prospect of a doctor directly inducing a patient's death.

Around 57 percent of U.S. physicians believe that physician-assisted suicide should be available to terminally ill patients (Lowes, 2016). At the same time, fewer than 20 percent of all U.S. physicians have received requests for such assistance and fewer than 5 percent have ever provided it (Emanuel et al., 2016).

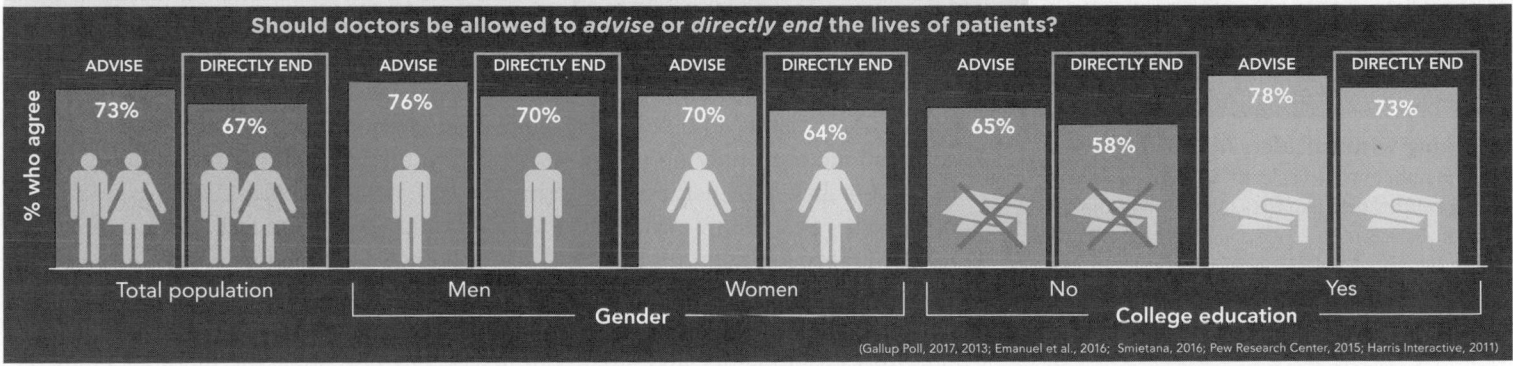

(Gallup Poll, 2017, 2013; Emanuel et al., 2016; Smietana, 2016; Pew Research Center, 2015; Harris Interactive, 2011)

WHERE IS EUTHANASIA AND PHYSICIAN-ASSISTED SUICIDE LEGAL?

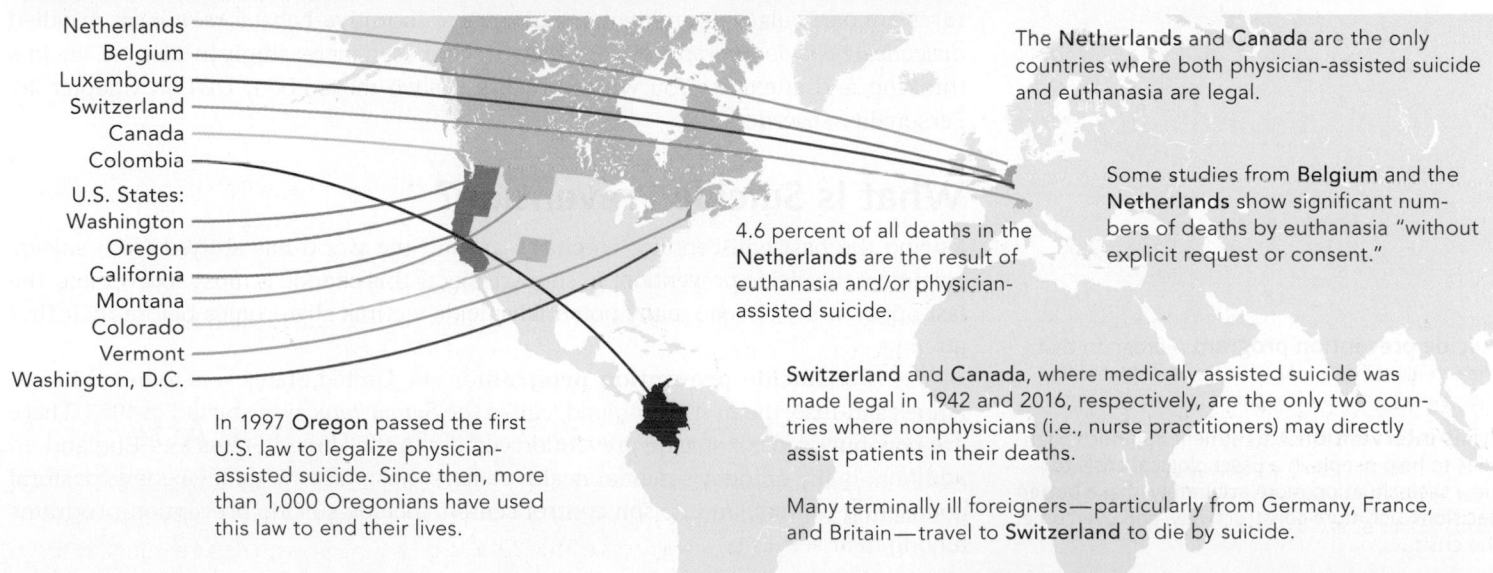

Netherlands
Belgium
Luxembourg
Switzerland
Canada
Colombia
U.S. States:
Washington
Oregon
California
Montana
Colorado
Vermont
Washington, D.C.

The **Netherlands** and **Canada** are the only countries where both physician-assisted suicide and euthanasia are legal.

Some studies from **Belgium** and the **Netherlands** show significant numbers of deaths by euthanasia "without explicit request or consent."

4.6 percent of all deaths in the **Netherlands** are the result of euthanasia and/or physician-assisted suicide.

Switzerland and **Canada**, where medically assisted suicide was made legal in 1942 and 2016, respectively, are the only two countries where nonphysicians (i.e., nurse practitioners) may directly assist patients in their deaths.

In 1997 **Oregon** passed the first U.S. law to legalize physician-assisted suicide. Since then, more than 1,000 Oregonians have used this law to end their lives.

Many terminally ill foreigners—particularly from Germany, France, and Britain—travel to **Switzerland** to die by suicide.

(Emanuel, 2017; Quill & Battin, 2017; Emanuel et al., 2016; Onwuteaka-Philipsen et al., 2012; Schadenberg, 2012; Thomasson, 2012)

Working with suicide After persuading this man to not jump to his death, California Highway Patrol officers help him back over a rail of the Golden Gate Bridge. Police departments across the world typically provide special crisis intervention training so that officers can develop the skills to help suicidal individuals.

damage, or other medical problems. Once the physical damage is treated, psychotherapy or drug therapy may begin, on either an inpatient or outpatient basis.

Unfortunately, even after trying to kill themselves, many suicidal people fail to receive systematic follow-up care (Stanley et al., 2015; Bridge et al., 2012). This is particularly striking, given that individuals who survive a suicide attempt are 6 times as likely as other people to make future suicide attempts (Schreiber & Culpepper, 2016). The likelihood of a future attempt is especially high among individuals who have used guns or other violent techniques in their first attempt (Olfson et al., 2017). Overall, around half of all people who die from suicide have made a previous attempt (Schreiber & Culpepper, 2016). In some cases, health care professionals are at fault for the lack of follow-up care. In others, the person who has attempted suicide refuses therapy. According to one review, the average number of therapy sessions attended by teenagers who receive follow-up care is 8; around 18 percent of such teens terminate treatment against their therapists' advice (Spirito et al., 2011).

The goals of therapy for those who have attempted suicide are to keep the individuals alive, reduce their psychological pain, help them achieve a nonsuicidal state of mind, provide them with hope, and guide them to develop better ways of handling stress (Sun et al., 2018; Rudd & Brown, 2011). Studies indicate that people who receive therapy after their suicide attempts have a lower risk of future suicide attempts and deaths than do attempters who do not receive such therapy (Kennebeck & Bonin, 2017; Schreiber & Culpepper, 2016). Various therapies have been employed, including drug, psychodynamic, cognitive-behavioral, group, and family therapies (Kennebeck & Bonin, 2017; Baldessarini & Tondo, 2011, 2007; Spirito et al., 2011).

Research indicates that cognitive-behavioral therapy may be particularly helpful (Asarnow et al., 2017; Rudd et al., 2015; Brown et al., 2011, 2010). When clients are suicidal, the approach focuses largely on the painful thoughts, sense of hopelessness, dichotomous thinking, poor coping skills, weak problem-solving abilities, and other cognitive and behavioral features that characterize suicidal people. Using elements of Beck's cognitive-behavioral therapy (see pages 225–227), the therapists may help their suicidal clients to assess, challenge, and change many of their negative attitudes and illogical thinking processes. Applying the principles of *mindfulness-based* cognitive-behavioral therapy (see pages 65, 122), the therapists may also guide the clients to become keenly aware of the various painful thoughts and feelings that keep streaming through their minds and to *accept* many such thoughts and feelings rather than try to eliminate them. Acceptance of this kind is expected to increase the clients' tolerance of psychological distress. Finally, employing a number of therapy exercises, homework assignments, and other cognitive-behavioral tools, the therapists may try to teach clients better coping and problem-solving skills. All of these treatment features are particularly prominent in a new-wave cognitive-behavioral approach called *dialectical behavior therapy (DBT),* which is being used increasingly in cases of suicidal thinking and attempts. You will be reading much more about DBT in Chapter 16, Personality Disorders.

What Is Suicide Prevention?

During the past half-century, emphasis around the world has shifted from suicide treatment to suicide prevention. In some respects this change is most appropriate: the last opportunity to keep many potential suicide victims alive comes before their first attempt.

The first **suicide prevention program** in the United States was founded in Los Angeles in 1955; the first in England, called the *Samaritans,* was started in 1953. There are now hundreds of suicide prevention centers in the United States and England. In addition, many of today's mental health centers, hospital emergency rooms, pastoral counseling centers, and poison control centers include suicide prevention programs among their services.

suicide prevention program A program that tries to identify people who are at risk of killing themselves and to offer them crisis intervention.

crisis intervention A treatment approach that tries to help people in a psychological crisis to view their situation more accurately, make better decisions, act more constructively, and overcome the crisis.

John Storey/San Francisco Chronicle/Polaris

There are also hundreds of *suicide hotlines,* 24-hour-a-day telephone services, in the United States. Callers reach a counselor, typically a *paraprofessional*—a person trained in counseling but without a formal degree—who provides services under the supervision of a mental health professional.

Suicide prevention programs and hotlines respond to suicidal people as individuals *in crisis*—that is, under great stress, unable to cope, feeling threatened or hurt, and interpreting their situations as unchangeable. Thus the programs offer **crisis intervention:** they try to help suicidal people see their situations more accurately, make better decisions, act more constructively, and overcome their crises (Lester, 2011). Because crises can occur at any time, the centers advertise their hotlines and also welcome people who walk in without appointments. A growing number of centers also offer their services through modalities such as text messaging and Internet chat (Predmore et al., 2017; Naurert, 2016).

Telling his story College student Bryce Mackie watches as his film, *Eternal High,* is played for a group of mental health professionals in Ohio. He made the film in high school, chronicling his struggle with bipolar disorder and suicidal thoughts. His presentations and discussions of the film to young people around the country reflect the field's special emphasis on education as the ultimate form of suicide prevention.

One nonprofit service, the Crisis Text Line, has been offering text counseling since 2013, in partnership with a number of hotlines across the United States (Park, 2016; Kaufman, 2014; Lublin, 2014). In the first half year of operation, it exchanged nearly a million texts with 19,000 teenagers, with only minimal advertising, and by 2017 it had processed a total of 28 million texts. As you read earlier, Facebook and Google now link suicidal users or friends and relatives of suicidal persons to this service (Guynn, 2017).

> **What limitations or problems might result from attempts to prevent suicides by the use of texting?**

Some prevention centers and hotlines reach out to particular suicidal populations. The *Trevor Lifeline,* for example, is a nationwide, around-the-clock hotline available for LGBTQ teenagers who are thinking about suicide. This hotline is one of several services offered by the *Trevor Project,* a wide-reaching organization dedicated to providing support, guidance, and information and promoting acceptance of LGBTQ teens.

The public sometimes confuses suicide prevention centers and hotlines with online chat rooms and forums (message boards) to which some suicidal people turn. However, chat rooms and forums operate quite differently, and in fact, most of them do not seek out suicidal people or try to prevent suicide. Typically, these sites are not prepared to deal with suicidal people, do not offer face-to-face support, do not involve professionals or paraprofessionals, and do not have ways of keeping out malicious users.

Today, suicide prevention takes place not only at prevention centers and hotlines but also in therapists' offices. Suicide experts encourage all therapists to look for and address signs of suicidal thinking in their clients, regardless of the broad reasons that the clients are seeking treatment (McGlothlin, 2008). With this in mind, a number of guidelines have been developed to help therapists effectively uncover, assess, prevent, and treat suicidal thinking and behavior in their daily work (de Beurs et al., 2015; Van Orden et al., 2008; Shneidman & Farberow, 1968).

Although specific techniques vary from therapist to therapist and from prevention center to prevention center, the approach developed originally by the Los Angeles Suicide Prevention Center continues to reflect the goals and techniques of many clinicians and organizations. During the initial contact at the center, the counselor has several tasks:

Establish a Positive Relationship As callers must trust counselors in order to confide in them and follow their suggestions, counselors try to set a positive and comfortable tone for the discussion. They convey that they are listening, understanding, interested, nonjudgmental, and available.

#HeightenedRisk

Some studies find that birthdays are associated with a greater risk of suicide. People are significantly more likely to complete suicide on their birthday (Stickley et al., 2016).

Understand and Clarify the Problem Counselors first try to understand the full scope of the caller's crisis and then help the person see the crisis in clear and constructive terms. In particular, they try to help callers see the central issues and the transient nature of their crises and recognize the alternatives to suicide.

Assess Suicide Potential Crisis workers at the Los Angeles Suicide Prevention Center fill out a questionnaire, often called a *lethality scale,* to estimate the caller's potential for suicide. It helps them determine the degree of stress the caller is under, the caller's relevant personality characteristics, how detailed the suicide plan is, the severity of symptoms, and the coping resources available to the caller.

Assess and Mobilize the Caller's Resources Although they may view themselves as ineffectual, helpless, and alone, people who are suicidal usually have many strengths and resources, including relatives and friends. It is the counselor's job to recognize, point out, and activate those resources.

Formulate a Plan Together the crisis worker and caller develop a plan of action. In essence, they are agreeing on a way out of the crisis, an alternative to suicidal action. Most plans include a series of follow-up counseling sessions over the next few days or weeks, either in person at the center or by phone. Each plan also requires the caller to take certain actions and make certain changes in his or her personal life. Counselors usually negotiate a *no-suicide contract* with the caller—a promise not to attempt suicide, or at least a promise to reestablish contact if the caller again considers suicide. Although such contracts are popular, their effectiveness has been called into question in recent years (Schreiber & Culpepper, 2016; Rudd et al., 2006). In addition, if callers are in the midst of a suicide attempt, counselors try to find out their whereabouts and get medical help to them immediately.

Although crisis intervention may be sufficient treatment for some suicidal people, longer-term therapy is needed for most (Lester et al., 2007). If a crisis intervention center does not offer this kind of therapy, its counselors will refer the clients elsewhere.

As the suicide prevention movement spread during the 1960s, many clinicians came to believe that crisis intervention techniques should also be applied to problems other than suicide. Crisis intervention has emerged during the past several decades as a respected form of treatment for such wide-ranging problems as drug and alcohol abuse, rape, and spouse abuse.

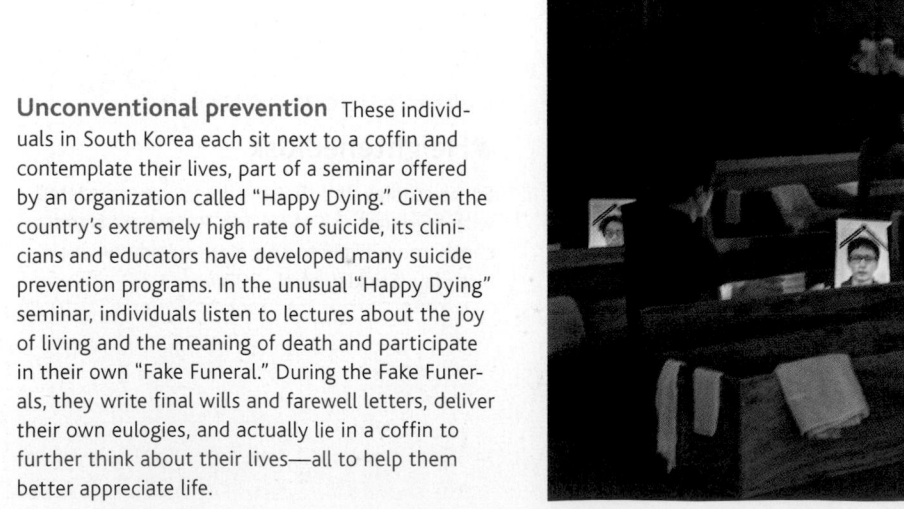

#TwitterAlert

Numerous tweeters express suicidality on Twitter. All suicide-related tweets should be taken seriously, but research has found that those with a higher word count, greater use of first-person pronouns, and more references to death may be of particular concern (O'Dea et al., 2018).

Unconventional prevention These individuals in South Korea each sit next to a coffin and contemplate their lives, part of a seminar offered by an organization called "Happy Dying." Given the country's extremely high rate of suicide, its clinicians and educators have developed many suicide prevention programs. In the unusual "Happy Dying" seminar, individuals listen to lectures about the joy of living and the meaning of death and participate in their own "Fake Funeral." During the Fake Funerals, they write final wills and farewell letters, deliver their own eulogies, and actually lie in a coffin to further think about their lives—all to help them better appreciate life.

Yet another way to help prevent suicide may be to reduce the public's access to particularly lethal and common means of suicide through measures such as gun control, safer medications, better bridge barriers, and car emission controls (Anestis & Houtsma, 2018; Zalsman et al., 2016). In 1960, for example, around 12 of every 100,000 people in Britain killed themselves by inhaling coal gas (which contains carbon monoxide). In the 1960s, Britain replaced coal gas with natural gas (which contains much less carbon monoxide) as an energy source, and by the mid-1970s the rate of coal gas suicide fell to 0 (Maris, 2001). In fact, England's overall rate of suicide, at least for older people, dropped as well. On the other hand, the Netherlands' drop in gas-induced suicides was compensated for by an increase in other methods, particularly drug overdoses.

Similarly, ever since Canada passed a law in the 1990s restricting the availability of and access to certain firearms, there has been a decrease in firearm suicides across the country (Leenaars, 2007). Some, but not all, studies suggest that this decrease has not been displaced by increases in other kinds of suicides (Caron, Julien, & Huang, 2008).

Do Suicide Prevention Programs Work?

It is difficult for researchers to measure the effectiveness of suicide prevention programs (Sanburn, 2013; Lester, 2011). There are many kinds of programs, each with its own procedures and each serving populations that vary in number, age, and the like. Communities with high suicide risk factors, such as a high elderly population or economic problems, may continue to have higher suicide rates than other communities regardless of the effectiveness of their local prevention centers.

Do suicide prevention centers reduce the number of suicides in a community? Clinical researchers do not know (Sanburn, 2013). Studies comparing local suicide rates before and after the establishment of community prevention centers have yielded different findings. Some find a decline in a community's suicide rates, others no change, and still others an increase (De Leo & Evans, 2004; Leenaars & Lester, 2004). Of course, even an increase may represent a positive impact, if it is lower than the larger society's overall increase in suicidal behavior.

Do suicidal people contact prevention centers? Apparently only a small percentage do (Sanburn, 2013). Moreover, the typical caller to an urban prevention center appears to be young, African American, and female, whereas the greatest number of suicides are carried out by older non-Hispanic white men (Maris, 2001). On the other hand, prevention programs do seem to reduce the number of suicides among those high-risk people who do call. One famous study identified 8,000 high-risk individuals who contacted the Los Angeles Suicide Prevention Center (Farberow & Litman, 1970). Approximately 2 percent of these callers later killed themselves, compared with the 6 percent suicide rate usually found in similar high-risk groups. Clearly, centers need to be more visible and available to people who are thinking of suicide. The growing number of advertisements and announcements on the Web, television, radio, and billboards indicate movement in this direction.

A key difficulty for suicide prevention programs is that they depend on accurate assessments of suicide risk, and accurate assessments are elusive. People who are suicidal do not necessarily admit to or talk about their true feelings in discussions with professionals. With this in mind, some researchers are working to develop tools of suicide assessment that rely less on verbal self-reports and more on non-verbal behaviors, psychophysiological measures, brain scans, and the like.

A different kind of military threat Concerned about the growing number of military suicides, the U.S. Army has set up suicide-prevention programs for soldiers around the world, centering on the theme of this anti-suicide poster. Research indicates that 80 percent of soldiers who have died by suicide had a current or prior psychological disorder at the time of their act (Nock et al., 2017, 2014).

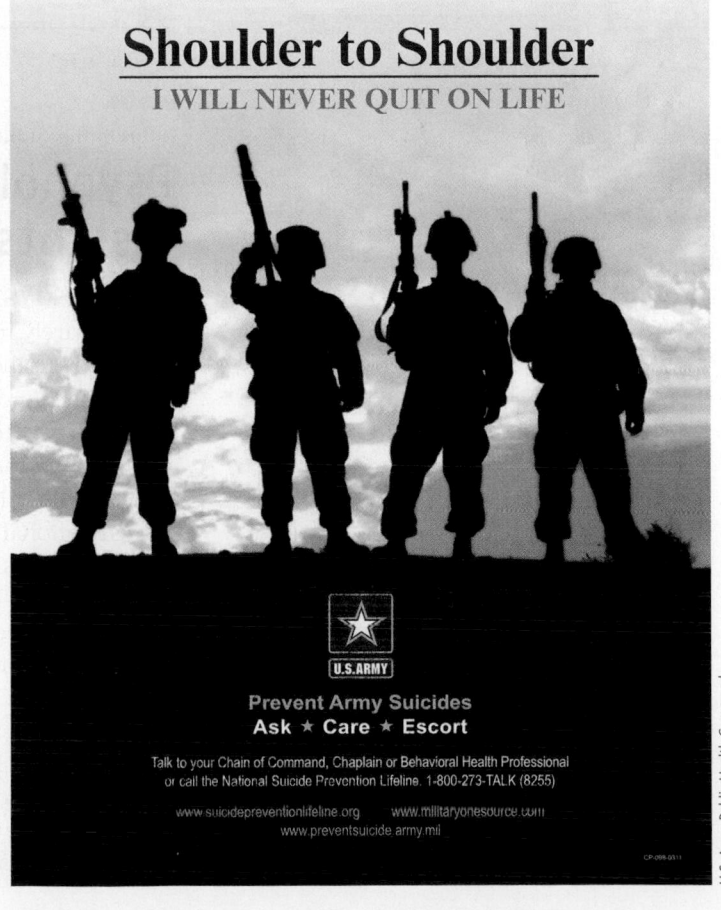

One alternative assessment approach is the Self-Injury Implicit Association Test, developed by researcher Matthew Nock. Rather than asking people if they plan to attempt suicide, this cognitive test simply instructs them to pair various suicide-related words (for example, "dead", "lifeless", "suicide") with words that are personally relevant ("I", "myself", "mine") and with words that are not personally relevant ("they", "them", "other"). It turns out that individuals who are inclined to attempt suicide pair the suicide-related words with personally relevant words much more quickly than with nonpersonally relevant words. In a number of studies, this test has detected and predicted past and future suicide behavior more accurately than traditional self-report assessment scales (Barnes et al., 2017; Glenn et al., 2017; Nock et al., 2010). Needless to say, this promising approach to assessment has captured the attention of many suicide researchers and clinicians.

> **Why might some schools be reluctant to offer suicide education programs, especially if they have never experienced a suicide attempt by one of their students?**

While the field awaits more accurate assessment tools and more effective interventions, many theorists believe that public education about suicide is the ultimate form of prevention—and a number of *suicide education programs* have emerged. Most of these programs take place in schools and concentrate on students and their teachers (Zalsman et al., 2016; Joshi et al., 2015). There are also a growing number of online sites that provide education about suicide—targeting troubled persons, their family members, and friends (Lai et al., 2014). These offerings agree with the following statement by Shneidman:

The primary prevention of suicide lies in education. The route is through teaching one another and . . . the public that suicide can happen to anyone, that there are verbal and behavioral clues that can be looked for . . . and that help is available. . . .
In the last analysis, the prevention of suicide is everybody's business.

(Shneidman, 1985, p. 238)

#FatalAccess

The rate of gun-related suicide is 11 times higher in the United States than in all other industrialized countries.

People who die by suicide are at least twice as likely to have a gun in their house as people who survive their suicide attempts.

Suicide rates increase 4 to 10 times among teenagers who live in a house with a gun.

(Anestis & Houtsma, 2018; Kennebeck & Bonin, 2016; Schreiber & Culpepper, 2016).

Psychological and Biological Insights Lag Behind

ONCE A MYSTERIOUS AND HIDDEN problem, hardly acknowledged by the public and barely investigated by professionals, suicide today is the focus of much attention. During the past 50 years in particular, investigators have learned a great deal about this life-or-death problem.

In contrast to most other problems covered in this textbook, suicide has received much more examination from the sociocultural model than from any other. Sociocultural theorists have, for example, highlighted the importance of societal change and stress, national and religious affiliation, marital status, gender, race, and the mass media. The insights and information gathered by psychological and biological researchers have been more limited.

Although sociocultural factors certainly shed light on the general background and triggers of suicide, they typically leave us unable to predict that a given person will attempt suicide. Clinicians do not yet fully understand why some people kill themselves while others in similar circumstances manage to find better ways of addressing their problems. Psychological and biological insights must catch up to the sociocultural insights if clinicians are truly to explain and understand suicide.

At the same time, the growth in the amount of research on suicide offers great promise. And perhaps most promising of all, clinicians are now enlisting the public in the fight against this problem. They are calling for broader public education about suicide—for programs aimed at both young and old. It is reasonable to expect that the current commitment will lead to a better understanding of suicide and to more successful interventions. Such goals are of importance to everyone. Although suicide itself is typically a lonely and desperate act, the impact of such acts is very broad indeed.

♀... SUMMING UP

» What Is Suicide? *Suicide* is a self-inflicted death in which a person makes an intentional, direct, and conscious effort to end his or her life. Four kinds of people who intentionally end their lives have been distinguished: the *death seeker,* the *death initiator,* the *death ignorer,* and the *death darer. pp. 250–253*

» Research Strategies Two major strategies are used in the study of suicide: *retrospective analysis* (a psychological autopsy) and the *study of people who survive suicide attempts,* on the assumption that they are similar to those who carry out fatal suicides. Each strategy has limitations.

Suicide ranks among the top 10 causes of death in Western societies. Rates vary from country to country. One reason seems to be cultural differences in *religious affiliation, beliefs,* and *degree of devoutness.* Suicide rates also vary according to *race, gender,* and *marital status. pp. 253–255*

» What Triggers a Suicide? Many suicidal acts are triggered by the current events or conditions in a person's life. The acts may be triggered by *recent stressors,* such as loss of a loved one and job loss, or *long-term stressors,* such as serious illness, an abusive environment, and job stress. They may also be preceded by *changes in mood or thought,* particularly increases in one's sense of *hopelessness.* In addition, the *use of alcohol or other kinds of substances, mental disorders,* or *news of another's suicide* may precede suicide attempts. *pp. 256–261*

» What Are the Underlying Causes of Suicide? The leading explanations for suicide come from the psychodynamic, sociocultural, and biological models. *Psychodynamic* theorists believe that suicide usually results from depression and self-directed anger. Emile Durkheim's *sociocultural* theory defines three categories of suicide, based on the person's relationship with society: *egoistic, altruistic,* and *anomic* suicides. A more recent theory, the *interpersonal theory,* asserts that people with *perceived burdensomeness, thwarted belongingness,* and a psychological *capability* to carry out suicide are more likely to attempt suicide. And *biological* theorists suggest that low serotonin activity and abnormalities in the depression-related brain circuit contribute to suicide. *pp. 261–266*

» Is Suicide Linked to Age? The likelihood of suicide varies with age. It is uncommon among *children,* although it has been rising in that group during the past several decades. Adolescent suicide has been linked to clinical depression, anger, impulsiveness, major stress, and adolescent life itself. *Suicide attempts* by this age group are numerous. The high attempt rate among adolescents and young adults may be related to the growing number and proportion of young people in the general population, the weakening of family ties, the increased availability and use of drugs among young people, and the broad media coverage of suicide attempts by the young. The rate of suicide among American Indian teens is twice as high as that among non-Hispanic white American teens and three times as high as those of African, Hispanic, and Asian American teens.

In Western societies, the *elderly* are more likely to end their lives than people in most other age groups. The loss of health, friends, control, and status may produce feelings of hopelessness, loneliness, depression, or inevitability in this age group. *pp. 266–274*

» Treatment and Suicide Treatment may *follow* a suicide attempt. When it does, therapists try to help the person achieve a nonsuicidal state of mind and develop better ways of handling stress and solving problems.

Over the past half century, emphasis has shifted to *suicide prevention.* Suicide prevention programs include 24-hour-a-day hotlines and walk-in centers staffed largely by *paraprofessionals.* During their initial contact with a suicidal person, counselors try to establish a positive relationship, understand and clarify the problem, assess the potential for suicide, assess and mobilize the caller's resources, and formulate a plan for overcoming the crisis. Beyond such *crisis intervention,* most suicidal people also need *longer-term therapy.* In a still broader attempt at prevention, *suicide education programs* for the public are on the increase. *pp. 274–280*

Visit *LaunchPad*
to access the e-Book, Clinical Choices, videos, activities, and LearningCurve, as well as study aids including flashcards, FAQs, and research exercises.

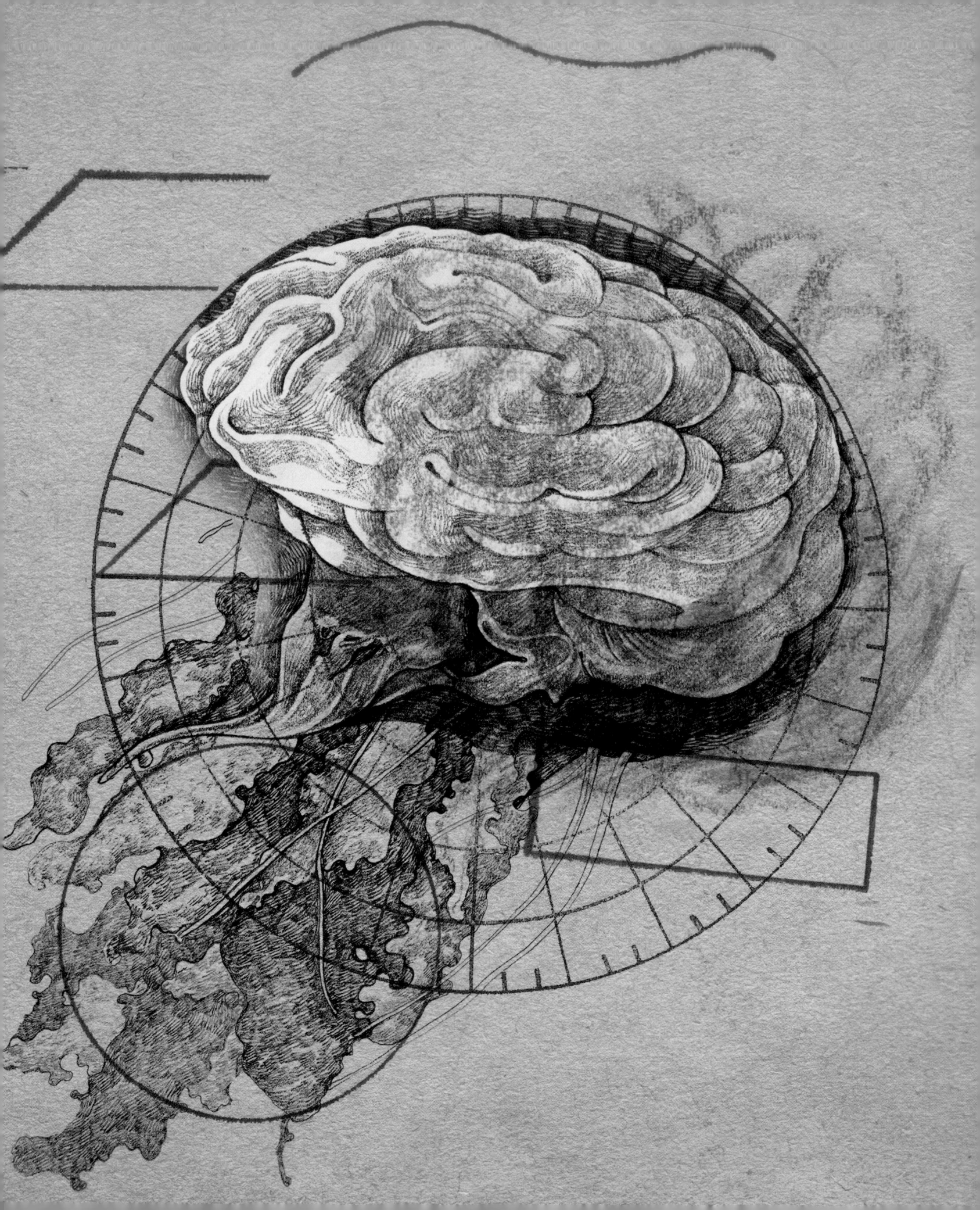

⚲...Disorders Featuring Somatic Symptoms

It was Wednesday. The big day. Midterms in history and physics back to back, beginning at 11:30, and an oral presentation in psych at 3:30. Jarell had been preparing for, and dreading, this day for weeks, calling it "D-Day" to his friends. He had been up until 3:30 a.m. the night before, studying, trying to nail everything down. It seemed like he had fallen asleep only minutes ago, yet here it was 9:30 a.m. and the killer day was under way.

As soon as he woke, Jarell felt a tight pain grip his stomach. He also noticed buzzing in his ears, a lightheadedness, and even aches throughout his body. He wasn't surprised, given the day he was about to face. One test might bring a few butterflies of anxiety; two and a presentation were probably good for a platoon of dragonflies.

As he tried to get going, however, Jarell began to suspect that this was more than butterflies. His stomach pain soon turned to spasms, and his lightheadedness became outright dizziness. He could barely make it to the bathroom without falling. Thoughts of breakfast made him nauseous. He knew he couldn't keep anything down.

Jarell began to worry, even panic. This was hardly the best way to face what was in store for him today. He tried to shake it off, but the symptoms stayed. Finally, his roommate convinced him that he had better go to a doctor. At 10:30, just an hour before the first exam, he entered the big brick building called "Student Health." He felt embarrassed, like a wimp, but what could he do? Persevering and taking two tests under these conditions wouldn't prove anything—except maybe that he was foolish.

Psychological factors may contribute to somatic, or bodily, illnesses in a variety of ways. The physician who sees Jarell has some possibilities to sort out. Jarell could be *faking* his pain and dizziness to avoid taking some tough tests. Alternatively, he may be *imagining* his illness, that is, faking to himself. Or he could be *overreacting* to his pain and dizziness. Then again, his physical symptoms could be both real and significant, yet triggered by *stress:* whenever he feels extreme pressure, such as a person can feel before an important test, Jarell's gastric juices may become more active and irritate his intestines, and his blood pressure may rise and cause him to become dizzy. Finally, he may be coming down with the flu. Even this "purely medical" problem, however, could be linked to psychological factors. Perhaps weeks of constant worry about the exams and presentation have weakened Jarell's body so that he was not able to fight off the flu virus. Whatever the diagnosis, Jarell's state of mind is affecting his body. The physician's view of the role played by psychological factors will in turn affect the treatment Jarell receives.

You have observed throughout the book that psychological disorders frequently have physical causes. Dysfunctional brain circuits and abnormal neurotransmitter activity, for example, contribute to generalized anxiety disorder, panic disorder, and posttraumatic stress disorder. Is it surprising, then, that bodily illnesses may have psychological causes? Today's clinicians recognize the wisdom of Socrates' assertion made many centuries ago: "You should not treat body without soul."

The idea that psychological factors may contribute to somatic illnesses has ancient roots, yet it had few proponents before the twentieth century. It was particularly unpopular during the Renaissance, when medicine began to be a physical science and scientists became committed to the pursuit of objective "fact" (Conti, 2014). At that time, the mind was considered the territory of priests and philosophers, not of physicians and scientists. By the seventeenth century, the French philosopher René Descartes went so far as to claim that the mind, or soul, is totally separate from the body—a position called *mind-body dualism*. Over the course of the twentieth century, however, numerous studies convinced medical and clinical researchers that psychological factors such as stress, worry, and perhaps even unconscious needs can contribute in major ways to bodily illness.

DSM-5 lists a number of psychological disorders in which bodily symptoms or concerns are the primary features of the disorders. These include *factitious disorder*, in which patients intentionally produce or feign physical symptoms; *conversion disorder*, which is characterized by medically unexplained physical symptoms that affect voluntary motor or sensory functioning; *somatic symptom disorder*, in which people become disproportionately concerned, distressed, and disrupted by bodily symptoms; *illness anxiety disorder*, in which people who are anxious about their health become preoccupied with the notion that they are seriously ill despite the absence of bodily symptoms; and *psychological factors affecting other medical conditions*, disorders in which psychological factors adversely affect a person's general medical condition. ■

Factitious Disorder

LIKE JARELL, PEOPLE WHO become physically sick usually go to a physician. Sometimes, however, the physician cannot find a medical cause for the problem and may suspect that other factors are involved. Perhaps the patient is *malingering*—intentionally feigning illness to achieve some external gain, such as financial compensation or deferment from military service (Greenberg, 2016; Irwin & Bursch, 2016).

Alternatively, a patient may intentionally produce or feign physical symptoms from a wish to be a patient; that is, the motivation for assuming the sick role may be the role itself (Weis et al., 2016). Physicians would then decide that the patient is manifesting **factitious disorder** (see **Table 10-1**). Consider, for example, the symptoms of Adia, a patient with bacteremia—presence of bacteria in the blood, which can, if not corrected, lead to the life-threatening condition called sepsis. As you will see, the medical team's handling of Adia's right to privacy raises ethical issues, but the case itself illustrates the features of factitious disorder.

[Adia] was referred to [the medical center] for evaluation of recurrent urinary tract infections and bacteremia. . . . She also had a skin disorder with blisters. An extensive workup showed no evidence of immunocompromise, no source of sepsis, and a completely normal genitourinary tract. . . . She was employed as a medical technologist and was married, with two children. She had no history of narcotic abuse.

Based on these clinical and social features, one of the several doctors on this case suspected that the patient was inducing her own illness, and he decided to secretly search her personal possessions. [Such a search] is always done with trepidation. In this case, the upside would be discovery of materials that indicate self-induced disease, which would provide an explanation for her recurrent [problem]. The downside is that the doctor may find nothing unusual [although] his intentions were honorable. It's not a comfortable feeling.

While the patient was having an x-ray, her room was searched. Her purse contained a Petri dish with growing bacterial colonies, as well as needles, a syringe, and a tourniquet. The colonies were subcultured and the Petri dish replaced. Later that day, the patient was asked whether she might be harming herself by injection [of bacteria into her body]. She denied this, saying that she wanted to get better. Still later that day, the doctor told the patient that he knew she had some incriminating items in her purse. She then opened her

factitious disorder A disorder in which a person feigns or induces physical symptoms, typically for the purpose of assuming the role of a sick person.

purse so the doctor could see inside, and the items were apparently no longer present. To prove her point, the patient turned her purse upside down. At that point, one needle and a syringe fell out, which she had apparently overlooked when she returned from her x-ray and suspected that someone had searched her purse. The patient was upset about the room search but not visibly angry. She readily agreed to see a psychiatrist but continued to deny self-injection.

The next day, the patient tearfully confessed that she had had bacteriological materials in her purse, but she said she used them only to aspirate and culture some blisters on her skin. She still denied self-injection with bacteria and said she wanted the doctors to "keep looking for the cause of my problems."

(Savino & Fordtran, 2006, pp. 201–202)

Factitious disorder is known popularly as *Munchausen syndrome,* a label derived from the exploits of Baron von Münchhausen, an eighteenth-century cavalry officer who journeyed from tavern to tavern in Europe telling fantastical tales about his supposed military adventures (Ayoub, 2010). People with factitious disorder often go to extremes to create the appearance of illness (APA, 2013). Many give themselves medications secretly. Some, like the woman just described, inject drugs to cause bleeding, infections, or other problems (Yates & Feldman, 2016). Still others use laxatives to produce chronic diarrhea. High fevers are especially easy to create. In studies of patients with a prolonged mysterious fever, 9 percent were eventually diagnosed with factitious disorder (Irwin & Bursch, 2016).

People with factitious disorder often research their supposed ailments and are impressively knowledgeable about medicine. Many eagerly undergo painful testing or treatment, even surgery (McDermott et al., 2012). When confronted with evidence that their symptoms are factitious, they typically deny the charges and leave the hospital; they may enter another hospital the same day.

Clinical researchers have had a hard time determining the prevalence of factitious disorder, since patients with the disorder hide the true nature of their problem (Kapfhammer, 2017). Overall, the pattern appears to be more common in women than men. Men, however, may more often have severe cases. The disorder usually begins during early adulthood.

Factitious disorder seems to be particularly common among people who (1) received extensive treatment for a medical problem as children, (2) carry a grudge against the medical profession, or (3) have worked as a nurse, laboratory technician, or medical aide (Yates & Feldman, 2016). A number have poor social support, few enduring social relationships, and little family life (Irwin & Bursch, 2016; McDermott et al., 2012).

The precise causes of factitious disorder are not understood, although clinical reports have pointed to factors such as depression, unsupportive parental relationships during childhood, and extreme needs for attention and/or social support that are not otherwise available (Irwin & Bursch, 2016; Yates & Feldman, 2016). Nor have clinicians been able to develop dependably effective treatments for this disorder.

Psychotherapists and medical practitioners often report feelings of annoyance or anger toward people with factitious disorder, feeling that these people are, at the very least, wasting their time (Greenberg, 2016; Weis et al., 2016). Yet people with the disorder feel they have no control over the problem, and they often experience great distress.

TABLE: 10-1
Dx Checklist

Factitious Disorder Imposed on Self

1. False creation of physical psychological symptoms, or deceptive production of injury or disease, even without external rewards for such ailments.

2. Presentation of oneself as ill, damaged, or hurt.

Factitious Disorder Imposed on Another

1. False creation of physical or psychological symptoms, or deceptive production of injury or disease, in another person, even without external rewards for such ailments.

2. Presentation of another person (victim) as ill, damaged, or hurt.

Information from: APA, 2013.

"My back is fine. My mind went out."

In a related pattern, *factitious disorder imposed on another,* known popularly as *Munchausen syndrome by proxy,* parents or caretakers make up or produce physical illnesses in their children, leading in some cases to repeated painful diagnostic tests, medication, and surgery (Gomila et al., 2016; Koetting, 2015) (see Table 10-1 again). If the children are removed from their parents and placed in the care of others, their symptoms disappear (see *PsychWatch*).

PSYCH WATCH

Munchausen Syndrome by Proxy

Tanya, a mere 8 years old, had been hospitalized 127 times over the past five years and undergone 28 different medical procedures—from removal of her spleen to exploratory surgery of her intestines. Two months ago, her mother was arrested, charged with child endangerment. When Tanya's grandmother gently tried to talk to the girl about her mother's arrest (or, as she put, "Mommy's going away"), Tanya was upset and confused.

"I miss Mommy so much. She's the best person in the world. She spent all her time with me in the hospital. They say Mommy was making me feel bad, putting bad stuff in my tube. But there's no way Mommy made me feel that bad."

Cases like Tanya's have horrified the public and called attention to *Munchausen syndrome by proxy*. This form of factitious disorder is caused by a caregiver who uses various techniques to induce symptoms in a child—giving the child drugs, tampering with medications, contaminating a feeding tube, or even smothering the child, for example (Gomila et al., 2016; Akin et al., 2016). The illness can take almost any form, but the most common symptoms are bleeding, seizures, asthma, comas, diarrhea, vomiting, "accidental" poisonings, infections, fevers, and sudden infant death syndrome (Wittkowski et al., 2017).

Between 6 and 30 percent of the victims of Munchausen syndrome by proxy die as a result of their symptoms, and 8 percent of those who survive are permanently disfigured or physically impaired (Braham et al., 2017; Ayoub, 2006). Psychological, educational, and physical development are also affected (Bass & Glaser, 2014; Schreier et al., 2010).

The syndrome is very hard to diagnose and may be more common than clinicians once thought (Ashraf & Thevasagayam, 2014; Scheuerman et al., 2013). The parent

Convalescent, 1867, by Frank Holl

Frank Holl, Convalescent. Private Collection ©Christopher Wood Gallery, London, UK /Bridgeman Images

(usually the mother) seems to be so devoted and caring that others sympathize with and admire her. Yet the physical problems disappear when the child and parent are separated (Roesler & Jenny, 2016; Koetting, 2015). In many cases, siblings of the sick child are also victimized (Braham et al., 2017; Ayoub, 2010, 2006).

> **Should society treat or punish those parents who produce Munchausen syndrome by proxy in their children?**

What kind of parent carefully inflicts pain and illness on her own child? The typical Munchausen mother is emotionally needy: she craves the attention and praise she receives for her devoted care of her sick child (Ashraf & Thevasagayam, 2014; Noeker, 2004). She may have little social support outside the medical system. Often the mothers have a medical background of some kind—perhaps having worked

formerly in a doctor's office. A number have medically unexplained physical problems of their own (Roesler & Jenny, 2016). Typically they deny their actions, even in the face of clear evidence, and initially may refuse to undergo therapy.

Law enforcement authorities approach Munchausen syndrome by proxy as a crime—a carefully planned form of child abuse (Irwin & Bursch, 2016). They almost always require that the child be separated from the mother (Koetting, 2015; Ayoub, 2010, 2006). At the same time, a parent who resorts to such actions is seriously disturbed and greatly in need of clinical help. In the majority of cases, particularly those that are of moderate or modest severity, treatment makes it possible for the parent to be reintegrated into the family (Roesler & Jenny, 2016). Currently, clinical researchers and practitioners are working to develop still clearer insights and more effective treatments for such parents and their young victims.

Conversion Disorder and Somatic Symptom Disorder

WHEN A BODILY AILMENT HAS an excessive and disproportionate impact on the person, has no apparent medical cause, or is inconsistent with known medical diseases, physicians may suspect a *conversion disorder* or a *somatic symptom disorder*. Consider the plight of Brian:

Brian was spending Saturday sailing with his wife, Helen. The water was rough but well within what they considered safe limits. They were having a wonderful time and really didn't notice that the sky was getting darker, the wind blowing harder, and the sailboat becoming more difficult to control. After a few hours of sailing, they found themselves far from shore in the middle of a powerful and dangerous storm.

The storm intensified very quickly. Brian had trouble controlling the sailboat amidst the high winds and wild waves. He and Helen tried to put on the safety jackets they had neglected to wear earlier, but the boat turned over before they were finished. Brian, the better swimmer of the two, was able to swim back to the overturned sailboat, grab the side, and hold on for dear life, but Helen simply could not overcome the rough waves and reach the boat. As Brian watched in horror and disbelief, his wife disappeared from view.

After a time, the storm began to lose its strength. Brian managed to right the sailboat and sail back to shore. Finally he reached safety, but the personal consequences of this storm were just beginning. The next days were filled with pain and further horror: the Coast Guard finding Helen's body . . . texts, emails, and conversations with family members and friends . . . self-blame . . . grief . . . and more. Compounding this horror, the accident had left Brian with a severe physical impairment—he could not walk properly. He first noticed this terrible impairment when he sailed the boat back to shore, right after the accident. As he tried to run from the sailboat to get help, he could hardly make his legs work. By the time he reached the nearby beach restaurant, all he could do was crawl. Two patrons had to lift him to a chair, and after he told his story and the authorities were alerted, he had to be taken to a hospital.

At first Brian and the hospital physician assumed that he must have been hurt during the accident. One by one, however, the hospital tests revealed nothing—no broken bones, no spinal damage, nothing. Nothing that could explain such severe impairment.

By the following morning, the weakness in his legs had become near paralysis. Because the physicians could not pin down the nature of his injuries, they decided to keep his activities to a minimum. He was not allowed to talk long with the police. To his deep regret, he was not even permitted to attend Helen's funeral.

The mystery deepened over the following days and weeks. As Brian's paralysis continued, he became more and more withdrawn, unable to see more than a few friends and family members and unable to take care of the many unpleasant tasks attached to Helen's death. He could not bring himself to return to work or get on with his life. Texting, emailing, and phone conversations slowly came to a halt. At most, he was able to go online and surf the Internet. Almost from the beginning, Brian's paralysis had left him self-absorbed and drained of emotion, unable to look back and unable to move forward.

Conversion Disorder

Eventually, Brian received a diagnosis of **conversion disorder** (see **Table 10-2**). People with this disorder display physical symptoms that affect voluntary motor or sensory functioning, but the symptoms are inconsistent with known medical diseases (APA, 2013). In short, they have neurological-like symptoms—for example, paralysis, blindness, or loss of feeling—that have no neurological basis.

#SeekingRelief

Research suggests that 17 percent of patients under the care of family physicians display physical symptoms that have no apparent physical cause (Greenberg, 2016).

conversion disorder A disorder in which a person's bodily symptoms affect his or her voluntary motor and sensory functions, but the symptoms are inconsistent with known medical diseases.

Conversion disorder often is hard, even for physicians, to distinguish from a genuine medical problem (Tsui, Deptula, & Yuan, 2017; Ali et al., 2015). In fact, it is always possible that a diagnosis of conversion disorder is a mistake and that the patient's problem has an undetected neurological or other medical cause (Greenberg, 2016; Stone & Sharpe, 2016, 2015). Because conversion disorders are so similar to "genuine" medical ailments, physicians sometimes rely on oddities in the patient's medical picture to help distinguish the two (Tsui et al., 2017). The symptoms of a conversion disorder may, for example, be at odds with the way the nervous system is known to work. In a conversion symptom called *glove anesthesia,* numbness begins sharply at the wrist and extends evenly right to the fingertips. As **Figure 10-1** shows, real neurological damage is rarely as abrupt or evenly spread out.

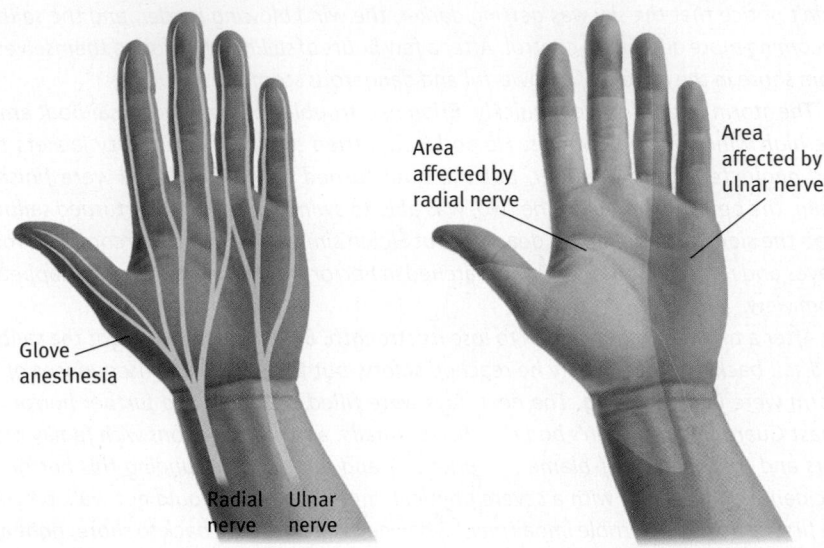

FIGURE 10-1

Glove Anesthesia

In this conversion symptom (left figure) the entire hand, extending from the fingertips to the wrist, becomes numb. Actual physical damage (right figure) to the ulnar nerve, in contrast, causes anesthesia in the ring finger and little finger and beyond the wrist partway up the arm; damage to the radial nerve causes loss of feeling only in parts of the ring, middle, and index fingers and the thumb and partway up the arm. (Information from: Gray, 1959.)

Area affected by radial nerve

Area affected by ulnar nerve

Glove anesthesia

Radial nerve   Ulnar nerve

The physical effects of a conversion disorder may also differ from those of the corresponding medical problem (Stone & Sharpe, 2016, 2015; Ali et al., 2015). For example, when paralysis from the waist down, or paraplegia, is caused by damage to the spinal cord, a person's leg muscles may *atrophy,* or waste away, unless physical therapy is applied. The muscles of people whose paralysis is the result of a conversion disorder, in contrast, do not usually atrophy. Perhaps those with a conversion disorder exercise their muscles without being aware that they are doing so. Similarly, people with conversion blindness have fewer accidents than people who are organically blind, an indication that they have at least some vision even if they are unaware of it.

Unlike people with factitious disorder, those with conversion disorder do not consciously want or purposely produce their symptoms. Like Brian, they almost always believe that their problems are genuinely medical (Greenberg, 2016). This pattern is called "conversion" disorder because clinical theorists used to believe that individuals with the disorder are converting psychological needs or conflicts into their neurological-like symptoms (Ding & Kanaan, 2017). Although some theorists still believe that conversion is at work in the disorder, others prefer alternative kinds of explanations, as you'll see later.

Conversion disorder usually begins between late childhood and young adulthood; it is diagnosed at least twice as often in women as in men (Raj et al., 2014). It often appears suddenly, at times of extreme stress. In some, but far from all, cases, conversion disorder lasts a matter of weeks (Stone & Sharpe, 2016, 2015; Kukla et al., 2010). Some research suggests that people who develop the disorder tend to be generally suggestible (see **MindTech**); many are highly susceptible to hypnotic procedures, for example (Tsui et al., 2017; Roelofs et al., 2002). It is thought to be a rare problem, occurring in at most 5 of every 1,000 persons (Stone & Sharpe, 2016, 2015).

TABLE: 10-2

Dx Checklist

Conversion Disorder

1. Presence of at least one symptom or deficit that affects voluntary or sensory function.

2. Symptoms are found to be inconsistent with known neurological or medical disease.

3. Significant distress or impairment.

Information from: APA, 2013.

Can Social Media Spread "Mass Hysteria"?

In Chapter 1, you read about outbreaks during the Middle Ages of *mass madness*, also called *mass hysteria* or *mass psychogenic illness*, in which large numbers of people would share psychological or physical maladies that had no apparent cause (see page 9). Periodic outbreaks of mysterious illnesses are not a thing of the past. In fact, the number of such cases currently seems to be on the increase (Boissoneault, 2017; Sample, 2015). Most of today's clinicians consider these outbreaks to be a form of conversion disorder.

New Zealand sociologist Robert Bartholemew (2014) has been studying mass psychogenic illnesses that date back over 400 years, and he argues that social media is a major factor in the current increase. One notable 2011 outbreak in Le Roy, New York, demonstrates the suggestive role played by social media (Goldstein & Hall, 2015; Vitelli, 2013; Dominus, 2012). A local high school student began having facial spasms. After several weeks, others started having similar symptoms, and eventually 18 girls from the high school were affected. Apparently, a number of these teenagers began to show symptoms after they saw a YouTube video featuring a girl from a nearby town who had significant tics. Doctors eventually concluded that this was an example of mass psychogenic illness.

An unusual aspect of the Le Roy case that further points to the likely role of social media is that in addition to the 18 high school girls, a 36-year-old woman with no connection to the teenage girls also began

Modern mass hysteria? A "flash mob" gathers around a security officer at Moscow's International Airport, waving their hands and arms. Some theorists believe that these increasingly common gatherings of numerous people are a form of mass hysteria—especially those flash mobs that are sudden, unplanned, and characterized by chaotic dance moves and flailing limbs.

Sergei Bobylev\TASS via Getty Images

having the same symptoms during the same period of time (NBC, 2012). She stated that she first saw the facts of the case on a Facebook post.

> In what ways could social media itself help prevent or reduce cases of mass psychogenic illness?

This case mirrors others in recent years, such as an outbreak of hiccups and vocal tics in 2013 among teenagers in Danvers, Massachusetts, and the case of 400 garment workers in a Bangladesh factory who had severe gastrointestinal symptoms for

which there was ultimately no physical explanation (Boissoneault, 2017; Vitelli, 2013). In these and other cases, the symptoms seemed to be spread, at least in part, by social media exposure.

Bartholomew (2014) believes that due to the power of social media, future outbreaks may be more numerous, wide ranging, and severe than any yet recorded. He observes that in the distant past "the local priests, who were . . . summoned to [treat mass psychogenic illnesses], faced a daunting task . . . but they were fortunate in one regard: they did not have to contend with mobile phones, Twitter, and Facebook."

Somatic Symptom Disorder

People with **somatic symptom disorder** become excessively distressed, concerned, and anxious about bodily symptoms that they are experiencing, and their lives are greatly disrupted by those symptoms (APA, 2013) (see **Table 10-3**). The symptoms last longer but are less dramatic than those found in conversion disorder. In some cases, the somatic symptoms have no known cause; in others, the cause can be identified. Either way, the person's concerns are disproportionate to the seriousness of the bodily problems.

Two patterns of somatic symptom disorder have received particular attention. In one, sometimes called a *somatization pattern,* the individual experiences a large and

somatic symptom disorder A disorder in which people become excessively distressed, concerned, and anxious about bodily symptoms they are experiencing, and their lives are disproportionately disrupted by the symptoms.

TABLE: 10-3

Dx Checklist

Somatic Symptom Disorder

1. Person experiences at least one upsetting or repeatedly disruptive physical (somatic) symptom.

2. Person experiences an unreasonable number of thoughts, feelings, and behavior regarding the nature or implications of the physical symptoms, including one of the following:
   (a) Repeated, excessive thoughts about their seriousness.
   (b) Continual high anxiety about their nature or health implications.
   (c) Disproportionate amounts of time and energy spent on the symptoms or their health implications.

3. Physical symptoms usually continue to some degree for more than 6 months.

Information from: APA, 2013.

varied number of bodily symptoms. In the other, called a *predominant pain pattern,* the person's primary bodily problem is the experience of pain.

Somatization Pattern Sheila baffled medical specialists with the wide range of her symptoms:

> *Sheila reported having abdominal pain since age 17, necessitating exploratory surgery that yielded no specific diagnosis. She had several pregnancies, each with severe nausea, vomiting, and abdominal pain; she ultimately had a hysterectomy for a "tipped uterus." Since age 40 she had experienced dizziness and "blackouts," which she eventually was told might be multiple sclerosis or a brain tumor. She continued to be bedridden for extended periods of time, with weakness, blurred vision, and difficulty urinating. At age 43 she was worked up for a hiatal hernia because of complaints of bloating and intolerance of a variety of foods. She also had additional hospitalizations for neurological, hypertensive, and renal workups, all of which failed to reveal a definitive diagnosis.*
>
> *(Spitzer et al., 1994, 1981, pp. 185, 260)*

Like Sheila, people with a somatization pattern of somatic symptom disorder experience many long-lasting physical ailments—ailments that typically have little or no physical basis. This pattern, first described by Pierre Briquet in 1859, is also known as *Briquet's syndrome*. A sufferer's ailments often include pain symptoms (such as headaches or chest pain), gastrointestinal symptoms (such as nausea or diarrhea), sexual symptoms (such as erectile or menstrual difficulties), and neurological-type symptoms (such as double vision or paralysis).

People with a somatization pattern usually go from doctor to doctor in search of relief. They often describe their many symptoms in dramatic and exaggerated terms. Most also feel anxious and depressed (Walentynowicz et al., 2017). The pattern typically lasts for many years, fluctuating over time but rarely disappearing completely without therapy (Greenberg, 2016; Abbey, 2005).

As many as 4 percent of all people in the United States may experience a somatization pattern in any given year, women much more commonly than men (Greenberg, 2016; North, 2005). The pattern often runs in families; as many as 20 percent of the close female relatives of women with the pattern also develop it. It usually begins between adolescence and young adulthood. Apparently, victims of childhood or recent sexual abuse are more likely than nonvictims to develop this pattern in adulthood.

Mind over matter The opposite of conversion and somatic symptom disorders—although again demonstrating the power of psychological processes—are instances in which people "ignore" pain or other physical symptoms. Here a London performance artist manages to smile comfortably at onlookers while her skin is being pierced with sharp hooks that help suspend her from the ceiling above. Her action was part of a protest to end shark finning—the practice of cutting off a shark's fin and throwing its still-living body back into the sea so that the fins can be used in the production of shark fin soup (a food delicacy) and other goods.

AP Photo/Lefteris Pitarakis

Predominant Pain Pattern If the primary feature of somatic symptom disorder is pain, the person is said to have a predominant pain pattern. Patients with conversion disorder or another pattern of somatic symptom disorder may also experience pain, but it is the key symptom in this pattern. The source of the pain may be known or unknown. Either way, the concerns and disruption produced by the pain are disproportionate to its severity and seriousness.

Although the precise prevalence has not been determined, this pattern appears to be fairly common (Cozzi et al., 2017; Klein, 2015). It may begin at any age, and women seem more likely than men to experience it. Often it develops after an accident or during an illness that has caused genuine pain, which then takes on a life of its own. For example, Laura, a 36-year-old woman, reported pains that went far beyond the usual symptoms of her tubercular disease, called sarcoidosis:

> *Before the operation I would have little joint pains, nothing that really bothered me that much. After the operation I was having severe pains in my chest and in my ribs, and those were the type of problems I'd been having after the operation, that I didn't have before. . . . I'd go to an emergency room at night, 11:00, 12:00, 1:00 or so. I'd take the medicine, and the next day it stopped hurting, and I'd go back again. In the meantime this is when I went to the other doctors, to complain about the same thing, to find out what was wrong; and they could never find out what was wrong with me either. . . .*
>
> *. . . At certain points when I go out or my husband and I go out, we have to leave early because I start hurting. . . . A lot of times I just won't do things because my chest is hurting for one reason or another. . . . Two months ago when the doctor checked me and another doctor looked at the x-rays, he said he didn't see any signs of the sarcoid then and that they were doing a study now, on blood and various things, to see if it was connected to sarcoid. . . .*
>
> *(Green, 1985, pp. 60–63)*

What Causes Conversion and Somatic Symptom Disorders?

For many years, conversion and somatic symptom disorders were referred to as *hysterical* disorders. This label was meant to convey the prevailing belief that excessive and uncontrolled emotions underlie the bodily symptoms found in these disorders.

Work by Ambroise-Auguste Liébault and Hippolyte Bernheim in the late nineteenth century helped foster the notion that such psychological factors were at the root of hysterical disorders. These researchers founded the Nancy School in Paris for the study and treatment of mental disorders. There they were able to produce hysterical symptoms in normal people—deafness, paralysis, blindness, and numbness—by hypnotic suggestion, and they could remove the symptoms by the same means (see Chapter 1). If hypnotic suggestion could both produce and reverse physical dysfunctions, they concluded, hysterical disorders might themselves be caused by psychological processes.

> **Why do the terms "hysteria" and "hysterical" currently have such negative connotations in our society, as in "mass hysteria" and "hysterical personality"?**

Today's leading explanations for conversion and somatic symptom disorders come from the psychodynamic, cognitive-behavioral, and multicultural models. None has received much research support, however, and the disorders are still poorly understood (Stone & Sharpe, 2016, 2015).

The Psychodynamic View As you read in Chapter 1, Freud's theory of psychoanalysis began with his efforts to explain hysterical symptoms. Indeed, he was one of the few clinicians of his day to treat patients with these symptoms seriously, as people

Electra complex goes awry Freud argued that a hysterical disorder may result when parents overreact to their daughter's early displays of affection for her father, by repeatedly punishing her, for example. The child may go on to exhibit sexual repression in adulthood and convert sexual feelings into physical ailments.

with genuine problems. After studying hypnosis in Paris, Freud became interested in the work of an older physician, Josef Breuer (1842–1925). Breuer had successfully used hypnosis to treat a woman he called Anna O., who suffered from hysterical deafness, disorganized speech, and paralysis (Ellenberger, 1972). On the basis of this and similar cases, Freud (1894) came to believe that hysterical disorders represented a *conversion* of underlying emotional conflicts into physical symptoms and concerns (Ding & Kanaan, 2017).

Observing that most of his patients with hysterical disorders were women, Freud centered his explanation of such disorders on the needs of girls during their *phallic stage* (ages 3 through 5). At that time in life, he believed, all girls develop a pattern of desires called the *Electra complex:* each girl experiences sexual feelings for her father and at the same time recognizes that she must compete with her mother for his affection. However, aware of her mother's more powerful position and of cultural taboos, the child typically represses her sexual feelings and rejects these early desires for her father.

Freud believed that if a child's parents overreact to her sexual feelings—with strong punishments, for example—the Electra conflict will be unresolved and the child may reexperience sexual anxiety throughout her life. Whenever events trigger sexual feelings, she may feel an unconscious need to hide them from both herself and others. Freud concluded that some women hide their sexual feelings by unconsciously converting them into physical symptoms and concerns.

Most of today's psychodynamic theorists take issue with parts of Freud's explanation of conversion and somatic symptom disorders, but they continue to believe that sufferers of the disorders have unconscious conflicts carried forth from childhood, which arouse anxiety, and that they convert this anxiety into "more tolerable" physical symptoms (Greenberg, 2016; Kaplan, 2016).

Psychodynamic theorists propose that two mechanisms are at work in these disorders—primary gain and secondary gain. People derive **primary gain** when their bodily symptoms keep their internal conflicts out of awareness. During an argument, for example, a man who has underlying fears about expressing anger may develop a conversion paralysis of the arm, thus preventing his feelings of rage from reaching consciousness. People derive **secondary gain** when their bodily symptoms further enable them to avoid unpleasant activities or to receive sympathy from others. When, for example, a conversion paralysis allows a soldier to avoid combat duty or conversion blindness prevents the breakup of a relationship, secondary gain may be at work. Similarly, the conversion paralysis of Brian, the man who lost his wife in the boating accident, seemed to help him avoid many painful duties after the accident, such as attending her funeral and returning to work.

primary gain In psychodynamic theory, the gain people derive when their somatic symptoms keep their internal conflicts out of awareness.

secondary gain In psychodynamic theory, the gain people derive when their somatic symptoms elicit kindness from others or provide an excuse to avoid unpleasant activities.

The Cognitive-Behavioral View Cognitive-behavioral theorists point to rewards and communication skills to help explain conversion and somatic symptom disorders. Regarding *rewards*, they propose that the physical symptoms of these disorders yield important benefits to sufferers (see **Table 10-4**). Perhaps the symptoms remove the individuals from an unpleasant relationship or perhaps the symptoms bring attention from other people (Greenberg, 2016; Witthöft & Hiller, 2010). In response to such rewards, the sufferers learn to display the bodily symptoms more and more prominently. The theorists also hold that people who are familiar with an illness will more readily adopt its physical symptoms. In fact, studies find that many sufferers develop their bodily symptoms after they or their close relatives or friends have had similar medical problems (Stone & Sharpe, 2016, 2015; Marshall et al., 2007).

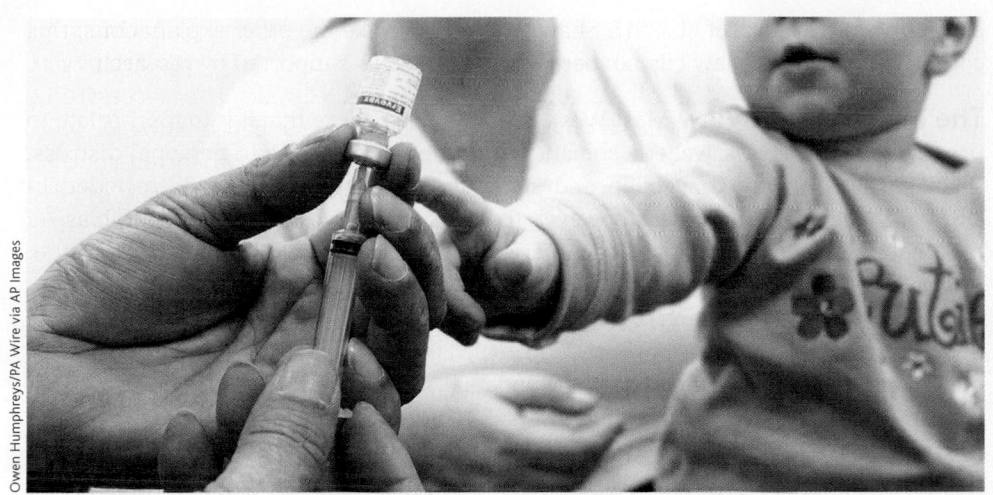

Owen Humphreys/PA Wire via AP Images

Can pain be learned? This baby is about to be given a vaccination. How much pain will she feel? According to research, it depends in large part on her mother. Infants of first-time mothers express significantly more pain before and during vaccine injections than do infants of experienced mothers. Apparently, through facial gestures, body language, modeling, or other conditioning processes, new mothers actually help produce more pain in their children.

Clearly, this focus on the role of rewards is similar to the psychodynamic notion of secondary gain. The key difference is that psychodynamic theorists view the gains as indeed secondary—that is, as gains that come only after underlying conflicts produce the disorders. Cognitive-behavioral theorists view them as the primary cause of the development of the disorders.

Like the psychodynamic explanation, the reward explanation of conversion and somatic symptom disorders has received little research support. Even clinical case reports only occasionally support this position. In many cases the pain and upset that surround the disorders seem to outweigh any rewards the symptoms might bring.

In the *communication* realm, some cognitive-behavioral theorists propose that conversion and somatic symptom disorders are forms of self-expression, providing a means for people to reveal emotions that would otherwise be difficult for them to convey (Farooq & Yousaf, 2016; Koo et al., 2014). Like their psychodynamic colleagues, these theorists hold that the emotions of people with the disorders are being converted into physical symptoms. They suggest, however, that the purpose of the conversion is not to defend against anxiety but to communicate extreme feelings—anger, fear, depression, guilt, jealousy—in a "physical language" that is familiar and comfortable for the person with the disorder.

According to this view, people who find it particularly hard to recognize or express their emotions are candidates for conversion and somatic symptom disorders. So are those who "know" the language of physical symptoms through firsthand experience with a genuine physical ailment. Because children are less able to express their emotions verbally, they are particularly likely to develop physical symptoms as a form of

TABLE: 10-4

Disorders That Have Somatic Symptoms

Disorder	Voluntary Control of Symptoms?	Symptoms Linked to Psychosocial Factor?	An Apparent Goal?
Malingering	Yes	Maybe	Yes
Factitious disorder	Yes	Yes	No*
Conversion disorder	No	Yes	Maybe
Somatic symptom disorders	No	Yes	Maybe
Illness anxiety disorder	No	Yes	No
Psychophysiological disorder	No	Yes	No
Physical illness	No	Maybe	No

*Except for medical attention.

communication (Cozzi et al., 2017; Shaw et al., 2010). Like the other explanations, this cognitive-behavioral view has not been widely tested or supported by research.

The Multicultural View Most Western clinicians believe that it is inappropriate to produce or focus excessively on somatic symptoms in response to personal distress. That is, in part, why conversion and somatic symptom disorders are included in DSM-5. Some theorists believe, however, that this position reflects a Western bias—a bias that sees somatic reactions as an *inferior* way of dealing with emotions (Bagayogo, Interian, & Escobar, 2013; Shaw et al., 2010; Moldavsky, 2004).

In fact, the transformation of personal distress into somatic complaints is the norm in many non-Western cultures (Bagayogo et al., 2013; Draguns, 2006). In such cultures, the formation of such complaints is viewed as a socially and medically correct—and less stigmatizing—reaction to life's stressors. Studies have found very high rates of stress-caused bodily symptoms in non-Western medical settings throughout the world, including those in China, Japan, and Arab countries (Matsumoto & Juang, 2016; Zhou et al., 2015). People throughout Latin America seem to display the most somatic reactions (Escobar, 2004, 1995). Even within the United States, Hispanic Americans display more somatic reactions in the face of stress than do other populations.

The lesson to be learned from such multicultural findings is not that somatic reactions to stress are superior to psychological ones or vice versa, but rather, once again, that both bodily and psychological reactions to life events are often influenced by one's culture. Overlooking this point can lead to knee-jerk mislabels or misdiagnoses.

How Are Conversion and Somatic Symptom Disorders Treated?

People with conversion and somatic symptom disorders usually seek psychotherapy only as a last resort. They believe that their problems are completely medical and at first reject all suggestions to the contrary (Greenberg, 2016; Lahmann et al., 2010). When a physician tells them that their symptoms or concerns have a psychological dimension, they often go to another physician. Eventually, however, many patients with these disorders do consent to psychotherapy, psychotropic drug therapy, or both (Greenberg, 2016; Raj et al., 2014).

Many therapists focus on the *causes* of these disorders (the trauma or anxiety tied to the physical symptoms) and apply insight, exposure, and drug therapies (Ali et al., 2015; Boone, 2011). Psychodynamic therapists, for example, try to help those with somatic symptoms become conscious of and resolve their underlying fears, thus eliminating the need to convert anxiety into physical symptoms (Kaplan, 2016; Hawkins, 2004). Alternatively, cognitive-behavioral therapists use exposure treatments. They expose clients to features of the horrific events that first triggered their physical symptoms, expecting that the clients will become less anxious over the course of repeated exposures and more able to face those upsetting events directly rather than through physical channels (Tsui et al., 2017; Stuart et al., 2008). And biological therapists most often use antidepressant drugs to help reduce anxiety and depression in patients with these disorders (Kurlansik & Maffei, 2016; Raj et al., 2014).

Other therapists try to address the *physical symptoms* of these disorders rather than the causes, using techniques such as education, reinforcement, and cognitive restructuring. Those who employ *education* explain the disorder to patients, while also offering emotional support and hope that the physical symptoms may soon disappear. Therapists who take a *reinforcement* approach arrange for the removal of rewards for a client's "sickness" symptoms and an increase of rewards for healthy behaviors. And those who offer

"Try falling down and scraping your knee. Then you can talk to me about pain."

Bruce Eric Kaplan The New Yorker Collection/TheCartoon Bank

cognitive restructuring guide clients to think differently about the nature and causes of physical symptoms and illness (Dallocchio et al., 2016). Researchers have not fully evaluated the effects of these approaches on conversion and somatic symptom disorders, however, several studies have found them to be useful interventions (Tsui et al., 2017; Stone & Sharpe, 2016, 2015; Ali et al., 2015). It is also the case that antidepressant medications sometimes help alleviate the physical symptoms of people with these disorders in addition to reducing their feelings of anxiety and depression (Greenberg, 2016).

Illness Anxiety Disorder

PEOPLE WITH ILLNESS ANXIETY DISORDER, previously known as *hypochondriasis,* are chronically anxious about their health and are convinced that they have or are developing a serious medical illness, despite the absence of somatic symptoms (see **Table 10-5**). They repeatedly check their body for signs of illness and misinterpret various bodily events as signs of serious medical problems. Typically the events are merely normal bodily changes, such as occasional coughing, sores, or sweating. Those with illness anxiety disorder persist in such misinterpretations no matter what friends, relatives, and physicians say. Some such people recognize that their concerns are excessive, but many do not.

Although illness anxiety disorder can begin at any age, it starts most often in early adulthood, among men and women in equal numbers. Between 1 and 5 percent of all people experience the disorder (Weck et al., 2015; Abramowitz & Braddock, 2011). Their symptoms tend to rise and fall over the years (Greenberg, 2016). Physicians report seeing many cases. As many as 5 percent of all patients seen by primary care physicians may display the disorder (Levenson, 2015; Dimsdale et al., 2011).

Theorists typically explain illness anxiety disorder much as they explain anxiety-related disorders (see Chapter 5). Cognitive-behavioral theorists, for example, believe (1) that the illness fears are acquired through classical conditioning or modeling, and (2) that people with the disorder are so sensitive to and threatened by bodily cues that they come to misinterpret them (Greenberg, 2016; Marshall et al., 2007).

People with illness anxiety disorder usually receive the kinds of treatments that are used to treat obsessive-compulsive disorder (see pages 142–146). Studies reveal, for example, that clients with the disorder often improve considerably when given the same *antidepressant drugs* that are helpful in cases of obsessive-compulsive disorder (Greenberg, 2016; Levenson, 2015). Many clients also improve when treated with the cognitive-behavioral approach of *exposure and response prevention* (Levenson, 2015; Weck et al., 2015). The therapists repeatedly point out bodily variations to the clients while, at the same time, preventing them from seeking their usual medical attention. In addition, the cognitive-behavioral therapists guide the clients to identify, challenge, and change their beliefs about illness that are helping to maintain their disorder (Greenberg, 2016; Hedman et al., 2016).

illness anxiety disorder A disorder in which people are chronically anxious about and preoccupied with the notion that they have or are developing a serious medical illness, despite the absence of somatic symptoms.

#StrangeCoincidence?

On February 17, 1673, French actor-playwright Molière collapsed onstage and died while performing in *Le Malade Imaginaire* (*The Hypochondriac*).

TABLE: **10-5**

Dx Checklist

Illness Anxiety Disorder
1. Person is preoccupied with thoughts about having or getting a significant illness. In reality, person has no or, at most, mild somatic symptoms.
2. Person has easily triggered high anxiety about health.
3. Person displays unduly high number of health-related behaviors (e.g., keeps focusing on body) or dysfunctional health-avoidance behaviors (e.g., avoids doctors).
4. Person's concerns continue to some degree for at least 6 months.

Information from: APA, 2013.

psychophysiological disorders Disorders in which biological, psychological, and sociocultural factors interact to cause or worsen a physical illness. Also known as *psychological factors affecting other medical conditions*.

ulcer A lesion that forms in the wall of the stomach or of the duodenum.

asthma A disease marked by narrowing of the trachea and bronchi, resulting in shortness of breath, wheezing, coughing, and a choking sensation.

insomnia Difficulty falling or staying asleep.

muscle contraction headache A headache caused by a narrowing of muscles surrounding the skull. Also known as *tension headache*.

migraine headache A very severe headache that occurs on one side of the head, often preceded by a warning sensation and sometimes accompanied by dizziness, nausea, or vomiting.

hypertension Chronic high blood pressure.

Psychophysiological Disorders: Psychological Factors Affecting Other Medical Conditions

ABOUT 85 YEARS AGO, clinicians identified a group of physical illnesses that seemed to be caused or worsened by an *interaction* of biological, psychological, and sociocultural factors (Dunbar, 1948; Bott, 1928). Early editions of the DSM labeled these illnesses **psychophysiological,** or **psychosomatic, disorders,** but DSM-5 labels them as **psychological factors affecting other medical conditions** (see **Table 10-6**). The more familiar term "psychophysiological" will be used in this chapter.

It is important to recognize that significant medical symptoms and conditions are involved in psychophysiological disorders and that the disorders often result in serious physical damage (APA, 2013). They are different from the factitious, conversion, and illness anxiety disorders that are accounted for primarily by psychological factors.

Traditional Psychophysiological Disorders

Before the 1970s, clinicians believed that only a limited number of illnesses were psychophysiological. The best known and most common of these disorders were ulcers, asthma, insomnia, chronic headaches, high blood pressure, and coronary heart disease. Recent research, however, has shown that many other physical illnesses—including bacterial and viral infections—may also be caused by an interaction of psychosocial and physical factors. Let's look first at the traditional psychophysiological disorders and then at the illnesses that are newer to this category.

Ulcers are lesions (holes) that form in the wall of the stomach or of the duodenum, resulting in burning sensations or pain in the stomach, occasional vomiting, and stomach bleeding. More than 25 million people in the United States have ulcers at some point during their lives, and ulcers cause an estimated 6,500 deaths each year (Stratemeier & Vignogna, 2014; Simon, 2013). Ulcers often are caused by an interaction of stress factors, such as environmental pressure or intense feelings of anger or anxiety (see **Figure 10-2**), and physiological factors, such as the bacteria *H. pylori* (Lanas & Chan, 2017; Marks, 2014).

Asthma causes the body's airways (the trachea and bronchi) to narrow periodically, making it hard for air to pass to and from the lungs. The resulting symptoms are shortness of breath, wheezing, coughing, and a terrifying choking sensation. Some 235 million people in the world—25 million in the United States alone—currently suffer from asthma (CDC, 2017; WHO, 2017), and most were children or young teenagers at the time of the first attack. Seventy percent of all cases appear to be caused by an interaction of stress factors, such as environmental pressures or anxiety, and physiological factors, such as allergies to specific substances, a slow-acting sympathetic nervous system, or a weakened respiratory system (Fanta, 2017; WHO, 2017).

Insomnia, difficulty falling asleep or maintaining sleep, plagues 30 percent of the population each year (ASA, 2017). Although many of us have temporary bouts of insomnia that last a few nights or so, a large number of people—10 percent of the population—have insomnia that lasts months or years (see ***InfoCentral*** on page 298). Chronic insomniacs feel as though they are almost constantly awake. They often are very sleepy during the day and may have difficulty functioning. Their problem may be caused by a combination of psychosocial factors, such as high levels of anxiety or depression, and physiological problems, such as an overactive arousal system or certain medical ailments (Bonnet & Arand, 2017, 2015; Trauer et al., 2015).

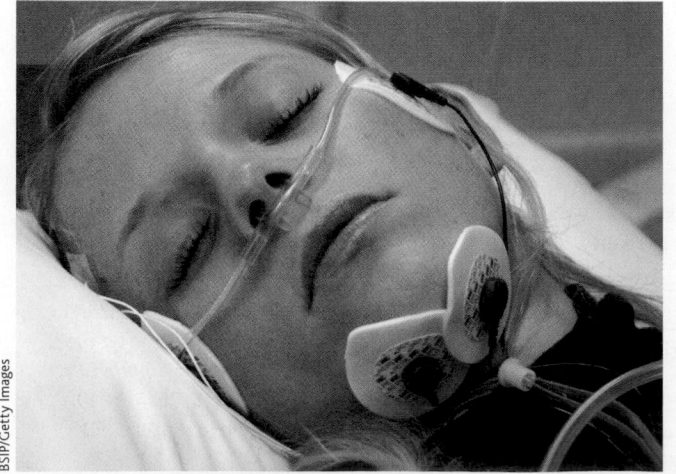

Studying sleep Clinicians use special techniques to assess sleep disorders. This woman is undergoing a *polysomnographic* examination, a procedure that measures physiological activity during sleep, including measurements of brain, eye, lung, and heart activity.

BSIP/Getty Images

Chronic headaches are frequent intense aches of the head or neck that are not caused by another physical disorder. There are two major types. **Muscle contraction,** or **tension, headaches** are marked by pain at the back or front of the head or the back of the neck. These occur when the muscles surrounding the skull tighten, narrowing the blood vessels. Approximately 45 million Americans suffer from such headaches (CDC, 2015, 2010).

Migraine headaches are extremely severe, often nearly paralyzing headaches that are located on one side of the head and are sometimes accompanied by dizziness, nausea, or vomiting. Migraine headaches are thought by some medical theorists to develop in two phases: (1) blood vessels in the brain narrow, so that the flow of blood to parts of the brain is reduced, and (2) the same blood vessels later expand, so that blood flows through them rapidly, stimulating many neuron endings and causing pain. Twenty-three million people in the United States suffer from migraines.

Research suggests that chronic headaches are caused by an interaction of stress factors, such as environmental pressures or general feelings of helplessness, anger, anxiety, or depression, and physiological factors, such as abnormal activity of the neurotransmitter serotonin, vascular problems, or muscle weakness (Taylor, 2016; Bruffaerts et al., 2015).

Hypertension is a state of chronic high blood pressure. That is, the blood pumped through the body's arteries by the heart produces too much pressure against the artery walls. Hypertension has few outward signs, but it interferes with the proper functioning of the entire cardiovascular system, greatly increasing the likelihood of stroke, heart disease, and kidney problems. It is estimated that 77 million people in the United States have hypertension, thousands die directly from it annually, and millions more perish because of illnesses caused by it (CDC, 2017, 2011; Basile & Bloch, 2016). Around 10 percent of all cases are caused by physiological abnormalities alone; the rest result from a combination of psychological and physiological factors and are called *essential hypertension.* Some of the leading psychosocial causes of essential hypertension are

TABLE: 10-6
Dx Checklist
Psychological Factors Affecting Other Medical Conditions

1. The presence of a medical condition.
2. Psychological factors negatively affect the medical condition by:
   • Affecting the course of the medical condition.
   • Providing obstacles for the treatment of the medical condition.
   • Posing new health risks.
   • Triggering or worsening the medical condition.

Information from: APA, 2013.

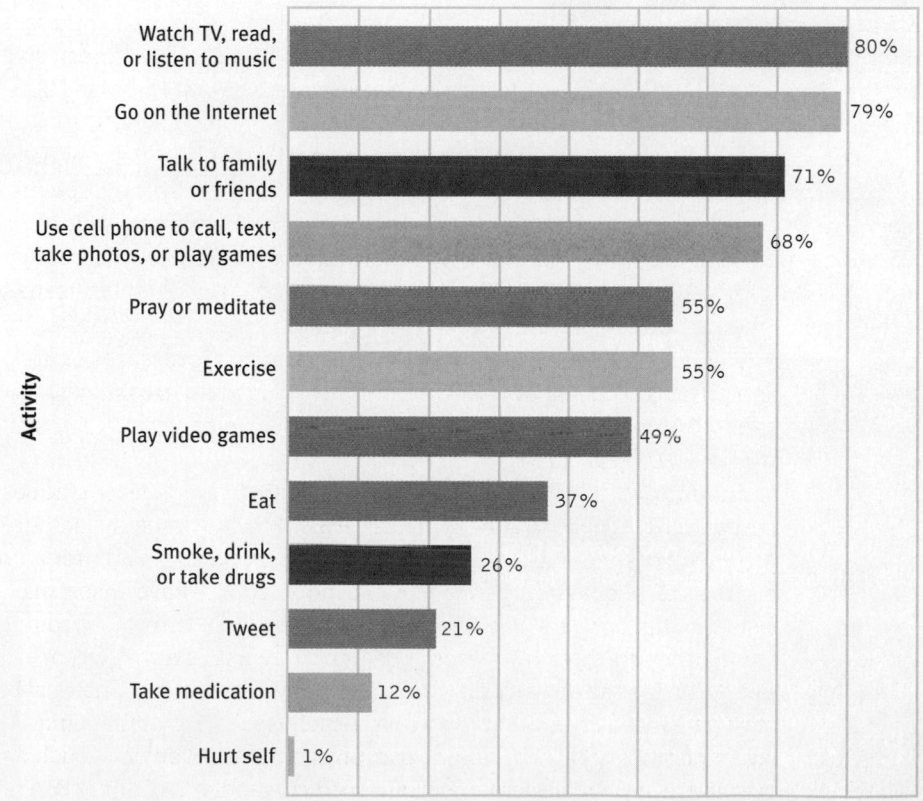

Percentage Who Perform Activity When Stressed

FIGURE 10-2

What Do People Do to Relieve Stress?

According to surveys, most of us go on the Internet, watch television, read, or listen to music. Tweeting is on the rise. (Information from: BLS, 2016; Pew Research Center, 2016, 2011, 2010; Wagstaff, 2015; IWS, 2011; MHA, 2008; NPD Group, 2008.)

SLEEP AND SLEEP DISORDERS

Sleep is a naturally recurring state that features altered consciousness, suspension of voluntary bodily functions, muscle relaxation, and reduced perception of environmental stimuli. Researchers have acquired much data about the stages, cycles, brain waves, and mechanics of sleep, but they do not fully understand its precise purpose. We do know, however, that humans and other animals need sleep to survive and function properly.

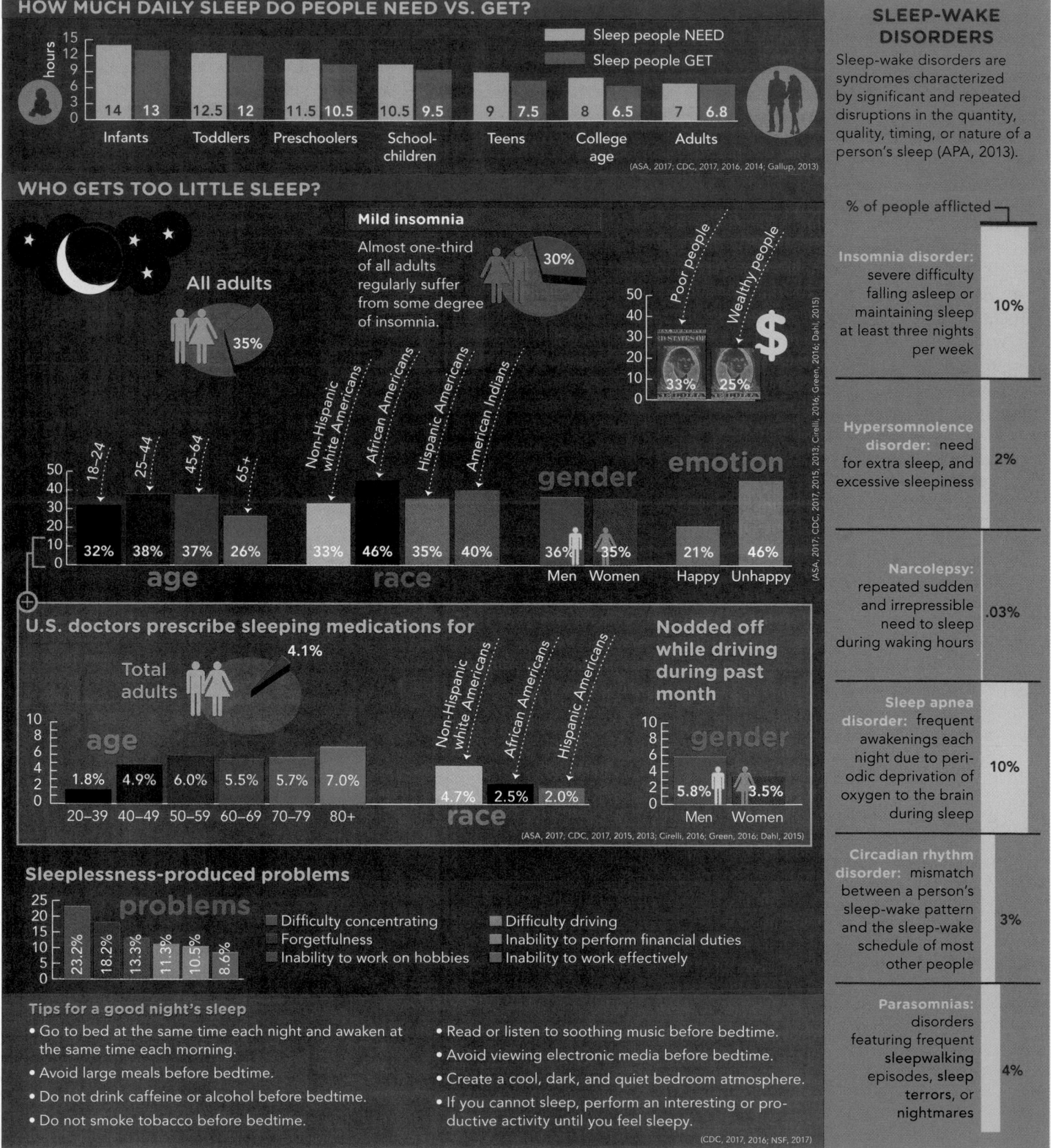

HOW MUCH DAILY SLEEP DO PEOPLE NEED VS. GET?

- Sleep people NEED
- Sleep people GET

	Infants	Toddlers	Preschoolers	School-children	Teens	College age	Adults
NEED	14	12.5	11.5	10.5	9	8	7
GET	13	12	10.5	9.5	7.5	6.5	6.8

(ASA, 2017; CDC, 2017, 2016, 2014; Gallup, 2013)

WHO GETS TOO LITTLE SLEEP?

All adults
35%

Mild insomnia
Almost one-third of all adults regularly suffer from some degree of insomnia.
30%

Poor people 33%
Wealthy people 25%

age
- 18–24: 32%
- 25–44: 38%
- 45–64: 37%
- 65+: 26%

race
- Non-Hispanic white Americans: 33%
- African Americans: 46%
- Hispanic Americans: 35%
- American Indians: 40%

gender
- Men: 36%
- Women: 35%

emotion
- Happy: 21%
- Unhappy: 46%

(ASA, 2017; CDC, 2017, 2015, 2013; Cirelli, 2016; Green, 2016; Dahl, 2015)

U.S. doctors prescribe sleeping medications for

Total adults: 4.1%

age
- 20–39: 1.8%
- 40–49: 4.9%
- 50–59: 6.0%
- 60–69: 5.5%
- 70–79: 5.7%
- 80+: 7.0%

race
- Non-Hispanic white Americans: 4.7%
- African Americans: 2.5%
- Hispanic Americans: 2.0%

Nodded off while driving during past month

gender
- Men: 5.8%
- Women: 3.5%

(ASA, 2017; CDC, 2017, 2015, 2013; Cirelli, 2016; Green, 2016; Dahl, 2015)

Sleeplessness-produced problems

problems
- 23.2%
- 18.2%
- 13.3%
- 11.3%
- 10.5%
- 8.6%

- Difficulty concentrating
- Forgetfulness
- Inability to work on hobbies
- Difficulty driving
- Inability to perform financial duties
- Inability to work effectively

Tips for a good night's sleep

- Go to bed at the same time each night and awaken at the same time each morning.
- Avoid large meals before bedtime.
- Do not drink caffeine or alcohol before bedtime.
- Do not smoke tobacco before bedtime.
- Read or listen to soothing music before bedtime.
- Avoid viewing electronic media before bedtime.
- Create a cool, dark, and quiet bedroom atmosphere.
- If you cannot sleep, perform an interesting or productive activity until you feel sleepy.

(CDC, 2017, 2016; NSF, 2017)

SLEEP-WAKE DISORDERS

Sleep-wake disorders are syndromes characterized by significant and repeated disruptions in the quantity, quality, timing, or nature of a person's sleep (APA, 2013).

% of people afflicted

Insomnia disorder: severe difficulty falling asleep or maintaining sleep at least three nights per week — 10%

Hypersomnolence disorder: need for extra sleep, and excessive sleepiness — 2%

Narcolepsy: repeated sudden and irrepressible need to sleep during waking hours — .03%

Sleep apnea disorder: frequent awakenings each night due to periodic deprivation of oxygen to the brain during sleep — 10%

Circadian rhythm disorder: mismatch between a person's sleep-wake pattern and the sleep-wake schedule of most other people — 3%

Parasomnias: disorders featuring frequent **sleepwalking** episodes, **sleep terrors**, or **nightmares** — 4%

(ASA, 2017; Foldvary-Schaefer, 2017; Strohl, 2016; APA, 2013)

constant stress, environmental danger, and general feelings of anger or depression. Physiological factors include obesity, smoking, poor kidney function, and an unusually high proportion of the gluey protein *collagen* in a person's blood vessels (Basile & Bloch, 2016; Hu et al., 2015).

Coronary heart disease is caused by a blocking of the *coronary arteries,* the blood vessels that surround the heart and are responsible for carrying oxygen to the heart muscle. The term actually refers to several problems, including blockage of the coronary arteries and *myocardial infarction* (a "heart attack"). In the United States, more than 16 million people currently have some form of coronary heart disease. It is the leading cause of death for both men and women, accounting for 17 million deaths around the world each year, 600,000 of them in the United States—around one-third of all deaths (Wilson & Douglas, 2017; CDC, 2016). Approximately half of all middle-aged men and one-third of middle-aged women develop coronary heart disease at some point in their lives. The majority of all cases of this disease are related to an interaction of psychosocial factors, such as job stress or high levels of anger or depression, and physiological factors, such as high cholesterol, obesity, hypertension, smoking, or lack of exercise (CDC, 2016; Levenson, 2016; Rheaume et al., 2014).

> Which jobs in our society might be particularly stressful and traumatizing? Might certain lifestyles be more stressful than others?

coronary heart disease Illness of the heart caused by a blockage in the coronary arteries.

What Factors Contribute to Psychophysiological Disorders? Over the years, clinicians have identified a number of variables that may generally contribute to the development of psychophysiological disorders. You may notice that several of these variables are the same as those that contribute to the onset of acute and post-traumatic stress disorders (see Chapter 6). The variables can be grouped as biological, psychological, and sociocultural factors, respectively.

BIOLOGICAL FACTORS You saw in Chapter 6 that one way the brain activates body organs is through the operation of the *autonomic nervous system* (*ANS*), the network of nerve fibers that connect the central nervous system to the body's organs. Defects in this system are believed to contribute to the development of psychophysiological disorders (Ackland et al., 2016; Lundberg, 2011). If one's ANS is stimulated too easily, for example, it may overreact to situations that most people find only mildly stressful, eventually damaging certain organs and causing a psychophysiological disorder. Other more specific biological problems may also contribute to psychophysiological disorders. A person with a weak gastrointestinal system, for example, may be a prime candidate for an ulcer, whereas someone with a weak respiratory system may develop asthma readily.

In a related vein, people may display favored biological reactions that raise their chances of developing psychophysiological disorders. Some individuals perspire in response to stress, others develop stomachaches, and still others have a rise in blood pressure. Research has indicated, for example, that some people are particularly likely to have temporary rises in blood pressure when stressed (Su et al., 2014; Lundberg, 2011). It may be that they are prone to develop hypertension.

PSYCHOLOGICAL FACTORS According to many theorists, certain needs, attitudes, emotions, or coping styles may cause people to overreact repeatedly to stressors, and so increase their chances of developing psychophysiological disorders. Researchers have found, for example, that men with a *repressive coping style* (a reluctance to express discomfort, anger, or hostility) tend to have a particularly sharp rise in blood pressure and heart rate when they are stressed (Howard, Myers, & Hughes, 2017; Trapp et al., 2014).

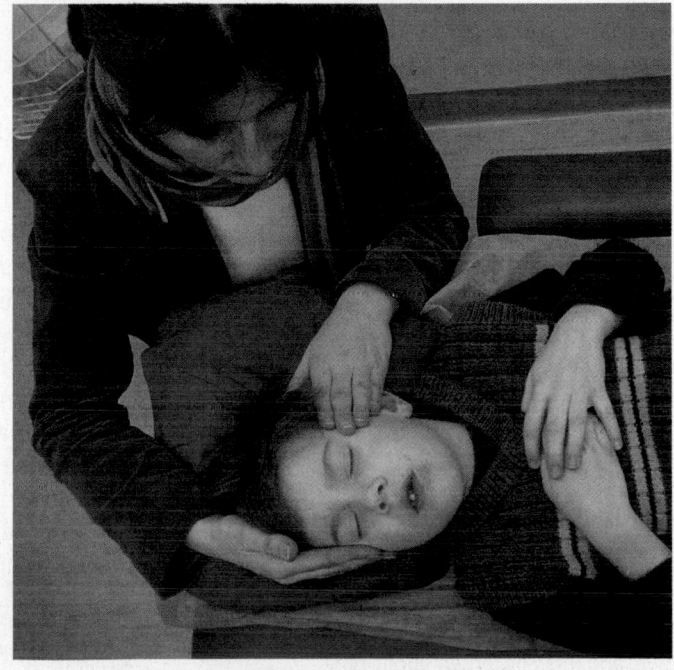

More than head pain Migraine headaches produce much more pain and a wider range of symptoms than most other kinds of headaches. Here, at a program in Stockholm, Sweden, a mother massages the head of her young son, who suffers from migraines. Systematic massaging is partially helpful to him during particularly severe episodes.

Rob Schoenbaum / Polaris

A Type B sea turtle Most people have a pretty clear picture of a Type A personality, but they have difficulty spotting a Type B personality. They need look no farther than *Crush*, the ever so relaxed and laid-back sea turtle in the animation films *Finding Nemo* and *Finding Dori*. Crush always goes with the flow and surfs the seas at his own comfortable pace, repeatedly using terms like "Righteous" and "Duuuude" along the way.

Type A personality style A personality pattern characterized by hostility, cynicism, drivenness, impatience, competitiveness, and ambition.

Type B personality style A personality pattern in which a person is more relaxed, less aggressive, and less concerned about time.

Another personality style that may contribute to psychophysiological disorders is the **Type A personality style,** an idea introduced a half-century ago by two cardiologists, Meyer Friedman and Ray Rosenman (1959). People with this style are said to be consistently angry, cynical, driven, impatient, competitive, and ambitious. They interact with the world in a way that, according to Friedman and Rosenman, produces continual stress and often leads to coronary heart disease. People with a **Type B personality style,** by contrast, are thought to be more relaxed, less aggressive, and less concerned about time and thus are less likely to develop cardiovascular deterioration.

The link between the Type A personality style and coronary heart disease has been supported by many studies. In one well-known investigation of more than 3,000 people, Friedman and Rosenman (1974) separated healthy men in their forties and fifties into Type A and Type B categories and then followed their health over the next eight years. More than twice as many Type A men developed coronary heart disease. Later studies found that Type A functioning correlates similarly with heart disease in women (Haynes et al., 1980).

Recent studies indicate that the link between the Type A personality style and heart disease may not be as strong as the earlier studies suggested. These studies do suggest, however, that several of the characteristics that supposedly make up the Type A style, particularly *hostility, competitiveness,* and *time urgency,* may indeed be strongly related to heart disease (Jennings et al., 2017; Lohse et al., 2017).

SOCIOCULTURAL FACTORS: THE MULTICULTURAL PERSPECTIVE Adverse social conditions may set the stage for psychophysiological disorders. Such conditions produce ongoing stressors that trigger and interact with the biological and personality factors just discussed. One of society's most negative social conditions, for example, is poverty. In study after study, it has been found that impoverished people have more psychophysiological disorders, poorer health in general, and poorer health outcomes than wealthier people (Robinson-Papp et al., 2017; Singh & Siahpush, 2014; Chandola & Marmot, 2011). One obvious reason for this relationship is that poor people typically experience higher rates of crime, unemployment, overcrowding, and other negative stressors than wealthier people. In addition, they typically receive inferior medical care.

The relationship between race and psychophysiological and other health problems is complicated. On the one hand, as one might expect from the economic trends just discussed, African Americans have more health problems than do non-Hispanic white Americans. African Americans have, for example, higher rates of high blood pressure, high cholesterol, diabetes, and asthma (CDC, 2017, 2016, 2014). They are also more likely to die of heart disease and stroke. Certainly, economic factors may help explain this racial difference. Many African Americans live in poverty; those who do often must contend with the high rates of crime and unemployment that often result in poor health conditions (Greer et al., 2014).

Research further suggests that the high rate of psychophysiological and other medical disorders among African Americans probably extends beyond economic factors. Consider, for example, the finding that 44 percent of African Americans have high blood pressure, compared with 33 percent of non-Hispanic white Americans (CDC, 2016, 2011). Although this difference may be explained in part by the dangerous environments in which many African Americans live and the unsatisfying jobs at which many must work (Marden et al., 2016; Gilbert et al., 2011), other factors may also be operating (Muntner et al., 2017). A physiological predisposition among African Americans may, for example, increase their risk of developing high blood pressure. Or it may be that repeated experiences of racial discrimination constitute special stressors that help raise the blood pressure of African Americans (see **Figure 10-3**). Studies have found, for example, that the more discrimination people experience over a 1-year period, the greater their daily rise in blood pressure, and the more discrimination African Americans experience over the course of their lives, the more likely they are

"I can't watch. It makes me sick." These fans are "watching" the 2010 World Cup match between Spain and Germany. The stress of big games in soccer and other sports causes many fans to develop a range of physical symptoms, such as fainting, throwing up, stomach pain, headaches, and chest pains. No wonder these people closed their eyes as the tension mounted.

Tobias Schwarz / Reuters

to have high blood pressure in middle age and old age (Beatty Moody et al., 2016; Dolezsar et al., 2014; Smart-Richman et al., 2010).

Looking at the health picture of African Americans, one might expect to find a similar trend among Hispanic Americans. After all, a high percentage of Hispanic Americans also live in poverty, are exposed to discrimination, are affected by high rates of crime and unemployment, and receive inferior medical care (U.S. Census Bureau, 2016, 2010; BLS, 2015). However, despite such disadvantages, the health of Hispanic Americans is, on average, at least as good and often better than that of both non-Hispanic white Americans and African Americans (CDC, 2017, 2016, 2015). For example, Hispanic Americans have lower rates of high blood pressure and asthma and live longer than non-Hispanic white Americans and African Americans do.

The relatively positive health picture for Hispanic Americans in the face of clear economic disadvantage has been referred to in the clinical field as the "Hispanic Health Paradox." Generally, researchers are puzzled by this pattern, but a few explanations have been offered (Giuntella, 2016; Dubowitz et al., 2010; Gallo et al., 2009). It may be, for example, that the strong emphasis on social relationships, family support, and religiousness that often characterize Hispanic American cultures increase health resilience among their members. Or Hispanic Americans may have a physiological predisposition that improves their likelihood of having better health outcomes.

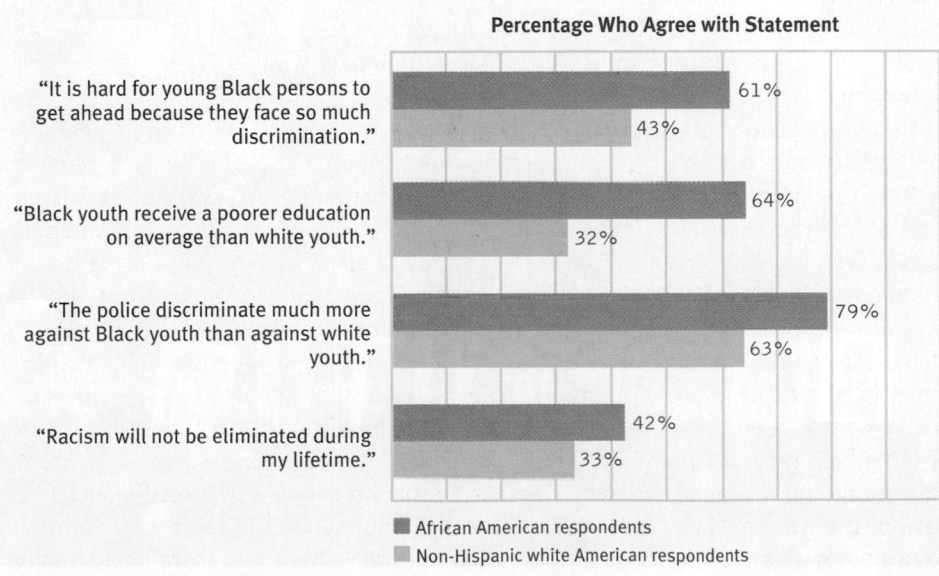

Percentage Who Agree with Statement

"It is hard for young Black persons to get ahead because they face so much discrimination." — 61% / 43%

"Black youth receive a poorer education on average than white youth." — 64% / 32%

"The police discriminate much more against Black youth than against white youth." — 79% / 63%

"Racism will not be eliminated during my lifetime." — 42% / 33%

■ African American respondents
■ Non-Hispanic white American respondents

FIGURE 10-3

How Much Discrimination Do Racial Minority Teenagers Face?

It depends on who's being asked the question. In surveys of teenagers and young adults, African American respondents were more likely than non-Hispanic white American respondents to recognize that African American teens experience various forms of discrimination. (Information from: OA, 2017; Black Youth Project, 2016, 2011.)

psychoneuroimmunology The study of the connections between stress, the body's immune system, and illness.

immune system The body's network of activities and cells that identify and destroy antigens and cancer cells.

antigen A foreign invader of the body, such as a bacterium or virus.

lymphocytes White blood cells that circulate through the lymph system and bloodstream, helping the body identify and destroy antigens and cancer cells.

New Psychophysiological Disorders

Clearly, biological, psychological, and sociocultural factors combine to produce psychophysiological disorders. In fact, the interaction of such factors is now considered the *rule* of bodily functioning, not the exception (Levenson, 2016). As the years have passed, more and more illnesses have been added to the list of traditional psychophysiological disorders and researchers have found many links between psychosocial stress and a wide range of physical illnesses. Let's look at how these links were established and then at *psychoneuroimmunology,* the area of study that ties stress and illness to the body's immune system.

Are Physical Illnesses Related to Stress? Back in 1967 two researchers, Thomas Holmes and Richard Rahe, developed the *Social Readjustment Rating Scale,* which assigns numerical values to the stresses that most people experience at some time in their lives (see **Table 10-7**). Answers given by a large sample of participants indicated that the most stressful event on the scale is the death of a spouse, which receives a score of 100 *life change units* (*LCUs*). Lower on the scale is retirement (45 LCUs), and still lower is a minor violation of the law (11 LCUs). This scale gave researchers a yardstick for measuring the total amount of stress a person faces over a period of time. If, for example, in the course of a year a woman started a new business (39 LCUs), sent her son off to college (29 LCUs), moved to a new house (20 LCUs), and had a close friend die (37 LCUs), her stress score for the year would be 125 LCUs, a considerable amount of stress for such a period of time.

With this scale in hand, Holmes and Rahe (1989, 1967) examined the relationship between life stress and the onset of illness. They found that the LCU scores of sick people during the year before they fell ill were much higher than those of healthy people. If a person's life changes totaled more than 300 LCUs over the course of a year, he or she was particularly likely to develop serious health problems.

Using the Social Readjustment Rating Scale or similar scales, studies have since linked stresses of various kinds to a wide range of physical conditions, from trench mouth and upper respiratory infections to cancer (Harkness & Monroe, 2016; Baum et al., 2011; Rook et al., 2011). Overall, the greater the amount of life stress, the greater the likelihood of illness (see **Figure 10-4**). Researchers even have found a relationship between traumatic stress and death. Widows and widowers, for example, display an

Religious protection? In this famous photo of a 2015 prayer vigil, church congregants hold up pictures of 9 Bible study participants who had been shot and killed two days earlier at the Emanuel African Methodist Episcopal Church in Charleston, South Carolina. Some relatives of the victims later talked directly to the mass murderer, telling him they forgave him and were praying for him. Research indicates that people with strong institutional, religious, and social ties often recover more readily and healthfully from the effects of traumatic events.

Win McNamee/Getty Images

increased risk of death during their period of bereavement (King et al., 2017; Moon et al., 2014).

One shortcoming of Holmes and Rahe's Social Readjustment Rating Scale is that it does not take into consideration the particular life stress reactions of specific populations. For example, in their development of the scale, the researchers sampled non-Hispanic white Americans predominantly. Few of the respondents were African Americans or Hispanic Americans. But since their ongoing life experiences often differ in key ways, might not members of minority groups and non-Hispanic white Americans differ in their stress reactions to various kinds of life events? Research indicates that indeed they do (Oates, 2016; Bennett & Olugbala, 2010). One recent study found, for example, that African American and Hispanic American teachers perceived and reacted to occupational stressors (for example, heavy workload and administrator pressure) very differently than did non-Hispanic white American teachers (Rauscher & Wilson, 2017).

Finally, college students may face stressors that are different from those listed in the Social Readjustment Rating Scale. Instead of having marital difficulties, being fired, or applying for a job, a college student may have trouble with a roommate, fail a course, or apply to graduate school. When researchers use special scales to measure life events in this population, they find the expected relationships between stressful events and illness (Amirkhan et al., 2015; Anders et al., 2012) (see Table 10-7 again).

Psychoneuroimmunology How do stressful events result in a viral or bacterial infection? Researchers in an area of study called **psychoneuroimmunology** seek to answer this question by uncovering the links between psychosocial stress, the immune system, and health. The **immune system** is the body's network of activities and cells that identify and destroy **antigens**—foreign invaders, such as bacteria, viruses, fungi, and parasites—and cancer cells. Among the most important cells in this system are billions of **lymphocytes,** white blood cells that circulate through the lymph system and the bloodstream. When stimulated by antigens, lymphocytes spring into action to help the body overcome the invaders.

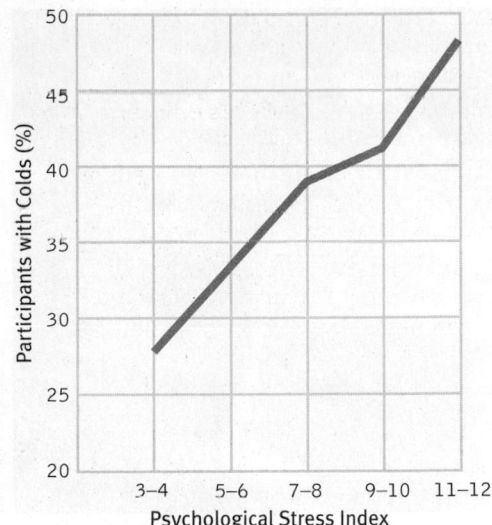

FIGURE 10-4

Stress and the Common Cold

In a landmark study, healthy participants were administered nasal drops containing common cold viruses. In turn, the participants who had recently experienced more stressors came down with more colds than did participants with fewer recent stressors. (Information from: Cohen et al., 1991.)

TABLE: 10-7

Most Stressful Life Events

Adults: Social Readjustment Rating Scale*	Students: Undergraduate Stress Questionnaire†
1. Death of spouse	1. Death (family member or friend)
2. Divorce	2. Had a lot of tests
3. Marital separation	3. It's finals week
4. Jail term	4. Applying to graduate school
5. Death of close family member	5. Victim of a crime
6. Personal injury or illness	6. Assignments in all classes due the same day
7. Marriage	7. Breaking up with boy/girlfriend
8. Fired at work	8. Found out boy/girlfriend cheated on you
9. Marital reconciliation	9. Lots of deadlines to meet
10. Retirement	10. Property stolen
11. Change in health of family member	11. You have a hard upcoming week
12. Pregnancy	12. Went into a test unprepared

*Full scale has 43 items.

(Reprinted from *Journal of Psychosomatic Research,* Vol. 11, Holmes, T. H., & Rahe, R. H., The Social Readjustment Rating Scale, 213–218, Copyright 1967, with permission from Elsevier.)

†Full scale has 83 items.

(Information from: Crandall, C. S., Preisler, J. J., & Aussprung, J. (1992). Measuring life event stress in the lives of college students: The Undergraduate Stress Questionnaire (USQ). *Journal of Behavioral Medicine,* 15(6), 627–662.)

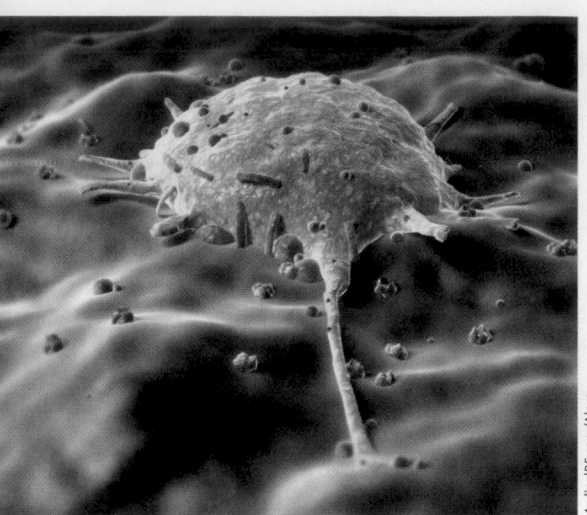

MedicalRF.com/Alamy

First line of defense How do lymphocytes meet up with invading antigens? The lymphocytes are first alerted by *macrophages*, big white blood cells in the immune system that recognize an antigen, engulf it, break it down, and hand off its dissected parts to the lymphocytes. Here a macrophage stretches its long "arms" (pseudopods) to detect and capture the suspected antigens.

#MaritalStress

During and after marital spats, women typically release more stress hormones than men, and so have poorer immune functioning (Jaremka et al., 2013; Gouin et al., 2009; Kiecolt-Glaser et al., 1996).

One group of lymphocytes, called *helper T-cells,* identifies antigens and then multiplies and triggers the production of other kinds of immune cells. Another group, *natural killer T-cells,* seeks out and destroys body cells that have already been infected by viruses, thus helping to stop the spread of a viral infection. A third group of lymphocytes, *B-cells,* produces *antibodies,* protein molecules that recognize and bind to antigens, mark them for destruction, and prevent them from causing infection.

Researchers now believe that stress can interfere with the activity of lymphocytes and other parts of the immune system, slowing them down and thus increasing a person's susceptibility to viral and bacterial infections (Peters et al., 2017; Levenson, 2016; Dhabhar, 2014, 2011). In a landmark study, investigator Roger Bartrop and his colleagues (1977) in New South Wales, Australia, compared the immune systems of 26 people whose spouses had died 8 weeks earlier with those of 26 matched control group participants whose spouses had not died. Blood samples revealed that lymphocyte functioning was much lower in the bereaved people than in the controls. Still other studies have shown poor immune functioning in people who are exposed to long-term stress (Reed et al., 2016). For example, researchers have found poorer immune functioning among those who provide ongoing care for a relative with Alzheimer's disease (Hirano et al., 2016; Fonareva & Oken, 2014).

These studies seem to be telling a remarkable story. During periods when healthy people happened to have unusual levels of stress, they remained healthy on the surface, but their stressors apparently slowed their immune systems so that they became susceptible to illness. If stress affects our capacity to fight off illness, it is no wonder that researchers have repeatedly found a relationship between life stress and illnesses of various kinds. But why and when does stress interfere with the immune system? Several factors influence whether stress will result in a slowdown of the system, including *biochemical activity, behavioral changes, personality style,* and *degree of social support.*

BIOCHEMICAL ACTIVITY As you'll recall from Chapter 6, there are two biological stress pathways by which stressors produce arousal throughout the brain and body (see pages 155–156). One is the *sympathetic nervous system,* which, among its many actions, triggers the release of the neurotransmitter *norepinephrine.* It turns out that in addition to its role in producing arousal, an extended release of norepinephrine can influence the immune system adversely. Research indicates that if stress continues for too long a period, norepinephrine eventually travels to receptors on certain lymphocytes and gives them an *inhibitory message* to stop their activity, thus slowing down immune functioning (Takenaka et al., 2016; Dhabhar, 2014).

Recall also that the other biological stress pathway is the *hypothalamic-pituitary-adrenal (HPA)* pathway, which, among its various actions, triggers the release of *cortisol* and other stress hormones. Apparently, in addition to producing bodily arousal, an extended release of cortisol and other stress hormones can contribute to poorer immune system functioning. As in the case of norepinephrine, if stress continues for too long, the stress hormones travel to receptor sites located on certain lymphocytes and give an inhibitory message, again causing a slowdown of the activity of the lymphocytes (Ciliberti et al., 2017; Huo et al., 2017).

Research has further indicated that another action of norepinephrine and the various stress hormones is to trigger an increase in the production of *cytokines,* proteins that bind to receptors throughout the body. At moderate levels of stress, the cytokines, another key player in the immune system, help combat infection. But as stress continues and more norepinephrine and stress hormones are released, the growing production and spread of cytokines lead to *chronic inflammation* throughout the body, contributing at times to heart disease, stroke, and other illnesses (Huo et al., 2017; Takenaka et al., 2016).

BEHAVIORAL CHANGES Stress may set in motion a series of behavioral changes that indirectly affect the immune system. Some people under stress may, for example, become anxious or depressed, perhaps even develop an anxiety or depressive disorder. As a result, they may sleep badly, eat poorly, exercise less, or smoke or drink more behaviors known to slow down the immune system (Levenson, 2016; Brooks et al., 2011).

PERSONALITY STYLE According to research, people who generally respond to life stress with optimism, constructive coping, and resilience—that is, people who welcome challenges and are willing to take control in their daily encounters—experience better immune system functioning and are better prepared to fight off illness (Pandey & Shrivastava, 2017; Kim et al., 2014). Some studies have found, for example, that people with "hardy" or resilient personal styles remain healthy after stressful events, while those whose personalities are less hardy seem more susceptible to illness (Van Schrojenstein Lantman et al., 2017; Bonanno & Mancini, 2012). Researchers have even discovered that men with a general sense of hopelessness die at above-average rates from heart disease and critical illnesses (Orwelius et al., 2017; Kangelaris et al., 2010). Similarly, a growing body of research suggests that people who are spiritual tend to be healthier than people without spiritual beliefs, and a few studies have linked spirituality to better immune system functioning (Roth et al., 2016; Jackson & Bergeman, 2011).

In related work, researchers have found a relationship between certain personality characteristics and a person's ability to cope effectively with cancer (Smith et al., 2016; Baum et al., 2011; Floyd et al., 2011). They have found, for example, that patients with certain forms of cancer who display a helpless coping style and who cannot easily express their feelings, particularly anger, tend to have a poorer quality of life in the face of their disease than patients who do express their emotions. A few investigators have even suggested a relationship between personality and cancer *outcome,* but this claim has not been supported clearly by research (Pillay et al., 2014; Urcuyo et al., 2005).

SOCIAL SUPPORT Finally, people who have few social supports and feel lonely tend to have poorer immune functioning in the face of stress than people who do not feel lonely (Pandey & Shrivastava, 2017; Hicks, 2014). In a pioneering study, medical students were given the *UCLA Loneliness Scale* and then divided into "high" and "low"

The ultimate body-mind connection? Psychologists have studied the relationship between psychological trauma and immediate death—sometimes called the *sudden death,* or *"giving-up,"* phenomenon. Although relatively rare, sudden deaths tend to occur among people who have just experienced the death of a loved one, extreme danger, or a severe loss of status (Cohen et al, 2013; Engel, 1971, 1968). In 2017, movie legend Debbie Reynolds (right) died just one day after the death of her daughter, actress and writer Carrie Fisher (left). According to Reynolds's son, "She literally said 'I want to be with Carrie' and closed her eyes and went to sleep."

The power of support Cancer survivors clasp hands at the Susan G. Komen "Race for the Cure," a 5K run held annually throughout the world, with a total of 1.6 million participants. The run, begun almost 30 years ago, not only raises funds and increases awareness about cancer, it helps survivors support and encourage one other—applying research findings that social support can affect the immune system and help facilitate recovery from various illnesses.

behavioral medicine A field that combines psychological and physical interventions to treat or prevent medical problems.

relaxation training A treatment procedure that teaches clients to relax at will so they can calm themselves in stressful situations.

biofeedback A technique in which a client is given information about physiological reactions as they occur and learns to control the reactions voluntarily.

electromyograph (EMG) A device that provides feedback about the level of muscular tension in the body.

loneliness groups (Kiecolt-Glaser et al., 1984). The high-loneliness group showed lower lymphocyte responses during a final exam period.

Other studies have found that social support and affiliation may actually help protect people from stress, poor immune system functioning, and subsequent illness, or help speed up recovery from illness or surgery (Hicks, 2014; Rook et al., 2011). Similarly, some studies have suggested that patients with certain forms of cancer who receive social support in their personal lives or supportive therapy often have better immune system functioning and more successful recoveries than patients without such supports (Muscatell et al., 2016; Hulett et al., 2015).

||||||||||||||||||||||||||||||||||||||||||||||||||||||||||||||||||||||||||||||||||||

Psychological Treatments for Physical Disorders

AS CLINICIANS HAVE DISCOVERED that stress and related psychological and sociocultural factors may contribute to physical disorders, they have applied psychological treatments to more and more medical problems. The most common of these interventions are relaxation training, biofeedback, meditation, hypnosis, cognitive interventions, support groups, and therapies to increase awareness and expression of emotions. The field of treatment that combines psychological and physical approaches to treat or prevent medical problems is known as **behavioral medicine.**

Relaxation Training

As you saw in Chapter 5, therapists sometimes teach clients to relax their muscles at will. The notion behind such **relaxation training** is that physical relaxation will lead to a state of psychological relaxation. In one version, therapists teach clients to identify individual muscle groups, tense them, release the tension, and ultimately relax the whole body. With continued practice, they can bring on a state of deep muscle relaxation. Given that relaxation training is useful in the treatment of phobias and other anxiety disorders, clinicians believe that it can also help prevent or treat medical illnesses that are related to stress.

Relaxation training, often in combination with medication, has been widely used in the treatment of high blood pressure (Aalami et al., 2016). It has also been of some

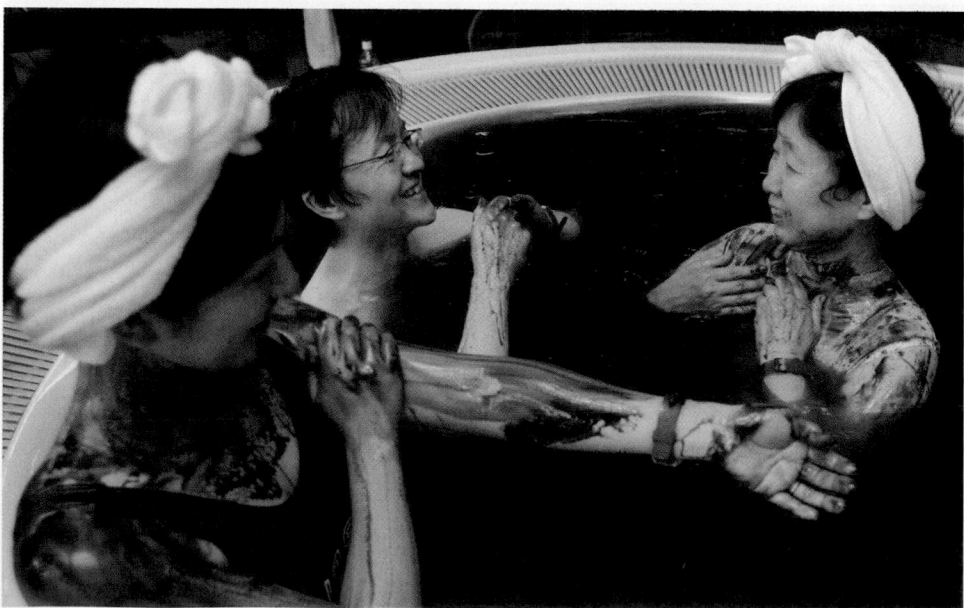

Relaxing—and delicious! New stress-relief programs, techniques, and products are constantly being introduced to the marketplace. These three individuals, for example, are able to unwind and relax in a chocolate spa at the Hakone Yunessun spa resort in Japan.

AP Photo/Itsuo Inouye

help in treating somatic symptom disorder, headaches, insomnia, asthma, diabetes, pain, certain vascular diseases, and the undesirable effects of certain cancer treatments (Greenberg, 2016; Kim et al., 2016; Gagnon et al., 2013).

Biofeedback

In **biofeedback,** therapists use electrical signals from the body to train people to control physiological processes such as heart rate or muscle tension. Clients are connected to a monitor that gives them continuous information about their bodily activities. By attending to the signals from the monitor, they may gradually learn to control even seemingly involuntary physiological processes.

The most widely applied method of biofeedback uses a device called an **electromyograph (EMG),** which provides feedback about the level of muscular tension in the body. Electrodes are attached to the client's muscles—usually the forehead muscles—where they detect the minute electrical activity that accompanies muscle tension (see **Figure 10-5**). The device then converts the electric energy, or *potentials,* coming from the muscles into an image, such as lines on a screen, or into a tone whose pitch changes along with changes in muscle tension. Thus clients "see" or "hear" when their muscles are becoming more or less tense. Through repeated trial and error, the individuals become skilled at voluntarily reducing muscle tension.

In a classic study, EMG feedback was used to treat 16 patients who had facial pain caused in part by tension in their jaw muscles (Dohrmann & Laskin, 1978). Changes in the pitch and volume of the tone indicate changes in muscle tension. After "listening" to EMG feedback repeatedly, the 16 patients in this study learned how to relax their jaw muscles at will and later reported that they had less facial pain.

EMG feedback has also been used successfully in the treatment of headaches and muscular disabilities caused by strokes or accidents. Still other forms of biofeedback training have been of some help in the treatment of heartbeat irregularities, asthma, high blood pressure, stuttering, and pain (Garbacz & Butz, 2016; McKenna et al., 2015; Young & Kemper, 2013).

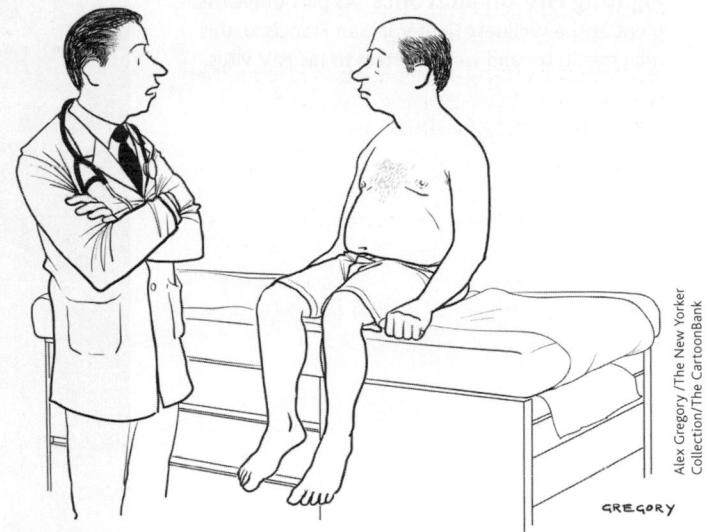

"Stress is killing you—you need an easier job, a smaller house, and a different family."

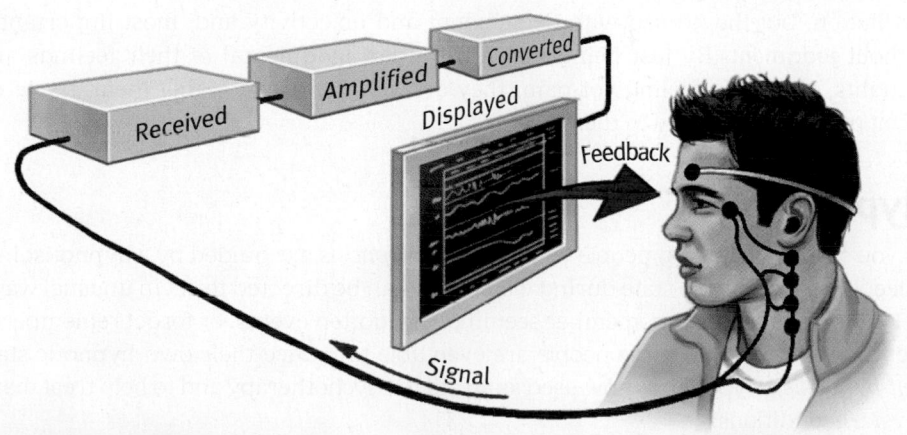

FIGURE 10-5

Biofeedback at Work This biofeedback system records tension in the forehead muscles of a person with severe headaches. The system receives, amplifies, converts, and displays information about the tension, allowing the client to "observe" it and to try to reduce his tension responses.

Fighting HIV on all fronts As part of his treatment at the Wellness Center in San Francisco, this man meditates and writes letters to his HIV virus.

Joe McNally/The LIFE Picture Collection/Getty Images

Meditation

Although meditation has been practiced since ancient times, Western health care professionals have only recently become aware of its effectiveness in relieving physical distress. *Meditation* is a technique of turning one's concentration inward, achieving a slightly changed state of consciousness, and temporarily ignoring all stressors. Typically, meditators go to a quiet place, assume a comfortable posture, utter or think a particular sound (called a *mantra*) to help focus their attention, and allow their mind to turn away from all outside thoughts and concerns. Many people who meditate regularly report feeling more peaceful, engaged, and creative. Meditation has been used to help manage pain and to treat high blood pressure, heart problems, asthma, skin disorders, diabetes, insomnia, and even viral infections (Park & Han, 2017; Manchanda & Madan, 2014; Stein, 2003).

One form of meditation that has been used in particular by patients suffering from severe pain is *mindfulness meditation* (Anheyer et al., 2017; Barker, 2014; Kabat-Zinn, 2005). Here, as you read in Chapters 3 and 5, mindfulness meditators pay attention to the feelings, thoughts, and sensations that are flowing through their mind during meditation, but they do so with detachment and objectivity and, most importantly, without judgment. By just being mindful but not judgmental of their feelings and thoughts, including feelings of pain, they are less inclined to label them, fixate on them, or react negatively to them.

Hypnosis

As you saw in Chapter 1, people who undergo *hypnosis* are guided by a hypnotist into a sleeplike, suggestible state during which they can be directed to act in unusual ways, feel unusual sensations, remember seemingly forgotten events, or forget remembered events. With training, some people are even able to induce their own hypnotic state (*self-hypnosis*). Hypnosis is now used as an aid to psychotherapy and to help treat many physical conditions.

Hypnosis seems to be particularly helpful in the control of pain (Mendoza et al., 2016; Jensen et al., 2014, 2011). A breakthrough case study described a patient who underwent dental surgery under hypnotic suggestion: After a hypnotic state was induced, the dentist suggested to the patient that he was in a pleasant and relaxed setting listening to

BSIP/Getty Images

The hypnotic way Hypnosis is now widely used in medical procedures, particularly to help reduce and control pain. Here, an anesthesiologist hypnotizes a patient undergoing major surgery at the University Hospital Center of Liege in Belgium. Many surgeries at the hospital are conducted using a combination of hypnosis and a local anesthetic rather than general anesthesia.

a friend describe his own success at undergoing similar dental surgery under hypnosis. The dentist then proceeded to perform a successful 25-minute operation (Gheorghiu & Orleanu, 1982). Although only some people are able to go through surgery while anesthetized by hypnosis alone, hypnosis combined with chemical forms of anesthesia is apparently helpful to many patients. Beyond its use in the control of pain, hypnosis has been used successfully to help treat such problems as skin diseases, asthma, insomnia, high blood pressure, warts, and other forms of infection (Sawni & Breuner, 2017; Becker, 2015).

Cognitive-Behavioral Interventions

People with physical ailments have sometimes been taught new attitudes or cognitive responses toward their ailments as part of treatment (Sandler et al., 2017; Hampel et al., 2014). For example, an approach called *self-instruction training,* or *stress inoculation training,* has helped patients cope with severe pain (Meichenbaum, 2017, 1993, 1975). In this training, therapists teach people to identify and eventually rid themselves of unpleasant thoughts that keep emerging during pain episodes (so-called *negative self-statements,* such as "Oh no, I can't take this pain") and to replace them with *coping self-statements* instead (for example, "When pain comes, just pause; keep focusing on what you have to do").

Support Groups and Emotion Expression

If anxiety, depression, anger, and the like contribute to a person's physical ills, interventions to reduce these negative emotions should help reduce the ills. Thus it is not surprising that some medically ill people have profited from support groups, including online support groups, and from therapies that guide them to become more aware of and express their emotions and needs (Gabbe et al., 2017; Cacioppo et al., 2016). Research suggests that the discussion, or even the writing down, of past and present emotions or upsets may help improve a person's health, just as it may help one's psychological functioning (Krupnick et al., 2016; Corter & Petrie, 2011; Smyth & Pennebaker, 2001). In one study, asthma and arthritis patients who wrote down their thoughts and feelings about stressful events for a handful of days showed lasting improvements in their conditions. Similarly, stress-related writing was found to be beneficial for patients with either HIV or cancer.

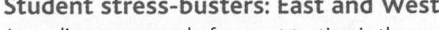

#FunnyRemedy

After watching a humorous video, research participants who laughed at the video showed decreases in stress and improvements in natural killer cell activity (Radcliff, 2017; Bennett, 1998).

Student stress-busters: East and West
According to research, frequent testing is the second-most-stressful life event for high school and college students. To reduce such stress, college applicants from Beijing give one another head massages in preparation for China's college entrance exams (left). In the meantime, students at a dorm at Northwestern University in the United States try to blow off steam by performing "primal screams" during their final exam period (right).

The power of distraction Researchers in New Jersey had this 10-year-old girl and other young patients play with handheld Game Boys while waiting for their anesthesia to take effect before their surgery. Such game-playing was found to be more effective at relaxing the young patients than antianxiety drugs or holding hands with parents. Additional research suggests that patients who are more relaxed often have better surgical outcomes.

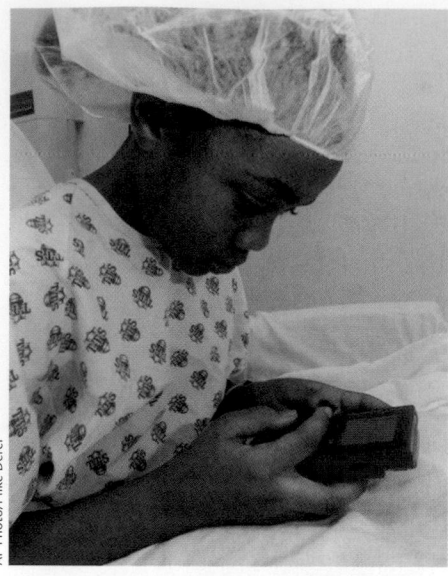

Combination Approaches

Studies have found that the various psychological interventions for physical problems tend to be equally effective (Sawni & Breuner, 2017; Devineni & Blanchard, 2005). Relaxation and biofeedback training, for example, are equally helpful (and more helpful than placebos) in the treatment of high blood pressure, headaches, and asthma. Psychological interventions are, in fact, often most helpful when they are combined with other psychological interventions and with medical treatments (Sandler et al., 2017; Mendoza et al., 2016). In a classic study, ulcer patients who were given relaxation, self-instruction, and assertiveness training along with medication were found to be less anxious and more comfortable, to have fewer symptoms, and to have a better long-term outcome than patients who received medication only (Brooks & Richardson, 1980). Combination interventions have also been helpful in changing Type A patterns and in reducing the risk of coronary heart disease among people who display Type A kinds of behavior (Burke & Riley, 2010; Harlapur et al., 2010).

Clearly, the treatment picture for physical illnesses has been changing dramatically. While medical treatments continue to dominate, today's medical practitioners are traveling a course far removed from that of their counterparts in centuries past.

Expanding the Boundaries of Abnormal Psychology

ONCE CONSIDERED OUTSIDE THE field of abnormal psychology, bodily ailments and physical illnesses are now seen as problems that fall squarely within its boundaries. Just as physical factors have long been recognized as playing a role in abnormal mental functioning, psychological conditions are now considered important contributors to abnormal physical functioning. In fact, many of today's clinicians believe that psychological and sociocultural factors contribute to some degree to the onset and course of virtually all physical ailments.

The number of studies devoted to this relationship has risen steadily during the past 40 years. What researchers once saw as a vague connection between stress and physical illness is now understood as a complex interaction of many variables. Such factors as life changes, a person's particular psychological state, social support, biochemical activity, and slowing of the immune system are all recognized as contributors to disorders once considered purely physical.

One of the most exciting aspects of these recent developments is the field's growing emphasis on the *interrelationship* of the social environment, the brain, and the rest of the body. Researchers have observed repeatedly that mental disorders are often best understood and treated when sociocultural, psychological, and biological factors are all taken into consideration. They now know that this interaction also helps explain medical problems. We are reminded that the brain is part of the body and that both are part of a social context. For better and for worse, the three are intertwined.

CLINICAL CHOICES

Now that you've read about disorders featuring somatic symptoms, try the interactive case study for this chapter. See if you are able to identify Joanne's symptoms and suggest a diagnosis based on her symptoms. What kind of treatment would be most effective for Joanne? Go to **Launch**Pad to access *Clinical Choices*.

♀... SUMMING UP

» **Disorders Focusing on Somatic Symptoms** Several DSM-5 categories focus on somatic symptoms, including *factitious disorder, conversion disorder, somatic symptom disorder,* and *illness anxiety disorder.* In these disorders, the somatic symptoms are primarily caused by psychosocial factors, or the symptoms trigger excessive anxiety or concern. *pp. 283–284*

» **Factitious Disorder** People with *factitious disorder* feign or induce physical disorders, typically for the purpose of assuming the role of a sick person. In a related pattern, *factitious disorder imposed on another,* a parent fabricates or induces a physical illness in his or her child. *pp. 284–286*

» **Conversion and Somatic Symptom Disorders** *Conversion disorder* involves bodily symptoms that affect voluntary motor and sensory functions, but the symptoms are inconsistent with known medical diseases. Diagnosticians are sometimes able to distinguish conversion disorder from a "true" medical problem by observing oddities in the patient's medical picture. In *somatic symptom disorder,* people become excessively distressed, concerned, and anxious about bodily symptoms that they are experiencing, and their lives are greatly and disproportionately disrupted by the symptoms.

Freud developed the initial psychodynamic view of conversion and somatic symptom disorders, proposing that the disorders represent a conversion of underlying emotional conflicts into physical symptoms. According to cognitive-behavioral theorists, the physical symptoms of these disorders bring rewards to the sufferer, and such reinforcement helps maintain the symptoms. Some cognitive-behavioral theorists further propose that the disorders are forms of *communication* and that people express their emotions through their physical symptoms. Treatments for these disorders include insight, exposure, and drug therapies and may include techniques such as education, reinforcement, or cognitive restructuring. *pp. 287–295*

» **Illness Anxiety Disorder** People with *illness anxiety disorder* are chronically anxious about and preoccupied with the notion that they have or are developing a serious medical illness, despite the absence of substantial somatic symptoms. Theorists explain this disorder much as they do anxiety disorders. Treatment includes drug and cognitive-behavioral approaches originally developed for obsessive-compulsive disorder. *p. 295*

» **Psychophysiological Disorders** *Psychological factors affecting other medical conditions,* known commonly as *psychophysiological disorders,* are those in which biological, psychosocial, and sociocultural factors interact to cause or worsen a physical problem. Factors linked to these disorders are biological factors, such as defects in the autonomic nervous system or particular organs; psychological factors, such as particular needs, attitudes, or personality styles; and sociocultural factors, such as aversive social conditions and cultural pressures.

For years, clinical researchers singled out a limited number of physical illnesses as psychophysiological, such as *ulcers* and *hypertension.* Recently many other psychophysiological disorders have been identified. Indeed, scientists have linked many physical illnesses to stress and have developed a new area of study called *psychoneuroimmunology.* Stress can slow *lymphocyte* activity, thereby interfering with the immune system's ability to protect against illness during times of stress. Factors that seem to affect immune functioning include *norepinephrine and cortisol activity, behavioral changes, personality style,* and *social support. pp. 296–306*

» **Psychological Treatments for Physical Disorders** *Behavioral medicine* combines psychological and physical interventions to treat or prevent medical problems. Psychological approaches such as *relaxation training, biofeedback training, meditation, hypnosis, cognitive-behavioral techniques, support groups, and therapies that heighten the awareness and expression of emotions and needs* are increasingly being included in the treatment of various medical problems. *pp. 306–310*

Visit *LaunchPad*
to access the e-Book, Clinical Choices, videos, activities, and LearningCurve, as well as study aids including flashcards, FAQs, and research exercises.

LaunchPad
macmillan learning

◉…Eating Disorders

Shani, age 15: While I was learning to resist the temptation of hunger, I walked into the kitchen when no one was around, took a slice of bread out the packet, toasted it, spread butter on it, took a deep breath and bit. Guilty. I spat it in the trash and tossed the rest of it in and walked away. Seconds later I longed for the toast, walked back to the trash, popped open the lid and sifted around in the debris. I found it and contemplated, for minutes, whether to eat it. I brought it close to my nose and inhaled the smell of melted butter. Guilty. Guilty for trashing it. Guilty for craving it. Guilty for tasting it. I threw it back in the trash and walked away. No is no, I told myself. No is no.

. . . And no matter how hard I would try to always have The Perfect Day in terms of my food, I would feel the guilt every second of every day. . . It was my desire to escape the guilt that perpetuated my compulsion to starve.

In time I formulated a more precise list of "can" and "can't" in my head that dictated what I was allowed or forbidden to consume. . . . It became my way of life. My manual. My blueprint. But more than that, it gave me false reassurance that my life was under control. I was managing everything because I had this list in front of me telling me what—and what not—to do. . . .

In the beginning, starving was hard work. It was not innate. Day by day I was slowly lured into another world, a world that was. . . as rewarding as it was challenging. . . .

That summer, despite the fact that I had lost a lot of weight, my mother agreed to let me go to summer camp with my fifteen-year-old peers, after I swore to her that I would eat. I broke that promise as soon as I got there. . . . At breakfast time when all the teens raced into the dining hall to grab cereal boxes and bread loaves and jelly tins and peanut butter jars, I sat alone cocooned in my fear. I fingered the plastic packet of a loaf of white sliced bread, took out a piece and tore off a corner, like I was marking a page in a book, onto which I dabbed a blob of peanut butter and jelly the size of a Q-tip. That was my breakfast. Every day. For three weeks.

I tried to get to the showers when everyone else was at the beach so nobody would see me. I heard girls behind me whispering, "That's the girl I told you about that looks so disgusting." Someone invariably walked in on me showering and covered her mouth with her hand like I was a dead body. I wished I could disappear into the drain like my hair that was falling out in chunks. . . .

While everyone else was out there swimming, tanning, making out, playing sports, volunteering and team building, I hid in my tent and wrote letters to my mother reassuring her that I was eating. I told her that I ate peanut butter and jelly sandwiches every morning for breakfast. . . .

[Upon returning to school] I was labeled the "concentration camp victim." On my return, over the months everyone watched my body shrink as though it were being vacuum packed in slow motion. . . . At my lowest weight my hipbones protruded like knuckle bones under my dress and I had to minimize the increments of the belt holes until there was so much extra belt material dangling down that I did away with the belt completely. My shoes were too big for my feet; my ankles were so thin that I wore three pairs of socks at a time and still my shoes would slide off my heels. And my panties were so baggy I secured them with safety pins on the sides so they wouldn't fall down. . . .

On the home front things were worse than ever. . . I locked my door and forbade anyone from entering. Even so, my mother and I had screaming matches every day, with her trying to convince me that "your body needs food as fuel" and me retaliating with "I'm not hungry."...

For nine months my mother stood by, forbidden to interfere, while I starved myself. She had no idea what was going on, nor did I... She watched me transform from an innocent, soft, kind, loving girl into a reclusive, vicious, aggressive, defiant teenager.... And there was nothing she could say or do to stop me....

(Raviv, 2010)

It has not always done so, but Western society today equates thinness with health and beauty. In fact, in the United States thinness has become a national obsession. Most of us are as preoccupied with how much we eat as with the taste and nutritional value of our food. Thus it is not surprising that during the past three decades we have also witnessed an increase in two eating disorders that have at their core a morbid fear of gaining weight. Sufferers of *anorexia nervosa*, like Shani, are convinced that they need to be extremely thin, and they lose so much weight that they may starve themselves to death. People with *bulimia nervosa* go on frequent eating binges, during which they uncontrollably consume large quantities of food, and then force themselves to vomit or take other extreme steps to keep from gaining weight. A third eating disorder, *binge-eating disorder*, in which people frequently go on eating binges but do not force themselves to vomit or engage in other such behaviors, also is on the rise. People with binge-eating disorder do not fear weight gain to the same degree as those with anorexia nervosa and bulimia nervosa, but they do have many of the other features found in those disorders (NIMH, 2017).

The news media have published many reports about eating disorders. One reason for the surge in public interest is the frightening medical consequences that can result from the disorders. The public first became aware of such consequences in 1983 when Karen Carpenter died from medical problems related to anorexia. Carpenter, the 32-year-old lead singer of the soft-rock brother-and-sister duo called the Carpenters, had been enormously successful and was admired by many as a wholesome and healthy model to young women everywhere. Another reason for the current concern is the disproportionate prevalence of anorexia nervosa and bulimia nervosa among adolescent girls and young women (NIMH, 2017). ■

> Are girls and women in Western society destined to struggle with at least some issues of eating and appearance?

Anorexia Nervosa

SHANI, 15 YEARS OLD AND in the ninth grade, displays many symptoms of **anorexia nervosa** (APA, 2013). She purposely maintains a significantly low body weight, intensely fears becoming overweight, has a distorted view of her weight and shape, and is excessively influenced by her weight and shape in her self-evaluations (see **Table 11–1**).

Like Shani, at least half of the people with anorexia nervosa reduce their weight by restricting their intake of food, a pattern called *restricting-type anorexia nervosa*. First they tend to cut out sweets and fattening snacks; then, increasingly, they eliminate other foods. Eventually people with this kind of anorexia nervosa show almost no variability in diet. Others, however, lose weight by forcing themselves to vomit after meals or by abusing laxatives or diuretics, and they may even engage in eating binges, a pattern called *binge-eating/purging-type anorexia nervosa*, which you will read about in more detail in the section on bulimia nervosa.

Between 75 and 90 percent of all cases of anorexia nervosa occur in females (NIMH, 2017). Although the disorder can appear at any age, the peak age of onset is between 14 and 20 years. Between 0.6 and 4.0 percent of all females in Western countries develop the disorder in their lifetime, and many more display at least some of its symptoms

---

TABLE: 11-1

Dx Checklist

Anorexia Nervosa

1. Individual purposely takes in too little nourishment, resulting in body weight that is very low and below that of other people of similar age and gender.

2. Individual is very fearful of gaining weight, or repeatedly seeks to prevent weight gain despite low body weight.

3. Individual has a distorted body perception, places inappropriate emphasis on weight or shape in judgments of herself or himself, or fails to appreciate the serious implications of her or his low weight.

Information from: APA, 2013.

(NIMH, 2017; Forman, 2016). It seems to be on the increase in North America, Europe, and Japan.

Typically the disorder begins after a person who is slightly overweight or of normal weight has been on a diet (APA, 2015; Stice & Presnell, 2010). The escalation toward anorexia nervosa may follow a stressful event such as separation of parents, a move away from home, or an experience of personal failure (APA, 2015; Wilson et al., 2003). Although most people with the disorder recover, as many as 6 percent of them become so seriously ill that they die, usually from medical problems brought about by starvation, or from suicide (Mehler, 2017). The suicide rate among people with anorexia nervosa is five times the rate found in the general population (Klein & Attia, 2017).

anorexia nervosa A disorder marked by the pursuit of extreme thinness and by extreme weight loss.

The Clinical Picture

Becoming thin is the key goal for people with anorexia nervosa, but *fear* provides their motivation. People with this disorder are afraid of becoming obese, of giving in to their growing desire to eat, and more generally of losing control over the size and shape of their bodies. In addition, despite their focus on thinness and the severe restrictions they may place on their food intake, people with anorexia are *preoccupied with food*. They may spend considerable time thinking and even reading about food and planning their limited meals (Klein & Attia, 2017; Knudson, 2006). Many report that their dreams are filled with images of food and eating.

This preoccupation with food may in fact be a result of food deprivation rather than its cause. In a famous "starvation study" conducted in the late 1940s, 36 normal-weight conscientious objectors were put on a semistarvation diet for six months (Keys et al., 1950). Like people with anorexia nervosa, the volunteers became preoccupied with food and eating. They spent hours each day planning their small meals, talked more about food than about any other topic, studied cookbooks and recipes, mixed food in odd combinations, and dawdled over their meals. Many also had vivid dreams about food.

Persons with anorexia nervosa also *think in distorted ways*. They usually have a low opinion of their body shape, for example, and consider themselves unattractive (Klein & Attia, 2017; Boone et al., 2014). In addition, they are likely to overestimate their actual proportions. While most women in Western society overestimate their body size, the estimates of those with anorexia nervosa are particularly high. In one of her classic books on eating disorders, Hilde Bruch, a pioneer in this field, recalled the self-perceptions of a 23-year-old patient:

Laboratory starvation Thirty-six conscientious objectors who were put on a semistarvation diet for six months developed many of the symptoms seen in anorexia nervosa and bulimia nervosa (Keys et al., 1950).

> *I look in a full-length mirror at least four or five times daily and I really cannot see myself as too thin. Sometimes after several days of strict dieting, I feel that my shape is tolerable, but most of the time, odd as it may seem, I look in the mirror and believe that I am too fat.*
>
> *(Bruch, 1973)*

This tendency to overestimate body size has been tested in the laboratory (Klein & Attia, 2017; Delinsky, 2011). In a popular assessment technique, research participants look at a photograph of themselves through an adjustable lens. They are asked to adjust the lens until the image that they see matches their actual body size. The image can be made to vary from 20 percent thinner to 20 percent larger than actual appearance. In one study, more than half of the individuals with anorexia nervosa overestimated their body size, stopping the lens when the image was larger than they actually were.

The distorted thinking of anorexia nervosa also takes the form of certain maladaptive attitudes and misperceptions (Alvarenga et al., 2014). Sufferers tend to hold such beliefs as "I must be perfect in every way"; "I will become a better person if I deprive myself"; and "I can avoid guilt by not eating."

People with anorexia nervosa also have certain *psychological problems,* such as depression, anxiety, low self-esteem, and insomnia or other sleep disturbances (Klein & Attia, 2017; Boone et al., 2014). A number grapple with substance abuse. And many display obsessive-compulsive patterns. They may set rigid rules for food preparation or even cut food into specific shapes. Broader obsessive-compulsive patterns are common as well. Many, for example, exercise compulsively, prioritizing exercise over most other activities in their lives. In some research, people with anorexia nervosa and others with obsessive-compulsive disorder score equally high for obsessiveness and compulsiveness. Finally, persons with anorexia nervosa tend to be perfectionistic, a characteristic that typically precedes the onset of the disorder.

Medical Problems

The starvation habits of anorexia nervosa cause medical problems (Mehler, 2017; Lawson & Miller, 2016). Women develop **amenorrhea,** the absence of menstrual cycles. Other problems include lowered body temperature, low blood pressure, body swelling, reduced bone mineral density, and slow heart rate. Metabolic and electrolyte imbalances also may occur and can lead to death by heart failure or circulatory collapse. The poor nutrition of people with anorexia nervosa may also cause skin to become rough, dry, and cracked; nails to become brittle; and hands and feet to be cold and blue. Some people lose hair from the scalp, and some grow *lanugo* (the fine, silky hair that covers some newborns) on their trunk, extremities, and face. Shani, the young woman whose self-description opened this chapter, recalls how her body deteriorated as her disorder was progressing:

Nobody knew that I was always cold no matter how many layers I wore. And that my hair came out in thick wads whenever I wet it or washed it. That I stopped menstruating. That at night I lay awake agonizing over thoughts of the day's consumption. That the guilt I carried every day weighed on me like lead. That my hipbones hurt to lie on my stomach and my coccyx hurt to sit on the floor. And that the concave feeling in my stomach of dying hunger left in its place an anger that would destroy all feeling.

(Raviv, 2010)

Bulimia Nervosa

PEOPLE WITH BULIMIA NERVOSA—a disorder also known as **binge-purge syndrome**—engage in repeated episodes of uncontrollable overeating, or **binges.** A binge episode takes place over a limited period of time, often two hours, during which the person eats much more food than most people would eat during a similar time span (APA, 2013). In addition, people with this disorder repeatedly perform inappropriate *compensatory behaviors,* such as forcing themselves to vomit; misusing laxatives, diuretics, or enemas; fasting; or exercising excessively (see **Table 11-2**). Lindsey, a woman who has since recovered from bulimia nervosa, describes a morning during her disorder:

Today I am going to be really good and that means eating certain predetermined portions of food and not taking one more bite than I think I am allowed. I am very careful to see that I don't take more than Doug does. I judge by his body. I can feel the tension building. I wish Doug would hurry up and leave so I can get going!

As soon as he shuts the door, I try to get involved with one of the myriad of responsibilities on the list. I hate them all! I just want to crawl into a hole. I don't want to do

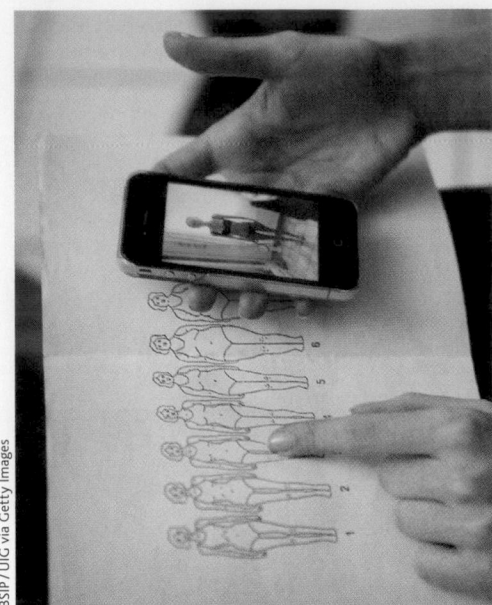

Seeing is deceiving In one assessment and research technique, people look at drawings of bodies, ranging from very thin to obese, then select the silhouette they believe represents their own body size. Individuals with anorexia nervosa typically pick the wrong body size even if they hold photos of themselves during the task.

TABLE: 11-2

Dx Checklist

Bulimia Nervosa

1. Repeated binge eating episodes.

2. Repeated performance of ill-advised compensatory behaviors (e.g., forced vomiting) to prevent weight gain.

3. Symptoms take place at least weekly for a period of 3 months.

4. Inappropriate influence of weight and shape on appraisal of oneself.

Information from: APA, 2013.

anything. I'd rather eat. I am alone, I am nervous, I am no good, I always do everything wrong anyway, I am not in control, I can't make it through the day, I just know it. It has been the same for so long.

I remember the starchy cereal I ate for breakfast. I am into the bathroom and onto the scale. It measures the same, but I don't want to stay the same! I want to be thinner! I look in the mirror, I think my thighs are ugly and deformed looking. I see a lumpy, clumsy, pear-shaped wimp. There is always something wrong with what I see. I feel frustrated trapped in this body and I don't know what to do about it.

I float to the refrigerator knowing exactly what is there. I begin with last night's brownies. I always begin with the sweets. At first I try to make it look like nothing is missing, but my appetite is huge and I resolve to make another batch of brownies. I know there is half of a bag of cookies in the bathroom, thrown out the night before, and I polish them off immediately. I take some milk so my vomiting will be smoother. I like the full feeling I get after downing a big glass. I get out six pieces of bread and toast one side in the broiler, turn them over and load them with patties of butter and put them under the broiler again till they are bubbling. I take all six pieces on a plate to the television and go back for a bowl of cereal and a banana to have along with them. Before the last toast is finished, I am already preparing the next batch of six more pieces. Maybe another brownie or five, and a couple of large bowlfuls of ice cream, yogurt or cottage cheese. My stomach is stretched into a huge ball below my ribcage. I know I'll have to go into the bathroom soon, but I want to postpone it. I am in never-never land. I am waiting, feeling the pressure, pacing the floor in and out of the rooms. Time is passing. Time is passing. It is getting to be time.

I wander aimlessly through each of the rooms again tidying, making the whole house neat and put back together. I finally make the turn into the bathroom. I brace my feet, pull my hair back and stick my finger down my throat, stroking twice, and get up a huge pile of food. Three times, four and another pile of food. I can see everything come back. I am glad to see those brownies because they are SO fattening. The rhythm of the emptying is broken and my head is beginning to hurt. I stand up feeling dizzy, empty and weak. The whole episode has taken about an hour.

(Hall & Cohn, 2010, p. 1)

Like anorexia nervosa, bulimia nervosa usually occurs in females, again in 75 to 90 percent of the cases (NIMH, 2017; Forman, 2016). It begins in adolescence or young adulthood (most often between 15 and 20 years of age) and often lasts for years, with periodic letup. The weight of people with bulimia nervosa usually stays within a normal range, although it may fluctuate markedly within that range. Some people with this disorder, however, become seriously underweight and may eventually qualify for a diagnosis of anorexia nervosa instead (see **Figure 11-1**).

amenorrhea The absence of menstrual cycles.

bulimia nervosa A disorder marked by frequent eating binges followed by forced vomiting or other extreme compensatory behaviors to avoid gaining weight. Also known as *binge-purge syndrome*.

binge An episode of uncontrollable eating during which a person ingests a very large quantity of food.

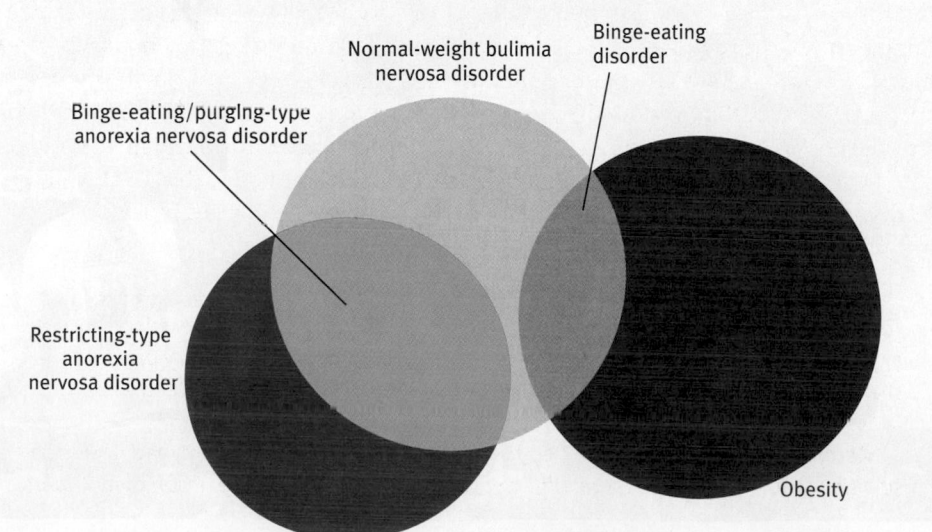

FIGURE 11.1

Overlapping Patterns of Anorexia Nervosa, Bulimia Nervosa, and Obesity

Some people with anorexia nervosa binge and purge their way to weight loss, and some obese people binge eat. However, most people with bulimia nervosa are not obese, and most overweight people do not binge eat.

Many teenagers and young adults go on occasional eating binges or experiment with vomiting or laxatives after they hear about these behaviors from their friends or the media. Indeed, according to global studies, 25 to 50 percent of all students report periodic binge eating or self-induced vomiting (Ekern, 2014; McDermott & Jaffa, 2005). Only some of these individuals, however, qualify for a diagnosis of bulimia nervosa. Surveys in several Western countries suggest that between 0.5 and 5.0 percent of women develop the full syndrome (Engel, Steffen, & Mitchell, 2017; NIMH, 2017; Ekern, 2014). Among college students the rate seems to be particularly high (Zerbe, 2008).

Binges

People with bulimia nervosa may have between 1 and 30 binge episodes per week (Fairburn et al., 2008). In most cases, they carry out the binges in secret. The person eats massive amounts of food very rapidly, with minimal chewing—usually sweet, high-calorie foods with a soft texture, such as ice cream, cookies, doughnuts, and sandwiches. The food is hardly tasted or thought about. Binge eaters consume an average of 2,000 to 3,400 calories during an episode (Engel et al., 2017). Some individuals consume as many as 10,000 calories.

Binges are usually preceded by feelings of great tension. The person feels irritable, "unreal," and powerless to control an overwhelming need to eat "forbidden" foods. During the binge, the person feels unable to stop eating (APA, 2013). Although the binge itself may be experienced as pleasurable in the sense that it relieves the unbearable tension, it is followed by feelings of extreme self-blame, shame, guilt, and depression, as well as fears of gaining weight and being discovered (Engel et al., 2017; Sanftner & Tantillo, 2011).

Compensatory Behaviors

After a binge, people with bulimia nervosa try to compensate for and undo its effects. Many resort to vomiting, for example. But vomiting actually fails to prevent the absorption of half of the calories consumed during a binge. Furthermore, because repeated vomiting affects one's general ability to feel satiated, it leads to greater hunger and more frequent and intense binges. Similarly, the use of laxatives or diuretics largely fails to undo the caloric effects of bingeing (Mitchell, 2016).

Curtis Means/NBC NewsWire/Getty Images

Eating for sport Many people go on occasional eating binges. In fact, sometimes binges are officially endorsed, as you see in this photo from the annual Nathan's Famous International Hot Dog Eating Contest in Brooklyn's Coney Island, New York. However, people are considered to have an eating disorder only when the binges recur, the pattern endures, and the issues of weight or shape dominate self-evaluation.

Vomiting and other compensatory behaviors may temporarily relieve the uncomfortable physical feelings of fullness or reduce the feelings of anxiety and self-disgust attached to binge eating (Stewart & Williamson, 2008). Over time, however, a cycle develops in which purging allows more bingeing, and bingeing necessitates more purging (Mitchell, 2016). The cycle eventually causes people with the disorder to feel powerless and disgusted with themselves (Engel et al., 2017). Most recognize fully that they have an eating disorder. Lindsey, the woman we met earlier, recalls how the pattern of binge eating, purging, and self-disgust took hold while she was a teenager in boarding school.

> *Every bite that went into my mouth was a naughty and selfish indulgence, and I became more and more disgusted with myself. . . .*
>
> *The first time I stuck my fingers down my throat was during the last week of school. I saw a girl come out of the bathroom with her face all red and her eyes puffy. She had always talked about her weight and how she should be dieting even though her body was really shapely. I knew instantly what she had just done and I had to try it. . . .*
>
> *I began with breakfasts which were served buffet-style on the main floor of the dorm. I learned which foods I could eat that would come back up easily. When I woke in the morning, I had to make the decision whether to stuff myself for half an hour and throw up before class, or whether to try and make it through the whole day without overeating. . . . I always thought people noticed when I took huge portions at mealtimes, but I figured they assumed that because I was an athlete, I burned it off. . . . Once a binge was under way, I did not stop until my stomach looked pregnant and I felt like I could not swallow one more time.*
>
> *That year was the first of my nine years of obsessive eating and throwing up. . . . I didn't want to tell anyone what I was doing, and I didn't want to stop. . . . [Though] being in love or other distractions occasionally lessened the cravings, I always returned to the food.*
>
> (Hall & Cohn, 2010, p. 55)

As with anorexia nervosa, a bulimic pattern typically begins during or after a period of intense dieting, often one that has been successful and earned praise from family members and friends (APA, 2015; Couturier & Lock, 2006). Studies of both animals and humans have found that normal research participants placed on very strict diets also develop a tendency to binge (Pankevich et al., 2010; Eifert et al., 2007). Some of the participants in the conscientious objector "starvation study," for example, later binged when they were allowed to return to regular eating, and a number of them continued to be hungry even after large meals (Keys et al., 1950).

Bulimia Nervosa Versus Anorexia Nervosa

Bulimia nervosa is similar to anorexia nervosa in many ways. Both disorders typically begin after a period of dieting by people who are fearful of becoming obese; driven to become thin; preoccupied with food, weight, and appearance; and struggling with depression, anxiety, obsessiveness, and the need to be perfect (Engel et al., 2017; Klein & Attia, 2017; Boone et al., 2014). People with either of the disorders have a heightened risk of suicide attempts and fatalities. Substance abuse may accompany either disorder, perhaps beginning with the excessive use of diet pills. People with either disorder believe that they weigh too much and look too heavy regardless of their actual weight or appearance (see *InfoCentral* on the next page). And both disorders are marked by disturbed attitudes toward eating.

#RoyalBulimia

During her three years as queen of England, Anne Boleyn, King Henry VIII's second wife, displayed a habit, first observed during her coronation banquet, of vomiting during meals. In fact, she assigned a lady-in-waiting the task of holding up a sheet when the queen looked likely to vomit (Shaw, 2004).

Across the generations When television journalist Katie Couric interviewed singer Demi Lovato in 2012, it turned out that the two had an important thing in common—eating disorders. Lovato has spoken openly for years about her body image issues and eating struggles, but not until this interview did Couric reveal that she had experienced similar problems in the past. She noted, "I wrestled with bulimia all through college and for two years after that."

Ida Mae Astute/Disney-ABC via Getty Images

BODY DISSATISFACTION

People who evaluate their weight and shape negatively are experiencing **body dissatisfaction**. Around 73% of all girls and women are dissatisfied with their bodies, compared with 56% of all boys and men (Pop, 2016; Swami et al., 2016; Mintem et al., 2014). The vast majority of dissatisfied females believe they are overweight; in contrast, half of dissatisfied males consider themselves overweight and half consider themselves underweight. The factors most closely tied to body dissatisfaction are perfectionism and unrealistic expectations. Body dissatisfaction is the single most powerful contributor to dieting and to the development of eating disorders.

BODY DISSATISFACTION CORRELATES WITH...

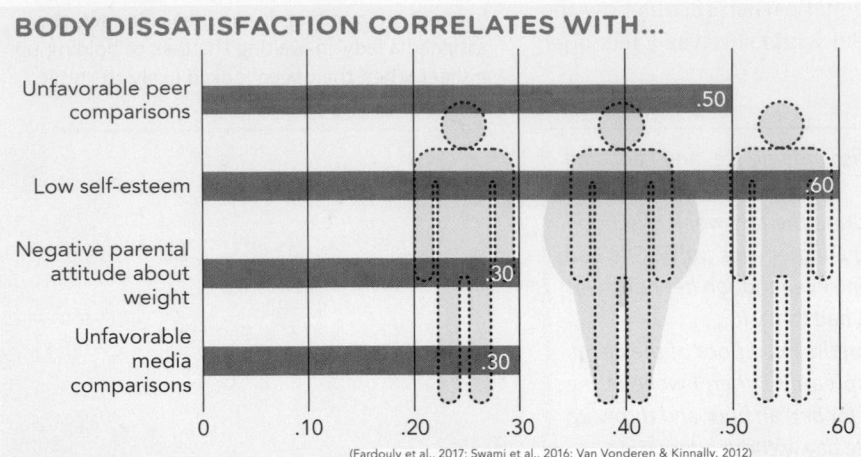

Unfavorable peer comparisons	.50
Low self-esteem	.60
Negative parental attitude about weight	.30
Unfavorable media comparisons	.30

0   .10   .20   .30   .40   .50   .60

(Fardouly et al., 2017; Swami et al., 2016; Van Vonderen & Kinnally, 2012)

PEOPLE WITH HIGH BODY DISSATISFACTION ARE MORE PRONE TO...

- Eating disorders
- Depressive disorders
- Anxiety disorders
- Body dysmorphic disorder
- Problems in interpersonal relationships
- Difficulties at work

(Griffiths et al., 2017; Frederick et al., 2016; Marques et al., 2012; Dyl et al., 2006; Ohring et al., 2002)

ADULTS AND BODY DISSATISFACTION

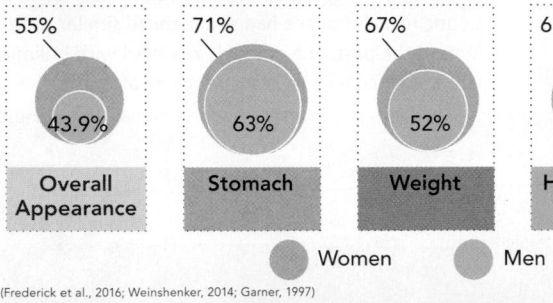

Overall Appearance	Stomach	Weight	Hips/Thighs
55%	71%	67%	61%
43.9%	63%	52%	29%

● Women ● Men

(Frederick et al., 2016; Weinshenker, 2014; Garner, 1997)

NEGATIVE BODY THOUGHTS

97% of women have at least one negative thought about their bodies each day.

On average, a woman has 13 negative body thoughts each day.

Examples of negative body thoughts:

● ● ● "I hate my thighs, my stomach, and my arms."

"I look disgusting." ● ● ●

● ● ● "I'm obese. All the pretty girls are size 2."

(Brodeur, 2016; Dreisbach, 2011)

ADOLESCENTS AND BODY DISSATISFACTION

Females of all ages tend to be dissatisfied with their bodies, but the biggest leap in dissatisfaction occurs when girls transition from early to mid-adolescence.

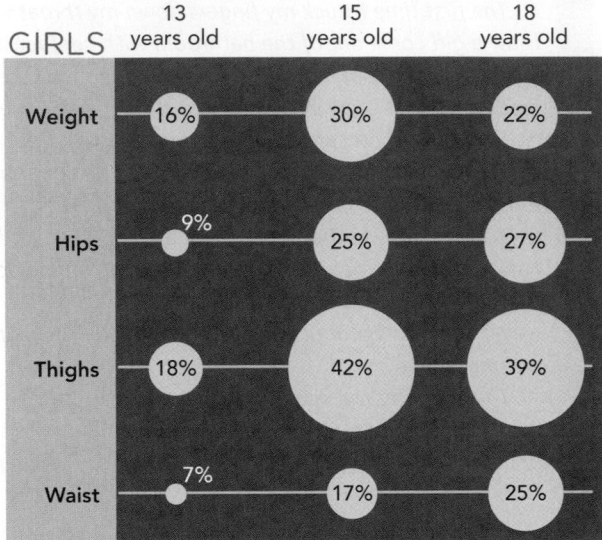

Dissatisfaction

GIRLS	13 years old	15 years old	18 years old
Weight	16%	30%	22%
Hips	9%	25%	27%
Thighs	18%	42%	39%
Waist	7%	17%	25%

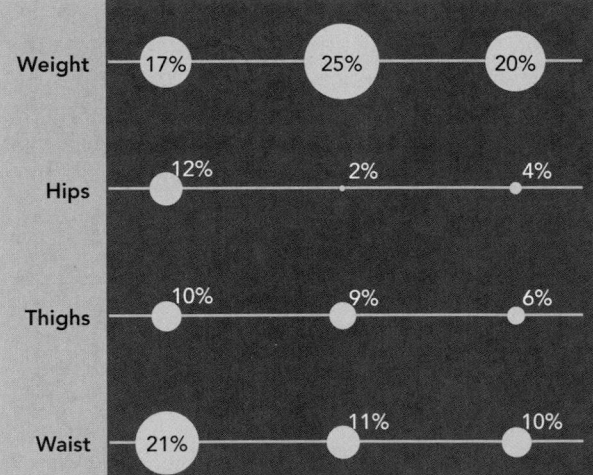

BOYS			
Weight	17%	25%	20%
Hips	12%	2%	4%
Thighs	10%	9%	6%
Waist	21%	11%	10%

(Griffiths et al., 2017; Mäkinen et al., 2015, 2012; Weinshenker, 2014; Rosenblum & Lewis, 1999)

SOCIAL MEDIA AND BODY DISSATISFACTION

- The more time teenage girls spend on social media, the higher their body dissatisfaction.
- Most teens say that social network sites hurt their body confidence.

(Dove, 2016; Kim & Chock, 2016; Tiggemann & Slater, 2013; Proud2Bme, 2012)

Yet the two disorders also differ in important ways. Although people with either disorder worry about the opinions of others, those with bulimia nervosa tend to be more concerned about pleasing others, being attractive to others, and having intimate relationships (Zerbe, 2010, 2008). They also tend to be more sexually experienced and active than people with anorexia nervosa (Gonidakis et al., 2014). Particularly troublesome, they are more likely to have long histories of mood swings, become easily frustrated or bored, and have trouble coping effectively or controlling their impulses and strong emotions (Engel et al., 2017; Lilenfeld, 2011). More than one-third of those with bulimia nervosa display the characteristics of a personality disorder, particularly borderline or avoidant personality disorder, which you will be looking at more closely in Chapter 16.

Another difference is the nature of the medical complications that accompany the two disorders (Forman, 2016; Mitchell & Zunker, 2016). Only half of women with bulimia nervosa are amenorrheic or have very irregular menstrual periods, compared with almost all of those with anorexia nervosa. On the other hand, repeated vomiting bathes teeth and gums in hydrochloric acid, leading some women with bulimia nervosa to have serious dental problems, such as breakdown of enamel and even loss of teeth. Moreover, frequent vomiting or chronic diarrhea (from the use of laxatives) can cause a host of serious medical problems, including dangerous potassium deficiencies, which may lead to weakness, intestinal disorders, kidney disease, or heart damage.

"What do you eat for anxiety?"

Binge-Eating Disorder

LIKE THOSE WITH BULIMIA NERVOSA, people with **binge-eating disorder** engage in repeated eating binges during which they feel no control over their eating (APA, 2013). However, they do *not* perform inappropriate compensatory behavior (see **Table 11-3**). As a result of their frequent binges, around half of people with binge-eating disorder become overweight or even obese (Forman, 2016; Sysko & Devlin, 2016).

Binge-eating disorder was first identified 60 years ago as a pattern common among many overweight people (Stunkard, 1959). It is important to recognize, however, that most overweight people do not engage in repeated binges; their weight results from frequent overeating and/or a combination of biological, psychological, and sociocultural factors (ANAD, 2014).

Between 2 and 7 percent of the population have binge-eating disorder (NIMH, 2017; Brownley et al., 2015). As with the other eating disorders, women with this disorder outnumber men; at least 64 percent of sufferers are female (NIMH, 2017; Forman, 2016) (see **Table 11-4**). In addition, the binges that characterize this pattern are similar to those seen in bulimia nervosa, particularly the amount of food eaten and the sense of loss of control experienced during the binge. Moreover, like people with bulimia nervosa or anorexia nervosa, those with binge-eating disorder typically are preoccupied with food, weight, and appearance; base their evaluation of themselves largely on their weight and shape; misperceive their body size and are extremely dissatisfied with their body; struggle with feelings of depression, anxiety, and perfectionism; and may abuse substances (NIMH, 2017; Sysko & Devlin, 2016). On the other hand, although they aspire to limit their eating, people with binge-eating disorder are not as driven to thinness as those with anorexia nervosa and bulimia nervosa. Unlike the

binge-eating disorder A disorder marked by frequent binges without extreme compensatory acts.

TABLE: 11-3
Dx Checklist
Binge-Eating Disorder
1. Recurrent binge eating episodes
2. Binge-eating episodes include at least three of these features: • Unusually fast eating • Absence of hunger • Uncomfortable fullness • Secret eating due to sense of shame • Subsequent feelings of self-disgust, depression, or severe guilt
3. Significant distress
4. Binge-eating episodes take place at least weekly over the course of 3 months
5. Absence of excessive compensatory behaviors

Information from: APA, 2013.

TABLE 11-4

Comparing the Eating Disorders

	One-Year Prevalence	Percentage Who Are Female	Typical Age at Onset	Percentage Who Receive Treatment	Successful Long-Term Recovery After Treatment
Anorexia nervosa	0.6–4.0%	75–90%	14–20 years	34%	75%
Bulimia nervosa	0.5–5.0%	75–90%	15–20 years	43%	75%
Binge-eating disorder	2.0–7.0%	64–70%	22–30 years	44%	60%

Information from: Engel et al., 2017; Klein & Attia, 2017; NIMH, 2017; Forman, 2016; Ekern, 2014.

other eating disorders, binge-eating disorder does not necessarily begin with efforts at extreme dieting. And people with this disorder typically first develop it later than those with the other eating disorders; most often they are in their twenties (NIMH, 2017; Forman, 2016).

What Causes Eating Disorders?

MOST OF TODAY'S THEORISTS AND RESEARCHERS use a **multidimensional risk perspective** to explain eating disorders. That is, they identify several key factors that place a person at risk for these disorders (Stice et al., 2017; Allen et al., 2016; Stice, 2016). Generally, the more of these factors that are present, the more likely it is that a person will develop an eating disorder. The most common of these are psychological, biological, and sociocultural factors. The multidimensional risk perspective for eating disorders does not yet have the specificity and research support that the developmental psychopathology perspective offers in its explanations of anxiety, posttraumatic stress, and depressive disorders, but it does share many of the principles of the developmental psychopathology perspective. That is, it contends that the risk factors for eating disorders unfold over the course of development, that some such factors may be particularly important, that interactions between these factors are key, and that different risk factors and combinations of factors may lead to the same eating disorders (Stice et al., 2017).

As you will see, most of the risk factors that have been cited and investigated center on anorexia nervosa and bulimia nervosa. Binge-eating disorder, formally identified as a clinical syndrome more recently, is only now being broadly investigated. The factors that are also at work in this "newer" disorder will probably become clear in the coming years.

Psychodynamic Factors: Ego Deficiencies

Hilde Bruch, a pioneer in the study and treatment of eating disorders, was mentioned earlier in this chapter. Bruch developed a largely psychodynamic theory of the disorders. She argued that disturbed mother–child interactions lead to serious *ego deficiencies* in the child (including a poor sense of independence and control) and to severe *perceptual disturbances* that jointly help produce disordered eating (Treasure & Cardi, 2017; Bruch, 2001, 1991, 1962).

According to Bruch, parents may respond to their children either effectively or ineffectively. *Effective parents* accurately attend to their children's biological and emotional needs, giving them food when they are crying from hunger and comfort when they are crying out of fear. *Ineffective parents,* by contrast, fail to attend to their children's needs, deciding that their children are hungry, cold, or tired without correctly

A dangerous trip back When actress and model Zoe Kravitz agreed to play the part of an anorexic woman in the movie *The Road Within*, she believed that her past history with eating disorders would be an asset to her performance. However, Kravitz reported that dieting down to 90 pounds for the movie "triggered some old stuff." She had difficulty calling an end to the weight loss and, later, did not want to regain the newly lost weight (Takeda, 2015).

Jeff Kravitz/Getty Images

interpreting the children's actual condition. They may feed their children when their children are anxious rather than hungry, or comfort them when they are tired rather than anxious. Children who receive such parenting may grow up confused and unaware of their own internal needs, not knowing for themselves when they are hungry or full and unable to identify their own emotions.

Because they cannot rely on internal signals, these children turn instead to external guides, such as their parents. They seem to be "model children," but they fail to develop genuine self-reliance and to "experience themselves as not being in control of their behavior, needs, and impulses, as not owning their own bodies" (Bruch, 1973, p. 55). Adolescence increases their basic desire to establish independence, yet they feel unable to do so. To overcome their sense of helplessness, they seek excessive control over their body size and shape and over their eating habits. Helen, an 18-year-old patient of Bruch's, described such needs and efforts:

> *There is a peculiar contradiction—everybody thinks you're doing so well and everybody thinks you're great, but your real problem is that you think that you are not good enough. You are afraid of not living up to what you think you are expected to do. You have one great fear, namely that of being ordinary, or average, or common—just not good enough. This peculiar dieting begins with such anxiety. You want to prove that you have control, that you can do it. The peculiar part of it is that it makes you feel good about yourself, makes you feel "I can accomplish something." It makes you feel "I can do something nobody else can do."*
>
> *(Bruch, 1978, p. 128)*

Clinical reports and research have provided some support for Bruch's theory (Treasure & Cardi, 2017: Holtom-Viesel & Allan, 2014; Schulz & Laessle, 2012). Clinicians have observed that the parents of teenagers with eating disorders do tend to define their children's needs rather than allow the children to define their own needs (Ihle et al., 2005). When Bruch interviewed the mothers of 51 children with anorexia nervosa, many proudly recalled that they had always "anticipated" their young child's needs, never permitting the child to "feel hungry" (Bruch, 1973).

Research has also supported Bruch's belief that people with eating disorders perceive internal cues, including emotional cues, inaccurately (Treasure & Cardi, 2017; Lavender et al., 2014). When research participants with an eating disorder are anxious or upset, for example, many of them mistakenly think they are also hungry (see **Figure 11-2**), and they respond as they might respond to hunger—by eating. In fact, people with eating disorders are often described by clinicians as *alexithymic*, meaning they have great difficulty putting descriptive labels on their feelings (D'Agata et al., 2015; Zerbe, 2010, 2008). And finally, studies support Bruch's argument that people with eating disorders rely excessively on the opinions, wishes, and views of others (see **MindTech**). They are more likely than other people to worry about how others view them, to seek approval, to be conforming, and to feel a lack of control over their lives (Treasure & Cardi, 2017; Travis & Meltzer, 2008).

Cognitive-Behavioral Factors

If you look closely at Bruch's explanation of eating disorders, you'll see that it contains several *cognitive-behavioral* ideas. She held, for example, that as a result of ineffective parenting, people with eating disorders improperly label their internal sensations and needs, generally feel little control over their

multidimensional risk perspective A theory that identifies several kinds of risk factors that are thought to combine to help cause a disorder. The more factors present, the greater the risk of developing the disorder.

FIGURE 11.2

When Do People Seek Junk Food?

Apparently, when they feel bad. People who eat junk food when they are feeling bad outnumber those who eat nutritional food under similar circumstances. In contrast, more people seek nutritional food when they are feeling good. (Information from: Isasi et al., 2013; Haberman, 2007; Rowan, 2005; Hudd et al., 2000; Lyman, 1982.)

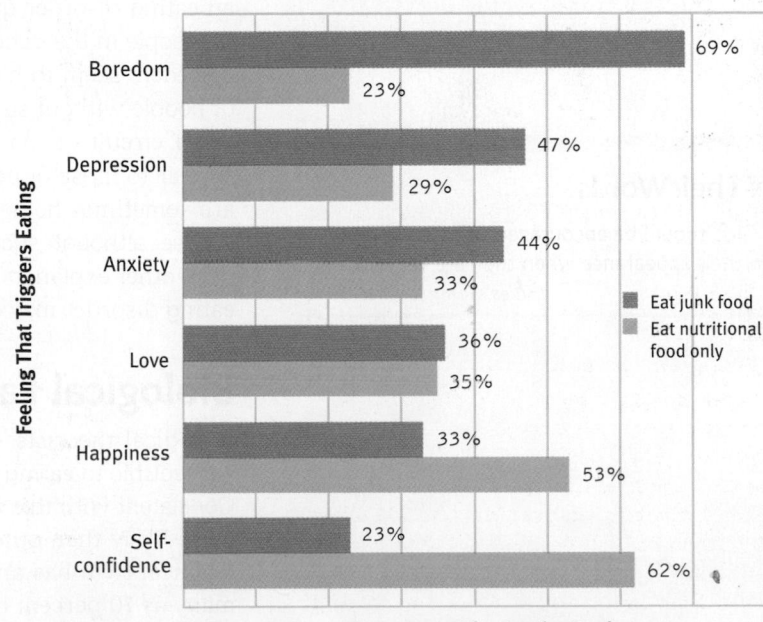

Percentage Who Eat the Food

(Feeling That Triggers Eating)

Boredom — Eat junk food 69%, Eat nutritional food only 23%
Depression — Eat junk food 47%, Eat nutritional food only 29%
Anxiety — Eat junk food 44%, Eat nutritional food only 33%
Love — Eat junk food 36%, Eat nutritional food only 35%
Happiness — Eat junk food 33%, Eat nutritional food only 53%
Self-confidence — Eat junk food 23%, Eat nutritional food only 62%

Downward spiral Over the course of several months in 2015, Australian teenager Christie Swadling transformed from a healthy-weight individual (left) into a 70-pound hospital patient suffering from anorexia nervosa (right). Aspiring to look like a Victoria's Secret model, the teenager restricted her food intake to as little as 200 calories a day. Now recovered, she speaks out on social media about her downward spiral and the dangers of disordered eating.

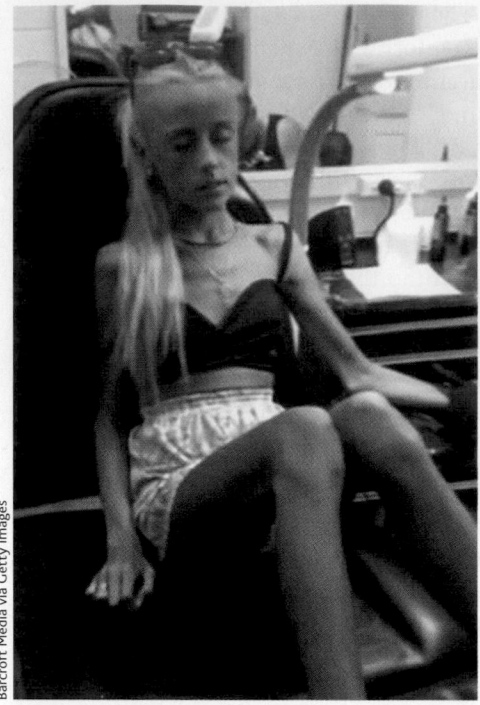

lives, and in turn, want to have excessive levels of control over their body size, shape, and eating habits. According to cognitive-behavioral theorists, these deficiencies contribute to a broad cognitive distortion that lies at the center of disordered eating, namely, people with anorexia nervosa and bulimia nervosa judge themselves—often exclusively—based on their shape and weight and their ability to control them (Mitchell, 2016; Fairburn et al., 2015, 2008). This "core pathology," say cognitive-behavioral theorists, contributes to all other aspects of the disorders, including the repeated efforts to lose weight and the preoccupation with shape, weight, and eating.

As you saw earlier in the chapter, research indicates that people with eating disorders do indeed display such cognitive deficiencies (Klein & Attia, 2017). Although studies have not clarified that the deficiencies are the *cause* of eating disorders, many cognitive-behavioral therapists proceed from this assumption and center their treatment for the disorders on correcting the clients' cognitive distortions and their accompanying behaviors. As you'll soon see, cognitive-behavioral therapies are among the most widely used of all treatments for eating disorders (Mitchell, 2016; Fairburn et al., 2015, 2008).

Depression

Many people with eating disorders, particularly those with bulimia nervosa, have symptoms of depression (Klein & Attia, 2017; Harrington et al., 2015). This finding has led some theorists to suggest that depressive disorders help set the stage for eating disorders.

Their claim is supported by four kinds of evidence. First, many more people with an eating disorder qualify for a clinical diagnosis of major depressive disorder than do people in the general population. Second, the close relatives of people with eating disorders seem to have a higher rate of depressive disorders than do close relatives of people without such disorders. Third, as you will soon see, the depression-related brain circuit of many people with eating disorders shows abnormalities that are similar to those of people with depression. And finally, people with eating disorders are sometimes helped by the same antidepressant drugs that reduce depression. Of course, although such findings suggest that depression may help cause eating disorders, other explanations are possible. For example, the pressure and pain of having an eating disorder may *cause* depression.

Biological Factors

Biological theorists suspect that certain genes may leave some people particularly susceptible to eating disorders (Bulik, Kleiman, & Yilmaz, 2016; Starr & Kreipe, 2014). Consistent with this idea, relatives of people with eating disorders are up to six times more likely than other people to develop the disorders themselves. Moreover, if one identical twin has anorexia nervosa, the other twin also develops the disorder in as many as 70 percent of cases; in contrast, the rate for fraternal twins, who are genetically less similar, is 20 percent. Similarly, in the case of bulimia nervosa, identical

#TheirWords

"Girls should be encouraged to take an interest in their appearance when they are very young."
Ladies' Home Journal, 1940

MINDTECH

Dark Sites of the Internet

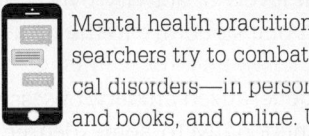

Mental health practitioners and researchers try to combat psychological disorders—in person, in journals and books, and online. Unfortunately, today there are also other—more negative—forces that run counter to the work of these professionals. Among the most common are so-called *dark sites* of the Internet—sites with the goal of promoting behaviors that the clinical community, and most of society, consider abnormal and destructive. *Pro-anorexia sites* are a prime example of this phenomenon (Chang & Bazarova, 2016).

By conservative estimates, there are at least 600 pro-anorexia Internet sites, with names such as "Dying to Be Thin" and "Starving for Perfection" (Yom-Tov, 2016; Borzekowski et al., 2010). These sites are commonly called *pro-Ana* sites, using a girl named Ana as the personification of this eating disorder. Some of the sites view anorexia nervosa (and bulimia nervosa) as lifestyles rather than psychological disorders; others present themselves as non-judgmental sites for people with anorexic symptoms. Either way, the sites are enormously popular and appear to outnumber "pro-recovery" Web sites.

Jean Claude Moshetti/REA/Redux

> **Besides promoting eating disorders, might there be other ways in which pro-Ana sites are potentially harmful to regular visitors?**

Many users of the sites exchange tips on how they can starve themselves and disguise their weight loss from family, friends, and doctors (Boepple & Thompson, 2016; Griffiths et al., 2015). The sites also offer support and feedback about starvation diets. Many offer mottos, emotional messages, and photos and videos of extremely thin actresses and models as "thinspiration."

As with the pro-suicide Web sites you read about in Chapter 9, the pro-Ana movement and its messages appear across the Internet—for example, on Web forums and chat groups; social networks such as Facebook, Tumblr, and LiveJournal; and video platforms such as YouTube and Vimeo (Sagan, 2015). Most social networks try to seek out and delete pro-Ana material and groups, taking the position that such messages promote self-harm. However, despite these efforts, the sites—and their pro-Ana messages—continue to flourish. A few years ago, for example, Instagram banned hashtags that glorify self-harm and threatened to disable those accounts. However, the accounts simply switched to more neutral hashtags such as #anorexia and #bulimia or to hashtags with modified spellings such as #thinspooooo and #thygap. What they did not change was their glorification of disordered eating and ultra-thinness.

Research suggests that, on average, regular visitors to the sites experience a rise in body dissatisfaction and depression, increase their dieting behavior, display more disordered eating, and attempt more self-harm as a result of their many visits (Gale et al., 2016; Rodgers et al., 2016; Yom-Tov et al., 2016). This worries professionals and parents alike. On the other hand, it is not clear what negative effects, if any, the sites have on infrequent visitors (Rodgers et al., 2016; Yom-Tov et al., 2016).

Many people worry that pro-Ana sites place vulnerable people at great risk, and they have called for more active efforts to ban these sites. Others argue, however, that despite their potential dangers, the sites represent basic freedoms that should not be violated—freedom of speech, for example, and perhaps even the freedom to do oneself harm. 💬

twins display a concordance rate of 23 percent, compared with a rate of 9 percent among fraternal twins (Kendler et al., 2018, 1995, 1991; Thornton et al., 2011).

One factor that has captured the attention of investigators is the possible role of dysfunctional *brain circuits* in people with eating disorders (Monteleone et al., 2018). As you have read throughout this book, a brain circuit is a network of particular brain structures that work together, triggering each other into action to produce a distinct kind of behavioral, cognitive, or emotional reaction (see pages 48–49). And as you read in Chapters 5, 6, and 7, studies over the past decade have increasingly tied each

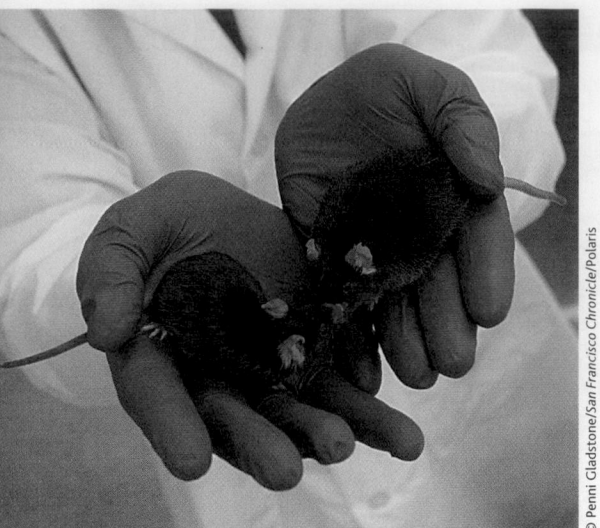

Laboratory obesity Biological theorists believe that certain genes leave some individuals particularly susceptible to eating disorders. To help support this view, researchers have created mutant ("knockout") mice—mice without certain genes. The mouse on the left is missing a gene that helps produce obesity, and it is thin. In contrast, the mouse on the right, which retains that gene, is obese.

hypothalamus A part of the brain that helps regulate various bodily functions, including eating and hunger.

lateral hypothalamus (LH) A brain region that produces hunger when activated.

ventromedial hypothalamus (VMH) A brain region that depresses hunger when activated.

weight set point The weight level that a person is predisposed to maintain, controlled in part by the hypothalamus.

psychological disorder to dysfunction by a particular brain circuit. Specifically, each disorder has been linked to abnormal communications (called *interconnectivity* problems) between the structures in a particular circuit, abnormal anatomy or operation of the individual structures in that circuit, or abnormal levels of activity by the neurotransmitters that carry messages from the neurons in one structure to the neurons in another.

Research suggests that each of the circuits linked to generalized anxiety, obsessive-compulsive, and depressive disorders also acts dysfunctionally to some degree in people with eating disorders (Forman, 2016). For example, among individuals with eating disorders, the *insula* (a structure in the anxiety-related circuit) is abnormally large and active (Frank et al., 2013), the *orbitofrontal cortex* (a structure in the obsessive-compulsive-related circuit) is uncommonly large (Frank et al., 2013), the *striatum* (another structure in the obsessive-compulsive-related circuit) is hyperactive (Foerde et al., 2015), and the *prefrontal cortex* (a structure at work in the anxiety-related, obsessive-compulsive-related, *and* depression-related circuits) is unusually small (Marsh et al., 2015). Similarly, the activity levels of serotonin, dopamine, and glutamate (key neurotransmitters in the anxiety-related, obsessive-compulsive-related, and depression-related circuits) are abnormal in people with eating disorders (Godlewska et al., 2017; Phillips et al., 2014; Kaye et al., 2013).

Given such findings, some researchers believe that dysfunction across or within the brain circuits tied to generalized anxiety, obsessive-compulsive, and depressive disorders collectively help cause eating disorders. However, at this early stage of research, it is just as possible that the dysfunctions in those circuits are actually the *result* of eating disorders (Forman, 2016). Alternatively, the observed circuit dysfunctions may be neither a direct cause nor a direct result of eating disorders. They may simply reflect the fact that many people with eating disorders also suffer from anxiety, obsessive-compulsive, and/or depressive disorders (Engel et al., 2017; Klein & Attia, 2017).

Finally, a number of biological theorists focus their explanation of eating disorders on one part of the brain in particular, the **hypothalamus,** a structure that regulates many bodily functions (Gao et al., 2017; Ogawa et al., 2017; Tandon et al., 2017). Researchers have located two separate areas in the hypothalamus that help control eating. One, the **lateral hypothalamus (LH),** consisting of the side areas of the hypothalamus, produces hunger when it is activated. When the LH of a laboratory animal is stimulated electrically, the animal eats, even if it has been fed recently. In contrast, another area, the **ventromedial hypothalamus (VMH),** consisting of the bottom and middle of the hypothalamus, reduces hunger when it is activated. When the VMH is electrically stimulated, laboratory animals stop eating.

These areas of the hypothalamus and related brain structures are apparently activated by chemicals from the brain and body, depending on whether the person is eating or fasting. One such brain chemical is the natural appetite suppressant *glucagon-like peptide-1* (*GLP-1*) (Harada et al., 2017; Dossat et al., 2014; Turton et al., 1996). When one team of researchers collected and injected GLP-1 into the brains of rats, the chemical traveled to receptors in the hypothalamus and caused the rats to reduce their food intake almost entirely even though they had not eaten for 24 hours. Conversely, when "full" rats were injected with a substance that blocked the reception of GLP-1 in the hypothalamus, they more than doubled their food intake.

Some researchers believe that the hypothalamus, related brain structures, and chemicals such as GLP-1, working together, comprise a "weight thermostat" of sorts in the body, which is responsible for keeping an individual at a particular weight level called the **weight set point.** Genetic inheritance and early eating practices seem to determine each person's weight set point (Yu, 2017; Chhabra et al., 2016; Sullivan et al., 2011). When a person's weight falls below his or her particular set point, the LH and certain other brain areas are activated and seek to restore the lost weight by producing hunger and lowering the body's *metabolic rate,* the rate at which the body expends energy. When a person's weight rises above his or her set point, the VMH and certain other brain areas are activated, and they try to remove the excess weight by reducing hunger and increasing the body's metabolic rate.

According to the weight set point theory, when people diet and fall to a weight below their weight set point, their brain starts trying to restore the lost weight. Hypothalamic and related brain activity produce a preoccupation with food and a desire to binge. They also trigger bodily changes that make it harder to lose weight and easier to gain weight, however little is eaten (Yu, 2017; Chhabra et al., 2016; Higgins & George, 2007). Once the brain and body begin conspiring to raise weight in this way, dieters actually enter into a battle against themselves. Some people apparently manage to shut down the inner "thermostat" and control their eating almost completely. These people move toward restricting-type anorexia nervosa. For others, the battle spirals toward a binge-purge or binge-only pattern. Although the weight set point explanation has received considerable debate in the clinical field, it continues to be accepted by many theorists and practitioners.

Societal Pressures

Eating disorders are more common in Western countries than in other parts of the world. Thus, many theorists believe that Western standards of female attractiveness are partly responsible for the emergence of the disorders (Forman, 2016; MacNeill & Best, 2015). Western standards of female beauty have changed throughout history, with a noticeable shift in preference toward a thin female frame over the past 60 years or so. For example, some "pioneering" studies conducted throughout the second half of the twentieth century tracked the weight, bust, and hip measurements of *Playboy* magazine centerfold models and Miss America Pageant contestants and found a steady year-by-year decrease in those measurements that has continued into the current century (Gilbert et al., 2005; Rubinstein & Caballero, 2000; Garner et al., 1980).

Because thinness is especially valued in the subcultures of performers, fashion models, and certain athletes, members of these groups are likely to be particularly concerned and/or criticized about their weight. For example, after undergoing an inpatient treatment program for eating disorders, the popular singer and rapper Kesha recently wrote, "The music industry has set unrealistic expectations for what a body is supposed to look like, and I started becoming overly critical of my own body because of that" (Sebert, 2014).

Studies have found that performers, models, and athletes are indeed more prone than others to anorexia nervosa and bulimia nervosa (Forman, 2016; Arcelus et al., 2014). In fact, many famous young women from these fields have publicly acknowledged grossly disordered eating patterns over the years. Surveys of athletes at colleges around the United States reveal that more than 9 percent of female college athletes suffer from an eating disorder and at least another 33 percent display eating behaviors that put them at risk for such disorders (Ekern, 2014; Van Durme et al., 2012; Kerr et al., 2007). By some estimates, a full 20 percent of gymnasts may have an eating disorder.

Why do you think that fashion models, often called super-models, have risen to celebrity status in recent decades?

#DietBusiness

Americans spend $60 billion each year on weight-reduction foods, products, and services. The vast majority of that amount is spent on diet foods (Fooducate, 2016).

The first diet book was published in England, in the mid-1800s (Herman, 2015).

Dangerous professions Certain occupations—fashion modeling, dancing, acting, and sports—place a premium on thinness, thus putting their professionals at particular risk for eating disorders. In a recent autobiography, *Dancing Throughout*, famous ballet artist Jenifer Ringer (performing here in the ballet *The Nutcracker*) described her struggles with eating disorders, both prior to and during her successful career as a principal dancer with the New York City Ballet.

Paul J. Kolnik

Donald Kravitz/Getty Images

Miss America speaks out During her 2008 reign as Miss America, Kirsten Haglund openly acknowledged her past struggles with anorexia nervosa. In recent years, she has continued to speak out about body-image issues and has started a foundation to provide treatment services for women with eating disorders.

Attitudes toward thinness may also help explain economic differences in the rates of eating disorders. In the past, women in the upper socioeconomic classes expressed more concern about thinness and dieting than women of the lower socioeconomic classes (Margo, 1985). Correspondingly, anorexia nervosa and bulimia nervosa were more common among women higher on the socioeconomic scale (Foreyt et al., 1996; Rosen et al., 1991). In recent years, however, dieting and a preoccupation with thinness have increased to some degree in all socioeconomic classes, as has the prevalence of these eating disorders (Javier, Moore, & Belgrave, 2016; Starr & Kreipe, 2014).

Western society not only glorifies thinness but also creates a climate of prejudice against overweight people (Puhl et al., 2015). Whereas slurs based on ethnicity, race, and gender are considered unacceptable, cruel jokes about obesity are standard fare on the Web and television and in movies, books, and magazines. Research indicates that the prejudice against obese people is deep-rooted (Grilo et al., 2005). Prospective parents who were shown pictures of a chubby child and a medium-weight or thin child rated the former as less friendly, energetic, intelligent, and desirable than the latter. In another study, preschool children who were given a choice between a chubby and a thin rag doll chose the thin one, although they could not say why. Thus it is small wonder that the number of children under 12 years who develop a full eating disorder is growing, especially among girls (NIMH, 2017; Ekern, 2014).

> How might you explain the finding that eating disorders tend to be less common in cultures that restrict a woman's freedom to make decisions about her life?

Given these trends, it is not totally surprising that one survey of 248 adolescent girls directly tied eating disorders and body dissatisfaction to social networking, Internet activity, and television browsing (Latzer, Katz, & Spivak, 2011). The survey found that the respondents who spent more time on Facebook were more likely to display eating disorders, have negative body image, eat in dysfunctional ways, and want to diet (see **Figure 11-3**). Those who spent more time on fashion and music Web sites and those who viewed more gossip- and leisure-related television programs showed similar tendencies.

Family Environment

Families may play an important role in the development and maintenance of eating disorders (Anastasiadou et al., 2016; Hoste et al., 2014). Research suggests that as many as half of the families of people with anorexia nervosa or bulimia nervosa have

FIGURE 11.3

What Does Teenage Eating Look Like?

Teenage eating habits are not particularly healthful in general and are, in fact, poor for many teens, according to research. Small wonder that the majority of adolescents fail to meet dietary recommendations for nutrient intake. (Information from: Demory-Luce & Motil, 2016; Lehman, 2016; CDC, 2015; Johnson, 2011; Sebastian et al., 2010.)

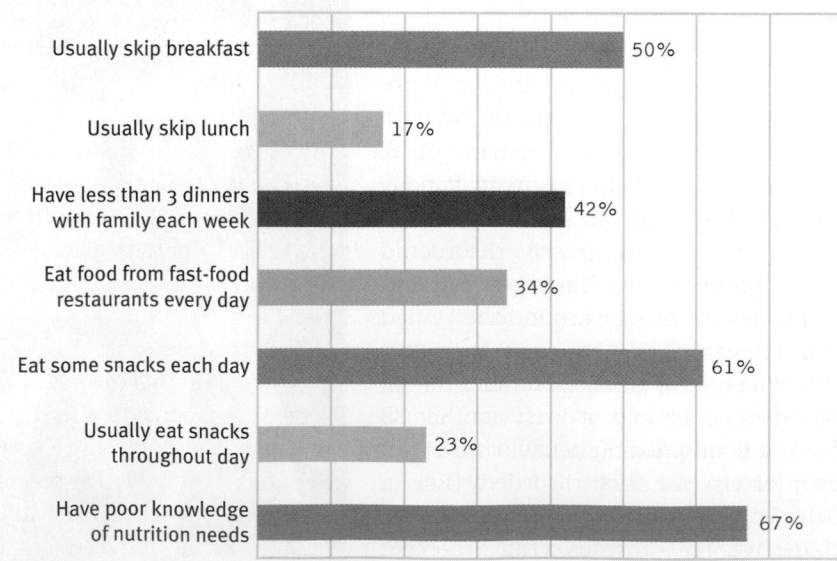

Eating pattern	Percentage
Usually skip breakfast	50%
Usually skip lunch	17%
Have less than 3 dinners with family each week	42%
Eat food from fast-food restaurants every day	34%
Eat some snacks each day	61%
Usually eat snacks throughout day	23%
Have poor knowledge of nutrition needs	67%

Percentage of teenagers who display eating pattern

a long history of emphasizing thinness, physical appearance, and dieting. In fact, the mothers in these families are more likely to diet themselves and to be generally perfectionistic than are the mothers in other families (Zerbe, 2008; Woodside et al., 2002). Tina, a 16-year-old, describes her view of the roots of her eating disorder:

> When I was a kid, say 6 or 7, my Mom and I would go to the drugstore all the time. She was heavy and bought all kinds of books and magazines on how to lose weight. Whenever we talked, like after I got home from school, it was almost always about dieting and how to lose weight. . . . I [went] on diets with my Mom, to keep her company.
>
> I just got better at it than she did. My eating disorder is my Mom's therapy. . . . It's also the way we have time together—working on the diets and exercise and all of that. We've stopped talking about diets since I got anorexia, and now I don't know what we can talk about.
>
> (Zerbe, 2008, pp. 20–21)

Abnormal interactions and forms of communication within a family may also set the stage for an eating disorder (Anastasiadou et al., 2016; Holtom-Viesel, & Allan, 2014). Family systems theorists argue that the families of people who develop eating disorders are often dysfunctional to begin with and that the eating disorder of one member is a reflection of the larger problem. Influential family theorist Salvador Minuchin, for example, believes that what he calls an **enmeshed family pattern** often leads to eating disorders (Minuchin et al., 2017, 2006).

In an enmeshed system, family members are overinvolved in each other's affairs and overconcerned with the details of each other's lives. On the positive side, enmeshed families can be affectionate and loyal. On the negative side, they can be clingy and foster dependency. Parents are too involved in the lives of their children, allowing little room for individuality and independence. Minuchin argues that adolescence poses a special problem for these families. The teenager's normal push for independence threatens the family's apparent harmony and closeness. In response, the family may subtly force the child to take on a "sick" role—to develop an eating disorder or some other illness. The child's disorder enables the family to maintain its appearance of harmony. A sick child needs her family, and family members can rally to protect her. Some studies have supported such family systems explanations (Anastasiadou et al., 2016), but have failed to show that particular family patterns consistently set the stage for the development of eating disorders (Holtom-Viesel & Allan, 2014).

Multicultural Factors: Racial and Ethnic Differences

In 1995 there was a popular movie named *Clueless* in which Cher and Dionne, wealthy teenage friends of different races, had similar tastes, beliefs, and values about everything from boys to schoolwork. In particular, they had the same kinds of eating habits and beauty ideals, and they were even similar in weight and physical form. But did the story of these young women reflect the realities of non-Hispanic white American and African American females in our society?

In the early 1990s, the answer to this question appeared to be a resounding no. Most studies conducted up to the time of *Clueless* indicated that the eating behaviors, values, and goals of young African American women were considerably healthier than those of young non-Hispanic white American women (Lovejoy, 2001; Cash & Henry, 1995; Parker et al., 1995). A widely publicized 1995 study at the University of Arizona, for example, found that the eating behaviors and attitudes of young African American women were more positive than those of young non-Hispanic white American women. It found, specifically, that "only" 70 percent of the African American respondents were

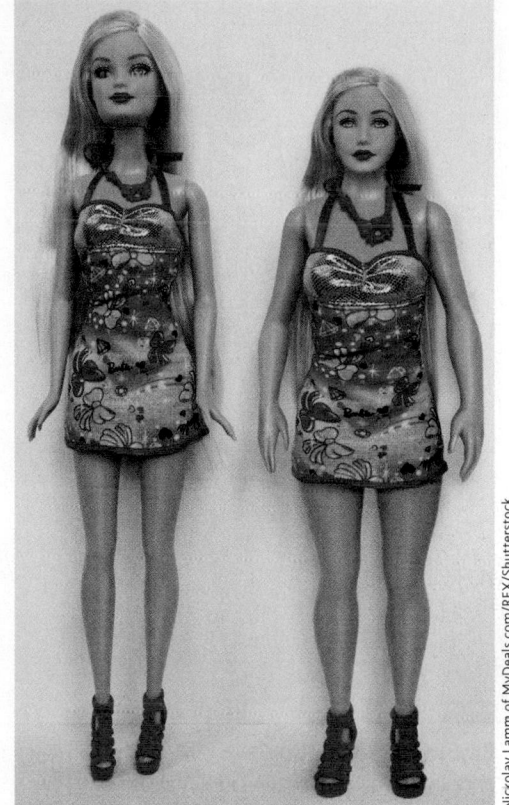

Nickolay Lamm of MyDeals.com/REX/Shutterstock

"Normal Barbie" For years, the ultra-slim measurements and proportions of the widely popular Barbie doll have introduced women to an unattainable ideal at a very young age. Hoping to demonstrate instead that "average is beautiful," artist Nickolay Lamm recently designed a Normal Barbie (right), using the CDC measurements of the average 19-year-old American woman. Normal Barbie turns out to be shorter, curvier, and bustier than the doll sitting on store shelves around the world.

enmeshed family pattern A family system in which members are overinvolved with each other's affairs and overly concerned about each other's welfare.

Chris Moore/Catwalking/Getty Images

Embracing diversity? The fashion industry prides itself on the range of nationalities now represented in its ranks. However, the Western ideal of extreme thinness remains the standard for all models, regardless of their cultural background. Many psychologists worry that the success of supermodels such as Ethiopia's Liya Kebede (shown here) and Sudan's Alek Wek may contribute to thinner body ideals, more body dissatisfaction, and more eating disorders in their African countries.

#

#TheirWords

"To be born woman is to know—Although they do not talk of it at school—Women must labour to be beautiful."

W. B. Yeats, 1904

dissatisfied with their weight and body shape, compared with nearly 90 percent of the non-Hispanic white American teens.

The study also suggested that non-Hispanic white American and African American adolescent girls had different ideals of beauty. The former teens, asked to define the "perfect girl," described a girl of 5'7" weighing between 100 and 110 pounds—proportions that mirror those of so-called supermodels. Attaining a perfect weight, many said, was the key to being happy and popular. In contrast, the African American respondents emphasized personality traits over physical characteristics. They defined the "perfect" African American girl as smart, fun, easy to talk to, not conceited, and funny; she did not necessarily need to be "pretty," as long as she was well groomed. The body dimensions the African American teens described were more attainable for the typical girl; they favored fuller hips, for example. Moreover, the African American respondents were less likely than the non-Hispanic white American respondents to diet for extended periods.

Unfortunately, research conducted over the past two decades suggests that body image concerns, dysfunctional eating patterns, and anorexia nervosa and bulimia nervosa are on the rise among young African American women as well as among women of other minority groups (Javier et al., 2016; Starr & Kreipe, 2014; Gilbert, 2011). For example, in a frequently cited survey conducted by *Essence*, a popular magazine geared toward African Americans, 65 percent of African American respondents reported dieting, 39 percent said that food controlled their lives, 19 percent avoided eating when hungry, 17 percent used laxatives, and 4 percent vomited to lose weight.

The shift in the eating behaviors and eating problems of African American women appears to be partly related to their *acculturation* (Kroon Van Diest et al., 2014; Ford, 2000). One study compared African American women at a predominately non-Hispanic white American university with those at a predominately African American university. Those at the former school had significantly higher depression scores, and those scores were positively correlated with eating problems.

Still other studies indicate that Hispanic American female adolescents and young adults engage in disordered eating behaviors (particularly bingeing behavior) and express body dissatisfaction at rates about equal to those of non-Hispanic white American women (Perez, Ohrt, & Hoek, 2016; Blow & Cooper, 2014; Cachelin et al., 2006). Moreover, those who consider themselves more oriented to non-Hispanic white American culture have particularly high rates of anorexia nervosa and bulimia nervosa. These eating disorders also appear to be on the increase among young Asian American women and young women in several Asian countries (Pike et al., 2013; Stewart & Williamson, 2008).

Multicultural Factors: Gender Differences

Males account for only 10 percent of all people with anorexia nervosa and bulimia nervosa. The reasons for this striking gender difference are not entirely clear, but Western society's double standard for attractiveness is, at the very least, one reason. Our society's emphasis on a thin appearance is clearly aimed at women much more than men, and some theorists believe that this difference has made women much more inclined to diet and more prone to eating disorders. Surveys of college men have, for example, found that the majority select "muscular, strong and broad shoulders" to describe the ideal male body and "thin, slim, slightly underweight" to describe the ideal female body (Mayo & George, 2014).

A second reason for the different rates of anorexia nervosa and bulimia nervosa between men and women may be the different methods of weight loss favored by the two genders. According to some clinical observations and studies, men are more likely to use exercise to lose weight, whereas women more often diet (Nurkkala et al., 2016; Thackray et al., 2016; Gadalla, 2009). And, as you have read, dieting often precedes the onset of these eating disorders.

BEI / REX / Shutterstock

Blend Images/Alamy

Not for women only A growing number of today's men are developing eating disorders. Some of them aspire to a very lean body shape and develop anorexia nervosa or bulimia nervosa. Singer Zayn Malik (left) has acknowledged falling into this pattern when he was a member of the boy band One Direction. Other men want the ultramuscular look displayed by bodybuilders (above) and may develop an eating disorder called *muscle dysmorphia*. These individuals inaccurately consider themselves to be scrawny and small and keep striving for a "perfect" body through excessive weight lifting and abuse of steroids.

Why do some men develop anorexia nervosa or bulimia nervosa? In a number of cases, the disorder is linked to the *requirements and pressures of a job or sport* (Cottrell & Williams, 2016; Thompson & Sherman, 2010; Braun, 1996). According to one study, 37 percent of men with these eating disorders had jobs or played sports for which weight control was important, compared with 13 percent of women with such disorders. The highest rates of male eating disorders have been found among jockeys, wrestlers, distance runners, body builders, and swimmers. Jockeys commonly spend hours before a race in a sauna, shedding up to seven pounds of weight, and may restrict their food intake, abuse laxatives and diuretics, and force vomiting (Kerr et al., 2007).

For other men who develop anorexia nervosa or bulimia nervosa, *body image* appears to be a key factor, just as it is in women (Lavender et al., 2017; Mayo & George, 2014). Many report that they want a "lean, toned, thin" shape similar to the ideal female body, rather than the muscular, broad-shouldered shape of the typical male ideal (Morgan, 2012; Hildebrandt & Alfano, 2009).

Still other men seem to be caught up in a different kind of eating disorder, called *reverse anorexia nervosa* or *muscle dysmorphia*. Men with this disorder are very muscular but still see themselves as scrawny and small and therefore continue to strive for a "perfect" body through extreme measures such as excessive weight lifting or the abuse of steroids (Lavender et al., 2017; Stewart & Williamson, 2008). People with muscle dysmorphia typically feel shame about their bodies, and many have a history of depression, anxiety, and self-destructive compulsive behavior. About one-third of them also engage in related dysfunctional behaviors such as binge eating.

> Why do you think that the prevalence of eating disorders among men has been on the increase in recent years?

How Are Eating Disorders Treated?

TODAY'S TREATMENTS FOR EATING disorders have two goals. The first is to correct the dangerous eating pattern as quickly as possible. The second is to address the broader psychological and situational factors that have led to and maintain the eating problem. Family and friends can also play an important role in helping to overcome the disorder.

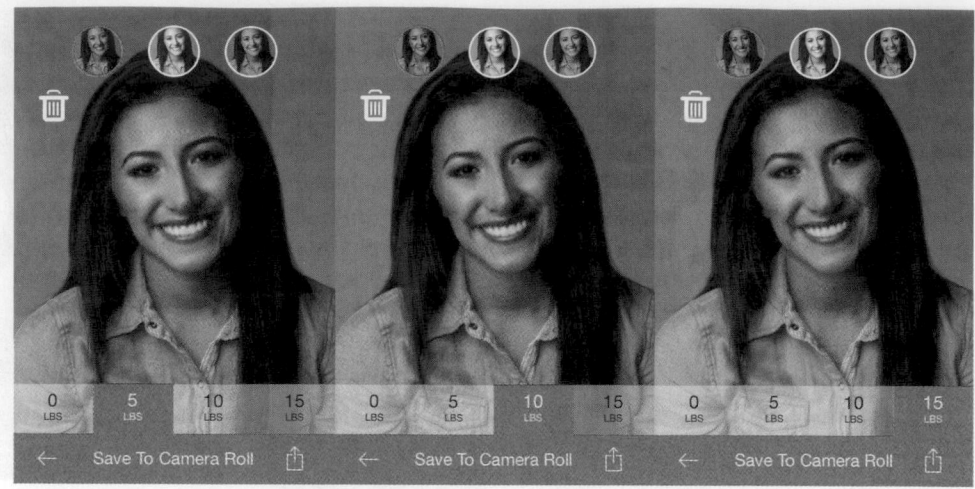

Medavia/ZUMA Press/Newscom

It was only a matter of time A new app hit the marketplace a few years ago enabling users to "doctor" their selfies before posting them. Like the woman in this app demonstration, a user's appearance can, through facial recognition software, be made to look lighter by 5 pounds (left), 10 pounds (center), or 15 pounds (right). Critics worry that the app, whose sales have boomed, is likely to further fuel body dissatisfaction and eating disorders.

Treatments for Anorexia Nervosa

Around one-third of those with anorexia nervosa receive treatment (NIMH, 2017). The immediate aims of treatment for anorexia nervosa are to help people regain their lost weight, recover from malnourishment, and eat normally again (Mehler, 2017). Therapists must then help them to make psychological and perhaps family changes to lock in those gains.

How Are Proper Weight and Normal Eating Restored? A variety of treatment methods are used to help patients with anorexia nervosa gain weight quickly and return to health within weeks, a phase of treatment called *nutritional rehabilitation* (Steinglass, 2016). In the past, treatment almost always took place in a hospital, but now it is often offered in day hospitals or outpatient settings (Raveneau et al., 2014).

In life-threatening cases, clinicians may need to force *tube and intravenous feedings* on a patient who refuses to eat (Rocks et al., 2014). Unfortunately, this use of force may cause the client to distrust the clinician. In contrast, clinicians using behavioral weight-restoration approaches offer *rewards* whenever patients eat properly or gain weight and offer no rewards when they eat improperly or fail to gain weight.

Perhaps the most popular nutritional rehabilitation approach is a combination of supportive nursing care, nutritional counseling, and a relatively high-calorie diet (Steinglass, 2016). Here nurses and other staff members *gradually* increase a patient's diet over the course of several weeks, to more than 3,000 calories a day (Zerbe, 2010, 2008). The nurses educate patients about the program, track their progress, provide encouragement, and help them appreciate that their weight gain is under control and will not lead to obesity. In some programs, the nurses also use **motivational interviewing**, an intervention that uses a mixture of empathy and inquiring review to help motivate clients to recognize they have a serious eating problem and commit to making constructive choices and behavior changes (Pike, 2017; Dray et al., 2014). Studies find that patients in nutritional rehabilitation programs usually gain the necessary weight over 8 to 12 weeks.

How Are Lasting Changes Achieved? Clinical researchers have found that people with anorexia nervosa must overcome their underlying psychological problems in order to create lasting improvement. Therapists typically use a combination of education, psychotherapy, and family therapy to help reach this broader goal (Knatz et al., 2015; Wade & Watson, 2012). Psychotropic drugs, particularly antipsychotic drugs, are sometimes used when patients do not respond to the other forms of treatments, but research has found that such medications are typically of limited benefit (Walsh, 2017).

motivational interviewing A treatment intervention that uses a mixture of empathy and inquiring review to help motivate clients to recognize they have a serious psychological problem and commit to making constructive choices and behavior changes.

COGNITIVE-BEHAVIORAL THERAPY A combination of cognitive and behavioral interventions are included in most treatment programs for anorexia nervosa. Such techniques are designed to help clients appreciate and alter the behaviors and thought processes that help keep their restrictive eating going (Pike, 2017). On the behavioral side, clients are typically required to monitor (perhaps by keeping a diary) their feelings, hunger levels, and food intake and the ties between these variables. On the cognitive side, they are taught to identify their "core pathology"—the deep-seated belief that they should in fact be judged by their shape and weight and by their ability to control these physical characteristics. The clients may also be taught alternative ways of coping with stress and of solving problems.

The therapists who provide cognitive-behavioral therapy are particularly careful to help patients with anorexia nervosa recognize their need for independence and teach them more appropriate ways to exercise control (Pike, 2017). The therapists may also teach them to better identify and trust their internal sensations and feelings. In the following session, a therapist tries to help a 15-year-old client recognize and share her feelings:

"You can't keep comparing yourself to those skinny little aliens you see in movies."

Bruce Eric Kaplan/The New Yorker Collection/The Cartoon Bank

Patient: *I don't talk about my feelings; I never did.*

Therapist: *Do you think I'll respond like others?*

Patient: *What do you mean?*

Therapist: *I think you may be afraid that I won't pay close attention to what you feel inside, or that I'll tell you not to feel the way you do—that it's foolish to feel frightened, to feel fat, to doubt yourself, considering how well you do in school, how you're appreciated by teachers, how pretty you are.*

Patient: *(Looking somewhat tense and agitated) Well, I was always told to be polite and respect other people, just like a stupid, faceless doll. (Affecting a vacant, doll-like pose)*

Therapist: *Do I give you the impression that it would be disrespectful for you to share your feelings, whatever they may be?*

Patient: *Not really; I don't know.*

Therapist: *I can't, and won't, tell you that this is easy for you to do. . . . But I can promise you that you are free to speak your mind, and that I won't turn away.*

(Strober & Yager, 1985, pp. 368–369)

Finally, cognitive-behavioral therapists seek to help clients with anorexia nervosa change their attitudes about eating and weight (Pike, 2017; Fairburn & Cooper, 2014) (see **Table 11-5**). The therapists may guide the clients to identify, challenge, and change maladaptive assumptions, such as "I must always be perfect" or "My weight and shape determine my value" (Fairburn et al., 2015, 2008). They may also educate the clients about the body distortions typical of anorexia nervosa and help them see that their own assessments of their size are incorrect. Even if a client never learns to judge her body shape accurately, she may at least reach a point where she says, "I know that a key feature of anorexia nervosa is a misperception of my own size, so I can expect to feel fat regardless of my actual size."

According to research, cognitive-behavioral techniques are often very effective in cases of anorexia nervosa, more effective than psychodynamic therapies, psychoeducation, or supportive therapy alone (Pike, 2017; Zerbe, 2010, 2008). The approach helps many individuals to restore their weight, overcome their fear of becoming overweight, develop greater self-esteem, correct their body distortions and dissatisfaction, adopt

#TheirWords

"Nothing tastes as good as skinny feels."

Kate Moss, model

TABLE 11-5

Sample Items from the Eating Disorder Inventory

For each item, decide if the item is true about you ALWAYS (A), USUALLY (U), OFTEN (O), SOMETIMES (S), RARELY (R), or NEVER (N). Circle the letter that corresponds to your rating.						
A	U	O	S	R	N	I eat when I am upset.
A	U	O	S	R	N	I stuff myself with food.
A	U	O	S	R	N	I think about dieting.
A	U	O	S	R	N	I think that my thighs are too large.
A	U	O	S	R	N	I feel extremely guilty after overeating.
A	U	O	S	R	N	I am terrified of gaining weight.
A	U	O	S	R	N	I get confused as to whether or not I am hungry.
A	U	O	S	R	N	I have the thought of trying to vomit in order to lose weight.
A	U	O	S	R	N	I think my buttocks are too large.
A	U	O	S	R	N	I eat or drink in secrecy.

Information from: Clausen et al., 2011; Garner, 2005; Garner, Olmsted, & Polivy, 2004, 1991, 1984.

more accurate and adaptive eating attitudes, acquire more appropriate eating and exercise habits, develop better problem-solving skills. The treatment is most successful at preventing relapses when it continues for at least a year beyond a patient's recovery—the *maintenance* therapy strategy that you read about in Chapter 8 (see page 240). At the same time, studies further suggest that the cognitive-behavioral approach brings the best results when it is supplemented by other approaches. In particular, family therapy is often included in treatment.

CHANGING FAMILY INTERACTIONS Family therapy can be an invaluable part of treatment for anorexia nervosa, particularly for children and adolescents with the disorder (Pike, 2017). As in other family therapy situations, the therapist meets with the family as a whole, points out troublesome family patterns, and helps the members make appropriate changes. In particular, family therapists may try to help the person with anorexia nervosa separate her feelings and needs from those of other members of her family. Although the role of family in the development of anorexia nervosa is not yet clear, research strongly suggests that family therapy (or at least parent counseling) can be helpful in the treatment of this disorder (Cook-Darzens, 2016; Jewell et al., 2016).

#FamilyTeasing

Researchers have found that adolescents teased about their weight by family members are twice as likely as nonteased teens of similar weight to become overweight within five years and 1.5 times more likely to become binge eaters and use extreme weight control measures (Saltzman & Liechty, 2016; Neumark-Sztainer et al., 2007).

Mother:	*I think I know what [Susan] is going through: all the doubt and insecurity of growing up and establishing her own identity. (Turning to the patient, with tears) If you just place trust in yourself, with the support of those around you who care, everything will turn out for the better.*
Therapist:	*Are you making yourself available to her? Should she turn to you, rely on you for guidance and emotional support?*
Mother:	*Well, that's what parents are for.*
Therapist:	*(Turning to patient) What do you think?*
Susan:	*(To mother) I can't keep depending on you, Mom, or everyone else. That's what I've been doing, and it gave me anorexia. . . .*
Therapist:	*Do you think your mom would prefer that there be no secrets between her and the kids—an open door, so to speak?*
Older sister:	*Sometimes I do.*

Therapist:	*(To patient and younger sister) How about you two?*
Susan:	*Yeah. Sometimes it's like whatever I feel, she has to feel.*
Younger sister:	*Yeah.*

(Strober & Yager, 1985, pp. 381–382)

What Is the Aftermath of Anorexia Nervosa? The use of combined treatment approaches, with cognitive-behavioral therapy typically at the center, has greatly improved the outlook for people with anorexia nervosa, although the road to recovery can be difficult. The course and outcome of this disorder vary from person to person, but researchers have noted certain trends.

On the positive side, weight is often quickly restored once treatment for the disorder begins, and treatment gains may continue for years. As many as 75 percent of patients continue to show improvement—either full or partial—when they are interviewed several years or more after their initial recovery (Klein & Attia, 2017; Isomaa & Isomaa, 2014).

Another positive note is that most females with anorexia nervosa menstruate again when they regain their weight, and other medical improvements follow (Mehler, 2016). Also encouraging is that the death rate from anorexia nervosa seems to be falling. Earlier diagnosis and safer and faster weight-restoration techniques may account for this trend. Deaths that do occur are usually caused by suicide, starvation, infection, gastrointestinal problems, or electrolyte imbalance (Mehler, 2017).

On the negative side, as many as 25 percent of persons with anorexia nervosa remain seriously troubled for years (Klein & Attia, 2017; Isomaa & Isomaa, 2014). Furthermore, recovery, when it does occur, is not always permanent. At least one-third of recovered patients have recurrences of anorexic behavior, usually triggered by new stresses, such as marriage, pregnancy, or a major relocation (Stice et al., 2017, 2013; Fennig et al., 2002). Even years later, many who have recovered continue to express concerns about their weight and appearance (Klein & Attia, 2017). Some still restrict their diets to a degree, feel anxiety when they eat with other people, or hold some distorted ideas about food, eating, and weight (Isomaa & Isomaa, 2014; Fairburn et al., 2008).

About half of those who have suffered from anorexia nervosa continue to have certain psychological problems—particularly depression, obsessiveness, and social anxiety—years after treatment. Such problems are particularly common in those who had not reached a fully normal weight by the end of treatment (Steinglass, 2016; Bodell & Mayer, 2011).

The more weight persons have lost and the more time that passes before they enter treatment, the poorer the recovery rate (Klein & Attia, 2017; Fairburn et al., 2008). People who had psychological or sexual problems before the onset of the disorder tend to have a poorer recovery rate than those without such a history (Zerwas et al., 2013; Amianto et al., 2011). People whose family or interpersonal relationships are troubled have less positive treatment outcomes (Klein & Attia, 2017; Holtom-Viesel & Allan, 2014). Younger sufferers seem to have a better recovery rate than older patients (Klein & Attia, 2017).

Exercising for health Student Antonia Carusa practices jumps with the Scarborough High School cheering squad in 2015 after having overcome anorexia nervosa. The teenager had developed the disorder in the first place by severely restricting her eating and exercising excessively. Exercise—to a proper degree—also helped her to recover, as she used weight training, along with other treatment interventions, to heal her body.

Treatments for Bulimia Nervosa

Around 43 percent of those with bulimia nervosa receive treatment (NIMH, 2017). Treatment programs for the disorder are often offered in eating disorder clinics (Henderson et al., 2014). Such programs offer (1) nutritional rehabilitation, which, for bulimia nervosa, means helping clients to eliminate their binge-purge patterns and establish good eating habits, and (2) a combination of therapies aimed at eliminating the

The beginning of a movement An early effort at responsible advertising regarding body shape and eating disorders occurred back in 2007 when the Nolita clothing brand launched a major ad campaign against excessive thinness. One of the brand's billboards featured an emaciated naked woman appearing beneath the words "No Anorexia." The billboard model Isabelle Caro died in 2010 of complications from anorexia nervosa.

underlying causes of bulimic patterns (Crow, 2016). The programs emphasize education as much as therapy (Mitchell, 2016; Fairburn & Cooper, 2014). Cognitive-behavioral therapy is particularly helpful in cases of bulimia nervosa—perhaps even more helpful than in cases of anorexia nervosa (Fairburn & Cooper, 2014; Wonderlich et al., 2014). And antidepressant drug therapy, which is of limited help to people with anorexia nervosa, appears to be quite effective in many cases of bulimia nervosa (Crow, 2016).

Cognitive-Behavioral Therapy When treating clients with bulimia nervosa, cognitive-behavioral therapists employ many of the same techniques that they use to help treat people with anorexia nervosa. However, they tailor the techniques to the unique features of bulimia (for example, bingeing and purging) and to the specific beliefs at work in bulimia nervosa (Mitchell, 2016).

The therapists often instruct clients with bulimia nervosa to keep diaries of their eating behavior, changes in sensations of hunger and fullness, and the ebb and flow of other feelings (Mitchell, 2016). This helps the clients to observe their eating patterns more objectively and recognize the emotions and situations that trigger their desire to binge. Smartphone apps have been particularly useful in keeping track of such changes throughout the day.

One team of researchers studied the effectiveness of an online version of the diary technique (Shapiro et al., 2010). They had 31 clients with bulimia nervosa, each an outpatient in a 12-week cognitive-behavioral therapy program, send nightly texts to their therapists, reporting on their bingeing and purging urges and episodes. The clients received feedback messages, including reinforcement and encouragement for the treatment goals they had been able to reach that day. The clinical researchers reported that by the end of therapy, the clients showed significant decreases in binges, purges, other bulimic symptoms, and feelings of depression.

Cognitive-behavioral therapists may also use the behavioral technique of *exposure and response prevention* to help break the binge-purge cycle. As you read in Chapter 5, this approach consists of exposing people to situations that would ordinarily raise anxiety and then preventing them from performing their usual compulsive responses until they learn that the situations are actually harmless and their compulsive acts unnecessary. For bulimia nervosa, the therapists require clients to eat particular kinds and amounts of food and then prevent them from vomiting to show that eating can be a harmless and even constructive activity that needs no undoing (Mitchell, 2016; Wilson, 2010). Typically the therapist sits with the client while the client eats the forbidden foods and stays until the urge to purge has passed. Studies find that this treatment often helps reduce eating-related anxieties, bingeing, and vomiting.

Beyond such behavioral techniques, a primary focus of cognitive-behavioral therapists is to help clients with bulimia nervosa recognize and change their maladaptive attitudes toward food, eating, weight, and shape (Fairburn & Cooper, 2014; Waller et al., 2014). The therapists typically teach the clients to identify and challenge the negative thoughts that regularly precede their urge to binge—I have no self-control; I might as well give up; I look fat. They may also guide clients to recognize, question, and eventually change their perfectionistic standards, sense of helplessness, and low self-concept (see *Trending* on page 338). Cognitive-behavioral approaches help as many as 75 percent of patients stop or reduce bingeing and purging to a point where they no longer meet the diagnostic criteria for the disorder (Mitchell, 2016; Poulsen et al., 2014).

Other Forms of Psychotherapy Because of its effectiveness in the treatment of bulimia nervosa, cognitive-behavioral therapy is often tried first, before other therapies are considered. If clients do not respond to it, other approaches with promising but less impressive track records may then be tried (Crow, 2016; Mitchell, 2016). A

Catherine Wylie/Press Association via AP Images

i-Images/Polaris

common alternative is *interpersonal psychotherapy,* the treatment that is used to help improve interpersonal functioning (Thompson-Brenner, 2016; Fairburn et al., 2015). *Psychodynamic therapy* has also been used in cases of bulimia nervosa, but only a few research studies have tested and supported its effectiveness (Thompson-Brenner, 2016; Tasca et al., 2014). The various forms of psychotherapy—cognitive-behavioral, interpersonal, and psychodynamic—are often supplemented by family therapy (Jewell et al., 2016; Mitchell, 2016).

Cognitive-behavioral, interpersonal, and psychodynamic therapy may each be offered in either an individual or a group therapy format. Group formats, including self-help groups, give clients with bulimia nervosa an opportunity to share their concerns and experiences with one another. Group members learn that their disorder is not unique or shameful, and they receive support from one another, along with honest feedback and insights. In the group they can also work directly on underlying fears of displeasing others or being criticized. Research suggests that group formats are at least somewhat helpful for as many as 75 percent of people with bulimia nervosa (Mitchell, 2016; Valbak, 2001).

Antidepressant Medications During the past 15 years, antidepressant drugs—all forms of antidepressant drugs—have been used to help treat bulimia nervosa. In contrast to people with anorexia nervosa, those with bulimia nervosa are often helped considerably by these drugs (Crow, 2016; Starr & Kreipe, 2014). According to research, the drugs help as many as 40 percent of patients, reducing their binges by an average of 67 percent and vomiting by 56 percent. Once again, drug therapy seems to work best in combination with other forms of therapy, particularly cognitive-behavioral therapy. Alternatively, some therapists wait to see whether cognitive-behavioral therapy or another form of psychotherapy is effective before trying antidepressants (Wilson, 2010, 2005). Studies suggest that psychotherapy is more effective than antidepressant drugs, but that a combination of the two is more effective than either form of treatment alone (Crow, 2016).

What Is the Aftermath of Bulimia Nervosa? Left untreated, bulimia nervosa can last for years, sometimes improving temporarily but then returning. Treatment, however, produces immediate, significant improvement in approximately 40 percent of clients: they stop or greatly reduce their bingeing and purging, eat properly, and maintain a normal weight (Mitchell, 2016; Isomaa & Isomaa, 2014). Another 40 percent show a moderate response—at least some decrease in binge eating and purging. Follow-up studies, conducted years after treatment, suggest that around 75 percent of people with bulimia nervosa have recovered, either fully or partially (Engel et al., 2017; Mitchell, 2016).

> Why might some people who recover from anorexia nervosa and bulimia nervosa remain vulnerable to relapse even after recovery?

Shame on Body Shamers

"What happened to . . . . .? Did she eat all her back-up singers?" Thousands of cruel tweets like this one about a popular singer's weight appear on social media every day. They are examples of body shaming, the practice of criticizing people publicly for being overweight, or, less frequently, underweight.

Body shaming itself is not new. It has been around since the mid-nineteenth century (Herman, 2015). What is new is the

Responding to shamers As Lady Gaga was giving a universally acclaimed half-time performance at the 2017 Super Bowl (above), many viewers took to social media to criticize her for daring to wear a crop-top and displaying the "flab" on her stomach. In an Instagram post, the superstar responded, "I'm proud of my body and you [i.e., all people] should be proud of yours too. No matter who you are or what you do."

Timothy A. Clary/AFP/Getty Images

current and ever-increasing volume of this practice. Our world of tweets, social networking, blogging, provocative Web sites, opinionated talk shows, and the like, has provided numerous platforms for cruel comments, including ones about people's appearance (Abate, 2016). As one eating disorder expert has said, "We are learning the language of body shaming from the mass media culture" (Mysko, 2016).

Of course, the body shaming of celebrities receives the most attention, but widely read comments of that kind have opened the door to an onslaught of body shaming in smaller circles and in everyday life. A recent survey revealed that a staggering 94 percent of today's teenage girls and 64 percent of teenage boys have been body shamed in one form or another (Miller, 2016).

Body shaming can bring great personal pain to the victims of such comments (Webb et al., 2016). In addition, the practice appears to be contributing, along with other factors, to an increase in body dissatisfaction and disordered eating throughout our society, especially among women (Kolata, 2016).

The good news is that a counter-trend is currently also taking place across society—growing concern and anger by millions of people, including clinicians and educators, over the unacceptability and harmful impact of these forms of communication, along with a determination to fight back. In the legal arena, for example, criminal charges have been brought against body shamers whose actions have been particularly ugly, invasive of privacy, and/or damaging. The prosecuting attorney for one such case said, "What really matters [in these cases] is our character and humanity" (Feuer, 2016).

Perhaps the most important development in the fight against body shaming is that

hundreds of influential celebrities are now calling out the perpetrators. Over the past year, for example, in response to negative tweets or posts about their bodies, celebrities have posted self-affirming messages such as the following:

"I will never conform to your skinny standards."
—Reality TV star Kim Kardashian

"I am not a woman whose self-worth comes from her chest size."
—Actress Kristen Bell

"I am so proud of what my body has done for me."
—Actress Gabourey Sidibe

"I'm healthy and happy, and if you're hating on my weight, you obviously aren't."
—Singer Demi Lovato

"[Body shaming] lets you know something's wrong with our culture and we all need to work together to change it."
—Comedian Amy Schumer

"People come on my page and body shame me because . . . I'm not good enough for their standards . . . But at the end of the day I'm good enough for me.
—Model Ashley Graham

"I love being happy with me."
—Singer and actress Selena Gomez

These are but a small fraction of the countershaming messages being posted by celebrities every day. Hopefully, the self-acceptance, independent thinking, and body satisfaction contained in such responses will come to influence readers more than the body-shaming messages themselves.

Relapse can be a problem even among people who respond successfully to treatment (Engel et al., 2017; Stice et al., 2013). As with anorexia nervosa, relapses are usually triggered by a new life stress, such as an upcoming exam, a job change, marriage, or divorce (Liu, 2007). One study found that 28 percent of those who had recovered from bulimia nervosa relapsed within six months (Olmsted et al., 2015). Relapse is more likely among people who had longer histories of bulimia nervosa before treatment, had vomited more frequently during their disorder, continued to vomit at the end of treatment, had histories of substance abuse, made slower progress in the early stages of treatment, and continue to be lonely or to distrust others after treatment (Engel et al., 2017; Vall & Wade, 2015).

Treatments for Binge-Eating Disorder

Approximately 44 percent of people with binge-eating disorder receive treatment (NIMH, 2017). Given the key role of binges in both this disorder (bingeing without purging) and bulimia, today's treatments for binge-eating disorder are often similar to those for bulimia nervosa. In particular, cognitive-behavioral therapy, other forms of psychotherapy, and in some cases, antidepressant medications are provided to help reduce or eliminate the binge-eating patterns and to change disturbed thinking such as being overly concerned with weight and shape (Sysko & Devlin, 2016; Fischer et al., 2014). According to research, psychotherapy is generally more helpful than antidepressants.

Evidence is emerging that these kinds of interventions are indeed often effective, at least in the short run. As many as 60 percent of clients no longer fit the criteria for binge-eating disorder by the end of treatment (Sysko & Devlin, 2016). Follow-up studies indicate that many of these early gains may continue for years, particularly with regard to binge eating. However, only around one-third of the recovered individuals showed total improvement in those follow-up studies. As with the other eating disorders, many of those who initially recover from binge-eating disorder continue to have a relatively high risk of relapse (Sysko & Devlin, 2016; ANAD, 2014).

Of course, many people with binge-eating disorder also are overweight, a problem that requires additional kinds of intervention. Their weight problems are often resistant to long-term improvement, even if regular binge-eating is reduced or eliminated (Sysko & Devlin, 2016; Grilo et al., 2014). In one follow-up study of hospitalized patients with severe symptoms of binge-eating disorder, 36 percent of those who had been treated were still significantly overweight 12 years after hospitalization (Fichter et al., 2008).

Cityfiles/Polaris

"The Biggest Loser" phenomenon These men participate in a group exercise program as part of the reality television show *Peso Pesado* (English: *Heavy Weight*), the Portuguese version of the remarkably successful American series *The Biggest Loser*. In these shows, overweight contestants compete to lose the most weight for cash prizes. Most overweight people do not display binge-eating disorder, but most people with the disorder are overweight.

Prevention of Eating Disorders: Wave of the Future

CLEARLY, EATING DISORDERS ARE profoundly destructive. Moreover, the various treatments for these disorders, while improving greatly in recent years, do not bring about a full recovery (or, in some instances, any recovery) for many people with these disorders. Thus, some clinical theorists believe that researchers must invest more work into the development of programs that *prevent* the onset of eating disorders (Atkinson & Wade, 2016).

One of today's promising prevention programs is called *Body Project*, a program developed and expanded by psychologists Eric Stice and Carolyn Black Becker and their colleagues (Becker et al., 2017; Stice et al., 2017, 2015. 2013). Keeping in mind the key factors that predispose people to the development of eating disorders, Body Project offers a total of four weekly group sessions for high school and college-age women. In these sessions, group members are guided through a range of intense verbal, written, role playing, and behavioral exercises that critique Western society's ultra-thin ideal. The participants also engage in body acceptance exercises, eating and related

\#

#FashionDownsizing

In 1968, the average fashion model was 8 percent thinner than the typical woman. In 2016, models were 32 percent thinner (Firger, 2016; Tashakova, 2011).

Shannon Stapleton/Reuters/Newscom

SPARK Movement Members of SPARK Movement, a group of high school girls dedicated to changing how female shapes and weight are portrayed in the media, recently conducted a mock fashion show on the streets of New York City. The group called on the editors of *Teen Vogue* magazine to stop altering the bodies and faces of girls displayed in the magazine's photos.

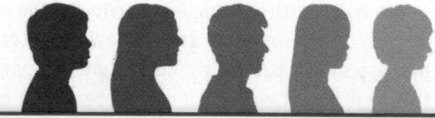

CLINICAL CHOICES

Now that you've read about eating disorders, try the interactive case study for this chapter. See if you are able to identify Jenny's symptoms and suggest a diagnosis based on her symptoms. What kind of treatment would be most effective for Jenny? Go to **Launch**Pad to access *Clinical Choices*.

activities that run counter to the ultra-thin ideal, motivation enhancement techniques, skill-building training, and social support exercises.

The principle behind this program is *cognitive dissonance theory*. According to this social psychology theory, when people adopt new attitudes (in this case, anti-thinness attitudes) that contradict their other attitudes and behaviors (for example, pro-thinness and pro-weight-loss attitudes), they will experience emotional discomfort—a state of dissonance that they implicitly seek to eliminate by changing their old attitudes and behaviors.

Although early in its development, the Body Project prevention program has performed well in research (Stice et al., 2017, 2015). In comparison to other young women who received education-only prevention programs or no prevention programs at all, participants in Body Project develop fewer eating disorders, hold more realistic and healthful appearance ideals, display fewer maladaptive eating attitudes and behaviors, have greater body satisfaction, and experience more positive emotions in follow-up studies conducted a year or more after the program.

Clearly, this program is promising and important. Whether in the form of Body Project or other such undertakings, prevention programs address a critical need in the clinical field's commitment to overcome eating disorders and are likely to increase in the years to come.

⚲... SUMMING UP

» Eating Disorders Rates of eating disorders have increased dramatically as thinness has become a national obsession. Two leading disorders in this category, *anorexia nervosa* and *bulimia nervosa*, share many similarities, as well as key differences. A third eating disorder, *binge-eating disorder*, also seems to be on the rise. *pp. 313–314*

» Anorexia Nervosa People with anorexia nervosa pursue extreme thinness and lose dangerous amounts of weight. They may follow a pattern of *restricting-type anorexia nervosa* or *binge-eating/purging-type anorexia nervosa*. The central features of anorexia nervosa are a drive for thinness, intense fear of weight gain, and disturbed body perception and other cognitive disturbances. People with this disorder develop various medical problems, particularly *amenorrhea*. As many as 90 percent of all cases of anorexia nervosa occur among females. Typically the disorder begins after a person who is slightly overweight or of normal weight has been on a diet. *pp. 314–316*

» **Bulimia Nervosa** People with bulimia nervosa go on frequent *eating binges* and then force themselves to vomit or perform other inappropriate *compensatory behaviors*. The binges are often in response to increasing tension and are followed by feelings of guilt and self-blame. Compensatory behavior is at first reinforced by the temporary relief from uncomfortable feelings of fullness or the reduction of feelings of anxiety, self-disgust, and loss of control attached to bingeing. Over time, however, sufferers generally feel disgusted with themselves, depressed, and guilty.

Once again, as many as 90 percent of all cases of bulimia nervosa occur among females. People with the disorder may have mood swings or have difficulty controlling their impulses. Some display a personality disorder. Around half are amenorrheic, a number develop dental problems, and some develop a potassium deficiency. *pp. 316–321*

» **Binge-Eating Disorder** People with binge-eating disorder have frequent binge eating episodes but do not display inappropriate compensatory behaviors. Although most overweight people do not have binge-eating disorder, half of those with binge-eating disorder become overweight. Between 2 and 7 percent of the population have binge-eating disorder. Unlike anorexia nervosa and bulimia nervosa, this disorder is somewhat more evenly distributed among males and females. *pp. 321–322*

» **Explanations for Eating Disorders** Most theorists now use a *multidimensional risk perspective* to explain eating disorders and to identify several key contributing factors. Principal among these are *ego deficiencies; cognitive factors; depression; biological factors* such as dysfunctional brain circuits, problematic activity of the *hypothalamus,* and disturbances of the body's weight set point; society's emphasis on thinness and bias against obesity; family environment; racial and ethnic differences; and gender differences. *pp. 322–331*

» **Treatments for Eating Disorders** The first step in treating *anorexia nervosa* is to increase calorie intake and quickly restore the person's weight, a part of treatment called *nutritional rehabilitation*. The second step is to deal with the underlying psychological and family problems, often using a combination of *education, cognitive-behavioral approaches,* and *family therapy*. As many as 75 percent of people who are successfully treated for anorexia nervosa continue to show full or partial improvements years later. However, some of them relapse along the way, many continue to worry about their weight and appearance, and half continue to have some emotional problems. Most menstruate again when they regain weight.

Treatments for *bulimia nervosa* focus first on stopping the binge-purge pattern (nutritional rehabilitation) and then on addressing the underlying causes of the disorder. Often several treatment strategies are combined, including *education, psychotherapy* (particularly *cognitive-behavioral therapy*), and, in some cases, *antidepressant medications*. As many as 75 percent of those who receive treatment eventually improve either fully or partially. While relapse can be a problem and may be precipitated by a new stress, treatment leads to lasting improvements in psychological and social functioning for many people. Similar treatments are used to help people with *binge-eating disorder*. These individuals, however, may also require interventions to address their excessive weight.

Prevention programs are becoming more common and more effective in addressing anorexia nervosa and bulimia nervosa. *pp. 331–340*

Visit *LaunchPad*
to access the e-Book, Clinical Choices, videos, activities, and LearningCurve, as well as study aids including flashcards, FAQs, and research exercises.

LaunchPad
macmillan learning

Substance Use and Addictive Disorders

"I am Duncan. I am an alcoholic." The audience settled deeper into their chairs at these familiar words. Another chronicle of death and rebirth would shortly begin [at] Alcoholics Anonymous. . . .

"I must have been just past my 15th birthday when I had that first drink that everybody talks about. And like so many of them . . . it was like a miracle. With a little beer in my gut, the world was transformed. I wasn't a weakling anymore, I could lick almost anybody on the block. And girls? Well, you can imagine how a couple of beers made me feel like I could have any girl I wanted. . . .

"Though it's obvious to me now that my drinking even then, in high school, and after I got to college, was a problem, I didn't think so at the time. After all, everybody was drinking and getting drunk and acting stupid, and I didn't really think I was different. . . . I guess the fact that I hadn't really had any blackouts and that I could go for days without having to drink reassured me that things hadn't gotten out of control. And that's the way it went, until I found myself drinking even more—and more often—and suffering more from my drinking, along about my third year of college. . . . "My roommate, a friend from high school, started bugging me about my drinking. It wasn't even that I'd have to sleep it off the whole next day and miss class, it was that he had begun to hear other friends talking about me, about the fool I'd made of myself at parties. He saw how shaky I was the morning after, and he saw how different I was when I'd been drinking a lot—almost out of my head was the way he put it. And he could count the bottles that I'd leave around the room, and he knew what the drinking and carousing was doing to my grades. . . . [P]artly because I really cared about my roommate and didn't want to lose him as a friend, I did cut down on my drinking by half or more. I only drank on weekends—and then only at night. . . . And that got me through the rest of college and, actually, through law school as well. . . .

"Shortly after getting my law degree, I married my first wife, and . . . for the first time since I started, my drinking was no problem at all. I would go for weeks at a time without touching a drop. . . .

"My marriage started to go bad after our second son, our third child, was born. I was very much career- and success-oriented, and I had little time to spend at home with my family. . . . My traveling had increased a lot, there were stimulating people on those trips, and, let's face it, there were some pretty exciting women available, too. So home got to be little else but a nagging, boring wife and children I wasn't very interested in. My drinking had gotten bad again, too, with being on the road so much, having to do a lot of entertaining at lunch when I wasn't away, and trying to soften the hassles at home. I guess I was putting down close to a gallon of very good scotch a week, with one thing or another.

"And as that went on, the drinking began to affect both my marriage and my career. With enough booze in me and under the pressures of guilt over my failure to carry out my responsibilities to my wife and children, I sometimes got kind of rough physically with them. I would break furniture, throw things around, then rush out and drive off in the car. I had a couple of wrecks, lost my license for two years because of one of them. Worst of all was when I tried to stop. By then I was totally hooked, so every time I tried to stop drinking, I'd experience withdrawal in all its horrors . . . with the vomiting and the 'shakes' and being unable to sit still or to lie down. And that would go on for days at a time. . . .

"Then, about four years ago, with my life in ruins, my wife given up on me and the kids with her, out of a job, and way down on my luck, [Alcoholics Anonymous] and I found each other. . . . I've been dry now for a little over two years, and with luck and support, I may stay sober. . . ."

(Spitzer et al., 1983, pp. 87–89)

TABLE: 12-1

Dx Checklist

Substance Use Disorder

1. Individual displays a maladaptive pattern of substance use leading to significant impairment or distress

2. Presence of at least 2 of the following symptoms within a 1-year period

   a. Substance is often taken in larger amounts or over a longer period than intended

   b. Unsuccessful efforts or persistent desire to reduce or control substance use

   c. Much time spent trying to obtain, use, or recover from the effects of substance use

   d. Failure to fulfill major role obligations at work, school, or home as a result of repeated substance use

   e. Continued use of substance despite persistent social or interpersonal problems caused by it

   f. Cessation or reduction of important social, occupational, or recreational activities because of substance use

   g. Continuing to use substance in situations in which use poses physical risks

   h. Continuing to use substance despite awareness that it is causing or worsening a physical or psychological problem

   i. Craving for substance

   j. Tolerance effects

   k. Withdrawal reactions

(Information from: APA, 2013.)

H uman beings enjoy a remarkable variety of foods and drinks. Every substance on earth probably has been tried by someone, somewhere, at some time. We also have discovered substances that have interesting effects—both medical and pleasurable—on our brains and the rest of our bodies. We may swallow an aspirin to quiet a headache, an antibiotic to fight an infection, or a tranquilizer to calm us down. We may drink coffee to get going in the morning or wine to relax with friends. We may smoke cigarettes to soothe our nerves. However, many of the substances we consume can harm us or disrupt our behavior or mood. The misuse of such substances has become one of society's biggest problems; it has been estimated that the cost of substance misuse is $740 billion each year in the United States alone (NIDA, 2017).

Not only are numerous substances available in our society, new ones are introduced almost every day. Some are harvested from nature, others derived from natural substances, and still others produced in the laboratory. Some, such as antianxiety drugs, require a physician's prescription for legal use. Others, such as alcohol and nicotine, are legally available to adults. Still others, such as heroin, are illegal under all circumstances. In 1962, only 4 million people in the United States had ever used marijuana, cocaine, heroin, or another illegal substance; today the number has climbed to 131 million (SAMHSA, 2017; NSDUH, 2016). In fact, 27 million people have used illegal substances within the past month. A quarter of all teenagers have used an illegal substance.

A *drug* is defined as any substance other than food that affects our bodies or minds. It need not be a medicine or be illegal. The term "substance" is now frequently used in place of "drug," in part because many people fail to see that such substances as alcohol, tobacco, and caffeine are drugs, too. When a person ingests a substance—whether it be alcohol, cocaine, marijuana, or some form of medication—trillions of powerful molecules surge through the bloodstream and into the brain. Once there, the molecules set off a series of biochemical events that disturb the normal operation of the brain and body. Not surprisingly, then, substance misuse may lead to various kinds of abnormal functioning.

Substances may cause *temporary* changes in behavior, emotion, or thought; this cluster of changes is called **substance intoxication** in DSM-5. As Duncan found out, for example, an excessive amount of alcohol may lead to *alcohol intoxication,* a temporary state of poor judgment, mood changes, irritability, slurred speech, and poor coordination. Similarly, drugs such as LSD may produce *hallucinogen intoxication,* sometimes called *hallucinosis,* which consists largely of perceptual distortions and hallucinations.

Some substances can also lead to *long-term* problems. People who regularly ingest them may develop **substance use disorders,** patterns of maladaptive behaviors and reactions brought about by the repeated use of substances (APA, 2013). People with a substance use disorder may come to crave a particular substance and rely on it excessively, resulting in damage to their family and social relationships, poor functioning at work, and/or danger to themselves or others (see **Table 12-1**). In many cases, people with such a disorder also become physically dependent on the substance, developing a *tolerance* for it and experiencing *withdrawal* reactions. When people develop **tolerance,** they need increasing doses of the substance to produce the desired effect. **Withdrawal** reactions consist of unpleasant and sometimes dangerous symptoms—cramps, anxiety attacks, sweating, nausea—that occur when the person suddenly stops taking or cuts back on the substance. Duncan, who described his problems to fellow members at an Alcoholics Anonymous meeting, was caught in a form of substance use disorder called *alcohol use disorder*. When he was a college student and later a lawyer, alcohol damaged his family, social, academic, and work life. He also built up a tolerance for alcohol over time and had withdrawal symptoms such as vomiting and shaking when he tried to stop using it.

In any given year, 7.8 percent of all teens and adults in the United States, around 21 million people, have a substance use disorder (SAMHSA, 2017; NSDUH, 2016). American Indians have the highest rate of substance use disorders in the United States (11.6 percent), while Asian Americans have the lowest (3.8 percent). Non-Hispanic white Americans, Hispanic Americans, and African Americans have rates between 7 and 8.2 percent (SAMHSA, 2017; NSDUH, 2016) (see **Figure 12-1**). Only 18 percent of all those with substance use disorders receive treatment from a mental health professional.

The substances people misuse fall into several categories: *depressants, stimulants, hallucinogens,* and *cannabis.* In this chapter you will read about some of the most problematic substances and the abnormal patterns they may produce. In addition, at the end of the chapter, you'll read about *gambling disorder,* a problem that DSM-5 lists as an additional addictive disorder. By listing this behavioral pattern alongside the substance use disorders, DSM-5 is suggesting that this problem has addictive-like symptoms and causes that share more than a passing similarity to those at work in substance use disorders. ∎

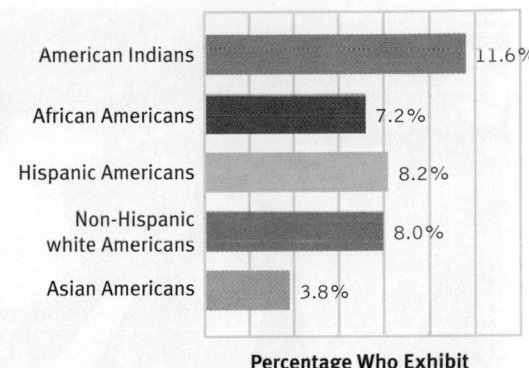

Percentage Who Exhibit Substance Use Disorders

FIGURE 12-1

How Do Racial/Ethnic Groups Differ in Substance Use Disorders?

In the United States, American Indians are more likely than members of other ethnic or cultural groups to have substance use disorders. (Information from: SAMHSA, 2017; NSDUH, 2016.)

|||||||||||||||||||||||||||||||||||||||||||||||||||||||||||||||||||||||||||||||||

Depressants

DEPRESSANTS SLOW THE ACTIVITY of the central nervous system. They reduce tension and inhibitions and may interfere with a person's judgment, motor activity, and concentration. The three most widely used groups of depressants are *alcohol, sedative-hypnotic drugs,* and *opioids.*

Alcohol

The World Health Organization estimates that 2 billion people worldwide consume **alcohol.** In the United States more than half of all residents at least from time to time drink beverages that contain alcohol (SAMHSA, 2017; NSDUH, 2016). Purchases of beer, wine, and liquor amount to tens of billions of dollars each year in the United States alone.

When people consume five or more drinks on a single occasion, it is called a *binge drinking* episode. Twenty-five percent of people in the United States over the age of 11, most of them male, binge drink each month (SAMHSA, 2017; NSDUH, 2016). Around 6.5 percent of people over 11 years of age binge drink at least five times each month. They are considered heavy drinkers. Among heavy drinkers, males outnumber females by at least 2 to 1.

All alcoholic beverages contain *ethyl alcohol,* a chemical that is quickly absorbed into the blood through the lining of the stomach and the intestine. The ethyl alcohol immediately begins to take effect as it is carried in the bloodstream to the central nervous system (the brain and spinal cord), where it acts to depress, or slow, functioning by binding to various neurons. One important group of neurons to which ethyl alcohol binds are those that normally receive the neurotransmitter GABA. As you saw in Chapter 5, GABA carries an *inhibitory* message—a message to stop firing—when it is received at certain neurons. When alcohol binds to receptors on those neurons, it apparently helps GABA to shut down the neurons, thus helping to relax the drinker (Gondré-Lewis et al., 2016; Nace, 2011, 2005).

substance intoxication A cluster of temporary undesirable behavioral or psychological changes that develop during or shortly after the ingestion of a substance.

substance use disorder A pattern of long-term maladaptive behaviors and reactions brought about by repeated use of a substance.

tolerance The brain and body's need for ever-larger doses of a drug to produce earlier effects.

withdrawal Unpleasant, sometimes dangerous reactions that may occur when people who use a drug regularly stop taking it or reduce the dosage.

alcohol Any beverage containing ethyl alcohol, including beer, wine, and liquor.

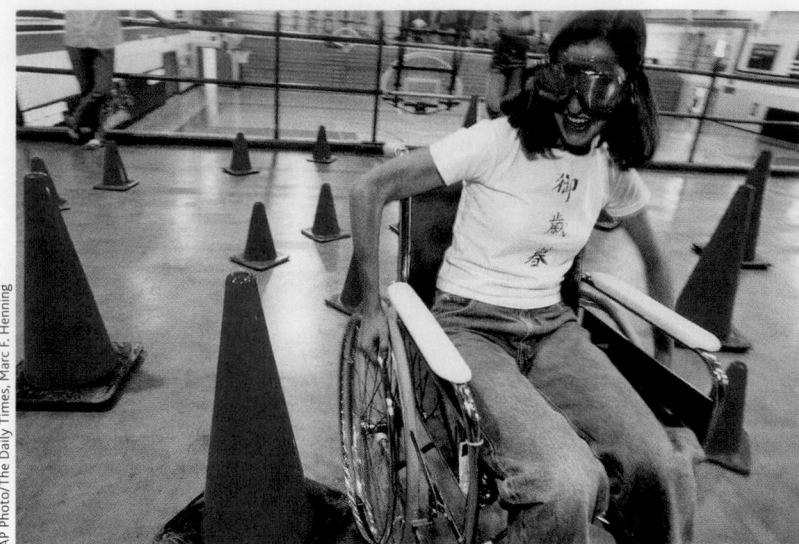

Simulating alcohol's effects A 16-year-old student weaves her way through an obstacle course while wearing a pair of goggles that produce alcohol-like impairment. The exercise is part of a DUI-prevention program at her New Mexico high school, designed to give students hands-on experience with alcohol's effects on vision and balance.

AP Photo/The Daily Times, Marc F. Henning

At first ethyl alcohol depresses the areas of the brain that control judgment and inhibition; people become looser, more talkative, and often more friendly. As their inner control breaks down, they may feel relaxed, confident, and happy. When more alcohol is absorbed, it slows down additional areas in the central nervous system, leaving the drinkers less able to make sound judgments, their speech less careful and less coherent, and their memory weaker. Many people become highly emotional and perhaps loud and aggressive.

Motor difficulties increase as a person continues drinking, and reaction times slow. People may be unsteady when they stand or walk and clumsy in performing even simple activities. They may drop things, bump into doors and furniture, and misjudge distances. Their vision becomes blurred, particularly their peripheral, or side, vision, and they have trouble hearing. As a result, people who have drunk too much alcohol may have great difficulty driving or solving simple problems.

The extent of the effect of ethyl alcohol is determined by its *concentration,* or proportion, in the blood. Thus a given amount of alcohol has less effect on a large person than on a small one. Gender also affects the concentration of alcohol in the blood. Women have less of the stomach enzyme *alcohol dehydrogenase,* which breaks down alcohol in the stomach before it enters the blood. So women become more intoxicated than men on equal doses of alcohol, and women may be at greater risk for physical and psychological damage from alcohol than men who drink similar quantities of alcohol (Mukamal, 2016).

Levels of impairment are closely related to the concentration of ethyl alcohol in the blood. When the alcohol concentration reaches 0.06 percent of the blood volume, a person usually feels relaxed and comfortable. By the time it reaches 0.09 percent, however, the drinker crosses the line into intoxication. If the level goes as high as 0.55 percent, the drinker will likely die. Most people lose consciousness before they can drink enough to reach this level; nevertheless, more than 1,000 people in the United States die each year from too high a blood alcohol level (Mukamal, 2016; Hart & Ksir, 2015).

The effects of alcohol subside only when the alcohol concentration in the blood declines. Most of the alcohol is broken down, or *metabolized,* by the liver into carbon dioxide and water, which can be exhaled and excreted. The average rate of this metabolism is 25 percent of an ounce per hour, but different people's livers work at different speeds; thus rates of "sobering up" vary. Despite popular belief, only time and metabolism can make a person sober. Drinking black coffee, splashing cold water on one's face, or "pulling oneself together" cannot hurry the process.

Alcohol Use Disorder Though legal, alcohol is actually one of the most dangerous of recreational drugs, and its reach extends across the life span. In fact, around 23 percent of middle school students admit to some alcohol use, while 33 percent of high school seniors drink alcohol each month (most to the point of intoxication) and 1.3 percent report drinking every day (Johnston et al., 2017). Alcohol misuse is also a major problem on college campuses (see **PsychWatch**).

Surveys indicate that over a one-year period, 5.9 percent of all people over 11 years of age in the United States display *alcohol use disorder,* known in popular terms as *alcoholism* (SAMHSA, 2017; NSDUH, 2016). For teenagers specifically, the rate is 2.5 percent. Men with this disorder outnumber women by 2 to 1.

The current prevalence of alcoholism is around 6.1 percent for non-Hispanic white Americans, 6.4 percent for Hispanic Americans, and 4.9 percent for African Americans (SAMHSA, 2017; NSDUH, 2016). American Indians, particularly men, tend to display a higher rate of alcohol use disorder than any of these groups. Overall, 9.7 percent of

---

# #

#DiagnosticControversy

Is All Drug Misuse the Same?

DSM-5 has combined two past disorders, *substance abuse* (excessive and chronic reliance on drugs) and *substance dependence* (excessive reliance accompanied by tolerance and withdrawal symptoms) into a single category—*substance use disorder.* Critics worry that clinicians may now fail to recognize and address the different prognoses and treatment needs of people who abuse substances and those who depend on substances.

College Binge Drinking: An Extracurricular Crisis

Drinking large amounts of alcohol in a short time, or *binge drinking*, is a serious problem on college campuses, as well as in many other settings. Studies show that 38 percent of college students binge drink at least once each month, one-third of them six times or more per month (NIAAA, 2017; NSDUH, 2016). In many circles, alcohol use is an accepted part of college life, but consider some of the following statistics;

- Alcohol-related arrests account for 83 percent of all campus arrests.

- More than half of all sexual assaults on college campuses involve the heavy consumption of alcohol.

- Alcohol is a factor in at least 25 percent of academic problems and 28 percent of all instances of dropping out of college.

- Approximately 700,000 students each year are physically or emotionally traumatized or assaulted by a student drinker.

- Half of college students say "drinking to get drunk" is an important reason for drinking.

- Binge drinking often has a lingering effect on mood, memory, brain functioning, and heart functioning.

- Binge drinking is tied to 4,300 deaths among college-age persons every year.

- The number of female binge drinkers among college students has increased 31 percent over the past decade.

    (CDC, 2017, 2016; NIAAA, 2017; Nourse et al., 2017; NCASA, 2007; Abbey, 2002)

These findings have led some educators to describe binge drinking as "the number

© Andrew Lichtenstein / Sygma via Getty Images

Testing the limits College binge drinking, which involves behaviors similar to that shown here, has led to a number of deaths in recent years.

one public health hazard" for full-time college students, and many researchers and clinicians have turned their attention to it. Studies have collectively surveyed more than 100,000 students at college campuses around the United States (CDC, 2017; Greene & Maggs, 2017; NIAAA, 2017; AC, 2015; Wechsler et al., 2004, 1995, 1994). Among other useful information, the surveys have found that the students most likely to binge drink are those who live in a fraternity or sorority house, pursue a party-centered lifestyle, and engage in high-risk behaviors such as substance misuse. The surveys have also suggested that students

who are binge drinkers in high school are more likely to binge drink in college.

Efforts to change such patterns have begun. For example, many universities now provide substance-free dorms. Studies indicate that the rate of binge drinking by residents in these college housing facilities is half the rate displayed by students who live in a fraternity or sorority house (Lippy & DeGue, 2016; Wechsler et al., 2002). This and other current research efforts are promising. However, most people in the clinical field agree that much more work is needed to help us fully understand, prevent, and treat what has become a major societal problem.

them experience the disorder, although specific prevalence rates differ widely across the various American Indian reservation communities. Generally, Asians in the United States and elsewhere have a lower rate of alcoholism (3.2 percent) than do people from other cultures. As many as half of these individuals have a deficiency of alcohol dehydrogenase, the chemical responsible for breaking down alcohol, so they react quite negatively to even a modest intake of alcohol. Such reactions in turn help prevent extended use (Chang, Hsiao, & Chen, 2017).

If alcohol is highly addictive and capable of causing so many psychological, physical, social, and personal problems, why does it remain legal in most countries?

CLINICAL PICTURE Generally speaking, people with alcohol use disorder drink large amounts regularly and rely on it to enable them to do things that would otherwise make them anxious. Eventually the drinking interferes with their social behavior and ability to think and work. They may have frequent arguments with family members or friends, miss work repeatedly, and even lose their jobs. MRI scans of chronic heavy drinkers have revealed damage in various structures of their brains and, correspondingly, impairments in their memory, speed of thinking, attention skills, and balance (Tetrault & O'Connor, 2017; Sifferlin, 2014).

Individually, people's patterns of alcoholism vary. Some drink large amounts of alcohol every day and keep drinking until intoxicated. Others go on periodic binges of heavy drinking that can last weeks or months. They may remain intoxicated for days and later be unable to remember anything about the period. Still others may limit their excessive drinking to weekends, evenings, or both.

TOLERANCE AND WITHDRAWAL For many people, alcohol use disorder includes the symptoms of tolerance and withdrawal reactions (Tetrault & O'Connor, 2017; McCrady, 2014). As their bodies build up a tolerance for alcohol, they need to drink ever larger amounts to feel its effects. In addition, they have withdrawal symptoms when they stop drinking. Within hours their hands, tongue, and eyelids begin to shake; they feel weak and nauseated; they sweat and vomit; their heart beats rapidly; and their blood pressure rises. They may also become anxious, depressed, unable to sleep, or irritable (APA, 2013).

A small percentage of people with alcohol use disorder go through a particularly dramatic withdrawal reaction called **delirium tremens ("the DTs").** It consists of terrifying visual hallucinations that begin within three days after they stop or reduce their drinking. Some people see small, frightening animals chasing or crawling on them or objects dancing about in front of their eyes. Like most other alcohol withdrawal symptoms, the DTs usually run their course in 2 to 3 days. However, people who have severe withdrawal reactions such as this may also have seizures, lose consciousness, suffer a stroke, or even die. Today certain medical procedures can help prevent or reduce such extreme reactions.

What Are the Personal and Social Impacts of Alcoholism? Alcoholism destroys millions of families, social relationships, and careers (Mukamal, 2016). Medical treatment, lost productivity, and losses due to deaths from alcoholism cost society many billions of dollars annually. The disorder also plays a role in more than one-third of all suicides, homicides, assaults, rapes, and accidental deaths, including 29 percent of all fatal automobile accidents in the United States (CDC, 2017; Gifford et al., 2010). Altogether, intoxicated drivers are responsible for more than 10,000 deaths each year. Around 10 percent of all adults have driven while intoxicated at least once in the past year (SAMHSA, 2017; NSDUH, 2016). Although this is a frightening number, it represents a significant drop since 2002 when 14 percent of adults had driven in an intoxicated state.

Alcoholism has serious effects on the 30 million children of people with this disorder. Home life for these children is likely to include much conflict and perhaps sexual or other forms of abuse. In turn, the children themselves have higher rates of psychological problems (Gold, 2016; Kelley et al., 2014). Many have low self-esteem, poor communication skills, poor sociability, and marital problems.

Long-term excessive drinking can also seriously damage a person's physical health (Mukamal, 2016; Nace, 2011, 2005). It so overworks the liver that people may develop an irreversible condition called *cirrhosis,* in which the liver becomes scarred and dysfunctional. Cirrhosis accounts for more than 38,000 deaths each year (CDC, 2017). Alcohol use disorder may also damage the heart and lower the immune system's ability to fight off cancer, bacterial infections, and AIDS.

Long-term excessive drinking also causes major nutritional problems. Alcohol makes people feel full and lowers their desire for food, yet it has no nutritional value. As a result, chronic

Substance misuse and sports fans
A problem that has received growing attention in recent years is excessive drinking by fans at sports events. While two soccer players were jumping for a high ball at this playoff game in Athens, Greece, fans—many of them intoxicated—ripped out plastic seats, threw flares on the field, and hurled coins and rocks at the players.

AP Photo/Aris Messinis

drinkers become malnourished, weak, and prone to disease. Their vitamin and mineral deficiencies may also cause problems. An alcohol-related deficiency of vitamin B (thiamine), for example, may lead to **Korsakoff's syndrome,** a disease marked by extreme confusion, memory loss, and other neurological symptoms (Mukamal, 2016; Nace, 2011, 2005). People with Korsakoff's syndrome cannot remember the past or learn new information and may make up for their memory losses by *confabulating*—reciting made-up events to fill in the gaps.

Women who drink during pregnancy place their fetuses at risk (Popova et al., 2017). Excessive alcohol use during pregnancy may cause a baby to be born with **fetal alcohol syndrome,** a pattern of abnormalities that can include intellectual disability disorder, hyperactivity, head and face deformities, heart defects, and slow growth. It has been estimated that in the overall population, around 1 of every 1,000 babies is born with this syndrome (CDC, 2017). The rate may increase to as many as 67 of every 1,000 babies of women who are problem drinkers (Popova et al., 2017). If all alcohol-related birth defects (known as *fetal alcohol spectrum disorder*) are counted, the rate becomes 80 to 200 such births per 1,000 heavy-drinking women. In addition, heavy drinking early in pregnancy often leads to a miscarriage. According to surveys, 9.3 percent of pregnant American women have drunk alcohol during the past month and 4.6 percent of pregnant women have had binge drinking episodes (SAMHSA, 2017; NSDUH, 2016).

Sedative-Hypnotic Drugs

Sedative-hypnotic drugs, also called **anxiolytic** (meaning "anxiety-reducing") **drugs,** produce feelings of relaxation and drowsiness. At low dosages, the drugs have a calming or sedative effect. At higher dosages, they are sleep inducers, or hypnotics. For the first half of the twentieth century, a group of drugs called **barbiturates** were the most widely prescribed sedative-hypnotic drugs. Although still prescribed by some physicians, these drugs have been largely replaced by **benzodiazepines,** which are generally safer and less likely to lead to intoxication, tolerance effects, and withdrawal reactions.

As Chapter 5 noted, benzodiazepines, developed in the 1950s, are the most popular sedative-hypnotic drugs available. Xanax, Ativan, and Valium are just three of the dozens of these compounds in clinical use. Altogether, 130 million prescriptions are written annually for benzodiazepines (Soyka, 2017; Bachhuber et al., 2016). Like alcohol and barbiturates, they calm people by binding to receptors on the neurons that receive GABA and by increasing GABA's activity at those neurons (Tietze & Fuchs, 2017). Benzodiazepines relieve anxiety without making people as drowsy as other kinds of sedative-hypnotics. They are also less likely to slow a person's breathing, so they are less likely to cause death in the event of an overdose.

When benzodiazepines were first discovered, they seemed so safe and effective that physicians prescribed them generously, and their use spread. Eventually it became clear that in high enough doses the drugs can cause intoxication and lead to *sedative-hypnotic use disorder*, a pattern marked by craving for the drugs, tolerance effects, and withdrawal reactions. Over a one-year period, 0.4 percent of all adults in the United States display this disorder (SAMHSA, 2017; NSDUH, 2016).

Opioids

Opioids include opium, which is taken from the sap of the opium poppy; drugs derived from opium, such as heroin, morphine, and codeine; and similar *synthetic* (laboratory-blended) drugs. **Opium** itself has been in use for thousands of years. In the past it

delirium tremens (DTs) A dramatic withdrawal reaction that some people dependent on alcohol have. It consists of confusion, clouded consciousness, and terrifying visual hallucinations.

Korsakoff's syndrome An alcohol-related disorder marked by extreme confusion, memory impairment, and other neurological symptoms.

fetal alcohol syndrome A cluster of problems in a child, including low birth weight, irregularities in the head and face, and intellectual deficits, caused by excessive alcohol intake by the mother during pregnancy.

sedative-hypnotic drug A drug used in low doses to reduce anxiety and in higher doses to help people sleep. Also called an *anxiolytic drug*.

barbiturates Addictive sedative-hypnotic drugs that reduce anxiety and help people sleep.

benzodiazepines The most common group of antianxiety drugs; includes Xanax.

opioid Opium, drugs derived from opium, and similar synthetic drugs.

opium A highly addictive substance made from the sap of the opium poppy.

Purer blend Heroin, derived from poppies such as this one in a poppy field in southern Afghanistan, is purer and stronger today than it was three decades ago (65 percent pure versus 5 percent pure).

Stringer /EPA/ Newscom

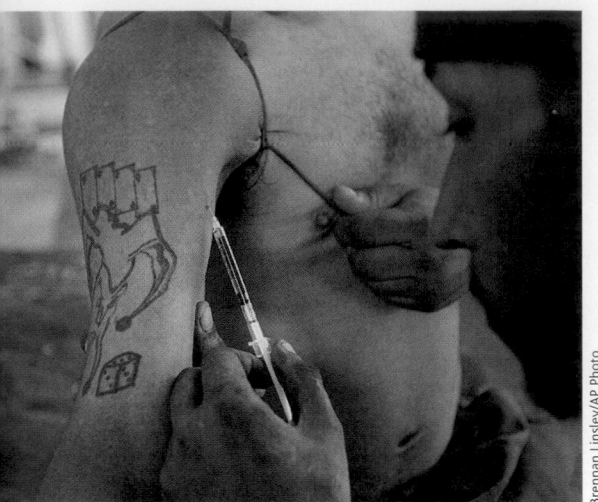

Injecting heroin Opioids may be taken by mouth, inhaled, snorted, injected just beneath the surface of the skin, or injected intravenously. Here, one addict injects another with heroin inside one of the many so-called shooting galleries where addicts gather in downtown San Juan, Puerto Rico.

was used widely in the treatment of medical disorders because of its ability to reduce both physical and emotional pain. Eventually, however, physicians discovered that the drug was addictive.

In 1804 a new substance, **morphine,** was derived from opium. Named after Morpheus, the Greek god of sleep, this drug relieved pain even better than opium did and initially was considered safe. However, wide use of the drug eventually revealed that it, too, could lead to addiction. So many wounded soldiers in the United States received morphine injections during the Civil War that morphine addiction became known as "soldiers' disease."

In 1898, morphine was converted into yet another new pain reliever, **heroin.** For several years heroin was viewed as a wonder drug and was used as a cough medicine and for other medical purposes. Eventually, however, physicians learned that heroin is even more addictive than the other opioids. By 1917, the U.S. Congress had concluded that all drugs derived from opium were addictive, and it passed a law making opioids illegal except for medical purposes.

Still other drugs have been derived from opium, and, as noted above, synthetic opioids such as *methadone* have also been developed. These various opioid drugs are also known collectively as *narcotics*. Each drug has a different strength, speed of action, and tolerance level. Morphine, *codeine,* and *oxycodone* (the key ingredient in OxyContin and Percocet) are medical opioids usually prescribed to relieve pain. In contrast to these opioids, heroin is illegal in the United States in all circumstances.

> Can you think of other substances or activities that, like opioids, can be helpful in controlled portions but dangerous when used excessively or uncontrollably?

Most opioids are smoked, inhaled, snorted, injected, or, as in the case of many pain relievers, swallowed in pill or liquid form. In injections, the opioid may be deposited just beneath the skin ("skin-popping"), deep into a muscle, or directly into a vein ("mainlining"). An injection quickly brings on a *rush*—a spasm of warmth and ecstasy that is sometimes compared with orgasm. The brief spasm is followed by several hours of a pleasant feeling called a *high* or *nod*. During a high, the drug user feels relaxed, happy, and unconcerned about food, sex, or other bodily needs.

Opioids create these effects by depressing the central nervous system, particularly the centers that help control emotion. The drugs attach to brain receptor sites that ordinarily receive **endorphins**—neurotransmitters that help relieve pain and reduce emotional tension (Stephan & Parsa, 2016). When neurons at these receptor sites receive opioids, they produce pleasurable and calming feelings just as they would do if they were receiving endorphins. In addition to reducing pain and tension, opioids cause nausea, narrowing of the pupils ("pinpoint pupils"), and constipation—bodily reactions that can also be brought about by releases of endorphins in the brain.

Opioid Use Disorder Heroin use exemplifies the kinds of problems posed by opioids. After taking heroin repeatedly for just a few weeks, users may develop *opioid use disorder*. Their heroin use interferes significantly with their social and occupational functioning, and their lives center around the drug. They may also build a tolerance for heroin and experience a withdrawal reaction when they stop taking it (Strain, 2017; Yin, 2016). At first the withdrawal symptoms are anxiety, restlessness, sweating, and rapid breathing; later they include severe twitching, aches, fever, vomiting, diarrhea, loss of appetite, high blood pressure, and weight loss of up to 15 pounds (due to loss of bodily fluids). These symptoms usually peak by the third day, gradually subside, and disappear by the eighth day. A person in heroin withdrawal can either wait out the symptoms or end withdrawal by taking the drug again.

Such people soon need heroin just to avoid going into withdrawal, and they must continually increase their doses in order to achieve even that relief. The temporary high becomes less intense and less important. Heroin users may spend much of their time planning their next dose, in many cases turning to criminal activities, such as

morphine A highly addictive substance derived from opium that is particularly effective in relieving pain.

heroin One of the most addictive substances derived from opium.

endorphins Neurotransmitters that help relieve pain and reduce emotional tension. They are sometimes referred to as the body's own opioids.

theft and prostitution, to support the expensive "habit" (Hart & Ksir, 2015; Cadet, Bisagno, & Milroy, 2014).

Surveys suggest that more than 1 percent of adults in the United States, a total of 2.6 million people, display an opioid use disorder within a given year (SAMHSA, 2017; NSDUH, 2016). Among teenagers specifically, the prevalence may be even higher (Johnston et al., 2017). Most of these persons (80 percent) are addicted to pain-reliever opioids, prescription drugs such as oxycodone (see **Figure 12-2**). Around 20 percent of those with opioid use disorder are addicted to heroin. The rate of opioid dependence dropped considerably during the 1980s, rose in the early 1990s, fell in the late 1990s, and now is high once again. Indeed, the accelerated increase of this rate over the past several years—including the increase among teenagers—and the growing number of deaths caused by opioid overdoses have many clinicians referring to it as an epidemic (see *Trending*). According to some studies, the mortality rate of untreated persons with opioid use disorder is 63 times the rate of other persons (Strain, 2017).

What Are the Dangers of Opioid Use? The most immediate danger of opioid use is an overdose, which closes down the respiratory center in the brain, almost paralyzing breathing and in many cases causing death (Coffin, 2017; Stolbach & Hoffman, 2017). Death is particularly likely during sleep, when a person is unable to fight this effect by consciously working to breathe. People who resume heroin or pain reliever use after having avoided it for some time often make the fatal mistake of taking the same dose they had built up to before. Because their bodies have been without such opioids for some time, however, they can no longer tolerate this high level. There has been a 400 percent increase in the number of deaths caused by opioid overdoses in the past decade (CDC, 2017). Currently, approximately 20,000 people in the United States die from pain reliever overdoses each year and 13,000 die from heroin overdoses (Coffin, 2017; ASAM, 2016). These numbers represent two-thirds of all drug overdose deaths.

Heroin users run other risks as well. Drug dealers often mix heroin with a cheaper drug or even a deadly substance such as cyanide or battery acid. In addition, dirty needles and other unsterilized equipment spread infections such as AIDS, hepatitis C, and skin abscesses (Strain, 2017). In some areas of the United States, the HIV infection rate among active heroin users is reported to be as high as 60 percent.

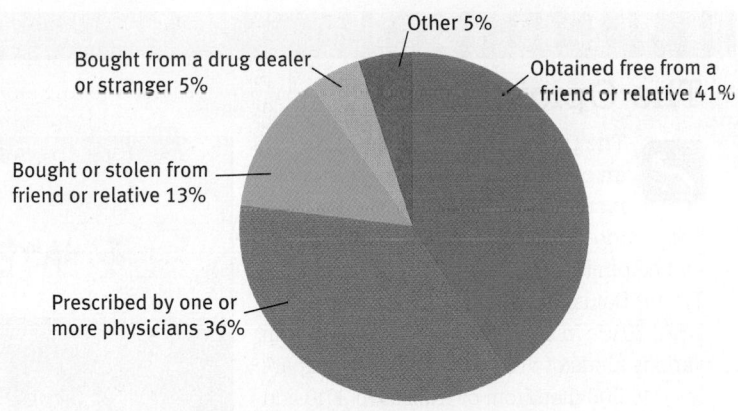

Other 5%

Bought from a drug dealer or stranger 5%

Obtained free from a friend or relative 41%

Bought or stolen from friend or relative 13%

Prescribed by one or more physicians 36%

FIGURE 12-2

Where Do People Obtain Pain Killers for Nonmedical Use?

More than 40 percent get the drugs from friends or relatives and 36 percent obtain them from a doctor. Only 5 percent buy them from a drug dealer. (Information from: SAMHSA, 2017; NSDUH, 2016.)

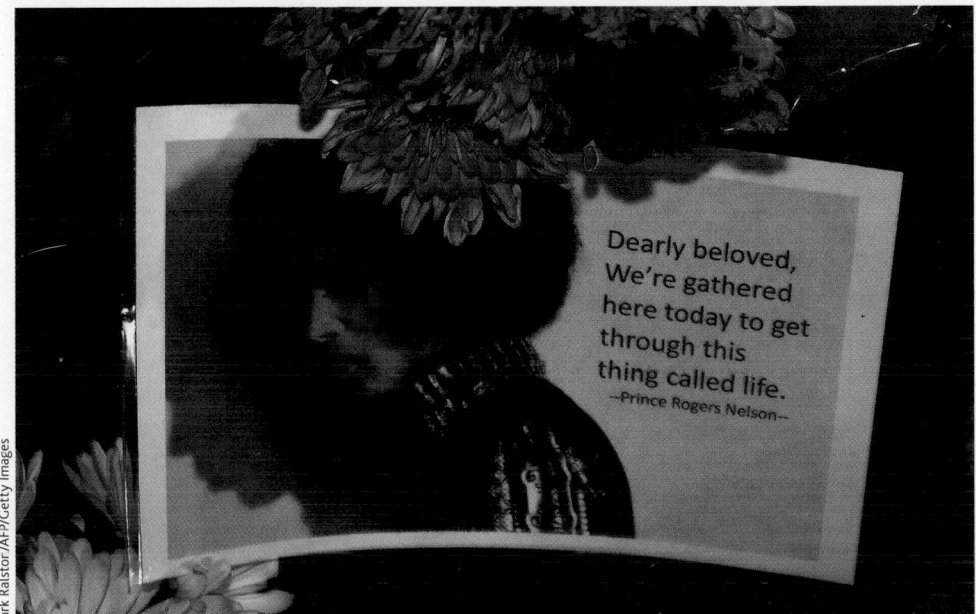

Mark Ralstor/AFP/Getty Images

Dearly beloved, We're gathered here today to get through this thing called life. ~Prince Rogers Nelson~

Deadly effects In 2016 music giant Prince died at the age of 57 from an overdose of the opioid drug *fentanyl*, an extremely powerful prescription pain reliever. Immediately after his death, fans started leaving messages outside his residential compound in Minnesota, including this one with apt lyrics from Prince's song "Let's Go Crazy."

The Opioid Crisis

The United States is in the midst of an opioid epidemic—a staggering increase in the number of addictions and overdose deaths related to painkillers and heroin (Stevens et al., 2018; CDC 2017; Trotter Davis, Bateman, & Avorn, 2017; DEA, 2015). In 2016, 62,000 people died from various kinds of drug overdoses; by comparison, 16,000 died from overdoses in 2010 and 4,000 in 1999 (Katz, 2017; NIDA, 2014). Two-thirds of all such drug deaths involve opioids. The opioid epidemic is predominantly an American problem because 80 percent of the world's opioids are consumed in the United States (Gusovsky, 2016). The last drug epidemic of this magnitude was the crack epidemic of the 1980s, which witnessed a comparable number of annual deaths if one calculates both overdoses and crack-related homicides (Regier, 2016).

How did the current opioid epidemic emerge? Several factors have contributed. First is the painkiller factor (Stanos, 2017; Trotter et al., 2017). Back in the 1990s, the number of Americans diagnosed with some form of chronic pain rose to one hundred million (a third of the population), leading to increased prescriptions of several powerful pain medications such as Percocet, Vicodin, and Oxycontin—drugs more powerful than morphine or heroin (CDC, 2017). These medications soon became overprescribed, despite the good intentions of physicians, and between 1991 and 2011, the number of U.S prescriptions for painkillers tripled to 219 million per year (Trotter Davis et al., 2017; Voon, Karamouzian, & Kerr, 2017; U.S. Surgeon General, 2016). Many patients developed a painkiller use disorder, and, as word about the opioid impact of these drugs spread, the illicit acquisition and use of prescription painkillers rose as well.

While the use of painkillers was increasing between 1991 and 2011, so was their potency, as pharmaceutical companies sought to develop more effective and powerful painkillers. One of the most powerful pain relief drugs is *fentanyl,* which is 50 to 100 times more powerful than morphine, 20 to 35 times more powerful than heroin, and, correspondingly, more dangerous than either (Caldwell, 2017; EMCDDA, 2017).

John Moore/Getty Images

"Fed Up!" At the National Mall in Washington, D.C., this man and thousands of other activists and family members rally for federal funding to help end the opioid epidemic. The rally was organized by Fed Up!, a coalition that is working for an end to the epidemic of opioid addictions and overdoses.

Given its exceptional potency, rapid onset, and short duration, fentanyl became a very popular street drug. Illegal—and, thus, uncontrolled—manufacture of this drug escalated correspondingly (CDC, 2017; Beletsky & Davis, 2017; Goggin, Nguyen, & Janis, 2017). Fentanyl is by far the painkiller most commonly linked to overdose deaths. (The 2016 death of the iconic musical performer Prince was caused by a fentanyl overdose.)

A second and related factor in the opioid explosion is the rising availability of heroin. As painkiller prescriptions were tripling between 1991 and 2011, foreign drug cartels recognized the growing thirst of the United States population for opioids, and, in turn, they flooded the United States marketplace with heroin (CRS, 2016; Nolan & Amico,

2016). This increased heroin availability led, in turn, to lower heroin prices, much easier acquisition, and greater heroin use.

Since 2011, the increased affordability, availability, and potency of opioid drugs have produced a still greater demand for opioids—both illicitly acquired painkillers and heroin—that has resulted in the current opioid epidemic. As the head of the CDC observed recently, "America is awash in opioids" (Frieden, 2016). Moreover, heroin and painkillers are not necessarily competing with each other in the U.S. marketplace. Rather, they are often combined or intermixed for users—a phenomenon that has multiplied their dangers exponentially. Fentanyl-laced heroin is, for example, now common on the streets (Perry, 2017). Users who think they are taking heroin at their usual dose often are taking the much more powerful fentanyl—a misperception that can readily lead to their death. Similarly, illegal manufacturers of painkillers often make the pain drugs look identical—although their potencies differ significantly. As one U.S. attorney has stated, purposeful disguises of this kind represent "an overdose waiting to happen" (STAT, 2016).

The opioid epidemic is currently being fought on all fronts: federal and state legislatures have, for example, passed laws calling for more funding to fight the opioid epidemic, greater efforts to combat international opioid trafficking, more coordination between the states, more monitoring of doctors' prescription practices, more accountability from pharmaceutical companies, and better funding of opioid treatment programs (CDC, 2017; Trotter Davis et al., 2017; DeBonis, 2016; Dowell et al., 2016; NGA, 2016). In addition, the clinical field is devoting a greater portion of its professionals and resources to the prevention and treatment of opioid use disorders. With such efforts in place, authorities and clinicians are hopeful that the epidemic will soon recede, but unfortunately, how soon and how much it will recede are far from clear at the present time (Stevens et al., 2018; Davis, Green, & Beletsky, 2017; Stanos, 2017; Volkow & Collins, 2017).

Stimulants

STIMULANTS ARE SUBSTANCES that increase the activity of the central nervous system, resulting in increased blood pressure and heart rate, more alertness, and sped-up behavior and thinking. Among the most troublesome stimulants are *cocaine* and *amphetamines,* whose effects on people are very similar. When users report different effects, it is often because they have ingested different amounts of the drugs. Two other widely used and legal stimulants are *caffeine* and *nicotine* (see *InfoCentral* on page 355).

cocaine An addictive stimulant obtained from the coca plant. It is the most powerful natural stimulant known.

Cocaine

Cocaine—the central active ingredient of the coca plant, found in South America—is the most powerful natural stimulant now known (Nelson & Odujebe, 2017). The drug was first separated from the plant in 1865. Native people of South America, however, have chewed the leaves of the plant since prehistoric times for the energy and alertness the drug offers. Processed cocaine (*hydrochloride powder*) is an odorless, white, fluffy powder. For recreational use, it is most often snorted so that it is absorbed through the mucous membrane of the nose. Some users prefer the more powerful effects of injecting cocaine intravenously or smoking it in a pipe or cigarette.

For years people believed that cocaine posed few problems aside from intoxication and, on occasion, temporary psychosis (see **Table 12-2**). Only later did researchers come to appreciate its many dangers (Gorelick, 2017). Their insights came after society witnessed a dramatic surge in the drug's popularity and in problems related to its use. In the early 1960s, an estimated 10,000 people in the United States had tried cocaine. Today 39 million people have tried it, and 1.9 million—most of them teenagers or young adults—are using it currently (SAMHSA, 2017; NSDUH, 2016).

Cocaine brings on a euphoric rush of well-being and confidence. Given a high enough dose, this rush can be almost orgasmic, like the one produced by heroin. At first cocaine stimulates the higher centers of the central nervous system, making users feel excited, energetic, talkative, and even euphoric. As more is taken, it stimulates other centers of the central nervous system, producing a faster pulse, higher blood pressure, faster and deeper breathing, and further arousal and wakefulness.

Cocaine apparently produces these effects largely by increasing supplies of the neurotransmitter *dopamine* at key neurons throughout the brain (Gorelick, 2017).

TABLE: 12-2

Risks and Consequences of Drug Misuse

	Potential Intoxication	Addiction Potential	Risk of Organ Damage or Death	Risk of Severe Social or Economic Consequences	Risk of Severe or Long-Lasting Mental & Behavioral Change
Opioids	High	High	Moderate	High	Low to Moderate
Sedative-Hypnotics Barbiturates Benzodiazepines	Moderate Moderate	Moderate to High Moderate	Moderate to High Low	Moderate to High Low	Low Low
Stimulants (cocaine, amphetamines)	High	High	Moderate	Low to Moderate	Moderate to High
Alcohol	High	Moderate	High	High	High
Cannabis	High	Low to Moderate	Low	Low to Moderate	Low
Mixed drugs	High	High	High	High	High

Information from: Mukamal, 2016; Hart & Ksir, 2015; APA, 2013; Hart et al., 2010.

freebase A technique for ingesting cocaine in which the pure cocaine basic alkaloid is chemically separated from processed cocaine, vaporized by heat from a flame, and inhaled with a pipe.

crack A powerful, ready-to-smoke freebase cocaine.

Excessive amounts of dopamine travel to receiving neurons throughout the central nervous system and overstimulate them. Cocaine appears to also increase the activity of the neurotransmitters *norepinephrine* and *serotonin* in some areas of the brain.

High doses of the drug produce *cocaine intoxication,* whose symptoms are poor muscle coordination, grandiosity, bad judgment, anger, aggression, compulsive behavior, anxiety, and confusion (Nelson & Odujebe, 2017). Some people have hallucinations, delusions, or both, a condition called *cocaine-induced psychosis.*

A young man described how, after free-basing, he went to his closet to get his clothes, but his suit asked him, "What do you want?" Afraid, he walked toward the door, which told him, "Get back!" Retreating, he then heard the sofa say, "If you sit on me, I'll kick your ass." With a sense of impending doom, intense anxiety, and momentary panic, the young man ran to the hospital where he received help.

(Allen, 1985, pp. 19–20)

As the stimulant effects of cocaine subside, the user goes through a depression-like letdown, popularly called *crashing,* a pattern that may also include headaches, dizziness, and fainting (Gorelick, 2017). For occasional users, the aftereffects usually disappear within 24 hours, but they may last longer for people who have taken a particularly high dose. These people may sink into a stupor, deep sleep, or, in some cases, coma.

Ingesting Cocaine In the past, cocaine use and impact were limited by the drug's high cost. Moreover, cocaine was usually snorted, a form of ingestion that has less powerful effects than either smoking or injection (NIDA, 2016; Haile, 2012). Since 1984, however, the availability of newer, more powerful, and sometimes cheaper forms of cocaine has produced an enormous increase in the use of the drug. For example, many people now ingest cocaine by **freebasing,** a technique in which the pure cocaine basic alkaloid is chemically separated, or "freed," from processed cocaine, vaporized by heat from a flame, and inhaled through a pipe.

Millions more people use **crack,** a powerful form of freebase cocaine that has been boiled down into crystalline balls. It is smoked with a special pipe and makes a crackling sound as it is inhaled (hence the name). Crack is sold in small quantities at a fairly low cost. Back in the 1980s, its affordability led to an epidemic of use among people who previously could not have afforded cocaine, primarily those in poor, urban areas (Turner, 2017; Acosta et al., 2011, 2005). Although the prevalence of crack use has declined over the past two decades, around .3 percent of all people over the age of 11 (almost 1 million individuals) have used it within the past year (SAMHSA, 2017; NSDUH, 2016).

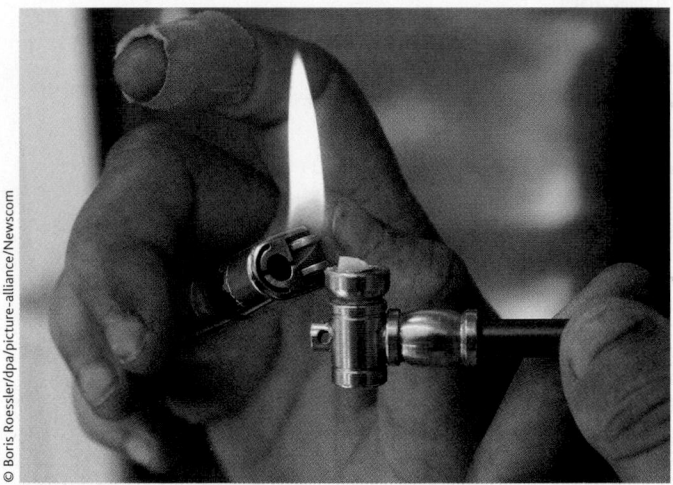

Smoking crack Crack, a powerful form of freebase cocaine, is produced by boiling cocaine down into crystalline balls and is smoked with a crack pipe.

© Boris Roessler/dpa/picture-alliance/Newscom

What Are the Dangers of Cocaine? Aside from cocaine's harmful effects on behavior, cognition, and emotion, the drug poses serious physical dangers (Chang, 2017; Mechem, 2016). The growth in the use of the powerful forms of cocaine has caused the annual number of cocaine-related emergency room incidents in the United States to multiply more than 125 times since 1982, from around 4,000 cases to 505,000 (Gorelick, 2017). Cocaine use has also been linked to many suicides.

The greatest danger of cocaine use is an overdose (Nelson & Odujebe, 2017). Excessive doses have a strong effect on the respiratory center of the brain, at first stimulating it and then depressing it to the point where breathing may stop. Cocaine can also create major, even fatal, heart irregularities or brain seizures that bring breathing or heart functioning to a sudden stop (Mechem, 2016; Morgan, 2015). In addition, pregnant women who use cocaine run the risk of having a miscarriage and of having children with predispositions to later drug use and with abnormalities in immune functioning, attention and learning, thyroid size, and dopamine and serotonin activity in the brain (Jansson, 2017; Minnes et al., 2014).

SMOKING, TOBACCO, AND NICOTINE

Around **24%** percent of all Americans over the age of 11 regularly smoke tobacco—a total of **63 million** people (NSDUH, 2017).

Similarly, **20%** of the world population over 11 smoke regularly—a total of **1.1 billion** people (WHO, 2017).

WHO SMOKES REGULARLY IN THE UNITED STATES?

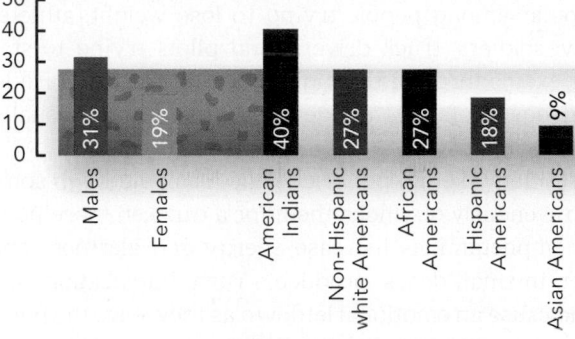

Category	%
Males	31%
Females	19%
American Indians	40%
Non-Hispanic white Americans	27%
African Americans	27%
Hispanic Americans	18%
Asian Americans	9%
Age 12–17	5%
Age 18–25	30%
Age 26 +	25%
Some high school	32%
High school graduate	33%
Some college	28%
College graduate	14%
Employed people	24%
Unemployed people	42%

(NSDUH, 2017)

SMOKING AND HEALTH

480,000 Annual U.S. deaths caused by smoking-related diseases

7 million Annual worldwide deaths caused by smoking-related diseases

41,000 Annual U.S. deaths caused by secondhand cigarette smoke

890,000 Annual worldwide deaths caused by secondhand cigarette smoke

(CDC, 2017, 2016; WHO, 2017)

WHY DO PEOPLE CONTINUE TO SMOKE?

As many as 75% of smokers keep smoking because they are addicted to **nicotine**, the active substance in tobacco (WHO, 2017, 2014). Nicotine is a stimulant of the central nervous system that acts on the same neurotransmitters and reward centers in the brain as amphetamines and cocaine. It is as addictive as those drugs and heroin. Smokers addicted to nicotine are said to have **tobacco use disorder** (APA, 2013).

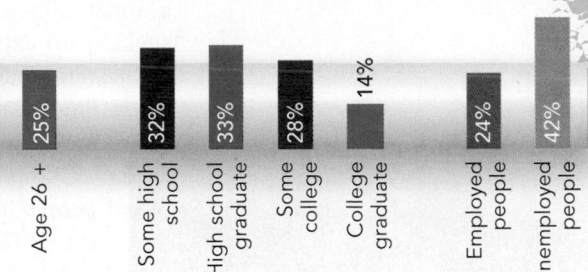

U.S. smokers with tobacco use disorder: 28.9 million

Worldwide smokers with tobacco use disorder: 770 million

10.7% ←→ population (over 11 years old) →→ 15.1%

(NSDUH, 2017; WHO, 2017, 2014)

QUITTING SMOKING

More and more smokers try to quit each year. One reason is that many studies have identified the severe health dangers smoking poses. Another is the outstanding job that health agencies have done spreading the word about these dangers. With the declining acceptability of smoking, a market for products and techniques to help people kick the habit has emerged.

Getting the Message

Teens who believe that smoking is harmful

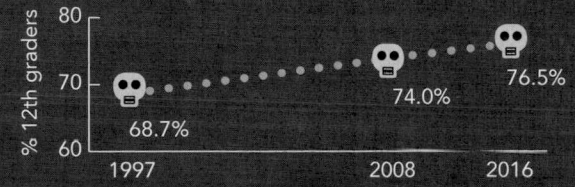

% 12th graders

1997	2008	2016
68.7%	74.0%	76.5%

(Johnston et al., 2017)

Common Aids for Quitting

NICOTINE GUM — Releases nicotine when chewed

NICOTINE PATCH — Releases nicotine through the skin

NICOTINE LOZENGES — Dissolves in the mouth and releases nicotine

NASAL SPRAY — Delivers aerosol nicotine into the nostrils

PSYCHOTROPIC DRUGS (VARENICLINE, BUPROPION, AND NORTRIPTYLINE) — Reduce craving for nicotine

SELF-HELP GROUPS — Offer psychological support

BEHAVIORAL COUNSELING — Teaches alternative behaviors

(CDC, 2017; Rigotti, 2017; Park, 2016)

Trying to Stop

% of smokers

Want to stop smoking	Make an attempt to quit each year	Eventually able to stop permanently
70%	50%	50%

(CDC, 2017, 2014; NSDUH, 2017, 2013; Rigotti, 2017)

E-Cigarettes: Battery-Operated Electronic Vaping

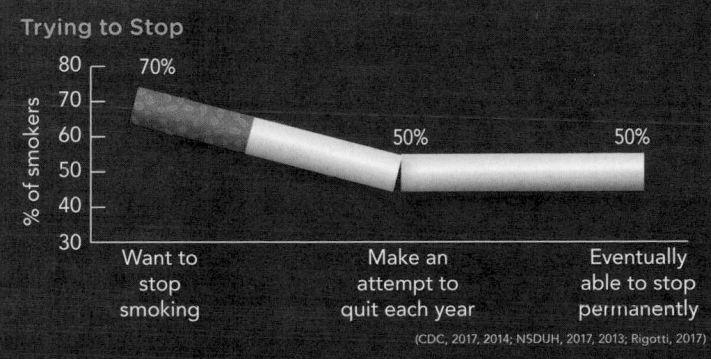

LED end glows when smoker inhales

Heater vaporizes nicotine

Smoker exhales a cloud of vapor

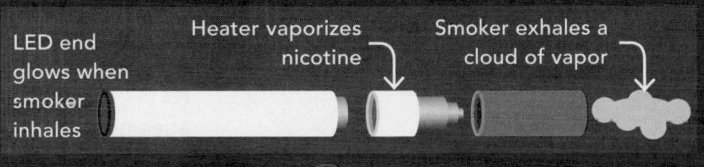

Tobacco Cigarette	vs.	E-Cigarette
Smoked by 24% of U.S. adults	○	Smoked by 4% of U.S. adults
Smoke poses biggest danger	○	No actual burning or smoke
Very addictive	○	Addiction depends on nicotine level
$117 billion annual U.S. revenues	○	$600 million annual U.S. revenues

(CDC, 2017; CSP, 2017; Maloney & Chaudhuri, 2017; Rigotti & Kalkhoran, 2017; Griffin, 2014)

Amphetamines

Amphetamines are stimulant drugs that are manufactured in the laboratory. Some common examples are amphetamine (Benzedrine), dextroamphetamine (Dexedrine), and methamphetamine (Methedrine). First produced in the 1930s to help treat asthma, amphetamines soon became popular among people trying to lose weight; athletes seeking an extra burst of energy; soldiers, truck drivers, and pilots trying to stay awake; and students studying for exams through the night (Hart & Ksir, 2015; Haile, 2012). Physicians now know the drugs are far too dangerous to be used so casually, and they prescribe them much less freely.

Amphetamines are most often taken in pill or capsule form, although some people inject the drugs intravenously or smoke them for a quicker, more powerful effect. Like cocaine, amphetamines increase energy and alertness and reduce appetite when taken in small doses; produce a rush, intoxication, and psychosis in high doses; and cause an emotional letdown as they leave the body. Also like cocaine, amphetamines stimulate the central nervous system by increasing the release of the neurotransmitters dopamine, norepinephrine, and serotonin throughout the brain, although the actions of amphetamines differ somewhat from those of cocaine (Carpenter et al., 2017; Hart & Ksir, 2015).

One kind of amphetamine, **methamphetamine** (nicknamed *crank*), has surged in popularity over the past decade and so warrants special focus. Almost 6 percent of all people over the age of 11 in the United States have used methamphetamine at least once (SAMHSA, 2017; NSDUH, 2016). Around 0.3 currently have methamphetamine use disorder. The drug is available in the form of crystals (also known by the street names *ice* and *crystal meth*), which users smoke.

Most of the nonmedical methamphetamine in the United States is made in small "stovetop laboratories," which typically operate for a few days in a remote area and then move on to a new—safer—location (Boyer et al., 2017). Such laboratories have been around since the 1960s, but they have increased eightfold—in number, production, and in being confiscated by authorities—this century. A major health concern is that the secret laboratories expel dangerous fumes and residue.

Since 1989, when the media first began reporting about the dangers of smoking methamphetamine crystals, the rise in usage has been dramatic. Until recently, it had been much more prevalent in western parts of the United States, but its use has now spread east as well. Methamphetamine-linked emergency room visits are rising in hospitals throughout all parts of the country (SAMHSA, 2017; NSDUH, 2016).

Methamphetamine is about as likely to be used by women as men. Around 40 percent of current users are women (Paulus, 2017). The drug is popular today among a wide range of people, from biker gangs to rural Americans to urban gay communities, and it has gained wide use as a "club drug," the term for those drugs that regularly find their way to all-night dance parties, or "raves" (Nordqvist, 2016; Hopfer, 2011).

Like other kinds of amphetamines, methamphetamine increases activity of the neurotransmitters dopamine, serotonin, and norepinephrine, producing increased arousal, attention, and related effects (Paulus, 2017). It can have serious negative effects on a user's physical, mental, and social life. Of particular concern is that it damages nerve endings, a problem called *neurotoxicity* (Moszczynska & Callan, 2017). But users focus more on methamphetamine's immediate positive impact, including perceptions by many that it makes them feel hypersexual and uninhibited (Paulus, 2017).

DON'T LET DRUG DEALERS CHANGE THE FACE OF YOUR NEIGHBOURHOOD.
Call Crimestoppers anonymously on 0800 555 111.

Methamphetamine dependence: Spreading the word This powerful ad shows the degenerative effects of methamphetamine addiction on a woman over a 4-year period—from age 36 in the top photo to age 40 in the bottom one.

Stimulant Use Disorder

Regular use of either cocaine or amphetamines may lead to *stimulant use disorder*. The stimulant comes to dominate the person's life, and the person may remain under the drug's effects much of each day and function poorly in social relationships and at work. People may develop tolerance and withdrawal reactions to the drug—in order to gain the desired effects, they must take higher doses, and when they stop taking it, they may go through deep depression, fatigue, sleep problems, irritability, and anxiety (Gorelick, 2017, NIDA, 2016). These withdrawal symptoms can last for weeks or even months after drug use has ended. In a given year, 0.1 percent of all people over the age of 11 years display stimulant use disorder that is centered on cocaine, and 0.3 percent display stimulant use disorder centered on amphetamines (SAMHSA, 2017; NSDUH, 2016).

Caffeine

Caffeine is the world's most widely used stimulant. Around 90 percent of the world's population consumes it daily (Bordeaux & Lieberman, 2017). Most of this caffeine is taken in the form of coffee (from the coffee bean); the rest is consumed in tea (from the tea leaf), cola (from the kola nut), so-called *energy drinks,* chocolate (from the cocoa bean), and numerous prescription and over-the-counter medications, such as Excedrin.

Around 99 percent of ingested caffeine is absorbed by the body and reaches its peak concentration within an hour. It acts as a stimulant of the central nervous system, again producing a release of the neurotransmitters dopamine, serotonin, and norepinephrine in the brain. Thus it raises a person's arousal and motor activity, enhances physical stamina, and reduces fatigue. It can also disrupt mood, fine motor movement, and reaction time and may interfere with sleep (McLellan et al., 2016; Juliano et al., 2011). At high doses, it increases gastric acid secretions in the stomach and the rate of breathing.

More than 250 milligrams of caffeine (that is, two to three cups of brewed coffee, six cans of cola, or three cans of Red Bull or a comparable energy drink) can produce caffeine intoxication, which may include such symptoms as restlessness, nervousness, anxiety, stomach disturbances, twitching, and a faster heart rate (Bordeaux & Lieberman, 2017; Juliano et al., 2011; Paton & Beer, 2001). Doses larger than 10 grams of caffeine (about 100 cups of coffee) can cause grand mal seizures and fatal respiratory failure.

Many people who suddenly stop or cut back on their usual intake of caffeine—even those whose regular consumption is low (two and a half cups of coffee daily or seven cans of cola)—have withdrawal symptoms (Bordeaux & Lieberman, 2017; Juliano & Griffiths, 2004). A breakthrough study on this subject had adult participants consume their usual caffeine-filled drinks and foods for 2 days, then abstain from all caffeine-containing foods for 2 days while taking placebo pills that they thought contained caffeine, and then abstain from such foods for 2 days while taking actual caffeine pills (Silverman et al., 1992). More participants had headaches (52 percent), depression (11 percent), anxiety (8 percent), and fatigue (8 percent) during the 2-day placebo period than during the caffeine periods. In addition, people used more unauthorized medications (13 percent) and performed experimental tasks more slowly during the placebo period than during the caffeine periods.

Although DSM-5 acknowledges that many people go through caffeine intoxication and caffeine withdrawal, it does not go so far as to list *caffeine use disorder* as an official category (APA, 2013). Instead, it views this disorder as a condition that may warrant official classification in a future edition of the DSM, depending on the outcome of future studies. If added to the DSM, the key criteria for this disorder would be a 1-year pattern of problematic caffeine use, unsuccessful efforts to reduce caffeine use, awareness that one's continued caffeine use is causing a repeated physical or psychological problem, withdrawal symptoms if one stops caffeine use, and significant impairment or distress.

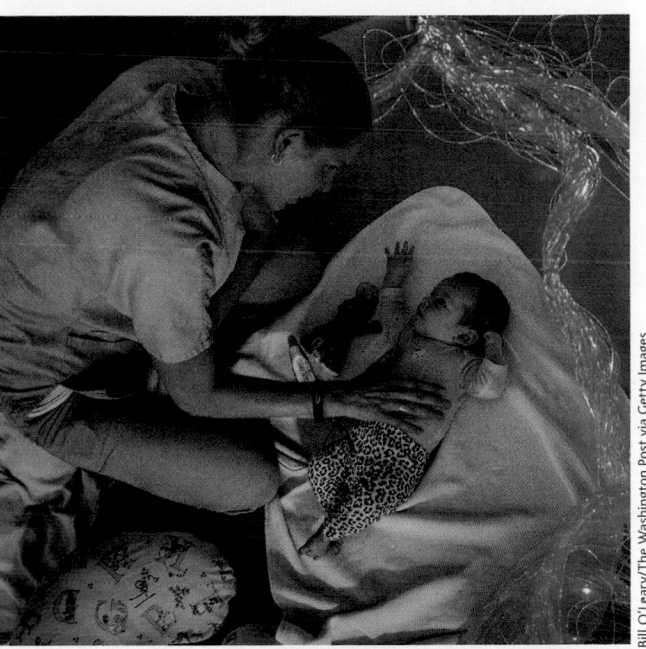

Bill O'Leary/The Washington Post via Getty Images

Addicted at birth Babies of mothers who have opioid or stimulant use disorders during pregnancy may be born with significant physical and psychological problems, including drug addiction. Here, at a pediatric hospital that specializes in weaning newborns off of heroin and methadone, a recreational therapist examines one such infant.

amphetamine A stimulant drug that is manufactured in the laboratory.

methamphetamine A powerful amphetamine drug that has surged in popularity in recent years, posing major health and law enforcement problems

caffeine The world's most widely used stimulant, most often consumed in coffee.

"Nowadays, Hal is ninety-nine per cent caffeine-free."

Mort Gerberg/The New Yorker Collection/The Cartoon Bank

Investigators often assess caffeine's impact by measuring coffee consumption, yet coffee also contains other chemicals that may be dangerous to a person's health. Thus research has really not clarified whether regular caffeine consumption can contribute to significant medical problems. In particular, concerns about possible ties between repeated high doses of caffeine and heart disease, cancer, infertility, or pregnancy outcomes have not been clearly supported in various studies (Bordeaux & Lieberman, 2017; Nisenblat & Norman, 2016; Juliano et al., 2011).

Hallucinogens, Cannabis, and Combinations of Substances

OTHER KINDS OF SUBSTANCES MAY also cause problems for their users and for society. *Hallucinogens* produce delusions, hallucinations, and other sensory changes. *Cannabis* produces sensory changes, but it also has depressant and stimulant effects, and so it is considered apart from hallucinogens in DSM-5. And many people take *combinations of substances.*

Hallucinogens

Hallucinogens are substances that cause powerful changes in sensory perception, from strengthening a person's normal perceptions to inducing illusions and hallucinations. They produce sensations so out of the ordinary that they are sometimes called "trips." The trips may be exciting or frightening, depending on how a person's mind interacts with the drugs. Also called *psychedelic drugs,* the hallucinogens include LSD, mescaline, psilocybin, and MDMA (Ecstasy) (see *PsychWatch*). Many of these substances come from plants or animals; others are produced in laboratories.

> Why do various club drugs (for example, Ecstasy and crystal meth), often used at "raves," fall in and out of favor rather quickly?

LSD (lysergic acid diethylamide), one of the most famous and most powerful hallucinogens, was derived by Swiss chemist Albert Hoffman in 1938 from a group of naturally occurring drugs called *ergot alkaloids.* During the 1960s, a decade of social rebellion and experimentation, millions of people turned to the drug as a way of expanding their experience. Within 2 hours of being swallowed, LSD brings on a

hallucinogen A substance that causes powerful changes primarily in sensory perception, including strengthening perceptions and producing illusions and hallucinations. Also called a *psychedelic drug.*

LSD (lysergic acid diethylamide) A hallucinogenic drug derived from ergot alkaloids.

Club Drugs: X Marks the (Wrong) Spot

You probably know of the drug *MDMA (3,4-methylenedioxymeth-amphetamine)* by its common street name, *Ecstasy.* It is also known as X, Adam, hug, beans, and love drug. This laboratory-produced drug is technically a *stimulant,* similar to amphetamines, but it also produces hallucinogenic effects and so is often considered a *hallucinogenic* drug (Litjens et al., 2014; McDowell, 2011, 2005). MDMA was developed as far back as 1910, but only in the past 25 years has it gained life as a club drug. Today, in the United States alone, consumers collectively take hundreds of thousands of doses of MDMA weekly (Johnston et al., 2017). Altogether, 18 million Americans over the age of 11 have now tried MDMA at least once in their lifetime, 1.5 million in the past year (SAMHSA, 2017; NSDUH, 2016). Around 3.6 percent of all high school seniors have used it within the past year (Johnston et al., 2017).

What is Ecstasy's allure? As a stimulant and hallucinogen, it helps to raise the mood of many partygoers and provides them with an energy boost that enables them to keep dancing and partying. It may also produce strong feelings of attachment and connectedness in users. However, it can be a dangerous drug, particularly when taken repeatedly.

What Are the Dangers of Using Ecstasy?

As MDMA has become more widely used, it has received more research scrutiny. As it turns out, the mood and energy lift produced by MDMA comes at a high price (Fonseca et al., 2018; Baggott et al., 2016; Parrott et al., 2014; Wiegand et al., 2008). The problems that the drug may cause include the following:

- Immediate psychological problems such as confusion, depression, sleep difficul-

Feeling the effects
Shortly after taking MDMA at a rave, this couple manifests a shift in mood, energy, and behavior.

Scott Houston/Polaris

ties, severe anxiety, and paranoid thinking. These symptoms may also continue for weeks after ingestion of MDMA.

- Significant impairment of memory and other cognitive skills.

- Physical symptoms such as muscle tension, nausea, blurred vision, faintness, and chills or sweating.

- Increases in heart rate and blood pressure, which place people with heart disease at special risk.

- Reduced sweat production. At a hot, crowded dance party, taking Ecstasy can even cause heat stroke, or *hyperthermia.* Users generally try to remedy this problem by drinking lots of water, but since the body cannot sweat under the drug's influence, the excess fluid intake can result in an equally perilous condition known as *hyponatremia,* or "water intoxication."

- Potential liver damage.

How Does MDMA Operate in the Brain?

MDMA works by causing the neurotransmitters *serotonin* and (to a lesser extent) *dopamine* to be released all at once through-

out the brain, at first increasing and then depleting a person's overall supply of the neurotransmitters. MDMA also interferes with the body's ability to produce new supplies of serotonin. With repeated use, the brain eventually produces less and less serotonin (Cadoni et al., 2017; Mercer et al., 2017; Lizarraga et al., 2014; McDowell, 2011, 2005). Ecstasy's impact on these neurotransmitters accounts for its various psychological effects and associated problems.

End of the Honeymoon?

The dangers of MDMA do not yet seem to outweigh its pleasures in the minds of many people. Although it is no longer used as much as it was in the early 2000s, MDMA seems to have regained considerable popularity in recent years—particularly in the form of "Molly," marketed as pure MDMA—finding its way back to raves, dance clubs, and various college settings (Johnston et al., 2017; Palamar et al., 2017). Clearly, despite the research results, the honeymoon for MDMA is not yet over.

state of *hallucinogen intoxication,* sometimes called *hallucinosis,* marked by a general strengthening of perceptions, particularly visual perceptions, along with psychological changes and physical symptoms. People may focus on small details—the pores of the skin, for example, or individual blades of grass. Colors may seem enhanced or take on a shade of purple. People may have illusions in which objects seem distorted and appear to move, breathe, or change shape. A person under the influence of LSD may also hallucinate—seeing people, objects, or forms that are not actually present.

Lingering popularity Although less popular than in the 1960s, LSD continues to be a drug of some favor, especially among younger people at many raves, rock concerts, and similar events. This participant at the annual Burning Man art festival in Nevada's Black Rock Desert has a message written on her back that leaves no doubt about how important the drug is to her.

Hallucinosis may also cause one to hear sounds more clearly, feel tingling or numbness in the limbs, or confuse the sensations of hot and cold. Some people have been badly burned after touching flames that felt cool to them under the influence of LSD. The drug may also cause different senses to cross, an effect called *synesthesia*. Colors, for example, may be "heard" or "felt."

LSD can also induce strong emotions, from joy to anxiety or depression. The perception of time may slow dramatically. Long-forgotten thoughts and feelings may resurface. Physical symptoms can include sweating, palpitations, blurred vision, tremors, and poor coordination. All of these effects take place while the user is fully awake and alert, and they wear off in about 6 hours.

It seems that LSD produces these symptoms primarily by binding to some of the neurons that normally receive the neurotransmitter *serotonin,* changing the neurotransmitter's activity at those sites (Delgado, 2017). These neurons ordinarily help the brain send visual information and control emotions (as you saw in Chapter 7); thus LSD's activity there produces various visual and emotional symptoms.

More than 15 percent of all people in the United States have used LSD or another hallucinogen at some point in their lives. Around 0.5 percent, or 1.2 million people, are currently using them (SAMHSA, 2017; NSDUH, 2016). Although people do not usually develop tolerance to LSD or have withdrawal symptoms when they stop taking it, the drug poses dangers for both one-time and long-term users. It is so powerful that any dose, no matter how small, is likely to produce enormous perceptual, emotional, and behavioral reactions. Sometimes the reactions are extremely unpleasant—a so-called bad trip (when LSD users injure themselves or others, for instance, they are usually in the midst of a bad trip). Witness, for example, this description of a young woman who took LSD during the 1960s when so many people thought of the drug as a problem-free mind expander, only to learn about its dark side through personal use:

 A 21-year-old woman was admitted to the hospital along with her lover. He had had a number of LSD experiences and had convinced her to take it to make her less constrained sexually. About half an hour after ingestion of approximately 200 microgm., she noticed that the bricks in the wall began to go in and out and that light affected her strangely. She became frightened when she realized that she was unable to distinguish her body from the chair she was sitting on or from her lover's body. Her fear became more marked after she thought that she would not get back into herself. At the time of admission she was hyperactive and laughed inappropriately. Her stream of talk was illogical and affect labile. Two days later, this reaction had ceased.

(Frosch, Robbins, & Stern, 1965)

Another danger is the long-term effect that LSD may have. Some users eventually develop psychosis or a mood or anxiety disorder. And a number have *flashbacks*—a recurrence of the sensory and emotional changes after the LSD has left the body. Flashbacks may occur days or even months after the last LSD experience (Delgado, 2017).

Cannabis

Cannabis sativa, the hemp plant, grows in warm climates throughout the world. The drugs produced from varieties of hemp are, as a group, called **cannabis.** The most powerful of them is *hashish;* the weaker ones include the best-known form of cannabis, **marijuana,** a mixture derived from the buds, crushed leaves, and flowering tops of hemp plants. More than 22 million people over the age of 11 (8.3 percent of the population) currently smoke marijuana at least monthly (SAMHSA, 2017; NSDUH, 2016).

Each of the cannabis drugs is found in various strengths because the potency of a cannabis drug is greatly affected by the climate in which the plant is grown, the way it was prepared, and the manner and duration of its storage. Of the several hundred

cannabis drugs Drugs produced from the varieties of the hemp plant *Cannabis sativa.* They cause a mixture of hallucinogenic, depressant, and stimulant effects.

marijuana One of the cannabis drugs, derived from the buds, leaves, and flowering tops of the hemp plant *Cannabis sativa.*

tetrahydrocannabinol (THC) The main active ingredient of cannabis substances.

active chemicals in cannabis, **tetrahydrocannabinol (THC)** appears to be the one most responsible for its effects. The higher the THC content, the more powerful the cannabis; hashish contains a large portion, while marijuana's is small.

When smoked, cannabis produces a mixture of hallucinogenic, depressant, and stimulant effects (Wang, 2016). At low doses, the smoker typically has feelings of joy and relaxation and may become either quiet or talkative. Some smokers, however, become anxious, suspicious, or irritated, especially if they have been in a bad mood or are smoking in an upsetting environment. Many smokers report sharpened perceptions and fascination with the intensified sounds and sights around them. Time seems to slow down, and distances and sizes seem greater than they actually are. This overall "high" is technically called *cannabis intoxication*. Physical changes include reddening of the eyes, fast heartbeat, increases in blood pressure and appetite, dryness in the mouth, and dizziness. Some people become drowsy and may fall asleep.

In high doses, cannabis produces odd visual experiences, changes in body image, and hallucinations. Smokers may become confused or impulsive. Some worry that other people are trying to hurt them. Most of the effects of cannabis last 2 to 6 hours. The changes in mood, however, may continue longer.

Cannabis Use Disorder

Until the early 1970s, the use of marijuana, the weak form of cannabis, rarely led to a pattern of *cannabis use disorder*. Today, however, many people, including large numbers of high school students, are developing the disorder, getting high on marijuana regularly and finding their social and occupational or academic lives very much affected (Kerridge et al., 2018) (see **Figure 12-3**). Many regular users also develop a tolerance for marijuana and may feel restless and irritable and have flulike symptoms when they stop smoking (Gorelick, 2016). Around 4 million people, 1.5 percent of all teenagers and adults in the United States, have displayed cannabis use disorder within the past year (SAMHSA, 2017; NSDUH, 2016).

Why have more and more marijuana users developed cannabis use disorder over the past three decades? Mainly because marijuana has changed. The marijuana widely available in the United States today is at least four times more powerful than that used in the early 1970s. The average THC content of today's marijuana is 8 percent, compared with 2 percent in the late 1960s. Marijuana is now grown in places with a hot, dry climate, which increases the THC content.

Is Marijuana Dangerous?

As the strength and use of marijuana have increased, researchers have discovered that smoking it may pose certain dangers (Wang, 2016; Price, 2011). It occasionally causes panic reactions similar to the ones caused by hallucinogens, and some smokers may fear they are losing their minds. Typically such reactions end in 2 to 6 hours, along with marijuana's other effects.

The source of marijuana Marijuana is made from the leaves of the hemp plant, *Cannabis sativa*, such as the plants being cultivated in this grow room at a medical marijuana dispensary in Massachusetts. *Cannabis sativa* is grown in a wide range of altitudes, climates, and soils.

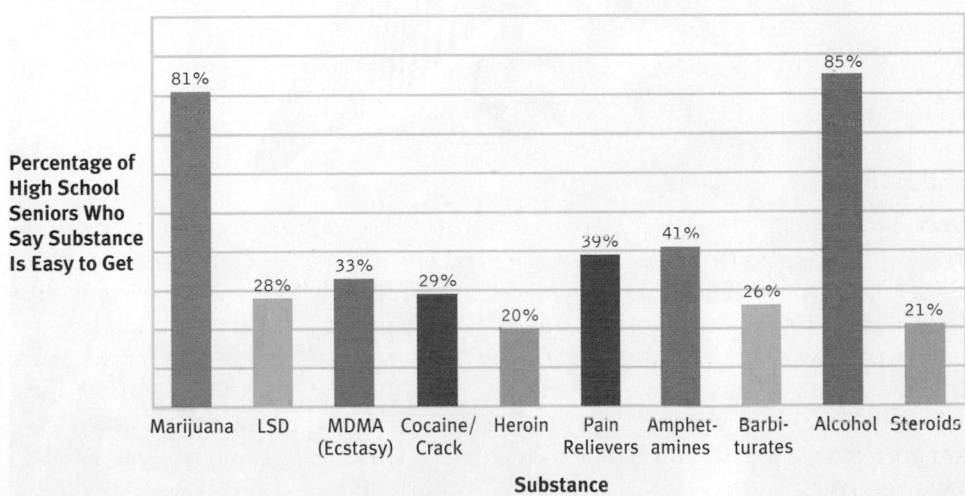

Percentage of High School Seniors Who Say Substance Is Easy to Get

Substance	%
Marijuana	81%
LSD	28%
MDMA (Ecstasy)	33%
Cocaine/Crack	29%
Heroin	20%
Pain Relievers	39%
Amphetamines	41%
Barbiturates	26%
Alcohol	85%
Steroids	21%

FIGURE 12-3

How Easy Is It for Teenagers to Acquire Substances?

Most surveyed high school seniors say it is easy to get alcohol and marijuana, and more than a third say it is easy to get amphetamines, pain relievers, and Ecstasy. (Information from: Johnston et al., 2017.)

#ChangingCourse

In 1907, California was the first state to declare marijuana a poison and to criminalize its sale or possession.

In 1996, California was the first state to legalize medical marijuana.

In 2016, California was the fifth state to legalize recreational marijuana.

Because marijuana can interfere with the performance of complex sensorimotor tasks and with cognitive functioning, it has caused many automobile accidents (Wang, 2016; Brady & Li, 2014). And, indeed, 4 percent of adults have driven while under the influence of marijuana at least once during the past year (SAMHSA, 2017; NSDUH, 2016). Furthermore, people on a marijuana high often fail to remember information, especially anything that has been recently learned, no matter how hard they try to concentrate; thus heavy marijuana smokers are at a serious disadvantage at school or work (Gorelick, 2016; Budney et al., 2011).

One study compared blood flow in the brain arteries of chronic marijuana users and nonusers (Herning et al., 2005). After one month of abstinence from smoking marijuana, chronic users continued to have higher blood flow than nonusers. Though still higher than normal, the blood flow of light marijuana users (fewer than 16 smokes per week) and of moderate users (fewer than 70 smokes per week) did improve somewhat over the course of the abstinence month. The blood flow of heavy users, however, showed no improvement. This lingering effect may help explain the memory and thinking problems of chronic heavy users of marijuana.

There are research indications that regular marijuana smoking may also lead to long-term health problems (Gorelick, 2016; Hartney, 2014; Pletcher et al., 2012). It may, for example, contribute to lung disease, although there is considerable debate on this issue. Some studies suggest that marijuana smoking reduces the ability to expel air from the lungs, perhaps even more than tobacco smoking does. Another concern is the effect of regular marijuana smoking on human reproduction. Studies since the late 1970s have discovered lower sperm counts in men who are chronic smokers and abnormal ovulation in women who are chronic smokers.

Efforts to educate the public about the dangers of repeated marijuana use appeared to have paid off throughout the 1980s. The percentage of high school seniors who smoked marijuana on a daily basis decreased from 11 percent in 1978 to 2 percent in 1992. Today, however, 6 percent of high school seniors smoke it daily, and 69 percent of seniors do not believe that regular use poses a great risk (Johnston et al., 2017).

Cannabis and Society: A Rocky Relationship For centuries, cannabis played a respected role in medicine. It was recommended as a surgical anesthetic by Chinese physicians 2,000 years ago and was used in other lands to treat cholera, malaria, coughs, insomnia, and rheumatism. When cannabis entered the United States in the early twentieth century, mainly in the form of marijuana, it was likewise used

Creative protesting People hold a huge cannabis cigarette, or "joint," during a march in Brazil calling for the legalization of marijuana—for both medical and recreational uses.

for various medical purposes. Soon, however, more effective medicines replaced it, and the favorable view of cannabis began to change. Marijuana began to be used as a recreational drug, and its illegal distribution became a law enforcement problem. Authorities assumed it was highly dangerous and outlawed the "killer weed."

In the 1980s, researchers developed precise techniques for measuring THC and for extracting pure THC from cannabis; they also developed laboratory forms of THC. These inventions opened the door to new medical applications for cannabis (Wang, 2016), such as its use in treating glaucoma, a severe eye disease. Cannabis was also found to help patients with chronic pain or asthma, to reduce the nausea and vomiting of cancer patients in chemotherapy, and to improve the appetites of people with AIDS and so help them combat weight loss.

In light of these findings, several interest groups campaigned during the late 1980s for the *medical legalization* of marijuana, which operates on the brain and body more quickly than the THC capsules developed in the laboratory. Government agencies resisted this movement, saying prescriptions for pure THC served all needed medical functions. However, medical marijuana advocates pressed on, and in 2009 the U.S. Attorney General directed federal prosecutors to not pursue cases against medical marijuana users or their caregivers who are complying with state laws. Currently, 29 states (plus Washington, D.C., Guam, and Puerto Rico) have laws allowing marijuana to be used for medical purposes, and several more have such laws pending (NCSL, 2017). Medical marijuana is now legal in about a dozen countries (Gorelick, 2016).

Heartened by such developments in the realm of medical marijuana, the U.S. movement to legalize the *recreational* use of marijuana has gained enormous momentum in recent years. In fact, since 2012 residents in eight states have voted to legalize marijuana for use of any kind—although such state measures still can be blocked by the federal government (Robinson, 2017). Moreover, according to recent polls, 57 percent believe that marijuana should be made legal, up from 12 percent in 1969 and 41 percent in 2010 (Pew Research Center, 2016). In such polls, more than half of all respondents acknowledge they have tried marijuana and most say that the federal government should not enforce federal antimarijuana laws in states where marijuana is legal. Several other countries have moved faster than the United States with regard to the recreational use of marijuana. In 2017, for example, Canada's prime minister introduced legislation to completely legalize marijuana as a consumer product, for any purpose—legislation that is expected to allow legal sales throughout the country by the middle of 2018 (Austen, 2017).

Choosing carefully A woman shops at a licensed marijuana dispensary in Oregon. In 2015, Oregon became one of several states to legalize the purchase of limited amounts of recreational marijuana.

Josh Edelson/AFP/Getty Images

Combinations of Substances

Because people often take more than one drug at a time, a pattern called *polysubstance use*, researchers have studied the ways in which drugs interact with one another (Jarlenski et al., 2017; Anthony et al., 2016). Two important discoveries have emerged from this work: the phenomena of *cross-tolerance* and *synergistic effects*.

Sometimes two or more drugs are so similar in their actions on the brain and the body that as people build a tolerance for one drug, they are simultaneously developing a tolerance for the other, even if they have never taken the latter. Correspondingly, users who display **cross-tolerance** can reduce the symptoms of withdrawal from one drug by taking the other (Adams, 2017). Alcohol and antianxiety drugs are cross-tolerant, for example, so it is sometimes possible to reduce the alcohol withdrawal reaction of delirium tremens by administering benzodiazepines, along with vitamins and electrolytes (Hart & Ksir, 2015).

cross-tolerance Tolerance for a substance one has not taken before as a result of using another substance similar to it.

synergistic effect In pharmacology, an increase of effects that occurs when more than one substance is acting on the body at the same time.

When different drugs are in the body at the same time, they may *multiply*, or potentiate, each other's effects. The combined impact, called a **synergistic effect,** is often greater than the sum of the effects of each drug taken alone: a small dose of one drug mixed with a small dose of another can produce an enormous change in body chemistry.

One kind of synergistic effect occurs when two or more drugs have *similar actions* (Buckley et al., 2017). For instance, alcohol, benzodiazepines, barbiturates, and opioids—all depressants—may severely depress the central nervous system when mixed (Anthony et al., 2016). Combining them, even in small doses, can lead to extreme intoxication, coma, and even death. A young man may have just a few alcoholic drinks at a party, for example, and shortly afterward takes a moderate dose of barbiturates to help him fall asleep. He believes he has acted with restraint and good judgment—yet he may never wake up.

A different kind of synergistic effect results when drugs have *opposite*, or *antagonistic, actions.* Stimulant drugs, for example, interfere with the liver's usual disposal of barbiturates and alcohol. Thus people who combine barbiturates or alcohol with cocaine or amphetamines may build up toxic, even lethal, levels of the depressant drugs in their systems. Students who take amphetamines to help them study late into the night and then take barbiturates to help them fall asleep are unknowingly placing themselves in serious danger.

Each year tens of thousands of people are admitted to hospitals with a multiple-drug emergency, and several thousand of them die (SAMHSA, 2017; NSDUH, 2016). Sometimes the cause is carelessness or ignorance. Often, however, people use multiple drugs precisely because they enjoy the synergistic effects (Patrick et al., 2018). In fact, as many as 90 percent of those who use one illegal drug are also using another to some extent (Jarlenski et al., 2017; Rosenthal & Levounis, 2011, 2005).

Fans mourn the deaths of many celebrities who have died from polysubstance use. In the past several years, for example, medical examiners have found multiple drugs in the bodies of actress Carrie Fisher, actor Philip Seymour Hoffman, *Glee* star Cory Monteith, and singers Whitney Houston and Michael Jackson—mixtures that may have contributed to their deaths. In the more distant past, Elvis Presley's delicate balancing act of stimulants and depressants, Janis Joplin's mixtures of wine and heroin, and John Belushi's and Chris Farley's liking for the combined effect of cocaine and opioids ("speedballs") each ended in tragedy.

> Who has more impact on the drug behaviors of teenagers and young adults: rock performers who speak out against drugs or rock performers who praise drugs?

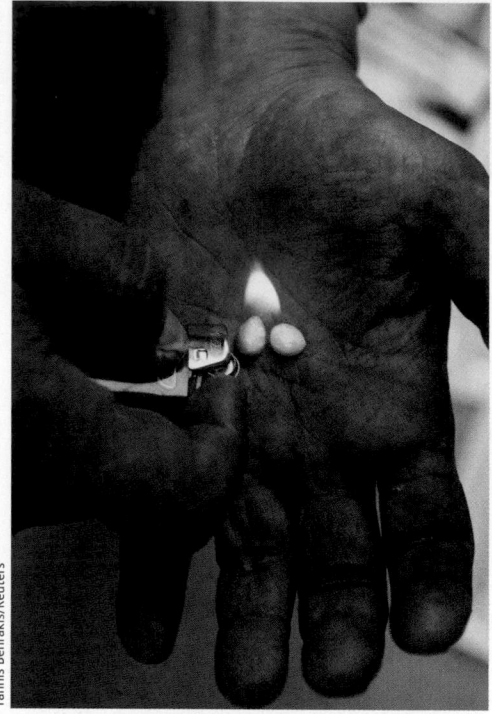

Easy to make, dangerous to take A drug user in Greece prepares a cocktail known as a speedball, a mixture of cocaine and heroin. The pink capsule in her hand contains heroin and the blue one contains cocaine. Speedballs have been linked to numerous polysubstance deaths.

Yannis Behrakis/Reuters

What Causes Substance Use Disorders?

CLINICAL THEORISTS HAVE DEVELOPED sociocultural, psychological, and biological explanations for why people develop substance use disorders. No single explanation, however, has gained broad support. Like so many other disorders, excessive and chronic drug use is increasingly viewed as the result of a combination of these factors.

Sociocultural Views

A number of sociocultural theorists propose that people are most likely to develop substance use disorders when they live under stressful socioeconomic conditions. Studies have found that regions with higher unemployment levels have higher rates of alcohol or opioid use disorder (Khazan, 2017; Marsiglia & Smith, 2010). Similarly, people in lower socioeconomic classes have rates of substance use disorder that are

Steven Rubin/The Image Works

Common substance, uncommon danger
A 13-year-old boy sniffs glue as he lies dazed near a garbage heap. In the United States, at least 6 percent of all people have tried to get high by inhaling the hydrocarbons found in common substances such as glue, gasoline, paint thinner, cleaners, and spray-can propellants (APA, 2013). Such behavior may lead to *inhalant use disorder* and poses a number of serious medical dangers.

higher than those of the other classes. In a related vein, 18 percent of unemployed adults currently use an illegal drug, compared with 11 percent of full-time employed workers and 13 percent of part-time employees (SAMHSA, 2017; NSDUH, 2016).

Sociocultural theorists hold that people confronted regularly by other kinds of stress also have a heightened risk of developing substance use disorders. A range of studies conducted with Hispanic and African American people, for example, find higher rates of substance use disorders among those participants who live or work in environments of particularly intense discrimination (Thompson, Goodman, & Kwate, 2016; Clark, 2014; Hurd et al., 2014).

Still other sociocultural theorists propose that people are more likely to develop substance use disorders if they are part of a family or social environment in which substance use is valued or at least accepted (Washburn et al., 2014). Researchers have learned that problem drinking is more common among teenagers whose parents and peers drink, as well as among teenagers whose family environments are stressful and unsupportive (Calhoun et al., 2018; Wilens et al., 2014; Andrews & Hops, 2010). Moreover, lower rates of alcoholism are found among Jews and Protestants, groups in which drinking is typically acceptable only as long as it remains within clear limits, whereas alcoholism rates are higher among the Irish and Eastern Europeans, who do not, in general, draw as clear a line (Hart & Ksir, 2015; Ledoux et al., 2002).

> What factors might explain the finding that different ethnic, religious, and national groups have different rates of alcohol use disorder?

Psychodynamic Views

Psychodynamic theorists believe that people with substance use disorders have powerful *dependency* needs that can be traced to their early years (Bressert, 2016; Dodes & Khantzian, 2011, 2005). They suggest that when parents fail to satisfy a young child's need for nurturance, the child is likely to grow up depending excessively on others for help and comfort, trying to find the nurturance that was lacking during the early years. If this search for outside support includes experimentation with a drug, the person may well develop a dependent relationship with the substance.

Some psychodynamic theorists also believe that certain people respond to their early deprivations by developing a *substance abuse personality* that leaves them particularly prone to drug abuse. Personality inventories, patient interviews, and even animal studies have in fact indicated that individuals who abuse drugs tend to be more dependent, antisocial, impulsive, novelty-seeking, risk-taking, and depressive than other individuals (Martino et al., 2017; Hicks et al., 2014). However, these findings are correlational (at least, the findings from human studies are), and do not clarify whether such traits lead to chronic drug use or whether repeated drug use causes people to be dependent, impulsive, and the like.

In an effort to establish clearer causation, one pioneering longitudinal study measured the personality traits of a large group of nonalcoholic young men and then kept track of each man's development (Littlefield & Sher, 2010; Jones, 1971, 1968). Years later, the traits of the men who developed alcohol problems in middle age were compared with the traits of those who did not. The men who developed alcohol problems had been more impulsive as teenagers and continued to be so in middle age, a finding suggesting that impulsive men are indeed more prone to develop alcohol problems. Similarly, in various laboratory investigations, "impulsive" rats—those that generally have trouble delaying their rewards—have been found to drink more alcohol when offered it than other rats (Spoelder et al., 2017; Bari et al., 2011).

A major weakness of this line of argument is the wide range of personality traits that have been tied to substance use disorders. Different studies point to different "key" traits. Inasmuch as some people with these disorders appear to be dependent, others impulsive, and still others antisocial, researchers cannot presently conclude that any one personality trait or group of traits stands out in the development of the disorders (Garofalo & Wright, 2017; Wills & Ainette, 2010; Chassin et al., 2001).

Cognitive-Behavioral Views

According to cognitive-behavioral theorists, *operant conditioning* may play a key role in substance use disorders. They argue that the temporary reduction of tension or raising of spirits produced by a drug has a rewarding effect, thus increasing the likelihood that the user will seek this reaction again (Dennhardt et al., 2016; Urošević et al., 2015). Similarly, the rewarding effects may eventually lead users to try higher dosages or more powerful methods of ingestion (see **Table 12-3**). Beyond these conditioning explanations, cognitive-behavioral theorists further argue that such rewards eventually produce an *expectancy* that substances will be rewarding, and this expectation helps motivate people to increase drug use at times of tension (Montes et al., 2017).

In support of these views, studies have found that many people do drink more alcohol or seek heroin when they feel tense (Collins et al., 2018; Frone, 2016; Marlatt et al.,

TABLE: 12-3

Methods of Taking Substances

Method	Route	Time to Reach Brain
Inhaling	Drug in vapor form is inhaled through mouth and lungs into circulatory system	7 seconds
Snorting	Drug in powdered form is snorted into the nose. Some of the drug lands on the nasal mucous membranes, is absorbed by blood vessels, and enters the bloodstream.	4 minutes

Injection	Drug in liquid form directly enters the body through a needle. Injection may be intravenous or intramuscular (subcutaneous)
	    Intravenous
	    Intramuscular
		
		20 seconds
		4 minutes

Oral ingestion	Drug in solid or liquid form passes through esophagus and stomach and finally to the small intestines. It is absorbed by blood vessels in the intestines.	30 minutes
Other routes	Drugs can be absorbed through areas that include mucous membranes. Drugs can be placed under the tongue, inserted anally and vaginally, and administered as eye drops.	Variable

Information from: Hart & Ksir, 2015; Landry, 1994.

1975). In one study, as participants worked on a difficult anagram task, a confederate planted by the researchers unfairly criticized and belittled them. The participants were then asked to participate in an "alcohol taste task," supposedly to compare and rate alcoholic beverages. Those who had been harassed drank more alcohol during the taste task than did the control participants who had not been criticized.

In a manner of speaking, the cognitive-behavioral theorists are arguing that many people take drugs to "medicate" themselves when they feel tense. If so, one would expect higher rates of substance use disorders among people who suffer from anxiety, depression, and other such problems. And, in fact, at least 20 percent of all adults who suffer from psychological disorders also display substance use disorders (Dworkin et al., 2018; SAMHSA, 2017; NSDUH, 2016).

A number of cognitive-behavioral theorists have proposed that *classical conditioning* may also play a role in these disorders (Goltseker et al., 2017; O'Brien, 2013; O'Brien et al., 1975). As you'll remember from Chapters 3 and 5, classical conditioning occurs when two stimuli that appear close together in time become connected in a person's mind, so that eventually, the person responds similarly to each stimulus. Cues or objects present in the environment at the time a person takes a drug may act as classically conditioned stimuli and come to produce some of the same pleasure brought on by the drugs themselves. Just the sight of a hypodermic needle, drug buddy, or regular supplier, for example, has been known to comfort people who are addicted to heroin or amphetamines and to relieve their withdrawal symptoms. In a similar manner, cues or objects that are present during withdrawal distress may *produce* withdrawal-like symptoms. One man who had formerly been dependent on heroin became nauseated and had other withdrawal symptoms when he returned to the neighborhood where he had gone through withdrawal in the past—a reaction that led him to start taking heroin again. Although classical conditioning certainly appears to be at work in particular cases of substance use disorder, it has not received widespread research support as the *key* factor in such disorders.

Biological Views

Over the past few decades, researchers have become clear that biological factors play a major role in drug misuse (Volkow, Koob, & McLellan, 2016). Studies on *genetic predisposition, neurotransmitters*, and *brain circuits* have all pointed in this direction.

Genetic Predisposition For years, breeding experiments have been conducted to see whether certain animals are genetically predisposed to become addicted to drugs (Saba et al., 2015; Weiss, 2011). In several studies, for example, investigators have first identified animals that prefer alcohol to other beverages and then mated them to one another. Generally, the offspring of these animals have been found also to display an unusual preference for alcohol.

Similarly, research with human twins has suggested that people may inherit a predisposition to misuse substances (Stickel et al., 2017; Ystrom et al., 2014). Numerous studies have found an alcoholism *concordance* rate of around 50 percent in identical twins; that is, if one identical twin displays alcoholism, the other twin also does in 50 percent of the cases. In contrast, in these same studies, fraternal twins have a concordance rate of only 30 percent. As you have read, however, such findings do not rule out other interpretations. For one thing, the parenting received by two identical twins may be more similar than that received by two fraternal twins.

A clearer indication that genetics may play a role in substance use disorders comes from studies of alcoholism rates in people adopted shortly after birth (Stickel et al., 2017; Samek et al., 2014). These studies have compared adoptees whose biological parents abuse alcohol

#PopularTitles

Substance use is a popular theme in music. Hit songs include Amy Winehouse's "Rehab," the Velvet Underground's "Heroin," Evanescence's "Call Me When You're Sober," the Rolling Stones' "Sister Morphine," Snoop Dogg's "Gin and Juice," Eric Clapton's "Cocaine," Cyprus Hill's "I Wanna Get High," Eminem's "Drug Ballad," and Lil' Kim's "Drugs."

Crack cookies? Researchers at Connecticut College found that the lab-induced addiction of rats to Oreo cookies—particularly the creamy center—was as strong as their lab-induced addiction to cocaine and morphine in many ways. The study was conducted to test the growing theory that many high-fat, high-sugar foods stimulate the brain in the same ways and locations that addictive drugs do.

Photo by Bob MacDonnell, courtesy Connecticut College

reward circuit A dopamine-rich circuit in the brain that produces feelings of pleasure when activated.

with adoptees whose biological parents do not. By adulthood, the individuals whose biological parents abuse alcohol typically show higher rates of alcoholism than those with nonalcoholic biological parents.

Genetic linkage strategies and *molecular biology* techniques provide more direct evidence in support of a genetic explanation (Way et al., 2017; Pieters et al., 2012). One line of investigation has found an abnormal form of the so-called *dopamine-2 (D2) receptor gene* in a majority of research participants with substance use disorders but in less than 20 percent of participants who do not have such disorders (Blum et al., 2018, 2015, 1996, 1990). Other studies have tied still other genes to substance use disorders (Patriquin et al., 2017; Rezaei et al., 2017).

Neurotransmitters Over the past few decades, some researchers have pieced together a neurotransmitter-focused explanation of drug tolerance and withdrawal symptoms (Lohani et al., 2017; Byrne et al., 2016; Kosten et al., 2011, 2005). These theorists contend that when a particular drug is ingested, it increases the activity of certain neurotransmitters whose normal purpose is to calm, reduce pain, lift mood, or increase alertness. When a person keeps on taking the drug, the brain apparently makes an adjustment and reduces its own production of the neurotransmitters. Because the drug is increasing neurotransmitter activity or efficiency, the brain's release of the neurotransmitter is less necessary. As drug intake increases, the body's production of the neurotransmitters continues to decrease, leaving the person in need of progressively more of the drug to achieve its effects. In this way, drug takers build tolerance for a drug, becoming more and more reliant on it rather than on their own biological processes to feel comfortable, happy, or alert. If they suddenly stop taking the drug, their natural supply of neurotransmitters will be low for a time, producing the symptoms of withdrawal. Withdrawal continues until the brain resumes its normal production of the neurotransmitters.

To some extent, the abused substance dictates which neurotransmitters will be affected. Repeated and excessive use of alcohol or benzodiazepines may lower the brain's production of the neurotransmitter GABA, regular use of opioids may reduce the brain's production of endorphins, and regular use of cocaine or amphetamines may lower the brain's production of dopamine (Vaquero et al., 2017; Kosten et al., 2011, 2005). In addition, researchers have identified a neurotransmitter called *anandamide* that operates much like THC; excessive use of marijuana may reduce the production of anandamide.

The Brain's Reward Circuit The neurotransmitter-focused explanation of substance abuse helps explain why people who regularly take substances have tolerance and withdrawal reactions. But why are drugs so rewarding, and why do certain people turn to them in the first place? Brain-imaging studies conducted in recent years answer these questions by pointing to the operation of a particular brain circuit—the circuit within which the neurotransmitters under discussion do their work. As you've read earlier, a brain circuit is a network of brain structures that work together, triggering each other into action to produce a distinct behavioral, cognitive, or emotional reaction. The circuit that has been tied to substance misuse is the **reward circuit**, also called the *reward center* and the *pleasure pathway* (Volkow et al., 2016).

Apparently, whenever a person ingests a substance (from foods to drugs), the substance eventually activates the brain's reward circuit (Hadar et al., 2017; Lohani et al., 2017). This reward circuit features the brain structure called the *ventral tegmental area* (in the midbrain), a structure known as the *nucleus accumbens,* and the *prefrontal cortex* (see **Figure 12-4**). In addition, the circuit includes the striatum, hippocampus, and several other import-

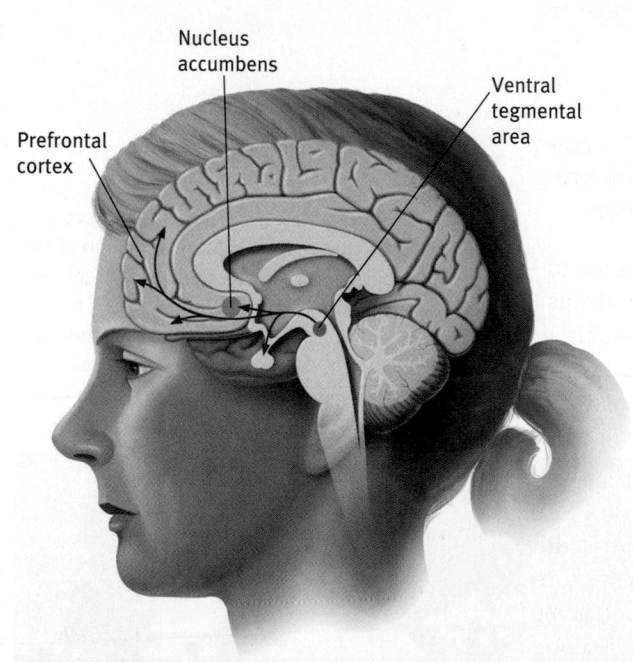

Nucleus accumbens

Ventral tegmental area

Prefrontal cortex

FIGURE 12-4

Pleasure Center in the Brain

One of the reasons substances produce feelings of pleasure is because they increase the activity of the neurotransmitter dopamine in the brain's reward circuit. Chronic dysfunction of this circuit—which includes the ventral tegmental area, nucleus accumbens, and prefrontal cortex—can lead to a substance use disorder.

ant structures (Byrne et al., 2016). The key neurotransmitter in this circuit is *dopamine* (Volkow et al., 2016; Ernst & Luciana, 2015). When dopamine is activated throughout this circuit, a person feels pleasure. Music may activate dopamine in the reward circuit. So may a hug or a word of praise. And so do drugs. Although other neurotransmitters also play roles in the reward circuit, dopamine is the primary one.

Certain drugs directly stimulate the structures in the reward circuit. Remember that cocaine and amphetamines directly increase dopamine activity. Other drugs seem to stimulate it in roundabout ways. The biochemical reactions triggered by alcohol, opioids, and marijuana set in motion a series of chemical events that eventually lead to increased dopamine activity in the reward circuit and, in turn, excessive communications (that is, heightened interconnectivity) between the structures in the reward circuit (Hadar et al., 2017; Vaquero et al., 2017; Carboni et al., 2016).

A number of theorists further believe that as substances repeatedly stimulate this reward circuit, the circuit develops a hypersensitivity to the substances. Neurons in the circuit fire more readily when stimulated by the substances, contributing to future desires for them. This theory, called the *incentive-sensitization theory* of addiction, has received considerable support in both animal and human studies (Moeller & Paulus, 2018; Berridge & Robinson, 2016). Still other theorists suspect that people who chronically use drugs may suffer from a *reward deficiency syndrome:* their reward circuit is not readily activated by the usual events in their lives, so they turn to drugs to stimulate this pleasure pathway, particularly in times of stress (Blum et al., 2018, 2017, 2016, 2000). Abnormal genes, such as the abnormal D2 receptor gene, have been cited as possible contributors to this syndrome. In short, the chronic intake of certain substances helps to produce a dysfunctional reward circuit in the brain and, along with that, the symptoms of a substance use disorder.

The Developmental Psychopathology View

Over the years, the explanatory factors for substance use disorders have each been studied independently. A list of variables that relate to substance use disorders has unfolded, but no single variable fully predicts or explains the disorders. Thus, as with other psychological disorders, a number of substance use theorists have tried to integrate the variables identified by each of the models. Once again, developmental psychopathology theorists have been active in this endeavor.

According to this perspective, the road to substance use disorders begins with genetically inherited predispositions—predispositions characterized by a less-than-optimal reward circuit in the brain and by a problematic temperament featuring some of the negative traits discussed earlier in this chapter. Developmental psychopathologists contend that such predispositions will eventually result in a substance use disorder if the individual further experiences numerous stressors throughout childhood, inadequate parenting (for example, substance misuse modeling), rewarding substance use experiences, relationships with peers who use drugs, and/or significant adult stressors (Forster et al., 2018; Chassin et al., 2016; Zucker et al, 2016). At the same time, individuals who experience *manageable* adversities throughout childhood and adolescence can develop a level of resilience that may help them counter such unfavorable predispositions, adversities, and negative family and peer influences.

	Control Subject	Drug Abuser
Cocaine		
METH		
Alcohol		

Victims of a reward deficiency syndrome? The brain reward circuits of people who develop substance use disorders may be inadequately activated by events in life—a problem called the *reward deficiency syndrome*. With the colors red and orange indicating more brain activity, these PET scans show that before abusers of cocaine, methamphetamine, and alcohol take those substances, their reward circuits (right) are generally less active than the reward circuits of nonabusers (left) (Volkow et al., 2016, 2004, 2002).

Reprinted from Neurobiology of Learning and Memory, N. D. Volkow et al. Role of Dopamine, the Frontal Cortex and Memory Circuits in Drug Addiction: Insight from Imaging Studies, 610–624, © 2002, with permission from Elsevier.

#StreetTags

Alcohol	booze, brew
Cocaine	blow, Charlie, rock, snow
Heroin	black tar, horse, smack
Marijuana	grass, Mary Jane, reefer, weed
Amphetamines	bennies, speed, uppers
MDMA	ecstasy, X, beans, hug
Methamphetamine	meth, crank, crystal, ice
Pain relievers	Oxy, Percs, Vikes

In short, as it does for other disorders, the developmental psychopathology perspective provides a framework for understanding why the factors discussed in this chapter sometimes lead to substance use disorders and sometimes do not. But the perspective also does more than this: it offers an explanation for seeming contradictions in the substance abuse research literature. Recall, for example, our earlier discussion of substance abuse personalities (see pages 365–366). As you read, a variety of personality traits have been linked to substance use disorders—dependency, antisocial inclinations, impulsivity, novelty seeking, risk taking, and depressive functioning—but different studies have tied different such traits to the disorders. These findings are not conflicting at all, according to developmental psychopathology theorists.

The theorists propose that either of two very different temperaments may set the stage for later substance abuse. On the one hand, some individuals may begin with a *disinhibited* temperament, also called an *externalizing* temperament—featuring impulsivity, aggressiveness, overactivity, limited persistence, low frustration tolerance, and inattention (Chassin et al., 2016; Zucker et al., 2016, 1996; Tarter et al., 1985). These individuals have great difficulty controlling their behaviors, thus increasing their risk of having early family conflicts, behavioral problems, and school difficulties—variables that may, in turn, lead to social problems, relationships with undesirable peers, access to alcohol and drugs from those peers, rewards from those peers for repeated drug use, and, ultimately, the onset of substance use disorders. A large number of developmental studies have confirmed that this cluster and sequence of variables does indeed unfold in many cases of substance use disorder (Chassin et al., 2016; Lopez-Vergara et al., 2012; King et al., 2004).

On the other hand, according to the developmental psychopathology perspective, other individuals may begin with a temperament of *inhibition* and *negative affectivity,* sometimes called an *internalizing* temperament—characterized by multiple fears, depression, negative thinking, and dependence (see pages 149 and 210). This temperament may contribute to worrying and sadness throughout the individuals' development, low self-concept, a sense of helplessness, and interpersonal rejections. These individuals may eventually turn to alcohol and drugs largely because the substances reduce their emotional pain, quiet their troublesome thoughts, and help them through interpersonal difficulties. A number of developmental studies have indicated that this cluster and sequence of variables may also lead to substance use disorders (Chassin et al., 2016; Hussong et al., 2011; Colder et al., 2010).

As you may recall, this notion that different temperaments may trigger and interact with different developmental factors to bring about substance use disorders is consistent with one of the key principles of the developmental psychopathology perspective, *equifinality*—the principle that different developmental pathways can lead to the same psychological disorder (see page 81). In short, identifying key factors in substance use disorders is only part of a comprehensive explanation. It is also necessary to identify when and how those factors interact.

End of a dream In 2016, Florida Marlins star pitcher Jose Fernandez was killed along with two passengers when he plowed his 32-foot boat into a jetty. A toxicology report showed that the 24-year-old Fernandez, who defected from Cuba in 2008, was very intoxicated (blood-alcohol level of 0.147) and had cocaine in his system at the time of the pre-dawn accident.

Christian Petersen/Getty Images

How Are Substance Use Disorders Treated?

MANY APPROACHES HAVE BEEN used to treat substance use disorders, including psychodynamic, cognitive-behavioral, and biological approaches, along with several sociocultural therapies. These various approaches are often combined with *motivational interviewing* (see page 332) in which therapists help motivate the clients to make constructive choices and behavioral changes (Ingersoll, 2017). Although treatment sometimes meets with great success, more often it is only moderately helpful (Kampman, 2017; Peavy, 2017; Strain, 2017). Today the various treatments are typi-

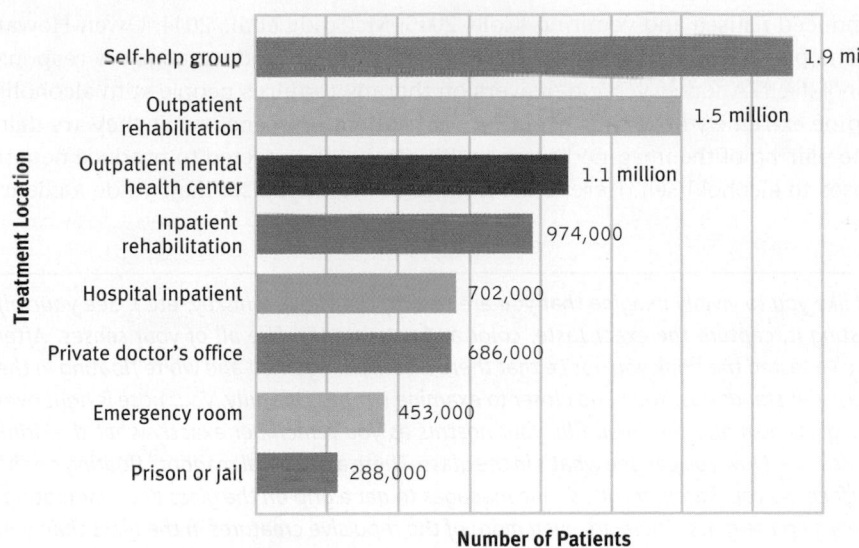

Number of Patients

FIGURE 12-5

Where Do People Receive Treatment?
Most people receive treatment for substance use disorders in a self-help group, rehabilitation program, or mental health center. (Information from: SAMHSA, 2017; NSDUH, 2016.)

cally used on either an outpatient or inpatient basis or a combination of the two (see **Figure 12-5**).

The effectiveness of treatment for substance use disorders can be difficult to determine. There are several reasons for this (Davis et al., 2017; Belendiuk & Riggs, 2014). First, different substance use disorders pose different problems. Second, many people with such disorders drop out of treatment very early. Third, some people recover without any intervention at all while many others recover and then relapse. And, fourth, different criteria are used by different clinical researchers. How long, for example, must a person refrain from substance use in order to be called a treatment success? And is total abstention the only criterion, or is a reduction of drug use acceptable?

Psychodynamic Therapies

Psychodynamic therapists first guide clients to uncover and work through the underlying needs and conflicts that they believe have led to the substance use disorder. The therapists then try to help the clients change their substance-related styles of living. Although this approach is often used, it has not been found to be particularly effective (McCrady et al., 2014; Lightdale et al., 2011, 2008). It may be that substance use disorders, regardless of their causes, eventually become stubborn independent problems that must be the direct target of treatment if people are to become drug-free. Psychodynamic therapy tends to be of more help when it is combined with other approaches in a multidimensional treatment program.

Cognitive-Behavioral Therapies

Cognitive-behavioral treatments for substance use disorders help clients identify and change the behaviors and cognitions that keep contributing to their patterns of substance misuse (Peavy, 2017; Stitzer & Cunningham, 2016). The leading cognitive-behavioral interventions for these disorders are *aversion therapy*, *contingency management*, *relapse prevention training*, and *acceptance and commitment therapy (ACT)*.

Aversion Therapy In **aversion therapy,** a widely used approach based on the behavioral principles of classical conditioning, clients are repeatedly presented with an unpleasant stimulus (for example, an electric shock) at the very moment that they are taking a drug. After repeated pairings, they are expected to react negatively to the substance itself and to lose their craving for it.

Aversion therapy has been used to treat alcoholism more often than it has to treat other substance use disorders. In one version of this therapy, drinking is paired with

aversion therapy A treatment in which clients are repeatedly presented with unpleasant stimuli while they are performing undesirable behaviors such as taking a drug.

drug-induced nausea and vomiting (Cole, 2016; McCrady et al., 2014; Owen-Howard, 2001). The pairing of nausea with alcohol is expected to produce negative responses to alcohol itself. Another version of aversion therapy requires people with alcoholism to imagine extremely upsetting, repulsive, or frightening scenes while they are drinking. The pairing of the imagined scenes with alcohol is expected to produce negative responses to alcohol itself. Here is the kind of scene therapists may guide a client to imagine:

> I'd like you to vividly imagine that you are tasting the (beer, whiskey, etc.). See yourself tasting it, capture the exact taste, color and consistency. Use all of your senses. After you've tasted the drink you notice that there is something small and white floating in the glass—it stands out. You bend closer to examine it more carefully, your nose is right over the glass now and the smell fills your nostrils as you remember exactly what the drink tastes like. Now you can see what's in the glass. There are several maggots floating on the surface. As you watch, revolted, one manages to get a grip on the glass and, undulating, creeps up the glass. There are even more of the repulsive creatures in the glass than you first thought. You realise that you have swallowed some of them and you're very aware of the taste in your mouth. You feel very sick and wish you'd never reached for the glass and had the drink at all.
>
> *(Clarke & Saunders, 1988, pp. 143–144)*

Aversion therapy for substance use disorders has had only limited success when it is the sole form of treatment (Belendiuk & Riggs, 2014; Carroll, 2008). A major problem is that the approach can be effective only if people are motivated to subject themselves to multiple sessions of this unpleasant procedure, and many people are not.

Contingency Management Based on the behavioral principles of operant conditioning, *contingency management* programs offer clients incentives (such as vouchers, prizes, cash, or privileges) that are contingent on the submission of drug-free urine specimens (Rash et al., 2017; Stitzer & Cunningham, 2016, 2015). In essence, this procedure—usually lasting 8 to 16 weeks—is rewarding clients for abstaining from the use of the substances upon which they are dependent.

Studies indicate that clients in contingency management programs maintain a higher attendance record than those in other kinds of programs. However, unless the programs are part of a larger treatment approach, they are at best moderately effective at helping clients abstain from substances for an extended period (Rash et al., 2017; Stitzer & Cunningham, 2016, 2015). As with aversion therapy, a major limitation is that the approach can be effective only when people are motivated to continue despite its unpleasantness or demands. Contingency management programs are most useful in the treatment of stimulant use disorder and opioid use disorder.

True to the principles of operant conditioning, research has found that the larger the rewards offered in a contingency management program, the greater a client's improvement, at least temporarily. For example, a study of two cocaine-focused contingency management programs—one offering a total incentive of $2,000 and the other offering a $500 incentive—found that twice as many clients in the former program were abstinent at the end 24 weeks (Stitzer & Cunningham, 2016; Higgins et al., 2007).

Relapse-Prevention Training One of the most prominent cognitive-behavioral approaches to substance misuse is **relapse-prevention training** (Swanson & Cooper, 2016; Takano et al., 2016; Daley et al., 2011). The overall goal of this approach is for clients to gain *control* over their substance-related behaviors. To help reach this goal, clients are taught to identify high-risk situations, appreciate the range of decisions that confront them in such situations, change their dysfunctional lifestyles, and learn from mistakes and lapses.

#FamousFatalities

Substance Overdose Deaths in the Twenty-first Century

Carrie Fisher, actress (polydrug and sleep apnea, 2017)

Prince, singer and songwriter (opioid, 2016)

Philip Seymour Hoffman, actor (polydrug, 2014)

Cory Monteith, actor (polydrug, 2013)

Whitney Houston, singer (cocaine and heart disease, 2012)

Amy Winehouse, singer (alcohol poisoning, 2011)

Michael Jackson, performer and songwriter (prescription polydrug, 2009)

Heath Ledger, actor (prescription polydrug, 2008)

Anna Nicole Smith, model (prescription polydrug, 2007)

Ol' Dirty Bastard, rapper, Wu-Tang Clan (polydrug, 2004)

Rick James, singer (cocaine, 2004)

Better ways to cope Several treatments for substance use disorders, including relapse-prevention training, teach clients alternative—more functional—ways of coping with stress and negative emotions. In that spirit, this patient at a drug rehabilitation center in China developed the practice of kicking a punching dummy to help release his pent-up anger.

Several strategies typically are included in relapse-prevention training for alcohol use disorder: (1) *Therapists have clients keep track of their drinking.* By writing down the times, locations, emotions, bodily changes, and other circumstances of their drinking, people become more aware of the situations that place them at risk for excessive drinking. (2) *Therapists teach clients coping strategies to use when such situations arise.* Clients learn, for example, to recognize when they are approaching their drinking limits; to control their rate of drinking (perhaps by spacing their drinks or by sipping them rather than gulping); and to practice relaxation techniques, assertiveness skills, and other coping behaviors in situations in which they would otherwise be drinking. (3) *Therapists teach clients to plan ahead of time.* Clients may, for example, determine beforehand how many drinks are appropriate, what to drink, and under which circumstances to drink.

Relapse-prevention training has been found to lower some people's frequency of intoxication and of binge drinking, although such gains are often made only after repeated relapse-prevention treatments (Swanson & Cooper, 2016; Jhanjee, 2014; Borden et al., 2011). People who are young and do not have the tolerance and withdrawal features of chronic alcohol use seem to do best with this approach (Hart & Ksir, 2015; Deas et al., 2008). Relapse-prevention training has also been used in cases of marijuana and cocaine abuse as well as with other kinds of disorders, such as sexual paraphilic disorders (see Chapter 13).

Acceptance and Commitment Therapy Another form of cognitive-behavioral treatment that has been used in cases of substance use disorder is *acceptance and commitment therapy (ACT)*. As you read in Chapters 3 and 5, ACT therapists use a mindfulness-based approach to help clients become *aware* of their streams of thoughts as they are occurring and to accept such thoughts as mere events of the mind. For people with substance use disorders, that means increasing their awareness and acceptance of their drug cravings, worries, and depressive thoughts. By accepting such thoughts rather than trying to eliminate them, the clients are expected to be less upset by them and less likely to act on them by seeking out drugs. Research indicates that ACT is more effective than placebo treatments and at least as effective as other cognitive-behavioral treatments for substance use disorders, and sometimes more effective (Smallwood et al., 2016; Lee et al., 2015; Bowen et al., 2014). In many cases, ACT has been combined with relapse-prevention training or other cognitive-behavioral approaches, a combination that typically yields more success than either approach alone (Black, 2014).

relapse-prevention training A cognitive-behavioral approach to treating alcohol use disorder in which clients are taught to keep track of their drinking behavior, apply coping strategies in situations that typically trigger excessive drinking, and plan ahead for risky situations and reactions.

#BadAge

By a strange coincidence, several of rock's most famous stars and substance abusers have died at age 27. They include Jimi Hendrix, Jim Morrison, Janis Joplin, Kurt Cobain, Brian Jones, and Amy Winehouse. The phenomenon has been called "The 27 Club" in some circles.

Biological Treatments

Biological treatments may be used to help people withdraw from substances, abstain from them, or simply maintain their level of use without increasing it further. As with the other forms of treatment, biological approaches alone rarely bring long-term improvement, but they can be helpful when combined with other approaches.

Detoxification Detoxification is systematic and medically supervised withdrawal from a drug. Some detoxification programs are offered on an outpatient basis. Others are located in hospitals and clinics and may also include individual and group therapy, a "full-service" institutional approach that has become popular. One detoxification approach is to have clients withdraw gradually from the substance, taking smaller and smaller doses until they are off the drug completely. A second—often medically preferred—detoxification strategy is to give clients other drugs that reduce the symptoms of withdrawal (Swift, 2016; Day & Strang, 2011). Antianxiety drugs, for example, are sometimes used to reduce severe alcohol withdrawal reactions such as delirium tremens and seizures. Detoxification programs seem to help motivated people withdraw from drugs. However, relapse rates tend to be high for those who do not receive a follow-up form of treatment—psychological, biological, or sociocultural—after successfully detoxifying (Strain, 2017; Blodgett et al., 2014).

Antagonist Drugs After successfully stopping a drug, people must avoid falling back into a pattern of chronic use. As an aid to resisting temptation, some people with substance use disorders are given **antagonist drugs,** which block or change the effects of the addictive drug (Sofin et al., 2017; Strain, 2017). *Disulfiram* (Antabuse), for example, is often given to people who are trying to stay away from alcohol. By itself, a low dose of disulfiram seems to have few negative effects, but a person who drinks alcohol while taking it will have intense nausea, vomiting, blushing, a faster heart rate, dizziness, and perhaps fainting. People taking disulfiram are less likely to drink alcohol because they know the terrible reaction that awaits them should they have even one drink. Disulfiram has proved helpful, but again only with people who are motivated to take it as prescribed (Sofin et al., 2017). In addition to disulfiram, several other antagonist drugs are now being tested.

For substance use disorders centered on opioids, several *opioid antagonist drugs,* such as **naloxone,** are used (Strain, 2017; Sevarino, 2016). These antagonists attach to *endorphin* receptor sites throughout the brain and make it impossible for the opioids to have their usual effect. Without the rush or high, continued drug use becomes point-

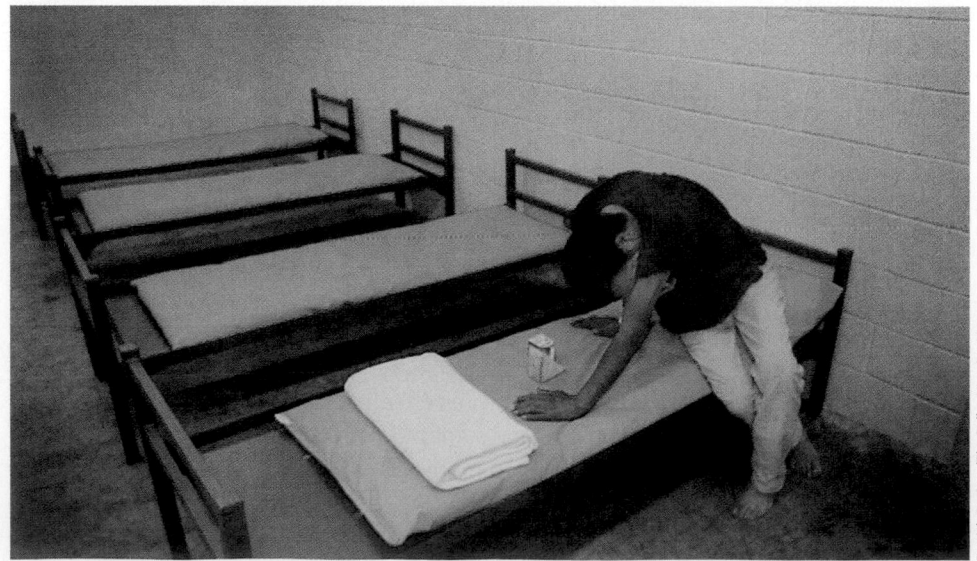

Forced detoxification Abstinence is not always medically supervised, nor is it necessarily planned or voluntary. This person, who is suffering from alcoholism, begins to have symptoms of withdrawal soon after being imprisoned for public intoxication.

Patrick Davison/The Dallas Morning News

less. In addition, by blocking endorphin receptors during an opioid overdose, opioid antagonists can actually reverse the deadly effect of respiratory depression, thus saving the user's life.

So-called *partial antagonists,* opioid antagonists that produce less severe withdrawal symptoms, have also been developed (Sevarino, 2016; Dijkstra et al., 2010). Many clinicians now prefer partial antagonists over full antagonists to help people withdraw from opioid use. The use of antagonists to help people withdraw is often called *rapid detoxification* because the antagonists speed things along. The full antagonists remain the treatment of choice in emergency cases of overdose.

Research indicates that opioid antagonists may also be useful in the treatment of substance use disorders involving alcohol or cocaine (Busch et al., 2017; Harrison & Petrakis, 2011; O'Malley et al., 2000, 1996, 1992). In some studies, for example, the opioid antagonist *naltrexone* has helped reduce cravings for alcohol. Why should opioid antagonists, which operate at the brain's endorphin receptors, help with alcoholism, which has been tied largely to activity at GABA sites? The answer may lie in the reward circuit of the brain. If various drugs eventually stimulate the same pleasure pathway, it seems reasonable that antagonists for one drug may, in a roundabout way, affect the impact of other drugs as well.

In case of an emergency In 2017 the New York City Health Department launched the "I Saved a Life" public awareness campaign, which urges people to carry the opioid antagonist drug *naloxone* for possible use in opioid-overdose crises. The campaign features powerful posters and stories about real-life people who were able to save the life of a friend or relative by using naloxone. This medication is now available in pharmacies throughout the city.

Drug Maintenance Therapy A drug-related lifestyle may be a bigger problem than the drug's direct effects. Much of the damage caused by heroin addiction, for example, comes from overdoses, unsterilized needles, and an accompanying life of crime. Thus clinicians were very enthusiastic when **methadone maintenance programs** were developed in the 1960s to treat heroin addiction (Dole & Nyswander, 1967, 1965). In these programs, people with an addiction are given the laboratory opioid *methadone* as a substitute, or *agonist,* for heroin. Although they then become dependent on methadone, their new addiction is maintained under safe medical supervision. Unlike heroin, methadone produces a moderate high, can be taken by mouth (thus eliminating the dangers of needles), and needs to be taken only once a day.

At first, methadone programs seemed very effective, and many of them were set up throughout the United States, Canada, and England. These programs became less popular during the 1980s, however, because of the dangers of methadone itself. Many clinicians came to believe that substituting one addiction for another is not an acceptable "solution" for a substance use disorder, and many people with an addiction complained that methadone addiction was creating an additional drug problem that simply complicated their original one (Dalsbø et al., 2017; Day & Strang, 2011; McCance-Katz & Kosten, 2005). Methadone is sometimes harder to withdraw from than heroin because the withdrawal symptoms can last longer.

> Why has the legal, medically supervised use of heroin (in Great Britain) or heroin substitutes (in the United States) sometimes failed to combat drug problems?

Despite such concerns, maintenance treatment with methadone has again sparked interest among clinicians in recent years, partly because of new research support (Strain, 2017; Balhara, 2014) and partly because of the rapid spread of the HIV and hepatitis C viruses among intravenous drug abusers and their sex partners and children (Kharasch, 2017; Lambdin et al., 2014). Not only is methadone treatment safer than street opioid use, but many methadone programs now include AIDS education and other health instructions in their services. Research suggests that methadone maintenance programs are most effective when they are combined with education, psychotherapy, family therapy, and employment counseling (Strain, 2017; Jhanjee, 2014). Today thousands of clinics provide methadone treatment across the United States.

detoxification Systematic and medically supervised withdrawal from a drug.

antagonist drugs Drugs that block or change the effects of an addictive drug.

naloxone One of the most widely used opioid antagonist drugs.

methadone maintenance program A treatment approach in which clients are given legally and medically supervised doses of methadone—a heroin substitute—to treat various opioid use disorders.

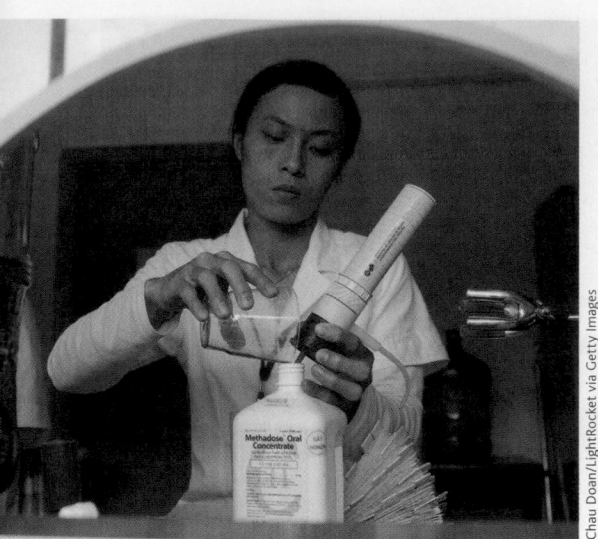

Drug use ... under medical supervision
Methadone is itself an opioid that can be as dangerous as other opioids when not taken under safe medical supervision. Here a nurse at a methadone treatment facility prepares the drug for administration to clients.

#StayingSober

48% of current AA members have been sober for more than 5 years.

24% of current AA members have been sober for 1–5 years.

37% of current AA members have been sober for less than 1 year.

(Information from: AA World Services, 2017.)

Another opioid substitute drug, *buprenorphine*, has been gaining momentum as a form of maintenance therapy during the past decade (SAMHSA, 2017, 2016). Like methadone, this drug is itself an opioid that is administered to patients as a safer alternative to heroin, painkillers, and the like. However, according to research, buprenorphine is a less potent substitute drug than methadone and produces less tolerance and fewer withdrawal reactions (Gowing et al., 2017; Thomas et al., 2014). For these reasons, buprenorphine is permitted by law to be prescribed by physicians in their offices rather than as part of a highly structured clinic program—offering a level of accessibility that is not possible with methadone treatment.

Sociocultural Therapies

As you have read, sociocultural theorists—both *family-social* and *multicultural* theorists—believe that psychological problems emerge in a social setting and are best treated in a social context. Three sociocultural approaches have been used to help people overcome substance use disorders: (1) *self-help programs,* (2) *culture- and gender-sensitive programs,* and (3) *community prevention programs.*

Self-Help and Residential Treatment Programs Many people with substance use disorders have organized among themselves to help one another recover without professional assistance (Lembke & Humphreys, 2016). The drug self-help movement dates back to 1935, when two Ohio men suffering from alcoholism met and wound up discussing alternative treatment possibilities. The first discussion led to others and to the eventual formation of a self-help group whose members discussed alcohol-related problems, traded ideas, and provided support. The organization became known as **Alcoholics Anonymous (AA).**

Today AA has approximately 2 million members in 110,000 groups across the world (AA World Services, 2017). It offers peer support along with moral and spiritual guidelines to help people overcome alcoholism. Different members apparently find different aspects of AA helpful. For some it is the peer support; for others it is the spiritual dimension (Kelly, 2017). Meetings take place regularly, and members are available to help each other 24 hours a day.

By offering guidelines for living, the organization helps members abstain "one day at a time," urging them to accept as "fact" the idea that they are powerless over alcohol and that they must stop drinking entirely and permanently if they are to live normal lives. AA views alcoholism as a disease and takes the position that "Once an alcoholic, always an alcoholic." Related self-help organizations, *Al-Anon* and *Alateen,* offer support for people who live with and care about people with alcoholism. Self-help programs such as *Narcotics Anonymous* and *Cocaine Anonymous* have been developed for other substance use disorders (Peavy, 2017; Lembke & Humphreys, 2016).

It is worth noting that the abstinence goal of AA is in direct opposition to the controlled-drinking goal of relapse-prevention training and several other interventions for substance misuse (see pages 372–373). In fact, this issue—abstinence versus controlled drinking—has been debated for years (Zemore, 2017; Rosenthal, 2011). Feelings about it have run so strongly that in the 1980s the people on one side challenged the motives and honesty of those on the other (Sobell & Sobell, 1984, 1973; Pendery et al., 1982).

Research indicates, however, that both controlled drinking and abstinence may be useful treatment goals, depending on the nature of the particular drinking problem (Best, 2017). Studies suggest that abstinence may be a more appropriate goal for people who have a long-standing alcohol use disorder, whereas controlled drinking can be helpful to younger drinkers whose pattern does not include tolerance and withdrawal reactions. Those in the latter group may indeed need to be taught a nonabusive form of drinking (Zemore, 2017; Witkiewitz & Marlatt, 2007, 2004). Studies also suggest that abstinence is appropriate for people who believe that it is the only answer for them, as they are more likely to relapse after having just one drink (Zemore, 2017; Rosenthal, 2011).

Many self-help programs have expanded into **residential treatment centers,** or **therapeutic communities**—such as *Daytop Village* and *Phoenix House*—where people formerly addicted to drugs live, work, and socialize in a drug-free environment while undergoing individual, group, and family therapies and making a transition back to community life (Gruenewald et al., 2016; Lembke & Humphreys, 2016; O'Brien et al., 2011).

The evidence that keeps self-help and residential treatment programs going comes largely in the form of individual testimonials. Many tens of thousands of people have revealed that they are members of these programs and credit them with turning their lives around. Studies of the programs have also had favorable findings, but the number of such studies has been limited (Best, 2017; Peavy, 2017; Lembke & Humphreys, 2016).

Culture- and Gender-Sensitive Programs
Many people with substance use disorders live in a poor and perhaps violent setting. A growing number of today's treatment programs try to be sensitive to the special sociocultural pressures and problems faced by drug abusers who are poor, homeless, or members of minority groups (McKinney & Caetano, 2016; Hadland & Baer, 2014; Hurd et al., 2014). Therapists who are sensitive to their clients' life challenges can do more to address the stresses that often lead to relapse.

> What different kinds of issues might be confronted by drug abusers from different minority groups or genders?

Similarly, therapists have become more aware that women often require treatment methods different from those designed for men (Gamboa, 2017; Greenfield et al., 2011). Women and men often have different physical and psychological reactions to drugs, for example. In addition, treatment of women with substance use disorders may be complicated by the impact of sexual abuse, the possibility that they may be or may become pregnant while taking drugs, the stresses of raising children, and the fear of criminal prosecution for abusing drugs during pregnancy (SAMHSA, 2017). Thus many women with such disorders feel more comfortable seeking help at gender-sensitive clinics or residential programs; some such programs also allow children to live with their recovering mothers.

Community Prevention Programs
Perhaps the most effective approach to substance use disorders is to prevent them (Gruenewald et al., 2016; Sandler et al., 2014). The first drug-prevention programs were conducted in schools (D'Amico et al., 2016). Today such programs are also offered in workplaces, activity centers, and other community settings and even through the media (SAMHSA, 2017; NSDUH, 2016, 2013). Around 12 percent of adolescents report that they have participated in drug prevention programs outside school within the past year. Around 75 percent have seen or heard a substance use–prevention message. And almost 60 percent have talked to their parents in the past year about the dangers of alcohol and other drugs.

Some prevention programs are based on a total abstinence model, while others teach responsible use. Some seek to interrupt drug use; others try to delay the age at which people first experiment with drugs. Programs may also differ in whether they offer drug education, teach alternatives to drug use, try to change the psychological state of the potential user, help people change their peer relationships, or combine these techniques.

Prevention programs may focus on the *individual* (for example, by providing education about unpleasant drug effects), the *family* (by teaching parenting skills), the

Peter Kovalev/TASS via Getty Images

Coming together In the tradition of Alcoholics Anonymous and therapeutic communities, these individuals hold a meeting at an alcohol and substance use disorder center in a remote Russian village. The individuals and their families provide support for each other and also seek to address moral and spiritual needs as they try to overcome their disorders.

Alcoholics Anonymous (AA) A self-help organization that provides support and guidance for people with alcohol use disorder.

residential treatment center A place where people formerly addicted to drugs live, work, and socialize in a drug-free environment. Also called a *therapeutic community.*

Fighting drug abuse while in prison Inmates shake hands during a drug counseling session at a prison in Utah. The session is part of a statewide program—for people living in communities, rehabilitation centers, and prisons—called Addict II Athlete (pronounced "addict-to-athlete"). The program emphasizes exercise and athletic endeavors as an alternative to drug-related behaviors, while also providing support, psychoeducation, and other interventions to help individuals address their substance use disorders.

Jonathan Newton / The Washington Post via Getty Images

peer group (by teaching resistance to peer pressure), the *school* (by setting up firm enforcement of drug policies), or the *community* at large. The most effective prevention efforts focus on several of these areas in order to provide a consistent message about drug misuse in all areas of people's lives (Gruenewald et al., 2016; Hansen et al., 2010). Some prevention programs have even been developed for preschool children.

Two of today's leading community-based prevention programs are TheTruth.com and Above the Influence. The Truth is an antismoking campaign, aimed at young people in particular, that has "edgy" ads on the Web (on YouTube, for instance), on television, and in magazines and newspapers. Above the Influence is a similar advertising campaign that focuses on a range of substances abused by teenagers. Originally created by the U.S. Office of National Drug Control Policy, Above the Influence became a private, not-for-profit program in 2014.

> What impact might admissions by celebrities about past drug use have on people's willingness to seek treatment for a substance use disorder?

Community-based prevention programs are not always effective, no matter how powerful and clever their ads may be (Allara et al., 2014). For example, after a 5-year study, the Government Accountability Office concluded in 2006 that the highly regarded My Anti-Drug campaign of the late 1990s and early 2000s had been largely ineffective. Thus, it is encouraging that a number of studies are now being conducted to assess the actual impact of the various community-based prevention programs (Allara et al., 2014). One nationwide survey of 3,000 students, for example, suggested that watching Above the Influence ads helped reduce marijuana use by teenagers (Slater et al., 2011). The survey found that 8 percent of eighth-graders familiar with the campaign have taken up marijuana use, in contrast to 12 percent of students who have never seen the ads.

Other Addictive Disorders

AS YOU READ AT THE BEGINNING of this chapter, DSM-5 lists **gambling disorder** as an addictive disorder alongside the substance use disorders. This represents a significant broadening of the concept of addiction, which in previous editions of the

gambling disorder A disorder marked by persistent and recurrent gambling behavior, leading to a range of life problems.

DSM referred only to the misuse of substances. In essence, DSM-5 is suggesting that people may become addicted to behaviors and activities beyond substance use.

Gambling Disorder

It is estimated that as many as 4 percent of adults and 3 to 10 percent of teenagers and college students suffer from *gambling disorder* (Choi et al., 2017; Nowak & Aloe, 2014). Clinicians are careful to distinguish between this disorder and social gambling (APA, 2013). Gambling disorder is defined less by the amount of time or money spent gambling than by the addictive nature of the behavior. People with gambling disorder are preoccupied with gambling and typically cannot walk away from a bet. When they lose money repeatedly, they often gamble more in an effort to win the money back, and continue gambling even in the face of financial, social, occupational, educational, and health problems (see **Table 12-4**). They usually gamble more when feeling distressed, and often lie to cover up the extent of their gambling. Many people with gambling disorder need to gamble with ever-larger amounts of money to reach the desired excitement, and they feel restless or irritable when they try to reduce or stop gambling—symptoms that are similar to the tolerance and withdrawal reactions often associated with substance use disorder (APA, 2013).

The explanations proposed for gambling disorder often parallel those for substance use disorders (Nautiyal et al., 2017; van Holst et al., 2017; Leeman et al., 2014). Some studies suggest, for example, that people with gambling disorder may: (1) inherit a genetic predisposition to develop the disorder; (2) experience heightened dopamine activity and dysfunction of the brain's reward circuit when they gamble; (3) have impulsive, novelty-seeking, and other personality styles that leave them prone to gambling disorder; and (4) make repeated and cognitive mistakes such as inaccurate expectations and misinterpretations of their emotions and bodily states. However, the research on these theories has been limited thus far, leaving such explanations tentative for now.

Several of the leading treatments for substance use disorders have been adapted for use with gambling disorder (Choi et al., 2017; Jabr, 2013). These treatments include cognitive-behavioral approaches like relapse-prevention training, and biological approaches such as opioid antagonists. In addition, the self-help group program *Gamblers Anonymous,* a network modeled after *Alcoholics Anonymous,* is available to the many thousands of people with gambling disorder (Marceaux & Melville, 2011). People who attend such groups seem to have a better recovery rate.

Increase in gambling venues This woman is playing a slot machine while vacationing on a cruise ship—harmless fun for her, but not for everyone. Some theorists believe the recent increases in the prevalence of gambling disorder are related to the explosion of new gambling venues, in particular the many casinos that have been built in every part of the country, and the legalization and spread of online gambling.

David Sacks/Getty Images

TABLE: 12-4

Dx Checklist

Gambling Disorder

1. Individual displays a maladaptive pattern of gambling, featuring at least four of the following symptoms over the course of a full year:
   a. Can achieve desired excitement only by gambling more and more money
   b. Feels restless or irritable when tries to reduce gambling
   c. Repeatedly tries and fails at efforts to control, reduce, or cease gambling
   d. Consumed with gambling thoughts or plans
   e. Gambling is often triggered by upset feelings
   f. Frequently returns to gambling to try and recoup previous losses
   g. Covers up amount of gambling by lying
   h. Gambling has put important relationships, job, or educational/career opportunities at risk
   i. Seeks money from others to address gambling-induced financial problems

2. Individual experiences significant distress or impairment.

(Information from: APA, 2013.)

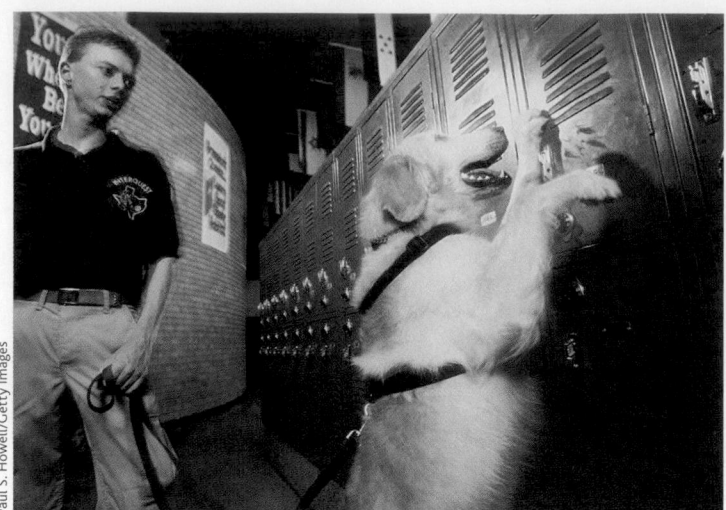

Sniffing for drugs An increasingly common scene in schools, airports, storage facilities, and similar settings is that of trained dogs sniffing for marijuana, cocaine, opioids, and other substances. Here one such animal sniffs lockers at a school in Texas to see whether students have hidden any illegal substances among their books or other belongings.

Internet Gaming Disorder: Awaiting Official Status

As people increasingly turn to the Internet for activities that used to take place in the "real world"—communicating, networking, shopping, playing games, and participating in a community—a new psychological problem has emerged: an uncontrollable need to be online (Cerniglia et al., 2017; Young, 2017). This pattern has been called *Internet use disorder, Internet addiction,* and *problematic Internet use,* among other names.

For people who have this pattern—at least 1 percent of all people—the Internet has become a black hole. They spend all or most of their waking hours texting, tweeting, networking, gaming, Internet browsing, e-mailing, blogging, visiting virtual worlds, shopping online, or viewing online pornography (McNicol & Thorsteinsson, 2017; Yoo et al., 2014). Specific symptoms of this pattern parallel those found in substance use disorders and gambling disorder, extending from the loss of outside interests to possible withdrawal reactions when Internet use is not possible (APA, 2013).

Although clinicians, the media, and the public have shown enormous interest in this problem, it is not included as a disorder in DSM-5. Rather, the DSM workgroup has recommended that one version of the pattern, which it calls *Internet gaming disorder,* receive further study for possible inclusion in future editions (APA, 2013). Time—and research—will tell whether this pattern reaches the status of a formal clinical disorder.

||||||||||||||||||||||||||||||||||||||||||||||||||||||||||||||||||||||||||||||||||||||||||||||||||||||||

New Wrinkles to a Familiar Story

IN SOME RESPECTS, THE STORY of the misuse of drugs is the same today as in the past. Substance use is still rampant, often creating damaging psychological disorders. New drugs keep emerging, and the public goes through periods of believing, naïvely, that the new drugs are "safe." Only gradually do people learn that these, too, pose dangers. And treatments for substance-related disorders continue to have only limited effect.

Yet there are positive new wrinkles in this familiar story. Researchers have begun to develop a clearer understanding of how drugs act on the brain and body. In treatment, self-help groups and rehabilitation programs are flourishing. And preventive education to make people aware of the dangers of drug misuse is also expanding and seems to be having an effect. One reason for these improvements is that investigators and clinicians have stopped working in isolation and are instead looking for intersections between their own work and work from other models. They have come to recognize that social pressures, personality characteristics, rewards, and genetic predispositions all play roles in substance use disorders, and in fact they operate together. Similarly, the various forms of treatment seem to work best when they are combined with approaches from the other models, making integrated treatment the most productive approach.

Yet another new wrinkle to the addiction story is that the clinical field has now formally proclaimed that substances are not the only things to which people may develop an addiction. By grouping gambling disorder with the substance use disorders and targeting Internet gaming disorder for possible inclusion in the future, DSM-5 has opened the door for a broader view and perhaps broader treatments of addictive patterns—whether they are induced by substances or by other kinds of experiences.

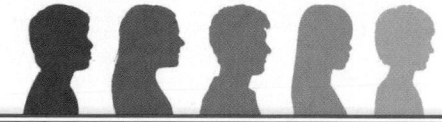

CLINICAL CHOICES

Now that you've read about substance use and addictive disorders, try the interactive case study for this chapter. See if you are able to identify Jorge's symptoms and suggest a diagnosis based on his symptoms. What kind of treatment would be most effective for Jorge? Go to **Launch**Pad to access *Clinical Choices.*

◈... SUMMING UP

» **Substance Misuse** The misuse of *substances* (or *drugs*) may lead to temporary changes in behavior, emotions, or thoughts; this cluster of changes is called *intoxication*. Chronic and excessive use can lead to *substance use disorders*. Many people with such disorders also develop a *tolerance* for the substance in question and/or have unpleasant *withdrawal symptoms* when they abstain from it. *pp. 344–345*

» **Depressants** *Depressants* are substances that slow the activity of the central nervous system. Chronic and excessive use of these substances can lead to problems such as *alcohol use disorder, sedative-hypnotic use disorder,* or *opioid use disorder.*

Alcohol intoxication occurs when the concentration of alcohol in the bloodstream reaches 0.09 percent. Among other actions, alcohol increases the activity of the neurotransmitter GABA at key sites in the brain. The *sedative-hypnotic drugs,* which produce feelings of relaxation and drowsiness, include *barbiturates* and *benzodiazepines.* These drugs also increase the activity of GABA. *Opioids* include *opium* and drugs derived from it, such as *morphine* and *heroin,* as well as laboratory-made opioids. They all reduce tension and pain and cause other reactions. Opioids operate by binding to neurons that ordinarily receive *endorphins. pp. 345–352*

» **Stimulants** *Stimulants,* including *cocaine, amphetamines, caffeine,* and *nicotine,* are substances that increase the activity of the central nervous system. Abnormal use of cocaine or amphetamines can lead to *stimulant use disorder.* Stimulants produce their effects by increasing the activity of dopamine, norepinephrine, and serotonin in the brain. *pp. 353–358*

» **Hallucinogens** *Hallucinogens,* such as *LSD,* are substances that cause powerful changes primarily in sensory perception. People's perceptions are intensified and they may have illusions and hallucinations. LSD apparently causes such effects by disturbing the release of the neurotransmitter serotonin. *pp. 358–360*

» **Cannabis** The main ingredient of *Cannabis sativa,* a hemp plant, is *tetrahydrocannabinol* (*THC*). *Marijuana,* the most popular form of cannabis, is more powerful today than it was in years past. It can cause intoxication, and regular use can lead to *cannabis use disorder. pp. 360–363*

» **Combinations of Substances** Many people take more than one drug at a time, and the drugs interact. The use of two or more drugs at the same time—*polysubstance use*—has become increasingly common. *pp. 363–364*

» **Explanations for Substance Use Disorders** Several explanations for substance use disorders have been put forward. Together they are beginning to shed light on the disorders. According to *sociocultural* theorists, the people most likely to develop these disorders are those living in socioeconomic conditions that generate stress or whose families value or tolerate drug use. In the *psychodynamic view,* people who develop substance use disorders have excessive *dependency* needs traceable to the early stages of life. Some psychodynamic theorists also believe that certain people have a *substance abuse personality* that makes them prone to drug use. In the leading *cognitive-behavioral* views, drug use is seen as being reinforced initially because it reduces tensions, and such reductions lead to an *expectancy* that drugs will be comforting and helpful.

The *biological* explanations are supported by twin, adoptee, and genetic studies, suggesting that people may inherit a predisposition to the disorders. Researchers have also learned that drug tolerance and withdrawal symptoms may be caused by cutbacks in the brain's production of particular neurotransmitters during excessive and chronic drug use. Biological studies suggest that many, perhaps all, drugs may ultimately lead to increased *dopamine* activity in the brain's *reward circuit.*

Developmental psychopathology theorists suggest that a genetically inherited biological predisposition and *temperamental* predisposition may interact with life stressors, problematic parenting, and/or other environmental factors to bring about a substance use disorder. *pp. 364–370*

» **Treatments for Substance Use Disorders** Usually several approaches are combined to treat substance use disorders. *Psychodynamic* therapists try to help clients become aware of and correct the underlying needs and conflicts that may have led to their use of drugs. *Cognitive-behavioral* techniques include *aversion therapy, contingency management, relapse-prevention training,* and *acceptance and commitment therapy.* Biological treatments include *detoxification, antagonist drugs,* and *drug maintenance therapy.* Sociocultural treatments approach substance use disorders in a social context by means of *self-help groups* (e.g., *Alcoholics Anonymous*), *residential treatment programs, culture-* and *gender-sensitive treatments,* and *community prevention programs. pp. 370–378*

» **Other Addictive Disorders** DSM-5 groups *gambling disorder* alongside the substance use disorders as an addictive disorder. Treatments for gambling disorder include cognitive-behavioral approaches, opioid antagonists, and self-help groups. *pp. 378–380*

Visit *LaunchPad*
to access the e-Book, Clinical Choices, videos, activities, and LearningCurve, as well as study aids including flashcards, FAQs, and research exercises.

LaunchPad
macmillan learning

?...Sexual Disorders and Gender Variations

> *Robert, a 57-year-old man, came to sex therapy with his wife because of his inability to get erections. He had not had a problem with erections until six months earlier, when they attempted to have sex after an evening out, during which he had had several drinks. They attributed his failure to get an erection to his being "a little drunk," but he found himself worrying over the next few days that he was perhaps becoming impotent. When they next attempted intercourse, he found himself unable to get involved in what they were doing because he was so intent on watching himself to see if he would get an erection. Once again he did not, and they were both very upset. His failure to get an erection continued over the next few months. Robert's wife was very upset and frustrated, accusing him of having an affair, or of no longer finding her attractive. Robert wondered if he was getting too old, or if his medication for high blood pressure, which he had been taking for about a year, might be interfering with erections. When they came for sex therapy, they had not attempted any sexual activity for over two months.*

Sexual behavior is a major focus of both our private thoughts and public discussions. Sexual feelings are a crucial part of our development and daily functioning, sexual activity is tied to the satisfaction of our basic needs, and sexual performance is linked to our self-esteem. Most people are fascinated by the abnormal sexual behavior of others and worry about the normality of their own sexuality.

Experts recognize two general categories of sexual disorders: sexual dysfunctions and paraphilic disorders. People with *sexual dysfunctions* have problems with their sexual responses. Robert, for example, had a dysfunction known as erectile disorder, a repeated failure to attain or maintain an erection during sexual activity. People with *paraphilic disorders* have repeated and intense sexual urges or fantasies in response to objects or situations that society deems inappropriate, and they may behave inappropriately as well. They may be aroused by the thought of sexual activity with a child, for example, or of exposing their genitals to strangers, and they may act on those urges.

As you will see throughout this chapter, relatively little is known about racial and other cultural differences in sexuality. This is true for normal sexual patterns, sexual dysfunctions, and paraphilic disorders alike. Although different cultural groups have for years been labeled hypersexual, "hot blooded," exotic, passionate, submissive, and the like, such incorrect stereotypes have grown strictly from ignorance or prejudice, not from objective observations or research (McGoldrick et al., 2007). In fact, sex therapists and sex researchers have only recently begun to attend systematically to the importance of culture and race.

After examining the sexual disorders, this chapter will turn to a discussion of *variations in gender*, specifically *transgender* functioning. Transgender people have a sense that their *gender identity* (one's personal experience of one's gender) is different from the gender they were assigned at birth. DSM-5 does not consider such individuals to be abnormal; however, it does include a diagnostic category called *gender dysphoria*, a pattern in which individuals experience significant distress or impairment as a consequence of their transgender feelings. As you will see, the inclusion of this category in the DSM is very controversial.

#SexualCensus

The World Health Organization estimates that around 115 million acts of sexual intercourse occur each day.

By convention, sexual disorders and issues of gender are often discussed in the same chapter, and we shall do the same in this chapter. At the same time, it is important to be clear that issues of sex are different from issues of gender. Sexual functioning refers to how one reacts and performs in the sexual realm, whereas gender identity is about whether one considers oneself male or female. ■

Sexual Dysfunctions

SEXUAL DYSFUNCTIONS, DISORDERS IN WHICH people cannot respond normally in key areas of sexual functioning, make it difficult or impossible to enjoy sexual intercourse. Studies suggest that as many as 30 percent of men and 45 percent of women around the world suffer from such a dysfunction during their lives (Cunningham & Rosen, 2016). Sexual dysfunctions are typically very distressing, and they often lead to sexual frustration, guilt, loss of self-esteem, and interpersonal problems. Often these dysfunctions are interrelated; many patients with one dysfunction have another as well. Sexual dysfunction is described here for heterosexual couples, the majority of couples seen in therapy. Gay and lesbian couples have the same dysfunctions, however, and therapists use the same basic techniques to treat them.

The human sexual response can be described as a *cycle* with four phases: *desire, excitement, orgasm,* and *resolution* (Shifren, 2016; Hayes, 2011) (see **Figure 13-1** and **Figure 13-2**). Sexual dysfunctions affect one or more of the first three phases. Resolution consists simply of the relaxation and reduction in arousal that follow orgasm. Some people struggle with a sexual dysfunction their whole lives (labeled *lifelong type*); in other cases, normal sexual functioning preceded the dysfunction (*acquired type*). In some cases the dysfunction is present during all sexual situations (*generalized type*); in others it is tied to particular situations (*situational type*) (APA, 2013).

> Rates for sexual behavior are typically based on population surveys. What factors might affect the accuracy of such surveys?

Disorders of Desire

The **desire phase** of the sexual response cycle consists of an interest in or urge to have sex, sexual attraction to others, and for many people, sexual fantasies. Two dysfunctions affect the desire phase—*male hypoactive sexual desire disorder* and *female sexual interest/arousal disorder*. The latter disorder actually cuts across both the desire and excitement phases of the sexual response cycle. It is considered a single disorder in

FIGURE 13-1

The Normal Sexual Response Cycle

Researchers have found a similar sequence of phases in both males and females. Sometimes, however, women do not experience orgasm; in that case, the resolution phase is less sudden. And sometimes women have two or more orgasms in succession before the resolution phase. (Information from: Kaplan, 1974; Masters & Johnson, 1970, 1966.)

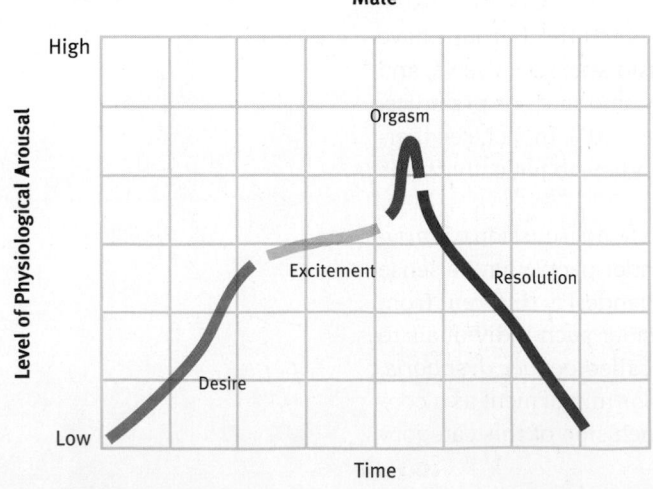

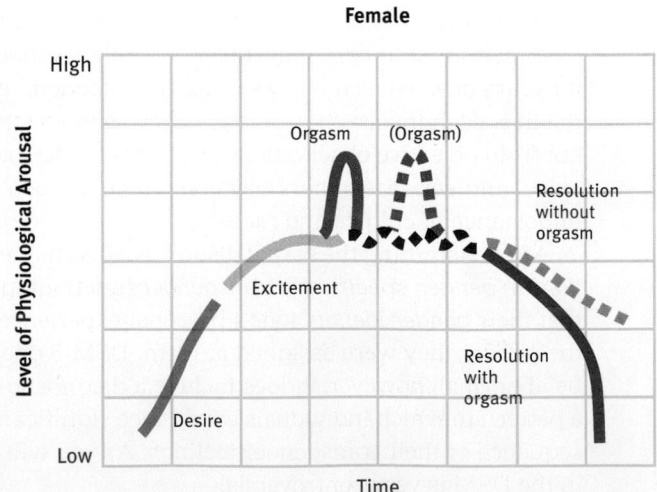

DSM-5 because, according to research, desire and arousal overlap particularly highly for women, and many women express difficulty distinguishing feelings of desire from those of arousal (APA, 2013).

A number of people have normal sexual interest but choose, as a matter of lifestyle rather than sexual desire, to avoid engaging in sexual relations (see *InfoCentral* on page 387). These people are not diagnosed as having one of the sexual desire disorders.

Men with **male hypoactive sexual desire disorder** persistently lack or have reduced interest in sex and engage in little sexual activity (see **Table 13-1**). Nevertheless, when they do have sex, their physical responses may be normal and they may enjoy the experience. While most cultures portray men as wanting all the sex they can get, as many as 18 percent of men worldwide have this disorder, and the number seeking therapy has increased during the past decade (Cunningham & Rosen, 2016; Martin et al., 2014).

Women with **female sexual interest/arousal disorder** also lack normal interest in sex and rarely initiate sexual activity (see Table 13-1 again). In addition, many such women feel little excitement during sexual activity, are unaroused by erotic cues, and have few genital or nongenital sensations during sexual activity (APA, 2013). As many as 39 percent of women worldwide have reduced sexual interest and arousal (Shifren, 2016; Christensen et al., 2011; Lewis et al., 2010). Around half of those individuals feel significant distress due to their level of arousal, and, as such, they qualify for a diagnosis of female sexual interest/arousal disorder. It is important to note that many sex researchers and therapists believe it is inaccurate to combine desire and excitement symptoms into a single female disorder (Sungur & Gündüz, 2014). They would have preferred that DSM-5 continue the past DSM tradition of listing two separate dysfunctions—*female hypoactive sexual desire disorder* and *female sexual arousal disorder*.

A person's sex drive is determined by a combination of biological, psychological, and sociocultural factors, any of which may reduce sexual desire (Rosian et al., 2017). Most cases of low sexual desire are caused primarily by sociocultural and psychological factors, but biological conditions can also lower sex drive significantly.

Biological Causes of Low Sexual Desire A number of hormones interact to help produce sexual desire and behavior, and abnormalities in their activity can lower a person's sex drive (Cunningham & Rosen, 2016; Shifren, 2016). In both men and women, a high level of the hormone *prolactin*, a low level of the male sex hormone *testosterone*, and either a high or low level of the female sex hormone *estrogen* can lead to low sex drive. Low sex drive has been linked to the high levels of estrogen contained in some birth control pills, for example. Conversely, it has also been tied to

sexual dysfunction A disorder marked by a persistent inability to function normally in some area of the sexual response cycle.

desire phase The phase of the sexual response cycle consisting of an urge to have sex, sexual fantasies, and sexual attraction to others.

male hypoactive sexual desire disorder A male dysfunction marked by a persistent reduction or lack of interest in sex and hence a low level of sexual activity.

female sexual interest/arousal disorder A female dysfunction marked by a persistent reduction or lack of interest in sex and low sexual activity, as well as, in some cases, limited excitement and few sexual sensations during sexual activity.

FIGURE 13-2

Normal Female Sexual Anatomy

Changes in the female anatomy take place during the different phases of the sexual response cycle. (Information from: Hyde, 1990, p. 200.)

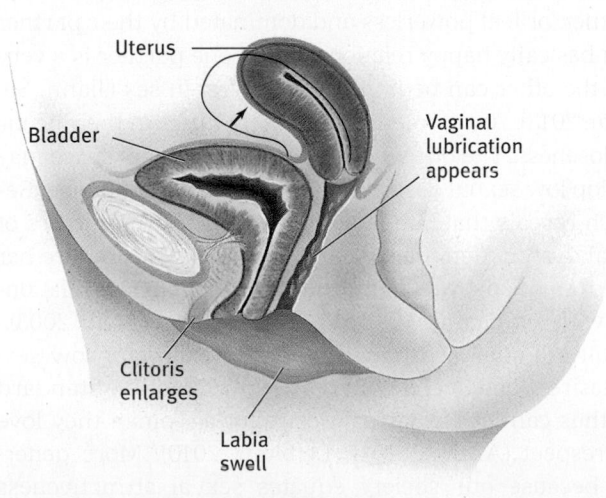

Desire

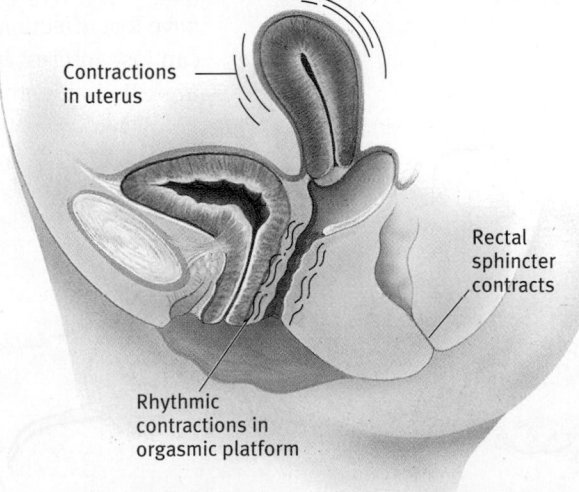

Orgasm

TABLE: 13-1

Dx Checklist

Male Hypoactive Sexual Desire Disorder

1. For at least 6 months, individual repeatedly experiences few or no sexual thoughts, fantasies, or desires.

2. Individual experiences significant distress about this.

Female Sexual Interest/Arousal Disorder.

1. For at least 6 months, individual usually displays reduced or no sexual interest and arousal, characterized by the reduction or absence of at least three of the following: • Sexual interest • Sexual thought or fantasies • Sexual initiation or receptiveness • Excitement or pleasure during sex • Responsiveness to sexual cues • Genital or nongenital sensations during sex.

2. Individual experiences significant distress.

(Information from: APA, 2013.)

the low level of estrogen found in many postmenopausal women or women who have recently given birth.

Recent investigations also have suggested that low sexual desire may be linked to excessive activity of the neurotransmitters *serotonin* and *dopamine* (Rosian et al., 2017). In one study, for example, female rats were administered *apomorphine,* a drug known to increase dopamine activity in certain areas of the brain (Snoeren et al., 2011). These rats then avoided sexual contact with male rats.

Clinical practice and research have further indicated that sex drive can be lowered by certain pain medications, psychotropic drugs, and illegal drugs such as cocaine, marijuana, amphetamines, and heroin (Hirsch & Birnbaum, 2016; Glina, Sharlip, & Hellstrom, 2013). Low levels of alcohol may enhance the sex drive by lowering a person's inhibitions, but high levels may reduce it (Cunningham & Khera, 2016).

Long-term physical illness can also lower a person's sex drive (Cunningham & Rosen, 2016). The reduced drive may be a direct result of the illness or an indirect result because of stress, pain, or depression brought on by the illness.

Psychological Causes of Low Sexual Desire A general increase in anxiety, depression, or anger may reduce sexual desire in both men and women (Shifren, 2016; Rubio-Aurioles & Bivalacqua, 2013). Frequently, as cognitive theorists have noted, people with low sexual desire have particular attitudes, fears, or memories that contribute to their dysfunction, such as a belief that sex is immoral or dangerous (Popov et al., 2015; Giraldi et al., 2013). Other people are so afraid of losing control over their sexual urges that they try to resist them completely. And still others fear pregnancy.

Certain psychological disorders may also contribute to low sexual desire. Even a mild level of depression can interfere with sexual desire, and some people with obsessive-compulsive symptoms find contact with another person's body fluids and odors to be highly unpleasant (Cunningham & Rosen, 2016; Rubio-Aurioles & Bivalacqua, 2013).

Sociocultural Causes of Low Sexual Desire The attitudes, fears, and psychological disorders that contribute to low sexual desire occur within a social context, and thus certain sociocultural factors have also been linked to disorders of sexual desire. Many people who have low sexual desire are feeling situational pressures—divorce, a death in the family, job stress, infertility difficulties, having a baby (Shifren, 2016; Hamilton & Meston, 2013). One study found, for example, that men who had experienced more job difficulties over the past year were almost twice as likely as men who were content at work to have low sexual desire or other sexual dysfunctions (Štulhofer et al., 2013). Other people may be having problems in their relationships (Cunningham & Rosen, 2016; Giraldi et al., 2013). People who are in an unhappy relationship, have lost affection for their partner, or feel powerless and dominated by their partner can lose interest in sex. Even in basically happy relationships, if one partner is a very unskilled, unenthusiastic lover, the other can begin to lose interest in sex (Jiann, Su, & Tsai, 2013). And sometimes partners differ in their needs for closeness. The one who needs more personal space may develop low sexual desire as a way of keeping distance. Research reveals that, among women, the best predictors of sexual dysfunction, particularly low sexual desire, are her level of emotional well-being and the quality of her relationship with her partner (Shifren, 2016; Bancroft et al., 2003).

Cultural standards can also set the stage for low sexual desire. Some men adopt our culture's double standard and thus cannot feel sexual desire for a woman they love and respect (Antfolk, 2017; Leiblum, 2010). More generally, because our society equates sexual attractiveness with youthfulness, many middle-aged and older men and

Carolita Johnson/The New Yorker Collection/www.cartoonbank.com

"It's not you, babe—I've been neutered."

SEX THROUGHOUT THE LIFE CYCLE

Sexual dysfunctions are different from the usual patterns of sexual functioning. But in the sexual realm, what is "the usual?" Studies conducted over the past two decades have provided a wealth of enlightening information about sexual behavior in the "normal" populations of North America. As you might expect, sexual behavior often differs by age and by gender.

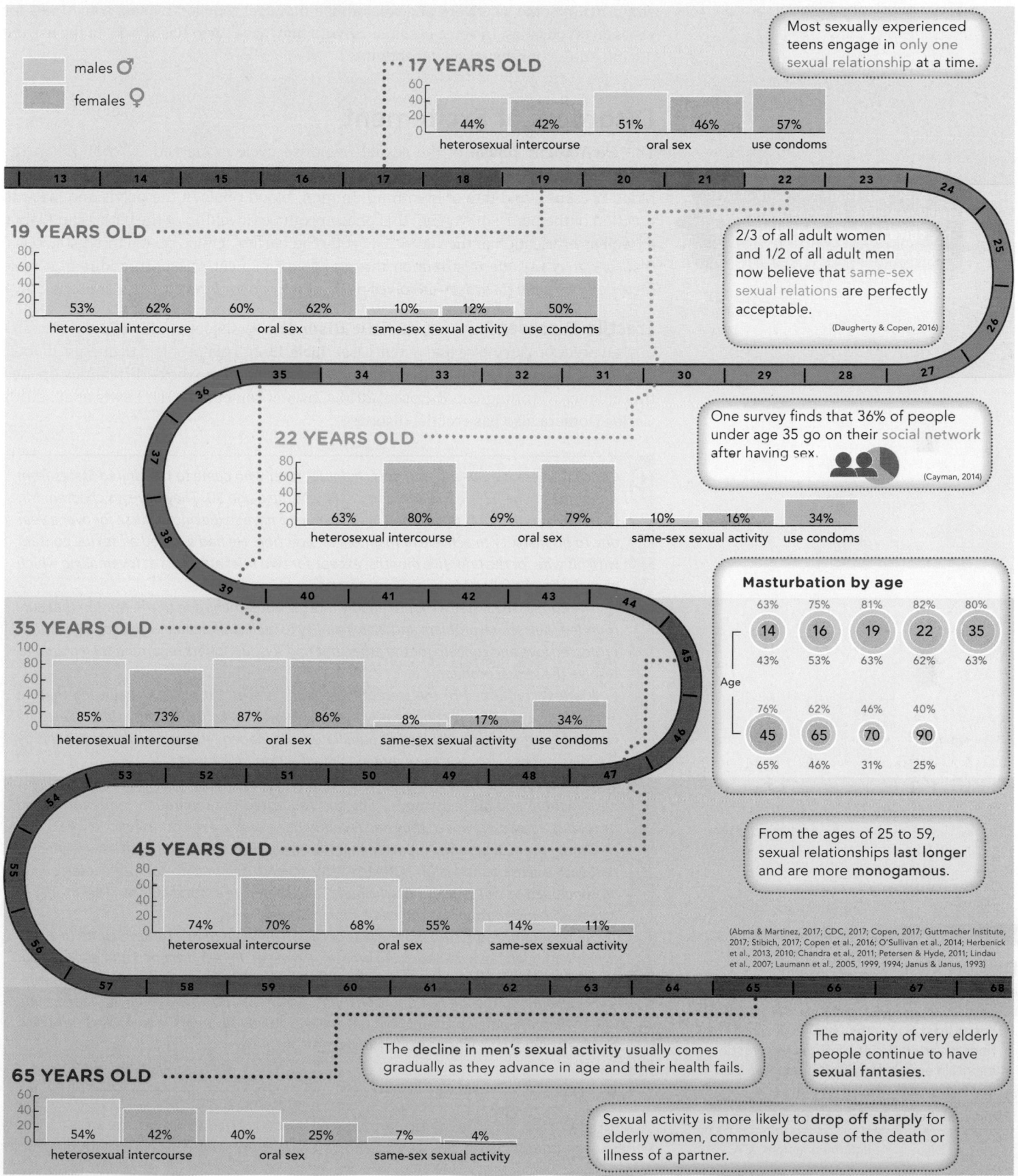

males ♂
females ♀

Most sexually experienced teens engage in only one sexual relationship at a time.

17 YEARS OLD

heterosexual intercourse		oral sex		use condoms
44%	42%	51%	46%	57%

19 YEARS OLD

heterosexual intercourse		oral sex		same-sex sexual activity		use condoms
53%	62%	60%	62%	10%	12%	50%

2/3 of all adult women and 1/2 of all adult men now believe that same-sex sexual relations are perfectly acceptable.
(Daugherty & Copen, 2016)

One survey finds that 36% of people under age 35 go on their social network after having sex.
(Cayman, 2014)

22 YEARS OLD

heterosexual intercourse		oral sex		same-sex sexual activity		use condoms
63%	80%	69%	79%	10%	16%	34%

35 YEARS OLD

heterosexual intercourse		oral sex		same-sex sexual activity		use condoms
85%	73%	87%	86%	8%	17%	34%

Masturbation by age

63%	75%	81%	82%	80%
14	16	19	22	35
43%	53%	63%	62%	63%

Age

76%	62%	46%	40%
45	65	70	90
65%	46%	31%	25%

From the ages of 25 to 59, sexual relationships last longer and are more monogamous.

45 YEARS OLD

heterosexual intercourse		oral sex		same-sex sexual activity	
74%	70%	68%	55%	14%	11%

(Abma & Martinez, 2017; CDC, 2017; Copen, 2017; Guttmacher Institute, 2017; Stibich, 2017; Copen et al., 2016; O'Sullivan et al., 2014; Herbenick et al., 2013, 2010; Chandra et al., 2011; Petersen & Hyde, 2011; Lindau et al., 2007; Laumann et al., 2005, 1999, 1994; Janus & Janus, 1993)

The decline in men's sexual activity usually comes gradually as they advance in age and their health fails.

The majority of very elderly people continue to have sexual fantasies.

65 YEARS OLD

heterosexual intercourse		oral sex		same-sex sexual activity	
54%	42%	40%	25%	7%	4%

Sexual activity is more likely to drop off sharply for elderly women, commonly because of the death or illness of a partner.

women lose interest in sex as their self-image or their attraction to their partner diminishes with age.

The trauma of sexual molestation or assault is especially likely to produce the fears, attitudes, and memories found in disorders of sexual desire (Shifren, 2016; Giraldi et al., 2013). Some survivors of sexual abuse may feel repelled by sex, sometimes for years, even decades. In some cases, survivors may have vivid flashbacks of the assault during adult consensual sexual activity.

Disorders of Excitement

The **excitement phase** of the sexual response cycle is marked by changes in the pelvic region, general physical arousal, and increases in heart rate, muscle tension, blood pressure, and rate of breathing. In men, blood pools in the pelvis and leads to erection of the penis; in women, this phase produces swelling of the clitoris and labia, as well as lubrication of the vagina. As you read earlier, female sexual interest/arousal disorder may include dysfunction during the excitement phase. In addition, a male disorder—*erectile disorder*—involves dysfunction during the excitement phase only.

Erectile Disorder Men with **erectile disorder** persistently fail to attain or maintain an erection during sexual activity (see **Table 13-2**). This problem occurs in 15 to 25 percent of the male population, including Robert, the man whose difficulties opened this chapter (Cunningham & Rosen, 2016; Christensen et al., 2011; Lewis et al., 2010). Carlos Domera also has erectile disorder:

> *Carlos Domera is a 30-year-old dress manufacturer who came to the United States from Argentina at age 22. He is married to . . . Phyllis, also age 30. They have no children. Mr. Domera's problem was that he had been unable to have sexual intercourse for over a year due to his inability to achieve or maintain an erection. He had avoided all sexual contact with his wife for the prior five months, except for two brief attempts at lovemaking which ended when he failed to maintain his erection.*
>
> *The couple separated a month ago by mutual agreement due to the tension that surrounded their sexual problem and their inability to feel comfortable with each other. Both professed love and concern for the other, but had serious doubts regarding their ability to resolve the sexual problem. . . .*
>
> *[Carlos] conformed to the stereotype of the "macho Latin lover," believing that he "should always have erections easily and be able to make love at any time." Since he couldn't "perform" sexually, he felt humiliated and inadequate, and he dealt with this by avoiding not only sex, but any expression of affection for his wife.*
>
> *[Phyllis] felt "he is not trying; perhaps he doesn't love me, and I can't live with no sex, no affection, and his bad moods." She had requested the separation temporarily, and he readily agreed. However, they had recently been seeing each other twice a week. . . .*
>
> *During the evaluation he reported that the onset of his erectile difficulties was concurrent with a tense period in his business. After several "failures" to complete intercourse, he concluded he was "useless as a husband" and therefore a "total failure." The anxiety of attempting lovemaking was too much for him to deal with.*
>
> *He reluctantly admitted that he was occasionally able to masturbate alone to a full, firm erection and reach a satisfying orgasm. However, he felt ashamed and guilty about this, from both childhood masturbatory guilt and a feeling that he was "cheating" his wife. It was also noted that he had occasional firm erections upon awakening in the morning. Other than the antidepressant, the patient was taking no drugs, and he was not using much alcohol. There was no evidence of physical illness.*
>
> *(Spitzer et al., 1983, pp. 105–106)*

Unlike Carlos, most men with an erectile disorder are over the age of 50, largely because so many cases are associated with ailments or diseases of older adults

---

Why do you think the clinical field has been slow to investigate possible cultural and racial differences in sexual behaviors?

TABLE: 13-2

Dx Checklist

Erectile Disorder

1. For at least 6 months, individual usually finds it very difficult to obtain an erection, maintain an erection, and/or achieve past levels of erectile rigidity during sex.

2. Individual experiences significant distress.

(Information from: APA, 2013.)

(Agronin, 2016; Cameron et al., 2005). Around 7 percent of men in their twenties also have the disorder; that number increases to as many as 40 percent of men in their sixties and early seventies and 70 percent of those in their late seventies and older (Cunningham & Rosen, 2016; Lewis et al., 2010). Moreover, according to surveys, half of all adult men experience erectile difficulty during intercourse at least some of the time. Most cases of erectile disorder result from an interaction of biological, psychological, and sociocultural processes (Berry & Berry, 2013; Rowland, 2012).

BIOLOGICAL CAUSES The same hormonal imbalances that can cause male hypoactive sexual desire disorder can also produce erectile disorder (Cunningham & Rosen, 2016; Hyde, 2005). More commonly, however, vascular problems—problems with the body's blood vessels—are involved (Lewis et al., 2010; Wincze et al., 2008). An erection occurs when the chambers in the penis fill with blood, so any condition that reduces blood flow into the penis, such as heart disease or clogging of the arteries, may lead to erectile disorder (Cunningham & Rosen, 2016; Berry & Berry, 2013; Glina et al., 2013). It can also be caused by damage to the nervous system as a result of diabetes, spinal cord injuries, multiple sclerosis, kidney failure, or treatment by dialysis. In addition, as is the case with male hypoactive sexual desire disorder, the use of certain medications and various forms of substance abuse, from alcohol abuse to cigarette smoking, may interfere with erections (Hirsch & Birnbaum, 2016; Glina et al., 2013).

Medical procedures, including ultrasound recordings and blood tests, have been developed for diagnosing biological causes of erectile disorder. Measuring **nocturnal penile tumescence (NPT),** or erections during sleep, is particularly useful in assessing whether physical factors are responsible. Men typically have erections during *rapid eye movement (REM) sleep,* the phase of sleep in which dreaming takes place. A healthy man is likely to have two to five REM periods each night, and several penile erections as well. Abnormal or absent nightly erections usually (but not always) indicate some physical basis for erectile failure. As a rough screening device, a patient may be instructed to fasten a simple "snap gauge" band around his penis before going to sleep and then check it the next morning. A broken band indicates that he has had an erection during the night. An unbroken band indicates that he did not have nighttime erections and suggests that his general erectile problem may have a physical basis. A newer version of this device further attaches the band to a computer, which provides precise measurements of erections throughout the night (Li et al., 2017). Such assessment devices are less likely to be used in clinical practice today than in past years. As you'll see later in the chapter, Viagra and other drugs for erectile disorder are typically given to patients without much formal evaluation of their problem.

PSYCHOLOGICAL CAUSES Any of the psychological causes of male hypoactive sexual desire disorder can also interfere with arousal and lead to erectile disorder (Cunningham & Rosen, 2016; Rowland, Georgoff, & Burnett, 2011). As many as 90 percent of all men with severe depression, for example, experience some degree of erectile dysfunction (Cunningham & Rosen, 2016; Montejo et al., 2011; Stevenson & Elliott, 2007).

One well-supported psychological explanation for erectile disorder is the cognitive-behavioral theory developed by William Masters and Virginia Johnson (1970). The explanation emphasizes **performance anxiety** and the **spectator role.** Once a man begins to have erectile problems, for whatever reason, he becomes fearful about failing to have an erection and worries during each sexual encounter (Cunningham & Rosen, 2016; Carvalho & Nobre, 2011). Instead of relaxing and enjoying the sensations

Joe Dator/The New Yorker Collection/The CartoonBank

"Well, how convenient."

excitement phase The phase of the sexual response cycle marked by changes in the pelvic region, general physical arousal, and increases in heart rate, muscle tension, blood pressure, and rate of breathing.

erectile disorder A dysfunction in which a man repeatedly fails to attain or maintain an erection during sexual activity.

nocturnal penile tumescence (NPT) Erection during sleep.

performance anxiety The fear of performing inadequately and a related tension that are experienced during sex.

spectator role A state of mind that some people experience during sex, focusing on their sexual performance to such an extent that their performance and their enjoyment are reduced.

Sexual pioneers William Masters and Virginia Johnson work with a couple in their office. The two researchers, the field's most important figures in the study of the human sexual response and the treatment of sexual dysfunctions, conducted their work from 1967 until the 1990s, writing two classic books, *Human Sexual Response* and *Human Sexual Inadequacy*.

George Tames/The New York Times/Redux

of sexual pleasure, he remains distanced from the activity, watching himself and focusing on the goal of reaching erection. Instead of being an aroused participant, he becomes a judge and spectator. Whatever the initial reason for the erectile dysfunction, the resulting spectator role becomes the reason for the ongoing problem. In this vicious cycle, the original cause of the erectile failure becomes less important than fear of failure.

> Are there other problem areas in life that might also be explained by performance anxiety and the spectator role?

SOCIOCULTURAL CAUSES Each of the sociocultural factors that contribute to male hypoactive sexual desire disorder has also been tied to erectile disorder. Men who have lost their jobs and are under financial stress, for example, are more likely to develop erectile difficulties than other men (Nobre, 2017). Marital stress, too, has been tied to this dysfunction (Cunningham & Rosen, 2016; Brenot, 2011; LoPiccolo, 2004, 1991). Two relationship patterns in particular may contribute to it. In one, a wife provides too little physical stimulation for her aging husband, who, because of normal aging changes, now requires more intense, direct, and lengthy physical stimulation of the penis in order to have an erection. In the second relationship pattern, a couple believes that only intercourse can give the wife an orgasm. This idea increases the pressure on the man to have an erection and makes him more vulnerable to erectile dysfunction. If the wife reaches orgasm manually or orally during their sexual encounter, his pressure to perform is reduced.

Disorders of Orgasm

During the **orgasm phase** of the sexual response cycle, a person's sexual pleasure peaks and sexual tension is released as the muscles in the pelvic region contract, or draw together, rhythmically (see **Figure 13-3**). The man's semen is ejaculated, and the outer third of the woman's vaginal wall contracts. Dysfunctions of this phase of the sexual response cycle are *early ejaculation* and *delayed ejaculation* in men and *female orgasmic disorder* in women.

Premature Ejaculation Eduardo is typical of many men in his experience of premature ejaculation:

orgasm phase The phase of the sexual response cycle during which a person's sexual pleasure peaks and sexual tension is released as muscles in the pelvic region contract rhythmically.

premature ejaculation A dysfunction in which a man persistently reaches orgasm and ejaculates within 1 minute of beginning sexual activity with a partner and before he wishes to. Also called *early* or *rapid* ejaculation.

Eduardo, a 20-year-old student, sought treatment after his girlfriend ended their relationship because his premature ejaculation left her sexually frustrated. Eduardo had had only one previous sexual relationship, during his senior year in high school. With two friends he would drive to a neighboring town and find a certain prostitute. After picking her up, they would drive to a deserted area and take turns having sex with her, while the others waited outside the car. Both the prostitute and his friends urged him to hurry up because they feared discovery by the police, and besides, in the winter it was cold. When Eduardo began his sexual relationship with his girlfriend, his entire sexual history consisted of this rapid intercourse, with virtually no foreplay. He found caressing his girlfriend's breasts and genitals and her touching of his penis to be so arousing that he sometimes ejaculated before complete entry of the penis, or after at most only a minute or so of intercourse.

#NightlyVisits

People can sometimes have an orgasm during sleep. Ancient Babylonians said that such nocturnal orgasms were caused by a "maid of the night" who visited men in their sleep and a "little night man" who visited women (Kahn & Fawcett, 1993).

A man suffering from **premature ejaculation** (also called *early,* or *rapid,* ejaculation) persistently reaches orgasm and ejaculates within 1 minute of beginning sexual activity with a partner and before he wishes to (see **Table 13-3** on page 392). As many as 30 percent of men worldwide ejaculate early at some time (Cunningham & Rosen, 2016; Lewis et al., 2010). The typical duration of intercourse in our society has increased over the past several decades, which has caused more distress among men who ejaculate prematurely. Although many young men certainly contend with the dysfunction, research suggests that men of any age may suffer from it (Chung et al., 2015).

Psychological, particularly cognitive-behavioral, explanations of premature ejaculation have received more research support than other kinds of explanations. The dysfunction is common, for example, among young, sexually inexperienced men such as Eduardo, who simply have not learned to slow down, control their arousal, and extend the pleasurable process of making love (Cunningham & Rosen, 2016; Althof, 2007). In fact, young men often ejaculate prematurely during their first sexual encounter. With continued sexual experience, most men acquire more control over their sexual responses. Men of any age who have sex only occasionally are also prone to ejaculate early.

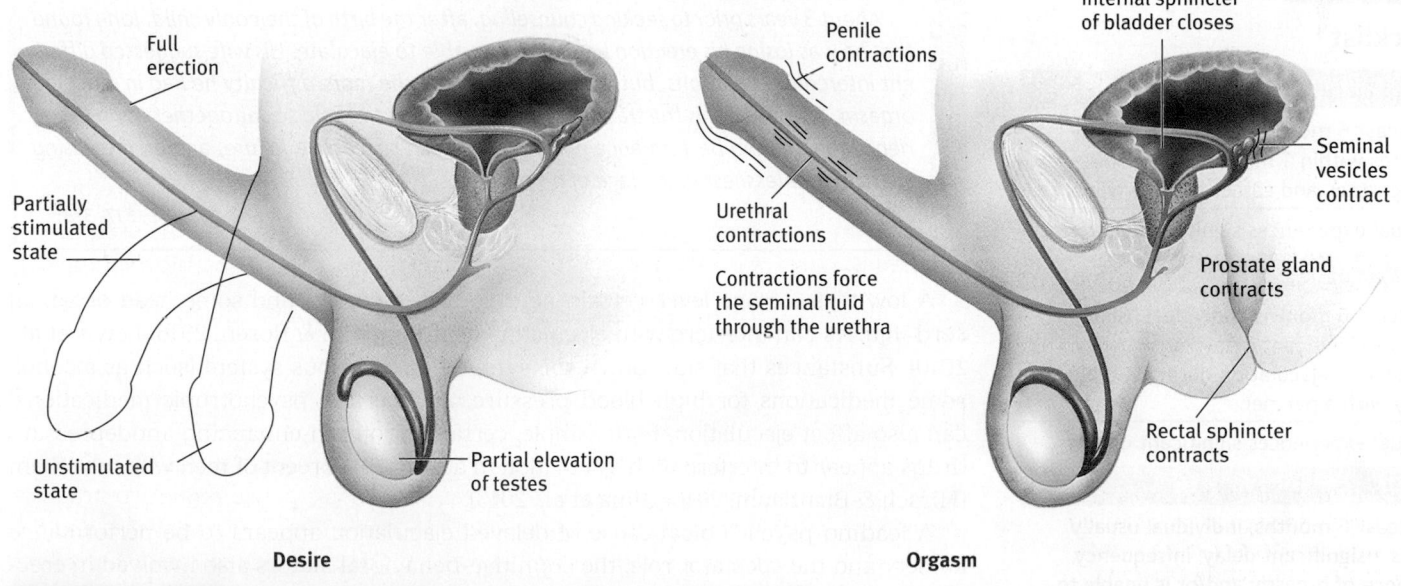

FIGURE 13-3

Normal Male Sexual Anatomy

Changes in the male anatomy occur during the different phases of the sexual response cycle. (Information from: Hyde, 1990, p. 199.)

Grooming is key Humans are not the only animals that follow a sexual response cycle or, for that matter, display sexual dysfunctions. Here a male macaque monkey grooms a female monkey while they sit in a hot spring in the snow in central Japan. Such grooming triples the likelihood that the female will engage in sexual activity with the male.

Clinicians have also suggested that premature ejaculation may be related to anxiety, hurried masturbation experiences during adolescence (in fear of being "caught" by parents), or poor recognition of one's own sexual arousal (Cunningham & Rosen, 2016; Althof, 2007). However, these theories have only sometimes received clear research support.

There is a growing belief among many clinical theorists that biological factors may also play a key role in many cases of premature ejaculation. Three biological theories have emerged from the limited investigations done so far. One theory states that some men are born with a genetic predisposition to develop this dysfunction. Indeed, one study found that 91 percent of a small sample of men suffering from early ejaculation had first-degree relatives who also had the dysfunction. A second theory, based on animal studies, argues that the brains of men who ejaculate prematurely contain certain serotonin receptors that are overactive and others that are underactive. A third explanation holds that men with this dysfunction have greater sensitivity or nerve conduction in the area of their penis, a notion that has received inconsistent research support thus far (Cunningham & Rosen, 2016; Althof, 2007).

Delayed Ejaculation A man with **delayed ejaculation** (previously called *male orgasmic disorder* or *inhibited male orgasm*) persistently is unable to ejaculate or has very delayed ejaculations during sexual activity with a partner (see Table 13-3 again). As many as 10 percent of men worldwide have this disorder (Di Sante et al., 2016; Lewis et al., 2010). It is typically a source of great frustration and upset, as in the case of John:

> *John, a 38-year-old sales representative, had been married for 9 years. At the insistence of his 32-year-old wife, the couple sought counseling for their sexual problem—his inability to ejaculate during intercourse. During the early years of the marriage, his wife had experienced difficulty reaching orgasm until he learned to delay his ejaculation for a long period of time. To do this, he used mental distraction techniques and regularly smoked marijuana before making love. Initially, John felt very satisfied that he could make love for longer and longer periods of time without ejaculation and regarded his ability as a sign of masculinity.*
>
> *About 3 years prior to seeking counseling, after the birth of their only child, John found that he was losing his erection before he was able to ejaculate. His wife suggested different intercourse positions, but the harder he tried, the more difficulty he had in reaching orgasm. Because of his frustration, the couple began to avoid sex altogether. John experienced increasing performance anxiety with each successive failure, and an increasing sense of helplessness in the face of his problem.*
>
> *(Rosen & Rosen, 1981, pp. 317–318)*

A low testosterone level, certain neurological diseases, and some head or spinal cord injuries can interfere with ejaculation (Cunningham & Rosen, 2016; Lewis et al., 2010). Substances that slow down the sympathetic nervous system (such as alcohol, some medications for high blood pressure, and certain psychotropic medications) can also affect ejaculation. For example, certain serotonin-enhancing antidepressant drugs appear to interfere with ejaculation in at least 30 percent of men who take them (Hirsch & Birnbaum, 2016; Glina et al., 2013).

A leading psychological cause of delayed ejaculation appears to be performance anxiety and the spectator role, the cognitive-behavioral factors also involved in erectile disorder (Carvalho & Nobre, 2011; Kashdan et al., 2011). Once a man begins to focus on reaching orgasm, he may stop being an aroused participant in his sexual activity and instead become an unaroused, self-critical, and fearful observer (Rowland, 2012; Hartmann & Waldinger, 2007; Wiederman, 2001). Another psychological cause

---

TABLE: 13-3

Dx Checklist

Premature Ejaculation

1. For at least 6 months, individual usually ejaculates within 1 minute of beginning sex with a partner, and earlier than he wants to.

2. Individual experiences significant distress.

Delayed Ejaculation

1. For at least 6 months, individual usually displays a significant delay, infrequency, or absence of ejaculation during sexual activity with a partner.

2. Individual experiences significant distress.

Female Orgasmic Disorder

1. For at least 6 months, individual usually displays a significant delay, infrequency, or absence of orgasm, and/or is unable to achieve past orgasmic intensity.

2. Individual experiences significant distress.

(Information from: APA, 2013.)

of delayed ejaculation may be past masturbation habits. If, for example, a man has masturbated all his life by rubbing his penis against sheets, pillows, or other such objects, he may have difficulty reaching orgasm in the absence of the sensations tied to those objects (Wincze et al., 2008). Finally, delayed ejaculation may develop out of male hypoactive sexual desire disorder. A man who engages in sex without any real desire for it may not get aroused enough to ejaculate.

Female Orgasmic Disorder Janel and Isaac, married for 3 years, went for sex therapy because of her lack of orgasm.

> Janel had never had an orgasm in any way, but because of Isaac's concern, she had been faking orgasm during intercourse until recently. Finally she told him the truth, and they sought therapy together. Janel had been raised by a strictly religious family. She could not recall ever seeing her parents kiss or show physical affection for each other. She was severely punished on one occasion when her mother found her looking at her own genitals, at about age 7. Janel received no sex education from her parents, and when she began to menstruate, her mother told her only that this meant that she could become pregnant, so she mustn't ever kiss a boy or let a boy touch her. Her mother restricted her dating severely, with repeated warnings that "boys only want one thing." While her parents were rather critical and demanding of her (asking her why she got one B among otherwise straight A's on her report card, for example), they were loving parents and their approval was very important to her.

Women with **female orgasmic disorder** persistently fail to reach orgasm, have very low intensity orgasms, or have a very delayed orgasm (see Table 13-3 again). Around 21 percent of women apparently experience this pattern to some degree (Shifren, 2016; Heiman, 2007, 2002). Approximately half of them report feeling distressed about it (Faubion & Rullo, 2015). Studies indicate that 10 percent or more of women have never had an orgasm, either alone or during intercourse, and at least another 9 percent rarely have orgasms (Bancroft et al., 2003). At the same time, 50 to 70 percent of all women experience orgasm in intercourse at least fairly regularly (Castleman, 2016). Women who are more sexually assertive and more comfortable with masturbation tend to have orgasms more regularly (Carrobles et al., 2011). In one study, when participants with female orgasmic disorder were asked to pick a word that best describes their feelings about it, two-thirds of them chose "frustration" (Kingsberg et al., 2013).

> Some theorists believe that the women's movement has helped to enlighten clinical views of sexual disorders. How might this be so?

Most clinicians agree that orgasm during intercourse is not mandatory for normal sexual functioning (Shifren, 2016; Meana, 2012; Wincze et al., 2008). Many women instead reach orgasm with their partners by direct stimulation of the clitoris. Although early psychoanalytic theory considered a lack of orgasm during intercourse to be pathological, evidence suggests that women who rely on stimulation of the clitoris for orgasm are entirely normal and healthy (Laan et al., 2013; Heiman, 2007). It is important to note that a number of clinicians further believe that the achievement of orgasm, under any circumstance, is not a defining feature of an acceptable and normal sex life (Shifren, 2017).

Biological, psychological, and sociocultural factors may combine to produce female orgasmic disorder. Because arousal plays a key role in orgasms, arousal difficulties often are featured prominently in explanations of female orgasmic disorder (Shifren, 2016; Laan et al., 2013).

delayed ejaculation A male dysfunction characterized by persistent inability to ejaculate or very delayed ejaculations during sexual activity with a partner.

female orgasmic disorder A dysfunction in which a woman persistently fails to reach orgasm, has very low intensity orgasms, or has very delayed orgasms.

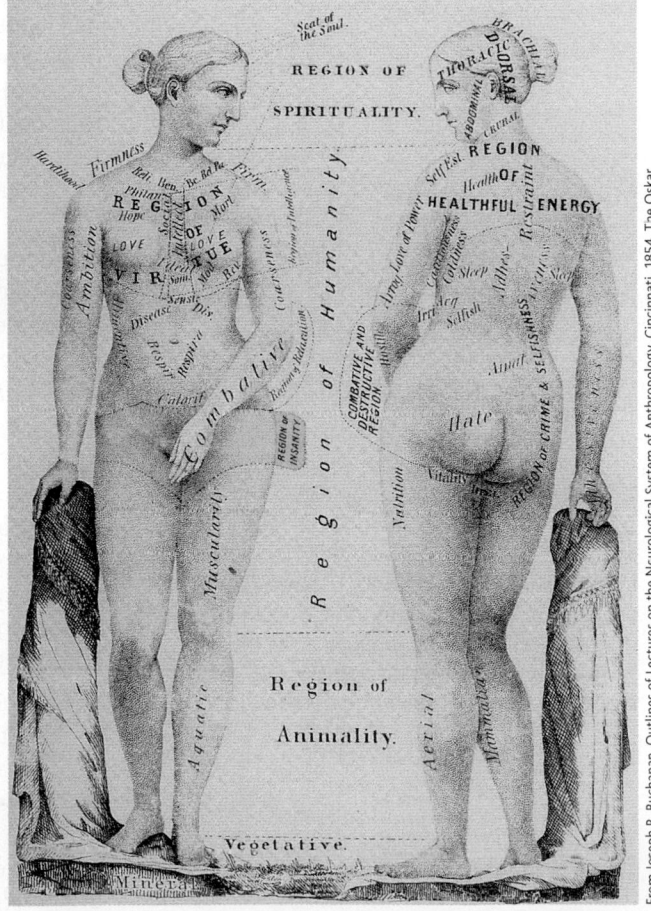

"The region of insanity" Medical authorities described "excessive passion" in Victorian women as dangerous and as a possible cause of insanity (Gamwell & Tomes, 1995). This illustration from a nineteenth-century medical textbook even labels a woman's reproductive organs as her "region of insanity."

"Since we're both being honest, I should tell you I have fleas."

Bruce Eric Kaplan/The New Yorker
Collection/The Cartoon Bank

BIOLOGICAL CAUSES A variety of physiological conditions can affect a woman's orgasm. Diabetes can damage the nervous system in ways that interfere with arousal, lubrication of the vagina, and orgasm. Lack of orgasm has sometimes been linked to multiple sclerosis and other neurological diseases, to the same drugs and medications that may interfere with ejaculation in men, and to changes, often postmenopausal, in skin sensitivity and structure of the clitoris, vaginal walls, or the labia—the folds of skin on each side of the vagina (Hirsch & Birnbaum, 2016; Shifren, 2016).

PSYCHOLOGICAL CAUSES The psychological causes of female sexual interest/arousal disorder, including depression, may also lead to female orgasmic disorder (Laan et al., 2013; Kim et al., 2011). In addition, as both psychodynamic and cognitive theorists might predict, memories of childhood traumas and relationships have sometimes been associated with orgasm problems (Carpenter et al., 2017; Laan et al., 2013). In one large study, memories of an unhappy childhood or loss of a parent during childhood were tied to lack of orgasm in adulthood (Raboch & Raboch, 1992). In other studies, childhood memories of a dependable father, a positive relationship with one's mother, affection between the parents, the mother's positive personality, and the mother's expression of positive emotions were all predictors of positive orgasm outcomes (Heiman, 2007).

SOCIOCULTURAL CAUSES For years many clinicians have believed that female orgasmic problems may result from society's recurrent message to women that they should repress and deny their sexuality, a message that has often led to "less permissive" sexual attitudes and behavior among women than among men. In fact, many women with both arousal and orgasmic difficulties report that they had an overly strict religious upbringing, were punished for childhood masturbation, received no preparation for the onset of menstruation, were restricted in their dating as teenagers, and were told that "nice girls don't" (Laan et al., 2013; LoPiccolo & Van Male, 2000).

A sexually restrictive history, however, is just as common among women who function well during sexual activity (LoPiccolo, 2002). In addition, cultural messages about female sexuality have been more positive in recent years, while the rate of arousal and orgasmic problems remains the same for women. Why, then, do some women and not others develop such problems? Researchers suggest that unusually stressful events, traumas, or relationships may help produce the fears, memories, and attitudes that often characterize these sexual problems (Carpenter et al., 2017; Meana, 2012). For example, many women molested as children or raped as adults have female orgasmic disorder (Hall, 2017, 2007).

Research has also related orgasmic behavior to certain qualities in a woman's intimate relationships (Carpenter et al., 2017; Laan et al., 2013; Brenot, 2011). Studies have found, for example, that the likelihood of reaching orgasm may be tied to how much emotional involvement a woman had during her first experience of intercourse and how long that relationship lasted, the pleasure the woman felt during the experience, her current attraction to her partner's body, and her relationship happiness. Interestingly, the same studies have found that orgasmic women more often have erotic fantasies during sex with their current partner than do nonorgasmic women.

#EarlyPleasure

In some studies, the majority of female participants from sexually healthy and generally positive marriages reported that *foreplay* is the most satisfying component of sexual activity with their partner (Basson, 2007; Hurlbert, 1993).

Disorders of Sexual Pain

Certain sexual dysfunctions are characterized by enormous physical discomfort during intercourse, a difficulty that does not fit neatly into a specific part of the sexual response cycle. Women have such dysfunctions, collectively called **genito-pelvic**

pain/penetration disorder, much more often than men do (Hellstrom & DeLay, 2017; Rezaee et al., 2016).

For some women with genito-pelvic pain/penetration disorder the muscles around the outer third of the vagina involuntarily contract, preventing entry of the penis (see **Table 13-4**). This problem, known in medical circles as *vaginismus* or *pelvic floor hypertonus,* can prevent a couple from ever having intercourse. The problem has received relatively little research, but estimates are that fewer than 1 percent of all women have vaginismus (Stewart, 2015; Christensen et al., 2011). A number of women with vaginismus enjoy sex greatly, have a strong sex drive, and reach orgasm with stimulation of the clitoris (Meana et al., 2017). They just fear the discomfort of penetration of the vagina.

Most clinicians agree with the cognitive-behavioral position that this form of genito-pelvic pain/penetration disorder is usually a learned fear response, set off by a woman's expectation that intercourse will be painful and damaging (Meana et al., 2017; Fugl-Meyer et al., 2013). A variety of factors apparently can set the stage for this fear, including anxiety and ignorance about intercourse, exaggerated stories about how painful and bloody the first occasion of intercourse is for women, trauma caused by an unskilled lover who forces his penis into the vagina before the woman is aroused and lubricated, and the trauma of childhood sexual abuse or adult rape (Jiann, Su, & Tsai, 2013; Binik, 2010).

Alternatively, women may have this form of genito-pelvic pain/penetration disorder because of an infection of the vagina or urinary tract, a gynecological disease such as herpes simplex, or the physical effects of menopause (Rezaee et al., 2016; Stewart, 2015). In such cases, the dysfunction can be overcome only if the women receive medical treatment for these conditions.

Other women with genito-pelvic pain/penetration disorder do not have involuntary contractions of their vaginal muscles, but they do experience severe vaginal or pelvic pain during sexual intercourse, a pattern known medically as *dyspareunia* (from Greek words meaning "painful mating"). Surveys suggest that 14 to 16 percent of all women (and 40 percent of all postmenopausal women) suffer from this problem to some degree (Rezaee et al., 2016; Shifren, 2016). Women with dyspareunia typically enjoy sex and get aroused but find their sex lives very limited by the pain that accompanies what used to be a positive event (Meana et al., 2017; Huijding et al., 2011).

This form of genito-pelvic pain/penetration disorder usually has a physical cause (Rezaee et al., 2016; Fugl-Meyer et al., 2013). Among the most common is an injury (for example, to the vagina or pelvic ligaments) during childbirth. The scar left by an episiotomy (a cut often made to enlarge the vaginal entrance and ease delivery) also can cause pain. Around 16 percent of women have severe vaginal or pelvic pain during intercourse for up to a year after giving birth (Bertozzi et al., 2010). More generally, such pain has also been tied to the penis colliding with remaining parts of the hymen, vaginal infections, wiry pubic hair rubbing against the labia during intercourse, pelvic diseases, tumors, cysts, allergic reactions to the chemicals in vaginal douches and contraceptive creams, the rubber in condoms and diaphragms, and the protein in semen (Rezaee et al., 2016; Tripoli et al., 2011).

Although psychological factors (for instance, heightened anxiety or overattentiveness to one's body) or relationship problems may contribute to dyspareunia, psychosocial factors alone are rarely responsible for it (Rezaee et al., 2016; Granot et al., 2011; Dewitte et al., 2011). In cases that are truly psychogenic, the woman may in fact be suffering from female sexual interest/arousal disorder. That is, penetration into an unaroused, unlubricated vagina is painful (Fugl-Meyer et al., 2013). It also is the case that 1 to 5 percent of men suffer from pain in the genitals during intercourse, and many of these men also qualify for a diagnosis of genito-pelvic pain/penetration disorder (Hellstrom & DeLay, 2017).

TABLE: 13-4
Dx Checklist
Genito-Pelvic Pain/Penetration Disorder
1. For at least 6 months, individual repeatedly experiences at least one of the following problems: • Difficulty having vaginal penetration during intercourse • Significant vaginal or pelvic pain when trying to have intercourse or penetration • Significant fear that vaginal penetration will cause vaginal or pelvic pain • Significant tensing of the pelvic muscles during vaginal penetration.
2. Individual experiences significant distress from this.

(Information from: APA, 2013.)

genito-pelvic pain/penetration disorder A sexual dysfunction characterized by significant physical discomfort during intercourse.

Treatments for Sexual Dysfunctions

THE LAST 40 YEARS HAVE BROUGHT major changes in the treatment of sexual dysfunctions. For the first half of the twentieth century, the leading approach was long-term psychodynamic therapy. Clinicians assumed that sexual dysfunction was caused by failure to progress properly through the psychosexual stages of development, and they used techniques of free association and therapist interpretations to help clients gain insight about themselves and their problems. Although it was expected that broad personality changes would lead to improvement in sexual functioning, psychodynamic therapy was typically unsuccessful (Bergler, 1951).

In the 1950s and 1960s, behavioral therapists offered new treatments for sexual dysfunctions. Usually they tried to reduce the fears that they believed were causing the dysfunctions. They did so through such procedures as relaxation training and systematic desensitization (Lazarus, 1965; Wolpe, 1958). These approaches had some success, but they failed to work in cases where the key problems included misinformation, negative attitudes, and lack of effective sexual techniques (LoPiccolo, 2002).

A revolution in the treatment of sexual dysfunctions took place with the publication of William Masters and Virginia Johnson's landmark book *Human Sexual Inadequacy* in 1970. The *sex therapy* program they introduced has evolved into a complex approach, which now includes interventions from the various models, particularly cognitive-behavioral, couple, and family systems therapies (Avery-Clark & Weiner, 2017; Leiblum, 2010, 2007). The goal of sex therapy is to help clients function better sexually and to achieve a higher level of sexual satisfaction and psychological well-being (Peterson, 2017). In recent years, biological interventions, particularly drug therapies, have been added to the treatment arsenal (McCarthy & Wald, 2017; Berry & Berry, 2013).

> Sex is one of the topics most commonly searched on the Internet. Why might it be such a popular search topic?

What Are the General Features of Sex Therapy?

Modern sex therapy is short-term and instructive, typically lasting 15 to 20 sessions. It centers on specific sexual problems rather than on broad personality issues (Peterson, 2017). Carlos Domera, the Argentinian man with erectile disorder whom you met earlier, responded successfully to the multiple techniques of modern sex therapy:

At the end of the evaluation session the psychiatrist reassured the couple that Mr. Domera had a "reversible psychological" sexual problem that was due to several factors, including his depression, but also more currently his anxiety and embarrassment, his high standards, and some cultural and relationship difficulties that made communication awkward and relaxation nearly impossible. The couple was advised that a brief trial of therapy, focused directly on the sexual problem, would very likely produce significant improvement within ten to fourteen sessions. They were assured that the problem was almost certainly not physical in origin, but rather psychogenic, and that therefore the prognosis was excellent.

Mr. Domera was shocked and skeptical, but the couple agreed to commence the therapy on a weekly basis, and they were given a typical first "assignment" to do at home: a caressing massage exercise to try together with specific instructions not to attempt genital stimulation or intercourse at all, even if an erection might occur.

Not surprisingly, during the second session Mr. Domera reported with a cautious smile that they had "cheated" and had had intercourse "against the rules." This was their first successful intercourse in more than a year. Their success and happiness were acknowledged by the therapist, but they were cautioned strongly that rapid initial improvement often occurs, only to be followed by increased performance anxiety in subsequent weeks and a return of the initial problem. They were humorously chastised and encouraged to try again to have sexual contact involving caressing and nondemand light genital stimulation, without an expectation of erection or orgasm, and to avoid intercourse.

During the second and fourth weeks [Carlos] did not achieve erections during the love play, and the therapy sessions dealt with helping him to accept himself with or without erections and to learn to enjoy sensual contact without intercourse. His wife helped him to believe genuinely that he could please her with manual or oral stimulation and that, although she enjoyed intercourse, she enjoyed these other stimulations as much, as long as he was relaxed.

[Carlos] struggled with his cultural image of what a "man" does, but he had to admit that his wife seemed pleased and that he, too, was enjoying the nonintercourse caressing techniques. He was encouraged to view his new lovemaking skills as a "success" and to recognize that in many ways he was becoming a better lover than many husbands, because he was listening to his wife and responding to her requests.

By the fifth week the patient was attempting intercourse successfully with relaxed confidence, and by the ninth session he was responding regularly with erections. If they both agreed, they would either have intercourse or choose another sexual technique to achieve orgasm. Treatment was terminated after ten sessions.

(Spitzer et al., 1983, pp. 106–107)

As Carlos Domera's treatment indicates, modern sex therapy includes a variety of principles and techniques. The following ones are used in almost all cases, regardless of the dysfunction:

1. **Assessing and conceptualizing the problem.** Patients are initially given a medical examination and are interviewed concerning their "sex history." The therapist's focus during the interview is on gathering information about past life events and, in particular, current factors that are contributing to the dysfunction (Shifren, 2017; Bradford, 2016; Cunningham & Khera, 2016). Sometimes proper assessment requires a team of specialists, perhaps including a psychologist, urologist, and neurologist.

2. **Mutual responsibility.** Therapists stress the principle of *mutual responsibility*. Both partners in the relationship share the sexual problem, regardless of who has the actual dysfunction, so treatment is likely to be more successful when both are in therapy (Shifren, 2017; Laan et al., 2013).

3. **Education about sexuality.** Many patients who suffer from sexual dysfunctions know very little about the physiology and techniques of sexual activity (Shifren, 2017; Cunningham & Khera, 2016). Thus sex therapists may discuss these topics and offer educational materials, including instructional books, videos, and Internet sites (van Lankveld, 2017).

4. **Emotion identification.** Sex therapists help patients identify and express upsetting emotions tied to past events that may keep interfering with sexual arousal and enjoyment (Johnson, 2017; Kleinplatz, 2010).

5. **Attitude change.** Following a cardinal principle of cognitive therapy, sex therapists help patients examine and change any beliefs about sexuality that are preventing sexual arousal and pleasure (Bradford, 2016; McCarthy & McCarthy, 2012). Some of these mistaken beliefs are widely shared in our society and can result from past traumatic events, family attitudes, or cultural ideas.

6. **Elimination of performance anxiety and the spectator role.** Therapists often teach couples sensate focus, or *nondemand pleasuring*, a series of sensual tasks,

"When I touch him he rolls into a ball."

Helping sexual arousal along *Peacocking* involves dressing with enormous flare—often in ostentatious ways with accessories like scarves, dyed hair, and piercings—in order to attract sexual partners. The strategy is so-named because of its similarity to the behavior of male peacocks who expand and fan their bright and beautiful feathers to attract mates.

Adrian Lourie / Evening Standard/Redux

sometimes called "petting" exercises, in which the partners focus on the sexual pleasure that can be achieved by exploring and caressing each other's body at home, without demands to have intercourse or reach orgasm—demands that may be interfering with arousal. Couples are told at first to refrain from intercourse at home and to restrict their sexual activity to kissing, hugging, and sensual massage of various parts of the body, but not of the breasts or genitals. Over time, they learn how to give and receive greater sexual pleasure and they build back up to the activity of sexual intercourse (Avery-Clark & Weiner, 2017; Cunningham & Khera, 2016).

7. **Increasing sexual and general communication skills.** Couples are taught to use their sensate-focus skills and apply new sexual techniques and positions at home (Shifren, 2017; Bradford, 2016). They may, for example, try sexual positions in which the person being caressed can guide the other's hands and control the speed, pressure, and location of sexual contact (Heiman, 2007). Couples are also taught to give instructions to each other in a nonthreatening, informative manner ("It feels better over here, with a little less pressure"), rather than a threatening uninformative manner ("The way you're touching me doesn't turn me on"). Moreover, couples are often given broader training in how best to communicate with each other (Cunningham & Khera, 2016; Brenot, 2011).

8. **Changing destructive lifestyles and couple interactions.** A therapist may encourage a couple to change their lifestyle or take other steps to improve a situation that is having a destructive effect on their relationship—to distance themselves from interfering in-laws, for example, or to change a job that is too demanding. Similarly, if the couple's general relationship is marked by conflict, the therapist will try to help them improve it, often before work on the sexual problems per se begins (Brenot, 2011; Rosen, 2007).

9. **Addressing physical and medical factors.** Systematic increases in physical activity have proved helpful for persons with various kinds of sexual dysfunctions (Cunningham & Khera, 2016; Lewis et al., 2010). In addition, when sexual dysfunctions are caused by a medical problem, such as disease, injury, medication, or substance abuse, therapists try to address that problem (Shifren, 2017; Korda et al., 2010). If antidepressant medications are causing erectile disorder, for example, the clinician may suggest lowering the dosage of the medication, changing the time of day when the drug is taken, or turning to a different antidepressant.

What Techniques Are Used to Treat Particular Dysfunctions?

In addition to the general components of sex therapy, specific techniques can help in each of the sexual dysfunctions.

Disorders of Desire Male hypoactive sexual desire disorder and female sexual interest/arousal disorder are among the most difficult dysfunctions to treat because of the many issues that may feed into them (Both et al., 2017; Leiblum, 2010). Thus therapists typically use a combination of techniques (Althof & Needle, 2017; Cunningham & Khera, 2016). In a technique called *affectual awareness,* patients visualize sexual scenes in order to discover any feelings of anxiety, vulnerability, and other negative emotions they may have concerning sex. In another technique, patients receive cognitive *self-instruction training* to help them change their negative reactions to sex. That is, they learn to replace negative statements during sex with "coping statements," such as "I can allow myself to enjoy sex; it doesn't mean I'll lose control."

Therapists may also use behavioral approaches to help heighten a patient's sex drive. They may instruct clients to keep a "desire diary" in which they record sexual thoughts and feelings, to read books and view films with erotic content, and to fantasize about sex. They also may encourage pleasurable shared activities such as dancing and walking together (Rubio-Aurioles & Bivalacqua, 2013; LoPiccolo, 2002). If the reduced sexual desire has resulted from sexual assault or childhood molestation, additional techniques may be needed (Shifren, 2017; Hall, 2017, 2010, 2007). A patient may, for example, be encouraged to remember, talk about, and think about the assault until the memories no longer arouse fear or tension. These and related psychological approaches apparently help many women and men with low sexual desire eventually to have intercourse more than once a week (Both et al., 2017; Cunningham & Khera, 2016). However, only a few controlled studies have been conducted.

Finally, biological interventions, such as *hormone* treatments, have been used, particularly for women whose problems arose after removal of their ovaries or later in life. These interventions have received some research support (Shifren, 2017; Rubio-Aurioles & Bivalacqua, 2013). In addition, several pharmaceutical drugs have been developed specifically for the treatment of these disorders (Cunningham & Khera, 2016; Giraldi et al., 2013).

Erectile Disorder Treatments for erectile disorder focus on reducing a man's performance anxiety, increasing his stimulation, or both, using a range of behavioral, cognitive, and relationship interventions (Nobre, 2017; Cunningham & Khera, 2016). In one technique, the couple may be instructed to try the *tease technique* during sensate-focus exercises: the partner keeps caressing the man, but if the man gets an erection, the partner stops caressing him until he loses it. This exercise reduces pressure on the man to perform and at the same time teaches the couple that erections occur naturally in response to stimulation, as long as the partners do not keep focusing on performance. In another technique, the couple may be instructed to use manual or oral sex to try to achieve the woman's orgasm, again reducing pressure on the man to perform (LoPiccolo, 2004, 2002).

Biological approaches gained great momentum with the development in 1998 of *sildenafil* (trade name Viagra) (Nobre, 2017; Rosen, 2007). This drug increases blood flow to the penis within one hour of ingestion; the increased blood flow enables the user to attain an erection during sexual activity (see **PsychWatch** on page 401). In general, sildenafil appears to be safe; however, it may not be so for men with certain coronary heart diseases and cardiovascular diseases, particularly those who are taking nitroglycerin and other heart medications (Cunningham & Khera, 2016; Stevenson & Elliott, 2007). Soon after Viagra emerged, two other erectile dysfunction drugs were also approved—*tadalafil* (Cialis) and *vardenafil* (Levitra)—and, more recently, yet another such drug, *avanafil* (Stendra), was added to the mix. The four drugs are now actively competing for a share of the lucrative marketplace. Collectively, the drugs are the most common form of treatment for erectile disorder. They effectively restore erections and enable sexual intercourse in 60 to 80 percent of men who use them, compared to a rate of 21 percent among men taking placebo drugs (Cunningham & Khera, 2016). Some research, though, suggests that a combination of one of these erectile dysfunction drugs and a psychological intervention such as those mentioned above may be more helpful than either kind of treatment alone (Nobre, 2017; Schmidt et al., 2014).

Prior to the development of Viagra, Cialis, Levitra, and Stendra, a range of other medical procedures were developed for erectile disorder. These procedures are now viewed as "second line"—often costly—treatments that are used primarily when the medications are unsuccessful or too risky for individuals (Cunningham & Khera, 2016; Lazarou, 2016). Such treatments include gel suppositories, injections of drugs into the penis, a surgical implantation of a penile prosthesis, and a *vacuum erection*

Jens Büttner/picture-alliance/dpa/AP Images

Is ASMR sexual? A growing number of individuals are pursuing experiences of *ASMR* (autonomous sensory meridian response), a tingling sensation on the skin that extends from the scalp to the neck and upper spine. This sensation supposedly can be triggered by auditory and visual stimulation without the body being touched. Here, Maria, known to a half-million YouTube subscribers as *Gentle Whispering*, reaches out to the camera and "massages" the temples of viewers to help them experience ASMR. In other videos, she uses additional triggers such as whispering to viewers and making quiet repetitive sounds. A major question is whether ASMR sensations are sexual (some people call them "brain orgasms") or nonsexual.

#TheirWords

"Erection is chiefly caused by scuraum, eringoes, cresses, crymon, parsnips, artichokes, turnips, asparagus, candied ginger, acorns bruised to powder and drank in muscadel, scallion, sea shell fish, etc."

Aristotle's Masterpiece, 1684

AP Photo/Amr Nabil

Viagra around the world Few drugs have had the worldwide impact of Viagra and related erectile dysfunction drugs. Here technicians at a pharmaceutical factory in Cairo sort thousands of Viagra pills for distribution and marketing in Egypt's pharmacies.

directed masturbation training A sex therapy approach that teaches women with female arousal or orgasmic problems how to masturbate effectively and eventually to reach orgasm during sexual interactions.

device (*VED*), a hollow cylinder that is placed over the penis. For the VED, a man uses a hand pump to pump air out of the cylinder, drawing blood into his penis and producing an erection.

Premature Ejaculation Early ejaculation has been treated successfully for years by behavioral procedures (Rowland & Cooper, 2017; Cunningham & Khera, 2016). In one such approach, the *stop-start,* or *pause, procedure,* the penis is manually stimulated until the man is highly aroused. The couple then pauses until his arousal subsides, after which the stimulation is resumed. This sequence is repeated several times before stimulation is carried through to ejaculation, so the man ultimately experiences much more total time of stimulation than he has ever experienced before (LoPiccolo, 2004). Eventually the couple progresses to putting the penis in the vagina, making sure to withdraw it and to pause whenever the man becomes too highly aroused. According to clinical reports, after 2 or 3 months, many couples can enjoy prolonged intercourse without any need for pauses (Althof, 2007; LoPiccolo, 2004, 2002).

Many clinicians treat premature ejaculation with SSRIs, the serotonin-enhancing antidepressant drugs (Cunningham & Khera, 2016). Because these drugs often reduce sexual arousal or orgasm, the reasoning goes, they may be helpful to men who ejaculate prematurely. Many studies report positive results with this approach (McMahon et al., 2013; Althof, 2007). The effect of this approach is consistent with the biological theory, mentioned earlier, that serotonin receptors in the brains of men with early ejaculation may function abnormally.

Delayed Ejaculation Therapies for delayed ejaculation include techniques to reduce performance anxiety and increase stimulation (Rowland & Cooper, 2017; Hartmann & Waldinger, 2007). In one of many such techniques, a man may be instructed to masturbate to orgasm in the presence of his partner or to masturbate just short of orgasm before inserting his penis for intercourse (Marshall, 1997). This increases the likelihood that he will ejaculate during intercourse. He then is instructed to insert his penis at ever earlier stages of masturbation.

When delayed ejaculation is caused by physical factors such as neurological damage or injury, treatment may include a drug to increase arousal of the sympathetic nervous system (Rowland & Cooper, 2017; Cunningham & Khera, 2016; Stevenson & Elliott, 2007). However, few studies have systematically tested the effectiveness of such treatments.

Female Orgasmic Disorder Specific treatments for female orgasmic disorder include cognitive-behavioral techniques, self-exploration, enhancement of body awareness, and directed masturbation training (Carpenter et al., 2017; Bradford, 2016; Laan et al., 2013). These procedures are especially useful for women who have never had an orgasm under any circumstances. Biological treatments, including hormone therapy or the use of sildenafil (Viagra), have also been tried, but research has not consistently found these to be helpful (Shifren, 2017; Bradford, 2016).

In **directed masturbation training,** a woman is taught step by step how to masturbate effectively and eventually to reach orgasm during sexual interactions. The training includes the use of diagrams and reading material, private self-stimulation, erotic material and fantasies, "orgasm triggers" such as holding her breath or thrusting her pelvis, sensate focus with her partner, and sexual positioning that produces stimulation of the clitoris during intercourse. This training program appears to be highly effective: over 90 percent of female clients learn to have an orgasm during masturbation, about 80 percent during caressing by their partners, and about 30 percent during intercourse (Shifren, 2017; Bradford, 2016; Laan et al., 2013).

As you read earlier, a lack of orgasm during intercourse is not necessarily a sexual dysfunction, provided the woman enjoys intercourse (Shifren, 2017, 2016). For this

PSYCH**WATCH**

Sexism, Viagra, and the Pill

Most of us would like to believe that we live in an enlightened world, where sexism is declining and where health care and benefits are available to men and women in equal measure. Periodically, however, such illusions are shattered (Goldstein, 2014). The responses of government agencies and insurance companies to the discovery and marketing of Viagra in 1998 may be a case in point.

Consider, first, the nation of Japan. In early 1999, just 6 months after it was introduced in the United States, Viagra was approved for use among men in Japan (Goldstein, 2014). In contrast, low-dose contraceptives—"the pill"—were not approved for use among women in Japan until later that same year—a full 40 years after their introduction elsewhere! Some observers believe that birth control pills would still be unavailable to women in Japan had

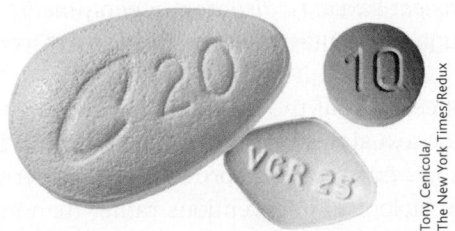

"The pills": Cialis, Viagra, and Levitra

Tony Cenicola/
The New York Times/Redux

Viagra not received its quick approval.

Has the United States been able to avoid such an apparent double standard in its health care system? Not really. Before Viagra was introduced, insurance companies were not required to reimburse women for the cost of prescription contraceptives. As a result, women had to pay 68 percent more out-of-pocket expenses for health care than did men, largely because of uncovered reproductive health care costs (Hollander, 2006; Hayden, 1998). Some legislators had tried to correct this problem by requiring contraceptive coverage in health insurance plans, but their efforts failed in state after state for more than a decade.

In contrast, when Viagra was introduced in 1998, many insurance companies readily agreed to cover it, and many states included Viagra as part of Medicaid coverage. As the public outcry grew over the contrast between coverage of Viagra for men and lack of coverage of oral contraceptives for women, laws across the country finally

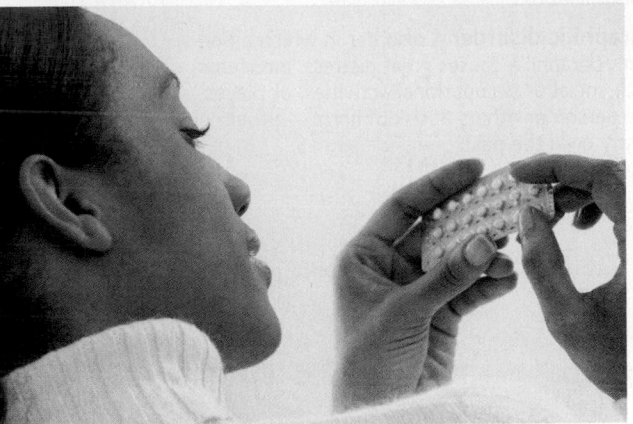

"The pill"

BSIP SA/Alamy

began to change. By the end of 1998, nine states required prescription contraceptive coverage. Today 28 states require such coverage by private insurance companies (Guttmacher Institute, 2017). The Affordable Care Act (ACA)—the federal health care law passed in 2010 and enacted a few years later—includes provisions that require *all* insurance companies to cover contraceptives. However, with Congress repeatedly considering the repeal of the ACA—and possibly, along with it, the elimination of contraceptive coverage requirements—the future of contraceptive insurance coverage is very much at risk.

reason some therapists believe that the wisest course is simply to educate women whose only concern is lack of orgasm during intercourse, informing them that they are quite normal, and to further teach them how to reach orgasm, if they wish, through caressing by their partner or by herself.

Genito-Pelvic Pain/Penetration Disorder Specific treatment for involuntary contractions of the muscles around the vagina typically involves two approaches (Meana et al., 2017; Shifren, 2017). First, a woman may practice tightening and relaxing her vaginal muscles until she gains more voluntary control over them. Second, she may receive gradual behavioral exposure treatment to help her overcome her fear of penetration, beginning, for example, by inserting increasingly large dilators in her vagina at home and at her own pace and eventually ending with the insertion of her partner's penis. Most clients treated with such procedures eventually have pain-free intercourse (Shifren, 2017; Engman et al., 2010). Some medical interventions have also been used. For example, several clinical investigators have injected the problematic vaginal muscles with Botox to help reduce spasms in those muscles (Fugl-Meyer et al., 2013). However, studies of this approach have been unsystematic.

paraphilias Patterns in which a person has recurrent and intense sexual urges, fantasies, or behaviors involving nonhuman objects, children, nonconsenting adults, or experiences suffering or humiliation.

paraphilic disorder A disorder in which a person's paraphilia causes great distress, interferes with social or occupational activities, or places the person or others at risk of harm—either currently or in the past.

Different approaches are used to treat the other form of genito-pelvic pain/penetration disorder—severe vaginal or pelvic pain during intercourse. As you saw earlier, the most common cause of this problem is physical, such as pain-causing scars, lesions, or infection aftereffects. When the cause is known, pain management procedures (see pages 306–310) and sex therapy techniques may be tried, including helping a couple to learn intercourse positions that avoid putting pressure on the injured area (Meana et al., 2017; Fugl-Meyer et al., 2013). Medical interventions—from topical creams to surgery—may also be tried, but typically they must be combined with other sex therapy techniques to overcome the years of sexual anxiety and lack of arousal (Shifren, 2017; Goodman, 2013). Many experts believe that, in most cases, both forms of genito-pelvic pain/penetration disorder are best assessed and treated by a *team* of professionals, including a gynecologist, physical therapist, and sex therapist or other mental health professional (Shifren, 2017; Berry & Berry, 2013).

What Are the Current Trends in Sex Therapy?

Sex therapists have now moved well beyond the approach first developed by Masters and Johnson. For example, today's sex therapists regularly treat partners who are living together but not married. They also treat sexual dysfunctions that arise from psychological disorders such as depression, mania, schizophrenia, and certain personality disorders (Buehler, 2017; Leiblum, 2010, 2007). In addition, sex therapists no longer screen out LGBTQ clients, individuals with severe relationship discord, the elderly, the medically ill, the physically handicapped, the intellectually disabled, or individuals who have no long-term sex partner (Cohen & Savin-Williams, 2017; Hough et al., 2017; Zhou & Bober, 2017). Sex therapists are also paying more attention to excessive sexuality, sometimes called *persistent sexuality disorder, hypersexuality,* or *sexual addiction* (Grubbs et al., 2017), although this condition is not listed as a disorder in DSM-5.

Many sex therapists have expressed concern about the sharp increase in the use of drugs and other medical interventions for sexual dysfunctions, particularly for the disorders characterized by low sexual desire and erectile disorder. Their concern is that therapists will increasingly choose the biological interventions rather than integrating biological, psychological, and sociocultural interventions. In fact, a narrow approach of any kind probably cannot fully address the complex factors that cause most sexual problems (McCarthy & Wald, 2017). It took sex therapists years to recognize the considerable advantages of an integrated approach to sexual dysfunctions. The development of new medical interventions should not lead to its abandonment.

‖‖‖

Paraphilic Disorders

PARAPHILIAS ARE PATTERNS IN which people repeatedly have intense sexual urges or fantasies or display sexual behaviors that involve objects or situations outside the usual sexual norms. The sexual focus may, for example, involve nonhuman objects or the experience of suffering or humiliation. Many people with a paraphilia can become aroused only when a paraphilic stimulus is present, fantasized about, or acted out. Others need the stimulus only during times of stress or under other special circumstances. Some people with one kind of paraphilia have others as well (Anupama et al., 2016; Seto et al., 2014). The large consumer market in paraphilic pornography and growing trends such as sexting and cybersex lead clinicians to suspect that paraphilias may be far more common than previously thought (see *MindTech*).

According to DSM-5, a diagnosis of **paraphilic disorder** should be applied when paraphilias cause a person significant distress or impairment *or* when the satisfaction of the paraphilias places the person or other people at risk of harm—either currently or

> Is the abundance of sexual material on the Internet psychologically healthy or damaging?

MINDTECH

"Sexting": Healthy or Pathological?

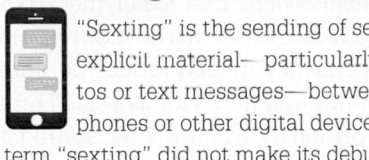

"Sexting" is the sending of sexually explicit material— particularly photos or text messages—between cell phones or other digital devices. The term "sexting" did not make its debut until 2005.

A recent survey of almost 6,000 single adults found that 21 percent of cell phone users have sent a sexually explicit text message and 16 percent have texted a sexually explicit photo of themselves. On the other side of the coin, 28 percent of users have received sext messages and 23 percent have received sexual photos (Garcia et al., 2016). In general, half of all people save the sexual images and text messages they receive, and a quarter of recipients—men much more than women —forward the sexual photos that they receive to others (Strassberg et al., 2017, 2013; Garcia et al., 2016; McAfee, 2014).

Naïve behavior? Not always. The majority of all sexters say they recognize that the act could lead to legal, social, career, or personal problems (Garcia et al., 2016). They are also aware that sexted images sometimes wind up on "revenge porn"—images that are posted on social media by vengeful former friends or relationship partners for all the world to see (LeBlanc, 2017; Recupero, 2016). Young adults (18 to 24 years old) are the largest group of sexters. And males sext more often than females by a 3 to 2 margin.

Is sexting a symptom of abnormal functioning? It depends. Certainly, some sexters fit the criteria for *exhibitionistic disorder*, the paraphilic pattern in which people act on urges to expose their genitals to others. Sixteen percent of sexters send sexual photos of themselves to complete strangers (McAfee, 2014). And like other forms of ex-

hibitionism, sexting can cause psychological stress for nonconsenting recipients.

There are yet other ways in which sexting may reflect psychological or relationship problems (Weisskirch et al., 2017; Drouin & Landgraff, 2012). According to one study, people who sext to strangers or other nonconsenting recipients are more likely to have general problems with attachment or intimacy than other people. In addition, research indicates that sexting (when done outside of one's marriage or monogamous relationship) is often a step toward infidelity. Some psychologists believe that sexting is itself a form of infidelity even though it does not involve physical contact. It has even been the

> **What texting activities outside the sexual realm might also have either a negative or positive psychological impact depending on how and when they are performed?**

grounds for divorce in some cases (Cable, 2008; Siemaszko, 2006).

On the other side of the coin, sexting can be a constructive activity, according to some psychologists (McDaniel & Drouin, 2015; Drouin & Landgraff, 2012). Many couples engage in it as an added dimension to their relationship. According to surveys, more than half of all couples have texted sexual photos or messages to their partners at least once; one-third more than once. Research suggests that this often enhances the in-person romantic relationship, creates more bonding, and heightens sexual satisfaction in the relationship (Wiederhold, 2015; Parker et al., 2012).

Putting sexting on the map In response to media revelations about his multiple episodes of sexting in 2011 and 2016, former New York congressman Anthony Weiner had to resign his congressional seat and, eventually, give up his political ambitions.

in the past (APA, 2013) (see **Table 13-5**). People who initiate sexual contact with children, for example, warrant a diagnosis of *pedophilic disorder* regardless of how troubled the individuals may or may not be over their behavior. People whose paraphilic disorder involves children or nonconsenting adults often come to the attention of clinicians as a result of legal issues generated by their inappropriate actions (Thibaut et al., 2016).

Although theorists have proposed various explanations for paraphilic disorders, there is little formal evidence to support such explanations (Martin & Levine, 2016; Becker et al., 2012). Moreover, none of the many treatments applied to these disorders

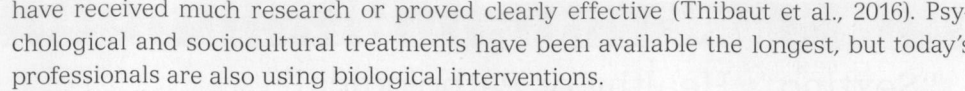

TABLE: 13-5

Dx Checklist

Paraphilic Disorder

1. For at least 6 months, individual experiences recurrent and intense sexually arousing fantasies, urges, or behaviors involving objects or situations outside the usual sexual norms (nonhuman objects; nongenital body parts; the suffering or humiliation of oneself or one's partner; or children or other nonconsenting persons).

2. Individual experiences significant distress or impairment over the fantasies, urges, or behaviors. (In some paraphilic disorders—pedophilic disorder, exhibitionistic disorder, voyeuristic disorder, frotteuristic disorder, and sexual sadism disorder—the performance of the paraphilic behaviors indicates a disorder, even in the absence of distress or impairment.)

(Information from: APA, 2013.)

#TheirWords

"Whoever called it 'necking' was a poor judge of anatomy."

Groucho Marx, comedian and actor

have received much research or proved clearly effective (Thibaut et al., 2016). Psychological and sociocultural treatments have been available the longest, but today's professionals are also using biological interventions.

Some practitioners administer drugs called *antiandrogens* that lower the production of testosterone, the male sex hormone, and reduce the sex drive (Konrad et al., 2015; Korda & Sommer, 2010). Although antiandrogens may indeed reduce paraphilic patterns, several of them disrupt normal sexual feelings and behavior as well (Thibaut et al., 2016, 2010). Thus the drugs tend to be used primarily when the paraphilic disorders are of particular danger either to the individuals themselves or to other people. Clinicians are also increasingly prescribing SSRIs, the serotonin-enhancing antidepressant medications, to treat people with paraphilic disorders, hoping that the SSRIs will reduce these compulsion-like sexual behaviors just as they help reduce other kinds of compulsions (Anupama et al., 2016; Thibaut et al., 2016). In addition, of course, a common effect of the SSRIs is to lower sexual arousal.

A word of caution is in order before examining the various paraphilic disorders. The definitions of these disorders, like those of sexual dysfunctions, are strongly influenced by the norms of the particular society in which they occur (McManus et al., 2013). Some clinicians argue that except when other people are hurt by them, at least some paraphilic behaviors should not be considered disorders at all (Giami, 2015; Joyal, 2015). Especially in light of the stigma associated with sexual disorders and the self-revulsion that many people feel when they believe they have such a disorder, we need to be very careful about applying these labels to others or to ourselves (McManus et al., 2013). Keep in mind that for years clinicians considered homosexuality a paraphilic disorder, and their judgment was used to justify laws and even police actions against gay people. Only in 1987, when the gay rights movement helped change society's understanding of and attitudes toward homosexuality did clinicians officially stop considering it a disorder and remove it entirely from the DSM. Even then, as you read in Chapter 2, many clinicians continued for years to recommend and offer *conversion,* or *reparative, therapy* to "fix" the sexual orientation of gay people. In the meantime, the clinical field had unintentionally contributed to the persecution, anxiety, and humiliation of millions of people because of personal sexual behavior that differed from the conventional norms.

Fetishistic Disorder

One relatively common paraphilic disorder is **fetishistic disorder.** Key features of this disorder are recurrent intense sexual urges, sexually arousing fantasies, or behaviors that involve the use of a nonliving object or nongenital body part, often to the exclusion of all other stimuli (APA, 2013). Usually the disorder, which is far more common in men than in women, begins in adolescence (Martin & Levine, 2016). Almost anything can be a fetish; women's underwear, shoes, and boots are particularly common. Some people with this disorder steal in order to collect as many of the desired objects as possible. The objects may be touched, smelled, worn, or used in some other way while the person masturbates, or the person may ask a partner to wear the object when they have sex (Martin & Levine, 2016; Marshall et al., 2008). Some of these features are seen in the case of Jaylen, a teenager whose mother, Kiara, discovered his fetishistic disorder over the course of six months:

[Kiara] reported that she first recognized [Jaylen's] sexual interest in women's shoes six months ago. He started to disappear repeatedly from their apartment and [one day, Kiara] found him on the stairs . . . handling the shoes of a female neighbor. Later on, [Kiara] came across [Jaylen] rubbing and smelling the shoes in such a fascinated manner that he did not even recognize his mother's presence. . . . [Kiara] also noticed that [Jaylen] was increasingly staying within their apartment building, taking the neighbor's shoes down to

the ground floor rather than going outside. . . . After a week [Jaylen] visited the neighbor's home while helping her carry shopping goods. After an apparently normal visit, the neighbor recognized that her shoes were missing. [Kiara] tried to talk with [her son], but he became agitated and refused to talk. After several weeks, she recognized that her own shoes were missing . . . The mother then started keeping track of [Jaylen] and recognized that he was awaking at night and was . . . rubbing and smelling her shoes. [Kiara] did not recognize the sexual nature of his behaviors and thought that he had a compulsive interest in shoes. [However, one day] she entered the bathroom and found [Jaylen] there masturbating while he was holding and rubbing her shoe in his hand. At that point, she recognized the sexual nature of his interest in shoes for the first time. Subsequently she came across some videos on his mobile phone. They were recordings of young women's feet with or without shoes, including videos of [Kiara's own] naked feet. There were dozens of these videos, . . . dating back four months.

(Coskun & Ozturk, 2013, p. 199)

fetishistic disorder A paraphilic disorder consisting of recurrent and intense sexual urges, fantasies, or behaviors that involve the use of a nonliving object or nongenital part, often to the exclusion of all other stimuli, accompanied by clinically significant distress or impairment.

Researchers have not been able to pinpoint the causes of fetishistic disorder. Psychodynamic theorists view fetishes as defense mechanisms that help people avoid the anxiety produced by normal sexual contact. Psychodynamic treatment for this problem, however, has met with little success (Martin & Levine, 2016; Öncü et al., 2009; Zurolo & Napolitano, 2008).

Viewing fetishes as learned behaviors, cognitive-behavioral theorists propose that fetishes are acquired through classical conditioning (Martin & Levine, 2016; Roche & Quayle, 2007). In a pioneering behavioral study, male participants were shown a series of slides of nude women along with slides of boots (Rachman, 1966). After many trials, the participants became aroused by the boot photos alone. If early sexual experiences similarly occur in the presence of particular objects, perhaps the stage is set for the development of fetishes.

Cognitive-behavioral therapists have sometimes treated fetishistic disorder with *aversion therapy* (Thibaut et al., 2016; Plaud, 2007). In a famous study, an electric shock was administered to the arms or legs of participants with this disorder while they imagined their objects of desire (Marks & Gelder, 1967). After 2 weeks of therapy all men in the study showed at least some improvement. In another aversion technique,

Mrs. Robinson's stockings The 1967 film *The Graduate* helped define a generation by focusing on the personal confusion, apathy, and sexual adventures of a young man in search of meaning. Marketers promoted this film by using a fetishistic-like photo of Mrs. Robinson putting on her stockings under Benjamin's watchful eye, a scene forever identified with the movie.

transvestic disorder A paraphilic disorder consisting of repeated and intense sexual urges, fantasies, or behaviors that involve dressing in clothes of the opposite sex, accompanied by clinically significant distress or impairment. Also known as *transvestism* or *cross-dressing*.

exhibitionistic disorder A paraphilic disorder in which persons have repeated sexually arousing urges or fantasies about exposing their genitals to others, and either act on these urges with nonconsenting individuals or experience clinically significant distress or impairment.

voyeuristic disorder A paraphilic disorder in which a person has repeated and intense sexual desires to observe unsuspecting people in secret as they undress or to spy on couples having intercourse, and either acts on these urges with nonconsenting people or experiences clinically significant distress or impairment.

covert sensitization, people with fetishistic disorder are guided to *imagine* the pleasurable object and repeatedly to pair this image with an *imagined* aversive stimulus until the object of sexual pleasure is no longer desired.

Another cognitive-behavioral treatment for fetishistic disorder is *masturbatory satiation* (Thibaut et al., 2016; Plaud, 2007). In this method, the client masturbates to orgasm while fantasizing about a sexually appropriate object, then switches to fantasizing in detail about fetishistic objects while masturbating again and continues the fetishistic fantasy for an hour. The procedure is meant to produce a feeling of boredom, which in turn becomes linked to the fetishistic object.

Transvestic Disorder

A person with **transvestic disorder,** also known as **transvestism** or **cross-dressing,** feels recurrent and intense sexual arousal from dressing in clothes of the opposite gender—arousal expressed through fantasies, urges, or behaviors (APA, 2013). In the following passage, a 42-year-old married father describes his pattern:

> I have been told that when I dress in drag, at times I look like Whistler's Mother [laughs], especially when I haven't shaved closely. I usually am good at detail, and I make sure when I dress as a woman that I have my nails done just so, and that my colors match. Honestly, it's hard to pin a date on when I began cross dressing. . . . If pressed, I would have to say it began when I was about 10 years of age, fooling around with and putting on my mom's clothes. . . . In 18 years of doing this in her home, my mother never, I mean never, suspected, or questioned me about putting on her clothes.
>
> I belong to a transvestite support group . . . Most of [the men in the group] have told their families about their dressing inclinations, but those that are married are a mixed lot; some wives know and some don't, they just suspect. I . . . told my wife about this before we were married. We're separated now. . . It took her some time to be comfortable with me wearing feminine underwear . . . I wear it while making love, it just makes it . . . . exciting.
>
> *(Janus & Janus, 1993, p. 121)*

Once again, transvestic needs and behaviors, such as those described by this man, must cause significant distress or impairment to warrant a diagnosis of transvestic disorder, Like this man, the typical person with the disorder, almost always a heterosexual male, begins cross-dressing in childhood or adolescence (Thibaut et al., 2016; Marshall et al., 2008). He may be the picture of characteristic masculinity in everyday life and is usually alone when he cross-dresses. A small percentage of such men cross-dress to visit bars or social clubs. Some wear a single item of women's clothing, such as underwear or hosiery, under their masculine clothes. Others wear makeup and dress fully as women. Some married men with transvestic disorder involve their wives in their cross-dressing.

Transvestic disorder is often confused with *transgender* feelings and behaviors, but, as you will see, they are two separate patterns that overlap only in some individuals (Martin & Levine, 2016; Zucker et al., 2012). Specifically, a transvestic disorder is about the sexual arousal certain persons feel when they dress in opposite-gender clothes, whereas transgender functioning is about the gender a person considers himself or herself to be.

Playful context Dressing in clothes of the opposite sex does not necessarily convey a paraphilia. Here two members—both male—of Harvard University's Hasty Pudding Theatricals Club, known for staging musicals in which male undergraduates dress like women, plant a kiss on actress Kerry Washington. Washington was receiving the club's 2016 Woman of the Year award.

Darren McCollester/Getty Images

As with fetishes, cognitive-behavioral theorists view transvestic arousal and behavior as learned responses, acquired most often through classical conditioning. That is, if early sexual experiences occur while a person is—out of curiosity, playfulness, or the like—wearing the attire of the other gender, the stage may be set for transvestic arousal and related reactions throughout life. This explanation has, however, received little support in clinical reports or research (Anupama et al., 2016).

Exhibitionistic Disorder

A person with **exhibitionistic disorder** experiences recurrent and intense sexual arousal from exposing his genitals to an unsuspecting individual—arousal reflected by fantasies, urges, or behaviors (APA, 2013). Most often, the person wants to provoke shock or surprise rather than initiate sexual activity with the victim. Sometimes an exhibitionist will expose himself in a particular neighborhood at particular hours. In a survey of 2,800 men, 4.3 percent of them reported that they perform exhibitionistic behavior (Långström & Seto, 2006). Yet between one-third and half of all women report having seen or had direct contact with an exhibitionist, or so-called flasher (Marshall et al., 2008). The urge to exhibit typically becomes stronger when the person has free time or is under significant stress.

Generally, exhibitionistic disorder begins before age 18 and usually, but not always, is found among men (Thibaut et al., 2016; APA, 2013; Holtzman & Kulish, 2012). Some studies suggest that those with the disorder are typically immature in their dealings with the opposite sex and have difficulty in interpersonal relationships (Marshall et al., 2008; Murphy & Page, 2006). Around 30 percent of them are married and another 30 percent divorced or separated; their sexual relations with their wives are not usually satisfactory (Doctor & Neff, 2001). Many have doubts or fears about their masculinity, and some seem to have a strong bond to a possessive mother. As with other paraphilic disorders, treatment generally includes aversion therapy, masturbatory satiation, social skills training, and some form of insight therapy (Marshall & Marshall, 2016; Thibaut et al., 2016; Federoff & Marshall, 2010).

Voyeuristic Disorder

A person with **voyeuristic disorder** experiences recurrent and intense sexual arousal from observing an unsuspecting individual who is naked, disrobing, or engaging in sexual activity. As with other paraphilic disorders, this arousal takes the form of fantasies, urges, or behaviors (APA, 2013). The disorder usually begins before the age of 15 and tends to persist (APA, 2013).

A person with voyeuristic disorder may masturbate during the act of observing or when thinking about it afterward but does not generally seek to have sex with the person being spied on. The vulnerability of the people being observed and the probability that they would feel humiliated if they knew they were under observation are often part of the enjoyment. In addition, the risk of being discovered adds to the excitement, as you can see in 25-year-old Sam's description of his disorder during an interview:

Lady Godiva and "Peeping Tom" According to legend, Lady Godiva (shown in this 1890 illustration) rode naked through the streets of Coventry, England, in order to persuade her husband, the earl of Mercia, to stop taxing the city's poor. Although all townspeople were ordered to stay inside their homes with shutters drawn during her eleventh-century ride, a tailor named Tom "could not contain his sexual curiosity and drilled a hole in his shutter in order to watch Lady Godiva pass by" (Mann et al., 2008). Since then, the term "Peeping Tom" has been used to refer to people with voyeuristic disorder.

imagebroker/Alamy

frotteuristic disorder A paraphilic disorder in which a person has repeated and intense sexual urges or fantasies that involve touching and rubbing against a nonconsenting person, and either acts on these urges with the nonconsenting person or experiences clinically significant distress or impairment.

pedophilic disorder A paraphilic disorder in which a person has repeated and intense sexual urges or fantasies about watching, touching, or engaging in sexual acts with children, and either acts on these urges or experiences clinically significant distress or impairment.

 I've had girlfriends, but it's not the same. It's fun at first, but I get bored after a while in relationships. I never get that kick, that excitement, that I do when I look at others. There's no way that it could be the same with someone who actually knows I'm there.

The biggest thrill is when I'm watching my neighbor having sex with one of her boyfriends, or maybe watching Zoe down the block changing her clothes. Neither of them fully shuts their drapes, so there's always a little angle where I can see into their rooms if I get in just the right position on the lawn. Everything about it turns me on—learning their schedules, waiting until it's just dark enough not to be seen, finding the right spot to look from, making sure I'm very quiet so no one hears me. Sometimes I'll take a walk and try to find someone I haven't watched before. If I hit the jackpot, that can be even more exciting, because I don't know their routines, I don't know what's coming next, and I'm a little more nervous that I might get caught.

Thinking about it afterwards, I also get excited, especially if I came close to getting caught. I realize what a chance I was taking, and it gets my heart going and gets the rest of me going as well. Sometimes I'll make up extra details when remembering what happened, especially details about barely getting away at the last second or even being spotted, and that makes it even better. Of course, if I ever did get caught, it would be horrible. I'd die if that ever happened.

Voyeurism, like exhibitionism, is often a source of sexual excitement in fantasy; it can also play a role in normal sexual interactions if a partner consents to voyeuristic-like behaviors. The clinical disorder of voyeuristic disorder is marked by the repeated invasion of other people's privacy. Some people with the disorder are unable to have normal sexual relations; others have a normal sex life apart from their disorder.

Many psychodynamic clinicians propose that people with voyeuristic disorder are seeking by their actions to gain power over others, possibly because they feel inadequate or are sexually or socially shy (Pfafflin, 2016; Metzl, 2004). Cognitive-behavioral theorists explain the disorder as a learned behavior that can be traced to a chance and secret observation of a sexually arousing scene (Lavin, 2008). If the onlookers observe such scenes on several occasions while masturbating, they may develop a voyeuristic pattern.

Frotteuristic Disorder

A person with **frotteuristic disorder** experiences repeated and intense sexual arousal from touching or rubbing against a nonconsenting person. The arousal may, like with the other paraphilic disorders, take the form of fantasies, urges, or behaviors. Frottage (from French *frotter*, "to rub") is usually committed in a crowded place, such as a subway or a busy sidewalk (Guterman, Martin, & Rudes, 2011). The person, almost always a male, may rub his genitals against the victim's thighs or buttocks or fondle her genital area or breasts with his hands. Typically he fantasizes during the act that he is having a caring relationship with the victim. This paraphilia usually begins in the teenage years or earlier, often after the person observes others committing an act of frottage. After the age of about 25, people gradually decrease and often cease their acts of frottage (APA, 2000).

Pedophilic Disorder

A person with **pedophilic disorder** experiences equal or greater sexual arousal from children than from physically mature people. This arousal is expressed through fantasies, urges, or behaviors (APA, 2013). Those with the disorder may be attracted to prepubescent children (*classic* type), early pubescent children (*hebephilic* type), or both (*pedohebephilic* type). Some people with pedophilic disorder are satisfied by child pornography or seemingly innocent material such as children's underwear ads;

 #

#LegalOption

In 1996 the California state legislature passed the first law in the United States allowing state judges to order *antiandrogen* drug treatments, often referred to as "chemical castration," for repeat sex crime offenders, such as men who repeatedly commit pedophilic acts or rape. Since then, at least eight other states also have passed laws permitting some form of coerced antiandrogen drug treatment.

Francis Demange/Gamma-Rapho via Getty Images

Pedophilia, abuse, and justice People enter the courthouse in Angers, France, in 2005, to witness the largest child abuse trial ever held in France. The court found 65 defendants (39 men and 26 women) guilty of raping, molesting, and prostituting children. The victims ranged in age from 6 months to 14 years, and the defendants ranged from 27 to 73 years.

others are driven to actually watch, touch, fondle, or engage in sexual intercourse with children (Babchishin, Hanson, & VanZuylen, 2014; Schmidt et al., 2014). Some people with the disorder are attracted only to children; others are attracted to adults as well (Schmidt, Mokros, & Banse, 2013; Roche & Quayle, 2007). Both boys and girls can be pedophilic victims, but there is evidence suggesting that two-thirds are girls (Seto, 2008; Koss & Heslet, 1992).

People with pedophilic disorder usually develop their pattern of sexual need during adolescence (Thibaut et al., 2016; Farkas, 2013). Some were themselves sexually abused as children (Thibaut et al., 2016; Nunes et al., 2013), and many were neglected, excessively punished, or deprived of genuinely close relationships during their childhood. It is not unusual for them to be married and to have sexual difficulties or other frustrations in life that lead them to seek an area in which they can be masters. Often these individuals are immature: their social and sexual skills may be underdeveloped, and thoughts of normal sexual relationships fill them with anxiety (Worthen, 2016; Seto, 2008; McAnulty, 2006).

Some people with pedophilic disorder also have distorted thinking, such as, "It's all right to have sex with children as long as they agree" (O Ciardha et al., 2016; Durkin & Hundersmarck, 2008; Abel et al., 2001). It is not uncommon for pedophiles to blame the children for adult–child sexual contacts or to assert that the children benefited from the experience.

While many people with this disorder believe that their feelings are indeed wrong and abnormal, others consider adult sexual activity with children to be acceptable and normal. Some even have joined pedophile organizations that advocate abolishing the age-of-consent laws. The Internet has opened the channels of communication among such people, and there is now a wide range of Web sites, newsgroups, chat rooms, forums, and message boards centered on pedophilia and adult–child sex (Durkin & Hundersmarck, 2008).

Studies have found that most men with pedophilic disorder also display at least one additional psychological disorder (Farkas, 2013; McAnulty, 2006). Some theorists have proposed that pedophilic disorder may be related to biochemical or brain structure abnormalities such as irregular patterns of activity in the amygdala or in the frontal areas of the brain, but such abnormalities have yet to receive consistent research support (Cantor et al., 2016; Lucka & Dziemian, 2014; Wiebking & Northoff, 2013).

Remembering the victims A large bronze monument, created by sculptor Michael Irving, memorializes the victims of a notorious pedophile ring that operated decades ago at Maple Leaf Gardens, a historic building in Toronto, Canada. The powerful monument has 300 squares, each featuring the handprint of a victim, including this square dedicated to Martin Kruze, a victim who died by suicide in 1997. The goal of the undertaking is not only to remember the victims, but to also increase public awareness of their pain and their continuing scars.

Carlos Osorio/Getty Images

Most pedophilic offenders are imprisoned or forced into treatment if they are caught (Thibaut et al., 2016; Staller & Faller, 2010). After all, they are committing child sexual abuse when they take any steps toward sexual contact with a child (Farkas, 2013). There are now many residential registration and community notification laws across the United States that help law enforcement agencies and the public account for and control where convicted child sex offenders live and work (OJJDP, 2010).

Treatments for pedophilic disorder include those already mentioned for other paraphilic disorders, such as aversion therapy, masturbatory satiation, cognitive-behavioral therapy, and antiandrogen drugs (Marshall & Marshall, 2016, 2015; Thibaut et al., 2016; Fromberger et al., 2013). One widely applied cognitive-behavioral treatment for this disorder, *relapse-prevention training,* is modeled after the relapse-prevention training programs used in the treatment of substance use disorders (see pages 372–373). In this approach, clients identify the kinds of situations that typically trigger their pedophilic fantasies and actions (such as depressed mood or distorted thinking). They then learn strategies for avoiding those situations or coping with them more appropriately and effectively. Relapse-prevention training has sometimes, but not consistently, been of help in this and certain other paraphilic disorders (Laws, 2016; Thibaut et al., 2016; Federoff & Marshall, 2010).

A celebration of S/M Sexual sadism and sexual masochism have been viewed by the public with either bemusement or horror, depending on the circumstances and events that surround particular acts of these paraphilias. On the light side, the annual Folsom Street Fair in San Francisco is a very large event that celebrates S/M and invites people (like this participant) to go on stage, display their trademark outfits, and in some cases, participate in whippings or spankings.

Sexual Masochism Disorder

A person with **sexual masochism disorder** is repeatedly and intensely sexually aroused by the act of being humiliated, beaten, bound, or otherwise made to suffer (APA, 2013). Again, this arousal may take such forms as fantasies, urges, or behaviors. Many people have fantasies of being forced into sexual acts against their will, but only those who are very distressed or impaired by the fantasies receive this diagnosis. Some people with the disorder act on the masochistic urges by themselves, perhaps tying, sticking pins into, or even cutting themselves. Others have their sexual partners restrain, tie up, blindfold, spank, paddle, whip, beat, electrically shock, "pin and pierce," or humiliate them (APA, 2013).

An industry of products and services has arisen to meet the desires of people with the paraphilia or the paraphilic disorder of sexual masochism. Here a 34-year-old woman describes her work as the operator of a facility that meets those desires:

I get people here who have been all over looking for the right kind of pain they feel they deserve. Don't ask me why they want pain, I'm not a psychologist; but when they have found us, they usually don't go elsewhere. It may take some of the other girls an hour or even two hours to make these guys feel like they've had their treatment—I can achieve that in about 20 minutes. . . . Remember, these are businessmen, and they are not only buying my time, but they have to get back to work, so time is important.

Among the things I do, that work really quickly and well, are: I put clothespins on their nipples, or pins in their [testicles]. Some of them need to see their own blood to be able to get off. . . .

All the time that a torture scene is going on, there is constant dialogue. . . . I scream at the guy, and tell him what a no-good rotten bastard he is, how this is even too good for him, that he knows he deserves worse, and I begin to list his sins. It works every time. Hey, I'm not nuts, I know what I'm doing. I act very tough and hard, but I'm really a very sensitive woman. But you have to watch out for a guy's health . . . you must not kill him, or have him get a heart attack. . . . I know of other places that have had guys die there. I've never lost a customer to death, though they may have wished for it during my "treatment." Remember, these are repeat customers. I have a clientele and a reputation that I value.

(Janus & Janus, 1993, p. 115)

In one form of sexual masochism disorder, *hypoxyphilia,* people strangle or smother themselves (or ask their partner to strangle them) in order to enhance their sexual pleasure. There have, in fact, been a disturbing number of clinical reports of *autoerotic asphyxia,* in which people, usually males and as young as 10 years old, may accidentally induce a fatal lack of oxygen by hanging, suffocating, or strangling themselves while masturbating (Coluccia et al., 2016; Hucker, 2011, 2008). There is some debate as to whether the practice should be characterized as sexual masochism disorder, but it is at least sometimes accompanied by other acts of bondage.

Most masochistic sexual fantasies begin in childhood. However, the person does not act out the urges until later, usually by early adulthood. The pattern typically continues for many years. Some people practice more and more dangerous acts over time or during times of particular stress (Frias et al., 2017; Krueger, 2010).

In many cases, sexual masochism disorder seems to have developed through the learning process of classical conditioning (Stekel, 2010; Akins, 2004). A classic case study tells of a teenage boy with a broken arm who was caressed and held close by an attractive nurse as the physician set his fracture, a procedure done in the past without anesthesia (Gebhard, 1965). The powerful combination of pain and sexual arousal the boy felt then may have been the cause of his later masochistic urges and acts.

Sexual Sadism Disorder

A person with **sexual sadism disorder,** usually male, is repeatedly and intensely sexually aroused by the physical or psychological suffering of another individual (APA, 2013). This arousal may be expressed through fantasies, urges, or behaviors, including acts such as dominating, restraining, blindfolding, cutting, strangling, mutilating, or even killing the victim (Marshall & Marshall, 2016; Nitschke et al., 2013). The label is derived from the name of the famous Marquis de Sade (1740–1814), who tortured others in order to satisfy his sexual desires.

People who fantasize about sexual sadism typically imagine that they have total control over a sexual victim who is terrified by the sadistic act. Many carry out sadistic acts with a consenting partner, often a person with sexual masochism disorder. Some, however, act out their urges on nonconsenting victims (Mokros et al., 2014). A number of rapists and sexual murderers, for example, exhibit sexual sadism disorder (Marshall & Marshall, 2016, 2015; Worthen, 2016; Knecht, 2014). In all cases, the real or fantasized victim's suffering is the key to arousal.

Fantasies of sexual sadism, like those of sexual masochism, may first appear in childhood or adolescence (Thibaut et al., 2016; Stone, 2010). People who engage in sadistic acts begin to do so by early adulthood (APA, 2013). The pattern is long-term. Some people with the disorder engage in the same level of cruelty in their sadistic acts over time, but often their sadism becomes more and more severe over the years (Marshall & Marshall, 2016, 2015; Robertson & Knight, 2014). Obviously, people with severe forms of the disorder may be highly dangerous to others.

Some cognitive-behavioral theorists believe that classical conditioning is at work in sexual sadism disorder (Akins, 2004). While inflicting pain, perhaps unintentionally, on an animal or person, a teenager may feel intense emotions and sexual arousal. The association between inflicting pain and being aroused sexually sets the stage for a pattern of sexual sadism. Cognitive-behavioral theorists also propose that the disorder may result from modeling, when adolescents observe others achieving sexual satisfaction by inflicting pain. The many Internet sex sites and sexual videos, magazines,

sexual masochism disorder A paraphilic disorder in which a person has repeated and intense sexual urges, fantasies, or behaviors that involve being humiliated, beaten, bound, or otherwise made to suffer, accompanied by clinically significant distress or impairment.

sexual sadism disorder A paraphilic disorder in which a person has repeated and intense sexual urges or fantasies that involve inflicting suffering on others, and either acts on these urges with nonconsenting individuals or experiences clinically significant distress or impairment.

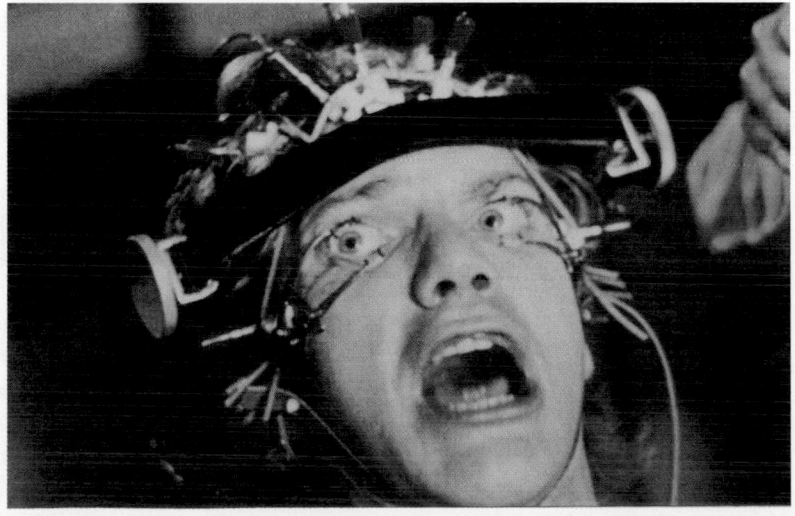

Cinematic introduction In one of filmdom's most famous scenes, Alex, the sexually sadistic character in *A Clockwork Orange*, is forced to observe violent images while he experiences painful stomach spasms.

The Everett Collection

transgender Individuals who have a strong sense that their gender identity is different from their birth anatomy.

gender dysphoria A disorder in which a person persistently feels clinically significant distress or impairment due to his or her assigned gender and strongly wishes to be a member of another gender.

and books in our society make such models readily available (Thibaut et al., 2016; Brophy, 2010).

Both psychodynamic and cognitive-behavioral theorists further suggest that people with sexual sadism disorder inflict pain in order to achieve a sense of power or control, necessitated perhaps by underlying feelings of sexual inadequacy. The sense of power in turn increases their sexual arousal (Marshall & Marshall, 2016, 2015; Stekel, 2010). Alternatively, certain biological studies have found signs of possible brain and hormonal abnormalities in people with sexual sadism (Harenski et al., 2012; Jacobs, 2011; Bradford et al., 2008). None of these explanations, however, has been thoroughly investigated.

Cognitive-behavioral therapists have treated the disorder with aversion therapy (Thibaut et al., 2016). The public's view of and distaste for this procedure have been influenced by the novel and 1971 movie *A Clockwork Orange,* which depicts simultaneous presentations of violent images and drug-induced stomach spasms to a sadistic young man until he is conditioned to feel nausea at the sight of such images. It is not clear that aversion therapy is helpful in cases of sexual sadism disorder. However, relapse-prevention training, used in some criminal cases, may be of value (Laws, 2016; Marshall & Marshall, 2016, 2015; Thibaut et al., 2016).

Gender Variations

AS CHILDREN AND ADULTS, most people feel like and identify themselves as males or females—a feeling and identity that is consistent with their *assigned gender* (or *birth anatomy)*, the gender to which they are born. But society has come to appreciate that many people do not experience such gender clarity. These people are **transgender**, individuals who have a sense that their *gender identity* (one's personal experience of one's gender) is different from their assigned gender. It is estimated that 25 million people in the world are transgender— 0.8% of the adult population (Tangpricha & Safer, 2017, 2016; Winter et al., 2016; Reisner et al., 2014). Many transgender people come to terms with their gender inconsistencies. They accept the incongruence or seek out interventions, such as hormone therapy or surgery, to change their birth anatomy into physical characteristics that fit their *gender identity*. Some transgender people, however, may experience extreme distress over the incongruence and/or find themselves impaired by it in their social relationships, at work, or at school. DSM-5 categorizes these latter people as having **gender dysphoria** (see **Table 13-6**).

The DSM-5 categorization of gender dysphoria is controversial. Many argue that since a transgender pattern reflects an alternative—not pathological—way of experiencing one's gender identity, it should never be considered a psychological disorder, even if it is accompanied by significant unhappiness. Indeed, this is rapidly becoming the dominant view in the clinical field (Russo, 2017; Belluck, 2016; Love, 2016). For example, the developers of the International Classification of Diseases, the classification system used in most countries outside of North America (see pages 100–101), are strongly considering removing all transgender-related behavior, thinking, and feelings—including transgender-related dysphoria—from the list of psychological disorders in its upcoming edition ICD-11. Denmark's Parliament is not waiting for that to occur. In 2017 it became the first country to rule that transgender individuals are no longer considered mentally ill in its mental health system.

> Why might labeling transgender people as mentally ill be harmful to them?

In this climate, it is expected that the category of gender dysphoria may be dropped from the next revision of DSM-5. If so, the DSM would be following a route that it travelled in past times with regard to homosexuality. As you read earlier (see page 404), in its first two editions, the developers of the DSM listed homosexuality as a sexual

---

TABLE: 13-6

Dx Checklist

Gender Dysphoria in Adolescents and Adults

1. For 6 months or more, an individual's gender-related feelings and/or behaviors are at odds with those of his or her assigned gender, as indicated by two or more of the following symptoms: • Gender-related feelings and/or behaviors clearly contradict the individual's primary or secondary sex characteristics • Powerful wish to eliminate one's sex characteristics • Yearning for the sex characteristics of another gender • Powerful wish to be a member of another gender • Yearning to be treated as a member of another gender • Firm belief that one's feelings and reactions are those that characterize another gender.

2. Individual experiences significant distress or impairment.

(Information from: APA, 2013.)

disorder, such as a paraphilic disorder. Protests by gay activist groups and many clinicians eventually led to the DSM's 1973 elimination of this category as a sexual disorder per se, but the DSM did retain a category called *ego dystonic homosexuality*—the experience of extreme distress over one's homosexual orientation. Finally, this latter category too was dropped in a 1987 revision of the DSM. Similarly, in early editions of the DSM, persons with transgender thoughts and needs qualified for a diagnosis of *transgender identity disorder*. This classification was dropped when DSM-5 was published in 2013 and replaced by the current category *gender dysphoria*.

To help distinguish what is known about transgender functioning (an alternative, but not abnormal, pattern) from what is known about gender dysphoria (an abnormal pattern, according to DSM-5), let us look first at transgender functioning, then turn to gender dysphoria.

Transgender Functioning

Given their gender identity, many transgender people would like to get rid of their primary and secondary sex characteristics—some of them find their own genitals repugnant—and to acquire characteristics that correspond to their gender identity (APA, 2013). *Transgender women* (that is, people who identify as female but were assigned male at birth) outnumber *transgender men* (people who identify as male but were assigned female at birth) by around 2 to 1.

Sometimes transgender feelings emerge in children (Olson-Kennedy & Forcier, 2017; Russo, 2016). Like transgender adults, the children feel uncomfortable with their assigned gender and yearn to be members of another gender. This childhood pattern often disappears by adolescence or adulthood, but in some cases the individuals do become transgender adults (Forcier & Olson-Kennedy, 2017; Cohen-Kettenis, 2001). Thus transgender adults may have had transgender feelings when they were children, but many children with transgender feelings do not become transgender adults. Surveys of mothers indicate that about 1.5 percent of young boys wish to be a girl, and 3.5 percent of young girls wish to be a boy (Carroll, 2007; Zucker & Bradley, 1995), yet, as we noted earlier, less than 1 percent of adults are transgender (Zucker, 2010). This age shift is, in part, why many experts on transgender functioning strongly recommend against any form of irreversible physical procedures for this pattern until the individual is at least 14 to 16 years of age, except in extraordinary instances (Forcier & Olson-Kennedy, 2017; Levine, 2017). Certain kinds of pharmacological interventions are, however, considered acceptable and are being administered increasingly to transgender adolescents (Nahata et al., 2017; Bechard et al., 2016; Leibowitz & de Vries, 2016).

A delicate matter A 5-year-old boy (left), who identifies and dresses as a girl and asks to be called "she," plays with a female friend. Sensitive to the gender identity rights movement and to the special needs of children with transgender feelings, a growing number of parents, educators, and clinicians are now supportive of children like this.

Jim Wilson /The New York Times/Redux

Explanations of Transgender Functioning
Increasingly, today's medical and psychological theorists believe that biological factors—perhaps genetic or prenatal—are key to transgender functioning (Cortés-Cortés et al., 2017; Zucker et al., 2016; Rametti et al., 2011). Consistent with a genetic explanation, transgender functioning does sometimes run in families. Research indicates, for example, that people with transgender siblings are more likely to be transgender than are people without such siblings (Gómez-Gil et al., 2010). Indeed, one study of identical twins found that when one of the twins was transgender, the other twin was as well in 9 out of 23 pairs (Heylens et al., 2012).

Biological investigators have uncovered some interesting findings when they examine and compare the brains of transgender and nontransgender individuals. Keeping

Lea T. Transgender model Lea T. emerged in 2010 as the face of Givenchy, the famous French fashion brand. Born with an assigned gender of male, the Brazilian model has become a leading female figure in runway fashion shows and magazines, including *Vogue Paris*, *Cover* magazine, and *Love* magazine, and she is currently the face of the hair-care brand Redken. In 2012 she underwent gender reassignment surgery.

in mind that male and female brains usually differ slightly, researchers have looked for indications that the brains of transgender people are more similar to brains of the gender with which they identify than the gender to which they were assigned at birth (Russo, 2016). For example, using MRI scanning, one team of researchers found that the brains of transgender men (people who identify as male but were assigned female at birth) have relatively thin subcortical areas, much like those of nontransgender men, and the brains of transgender women (people who identify as female but were assigned male at birth) have relatively thin cortical regions in the right hemisphere, much like those of nontransgender women (Guillamon et al., 2016; Russo, 2016; Luders et al. 2012). Correspondingly, other research has found similarities between transgender individuals and their nontransgender counterparts with regard to the activity and size of brain structures such as the insula, anterior cingulate cortex, and bed nucleus of stria terminalis (BST)—structures known to play roles in gender functioning and consciousness (Nawata et al., 2010; Zhou et al., 1997, 1995).

Similar results have been uncovered in studies of brain reactions to strong unpleasant odors. In general, male and female brains react to strong smells differently, particularly in the hypothalamus. Here again, transgender studies have found that, when exposed to strong unpleasant smells, the hypothalamic responses of transgender males are similar to those of nontransgender males, whereas the hypothalamic responses of transgender females are similar to those of nontransgender females (Burke et al., 2014). Brain response similarities between transgender individuals and their nontransgender counterparts have likewise been found in studies that expose participants to certain sounds, visual stimuli, and memory challenges (Burke et al., 2016, 2014). These findings are particularly telling, because the kinds of odor, sound, and visual responses examined in these studies are not typically influenced by training or experience, suggesting that predispositions to transgender functioning may indeed be inborn (Kreukels, 2016).

Based on such findings, it might be tempting to conclude that transgender people are individuals whose male brain is simply trapped inside a female body or whose female brain is trapped inside a male body, but, as researcher Antonio Guillamon cautions, "Trans people have brains that are different from males and females, a *unique* kind of brain" (Guillamon, 2016). That is, they do not have a male or female brain, but rather a transgender brain.

Options for Transgender Individuals As you read earlier, transgender people often address the incongruence between their gender identity and birth anatomy through biological procedures. For example, many change their sexual characteristics by means of *hormone administration* (Tangpricha & Safer, 2017, 2016; Wierckx et al., 2014). Physicians prescribe the female sex hormone *estrogen* for transgender females, as well as other medications designed to suppress their bodies' production of the male sex hormone testosterone. This leads to breast development, loss of body and facial hair, and changes in body fat distribution. Some of these patients also go to speech therapy, raising their tenor voice to alto through training, and some have facial feminization surgery (Tangpricha & Safer, 2017; Capitán et al., 2014; Steinmetz, 2014). In contrast, transgender men are administered the male sex hormone *testosterone*, resulting in a deeper voice, increased muscle mass, and changes in facial and body hair (Tangpricha & Safer, 2016).

Hormone administration enables many transgender persons to lead a fulfilling life in the gender that fits them. For others, however, this is not enough, and they may seek out **gender reassignment surgery,** or **gender change surgery**—also called *gender confirmation surgery* or *gender-affirming surgery* (Tangpricha & Safer, 2017, 2016). Such surgery is usually preceded by 1 to 2 years of hormone administration. For transgender women, the surgery can involve one or more of the following procedures: face-changing plastic surgery, breast augmentation, and genital reconstruction (partial removal of the penis and restructuring of its remaining parts into a clitoris

gender reassignment surgery A surgical procedure that changes a person's sex organs and gender features. Also known as *gender change surgery*.

and vagina). For transgender men, surgery may include a bilateral mastectomy, chest reconstruction, a hysterectomy, and/or genital reconstruction (the formation of a functioning penis—a procedure not yet perfected—or a silicone prosthesis that can give the appearance of male genitals). Genital reconstruction is performed much less often than the other surgical procedures, especially among transgender men (ASPS, 2017; Mainwaring, 2017). According to a report by the American Society of Plastic Surgeons, more than 3,200 gender reassignment surgeries were performed in the United States in 2016, an increase of 20 percent over the number in 2015. The surgeries were conducted on more transgender women than transgender men. Some insurance companies refuse to cover these (or even nonsurgical) biological treatments for transgender people, but a growing number of states now prohibit such insurance exclusions (Sifferlin, 2017; Steimetz, 2014).

Clinicians have debated whether gender change surgery is an appropriate option for transgender persons (à Campo & Nijman, 2016; Gozlan, 2011). Some consider it a humane procedure, perhaps the most satisfying one to many transgender people. Others argue that gender change surgery is a "drastic nonsolution" for a complex issue. Either way, as indicated above, such surgery appears to be on the increase (ASPS, 2017; à Campo & Nijman, 2016).

Research into the outcomes of gender reassignment surgery has yielded generally positive findings. Across a number of studies, at least 70 percent of patients report satisfaction with the outcome of the surgery, improvement in the quality of their lives, a better psychological state, greater self-satisfaction, more positive body satisfaction, better interpersonal interactions, and improvements in sexual functioning (Lindqvist et al., 2017; Tangpricha & Safer, 2017, 2016; van de Grift et al., 2017). On the other hand, several studies have yielded less favorable findings. A long-term follow-up study in Sweden, for example, found that gender-reassigned participants had a higher rate of psychological disorders and of suicide attempts than the general population (Dhejne et al., 2011). People with serious pretreatment psychological disturbances (for example, a personality disorder) seem most likely to later regret the surgery (Carroll, 2007). All of this argues for careful screening prior to surgical interventions, continued research to better understand the long-term impact of the surgical procedures, and, more generally, improved medical and clinical care for transgender people.

#GenderTerms

Trans: Short for transgender

Gender identity: Your personal sense of your gender

Assigned gender: Your gender at birth, based on your genitals

Cisgender persons: Individuals whose gender identity matches their assigned gender

A new audience When he won the gold medal for the decathlon at the 1976 Olympics (left), Bruce Jenner became a national hero and was widely viewed as the personification of masculinity—the world's best male athlete. When in 2015 Jenner appeared in *Vanity Fair* magazine (right) as a transgender woman, Caitlyn, transgender persons across the country hoped that this high-profile revelation would help reduce the public's prejudice against transgender individuals.

Every walk of life As society is coming to appreciate, transgender functioning is not confined to people with one kind of family history, personality, or occupation. In 2012, Thomas Gabel (left), the founder and lead singer of the punk rock band Against Me!, came out as a transgender woman named Laura Jane Grace (right). Although the punk rock community was initially divided in its support of the transition, Laura Jane Grace has been steadfastly vocal about her early life struggles with gender identity issues. A year after her transition, the band released *Transgender Dysphoria Blues*, one of their most acclaimed and highest-selling albums.

Gender Dysphoria

Surveys reveal that 90 percent of transgender persons experience at least a moderate degree of distress or dysfunction at home, school, or work, or in social relationships, especially during adolescence (Robles et al., 2016). As you have read, if that level of distress and impairment becomes significant, DSM-5 categorizes the pattern as gender dysphoria. Some individuals with this disorder—children, adolescents, and adults—feel severe anxiety or depression, display substance abuse, and may have thoughts of suicide (Schulman & Erickson-Schroth, 2017; Aitken et al., 2016).

Although such features of dysphoria have been documented, the cause of gender dysphoria has been hard to sort out (Zucker et al., 2016). On the one hand, most transgender people do indeed report that the incongruence between their gender identity and birth anatomy directly causes them some distress (Robles et al., 2016). On the other hand, surveys suggest that the primary cause for intense dysphoric reactions is the enormous prejudice that transgender persons typically face. According to surveys across the United States and other countries, for example, 80 to 90 percent of transgender people have been harassed or attacked in their schools, workplaces, or communities (some have even been murdered); 50 percent have been fired from a job, not hired, or not promoted; and 20 percent have been denied a place to live (Winter et al., 2016; Steinmetz, 2014). Many have been stigmatized, excluded from social groups, and denied access to appropriate health care (both general health care and care related to their gender needs). This is why so many clinicians favor the elimination of gender dysphoria from the DSM. That is, society's reactions to a transgender person may be much more responsible for the individual's psychological pain than the individual's dismay over transgender issues themselves, difficult though they may be. In fact, more and more studies are finding that when transgender individuals are supported in their identities by their family members and friends, they typically do not experience significant mental health problems (Durwood et al., 2017; Olson et al., 2016).

That said, people in psychological pain still need help, and, indeed, many individuals with gender dysphoria receive psychotherapy (Majumber & Sanyal, 2017, 2016; Affatati et al., 2004). Here, they typically try to become more aware of their needs and feelings; reduce their feelings of anxiety, depression, and anger; improve their self-image; learn how to cope with the stress caused by their gender issues; develop better problem-solving skills; and develop a sense of self that also extends beyond gen-

A special bond Two men, 64-year-old Juani Santos (left) and 28-year-old Liam Duran (right), catch up on recent events at a cafe in Cuba. Despite a significant age difference, they are close friends, partly because they share an important gender identity experience—they are both transgender men. Santos, one of Cuba's oldest documented transgender individuals, had gender reassignment surgery just a few years ago. He says he first knew he was a boy at the age of 5.

der identity. No single form of psychotherapy has been more widely used than other forms in cases of gender dysphoria. Nor has research indicated that psychotherapy alone consistently brings significant psychological improvement in cases of gender dysphoria.

Actually, the interventions that seem to be of greater help to people with gender dysphoria are the biological gender-change procedures that so many transgender persons undergo. In a meta-analysis of 28 studies—some of them long-term follow-up studies—with a total of 1,833 transgender individuals who received hormone therapy and/or gender reassignment surgery, it was found that 80 percent of participants experienced significant improvements in their symptoms of gender dysphoria as a result of the biological interventions (Tangpricha & Safer, 2017, 2016; Murad et al., 2010).

Finally, two positive developments in recent years have been the emergence and growth of transgender education programs and an increase in support programs for transgender people (Morrison et al., 2017; McPhail et al., 2016). Across the world, there has been a concerted effort to broaden knowledge about and awareness of transgender functioning. Many hundreds of educational programs, which are offered in locations ranging from schools to workplaces to the Internet, now target transgender persons themselves (both young and old), health care professionals, family members, and the general public. Similarly, numerous support, or mutual help, groups—both in-person and online—are now available for transgender adolescents and adults, providing social support, advice, and relevant information. Research indicates that these various programs help prevent or reduce gender dysphoria or other forms of psychological distress among transgender participants (Cipolletta et al., 2017; Logie et al., 2016; McConnell et al., 2016).

Personal Topics Draw Public Attention

AT THE BEGINNING of this chapter, we noted that sexual disorders and gender variations are, in fact, very different topics. However, they do share two things. They have both received considerable study over the past few decades, and a key to progress in both areas appears to be public education.

#

#KeyDistinction

Sexual orientation is about whom one is sexually attracted to. *Gender identity* is about whether one considers oneself male or female.

As a result of research in the realm of sexual disorders, people with sexual dysfunctions are no longer doomed to a lifetime of sexual frustration. Studies of sexual dysfunctions have uncovered many psychological, sociocultural, and biological causes. Correspondingly, important progress has been made in the treatment of sexual dysfunctions, and people with such problems are now often helped greatly by therapy. At the same time, it has become clear that education about sexual dysfunctions can be as important as therapy. When taken seriously, sexual myths often lead to feelings of shame, self-hatred, isolation, and hopelessness—feelings that themselves contribute to sexual difficulty. Thus public education about sexual functioning—through the Internet, books, television and radio, school programs, group presentations, and the like—has become a major clinical focus.

Similarly, as a result of research in the realm of gender diversity, transgender persons are no longer doomed to a life of gender confusion and frustration. In addition, the clinical field is now clear that transgender functioning does not represent a mental disorder. And, finally, it has become clear that public education about gender variations is a key to further understanding and progress in this realm. Recent increases in such educational programs have already begun to make some difference in the levels of discrimination, stigmatization, harassment, and hardship that are faced regularly by transgender people. Clearly, more such education is needed.

CLINICAL CHOICES

Now that you've read about sexual disorders and gender variations, try the interactive case study for this chapter. See if you are able to identify Cheryl's issues and suggest a possible diagnosis based on them. What kind of interventions might be most helpful for Cheryl? Go to **Launch**Pad to access *Clinical Choices*.

♀... SUMMING UP

» **Sexual Dysfunctions** The *human sexual response cycle* consists of four phases: *desire, excitement, orgasm,* and *resolution. Sexual dysfunctions,* disorders in which people cannot respond normally in a key area of sexual functioning, make it difficult or impossible for a person to have or enjoy sexual activity. *p. 384*

» **Disorders of Desire** DSM-5 lists two disorders of the *desire phase* of the *sexual response cycle: male hypoactive sexual desire disorder* and *female sexual interest/arousal disorder.* Men with the former disorder persistently lack or have reduced interest in sex and, in turn, engage in little sexual activity. Women with the latter disorder lack normal interest in sex, rarely initiate sexual activity, and may also feel little excitement during sexual activity or in the presence of erotic cues. Biological causes for these disorders include abnormal hormone levels, certain drugs, and some medical illnesses. Psychological and sociocultural causes include specific fears, situational pressures, relationship problems, and the trauma of having been sexually molested or assaulted. *pp. 384–388*

» **Disorders of Excitement** Disorders of the *excitement phase* include *erectile disorder,* a repeated inability to attain or maintain an erection during sexual activity. Biological causes of erectile disorder include abnormal hormone levels, vascular problems, medical conditions, and certain medications. Psychological and sociocultural causes include the combination of *performance anxiety* and the *spectator role,* situational pressures such as job loss, and relationship problems. *pp. 388–390*

» **Disorders of Orgasm** *Premature ejaculation* has been attributed most often to behavioral causes, such as inappropriate early learning and inexperience. In recent years, possible biological factors have been identified as well. *Delayed ejaculation,* a repeated absence of or long delay in reaching orgasm, can have biological causes, such as low testosterone levels, neurological diseases, and certain drugs, and psychological causes, such as performance anxiety and the spectator role. The dysfunction may also develop from male hypoactive sexual desire disorder.

Female orgasmic disorder, which is often accompanied by arousal difficulties, has been tied to biological causes such as medical diseases and changes that occur after menopause, psychological causes such as memories of childhood traumas, and sociocultural causes such as relationship problems. Most clinicians agree that orgasm during intercourse is not critical to normal sexual functioning, provided a woman can reach orgasm with her partner during direct stimulation of the clitoris. *pp. 390–394*

» **Sexual Pain Disorders** *Genito-pelvic pain/penetration disorder* involves significant pain during intercourse. In one form of this disorder, *vaginismus,* involuntary contractions of the muscles around the outer third of the vagina prevent entry of the penis. In another form, *dyspareunia,* the person has severe vaginal or pelvic pain during intercourse. This form of the disorder usually occurs in women and typically has a physical cause, such as injury resulting from childbirth. *pp. 394–395*

» **Treatments for Sexual Dysfunctions** In the 1970s, the work of William Masters and Virginia Johnson led to the development of *sex therapy.* Today sex therapy combines a variety of cognitive, behavioral, couple, and family systems therapies. It generally includes features such as careful assessment, education, acceptance of mutual responsibility, attitude changes, *sensate-focus* exercises, improvements in communication, and couple therapy. In addition, specific techniques have been developed for each of the sexual dysfunctions. The use of biological treatments for sexual dysfunctions is also increasing. *pp. 396–402*

» Paraphilic Disorders

Paraphilias are patterns characterized by recurrent and intense sexual urges, fantasies, or behaviors involving objects or situations outside the usual sexual norms—for example, nonhuman objects, children, nonconsenting adults, or experiences of suffering or humiliation. When an individual's paraphilia causes great distress, interferes with social or occupational functioning, or places the individual or others at risk of harm, a diagnosis of *paraphilic disorder* is applied. Paraphilic disorders are found primarily in men.

Fetishistic disorder consists of recurrent and intense sexual fantasies, urges, or behaviors that involve the use of a nonliving object or nongenital part. *Transvestic disorder*, also known as *transvestism* or *cross-dressing*, is characterized by repeated and intense sexual fantasies, urges, or behaviors that involve dressing in clothes of the opposite sex. *Exhibitionistic disorder* features repeated and intense sexual fantasies, urges, or behaviors that involve exposing one's genitals to others. In *voyeuristic disorder*, a person has repeated and intense sexual fantasies, urges, or behaviors that involve secretly observing unsuspecting people who are naked, undressing, or engaging in sexual activity. In *frotteuristic disorder*, a person has repeated and intense sexual fantasies, urges, or behaviors that involve touching or rubbing against a nonconsenting person. In *pedophilic disorder*, a person has repeated and intense sexual fantasies, urges, or behaviors that involve watching, touching, or engaging in sexual acts with children. *Sexual masochism disorder* is characterized by repeated and intense sexual fantasies, urges, or behaviors that involve being humiliated, beaten, bound, or otherwise made to suffer. *Sexual sadism disorder* is characterized by repeated and intense sexual fantasies, urges, or behaviors that involve inflicting suffering on others.

Although various explanations have been proposed for paraphilic disorders, research has revealed little about their causes. A range of treatments have been tried, including *aversion therapy, masturbatory satiation,* and *relapse-prevention training. pp. 402–412*

» Gender Variations

DSM-5 does not consider *transgender* functioning to be a psychological disorder, but it does categorize *gender dysphoria*—a pattern of significant distress or impairment due to one's transgender feelings and thoughts—as a disorder. It is possible, however, that gender dysphoria will be eliminated from the list of disorders in the next DSM revision. Transgender feelings and thoughts in children often disappear by adolescence or adulthood, but in some cases, children with such feelings develop into transgender adults. *Hormone treatments* have been used to help some people adopt the gender role they believe to be right for them. *Gender change surgery* has also been performed. *pp. 412–417*

Visit *LaunchPad*
to access the e-Book, Clinical Choices, videos, activities, and LearningCurve, as well as study aids including flashcards, FAQs, and research exercises.

 **LaunchPad** macmillan learning

...Schizophrenia and Related Disorders

Laura, 40 years old: Laura's desire was to become independent and leave home . . . as soon as possible. . . . She became a professional dancer at the age of 20 . . . and was booked for . . . theaters in many European countries. . . .

It was during one of her tours in Germany that Laura met her husband. . . . They were married and went to live in a small . . . town in France where the husband's business was. . . . She spent a year in that town and was very unhappy. . . . [Finally] Laura and her husband decided to emigrate to the United States. . . .

They had no children, and Laura . . . showed interest in pets. She had a dog to whom she was very devoted. The dog became sick and partially paralyzed, and veterinarians felt that there was no hope of recovery. . . . Finally [her husband] broached the problem to his wife, asking her "Should the dog be destroyed or not?" From that time on Laura became restless, agitated, and depressed. . . .

Later Laura started to complain about the neighbors. A woman who lived on the floor beneath them was knocking on the wall to irritate her. According to the husband, this woman had really knocked on the wall a few times; he had heard the noises. However, Laura became more and more concerned about it. She would wake up in the middle of the night under the impression that she was hearing noises from the apartment downstairs. She would become upset and angry at the neighbors. . . . Later she became more disturbed. She started to feel that the neighbors were now recording everything she said; maybe they had hidden wires in the apartment. She started to feel "funny" sensations. There were many strange things happening, which she did not know how to explain; people were looking at her in a funny way in the street. . . . She felt that people were planning to harm either her or her husband. . . . In the evening when she looked at television, it became obvious to her that the programs referred to her life. Often the people on the programs were just repeating what she had thought. They were stealing her ideas. She wanted to go to the police and report them.

(Arieti, 1974, pp. 165–168)

Richard, 23 years old: In high school, Richard was an average student. After graduation from high school, he [entered] the army. . . . Richard remembered [the] period . . . after his discharge from the army . . . as one of the worst in his life. . . . Any, even remote, anticipation of disappointment was able to provoke attacks of anxiety in him. . . .

Approximately two years after his return to civilian life, Richard left his job because he became overwhelmed by these feelings of lack of confidence in himself, and he refused to go look for another one. He stayed home most of the day. His mother would nag him that he was too lazy and unwilling to do anything. He became slower and slower in dressing and undressing and taking care of himself. When he went out of the house, he felt compelled "to give interpretations" to everything he looked at. He did not know what to do outside the house, where to go, where to turn. If he saw a red light at a crossing, he would interpret it as a message that he should not go in that direction. If he saw an arrow, he would follow the arrow interpreting it as a sign sent by God that he should go in that direction. Feeling lost and horrified, he would go home and stay there, afraid to go out because going out meant making decisions or choices that he felt unable to make. He reached the point where he stayed home most of the time. But even at home, he was tortured by his symptoms. He could not act; any motion that he felt like making seemed to him an insurmountable obstacle, because he did not know whether he should make it or not. He was increasingly afraid of doing the wrong thing. Such fears prevented him from

schizophrenia A psychotic disorder in which personal, social, and occupational functioning deteriorate as a result of unusual perceptions, odd thoughts, disturbed emotions, and motor abnormalities.

psychosis A state in which a person loses contact with reality in key ways.

dressing, undressing, eating, and so forth. He felt paralyzed and lay motionless in bed. He gradually became worse, was completely motionless, and had to be hospitalized. . . . Being undecided, he felt blocked, and often would remain mute and motionless, like a statue, even for days.

(Arieti, 1974, pp. 153–155)

Eventually, Laura and Richard each received a diagnosis of **schizophrenia** (APA, 2013). People with schizophrenia, though they previously functioned well or at least acceptably, deteriorate into an isolated wilderness of unusual perceptions, odd thoughts, disturbed emotions, and motor abnormalities. In Chapter 15 you will see that schizophrenia is no longer the hopeless disorder of times past and that some sufferers, though certainly not all, now make remarkable recoveries. However, in this chapter let us first take a look at the symptoms of the disorder and at the theories that have been developed to explain them.

Like Laura and Richard, people with schizophrenia experience **psychosis,** a loss of contact with reality. Their ability to perceive and respond to the environment becomes so disturbed that they may not be able to function at home, with friends, in school, or at work (Marder & Davis, 2016). They may have hallucinations (false sensory perceptions) or delusions (false beliefs), or they may withdraw into a private world. DSM-5 calls for a diagnosis of schizophrenia only after the symptoms continue for six months or more (see **Table 14-1**).

As you saw in Chapter 12, taking LSD or abusing amphetamines or cocaine may also produce psychosis (see *PsychWatch*). So may injuries or diseases of the brain. And so may other severe psychological disorders, such as major depressive disorder or bipolar disorder. Most commonly, however, psychosis appears in the form of schizophrenia. The term schizophrenia comes from the Greek words for "split mind."

Approximately 1 of every 100 people in the world suffers from schizophrenia during his or her lifetime (Fischer & Buchanan, 2017). An estimated 21 million people worldwide are afflicted with it, including 3.6 million in the United States (NIMH, 2017; WHO, 2016). Equal numbers of men and women experience the disorder. The average age of onset for men is 23 years, compared with 28 years for women.

The financial cost of schizophrenia is enormous, and the emotional cost is even greater. As you read in Chapter 9, people with this disorder are much more likely to attempt suicide than the general population. It is estimated that as many as 25 percent

#

#WrongSplit

Despite popular misconceptions, people with schizophrenia do not have a "split" or multiple personality. That pattern is indicative of dissociative identity disorder.

TABLE: 14-1

Dx Checklist

Schizophrenia

1. For 1 month, individual displays two or more of the following symptoms much of the time:
   (a) Delusions
   (b) Hallucinations
   (c) Disorganized speech
   (d) Very abnormal motor activity, including catatonia
   (e) Negative symptoms

2. At least one of the individual's symptoms must be delusions, hallucinations, or disorganized speech.

3. Individual functions much more poorly in various life spheres than was the case prior to the symptoms.

4. Beyond this 1 month of intense symptomology, individual continues to display some degree of impaired functioning for at least 5 additional months.

(Information from: APA, 2013.)

Mentally Ill Chemical Abusers

During the 1990s, Larry Hogue, nicknamed the "Wild Man of West 96th Street" by neighbors, became the best-known *mentally ill chemical abuser* (*MICA*) in the United States. MICAs, also known as *dual diagnosis* patients, are people who display both a severe mental disorder *and* a substance use disorder.

Hogue, a homeless man who lived on the streets of New York City's Upper West Side, suffered from a combination of schizophrenia and cocaine and alcohol use disorders. As long as he did not abuse these substances, his schizophrenic disorder was responsive to treatment. But Hogue was unable to resist cocaine and alcohol, and the substances combined with his schizophrenia to produce a pattern of severe psychosis. While on the streets, particularly West 96th Street, Hogue behaved bizarrely. He would roam the streets in a menacing way, scream at passers-by, attack and threaten those who crossed his path, commit crimes against property, and strike fear into the hearts of the Upper West Side residents.

Hogue was arrested more than 30 times and imprisoned at least six times. In prison, with substances out of reach, he would quickly calm down, become more coherent, and seem ready for treatment in the community. However, once back in the community, he would seek alcohol and cocaine instead of treatment, and the whole pattern would begin again. Only after the case gained national attention was Hogue committed to a mental health facility for treatment of his dual diagnosis problem.

Although Larry Hogue eventually received proper attention, today the MICA problem in the United States appears to be bigger than ever (Campbell et al., 2016; Chakraborty et al., 2014). Between 20 and 50 percent of all people with schizophrenia or other severe mental disorders may be MICAs.

MICAs tend to be young and male. They often rate below average in social functioning and school achievement and above average in poverty, acting-out behavior, emergency room visits, and encounters with the criminal justice system (Robertson et al., 2014). MICAs commonly report more dis-

Wild Man of West 96th Street Larry Hogue, the so-called Wild Man of West 96th Street, roams the streets in the 1990s while displaying the combined effects of schizophrenia and substance abuse.

tress, have poorer treatment outcomes, and relapse more often than people with mental disorders who do not abuse substances (Campbell et al., 2016; Large et al., 2014).

The relationship between substance abuse and mental dysfunction is complex. A person's mental disorder may precede his or her substance abuse, and he or she may take a drug as a form of self-medication or as a result of impaired judgment. Conversely, substance abuse may cause or exacerbate psychopathology. Cocaine and amphetamines, for example, exacerbate the symptoms of psychosis and can quickly intensify the symptoms of schizophrenia, as in Larry Hogue's case (Li et al., 2014). Whichever begins first, substance abuse and mental disorders interact to create a complex and distinct problem that is greater than the sum of its parts (Campbell et al., 2016; Chakraborty et al., 2014). The course and outcome of each disorder can be significantly influenced by the other.

Treatment of MICAs has been undermined by the tendency of patients to hide their drug abuse problems and for clinicians to overlook such problems (Bahorik et al., 2014). Unrecognized substance abuse may lead to misdiagnosis and misunderstanding of the disorders. The treatment of MICAs is further complicated by the fact that

many treatment facilities are designed and funded to treat *either* mental disorders *or* substance abuse; only some are equipped or willing to treat both (De Witte et al., 2014). As a result, it is not uncommon for MICA patients to be rejected as inappropriate for treatment in both substance abuse and mental health programs. Many such patients fall through the cracks in this way and find themselves in jail, like Larry Hogue, or in homeless shelters for want of the treatment they sought in vain.

The problem of falling through the cracks is perhaps most poignantly seen in the case of *homeless* MICAs (Campbell et al., 2016; Kooyman & Walsh, 2011). Researchers estimate that 10 to 20 percent of the homeless population may be MICAs. MICAs typically remain homeless longer than other homeless people and are more likely to have to contend with extremely harsh conditions, such as living on the winter streets rather than in a homeless shelter. Homeless MICAs need treatment programs committed to building trust and providing intensive case management (Campbell et al., 2016; Coldwell & Bender, 2007). In short, therapists must tailor treatment programs to MICAs' unique combination of problems rather than expecting the MICAs to adapt to traditional forms of care.

of people with schizophrenia attempt suicide and 5 percent die from suicide (Fischer & Buchanan, 2017). Given this high risk, it is strongly recommended that patients with schizophrenia receive thorough suicide risk assessments during treatment and when they are discharged from treatment programs (Pedersen et al., 2014). In addition, people with the disorder have an increased risk of physical—often fatal—illness. On average, they live 10 to 20 fewer years than other people (Fischer & Buchanan, 2017; Laursen et al., 2014).

Although schizophrenia appears in all socioeconomic groups, it is found more frequently in the lower levels (Gruebner et al., 2017; Uher & Zwicker, 2017; Sareen et al., 2011) (see **Figure 14-1**). This has led some theorists to believe that the stress of poverty is itself a cause of the disorder. However, it could be that schizophrenia causes its sufferers to fall from a higher to a lower socioeconomic level or to remain poor because they are unable to function effectively. This is sometimes called the *downward drift* theory.

People have long shown great interest in schizophrenia, flocking to plays and movies that explore or exploit our fascination with the disorder. Yet, as you will read, all too many people with schizophrenia are neglected in our country, their needs almost entirely ignored. Although effective interventions have been developed, many sufferers live without adequate treatment and never fully achieve their potential as human beings. ■

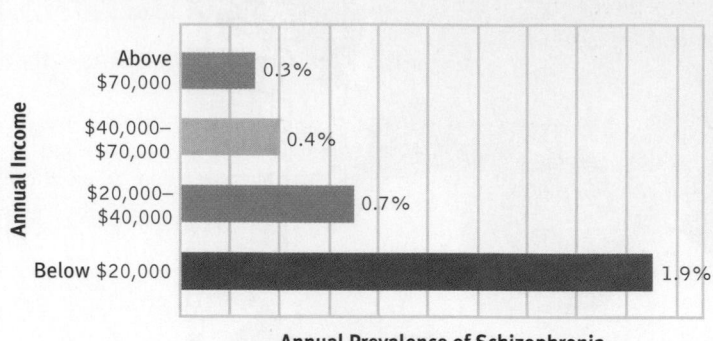

FIGURE 14-1

Socioeconomic Class and Schizophrenia

Poor people in the United States are more likely than wealthy people to experience schizophrenia. (Information from: Gruebner et al., 2017; Uher & Zwicker, 2017; Sareen et al., 2011.)

The Clinical Picture of Schizophrenia

FOR YEARS, SCHIZOPHRENIA WAS a "wastebasket category" for diagnosticians, particularly for those in the United States, where the label was at times assigned to anyone who acted unpredictably or strangely. The disorder is defined more precisely today, but still its symptoms vary greatly, and so do its triggers, course, and responsiveness to treatment (APA, 2013). In fact, most of today's clinicians believe that schizophrenia is actually a group of distinct disorders that happen to have some features in common (Fischer & Buchanan, 2017).

Regardless of whether schizophrenia is a single disorder or several disorders, the lives of people who struggle with its symptoms are filled with pain and turmoil. One particularly coherent and articulate patient described what it is like to live with this disorder:

 What . . . does schizophrenia mean to me? It means fatigue and confusion, it means trying to separate every experience into the real and the unreal and sometimes not being aware of where the edges overlap. It means trying to think straight when there is a maze of experiences getting in the way, and when thoughts are continually being sucked out of your head so that you become embarrassed to speak at meetings. It means feeling sometimes that you are inside your head and visualizing yourself walking over your brain, or watching another girl wearing your clothes and carrying out actions as you think them. It means knowing that you are continually "watched," that you can never succeed in life because the laws are all against you and knowing that your ultimate destruction is never far away.

(Rollin, 1980, p. 162)

What Are the Symptoms of Schizophrenia?

Think back to Laura and Richard, the two people described at the beginning of the chapter. Both of them deteriorated from a normal level of functioning to become ineffective in dealing with the world. Each had some of the symptoms found in schizophrenia. The symptoms can be grouped into three categories: *positive symptoms* (excesses of thought, emotion, and behavior), *negative symptoms* (deficits of thought, emotion, and behavior), and *psychomotor symptoms* (unusual movements or gestures). Some people with schizophrenia are more dominated by positive symptoms and others by negative symptoms, although most tend to have both kinds of symptoms to some degree. In addition, around half of those with schizophrenia have significant difficulties with memory and other kinds of cognitive functioning (Fischer & Buchanan, 2017; Ragland et al., 2015).

Positive Symptoms Positive symptoms are "pathological excesses," or bizarre additions, to a person's behavior. *Delusions, disorganized thinking and speech, heightened perceptions and hallucinations,* and *inappropriate affect* are the ones most often found in schizophrenia.

DELUSIONS Many people with schizophrenia develop **delusions,** ideas that they believe wholeheartedly but that have no basis in fact. The deluded person may consider the ideas enlightening or may feel confused by them. Some people hold a single delusion that dominates their lives and behavior; others have many delusions. *Delusions of persecution* are the most common in schizophrenia (APA, 2013). People with such delusions believe they are being plotted or discriminated against, spied on, slandered, threatened, attacked, or deliberately victimized. Laura believed that her neighbors were trying to irritate her and that other people were trying to harm her and her husband.

People with schizophrenia may also have *delusions of reference:* they attach special and personal meaning to the actions of others or to various objects or events. Richard, for example, interpreted arrows on street signs as indicators of the direction he should take. People with *delusions of grandeur* believe themselves to be great inventors, religious saviors, or other specially empowered persons. And those with *delusions of control* believe their feelings, thoughts, and actions are being controlled by other people.

DISORGANIZED THINKING AND SPEECH People with schizophrenia may not be able to think logically and may speak in peculiar ways. These difficulties, collectively called **formal thought disorders,** can cause the sufferer great confusion and make communication extremely difficult. Often such thought disorders take the form of positive symptoms (pathological excesses), as in *loose associations, neologisms, perseveration,* and *clang.*

People who have **loose associations,** or **derailment,** the most common formal thought disorder, rapidly shift from one topic to another, believing that their incoherent statements make sense. A single, perhaps unimportant word in one sentence becomes the focus of the next. One man with schizophrenia, asked about his itchy arms, responded:

 The problem is insects. My brother used to collect insects. He's now a man 5 foot 10 inches. You know, 10 is my favorite number. I also like to dance, draw, and watch television.

Some people with schizophrenia use *neologisms,* made-up words that typically have meaning only to the person using them. One person said, for example, "I am here from a foreign university . . . and you have to have a *'plausity'* of all acts of amendment to go through for the children's code . . . it is an *'amorition'* law . . . the children have to have this *'accentuative'* law so they don't go into the *'mortite'* law of the church" (Vetter, 1969, p. 189). Others may have the formal thought disorder of *perseveration,* in which they repeat their words and statements again and again. Finally, some use *clang,* or rhyme, to think or express themselves. When asked how he was feeling, one man replied, "Well, hell, it's well to tell." Another described the weather as "So hot, you know it runs on a cot." Research suggests that some people may have disorganized speech or thinking long before their full pattern of schizophrenia unfolds (Remington et al., 2014).

positive symptoms Symptoms of schizophrenia that seem to be excesses of or bizarre additions to normal thoughts, emotions, or behaviors.

delusion A strange false belief firmly held despite evidence to the contrary.

formal thought disorder A disturbance in the production and organization of thought.

loose associations A common thinking disturbance in schizophrenia, characterized by rapid shifts from one topic of conversation to another. Also known as *derailment.*

Philosopher Friedrich Nietzsche said, "Insanity in individuals is something rare—but in groups, parties, nations and epochs, it is the rule." What did he mean?

Delusions of grandeur In 1892, an artist who was a patient at a mental hospital claimed credit for this painting, *Self-Portrait as Christ.* Although few people with schizophrenia have his artistic skill, a number have similar delusions of grandeur.

Mütter Museum, College of Physicians of Philadelphia

hallucination The experiencing of sights, sounds, or other perceptions in the absence of external stimuli.

HEIGHTENED PERCEPTIONS AND HALLUCINATIONS A deranged character in Edgar Allan Poe's "The Tell-Tale Heart" asks, "Have I not told you that what you mistake for madness is but the overacuteness of the senses?" Similarly, the perceptions and attention of some people with schizophrenia seem to intensify (Rossi-Arnaud et al., 2014). The persons may feel that their senses are being flooded by all the sights and sounds that surround them (Galderisi et al., 2014). This makes it almost impossible for them to attend to anything important:

 Everything seems to grip my attention. . . . I am speaking to you just now, but I can hear noises going on next door . . . I find it difficult to shut these out, and it makes it more difficult for me to concentrate on what I am saying to you.

(McGhie and Chapman, 1961)

Laboratory studies repeatedly have found problems of perception and attention among people with schizophrenia (Fischer & Buchanan, 2017; Bozikas et al., 2014). In one early study, participants were instructed to listen for a particular syllable recorded against an ongoing background of speech (Harris et al., 1985). As long as the background speech was kept simple, participants with and without schizophrenia were equally successful at picking out the syllable in question; but when the background speech was made more distracting, those with schizophrenia became less able to identify the syllable. In many studies, people with schizophrenia have also demonstrated deficiencies in *smooth pursuit eye movement,* weaknesses that may be related again to attention problems. When asked to keep their head still and track a moving object back and forth with their eyes, research participants with schizophrenia tend to perform more poorly than those without schizophrenia (Demily et al., 2016; Franco et al., 2014).

The various perception and attention problems that people with schizophrenia have may develop years before the onset of the actual disorder (Fischer & Buchanan, 2017; Remington et al., 2014). It is also possible that such problems further contribute to the memory impairments that are common to many people with schizophrenia (Ordemann et al., 2014).

Another kind of perceptual problem in schizophrenia consists of **hallucinations,** perceptions that a person has in the absence of external stimuli (see *InfoCentral* on the next page). People who have *auditory* hallucinations, by far the most common kind in schizophrenia, hear sounds and voices that seem to come from outside their heads. The voices may talk directly to the hallucinator, perhaps giving commands or warning of dangers, or they may be experienced as overheard:

 The voices . . . were mostly heard in my head, though I often heard them in the air, or in different parts of the room. Every voice was different, and each beautiful, and generally, speaking or singing in a different tone and measure, and resembling those of relations or friends. There appeared to be many in my head, I should say upwards of fourteen. I divide them, as they styled themselves, or one another, into voices of contrition and voices of joy and honour.

("Perceval's Narrative," in Bateson, 1974)

Poor tracking A clinical researcher demonstrates a device that reveals how well a person's eyes track a moving laser dot. People with schizophrenia tend to perform poorly on this and other eye-pursuit tasks.

Research suggests that people with auditory hallucinations actually produce the nerve signals of sound in their brains, "hear" them, and then believe that external sources are responsible (Chun et al., 2014). One line of research has measured blood flow in *Broca's area,* the region of the brain that helps people produce speech (Cui et al., 2016; Homan et al., 2014; McGuire et al., 1996). The investigators have found more blood flow in Broca's area while patients are having auditory hallucinations. A related study instructed six men with schizophrenia to press a button whenever they had an auditory hallucination (Silbersweig et al., 1995). PET scans revealed increased

HALLUCINATIONS

Hallucinations are the experiencing of sights, sounds, smells, and other perceptions that occur in the absence of external stimuli.

TYPES OF HALLUCINATIONS

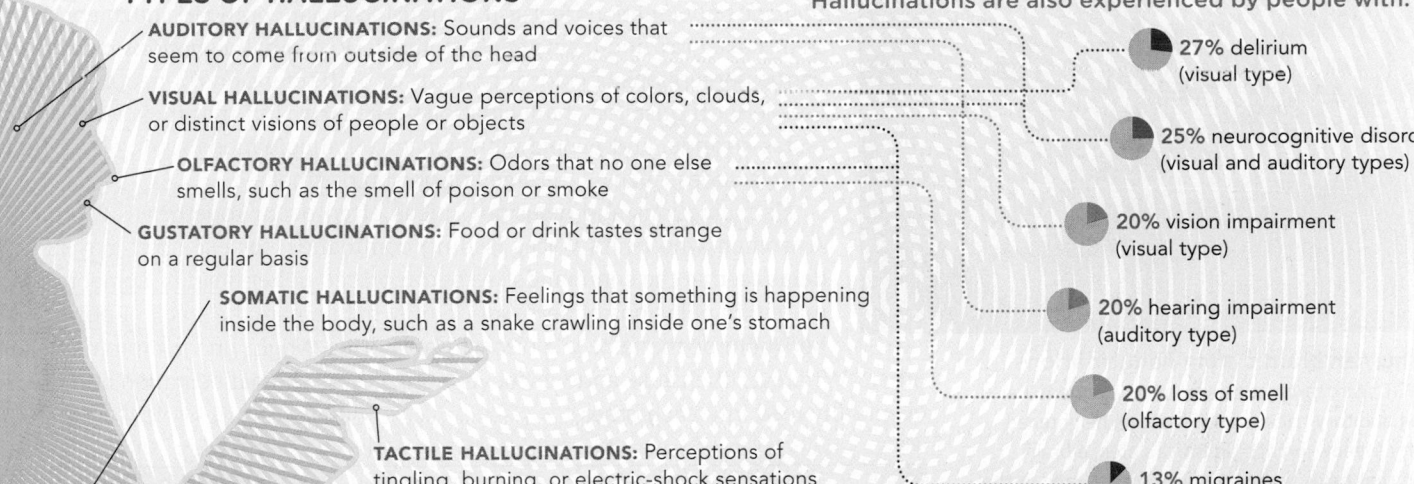

AUDITORY HALLUCINATIONS: Sounds and voices that seem to come from outside of the head

VISUAL HALLUCINATIONS: Vague perceptions of colors, clouds, or distinct visions of people or objects

OLFACTORY HALLUCINATIONS: Odors that no one else smells, such as the smell of poison or smoke

GUSTATORY HALLUCINATIONS: Food or drink tastes strange on a regular basis

SOMATIC HALLUCINATIONS: Feelings that something is happening inside the body, such as a snake crawling inside one's stomach

TACTILE HALLUCINATIONS: Perceptions of tingling, burning, or electric-shock sensations

Hallucinations are also experienced by people with:

- 27% delirium (visual type)
- 25% neurocognitive disorder (visual and auditory types)
- 20% vision impairment (visual type)
- 20% hearing impairment (auditory type)
- 20% loss of smell (olfactory type)
- 13% migraines (visual and olfactory types)

(Pelak, 2016; AFA, 2014; Mandal, 2014; Sacks, 2012; Knott, 2011; Norton, 2011; Frey, 2005)

Hallucinations are different from:

Illusions: Distorted or misinterpreted real perceptions

Imagery: Under voluntary control and does not mimic real perception

Dreaming: Occurs when person is asleep

Pseudohallucinations: Internally triggered, vivid perceptions that are recognized by individual as unreal, and partly under voluntary control

HALLUCINATIONS CAN BE "NORMAL"

Many people experience hallucinations that are unrelated to disorders or substance ingestion. These hallucinations...

- affect as many as 10–12% of the population
- occur every 3 days, on average
- last for 2–3 minutes
- can be controlled around 60% of the time
- cause little distress or disruption, unless misinterpreted

(Sheikh, 2017; Read, 2016; de Leede-Smith & Barkus, 2013; Daalman et al., 2011)

SCHIZOPHRENIC HALLUCINATIONS

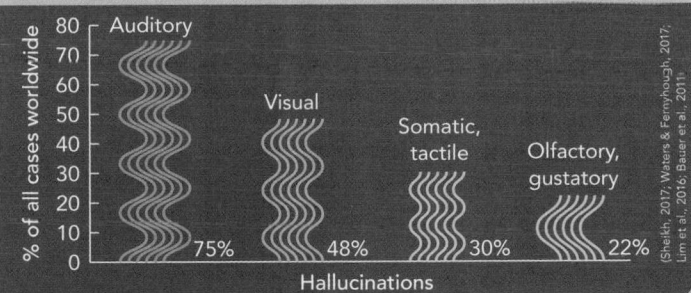

% of all cases worldwide — Hallucinations

Auditory 75% — Visual 48% — Somatic, tactile 30% — Olfactory, gustatory 22%

(Sheikh, 2017; Waters & Fernyhough, 2017; Lim et al., 2016; Bauer et al. 2011)

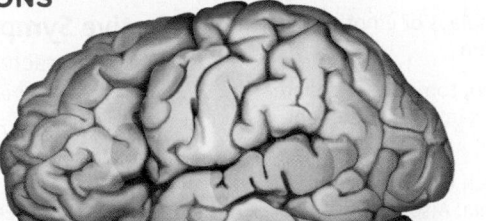

37% Hypnagogic hallucinations Geometric patterns, faces, or landscapes experienced by some people falling asleep

12.5% Hypnopompic hallucinations Geometric patterns, faces, or landscapes experienced by some people as they are awakening

(Pelak, 2016; de Leede-Smith & Barkus, 2013; Daalman et al., 2011)

BRAIN EXPLANATIONS FOR AUDITORY HALLUCINATIONS

ABNORMAL ACTIVATION of the primary **auditory cortex**.

FAILURE to recognize **internally generated speech** as one's own. Cross-activation with the **auditory areas**, so what most people experience as thoughts become "voiced."

ABNORMAL ATTENTION to the **subvocal stream** that accompanies verbal thinking.

MUSICAL HALLUCINATIONS result from activation of the brain network involving **auditory areas**, the **motor cortex**, **visual areas**, **basal ganglia**, **cerebellum**, **hippocampus**, and **amygdala**.

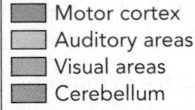

- Motor cortex
- Auditory areas
- Visual areas
- Cerebellum

HALLUCINATIONS OVER THE AGES

Ancient times: Attributed to gifts from the gods or the Muses

Prior to 18th century: Caused by supernatural forces, such as gods or demons, angels or djinns

Middle of 18th century: Caused by the overactivity of certain centers in the brain

1990s: Resulting from a circuit of cortical and subcortical structures

(Groopman, 2017; Sacks, 2012; Shergill et al., 2000)

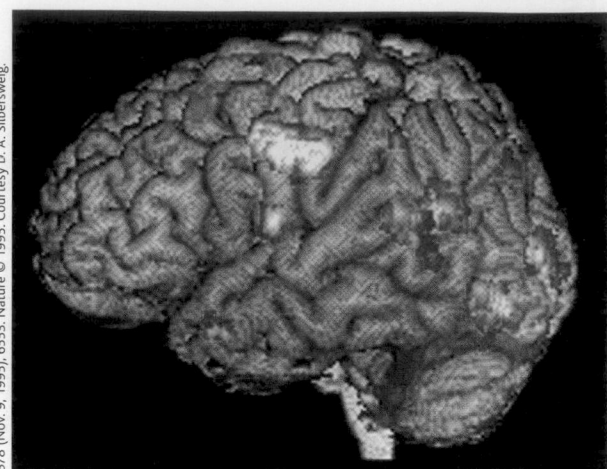

The human brain during hallucinations

This PET scan, taken at the moment a patient was having auditory hallucinations, shows heightened activity (yellow-orange) in Broca's area, a brain region that helps people produce speech, and in the auditory cortex, the brain area that helps people hear sounds. Conversely, the front of the brain, which is responsible for determining the source of sounds, was quiet during the hallucinations. Thus people who are hallucinating seem to hear sounds produced by their own brains, but their brains cannot recognize that the sounds are actually coming from within (Juckel, 2014; Silbersweig et al., 1995).

activity near the surfaces of their brains, in the tissues of the auditory cortex, the brain's hearing center, when they pressed the button.

Hallucinations can also involve any of the other senses. *Tactile* hallucinations may take the form of tingling, burning, or electric-shock sensations. *Somatic* hallucinations feel as if something is happening inside the body, such as a snake crawling inside one's stomach. *Visual* hallucinations may produce vague perceptions of colors or clouds or distinct visions of people or objects. People with *gustatory* hallucinations regularly find that their food or drink tastes strange, and people with *olfactory* hallucinations smell odors that no one else does, such as the smell of poison or smoke.

Hallucinations and delusional ideas often occur together (Cutting, 2015). A woman who hears voices issuing commands, for example, may have the delusion that the commands are being placed in her head by someone else. A man with delusions of persecution may hallucinate the smell of poison in his bedroom or the taste of poison in his coffee. Might one symptom cause the other? Whatever the cause and whichever comes first, the hallucination and delusion eventually feed into each other.

 I thought the voices I heard were being transmitted through the walls of my apartment and through the washer and dryer and that these machines were talking and telling me things. I felt that the government agencies had planted transmitters and receivers in my apartment so that I could hear what they were saying and they could hear what I was saying.

(Anonymous, 1996, p. 183)

INAPPROPRIATE AFFECT Many people with schizophrenia display **inappropriate affect,** emotions that are unsuited to the situation (Fischer & Buchanan, 2017; Taylor et al., 2014). They may smile when making a somber statement or upon being told terrible news, or they may become upset in situations that should make them happy. They may also undergo inappropriate shifts in mood. During a tender conversation with his wife, for example, a man with schizophrenia suddenly started yelling obscenities at her and complaining about her inadequacies.

In at least some cases, these emotions may be merely a response to other features of the disorder. Consider a woman with schizophrenia who smiles when told of her husband's serious illness. She may not actually be happy about the news; in fact, she may not be understanding or even hearing it. She could, for example, be responding instead to another of the many stimuli flooding her senses, perhaps a joke coming from an auditory hallucination.

inappropriate affect Displays of emotions that are unsuited to the situation.

negative symptoms Symptoms of schizophrenia that seem to be deficits in normal thought, emotions, or behaviors.

alogia A decrease in speech or speech content; a symptom of schizophrenia. Also known as *poverty of speech*.

flat affect A marked lack of apparent emotions; a symptom of schizophrenia.

avolition A symptom of schizophrenia marked by apathy and an inability to start or complete a course of action.

catatonia A pattern of extreme psychomotor symptoms, found in some forms of schizophrenia, which may include catatonic stupor, rigidity, or posturing.

Negative Symptoms

Negative symptoms are those that seem to be "pathological deficits," characteristics that are lacking in a person. *Poverty of speech, blunted and flat affect, loss of volition,* and *social withdrawal* are commonly found in schizophrenia (Fischer & Buchanan, 2017; Haas et al., 2014; Rocca et al., 2014). Such deficits greatly affect one's life and activities.

POVERTY OF SPEECH People with schizophrenia often have **alogia,** or **poverty of speech**, a reduction in speech or speech content. Some people with this negative kind of formal thought disorder think and say very little. Others say quite a bit but still manage to convey little meaning. These problems are revealed in the following diary entry written in 1919 by Vaslav Nijinsky, one of the twentieth century's great ballet dancers, as his pattern of schizophrenia was unfolding:

 I do not wish people to think that I am a great writer or that I am a great artist nor even that I am a great man. I am a simple man who has suffered a lot. I believe I suffered

> *more than Christ. I love life and want to live, to cry but cannot—I feel such a pain in my soul—a pain which frightens me. My soul is ill. My soul, not my mind. The doctors do not understand my illness. I know what I need to get well. My illness is too great to be cured quickly. I am incurable. Everyone who reads these lines will suffer—they will understand my feelings. I know what I need. I am strong, not weak. My body is not ill—it is my soul that is ill. I suffer, I suffer. Everyone will feel and understand. I am a man, not a beast. I love everyone, I have faults, I am a man—not God. I want to be God and therefore I try to improve myself. I want to dance, to draw, to play the piano, to write verses, I want to love everybody. That is the object of my life.*
>
> *(Nijinsky, 1936)*

RESTRICTED AFFECT Many people with schizophrenia have a *blunted affect*—they display less anger, sadness, joy, and other feelings than most people. Indeed, a number show almost no emotions at all, a condition known as **flat affect.** Their faces are still, their eye contact is poor, and their voices are monotonous.

#TheirWords

"No great genius was ever without some tincture of madness."

Aristotle

Restricted affect of this kind may actually reflect an inability to *express* emotions as others do. One study had participants view very emotional film clips. The participants with schizophrenia showed less facial expression than the others; however, they reported feeling just as much positive and negative emotion and in fact displayed more skin arousal (Kring & Neale, 1996). There is, in fact, a growing recognition in the clinical field that many people with schizophrenia not only experience emotions internally, they grapple with high levels of anxiety and/or depression (Siris & Braga, 2017, 2016).

LOSS OF VOLITION Many people with schizophrenia experience **avolition,** or apathy, feeling drained of energy and of interest in normal goals and unable to start or follow through on a course of action. This problem is particularly common in people who have had schizophrenia for many years, as if they have been worn down by it. Similarly, people with schizophrenia may feel *ambivalence,* or conflicting feelings, about most things. The avolition and ambivalence of Richard, the young man you read about earlier, made eating, dressing, and undressing impossible ordeals for him.

SOCIAL WITHDRAWAL People with schizophrenia may withdraw from their social environment and attend only to their own ideas and fantasies (Swain et al., 2017). Because their ideas are illogical and confused, the withdrawal has the effect of distancing them still further from reality. The social withdrawal seems also to lead to a breakdown of social skills, including the ability to recognize other people's needs and emotions accurately (Fischer & Buchanan, 2017; Lysaker et al., 2014).

A catatonic pose These patients, photographed in the early 1900s, show features of catatonia, including catatonic posturing, in which they assume bizarre positions for long periods of time.

Psychomotor Symptoms

People with schizophrenia sometimes experience *psychomotor symptoms*. Many move relatively slowly, and a number make awkward movements or repeated grimaces and odd gestures that seem to have a private purpose—perhaps ritualistic or magical (Grover et al., 2015).

The psychomotor symptoms of schizophrenia may take certain extreme forms, collectively called **catatonia.** People in a *catatonic stupor* stop responding to their environment, remaining motionless and silent for long stretches of time. Recall how Richard would lie motionless and mute in bed for days. People with *catatonic rigidity* maintain a rigid, upright posture for hours and resist efforts to be moved. Still others exhibit *catatonic posturing*, assuming awkward, bizarre positions for long periods of time. They may, for example, spend hours holding their arms out at a 90-degree angle or balancing in a squatting position. Finally, people with

catatonic excitement, a different form of catatonia, move excitedly, sometimes wildly waving their arms and legs.

Around 10 percent of people with schizophrenia experience some degree of catatonia (Coffey, 2017, 2016). Individuals with other severe psychological disorders, such as major depressive disorder or bipolar disorder, may also experience these symptoms.

What Is the Course of Schizophrenia?

Schizophrenia usually first appears between the person's late teens and mid-thirties (Fischer & Buchanan, 2017; Häfner, 2015). Although its course varies widely from case to case, many sufferers seem to go through three phases—prodromal, active, and residual (Fukumoto et al., 2014). During the *prodromal phase,* symptoms are not yet obvious, but the person is beginning to deteriorate. He or she may withdraw socially, speak in vague or odd ways, develop strange ideas, or express little emotion. During the *active phase,* symptoms become apparent. Sometimes this phase is triggered by stress or trauma in the person's life (Bebbington & Kuipers, 2011). For Laura, the middle-aged woman described earlier, the immediate trigger was the loss of her cherished dog.

Many people with schizophrenia eventually enter a *residual phase* in which they return to a prodromal-like level of functioning. They may retain some negative symptoms, such as blunted emotion, but have a lessening of the striking symptoms of the active phase. Although 25 percent or more of patients recover completely from schizophrenia, the majority continue to have at least some residual problems for the rest of their lives (Fischer & Buchanan, 2017; an der Heiden & Häfner, 2011).

Each of these phases may last for days or for years. A fuller recovery from schizophrenia is more likely in people who functioned quite well before the disorder (had good *premorbid functioning*); whose initial disorder is triggered by stress, comes on abruptly, or develops during middle age; and who receive early treatment, preferably during the prodromal phase (Remberk et al., 2014). Relapses are apparently more likely during times of life stress (Lange et al., 2017).

Diagnosing Schizophrenia

As you read earlier, DSM-5 calls for a diagnosis of schizophrenia only after symptoms of the disorder continue for six months or more (APA, 2013). In at least one of those months, the person must be in an active phase, marked by significant delusions, hallucinations, or disorganized speech. In addition, there must be a deterioration in the person's work, social relations, and ability to care for him or herself (see again Table 14-1). In 80 to 85 percent of cases, the disorder is dominated by positive symptoms, such as delusions, hallucinations, and certain formal thought disorders—a clinical picture sometimes called *Type I* schizophrenia (Crow, 2008, 1995, 1985, 1980). In 15 to 20 percent of cases, the individual displays mostly negative symptoms, such as restricted affect, poverty of speech, and loss of volition—a picture called *Type II* schizophrenia. Type I patients generally seem to have been better adjusted prior to their disorder, to have later onset of symptoms, and to be more likely to show improvement, especially when treated with medications (Fischer & Buchanan, 2017; Mitra et al., 2016).

There are, in fact, a number of schizophrenia-like disorders listed in DSM-5, each distinguished by particular durations and sets of symptoms (see **Table 14-2**). Because these psychotic disorders all bear a similarity to schizophrenia,

Famous, but rare, delusion In MTV's long-running show *Teen Wolf,* a possessed man cries out in terror as his body changes into that of a wolf. *Lycanthropy,* the delusion of being an animal, is a rare psychological syndrome, but it has been the subject of many profitable books, movies, and TV shows over the years.

TABLE: 14-2

Schizophrenia Spectrum Disorders: An Array of Psychosis

Disorder	Key Features	Duration	Lifetime Prevalence
Schizophrenia	Various psychotic symptoms, such as delusions, hallucinations, disorganized speech, restricted or inappropriate affect, and catatonia	6 months or more	1.0%
Brief psychotic disorder	Various psychotic symptoms, such as delusions, hallucinations, disorganized speech, restricted or inappropriate affect, and catatonia	Less than 1 month	Unknown
Schizophreniform disorder	Various psychotic symptoms, such as delusions, hallucinations, disorganized speech, restricted or inappropriate affect, and catatonia	1 to 6 months	0.2%
Schizoaffective disorder	Marked symptoms of both schizophrenia and a major depressive episode or a manic episode	6 months or more	Unknown
Delusional disorder	Persistent delusions that are not bizarre and not due to schizophrenia; persecutory, jealous, grandiose, and somatic delusions are common	1 month or more	0.1%
Psychotic disorder due to another medical condition	Hallucinations, delusions, or disorganized speech caused by a medical illness or brain damage	No minimum length	Unknown
Substance/medication-induced psychotic disorder	Hallucinations, delusions, or disorganized speech caused directly by a substance, such as an abused drug	No minimum length	Unknown

(Information from: APA, 2013.)

they—along with schizophrenia itself—are collectively called *schizophrenia spectrum disorders* (APA, 2013). Schizophrenia is the most prevalent of these disorders. Clinical theorists believe that most of the explanations and treatments offered for schizophrenia are applicable to the other disorders as well, especially to *schizophreniform disorder* and *schizoaffective disorder*, the schizophrenia spectrum disorders that are most similar to schizophrenia in severity and duration (Bole et al., 2017; Mojtabai, 2016; Manschreck, 2015). This broader scope is important to keep in mind as you read the following section on explanations and the next chapter on treatments for schizophrenia.

How Do Theorists Explain Schizophrenia?

As with many other kinds of disorders, biological, psychological, and sociocultural theorists have each proposed explanations for schizophrenia. So far, the biological explanations have received by far the most research support. This is not to say that psychological and sociocultural factors play no role in the disorder. Rather, a *diathesis–stress relationship* may be at work: people with a biological predisposition will develop schizophrenia only if certain kinds of events or stressors are also present (Pruessner et al., 2017; Winchester et al., 2014). Similarly, a diathesis–stress relationship often seems to be operating in the development of other kinds of psychotic disorders (see **PsychWatch** on page 433).

Biological Views

What is arguably the most enlightening research on schizophrenia during the past several decades has come from genetic and biological investigations. These studies have revealed the key roles of inheritance and brain activity in the development of schizophrenia and have opened the door to important treatment changes.

#

#PrivateNotions

Surveys suggest that 22 to 37 percent of people in the United States and Britain believe Earth has been visited by aliens from outer space.

Twenty percent of people worldwide believe that aliens walk on Earth disguised as humans.

(MacIsaac, 2014; Reuters, 2010; Spanton, 2008; Andrews, 1998)

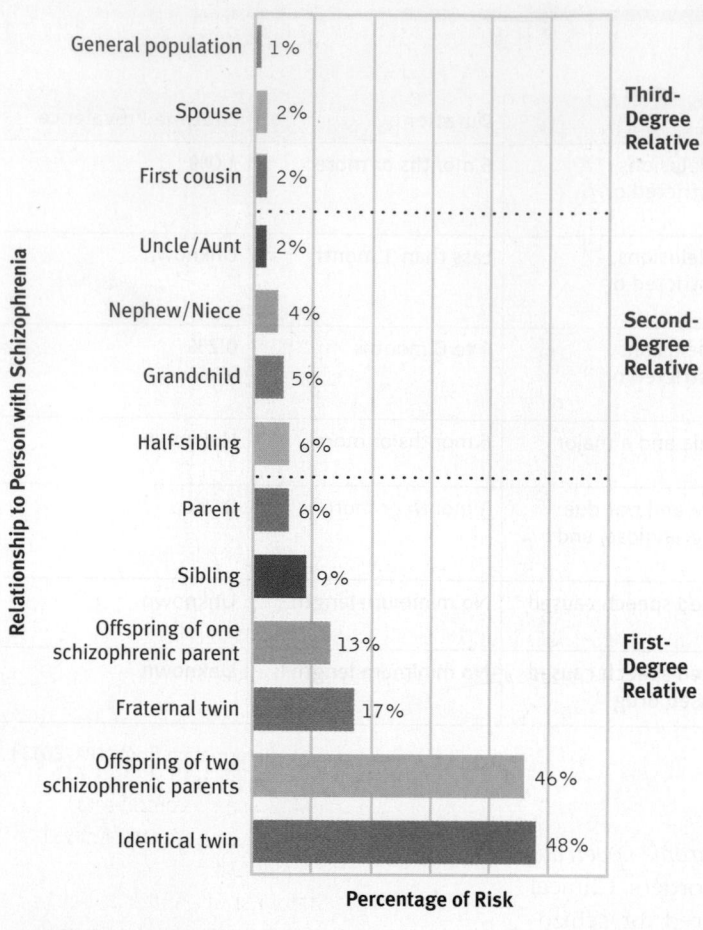

Relationship to Person with Schizophrenia

Relationship	Percentage of Risk	Degree
General population	1%	
Spouse	2%	Third-Degree Relative
First cousin	2%	
Uncle/Aunt	2%	
Nephew/Niece	4%	Second-Degree Relative
Grandchild	5%	
Half-sibling	6%	
Parent	6%	
Sibling	9%	
Offspring of one schizophrenic parent	13%	First-Degree Relative
Fraternal twin	17%	
Offspring of two schizophrenic parents	46%	
Identical twin	48%	

Percentage of Risk

FIGURE 14-2

Family Links

People who are biologically related to someone with schizophrenia have a heightened risk of developing the disorder during their lifetimes. The closer the biological relationship (that is, the more similar the genetic makeup), the greater the risk of developing the disorder. (Information from: Henriksen et al., 2017; Bhatia et al., 2016; Gottesman, 1991, p. 96.)

Genetic Factors Following the principles of the diathesis–stress perspective, genetic researchers believe that some people inherit a biological predisposition to schizophrenia and develop the disorder later when they face extreme stress, usually during late adolescence or early adulthood. The genetic view has been supported by studies of (1) relatives of people with schizophrenia, (2) twins with schizophrenia, and (3) people with schizophrenia who are adopted, and by (4) direct genetic research.

ARE RELATIVES VULNERABLE? Family pedigree studies have found repeatedly that schizophrenia and schizophrenia-like brain abnormalities are more common among relatives of people with the disorder (Henriksen et al., 2017; Bhatia et al., 2016; Gottesman & Reilly, 2003). And the more closely related the relatives are to the person with schizophrenia, the more likely they are to develop the disorder (see **Figure 14-2**).

As you saw earlier, 1 percent of the general population develops schizophrenia. The prevalence rises to 3 percent among second-degree relatives with the disorder—that is, half-siblings, uncles, aunts, nephews, nieces, and grandchildren—and it reaches an average of 10 percent among first-degree relatives (parents, siblings, and children). Of course, this trend by itself does not establish a genetic basis for the disorder. As the famous neuroscientist Solomon Snyder (1980) once pointed out, "Attendance at Harvard University also runs in families but would hardly be considered a genetic trait" (Snyder, 1980). Close family members are exposed to many of the same environmental influences as the person with schizophrenia, and it may be these influences that lead to the disorder.

IS AN IDENTICAL TWIN MORE VULNERABLE THAN A FRATERNAL TWIN? Twins, who are among the closest of relatives, have in particular been studied by schizophrenia researchers. If both members of a pair of twins have a particular trait, they are said to be *concordant* for that trait. If genetic factors are at work in schizophrenia, identical twins (who share all their genes) should have a higher concordance rate for schizophrenia than fraternal twins (who share only some genes). This expectation has been supported consistently by research (Fischer & Buchanan, 2017; Ritsner & Gottesman, 2011; Gottesman, 1991). Studies have found that if one identical twin develops schizophrenia, there is a 48 percent chance that the other twin will do so as well. If the twins are fraternal, on the other hand, the second twin has approximately a 17 percent chance of developing the disorder.

Once again, however, factors other than genetics may explain these concordance rates. For example, if one twin is exposed to a particular danger during the prenatal period, such as an injury or virus, the other twin is likely to be exposed to it as well. This is especially true for identical twins, whose prenatal environment is especially similar. Thus a predisposition to schizophrenia could be the result of a prenatal problem, and twins, particularly identical twins, would still be expected to have a higher concordance rate.

> What factors, besides genetic ones, might account for the elevated rate of schizophrenia among relatives of people with this disorder?

ARE THE BIOLOGICAL RELATIVES OF AN ADOPTEE VULNERABLE? Adoption studies look at adults with schizophrenia who were adopted as infants and compare them with both their biological and their adoptive relatives. Because they were reared apart from their biological relatives, similar symptoms in those relatives would indicate genetic influences. Conversely, similarities to their adoptive relatives would suggest environ-

Postpartum Psychosis: A Dangerous Syndrome

On the morning of June 20, 2001, the nation's television viewers watched in horror as officials escorted 36-year-old Andrea Yates to a police car. Just minutes before, she had called police and explained that she had drowned her five children in the bathtub because "they weren't developing correctly" and because she "realized [she had not been] a good mother to them."

Homicide sergeant Eric Mehl described how she looked him in the eye, nodded, answered with a polite "Yes, sir" to many of his questions, and twice recounted the order in which the children had died: first 3-year-old Paul, then 2-year-old Luke, followed by 5-year-old John and 6-month-old Mary. She then described how she had had to drag 7-year-old Noah to the bathroom and how he had come up twice as he fought for air. Later she told doctors she wanted her hair shaved so she could see the number 666—the mark of the Antichrist—on her scalp (Roche, 2002).

In Chapter 7 you read that as many as 80 percent of mothers experience "baby blues" soon after giving birth, while between 10 and 30 percent display the clinical syndrome of *postpartum depression*. Yet another postpartum disorder that has become all too familiar to the public in recent times, by way of cases such as that of Andrea Yates, is *postpartum psychosis* (Denno, 2017; Engqvist & Nilsson, 2014).

Postpartum psychosis affects about 1 to 2 of every 1,000 mothers who have recently given birth (Payne, 2016). The symptoms apparently are triggered, in part, by the enormous shift in hormone levels that takes place after delivery (Payne, 2016; Jones et al., 2014; Meinhard et al., 2014). Within days or weeks, the woman develops signs of losing touch with reality, such as delusions (for example, she may become convinced that her baby is the devil); hallucinations (perhaps hearing voices); extreme anxiety, confusion,

Family tragedy In this undated photograph, Andrea Yates poses with her husband and four of the five children she later drowned.

Photo Courtesy of Yates Family/Getty Images

and disorientation; disturbed sleep; and illogical or chaotic thoughts (for example, thoughts about killing herself or her child). Typically, treatment consists of antipsychotic drugs and psychotherapy, although the effectiveness of this approach has not received much research (Marder, 2016).

Women with a history of bipolar disorder, schizophrenia, or major depressive disorder are particularly vulnerable to the disorder (Payne, 2016; Di Florio et al., 2014). Women who have previously experienced postpartum depression or postpartum psychosis have an increased likelihood of developing postpartum psychosis after subsequent births (Payne, 2016; Bergink et al., 2012). Andrea Yates, for example, had developed signs of postpartum depression (and perhaps postpartum psychosis) and attempted suicide after the birth of her fourth child (Denno, 2017). At that time, however, she appeared to respond well to a combination of medications, including antipsychotic drugs, and so she and her husband later decided to conceive a fifth child. Although they were warned that she was at risk for

serious postpartum symptoms once again, they believed that the same combination of medications would help if the symptoms were to recur (King, 2002).

After the birth of her fifth child, the symptoms did in fact recur, along with features of psychosis. Yates again attempted suicide. Although she was hospitalized twice and treated with various medications, her condition failed to improve. Six months after giving birth to Mary, her fifth child, she drowned all five of her children. Although relatively few women with the disorder actually try to harm their children (estimates run as high as 4 percent), the Yates case reminds us that such an outcome is possible (Gressier et al., 2015; Posmontier, 2010). The case also reminds us that early detection and treatment are critical (Marder, 2016; O'Hara & Wisner, 2014).

On July 26, 2006, after an initial conviction for murder was overturned by an appeals court, Yates was found *not guilty by reason of insanity* and sent to a state mental hospital, where she continues to receive treatment today (Denno, 2017).

mental influences. Researchers have repeatedly found that the biological relatives of adoptees with schizophrenia are more likely than their adoptive relatives to develop schizophrenia or another schizophrenia spectrum disorder (Henriksen et al., 2017; Andreasen & Black, 2006; Kety, 1988; Kety et al., 1968).

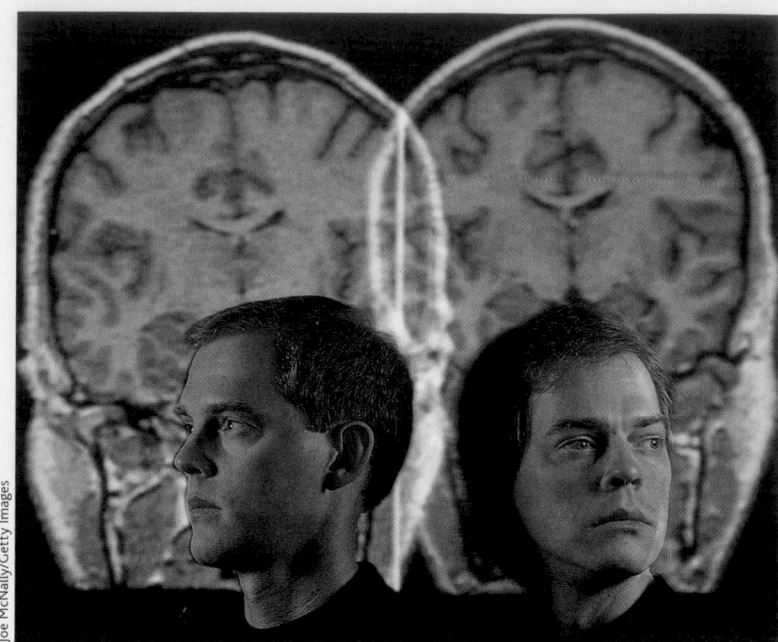

Not-so-identical twins The man on the left does not have schizophrenia, while his identical twin, on the right, does. MRI scans, shown in the background, clarify that the brain of the twin with schizophrenia is smaller overall than his brother's and has larger ventricles, indicated by the dark, butterfly-shaped spaces. Ventricles, cavities throughout the brain and spinal cord that contain fluid, tend to be larger in the brains of people with schizophrenia.

dopamine hypothesis The theory that schizophrenia results from excessive activity of the neurotransmitter dopamine.

antipsychotic drugs Drugs that help correct grossly confused or distorted thinking.

phenothiazines A group of antihistamine drugs that became the first group of effective antipsychotic medications.

second-generation antipsychotic drugs A relatively new group of antipsychotic drugs whose biological action is different from that of the first-generation antipsychotic drugs. Also known as *atypical antipsychotic drugs*.

WHAT DO GENETIC STUDIES SUGGEST? As with bipolar disorders (see Chapter 7), researchers have run studies of *genetic linkage* and *molecular biology* to pinpoint the possible genetic factors in schizophrenia (Henriksen et al., 2017; Uher & Zwicker, 2017). In one approach, they select large families in which schizophrenia is very common, take blood and DNA samples from all members of the families, and then compare gene fragments from members with and without schizophrenia. Using this and various other genetic research procedures, studies have identified possible gene defects on chromosomes 1, 2, 6, 8, 10, 13, 15, 18, 20, and 22 and on the X chromosome, each of which may help predispose a person to develop this disorder (Xu et al., 2018; Zhao et al., 2018). Altogether, the number of specific gene sites linked to schizophrenia is no fewer than 281 to date (Tartakovsky, 2016)!

These varied findings may indicate that some of the suspected gene sites are cases of mistaken identity and do not actually contribute to schizophrenia. Alternatively, it may be that different kinds of schizophrenia are linked to different genes. It is most likely, however, that schizophrenia, like a number of other disorders, is a *polygenic disorder*, caused by a combination of gene defects (Fischer & Buchanan, 2017).

How might genetic factors lead to the development of schizophrenia? Research has pointed to two kinds of biological abnormalities that could conceivably be inherited—*biochemical abnormalities* and *dysfunctional brain circuitry*.

Biochemical Abnormalities As you have read, the brain is made up of neurons whose electrical impulses (or "messages") are transmitted from one to another by neurotransmitters. After an impulse arrives at a receiving neuron, it travels down the axon of that neuron until it reaches the nerve ending. The nerve ending then releases neurotransmitters that travel across the synaptic space and bind to receptors on yet another neuron, thus relaying the message to the next "station." This neuron activity is known as "firing."

Over the past four decades, researchers have developed a **dopamine hypothesis** to explain their findings on schizophrenia: certain neurons that use the neurotransmitter dopamine fire too often and transmit too many messages, thus producing the symptoms of schizophrenia (Brisch et al., 2014; Düring et al., 2014). This hypothesis has undergone challenges and adjustments in recent years, but it is still very influential (Rao & Remington, 2014). The chain of events leading to this hypothesis began with the accidental discovery of **antipsychotic drugs,** medications that help remove the symptoms of schizophrenia. As you will see in Chapter 15, the first group of antipsychotic medications, the **phenothiazines,** were discovered in the 1950s by researchers who were looking for better *antihistamine* drugs to combat allergies. Although phenothiazines failed as antihistamines, it soon became obvious that they were effective in reducing schizophrenic symptoms, and clinicians began to prescribe them widely (Adams et al., 2014).

Researchers later learned that these early antipsychotic drugs often produce troublesome muscular tremors, symptoms that are identical to the central symptom of *Parkinson's disease,* a disabling neurological illness. This undesired reaction to antipsychotic drugs offered the first important clue to the biology of schizophrenia. Scientists already knew that people who suffer from Parkinson's disease have abnormally low levels of the neurotransmitter dopamine in some areas of the brain and that lack of dopamine is the reason for their uncontrollable shaking. If antipsychotic drugs produce Parkinsonian symptoms in people with schizophrenia while removing their psychotic symptoms, perhaps the drugs reduce dopamine activity. And, scientists reasoned further, if lowering dopamine activity helps remove the symptoms of schizophrenia, perhaps schizophrenia is related to excessive dopamine activity in the first place.

Since the 1960s, research has supported and helped clarify the dopamine hypothesis. It has been found, for example, that some people with Parkinson's disease develop schizophrenia-like symptoms if they take too much *L-dopa*, a medication that raises Parkinson's patients' dopamine levels (Brunelin et al., 2013). The L-dopa apparently raises the dopamine activity so much that it produces psychosis. Support has also come from research on *amphetamines*, drugs that, as you saw in Chapter 12, stimulate the central nervous system by increasing dopamine activity in the brain. Clinical investigators have observed that people who take high doses of amphetamines may develop *amphetamine psychosis*—a syndrome very similar to schizophrenia (Hawken & Beninger, 2014; Li et al., 2014).

Researchers have located areas of the brain that are rich in dopamine receptors and have found that phenothiazines and related antipsychotic drugs bind to many of these receptors (Yoshida et al., 2014). Apparently the drugs are dopamine *antagonists*—drugs that bind to dopamine receptors, *prevent* dopamine from binding there, and so prevent the neurons from firing. Researchers have identified five kinds of dopamine receptors in the brain—called the D-1, D-2, D-3, D-4, and D-5 receptors—and have found that phenothiazines bind most strongly to the *D-2 receptors* (Chun et al., 2014; Seeman, 2011).

These and related findings suggest that in schizophrenia, messages traveling from dopamine-sending neurons to dopamine receptors on other neurons, particularly to the D-2 receptors, may be transmitted too easily or too often. This theory is appealing because certain dopamine neurons are known to play a key role in guiding attention (Brisch et al., 2014). People whose attention is severely disturbed by excessive dopamine activity might well be expected to suffer from some of the attention, perception, and thought problems that characterize schizophrenia.

Though enlightening, the dopamine hypothesis has certain problems. The biggest challenge to it has come with the recent discovery of a new group of antipsychotic drugs, initially referred to as *atypical antipsychotic drugs* and now called **second-generation antipsychotic drugs**, which are often more effective than the phenothiazines and related early drugs, now collectively called *first-generation antipsychotic drugs*. The newer drugs bind not only to D-2 dopamine receptors, like the first-generation antipsychotic drugs, but also to many D-1 receptors and to receptors for other neurotransmitters such as *serotonin, glutamate,* and *GABA* (Fischer & Buchanan, 2017). Thus, it may be that schizophrenia is related to abnormal activity or interactions of both dopamine and other neurotransmitters, rather than to abnormal dopamine activity alone (Fischer & Buchanan, 2017; Juckel, 2014).

Dysfunctional Brain Structures and Circuitry In recent years, biological researchers have increasingly sought to identify the *brain circuit* that may be contributing to schizophrenia. As you have read, reactions of various kinds are tied to brain circuits—networks of brain structures that work together, triggering each other into action and producing particular behaviors, cognitions, or emotions. Although research is far from complete, the brain circuit whose dysfunction contributes to schizophrenia has begun to emerge (Chen et al., 2017; Sigurdsson, 2016). The structures that comprise this schizophrenia-related circuit include the prefrontal cortex, hippocampus, amygdala, thalamus, striatum, and substantia nigra, among other brain regions (see **Figure 14-3**). You may notice, once again, that several of the structures in this circuit are also members of brain circuits that contribute to other disorders, but in cases of schizophrenia the structures function and interconnect in problematic ways that are, collectively, unique to this disorder.

Barcroft Irdia/Barcroft Media via Getty Images

Delusional harm These coins, pellets, nuts, and bolts—13 pounds of metal in all—were surgically removed by stunned doctors from the stomach of a man with schizophrenia. The man, a resident of India, had the delusion that he should consume iron objects, and he had been doing so for more than nine months. The surgery failed to save his life.

#PaternalImpact

People whose fathers were over 50 years of age when they were born are more likely to develop schizophrenia than people who are born to fathers under 50 years old. As in cases of bipolar disorder, this phenomenon may be explained by the tendency of aging men to produce increased genetic mutations during the manufacture of sperm cells (Stovall, 2016; Crystal et al., 2012; Petersen et al, 2011).

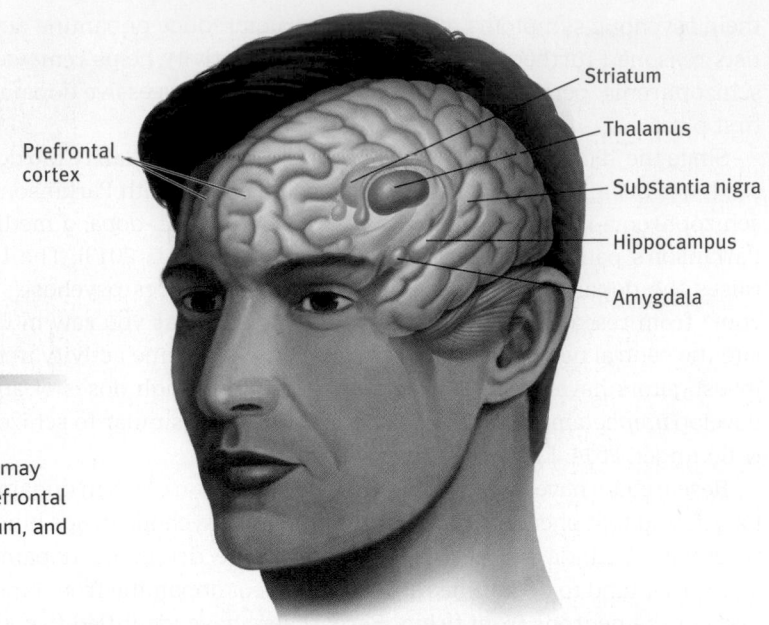

Prefrontal
cortex

Striatum

Thalamus

Substantia nigra

Hippocampus

Amygdala

FIGURE 14-3

Biology of Schizophrenia

Studies suggest that a dysfunctional brain circuit may lead to schizophrenia. This circuit includes the prefrontal cortex, hippocampus, amygdala, thalamus, striatum, and substantia nigra, among other structures.

The dysfunction of this schizophrenia-related circuit cannot be characterized in broad terms as, for example, a generally "hyperactive" or generally "underactive" circuit. But numerous studies suggest that the circuit does indeed operate abnormally in persons with schizophrenia. Brain scans have shown repeatedly that the circuits of schizophrenic and nonschizophrenic individuals differ significantly whether study participants are at rest, performing cognitive tasks, or experiencing hallucinations (Han et al., 2018; Wang et al., 2017).

Studies have found, for example, that under certain circumstances, particular structures in the circuit may be hyperactive (for example, the substantia nigra) or underactive (for example, the prefrontal cortex) among people with schizophrenia (Schoonover et al., 2017; Yoon et al., 2014, 2013). In addition, and perhaps most important, research indicates that the *interconnectivity* (flow of communication) between particular structures in the circuit is typically excessive or diminished for people with schizophrenia. Studies have found, for example, that interconnectivity is abnormally low between their substantia nigra and prefrontal cortex and between their striatum and thalamus, while it is abnormally high between their substantia nigra and striatum, their thalamus and prefrontal cortex, and their hippocampus and prefrontal cortex (Martino et al., 2018; Wang et al., 2017; Amad et al., 2014; Yoon et al., 2014, 2013).

Just to complicate things a bit more, recent research suggests that the schizophrenia-related circuit may actually be two distinct subcircuits whose various structures sometimes overlap. Dysfunction by one of the subcircuits (which includes the substantia nigra and striatum) might be more responsible for cases of schizophrenia that are characterized by positive symptoms such as hallucinations and delusions. In contrast, dysfunction by the other subcircuit (which includes the hippocampus and amygdala) might be responsible for cases of schizophrenia that are dominated by negative symptoms like flat affect and poverty of speech (Mitra et al., 2016; Shaffer et al., 2015).

Keep in mind that this focus on brain circuitry is fairly compatible with the dopamine hypothesis of schizophrenia that monopolized biological explanations for so many years. After all, dopamine activity is very prominent throughout the schizophrenia-related brain circuit, particularly in the substantia nigra and striatum structures. The key difference between the dopamine hypothesis and the newer brain circuit view is that abnormal activity by this neurotransmitter is now seen as *part of* a broader circuit dysfunction that can propel people toward schizophrenia.

Making a comeback For years, rats were preferred over mice as animal lab subjects. However, in 1989, scientists developed a technique to make "knockout mice"—mice with specific genes eliminated—and mice became the preferred animals in studies on the causes of schizophrenia and other disorders. Until 2010, that is. With the relatively recent discovery of techniques to make "knockout rats," rats are now beginning to regain their elite laboratory status.

Viral Problems What might cause the biochemical and structural abnormalities found in many cases of schizophrenia? Various studies have pointed to genetic factors, poor nutrition, fetal development, birth complications, immune reactions, and toxins (Fischer & Buchanan, 2017; Uher & Zwicker, 2017). In addition, some investigators suggest that the brain abnormalities may result from exposure to *viruses* before birth. Perhaps a viral infection triggers an immune system response in the mother, is passed on to the developing fetus, enters his or her brain, and interrupts proper brain development.

Some of the evidence for the viral theory comes from animal model investigations, and other evidence is circumstantial, such as the finding that an unusually large number of people with schizophrenia are born during the late winter (Fischer & Buchanan, 2017; Patterson, 2012). The late winter birth rate among people with schizophrenia is 5 to 8 percent higher than among other people. This could be because of an increase in fetal or infant exposure to viruses at that time of year.

More direct evidence for the viral theory of schizophrenia comes from studies showing that mothers of people with schizophrenia were more likely to have been exposed to the influenza virus during pregnancy than were mothers of people without schizophrenia (Fischer & Buchanan, 2017; Canetta et al., 2014). Still other studies have found antibodies to suspicious viruses in the blood of 40 percent of research participants with schizophrenia (Fischer & Buchanan, 2017; Leweke et al., 2004). The presence of such antibodies suggests that these people had at some time been exposed to those particular viruses.

Together, the biochemical, brain circuit, and viral findings are shedding much light on the mysteries of schizophrenia. At the same time, it is important to recognize that many people who have these biological abnormalities never develop schizophrenia. Why not? Possibly, as you read earlier, because biological factors merely set the stage for schizophrenia, while key psychological and sociocultural factors must be present for the disorder to appear.

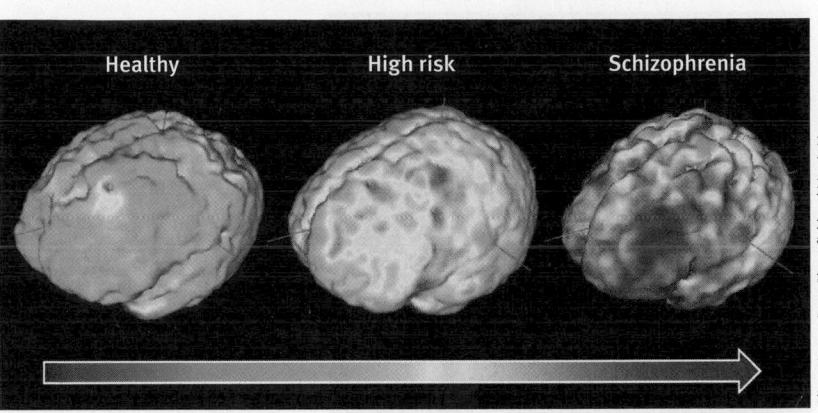

Healthy   High risk   Schizophrenia

Oliver Howes, Peter Bloomfield and Mattia Veronese

Involvement of the immune system Consistent with explanations that point to viral infections and immune system reactions, researchers have found that *microglia* are especially active in the brains of people with schizophrenia. Microglia are brain immune cells that provide a first line of defense against brain infections and inflammation. These PET scans show that the microglia activity (orange) of research participants at risk for schizophrenia is higher than that of healthy participants. The microglia activity of participants *with* schizophrenia is higher still.

Psychological Views

When schizophrenia investigators began to identify genetic and biological factors during the 1950s and 1960s, many clinicians abandoned the psychological theories of the disorder. During the past few decades, however, the tables have been turned and psychological factors are once again being considered as important pieces of the schizophrenia puzzle (Uher & Zwicker, 2017). The leading psychological theories come from the psychodynamic and cognitive-behavioral perspectives.

The Psychodynamic Explanation In the middle of the twentieth century, noted psychodynamic clinician Frieda Fromm-Reichmann (1948) elaborated on an earlier notion by Sigmund Freud (1924, 1915, 1914) that cold or unnurturing parents may set schizophrenia in motion. Based on her clinical observations, Fromm-Reichmann described the mothers of people who develop the disorder as cold, domineering, and uninterested in their children's needs. She claimed that these mothers may appear to be self-sacrificing but are actually using their children to meet their own needs. At once overprotective and rejecting, they confuse their children and set the stage for schizophrenic functioning. She called them **schizophrenogenic** (schizophrenia-causing) **mothers**.

> Why have parents and family life so often been blamed for schizophrenia, and why do such explanations continue to be influential?

schizophrenogenic mother A type of mother—supposedly cold, domineering, and uninterested in the needs of her children—who was once thought to cause schizophrenia in her child.

Paul Brown/REX/Shutterstock

Shared delusions When two or more persons share a delusion or hallucination, it is called *folie à deux* or *shared psychosis*. An Internet version of this phenomenon seems to be the online preoccupation by many users with *Slender Man*, a mythical "boogie man" whom communities of people report seeing and fearing in their everyday lives. (He is portrayed here at a science fiction convention.) In an infamous case, two 12-year-old girls recently stabbed a classmate multiple times, saying they were trying to appease and impress Slender Man. Clinicians later testified that each assailant had a schizophrenia spectrum disorder.

Although famous, Fromm-Reichmann's theory has received little research support (Harrington, 2012; Willick, 2001). The majority of people with schizophrenia do not appear to have mothers who fit the schizophrenogenic description. Thus most of today's psychodynamic theorists have rejected Fromm-Reichmann's view. Indeed, they typically assign a role to biological predispositions in their psychodynamic explanations of schizophrenia. For example, *self theorists*, those psychodynamic theorists who believe that the most basic human motive is to strengthen the wholeness of the self (see pages 55–56), suggest that biological deficiencies cause people with schizophrenia to develop a fragmented, rather than integrated, self (Lysaker & Hermans, 2007).

Cognitive-Behavioral Explanations Cognitive-behavioral theorists have offered two explanations of how and why people develop schizophrenia. One focuses largely on the behaviors of people with schizophrenia and applies the principles of *operant conditioning*. The other focuses on the unusual thoughts of such individuals and stresses the possible role of *misinterpretations*.

OPERANT CONDITIONING As you have read, operant conditioning is the process by which people learn to perform behaviors for which they have been rewarded frequently. The operant explanation of schizophrenia begins with the general observation that most people in life become quite proficient at reading and responding to social cues—that is, other people's smiles, frowns, and comments. People who respond to such cues in a socially acceptable way are better able to satisfy their own emotional needs and reach their goals. Some people, however, are not reinforced for their attention to social cues, either because of unusual circumstances or because important figures in their lives are socially inadequate. As a result, they stop attending to such cues and focus instead on irrelevant cues—the brightness of light in a room, a bird flying above, or the sound of a word rather than its meaning. As they attend to irrelevant cues more and more, their responses become increasingly bizarre (Pinkham, 2014). Because the bizarre responses are rewarded with attention or other types of reinforcement, they are likely to be repeated again and again.

Support for this operant explanation of schizophrenia has been circumstantial. As you'll see in Chapter 15, researchers have found that patients with schizophrenia are capable of learning at least some appropriate verbal and social behaviors if hospital personnel consistently ignore their bizarre responses and reward normal responses with cigarettes, food, attention, or other rewards (Ivy et al., 2017; Kopelowicz et al., 2007). If bizarre verbal and social responses can be eliminated by appropriate reinforcements, perhaps they were acquired through improper learning in the first place. Of course, an effective treatment does not necessarily indicate the cause of a disorder. Today the operant view is usually considered at best a partial explanation for schizophrenia. Although it may help explain why a given person displays more psychotic behavior in some situations than in others, it is too limited, in the opinion of many, to account for schizophrenia's origins and its many symptoms.

Charles Barsotti/The New Yorker Collection/The Cartoon Bank

"I can't explain it—it's just a funny feeling that I'm being Googled."

MISINTERPRETING UNUSUAL SENSATIONS The misinterpretation explanation of schizophrenia begins by accepting the biological position that the brains of people with schizophrenia are actually producing strange and unreal sensations—sensations triggered by biological factors—when they have hallucinations and related perceptual experiences. According to the cognitive-behavioral explanation, however, when the individuals attempt to understand their unusual experiences, more features of their disorder emerge (Waters & Fernyhough, 2017; Howes & Murray, 2014). When first confronted by voices or other troubling sensations, these people turn to friends and relatives. Naturally, the friends and relatives deny the reality of the sensations, and eventually the sufferers conclude that the others are trying to hide the truth. They begin to reject all feedback, and some develop beliefs (delusions) that they are being persecuted. In short, according to this theory, people with schizophrenia take a "rational path to madness" (Zimbardo, 1976). This process of drawing incorrect and bizarre conclusions (delusions) may be helped along by a cognitive bias that many people with schizophrenia have—a tendency to jump to conclusions (Sarin & Wallin, 2014).

David X Prutting/BFA/REX/Shutterstock

Relationships of the mind Like Taylor Swift, most celebrities grow used to the constant crush of fans, reporters, crew members, and curious onlookers. However when they are stalked—repeatedly followed and harassed by an individual—the matter grows more serious. Some stalkers have *erotomanic delusions*, false beliefs that they are loved by and in a relationship with the object of their attention. In recent years, Swift, Mila Kunis, Sandra Bullock, and other celebrities have had to seek court protection against stalkers who are constantly following them, trying to enter their premises, bombarding them with phone calls and messages, seeking expressions of love, threatening them, and the like.

Researchers have established that people with schizophrenia do indeed experience sensory and perceptual problems. As you saw earlier, many have hallucinations and most have trouble keeping their attention focused. But researchers have yet to provide clear, direct support for the cognitive-behavioral notion that misinterpretations of such sensory problems actually produce a syndrome of schizophrenia.

Sociocultural Views

Sociocultural theorists, recognizing that people with mental disorders are subject to a wide range of social and cultural forces, believe that *multicultural factors, social labeling,* and *family dysfunction* all contribute to schizophrenia. Research has yet to clarify what the precise causal relationships might be.

Multicultural Factors Rates of schizophrenia appear to differ between racial and ethnic groups, particularly between African Americans and non-Hispanic white Americans (Coleman et al., 2016; Schwartz & Blankenship; 2014; Folsom et al., 2006). As many as 2.1 percent of African Americans receive a diagnosis of schizophrenia, compared with 1.4 percent of non-Hispanic white Americans. Research also suggests that African Americans with schizophrenia are overrepresented in state hospitals (Durbin el al., 2014; Barnes, 2004). For example, in Tennessee's state hospitals, 48 percent of those with a diagnosis of schizophrenia are African American, although only 16 percent of the state population is African American.

> How might bias by diagnosticians contribute to race-linked and culture-linked differences in the diagnosis of schizophrenia?

It is not clear why African Americans are more likely than non-Hispanic white Americans to receive this diagnosis. One possibility is that African Americans are more prone to develop schizophrenia. Another is that clinicians from majority groups are unintentionally biased in their diagnoses of African Americans or misread cultural differences as symptoms of schizophrenia.

Silvia Izquierdo/AP Photo

Coming together Different countries and cultures each have their own way of viewing and interacting with people suffering from schizophrenia and other mental disturbances. Here patients and members of the community come together and dance during the annual Carnival parade in front of the Psychiatric Institute in Rio de Janeiro, Brazil. The goal of the carnival is to promote public acceptance by blurring the lines between normal and abnormal functioning.

\#

#TheirWords

"I shouldn't precisely have chosen madness if there had been any choice, but once such a thing has taken hold of you, you can't very well get out of it."

Vincent van Gogh, 1889

Yet another explanation for the difference between African Americans and non-Hispanic white Americans may lie in the economic sphere. On average, African Americans are more likely to be poor; when economic differences are controlled for, the prevalence rates of schizophrenia become closer for the two racial groups. Consistent with the economic explanation is the finding that Hispanic Americans, who also tend to be economically disadvantaged, appear to be more likely to be diagnosed with schizophrenia than non-Hispanic white Americans, although their diagnostic rate is not as high as that of African Americans (Coleman et al., 2016; Blow et al., 2004).

It also appears that schizophrenia differs from country to country in key ways (Dein, 2017; McLean et al., 2014). Although the overall prevalence of this disorder is stable—around 1 percent—in countries across the world, the *course* and *outcome* of the disorder may vary considerably. According to a 10-country study conducted by the World Health Organization (WHO), the 25 million schizophrenic patients who live in *developing* countries have better recovery rates than schizophrenic patients in Western and other *developed* countries (Dein, 2017; Vahia & Vahia, 2008; Jablensky, 2000). The WHO study followed the progress of 467 patients from developing countries (Colombia, India, and Nigeria) over a two-year period and compared it with that of 603 patients from developed countries (the Czech Republic, Denmark, Ireland, Japan, Russia, the United Kingdom, and the United States). As you can see in **Figure 14-4**, during the course of the study, the schizophrenic patients from the developing countries were more likely than those in the developed countries to recover from their disorder and less likely to have continuous or episodic symptoms, to have impaired social functioning, or to require heavy antipsychotic drugs or hospitalization.

Some clinical theorists believe that these differences partly reflect genetic differences from population to population. However, others argue that the psychosocial environments of developing countries tend to be more supportive and therapeutic than those of developed countries, leading to more favorable outcomes for people with schizophrenia (Dein, 2017; Vahia & Vahia, 2008; Jablensky, 2000). In developing countries, for example, there may be more family and social support for people with schizophrenia; more relatives and friends available to help care for such people; and less judgmental, critical, and hostile attitudes toward people with schizophrenia. The Nigerian culture, for example, is generally more tolerant of the presence of voices than are Western cultures (Matsumoto & Juang, 2016).

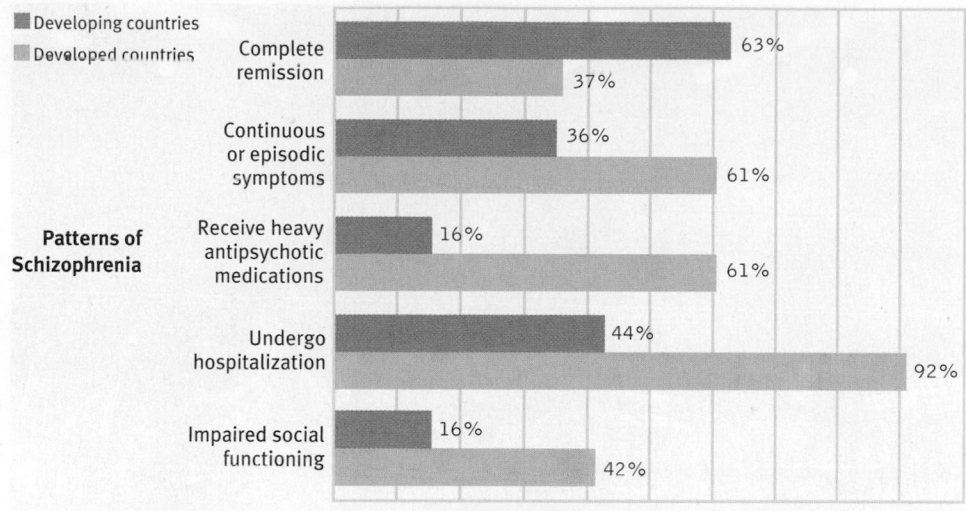

■ Developing countries
■ Developed countries

Patterns of Schizophrenia

Complete remission — 63% / 37%
Continuous or episodic symptoms — 36% / 61%
Receive heavy antipsychotic medications — 16% / 61%
Undergo hospitalization — 44% / 92%
Impaired social functioning — 16% / 42%

Percentage of Patients Who Display Pattern

FIGURE 14-4

Do the Course and Outcome of Schizophrenia Differ from Country to Country?

Yes, according to a World Health Organization study. In developing countries, patients with schizophrenia seem to recover more quickly, more often, and more completely than patients in developed countries. (Information from: Dein, 2017; Jablensky, 2000.)

Social Labeling Many sociocultural theorists believe that the features of schizophrenia are influenced by the diagnosis itself. In their opinion, society assigns the label "schizophrenic" to people who fail to conform to certain norms of behavior. Once the label is assigned, justified or not, it becomes a self-fulfilling prophecy that promotes the development of many schizophrenic symptoms. Certainly sufferers of schizophrenia have attested to the power that labeling has had on their lives:

Like any worthwhile endeavor, becoming a schizophrenic requires a long period of rigorous training. My training for this unique calling began in earnest when I was six years old. At that time my somewhat befuddled mother took me to the University of Washington to be examined by psychiatrists in order to find out what was wrong with me. These psychiatrists told my mother: "We don't know exactly what is wrong with your son, but whatever it is, it is very serious. We recommend that you have him committed immediately or else he will be completely psychotic within less than a year." My mother did not have me committed since she realized that such a course of action would be extremely damaging to me. But after that ominous prophecy my parents began to view and treat me as if I were either insane or at least in the process of becoming that way. Once, when my mother caught me playing with some vile muck I had mixed up—I was seven at the time—she gravely told me, "They have people put away in mental institutions for doing things like that." Fear was written all over my mother's face as she told me this. . . . The slightest odd behavior on my part was enough to send my parents into paroxysms of apprehension. My parents' apprehensions in turn made me fear that I was going insane. . . . My fate had been sealed not by my genes, but by the attitudes, beliefs, and expectations of my parents. . . . I find it extremely difficult to condemn my parents for behaving as if I were going insane when the psychiatric authorities told them that this was an absolute certainty.

(Modrow, 1992, pp. 1–2)

Like this man, people who are labeled schizophrenic may be viewed and treated as "crazy" (Fischer & Buchanan, 2017; Farrelly et al., 2014). Perhaps the expectations of other people subtly encourage the individuals to display psychotic behaviors, and they come to accept their assigned role and learn to play it convincingly.

We have already seen the very real dangers of diagnostic labeling. In the famous Rosenhan (1973) study, discussed in Chapter 3, eight normal people presented themselves at various mental hospitals, complaining that they had been hearing voices utter the words "empty," "hollow," and "thud." They were quickly diagnosed as schizophrenic, and all eight were hospitalized. Although the pseudopatients then dropped

#TheirWords

"If you talk to God, you are praying. If God talks to you, you have schizophrenia."

Thomas Szasz, psychiatric theorist

What's in a name? The British band Madness entertains 15,000 people in a Liverpool concert, just as they have entertained millions of fans during their four decades of performing. Some social critics worry that band names like Madness, Bad Brains, the Insane Clown Posse, the Schizos, and Bark Psychosis serve to trivialize or romanticize the plight of people with schizophrenia and other psychotic disorders—thus reducing the public's awareness of the pain and suffering that accompany these disorders.

Paul Warburton / Alamy

all symptoms and behaved normally, they had great difficulty getting rid of the label and gaining release from the hospital.

The pseudopatients reported that staff members were authoritarian in their behavior toward patients, spent limited time interacting with them, and responded curtly and uncaringly to questions. They generally treated patients as though they were invisible. "A nurse unbuttoned her uniform to adjust her brassiere in the presence of an entire ward of viewing men. One did not have the sense that she was being seductive. Rather, she didn't notice us." In addition, the pseudopatients described feeling powerless, bored, tired, and uninterested. The deceptive design and possible implications of this study have aroused the emotions of clinicians and researchers, pro and con. The investigation does demonstrate, however, that the label "schizophrenic" can itself have a negative effect not just on how people are viewed but also on how they themselves feel and behave.

> Rosenhan's study is one of the most controversial in the field. What kinds of ethical, legal, and therapeutic concerns does it raise?

Family Dysfunction Many studies suggest that schizophrenia, like a number of other mental disorders, is often linked to *family stress* (Gurak & Weisman de Mamani, 2016; Cullen et al., 2014). Parents of people with schizophrenia often (1) display more conflict, (2) have more difficulty communicating with one another, and (3) are more critical of and overinvolved with their children than other parents.

Family theorists have long recognized that some families are high in **expressed emotion**—that is, members frequently express criticism, disapproval, and hostility toward each other and intrude on one another's privacy. People who are trying to recover from schizophrenia are almost four times more likely to relapse if they live with such a family than if they live with one low in expressed emotion (Sadiq et al., 2017; Koutra et al., 2015). Do such findings mean that family dysfunction helps cause and maintain schizophrenia? Not necessarily. It is also the case that people with schizophrenia greatly disrupt family life (Gurak & Weisman de Mamani, 2016; Swain et al., 2017). In so doing, they themselves may help produce the family problems that clinicians and researchers continue to observe (McFarlane, 2016, 2011; Hsiao et al., 2014).

Bruce Eric Kaplan/The New Yorker Collection/The Cartoon Bank

"Bad news—we're all out of our minds. You're going to have to be the lone healthy person in this family."

Developmental Psychopathology View

As they do with other psychological disorders, developmental psychopathology theorists offer an integrative and developmental framework to explain why and how the factors discussed in this chapter may lead to schizophrenia. The theorists contend that the road to schizophrenia begins with a genetically inherited predisposition to the disorder—a predisposition that is expressed by the dysfunctional brain circuit you read about earlier (Nivard et al., 2018; Walker et al., 2016). The theorists further argue that this genetic predisposition may eventually lead to schizophrenia if, over the course of an individual's development, he or she experiences significant life stressors, difficult family interactions, and/or other negative environmental factors (Mayo et al., 2017; Vallejos et al., 2017).

Of course, as you read earlier, theorists of all kinds have, for years, proposed that a *diathesis–stress* relationship is at work in schizophrenia—that is, people with a biological predisposition to this disorder will develop it if they further experience significant life stress or other negative events. Thus, the developmental psychopathology perspective does not represent a totally new way of understanding schizophrenia. What theorists and researchers from this perspective have done, however, is provide much more detail about the diathesis–stress processes at work in schizophrenia. In particular, they have clarified two key points:

1. Schizophrenia typically begins to unfold long before the actual onset of the disorder in young adulthood. Previously, you read that people with this disorder often display cognitive, perception, and attention problems earlier in their lives (Jansen et al., 2018; Fischer & Buchanan, 2017). Developmental psychopathology researchers have found that such people also tend to be more socially withdrawn, disagreeable, and disobedient, and to have more motor difficulties, throughout their early development (Walker et al., 2016; Dickson et al., 2012). Some of those early problems seem to result largely from the individual's inherited predisposition, but, according to research, they may also be due to repeated experiences of childhood stress, family dysfunction, and/or difficult social interactions (Kraan et al., 2018; Walker et al., 2016).

2. One of the key ways that a dysfunctional brain circuit may adversely affect the functioning of people who later become schizophrenic is through the circuit's impact on the operation of the *hypothalamic-pituitary-adrenal (HPA)* stress pathway (see page 156). As you'll recall, whenever we are stressed, the brain's hypothalamus activates this brain–body pathway, leading, in turn, to the secretion of cortisol and other stress hormones and to a broad experience of arousal. Developmental psychopathology researchers have found that dysfunction by the schizophrenia-related brain circuit leads to repeated overreactions by the HPA pathway in the face of stress (Walker, et al., 2016, 2010, 2008). Such chronic overreactions leave individuals highly sensitive to and unsettled by stressors throughout their development. The individuals become all the more inclined to later develop schizophrenia in the face of stress (Pruessner et al., 2017).

Developmental psychopathology researchers and other investigators have further discovered that an overreactive HPA stress pathway and chronic stress reactions lead to the development of a dysfunctional *immune system*, characterized by heightened inflammation throughout the brain (Muller et al., 2015). Thus it is not surprising that numerous studies conducted over the past several years have found significant immune system problems and chronic inflammation throughout the brains of people with schizophrenia (Howes & McCutcheon, 2017).

expressed emotion The general level of criticism, disapproval, and hostility expressed in a family. People recovering from schizophrenia are considered more likely to relapse if their families rate high in expressed emotion.

"The Devil and Daniel Johnston" For decades, singer-songwriter Daniel Johnston has been very influential in the *outsider* and *alternative* music genres. At the same time, he suffers from schizophrenia and bipolar disorder and has been institutionalized several times for these problems. His disorders and their effect on his life and career are chronicled in the film documentary *The Devil and Daniel Johnston*.

Jordi Vidal/Redferns via Getty Images

In addition to adding depth to the diathesis–stress view of schizophrenia, the developmental psychopathology perspective provides an important service by emphasizing the advantages of *prevention* in dealing with this disorder (Seidman & Nordentoft, 2015; Stafford et al., 2013). According to this perspective, each of the factors discussed in this chapter (from brain circuit dysfunction to family dynamics to stress reactions) can affect each other. Just as children's overreactive HPA stress pathways can make them particularly vulnerable to stress, so too can their acquisition of resilience and coping skills improve the operation of their HPA pathways. This two-way relationship argues for better identification of children at risk for schizophrenia and for stronger preventive interventions that might reverse the factors predisposing them to schizophrenia (Mayo et al., 2017; Seidman & Nordentoft, 2015). Unfortunately, as you will see in the next chapter, most of today's approaches to schizophrenia involve treatment after the onset of the disorder rather than prevention.

Psychological and Sociocultural Models Lag Behind

SCHIZOPHRENIA—A BIZARRE AND FRIGHTENING disorder—was studied intensively throughout the twentieth century. Only since the discovery of antipsychotic drugs, however, have clinicians acquired any practical insight into its course and causes. Theories abounded before that time, but they typically failed to find empirical support and, in fact, contributed to inaccurate stereotyping of people with schizophrenia and their parents.

As they do with other psychological disorders, most clinical theorists now believe that schizophrenia is caused by a combination of factors, though researchers have been far more successful in identifying the biological influences than the psychological and sociocultural ones. While biological investigations have closed in on specific genes, abnormalities in brain biochemistry and brain circuits, and even viral infections, most of the psychological and sociocultural research has been able to cite only general factors, such as the roles of family conflict and diagnostic labeling. Clearly, researchers must identify psychological and sociocultural factors with greater precision if we are to gain a full understanding of schizophrenia. The exciting progress now being made in the biological study of schizophrenia is impressive, but it must not blind us to the significant gaps and uncertainties that continue to obscure our view.

CLINICAL CHOICES

Now that you've read about schizophrenia, try the interactive case study for this chapter. See if you are able to identify Randy's symptoms and suggest a diagnosis based on his symptoms. What kind of treatment would be most effective for Randy? Go to **Launch**Pad to access *Clinical Choices*.

♀... SUMMING UP

» **The Clinical Picture of Schizophrenia** *Schizophrenia* is a disorder in which personal, social, and occupational functioning deteriorate as a result of disturbed thought processes, distorted perceptions, unusual emotions, and motor abnormalities. Approximately 1 percent of the world's population suffers from this disorder. *pp. 422–424*

» **Symptoms of Schizophrenia** The symptoms of schizophrenia fall into three groupings. *Positive symptoms* include *delusions*, certain *formal thought disorders*, *hallucinations* and other *disturbances in perception and attention*, and *inappropriate affect*. *Negative symptoms* include *poverty of speech*, *restricted affect*, *loss of volition*, and *social withdrawal*. Schizophrenia may also include *psychomotor symptoms*, collectively called *catatonia* in their extreme form. Schizophrenia usually emerges during late adolescence or early adulthood and tends to progress through three phases: *prodromal*, *active*, and *residual*. *pp. 424–430*

» **Diagnosing Schizophrenia** DSM-5 calls for a diagnosis of schizophrenia after symptoms of the disorder continue for *six months* or more. This diagnosis also requires that people have active symptoms for at least one of those months and show a deterioration from previous levels of functioning. *Type I schizophrenia* is often distinguished from *Type II schizophrenia*. Patients with the former type seem to be dominated by positive symptoms, and those with the latter type seem to display more negative ones. *pp. 430–431*

» **Biological Explanations** The biological explanations of schizophrenia point to genetic, biochemical, brain structure and circuitry, and viral causes. The *genetic* view is supported by studies of relatives, twins, adoptees, and genes. The leading *biochemical* explanation holds that *dopamine* may be overactive in the brains of people with schizophrenia. Studies have also identified a *brain circuit* whose dysfunction may lead to schizophrenia. The circuit includes structures such as the prefrontal cortex, hippocampus, amygdala, thalamus, striatum, and substantia nigra. Finally, some researchers believe that schizophrenia is related to a *virus* that settles in the fetus. *pp. 431–437*

» **Psychological Explanations** The leading psychological explanations for schizophrenia come from the psychodynamic and cognitive-behavioral models. One influential *psychodynamic* explanation has contended that *schizophrenogenic mothers* help produce schizophrenia. Contemporary psychodynamic theorists, however, typically ascribe the disorder to a combination of biological and psychodynamic factors. *Cognitive-behavioral* theorists suggest that people with schizophrenia (1) fail to learn to attend to appropriate social cues and/or (2) misinterpret their strange biological sensations in ways that foster delusional thinking. None of these theories have received compelling research support. *pp. 437–439*

» **Sociocultural Explanations** One sociocultural explanation holds that *multicultural* differences may influence the prevalence and character of schizophrenia, as well as recovery from this disorder, both within the United States and around the world. Another sociocultural explanation says that society expects people who are *labeled* as having schizophrenia to behave in certain ways and that these expectations actually lead to further symptoms. Other sociocultural theorists point to *family dysfunction,* including *family stress and conflict,* as a cause of schizophrenia. *pp. 439–442*

» **Developmental Psychopathology View** Applying an integrative and developmental framework, *developmental psychopathology* theorists contend that an individual's *genetic predisposition*—implemented by a dysfunctional brain circuit—may eventually lead to schizophrenia if, over the course of the person's development, he or she experiences significant life stressors, difficult family interactions, and/or other negative environmental factors. *pp. 443–444*

Treatments for Schizophrenia and Other Severe Mental Disorders

During [Cathy's] second year in college . . . her emotional troubles worsened. . . . Her thoughts about sex gradually bloomed into a fantasy about Steve Martin, the comedian. Unable to sleep through the night, she would awaken at four a.m. and go for walks, and at times, it seemed that Steve Martin was there on campus, stalking her. "I thought he was in love with me and was running through the bushes just out of sight," she says. "He was looking for me."

. . . The breaking point came one evening when she threw a glass object against the wall in her dorm room. "I didn't clean it up, but instead was walking around in it. I was, you know, taking the glass out of my feet. I was completely out of my mind." . . . She was . . . informed that she suffered from a chemical imbalance in the brain, and [was] put on Haldol and lithium.

For the next sixteen years, Cathy cycled in and out of hospitals. She "hated the meds"—Haldol stiffened her muscles and caused her to drool, while the lithium made her depressed—and often she would abruptly stop taking them. . . . The problem was that off the drugs, she would "start to decompensate and become disorganized."

In early 1994, she was hospitalized for the fifteenth time. She was seen as chronically mentally ill, occasionally heard voices now . . . and was on a cocktail of drugs: Haldol, Ativan, Tegretol, Halcion, and Cogentin, the last drug an antidote to Haldol's nasty side effects. But after she was released that spring, a psychiatrist told her to try Risperdal, a new antipsychotic that had just been approved by the FDA. "Three weeks later, my mind was much clearer," she says. "The voices were going away. I got off the other meds and took only this one drug. I got better. I could start to plan. I wasn't talking to the devil anymore. Jesus and God weren't battling it out in my head." Her father put it this way: "Cathy is back." . . .

She went back to school and earned a degree in radio, film, and television. . . . In 1998, she began dating the man she lives with today. . . . In 2005, she took a part-time job. . . . Still, she remains on SSDI (Social Security Disability Insurance)—"I am a kept woman," she jokes—and although there are many reasons for that, she believes that Risperdal, the very drug that has helped her so much, nevertheless has proven to be a barrier to full-time work. Although she is usually energetic by the early afternoon, Risperdal makes her so sleepy that she has trouble getting up in the morning. The other problem is that she has always had trouble getting along with other people, and Risperdal exacerbates that problem, she says. . . . "The drugs may take care of aggression and anxiety and some paranoia, those sorts of symptoms, but they don't help with the empathy that helps you get along with people."

Risperdal has also taken a physical toll. . . . She has . . . developed some of the metabolic problems, such as high cholesterol, that the atypical antipsychotics regularly cause. "I can go toe-to-toe with an old lady with a recital of my physical problems," she says. "My feet, my bladder, my heart, my sinuses, the weight gain—I have it all." . . . But she can't do well without Risperdal. . . .

Such has been her life's course on medications. Sixteen terrible years, followed by fourteen pretty good years on Risperdal. She believes that this drug is essential to her mental health today, and indeed, she could be seen as a local poster child for promoting the wonders of that drug. Still, if you look at the long-term course of her illness . . . you have to ask: Is hers a story of a life made better by our drug-based . . . care for mental disorders, or a story of a life made worse? . . .

A graphic reminder During the 1800s and 1900s, tens of thousands of patients with severe mental disorders were abandoned by their families and spent the rest of their lives in the back wards of the public mental institutions. We are reminded of their tragic situation by the 3,500 copper urns filled with unclaimed ashes currently stored in a building at Oregon State Hospital.

ZUMA Press, Inc./Alamy Stock Photo

> Cathy believes that this is a question that psychiatrists never contemplate. "They don't have any sense about how these drugs affect you over the long term. They just try to stabilize you for the moment, and look to manage you from week to week, month to month. That's all they ever think about."
>
> (Whitaker, 2010)

In many ways, Cathy's clumsy journey is typical of that of hundreds of thousands of people with schizophrenia and other severe mental disorders. To be sure, there are other patients whose efforts to overcome such disorders go more smoothly. And at the other end of the spectrum, there are many whose struggles against severe mental dysfunction never come close to Cathy's level of success. But in between, there are the Cathys.

This is today's treatment picture for schizophrenia and other severe mental disorders. For some, it involves miraculous triumphs; for others, modest success; and for still others, heartbreaking failure. Treatment is typically characterized by medications, medication-linked health problems, compromised lifestyles, and a mixture of hope and frustration. Despite this, today's treatment outlook for schizophrenia and other severe mental disorders is vastly superior to that of past years. In fact, for much of human history, people with such disorders were considered beyond help. Few returned to any semblance of normal or functional living. Indeed, few returned home from the institutions to which they were sent.

Schizophrenia is still extremely difficult to treat, but clinicians are much more successful at doing so today than they were in the past. Much of the credit goes to *antipsychotic drugs*—imperfect, troubling, and even dangerous though they may be. These medications help many people with schizophrenia and other psychotic disorders to think clearly and profit from psychotherapies that previously would have had little effect for them (Bustillo & Weil, 2016).

As you will see, each of the models offers treatments for schizophrenia, and all have been influential at one time or another. However, a mere description of the different approaches cannot convey the pain suffered by those with this disorder as the various methods of treatment evolved over the years. People with schizophrenia have been subjected to more mistreatment and indifference than perhaps any other group of patients. Even today, at least 40 percent of them do not receive adequate care (NIMH, 2017). To better convey the plight of people with schizophrenia, this chapter will depart from the usual format and discuss the treatments from a historical perspective.

As you saw in Chapter 14, throughout much of the twentieth century the label "schizophrenia" was assigned to most people with psychosis. However, clinical theorists now realize that many people with psychotic symptoms are instead manifesting a severe form of bipolar disorder or major depressive disorder and that such people were in past times inaccurately diagnosed with schizophrenia (Tondo et al., 2015; Lake, 2012). Thus, our discussions of past treatments for schizophrenia, particularly the failures of institutional care, are as applicable to those other severe mental disorders as they are to schizophrenia (Bustillo & Weil, 2017). And our discussions about current approaches to schizophrenia, such as the community mental health movement, often apply to other severe mental disorders as well. ●

Institutional Care in the Past

FOR MORE THAN HALF of the twentieth century, most people diagnosed with schizophrenia were *institutionalized* in a public mental hospital. Because patients with schizophrenia did not respond to traditional therapies, the primary goals of these hospitals were to restrain them and give them food, shelter, and clothing. Patients rarely

state hospitals Public mental hospitals in the United States, run by the individual states.

saw therapists and generally were neglected. Many were abused. Oddly enough, this state of affairs unfolded in an atmosphere of good intentions.

As you read in Chapter 1, the move toward institutionalization in hospitals began in 1793 when French physician Philippe Pinel "unchained the insane" at La Bicêtre asylum and began the practice of "moral treatment." For the first time in centuries, patients with severe disturbances were viewed as human beings who should be cared for with sympathy and kindness. As Pinel's ideas spread throughout Europe and the United States, they led to the creation of large mental hospitals rather than asylums to care for those with severe mental disorders (Goshen, 1967).

These new mental hospitals, typically located in isolated areas where land and labor were cheap, were meant to protect patients from the stresses of daily life and offer them a healthful psychological environment in which they could work closely with therapists (Grob, 1966). States throughout the United States were even required by law to establish public mental institutions, **state hospitals,** for patients who could not afford private ones.

Eventually, however, the state hospital system encountered serious problems. Between 1845 and 1955, nearly 300 state hospitals opened in the United States, and the number of hospitalized patients on any given day rose from 2,000 in 1845 to nearly 600,000 in 1955. During this expansion, wards became overcrowded, admissions kept rising, and state funding was unable to keep up. Too many aspects of treatment became the responsibility of nurses and attendants, whose knowledge and experience at that time were limited.

The priorities of the public mental hospitals, and the quality of care they provided, changed over those 110 years. In the face of overcrowding and understaffing, the emphasis shifted from giving humanitarian care to keeping order. In a throwback to the asylum period, difficult patients were restrained, isolated, and punished; individual attention disappeared. Patients were transferred to *back wards,* or chronic wards, if they failed to improve quickly (Bloom, 1984). Most of the patients on these wards suffered from schizophrenia (Häfner & an der Heiden, 1988). The back wards were human warehouses filled with hopelessness. Staff members relied on straitjackets and handcuffs to deal with difficult patients. More "advanced" forms of treatment included medical approaches such as *lobotomy* (see **PsychWatch** on page 450).

> Why have people with schizophrenia so often been victims of horrific treatments such as overcrowded wards, lobotomy, and, later, deinstitutionalization?

John Stanmeyer/VII/Redux

Institutional life In a scene reminiscent of public mental hospitals in the United States during the first half of the twentieth century, these patients spend their days crowded together on a hospital ward in central Shanghai. Because of a shortage of therapists, only a small fraction of Chinese people with psychological disorders receive proper professional care today.

PSYCHWATCH

Lobotomy: How Could It Happen?

In 1935, a Portuguese neurologist named Egas Moniz performed a revolutionary new surgical procedure, which he called a *prefrontal leucotomy,* on a patient with severe mental dysfunction (Wright, 2017; Raz, 2013). The procedure, the first form of *lobotomy,* consisted of drilling two holes in either side of the skull and inserting an instrument resembling an icepick into the brain tissue to cut or destroy nerve fibers. Moniz believed that severe abnormal thinking—such as that on display in schizophrenia, depression, and obsessive-compulsive disorder—was the result of nerve pathways that carried such thoughts from one part of the brain to another. By cutting these pathways, Moniz believed, he could stop the abnormal thinking in its tracks and restore normal mental functioning.

A year after his first leucotomy, Moniz published a monograph in Europe describing his successful use of the procedure on 20 patients (Raz, 2013). An American neurologist, Walter Freeman, read the monograph, called the procedure to the attention of the medical community in the United States, performed the procedure on many patients, and became its foremost supporter. In 1947 he developed a second kind of lobotomy called the *transorbital lobotomy,* in which the surgeon inserted a needle into the brain through the eye socket and rotated it in order to destroy the brain tissue (Collins & Stam, 2015).

From the early 1940s through the mid-1950s, the lobotomy was viewed as a miracle cure by most doctors and became a mainstream part of psychiatry (Wright, 2017; Levinson, 2011). An estimated 50,000 people in the United States alone eventually received lobotomies (Johnson, 2005).

We now know that the lobotomy was hardly a miracle treatment. Far from "curing" people with mental disorders, the procedure left thousands upon thousands extremely withdrawn, subdued, and even stuporous. Why then was the procedure so enthusiastically accepted by the medical

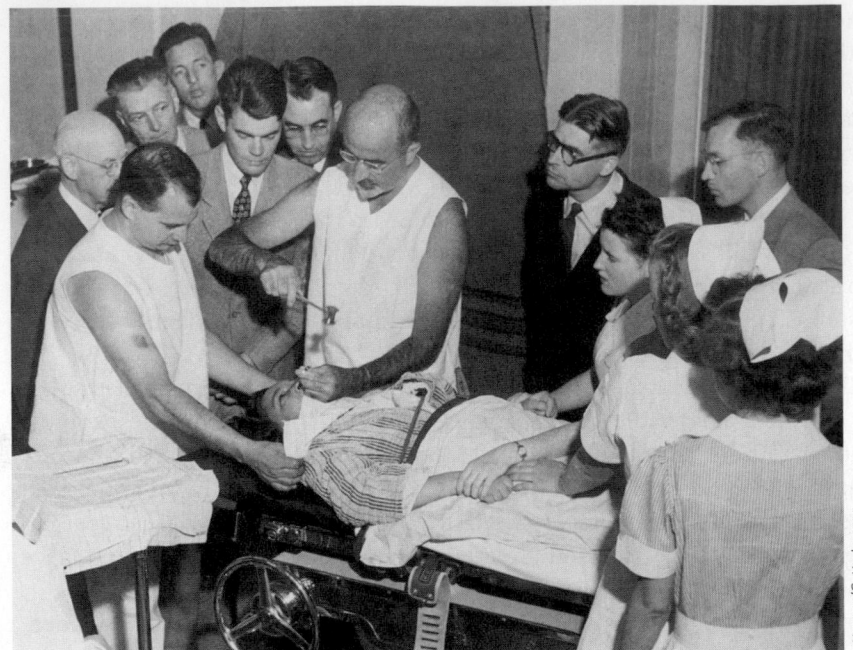

Bettmann/Getty Images

Lessons in psychosurgery Neuropsychiatrist Walter Freeman performs a lobotomy in 1949 before a group of interested onlookers by inserting a needle through a patient's eye socket into the brain.

community in the 1940s and 1950s? Neuroscientist Elliot Valenstein (1986) points first to the extreme overcrowding in mental hospitals at the time. This crowding was making it difficult to maintain decent standards in the hospitals. Valenstein also points to the personalities of the inventors of the procedure as important factors. Although these individuals were gifted and dedicated physicians—in 1949 Moniz was awarded the Nobel Prize for his work—Valenstein believes that their professional ambitions led them to move too quickly and boldly in applying the procedure.

The prestige of Moniz and Freeman were so great and the field of neurology was so small that their procedures drew little criticism. Physicians may also have been misled by the seemingly positive findings of early studies of the lobotomy, which, as it turned out, were not based on sound methodology (Wright, 2017; Cooper, 2014).

By the 1950s, better studies revealed that in addition to having a fatality rate of

1.5 to 6 percent, lobotomies could cause serious problems such as brain seizures, huge weight gain, loss of motor coordination, partial paralysis, incontinence, endocrine malfunctions, and very poor intellectual and emotional responsiveness (Lapidus et al., 2013). The discovery of effective antipsychotic drugs helped put an end to this inhumane treatment for mental disorders (Krack et al., 2010).

Today's psychosurgical procedures are greatly refined and hardly resemble the lobotomies of 60 years back. Moreover, the procedures are usually used only as a last resort: they are reserved for the most severe cases of disorders such as OCD and depression (Neumaier et al., 2018, 2016; Nair et al., 2014). Even so, many professionals believe that any kind of surgery that destroys brain tissue is inappropriate and perhaps unethical and that it keeps alive one of the clinical field's most shameful and ill-advised efforts at cure.

Many patients not only failed to improve under these conditions but also developed additional symptoms, apparently as a result of institutionalization itself (see *InfoCentral* on the next page). The most common pattern of decline was called the *social breakdown syndrome:* extreme withdrawal, anger, physical aggressiveness, and loss of interest in personal appearance and functioning (Oshima et al., 2005). Often more troublesome than the patients' original symptoms, this new syndrome made it impossible for patients to return to society even if they somehow recovered from the symptoms that had first brought them to the hospital.

milieu therapy A humanistic approach to institutional treatment based on the premise that institutions can help patients recover by creating a climate that promotes self-respect, responsible behavior, and meaningful activity.

Institutional Care Takes a Turn for the Better

IN THE 1950s, CLINICIANS developed two institutional approaches that finally brought some hope to patients who had lived in institutions for years: *milieu therapy,* based on humanistic principles, and the *token economy program,* based on behavioral principles. These approaches particularly helped improve the personal care and self-image of patients, problem areas that had been worsened by institutionalization. The approaches were soon adapted by many institutions and are now standard features of institutional care.

Milieu Therapy

In the opinion of humanistic theorists, institutionalized patients deteriorate because they are deprived of opportunities to exercise independence, responsibility, and positive self-regard, and to engage in meaningful activities. Thus the premise of **milieu therapy** is that institutions cannot be of help to patients unless they can somehow create a social climate, or milieu, that promotes productive activity, self-respect, and individual responsibility.

The pioneer of this approach was Maxwell Jones, a London psychiatrist who in 1953 converted a ward of patients with various psychological disorders into a therapeutic community. The patients were referred to as "residents" and were regarded as capable

Eitan Abramovich/Getty Images

Milieu philosophy Although not as prominent as it was a half-century ago, a milieu philosophy continues to influence programs in mental hospitals around the world. At the Borda psychiatric hospital in Buenos Aires, Argentina, patients, therapists, and volunteers take a tango workshop together—not only to provide an exercise opportunity, but to instill in patients a sense of equality, self-respect, and competence.

INSTITUTIONS FOR PSYCHOLOGICAL CARE

Prior to the 1960s, most people with severe mental disorders resided in institutions until they improved. Sadly, many were never released. Today, a much smaller number of people are institutionalized. Moreover, the nature and patient census of psychiatric institutionalization has changed significantly over the past 60 years.

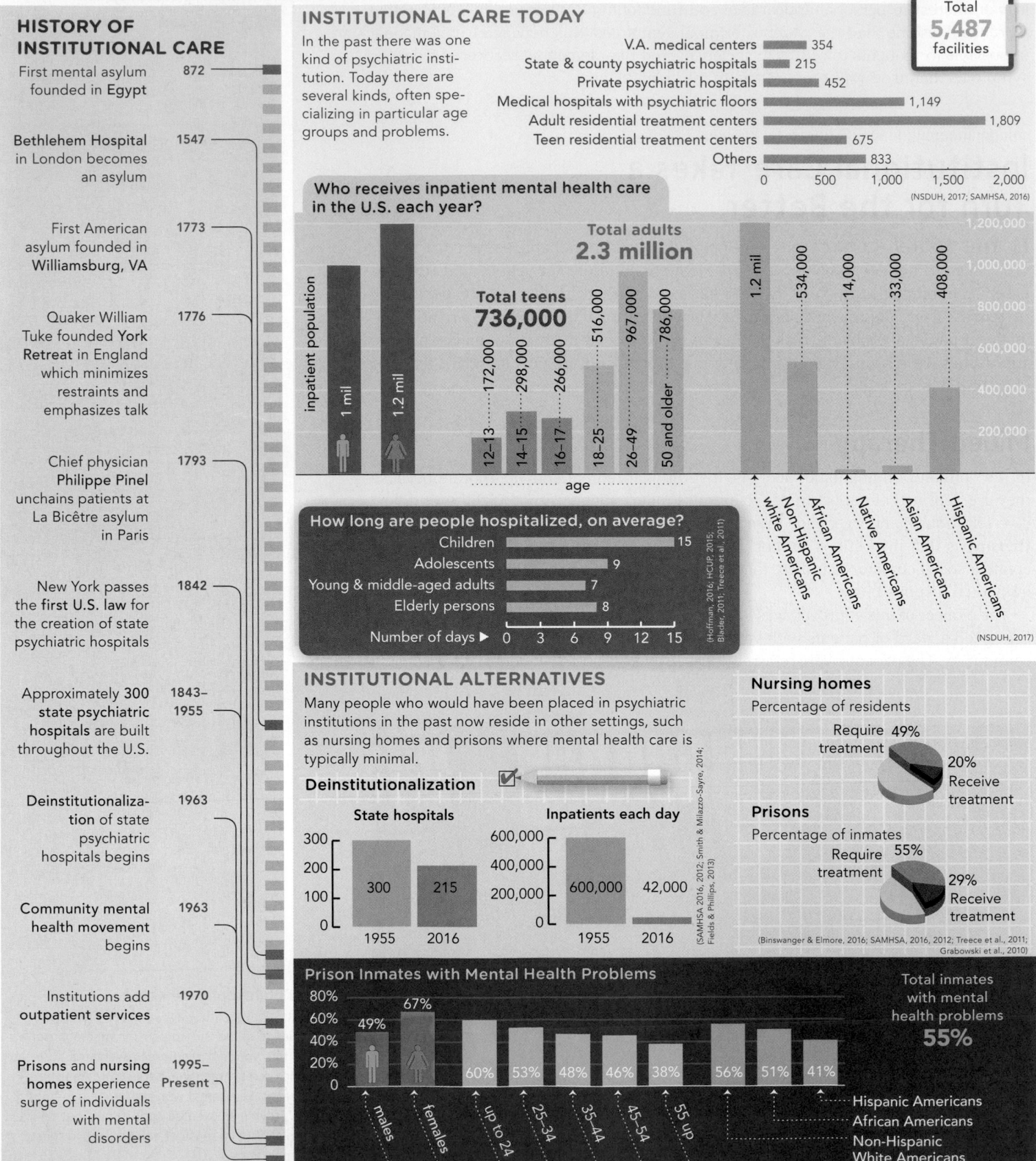

HISTORY OF INSTITUTIONAL CARE

First mental asylum founded in **Egypt**	872
Bethlehem Hospital in London becomes an asylum	1547
First American asylum founded in **Williamsburg, VA**	1773
Quaker William Tuke founded **York Retreat** in England which minimizes restraints and emphasizes talk	1776
Chief physician **Philippe Pinel** unchains patients at La Bicêtre asylum in Paris	1793
New York passes the **first U.S. law** for the creation of state psychiatric hospitals	1842
Approximately **300 state psychiatric hospitals** are built throughout the U.S.	1843–1955
Deinstitutionalization of state psychiatric hospitals begins	1963
Community mental health movement begins	1963
Institutions add **outpatient services**	1970
Prisons and **nursing homes** experience surge of individuals with mental disorders	1995–Present

(Binswanger & Elmore, 2016; Treece et al., 2011; Bloom, 1984)

INSTITUTIONAL CARE TODAY

In the past there was one kind of psychiatric institution. Today there are several kinds, often specializing in particular age groups and problems.

Total 5,487 facilities

Facility	Count
V.A. medical centers	354
State & county psychiatric hospitals	215
Private psychiatric hospitals	452
Medical hospitals with psychiatric floors	1,149
Adult residential treatment centers	1,809
Teen residential treatment centers	675
Others	833

(NSDUH, 2017; SAMHSA, 2016)

Who receives inpatient mental health care in the U.S. each year?

Total adults 2.3 million

inpatient population: 1 mil (male), 1.2 mil (female)

Total teens 736,000

By age:
- 12–13: 172,000
- 14–15: 298,000
- 16–17: 266,000
- 18–25: 516,000
- 26–49: 967,000
- 50 and older: 786,000

By group:
- Non-Hispanic white Americans: 1.2 mil
- African Americans: 534,000
- Native Americans: 14,000
- Asian Americans: 33,000
- Hispanic Americans: 408,000

(NSDUH, 2017)

How long are people hospitalized, on average?

	Number of days
Children	15
Adolescents	9
Young & middle-aged adults	7
Elderly persons	8

(Hofman, 2016; HCUP, 2015; Blader, 2011; Treece et al., 2011)

INSTITUTIONAL ALTERNATIVES

Many people who would have been placed in psychiatric institutions in the past now reside in other settings, such as nursing homes and prisons where mental health care is typically minimal.

Deinstitutionalization

State hospitals
- 1955: 300
- 2016: 215

Inpatients each day
- 1955: 600,000
- 2016: 42,000

(SAMHSA 2016, 2012; Smith & Milazzo-Sayre, 2014; Fields & Phillips, 2013)

Nursing homes
Percentage of residents
- Require treatment: 49%
- Receive treatment: 20%

Prisons
Percentage of inmates
- Require treatment: 55%
- Receive treatment: 29%

(Binswanger & Elmore, 2016; SAMHSA, 2016, 2012; Treece et al., 2011; Grabowski et al., 2010)

Prison Inmates with Mental Health Problems

Total inmates with mental health problems 55%

- males: 49%
- females: 67%
- up to 24: 60%
- 25–34: 53%
- 35–44: 48%
- 45–54: 46%
- 55 up: 38%
- Hispanic Americans: 56%
- African Americans: 51%
- Non-Hispanic White Americans: 41%

of running their own lives and making their own decisions. They participated in community government, working with staff members to establish rules and determine sanctions. Residents and staff members alike were valued as important therapeutic agents. The atmosphere was one of mutual respect, support, and openness. Patients could also take on special projects, jobs, and recreational activities. In short, their daily schedule was designed to resemble life outside the hospital.

Milieu-style programs have since been set up in institutions throughout the Western world. The programs vary from setting to setting, but at a minimum, staff members try to encourage interactions (especially group interactions) between patients and staff, to keep patients active, and to raise their expectations about what they can accomplish.

Research over the years has shown that people with schizophrenia and other severe mental disorders in milieu hospital programs often improve and that they leave the hospital at higher rates than patients in programs offering primarily custodial care (Paul, 2000; Paul & Lentz, 1977). Many remain impaired, however, and must live in sheltered settings after their release. Despite its limitations, milieu therapy continues to be practiced in many institutions, often combined with other hospital approaches (Smith & Spitzmueller, 2016). Moreover, you will see later in this chapter that many of today's halfway houses and other community programs for people with severe mental disorders are run in accordance with the same principles of resident self-government and work schedules that have proved effective in hospital milieu programs.

The Token Economy

In the 1950s, clinicians interested primarily in behaviors and in principles of conditioning had little status in mental institutions and were permitted to work only with patients whose problems seemed hopeless. Among the "hopeless" were patients diagnosed with schizophrenia. Through years of experimentation, behavior-focused researchers discovered that the systematic use of *operant conditioning* techniques on hospital wards could help change the behaviors of these patients (Ayllon, 1963; Ayllon & Michael, 1959). Programs that apply these techniques are called **token economy programs.**

In token economies, patients are rewarded when they behave acceptably and are not rewarded when they behave unacceptably. The immediate rewards for acceptable behavior are often tokens that can later be exchanged for food, cigarettes, hospital privileges, and other desirable items, all of which compose a "token economy." Acceptable behaviors likely to be included are caring for oneself and for one's possessions (making the bed, getting dressed), going to a work program, speaking normally, following ward rules, and showing self-control.

How Effective Are Token Economy Programs? Researchers have found that token economies do help reduce psychotic and related behaviors (Ivy et al., 2017; Swartz et al., 2012). In one early program, Gordon Paul and Robert Lentz (1977) set up a hospital token economy for 28 patients diagnosed with chronic schizophrenia, most of whom improved greatly. After four and a half years, 98 percent of the patients had been released, mostly to sheltered-care facilities, compared with 71 percent of patients treated in a milieu program and 45 percent of patients who received custodial care only.

What Are the Limitations of Token Economies? Some clinicians have voiced reservations about the claims made regarding token economy programs. One problem is that many token economy studies, unlike Paul and Lentz's, are uncontrolled. When administrators set up a token economy, they usually bring all ward patients into the program rather than dividing the ward into a token economy group and a control group. As a result, patients' improvements can be compared only with their own past

token economy program A program in which a person' are reinforced systemat' of tokens that can be exc. privileges.

behaviors—a comparison that may be misleading. Changes in the physical setting, for example, or a general increase in staff attention could be causing patients' improvement, rather than the token economy.

Many clinicians have also raised ethical and legal concerns. If token economy programs are to be effective, administrators need to control the important rewards in a patient's life, perhaps including such basic ones as food and a comfortable bed. But aren't there some things in life to which all human beings are entitled? Court decisions have now ruled that patients do indeed have certain basic rights that clinicians cannot violate, regardless of the positive goals of a treatment program. They have a right to food, storage space, and furniture, as well as freedom of movement.

Still other clinicians have questioned the quality of the improvements made under token economy programs. Are operant conditioning procedures changing a patient's psychotic thoughts and perceptions or simply improving the patient's ability to imitate normal behavior? This issue is illustrated by the case of a middle-aged man named John, who had the delusion that he was the U.S. government. Whenever he spoke, he spoke as the government. "We are happy to see you. . . . We need people like you in our service. . . . We are carrying out our activities in John's body." When John's hospital ward converted to using a token economy, the staff members targeted his delusional statements and required him to identify himself properly to earn tokens. If he called himself John, he received tokens; if he described himself as the government, he received nothing. After a few months on the token economy program, John stopped referring to himself as the government. When asked his name, he would say, "John." Although staff members were understandably pleased with his improvement, John himself had a different view of the situation. In a private discussion he said:

We're tired of it. Every damn time we want a cigarette, we have to go through their bullshit. "What's your name? . . . Who wants the cigarette? . . . Where is the government?" Today, we were desperate for a smoke and went to Simpson, the damn nurse, and she made us do her bidding. "Tell me your name if you want a cigarette. What's your name?" Of course, we said, "John." We needed the cigarettes. If we told her the truth, no cigarettes. But we don't have time for this nonsense. We've got business to do, international business, laws to change, people to recruit. And these people keep playing their games.

(Comer, 1973)

Critics of token economies would argue that John was still delusional and therefore as psychotic as before. However, proponents of these programs would argue that at the very least, John's judgment about the consequences of his behavior had improved. Learning to keep his delusion to himself might even be a step toward changing his private thinking.

Last, it has often been difficult for patients to make a satisfactory transition from hospital token economy programs to community living. In an environment where rewards are contingent on proper conduct, proper conduct becomes contingent on continued rewards. Some patients who find that the real world doesn't reward them so concretely abandon their newly acquired behaviors.

Nevertheless, token economies have had a most important effect on the treatment of people with schizophrenia and other severe mental disorders. They were among the first hospital treatments that actually changed psychotic symptoms and got chronic patients moving again. These programs are no longer as popular as they once were, but they are still used in many mental hospitals, usually along with medication, and in many community residences as well (Ivy et al., 2017; Kopelowicz et al., 2008). The approach has also been applied to other clinical problems, including intellectual disability, delinquency, and hyperactivity, as well as in other fields, such as education and business (Ivy et al., 2017; Spiegler & Guevremont, 2015).

Antipsychotic Drugs

MILIEU THERAPY AND token economy programs helped improve the gloomy outlook for patients diagnosed with schizophrenia, but it was the discovery of **antipsychotic drugs** in the 1950s that truly revolutionized treatment for schizophrenia. These drugs eliminate many of its symptoms and today are almost always a part of treatment (Jibson, 2017; Bustillo & Weil, 2016).

The discovery of antipsychotic medications dates back to the 1940s, when researchers developed the first *antihistamine drugs* to combat allergies. The French surgeon Henri Laborit soon discovered that one group of antihistamines, *phenothiazines,* could also be used to help calm patients about to undergo surgery. After experimenting with several phenothiazine antihistamines and becoming most impressed with one called *chlorpromazine,* Laborit reported, "It provokes not any loss of consciousness, not any change in the patient's mentality but a slight tendency to sleep and above all 'disinterest' for all that goes on around him."

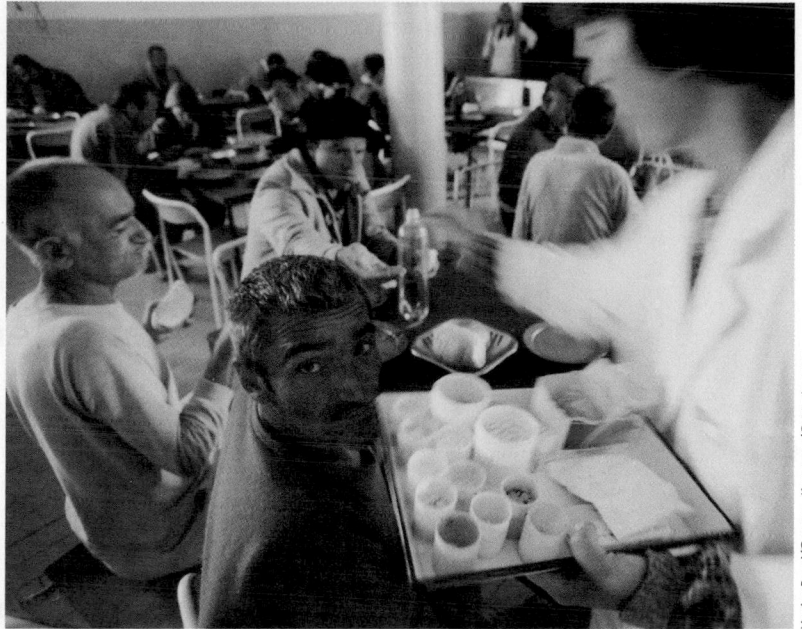

The drug revolution Since the 1950s, medications have become a central part of treatment for patients with schizophrenia and other severe mental disorders. The medications have resulted in shorter hospitalizations that now last weeks rather than years.

Laborit suspected that chlorpromazine might also have a calming effect on people with severe psychological disorders. Psychiatrists Jean Delay and Pierre Deniker (1952) tested the drug on six patients with psychotic symptoms and did indeed observe a sharp reduction in their symptoms. In 1954, chlorpromazine was approved for sale in the United States as an antipsychotic drug under the trade name Thorazine.

Since the discovery of the phenothiazines, other kinds of antipsychotic drugs have been developed. The ones developed throughout the 1960s, 1970s, and 1980s are now referred to as *first-generation antipsychotic drugs* (also called *conventional* antipsychotic drugs) in order to distinguish them from the *second-generation antipsychotics* (also called *atypical* antipsychotic drugs) that have been developed subsequently. The first-generation drugs are also known as **neuroleptic drugs** because they often produce undesired movement effects similar to the symptoms of neurological diseases. Among the best known such drugs are *thioridazine* (Mellaril), *fluphenazine* (Prolixin), *trifluoperazine* (Stelazine), and *haloperidol* (Haldol). As you saw in Chapter 14, antipsychotic drugs reduce psychotic symptoms at least in part by blocking excessive activity of the neurotransmitter *dopamine* (Jibson, 2017; Chun et al., 2014).

How Effective Are Antipsychotic Drugs?

Research has shown that antipsychotic drugs reduce symptoms in around 70 percent of patients diagnosed with schizophrenia (Stroup & Marder, 2017). Moreover, in direct comparisons the drugs appear to be a more effective treatment for schizophrenia than any of the other approaches used alone, such as psychotherapy, milieu therapy, or electroconvulsive therapy.

For patients helped by the drugs, the medications bring about clear improvement within a period of weeks and maximum improvement within six months (Jibson, 2017; Rabinowitz et al., 2014). However, symptoms may return if the patients stop taking the drugs too soon (Razali & Yusoff, 2014). In one pioneering study, when the antipsychotic medications of people with chronic schizophrenia were changed to a placebo after 5 years, 75 percent of the patients relapsed within a year, compared with 33 percent of similar patients who continued to receive medication (Sampath et al., 1992).

As you read in Chapter 14, antipsychotic drugs, particularly the first-generation ones, reduce the positive symptoms of schizophrenia (such as hallucinations and

antipsychotic drugs Drugs that help correct grossly confused or distorted thinking.

neuroleptic drugs First-generation antipsychotic drugs, so called because they often produce undesired effects similar to the symptoms of neurological disorders.

extrapyramidal effects Unwanted movements, such as severe shaking, bizarre-looking grimaces, twisting of the body, and extreme restlessness, sometimes produced by antipsychotic drugs.

tardive dyskinesia Extrapyramidal effects involving involuntary movements that some patients have after they have taken antipsychotic drugs for an extended time.

delusions) more completely, or at least more quickly, than the negative symptoms (such as restricted affect, poverty of speech, and loss of volition) (Jibson, 2017; Millan, et al., 2014). Correspondingly, people whose symptoms are largely positive generally have better rates of recovery from schizophrenia than those with predominantly negative symptoms (Stroup & Marder, 2017).

Although antipsychotic drugs are now widely accepted, patients often dislike the powerful effects of the drugs—both intended and unintended—and some refuse to take them (Liersch-Sumskis et al., 2014; Mohamed et al., 2014).

The Unwanted Effects of First-Generation Antipsychotic Drugs

In addition to reducing psychotic symptoms, the first-generation antipsychotic drugs sometimes produce disturbing movement problems (Jibson, 2017; Marder & Stroup, 2016). These effects are called **extrapyramidal effects** because they appear to be caused by the drugs' impact on the extrapyramidal areas of the brain, areas that help control motor activity. These undesired effects include *Parkinsonian and related symptoms, neuroleptic malignant syndrome,* and *tardive dyskinesia.*

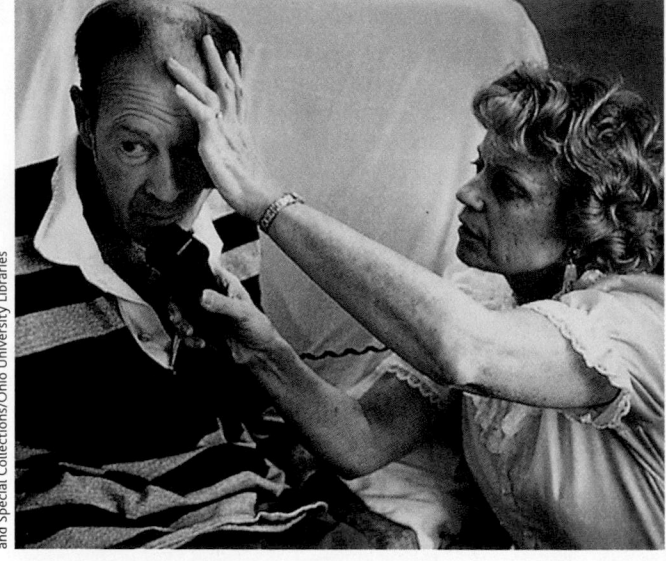

Lynn Johnson Collection/Mahn Center for Archives and Special Collections/Ohio University Libraries

Unwanted effects This man has a severe case of Parkinson's disease, a disorder caused by low dopamine activity, and his muscle tremors prevent him from shaving himself. Antipsychotic drugs, particularly the first-generation drugs, often produce similar Parkinsonian symptoms.

Parkinsonian and Related Symptoms The most common extrapyramidal effects are *Parkinsonian symptoms,* reactions that closely resemble the features of the neurological disorder Parkinson's disease. At least half of patients on conventional antipsychotic drugs have muscle tremors and muscle rigidity at some point in their treatment; they may shake, move slowly, shuffle their feet, and show little facial expression (Marder & Stroup, 2016). Some also have related symptoms such as movements of the face, neck, tongue, and back; and a number experience significant restlessness and discomfort in their limbs, which causes them to move their arms and legs continually in search of relief.

The Parkinsonian and related symptoms seem to be the result of medication-induced reductions of dopamine activity in the *striatum,* the brain structure that coordinates movement and posture, among other functions (Tarsy, 2016). In most cases, the symptoms can be reversed if the person takes an anti-Parkinsonian drug along with the antipsychotic drug (Marder & Stroup, 2016). Alternatively, clinicians may have to reduce the dose of the antipsychotic drug or stop it altogether.

Neuroleptic Malignant Syndrome In as many as 1 percent of patients, particularly those who are elderly, first-generation antipsychotic drugs produce *neuroleptic malignant syndrome,* a severe, potentially fatal reaction consisting of muscle rigidity, fever, altered consciousness, and improper functioning of the autonomic nervous system (Lavonas, 2016). If a person is identified as having the syndrome, he or she is immediately taken off the drug and each neuroleptic symptom is treated medically. In addition, the patient may be given dopamine-enhancing drugs.

Tardive Dyskinesia Whereas most undesired drug effects appear within days or weeks, a reaction called **tardive dyskinesia** (meaning "late-appearing movement disorder") does not usually unfold until after a person has taken first-generation antipsychotic drugs for more than six months (Tarsy, 2016). Sometimes it does not even appear until after the medications are stopped. This syndrome may include involuntary writhing or ticlike movements of the tongue, mouth, face, or whole body; involuntary chewing, sucking, and lip smacking; and jerky movements of the arms, legs, or entire body.

Most cases of tardive dyskinesia are mild and involve a single symptom, such as tongue flicking; however, some are severe and include such features as continual rocking back and forth, irregular breathing, and grotesque twisting of the face and body. It is believed that more than 15 percent of the people who take first-generation antipsychotic drugs, especially the most powerful ones, for an extended time develop tardive dyskinesia to some degree, and the longer the drugs are taken, the higher the risk becomes (Tarsy, 2016; Achalia et al., 2014). Patients over 50 years of age are at greater risk—perhaps 3 to 5 times the risk of younger patients.

Tardive dyskinesia can be difficult, sometimes impossible, to eliminate (Tarsy, 2016; Combs et al., 2008). If it is discovered early and the first-generation drugs are stopped immediately, it eventually disappears in as many as 90 percent of cases. Early detection, however, is elusive because some of the symptoms are similar to psychotic symptoms. Clinicians may easily overlook them, continue to administer the drugs, and unintentionally create a more serious case of tardive dyskinesia. If detection is late, the symptoms of tardive dyskinesia disappear in fewer than 40 percent of cases (Tarsy, 2016). Researchers do not fully understand why first-generation antipsychotic drugs cause tardive dyskinesia; however, they suspect that, once again, the problem is related to the drugs' effect on dopamine receptors in the striatum, particularly the D-2 receptors (Tarsy, 2016).

How Should First-Generation Antipsychotic Drugs Be Prescribed? Today clinicians are more knowledgeable and more cautious about prescribing first-generation antipsychotic drugs than they were in the past (Stroup & Marder, 2017) (see **Table 15-1**). Previously, when patients did not improve with such a drug, their clinician would keep increasing the dose; today a clinician will typically add an additional drug to achieve a synergistic effect (called *polypharmacy*), stop the drug and try an alternative one, or stop all medications (Stroup & Marder, 2017; Roh et al., 2014). Today's clinicians also try to prescribe the lowest effective doses for each patient and to gradually reduce medications weeks or months after the patient begins functioning normally. Research indicates that, for many such patients, reductions of this kind do not lead to a return of symptoms. For others, however, only small reductions in dosage are possible, and treatment for these patients typically involves the long-term use of carefully monitored high dosages of antipsychotic drugs (Stroup & Marder, 2017; Deutschenbaur et al., 2014).

Second-Generation Antipsychotic Drugs

Chapter 14 noted that *second-generation* ("atypical") antipsychotic drugs have been developed. The most widely used of these newer drugs are *clozapine* (trade name Clozaril), *risperidone* (Risperdal), *olanzapine* (Zyprexa), *quetiapine* (Seroquel), *ziprasidone* (Geodon), and *aripiprazole* (Abilify). As you have read, the drugs were called *atypical* initially because their biological operation differs from that of the first-generation antipsychotic medications: the second-generation drugs are received at fewer dopamine D-2 receptors and more D-1, D-4, and serotonin receptors than the others (Tarsy, 2016; Nord & Farde, 2011).

Second-generation antipsychotic drugs appear to be at least as effective, and often more effective, than the first-generation drugs (Jibson, 2017; Stroup & Marder, 2017). Clozapine is often the most effective such drug, but the other second-generation drugs also bring significant change for many people. Recall, for example, Cathy, the woman whom we met at the beginning of this chapter, and how well she responded to risperidone after years of doing poorly on first-generation antipsychotic drugs. Unlike the first-generation drugs, the newer drugs reduce not only the positive symptoms of schizophrenia, but—to a small degree—the negative ones as well (Millan et al., 2014; Waddington et al., 2011). Another major benefit of the second-generation antipsychotics is that they cause fewer extrapyramidal symptoms and seem less likely to produce tardive dyskinesia (Jibson, 2017; Tarsy, 2016) (see **Figure 15-1**). Approximately 5 percent of patients who take second-generation antipsychotics for an extended time

> Why did psychiatrists in the past keep administering high dosages of antipsychotic drugs to patients who had adverse effects from the medications?

TABLE: 15-1

Some Antipsychotic Drugs

Generic Name	Trade Name
First-generation antipsychotics	
Chlorpromazine	*Thorazine*
Trifluoperazine	*Stelazine*
Fluphenazine	*Prolixin*
Perphenazine	*Trilafon*
Acetophenazine	*Tindal*
Chlorprothixene	*Taractan*
Thiothixene	*Navane*
Haloperidol	*Haldol*
Loxapine	*Loxitane*
Pimozide	*Orap*
Second-generation antipsychotics	
Risperidone	*Risperdal*
Clozapine	*Clozaril*
Olanzapine	*Zyprexa*
Quetiapine	*Seroquel*
Ziprasidone	*Geodon*
Aripiprazole	*Abilify*
Iloperidone	*Fanapt*
Lurasidone	*Latuda*
Paliperidone	*Invega*
Asenapine	*Saphris*

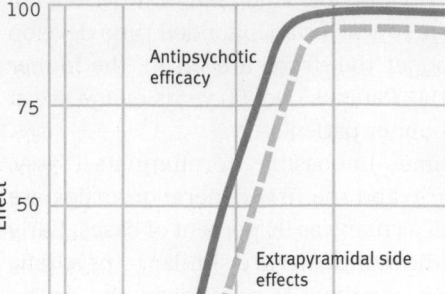

FIGURE 15-1

The Side Effect Advantage

First-generation antipsychotic drugs are much more likely than second-generation drugs to produce undesired extrapyramidal symptoms. (A) The dose-response curve for first-generation antipsychotics shows that, beginning with low doses of the drugs, extrapyramidal side effects emerge and keep intensifying right along with increases in the drug doses. (B) In contrast, the dose-response curve for second-generation antipsychotics indicates that extrapyramidal side effects typically do not even appear until a patient is taking relatively high doses of the drugs. (Information from Casey, 1995, p. 107.)

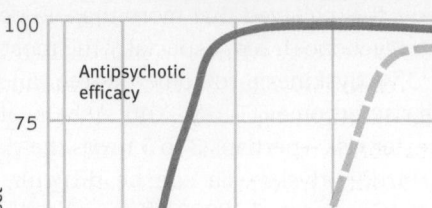

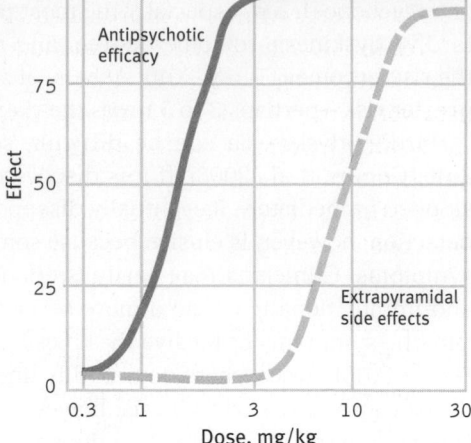

develop tardive dyskinesia (in contrast to 15 percent of those on the first-generation drugs). This lower rate may be because the second-generation drugs are less likely to be received by D-2 receptors, the dopamine receptors that, as we just discussed, are particularly involved in the development of tardive dyskinesia (Tarsy, 2016). Clozapine is, by far, the least likely of the second-generation drugs to cause tardive dyskinesia (Jibson, 2017).

Given such advantages, more than half of all patients with schizophrenia who are medicated now take the second-generation drugs, which are considered the first line of treatment for the disorder (Jibson, 2017; Barnes & Marder, 2011). Many patients with bipolar or other severe mental disorders also seem to be helped by several of these antipsychotic drugs (Jibson, 2017). Studies indicate, for example, that olanzapine, prescribed alone or in combination with mood-stabilizing drugs, is very effective in cases of acute mania. Clinicians use the same general prescription strategies for the second-generation antipsychotic drugs as they do for the first-generation drugs (Stroup & Marder, 2017).

Yet the second-generation antipsychotic drugs have serious problems as well. For example, people who use one of these drugs, clozapine, have around a 1 to 1.5 percent risk of developing **agranulocytosis,** a life-threatening drop in white blood cells (other atypical antipsychotic drugs do not produce this undesired effect) (Coates, 2016). Patients who take clozapine must therefore have frequent blood tests so that agranulocytosis can be spotted early and the drug stopped (Freudenreich & McEvoy, 2017). In addition, some of the second-generation antipsychotic drugs may cause weight gain, particularly among women; dizziness; metabolic problems; sexual dysfunctions; cardiovascular changes; and significant elevations in blood sugar, as we also saw in the case of Cathy (Jibson, 2017; Marder & Stroup, 2016). Also, research indicates that although these medications do often reduce the symptoms of psychosis, they, like the first-generation antipsychotics, typically produce only modest changes in overall life satisfaction among those who have chronic schizophrenia (Fervaha et al., 2014).

Psychotherapy

BEFORE THE DISCOVERY OF antipsychotic drugs, psychotherapy was not really an option for people with schizophrenia. Most were too far removed from reality to profit from it. Only a handful of therapists, apparently blessed with extraordinary patience and skill, specialized in the psychotherapeutic treatment of this disorder and reported

agranulocytosis A life-threatening drop in white blood cells. This condition is sometimes produced by the second-generation antipsychotic drug *clozapine*.

a measure of success (Will, 1967, 1961; Sullivan, 1962, 1953; Fromm-Reichmann, 1950, 1948, 1943). These therapists believed that the first task of such therapy was to win the trust of patients with schizophrenia and build a close relationship with them.

Well-known clinical theorist and therapist Frieda Fromm-Reichmann, for example, would initially tell her patients that they could continue to exclude her from their private world and hold onto their disorder as long as they wished. She reported that eventually, after much testing and acting out, the patients would accept, trust, and grow attached to her and begin to talk to her about their problems. Case studies seemed to attest to the effectiveness of such approaches and to the importance of trust and emotional bonding in treatment. Here a recovered woman tells her therapist how she had felt during their early interactions:

> At the start, I didn't listen to what you said most of the time but I watched like a hawk for your expression and the sound of your voice. After the interview, I would add all this up to see if it seemed to show love. The words were nothing compared to the feelings you showed. I sense that you felt confident I could be helped and that there was hope for the future. . . .
>
> The problem with schizophrenics is that they can't trust anyone. They can't put their eggs in one basket. The doctor will usually have to fight to get in no matter how much the patient objects. . . .
>
> Loving is impossible at first because it turns you into a helpless little baby. The patient can't feel safe to do this until he is absolutely sure the doctor understands what is needed and will provide it.
>
> *(Hayward & Taylor, 1965)*

Today, psychotherapy is successful in many more cases of schizophrenia (Spaulding & Sullivan, 2016; Miller et al., 2012; Swartz et al., 2012). By helping to relieve thought and perceptual disturbances, antipsychotic drugs allow people with schizophrenia to learn about their disorder, participate actively in therapy (see *MindTech* on page 461), think more clearly about themselves and their relationships, make changes in their behavior, and cope with stressors in their lives. The most helpful forms of psychotherapy include cognitive-behavioral therapy and two sociocultural interventions—family therapy and social therapy. Often the various approaches are combined.

"Yes, you've mentioned this 'Facebook' in the past—tell me, is 'Facebook' saying anything right now?"

Sara Lautman The New Yorker Collection/The Cartoon Bank

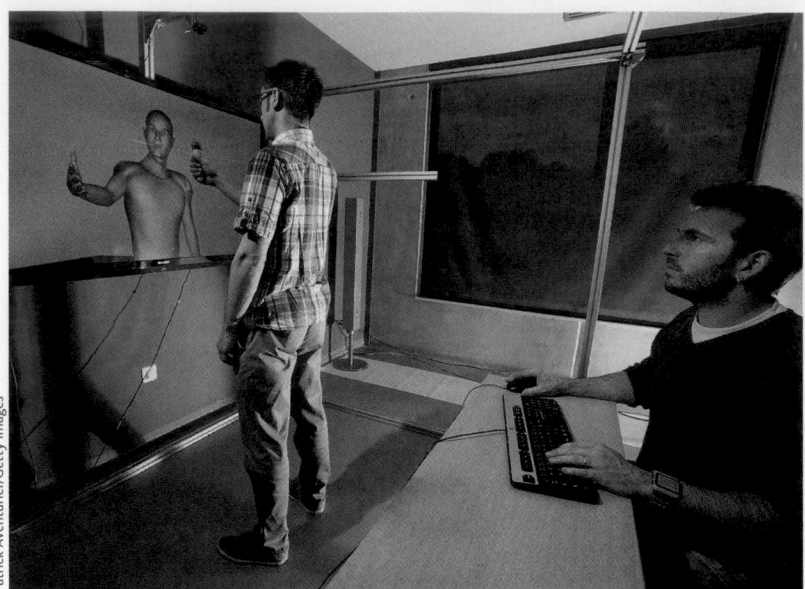

A therapist like myself The AlterEgo project at France's Hospital of Montpellier, uses computer-based technology to help people with schizophrenia. Based on the premise that people relate better with and learn more from individuals who resemble them, the program has clients interact with avatars similar to themselves. Here a client helps to program the avatar with whom he will be working by having his body and movements scanned.

Cognitive-Behavioral Therapies

Two kinds of cognitive-behavior therapy are now used for people with schizophrenia, (1) *cognitive remediation* and (2) *hallucination reinterpretation and acceptance*. Research indicates that both approaches are helpful, each in a different way (Bustillo & Weil, 2016).

Cognitive Remediation Cognitive remediation is an approach that focuses on the cognitive impairments that often characterize people with schizophrenia—particularly their difficulties in attention, planning, and memory (John et al., 2017; Vinogradov et al., 2012). Here clients are required to complete increasingly difficult information-processing tasks on a computer. They may start with a simple task such as responding as quickly as possible to various stimuli that are flashed on the screen—a task designed to improve their attention skills. Once they can perform this task with considerable speed, they move on to more complex computer tasks, such as tasks that challenge their short-term memory. As they master each computer task, they keep moving up the ladder until eventually reaching computer tasks that require planning and social awareness.

Studies indicate that, for many people with schizophrenia, cognitive remediation brings about moderate improvements in attention, planning, memory, and problem-solving—improvements that surpass those produced by other treatment interventions (Bustillo & Weil, 2016; Wykes et al., 2011). Moreover, these improvements extend to the client's everyday life and social relationships.

Hallucination Reinterpretation and Acceptance As you read in Chapter 14, the cognitive-behavioral explanation for schizophrenia starts with the premise that people with the disorder do indeed actually hear voices (or experience other kinds of hallucinations) as a result of biologically triggered sensations. According to this theory, the journey into schizophrenia takes shape when people try to make sense of these strange sensations and conclude incorrectly that the voices are coming from external sources, that they are being persecuted, or another such notion. These misinterpretations are essentially delusions.

With this explanation in mind, many clinicians now employ a cognitive-behavioral treatment for schizophrenia that is designed to help change how people view and react to their hallucinations (Bustillo & Weil, 2016; Howes & Murray, 2014). The therapists believe that if people can be guided to interpret such experiences in a more accurate way, they will not suffer the fear and confusion produced by their delusional misinterpretations. Thus, the therapists use a combination of behavioral and cognitive techniques:

1. They provide clients with education and evidence about the biological causes of hallucinations.

2. They help clients learn more about the "comings and goings" of their own hallucinations and delusions. The clients learn, for example, to identify which kinds of events and situations trigger the voices in their heads.

3. The therapists challenge their clients' inaccurate ideas about the power of their hallucinations, such as the idea that the voices are all-powerful and uncontrollable and must be obeyed. The therapists also have the clients conduct behavioral experiments to put such notions to the test. What happens, for example, if the clients occasionally resist following the orders from their hallucinatory voices?

cognitive remediation A treatment that focuses on the cognitive impairments that often characterize people with schizophrenia—particularly their difficulties in attention, planning, and memory.

MINDTECH

Putting a Face on Auditory Hallucinations

 In Chapter 3, you read that a growing number of therapists are using *avatar therapy* to help clients overcome their psychological problems. In this form of virtual reality therapy, clinicians have the clients interact with computer-generated on-screen virtual human figures. Perhaps the boldest application of avatar therapy is its use with people suffering from schizophrenia. Clinical researcher Julian Leff and several colleagues have developed an approach that seems to offer particular promise for such individuals (Craig, Ward, & Rus-Callafel, 2016; Leff et al., 2014; 2013).

For a pilot study, the researchers selected 16 participants who were being tormented by imaginary voices (auditory hallucinations). In each case, the therapist presented the individual with a mean-sounding and mean-looking avatar. The avatar's voice pitch and appearance were designed based on the patient's description of what he or she was hearing and what the patient believed would be a corresponding face.

The patient was placed alone in a room with the computer simulation while the therapist generated the on-screen avatar from another room. Initially, the avatar spewed all sorts of frightening and upsetting statements at the patient. Then, the therapist encouraged the patient to fight back—to tell the avatar things such as "I will not put up with this, what you are saying is nonsense, I don't believe these things, you must go

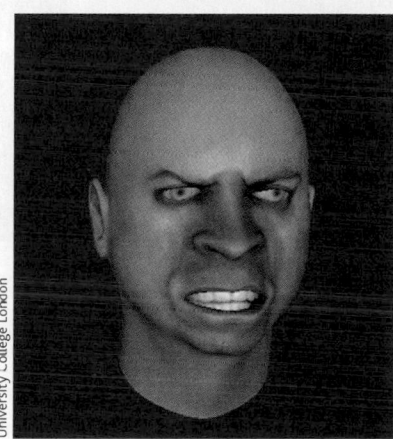

University College London

Voices spring to virtual life This is one of the sinister-looking avatars developed by clinical researcher Julian Leff and his colleagues in their treatment for people with schizophrenia.

away and leave me alone, and I do not need this kind of torment" (Rus-Calafell et al., 2015; Kedmey, 2013; Leff et al., 2014, 2013).

> Can you think of any negative effects—short-term or long-term—that might result from putting a face on auditory hallucinations?

After seven 30-minute sessions, most of the participants in the pilot study had less frequent and less intense auditory hallucinations and reported being less upset by the voices they did continue to hear. The participants also reported improvements in their feelings of depression and suicidal thinking. Three of the 16 actually reported a total cessation of their auditory hallucinations after the sessions. These promising results have now been followed up by larger studies with more participants – each producing similar findings (Craig et al., 2016). The collective results of these studies suggest that confronting one's hallucinations in a virtual world can indeed help at least some people with schizophrenia.

4. The therapists teach clients to reattribute and more accurately interpret their hallucinations. Clients may, for example, adopt and apply alternative conclusions such as "It's not a real voice, it's my illness."

5. The therapists teach clients techniques for coping with their unpleasant sensations (hallucinations). The clients may, for example, learn ways to reduce the physical arousal that accompanies hallucinations—using special breathing and relaxation techniques, positive self-statements, and the like. Similarly, they may learn to refocus or distract themselves whenever the hallucinations occur. In one reported case, a therapist repeatedly walked behind his schizophrenic client and made harsh and critical statements, seeking to simulate the clients' auditory hallucinations and then guiding him to focus his attention past the voices and on to the task at hand (Veiga-Martínez et al., 2008).

These cognitive-behavioral techniques often help people with schizophrenia feel more control over their hallucinations and reduce their delusional ideas (Bustillo & Weil, 2016). But they do not eliminate the hallucinations. They simply render the hallucinations less powerful and less destructive. Can anything be done further to lessen the hallucinations' unpleasant impact on the person? Yes, say *new-wave cognitive-behavioral therapists,* including practitioners of *acceptance and commitment therapy.*

As you read in Chapters 3 and 5, new-wave cognitive-behavioral therapists believe that the most useful goal of treatment is often to help clients *accept* their streams

#TreatmentDelay

The average length of time between the first appearance of psychotic symptoms and the initiation of treatment is two years. (Brunet & Birchwood, 2010)

AP Photo/Paul Sakuma

Art that heals Art and other creative activities can be therapeutic for people with severe mental disorders. Here, artist William Scott paints a San Francisco cityscape at the Creative Growth Art Center in California. Scott, who has been diagnosed with schizophrenia and autism, has sold paintings and sculptures around the world.

#

#TheirWords

"What's so great about reality?"
                Person with schizophrenia, 1988

of problematic thoughts rather than to judge them, act on them, or try fruitlessly to change them (Davison et al., 2016; Hayes, 2016). The therapists, for example, help highly anxious individuals to become simply *mindful* of the worries that engulf their thinking and to *accept* such negative thoughts as harmless events of the mind (see page 122). Similarly, in cases of schizophrenia, new-wave cognitive-behavioral therapists try to help clients become detached and comfortable observers of their hallucinations—merely mindful of the unusual sensations and accepting of them—while otherwise moving forward with the tasks and events of their lives (Gaudiano et al., 2017; Bacon et al., 2014).

Studies indicate that these various cognitive-behavioral treatments are often very helpful to clients with schizophrenia (Bustillo & Weil, 2016; Morrison et al., 2014). Many clients who receive such treatments report that they feel less distressed by their hallucinations and that they have fewer delusions. Indeed, they are often able to shed the diagnosis of schizophrenia. Rehospitalizations decrease by 50 percent among clients treated with cognitive-behavioral therapy.

The cognitive-behavioral view that hallucinations should be accepted (rather than misinterpreted or overreacted to) is compatible with a notion already held by some people who hallucinate. There are a number of self-help groups comprised of people with auditory hallucinations whose guiding principles are that hallucinations themselves are harmless and valid experiences and that those who have auditory hallucinations often do best if they simply can accept and learn to live with them.

Family Therapy

Many persons who are recovering from schizophrenia and other severe mental disorders live with their families: parents, siblings, spouses, or children. Such situations create special pressures; even if family stress was not a factor in the onset of the disorder, a patient's recovery may be strongly influenced by the behavior and reactions of his or her relatives at home (Bustillo & Weil, 2016; Macleod et al., 2011).

Generally speaking, people with schizophrenia who feel positive toward their relatives do better in treatment (Okpokoro et al., 2014). As you saw in Chapter 14, recovered patients living with relatives who display high levels of *expressed emotion*—that is, relatives who are very critical, emotionally overinvolved, and hostile—often have a much higher relapse rate than those living with more positive and supportive relatives.

Moreover, for their part, family members may be very upset by the social withdrawal and unusual behaviors of a relative with schizophrenia (Friedrich et al., 2014; Quah, 2014).

To address such issues, clinicians now commonly include family therapy in their treatment of schizophrenia, providing family members with guidance, training, practical advice, psychoeducation about the disorder, and emotional support and empathy (Bustillo & Weil, 2016; Burbach, Fadden, & Smith, 2010). In family therapy, relatives develop more realistic expectations and become more tolerant, less guilt-ridden, and more willing to try new patterns of communication. Family therapy also helps the person with schizophrenia cope with the pressures of family life, make better use of family members, and avoid troublesome interactions.

Research has found that family therapy—particularly when it is combined with drug therapy—helps reduce tensions within the family and so helps relapse rates and hospital readmissions go down (Bustillo & Weil, 2016; Giron et al., 2015; Okpokoro et al., 2014). The principles of this approach are evident in the following description:

Robert Gauthier/Los Angeles Times via Getty Images

Engaging the family Research indicates that people with schizophrenia make more progress in treatment when they feel positive toward their family. Thus, family involvement, including family therapy, is now often a significant part of treatment. Here a loving mother, Maria Orduna, caresses her son Alfredo during his visit to her apartment. Alfredo has suffered through homelessness, poverty, and jail, largely because of his schizophrenic disorder.

Mark was a 32-year-old single man living with his parents. He had a long and stormy history of schizophrenia with many episodes of psychosis, interspersed with occasional brief periods of good functioning. Mark's father was a bright but neurotically tormented man gripped by obsessions and inhibitions. Mark's mother appeared weary, detached, and embittered. Both parents felt hopeless about Mark's chances of recovery and resentful that needing to care for him would always plague their lives. They acted as if they were being intentionally punished. It gradually emerged that the father, in fact, was riddled with guilt and self-doubt; he suspected that his wife had been cold and rejecting toward Mark as an infant and that he had failed to intervene, due to his unwillingness to confront his wife and the demands of graduate school that distanced him from home life. He entertained the fantasy that Mark's illness was a punishment for this. Every time Mark did begin to show improvement—both in reduced symptoms and in increased functioning—his parents responded as if it were just a cruel torment designed to raise their hopes and then to plunge them into deeper despair when Mark's condition deteriorated. This pattern was especially apparent when Mark got a job. As a result, at such times, the parents actually became more critical and hostile toward Mark. He would become increasingly defensive and insecure, finally developing paranoid delusions, and usually would be hospitalized in a panicky and agitated state.

All of this became apparent during the psychoeducational sessions. When the pattern was pointed out to the family, they were able to recognize their self-fulfilling prophecy and were motivated to deal with it. As a result, the therapist decided to see the family together. Concrete instances of the pattern and its consequences were explored, and alternative responses by the parents were developed. The therapist encouraged both the parents and Mark to discuss their anxieties and doubts about Mark's progress, rather than to stir up one another's expectations of failure. The therapist had regular individual sessions with Mark as well as the family sessions. As a result, Mark has successfully held a job for an unprecedented 12 months.

(Heinrichs & Carpenter, 1983, pp. 284–285)

The families of people with schizophrenia and other severe mental disorders may also turn to *family support groups* and *family psychoeducational programs* for encouragement and advice (Bademli & Duman, 2016; Fallahi Khoshknab et al., 2014). In such programs, family members meet with others in the same situation to share their thoughts and emotions, provide mutual support, and learn about schizophrenia. Although research has yet to fully determine the usefulness of these groups, the approach has become popular.

#TheirWords

"Her face was a solemn mask, and she could neither give nor receive affection."

Mother, 1991, describing her daughter who has schizophrenia

deinstitutionalization The discharge of large numbers of patients from long-term institutional care so that they might be treated in community programs.

community mental health center A treatment facility that provides medication, psychotherapy, and emergency care for psychological problems and coordinates treatment in the community.

aftercare A program of posthospitalization care and treatment in the community.

day center A program that offers hospital-like treatment during the day only. Also known as a *day hospital*.

Social Therapy

Many clinicians believe that the treatment of people with schizophrenia should include techniques that address social and personal difficulties in the clients' lives. These clinicians offer practical advice; work with clients on problem solving, memory enhancement, decision making, and social skills; make sure that the clients are taking their medications properly; and may even help them find work, financial assistance, appropriate health care, and proper housing (Granholm et al., 2014).

Research finds that this practical, active, and broad approach, called *social therapy* or *personal therapy,* does indeed help keep people out of the hospital (Bustillo & Weil, 2017, 2016; Haddock & Spaulding, 2011). One study compared the progress of four groups of patients with chronic schizophrenia after their discharge from a state hospital (Hogarty et al., 2006, 1986, 1974). One group received both antipsychotic medications and social therapy in the community, while the other groups received medication only, social therapy only, or no treatment of any kind. The researchers' first finding was that chronic patients need to continue taking medication after being released in order to avoid rehospitalization. Over a two-year period, 80 percent of those who did not continue medication needed to be hospitalized again, compared with 48 percent of those who received medication. They also found that among the patients on medication, those who also received social therapy adjusted to the community and avoided rehospitalization most successfully. Other studies tell a similar story (Bustillo & Weil, 2017, 2016; Razali & Yusoff, 2014). Clearly, social therapy played an important role in their recovery.

||||||||||||||||||||||||||||||||||||||||||||||||||||||||||||||||||||||||||||||

The Community Approach

THE BROADEST APPROACH FOR THE TREATMENT of schizophrenia and other severe mental disorders is the *community approach*. In 1963, partly in response to the terrible conditions in public mental institutions and partly because of the emergence of antipsychotic drugs, the U.S. government ordered that patients be released and treated in the community. Congress passed the *Community Mental Health Act,* which stipulated that patients with psychological disorders were to receive a range of mental health services—outpatient therapy, inpatient treatment, emergency care, preventive care, and aftercare—in their communities rather than being transported to institutions far from home. The act was aimed at a variety of psychological disorders, but patients diagnosed with schizophrenia and other severe disorders, especially those who had been institutionalized for years, were affected most. Other countries around the world put similar sociocultural treatment programs into action shortly thereafter (Wiley-Exley, 2007).

Thus began several decades of **deinstitutionalization,** an exodus of hundreds of thousands of patients with schizophrenia and other long-term mental disorders from state institutions into the community. On a given day in 1955, close to 600,000 patients were living in state institutions; today 42,000 patients live in such facilities (Smith & Milazzo-Sayre, 2014). Clinicians have learned that patients recovering from schizophrenia and other severe disorders can profit greatly from community programs (Bustillo & Weil, 2017, 2016). As you will see, however, the actual quality of community care for these people has often been inadequate throughout the United States. The result is a

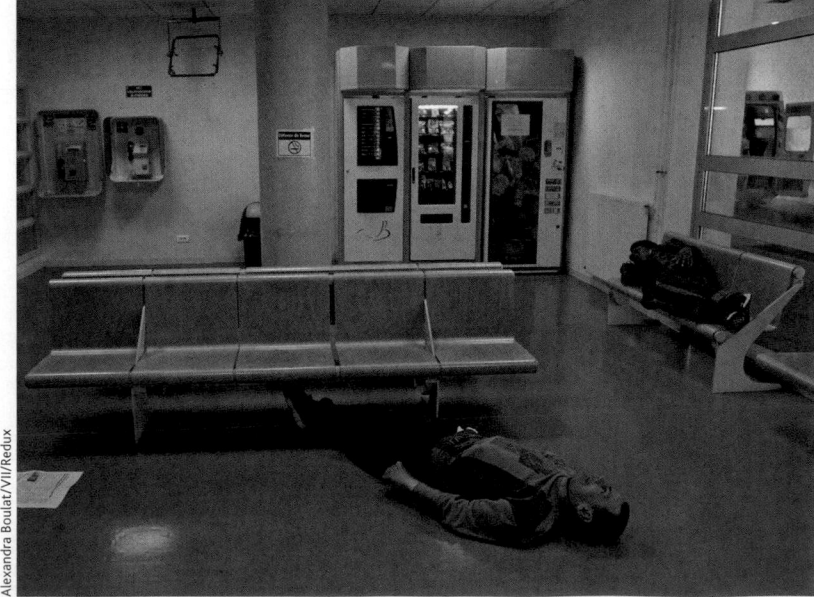

A long way to go A man with schizophrenia lies on the floor of the emergency room waiting area at Delafontaine Hospital near Paris, France. The plight of this patient is a reminder that, despite the development of various effective interventions, the overall treatment picture for many people with severe mental disorders leaves much to be desired.

Alexandra Boulat/VII/Redux

"revolving door" pattern for many patients. They are released to the community, re-admitted to an institution within months, released a second time, admitted yet again, and so on, over and over (Chi et al., 2016; Duhig et al., 2015; Burns & Drake, 2011).

> How might the "revolving door" pattern itself worsen the symptoms and outlook of people with schizophrenia?

What Are the Features of Effective Community Care?

People recovering from schizophrenia and other severe disorders need medication, psychotherapy, help in handling daily pressures and responsibilities, guidance in making decisions, social skills training, residential supervision, and vocational coun-seling—a combination of services called *assertive community treatment* (Bustillo & Weil, 2017, 2016; Gaudiano et al., 2017; Keller et al., 2014). Those whose communities help them meet these needs make more progress than those living in other commu-nities (Malm et al., 2014; Swartz et al., 2012). Some of the key features of effective community care programs are (1) coordination of patient services, (2) short-term hos-pitalization, (3) partial hospitalization, (4) supervised residencies, and (5) occupational training.

Coordinated Services When the Community Mental Health Act was first passed, it was expected that community care would be provided by **community mental health centers,** treatment facilities that would supply medication, psychotherapy, and inpa-tient emergency care to people with severe disturbances, as well as coordinate the services offered by other community agencies. When community mental health cen-ters are available and do provide these services, patients with schizophrenia and other severe disorders often make significant progress (Bustillo & Weil, 2017, 2016; Burns & Drake, 2011). Coordination of services is particularly important for so-called *mentally ill chemical abusers* (*MICAs*), patients with psychotic disorders as well as substance use disorders (Campbell et al., 2016; Drake et al., 2015).

Short-Term Hospitalization When people develop severe psychotic symptoms, today's clinicians first try to treat them on an outpatient basis, usually with a combi-nation of antipsychotic medication and psychotherapy. If this approach fails, they may try *short-term hospitalization* –in a mental hospital or a general hospital's psychiatric unit—that lasts a few weeks (rather than months or years) (Gaudiano et al., 2017; Craig & Power, 2010). Soon after the patients improve, they are released for **aftercare,** a general term for follow-up care and treatment in the community. Because short-term hospitalization usually leads to more improvement and a lower rehospitalization rate than extended institutionalization (Soliman et al., 2008), countries throughout the world now favor it over long-term institutionalization.

Partial Hospitalization People's needs may fall between full hospitalization and outpatient therapy, and so some com-munities offer **day centers,** or **day hospitals,** all-day pro-grams in which patients return to their homes for the night. Such programs actually originated in Moscow in 1933, when a shortage of hospital beds necessitated the premature release of many patients. Today's day centers provide patients with daily supervised activities, therapy, and programs to improve social skills. People recovering from severe disorders in day centers often do better and have fewer relapses than those who spend extended periods in a hospital or in traditional outpatient ther-apy (Bustillo & Weil, 2017, 2016; Bales et al., 2014).

Another kind of institution that has become a popular set-ting for the treatment of people with schizophrenia and other

They met at a day center Sunday and Sam Duncan pose for a portrait at their home in La Junta, Colorado. The married couple, both of whom have suffered from schizophrenia, met in a day center at Southeast Mental Health Services and, according to them, fell in love at first sight. The day center has received national awards for its innovative approach to schizophrenia.

Craig F. Walker/The Denver Post via Getty Images

AP Photo/M. Spencer Green

A place to call home This man, recovering from schizophrenia and bipolar disorder, joyfully assumes a yoga pose in the living room of his new Chicago apartment. He found the residence with the help of a program called Direct Connect, which has helped many such people move into their own apartments.

severe disorders is the *semihospital,* or *residential crisis center.* These are houses or other structures in the community that provide 24-hour nursing care for people with severe mental disorders. Many individuals who would otherwise be cared for in state hospitals are now being transferred to these semihospitals (Zarzar et al., 2018; Soliman et al., 2008).

Supervised Residences Many people do not require hospitalization but are unable to live alone or with their families. **Halfway houses,** also known as *crisis houses* or *group homes,* often serve individuals well (MHA, 2017; Lindenmayer & Khan, 2012; Levy et al., 2005). Such residences may shelter between one and two dozen people. The live-in staff usually are *paraprofessionals*—lay people who receive training and ongoing supervision from outside mental health professionals. The houses are usually run with a *milieu therapy* philosophy that emphasizes mutual support, resident responsibility, and self-government. Research indicates that halfway houses help many people recovering from schizophrenia and other severe disorders adjust to community life and avoid rehospitalization (MHA, 2017; Hansson et al., 2002). Here is how one woman described living in a halfway house after 10 hospitalizations in 12 years:

The halfway house changed my life. First of all, I discovered that some of the staff members had once been clients in the program! That one single fact offered me hope. For the first time, I saw proof that a program could help someone, that it was possible to regain control over one's life and become independent. The house was democratically run; all residents had one vote and the staff members, outnumbered 5 to 22, could not make rules or even discharge a client from the program without majority sentiment. There was a house bill of rights that was strictly observed by all. We helped one another and gave support. When residents were in a crisis, no staff member hustled them off or increased their medication to calm them down. Residents could cry, be comforted and hugged until a solution could be found, or until they accepted that it was okay to feel bad. Even anger was an acceptable feeling that did not have to be feared, but could be expressed and turned into constructive energy. If you disliked some aspect of the program or the behavior of a staff member, you could change things rather than passively accept what was happening. Choices were real, and failure and success were accepted equally. . . . Bit by bit, my distrust faltered and the fears lessened. I slept better and made friends. . . . Other residents and staff members who had hallucinated for years and now were able to control their hallucinations shared with me some of the techniques that had worked for them. Things like diet . . . and interpersonal relationships became a few of my tools.

(Lovejoy, 1982, pp. 605–609)

halfway house A residence for people with schizophrenia or other severe problems, often staffed by paraprofessionals. Also known as a *group home* or *crisis house.*

sheltered workshop A supervised workplace for people who are not yet ready for competitive jobs.

case manager A community therapist who offers and coordinates a full range of services for people with schizophrenia or other severe disorders, including therapy, advice, medication, guidance, and protection of patients' rights.

Occupational Training and Support Paid employment provides income, independence, self-respect, and the stimulation of working with others. It also brings companionship and order to one's daily life. For these reasons, occupational training and placement are important services for people with schizophrenia and other severe mental disorders (Bustillo & Weil, 2017, 2016; Johnson et al., 2014).

Many people recovering from such disorders receive occupational training in a **sheltered workshop**—a supervised workplace for employees who are not ready for competitive or complicated jobs. The workshop replicates a typical work environment: products such as toys or simple appliances are manufactured and sold, workers are paid according to performance and are expected to be at work regularly and on time. For some, the sheltered workshop becomes a permanent workplace. For others, it is an important step toward better-paying and more demanding employment or a return to a previous job (Becker, 2008; Chalamat et al., 2005). In the United States, however, occupational training is not consistently available to people with severe mental disorders.

Everything counts Assertive community treatment programs seek to address *all* areas of need for people with severe mental disorders—from cognitive, emotional, and social functioning to the mastery of everyday skills. Here a community care staff member teaches a client how to use kitchen appliances and prepare his meals.

An alternative work opportunity for people with severe psychological disorders is *supported employment,* in which vocational agencies and counselors help clients find competitive jobs in the community and provide psychological support while the clients are employed (Bustillo & Weil, 2017, 2016; Solar, 2014). Like sheltered workshops, supported employment opportunities are often in short supply. Fewer than 20 percent of individuals with severe psychological disorders have jobs in the competitive job market (Bustillo & Weil, 2017, 2016).

How Has Community Treatment Failed?

There is no doubt that effective community programs can help people with schizophrenia and other severe mental disorders recover. However, fewer than half of all the people who need them receive appropriate community mental health services (Addington et al., 2015; Burns & Drake, 2011). In fact, in any given year, 40 to 60 percent of all people with schizophrenia and other severe mental disorders receive no treatment at all (NIMH, 2017; Torrey, 2001). Two factors are primarily responsible: *poor coordination* of services and a *shortage* of services.

Poor Coordination of Services The various mental health agencies in a community often fail to communicate with one another. There may be an opening at a nearby halfway house, for example, and the therapist at the community mental health center may not know about it. In addition, even within a community agency a patient may not have continuing contacts with the same staff members and may fail to receive consistent services. Still another problem is poor communication between state hospitals and community mental health centers, particularly at times of discharge (Bonsack et al., 2016; Torrey, 2001).

To help deal with such problems in communication and coordination, a growing number of community therapists have become **case managers** for people with schizophrenia and other severe mental disorders (Bustillo & Weil, 2017, 2016; Burns, 2010). They try to coordinate available community services, guide clients through the community system, and help protect clients' legal rights. Like the social therapists described earlier, they also offer therapy and advice, teach problem-solving and social skills, ensure that clients are taking their medications properly, and keep an eye on possible health care needs. Many professionals now believe that effective case management is the key to success for a community program.

#PrisonPopulation

There are more people with schizophrenia and other severe mental disorders in jails and prisons than there are in all hospitals and other treatment facilities.

Inmates in jails and prisons have rates of schizophrenia that are four times higher than that of the general public.

Chicago's Cook County Jail, where several thousand of the inmates require daily mental health services, is now in effect the largest mental institution in the United States.

(Binswanger & Elmore, 2016; Pruchno, 2014; Balassone, 2011; Morrissey & Cuddeback, 2008)

Changing the unacceptable A resident of a group home holds a sign during a rally in New York to protest the shortage of appropriate community residences for people with severe mental disorders. This shortage is one of the reasons that many such people have become homeless and/or imprisoned.

Shortage of Services The number of community programs—community mental health centers, halfway houses, sheltered workshops—available to people with severe mental disorders falls woefully short (NIMH, 2017; Zipursky, 2014; Burns & Drake, 2011). In addition, a number of the community mental health centers that do exist generally fail to provide adequate services for people with severe disorders. They tend to devote their efforts and money to people with less disabling problems, such as anxiety disorders or problems in social adjustment. Only a fraction of the patients treated by such community mental health centers suffer from schizophrenia or other disorders marked by psychosis (NIMH, 2017; Torrey, 2001).

There are various reasons for this shortage of services. Perhaps the primary one is economic. On the one hand, more public funds are available for people with psychological disorders now than in the past. In 1963 a total of $1 billion was spent in this area, whereas in 2017 approximately $152 billion in public funding was devoted each year to people with mental disorders (SAMHSA, 2017, 2014). This represents a significant increase even when inflation and so-called real dollars are factored in. On the other hand, rather little of the additional money is going to community treatment programs for people with severe disorders. Much of it goes instead to prescription drugs, monthly income payments such as social security disability income, services for people with mental disorders in nursing homes and general hospitals, and community services for people who are less disturbed (SAMHSA, 2017, 2014). Today, the financial burden of providing community treatment for people with long-term severe disorders often falls on local governments and nonprofit organizations rather than the federal or state government, and such local resources, which provided a total of $88 billion for mental health care in 2017, cannot always meet this challenge (SAMHSA, 2017, 2014; Feldman et al., 2014; Rampell, 2013).

What Are the Consequences of Inadequate Community Treatment? What happens to people with schizophrenia and other severe disorders whose communities do not provide the services they need and whose families cannot afford private treatment (see **Figure 15-2**)? As you have read, at least 40 percent receive no treatment at all; many others spend a short time in a state hospital or semihospital and are then discharged prematurely, often without adequate follow-up treatment (NIMH, 2017; Burns & Drake, 2011).

These individuals live in various settings (MIP, 2017; Torrey, 2014, 2001). Many return to their families and receive medication and perhaps emotional and financial support, but little else in the way of treatment. Around 8 percent enter an alternative institution such as a nursing home or rest home, where they receive only custodial care

AP Photo/Lynsey Addario

FIGURE 15-2

Where Do People with Schizophrenia Live?

More than one-third live in unsupervised residences, 6 percent are in jails, and 5 percent are homeless. (Information from Allison et al., 2017; MIP, 2017; Torrey, 2014, 2001; Kooyman & Walsh, 2011)

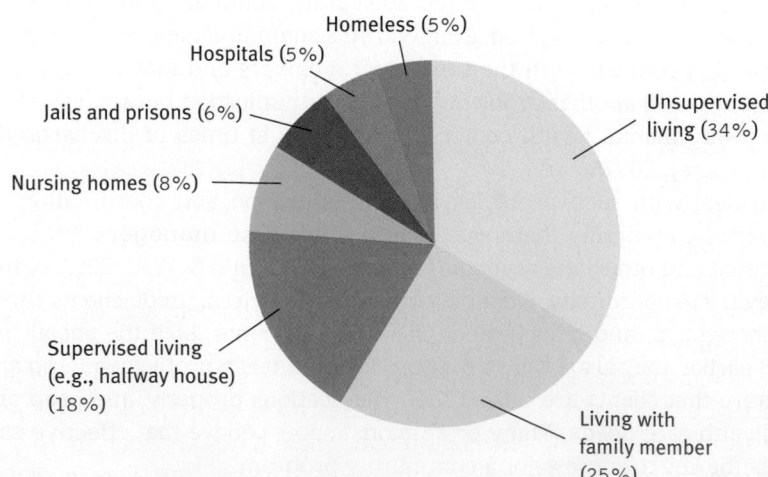

Homeless (5%)

Hospitals (5%)

Jails and prisons (6%)

Nursing homes (8%)

Supervised living (e.g., halfway house) (18%)

Unsupervised living (34%)

Living with family member (25%)

and medication. As many as 18 percent are placed in privately run residences where supervision often is provided by untrained staff—foster homes (small or large), boardinghouses, care homes, and similar facilities. These residences vary greatly in quality. Some of them are legitimate "bed and care" facilities, providing three meals a day, medication reminders, and at least a small degree of staff supervision. However, many do not offer even these minimal services.

Another 34 percent of people with schizophrenia and other severe disorders live in totally unsupervised settings. Some are equal to the challenge of living alone, supporting themselves effectively, and maintaining nicely furnished apartments. But others cannot really function independently and wind up in rundown single-room occupancy hotels (SROs) or rooming houses. They may live in conditions that are substandard and unsafe, which may exacerbate their disorder. Many survive on government disability payments, and a number spend their days wandering through neighborhood streets.

Community outreach Homeless people are more likely to develop schizophrenia, and having schizophrenia increases one's chances of becoming homeless. Thus, extraordinary University of Central Florida graduate student Briana Daniel founded and directs the Street Team Movement, a volunteer program that helps homeless people in Orlando address their clothing, laundry, hygiene, and mental health needs. The 25-year-old woman plans to eventually take the program nationwide.

Finally, a great number of people with schizophrenia and other severe disorders have become homeless. There are 565,000 homeless people in the United States, and approximately one-fourth of them—a total of 140,000 homeless people—have a severe mental disorder, commonly schizophrenia (MIP, 2017). Many have been released from hospitals. Others are young adults who were never hospitalized in the first place. Another 440,000 or more people with severe mental disorders are in prisons and jails, often because their disorders have led them to break the law (Allison, Bastiampillai, & Fuller, 2017). As many as 26 percent of all persons imprisoned in the United States suffer from schizophrenia or another severe mental disorder (Binswanger & Elmore, 2016). Certainly deinstitutionalization and the community mental health movement have failed these individuals, and many report actually feeling relieved if they are able to return to hospital life.

> **Why do so many people continue to perceive most people with schizophrenia as dangerous and violent, despite evidence to the contrary?**

The Promise of Community Treatment

Despite these very serious problems, proper community care has shown great potential for assisting people in recovering from schizophrenia and other severe disorders, and clinicians and many government officials continue to press to make it more available. Indeed, in one meta-analysis of 34 effective community programs across 21 states—programs that properly provide a combination of services (medication, psychotherapy, case management, integrated staffing and services, and assertive community treatment)— clients with schizophrenia were found to make more improvements in their quality of life, symptom reduction, and participation at work and school than did comparable clients in other kinds of treatment or in less-comprehensive community programs (Kane et al, 2016). Moreover, these well-run community programs managed to achieve their success with the limited funding and reimbursement mechanisms currently available.

In addition, a number of *national interest groups* have formed in countries around the world that push for better community treatment (Frese, 2008). In the United States, for example, the *National Alliance on Mental Illness (NAMI)* began in 1979 with 300 members and has expanded to 200,000 members in more than 1,000 chapters (NAMI,

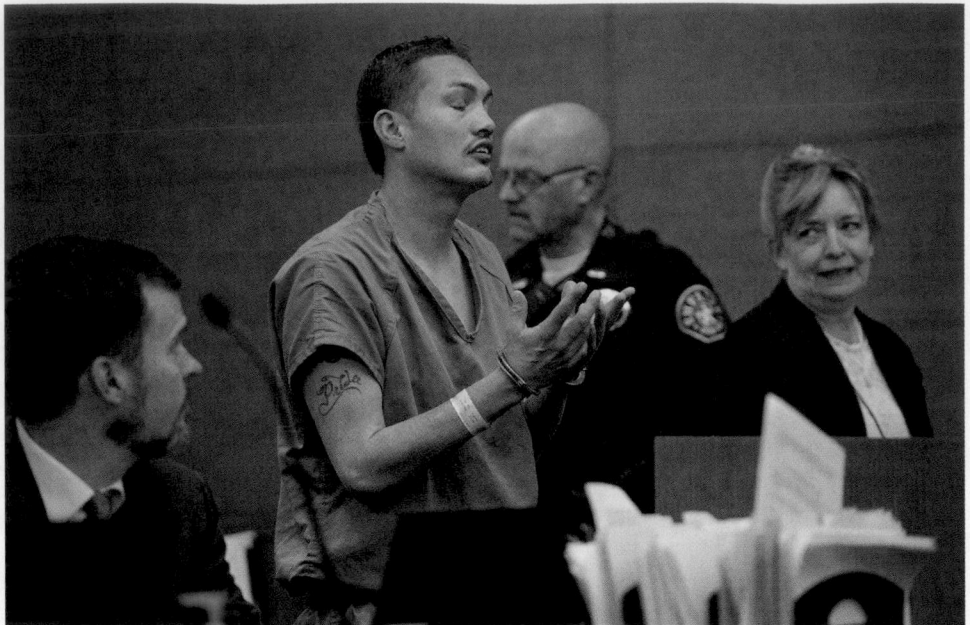

Craig F. Walker/Getty Images

"Court to Community" Denver, Colorado, has established a program called *Court to Community*, which diverts people with severe mental disorders—especially those who keep committing misdemeanor offenses—into court-monitored mental health programs rather than jails and prisons. Repeat criminal offenders, like this schizophrenic man who has been in jail more than 30 times, plead their cases to the program's judges, who determine whether the individuals are taking their medications, avoiding street drugs, and attending therapy sessions. Although life in the community is preferable to jail, it too is difficult. This man told the judge, "I feel like I'm in prison when I'm out there."

2014). Made up largely of families and people affected by severe mental disorders (particularly schizophrenia, bipolar disorders, and major depressive disorder), NAMI has become not only a source of information, support, and guidance for its members but also a powerful lobbying force in state and national legislatures; and it has pressured community mental health centers to treat more people with schizophrenia and other severe disorders.

Today, community care is a major feature of treatment for people recovering from severe mental disorders in countries around the world. Both in the United States and abroad, well-coordinated community treatment is seen as an important part of the solution to the problem of severe mental dysfunction (Bustillo & Weil, 2017, 2016).

An Important Lesson

AFTER YEARS OF FRUSTRATION and failure, clinicians now have an arsenal of weapons to use against schizophrenia and other disorders marked by psychosis—medication, institutional programs, psychotherapy, and community programs. It has become clear that antipsychotic medications open the door for recovery from these disorders, but in most cases other kinds of treatment are also needed to help the recovery process along. The various approaches must be combined in a way that meets each individual's specific needs.

Working with schizophrenia and other severe disorders has taught therapists an important lesson: no matter how compelling the evidence for biological causation may be, a strictly biological approach to the treatment of psychological disorders is a mistake more often than not. Largely on the basis of biological discoveries and pharmacological advances, hundreds of thousands of patients with schizophrenia and other severe mental disorders were released to their communities in the 1960s. Little attention was paid to their psychological and sociocultural needs, and many have been trapped in their pathology ever since. Clinicians must remember this lesson, especially in today's climate, when managed care and government priorities often promote medication as the sole treatment for psychological problems.

When the pioneering clinical researcher Emil Kraepelin described schizophrenia at the end of the nineteenth century, he estimated that only 13 percent of its victims

#EasyTargets

Adults with schizophrenia are at far greater risk of dying by homicide than other people.

In the United States, more than one-third of adults with schizophrenia are victims of violent crime.

In the United States, adults with schizophrenia are 14 times more likely to be victims of violent crime than to be arrested for committing such a crime.

(MIP, 2017; Kooyman & Walsh, 2011; Cuvelier, 2002; Hiroeh et al., 2001)

ever improved. Today, even with shortages in community care, many more people with schizophrenia—at least three times as many—show improvement. Certainly the clinical field has advanced considerably since Kraepelin's day, but it still has far to go. Studies suggest that the recovery rates—both partial and full—could be considerably higher. It is unacceptable that so many people with this and other severe mental disorders receive few or none of the effective community interventions that have been developed, worse still that tens of thousands have become homeless or imprisoned. It is now up to clinicians, along with public officials, to address the needs of all people with schizophrenia and other severe disorders.

?... SUMMING UP

» **Overview of Treatment** For years, all efforts to treat schizophrenia brought only frustration. Schizophrenia is still difficult to treat, but today's therapies are more successful than those of the past. *p. 448*

» **Past Institutional Care** For more than half of the twentieth century, the main treatment for schizophrenia and other severe mental disorders was *institutionalization* and *custodial care*. Because patients failed to respond to traditional therapies, they were usually placed in overcrowded public institutions (*state hospitals* in the United States), typically in *back wards* where the primary goal was to maintain and restrain them. Between 1845 and 1955 the number of state hospitals and mental patients rose steadily, while the quality of care declined. *pp. 448–451*

» **Improved Institutional Care** In the 1950s, two in-hospital approaches were developed, *milieu therapy* and *token economy programs*. They often brought improvement and particularly helped patients to care for themselves and feel better about themselves. *pp. 451–454*

» **Antipsychotic Drugs** The discovery of *antipsychotic drugs* in the 1950s revolutionized the treatment of schizophrenia and other disorders marked by psychosis. Today they are almost always a part of treatment. Theorists believe that the first generation of antipsychotic drugs operate by reducing excessive dopamine activity in the brain. These drugs reduce the positive symptoms of schizophrenia more completely, or more quickly, than they do the negative symptoms.

The *first-generation* antipsychotic drugs can also produce dramatic unwanted effects, particularly movement abnormalities called *extrapyramidal effects*, which include *Parkinsonian and related symptoms*, *neuroleptic malignant syndrome*, and *tardive dyskinesia*. Around 15 percent of the people who take first-generation antipsychotic drugs for an extended time develop *tardive dyskinesia*, a syndrome that can be difficult or impossible to eliminate if not detected early, even

when the drugs are stopped. More recently, *second-generation* antipsychotic drugs (such as clozapine, risperidone, and olanzapine) have been developed; these cause fewer extrapyramidal effects. *pp. 455–458*

» **Psychotherapy** *Psychotherapy* is often employed successfully in combination with antipsychotic drugs. Helpful forms include *cognitive-behavioral therapy*, *family therapy*, and *social therapy*. *Family support groups* and *family psychoeducational programs* are also growing in number. *pp. 458–464*

» **The Community Approach** A *community approach* to the treatment of schizophrenia and other severe mental disorders began in the 1960s, when a policy of *deinstitutionalization* in the United States brought about a mass exodus of hundreds of thousands of patients from state institutions into the community. Among the key elements of effective community care programs are coordination of patient services by a *community mental health center*, *short-term hospitalization* (followed by *aftercare*), *day centers*, *halfway houses*, *occupational training and support*, and *case management*.

Unfortunately, the quality and funding of community care for people with schizophrenia and other severe disorders have been inadequate throughout the United States, often resulting in a "revolving door" pattern. One consequence is that many people with such disorders are now homeless or in prison. Still others live in *nursing homes* or *rest homes* where they do not receive effective treatment, and many live in *boardinghouses* or *single-room-occupancy hotels*. *pp. 464–469*

» **The Promise of Community Treatment** The potential of proper community care to help people recovering from schizophrenia and other severe disorders continues to capture the interest of clinicians and policy makers. One major development has been the formation of *national interest groups* that are successfully promoting community treatment for people with these disorders. *pp. 469–470*

Visit *LaunchPad*
to access the e-Book, Clinical Choices, videos, activities, and LearningCurve, as well as study aids including flashcards, FAQs, and research exercises.

♀...Personality Disorders

> *While interviewing for the job of editor of a start-up news Web site, Frederick said, "This may sound self-serving, but I am extraordinarily gifted. I am certain that I will do great things in this position. I and the Osterman Post will soon set the standard for journalism and blogging in the country. Within a year, we'll be looking at the Huffington Post in the rearview mirror." The committee was impressed. Certainly, Frederick's credentials were strong, but even more important, his self-confidence and boldness had wowed them.*
>
> *A year later, many of the same individuals were describing Frederick differently—arrogant, self-serving, cold, ego-maniacal, draining. He had performed well as editor (though not as spectacularly as he seemed to think), but that performance could not outweigh his impossible personality. Colleagues below and above him had grown weary of his manipulations, his emotional outbursts, his refusal ever to take the blame, his non-stop boasting, and his grandiose plans. Once again Frederick had outworn his welcome.*
>
> *To be sure, Frederick had great charm, and he knew how to make others feel important, when it served his purpose. Thus he always had his share of friends and admirers. But in reality they were just passing through, until Frederick would tire of them or feel betrayed by their lack of enthusiasm for one of his self-serving interpretations or grand plans. Or until they simply could take Frederick no longer.*
>
> *Bright and successful though he was, Frederick always felt entitled to more than he was receiving—to higher grades at school, greater compensation at work, more attention from girlfriends. If criticized even slightly, he reacted with fury, and was certain that the critic was jealous of his superior intelligence, skill, or looks. At first glance, Frederick seemed to have a lot going for him socially. Typically, he could be found in the midst of a deep, meaningful romantic relationship—in which he might be tender, attentive, and seemingly devoted to his partner. But Frederick would always tire of his partner within a few weeks or months and would turn cold or even mean. Often he started affairs with other women while still involved with the current partner. The breakups—usually unpleasant and sometimes ugly—rarely brought sadness or remorse to him, and he would almost never think about his former partner again. He always had himself.*

Each of us has a *personality*—a set of uniquely expressed characteristics that influence our behaviors, emotions, thoughts, and interactions. Our particular characteristics, often called *personality traits,* lead us to react in fairly predictable ways as we move through life. Yet our personalities are also flexible. We learn from experience. As we interact with our surroundings, we try out various responses to see which feel better and which are more effective. This is a flexibility that people who suffer from a personality disorder usually do not have.

People with a **personality disorder** display an enduring, rigid pattern of inner experience and outward behavior that impairs their sense of self, emotional experiences, goals, capacity for empathy, and/or capacity for intimacy (APA, 2013) (see **Table 16-1**). Put another way, they have personality traits that are much more extreme and dysfunctional than those of most other people in their culture, leading to significant problems and psychological pain for themselves or others.

Frederick appears to display a personality disorder. For most of his life, his extreme narcissism, grandiosity, and insensitivity have led to poor functioning in both the personal and social realms. They have caused him to repeatedly feel angry and

TABLE: 16-1

Dx Checklist

Personality Disorder

1. Individual displays a long-term, rigid, and wide-ranging pattern of inner experience and behavior that leads to dysfunction in at least two of the following realms: • Cognition • Emotion • Social interactions • Impulsivity.

2. The individual's pattern is significantly different from ones usually found in his or her culture.

3. Individual experiences significant distress or impairment.

Information from: APA, 2013.

personality disorder An enduring, rigid pattern of inner experience and outward behavior that repeatedly impairs a person's sense of self, emotional experiences, goals, capacity for empathy, and/or capacity for intimacy.

paranoid personality disorder A personality disorder marked by a pattern of distrust and suspiciousness of others.

unappreciated, deprived him of close personal relationships, and brought considerable pain to others. Witness the upset and turmoil felt by Frederick's coworkers and girlfriends.

The symptoms of personality disorders last for years and typically become recognizable in adolescence or early adulthood, although some start during childhood (Skodol, 2016; APA, 2013). These disorders are among the most difficult psychological disorders to treat. Many people with the disorders are not even aware of their personality problems and fail to trace their difficulties to their maladaptive style of thinking and behaving. Surveys indicate that around 15 percent all adults in the United States display a personality disorder at some point in their lives (Skodol, 2016).

It is common for a person with a personality disorder to also suffer from another disorder, a relationship called *comorbidity*. As you will see later in this chapter, for example, many people with avoidant personality disorder, who fearfully shy away from all relationships, also display social anxiety disorder. Perhaps avoidant personality disorder predisposes people to develop social anxiety disorder. Or perhaps social anxiety disorder sets the stage for the personality disorder. Then again, some biological factor may create a predisposition to both the personality disorder and the anxiety disorder. Whatever the reason for the relationship, research indicates that the presence of a personality disorder complicates a person's chances for a successful recovery from other psychological problems (Caligor & Petrini, 2016; Fok et al., 2014).

DSM-5 identifies 10 personality disorders (APA, 2013). Often these disorders are separated into three groups, or *clusters*. One cluster, marked by odd or eccentric behavior, consists of the *paranoid, schizoid,* and *schizotypal* personality disorders. A second cluster features dramatic behavior and consists of the *antisocial, borderline, histrionic,* and *narcissistic* personality disorders. The final cluster features a high degree of anxiety and includes the *avoidant, dependent,* and *obsessive-compulsive* personality disorders.

These 10 personality disorders are each characterized by a group of problematic personality symptoms. For example, as you will soon see, *paranoid personality disorder* is diagnosed when a person has unjustified suspicions that others are harming him or her, has persistent unfounded doubts about the loyalty of friends, reads threatening meanings into benign events, persistently bears grudges, and has recurrent unjustified suspicions about the faithfulness of life partners.

The DSM's listing of 10 distinct personality disorders is called a *categorical* approach. Like a light switch that is either on or off, this kind of approach assumes that (1) problematic personality traits are either present or absent in people, (2) a personality disorder is either displayed or not displayed by a person, and (3) a person who suffers from a personality disorder is not markedly troubled by personality traits outside of that disorder.

It turns out, however, that these assumptions are frequently contradicted in clinical practice. In fact, the symptoms of the personality disorders listed in DSM-5 overlap so much that clinicians often find it difficult to distinguish one disorder from another, resulting in frequent disagreements about which diagnosis is correct for a person with a personality disorder. Diagnosticians sometimes even determine that particular people have more than one personality disorder (Black, 2016; Eaton et al., 2016). This lack of agreement has raised serious questions about the *validity* (accuracy) and *reliability* (consistency) of the 10 DSM-5 personality disorder categories.

Given this state of affairs, many theorists have challenged the use of a categorical approach to personality disorders. They believe that personality disorders differ more in *degree* than in type of dysfunction and should instead be classified by the severity of personality traits rather than by the presence or absence of specific traits—a procedure called a *dimensional* approach (Anderson et al., 2018, 2014). In a dimensional approach, each trait is seen as varying along a continuum extending from nonproblematic to extremely problematic. People with a personality disorder are those who display extreme degrees of problematic traits—degrees not commonly found in the general population.

Given the inadequacies of a categorical approach and the growing enthusiasm for a dimensional one, the framers of DSM-5 initially proposed significant changes in how personality disorders should be classified. They proposed a largely dimensional system that would allow many additional kinds of personality problems to be classified as personality disorders and would require clinicians to assess the severity of each problematic trait exhibited by a person who receives a diagnosis of personality disorder. However, this proposal itself produced enormous concern and criticism in the clinical field, leading the framers of DSM-5 to change their mind and to retain, for now, a classic 10-disorder categorical approach in the new DSM. At the same time, the framers acknowledged the likely future direction of personality disorder classifications by also describing an *alternative* dimensional approach.

Most of the discussions in this chapter are organized around the 10-disorder categorical approach currently used in DSM-5. Later in the chapter, however, we will examine possible alternative—dimensional—approaches of the future, including the one presented in DSM-5.

As you read about the various personality disorders, you should be clear that diagnoses of such disorders can be assigned too often. We may catch glimpses of ourselves or of people we know in the descriptions of these disorders and be tempted to conclude that we or they have a personality disorder. In the vast majority of instances, such interpretations are incorrect. We all display personality traits. Only occasionally are they so maladaptive, distressing, and inflexible that they can be considered disorders. ■

> **Why do you think personality disorders attract so many efforts at amateur psychology?**

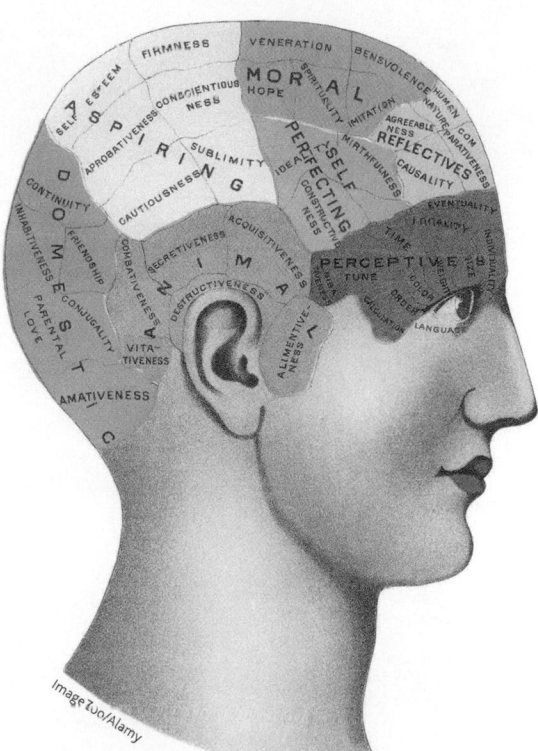

Early notions of personality In the popular nineteenth-century theory of phrenology, Franz Joseph Gall (1758–1828) suggested that the brain consists of distinct portions, each responsible for some aspect of personality. Phrenologists tried to assess personality by feeling bumps and indentations on a person's head.

"Odd" Personality Disorders

THE CLUSTER OF "ODD" PERSONALITY DISORDERS consists of the *paranoid, schizoid,* and *schizotypal* personality disorders. People with these disorders typically have odd or eccentric behaviors that are similar to but not as extensive as those seen in schizophrenia, including extreme suspiciousness, social withdrawal, and peculiar ways of thinking and perceiving things. Such behaviors often leave the person isolated. Some clinicians believe that these personality disorders are related to schizophrenia. In fact, schizotypal personality disorder is listed twice in DSM-5—as one of the schizophrenia spectrum disorders and as one of the personality disorders. Directly related or not, people with an odd-cluster personality disorder often qualify for an additional diagnosis of schizophrenia or have close relatives with schizophrenia (Rosell, 2017; Chemerinski & Siever, 2011).

Clinicians have learned much about the symptoms of the odd-cluster personality disorders but have not been so successful in determining their causes or how to treat them. In fact, as you'll soon see, people with these disorders rarely seek treatment.

Paranoid Personality Disorder

As you read earlier, people with **paranoid personality disorder** deeply distrust other people and are suspicious of others' motives (APA, 2013). Because they believe that everyone intends them harm, they shun close relationships. Their trust in their own ideas and abilities can be excessive, though, as you can see in the case of Eduardo:

For Eduardo, a researcher at a genetic engineering company, this was the last straw. He had been severely chastised by his supervisor for deviating from the research procedure on a major study. He knew where this was coming from. He had been "ratted out" by

(continued on the next page)

his jealous, conniving lab colleagues. This time, Eduardo would not sit back quietly. He demanded a meeting with his supervisor and the three other researchers in the lab.

At the outset of the meeting, Eduardo insisted that he would not leave the room until he was told the name of the person who had ratted him out. He acknowledged that he had, in fact, changed the study's design in key ways, maintaining that these changes would open the door to enormous medical gains. Eduardo quickly shifted the focus onto his lab colleagues. He stated that the other scientists were intimidated by his visionary ideas, and he accused them of trying to get him out of the way so they could continue to work in an unproductive, low-pressure atmosphere. He said that their desire to get rid of him was always apparent to him, revealed by their coldness toward him each and every day and their outright nastiness whenever he tried to correct them or offer constructive criticism. Nor did it escape his attention that they were always laughing at him, talking about him behind his back, and, on more than one occasion, trying to copy or destroy his notes.

The other researchers were aghast as Eduardo laid out his suspicions. They pointed out that it was Eduardo, not they, who was always behaving in an unfriendly manner. He had stopped speaking to all of them two months ago and he regularly tried to antagonize them—giving them dirty looks and slamming doors.

Next, Eduardo's supervisor, Lisa, spoke up. She said that in her objective opinion, none of Eduardo's accusations were true. First, none of his colleagues had informed on him. She herself had reviewed videos from the lab cameras as a matter of routine and had noticed him feeding rats that were supposed to be left hungry. Second, she said that it was his co-workers' account, not Eduardo's, that rang true. In fact, she had received many complaints from people outside the lab about Eduardo's cold and aloof manner.

Later, in the privacy of her office, Lisa told Eduardo that she had no choice but to let him go. Eduardo was furious, but not completely surprised. His past two jobs had ended badly as well.

Is hatred a disorder? With the term "Skinhead" tattooed on the back of his head, this man awaits trial in Germany for committing neo-Nazi crimes against foreigners and liberals. Clinicians sometimes confront extreme racism and intolerance in their practices, particularly among clients with paranoid, antisocial, and certain other personality disorders. There is a small, but growing movement in the clinical field to classify extreme hatred and prejudice as a psychological disorder.

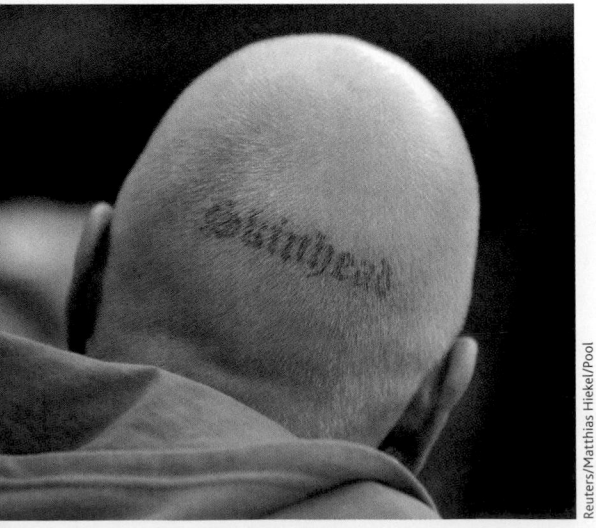

Reuters/Matthias Hiekel/Pool

Ever on guard and cautious and seeing threats everywhere, people like Eduardo continually expect to be the targets of some trickery (see **Figure 16-1**). They find "hidden" meanings, which are usually belittling or threatening, in everything. In an early study that required people to role-play, participants with paranoia were more likely than control participants to read hostile intentions into the actions of others (Turkat et al., 1990). In addition, they more often chose anger as the appropriate role-play response.

Quick to challenge the loyalty or trustworthiness of acquaintances, people with paranoid personality disorder remain cold and distant. A woman might avoid confiding in anyone, for example, for fear of being hurt; or a husband might, without any justification, persist in questioning his wife's faithfulness. Although inaccurate and inappropriate, their suspicions are not usually *delusional;* the ideas are not so bizarre or so firmly held as to clearly remove the individuals from reality (Kellett & Hardy, 2014).

People with this disorder are critical of weakness and fault in others, particularly at work (McGurk et al., 2013). They are unable to recognize their own mistakes, though, and are extremely sensitive to criticism. They often blame others for the things that go wrong in their lives, and they repeatedly bear grudges (Rotter, 2011). As many as 4.4 percent of adults experience this disorder, which is apparently more common in men than in women (Quirk et al., 2017, 2016; APA, 2013; Sansone & Sansone, 2011).

How Do Theorists Explain Paranoid Personality Disorder? The theories that have been proposed to explain paranoid personality disorder, like those about most other personality disorders, have received little systematic research (Triebwasser et al., 2013). Psychodynamic theories, the oldest of these explanations, trace the pattern to early interactions with demanding parents, particularly distant, rigid fathers and overcontrolling, rejecting mothers (Kellett & Hardy, 2014; Caligor & Clarkin, 2010; Williams, 2010). (You will see that psychodynamic explanations for almost all the personality disorders begin the same way—with repeated mistreatment during childhood and lack of love.) According to one psychodynamic view, some people come to view their environment as hostile as a result of their parents' persistently unreasonable demands. They must always be on the alert because they cannot trust others, and they are likely to develop feelings of extreme anger. They also project these feelings onto others and, as a result, feel increasingly persecuted (Geoffreys, 2015; Koenigsberg et al., 2001). Similarly, some cognitive-behavioral theorists suggest that people with paranoid personality disorder generally hold broad maladaptive assumptions, such as "People are evil" and "People will attack you if given the chance" (Beck & Weishaar, 2014; Weishaar & Beck, 2006).

Biological theorists propose that paranoid personality disorder has genetic causes (Haghighatfard et al., 2018; Bernstein & Useda, 2007). A widely reported study that looked at self-reports of suspiciousness in 3,810 Australian twin pairs found that if one twin was excessively suspicious, the other had an increased likelihood of also being suspicious (Kendler et al., 1987). Once again, however, it is important to note that such similarities between twins might also be the result of common environmental experiences.

Treatments for Paranoid Personality Disorder People with paranoid personality disorder do not typically see themselves as needing help, and few come to treatment willingly (Bressert, 2016; Skodol, 2016; Kellett & Hardy, 2014). Furthermore, many who are in treatment view the role of patient as inferior and distrust and rebel against their therapists. Thus it is not surprising that therapy for this disorder, as for most other personality disorders, has limited effect and moves very slowly.

Object relations therapists—the psychodynamic therapists who give center stage to relationships—try to see past the patient's anger and work on what they view as his or her deep wish for a satisfying relationship (Caligor & Clarkin, 2010). Self-therapists—the psychodynamic clinicians who focus on the need for a healthy and unified self—try to help clients reestablish self-cohesion (a unified personality), which they believe has been lost in the person's continuing negative focus on others (Vermote et al., 2010; Silverstein, 2007). Cognitive-behavioral therapy has also been used to treat people with paranoid personality disorder. On the behavioral side, therapists help clients to master anxiety-reduction techniques and to improve their skills at solving interpersonal problems. On the cognitive side, therapists guide the clients to develop

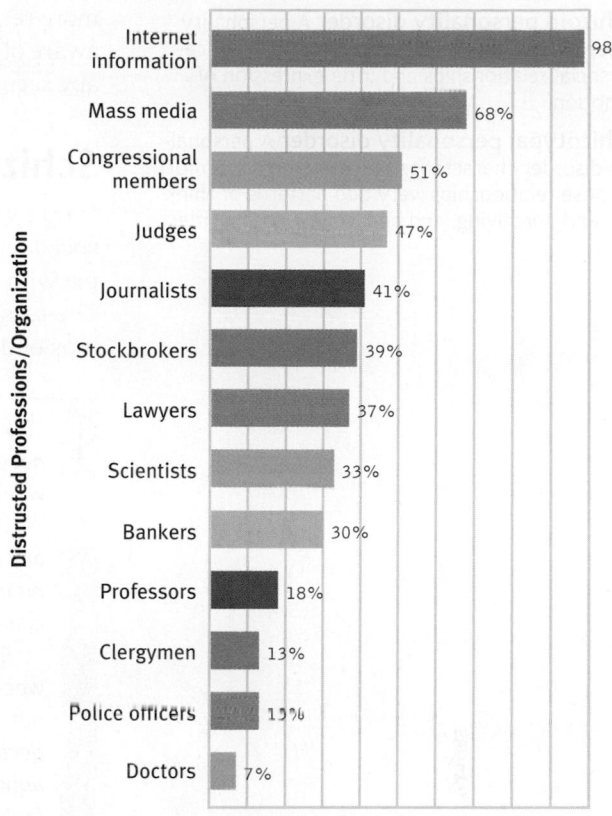

Distrusted Professions/Organization

Profession/Organization	Percentage Who Distrust Them
Internet information	98%
Mass media	68%
Congressional members	51%
Judges	47%
Journalists	41%
Stockbrokers	39%
Lawyers	37%
Scientists	33%
Bankers	30%
Professors	18%
Clergymen	13%
Police officers	13%
Doctors	7%

Percentage Who Distrust Them

FIGURE 16-1

Whom Do You Distrust?

Although distrust and suspiciousness are the hallmarks of paranoid personality disorder, even people without this disorder are often untrusting. In various surveys, the majority of respondents have said they distrust Internet information, the mass media (newspapers, TV, and radio), and members of Congress. (Information from: Bernstein, 2017; Pew Research, 2017, 2016; Gallup Poll, 2016, 2015; Swift, 2016; Ho, 2012.)

DO CARS JUST HATE ME?

schizoid personality disorder A personality disorder characterized by persistent avoidance of social relationships and little expression of emotion.

schizotypal personality disorder A personality disorder characterized by extreme discomfort in close relationships, very odd patterns of thinking and perceiving, and behavioral eccentricities.

more realistic interpretations of other people's words and actions and to become more aware of other people's points of view (Kellett & Hardy, 2014). Antipsychotic drug therapy seems to be of limited help (Skodol, 2016; Birkeland, 2013).

Schizoid Personality Disorder

People with **schizoid personality disorder** persistently avoid and are removed from social relationships and demonstrate little in the way of emotion (APA, 2013). Like people with paranoid personality disorder, they do not have close ties with other people. The reason they avoid social contact, however, has nothing to do with paranoid feelings of distrust or suspicion; it is because they genuinely prefer to be alone. Take Eli:

Eli, a student at the local technical institute, had been engaged in several different Internet certificate programs over the past few years, and was about to engage in yet another, when his mother, confused as to why he would not apply for a traditional degree at a "real" college, insisted he seek therapy. A loner by nature, Eli preferred not to socialize in any traditional sense, having little to no desire to get to know much about the people in his immediate social context. The way Eli saw it, . . . "at least at my school you just go to class and go home."

Routinely, he slept through much of his day and then spent his evenings, nights, and weekends at the school's computer lab, "chatting" with others over the Internet while not in class. Notably, people that he chatted with often sought to meet Eli, but he always declined these invitations, stating that he didn't really have any desire to learn more about them than what they shared over the computer in the chat rooms. He described a family life that was similar to that of his social surroundings; he was mostly oblivious of his younger brother and sister, two outgoing teens, despite the fact that they seemed to hold him in the highest regard, and he had recently alienated himself entirely from his father, who had left the family several years earlier. . . .

A marked deficit in social interest was notable in Eli, as were frequent behavioral eccentricities. . . . At best, he had acquired a peripheral . . . role in social and family relationships. . . . Rather than venturing outward, he had increasingly removed himself from others and from sources of potential growth and gratification. Life was uneventful, with extended periods of solitude interspersed.

(Millon, 2011)

People like Eli, often described as "loners," make no effort to start or keep friendships, take little interest in having sexual relationships, and even seem indifferent to their families. They seek out jobs that require little or no contact with others. When necessary, they can form work relations to a degree, but they prefer to keep to themselves. Many live by themselves as well. Not surprisingly, their social skills tend to be weak. If they marry, their lack of interest in intimacy may create marital or family problems.

People with schizoid personality disorder focus mainly on themselves and are generally unaffected by praise or criticism. They rarely show any feelings, expressing neither joy nor anger. They seem to have no need for attention or acceptance; are typically viewed as cold, humorless, or dull; and generally succeed in being ignored. This disorder is present in 3.1 percent of the adult population (APA, 2013; Sansone & Sansone, 2011). Men are slightly more likely to experience it than are women, and men may also be more impaired by it.

How Do Theorists Explain Schizoid Personality Disorder? Many psychodynamic theorists, particularly object relations theorists, propose that schizoid personality disorder has its roots in an unsatisfied need for human contact (Rosa, 2015; Caligor & Clarkin, 2010). The parents of people with this disorder, like those of people with paranoid personality disorder, are believed to have been unaccepting or even abusive of their children. Whereas people with paranoid symptoms react to such parenting chiefly with distrust, those with schizoid personality disorder are left unable to give or receive love. They cope by avoiding all relationships.

Cognitive-behavioral theorists propose, not surprisingly, that people with schizoid personality disorder suffer from deficiencies in their thinking. Their thoughts tend to be vague, empty, and without much meaning, and they have trouble scanning the environment to arrive at accurate perceptions (Chadwick, 2014; Kramer & Meystre, 2010). Unable to pick up emotional cues from others, they simply cannot respond to emotions. As this theory might predict, children with schizoid personality disorder develop language and motor skills very slowly, whatever their level of intelligence (APA, 2013).

Treatments for Schizoid Personality Disorder Their social withdrawal prevents most people with schizoid personality disorder from entering therapy unless some other disorder, such as alcoholism, makes treatment necessary (Skodol & Bender, 2016; Mittal et al., 2007). These clients are likely to remain emotionally distant from the therapist, seem not to care about their treatment, and make limited progress at best (Bressert, 2016; Colli et al., 2014).

Cognitive-behavioral therapists have sometimes been able to help people with this disorder experience more positive emotions and more satisfying social interactions (Bressert, 2016; Weishaar & Beck, 2006; Beck et al., 2004). On the cognitive end, their techniques include presenting clients with lists of emotions to think about or having them write down and remember pleasurable experiences. On the behavioral end, therapists have sometimes had success teaching social skills to such clients, using role-playing, exposure techniques, and homework assignments as tools. Group therapy is apparently useful when it offers a safe setting for social contact, although people with schizoid personality disorder may resist pressure to take part (Bressert 2016; Piper & Joyce, 2001). As with paranoid personality disorder, drug therapy seems to offer limited help (Skodol, 2016; Silk & Jibson, 2010).

Warner Bros/DC Comics/Kobal/REX/Shutterstock

A darker knight In recent years, Batman movies have presented the crime fighter as a singularly driven loner incapable of forming or sustaining relationships, a portrayal true to the original comic book presentation. In the 2016 film *Batman v Superman: Dawn of Justice*, for example, Batman's asocial personality, including his hatred and distrust of Superman, is evident. A number of clinical observers have argued that in these recent presentations, Batman displays some of the symptoms of schizoid personality disorder.

Schizotypal Personality Disorder

People with **schizotypal personality disorder** display a range of interpersonal problems marked by extreme discomfort in close relationships, very odd patterns of thinking and perceiving, and behavioral eccentricities (APA, 2013). Anxious around others, they seek isolation and have few close friends. Some feel intensely lonely. The disorder is more severe than the paranoid and schizoid personality disorders, as we see in the case of 41-year-old Kevin:

> *Kevin was a night security guard at a warehouse, where he had worked since his high school graduation more than 20 years ago. His parents, both successful professionals, had been worried for many years, as Kevin seemed entirely disconnected from himself and his surroundings and had never taken initiative to make any changes, even toward a shift supervisory position. They therefore made the referral for therapy, and Kevin simply acquiesced. He explained that he liked his work, as it was a place where he could be by himself in a quiet atmosphere, away from anyone else. He described where he worked as "an empty warehouse; they don't use it no more but they don't want no one in there. It's nice; 'homey.'"*
>
> *Throughout the . . . interview, Kevin remained aloof, never once looking at the counselor, usually answering questions with either one-word responses or short phrases, and*

(continued on the next page)

usually waiting to respond until a second question was asked or the first question was repeated. He described, in . . . short, bizarre answers, a life devoid of almost any human interconnectedness, almost his only tangible contact being his brother, whom he saw only during major holidays. Living alone, he could only remember one significant relationship, and that was with a girl in high school. Very simply, he stated, "We graduated, and then I didn't see her anymore." He expressed no apparent loneliness, however, and appeared entirely emotionless regarding any aspect of his life. . . .

Kevin . . . often seemed to experience a separation between his mind and his physical body. There was a strange sense of nonbeing or nonexistence, as if his floating conscious awareness carried with it a depersonalized or identityless human form. Behaviorally, his tendency was to be drab, sluggish, and inexpressive. He . . . appeared bland, indifferent, unmotivated, and insensitive to the external world. . . . Most people considered him to be [a] strange person . . . who faded into the background, self-absorbed . . . and lost to the outside world. . . . Bizarre "telepathic" powers enabled him to communicate with mythical or distant others. . . . Kevin also occasionally decompensated when faced with too much, rather than too little, stimulation. . . . He would simply fade out, becoming blank, losing conscious awareness, and turning off the pressures of the outer world.

(Millon, 2011)

As with Kevin, the thoughts and behaviors of people with schizotypal personality disorder can be noticeably disturbed. These symptoms may include *ideas of reference*—beliefs that unrelated events pertain to them in some important way—and *bodily illusions,* such as sensing an external "force" or presence. A number of people with this disorder see themselves as having special extrasensory abilities, and some believe that they have magical control over others. Examples of schizotypal eccentricities include repeatedly arranging cans to align their labels, organizing closets extensively, or wearing an odd assortment of clothing. The emotions of these individuals may be inappropriate, flat, or humorless.

People with schizotypal personality disorder often have great difficulty keeping their attention focused. Correspondingly, their conversation is typically digressive and vague, even sprinkled with loose associations (Rabella et al., 2016; Millon, 2011). Like Kevin, they tend to drift aimlessly and lead an idle, unproductive life (Hengartner et al., 2014). They are likely to choose undemanding jobs in which they can work below their capacity and are not required to interact with other people. Surveys suggest that 3.9 percent of adults—slightly more males than females—display schizotypal personality disorder (Rosell, 2017).

Sipa Press

When personality disorders explode In this 2007 video, Seung-Hui Cho, a student at Virginia Tech, described the slights he experienced throughout his life. After mailing the video to NBC News, he proceeded to kill 32 people, including himself, and to wound 25 others in a massive campus shooting. Most clinical observers agree that he displayed a combination of features from the antisocial, borderline, paranoid, schizoid, schizotypal, and narcissistic personality disorders, including boundless fury and hatred, extreme social withdrawal, persistent distrust, strange thinking, intimidating behavior and arrogance, and disregard for others.

How Do Theorists Explain Schizotypal Personality Disorder? Because the symptoms of schizotypal personality disorder so often resemble those of schizophrenia, researchers have hypothesized that similar factors may be at work in both disorders. A wide range of studies have supported such expectations (Rosell, 2017; Zhu et al., 2017; Asai, 2016). Investigators have found that schizotypal symptoms, like schizophrenic patterns, are often linked to family conflicts and to psychological disorders in parents. They have also learned that defects in attention and short-term memory may contribute to schizotypal personality disorder, just as they apparently do to schizophrenia. For example, research participants with either disorder perform poorly on *backward masking,* a laboratory test of attention that requires a person to identify a visual stimulus immediately after a previous stimulus has flashed on and off the screen. People with these disorders have a hard time shutting out the first stimulus in order to focus on the second. Finally, researchers have linked schizotypal personality disorder to some of the same biological factors found in schizophrenia, such as high activity of the neurotransmitter dopamine, enlarged brain ventricles, smaller temporal lobes, and loss of gray matter (Rosell, 2017; Rabella et al., 2016; Lener et al., 2015). As you read in Chapter 14, there are indications that these biological factors may have a genetic basis (Walter et al., 2016).

Although these findings do suggest a close relationship between schizotypal personality disorder and schizophrenia, the personality disorder also has been linked to disorders of mood. Around two-thirds of people with schizotypal personality disorder also suffer from major depressive disorder or bipolar disorder at some point in their lives (Rosell, 2017). Moreover, relatives of people with depression have a higher than usual rate of schizotypal personality disorder, and vice versa. Thus, at the very least, this personality disorder is not tied exclusively to schizophrenia.

Treatments for Schizotypal Personality Disorder Therapy is as difficult in cases of schizotypal personality disorder as it is in cases of paranoid and schizoid personality disorders. Most therapists agree on the need to help these clients "reconnect" with the world and recognize the limits of their thinking and their powers. The therapists may thus try to set clear limits—for example, by requiring punctuality—and work on helping the clients recognize where their views end and those of the therapist begin. Other therapy goals are to increase positive social contacts, ease loneliness, reduce overstimulation, and help the individuals become more aware of their personal feelings (Colli et al., 2014; Sperry, 2003).

Cognitive-behavioral therapists further combine cognitive and behavioral techniques to help people with schizotypal personality disorder function more effectively. Using cognitive interventions, they try to teach clients to evaluate their unusual thoughts or perceptions objectively and to ignore the inappropriate ones (Beck & Weishaar, 2014; Weishaar & Beck, 2006). Therapists may keep track of clients' odd or magical predictions, for example, and later point out their inaccuracy. When clients are speaking and begin to digress, the therapists might ask them to sum up what they are trying to say. In addition, specific behavioral methods, such as speech lessons, social skills training, and tips on appropriate dress and manners, have sometimes helped clients learn to blend in better with and be more comfortable around others (Bressert, 2016; Skodol, 2016).

Antipsychotic drugs have been given to people with schizotypal personality disorder, again because of the disorder's similarity to schizophrenia. In low doses the drugs appear to have helped some people, usually by reducing certain of their thought problems (Jakobsen et al., 2017; Skodol, 2016).

"Dramatic" Personality Disorders

THE CLUSTER OF "DRAMATIC" PERSONALITY DISORDERS includes the *antisocial, borderline, histrionic,* and *narcissistic* personality disorders. The behaviors of people with these problems are so dramatic, emotional, or erratic that it is almost impossible for them to have relationships that are truly giving and satisfying.

These personality disorders are more commonly diagnosed than the others. However, only the antisocial and borderline personality disorders have received much study, partly because they create so many problems for other people. The causes of the disorders, like those of the odd personality disorders, are not well understood. Treatments range from ineffective to moderately effective.

Antisocial Personality Disorder

Sometimes described as "psychopaths" or "sociopaths," people with **antisocial personality disorder** persistently disregard and violate others' rights (APA, 2013). Aside

antisocial personality disorder A personality disorder marked by a general pattern of disregard for and violation of other people's rights.

from substance use disorders, this is the disorder most closely linked to adult criminal behavior. DSM-5 stipulates that a person must be at least 18 years of age to receive this diagnosis; however, most people with antisocial personality disorder displayed some patterns of misbehavior before they were 15, including truancy, running away, cruelty to animals or people, and destroying property.

Robert Hare, a leading clinician and researcher in this realm, recalls an early professional encounter with a prison inmate named Ray:

Notorious disregard In 2009, financier Bernard Madoff was sentenced to 150 years in prison after defrauding thousands of investors, including many charities, of billions of dollars. Given his overwhelming disregard for people and other such qualities, some clinicians suggest that Madoff displays antisocial personality disorder.

In the early 1960s, I found myself employed as the sole psychologist at the British Columbia Penitentiary. . . . I wasn't in my office for more than an hour when my first "client" arrived. He was a tall, slim, dark-haired man in his thirties. The air around him seemed to buzz, and the eye contact he made with me was so direct and intense that I wondered if I had ever really looked anybody in the eye before. That stare was unrelenting—he didn't indulge in the brief glances away that most people use to soften the force of their gaze.

Without waiting for an introduction, the inmate—I'll call him Ray—opened the conversation: "Hey, Doc, how's it going? Look, I've got a problem. I need your help. I'd really like to talk to you about this."

Eager to begin work as a genuine psychotherapist, I asked him to tell me about it. In response, he pulled out a knife and waved it in front of my nose, all the while smiling and maintaining that intense eye contact.

Once he determined that I wasn't going to push the button, he explained that he intended to use the knife not on me but on another inmate who had been making overtures to his "protégé," a prison term for the more passive member of a homosexual pairing. Just why he was telling me this was not immediately clear, but I soon suspected that he was checking me out, trying to determine what sort of a prison employee I was. . . .

From that first meeting on, Ray managed to make my eight-month stint at the prison miserable. His constant demands on my time and his attempts to manipulate me into doing things for him were unending. On one occasion, he convinced me that he would make a good cook . . . and I supported his request for a transfer from the machine shop (where he had apparently made the knife). What I didn't consider was that the kitchen was a source of sugar, potatoes, fruit, and other ingredients that could be turned into alcohol. Several months after I had recommended the transfer, there was a mighty eruption below the floorboards directly under the warden's table. When the commotion died down, we found an elaborate system for distilling alcohol below the floor. Something had gone wrong and one of the pots had exploded. There was nothing unusual about the presence of a still in a maximum-security prison, but the audacity of placing one under the warden's seat shook up a lot of people. When it was discovered that Ray was the brains behind the bootleg operation, he spent some time in solitary confinement.

Once out of "the hole," Ray appeared in my office as if nothing had happened and asked for a transfer from the kitchen to the auto shop—he really felt he had a knack, he saw the need to prepare himself for the outside world, if he only had the time to practice he could have his own body shop on the outside. . . . I was still feeling the sting of having arranged the first transfer, but eventually he wore me down.

Soon afterward I decided to leave the prison to pursue a Ph.D. in psychology, and about a month before I left Ray almost persuaded me to ask my father, a roofing contractor, to offer him a job as part of an application for parole.

Ray had an incredible ability to con not just me but everybody. He could talk, and lie, with a smoothness and a directness that sometimes momentarily disarmed even the most experienced and cynical of the prison staff. When I met him he had a long criminal record behind him (and, as it turned out, ahead of him); about half his adult life had been spent in prison, and many of his crimes had been violent. . . . He lied endlessly, lazily, about everything, and it disturbed him not a whit whenever I pointed out something in his file that contradicted one of his lies. He would simply change the subject and spin off in a different direction. Finally convinced that he might not make the perfect job candidate in my father's firm, I turned down Ray's request—and was shaken by his nastiness at my refusal.

#PreviousIdentity

Antisocial personality disorder was referred to as "moral insanity" during the nineteenth century (Jones, 2017).

> *Before I left the prison for the university, I took advantage of the prison policy of letting staff have their cars repaired in the institution's auto shop—where Ray still worked, thanks (he would have said no thanks) to me. The car received a beautiful paint job and the motor and drivetrain were reconditioned.*
>
> *With all our possessions on top of the car and our baby . . . in the backseat, my wife and I headed for Ontario. The first problems appeared soon after we left Vancouver, when the motor seemed a bit rough. Later, when we encountered some moderate inclines, the radiator boiled over. A garage mechanic discovered ball bearings in the carburetor's float chamber; he also pointed out where one of the hoses to the radiator had clearly been tampered with. These problems were repaired easily enough, but the next one, which arose while we were going down a long hill, was more serious. The brake pedal became very spongy and then simply dropped to the floor—no brakes, and it was a long hill. Fortunately, we made it to a service station, where we found that the brake line had been cut so that a slow leak would occur. Perhaps it was a coincidence that Ray was working in the auto shop when the car was being tuned up, but I had no doubt that the prison [pipeline] had informed him of the owner of the car.*
>
> *(Hare, 1993)*

Like Ray, people with antisocial personality disorder lie repeatedly (APA, 2013). Many cannot work consistently at a job; they are absent frequently and are likely to quit their jobs altogether (Black, 2016; Hengartner et al., 2014). Usually they are also careless with money and frequently fail to pay their debts. They are often impulsive, taking action without thinking of the consequences (Olson & Patrick, 2018; Black, 2017). Correspondingly, they may be irritable, aggressive, and quick to start fights. Many travel from place to place.

> **How do various institutions in our society—business, government, science, religion—view lying? How might such views affect lying by individuals?**

Recklessness is another common trait: people with antisocial personality disorder have little regard for their own safety or for that of others, even their children. They are self-centered as well, and are likely to have trouble maintaining close relationships. Usually they develop a knack for gaining personal profit at the expense of other people. Because the pain or damage they cause seldom concerns them, clinicians commonly say that they lack a moral conscience (see **Table 16-2**). They think of their victims as weak and deserving of being conned, robbed, or even physically harmed (see *Trending* on the next page).

Surveys indicate that 3.6 percent of adults in the United States meet the criteria for antisocial personality disorder (Black, 2016). The disorder is as much as four times more common among men than women.

Because people with this disorder are often arrested, researchers frequently look for people with antisocial patterns in prison populations (Black, 2016; Pondé et al., 2014; Naidoo & Mkize, 2012). It is estimated that at least 35 percent of people in prison meet the diagnostic criteria for this disorder. Among men in urban jails, the antisocial personality pattern has been linked strongly to past arrests for crimes of violence (De Matteo et al., 2005). The criminal behavior of many people with this disorder declines after the age of 40; some, however, continue their criminal activities throughout their lives (APA, 2013).

Studies and clinical observations also indicate that people with antisocial personality disorder have higher rates of alcoholism and other substance use disorders than do the rest of the population (Brook et al., 2014). Indeed, some research indicates that more than 80 percent of people with this personality disorder display a substance use disorder at some point in their lives (Black, 2016). Perhaps intoxication and substance misuse help trigger the development of antisocial personality disorder by loosening a person's inhibitions. Perhaps this personality disorder somehow makes a person more prone to abuse substances. Or perhaps antisocial personality disorder and substance use disorders both have the same cause, such as a deep-seated need to take risks. Interestingly, drug users with the personality disorder often cite the recreational

TABLE: 16-2

Annual Hate Crimes in the United States

Group Attacked	Number of Reported Incidents
Racial/ethnic groups	4,216
LGBT groups	1,410
Religious groups	1,402
Groups with disability	85

Information from: U.S. Department of Justice, Federal Bureau of Investigation, 2016.

Mass Murders: Where Does Such Violence Come From?

At 2:00 A.M. on June 12, 2016, a 29-year-old man entered Pulse, a gay nightclub in Orlando, Florida, and, using two semi-automatic weapons, proceeded to shoot 100 patrons, killing 49 of them. The mass killing, considered a terrorist-hate attack, was one of the deadliest by a single shooter in U.S. history. But it was certainly not the only mass killing. The Orlando horror has been followed by numerous other mass shootings, including an even more deadly one in 2017 at a country music concert in Las Vegas, Nevada, and it was preceded by numerous mass killings across the country and the world, including the 2015 killings of 9 Bible study members at a church in Charleston, South Carolina, the 2012 killings of 26 students and teachers at the Sandy Hook Elementary School in Newtown, Connecticut, and the 2012 murders of 12 movie-goers at a *Batman* movie in Aurora, Colorado.

These numbers are numbing, and the public has looked to the clinical field to help it understand why mass killings occur and why they are on the increase. Clinical theorists and researchers have offered various theories about why individuals commit such murders, but enlightening research and effective interventions have been elusive (Abe, 2017; Smith & Hughes, 2016; Wilson, 2016).

What do we know about mass killings? We know they involve, by definition, the murder of four or more people in the same location and at around the same time. FBI records also indicate that, on average, mass killings occur in the United States every two weeks, 75 percent of them feature a lone killer, 67 percent involve the use of guns, and most are committed by males (FBI, 2017; Hoyer & Heath, 2012).

We also know that despite public perceptions, mass killings are not a new phenomenon. They have occurred—with regularity—for centuries (Bonn, 2017, 2015; Duwe, 2016). What is new, however, is the increasing frequency of mass *public* shootings (for example, schools, shopping malls, and workplaces) and the emergence of certain patterns of mass murder (Wilson, 2016). Although specific issues vary from mass murder to mass murder—racial or religious hatred, for example—two general patterns are on the rise (Abe, 2017). In one pattern,

so-called "pseudocommando" mass murders, the murderer "kills in public, often during the daytime, plans his offense well in advance, and comes prepared with a powerful arsenal of weapons. He has no escape planned and expects to be killed during the incident" (Knoll, 2010). In another pattern, "autogenic" (self-generated) massacres, individuals kill people indiscriminately to fulfill a personal agenda.

Theorists have suggested a number of factors to help explain pseudocommando, autogenic, and other mass killings, including the availability of guns, bullying behavior, substance abuse, the proliferation of violent media and video games, dysfunctional homes, and contagion effects (Lankford & Tomek, 2018; Abe, 2017; Singal, 2017). Moreover, regardless of one's position on gun control, media violence, or the like, almost everyone, including most clinicians, believe that mass killers typically suffer from a mental disorder (Fox & Levin, 2016, 2014; Winegard & Ferguson, 2016). Which mental disorder? On this, there is little agreement (Carey, 2016). Each of the following has been suggested:

- Antisocial, borderline, paranoid, or schizotypal personality disorder
- Schizophrenia or severe bipolar disorder
- Intermittent explosive disorder—an impulse-control disorder featuring

repeated, unprovoked verbal and/or behavioral outbursts
- Severe depression, stress, or anxiety

Although these and yet other disorders have been proposed, none has received clear support in the limited research conducted on mass killings. On the other hand, several psychological variables have emerged as a common denominator across the various studies: severe feelings of anger and resentment, feelings of being persecuted or grossly mistreated, and desires for revenge (Fox & Levin, 2016, 2014). That is, regardless of which mental disorder a mass killer may display, he usually is driven by this set of feelings. For a growing number of clinical researchers, this repeated finding suggests that research should focus less on diagnosis and much more on identifying and understanding these particular feelings.

Clearly, clinical research must expand its focus on this area of enormous social concern. It is a difficult problem to investigate, partly because so few mass killers survive their crimes, but the clinical field has managed to gather useful insights about other elusive areas. And, indeed, in the aftermath of the horrific murders mentioned at the beginning of this box, a wave of heightened determination and commitment seems to have seized the clinical community.

Unthinkable Friends of the victims of the 2016 mass shooting at Pulse nightclub gather in downtown Orlando to embrace, cry, and show support for those who died or were injured in the mass murder.

Melissa Lyttle for The Washington Post via Getty Images

aspects of drug use as their reason for starting and continuing it. Consistent with this risk-focused explanation, a number of people with antisocial personality disorder also display gambling disorder. In fact, the personality disorder is manifested by 23 percent of all people with gambling disorder (Black, 2016; Grant et al., 2004).

It appears that children with conduct disorder and an accompanying attention-deficit/hyperactivity disorder have a heightened risk of developing antisocial personality disorder (Black, 2016; APA, 2013). These two childhood disorders, which you will read about in Chapter 17, often bear similarities to antisocial personality disorder. Like adults with antisocial personality disorder, children with a conduct disorder persistently lie and violate rules and other people's rights, and children with attention-deficit/hyperactivity disorder lack foresight and judgment and fail to learn from experience. Intriguing as these observations may be, however, the precise connection between the childhood disorders and antisocial personality disorder has been difficult to pinpoint.

How Do Theorists Explain Antisocial Personality Disorder? Most explanations of antisocial personality disorder come from the psychodynamic, cognitive-behavioral, and biological models. In fact, a number of factors have been linked to this disorder by researchers, but complete explanations have been elusive.

PSYCHODYNAMIC FACTORS As with many other personality disorders, psychodynamic theorists propose that this one begins with an absence of parental love during infancy, leading to a lack of basic trust (Meloy & Yakeley, 2010; Sperry, 2003). In this view, some children—the ones who develop antisocial personality disorder—respond to the early inadequacies by becoming emotionally distant, and they bond with others through the use of power and destructiveness. In support of the psychodynamic explanation, researchers have found that people with this disorder are more likely than others to have had significant stress in their childhoods, particularly in such forms as family poverty, family violence, child abuse, and parental conflict or divorce (Black, 2016; Kumari et al., 2014).

COGNITIVE-BEHAVIORAL FACTORS On the behavioral side, many theorists have suggested that antisocial symptoms may be learned through principles of conditioning, particularly *modeling*, or imitation (Cabrera et al., 2017). As evidence, they point to the higher rate of antisocial personality disorder found among the parents and close relatives of people with this disorder (Black, 2016; APA, 2013). The modeling explanation is also supported by studies of friends and associates of people with antisocial personality disorder. For example, one investigation found that middle school students who were attracted to antisocial peers went on to engage in antisocial behavior themselves in order to gain acceptance (Juvonen & Ho, 2008).

Other theorists have pointed to another principle of conditioning, *operant conditioning*, to help explain antisocial personality disorder. These theorists suggest that some parents unintentionally teach antisocial behavior by regularly rewarding a child's aggressive behavior (Black, 2016; Kazdin, 2005). When the child misbehaves or becomes violent in reaction to the parents' requests or orders, for example, the parents may give in to restore peace. Without meaning to, they may be teaching the child to be stubborn and perhaps even violent.

On the cognitive side, a number of theorists say that people with antisocial personality disorder hold attitudes that trivialize the importance of other people's needs (Elwood et al., 2004). Such a philosophy of life, the theorists suggest, may be far more common in our society than people recognize. In another explanation that emphasizes

Hardly a new disorder A worker attaches a tag that translates as "Killer of a Wife" to a wax-covered head at the Lombroso Museum in Turin, Italy. Hundreds of such heads, taken from prisons throughout Europe, line the museum's shelves, each with the tags like "Ladro" ("Thief") or "Omicida" ("Murderer"). The display comes from nineteenth-century psychiatrist Cesare Lombroso's crude but pioneering research into the nature of criminal and related antisocial behavior.

Popular sociopaths Television audiences seem to love characters with the symptoms of antisocial personality disorder. Legendary character Walter White (above), the ruthless meth manufacturer and dealer in *Breaking Bad,* and the equally legendary Joffrey Baratheon (below), the amoral and cruel king in *Game of Thrones*, are two of this decade's most popular villains.

cognitive functioning, some theorists propose that people with this disorder have genuine difficulty recognizing points of view or feelings other than their own (Herpertz & Bertsch, 2014).

BIOLOGICAL FACTORS A wide range of studies suggest that biological factors play an important role in antisocial personality disorder. First, there are indications that people may inherit a biological predisposition to the disorder. For example, twin research has found that 67 percent of the identical twins of people with antisocial personality disorder also display the disorder themselves, in contrast to 31 percent of fraternal twins of people with the disorder. In a similar vein, some genetic research suggests that the disorder may be linked to particular genes (Black, 2016; Foley et al., 2004; Caspi et al., 2002).

Biological researchers have found that antisocial people, particularly those who are highly impulsive and aggressive, have lower serotonin activity than other people (Thompson, Ramos, & Willett, 2014). As you'll recall (see page 266), both impulsivity and aggression also have been linked to low serotonin activity in other kinds of studies, so the presence of this biological factor in people with antisocial personality disorder is not surprising.

In related work, studies indicate that individuals with this disorder display deficient functioning in their *prefrontal cortex* and *anterior cingulate cortex* (Glenn et al., 2017; Black, 2016; Liu et al., 2014). Among other duties, these brain structures help people to plan and execute realistic strategies and to have personal characteristics such as sympathy, judgment, and empathy. These are, of course, all qualities found wanting in people with antisocial personality disorder. Similar research has found deficient functioning in the *amygdala, hippocampus,* and *temporal cortex* of people with this disorder, brain structure problems that may contribute to the individuals' inability to follow rules (Aghajani et al., 2017; Volman et al., 2016).

A different line of biological research has found that research participants with this disorder often respond to warnings or expectations of stress with low brain and bodily arousal, such as slow autonomic arousal and slow EEG waves (Thompson et al., 2014; Perdeci et al., 2010). It is believed that such underarousal in response to stress enables people with the disorder to readily tune out threatening or emotional situations and so be unaffected by them. This could help explain a phenomenon often observed by clinicians—that people with antisocial personality disorder seem to feel less anxiety than other people, and so lack a key ingredient for learning from negative life experiences or tuning in to the emotional cues of others (Black, 2016; Blair et al., 2005).

It could also be argued that because of their physical underarousal, people with antisocial personality disorder are more likely than other people to take risks and seek thrills. That is, they may be drawn to antisocial activity precisely because it meets an underlying biological need for more excitement and arousal. In support of this idea, as you read earlier, antisocial personality disorder often goes hand in hand with sensation-seeking behavior.

These various biological factors may be tied together more closely than first meets the eye. Consistent with the field's increasing emphasis on dysfunctional brain circuits, many theorists now suspect that antisocial personality disorder is ultimately related to poor functioning by a brain circuit consisting of the prefrontal cortex, anterior cingulate cortex, amygdala, hippocampus, and temporal cortex, among other structures. Poor communication (that is, poor *interconnectivity*) between the structures in this circuit may produce chronic low reactions to stress by the two brain–body stress pathways—the *sympathetic nervous system pathway* and the *hypothalamic-pituitary-adrenal pathway*—leading, in turn, to a state of low arousal, weak stress reactions, poor empathy for the pain of others, and other features of antisocial personality disorder (Aghajani et al., 2017; Glenn et al., 2017, 2015; Sobhani et al., 2015). Although enthusiasm for this circuit-centered explanation is growing, research regarding its specifics and merits has been limited to date.

Treatments for Antisocial Personality Disorder Treatments for people with antisocial personality disorder are typically ineffective (Skodol & Bender, 2016). Major obstacles to treatment include the individual's lacking a conscience, a desire to change, or respect for therapy (Colli et al., 2014). Most of those in therapy have been forced to participate by an employer, their school, or the law, or they come to the attention of therapists when they also develop another psychological disorder (Bressert, 2016).

Some cognitive-behavioral therapists try to guide clients with antisocial personality disorder to think about moral issues and about the needs of other people. However, research has not found this approach to be particularly helpful (Black, 2017). In a similar vein, a number of hospitals and prisons have tried to create a therapeutic community for people with this disorder, a structured environment that teaches responsibility toward others (Bressert, 2016). Some patients seem to profit from such approaches, but it appears that most do not. In recent years, clinicians have also used psychotropic medications, particularly antipsychotic drugs, to treat people with antisocial personality disorder. However, research has not found medication to be consistently useful in addressing the overall antisocial pattern (Black, 2017).

Borderline Personality Disorder

People with **borderline personality disorder** display great instability, including major shifts in mood, an unstable self-image, and impulsivity (APA, 2013). These characteristics combine to make their relationships very unstable as well (Paris, 2018; Miano et al., 2017). In her first treatment session, Dal displays or reveals all of these difficulties, as described by her therapist:

> Dal . . . seems to be unable to maintain a stable sense of self-worth and self-esteem. Her confidence in her ability to "hold on to men" is at a low ebb, having just parted ways with "the love of her life." In the last year alone she confesses to having had six "serious relationships."
>
> . . . The commencement of each affair was "a dream come true" and the men were all and one "Prince Charming." But then she invariably found herself in the stormy throes of violent fights over seeming trifles. She tried to "hang in there," but the more she invested in the relationships, the more distant and "vicious" her partners became. Finally, they abandoned her . . . .
>
> She shrugs and . . . her posture [becomes] almost violent: "No one f***s with me. I stand my ground, you get my meaning?" She admits that she physically assaulted three of her last six paramours, hurled things at them, and, amidst uncontrollable rage attacks and temper tantrums, even threatened to kill them. What made her so angry? She can't remember now . . .
>
> As she recounts these sad exploits, she alternates between boastful swagger and self-chastising, biting criticism of her own traits and conduct. Her affect swings wildly, in the confines of a single therapy session, between exuberant and fantastic optimism and unbridled gloom.
>
> One minute she can conquer the world, careless and "free at last" ("It's their loss. . . .") —the next instant, she hyperventilates with unsuppressed anxiety, bordering on a panic attack . . .
>
> Dal likes to "live dangerously, on the edge." She does drugs occasionally—"not a habit, just for recreation," she assures me. She is a shopaholic and often finds herself mired in debts. She went through three personal bankruptcies . . . She also binges on food, especially when she is stressed or depressed which seems to occur quite often.
>
> She sought therapy because she is having intrusive thoughts about killing herself. [She often performs] self-injury and self-mutilation (she shows me a pair of pale, patched wrists, more scratched than slashed).
>
> *(Vaknin, 2016, 2015)*

#CharacterIngestion

As late as the Victorian era, many English parents believed babies absorbed personality and moral uprightness as they took in milk. Thus, if a mother could not nurse, it was important to find a wet nurse of good character (Asimov, 1997).

borderline personality disorder A personality disorder characterized by repeated instability in interpersonal relationships, self-image, and mood and by impulsive behavior.

Like Dal, people with borderline personality disorder swing in and out of very depressive, anxious, and irritable states that last anywhere from a few hours to a few days or more (see **Table 16-3**). Their emotions seem to be always in conflict with the world around them. They are prone to bouts of anger, which sometimes result in physical aggression and violence (Paris, 2018; Martino et al., 2015). Just as often, however, they direct their impulsive anger inward and inflict bodily harm on themselves. Many seem troubled by deep feelings of emptiness.

Borderline personality disorder is a complex disorder, and it is fast becoming one of the more common conditions seen in clinical practice. As many as 85 percent of individuals with this syndrome also experience another psychological disorder at some point in their lives, most often major depressive disorder, PTSD, an eating disorder, bipolar disorder, and/or another personality disorder (Skodol, 2017; Zanarini et al., 2016, 2011). Their impulsive, self-destructive activities may range from alcohol and substance abuse to delinquency, unsafe sex, and reckless driving (Kienast et al., 2014; Coffey et al., 2011). Many engage in self-injurious or self-mutilation behaviors, such as cutting or burning themselves or banging their heads (Turner et al., 2015). As you saw in Chapter 9, such behaviors typically cause immense physical suffering, but those with borderline personality disorder often feel as if the physical discomfort offers relief from their emotional suffering. It may serve as a distraction from their emotional or interpersonal upsets, "snapping" them out of an "emotional overload" (Skodol, 2017; Sadeh et al., 2014). Many try to hurt themselves as a way of dealing with their chronic feelings of emptiness, boredom, and identity confusion. Scars and bruises also may provide them with a kind of concrete evidence of their emotional distress (Paris, 2018).

Suicidal threats and actions are also common (Sher et al., 2016; Amore et al., 2014). Studies suggest that around 75 percent of people with borderline personality disorder attempt suicide at least once in their lives; as many as 10 percent actually die of suicide. It is common for people with this disorder to enter clinical treatment by way of the emergency room after a suicide attempt (Hong, 2016).

People with borderline personality disorder frequently form intense, conflict-ridden relationships in which their feelings are not necessarily shared by the other person (Skodol, 2017). They may come to idealize another person's qualities and abilities after just a brief first encounter. They also may violate the boundaries of relationships (Lazarus et al., 2014). Thinking in dichotomous (black-and-white) terms, they quickly feel rejected and become furious when their expectations are not met; yet they remain very attached to the relationships (Miano et al., 2017; Berenson et al., 2011). In fact, they have recurrent fears of impending abandonment and frequently engage in frantic efforts to avoid real or imagined separations from important people in their lives (Skodol, 2017; Gunderson, 2011). Sometimes they cut themselves or carry out other self-destructive acts to prevent partners from leaving.

People with borderline personality disorder typically have dramatic identity shifts. Because of this unstable sense of self, their goals, aspirations, friends, and even sexual orientation may shift rapidly. They may also occasionally have a sense of dissociation, or detachment, from their own thoughts or bodies (Krause-Utz et al., 2017; Zanarini et al., 2016, 2011). At times they may have no sense of themselves at all, leading to the feelings of emptiness described earlier.

According to surveys, 5.9 percent of the adult population display borderline personality disorder (Skodol, 2017, 2016; Zanarini et al., 2016, 2011). Close to 75 percent of the patients who receive the diagnosis

TABLE: 16-3

Comparison of Personality Disorders

	Cluster	Similar Disorders	Responsiveness to Treatment
Paranoid	Odd	Schizophrenia; delusional disorder	Modest
Schizoid	Odd	Schizophrenia; delusional disorder	Modest
Schizotypal	Odd	Schizophrenia; delusional disorder	Modest
Antisocial	Dramatic	Conduct disorder	Poor
Borderline	Dramatic	Depressive disorder; bipolar disorder	Moderate
Histrionic	Dramatic	Somatic symptom disorder; depressive disorder	Modest
Narcissistic	Dramatic	Cyclothymic disorder (mild bipolar disorder)	Poor
Avoidant	Anxious	Social anxiety disorder	Moderate
Dependent	Anxious	Separation anxiety disorder; depressive disorder	Moderate
Obsessive-Compulsive	Anxious	Obsessive-compulsive disorder	Moderate

Troubled princess Princess Diana, shown here embracing schoolchildren at a Hindu temple in northern London, was admired by millions during her short life, particularly for her numerous charitable efforts and humane acts. However, she also had a range of psychological problems that she herself disclosed in books and interviews. Diagnosing and explaining the princess's problems has become a common practice—both inside and outside the clinical field—since her death in 1997. Her self-cutting, possible borderline personality functioning, and disordered eating behaviors have received the most attention.

are women. The course of the disorder varies from person to person. In the most common pattern, the person's instability and risk of suicide peak during young adulthood and then gradually wane with advancing age (Skodol, 2017; APA, 2013). Given the chaotic and unstable relationships characteristic of borderline personality disorder, it is not surprising that the disorder tends to interfere with job performance even more than most other personality disorders do (Hengartner et al., 2014).

How Do Theorists Explain Borderline Personality Disorder? Theorists have pointed to a range of possible psychological, biological, and sociocultural factors in their explanations of borderline personality disorder. In addition, over the past several years, there have been productive efforts to determine how such factors may interact to produce the disorder.

PSYCHOLOGICAL FACTORS Because a fear of abandonment tortures so many people with borderline personality disorder, psychodynamic theorists have looked once again to early parental relationships to explain the disorder. Object relations theorists, for example, propose that an early lack of acceptance by parents may lead to a loss of self-esteem, increased dependence, and an inability to cope with separation (Huprich et al., 2017; Caligor & Clarkin, 2010; Gabbard, 2010).

Research has found that this is consistent with the early childhoods of people with borderline personality disorder. In many cases, when they were children, their parents neglected or rejected them, verbally abused them, or otherwise behaved inappropriately (Skodol, 2017; Martín-Blanco et al., 2014). Their childhoods were often marked by multiple parent substitutes, divorce, death, or traumas such as physical or sexual abuse. Indeed, research suggests that early sexual abuse is a common contributor to the development of borderline personality disorder (Newnham & Janca, 2014; Huang, Yang, & Wu, 2010). Children who experience such abuse are four times more likely to develop the disorder than those who do not experience abuse (Zelkowitz et al., 2001). At the same time, it is important to recognize that the vast majority of people with histories of physical, sexual, or psychological abuse do not go on to develop borderline personality disorder (Skodol, 2017).

BIOLOGICAL FACTORS There are indications that people may inherit a biological predisposition to develop borderline personality disorder, although the impact of this

#WhitherBorderline?

In 1938 the term "borderline" was introduced by psychoanalyst Adolph Stern. He used it to describe patients who were more disturbed than "neurotic" patients, yet not psychotic (Bateman, 2011; Stern, 1938). The term has since evolved to its present usage.

"I wish my identity weren't so wrapped up with who I am."

factor seems to be less influential for this disorder than for antisocial personality disorder. In twin research, for example, it has been found that 35 percent of the identical twins of people with borderline personality disorder also display the disorder themselves, in contrast to 19 percent of fraternal twins of people with the disorder (Skodol, 2017; Kendler et al., 2008; Torgersen et al., 2000). Similarly, research has revealed that close relatives of those with borderline personality disorder are five times more likely than the general population to have the same personality disorder (Amad et al., 2014). In a similar vein, some genetic research suggests that the disorder may be linked to particular genes (Agha et al., 2017).

Beyond genetic studies, researchers have found that people with borderline personality disorder, particularly those who are most impulsive—individuals who attempt suicide or are very aggressive toward others—have lower brain serotonin activity (Skodol, 2017; Soloff et al., 2014). As you may recall from Chapters 7 and 9, low serotonin activity has been linked repeatedly to depression, suicide, aggression, and impulsivity (see pages 196–198 and 265–266).

Borderline personality disorder also has been tied to abnormal activity and anatomy of certain brain structures, including the amygdala (hyperactive), hippocampus (underactive), prefrontal cortex (underactive), and other structures in the frontal lobes (Skodol, 2017; Ruocco & Carcone, 2016; Mitchell et al., 2014). The frontal lobes—located in the outermost layer of the brain—are comprised of numerous structures that collectively control our abilities to plan well, form accurate judgments, make good decisions, exercise self-control, and express our emotions properly. Many of today's theorists believe that the various structures mentioned above are members of a particular brain circuit and that the problems displayed by each structure actually reflect dysfunction throughout that entire brain circuit (Agha et al., 2017). Specifically, they believe that the structures in this circuit communicate poorly with each other (they have poor *interconnectivity*) for people with borderline personality disorder, leading to the frequent emotional outbursts, impulsive acts, wrong judgments, and bad decisions that characterize this disorder. As with the brain circuit explanation for antisocial personality disorder, research has not yet fully sorted out all of the specifics or possible merits of this explanation for borderline personality disorder, although numerous specific findings seem to point in this direction (Agha et al., 2017; Krause-Utz et al., 2017; Ruocco & Carcone, 2016).

SOCIOCULTURAL FACTORS Some sociocultural theorists suggest that cases of borderline personality disorder are particularly likely to emerge in cultures that change rapidly. As a culture loses its stability, they argue, it inevitably leaves many of its members with problems of identity, a sense of emptiness, high anxiety, and fears of abandonment. Family units may come apart, leaving people with little sense of belonging. Changes of this kind in society today may explain growing reports of the disorder (Paris, 2018, 2010; Lazzari et al., 2017).

INTEGRATIVE EXPLANATIONS In recent years, two explanations—the *biosocial* and the *developmental psychopathology* explanations—have examined how these various factors, particularly the psychological and biological factors, might intersect to more fully account for borderline personality disorder. As you will see, the two explanations are quite compatible and often overlap.

According to the *biosocial* explanation (Neacsiu & Linehan, 2014), borderline personality disorder results from a combination of internal forces (for example, difficulty identifying and controlling one's emotions, social skill deficits, abnormal neurotransmitter activity) and external forces (for example, an environment in which a child's emotions are punished, ignored, trivialized, or disregarded). Parents may, for instance,

#VentingMyth

Contrary to the notion that "letting off steam" reduces anger, angry participants in one study acted much more aggressively after hitting a punching bag than did angry participants who first sat quietly for a while (Bushman et al., 1999).

misinterpret their child's intense emotions as exaggerations or attempts at manipulation rather than as serious expressions of unsettled internal states. According to the biosocial theory, if children have intrinsic difficulty identifying and controlling their emotions and if their parents teach them to ignore their intense feelings, they may never learn how properly to recognize and control their emotional arousal, how to tolerate emotional distress, or when to trust their emotional responses (Herpertz & Bertsch, 2014; Lazarus et al., 2014). Such children will be at risk for the development of borderline personality disorder. This theory has received some, but not consistent, research support (Gill & Warburton, 2014).

Note that the biosocial theory is similar to one of the leading explanations for eating disorders. As you saw in Chapter 11, pioneering theorist Hilde Bruch proposed that children whose parents do not respond accurately to the children's internal cues may never learn to identify cues of hunger, thus increasing their risk of developing an eating disorder (see pages 322–323). Small wonder that a large number of people with borderline personality disorder also have an eating disorder (Gabriel & Waller, 2014). Recall, for example, Dal's binge eating behaviors.

Proponents of the other integrative explanation of borderline personality disorder, the *developmental psychopathology* explanation, build on and add details to the biosocial view. Like the biosocial theorists, developmental psychopathologists believe that internal and external factors intersect over the course of a person's life to help produce this disorder (Fonagy & Luyten, 2018, 2016; Lenzenweger & Depue, 2016; Tackett et al., 2016). While these theorists are interested in all such factors—from genetic to environmental—they believe that early parent–child relationships are particularly influential in the development of borderline personality disorder. Consistent with the psychodynamic model's *object relations* theorists, developmental psychopathologists contend that children who experience early trauma and abuse and whose parents are markedly inattentive, uncaring, confusing, threatening, and dismissive, are likely to develop a *disorganized attachment style* (Fonagy & Luyten, 2018, 2016). That is, their attachments to other people throughout life will parallel their problematic attachments to their parents and will be filled with anxiety, emotional instability, and inconsistency.

In short, according to the developmental psychopathology explanation, individuals whose early childhoods are marked by traumas and dysfunctional attachments with their parents are likely to enter adulthood with a severely flawed capacity for healthy relationships—a disorganized attachment style—unless they are fortunate enough to further experience significant positive factors (positive genetic predispositions, positive life events, sensitive role models, opportunities to build resilience, and the like) that help counter their early negative experiences (Fonagy et al., 2017). Individuals who do not experience such positive factors are, say developmental psychopathologists, high risk candidates for borderline personality disorder. Studies repeatedly confirm that, on average, people with borderline personality disorder display a disorganized attachment style and have indeed experienced unfavorable parenting and early childhood traumas (Fonagy & Luyten, 2018, 2016; Beeney et al., 2017).

In recent years, a number of theorists, particularly developmental psychopathologists, have also come to believe that the central psychological deficit in borderline personality disorder may be the person's inability to *mentalize* (Bateman & Fonagy, 2016, 2012, 2010). **Mentalization** refers to people's capacity to understand their own mental states and those of other people—that is, to recognize needs, desires, feelings, beliefs, and goals. When people mentalize effectively, they can better understand and predict the behaviors of other people, and they can react to others in appropriate and trusting ways. Many developmental psychopathologists suspect that persons subjected to early dysfunctional attachment relationships emerge from their childhood with a weakened ability to mentalize and, correspondingly, a poor ability to control their emotions, attention, thinking, and behavior (Quek et al., 2017; Fonagy & Luyten, 2018, 2016; Sroufe et al., 2005). They cannot accurately understand either their own or other people's underlying mental states. As one theorist has stated, a mind that repeatedly

---

#AllOut

Expressions of Anger

12	Percent of adults who say they have trouble controlling their own anger.
23	Percent who report openly expressing their anger.
23	Percent who walk away to try to collect themselves.
28	Percent who say they worry about how angry they sometimes feel.
39	Percent who say they hide or contain their anger.
20	Percent who say they have ended a relationship or friendship with someone because of how they behaved when they were angry.

(Information from: BAAM, 2016; Kanner, 2005, 1995)

---

mentalization The capacity to understand one's own mental states and those of other people.

misinterprets itself is going to misinterpret others as well (Bateman & Fonagy, 2016, 2012, 2010). Several psychological disorders have been linked to poor mentalization skills, but those skills seem particularly flawed in people with borderline personality disorder, according to research (Badoud et al., 2018; Fonagy et al., 2017).

The developmental psychopathology notions about borderline personality disorder have excited many in the clinical field, just as the perspective's explanations of other psychological disorders have aroused enthusiasm. Moreover, studies have found clear relationships between poor parent–child attachments and the development of disorganized attachment styles and between disorganized attachment styles and borderline personality disorders (Beeney et al., 2017; Bateman & Fonagy, 2016, 2012, 2010). However, it is not necessarily the case that early parent–child attachments are the *primary* factor in the development of this disorder. Nor is it clear that mentalization deficits are at the center of the disorder. Those important issues are currently being investigated in a range of studies.

Treatments for Borderline Personality Disorder It appears that psychotherapy can eventually lead to some degree of improvement for people with borderline personality disorder (Livesley, 2017; Choi-Kain et al., 2016; McMain, 2015). It is, however, extraordinarily difficult for a therapist to strike a balance between empathizing with the borderline client's dependency and anger and challenging his or her way of thinking (Skodol, 2016; Goodman et al., 2014). The wildly fluctuating interpersonal attitudes of clients with the disorder can also make it difficult for therapists to establish collaborative working relationships with them. Moreover, clients with borderline personality disorder may violate the boundaries of the client–therapist relationship (for example, calling the therapist's emergency contact number to discuss matters of a less urgent nature) (Skodol, 2016; Colli et al., 2014).

Traditional psychoanalytic therapy has not been effective with people with borderline personality disorder (Doering et al., 2010). The clients often experience the psychoanalytic therapist's reserved style and use of free association as suggesting disinterest and abandonment. The clients may also have difficulty tolerating interpretations made by psychoanalytic therapists and see them as attacks.

On the other hand, contemporary psychodynamic approaches, particularly *relational psychoanalytic therapy* (see page 58), in which therapists take a more supportive posture and focus primarily on the therapist–patient relationship, have been more effective than traditional psychoanalytic approaches. In approaches of this kind, therapists work to provide an empathic setting within which borderline clients can explore their unconscious conflicts and pay attention to their central relationship disturbance, poor sense of self, and pervasive loneliness and emptiness (Cristea et al., 2017; Goodman et al., 2014; Gabbard, 2010, 2001). Research has found that relational psychoanalytic therapy and other contemporary psychodynamic treatments may help reduce suicide attempts, self-harm behaviors, and the number of hospitalizations, and bring at least some improvement to those with the disorder (Skodol, 2016; Clarkin et al., 2010, 2001; Doering et al., 2010).

Over the past two decades, a new-wave cognitive-behavioral therapy for borderline personality disorder, called **dialectical behavior therapy (DBT),** has received considerable research support and is now considered the treatment of choice for people with borderline personality disorder (Robins et al., 2018; Rudge et al., 2018; Linehan et al., 2015, 2002, 2001). DBT, developed by psychologist Marsha Linehan, consists of weekly individual therapy and group skill-building sessions that last for approximately one year. While targeting all of the features of borderline personality disorder, DBT places special emphasis on clients' efforts at self-harm and/or suicide.

The individual therapy sessions include many of the same behavioral and cognitive techniques that are applied to other disorders: homework assignments, psychoeducation, the teaching of coping and related skills, modeling by the therapist, clear goal setting, reinforcements for appropriate behaviors, mindfulness skill training, ongo-

dialectical behavior therapy A comprehensive treatment approach, applied particularly in cases of borderline personality disorder and/or suicidal intent; includes both individual therapy sessions (featuring cognitive-behavioral interventions) and group sessions (featuring social skill–building and support).

histrionic personality disorder A personality disorder characterized by a pattern of excessive emotionality and attention seeking. Once called *hysterical personality disorder.*

ing assessment of the client's behaviors and treatment progress, and collaborative examinations by the client and therapist of the client's ways of thinking.

Although primarily cognitive-behavioral, the individual DBT sessions also borrow heavily from the humanistic and contemporary psychodynamic approaches, placing the client–therapist relationship itself at the center of treatment interactions, making sure that appropriate treatment boundaries are adhered to, and providing an environment of acceptance and validation of the client. Indeed, DBT therapists regularly empathize with their borderline clients and with the emotional turmoil they are experiencing; locate kernels of truth in the clients' complaints or demands; and examine alternative ways for them to address valid needs (Skodol, 2016).

DBT clients also participate in social skill–building groups (Kramer, 2017; Roney & Cannon, 2014). In these groups, clients practice new ways of relating to other people in a safe environment and receive validation and support from other group members.

DBT has received more research support than any other treatment for borderline personality disorder (Rudge et al., 2018; Livesley, 2017; Neacsiu & Linehan, 2014). Many clients who undergo DBT become more able to tolerate stress, develop more social skills, respond more effectively to life situations, and develop a more stable identity. They also display significantly fewer self-harm and suicidal behaviors and require fewer hospitalizations than those who receive other forms of treatment. In addition, they are more likely to remain in treatment and to report less anger, more social gratification, improved work performance, and reductions in substance abuse (Skodol, 2016; Linehan et al., 2015; Rizvi et al., 2011).

Antidepressant, antibipolar, antianxiety, and antipsychotic drugs have helped calm the emotional and aggressive storms of some people with borderline personality disorder (Bridler et al., 2015). However, given the numerous suicide attempts by people with this disorder, some clinicians believe that the use of drugs on an outpatient basis is unwise (Gunderson, 2011). Most professionals believe that psychotropic drug treatment for borderline personality disorder should be used largely as an adjunct to psychotherapy approaches, and indeed many clients seem to benefit from a combination of psychotherapy and drug therapy (Skodol, 2016; Omar et al., 2014).

"Zero Degrees of Empathy" Psychologist Simon Baron-Cohen has argued in his book *Zero Degrees of Empathy* that a common element in most of the "odd" and "dramatic" personality disorders is a total lack of empathy. In fact, many people without such disorders also have empathy difficulties. Thus, in 2017, as part of a film project called "See Yourself in Others," 20 actors walked around New York City wearing mirrored cubes over their heads. Passers-by saw only their own reflected faces while they were observing and interacting with the actors—an exercise designed to increase the pedestrians' empathy for others by forcing them to "see themselves in others."

Histrionic Personality Disorder

People with **histrionic personality disorder**, once called **hysterical personality disorder**, are extremely emotional—they are typically described as "emotionally charged"—and continually seek to be the center of attention (APA, 2013). Their exaggerated moods and neediness can complicate life considerably, as we see in the case of Lucinda:

Unhappy over her impending divorce, Lucinda decided to seek counseling. She arrived at her first session wearing a very provocative outfit, including a revealing blouse and extremely short skirt. Her hair had been labored over, and she had on an excessive amount of makeup—very carefully applied.

When asked to discuss her separation, Lucinda first insisted that the therapist call her Cindy, saying, "All my close friends call me that, and I like to think that you and I will become very good friends here." She said that her husband, Morgan, had suddenly

(continued on the next page)

#VainPortrait

King Frederick V, ruler of Denmark from 1746 to 1766, had his portrait painted at least 70 times by the same artist, Carl Pilo (Shaw, 2004).

abandoned her—"probably brainwashed by some young trollop." She proceeded to describe their break-up in a theatrical manner. Over a span of five minutes, her voice ranged from whispers to cries of agony and back again to whispers; she waved her arms dramatically while making some points and sat totally still while making others.

Lucinda said that when Morgan first told her that he wanted a divorce, she did not know whether she could go on. The pain was palpable. After all, they had been so "incredibly and irrevocably" close, and he had been so very devoted to her. She said that initially she even had thoughts of doing away with herself. But, of course, she knew that she had to pull herself together. So many people needed her to be strong. So many people relied on her, particularly her "dear friends" and her sister. She had deep and special relationships with them all.

She told the therapist that without Morgan she would now need a man to take care of her—emotionally and every other way. She asked the therapist if she looked like a 30-year-old woman. When he declined to answer, she said, "I know you're not supposed to say."

When the therapist attempted to steer the conversation back to Morgan, Lucinda became petulant and asked, "Do we really need to talk about that abusive lout?" Pressed on the word "abusive," Lucinda replied that she was referring to "mental cruelty." Morgan had, after all, called her inadequate and worthless throughout their marriage and told her that everything good in her life had been due to him. When her therapist pointed out that this seemed to contradict the rosy picture she had just painted of Morgan and their married life, she quickly changed the subject.

As the session came to a close, Lucinda's therapist suggested that it might be useful for him to meet with Morgan. She loved the idea, saying, "Then he'll know the competition he has!"

When he met with Morgan a few days later, the therapist heard a very different story than the one presented by Lucinda. Morgan said, "I really loved Cindy—still do—but she was always flying off the handle, telling me I'm no good or that I didn't care about her. She would often complain that I spent too much time at work—keep in mind that I never work more than 30 hours a week—and too little time attending to her and her needs. I just can't take life with her anymore. It's too draining."

Morgan also indicated that Lucinda had virtually no close friends. She and her sister might talk on the phone once a month and get together in person twice a year. He acknowledged that she drew a lot of attention from people. But, he noted. "Look at the way she dresses and her constant flirting. That'll certainly get people's attention, keep them around for a while."

#TheirWords

"The hysterical find too much significance in things. The depressed find too little."

Mason Cooley, American aphorist

People with histrionic personality disorder are always "on stage," using theatrical gestures and mannerisms and grandiose language to describe ordinary everyday events. Like chameleons, they keep changing themselves to attract and impress an audience, and in their pursuit they change not only their surface characteristics—according to the latest fads—but also their opinions and beliefs. In fact, their speech is actually scanty in detail and substance, and they seem to lack a sense of who they really are.

Approval and praise are their lifeblood; they must have others present to witness their exaggerated emotional states. Vain, self-centered, demanding, and unable to delay gratification for long, they overreact to any minor event that gets in the way of their quest for attention. Some make suicide attempts, often to manipulate others (Bressert, 2016; APA, 2013).

People with histrionic personality disorder may draw attention to themselves by exaggerating their physical illnesses or fatigue (Kayhan et al., 2016). They may also behave very provocatively and try to achieve their goals through sexual seduction. Most obsess over how they look and how others will perceive them, often wearing bright, eye-catching clothes. They exaggerate the depth of their relationships, considering themselves to be the intimate friends of people who see them as no more than casual acquaintances. Often they become involved with romantic partners who may be exciting but who do not treat them well.

This disorder was once believed to be more common in women than in men, and clinicians long described the "hysterical wife" (Novais et al., 2015; Anderson et al., 2001). Research, however, has revealed gender bias in past diagnoses (APA, 2013). When evaluating case studies of people with a mixture of histrionic and antisocial traits, clinicians in several studies gave a diagnosis of histrionic personality disorder to women more than men. Surveys suggest that 1.8 percent of adults have this personality disorder, with males and females equally affected (APA, 2013; Sansone & Sansone, 2011).

How Do Theorists Explain Histrionic Personality Disorder? The psychodynamic perspective was originally developed to help explain cases of hysteria (see Chapter 10), so it is no surprise that psychodynamic theorists continue to have a strong interest in histrionic personality disorder. Most psychodynamic theorists believe that as children, people with this disorder had cold and controlling parents who left them feeling unloved and afraid of abandonment (Novais et al., 2015; Horowitz & Lerner, 2010). To defend against deep-seated fears of loss, the children learned to behave dramatically, inventing crises that would require other people to act protectively.

Cognitive-behavioral explanations look instead at the lack of substance and extreme suggestibility that people with histrionic personality disorder have (Novais et al., 2015; Blagov et al., 2007). Cognitive-behavioral theorists see these people as becoming less and less interested in knowing about the world at large because they are so self-focused and emotional. With no detailed memories of what they never learned, they must rely on hunches or on other people to provide them with direction in life. Some cognitive theorists also believe that people with this disorder hold a general assumption that they are helpless to care for themselves, and so they constantly seek out others who will meet their needs (Weishaar & Beck, 2006; Beck et al., 2004).

Transient hysterical symptoms These avid Harry Potter fans expressed themselves with exaggerated emotionality and lack of restraint at the midnight launch of one of the books in the series. Similar reactions, along with fainting, tremors, and even convulsions, have been common at concerts by musical idols dating back to the 1940s. Small wonder that expressive fans of this kind are regularly described as "hysterical" or "histrionic" by the press—the same labels applied to the personality disorder that is marked by such behaviors and symptoms.

Sociocultural, particularly multicultural, theorists believe that histrionic personality disorder is produced in part by cultural norms and expectations (Novais et al., 2015; Fowler et al., 2007). Until recent decades, our society encouraged girls to hold on to childhood and dependency as they grew up. The vain, dramatic, and selfish behavior of the histrionic personality may actually be an exaggeration of femininity as our culture once defined it. Similarly, some clinical observers claim that histrionic personality disorder is diagnosed less often in Asian and other cultures that discourage overt sexualization and more often in Hispanic American and Latin American cultures that are more tolerant of overt sexualization (Patrick, 2007; Trull & Widiger, 2003). Researchers have not, however, investigated this claim systematically.

Treatments for Histrionic Personality Disorder People with histrionic personality disorder are more likely than those with most other personality disorders to seek out treatment on their own (Bressert, 2016). Working with them can be very difficult, however, because of the demands, tantrums, and seductiveness they are likely to deploy. Another problem is that these clients may pretend to have important insights or to change during treatment merely to please the therapist. To head off such problems, therapists must remain objective and maintain strict professional boundaries (Bressert, 2016; Colli et al., 2014).

Cognitive-behavioral therapists have tried to help people with this disorder to change their belief that they are helpless and also to develop better, more deliberate ways of thinking and solving problems (Bressert, 2016; Beck & Weishaar, 2014;

narcissistic personality disorder A personality disorder marked by a broad pattern of grandiosity, need for admiration, and lack of empathy.

Weishaar & Beck, 2006). Psychodynamic therapy and various group therapy formats have also been used (Novais et al., 2015; Horowitz & Lerner, 2010). In all these approaches, therapists ultimately aim to help the clients recognize their excessive dependency, find inner satisfaction, and become more self-reliant. Clinical case reports suggest that each of the approaches can be useful. Drug therapy appears less successful except as a means of relieving the depressive symptoms that some patients have (Skodol, 2016; Bock et al., 2010; Grossman, 2004).

Narcissistic Personality Disorder

People with **narcissistic personality disorder** are generally grandiose, need much admiration, and feel no empathy with others (APA, 2013). Convinced of their own great success, power, or beauty, they expect constant attention and admiration from those around them. Frederick, the man whom we met at the beginning of this chapter, was one such person. So is Steven, a 30-year-old artist, married, with one child:

> Steven came to the attention of a therapist when his wife insisted that they seek marital counseling. According to her, Steven was "selfish, ungiving and preoccupied with his work." Everything at home had to "revolve about him, his comfort, moods and desires, no one else's." She claimed that he contributed nothing to the marriage, except a rather meager income. He shirked all "normal" responsibilities and kept "throwing chores in her lap," and she was "getting fed up with being the chief cook and bottlewasher, tired of being his mother and sleep-in maid."
>
> On the positive side, Steven's wife felt that he was basically a "gentle and good-natured guy with talent and intelligence." But this wasn't enough. She wanted a husband, someone with whom she could share things. In contrast, he wanted, according to her, "a mother, not a wife"; he didn't want "to grow up, he didn't know how to give affection, only to take it when he felt like it, nothing more, nothing less."
>
> Steven presented a picture of an affable, self-satisfied and somewhat disdainful young man. He was employed as a commercial artist, but looked forward to his evenings and weekends when he could turn his attention to serious painting. He claimed that he had to devote all of his spare time and energies to "fulfill himself," to achieve expression in his creative work. . . .
>
> His relationships with his present co-workers and social acquaintances were pleasant and satisfying, but he did admit that most people viewed him as a "bit self-centered, cold and snobbish." He recognized that he did not know how to share his thoughts and feelings with others, that he was much more interested in himself than in them and that perhaps he always had "preferred the pleasure" of his own company to that of others.
>
> (Millon, 1969, pp. 261–262)

In the Greek myth, Narcissus died enraptured by the beauty of his own reflection in a pool, pining away with longing to possess his own image. His name has come to be synonymous with extreme self-involvement, and indeed people with narcissistic personality disorder have a grandiose sense of self-importance. They exaggerate their achievements and talents, expecting others to recognize them as superior, and often appear arrogant. They are very choosy about their friends and associates, believing that their problems are unique and can be appreciated only by other "special," high-status people. Because of their charm, they often make favorable first impressions, yet they can rarely maintain long-term relationships (Caligor & Petrini, 2016; Campbell & Miller, 2011).

Why do people often admire arrogant deceivers—art forgers, jewel thieves, or certain kinds of "con" artists, for example?

Like Steven, people with narcissistic personality disorder are seldom interested in the feelings of others. They may not even be able to empathize with such feelings (Bressert, 2016; Marcoux et al., 2014). Many take advantage of other people to achieve their own ends, perhaps partly out of envy; at the same time they believe others envy them. Though grandiose, some react to criticism or frustration with bouts of rage, humiliation, or embitterment (Miller et al., 2017; Caligor & Petrini, 2016). Others may react with cold indifference. And still others become extremely pessimistic and filled with depression (Gore & Widiger, 2016). They may have periods of zest that alternate with periods of disappointment (Ronningstam, 2017, 2011).

As many as 6.2 percent of adults display narcissistic personality disorder, up to 75 percent of them men (Caligor & Petrini, 2016; APA, 2013). Narcissistic-type behaviors and thoughts are common and normal among teenagers and do not usually lead to adult narcissism (see *MindTech* on page 498).

How Do Theorists Explain Narcissistic Personality Disorder?

Psychodynamic theorists more than others have theorized about narcissistic personality disorder, and they again propose that the problem begins with cold, rejecting parents (Miller at al., 2017; Roepke & Vater, 2014). They argue that some people with this background spend their lives defending against feeling unsatisfied, rejected, unworthy, ashamed, and wary of the world. They do so by repeatedly telling themselves that they are actually perfect and desirable, and also by seeking admiration from others. Object relations theorists—the psychodynamic theorists who emphasize relationships—interpret the grandiose self-image as a way for these people to convince themselves that they are totally self-sufficient and without need of warm relationships with their parents or anyone else (Miller at al., 2017; Celani, 2014). In support of the psychodynamic theories, research has found that children who are neglected and/or abused or who lose parents through adoption, divorce, or death are at particular risk for the later development of narcissistic personality disorder (Caligor & Petrini, 2016; Kernberg, 2010, 1992, 1989). Studies also show that people with this disorder do indeed earn relatively high shame and rejection scores on various scales and believe that other people are basically unavailable to them (Miller at al., 2017; Ritter et al., 2014).

A number of cognitive-behavioral theorists propose that narcissistic personality disorder may develop when people are treated *too positively* rather than too negatively in early life. They hold that certain children acquire a superior and grandiose attitude when their "admiring or doting parents" teach them to "overvalue their self-worth," repeatedly rewarding them for minor accomplishments or for no accomplishment at all (Miller at al., 2017; Caligor & Petrini, 2016).

Many sociocultural theorists see a link between narcissistic personality disorder and "eras of narcissism" in society (Paris, 2014). They suggest that family values and social ideals in certain societies periodically break down, producing generations of young people who are self-centered and materialistic and have short attention spans. Western cultures in particular, which encourage self-expression, individualism, and competitiveness, are considered likely to produce such generations of narcissism. In fact, one worldwide study conducted on the Internet found that respondents from the United States had the highest narcissism scores, followed, in descending order, by those from Europe, Canada, Asia, and the Middle East (Foster, Campbell, & Twenge, 2003).

Treatments for Narcissistic Personality Disorder Narcissistic personality disorder is one of the most difficult personality patterns to treat because the clients are unable to acknowledge weaknesses, to appreciate the effect of their behavior on others, or to incorporate feedback from others (Tanzilli et al., 2017; Ronningstam, 2017).The clients who consult therapists usually do so because of a related disorder such as depression (Caligor & Petrini, 2016). Once in treatment, the clients may try to manipulate the therapist into supporting their sense of superiority (Skodol & Bender, 2016). Some also seem to project their grandiose attitudes onto their therapists and develop a love-hate stance toward them (Colli et al., 2014; Shapiro, 2004).

Richard Cline The New Yorker Collection/The Cartoon Bank

"I'm attracted to you, but then I'm attracted to me, too."

#StolenGlances

22% Percentage of people who regularly check their reflections in store windows and the like

69% Those who steal glances at least occasionally

9% Those who never look at themselves in public mirrors or windows

(Information from: Kanner, 2005, 1995)

Selfies: Narcissistic or Not?

In the art world, people have been drawing self-portraits for centuries. In recent years, however, digital technology has ushered in the era of the *selfie,* a cousin to the self-portrait. Safe to say, just about every cell phone user has taken a selfie. In fact, more than 90 percent of all teens have now posted a photo of themselves online (SMA, 2017; Pew Research Center, 2014), and, according to some estimates, 93 million selfies are posted online every day (Whitbourne, 2016). These self-photos have created such a stir that the word "selfie" was elected "Word of the Year" by the Oxford English Dictionary a few years back.

Peter Bernik/Shutterstock

As the selfie phenomenon has grown, opinions about selfies have intensified (Diefenbach & Christoforakos, 2017). It seems like people either love them or hate them. This is true in the field of psychology as well. Some psychologists view taking selfies as a form of narcissistic behavior, while others view them more positively.

> **What other trends in behavior—digital or otherwise—might suggest that our society is currently in an era of narcissism?**

First, the negative perspective. Many sociocultural theorists see a link between narcissistic personality disorder and "eras of narcissism" in society (Paris, 2014). They suggest that social values in society break down periodically, producing generations of self-centered, materialistic youth. Some of these theorists consider today's selfie generation a perfect example of a current era of narcissism. This theory has gained a large following, but it is not supported by research. Several teams of investigators have found no relationship at all between how many selfies people post and how high they score on narcissism personality scales (Etgar & Amichai-Hamburger, 2017; Alloway, 2014; Alloway et al., 2014). Other researchers have found that people who score high on narcissism scales do, on average, like to take selfies, but many such individuals do not (Kim et al., 2016; Whitbourne, 2016). Moreover, the vast majority of people who post selfies do not score especially high on narcissism scales.

This lack of support for the narcissism viewpoint does not mean that selfies, especially repeated selfie behaviors, are completely harmless. Sherry Turkle, an influential technology psychologist, believes that the near-reflexive instinct to photograph oneself may limit deeper engagements with the environment or prevent a full experience of events (Turkle, 2015, 3013; Eisold, 2013). Turkle also suggests that people who post an endless stream of selfies are often seeking external validation of their self-worth, even if that pursuit may not rise to a level of clinical narcissism.

Psychologists also observe that posting too many "selfies" may alienate those who view the poster's social media profile (Miller, 2013). Studies have found, for example, that people often take a negative view of friends and family members who excessively post photos to their Facebook sites (Houghton, 2013).

On the positive side, a number of psychologists believe that the criticisms and concerns about the selfie movement have been overstated. They agree with media psychologist Pamela Rutledge (2013) that, for the most part, selfies are an inevitable by-product of "technology-enabled self-expression." Rutledge contends that selfie behaviors are simply confusing to individuals of a predigital generation. Moreover, she concludes that the selfie trend can enhance explorations of identity, help identify one's interests, develop artistic expression, help people craft a meaningful narrative of their life experiences, and even reflect more realistic body images (for example, posting "selfies" without makeup). Indeed, several studies have supported these points and have also uncovered additional positive motives and effects of selfie taking (Christensen, 2017; Holiday et al., 2016; Kim et al., 2016).

In short, like other technological trends you've read about, the selfie phenomenon has received mixed grades from psychology researchers and practitioners so far.

Psychodynamic therapists seek to help people with this disorder recognize and work through their basic insecurities and defenses (Bressert, 2016; Diamond & Meehan, 2013). Cognitive-behavioral therapists, focusing on the self-centered thinking of such individuals, try to redirect the clients' focus onto the opinions of others, teach them to interpret criticism more rationally, increase their ability to empathize, and change their all-or-nothing notions (Caligor & Petrini, 2016; Weishaar & Beck, 2006; Beck et al., 2004). None of the approaches have had clear success, however (Paris, 2014).

"Anxious" Personality Disorders

THE CLUSTER OF "ANXIOUS" PERSONALITY DISORDERS includes the *avoidant, dependent,* and *obsessive-compulsive personality disorders*. People with these patterns typically display anxious and fearful behavior. Although many of the symptoms of these personality disorders are similar to those of the anxiety and depressive disorders, researchers have not found direct links between this cluster and those disorders (O'Donohue et al., 2007). As with most of the other personality disorders, research support for the various explanations is very limited. At the same time, treatments for these disorders appear to be modestly to moderately helpful—considerably better than for other personality disorders.

avoidant personality disorder A personality disorder characterized by consistent discomfort and restraint in social situations, overwhelming feelings of inadequacy, and extreme sensitivity to negative evaluation.

Avoidant Personality Disorder

People with **avoidant personality disorder** are very uncomfortable and inhibited in social situations, overwhelmed by feelings of inadequacy, and extremely sensitive to negative evaluation (APA, 2013). They are so fearful of being rejected that they give no one an opportunity to reject them—or to accept them either:

Perhaps what made Malcolm pursue counseling was the painful awareness of his inability to socialize at a party hosted by a professor. A first-semester computer science graduate student, Malcolm watched other new students in his program fraternize at this gathering while he suffered in silence. He wanted desperately to join [in], but, as he described it, "I was totally at a loss as to how to go about talking to anyone." The best feeling in the world, he stated, was getting out of there. The following Monday, he came to the university counseling center, realizing he would have to be able to function in this group, but not before his first teaching experience that morning, which he described as "the most terrifying feeling I have ever encountered." As an undergrad, he spent most of his time alone in the computer lab working on new programs, which was what he most enjoyed as "no one was looking over my shoulder or judging me." In contrast to this, with his teaching assistantship duties . . . he felt he constantly ran the risk of being made to look like a fool in front of a large audience.

When asked about personal relationships he had previously enjoyed, Malcolm admitted that any interaction was a source of frustration and worry. From the moment he left home for undergraduate school, he lived alone, attended functions alone, and found it nearly impossible to make conversation with anyone. . . . The expectancy that people would be rejecting . . . precipitated profound gloom. . . . Despite a longing to relate and be accepted, Malcolm . . . maintained a safe distance from all emotional involvement. [He] became remote from others and from needed sources of support. He . . . had learned to be watchful, on guard against ridicule, and ever alert . . . to the most minute traces of annoyance expressed by others.

(Millon, 2011)

People like Malcolm actively avoid occasions for social contact. At the center of this withdrawal lies not so much poor social skills as a dread of criticism, disapproval, or rejection. They are timid and hesitant in social situations, afraid to say something foolish or to embarrass themselves by blushing or acting nervous. Even in intimate relationships they express themselves very carefully, afraid of being shamed or ridiculed.

People with this disorder believe themselves to be unappealing or inferior to others. They exaggerate the potential difficulties of new situations, so they seldom take risks or try out new activities. They usually have few or no close friends, though they actually yearn for intimate relationships, and frequently feel depressed and lonely. As a substitute, some develop an inner world of fantasy and imagination (Bressert, 2017; Millon, 2011).

#ShynessAlert

Between 40 and 60 percent of people in the United States consider themselves to be shy (Bressert, 2016).

Avoidant personality disorder is similar to *social anxiety disorder* (see Chapter 5), and many people with one of these disorders also experience the other (Eikenaes et al., 2016, 2013; Lampe, 2016). The similarities include a fear of humiliation and low confidence. Some theorists believe that there is a key difference between the two disorders—namely, that people with social anxiety disorder primarily fear social *circumstances,* while people with the personality disorder tend to fear close social *relationships.* Other theorists, however, believe that the two disorders reflect the same core of psychopathology and should be combined.

At least 2.4 percent of adults have avoidant personality disorder, men as frequently as women (NIMH, 2017; APA, 2013; Sansone & Sansone, 2011). Many children and teenagers are also painfully shy and avoid other people, but this is usually just a normal part of their development.

How Do Theorists Explain Avoidant Personality Disorder?
Theorists often assume that avoidant personality disorder has the same causes as anxiety disorders—such as early traumas, conditioned fears, upsetting beliefs, or biochemical abnormalities. However, with the exception of social anxiety disorder, research has not clearly tied the personality disorder directly to the anxiety disorders (Herbert, 2007). Psychodynamic and cognitive-behavioral explanations of avoidant personality disorder are the most popular among clinicians.

Psychodynamic theorists focus mainly on the general feelings of shame and insecurity that people with avoidant personality disorder have (Guina, 2016; Svartberg & McCullough, 2010). Some trace the shame to childhood experiences such as early bowel and bladder accidents. If parents repeatedly punish or ridicule a child for having such accidents, the child may develop a negative self-image. This may lead to the child's feeling unlovable throughout life and distrusting the love of others.

Similarly, cognitive-behavioral theorists believe that harsh criticism and rejection in early childhood may lead certain people to assume that others in their environment will always judge them negatively. These people come to expect rejection, misinterpret the reactions of others to fit that expectation, discount positive feedback, and generally fear social involvements—setting the stage for avoidant personality disorder (Lampe, 2015; Weishaar & Beck, 2006). In several studies, when participants with this disorder were asked to recall their childhood, their descriptions supported both the psychodynamic and cognitive-behavioral predictions (Carr & Francis, 2010; Herbert, 2007). They remembered, for example, feeling criticized, rejected, and isolated; receiving little encouragement from their parents; and experiencing few displays of parental love or pride.

Cognitive-behavioral theorists also suggest that most people with avoidant personality disorder fail to develop effective social skills, a failure that helps maintain the disorder. In support of this position, several studies have found social skills deficits among people with avoidant personality disorder (Moroni et al., 2016; Kantor, 2010; Herbert, 2007). Most of the theorists agree, however, that these deficits first develop as a result of the individuals avoiding so many social situations.

Treatments for Avoidant Personality Disorder
People with avoidant personality disorder come to therapy in the hope of finding acceptance and affection. Keeping them in treatment can be a challenge, however, for many of them soon begin to avoid the sessions. Often they distrust the therapist's sincerity and start to fear his or her rejection (Skodol & Bender, 2016). Thus, as with several of the other personality

Michael Prince

Just a stage This child sits alone on the steps of his school as other children pass by. That behavior could be a sign of being painfully shy, withdrawn, easily embarrassed, and uncomfortable with people. Early temperament is often linked to adult personality traits, but research has not shown that extreme shyness, a common and normal part of childhood, necessarily predicts the development of avoidant or dependent personality disorder in adulthood.

disorders, a key task of the therapist is to gain the person's trust (Skodol, 2016; Colli et al., 2014).

Beyond building trust, therapists tend to treat people with avoidant personality disorder much as they treat people with social anxiety disorder and other anxiety disorders. Such approaches have had at least modest success (Bernecker et al., 2017; Kikkert et al., 2016; Lampe, 2016). Psychodynamic therapists try to help clients recognize and resolve the unconscious conflicts that may be operating (Guina, 2016; Leichsenring & Salzer, 2014). Cognitive-behavioral therapists help them change their distressing beliefs and thoughts, carry on in the face of painful emotions, and improve their self-image (Lampe, 2016; Rees & Pritchard, 2013). They also provide social skills training and exposure treatments that require people to gradually increase their social contacts (Kampmann et al., 2016). Group therapy formats, especially groups that follow cognitive and behavioral principles, have the added advantage of providing clients with practice in social interactions (Balje et al., 2016; Bressert, 2017; Herbert et al., 2005). Antianxiety and antidepressant drugs are sometimes useful in reducing the social anxiety of people with the disorder, although the symptoms may return when medication is stopped (Nordahl et al., 2016; Skodol, 2016).

Dependent Personality Disorder

People with **dependent personality disorder** have a pervasive, excessive need to be taken care of (APA, 2013). As a result, they are clinging and obedient, fearing separation from their parent, spouse, or other person with whom they are in a close relationship. They rely on others so much that they cannot make the smallest decision for themselves. Lucas is a case in point.

> *Lucas, an assistant graphics programmer, is a 42-year-old single man who lives with his father. He is currently grappling with significant feelings of depression and anxiety. These feelings began when he ended his relationship of two years with Orena, whom he had viewed as the woman of his dreams and his future wife. But Lucas's father just didn't like Orena, and he certainly didn't like the idea of Lucas marrying her. In fact, he forbid it—forbid his middle-aged son from marrying the woman of his dreams.*
>
> *Inside, Lucas was furious at his father, although he knew he could never express his anger. Not that he was afraid of his father physically. His fear was in the psychological sphere. He simply could not—now or ever—risk his father getting angry at him, being disappointed in him, not talking to him, or being unsupportive. Then he might have to fend for himself, and that was unthinkable. At some level, he also thought that maybe his father was right, maybe he should not marry Orena. He always went along with his father's advice and decisions. He thought of himself as a person of poor judgment—too poor to make a decision, big or small, on his own.*
>
> *So eventually Lucas did what he always knew he would have to do—he broke up with Orena. He was more than ashamed and critical of himself, for hurting Orena, for being such a weakling, for giving up his dream so readily. But what could he do? He felt helpless and incapable of taking any other course of action.*
>
> *Lucas is not particularly accomplished in the various areas of his life. His job of 15 years is at least two levels below what he is capable of. Over the years, he has rejected promotion offers and has not responded to overtures from other graphic design companies. The reason was always the same: he didn't want—no, he was afraid to take on—additional responsibilities, especially responsibilities for making decisions and leading a team of workers. So he continues to work at the same job, for the same boss, in the same routine. He is considered dependable and hard-working—a never-changing fixture in the work setting.*
>
> *His social life is similarly modest and uneventful. Outside of Orena, his social life is limited to a single life-long friend. They get together for dinner and an activity three nights a week. If his friend ever cancels, Lucas feels lost.*

(continued on the next page)

#ShynessRocks

In recent years, rock music has been strongly influenced by stars with extremely shy, reticent demeanors.

The alternative rock band My Bloody Valentine often plays with their backs to the audience and spearheaded an influential pop movement called "shoegaze" based on their tendency to look away or at the floor during shows.

For many of her initial concerts, folk singer Cat Power (Chan Marshall) would not look at the audience and would weep or run offstage during shows.

dependent personality disorder A personality disorder characterized by a pattern of clinging and obedience, fear of separation, and an ongoing need to be taken care of.

> *Growing up, Lucas's older sisters, mother, and father always pampered and protected him, catering to his every need. Still he remembers being fearful and tentative throughout his childhood, always wanting to hold a family member's hand, afraid to do anything on his own. When his sisters grew older and moved away and after his mother died, it became just him and his father. Going away to college in another city was unthinkable. Without question, his father is now the most important person in his life. Although more than a little domineering, he loves Lucas and continues the family tradition of protecting and guiding him.*

It is normal and healthy to depend on others, but those with dependent personality disorder constantly need assistance with even the simplest matters and have extreme feelings of inadequacy and helplessness. Afraid that they cannot care for themselves, they cling desperately to friends or relatives.

As you observed previously, people with avoidant personality disorder have difficulty *initiating* relationships. In contrast, people with dependent personality disorder have difficulty with *separation*. They feel completely helpless and devastated when a close relationship ends, and they quickly seek out another relationship to fill the void. Many cling persistently to relationships with partners who physically or psychologically abuse them (Leemans & Loas, 2016; Loas et al., 2015, 2011).

Lacking confidence in their own ability and judgment, people with this disorder seldom disagree with others and allow even important decisions to be made for them (Bressert, 2017; Gore & Widiger, 2015). They may depend on a parent or spouse to decide where to live, what job to have, and which neighbors to befriend. Because they so fear rejection, they are overly sensitive to disapproval and keep trying to meet other people's wishes and expectations, even if it means volunteering for unpleasant or demeaning tasks.

Many people with dependent personality disorder feel distressed, lonely, and sad; often they dislike themselves. Thus they are at risk for depressive, anxiety, and eating disorders (Bornstein, 2012, 2007). Their fear of separation and their feelings of helplessness may leave them particularly prone to suicidal thoughts, especially when they believe that a relationship is about to end (Bornstein, 2012; Kiev, 1989).

Surveys suggest that fewer than 1 percent of the population experience dependent personality disorder (APA, 2013; Sansone & Sansone, 2011). For years, clinicians have believed that more women than men display this pattern, but some research suggests that the disorder is just as common in men (APA, 2013).

How Do Theorists Explain Dependent Personality Disorder? Psychodynamic explanations for dependent personality disorder are very similar to those for depression (Svartberg & McCullough, 2010). Freudian theorists argue, for example, that unresolved conflicts during the oral stage of development can give rise to a lifelong need for nurturance, thus heightening the likelihood of a dependent personality disorder (Bornstein, 2012, 2007, 2005). Similarly, object relations theorists say that early parental loss or rejection may prevent normal experiences of *attachment* and *separation,* leaving some children with fears of abandonment that persist throughout their lives (Caligor & Clarkin, 2010). Still other psychodynamic theorists suggest that, to the contrary, many parents of people with this disorder were overinvolved and overprotective, thus increasing their children's dependency, insecurity, and separation anxiety (Sperry, 2003).

Cognitive-behavioral theorists point to both behavioral and cognitive factors in their explanation of dependent personality disorder. In the behavioral realm, they propose that parents of people with dependent personality disorder unintentionally rewarded their children's clinging and "loyal" behavior, while at the same time punishing acts of independence, perhaps through the withdrawal of love. Alternatively, some parents' own dependent behaviors may have served as models for their children

(Bornstein, 2012, 2007). In the cognitive realm, the theorists identify two maladaptive attitudes as further helping to produce and maintain this disorder: (1) "I am inadequate and helpless to deal with the world," and (2) "I must find a person to provide protection so I can cope." Dichotomous (black-and-white) thinking may also play a key role: "If I am to be dependent, I must be completely helpless," or "If I am to be independent, I must be alone." Such thinking prevents sufferers from making efforts to be autonomous (Borge et al., 2010; Weishaar & Beck, 2006).

Treatments for Dependent Personality Disorder In therapy, people with dependent personality disorder usually place all responsibility for their treatment and well-being on the clinician. Thus a key task of therapy is to help patients accept responsibility for themselves (Bressert, 2017; Colli et al., 2014). Because the domineering behaviors of a spouse or parent may help foster a patient's symptoms, some clinicians suggest couple or family therapy as well, or even separate therapy for the partner or parent (Lebow & Uliaszek, 2010; Nichols, 2004).

"My self-esteem was so low I just followed her around everywhere she would go."

Treatment for dependent personality disorder can be at least modestly helpful. Psychodynamic therapy for this pattern focuses on many of the same issues as therapy for depressed people, including the *transference* of dependency needs onto the therapist (Svartberg & McCullough, 2010). Cognitive-behavioral therapists combine behavioral and cognitive interventions to help the clients take control of their lives. On the behavioral end, the therapists often provide assertiveness training to help the individuals better express their own wishes in relationships (Bressert, 2017; Farmer & Nelson-Gray, 2005). On the cognitive end, the therapists also try to help the clients challenge and change their assumptions of incompetence and helplessness (Bressert, 2017; Borge et al., 2010; Beck et al., 2004). Antidepressant drug therapy has been helpful for people whose personality disorder is accompanied by depression (Skodol, 2016; Fava et al., 2002).

As with avoidant personality disorder, a group therapy format can be helpful because it provides opportunities for the client to receive support from a number of peers rather than from a single dominant person (Bressert, 2017; Perry, 2005). In addition, group members may serve as models for one another as they practice better ways to express feelings and solve problems.

Obsessive-Compulsive Personality Disorder

People with **obsessive-compulsive personality disorder** are so preoccupied with order, perfection, and control that they lose all flexibility, openness, and efficiency (APA, 2013). Their concern for doing everything "right" impairs their productivity, as in the case of Joseph:

 Joseph was advised to seek assistance from a therapist following several months of relatively sleepless nights and a growing immobility and indecisiveness at his job. When first seen, he reported feelings of extreme self-doubt and guilt and prolonged periods of tension and diffuse anxiety. It was established early in therapy that he always had experienced these symptoms; they were now merely more pronounced than before.

The precipitant for this sudden increase in discomfort was a forthcoming change in his academic post. New administrative officers had assumed authority at the college, and he was asked to resign his deanship to return to regular departmental instruction. In the early sessions, Joseph spoke largely of his fear of facing classroom students again, wondered if he could organize his material well, and doubted that he could keep classes disciplined

obsessive-compulsive personality disorder A personality disorder marked by such an intense focus on orderliness, perfectionism, and control that the person loses flexibility, openness, and efficiency.

(continued on the next page)

and interested in his lectures. It was his preoccupation with these matters that he believed was preventing him from concentrating and completing his present responsibilities.

At no time did Joseph express anger toward the new college officials for the demotion he was asked to accept; he repeatedly voiced his "complete confidence" in the "rationality of their decision." Yet, when face-to-face with them, he observed that he stuttered and was extremely tremulous.

Joseph was the second of two sons, younger than his brother by three years. His father was a successful engineer, and his mother a high school teacher. Both were "efficient, orderly, and strict" parents. Life at home was "extremely well planned," with "daily and weekly schedules of responsibility posted" and "vacations arranged a year or two in advance." Nothing apparently was left to chance. . . . Joseph adopted the "good boy" image. Unable to challenge his brother either physically, intellectually, or socially, he became a "paragon of virtue." By being punctilious, scrupulous, methodical, and orderly, he could avoid antagonizing his perfectionistic parents, and would, at times, obtain preferred treatment from them. He obeyed their advice, took their guidance as gospel, and hesitated making any decision before gaining their approval. Although he recalled "fighting" with his brother before he was 6 or 7, he "restrained my anger from that time on and never upset my parents again."

(Millon, 2011, 1969, pp. 278–279)

#CriticalDifference

People with obsessive-compulsive disorder typically do not want or like their symptoms; those with obsessive-compulsive personality disorder often embrace their symptoms and rarely wish to resist them.

In Joseph's concern with rules and order and doing things right, he has trouble seeing the larger picture. When faced with a task, he and others who have obsessive-compulsive personality disorder may become so focused on organization and details that they fail to grasp the point of the activity. As a result, their work is often behind schedule (some seem unable to finish any job), and they may neglect leisure activities and friendships.

People with this personality disorder set unreasonably high standards for themselves and others. Their behaviors extend well beyond the realm of conscientiousness. They can never be satisfied with their performance, but they typically refuse to seek help or to work with a team, convinced that others are too careless or incompetent to do the job right. Because they are so afraid of making mistakes, they may be reluctant to make decisions (Wheaton & Pinto, 2017).

They also tend to be rigid and stubborn, particularly in their morals, ethics, and values. They live by a strict personal code and use it as a yardstick for measuring others. They may have trouble expressing much affection, and their relationships are sometimes stiff and superficial (Cain et al., 2015). In addition, they are often stingy with their time or money. Some cannot even throw away objects that are worn out or useless (Riddle et al., 2016; APA, 2013).

According to surveys, as many as 7.9 percent of the adult population display obsessive-compulsive personality disorder, with white, educated, married, and employed people receiving the diagnosis most often (APA, 2013; Sansone & Sansone, 2011). Men are twice as likely as women to display the disorder.

Many clinicians believe that obsessive-compulsive personality disorder and *obsessive-compulsive disorder* are closely related. Certainly, the two disorders share a number of features, and many people who suffer from one of the disorders meet the diagnostic criteria for the other disorder (Starcevic & Brakoulias, 2017; Gordon et al., 2016). However, it is worth noting that people with the personality disorder are more likely to suffer from either major depressive disorder, an anxiety disorder, or a substance use disorder than from obsessive-compulsive disorder (Brakoulias et al., 2017; APA, 2013). In fact, researchers have not consistently found a specific link between obsessive-compulsive personality disorder and obsessive-compulsive disorder (Starcevic & Brakoulias, 2017, 2014).

"You'll have to excuse me—I'm myself today."

How Do Theorists Explain Obsessive-Compulsive Personality Disorder?

Most explanations of obsessive-compulsive personality disorder borrow heavily from those of obsessive-compulsive disorder, despite the doubts concerning a link between the two disorders. As with so many of the personality disorders, psychodynamic explanations dominate and research evidence is limited.

Freudian theorists suggest that people with obsessive-compulsive personality disorder are *anal retentive*. That is, because of overly harsh toilet training during the anal stage, they become filled with anger, and they remain *fixated* at this stage. To keep their anger under control, they persistently resist both their anger and their instincts to have bowel movements. In turn, they become extremely orderly and restrained; many become passionate collectors. Other psychodynamic theorists suggest that any early struggles with parents over control and independence may ignite the aggressive impulses at the root of this personality disorder (Kanehisa et al., 2017; Bartz et al., 2007).

Cognitive-behavioral theorists have little to say about the origins of obsessive-compulsive personality disorder, but they do propose that illogical thinking processes help keep it going (Paast et al., 2016; Weishaar & Beck, 2006; Beck et al., 2004). They point, for example, to dichotomous thinking, which may produce rigidity and perfectionism. Similarly, they note that people with this disorder tend to misread or exaggerate the potential outcomes of mistakes or errors.

Treatments for Obsessive-Compulsive Personality Disorder People with obsessive-compulsive personality disorder do not usually believe there is anything wrong with them. They therefore are not likely to seek treatment unless they are also suffering from another disorder, most frequently an anxiety disorder or depression, or unless someone close to them insists that they get treatment (Bartz et al., 2007). Because of this, therapists often feel as though they must "win over" and engage the clients in the therapy process (Colli et al., 2014).

People with obsessive-compulsive personality disorder often respond well to psychodynamic or cognitive-behavioral therapy (Smith et al., 2017; Kikkert et al., 2016; Weishaar & Beck, 2006). Psychodynamic therapists typically try to help these clients recognize, experience, and accept their underlying feelings and insecurities, and perhaps take risks and accept their personal limitations (Bressert, 2016). Cognitive therapists focus on helping the clients to change their dichotomous—"all or nothing"—thinking, perfectionism, indecisiveness, procrastination, and chronic worrying (Bressert, 2016). A number of clinicians report that people with obsessive-compulsive personality disorder, like those with obsessive-compulsive disorder, respond well to SSRIs, the serotonin-enhancing antidepressant drugs; however, researchers have yet to study this issue fully (Pinto et al., 2008).

Toilet trouble According to Freud, toilet training often produces rage in a child. If parents are too harsh in their approach, the child may become fixated at the anal stage and prone to obsessive-compulsive functioning later in life.

Multicultural Factors: Research Neglect

ACCORDING TO THE CURRENT CRITERIA of DSM-5, a pattern diagnosed as a personality disorder must "deviate markedly from the expectations of the individual's culture" (APA, 2013). Given the importance of culture in this diagnosis, and given the enormous clinical interest in personality disorders, it is striking how little multicultural research has been conducted on these problems. Clinical theorists have suspicions but little compelling evidence that there are cultural differences in this realm (Ascoli et al., 2017; NIMH, 2017; Iacovino et al., 2014).

The lack of multicultural research is of special concern with regard to borderline personality disorder, the pattern characterized by extreme mood fluctuations, outbursts of intense anger, self-injurious behavior, fear of abandonment, feelings of emptiness, problematic relationships, and identity confusion, because many theorists are

#PersonalityDemographics

6%	People with severe personality disorders who are unemployed
23%	People with severe personality disorders who have never married
59%	People with severe personality disorders who are male

(Information from: Sareen et al., 2011; Cloninger & Svrakic, 2005)

Too little attention As illustrated by this diverse group of people, we live in a multicultural nation and world. The field of psychology has devoted considerable study to a range of cultural and racial differences. However, it has given relatively little attention to multicultural differences in the development, features, and treatment of personality disorders.

convinced that gender and other cultural differences may be particularly important in both the development and diagnosis of this disorder.

As you read earlier, around 75 percent of all people who receive a diagnosis of borderline personality disorder are female (Skodol, 2017, 2016). Although it may be that women are biologically more prone to the disorder or that diagnostic bias is at work, this gender difference may instead be a reflection of the extraordinary traumas to which many women are subjected as children (Daigre et al., 2015). Recall, for example, that the childhoods of some people with borderline personality disorder are filled with emotional trauma, victimization, violence, and abuse, at times sexual abuse. It may be, a number of theorists argue, that experiences of this kind are *prerequisites* to the development of borderline personality disorder, that women in our society are particularly subjected to such experiences, and that, in fact, the disorder should more properly be viewed and treated as a special form of posttraumatic stress disorder (Kulkarni, 2017; Sherry & Whilde, 2008; Hodges, 2003). In the absence of systematic research, however, alternative explanations like this remain untested and corresponding treatments undeveloped.

In a related vein, given the childhood experiences that typically precede borderline personality disorder, some multicultural theorists believe that the disorder may actually be a reaction to persistent feelings of marginality, powerlessness, and social failure (Sherry & Whilde, 2008; Miller, 1999, 1994). That is, the disorder may be attributable more to social inequalities (including sexism, racism, or homophobia) than to psychological factors.

Given such possibilities, it is most welcome that a few multicultural studies of borderline personality disorder have been conducted over the past decade (Skodol, 2017; De Genna & Feske, 2013). In these undertakings, researchers assessed the prevalence of the personality disorder in diverse clinical populations (Meaney et al., 2016; Trull et al., 2010; Chavira et al., 2003). They found that Hispanic American individuals qualified for a diagnosis of borderline personality disorder more often than non-Hispanic white American or African American individuals did. Could it be that Hispanic Americans generally are more likely than other cultural groups to display this disorder, and—if so—why? Questions of this kind underline once again the need for more multicultural research into personality disorders.

Are There Better Ways to Classify Personality Disorders?

THE LEADING CRITICISM OF DSM-5'S approach to personality disorders is, as you read earlier, that the classification system defines such disorders by using *categories*—rather than *dimensions*—of personality. Many of today's theorists believe that personality disorders differ more in *degree* than in type of dysfunction. Therefore, they propose that the disorders should be classified by the severity of key personality traits (or dimensions) rather than by the presence or absence of specific traits (Anderson et al., 2018, 2016; Carvalho et al., 2017). In such an approach, each key trait (for example, disagreeableness, dishonesty, or self-absorption) would be seen as varying along a continuum in which there is no clear boundary between normal and abnormal. People with a personality disorder would be those who display extreme degrees of several of these key traits—degrees not commonly found in the general population (see *InfoCentral* on the next page).

> Why do some observers suggest that personality disorders are little more than descriptions of undesirable personal styles?

#BigOverlap

Suspiciousness, self-absorption, anxiety, and depression are prominent features in almost all 10 personality disorders in DSM-5.

Hostility, oversensitivity, and being controlling are prominent features in at least half of the 10 personality disorders in DSM-5.

THE DARK TRIAD

Over the past 15 years, researchers have studied the **Dark Triad**, a trio of "malicious" traits that work together to produce socially offensive behaviors (Muris et al., 2017; Paulhus & Williams, 2002). People with these traits—*narcissism*, *psychopathy*, and *Machiavellianism*—tend to undermine others, perhaps secretly, to achieve their own ends (Whitbourne, 2013).

Individuals with just one of these traits often offend, manipulate, or disregard the needs of others. But those with **all three** traits are particularly self-absorbed and create serious problems for others. People who score high on Dark Triad rating scales may display a personality disorder, but more often, they experience little distress or impairment and function adequately, sometimes quite effectively, in the personal, social, and occupational realms.

WHAT IS THE DARK TRIAD?

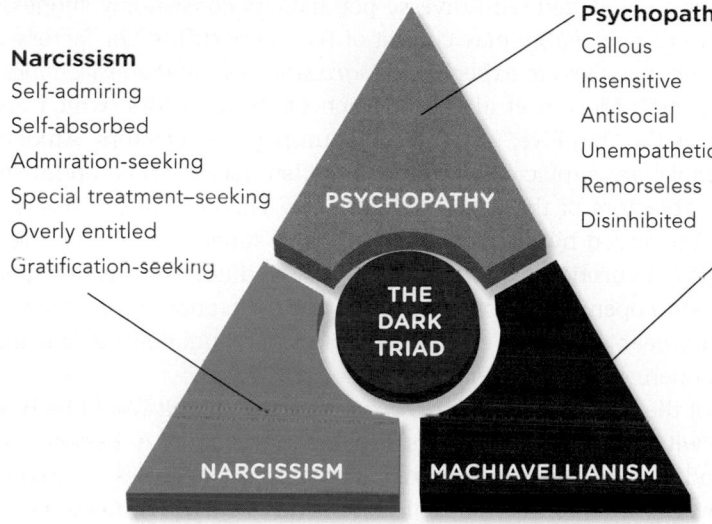

Narcissism
Self-admiring
Self-absorbed
Admiration-seeking
Special treatment–seeking
Overly entitled
Gratification-seeking

PSYCHOPATHY

THE DARK TRIAD

NARCISSISM MACHIAVELLIANISM

Psychopathy
Callous
Insensitive
Antisocial
Unempathetic
Remorseless
Disinhibited

Machiavellianism
Manipulative
Self-interested
Duplicitous
Cynical
Amoral
Focused on personal gain

(Jonason & Paulhus, 2017; Muris et al., 2017; Whitbourne, 2013)

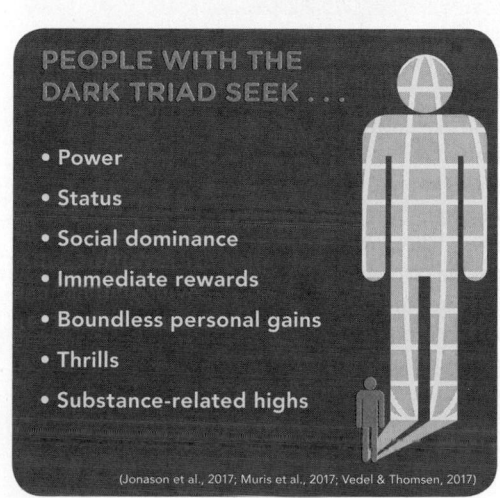

PEOPLE WITH THE DARK TRIAD SEEK . . .

• Power
• Status
• Social dominance
• Immediate rewards
• Boundless personal gains
• Thrills
• Substance-related highs

(Jonason et al., 2017; Muris et al., 2017; Vedel & Thomsen, 2017)

THE DARK TRIAD AFFECTS ALL SPHERES OF LIFE

The PERSONAL realm
People are more likely to be...

Immodest   Dishonest
Disagreeable   Substance abusers
Greedy   Aggressive drivers
Suspicious

(Jones & Paulhus, 2017; Muris et al., 2017; Burtăverde et al., 2016; Sabouri et al., 2016; Furnham et al., 2013)

THE DARK TRIAD

The SOCIAL sphere
People are more likely to be...

Dominant   Bullies
Prejudiced   Extroverted
Unethical   Aggressive
                Insensitive

(Muris et al., 2017; Furnham et al., 2013)

The SEXUAL realm
People are more likely to...

Pursue quick gratification   Seek more sexual partners
Seek casual sex   Commit sexual infidelities
Display aggressive strategies   Poach mates from others
Exhibit sexual opportunism

(Jonason et al., 2017, 2011, 2010, 2009; Furnham et al., 2013; Whitbourne, 2013)

At WORK
People are more likely to...

Have troubled work relationships   Commit sexual harassment
Exhibit toxic leadership   Hinder career success of
Ruthlessly seek self-advancement   subordinates
Cheat   Adversely affect personal well-
                                    being of subordinates

(Jones & Paulhus, 2017; Muris et al., 2017; Volmer et al., 2016; Zeigler-Hill et al., 2016; Furnham et al., 2013)

WHO IS MORE LIKELY TO DISPLAY THE DARK TRIAD?

THE DARK TRIAD

Men > Women

Non-Hispanic white Americans > Ethnic/racial minorities

CEOs/upper managers > Nonmanagement workers

Internet trolls > Nonmalevolent users

(Lopes & Yu, 2017; Muris et al., 2017; Vedel & Thomsen, 2017; Dahling et al., 2008; Twenge & Foster, 2008)

THE DARK TRIAD AND SUCCESS

People tend to...

• Attain leadership positions
• Earn higher salaries
• Experience career satisfaction
• Negotiate effectively

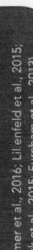

THE DARK TRIAD

(Volmer et al., 2016; Lilienfeld et al., 2015; Spurk et al., 2015; Furnham et al., 2013)

Which key personality dimensions should clinicians use to help identify people with personality problems? Some theorists believe that they should rely on the dimensions identified in the "Big Five" theory of personality, dimensions that have received enormous attention by personality psychologists over the years.

The "Big Five" Theory of Personality and Personality Disorders

A large body of research conducted with diverse populations consistently suggests that the basic structure of personality may consist of five "supertraits," or factors—*neuroticism, extroversion, openness to experiences, agreeableness,* and *conscientiousness* (Chapman et al., 2017; Morton et al., 2016). Each of these factors, which are frequently referred to as the "Big Five," consists of a number of subfactors. Anxiety and hostility, for example, are subfactors of the neuroticism factor, while optimism and friendliness are subfactors of the extroversion factor. Theoretically, everyone's personality can be summarized by a combination of these supertraits. One person may display high levels of neuroticism and agreeableness, medium extroversion, and low conscientiousness and openness to experiences. In contrast, another person may display high levels of agreeableness and conscientiousness, medium neuroticism and extroversion, and low openness to experiences. And so on.

Many proponents of the Big Five model have argued further that it would be best to describe all people with personality disorders as being high, low, or in between on the five supertraits and to drop the use of personality disorder categories altogether (Song & Shi, 2017; Glover et al., 2011; Lawton et al., 2011). Thus a particular person who currently qualifies for a diagnosis of avoidant personality disorder might instead be described as displaying a high degree of neuroticism, medium degrees of agreeableness and conscientiousness, and very low degrees of extroversion and openness to new experiences. Similarly, a person currently diagnosed with narcissistic personality disorder might be described in the Big Five approach as displaying very high degrees of neuroticism and extroversion, medium degrees of conscientiousness and openness to new experiences, and a very low degree of agreeableness.

"Personality Disorder—Trait Specified": DSM-5's Proposed Dimensional Approach

The "Big Five" approach to personality disorders has received considerable study, and some theorists would like it to be used as the official classification approach in the United States and around the world. Instead, the framers of the ICD (the classification system used in most countries outside the United States) and the DSM (the classification system used in the United States) have each developed their own dimensional approach for classifying personality disorders, and they plan to use those approaches in their future editions. Indeed, as you read earlier, the DSM-5 framers have already included a detailed description of their proposed dimensional approach in DSM-5, so that it can be examined by clinicians and studied and tested by researchers.

DSM-5's proposed dimensional approach to personality disorders begins with the notion that people whose traits significantly impair their functioning should receive a diagnosis called **personality disorder—trait specified (PDTS)** (APA, 2013). When assigning this diagnosis, clinicians would also identify and list the problematic traits and rate the severity of impairment caused by them. According to the proposal, five groups of problematic traits would be eligible for a diagnosis of PDTS: *negative affectivity, detachment, antagonism, disinhibition,* and *psychoticism.*

- **Negative Affectivity** People who display negative affectivity experience negative emotions frequently and intensely. In particular, they exhibit one or more of the following traits: *emotional lability* (unstable emotions), *anxiousness, separation*

#AsSuspected

For years, people have suspected that individuals who like dogs may be psychologically different from those who like cats. Research supports such speculation (Cherry, 2017; Gossling et al., 2015). Almost 5,000 participants filled out a Big Five personality inventory. On average, the "dog people" scored higher than the "cat people" on extroversion, agreeableness, and conscientiousness. In contrast, the cat people scored higher on introversion and curiosity (i.e., openness to experiences).

#AnimalTraits

Researchers have found that animals of every kind—from spiders to lions—display distinct differences in their personalities, behaviors, and preferences. Among sheep, for example, some are leaders and others followers. Similarly, sheep differ in their individual levels of fearfulness, vocalization, friendliness, and distraction. These differences often hold steady throughout their lives (Cherry, 2017; Angier, 2010).

Dysfunctional toons Today's animated film characters often display significant personality flaws or disorders. Some have a single dysfunctional trait, as is the case for Angry Birds, while others may have "clusters" of problematic traits, as shown by the *South Park* kids. Some observers suggest that the latter (especially Cartman, second from left) show enduring grumpiness, disrespect for authority, irreverence, self-absorption, disregard for the feelings of others, general lack of conscience, and a tendency to get into trouble.

insecurity, perseveration (repetition of certain behaviors despite repeated failures), *submissiveness, hostility, depressivity, suspiciousness,* and *strong emotional reactions* (overreactions to emotionally arousing situations).

- **Detachment** People who manifest detachment tend to withdraw from other people and social interactions. They may exhibit any of the following traits: *restricted emotional reactivity* (little reaction to emotionally arousing situations), *depressivity, suspiciousness, withdrawal, anhedonia* (inability to feel pleasure or take interest in things), and *intimacy avoidance.* You'll note that two of the traits in this group— depressivity and suspiciousness—are also found in the negative affectivity group.

- **Antagonism** People who display antagonism behave in ways that put them at odds with other people. They may exhibit any of the following traits: *manipulativeness, deceitfulness, grandiosity, attention seeking, callousness,* and *hostility.* Hostility is also found in the negative affectivity group.

- **Disinhibition** People who manifest disinhibition behave impulsively, without reflecting on potential future consequences. They may exhibit any of the following traits: *irresponsibility, impulsivity, distractibility, risk taking,* and *imperfection/ disorganization.*

- **Psychoticism** People who display psychoticism have unusual and bizarre experiences. They may exhibit any of the following traits: *unusual beliefs and experiences, eccentricity,* and *cognitive and perceptual dysregulation* (odd thought processes and sensory experiences).

If a person is impaired significantly by any of the five trait groups, or even by just 1 of the 25 traits that make up those groups, he or she would qualify for a diagnosis of *personality disorder—trait specified.* In such cases, the diagnostician would indicate which traits are impaired.

Consider, for example, Lucas, the unhappy 42-year-old assistant graphics programmer described on page 501. As you'll recall, Lucas meets the criteria for a diagnosis of dependent personality disorder under DSM-5's current categorical approach, based largely on his lifetime of extreme dependence on his father, mother, sisters, friends, and coworkers. Using the alternative dimensional approach presented in DSM-5, a diagnostician would instead observe that Lucas is significantly impaired by several of the traits that characterize the negative affectivity trait group. He is, for example, greatly impaired by "separation insecurity." This trait has prevented him from ever living on his own, marrying his girlfriend, disagreeing with his father, advancing at work, and broadening his social life. In addition, Lucas seems to be impaired significantly by the traits of "submissiveness," "anxiousness," and "depressivity." Given

personality disorder—trait specified (PDTS) A personality disorder currently undergoing study for possible inclusion in a future revision of DSM-5. People would receive this diagnosis if they had significant impairment in their functioning as a result of one or more very problematic traits.

"Today I'm going to be unaware, uninvolved, uncommitted and self-centered."

this picture, his therapist might assign him a diagnosis of *personality disorder—trait specified, with problematic traits of separation insecurity, submissiveness, anxiousness, and depressivity.*

According to this dimensional approach, when clinicians assign a diagnosis of personality disorder—trait specified, they also must rate the degree of dysfunction caused by each of the person's traits, using a five-point scale ranging from "little or no impairment" (Rating = 0) to "extreme impairment" (Rating = 4).

Consider Lucas once again. He would probably warrant a rating of "0" on most of the 25 traits listed in the DSM-5 proposal, a rating of "3" on the traits of anxiousness and depressivity, and a rating of "4" on the traits of separation insecurity and submissiveness. Altogether, he would receive the following cumbersome, but informative, diagnosis:

Diagnosis: *Personality Disorder—Trait Specified*

Separation insecurity: Rating 4

Submissiveness: Rating 4

Anxiousness: Rating 3

Depressivity: Rating 3

Other traits: Rating 0

This dimensional approach to personality disorders may indeed prove superior to DSM-5's current categorical approach. Thus far, however, it has caused its own stir in the clinical community. Many clinicians believe that the proposed changes would give too much latitude to diagnosticians—allowing them to apply diagnoses of personality disorder to an enormous range of personality patterns. Still others worry that the requirements of the newly proposed system are too cumbersome or complicated. Thus a number of researchers are currently conducting studies to clarify the merits and drawbacks of the proposed system (Anderson et al., 2018, 2016; Rojas & Widiger, 2016). Only time and continued research will determine whether the alternative system is indeed a useful approach to the classification and diagnosis of personality disorders.

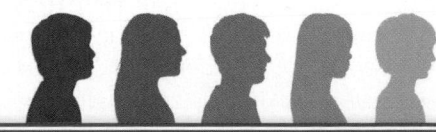

CLINICAL CHOICES

Now that you've read about personality disorders, try the interactive case study for this chapter. See if you are able to identify Alicia's symptoms and suggest a diagnosis based on her symptoms. What kind of treatment would be most effective for Alicia? Go to **Launch**Pad to access *Clinical Choices*.

||||||||||||||||||||||||||||||||||||||||||||||||||||||||||||||||||||||||||||||||||

Rediscovered, Then Reconsidered

DURING THE FIRST HALF OF the twentieth century, clinicians believed deeply in the unique, enduring patterns we call personality, and they tried to define important personality traits. They then discovered how readily people can be shaped by the situations in which they find themselves, and a backlash developed. The concept of personality seemed to lose legitimacy, and for a while it became almost an obscene word in some circles. The clinical category of personality disorders went through a similar rejection. When psychodynamic and humanistic theorists dominated the clinical field, *neurotic character disorders*—a set of diagnoses similar to today's personality disorders—were considered useful clinical categories, but their popularity declined as other models grew in influence.

During the past 25 years, serious interest in personality and personality disorders has rebounded. In case after case, clinicians have concluded that rigid personality traits do seem to pose special problems, and they have developed new objective tests and interview guides to assess these disorders, setting in motion a wave of systematic research (Clarkin et al., 2018). So far, only the antisocial and borderline personality disorders have received much study. However, with DSM-5 now considering a new—dimensional—classification approach for possible use in the future, additional research is likely to follow. This may allow clinicians to better answer some pressing questions: How common are the various personality disorders? How useful are personality disorder categories? How effective is a dimensional approach to diagnosing these disorders? And which treatments are most effective?

In short, DSM-5's proposal of a dimensional classification approach eventually may lead to major changes in the field's understanding, diagnosis, and treatment of personality disorders. Now that clinicians have rediscovered personality disorders, they must determine the most appropriate ways to think about, explain, and treat them.

♥... SUMMING UP

» **Personality Disorders and DSM-5** People with a *personality disorder* display an enduring, rigid pattern of inner experience and outward behavior. Their personality traits are much more extreme and dysfunctional than those of most other people in their culture, resulting in significant problems for them or those around them. It has been estimated that as many as 15 percent of adults develop such a disorder at some point in their lives. DSM-5 uses a *categorical approach* that lists 10 distinct personality disorders. In addition, the framers of DSM-5 have proposed a *dimensional approach* to the classification of personality disorders. *pp. 473–475*

» **"Odd" Personality Disorders** Three of the personality disorders in DSM-5 are marked by the kinds of odd or eccentric behavior often seen in schizophrenia. People with *paranoid personality disorder* display a broad pattern of distrust and suspiciousness. Those with *schizoid personality disorder* persistently avoid social relationships, have little or no social interest, and show little emotional expression. People with *schizotypal personality disorder* display a range of interpersonal problems marked by extreme discomfort in close relationships, very odd forms of thinking and behavior, and behavioral eccentricities. People with these three kinds of disorders usually are resistant to treatment, and treatment gains tend to be modest at best. *pp. 475–481*

» **"Dramatic" Personality Disorders** Four of the personality disorders in DSM-5 are marked by highly dramatic, emotional, or erratic symptoms. People with *antisocial personality disorder* display a pattern of disregard for and violation of the rights of others. No known treatment is notably effective. People with *borderline personality disorder* display a pattern of instability in interpersonal relationships, self-image, and mood, along with extreme impulsivity. Treatment apparently can be helpful and lead to some improvement. People with

histrionic personality disorder display a pattern of extreme emotionality and attention seeking. Clinical case reports suggest that treatment is helpful on occasion. Finally, people with *narcissistic personality disorder* display a pattern of grandiosity, need for admiration, and lack of empathy. It is one of the most difficult disorders to treat. *pp. 481–498*

» **"Anxious" Personality Disorder** Three of the personality disorders in DSM-5 are marked by anxious and fearful behavior. People with *avoidant personality disorder* are consistently uncomfortable and inhibited in social situations, overwhelmed by feelings of inadequacy, and extremely sensitive to negative evaluation. People with *dependent personality disorder* have a persistent need to be taken care of, are submissive and clinging, and fear separation. People with *obsessive-compulsive personality disorder* are so preoccupied with order, perfection, and control that they lose their flexibility, openness, and efficiency. A variety of treatment strategies have been used for people with these disorders and apparently have been modestly to moderately helpful. *pp. 499–505*

» **Multicultural Factors** Despite the field's growing focus on personality disorders, relatively little research has been done on gender and other *multicultural* influences. *pp. 505–506*

» **Are There Better Ways to Classify Personality Disorders?** Given the significant problems posed by DSM-5's current *categorical approach*, a number of today's theorists believe that personality disorders should instead be described and classified by a *dimensional approach*. Thus, the framers of DSM-5 have developed a dimensional approach called the *"personality disorder—trait specified"* model. A description of this approach is under study for possible inclusion in a future revision of DSM-5. *pp. 506–510*

Visit *LaunchPad*
to access the e-Book, Clinical Choices, videos, activities, and LearningCurve, as well as study aids including flashcards, FAQs, and research exercises.

LaunchPad
macmillan learning

⚲...Disorders Common Among Children and Adolescents

When Cameron was eight years old, his mother started to worry about him. Not so coincidentally, his teacher was becoming concerned at the same time. What they both saw was a sad, and seemingly lost, little boy. At home Cameron just wanted to lie around and watch TV. He would do his chores, and answer his parents' questions—in as few words as possible— but he initiated almost nothing. He ate only when told to eat. He showed little interest in his beloved iPad, and stopped playing computer games. Nor did Cameron seek out playmates anymore. His mother had to virtually drag him to their houses. Nothing gave him pleasure. Cameron also seemed to have more than a few physical problems—from headaches to stomach pains, it was always something, yet the doctor said he checked out fine.

The story was similar at school. Cameron was obedient and compliant, always did what his teacher asked, but he seemed sad and joyless. He rarely joined in class discussions. He stayed in a group with the other kids as they travelled from the classroom to the cafeteria or the schoolyard, but he interacted very little with anyone in particular. When the school psychologist interviewed him, she noticed that he made no eye contact, offered little, and rarely smiled.

When the counselor asked Cameron's mother and teacher if anything special had triggered his unhappiness, they both pointed to the departure of his two best friends—twins who had moved to another state two months ago. But, at the same time, the more they thought about it, that was not really the beginning of Cameron's slide. It certainly worsened things, but his sad mood, inactivity, and isolation had been increasing for quite a while before that.

Ricky Smith was a 7-year-old. . . . During her initial call to the clinic, Mrs. Smith said her son was "out of control." She said Ricky "was all over the place" and "constantly getting into trouble." . . .

Ricky . . . said his teacher, Mrs. Candler, was always yelling at him and sending notes home to his mother. Ricky initially said he did not know why the teacher yelled at him but then said it was mostly about not paying attention or following class rules. . . .

Ricky . . . said he had a few friends but often had to keep to himself. This was because Mrs. Candler made him spend much of the school day in a corner of the classroom to complete his work. Unfortunately, little of the work was successfully finished. Ricky said he felt bored, sad, tired, and angry in the classroom. . . .

Ricky said his mother yelled at him a lot. . . . He said he felt happiest when riding his bike because nobody yelled at him and he could "go wherever I want." . . .

Mrs. Smith said Ricky was almost intolerable in the classroom, . . . crying when asked to do something, stomping his feet, and being disrespectful to the teacher. . . . [She also said] her son was generally "out of control" at home. He would not listen to her commands and often ran around the house until he got what he wanted. She and her son often argued about his homework, chores, [and] misbehavior. . . [In addition,] Ricky often fidgeted and lost many of his school materials. He was disorganized and paid little attention to long-term consequences. The child was also difficult to control in public places, such as a supermarket or church. . . .

Ricky's teacher . . . added that Ricky's academic performance was below average. . . He understood and completed his reading and math assignments when motivated to do so but his attention was sporadic and insufficient. . . . Ricky was [also] getting out of his seat more and more, requiring a constant response. . . .

(Kearney, 2013, pp. 62–64)

Cameron and Ricky are both displaying psychological disorders. Their disorders are disrupting the boys' family ties, school performances, and social relationships, but each disorder does so in a particular way and for particular reasons. Cameron, who may qualify for a diagnosis of *major depressive disorder*, struggles constantly with sadness, disinterest in other people and activities, and lack of pleasure, along with stomachaches and other physical ailments. Ricky's main problems, on the other hand, are that he cannot concentrate and is overly active and impulsive—difficulties that characterize attention-deficit/hyperactivity disorder (ADHD).

Abnormal functioning can occur at any time in life. Some patterns of abnormality, however, are more likely to emerge during particular periods—during childhood for example, or, at the other end of the spectrum, during old age. In this chapter you will read about disorders that commonly have their onset during childhood or early adolescence. In the next chapter you'll learn about problems that are more prevalent among the elderly. ▪

Childhood and Adolescence

PEOPLE OFTEN THINK OF CHILDHOOD as a carefree and happy time—yet it can also be frightening and upsetting (see **Figure 17-1**). In fact, children of all cultures typically have at least some emotional and behavioral problems as they encounter new people and situations. Surveys reveal that *worry* is a common experience: close to half of all children in the United States have multiple fears, particularly concerning school, health, and personal safety (Jovanovic et al., 2014; Szabo & Lovibond, 2004). Bed-wetting, nightmares, temper tantrums, and restlessness are other problems that many children contend with. Adolescence can also be a difficult period. Physical and sexual changes, social and academic pressures, school violence, personal doubts, and temptations cause many teenagers to feel nervous, confused, and depressed.

A particular concern among children and adolescents is that of being bullied (see *InfoCentral* on the next page). Surveys throughout the world have revealed repeatedly that bullying ranks as a major problem in the minds of most young respondents, often a bigger problem than racism, AIDS, and peer pressure to try sex or alcohol (Hymel & Swearer, 2015). More generally, over 20 percent of students report being bullied frequently, and more than 50 percent report having been bullied at least once (DTL, 2017). Typically, kids who have been bullied react with feelings of humiliation, anxiety, or dislike for school. In extreme cases, they may attempt suicide (Barzilay et al., 2017; Ford et al., 2017). Moreover, the psychological effects of being bullied can reach far into adulthood (Arseneault, 2017; Takizawa, Maughan, & Arseneault, 2014). Also troubling, the technological advances of today's world have broadened the ways in which children and adolescents can be bullied, and *cyberbullying*—bullying and humiliating by e-mail, text messages, and social media—is now on the rise (Kim et al., 2018).

> Most people who are bullied are upset by it, but some seem to be more traumatized by the experience than others. Why might this be so?

Beyond these common concerns and psychological difficulties, at least one-fifth of all children and adolescents in North America also experience a diagnosable psychological disorder (Costello & Angold, 2016; Costello et al., 2016). Boys with disorders outnumber girls, even though most of the adult psychological disorders are more common among women.

FIGURE 17-1

Are Parents Aware of Their Children's Stress?

Not always, according to a large survey of parents and their children aged 8 to 17. For example, although 44 percent of the child respondents report that they worry about school, only 34 percent of the parent respondents believe that their children are worried about school. (Information from: Munsey, 2010.)

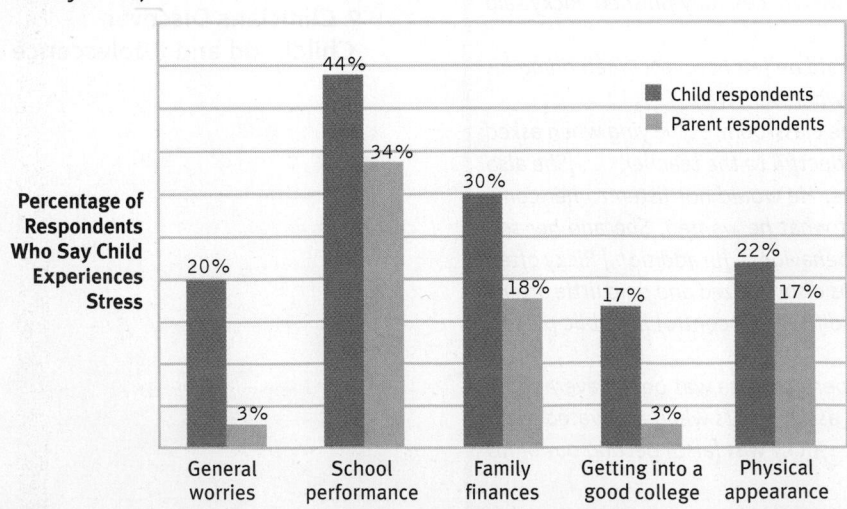

CHILD AND ADOLESCENT BULLYING

Bullying is the repeated infliction of force, threats, or coercion in order to intimidate, hurt, or dominate another, less powerful person. It is particularly common among children and adolescents. Members of certain minority groups, such as LGBTQ individuals, are much more likely to be bullied. Over the past decade, clinicians and educators have learned that bullying is much more common and more harmful than previously thought.

(USDHHS, 2017)

TYPES OF BULLYING

Physical — hitting, pushing, tripping

Verbal — name-calling, mean taunting, sexual comments, threatening

spreading rumors, posting embarrassing images, rejecting from group

Relational/Social

BULLIES TEND TO:
Display antisocial behaviors
Perform poorly in school
Drop out of school
Bring weapons to school
Drink alcohol
Smoke cigarettes
Use drugs

(BSA, 2017; CDC, 2017; Hertz & Donato, 2013)

EFFECTS OF BULLYING
Depression
Suicidal thinking and attempts
Anxiety
Low self-esteem
Sleep problems
Somatic symptoms
Substance use and abuse
School problems and/or phobias
Antisocial behavior

(APA, 2017; Barzilay et al., 2017; BSA, 2017; CDC, 2017, 2015; CRC, 2017; UNESCO, 2017)

BULLYING IS ON THE RISE...
39% over age 50
54% under age 50
people bullied as teenagers

(DTL, 2017; Harris Interactive, 2014; Ratcliffe, 2014; NFER, 2010)

SCHOOL BULLYING

Much bullying takes place at school. Around **2/3** of all school bullying occurs in hallways, schoolyards, bathrooms, cafeterias, or buses. A full **1/3** occurs in classrooms, while teachers are present (BSA, 2014). It is estimated that **30% to 40%** of school bullying goes unreported. (BSA, 2017; NB, 2017; UNESCO, 2017; USDHHS, 2017)

The Nature of School Bullying

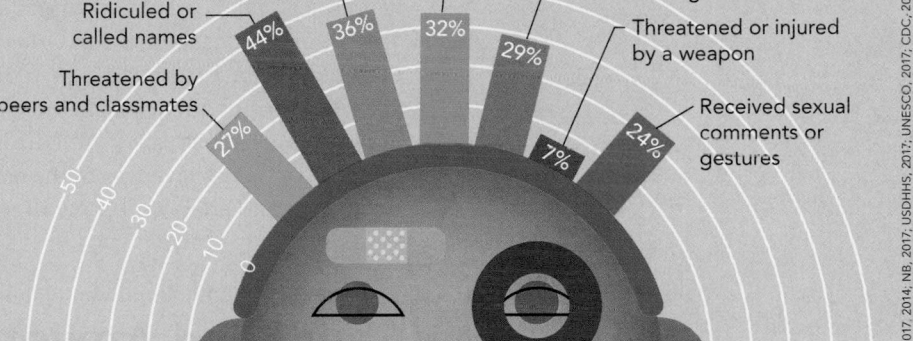

Slandered by lies and rumors — 44%
Ridiculed or called names — 36%
Pushed and shoved — 32%
Left out or ignored — 29%
Threatened or injured by a weapon — 7%
Threatened by peers and classmates — 27%
Received sexual comments or gestures — 24%

(BSA, 2017, 2014; NB, 2017; USDHHS, 2017; UNESCO, 2017; CDC, 2013)

Features of School Anti-Bullying Programs
- Increased supervision of students
- Delivery of consequences for bullying
- School-wide implementation of anti-bullying policies
- Cooperation among school staff, parents, and professionals across disciplines
- Identification of risk factors for bullying

Bullying prevention programs in schools reduce bullying between **25% and 50%**.
(NB, 2017, 2016; UNESCO, 2017; NBPC, 2016)

(CDC, 2017, 2013)

CYBERBULLYING

Cyberbullying takes place through e-mail, text messaging, Web sites and apps, instant messaging, chat rooms, or posted videos or photos. Between **40% and 50%** of all children and teens have been bullied online at least once. About **21%** are bullied online frequently. Girls are at least **50%** more likely than boys to be cyberbullied on a regular basis. (Kim et al., 2018; DTL, 2017; EIE, 2017; NB, 2017; Pew Research Center, 2017; CRC, 2016; BSA, 2014; NSPCC, 2013; Sedghi, 2013)

 Like

Why Do Teens Cyberbully?

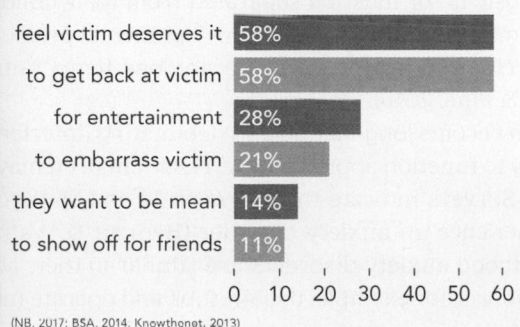

feel victim deserves it — 58%
to get back at victim — 58%
for entertainment — 28%
to embarrass victim — 21%
they want to be mean — 14%
to show off for friends — 11%

0 10 20 30 40 50 60

(NB, 2017; BSA, 2014, Knowthenet, 2013)

Social Media and Cyberbullying

37% victims report incidents to their social network
40% victims tell their parent or another adult
90% users who witness cyberbullying on their social media site
35% witnesses who usually ignore cyberbullying on their social media site

100 80 60 40 20 0

(EIE, 2017; NB, 2017; Pew Research Center, 2017; BSA, 2014; Knowthenet, 2013)

Jason Szenes/EPA/Redux

It gets better Gay activist author and journalist Dan Savage accepts a Webby Special Achievement award for co-founding the "It Gets Better" project—an Internet outreach program that tells LGBTQ teenagers their lives will get better as they move toward adulthood and find support from their communities. The project was started in 2010 by Savage and his husband Terry Miller after a number of gay teens had killed themselves in response to bullying. It now has a website featuring more than 50,000 messages of support and inspiration to beleaguered LGBTQ teens—messages that have received 50 million views.

Some disorders displayed by children—childhood anxiety disorders, childhood depression, and disruptive disorders—have adult counterparts, although they are also distinct in certain ways. Other childhood disorders—elimination disorders, for example—usually disappear or radically change form by adulthood. There are also disorders that begin at birth or in childhood and persist in stable forms into adult life. These include autism spectrum disorder and intellectual disability, the former marked by a lack of responsiveness to the environment, the latter by an extensive disturbance in intellect and adaptive functioning.

Childhood Anxiety Disorders

ANXIETY IS, TO A DEGREE, A NORMAL part of childhood. Since children have had fewer experiences than adults, their world is often new and scary. They may be frightened by common events, such as the beginning of school, or by special upsets, such as moving to a new house or becoming seriously ill. In addition, each generation of children is confronted by new sources of anxiety. Today's children, for example, are repeatedly warned, both at home and at school, about the dangers of Internet browsing and online predators, child abduction, drugs, school shootings, and terrorism. They are bombarded by violent images on the Web and television. Even children's books and family movies, such as animated films, often contain frightening images that upset many children.

Children may also be strongly affected by parental problems or inadequacies. If, for example, parents typically react to events with high levels of anxiety or uncertainty, or if they overprotect their children, the children may be more likely to respond to the world with anxiety (Kerns et al., 2017, 2014; Sanchez, Kendall, & Comer, 2016). And if parents are divorced, become seriously ill, or must be separated from their children for a long period, childhood anxiety may result. Beyond such environmental problems, genetic studies suggest that some children are prone to an anxious temperament (Sylvester & Pine, 2016; Tone, Garn, & Pine, 2016).

For some children, these anxieties become long-lasting and debilitating, interfering with their daily lives and their ability to function appropriately. These children may be suffering from an *anxiety disorder*. Surveys indicate that between 14 and 25 percent of all children and adolescents experience an anxiety disorder (Bennett & Walkup, 2016; Mian, 2014). Some of the childhood anxiety disorders are similar to their adult counterparts. Childhood specific phobias, for example, usually look and operate much

separation anxiety disorder A disorder marked by excessive anxiety, even panic, whenever the person is separated from home, a parent, or another attachment figure.

selective mutism A disorder marked by failure to speak in certain social situations when speech is expected, despite ability to speak in other situations.

like the phobias of adulthood (Oar et al., 2016), and a number of untreated childhood phobias grow into adult ones.

More often, however, the anxiety disorders of childhood take on a different character from that of adult anxiety disorders. Consider *generalized anxiety disorder*, marked by constant worrying, and *social anxiety disorder*, marked by fears of embarrassing oneself in front of others. In order to have such disorders, people must be able to anticipate future negative events (losing one's job, having a car accident, fainting in front of others), take the perspective of other people, and/or recognize that the thoughts and beliefs of others differ from their own. These cognitive skills are commonly beyond the capacity of very young children, and so many of the more cognitive symptoms that characterize generalized anxiety disorder and social anxiety disorder in adulthood do not usually appear in earnest until children are 7 years old or older. In short, odd as it may sound, some patterns of anxiety cannot fully unfold until children are afforded the "benefits" of cognitive, physical, and emotional growth (Sanchez et al., 2017).

What, then, do the anxiety disorders of young children look like? Typically they are dominated by behavioral and somatic symptoms rather than cognitive ones—symptoms such as clinging, sleep difficulties, avoidance, irritability, and stomach pains (Whalen et al., 2017; Cornacchio et al., 2016; Schlarb et al., 2016). They tend to center on specific, sometimes imaginary, objects and events, such as monsters, ghosts, or thunderstorms, rather than broad concerns about the future or one's place in the world (APA, 2013). Similarly, the anxiety symptoms are more often than not triggered by immediate situations and surroundings, rather than by thoughts about events that could happen in the future (Felix et al., 2011).

Never too young? Young campers at the Camp Honey Shine in Miami, Florida, learn mindfulness meditation and other techniques for dealing with stress.

Al Diaz/Miami Herald/TNS via Getty Images

Separation Anxiety Disorder and Selective Mutism

Two patterns of childhood anxiety, *separation anxiety disorder* and *selective mutism*, have received considerable attention in recent years, partly because they cause children emotional pain and partly because they leave the parents feeling helpless as they try to help their children.

Separation anxiety disorder, which you read about in Chapter 5, is one of the most common anxiety disorders among children (see page 116). The disorder often begins as early as the preschool years, and at least 4 percent of all children experience it (Baldwin et al., 2016). As you'll recall, children suffering from this disorder have enormous difficulty being away from their parents or other major attachment figures, and they are often reluctant—or outright refuse—to go anywhere where they might be separated from their parents—friends' houses, birthday parties, or even their own bedrooms. Children with the disorder often worry that when separated, their parents might get seriously hurt or die or that they themselves might get kidnapped or lost, preventing them from ever seeing their parents again. Separation anxiety disorder in childhood may further take the form of *school refusal,* in which children fear going to school and often stay home for a long period (APA, 2013). However, many cases of school refusal, particularly those in later childhood, have causes other than separation fears, such as social or academic concerns, depression, fears of specific objects or persons at school, or a desire to be defiant.

In **selective mutism**, children consistently fail to speak in certain social situations, but show no difficulty at all speaking in others (Muris & Ollendick, 2015). A child with this disorder may have no problem talking, laughing, or singing at home with family members, but will offer absolutely no words in other key situations, such as the classroom (see **Table 17-1**). Some go an entire school year without speaking a word to their teacher or classmates. Many have a special friend in the classroom to whom

TABLE: 17-1

Dx Checklist

Selective Mutism

1. Individual persistently does not speak in certain social situations in which speech is expected, although speaking in other situations presents no problem.

2. Academic or social interference.

3. Individual's symptoms last 1 month or more, and are not limited to the first 4 weeks of a new school year.

4. Symptoms not due to autism spectrum disorder, thought disorder, or language or communication disorder.

Information from: APA, 2013.

Reluctant to speak Children with selective mutism fail to speak in their classrooms and/or other social situations. Often the children use whispering, either directly to a teacher or through a go-between, to communicate important messages. Here, a child with the disorder whispers to her counselor at Florida International University's Center for Children and Families.

they will discreetly whisper important things to be communicated to the class, such as answers to a teacher's questions or the need to use the restroom. People who only see a selectively mute child at school often find it hard to believe that the child is an absolute chatterbox at home. Almost 1 percent of all children display this disorder (Hua & Major, 2016).

Many researchers believe that selective mutism is an early version of *social anxiety disorder*, appearing in children before they have fully developed the cognitive capacities to worry about future embarrassment or anticipate potential judgment from others (see pages 132–134). Indeed, some, but far from all, older children with selective mutism do develop social anxiety disorder (Muris & Ollendick, 2015). At the same time, there are many features unique to selective mutism. For example, some children with this disorder have significant delays in their development of communication and language skills (Hua & Major, 2016; Klein, Armstrong, & Shipon-Blum, 2013).

Educators and clinicians can underestimate a child's capabilities when he or she refuses to speak during an evaluation. Thus some children with selective mutism are misclassified as having an *intellectual disability* (which you will read about later in this chapter). This can, in turn, lead to incorrect interventions that focus on intellectual functioning and language development rather than on anxiety difficulties.

Treatments for Childhood Anxiety Disorders

Despite the high prevalence of childhood and adolescent anxiety disorders, around two-thirds of anxious children go untreated (NIMH, 2017). Among the children who do receive treatment, psychodynamic, cognitive-behavioral, family, and group therapies, separately or in combination, have been used most often. Each approach has had some degree of success; however, studies have found that cognitive-behavioral therapy fares best (Cornacchio et al., 2017; Higa-McMillan et al., 2016). These various therapies parallel the adult anxiety approaches you read about in Chapter 5, but they are tailored to the child's cognitive abilities, unique life situation, and limited control over his or her life. In addition, clinicians may offer psychoeducation, provide parent training, and arrange school interventions to treat anxious children (Cornacchio et al., 2017; Warner et al., 2016).

Clinicians have also used drug therapy in a number of cases of childhood anxiety disorders, often in combination with psychotherapy. Not only do they prescribe anti-anxiety drugs, but antidepressant and antipsychotic drugs as well (Comer et al., 2011, 2010). Studies suggest that antidepressant drugs, in particular, are helpful for severely anxious children, often as helpful as cognitive-behavioral therapy (Albano et al., 2017). In a landmark study called the *Child/Adolescent Anxiety Multimodal Study (CAMS)*, clinicians treated almost 500 children and adolescents with anxiety disorders across the United States, and compared the effectiveness of cognitive-behavioral therapy alone, antidepressant therapy alone, cognitive-behavioral and antidepressant therapy combined, and placebo therapy. They found that combining cognitive-behavioral therapy and antidepressant drug therapy led to the most favorable outcomes. Around 80 percent of the anxious children and adolescents receiving the combination treatment showed substantial clinical improvements (Piacentini et al., 2014; Walkup et al., 2008).

Because children typically have difficulty recognizing and understanding their feelings and motives, many therapists, particularly psychodynamic therapists, use **play therapy** as part of treatment. In this approach, the children play with toys, draw, and make up stories; in doing so, they are thought to reveal the conflicts in their lives and their related feelings. Over the course of therapy, the therapists introduce more play

Constructive play During play therapy, young children like this 6-year-old play with toys, draw, and make up stories, and in doing so, reveal their feelings and thoughts.

and fantasy to help the children work through their conflicts and change their emotions and behavior. In addition, humanistic therapists conduct *child-centered therapy* with anxious children, in which, as you read in Chapter 3, the clinician listens carefully to the child, reflects on what the child is saying, shows empathy, and gives unconditional positive regard (Silk et al., 2018).

play therapy An approach to treating childhood disorders that helps children express their conflicts and feelings indirectly by drawing, playing with toys, and making up stories.

Depressive and Bipolar Disorders During Childhood

LIKE CAMERON, THE BOY YOU READ ABOUT at the beginning of this chapter, around 2 percent of children and 8 percent of adolescents currently experience a major depressive disorder (NIMH, 2016; Avenevoli et al., 2015). As many as 20 percent of adolescents experience at least one depressive episode during their teen years. In addition, a number of clinicians believe that children can experience a bipolar disorder.

Major Depressive Disorder

As with anxiety disorders, very young children lack some of the cognitive skills that help produce clinical depression, thus accounting for the relatively low rate of depression among the very young (Wesselhoeft et al., 2016). For example, in order to experience the sense of hopelessness typically found in depressed adults, children must be able to hold expectations about the future, a skill rarely in full bloom before the age of 7.

Nevertheless, if life situations or biological predispositions are significant enough, even very young children sometimes have severe downward turns of mood (Whalen et al., 2017; Wesselhoeft et al., 2016). Depression in the young may be triggered by negative life events (particularly losses), major changes, rejection, or ongoing abuse (see **PsychWatch** on the next page). Childhood depression commonly features symptoms such as irritability, headaches, stomach pain, and a disinterest in toys and games (Whalen et al., 2017; Vidal-Ribas et al., 2016).

Clinical depression is much more common among teenagers than among young children. Adolescence is, under the best of circumstances, a difficult and confusing time, marked by angst, hormonal and bodily changes, mood changes, complex relationships, and new explorations. For some teens, these "normal" upsets of adolescence cross the line into clinical depression. As you read in Chapter 9, suicidal thoughts and attempts are particularly common among adolescents—one in eight teens persistently thinks about suicide each year—and depression is the leading cause of such thoughts and attempts (Kennebeck & Bonin, 2017, 2016; Nock et al., 2013).

Interestingly, while there is no difference between the rates of depression in boys and girls before the age of 13, girls are twice as likely as boys to be depressed by the age of 16 (Breslau et al., 2017; Salk et al., 2016). Why this gender shift? Several factors have been suggested, including hormonal changes, the fact that females increasingly experience more stressors than males, and the tendency of girls to become more emotionally invested than boys in social and intimate relationships as they mature. One explanation also focuses on teenage girls' growing dissatisfaction with their bodies. Whereas boys tend to like the increase in muscle mass and other body changes that accompany puberty, girls often detest the increases in body fat and weight gain that they experience during puberty and beyond. Raised in a society that values and demands extreme thinness as the aesthetic female ideal, many adolescent girls feel imprisoned by their own bodies, have low self-esteem, and become depressed (Klein & Attia, 2017; Stice et al., 2000). Many also develop eating disorders, as you saw in Chapter 11.

AP Photo/The Free Lance-Star, Mike Morones

Separation and depression This 3-year-old boy hugs his father as the soldier departs for deployment to Iraq. Given research evidence that extended family separations often produce depression in children, clinical theorists have been particularly worried about the thousands of children from military families who were left behind during the wars in Afghanistan and Iraq.

Child Abuse

A problem that affects all too many children and has an enormous impact on their psychological development is *child abuse,* the nonaccidental use of excessive physical or psychological force by an adult on a child, often with the intention of hurting or destroying the child. Between 5 and 16 percent of children in the United States are physically abused each year (Boos, 2017; Cicchetti & Toth, 2016). Surveys suggest that 1 of every 10 children is the victim of severe violence, such as being kicked, bitten, hit, beaten, or threatened with a knife or a gun. In fact, it is estimated that 13 percent of all child deaths are due to abuse.

Overall, girls and boys are physically abused at approximately the same rate. Although such abuse is perpetrated in all socioeconomic groups, it is apparently more common among the poor (Boos, 2017; Romero-Martínez et al., 2014).

Abusers are usually the child's parents (Christian & Greenbaum, 2016; Ben-Natan et al., 2014). Clinical investigators have learned that abusive parents often have poor impulse control, low self-esteem, higher levels of depression, and weak parenting skills (Boos, 2017; Easterbrooks et al., 2013). Many were abused themselves as children and have had poor role models. In some cases, they are dealing with stressors such as marital discord or unemployment (Bor et al., 2013).

Studies suggest that the victims of child abuse may suffer both immediate and long-term psychological effects (Kolko & Berkout, 2017). Research has shown, for example, that they may have psychological symptoms such as anxiety, depression, or bed-wetting, and that they tend to display more performance and behavior problems in school (Kolko & Berkout, 2017; Keeshin et al., 2014; Buckingham & Daniolos, 2013). Long-term negative effects include lack of social acceptance, a higher number of medical and psychological disorders during adulthood, more

Lingering impact A mother prepares her adopted 5-year-old son for pajama day at a trauma treatment program in which the child participates. The program addresses issues that the boy is still dealing with as a result of abuse or neglect in an earlier family.

Jill Toyoshiba/Kansas City Star/TNS via Getty Images

abuse of alcohol and other substances, more impulsive and risk-taking behaviors, more arrests during adolescence and adulthood, a greater risk of becoming criminally violent, a higher unemployment rate, and a higher suicide rate (Kolko & Berkout, 2017; Afifi et al, 2014; Sujan et al., 2014). Finally, as many as one-third of those who are abused grow up to be abusive, neglectful, or inadequate parents themselves (Romero-Martínez et al., 2014; Yaghoubi-Doust, 2013).

Two forms of child abuse have received special attention: psychological and sexual abuse. *Psychological abuse* may include severe rejection, excessive discipline, scapegoating and ridicule, isolation, and refusal to provide help for a child with psychological problems (Endom, 2017). It probably accompanies all forms of physical abuse and neglect and often occurs by itself. *Child sexual abuse,* the use of a child for gratification of adult sexual desires, may occur out-

side or within the home (Bechtel & Bennett, 2017; Murray, Nguyen, & Cohen, 2014). Surveys suggest that, worldwide, as many as 25 percent of women were forced into sexual contact with an adult male during childhood, many of them with a parent or stepparent. As many as 9 percent of men were also sexually abused during childhood. Child sexual abuse appears to be equally common across all socioeconomic classes, races, and ethnic groups.

A variety of therapies have been used in cases of child abuse, including groups sponsored by *Parents Anonymous,* which help parents to develop insight into their behavior, provide training on alternatives to abuse, and teach coping and parenting skills (PA, 2017; Miller et al., 2007; Tolan et al., 2006). In addition, prevention programs, often in the form of home visitations and parent training, have proved promising (Beasley et al., 2014; Rubin et al., 2014).

Research suggests that the psychological needs of children who have been abused should be addressed as early as possible (PA, 2017; Murray et al., 2014; Roesler & McKenzie, 1994). Clinicians and educators have launched valuable *early detection programs* that (1) educate all children about child abuse, (2) teach them skills for avoiding or escaping from abusive situations, (3) encourage children to tell another adult if they are abused, and (4) assure them that abuse is never their own fault (PA, 2017; Miller et al., 2007; Finkelhor et al., 1995).

For years, it was generally believed that childhood and teenage depression would respond well to some of the same treatments that have been of help to depressed adults—particularly, cognitive-behavioral therapy, interpersonal psychotherapy, and antidepressant drugs—and, in fact, many studies have indicated the effectiveness of such approaches (Weersing et al., 2017). Moreover, clinicians have often found success treating children and adolescents with family-focused approaches that aim to improve parent–child relationships, increase shared family activities, and build child coping skills (Tompson et al., 2017). At the same time, some studies and events over the past decade or so, have raised questions about the best approaches for teenagers.

In one development, the National Institute of Mental Health sponsored a massive multi-year study called the *Treatment for Adolescents with Depression Study* (*TADS*), which compared the effectiveness of cognitive-behavioral therapy alone, antidepressant therapy alone, cognitive-behavioral and antidepressant therapy combined, and placebo therapy for teenage depression (TADS, 2010, 2007, 2004). Three major surprises emerged from this large-scale study. First, neither antidepressants alone nor cognitive-behavioral therapy alone was as effective for teenage depression as was a combination of antidepressants and cognitive-behavioral therapy—a finding similar to the CAMS study of treatments for anxious adolescents discussed earlier. Second, antidepressants alone tended to be more helpful to depressed teens than cognitive-behavioral therapy alone. And third, cognitive-behavioral therapy alone was barely more helpful than placebo therapy. Many researchers believe that certain peculiarities in the participant population of the TADS study may have been responsible for the poor showing of cognitive-behavioral therapy. However, other clinical theorists believe that the TADS investigation is a definitive research undertaking and that many depressed teens may in fact respond less well to cognitive-behavioral therapy than adults do.

A second development in recent years has been the discovery that antidepressant drugs may be dangerous for some depressed children and teenagers. Throughout the 1990s, most psychiatrists believed that second-generation antidepressants were safe and effective for children and adolescents, and they prescribed them readily (Cooper et al., 2014). However, as you read in Chapter 9, the U.S. Food and Drug Administration (FDA) concluded in 2004, based on a number of clinical reports, that the drugs may produce a real, though small, increase in the risk of suicidal behavior for certain children and adolescents, especially during the first few months of treatment. Thus, the FDA ordered that all antidepressant containers carry "black box" warnings stating that the drugs "increase the risk of suicidal thinking and behavior in children."

Arguments about the wisdom of this FDA order have since ensued. Although most clinicians agree that the drugs may increase the risk of suicidal thoughts and attempts in as many as 2 percent of young patients, some have noted that the overall risk of suicide may actually be reduced for the vast majority of children who take the drugs (Pozzi et al., 2016; Christiansen et al., 2015; Isacsson & Rich, 2014). They point out, for example, that suicides among children and teenagers decreased by 30 percent in the decade leading up to 2004, as the number of antidepressant prescriptions provided to children and teenagers was soaring.

While the findings of the TADS investigation and questions about antidepressant drug safety continue to be sorted out, these two developments serve to highlight once again the importance of research, particularly in the treatment realm. We are reminded that treatments that work for individuals of a certain age, gender, race, or ethnic background may be ineffective or even dangerous for other groups of people.

Grief camp A number of "grief camps" have been developed around the country for children and teenagers who have lost a loved one. At one such program, this young girl, whose uncle was killed while fighting in Iraq, puts a clipping representing what she feels about his death into a bag.

Bipolar Disorder and Disruptive Mood Dysregulation Disorder

For decades, bipolar disorder was thought to be almost exclusively an *adult* disorder, and that its earliest age of onset is the late teens (APA, 2013). However, beginning in the mid-1990s, clinical theorists did an about-face, and a rapidly growing number of them came to believe that many children display bipolar disorder (Van Meter et al.,

Are children being medicated properly?
Two 12-year-olds hand out pamphlets at the American Psychiatric Association Convention while wearing shirts that call attention to the practice of prescribing high-dosage medications to children with psychological disorders. The pamphlets asked people to protest against the "psychiatric drug abuse" of children.

2016). For example, one review of national diagnostic trends from 1994 through 2003 found that the number of children and adolescents diagnosed and treated for bipolar disorder in the United States increased 40-fold, from 25 such diagnoses per 100,000 individuals in 1994 to 1,000 per 100,000 individuals in 2003 (Moreno et al., 2007). Correspondingly, the number of private office visits for children with bipolar disorders increased from 20,000 in 1994 to 800,000 in 2003 over the same period of time. Moreover, this trend continued during the decade following that diagnostic review (Mash & Wolfe, 2018, 2015).

During that 20-year period, many theorists came to suspect that such increases reflected not a rise in the prevalence of bipolar disorders among children but rather a new—often inaccurate—diagnostic trend (Van Meter et al., 2016; Paris, 2014). They believed that the diagnosis of bipolar disorder was being overapplied to children and adolescents and being assigned to the majority of extremely explosive, aggressive children. In support of these claims, studies revealed that symptoms of rage and aggression, along with depression, were in fact dominating the clinical picture of most children who were receiving a bipolar diagnosis (Van Meter et al., 2016; Roy et al., 2013). Many such children were not even displaying the symptoms of mania or the mood swings that characterize adult bipolar disorder. Moreover, two-thirds of the children and adolescents who were receiving a bipolar diagnosis were boys, while adult men and women have bipolar disorder in equal numbers.

Based on a range of research findings, the task force of DSM-5 came to the same conclusion—that the childhood bipolar label had been overapplied. In an attempt to rectify this, DSM-5 now includes a new category, **disruptive mood dysregulation disorder,** which is used to describe children with patterns of severe rage (see **Table 17-2**). It is hoped that, henceforth, children with severe anger and temper outbursts will receive this diagnosis and that the number of childhood bipolar disorder diagnoses will decrease correspondingly. It is also hoped that the inclusion of this new category in DSM-5 will help clinicians clarify whether certain young adolescents do, in fact, suffer from the early stages of bipolar disorder. A growing body of longitudinal studies suggests that the symptoms of many adults with bipolar disorder may have begun well before the age of 18 (Van Meter et al., 2016).

These diagnostic issues are particularly important because the rise in diagnoses of bipolar disorder has been accompanied by an increase in the number of children prescribed medications (Cervesi et al., 2017; Toteja et al., 2014). Although a number of psychological approaches seem to be helpful for children with a diagnosis of bipolar disorder, fully half of those in treatment receive an antipsychotic drug, a third receive an antibipolar drug, and many others receive antidepressant or stimulant drugs (Vallarino et al., 2015). Yet relatively few of these drugs or drug combinations have been tested for such use with children.

TABLE: 17-2

Dx Checklist

Disruptive Mood Dysregulation Disorder

1. For at least a year, individual repeatedly displays severe outbursts of temper that are extremely out of proportion to triggering situations and different from ones displayed by most other individuals of his or her age.

2. The outbursts occur at least three times per week and are present in at least two settings (home, school, with peers).

3. Individual repeatedly displays irritable or angry mood between the outbursts.

4. Individual receives initial diagnosis between 6 and 18 years of age.

Information from: APA, 2013.

||||||||||||||||||||||||||||||||||||||||||||||||||||||||||||||||||||||||||||||

Oppositional Defiant Disorder and Conduct Disorder

MOST CHILDREN BREAK RULES OR MISBEHAVE on occasion. If they consistently display extreme hostility and defiance, however, they may qualify for a diagnosis of oppositional defiant disorder or conduct disorder. Those with **oppositional defiant disorder** are argumentative and defiant, angry, and irritable, and in some cases, vindictive (Matthys & Lochman, 2017). They may argue repeatedly with adults, ignore adult rules and requests, deliberately annoy other people, and feel much anger and resentment. As many as 10 percent of children qualify for a diagnosis of oppositional defiant disorder (Mash & Wolfe, 2018, 2015). The disorder is more common in boys than in girls before puberty but equal in both genders after puberty.

Children with **conduct disorder,** a more severe problem, repeatedly violate the basic rights of others (APA, 2013). They are often aggressive and may be physically cruel to people or animals, deliberately destroy other people's property, steal or lie, skip school, or run away from home (see **Table 17-3**). Many threaten or harm their victims, committing such crimes as firesetting, shoplifting, forgery, breaking into buildings or cars, mugging, and armed robbery. As they get older, their acts of physical violence may include rape or, in rare cases, homicide. The symptoms of conduct disorder are apparent in this summary of a clinical interview with a 15-year-old boy named Derek:

Questioning revealed that Derek was getting into . . . serious trouble of late, having been arrested for shoplifting 4 weeks before. Derek was caught with one other youth when he and a dozen friends swarmed a convenience store and took everything they could before leaving in cars. This event followed similar others at [an electronics] store and a . . . clothing store. Derek blamed his friends for his arrest because they apparently left him behind as he straggled out of the store. He was charged only with shoplifting, however, after police found him holding just three candy bars and a bag of potato chips. Derek expressed no remorse for the theft or any care for the store clerk who was injured when one of the teens pushed her into a glass case. When informed of the clerk's injury, for example, Derek replied, "I didn't do it, so what do I care?"

The psychologist questioned Derek further about other legal violations and discovered a rather extended history of trouble. Derek was arrested for vandalism 10 months earlier for breaking windows and damaging cars on school property. He received probation for 6 months because this was his first offense. Derek also boasted of other exploits for which he was not caught, including several shoplifting episodes, . . . joyriding, and missing school. Derek missed 23 days (50 percent) of school since the beginning of the academic year. In addition, he described break-in attempts of his neighbors' apartments. . . . Only rarely during the interview did Derek stray from his bravado.

(Kearney, 2013, pp. 87–88)

Conduct disorder usually begins between 7 and 15 years of age (APA, 2013). Between 5 and 10 percent of children, three-quarters of them boys, qualify for this diagnosis (Matthys & Lochman, 2017; Boat & Wu, 2015). Children with a relatively mild conduct disorder often improve over time, but a severe case may continue into adulthood and develop into antisocial personality disorder, another psychological problem, and/or a criminal lifestyle (Mash & Wolfe, 2018, 2015; Dishion & Patterson, 2016). Usually, the earlier the onset of the conduct disorder, the poorer the eventual outcome. Research indicates that more than 80 percent of those who develop this disorder first display a pattern of oppositional defiant disorder (APA, 2013; Lahey, 2008). More than one-third of children with conduct disorder also display attention-deficit/hyperactivity disorder (ADHD), a disorder that you will read about shortly, and a number experience depression and anxiety (Wichstrom, Belsky, & Steinsbekk, 2017; Harvey et al., 2016).

Some clinical theorists believe that there are actually several kinds of conduct disorder, including (1) the *overt-destructive* pattern, in which individuals display openly aggressive and confrontational behaviors; (2) the *overt-nondestructive* pattern, dominated by openly offensive but nonconfrontational behaviors such as lying; (3) the *covert-destructive* pattern, characterized by secretive destructive behaviors such as violating other people's property, breaking and entering, and setting fires;

TABLE: 17-3

Dx Checklist

Conduct Disorder

1. Individual repeatedly behaves in ways that violate the rights of other people or ignores the norms or rules of society, beyond the violations displayed by most other people of his or her age.

2. At least three of the following features are present over the past year (and at least one in the past 6 months): • Frequent bullying or threatening of others • Frequent provoking of physical fights • Using dangerous weapons • Physical cruelty to people • Physical cruelty to animals • Stealing during confrontations with a victim • Forcing someone into sexual activity • Fire-setting • Deliberately destroying others' property • Breaking into a house, building, or car • Frequent lying • Stealing items of value under nonconfrontational circumstances • Frequent staying out beyond curfews, starting before the age of 13 • Running away from home overnight at least twice • Frequent truancy from school, starting before the age of 13.

3. Significant impairment.

Information from: APA, 2013.

disruptive mood dysregulation disorder A childhood disorder marked by severe recurrent temper outbursts along with a persistent irritable or angry mood.

oppositional defiant disorder A disorder in which children are repeatedly argumentative, defiant, angry, irritable, and perhaps vindictive.

conduct disorder A disorder in which children repeatedly violate the basic rights of others and display significant aggression.

#GenderGap

Today, one of every five teens arrested for violent crimes is female (DOJ, 2017).

Antisocial behavior and the law Many children and adolescents with conduct disorder wind up incarcerated in *juvenile detention,* or *juvenile training, centers* when their antisocial behaviors place them in conflict with the law. Here inmates at one such center in Holland spend many hours sitting around, staring, and thinking—hardly a prescription for improvements in their behaviors or mental health.

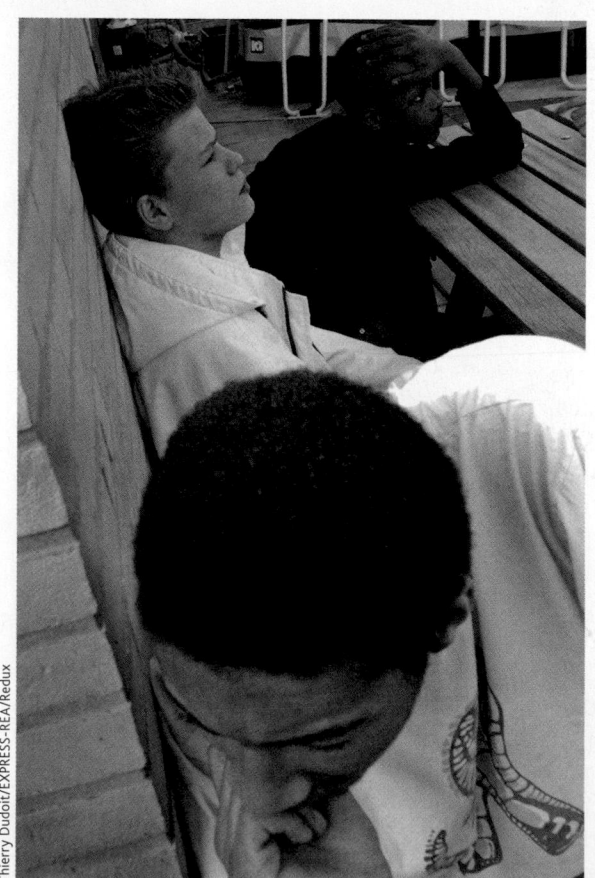

and (4) the *covert-nondestructive* pattern, in which individuals secretly commit non-aggressive behaviors, such as being truant from school (McMahon et al., 2010; McMahon & Frick, 2007, 2005). It may be that the different patterns have different causes. In a similar vein, DSM-5 instructs diagnosticians to distinguish those individuals whose conduct disorder is marked by particularly callous and unemotional behaviors, as they may be qualitatively different from others with the disorder (Eisenbarth et al., 2016; APA, 2013).

A number of researchers distinguish yet another pattern of aggression found in certain cases of conduct disorder, *relational aggression,* in which the individual is socially isolated and primarily performs social misdeeds such as slandering others, spreading rumors, and manipulating friendships (Perry & Ostrov, 2018; Murray-Close et al., 2016). Relational aggression is more common among girls than boys.

Many children with conduct disorder are suspended from school, placed in foster homes, or incarcerated (Matthys & Lochman, 2017). When children between the ages of 8 and 18 break the law, the legal system often labels them *juvenile delinquents* (Krisberg, 2018). More than half of the juveniles who are arrested each year are *recidivists,* meaning they have a history of having been arrested. Boys are much more involved in juvenile crime than girls, although the gap between them is narrowing. Girls are most likely to be arrested for drug use, sexual offenses, and running away, boys for drug use and crimes against property. Although any number is too high, it is encouraging that the number of arrests of teenagers for serious crimes has fallen by one-third since the turn of the century (U.S. Department of Justice, 2014, 2010).

What Are the Causes of Conduct Disorder?

Many cases of conduct disorder, particularly those marked by destructive behaviors, have been linked to genetic and biological factors (Matthys & Lochman, 2017; Wallace et al., 2014). A number of cases have also been tied to drug abuse, poverty, traumatic events, and exposure to violent peers or community violence (Wymbs et al., 2014; Weyandt et al., 2011). In addition, conduct disorder is often related to troubled parent–child relationships, inadequate parenting, family conflict, marital conflict, and family hostility (Mash & Wolfe, 2018, 2015; Dishion & Patterson, 2016). Children whose parents reject, leave, coerce, or abuse them or fail to provide appropriate and consistent supervision are apparently more likely to develop conduct problems. Children also seem more prone to this disorder when their parents themselves are antisocial, display excessive anger, or have substance use, mood, or schizophrenic disorders (Wilson, 2017; Advokat et al., 2014).

As they do with regard to other psychological disorders, developmental psychopathologists explain conduct disorder by pointing to *interactions* between these various factors (Holz et al., 2018; Dishion & Patterson, 2016). Research shows, for example, that some, but not all, children who are maltreated go on to develop conduct disorder. Why only some? According to several influential studies, maltreated individuals are especially likely to develop conduct problems if they were also born with a particular variation of a gene called the *MAOA gene* (nicknamed the "human warrior gene") (Taylor & Kim-Cohen, 2007; Caspi et al., 2002). On the other hand, children who are similarly maltreated but who do *not* carry this particular genetic vulnerability are not nearly as likely to develop conduct disorder. And, finally, *unless* they are maltreated, people with this genetic variability do not have a particularly high risk for developing conduct disorder. In short, children with a problematic variation of the MAOA gene *and* a childhood filled with maltreatment are at high risk for conduct disorder, but children with only one of these factors are significantly less likely to develop the disorder.

How Do Clinicians Treat Conduct Disorder?

Because aggressive behaviors become more locked in with age, treatments for conduct disorder are generally most effective with children younger than age 13 (Cornacchio et al., 2017; Webster-Stratton, 2016; Comer et al., 2013). A number of interventions, from sociocultural to child-focused, have been developed to treat children with the disorder. As you will see, several of these have had moderate success, but clearly no one of them alone is the answer for this difficult problem. Today's clinicians are increasingly combining several approaches into a wide-ranging treatment program.

Parent Management Training Given the importance of family factors in conduct disorder, many therapists use a combination of family and cognitive-behavioral interventions, collectively known as **parent management training,** to help improve family functioning and help parents deal with their children more effectively (Kaminski & Claussen, 2017). Parent management training takes different forms, depending on the age of the child with conduct problems.

One form of parent management training, used with preschoolers, is called *parent–child interaction therapy* (Elkins et al., 2017; Hembree-Kigin & McNeil, 2013). Here therapists teach parents to work with their child positively, set appropriate limits, act consistently, be fair and structured in their discipline, and establish appropriate expectations regarding the child. Ideally, these efforts strengthen the parent–child relationship, improve the parents' attitudes, increase parental control, promote a consistent home environment, and produce improvements in the child's behavior. A related family intervention for preschoolers, *video modeling,* uses video tools to help achieve the same goals (Webster-Stratton, 2016).

In recent years, researchers have successfully used *videoconferencing* technology to offer parent–child interaction therapy in the actual homes of children with severe conduct problems. Using webcams, parents stream their home family interactions in real-time to a therapist located elsewhere, and the therapist, in turn, coaches the parents through a Bluetooth earpiece (Comer et al., 2015). Initial research suggests that this videoconferencing technique may lead to even more positive child improvements than those seen in parent–child interaction therapy delivered in a clinic (Comer et al., 2017).

> **Why might some children show more positive improvements when their therapist uses technology to treat them in their own homes instead of in a clinic?**

If children with conduct problems are of school age, an important ingredient is added to parent management training. In addition to teaching the parents more effective ways of dealing with their children, therapists may also engage the children more directly, particularly in the form of family therapy (Kazdin, 2012, 2010, 2002; Forgatch & Patterson, 2010). They may further hold individual treatment sessions with the children. Using cognitive and behavioral techniques, the therapists may first guide the family to identify behaviors that are in need of change. Then, with the aid of written manuals, rehearsals, practice, and homework, they teach the parents how to stop rewarding unwanted behaviors and consistently reward proper behaviors. Like parent management training for preschoolers, this approach to school-age children with conduct disorder has often achieved a measure of success (Kaminski & Claussen, 2017; Kazdin, 2012; Forgatch & Patterson, 2010).

One increasingly popular and supported approach for treating child conduct disorder, *multisystemic therapy,* aims to make needed changes across multiple contexts of children's lives.

parent management training A treatment approach for conduct disorder in which therapists combine family and cognitive-behavioral interventions to help improve family functioning and help parents deal with their children more effectively.

"Is this the story you want to tell on your college application?"

Lee Lorenz The New Yorker Collection/The Cartoon Bank

AP Photo/Charles Krupa

Multiple traumas A number of children in the Boston area developed posttraumatic stress disorder and/or other psychological disorders in the aftermath of the Boston Marathon bombing in 2013. It turns out that their disorders were triggered not only by witnessing (in person or on television) the devastation produced by the bombing, but also by the door-to-door searches for the suspects conducted by police in the days following the bombing (Comer, 2014). Here a woman carries her child from their home as a SWAT team enters to conduct one such search.

Multisystemic therapists treat family dynamics, but they also make adjustments in children's schools, social lives, and the broader community. These therapists deliver parent management training in hopes of improving family cohesion and promoting effective discipline, while also working to increase the amount of time children spend with positive children and role models instead of delinquent peers. Treatment goals often include improving grades or helping the child develop vocational skills, as well as promoting the child's participation in positive and structured activities, such as sports, school clubs, or neighborhood organizations. Despite the fact that multisystemic therapy is typically applied to some of the more severe and complex cases of child conduct disorder, research finds this integrative approach can result in small, but long-lasting positive effects (van der Stouwe et al., 2014).

Child-Focused Treatments Treatments that focus primarily on the child with conduct disorder, particularly cognitive-behavioral interventions, have had some degree of success (Kaminski et al., 2017). In an approach called *problem-solving skills training,* therapists combine modeling, practice, role-playing, and systematic rewards to help teach children constructive thinking and positive social behaviors. During therapy sessions, the therapists may play games and solve tasks with the children, and later help them apply the lessons and skills derived from the games and tasks to real-life situations.

In another child-focused approach, the *Coping Power Program,* children with conduct problems participate in group sessions that teach them to manage their anger more effectively, view situations in perspective, solve problems, become aware of their emotions, build social skills, set goals, and handle peer pressure. Studies indicate that child-focused approaches such as these do indeed help reduce aggressive behaviors and prevent substance use in adolescence (Powell et al., 2017; Lochman et al., 2011, 2010).

Drug therapy has also been used for some children with conduct disorder. Studies suggest that *stimulant drugs* may help reduce their aggressive behaviors at home and at school, particularly if the children's symptoms further include impulsivity and overactivity (Haggerty, 2017; Levy & Bloch, 2012),

Residential Treatment Residential treatment in the community and programs at school have also helped some children improve. In one such approach, *treatment foster*

care, delinquent boys and girls with conduct disorder are assigned to a foster home in the community by the juvenile justice system (Henggeler & Sheidow, 2012). While there, the children, foster parents, and birth parents all receive training and treatment interventions, including family therapy with both sets of parents, individual treatment for the child, and meetings with the school and with parole and probation officers. In addition, the children and their parents continue to receive treatment and support after the children leave foster care. This program is apparently most beneficial when all the intervention components are applied simultaneously.

In contrast to this form of residential treatment, institutionalization in so-called *juvenile training centers* has not met with much success (Stahlberg et al., 2010; Heilbrun et al., 2005). In fact, such institutions frequently serve to strengthen delinquent behavior rather than resocialize young offenders.

> How might juvenile training centers themselves contribute to the high recidivism rate among teenage criminal offenders?

Prevention It may be that the best hope for dealing with the problem of conduct disorder lies in *prevention* programs that begin in the earliest stages of childhood (Pasalich et al., 2016; Toth et al., 2016). These programs try to change unfavorable social conditions before a conduct disorder is able to develop. Typically, the programs offer training opportunities for young people, recreational facilities, and health care. They may also seek to ease the stresses of poverty, promote more positive school environments, and improve parents' child-rearing skills. All such approaches work best when they educate and involve the family.

Elimination Disorders

CHILDREN WITH ELIMINATION DISORDERS repeatedly urinate or pass feces in their clothes, in bed, or on the floor. They already have reached an age at which they are expected to control these bodily functions, and their symptoms are not caused by physical illness.

Enuresis

Enuresis is repeated involuntary (or in some cases intentional) bed-wetting or wetting of one's clothes. It typically occurs at night during sleep but may also occur during the day. Children must be at least 5 years of age to receive this diagnosis (Tu, Baskin, & Arnhym, 2017; APA, 2013). The problem may be triggered by stressful events, such as a hospitalization, entrance into school, or family problems.

The prevalence of enuresis decreases with age. As many as 33 percent of 5-year-old children have some bed-wetting and 16 percent meet the criteria for enuresis; in contrast, 5 percent of 10-year-olds and 1 to 2 percent of 15-year-olds have enuresis (Tu et al., 2017; Mash & Wolfe, 2015; APA, 2013). Boys with the disorder outnumber girls by 2 to 1. Those with enuresis typically have a close relative (parent, sibling) who has had or will have the same disorder.

Research has not favored one explanation for enuresis over the others (Tu et al., 2017; Kim et al., 2014; Friman, 2008). Psychodynamic theorists explain it as a symptom of broader anxiety and underlying conflicts. Family theorists point to disturbed family interactions. Cognitive-behavioral theorists view the problem as the result of improper, unrealistic, or coercive toilet training. And biological theorists suspect that children with this disorder often have a small bladder capacity, weak bladder muscles, and/or disturbed sleep patterns.

enuresis A childhood disorder marked by repeated bed-wetting or wetting of one's clothes.

"This weekend I'm going to finally go through that closet and get rid of all those monsters."

The Bedwetter Outrageous comedian Sarah Silverman holds up a copy of her best-selling book *The Bedwetter*. In this memoir, she writes extensively about her childhood experiences with enuresis and other emotional difficulties—always with a blend of self-revelation, pain, and humor.

Most cases of enuresis correct themselves even without treatment. However, treatments, particularly cognitive-behavioral therapy, can speed up the process (Tu & Baskin, 2017; Axelrod et al., 2014; Christophersen & Friman, 2010). In a widely used classical conditioning approach, the *bell-and-battery technique,* a bell and a battery are wired to a pad consisting of two metallic foil sheets, and the entire apparatus is placed under the child at bedtime (Mowrer & Mowrer, 1938). A single drop of urine sets off the bell, awakening the child as soon as he or she starts to wet. Thus the bell (unconditioned stimulus) paired with the sensation of a full bladder (conditioned stimulus) produces the response of waking. Eventually, a full bladder alone awakens the child.

Another effective cognitive-behavioral treatment method is *dry-bed training,* in which children receive training in cleanliness and retention control, are awakened periodically during the night, practice going to the bathroom, and are appropriately rewarded. Like the bell-and-battery technique, this behavioral approach is often effective.

Encopresis

Children with **encopresis,** also called soiling, repeatedly defecate into their clothing. The disorder is less common than enuresis, and it is also less well researched (Mash & Wolfe, 2018, 2015; Sood, 2017, 2016; APA, 2013). This problem seldom occurs at night during sleep. It is usually involuntary, starts at the age of 4 or older, and affects about 1.5 to 4 percent of all children (see **Table 17-4**). The disorder is much more common in boys than in girls.

Encopresis causes intense social problems, shame, and embarrassment (Sood, 2017, 2016; NLM, 2015; Mosca & Schatz, 2013). Children who suffer from it usually try to hide their condition and to avoid situations, such as camp or school, in which they might embarrass themselves. It may stem from biological factors such as constipation, stress, improper toilet training, or a combination of these factors (Sood, 2017, 2016). Constipation, by far the most common cause, is a factor in 80 percent of cases. Because physical problems are so often linked to this disorder, a medical examination is typically conducted first.

The most common and successful treatments for encopresis are cognitive-behavioral and medical approaches or a combination of the two (Sood, 2017, 2016; NLM, 2015; Collins et al., 2012). Treatment may include interventions to eliminate the children's constipation; biofeedback training (see page 307) to help the children better detect when their bowels are full; and the stimulation of regular bowel functioning with high-fiber diets, mineral oil, laxatives, and lubricants. Family therapy has also proved helpful.

TABLE: 17-4

Comparison of Childhood Disorders

Disorder	Usual Age of Identification	Prevalence Among All Children	Gender with Greater Prevalence	Elevated Family History	Recovery by Adulthood
Separation anxiety disorder	Before 12 years	4%–10%	Females	Yes	Usually
Selective mutism	2–4 years	1%	Females	Yes	Often
Conduct disorder	7–15 years	5%–10%	Males	Yes	Often
Enuresis	5–8 Years	7%	Males	Yes	Usually
Encopresis	After 4 years	1.5%–4%	Males	Unclear	Usually
ADHD	Before 12 years	7%	Males	Yes	Often
Autism spectrum disorder	0–3 years	2%	Males	Yes	Sometimes
Specific learning disorders	6–9 years	5%–10%	Males	Yes	Often
Intellectual disability	Before 10 years	1%–3%	Males	Unclear	Sometimes

Neurodevelopmental Disorders

NEURODEVELOPMENTAL DISORDERS ARE a group of disabilities in the functioning of the brain that emerge at birth or during very early childhood and affect the individual's behavior, memory, concentration, and/or ability to learn. As you read at the beginning of this chapter, some disorders first displayed during childhood subside as the person ages. However, the neurodevelopmental disorders often have a significant impact throughout the person's life. For example, at least half of those with *attention-deficit/hyperactivity disorder,* one of the neurodevelopmental disorders, carry some version of their disorder with them into adulthood. Moreover, the vast majority of those with *autism spectrum disorder* and *intellectual disability,* two other neurodevelopmental disorders, continue to display the symptoms of their disorders in largely unchanged form throughout adulthood.

Researchers have investigated each of the neurodevelopmental disorders extensively. In addition, although this was not always so, clinicians now have a range of treatment approaches that can make a major difference in the lives of people with these problems.

Attention-Deficit/Hyperactivity Disorder

Children with **attention-deficit/hyperactivity disorder (ADHD)** have great difficulty attending to tasks, or behave overactively and impulsively, or both (APA, 2013) (see **Table 17-5**). Because all children are inattentive and impulsive to a certain extent, the symptoms must be beyond what is developmentally normal in order to qualify for a diagnosis of ADHD (Nigg, 2016). ADHD often appears before the child starts school, as with Ricky, one of the boys we met at the beginning of this chapter. Steven is another child whose symptoms began very early in life:

> *Steven's mother cannot remember a time when her son was not into something or in trouble. As a baby he was incredibly active, so active in fact that he nearly rocked his crib apart. All the bolts and screws became loose and had to be tightened periodically. Steven was also always into forbidden places, going through the medicine cabinet or under the kitchen sink. He once swallowed some washing detergent and had to be taken to the emergency room. As a matter of fact, Steven had many more accidents and was more clumsy than his older brother and younger sister. . . . He always seemed to be moving fast. His mother recalls that Steven progressed from the crawling stage to a running stage with very little walking in between.*
>
> *Trouble really started to develop for Steven when he entered kindergarten. Since his entry into school, his life has been miserable and so has the teacher's. Steven does not seem capable of attending to assigned tasks and following instructions. He would rather be talking to a neighbor or wandering around the room without the teacher's permission. When he is seated and the teacher is keeping an eye on him to make sure that he works, Steven's body still seems to be in motion. He is either tapping his pencil, fidgeting, or staring out the window and daydreaming. Steven hates kindergarten and has few long-term friends; indeed, school rules and demands appear to be impossible challenges for him. The effects of this mismatch are now showing in Steven's schoolwork and attitude. He has fallen behind academically and has real difficulty mastering new concepts; he no longer follows directions from the teacher and has started to talk back.*
>
> *(Gelfand, Jenson, & Drew, 1982, p. 256)*

The symptoms of ADHD often feed into one another. Children who have trouble focusing attention may keep turning from task to task until they end up trying to run in several directions at once. Similarly, children who move constantly may find it hard

encopresis A childhood disorder characterized by repeated defecating in inappropriate places, such as one's clothing.

neurodevelopmental disorders A group of disabilities—including ADHD, autism spectrum disorder, and intellectual disability—in the functioning of the brain that emerge at birth or during very early childhood and affect a person's behavior, memory, concentration, and/or ability to learn.

attention-deficit/hyperactivity disorder (ADHD) A disorder marked by the inability to focus attention, or overactive and impulsive behavior, or both.

#SchoolPerformance

More than 90 percent of children with ADHD underachieve scholastically.

Between 23 and 32 percent of children with ADHD do not complete high school.

Of people with ADHD, 22 percent are admitted to college.

(ADDitude, 2017; Dendy, 2016; Rapport et al., 2008)

TABLE: 17-5

Dx Checklist

Attention-Deficit/Hyperactivity Disorder

1. Individual presents one or both of the following patterns:

   (a) For 6 months or more, individual frequently displays at least six of the following symptoms of inattention, to a degree that is maladaptive and beyond that shown by most similarly aged persons: • Unable to properly attend to details, or frequently makes careless errors • Finds it hard to maintain attention • Fails to listen when spoken to by others • Fails to carry out instructions and finish work • Disorganized • Dislikes or avoids mentally effortful work • Loses items that are needed for successful work • Easily distracted by irrelevant stimuli • Forgets to do many everyday activities.

   (b) For 6 months or more, individual frequently displays at least six of the following symptoms of hyperactivity and impulsivity, to a degree that is maladaptive and beyond that shown by most similarly aged persons: • Fidgets, taps hands or feet, or squirms • Inappropriately wanders from seat • Inappropriately runs or climbs • Unable to play quietly • In constant motion • Talks excessively • Interrupts questioners during discussions • Unable to wait for turn • Barges in on others' activities or conversations.

2. Individual displayed some of the symptoms before 12 years of age.

3. Individual shows symptoms in more than one setting.

4. Individual experiences impaired functioning.

Information from: APA, 2013.

to attend to tasks or show good judgment. In many cases, one of these symptoms stands out much more than the other. About half of the children with ADHD also have learning or communication problems; many perform poorly in school; a number have difficulty interacting with other children, and about 80 percent misbehave, often quite seriously (Mash & Wolfe, 2018, 2015). The children may also have great difficulty controlling their emotions, and some have anxiety or mood problems (Musser & Nigg, 2018; Jarrett et al., 2016; Graziano & Garcia, 2016).

Around 7 percent of all children display ADHD at any given time, as many as 70 percent of them boys (Krull, 2017; APA, 2013). Those whose parents have had ADHD are more likely than others to develop it. The disorder usually persists throughout childhood. Many children show a lessening of symptoms as they move into mid-adolescence, but as many as 60 percent of them, particularly those with more severe symptoms, continue to have ADHD as adults (Roy et al., 2016; APA, 2013). The symptoms of restlessness and overactivity are not usually as pronounced in adult cases. Adults with ADHD have higher than average rates of substance misuse, risky sexual behavior, driving accidents, and job changes, and they tend to earn a lower income (Hechtman et al., 2016).

ADHD is a difficult disorder to assess properly (Sibley, Campez, & Raiker, 2018; Pelham et al., 2005). Ideally, the child's behavior should be observed in several environments (school, home, with friends) because the symptoms of hyperactivity and inattentiveness must be present across multiple settings in order for ADHD to be diagnosed (APA, 2013). Because children with ADHD often give poor descriptions of their symptoms, it is important to obtain reports of the symptoms from parents and teachers (Raiker et al., 2017). And, finally, although diagnostic interviews, ratings scales, and psychological tests can be helpful in the assessment of ADHD, studies suggest that many children receive their diagnosis from pediatricians or family physicians rather than mental health professionals and that at most one-third of such diagnoses are based on psychological or educational testing (Millichap, 2010).

What Are the Causes of ADHD? Most of today's clinicians consider ADHD to result from several interacting causes. Biological factors have been identified in many cases, with genetic studies suggesting that certain children have a predisposition to display inattention, impulsivity, and overactivity (Krull, 2017; Chang et al., 2013).

To appreciate the brain factors that may contribute to ADHD, it is necessary to first understand normal human cognition. There are two complementary processes that make up our moment-to-moment attention (Nigg, 2016). *Type 1 attention processes* are beyond our voluntary control and focus our attention on unexpected things that occur in our surroundings, such as sudden sounds or startling information. In contrast, *Type 2 attention processes* are mental activities that we control, and they involve our effortful focus of attention. In order to attend to our environment properly, we must have an appropriate interplay between our Type 1 and Type 2 attention processes. In many situations, for example, it is important that our Type 2 attention processes suppress our Type 1 attention alerts so that we can achieve our goals. If you were reading a book and suddenly there was lightning and thunder outside, your Type 1 attention processes might automatically reorient your focus momentarily to the unanticipated sight and sound. In order to resume reading, however, you would need to engage your Type 2 attention processes to consciously divert your attention from the distracting weather outside back to your book.

The symptoms of poor attention that characterize ADHD are commonly understood as a breakdown in the balance between Type 1 and Type 2 attention processes (Nigg, 2016). Children with ADHD have particular difficulty engaging Type 2 attention processes to override Type 1 "emergency alarms," and as a result they have trouble deliberately refocusing their attention to successfully function at home, at school, and in social situations. If there is a loud lawn mower running outside of a classroom, most students can keep their focus on the teacher despite the distraction. In contrast, students with ADHD will have difficulty recruiting Type 2 attention processes to return their focus back to the teacher.

Brain scan studies have identified an *attention circuit*—a number of structures that work together throughout the brain to bring about attention and to maintain a proper balance between Type I and Type 2 attention processes (Gehricke et al., 2017). You have read about some of the brain structures in this circuit (the *prefrontal cortex*, *anterior cingulate*, and *striatum*, for example) in our earlier discussions of other brain circuits. Other structures in the attention circuit, such as the *corona radiata* and the *longitudinal fasciculus*, are new to your reading and are tied to a narrower range of behaviors and cognitive processes, including attention. Research on the possible ties between the attention circuit and ADHD is still unfolding, but indications are that individuals with ADHD have a dysfunctional attention circuit, marked by poor communication (that is, low *interconnectivity*) between the structures in this circuit, as well as by abnormal activity of the neurotransmitter *dopamine* throughout the circuit (Gehricke et al., 2017; Nigg, 2016). Given the dysfunctional attention circuit of these individuals, their Type 2 attention processes are, more often than not, simply unable to override their Type 1 attention processes.

In addition to biological factors, ADHD has been linked to high levels of stress and to family dysfunction (Krull, 2017; DuPaul & Kern, 2011). In fact, some studies suggest that these negative factors interfere with the development of effective Type 2 attention processes (Nigg, 2016). In addition, sociocultural theorists have noted that ADHD symptoms and a diagnosis of ADHD may themselves create interpersonal problems and produce further symptoms in the child. That is, children who are hyperactive tend to be viewed negatively by their peers and parents, have impaired peer relationships, and, in turn, come to view themselves negatively (Ros & Graziano, 2018).

How Is ADHD Treated?

Almost 80 percent of all children and adolescents with ADHD receive treatment (Winter & Bienvenu, 2011). There is, however, disagreement in the field about which kind of treatment is most effective. The most commonly used approaches are drug therapy, cognitive-behavioral therapy, or a combination of the two (Krull, 2017; Sibley et al., 2014).

DRUG THERAPY Like Tom, the child described in the following case, millions of children and adults with ADHD are currently treated with **methylphenidate,** a stimulant drug that actually has been available for decades, or with certain other stimulants.

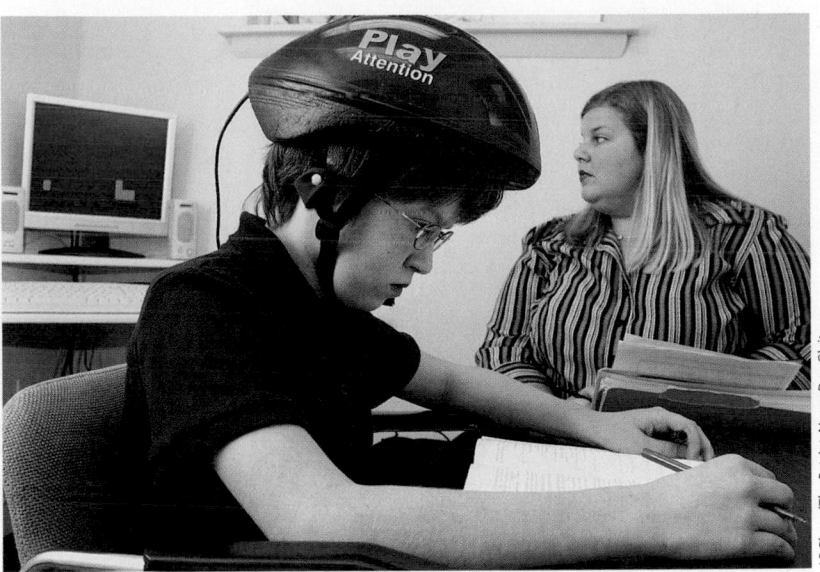

"Playing" attention A range of techniques have been used to help understand and treat children with ADHD, including a computer program called *Play Attention*. Here, under the watchful eye of a behavior specialist, a child wears a bike helmet that measures brain waves while she performs tasks that require attention.

When Tom was born, he acted like a "crack baby," his mother, Ann, says. "He responded violently to even the slightest touch, and he never slept." Shortly after Tom turned two, the . . . day care center asked Ann to withdraw him. They deemed his behavior "just too aberrant," she remembers. Tom's doctors ran a battery of tests to screen for brain damage, but they found no physical explanation for his lack of self-control. In fact, his IQ was high—even though he performed poorly in school. Eventually, Tom was diagnosed with attention-deficit/hyperactivity disorder (ADHD). . . . The psychiatrist told Ann that in terms of severity, Tom was 15 on a scale of one to 10. As therapy, this doctor prescribed methylphenidate, a drug better known by its brand name, Ritalin.

(Leutwyler, 1996, p. 13)

methylphenidate A stimulant drug, known better by the trade names *Ritalin* or *Concerta*, commonly used to treat ADHD.

Competition of another kind Simone Biles, the most decorated American gymnast in history, performs in the balance beam competition at the 2016 Olympic Games at the age of 19. After hackers revealed her medical records, Biles proudly announced that she suffers from ADHD and has received an exemption from the World Anti-Doping Association (WADA) to take methylphenidate for her condition. She tweeted: "Having ADHD and taking medicine for it is nothing to be ashamed of."

Although a variety of manufacturers now produce methylphenidate, the drug is often known to the public by its famous trade names, *Ritalin* or *Concerta*. As researchers have confirmed methylphenidate's quieting effects on children with ADHD and its ability to help them focus, solve complex tasks, perform better at school, and control aggression, use of the drug has increased enormously—according to some estimates, at least a threefold increase since 1990 alone (Mash & Wolfe, 2018, 2015; Krull, 2017). This increase in use also extends to preschoolers.

Around 2.2 million children in the United States, 3 percent of all schoolchildren, regularly take methylphenidate for ADHD, a number that is still rising (Bachmann et al., 2017; Burcu et al., 2016; Olfson et al., 2016). It is now the most common treatment for the disorder, although amphetamines such as *Adderall* are being increasingly prescribed for children with ADHD and are now the medication of choice to treat adult ADHD (Safer, 2016). It is worth noting that, although methylphenidate and amphetamines are both stimulant drugs, they are somewhat different in structure and certain actions. Many clinicians worry about the possible long-term effects of these various stimulants, and others question whether the favorable findings of the drug studies (most of which have been done on white non-Hispanic American children) are applicable to children from minority groups (Biederman et al., 2005, 2004).

Extensive investigations indicate that ADHD is overdiagnosed in the United States, so many children who are receiving stimulants may in fact have been inaccurately diagnosed (Batstra et al., 2014; Rapport et al., 2008). In addition, a number of clinicians and parents have questioned the safety of the stimulants. During the late 1980s, several lawsuits were filed against physicians, schools, and even the American Psychiatric Association, claiming misuse of these drugs (Safer, 1994). Most of the suits were dismissed, but the media blitz that surrounded them affected public perceptions. As you read in Chapter 12, the stimulants used to treat ADHD have also become popular recreational drugs among teenagers and young adults; some snort them to get high, others use them to stay alert or improve their performance at school or work. A number of young people become dependent on the stimulants, further raising public concerns about the drugs. Moreover, although stimulant medication can improve children's attention and behavioral control in the short term, studies do not find that such treatment necessarily leads to meaningful long-term improvements, or to positive changes in academic performance, peer relationships, or family dynamics. Yet these latter concerns are often the very reasons parents initially bring children with ADHD in for treatment.

> **Why has there been a sizable increase in the diagnosis and treatment of ADHD over the past few decades?**

On the positive side, stimulant medications are apparently very helpful, at least in the short term, to children and adults who suffer from ADHD (Sibley et al., 2014). As you will see, behavioral programs are also effective in many cases but not in all, and tend to be most effective when they are used in concert with stimulant drugs. When children with ADHD are taken off the drugs, many fare badly.

Most studies to date have indicated that the stimulant medications are safe for the majority of people with ADHD (Krull, 2017; Berg et al., 2014). Their undesired effects are usually no worse than insomnia, stomachaches, headaches, or loss of appetite. However, some research and case reports suggest that, in a small number of cases, the medications may increase the risk of developing mild tremors or tics (Krull, 2017; Waugh, 2013), developing psychotic symptoms (Schwarz & Cohen, 2013), or having a heart attack—among people (primarily adults) who already have cardiac problems

Laurence Griffiths/Getty Images

or high blood pressure (Berg et al., 2014). They also apparently can affect the growth of some children (Swanson et al., 2017); to prevent this, children must take periodic breaks from the medications in what are called "drug holidays."

COGNITIVE-BEHAVIORAL THERAPY AND COMBINATION THERAPIES Cognitive-behavioral therapy, particularly interventions that seek to change and/or manage specific behaviors, is often used for individuals with ADHD. In many cases, parents and teachers are taught how to apply the principles of operant conditioning—systematically rewarding the children for attentiveness or self-control. They may, for example, set up a *token economy program* in which the children receive tokens whenever they attend and respond appropriately—tokens that can later be exchanged for rewards of various kinds (Krull, 2017; Sibley et al., 2014).

Parents of children with ADHD may also receive *parent management training*, in which cognitive-behavioral techniques are combined with family interventions to help them deal with their children more effectively, similar to the training received by parents of children with conduct disorder. Moreover, parent management training and operant techniques may be further combined with *school interventions*. In one such combination program, the *Daily Report Card (DRC)*, a child's target behaviors—staying in his or her classroom seat, raising a hand to speak, and using an "inside voice"—are carefully evaluated, recorded on a DRC, and reinforced by teachers throughout the school day. At the end of the day, the teacher further provides the report card for the parents to see, and, if a sufficient number of target behaviors had been performed satisfactorily that day, the child is also given rewards at home (Cornacchio et al., 2017). For example, the child may be able to select a treat at home for every 10 DRC "checks" from the teacher.

Many children with ADHD also participate in summer treatment programs. Typically, these programs take the form of an eight-week therapeutic camp that provides systematic cognitive-behavioral interventions in classroom-like formats (Evans, Owens, & Bunford, 2014).

Research suggests that children with ADHD may improve most when they receive a combination of stimulant drug therapy and the cognitive-behavioral treatments we have been discussing (Pelham et al., 2016; Evans et al., 2014). Combining drug therapies and cognitive-behavioral therapy is also desirable because, according to research, children who receive both treatments require lower levels of medication, meaning, of course, that they are less subject to the medication's undesired effects (Page et al., 2016; Hoza et al., 2008).

Multicultural Factors and ADHD Throughout this book, you have seen that race and ethnicity often affect how people are diagnosed and treated for various psychological disorders. Thus, you should not be totally surprised that race and ethnicity also seem important with regard to ADHD.

A number of studies indicate that African American and Hispanic American children with significant attention and activity problems are less likely than non-Hispanic white American children with similar symptoms to be assessed for ADHD, receive a diagnosis of ADHD, or undergo treatment for it (Coker et al., 2016; Morgan & Farkas, 2016). Moreover, among those who do receive such a diagnosis and treatment, children from racial/ethnic minorities are less likely than non-Hispanic white American children to be treated with stimulant drugs or a combination of stimulants and cognitive-behavioral therapy—the interventions that seem to be of most help to those with ADHD (Pham et al., 2010; Stevens et al., 2005). Finally, among those children who do receive stimulant drug treatment for ADHD, children from racial/ethnic minorities are also less likely to receive adequate follow-up care to monitor their medication responses (Cummings et al., 2017).

In part, these racial and ethnic differences are tied to economic factors. Studies consistently show that poorer children are less likely than wealthier ones to be

Jose Azel/Aurora

Cognitive-behavioral interventions Educational programs often use operant conditioning principles that clearly spell out targeted behaviors and rewards and systematically reinforce appropriate behaviors. Such programs can be particularly helpful for children with ADHD.

#CounselingDeficit

Currently there is 1 school counselor for every 491 students in the United States. The recommended ratio is 1 per 250 students (ASCA, 2017, 2016).

TABLE: 17-6

Dx Checklist

Autism Spectrum Disorder

1. Individual displays continual deficiencies in various areas of communication and social interaction, including the following:
   • Social-emotional reciprocity • Nonverbal communication • Development and maintenance of relationships.

2. Individual displays significant restriction and repetition in behaviors, interests, or activities, including two or more of the following: • Exaggerated and repeated speech patterns, movements, or object use • Inflexible demand for same routines, statements, and behaviors • Highly restricted, fixated, and overly intense interests • Over- or underreactions to sensory input from the environment.

3. Individual develops symptoms by early childhood.

4. Individual experiences impaired functioning.

Information from: APA, 2013.

---

identified as having ADHD and are less likely to receive effective treatment, and racial/ethnic minority families have, on average, relatively lower incomes and weaker insurance coverage. Consistent with this point, one study found that privately insured African American children with ADHD received higher, more effective doses of stimulant drugs than did Medicaid-insured African American children with ADHD (Lipkin et al., 2005).

Some clinical theorists further believe that social bias and stereotyping may contribute to these racial and ethnic differences in diagnosis and treatment. They argue that our society often views the symptoms of ADHD as medical problems when exhibited by non-Hispanic white American children, but as indicators of poor parenting, lower IQ, substance use, or violence when displayed by African American and Hispanic American children (Duval-Harvey & Rogers, 2010; Kendall & Hatton, 2002). This notion has been supported by the finding that, all symptoms being equal, teachers are more likely to conclude that overactive non-Hispanic white American children have ADHD, but that overactive African American or Hispanic American children have other kinds of difficulties. Similarly, non-Hispanic white American parents of children with ADHD are more likely than African American and Hispanic American parents to believe that their children have ADHD or to seek ADHD evaluations and treatments for their children (Alvarado & Modesto-Lowe, 2017; Hillemeier et al., 2007; Raymond, 1997).

Whatever the precise reasons may be, it appears that children from racial/ethnic minority groups are less likely to receive a proper ADHD diagnosis and treatment. While many of today's clinical theorists correctly alert us to the possibility that ADHD may be generally overdiagnosed and overtreated, it is important to also recognize that children from minority backgrounds may, in fact, be underdiagnosed and undertreated.

Autism Spectrum Disorder

Autism spectrum disorder, a pattern first identified by psychiatrist Leo Kanner in 1943, is marked by extreme unresponsiveness to other people, severe communication deficits, and highly rigid and repetitive behaviors, interests, and activities (APA, 2013) (see **Table 17-6**). These symptoms appear early in life, typically before 3 years of age. Just two decades ago, the disorder seemed to affect around 1 out of every 2,000 children. However, in recent years there has been a steady increase in the number of children diagnosed with autism spectrum disorder, and it now appears that as many as 1 in 50 children display this pattern (Augustyn, 2017). Jennie is one such child:

Ms. D'Angelo [a special education teacher] first observed Jennie [Hobson] in a small classroom over a 5-day period. Jennie was often nonresponsive to others, especially her classmates, and rarely made eye contact with anyone. When left alone, Jennie would usually stand, put her hands over her throat, stick out her tongue, and make strange but soft noises. This would last for hours if she were left alone. When seated, Jennie rocked back and forth in her chair but never fell. Her motor skills seemed excellent and she could use crayons and manipulate paper when asked to do so. Her dexterity was also evident in her aggression, however. Jennie often grabbed people's jewelry and eyeglasses and flung them across the room. She moved quickly enough to accomplish this in less than two seconds. . . . Ms. D'Angelo noticed that Jennie was most aggressive when introduced to something or someone new. . . .

Ms. D'Angelo noticed that Jennie did not speak and vocalized only when making her soft sounds. The volume of her sounds rarely changed but she appeared to make the sounds when bored or anxious. Jennie made no effort to communicate with others and was often oblivious to others. She was sometimes startled when asked to do something. Despite her lack of expressiveness, Jennie did understand and adhere to simple requests from others. She complied readily when told to get her lunch, use the bathroom, or retrieve an item in the classroom. . . .

Jennie had a "picture book" with photographs of items she might want or need. Jennie never picked up the book or presented it to anyone but did follow directions to use the book to make requests. When shown the book and asked to point, Jennie either pushed the book onto the desk if she did not want anything or pointed to one of five photographs (i.e., a lunch box, cookie, glass of water, favorite toy, or toilet) if she did want something. . . .

Following her classroom observations of Jennie, Ms. D'Angelo had an extensive conversation with Mr. and Mrs. Hobson. They said Jennie "had always been like this" and gave examples of her early impairment. Both said Jennie was "different" as a baby when she resisted being held and when she failed to talk by age 3 years. . . . Mr. and Mrs. Hobson had enrolled their daughter in her current school when she was 4 years old.

(Kearney, 2013, pp. 125–126)

autism spectrum disorder A developmental disorder marked by extreme unresponsiveness to others, severe communication deficits, and highly repetitive and rigid behaviors, interests, and activities.

Around 80 percent of all cases of autism spectrum disorder occur in boys. As many as 90 percent of children with the disorder remain significantly disabled into adulthood. They have enormous difficulty maintaining employment, performing household tasks, and leading independent lives (Sicile-Kira, 2014). Even the highest-functioning adults with autism typically have problems with closeness and empathy and have restricted interests and activities.

The individual's *lack of responsiveness and social reciprocity*—extreme aloofness, lack of interest in other people, low empathy, and inability to share attention with others—has long been considered a central feature of autism. Like Jennie, children with this disorder typically do not reach for their parents during infancy. Instead they may arch their backs when they are held and appear not to recognize or care about those around them. In a similar vein, unlike other children of the same age, children with autism typically do not include others in their play and do not represent social experiences when they are playing; they often fail to see themselves as others see them and have no desire to imitate or be like others (Augustyn, 2017; Bodison, 2015).

Communication problems take various forms in autism spectrum disorder (Bernier & Dawson, 2016). Many people with the disorder have great difficulty understanding speech or using language for conversational purposes. In fact, like Jennie, at least a third fail to speak or develop language skills (Autism Speaks, 2017; Paul & Gilbert, 2011). Those who do talk may have rigid and repetitive speech patterns. One of the most common speech peculiarities is *echolalia*, the exact echoing of phrases spoken by others. The individuals repeat the words with the same accent or inflection, but with no sign of understanding or intent of communicating. Some even repeat a sentence days after they have heard it (*delayed echolalia*). Another speech oddity is *pronominal reversal*, or confusion of pronouns—for example, the use of "you" instead of "I." When hungry, a child with autism spectrum disorder might say, "Do you want dinner?"

The nonverbal behaviors of these individuals are often at odds with their efforts at verbal communication. They may not, for example, use a proper tone when talking. They may display few or no facial expressions or body gestures. And they may be incapable of maintaining proper eye contact during interactions. Recall, for example, that Jennie "rarely made eye contact with anyone."

People with autism also display a wide range of *highly rigid and repetitive behaviors, interests, and activities* that extend beyond speech patterns (Bernier & Dawson, 2016). Typically they become very upset at minor changes in objects, persons, or routines and resist any efforts to change their own repetitive behaviors. Jennie's special education teacher noticed that she was most aggressive when introduced to something or someone new.

Blocking out the world An 8-year-old child with autism spectrum disorder peers vacantly through a hole in the netting of a baseball batting cage, seemingly unaware of other children and activities at the playground.

© Robin Rayne Nelson/ZUMAPRESS.com

Similarly, some children with the disorder react with tantrums if a parent wears an unfamiliar pair of glasses, a chair is moved to a different part of the room, or a word in a song is changed. Kanner (1943) labeled such reactions a *perseveration of sameness*. Many also become strongly attached to particular objects—plastic lids, rubber bands, buttons, water. They may collect these objects, carry them, or play with them constantly. Some are fascinated by movement and may watch spinning objects, such as fans, for hours.

People with autism may display *motor movements* that are unusual, rigid, and repetitive. They may jump, flap their arms, twist their hands and fingers, rock, walk on their toes, spin, and make faces. These acts are called *self-stimulatory behaviors*. Some individuals with the disorder also perform *self-injurious behaviors*, such as repeatedly lunging into or banging their head against a wall, pulling their hair, or biting themselves (Oliver et al., 2017; Aman & Farmer, 2011).

The symptoms of autism spectrum disorder suggest a very disturbed and contradictory pattern of reactions to stimuli. Sometimes the individuals seem overstimulated by sights and sounds and appear to be trying to block them out (called *hyperreactivity*), while at other times they seem understimulated and appear to be performing self-stimulatory actions (called *hyporeactivity*). They may, for example, fail to react to loud noises yet turn around when they hear soda being poured.

What Are the Causes of Autism Spectrum Disorder? A variety of explanations have been offered for autism spectrum disorder. This is one disorder for which sociocultural explanations have probably been overemphasized. In fact, such explanations initially led investigators in the wrong direction. More recent work in the psychological and biological spheres has persuaded clinical theorists that cognitive limitations and brain abnormalities are the primary causes of the disorder.

SOCIOCULTURAL CAUSES At first, theorists thought that family dysfunction was the primary cause of autism spectrum disorder. When he first identified this disorder, for example, Kanner argued that particular personality characteristics of the parents created an unfavorable climate for development and contributed to the disorder (Kanner, 1954, 1943). He saw these parents as very intelligent yet cold—"refrigerator parents." These claims had enormous influence on the public and on the self-image of the parents themselves, but research has totally failed to support a picture of rigid, cold, rejecting, or disturbed parents (Sicile-Kira, 2014; Vierck & Silverman, 2011).

PSYCHOLOGICAL CAUSES According to certain theorists, people with autism spectrum disorder have a central cognitive disturbance that makes normal communication and interactions impossible. One influential explanation holds that those with the disorder fail to develop a **theory of mind**—an awareness that other people base their behaviors on their own beliefs, intentions, and other mental states, not on information that they have no way of knowing (Mazza et al., 2017; Begeer et al., 2015). (You may notice that theory of mind is similar to *mentalization*, which was discussed on pages 491–492 in Chapter 16).

By 3 to 5 years of age, most normal children can take the perspective of another person into account and use it to anticipate what the person will do. In a way, they learn to read others' minds. Let us say, for example, that we watch Jessica place a marble in a container and then we observe Frank move the marble to a nearby room while Jessica is taking a nap. We know that later Jessica will search first in the container for the marble because she is not aware that Frank moved it. We know that because we take Jessica's perspective into account. A normal child would also anticipate Jessica's

Special insights One of the highest-achieving people with autism in the world is Dr. Temple Grandin, a professor at Colorado State University. Applying her personal perspective and unique visualization skills, she has developed insight into the minds and sensitivities of cattle and has designed more humane animal-handling equipment and facilities. She argues that animals and high-functioning people with autism share cognitive similarities.

Imke Lass/Redux Pictures

Linda Davidson/The Washington Post via Getty Images

Autistic and artistic High school student Austin Morrison (standing) rehearses for the play *Nerdicus (My Brother with Autism)*. Morrison, who himself has autism, stars in the play, which is about a child whose intellectual, adaptive, and language skills remain relatively strong despite his severe social interaction deficits and his highly rigid and repetitive behaviors. This higher-functioning pattern of autism was previously called *Asperger's disorder*, but it is now classified as autism spectrum disorder along with lower-functioning patterns.

search correctly. A child with autism would not. He or she would expect Jessica to look in the nearby room because that is where the marble actually is. Jessica's own mental processes would be unimportant to the child.

Studies show that people with autism spectrum disorder do indeed have this kind of "mind-blindness," although they are not the only kinds of individuals with this limitation (Loukusa et al., 2014). They thus have great difficulty taking part in make-believe play, using language in ways that include the perspectives of others, developing relationships, or participating in human interactions.

People with autism also display deficiencies in **joint attention**, a cognitive limitation that is probably related to their theory of mind deficiency. They have great difficulty sharing focus with other people on items and events in their immediate surroundings, through mutual eye-gazing, making reference to observed objects, pointing, or other such acts (Van Hecke, Oswald, & Mundy, 2016). When individuals with severe autism are around other people, they simply are not having a "shared" experience. Deficiencies in joint attention can greatly impair proper language development, since a core function of language is to direct someone else's attention.

Why do people with autism have these cognitive limitations? Most theorists point to biological factors that prevent proper cognitive development and functioning.

BIOLOGICAL CAUSES For years researchers have tried to determine what biological abnormalities might cause theory-of-mind deficits and the other features of autism spectrum disorder. They have not yet developed a complete biological explanation, but they have uncovered promising leads. First, examinations of the relatives of people with autism keep suggesting a *genetic factor* in this disorder. The prevalence of autism among their siblings, for example, is 10 to 20 percent, a rate much higher than the general population's (Bernier & Dawson, 2016; Risch et al., 2014). Moreover, the prevalence of autism among the identical twins of people with the disorder is 60 percent. Genetic studies are increasingly identifying specific genes that, in combination, increase the likelihood of developing autism spectrum disorder (Fakhoury, 2018).

Some studies have also linked autism spectrum disorder to *prenatal difficulties* or *birth complications* (Bernier & Dawson, 2016; Reichenberg et al., 2011). For example, the chances of developing the disorder are higher when the mother had rubella (German measles) during pregnancy, was exposed to toxic chemicals before or during pregnancy, or had complications during labor or delivery.

theory of mind An awareness that other people base their behaviors on their own beliefs, intentions, and other mental states, not on information that they have no way of knowing.

joint attention Sharing focus with other people on items or events in one's immediate surroundings, whether through shared eye-gazing, pointing, referencing, or other verbal or nonverbal indications that one is paying attention to the same object.

#StunningNumbers

Approximately 100 individuals are diagnosed with autism every day in the United States.

Each year, more children are diagnosed with autism than with cancer, diabetes, and AIDS combined.

Information from: TACA, 2017

Finally, researchers have identified specific *biological factors* that may contribute to autism spectrum disorder. Initially, investigators searched for a single brain structure whose abnormal anatomy or activity might produce the symptoms of autism spectrum disorder. One early line of research found, for example, that the *cerebellum* of people with this disorder develops and functions abnormally beginning very early in life (Bernier & Dawson, 2016; Mosconi et al., 2015; Pierce & Courchesne, 2002, 2001). Because this brain structure helps control a person's ability to rapidly shift attention, among other important responsibilities, some theorists concluded that it might be the key contributor to the attention problems and related social deficiencies of individuals with autism.

Cerebellum abnormalities are still considered a possible factor in the development of this disorder, but a large body of animal research and brain scan studies conducted over the past two decades has also tied autism spectrum disorder to the abnormal activities and/or anatomies of numerous other brain structures, including the *corpus callosum, prefrontal cortex, amygdala, orbitofrontal cortex, cingulate cortex, striatum,* and *thalamus* (Hegarty et al., 2017; Twining et al., 2017; Kim et al., 2016; Zeliadt, 2015). Dysfunction by any of these brain structures may contribute to the disorder. However, in line with scientists' growing appreciation of the importance of brain circuits, a growing number of theorists believe that flawed communication (that is, flawed *interconnectivity*) among these and perhaps other brain structures may be the key to autistic spectrum disorder. In support of this belief, many studies of people with autism and of animals that display autistic-like behavior have indeed revealed poor interconnectivity—sometimes hyperconnectivity and sometimes hypoconnectivity—between these various structures (Fingher et al., 2017; Cantani et al., 2016; Solso et al., 2016).

It is tempting to conclude from these findings that there is an autism-related brain circuit whose dysfunction is the key to autism spectrum disorder. But, given the large number of brain structures implicated by research and the wide range of symptoms that characterize autism, it is more likely that two or more circuits in the brain are dysfunctional in people with this disorder. It may be, for example, that one dysfunctional circuit (consisting of the striatum, thalamus, and orbitofrontal cortex, among other structures) is related to the severe repetitive and restrictive behaviors and interests of persons with autism, while another dysfunctional circuit (consisting of the amygdala and prefrontal cortex, among other structures) helps produce the severe communication and social deficiencies of these individuals (Twining et al., 2017; Fuccillo, 2016; Kim et al., 2016).

A special bond Given the hard road they must travel together, the bond between children with autism and their parents is often especially close and intense. Here Gordy Baylinson, who has autism and is nonverbal, reaches back to caress the face of his father during a therapy session at Growing Kids Therapy Center in Herndon, Virginia.

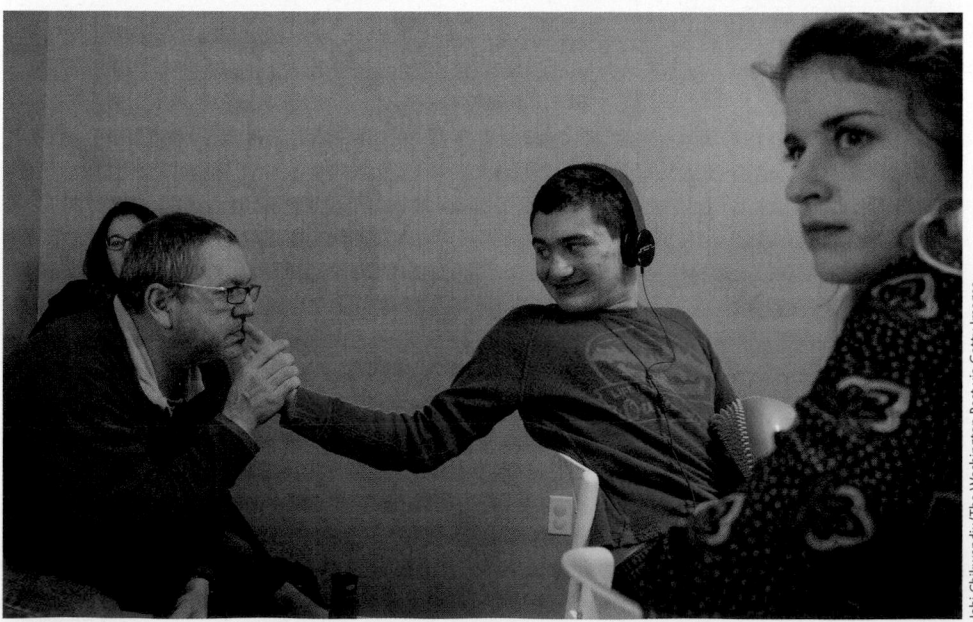

Jahi Chikwendiu/The Washington Post via Getty Images

Finally, because it has received so much attention over the past 20 years, it is worth mentioning a biological explanation for autism spectrum disorder that has *not* been borne out—the *MMR vaccine* theory. In 1998 a team of investigators published a study suggesting that a *postnatal event*—the vaccine for measles, mumps, and rubella (*MMR vaccine*)—might produce autistic symptoms in some children (Wakefield et al., 1998). Specifically, the researchers thought that for certain children, this vaccine, which is usually given to children between the ages of 12 and 15 months, produces an increase in the measles virus throughout the body, which in turn causes the onset of a powerful stomach disease and, ultimately, autism spectrum disorder.

However, virtually all research conducted since 1998 has argued against this theory (Drutz, 2017; Taylor, Swerdfeger, & Eslick, 2014; Ahearn, 2010). First, epidemiological studies repeatedly have found that children throughout the world who receive the MMR vaccine have the same prevalence of autism as those who do not receive the vaccine. Second, according to research, children with autism do not have more measles viruses in their bodies than children without autism. Third, children with autism do not have the special stomach disease proposed by this theory. Finally, careful reexaminations of the original study have indicated that it was methodologically flawed and perhaps even manipulated and that it failed to demonstrate any relationship between the MMR vaccine and the development of autism spectrum disorder (*Lancet*, 2010). Unfortunately, despite this clear refutation, many concerned parents now choose to withhold the MMR vaccine from their young children, leaving them highly vulnerable to diseases that can be very dangerous.

> Why do many people still believe that the MMR vaccine causes autism spectrum disorder, despite so much evidence to the contrary?

The iPad breakthrough A child works on an iPad as his teacher looks on. A major new trend in the training and treatment of autism spectrum disorder is the use of electronic tablets. They are effective augmentative communication systems, and they also seem to provide enormous cognitive stimulation and pleasure for people with autism.

AP Photo/Daily Herald, Bev Horne

How Do Clinicians and Educators Treat Autism Spectrum Disorder?

Treatment can help people with autism spectrum disorder adapt better to their environment, although no treatment yet known totally reverses the autistic pattern. Treatments of particular help are *cognitive-behavioral therapy, communication training, parent training,* and *community integration.* In addition, psychotropic drugs and certain vitamins have sometimes helped when combined with other approaches (Weissman & Bridgemohan, 2017; Sicile-Kira, 2014).

COGNITIVE-BEHAVIORAL THERAPY For more than 50 years, cognitive-behavioral approaches have been used in cases of autism, particularly behavior-focused interventions that teach the individuals new, appropriate behaviors—including speech, social skills, classroom skills, and self-help skills—while seeking to reduce their negative, dysfunctional behaviors. Using the principles of *modeling,* therapists often demonstrate desired behaviors and guide the persons with autism to imitate them. Using the principles of *operant conditioning,* the clinicians reinforce desired behaviors, first by "shaping" them—breaking them down so they can be learned step by step—and then rewarding each step clearly and consistently. With careful planning and execution, these procedures often produce new, more functional behaviors.

A pioneering, long-term study compared the progress of two groups of children with autism spectrum disorder (Lovaas, 2003, 1987; McEachin et al., 1993). Nineteen received the treatments described above, and 19 served as a control group. Treatment began when the children were 3 years old and continued until they were 7. By the age of 7, the group that received behavior-focused interventions was doing better in school and scoring higher on intelligence tests than the control group. Many were able to go to school in regular classrooms. The gains continued into the research participants' teenage years. Given the favorable findings of this and similar studies, many clinicians now consider early intensive behavior-focused programs to be the preferred treatment for autism spectrum disorder (Bernier & Dawson, 2016; Smith & Iadarola, 2015).

#

#TheirWords

"The one common denominator for all of the young children [with autism] is that early intervention does work, and it seems to improve the prognosis."

Temple Grandin, professor and individual with autism

augmentative communication system A method for enhancing the communication skills of people with autism spectrum disorder, intellectual disability, or cerebral palsy by teaching them to point to pictures, symbols, letters, or words on a communication board or computer.

Therapies for individuals with this disorder tend to provide the most benefit when they are started early in life (Bernier & Dawson, 2016; Smith & Iadarola, 2015). Very young children with autism often begin with services at home, but ideally, by the age of 3 they attend special programs outside the home. Typically, services are provided by education, health, or social service agencies until the children reach 3; then the department of education for each state determines which specific services the children will receive. A federal law lists autism spectrum disorder as one of 10 disorders for which school districts must provide a free special education program from birth to age 22, in the least restrictive or most appropriate setting possible. Each child with autism, like those with the other listed disabilities, receives an *Individualized Education Program* (IEP), a legal document that details the support services, therapies, and special accommodations to be afforded the child in order for him or her to achieve appropriate educational goals. The IEP is re-evaluated each year and is adjusted if the educational goals are not being achieved.

Given the recent increases in the prevalence of this disorder, many school districts are now trying to provide education and training for the children in special classes that operate at the district's own facilities (Iadarola et al., 2015). However, most school districts remain ill-equipped to meet the profound needs of students with autism. The most fortunate of these students are sent by their school districts to attend special schools, where education and therapy are combined. At such schools, specially trained teachers help the children improve their skills, behaviors, and interactions with the world. Higher-functioning students with autism may eventually spend at least part of their school day returning to standard classrooms in their own school district (Weissman & Bridgemohan, 2017; Hartford & Marcus, 2011).

COMMUNICATION TRAINING As you read earlier, even when given intensive treatment, at least a third of people with autism spectrum disorder remain speechless. To help address this, they are often taught other forms of communication, including *sign language* and *simultaneous communication,* a method combining sign language and speech. They may also learn to use **augmentative communication systems,** such as "communication boards" or computers that use pictures, symbols, or written words to represent objects or needs (Reichle et al., 2016). A child may point to a picture of a fork to give the message "I am hungry," for instance, or point to a radio for "I want music." Recall, for example, the use of a "picture book" by Jennie, the child whose case introduced this section.

Some programs now use *child-initiated interactions* to help improve the communication skills of children with autism. In such programs, teachers try to identify *intrinsic* reinforcers rather than trivial ones like food or candy. The children are first encouraged to choose items that they are interested in, and they then learn to initiate questions ("What's that?" "Where is it?" "Whose is it?") in order to obtain the items. Studies find that child-directed interventions of this kind often increase self-initiated communications, language development, and social participation (Houghton et al., 2013; Koegel et al., 2010, 2005).

Finally, some programs try to improve language and communication skills by working on the individual's capacity for *joint attention*, the cognitive ability that you read about above (Van Hecke, Oswald, & Mundy, 2016). The clinician teaches the individual to gaze into the eyes of others, make reference to observed objects, point at objects, and perform other "sharing" behaviors when he or she is involved in joint activities with other people. Studies have found that treating joint attention deficiencies during the preschool years can have a positive impact on communication and language development as well as other features of autism (Shire et al., 2017; Chang et al., 2016).

Learning to communicate Cognitive-behavioral clinicians and educators have had success teaching many children with autism spectrum disorder to communicate. Here a speech language specialist combines cognitive-behavioral techniques with the use of a communication board to teach a 3-year-old child how to express herself better and understand others.

AP Photo/Albuquerque Journal, Pat Vasquez-Cunningham

AP Photo/Javier Galeano

Animal connection At the National Aquarium in Havana, Cuba, therapists host regular sessions of stroking and touching dolphins, sea tortoises, and sea lions for children. These sessions have helped many children with autism spectrum disorder and others with intellectual disability to become more spontaneous, independent, and sociable.

PARENT TRAINING Today's treatment programs for autism spectrum disorder involve parents in a variety of ways. Cognitive-behavioral programs, for example, often train parents so that they can apply conditioning and skill-building techniques at home (Ginn et al., 2017; Masse et al., 2016). Instruction manuals for parents and home visits by teachers and other professionals are typically included in such programs. Research consistently has demonstrated that the behavior improvements produced by trained parents are often equal to or greater than those generated by teachers.

In addition to parent-training programs, individual therapy and support groups are becoming more available to help the parents of children with autism deal with their own emotions and needs (Da Paz & Wallander, 2017). A number of parent associations and lobbies also offer emotional support and practical help.

COMMUNITY INTEGRATION Many of today's school-based and home-based programs for autism spectrum disorder teach self-help, self-management, and living, social, and work skills as early as possible to help the individuals function better in their communities. In addition, greater numbers of carefully run *group homes* and *sheltered workshops* are now available for teenagers and adults with autism. These and related programs help the individuals become a part of their community; they also reduce the concerns of aging parents whose children will always need supervision.

#FamilyCost

On average, the lifetime cost of rearing an individual with autism ranges from $3.5 million to $5 million—at least 3 times the cost of rearing a nonautistic individual (Autism Speaks, 2017; NAN, 2017)

Intellectual Disability

Ed Murphy, aged 26, can tell us what it's like to be considered intellectually disabled or, as it was called in his day, "mentally retarded":

> *What is retardation? It's hard to say. I guess it's having problems thinking. Some people think that you can tell if a person is retarded by looking at them. If you think that way you don't give people the benefit of the doubt. You judge a person by how they look or how they talk or what the tests show, but you can never really tell what is inside the person.*
>
> *(Bogdan & Taylor, 1976, p. 51)*

For much of his life Ed was considered intellectually disabled and was educated and cared for in special institutions. During his adult years, clinicians discovered that

TABLE: 17-7

Dx Checklist

Intellectual Disability

1. Individual displays deficient intellectual functioning in areas such as reasoning, problem-solving, planning, abstract thinking, judgment, academic learning, and learning from experience. The deficits are reflected by clinical assessment and intelligence tests.

2. Individual displays deficient adaptive functioning in at least one area of daily life, such as communication, social involvement, or personal independence, across home, school, work, or community settings. The limitations extend beyond those displayed by most other persons of his or her age and necessitate ongoing support at school or work, or with independent living.

3. The deficits begin during the developmental period (before the age of 18).

Information from: APA, 2013.

Getting a head start Studies suggest that IQ scores and school performances of children from poor neighborhoods can be improved by enriching their daily environments at a young age. The teachers in this classroom try to stimulate further and enrich the lives of preschool children in a Head Start program in Oregon.

Don Ryan/AP Photo

Ed's intellectual ability was in fact higher than had been assumed. In the meantime, however, he had lived the childhood and adolescence of an intellectually disabled person, and his statement reveals the kinds of difficulties often faced by people with this disability.

In 2010, President Obama signed legislation known as "Rosa's Law" requiring the federal government and all public health, education, and workforce policies to replace the term "mental retardation" with "intellectual disability." Correspondingly, DSM-5 changed the diagnostic category of mental retardation to *intellectual disability*. This term is applied to a varied population, including children in institutional wards who rock back and forth, young people who work in special job programs, and men and women who raise and support their families by working at jobs that are modestly demanding. As many as 3 of every 100 people meet the criteria for this diagnosis (Baldor, 2017; APA, 2013). Around three-fifths of them are male, and the vast majority display a *mild* level of the disability (Reichenberg et al., 2016).

People receive a diagnosis of **intellectual disability (ID)** when they display general *intellectual functioning* that is well below average, in combination with poor *adaptive behavior* (APA, 2013). That is, in addition to having a low IQ (a score of 70 or below), a person with ID has great difficulty in areas such as communication, home living, self-direction, work, or safety (APA, 2013). The symptoms also must appear before the age of 18 (see **Table 17-7**).

Assessing Intelligence Educators and clinicians administer intelligence tests to measure intellectual functioning (see Chapter 4). These tests consist of a variety of questions and tasks that rely on different aspects of intelligence, such as knowledge, reasoning, and judgment. Having difficulty in just one or two of these subtests or areas of functioning does not necessarily reflect low intelligence (see *PsychWatch* on the next page). It is an individual's overall test score, or **intelligence quotient (IQ),** that is thought to indicate general intellectual ability.

> Are there other kinds of intelligence that IQ tests might fail to assess? What might that suggest about the validity and usefulness of these tests?

Many theorists have questioned whether IQ tests are indeed valid. Do they actually measure what they are supposed to measure? The correlation between IQ and school performance is rather high—around .50—indicating that many children with lower IQs do, as one might expect, perform poorly in school, while many of those with higher IQs perform better (Sternberg et al., 2001). At the same time, the correlation also suggests that the relationship is far from perfect. That is, a particular child's school performance is often higher or lower than his or her IQ might predict. Moreover, the accuracy of IQ tests at measuring extremely low intelligence has not been evaluated adequately, so it is difficult to properly assess people with severe intellectual disability (AAIDD, 2017).

Intelligence tests also appear to be socioculturally biased, as you read in Chapter 4. Children reared in households at the middle and upper socioeconomic levels tend to have an advantage on the tests because they are regularly exposed to the kinds of language and thinking that the tests evaluate. The tests rarely measure the "street sense" needed for survival by people who live in poor, crime-ridden areas—a kind of know-how that certainly requires intellectual skills. Members of cultural

Reading and 'Riting and 'Rithmetic

Compared with their peers, around 15 to 20 percent of all children, boys more often than girls, develop slowly and function poorly in a single area such as learning, communication, or motor coordination (Allen & Casey, 2017; CDC, 2017; NIH, 2016; APA, 2013). The children do not suffer from intellectual disability, and in fact they are often very bright, yet their problems may interfere with school performance, daily living, and in some cases social interactions. Similar difficulties may be seen in the children's close biological relatives (von Hahn, 2017, 2016; APA, 2013). According to DSM-5, many of these children are suffering from a specific learning disorder, communication disorder, or developmental coordination disorder—each a kind of neurodevelopmental disorder.

Children with a *specific learning disorder* have significant difficulties in acquiring reading, writing, arithmetic, or mathematical reasoning skills. Across the United States, children with such problems comprise the largest subgroup of those placed in special education classes (von Hahn, 2017, 2016; Watson et al., 2008). Some of these children read slowly or inaccurately or have difficulty understanding the meaning of what they are reading, difficulties also known as *dyslexia* (Hamilton, 2017, 2016; Boets, 2014). Others spell or write very poorly. And still others have great trouble remembering number facts, performing calculations, or reasoning mathematically.

The *communication disorders* include language disorder, speech sound disorder, and childhood-onset fluency disorder

A special pair of glasses One of several explanations for dyslexia is that some people with this disorder have a significant visual processing problem. Thus various kinds of special 3D glasses, modeled here by this child, have been developed to help diagnose and treat the disorder.

Libor Sojka/CTK v a AP Images

(stuttering) (APA, 2013; Gillam & Petersen, 2011). Children with *language disorder* have persistent difficulties acquiring, using, or comprehending spoken or written language. They may, for example, have trouble using language to express themselves, struggle at learning new words, confine their speech to short simple sentences, or show a general lag in language development. Children with *speech sound disorder* have persistent difficulties in speech production or speech fluency. Some, for example, cannot make correct speech sounds at an appropriate age, resulting in speech that sounds like baby talk. People who display *stuttering*

have a disturbance in the fluency and timing of their speech, characterized by repeating, prolonging, or interjecting sounds, pausing before finishing a word, or having excessive tension in the muscles they use for speech.

Finally, children with *developmental coordination disorder* perform coordinated motor activities at a level well below that of others their age (Hamilton, 2017; APA, 2013). Younger children with this disorder are clumsy and slow to master skills such as tying shoelaces, buttoning shirts, and zipping pants. Older children with the disorder may have great difficulty assembling puzzles, building models, playing ball, and printing or writing.

Studies have linked these various disorders to genetic factors, brain abnormalities, birth injuries, lead poisoning, inappropriate diet, sensory or perceptual dysfunction, and poor teaching (Hamilton, 2017, 2016; von Hahn, 2017, 2016; APA, 2013). Research implicating each of these factors has been limited, however, and the precise causes of the disorders remain unclear.

Some of the disorders respond to special treatment approaches (Hamilton, 2016; McArthur et al., 2013; Miller, 2010). Reading therapy, for example, is very helpful in mild cases of dyslexia, and speech therapy brings about complete recovery in many cases of speech sound disorder. Furthermore, the various disorders often disappear before adulthood, even without any treatment.

---

minorities and people for whom English is a second language also often appear to be at a disadvantage in taking these tests.

If IQ tests do not always measure intelligence accurately and objectively, then the diagnosis of intellectual disability also may be biased. That is, some people may receive the diagnosis partly because of test inadequacies, cultural differences, discomfort with the testing situation, or the bias of a tester.

Assessing Adaptive Functioning Diagnosticians cannot rely solely on a cutoff IQ score of 70 to determine whether a person suffers from intellectual disability. Some people with a low IQ are quite capable of managing their lives and functioning

intellectual disability (ID) A disorder marked by intellectual functioning and adaptive behavior that are well below average. Previously called *mental retardation*.

intelligence quotient (IQ) A score derived from intelligence tests that theoretically represents a person's overall intellectual capacity.

mild ID A level of intellectual disability (IQ between 50 and 70) at which people can benefit from education and can support themselves as adults.

moderate ID A level of intellectual disability (IQ between 35 and 49) at which people can learn to care for themselves and can benefit from vocational training.

severe ID A level of intellectual disability (IQ between 20 and 34) at which people require careful supervision and can learn to perform basic work in structured and sheltered settings.

profound ID A level of intellectual disability (IQ below 20) at which people need a very structured environment with close supervision.

Down syndrome A form of intellectual disability caused by an abnormality in the 21st chromosome.

independently, while others are not. The cases of Brian and Jeffrey show the range of adaptive abilities.

Brian comes from a lower-income family. He always has functioned adequately at home and in his community. He dresses and feeds himself and even takes care of himself each day until his mother returns home from work. He also plays well with his friends. At school, however, Brian refuses to participate or do his homework. He seems ineffective, at times lost, in the classroom. Referred to a school psychologist by his teacher, he received an IQ score of 60.

Jeffrey comes from an upper-middle-class home. He was always slow to develop, and sat up, stood, and talked late. During his infancy and toddler years, he was put in a special stimulation program and given special help and attention at home. Still Jeffrey has trouble dressing himself today and cannot be left alone in the backyard lest he hurt himself or wander off into the street. Schoolwork is very difficult for him. The teacher must work slowly and provide individual instruction for him. Tested at age 6, Jeffrey received an IQ score of 60.

Brian seems well adapted to his environment outside school. However, Jeffrey's limitations are pervasive. In addition to his low IQ score, Jeffrey has difficulty meeting challenges at home and elsewhere. Thus a diagnosis of intellectual disability may be more appropriate for Jeffrey than for Brian.

Several scales have been developed to assess adaptive behavior. Here again, however, some people function better in their lives than the scales predict, while others fall short. Thus to properly diagnose intellectual disability, clinicians should probably observe the adaptive functioning of each individual in his or her everyday environment, taking both the person's background and the community's standards into account. Even then, such judgments may be subjective, as clinicians may not be familiar with the standards of a particular culture or community.

What Are the Features of Intellectual Disability? The most consistent feature of intellectual disability is that the person learns very slowly (AAIDD, 2017; Sturmey & Didden, 2014). Other areas of difficulty are attention, short-term memory, planning, and language (Burack et al., 2016). Those who are institutionalized with this disability are particularly likely to have these limitations. It may be that the unstimulating environment and minimal interactions with staff in many institutions contribute to such difficulties. Traditionally, four levels of intellectual disability have been distinguished: *mild* (IQ 50–70), *moderate* (IQ 35–49), *severe* (IQ 20–34), and *profound* (IQ below 20).

Mild ID Some 80 to 85 percent of all people with intellectual disability fall into the category of **mild ID** (IQ 50–70). This is sometimes called the "educable" level because the individuals can benefit from schooling and can support themselves as adults. Mild ID is not usually recognized until children enter school and are assessed there. These children demonstrate rather typical language, social, and play skills, but they need assistance when under stress—a limitation that becomes increasingly apparent as academic and social demands increase (Pivalizza, 2016). Interestingly, the intellectual performance of individuals with mild ID often seems to improve with age; some even seem to leave the label behind when they leave school, and they go on to function well in the community (Sturmey & Didden, 2014). Their jobs tend to be unskilled or semiskilled.

Research has often linked mild ID to sociocultural and psychological causes, particularly poor and unstimulating environments during a child's early years, inadequate parent–child interactions, and insufficient learning experiences (Pivalizza & Lalani, 2016; Sturmey & Didden, 2014). These relationships have been observed in studies comparing deprived and enriched environments (see **Figure 17-2**). In fact, some community programs have sent workers into the homes of young children with low IQ

#

#TheirWords

"The IQ test was invented to predict academic performance, nothing else. If we wanted something that would predict life success, we'd have to invent another test completely."

Robert Zajonc, psychologist, 1984

scores to help enrich the environment there, and their interventions have often improved the children's functioning. When continued, programs of this kind also help improve the person's later performance in school and adulthood (Ramey et al., 2012; Ramey & Ramey, 2007, 2004).

Although sociocultural and psychological factors seem to be key causes of mild ID, at least some biological factors also may be operating (Reichenberg et al., 2016). Studies suggest, for example, that a mother's moderate drinking, drug use, or malnutrition during pregnancy may lower her child's intellectual potential (CDC, 2017; Popova et al., 2017). Malnourishment during a child's early years also may hurt his or her intellectual development, although this effect can usually be reversed at least partly if a child's diet is improved before too much time goes by.

Moderate, Severe, and Profound ID

Approximately 10 percent of those with intellectual disability function at a level of **moderate ID** (IQ 35–49). They typically receive their diagnosis earlier in life than do individuals with mild ID, as they demonstrate clear deficits in language development and play during their preschool years. By middle school they further show significant delays in their acquisition of reading and number skills and adaptive skills. By adulthood, however, many individuals with moderate ID manage to develop a fair degree of communication skill, learn to care for themselves, benefit from vocational training, and can work in unskilled or semiskilled jobs, usually under supervision. Most also function well in the community if they have supervision (AAIDD, 2017).

Approximately 3 to 4 percent of people with intellectual disability display **severe ID** (IQ 20–34). They typically demonstrate basic motor and communication deficits during infancy. Many also show signs of neurological dysfunction and have an increased risk for brain seizure disorder. In school, they may be able to string together only two or three words when speaking. They usually require careful supervision, profit somewhat from vocational training, and can perform only basic work tasks in structured and sheltered settings. Their understanding of communication is usually better than their speech. Most are able to function well in the community if they live in group homes, in community nursing homes, or with their families (AAIDD, 2017).

Around 1 to 2 percent of all people with intellectual disability function at a level of **profound ID** (IQ below 20). This level is very noticeable at birth or early infancy. With training, people with profound ID may learn or improve basic skills such as walking, some talking, and feeding themselves. They need a very structured environment, with close supervision and considerable help, including a one-to-one relationship with a caregiver, in order to develop to the fullest (AAIDD, 2017).

Severe and profound levels of intellectual disability often appear as part of larger syndromes that include severe physical handicaps. The physical problems are often even more limiting than the individual's low intellectual functioning and in some cases can be fatal.

What Are the Biological Causes of Intellectual Disability?

As you read earlier, the primary causes of mild ID are environmental, although biological factors may also be operating in many cases. In contrast, the main causes of moderate, severe, and profound ID are biological, although people who function at these levels also are strongly affected by their family and social environment (Reichenberg et al., 2016; Sturmey & Didden, 2014). The leading biological causes of intellectual disability are chromosomal abnormalities, metabolic disorders, prenatal problems, birth complications, and childhood diseases and injuries.

CHROMOSOMAL CAUSES The most common of the chromosomal disorders that lead to intellectual disability is **Down syndrome,** named after Langdon Down, the British

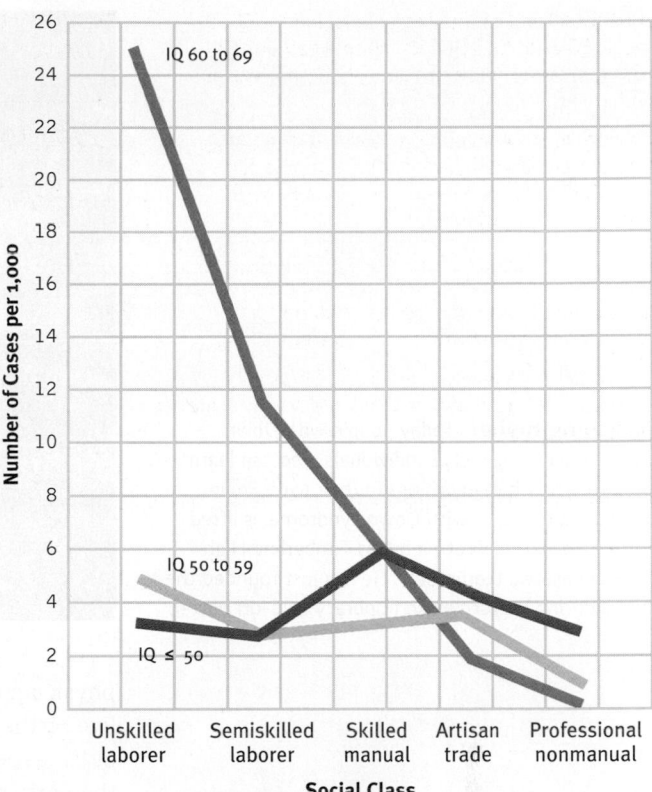

FIGURE 17-2

Intellectual Disability and Socioeconomic Class

The prevalence of mild ID is much higher in the lower socioeconomic classes than in the upper classes. In contrast, other levels of intellectual disability are evenly distributed among the various socioeconomic classes.

AP Photo/The Idaho Statesman, Kyle Green

Reaching higher Today people with Down syndrome are viewed as individuals who can learn and accomplish many things in their lives. Eddie Gordon, a teenager with Down syndrome, is lifted into the air in celebration by his Timberline High School baseball teammates. He has just rounded the bases during his turn as an honorary lead-off batter.

physician who first identified it. Down syndrome occurs in fewer than 1 of every 1,000 live births, but the rate increases significantly when the mother's age is over 35. Many older expectant mothers are now encouraged to undergo prenatal testing during the early months of pregnancy to identify Down syndrome and other chromosomal abnormalities.

People with Down syndrome may have a small head, flat face, slanted eyes, high cheekbones, and, in some cases, protruding tongue. The latter may affect their ability to pronounce words clearly. They are often very affectionate with family members but in general display the same range of personality characteristics as people in the general population.

Several types of chromosomal abnormalities may cause Down syndrome (NICHD, 2015). The most common type (94 percent of cases) is *trisomy 21,* in which the person has three free-floating 21st chromosomes instead of two. Most people with Down syndrome range in IQ from 35 to 55. The individuals appear to age early, and many even show signs of neurocognitive decline as they approach 40 (Rosalyn et al., 2017; Powell et al., 2014). It appears that Down syndrome and early neurocognitive decline often occur together because the genes that produce them are located close to each other on chromosome 21 (Hithersay et al., 2017; Rohn et al., 2014).

Fragile X syndrome is the second most common chromosomal cause of intellectual disability. Children born with a fragile X chromosome (that is, an X chromosome with a genetic abnormality that leaves it prone to breakage and loss) generally display mild to moderate degrees of intellectual dysfunction, language impairments, and in some cases, behavioral problems (Karmiloff-Smith et al., 2016). Typically, they are shy and anxious.

METABOLIC CAUSES In metabolic disorders, the body's breakdown or production of chemicals is disturbed. The metabolic disorders that affect intelligence and development are typically caused by the pairing of two defective *recessive* genes, one from each parent. Although one such gene would have no influence if it were paired with a normal gene, its pairing with another defective gene leads to major problems for the child.

The most common metabolic disorder to cause intellectual disability is *phenylketonuria (PKU),* which strikes 1 of every 14,000 children. Babies with PKU appear normal at birth but cannot break down the amino acid *phenylalanine.* The chemical builds up and is converted into substances that poison the system, causing severe

#SexChromosomes

The 23rd chromosome, whose abnormality causes Fragile X syndrome, is the smallest human chromosome.

The 23rd chromosome determines a person's sex and thus is also referred to as the sex chromosome.

In males, the 23rd chromosome pair consists of an X chromosome and a Y chromosome.

In females, the 23rd chromosome pair consists of two X chromosomes.

intellectual dysfunction and several other symptoms (NICHD, 2015; Waisbren, 2011). Today infants can be screened for PKU, and if started on a special diet before 3 months of age, they may develop normal intelligence (van Spronsen et al., 2017).

Children with *Tay-Sachs disease,* another metabolic disorder resulting from a pairing of recessive genes, progressively lose their mental functioning, vision, and motor ability over the course of two to four years, and eventually die. One of every 30 persons of Eastern European Jewish ancestry carries the recessive gene responsible for this disorder, so that 1 of every 900 Jewish couples is at risk for having a child with Tay-Sachs disease.

PRENATAL AND BIRTH-RELATED CAUSES As a fetus develops, major physical problems in the pregnant mother can threaten the child's prospects for a normal life (AAIDD, 2017; Bebko & Weiss, 2006). When a pregnant woman has too little iodine in her diet, for example, her child may be born with *cretinism,* also called *severe congenital hypothyroidism,* marked by an abnormal thyroid gland, slow development, intellectual disability, and a dwarflike appearance. This condition is rare today because the salt in most diets now contains extra iodine. Also, any infant born with this problem may quickly be given thyroid extract to bring about normal development.

Other prenatal problems may also cause intellectual disability. As you read in Chapter 12, children whose mothers drink too much alcohol during pregnancy may be born with **fetal alcohol syndrome,** a group of very serious problems that includes mild to severe ID (CDC, 2017; Popova et al., 2017). It is estimated that 120,000 children are born with fetal alcohol syndrome each year (Popova et al., 2017). In fact, a generally safe level of alcohol consumption during pregnancy has not been established by research. In addition, certain maternal infections during pregnancy—*rubella* (German measles) and *syphilis,* for example—may cause childhood problems that include intellectual disability.

Birth complications also can lead to problems in intellectual functioning. A prolonged period without oxygen (*anoxia*) during or after delivery can cause brain damage and intellectual disability in a baby. In addition, although premature birth does not necessarily lead to long-term problems for children, researchers have found that some babies with a premature birth weight of less than 3.5 pounds display low intelligence (Howe et al., 2016; Oudgenoeg-Paz et al., 2017; Howe et al., 2016).

CHILDHOOD PROBLEMS After birth, particularly up to age 6, certain injuries and accidents can affect intellectual function and in some cases lead to intellectual disability. Poisonings, serious head injuries caused by accident or abuse, excessive exposure to X-rays, and excessive use of certain drugs pose special dangers (Kirkham, 2017; Yorifuji et al., 2016). For example, a serious case of *lead poisoning,* from eating lead-based paints or inhaling high levels of automobile fumes, can cause ID in children. Mercury, radiation, nitrite, and pesticide poisoning may do the same. In addition, certain infections, such as *meningitis* and *encephalitis,* can lead to intellectual disability if they are not diagnosed and treated in time (Khandaker et al., 2016).

Interventions for People with Intellectual Disability

The quality of life attained by people with intellectual disability depends largely on sociocultural factors: where they live and with whom, how they are educated, and the growth opportunities available at home and in the community. Thus intervention programs for these individuals try to provide comfortable and stimulating residences, a proper education, and social and economic opportunities. At the same time, the programs seek to improve the self-image and self-esteem of those with intellectual disability. Once these needs are met, formal psychological or biological treatments are also of help in some cases.

fetal alcohol syndrome A group of problems in a child, including lower intellectual functioning, low birth weight, and irregularities in the hands and face, that result from excessive alcohol intake by the mother during pregnancy.

Normal needs People with intellectual disability have normal interpersonal and sexual needs—needs for which they may receive training and supervision in various clinical programs, especially those that adhere to the principle of normalization. Here a couple with Down syndrome twirl each other on the dance floor during the Night to Shine—a dance party in Portland, Maine, for people with special needs.

Ben McCanna/Portland Press Herald via Getty Images

Attila Balazs/EPA/Redux

The power of mainstreaming The goal of mainstreaming, or inclusion, programs—in which children with intellectual disability are placed in regular classes with the general school population—is apparent in this photo. Here, Nandor Szecsi (front), who has Down syndrome and is mainstreamed, is hugged lovingly by his primary school classmate in Budapest, Hungary.

> What might be the benefits of mainstreaming compared with special education classes, and vice versa?

WHAT IS THE PROPER RESIDENCE? Until recent decades, parents of children with intellectual disability would send them to live in public institutions—**state schools**—as early as possible (Harris, 2010). These overcrowded institutions provided basic care, but residents were neglected, often abused, and isolated from society.

During the 1960s and 1970s, the public became more aware of these sorry conditions and, as part of the broader *deinstitutionalization* movement (see Chapter 15), demanded that many people with intellectual disability be released from the state schools (Harris, 2010). In many cases, the releases were done without adequate preparation or supervision. Like people with schizophrenia who were suddenly deinstitutionalized, those with intellectual disability were virtually dumped into the community. Often they failed to adjust and had to be institutionalized once again.

Since that time, reforms have led to the creation of *small institutions* and other *community residences* that teach self-sufficiency, devote more staff time to patient care, and offer educational and medical services. The community residences range from group homes with 24-hour support staff to local branches of larger institutions to more autonomous, semi-independent residences with part-time staff providing support only as needed. Many of these settings follow the principles of **normalization** first started in Denmark and Sweden—they attempt to provide living conditions similar to those enjoyed by the rest of society; flexible routines; and normal developmental experiences, including opportunities for self-determination, sexual fulfillment, and economic freedom (Pivalizza, 2016; Merrick et al., 2014; Hemmings, 2010).

Today the vast majority of children with intellectual disability live at home rather than in an institution. During adulthood and as their parents age, however, some people with intellectual disability require levels of assistance and opportunities that their families are unable to provide. A community residence becomes an appropriate alternative for them. Most people with intellectual disability, including almost all with mild ID, now spend their adult lives either in the family home or in a community residence (Sturmey & Didden, 2014; Sturmey, 2008). The type of community residence is typically determined by the extent of the individual's disability, the preferences of the individual and family, and available resources.

WHICH EDUCATIONAL PROGRAMS WORK BEST? Because early intervention seems to offer such great promise, educational programs for people with intellectual disability may begin during the earliest years. The appropriate education depends on the person's level of functioning. Educators hotly debate whether special classes or mainstreaming is most effective once the children enter school (Malki & Einat, 2017; Bouck & Park, 2016; McKenzie, McConkey, & Adnams, 2014). In **special education,** children with intellectual disability are grouped together in a separate, specially designed educational program. In contrast, in **mainstreaming,** or **inclusion,** they are placed in regular classes with students from the general school population. Neither approach seems consistently superior. It may well be that mainstreaming is better for some areas of learning and for some children, and special classes are better for others.

Teacher preparedness is another factor that may play into decisions about mainstreaming and special education classes. Many teachers report feeling inadequately prepared to provide training and support for children with intellectual disability, especially children who have additional problems (Scheuermann et al., 2003). Brief training courses for teachers appear to address such concerns (Mader, 2017; Callanan, 2012; Campbell et al., 2003).

Teachers who work with students with intellectual disability often use operant conditioning principles to improve their students' self-help, communication, social, and academic skills (Pivalizza, 2016; Sturmey, 2008; Ardoin et al., 2004). They break learning tasks down into small steps, giving positive reinforcement for each increment of progress. Additionally, many institutions, schools, and private homes have set up *token economy programs*—the operant conditioning programs that have also been used to treat children with ADHD and institutionalized patients who have schizophrenia.

Like autism, intellectual disability is listed by federal law as one of the disabilities for which school districts must provide a free, appropriate educational program from birth to age 22, in the least restrictive or most appropriate setting possible. Here too, each child with intellectual disability receives an *Individualized Education Program* (IEP) that details the support services, therapies, and special accommodations to be afforded the child in order for him or her to achieve proper educational goals—a legal document that is re-evaluated and, if necessary, adjusted each year.

WHEN IS THERAPY NEEDED? Like anyone else, people with intellectual disability sometimes have emotional and behavioral problems. Around 30 percent or more have a psychological disorder other than intellectual disability (Sturmey & Didden, 2014; Bouras & Holt, 2010). Furthermore, some suffer from low self-esteem, interpersonal problems, and difficulties adjusting to community life. These problems are helped to some degree by either individual or group therapy. Large numbers of people with intellectual disability also take psychotropic medications (Bowring et al., 2017; Park et al., 2016). Many clinicians argue, however, that too often the medications are used simply for the purpose of making the individuals easier to manage.

HOW CAN OPPORTUNITIES FOR PERSONAL, SOCIAL, AND OCCUPATIONAL GROWTH BE INCREASED? People need to feel effective and competent in order to move forward in life. Those with intellectual disability are most likely to feel effective and competent if their communities allow them to grow and to make many of their own choices. Denmark and Sweden, where the normalization movement began, have again been leaders in this area, developing youth clubs that encourage those with intellectual disability to take risks and function independently. The Special Olympics program has also encouraged those with intellectual disability to be active in setting goals, to participate in their environment, and to interact socially with others (Tint et al., 2017; Crawford et al., 2015).

Socializing, sex, and marriage are difficult issues for people with intellectual disability and their families, but with proper training and practice, they usually can learn to use contraceptives and carry out responsible family planning (Roy, 2016). National advocacy organizations and a number of clinicians currently offer guidance in these matters, and some have developed *dating skills programs* (AAIDD, 2017; Segal, 2008).

Some states restrict marriage for people with intellectual disability. These laws are rarely enforced, though, and in fact many people with mild ID marry. Contrary to popular myths, the marriages can be very successful. And although some may be

state school A state-supported institution for people with intellectual disability.

normalization The principle that institutions and community residences for people with intellectual disability should provide living conditions and opportunities similar to those enjoyed by the rest of society.

special education An approach to educating children with intellectual disability in which they are grouped together and given a separate, specially designed education.

mainstreaming The placement of children with intellectual disability in regular school classes. Also known as *inclusion*.

Diego Lima/AFP/Getty Images

Breaking the barrier Thirty-one-year-old Noelia Garella (center) reads a book to her kindergarten students in Cordoba, Argentina. She is one of but a few persons in the world with intellectual disability who work as a public school teacher. When she was a child, a nursery school rejected her as "a monster."

Working for money, independence, and self-respect Simone Ippoliti pours a beer for a patron at Locanda dei Sunflowers, a restaurant in Rome. The restaurant promotes the employment of individuals with intellectual disability, like Simone—providing them with job opportunities and dignity through training and placement.

incapable of raising children, many are quite able to do so, either on their own or with special help and community services (McConnell et al., 2017).

Finally, adults with intellectual disability—whatever the severity—need the personal and financial rewards that come with holding a job (AAIDD, 2017; Kiernan, 2000). Many work in *sheltered workshops,* protected and supervised workplaces that train them at a pace and level tailored to their abilities. After training in the workshops, a number of people with mild or moderate ID move on to hold regular jobs.

Although training programs for people with intellectual disability have improved greatly in quality over the past 40 years, there are too few of them. Consequently, most participants do not receive a complete range of educational and occupational training services. Additional programs are required so that more people with intellectual disability may achieve their full potential, as workers and as human beings.

Clinicians Discover Childhood and Adolescence

EARLY IN THE TWENTIETH CENTURY, mental health professionals virtually ignored children. At best, they viewed them as small adults and treated their psychological disorders as they would adult problems. Today the problems and needs of young people have caught the attention of researchers and clinicians. Although the leading models have been used to help explain and treat these problems, the sociocultural perspective—especially the family perspective—is considered to play a special role.

Because children and adolescents have limited control over their lives, they are particularly affected by the attitudes and reactions of family members. Clinicians must therefore deal with those attitudes and reactions as they try to address the problems of the young. Treatments for conduct disorder, ADHD, intellectual disability, and other problems of childhood and adolescence typically fall short unless clinicians educate and work with the family as well.

At the same time, clinicians who work with children and adolescents have learned that a narrow focus on any one model can lead to problems. For years, autism spectrum disorder was explained exclusively by family factors, misleading theorists and therapists alike and adding to the pain of parents already devastated by their child's disorder. In addition, in the past, the sociocultural model often led professionals to wrongly accept anxiety among young children and depression among teenagers as inevitable, given the many new experiences confronted by the former and the latter group's preoccupation with peer approval.

The increased clinical focus on the young has also been accompanied by more attention to young people's human and legal rights. More and more clinicians have called on government agencies to protect the rights and safety of this often powerless group. In doing so, they hope to fuel the fights for better educational resources and against child abuse and neglect, sexual abuse, malnourishment, and fetal alcohol syndrome.

As the problems and, at times, mistreatment of young people receive more attention, the special needs of these individuals are becoming more visible. Thus the study and treatment of psychological disorders among children and adolescents are likely to continue at a rapid pace. Now that clinicians and public officials have "discovered" this population, they are not likely to underestimate their needs and importance again.

CLINICAL CHOICES

Now that you've read about disorders common among children and adolescents, try the interactive case study for this chapter. See if you are able to identify Gabriel's symptoms and suggest a diagnosis based on his symptoms. What kind of treatment would be most effective for Gabriel? Go to **Launch**Pad to access *Clinical Choices.*

SUMMING UP

» Disorders Common Among Children and Adolescents

Emotional and behavioral problems are common in childhood and adolescence, but in addition, at least 20 percent of all children and adolescents in the United States have a diagnosable psychological disorder. A particular concern among children is that of being *bullied*. According to surveys, more than 25 percent of students are bullied frequently and more than 70 percent have been victims of bullying at least once. *Cyberbullying* is on the rise. *pp. 514–516*

» Childhood Anxiety Disorders

Anxiety disorders are particularly common among children and adolescents. This group of problems includes adultlike disorders, such as social anxiety disorder and generalized anxiety disorder; the childhood form of *separation anxiety disorder*, which is characterized by excessive anxiety, often panic, whenever a child is separated from a parent; and *selective mutism* in which children fail to speak in certain social situations, such as in the classroom or in the company of other children, but have no difficulty speaking at home, when with family members, or in other such situations. *pp. 516–519*

» Depression and Bipolar Disorders

Two percent of children and 8 percent of adolescents experience *depression*. Childhood depression is often characterized by such symptoms as irritability, headaches, stomach pain, and a disinterest in toys and games. In addition, over the past two decades, there has also been an enormous increase in the number of children and adolescents who receive diagnoses of *bipolar disorder*. Such diagnoses are expected to decrease now that DSM-5 has added a new childhood category, *disruptive mood dysregulation disorder*. *pp. 519–522*

» Oppositional Defiant Disorder and Conduct Disorder

Children with *oppositional defiant disorder* and *conduct disorder* exceed the normal breaking of rules and act very aggressively. Those with oppositional defiant disorder argue repeatedly with adults, ignore adult rules and requests, and feel intense anger and resentment. Those with conduct disorder, a more severe pattern, repeatedly violate the basic rights of others. Children with this disorder often are violent and cruel and may deliberately destroy property, steal, and run away. Several types of conduct disorders have been identified. Clinicians have treated children with conduct disorders by using approaches such as *parent management training*, including *parent–child interaction therapy*; multisystemic therapy; *problem-solving skills training*; the *Coping Power Program*; and *treatment foster care*. Some individuals with this disorder have been institutionalized in *juvenile training centers*. A number of *prevention* programs have also been developed. *pp. 522–527*

» Elimination Disorders

Children with an *elimination disorder*— *enuresis* or *encopresis*—repeatedly urinate or pass feces in inappropriate places. Cognitive-behavioral approaches, such as the *bell-and-battery technique*, are effective treatments for enuresis. *pp. 527–528*

» Neurodevelopmental Disorders

Neurodevelopmental disorders are a group of disabilities in the functioning of the brain that emerge at birth or during very early childhood and affect the person's behavior, memory, concentration, and/or ability to learn. They often have a significant impact throughout the person's life.

Children with *attention-deficit/hyperactivity disorder* (*ADHD*) attend poorly to tasks, behave overactively and impulsively, or both. Many of the attention difficulties seen in ADHD may be associated with a *dysfunctional attention brain circuit* whose structures display *problematic interconnectivity*. Drug therapy—*methylphenidate*, *amphetamine*, or other *stimulant drugs*—and *cognitive-behavioral programs* can be effective treatments.

People with *autism spectrum disorder* are *extremely unresponsive to others, have severe communication deficits*, and *display very rigid and repetitive behaviors, interests*, and *activities*. The leading explanations of this disorder point to cognitive deficits, such as failure to develop a *theory of mind* and *joint attention skills*, and biological abnormalities, such as one or more *dysfunctional brain circuits* (that is, circuits whose structures have *problematic interconnectivity*). Although no treatment totally reverses the autistic pattern, significant help is available in the form of *cognitive-behavioral treatments, communication training, training and treatment for parents*, and *community integration*.

People with *intellectual disability* are significantly below average in *intelligence* and *adaptive ability*. *Mild ID*, by far the most common level of intellectual disability, has often been linked to environmental factors such as unstimulating environments during a child's early years, inadequate parent–child interactions, and insufficient learning experiences. *Moderate, severe*, and *profound ID* are caused primarily by biological factors, although people who function at these levels also are affected enormously by their family and social environment. The leading biological causes of intellectual disability are *chromosomal abnormalities, metabolic disorders, prenatal problems, birth complications*, and *childhood diseases* and *injuries*.

Today's intervention programs for people with intellectual disability typically emphasize the importance of a comfortable and stimulating residence—either the family home, a small institution or group home, or a semi-independent residence—that follows the principles of *normalization*. Other important interventions include *proper education, therapy for psychological problems*, and *programs offering training in socializing, sex, marriage, parenting*, and *occupational skills*. One of the most intense debates in the field of education centers on whether people with intellectual disability profit more from *special classes* or from *mainstreaming*. Research has not consistently favored one approach over the other. *pp. 529–550*

Visit *LaunchPad*

to access the e-Book, Clinical Choices, videos, activities, and LearningCurve, as well as study aids including flashcards, FAQs, and research exercises.

LaunchPad macmillan learning

...Disorders of Aging and Cognition

Harry appeared to be in perfect health at age 58. . . . He worked in the municipal water treatment plant of a small city, and it was at work that the first overt signs of Harry's mental illness appeared. While responding to a minor emergency, he became confused about the correct order in which to pull the levers that controlled the flow of fluids. As a result, several thousand gallons of raw sewage were discharged into a river. Harry had been an efficient and diligent worker, so after puzzled questioning, his error was attributed to the flu and overlooked.

Several weeks later, Harry came home with a baking dish his wife had asked him to buy, having forgotten that he had brought home the identical dish two nights before. Later that week, on two successive nights, he went to pick up his daughter at her job in a restaurant, apparently forgetting that she had changed shifts and was now working days. A month after that, he quite uncharacteristically argued with . . . the phone company; he was trying to pay a bill that he had already paid three days before. . . .

Months passed and Harry's wife was beside herself. She could see that his problem was worsening. Not only had she been unable to get effective help, but Harry himself was becoming resentful and sometimes suspicious of her attempts. He now insisted there was nothing wrong with him, and she would catch him narrowly watching her every movement. . . . Sometimes he became angry—sudden little storms without apparent cause. . . . More difficult for his wife was Harry's repetitiveness in conversation: He often repeated stories from the past and sometimes repeated isolated phrases and sentences from more recent exchanges. There was no context and little continuity to his choice of subjects. . . .

Two years after Harry had first allowed the sewage to escape, he was clearly a changed man. Most of the time he seemed preoccupied; he usually had a vacant smile on his face, and what little he said was so vague that it lacked meaning. . . . Gradually his wife took over getting him up, toileted, and dressed each morning. . . .

Harry's condition continued to worsen slowly. When his wife's school was in session, his daughter would stay with him some days, and neighbors were able to offer some help. But occasionally he would still manage to wander away. On those occasions he greeted everyone he met—old friends and strangers alike—with "Hi, it's so nice." That was the extent of his conversation, although he might repeat "nice, nice, nice" over and over again. . . . When Harry left a coffee pot on a unit of the electric stove until it melted, his wife, desperate for help, took him to see another doctor. Again Harry was found to be in good health. [However] the doctor ordered a [brain scan and eventually concluded] that Harry had "Pick-Alzheimer disease." . . . Because Harry was a veteran . . . [he qualified for] hospitalization in a . . . veterans' hospital about 400 miles away from his home. . . .

At the hospital the nursing staff sat Harry up in a chair each day and, aided by volunteers, made sure he ate enough. Still, he lost weight and became weaker. He would weep when his wife came to see him, but he did not talk, and he gave no other sign that he recognized her. After a year, even the weeping stopped. Harry's wife could no longer bear to visit. Harry lived on until just after his sixty-fifth birthday, when he choked on a piece of bread, developed pneumonia as a consequence, and soon died.

(Heston, 1992, pp. 87–90)

Harry suffered from a form of *Alzheimer's disease*. This term is familiar to almost everyone in our society. It seems as if each decade is marked by a disease that everyone dreads—a diagnosis no one wants to hear because it feels like a death sentence. Cancer used to be such a diagnosis, then AIDS. But medical science has made remarkable strides with those diseases, and patients who now develop them have reason for great hope. Alzheimer's disease, on the other hand, remains incurable and almost untreatable, although, as you will see later, researchers are currently making enormous progress toward understanding it and reversing, or at least slowing, its march.

What makes Alzheimer's disease particularly frightening is that it means not only eventual physical death but also, as in Harry's case, a slow psychological death—a progressive deterioration of one's memory and related cognitive faculties. Significant cognitive deterioration, previously called *dementia*, is now categorized as *neurocognitive disorder*. There are many types of neurocognitive disorders listed in DSM-5 (APA, 2013). Alzheimer's disease is the most common one (Wolk & Dickerson, 2017).

Although neurocognitive disorders are currently the most publicized and feared psychological problems among the elderly, they are hardly the only ones. A variety of psychological disorders are tied closely to later life. As with childhood disorders, some of the disorders of old age are caused primarily by pressures that are particularly likely to appear at that time of life, others by unique traumatic experiences, and still others—like neurocognitive disorders—by biological abnormalities. ■

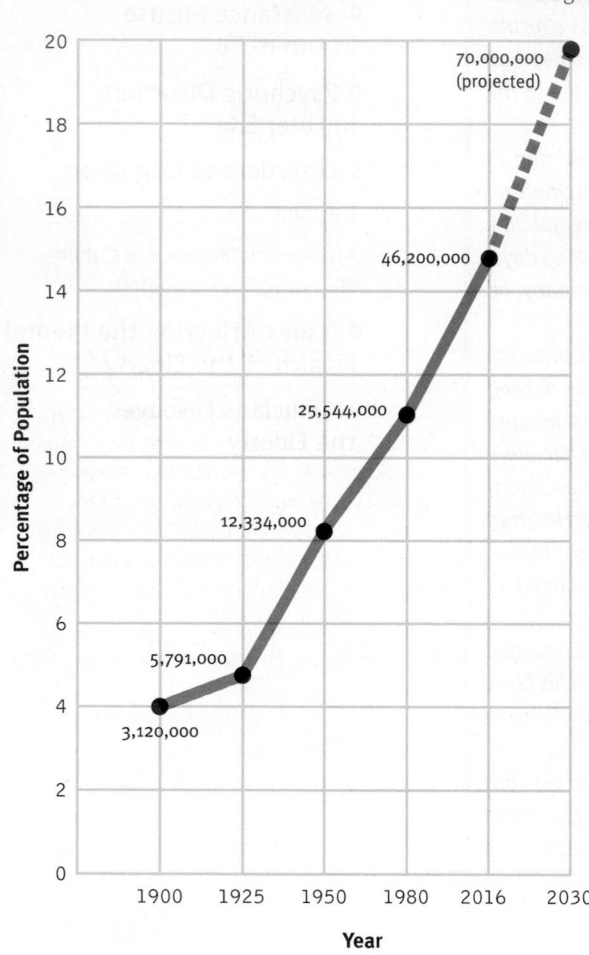

FIGURE 18-1

On the Rise

The population of people aged 65 and older in the United States has increased 15-fold since the beginning of the twentieth century. The percentage of elderly people in the population increased from 4 percent in 1900 to 14.5 percent in 2016. It is expected to be more than 20 percent in 2030. (Information from: CDC, 2017, 2016, 2014; Heflin, 2017; U.S. Census Bureau, 2016; Mather, 2016.)

Old Age and Stress

OLD AGE IS USUALLY DEFINED in our society as the years past age 65. By this account, around 46 million people in the United States are "old," representing 14.5 percent of the total population; this is a 15-fold increase since 1900 (U.S. Census Bureau, 2016; Mather, 2016) (see **Figure 18-1**). It has also been estimated that there will be 70 million elderly people in the United States by the year 2030—21 percent of the population. Not only is the overall population of the elderly on the rise, but also the number of people over 85 will double in the next 10 years. Indeed, people over 85 represent the fastest-growing segment of the population in the United States and in most countries around the world. Older women outnumber older men by almost 3 to 2.

Like childhood, old age brings special pressures, unique upsets, and major biological changes (Heflin, 2017; Espinoza & Unützer, 2016; Murayama et al., 2014). People become more prone to illness and injury as they age. About half of adults over 65 have two or three chronic illnesses, and 15 percent have four or more. And at least half of elderly people have some measure of insomnia or other sleep problems (APA, 2017). In addition, elderly people are likely to be contending with the stress of loss—the loss of spouses, friends, and adult children; of former activities and roles; of hearing and vision. Many lose their sense of purpose after they retire. Some also have to adjust to the loss of favored pets and possessions.

The stresses of aging need not necessarily cause psychological problems (see **PsychWatch**). In fact, some older people, particularly those who seek social contacts and those who maintain a sense of control over their lives, use the changes that come with aging as opportunities for learning and growth (Espinoza & Unützer, 2016). For example, two-thirds of elderly people now use the Internet to connect with people of similar ages and interests, a 16-fold increase since

> What kinds of attitudes and activities might help people enter old age with peace of mind and positive anticipation?

The Oldest Old

Clinicians suggest that aging need not inevitably lead to psychological problems. Nor apparently does it always lead to physical problems.

There are currently 72,000 *centenarians* in the United States—people who are 100 years old or older. When researchers have studied these people—often called the "oldest old"—they have been surprised to learn that centenarians are on average more healthy, positive, clearheaded, and agile than those in their 80s and early 90s (Etxeberria et al., 2018; Rea, 2017). Although some certainly experience cognitive decline, more than half remain perfectly alert. Many of the oldest old are, in fact, still employed, sexually active, and able to enjoy the outdoors and the arts. What is their greatest fear? The fear of significant cognitive decline. According to some studies, many people in their 90s and older fear the prospect of mental deterioration more than they fear death (Arosio et al., 2017; Boeve et al., 2003).

Some scientists believe that people who live this long carry "longevity" genes that make them resistant to disabling or terminal infections (He et al., 2016, 2014; Rea, 2017). In fact, centenarians are 20 times more likely than other elderly people to have had a relative who also lived to a very old age (He et al., 2016; D.I., 2014).

© Lawrence Jackson/White House/ZUMAPRESS.com

Other research points to engaged lifestyles and "robust" personalities that help the oldest old meet life's challenges with optimism and a sense of challenge (Etxeberria et al., 2018; da Rosa et al., 2014). The centenarians themselves often credit a good frame of mind or regular behaviors that they have maintained for many years—for example, eating healthful food, getting regular exercise, and not smoking (Rea, 2017; D.I., 2014). Said one very elderly retired math and science teacher, "You can't sit. . . . You have to keep moving" (Duenwald, 2003).

Dream of a (long) lifetime Since 2008, it had been 107-year-old Virginia McLaurin's dream to meet President Barack Obama. That wish came true in 2016 when the centenarian was invited to a reception at the White House celebrating African American History Month. McLaurin not only met with then-President Obama, but got to dance with then-First Lady Michelle Obama.

---

the year 2000 (Pew Research Center, 2017; Oinas-Kukkonen & Mantila, 2010). Indeed, 34 percent of persons over age 65 use social media. For other elderly people, however, the stresses of old age do lead to psychological difficulties. Studies indicate that more than 20 percent of elderly people meet the criteria for a mental disorder and as many as half of all elderly people would benefit from some degree of mental health services, yet fewer than 20 percent actually receive them (APA, 2017). **Geropsychology,** the field of psychology dedicated to the mental health of elderly people, has developed almost entirely within the last four decades, and at present only 4.2 percent of clinicians work primarily with elderly persons (APA, 2017).

The psychological problems of elderly people may be divided into two groups. One group consists of disorders that may be common among people in all age groups but are often connected to the process of aging when they occur in an elderly person. These include *depressive, anxiety,* and *substance use disorders.* The other group consists of disorders of cognition, such as *delirium, mild neurocognitive disorders,* and *major neurocognitive disorders* that result from brain abnormalities. As in Harry's case, these brain abnormalities are most often tied to aging, but they also can sometimes occur when people are younger. Elderly people with one of these psychological problems often display other such problems. For example, many who suffer from neurocognitive disorders also deal with depression and anxiety (Lebedeva et al., 2014; Abdel-Rahman, 2012).

geropsychology The field of psychology concerned with the mental health of elderly people.

#SpousalLoss

9.0 million   Number of widows in the U.S.

2.1 million   Number of widowers in the U.S.

(Information from: U.S. Census Bureau, 2017)

Depression in Later Life

DEPRESSION IS ONE OF the most common mental health problems of older adults. The features of depression are the same for elderly people as for younger people, including feelings of profound sadness and emptiness; low self-esteem, guilt, and pessimism; and loss of appetite and sleep disturbances. Depression is particularly common among those who have recently undergone a trauma, such as the loss of a spouse or close friend or the development of a serious physical illness (Espinoza & Unützer, 2016; Draper, 2014).

> *[Oscar] was an 83-year-old married man with an episode of major depressive disorder. . . . He said that about one and one-half years prior to beginning treatment, his brother had died. In the following months, two friends whom he had known since childhood died. Following these losses, he became increasingly anxious [and] grew more and more pessimistic. Reluctantly, he acknowledged, "I even thought about ending my life." Review of his symptoms indicated that while . . . anxiety was a prominent part of his clinical picture, so was depression. . . .*
>
> *During . . . treatment, [Oscar] discussed his relationship with his brother. He discussed how distraught he was to watch his brother's physical deterioration from an extended illness. He described the scene at his brother's deathbed and the moment "when he took his final breath." He experienced guilt over the failure to carry out his brother's funeral services in a manner he felt his brother would have wanted. While initially characterizing his relationship with his brother as loving and amiable, he later acknowledged that he disapproved of many ways in which his brother acted. Later in therapy, he also reviewed different facets of his past relationships with his two deceased friends. He expressed sadness that the long years had ended. . . . [Oscar's] life had been organized around visits to his brother's home and outings with his friends. . . . [While] his wife had encouraged him to visit with other friends and family, it became harder and harder to do so as he became more depressed.*
>
> *(Hinrichsen, 1999, p. 433)*

Overall, as many as 20 percent of people become depressed at some point during old age (APA, 2017). The rate is highest in older women. This rate among the elderly is about the same as that among younger adults—even lower, according to some studies. However, it climbs much higher (32 percent or more) among aged people who live

Making a difference To help prevent feelings of unimportance and low self-esteem, some older people now offer their expertise to young people who are trying to master new skills, undertake business projects, and the like. This elderly man, who volunteers regularly at an elementary school, is teaching math to a first-grader.

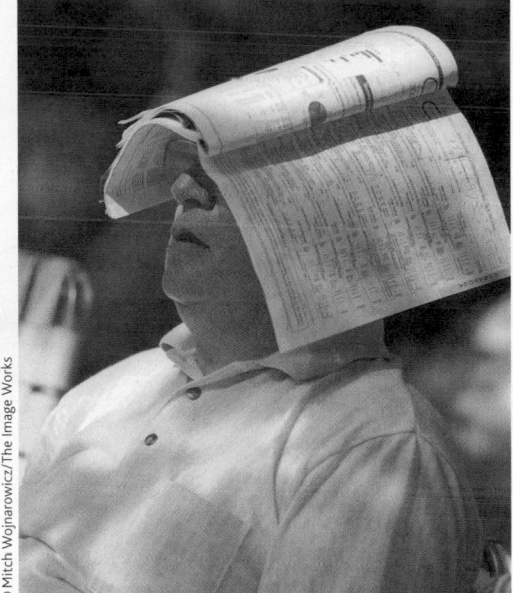

Racing to mental health Gerontologists propose that elderly people need to pursue pleasurable and personally meaningful activities. The elderly women on the left compete in a race at the National Senior Games. In contrast, the elderly gentleman on the right, also interested in racing, watches a competition at the Saratoga Springs horse racing track with the daily racing form on his head. Which of these two activities might be more likely to contribute to successful psychological functioning during old age?

in nursing homes, as opposed to those in the community (Espinoza & Unützer, 2016; Seitz, et al., 2010).

Several studies suggest that depression raises an elderly person's chances of developing significant medical problems (Heflin, 2017; Taylor, 2014). For example, older depressed people with high blood pressure are almost three times as likely to suffer a stroke as older nondepressed people with the same condition. Similarly, elderly people who are depressed recover more slowly and less completely from heart attacks, hip fractures, pneumonia, and other infections and illnesses. Small wonder that among the elderly, increases in clinical depression are tied to increases in the mortality rate (Heflin, 2017).

> **Is it more likely that positive thinking leads to good health or that good health produces positive thinking?**

As you read in Chapter 9, elderly people are also more likely to die from suicide than young people, and often their suicides are related to depression. The overall rate of suicide in the United States is 12.6 per 100,000 people; among those over 65 years of age, it is more than 16 per 100,000, and among those over 75, it is more than 24 per 100,000 (CDC, 2017, 2016; WHO, 2017).

Like younger adults, older people who are depressed may be helped by cognitive-behavioral therapy, interpersonal psychotherapy, antidepressant medications, or a combination of these approaches (Espinoza & Unützer, 2016; Dines et al., 2014). Both individual and group therapy formats have been used. More than half of elderly patients with depression improve with these various treatments. It is, however, sometimes difficult for older people to use antidepressant drugs effectively and safely because the body breaks the drugs down differently in later life (Rochon, 2017; Dubovsky & Dubovsky, 2011). Moreover, among elderly people, antidepressant drugs have a higher risk of causing some cognitive impairment. Electroconvulsive therapy, applied with certain modifications, has been used for elderly people who are severely depressed and have not been helped by other approaches (Kellner et al., 2016; Coffey & Kellner, 2011).

Some elderly people experience depression as part of a bipolar disorder rather than a unipolar type of depressive disorder (Sajatovic & Chen, 2017). Around 1 percent of all persons over 65 years of age display a bipolar disorder in any given year. For more than 70 percent of them, the disorder began well before they reached old age. In most cases, the individuals receive the kinds of treatment that younger individuals with bipolar disorder receive—mood-stabilizing medications and adjunctive psychotherapy (Sajatovic & Chen, 2017).

#LifeExpectancy

Aging and Race

82.0 years	Hispanic American average life expectancy
78.7 years	Non-Hispanic white American average life expectancy
75.1 years	African American average life expectancy

(Information from: CDC, 2017)

"All of a sudden, everyone seems younger than I am."

Mike Twohy/The New Yorker Collection/www.cartoonbank.com

Anxiety Disorders in Later Life

ANXIETY IS ALSO COMMON AMONG elderly people (APA, 2017). At any given time, as many as 11 percent of elderly individuals in the United States experience at least one of the anxiety disorders (ADAA, 2017; Zhang et al., 2015). Surveys indicate that generalized anxiety disorder is particularly common. The prevalence of anxiety also increases throughout old age. For example, people over 85 years of age report higher rates of anxiety than those between 65 and 84 years. In fact, all of these numbers may be low, as anxiety in the elderly tends to be underreported (APA, 2017). Both the elderly patient and the clinician may interpret physical symptoms of anxiety, such as heart palpitations and perspiring, as symptoms of a medical condition.

There are many things about aging that may heighten the anxiety levels of certain people (APA, 2017; Bower et al., 2015). Declining health, for example, has often been pointed to, and in fact, older persons who have significant medical illnesses or injuries report more anxiety than those who are healthy or injury-free. Researchers have not, however, been able to determine why some people who face such problems in old age become anxious while others in similar circumstances remain relatively calm (see *InfoCentral* on the next page).

Older adults with anxiety disorders have been treated with psychotherapy of various kinds, particularly cognitive-behavioral therapy (APA, 2017; Hyams & Scogin, 2016; Bower et al., 2015). Many also receive benzodiazepines or other antianxiety medications, just as younger sufferers do. And a number are treated with serotonin-enhancing antidepressant drugs. Again, however, all such drugs must be used cautiously with older people (Rochon, 2017; Dubovsky & Dubovsky, 2011).

Substance Misuse in Later Life

ALTHOUGH ALCOHOL USE DISORDER and other substance use disorders are significant problems for many older persons, the prevalence of such patterns actually appears to decline after age 65, perhaps because of declining health or reduced income (APA, 2017; Li & Caltabiano, 2017). The majority of older adults do not misuse alcohol or other substances, despite the fact that aging can sometimes be a time of considerable stress and in our society people often turn to alcohol and drugs during times of stress. Accurate data about the rate of substance abuse among older adults are difficult to gather because many elderly people do not suspect or admit that they have such a problem.

Surveys find that 3 to 7 percent of older people, particularly men, have alcohol use disorder in a given year (Li & Caltabiano, 2017; Trevisan, 2014). Men under 30 are four times as likely as men over 60 to display a behavioral problem associated with excessive alcohol use, such as repeated falling, spells of dizziness or blacking out, secretive drinking, or social withdrawal. Older patients who are institutionalized, however, do display high rates of problem drinking. For example, alcohol problems among older people admitted to general and mental hospitals are at least 15 percent, and estimates of alcohol-related problems among patients in nursing homes are as high as 50 percent (Li & Caltabiano, 2017; McConnaughey, 2014).

Researchers often distinguish between older problem drinkers who have had alcohol use disorder for many years, perhaps since their 20s, and those who do not start abusing alcohol until their 50s or 60s (in what is sometimes called "late-onset alcoholism"). The latter group typically begins abusive drinking as a reaction to the

---

#

#LateLifeMeds

66%	Percentage of elderly persons who take blood pressure drugs
47%	Percentage of elderly persons who take cholesterol drugs
19%	Percentage of elderly persons who take diabetes drugs
17%	Percentage of elderly persons who take antidepressant drugs
9%	Percentage of elderly persons who take antianxiety drugs

(Information from: Kantor et al., 2015)

THE AGING POPULATION

The number and proportion of elderly people in the United States and around the world are ever-growing. This acceleration has important consequences, requiring each society to pay particular attention to aging-related issues in healthcare, housing, the economy, and other such realms. In particular, as the number and proportion of elderly people increases, so too do the number and proportion of the population who experience aging-related psychological difficulties.

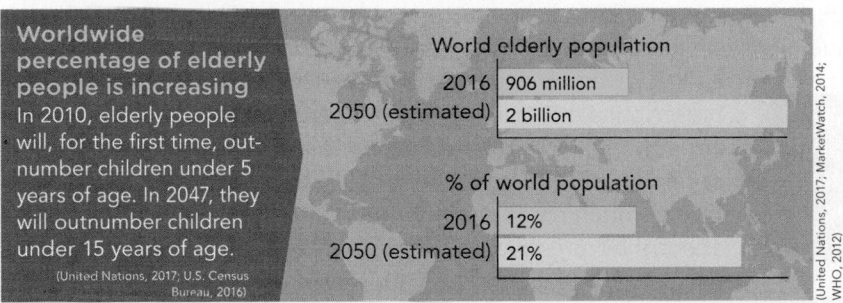

Worldwide percentage of elderly people is increasing
In 2010, elderly people will, for the first time, outnumber children under 5 years of age. In 2047, they will outnumber children under 15 years of age.
(United Nations, 2017; U.S. Census Bureau, 2016)

World elderly population
2016 | 906 million
2050 (estimated) | 2 billion

% of world population
2016 | 12%
2050 (estimated) | 21%

(United Nations, 2017; MarketWatch, 2014; WHO, 2012)

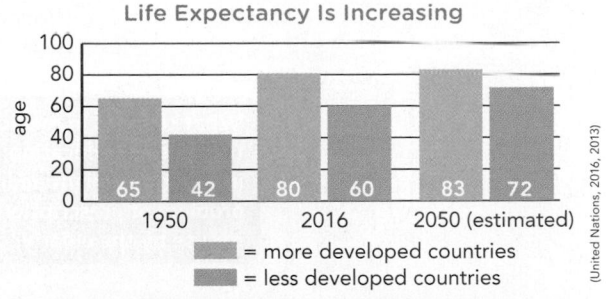

Life Expectancy Is Increasing

1950: 65, 42
2016: 80, 60
2050 (estimated): 83, 72

= more developed countries
= less developed countries
(United Nations, 2016, 2013)

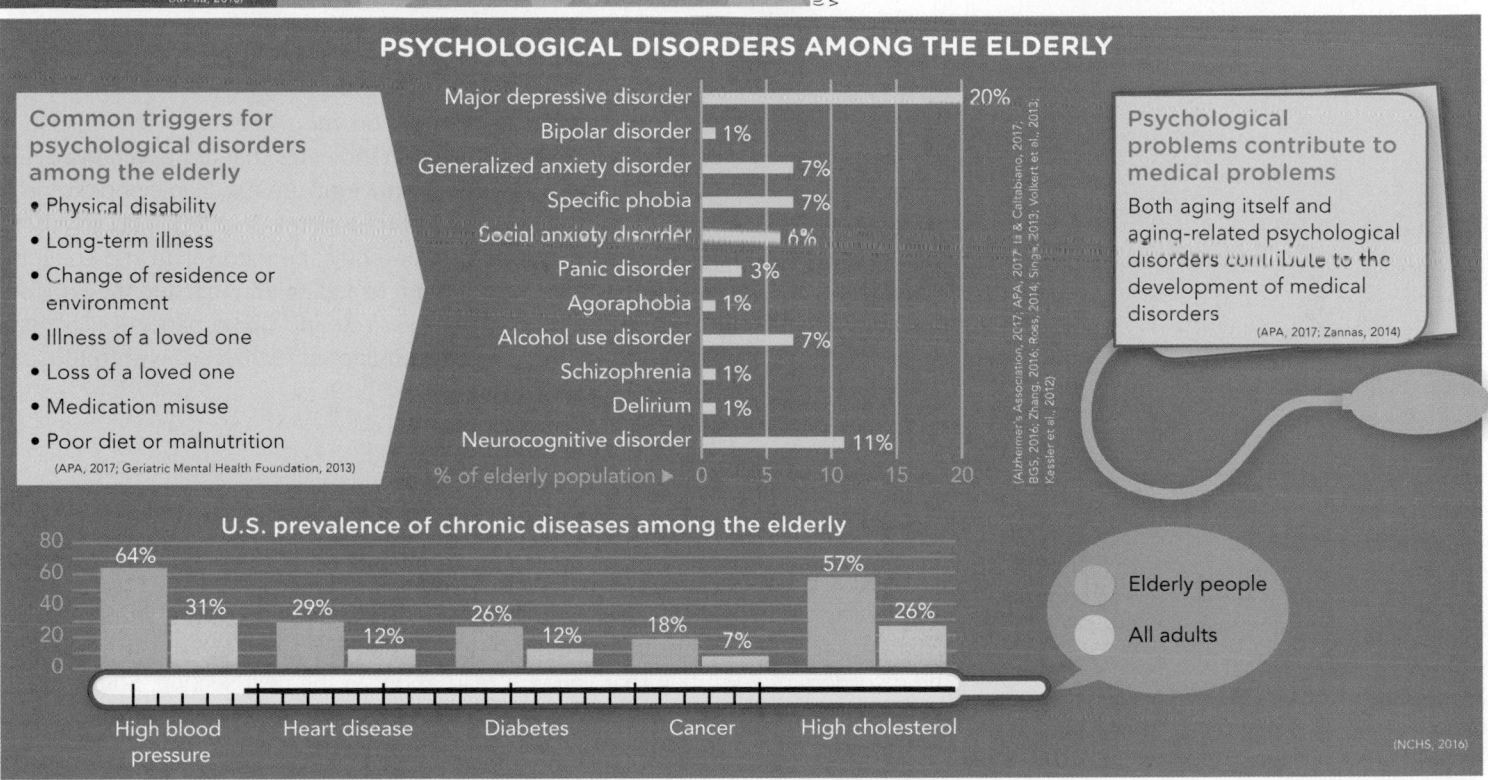

PSYCHOLOGICAL DISORDERS AMONG THE ELDERLY

Common triggers for psychological disorders among the elderly
- Physical disability
- Long-term illness
- Change of residence or environment
- Illness of a loved one
- Loss of a loved one
- Medication misuse
- Poor diet or malnutrition

(APA, 2017; Geriatric Mental Health Foundation, 2013)

Major depressive disorder — 20%
Bipolar disorder — 1%
Generalized anxiety disorder — 7%
Specific phobia — 7%
Social anxiety disorder — 6%
Panic disorder — 3%
Agoraphobia — 1%
Alcohol use disorder — 7%
Schizophrenia — 1%
Delirium — 1%
Neurocognitive disorder — 11%

% of elderly population ▶ 0 5 10 15 20

(Alzheimer's Association, 2017; APA, 2017; BGS, 2016, Zhang, 2016; Roos, 2014, Singh, 2013, Volkert et al., 2013; Iä & Cattabiano, 2017; Kessler et al., 2012)

Psychological problems contribute to medical problems
Both aging itself and aging-related psychological disorders contribute to the development of medical disorders
(APA, 2017; Zannas, 2014)

U.S. prevalence of chronic diseases among the elderly
High blood pressure: 64%, 31%
Heart disease: 29%, 12%
Diabetes: 26%, 12%
Cancer: 18%, 7%
High cholesterol: 57%, 26%

Elderly people
All adults
(NCHS, 2016)

THE ELDERLY POPULATION IS ITSELF AGING

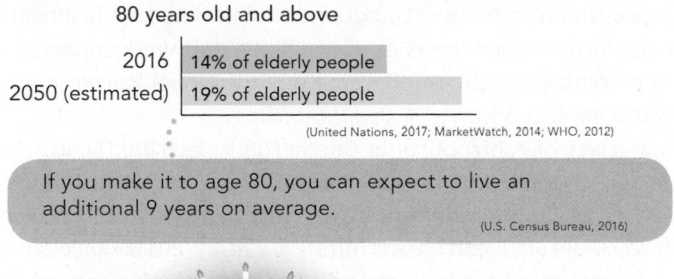

80 years old and above
2016 | 14% of elderly people
2050 (estimated) | 19% of elderly people
(United Nations, 2017; MarketWatch, 2014; WHO, 2012)

If you make it to age 80, you can expect to live an additional 9 years on average. (U.S. Census Bureau, 2016)

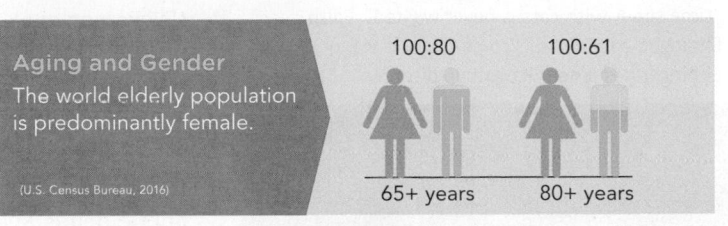

Aging and Gender
The world elderly population is predominantly female.
(U.S. Census Bureau, 2016)

100:80 — 65+ years
100:61 — 80+ years

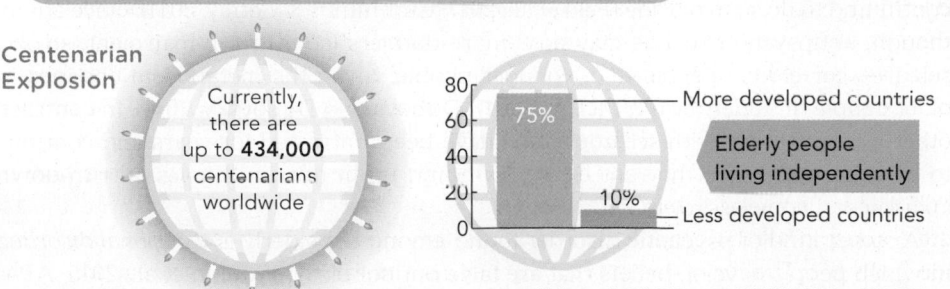

Centenarian Explosion
Currently, there are up to **434,000** centenarians worldwide
(United Nations, 2017)

75% More developed countries
Elderly people living independently
10% Less developed countries
(Al-Shaqi et al., 2016; NAELA, 2016, 2014; United Nations, 2016; 2013)

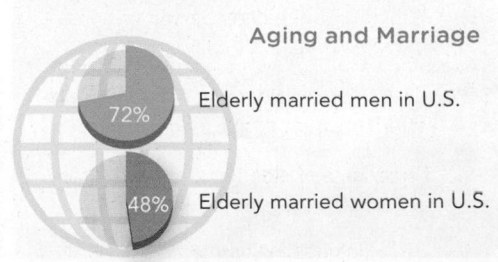

Aging and Marriage
72% Elderly married men in U.S.
48% Elderly married women in U.S.
(Mather, 2016; Mather et al., 2015)

delirium A rapidly developing, acute disturbance in attention and orientation that makes it very difficult to concentrate and think in a clear and organized manner

negative events and pressures of growing older, such as the death of a spouse, living alone, or unwanted retirement. Alcohol use disorder in elderly people is treated much as it is in younger adults (see Chapter 12): through such interventions as detoxification, Antabuse, Alcoholics Anonymous (AA), and cognitive-behavioral therapy (APA, 2017).

A leading substance problem in the elderly is the *misuse of prescription drugs* (Rochon, 2017). Most often the misuse is unintentional. In the United States, people over the age of 65 buy more than one-third of all prescription drugs (NIDA, 2016).

> What changes in medical practice, patient education, or family interactions might address the problem of prescription drug misuse by the elderly?

At any given time, elderly people are taking, on average, 3 to 5 prescription drugs and two over-the-counter drugs (Heflin, 2017; NCHS, 2014). Thus their risk of confusing medications or skipping doses is high. To help address this problem, physicians and pharmacists often try to simplify medications, educate older patients about their prescriptions, clarify directions, and teach them to watch for undesired effects. However, physicians themselves are sometimes to blame in cases of prescription drug misuse, perhaps overprescribing medications for elderly patients or unwisely mixing certain medicines (Rochon, 2017; Metsälä & Vaherkoski, 2014).

Yet another drug-related problem, apparently on the increase, is the misuse of powerful medications at nursing homes. Research indicates that antipsychotic drugs are currently being given to almost 30 percent of the total nursing home population in the United States, despite the fact that many of the residents do not display psychotic functioning (Rochon, 2017; Mort et al., 2014). Apparently, these powerful and (for some elderly patients) dangerous drugs are often given to sedate and manage the patients. Indeed, research suggests that 17 percent of new nursing home patients who have never before taken an antipsychotic drug are administered such drugs within 100 days of admission (Rochon, 2017; Bronskill et al., 2004).

Psychotic Disorders in Later Life

Elderly people have a higher rate of psychotic symptoms than younger people (Soares et al., 2017; Colijn et al., 2015). Among aged people, these symptoms are usually caused by underlying medical conditions such as neurocognitive disorders, the disorders of cognition that you will read about in the next section. Some elderly people, though, suffer from *schizophrenia* or *delusional disorder,* one of the other schizophrenia spectrum disorders.

Affection is not forgotten Clinicians have found that elderly people in senior care facilities are uplifted and stimulated by interactions with cats, dogs, parakeets, and other pets. In apparent agreement with Sigmund Freud's declaration that "time spent with cats is never wasted," Edith Ehninger, age 95, talks to her regular visitor Mogli. Ehninger has a neurocognitive disorder.

Actually, schizophrenia is less common in older people than in younger ones. In fact, many people with schizophrenia find that their symptoms lessen in later life (Dickerson et al., 2014). Improvement can occur in people who have had schizophrenia for 30 or more years, particularly in such areas as social skills and work capacity, as we are reminded by the remarkable late-life improvement of the Nobel Prize recipient John Nash, the subject of the book and movie *A Beautiful Mind.*

It is uncommon for *new* cases of schizophrenia to emerge in late life (Devanand, 2011). Thus some of the elderly people with schizophrenia began receiving antipsychotic drugs and psychotherapeutic interventions many years earlier in life and are continuing to do so in old age (Feki et al., 2017; Cummings & Coffey, 2011). Once again, though, antipsychotic drugs may pose more dangers (cognitive impairment, stroke, seizures) for elderly people than younger people, given the metabolism changes in older people (Freudenreich & McEvoy, 2017; Dubovsky & Dubovsky, 2011). In contrast, other elderly people with schizophrenia have been untreated for years and continue to be untreated when they are elderly, winding up in nursing homes, in run-down apartments, homeless, or in jail.

Another kind of psychotic disorder found among the elderly is *delusional disorder,* in which people develop beliefs that are false but not bizarre (Colijn et al., 2015; APA,

Sean Gallup/Getty Images

2013). This disorder, which you read about in Chapter 14, is rare in most age groups—around 2 of every 1,000 persons—but its prevalence appears to increase in the elderly population. Older people with a delusional disorder may develop deeply held suspicions of persecution; they believe that other people—often family members, doctors, or friends—are conspiring against, cheating, spying on, or maligning them. They may become irritable, angry, or depressed or pursue legal action because of such ideas. It is not clear why this disorder increases among elderly people, but some clinicians suggest that the rise is related to the deficiencies in hearing, the social isolation, the greater stress, or the heightened poverty with which many elderly persons contend.

Disorders of Cognition

MOST OF US WORRY FROM time to time that we are losing our memory and other mental abilities (Glauberman, 2014). You rush out the door without your keys, you meet a familiar person and cannot remember her name, or you forget that you have seen a particular film. Actually such mishaps are a common and quite normal feature of stress or of aging. As people move through middle age, these memory difficulties and lapses of attention increase, and they may occur regularly by the age of 60 or 70 (see *MindTech* on page 562). Sometimes, however, people have memory and other cognitive changes that are far more extensive and problematic.

In Chapter 6 you saw that problems in memory and related cognitive processes can occur without biological causes, in the form of *dissociative disorders*. More often, though, cognitive problems do have organic roots, particularly when they appear late in life. The leading such disorders among the elderly are *delirium, major neurocognitive disorder*, and *mild neurocognitive disorder*.

Delirium

Delirium is a major disturbance in attention and orientation to the environment (see **Table 18-1**). As the person's focus becomes less clear, he or she has great difficulty concentrating and thinking in an organized way, leading to misinterpretations, illusions, and on occasion, hallucinations. Sufferers may believe that it is morning in the middle of the night or that they are home when actually they are in a hospital room.

This state of massive confusion typically develops over a short period of time, usually hours or days (APA, 2013). Delirium may occur in any age group, including children, but is most common in elderly people. Fewer than 0.5 percent of the nonelderly population experience delirium, compared with 1 percent of people over 55 years of age and 14 percent of those over 85 years of age (BGS, 2016; Tune & DeWitt, 2011). When elderly people enter a hospital—which represents a major change in their environment and routine—to be treated for a general medical condition, 10 percent of them show the symptoms of delirium (Paulo et al., 2017). At least another 10 to 20 percent develop delirium during their stay in the hospital (Bagnall & Faiz, 2014; Francis & Young, 2014). Around 17 percent of elderly patients admitted for surgery develop delirium (Wang et al., 2017; de Castro et al., 2014). That number rises to 23 percent among those admitted suddenly for acute surgery. Between 18 and 50 percent of elderly nursing home residents have some delirium (Forsberg, 2017; Tune & DeWitt, 2011).

Fever, certain diseases and infections, poor nutrition, head injuries, strokes, and stress (including the trauma of surgery) may all cause delirium (Paulo et al., 2017; Lawlor & Bush, 2014). So may intoxication by certain substances, such as prescription drugs. Partly because older people face so many of these problems, they are more likely than younger ones to experience delirium. If a clinician accurately identifies

BSIP/UIG via Getty Images

A therapeutic environment Some long-term care facilities have designed their buildings so that the settings address the cognitive and emotional needs of the elderly residents. In this facility, a woman with Alzheimer's disease is drawn to and touches some of her room's stimulating objects and is, at the same time, comforted by the room's soothing colors and decorations.

TABLE: 18-1

Dx Checklist

Delirium

1. Over the course of hours or a few days, individual experiences fast-moving and fluctuating disturbances in attention and orientation to the environment.

2. Individual also displays a significant cognitive disturbance.

Information from: APA, 2013.

MINDTECH

Remember to Tweet; Tweet to Remember

Social media sites, and the Internet in general, are often thought of as the province of the young. However, elderly people are also going online and joining social networking sites at increasing rates. Two-thirds of people over age 65 now use the Internet, and 62 percent of those users are Facebook members (Pew Research Center, 2017; Wayne, 2017).

Social networking among the elderly is much more than just an interesting statistic, it may be downright therapeutic. Several studies have found that online activity actually helps elderly people maintain and possibly improve their cognitive skills, coping skills, social pleasures, and emotions (GCBH, 2017; Wayne, 2017; Szalavitz, 2013). In one study, for example, researchers recruited 42 adults, aged 68 to 91, and trained 14 of them on Facebook. The study found a 25 percent improvement in the cognitive performances of the 14 participants, including improvements in their mental "updating" skills—the ability to quickly add or delete material from their working memory (Piatt, 2013; Wohltmann, 2013).

Clinical theorists have offered several explanations for the positive effects of social media on elderly people. It may be, for example, that the cognitive stimulation derived from Internet use activates memory and other cognitive faculties or that the engagement with the world and family provided by the Internet directly satisfies

A new world A young volunteer teaches this elderly man how to use modern communication devices such as computers and smartphones.

Dieter Nagl/AFP/Getty Images

social and emotional needs. Whatever the reason, more and more studies indicate that elderly people who are online often function and feel better that those who do not pursue online activities.

> **What other factors might help explain the link between social networking and better coping, social functioning, and emotions among the elderly?**

Of course, just as social networking does not always produce positive results for younger people, it can sometimes be problematic for the elderly. One older user—a clinical psychologist!—put it this way, "Even at my age, it's easy to feel competi-

tive, jealous, left out on social media . . . It stirs up those feelings and juvenile thoughts of 'I'm not cool' that I might have had when I was younger. You think you've outgrown those decades ago, but, no, they're right there, waiting to pop out" (Pennoyer, 2017).

Perhaps because of concerns like this or simply because older persons often find it intimidating to go online, many elderly people resist the Internet and social networking, saying things like "It's not for me," "It overwhelms me," or "You can't teach an old dog new tricks." However, the growing body of research suggests that they may want to embrace social networking and the Internet for better functioning and for better mental health. 💬

delirium, it can often be relatively easy to correct—by treating the underlying infection, for example, or changing the patient's drug prescription. However, the syndrome typically fails to be recognized for what it is (Numan et al., 2017; Traynor et al., 2015). One pioneering study on a medical ward, for example, found that admission doctors detected only 1 of 15 consecutive cases of delirium (Cameron et al., 1987). Incorrect diagnoses of this kind may contribute to a high death rate for older people with delirium (Forsberg, 2017; Wang et al., 2017).

Alzheimer's Disease and Other Neurocognitive Disorders

People with a **neurocognitive disorder** experience a significant decline in at least one (often more than one) area of cognitive functioning, such as memory, attention, visual perception, planning and decision making, language ability, or social awareness (APA, 2013). Those who have certain types of neurocognitive disorders may also

TABLE: 18-2

Dx Checklist

Major Neurocognitive Disorder

1. Individual displays substantial decline in at least one of the following areas of cognitive function: • Memory and learning • Attention • Perceptual-motor skills • Planning and decision-making • Language ability • Social awareness.

2. Cognitive deficits interfere with the individual's everyday independence.

Mild Neurocognitive Disorder

1. Individual displays modest decline in at least one of the following areas of cognitive function: • Memory and learning • Attention • Perceptual-motor skills • Planning and decision-making • Language ability • Social awareness.

2. Cognitive deficits do not interfere with the individual's everyday independence.

Information from: APA, 2013.

undergo personality changes—they may behave inappropriately, for example—and their symptoms may worsen steadily.

If the person's cognitive decline is substantial and interferes significantly with his or her ability to be independent, a diagnosis of **major neurocognitive disorder** is in order. If the decline is modest and does not interfere with independent functioning, the appropriate diagnosis is **mild neurocognitive disorder** (see Table 18-2).

There are currently 47 million people with neurocognitive disorders around the world, with 4.6 million new cases emerging each year (Keene, Montine, & Kuller, 2017). The number of cases is expected to reach 135 million by 2050 unless a cure is found. The occurrence of neurocognitive disorders is closely related to age (see **Figure 18-2**). Among people 65 years of age, the prevalence is around 1 to 2 percent, increasing to as much as 50 percent for those over the age of 85 (Heflin, 2017; Zhao et al., 2014).

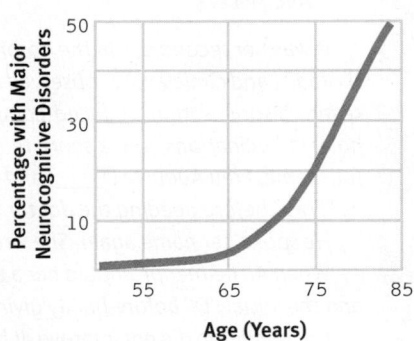

FIGURE 18-2

Substantial Cognitive Decline and Age

The occurrence of substantial cognitive decline is closely related to age. Fewer than 1 percent of all 60-year-olds have major neurocognitive disorders, compared with as many as 50 percent of those who are 85. (Information from: Heflin, 2017; Keene et al., 2017; Wolk & Dickerson, 2017)

As you read earlier, **Alzheimer's disease** is the most common type of neurocognitive disorder, accounting for at least two-thirds of all cases. Around 5.4 million people in the United States currently have this disease, a number that is expected to triple by the year 2050 (Alzheimer's Association, 2017; Keene et al., 2017). Alzheimer's disease sometimes appears in middle age (early onset), but in the vast majority of cases it occurs after the age of 65 (late onset), and its prevalence increases markedly among people in their late 70s (Wolk & Dickerson, 2017). Altogether, 11 percent of all people over 65 have Alzheimer's disease (Alzheimer's Association, 2017).

African Americans and Hispanic Americans are twice as likely as non-Hispanic white Americans to develop this disease (Alzheimer's Association, 2017). The reasons for this significant difference are not known. Some of it may be due to racial/ethnic differences in the genetic factors that relate to Alzheimer's disease, which you will be reading about shortly. A large part of the difference may be due to racial/ethnic differences in general health, particularly cardiovascular disease and diabetes, diseases that appear to heighten a person's risk of developing Alzheimer's disease (Keene et al., 2017; Larson, 2017).

Alzheimer's disease is a gradually progressive disease in which memory impairment is, by far, the most prominent cognitive dysfunction. Technically, sufferers receive a DSM-5 diagnosis of *mild neurocognitive disorder due to Alzheimer's disease*

neurocognitive disorder A disorder marked by a significant decline in at least one area of cognitive functioning.

major neurocognitive disorder A neurocognitive disorder in which the decline in cognitive functioning is substantial and interferes with a person's ability to be independent.

mild neurocognitive disorder A neurocognitive disorder in which the decline in cognitive functioning is modest and does not interfere with a person's ability to be independent.

Alzheimer's disease The most common type of neurocognitive disorder, usually occurring after the age of 65, marked most prominently by memory impairment.

Slipping away Because of their short-term memory problems, people with advanced cases of Alzheimer's disease are often unable to easily draw or paint or do simple tasks. In addition, their long-term memory deficits may prevent them from recognizing even close relatives or friends.

during the early and mild stages of the syndrome and *major neurocognitive disorder due to Alzheimer's disease* during the later, more severe stages (see **Table 18-3**).

Alzheimer's disease is named after Alois Alzheimer, the German physician who formally identified it in 1907. Alzheimer first became aware of the syndrome in 1901 when a new patient, Auguste D., was placed under his care:

> On November 25, 1901, a . . . woman with no personal or family history of mental illness was admitted to a psychiatric hospital in Frankfurt, Germany, by her husband, who could no longer ignore or hide quirks and lapses that had overtaken her in recent months. First, there were unexplainable bursts of anger, and then a strange series of memory problems. She became increasingly unable to locate things in her own home and began to make surprising mistakes in the kitchen. By the time she arrived at Städtische Irrenanstalt, the Frankfurt Hospital for the Mentally Ill and Epileptics, her condition was as severe as it was curious. The attending doctor, senior physician Alois Alzheimer, began the new file with these notes. . . .
>
> > She sits on the bed with a helpless expression.
> > "What is your name?"
> > Auguste.
> > "Last name?"
> > Auguste.
> > "What is your husband's name?"
> > Auguste, I think.
> > "How long have you been here?"
> > (She seems to be trying to remember.)
> > Three weeks.
>
> It was her second day in the hospital. Dr. Alzheimer, a thirty-seven-year-old neuropathologist and clinician, . . . observed in his new patient a remarkable cluster of symptoms: severe disorientation, reduced comprehension, aphasia (language impairment), paranoia, hallucinations, and a short-term memory so incapacitated that when he spoke her full-name, Frau Auguste D____, and asked her to write it down, the patient got only as far as "Frau" before needing the doctor to repeat the rest.
>
> He spoke her name again. She wrote "Augu" and again stopped.
>
> When Alzheimer prompted her a third time, she was able to write her entire first name and the initial "D" before finally giving up, telling the doctor, "I have lost myself."
>
> Her condition did not improve. It became apparent that there was nothing that anyone at this or any other hospital could do for Frau D. except to insure her safety and try to keep her as clean and comfortable as possible for the rest of her days. Over the next four and a half years, she became increasingly disoriented, delusional, and incoherent. She was often hostile.
>
> "Her gestures showed a complete helplessness," Alzheimer later noted in a published report. "She was disoriented as to time and place. From time to time she would state that she did not understand anything, that she felt confused and totally lost. . . . Often she would scream for hours and hours in a horrible voice."
>
> By November 1904, three and a half years into her illness, Auguste D. was bedridden, incontinent, and largely immobile. . . . Notes from October 1905 indicate that she had become permanently curled up in a fetal position with her knees drawn up to her chest, muttering but unable to speak, and requiring assistance to be fed.
>
> (Shenk, 2001, pp. 12–14)

Although some people with Alzheimer's disease may survive for as many as 20 years, the time between onset and death is typically 3 to 8 years (Wolk & Dickerson, 2017). It usually begins with mild memory problems, lapses of attention, and difficulties in language and communication. As symptoms worsen, the person has trouble completing complicated tasks or remembering important appointments. Eventually

---

TABLE: 18-3

Dx Checklist

Neurocognitive Disorder Due to Alzheimer's Disease

1. Individual displays the features of major or mild neurocognitive disorder.

2. Memory impairment is a prominent feature.

3. Genetic indications or family history of Alzheimer's disease underscore diagnosis, but are not essential to diagnosis.

4. Symptoms are not due to other types of disorders or medical problems.

Information from: APA, 2013.

sufferers also have difficulty with simple tasks, forget distant memories, and have changes in personality that often become very noticeable. For example, a gentle man may become uncharacteristically aggressive.

People with Alzheimer's disease may at first deny that they have a problem, but they soon become anxious or depressed about their state of mind; many also become agitated. At least 17 percent of them develop major depressive disorder (Chi et al., 2014). A woman from Virginia describes her memory loss as the disease progresses:

> *Very often I wander around looking for something which I know is very pertinent, but then after a while I forget about what it is I was looking for. . . . Once the idea is lost, everything is lost and I have nothing to do but wander around trying to figure out what it was that was so important earlier.*
>
> *(Shenk, 2001, p. 43)*

As the neurocognitive symptoms intensify, people with Alzheimer's disease show less and less awareness of their limitations. They may withdraw from others during the late stages of the disorder, become more confused about time and place, wander, speak little, and show very poor judgment (Wolk & Dickerson, 2017). Eventually they become fully dependent on other people. They may lose almost all knowledge of the past and fail to recognize the faces of even close relatives. They also become increasingly uncomfortable at night and take frequent naps during the day (Ferman et al., 2014). During the late phases of the disorder, they require constant care.

People with Alzheimer's usually remain in fairly good health until the later stages of the disease. As their mental functioning declines, however, they become less active and spend much of their time just sitting or lying in bed. This makes them prone to develop serious infections such as pneumonia, which can result in death (Mitchell, 2017). Alzheimer's disease is currently responsible for almost 94,000 deaths each year in the United States, a number more than 40 percent higher than it was a decade ago (CDC, 2017, 2015). It is the sixth leading cause of death in the country, the third leading cause among the elderly.

In most cases, Alzheimer's disease can be diagnosed with certainty only after death, when structural changes in the person's brain, such as excessive *senile plaques* and *neurofibrillary tangles,* can be fully examined. **Senile plaques** are sphere-shaped deposits of a small molecule known as the *beta-amyloid protein* that form in the spaces *between* neurons in the hippocampus, cerebral cortex, and certain other brain structures, as well as in some nearby blood vessels. The formation of plaques is a normal part of aging, but it is exceptionally high in people with Alzheimer's disease (Keene et al., 2017). **Neurofibrillary tangles,** twisted protein fibers found *within* the neurons of the hippocampus and certain other brain structures, also occur in all people as they age, but again people with Alzheimer's disease form an extraordinary number of them.

Scientists do not fully understand what role excessive numbers of plaques and tangles play in Alzheimer's disease, but most agree that they both do their ultimate damage by contributing to the death of neurons. The plaques (which occur between neurons) accomplish this by interfering with neuron-to-neuron communications, while the tangles (which occur inside neurons) accomplish it by blocking the transportation of essential molecules within neurons (Alzheimer's Association, 2017). Today's leading explanations for Alzheimer's disease center on plaques and tangles and on the various factors that may contribute to their formation and excessive buildup.

What Are the Genetic Causes of Alzheimer's Disease?

To understand the genetic theories of Alzheimer's disease, we must first appreciate the nature and role of *proteins*. Proteins are fundamental components of all living cells, including, of course, brain cells. They are large molecules made up of chains of carbon, hydrogen, oxygen,

senile plaques Sphere-shaped deposits of beta-amyloid protein that form in the spaces between certain neurons and in certain blood vessels of the brain as people age. People with Alzheimer's disease have an excessive number of such plaques.

neurofibrillary tangles Twisted protein fibers that form within certain neurons as people age. People with Alzheimer's disease have an excessive number of such tangles.

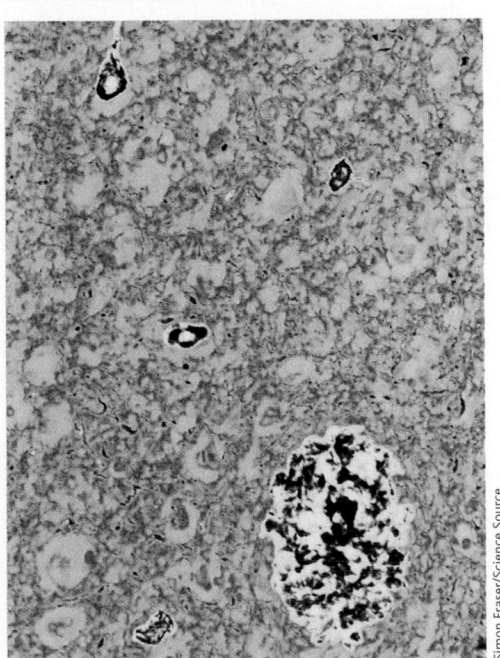

Simon Fraser/Science Source

Biological culprits Tissue from the brain of a person with Alzheimer's disease shows excessive amounts of plaque (large yellow black sphere at lower right of photo) and neurofibrillary tangles (several smaller yellow blobs throughout photo).

nitrogen, and sulfur. There are many different kinds of proteins, each with a different function. Collectively, they are essential for the proper functioning of an organism.

The plaques and tangles that are so plentiful in the brains of Alzheimer's patients seem to occur when two important proteins start acting in a frenzied manner. Abnormal activity by the beta-amyloid protein is, as you just read, key to the repeated formation of plaques. Abnormal activity by another protein, *tau,* is key to the excessive formation of tangles. One of the leading theories holds that the many plaques formed by beta-amyloid proteins also cause tau proteins within neurons to start breaking down, resulting in tangles and the death of many neurons (Keene et al., 2017; Khan, 2015; Hughes, 2011).

What causes this chain of events? Genetic factors are a major culprit. However, the genetic factors that are responsible differ for the early-onset and late-onset types of Alzheimer's disease.

EARLY-ONSET ALZHEIMER'S DISEASE Alzheimer's disease occurs before the age of 65 in fewer than one percent of cases. This relatively rare form of the disorder typically runs in families. Researchers have learned that it is caused by abnormalities in genes responsible for the production of two proteins—the beta-amyloid precursor protein (beta-APP) and the presenilin protein. Apparently, some families transmit mutations, or abnormal forms, of one or both of these genes—mutations that lead ultimately to abnormal beta-amyloid protein buildups and, in turn, to plaque formations (Brosch & Farlow, 2017; Wolk & Dickerson, 2017).

LATE-ONSET ALZHEIMER'S DISEASE The vast majority of Alzheimer cases develop after the age of 65 and do not typically run in families (Wolk & Dickerson, 2017). This late-onset form of the disease appears to result from a combination of genetic, environmental, and lifestyle factors. However, the genetic factors at play in late-onset Alzheimer's disease are different from those involved in early-onset Alzheimer's disease. The genetic factor that has received the most attention from clinical theorists and researchers is a gene called the apolipoprotein E (ApoE) gene.

An early good-bye Lyndon Blackbird (left) takes a leave of absence from work to spend what he suspects will be the last summer with his 54-year-old wife, Evelyn Davis. Davis suffers from early-onset Alzheimer's disease, a relatively uncommon form of this neurocognitive disorder.

The ApoE gene, located on chromosome 19, is normally responsible for the production of a protein that helps carry various fats into the bloodstream. This gene comes in various forms. About 30 percent of the population inherit the form called ApoE-4, and those people may be particularly vulnerable to the development of Alzheimer's disease (Keene et al., 2017; Sherva & Kowall, 2016). Apparently, this ApoE-4 gene form promotes the excessive formation of beta-amyloid proteins, helping to spur the formation of plaques and, in turn, the breakdown of the tau protein, the formation of numerous tangles, the death of many neurons, and, ultimately, the onset of Alzheimer's disease.

Although the ApoE-4 gene form appears to be a major contributor to the development of Alzheimer's disease, it is important to recognize that not everyone with this form of the gene develops the disease. Other factors—perhaps environmental, lifestyle, or stress-related—may also have a significant impact in the development of late-onset Alzheimer's disease (Alzheimer's Association, 2017; Chin-Chan et al., 2015).

AN ALTERNATIVE GENETIC THEORY OF ALZHEIMER'S DISEASE As you have just read, a number of genetic theories of Alzheimer's disease point to gene forms—most often ApoE-4—that produce abnormal beta-amyloid protein buildups and plaque formations. These gene forms, in turn, lead to abnormal activity of tau proteins and the formation of numerous tangles. In recent years, however, some researchers have come to believe that abnormal tau protein activity is not always the result of these abnormal beta-amyloid protein buildups (Peterson et al., 2014; Karch, Jeng, & Goate, 2013). These researchers have identified other gene forms in Alzheimer's patients that seem to be directly associated with tau protein abnormalities and tangle formations within neurons. Thus it may be that there are multiple genetic causes for the formation of numerous tangle formations and the onset of Alzheimer's disease: (1) gene forms that start the ball rolling by first promoting beta-amyloid protein formations and plaques, and (2) gene forms that more directly promote tau protein abnormalities and tangle formations.

How Does Brain Structure Relate to Alzheimer's Disease? Granting that genetic factors may predispose people to Alzheimer's disease, we still need to know what abnormalities in brain structure eventually result from such factors and help promote Alzheimer's disease. Researchers have identified a number of possibilities.

Certain brain structures seem to be especially important in memory. Among the most important structures in short-term memory is the *prefrontal cortex*. When animals or humans acquire new information, their prefrontal cortex becomes more active, enabling them to hold information temporarily and to continue working with the information as long as it is needed. Among the most important structures in transforming short-term memory into long-term memory are the *temporal lobes* (which include the *hippocampus* and *amygdala*) and the *diencephalon* (which includes the *mammillary bodies, thalamus,* and *hypothalamus*). Research indicates that Alzheimer's disease involves improper functioning of one or more of these brain structures (Wolk & Dickerson, 2017) (see **Figure 18-3**).

What Biochemical Changes in the Brain Relate to Alzheimer's Disease? In order for new information to be acquired and remembered, certain proteins must be produced in key brain cells. Several brain chemicals—for example, *acetylcholine, glutamate, RNA* (*ribonucleic acid*), and *calcium*—are responsible for the production of the memory-linked proteins. If the activity of any of these chemicals is disturbed, the proper production of proteins may be prevented and the formation of memories

#BetterBrains

Busy Mind, Healthier Brain

Researchers have found fewer plaques and tangles in the brains of lab mice that live in intellectually and physically stimulating environments—with chew toys, running wheels, and tunnels—than in those of mice that live in less stimulating settings (Li et al., 2017; Lazarov et al., 2005).

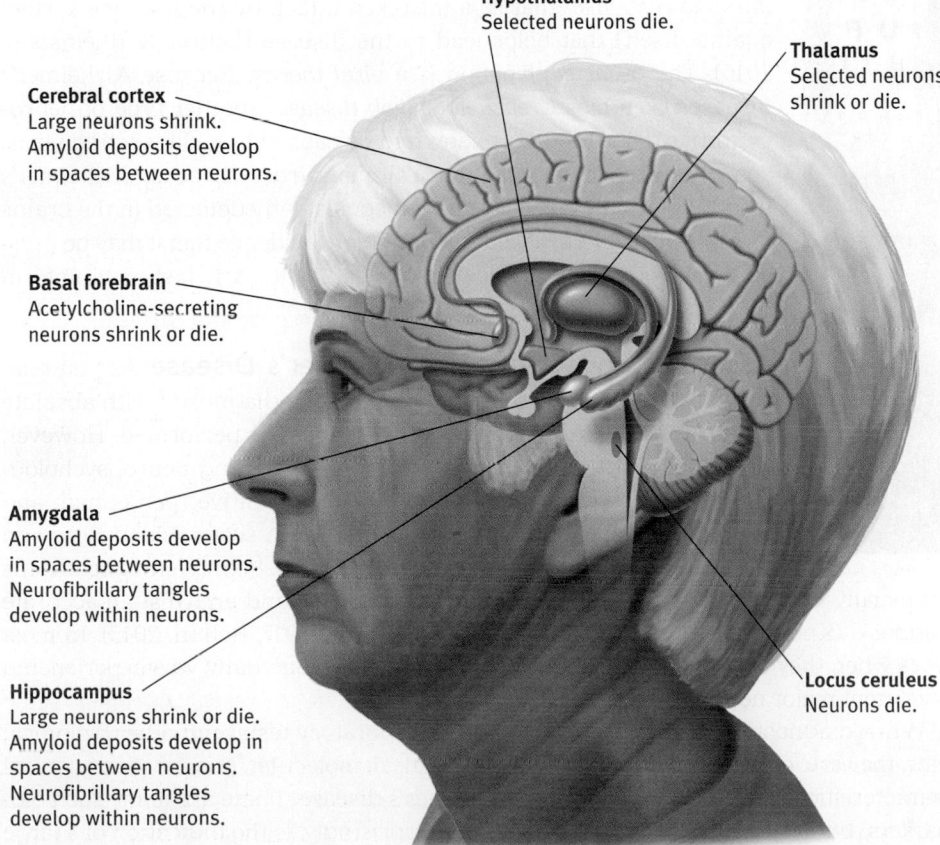

Hypothalamus
Selected neurons die.

Thalamus
Selected neurons shrink or die.

Cerebral cortex
Large neurons shrink.
Amyloid deposits develop in spaces between neurons.

Basal forebrain
Acetylcholine-secreting neurons shrink or die.

Amygdala
Amyloid deposits develop in spaces between neurons. Neurofibrillary tangles develop within neurons.

Hippocampus
Large neurons shrink or die. Amyloid deposits develop in spaces between neurons. Neurofibrillary tangles develop within neurons.

Locus ceruleus
Neurons die.

FIGURE 18-3

The aging brain

In old age, the brain undergoes changes that affect cognitive functions such as memory, learning, and reasoning to some degree. The same changes occur to an excessive degree in people with Alzheimer's disease. (Information from: Mu et al., 2017; Nomi et al., 2017; Zheng et al., 2017; Selkoe, 2011, 1992.)

biomarkers Biochemical, molecular, genetic, or structural characteristics that usually accompany a disease.

interrupted (Canas et al., 2014). In fact, animal researchers have been able to impede short-term memory by blocking the activity of glutamate, and they have interrupted the formation of long-term memories by blocking the cellular production of RNA and calcium (Berridge, 2011).

Researchers have further linked abnormal activity by these various chemicals to Alzheimer's disease. Studies have found, for example, deficient activity levels of acetylcholine and glutamate in the brains of Alzheimer's victims, as well as irregularities in the breakdown of *calcium* (Canas et al., 2014).

Other Explanations of Alzheimer's Disease Several lines of investigation suggest that certain substances found in nature may act as toxins, damage the brain, and contribute to the development of Alzheimer's disease. For example, researchers have detected high levels of *zinc* in the brains of some Alzheimer's patients (Khan, 2016; Schrag et al., 2011). This finding has gained particular attention because in some animal studies zinc has been observed to trigger a clumping of the beta-amyloid protein, similar to the plaques found in the brains of Alzheimer's patients.

Still other studies suggest that the environmental toxin *lead* may contribute to the development of Alzheimer's disease (Lee & Freeman, 2016, 2014; Ritter, 2008). Lead was phased out of gasoline products between 1976 and 1991, leading to an 80 percent drop of lead levels in people's blood. However, many of today's elderly were exposed to high levels of lead in the 1960s and 1970s, regularly inhaling air pollution from vehicle exhausts—an exposure that might have damaged or destroyed many of their neurons. Several studies suggest that this earlier absorption of lead and other pollutants may be having a negative effect on the current cognitive functioning of these individuals (Richardson et al., 2014).

Two other explanations for Alzheimer's disease have also been offered. One is the *autoimmune theory*. On the basis of certain irregularities found in the immune systems of people with Alzheimer's disease, several researchers have speculated that changes in aging brain cells may trigger an *autoimmune response* (that is, a mistaken attack by the immune system against itself) that helps lead to the disease (Lehrer & Rheinstein, 2015). The other explanation is a *viral theory*. Because Alzheimer's disease resembles *Creutzfeldt-Jakob disease*, another type of neurocognitive disorder that is known to be caused by a slow-acting virus, some researchers propose that a similar virus may cause Alzheimer's disease. Such a virus has not been consistently detected in the brains of Alzheimer's victims, but there is some evidence that it may be present in the brains of people who have a particularly fast-moving form of the disease (Zafar et al., 2017; Head, 2013).

Assessing and Predicting Alzheimer's Disease As you read earlier, cases of Alzheimer's disease can be diagnosed with absolute certainty only after death, when an autopsy is performed. However, by using a battery of assessment tools—including neuropsychological tests (tests that measure a person's cognitive, perceptual, and motor performances on certain tasks), brain scans, blood tests and other laboratory work, and careful history taking—diagnosticians are usually able to build a very strong circumstantial case and arrive at an accurate diagnosis (Knezevic & Mizrahi, 2018; Wolk & Dickerson, 2017; Relkin, 2015). In most cases when they are wrong, it turns out that the individual actually was experiencing a different major neurocognitive disorder.

When diagnosticians administer brain scans, laboratory tests, and other biological tests, they are looking for **biomarkers**—biochemical, molecular, genetic, or structural characteristics that usually accompany Alzheimer's disease. There are many such biomarkers, but one that is always important, not surprisingly, is the indication of a large

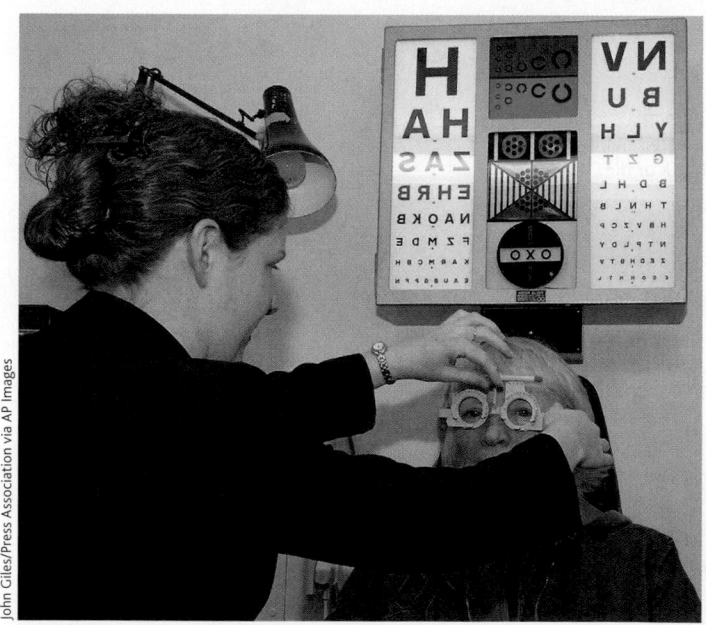

John Giles/Press Association via AP Images

Screening for Alzheimer's disease To better predict and/or assess neurocognitive disorders, clinical researchers are always trying to identify *biomarkers*, biological characteristics that may accompany or predate the disorders. Some research has found that people with cognitive deficits have thinner retinal nerves, sparking the belief that a relatively simple eye test may eventually be able to predict neurocognitive disorders years before their onset.

number of beta-amyloid proteins and tau proteins, the building blocks for plaques and tangles (Wolk & Dickerson, 2017).

It turns out that many of these biomarkers appear in the brain long before the obvious onset of Alzheimer's disease. Thus many researchers have tried to determine whether certain combinations of biomarkers might be able to *predict* cases of Alzheimer's disease and other types of neurocognitive disorders. Apparently they sometimes can, although further research needs to be done (Sheng et al., 2018). One promising line of work, for example, comes from the laboratory of neuroscientist Lisa Mosconi and her colleagues (Walters et al., 2017; Li et al., 2015; Mosconi et al., 2014, 2010, 2008).

> **Would people be better off knowing that they will eventually develop a disease that has no known cure?**

Using brain scans and other biological tests, this research team measured a combination of biomarkers in dozens of elderly research participants—all of them seemingly healthy— and then conducted follow-up studies of them for up to 24 years. Eventually, 43 percent of the study's participants developed either a mild or major neurocognitive disorder due to Alzheimer's disease. The researchers found that those who developed such disorders had displayed more biomarker abnormalities, including low hippocampus activity, on their initial brain tests than the participants who remained healthy. (Recall that the hippocampus plays a major role in memory.) Overall, the biomarker tests, administered years before the onset of symptoms, predicted mild neurocognitive impairment with an accuracy rate of 71 percent and major neurocognitive impairment with an accuracy rate of 83 percent.

As you will see shortly, the most effective interventions for Alzheimer's disease and other neurocognitive disorders are those that help *prevent* these problems, or at least ones that are applied early. Clearly, then, it is essential to have tools that identify the disorders as early as possible, preferably years before the onset of symptoms (Perpetuini et al., 2018). That is what makes the research advances in assessment and diagnosis so exciting.

Other Types of Neurocognitive Disorders There are a number of neurocognitive disorders in addition to Alzheimer's disease (APA, 2013) (see *Trending* on page 571). *Vascular neurocognitive disorder,* for example, follows a cerebrovascular accident, or *stroke,* during which blood flow to specific areas of the brain was cut off, thus damaging the areas (Wright, 2017). In many cases, the patient may not even be

#AfflictionAwareness
Would You Want to Know?

78% Percentage of U.S. adults who would want to have a test done to diagnose a disease even if there were no treatment or cure available

22% Percentage of U.S. adults who would not want to know

(Information from: Siemens Healthcare, 2013)

Jens Büttner/picture-alliance/dpa/AP Images

More than a dance Carmen Dunkelmann, who suffers from an advanced neurocognitive disorder, dances with her husband Peter at the "dance cafe" of her treatment center. The couple always loved dancing and, as Carmen's memories and abilities slip away all too fast, this is an activity and form of intimacy they can still share. In addition, the exercise, stimulation, and joy that accompany dancing are thought to be helpful in Carmen's struggle against her progressive disorder.

#NormalDecline?

DSM-5 has added the category *mild neurocognitive disorder,* characterized by modest declines in memory or other cognitive functions, in order to help clinicians detect individuals in the early stages of *major neurocognitive disorder (e.g., Alzheimer's disease).* Critics worry, however, that many people who display normal forgetfulness and other common features of growing older will incorrectly receive a diagnosis of mild neurocognitive disorder.

aware of the stroke. Like Alzheimer's disease, this disorder is progressive, but its symptoms begin suddenly rather than gradually. Moreover, the person's cognitive functioning may continue to be normal in areas of the brain that have not been affected by the stroke, in contrast to the broad cognitive deficiencies usually displayed by Alzheimer's patients. Some people have both Alzheimer's disease and vascular neurocognitive disorder.

Frontotemporal neurocognitive disorder, also known as *Pick's disease,* is a rare disorder that affects the frontal and temporal lobes (Che et al., 2018; Lee & Miller, 2016). It has a clinical picture similar to Alzheimer's disease, but the two diseases can be distinguished at autopsy.

Neurocognitive disorder due to prion disease, also called *Creutzfeldt-Jakob disease,* has symptoms that include spasms of the body. As we observed earlier, this disorder is caused by a slow-acting virus that may live in the body for years before the disease develops. Once launched, however, the disease has a rapid course.

Neurocognitive disorder due to Huntington's disease is an inherited progressive disease in which memory problems, along with personality changes and mood difficulties, worsen over time. People with Huntington's have movement problems, too, such as severe twitching and spasms. Children of people with Huntington's disease have a 50 percent chance of developing it.

Parkinson's disease, the slowly progressive neurological disorder marked by tremors, rigidity, and unsteadiness, can result in *neurocognitive disorder due to Parkinson's disease,* particularly in older people or those whose cases are advanced (Rodnitzky, 2017). In recent years, it has become clear that many people who used to receive this diagnosis were, in fact, suffering from *neurocognitive disorder due to Lewy body disease.* Lewy body disease involves the buildup of clumps of protein deposits, called Lewy bodies, within many neurons. In addition to progressive cognitive problems, this disease features significant movement difficulties, visual hallucinations, and sleep disturbances. Once thought to be rare, it is now recognized as the second most common neurocognitive disorder, affecting close to 1 percent of people over age 65 (Farlow, 2017).

Yet other neurocognitive disorders may be caused by *HIV infections, traumatic brain injury, substance abuse,* or various *medical conditions* such as meningitis or advanced syphilis.

What Treatments Are Currently Available for Alzheimer's Disease and Other Neurocognitive Disorders? Treatments for the cognitive features of Alzheimer's disease and most other types of neurocognitive disorders have been at best modestly helpful. A number of approaches have been applied, including drug therapy, cognitive-behavioral interventions, support for caregivers, and sociocultural

Rejoining the world, virtually Virtual reality technology can help improve the cognitive and physical functioning of elderly people and Alzheimer's sufferers. Using a virtual reality app, this retirement home resident takes a bike ride through various environments, remembers and revisits old haunts, and performs valuable exercise (she's also on a stationary bike).

Damaging the Brain

 Tens of millions of people in the United States build their Sunday schedules around professional football. They watch their favorite National Football League (NFL) teams go "head-to-head" in what has arguably become America's favorite viewer pastime. For years it was generally believed that the obvious dangers of this sport were outweighed by the enjoyment it brought to so many and the riches it offered the players. But that thinking has changed dramatically over the past decade. The reason? The discovery that *chronic traumatic encephalopathy (CTE),* a degenerative brain disease, is suffered by many NFL players, largely as a result of the repeated head blows they receive over the course of their years in the game (Lindsley, 2017; Mez et al., 2017; Rabinovici, 2017).

Research has clarified that, like various other neurocognitive disorders, CTE features excessive formations of *tangles*—produced by the *tau protein*—in neurons throughout the brain (Ling, 2018). These tangles, along with related abnormalities in brain structures such as the hippocampus, thalamus, substantia nigra, and amygdala, produce a range of neurocognitive symptoms that unfold over a period of years—disorientation, memory loss, erratic behavior, personality changes, progressive cognitive decline, suicidal thinking, and death (Brosch & Farlow, 2017; Larson, 2017).

CTE and its lethal impact were not identified until 2005 when neuropathologist Bennet Omalu was conducting an autopsy on former NFL player Mike Webster and discovered indications of this "new" disease in Webster's brain. Webster had displayed severe cognitive, behavioral, and emotional deterioration prior to his death, but his symptoms had been a mystery to medical professionals. Since Omalu's breakthrough discovery, CTE has been identified in the autopsied brains of many dozens of former football, hockey, soccer, and rugby players, as well as boxers, wrestlers, martial artists, and military personnel (Lindsley, 2017).

The recognition of CTE and its impact unfolded slowly for several reasons (Mez et al., 2017). One, it is caused by multiple relatively mild concussions and mild blows to the head, rather than by one obvious episode of major brain trauma. Two, brain scans of living persons cannot detect the disease in progress because mild concussions do not result in bleeding or obvious brain structure damage. Like Alzheimer's disease, a definitive diagnosis of CTE can be made only when the brain is examined after death. However, what *is* clear while the sufferers are still alive is that something profoundly wrong is happening to them.

Now that CTE is "on the map," a growing number of precautions and actions are being taken—by individuals and officials alike (Lindsley, 2017). For example, the NFL has changed its "return-to-play" procedures, making sure that players fully recover from all symptoms of even mild concussions before they resume playing. The league has also reduced the number of "contact" practice sessions a team may conduct. Moreover, the NFL has created a multimillion-dollar CTE compensation fund from which former players and their families can collect as their symptoms unfold and/or after their deaths. Changes of this kind did not necessarily come about easily or cooperatively—multiple lawsuits and collective bargaining pressures preceded them. Nevertheless, they and other such improvements are now unfolding.

In the meantime, we are reminded all too well that neurocognitive disorders are not only the result of genetic and/or lifestyle factors. They can also be brought about by head injuries—even seemingly mild ones—or, for that matter, by drugs, brain surgery, or factors yet to be determined.

Part of the game? National Football League great John Mackey shows off his Super Bowl V and Hall of Fame rings. Mackey died at age 69 in 2011 of a major neurocognitive disorder, apparently caused by repeated sports injuries to his head. The link between football and such disorders was implicitly acknowledged by the NFL with their implementation of the "88 Plan" (named after Mackey's jersey number), which helps pay the cost of nursing home care and day care for football veterans with such problems.

AP Photo/Steve Ruark

approaches. None of these interventions stops the progression of the disorder (Wolk & Dickerson, 2017).

DRUG TREATMENT The drugs currently prescribed for Alzheimer's patients are designed to affect acetylcholine and glutamate, the neurotransmitters that play important roles in memory. Such drugs include donepezil (Aricept), rivastigmine (Exelon), galantamine (Reminyl), and memantine (Namenda). The short-term memory and

#CostlyDisease

In the United States, the total annual cost for Alzheimer's disease and other neurocognitive disorders is $236 billion (Alzheimer's Association, 2017).

reasoning ability of some Alzheimer's patients who take these drugs improve slightly, as do their use of language and their ability to cope under pressure (Press & Alexander, 2017; Jessen, 2014). Although the benefits of the drugs are limited and their side effects can be problematic, they have been approved by the FDA. Clinicians believe that they may be of greatest use to people in the early, mild stage of Alzheimer's disease. There is a popular belief that another approach, taking vitamin E, either alone or in combination with one of these drugs, will help slow down some of the cognitive difficulties experienced by people in the mild stage of Alzheimer's disease; however, as it turns out, this notion is, at best, modestly supported by various studies (Press & Alexander, 2017).

The drugs just discussed are each prescribed *after* a person has developed Alzheimer's disease. In contrast, studies suggest that certain substances now available on the marketplace for other kinds of problems may help prevent or delay the onset of Alzheimer's disease. For example, some studies have found that women who took *estrogen,* the female sex hormone, for years after menopause cut their risk of developing Alzheimer's disease in half (Li et al., 2017, 2014). Other studies have suggested that the long-term use of *nonsteroidal anti-inflammatory drugs* such as *ibuprofen* and *naprosyn* (drugs found in Advil, Motrin, Nuprin, and other pain relievers) may help reduce the risk of Alzheimer's disease, although recent findings on this possibility have been mixed (Press & Alexander, 2017).

COGNITIVE-BEHAVIORAL TECHNIQUES Cognitive-behavioral treatments have been used in cases of Alzheimer's disease, with some degree of success. In Japan, for example, a number of people with the disease meet regularly in classes, performing simple calculations and reading essays and novels aloud. Similarly, research suggests that cognitive activities, including computer-based cognitive stimulation programs, sometimes help prevent or delay the onset of Alzheimer's disease (Li et al., 2017; Press & Alexander, 2017; Szalavitz, 2013). For example, one study of 700 people in their 80s found that those research participants who had pursued cognitive activities over a five-year period (for example, writing letters, following the news, reading books, or attending concerts or plays) were less likely to develop Alzheimer's disease than were mentally inactive participants (Wilson et al., 2012, 2007).

Interestingly, cognitive-behavioral strategies that focus primarily on behaviors rather than on cognitions seem to be even more useful in preventing and managing this disease. It has become clear across many studies that physical exercise helps improve cognitive functioning—for people of all ages and states of health. There is evidence that regular physical exercise may also help reduce the risk of developing

Fitness of all kinds In recent years, clinicians have stressed the value of *cognitive fitness* to help prevent or slow down the cognitive decline seen in old age and/or neurocognitive disorders. Thus, many senior community programs now include facilities (left) where elderly people can work on cognitive computer programs. At the same time, research suggests that *physical exercise* may be even more effective at slowing down cognitive decline. Thus, the elderly identical twins on the right, both of whom have Alzheimer's disease, participate regularly in a physical exercise program.

Alzheimer's disease and other neurocognitive disorders (Keene et al., 2017; Press & Alexander, 2017). Correspondingly, physical exercise is often a part of treatment programs for people with the disorders.

Behavior-focused interventions of a different kind have been used to help improve specific symptoms displayed by Alzheimer's patients. The approaches typically focus on changing everyday patient behaviors that are stressful for the family, such as wandering at night, loss of bladder control, demands for attention, and inadequate personal care (Press & Alexander, 2017; Lancioni et al., 2011). The therapists use a combination of role-playing exercises, modeling, and practice to teach family members how and when to use reinforcement in order to shape more positive behaviors.

SUPPORT FOR CAREGIVERS Caregiving can take a heavy toll on the close relatives of people with Alzheimer's disease and other neurocognitive disorders (Alzheimer's Association, 2017; Kang et al., 2014). Almost 90 percent of all people with Alzheimer's disease are cared for by their relatives, usually their adult children or spouses. The majority of these relatives say they provide this heavy-duty assistance because they feel an obligation to their family member and want dearly to keep him or her at home (Alzheimer's Association, 2017). But it is hard to take care of someone who is becoming increasingly lost, helpless, and medically ill. And it is very painful to witness mental and physical decline in someone you love.

© Jodi Cobb/National Geographic Creative

Toll on caregivers A woman comforts her twin sister, who suffers from Alzheimer's disease. The psychological and physical burdens of caring for close relatives with neurocognitive disorders typically take a heavy toll on caregivers.

I have really struggled with the honesty issue. What do you say to someone who sits on her bed and says that she has never stayed out overnight without letting her parents know where she is? What do you say to someone who thinks she is a teacher and if she doesn't get home and into her classroom there will be a whole class of children left unattended? What do you say to someone who thinks she has no money to pay bills and will lose everything she owns if she doesn't get home to a job that you know she has been retired from for years? I couldn't find any reason for telling her over and over that she has a horrible terrible degenerating disease that was making her feel the way she does.

I found that she became less anxious if I just listened to what she was saying and feeling. Sometimes saying nothing was better than anything I could say. Telling her that I would take care of some of these things put her a bit more at ease. It may feel better for me to verbalize the facts, but what she needs is comfort and security—not the truth. The truth won't change anything.

(Shenk, 2001, p. 147)

One of the most frequent reasons for the institutionalization of people with Alzheimer's disease is that overwhelmed caregivers can no longer cope with the difficulties of keeping them at home (Alzheimer's Association, 2017; Di Rosa et al., 2011). Many caregivers experience anger and depression, and their own physical and mental health often declines (Kang et al., 2014). A number of them are, in fact, "sandwich generation" caregivers, meaning they must care not only for their parents with Alzheimer's disease, but also for their teenage children. Clinicians now recognize that one of the most important aspects of treating Alzheimer's disease and other types of neurocognitive disorders is to focus on the emotional needs of the caregivers, including their needs for regular time out, education about the disease, and psychotherapy (Mittelman & Bartels, 2014). Some clinicians also provide caregiver support groups (Press & Alexander, 2017).

#GenderPressure

Two-thirds of caregivers for Alzheimer sufferers are women.

One-third of caregivers for Alzheimer sufferers are daughters.

Daughters provide an average of 102 caregiving hours per month for their parents with Alzheimer's disease. Sons provide 80 hours per month.

(Information from: Alzheimer's Association, 2017)

Kyodo News/Getty Images

First things first Proper self-care and self-concern may decline significantly over the course of a major neurocognitive disorder. Thus some treatment programs emphasize hygiene, appearance, and other daily needs. These elderly women at a care facility in Japan are receiving make-up lessons, part of their "cosmetic therapy program."

#PovertyLine

10%	Percentage of elderly non-Hispanic white Americans who live below the poverty line
21%	Percentage of elderly Hispanic Americans who live below the poverty line
24%	Percentage of elderly African Americans who live below the poverty line

(Information from: Heflin, 2017)

SOCIOCULTURAL APPROACHES Sociocultural approaches play an important role in treatment (Alzheimer's Association, 2017; Pongan et al., 2012). A number of day-care facilities for patients with neurocognitive disorders have been developed, providing treatment programs and activities for outpatients during the day and returning them to their homes and families at night. There are also many assisted-living facilities in which those suffering from neurocognitive impairment live in cheerful apartments, receive needed supervision, and take part in various activities that bring more joy and stimulation to their lives. These apartments are typically designed to meet the special needs of the residents—providing more light, for example, or enclosing gardens with circular paths so the residents can go for strolls alone without getting lost. Studies suggest that such facilities bring some degree of improvement to the cognitive deficits of residents and enhance their enjoyment of life. In addition, a growing number of practical devices, such as tracking beacons worn on the wrists of Alzheimer's patients and shoes that contain a GPS tracker, have been developed to help locate patients who may wander off (Press & Alexander, 2017; Cavallo et al., 2015; Schiller, 2014).

> If Alzheimer's disease is a cognitive disorder, and biologically caused, why would increasing patients' comfort levels make a difference?

Given the progress now unfolding in the understanding and treatment of Alzheimer's disease and other neurocognitive disorders, researchers are looking forward to life-changing advances in the coming years. The brain changes responsible for these disorders are tremendously complex, but most investigators believe that exciting breakthroughs are just over the horizon. Ironically, just when significant progress is being made, the public seems to be losing patience. In one survey of 1,000 adults across the United States, only 22 percent of the respondents believed that a major breakthrough or cure will be coming in the next decade or so (Rasmussen, 2014).

Issues Affecting the Mental Health of the Elderly

AS THE STUDY AND TREATMENT of elderly people have progressed, three issues have raised concern among clinicians: the special problems faced by elderly members of racial and ethnic minority groups, the inadequacies of long-term care, and the need for a health-maintenance approach to medical care in an aging world.

First, *discrimination based on race and ethnicity* has long been a problem in the United States (see Chapter 3), and many people suffer as a result, particularly those who are old. To be both old and a member of a minority group is considered a kind of "double jeopardy" by many observers. For older women in minority groups, the difficulties are sometimes termed "triple jeopardy," as many more older women than older men live alone, are widowed, and are poor. Clinicians must take into account their older patients' race, ethnicity, and gender as they try to diagnose and treat their mental health problems (Heflin, 2017; Ng et al., 2014; Sirey et al., 2014) (see **Figure 18-4**).

Some elderly people in minority groups face language barriers that interfere with their medical and mental health care. Others may hold cultural beliefs that prevent them from seeking services. Additionally, many members of minority groups do not trust the majority establishment or do not know about medical and mental health services that are sensitive to their culture and their particular needs (Lines & Wiener, 2014; Ayalon & Huyck, 2001). As a result, it is common for elderly members of racial and ethnic minority groups to rely largely on family members or friends for remedies and

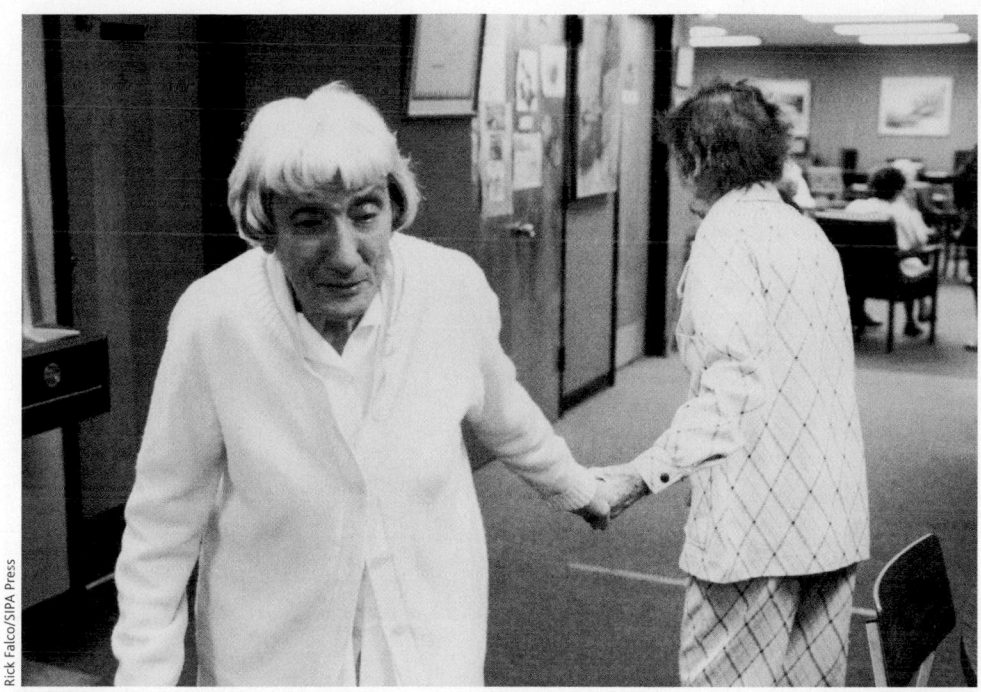

Day treatment Two women touch hands as they go their separate ways in a New Jersey day-care facility for patients with Alzheimer's disease. They return to their families each night.

health care. Today, around 20 percent of all elderly people live with their children or other relatives, usually because of increasing health problems (Pew Research Center, 2017; Keefer, 2015). In the United States, this living arrangement is more common for families from racial and ethnic minority groups.

Second, many older people require *long-term care,* a general term that may refer variously to the services offered outside the family in a partially supervised apartment, a senior housing complex for mildly impaired elderly persons, or a nursing home where skilled medical and nursing care is available around the clock (Samos et al., 2010). The quality of care in such residences varies widely.

At any given time in the United States, only about 4 percent of the entire elderly population actually live in nursing homes (1.5 million people), but as many as 20 percent of people 85 years and older do eventually wind up being placed in such facilities (CDC, 2017). Thus many older adults live in fear of being "put away." They fear having to move, losing independence, and living in a medical environment. Many also worry about the cost of long-term care facilities. Around-the-clock nursing care is expensive, and nursing home costs continue to rise. The average cost for a private room in a

FIGURE 18-4

Ethnicity and old age

The elderly population is becoming racially and ethnically more diverse. In the United States today, almost 80 percent of all people over the age of 65 are non-Hispanic white Americans. By 2060, non-Hispanic white Americans will comprise only 55 percent of the elderly. (Information from: Mather, 2016; PRB, 2015.)

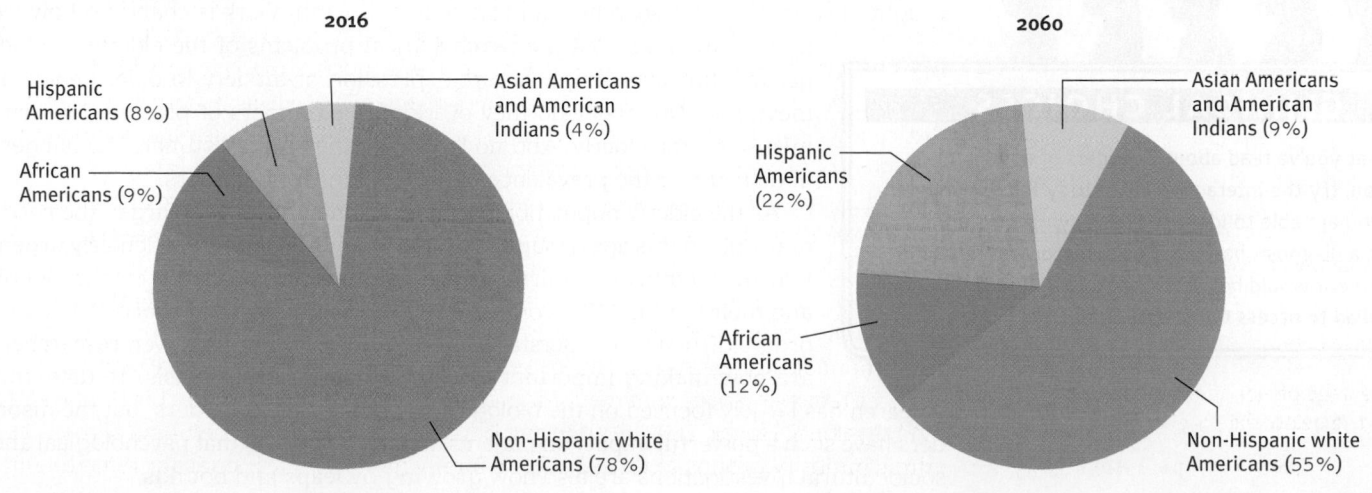

2016

Hispanic Americans (8%)

African Americans (9%)

Asian Americans and American Indians (4%)

Non-Hispanic white Americans (78%)

2060

Hispanic Americans (22%)

African Americans (12%)

Asian Americans and American Indians (9%)

Non-Hispanic white Americans (55%)

Every little bit helps In line with research findings that all kinds of physical exercise may help improve cognitive functioning and help prevent or slow down cognitive decline, these elderly persons participate in an "armchair" exercise program at the Dominica Association, a community center in Bradford, West Yorkshire, in the United Kingdom.

nursing home in the United States is over $90,000 per year; for a semi-private room it is over $80,000 (Alzheimer's Association, 2017). Most health insurance plans available today do not adequately cover the costs of long-term or permanent placement. Worry over these issues can greatly harm the mental health of older adults, perhaps leading to depression and anxiety as well as family conflict.

Finally, clinical scientists suggest that the current generation of young adults should take a *health-maintenance,* or *wellness promotion, approach* to their own aging process (Heflin, 2017; Libman et al., 2017; Press & Alexander, 2017). In other words, they should do things that promote physical and mental health—avoid smoking, eat well-balanced and healthful meals, exercise regularly, engage in positive social relationships, and take advantage of psycho-educational, stress management, and other mental health programs. There is a growing belief that older adults will adapt more readily to changes and negative events if their physical and psychological health is good.

Clinicians Discover the Elderly

JUST A HALF CENTURY AGO, mental health professionals focused relatively little on the elderly. But like the problems of children, those of aging people have now caught the attention of researchers and clinicians. Current work is changing how we understand and treat the psychological problems of the elderly. No longer do clinicians simply accept depression or anxiety in older people as inevitable. No longer do they overlook the dangers of prescription drug misuse by the elderly. And no longer do they underestimate the dangers of delirium or the prevalence of neurocognitive disorders.

As the elderly population lives longer and grows ever larger, the needs of people in this age group are becoming more visible. Particularly urgent is neurocognitive impairment and its devastating impact on the elderly and their families. The complexity of the brain makes neurocognitive disorders difficult to understand, diagnose, and treat. However, researchers are now making important discoveries on a regular basis. To date, this research has largely focused on the biological aspects of the disorders, but the disorders have such a powerful impact on patients and their families that psychological and sociocultural investigations are also now growing by leaps and bounds.

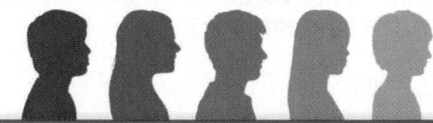

CLINICAL CHOICES

Now that you've read about disorders of aging and cognition, try the interactive case study for this chapter. See if you are able to identify Fred's symptoms and suggest a diagnosis based on his symptoms. What kind of treatment would be most effective for Fred? Go to **Launch**Pad to access *Clinical Choices*.

♥... SUMMING UP

» Disorders of Later Life The problems of elderly people are often linked to the losses and other stresses and changes that accompany advancing age. As many as 50 percent of the elderly would benefit from mental health services, yet fewer than 20 percent receive them. *Depression* is a common mental health problem among those in this age group. Older people may also suffer from *anxiety disorders*. Between 3 and 7 percent exhibit *alcohol use disorder* in any given year, and many others *misuse prescription drugs*. In addition, some elderly people display psychotic disorders such as *schizophrenia* or *delusional disorder*. pp. 554–561

» Disorders of Cognition Older people are more likely than people of other age groups to experience *delirium*, a fast-developing disturbance marked by great difficulty focusing attention, staying oriented, concentrating, and following an orderly sequence of thought.

Neurocognitive disorders, characterized by a significant decline in cognitive function, become increasingly common in older age groups. There are many types of neurocognitive disorders, the most common being *Alzheimer's disease*. Alzheimer's disease has been linked to an unusually high number of *senile plaques* and *neurofibrillary tangles* in the brain. According to a leading explanation of late-onset Alzheimer's disease—by far, the most common kind of Alzheimer's disease—people who inherit *ApoE-4*, a particular form of the *apolipoprotein E (ApoE) gene*, are particularly vulnerable to the development of Alzheimer's disease. Apparently, the ApoE-4 gene form promotes the excessive formation of *beta-amyloid proteins*, helping to spur the formation of plaques and, in turn, the breakdown of the *tau protein*, the formation of numerous tangles, the death of many neurons, and ultimately, the onset of Alzheimer's disease.

A number of other causes have also been proposed for this disease, including high levels of *zinc, lead*, or *other toxins; immune system problems;* and a *virus* of some kind.

Researchers are making significant strides at better assessing Alzheimer's disease and other types of neurocognitive disorders and even at identifying those who will eventually develop these disorders. Drug therapy and cognitive-behavioral therapies have been used to treat Alzheimer's disease, with limited success. Addressing the needs of *caregivers* is now also recognized as a key part of treatment. In addition, sociocultural approaches such as day-care facilities are on the rise. Major treatment breakthroughs are expected in the coming years. *pp. 561–574*

» Key Issues In studying and treating the problems of old age, clinicians have become concerned about three issues: *the problems of elderly members of racial and ethnic minority groups, inadequacies of long-term care,* and *the need for health maintenance by young adults.* pp. 574–576

Visit *LaunchPad* to access the e-Book, Clinical Choices, videos, activities, and LearningCurve, as well as study aids including flashcards, FAQs, and research exercises.

LaunchPad
macmillan learning

◦...Law, Society, and the Mental Health Profession

> *Dear Jodie:*
>
> *There is a definite possibility that I will be killed in my attempt to get Reagan. It is for this very reason that I am writing you this letter now. As you well know by now, I love you very much. The past seven months I have left you dozens of poems, letters and messages in the faint hope you would develop an interest in me. . . . Jodie, I would abandon this idea of getting Reagan in a second if I could only win your heart and live out the rest of my life with you, whether it be in total obscurity or whatever. I will admit to you that the reason I'm going ahead with this attempt now is because I just cannot wait any longer to impress you. I've got to do something now to make you understand in no uncertain terms that I am doing all of this for your sake. By sacrificing my freedom and possibly my life I hope to change your mind about me. This letter is being written an hour before I leave for the Hilton Hotel. Jodie, I'm asking you please to look into your heart and at least give me the chance with this historical deed to gain your respect and love. I love you forever.*
>
> *John Hinckley*

John W. Hinckley Jr. wrote this letter to actress Jodie Foster in March 1981. Soon after writing it, he stood waiting, pistol ready, outside the Washington Hilton Hotel. Moments later, President Ronald Reagan came out of the hotel, and the popping of pistol fire was heard. As Secret Service agents pushed Reagan into the limousine, a police officer and the president's press secretary fell to the pavement. The president had been shot, and by nightfall most of America had seen the face and heard the name of the disturbed young man from Colorado.

As you have seen throughout this book, the psychological dysfunction of an individual does not occur in isolation. It is influenced—sometimes caused—by societal and social factors, and it affects the lives of relatives, friends, and acquaintances. The case of John Hinckley demonstrates in powerful terms that individual dysfunction may, in some cases, also affect the well-being and rights of people the person does not know.

By the same token, clinical scientists and practitioners do not conduct their work in isolation. As they study and treat people with psychological problems, they affect and are affected by other institutions of society. We have seen, for example, how the government regulates the use of psychotropic medications, how clinicians helped carry out the government's policy of deinstitutionalization, and how clinicians have called the psychological ordeals of Vietnam, Iraq, and Afghanistan combat veterans to the attention of society.

In short, like their clients, clinical professionals operate within a complex social system—for clinicians, it is the system that defines and often regulates their professional responsibilities. Just as we must understand the social context in which abnormal behavior occurs in order to understand the behavior, so must we understand the context in which this behavior is studied and treated. This chapter focuses on the relationship between the mental health field and three major forces in society—the *legislative/judicial system,* the *business/economic* arena, and the world of *technology.* ▪

#TheirWords

"I think John Hinckley will be a threat the rest of his life. He is a time bomb."

U.S. Attorney, 1982

"Without doubt, [John Hinckley] is the least dangerous person on the planet."

Attorney for John Hinckley, 2003

forensic psychology The branch of psychology concerned with intersections between psychological practice and research and the judicial system. Also related to the field of *forensic psychiatry*.

criminal commitment A legal process by which people accused of a crime are instead judged mentally unstable and sent to a treatment facility.

not guilty by reason of insanity (NGRI) A verdict stating that defendants are not guilty of a crime because they were insane at the time of the crime.

M'Naghten test A legal test that holds people to be insane at the time they committed a crime if, because of a mental disorder, they did not know the nature of the act or did not know right from wrong.

irresistible impulse test A legal test that holds people to be insane at the time they committed a crime if they were driven to do so by an uncontrollable "fit of passion."

Durham test A legal test that holds people to be insane at the time they committed a crime if their act was the result of a mental disorder.

Law and Mental Health

TWO SOCIAL INSTITUTIONS HAVE a particularly strong impact on the mental health profession: the legislative and judicial systems. These institutions—collectively, the *legal field*—have long been responsible for protecting both the public good and the rights of individuals. Sometimes the relationship between the legal field and the mental health field has been friendly, and those in the two fields have worked together to protect the rights and meet the needs of troubled people and of society at large. At other times they have clashed, and one field has imposed its will on the other.

This relationship has two distinct aspects. On the one hand, mental health professionals often play a role in the criminal justice system, as when they are called upon to help the courts assess the mental stability of people accused of crimes. They responded to this call in the Hinckley case, as you will see, and in thousands of other cases. This aspect of the relationship is sometimes termed *psychology in law*; that is, clinical practitioners and researchers operate within the legal system. On the other hand, there is another aspect to the relationship, called *law in psychology*. The legislative and judicial systems act upon the clinical field, regulating certain aspects of mental health care. The courts may, for example, force some people to enter treatment, even against their will. In addition, the law protects the rights of patients.

The intersections between the mental health field and the legal and judicial systems are collectively referred to as **forensic psychology** (Ryan, 2016). Forensic psychologists or psychiatrists (or related mental health professionals) may perform such varied activities as testifying in trials, researching the reliability of eyewitness testimony, or helping police profile the personality of a serial killer on the loose.

Psychology in Law: How Do Clinicians Influence the Criminal Justice System?

To arrive at just and appropriate punishments, the courts need to know whether defendants are *responsible* for the crimes they commit and *capable* of defending themselves in court. If not, it would be inappropriate to find defendants guilty or punish them in the usual manner. The courts have decided that in some instances people who suffer from severe *mental instability* may not be responsible for their actions or may not be able to defend themselves in court, and so should not be punished in the usual way. Although the courts make the final judgment as to mental instability, their decisions are guided to a large degree by the opinions of mental health professionals.

When people accused of crimes are judged to be mentally unstable, they are usually sent to a mental institution for treatment, a process called **criminal commitment.** Actually there are several forms of criminal commitment. In one, people are judged mentally unstable *at the time of their crimes* and so innocent of wrongdoing. They may plead **not guilty by reason of insanity (NGRI)** and bring mental health professionals into court to support their claim. When people are found not guilty on this basis, they are committed for treatment until they improve enough to be released (Gowensmith et al., 2017).

In a second form of criminal commitment, people are judged mentally unstable *at the time of their trial* and so are considered unable to understand the trial procedures and defend themselves in court. They are committed for treatment until they are competent to stand trial. Once again, the testimony of mental health professionals helps determine the defendant's psychological functioning.

These judgments of mental instability have stirred many arguments. Some people consider the judgments to be loopholes in the legal system that allow criminals to escape proper punishment for wrongdoing. Others argue that a legal system simply cannot be just unless it allows for extenuating circumstances, such as mental instability.

The practice of criminal commitment differs from country to country. In this chapter you will see primarily how it operates in the United States. Although the specific principles and procedures of each country may differ, most countries grapple with the same issues, concerns, and decisions that you will read about here.

Criminal Commitment and Insanity During Commission of a Crime Consider once again the case of John Hinckley. Was he insane at the time he shot the president? If insane, should he be held responsible for his actions? On June 21, 1982, fifteen months after he shot four men in the nation's capital, a jury pronounced Hinckley not guilty by reason of insanity. Hinckley thus joined Richard Lawrence, a house painter who shot at Andrew Jackson in 1835, and John Schrank, a saloonkeeper who shot former president Teddy Roosevelt in 1912, as a would-be assassin who was found not guilty by reason of insanity.

Although most Americans were shocked by the Hinckley verdict, those familiar with the insanity defense were not so surprised. In this case, as in other federal court cases at that time, the prosecution had the burden of proving beyond a reasonable doubt that the defendant was sane. Many state courts placed a similar responsibility on the prosecution. To present a clear-cut demonstration of sanity can be difficult, especially when the defendant has exhibited bizarre behavior in other areas of life. A few years after the Hinckley verdict, Congress passed a law making it the defense's burden in federal cases to prove that defendants are insane, rather than the prosecution's burden to prove them sane. Around 75 percent of state legislatures have since followed suit (Gandhi & Prabbu, 2017).

It is important to recognize that "insanity" is a *legal* term (Hallevy, 2017). That is, the definition of "insanity" used in criminal cases was written by legislators, not by clinicians. Defendants may have mental disorders but not necessarily qualify for a legal definition of insanity. Modern Western definitions of insanity can be traced to the murder case of Daniel M'Naghten in England in 1843. M'Naghten shot and killed Edward Drummond, the secretary to British prime minister Robert Peel, while trying to shoot Peel. Because of M'Naghten's apparent delusions of persecution, the jury found him to be not guilty by reason of insanity. The public was outraged by this decision, and their angry outcry forced the British law lords to define the insanity defense more clearly. This legal definition, known as the **M'Naghten test,** or **M'Naghten rule,** stated that having a mental disorder at the time of a crime does not by itself mean that the person was insane; the defendant also had to be *unable to know right from wrong.* The state and federal courts in the United States adopted this test as well.

In the late nineteenth century some state and federal courts in the United States, dissatisfied with the M'Naghten rule, adopted a different test—the **irresistible impulse test.** This test, which had first been used in Ohio in 1834, emphasized the inability to control one's actions. A person who committed a crime during an uncontrollable "fit of passion" was considered insane and not guilty under this test.

For years state and federal courts chose between the M'Naghten test and the irresistible impulse test to determine the sanity of criminal defendants. For a while a third test, called the **Durham test,** also became popular, but it was soon replaced in most courts. This test, based on a decision handed down by the Supreme Court in 1954 in the case of *Durham v. United States,* stated simply that people are not criminally responsible if their "unlawful act was the product of mental disease or mental defect." This test was meant to offer more flexibility in court decisions, but it proved too flexible. Insanity defenses could point to such problems as alcoholism or other forms of substance abuse and conceivably even headaches or ulcers, which were listed as psychophysiological disorders in DSM-I (Covey, 2017).

AP Photo

Would-be assassin Few courtroom decisions have spurred as much debate or legislative action as the jury's verdict that John Hinckley, having been captured in the act of shooting President Ronald Reagan, was not guilty by reason of insanity.

> Which burden of proof is more appropriate—that defense attorneys must prove defendants "insane" or that prosecutors must prove defendants "not insane"?

#TheAftermath

Daniel M'Naghten Judged not guilty by reason of insanity in 1843, M'Naghten lived in a mental hospital until his death 22 years later.

John Hinckley Judged not guilty by reason of insanity in 1982, Hinckley lived in a mental hospital until his release by a federal judge in 2016.

In 1955 the American Law Institute (ALI) formulated a test that combined aspects of the M'Naghten, irresistible impulse, and Durham tests. The **American Law Institute test** held that people are not criminally responsible if at the time of a crime they had a mental disorder or defect that prevented them from knowing right from wrong *or* from being able to control themselves and to follow the law. For a time the new test became the most widely accepted legal test of insanity. After the Hinckley verdict, however, there was a public uproar over the "liberal" ALI guidelines, and people called for tougher standards.

Partly in response to this uproar, the American Psychiatric Association recommended in 1983 that people should be found not guilty by reason of insanity *only* if they did not know right from wrong at the time of the crime; an inability to control themselves and to follow the law should no longer be sufficient grounds for a judgment of insanity. In short, the association was calling for a return to the M'Naghten test.

This test now is used in all cases tried in federal courts and in about half of the state courts. The more liberal ALI standard is still used in the remaining state courts, except in Idaho, Kansas, Montana, and Utah, which have more or less done away with the insanity plea altogether.

People suffering from severe mental disorders in which confusion is a major feature may not be able to tell right from wrong or to control their behavior. It is therefore not surprising that more than 80 percent of defendants who are acquitted of a crime by reason of insanity qualify for a diagnosis of schizophrenia or another form of psychosis (Melton et al., 2017, 2007; Steadman et al., 1993). The majority of these acquitted defendants have a history of past hospitalization, arrest, or both. About half who successfully plead insanity are white, and 86 percent are male. Their mean age is 32 years. The crimes for which defendants are found not guilty by reason of insanity vary greatly, although approximately 70 percent are violent crimes of some sort. At least 15 percent of those acquitted are accused specifically of murder (see **Figure 19-1**).

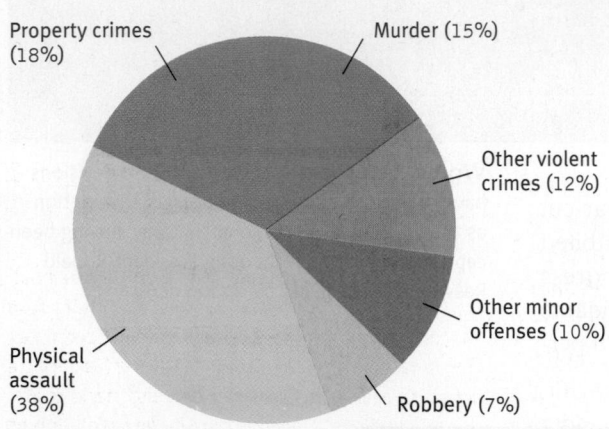

Property crimes (18%) · **Murder (15%)** · **Other violent crimes (12%)** · **Other minor offenses (10%)** · **Robbery (7%)** · **Physical assault (38%)**

FIGURE 19-1

Crimes for Which People Are Found Not Guilty by Reason of Insanity (NGRI)

Reviews of NGRI verdicts in a number of states show that most people who are acquitted on this basis had been charged with a violent crime. (Information from: Melton et al., 2017, 2007; Perlin, 2017; Steadman et al., 1993; Callahan et al., 1991.)

WHAT CONCERNS ARE RAISED BY THE INSANITY DEFENSE? Despite the changes in the insanity criteria, criticism of the insanity defense continues (Perlin, 2017; Greene & Heilbrun, 2013; Pouncey & Lukens, 2010). One concern is the fundamental difference between the law and the science of human behavior. The law assumes that individuals have free will and are generally responsible for their actions. Several models of human behavior, in contrast, assume that physical or psychological forces act to determine the individual's behavior. Inevitably, then, legal definitions of insanity and responsibility will differ from those suggested by clinical research.

A second criticism points to the uncertainty of scientific knowledge about abnormal behavior. During a typical insanity defense trial, the testimony of defense clinicians conflicts with that of clinicians hired by the prosecution, and so the jury must weigh the claims of "experts" who disagree in their assessments. Some people see this lack of professional agreement as evidence that clinical knowledge in some areas may be too incomplete to be allowed to influence important legal decisions. Others counter that the field has made great strides—for example, developing several psychological scales to help clinicians discriminate more consistently between the sane and insane as defined by the M'Naghten standard (Melton et al., 2017, 2007; Xue et al., 2015; Rogers, 2008).

Even with helpful scales in hand, however, clinicians making judgments of legal insanity face a problem that is difficult to overcome: They must evaluate a defendant's state of mind during an event that took place weeks, months, or years earlier. Because mental states can and do change over time and across situations, clinicians can never be entirely certain that their assessments of mental instability at the time of the crime are accurate.

Perhaps the most common criticism of the insanity defense is that it allows criminals to escape punishment. Granted, some people who successfully plead insanity are released from treatment facilities just months after their acquittal. Yet the number of such cases is quite small (Melton et al., 2017, 2007; Steadman et al., 1993; Callahan et al., 1991). According to surveys, the public dramatically overestimates the percentage of defendants who plead insanity, guessing it to be 30 to 40 percent, when in fact it is less than 1 percent. Moreover, only a minority of these defendants fake or exaggerate their psychological symptoms, and only 26 percent of those who plead insanity are actually found not guilty on this basis. In all, less than 1 of every 400 defendants in the United States is found not guilty by reason of insanity (see **PsychWatch** on page 585). It is also worth noting that in 80 percent of those cases in which defendants are acquitted by reason of insanity, the prosecution has agreed to the appropriateness of the plea.

> After patients have been criminally committed to institutions, why might clinicians be hesitant to later declare them unlikely to commit the same crime again?

During most of U.S. history, a successful insanity plea amounted to the equivalent of a long-term prison sentence. In fact, on average, treatment in a mental hospital resulted in confinement that was twice as long as imprisonment for the same crime would have brought (Perlin, 2017). Because hospitalization resulted in little if any improvement, clinicians were reluctant to predict that the offenders would not repeat their crimes.

Today, however, offenders are being released from mental hospitals earlier and earlier. This trend is the result of the increasing effectiveness of drug therapy and other treatments in institutions, the growing reaction against extended institutionalization, and more emphasis on patients' rights (Gowensmith et al., 2017; Slovenko, 2011, 2009, 2004). In 1992, in the case of *Foucha v. Louisiana,* the U.S. Supreme Court clarified that the *only* acceptable basis for determining the release of hospitalized offenders is whether or not they are still "insane"; they cannot be kept indefinitely in mental hospitals solely because they are dangerous. Some states are able to maintain control over offenders even after their release from hospitals. Adopting a procedure called "outpatient commitment," the states may insist on community treatment, monitor the patients closely, and rehospitalize them if necessary (Gowensmith et al., 2017; Norko et al., 2016).

WHAT OTHER VERDICTS ARE AVAILABLE? Over the past four decades, at least 20 states have added another verdict option—**guilty but mentally ill.** Defendants who receive this verdict are found to have had a mental illness at the time of their crime, but the illness was not fully related to or responsible for the crime. The option of guilty but mentally ill enables jurors to convict a person they view as dangerous while also suggesting that the individual receive needed treatment. Defendants found to be guilty but mentally ill are given a prison term with the added recommendation that they also undergo treatment if necessary.

After initial enthusiasm for this verdict option, legal and clinical theorists have increasingly found it unsatisfactory. According to research, it has not reduced the number of not guilty by reason of insanity verdicts, and it often confuses jurors (Bartol & Bartol, 2015; Frierson et al., 2015). In addition, as critics point out, appropriate mental health care is supposed to be available to all prisoners anyway, regardless of the verdict (Binswanger & Elmore, 2016). That is, the verdict of guilty but mentally ill may differ from a guilty verdict in name only.

Some states allow still another kind of defense, *guilty with diminished capacity,* in which a defendant's mental dysfunction is viewed as an extenuating circumstance that the court should take into consideration in determining the precise crime of which he or she is guilty (ABA, 2017; Slovenko, 2011). The defense lawyer argues that because of mental dysfunction, the defendant could not have *intended* to commit a particular crime. The person can then be found guilty of a lesser crime—of manslaughter (unlawful killing without intent), say, instead of murder in the first degree (planned murder).

AP Photo/Douglas D. Pizac

"Effectively misleading psychopath" In 2002 Brian David Mitchell abducted a 14-year-old teenager named Elizabeth Smart at knifepoint from her home and held her until she was rescued nine months later. For seven years following his capture, Mitchell was declared incompetent to stand trial. Finally, in 2010, a federal court judge called him an "effectively misleading psychopath" and scheduled him for trial. Mitchell was found guilty of kidnapping and sentenced to life in prison, despite his not guilty by reason of insanity plea.

American Law Institute test A legal test for insanity that holds people to be insane at the time they committed a crime if, because of a mental disorder, they did not know right from wrong or could not resist an uncontrollable impulse to act.

guilty but mentally ill A verdict stating that defendants are guilty of committing a crime but are also suffering from a mental illness that should be treated during their imprisonment.

Justice served? People held mass protests in San Francisco after Dan White was convicted of voluntary manslaughter rather than premeditated murder in the 1978 killings of Mayor George Moscone and Supervisor Harvey Milk, who was one of the nation's leading gay activists. The verdict highlighted the serious pitfalls of the "diminished capacity" defense and has led to a significant decrease in its use.

Bill Nation

The famous case of Dan White, who shot and killed Mayor George Moscone and City Supervisor Harvey Milk of San Francisco in 1978, illustrates the use of this verdict.

> *Defense attorney Douglas Schmidt argued that a patriotic, civic-minded man like Dan White—high school athlete, decorated war veteran, former fireman, policeman, and city supervisor—could not possibly have committed such an act unless something had snapped inside him. The brutal nature of the two final shots to each man's head only proved that White had lost his wits. White was not fully responsible for his actions because he suffered from "diminished capacity." Although White killed Mayor George Moscone and Supervisor Harvey Milk, he had not planned his actions. On the day of the shootings, White was mentally incapable of planning to kill, or even of wanting to do such a thing.*
>
> *Well known in forensic psychiatry circles, Martin Blinder, professor of law and psychiatry at the University of California's Hastings Law School in San Francisco, brought a good measure of academic prestige to White's defense. White had been, Blinder explained to the jury, "gorging himself on junk food: Twinkies, Coca-Cola. . . . The more he consumed, the worse he'd feel and he'd respond to his ever-growing depression by consuming ever more junk food." Schmidt later asked Blinder if he could elaborate on this. "Perhaps if it were not for the ingestion of this junk food," Blinder responded, "I would suspect that these homicides would not have taken place." From that moment on, Blinder became known as the author of the Twinkie defense. . . .*
>
> *Dan White was convicted only of voluntary manslaughter, and was sentenced to seven years, eight months. (He was released on parole January 6, 1984.) Psychiatric testimony convinced the jury that White did not wish to kill George Moscone or Harvey Milk.*
>
> *The angry crowd that responded to the verdict by marching, shouting, trashing City Hall, and burning police cars was in good part homosexual. Gay supervisor Harvey Milk had worked well for their cause, and his loss was a serious setback for human rights in San Francisco. Yet it was not only members of the gay community who were appalled at the outcome. Most San Franciscans shared their feelings of outrage.*
>
> *(Coleman, 1984, pp. 65–70)*

#FollowUp

Released from prison in 1984, Dan White died by suicide in 1985.

Because of possible miscarriages of justice, many legal experts have argued against the "diminished capacity" defense. A number of states have even eliminated it, including California shortly after the Dan White verdict (Hallevy, 2016; Gado, 2008).

Famous Insanity Defense Cases

Although the plea of not guilty by reason of insanity is used infrequently, some of the most famous cases in history have featured this defense strategy. You have already read about the cases of John Hinckley (see page 581) and Andrea Yates (see page 433). Here are some other famous insanity defense cases:

1977 In Michigan, Francine Hughes poured gasoline around the bed where her husband, Mickey, lay in a drunken stupor. Then she lit a match and set him on fire. At her trial she explained that he had beaten her repeatedly for 14 years and had threatened to kill her if she tried to leave him. The jury found her not guilty by reason of temporary insanity, making her into a symbol for many abused women across the nation.

1978 David "Son of Sam" Berkowitz, a serial killer in New York City, explained that a barking dog had sent him demonic messages to kill. Although two psychiatrists assessed him as psychotic, he was found guilty of his crimes. Long after his trial, he said that he had actually made up the delusions.

1979 Kenneth Bianchi, one of the pair known as the Hillside Strangler, entered a plea of not guilty by reason of insanity but was found guilty along with his cousin of sexually assaulting and murdering women in the Los Angeles area in late 1977 and early 1978. He claimed that he had multiple personalities.

1980 In December, Mark David Chapman murdered John Lennon. Chapman later explained that he had killed the rock music legend because he believed Lennon to be a "sell-out." Pleading not guilty by reason of insanity, he also described hearing the voice of God and compared himself with Moses. Chapman was convicted of murder.

1992 Jeffrey Dahmer, a 31-year-old mass murderer in Milwaukee, was tried for the killings of 15 young men. Dahmer drugged some of his victims, performed crude lobotomies on them, and dismembered their bodies and stored their parts to be eaten. Despite a plea of not guilty by reason of insanity, the jury found him guilty as charged. He was beaten to death by another inmate in 1995.

1994 On June 23, 1993, twenty-four-year-old Lorena Bobbitt cut off her husband's penis with a 12-inch kitchen knife while he slept. During her trial, defense attorneys argued that after years of abuse by John Bobbitt, his wife suffered a brief psychotic episode and was seized by an "irresistible impulse" to cut off his penis after he raped her. In 1994, the jury found her not guilty by reason of temporary insanity. She was committed to a state mental hospital and released a few months later.

2011 In 2002, Brian David Mitchell abducted a 14-year-old teenager named Elizabeth Smart from her home and held her until she was rescued nine months later. After years of trial delays, Mitchell was tried for kidnapping in 2010. He pleaded not guilty by reason of insanity, saying that he was acting out delusions ("revelations from God") when he committed this crime. The jury found him guilty of kidnapping in 2011 and sentenced him to life in prison without parole.

2015 In 2012, James Holmes, a 25-year-old neuroscience doctoral student, entered a cinema in Aurora, Colorado, and opened fire on the moviegoers, killing 12 and wounding 20. In the months after his arrest, Holmes, who had no prior criminal record, tried to kill himself three times. Although Holmes pleaded not guilty by reason of insanity, a jury found him guilty of murder in 2015

Plea Rejected James Holmes sits in a courtroom in Colorado in 2012, a few days after killing 12 moviegoers and wounding 20 in the town of Aurora. In 2015, a jury rejected his plea of not guilty by reason of insanity and instead found him guilty of murder and attempted murder.

and sentenced him to life in prison without parole.

2017 In 2014 two 12-year-old girls stabbed a classmate multiple times, saying they were trying to appease and impress Slender Man, a mythical "boogie man" whom a number of Internet users report seeing and fearing in their everyday lives. In separate 2017 trials, each of the assailants pleaded guilty to attempted intentional homicide, but in each case they were further deemed to have been mentally ill at the time of the attack and were assigned to extended treatment in a mental hospital rather than imprisonment.

AF Photo/Denver Post, RJ Sangosti

WHAT ARE SEX-OFFENDER STATUTES? Since 1937, when Michigan passed the first "sexual psychopath" law, a number of states have placed sex offenders in a special legal category (Sanders, 2016; Perillo et al., 2014). These states believe that some of those who are repeatedly found guilty of sex crimes have a mental disorder, so the states categorize them as *mentally disordered sex offenders.*

mental incompetence A state of mental instability that leaves defendants unable to understand the legal charges and proceedings they are facing and unable to prepare an adequate defense with their attorney.

People classified in this way are convicted of a criminal offense and are thus judged to be responsible for their actions. Nevertheless, mentally disordered sex offenders are sent to a mental health facility instead of a prison. In part, such laws reflect a belief held by many legislators that such sex offenders are psychologically disturbed. On a practical level, the laws help protect sex offenders from the physical abuse that they often receive in prison society.

Over the past two decades, however, most states have been changing or abolishing their mentally disordered sex offender laws, and at this point only a handful still have them. There are several reasons for this trend. First, the state laws often declare that in order to be classified as a mentally disordered sex offender, the person must be a good candidate for treatment, another judgment that is difficult for clinicians to make, especially for this population (Marshall & Marshall, 2016; Marshall et al., 2011). Second, there is evidence that racial bias often affects the use of the mentally disordered sex offender classification. From a defendant's perspective, this classification is considered an attractive alternative to imprisonment—an alternative available to non-Hispanic white Americans much more often than to members of racial and ethnic minority groups. Non-Hispanic white Americans are twice as likely as African Americans or Hispanic Americans who have been convicted of similar crimes to be granted mentally disordered sex offender status.

But perhaps the primary reason that mentally disordered sex offender laws have lost favor is that state legislatures and courts are now less concerned than they used to be about the rights and needs of sex offenders, given the growing number of sex crimes taking place across the country (Feldman, 2017; Sanders, 2016), particularly ones in which children are victims. In fact, in response to public outrage over the high number of sex crimes, 21 states and the federal government have instead passed *sexually violent predator* laws (or *sexually dangerous persons* laws) (MHA, 2017). These relatively new laws call for certain sex offenders who have been convicted of sex crimes and have served their sentence in prison to be removed from prison before their release and committed involuntarily to a mental hospital for treatment if a court judges them likely to engage in further "predatory acts of sexual violence" as a result of "mental abnormality" or "personality disorder" (MHA, 2017; Perillo et al., 2014). That is, in contrast to the mentally disordered sex offender laws, which call for sex offenders to receive treatment *instead* of imprisonment, the sexually violent predator laws require certain sex offenders to receive imprisonment and then, *in addition,* be committed for a period of involuntary treatment. The constitutionality of the sexually violent predator laws was upheld by the Supreme Court in the 1997 case of *Kansas v. Hendricks* by a 5-to-4 margin.

Incompetent to stand trial In 2014, Alton Nolen beheaded a co-worker and tried to behead another at a food plant in Oklahoma. The defendant was ruled incompetent to stand trial until 2017, at which time he pled guilty and requested to receive the death penalty.

AP Photo/Sue Ogrocki

Criminal Commitment and Incompetence to Stand Trial

Regardless of their state of mind at the time of a crime, defendants may be judged to be **mentally incompetent** to stand trial. The competence requirement is meant to ensure that defendants understand the charges they are facing and can work with their lawyers to prepare and conduct an adequate defense (Hallevy, 2017; Reisner et al., 2013). This minimum standard of competence was specified by the Supreme Court in the case of *Dusky v. United States* (1960).

The issue of competence is most often raised by the defendant's attorney, although prosecutors, arresting police officers, and even the judge may raise it as well (Roesch, 2016; Reisner et al., 2013). When the issue of competence is raised, the judge orders a psychological evaluation, usually on an inpatient basis (see **Table 19-1**). As many as 60,000 competency evaluations are conducted in the United States each year (Faubion, 2016; Bartol & Bartol, 2015). Approximately 20 to 25 percent of defendants who receive such an evaluation are found to be incompetent to stand trial. If the court decides that the defendant is incompetent, he or she is typically assigned to a mental health facility until competent to stand trial.

TABLE: 19-1

Race and Forensic Psychology

Racial/Ethnic Minority Individuals	Non-Hispanic White Individuals
• Psychologically disturbed law breakers *more* likely to be sent to prison.	• Psychologically disturbed law breakers *more* likely to be sent to mental health facilities.
• Defendants *more* likely to be judged incompetent to stand trial.	• Defendants *less* likely to be judged incompetent to stand trial.
• Individuals *more* likely to be referred for involuntary commitment evaluations.	• Individuals *less* likely to be referred for involuntary commitment evaluations.
• Individuals *more* likely to be ordered into involuntary mental hospital commitment.	• Individuals *less* likely to be ordered into involuntary mental hospital commitment.
• Individuals *more* likely to be ordered into involuntary outpatient commitment.	• Individuals *less* likely to be ordered into involuntary outpatient commitment.

Information from: APA, 2017; Fraser, 2016; NCBH, 2015; Zaejian, 2014; Swanson et al., 2009; Haroules, 2007; Pinals et al., 2004.

A famous case of incompetence to stand trial is that of Jared Lee Loughner. On January 8, 2011, Loughner went to a political gathering at a shopping center in Tucson, Arizona, and opened fire on 20 persons. Six people were killed and 14 injured, including U.S. representative Gabrielle Giffords. Giffords, the apparent target of the attack, survived, although she was shot in the head. After Loughner underwent five weeks of psychiatric assessment, a judge ruled that he was incompetent to stand trial. It was not until 18 months later, after extended treatment with antipsychotic drugs, that Loughner was ruled competent to stand trial. In November 2012, he pleaded guilty to murder and was sentenced to life imprisonment.

Sometimes, incompetence rulings can continue even longer. In another famous case, a man named Russell Weston entered the U.S. Capitol building in 1998, apparently seeking out then–House Majority Whip Tom DeLay, among others, and shot two police officers to death. In 1999, Weston, who had stopped taking medications for his severe psychosis, was found incompetent to stand trial and sent to a psychiatric institution. In 2001, a judge ruled that he should be forced to take medications again, but even with such drugs Weston continued to have severe symptoms and to this day remains incompetent to stand trial for the 1998 shootings.

Many more cases of criminal commitment result from decisions of mental incompetence than from verdicts of not guilty by reason of insanity (Roesch, 2016; Roesch et al., 2010). However, the majority of criminals currently institutionalized for psychological treatment in the United States are not from either of these two groups. Rather, they are convicted inmates whose psychological problems have led prison officials to decide they need treatment, either in mental health units within the prison or in mental hospitals (Ollove, 2017; Fazel et al., 2016) (see **Figure 19-2**).

It is possible that an innocent defendant, ruled incompetent to stand trial, could spend years in a mental health facility with no opportunity to disprove the criminal accusations against him or her. Some defendants have, in fact, served longer "sentences" in mental health facilities awaiting a ruling of competence than they would have served in prison had they been convicted. Such a possibility was reduced when the Supreme Court ruled, in the case of *Jackson v. Indiana* (1972), that an incompetent defendant

FIGURE 19-2

Prison and Mental Health

According to studies conducted in several Western countries, psychological disorders are much more prevalent in prison populations than in the general population. For example, schizophrenia and personality disorders (particularly antisocial personality disorder) are each four times more common among prisoners than among nonprisoners. (Information from: Fischer & Buchanan, 2017; Krishnan, 2017; NIMH, 2017; SAMHSA, 2017; Bukstein, 2016; Fazel et al., 2016; NSDUH, 2016; Skodol, 2016; Khazan, 2015; Aufderheide, 2014.)

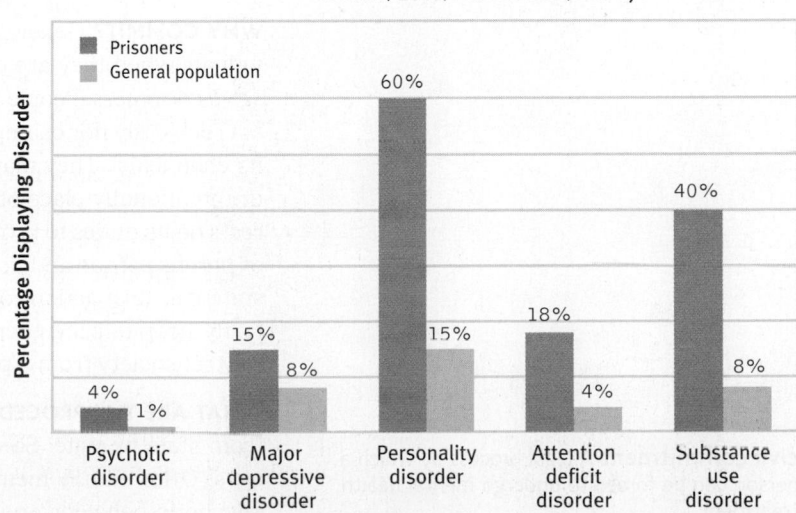

cannot be indefinitely committed. After a reasonable amount of time, he or she should either be found competent and tried, set free, or transferred to a mental health facility under *civil* commitment procedures.

Until the early 1970s, most states required that mentally incompetent defendants be committed to maximum security institutions for the "criminally insane." Under current law, however, the courts have more flexibility. In fact, when the charges are relatively minor, such defendants are often treated on an outpatient basis, an arrangement often called *jail diversion* because the disturbed person is "diverted" from jail to the community for mental health care (Alarid & Rubin, 2016; Becker, 2016).

Brian van der Brug/Los Angeles Times via Getty Images

"The Taser solution" Police often use Tasers—stun guns that affect neuromuscular control and temporarily incapacitate individuals—to subdue people with mental disorders. To help officers appreciate the impact of this weapon, the Los Angeles Police Department has new recruits—such as Officer Vanessa Lopez—receive a Taser charge during training. Mental health advocates view Tasers as an inhumane intervention when dealing with extremely confused or frightened people.

Law in Psychology: How Do the Legislative and Judicial Systems Influence Mental Health Care?

Just as clinical science and practice have influenced the legal system, so the legal system has had a major impact on clinical practice. First, courts and legislatures have developed the process of **civil commitment,** which allows certain people to be forced into mental health treatment. Although many people who show signs of mental disturbance seek treatment voluntarily, a large number are not aware of their problems or are simply not interested in undergoing therapy. For such people, civil commitment procedures may be put into action.

Second, the legal system, on behalf of the state, has taken on the responsibility of protecting patients' rights during treatment. This protection extends not only to patients who have been involuntarily committed but also to those who seek treatment voluntarily, even on an outpatient basis.

Civil Commitment Every year in the United States, large numbers of people with mental disorders are involuntarily committed to treatment. Typically they are committed to *mental institutions,* but 46 states also have some form of *outpatient* civil commitment laws that allow patients to be forced into community treatment programs (TAC, 2017; Miller & Hanson, 2016; Zilber, 2016). Canada and Great Britain have similar laws. Civil commitments have long caused controversy and debate. In some ways the law provides more protection for people suspected of being criminals than for people suspected of being psychotic (Strachan, 2008; Burton, 1990).

WHY COMMIT? Generally our legal system permits involuntary commitment of individuals when they are considered to be *in need of treatment* and *dangerous to themselves or others.* People may be dangerous to themselves if they are suicidal or if they act recklessly (for example, drinking a drain cleaner to prove that they are immune to its chemicals). They may be dangerous to others if they seek to harm them or if they unintentionally place others at risk. The state's authority to commit disturbed people rests on its duties to protect the interests of the individual and of society: the principles of *parens patriae* and *police power.* Under *parens patriae* ("parent of the country"), the state can take action to protect patients from self-harm, including through involuntarily hospitalizing them. Conversely, *police power* allows the state to take steps to protect society from a person who is dangerous.

WHAT ARE THE PROCEDURES FOR CIVIL COMMITMENT? Civil commitment laws vary from state to state. Some basic procedures, however, are common to most of these laws. Often family members begin commitment proceedings. In response to a son's psychotic behavior and repeated assaults on other people, for example, his parents

civil commitment A legal process by which a person can be forced to undergo mental health treatment.

may try to persuade him to seek admission to a mental institution. If the son refuses, the parents may go to court and seek an involuntary commitment order. If the son is a minor, the process is straightforward. The Supreme Court, in the case of *Parham v. J. R.* (1979), has ruled that a hearing is not necessary in such cases, as long as a qualified mental health professional considers commitment necessary. If the son is an adult, however, the process is more involved. The court usually will order a mental examination and allow the person to contest the commitment in court, often represented by a lawyer.

The Supreme Court has ruled that before an individual can be committed, there must be "clear and convincing" proof that he or she is mentally ill and has met the state's criteria for involuntary commitment. The ruling does not suggest what criteria should be used (Hille, 2017). That matter is still left to each state. But, whatever the state's criteria, clinicians must offer clear and convincing proof that the person meets those criteria. When is proof clear and convincing, according to the court? When it provides 75 percent certainty that the criteria of commitment have been met. This is far less than the near-total certainty ("beyond a reasonable doubt") required to convict people of committing a crime.

EMERGENCY COMMITMENT Many situations require immediate action; no one can wait for commitment proceedings when a life is at stake. Consider, for example, an emergency patient who is suicidal or hearing voices demanding hostile actions against others. He or she may need immediate treatment and round-the-clock supervision. If treatment could not be given in such situations without the patient's full consent, the consequences could be tragic.

Therefore, many states give clinicians the right to certify that certain patients need temporary commitment and medication. In past years, these states required certification by two *physicians* (not necessarily psychiatrists in some of the states). Today states may allow certification by other mental health professionals as well. The clinicians must declare that the state of mind of the patients makes them dangerous to themselves or others. By tradition, the certifications are often referred to as *two-physician certificates,* or *2 PCs.* The length of such emergency commitments varies from state to state, but three days is often the limit (Hedman et al., 2016). Should clinicians come to believe that a longer stay is necessary, formal commitment proceedings may be initiated during the period of emergency commitment.

WHO IS DANGEROUS? In the past, people with mental disorders were actually less likely than others to commit violent or dangerous acts. This low rate of violence was apparently related to the fact that so many such people lived in institutions. As a result of deinstitutionalization, however, hundreds of thousands of people with severe disturbances now live in the community, and many of them receive little, if any, treatment. Some are indeed dangerous to themselves or others.

It is important to be clear that, according to research, the vast majority of people with mental disorders (90 percent) are in no way violent or dangerous, and only a small percentage of all violent acts (3 percent) are committed by people with mental disorders (HHS, 2017; Frances, 2016; Beckett, 2014). That said, recent studies do suggest that people with severe mental disorders are somewhat more likely than the general population to perform violent behaviors (Miller & Hanson, 2016; Beckett, 2014). The disorders with the strongest relationships to violence are severe substance use disorder, impulse control disorder, antisocial personality disorder, and psychotic disorders (Bonnet et al., 2017; Moore & Pfaff, 2017; Alniak et al., 2016). Of these, substance use

#BetterInterventions

Many police now receive *Crisis Intervention Team (CIT)* training to help them respond more knowledgeably and effectively when dealing with people who have mental disorders. The police undergo 40 hours of intensive training regarding mental conditions, medications, and community resources, and they develop skills at *verbal de-escalation.* There are now 2,800 CIT programs across the United States—offered in 15 percent of all police jurisdictions (Lucas, 2016).

Failure to predict A school surveillance camera shows Dylan Klebold and Eric Harris in the midst of their killing rampage at Columbine High School in Littleton, Colorado, in 1999. Although the teenagers had built a violent Web site, threatened other students, had problems with the law, and, in the case of one of the boys, received treatment for psychological problems, professionals were not able to predict or prevent their violent behavior.

AFP/Getty Images

Dangerous to oneself The public often thinks that the term "dangerous to oneself" refers exclusively to those who are suicidal. There are, however, other ways that people may pose a danger to themselves, be in need of treatment, and be subject to civil commitment. This sequence of photos shows a man being attacked by a lion at the zoo after he crossed a barbed wire fence to "preach" to two of the animals.

disorder appears to be the single most influential factor. For example, schizophrenia compounded by substance use disorder has a stronger relationship to violence than schizophrenia alone does.

A determination of *dangerousness* is often required for involuntary civil commitment. But can mental health professionals accurately predict who will commit violent acts? Research suggests that psychiatrists and psychologists are wrong more often than right when they make *long-term* predictions of violence (Galán et al., 2018; Miller & Hanson, 2016; Mills et al., 2011). Most often they overestimate the likelihood that a patient will eventually be violent. Their *short-term* predictions—that is, predictions of imminent violence—tend to be more accurate (Fazel et al., 2017; O'Shea & Dickens, 2016). Researchers are now working, with some success, to develop new assessment techniques that use statistical approaches and are more objective in their predictions of dangerousness than are the subjective judgments of clinicians (Fazel et al., 2017; Murray et al., 2016; O'Shea & Dickens, 2016).

> How are people who have been institutionalized viewed and treated by other people in society today?

WHAT ARE THE PROBLEMS WITH CIVIL COMMITMENT? Civil commitment has been criticized on several grounds (Miller & Hanson, 2016; Winick, 2008). First is the difficulty of assessing a person's dangerousness. If judgments of dangerousness are often inaccurate, how can one justify using them to deprive people of liberty? Second, the legal definitions of "mental illness" and "dangerousness" are vague. The terms may be defined so broadly that they could be applied to almost anyone an evaluator views as undesirable. Indeed, many civil libertarians worry about involuntary commitment being used to control people, as is often done in countries ruled by authoritarian governments, where mental hospitals house people with unpopular political views. A third problem is the sometimes questionable therapeutic value of civil commitment. Research suggests that many people committed involuntarily do not respond well to therapy.

On the basis of these and other arguments, some clinicians suggest that involuntary commitment should be abolished (Miller & Hanson, 2016; McSherry & Weller, 2010). Others, however, advocate finding a more systematic way to evaluate dangerousness when decisions are to be made about commitment (Miller & Hanson, 2016; Heilbrun

#HomelessArrests

Many homeless people with severe mental disorders wind up in jail rather than in treatment. Most are charged with such infractions as disorderly conduct, public intoxication, trespassing, not paying for a meal, menacing panhandling, loitering, or "lewd and lascivious behavior" (for example, urinating on a street corner) (Fuller et al., 2017; Treatment Advocacy Center, 2007).

& Erickson, 2007). Some suggest instituting a process of *risk assessment* that would arrive at statements such as, "The patient is believed to have *X* likelihood of being violent to the following people or under the following conditions over *Y* period of time." Proponents argue that this would be a more useful and appropriate way of deciding where and how people with psychological disorders should be treated.

TRENDS IN CIVIL COMMITMENT The flexibility of the involuntary commitment laws probably reached a peak in 1962. That year, in the case of *Robinson v. California,* the Supreme Court ruled that imprisoning people who suffered from substance use disorders might violate the Constitution's ban on cruel and unusual punishment, and it recommended involuntary civil commitment to a mental hospital as a more reasonable action. This ruling encouraged the civil commitment of many kinds of "social deviants," and many such individuals found it difficult to obtain release from the hospitals to which they were committed.

During the late 1960s and early 1970s, reporters, novelists, civil libertarians, and others spoke out against the ease with which so many people were being unjustifiably committed to mental hospitals. As the public became more aware of these issues, state legislatures started to pass stricter standards about involuntary hospital commitment, and, as mentioned earlier, many launched outpatient commitment programs in which courts may order people with severe mental disorders into community treatment (Miller & Hanson, 2016). In turn, rates of involuntary hospital commitment declined, and release rates rose. Fewer people are institutionalized through civil commitment procedures today than in the past.

Protecting Patients' Rights

Over the past two decades, court decisions and state and federal laws have significantly expanded the rights of patients with mental disorders, in particular the *right to treatment* and the *right to refuse treatment* (Miller & Hanson, 2016; OPA, 2016; Lepping & Raveesh, 2014).

HOW IS THE RIGHT TO TREATMENT PROTECTED? When people are committed to mental institutions and do not receive treatment, the institutions become, in effect, prisons for the unconvicted. To many patients in the late 1960s and the 1970s, large state mental institutions were just that, and some patients and their attorneys began to demand that the state honor the patients' **right to treatment.** In the landmark case of *Wyatt v. Stickney,* a suit on behalf of institutionalized patients in Alabama in 1972, a federal court ruled that the state was constitutionally obligated to provide "adequate treatment" to all people who had been committed involuntarily. Because conditions in the state's hospitals were so terrible, the judge laid out goals that state officials had to meet, including more therapists, better living conditions, more privacy, more social interactions and physical exercise, and a more proper use of physical restraint and medication. Other states have since adopted many of these standards.

Another important decision was handed down in 1975 by the Supreme Court in the case of *O'Connor v. Donaldson.* After being held in a Florida mental institution for more than 14 years, Kenneth Donaldson sued for release. Donaldson repeatedly had sought release and had been overruled by the institution's psychiatrists. He argued that he and his fellow patients were receiving poor treatment, were being largely ignored by the staff, and were allowed little personal freedom. The Supreme Court ruled in his favor, fined the hospital's superintendent, and said that such institutions must review patients' cases periodically. The justices also ruled that the state

right to treatment The legal right of patients, particularly those who are involuntarily committed, to receive adequate treatment.

Hospital neglect While some countries increasingly have attended to the rights of patients, including their rights to treatment and to humane treatment conditions, other countries, especially poor ones, have lagged behind. For example, although the government of Indonesia banned *pasung*—the chaining or close-quarter confinement of mentally ill persons—back in 1977, the practice apparently continues today. This scene inside a center for mental patients in Jakarta underscores the point.

Don Bartletti/Los Angeles Times via Getty Images

Prisoners also have a right to treatment
These prisoners, all military veterans, at the San Diego County jail are receiving day-long classes on subjects like anger management and PTSD. Many prisoners in the U.S. have psychological disorders, and the Supreme Court has upheld their right to receive treatment during their incarceration. However, prison systems are often ill-equipped to provide proper care.

#

#NoVote

Thirty-nine states deny or place restrictions on the voting privileges of certain people with mental disorders. The wording in some of the state laws refers to the ineligible individuals as "incompetent," "insane," "incapacitated," "idiot," "lunatic," and of "unsound mind" (Bazelon Center, 2016, 2008).

cannot continue to institutionalize people against their will if they are not dangerous and are capable of surviving on their own or with the willing help of responsible family members or friends.

To help protect the rights of patients, Congress passed the Protection and Advocacy for Mentally Ill Individuals Act in 1986. This law set up *protection and advocacy systems* in all states and U.S. territories and gave public advocates who worked for patients the power to investigate possible abuse and neglect and to correct those problems legally.

In more recent years, public advocates have argued that the right to treatment also should be extended to the tens of thousands of people with severe mental disorders who are repeatedly released from hospitals into communities ill-equipped to care for them. Many such people have no place to go and are unable to care for themselves, often winding up homeless or in prisons (Allison et al., 2017; MIP, 2017). A number of advocates are now suing federal and state agencies throughout the country, demanding that they fulfill the promises of the community mental health movement (see Chapter 15).

HOW IS THE RIGHT TO REFUSE TREATMENT PROTECTED? During the past two decades, the courts have also decided that patients, particularly those in institutions, have the **right to refuse treatment.** The courts have been reluctant to make a single general ruling on this right because there are so many different kinds of treatment, and a general ruling based on one of them might have unintended effects. Therefore, rulings usually target one specific treatment at a time.

Most of the right-to-refuse-treatment rulings center on *biological treatments*. These treatments are easier to impose on patients without their cooperation than psychotherapy, and they often are more hazardous. For example, state rulings have consistently granted patients the right to refuse *psychosurgery*, the most irreversible form of physical treatment—and often the most dangerous.

Some states have also acknowledged a patient's right to refuse *electroconvulsive therapy (ECT)*, the treatment used in many cases of severe depression (see Chapter 8). However, the right-to-refuse issue is more complex with regard to ECT than to psychosurgery. ECT is very effective for many people with severe depression, but it can cause great upset and can also be misused. Today many states grant patients—particularly voluntary patients—the right to refuse ECT (Miller & Hanson, 2016; OPA, 2016). Usually a patient must be informed fully about the nature of the treatment and must give written consent to it. A number of states continue to permit ECT to be forced on committed patients, whereas others require the consent of a close relative or other third party in such cases.

In the past, patients did not have the right to refuse *psychotropic medications*. As you have read, however, many psychotropic drugs are very powerful, and some produce effects that are unwanted and dangerous. As these harmful effects have become more apparent, some states have granted patients the right to refuse medication (Dunlop & Pinals, 2016; OPA, 2016). Typically, these states require physicians to explain the purpose of the medication to patients and obtain their written consent. If a patient's refusal is considered incompetent, dangerous, or irrational, the state may allow it to be overturned by an independent psychiatrist, medical committee, or local court. However, the refusing patient is supported in this process by a lawyer or other patient advocate (OPA, 2016).

WHAT OTHER RIGHTS DO PATIENTS HAVE? Court decisions have protected still other patient rights over the past several decades. Patients who perform work in mental institutions, particularly private institutions, are now guaranteed at least a *minimum wage*. In addition, according to a court decision, patients released from state mental hospitals have a right to *aftercare* and to an *appropriate community residence*, such as a group home. And, more generally, people with psychological disorders should receive treatment in the *least restrictive facility* available. If an inpatient program at a community mental health center is available and appropriate, for example, then that is the facility to which they should be assigned, not a mental hospital.

THE "RIGHTS" DEBATE Certainly, people with psychological disorders have civil rights that must be protected at all times. However, many clinicians express concern that the patients' rights rulings and laws may unintentionally deprive these patients of opportunities for recovery. Consider the right to refuse medication. If medications can help a patient with a severe mental disorder to recover, doesn't the patient have the right to that recovery? If confusion causes the patient to refuse medication, can clinicians in good conscience delay medication while legal channels are being cleared?

Despite such legitimate concerns, keep in mind that the clinical field has not always done an effective job of protecting patients' rights. Over the years, many patients have been overmedicated and received improper treatments. Furthermore, one must ask whether the field's present state of knowledge justifies clinicians' overriding of patients' rights. Can clinicians confidently say that a given treatment will help a patient? Can they predict when a treatment will have harmful effects? Since clinicians themselves often disagree, it seems appropriate for patients, their advocates, and outside evaluators to also play key roles in decision making.

Executing the mentally ill Charles Singleton, a man who killed a store clerk in Arkansas, was sentenced to death in 1979, and then developed schizophrenia at some point after the trial. Since the United States does not allow executions if persons cannot understand why they are being executed, state officials wanted Singleton to take medications to clear up his psychosis. Eventually, Singleton chose to take medications voluntarily, showed psychological improvement, and was executed by lethal injection in 2004. The U.S. Supreme Court has never ruled on whether states have the right to force a "death row" inmate to receive treatment.

In What Other Ways Do the Clinical and Legal Fields Interact?

Mental health and legal professionals may influence each other's work in other ways as well. During the past 25 years, their paths have crossed in four key areas: *malpractice suits, professional boundaries, jury consultation,* and *psychological research of legal topics.*

Malpractice Suits The number of **malpractice suits** against therapists has risen sharply in recent years. Claims have been made against clinicians in response to a patient's attempted suicide, sexual activity with a patient, failure to obtain informed consent for a treatment, negligent drug therapy, omission of drug therapy that would speed improvement, improper termination of treatment, and wrongful commitment (Pope & Vasquez, 2016; Sher, 2015; Reich & Schatzberg, 2014). Studies suggest that malpractice suits, or the fear of them, can have significant effects on clinical decisions and practice, for better or for worse (Appelbaum, 2011).

Professional Boundaries Over the past 25 years, the legislative and judicial systems have helped change the *boundaries* that distinguish one clinical profession from another. In particular, they have given more authority to psychologists and blurred the lines that once separated psychiatry from psychology. A growing number of states, for example, are ruling that psychologists can admit patients to the state's hospitals, a power previously held only by psychiatrists.

In 1991, with the blessing of Congress, the Department of Defense (DOD) started to reconsider the biggest difference of all between the practices of psychiatrists and psychologists—the authority to prescribe drugs, a role previously denied to psychologists. The DOD set up a trial training program for Army psychologists. Given the apparent success of this trial program, the American Psychological Association later recommended that all psychologists be allowed to pursue extensive educational and

right to refuse treatment The legal right of patients to refuse certain forms of treatment.

malpractice suit A lawsuit charging a therapist with improper conduct in the course of treatment.

training programs in prescription services and receive certification to prescribe medications if they pass. New Mexico, Louisiana, Illinois, Iowa, Idaho, and the U.S. territory of Guam now do grant prescription privileges to psychologists who receive special pharmacology training (APA, 2017).

> Most psychiatrists oppose the idea of prescription rights for psychologists. Why do some psychologists also oppose this idea?

As the action by the American Psychological Association suggests, the legislative and judicial systems do not simply take it upon themselves to interfere in the affairs of clinical professionals. Professional associations of psychologists, psychiatrists, and social workers actually lobby in state legislatures across the country for laws and decisions that may increase the authority of their members, a further demonstration of the way the mental health system interacts with other sectors of our society.

Jury Consultation During the past 30 years, more and more lawyers have turned to clinicians for psychological advice in conducting trials (Gomez, 2016; Crouter, 2015). A new breed of clinical specialists, known as "jury specialists," has evolved. They advise lawyers about which potential jurors are likely to favor their side and which strategies are likely to win jurors' support during trials. The jury specialists make their suggestions on the basis of surveys, interviews, analyses of jurors' backgrounds and attitudes, and laboratory simulations of upcoming trials. However, it is not clear that a clinician's advice is more valid than a lawyer's instincts or that the judgments of either are particularly accurate.

Psychological Research of Legal Topics Psychologists have sometimes conducted studies and developed expertise on topics of great importance to the criminal justice system. In turn, these studies influence how the system carries out its work. Psychological investigations of two topics, *eyewitness testimony* and *patterns of criminality,* have gained particular attention.

Chuck Burton/AP Photo

Eyewitness error Psychological research indicates that eyewitness testimony is often invalid. Here a woman talks to the man whom she had identified as her rapist back in 1984. DNA testing eventually proved that a different person had raped her, and the incorrectly identified man was released. In the meantime, however, he had served 11 years of a life sentence in prison.

EYEWITNESS TESTIMONY In criminal cases, testimony by eyewitnesses is extremely influential. It often determines whether a defendant will be found guilty or not guilty. But how accurate is eyewitness testimony? This question has become urgent, as a troubling number of prisoners (many on death row) have had their convictions overturned after DNA evidence revealed that they could not have committed the crimes of which they had been convicted. It turns out that more than 70 percent of such wrongful convictions were based in large part on mistaken eyewitness testimony (Innocence Project, 2017; Wise et al., 2014).

Most eyewitnesses undoubtedly try to tell the truth about what or who they saw. Yet research indicates that eyewitness testimony can be highly unreliable, partly because eyewitnesses sometimes hold subtle biases and partly because most crimes are unexpected and fleeting and therefore not the sort of events remembered well (Carpenter & Krendl, 2016; Houston et al., 2013). During the crime, for example, lighting may be poor or other distractions may be present. Witnesses may have had other things on their minds, such as concern for their own safety or that of bystanders. Such concerns may greatly impair later memory.

In laboratory studies, researchers have found it easy to fool participants who are trying to recall the details of an observed event simply by introducing misinformation (Loftus, 2017; Rindall et al., 2017; Morgan et al., 2013). After a suggestive description by the researcher, stop signs can be transformed into yield signs, white cars into blue ones, and Mickey Mouse into Minnie Mouse. In addition, laboratory studies indicate that persons who are highly suggestible have the poorest recall of observed events (Liebman et al., 2002).

As for identifying actual perpetrators, research has found that accuracy is heavily influenced by the method used in identification (Wixted & Wells, 2017; Bartol & Bartol, 2015). For example, police lineups, particularly ones conducted poorly, are not always reliable, and the errors that witnesses make when looking at lineups tend to stick (Miura & Itoh, 2016; Wixted et al., 2016; Wells et al., 2015, 2011). Researchers have also learned that the confidence of witnesses is not consistently related to accuracy (Wixted & Wells, 2017; Wise et al., 2014). Witnesses who are "absolutely certain" may be no more correct in their recollections than those who are only "fairly sure." Yet the degree of a witness's confidence often influences whether jurors believe his or her testimony (Loftus & Greenspan, 2017).

Psychological investigations into the memories of eyewitnesses have not yet undone the judicial system's reliance on or respect for those witnesses' testimony. Nor should it. The distance between laboratory studies and real-life events is often great, and the findings from such studies must be applied with care. Still, eyewitness research has begun to make an impact. Instructions to jurors about the accuracy of eyewitness confidence may now be included in eyewitness cases (Cash & Lane, 2017; Safer et al., 2016). In addition, studies of hypnosis and of its ability to create false memories have led most states to prohibit eyewitnesses from testifying about events or details if their recall of the events was initially helped by hypnosis.

PATTERNS OF CRIMINALITY A growing number of television shows, movies, and books suggest that clinicians often play a major role in criminal investigations by providing police with *psychological profiles* of perpetrators—"He's probably white, in his thirties, has a history of animal torture, has few friends, and is subject to emotional outbursts." The study of criminal behavior patterns and of profiling has increased in recent decades; however, it is not nearly as revealing or influential as the media and the arts would have us believe (Kapardis, 2017; Kocsis & Palermo, 2016, 2013).

On the positive side, researchers have gathered information about the psychological features of various criminals, and they have indeed found that perpetrators of particular kinds of crimes—serial murder or serial sexual assault, for example—frequently share a number of traits and background features (see **PsychWatch** on page 596). But while such traits are *often* present, they are not *always* present, and so applying profile information to a particular crime can be wrong and misleading (Kapardis, 2017). Increasingly, police are consulting psychological profilers, and this

#TVProfilers

Criminal Minds (current)

Mindhunter (current)

Luther (current)

Law and Order: SVU (current)

The Mentalist (recent)

Psych (recent)

Misleading profile Police search for clues outside a Home Depot in Virginia in 2002, hoping to identify and capture the serial sniper who killed 10 people and terrorized residents throughout Washington, DC, Maryland, and Virginia. As it turned out, psychological profiling in this famous case offered little help and even misled the police.

AP Photo/Doug Mills

Serial Murderers: Madness or Badness?

Over the course of a decade, between 2003 and 2014, an eccentric history buff named Charles Severance killed three individuals in Alexandria, Virginia. Severance shot the victims—people he had never met—in their homes, simply because they were relatively affluent. In his private journals, the murderer had repeatedly expressed a desire to kill the local elite—members of the ruling class, as he put it. He was convicted of these crimes and sentenced to life in prison in 2016, joining a growing list of serial killers who have fascinated and horrified the public over the years: Bruce Ivins ("anthrax killer"), Theodore Kaczynski ("Unabomber"), Ted Bundy, David Berkowitz ("Son of Sam"), Albert DeSalvo ("Boston Strangler"), John Wayne Gacy ("Killer Clown"), Jeffrey Dahmer ("Milwaukee Cannibal"), Dennis Rader ("BTK killer"), and more.

By definition, serial killers commit a series of murders (3 or more) in separate incidents over an extended period of time. They are different from mass killers, whom you read about in Chapter 16—individuals who murder four or more people at a single time, usually in a single location (see page 484).

The FBI estimates that there are between 25 and 50 serial killers at large in the United States at any given time (FBI, 2017, 2014). Worldwide, 4,500 such killers have been identified since the year 1900 (Aamodt, 2016, 2014).

Each serial killer follows his or her own pattern, but many of them appear to have certain characteristics in common (FBI,

Serial sentences for serial murders Serial murderer Charles Severance, who killed three affluent people over the course of a decade, is watched closely by court deputies during his trial. In 2016, Severance was found guilty for his serial killings and sentenced to three consecutive life sentences.

Bill O'Leary/The Washington Post via Getty Images

2017, 2014; Johnston, 2017; Becker, 2016). The majority—but certainly not all—are non-Hispanic white males between 30 and 45 years old, of average to high intelligence, seemingly clean-cut, smooth-talking, attractive, and skillful manipulators.

Close to half of serial killers seem to have severe personality disorders (FBI, 2017, 2014; Becker, 2016; Hickey, 2015). Lack of conscience and an utter disregard for people and the rules of society—key features of antisocial personality disorder—are typical. Narcissistic thinking is quite common as well. Feelings of being special may even give the killers an unrealistic belief that they will not get caught (Kocsis, 2008; Wright et al., 2006). Often it is this sense of invincibility that leads to their capture.

Sexual dysfunctions, paraphilic disorders, and fantasies also seem to play a part (FBI, 2017, 2014; Becker, 2016). Studies have

found that vivid fantasies, often sexual and sadistic, may help drive the killer's behavior. Some clinicians also believe that the killers may be trying to overcome general feelings of powerlessness by controlling, hurting, or eliminating those who are momentarily weaker. A number of the killers were abused as children—physically, sexually, and/or emotionally.

Law enforcement agencies and behavioral researchers have gathered an impressive body of statistical information about serial killings and killers in recent years. This data is often of help to criminal investigators as they seek to capture these repeat perpetrators of particularly heinous acts. At the same time, it would be inaccurate to say that clinical theorists understand why serial killers behave as they do.

practice appears to be helpful as long as the limitations of profiling are recognized (Kocsis & Palermo, 2016, 2013).

A reminder of the limitations of profiling comes from the case of the snipers who terrorized the Washington, DC, area for three weeks in October 2002, shooting 10 people dead and seriously wounding 3 others. Most of the profiling done by FBI psychologists had suggested that the sniper was acting alone; it turned out that the attacks were conducted by a pair: a middle-aged man, John Allen Muhammad, and a teenage boy, Lee Boyd Malvo. Although profiles had suggested a young thrill-seeker, Muhammad was 41. Profilers had believed the attacker to be non-Hispanic white but neither Muhammad nor Malvo was white. The prediction of a *male* attacker was correct, but then again female serial killers are relatively rare.

What Ethical Principles Guide Mental Health Professionals?

DISCUSSIONS OF THE LEGAL AND mental health systems may sometimes give the impression that clinicians as a group are uncaring and are considerate of patients' rights and needs only when they are forced to be. This, of course, is not true. Most clinicians care greatly about their clients and strive to help them while at the same time respecting their rights and dignity (Pope & Vasquez, 2016, 2011). In fact, clinicians do not rely exclusively on the legislative and court systems to ensure proper and effective clinical practice. They also regulate themselves by continually developing and revising ethical guidelines for their work and behavior. Many legal decisions do nothing more than place the power of the law behind these already existing professional guidelines.

Each profession within the mental health field has its own **code of ethics.** The code of the American Psychological Association (2017, 2010, 2002) is typical. This code, highly respected by other mental health professionals and public officials, includes specific guidelines:

1. **Psychologists are permitted to offer advice** in self-help books, on DVDs, on television and radio programs, in newspapers and magazines, through mailed material, and in other places, provided they do so responsibly and professionally and base their advice on appropriate psychological literature and practices. Psychologists are bound by these same ethical requirements when they offer advice and ideas online, whether on individual Web pages, blogs, bulletin boards, or chat rooms. Internet-based professional advice has proved difficult to regulate, however, because the number of such offerings keeps getting larger and larger and so many advice-givers do not appear to have any professional training or credentials.

2. **Psychologists may not conduct fraudulent research, plagiarize the work of others, or publish false data.** During the past 30 years cases of scientific fraud or misconduct have been discovered in all of the sciences, including psychology. These acts have led to misunderstandings of important issues, taken scientific research in the wrong direction, and damaged public trust. Unfortunately, the impressions created by false findings may continue to influence the thinking of both the public and other scientists for years.

3. **Psychologists must acknowledge their limitations** with regard to patients who are disabled or whose gender, ethnicity, language, socioeconomic status, or sexual orientation differs from that of the therapist. This guideline often requires psychotherapists to obtain additional training or supervision, consult with more knowledgeable colleagues, or refer clients to more appropriate professionals.

4. **Psychologists who make evaluations and testify in legal cases must base their assessments on sufficient information and substantiate their findings appropriately.** If an adequate examination of the individual in question is not possible, psychologists must make clear the limited nature of their testimony.

5. **Psychologists may not participate or assist in torture—acts in which severe pain, suffering, or degradation is intentionally inflicted on people.** This guideline was added to the code of ethics in 2017, a year after an APA-sponsored report revealed that, over a period of several years, the APA had aided and advised the Department of Defense and the Central Intelligence Agency in the

code of ethics A body of principles and rules for ethical behavior, designed to guide decisions and actions by members of a profession.

Barry Brecheisen/Getty Images

The ethics of giving professional advice Today's psychologists are bound by the field's ethics code to base their advice on psychological theories and findings. In 2006, the enormously popular Phil McGraw ("Dr. Phil") surrendered his Texas psychologist license so that he could be free to use his own best judgment when giving advice on television and in books.

confidentiality The principle that certain professionals will not divulge the information they obtain from a client.

duty to protect The principle that therapists must break confidentiality in order to protect a person who may be the intended victim of a client.

development of "enhanced interrogation" techniques (that is, torture-based questioning) and had adjusted professional guidelines to allow psychologist involvement in such interrogations (see *Trending*).

6. **Psychologists may not take advantage of clients and students, sexually or otherwise.** This guideline relates to the widespread social problem of sexual harassment, as well as the problem of therapists who take sexual advantage of clients in therapy. The code specifically forbids a sexual relationship with a present or former therapy client for at least two years after the end of treatment—and even then such a relationship is permitted only in "the most unusual circumstances." Furthermore, psychologists may not accept as clients people with whom they have previously had a sexual relationship.

Research has clarified that clients may suffer great emotional damage from sexual involvement with their therapists (Pope & Vasquez, 2016, 2011; Pope & Wedding, 2014). How many therapists actually have a sexual relationship with a client? On the basis of various surveys, reviewers have estimated that 4 to 5 percent of today's therapists engage in some form of sexual misconduct with patients, down from 10 percent more than a decade ago.

Although the vast majority of therapists do not engage in sexual behavior of any kind with clients, their ability to control private feelings is apparently another matter. In surveys, more than 80 percent of therapists reported having been sexually attracted to a client, at least on occasion (Pope & Vasquez, 2016, 2011; Pope & Wedding, 2014). Although few of these therapists acted on their feelings, most of them felt guilty, anxious, or concerned about the attraction. Given such issues, it is not surprising that sexual ethics training is given high priority in many of today's clinical training programs.

7. **Psychologists must adhere to the principle of confidentiality.** All of the state and federal courts have upheld laws protecting therapist **confidentiality** (Fisher, 2016, 2013). For peace of mind and to ensure effective therapy, clients must be able to trust that their private exchanges with a therapist will not be repeated to others (Skodol & Bender, 2016). There are times, however, when the principle of confidentiality must be compromised (Middleman & Olson, 2017; Pope & Vasquez, 2016, 2011). A therapist in training, for example, must discuss cases on a regular basis with a supervisor, and clients must be informed that such discussions are taking place.

A second exception arises in cases of outpatients who are clearly dangerous. The 1976 case of *Tarasoff v. Regents of the University of California*, one of the most important cases to affect client–therapist relationships, concerned an outpatient at a University of California hospital. He had confided to his therapist that he wanted to harm his former girlfriend, Tanya Tarasoff. Several days after ending therapy, the former patient fulfilled his promise. He stabbed Tanya Tarasoff to death.

Should confidentiality have been broken in this case? The therapist, in fact, felt that it should. Campus police were notified, but the patient was released after some questioning. In their suit against the hospital and therapist, the victim's parents argued that the therapist should have also warned them and their daughter that the patient intended to harm Ms. Tarasoff. The California Supreme Court agreed: "The protective privilege ends where the public peril begins."

The current code of ethics for psychologists thus declares that therapists have a **duty to protect**—a responsibility to break confidentiality, even without the client's consent, when it is necessary "to protect the client or others from harm." Since the *Tarasoff* ruling, most states have adopted the California court rulings or similar ones, and a number have passed "duty to protect" bills that clarify the rules of confidentiality for therapists and protect them from certain

#LegalKnowledge

75%   Percentage of psychologists who are misinformed about their legal responsibilities regarding potentially dangerous clients.

90%   Percentage of same psychologists who feel confident that their legal knowledge in this realm is accurate.

(Information from: Thomas, 2014)

Doctor, Do No Harm

The Hippocratic Oath requires that doctors, first and foremost, "do no harm"—a principle also embraced by the code of ethics for each mental health profession. However, recent developments suggest that in the realm of torture, some psychologists have indeed done harm to individuals.

A 2014 book entitled *Pay Any Price,* a 2015 Senate Select Committee investigation, a 2015 report called the Hoffman Report, and a 2017 lawsuit have collectively indicated that certain psychologists and, indeed, the American Psychological Association (APA), participated for several years in the Central Intelligence Agency's program of *enhanced interrogation,* or *torture-based questioning,* to obtain information from suspected terrorists (APA, 2017; Bailey, 2017; Fink & Risen, 2017; Melechi, 2016; Patel & Elkin, 2015). Here are key events revealed by these sources:

1. In 2002, shortly after the September 11, 2001 terrorist attacks in New York City and Washington, DC, the White House gave approval to a CIA program of "enhanced interrogation" of national security prisoners, or "detainees." In a series of so-called torture memos, it stated that enhanced interrogations could indeed proceed if consulting mental health experts indicated the procedures were not causing or likely to cause significant physical injury or severe mental distress.

2. Later in 2002, two psychologists, commissioned by the CIA, developed a package of enhanced interrogation procedures (including sleep deprivation, repeated waterboarding, physical assault, binding in stressful positions, deafening noise, and imprisonment in a box), and the CIA tested those procedures on a prisoner with possible ties to the terrorist organization Al Qaeda. Officials declared the test a success and, from that point forward, enhanced interrogations became an accepted national security policy. The two psychologists continued to serve as major advisers for the CIA program.

3. In order for the enhanced interrogation program to proceed, the CIA needed a number of psychologists to observe the interrogations and declare them acceptable, as well as ongoing advice and input from

No place for psychologists Protestors at an APA conference rally against psychologist involvement in CIA enhanced interrogation programs.

various psychologists to further develop the program. As a result, the CIA and key administrators at the APA developed a cooperative relationship that continued for several years. Although the APA did not participate in the actual administration of torture procedures, some of its administrators did have a series of communications, discussions, and brainstorming sessions with the CIA about the enhanced interrogation program and the possible role of psychologists.

4. Perhaps most damning, certain APA administrators manipulated the language of the organization's code of ethics, apparently to allow individual psychologists to participate in the enhanced interrogation program without fear of professional wrongdoing or reprisal. After all, psychologists could not work with the program if that meant they were violating their profession's ethical standards. This concern disappeared in 2005 when the APA's "Presidential Task Force on Ethics and National Security" (PENS) ruled, in subtle language, that psy-

chologists are not violating their "do no harm" obligation if they do not break any laws in their work, including possible work in the realm of enhanced interrogations. That is, even if their enhanced interrogation involvement contributed to the development of PTSD, anxiety disorders, depression, or the like, the psychologists would not be violating their profession's ethical principles.

5. Although many members of the APA did not recognize that the subtly worded PENS ruling allowed psychologists to participate in the CIA torture-based program, some did appreciate this important implication. In the ensuing years, as the relationship between certain APA officials and the CIA continued and while the APA continued to deny the organization's involvement in or endorsement of the torture-based program, these astute APA members and a number of colleagues vociferously protested the APA's likely involvement with the CIA.

All this came to a head in 2014, when the stunning developments mentioned earlier began to unfold in quick succession. Since those revelations, several key APA administrators have resigned, apparently because of their roles in the enhanced interrogation discussions and decisions. (In 2017, those former administrators sued the authors of the Hoffman report for incorrectly characterizing their actions and for defaming them.) Also in 2017, the two psychologists who initiated and implemented the CIA's enhanced interrogation program beginning back in 2002 reached a court settlement with three tortured national security prisoners who had sued them.

Finally, the APA, with its members now fully informed about what had unfolded, sought to end this ugly episode and to ensure that it would not occur again. Most importantly, the entire APA membership voted to bar psychologists from direct and indirect involvement in any national security interrogations—both enhanced and noncoercive. In so doing, it was reaffirming that, even in a complex and dangerous world, a primary obligation of psychologists is to "do no harm" of any kind to individuals.

employee assistance program A mental health program offered by a business to its employees.

stress-reduction and problem-solving program A workshop or series of group sessions offered by a business, in which mental health professionals teach employees how to cope with and solve problems and reduce stress.

managed care program An insurance program in which the insurance company decides the cost, method, provider, and length of treatment.

civil suits (Middleman & Olson, 2017; Knoll, 2015). Many such bills further rule that therapists must also protect people who are close to a client's intended victim and thus in danger. A child, for example, is likely to be at risk when a client plans to assault the child's mother.

Mental Health, Business, and Economics

THE LEGISLATIVE AND JUDICIAL SYSTEMS are not the only social institutions with which mental health professionals interact. *Business* and *economic* fields are two other sectors that influence and are influenced by clinical practice and study.

Bringing Mental Health Services to the Workplace

According to numerous surveys, work is by far the leading source of stress for people (AIS, 2017). Over 40 percent of workers find their jobs very stressful and believe them to be bad for their mental health and general health (AIS, 2017, Harvard School of Public Health, 2016; Pazzanese, 2016). Stressed-out workers report that the primary causes of their upsets are excessive workload (46 percent of workers), people and personnel issues (28 percent), difficulties balancing work with home life (20 percent), and lack of job security (6 percent) (AIS, 2017).

All this stress not only affects the home life and personal functioning of employees. It also impairs performance and productivity in the workplace. Stress and mental health problems are the third leading cause of work absences, behind minor sicknesses and back and neck pain (ONS, 2017). Keeping in mind that job stress often contributes to medical problems such as high blood pressure and cardiovascular issues, 60 percent of absences from work can be traced, directly or indirectly, to stress and related mental health issues (AIS, 2017; Harvard School of Public Health, 2016). Altogether, it is estimated that businesses in the United States lose $30 billion to lost work days and $12 billion to extra health care expenses (Harvard School of Public Health, 2016; Pazzanese, 2016; White, 2015). Furthermore, studies find that stress at work contributes to poorer productivity and more accidents, employee mistakes, employee departures, insurance costs, and worker compensation expenses (AIS, 2017; White, 2015).

For both humane and financial reasons, many employers try to address the work-related stress and other mental health needs of their employees. Two common approaches, provided by about half of employers, are *employee assistance programs* and *stress reduction programs* (Harvard School of Public Health, 2016; Richmond et al., 2016; Waehrer et al., 2016). **Employee assistance programs** are mental health services made available by a place of business. They are run either by mental health professionals who work directly for a company or by outside mental health agencies. **Stress-reduction and problem-solving programs** are workshops or group sessions in which mental health professionals teach employees techniques for coping, solving problems, and handling and reducing stress. As you read in Chapter 3, one of today's most common such techniques is *mindfulness training*, offered by around one-third of employers (see pages 65–66). Stress-reduction programs are just as likely to be aimed at high-level executives as at assembly-line workers. Often employees are required to attend such programs, and they are given time off from their jobs to do so. Businesses believe that employee assistance and stress reduction programs save them money in the long run by preventing psychological problems from interfering with work performance and by reducing employee insurance claims, a notion that

"My life has become a tangled web of fictitious user names and fiendishly clever passwords."

William Haefeli The New Yorker Collection/The Cartoon Bank

has been supported in various studies (Richmond et al., 2016; Waehrer et al., 2016). And, for their part, at least half of workers agree that they need help learning how to manage stress (AIS, 2017).

The Economics of Mental Health

You have already seen how economic decisions by the government may influence the clinical field's treatment of people with severe mental disorders. For example, the desire of the state and federal governments to reduce costs was an important consideration in the country's deinstitutionalization movement, which contributed to the premature release of hospital patients into the community. Economic decisions by government agencies may affect other kinds of clients and treatment programs as well.

As you read in Chapter 15, government funding for services to people with psychological disorders has risen sharply over the past five decades, from $1 billion in 1963 to around $152 billion today (SAMHSA, 2017, 2014). Around 28 percent of that money is spent on prescription drugs, but much of the rest is targeted for income support, housing subsidies, and other such expenses rather than direct mental health services. The result is that government funding for mental health services is, in fact, insufficient. People with severe mental disorders are hit hardest by the funding shortage. The number of people on waiting lists for community-based services grew from 200,000 in 2002 to 393,000 in 2008, and that number has increased still more over the past decade, according to individual state reports (Morris, 2017; NCBH, 2017; Daly, 2010).

Government funding currently covers 63 percent of all mental health services, leaving a mental health expense of tens of billions of dollars for individual patients and their private insurance companies (SAMHSA, 2017, 2014). This large economic role of private insurance companies has had a significant effect on the way clinicians go about their work. As you'll remember from Chapter 1, to reduce their expenses, most of these companies have developed **managed care programs,** in which the insurance company determines which therapists clients may choose from, the cost of sessions, and the number of sessions for which a

> **What are the costs to clients and practitioners when insurance companies make decisions about the methods, frequency, and duration of treatment?**

AP Photo/Gerry Eroome

Caught in an economic spiral Group home residents and mental health advocates rally at the legislative office building in Raleigh, North Carolina, to protest a Medicaid payment law change. This change could result in residents with severe mental disorders losing their group homes and having nowhere to live.

#MoneyMatters

Psychiatrists Nix Insurance Payments

55% Percentage of psychiatrists willing to accept insurance payments.

93% Percentage of all other kinds of physicians who accept insurance payments.

43% Percentage of psychiatrists willing to accept Medicaid, insurance for low-income people.

75% Percentage of all other kinds of physicians who accept Medicaid.

(Information from: Pettypiece, 2015; Pear, 2013)

client may be reimbursed (Bowers et al., 2016). These and other insurance plans may also control expenses through the use of **peer review systems,** in which clinicians who work for the insurance company periodically review a client's treatment program and recommend that insurance benefits be either continued or stopped. Typically, insurers require reports or session notes from the therapist, often including intimate personal information about the patient.

As you also read in Chapter 1, many therapists and clients dislike managed care programs and peer reviews (Decker, 2016; Lustig et al., 2013). They believe that the reports required of therapists breach confidentiality, even when efforts are made to protect anonymity, and that the importance of therapy in a given case is sometimes difficult to convey in a brief report. They also argue that the priorities of managed care programs inevitably shorten therapy, even if longer-term treatment would be advisable in particular cases. The priorities may also favor treatments that offer short-term results (for example, drug therapy) over more costly approaches that might yield more promising long-term improvement (Bowers et al., 2016). As in the medical field, there are disturbing stories about patients who are prematurely cut off from mental health services by their managed care programs. In short, many clinicians fear that the current system amounts to regulation of therapy by insurance companies rather than by therapists.

Yet another major problem with insurance coverage in the United States—whether managed care or other kinds of insurance programs—is that reimbursements for mental disorders are, on average, lower than those for physical disorders, placing people with psychological difficulties at a significant disadvantage (McGuire, 2016; Sipe et al., 2015). As you have read, the federal government tried to address this problem from 2008 through 2016 (see pages 16–18). In 2008 Congress passed a *parity* law that mandated equal insurance coverage for mental and physical problems, and in 2014 the mental health provisions of the Affordable Care Act ("Obamacare") expanded the reach of the earlier bill. If, however, efforts in Congress to change or repeal the Affordable Care Act eventually succeed, it is possible that the federal mandates for parity in mental health insurance coverage will, likewise, be discontinued.

Technology and Mental Health

AS YOU HAVE SEEN THROUGHOUT this book, today's ever-changing technology has had significant effects—both positive and negative—on the mental health field, and it will undoubtedly affect the field even more in the coming years.

Our digital world provides new *triggers* for the expression of abnormal behavior. The maladaptive functioning of many persons with gambling disorder, for example, has been exacerbated by the ready availability of Internet gambling (see page 379). Similarly, the Internet, texting, and social networking are now used frequently by those who wish to stalk or bully others, express sexual exhibitionism, pursue pedophilic desires, or satisfy other paraphilic disorders (see pages 403, 515). And, in the opinion of many clinicians, constant texting, tweeting, and Internet browsing may help shorten people's attention spans and establish a foundation for attention problems.

Beyond providing new triggers for abnormal behavior, research indicates that today's technology also is helping to produce *new* psychological disorders. As you read in Chapter 12, one such pattern is *Internet use disorder,* a problem marked by excessive and dysfunctional levels of texting, tweeting, networking, Internet browsing, e-mailing, blogging, online shopping, or online pornographic use (McNicol & Thorsteinsson, 2017) (see page 380). The framers of DSM-5 have suggested that this disorder be considered for possible inclusion in future revisions of the DSM. Similarly, the Internet has brought a new exhibitionistic feature to certain kinds of abnormal behavior. For example, as you read in Chapter 9, a growing number of people now use

peer review system A system by which clinicians paid by an insurance company may periodically review a patient's progress and recommend the continuation or termination of insurance benefits.

social networking to post videos of themselves engaging in self-cutting or suicidal acts, acts that traditionally had been conducted in private (see pages 253–254).

There is also a growing recognition among clinical practitioners and researchers that even everyday social networking can contribute to psychological dysfunction. In addition to its many virtues, social networking may, according to research, provide a new venue for peer pressure and social anxiety in some adolescents (Houston, 2016; Nesi & Prinstein, 2015). It may, for example, cause some people to develop fears that others in their network will exclude them socially. Similarly, clinicians worry that social networking may lead shy or socially anxious people to withdraw from valuable face-to-face relationships.

As you have read throughout this textbook, the face of clinical treatment has also expanded in our fast-moving digital world. *Telemental health,* the use of various technologies to deliver mental health services without the therapist being physically present, is now common (Comer et al., 2017; Maheu et al., 2017). It takes such forms as long-distance therapy between clients and therapists using videoconferencing (see page 65), therapy offered by computer programs (see page 20), treatment enhanced by the use of video game–like avatars and other virtual reality experiences (see page 169), and Internet-based support groups (see pages 20, 74). In addition, of the hundreds of thousands of new apps created over the past five years, a number are devoted to helping people relax, cheer up, or track their shifting moods and thoughts (see page 225). And many computer exercise programs—cognitive and physical—have been developed with the goal of improving both mental health (particularly, cognitive functioning and mood) and physical health (see pages 572–576).

> **What ethical concerns or problems might emerge as a result of the mental health field's increasing use of new technologies?**

Similarly, numerous websites now offer useful mental health information, enabling people to better inform themselves, their friends, and their family members about psychological problems and treatment options (see page 20). Unfortunately, along

"I can't wait to see what you're like online."

Paul Noth The New Yorker Collection/The Cartoon Bank

AP Photo/Nati Harnik

Extending psychology's reach A child meets with a psychologist (left on screen) and physician (right) located several towns away. Long-distance therapy by videoconferencing is an increasingly used form of telemental health.

with this wealth of online information comes considerable misinformation about psychological problems and their treatments, offered by persons and sites that are far from knowledgeable or noble. The issue of quality control is also a major problem for Internet-based therapy, support groups, and the like, and there are now numerous antitreatment networks, such as the pro-suicide and pro-Ana networks you read about in Chapters 9 and 11, that try to guide people away from seeking help for their psychological problems (see pages 254, 325).

Clearly, the growing impact of technological change on the mental health field presents formidable challenges for clinicians and researchers alike. Few of the technological applications discussed throughout this book are well understood, and few have been subjected to comprehensive research. Yet, as we mentioned earlier, the relationship between technology and mental health is growing precipitously. It behooves everyone in the field to understand this growth and its implications.

The Person Within the Profession

THE ACTIONS OF CLINICAL RESEARCHERS and practitioners not only influence and are influenced by other forces in society but also are closely tied to their personal needs and goals (see *InfoCentral* on the next page). You have seen that the human strengths, imperfections, wisdom, and clumsiness of clinical professionals may affect their theoretical orientations, their interactions with clients, and the kinds of clients with whom they choose to work. You have also seen how personal leanings may sometimes override professional standards and scruples and, in extreme cases, lead clinical scientists to commit research fraud and clinical practitioners to engage in sexual misconduct with clients.

Surveys of the mental health of therapists have found that as many as 84 percent report having been in therapy at least once (Pope & Vasquez, 2016; Bearse et al., 2014; Pope & Wedding, 2014). Their reasons are largely the same as those of other clients, with relationship problems, depression, and anxiety topping the list. And, like other people, therapists often are reluctant to acknowledge their psychological problems.

It is not clear why so many therapists have psychological problems. Perhaps it is because their jobs are highly stressful; research suggests that therapists often experience some degree of job burnout (BPS, 2016). Or perhaps therapists are simply more aware of their own negative feelings or are more likely to pursue treatment for their problems. Alternatively, people with personal concerns may be more inclined to choose clinical work as a profession. Whatever the reason, clinicians bring to their work a set of psychological issues that may, along with other important factors, affect how they listen and respond to clients.

The science and profession of abnormal psychology seek to understand, predict, and change abnormal functioning. But we must not lose sight of the fact that mental health researchers and clinicians are human beings, living within a society of human beings, working to serve human beings. The mixture of discovery, misdirection, promise, and frustration that you have encountered throughout this book is thus to be expected. When you think about it, could the study and treatment of human behavior really proceed in any other way?

An early start Deciding at age 11 that clinical psychology was the field for him, Ciro Ortiz set up a therapy office each week on a New York City subway platform. Calling himself the Emotional Advice Kid, the sixth grader talked to clients of all ages with various kinds of psychological issues, charging 2 dollars for a five-minute session and using his earnings to buy food for schoolmates who could not afford it.

Courtesy Adam Ortiz

Within a Larger System

AT ONE TIME, CLINICAL RESEARCHERS and professionals conducted their work largely in isolation. Today their activities have numerous ties to the legislative, judicial, and economic systems, and to technological forces as well. One reason for this growing

PERSONAL AND PROFESSIONAL ISSUES

Like everyone else, clinicians have personal needs, perspectives, goals, and problems, each of which may affect their work. Therapists typically try to minimize the impact of such variables on their interactions with clients—called **countertransference** by Freud. However, research suggests that, to at least some degree, personal therapist issues influence how clinicians deal with clients.

THE EARLY YEARS

Common events in the early lives of therapists

- Experiencing personal distress
- Witnessing the distress of others
- Observing the behaviors and emotions of others; becoming psychologically minded
- Reading
- Being in therapy
- Being a confidant to others
- Modeling the behavior of others
- Learning from a mentor

(Miller, 2017; Pope & Vasquez, 2016; Farber et al., 2005)

Top 5 reasons people become therapists

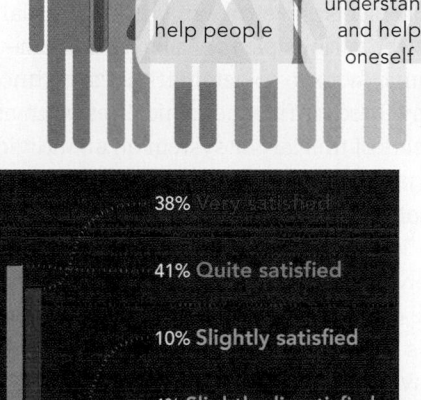

help people · understand and help oneself · understand others · intellectual stimulation · professional autonomy

(Miller, 2017; Waters, 2015; Farber et al., 2005; Norcross & Farber, 2005)

CLINICAL CAREERS

How satisfied are clinical psychologists with their careers?

- 38% Very satisfied
- 41% Quite satisfied
- 10% Slightly satisfied
- 4% Slightly dissatisfied
- 5% Quite dissatisfied
- 3% Very dissatisfied

(Goetz et al., 2018; Rupert et al., 2012; Norcross et al., 2005)

How do clinical psychologists spend their professional time?

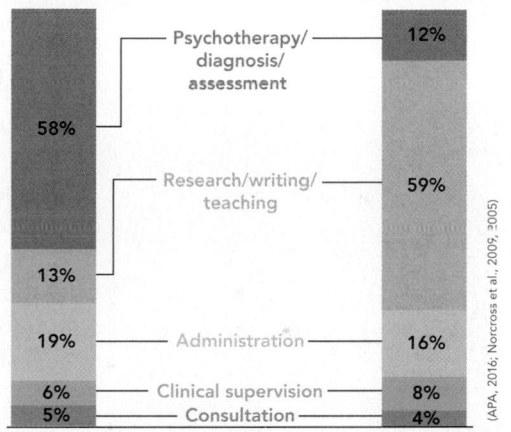

	Private practitioners	Academic psychologists
Psychotherapy/diagnosis/assessment	58%	12%
Research/writing/teaching	13%	59%
Administration	19%	16%
Clinical supervision	6%	8%
Consultation	5%	4%

(APA, 2016; Norcross et al., 2009, 2005)

ETHICS IN CLINICAL PRACTICE

Although the field's code of ethics explicitly forbids it, some therapists engage in sexual relationships with their clients. This is the profession's most egregious violation of trust and boundaries and typically causes significant psychological harm to clients.

Who has had a sexual relationship with a client?

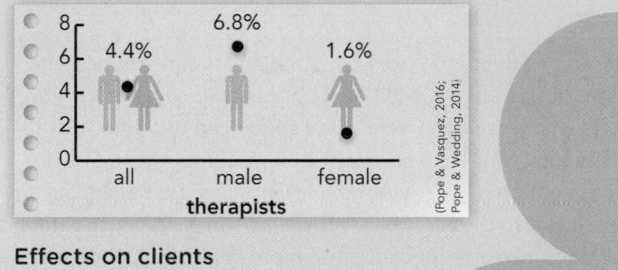

4.4% all · 6.8% male · 1.6% female — therapists

(Pope & Vasquez, 2016; Pope & Wedding, 2014; Pope, 1994, 1988)

Effects on clients

- Ambivalence
- Guilt
- Emptiness and isolation
- Sexual confusion
- Inability to trust
- Confusion of roles and boundaries
- Emotional damage
- Suppressed rage
- Heightened risk of suicide
- Cognitive dysfunction

(Pope & Vasquez, 2015; Pope & Wedding, 2014; Pope, 1994)

CLINICIANS IN THERAPY

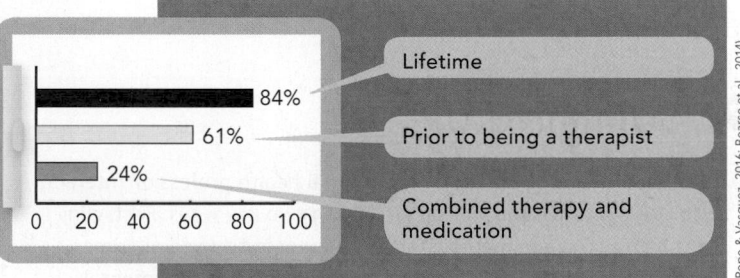

- 84% Lifetime
- 61% Prior to being a therapist
- 24% Combined therapy and medication

(Pope & Vasquez, 2016; Bearse et al., 2014)

Top qualities clinicians look for in choosing a therapist

- Competence
- Warmth and caring
- Clinical experience and professional reputation
- Openness
- Active therapeutic style
- Flexibility

(Hill et al., 2017; Norcross et al., 2009, 2005)

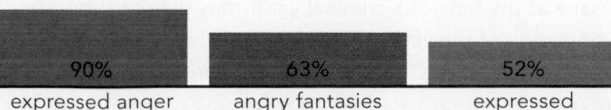

THE EMOTIONAL SIDE

Therapists' fears regarding clients

- 97% might commit suicide
- 91% condition might worsen
- 88% colleagues might criticize their work
- 66% malpractice complaint

Therapists' anger toward clients

- 90% expressed anger toward a client
- 63% angry fantasies regarding a client
- 52% expressed disappointment toward a client

(Pope & Vasquez, 2016; Pope & Tabachnick, 1993; Pope et al., 1987)

#TheirWords

"I spent . . . two hours chatting with Einstein. . . . He is cheerful, assured and likable, and understands as much about psychology as I do about physics, so we got on together very well."

Sigmund Freud, 1927

interconnectedness is that the clinical field has reached a high level of respect and acceptance in our society. Clinicians now serve millions of people in many ways. They have much to say about almost every aspect of society, from education to ecology, and are widely looked to as sources of expertise. When a field becomes so prominent, it inevitably affects how other institutions are run. It also attracts public scrutiny, and various institutions begin to keep an eye on its activities.

When people with psychological problems seek help from a therapist, they are entering a complex system consisting of many interconnected parts. Just as their personal problems have grown within a social structure, so will their treatment be affected by the various parts of a larger system—the therapist's values and needs, legal and economic factors, societal attitudes, technological changes, and yet other forces. These many forces influence clinical research as well.

The effects of this larger system on an individual's psychological needs can be positive or negative, like a family's impact on each of its members. When the system protects a client's rights and confidentiality, for example, it is serving the client well. When economic, legal, or other societal forces limit treatment options, cut off treatment prematurely, or stigmatize a person, the system is adding to the person's problems.

Because of the enormous growth and impact of the mental health profession in our society, it is important that we understand the profession's strengths and weaknesses. As you have seen throughout this book, the field has gathered much knowledge, especially during the past several decades. What mental health professionals do not know and cannot do, however, still outweighs what they do know and can do. Everyone who turns to the clinical field—directly or indirectly—must recognize that it is young and imperfect. Society is vastly curious about behavior and often in need of information and help. What we as a society must remember, however, is that the field is still unfolding.

♀... SUMMING UP

» **Law and Mental Health** The mental health profession interacts with the *legislative and judicial systems* in two key ways. First, clinicians help assess the mental stability of people accused of crimes. Second, the legislative and judicial systems help regulate mental health care. *pp. 579–580*

» **Criminal Commitment** The punishment of people convicted of crimes rests on the assumption that individuals are *responsible for their acts* and are *capable of defending themselves in court.* Evaluations by clinicians may help judges and juries decide the culpability of defendants and sometimes result in criminal commitment.

If defendants are judged to have been *mentally unstable at the time they committed a crime*, they may be found *not guilty by reason of insanity* and placed in a treatment facility rather than a prison. "Insanity" is a legal term, one defined by legislators, not by clinicians. In federal courts and about half the state courts, insanity is judged in accordance with the *M'Naghten test*, which holds that defendants were insane at the time of a criminal act if they did not know the nature or quality of the act or did not know right from wrong at the time they committed it. Other states use the broader *American Law Institute test*.

The insanity defense has been criticized on several grounds, and some states have added an additional option, *guilty but mentally ill*. Defendants who receive this verdict are sentenced to prison with the proviso that they will also receive psychological treatment. Still another verdict option is *guilty with diminished capacity*. Depending on state laws, it is also the case that *sex offenders* may receive treatment as *mentally disordered sex offenders*, or, more commonly, under the state's *sexually violent predator law*.

Regardless of their state of mind at the time of the crime, defendants may be found *mentally incompetent to stand trial*, that is, incapable of fully understanding the charges or legal proceedings that confront them. These defendants are commonly sent to a mental hospital until they are competent to stand trial. *pp. 580–588*

» **Civil Commitment** The legal system also influences the clinical profession. Courts may be called upon to commit noncriminals to mental hospitals for treatment, a process called *civil commitment*. Society allows involuntary commitment of people considered to be *in need of treatment* and *dangerous to themselves or others.* Laws governing civil commitment procedures vary from state to state, but the Supreme Court has ruled that in order for individuals to be committed, there must be *clear and convincing* proof that they are mentally ill and meet their state's criteria for involuntary commitment. In addition to mental hospital commitment, many states have established *outpatient civil commitment* programs. *pp. 588–591*

» **Protecting Patients' Rights** The courts and legislatures significantly affect the mental health profession by specifying legal rights to which patients are entitled. The rights that have received the most attention are the *right to treatment* and the *right to refuse treatment*. *pp. 591–593*

» **Other Clinical–Legal Interactions** Mental health and legal professionals also cross paths in four other areas. First, *malpractice suits* against therapists have increased in recent years. Second, the legislative and judicial systems help define *professional boundaries*. Third, lawyers may solicit the advice of mental health professionals regarding the *selection of jurors* and *case strategies*. Fourth, psychologists may *investigate legal phenomena* such as *eyewitness testimony* and *patterns of criminality*. *pp. 593–596*

» **Ethical Principles** Each clinical profession has a *code of ethics*. The psychologists' code includes prohibitions against *engaging in fraudulent research, taking advantage of clients and students (sexually or otherwise)*, and *participating or assisting in enhanced interrogation programs*. It also establishes guidelines for respecting patient *confidentiality*. The case of *Tarasoff v. Regents of the University of California* helped determine the circumstances in which therapists have a *duty to protect* the client or others from harm and must break confidentiality. *pp. 597–600*

» **Mental Health, Business, and Economics** Clinical practice and study also intersect with the business and economic worlds. Clinicians often help to address psychological problems in the workplace, for example, through *employee assistance programs* and *stress-reduction and problem-solving programs*.

Reductions in government funding of clinical services have left much of the expense for these services to be paid by insurance companies. Private insurance companies are setting up *managed care programs* whose structure and reimbursement procedures influence and often reduce the duration and focus of therapy. Their procedures, which include *peer review systems*, may also compromise patient confidentiality and the quality of therapy services. *pp. 600–602*

» **Technology and Mental Health** The remarkable technological advances of recent times have affected the mental health field, just as they have affected all other fields and professions. In particular, these advances have contributed to new *triggers* for psychopathology, new *forms* of psychopathology, and various kinds of *telemental health*. *pp. 602–604*

» **The Person Within the Profession** Mental health activities are affected by the personal needs, values, and goals of the human beings who provide the clinical services. These factors inevitably affect the choice, direction, and even quality of their work. *p. 604*

Glossary

ABAB design A single-subject experimental design in which behavior is measured during a baseline period, after a treatment has been applied, after baseline conditions have been reintroduced, and after the treatment has been reintroduced. Also called a *reversal design*.

Abnormal psychology The scientific study of abnormal behavior undertaken to describe, predict, explain, and change abnormal patterns of functioning.

Acceptance and commitment therapy (ACT) A cognitive-behavioral therapy that teaches clients to accept and be mindful of (i.e., just notice) their dysfunctional thoughts or worries.

Acetylcholine A neurotransmitter that has been linked to depression and dementia.

Acute stress disorder A disorder in which fear and related symptoms are experienced soon after a traumatic event and last less than a month.

Addiction Persistent, compulsive dependence on a substance or behavior.

Adjustment disorders Disorders characterized by clinical symptoms such as depressed mood or anxiety in response to significant stressors.

Affect An experience of emotion or mood.

Aftercare A program of post-hospitalization care and treatment in the community.

Agoraphobia An anxiety disorder in which a person is afraid to be in public places or situations from which escape might be difficult (or embarrassing) or help unavailable if panic-like symptoms were to occur.

Agranulocytosis A life-threatening drop in white blood cells. This condition is sometimes produced by the second-generation antipsychotic drug *clozapine*.

Alcohol Any beverage containing ethyl alcohol, including beer, wine, and liquor.

Alcohol dehydrogenase An enzyme that breaks down alcohol in the stomach before it enters the blood.

Alcohol use disorder A pattern of behavior in which a person repeatedly abuses or depends on alcohol. Also known as *alcoholism*.

Alcoholics Anonymous (AA) A self-help organization that provides support and guidance for people with alcoholism.

Alcoholism A pattern of behavior in which a person repeatedly abuses or depends on alcohol. Also known as *alcohol use disorder*.

Alogia A decrease in speech or speech content; a symptom of schizophrenia. Also known as *poverty of speech*.

Alprazolam A benzodiazepine drug shown to be effective in the treatment of anxiety disorders. Marketed as *Xanax*.

Altruistic suicide Suicide committed by people who intentionally sacrifice their lives for the well-being of society.

Alzheimer's disease The most common type of neurocognitive disorder, usually occurring after the age of 65, marked most prominently by memory impairment.

Amenorrhea The absence of menstrual cycles.

American Law Institute test A legal test for insanity that holds people to be insane at the time of committing a crime if, because of a mental disorder, they did not know right from wrong or could not resist an uncontrollable impulse to act.

Amnesia Loss of memory.

Amniocentesis A prenatal procedure used to test the amniotic fluid that surrounds the fetus for the possibility of birth defects.

Amphetamines Stimulant drugs that are manufactured in the laboratory.

Amphetamine psychosis A syndrome characterized by psychotic symptoms brought on by high doses of amphetamines. Similar to *cocaine psychosis*.

Amygdala A structure in the brain that plays a key role in emotion and memory.

Analog observation A method for observing behavior in which people are observed in artificial settings such as clinicians' offices or laboratories.

Analogue experiment A research method in which the experimenter produces abnormal-like behavior in laboratory participants and then conducts experiments on the participants.

Anal stage In psychoanalytic theory, the second 18 months of life, during which the child's focus of pleasure shifts to the anus.

Anesthesia A lessening or loss of sensation of touch or of pain.

Anomic suicide Suicide committed by individuals whose social environment fails to provide stability, thus leaving them without a sense of belonging.

Anorexia nervosa A disorder marked by the pursuit of extreme thinness and by an extreme loss of weight.

Anoxia A complication of birth in which the baby is deprived of oxygen.

Antabuse (disulfiram) A drug that causes intense nausea, vomiting, increased heart rate, and dizziness when taken with alcohol. It is often taken by people who are trying to refrain from drinking alcohol.

Antagonist drugs Drugs that block or change the effects of an addictive drug.

Antianxiety drugs Psychotropic drugs that help reduce tension and anxiety. Also called *minor tranquilizers* or *anxiolytics*.

Antibipolar drugs Psychotropic drugs that help stabilize the moods of people suffering from a bipolar disorder. Also known as *mood stabilizers*.

Antibodies Bodily chemicals that seek out and destroy foreign invaders such as bacteria or viruses.

Antidepressant drugs Psychotropic drugs that improve the mood of people with depression.

Antigen A foreign invader of the body, such as a bacterium or virus.

Antipsychotic drugs Drugs that help correct grossly confused or distorted thinking.

Antisocial personality disorder A personality disorder marked by a general pattern of disregard for and violation of other people's rights.

Anxiety The central nervous system's physiological and emotional response to a vague sense of threat or danger.

Anxiety disorder A disorder in which anxiety is a central symptom.

Anxiety sensitivity A tendency to focus on one's bodily sensations, assess them illogically, and interpret them as harmful.

Anxiolytics Drugs that reduce anxiety.

ApoE-4 gene One form of the ApoE gene that is inherited by about 30 percent of the population. Those people may be particularly vulnerable to the development of Alzheimer's disease.

Arbitrary inference An error in logic in which a person draws negative conclusions on the basis of little or even contrary evidence.

Aripiprazole A second-generation antipsychotic drug whose brand name is Abilify.

Asperger's disorder The term previously applied to persons with autism spectrum disorder who display profound social impairment yet maintain a relatively high level of cognitive functioning and language skills.

Assertiveness training A cognitive-behavioral approach to increasing assertive behavior that is socially desirable.

Assessment The process of collecting and interpreting relevant information about a client or research participant.

Asthma A medical problem marked by narrowing of the trachea and bronchi, which results in shortness of breath, wheezing, coughing, and a choking sensation.

Asylum A type of institution that first became popular in the sixteenth century to provide care for persons with mental disorders. Most became virtual prisons.

Attention circuit A number of brain structures that work together to bring about attention and to maintain a proper balance between Type 1 and Type 2 attention processes.

Attention-deficit/hyperactivity disorder (ADHD) A disorder marked by the inability to focus attention, or overactive and impulsive behavior, or both.

Attribution An explanation of things we see going on around us that points to particular causes.

Atypical antipsychotic drugs A relatively new group of antipsychotic drugs whose biological action is different from that of the first-generation antipsychotic drugs. Also known as *second-generation antipsychotic drugs*.

Auditory hallucination A hallucination in which a person hears sounds or voices that are not actually present.

Augmentative communication system A method for enhancing the communication skills of people with autism spectrum disorder, intellectual developmental disorder, or cerebral palsy by teaching them to point to pictures, symbols, letters, or words on a communication board or computer.

Aura A warning sensation that may precede a migraine headache.

Autism spectrum disorder A developmental disorder marked by extreme unresponsiveness to others, severe communication deficits, and highly repetitive and rigid behaviors, interests, and activities.

Autoerotic asphyxia A fatal lack of oxygen that people may unintentionally produce while hanging, suffocating, or strangling themselves during masturbation.

Autogenic mass killing Mass murder in which an individual kills people indiscriminately to fulfill a personal agenda.

Automatic thoughts Numerous unpleasant thoughts that help to cause or maintain depression, anxiety, or other forms of psychological dysfunction.

Autonomic nervous system (ANS) The network of nerve fibers that connect the central nervous system to all the other organs of the body.

Aversion therapy A treatment in which clients are repeatedly presented with unpleasant stimuli while performing undesirable behaviors such as taking a drug.

Avoidant personality disorder A personality disorder characterized by consistent discomfort and restraint in social situations, overwhelming feelings of inadequacy, and extreme sensitivity to negative evaluation.

Avolition A symptom of schizophrenia marked by apathy and an inability to start or complete a course of action.

Axon A long fiber extending from the body of a neuron.

Barbiturates One group of sedative-hypnotic drugs that reduces anxiety and helps produce sleep.

Baseline data A person's initial response level on a test or scale.

Basic irrational assumptions The inaccurate and inappropriate beliefs held by people with various psychological problems, according to Albert Ellis.

Battery A series of tests, each of which measures a specific skill area.

B-cell A lymphocyte that produces antibodies.

Behavioral activation A therapy for depression in which the client is guided to systematically increase the number of constructive and pleasurable activities and events in his or her life.

Behavioral medicine A field that combines psychological and physical interventions to treat or prevent medical problems.

Behavior-focused therapy A therapeutic approach that seeks to identify problem-causing behaviors and change them. Also known as *behavior modification*.

Behaviors The responses an organism makes to its environment.

Bender Visual-Motor Gestalt Test A neuropsychological test in which a subject is asked to copy a set of nine simple designs and later reproduce the designs from memory.

Benzodiazepines The most common group of antianxiety drugs, which includes Valium and Xanax.

Bereavement The process of working through the grief that one feels when a loved one dies.

Beta-amyloid protein A small molecule that forms sphere-shaped deposits called senile plaques, linked to aging and to Alzheimer's disease.

"Big Five" theory of personality A leading theory that holds that personality can be effectively organized and described by five broad dimensions of personality—openness, conscientiousness, extraversion, agreeableness, and neuroticism.

Binge An episode of uncontrollable eating during which a person ingests a very large quantity of food.

Binge drinking A pattern of alcohol consumption in which a person consumes five or more drinks on a single occasion.

Binge-eating disorder A disorder marked by frequent binges but not extreme compensatory behaviors.

Binge-eating/purging-type anorexia nervosa A type of anorexia nervosa in which people have eating binges but still lose excessive weight by forcing themselves to vomit after meals or by abusing laxatives or diuretics.

Biofeedback A technique in which a client is given information about physiological reactions as they occur and learns to control the reactions voluntarily.

Biological challenge test A procedure used to produce panic in participants or clients by having them exercise vigorously or perform some other potentially panic-inducing task in the presence of a researcher or therapist.

Biological model The theoretical perspective that points to biological processes as the key to human behavior.

Biological therapy The use of physical and chemical procedures to help people overcome psychological problems.

Biomarkers Biochemical, molecular, genetic, or structural characteristics that usually accompany a disease.

Biopsychosocial theories Explanations that attribute the cause of abnormality to an interaction of genetic, biological, developmental, emotional, behavioral, cognitive, social, and societal influences.

Bipolar disorder A disorder marked by alternating or intermixed periods of mania and depression.

Bipolar I disorder A type of bipolar disorder marked by full manic and major depressive episodes.

Bipolar II disorder A type of bipolar disorder marked by mild manic (hypomanic) and major depressive episodes.

Birth complications Problematic biological conditions during birth that can affect the physical and psychological well-being of the child.

Blind design An experiment in which participants do not know whether they are in the experimental or the control condition. Also known as *masked design*, now the preferred term.

Blunted affect A symptom of schizophrenia in which a person shows less emotion than most people.

Body dysmorphic disorder A disorder in which individuals become preoccupied with the belief that they have certain defects or flaws in their physical appearance. The perceived defects or flaws are imagined or greatly exaggerated.

Body shaming The practice of criticizing people publicly for being overweight, or, less frequently, underweight.

Borderline personality disorder A personality disorder characterized by repeated instability in interpersonal relationships, self-image, and mood, and by impulsive behavior.

Brain circuit A network of particular brain structures that work together, triggering each other into action to produce a distinct kind of behavioral, cognitive, or emotional reaction.

Brain stimulation Interventions that directly or indirectly stimulate the brain in order to bring about psychological improvement.

Brain structure A distinct area or region of the brain formed by a large group of neurons.

Brain wave The fluctuations of electrical potential that are produced by neurons in the brain.

Breathing-related sleep disorder A sleep disorder in which sleep is frequently disrupted by a breathing problem, causing excessive sleepiness or insomnia.

Brief psychotic disorder Psychotic symptoms that appear suddenly after a very stressful event or a period of emotional turmoil and last anywhere from a few hours to a month.

Brodmann Area 25 A brain structure whose abnormal activity has been linked to depression. Also called the *subgenual cingulate*.

Bulimia nervosa A disorder marked by frequent eating binges that are followed by forced vomiting or other extreme compensatory behaviors to avoid gaining weight. Also known as binge-purge syndrome.

Buprenorpine An opioid substitute drug that is administered as a form of maintenance therapy for substance use disorder.

Caffeine The world's most widely used stimulant, most often consumed in coffee.

Cannabis Substance produced from the varieties of the hemp plant, *Cannabis sativa*. It causes a mixture of hallucinogenic, depressant, and stimulant effects.

Case manager A community therapist who offers a full range of services for people with schizophrenia or other severe disorders, including therapy, advice, medication, guidance, and protection of patients' rights.

Case study A detailed account of a person's life and psychological problems.

Catatonia A pattern of extreme psychomotor symptoms, found in some forms of schizophrenia, which may include catatonic stupor, rigidity, or posturing.

Catatonic excitement A form of catatonia in which a person moves excitedly, sometimes with wild waving of the arms and legs.

Catatonic stupor A symptom associated with schizophrenia in which a person becomes almost totally unresponsive to the environment, remaining motionless and silent for long stretches of time.

Catharsis The reliving of past repressed feelings in order to settle internal conflicts and overcome problems.

Caudate nuclei Structures in the brain, within the region known as the basal ganglia, that help convert sensory information into thoughts and actions.

Central nervous system The brain and spinal cord.

Cerebellum An area of the brain that coordinates movement in the body and perhaps helps control a person's ability to shift attention rapidly.

Checking compulsion A compulsion in which people feel compelled to check the same things over and over.

Child abuse The nonaccidental use of excessive physical or psychological force by an adult on a child, often aimed at hurting or destroying the child.

Chlorpromazine A phenothiazine drug commonly used for treating schizophrenia. Marketed as *Thorazine*.

Chromosomes The structures, located within a cell, that contain genes.

Chronic headaches A medical problem marked by frequent intense aches in the head or neck that are not caused by another medical disorder.

Chronic traumatic encephalopathy (CTE) A degenerative brain disease that is suffered by many NFL players, among others, that is caused by repeated head blows over the course of time.

Circadian rhythm disorder A sleep-wake disorder characterized by a mismatch between a person's sleep-wake pattern and the sleep-wake schedule of most other people.

Circadian rhythms Internal "clocks" consisting of repeated biological fluctuations.

Cirrhosis An irreversible condition, often caused by excessive drinking, in which the liver becomes scarred and begins to change in anatomy and functioning.

Civil commitment A legal process by which an individual can be forced to undergo mental health treatment.

Clang A rhyme used by some people with schizophrenia as a guide to forming thoughts and statements.

Classical conditioning A process of learning in which two events that repeatedly occur close together in time become tied together in a person's mind and so produce the same response.

Classification system A list of disorders, along with descriptions of symptoms and guidelines for making appropriate diagnoses.

Cleaning compulsion A common compulsion in which people feel compelled to keep cleaning themselves, their clothing, and their homes.

Client-centered therapy The humanistic therapy developed by Carl Rogers in which clinicians try to help clients by being accepting, empathizing accurately, and conveying genuineness.

Clinical interview A face-to-face encounter in which clinicians ask questions of clients, weigh their responses and reactions, and learn about them and their psychological problems.

Clinical psychologist A mental health professional who has earned a doctorate in clinical psychology.

Clinical psychology The study, assessment, treatment, and prevention of abnormal behavior.

Clitoris The female sex organ located in front of the urinary and vaginal openings. It becomes enlarged during sexual arousal.

Clozapine A commonly prescribed second-generation antipsychotic drug.

Cocaine An addictive stimulant obtained from the coca plant. It is the most powerful natural stimulant known.

Code of ethics A body of principles and rules for ethical behavior, designed to guide decisions and actions by members of a profession.

Cognition The capacity to think, remember, and anticipate.

Cognitive-behavioral model A theoretical perspective that emphasizes both behavior and the process and content of thinking as causes of psychological problems.

Cognitive-behavioral therapies Therapy approaches that seek to help clients change both counterproductive behaviors and dysfunctional ways of thinking.

Cognitive processing therapy A cognitive-focused intervention for people with PTSD in which therapists guide individuals to examine and change the dysfunctional attitudes and styles of interpretation they have developed as a result of their traumatic experiences, thus enabling them to deal with difficult memories and feelings.

Cognitive remediation A treatment that focuses on the cognitive impairments that often characterize people with schizophrenia, particularly their difficulties in attention, planning, and memory.

Cognitive therapy A therapy developed by Aaron Beck that helps people identify and change the maladaptive assumptions and ways of thinking that help cause their psychological disorders.

Cognitive triad The three forms of negative thinking that theorist Aaron Beck theorizes lead people to feel depressed. The triad consists of a negative view of one's experiences, oneself, and the future.

Coitus Sexual intercourse.

Communication disorders Neurodevelopmental disorders characterized by marked impairment in language and/or speech.

Community mental health center A treatment facility that provides medication, psychotherapy, and emergency care to patients and coordinates treatment in the community.

Community mental health treatment A treatment approach that emphasizes community care.

Comorbidity The occurrence of two or more disorders in the same person.

Compulsion A repetitive and rigid behavior or mental act that persons feel driven to perform in order to prevent or reduce anxiety.

Compulsive ritual A detailed, often elaborate, set of actions that a person often feels compelled to perform, always in an identical manner.

Computerized axial tomography (CT scan) A composite image of the brain created by compiling X-ray images taken from many angles.

Concerta A trade name of methylphenidate, a stimulant drug that is helpful in many cases of attention-deficit/hyperactivity disorder (ADHD).

Concordance A statistical measure of the frequency with which family members (often both members of a pair of twins) have the same particular characteristic.

Concurrent validity The degree to which the measures gathered from one assessment tool agree with the measures gathered from other assessment techniques.

Conditioned response (CR) A response previously associated with an unconditioned stimulus that comes to be produced by a conditioned stimulus.

Conditioned stimulus (CS) A previously neutral stimulus that comes to be associated with a nonneutral stimulus, and can then produce responses similar to those produced by the nonneutral stimulus.

Conditioning A simple form of learning.

Conditions of worth According to client-centered theorists, the internal standards by which a person judges his or her own lovability and acceptability, determined by the standards to which the person was held as a child.

Conduct disorder A disorder in which a child repeatedly violates the basic rights of others and displays aggression, characterized by symptoms such as physical cruelty to people or animals, the deliberate destruction of other people's property, and the commission of various crimes.

Confabulation A made-up description of one's experience to fill in a gap in one's memory.

Confederate An experimenter's accomplice, who helps create a particular impression in a study while pretending to be just another research participant.

Confidentiality The principle that certain professionals will not divulge the information they obtain from a client.

Confound In an experiment, a variable other than the independent variable that is also acting on the dependent variable.

Contingency management An operant conditioning treatment program that offers clients incentives (such as vouchers, prizes, cash, or privileges) that are contingent on the submission of drug-free urine specimens.

Continuous amnesia An inability to recall newly occurring events as well as certain past events.

Control group In an experiment, a group of participants who are not exposed to the independent variable.

Conversion disorder A disorder in which bodily symptoms affect voluntary motor and sensory functions, but the symptoms are inconsistent with known medical diseases.

Conversion therapy A treatment approach, widely discredited, that attempts to change the sexual orientation of a person from homosexual or bisexual to heterosexual. Also called *reparative therapy*.

Convulsion A brain seizure.

Coronary arteries Blood vessels that surround the heart and are responsible for carrying oxygen to the heart muscle.

Coronary heart disease Illness of the heart caused by a blockage in the coronary arteries.

Correlation The degree to which events or characteristics vary along with each other.

Correlation coefficient (r) A statistical term that indicates the direction and the magnitude of a correlation, ranging from −1.00 to +1.00.

Correlational method A research procedure used to determine how much events or characteristics vary along with each other.

Corticosteroids A group of hormones, including cortisol, released by the adrenal glands at times of stress.

Cortico-striato-thalamo-cortical brain circuit A brain circuit that includes such brain structures as the orbitofrontal cortex (just above each eye), cingulate cortex, striatum (including the caudate nucleus and putamen, two other structures at the back of the striatum), and thalamus. The circuit is hyperactive in people with obsessive-compulsive disorder, making it difficult for them to turn off or dismiss their various impulses, needs, and related thoughts.

Cortisol A hormone released by the adrenal glands when a person is under stress.

Counseling psychology A mental health specialty similar to clinical psychology that offers its own graduate training program.

Countertransference A phenomenon of psychotherapy in which therapists' own feelings, history, and values subtly influence the way they interpret a patient's problems.

Couple therapy A therapy format in which the therapist works with two people who share a long-term relationship.

Covert desensitization Desensitization that focuses on imagining confrontations with frightening objects or situations while in a state of relaxation.

Covert sensitization A treatment for eliminating unwanted behavior by pairing the behavior with unpleasant mental images.

Crack A powerful, ready-to-smoke freebase cocaine.

C-reactive protein (CRP) A protein that spreads throughout the body and causes inflammation and various illnesses and disorders.

Cretinism A disorder marked by intellectual deficiencies and physical abnormalities; caused by low levels of iodine in the mother's diet during pregnancy. Also known as *severe congenital hypothyroidism*.

Creutzfeldt–Jakob disease A form of neurocognitive disorder caused by a slow-acting virus that may live in the body for years before the disease unfolds.

Criminal commitment A legal process by which people accused of a crime are instead judged mentally unstable and sent to a mental health facility for treatment.

Crisis intervention A treatment approach that tries to help people in a psychological crisis view their situation more accurately, make better decisions, act more constructively, and overcome the crisis.

Critical incident stress debriefing Training in how to help victims of disasters or other horrifying events talk about their feelings and reactions to the traumatic incidents.

Cross-tolerance Tolerance that a person develops for a substance as a result of regularly using another substance similar to it.

Culture A people's common history, values, institutions, habits, skills, technology, and arts.

Culture-sensitive therapies Approaches that are designed to address the unique issues faced by members of minority groups.

Cyberbullying The use of e-mail, texting, chat rooms, cell phones, or other digital devices to harass, threaten, or intimidate people.

Cyclothymic disorder A disorder marked by numerous periods of hypomanic symptoms and mild depressive symptoms.

Daily Report Card (DRC) A treatment for ADHD in which a child's target classroom behaviors—staying in his or her classroom seat, raising a hand to speak, and using an "inside voice"—are carefully evaluated, recorded on a DRC, and reinforced by teachers throughout the school day. At the end of the day, the teacher further provides the report card for the parents to see, and, if a sufficient number of target behaviors had been performed satisfactorily that day, the child is also given rewards at home.

Day center A program that offers hospital-like treatment during the day only. Also known as a *day hospital*.

Death darer A person who is ambivalent about the wish to die even as he or she attempts suicide.

Death ignorer A person who attempts suicide without recognizing the finality of death.

Death initiator A person who attempts suicide believing that the process of death is already under way and that he or she is simply quickening the process.

Death seeker A person who clearly intends to end his or her life at the time of a suicide attempt.

Deep brain stimulation (DBS) A treatment procedure for depression in which a pacemaker powers electrodes that have been implanted in the subgenual cingulate, thus stimulating that brain structure.

Deinstitutionalization The discharge, begun during the 1960s, of large numbers of patients from long-term institutional care so that they might be treated in community programs.

Déjà vu The haunting sense of having previously seen or experienced a new scene or situation.

Delayed ejaculation A male dysfunction characterized by persistent inability to ejaculate or very delayed ejaculations during sexual activity with a partner.

Delirium A rapidly developing, acute disturbance in attention and orientation that makes it very difficult to concentrate and think in a clear and organized manner.

Delirium tremens (DTs) A dramatic withdrawal reaction experienced by some people with alcohol use disorder. It consists of confusion, clouded consciousness, and terrifying visual hallucinations.

Delusion A strange false belief firmly held despite evidence to the contrary.

Delusion of control The belief that one's impulses, feelings, thoughts, or actions are being controlled by other people.

Delusion of grandeur The belief that one is a great inventor, historical figure, or other specially empowered person.

Delusion of persecution The belief that one is being plotted or discriminated against, spied on, slandered, threatened, attacked, or deliberately victimized.

Delusion of reference A belief that attaches special and personal meaning to the actions of others or to various objects or events.

Delusional disorder A disorder consisting of persistent, nonbizarre delusions that are not part of a schizophrenic disorder.

Demonology The belief that abnormal behavior results from supernatural causes such as evil spirits.

Dendrite An extension located at one end of a neuron that receives impulses from other neurons.

Denial An ego defense mechanism in which a person fails to acknowledge unacceptable thoughts, feelings, or actions.

Dependent personality disorder A personality disorder characterized by a pattern of clinging and obedience, fear of separation, and an ongoing need to be taken care of.

Dependent variable The variable in an experiment that is expected to change as the independent variable is manipulated.

Depersonalization–derealization disorder A dissociative disorder marked by the presence of persistent and recurrent episodes of depersonalization, derealization, or both.

Depressant A substance that slows the activity of the central nervous system and in sufficient dosages causes a reduction of tension and inhibitions.

Depression A low, sad state marked by significant levels of sadness, lack of energy, low self-worth, guilt, or related symptoms.

Depression-related brain circuit A brain circuit whose dysfunction contributes to unipolar depression. It includes the prefrontal cortex, hippocampus, amygdala, and subgenual cingulate (also called Brodmann Area 25), among other structures.

Depressive disorders The group of disorders marked by unipolar depression.

Derailment A common thinking disturbance in schizophrenia, involving rapid shifts from one topic of conversation to another. Also called *loose associations*.

Desensitization *See* Systematic desensitization.

Desire phase The phase of the sexual response cycle consisting of an urge to have sex, sexual fantasies, and sexual attraction.

Detoxification Systematic and medically supervised withdrawal from a drug.

Developmental coordination disorder Neurodevelopmental disorder characterized by marked impairment in the development and performance of coordinated motor activities.

Developmental psychopathology A perspective that uses a developmental framework to understand how factors and principles from the various models may intersect at points throughout the lifespan to help produce both normal and abnormal functioning.

Deviance Variance from common patterns of behavior.

Diagnosis A determination that a person's problems reflect a particular disorder.

Diagnostic and Statistical Manual of Mental Disorders (DSM) The classification system for mental disorders developed by the American Psychiatric Association.

Dialectical behavior therapy (DBT) A comprehensive treatment approach developed by psychologist Marsha Linehan, applied particularly in cases of borderline personality disorder and/or suicidal intent. The approach includes both individual therapy sessions and group sessions and features cognitive-behavioral techniques, social skill building, and various emotion regulation, mindfulness, humanistic, and other techniques.

Diathesis–stress view The view that a person must first have a predisposition to a disorder and then be subjected to immediate psychosocial stress in order to develop the disorder.

Diazepam A benzodiazepine drug, marketed as *Valium*.

Dichotomous thinking Viewing problems and solutions in rigid "either/or" terms.

Diencephalon A brain area (consisting of the mammillary bodies, thalamus, and hypothalamus) that plays a key role in transforming short-term to long-term memory, among other functions.

Directed masturbation training A sex therapy approach that teaches women with female arousal or orgasmic disorders how to masturbate effectively and eventually reach orgasm during sexual interactions.

Disaster Response Network (DRN) A network of thousands of volunteer mental health professionals who mobilize to provide free emergency psychological services at disaster sites throughout North America.

Displacement An ego defense mechanism that channels unacceptable id impulses toward another, safer substitute.

Disruptive mood dysregulation disorder A childhood disorder marked by severe recurrent temper outbursts along with a persistent irritable or angry mood.

Dissociative amnesia A dissociative disorder marked by an inability to recall important personal events and information.

Dissociative disorders A group of disorders in which some parts of one's memory or identity seem to be dissociated, or separated, from other parts of one's memory or identity.

Dissociative fugue A form of dissociative amnesia in which a person travels to a new location and may assume a new identity, simultaneously forgetting his or her past.

Dissociative identity disorder A disorder in which a person develops two or more distinct personalities. Previously known as *multiple personality disorder*.

Disulfiram (Antabuse) An antagonist drug used in treating alcohol abuse or dependence.

Dopamine The neurotransmitter whose high activity has been shown to be related to schizophrenia.

Dopamine hypothesis The theory that schizophrenia results from excessive activity of the neurotransmitter dopamine.

Double-bind hypothesis A theory that some parents repeatedly communicate pairs of messages that are mutually contradictory, helping to produce schizophrenia in their children.

Double-masked design Experimental procedure in which neither the participant nor the experimenter knows whether the participant has received the experimental treatment or a placebo.

Down syndrome A form of intellectual disability caused by an abnormality in the 21st chromosome.

Dream A series of ideas and images that form during sleep.

Drug Any substance other than food that affects the body or mind.

Drug maintenance therapy An approach to treating substance dependence in which clients are given legally and medically supervised doses of the drug on which they are dependent or a substitute drug.

Drug therapy The use of psychotropic drugs to reduce the symptoms of psychological disorders.

DSM-5 (*Diagnostic and Statistical Manual of Mental Disorders,* Fifth Edition) The newest edition of the DSM, published in 2013.

Durham test A legal test for insanity that holds people to be insane at the time they committed a crime if their act was the result of a mental disorder or defect.

Duty to protect The principle that therapists must break confidentiality in order to protect a person who may be the intended victim of a client.

Dyslexia A type of specific learning disorder in which people show a marked impairment in the ability to recognize words and to comprehend what they read.

Dyssomnias Sleep-wake disorders, such as insomnia disorder and hypersomnolence disorder, in which the amount, quality, or timing of sleep is disturbed.

Dysthymia A pattern of persistent depressive disorder that is chronic but less severe and less disabling than repeated episodes of major depression.

Early-onset Alzheimer's disease A relatively rare form of Alzheimer's disease that occurs before the age of 65. It typically runs in families.

Eccentric A person who deviates from conventional norms in odd, irregular, or even bizarre ways, but is not displaying a psychological disorder.

Echolalia A symptom of autism or schizophrenia in which a person responds to statements by repeating the other person's words.

Ecstasy (MDMA) A drug chemically related to amphetamines and hallucinogens, used illicitly for its euphoric and hallucinogenic effects.

Ego According to Freud, the psychological force that employs reason and operates in accordance with the reality principle.

Ego defense mechanisms According to psychoanalytic theory, strategies developed by the ego to control unacceptable id impulses and to avoid or reduce the anxiety they arouse.

Egoistic suicide Suicide committed by people over whom society has little or no control, people who are not concerned with the norms or rules of society.

Eidetic imagery A strong visual image of an object or scene that persists in some persons long after the object or scene is removed.

Ejaculation Contractions of the muscles at the base of the penis that cause sperm to be ejected.

Electra complex According to Freud, the pattern of desires all girls experience during the phallic stage, in which they develop a sexual attraction to their father.

Electroconvulsive therapy (ECT) A treatment for depression in which electrodes attached to a patient's head send an electrical current through the brain, causing a seizure.

Electroencephalograph (EEG) A device that records electrical impulses in the brain.

Electromyograph (EMG) A device that provides feedback about the level of muscular tension in the body.

Emergency commitment The temporary commitment to a mental hospital of a patient who is behaving in a bizarre or violent way.

Empirically supported treatment A movement in the clinical field that seeks to identify which therapies have received clear research support for each disorder, to develop corresponding treatment guidelines, and to spread such information to clinicians. Also known as *evidence-based treatment*.

Employee assistance program A mental health program offered by a business to its employees.

Encopresis A disorder characterized by repeated defecating in inappropriate places, such as one's clothing.

Endocrine system The system of glands located throughout the body that help control important activities such as growth and sexual activity.

Endogenous depression A depression that appears to develop without external reasons and is assumed to be caused by internal factors.

Endorphins Neurotransmitters that help relieve pain and reduce emotional tension. They are sometimes referred to as the body's own opioids.

Enhanced interrogation program A torture-based form of questioning that has been used to try to obtain information from suspected terrorists.

Enmeshed family pattern A family system in which members are overinvolved with each other's affairs and overconcerned about each other's welfare.

Enuresis A disorder marked by repeated bed-wetting or wetting of one's clothes.

Epidemiological study A study that measures the incidence and prevalence of a disorder in a given population.

Equifinality The principle that a number of different developmental pathways can lead to the same psychological disorder.

Erectile disorder A dysfunction in which a man persistently fails to attain or maintain an erection during sexual activity.

Ergot alkaloid A naturally occurring compound from which LSD is derived.

Erotomanic delusions Delusional beliefs held by some individuals that they are loved by and in a relationship with a person on whom they focus their attention (for example, a celebrity), a person with whom they have no relationship.

Essential hypertension High blood pressure caused by a combination of psychosocial and physiological factors.

Estrogen The primary female sex hormone.

Ethyl alcohol The chemical compound in all alcoholic beverages that is rapidly absorbed into the blood and immediately begins to affect the person's functioning.

Evoked potentials The brain response patterns recorded on an electroencephalograph while a person performs a task such as observing a flashing light.

Excitement phase The phase of the sexual response cycle marked by changes in the pelvic region, general physical arousal, and increases in heart rate, muscle tension, blood pressure, and rate of breathing.

Excoriation disorder A disorder in which persons repeatedly pick at their skin, resulting in significant sores or wounds. Also called *skin-picking disorder*.

Exhibitionistic disorder A paraphilic disorder in which persons have repeated sexually arousing urges or fantasies about exposing their genitals to others, and either act on these urges with nonconsenting individuals or experience clinically significant distress or impairment.

Existential anxiety According to existential theorists, a universal fear of the limits and responsibilities of one's existence.

Existential model The theoretical perspective that human beings are born with the total freedom either to face up to one's existence and give meaning to one's life or to shrink from that responsibility.

Existential therapy A therapy that encourages clients to accept responsibility for their lives and to live with greater meaning and value.

Exorcism The practice, common in early societies, of treating abnormality by coaxing evil spirits to leave the person's body.

Experiment A research procedure in which a variable is manipulated and the effect of the manipulation is observed.

Experimental group In an experiment, the participants who are exposed to the independent variable under investigation.

Exposure and response prevention A treatment for obsessive-compulsive disorder that exposes a client to anxiety-arousing thoughts or situations and then prevents the client from performing his or her compulsive acts. Also called *exposure and ritual prevention*.

Exposure therapy A behavior-focused intervention in which fearful persons are repeatedly exposed to the objects or situations they dread.

Expressed emotion The general level of criticism, disapproval, hostility, and intrusiveness expressed in a family. People recovering from schizophrenia are considered more likely to relapse if their families rate high in expressed emotion.

External validity The degree to which the results of a study may be generalized beyond that study.

Extrapyramidal effects Unwanted movements, such as severe shaking, bizarre-looking grimaces, twisting of the body, and extreme restlessness, sometimes produced by antipsychotic drugs.

Eye movement desensitization and reprocessing (EMDR) An exposure treatment in which clients move their eyes in a rhythmic manner from side to side while flooding their minds with images of objects and situations they ordinarily avoid.

Factitious disorder A disorder in which a person feigns or induces symptoms, typically for the purpose of assuming the role of a sick person.

Family pedigree study A research design in which investigators determine how many and which relatives of a person with a disorder have the same disorder.

Family systems theory A theory that views the family as a system of interacting parts whose interactions exhibit consistent patterns and unstated rules.

Family therapy A therapy format in which the therapist meets with all members of a family and helps them to change in therapeutic ways.

Fantasy An ego defense mechanism in which a person uses imaginary events to satisfy unacceptable impulses.

Fear The central nervous system's physiological and emotional response to a serious threat to one's well-being.

Fear brain circuit The brain circuit that produces and manages fear reactions. Generalized anxiety disorder is related to dysfunction in this circuit, which includes such brain structures as the prefrontal cortex, anterior cingulate cortex, insula, and amygdala.

Fear hierarchy A list of objects or situations that frighten a person, starting with those that are slightly feared and ending with those that are feared greatly; used in systematic desensitization.

Female orgasmic disorder A dysfunction in which a woman persistently fails to reach orgasm, has very low intensity orgasms, or has very delayed orgasms.

Female sexual interest/arousal disorder A female dysfunction marked by a persistent reduction or lack of interest in sex and low sexual activity, as well as, in some cases, limited excitement and few sexual sensations during sexual activity.

Fentanyl A powerful opioid pain relief drug that is 50 to 100 times more powerful than morphine and 20 to 35 times more powerful than heroin. It is by far the painkiller most commonly linked to overdose deaths.

Fetal alcohol syndrome A cluster of problems in a child, including low birth weight, irregularities in the hands and face, and intellectual deficits, caused by excessive alcohol intake by the mother during pregnancy.

Fetishistic disorder A paraphilic disorder consisting of recurrent and intense sexual urges, fantasies, or behaviors that involve the use of a nonliving object or nongenital part, often to the exclusion of all other stimuli, accompanied by significant distress or impairment.

First-generation antipsychotic drugs A group of drugs, including phenothiazines, that comprised the first wave of antipsychotic drugs and are still in use today.

Fixation According to Freud, a condition in which the id, ego, and superego do not mature properly and are frozen at an early stage of development.

Flashback The recurrence of LSD-induced sensory and emotional changes long after the drug has left the body, or, in posttraumatic stress disorder, the reexperiencing of past traumatic events.

Flat affect A symptom of schizophrenia in which the person shows almost no emotion at all.

Flooding An exposure therapy in which clients are exposed repeatedly and intensively to a feared object and made to see that it is actually harmless.

Forensic psychology The branch of psychology concerned with intersections between psychological practice and research and the judicial system. Also related to the field of *forensic psychiatry*.

Formal thought disorder A disturbance in the production and organization of thought.

Free association A psychodynamic technique in which the patient describes any thought, feeling, or image that comes to mind, even if it seems unimportant.

Freebase A technique for ingesting cocaine in which the pure cocaine basic alkaloid is chemically separated from processed cocaine, vaporized by heat from a flame, and inhaled through a pipe.

Free-floating anxiety Chronic and persistent feelings of anxiety that are not clearly attached to a specific, identifiable threat.

Frotteuristic disorder A paraphilic disorder in which a person has repeated and intense sexual urges or fantasies that involve touching and rubbing against a nonconsenting person, and either acts on these urges with nonconsenting individuals or experiences clinically significant distress or impairment.

Functional magnetic resonance imaging (fMRI) A neuroimaging technique used to visualize internal functioning of the brain or body.

Fusion The final merging of two or more subpersonalities in multiple personality disorder.

GABA *See* Gamma-aminobutyric acid.

Gambling disorder A disorder marked by persistent and recurrent gambling behavior, leading to a range of life problems.

Gamma-aminobutyric acid (GABA) A neurotransmitter whose low activity has been linked to generalized anxiety disorder.

Gender-change surgery A surgical procedure that changes a person's sex organs and gender features. Also known as *gender reassignment surgery*, *gender confirmation surgery*, and *gender-affirming surgery*.

Gender dysphoria A disorder in which a transgender individual persistently experiences clinically significant distress or impairment due to his or her assigned gender.

Gender reassignment surgery A surgical procedure that changes a person's sex organs and gender features. Also known as *gender change surgery*, *gender confirmation surgery*, and *gender-affirming surgery*.

Gender-sensitive therapies Approaches geared to the pressures of being a woman in Western society. Also called *feminist therapies*.

Gene Chromosome segments that control the characteristics and traits we inherit.

General paresis An irreversible medical disorder whose symptoms include psychological abnormalities, such as delusions of grandeur; caused by syphilis.

Generalized amnesia A loss of memory for events that occurred over a limited period of time as well as for certain events that occurred prior to that period.

Generalized anxiety disorder A disorder marked by persistent and excessive feelings of anxiety and worry about numerous events and activities.

Generic drug A marketed drug that is comparable to a trade-named drug in dosage form, strength, and performance.

Genetic linkage study A research approach in which extended families with high rates of a disorder over several generations are observed in order to determine whether the disorder closely follows the distribution pattern of other family traits.

Genital stage In Freud's theory, the stage beginning at approximately 12 years old, when the child begins to find sexual pleasure in heterosexual relationships.

Genito-pelvic pain/penetration disorder A sexual dysfunction characterized by significant physical discomfort during intercourse.

Geropsychology The field of psychology concerned with the mental health of elderly people.

Gestalt therapy The humanistic therapy developed by Fritz Perls in which clinicians actively move clients toward self-recognition and self-acceptance by using techniques such as role playing and self-discovery exercises.

Glia Brain cells that support the neurons.

Glutamate A common neurotransmitter that has been linked to memory and to dementia.

Grief The reaction a person experiences when a loved one is lost.

Group home A special home where people with disorders or disabilities live and are taught self-help, living, and working skills.

Group therapy A therapy format in which a group of people with similar problems meet together with a therapist to work on those problems.

Guided participation A modeling technique in which a client systematically observes and imitates the therapist while the therapist confronts feared items.

Guilty but mentally ill A verdict stating that defendants are guilty of committing a crime but are also suffering from a mental illness that should be treated during their imprisonment.

Guilty with diminished capacity A legal defense argument that states that because of limitations posed by mental dysfunction, a defendant could not have intended to commit a particular crime and thus should be convicted of a lesser crime.

Halfway house A residence for people with schizophrenia or other severe problems, often staffed by paraprofessionals. Also known as a *group home* or *crisis house*.

Hallucination The experiencing of imagined sights, sounds, or other perceptions in the absence of external stimuli.

Hallucinogen A substance that causes powerful changes primarily in sensory perception, including strengthening perceptions and producing illusions and hallucinations. Also called a *psychedelic drug*.

Hallucinosis A form of intoxication caused by hallucinogens, consisting of perceptual distortions and hallucinations.

Hardiness A set of positive attitudes and reactions in response to stress.

Health maintenance The principle that young adults should act to promote their physical and mental health to best prepare for the aging process. Also called *wellness*.

Helper T-cell A lymphocyte that identifies foreign invaders and then both multiplies and triggers the production of other kinds of immune cells.

Heroin One of the most addictive substances derived from opium.

High The pleasant feeling of relaxation and euphoria that follows the rush from certain recreational drugs.

Hippocampus A brain structure located below the cerebral cortex that is involved in memory.

Histrionic personality disorder A personality disorder in which an individual displays a pattern of excessive emotionality and attention seeking. Once called *hysterical personality disorder*.

Hoarding disorder A disorder in which people feel compelled to save items and experience significant distress if they try to discard them, resulting in an excessive accumulation of items and possessions.

Hopelessness A pessimistic belief that one's present circumstances, problems, or mood will not change.

Hormones The chemicals released by endocrine glands into the bloodstream.

Humanistic model The theoretical perspective that human beings are born with a natural inclination to be friendly, cooperative, and constructive and are driven to self-actualize.

Humanistic therapy A system of therapy in which clinicians try to help clients look at themselves accurately and acceptingly so that they can fulfill their positive inborn potential.

Humors According to the Greeks and Romans, bodily chemicals that influence mental and physical functioning.

Huntington's disease An inherited disease, characterized by progressive problems in cognition, emotion, and movement, which results in neurocognitive disorder.

Hypersomnolence disorder A sleep-wake disorder characterized by an extreme need for extra sleep and feelings of excessive sleepiness.

Hypertension Chronic high blood pressure.

Hypnosis A sleeplike suggestible state during which a person can be directed to act in unusual ways, to experience unusual sensations, to remember seemingly forgotten events, or to forget remembered events.

Hypnotic amnesia Loss of memory produced by hypnotic suggestion.

Hypnotic therapy A treatment in which the patient undergoes hypnosis and is then guided to recall forgotten events or perform other therapeutic activities. Also known as *hypnotherapy*.

Hypnotism A procedure that places people in a trancelike mental state during which they become extremely suggestible.

Hypochondriasis A disorder in which people mistakenly fear that minor changes in their physical functioning indicate a serious disease. Now known as *illness anxiety disorder*.

Hypomanic episode An episode of mania in which the symptoms cause relatively little impairment.

Hypomanic pattern A pattern in which a person displays symptoms of mania, but the symptoms are less severe and cause less impairment than those of a manic episode.

Hypothalamic-pituitary-adrenal (HPA) pathway One of the two major routes by which the brain and body produce arousal and fear.

Hypothalamus A brain structure that helps maintain various bodily functions, including eating and hunger.

Hypothesis A hunch or prediction that certain variables are related in certain ways.

Hypoxyphilia A pattern in which people strangle or smother themselves, or ask their partners to strangle or smother them, to increase their sexual pleasure.

Hysteria A term once used to describe what are now known as conversion disorder, somatic symptom disorder, and illness anxiety disorder.

Hysterical disorder A disorder in which physical functioning is changed or lost, without an apparent physical cause.

Iatrogenic Produced or caused inadvertently by a clinician.

Id According to Freud, the psychological force that produces instinctual needs, drives, and impulses.

Ideas of reference Beliefs that unrelated events pertain to oneself in some important way.

Identification Unconsciously incorporating the values and feelings of one's parents and fusing them with one's identity. Also, an ego defense mechanism in which a person takes on the values and feelings of a person who is causing them anxiety.

Idiographic understanding An understanding of the behavior of a particular individual.

Illness anxiety disorder A disorder in which people are chronically anxious about and preoccupied with the notion that they have or are developing a serious medical illness, despite the absence of somatic symptoms. Previously known as *hypochondriasis*.

Illogical thinking According to cognitive theories, illogical ways of thinking that may lead to self-defeating conclusions and psychological problems.

Immune system The body's network of activities and cells that identify and destroy antigens and cancer cells.

Inappropriate affect Display of emotions that are unsuited to the situation; a symptom of schizophrenia.

Incest Sexual relations between closely related individuals.

Incidence The number of new cases of a disorder occurring in a population over a specific period of time.

Independent variable The variable in an experiment that is manipulated to determine whether it has an effect on another variable.

Individual therapy A therapeutic approach in which a therapist sees a client alone for sessions that may last from 15 minutes to 2 hours.

Informed consent The requirement that researchers provide sufficient information to participants about the purpose, procedure, risks, and benefits of a study.

Insanity defense A legal defense in which a person charged with a criminal offense claims to be not guilty by reason of insanity at the time of the crime.

Insomnia Difficulty falling or staying asleep.

Insomnia disorder A sleep-wake disorder characterized by severe difficulty falling asleep or maintaining sleep at least three nights per week.

Institutional Review Board (IRB) An ethics committee formed in a research facility that is empowered to protect the rights and safety of human research participants. It reviews and may require changes in each proposed study at the facility before approving or disapproving the study.

Integrity test A test that is designed to measure whether the test taker is generally honest or dishonest.

Intellectual disability (ID) A disorder marked by intellectual functioning and adaptive behavior that are well below average. Previously called *mental retardation*.

Intelligence quotient (IQ) A score derived from intelligence tests that theoretically represents a person's overall intellectual capacity.

Intelligence test A test designed to measure a person's intellectual ability.

Intermittent explosive disorder An impulse-control disorder in which people periodically fail to resist aggressive impulses and commit serious assaults on others or destroy property.

Internal validity The accuracy with which a study can pinpoint one of various possible factors as the cause of a phenomenon.

International Classification of Diseases (ICD) The classification system for medical and mental disorders that is used by the World Health Organization.

Internet gaming disorder A disorder marked by persistent, recurrent, and excessive Internet gaming activity. Recommended for further study by the DSM-5 study group.

Interpersonal psychotherapy (IPT) A treatment for unipolar depression that is based on the belief that clarifying and changing one's interpersonal problems will help lead to recovery.

Interpersonal theory of suicide A theory asserting that people with perceived burdensomeness, thwarted belongingness, and a psychological capability to carry out suicide are the most likely to attempt suicide. Also called *interpersonal-psychological theory*.

Interrater reliability A measure of the reliability of a test or of research results in which the consistency of evaluations across different judges is assessed. Also called *interjudge reliability*.

Intolerance of uncertainty theory An explanation for generalized anxiety disorder that states that certain individuals cannot tolerate the knowledge that negative events may occur, even if the possibility of occurrence is very small.

Intoxication A cluster of undesirable behavioral or psychological changes, such as slurred speech or mood changes, that may develop during or shortly after the ingestion of a substance.

In vivo desensitization Desensitization that makes use of actual objects or situations, as opposed to imagined ones.

Ion An atom or group of atoms that has a positive or negative electrical charge.

Irresistible impulse test A legal test for insanity that holds people to be insane at the time they committed a crime if they were driven to do so by an uncontrollable "fit of passion."

Isolation An ego defense mechanism in which people unconsciously isolate and disown undesirable and unwanted thoughts, experiencing them as foreign intrusions.

Jail diversion An arrangement in which mentally disturbed criminal defendants are treated for their disorders on an outpatient basis. That is, they are diverted from jail to the community for mental health care.

Joint attention Sharing focus with other people on items or events in one's immediate surroundings, through shared eye-gazing, pointing, referencing, or other verbal or non-verbal indications that one is paying attention to the same object.

Kleptomania An impulse-control disorder characterized by the recurrent failure to resist impulses to steal objects not needed for personal use or monetary value.

Korsakoff's syndrome An alcohol-related disorder marked by extreme confusion, memory impairment, and other neurological symptoms.

Late-onset Alzheimer's disease By far, the most common form of Alzheimer disease, developing after the age of 65 and not typically running in families.

Latent content The symbolic meaning behind a dream's content.

Lateral hypothalamus (LH) A brain region that produces hunger when activated.

L-dopa A drug used in the treatment of Parkinson's disease, a disease in which dopamine is low.

Learned helplessness The perception, based on past experiences, that one has no control over one's reinforcements.

Lewy body disease A type of neurocognitive disorder that involves a buildup of clumps of protein deposits, called Lewy bodies, within many neurons. In addition to progressive cognitive problems, this disease features significant movement difficulties.

Libido The sexual energy that fuels the id.

Life change units (LCUs) A system for measuring the stress associated with various life events.

Light therapy A treatment for seasonal affective disorder in which patients are exposed to extra light for several hours. Also called *phototherapy*.

Lithium A metallic element that occurs in nature as a mineral salt and is an effective treatment for bipolar disorders.

Lobotomy Psychosurgery in which a surgeon cuts the connections between the brain's frontal lobes and the lower centers of the brain.

Localized amnesia An inability to recall any of the events that occurred over a limited period of time.

Locus ceruleus A small brain structure that seems to be active in the regulation of emotions. Many of its neurons use norepinephrine.

Longitudinal study A study that observes the same participants on many occasions over a long period of time.

Long-term care Extended personal and medical support provided to elderly and other persons who may be impaired. It may range from partial support in a supervised apartment to intensive care at a nursing home.

Long-term memory The memory system that contains all the information that a person has stored over the years.

Loose associations A common thinking disturbance in schizophrenia, characterized by rapid shifts from one topic of conversation to another. Also known as *derailment*.

LSD (lysergic acid diethylamide) A hallucinogenic drug derived from ergot alkaloids.

Lycanthropy A condition in which persons believe themselves to be possessed by wolves or other animals.

Lymphocytes White blood cells that circulate through the lymph system and bloodstream, helping the body identify and destroy antigens and cancer cells.

Magnetic resonance imaging (MRI) A neuroimaging technique used to visualize internal structures of the brain or body.

Mainstreaming The placement of children with intellectual disability in regular school classes. Also known as *inclusion*.

Major depressive disorder A severe pattern of unipolar depression that is disabling and is not caused by such factors as drugs or a general medical condition.

Major neurocognitive disorder A neurocognitive disorder in which the decline in cognitive functioning is substantial and interferes with the ability to be independent.

Male hypoactive sexual desire disorder A male dysfunction marked by a persistent reduction or lack of interest in sex and hence a low level of sexual activity.

Malingering Intentionally faking illness to achieve some external gains, such as financial compensation or military deferment.

Malpractice suit A lawsuit charging a therapist with improper conduct or decision making in the course of treatment.

Managed care program A system of health care coverage in which the insurance company largely controls the nature, scope, and cost of medical or psychological services.

Mania A state or episode of euphoria or frenzied activity in which people may have an exaggerated belief that the world is theirs for the taking.

Manifest content The consciously remembered content of a dream.

Mantra A sound, uttered or thought, used to focus one's attention and to turn away from ordinary thoughts and concerns during meditation.

MAO inhibitor An antidepressant drug that prevents the action of the enzyme monoamine oxidase.

Marijuana One of the cannabis drugs, derived from the buds, leaves, and flowering tops of the hemp plant *Cannabis sativa*.

Marital therapy A therapy approach in which the therapist works with two people who share a long-term relationship. Also known as *couple therapy*.

Masked design An experiment in which participants do not know whether they are in the experimental or the control condition. Previously called a *blind design*.

Masturbation Self-stimulation of the genitals to achieve sexual arousal.

Masturbatory satiation A behavioral treatment in which a client masturbates for a very long period of time while fantasizing in detail about a paraphilic object. The procedure is expected to produce a feeling of boredom that becomes linked to the object.

Matched design A research design that matches the experimental participants with control participants who are similar on key characteristics.

Mean The average of a group of scores.

Meditation A technique of turning one's concentration inward and achieving a slightly changed state of consciousness.

Melancholia A condition described by early Greek and Roman philosophers and physicians as consisting of unshakable sadness. Today it is known as *depression*.

Melatonin A hormone released by the pineal gland when a person's surroundings are dark.

Memory The faculty for recalling past events and past learning.

Mental incompetence A state of mental instability that leaves defendants unable to understand the legal charges and proceedings they are facing and unable to prepare an adequate defense with their attorney.

Mentalization The capacity to understand one's own mental states and those of other people.

Mental status exam A set of interview questions and observations designed to reveal the degree and nature of a client's psychological functioning.

Mentally disordered sex offender A legal category that some states apply to certain people who are repeatedly found guilty of sex crimes.

Mentally ill chemical abusers (MICAs) People suffering from both schizophrenia (or another severe psychological disorder) and a substance use disorder. Also called *dual-diagnosis patients*.

Mesmerism The method employed by Austrian physician F. A. Mesmer to treat hysterical disorders; a precursor of *hypnotism*.

Meta-analysis A statistical method that combines results from multiple independent studies.

Metabolism An organism's chemical and physical breakdown of food and the process of converting it into energy. Also, an organism's biochemical transformation of various substances, as when the liver breaks down alcohol into acetylaldehyde.

Metacognitive theory A theory suggesting that people with generalized anxiety disorder implicitly hold both positive and negative beliefs about worrying.

Metaworry Worrying about the fact that one is worrying so much.

Methadone A laboratory-made opioid-like drug.

Methadone maintenance program An approach to treating opioid-centered substance use in which clients are given legally and medically supervised doses of a substitute drug, methadone.

Methamphetamine A powerful amphetamine drug that has experienced a surge in popularity in recent years, posing major health and law enforcement problems.

Methylphenidate A stimulant drug, known better by the trade names *Ritalin* and *Concerta*, commonly used to treat ADHD.

Migraine headache A very severe headache that occurs on one side of the head, often preceded by a warning sensation and sometimes accompanied by dizziness, nausea, or vomiting.

Mild intellectual disability A level of intellectual disability (IQ between 50 and 70) at which people can benefit from education and can support themselves as adults.

Mild neurocognitive disorder Neurocognitive disorder in which the decline in cognitive functioning is modest and does not interfere with the ability to be independent.

Milieu therapy A humanistic approach to institutional treatment based on the premise that institutions can help patients recover by creating a climate that promotes self-respect, individual responsible behavior, and meaningful activity.

Mind-body dualism The position advocated by the seventeenth century French philosopher René Descartes that the mind is separate from the body.

Mindfulness-based cognitive-behavioral therapy A type of therapy that teaches clients to be mindful of (just notice and accept) their dysfunctional thoughts or worries.

Mindfulness meditation A type of meditation in which people are mindful of (just notice) the various thoughts, emotions, sensations, and other private experiences that pass through their minds and bodies.

Minnesota Multiphasic Personality Inventory (MMPI) A widely used personality inventory consisting of a large number of statements that subjects mark as being true or false for them.

Mixed design A research design that intermixes elements of both experimental and correlational studies. Also known as *quasi-experimental design*.

M'Naghten test A widely used legal test for insanity that holds people to be insane at the time they committed a crime if, because of a mental disorder, they did not know the nature of the act or did not know right from wrong. Also known as the *M'Naghten rule*.

Model A set of assumptions and concepts that help scientists explain and interpret observations. Also called a *paradigm*.

Modeling A process of learning in which a person acquires responses by observing and imitating others. Also, a therapy approach based on the same principle.

Moderate intellectual disability A level of intellectual disability (IQ between 35 and 49) at which people can learn to care for themselves and can benefit from vocational training.

Monoamine oxidase (MAO) A body chemical that destroys the neurotransmitter norepinephrine.

Monoamine oxidase (MAO) inhibitors Antidepressant drugs that lower MAO activity and thus increase the level of norepinephrine activity in the brain.

Mood disorder A disorder affecting one's emotional state, including major depressive disorder and bipolar disorders.

Mood stabilizing drugs Psychotropic drugs that help stabilize the moods of people suffering from a bipolar disorder. Also known as *antibipolar drugs*.

Moral treatment A nineteenth-century approach to treating people with mental dysfunction that emphasized moral guidance and humane and respectful treatment.

Morphine A highly addictive substance derived from opium that is particularly effective in relieving pain.

Motivational interviewing A treatment intervention that uses a mixture of empathy and inquiring review to help motivate clients to recognize they have a serious psychological problem and to commit to making constructive choices and behavior changes.

Multicultural perspective The view that each culture within a larger society has a particular set of values and beliefs, as well as special external pressures, that help account for the behavior and functioning of its members. Also called *culturally diverse perspective*.

Multicultural psychology The field of psychology that examines the impact of culture, race, ethnicity, gender, and similar factors on our behaviors and thoughts and focuses on how such factors may influence the origin, nature, and treatment of abnormal behavior.

Multidimensional risk perspective A theory that identifies several kinds of risk factors that are thought to combine to help cause a disorder. The more factors present, the greater the risk of developing the disorder.

Multifinality The principle that persons with a similar developmental history may nevertheless react to similar current situations in very different ways.

Munchausen syndrome An extreme and long-term form of factitious disorder in which a person produces symptoms, gains admission to a hospital, and receives treatment.

Munchausen syndrome by proxy A factitious disorder in which parents make up or produce physical illnesses in their children.

Muscle contraction headache A headache caused by the narrowing of muscles surrounding the skull. Also known as *tension headache*.

Muscle dysmorphia Disorder in which people become obsessed with the incorrect belief that they are not muscular enough.

Naloxone One of the most widely used opioid antagonist drugs.

Narcissistic personality disorder A personality disorder marked by a broad pattern of grandiosity, need for admiration, and lack of empathy.

Narcolepsy A sleep-wake disorder characterized by a repeated sudden and irrepressible need to sleep during waking hours.

Narcotic Any natural or synthetic opioid-like drug.

National Alliance on Mental Illness (NAMI) A nationwide grassroots organization that provides support, education, advocacy, and research for people with severe mental disorders and their families.

National interest groups Groups and organizations such as NAMI that have formed in countries around the world to push for better community treatment.

Natural experiment An experiment in which nature, rather than an experimenter, manipulates an independent variable.

Naturalistic observation A method of observing behavior, in which clinicians or researchers observe people in their everyday environments.

Negative correlation A statistical relationship in which the value of one variable increases while the other variable decreases.

Negative symptoms Symptoms of schizophrenia that seem to be deficits in normal thought, emotions, or behaviors.

Neologism A made-up word that has meaning only to the person using it.

Nerve ending The region at the end of a neuron from which an impulse is sent to a neighboring neuron.

Neurocognitive disorder A disorder marked by a significant decline in at least one area of cognitive functioning.

Neurodevelopmental disorders A group of disorders—including ADHD, autism spectrum disorder, and intellectual disability—in the functioning of the brain that emerge at birth or during very early childhood and affect an individual's behavior, memory, concentration, and/or ability to learn.

Neurofibrillary tangles Twisted protein fibers that form within certain brain cells as people age. People with Alzheimer's disease have an excessive number of such tangles.

Neuroimaging techniques Neurological tests that provide images of brain structure or activity, such as CT scans, PET scans, and MRIs. Also called *brain scans*.

Neuroleptic drugs An alternative term for first-generation antipsychotic drugs, so called because they often produce undesired effects similar to the symptoms of neurological disorders.

Neuroleptic malignant syndrome A severe, potentially fatal reaction to antipsychotic drugs, marked by muscle rigidity, fever, altered consciousness, and autonomic dysfunction.

Neurological Relating to the structure or activity of the brain.

Neurological test A test that directly measures brain structure or activity.

Neuromodulator A neurotransmitter that helps modify or regulate the effect of other neurotransmitters.

Neuron A nerve cell.

Neuropsychological test A test that detects brain impairment by measuring a person's cognitive, perceptual, and motor performances.

Neurosis Freud's term for disorders characterized by intense anxiety, attributed to failure of a person's ego defense mechanisms to cope with unconscious conflicts.

Neurotransmitter A chemical that, released by one neuron, crosses the synaptic space to be received at receptors on the dendrites of neighboring neurons

Neutralizing Attempting to eliminate thoughts that one finds unacceptable by thinking or behaving in ways that make up for those thoughts and so put matters right internally.

New wave cognitive-behavioral therapies A group of relatively new approaches, including acceptance and commitment therapy (ACT), that help clients to accept many of their problematic thoughts rather than judge them, act on them, or try fruitlessly to change them.

Nicotine An alkaloid (nitrogen-containing chemical) derived from tobacco or produced in the laboratory.

Nicotine patch A patch attached to the skin like a Band-Aid, with nicotine content that is absorbed through the skin, that supposedly eases the withdrawal reaction brought on by quitting cigarette smoking.

Nightmare disorder A parasomnia characterized by chronic distressful, frightening dreams.

Nocturnal penile tumescence (NPT) Erection during sleep.

Nomothetic understanding A general understanding of the nature, causes, and treatments of abnormal psychological functioning, in the form of laws or principles.

Nonsuicidal self-injury (NSSI) A disorder that is being studied for possible inclusion in a future edition of DSM-5, characterized by persons intentionally injuring themselves on five or more occasions over a 1-year period, without the conscious intent of killing themselves.

Norepinephrine A neurotransmitter whose abnormal activity is linked to panic disorder and depression.

Normalization The principle that institutions and community residences should provide people with intellectual disability types of living conditions and opportunities that are similar to those enjoyed by the rest of society.

Norms A society's stated and unstated rules for proper conduct.

Not guilty by reason of insanity (NGRI) A verdict stating that defendants are not guilty of committing a crime because they were insane at the time of the crime.

Nutritional rehabilitation An initial phase of treatment in a number of cases of anorexia nervosa that includes supportive nursing care, day-to-day increased caloric intake, nutrition counseling, support, and, in some programs, motivational interviewing.

Object relations theory The psychodynamic theory that views the desire for relationships as the key motivating force in human behavior.

Observer drift The tendency of an observer who is rating subjects in an experiment to change criteria gradually and involuntarily, thus making the data unreliable.

Obsession A persistent thought, idea, impulse, or image that is experienced repeatedly, feels intrusive, and causes anxiety.

Obsessive-compulsive disorder (OCD) A disorder in which a person has recurrent and unwanted thoughts and/or a need to perform repetitive and rigid actions.

Obsessive-compulsive personality disorder A personality disorder marked by such an intense focus on orderliness, perfectionism, and control that the person loses flexibility, openness, and efficiency.

Obsessive-compulsive-related disorders A group of disorders in which obsessive-like concerns drive people to repeatedly and excessively perform specific patterns of behavior that greatly disrupt their lives.

Oedipus complex In Freudian theory, the pattern of desires emerging during the phallic stage in which boys become attracted to their mother as a sexual object and see their father as a rival they would like to push aside.

Olanzapine A second generation antipsychotic drug whose brand name is Zyprexa.

Operant conditioning A process of learning in which behavior that leads to satisfying consequences is likely to be repeated.

Opioid Opium, drugs derived from opium, and similar synthetic drugs. Also known collectively as *narcotics*.

Opioid antagonist A substance that attaches to opioid receptors in the brain and, in turn, blocks the effects of opioids.

Opium A highly addictive substance made from the sap of the opium poppy seed.

Oppositional defiant disorder A disorder in which children are repeatedly argumentative and defiant, angry and irritable, and, in some cases, vindictive.

Oral stage The earliest developmental stage in Freud's conceptualization of psychosexual development, during which the infant's main gratification comes from feeding and from the body parts involved in feeding.

Orbitofrontal cortex A brain structure in which impulses involving excretion, sexuality, violence, and other primitive activities normally arise.

Orgasm A peaking of sexual pleasure, consisting of rhythmic muscular contractions in the pelvic region, during which a man's semen is ejaculated and the outer third of a woman's vaginal wall contracts.

Orgasm phase The phase of the sexual response cycle during which a person's sexual pleasure peaks and sexual tension is released as muscles in the pelvic region contract rhythmically.

Outpatient A person who receives a diagnosis or treatment in a clinic, hospital, or therapist's office but is not hospitalized overnight.

Outpatient civil commitment program A legal process in which courts order people with severe mental disorders into community treatment.

Oxycodone The key ingredient in OxyContin and Percocet, medical opioids prescribed to relieve pain.

Panic attacks Periodic, short bouts of panic that occur suddenly, reach a peak within minutes, and gradually pass.

Panic brain circuit The brain circuit that helps produce panic reactions, consisting of structures such as the amygdala, hippocampus, ventromedial nucleus of the hypothalamus, central gray matter, and locus coeruleus.

Panic disorder An anxiety disorder marked by recurrent and unpredictable panic attacks.

Paranoid personality disorder A personality disorder marked by a pattern of extreme distrust and suspiciousness of others.

Paraphilias Patterns in which a person has recurrent and intense sexual urges, fantasies, or behaviors involving nonhuman objects, children, nonconsenting adults, or experiences of suffering or humiliation.

Paraphilic disorder A disorder in which a person's paraphilia causes great distress, interferes with social or occupational activities, or places the person or others at risk of harm—either currently or in the past.

Paraprofessional A person without previous professional training who provides services under the supervision of a mental health professional.

Parasomnias Sleep-wake disorders, such as sleepwalking, sleep terrors, and nightmare disorder, characterized by the occurrence of abnormal events during sleep.

Parasuicide A suicide attempt that does not result in death.

Parasympathetic nervous system The nerve fibers of the autonomic nervous system that help return bodily processes to normal.

Parity laws Laws that direct insurance companies to provide equal coverage for mental and physical problems.

Parens patriae The principle by which the state can make decisions to promote the individual's best interests and protect him or her from self-harm or neglect.

Parent management training A treatment approach for conduct disorder in which therapists combine family and cognitive-behavioral interventions to improve family functioning and help parents deal with their children more effectively.

Parkinsonian symptoms Symptoms similar to those found in Parkinson's disease. Patients with schizophrenia who take antipsychotic medications may display one or more of these symptoms.

Parkinson's disease A slowly progressive neurological disease, marked by tremors and rigidity, that may also cause a neurocognitive disorder.

Participant An individual chosen to participate in a study. Also called a *subject*.

Participant modeling A behavioral treatment in which people with fears observe a therapist (model) interacting with a feared object and then interact with the object themselves.

Pedophilic disorder A paraphilic disorder in which a person has repeated and intense sexual urges or fantasies about watching, touching, or engaging in sexual acts with children, and either acts on these urges or experiences clinically significant distress or impairment.

Peer review system A system by which clinicians paid by an insurance company may periodically review a patient's progress and recommend the continuation or termination of insurance benefits.

Penile prosthesis A surgical implant consisting of a semirigid rod that produces an artificial erection.

Performance anxiety The fear of performing inadequately and a related tension experienced during sex.

Perseveration The persistent repetition of words and statements.

Persistent depressive disorder A chronic form of unipolar depression marked by ongoing and repeated symptoms of either major or mild depression.

Personality A unique and long-term pattern of inner experience and outward behavior that leads to consistent reactions across various situations.

Personality disorder An enduring, rigid pattern of inner experience and outward behavior that repeatedly impairs a person's sense of self, emotional experiences, goals, capacity for empathy, and/or capacity for intimacy.

Personality disorder—trait specified (PDTS) A personality disorder currently undergoing study for possible inclusion in a future revision of DSM-5. Individuals would receive this diagnosis if they display significant impairment in functioning as a result of one or more very problematic traits.

Personality inventory A test designed to measure broad personality characteristics, consisting of statements about behaviors, beliefs, and feelings that people evaluate as either characteristic or uncharacteristic of them.

Phallic stage In psychoanalytic theory, the period between the third and fourth years when the focus of sexual pleasure shifts to the genitals.

Phalloplasty A surgical procedure designed to create a functional penis.

Phenothiazines A group of antihistamine drugs that became the first group of effective antipsychotic medications.

Phenylketonuria (PKU) A metabolic disorder caused by the body's inability to break down the amino acid phenylalanine, resulting in intellectual disability and other symptoms.

Phobia A persistent and unreasonable fear of a particular object, activity, or situation.

Pick's disease A neurological disease that affects the frontal and temporal lobes, causing a neurocognitive disorder.

Placebo therapy A simulated treatment that the participant in an experiment believes to be genuine.

Play therapy An approach to treating childhood disorders that helps children express their conflicts and feelings indirectly by drawing, playing with toys, and making up stories.

Pleasure principle The pursuit of gratification that characterizes id functioning.

Plethysmograph A device used to measure sexual arousal.

Polygraph test A test that seeks to determine whether the test taker is telling the truth by measuring physiological responses such as respiration level, perspiration level, and heart rate. Also known as a *lie detector test*.

Polysubstance use The use of two or more substances at the same time.

Positive correlation A statistical relationship in which the values of two variables increase together or decrease together.

Positive psychology The study and enhancement of positive feelings, traits, and abilities.

Positive symptoms Symptoms of schizophrenia that seem to be excesses of or bizarre additions to normal thoughts, emotions, or behaviors.

Positron emission tomography (PET scan) A computer-produced motion picture showing rates of metabolism throughout the brain.

Postpartum depression An episode of depression experienced by some new mothers that begins within four weeks after giving birth.

Postpartum psychosis An episode of psychosis experienced by a small percentage of new mothers that begins within days or weeks after giving birth.

Posttraumatic stress disorder (PTSD) A disorder in which fear and related symptoms continue to be experienced long after a traumatic event.

Poverty of speech A decrease in speech or speech content found in some people with schizophrenia. Also known as *alogia*.

Predictive validity The ability of a test or other assessment tool to predict future characteristics or behaviors.

Predisposition An inborn or acquired vulnerability for developing certain symptoms or disorders.

Prefrontal lobes Structures of the brain that play a key role in short-term memory, among other functions.

Premature ejaculation A dysfunction in which a man persistently reaches orgasm and ejaculates within one minute of beginning sexual activity with a partner and before he wishes to. Also called *early* or *rapid ejaculation*.

Premenstrual dysphoric disorder A disorder marked by repeated experiences of significant depression and related symptoms during the week before menstruation.

Premenstrual syndrome (PMS) A common and normal cluster of psychological and physical discomforts that precede menses.

Premorbid The period prior to the onset of a disorder.

Preparedness A predisposition to develop certain fears.

Prevalence The total number of cases of a disorder occurring in a population over a specific period of time.

Prevention A key feature of community mental health programs that seek to prevent or minimize psychological disorders.

Primary gain In psychodynamic theory, the gain people achieve when their somatic symptoms keep their internal conflicts out of awareness.

Primary personality The subpersonality that appears more often than the others in individuals with dissociative identity disorder.

Primary prevention Prevention interventions that are designed to prevent disorders altogether.

Private psychotherapy An arrangement in which a person directly pays a therapist for counseling services.

Proband The person who is the focus of a genetic study.

Procedural memory Memory of learned skills that a person performs without needing to think about them.

Prodromal phase The period during which the symptoms of schizophrenia are not yet prominent, but the person has begun to deteriorate from previous levels of functioning.

Profound intellectual disability A level of intellectual disability (IQ below 20) at which people need a very structured environment with close supervision.

Projection An ego defense mechanism whereby individuals attribute to other people characteristics or impulses they do not wish to acknowledge in themselves.

Projective test A test consisting of ambiguous material that people interpret or respond to.

Prolonged exposure An exposure treatment in which clients confront not only trauma-related objects and situations, but also their painful memories of traumatic experiences.

Protection and advocacy system The system by which lawyers and advocates who work for patients may investigate the patients' treatment and protect their rights.

Prozac The trade name for fluoxetine, a second-generation antidepressant.

Pseudocommando mass killing Mass murder in which an individual kills in public, often during the daytime, plans his offense well in advance, and comes prepared with a powerful arsenal of weapons. The killer has no escape planned and expects to be killed during the incident.

Psychedelic drugs Substances such as LSD that cause profound perceptual changes. Also called *hallucinogenic drugs*.

Psychiatric social worker A mental health specialist who is qualified to conduct psychotherapy upon earning a master's degree or doctorate in social work.

Psychiatrist A physician who in addition to medical school has completed three to four years of residency training in the treatment of abnormal mental functioning.

Psychoanalysis Either the theory or the treatment of abnormal mental functioning that emphasizes unconscious psychological forces as the cause of psychopathology.

Psychodynamic model The theoretical perspective that sees all human functioning as being shaped by dynamic (interacting) psychological forces and explains people's behavior by reference to unconscious internal conflicts.

Psychodynamic therapy A system of therapy whose goals are to help clients uncover past traumatic events and the inner conflicts that have resulted from them, settle those conflicts, and resume personal development.

Psychogenic perspective The view that the chief causes of abnormal functioning are psychological.

Psychological autopsy A procedure used to analyze information about a deceased person, for example, in order to determine whether the person's death was a suicide.

Psychological debriefing A form of crisis intervention in which victims are helped to talk about their feelings and reactions to traumatic incidents. Also called *critical incident stress debriefing*.

Psychological profile A method of suspect identification that seeks to predict an unknown criminal's psychological, emotional, and personality characteristics based on the individual's pattern of criminal behavior and on research into the psychological characteristics of people who have committed similar crimes.

Psychology The study of mental processes and behaviors.

Psychomotor symptoms Disturbances in movement sometimes found in certain disorders such as schizophrenia.

Psychoneuroimmunology The study of the connections among stress, the body's immune system, and illness.

Psychopathology An abnormal pattern of functioning that may be described as deviant, distressful, dysfunctional, and/or dangerous.

Psychopathy *See* antisocial personality disorder.

Psychopharmacologist A psychiatrist who primarily prescribes medications. Also called *pharmacotherapist*.

Psychophysiological disorders Disorders in which biological, psychological, and sociocultural factors interact to cause or worsen a physical illness. Also known as *psychological factors affecting other medical conditions*.

Psychophysiological test A test that measures physical responses (such as heart rate and muscle tension) as possible indicators of psychological problems.

Psychosexual stages The developmental stages defined by Freud in which the id, ego, and superego interact.

Psychosis A state in which a person loses contact with reality in key ways.

Psychosurgery Brain surgery for mental disorders.

Psychotherapy A treatment system in which words and acts are used by a client (patient) and therapist in order to help the client overcome psychological difficulties.

Psychotropic medications Drugs that mainly affect the brain and reduce many symptoms of mental dysfunction.

Quasi-experimental design A research design that fails to include key elements of a "pure" experiment and/or intermixes elements of both experimental and correlational studies. Also called a *mixed design*.

Random assignment A selection procedure that ensures that participants are randomly placed either in the control group or in the experimental group.

Rap group The initial term for group therapy sessions among veterans, in which members meet to talk about and explore problems in an atmosphere of mutual support.

Rape Forced sexual intercourse or another sexual act committed against a nonconsenting person or intercourse with an underage person.

Rapid eye movement (REM) sleep The period of the sleep cycle during which the eyes move quickly back and forth, indicating that the person is dreaming.

Rapprochement movement An effort to identify a set of common strategies that run through the work of all effective therapists.

Rational-emotive therapy A cognitive-behavioral therapy developed by Albert Ellis that helps clients identify and change the irrational assumptions and thinking that help cause their psychological disorder.

Rationalization An ego defense mechanism in which one creates acceptable reasons for unwanted or undesirable behavior.

Reaction formation An ego defense mechanism whereby a person counters an unacceptable desire by taking on a lifestyle that directly opposes the unwanted impulse.

Reactive depression A depression that appears to be triggered by clear events. Also known as *exogenous depression*.

Reactivity The extent to which the very presence of an observer affects a person's behavior.

Reality principle The recognition, characterizing ego functioning, that we cannot always express or satisfy our id impulses.

Receptor A site on a neuron that receives a neurotransmitter.

Regression An ego defense mechanism in which a person returns to a more primitive mode of interacting with the world.

Reinforcement The desirable or undesirable stimuli that result from an organism's behavior.

Relapse-prevention training A cognitive behavioral approach to treating alcohol use disorder (and applied to certain other disorders) in which clients are taught to keep track of their drinking behavior, apply coping strategies in situations that typically trigger excessive drinking, and plan ahead for risky situations and reactions.

Relational psychoanalytic therapy A form of psychodynamic therapy that considers therapists to be active participants in the formation of patients' feelings and reactions and therefore calls for therapists to disclose their own experiences and feelings in discussions with patients.

Relaxation training A treatment procedure that teaches clients to relax at will so they can calm themselves in stressful situations.

Reliability A measure of the consistency of test or research results.

Repression A defense mechanism whereby the ego prevents unacceptable impulses from reaching consciousness.

Residential treatment center A place where people formerly addicted to drugs live, work, and socialize in a drug-free environment. Also called a *therapeutic community*.

Resiliency The ability to avoid or recover from the effects of negative circumstances.

Resistance An unconscious refusal to participate fully in therapy.

Resolution phase The fourth phase in the sexual response cycle, characterized by relaxation and a decline in arousal following orgasm.

Response inventories Tests designed to measure a person's responses in one specific area of functioning, such as affect, social skills, or cognitive processes.

Response set A particular way of responding to questions or statements on a test, such as always selecting "true," regardless of the actual questions.

Restricting-type anorexia nervosa A type of anorexia nervosa in which people reduce their weight by severely restricting their food intake.

Reticular formation The brain's arousal center, which helps people to be awake, alert, and attentive.

Retrograde amnesia A lack of memory about events that occurred before the event that triggered amnesia.

Retrospective analysis A psychological autopsy in which clinicians and researchers piece together information about a person's suicide from the person's past.

Reversal design A single-subject experimental design in which behavior is measured to provide a baseline (A), then again after the treatment has been applied (B), then again after the conditions during baseline have been reintroduced (A), and then once again after the treatment is reintroduced (B). Also known as *ABAB design*.

Reward A pleasurable stimulus given to an organism that encourages a specific behavior.

Reward circuit A dopamine-rich circuit in the brain that produces feelings of pleasure when activated.

Reward-deficiency syndrome A condition, suspected to be present in some people, in which the brain's reward circuit is not readily activated by the usual events in their lives.

Right to refuse treatment The legal right of patients to refuse certain forms of treatment.

Right to treatment The legal right of patients, particularly those who are involuntarily committed, to receive adequate treatment.

Risperidone A commonly prescribed atypical antipsychotic drug.

Ritalin A trade name of methylphenidate, a stimulant drug that is helpful in many cases of attention-deficit/hyperactivity disorder (ADHD).

Role play A therapy technique in which clients are instructed to act out roles assigned to them by the therapist.

Rorschach test A projective test, in which a person reacts to inkblots designed to help reveal psychological features of the person.

Rosenthal effect The general finding that the results of any experiment often conform to the expectations of the experimenter.

Rush A spasm of warmth and ecstasy that occurs when certain drugs, such as heroin, are ingested.

Savant A person with a mental disorder or significant intellectual deficits who has some extraordinary ability despite the disorder or deficits.

Schizoaffective disorder A disorder in which symptoms of both schizophrenia and a mood disorder are prominent.

Schizoid personality disorder A personality disorder in which a person persistently avoids social relationships and shows little emotional expression.

Schizophrenia A psychotic disorder in which personal, social, and occupational functioning deteriorate as a result of strange perceptions, disturbed thought processes, unusual emotions, and motor abnormalities.

Schizophrenia-related brain circuit A brain circuit whose dysfunction contributes to schizophrenia. It includes the prefrontal cortex, hippocampus, amygdala, thalamus, striatum, and substantia nigra, among other brain structures.

Schizophreniform disorder A disorder in which all of the key features of schizophrenia are present but last only between one and six months.

Schizophrenogenic mother A type of mother—supposedly cold, domineering, and uninterested in the needs of her children—who was once thought to cause schizophrenia in her child.

Schizotypal personality disorder A personality disorder characterized by extreme discomfort in close relationships, odd forms of thinking and perceiving, and behavioral eccentricities.

School refusal A pattern in which children fear going to school and often stay home for a long period of time. Also called *school phobia*.

Scientific method The process of systematically gathering and evaluating information through careful observations to gain an understanding of a phenomenon.

Seasonal affective disorder (SAD) A mood disorder in which mood episodes are related to changes in season.

Second-generation antidepressant drugs A relatively new group of antidepressant drugs that differ structurally from tricyclics and MAO inhibitors.

Second-generation antipsychotic drugs A relatively new group of antipsychotic drugs whose biological action is different from that of the first-generation antipsychotic drugs. Also known as *atypical antipsychotic drugs*.

Second messengers Chemical changes within a neuron just after the neuron receives a neurotransmitter message and just before it responds.

Secondary gain In psychodynamic theory, the gain people achieve when their somatic symptoms elicit kindness from others or provide an excuse for avoiding unpleasant activities.

Secondary prevention Prevention interventions that are designed to address disorders quickly, before they become more serious problems.

Sedative-hypnotic drugs Drugs used in low doses to calm people and in higher doses to help people sleep.

Selective amnesia An inability to recall some of the events that occurred over a limited period of time.

Selective mutism A disorder marked by failure to speak in certain social situations when speech is expected, despite ability to speak in other situations.

Selective serotonin reuptake inhibitors (SSRIs) A group of second-generation antidepressant drugs that increase serotonin activity specifically, without affecting other neurotransmitters.

Self-actualization The humanistic process by which people fulfill their potential for goodness and growth.

Self-efficacy The belief that one can master and perform needed behaviors whenever necessary.

Self-help group A group made up of people with similar problems who help and support one another without the direct leadership of a clinician. Also called a *mutual help group*.

Self-hypnosis The process of hypnotizing oneself, sometimes for the purpose of forgetting unpleasant events.

Self-Injury Implicit Association Test A cognitive test used to help assess suicidal risk. Rather than asking people if they plan to attempt suicide, this test instructs them to pair various suicide-related words (for example, "dead," "lifeless," "suicide") with words that are personally relevant ("I," "myself," "mine") and with words that are not personally relevant ("they," "them," "other").

Self-instruction training A treatment developed by Donald Meichenbaum that teaches people to use coping self-statements at times of stress, discomfort, or significant pain. Also called *stress inoculation training*.

Self-monitoring Clients' observation of their own behavior.

Self-statements According to some theorists, statements about oneself, sometimes counterproductive, that come to mind during stressful situations.

Self-theory The psychodynamic theory that emphasizes the role of the self—a person's unified personality.

Senile plaques Sphere-shaped deposits of beta-amyloid protein that form in the spaces between certain brain cells and in certain blood vessels as people age. People with Alzheimer's disease have an excessive number of such plaques.

Sensate focus A treatment for sexual disorders that instructs couples to take the focus away from orgasm or intercourse and instead spend time concentrating on the pleasure achieved by such acts as kissing, hugging, and mutual massage. Also known as *nondemand pleasuring*.

Separation anxiety disorder A disorder marked by excessive anxiety, even panic, whenever the individual is separated from home, a parent, or another attachment figure.

Serial murders A series of three or more killings carried out separately by the same individual(s) over a period of time—usually a month or more.

Serotonin A neurotransmitter whose abnormal activity is linked to depression, obsessive-compulsive disorder, and eating disorders.

Severe intellectual disability A level of intellectual disability (IQ between 20 and 34) at which individuals require careful supervision and can learn to perform basic work in structured and sheltered settings.

Sex offender statute The presumption by some state legislatures that people who are repeatedly found guilty of certain sex crimes have a mental disorder and should be categorized as "mentally disordered sex offenders." Such laws have been changed or abolished by many states over the past two decades.

Sexting The sending of sexually explicit material—particularly photos or text messages—between cell phones or other digital devices.

Sexual dysfunction A disorder marked by a persistent inability to function normally in some area of the human sexual response cycle.

Sexual masochism disorder A paraphilic disorder in which a person has repeated and intense sexual urges, fantasies, or behaviors that involve being humiliated, beaten, bound, or otherwise made to suffer, accompanied by clinically significant distress or impairment.

Sexual response cycle The general sequence of behavior and feelings that occurs during sexual activity, consisting of desire, excitement, orgasm, and resolution.

Sexual sadism disorder A paraphilic disorder in which a person has repeated and intense sexual urges or fantasies that involve inflicting suffering on others, and either acts on these urges with nonconsenting individuals or experiences clinically significant distress or impairment.

Sexually violent predator laws Laws passed by the federal government and many states that call for certain sex offenders who have been convicted of sex crimes and have served their sentence in prison to be removed from prison before their release and committed involuntarily to a mental hospital for treatment if a court judges them likely to engage in further acts of sexual violence due to a mental or personality abnormality. Also called *sexually dangerous persons laws*.

Shaping A learning procedure in which successive approximations of the desired behavior are rewarded until finally the exact and complete behavior is learned.

Sheltered workshop A supervised workplace for people who are not yet ready for competitive jobs.

Short-term memory The memory system that collects new information. Also known as *working memory*.

Shuttle box A box separated in the middle by a barrier that an animal can jump over in order to escape or avoid shock.

Sildenafil A drug used to treat erectile disorder that helps increase blood flow to the penis during sexual activity. Marketed as Viagra.

Single-subject experimental design A research method in which a single participant is observed and measured both before and after the manipulation of an independent variable.

Sleep apnea disorder A sleep-wake disorder characterized by frequent awakenings each night due to periodic deprivation of oxygen to the brain during sleep.

Sleep terror disorder A parasomnia in which a person awakens suddenly during the first third of sleep, screaming out in extreme fear and agitation.

Sleepwalking disorder A parasomnia in which people repeatedly leave their beds and walk around without being conscious of the episode or remembering it later.

Social anxiety disorder A severe and persistent fear of social or performance situations in which embarrassment may occur.

Social communication disorder A disorder marked by persistent problems in communication and social relationships, but without significant language difficulties or cognitive impairment. The communication and social problems are different in nature and less severe than those in autism spectrum disorder.

Social skills training A therapy approach that helps people learn or improve social skills and assertiveness through role playing and rehearsing of desirable behaviors.

Social therapy An approach to therapy in which the therapist makes practical advice and life adjustment a central focus of treatment for schizophrenia. Therapy also focuses on problem solving, decision making, memory enhancement, development of social skills, and management of medications. Also known as *personal therapy*.

Sociocultural model The theoretical perspective that emphasizes the effects of society, culture, and social and family groups on individual behavior.

Sociopathy *See* antisocial personality disorder.

Sodium amobarbital (Amytal) A drug used to put people into a near-sleep state during which some can better recall forgotten events.

Sodium pentobarbital (Pentothal) A drug used to put people into a near-sleep state during which some can better recall forgotten events.

Somatic symptom disorder A disorder in which people become excessively distressed, concerned, and anxious about bodily symptoms that they are experiencing, and their lives are greatly and disproportionately disrupted by the symptoms.

Somatogenic perspective The view that abnormal psychological functioning has physical causes.

Special education An approach to educating children with intellectual disability in which they are grouped together and given a separate, specially designed education.

Specific learning disorder A neurodevelopmental disorder marked by impairments in cognitive skills such as reading, writing, arithmetic, or mathematical skills.

Specific phobia A severe and persistent fear of a specific object or situation (does not include agoraphobia and social anxiety disorder).

Spectator role A state of mind that some people experience during sex, focusing on their sexual performance to such an extent that their performance and their enjoyment are reduced.

Standardization The process in which a test is administered to a large group of people whose performance then serves as a standard or norm against which any individual's score can be measured.

State-dependent learning Learning that becomes associated with the conditions under which it occurred, so that it is best remembered under the same conditions.

State hospitals Public mental institutions in the United States, run by the individual states.

State school A state-supported institution for people with intellectual disability.

Statistical analysis The application of principles of probability to the findings of a study in order to learn how likely it is that the findings have occurred by chance.

Statistical significance A measure of the probability that a study's findings occurred by chance rather than because of the experimental manipulation.

Stimulant drug A substance that increases the activity of the central nervous system.

Stimulus generalization A phenomenon in which responses to one stimulus are also produced by similar stimuli.

Stress brain circuit The brain circuit whose dysfunction contributes to PTSD. It includes such brain structures as the amygdala, prefrontal cortex, anterior cingulate cortex, insula, and hippocampus, among others.

Stress-management program An approach to treating generalized and other anxiety disorders that teaches clients techniques for reducing and controlling stress.

Stressor An event that creates a sense of threat by confronting a person with a demand or opportunity for change of some kind.

Stress-reduction and problem-solving programs Workshops or group sessions offered by a business, in which mental health professionals teach employees techniques for coping, solving problems, and handling and reducing stress.

Stress response A person's particular reactions to stress.

Structured interview An interview format in which the clinician asks prepared questions.

Subgenual cingulate A brain structure whose abnormal activity has been linked to depression. Also called *Brodmann Area 25*.

Subintentional death A death in which the victim plays an indirect, hidden, partial, or unconscious role.

Subject An individual chosen to participate in a study. Also called a *participant*.

Sublimation In psychoanalytic theory, the rechanneling of id impulses into endeavors that are both socially acceptable and personally gratifying. Sublimation can also be used as an ego defense mechanism.

Subpersonalities The two or more distinct personalities found in individuals suffering with dissociative identity disorder. Also known as *alternate personalities*.

Substance use disorder A pattern of maladaptive behaviors and reactions brought about by repeated use of a substance, sometimes also including tolerance for the substance and withdrawal reactions.

Suicidal behavior disorder A classification being studied for possible inclusion in a future revision of DSM-5, in which individuals have tried to die by suicide within the last two years.

Suicide A self-inflicted death in which the person acted intentionally, directly, and consciously.

Suicide education programs Suicide prevention programs that take place in schools and concentrate on students and their teachers. There are also a growing number of online sites that provide education about suicide—targeting troubled persons, their family members, and friends.

Suicide prevention program A program that tries to identify people who are at risk of killing themselves and to offer them crisis intervention.

Superego According to Freud, the psychological force that represents a person's values and ideals.

Symbolic loss According to Freudian theory, the loss of a valued object (for example, a loss of employment) that is unconsciously interpreted as the loss of a loved one. Also called *imagined loss*.

Sympathetic nervous system The nerve fibers of the autonomic nervous system that quicken the heartbeat and produce other changes experienced as arousal and fear. One of the two major routes by which the brain and body produce arousal and fear.

Symptom A physical or psychological sign of a disorder.

Synapse The tiny space between the nerve ending of one neuron and the dendrite of another.

Syndrome A cluster of symptoms that usually occur together.

Synergistic effect In pharmacology, an increase of effects that occurs when more than one substance is acting on the body at the same time.

Synesthesia A crossing over of sensory perceptions. For example, a loud sound may be seen or a color may be felt.

Systematic desensitization An exposure therapy that uses relaxation training and a fear hierarchy to help clients with phobias react calmly to the objects or situations they dread.

Tarantism A disorder occurring throughout Europe between 900 and 1800 A.D. in which people would suddenly start to jump around, dance, and go into convulsions. Also known as *St. Vitus's dance*.

Tardive dyskinesia Extrapyramidal effects that appear in some patients after they have taken antipsychotic drugs for an extended time.

Tay-Sachs disease A metabolic disorder that causes progressive loss of intellectual functioning, vision, and motor functioning, resulting in death.

Telemental health The use of digital technologies to deliver mental health services without the therapist being physically present.

Temporal lobes Regions of the brain that play a key role in transforming short-term memory to long-term memory, among other functions.

Tension headache *See* Muscle contraction headache.

Tertiary prevention Prevention interventions that are designed to provide effective treatment for moderate or severe disorders as soon as it is needed so that the disorders do not become long-term problems.

Test A device for gathering information about a few aspects of a person's psychological functioning from which broader information about the person can be inferred.

Testosterone The principal male sex hormone.

Tetrahydrocannabinol (THC) The main active ingredient of cannabis.

Thanatos According to the Freudian view, the basic death instinct that functions in opposition to the life instinct.

Thematic Apperception Test (TAT) A projective test consisting of pictures that show people in ambiguous situations that the client is asked to interpret.

Theory of mind One's awareness that other people base their behaviors on their own beliefs, intentions, and mental states, not on information they have no way of knowing.

Therapist A professional clinician who applies a system of therapy to help a person overcome psychological difficulties.

Therapy A systematic process for helping people overcome their psychological problems. Therapy consists of a client (patient), a trained therapist, and a series of contacts between them.

Token economy program A behavior-focused program in which a person's desirable behaviors are reinforced systematically throughout the day by the awarding of tokens that can be exchanged for goods or privileges.

Tolerance The adjustment that the brain and the body make to the regular use of certain drugs so that ever larger doses are needed to achieve the earlier effects.

Torture The use of brutal, degrading, and disorienting strategies to reduce victims to a state of utter helplessness.

Tranquilizer A drug that reduces anxiety.

Transcranial magnetic stimulation (TMS) A treatment procedure for depression and certain other disorders in which an electromagnetic coil, which is placed on or above a person's head, sends a current into the person's brain.

Transference According to psychodynamic theorists, the redirection toward the psychotherapist of feelings associated with important figures in a patient's life, now or in the past.

Transgender Individuals who have a strong sense that their gender identity is different from their birth anatomy.

Transvestic disorder A paraphilic disorder consisting of repeated and intense sexual urges, fantasies, or behaviors that involve dressing in clothes of the opposite sex, accompanied by clinically significant distress or impairment. Also known as *transvestism* or *cross-dressing*.

Treatment A systematic procedure designed to help change abnormal behavior into more normal behavior. Also called *therapy*.

Trephination An ancient operation in which a stone instrument was used to cut away a circular section of the skull, perhaps to treat abnormal behavior.

Trichotillomania A disorder in which people repeatedly pull out hair from their scalp, eyebrows, eyelashes, or other parts of their body. Also called *hair-pulling disorder*.

Tricyclic An antidepressant drug such as imipramine that has three rings in its molecular structure.

Trisomy A chromosomal abnormality in which a person has three chromosomes of one kind rather than the usual two.

Tube and intravenous feeding Forced nourishment sometimes provided to people with anorexia nervosa when their condition becomes life-threatening.

Type A personality style A personality pattern characterized by hostility, cynicism, drivenness, impatience, competitiveness, and ambition.

Type B personality style A personality pattern in which a person is more relaxed, less aggressive, and less concerned about time.

Type I schizophrenia According to some theorists, a type of schizophrenia dominated by positive symptoms, such as delusions, hallucinations, and certain formal thought disorders.

Type II schizophrenia According to some theorists, a type of schizophrenia dominated by negative symptoms, such as flat affect, poverty of speech, and loss of volition.

Tyramine A chemical that, if allowed to accumulate, can raise blood pressure dangerously. It is found in many common foods and is broken down by MAO.

Ulcer A lesion that forms in the wall of the stomach or of the duodenum.

Unconditional positive regard Full, warm acceptance of a person regardless of what he or she says, thinks, or feels; a critical component of client-centered therapy.

Unconditioned response (UCR) The natural, automatic response produced by an unconditioned stimulus.

Unconditioned stimulus (UCS) A stimulus that produces an automatic, natural response.

Unconscious The deeply hidden mass of memories, experiences, and impulses that is viewed in Freudian theory as the source of much behavior.

Undoing An ego defense mechanism in which a person unconsciously cancels out an unacceptable desire or act by performing another act.

Unilateral electroconvulsive therapy (ECT) A form of electroconvulsive therapy in which electrodes are attached to the head so that electrical current passes through only one side of the brain.

Unipolar depression Depression without a history of mania.

Unstructured interview An interview format in which the clinician asks spontaneous questions that are based on issues that arise during the interview.

Vagus nerve stimulation A treatment procedure for depression in which an implanted pulse generator sends regular electrical signals to a person's vagus nerve; the nerve, in turn, stimulates the brain.

Validity The accuracy of a test's or study's results; that is, the extent to which the test or study actually measures or shows what it claims.

Valium The trade name of diazepam, an anti-anxiety drug.

Variable Any characteristic or event that can vary across time, locations, or persons.

Ventromedial hypothalamus (VMH) A brain region that depresses hunger when activated.

Virtual reality treatment Cognitive-behavioral intervention that uses virtual reality—3D computer graphics that simulate real-world objects and situations—as an exposure tool.

Visual hallucinations Hallucinations in which a person may either experience vague visual perceptions, perhaps of colors or clouds, or have distinct visions of people, objects, or scenes that are not there.

Voyeuristic disorder A paraphilic disorder in which a person has repeated and intense sexual desires to observe unsuspecting people in secret as they undress or to spy on couples having intercourse, and either acts on these urges with nonconsenting individuals or experiences clinically significant distress or impairment.

Weight set point The weight level that a person is predisposed to maintain, controlled in part by the hypothalamus.

Withdrawal Unpleasant, sometimes dangerous reactions that may occur when people who use a drug regularly stop taking or reduce their dosage of the drug.

Working through The psychoanalytic process of facing conflicts, reinterpreting feelings, and overcoming one's problems.

References

AAFPRS (American Academy of Facial Plastic and Reconstructive Surgery). (2017, January 26). AAFPRS Annual Survey unveils rising trends in facial plastic surgery. Retrieved from http://www.aafprs.org/media/stats_polls/m_stats.html.

AAIDD (American Association of Intellectual and Developmental Disabilities). (2013). *Definition of intellectual disability.* Washington, DC: Author.

AAIDD (American Association of Intellectual and Developmental Disabilities). (2017). Definition of intellectual disability. *AAIDD.* Retrieved from http://www.aaidd.org.

Aalami, M., Jafarnejad, F., & Modarres Gharavi, M. (2016). The effects of progressive muscular relaxation and breathing control technique on blood pressure during pregnancy. *Iranian Journal of Nursing and Midwifery Research, 21*(3), 331–336.

Aamodt, M. G. (2014, September 6). *Serial killer statistics.* Retrieved from Aamodt website: http://maamodt. asp.radford.edu/serial_killer_information_center/project_description.htm.

Aamodt, M. G. (2016, September 4). *Serial killer statistics.* Retrieved from http://maamodt.asp.radford.edu/serial_killer_information_center/project description.htm.

AA World Services. (2017, April). Estimated worldwide A.A. individual and group membership (SM F-132). *A.A.* Retrieved from http://www.aa.org/assets.

Aaronson, S. T., Sears, P., Ruvunaq, F., Bunker, M., Conway, C. R., Dougherty, D. D., . . . Zajecka, J. M. (2017). A 5-year observational study of patients with treatment-resistant depression treated with vagus nerve stimulation or treatment as usual: Comparison of response, remission, and suicidality. *American Journal of Psychiatry, 174,* 640–648.

ABA (American Bar Association). (2017). *Court cases by diminished capacity/guilt.* Washington, DC: ABA (Center on Children and the Law).

Abate, C. (2016, November 17). Body shaming in an age of social media. *Healthline News.*

Abbey, A. (2002). Alcohol-related sexual assault: A common problem among college students. *Journal of Studies on Alcohol, 14,* 118–128.

Abbey, S. E. (2005). Somatization and somatoform disorders. In J. L. Levenson (Ed.), *The American Psychiatric Publishing textbook of psychosomatic medicine* (pp. 271–296). Washington, DC: American Psychiatric Publishing.

Abdel-Rahman, E. (Ed.) (2012). *Depression in the elderly.* Hauppauge, NY: Nova Science Publishers.

Abe, K. (2017). What is a serial killer? What is a mass murderer? How do they differ? *European Journal of Academic Essays, 4*(4), 187–198.

Abel, G. G., Jordan, A., Hand, C. G., Holland, L. A., & Phipps, A. (2001). Classification models of child molesters utilizing the Abel Assessment for child sexual abuse interest. *Child Abuse and Neglect, 25*(5), 703–718.

Abma, J. C., & Martinez, G. M. (2017, June 22). Sexual activity and contraceptive use among teenagers in the United States, 2011–2015. Atlanta, GA: CDC, National Health Statistics Report, No. 104.

Abraham, K. (1911). Notes on the psychoanalytic investigation and treatment of manic-depressive insanity and allied conditions. In *Selected papers on psychoanalysis* (pp. 137–156). New York: Basic Books. [Work republished 1960]

Abraham, K. (1916). The first pregenital stage of the libido. In *Selected papers on psychoanalysis* (pp. 248–279). New York: Basic Books. [Work republished 1960].

Abramowitz, J. (2016, June 23). Psychotherapy for obsessive-compulsive disorder in adults. *UpToDate.* Retrieved from http://www.uptodate.com.

Abramowitz, J. S., & Braddock, A. E. (2011). *Hypochondriasis and health anxiety. Advances in psychotherapy—Evidence-based practice.* Cambridge, MA: Hogrefe Publishing.

Abramson, L. Y., Alloy, L. B., Hankin, B. L., Haeffel, G. J., MacCoon, D. G., & Gibb, B. E. (2002). Cognitive vulnerability—Stress models of depression in a self-regulatory and psychobiological context. In I. H. Gotlib & C. L. Hammen (Eds.), *Handbook of depression* (pp. 268–294). New York: Guilford Press.

Abramson, L. Y., Metalsky, G. I., & Alloy, L. B. (1989). Hopelessness depression: A theory-based subtype of depression. *Psychological Review, 96*(2), 358–372.

Abramson, L. Y., Seligman, M. E., & Teasdale, J. D. (1978). Learned helplessness in humans: Critique and reformulation. *Journal of Abnormal Psychology, 87*(1), 49–74.

Abulizi, X., Pryor, L., Michel, G., Melchior, M., van der Waerden, J., & EDEN Mother–Child Cohort Study Group. (2017). Temperament in infancy and behavioral and emotional problems at age 5.5: The EDEN mother-child cohort. *PLOS ONE, 12*(2), e0171971.

AC (AddictionCenter). (2015, November 25). Drinking and drug abuse in Greek life. *Addiction Center.* Retrieved from https://www.addictioncenter.com.

à Campo, J. M. L. G., & Nijman, H. (2016). Gender dysphoria and psychiatric symptoms. *Journal of Nervous & Mental Disease, 204*(7), 558.

Achalia, R. M., Chaturvedi, S. K., Desai, G., Rao, G. N., & Prakash, O. (2014). Prevalence and risk factors associated with tardive dyskinesia among Indian patients with schizophrenia. *Asian Journal of Psychiatry, 9,* 31–35.

Acierno, R., Knapp, R., Tuerk, P., Gilmore, A. K., Lejuez, C., Ruggiero, K., . . . Foa, E. B. (2017). A non-inferiority trial of prolonged exposure for posttraumatic stress disorder: In person versus home-based telehealth. *Behaviour Research and Therapy, 89,* 57–65.

Ackerman, C. (2017, January 18). 22 mindfulness exercises, techniques & activities for adults (+PDF's). *Positive Psychology Program.* Retrieved from https://positivepsychologyprogram.com.

Ackland, G. L., Whittle, J., Toner, A., Machada, A., Del Arroyo, A. G., Sciuso, A., . . . Gourine, A. V. (2016). Molecular mechanisms linking autonomic dysfunction and impaired cardiac contractility in critical illness. *Critical Care Medicine, 44*(8), e614–e624.

ACOG (American Congress of Obstetricians and Gynecologists). (2016). *Committee opinion: Concerns regarding social media and health issues in adolescents and young adults* (No. 653). Washington, DC: ACOG.

Acosta, M. C., Haller, D. L., & Schnoll, S. H. (2005). Cocaine and stimulants. In R. J. Frances, A. H. Mack, & S. I. Miller (Eds.), *Clinical textbook of addictive disorders* (3rd ed., pp. 184–218). New York: Guilford Press.

Acosta, M. C., Haller, D. L., & Schnoll, S. H. (2011). Cocaine and stimulants. In R. J. Frances, A. H. Mack, & S. I. Miller (Eds.), *Clinical textbook of addictive disorders* (3rd ed., pp. 184–218). New York: Guilford Press.

Acri, M. C., Bornheimer, L. A., O'Brien, K., Sezer, S., Little, V., Cleek, A. F., & McKay, M. M. (2016) A model of integrated health care in a poverty-impacted community in New York City: Importance of early detection and addressing potential barriers to intervention implementation. *Social Work in Health Care, 55*(4), 314–327.

ADAA (Anxiety and Depression Association of America). (2017). *About ADA: Facts & statistics.* Silver Springs, MD: ADAA.

Adams, J. G. (2013). Sexual assault (Ch. 128). In J. G. Adams (Ed.). *Emergency medicine: Clinical essentials* (2nd ed.). Elsevier Health Services. [Kindle edition]

Adam, K. S., Bouckoms, A., & Streiner, D. (1982). Parental loss and family stability in attempted suicide. *Archives of General Psychiatry, 39* (9), 1081–1085.

Adamowicz, M. W. (2016). Psychological Testing. *Mentalhelp.net*

Adams, C. E., Awad, G. A., Rathbone, J., Thornley, B., & Soares-Weiser, K. (2014). Chlorpromazine versus placebo for schizophrenia. *Cochrane Database of Systematic Reviews, 1,* CD000284.

Adams, R. E., & Boscarino, J. A. (2005). Stress and well-being in the aftermath of the World Trade Center attack: The continuing effects of a communitywide disaster. *Journal of Community Psychology, 33*(2), 175–190.

Adams, S. (2017). Psychopharmacology of tobacco and alcohol comorbidity: A review of current evidence. *Current Addiction Reports, 4*(1), 25–34.

Addington, J., Heinssen, R. K., Robinson, D. G., Schooler, N. R., Marcy, P., Brunette, M. F., . . . Kane, J. M. (2015). Duration of untreated psychosis in community treatment settings in the United States. *Psychiatric Services* (Washington, D.C.), *66*(7), 753–756.

ADDitude. (2017). ADHD, by the numbers. *ADDitude Magazine.*

Advokat, C. D., Comaty, J. E., & Julien, R. M. (2014). *Julien's primer of drug action.* New York: Worth Publishers.

AFA (Alzheimer's Foundation of America). (2014). *About dementia.* New York: AFA.

Affatati, V., Di Nicola, V., Santoro, M., Bellomo, A., Todarello, G., & Todarello, O. (2004). Psychotherapy of gender identity disorder: Problems and perspectives. *Medica Psicosomatica, 49*(1–2), 57–64.

Afifi, T. O., MacMillan, H. L., Boyle, M., Taillieu, T., Cheung, K., & Sareen, J. (2014). Child abuse and mental disorders in Canada. *Canadian Medical Association Journal, 186*(9), E324–E332.

AFSP (American Foundation for Suicide Prevention). (2014). Facts and figures for 2010: Suicide deaths. Retrieved from https://www.afsp.org/understanding-suicide/facts-and-figures.

AFSP (American Foundation for Suicide Prevention). (2014). Facts and figures for 2011: Suicide deaths. Retrieved from https://www.afsp.org/understanding-suicide/facts-and-figures.

AFSP (American Foundation for Suicide Prevention). (2017). Suicide statistics. Retrieved from https://www.afsp.org/about-suicide/suicide-statistics/.

Agha, M., Nisar, A., Liaqat, H., Choudry, U. K., Choudry, A. K., & Shoaib, M. (2017). Neurophysiological perspectives of borderline personality disorders. Acta Psychopathologica, 3(3). 21.

Aghajani, M., Klapwijk, E. T., van der Wee, N. J., Veer, I. M., Rombouts, S. A. R. B., Boon, A. E., . . . Colins, O. F. (2017). Disorganized amygdala networks in conduct-disordered juvenile offenders with callous-unemotional traits. Biological Psychiatry, 82(4), 283–293.

Agras, S. (1985). Panic: Facing fears, phobias, and anxiety. New York: W. H. Freeman.

Agrawal, A., Tillman, R., Grucza, R. A., Nelson, E. C., McCutcheon, V. V., Few, L., . . . Bucholz, K. K. (2017). Reciprocal relationships between substance use and disorders and suicidal ideation and suicide attempts in the Collaborative Study of the Genetics of Alcoholism. Journal of Affective Disorders, 213, 96–104.

Agrawal, H. E., Gunderson, J. G., Holmes, B. M., & Lyons-Ruth, K. (2004). Attachment studies with borderline patients: A review. Harvard Review of Psychiatry, 12, 94–104.

Agronin, M. (2016, February 5). Sexual dysfunction in older adults. UpToDate. Retrieved from http://www.uptodate.com.

Aguilera, A., Bruehlman-Senecal, E., Demasi, O., & Avila, P. (2017). Automated text messaging as an adjunct to cognitive behavioral therapy for depression: A clinical trial. Journal of Medical Internet Research, 19(5), e148.

Ahearn, W. H. (2010). What every behavior analyst should know about the "MMR causes autism" hypothesis. Behavior Analysis in Practice, 3(1), 46–50.

Ahern, G. L., Herring, A. M., Labiner, D. M., Weinand, M. E., & Hutzler, R. (2000). Affective self-report during the intracarotid sodium amobarbital test: Group differences. Journal of the International Neuropsychological Society, 6(6), 659–667.

Ahmed, A. (2016, October 21). After hurricane, Haiti confronts scars from 2010 earthquake recovery. New York Times.

Ahn, R., Woodbridge, A., Abraham, A., Saba, S., Korenstein, D., Madden, E., . . . Keyhani, S. (2017, January 17). Financial ties of principal investigators and randomized controlled trial outcomes: Cross sectional study. BMJ, 356, i6770.

Aiken, L. R. (1985). Psychological testing and assessment (5th ed.). Boston: Allyn & Bacon.

AIPC (Australian Institute of Professional Counselors). (2015). The efficacy of CBT treatment for depression. Australia: AIPC.

AIS (American Institute of Stress). (2017). Transforming stress through awareness, education and collaboration. Fort Worth, TX: AIS.

Aitken, M., VanderLaan, D. P., Wasserman, L., Stojanovski, S., & Zucker, K. J. (2016). Self-harm and suicidality in children referred for gender dysphoria. Journal of the American Academy of Child and Adolescent Psychiatry, 55(6), 513–520.

Ajdacic-Gross, V., Ring, M., Gadola, E., Lauber, C., Bopp, M., Gutzwiller, F., & Rössler, W. (2008). Suicide after bereavement: An overlooked problem. Psychological Medicine, 38(5), 673–676.

Akhtar, S., Wig, N. H., Verma, V. K., Pershod, D., & Verma, S. K. (1975). A phenomenological analysis of symptoms in obsessive-compulsive neuroses. British Journal of Psychiatry, 127, 342–348.

Akin, O., Yesilkaya, E., Sari, E., Akar, C., Basbozkurt, G., Macit, C., . . . Gül, H. (2016). A rare reason of hyperinsulinism: Munchausen syndrome by proxy. Hormone Research in Paediatrics, 86(6), 416–419.

Akins, C. K. (2004). The role of Pavlovian conditioning in sexual behavior: A comparative analysis of human and nonhuman animals. International Journal of Comparative Psychology, 17(2–3), 241–262.

Alarid, L. F., & Rubin, M. (2016). Misdemeanor arrestees with mental health needs: Diversion and outpatient services as a recidivism reduction strategy. International Journal of Offender Therapy and Comparative Criminology. [Epub ahead of print]

Albala, I., Doyle, M., & Appelbaum, P. S. (2010). The evolution of consent forms for research: A quarter century of changes. IRB: Ethics & Human Research, 32(3), 7–11.

Albano, A. M., Comer, J. S., Compton, S. N., Piacentini, J., Kendall, P. C., Birmaher, B., Walkup, J. T., Ginsburg, G. S., Rynn, M. A., McCracken, J., Keeton, C., Sakolsky, D. J., & Sherrill, J. T. (2017). Secondary outcomes from the Child/Adolescent Anxiety Multimodal Study (CAMS): Implications for clinical practice. Evidence-Based Practice in Child and Adolescent Mental Health.

Albert, P. R., Vahid-Ansari, F., & Luckhart, C. (2014). Serotonin-prefrontal cortical circuitry in anxiety and depression phenotypes: Pivotal role of pre- and post-synaptic 5-HT1A receptor expression. Frontiers in Behavioral Neuroscience, 8, 199.

Alcántara, C., & Gone, J. P. (2008). Suicide in Native American communities: A transactional ecological formulation of the problem. In M. M. Leach & F. T. L. Leong (Eds.), Suicide among racial and ethnic minority groups: Theory, research, and practice (pp. 173–199). New York: Routledge/Taylor & Francis Group.

Alegría, M., Alvarez, K. Ishikawa, R. Z., DiMarzio, K., & McPeck, S. (2016). Removing obstacles to eliminating racial and ethnic disparities in behavioral health care. Health Affairs, 35(6), 991–999.

Alegría, M., Atkins, M., Farmer, E., Slaton, E., & Stelk, W. (2010). One size does not fit all: Taking diversity, culture and context seriously. Administration and Policy in Mental Health and Mental Health Service Research, 37(1-2), 48–60.

Alegría, M., Fortuna, L. R., Lin, J. Y., Norris, F. H., Gao, S., Takeuchi, D. T., . . . Valentine, A. (2013). Prevalence, risk, and correlates of posttraumatic stress disorder across ethnic and racial minority groups in the United States. Medical Care, 51(12), 1114–1123.

Alegría, M., Molina, K. M., & Chen, C. (2014). Neighborhood characteristics and differential risk for depressive and anxiety disorders across racial/ethnic groups in the United States. Depression and Anxiety, 31(1), 27–37.

Alexander, J. F., Sexton, T. L., & Robbins, M. S. (2002). The developmental status of family therapy in family psychology intervention science. In H. A. Liddle, D. A. Santiseban, R. F. Levant, & J. H. Bray (Eds.), Family psychology: Science-based interventions (pp. 17–40) Washington, DC: American Psychological Association.

Algars, M., Santtila, P., Jern, P., Johansson, A., Westerlund, M., & Sandnabba, N. K. (2011). Sexual body image and its correlates: A population-based study of Finnish women and men. International Journal of Sexual Health, 23(1), 26–34.

Ali, M. M., Dwyer, D. S., & Rizzo, J. A. (2011). The social contagion effect of suicidal behavior in adolescents: Does it really exist? Journal of Mental Health Policy and Economics, 14(1), 3–12.

Ali, S., Jabeen, S., Pate, R. J., Shahid, M., Chinala, S., Nathani, M., & Shah, R. (2015). Conversion disorder—mind versus body: A review. Innovations in Clinical Neuroscience, 12(5-6), 27–33.

Alisic, E., Barrett, A., Bowles, P., Conroy, R., & Mehl, M. R. (2016). Topical review: Families coping with child trauma: A naturalistic observation methodology. Journal of Pediatric Psychology, 41(1), 117–127.

Alisic, E., Zalta, A. K., van Wesel, F., Larsen, S. E., Hafstad, G. S., Hassanpour, K., & Smid, G. E. (2014). Rates of post-traumatic stress disorder in trauma-exposed children and adolescents: Meta-analysis. British Journal of Psychiatry, 204, 335–340.

Allara, E., Ferri, M., Bo, A., Gasparrini, A., & Faggiano, F. (2014). Are mass-media campaigns effective in preventing drug use: A Cochrane systematic review and meta-analysis. BMJ. Retrieved from http://bmjopen.bmj.com.

Allderidge, P. (1979). Hospitals, madhouses and asylums: Cycles in the care of the insane. British Journal of Psychiatry, 134, 321–334.

Allen, A. R., Newby, J. M., Mackenzie, A., Smith, J., Boulton, M., Loughnan, S. A., & Andrews, G. (2016). Internet cognitive-behavioural treatment for panic disorder: Randomized controlled trial and evidence of effectiveness in primary care. British Journal of Psychiatry Open, 2(2), 154–162.

Allen, D. F. (Ed.). (1985). The cocaine crisis. Plenum Press: New York.

Allen, K. L., Byrne, S. M., Crosby, R. D., & Stice, E. (2016). Testing for interactive and non-linear effects of risk factors for binge eating and purging eating disorders. Behaviour Research and Therapy. 87, 40–47.

Allen, S., & Casey, J. (2017). Developmental coordination disorders and sensory processing and integration: Incidence, associations and co-morbidities. British Journal of Occupational Therapy, 80(9), 549–557.

Allison, S., Bastiampillai, T., & Fuller, D. A. (2017). Mass incarceration and severe mental illness in the USA. *The Lancet, 390*(1009), 25.

Alloway, T. P. (2014, May 11). Selfies, Facebook, and narcissism: What's the link? *Psychology Today*.

Alloway, T. P., Runac, R., Qureshi, M., & Kemp, G. (2014). Is Facebook linked to selfishness? Investigating the relationships among social media use, empathy, and narcissism. *Social Networking, 3*(3), 150–158.

Alniak, I., Erkiran, M., & Mutlu, E. (2016). Substance use is a risk factor for violent behavior in male patients with bipolar disorder. *Journal of Affective Disorders, 193*, 89–93.

Alonzo, D., Thompson, R. G., Stohl, M., & Hasin, D. (2014). The influence of parental divorce and alcohol abuse on adult offspring risk of lifetime suicide attempt in the United States. *The American Journal of Orthopsychiatry, 84*(3), 316–320.

Alridge, J. (2012, May 17). How many people commit suicide due to depression? *Examiner .com*.

Al-Shaqi, R., Mourshed, M., & Rezgui, Y. (2016). Progress in ambient assisted systems for independent living by the elderly. *Springer-plus, 5*, 624.

Althof, S. E. (2007). Treatment of rapid ejaculation: Psychotherapy, pharmacotherapy, and combined therapy. In S. R. Leiblum, *Principles and practice of sex therapy* (4th ed., pp. 212–240). New York: Guilford Press.

Althof, S. E., & Needle, R. B. (2017). Treating low sexual desire in men. In Z. D. Peterson, *The Wiley-Blackwell handbook of sex therapy* (Ch. 3, pp. 32–39). Hoboken, NJ: Wiley-Blackwell.

Altinay, M., Karne, H., & Anand, A. (2018). Lithium monotherapy associated clinical improvement effects on amygdala-ventromedial prefrontal cortex resting state connectivity in bipolar disorder. *Journal of Affective Disorders, 225*, 4–12.

Alvarado, C., & Modesto-Lowe, V. (2017). Improving treatment in minority children with attention deficit/hyperactivity disorder. *Clinical Pediatrics, 56*, 171–176.

Alvarenga, M. S., Koritar, P., Pisciolaro, F., Mancini, M., Cordás, T. A., & Scagliusi, F. B. (2014). Eating attitudes of anorexia nervosa, bulimia nervosa, binge eating disorder and obesity without eating disorder female patients: Differences and similarities. *Physiology & Behavior, 131*, 99–104.

Alzheimer's Association. (2017). *2016 Alzheimer's disease facts and figures*. Chicago, IL: Alzheimer's Association.

AMA (American Medical Association). (2015). *AMA calls for ban on DTC ads of prescription drugs and medical devices*. Washington, DC: Author

Amad, A., Cachia, A., Gorwood, P., Pins, D., Delmaire, C., Rolland, B., . . . Jardri, R. (2014). The multimodal connectivity of the hippocampal complex in auditory and visual hallucinations. *Molecular Psychiatry, 19*, 184–191.

Amad, A., Ramoz, N., Thomas, P., Jardri, R., & Gorwood, P. (2014). Genetics of borderline personality disorder: Systematic review and proposal of an integrative model. *Neuroscience and Biobehavioral Reviews, 40*, 6–19.

Aman, M. G., & Farmer, C. A. (2011). Self-injury, aggression, and related problems.

In E. Hollander, A. Kolevzon & J. T. Coyle (Eds.), *Textbook of autism spectrum disorders*. (pp. 179–187). Arlington, VA: American Psychiatric Publishing, Inc.

Amianto, F., Abbate-Daga, G., Morando, S., Sobrero, C., & Fassino, S. (2011). Personality traits that differentiate individuals with anorexia nervosa and their healthy siblings. *Clinician's Research Digest, 29*(3).

Amini, A. (2008). The Minister of Magic: Adeel Amini delves into JK Rowling's chamber of secrets. *The Edinburgh Student*. Reported by Associated Press.

Amirkhan, J. H., Urizar, G. G., & Clark, S. (2015). Criterion validation of a stress measure: The Stress Overload Scale. *Psychological Assessment, 27*(3), 985–996.

Ammerman, B. A., Burke, T. A., Alloy, L. B., & McCloskey, M. S. (2016). Subjective pain during NSSI as an active agent in suicide risk. *Psychiatry Research, 236*, 80–85.

Amore, M., Innamorati, M., Vittorio, C. D., Weinberg, I., Turecki, G., Sher, L., . . . Pompili, M. (2014). Suicide attempts in major depressed patients with personality disorder. *Suicide and Life-Threatening Behavior, 44*(2), 155–166.

Anacker, C., O'Donnell, K. J., & Meaney, M. J. (2014). Early life adversity and the epigenetic programming of hypothalamic-pituitary adrenal function. *Dialogues in Clinical Neuroscience, 16*(3), 321–333.

ANAD (National Association of Anorexia Nervosa and Associated Disorders). (2014). *Binge eating disorder: The "new" eating disorder: Binge eating disorder (BED)*. Retrieved from http://www.anad.org/get-information/ get-informationbinge-eating.

Anastasiadou, D., Sepulveda, A. R., Parks, M., Cuellar-Flores, I., & Graell, M. (2016). The relationship between dysfunctional family patterns and symptom severity among adolescent patients with eating disorders: A gender-specific approach. *Women's Health, 56*(6), 695–712.

Anastasiadou, D., Sepulveda, A. R., Sánchez, J. C., Parks, M., Alvarez, T., & Graell, M. (2016). Family functioning and quality of life among families in eating disorders: A comparison with substance-related disorders and healthy controls. *European Eating Disorders Review, 24*(4), 294–303.

an der Heiden, W., & Häfner, H. (2011). Course and outcomes. In D. R. Weinberg & P. Harrison (Eds.), *Schizophrenia* (pp. 104–141). Hoboken, NJ: Wiley-Blackwell.

Anders, S. L., Frazier, P. A., & Shallcross, S. L. (2012). Prevalence and effects of life event exposure among undergraduate and community college students. *Journal of Counseling Psychology, 59*(3), 449–457.

Anderson, E., Schlueter, J. E., Carlson, J. F., & Geisinger, K. F. (Eds.). (2016). *Tests in Print IX*. Lincoln, NE: University of Nebraska Press.

Anderson, G. (2018). Linking the biological underpinnings of depression: Role of mitochondria interactions with melatonin, inflammation, sirtuins, tryptophan catabolites, DNA repair and oxidative and nitrosative stress, with consequences for classification and cognition. *Progress in Neuro-Psychopharmacology and Biological Psychiatry, 80*(Pt C), 255–266.

Anderson, G., Berk, M., Dean, O., Moylan, S., & Maes, M. (2014). Role of immune-inflammatory and oxidative and nitrosative stress pathways in the etiology of depression: Therapeutic implications. *CNS Drugs, 28*(1), 1–10.

Anderson, J., Snider, S., Sellbom, M., Krueger, R., & Hopwood, C. (2014). A comparison of the DSM-5 Section II and Section III personality disorder structures. *Psychiatry Research, 216*(3), 363–372.

Anderson, J. L., Sellbom, M., & Shealy, R. C. (2017). Clinician perspectives of antisocial and borderline personality disorders using DSM-5 Section III dimensional personality traits. *Journal of Personality Disorders, 31*, 1–15.

Anderson, J. L., Sellbomn, M., & Salekin, R. T. (2016, November 7). Utility of the personality inventory for DSM-5 Brief Form (PID-5-BF) in the measurement of maladaptive personality and psychopathology. *Assessment*. [Epub ahead of print]

Anderson, J. L., Wood, M. E., Tarescavage, A. M., Burchett, D., & Glassmire, D. M. (2018). The role of dimensional personality psychopathology in a forensic inpatient psychiatric setting. *Journal of Personality Disorders*. [Manuscript in press]

Anderson, K. G., Sankis, L. M., & Widiger, T. A. (2001). Pathology versus statistical in frequency: Potential sources of gender bias in personality disorder criteria. *Journal of Nervous and Mental Disease, 189*(10), 661–668.

Anderson, N. (2014, July 1). Sex offense statistics show U.S. college reports are rising. *Washington Post*.

Anderson, P. L., Price, M., Edwards, S. M., Obasaju, M. A., Schmertz, S. K., Zimand, E., & Calamaras, M. R. (2013). Virtual reality exposure therapy for social anxiety disorder: A randomized controlled trial. *Journal of Consulting and Clinical Psychology, 81*(5), 751–760.

Andrade, C. (2016). Antipsychotic drugs in schizophrenia: Relative effects in patients with and without treatment resistance. *Journal of Clinical Psychiatry, 77*(12), e1656–e1660.

Andreasen, N. C., & Black, D. W. (2006). *Introductory textbook of psychiatry* (4th ed.). Washington, DC: American Psychiatric Publishing.

Andrews, B., & Brewin, C.R. (2017). False Memories and Free Speech: Is Scientific Debate Being Suppressed? *Applied Cognitive Psychology, 31*(1), 45–49.

Andrews, J. A., & Hops, H. (2010). The influence of peers on substance use. In L. Scheier (Ed.), *Handbook of drug use etiology: Theory, methods, and empirical findings* (pp. 403–420). Washington, DC: American Psychological Association.

Andrews, V. (1998, December 14). Abducted by aliens? Or just a little schizoid? *HealthScout*.

Anestis, M. D., & Houtsma, C. (2018). The association between gun ownership and statewide overall suicide rates. *Suicide and Life-Threatening Behavior*. [Manuscript in press]

Anestis, M. D., Khazem, L. R., & Anestis, J. C. (2017). Differentiating suicide decedents who died using firearms from those who died using other methods. *Psychiatry Research, 252*, 23–28.

Angier, N. (2010, April 5). Even among animals: Leaders, followers and schmoozers. *New York Times*.

Anheyer, D., Haller, H., Barth, J., Lauche, R., Dobos, G., & Cramer, H. (2017, April 25). Mindfulness-based stress reduction for treating low back pain: A systematic review and meta-analysis. *Annals of Internal Medicine*, 1–9. [Epub ahead of print]

Anonymous. (1996). First person account: Social, economic, and medical effects of schizophrenia. *Schizophrenia Bulletin, 22*(1), 183.

Anonymous. (2006). On madness: A personal account of rapid cycling bipolar disorder. *British Journal of General Practice, 56*(530), 726–728.

Anson, P. (2017, February 9). Sex, poverty and education linked to chronic pain. *Pain News Network*. Retrieved from https://www.painnewsnetwork.org.

Antal, H., Hossain, M. J., Hassink, S., Henry, S., Fuzzell, L., Taylor, A., & Wysocki, T. (2015). Audio-video recording of health care encounters for pediatric chronic conditions: Observational reactivity and its correlates. *Journal of Pediatric Psychology, 40*(1), 144–153.

Antfolk, J. (2017, January 25). Age limits. *Evolutionary Psychology, 15*(1).

Anthony, J., Barondess, D. A., Radovanovic, J., Lopez-Quintero, C. (2016). Polydrug use: Research topics and issues. In K. J. Sher (Ed.). *Oxford handbook of substance use and substance use disorders* (Vol. 2, Ch. 2, pp. 29–59). New York: Oxford University Press.

Antony, M. M. (2014). Behavior therapy. In D. Wedding & R. J. Corsini (Eds.), *Current psychotherapies* (10th ed., pp. 193–230). Independence, KY: Cengage Publications.

Anupama, M., Gangadhar, K. H., Shetty, V. B., & Dip, P. B. (2016). Transvestism as a symptom: A case series. *Indian Journal of Psychological Medicine, 38*(1), 78–80.

APA (American Psychiatric Association). (2000). *DSM-IV text revision*. Washington, DC: Author.

APA (American Psychiatric Association). (2013, May 13). *DSM-5 field trials*. Washington, DC: Author.

APA (American Psychiatric Association). (2013). *Diagnostic and statistical manual of mental disorders* (5th ed.). Washington, DC: Author.

APA (American Psychiatric Association). (2013). *The people behind DSM-5*. Washington, DC: Author.

APA (American Psychiatric Association). (2017). *DSM history*. Arlington, VA: APA.

APA (American Psychological Association). (2002). *Ethical principles of psychologists and code of conduct*. Washington, DC: Author.

APA (American Psychological Association). (2010). *Ethical principles of psychologists and code of conduct*. Washington, DC: Author.

APA (American Psychological Association). (2010). *Introduction and applicability*. Washington, DC: Author.

APA (American Psychological Association). (2014). *Ethical principles of psychologists and code of conduct*. Washington, DC: Author.

APA (American Psychological Association). (2014, July/August). How many psychology doctorates are awarded by U.S. institutions? *Monitor, 45*(7), 13.

APA (American Psychological Association). (2014). *Mental and behavioral health and older Americans*. Washington, DC: American Psychiatric Publishing, Inc. Retrieved from http://www.apa.org/about/gr/issues/aging/mental-health.aspx.

APA (American Psychological Association). (2015). *2005–13: Demographics of the U.S. psychology workforce*. Washington, DC: American Psychological Association.

APA (American Psychological Association). (2015, February 4). Stress in America: Paying with our health. Washington, DC: Author.

APA (American Psychological Association). (2016, September). *2015 APA survey of psychology health service providers. Times Higher Education*. Retrieved from https://www.timeshighereducation.com.

APA (American Psychological Association). (2016). *Data on behavioral health in the United States*. Washington, DC: American Psychological Association.

APA (American Psychological Association). (2017, January 1). *Introduction and applicability (Amendment)*. Washington, DC: Author.

APA (American Psychological Association). (2017, January 30). *School bullying linked to lower academic achievement, research finds*. Retrieved from http://www.apa.org/news/press/releases.

APA (American Psychological Association). (2017, April 5). *Idaho becomes fifth state to allow psychologists to prescribe medications*. Washington, DC: Author.

APA (American Psychological Association). (2017, August 17). *APA reaction to settlement of torture case against psychologists Mitchell, Jessen*. Washington, DC: APA.

APA (American Psychological Association). (2017). *Data on behavioral health in the United States*. Washington, DC: American Psychological Association.

APA (American Psychological Association). (2017). *Depression*. Washington, DC: Author.

APA (American Psychological Association). (2017). *Ethical principles of psychologists and code of conduct*. Washington, DC: Author.

APA (American Psychological Association). (2017). *Ethnic and racial minorities & socioeconomic status*. Washington, DC: Author.

APA (American Psychological Association). (2017). *Mental and behavioral health and older Americans*. Washington, DC: APA.

Appelbaum, P. S. (2011). Law and psychiatry: Reforming malpractice: The prospects for change. *Psychiatric Services, 62*(1), 6–8.

Appelbaum, P. S. (2011). Law and psychiatry: SSRIs, suicide, and liability for failure to warn of medication risks. *Psychiatric Services, 62*(4), 347–349.

Apter, A., & Wasserman, D. (2007). Suicide in psychiatric disorders during adolescence. In R. Tatarelli, M. Pompili, & P. Girardi (Eds.), *Suicide in psychiatric disorders*. New York: Nova Science Publishers.

Arcelus, J., Witcomb, G. L., & Mitchell, A. (2014). Prevalence of eating disorders amongst dancers: A systemic review and meta-analysis. *European Eating Disorders Review, 22*(2), 92–101.

Archer, D. (2013). Reading between the (head) lines: Smartphone Addiction. *Psychology Today*. Retrieved from http://www.psychologytoday.com/blog/reading-between-the-headlines/2013077/smartphone-addiction.

Ardjmand, A., Rezayof, A., & Zarrindast, M-R. (2011). Involvement of central amygdala NMDA receptor mechanism in morphine state-dependent memory retrieval. *Neuroscience Research, 69*(1), 25–31.

Ardoin, S. P., Martens, B. K., Wolfe, L. A., Hilt, A. M., & Rosenthal, B. D. (2004). A method for conditioning reinforcer preferences in students with moderate mental retardation. *Journal of Developmental and Physical Disabilities, 16*(1), 33–51.

Arie, S. (2016, September 21). Beyond Bedlam. *BMJ, 354*:i5115.

Arieti, S. (1974). *Interpretation of schizophrenia*. New York: Basic Books.

Arieti, S., & Bemporad, J. R. (1978). *Severe and mild depression: The psychotherapeutic approach*. New York: Basic Books.

Aring, C. D. (1974). The Gheel experience: Eternal spirit of the chainless mind! *Journal of the American Medical Association, 230*(7), 998–1001.

Aring, C. D. (1975). Gheel: The town that cares. *Family Health, 7*(4), 54–55, 58, 60.

Arosio, B., Ostan, R., Mari, D., Damanti, S., Ronchetti, F., Arcudi, S., . . . Monti, D. (2017). Cognitive status in the oldest old and centenarians: A condition crucial for quality of life methodologically difficult to assess. *Mechanisms of Ageing and Development, 165 (Part B)*, 185–194.

Arseneault, L. (2017). The long-term impact of bullying victimization on mental health. *World Psychiatry, 16*, 27–28.

ASA (American Sleep Association). (2017). Sleep and sleep disorder statistics. *Sleep Association*. Retrieved from https://www.sleepassociation.org/sleep/sleep-statistics.

Asai, T. (2016). Self is "other", other is "self": Poor self-other discriminability explains schizotypal twisted agency judgment. *Psychiatry Research, 246*, 593–600.

ASAM (American Society of Addiction Medicine). (2016). Opioid addiction: 2016 facts and figures. *ASAM*. Retrieved from https://www.asam.org.

Asarnow, J. R., Hughes, J. L., Babeva, K., & Sugar, C. A. (2017). Cognitive-behavioral family treatment for suicide attempt prevention: A randomized controlled trial. *Journal of the American Academy of Child and Adolescent Psychiatry, 56*(6), 506–514.

Asberg, M., Traskman, L., & Thoren, P. (1976). 5 HIAA in the cerebrospinal fluid: A biochemical suicide predictor? *Archives of General Psychiatry, 33*(10), 1193–1197.

ASCA (American School Counselor Association). (2016). *Student-to-school-counselor ratio 2013–2014*. Alexandria, VA: ASCA.

ASCA (American School Counselor Association). (2017). *Student-to-school-counselor ratio*. Alexandria, VA: ASCA.

Ascoli, M., Lee, T., Warfa, N., Mairura, J., Persaud, A., & Bhui, K. (2017, March 31). Race, culture, ethnicity and personality disorder: Group Careif position paper. *Psycheblog*. Retrieved from http://psycheblog.uk.

Ash, R. (2001). *The top 10 of everything 2002* (American ed.). New York: DK Publishing.

Ashraf, N., & Thevasagayam, M. S. (2014). Munchausen syndrome by proxy presenting as hearing loss., *Journal of Laryngology and Otology, 128*(6), 540–542.

Ashton, J. R., & Donnan, S. (1981). Suicide by burning as an epidemic phenomenon: An analysis of 82 deaths and inquests in England and Wales in 1978–9. *Psychological Medicine, 11*(4), 735–739.

Asimov, I. (1997). *Isaac Asimov's book of facts*. New York: Random House (Wings Books).

Askew, C., Reynolds, G., Fielding-Smith, S., & Field, A. P. (2016). Inhibition of vicariously learned fear in children using positive modeling and prior exposure. *Journal of Abnormal Psychology, 125*, 279–291.

ASPS (American Society of Plastic Surgeons). (2017, May 22). *Gender confirmation surgeries rise 20% in first ever report*. Retrieved from https://www.plasticsurgery.org/news/press-releases.

ASPS (American Society of Plastic Surgeons). (2017). *2016 plastic surgery statistics*. Retrieved from https://www.plasticsurgery.org/news.

Asselmann, E., Stender, J., Grabe, H. J., König, J., Schmidt, C. O., Hamm, A. O., & Pané-Farré, C. A. (2018). Assessing the interplay of childhood adversities with more recent stressful life events and conditions in predicting panic pathology among adults from the general population. *Journal of Affective Disorders, 225*, 715–722.

Atkinson, M. J., & Wade, T. D. (2016). Does mindfulness have potential in eating disorders prevention? A preliminary controlled trial with young adult women. *Early Intervention in Psychiatry, 10*(3), 234–245.

Au, T. M., Dickstein, B. D., Comer, J. S., Salters-Pedneault, K., & Litz, B. T. (2013). The co-occurrence of posttraumatic stress and depressive symptoms after sexual assault: A latent profile analysis. *Journal of Affective Disorders, 149*, 209.

Aufderheide, D. (2014, April 1). Mental illness in America's jails and prisons: Toward a public safety/public health model. *Health Affairs Blog*. Retrieved from http://healthaffairs.org.

Augustyn, M. (2016, November 21). Autism spectrum disorder: Diagnosis. *UpToDate*. Retrieved from http://www.uptodate.com.

Augustyn, M. (2017, March 7). Autism spectrum disorder: Terminology, epidemiology, and pathogenesis. *UpToDate*. Retrieved from http://www.uptodate.com.

Augustyn, M. (2017, March 8). Autism spectrum disorder: Clinical features. *UpToDate*. Retrieved from http://www.uptodate.com.

Austen, I. (2017, April 13). Trudeau unveils bill legalizing recreational marijuana in Canada. *New York Times*.

Austin, J. (2015). More than half of Britons claim to have had contact with ghosts. *The Independent*. Retrieved from http://www.theindependentbd.com.

Avenevoli, S., Swendsen, J., He, J. P., Burstein, M., & Merikangas, K. R. (2015). Major depression in the National Comorbidity Survey-Adolescent Supplement: Prevalence, correlates, and treatment. *Journal of the American Academy of Child and Adolescent Psychiatry, 54*, 37–44.

Autism Speaks. (2017). *Facts about autism*. New York: Autism Speaks.

Autism Speaks. (2017). *What is autism?* New York: Autism Speaks.

Avery-Clark, C., & Weiner, L. (2017). A traditional Masters and Johnson behavioral approach to sex therapy. In Z. D. Peterson, *The Wiley-Blackwell handbook of sex therapy* (Ch. 11, pp. 165–189). Hoboken, NJ: Wiley-Blackwell.

Avraham, Y., Hants, Y., Vorobeiv, L., Staum, M., Abu Ahmad, W., Mankuta, D., . . . Arbel-Alon, S. (2017). Brain neurotransmitters in an animal model with postpartum depressive-like behavior. *Behavioural Brain Research, 326*, 307–321.

Axelrod, M. I., Tornehl, C., & Fontanini-Axelrod, A. (2014). Enhanced response using a multicomponent urine alarm treatment for nocturnal enuresis. *Journal for Specialists in Pediatric Nursing, 19*(2), 172–182.

Axelsson, E., Andersson, E., Ljótsson, B., Wallhed Finn, D., & Hedman, E. (2016). The Health Preoccupation Diagnostic Interview: Inter-rater reliability of a structured interview for diagnostic assessment of DSM-5 somatic symptom disorder and illness anxiety disorder. *Cognitive Behaviour Therapy, 45*(4), 259–269.

Ayalon, L., & Huyck, M. H. (2001). Latino caregivers of relatives with Alzheimer's disease. *Clinical Gerontology, 24*(3–4), 93–106.

Ayd, F. J., Jr. (1956). A clinical evaluation of Frenquel. *Journal of Nervous and Mental Disease, 124*, 507–509.

Ayhan, G., Arnal, R., Basurko, C., About, V., Pastre, A., Pinganaud, E., . . . Nacher, M. (2017). Suicide risk among prisoners in French Guiana: Prevalence and predictive factors. *BMC Psychiatry, 17*(1), 156.

Ayllon, T. (1963). Intensive treatment of psychotic behavior by stimulus satiation and food reinforcement. *Behavioral Research and Therapy, 1*, 53–62.

Ayllon, T., & Michael, J. (1959). The psychiatric nurse as a behavioural engineer. *Journal of Experimental Analytical Behavior, 2*, 323–334.

Ayoub, C. C. (2006). Munchausen by proxy. In T. G. Plante (Ed.), *Mental disorders of the new millenium: Biology and function* (Vol. 3, pp. 173–193). Westport, CT: Praeger Publishers/Greenwood Publishing.

Ayoub, C. C. (2010). Munchausen by proxy. In J. M. Brown & E. A. Campbell (Eds.), *The Cambridge handbook of forensic psychology* (pp. 690–699). New York: Cambridge University Press.

Ayoub, C. C. (2010). Munchausen by proxy. In R. J. Shaw & D. R. DeMaso (Eds.), *Textbook of pediatric psychosomatic medicine* (pp. 185–198). Arlington, VA: American Psychiatric Publishing.

BAAM (British Association Anger Management). (2016). Mental health organization: Boiling point report 2008. *BAAM*. Retrieved from https://www.angermanage.co.uk/anger-statistics.

Babchishin, K. M., Hanson, R. K., & VanZuylen, H. (2014). Online child pornography offenders are different: A meta-analysis of the characteristics of online and offline sex offenders against children. *Archives of Sexual Behavior*. [Manuscript submitted for publication]

Baca-Garcia, E., Perez-Rodriguez, M. M., Keyes, K. M., Oquendo, M. A., Hasin, D. S., Grant, B. F., & Blanco, C. (2011). Suicidal ideation and suicide attempts among Hispanic subgroups in the United States: 1991–1992 and 2001–2002. *Journal of Psychiatric Research, 45*(4), 512–518.

Bachhuber, M. A., Hennessy, S., Cunningham, C. O., & Starrels, J. L. (2016). Increasing benzodiazepine prescriptions and overdose mortality in the United States, 1996–2013. *American Journal of Public Health, 106*, 686–688.

Bachmann, C. J., Aagaard, L., Burcu, M., Glaeske, G., Kalverdijk, L. J., Petersen, I., . . . Hoffmann, F. (2016). Trends and patterns of antidepressant use in children and adolescents from five western countries, 2005–2012. *European Neuropsychopharmacology, 26*(3), 411–419.

Bachmann, C. J., Wijilaars, L. P., Kalverdijk, L. J., Burcu, M., Glaeske, G., Schuiling-Beninga, C. C. M., Hoffmann, F., Aagaard, L., & Zito, J. M. (2017). Trends in ADHD medication use in children and adolescents in five western countries, 2005–2012. *European Neuropsychopharmacology, 27*, 484–493.

Bacon, T., Farhall, J., & Fossey, E. (2014). The active therapeutic processes of acceptance and commitment therapy for persistent symptoms of psychosis: Clients' perspectives. *Behavioural and Cognitive Psychotherapy, 42*(4), 402–420.

Bademli, K., & Duman, Z. C. (2016). Emotions, ideas and experiences of caregivers of patients with schizophrenia about "family to family support program." *Archives of Psychiatric Nursing, 30*(3), 329–333.

Badoud, D., Prada, P., Nicastro, R., Germond, C., Luyten, P., Perroud, N., & Debbane, M. (2018). Attachment and reflective functioning in women with borderline personality disorder. *Journal of Personality Disorders*. [Manuscript in press]

Baer, L., & Blais, M. A. (Eds.). (2010). *Handbook of clinical rating scales and assessment in psychiatry and mental health*. Totowa, NJ: Humana Press.

Bagayogo, I. P., Interian, A., & Escobar, J. I. (2013). Transcultural aspects of somatic symptoms in the context of depressive disorders. *Advances in Psychosomatic Medicine, 33*, 64–74.

Bagby, E. (1922). The etiology of phobias. *Journal of Abnormal Psychology, 17*, 16–18.

Baggott, M. J., Garrison, K. J., Coyle, J. R., Galloway, G. P., Barnes, A. J., Hiestis, M. A., & Mendelson, J. E. (2016, June 14). MDMA impairs response to water intake in healthy volunteers. *Advances in Pharmacological Sciences*. [Epub ahead of print]

Bagnall, N., & Faiz, O. D. (2014). Delirium, frailty and IL-6 in the elderly surgical patient. *Langenbeck's Archives of Surgery / Deutsche Gesellschaft Für Chirurgie, 399*(6), 799–800.

Bagot, R. C., Cates, H. M., Purushothaman, I., Lorsch, Z. S., Walker, D. M., Wang, J., . . . Nestler, E. J. (2016). Circuit-wide transcriptional profiling reveals brain region-specific gene networks regulating depression susceptibility. *Neuron, 90*(5), 969–983.

Bahorik, A. L., Newhill, C. E., Queen, C. C., & Eack, S. M. (2014). Under-reporting of drug use among individuals with schizophrenia: Prevalence and predictors. *Psychological Medicine, 44*(1), 61–69.

Bailey, L. (2017, February 21). Psychologists refute report on collusion with Feds. *Courthouse News*. Retrieved from https://www.courthousenews.com.

Baillargeon, J., Binswanger, I. A., Penn, J. V., Williams, B. A., & Murray, O. J. (2009). Psychiatric disorders and repeat incarcerations: The revolving prison door. *American Journal of Psychiatry. 166*(1), 103–109.

Bakalar, N. (2013, July 31). Moon phases tied to sleep cycles. *New York Times*.

Baker, E., Baibazarova, E., Ktistaki, G., Shelton, K. H., & van Goozen, S. H. (2012). Development of fear and guilt in young children: Stability over time and relations with psychopathology. *Development and Psychopathology, 24*(3), 833–845.

Baker, K. (2010). From "it's not me" to "it was me, after all": A case presentation of a patient diagnosed with dissociative identity disorder. *Psychoanalytic Social Work, 17*(2), 79–98.

Balassone, M., (2011). Jails, prisons increasingly taking care of mentally ill. *Washington Post, 134*(49).

Baldessarini, R. J., & Tondo, L. (2007). Psychopharmacology for suicide prevention. In R. Tatarelli, M. Pompili, & P. Girardi (Eds.), *Suicide in psychiatric disorders*. New York: Nova Science Publishers.

Baldessarini, R. J., & Tondo, L. (2011). Psychopharmacology for suicide prevention. In M. Pompili & R. Tatarelli (Eds.), *Evidence-based practice in suicidology: A source book* (pp. 243–264). Cambridge MA: Hogrefe Publishing.

Baldinger, P., Lotan, A., Frey, R., Kasper, S., Lerer, B., & Lanzenberger, R. (2014). Neurotransmitters and electroconvulsive therapy. *The Journal of ECT, 30*(2), 116–121.

Baldor, R. (2017, January 4). Primary care of the adult with intellectual and developmental disabilities. *UpToDate*. Retrieved from http://www.uptodate.com.

Baldwin, D. S., Gordon, R., Abelli, M., & Pini, S. (2016). The separation of adult separation anxiety disorder. *CNS Spectrums, 21*(4), 289–294.

Bales, D. L., Timman, R., Andrea, H., Busschbach, J. V., Verheul, R., & Kamphuis, J. H. (2014). Effectiveness of day hospital mentalization-based treatment for patients with severe borderline personality disorder: A matched control study. *Clinical Psychology and Psychotherapy*. [Advance online publication]

Balhara, Y. S. (2014). A chart review based comparative study of retention rates for two dispensing regimens for buprenorphine for subjects with opioid dependence at a tertiary care substance use disorder treatment center. *Journal of Opioid Management, 10*(3), 200–206.

Balje, A., Greeven, A., van Giezen, A., Korrelboom, K., Arntz, A., & Spinhoven, P. (2016). Group schema therapy versus group cognitive behavioral therapy for social anxiety disorder with comorbid avoidant personality disorder: Study protocol for a randomized controlled trial. *Trials, 17*(1), 487.

Bancroft, J. (1989). *Human sexuality and its problems*. New York: Churchill-Livingstone.

Bancroft, J., Loftus, J., & Long, J. S. (2003). Distress about sex: A national survey of women in heterosexual relationships. *Archives of Sexual Behavior, 32*(3), 193–208.

Bandelow, B., & Michaelis, S. (2015). Epidemiology of anxiety disorders in the 21st century. *Dialogues in Clinical Neuroscience, 17*, 327–335.

Bandelow, B., Reitt, M., Röver, C., Michaelis, S., Görlich, Y., & Wedekind, D. (2015). Efficacy of treatments for anxiety disorders: A meta-analysis. *International Clinical Psychopharmacology, 30*(4), 183–192.

Bandura, A. (1971). Psychotherapy based upon modeling principles. In A. E. Bergin & S. L. Garfield (Eds.), *Handbook of psychotherapy and behavior change*. New York: Wiley.

Bandura, A. (1977). Self-efficacy: Toward a unifying theory of behavioral change. *Psychological Review, 84*(2), 191–215.

Bandura, A. (2011). But what about that gigantic elephant in the room? In R. M. Arkin (Ed.), *Most underappreciated: 50 prominent social psychologists describe their most unloved work* (pp. 51–59). New York: Oxford University Press.

Bandura, A., Adams, N. E., & Beyer, J. (1977). Cognitive processes mediating behavioral change. *Journal of Personality and Social Psychology, 35*(3), 125–139.

Bandura, A., & Rosenthal, T. (1966). Vicarious classical conditioning as a function of arousal level. *Journal of Personality and Social Psychology, 3*, 54–62.

Bareggi, S. R., Bianchi, L., Cavallaro, R., Gervasoni, M., Siliprandi, F., & Bellodi, L. (2004). Citalopram concentrations and response in obsessive-compulsive disorder: Preliminary results. *CNS Drugs, 18*(5), 329–335.

Bari, A., Robbins, T. W., & Dalley, J. W. (2011). Impulsivity. In M. C. Olmstead (Ed.), *Animal models of drug addiction. Springer protocols: Neuromethods* (pp. 379–401). Totowa, NJ: Humana Press.

Barker, K. K. (2014). Mindfulness meditation: Do-it-yourself medicalization of every moment. *Social Science and Medicine, 106*, 168–176.

Barlow, M. R., & Chu, J. A. (2014). Measuring fragmentation in dissociative identity disorder: The integration measure and relationship to switching and time in therapy. *European Journal of Psychotraumatology, 5*, 10.3402/ejpt. v5.22250

Barnes, A. (2004). Race, schizophrenia, and admission to state psychiatric hospitals. *Administration and Policy in Mental Health, 31*(3), 241–252.

Barnes, D. H. (2010). Suicide. In R. L. Hampton, T. P. Gullotta, & R. L. Crowel (Eds.), *Handbook of African American health* (pp. 444–460). New York: Guilford Press.

Barnes, M. (2017, March 14). Mom thought daughter's Facebook suicide was fake, posts cruel comment. *Rolling Out*. Retrieved from http://rollingout.com.

Barnes, N., Hattan, P., Black, D. S., & Schuman-Olivier, Z. (2016). An examination of mindfulness-based programs in US medical schools. *Biomind*. Retrieved from http://www. biomind.usc.edu.

Barnes, S. M., Bahraini, N. H., Forster, J. E., Stearns-Yoder, K. A., Hostetter, T. A. Smith, G., . . . Nock, M. K. (2017). Moving beyond self-report: Implicit associations about death/life prospectively predict suicidal behavior among veterans. *Suicide and Life-Threatening Behavior, 47*(1), 67–77.

Barnes, T. R. E., & Marder, S. R. (2011). Principles of pharmacological treatment in schizophrenia. In D. R. Weinberg & P. Harrison (Eds.), *Schizophrenia* (pp. 515–524). Hoboken, NJ: Wiley-Blackwell.

Barrera, T. L., Wilson, K. P., & Norton, P. J. (2010). The experience of panic symptoms across racial groups in a student sample. *Journal of Anxiety Disorders, 24*(8), 873–878.

Barsky, A. J. (2016). Assessing the new DSM-5 diagnosis of somatic symptom disorder. *Psychosomatic Medicine, 78*(1), 2–4.

Bartholomew, R. (2014). *Mass hysteria in schools: Worldwide since 1566*. Jefferson, NC: McFarland.

Bartol, C. R., & Bartol, A. M. (2015). *Psychology and Law: Research and Practice*. Los Angeles: Sage Publications.

Bartoli, F., Pompili, M., Lillia, N., Crocamo, C., Salemi, G., Clerici, M., Carrà, G. (2017). Rates and correlates of suicidal ideation among stroke survivors: A meta-analysis. *Journal of Neurology, Neurosurgery & Psychiatry, 88*, 498–504.

Barton, A. (2004).Women and community punishment: The probation hostel as a semipenal institution for female offenders. *The Howard Journal of Crime and Justice, 43*(2), 149–163.

Bartrop, R. W., Lockhurst, E., Lazarus, L., Kiloh, L. G., & Penny, R. (1977). Depressed lymphocyte function after bereavement. *Lancet, 1*, 834–836.

Bartz, J., Kaplan, A., & Hollander, E. (2007). Obsessive-compulsive personality disorder. In W. O'Donohue, K. A. Fowler, S. O. Lilienfeld (Eds.). *Personality disorders: Toward the DSM-V*. Los Angeles: Sage Publications.

Baruth, L. G., & Manning, M. L. (2016). *Multicultural counseling and psychotherapy: A lifespan approach*. (6th ed.). New York: Routledge.

Barzilay, S., Brunstein, K. A., Apter, A., Carli, V., Wasserman, C., et al. (2017). Bullying victimization and suicide ideation and behavior among adolescents in Europe: A 10-country study. *Journal of Adolescent Health, 61*(2), 179–186.

Basile, J., & Bloch, M. J. (2016, March 2). Overview of hypertension in adults. *UpToDate*. Retrieved from www.uptodate.com.

Basoglu, M., Jaranson, J. M., Mollica, R., & Kastrup, M. (2001). Torture and mental health: A research overview. In E. Gerrity, T. M. Keane, & F. Tuma (Eds.), *The mental health consequences of torture* (pp. 35–62). New York: Kluwer Academic/Plenum Publishers.

Bass, C., & Glaser, D. (2014). Early recognition and management of fabricated or induced illness in children. *Lancet, 383*(9926), 1412–1421.

Basson, R. (2007). Sexual desire/arousal disorders in women. In S. R. Leiblum (Ed.), *Principles and practice of sex therapy* (4th ed., pp. 25–53). New York: Guilford Press.

Bateman, A. W. (2011). Borderline personality disorder. In J. C. Norcross, G. R. VandenBos, & D. K. Freedheim (Eds.), *History of psychotherapy: Continuity and change* (2nd ed., pp. 588–600). Washington, DC: American Psychological Association.

Bateman, A. W., & Fonagy, P. (2010). Mentalization based treatment for borderline personality disorder. *World Psychiatry, 9*, 11–15.

Bateman, A. W., & Fonagy, P. (Eds.). (2012). *Handbook of mentalizing in mental health practice*. Washington, DC: American Psychiatric Publishing.

Bateman, A. W., & Fonagy, P. (2016). The role of mentalization in treatments for personality disorder. In W. J. Livesley, G. Dimaggio, & J. F. Clarkin (Eds.), *Integrated treatment for personality disorder: A modular approach*. Behavioral Tech, LLC; reprint edition.

Bates, G. W., Thompson, J. C., & Flanagan, C. (1999). The effectiveness of individual versus group induction of depressed mood. *Journal of Psychology, 133*(3), 245–252.

Bateson, G. (1974) *Perceval's narrative: A patient's account of his psychosis.* New York: William Morrow.

Batstra, L., Nieweg, E. H., Pij, S., Van Tol, D. G., & Haddeis-Algra, M. (2014). Childhood ADHD: A stepped diagnosis approach. *Journal of Psychiatric Practice, 20*(3),169–177.

Baucom, B. R., Atkins, D. C., Rowe, L. S., Doss, B. D., & Christensen, A. (2015). Prediction of treatment response at 5-year follow-up in a randomized clinical trial of behaviorally based couple therapies. *Journal of Consulting and Clinical Psychology, 83*(1), 103–114.

Baucom, D. H., Epstein, N. B., Kirby, J. S., & LaTaillade, J. J. (2010). Cognitive-behavioral couple therapy. In K. S. Dobson (Ed.), *Handbook of cognitive-behavioral therapies* (3rd ed., pp. 411–444). New York: Guilford Press.

Bauer, S. M., Schanda, H., Karakula, H., Olajossy-Hilkesberger, L., Rudaleviciene, P., Okribelashvili, N., Chaudhry, H. R., Idemudia, S. E., Gscheider, S., Ritter, K., & Stompe, T. (2011). Culture and the prevalence of hallucinations in schizophrenia. *Comprehensive Psychiatry, 52*(3), 319–325.

Baum, A., Trevino, L. A., & Dougall, A. L. (2011). Stress and the cancers. In R. J. Contrada & A. Baum (Eds.), *The handbook of stress science: Biology, psychology, and health* (pp. 411–423). New York: Springer Publishing.

Baune, B. T., Malhi, G. S., Morris, G., Outhred, T., Hamilton, A., Das, P., Bassett, D., Berk, M., Boyce, P., Lyndon, B., Mulder, R., Parker, G., & Singh, A. B. (2018). Cognition in depression: Can we THINC-it better? *Journal of Affective Disorders, 225,* 559–562.

Baxter, L. C. (2016, April 1). Appetite changes in depression. *American Journal of Psychiatry, 173*(4), 317–318.

Bazelon Center. (2008). *Vote: It's your right: A guide to the voting rights of people with mental disabilities.* Washington, DC: Author.

Bazelon Center. (2016). *It's your right: A guide to the voting rights of people with mental disabilities.* Washington, DC: Author.

Bearse, J. L., McMinn, M. R., Seegobin, W., & Free, K. (2014). Healing thyself: What barriers do psychologists face when considering personal psychotherapy and how can they be overcome? *APA, 45*(49), 62.

Beasley, L. O., Silovsky, J. F., Owora, A., Burris, L., Hecht, D., DeMoracs-Huffine, P., . . . Tolma, E. (2014). Mixed-methods feasibility study on the cultural adaptation of a child abuse prevention model. *Child Abuse and Neglect.* [Electronic publication]

Beatty Moody, D. L., Waldstein, S. R., Tobin, J. N., Cassells, A., Schwartz, J. C., & Brondolo, E. (2016). Lifetime racial/ethnic discrimination and ambulatory blood pressure: The moderating effect of age. *Health Psychology, 35*(4), 333–342.

Bebbington, P. E., & Kuipers, E. (2011). Schizophrenia and psychosocial stresses. In D. R. Weinberg & P. Harrison (Eds.), *Schizophrenia* (pp. 599–624). Hoboken, NJ: Wiley-Blackwell.

Bebko, J. M., & Weiss, J. A. (2006). Mental retardation. In M. Hersen & J. C. Thomas (Series Eds.) & R. T. Ammerman (Vol. Ed.), *Comprehensive handbook of personality and psychopathology, Vol. 3: Child psychopathology* (pp. 233–253). Hoboken, NJ: Wiley.

Beblo, T., Kater, L., Baetge, S., Driessen, M., & Piefke, M. (2017). Memory performance of patients with major depression in an everyday life situation. *Psychiatry Research. 248,* 28–34.

Bechard, M., VanderLaan, D. P., Wood, H., Wasserman, L., & Zucker, K. J. (2016, September 6). Psychosocial and psychological vulnerability in adolescents with gender dysphoria: A "proof of principle" study. *Journal of Sex & Marital Therapy.* [Epub ahead of print]

Bechtel, K., & Bennett, B. L. (2017, March 15). Evaluation of sexual abuse in children and adolescents. *UpToDate.* Retrieved from http://www.uptodate.com.

Beck, A. T. (1967). *Depression: Clinical, experimental and theoretical aspects.* New York: Harper & Row.

Beck, A. T. (2002). Cognitive models of depression. In R. L. Leahy & E. T. Dowd (Eds.), *Clinical advances in cognitive psychotherapy: Theory and application* (pp. 29–61). New York: Springer.

Beck, A. T. (2016). Cognitive therapy: Nature and relation to behavior therapy (Republished article). *Behavior Therapy, 47*(6), 776–784.

Beck, A. T., & Emery, G., with Greenberg, R. L. (1985). Differentiating anxiety and depression: A test of the cognitive content-specificity hypothesis. *Journal of Abnormal Psychology, 96,* 179–183.

Beck, A. T., Freeman, A., Davis, D. D., & Associates. (2004). *Cognitive therapy of personality disorders* (2nd ed.). New York: Guilford Press.

Beck, A. T., Rush, A. J., Shaw, B. F., & Emery, G. (1979). *Cognitive therapy of depression.* New York: Guilford Press.

Beck, A. T., Ward, C. H., Mendelson, M., Mock, J. E., & Erbaugh, J. (1962). Reliability of psychiatric diagnosis: 2. A study of consistency of clinical judgments and ratings. *American Journal of Psychiatry, 119,* 351–357.

Beck, A. T., & Weishaar, M. E. (2014). Cognitive therapy. In D. Wedding & R. J. Corsini (Eds.), *Current psychotherapies* (10th ed., pp. 231–264). Independence, KY: Cengage Publications.

Becker, C. B., Perez, M., Kilpela, L. S., Diedrichs, P. C., Trujillo, E., & Stice, E. (2017). Engaging stakeholder communities as body image intervention partners: The Body Project as a case example. *Eating Behaviors, 25,* 62–67.

Becker, D. R. (2008). Vocational rehabilitation. In K. T. Mueser & D. V. Jeste (Eds.), *Clinical handbook of schizophrenia* (pp. 261–267). New York: Guilford Press.

Becker, E. A. (2016). Mental health services in Texas jails. *TexMed, 112*(11), e1.

Becker, J. V., Johnson, B. R., Parthasarathi, U., & Hategan, A. (2012). Gender identity disorders and paraphilias. In J. A. Bourgeois, U. Parthasarathi, & A. Hategan (Eds.), *Psychiatry review and Canadian certification exam preparation guide* (pp. 305–315). Arlington, VA: American Psychiatric Publishing.

Becker, S. (2016, November 30). *Criminal psychology: The criminal mind of a serial killer (Criminal psychology, serial killers, criminal mind, dark psychology, Book 1).* Amazon Digital Services, LLC.

Beckett, L. (2014, June 10). Myth vs. fact: Violence and mental health. *Propublica.*

Beeney, J. E., Wright, A. G. C., Stepp, S. D. Hallquist, M. N., Lazarus, S. A., Beeney, J. R. S., . . . Pilkonis, P. A. (2017). Disorganized attachment and personality functioning in adults: A latent class analysis. *Personality Disorders, 8*(3), 206–216.

Beidel, D. C., Alfano, C. A., Kofler, M. J., Rao, P. A., Scharfstein, L., & Wong Sarver, N. (2014). The impact of social skills training for social anxiety disorder: A randomized controlled trial. *Journal of Anxiety Disorders, 28*(8), 908–918.

Beier, E. G., & Young, D. M. (1984). *The silent language of psychotherapy: Social reinforcement of the unconscious processes* (2nd ed.). Hawthorne, New York: Aldine.

Belendiuk, K. A., & Riggs, P. (2014). Treatment of adolescent substance use disorders. *Current Treatment Options in Psychiatry, 1*(2), 175–188.

Beletsky, L., & Davis, C. S. (2017). Today's fentanyl crisis: Prohibition's iron law, revisited. *International Journal of Drug Policy, 46,* 156–159.

Belluck, P. (2016, July 26). W.H.O. weighs dropping transgender identity from list of mental disorders. *New York Times.*

Beltz, A. M., Wright, A. G., Sprague, B. N., & Molenaar, P. C. (2016). Bridging the nomothetic and idiographic approaches to the analysis of clinical data. *Assessment, 23*(4), 447–458.

Bemporad, J. R. (1992). Psychoanalytically orientated psychotherapy. In E. S. Paykel (Ed.), *Handbook of affective disorders.* New York: Guilford Press.

Bender, E. (2006, June 16). APA, AACAP suggest ways to reduce high suicide rates in Native Americans. *Psychiatric News, 41*(12), 6.

Benes, F. M. (2011). The neurobiology of bipolar disorder: From circuits to cells to molecular regulation. In H. K. Manji & C. A. Zarate, Jr. (Eds.), *Behavioral neurobiology of bipolar disorders and its treatment. Current topics in behavioral neurosciences* (pp. 127–138). New York: Springer Science + Business Media.

Ben-Ezra, M., Leshem, E., & Goodwin, R. (2015). In the wake of national trauma: Psychological reactions following the Charlie Hebdo attack. *American Journal of Psychiatry, 172*(8), 795–796.

Ben-Natan, M., Sharon, I., Barbashov, P., Minasyan, Y., Hanukayev, I., Kajdan, D., & Klein-Kremer, A. (2014). Risk factors for child abuse: Quantitataive correlational design. *Journal of Pediatric Nursing, 29*(3), 220–227.

Bennett, M. D., & Olugbala, F. K. (2010). Don't bother me, I can't cope: Stress, coping, and problem behaviors among young African American males. In W. E. Johnson Jr. (Ed.), *Social work with African American males: Health, mental health, and social policy.* (pp. 179–194) New York: Oxford University Press.

Bennett, M. P. (1998). The effect of mirthful laughter on stress and natural killer cell cytotoxicity. *Dissertation Abstracts International: Section B: The Sciences and Engineering, 58*(7–B), 3553.

Bennett, S., & Walkup, J. T. (2016, January 20). Anxiety disorders in children and adolescents: Epidemiology, pathogenesis, clinical manifestations, and course. *UpToDate.* Retrieved from http://www.uptodate.com.

Bennett, S. M. (2015). Treatment of contamination obsessive-compulsive disorder. In E. Storch & A. Lewin (Eds.), *Clinical handbook of obsessive-compulsive and related disorders.* New York: Springer.

Benros, M. E., Nielsen, P. R., Nordentoft, M., Eaton, W. W., Dalton, S. O., & Mortensen, P. B. (2011). Medicine abstract for Reference 63 of "Schizophrenia in adults: Epidemiology and pathogenesis." *American Journal of Psychiatry, 168*(12), 1303–1310.

Berenson, K. R., Downey, G., Rafaeli, E., Coifman, K. G., & Leventhal Paquin, N. (2011). The rejection-rage contingency in borderline personality disorder. *Journal of Abnormal Psychology, 120*(3), 681–690.

Berg, A., Brätane, E., Odland, H. H., Brudvik, C., Rosland, B., & Hirth, A. (2014). Cardiovascular risk assessmet for the use of ADHD drugs in children. *Tidsskrift for den Norske Laegeforening, 134*(7), 710–714.

Bergink, V., Bouvy, P. F., Vervoort, J. P., Koorengevel, K. M., Steegers, E. P., & Kushner, S. A. (2012). Prevention of postpartum psychosis and mania in women at high risk. *American Journal of Psychiatry, 169*(6), 609–615.

Bergler, E. (1951). *Neurotic counterfeit sex.* New York: Grune & Stratton.

Bergner, R. M., & Bunford, N. (2014). *Mental disorder is a disability concept, not a behavioral one: An empirical investigation.* Athens, OH: Ohio University.

Berk, S. N., & Efran, J. S. (1983). Some recent developments in the treatment of neurosis. In C. E. Walker (Ed.), *The handbook of clinical psychology: Theory, research, and practice* (Vol. 2). Homewood, IL: Dow Jones-Irwin.

Berlim, M. T., McGirr, A., Van den Eynde, F., Fleck, M. P., & Giacobbe, P. (2014). Effectiveness and acceptability of deep brain stimulation (DBS) of the subgenual cingulate cortex for treatment-resistant depression: A systematic review and exploratory meta-analysis. *Journal of Affective Disorders, 159,* 31–38.

Berman, A. L. (1986). Helping suicidal adolescents: Needs and responses. In C. A. Corr & J. N. McNeil (Eds.), *Adolescence and death.* New York: Springer.

Berman, A. L. (2018). Risk factors proximate to suicide and suicide risk assessment in the context of denied suicide ideation. *Suicide and Life-Threatening Behavior.* [Manuscript in press]

Bernecker, S. L., Coyne, A. E., Constantino, M. J., & Ravitz, P. (2017). For whom does interpersonal psychotherapy work? A systematic review. *Clinical Psychology Review, 56,* 82–93.

Bernier, R., & Dawson, G. (2016). Autism spectrum disorders. In D. Cicchetti (ed.), *Developmental psychopathology, Vol. 3: Maladaptation and psychopathology* (3rd ed.). New York: Wiley.

Bernstein, D. P., & Useda, J.D (2007). Paranoid personality disorder. In W. O'Donohue, K. A. Fowler, & S. O. Lilienfeld (Eds.). *Personality disorders: Toward the DSM-V.* Los Angeles: Sage Publications.

Bernstein, L. (2017, February 14). Poll: Mainstream media continues to lose the public's trust. *WJLA.*

Berridge, K. C., & Robinson, T. E. (2016). Liking, wanting, and the incentive-sensitization theory of addiction. *American Psychologist, 71*(8), 670–679.

Berridge, M. J. (2011). Calcium signaling and Alzheimer's disease. *Neurochemical Research, 36*(7), 1149–1156.

Berry, M. D., & Berry, P. D. (2013). Contemporary treatment of sexual dysfunction: Reexamining the biopsychosocial model. *Journal of Sexual Medicine, 10,* 2627–2643.

Berry, S. M., Broglio, K., Bunker, M., Jayewardene, A., Olin, B., & Rush, A. J. (2013). A patient-level meta-analysis of studies evaluating vagus nerve stimulation therapy for treatment-resistant depression. *Medical Devices: Evidence and Research, 6,* 17–635.

Bertozzi, S., Londero, A. P., Fruscalzo, A., Driul, L., & Marchesoni, D. (2010). Prevalence and risk factors for dyspareunia and unsatisfying sexual relationships in a cohort of primiparous and secondiparous women after 12 months postpartum. *International Journal of Sexual Health, 22*(1), 47–53.

Besal, L., & Liu, D. (2013). In U.S., women's emotional health worse after heart attack: Emotional support programs may be key to post-heart attack care for women. Retrieved from Gallup website: http://www.gallup.com/poll/160418.

Best, D. (2017). Why the mechanisms of 12-step behaviour change should matter to clinicians. *Addiction, 112*(6), 938–939.

Betan, E., & Binder, J. (2016). Psychodynamic therapies in practice: Time-limited dynamic psychotherapy. In A. J. Consoli, L. E. Beutler, & B. Bongar (Eds.), *Comprehensive textbook of psychotherapy: Theory and practice* (2nd ed.), (pp. 45–60). New York: Oxford University Press.

Beutler, L. E., Clarkin, J. F., & Bongar, B. (2000). *Guidelines for the systematic treatment of the depressed patient.* New York: Oxford University Press.

Beutler, L. E., Consoli, A. J., Lenore, S., & Sheltzer, J. M. (2016). Integrative and eclectic therapies in practice: Systematic treatment selection. In A. J. Consoli, L. E. Beutler, & B. Bongar (Eds.), *Comprehensive textbook of psychotherapy: Theory and practice* (2nd ed., pp. 205–222). New York: Oxford University Press.

Beutler, L. E., Williams, R. E., Wakefield, P. J., & Entwistle, S. R. (1995). Bridging scientist and practitioner perspectives in clinical psychology. *American Psychologist, 50*(12), 984–994.

Bever, L. (2017, June 6). The disturbing trend of live-streamed suicides. *Chicago Tribune.*

BGS (British Geriatrics Society). (2016, February). Acute confusion/delirium. *BGS.* Retrieved from bgs.org.uk.

Bhatia, T., Gettig, E. A., Gottesman, I. I., Berliner, J., Mishra, N. N., Nimgaonkar, V. L., & Deshpande, S. N. (2016). Stratifying empiric risk of schizophrenia among first degree relatives using multiple predictors in two independent Indian samples. *Asian Journal of Psychiatry, 24,* 79–84.

Bhattacharya, R., Cross, S., & Bhugra, D. (Eds.). (2010). *Clinical topics in cultural psychiatry.* London: Royal College of Psychiatrists.

Bhui, K. (2016). Discrimination, poor mental health, and mental illness. *International Review of Psychiatry, 28*(4), 411–414.

Biederman, J., Spencer, T., & Wilens, T. (2004). Evidence-based pharmacotherapy for attention-deficit hyperactivity disorder. *International Journal of Neuropsychopharmacology, 7,* 77–97.

Biederman, J., Spencer, T., & Wilens, T. (2005). Evidence-based pharmacotherapy of attention-deficit hyperactivity disorder. In D. J. Stein, B. Lerer, & S. Stahl, *Evidence-based psychopharmacology* (pp. 255–289). New York: Cambridge University Press.

Bigdeli, T. B., Maher, B. S., Zhao, Z., Sun, J., Medeiros, H., Akula, N., . . . Fanous, A. H. (2013). Association study of 83 candidate genes for bipolar disorder in chromosome 6q selected using an evidence-based prioritization algorithm. *American Journal of Medical Genetics. Part B, Neuropsychiatric Genetics, 162B*(8), 898–906.

Bighelli, I., Trespidi, C., Castellazzi, M., Cipriani, A., Furukawa, T. A., Girlanda, F., . . . Barbui, C. (2016, September 12). Antidepressants and benzodiazepines for panic disorder in adults. *Cochrane Database of Systematic Reviews, 9.* [Epub ahead of print]

Bills, C. B., & Li, G. (2005). Correlating homicide and suicide. *International Journal of Epidemiology, 34*(4), 837–845.

Bina, R. (2014). Seeking help for postpartum depression in the Israeli Jewish orthodox community: Factors associated with use of professional and informal help. *Women and Health, 54*(5), 455–473.

Binet, A., & Simon, T. (1916). *The development of intelligence in children (The Binet-Simon Scale).* Baltimore: Williams & Wilkins.

Binik, Y. M. (2010). The DSM diagnostic criteria for vaginismus. *Archives of Sexual Behavior, 39*(2), 278–291.

Binswanger, I., & Elmore, J. G. (2016, November 22). Clinical care of incarcerated adults. *UpToDate.* Retrieved from http://www.uptodate.com.

Biran, J., Tahor, M., Wircer, E., & Levkowitz, G. (2015). Role of developmental factors in hypothalamic function. *Frontiers in Neuroanatomy, 9,* 47.

Birkeland, S. F. (2013). Psychopharmacological treatment and course in paranoid personality disorder: A case series. *International Clinical Psychopharmacology, 28*(5), 283–285.

Biron, M., & Link, S. (2014). Stress, appraisal and work routine in wartime: Do men and women differ? *Anxiety, Stress, and Coping, 27*(2), 229–240.

Bitter, J. R. (2013). *Theory and practice of family therapy and counseling.* Independence, KY: Cengage Learning.

BJS (Bureau of Justice Statistics). (2013, March 7). *Female victims of sexual violence, 1994–2010* (NCJ 240655). Retrieved from http://www.bjs.gov/index.cfm?tv=pbdetail&iid=4594.

BJS (Bureau of Justice Statistics). (2016, April). *Assessing inmate cause of death: Deaths in Custody Reporting Program and National Death Index* (NCJ 249568). Retrieved from http://www.bjs.gov.

BJS (Bureau of Justice Statistics). (2016, October). *Criminal victimization, 2015* (NCJ 250180). Washington, DC: BJS.

BJS (Bureau of Justice Statistics). (2016). *Data collection: National Crime Victimization Survey (NCVS).* Washington, DC: Author.

BJS (Bureau of Justice Statistics). (2017). *Victims and offenders.* Washington, DC: Author.

Black, D. S. (2014). Mindfulness-based interventions: An antidote to suffering in the context of substance use, misuse, and addiction. *Substance Use and Misuse, 49*(5), 487–491.

Black, D. W. (2016, February 5). Antisocial personality disorder: Epidemiology, clinical manifestations, course and diagnosis. *UpToDate.* Retrieved from http://www.uptodate.com.

Black, D. W. (2017, April 20). Treatment of antisocial personality disorder. *UpToDate.* Retrieved from http://www.uptodate.com.

Black, M. C., Basile, K. C., Breiding, M. J., Smith, S. G., Walters, M. L., Merrick. M. T., . . . Stevens, M. R. (2011) *The National Intimate Partner and Sexual Violence Survey (NISVS): 2010 summary report.* Atlanta, GA: National Center for Injury Prevention and Control, CDC.

Black Youth Project. (2011). The attitudes and behavior of young Black Americans: Research summary. Retrieved from Black Youth Project website: www.blackyouthproject.com/survey/findings.

Black Youth Project. (2016). *About us.* Chicago, IL: Author.

Blader, J. C. (2011). Acute inpatient care for psychiatric disorders in the United States, 1996 through 2007. *Archives of General Psychiatry, 68*(12), 1276–1283.

Blagov, P. S., Fowler K. A., & Lilienfeld, S. O. (2007). Histrionic personality disorder. In W. O'Donohue, K. A. Fowler, & S. O. Lilienfeld (Eds.). *Personality disorders: Toward the DSM-V.* Los Angeles: Sage Publications.

Blair, J., Mitchell, D., & Blair, K. (2005). *The psychopath: Emotion and the brain.* Malden, MA: Blackwell Publishing.

Blanchard, J. J., Bradshaw, K. R., Garcia, C. P., Nasrallah, H. A., Harvey, P. D., Casey, D., . . . O'Gorman, C. (2017). Examining the reliability and validity of the Clinical Assessment Interview for Negative Symptoms within the Management of Schizophrenia in Clinical Practice (MOSAIC) multisite national study. *Schizophrenia Research, 185,* 137–143.

Blashfield, R. K., Keele, J. W., Flanagan, E. H., & Miles, S. R. (2014). The cycle, of classification: DSM-I through DSM-5. *Annual Review of Clinical Psychology, 10,* 25–51.

Blass, R. B. (2014). On the "fear of death" as the primary anxiety: How and why Klein differs from Freud. *International Journal of Psycho-Analysis, 95*(4), 613–627.

Blass, R.B. (2015). Conceptualizing splitting: On the different meanings of splitting and their implications for the understanding of the person and the analytic process. *International Journal of Psychoanalysis, 96*(1), 123–139.

Blatt, S. J. (1995). The destructiveness of perfectionism. Implications for the treatment of depression. *American Psychologist., 50*(12), 1003–1020.

Blatt, S. J. (1999). Personality factors in brief treatment of depression: Further analyses of the NIMH-sponsored Treatment for Depression Collaborative Research Program. In D. S. Janowsky (Ed.), *Psychotherapy indications and outcomes.* Washington, DC: American Psychiatric Press.

Bleiberg, K. L., & Markowitz, J. C. (2014). Interpersonal psychotherapy for depression. In D. H. Barlow (Ed.), *Clinical handbook of psychological disorders: A step-by-step treatment manual* (5th ed., Ch. 8). New York: Guilford Press.

Bliss, E. L. (1980). *Multiple personality, allied disorders and hypnosis.* New York: Oxford University Press.

Block, J. (2015). Shortage of psychiatrists only getting worse. *Psychiatry Advisor.* Retrieved from http://www.psychiatryadvisor.com/shortage-of-psychiatrists-only-getting worse/printarticle/437233.

Blodgett, J. C., Maisel, N. C., Fuh, I. L., Wilbourne, P. L., & Finney, J. W. (2014). How effective is continuing care for substance use disorders? A meta-analytic review. *Journal of Substance Abuse Treatment, 46*(2), 87–97.

Bloom, B. L. (1984). *Community mental health: A general introduction* (2nd ed.). Monterey, CA: Brooks/Cole.

Blow, F. C., Zeber, J. E., McCarthy, J. F., Valenstein, M., Gillon, L., & Bingham, C. R. (2004). Ethnicity and diagnostic patterns in veterans with psychoses. *Social Psychiatry and Psychiatric Epidemiology, 39*(10), 841–851.

Blow, J., & Cooper, T. V. (2014). Predictors of body dissatisfaction in a Hispanic college student sample. *Eating Behaviors, 15*(1), 1–4.

BLS (Bureau of Labor Statistics). (2015). *Economic News Release. Table A-3. Employment status of the Hispanic or Latino population by sex and age.* Retrieved from http://www.bls.gov/news.release.empsit.t03.htm.

BLS (Bureau of Labor Statistics). (2016). *American time use survey – 2015 results.* Washington, DC: Author.

BLS (Bureau of Labor Statistics). (2016). *Occupational employment statistics. Occupational employment and wages, May 2015: 21-1014 Mental health counselors.* Retrieved from https://data.bls.gov/cgi-bin/print.pl/oes/current/oes211014.htm.

BLS (Bureau of Labor Statistics). (2016). *Occupational employment statistics. Occupational employment and wages, May 2015. 29-1066 Psychiatrists.* Retrieved from https://www.bls.gov/oes/current/oes291066.htm.

BLS (Bureau of Labor Statistics). (2016). *Occupational Outlook Handbook, 2016–17 Edition, Psychologists.* Washington, DC: U.S. Department of Labor. Retrieved from https://www.bls.gov/ooh/life-physical-and-social-science/psychologists.htm.

BLS (Bureau of Labor Statistics). (2016). *Occupational Outlook Handbook, 2016–17 Edition, Social Workers.* Washington, DC: U.S. Department of Labor. Retrieved from https://www.bls.gov/ooh/community-and-social-service/social-workers.htm.

BLS (Bureau of Labor Statistics). (2016). *Women's earnings 83 percent of men's, but vary by occupation.* January 15, 2016. Retrieved from https://data.bls.gov/opub/ted/2016/womens-earnings-83-percent-of-mens-but-vary-by-occupation.htm#bls-print.

Blum, K., Braverman, E. R., Holder, J. M., Lubar, J. F., Monastra, V. J., Miller, D., & Comings, D. E. (2000). Reward deficiency syndrome: A biogenetic model for the diagnosis and treatment of impulsive, addictive, and compulsive behaviors. *Journal of Psychoactive Drugs, 32*(Suppl.), 1–68.

Blum, K., Chen, A. L. C., Thanos, P. K., Febo, M., Demetrovics, Z., Dushaj, K., . . . Badgaiyan, R. D. (2018). Genetic addiction risk score (GARS)™, a predictor of vulnerability to opioid dependence. *Frontiers in Bioscience (Elite Edition), 10,* 175–196.

Blum, K., Cull, J. G., Braverman, E. R., & Comings, D. E. (1996). Reward deficiency syndrome. *American Scientist, 84*(2), 132–144.

Blum, K., Febo, M., & Badgaiyan, R. D. (2016, October 12). Fifty years in the development of a glutaminergic-dopaminergic optimization complex (KB220) to balance brain reward circuitry in reward deficiency syndrome: A pictorial. *Austin Addiction Science, 1*(2).

Blum, K., Gold, M., Demetrovics, A., Archer, T., Thanos, P. K., Baron, D., & Badgaiyan, R. D. (2017). Substance use disorder a bio-directional subset of reward deficiency syndrome. *Frontiers in Bioscience, 22,* 1534–1548.

Blum, K., Noble, E. P., Sheridan, P. J., Montgomery, A., Ritchie, T., Jagadeeswaran, P., . . . Cohn, J. B. (1990). Allelic association of human dopamine D2 receptor gene in alcoholism. *Journal of the American Medical Association, 263*(15), 2055–2060.

Blum, K., Simpatico, T., Badgaiyan, R. D., Demetrovics, Z., Fratantonio, J., Agan, C., . . . Gold, M. S. (2015). Coupling neurogenetics (GARS) and a nutrigenomic based dopaminergic agonist to treat Reward Deficiency Syndrome (RDS): Targeting polymorphic reward genes for carbohydrate addiction algorithms. *Journal of Reward Deficiency Syndrome, 1*(2), 75–80.

Boat, T. F., & Wu, J. T. (Eds.). (2015). *Mental disorders and disabilities among low-income children.* Washington, DC: National Academies Press.

Bobo, W. V., & Shelton, R. C. (2016, July 13). Bipolar disorder in adults: Treating major depression with antidepressants. *UpToDate.* Retrieved from www.uptodate.com.

Bock, C., Bukh, J. D., Vinberg, M., Gether, U., & Kessing, L. V. (2010). The influence of comorbid personality disorder and neuroticism on treatment outcome in first episode depression. *Psychopathology, 43*(3), 197–204.

Bodell, L. P., & Mayer, L. E. S. (2011). Percent body fat is a risk factor for relapse in anorexia nervosa: A replication study. *International Journal of Eating Disorders, 44*(2), 118–123.

Bodison, S. C. (2015). Developmental dyspraxia and the play skills of children with autism. *The American Journal of Occupational Therapy, 69*(5), 6905185060.

Bodnar, A., Krzywotulski, M., Lewandowska, A., Chlopocka-Wozniak, M., Bartkowska-Sniatkowska, A., Michalak, M., & Rybakowski, J. K. (2016). Electroconvulsive therapy and cognitive functions in treatment-resistant depression. *17*(2), 159–164.

Boepple, L., & Thompson, J. K. (2016). A content analytic comparison of fitspiration and thinspiration websites. *International Journal of Eating Disorders, 49*(1), 98–101.

Boer, D. P. (2016). *The Wiley handbook on the theories, assessment and treatment of sexual offending.* Hoboken, NJ: Wiley-Blackwell.

Boets, B. (2014, July 14). Dyslexia: Reconciling controversies within an integrative developmental perspective. *Trends in Cognitive Sciences.* [Electronic publication]

Boeve, B., McCormick, J., Smith, G., Ferman, T., Rummans, T., Carpenter, T., . . . Petersen, R. (2003). Mild cognitive impairment in the oldest old. *Neurology, 60*(3), 477–480.

Bogdan, R., & Taylor, S. (1976, January). The judged, not the judges: An insider's view of mental retardation. *American Psychologist., 31*(1), 47–52.

Bohart, A. C. (2015). From there and back again. *Journal of Clinical Psychology, 71*(11), 1060–1069.

Bohnert, K. M., Ilgen, M. A., Louzon, S., McCarthy, J. F., & Katz, I. R. (2017). Substance use disorders and the risk of suicide mortality among men and women in the U.S. Veterans Health Administration. *Addiction, 112,* 1193–1201.

Boissoneault, L. (2017, March 6). How a soap opera virus felled hundreds of students in Portugal. *Smithsonian Magazine.*

Bokor, G., & Anderson, P. D. (2014). Obsessive-compulsive disorder. *Journal of Pharmacy Practice, 27*(2), 116–130.

Bole, C. B., Pislar, M., Sen, M., Tavcar, R., & Mrhar, A. (2017). Original research paper. Switching antipsychotics: Results of 16-month non-interventional, prospective, observational clinical research of inpatients with schizophrenia spectrum disorders. *Acta Pharmaceutica, 67*(1), 99–112.

Bolgar, H. (1965). The case study method. In B. B. Wolman (Ed.), *Handbook of clinical psychology.* New York: McGraw-Hill.

Bonn, S. (2015, March 9). The history and rise of mass public shootings. *Psychology Today.*

Bonn, S. A. (2017, January 1). Why psychopaths are effective killers: Psychopaths are cold-blooded and calculating. *Psychology Today.*

Bonanno, G. A., & Mancini, A. D. (2012). Beyond resilience and PTSD: Mapping the heterogeneity of responses to potential trauma. *Psychological Trauma: Theory, Research, Practice, and Policy, 4*(1), 74–83.

Bonnet, M. H., & Arand, D. L. (2015, December 15). Clinical features and diagnosis of insomnia in adults. *UpToDate.* Retrieved from www.uptodate.com.

Bonnet, M. H., & Arand, D. L. (2017, May 11). Treatment of insomnia in adults. *UpToDate.* Retrieved from www.uptodate.com.

Bonnet, S., Lacambre, M., Schandrin, A., Capdevielle, D., & Courtet, P. (2017). Insight and psychiatric dangerousness: A review of the literature. *Encephale, 43*(2), 146–153.

Bonnet, S., Lacambre, M., Schandrin, A., Capdevielle, D., & Courtet, P. (2016). Insight and psychiatric dangerousness: A review of the literature. [French] *L'Encéphale.* Advance online publication.

Bonsack, C., Golay, P., Gibellini Manetti, S., Gebel, S., Ferrari, P., Besse, C., . . . Morandi, S. (2016). Linking primary and secondary care after psychiatric hospitalization: Comparison between transitional case management setting and routine care for common mental disorders. *Frontiers in Psychiatry, 7,* 96.

Boone, K. (2011). Somatoform disorders, factitious disorder, and malingering. In M. R. Schoenberg & J. G. Scott (Eds.), *The little black book of neuropsychology: Syndrome-based approach* (pp. 551–565). New York: Springer Science + Business Media.

Boone, L., Claes, L., & Luyten, P. (2014). Too strict or too loose? Perfectionism and impulsivity: The relation with eating disorder symptoms using a person-centered approach. *Eating Behaviors, 15*(1), 17–23.

Boone, L., Soenens, B., & Luyten, P. (2014). When or why does perfectionism translate into eating disorder pathology? A longitudinal examination of the moderating and mediating role of body dissatisfaction. *Journal of Abnormal Psychology, 123*(2), 412–418.

Boos, S. C. (2017, August 7). Physical child abuse: Diagnostic evaluation and management. *UpToDate.* Retrieved from http://www.uptodate.com.

Boos, S. C. (2017, February 15). Physical child abuse: Recognition. *UpToDate.* Retrieved from http://www.uptodate.com.

Bor, W., Stallman, H., Collerson, E., Boyle, C., Swenson, C. C., McDermott, B., & Lee, E. (2013). Therapy implications of child abuse in multi-risk families. *Australasian Psychiatry, 21*(4), 389–392.

Borchgrevink, C. P., Cha, J-M., Kim, S.-H. (2013). Hand washing practices in a college town environment. *Journal of Environmental Health, 75*(6), 18–24.

Bordeaux, B., & Lieberman, H. R. (2017, August 30). Benefits and risks of caffeine and caffeinated beverages. *UpToDate.* Retrieved from http://www.uptodate.com.

Borden, K. A. (2017). Contemporary assessment practices Part 1: General and diversity issues. *Professional Psychology: Research and Practice, 48*(2), 71–72.

Borden, L. A., Martens, M. P., McBride, M. A., Sheline, K. T., Bloch, K. K., & Dude, K. (2011). The role of college students' use of protective behavioral strategies in the relation between binge drinking and alcohol-related problems. *Psychology of Addictive Behaviors, 25*(2), 346–351.

Borge, F., Hoffart, A., Sexton, H., Martinsen, E., Gude, T., Hedley, L. M., & Abrahamsen, G. (2010). Pre-treatment predictors and in-treatment factors associated with change in avoidant and dependent personality disorder traits among patients with social phobia. *Clinical Psychology and Psychotherapy, 17*(2), 87–99.

Borkovec, T. D., Alcaine, O. M., & Behar, E. (2004). Avoidance theory of worry and generalized anxiety disorder. In R. G. Heimberg, C. L. Turk, & D. S. Mennin (Eds.), *Generalized anxiety disorder: Advances in research and practice* (pp. 77–108). New York: Guilford Press.

Bornstein, R. F. (2005). Psychodynamic theory and personality disorders. In S. Strack (Ed.), *Handbook of personality and psychopathology* (pp. 164–180). Hoboken, NJ: Wiley.

Bornstein, R. F. (2007). Dependent personality disorder. In W. O'Donohue, K. A. Fowler, S. O. Lilienfeld (Eds.). *Personality disorders: Toward the DSM-V.* Los Angeles: Sage Publications.

Bornstein, R. F. (2007). Might the Rorschach be a projective test after all: Social projection of an undesired trait alters Rorschach oral dependency scores. *Journal of Personality Assessment, 88*(3), 354–367.

Bornstein, R. F. (2012). Illuminating a neglected clinical issue: Societal costs of interpersonal dependency and dependent personality disorder. *Journal of Clinical Psychology, 68*(7), 766–781.

Borzekowski, D. L. G., Schenk, S., Wilson, J. L., & Peebles, R. (2010). e-Ana and e-Mia: A content analysis of pro-eating disorder web sites. *American Journal of Public Health, 100*(8), 1526–1534.

Botella, C., Pérez-Ara, M. Á., Bretón-López, J., Quero, S., Garcia-Palacios, A., & Baños, R. M. (2016). In vivo versus augmented reality exposure in the treatment of small animal phobia: A randomized controlled trial. *PLoS One, 11*(2), e0148237.

Both, S., Schultz, W. W., & Laan, E. (2017). Treating women's sexual desire and arousal problems. In Z. D. Peterson, *The Wiley-Blackwell handbook of sex therapy* (Ch. 2, pp. 11–31). Hoboken, NJ: Wiley-Blackwell.

Bott, E. (1928). Teaching of psychology in the medical course. *Bulletin of the Association of American Medical Colleges, 3,* 289–304.

Bouchard, S., Dumoulin, S., Robillard, G., Guitard, T., Klinger, E., Forget, H., . . . Roucaut, F. X. (2017). Virtual reality compared with in vivo exposure in the treatment of social anxiety disorder: A three-arm randomised controlled trial. *British Journal of Psychiatry, 210*(4), 276–283.

Bouck, E. C., & Park, J. (2016). Inclusion and students with an intellectual disability. In J. P. Bakken & F. E. Obiakor (Eds), *General and special education inclusion in an age of change: Impact on students with disabilities (Advances in Special Education, Vol. 31).* West Yorkshire, UK: Emerald Publishing Limited.

Bouman, T. K., Mulkens, S., & van der Lei, B. (2017). Cosmetic professionals' awareness of body dysmorphic disorder. *Plastic and Reconstructive Surgery, 139*(2), 336–342.

Bouras, N., & Holt, G. (Eds.). (2010). *Mental health services for adults with intellectual disability: Strategies and solutions. The Maudsley Series.* New York, Psychology Press.

Bourin, M., Malinge, M., & Guitton, B. (1995). Provocative agents in panic disorder. *Therapie 50*(4), 301–306. [French].

Bowden, S. C., Saklofske, D. H., & Weiss, L. G. (2011). Invariance of the measurement model underlying the Wechsler Adult Intelligence Scale-IV in the United States and Canada. *Educational and Psychological Measurement, 71*(1), 186–199.

Bowen, S., Witkiewitz, K., Clifasefi, S. L., Grow, J., Chawla, N., Hsu, S. H., . . . Larimer, M. E. (2014). Relative efficacy of mindfulness-based relapse prevention, standard relapse prevention, and treatment as usual for substance use disorders: A randomized clinical trial. *JAMA Psychiatry, 71*(5), 547–556.

Bower, B. (2013, November 2). The bright side of sadness. *Science News.*

Bower, E. S., Wetherell, J. L., Mon, T., & Lenze, E. J. (2015). Treating anxiety disorders in older adults: Current treatments and future directions. *Harvard Review of Psychiatry, 23*(5), 329–342.

Bower, G. H. (1981). Mood and memory. *American Psychologist, 36*(2), 129–148.

Bowerman, M. (2016, October 12). Survey reveals what Americans fear the most. *USA Today.*

Bowers, A., Owen, R., & Heller, T. (2016). Care coordination experiences of people with disabilities enrolled in Medicaid managed care. *Disability and Rehabilitation.* Retrieved from http://www.tandfonline.com.

Bowler, R. M., Adams, S. W., Schwarzer, R., Gocheva, V. V., Roels, H. A., Kim, Y., . . . Lobdell, D. T. (2018). Validity of self-reported concentration and memory problems: Relationship with neuropsychological assessment and depression. *Journal of Clinical and Experimental Neuropsychology*, 1–11.

Bowring, D. L., Totsika, V., Hastings, R. P., Toogood, S., & McMahon, M. (2017). Prevalence of psychotropic medication use and association with challenging behaviour in adults with an intellectual disability. A total population study. *Journal of Intellectual Disability Research, 61*, 604–617.

Boyer, E. W., Siefert, S. A., & Hernon, C. (2017, April 6). Methamphetamine: Acute intoxication. *UpToDate*. Retrieved from http://www.uptodate.com.

Boysen, G. A., & VanBergen, A. (2013). A review of published research on adult dissociative identity disorder: 2000–2010. *The Journal of Nervous and Mental Disease, 201*(1), 5–11.

Boysen, G. A., & VanBergen, A. (2014). Simulation of multiple personalities: A review of research comparing diagnosed and simulated dissociative identity disorder. *Clinical Psychology Review, 34*(1), 14–28.

Bozikas, V. P., Kosmidis, M. H., Giannakou, M., Kechayas, P., Tsotsi, S., Kiosscoglou, G., . . . Garyfallos, G. (2014). Controlled shifting of attention in schizophrenia and bipolar disorder through a dichotic listening paradigm. *Comprehensive Psychiatry, 55*(5), 1212–1219.

BPS (British Psychological Society). (2016). Wellbeing issues facing psychological professionals. *The Psychologist*.

Bradford, A. (2016, November 28). Treatment of female orgasmic disorder. *UpToDate*. Retrieved from http://www.uptodate.com.

Bradford, J. M. W., Fedoroff, P., & Firestone, P. (2008). Sexual violence and the clinician. In R. I. Simon & K. Tardiff (Eds.), *Textbook of violence assessment and management* (pp. 441–460). Arlington, VA: American Psychiatric Publishing.

Brady, J. E., & Li, G. (2014). Trends in alcohol and other drugs detected in fatally injured drivers in the United States, 1999–2010. *American Journal of Epidemiology, 179*(6), 1093.

Braham, M. Y., Jedidi, M., Chkirbene, Y., Hmila, I., El Khai, M. C., Souguir, M. K., & Ben Dhiab, M. (2017). Caregiver-fabricated illness in a child: A case report of three siblings. *Journal of Forensic Nursing, 13*(1), 39–42.

Brakoulias, V., Starcevic, V., Belloch, A., Brown, C., Ferrao, Y. A., Fontenelle, L. F., . . . Viswasam, K. (2017). Comorbidity, age of onset and suicidality in obsessive-compulsive disorder (OCD): An international collaboration. *Comprehensive Psychiatry, 76*, 79–86.

Bram, A. D. (2016, November 3). Reviving and refining psychodynamic interpretation of the Wechsler Intelligence Tests: The verbal comprehension subtests. *Journal of Personality Assessment*, 1–10. [Epub ahead of print]

Brand, B. L., Loewenstein, R. J., & Spiegel, D. (2014). Dispelling myths about dissociative identity disorder treatment: An empirically based approach. *Psychiatry, 77*(2), 169–189.

Brandon, S. (1981). *The history of shock treatment*. In R. L. Palmer (Ed.), *Electroconvulsive therapy: An appraisal* (pp. 3–10). Oxford, England: Oxford University Press.

Brannon, G. E. (2016). History and mental status examination. Retrieved from http://emedicine.medscape.com/article/293402–overview.

Bratskeir, K. (2013, September 16). The habits of supremely happy people. *Huffington Post*.

Braun, D. L. (1996, July 28). Interview. In S. Gilbert, More men may seek eating-disorder help. *New York Times*.

Braverman, D. W., Marcus, B. S., Wakim, P. G., Mercurio, M. R., & Kopf, G. S. (2017). Healthcare professionals' attitudes about physician-assisted death: An analysis of their justifications and the role of terminology and patient competency. *Journal of Pain and Symptom Management, 54*, 538–545.

Braxton, L. E., Calhoun, P. S., Williams, J. E., & Boggs, C. D. (2007). Validity rates of the Personality Assessment Inventory and the Minnesota Multiphasic Personality Inventory-2 in a VA medical center setting. *Journal of Personality Assessment, 88*(1), 5–15.

Bremner, J. D. (2002). *Does stress damage the brain? Understanding trauma-related disorders from a mind-body perspective*. New York: Norton.

Bremner, J. D. (2016). Traumatic stress from a multilevel developmental psychopathology perspective. In D. Cicchetti (Ed.), *Developmental psychopathology, maladaptation and psychopathology, Vol. 3: Maladaptation and psychopathology* (3rd ed., Chap. 9, pp. 1–39). New York: Wiley.

Bremner, J. D., & Charney, D. S. (2010). Neural circuits in fear and anxiety. In D. J. Stein, E. Hollander & B. O. Rothbaum (Eds.), *Textbook of anxiety disorders* (2nd ed., pp. 55–71). Arlington, VA: American Psychiatric Publishing.

Bremner, J. D., Vythilingam, M., Vermetten, E., Vaccarino, V., & Charney, D. S. (2004). Deficits in hippocampal and anterior cingulate functioning during verbal declarative memory encoding in midlife major depression. *American Journal of Psychiatry, 161*(4), 637–645.

Brenot, P. (2011). Can a sexual symptom be fixed without taking account of the couple? *Sexologies: European Journal of Sexology and Sexual Health, 20*(1), 20–22.

Brent, D. A. (2001). Assessment and treatment of the youthful suicidal patient. In H. Hendin & J. J. Mann (Eds.), *The clinical science of suicide prevention* (Vol. 932, pp. 106–131). New York: Annals of the New York Academy of Sciences.

Breslau, J., Gilman, S. E., Stein, B. D., Ruder, T., Gmelin, T., & Miller, E. (2017). Sex differences in recent first-onset depression in an epidemiological sample of adolescents. *Translational Psychiatry, 7*, e1139.

Bressert, S. (2016) Antisocial personality disorder treatment. *Psych Central*. Retrieved from https://psychcentral.com.

Bressert, S. (2016, May 18). Dependent personality disorder treatment. *Psych Central*. Retrieved from https://psychcentral.com.

Bressert, S. (2016). Histrionic personality disorder treatment. *Psych Central*. Retrieved from https://psychcentral.com.

Bressert, S. (2016). Narcissistic personality disorder treatment. *Psych Central*. Retrieved from https://psychcentral.com.

Bressert, S. (2016). Obsessive-compulsive personality disorder treatment. *Psych Central*. Retrieved from https://psychcentral.com.

Bressert, S. (2016). Paranoid personality disorder treatment. *Psych Central*. Retrieved from https://psychcentral.com.

Bressert, S. (2016). Schizotypal personality disorder. *Psych Central*. Retrieved from https://psychcentral.com.

Bressert, S. (2016, May 17). Facts about shyness. *Psych Central*. Retrieved from https://psychcentral.com.

Bressert, S. (2017). Avoidant personality disorder symptoms. *Psych Central*. Retrieved from https://psychcentral.com.

Bressert, S. (2017). Dependent personality disorder treatment. *Psych Central*. Retrieved from https://psychcentral.com.

Bressi, C., Nocito, E. P., Milanese, E. A., Fronza, S., Della Valentina, P., Castagna, L., . . . Capra, G. A. (2014). Efficacy of short-term psychodynamic psychotherapy vs treatment as usual in a sample of patients with anxiety and depressive disorders. *Rivista Di Psichiatria, 49*(1), 28–33.

Brewer, J. (2014). Mindfulness in the military. *American Journal of Psychiatry, 171*, 803–806.

Brewin, C. R., & Andrews, B. (2017). Creating memories for false autobiographical events in childhood; A systematic review. *Applied Cognitive Psychology, 31*(1), 2–23.

Bridge, J. A., Marcus, S. C., & Olfson, M. (2012). Outpatient care of young people after emergency treatment of deliberate self-harm. *Journal of the American Academy of Child and Adolescent Psychiatry, 51*, 213–222.

Bridler, R., Häberle, A., Müller, S. T., Cattapan, K., Grohmann, R., Toto, S., . . . Greil, W. (2015). Psychopharmacological treatment of 2195 in-patients with borderline personality disorder: A comparison with other psychiatric disorders. *European Neuropsychopharmacology, 25*(6), 763–772.

Briggs, S., Slater, T., & Bowley, J. (2017). Practitioners' experiences of adolescent suicidal behaviour in peer groups. *Journal of Psychiatric and Mental Health Nursing, 24*, 293–301.

Brinker, J., & Cheruvu, V. K. (2016). Social and emotional support as a protective factor against current depression along individuals with adverse childhood experiences. *Preventive Medicine Reports, 5*, 127–133.

Brisch, R., Saniotis, A., Wolf, R., Bielau, H., Bernstein, H., Steiner, J., . . . Gos, T. (2014). The role of dopamine in schizophrenia from a neurobiological and evolutionary perspective: Old fashioned, but still in vogue. *Frontiers in Psychiatry, 547*.

Britt, R. R. (2005, January 6). The odds of dying. *LiveScience.com*.

Brodeur, M. (2016, December 21). 10 negative body image thoughts you need to stop right now. *Verily Magazine*.

Bromwich, J. E. (2016, April 20). You've been washing your hands wrong. *New York Times*.

Bronskill, S. E., Anderson, G. M., Sykora, K., Wodchis, W. P., Gill, S., Shulman, K. I., & Rochon, P. A. (2004). Neuroleptic drug therapy in older adults newly admitted to nursing homes: Incidence, dose, and specialist contact. *Journal of the American Geriatrics Society, 52*(5), 749.

Brook, J. S., Lee, J. Y., Rubenstone, E., Brook, D. W., & Finch, S. J. (2014). Triple comorbid trajectories of tobacco, alcohol, and marijuana use as predictors of antisocial personality disorder and generalized anxiety disorder among urban adults. *American Journal of Public Health, 104*(8), 1413–1420.

Brooks, A. C. (2013, December 14). A formula for happiness. *New York Times*.

Brooks, G. R., & Richardson, F. C. (1980). Emotional skills training: A treatment program for duodenal ulcer. *Behavior Therapist, 11*(2), 198–207.

Brooks, L., McCabe, P., & Schneiderman, N. (2011). Stress and cardiometabolic syndrome. In R. J. Contrada & A. Baum (Eds.), *The handbook of stress science: Biology, psychology, and health* (pp. 399–409). New York: Springer Publishing.

Brookshire, B. (2013, May 8). Psychology is WEIRD. *Slate*. Retrieved from http://www.slate.com.

Brophy, M. (2010). Sex, lies, and virtual reality. In D. Monroe (Ed.), *Porn: How to think with kink, Philosophy for everyone* (pp. 204–218). Hoboken, NJ: Wiley-Blackwell.

Brosch, J. R., & Farlow, M. R. (2017, May 30). Early-onset dementia in adults. *UpToDate*. Retrieved from http://www.uptodate.com.

Brown, A. (2012, April 27). Chronic pain rates shoot up until Americans reach late 50s: Low-income and obese Americans more likely to have chronic pain. Retrieved from Gallup website: http://www.gallup.com/poll/154169.

Brown, C. H., Brincks, A., Huang, S., Perrino, T., Cruden, G., Pantin, H., . . . Sandler, I. (2016, December 24). Two-year impact of prevention programs on adolescent depression: An integrative data analysis approach. *Prevention Science*. [Epub ahead of print]

Brown, G. K., Stirman, S. W., & Spokas, M. (2010). Relapse prevention of suicide attempts: Application of cognitive therapy. In C. S. Richards & M. G. Perri (Eds.), *Relapse prevention for depression* (pp. 177–198). Washington, DC: American Psychological Association.

Brown, G. K., Wenzel, A., & Rudd, M. D. (2011). Cognitive therapy for suicidal patients. In K. Michel & D. A. Jobes (Eds.), *Building a therapeutic alliance with the suicidal patient* (pp. 273–291). Washington, DC: American Psychological Association.

Brown, G. W. (2002). Social roles, context and evolution in the origins of depression. *Journal of Health and Social Behavior, 43*(3), 255–276.

Brown, G. W., & Harris, T. O. (1978). *Social origins of depression: A study of psychiatric disorder in women*. London: Tavistock.

Brown, J. (2014, November 23). In mental health courtroom, emphasis is on treatment. *The Denver Post*.

Brown, J. (2016, July 8). Updated: In mental health courtroom, emphasis is on treatment. *The Denver Post*.

Brown, J. H., Henteleff, P., Barakat, S., & Rowe, C. J. (1986). Is it normal for terminally ill patients to desire death? *American Journal of Psychiatry, 143*(2), 208–211.

Brown, L., Beutler, L. E., Patterson, J. H., Bongar, B., & Holleran, L. (2016). Psychotherapy with people exposed to mass casualty events: Theory and practice. In A. J. Consoli, L. E. Beutler, & B. Bongar, *Comprehensive textbook of psychotherapy: theory and practice: Part II: Psychotherapy by modalities and populations* (Chap. 27). (2nd ed.). New York: Oxford University Press.

Brown, R. C., & Plener, P. L. (2017). Non-suicidal self-injury in adolescence. *Current Psychiatry Reports, 19*(3), 20.

Brown, S. A. (2017). The effects of direct-to-consumer-advertising on mental illness beliefs and stigma. *Community Mental Health Journal, 53*(5), 534–541.

Brownley, K. A., Peat, C. M., La Via, M., & Bulik, C. M. (2015). Pharmacological approaches to the management of binge eating disorder. *Drugs, 75*(1), 9–32.

Bruch, H. (1962). Perceptual and conceptual disturbances in anorexia nervosa. *Psychosomatic Medicine, 24,* 187–194.

Bruch, H. (1973). *Eating disorders: Obesity, anorexia nervosa and the person within*. New York: Basic Books.

Bruch, H. (1978). *The golden cage: The enigma of anorexia nervosa*. Cambridge, MA: Harvard University Press.

Bruch, H. (1991). The sleeping beauty: Escape from change. In S. I. Greenspan & G. H. Pollock (Eds.), *The course of life, Vol. 4: Adolescence*. Madison, CT: International Universities Press.

Bruch, H. (2001). *The golden cage: The enigma of anorexia nervosa*. Cambridge, MA: Harvard University Press.

Bruffaerts, R., Demyttenaere, K., Kessler, R. C., Tachimori, H., Bunting, B., Hu, C., . . . Scott, K. M. (2015). The associations between preexisting mental disorders and subsequent onset of chronic headaches: A worldwide epidemiologic perspective. *The Journal of Pain, 16*(1), 42–52.

Brühl, A. B., Delsignore, A., Komossa, K., & Weidt, S. (2014). Neuroimaging in social anxiety disorder—A meta-analytic review resulting in a new neurofunctional model. *Neuroscience & Biobehavioral Reviews, 47,* 260–280.

Brumberg, J. J. (1988). *Fasting girls: The history of anorexia nervosa*. New York: Penguin Books.

Brunelin, J., Fecteau, S., & Suaud-Chagny, M-F. (2013). Abnormal striatal dopamine transmission in schizophrenia. *Current Medicinal Chemistry, 20*(3), 397–404.

Brunet, K., & Birchwood, M. (2010). Duration of untreated psychosis and pathways to care. In P. French, J. Smith, D. Shiers, M. Reed, & M. Rayne (Eds.), *Promoting recovery in early psychosis: A practice manual* (pp. 9–16). Hoboken, NJ: Wiley-Blackwell.

Bryan, C. J., & Corso, K. A. (2011). Depression, PTSD, and suicidal ideation among active duty veterans in an integrated primary care clinic. *Psychological Services, 8*(2), 94–103.

Bryant, R. A., Creamer, M., O'Donnell, M., Silove, D., McFarlane, A. C., & Forbes, D. (2015). A comparison of the capacity of DSM-IV and DSM-5 acute stress disorder definitions to predict posttraumatic stress disorder and related disorders. *The Journal of Clinical Psychiatry, 76*(4), 391–397.

Bryant, R. A., Moulds, M. L., Guthrie, R. M., & Nixon, R. D. V. (2005). The additive benefit of hypnosis and cognitive-behavioral therapy in treating acute stress disorder. *Journal of Consulting and Clinical Psychology, 73*(2), 334–340.

Bryman, A. (2016). *Social research methods* (5th ed.). New York: Oxford University Press.

Bryner, J. (2011). Close friends less common today, study finds. *Live Science*. Retrieved from http://www.livescience.com/16879.

BSA (Boy Scouts of America). (2017). *Bullying awareness*. Retrieved from http://www. scouting.org/training/YouthProtection/bullying.aspx.

BSA (Bullying Statistics in America). (2014). A 2014 presentation of statistics and graphs on bullying.

BSA (Bullying Statistics in America). (2017). A 2017 presentation of statistics and graphs on bullying.

Bschor, T., & Kilarski, L. L. (2016). Are antidepressants effective? A debate on their efficacy for the treatment of major depression in adults. *Expert Review of Neurotherapeutics,16*(4), 367–374.

Buckingham, E. T., & Daniolos, P. (2013). Longitudinal outcomes for victims of child abuse. *Current Psychiatry Reports, 15*(2), 342.

Buckley, L., Bonar, E. E., Walton, M. A., Carter, P. M., Voloshyna, D., Ehrlich, P. F., & Cunningham, R. M. (2017). Marijuana and other substance use among male and female underage drinkers who drive after drinking and ride with those who drive after drinking. *Addictive Behaviors, 71,* 7–11.

Buckner, J. D., Lemke, A. W., Jeffries, E. R., & Shah, S. M. (2017). Social anxiety and suicidal ideation: Test of the utility of the Interpersonal-Psychological Theory of Suicide. *Journal of Anxiety Disorders, 45,* 60–63.

Budney, A. J., Vandrey, R. L., & Fearer, S. (2011). Cannabis. In J. H. Lowinson & P. Ruiz (Eds.), *Substance abuse: A comprehensive textbook* (5th ed.). Philadelphia, PA: Lippincott, Williams, & Wilkins.

Buehler, S. (2017). Treating sexual problems in clients with mental illness. In Z. D. Peterson, *The Wiley-Blackwell handbook of sex therapy* (Ch. 22, pp. 359–368). Hoboken, NJ: Wiley-Blackwell.

Bukalo, O., Pinard, C. R., & Holmes, A. (2014). Mechanisms to medicines: Elucidating neural and molecular substrates of fear extinction to identify novel treatments for anxiety disorders. *British Journal of Pharmacology, 171*(20), 4690–4718.

Bukstein, O. (2016, November 3). Attention deficit hyperactivity disorder in adults: Epidemiology, pathogenesis, clinical features, course, assessment, and diagnosis. *UpToDate*. Retrieved from http://www.uptodate.com.

Bulik, B. S. (2017). *The top 10 most-advertised prescription drug brands*. FiercePharma.

Bulik, C. M., Kleiman, S. C., & Yilmaz, Z. (2016). Genetic epidemiology of eating disorders. *Current Opinion in Psychiatry, 29*(6), 383–388.

Bunaciu, L., Feldner, M. T., Babson, K. A., Zvolensky, M. J., & Eifert, G. H. (2012). Biological sex and panic-relevant anxious reactivity to abrupt increases in bodily arousal as a function of biological challenge intensity. *Journal of Behavior Therapy and Experimental Psychiatry, 43*(1), 526–531.

Burack, J. A., Russo, N., Green, C. G., Landry, O., & Iarocci, G. (2016). Developments in the developmental approach to intellectual disability. In D. Cicchetti (Ed.), *Developmental psychopathology, Vol. 3: Maladaptation and psychopathology* (3rd ed.). New York: Wiley.

Burbach, F. R., Fadden, G., & Smith. J. (2010). Family interventions for first-episode psychosis. In P. French, J. Smith, D. Shiers, M. Reed, & M. Rayne (Eds.), *Promoting recovery in early psychosis: A practice manual* (pp. 210–225). Hoboken, NJ: Wiley-Blackwell.

Burcu, M., Zito, J. M., Metcalfe, L., Underwood, H., & Safer, D. J. (2016). Trends in stimulant medication use in commercially insured youths and adults, 2010–2014. *JAMA Psychiatry, 73,* 992–993.

Burke, K. (2016, May 24). 63 texting statistics that answer all your questions. *Text Request*. Retrieved from https://www.textrequest.com.

Burke, K., & Riley, J. (2010). Coronary artery disease. In C. Margereson & S. Trenoweth (Eds.), *Developing holistic care for long-term conditions* (pp. 255–273). New York: Routledge/Taylor &, Francis Group.

Burke, S. M., Cohen-Kettenis, P. T., Veltman, D. J., Klink, D. T., & Bakker, J. (2014). Hypothalamic response to the chemo-signal androstadienone in gender dysphoric children and adolescents. *Frontiers in Endocrinology, 5*, 60.

Burke, S. M., Kreukels, B. P., Cohen-Kettenis, P. T., Veltman, D. J., Klink, D. T., & Bakker, J. (2016). Male-typical visuospatial functioning in gynephilic girls with gender dysphoria: Organizational and activational effects of testosterone. *Journal of Psychiatry & Neuroscience, 41*(6), 395–404.

Burke, S. M., Menks, W. M., Cohen-Kettenis, P. T., Klink, D. T., & Bakker, J. (2014). Click-evoked otoacoustic emissions in children and adolescents with gender identity disorder. *Archives of Sexual Behavior, 43*(8), 1515–1523.

Burlingame, G. M., & Baldwin, S. (2011). Group therapy. In J. C. Norcross, G. R. VandenBos, & D. K. Freedheim (Eds.), *History of psychotherapy: Continuity and change* (2nd ed., pp. 505–515). Washington, DC: American Psychological Association.

Burns, T. (2010). Modern community care strategies for schizophrenia care: Impacts on outcome. In W. F. Gattaz & G. Busatto (Eds.), *Advances in schizophrenia research 2009* (pp. 417–427). New York: Springer Science + Business Media.

Burns, T., & Drake, B. (2011). Mental health services and patients with schizophrenia. In D. R. Weinberg & P. Harrison (Eds.), *Schizophrenia* (pp. 625–643). Hoboken, NJ: Wiley-Blackwell.

Burnsed, B. (2014, July 22). Rates of excessive drinking among student-athletes falling. *NCAA*. Retrieved from http://www.ncaa.org.

Burt, K. B., Coatsworth, J. D., & Masten, A. S. (2016). Competence and psychopathology in development. In D. Cicchetti (Ed.), *Developmental psychopathology, Vol. 4: Risk, resilience, and intervention* (3rd ed.). New York: Wiley.

Burtăverde, V., Chraif, M., Aniței, M., & Mihăilă, T. (2016). The incremental validity of the Dark Triad in predicting driving aggression. *Accident Analysis and Prevention, 96*, 1–11.

Burton, V. S. (1990). The consequences of official labels: A research note on rights lost by the mentally ill, mentally incompetent, and convicted felons. *Community Mental Health Journal, 26*(3), 267–276.

Busch, A. C., Denduluri, M., Glass, J., Hetzel, S., Gugnani, S. P., Gassman, M., . . . Brown, R. (2017). Predischarge injectable versus oral Naltrexone to improve postdischarge treatment engagement among hospitalized veterans with alcohol use disorder: A randomized pilot proof-of-concept study. *Alcoholism: Clinical and Experimental Research, 41*, 1352–1360.

Busch, A. M., Ciccolo, J. T., Puspitasari, A. J., Nosrat, S., Whitworth, J. W., & Stults-Kolehmainen, M. (2017). Preferences for exercise as a treatment for depression. *Mental Health and Physical Activity, 10*, 68–72.

Busch, F. N., Milrod, B. L., & Shear, K. (2010). Psychodynamic concepts of anxiety. In D. J. Stein, E. Hollander, & B. O. Rothbaum (Eds.), *Textbook of anxiety disorders* (2nd ed., pp. 117–128). Arlington, VA: American Psychiatric Publishing.

Busch, F. N., Rudden, M. G., & Shapiro, T. (2004). *Psychodynamic treatment of depression*. Washington, DC: American Psychiatric Publishing.

Bushman, B. J., Baumeister, R. F., & Stack, A. D. (1999). Catharsis, aggression, and persuasive influence: Self-fulfilling or self-defeating prophecies? *Journal of Personality and Social Psychology, 76*(3), 367–376.

Bustillo, J., & Weil, E. (2016, October 13). Psychosocial interventions for schizophrenia. *UpToDate*. Retrieved from http://www.uptodate.com.

Bustillo, J., & Weil, E. (2017, March 17). Psychosocial interventions for severe mental illness. *UpToDate*. Retrieved from http://www.uptodate.com.

Butcher, J. N. (2010). Personality assessment from the nineteenth to the early twenty-first century: Past achievements and contemporary challenges. *Annual Review of Clinical Psychology, 6*, 1–20.

Butcher, J. N. (2011). *A beginner's guide to the MMPI-2* (3rd ed.). Washington, DC: American Psychological Association.

Byers, A. L., Covinsky, K. E., Neylan, T. C., & Yaffe, K. (2014). Chronicity of posttraumatic stress disorder and risk of disability in older persons. *JAMA Psychiatry, 71*(5), 540–546.

Byrne, K. A., Patrick, C. J., & Worthy, D. A. (2016). Striatal dopamine, externalizing proneness, and substance abuse: Effects on wanting and learning during reward-based decision making. *Clinical Psychological Science, 4*(5), 760–774.

Bystritsky, A. (2016, April 25). Pharmacotherapy for generalized anxiety disorder in adults. *UpToDate*. Retrieved from http://www.uptodate.com.

Cable, A. (2008, November 14). Divorced from reality: All three accounts of the Second Life love triangle that saw a woman separate from her husband for having a cyber-affair. *Daily Mail, UK*.

Cabrera, F. J. P., Herrera, A. R. C., Rubalcava, S. J. A., & Martinez, K. I. M. (2017, June 2). Behavior patterns of antisocial teenagers interacting with parents and peers: A longitudinal study. *Frontiers in Psychology, 8*, 757.

Cachelin, F. M., Phinney, J. S., Schug, R. A., & Striegel-Moore, R. M. (2006). Acculturation and eating disorders in a Mexican American community sample. *Psychology of Women Quarterly, 30*(4), 340–347.

Cacioppo, C. N., Conway, L. J., Mehta, D., Krantz, I. D., & Noon, S. E. (2016). Attitudes about the use of internet support groups and the impact among parents of children with Cornelia de Lange syndrome. *American Journal of Medical Genetics Part C: Seminars in Medical Genetics, 172*(2), 229–236.

Cacioppo, J., & Freberg, L. (2016). *Discovering pychology: The science of mind* (2nd edition). Boston: Cengage Learning.

Cadet, J. L., Bisagno, V., & Milroy, C. M. (2014). Neuropathology of substance use disorders. *Acta Neuropathologica, 127*(1), 91–107.

Cadoni, C., Pisanu, A., Simola, N., Frau, L., Porceddu, P. F., Corongiu, S., . . . Chiara, G. (2017). Widespread reduction of dopamine cell bodies and terminals in adult rats exposed to a low dose regimen of MDMA during adolescence. *Neuropharmacology, 123*, 385–394.

Cain, N. M., Ansell, E. B., Simpson, H. B., & Pinto, A. (2015). Interpersonal functioning in obsessive-compulsive personality disorder. *Journal of Personality Assessment, 97*(1), 90–99.

Calarco, M. (2017). Does depression turn self-medication into addiction? *Psych Central*. Retrieved from https://psychcentral.com/blog/archives/2016/10/15/does-depression-turn-self-medication-into-addiction/

Caldwell, C. (2017, April). American carnage: The new landscape of opioid addiction. *First Things*.

Calhoun, B. H., Maggs, J. L., & Loken, E. (2018). Change in college students' perceived parental permissibility of alcohol use and its relation to college drinking. *Addictive Behaviors, 76*, 275–280.

Caligor, E., & Clarkin, J. F. (2010). An object relations model of personality and personality pathology. In J. F. Clarkin, P. Fonagy, & G. O. Gabbard (Eds.), *Psychodynamic psychotherapy for personality disorders: A clinical handbook* (pp. 3–36). Arlington, VA: American Psychiatric Publishing.

Caligor, E., & Petrini, M. J. (2016, December 9). Treatment of narcissistic personality disorder. *UpToDate*. Retrieved from http://www.uptodate.com.

Caligor, E., & Petrini, M. J. (2016, October 21). Narcissistic personality disorder: Epidemiology, pathogenesis, clinical manifestations, course, assessment, and diagnosis. *UpToDate*. Retrieved from http://www.uptodate.com.

Calkins, S. D., & Dollar, J. M. (2014). Emotion: Commentary. A biopsychosocial perspective on maternal psychopathology and the development of child emotion regulation. *Journal of Personality Disorders, 28*(1), 70–77.

Calkins, S. D., & Perry, N. B. (2016). The development of emotion regulation: Implications for child adjustment. In D. Cicchetti, *Developmental psychopathology, Vol. 3: Maladaptation and psychopathology* (3rd ed., Chapter 6). New York: Wiley

Callahan, L. A., Steadman, H. J., McGreevy, M. A., & Robbins, P. C. (1991). The volume and characteristics of insanity defense pleas: An eight-state study. *Bulletin of the American Academy of Psychiatry Law, 19*(4), 331–338.

Callanen, R. J. (2012). Teacher training for LRE mainstreaming and diverse classrooms. *Theses, dissertations, and other Capstone projects, Paper 78*. Mankato, MN: Cornerstone, Minnesota State University.

Cameron, A., Rosen, R. C., & Swindle, R. W. (2005). Sexual and relationship characteristics among an internet-based sample of U.S. men with and without erectile dysfunction. *Journal of Sex and Marital Therapy, 31*(3), 229–242.

Cameron, D. J., Thomas, R. I., Mulvihill, M., & Bronheim, H. (1987). Delirium: A test of the Diagnostic and Statistical Manual III criteria on medical inpatients. *Journal of the American Geriatrics Society, 35*, 1007–1010.

Cameron, E. E., Hunter, D., Sedov, I. D., & Tomfohr-Madsen, L. M. (2017). What do dads want? Treatment preferences for paternal postpartum depression. *Journal of Affective Disorders, 215,* 62–70.

Campbell, D. (2010). Pre-suicide states of mind. In P. Williams (Ed.), *The psychoanalytic therapy of severe disturbance, Psychoanalytic ideas* (pp. 171–183). London, England: Karnac Books.

Campbell, E. C., Caroff, S. N., & Mann, S. C. (2016, March 29). Co-occurring schizophrenia and substance use disorder: Epidemiology, pathogenesis, clinical manifestations, course, assessment and diagnosis. *UpToDate.* Retrieved from http://www.uptodate.com.

Campbell, E. C., Caroff, S. N., & Mann, S. C. (2016, April 27). Psychosocial interventions for co-occurring schizophrenia and substance use disorder. *UpToDate.* Retrieved from http://www.uptodate.com.

Campbell, E. C., Caroff, S. N., & Mann, S. C. (2016, May 16). Pharmacotherapy for co-occurring schizophrenia and substance use disorder. *UpToDate.* Retrieved from http://www.upto-date.com.

Campbell, J., Gilmore, L., & Cuskelly, M. (2003). Changing student teachers' attitudes towards disability and inclusion. *Journal of Intellectual and Developmental Disability, 28,* 369–379.

Campbell, K. (2016, March 23). The pitfalls of direct-to-consumer advertising in medicine. *U.S. News & World Report. Health Care.*

Campbell, W. K., & Miller, J. D. (Eds.). (2011). *The handbook of narcissism and narcissistic personality disorder: Theoretical approaches, empirical findings, and treatments.* Hoboken, NJ: John Wiley.

Campese, V. D., Sears, R. M., Moscarello, J. M., Diaz-Mataix, L., Cain, C. K., & LeDoux, J. E. (2016). The neural foundations of reaction and action in aversive motivation. *Current Topics in Behavioral Neurosciences, 27,* 171–195.

Canas, P. M., Simões, A. P., Rodrigues, R. J., & Cunha, R. A. (2014). Predominant loss of glutamatergic terminal markers in a b-amyloid peptide model of Alzheimers disease. *Neuropharmacology, 76 Pt A,* 51–56.

Canetta, S., Sourander, A., Surcel, H., Hinkka-Yli-Salomäki, S., Leiviskä, J., Kellendonk, C., . . . Brown, A. S. (2014). Elevated maternal C-reactive protein and increased risk of schizophrenia in a national birth cohort. *American Journal of Psychiatry, 171*(9), 960–968.

Cantani, M., Dell'Acqua, F., Budisavljevic, S., Howells, H., et al. (2016). Frontal networks in adults with autism spectrum disorder. *Brain, 139,* 616–630.

Cantor, J. M., Lafaille, S. J., Hannah, J., Kucyi, A., Soh, D. W., Girard, A., & Mikulis, D. J. (2016). Independent component analysis of resting-state functional magnetic resonance imaging in pedophiles. *Journal of Sexual Medicine, 13*(10), 1546–1554.

Cao, H., Zhou, N., Fang, X., & Fine, M. (2017). Marital well-being and depression in Chinese marriage: Going beyond satisfaction and ruling out critical confounders. *Journal of Family Psychology, 31,* 775–784.

Capitán, L., Simon, D., Kaye, K., & Tenorio, T. (2014). Facial feminization surgery: The forehead. Surgical techniques and analysis of results. *Plastic and Reconstructive Surgery, 134*(4), 609–619.

Carboni, L., Romoli, B., Romualdi, P., & Zoil, M. (2016). Repeated nicotine exposure modulates prodynorphin and pronociceptin levels in the reward pathway. *Drug and Alcohol Dependence, 166,* 150–158.

CareerBuilder. (2012, April 18). 37% of companies use social networks to research potential job candidates. *CareerBuilder.* Retrieved from http://www.careerbuilder.com/share/aboutus/pressreleasesdetail.

CareerBuilder. (2017). Number of employees using social media to screen candidates has increased 500 percent over the last decade. Chicago, IL: CareerBuilder. Retrieved from http://www.careerbuilder.com/share/aboutus/pressreleasedetail.

Carey, B. (2016, April 3). Investigating the minds of mass killers. *New York Times.*

Carey, C., Lieber, E., & Miller, S. (2015). *Drug firms' payments and physicians' prescribing behavior in Medicare Part D.* Retrieved from http://www.scholar.google.com.

Carey, C., Lieber, E. M. J., & Miller, S. (2016, December). *Drug firms' payments and physicians' prescribing behavior in Medicare Part D.* Presented at the 2016 annual meeting of the Association for Public Policy Analysis and Management, Washington, DC.

Carmichael, K. L., Sellborn, M., Liggett, J., & Smith, A. (2016). A personality and impairment approach to examine the similarities and differences between avoidant personality disorder and social anxiety disorder. *Personality and Mental Health, 10*(4), 337–347.

Caron, J., Julien, M., & Huang, J. H. (2008). Changes in suicide methods in Quebec between 1987 and 2000: The possible impact of Bill C-17 requiring safe storage of firearms. *Suicide and Life-Threatening Behavior, 38*(2), 195–208.

Carpenter, A. C., & Krendl, A. C. (2016, November 17). Are eyewitness accounts biased? Evaluating false memories for crimes involving in-group or out-group conflict. *Society for Neuroscience.* [Epub ahead of print]

Carpenter, C., Zestos, A. G., Altshuler, R., Sorenson, R. J., Guptaroy, B., Showalter, H. D., . . . Gnegy, M. E. (2017). Direct and systemic administration of a CNS-permeant tamoxifen analog reduces amphetamine-induced dopamine release and reinforcing effects. *Neuropsychopharmacology, 42,* 1940–1949.

Carpenter, K. M., Williams, K., & Worly, B. (2017). Treating women's orgasmic difficulties. In Z. D. Peterson (Ed.), *The Wiley-Blackwell handbook of sex therapy* (Ch. 5, pp. 57–71). Hoboken, NJ: Wiley-Blackwell.

Carr, S. N., & Francis, A. J. P. (2010). Do early maladaptive schemas mediate the relationship between childhood experiences and avoidant personality disorder features? A preliminary investigation in a non-clinical sample. *Cognitive Therapy and Research, 34*(4), 343–358.

Carrey, J. (2008, December 16). Cited in Celebrity News. *US Weekly Magazine.*

Carrey, J. (2013, November/December). Quoted in A. Richter, How Jim Carrey rolls. *Energy Times.*

Carrobles, J. A., Gámez-Guadix, M., & Almendros, C. (2011). Sexual functioning, sexual satisfaction, and subjective and psychological well-being in Spanish women. *Anals de Psicologia, 27*(1), 27–33.

Carroll, K. M. (2008). Cognitive-behavioral therapies. In H. D. Kleber & M. Galanter (Eds.), *The American Psychiatric Publishing textbook of substance abuse treatment* (4th ed., pp. 349–360). Arlington, VA: American Psychiatric Publishing.

Carroll, R. A. (2007). Gender dysphoria and transgender experiences. In S. R. Leiblum (Ed.), *Principles and practice of sex therapy* (4th ed., pp. 477–508). New York: Guilford Press.

Carroll, T. D., Currier, J. M., McCormick, W. H., & Drescher, K. D. (2017). Adverse childhood experiences and risk for suicidal behavior in male Iraq and Afghanistan veterans seeking PTSD treatment. *Psychological Trauma. 9,* 583–586.

Carvalho, J., & Nobre, P. (2011). Biopsychosocial determinants of men's sexual desire: Testing an integrative model. *Journal of Sexual Medicine, 8*(3), 754–763.

Carvalho, J., & Nobre, P. (2011). Predictors of men's sexual desire: The role of psychological, cognitive-emotional, relational, and medical factors. *Journal of Sex Research, 48*(2-3), 254–262.

Carvalho, L. F., Pianowski, G., & Filho, N. H. (2017). Establishing a clinically relevant cutoff to the Dependency Scale from the dimensional clinical personality inventory. *Psychiatry Research, 251,* 26–33.

Casey, D. E. (1995). Motor and mental aspects of EPS. *International Clinical Psychopharmacology, 10,* 105–114.

Cash, D. K., & Lane, S. M. (2017). Context influences interpretation of eyewitness confidence statements. *Law and Human Behavior, 41*(2), 180–190.

Cash, T. F., & Henry, P. E. (1995). Women's body images: The results of a national survey in the U. S. A. *Sex Roles, 33*(1/2), 19–28.

Caspi, A., McClay, J., Moffitt, T. E., Mill, J., Martin, J., Craig, I. W., . . . Poulton, R. (2002). Role of genotype in the cycle of violence in maltreated children. *Science, 297*(5582), 851.

Castleman, M. (2016, February 1). Why so many women don't have orgasms. *Psychology Today.*

Catanesi, R., Martino, V., Candelli, C., Troccoli, G., Grattagliano, I., Di Vella, G., & Carabellese, F. (2013). Posttraumatic stress disorder: Protective and risk factors in 18 survivors of a plane crash. *Journal of Forensic Sciences, 58*(5), 1388–1392.

Cavallo, F., Aquilano, M., & Arvati, M. (2015). An ambient assisted living approach in designing domiciliary services combined with innovative technologies for patients with Alzheimer's disease: A case study. *American Journal of Alzheimer's Disease and Other Dementias, 30*(1), 69–77.

Cavett, D. (1992, August 3). Goodbye darkness. *People Magazine.* Retrieved from //www.people.com/people/archive/article/0,20113244,00.html.

Cayman, S. (2014). *Sex facts: 369 facts to blow you away.* Chichester, UK: Summersdale.

CBC. (2008, May 13). The world's worst natural disasters: Calamities of the 20th and 21st centuries. *CBC News.*

CDC (Centers for Disease Control and Prevention). (2010, December 3). QuickStats:

Percentage of adults who had migraines or severe headaches, pain in the neck, lower back, or face/jaw. by sex. National Health Interview Survey, 2009. *Morbidity and Mortality Weekly Report, 59*(47), 1557.

CDC (Centers for Disease Control and Prevention). (2010). *Suicide rates among persons ages 10 years and older, by race/ethnicity and sex, United States, 2002–2006. National Suicide Statistics at a Glance.* Atlanta, GA: CDC.

CDC (Centers for Disease Control and Prevention). (2011). *High blood pressure facts.* Retrieved from http://www.cdc.gov/bloodpressure/facts.htm.

CDC (Centers for Disease Control and Prevention). (2013). *Suicide and self-inflicted injury.* Atlanta, GA: CDC.

CDC (Centers for Disease Controls and Prevention). (2014). *Data and statistics.* Washington, DC: CDC.

CDC (Centers for Disease Control and Prevention). (2014). *National diabetes statistics report: Estimates of diabetes and its burden in the United States, 2014.* Atlanta, GA: U.S. Department of Health and Human Services.

CDC (Centers for Disease Control and Prevention). (2014). *National suicide statistics at a glance.* Atlanta, GA: CDC.

CDC (Centers for Disease Controls and Prevention). (2014). *Older persons' health.* Washington, DC: CDC.

CDC (Centers for Disease Control and Prevention). (2015, March 17). *High cholesterol facts.* Retrieved from https://www.cdc.gov/cholesterol/facts.htm.

CDC (Centers for Disease Control). (2015, November 5). *Drowsy driving: Asleep at the wheel.* Atlanta, GA: Author.

CDC (Centers for Disease Control and Prevention). (2015). *Caloric intake from fast food among children and adolescents in the United States, 2011–2012.* Data Brief 213. Atlanta, GA: CDC.

CDC (Centers for Disease Control and Prevention). (2015). *Table 41 (page 1 of 3). Severe headache or migraine, low back, and neck pain among adults aged 18 and over, by selected characteristics: United States, selected years 1997–2014.* Retrieved from https://www.cdc.gov/nchs/data/hus/ 2015/041.pdf.

CDC (Centers for Disease Control and Prevention). (2016, January). *Mortality among centenarians in the United States, 2000–2014.* NCHS data brief No. 233. Hyattsville, MD: NCHS.

CDC (Centers for Disease Control and Prevention). (2016, February 18). *1 in 3 adults don't get enough sleep.* Atlanta, GA: Author.

CDC (Centers for Disease Control and Prevention). (2016, February 19). *Prevalence of healthy sleep duration among adults – United States, 2014.* Atlanta, GA: Author.

CDC (Centers for Disease Control and Prevention). (2016, April). *Suicide rates for females and males by race and ethnicity: United States, 1999 and 2014.* Hyattsville, MD: NCHS.

CDC (Centers for Disease Control and Prevention). (2016, June 6). *Chronic liver disease and cirrhosis.* Atlanta, GA: CDC.

CDC (Centers for Disease Control and Prevention). (2016, June 16). *Heart disease fact sheet.* Retrieved from https://www.cdc.gov/ dhdsp/data_statistics/fact_sheets/fs_heart_ disease.htm.

CDC (Centers for Disease Control and Prevention). (2016, July 15). *Tips for better sleep.* Atlanta, GA: Author.

CDC (Centers for Disease Control and Prevention). (2016, September 8). *Asthma surveillance data.* Retrieved from https://www.cdc. gov/asthma/asthmadata.htm.

CDC (Centers for Disease Control and Prevention). (2016, October 20). *Fact sheets– Underage drinking.* Atlanta, GA: CDC.

CDC (Centers for Disease Control and Prevention). (2016, November 30). *High blood pressure facts.* Retrieved from https://www.cdc. gov/bloodpressure/facts.htm.

CDC (Centers for Disease Control and Prevention). (2016, December 1). *Tobacco-related mortality.* Retrieved from https://www. cdc.gov/tobacco/data_statistics/fact_sheets/ health_effects/tobacco_related_mortality/ index.htm.

CDC (Centers for Disease Control and Prevention). (2016). *Serious psychological distress among adults: Early release of selected estimates based on data from the January–March 2016 national health interview survey.* Retrieved from https://www.cdc.gov/nchs/nhis/releases/ released201609.htm#13

CDC (Centers for Disease Control and Prevention). (2016). *10 leading causes of death by age group, United States–2014.* Retrieved from https://www.cdc.gov/injury/images/ k-charts/leading_causes_of_death_age_ group_2014_1050w760h.qtf.

CDC (Centers for Disease Control and Prevention). (2016). *Understanding bullying: Fact sheet.* Atlanta, GA: CDC.

CDC (Centers for Disease Control and Prevention). (2017, January 3). *Learning disorder.* Atlanta, GA: CDC.

CDC (Centers for Disease Control and Prevention). (2017, January 19). *Hypertension.* Retrieved from https://www.cdc.gov/nchs/fastats/ hypertension.htm.

CDC (Centers for Disease Control and Prevention). (2017, February 27). *Most recent asthma data.* Retrieved from https://www.cdc. gov/asthma/most_recent_data/htm.

CDC (Centers for Disease Control and Prevention). (2017, March 2). *How much sleep do I need?* Atlanta, GA: Author.

CDC (Centers for Disease Control and Prevention). (2017, March 6). *America's opioid epidemic is worsening. The Economist.*

CDC (Centers for Disease Control). (2017, March 9). *Sleep and sleep disorders.* Atlanta, GA: Author.

CDC (Centers for Disease Control and Prevention). (2017, March 17). *Accidents or unintentional injuries.* Retrieved from https://www.cdc.gov/nchs/fastats/accidental-injury.htm.

CDC (Centers for Disease Control and Prevention). (2017, March 17). *Assault or homicide.* Retrieved from https://www.cdc.gov/ nchs/fastats/homicide.htm.

CDC (Centers for Disease Control and Prevention). (2017, March 17). *Leading causes of death.* Retrieved from https://www.cdc.gov/ nchs/fastats/leading-causes-of-death.htm.

CDC (Centers for Disease Control and Prevention). (2017, March 17). *Suicide and self-inflicted injury.* Retrieved from https://www.cdc. gov/nchs/fastats/suicide.htm.

CDC (Centers for Disease Control and Prevention). (2017, March 29). *Fast facts: Diseases and death.* Atlanta, GA: CDC.

CDC (Centers for Disease Control and Prevention). (2017, April 24). *Are you getting enough sleep?* Atlanta, GA: Author.

CDC (Centers for Disease Control and Prevention). (2017, May 3). *Life expectancy: 78.8 years.* Retrieved from https://www.cdc.gov.

CDC (Centers for Disease Control and Prevention). (2017, May 12). *Youth bullying: What does the research say?* Atlanta, GA: CDC.

CDC (Centers for Disease Control and Prevention). (2017, June 1). *Adverse drug event monitoring.* Hyattsville, MD: NCHS.

CDC (Centers for Disease Control and Prevention). (2017, June 6). *Data and statistics: FASDs.* Atlanta, GA: CDC.

CDC (Centers for Disease Control and Prevention). (2017, June 7). *Binge drinking.* Atlanta, GA: CDC.

CDC (Centers for Disease Control and Prevention). (2017, June 16). *Impaired driving: Get the facts.* Atlanta, GA: CDC.

CDC (Centers for Disease Control and Prevention). (2017, July 6). *Press release: Opioid prescribing is still high and varies widely throughout the U.S.* Atlanta, GA: CDC.

CDC (Centers for Disease Control and Prevention). (2017). *Adolescent health.* Retrieved from https://www.cdc.gov/nchs/fastats/adolescent-health.htm.

CDC (Centers for Disease Control and Prevention). (2017). *Data overview: Drug overdose.* Atlanta, GA: CDC.

CDC (Centers for Disease Control and Prevention). (2017). *Economic trends in tobacco.* Atlanta, GA: CDC.

CDC (Centers for Disease Control and Prevention). (2017). *Fact sheets - Binge drinking.* Atlanta, GA: CDC.

CDC (Centers for Disease Control and Prevention). (2017). *Heroin overdose data.* Atlanta, GA: CDC.

CDC (Centers for Disease Control and Prevention). (2017). *National Survey of Family Growth: Key statistics.* Atlanta, GA: CDC.

CDC (Centers for Disease Control and Prevention). (2017). *Opioid data analysis. CDC.* Retrieved from https://www.cdc.gov.

CDC (Centers for Disease Control and Prevention). (2017). *QuickStats: Age-adjusted rate for suicide, by sex—National Vital Statistics System, United States, 1975–2015.* Retrieved from https://www-cdc-gov.ezproxy.princeton.edu/ mmwr/volumes/66/wr/mm6610a7.htm.

CDC (Centers for Disease Control and Prevention). (2017). *Quitting smoking.* Atlanta, GA: CDC.

CDC (Centers for Disease Control and Prevention). (2017). *Sexual risk behaviors: HIV, STD, & teen pregnancy prevention* Atlanta, GA: CDC.

Celani, D. P. (2014). A Fairbairnian structural analysis of the narcissistic personality disorder. *Psychoanalytic Review, 101*(3), 385–409.

Cerdá, M., Nandi, V., Frye, V., Egan, J.E., Rundle, A., Quinn, J.W., . . . Koblin, B. (2017, April 5). Neighborhood determinants of mood and anxiety disorders among men who have sex with men in New York City. *Social Psychiatry and Psychiatric Epidemiology.* [Epub ahead of print]

Cerletti, U., & Bini, L. (1938). L'elettroshock. *Archives of General Neurology, Psychiatry, and Psychoanalysis, 19,* 266–268.

Cerniglia, L., Zoratto, F., Cimino, S., Laviola, G., Ammaniti, M., & Adriani, W. (2017). Internet addiction in adolescence: Neurobiological, psychosocial and clinical issues. *Neuroscience & Biobehavioral Reviews, 76*(Pt A), 174–184.

Cervesi, C., Park, S. Y., Galling, B., Molteni, S., Masi, G., Gerhard, T., Olfson, M., & Correll, C. U. (2017). Extent, time course, and moderators of antipsychotic treatment in youth and mood disorders: Results of a meta-analysis and meta-regression analyses. *Journal of Clinical Psychiatry, 78,* 347–357.

Chacón, F., & Vecina, M. L. (2007). The 2004 Madrid terrorist attack: Organizing a large-scale psychological response. In E. K. Carll (Ed.), *Trauma psychology: Issues in violence, disaster, health, and illness* (Vol. 1). Westport, CT: Praeger Publishers.

Chadwick, P. K. (2014). Peer-professional first person account: Before psychosis—schizoid personality from the inside. *Schizophrenia Bulletin, 40*(3), 483–486.

Chakraborty, R., Chatterjee, A., & Chaudhury, S. (2014). Impact of substance use disorder on presentation and short-term course of schizophrenia. *Psychiatry Journal, 2014,* 280243.

Chalamat, M., Mihalopoulos, C., Carter, R., & Vos, T. (2005). Assessing cost-effectiveness in mental health: Vocational rehabilitation for schizophrenia and related conditions. *Australian and New Zealand Journal of Psychiatry, 39*(8), 693–700.

Chan, A. T., Sun, G. Y., Tam, W. W., Tsoi, K. K., & Wong, S. Y. (2017). The effectiveness of group-based behavioral activation in the treatment of depression: An updated meta-analysis of randomized controlled trial. *Journal of Affective Disorders, 208,* 345–354.

Chandola, T., & Marmot, M. G. (2011). Socioeconomic status and stress. In R. J. Contrada & A. Baum (Eds.), *The handbook of stress science: Biology, psychology, and health* (pp. 185–193). New York: Springer Publishing.

Chandra, A., Mosher, W.D., & Copen, C. (2011). Sexual behavior, sexual attraction, and sexual identity in the United States: Data from the 2006–2008 national survey of family growth. *National Health Statistics Reports, 36,* March 3.

Chang, G. (2017, April 18). Substance misuse in pregnant women. *UpToDate.* Retrieved from http://www.uptodate.com.

Chang, J. S., Hsiao, J-R., & Chen, C-H. (2017). *ALDH2* polymorphism and alcohol-related cancers in Asians: A public health perspective. *Journal of Biomedical Science, 24,* 19.

Chang, L. Y., Chang, H. Y., Lin, L. N., Wu, C. C., & Yen, L. L. (2017). Disentangling the effects of depression on trajectories of sleep problems from adolescence through young adulthood. *Journal of Affective Disorders. 217,* 48–54.

Chang, P. F., & Bazarova, N. N. (2016). Managing stigma: Disclosure-response communication patterns in pro-anorexia websites. *Health Communication, 31*(2), 217–229.

Chang, Z., Lichstein, P., Asherson, P. J., & Larsson, H. (2013). Developmental twin study of attention problems: High heritabilities throughout development. *Journal of the American Medical Association, 70,* 311–318.

Chapman, B. P., Benedict, R. H., Lin, F., Roy, S., Federoff, H. J., & Mapstone, M. (2017). Personality and performance in specific neurocognitive domains among older persons. *American Journal of Geriatric Psychiatry, 25*(8), 900–908.

Chaput, J-P., Weippert, M., LeBlanc, A. G., Hjorth, M. F., Michaelsen, K. F., Katzmarzyk, P. T., . . . Sjödin, A. M. (2016). Are children like werewolves? Full moon and its association with sleep and activity behaviors in an international sample of children. *Frontiers in Pediatrics, 4,* 24.

Charney, A. W., Ruderfer, D. M., Stahl, E. A., Moran, J. L., Chambert, K., Belliveau, R. A., . . . Sklar, P. (2017). Evidence for genetic heterogeneity between clinical subtypes of bipolar disorder. *Translational Psychiatry. 7*(1), e993.

Charney, D. S., Woods, S. W., Goodman, W. K., & Heninger, G. R. (1987). Neurobiological mechanisms of panic anxiety: Biochemical and behavioral correlates of yohimbine-induced anxiety. *American Journal of Psychiatry, 144*(8), 1030–1036.

Charney, D. S., Woods, S. W., Price, L. H., Goodman, W. K., Glazer, W. M., & Heninger, G. R. (1990). Noradrenergic dysregulation in panic disorder. In J. C. Ballenger (Ed.), *Neurobiology of panic disorder.* New York: Wiley-Liss.

Chase, M. (1993, May 28). Psychiatrists declare severe PMS a depressive disorder. *Wall Street Journal,* pp. B1, B6.

Chassin, L., Colder, C. R., Hussong, A., & Sher, K. J. (2016). Substance use and substance use disorders. In D. Cicchetti (Ed.), *Developmental psychopathology, Vol. 3: Maladaptation and psychopathology* (3rd ed., Ch. 19, pp. 833–897). Hoboken, NJ: John Wiley.

Chassin, L., Collins, R. L., Ritter, J., & Shirley, M. C. (2001). Vulnerability to substance use disorders across the life span. In R. E. Ingram & J. M. Price (Eds.), *Vulnerability to psychopathology: Risk across the lifespan* (pp. 165–172). New York: Guilford Press.

Chaturvedi, S. K., Desai, G., & Shaligram, D. (2010). Dissociative disorders in a psychiatric institute in India—A selected review and patterns over a decade. *International Journal of Social Psychiatry, 56*(5), 533–539.

Chaudhry, M., & Ready, R. (2012). Differential effects of test anxiety and stress on the WAIS-IV. *Journal of Young Investigators, 24*(5), 60–66.

Chavira, D. A., Grilo, C. M., Shea, M. T., Yen, S., Gunderson, J. G., Morey, L. C., . . . McGlashan, T. H. (2003). Ethnicity and four personality disorders. *Comprehensive Psychiatry, 44*(6), 483–491.

Che, X. Q., Song, N., Gao, Y., Ren, R. J., & Wang, G. (2018). Precision medicine of frontotemporal dementia: From genotype to phenotype. *Frontiers in Bioscience (Landmark Edition), 23,* 1144–1165.

Cheek, C., Bridgman, H., Fleming, T., Cummings, E., Ellis, L., Lucassen, M. F., Shepherd, M., & Skinner, T. (2014). Views of young people in rural Australia on SPARX, a fantasy world developed for New Zealand youth with depression. *JMIR Serious Games, 2*(1):e3.

Chekki, C. (2004, November 10). Treaty 3 cries for help. *The Chronicle Journal* (Thunder Bay, Ontario, Canada), p. A3.

Chemerinski, E., & Siever, L. J. (2011). The schizophrenia spectrum personality disorders. In D.R. Weinberger & P. Harrison (Eds.). *Schizophrenia.* Hoboken, NJ: Wiley-Blackwell.

Chen, C-H., Suckling, J., Lennox, B. R., Ooi, C., & Bullmore, E. T. (2011). A quantitative meta-analysis of fMRI studies in bipolar disorder. *Bipolar Disorders, 13*(1), 1–15.

Chen, L., Zhang, G., Hu, M., & Liang, X. (2015). Eye movement desensitization and reprocessing versus cognitive-behavioral therapy for adult posttraumatic stress disorder: Systematic review and metaanalysis. *The Journal of Nervous and Mental Disease, 203*(6), 443–451.

Chen, X., Jiang, Y., Chen, L., He, H., Dong, L., Hou, C., . . . Luo, C. (2017). Altered hippocampo-cerebello-cortical circuit in schizophrenia by a spatiotemporal consistency and causal connectivity analysis. *Frontiers in Neuroscience, 11,* 25.

Chen, X., & Liu, C. H. (2016). Culture, peer relationships, and developmental psychopathology. In D. Cicchetti (Ed.), *Developmental psychopathology, Vol. 3: Risk, resilience, and intervention* (3rd ed.). New York: Wiley.

Cheng, A. T. A., Hawton, K., Lee, C. T. C., & Chen, T. H. H. (2007). The influence of media reporting of the suicide of a celebrity on suicide rates: A population-based study. *International Journal of Epidemiology, 36*(6), 1229–1234.

Cherry, K. (2015). What is a projective test? *About Education.* Retrieved from About.com website: http:// psychology.about.com/od/ psychologicaltesting.

Cherry, K. (2015). What is personality testing? *About Education.* Retrieved from About.com website: http://psychology.about.com/od/ personality-testing.

Cherry, K. (2017, April 25). 10 fascinating facts about personality. *Verywell.* Retrieved from https://www.verywell.com/ facts-about-personality-2795436.

Chesnes, M., & Jin, G. Z. (2016). *Direct-to-consumer advertising and online search.* Federal Trade Commission.

Chhabra, K. H., Adams, J. M., Jones, G. L., Yamashita, M., Schlapschy, M., Skerra, A., . . . Low, M. J. (2016). Reprogramming the body weight set point by a reciprocal interaction of hydrothalamic leptin sensitivity and Pomc gene expression reverts extreme obesity. *Molecular Metabolism, 5*(10), 869–881.

Chi, M. H., Hsiao, C. Y., Chen, K. C., Lee, L. T., Tsai, H. C., Hui Lee, I., . . . Yang, Y. K. (2016). The readmission rate and medical cost of patients with schizophrenia after first hospitalization: A 10-year follow-up population-based study. *Schizophrenia Research, 170*(1), 184–190.

Chi, S., Yu, J., Tan, M., & Tan, L. (2014). Depression in Alzheimer's disease: Epidemiology, mechanisms, and management. *Journal of Alzheimer's Disease, 42*(3), 739–755.

Chin-Chan, M., Navarro-Yepes, J., & Quintanilla-Vega, B. (2015). Environmental pollutants as risk factors for neurodegenerative disorders: Alzheimer and Parkinson diseases. *Frontiers in Cellular Neuroscience, 9,* 124.

Chmielewski, M., Clark, L. A., Bagby, R. M., & Watson, D. (2015). Method matters: Understanding diagnostic reliability in DSM-IV and DSM-5. *Journal of Abnormal Psychology, 124*(3), 764–769.

Choi, S. W., Shin, Y. C., Kim, D. J., Choi, J. S., Kim, S., Kim, S. H., & Youn, H. (2017). Treatment modalities for patients with gambling disorder. *Annals of General Psychiatry, 16,* 23.

Choi, Y. S., Lee, E. J., & Cho, Y. (2017). The effect of Korean-group cognitive behavioural therapy among patients with panic disorder in clinic settings. *Journal of Psychiatric and Mental Health Nursing, 24*(1), 28–40.

Choi-Kain, L. W., Albert, E. B., & Gunderson, J. G. (2016). Evidence-based treatments for borderline personality disorder. *Harvard Review of Psychiatry, 24*(5), 342.

Chollet, J., Saragoussi, D., Clay, E., & François, C. (2013). A clinical research practice datalink analysis of antidepressant treatment patterns and health care costs in generalized anxiety disorder. *Value in Health, 16*(8), 1133–1139.

Chou, T., Carpenter, A., Kerns, C. E., Elkins, R. M., Green, J. G., & Comer, J. S. (2017). Disqualified qualifiers: Evaluating the utility of the revised DSM-5 definition of potentially traumatic events among area youth following the Boston Marathon bombing. *Depression and Anxiety, 34,* 367–373.

Chou, T., DeSerisy, M., Garcia, A.M., Freeman, J., & Comer, J. S. (2017). Obsessive-compulsive problems in very young children. In J.S. Abramowitz, D. McKay, & E. Storch (Eds.), *Handbook of obsessive-compulsive disorder across the lifespan.* New York: Wiley.

Chowdhary, N., Jotheeswaran, A. T., Nadkarni, A., Hollon, S. D., King, M., Jordans, M. J., . . . Patel, V. (2014). The methods and outcomes of cultural adaptations of psychological treatments for depressive disorders: A systematic review. *Psychological Medicine, 44*(6), 1131–1146.

Choy, Y. (2016, October 25). Treatment of specific phobias of clinical procedures in adults. *UpToDate.* Retrieved from http://www.uptodate.com.

Christensen, A. (2017, January 10). Most selfie takers aren't narcissists, study says. *PhysicsForums.* Retrieved from https://phys.org/news.

Christensen, A., Atkins, D. C., Baucom, B., & Yi, J. (2010). Marital status and satisfaction five years following an randomized clinical trial comparing traditional versus integrative behavioral couple therapy. *Journal of Consulting and Clinical Psychology, 78*(2), 225–235.

Christensen, A., & Doss, B. D. (2017). Integrative behavioral couple therapy. *Current Opinion in Psychology, 13,* 111–114.

Christensen, A., Doss, B. D., & Jacobson, N. S. (2014). *Reconcilable differences: Rebuild your relationship by, rediscovering the partner you love—without losing yourself* (2nd ed.). New York: Guilford Press.

Christensen, B. S., Gronbaek, M., Osler, M., Pedersen, B. V., Graugaard, C., & Frisch, M. (2011). Sexual dysfunctions and difficulties in Denmark: Prevalence and associated sociodemographic factors. *Archives of Sexual Behavior, 40*(1), 121–132.

Christian, C., & Greenbaum, V. J. (2010, May 31). Child abuse: Epidemiology, mechanisms, and types of abusive head trauma in infants and children. *UpToDate.* Retrieved from http://www.uptodate.com.

Christiansen, E., Agerbo, E., Bilenberg, N., & Stenager, E. (2016). SSRIs and risk of suicide attempts in young people A Danish observational register-based historical cohort study using propensity score. *Nordic Journal of Psychiatry, 70*(3), 167–175.

Christophersen, E. R., & Friman, P. C. (2010). *Elimination disorders in children and adolescents.* Cambridge, MA: Hogrefe Publishing.

Chu, C. S., Stubbs, B., Chen, T. Y., Tang, C. H., Li, D. J., Yang, W. C., Wu, C. K., Carvalho, A. F., Vieta, E., Miklowitz, D. J., Tseng, P. T., & Lin, P. Y. (2018). The effectiveness of adjunct mindfulness-based intervention in treatment of bipolar disorder: A systematic review and meta-analysis. *Journal of Affective Disorders, 225,* 234–245.

Chu, J., Leino, A., Pflum, S., & Sue, S. (2016). Psychotherapy with racial/ethnic minority groups: Theory and practice. In A. J. Consoli, L. E. Beutler, & B. Bongar (Eds.), *Comprehensive textbook of psychotherapy: Theory and practice* (2nd ed., pp. 346–362). New York: Oxford University Press.

Chudal, R., Gissler, M., Sucksdorff, D., Lehti, V., Suominen, A., Kinkka-Yli-Salomaki, S., . . . Sourander, A. (2014). Parental age and the risk of bipolar disorders. *Bipolar Disorders, 16,* 624–632.

Chun, S., Westmoreland, J. J., Bayazitov, I. T., Eddins, D., Pani, A. K., Smeyne, R. J., . . . Zakharenko, S. S. (2014). Specific disruption of thalamic inputs to the auditory cortex in schizophrenia models. *Science, 344*(6188), 1178–1182.

Chung, E., Gilbert, B., Perera, M., & Roberts, M. J. (2015). Premature ejaculation: A clinical review for the general physician. *Australian Family Physician, 44*(10), 737–743.

Chung, T., Sealy, L., Abraham, M., Ruglovsky, C., Schall, J., & Maisto, S. A. (2014). Personal network characteristics of youth in substance use treatment: Motivation for and perceived difficulty of positive network change. *Substance Abuse, 36*(3):380–8.

Cicchetti, D. (2016). *Developmental psychopathology* (3rd ed., 4 vols.). New York: Wiley.

Cicchetti, D. (2016). *Developmental psychopathology Vol. 1: Theory and method* (3rd ed.). New York: Wiley.

Cicchetti, D. (Ed.) (2016). *Developmental psychopathology, maladaptation and psychopathology, Vol. 3: Maladaptation and psychopathology* (3rd ed.). New York: Wiley.

Cicchetti, D., & Toth, S. L. (2016). Child maltreatment and developmental psychopathology: A multilevel perspective. In D. Cicchetti (Ed.), *Developmental psychopathology, Vol. 3: Maladaptation and psychopathology* (3rd ed., pp. 457–512). New York: Wiley.

Ciliberti, M. G., Albenzio, M., Inghese, C., Santillo, A., Marino, R., Sevi, A., & Caprese, M. (2017). Peripheral blood mononuclear cell proliferation and cytokine production in sheep as affected by cortisol level and duration of stress. *Journal of Dairy Science, 100*(1), 750–756.

Cipolletta, S., Votadoro, R., & Faccio, E. (2017). Online support for transgender people: An analysis of forums and social networks. *Health & Social Care in the Community, 25,* 1542–1551.

Ciraulo, D. A., Evans, J. A., Qiu, W. Q., Shader, R. I., & Salzman, C. (2011). Antidepressant treatment of geriatric depression. In D. A. Ciraulo & R. I. Shader (Eds.), *Pharmacotherapy for depression* (2nd ed., pp. 125–183). New York: Springer Science + Business Media.

Ciraulo, D. A., Shader, R. I., & Greenblatt, D. J. (2011). Clinical pharmacology and therapeutics of antidepressants. In D. A. Ciraulo & R. I. Shader (Eds.), *Pharmacotherapy of depression* (2nd ed., pp. 33–124). New York: Springer Science + Business Media.

Cirelli, C. (2016, December 8). Insufficient sleep: Definition, epidemiology, and adverse outcomes: *UpToDate.* Retrieved from http://www.uptodate.com.

CISCRP (Center for Information and Study on Clinical Research Participation). (2013). *Clinical trial facts and figures for health professionals.* Boston, MA: CISCRP.

CISCRP (Center for Information & Study on Clinical Research Participation). (2016). *Charts and statistics: Useful information about clinical research before participating in a trial.* Retrieved from http://www.ciscrp.org/education-center/charts-and-statistics/before-participation/

CISCRP (Center for Information & Study on Clinical Research Participation). (2016). *Charts and statistics: Useful information about clinical research while participating in a trial.* Retrieved from http://www.ciscrp.org/education-center/charts-and-statistics/during-participation/

Clark, D. A., & Beck, A. T. (2010). *Cognitive therapy of anxiety disorders: Science and practice.* New York: Guilford Press.

Clark, D. A., & Beck, A. T. (2012). *The anxiety and worry workbook: The cognitive behavioral solution.* New York: Guilford Press.

Clark, J. M. (2013, July 19). Importance of family structure in Hispanic families. *Livestrong.* Retrieved from http://www.livestrong.com/article/1005977.

Clarke, J. C., & Saunders, J. B. (1988). *Alcoholism and problem drinking: Theories and treatment.* Sydney, Australia: Pergamon Press.

Clarkin, J. F., Foelsch, P. A., Levy, K. N., Hull, J. W., Delaney, J. C., & Kernberg, O. F. (2001). The development of a psychodynamic treatment for patients with borderline personality disorder: A preliminary study of behavioral change. *Journal of Personality Disorders, 15,* 487–495.

Clarkin, J. F., Fonagy, P., & Gabbard, G. O. (Eds.). (2010). *Psychodynamic psychotherapy for personality disorders: A clinical handbook.* Arlington, VA: American Psychiatric Publishing.

Clarkin, J. F., Livesley, W. J., & Meehan, K. B. (2018). Clinical assessment. In W. J. Livesley & R. Larstone (Eds.), *Handbook of personality disorders: Theory, research, and treatment* (2nd ed.). New York: Guilford Press.

Clausen, H., Ruud, T., Odden, S., Saltyte Benth, J., Heiervang, K. S., Stuen, H. K., . . . Landheim, A. (2016). Hospitalisation of severely mentally ill patients with and without problematic substance use before and after Assertive Community Treatment: An observational cohort study. *BMC Psychiatry, 16,* 125.

Clausen, L., Rosenvinge J. H., Friborg, O., & Rokkedal, K. (2011). Validating the Eating

Disorder Inventory-3 (EDI-3): A comparison between 561 female eating disorders patients and 878 females from the general population. *Journal of Psychopathology and Behavioral Assessment, 33*(1), 101–110.

Clemence, M., & Leaman, J. (2016). Public attitudes to animal research in 2016. *Ipsos MORI, Social Research Institute*, July.

Clinton, A. B., Fernandez, L., & Alicea, G. (2010). Interviewing, bias, and cultural considerations in Prevention Program Evaluation. Paper presented at APA 118th Annual Convention, San Diego, California, August 12–15.

Cloninger, C. F., & Svrakic, D. M. (2005). Personality disorders. In E. H. Rubin & C. F. Zorumski (Eds.), *Adult psychiatry* (2nd ed., pp. 290–306). Oxford, England: Blackwell Publishing.

CMSAC (Central MN Sexual Assault Center). (2017). *Facts and statistics: Facts about sexual assault.* St. Cloud, MN: CMSAC.

Coates, T. D. (2016, August 1). Drug-induced neutropenia and agranulocytosis. *UpToDate.* Retrieved from http://www.uptodate.com.

Coffey, C. E., & Kellner, C. H. (2011). Electroconvulsive therapy. In C. E. Coffey, J. L. Cummings, M. S. George, & D. Weintraub (Eds.), *The American Psychiatric Publishing textbook of geriatric neuropsychiatry.* Arlington, VA: American Psychiatric Publishing, Inc.

Coffey, M. J. (2016, December 8). Catatonia in adults: Epidemiology, clinical features, assessment, and diagnosis. *UpToDate.* Retrieved from http://www.uptodate.com.

Coffey, M. J. (2017, March 31). Catatonia: Treatment and prognosis. *UpToDate.* Retrieved from http://www.uptodate.com.

Coffey, S. F., Schumacher, J. A., Baschnagel, J. S., Hawk, L. W., & Holloman, G. (2011). Impulsivity and risk-taking in borderline personality disorder with and without substance use disorders. *Personality Disorders: Theory, Research, and Treatment, 2*(2), 128–141.

Coffin, P. (2017, April 10). Prevention of lethal opioid overdose in the community. *UpToDate.* Retrieved from http://www.uptodate.com.

Cohen, K. M., & Savin-Williams, R. C. (2017). Treating sexual problems in lesbian, gay, and bisexual clients. In Z. D. Peterson (Ed.), *The Wiley-Blackwell handbook of sex therapy* (Ch. 17, pp. 269–290). Hoboken, NJ: Wiley-Blackwell.

Cohen, N. (2009, July 28). "A Rorschach cheat sheet on Wikipedia?" *New York Times,* p. A1.

Cohen, S., Daniel O'Leary, K., Foran, H. M., & Kliem, S. (2014). Mechanisms of change in brief couple therapy for depression. *Behavior Therapy, 45*(3), 402–417.

Cohen, S., Evans, G. W., Stokols, D., & Krantz, D. S. (2013). *Behavior, health, and environmental stress* (reprint of 1986 1st edition). New York: Springer Science + Business Media.

Cohen, S., Tyrrell, A. D., & Smith, A. P. (1991). Psychological stress and susceptibility to the common cold. *New England Journal of Medicine, 325,* 606–612.

Cohen-Kettenis, P. T. (2001). Gender identity disorder in DSM? *Journal of the American Academy of Child and Adolescent Psychiatry, 40*(4), 391.

Coker, T. R., Elliott, M. N., Toomey, S. L., Schwebel, D. C., Cuccaro, P., Emery, S. . . . Schuster, M. A. (2016). Racial and ethnic disparities in ADHD diagnosis and treatment. *Pediatrics, 138*(3).

Colburn, D. (1996, November 19). Singer's suicide doesn't lead to "copycat" deaths. *Washington Post Health,* p. 5.

Colder, C. R., Chassin, L. A., Lee, M. R., & Villalta, I. K. (2010). Developmental perspectives: Affect and adolescent substance use. In J. D. Kassel (Ed.), *Substance use and emotion* (pp. 109–135). Washington, DC: American Psychological Association.

Coldwell, C. M., & Bender, W. S. (2007). The effectiveness of assertive community treatment for homeless populations with severe mental illness: A meta-analysis. *American Journal of Psychiatry, 164*(3), 393–399.

Cole, K. (2013, October 6). Sinead O'Connor announces: "I'm not bipolar . . . I should never have been medicated." *Madinamerica.com.*

Cole, M. (2016, August 13). Aversion therapy and learning to overcome bad habits. *Today's Therapist.*

Coleman, K. J., Stewart, C., Waitzfelder, B. E., Zeber, J. E., Morales, L. S., Ahmed, A. T., . . . Simon, G. E. (2016). Racial-ethnic differences in psychiatric diagnoses and treatment across 11 health care systems in the mental health research network. *Psychiatry Services, 67*(7), 749–757.

Coleman, L. (1984). *The reign of error: Psychiatry, authority, and law.* Boston: Beacon.

Colijn, M. A., Nitta, B. H., & Grossberg, G. T. (2015). Psychosis in later life: A review and update. *Harvard Review of Psychiatry, 23*(5), 354–367.

Colletti, G., Lynn, S. J., & Laurence, J-R. (2010). Hypnosis and the treatment of dissociative identity disorder. In S. J. Lynn, J. W. Rhue, & I. Kirsch (Eds.), *Handbook of clinical hypnosis* (2nd ed., pp. 433–451). Washington, DC: American Psychological Association.

Colli, A., Tanzilli, A., Dimaggio, G., & Lingiardi, V. (2014). Patient personality and therapist response: An empirical investigation. *American Journal of Psychiatry, 171*(1), 102–108.

Collingwood, J. (2016). The link between bipolar disorder and creativity. *Psych Central.* Retrieved from https://psychcentral.com.

Collins, B. M., & Stam, H. J. (2015). Freeman's transorbital lobotomy as an anomaly: A material culture examination of surgical instruments and operational spaces. *History of Psychology, 18*(2), 119–131.

Collins, J. L., Thompson, K., Sherry, S. B., Glowacka, M., & Stewart, S. H. (2018). Drinking to cope with depression mediates the relationship between social avoidance and alcohol problems: A 3-wave, 18-month longitudinal study. *Addictive Behaviors, 76,* 182–187.

Collins, R. W., Levitt, M. A., Birnbaum, A. H., & Wruck, M. (2012). Encopresis: A medical and family approach. *Pediatric Nursing, 38*(4), 236–237.

Coluccia, M., Gabbrielli, M., Gualtieri, G., Ferretti, F., Pozza, A., & Fagiolini, A. (2016). Sexual masochism disorder in asphyxiophilia: A deadly yet underrecognized disease. *Case Reports in Psychiatry, 2016,* ID 5474862.

Comas-Díaz, L. (2011). Multicultural psychotherapies. In R. J. Corsini & D. Wedding (Eds.), *Current psychotherapies* (9th ed.). Belmont, CA: Brooks/Cole.

Comas-Díaz, L. (2011). Multicultural approaches to psychotherapy. In J. C. Norcross, G. R. VandenBos, & D. K. Freedheim (Eds.), *History of psychotherapy: Continuity and change* (2nd ed., pp. 243–267). Washington, DC: American Psychological Association.

Comas-Díaz, L. (2012). *Multicultural care: A clinician's guide to cultural competence. Psychologists in independent practice* (Div. 42). Washington, DC: American Psychological Association.

Comas-Díaz, L. (2014). Multicultural psychotherapy. In F. T. L. Leong (Ed.), *APA handbook of multicultural psychology* (Ch. 25). Washington, DC: American Psychological Association.

Comas-Díaz, L. (2014). Multicultural theories of psychotherapy. In D. Wedding & R. J. Corsini (Eds.), *Current psychotherapies* (10th ed., pp. 533–568). Independence, KY: Cengage Publications.

Comasco, E., Sylvén, S. M., Papadopoulos, F. C., Sundström-Poromaa, I., Oreland, L., & Skalkidou, A. (2011). Postpartum depression symptoms: A case-control study on monoaminergic functional polymorphisms and environmental stressors. *Psychiatric Genetics, 21*(1), 19–28.

Combs, D. R., Basso, M. R., Wanner, J. L., & Ledet, S. N. (2008). Schizophrenia. In M. Hersen & J. Rosqvist (Eds.), *Handbook of psychological assessment, case conceptualization and treatment, Vol. 1: Adults* (pp. 352–402). Hoboken, NJ: John Wiley & Sons.

Comer, J. S., Blanco, C., Grant, B., Hasin, D., Liu, S. M., Turner, J. B., & Olfson, M. (2011). Health-related quality of life across the anxiety disorders: Results from the National Epidemiologic Survey on Alcohol and Related Conditions. *Journal of Clinical Psychiatry, 72,* 43–50.

Comer, J. S., & Bry, L. J. (2017). Research methodology in clinical child and adolescent psychology. In T. H. Ollendick, S. W. White, & B. A. White (Eds.), *The Oxford Handbook of Clinical Child and Adolescent Psychology.* New York: Oxford University Press.

Comer, J. S., Bry, L., Poznanski, B., & Golik, A. M. (2016). Children's mental health in the context of terrorist attacks, ongoing threats, and possibilities of future terrorism. *Current Psychiatry Reports, 18,* 79.

Comer, J. S., Chow, C., Chan, P., Cooper-Vince, C., & Wilson, L. A. S. (2013). Psychosocial treatment efficacy for disruptive behavior problems in young children: A meta-analytic examination. *Journal of the American Academy of Child and Adolescent Psychiatry, 52,* 26–36.

Comer, J. S., Dantowitz, A., Chou, T., Edison, A. L., Elkins, R. M., Kerns, C., Brown, B., & Green, J. G. (2014). Adjustment among area youth after the Boston Marathon bombing and subsequent manhunt, *Pediatrics, 134*(1), 7–14.

Comer, J. S., Furr, J. M., Cooper-Vince, C., Madigan, R. J., Chow, C., Chan, P. T., . . . Eyberg, S. M. (2015). Rationale and considerations for the Internet-based delivery of parent-child interaction therapy. *Cognitive and Behavioral Practice, 22,* 302–316.

Comer, J. S., Furr, J. M., & Gurwitch, R. (2018). Terrorism exposure and the family:

Where we are, and where we go next. In B. Fiese (Ed.), *APA Handbook of Contemporary Family Psychology*. Washington, DC: APA.

Comer, J. S., Furr, J. M., Kerns, C. E., Miguel, E., Coxe, S., Elkins, R. M., . . . Freeman, J. B. (2017). Internet-delivered, family-based treatment for early-onset OCD: A pilot randomized trial. *Journal of Consulting and Clinical Psychology, 85*, 178–186.

Comer, J. S., Furr, J. M., Miguel, E., Cooper-Vince, C. E., Carpenter, A. L., Elkins, R. M., . . . Chase, R. (2017). Remotely delivering real-time parent training to the home: An initial randomized trial of Internet-delivered Parent-Child Interaction Therapy (I-PCIT). *Journal of Consulting and Clinical Psychology, 85*, 909–917.

Comer, J. S., Golik, A., & Martin, J. (In press). Learning from the past: Understanding children's mental health after 9/11 and after the Boston Marathon bombing. In S. Tyano, C. W. Hoven, & L. Amsel (Eds.), *Responses to children's mental health needs after major disasters: An international perspective*. New York: Springer.

Comer, J. S., Mojtabai, R., & Olfson, M. (2011). National trends in the antipsychotic treatment of psychiatric outpatients with anxiety disorders. *American Journal of Psychiatry, 168*(10), 1057–1065.

Comer, J. S., Olfson, M., & Mojtabai, R. (2010). National trends in child and adolescent psychotropic polypharmacy in office-based practice, 1996–2007. *Journal of the American Academy of Child & Adolescent Psychiatry, 49*(10), 1001–1010.

Comer, J. S., Pincus, D. B., & Hofmann, S. G. (2012). Generalized anxiety disorder and the proposed associated symptoms criterion change for DSM-5 in a treatment-seeking sample of anxious youth. *Depression and Anxiety, 29*, 994-1003.

Comer, R. (1973). *Therapy interviews with a schizophrenic patient*. Unpublished manuscript.

Conduct Problems Prevention Research Group (2011). The effects of the fast track preventive intervention on the development of conduct disorder across childhood. *Child Development, 82*, 331–345.

Conner, K. R., & Weisman, R. L. (2011). Embitterment in suicide and homicide-suicide. In M. Linden & A. Maercker (Eds.), *Embitterment: Societal, psychological, and clinical perspectives* (pp. 240–247). New York: Springer-Verlag Publishing.

Connor, J. P., Young, R. McD., Lawford, B. R., Ritchie, T. L., & Noble, E. P. (2002). D2 dopamine receptor (DRD2) polymorphism is associated with severity of alcohol dependence. *European Psychiatry, 17*(1), 17–23.

Conradi, H. J., Kamphuis, J. H., & de Jonge, P. (2018). Adult attachment predicts the seven-year course of recurrent depression in primary care. *Journal of Affective Disorders, 225*, 160–166.

Consoli, A. J., Beutler, L. E., & Bongar, B. (Eds.). (2016). *Comprehensive textbook of psychotherapy: theory and practice* (2nd ed.). New York: Oxford University Press.

Consoli, M. M., Wang, S. C., DeLucio, K., & Yakushko, O. (2016). Psychotherapy with immigrants and refugees: Theory and practice. In A. J. Consoli, L. E. Beutler, & B. Bongar, *Comprehensive textbook of psychotherapy: theory and practice: Part II: Psychotherapy by modalities and populations* (Chap. 24). (2nd ed.). New York: Oxford University Press.

Conti, A. A. (2014). Western medical rehabilitation through time: A historical and epistemological review. *The Scientific World Journal, 2014*, 432506.

Conti, C., Mennitto, C., De Francesco, G., Fraticelli, F., Vitacolonna, E., & Fulcheri, M. (2017). Clinical characteristics of diabetes mellitus and suicide risk. *Frontiers in Psychiatry, 8*, 40.

Conway, P. M., Erlangsen, A., Teasdale, T. W., Jakobsen, I. S., & Larsen, K. J. (2016, August 16). Predictive validity of the Columbia-Suicide Severity Rating Scale for short-term suicidal behavior: A Danish study of adolescents at a high risk of suicide. *Archives of Suicide Research*. [Epub ahead of print]

Cook, B. L., Zuvekas, S. H., Carson, N., Wayne, G. F., Vesper, A., & McGuire, T. G. (2014). Assessing racial/ethnic disparities in treatment across episodes of mental health care. *Health Services Research, 49*(1), 206–229.

Cook, C. H. (2014). Suicide and religion. *The British Journal of Psychiatry, 204*, 254–255.

Cook, N., Ayers, S., & Horsch, A. (2018). Maternal posttraumatic stress disorder during the perinatal period and child outcomes: A systematic review. *Journal of Affective Disorders, 225*, 18–31.

Cook-Darzens, S. (2016). The role of family meals in the treatment of eating disorders: A scoping review of the literature and implications. *Eating and Weight Disorders, 21*(3), 383–393.

Cool Infographics. (2013). Social network overload. Retrieved from http://www.coolinfographics.com/blog/2013/4/2/social-network-overload.

Coons, P. M., & Bowman, E. S. (2001). Ten-year follow-up study of patients with dissociative identity disorder. *Journal of Trauma and Dissociation, 2*(1), 73–89.

Cooper, A. A., Kline, A. C., Graham, B., Bedard-Gilligan, M., Mello, P. G., Feeny, N. C., & Zoellner, L. A. (2017). Homework "dose," type, and helpfulness as predictors of clinical outcomes in prolonged exposure for PTSD. *Behavior Therapy, 48*(2), 182–194.

Cooper, M. (2008). *Essential research findings in counselling and psychotherapy: The facts are friendly*. Los Angeles, CA: Sage Publications.

Cooper, M. (2016). *Existential therapies* (2nd ed.). Los Angeles: Sage Publications.

Cooper, R. (2014). On deciding to have a lobotomy: Either lobotomies were justified or decisions under risk should not always seek to maximize expected utility. *Medicine, Health Care, and Philosophy, 17*(1), 143–154.

Cooper, R. (2017, July 5). Where's the problem: Considering Laing and Esterson's account of schizophrenia, social models of disability, and extended mental disorder. *Theoretical Medicine and Bioethics*. [Epub ahead of print]

Cooper, W. O., Callahan, S. T., Shintani, A., Fuchs, D. C., Shelton, R. C., Dudley, J. A., . . . Ray, W. A. (2014). Antidepressants and suicide attempts in children. *Pediatrics, 133*(2), 204–210.

Cooper-Vince, C., Emmert-Aronson, B., Pincus, D. B., Comer, J. S. (2014). The diagnostic utility of separation anxiety disorder symptoms: An item response theory analysis. *Journal of Abnormal Child Psychology, 42*, 417–428.

Copen, C. (2017). *Condom use during sexual intercourse among women and men aged 15–44 in the United States: 2011–2015 National Survey of Family Growth*. Atlanta, GA: CDC, National Health Statistics Report, No. 105.

Copen, C. E., Chandra, A., & Febo-Vazquez, M. S. (2016, January 7). Sexual behavior, sexual attraction, and sexual orientation among adults aged 18–44 in the United States: Data from the 2011–2013 National Survey of Family Growth. Atlanta, GA: CDC, National Health Statistics Report, No. 88.

Copley, J. (2008, May 8). Psychology of heavy metal music. *Suite101.com*. Retrieved from http://www.suite101.com.

Corey, G. (2017). *Theory and practice of counseling and psychotherapy* (10th ed.). Independence, KY: Cengage Learning.

Cornacchio, D., Bry, L. J., Sanchez, A. L., Poznanski, B., & Comer, J. S. (2017). Psychosocial treatment and prevention of conduct problems in early childhood. In J. E. Lochman & W. Matthys (Eds.), *The Wiley handbook of disruptive and impulse-control disorders*. New York: Wiley.

Cornacchio, D., Crum, K. I., Coxe, S., Pincus, D. B., & Comer, J. S. (2016). Irritability and severity of anxious symptomatology among youth with anxiety disorders. *Journal of the American Academy of Child and Adolescent Psychiatry, 55*, 54–61.

Cornacchio, D., Sanchez, A. L., Chou, T., & Comer, J. S. (2017). Cognitive-behavioral therapy for children and adolescents. In S.G. Hofmann & G. Asmundson (Eds.), *The science of cognitive behavioral therapy: From theory to therapy*. New York: Elsevier.

Corral-Corral, I., & Corral-Corral, C. (2016). Tarantism in Spain in the eighteenth century: Iatrodectism and suggestion. [Spanish] *Revista de Neurologia, 63*(8), 370–379.

Corrie, S., & Callanan, M. M. (2001). Therapists' beliefs about research and the scientist-practitioner model in an evidence-based health care climate? A qualitative study. *British Journal of Medical Psychology, 74*(2), 135–149.

Corrigan, P. W., Schomerus, G., Shuman, V., Kraus, D., Perlick, D., Harnish, A., . . . Smelson, D. (2017). Developing a research agenda for reducing the stigma of addictions, Part II: Lessons from the mental health stigma literature. *American Journal on Addictions, 26*(1), 67–74.

Corter, A., & Petrie, K. J. (2011). Expressive writing in patients diagnosed with cancer. In I. Nyklicek, A. Vingerhoets, & M. Zeelenberg (Eds.), *Emotion regulation and well-being* (pp. 297–306). New York: Springer Science + Business Media.

Cortés-Cortés, J., Fernández, R., Teijeiro, N., Gómez-Gil, E., Esteva, I., Almaraz, M. C., . . . Pasaro, E. (2017). Genotypes and haplotypes of the estrogen receptor α gene (ESR1) are associated with female-to-male gender dysphoria. *Journal of Sexual Medicine, 14*(3), 464–472.

Coryell, W. (2016, December 21). Unipolar depression in adults: Course of illness. *UpToDate*. Retrieved from https://uptodate.com.

Coskun, M., & Ozturk, M. (2013). Sexual fetishism in adolescence: Report of two cases. *Journal of Psychiatry and Neurological Sciences, 26,* 199–205.

Costa, E. (1983). Are benzodiazepine recognition sites functional entities for the action of endogenous effectors or merely drug receptors? *Advances in Biochemistry and Psychopharmacology, 38,* 249–259.

Costa, E. (1985). Benzodiazepine-GABA interactions: A model to investigate the neurobiology of anxiety. In A. H. Tuma & J. Maser (Eds.), *Anxiety and the anxiety disorders.* Hillsdale, NJ: Lawrence Erlbaum.

Costa, R., Carvalho, M., Cantini, J., Freire, R., & Nardi, A. (2014). Demographics, clinical characteristics and quality of life of Brazilian women with driving phobia. *Comprehensive Psychiatry, 55*(2), 374–379.

Costantino, G., Dana, R. H., & Malgady, R. G. (2007). *TEMAS (Tell-Me-A-Story) assessment in multicultural societies.* Mahwah, NJ: Lawrence Erlbaum.

Costantino, G., Malgady, R. G., Colon-Malgady, G., & Bailey, J. (1992). Clinical utility of the TEMAS with nonminority children. *Journal of Personality Assessment, 59*(3), 433–438.

Costello, E. J. (2016). Early detection and prevention of mental health problems: Developmental epidemiology and systems of support. *Journal of Clinical Child & Adolescent Psychology. 45*(6), 710–717.

Costello, E. J., & Angold, A. (2016). Developmental epidemiology. In D. Cicchetti (Ed.), *Developmental psychology, Vol. 1: Theory and Method* (3rd ed.). New York: Wiley.

Costello, E. J., Copeland, W., & Angold, A. (2016). The Great Smoky Mountains Study: Developmental epidemiology in the southeastern United States. *Social Psychiatry and Psychiatric Epidemiology, 51,* 639–646.

Cottle, J. (2016, March 15). Facebook and mental health: Is social media hurting or helping? *MentalHelp.net.*

Cottler, L. B., Hu, H., Smallwood, B. A., Anthony, J. C., Wu, L. T., & Eaton, W. W. (2016). Nonmedical opioid pain relievers and all-cause mortality: A 27-year follow-up from the Epidemiologic Catchment Area Study. *American Journal of Public Health, 106*(3), 509–516.

Cottrell, D. B., & Williams, J. (2016). Eating disorders in men. *Nurse Practitioner, 41*(9), 49–55.

Couturier, J., & Lock, J. (2006). Eating disorders: Anorexia nervosa, bulimia nervosa, and binge eating disorder. In T. G. Plante (Ed.), *Mental disorders of the new millennium, Vol. 3: Biology and function.* Westport, CT: Praeger Publishers.

Covey, R. D. (2017). The temporary insanity defense. In M. D. White (Ed.), *The insanity defense: Multidisciplinary views on its history, trends, and controversies* (Chap. 2, pp. 23–60). Westport, CT: Praeger.

Cox, K. L., Nock, M. K., Biggs, Q. M., Borneman, J., Colpe, L. J., Dempsey, C. L., . . . Army STARRS Collaborators. (2017, July 22). An examination of potential misclassification of army suicides: Results from the Army Study to Assess Risk and Resilience in Servicemembers. *Suicide and Life-Threatening Behavior.* [Epub ahead of print]

Coyne, J. C. (2001). Depression and the response of others. In W. G. Parrott (Ed.), *Emotions in social psychology: Essential readings* (pp. 231–238). Philadelphia: Psychology Press/Taylor & Francis.

Cozzi, G., Minute, M., Skabar, A., Pirrone, A., Jaber, M., Neri, E., . . . Barbi, E. (2017). Somatic symptom disorder was common in children and adolescents attending an emergency department complaining of pain. *Acta Paediatrica, 106*(4), 586–593.

Crabtree, S. (2011). *U.S. seniors maintain happiness highs with less social time* (Gallup poll 151457). *Gallup.* Retrieved from http://www.gallup.com/poll/151457.

Craig, T., & Power, P. (2010). Inpatient provision in early psychosis. In P. French, J. Smith, D. Shiers, M. Reed, & M. Rayne (Eds.), *Promoting recovery in early psychosis: A practice manual* (pp. 17–26). Hoboken, NJ: Wiley-Blackwell.

Craig, T., Ward,T., & Rus-Calafell, M. (2016). AVATAR therapy for refractory auditory hallucinations. In B. Pradhan, N. Pinninti, & S. Rathod (Eds.), *Brief interventions for psychosis: A clinical compendium* (Chap. 4). London: Springer.

Cramer, P. (2017), Defense mechanism card pull in TAT stories. *Journal of Personality Assessment, 99*(1), 15–24.

Craske, C. M., & Barlow, D. H. (2014). Panic disorder and agoraphobia. In D. H. Barlow, *Clinical handbook of psychological disorders* (5th ed., pp. 1–61). New York: Guilford Press.

Craske, M. (2015, September 15). Psychotherapy for panic disorder in adults. *UpToDate.* Retrieved from http://www.uptodate.com.

Craske, M. (2016, September 1). Psychotherapy for generalized anxiety disorder in adults. *UpToDate.* Retrieved from http://www.uptodate.com.

Craske, M. G. (2017). *Cognitive-behavioral therapy.* Washington, DC: American Psychological Association.

Crawford, C., Burns, J., & Fernie, B. A. (2015). Psychosocial impact of involvement in the Special Olympics. *Research in Developmental Disabilities, 45-46,* 93–102.

CRC (Cyberbullying Research Center). (2016, November 26). *2016 cyberbullying data.*. Retrieved from https://cyberbullying.org.

CRC (Cyberbullying Research Center). (2017, January 3). *Millions of students skip school each year because of bullying.* Retrieved from https://cyberbullying.org.

CRC (Cyberbullying Research Center). (2017, June 2). *More on the link between bullying and suicide.* Retrieved from https://cyberbullying.org.

CRCC (Cleveland Rape Crisis Center). (2014). Sexual violence on college campuses. Retrieved from CRCC website: http://www.clevelandrapecrisis.org/resources/statistics/sexual-violence-on-college-campuses.

Creswell, J. D. (2017). Mindfulness interventions. *Annual Review of Psychology, 6i*(18), 18–26.

Cristea, I. A., Gentili, C., Cotet, C. D., Palomba, D., Barbui, C., & Cuijpers, P. (2017). Efficacy of psychotherapies for borderline personality disorder: A systematic review and meta-analysis. *JAMA Psychiatry, 74*(4), 319–328.

Cronin, E., Brand, B. L., & Mattanah, J. F. (2014). The impact of the therapeutic alliance on treatment outcome in patients with dissociative disorders. *European Journal of Psychotraumatology, 5d,* 22676.

Crosby, A. E., Espitia-Hardeman, V., Hill, H. A., Ortega, L., & Clavel-Arcas, C. (2009). Alcohol and suicide among racial/ethnic populations—17 states, 2005–2006. *Journal of the American Medical Association, 302*(7), 733–734.

Crouter, F. (2015). *The psychology of jury selection.* Koko Books. [Electronic publication]

Crow, S. J. (2016, January 14). Bulimia nervosa in adults: Pharmacotherapy. *UpToDate.* Retrieved from www.uptodate.com.

Crow, T. J. (1980). Positive and negative schizophrenic symptoms and the role of dopamine: II. *British Journal of Psychiatry, 137,* 383–386.

Crow, T. J. (1985). The two-syndrome concept: Origins and current status. *Schizophrenia Bulletin, 11*(3), 471–486.

Crow, T. J. (1995). Brain changes and negative symptoms in schizophrenia. *Psychopathology, 28*(1), 18–21.

Crow, T. J. (2008). The "big bang" theory of the origin of psychosis and the faculty of language. *Schizophrenia Research, 102*(1–3), 31–52.

CRS (Congressional Research Service). (2016, March 3). Heroin production in Mexico and U.S. policy. *CRS.* Retrieved from https://fas.org/sgp/crs/row/IN10456.pdf.

Crump, C., Sundquist, K., Sundquist, J., & Winkleby, M. A. (2014). Sociodemographic, psychiatric and somatic risk factors for suicide: A Swedish national cohort study. *Psychological Medicine, 44*(2), 279–289.

Crystal, S., Kleinhaus, K., Perrin, M., & Malaspina, D. (2012). Advancing paternal age and the risk of schizophrenia. In A. S. Brown & P. H. Patterson (Eds.), *The origins of schizophrenia* (pp. 140–155). New York: Columbia University Press.

CSP Daily News. (2017, March 7). *E-cig sales to hit $27 billion by 2022: Study.* Retrieved from http://www.cspdailynews.com.

Cui, L. B., Liu, K., Li, C., Wang, L. X., Guo, F., Tian, P., . . . Yin, H. Putamen-related regional and network functional deficits in first-episode schizophrenia with auditory verbal hallucinations. *Schizophrenia Research, 173*(1-2), 13–22.

Cuijpers, P., Centili, C., Banos, R. M., Garcia-Campayo, J., Botella, C., & Cristea, I. A. (2016). Relative effects of cognitive and behavioral therapies on generalized anxiety disorder, social anxiety disorder and panic disorder: A meta-analysis. *Journal of Anxiety Disorders, 43,* 79–89.

Cuijpers, P., Karyotaki, E., Weitz, E., Andersson, G., Hollon, S. D., & van Straten, A. (2014). The effects of psychotherapies for major depression in adults on remission, recovery and improvement: A meta-analysis. *Journal of Affective Disorders, 159,* 118–126.

Cuijpers, P., Sijbrandij, M., Koole, S., Huibers, M., Berking, M., & Andersson, G. (2014). Psychological treatment of generalized anxiety disorder: A meta-analysis. *Clinical Psychology Review, 34*(2), 130–140.

Cukrowicz, K. C., Cheavens, J. S., Van Orden, K. A., Ragain, R. M., & Cook, R. L. (2011). Perceived burdensomeness and suicide ideation in older adults. *Psychology and Aging, 26*(2), 331–338.

Cullen, A. E., Fisher, H. L., Roberts, R. E., Pariante, C. M., & Laurens, K. R. (2014).

Daily stressors and negative life events in children at elevated risk of developing schizophrenia. *British Journal of Psychiatry, 204,* 354–360.

Cullen, K. R., Klimes Dougan, B., Vu, D. P., Westlund Schreiner, M., Mueller, B. A., Eberly, L. E., . . . Lim, K. O. (2016). Neural correlates of antidepressant treatment response in adolescents with major depressive disorder. *Journal of Child and Adolescent Psychopharmacology, 26*(8), 705–712.

Culp, A. M., Clyman, M. M., & Culp, R. E. (1995). Adolescent depressed mood, reports of suicide attempts, and asking for help. *Adolescence, 30*(120), 827–837.

Culver, J. L., & Pratchett, L. C. (2010). Adjunctive psychosocial interventions in the management of bipolar disorders. In T. A. Ketter (Ed.), *Handbook of diagnosis and treatment of bipolar disorders* (pp. 661–676). Arlington, VA: American Psychiatric Publishing.

Cummings, J. L., & Coffey, C. E. (2011). Geriatric neuropsychiatry. In C.E. Coffey, J.L. Cummings, M.S. George, & D. Weintraub (Eds.), *The American Psychiatric Publishing textbook of geriatric neuropsychiatry.* Arlington, VA: American Psychiatric Publishing, Inc.

Cummings, J. R., Ji, X., Allen, L., Lally, C., & Druss, B. G. (2017). Racial and ethnic differences in ADHD treatment quality among Medicaid-enrolled youth. *Pediatrics, 139.*

Cunningham, G. R., & Khera, M. (2016, July 31). Treatment of male sexual dysfunction. *UpToDate.* Retrieved from http://www.uptodate.com.

Cunningham, G. R., & Rosen, R. C. (2016, May 11). Overview of male sexual dysfunction. *UpToDate.* Retrieved from http://www.uptodate.com.

Curtiss, J., Andrews, L., Davis, M., Smits, J., & Hofmann, S. G. (2017). A meta-analysis of pharmacotherapy for social anxiety disorder: An examination of efficacy, moderators, and mediators. *Expert Opinion on Pharmacotherapy, 18*(3), 243–251.

Cutler, D. M., Glaeser, E. L., & Norberg, K. E. (2001). Explaining the rise in youth suicide. In J. Gruber (Ed.), *Risky behavior among youths: An economic analysis* (pp. 219–269). Chicago: University of Chicago Press.

Cutright, P., & Fernquist, R. M. (2001). The relative gender gap in suicide: Societal integration, the culture of suicide and period effects in 20 developed countries, 1955–1994. *Social Science Research, 30*(1), 76–99.

Cutting, J. (2015). First rank symptoms of schizophrenia: Their nature and origin. *History of Psychiatry, 26*(2), 131–146.

Cuvelier, M. (2002). Victim, not villain. The mentally ill are six to seven times more likely to be murdered. *Psychology Today, 35*(3), 23.

Cynkar, A. (2007). The changing gender composition of psychology. *The Monitor, 38*(6), 46.

Czéh, B., Fuchs, E., Wiborg, O., & Simon, M. (2016). Animal models of major depression and their clinical implications. *Progress in Neuro-Psychopharmacology & Biological Psychiatry, 64,* 293–310.

Daalman, K., Boks, M. P., Diederen, K. M., de Weijer, A. D., Blom, J. D., Kahn, R. S., & Sommer, I. E. (2011). The same or different? A phenomenological comparison of auditory verbal hallucinations in healthy and psychotic individuals. *Journal of Clinical Psychiatry, 72*(3), 320–325.

D'Agata, F., Caroppo, P., Amianto, F., Spalatro, A., Caglio, M. M., Bergui, M., . . . Fassino, S. (2015). Brain correlates of alexithymia in eating disorders: A voxel-based morphometry study. *Psychiatry and Clinical Neurosciences. 69,* 708–716.

Daigre, C., Rodríguez-Cintas, L., Tarifa, N., Rodríguez-Martos, L., Grau-Lopez, L., Berenguer, M., . . . Roncero, C. (2015). History of sexual, emotional or physical abuse and psychiatric comorbidity in substance-dependent patients. *Psychiatry Research, 229*(3), 743–749.

Dahl, M. (2015, April 10). The more money you make, the more sleep you get. *NY Magazine.*

Dahling, J. J., Whitaker, B. G., & Levy, P. E. (2008). The development and validation of a new Machiavellianism scale. *Journal of Management, 35,* 219–257.

Dalby, J., T. (1997). Elizabethan madness: On London's stage. *Psychological Reports, 81,* 1331–1343.

Daley, D. C., Marlatt, G. A., & Douaihy, A. (2011). Relapse prevention. In J. H. Lowinson & P. Ruiz (Eds.), *Substance abuse: A comprehensive textbook* (5th ed.). Philadelphia, PA: Lippincott, Williams, & Wilkins.

Dallocchio, C., Tinazzi, M., Bombieri, F., Arnó, N., & Erro, R. (2016). Cognitive behavioural therapy and adjunctive physical activity for functional movement disorders (conversion disorder): A pilot, single-blinded, randomized study. *Psychotherapy and Psychosomatics, 85*(6), 381–383.

Dalsbø, T. K., Steiro, A., Strømme, H., & Reinar, L. M. (2017). Effectiveness of tapering from methadone or buprenorphine maintenance treatment compared to traditional maintenance treatment for people with opiate addiction: Systematic review. *Folkehelseinstitutet.* Retrieved from https://www.fhi.no/en.

Daly, M., Baumeister, R. F., Delaney, L., & MacLachlan, M. (2014). Self-control and its relation to emotions and psychobiology: Evidence from a Day Reconstruction Method study. *Journal of Behavioral Medicine, 37*(1), 81–93.

Daly, R. (2010). Shift to community care slowing in many states. *Psychiatric News, 45*(15), 8.

D'Amico, E. J., Osilla, K. C., & Stern, S. A. (2016). Prevention and intervention in the school setting. In K. J. Sher (Ed.). *Oxford handbook of substance use and substance use disorders* (Vol. 2, Chap. 23, pp. 675–727). New York: Oxford University Press.

Dana, R. H. (2000). Culture and methodology in personality assessment. In I. Cuellar & F. A. Paniagua (Eds.), Handbook of multicultural mental health (pp. 97–120). San Diego, CA: Academic Press.

Dana, R. H. (2005). *Multicultural assessment: Principles, applications, and examples.* Mahwah, NJ: Lawrence Erlbaum.

Dana, R. H. (Ed.). (2015). *Handbook of cross-cultural and multicultural personality assessment.* New York: Routledge.

Dance, A. (2015, November 24). News Feature: How online studies are transforming psychology research. *Proceedings of the National Academy of Sciences USA, 112*(47), 14399–14401.

Dando, C. (2017, January 26). I specialise in the psychology of torture, so I know the truth behind Trump's claims that waterboarding works. *The Independent Online.* Retrieved from http://www.independent.co.uk.

Danquah, M. N-A. (1998). *Willow weep for me: A black woman's journey through depression.* New York: W. W. Norton.

D'Antonio, A. C. (2016). Karl Abraham: The birth of object relations theory. By Isabel Sanfeliu (Kate Walters, trans.). *Psychoanalytic Quarterly, 85*(4), 1022–1026.

Da Paz, N. S., & Wallander, J. L. (2017). Interventions that target improvements in mental health for parents of children with autism spectrum disorders: A narrative review. *Clinical Psychology Review, 51,* 1–14.

Darke, S., Williamson, A., Ross, J., & Teesson, M. (2005). Attempted suicide among heroin users: 12-month outcomes from the Australian Treatment Outcome Study (ATOS). *Drug and Alcohol Dependence, 78*(2), 177–186.

da Rosa, G., Martin, P., Gondo, Y., Hirose, N., Ishioka, Y., & Poon, L. (2014). Examination of important life experiences of the oldest-old: Cross-cultural comparisons of U.S. and Japanese centenarians. *Journal of Cross-Cultural Gerontology, 29*(2), 109–130.

Daugherty, J., & Copen, C. (2016, March 17). Trends in attitudes about marriage, childbearing, and sexual behavior: United States, 2002, 2006–2010, and 2011–2013. Atlanta, GA: CDC, National Health Statistics Report, No. 92.

Daugherty, J. C., Puente, A. E., Fasfous, A. F., Hidalgo-Ruzzante, N., & Pérez-Garcia, M. (2017). Diagnostic mistakes of culturally diverse individuals when using North American neuropsychological tests. *Applied Neuropsychology: Adult, 24*(1), 16–33.

Davenport, L. (2017, August 30). Aerobic exercise improves cognition in depression. *Medscape.*

David, D. J., & Gourion, D. (2016). Antidepressant and tolerance: Determinants and management of major side effects. *Encephale, 42*(6), 553–561.

Davidson, L., & Chan, K. K. S. (2014). Common factors: Evidence-based practice and recovery. *Psychiatric Services, 65*(5), 675–677.

Davidson, L., Rakfeldt, J., & Strauss, J. (2010). *The roots of the recovery movement in psychiatry: Lessons learned.* Hoboken, NJ: John Wiley.

Davis, C., Green, T., & Beletsky, L. (2017). Action, not rhetoric, needed to reverse the opioid overdose epidemic. *Journal of Law, Medicine & Ethics, 45*(1 suppl), 20–23.

Davis, E., Burden, R., & Manning, R. (2010). Early intervention and vocational opportunities. In P. French, J. Smith, D. Shiers, M. Reed, & M. Rayne (Eds.), *Promoting recovery in early psychosis: A practice manual* (pp. 140–146). Hoboken, NJ: Wiley-Blackwell.

Davis, P., Patton, R., & Jackson, S. (2017). *Addiction: Psychology and treatment (BPS Textbooks in Psychology).* Hoboken, NJ: Wiley-Blackwell.

Davison, T. E., Eppingstall, B., Runci, S., & O'Connor, D. W. (2016, March 4). A pilot trial of acceptance and commitment therapy for symptoms of depression and anxiety in older adults residing in long-term care facilities. *Aging & Mental Health,* 1–8. [Epub ahead of print]

Day, E., & Strang, J. (2011). Outpatient versus inpatient opioid detoxification: A randomized controlled trial. *Journal of Substance Abuse Treatment, 40*(1), 56–66.

Dayan, J., Rauchs, G., & Guillery-Girard, B. (2017, February 1). Rhythms dysregulation: A new perspective for understanding PTSD? *Journal of Physiology Paris.* [Epub ahead of print]

DEA (Drug Enforcement Administration). (2015). 2015 National drug threat assessment summary. *DEA. Retrieved from https://www.dea.gov.*

Deacon, B. J., & Spielmans, G. I. (2017). Is the efficacy of "antidepressant" medications overrated? In S. O. Lilienfeld and I. D. Waldman (Eds.), *Psychological science under scrutiny: Recent challenges and proposed solutions* (Chap. 13). New Jersey: John Wiley.

DeAngelis, T. (1993, September). Controversial diagnosis is voted into latest DSM. *APA Monitor, 24*(9), 32–33.

Deas, D., Gray, K., & Upadhyaya, H. (2008). Evidence-based treatments for adolescent substance use disorders. In R. G. Steele, T. D. Elkin, M. C. Roberts (Eds.), *Handbook of evidence-based therapies for children and adolescents,* (pp. 429–444). New York: Springer.

de Beurs, D. P., Bosmans, J. E., de Groot, M. H., de Keijser, J., van Duijn, E., de Winter, R. P., & Kerkhof, A. M. (2015). Training mental health professionals in suicide practice guideline adherence: Cost-effectiveness analysis alongside a randomized controlled trial. *Journal of Affective Disorders, 186,* 203–210.

DeBonis, M. (2016, December 7). Congress passes 21st Century Cures Act, boosting research and easing drug approvals. *Washington Post.*

de Castro, S. M., Ünlü, Ç., Tuynman, J. B., Honig, A., van Wagensveld, B. A., Steller, E. P., & Vrouenraets, B. C. (2014). Incidence and risk factors of delirium in the elderly general surgical patient. *American Journal of Surgery, 208*(1), 26–32.

Decker, H. S. (2016). Cyclical swings: The bête noire of psychiatry. *History of Psychology, 19*(1), 52–56.

De Cort, K., Schroijen, M., Hurlemann, R., Claassen, S., Hoogenhout, J., Van den Bergh, O., . . . Schruers, K. (2017). Modeling the development of panic disorder with interoceptive conditioning. *European Neuropsychopharmacology, 27*(1), 59–69.

Deeley, Q. (2017). Hypnosis as therapy for functional neurologic disorders. *Handbook of Clinical Neurology, 139,* 585–595.

De Genna, N. M., & Feske, U. (2013). Phenomenology of borderline personality disorder: The role of race and socioeconomic status. *The Journal of Nervous and Mental Disease, 201*(12), 1027–1034.

Dein, S. (2017). Recent work on culture and schizophrenia: Epidemiological and anthropological approaches. *Global Journal of Archaeology & Anthropology, 1*(3), 1–5.

Deitz, S. M. (1977). An analysis of programming DRL schedules in educational settings. *Behavioral Research and Therapy, 15*(1), 103–111.

de Jonge, P., Roest, A. M., Lim, C. C., Florescu, S. E., Bromet, E. J., Stein, D. J., . . . Scott, K. M. (2016). Cross-national epidemiology of panic disorder and panic attacks in the world mental health surveys. *Depression and Anxiety, 33*(12), 1155–1177.

de Kloet, C. S., Vermetten, E., Geuze, E., Kavelaars, A., Heijnen, C. J., & Westerberg, H. G. (2006). Assessment of HPA-axis function in posttraumatic stress disorder: Pharmacological and non-pharmacological challenge tests, a review. *Journal of Psychiatric Research, 40*(6), 550–567.

Delay, J., & Deniker, P. (1952). Le traitement des psychoses par une méthode neurolytique dérivée d'hibernothérapie: Le 4560 RP utilisé seul en cure prolongée et continuée. *Congrès des médicins aliénistes et neurologistes de France et des pays du langue francaise, 50,* 503–513.

de Leede-Smith, S., & Barkus, E. (2013). A comprehensive review of auditory verbal hallucinations: Lifetime prevalence, correlates, and mechanisms in healthy and clinical individuals. *Frontiers in Human Neurosciences, 7,* 367.

De Leo, D., & Evans, R. (2004). *International suicide rates and prevention strategies.* Cambridge, MA: Hogrefe & Huber.

de l'Etoile, S. K. (2002). The effect of musical mood induction procedure on mood state-dependent word retrieval. *Journal of Music Therapy, 39*(2), 145–160.

Delgadillo, J., Asaria, M., Ali, S., & Gilbody, S. (2016). On poverty, politics and psychology: The socioeconomic gradient of mental healthcare utilisation and outcomes. *British Journal of Psychiatry, 209*(5), 429–430.

Delgado, J. (2017, March 2). Intoxication from LSD and other common hallucinogens. *UpToDate.* Retrieved from http://www.uptodate.com.

Delinsky, S. S. (2011). Body image and anorexia nervosa. In T. F. Cash & L. Smolak, *Body image: A handbook of science, practice, and prevention* (Chap. 32). New York: Guilford Press.

Dell, P. F. (2010). Involuntariness in hypnotic responding and dissociative symptoms. *Journal of Trauma & Dissociation, 11*(1), 1–18.

Delli Pizzi, S., Padulo, C., Brancucci, A., Bubbico, G., Edden, R. A., Ferretti, A., . . . Bonanni, L. (2016). GABA content within the ventromedial prefrontal cortex is related to trait anxiety. *Social Cognitive and Affective Neuroscience, 11*(5), 758–766.

De Luca, S. M., Blosnich, J. R., Hentschel, E. A.. King, W., & Amen, S. (2016). Mental health care utilization: How race, ethnicity and veteran status are associated with seeking help. *Community Mental Health Journal, 52*(2), 174–179.

De Matteo, D., Heilbrun, K., & Marczyk, G. (2005). Psychopathy, risk of violence, and protective factors in a noninstitutionalized and noncriminal sample. *International Journal of Forensic Mental Health, 4*(2), 147–157.

Demily, C., Louchart-de-la-Chapelle, S., Nkam, I., Ramoz, N., Denise, P., Nicolas, A., . . . Thibaut, F. (2016). Does COMT val-158met polymorphism influence P50 sensory gating, eye tracking or saccadic inhibition dysfunctions in schizophrenia? *Psychiatry Research, 246,* 738–744.

Demory-Luce, D., & Motil, K. J. (2016, August 2). Adolescent eating habits. *UpToDate.* Retrieved from http://www.uptodate.com.

De Nadia. A. S., Karver, M. S., Murphy, T. K., Cavitt, M. A., Alvaro, J. L., Bengtson, M., . . . Storch, E. A. (2017). Common factors in pediatric psychiatry: A review of essential and adjunctive mechanisms of treatment outcome. *Journal of Child and Adolescent Psychopharmacology, 27*(1), 10–18.

den Braber, A., Zilhão, N. R., Fedko, I. O., Hottenga, J. J., Pool, R., Smit, D. J., . . . Boomsma, D. I. (2016, February 9). Obsessive-compulsive symptoms in a large population-based twin-family sample are predicted by clinically based polygenic scores and by genome-wide SNPs. *Translational Psychiatry, 6.* [Online publication]

Dendy, C. A. Z. (2016, February 11). Impact of ADHD on school performance. *HealthyPlace.* Retrieved from https://www.healthyplace.com/adhd.

De Neve, J. E., & Ward, G. (2017) Happiness at work. In J. Helliwell, R. Layard, & J. Sacks (Ed.), *World happiness report 2017.* New York: Sustainable Development Solutions Network.

Denis, C. M., Gelernter, J., Hart, A. B., & Kranzler, H. R. (2015). Inter-observer reliability of DSM-5 substance use disorders. *Drug and Alcohol Dependence, 153,* 229–235.

Dennhardt, A. A., Murphy, J. G., McDevitt-Murphy, M. E., & Williams, J. L. (2016). Drinking motives mediate the relationship between alcohol reward value and alcohol problems in military veterans. *Psychology of Addictive Behaviors, 30*(8), 819–826.

Dennis, C. (2014). The process of developing and implementing a telephone-based peer support program for postpartum depression: Evidence from two randomized controlled trials. *Trials, 15,* 131.

Dennis, J. P., & Brown, G. K. (2011). Suicidal older adults: Suicide risk assessments, safety planning, and cognitive behavioral therapy. In K. H. Sorocco & S. Lauderdale (Eds.), *Cognitive behavior therapy with older adults: Innovations across care settings* (pp. 95–123). New York: Springer Publishing.

Denno, D. W. (2017). Andrea Yates: A continuing story about insanity. In M. D. White (Ed.), *The insanity defense: Multidisciplinary views on its history, trends, and controversies* (Chap. 12). Westport, CT: Praeger Publishers.

DePaulo, B. M. (2013, March 15). Marriage and happiness: 18 long-term studies. *Psychology Today.*

DePaulo, B. M. (2013, April 5). On getting married and (not) getting happier: What we know. Retrieved from http://belladepaulo.com/2013/04/05/on-getting-married-and-not-getting-happpier.

De Rosa, C., Del Vecchio, V., Del Gaudio, L., Sampogna, G., Luciano, M., Giacco, D., & Fiorillo, A. (2011). Suicide and the Internet: A search on Italian websites. *Italian Journal of Psychopathology, 17,* 376–382.

DeRubeis, R. J., & Strunk, D. R. (2017). *The Oxford handbook of mood disorders.* New York: Oxford University Press.

Desmet, M. (2013). Some preliminary notes on an empirical test of Freud's theory on depression. *Frontiers In Psychology, 4,* 158.

Detweiler, M. F., Comer, J. S., Crum, K. I., & Albanbo, A. M. (2014). Social anxiety in children and adolescents: Biological, developmental, and social considerations. In S. G. Hofmann & P. M. DiBartolo (Eds.), *Social anxiety* (3rd ed.), (Chap. 10, pp. 253–309). San Diego, CA: Academic Press.

Deutschenbaur, L., Lambert, M., Walter, M., Naber, D., & Huber, C. G. (2014). Long-term treatment of schizophrenia spectrum disorders: Focus on pharmacotherapy. *Der Nervenarzt, 85*(3), 363 375.

Devanand, D. P. (2011). Psychosis. In C. E. Coffey, J. L. Cummings, M. S. George, & D. Weintraub (Eds.), *The American Psychiatric Publishing textbook of geriatric neuropsychiatry.* Arlington, VA: American Psychiatric Publishing, Inc.

DeVeaugh-Geiss, J., Moroz, G., Biederman, J., Cantwell, D. P., Fontaine, R., Griest, J. H., . . . Landau, P. (1992). Clomipramine hydrochloride in childhood and adolescent obsessive compulsive disorder. A multicenter trial. *Journal of the American Academy of Child and Adolescent Psychiatry, 31*(1), 45–49.

Devineni, T., & Blanchard, E. B. (2005). A randomized controlled trial of an internet-based treatment for chronic headache. *Behavioral Research and Therapy, 43,* 277–292.

Dewey, C. (2014, July 1). 9 answers about Facebook's creepy emotional-manipulation experiment. *Washington Post.*

Dewitte, M., Van Lankveld, J., & Crombez, G. (2011). Understanding sexual pain: A cognitive-motivational account. *Pain, 152*(2), 251–253.

De Witte, N. A., Crunelle, C. L., Sabbe, B., Moggi, F., & Dom, G. (2014). Treatment for outpatients with comorbid schizophrenia and substance use disorders: A review. *European Addiction Research, 20*(3), 105–114.

Dhabhar, F. S. (2011). Effects of stress on immune function: Implications for immunoprotection and immunopathology. In R. J. Contrada & A. Baum (Eds.), *The handbook of stress science: Biology, psychology, and health* (pp. 47–63). New York: Springer Publishing.

Dhabhar, F. S. (2014). Effects of stress on immune function: The good, the bad, and the beautiful. *Immunologic Research, 58*(2-3), 193–210.

Dhejne, C., Lichtenstein, P., Boman, M., Johansson, A. L. V., Langström, N., & Landén, M. (2011). Long-term follow-up of transsexual persons undergoing sex reassignment surgery: Cohort study in Sweden. *PLoS ONE, 6*(2), e16885.

Dhejne, C., Van Vlerken, R., Heylens, G., & Arcelus, J. (2016). Mental health and gender dysphoria: A review of the literature. *International Review of Psychiatry, 28*(1), 44–57.

D.I. (Daily Infographic). (2014). Secrets of the world's oldest people. Retrieved from http://www.dailyinfographic.com.

Diamond, D., & Meehan, K. B. (2013). Attachment and object relations in patients with narcissistic personality disorder: Implications for therapeutic process and outcome. *Journal of Clinical Psychology, 69*(11), 1148–1159.

Dickerson, F., Schroeder, J., Stallings, C., Origoni, A., Katsafanas, E., Schwienfurth, L. A., . . . Yolken, R. (2014). A longitudinal study of cognitive functioning in schizophrenia: Clinical and biological predictors. *Schizophrenia Research, 156*(2/3), 248–253.

Dickson, H., Laurens, K. R., Cullen, A. E., & Hodgins, S. (2012). Meta-analyses of cognitive and motor function in youth aged 16 years and younger who subsequently develop schizophrenia. *Psychological Medicine, 42*(4), 743–755.

Didehbani, N., Munro Cullum, C., Mansinghani, S., Conover, H., & Hart, J., Jr. (2013). Depressive symptoms and concussions in aging retired NFL players. *Archives of Clinical Neuropsychology, 28*(5), 418–424.

Diefenbach, S., & Christoforakos, L. (2017). The selfie paradox: Nobody seems to like them yet everyone has reasons to take them. An exploration of psychological functions of selfies in self-presentation. *Frontiers in Psychology, 87,* 7.

Di Florio, A., Jones, L., Forty, L., Gordon-Smith, K., Blackmore, E. R., Heron, J., . . . Jones, I. (2014). Mood disorders and parity: A clue to the aetiology of the postpartum trigger. *Journal of Affective Disorders, 152-154,* 334–339.

DiGangi, J. A., Gomez, D., Mendoza, L., Jason, L. A., Keys, C. B., & Koenen, K. C. (2013). Pretrauma risk factors for posttraumatic stress disorder: A systematic review of the literature. *Clinical Psychology Review, 33*(6), 728–744.

Dijkstra, B. A. G., De Jong, C. A. J., Wensing, M., Krabbe, P. F. M., & Van Der Staak, C. P. F. (2010). Opioid detoxification: From controlled clinical trial to clinical practice. *American Journal on Addictions, 19*(3), 283–290.

Diliberto, R. A., & Kearney, C. A. (2016). Anxicity and oppositional behavior profiles among youth with selective mutism. *Journal of Communication Disorders, 59,* 16–23.

Dillard, D. A., Avey, J. P., Robinson, R. F., Smith, J. J., Beals, J., Manson, S. M., & Comtois, K. A. (2017). Demographic, clinical, and service utilization factors associated with suicide-related visits among Alaska native and American Indian adults. *Suicide and Life-Threatening Behavior, 47*(1), 27–37.

Dimidjian, S., Martell, C. R., Herman-Dunn, R., & Hubley, S. (2014). Behavioral activation for depression. In D. H. Barlow (Ed.), *Clinical handbook of psychological disorders* (5th ed., Chap. 9). New York: Guilford Press.

Di Narzo, A. F., Kozlenkov, A., Roussos, P., Hao, K., Hurd, Y., Lewis, D. A., . . . Dracheva, S. (2014). A unique gene expression signature associated with serotonin 2C receptor RNA editing in the prefrontal cortex and altered in suicide. *Human Molecular Genetics, 23*(18), 4801–4813.

Dines, P., Hu, W., & Sajatovic, M. (2014). Depression in later-life: An overview of assessment and management. *Psychiatria Danubina, 26*(Suppl. 1), 78–84.

Ding, J. M., & Kanaan, R. A. (2017). Conversion disorder: A systematic review of current terminology. *General Hospital Psychiatry, 45,* 51–55.

Ding, Y., Naganawa, M., Gallezot, J., Nabulsi, N., Lin, S., Ropchan, J., . . . Laruelle, M. (2014). Clinical doses of atomoxetine significantly occupy both norepinephrine and serotonin transports: Implications on treatment of depression and ADHD. *Neuroimage, 86,* 164–171.

Di Rosa, M., Kofahl, C., McKee, K., Bien, B., Lamura, G., Prouskas, C., Döhner, H., & Mnich, E. (2011). A typology of caregiving situations and service use in family careers of older people in six European countries: The EUROFAMCARE study. *GeroPsych: The Journal of Gerontopsychology and Geriatric Psychiatry, 24*(1), 5–18.

Di Sante, S., Mollaioli, D., Gravina, G. L., Ciocca, G., Limoncin, E., Carosa, E., . . . Jannini, E. A. (2016). Epidemiology of delayed ejaculation. *Translational Andrology and Urology, 5*(4), 541–548.

Dishion, T. J., & Patterson, G. R. (2016). The development and ecology of antisocial behavior: Linking etiology, prevention, and treatment. In D. Cicchetti (Ed.), *Developmental psychopathology, Vol. 3: Maladaptation and psychopathology* (3rd ed.). New York: Wiley.

Dittrich, K., Fuchs, A., Bermpohl, F., Meyer, J., Führer, D., Reichl, C., . . . Resch, F. (2018). Effects of maternal history of depression and early life maltreatment on children's health-related quality of life. *Journal of Affective Disorders, 225,* 280–288.

Dixon, L. B., & Schwarz, E. C. (2014). Fifty years of progress in community mental health in US: The growth of evidence–based practices. *Epidemiology and Psychiatric Sciences, 23*(1), 5–9.

Dobson, D., & Dobson, K. S. (2017). *Evidence-based practice of cognitive-behavioral therapy* (2nd ed.). New York: Guilford Press.

Doctor, R. M., & Neff, B. (2001). Sexual disorders. In H. S. Friedman (Ed.), *Specialty articles from the encyclopedia of mental health.* San Diego: Academic Press.

Dodes, L. M., & Khantzian, E. J. (2005). Individual psychodynamic psychotherapy. In R. J. Frances, A. H. Mack, & S. I. Miller (Eds.), *Clinical textbook of addictive disorders* (3rd ed., pp. 457–473). New York: Guilford Press.

Dodes, L. M., & Khantzian, E. J. (2011). Individual psychodynamic psychotherapy. In R. J. Frances, S. I. Miller, & A. H. Mack (Eds.), *Clinical textbook of addictive disorders* (3rd ed., Chap. 21). New York: Guilford Press.

Doering, S., Hörz, S., Rentrop, M., Fischer-Kern, M., Schuster, P., Benecke, C., . . . Buchheim, P. (2010). Transference-focused psychotherapy v. treatment by community psychotherapists for borderline personality disorder: Randomised controlled trial. *British Journal of Psychiatry, 196*(5), 389–395.

Dohrmann, R. J., & Laskin, D. M. (1978). An evaluation of electromyographic feedback in the treatment of myofascial pain dysfunction syndrome. *Journal of the American Medical Association, 96,* 656–666.

DOJ (U.S. Department of Justice). (2010). Arrests. *Crime in the United States 2009.* http://www.fbi.gov/ucr/cius2009/arrests/index.html.

DOJ (U.S. Department of Justice). (2010). National study of jail suicide: 20 years later. Washington, DC: National Institute of Corrections.

DOJ (U.S. Department of Justice). (2014). *Crime in the United States 2013.* http://www.fbi.gov/about-us/cjis/ucr/crime-in-the-u.s./2013.

DOJ (U.S. Department of Justice). (2016). *Criminal victimization, 2015.* October, 2016. Bureau of Justice Statistics.

DOJ (U.S. Department of Justice). (2017). *Statistical briefing book: Law enforcement & juvenile crime: Juvenile arrest rate trends.* Retrieved from https://www.ojjdp.gov/ojstatbb/crime/JAR.

Dole, V. P., & Nyswander, M. (1965). A medical treatment for heroin addiction. *Journal of the American Medical Association, 193,* 646–650.

Dole, V. P., & Nyswander, M. (1967). Heroin addiction, a metabolic disease. *Archives of Internal Medicine, 120,* 19–24.

Dolezsar, C. M., McGrath, J. J., Herzig, A. M., & Miller, S. B. (2014). Perceived racial discrimination and hypertension: A comprehensive systematic review. *Health Psychology, 33*(1), 20–34.

Dominus, S. (2012, March 7). What happened to the girls in Le Roy? *New York Times.*

Dorahy, M. J., Brand, B. L., Sar, V., Krüger, C., Stavropoulos, P., Martínez-Taboas, A., . . . Middleton, W. (2014). Dissociative identity disorder: An empirical overview. *The Australian and New Zealand Journal of Psychiatry, 48*(5), 402–417.

Dorahy, M. J., & Huntjens, R. J. C. (2007). Memory and attentional processes in dissociative identity disorder: A review of the empirical literature. In D. Spiegel, E. Vermetten, & M. Dorahy (Eds.), *Traumatic dissociation: Neurobiology and treatment* (pp. 55–75). Washington, DC: American Psychiatric Publishing.

Dorsey, S., McLaughlin, K. A., Kerns, S. E., Harrison, J. P., Lambert, H. K., Briggs, E. C., . . . Amaya-Jackson, L. (2016, October 19). Evidence base update for psychosocial treatments for children and adolescents exposed to traumatic events. *Journal of Clinical Child & Adolescent Psychology,* 1–28. [Epub ahead of print]

Dossat, A. M., Bodell, L. P., Williams, D. L., Eckel, L. A., & Keel, P. K. (2014). Preliminary examination of glucagon-like peptide-1 levels in women with purging disorder and bulimia nervosa. *International Journal of Eating Disorders.*

Dove. (2016). *Dove global beauty and confidence report.* Englewood Cliffs, NJ: Author.

Dowell, D., Haegerich, T., & Chou, R. (2016). CDC guideline for prescribing opioids for chronic pain—United States, 2016. *JAMA, 315,* 1624–1645.

Doyle, A. C. (1938). The sign of the four. In *The complete Sherlock Holmes.* Garden City, NY: Doubleday.

DPE (Department for Professional Employees). (2016). *Social service workers: An occupational overview. Fact sheet 2016.* Washington, DC: DPE, AFL-CIO.

Draguns, J. G. (2006). Culture in psychopathology—psychopathology in culture: Taking a new look at an old problem. In T. G. Plante (Ed.), *Mental disorders of the new millennium, Vol. 2: Public and social problems.* Westport, CT: Praeger Publishers.

Drain, K. (2016, August 13). The top Google health searches of the last 4 years and how they've changed. *MedicalDaily.com.* Retrieved from http://medicaldaily.com.

Drake, R. E., Luciano, A. E., Mueser, K. T., Covell, N. H., Essock, S. M., Xie, H., & McHugo, G. J. (2015). Longitudinal course of clients with co-occurring schizophrenia-spectrum and substance use disorders in urban mental health centers: A 7-year prospective study. *Schizophrenia Bulletin.* [Electronic publication]

Draper, B. M. (2014). Suicidal behaviour and suicide prevention in later life. *Maturitas, 79*(2), 179–183.

Dray, J., Gilchrist, P., Singh, D., Cheesman, G., & Wade, T. D. (2014). Training mental health nurses to provide motivational interviewing on an inpatient eating disorder unit. *Journal of Psychiatric and Mental Health Nursing, 21*(7), 652–657.

Dreisbach, S. (2011). Shocking body-image news: 97% of women will be cruel to their bodies today. *Glamour.* Retrieved from *Glamour* website: http://www.glamour.com/health-fitness/2011/02.

Driessen, E., Hollon, S. D., Bockting, C. L., Cuijpers, P., & Turner, E. H. (2015). Does publication bias inflate the apparent efficacy of psychological treatment for major depressive disorder? A systematic review and meta-analysis of US National Institutes of Health-funded trials. *PLoS ONE, 10*(9), e0137864.

Drouin, M., & Landgraff, C. (2012). Texting, sexting, attachment, and intimacy in college students' romantic relationships. *Computers in Human Behavior, 28,* 444–449.

Drutz, J. E. (2017, April 14). Autism spectrum disorder and chronic disease: No evidence for vaccines or thimerosal as a contributing factor. *UpToDate.* Retrieved from http://www.uptodate.com.

DTL (Ditch the Label). (2017). *The annual bullying survey 2017.* Los Angeles: Ditch the Label.

Du, L., Zeng, J., Liu, H., Tang, D., Meng, H., Li, Y., & Fu, Y. (2017). Fronto-limbic disconnection in depressed patients with suicidal ideation: A resting-state functional connectivity study. *Journal of Affective Disorders, 215,* 213–217.

Dubovsky, S., & Dubovsky, A. (2011). Geriatric neuropsychopharmacology: Why does age matter? In C. E. Coffey, J. L. Cummings, M.S. George, & D. Weintraub (Eds.), *The American Psychiatric Publishing textbook of geriatric neuropsychiatry.* Arlington, VA: American Psychiatric Publishing, Inc.

Dubowitz, T., Bates, L. M., & Acevedo-Garcia, D. (2010). The Latino health paradox: Looking at the intersection of sociology and health. In C. E. Bird, P. Conrad, A. M. Fremont, & S. Timmermans (Eds.), *Handbook of medical sociology* (6th ed., pp. 106–123). Nashville, TN: Vanderbilt University Press.

Dubrovina, N. I. (2016). GABA-receptors in modulation of fear memory extinction. *Zh Vyssh Nerv Deiat Im I P Pavlova, 66*(2), 131–147. [Article in Russian]

Duenwald, M. (2003, March 18). "Oldest old" still show alertness. *New York Times.*

Dugas, M. J., Brillon, P., Savard, P., Turcotte, J., Gaudet, A., Ladouceur, R., . . . Gervais, N. J. (2010). A randomized clinical trial of cognitive-behavioral therapy and applied relaxation for adults with generalized anxiety disorder. *Behavior Therapy, 41*(1), 46–58.

Dugas, M. J., Buhr, K., & Ladouceur, R. (2004). The role of intolerance of uncertainty in etiology and maintenance. In R. G. Heimberg, C. L. Turk, & D. S. Mennin (Eds.), *Generalized anxiety disorder: Advances in research and practice* (pp. 143–163). New York: Guilford Press.

Dugas, M. J., Laugesen, N., & Bukowski, W. M. (2012). Intolerance of uncertainty, fear of anxiety, and adolescent worry. *Journal of Abnormal Child Psychology, 40*(6), 863–870.

Duhig, M., Gunasekara, I., & Patterson, S. (2015). Understanding readmission to psychiatric hospital in Australia from the service user's perspective: A qualitative study. *Health & Social Care in the Community.* [Electronic publication]

Dukart, J., Regen, F., Kherif, F., Colla, M., Bajbouj, M., Heuser, I., . . . & Draganski, B. (2014). Electroconvulsive therapy-induced brain plasticity determines therapeutic outcome in mood disorders. *Proceedings of the National Academy of Sciences USA, 111*(3), 1156–1161.

Duman, R. S. (2014). Pathophysiology of depression and innovative treatments: Remodeling glutamatergic synaptic connections. *Dialogues in Clinical Neuroscience, 16*(1), 11–27.

Dunbar, F. (1948). *Synopsis of psychosomatic diagnosis and treatment.* St. Louis: Mosby.

Dunbar, R. I. (2016). Do online social media cut through the constraints that limit the size of offline social networks? *Royal Society Open Science, 3*(1), 150292.

Dundas, I., Thorsheim, T., Hjeltnes, A., & Binder, P. E. (2016). Mindfulness-based stress reduction for academic evaluation anxiety: A naturalistic longitudinal study. *Journal of College Student Psychotherapy, 30*(2), 114–131.

Dunlop, J., & Pinals, D. A. (2016). Criteria for increasing involuntary medication dosage for a committed insanity acquittee. *Journal of the American Academy of Psychiatry and the Law, 44*(4), 501–503.

Dunsmoor, J. E., Ahs, F., Zielinski, D. J., & LaBar, K. S. (2014). Extinction in multiple virtual reality contexts diminishes fear reinstatement in humans. *Neurobiology of Learning and Memory, 113,* 157–164.

DuPaul, G. J., & Kern, L. (2011). Assessment and identification of attention-deficit/hyperactivity disorder. In G. J. DuPaul & K. Lee. (2011). *Young children with ADHD: Early identification and intervention* (2nd ed., pp. 23–46). Washington, DC: American Psychological Association.

Durbin, A., Rudoler, D., Durbin, J., Laporte, A., & Callaghan, R. C. (2014). Examining patient race and area predictors of inpatient admission for schizophrenia among hospital users in California. *Journal of Immigrant and Minority Health, 16*(6), 1025–1034.

Düring, S., Glenthøj, B. Y., Andersen, G. S., & Oranje, B. (2014). Effects of dopamine d2/d3 blockade on human sensory and sensorimotor gating in initially antipsychotic-naive, first-episode schizophrenia patients. *Neuropsychopharmacology, 39*(13), 3000–3008.

Durisko, Z., Mulsant, B. H., McKenzie, K., & Andrews, P. W. (2016). Using evolutionary theory to guide mental health research. *Canadian Journal of Psychiatry, 61*(3), 159–165.

Durkheim, E. (1897). *Suicide.* New York: Free Press. (Work republished 1951)

Durkin, K. F., & Hundersmarck, S. (2008). Pedophiles and child molesters. In E. Goode & D. A. Vail (Eds.), *Extreme deviance.* Los Angeles: Pine Forge Press.

Durwood, L., McLaughlin, K. A., & Olson, K. R. (2017). Mental health and self-worth in socially transitioned transgender youth. *Journal* of the American Academy of Child and Adolescent Psychiatry, 56, 116–123.

Duval, E. R., Javanbakht, A., & Liberzon, I. (2015). Neural circuits in anxiety and stress disorders: A focused review. Therapeutics and Clinical Risk Management, 11, 115–126.

Duval-Harvey, J., & Rogers, K. M. (2010). Attention-deficit/hyperactivity disorder. In R. L. Hampton, T. P. Gullotta, & R. L. Crowel (Eds.), Handbook of African American health (pp. 375–418). New York: Guilford Press.

Duwe, G. (2016). The patterns and prevalence of mass public shootings in the United States, 1915–2013. In L. C. Wilson (Ed.). The Wiley handbook of the psychology of mass shootings (Chap. 2, pp. 20–35). Hoboken, NJ: Wiley-Blackwell.

Dworkin, E. R., Wanklyn, S., Stasiewicz, P. R., & Coffey, S. F. (2018). PTSD symptom presentation among people with alcohol and drug use disorders: Comparisons by substance of abuse. Addictive Behaviors, 76, 188–194.

Dyl, J., Kittler, J., Phillips, K. A., & Hunt, J. I. (2006). Body dysmorphic disorder and other clinically significant body image concerns in adolescent psychiatric inpatients: Prevalence and clinical characteristics. Child Psychiatry and Human Development, 36(4), 369–382.

Easterbrooks, M. A., Bartlett, J. D., Raskin, M., Goldberg, J., Contreras, M. M., Kotake, C., . . . Jacobs, F. H. (2013). Limiting home visiting effects: Maternal depression as a moderator of child maltreatment. Pediatrics, 132(2), 126–133.

Eaton, N. R., Rodriguez-Seijas, C., Krueger, R. F., Campbell, W. K., Grant, B. F., & Hasin, D. S. (2016, September 12). Narcissistic personality disorder and the structure of common mental disorders. Journal of Personality Disorders. [Epub ahead of print]

eBizMBA. (2015, July). Top 15 most popular social networking sites. Retrieved from eBizMBA website: http://www.ebizmba.com.

Eckler, P., Kalyango, Y., & Paasch, E. (2017). Facebook use and negative body image among U.S. college women. Women's Health, 57(2), 249–267.

Economist. (2010, December 16). Age and happiness: The U-bend of life. The Economist. Retrieved from http://www.economist.com/node/17722567.

Eftekhari, A., Ruzek, J. I., Crowley, J. J., Rosen, C. S., Greenbaum, M. A., & Karlin, B. E. (2017). Effectiveness of national implementation of prolonged exposure therapy in Veterans Affairs care. JAMA Psychiatry, 70(9), 949–955.

Eggers, A. E. (2014). Treatment of depression with deep brain stimulation works by altering in specific ways the conscious perception of the core symptoms of sadness or anhedonia, not by modulating network circuitry. Medical Hypotheses, 83(1), 62–64.

Ehnvall, A., Parker, G., Hadzi, P. D., & Malhi, G. (2008). Perception of rejecting and neglectful parenting in childhood relates to lifetime suicide attempts for females—but not for males. Acta Psychiatrica Scandinavica, 117(1), 50–56.

EIE (Enough Is Enough). (2017). Cyberbullying statistics. Retrieved from http://enough.org/stats_cyberbullying.

Eifert, G. H., Greco, L. A., Heffner, M., & Louis, A. (2007). Eating disorders: A new behavioral perspective and acceptance-based treatment approach. In D. W. Woods & J. W. Kanter (Eds.), Understanding behavior disorders: A contemporary behavioral perspective. Reno, NV: Context Press.

Eikenaes, I., Hummelen, B., Abrahamsen, G., Andrea, H., & Wilberg, T. (2013). Personality functioning in patients with avoidant personality disorder and social phobia. Journal of Personality Disorders, 27(6), 746–763.

Eikenaes, I., Pedersen, G., & Wilberg, T. (2016). Attachment styles in patients with avoidant personality disorder compared with social phobia. Psychology and Psychotherapy, 89(3), 245–260.

Eilenberg, T. (2016). Acceptance and Commitment Group Therapy (ACT-G) for health anxiety. Danish Medical Journal, 63(10).

Eisenbarth, H., Demetriou, C. A., Kyranides, M. N., & Fanti, K. A. (2016). Stability subtypes of callous-unemotional traits and conduct disorder symptoms and their correlates. Journal of Youth and Adolescence, 45, 1889–1901.

Eisold, K. (2013, December 21). Hidden motives: A look at the hidden factors that really drive our social interactions. Psychology Today.

Eker, C., Simsek, F., Yılmazer, E. E., Kitis, O., Cinar, C., Eker, O. D., . . . Gonul, A. S. (2014). Brain regions associated with risk and resistance for bipolar I disorder: A voxel-based MRI study of patients with bipolar disorder and their healthy siblings. Bipolar Disorders, 16(3), 249–261.

Ekern, J. (2014, April 28). Eating disorder statistics and research. Retrieved from http:www.eatingdisorderhope.com.

Elhai, J. D., Dvorak, R. D., Levine, J. C., & Hall, B. J. (2017). Problematic smartphone use: A conceptual overview and systematic review of relations with anxiety and depression psychopathology. Journal of Affective Disorders, 207, 251–259.

Elias, A., & Paradies, Y. (2016). Estimating the mental health costs of racial discrimination. BMC Public Health, 19(1), 1205.

Elkin, I. (1994). The NIMH Treatment of Depression Collaborative Research Program: Where we began and where we are. In A. E. Bergin & S. L. Garfield (Eds.), Handbook of psychotherapy and behavior change (4th ed.). New York: Wiley.

Elkin, I., Parloff, M. B., Hadley, S. W., & Autry, J. H. (1985). National Institute of Mental Health Treatment of Depression Collaborative Research Program: Background and research plan. Archives of General Psychiatry, 42, 305–316.

Elkin, I., Shea, M. T., Watkins, J. T., Imber, S. D., Sotsky, S.M., Collins, J. F., . . . Parloff, M. B. (1989). National Institute of Mental Health Treatment of Depression Collaborative Research Program: General effectiveness of treatments. Archives of General Psychiatry, 46(11), 971–982.

Elkins, R. M., Edson, A., Pincus, D. B., & Comer, J. S. (2014). Inattention symptoms and the diagnosis of comorbid attention-deficit/hyperactivity disorder among youth with generalized anxiety disorder. Journal of Anxiety Disorders, 28, 754–760.

Elkins, R. M., Mian, N. D., Comer, J. S., & Pincus, D. B. (2017). Parent-Child Interaction Therapy (PCIT) and its adaptations. In J. L. Luby (Ed.), Handbook of preschool mental health. Development, disorders, and treatment (2nd ed.). New York: Guilford.

Ellenberger, H. F. (1970). The discovery of the unconscious. New York: Basic Books.

Ellenberger, H. F. (1972). The story of "Anna O.": A critical review with new data. Journal of the History of the Behavioral Sciences, 8, 267–279.

Elliott, E., & Vollm, B. (2016, October 17). The utility of post-conviction polygraph testing among sexual offenders. Sexual Abuse. [Epub ahead of print]

Ellis, A. (1962). Reason and emotion in psychotherapy. Secaucus, NJ: Lyle Stuart.

Ellis, A. (2014). Rational emotive behavior. In D. Wedding & R. J. Corsini (Eds.), Current psychotherapies (10th ed., pp. 151–192). Independence, KY: Cengage Publications.

Ellis, A. (2016). How to stubbornly refuse to make yourself miserable about anything—Yes, anything! New York: Citadel Press.

Ellis, C. C., Peterson, M., Bufford, R., & Benson, J. (2014). The importance of group cohesion in inpatient treatment of combat-related PTSD. International Journal of Group Psychotherapy, 64(2), 208–226.

Ellis, H. (2015). Franz Mesmer: Pioneer in the treatment of functional disease or charlatan? British Journal of Hospital Medicine, 76(3), 170.

Elwood, C. E., Poythress, N. G., & Douglas, K. S. (2004). Evaluation of the Hare P-SCAN in a non-clinical population. Personality and Individual Differences, 36(4), 833–843.

Emanuel, E. (2017). Euthanasia and physician-assisted suicide: Focus on the data. Medical Journal of Australia, 206(8), 339–340.

Emanuel, E. J., Onwuteaka-Philipsen, B. D., Urwin, J. W., & Cohen, J. (2016). Attitudes and practices of euthanasia and physician-assisted suicide in the United States, Canada, and Europe. JAMA, 316(1), 79.

EMCDDA (European Monitoring Centre for Drugs and Drug Addiction). (2017). Fentanyl drug profile. EMCDDA. Retrieved from http://www.emcdda.europa.eu.

Emmelkamp, P. M. (1982). Exposure in vivo treatments. In A. Goldstein & D. Chambless (Eds.), Agoraphobia: Multiple perspectives on theory and treatment. New York: Wiley.

Enatescu, V., Enatescu, I., Craina, M., Gluhovschi, A., Papava, I., Romosan, R., . . . Bernad, E. (2014). State and trait anxiety as a psychopathological phenomenon correlated with postpartum depression in a Romanian sample: A pilot study. Journal of Psychosomatic Obstetrics and Gynaecology, 35(2), 55–61.

Endom, E. E. (2016, August 11). Child abuse: Social and medicolegal issues. UpToDate. Retrieved from http://www.uptodate.com.

Endom, E. E. (2017, March 22). Child neglect and emotional maltreatment. UpToDate. Retrieved from http://www.uptodate.com.

Engel, G. L. (1968). A life setting conducive to illness: The giving-up-given-up complex. Annals of Internal Medicine, 69, 293.

Engel, G. L. (1971). Sudden and rapid death during psychological stress, folklore or folkwisdom? Annals of Internal Medicine, 74, 771–774.

Engel, M., & Comstock, G. L. (Eds.). (2016). *The moral rights of animals.* Lexington Books.

Engel, S., Steffen, K., & Mitchell, J. E. (2017, March 6). Bulimia nervosa in adults: Clinical features, course of illness, assessment, and diagnosis. *UpToDate.* Retrieved from www.uptodate.com.

Englbrecht, M., Alten, R., Aringer, M., Baerwald, C. G., Burkhardt, H., Eby, N., . . . Wendler, J. (2017). Validation of standardized questionnaires evaluating symptoms of depression in rheumatoid arthritis patients: Approaches to screening for a frequent yet underrated challenge. *Arthritis Care & Research, 69*(1), 58–66.

Engman, M., Wijma, K., & Wijma, B. (2010). Long-term coital behaviour in women treated with cognitive behaviour therapy for superficial coital pain and vaginismus. *Cognitive Behaviour Therapy, 39*(3), 193–202.

Engqvist, I., & Nilsson, K. (2014). The recovery process of postpartum psychosis from both the woman's and next of kin's perspective: An interview study in Sweden. *Open Nursing Journal, 8,* 8–16.

Erikson, E. (1963). *Childhood and society.* New York: Norton.

Erlangsen, A., Vach, W., & Jeune, B. (2005). The effect of hospitalization with medical illnesses on the suicide risk in the oldest old: A population-based register study. *Journal of the American Geriatrics Society, 53*(5), 771–776.

Ernst, M., & Luciana, M. (2015). Neuroimaging of the dopamine/reward system in adolescent drug use. *CNS Spectrums, 20*(4), 427–441.

Erskine, H. E., Norman, R. E., Ferrari, A. J., Chan, G. C. K., Copeland, W. E., Whiteford, H. A., & Scott, J. G. (2016). Long-term outcomes of attention-deficit/hyperactivity disorder and conduct disorder: A systematic review and meta-analysis. *Journal of the American Academy of Child and Adolescent Psychiatry, 55,* 841–850.

Escobar, J. I. (1995). Transcultural aspects of dissociative and somatoform disorders. *Psychiatric Clinics of North America, 18*(3), 555–569.

Escobar, J. I. (2004, April 15). Transcultural aspects of dissociative and somatoform disorders. *Psychiatric Times, XXI*(5), p. 10.

Espinoza, R. T., & Unützer, J. (2016, July 28). Diagnosis and management of late-life unipolar depression. *UpToDate.* Retrieved from http://www.uptodate.com.

Etgar, S., & Amichai-Hamburger, Y. (2017). Not all selfies took alike: Distinct selfie motivations are related to different personality characteristics. *Frontiers in Psychology, 8,* 842.

Etkin, A. (2010). Functional neuroanatomy of anxiety: A neural circuit perspective. In M. B. Stein & T. Steckler (Eds.), *Behavioral neurobiology of anxiety and its treatment. Current topics in behavioral neurosciences* (pp. 251–277). New York: Springer Science + Business Media.

Euesden, J., Danese, A., Lewis, C. M., & Maughan, B. (2017). A bidirectional relationship between depression and the autoimmune disorders: New perspectives from the National Child Development Study. *PLoS ONE, 12*(3), e0173015.

Eustis, E. H., Hayes-Skelton, S. A., Roemer, L., & Orsillo, S. M. (2016). Reductions in experiential avoidance as a mediator of change in symptom outcome and quality of life in acceptance-based behavior therapy and applied relaxation for generalized anxiety disorder. *Behaviour Research and Therapy, 87,* 188–195.

Evans, M., Donelle, L., & Hume-Loveland, L. (2012). Social support and online postpartum depression discussion groups: A content analysis. *Patient Education and Counseling, 87*(3), 405–410.

Evans, R. W. (2015, April 29). Concussion and mild traumatic brain injury. *UpToDate.* Retrieved from http://www.uptodate.com.

Evans, S. C., Burke, J. D., Roberts, M. C., Fite, P. J., Lochman, J. E., de la Pena, F., & Reed, G. M. (2017). Irritability in child and adolescent psychopathology: An integrative review for ICD-11. *Clinical Psychology Review, 53,* 29–45.

Evans, S. W., Owens, J., & Bunford, N. (2014). Evidence-based psychosocial treatments for children and adolescents with attention-deficit/hyperactivity disorder. *Journal of Clinical Child and Adolescent Psychology, 43,* 527–551.

Etxeberria, I., Etxebarria, I., & Urdaneta, E. (2018). Profiles in emotional aging: Does age matter? *Aging & Mental Health.* [Manuscript in press]

Fábrega, H., Jr. (2010). Understanding the evolution of medical traditions: Brain/behavior influences, enculturation, and the study of sickness and healing. *Neuropsychoanalysis, 12*(1), 21–27.

Fairburn, C. G., Bailey-Straebler, S., Basden, S., Doll, H. A., Jones, R., Murphy, R., . . . Cooper, Z. (2015). A transdiagnostic comparison of enhanced cognitive behavior therapy (CBT-E) and interpersonal psychotherapy in the treatment of eating disorders. *Behavior Research and Therapy, 70,* 64–71.

Fairburn, C. G., & Cooper, Z. (2014). Eating disorders: A transdiagnostic protocol. In D. H. Barlow, *Clinical handbook of psychological disorders* (5th ed., Chap. 17). New York: Guilford Press.

Fairburn, C. G., Cooper, Z., Shafran, R., & Wilson, G. T. (2008). Eating disorders: A transdiagnostic protocol. In D. H. Barlow (Ed.), *Clinical handbook of psychological disorders: A step-by-step treatment manual* (4th ed.). New York: Guilford Press.

Fakhoury, M. (2018). Imaging genetics in autism spectrum disorders: Linking genetics and brain imaging in the pursuit of the underlying neurobiological mechanisms. *Progress in Neuro-Psychopharmacology and Biological Psychiatry, 80*(Pt B), 101–114.

Fallahi Khoshknab, M., Sheikhona, M., Rahgouy, A., Rahgozar, M., & Sodagari, F. (2014). The effects of group psychoeducational programme on family burden in caregivers of Iranian patients with schizophrenia. *Journal of Psychiatric and Mental Health Nursing, 21*(5), 438–446.

Fanelli, D. (2010). "Positive" results increase down the Hierarchy of the Sciences. *PLoS One, 5*(4), e10068.

Fanelli, D. (2010). Do pressures to publish increase scientists' bias? An empirical support from US states data. *PLoS One, 5*(4), e10271.

Fanelli, D. (2011). Negative results are disappearing from most disciplines and countries. *Scientometrics, 90,* 891–904.

Fanelli, D., Costas, R., & Ioannidis, J. P. (2017). Meta-assessment of bias in science. *Proceedings of the National Academy of Sciences USA, 114*(14), 3714–3719.

Fanta, C. H. (2017, March 6). Diagnosis of asthma in adolescents and adults. *UpToDate.* Retrieved from www.uptodate.com.

faqs.org. (2014). Asylums. Retrieved from http://www.faqs.org/health/topics/99/asylums.html.

Farber, B. A., Manevich, I., Metzger, J., & Saypol, E. (2005). Choosing psychotherapy as a career: Why did we cross that road? *Journal of Clinical Psychology, 61*(8), 1009–1031.

Farberow, N. L., & Litman, R. E. (1970). *A comprehensive suicide prevention program.* Unpublished final report, Suicide Prevention Center of Los Angeles, Los Angeles.

Fardouly, J., Pinkus, R. T., & Vartanian, L. R. (2017). The impact of appearance comparisons made through social media, traditional media, and in person in women's everyday lives. *Body Image, 20,* 31–39.

Farkas, M. (2013). Pedophilia. *Psychiatria Hungarica: A Magyar Pszichiátriai Társaság Tudományos Folyóirata, 28*(2), 180–188.

Farlow, M. R. (2017, March 13). Epidemiology, pathology, and pathogenesis of dementia with Lewy bodies. *UpToDate.* Retrieved from http://www.uptodate.com.

Farmer, R. F., & Chapman, A. L. (2015). *Behavioral interventions in cognitive behavior therapy: Practical guidance for putting theory into action* (2nd ed.). Washington, DC: APA Books.

Farmer, R. F., & Nelson-Gray, R. O. (2005). Behavioral treatment of personality disorders. In R. F. Farmer & R. O. Nelson-Gray (Eds.), *Personality-guided behavior therapy* (pp. 203–243). Washington, DC: American Psychological Association.

Farooq, A., & Yousaf, A. (2016). Childhood trauma and alexithymia in patients with conversion disorder. *Journal of the College of Physicians and Surgeons Pakistan, 26*(7), 606–610.

Farrelly, S., Clement, S., Gabbidon, J., Jeffery, D., Dockery, L., Lassman, F., . . . Thornicroft, G. (2014). Anticipated and experienced discrimination amongst people with schizophrenia, bipolar disorder and major depressive disorder: A cross sectional study. *BMC Psychiatry, 14*(1), 367–382.

Fauber, J., Fiore, K., Wynn, M. (2017, January 6). For one condition, the drugs came before the disorder. *Milwaukee Journal Sentinal* and *MedPage Today.*

Faubion, M. D. (2016, September-October). Evaluating defendants for competency and sanity. Austin, TX: Texas District & County Attorneys Association.

Faubion, S. S., & Rullo, J. E. (2015). Sexual dysfunction in women: A practical approach. *American Family Physician, 92*(4), 281–288.

Faugere, M., Micoulaud-Franchi, J. A., Faget-Agius, C., Lançon, C., Cermolacce, M., & Richieri, R. (2018). High C-reactive protein levels are associated with depressive symptoms in schizophrenia. *Journal of Affective Disorders, 225,* 671–675.

Fava, M., Farabaugh, A. H., Sickinger, A. H., Wright, E., Alpert, J. E., Sonawalla, S., . . . Worthington, J. J., III. (2002). Personality disorders and depression. *Psychological Medicine, 32*(6), 1049–1057.

Fawcett, J. (2007). What has the "black box" done to reduce suicide? *Psychiatric Annals, 37*(10), 657, 662.

Fay, B. P. (1995). The individual versus society: The cultural dynamics of criminalizing suicide. *Hastings International and Comparative Law Review, 18*, 591–615.

Fazel, S., Grann, M., Kling, B., & Hawton, K. (2011). Prison suicide in 12 countries: An ecological study of 861 suicides during 2003–2007. *Social Psychiatry and Psychiatric Epidemiology, 46*(3), 191–195.

Fazel, S., Hayes, A. J., Bartellas, K., Clerici, M., & Trestman, R. (2016). The mental health of prisoners: A review of prevalence, adverse outcomes and interventions. *Lancet Psychiatry, 3*(9), 871–881.

Fazel, S., Wolf, A., Larsson, H., Lichtenstein, P., Mallett, S., & Fanshawe, T. R. (2017). Identification of low risk of violent crime in severe mental illness with a clinical prediction tool (Oxford Mental Illness and Violence tool [OxMIV]): A derivation and validation study. *Lancet Psychiatry, 4*(6), 461–468.

FBI (Federal Bureau of Investigation). (2014) Ten-year arrest trends. Totals, 2003–2012. Washington, DC: Department of Justice, Criminal Justice Information Services.

FBI (Federal Bureau of Investigation). (2016, September 26). *Latest crime statistics released: Increase in violent crime, decrease in property crime.* Washington, DC: FBI.

FBI (Federal Bureau of Investigation). (2016, November 14). Latest hate crime statistics released: Annual report sheds light on serious issue. *FBI*. Retrieved from https://www.fbi.gov/news/stories/2015.

FBI (Federal Bureau of Investigation). (2017). *Active shooter resources.* Washington DC: FBI.

FBI (Federal Bureau of Investigation). (2017). *Resources: Reports and publications.* Washington, DC: FBI.

FBI (Federal Bureau of Investigation). (2017). *Serial murder: Pathways for investigations.* Washington, DC: FBI.

FDA (U.S. Food and Drug Administration). (2012, August). *Guidance for industry: Suicidal ideation and behavior: Prospective assessment of occurrence in clinical trials.* Retrieved from https://www.fda.gov/drugs/guidancecomplianceregulatoryinformation/guidances/ucm315156.htm.

FDA (U.S. Food and Drug Administration). (2014). Consumer update: Understanding antidepressant medications. Retrieved from http://www.fda.gov/forconsumers/consumerupdates/ucm095980.html.

FDA (Food and Drug Administration). (2015). *The impact of direct-to-consumer advertising.* Retrieved from https://www.fda.gov/drugs/ResourcesForYou/consumers/ucm143562.htm.

FDA (U.S. Food and Drug Administration). (2016). *The drug development process* (last updated 10/14/2016). Washington, DC: U.S. Department of Health and Human Services.

FDA (U.S. Food and Drug Administration). (2016). *The impact of direct-to-consumer advertising.* Washington, DC: U.S. Department of Health and Human Services.

FDA (U.S. Food and Drug Administration). (2016). *Keeping watch over direct-to-consumer ads.* (last updated 6/14/2016). Washington, DC: U.S. Department of Health and Human Services.

Fearon, P., Groh, A. M., Bakermans-Kranenburg, M. J., van IJzendoorn, M. H., & Roisman, G. I. (2016). Attachment and developmental psychopathology. In D. Cicchetti (Ed.), *Developmental psychopathology, Vol. 1. Theory and method* (3rd ed.). New York: Wiley.

Federoff, J. P., & Marshall, W. L. (2010). Paraphilias. In D. McKay, J. S. Abramowitz, & S. Taylor (Eds.), *Cognitive-behavioral therapy for refractory cases: Turning failure into success* (pp. 369–384). Washington, DC: American Psychological Association.

Feigelman, B., & Feigelman, W. (2011). Suicide survivor support groups: Comings and goings, Part I. *Illness, Crisis & Loss, 19*(1), 57–71.

Feki, I., Mdhaffar, K., Hentati, S., Sallemi, R., & Masmoudi, J. (2017). Depression in elderly patients with schizophrenia. *European Psychiatry, 41*(Suppl Apr), S654.

Feldman, N. (2017, January 4). Sex offender lockup should trouble court more. *Bloomberg View.*

Feldman, R., Bailey, R. A., Muller, J., Le, J., & Dirani, R. (2014). Cost of schizophrenia in the medicare program. *Population Health Management, 17*(3), 190–196.

Feldman, S. R., Moritz, S. H., & Benjamin, G. A. H. (2005). Suicide and the law: A practical overview for mental health professionals. *Women and Therapy, 28*(1), 95–103.

Felix, E., Hernández, L. A., Bravo, M., Ramirez, R., Cabiya, J., & Canino, G. (2011). Natural disaster and risk of psychiatric disorders in Puerto Rican children. *Journal of Abnormal Child Psychology, 39*(4), 589–600.

Fennig, S., Fennig, S., & Roe, D. (2002). Cognitive-behavioral therapy for bulimia nervosa: Time course and mechanisms of change. *General Hospital Psychiatry, 24*(2), 87–92.

Ferman, T. J., Smith, G. E., Dickson, D. W., Graff-Radford, N. R., Lin, S., Wszolek, Z., . . . Boeve, B. F. (2014). Abnormal daytime sleepiness in dementia with Lewy bodies compared to Alzheimer's disease using the Multiple Sleep Latency Test. *Alzheimer's Research & Therapy, 6*(9), 76.

Fernquist, R. M. (2007). How do Durkheimian variables impact variation in national suicide rates when proxies for depression and alcoholism are controlled? *Archives of Suicide Research, 11*(4), 361–374.

Ferrari, A. J., Norman, R. E., Freedman, G., Baxter, A. J., Pirkis, J. E., Harris, M. G., & Whiteford, H. A. (2014). The burden attributable to mental and substance use disorders as risk factors for suicide: Findings from the Global Burden of Disease Study 2010. *PLoS One, 9*(4), e91936.

Fervaha, G., Agid, O., Takeuchi, H., Foussias, G., & Remington, G. (2014). Effect of antipsychotic medication on overall life satisfaction among individuals with chronic schizophrenia: Findings from the NIMH CATIE study. *European Neuropsychopharmacology, 24*(7), 1078–1085.

Feuer, M. (2016, November 17). Interview. In C. Abate, Body shaming in an age of social media. *Healthline News.*

Fichter, M. M., Quadflieg, N., & Hedlund, S. (2008). Long-term course of binge eating disorder and bulimia nervosa: Relevance for nosology and diagnostic criteria. *International Journal of Eating Disorders, 41*, 577–586.

Field, A. P., & Purkis, H. M. (2012). Associative learning and phobias. In M. Haselgrove (Ed.), *Clinical applications of learning theory* (pp. 49–73). New York: Psychology Press.

Fields, G., & Phillips, E. E. (2013, September 25). The new asylums: Jails swell with mentally ill. *The Wall Street Journal.*

Fieve, R. R. (1975). *Moodswing.* New York: Morrow.

Figley, C. R. (1978). Symptoms of delayed combat stress among a college sample of Vietnam veterans. *Military Medicine, 143*(2), 107–110.

Finberg, J. P., & Rabey, J. M. (2016). Inhibitors of MAO-A and MAO-B in psychiatry and neurology. *Frontiers in Pharmacology, 7*, 340.

Fine, C. G., & Madden, N. E. (2000). Group psychotherapy in the treatment of dissociative identity disorder and allied dissociative disorders. In R. H. Klein & V. L. Schermer (Eds.), *Group psychotherapy for psychological trauma* (pp. 298–325). New York: Guilford Press.

Fingher, N., Dinstein, I., Ben-Shachar, M., Haar, S., Dale, A. M., Eyler, L., Pierce, K., & Courchesne, E. (2017). Toddlers later diagnosed with autism exhibit multiple structural abnormalities in temporal corpus callosum fibers. *Cortex.*

Fink, H. A., Mac Donald, R., Rutks, I. R., Nelson, D. B., & Wilt, T. J. (2002). Sildenafil for male erectile dysfunction: A systematic review and meta-analysis. *Archives of Internal Medicine, 162*(12), 1349–1360.

Fink, M. (2001). Convulsive therapy: A review of the first 55 years. *Journal of Affective Disorders, 63*(1–3), 1–15.

Fink, M. (2007). What we learn about continuation treatments from the collaborative electroconvulsive therapy studies. *Journal of ECT, 23*(4), 215–218.

Fink, M. (2014). What was learned: Studies by the consortium for research in ECT (CORE) 1997–2011. *Acta Psychiatrica Scandinavica, 129*(6), 417–426.

Fink, M., Kellner, C. H., & McCall, W. V. (2014). The role of ECT in suicide prevention. *The Journal of ECT, 30*(1), 5–9.

Fink, S., & Risen, J. (2017, June 21). Psychologists open a window on brutal C.I.A. interrogations. *New York Times.*

Finkelhor, D., Asdigian, N., & Dziuba-Leatherman, J. (1995). Victimization prevention programs for children: A follow-up. *American Journal of Public Health, 85*(12), 1684–1689.

Finley, E. P., Noël, P. H., Mader, M., Haro, E., Bernardy, N., Rosen, C. S., . . . Pugh, M. J. (2017). Community clinicians and the Veterans Choice Program for PTSD Care: Understanding provider interest during early implementation. *Medical Care, 55* Suppl 7, Suppl 1: S61–S70.

Firger, J. (2016, February 10). For runway models, high fashion means a dangerously low BMI. *Newsweek.*

Fischer, B. A. (2012). Maltreatment of people with serious mental illness in the early 20th century: A focus on Nazi Germany and eugenics in America. *The Journal of Nervous and Mental Disease, 200*(12), 1096–1100.

Fischer, B. A., & Buchanan, R. W. (2017, February 27). Schizophrenia in adults: Clinical manifestations, course, assessment, and diagnosis. *UpToDate.* Retrieved from http://www.uptodate.com.

Fischer, B. A., & Buchanan, R. W. (2017, March 17). Schizophrenia in adults: Epidemiology and pathogenesis. *UpToDate*. Retrieved from http://www.uptodate.com.

Fischer, M. S., Baucom, D. H., & Cohen, M. J. (2016). Cognitive-behavioral couple therapies: Review of the evidence for the treatment of relationship distress, psychopathology, and chronic health conditions. *Family Process, 55*(3), 423–442.

Fischer, S., Meyer, A. H., Dremmel, D., Schlup, B., & Munsch, S. (2014). Short-term cognitive-behavioral therapy for binge eating disorder: Long-term efficacy and predictors of long-term treatment success. *Behaviour Research and Therapy, 58,* 36–42.

Fisher, M. A. (2013). *The ethics of conditional confidentiality: A practical model for mental health professionals.* New York: Oxford University Press.

Fisher, M. A. (2016, March 14). *Confidentiality limits in psychotherapy: Ethics checklists for mental health professionals.* Washington, DC: APA.

Flavin, D. K., Franklin, J. E., & Frances, R. J. (1990). Substance abuse and suicidal behavior. In S. J. Blumenthal & D. J. Kupfer (Eds.), *Suicide over the life cycle: Risk factors, assessment, and treatment of suicidal patients.* Washington, DC: American Psychiatry Press.

Fleck, D. E., Keck, P. E., Corey, K. B., & Strakowski, S. M. (2005). Factors associated with medication adherence in African American and white patients with bipolar disorder. *Journal of Clinical Psychiatry, 66*(5), 646–652.

Flick, C. (2016). Informed consent and the Facebook emotional manipulation study. *Research Ethics, 12*(1), 14–28.

Floyd, A., Dedert, E., Ghate, S., Salmon, P., Weissbecker, I., Studts, J. L., . . . Sephton, S. E. (2011). Depression may mediate the relationship between sense of coherence and quality of life in lung cancer patients. *Journal of Health Psychology, 16*(2), 249–257.

Foa, E., Hembree, E., & Rothbaum, B. O. (2017). *Prolonged exposure therapy for PTSD: Emotional processing of traumatic experiences (treatments that work).* New York: Oxford University Press.

Foa, E. B. (2011). Prolonged exposure therapy: Past, present, and future. *Depression and Anxiety, 28*(12), 1043–1047.

Foa, E. B., & McLean, C. P. (2016). The efficacy of exposure therapy for anxiety-related disorders and its underlying mechanisms: The case of OCD and PTSD. *Annual Review of Clinical Psychology, 12,* 1–28.

Foerde, K., Steinglass, J. E., Shohamy, D., & Walsh, B. T. (2015). Neural mechanisms supporting maladaptive food choices in anorexia nervosa. *Nature Neuroscience, 18,* 1571.

Foldvary-Schaefer, N. (2017, July 28). Disorders of arousal from non-rapid eye movement sleep in adults. *UpToDate*. Retrieved from http://www.uptodate.com.

Foley, D. L., Eaves, L. J., Wormley, B., Silberg, J. L., Maes, H. H., Kohn, J., & Riley, B. (2004). Childhood adversity, monoamine oxidase A genotype, and risk for conduct disorder. *Archives of General Psychiatry, 61*(7), 738.

Folsom, D. P., Fleisher, A. S., & Depp, C. A. (2006). Schizophrenia. In D. V. Jeste & J. H. Friedman (Eds.), *Psychiatry for neurologists* (pp. 59–66). Totowa, NJ: Humana Press.

Fonagy, P. (2015). The effectiveness of psychodynamic psychotherapies: An update. *World Psychiatry, 14,* 137–150.

Fonagy, P., & Luyten, P. (2016). A multilevel perspective on the development of borderline personality disorder. In D. Cicchetti (Ed.), *Developmental psychopathology, Vol. 3: Maladaptation and psychopathology* (3rd ed., pp. 726–792). New York: Wiley.

Fonagy, P., & Luyten, P. (2018). Attachment, mentalizing, and the self. In W. J. Livesley & R. Larstone (Eds.), *Handbook of personality disorders: Theory, research, and treatment* (2nd ed.). New York: Guilford Press.

Fonagy, P., Luyten, P., Allison, E., & Campbell, C. (2017). What we have changed our minds about: Part 1. Borderline personality disorder as a limitation of resilience. *Borderline Personality Disorder and Emotion Dysregulation, 4,* 11.

Fonagy, P., Luyten, P., Allison, E., & Campbell, C. (2017). What we have changed our minds about: Part 2. Borderline personality disorder, epistemic trust and the developmental significance of social communication. *Borderline Personality Disorder and Emotion Dysregulation, 4,* 9.

Fonareva, I., & Oken, B. S. (2014). Physiological and functional consequences of caregiving for relatives with dementia. *International Psychogeriatrics, 26*(5), 725–747.

Fonseca, D. A., Guerra, A. F., Carvalho, F., Fernandes, E., Ferreira, L. M., Branco, P. S., . . . Cotrim, M. D. (2018). Hyperthermia severely affects the vascular effects of MDMA and metabolites in the human internal mammary artery in vitro. *Cardiovascular Toxicology.* [Manuscript in press]

Foo, X. Y., Alwi, M. M., Ismail, S. F., Ibrahim, N., & Osman, Z. J. (2014). Religious commitment, attitudes toward suicide, and suicidal behaviors among college students of different ethnic and religious groups in Malaysia. *Journal of Religion and Health, 53*(3), 731–746.

Fooducate. (2016, April 7). The weight loss industry by numbers. *Fooducate*. Retrieved from http://www.fooducate.com.

Foote, B. (2016, November 22). Dissociative identity disorder. *UpToDate*. Retrieved from http://www.uptodate.com.

Forcier, M., & Olson-Kennedy, J. (2017, April 4). Sexual minority youth: Epidemiology and health concerns. *UpToDate*. Retrieved from www.uptodate.com.

Forcier, M., & Olson-Kennedy, J. (2017, May 12). Gender development and clinical presentation of gender nonconformity in children and adolescents. *UpToDate*. Retrieved from http://www.uptodate.com.

Ford, R., King, T., Priest, N., & Kavanagh, A. (2017). Bullying and mental health and suicidal behavior among 14- to 15-year-olds in a representative sample of Australian children. *Australian and New Zealand Journal of Psychiatry, 51,* 897–908.

Ford, T. (2000). The influence of womanist identity on the development of eating disorders and depression in African American female college students. *Dissertation Abstracts International: Section A: Humanities and Social Sciences, 61,* 2194.

Foreyt, J. P., Poston, W. S. C., & Goodrick, G. K. (1996). Future directions in obesity and eating disorders. *Addictive Behavior, 21*(6), 767–778.

Forgas, J. F. (2013). Don't worry, be sad! On the cognitive, motivational, and interpersonal benefits of negative mood. *Current Directions in Psychological Science, 22*(3), 225–232.

Forgas, J. F. (2014, June 4). Four ways sadness may be good for you. *Greater Good.*

Forgas, J. F. (2017, May 14). Why bad moods are good for you: The surprising benefits of sadness. *The Conversation.*

Forgatch, M. S., & Patterson, G. R. (2010). Parent management training—Oregon model: An intervention for antisocial behavior in children and adolescents. In J. R. Weisz, & A. E. Kazdin (Eds.), *Evidence-based psychotherapies for children and adolescents* (2nd ed., pp. 159–177). New York: Guilford Press.

Forman, S. F. (2016, December 22). Eating disorders: Overview of treatment. *UpToDate*. Retrieved from www.uptodate.com.

Forman, S. F. (2016, July 27). Eating disorders: Overview of epidemiology, clinical features, and diagnosis. *UpToDate*. Retrieved from www.uptodate.com.

Forsberg, M. M. (2017). Delirium update for postacute care and long-term care settings: A narrative review. *Journal of the American Osteopathic Association, 117*(1), 32–38.

Forster, M., Grigsby, T. J., Rogers, C. J., & Benjamin, S. M. (2018). The relationship between family-based adverse childhood experiences and substance use behaviors among a diverse sample of college students. *Addictive Behaviors, 76,* 298–304.

Fortune, S. A., & Hawton, K. (2007). Suicide and deliberate self-harm in children and adolescents. *Paediatrics and Child Health, 17*(11), 443–447.

Fosse, R., Ryberg, W., Carlsson, M. K., & Hammer, J. (2017). Predictors of suicide in the patient population admitted to a locked-door psychiatric acute ward. *PLoS ONE, 12*(3), e0173958.

Foster, J. D., Campbell, W. K., & Twenge, J. M. (2003). Individual differences in narcissicm: Inflated self-views across the lifespan and around the world. *Journal of Research in Personality, 37,* 469–486.

Fouet, T. (2017). Psychological support for people bereaved by suicide. *Soins, 62*(814), 47–48. [French]

Fowler, K. A., O'Donohue, W., Lilienfeld, S. O. (2007). Introduction: Personality disorders in perspective. In W. O'Donohue, K. A. Fowler, S. O. Lilienfeld (Eds.). *Personality disorders: Toward the DSM-V.* Los Angeles: Sage Publications.

Fox, A. S., Oler, J. A., Shackman, A. J., Shelton, S. E., Raveendran, M., McKay, D. R., . . . Kalin, N. H. (2015). Intergenerational neural mediators of early-life anxious temperament. *Proceedings of the National Academy of Sciences USA, 112*(29), 9118–9122.

Fox, J. A., & Levin, J. (2014). *Extreme killing: Understanding serial and mass murder* (3rd ed.). Los Angeles: Sage Publications.

Fox, J. A., & Levin, J. (2016). Explaining mass shootings: Types, patterns, and theories. In L. C. Wilson (Ed.). *The Wiley handbook of the psychology of mass shootings* (Chap. 3, pp. 36–58). Hoboken, NJ: Wiley-Blackwell.

Fox, N. A., & Pine, D. S. (2012). Temperament and the emergence of anxiety disorders. *Journal of the American Academy of Child and Adolescent Psychiatry, 51,* 125–128.

França, K., Roccia, M. G., Castillo, D., Al Harbi, M., Tchernev, G., Chokoeva, A., . . . & Fioranelli, M. (2017, February 20). Body dysmorphic disorder: History and curiosities. *Wiener Medizinische Wochenschrift.* [Epub ahead of print]

Frances, A. (2015). Don't throw out the baby with the bath water. *Australian & New Zealand Journal of Psychiatry, 49*(6), 577.

Frances, A. (2016). A report card on the utility of psychiatric diagnosis. *World Psychiatry, 15*(1), 32–33.

Frances, A. J. (2013, July 3). Back to normal. *Psychology Today* Blogs: DSM 5 in distress. Retrieved from http://www.psychologytoday.com/blog/dsm5-in-distress/201307/back-normal

Frances, A. J. (2013, January 16). Bad news: DSM5 refuses to correct somatic symptom disorder. *Psychology Today* Blogs: DSM 5 in distress.

Frances, A. J. (2013). Frances's letter to editor. *New York Times,* RE DSM-5.

Frances, A. J. (2016, July 11). Mental illness, violence, and family homicides. *Psychology Today.*

Francis, J., Jr., & Young, G. B. (2014, August 22). Diagnosis of delirium and confusional states. *UpToDate.* Retrieved from http://www.uptodate.com.

Franco, A., Malhotra, N., & Simonovits, G. (2014). Social science. Publication bias in the social sciences: Unlocking the file drawer. *Science, 345*(6203), 1502–1505.

Franco, J. G., de Pablo, J., Gaviria, A. M., Sepúlveda, E., & Vilella, E. (2014). Smooth pursuit eye movements and schizophrenia: Literature review. *Archivos De La Sociedad Española De Oftalmología, 89*(9), 361–367.

Frank, G. K., Shott, M. E., Hagman, J. O., & Mittal, V. A. (2013). Alterations in brain structures related to taste reward circuitry in ill and recovered anorexia nervosa and in bulimia nervosa. *American Journal of Psychiatry, 170,* 1152.

Frank, J. D. (1973). *Persuasion and healing* (Rev. ed.). Baltimore: Johns Hopkins University Press.

Franklin, M. E., & Foa, E. B. (2014). Obsessive compulsive disorder. In D. H. Barlow (Ed.), (2014). *Clinical handbook of psychological disorders: A step-by-step treatment manual* (5th ed., pp. 155–205). New York: Guilford Press.

Franklin, T. (2017). Best practices in multicultural assessment of cognition. In R. S. McCallum, *Handbook of nonverbal assessment* (Chap. 4, pp. 39–46). New York: Springer.

Fraser, J. (2016, April 28). Involuntary mental health commitment. *Pittsburgh Today.*

Frederick, D. A., Sandhu, G., Morse, P. J., & Swami, V. (2016). Correlates of appearance and weight satisfaction in a U.S. National Sample: Personality, attachment style, television viewing, self-esteem, and life satisfaction. *Body Image, 17,* 191–203.

Frederickson, J. (2013). *Co-creating change: Effective dynamic therapy techniques.* Kansas City, MO: Seven Leaves Press.

French, A. P., & Berlin, I. N. (1979). *Depression in children and adolescents.* New York: Human Sciences Press.

Frese, F. J., III. (2008). Self-help activities. In D. V. Jeste, & K. T. Mueser (Eds.) *Clinical handbook of schizophrenia* (pp. 298–305). New York: Guilford Press.

Freud, S. (1894). The neuropsychoses of defense. In J. Strachey (Ed.), *The standard edition of the complete psychological works of Sigmund Freud* (Vol. 3). London: Hogarth Press. (Work republished 1962).

Freud, S. (1909). Analysis of a phobia in a five-year-old boy. In *Sigmund Freud: Collected papers* (Vol. 3). New York: Basic Books.

Freud, S. (1914). On narcissism. In *Complete psychological works* (Vol. 14). London: Hogarth Press. (Work republished 1957.)

Freud, S. (1915). A case of paranoia counter to psychoanalytic theory. In *Complete psychological works* (Vol. 14). London: Hogarth Press. [Work republished 1957]

Freud, S. (1917). *A general introduction to psychoanalysis* (J. Riviere, Trans.). New York: Liveright. (Work republished 1963).

Freud, S. (1917). Mourning and melancholia. In *Collected papers* (Vol. 4, pp. 152–172). London: Hogarth Press and the Institute of Psychoanalysis. (Work republished 1950).

Freud, S. (1920). Beyond the pleasure principle. In J. Strachey (Ed.), (1955), *The standard edition of the complete psychological works of Sigmund Freud, Volume XVIII (1920–1922): Beyond the pleasure principle, group psychology and other works.* London, England: The Hogarth Press and the Institute of Psychoanalysis.

Freud, S. (1924). The loss of reality in neurosis and psychosis. In *Sigmund Freud's collected papers* (Vol. 2, pp. 272–282). London: Hogarth Press.

Freud, S. (1933). *New introductory lectures on psychoanalysis.* New York: Norton.

Freud, S. (1961). *The future of an illusion.* New York: W. W. Norton.

Freudenreich, O., & Goff, D. C. (2011). Treatment of psychotic disorders. In D. A. Ciraulo & R. I. Shader (Eds.), *Pharmacotherapy of depression* (2nd ed., pp. 185–196). New York: Springer Science + Business Media.

Freudenreich, O., & McEvoy, J. (2017, February 2). Guidelines for prescribing clozapine in schizophrenia. *UpToDate.* Retrieved from http://www.uptodate.com.

Frey, R. (2005). Hallucination. In S. L. Chamberlin & B. Narins (Eds.), *Gale encyclopedia of neurological disorders.* PA: Thomson Gale.

Freytes, I. M., LeLaurin, J. H., Zickmund, S. L., Resende, R. D., & Uphold, C. R. (2017). Exploring the post-deployment reintegration experiences of veterans with PTSD and their significant others. *American Journal of Orthopsychiatry, 87*(2), 149–156.

Frias, A., Gonzalez, L., Palma, C., & Farriols, N. (2017). Is there a relationship between borderline personality disorder and sexual masochism in women. *Archives of Sexual Behavior, 46*(3), 747–754.

Frieden, T. (2016, December 17). How to end America's growing opioid epidemic. *Fox News.*

Friedman, M., Grawert, A., & Cullen, J. (2016, September 19). *Crime in 2016: A preliminary analysis.* New York: Brennan Center for Justice.

Friedman, M., & Rosenman, R. (1959). Association of specific overt behavior pattern with blood and cardiovascular findings. *Journal of the American Medical Association, 169,* 1286.

Friedman, M., & Rosenman, R. (1974). *Type A behavior and your heart.* New York: Knopf.

Friedrich, F., Gross, R., Wrobel, M., Klug, G., Unger, A., Fellinger, M., . . . Wancata, J. (2014). Burden of mothers and fathers of persons with schizophrenia. *Psychiatrische Praxis, 42*(4), 208–215.

Frierson, R. L., Boyd, M. S., & Harper, A. (2015). Mental illness and mental health defenses: Perceptions of the criminal bar. *Journal of the American Academy of Psychiatry and the Law. 43*(4), 483–491.

Friman, P. C. (2008). Evidence-based therapies for enuresis and encopresis. In R. G. Steele, T. D. Elkin, & M. C. Roberts (Eds.), *Handbook of evidence-based therapies for children and adolescents: Bridging science and practice.* New York: Springer.

Fristad, M. A., & MacPherson, H. A. (2013). Evidence-based psychosocial treatments for child and adolescent bipolar spectrum disorders. *Journal of Clinical Child and Adolescent Psychology, 43,* 339–355.

Fromberger, P., Jordan, K., & Müller, J. L. (2013). Pedophilia: Etiology, diagnostics and therapy. *Der Nervenarzt, 84*(9), 1123–1135.

Fromm-Reichmann, F. (1943). Psychotherapy of schizophrenia. *American Journal of Psychiatry, 111,* 410–419.

Fromm-Reichmann, F. (1948). Notes on the development of treatment of schizophrenia by psychoanalytic psychotherapy. *Psychiatry, 11,* 263–273.

Fromm-Reichmann, F. (1950). *Principles of intensive psychotherapy.* Chicago: University of Chicago.

Frone, M. R. (2016). Work stress and alcohol use: Developing and testing a biphasic self-medication model. *Work Stress, 30*(4), 374–394.

Frosch, W. A., Robbins, E. S., & Stern, M. (1965). Untoward reactions to lysergic acid diethylamide (LSD) resulting in hospitalization. *New England Journal of Medicine, 273,* 1235–1239.

Frost, R. O., Patronek, G., & Rosenfield, E. (2011). Comparison of object and animal hoarding. *Depression and Anxiety, 28,* 885.

Frydman, I., de Sales Andrade, J. B., Vigne, P., & Fontenelle, L. F. (2016). Can neuroimaging provide reliable biomarkers for obsessive-compulsive disorder? A narrative review. *Current Psychiatry Reports, 18*(10), 90.

Fu, R., Noguchi, H., Tachikawa, H., Aiba, M., Nakamine, S., Kawamura, A., Takahashi, H., & Tamiya, N. (2016). Relation between social network and psychological distress among middle-aged adults in Japan: Evidence from a national longitudinal survey. *Social Science & Medicine, 175,* 58–65.

Fuccillo, M.V. (2016). Striatal circuits as a common node for autism pathophysiology. *Frontiers in Neuroscience, 10,* 27.

Fugl-Meyer, K. S., Bohm-Starke, N., Petersen, C. D., Fugl-Meyer, A., Parish, S., & Giraldi, A. (2013). Standard operating procedures for female genital sexual pain. *Journal of Sexual Medicine, 10,* 83–93.

Fujiwara, T., Yagi, J., Homma, H., Mashiko, H., Nagao, K., Okuyama, M., Great Japan Earthquake Follow-up for Children Study Team. (2017). Suicide risk among young children after the Great East Japan earthquake: A follow-up study. *Psychiatry Research, 253,* 318–324.

Fukumoto, M., Hashimoto, R., Ohi, K., Yasuda, Y., Yamamori, H., Umeda-Yano, S., . . . Takeda, M. (2014). Relation between remission status and attention in patients with schizophrenia. *Psychiatry and Clinical Neurosciences, 68*(3), 234–241.

Fuller, D. A., Sinclair, E., Lamb, H. R., Cayce, J. D., & Snook, J. (2017). *Emptying the "new asylums": A beds capacity model to reduce mental illness behind bars.* Arlington, VA: Treatment Advocacy Center.

Furnham, A., Richards, S. C., & Paulhus, D. L. (2013). The Dark Triad of personality: A 10 year review. *Social and Personality Psychology Compass, 7,* 199–216.

Furr, J. M., Comer, J. S., Edmunds, J., & Kendall, P. C. (2010). Disasters and youth: A meta-analytic examination of posttraumatic stress. *Journal of Consulting and Clinical Psychology, 78,* 765–780.

Furr, J. M., Comer, J. S., Villodas, M., Poznanski, B., & Gurwitch, R. (2018). Trauma and child psychopathology: From risk and resilience to evidence-based intervention. In P. C. Kendall & J. Butcher (Eds.), *APA handbook of child psychopathology.* Washington, DC: APA.

Gabbard, G., & DeJean, V. (2016, July 20). Unipolar depression in adults: Psychodynamic psychotherapy. *UpToDate.* Retrieved from https://uptodate.com.

Gabbard, G. O. (2001). Psychoanalysis and psychoanalytic psychotherapy. In W. J. Livesley (Ed.), *Handbook of personality disorders: Theory, research, and treatment* (pp. 359–376). New York: Guilford Press.

Gabbard, G. O. (2010). Therapeutic action in the psychoanalytic psychotherapy of borderline personality disorder. In J. F. Clarkin, P. Fonagy, G. O. Gabbard (Eds.), *Psychodynamic psychotherapy for personality disorders: A clinical handbook.* Arlington, VA: American Psychiatric Publishing, Inc.

Gabbe, P. T., Reno, R., Clutter, C., Schottke, T. F., Price, T., Calhoun, K., . . . Lynch, C. D. (2017). Improving maternal and infant child health outcomes with community-based pregnancy support groups: Outcomes from Moms2B Ohio. *Maternal and Child Health, 21*(5), 1130–1138.

Gabriel, C., & Waller, G. (2014). Personality disorder cognitions in the eating disorders. *Journal of Nervous and Mental Disease, 202*(2), 172–176.

Gadalla, T. M. (2009). Eating disorders in men: A community-based study. *International Journal of Men's Health, 8*(1), 72–81.

Gado, M. (2008). The insanity defense: Twinkies as a defense. *trutv.com.* Retrieved from http://www.trutv.com/library/crime/criminal_mind/psychology/insanity.

Gagnon, C. M., Stanos, S. P., van der Ende, G., Rader, L. R., & Harden, R. N. (2013). Treatment outcomes for workers compensation patients in a U.S.-based interdisciplinary pain management program. *Pain Practice, 13*(4), 282–288.

Gainsbury, S. M. (2016, December 15). Cultural competence in the treatment of addictions: Theory, practice and evidence. *Clinical Psychology & Psychotherapy.* [Epub ahead of print]

Galán, C. A., Choe, D. E., Forbes, E. E., & Shaw, D. S. (2018). Interactions between empathy and resting heart rate in early adolescence predict violent behavior in late adolescence and early adulthood. *Journal of Child Psychology and Psychiatry.* [Manuscript in press]

Galderisi, S., Vignapiano, A., Mucci, A., & Boutros, N. N. (2014). Physiological correlates of positive symptoms in schizophrenia. *Current Topics in Behavioral Neurosciences, 21,* 103–128.

Gale, L., Channon, S., Larner, M., & James, D. (2016). Experiences of using pro-eating disorder websites: A qualitative study with service users in NHS eating disorder services. *Eating and Weight Disorders, 21*(3), 427–434.

Galea, S., Ahern, J., Resnick, H., Kilpatrick, D., Bucuvalas, M., Gold, J., & Vlahov, D. (2007). Psychological sequelae of the September 11 terrorist attacks in New York City. In B. Trappler (Ed.), *Modern terrorism and psychological trauma* (pp. 14–24). New York: Gordian Knot Books/Richard Altschulerr & Associates.

Galling, B., Garvia, M. A., Osuchukwu, U., Hagi, K., & Correll, C. U. (2015). Safety and tolerability of antipsychotic-mood stabilizer co-treatment in the management of acute bipolar disorder: Results from a systematic review and exploratory meta-analysis. *Expert Opinion on Drug Safety, 14*(8), 1181–1199.

Gallo, L. C., Penedo, F. J., de los Monteros, K. E., & Arguelles, W. (2009). Resiliency in the face of disadvantage: Do Hispanic cultural characteristics protect health outcomes? *Journal of Personality, 77*(6), 1707–1746.

Gallup Poll. (2005). Three in four Americans believe in paranormal. *Gallup News Service.* http://www.gallup.com/poll/16915/three-four-americans-believe-paranormal.aspx.

Gallup Poll. (2013). Most Americans practice charitable giving, volunteerism. Retrieved from Gallup website: http://www.gallup.com/poll/166250.

Gallup Poll. (2015, May 18). *In U.S., more say animals should have same rights as people.* Retrieved from Gallup website: http://www.gallup.com/poll/183275.

Gallup Poll. (2015, July 9). *Most U.S. smartphone owners check phone at least hourly.* Retrieved from http://www.gallup.com/poll/184046/smartphone-owners-check-phone-least-hourly.

Gallup Poll. (2015, September 18). Trust in U.S. judicial branch sinks to new low of 53%. *Gallup News.* Retrieved from http://www.gallup.com/poll/185528.

Gallup Poll. (2016, December 7-11). Honesty/ethics in professions. *Gallup News.* Retrieved from http://www.gallup.com/poll/1654.

Gallup Poll. (2017, June 12). Majority of Americans remain supportive of euthanasia. *Gallup.* Retrieved from http://www.gallup.com/poll/211928.

Galvez, J. F., Thommi, S., & Ghaemi, S. N. (2011). Positive aspects of mental illness: A review in bipolar disorder. *Journal of Affective Disorders, 28*(3), 185–190.

Gamble, A. L., Harvey, A. G., & Rapee, R. M. (2010). Specific phobia. In D. J. Stein, E. Hollander, & B. O. Rothbaum (Eds.), *Textbook of anxiety disorders* (2nd ed., pp. 525–541). Arlington, VA: American Psychiatric Publishing.

Gamboa, C. (2017, February 4). Women face unique challenges in overcoming opioid dependence. *Drug Addiction Now.* Retrieved from https://www.drugaddictionnow.com.

Gamwell, L., & Tomes, N. (1995). *Madness in America: Cultural and medical perceptions of mental illness before 1914.* Ithaca, NY: Cornell University Press.

Gander, F., Proyer, R. T., & Ruch, W. (2016). Positive psychology interventions addressing pleasure, engagement, meaning, positive relationships, and accomplishment increase well-being and ameliorate depressive symptoms: A randomized, placebo-controlled online study. *Frontiers in Pediatrics, 7,* 686.

Gandhi, T., & Prabhu, M. (2017). Jury instructions on the consequences of an insanity verdict. *Journal of the American Academy of Psychiatry and the Law, 45*(1), 121–122.

Gao, K., Kemp, D. E., Wang, Z., Ganocy, S. J., Conroy, C., Serrano, M. B., . . . Calabrese, J. R. (2010). Predictors of nonstabilization during the combination therapy of lithium and divalproex in rapid cycling bipolar disorder: A post-hoc analysis of two studies. *Psychopharmacology Bulletin, 43*(1), 23–38.

Gao, S., Guo, F., Sun, X., Zhang, N., Gong, Y., & Xu, L. (2017). The inhibitory effects of Nesfatin-1 in ventromedial hypothalamus on gastric function and its regulation by nucleus accumbens. *Frontiers in Physiology, 7,* 634.

Gao, T., Li, J., Zhang, H., Gao, J., Kong, Y., Hu, Y., & Mei, S. (2018). The influence of alexithymia on mobile phone addiction: The role of depression, anxiety and stress. *Journal of Affective Disorders, 225,* 761–766.

Garb, H. N. (2006). The conjunction effect and clinical judgment. *Journal of Social and Clinical Psychology, 25*(9), 1048–1056.

Garb, H. N. (2010). Clinical judgment and the influence of screening on decision making. In A. J. Mitchell & J. C. Coyne (Eds.), *Screening for depression in clinical practice: An evidence-based guide* (pp. 113–121). New York: Oxford University Press.

Garbacz, L., & Butz, C. (2016). Using a brief biofeedback treatment model for headache pain. *Journal of Pain, 17*(4S), S100.

Garber, K. (2008). Who's behind the bible of mental illness. *U.S. News & World Report,* December 31, 2007/ January 7, 2008, 25.

Garcia, J. R., Gesselman, A. N., Siliman, S. A., Perry, B. L., Coe, K., & Fisher, H. E. (2016, July 29). Sexting among singles in the USA: Prevalence of sending, receiving, and sharing sexual messages and images. *Sex Health.* [Epub ahead of print]

Garner, D. M. (1997). The 1997 body image survey results. *Psychology Today, 30*(1), 30–44.

Garner, D. M. (2005). *Eating Disorder Inventory TM-3 (EDI TM-3).* Lutz, Florida: Psychological Assessment Resources.

Garner, D. M., Garfinkel, P. E., Schwartz, D., & Thompson, M. (1980). Cultural expectations of thinness in women. *Psychological Reports, 47,* 483–491.

Garner, D. M., Olmsted, M. P., & Polivy, J. (1984). *The EDI.* Odessa, FL: Psychological Assessment Resources.

Garner, D. M., Olmsted, M. P., & Polivy, J. (1991). *The EDI-2.* Odessa, FL: Psychological Assessment Resources.

Garner, D. M., Olmsted, M. P., & Polivy, J. (2004). *The EDI-3*. Odessa, FL: Psychological Assessment Resources.

Garofalo, C., & Wright, A. G. C. (2017). Alcohol abuse, personality disorders, and aggression: The quest for a common underlying mechanism. *Aggression and Violent Behavior, 34*, 1–8.

Gaspersz, R., Lamers, F., Kent, J. M., Beekman, A. T., Smit, J. H., Van Hemert, A.M., . . . Penninx, B. W. (2016, March 29). Longitudinal predictive validity of the DSM-5 anxious distress specifier for clinical outcomes in a large cohort of patients with major depressive disorder. *Journal of Clinical Psychiatry*. [Epub ahead of print]

Gaudiano, B. A. (2013, September 29). Psychotherapy's image problem. *New York Times*.

Gaudiano, B. A., Davis, C. H., Epstein-Lubow, G., Johnson, J. E., Mueser, K. T., & Miller, I. W. (2017). Acceptance and commitment therapy for inpatients with psychosis (the REACH Study): Protocol for treatment development and pilot testing. *Healthcare, 5*, 23.

Gavric, D., Moscovitch, D. A., Rowa, K., & McCabe, R. E. (2017). Post-event processing in social anxiety disorder: Examining the mediating roles of positive metacognitive beliefs and perceptions of performance. *Behaviour Research and Therapy, 91*, 1–12.

Gay, P. (1999, March 29). Psychoanalyst Sigmund Freud. *Time*, pp. 66–69.

Gay, P. (2006). *Freud: A life for our time*. New York: W. W. Norton.

GCBH (Global Council on Brain Health). (2017). *The brain and social connectedness: GCBH recommendations on social engagement and brain health*. Retrieved from www.GlobalCouncilOnBrainHealth.org.

Gebhard, P. H. (1965). Situational factors affecting human sexual behavior. In F. Beach (Ed.), *Sex and behavior*. New York: Wiley.

Geddes, J. R., & Miklowitz, D. J. (2013). Treatment of bipolar disorder. *Lancet, 381*(9878), 1672–1682.

Geddes, S. D., Assadzada, S., Lemelin, D., Sokolovski, A., Bergeron, R., Haj-Dahmane, S., & Beique, J. C. (2016). Target-specific modulations of the descending prefrontal cortex inputs to the dorsal raphe nucleus by cannabinoids. *Proceedings of the National Academy of Sciences USA, 113*(19), 5429–5434.

Geerlings, M. I., & Gerritsen, L. (2017). Late-life depression, Hippocampal volumes, and hypothalamic-pituitary-adrenal axis regulation: A systematic review and meta-analysis. *Biological Psychiatry, 82*, 339–350.

Gehricke, J.-G., Kruggel, F., Thampipop, T., Alejo, S. D., Tatos, E., Fallon, J., & Muftuler, L. T. (2017). The brain anatomy of attention-deficit/hyperactivity disorder in young adults: a magnetic resonance imaging study. *PLoS One, 12*(4), e0175433.

Geison, G. (2008). Louis Pasteur. *Encyclopedia.com*. Retrieved from http://www.encyclopedia.com.

Gelfand, D. M., Jenson, W. R., & Drew, C. J. (1982). *Understanding child behavior disorders*. New York: Holt, Rinehart & Winston.

Gellatly, J., Pedley, R., Molloy, C., Butler, J., Lovell, K., & Bee, P. (2017). Low intensity interventions for obsessive-compulsive disorder (OCD): A qualitative study of mental health practitioner experiences. *BMC Psychiatry, 17*(1), 77.

Gentile, J. P., Dillon, K. S., & Gillig, P. M. (2013). Psychotherapy and pharmacotherapy for patients with dissociative identity disorder. *Innovations in Clinical Neuroscience, 10*(2), 22–29.

Gentile, J. P., Snyder, M., & Marie Gillig, P. (2014). Stress and trauma: Psychotherapy and pharmacotherapy for depersonalization/derealization disorder. *Innovations in Clinical Neuroscience, 11*(7–8), 37–41.

Gentile, S., & Fusco, M. L. (2017). Untreated perinatal paternal depression: Effects on offspring. *Psychiatry Research, 252*, 325–332.

Geoffreys, C. (2015). *Paranoid personality disorder: The ultimate guide to symptoms, treatment, and prevention (personality disorders)*. CreateSpace Independent Publishing Platform.

Gerardi, M., Rothbaum, B. O., Astin, M. C., & Kelley, M. (2010). Cortisol response following exposure treatment for PTSD in rape victims. *Journal of Aggression, Maltreatment and Trauma, 19*(4), 349–356.

Gerez, M., Suárez, E., Serrano, C., Castanedo, L., & Tello, A. (2016). The crossroads of anxiety: Distinct neurophysiological maps for different symptomatic groups. *Neuropsychiatric Disease and Treatment, 12*, 159–175.

Geriatric Mental Health Foundation. (2013, October 7). Causes and risk factors for senior mental illness. Retrieved from http://www.aplaceformom.com/blog.

Gernsbacher, L. M. (1985). *The suicide syndrome*. New York: Human Sciences Press.

Gerring, J. (2017). *Case study research: Principles and practices (strategies for social inquiry)* (2nd ed.). New York: Cambridge University Press.

Gesi, C., Carmassi, C., Shear, K. M., Schwartz, T., Ghesquiere, A., Khaler, J., & Dell'Osso, L. (2017). Adult separation anxiety disorder in complicated grief: An exploratory study on frequency and correlates. *Comprehensive Psychiatry, 72*, 6–12.

Ghafoori, B., Barragan, B., Tohidian, N., & Palinkas, L. (2013). Racial and ethnic differences in symptom severity of PTSD, GAD, and depression in trauma-exposed, urban, treatment-seeking adults. *Journal of Traumatic Stress, 25*(1), 106–110.

Gheorghiu, V. A., & Orleanu, P. (1982). Dental implant under hypnosis. *American Journal of Clinical Hypnosis, 25*(1), 68–70.

Giami, A. (2015). Between DSM and ICS: Paraphilias and the transformation of sexual norms. *Archives of Sexual Behavior, 44*(5), 1127–1138.

Giesbrecht, T., & Merckelbach, H. (2009). Betrayal trauma theory of dissociative experiences: Stroop and directed forgetting findings. *American Journal of Psychology, 122*(3), 337–340.

Gifford, M., Friedman, S., & Majerus, R. (2010). *Alcoholism*. Santa Barbara, CA: Greenwood Press/ABC-CLIO.

Gilbert, D. T., King, G., Pettigrew, S., & Wilson, T. D. (2016). Comment on "Estimating the reproducibility of psychological science." *Science, 351*(6277), 1037.

Gilbert, K. L., Quinn, S. C., Ford, A. F., & Thomas, S. B. (2011). The urban context: A place to eliminate health disparities and build organizational capacity. *Journal of Prevention & Intervention in the Community, 39*(1), 77–92.

Gilbert, S. (2011). Eating disorders in women of African descent. In J. Alexander & J. Treasure (Eds.), *A collaborative approach to eating disorders* (pp. 249–261). New York: Taylor & Francis.

Gilbert, S. C., Keery, H., & Thompson, J. K. (2005). The media's role in body image and eating disorders. In J. H. Daniel & E. Cole (Eds.), *Featuring females: Feminist analyses of media* (pp. 41–56). Washington, DC: American Psychological Association.

Gill, A. D. (1982). Vulnerability to suicide. In E. L. Bassuk, S. C. Schoonover, & A. D. Gill (Eds.), *Lifelines: Clinical perspectives on suicide*. New York: Plenum Press.

Gill, D., & Warburton, W. (2014). An investigation of the biosocial model of borderline personality disorder. *Journal of Clinical Psychology, 70*(9), 866–873.

Gillam, R. B., & Petersen, D. B. (2011). Language disorders in school-age children. In R. B. Gillam, T. P. Marquardt, & F. N. Martin (Eds.), *Communication sciences and disorders: From science to clinical practice* (2nd ed., pp. 245–270). Boston, MA: Jones and Bartlett Publishers.

Gilman, S. E. (2013). Commentary: The causal and nosological status of loss in major depression. *Epidemiology, 24*(4), 616–618.

Ginn, N. C., Clionsky, L. N., Eyberg, S. M., Warner-Metzger, C., & Abner, J. P. (2017). Child-Directed Interaction Training for young children with autism spectrum disorders: Parent and child outcomes. *Journal of Clinical Child and Adolescent Psychology, 46*, 101–109.

Giraldi, A., Rellini, A. H., Pfaus, J., & Laan, E. (2013). Female sexual arousal disorders. *Journal of Sexual Medicine, 10*, 58–73.

Girón, M., Nova-Fernández, F., Mañá-Alvarenga, S., Nolasco, A., Molina-Habas, A., Fernández-Yañez, A., . . . Gómez-Beneyto, M. (2015). How does family intervention improve the outcome of people with schizophrenia? *Social Psychiatry and Psychiatric Epidemiology, 50*(3), 379–387.

Giuntella, O. (2016). The Hispanic health paradox: New evidence from longitudinal data on second and third-generation birth outcomes. *Science Direct, 2*, 84–89.

Glauberman, N. (2014, January 29). On losing it (or not). *New York Times*.

Glenn, A. L., Han, H., Yang, Y., Raine, A., & Schug, R. A. (2017). Associations between psychopathic traits and brain activity during instructed false responding. *Psychiatry Research, 266*, 123–137.

Glenn, A. L., Remmel, R. J., Raine, A., Schug, R. A., Gao, Y., & Granger, D. A. (2015). Alpha-amylase reactivity in relation to psychopathic traits in adults. *Psychoneuroendocrinology, 54*, 14–23.

Glenn, J. J., Werntz, A. J., Slama, S. J., Steinman, S. A., Teachman, B. A., & Nock, M. K. (2017). Suicide and self-injury-related implicit cognition: A large-scale examination and replication. *Journal of Abnormal Psychology, 126*(2), 199–211.

Glina, S., Sharlip, I. D., & Hellstrom, W. J. G. (2013). Modifying risk factors to prevent and treat erectile dysfunction. *Journal of Sexual Medicine, 10*, 115–119.

Gloster, A. T., Klotsche, J., Gerlach, A. L., Hamm, A., Ströhle, A., Gauggel, S., . . . Wittchen, H. (2014). Timing matters: Change depends on the stage of treatment in cognitive behavioral therapy for panic disorder with agoraphobia. *Journal of Consulting and Clinical Psychology, 82*(1), 141–153.

Gloster, A. T., Sonntag, R., Hoyer, J., Meyer, A. H., Heinze, S., Ströhle, A., . . . Wittchen, H-U. (2015). Treating treatment-resistant patients with panic disorder and agoraphobia using psychotherapy: A randomized controlled switching trial. *Psychotherapy and Psychosomatics, 84*(2), 100–109.

Gloster, A. T., Wittchen, H-U., Einsle, F., Lang, T., Helbig-Lang, S., Fydrich, T., . . . Arolt, V. (2011). Psychological treatment for panic disorder with agoraphobia: A randomized controlled trial to examine the role of therapist-guided exposure in situ in CBT. *Journal of Consulting and Clinical Psychology, 79*(3), 406–420.

Glover, N. G., Crego, C., & Widiger, T. A. (2011). The clinical utility of the five factor model of personality disorder. *Personality Disorders, 3*(2), 176–184.

Glovin, D. (2014, September 9). Baseball caught looking as fouls injure 17,500 fans a year. *Bloomberg.*

Godlewska, B. R., Pike, A., Sharpley, A. L., Ayton, A., Park, R. J., Cowen, P. J., & Emir, U. E. (2017). Brain glutamate in anorexia nervosa: A magnetic resonance spectroscopy case control study at 7 Tesla. *Psychopharmacology, 234*(3), 421–426.

Goetz, K., Kleine-Budde, K., Bramesfeld, A., & Stegbauer, C. (2018). Working atmosphere, job satisfaction and individual characteristics of community mental health professionals in integrated care. *Health & Social Care in the Community.* [Manuscript in press]

Goff, P., Farnsley, A. E., II, & Thuesen, P. J. (2014, March 6). *The Bible in American life.* Indianapolis: Center for the Study of Religion and American Culture, Indiana University-Purdue University.

Goggin, M. M., Nguyen, A., & Janis, G. C. (2017). Identification of unique metabolites of the designer opioid furanyl fentanyl. *Journal of Analytical Toxicology, 41*(5), 367–375.

Gola, H., Engler, H., Schauer, M., Adenauer, H., Riether, C., Kolassa, S., . . . Kolassa, I. (2012). Victims of rape show increased cortisol responses to trauma reminders: A study in individuals with war- and torture-related PTSD. *Psychoneuroendocrinology, 37*(2), 213–220.

Golbeck, J. (2016, August 5). Social anxiety and Internet use: What we know. *Psychology Today.*

Gold, M. (2016). Children of alcoholics. *Psych Central.* Retrieved from https://psychcentral.com.

Gold, S. N., & Castillo, Y. (2010). Dealing with defenses and defensiveness in interviews. In D. L. Segal & M. Hersen (Eds.), *Diagnostic interviewing* (pp. 89–102). New York: Springer Publishing.

Goldenberg, I., Stanton, M., & Goldenberg, H. (2016). *Family therapy: An overview* (9th ed.). Belmont, CA: Brooks Cole.

Goldstein, D. M., & Hall, K. (2015). Mass hysteria in Le Roy, New York: How brain experts materialized truth and outscienced environmental inquiry. *Journal of the American Ethnological Society, 42*(4), 640–657.

Goldstein, I. (2014). Unfair: Government-approved sexual medicine treatments only available for men. *Journal of Sexual Medicine, 11,* 317–320.

Goldston, D. B., Molock, S. D., Whitbeck, L. B., Murakami, J. L., Zayas, L. H., & Hall, G. C. N. (2008). Cultural considerations in adolescent suicide prevention and psychosocial treatment. *American Psychologist, 63*(1), 14–31.

Golland, J. (2016, July 20). Psychoanalysis is scientific. *Division Review.* Retrieved from https://divisionreview.com/uncategorized/psychoanalysis-is-scientific

Goltseker, K., Bolotin, L., & Barak, S. (2017). Counterconditioning during reconsolidation prevents relapse of cocaine memories. *Neuropsychopharmacology, 42,* 716–726.

Gomez, M. M. (2016, March 30). *Jury trials outside in* (Kindle edition). LexisNexis.

Gómez-Gil, E., Esteva, I., Almaraz, M. C., Pasaro, E., Segovia, S., & Guillamon, A. (2010). Familiarity of gender identity disorder in non-twin siblings. *Archives of Sexual Behavior, 39*(2), 546–552.

Gomila, I., López-Corominas, V., Pellegrini, M., Quesada, L., Miravet, E., Pichini, S., & Barceló, B. (2016, September). Alimemazine poisoning as evidence of Munchausen syndrome by proxy: A pediatric case report. *Forensic Science International, 266,* e18–22.

Gondré-Lewis, M. C., Warnock, K. T., Wang, H., June, H. L., Jr., Bell, K. A., Rabe, H., . . . June, H. L., Sr. (2016). Early life stress is a risk factor for excessive alcohol drinking and impulsivity in adults and is mediated via a CRF/GABA(A) mechanism. *Stress, 19*(2), 235–247.

Gonidakis, F., Kravvariti, V., & Varsou, E. (2015). Sexual function of women suffering from anorexia nervosa and bulimia nervosa. *Journal of Sex and Marital Therapy, 41*(4), 368–378.

González, H. M., Tarraf, W., Whitfield, K. E., & Vega, W. A. (2010). The epidemiology of major depression and ethnicity in the United States. *Journal of Psychiatric Research, 44,* 1043–1051.

Goodman, G., Edwards, K., & Chung, H. (2014). Interaction structures formed in the psychodynamic therapy of five patients with borderline personality disorder in crisis. *Psychology and Psychotherapy, 87*(1), 15–31.

Goodman, M. (2013). Patient highlights: Female genital plastic/cosmetic surgery. *Journal of Sexual Medicine, 10*(8), 2125–2126.

Goodman, W. K. (2016, May 17). What causes obsessive-compulsive disorder (OCD)? *Psychcentral.com.* Retrieved from https://psychcentral.com.

Goodnough, A., & Atkinson, S. (2016). A potent side effect to the Flint water crisis: Mental health problems. *The New York Times,* April 30, 2016.

Goodwin, R., Kaniasty, K., Sun, S., & Ben-Ezra, M. (2017). Psychological distress and prejudice following terror attacks in France. *Journal of Psychiatric Research, 16*(91), 111–115.

Gordon, O. M., Salkovskis, P. M., & Bream, V. (2016). The impact of obsessive compulsive personality disorder on cognitive behaviour therapy for obsessive compulsive disorder. *Behavioural and Cognitive Psychotherapy, 44*(4), 444–459.

Gore, W. L., & Widiger, T. A. (2015). Assessment of dependency by the FFDI: Comparisons to the PID-5 and maladaptive agreeableness. *Personality and Mental Health, 9*(4), 258–276.

Gore, W. L., & Widiger, T. A. (2016). Fluctuation between grandiose and vulnerable narcissism. *Personality Disorders, 7*(4), 363–371.

Gorelick, D. A. (2016, December 9). Cannabis use and disorder: Clinical manifestations, course, assessment, and diagnosis. *UpToDate.* Retrieved from http://www.uptodate.com.

Gorelick, D. A. (2016, October 28). Cannabis use and disorder: Epidemiology, comorbidity, health consequences, and medico-legal status. *UpToDate.* Retrieved from http://www.uptodate.com.

Gorelick, D. A. (2016, October 28). Cannabis use and disorder: Pathogenesis and pharmacology. *UpToDate.* Retrieved from http://www.uptodate.com.

Gorelick, D. A. (2017, February 10). Cocaine use disorder in adults: Epidemiology, pharmacology, clinical manifestations, medical consequences, and diagnosis. *UpToDate.* Retrieved from http://www.uptodate.com.

Gorenstein, D. (2013, May 17). How much is the DSM-5 worth? *Marketplace.org.*

Gorlin, E. I., Dalrymple, K., Chelminski, I., & Zimmerman, M. (2016). Reliability and validity of a semi-structured DSM-based diagnostic interview module for the assessment of Attention Deficit Hyperactivity Disorder in adult psychiatric outpatients. *Psychiatry Research, 242,* 46–53.

Goshen, C. E. (1967). *Documentary history of psychiatry: A source book on historical principles.* New York: Philosophy Library.

Gosling, S. D., Sandy, C. J., & Potter, J. (2015, April 28). Personalities of self-identified "dog people" and "cat people." *Anthrozoös, 23*(3), 213–222.

Gosling, S. D., Vazire, S., Srivastava, S., & John, O. P. (2004, February–March). Should we trust web-based studies? A comparative analysis of six preconceptions about Internet questionnaires. *American Psychologist, 59*(2), 93–104.

Gottesman, I. I. (1991). *Schizophrenia genesis.* New York: Freeman.

Gottesman, I. I., & Reilly, J. L. (2003). Strengthening the evidence for genetic factors in schizophrenia (without abetting genetic discrimination). In M. F. Lenzenweger & J. M. Hooley (Eds.), *Principles of experimental psychopathology: Essays in honor of Brendan A. Maher* (pp. 31–44). Washington, DC: American Psychological Association.

Gottschalk, M. G., Leussis, M. P., Ruland, T., Gjeluci, K., Petryshen, T. L., & Bahn, S. (2017). Lithium reverses behavioral and axonal transport-related changes associated with ANK3 bipolar disorder gene disruption. *European Neuropsychopharmacology, 27*(3), 274–288.

Gouin, J-P, Glaser, R., Loving, T. J., Malarkey, W. B., Stowell, J., Houts, C., & Kiecolt-Glaser, J. K. (2009). Attachment avoidance predicts inflammatory responses to marital conflict. *Brain, Behavior, and Immunity, 23*(7), 898–904.

Gould, M. S., Kleinman, M. H., Lake, A. M., Forman, J., & Midle, J. B. (2014). Newspaper coverage of suicide and initiation of suicide clusters in teenagers in the USA, 1988–96: A retrospective, population-based case-control study. *Lancet Psychiatry, 1,* 34–43.

Gowensmith, W. N., Murrie, D. C., Boccaccini, M. T., & McNichols, B. J. (2017). Field reliability influences field validity: Risk assessment of individuals found not guilty by reason of insanity. *Psychological Assessment, 29*(6), 786–794.

Gowing, L., Ali, R., White, J. M., & Mbewe, D. (2017). Buprenorphine for managing opioid withdrawal. *Cochrane Database of Systematic Reviews, 2,* CD002025.

Gozlan, O. (2011). Transsexual surgery: A novel reminder and a navel remainder. *International Forum of Psychoanalysis, 20*(1), 45–52.

Grabowski, D. C., Aschbrenner, K. A., Rome, V. F., & Bartels, S. J. (2010). Quality of mental health care for nursing home residents: A literature review. *Medical Care Research and Review, 67*(7), 627–656.

Graham, J. R. (2006). *MMPI-2: Assessing personality and psychopathology* (4th ed.). New York: Oxford University Press.

Graham, J. R. (2014). *MMPI-2: Assessing personality and psychopathology.* New York: Oxford University Press.

Granholm, E., Holden, J., Link, P. C., & McQuaid, J. R. (2014). Randomized clinical trial of cognitive behavioral social skills training for schizophrenia: Improvement in functioning and experiential negative symptoms. *Journal of Consulting and Clinical Psychology.* [Manuscript submitted for publication]

Granitz, P. (2014, January 12). Four years after earthquake, many in Haiti remain displaced. *NPR.*

Granot, M., Zisman-Ilani, Y., Ram, E., Goldstick, O., & Yovell, Y. (2011). Characteristics of attachment style in women with dyspareunia. *Journal of Sex & Marital Therapy, 37*(1), 1–16.

Grant, B. F., Stinson, F. S., Dawson, D. A., Chou, S. P., Ruan, W. J., & Pickering, R. P. (2004). Co-occurrence of 12-month alcohol and drug use disorders and personality disorders in the United States: Results from the National Epidemiologic Survey on Alcohol and Related Conditions. *Archives of General Psychiatry, 61*(4), 361.

Grant, J. E., Odlaug, B. L., Chamberlain, S. R., Keuthen, N. J., Lochner, C., & Stein, D. (2012). Skin picking disorder. *The American Journal of Psychiatry, 169*(11), 1143–1149.

Grant, J. E., Redden, S. A., Leppink, E. W., & Chamberlain, S. R. (2017). Trichotillomania and co-occurring anxiety. *Comprehensive Psychiatry, 72,* 1–5.

Grant, J. E., Redden, S. A., Leppink, E. W., & Odlaug, B. L. (2015). Skin picking disorder with co-occurring body dysmorphic disorder. *Body Image, 15,* 44–48.

Gray, H. (1959). *Anatomy of the human body* (27th ed.). Philadelphia: Lea & Febiger.

Gray, J. A., & McNaughton, N. (1996). The neuropsychology of anxiety: Reprise. In D. A. Hope (Ed.), *The Nebraska symposium on motivation* (Vol. 43). Lincoln: University of Nebraska Press.

Gray, K. (2017, June 1). Here's why millennials are so dedicated to practicing mindfulness. *Brit+Co.* Retrieved from https://www.brit.co.

Gray, N. A., Zhou, R., Du, J., Moore, G. J., & Manji, H. K. (2003). The use of mood stabilizers as plasticity enhancers in the treatment of neuropsychiatric disorders. *Journal of Clinical Psychiatry, 64*(Suppl. 5), 3–17.

Grayson, J. (2014). *Freedom from obsessive-compulsive disorder.* (Updated ed.). Berkley, MI: Berkley Trade.

Graziano, P. A., & Garcia, A. (2016). Attention-deficit hyperactivity disorder and children's emotion dysregulation: A meta-analysis. *Clinical Psychology Review, 46,* 106–123.

Green, E. (2016, June 22). Sleeping pills – Do the benefits outweigh the risks? *No Sleepless Nights.* Retrieved from http://www.nosleeplessnights.com

Green, S. A. (1985). *Mind and body: The psychology of physical illness.* Washington, DC: American Psychiatric Press.

Greenberg, D. B. (2016, January 27). Somatization, epidemiology, pathogenesis, clinical features, medical evaluation, and diagnosis. *UpToDate.* Retrieved from www.uptodate.com.

Greenberg, D. B. (2016, November 15). Somatization: Treatment and prognosis. *UpToDate.* Retrieved from www.uptodate.com.

Greenberg, G. (2011, December 27). Inside the battle to define mental illness. *Wired Magazine.*

Greene, E., & Heilbrun, K. (2013). *Wrightman's psychology and the legal system* (8th ed.). Stanford, CT: Wadsworth Publishing.

Greene, K. M., & Maggs, J. L. (2017). Academic time during college: Associations with mood, tiredness, and binge drinking across days and semesters. *Journal of Adolescence, 56,* 24–33.

Greenfield, S. F., Back, S. E., Lawson, K., & Brady, K. T. (2011). Women and addiction. In J. H. Lowinson & P. Ruiz (Eds.), *Substance abuse: A comprehensive textbook* (5th ed.). Philadelphia, PA: Lippincott, Williams, & Wilkins.

Greening, L., Stoppelbein, L., Fite, P., Dhossche, D., Erath, S., Brown, J., Cramer, R., & Young, L. (2008). Pathways to suicidal behaviors in childhood. *Suicide and Life-Threatening Behavior, 38*(1), 35–45.

Greer, S., Kramer, M. R., Cook-Smith, J. N., & Casper, M. L. (2014). Metropolitan racial residential segregation and cardiovascular mortality: Exploring pathways. *Journal of Urban Health, 91*(3), 499–509.

Greger, H. K., Myhre, A. K., Lydersen, S., & Jozefiak, T. (2016, May 10). Child maltreatment and quality of life: A study of adolescents in residential care. *Health and Quality of Life Outcomes, 14:* 74.

Gregory, B., & Peters, L. (2017). Changes in the self during cognitive behavioural therapy for social anxiety disorder: A systematic review. *Clinical Psychology Review, 52,* 1–18.

Gressier, F., Letranchant, A., & Hardy, P. (2015). Post-partum psychosis. *La Revue Du Praticien, 65*(2), 232–234. [Article in French]

Griebel, G., & Holmes, A. (2013). 50 years of hurdles and hope in anxiolytic drug discovery. *Nature Reviews. Drug Discovery, 12*(9), 667–687.

Griffin, R. M. (2014). E-cigarettes 101. *Web*MD. Retrieved from http://www/webmd/com/smoking-cessation.

Griffiths, F., Dobermann, T., Cave, J. A. K., Thorogood, M., Johnson, S., Salamatian, K., . . . Goudge, J. (2015). The impact of online social networks on health and health systems: A scoping review and case studies. *Policy & Internet, 7*(4), 473–496.

Griffiths, S., Murray, S. B., Bentley, C., Gratwick-Sarll, K., Harrison, C., & Mond, J. M. (2017). Sex differences in quality of life impairment association with body dissatisfaction in adolescents. *Journal of Adolescent Health, 61*(1), 77–82.

Grigg, J. R. (1988). Imitative suicides in an active duty military population. *Military Medicine, 153*(2), 79–81.

Grigorenko, E. L., Bick, J., Campbell, D. J., Lewine, G., Abrams, J., Nguyen, V., & Chang, J. T. (2016). The trilogy of GXE: Conceptualization, operationalization, and application. In D. Cicchetti (Ed.), *Developmental psychopathology, Vol. 4: Developmental neuroscience* (3rd ed.). New York: Wiley.

Grilo, C. M., Masheb, R. M., Brody, M., Toth, C., Burke-Martindale, C. H., & Rothschild, B. S. (2005). Childhood maltreatment in extremely obese male and female bariatric surgery candidates. *Obesity Research, 13,* 123–130.

Grilo, C. M., Masheb, R. M., White, M. A., Gueorguieva, R., Barnes, R. D., Walsh, B. T., . . . Garcia, R. (2014). Treatment of binge eating disorder in racially and ethnically diverse obese patients in primary care: Randomized placebo-controlled clinical trial of self-help and medication. *Behaviour Research and Therapy, 58,* 1–9.

Grimm, D. (2013). Animal rights. Lawsuits seek 'personhood' for chimpanzees. *Science, 342*(6163), 1154–1155.

Grob, G. N. (1966). *The state and the mentally ill: A history of Worcester State Hospital in Massachusetts, 1830–1920.* Chapel Hill: University of North Carolina Press.

Grof, P. (2010). Sixty years of lithium responders. *Neuropsychobiology, 62*(1), 8–16.

Grohol, J. (2016). Treatment of phobias. *Psych Central.* Retrieved from http://psychcentral.com/disorders/treatment-of-phobias/.

Grohol, J. M. (2015). *6 surprising, bizarre facts you didn't know about Freud.* Retrieved from http://psychcentral.com/blog/archives/2015/07/09.

Groopman, J. (2017, January 9). The voices in our heads. *The New Yorker.*

Grossman, L. A. (2013). The origins of American health libertarianism. *Yale Journal of Health Policy, Law, and Ethics, 13*(1), 76–134.

Grossman, R. (2004). Pharmacotherapy of personality disorders. In J. J. Magnavita (Ed.), *Handbook of personality disorders: Theory and practice.* Hoboken, NJ: Wiley.

Groth-Marnat, G., & Wright, A. J. (2016). *Handbook of psychological assessment* (6th ed.). Hoboken, NJ: Wiley.

Grover, S., Chakrabarti, S., Ghormode, D., Agarwal, M., Sharma, A., & Avasthi, A. (2015). Catatonia in inpatients with psychiatric disorders: A comparison of schizophrenia and mood disorders. *Psychiatry Research, 229*(3), 919–925.

Grubbs, J. B., Hook, J. P., Griffin, B. J., Cushman, M. S., Hook, J. N., & Penberthy, J. K. (2017). Treating hypersexuality. In Z. D. Peterson (Ed.), *The Wiley-Blackwell handbook of sex therapy* (Chap. 8, pp. 115–128). Hoboken, NJ: Wiley-Blackwell.

Grubin, D. (2010). Polygraphy. In J. M. Brown & E. A. Campbell (Eds.), *The Cambridge handbook of forensic psychology* (pp. 276–282). New York: Cambridge University Press.

Gruebner, O., Rapp, M. A., Adli, M., Kluge, U., Galea, S., & Heinz, A. (2017). Cities and mental health. *Deutsches Ärzteblatt, 114*(8), 121–127.

Gruenewald, P. J., Treno, A. J., Holder, H. D., & LaScala, E. A. (2016) 18 Community-based approaches to the prevention of substance use-related problems. In K. J. Sher (Ed.). *Oxford handbook of substance use and substance use disorders* (Vol. 1, Chap. 18, pp. 600–624). New York: Oxford University Press.

Gruttadaro, D. (2005). Federal leaders call on schools to help. *NAMI Advocate, 3*(1), 7.

GSS (General Social Survey). (2016). General social survey. *NORC at the University of Chicago.*

Guarnieri, P. (2009). Towards a history of the family care of psychiatric patients. *Epidemiologia e Psichiatria Sociale, 18*(1), 34–39.

Gudin, J. A., Mogali, S., Jones, J. D., & Comer, S. D. (2016, March 8). The risks of combining opioids, benzodiazepines, and alcohol. *The Pain Practitioner.*

Guffanti, G., Gameroff, M., Warner, V., Talati, A., Glatt, C. E., Wickramaratne, P., & Weissman, M. M. (2016). Heritability of major depressive and comorbid anxiety disorders in multi-generational families at high risk for depression. *American Journal of Medical Genetics, 171B,* 1072–1079.

Guillamon, A. (2016). Quote cited in Russo, F. (2016, January 1). Is there something unique about the transgender brain? *Scientific American.*

Guillamon, A., Junque, C., & Gómez-Gil, E. (2016). A review of the status of brain structure research in transsexualism. *Archives of Sexual Behavior, 45,* 1615–1648.

Guina, J. (2016). The talking cure of avoidant personality disorder: Remission through earned-secure attachment. *American Journal of Psychotherapy, 70*(3), 233–250.

Guintivano, J., Arad, M., Gould, T. D., Payne, J. L., & Kaminsky, Z. A. (2014). Antenatal prediction of postpartum depression with blood DNA methylation biomarkers. *Molecular Psychiatry, 19*(5), 560–567.

Gulyaeva, N. V. (2017). Interplay between brain BDNF and glutamatergic systems: A brief state of the evidence and association with the pathogenesis of depression. *Biochemistry (Moscow), 82*(3), 301–307.

Gunderson, J. G. (2011). Borderline personality disorder. *New England Journal of Medicine, 364*(21), 2037–2042.

Gunnar, M. R., Frenn, K., Wewerka, S. S., & Van Ryzin, M. J. (2009). Moderate versus severe early life stress: Associations with stress reactivity and regulation in 10–12-year-old children. *Psychoneuroendocrinology, 34,* 62–75.

Gurak, K., & Weisman de Mamani, A. (2016). Risk and protective factors, perceptions of family environment, ethnicity, and schizophrenia symptoms. *Journal of Nervous and Mental Disease, 204*(8), 570–577.

Gurman, A. S., Lebow, J. L., & Snyder, D. K. (2015). *Clinical handbook of couple therapy* (5th ed.). New York: Guilford Press.

Gusovsky, D. (2016, April 27). Americans consume vast majority of the world's opioids. *CNBC.* Retrieved from http://www.cnbc.com

Guterman, J. T., Martin, C. V., & Rudes, J. (2011). A solution-focused approach to frotteurism. *Journal of Systemic Therapies, 30*(1), 59–72.

Gutman, D. A., & Nemeroff, C. B. (2011). Stress and depression. In R. J. Contrada & A. Baum (Eds.), *The handbook of stress science: Biology, psychology, and health* (pp. 345–357). New York: Springer Publishing.

Guttmacher Institute. (2017, July 1). *Insurance coverage of contraceptives.* New York: Guttmacher Institute.

Guttmacher Institute. (2017, July 6). *Insurance coverage of contraceptives.* Retrieved from https://www.guttmacher.org./state-policy.

Guttmacher Institute. (2017, September). *Adolescent sexual and reproductive health in the United States.* New York: Guttmacher Institute

Guynn, J. (2017, March 1). Facebook takes steps to stop suicides on Live. *USA Today.*

Gyani, A., Shafran, R., Rose, S., & Lee, M. J. (2015). A qualitative investigation of therapists' attitudes towards research: Horses for courses? *Behavioural and Cognitive Psychotherapy, 43*(4), 436–438.

Haagen, J. G., Smid, G. E., Knipscheer, J. W., & Kleber, R. J. (2015). The efficacy of recommended treatments for veterans with PTSD: A metaregression analysis. *Clinical Psychology Review, 40,* 184–194.

Haaken, J., & Reavey, P. (Eds.). (2010). *Memory matters: Contexts for understanding sexual abuse recollections.* New York: Routledge/Taylor & Francis Group.

Haas, M. H., Chance, S. A., Cram, D. F., Crow, T. J., Luc, A., & Hage, S. (2014). Evidence of pragmatic impairments in speech and proverb interpretation in schizophrenia. *Journal of Psycholinguistic Research.* [Manuscript submitted for publication]

Haberman, C. (2007). It's not the stress, it's how you deal with it. *New York Times, 156*(54), 109.

Hadar, R., Voget, M., Vengeliene, V., Haumesser, J. K., van Riesen, C., Avchalumov, Y., . . . Winter, C. (2017, January 1). Altered neural oscillations and elevated dopamine levels in the reward pathway during alcohol relapse. *Behavioural Brain Research, 316,* 131–135.

Haddock, G., & Spaulding, W. (2011). Psychological treatment of psychosis. In D. R. Weinberg & P. Harrison (Eds.), *Schizophrenia* (pp. 666–686). Hoboken, NJ: Wiley-Blackwell.

Hadland, S. E., & Baer, T. E. (2014). The racial and ethnic gap in substance use treatment: Implications for U.S. healthcare reform. *Journal of Adolescent Health, 54*(6), 627–628.

Häfner, H. (2015). What is schizophrenia? 25 years of research into schizophrenia—the Age Beginning Course Study. *World Journal of Psychiatry, 5*(2), 167–169.

Häfner, H., & an der Heiden, W. (1988). The mental health care system in transition: A study in organization, effectiveness, and costs of complementary care for schizophrenic patients. In C. N. Stefanis & A. D. Rabavilis (Eds.), *Schizophrenia: Recent biosocial developments.* New York: Human Sciences Press.

Hagen, R., Hjemdal, O., Solem, S., Kennair, L., Nordahl, H. M., Fisher, P., & Wells, A. (2017). Metacognitive therapy for depression in adults: A waiting list randomized controlled trial with six months follow-up. *Frontiers in Psychology, 8,* 1–10.

Haggerty, J. (2016). An overview of depression treatment options. *Psych Central.* Retrieved from https://psychcentral.com.

Haggerty, J. (2017). Treatment of ADHD in children. *Psych Central.* Retrieved from https://psychcentral.com.

Haghighatfard, A., Andalib, S., Amini Faskhodi, M., Sadeghi, S., Ghaderi, A. H., Moiradkhani, S., . . . Ghadimi, Z. (2018). Gene expression study of mitochondrial complex I in schizophrenia and paranoid personality disorder. *World Journal of Biological Psychiatry.* [Manuscript in press]

Hagihara, A., Abe, T., Omagari, M., Motoi, M., & Nabeshima, Y. (2014). The impact of newspaper reporting of hydrogen sulfide suicide on imitative suicide attempts in Japan. *Social Psychiatry and Psychiatric Epidemiology, 49*(2), 221–229.

Haile, C. N. (2012). History, use, and basic pharmacology of stimulants. In T. R. Kosten, T. F. Newton, De La Garza, R. II, & Haile, C. N. (Eds.), *Cocaine and methamphetamine dependence: Advances in treatment* (pp. 13–84). Arlington, VA: American Psychiatric Publishing.

Hales, S., Blackwell, S. E., Di Simplicio, M., Iyadurai, L., Young, K., & Holmes, E. A. (2015). Imagery-based cognitive-behavioral assessment. In G. P. Brown & D. A. Clark (Eds.), *Assessment in Cognitive Therapy (Internet)* (Chap. 4). New York: Guilford Press.

Haley, M., Golden, S. H., & Nate, R. D. (2016). Gestalt therapy. In D. Capuzzi & M. D. Stauffer, *Counseling and psychotherapy: Theories and interventions* (6th ed., pp. 195–226). Alexandria, VA: American Counseling Association.

Hall, G. C., Yip, T., & Zárate, M. A. (2016). On becoming multicultural in a monocultural research world: A conceptual approach to studying ethnocultural diversity. *American Psychologist, 71*(12), 40–51.

Hall, K. (2007). Sexual dysfunction and childhood sexual abuse: Gender differences and treatment implications. In S. R. Leiblum (Ed.), *Principles and practice of sex therapy* (4th ed., pp. 350–370). New York: Guilford Press.

Hall, K. (2010). The canary in the coal mine: Reviving sexual desire in long-term relationships. In S. R. Leiblum (Ed.), *Treating sexual desire disorders: A clinical casebook* (pp. 61–74). New York: Guilford Press.

Hall, K. (2017). Treating sexual problems in survivors of sexual trauma. In Z. D. Peterson (Ed.), *The Wiley-Blackwell handbook of sex therapy* (Chap. 24, pp. 389–406). Hoboken, NJ: Wiley-Blackwell.

Hall, L., & Cohn, L. (2010). *Bulimia: A guide to recovery.* Carlsbad, CA: Gurze Books.

Hallevy, D. (2016, November 4). *The matrix of insanity in modern criminal law.* New York: Springer Publishing.

Hallevy, G. (2017). The shadows of normality: Legal insanity under modern criminal law. In M. D. White (Ed.), *The insanity defense: Multidisciplinary views on its history, trends, and controversies* (Chap. 4, pp. 97–132). Westport, CT: Praeger.

Hall-Flavin, D. K. (2016). What does it mean to have a nervous breakdown? *Mayo Clinic, Mayo Foundation for Medical Education and Research.*

Hallgren, M., Vancampfort, D., & Stubbs, B. (2017). Exercise is medicine for depression: Even when the "pill" is small. *Neuropsychiatric Disease and Treatment, 12,* 2715–2721.

Hameed, M. A., & Lewis, A. J. (2016). Offspring of parents with schizophrenia: A systematic review of developmental features across childhood. *Harvard Review of Psychiatry, 24*(2), 104–117.

Hamilton, L. D., & Meston, C. M. (2013). Chronic stress and sexual function in women. *Journal of Sexual Medicine, 10,* 2443–2454.

Hamilton, S. S. (2016, November 16). Reading difficulty in children: Intervention. *UpToDate.* Retrieved from http://www.uptodate.com.

Hamilton, S. S. (2017, July 3). Reading difficulty in children: Normal reading development and etiology of reading difficulty. *UpToDate.* Retrieved from http://www.uptodate.com.

Hamilton, S. S. (2017, June 26). Developmental coordination disorder: Clinical features and diagnosis. *UpToDate.* Retrieved from http://www.uptodate.com.

Hammen, C. (2016). Depression and stressful environments: Identifying gaps in conceptualization and measurement. *Anxiety, Stress & Coping, 29*(4), 335–351.

Hammen, C. L., & Krantz, S. (1976). Effect of success and failure on depressive cognitions. *Journal of Abnormal Psychology, 85*(8), 577–588.

Hampel, P., Gemp, S., Mohr, B., Schulze, J., & Tlach, L. (2014). Long-term effects of a cognitive-behavioral intervention on pain coping among inpatient orthopedic rehabilitation of chronic low back pain and depressive symptoms. *Psychotherapie, Psychosomatik, Medizinische Psychologie, 64*(11), 439–447.

Han, S., Zong, X., Hu, M., Yu, Y., Wang, X., Long, Z., . . . Chen, H. (2018). Frequency-selective alteration in the resting-state corticostriatal-thalamo-cortical circuit correlates with symptoms severity in first-episode drug-naive patients with schizophrenia. *Schizophrenia Research.* [Manuscript in press]

Handel, R. W. (2016). An introduction to the Minnesota Multiphasic Personality Inventory-Adolescent-Restructured Form (MMPI-A-RF). *BMC Psychology, 23*(4), 361–373.

Hankin, B. L., Snyder, H. R., & Gulley, L. D. (2016). Cognitive risks in developmental psychopathology. In D. Cicchetti (Ed.), *Developmental psychopathology, Vol. 3: Maladaptation and psychopathology* (3rd ed.). New York: Wiley.

Hanna, D., Kershaw, K., & Chaplin, R. (2009) How specialist ECT consultants inform patients about memory loss. *Psychiatric Bulletin, 33*(11), 412–415.

Hanna, E., Ward, L. M., Seabrook, R. C., Jerald, M., Reed, L., Giaccardi, S., & Lippman, J. R. (2017). Contributions of social comparison and self-objectification in mediating associations between Facebook use and emergent adults' psychological well-being. *Cyberpsychology, Behavior, and Social Networking, 20*(3), 172–179.

Hansen, M., Ross, J., & Armour, C. (2017). Evidence of the dissociative PTSD subtype: A systematic literature review of latent class and profile analytic studies of PTSD. *Journal of Affective Disorders, 213,* 59–69.

Hansen, W. B., Derzon, J., Dusenbury, L., Bishop, D., Campbell, K., & Alford, A. (2010). Operating characteristics of prevention programs: Connections to drug use etiology. In L. Scheier (Ed.), *Handbook of drug use etiology: Theory, methods, and empirical findings* (pp. 597–616). Washington, DC: American Psychological Association.

Hansson, L., Middelboe, T., Sorgaard, K. W., Bengtsson, T. A., Bjarnason, O., Merinder, L., . . . Vinding, H. R. (2002). Living situation, subjective quality of life and social network among individuals with schizophrenia living in community settings. *Acta Pyschiatrica Scandinavica, 106*(5), 343–35.

Harada, K., Kitaguchi, T., Kamiya, T., Aung, K. H., Nakamura, K., Ohta, K., & Tsuboi, T. (2017). Lysophosphatidylinositol-induced activation of the cation channel TRPV2 triggers glucagon-like peptide-1 secretion in enteroendocrine L cells. *Journal of Biological Chemistry, 292,* 10855–10864.

Hardin, S. B., Weinrich, S., Weinrich, M., Garrison, C., Addy, C., & Hardin, T. L. (2002). Effects of a long-term psychosocial nursing intervention on adolescents exposed to catastrophic stress. *Issues in Mental Health Nursing, 23*(6), 537–551.

Hardman, M. L., Drew, C. J., & Egan, M. W. (2002). *Human exceptionality: Society, school and family.* Boston: Allyn & Bacon.

Hare, R. D. (1993). *Without conscience: The disturbing world of the psychopaths among us.* New York: Pocket Books.

Harenski, C. L., Thornton, D. M., Harenski, K. A., Decety, J., & Kiehl, K. A. (2012). Increased frontotemporal activation during pain observation in sexual sadism: Preliminary findings. *Archives of General Psychiatry, 69*(3), 283–292.

Harkness, K. L., & Monroe, S. M. (2016). The assessment and measurement of adult life stress: Basic premises, operational principles, and design requirements. *Journal of Abnormal Psychology, 125*(5), 727–745.

Harlapur, M., Abraham, D., & Shimbo, D. (2010). Cardiology. In J. M. Suls, K. W. Davidson, & R. M. Kaplan, (Eds.), *Handbook of health psychology and behavioral medicine* (pp. 411–425). New York: Guilford Press.

Haroules, B. (2007). Involuntary commitment is unconstitutional. In A. Quigley (Ed.), *Current controversies: Mental health.* Detroit: Greenhaven Press/Thomson Gale.

Harrington, A. (2012). The fall of the schizophrenogenic mother. *The Lancet, 379*(9823), 1292–1293.

Harrington, B. C., Jimerson, M., Haxton, C., & Jimerson, D. C. (2015). Initial evaluation, diagnosis, and treatment of anorexia nervosa and bulimia nervosa. *American Family Physician, 91*(1), 46–52.

Harris Interactive. (2011). *Large majorities support doctor assisted suicide for terminally ill patients in great pain.* (Harris Poll #9, January 25, 2011). New York: Harris Interactive.

Harris Interactive. (2013). *Are Americans still serving up family dinners?* (Harris Poll #82). New York: Harris Interactive.

Harris Interactive. (2014, February 19). *6 in 10 Americans say they or someone they know have been bullied.* (Harris Poll #17)., New York: Harris Interactive.

Harris Poll. (2013, May 30). *Are you happy? It may depend on age, race/ethnicity and other factors* (Harris Poll #30). New York: Harris Interactive.

Harris Poll. (2015, June 3). *Older Americans, those who are religious, and even political party members are happier* (Harris Poll #30). New York: Harris Interactive.

Harris Poll. (2016, July 8). *Latest happiness index reveals American happiness at all-time low* (Harris Poll #50). New York: Harris Interactive.

Harris, A. (2017, March 1). Facebook harnesses artificial intelligence to combat live suicide broadcasts. *Miami Herald.*

Harris, A., Ayers, T., & Leek, M. R. (1985). Auditory span of apprehension deficits in schizophrenia. *Journal of Nervous and Mental Disease, 173*(11), 650–657.

Harris, J. C. (2014). Exorcism: The miracles of St. Ignatius of Loyola: Peter Paul Rubens. *JAMA Psychiatry, 71*(8), 866–867.

Harris, J. C. (2010). *Intellectual disability: A guide for families and professionals.* New York: Oxford University Press.

Harrison, A., de la Cruz, L. F., Enander, J., Radua, J., & Mataix-Cols, D. (2016). Cognitive-behavioral therapy for body dysmorphic disorder: A systematic review and meta-analysis of randomized controlled trials. *Clinical Psychology Review, 48,* 43–51.

Harrison, E., & Petrakis, I. (2011). Naltrexone pharmacotherapy. In J. H. Lowinson & P. Ruiz (Eds.), *Substance abuse: A comprehensive textbook* (5th ed.). Philadelphia, PA: Lippincott, Williams, & Wilkins.

Hart, C. L., & Ksir, C. (2015). *Drugs, society, and human behavior* (16th ed.). New York: McGraw-Hill Publishing.

Hart, C., Ksir, C., & Ray, O. (2010). *Drugs, society, and human behavior.* New York: McGraw-Hill Humanities.

Hart, J., Jr., Kraut, M. A., Womack, K. B., Strain, J., Didehbani, N., Bartz, E., . . . Cullum, C. M. (2013). Neuroimaging of cognitive dysfunction and depression in aging retired National Football League players: A cross-sectional study. *JAMA Neurology. 70*(3), 326–335.

Hartford, D., & Marcus, L. M. (2011). Educational approaches. In E. Hollander, A. Kolevzon & J. T. Coyle (Eds.), *Textbook of autism spectrum disorders.* (pp. 537–553) Arlington, VA: American Psychiatric Publishing.

Harford, T. C., Yi, H. Y., Chen, C. M., & Grant, B. F. (2018). Substance use disorders and self- and other-directed violence among adults: Results from the National Survey on Drug Use and Health. *Journal of Affective Disorders, 225,* 365–373.

Hartley, T. A., Violanti, J. M., Fekedulegn, D., Andrew, M. E., & Burchfield, C. M. (2007). Associations between major life events, traumatic incidents, and depression among Buffalo police officers. *International Journal of Emergency Mental Health, 9*(1), 25–35.

Hartmann, U., & Waldinger, M. D. (2007). Treatment of delayed ejaculation. In S. R. Leiblum (Ed.), *Principles and practice of sex therapy* (4th ed., pp. 241–276). New York: Guilford Press.

Hartney, E. (2014). Additions: Can marijuana cause infertility? Retrieved from http://addictions.about.com/od/legalissues/f/Can-Marijuana-Cause-Infertility.htm.

Harvard School of Public Health. (2016, July). *The workplace and health.* Boston, MA: Harvard.

Harvey, E. A., Breaux, R. P., & Lugo-Candelas, C.I . (2016). Early development of comorbidity between symptoms of attention-deficit/hyperactivity disorder (ADHD) and oppositional defiant disorder (ODD). *Journal of Abnormal Psychology, 125,* 154–167.

Hausman, A. (2008). Direct-to-consumer advertising and its effect on prescription requests. *Journal of Advertising Research, 48*(1), 42–56.

Havinga, P. J., Boschloo, L., Bloemen, A. J., Nauta, M. H., de Vries, S. O., Penninx, B. W., . . . Hartman, C. A. (2017). Doomed for disorder? High incidence of mood and anxiety disorders in offspring of depressed and anxious patients: A prospective cohort study. *Journal of Clinical Psychiatry, 78*(1), e8–e17.

Hawken, E. R., & Beninger, R. J. (2014). The amphetamine sensitization model of schizophrenia symptoms and its effect on schedule-induced polydipsia in the rat. *Psychopharmacology, 231*(9), 2001–2008.

Hawkins, J. R. (2004). The role of emotional repression in chronic back pain: A study of chronic back pain patients undergoing psychodynamically oriented group psychotherapy as treatment for their pain. *Dissertation Abstracts International: Section B: The Sciences and Engineering, 64*(8-B), 4038.

Hawks, E., Blumenthal, H., Feldner, M. T., Leen-Feldner, E. W., & Jones, R. (2011). An examination of the relation between traumatic event exposure and panic-relevant biological challenge responding among adolescents. *Behavior Therapy, 42*(3), 427–438.

Hayden, E. P., Hankin, B. L., Mackrell, S. V. M., Sheikh, H. I., Jordan, P. L., Dozois, D. J. A., . . . Badanes, L. S. (2014). Parental depression and child cognitive vulnerability predict children's cortisol reactivity. *Development and Psychopathology, 26,* 1445–1460.

Hayden, L. A. (1998). Gender discrimination within the reproductive health care system: Viagra v. birth control. *Journal of Law and Health, 13,* 171–198.

Hayes, R. D. (2011). Circular and linear modeling of female sexual desire and arousal. *Journal of Sex Research, 48*(2-3), 130–141.

Hayes, S. C. (2016). Acceptance and commitment therapy, relational frame theory, and the third wave of behavioral and cognitive therapies (republished article). *Behavior Therapy. 47*(6), 869–885.

Haynes, S. G., Feinleib, M., & Kannel, W. B. (1980). The relationship of psychosocial factors to coronary heart disease in the Framingham study: III. Eight-year incidence of coronary heart disease. *American Journal of Epidemiology, 111,* 37–58.

Hays, P. A. (2016). *Addressing cultural complexities in practice: Assessment, diagnosis, and therapy* (3rd edition). Washington, DC: APA.

Hayward, M. D., & Taylor, J. E. (1965). A schizophrenic patient describes the action of intensive psychotherapy. *Psychiatric Quarterly, 30.*

Hazler, R. J. (2016). Person-centered therapy. In D. Capuzzi & M. D. Stauffer, *Counseling and psychotherapy: Theories and interventions* (6th ed., pp. 169–194). Alexandria, VA: American Counseling Association.

HCUP (Healthcare Cost and Utilization Project). (2015, June). *Hospitalizations involving mental and substance use disorders among adults, 2012* (Statistical Brief #2015). Rockville, MD: Agency for Healthcare Research and Quality.

He, Y., Lu, X., Wu, H., Cai, W., Yang, L., Xu, L., . . . Kong, Q. (2014). Mitochondrial DNA content contributes to healthy aging in Chinese: A study from nonagenarians and centenarians. *Neurobiology of Aging, 35*(7), 1779. e1–4.

He, Y. H., Chen, X. Q., Yan, D. J., Xiao, F. H., Lin, R., Liao, X. P., . . . Kong, Q. P. (2016). Familial longevity study reveals a significant association of mitochondrial DNA copy number between centenarians and their offspring. *Neurobiology of Aging, 47,* 218.

Head, M. W. (2013). Human prion diseases: Molecular, cellular and population biology. *Neuropathology, 33*(3), 221–236.

Headrick, J. P., Peart, J. N., Budiono, B. P., Shum, D. H., Neumann, D. L., & Stapelberg, N. J. (2017). The heartbreak of depression: "Psycho-cardiac" coupling in myocardial infarction. *Journal of Molecular and Cellular Cardiology, 106,* 14–28.

Healy, S., & Tyrrell, M. (2013). Importance of debriefing following critical incidents. *Emergency Nurse, 20*(10), 32–7.

Hébert, M., Langevin, R., & Oussaïd, E. (2018). Cumulative childhood trauma, emotion regulation, dissociation, and behavior problems in school-aged sexual abuse victims. *Journal of Affective Disorders, 225,* 306–312.

Hechtman, L., Swanson, J. M., Sibley, M. H., Stehili, A., Owens, E. B., et al. (2016). Functional adult outcomes 16 years after childhood diagnosis of attention-deficit/hyperactivity disorder: MTA results. *Journal of the American Academy of Child and Adolescent Psychiatry, 55,* 945–952.

Hedaya, R. J. (2011). Health matters: Connecting you to the sources of health. Panic disorders: Part 2. *Psychology Today.* Retrieved from http://www.psychologytoday.com/blog/health-matters/201102.

Hedman, E., Axelsson, E., Andersson, E., Lekander, M., & Ljotsson, B. (2016). Exposure-based cognitive-behavioural therapy via the Internet and as bibliotherapy for somatic symptom disorder and illness anxiety disorder: Randomised controlled trial. *British Journal of Psychiatry, 209*(5), 407–413.

Hedman, L. C., Petrila, J., Fisher, W. H., Swanson, J. W., Dingman, D. A., & Burris, S. (2016). State laws on emergency holds for mental health stabilization. *Psychiatry Services, 67*(5), 529–535.

Hefin, M. T. (2017, June 30). Geriatric health maintenance. *UpToDate.* Retrieved from http://www.uptodate.com.

Hegarty II, J. P., Gu, M., Spielman, D. M., Cleveland, S. C., Hallmayer, J. F., Lazzeroni, L. C., Raman, M. M., Frazier, T. W., Phillips, J. M., Reiss, A. L., & Hardan, A. Y. (2017). A proton MR spectroscopy study of the thalamus in twins with autism spectrum disorder. *Progress in Neuro-Psychopharmacology and Biological Psychiatry.* [Epub ahead of print]

Heilbrun, K., & Erickson, J. (2007). A behavioural science perspective on identifying and managing hindsight bias and unstructured judgement: Implications for legal decision making. In D. Carson, R. Milne, F. Pakes, K. Shalev, & A. Shawyer (Eds.), *Applying psychology to criminal justice.* Hoboken, NJ: John Wiley & Sons.

Heilbrun, K., Goldstein, N. E. S., & Redding, R. E. (Eds.). (2005). *Juvenile delinquency: Prevention, assessment, and intervention* (pp. 85–110). New York: Oxford University Press.

Heiman, J. R. (2002). Sexual dysfunction: Overview of prevalence, etiological factors, and treatments. *Journal of Sex Research, 39*(1), 73–78.

Heiman, J. R. (2007). Orgasmic disorders in women. In S. R. Leiblum (Ed.), *Principles and practice of sex therapy* (4th ed., pp. 84–123). New York: Guilford Press.

Heimberg, R. G., Brozovich, F. A., & Rapee, R. M. (2010). A cognitive-behavioral model of social anxiety disorder: Update and extension. In S. G. Hofmann & P. M. DiBartolo (Eds.), *Social anxiety: Clinical, developmental, and social perspectives.* New York: Academic Press.

Heimberg, R. G., & Magee, L. (2014). Social anxiety disorder. In D. H. Barlow (Ed.), *Clinical handbook of psychological disorders: A step-by-step treatment manual* (5th ed., pp. 114–154). New York: Guilford Press.

Heinrichs, D. W., & Carpenter, W. T., Jr. (1983). The coordination of family therapy with other treatment modalities for schizophrenia. In W. McFarlane (Ed.), *Family therapy in schizophrenia.* New York: Guilford Press.

Held, M. L., & Lee, S. (2016, August 5). Discrimination and mental health among Latinos: Variation by place of origin. *Journal of Mental Health,* 1–6. [Epub ahead of print]

Hellstrom, W. J. G., & DeLay, K. (2017, June 27). Male dyspareunia. *UpToDate.* Retrieved from http://www.uptodate.com.

Hembree-Kigin, T. L., & McNeil, C. B. (2013). *Parent-child interaction therapy (Clinical Child Psychology Library).* New York: Springer Science + Business Media.

Hemmings, C. (2010). Service use and outcomes. In N. Bouras (Ed.), *Mental health services for adults with intellectual disability: Strategies and solutions. The Maudsley Series* (pp. 75–88). New York: Psychology Press.

Henderson, K., Buchholz, A., Obeid, N., Mossiere, A., Maras, D., Norris, M., . . . Spettigue, W. (2014). A family-based eating disorder day treatment program for youth: Examining the clinical and statistical significance of short-term treatment outcomes. *Eating Disorders, 22*(1), 1–18.

Henderson, V. (2010). Diminishing dissociative experiences for war veterans in group therapy. In S. S. Fehr (Ed.), *101 interventions in group therapy* (rev. ed., pp. 217–220). New York: Routledge/Taylor & Francis Group.

Henderson, V. C., Kimmelman, J., Fergusson, D., Grimshaw, J. M., & Hackam, D. G. (2013). Threats to validity in the design and conduct of preclinical efficacy studies: A systematic review of guidelines for in vivo animal experiments. *PLoS Medicine, 10*(7), e1001489.

Hengartner, M., Müller, M., Rodgers, S., Rössler, W., & Ajdacic-Gross, V. (2014). Occupational functioning and work impairment in association with personality disorder trait-scores. *Social Psychiatry and Psychiatric Epidemiology, 49*(2), 327–335.

Henggeler, S. W., & Sheidow, A. J. (2012). Empirically supported family-based treatments for conduct disorder and delinquency in adolescents. *Journal of Marital and Family Therapy, 38*(1), 30–58.

Henn, F. (2013). Using brain imaging to understand the response to cognitive therapy in panic disorder. *American Journal of Psychiatry, 170*, 1235–1236.

Henrich, J., Heine, S. J., & Norenzayan, A. (2010, June). The weirdest people in the world? *Behavioral and Brain Sciences, 33*(2–3), 61–83; discussion, 83–135.

Henriksen, M. G., Nordgaard, J., & Jansson, L. B. (2017). Genetics of schizophrenia: Overview of methods, findings and limitations. *Frontiers in Human Neuroscience, 11*, 322.

Heppner, P. P., Wampold, B. E., Owen, J., Thompson, M. N., & Wang, K. T. (2016). *Research design in counseling* (4th ed.). Belmont, CA: Brooks Cole.

Herbenick, D., Reece, M., Schick, V., Sanders, S. A., Dodge, B., & Fortenberry, J. D. (2010). Sexual behavior in the United States: Results from a national probability sample of men and women ages 14–94. *Journal of Sexual Medicine, 7*(5), 255–265.

Herbenick, D., Schick, V., Reece, M., Sanders, S. A., Smith, N., Dodge, B., & Fortenberry, J. D. (2013). Characteristics of condom and lubricant use among a nationally representative probability sample of adults ages 18–59 in the United States. *Journal of Sexual Medicine, 10*, 474–483.

Herbert, J. D. (2007). Avoidant personality disorder. In W. O'Donohue, K. A. Fowler, S. O. Lilienfeld (Eds.). *Personality disorders: Toward the DSM-V.* Los Angeles: Sage Publications.

Herbert, J. D., Gaudiano, B. A., Rheingold, A., Harwell, V., Dalrymple, K., & Nolan, E. M. (2005). Social skills training augments the effectiveness of cognitive behavior group therapy for social anxiety disorder. *Behavior Therapy, 36*, 125–138.

Herculano-Houzel, S. (2016). *The human advantage: A new understanding of how our brain became remarkable.* MIT Press.

Herman, B. (2015, May 28). Fat-shaming and body-shaming, a history: Author talks thigh gaps, "Dad bods" and why we hate fat. *International Business Times.*

Hermes, E. A., Hoff, R., & Rosenheck, R. A. (2014). Sources of the increasing number of Vietnam era veterans with a diagnosis of PTSD using VHA services. *Psychiatric Services, 65*(6), 830–832.

Herne, M. A., Bartholomew, M. L., & Weahkee, R. L. (2014, June). Suicide mortality among American Indians and Alaska natives, 1999–2009. *American Journal of Public Health, 104* (Suppl. 3), S336–S342.

Herning, R. I., Better, W. E., Tate, K., & Cadet, J. L. (2005). Cerebrovascular perfusion in marijuana users during a month of monitored abstinence. *Neurology, 64*, 488–493.

Heron, M. (2016, June 30). Deaths: Leading causes for 2014. *National Vital Statistics Report, 65*(5).

Herpertz, S. C., & Bertsch, K. (2014). The social-cognitive basis of personality disorders. *Current Opinion in Psychiatry, 27*(1), 73–77.

Hertz, M. F., & Donato, I. (2013). Bullying and suicide: A public health approach *Journal of Adolescent Health, 53,* S1-S3.

Hess, A. (2009 June 16). *Huffington Post:* Sometimes a cigar is just a nipple is just sexist. *Washington City Paper.*

Hess, A. (2016, January 26). How "-phobic" became a weapon in the identity wars. *New York Times.*

Heston, L. L. (1992). *Mending minds: A guide to the new psychiatry of depression, anxiety, and other serious mental disorders.* New York: W. H. Freeman.

Heylens, G., De Cuyper, G., Zucker, K. J., Schelfaut, C., Elaut, E., Vanden Bossche, H., De Baere, E., & T'Sjoen, G. (2012). Gender identity disorder in twins: A review of the case report literature. *Journal of Sexual Medicine, 9*(3), 751–757.

HHS (U.S. Department of Health and Human Services). (2009). *Mental health and African Americans.* Washington, DC: Office of Minority Health.

HHS (U.S. Department of Health and Human Services). (2017). *Mental health myths and facts.* Washington, DC: USDHHS.

Hickey, E. W. (2015). *Serial murderers and their victims* (7th ed.). Belmont, CA: Wadsworth.

Hickling, E. J., & Blanchard, E. B. (2007). Motor vehicle accidents and psychological trauma. In E. K. Carll (Ed.), *Trauma psychology: Issues in violence, disaster, health, and illness* (Vol. 2). Westport, CT: Praeger Publishers.

Hicks, B. M., Iacono, W. G., & McGue, M. (2014). Identifying childhood characteristics that underlie premorbid risk for substance use disorders: Socialization and boldness. *Development and Psychopathology, 26*(1), 141–157.

Hicks, K. (2014). A biocultural perspective on fictive kinship in the Andes: Social support and women's immune function in El Alto, Bolivia. *Medical Anthropology Quarterly, 28*(3), 440–458.

Hieronymus, F., Emilsson, J. F., Nilsson, S., & Eriksson, E. (2016). Consistent superiority of selective serotonin reuptake inhibitors over placebo in reducing depressed mood in patients with major depression. *Molecular Psychiatry, 21*(4), 523–530.

Higa-McMillan, C. K., Francis, S. E., Rith-Najarian, L., & Chorpita, B. F. (2016). Evidence base update: 50 years of research on treatment for child and adolescent anxiety. *Journal of Clinical Child and Adolescent Psychology, 45*, 91–113.

Higgins, E. S., & George, M. S. (2007). *The neuroscience of clinical psychiatry: The pathophysiology of behavior and mental illness.* Philadelphia: Wolters Kluwer/Lippincott Williams & Wilkins.

Higgins, S. T., Heil, S. H., Dantona, R., Donham, R., Matthews, M., & Badger, G. J. (2007). Effects of varying the monetary value of voucher-based incentives on abstinence achieved during and following treatment among cocaine-dependent outpatients. *Addiction, 102*(2), 271–281.

Hildebrand, K. M., Johnson, D. J., Dewayne, J., & Bogle, K. (2001). Comparison of patterns of alcohol use between high school and college athletes and non-athletes. *College Student Journal, 35*, 358–365.

Hildebrandt, T., & Alfano, L. (2009). A review of eating disorders in males: Working towards an improved diagnostic system. *International Journal of Child and Adolescent Health, 2*(2), 185–196.

Hill, C. E., Spiegel, S. B., Hoffman, M. A., Kivlighan, D. M., & Gelso, C. J. (2017, January 30). Therapist expertise in psychotherapy revisited. *The Counseling Psychologist, 45*(1), 99–112.

Hill, R., & Harris, J. (2017). Relapse prevention: Underlying assumptions and current thinking. In P. Davis, R. Patton, & J. Jackson, *Addiction: Psychology and treatment (BPS Textbooks in Psychology),* (Chap. 15, pp. 245–261). Hoboken, NJ: Wiley-Blackwell.

Hille, R. B. (2017, January 6). *LexisNexis practice guide: New Jersey pleadings, 2017 edition.* LexisNexis.

Hillemeier, M. M., Foster, E. M., Heinrichs, B., & Heier, B. (2007). Racial differences in parental reports of attention-deficit/hyperactivity disorder behaviors. *Journal of Developmental and Behavioral Pediatrics, 28*(5), 353–361.

Hills, P. J., & Hill, D. M. (2018). Sad people are more accurate at expression identification with a smaller own-ethnicity bias than happy people. *Quarterly Journal of Experimental Psychology.* [Manuscript in press]

Hinrichsen, G. A. (1999). Interpersonal psychotherapy for late-life depression. In M. Duffy (Ed.), *Handbook of counseling and psychotherapy with older adults.* New York: Wiley.

Hirano, A., Umegaki, H., Suzuki, Y., Hayashi, T., & Kuzuya, M. (2016). Effects of leisure activities at home on perceived care burden and the endocrine system of caregivers of dementia patients: A randomized controlled study. *International Psychogeriatrics, 28*(2), 261–268.

Hiroeh, U., Appleby, L., Mortensen, P.-B., & Dunn, G. (2001). Death by homicide, suicide, and other unnatural causes in people with mental illness: A population-based study. *Lancet, 358*(9299), 2110–2112.

Hirsch, C. R., Hayes, S., Mathews, A., Perman, G., & Borkovec, T. (2012). The extent and nature of imagery during worry and positive thinking in generalized anxiety disorder. *Journal of Abnormal Psychology, 121*(1), 238–243.

Hirsch, M., & Birnbaum, R. J. (2016, August 22). Selective serotonin reuptake inhibitors: Pharmacology, administration, and side effects. *UpToDate.* Retrieved from www.uptodate.com.

Hirsch, M., & Birnbaum, R. J. (2016, February 11). Tricyclic and tetracyclic drugs: Pharmacology, administration, and side effects. *UpToDate.* Retrieved from www.uptodate.com.

Hirsch, M., & Birnbaum, R. J. (2016, January 9). Sexual dysfunction caused by selective serotonin reuptake inhibitors (SSRIs): Management. *UpToDate.* Retrieved from www.uptodate.com.

Hithersay, R., Hamburg, S., Knight, B., & Strydom, A. (2017). Cognitive decline and dementia in Down syndrome. *Current Opinion in Psychiatry, 30*(2), 102–107.

Ho, E. (2012, July 23). Almost everyone doesn't trust the Internet. *Time.*

Hodges, S. (2003). Borderline personality disorder and posttraumatic stress disorder: Time for integration? *Journal of Counseling & Development, 81*(4), 409–417.

Hodgetts, S., Gallagher, P., Stow, D., Ferrier, I. N., & O'Brien, J. T. (2017). The impact and measurement of social dysfunction in late-life depression: An evaluation of current methods with a focus on wearable technology. *International Journal of Geriatric Psychiatry, 32*(3), 247–255.

Hofer, H., Frigerio, S., Frischknecht, E., Gassmann, D., Gutbrod, K., & Müri, R. M. (2013). Diagnosis and treatment of an obsessive-compulsive disorder following traumatic brain injury: A single case and review of the literature. *Neurocase, 19*(4), 390–400.

Hoff, P. (2015). The Kraepelinian tradition. *Dialogues in Clinical Neuroscience, 17*(1), 31–41.

Hoffart, A., Ledley, L. M., Savøe, K., & Sexton, H. (2016). Cognitive and guided mastery therapies for panic disorder with agoraphobia: 18-year long-term outcome and predictors of long-term change. *Clinical Psychology & Psychotherapy, 23*(1), 1–13.

Hoffman, A. (2016, November 17). Length of stay in state hospitals for mental health treatment linked to likelihood of relapse. *NewsWorks*.

Hofmann, S. G., & Hinton, D. E. (2014). Cross-cultural aspects of anxiety disorders. *Current Psychiatry Reports, 16*(6), 450.

Hogan, R. A. (1968). The implosive technique. *Behavioral Research and Therapy, 6*, 423–431.

Hogan, T. P. (2014). *Psychological testing: A practical introduction* (3rd ed.). Hoboken, NJ: Wiley.

Hogarty, G. E., Anderson, C. M., Reiss, D. J., Kornblith, S. J., Greenwald, D. P., Javna, C. D., . . . Madonia, M. J. (1986). Family psychoeducation, social skills training, and maintenance chemotherapy in the aftercare treatment of schizophrenia: I. One-year effects of a controlled study on relapse and expressed emotion. *Archives of General Psychiatry, 43*(7), 633–642.

Hogarty, G. E., Goldberg, S. C., & Schooler, N.R. (1974). Drug and sociotherapy in the aftercare of schizophrenic patients: III. Adjustment of nonrelapsed patients. *Archives of General Psychiatry, 31*(5), 609–618.

Hogarty, G. E., Goldberg, S. C., Schooler, N. R., & Ulrich, R. F. (1974). Drug and sociotherapy in the aftercare of schizophrenic patients: II. Two-year relapse rates. *Archives of General Psychiatry, 31*(5), 603–608.

Hogarty, G. E., Greenwald, D. P., & Eack, S. M. (2006). Durability and mechanism of effects of cognitive enhancement therapy. *Psychiatric Services, 57*(12), 1751–1757.

Hoge, E. A., Bui, E., Palitz, S. A., Schwarz, N. R., Owens, M. E., Johnston, J. M., . . . Simon, N. M. (2018). The effect of mindfulness meditation training on biological acute stress responses in generalized anxiety disorder. *Psychiatry Research*. [Article in press]

Hoge, E. A., Guidos, B. M., Mete, M., Bui, E., Pollack, M. H., Simon, N. M., & Dutton, M. A. (2017). Effects of mindfulness meditation on occupational functioning and health care utilization in individuals with anxiety. *Journal of Psychosomatic Research, 95*, 7–11.

Hogebrug, J., Koopmans, P. P., van Oostrom, I., & Schellekens, A. (2013). Neurosyphilis, the great imitator: A diagnostic challenge. *Nederlands Tijdschrift Voor Geneeskunde, 157*(30), A6033.

Holiday, S., Lewis, M. J., Nielsen, R., Anderson, H. D., & Elinzano, M. (2016). The selfie-study: Archetypes and motivations in modern self-photography. *Visual Communication Quarterly, 23*(3), 175–187.

Holinger, P. C., & Offer, D. (1982). Prediction of adolescent suicide: A population model. *American Journal of Psychiatry, 139*, 302–307.

Holinger, P. C., & Offer, D. (1991). Sociodemographic, epidemiologic, and individual attributes. In L. Davidson & M. Linnoila (Eds.), *Risk factors for youth suicide*. New York: Hemisphere.

Holinger, P. C., & Offer, D. (1993). *Adolescent suicide*. New York: Guilford Press.

Hollander, I. (2006). Viagra's rise above women's health issues: An analysis of the social and political influences on drug approvals in the United States and Japan. *Social Science & Medicine, 62*(3), 683–693.

Holliday, R. P., Holder, N. D., Williamson, M. L. C., & Suris, A. (2017). Therapeutic response to cognitive processing therapy in white and black female veterans with military sexual trauma-related PTSD. *Cognitive Behavior Therapy, 46*, 432–444.

Hollon, S. D., & Ponniah, K. (2010). A review of empirically supported psychological therapies for mood disorders in adults. *Depression and Anxiety, 27*(10), 891–932.

Holmes, L. (2014, July 14). Sadness is not depression. *About.com*.

Holmes, T. H., & Rahe, R. H. (1967). The Social Readjustment Rating Scale. *Journal of Psychosomatic Research, 11*, 213–218.

Holmes, T. H., & Rahe, R. H. (1989). The Social Readjustment Rating Scale. In T. H. Holmes & E. M. David (Eds.), *Life change, life events, and illness: Selected papers*. New York: Praeger.

Holt, H., Beutler, L. E., Kimpara, S., Macias, S., Haug, N. A., Shiloff, N., . . . Stein, M. (2015). Evidence-based supervision: Tracking outcome and teaching principles of change in clinical supervision to bring science to integrative practice. *Psychotherapy (Chicago), 52*(2), 185–189.

Holtom-Viesel, A., & Allan, S. (2014). A systematic review of the literature on family functioning across all eating disorder diagnoses in comparison to control families. *Clinical Psychology Review, 34*(1), 29–43.

Holtzheimer, P. E. (2015, August 13). Unipolar depression in adults: Treatment with surgical approaches. *UpToDate*. Retrieved from www.uptodate.com.

Holtzheimer, P. E. (2015, August 13). Unipolar depression in adults: Treatment with transcranial magnetic stimulation (TMS). *UpToDate*. Retrieved from www.uptodate.com.

Holtzheimer, P. E. (2017, January 24). Depression in adults: Overview of neuromodulation procedures. *UpToDate*. Retrieved from www.uptodate.com.

Holtzman, D., & Kulish, N. (2012). Female exhibitionism: Identification, competition and camaraderie. *International Journal of Psychoanalysis, 93*(2), 271–292.

Holz, N. E., Zohsel, K., Laucht, M., Banaschewski, T., Hohmann, S., & Brandeis, D. (2018). Gene X environment interactions in conduct disorder: Implications for future treatments. *Neuroscience and Biobehavioral Reviews*. [Manuscript in press]

Homan, P., Vermathen, P., Van Swam, C., Federspiel, A., Boesch, C., Strik, W., . . . Kreis, R. (2014). Magnetic resonance spectroscopy investigations of functionally defined language areas in schizophrenia patients with and without auditory hallucinations. *Neuroimage, 94*, 23–32.

Hong, V. (2016). Borderline personality disorder in the emergency department. *Harvard Review of Psychiatry, 24*(5), 357.

Hopfer, C. (2011). Club drug, prescription drug, and over-the-counter medication abuse: Description, diagnosis, and intervention. In Y. Kaminer & K. C. Winters (Eds), *Clinical manual of adolescent substance abuse treatment* (pp. 187–212). Arlington, VA: American Psychiatric Publishing.

Hopkins, D. (2014, June). Benjamin Rush (1746–1813). *Journal of Mississippi State Medical Association, 55*(7), 245.

Hopko, D. R., Robertson, S. M. C., Widman, L., & Lejuez, C. W. (2008). Specific phobias. In M. Hersen & J. Rosqvist (Eds.), *Handbook of psychological assessment, case conceptualization, and treatment, Vol. 1: Adults* (pp. 139–170). Hoboken, NJ: John Wiley & Sons.

Hor, K., & Taylor, M. (2010). Suicide and schizophrenia: A systematic review of rates and risk factors. *Journal of Psychopharmacology, 24*(4 Suppl), 81.

Horney, K. (1937). *The neurotic personality of our time*. New York: Norton.

Horowitz, J. A., Damato, E. G., Duffy, M. E., & Solon, L. (2005). The relationship of maternal attributes, resources, and perceptions of postpartum experiences to depression. *Research in Nursing and Health, 28*(2), 159–171.

Horowitz, J. A., Damato, E., Solon, L., Metzsch, G., & Gill, V. (1995). Postpartum depression: Issues in clinical assessment. *Journal of Perinatal Medicine, 15*(4), 268–278.

Horowitz, M. J., & Lerner, U. (2010). Treatment of histrionic personality disorder. In J. F. Clarkin, P. Fonagy, & G. O. Gabbard (Eds.), *Psychodynamic psychotherapy for personality disorders: A clinical handbook* (pp. 3289–309). Arlington, VA: American Psychiatric Publishing.

Horton, S. E., Hughes, J. L., King, J. D., Kennard, B. D., Westers, N. J., Mayers, T. L., & Stewart, S. M. (2016). Preliminary examination of the Interpersonal Psychological Theory of Suicide in an adolescent clinical sample. *Journal of Abnormal Child Psychology, 44*(6), 1133–1144.

Horwitz, A. G., Czyz, E. K., & King, C. A. (2014). Predicting future suicide attempts among adolescent and emerging adult psychiatric emergency patients. *Journal of Clinical Child and Adolescent Psychology, 53*, 1–11.

Horwitz, A. V., & Wakefield, J. C. (2007, December 9). Sadness is not a disorder. *The Philadelphia Inquirer*, pp. C1, C5.

Horwitz, A. V., & Wakefield, J. C. (2012). *The loss of sadness: How psychiatry transforms normal sorrow into depressive disorder*. New York: Oxford University Press.

Horwitz, S. (2014, March 9). The hard lives—and high suicide rate—of Native American children on reservations. *The Washington Post*.

Hoste, R. R., Lebow, J., & Le Grange, D. (2014). A bidirectional examination of expressed emotion among families of adolescents with bulimia nervosa. *International Journal of Eating Disorders*.

Hou, Y., Hu, P., Zhang, Y., Lu, Q., Wang, D., Yin, L., . . . Zou, X. (2014). Cognitive behavioral therapy in combination with systemic family therapy improves mild to moderate postpartum depression. *Revista Brasileira De Psiquiatria, 36*(1), 47–52.

Hough, S., DenBoer, J. W., Crehan, E. T., Stone, M. T., & Hicks, T. (2017). Treating sexual problems in clients with cognitive and intellectual disabilities. In Z. D. Peterson (Ed.), *The Wiley-Blackwell handbook of sex therapy* (Chap. 21, pp. 345–358). Hoboken, NJ: Wiley-Blackwell.

Houghton, D. (2013, August 12). Cited in T. Miller, Too many selfies on Facebook can damage relationships: Study. *New York Daily News*.

Houghton, K., Schuchard, J., Lewis, C., & Thompson, C. K. (2013). Promoting child-initiated social-communication in children with autism: Son-Rise Program intervention effects. *Journal of Communication Disorders, 46*(5-6), 495–506.

Houle, J. N., & Light, M. T. (2014). The home foreclosure crisis and rising suicide rates, 2005 to 2010. *American Journal of Public Health, 104*(6), 1073–1079.

Houston, G. (2016). *Counsel Heal: Mental Health: 5 negative effects of social media on your mental health.* Retrieved from http://www.counselheal.com/articles/24341/20160518.

Houston, K. A., Clifford, B. R., Phillips, L. H., & Memon, A. (2013). The emotional eyewitness: The effects of emotion on specific aspects of eyewitness recall and recognition performance. *Emotion, 13*(1), 118–128.

Howard, M., Muris, P., Loxton, H., & Wege, A. (2016). Anxiety-proneness, anxiety symptoms, and the role of parental overprotection in young South African children. *Journal of Child and Family Studies, 26*(1), 262–270.

Howard, S., Myers, L. B., & Hughes, B. M. (2017, January 20). Repressive coping and cardiovascular reactivity to novel and recurrent stress. *Anxiety, Stress & Coping*, 1–13. [Epub ahead of print]

Howe, T. H., Sheu, C. F., Hsu, Y. W., Wang, T. N., & Wang, L. N. (2016). Predicting neurodevelopmental outcomes at preschool age for children with very low birth weight. *Research in Developmental Disabilities, 48*, 231–241.

Howell, E. F. (2011). *Understanding and treating dissociative identity disorder: A rational approach.* New York: Routledge/Taylor & Francis Group.

Howes, O. D., & McCutcheon, R. (2017). Inflammation and the neural diathesis-stress hypothesis of schizophrenia: A reconceptualization. *Translational Psychiatry, 7*(2), e1024.

Howes, O. D., & Murray, R. M. (2014). Schizophrenia: An integrated sociodevelopmental-cognitive model. *Lancet, 383*(9929), 1677–1687.

Howland, J., Rohsenow, D. J., Greece, J. A., Littlefield, C. A., Almeida, A., Heeren, T., Winter, M., Bliss, C. A., Hunt, S., & Hermos, J. (2010). The effects of binge drinking on college students' next-day academic test-taking performance and mood state. *Addiction, 105*(4), 655–665.

Howland, R. H. (2012). Dietary supplement drug therapies for depression. *Journal of Psychosocial Nursing and Mental Health Services, 50*(6), 13–16.

Howland, R. H. (2014). Vagus nerve stimulation. *Current Behavioral Neuroscience Reports, 1*(2), 64–73.

Hoyer, M., & Heath, B. (2012, December 19). A mass killing in U.S. occurs every 2 weeks. *USA Today*.

Hoza, B., Kaiser, N., & Hurt, E. (2008). Evidence-based treatments for attention-deficit/hyperactivity disorder (ADHD). In R. G. Steele, T. D. Elkin, & M. C. Roberts (Eds.), *Handbook of evidence-based therapies for children and adolescents: Bridging science and practice*. New York: Springer.

Hrenchir, T. (2015, September 2). 10 most-prescribed antidepressant medications. *Newsmax. Health*. Retrieved from http://www.newsmax.com/health/health-wire/most-prescribed-antidepressant-medications/2015/09/02/id/673123.

Hróbjartsson, A., Thomsen, A. S., Emanuelsson, F., Tendal, B., Rasmussen, J. V., Hilden, J., . . . Brorson, S. (2014). Observer bias in randomized clinical trials with time-to-event outcomes: Systematic review of trials with both blinded and non-blinded outcome assessors. *International Journal of Epidemiology, 43*(3), 937–948.

Hsu, J., Lirng, J., Wang, S., Lin, C., Yang, K., Liao, M., & Chou, Y. (2014). Association of thalamic serotonin transporter and interleukin-10 in bipolar I disorder: A SPECT study. *Bipolar Disorders, 16*(3), 241–248.

Hu, W., Zhou, P., Zhang, X., Xu, C., & Wang, W. (2015). Plasma concentrations of adrenomedullin and natriuretic peptides in patients with essential hypertension. *Experimental and Therapeutic Medicine, 9*(5), 1901–1908.

Hu, X., Kim, A., Siwek, N., & Wilder, D. (2017). The Facebook paradox: Effects of facebooking on individuals' social relationships and psychological well-being. *Frontiers in Psychology, 8*, 87.

Hua, A., & Major, N. (2016). Selective mutism. *Current Opinion in Pediatrics, 28*, 114–120.

Huang, J-J., Yang, Y-P., & Wu, J. (2010). Relationships of borderline personality disorder and childhood trauma. *Chinese Journal of Clinical Psychology, 18*(6), 769–771.

Huang, S., Zhu, Z., Shang, W., Chen, Y., & Zhen, S. (2017). Trait impulsivity components correlate differently with proactive and reactive control. *PLoS ONE, 12*(4), e0176102.

Hucker, S. J. (2008). Sexual masochism: Psychopathology and theory. In D. R. Laws & W. T. O'Donohue (Eds.), *Sexual deviance: Theory, assessment, and treatment* (2nd ed., pp. 250–263). New York: Guilford Press.

Hucker, S. J. (2011). Hypoxyphilia. *Archives of Sexual Behavior, 40*(6), 1323–1326.

Hudd, S., Dumlao, J., Erdmann-Sager, D., Murray, D., Phan, E., Soukas, N., & Yokozuka, N. (2000). Stress at college: Effects on health habits, health status and self-esteem. *Colege Student Journal, 34*(2), 217–227.

Hudson, J. I., Hiripi, E., Pope, H. G., Jr., & Kessler, R. C. (2007). The prevalence and correlates of eating disorders in the National Comorbidity Survey Replication. *Biological Psychiatry, 61*(3), 348–358.

Hughes, S. (2011). Untangling Alzheimer's. *The Pennsylvania Gazette, 109*(4), 30–41.

Huguet, A., Rao, S., McGrath, P. J., Wozney, L., Wheaton, M., Conrod, J., & Rozario, S. (2016, May 2). A systematic review of cognitive behavioral therapy and behavioral activation apps for depression. *PLoS ONE, 11*(5), e0154248.

Huh, J., Le, T., Reeder, B., Thompson, H. J., & Demiris, G. (2013). Perspectives on wellness self-monitoring tools for older adults. *International Journal of Medical Informatics, 82*(11), 1092–1103.

Huijding, J., Borg, C., Weijmar-Schultz, W., & de Jong, P. J. (2011). Automatic affective appraisal of sexual penetration stimuli in women with vaginismus or dyspareunia. *Journal of Sexual Medicine, 8*(3), 806–813.

Hulett, J. M., Armer, J. M., Stewart, B. R., & Wanchai, A. (2015). Perspectives of the breast cancer survivorship continuum: Diagnosis through 30 months post-treatment. *Journal of Personalized Medicine, 5*(2), 174–190.

Humphrey, J. A. (2006). *Deviant behavior.* Upper Saddle River, NJ: Pearson/Prentice Hall.

Hunsley, J., & Lee, C. M. (2014). *Introduction to clinical psychology: An evidence-based approach.* (2nd ed.). Hoboken, NJ: Wiley.

Huo, Y., Chu, Y., Guo, L. Liu, L., Xia, X., & Wang, T. (2017). Cortisol is associated with low frequency of interleukin 10-producing B cells in patients with atherosclerosis. *Cell Biochemistry and Function, 35*(3), 178–183.

Huprich, S. K., Nelson, S. M., Paggeot, A., Lengu, K., & Albright, J. (2017). Object relations predicts borderline personality disorder symptoms beyond emotional dysregulation, negative affect, and impulsivity. *Personality Disorders, 8*(1), 46–53.

Hurd, N. M., Varner, F. A., Caldwell, C. H., & Zimmerman, M. A. (2014). Does perceived racial discrimination predict changes in psychological distress and substance use over time? An examination among Black emerging adults. *Developmental Psychology, 50*(7), 1910–1918.

Hussain, A., Nygaard, E., Sigveland, J., & Heir, T. (2016). The relationship between psychiatric morbidity and quality of life: Interview study of Norwegian tsunami survivors 2 and 6 years post-disaster. *BMC Psychiatry, 16*, 173.

Hussong, A. M., Jones, D. J., Stein, G. L., Baucom, D. H., & Boeding, S. (2011). An internalizing pathway to alcohol use and disorder. *Psychology of Addictive Behaviors, 25*(3), 390–404.

Hyams, A., & Scogin, F. (2016). Psychotherapy with older adults: Theory and practice. In A. J. Consoli, L. E. Beutler, & B. Bongar (Eds.), *Comprehensive textbook of psychotherapy* (2nd ed.), (Part II, Chap. 19). New York: Oxford University Press.

Hyde, J. S. (1990). *Understanding human sexuality* (4th ed.). New York: McGraw-Hill.

Hyde, J. S. (2005). The genetics of sexual orientation. In J. S. Hyde (Ed.), *Biological substrates of human sexuality*. Washington, DC: American Psychological Association.

Hyland, P., Murphy, J., Shevlin, M., Vallières, F., McElroy, E., Elkit, A., . . . Cloitre, M. (2017). Variation in post-traumatic response: The role of trauma type in predicting ICD-11 PTSD and CPTSD symptoms. *Social Psychiatry and Psychiatric Epidemiology, 52*, 727–736.

Hymel, S., & Swearer, S. M. (2015). Four decades of research on school bullying: An introduction. *American Psychologist, 70*, 293–299.

Iacovino, J. M., Jackson, J. J., & Oltmanns, T. F. (2014). The relative impact of socioeconomic status and childhood trauma on Black-White differences in paranoid personality disorder symptoms. *Journal of Abnormal Psychology, 123*(1), 225–230.

Iadarola, S., Hetherington, S., Clinton, C., Dean, M., Reisinger, E., Huynh, L., & Kasari, C. (2015). Services for children with autism spectrum disorder in three, large urban school districts: Perspectives of parents and educators. *Autism; The International Journal of Research and Practice, 19*(6), 694–703.

Ibrahim, H., & Hassan, C. Q. (2017). Post-traumatic stress disorder symptoms resulting from torture and other traumatic events among Syrian Kurdish refugees in Kurdistan region, Iraq. *Frontiers in Psychology, 8,* 241.

ICLG (International Comparative Legal Guides) (2016). *USA copyright 2017.* London, UK.

Igwe, M. N. (2013). Dissociative fugue symptoms in a 28-year-old male Nigerian medical student: A case report. *Journal of Medical Case Reports, 7,* 143.

Ihle, W., Jahnke, D., Heerwagen, A., & Neuperdt, C. (2005). Depression, anxiety, and eating disorders and recalled parental rearing behavior. *Kindheit Entwicklung, 14*(1), 30–38.

Iglehart, J. K. (2016). Future of long-term care and the expanding role of Medicaid managed care. *New England Journal of Medicine, 374*(2), 182–187.

Infogalactic. (2016, January 11). *List of natural disasters by death toll.* Retrieved from http://infogalactic.com/info/List_of_natural_disasters_by_death_toll.

Ingersoll, K. (2017, March 2). Motivational interviewing for substance use disorders. *UpToDate.* Retrieved from http://www.uptodate.com.

Ingram, R. E., Nelson, T., Steidtmann, D. K., & Bistricky, S. L. (2007). Comparative data on child and adolescent cognitive measures associated with depression. *Journal of Consulting and Clinical Psychology, 75*(3), 390–403.

Innocence Project. (2017). *Eyewitness misidentification.* New York: Author.

Insel, T. (2017). Interview. In A. Rogers, Star neuroscientist Tom Insel leaves the Google-spawned verily for . . . a startup? *Wired.* Retrieved from https://www.wired.com.

Insel, T. R., & Lieberman, J. A. (2013). *DSM-5 and RDoC: Shared interests.* Retrieved from NIMH website: http://www.nimh.nih.gov/news/science-news/2013.

Irwin, M. R., & Bursch, B. (2016, January 15). Factitious disorder imposed on self (Munchausen syndrome). *UpToDate.* Retrieved from www.uptodate.com.

Isaac, M. (2016). Cross-cultural differences in caregiving: The relevance to community care in India. *Indian Journal of Social Psychiatry, 32*(1), 25–27.

Isacsson, G., Reutfors, J., Papadopoulos, F. C., Ösby, U., & Ahlner, J. (2010). Antidepressant medication prevents suicide in depression. *Acta Psychiatrica Scandinavica, 122*(6), 454–460.

Isacsson, G., & Rich, C. L. (2014). Antidepressant drugs and the risk of suicide in children and adolescents. *Pediatric Drugs, 16*(2), 115–122.

Isasi, C. R., Ostrovsky, N. W., & Wills, T. A. (2013). The association of emotion regulation with lifestyle behaviors in inner-city adolescents. *Eating Behaviors, 14*(4), 518–521.

Ishii, T., Hashimoto, E., Ukai, W., Kakutani, Y., Sasaki, R., & Saito, T. (2014). Characteristics of attempted suicide by patients with schizophrenia compared with those with mood disorders: A case-controlled study in northern Japan. *PLoS One, 9*(5), e96272.

Islam, M. M., Conigrave, K. M., Day, C. A., Nguyen, Y., & Haber, P. S. (2014). Twenty-year trends in benzodiazepine dispensing in the Australian population. *Internal Medicine Journal, 44*(1), 57–64.

Isomaa, R., and Isomaa, A-L. (2014). And then what happened? A 5-year follow-up of eating disorder patients. *Nordic Journal of Psychiatry, 68*(8), 567–572.

Itsonus.org. (2017). It's on us: Campaign organizing tools. Fall 2016. Retrieved from http://www.itsonus.org.

Ivy, J. W., Meindl, J. N., Overley, E., & Robson, K. M. (2017). Token economy: A systematic review of procedural descriptions. *Behavior Modification, 41,* 708–737.

IWS (Internet World Stats). (2011). Top 20 countries with the highest number of Internet users. Retrieved from http://www.internetworldstats.com/top20.htm.

Iza, M., Wall, M. M., Heimberg, R. G., Rodebaugh, T. L., Schneier, F. R., Liu, S., & Blanco, C. (2014). Latent structure of social fears and social anxiety disorders. *Psychological Medicine, 44*(2), 361–370.

Jablensky, A. (2000). Epidemiology of schizophrenia: The global burden of disease and disability. *European Archives of Psychiatry and Clinical Neuroscience, 250,* 274–285.

Jabr, F. (2013, October 15). How the brain gets addicted to gambling. *Scientific American.*

Jabr, F. (2017, January 1). Why exercise may be the best fix for depression. *Scientific American.*

Jackson, B. R., & Bergeman, C. S. (2011). How does religiosity enhance well being? The role of perceived control. *Psychology of Religion and Spirituality, 3*(2), 149–161.

Jackson-Koku, G. (2016). Beck Depression Inventory. *Occupational Medicine (London), 66*(2), 174–175.

Jacob, M., Larson, M., & Storch, E. (2014). Insight in adults with obsessive-compulsive disorder. *Comprehensive Psychiatry, 55*(4), 896–903.

Jacobs, D. (2011). *Analyzing criminal minds: Forensic investigative science for the 21st century. Brain, behavior, and evolution.* Santa Barbara, CA: Praeger/ABC-CLIO.

Jacobs, J. R., & Bovasso, G. B. (2009). Re-examining the long-term effects of experiencing parental death in childhood on adult psychopathology. *Journal of Nervous and Mental Disease, 197*(1), 24–27.

Jacobs, M. (2003). *Sigmund Freud.* London: Sage.

Jacobsen, K. H. (2016). *Introduction to health research methods* (2nd ed.). Burlington, MA: Jones & Bartlett Learning.

Jacobson, G. (1999). The inpatient management of suicidality. In D. G. Jacobs (Ed.), *The Harvard Medical School guide to suicide assessment and intervention.* San Francisco: Jossey-Bass.

Jacoby, N., Overfeld, J., Binder, E. B., & Heimb, C. M. (2016). Stress neurobiology and developmental psychopathology. In D. Cicchetti (Ed.), *Developmental psychopathology: Vol. 2, Developmental neuroscience* (3rd ed., Chap. 21, pp. 787–831). New York: Wiley.

Jager, L. R., & Leek, J. T. (2013). Empirical estimates suggest most published medical research is true. Ithaca, NY: Cornell University Library.

Jain, S. (2017, April 4). How to use exercise to manage depression. *WebMD.*

Jakob, J. M., Lamp, K., Rauch, S. A., Smith, E. R., & Buchholz, K. R. (2017). The impact of trauma type or number of traumatic events on PTSD diagnosis and symptom severity in treatment seeking veterans. *Journal of Nervous and Mental Disease, 205*(2), 83–86.

Jakobsen, K. D., Skyum, E., Hashemi, N., Schjerning, O., Fink-Jensen, A., & Nielsen, J. (2017). Antipsychotic treatment of schizotypy and schizotypal personality disorder: A systematic review. *Journal of Psychopharmacology, 31*(4), 397–405.

James, G. M., Baldinger-Melich, P., Philippe, C., Kranz, G. S., Vanicek, T., Hahn, A., . . . Lanzenberger, R. (2017, February 6). Effects of selective serotonin reuptake inhibitors on interregional relation of serotonin transporter availability in major depression. *Frontiers in Human Neuroscience, 11,* 48.

James, W. (1890). *Principles of psychology* (Vol. 1). New York: Holt, Rinehart & Winston.

Jamison, K. R. (1995, February). Manic-depressive illness and creativity. *Scientific American,* pp. 63–67.

Jamison, K. R. (1995). *An unquiet mind.* New York: Vintage Books.

Janicak, P. G. (2017, August 31). Bipolar disorder in adults and lithium: Pharmacology, administration, and side effects. *UpToDate.* Retrieved from http://www.uptodate.com.

Jansen, P. R., Polderman, T. J. C., Bolhuis, K., van der Ende, J., Jaddoe, V. W. V., Verhuist, F. C., . . . Tiemeier, H. (2018). Polygenic scores for schizophrenia and educational attainment are associated with behavioural problems in early childhood in the general population. *Journal of Child Psychology and Psychiatry.* [Manuscript in press]

Jansen, R., Penninx, B. H., Madar, V., Xia, K., Milaneschi, Y., Hottenga, J. J., . . . Sullivan, P. F. (2015). Gene expression in major depressive disorder. *Molecular Psychiatry.* [Electronic publication]

Jansson, L. M. (2017, August 8). Infants of mothers with substance use disorder. *UpToDate.* Retrieved from http://www.uptodate.com.

Janus, S. S., & Janus, C. L. (1993). *The Janus report on sexual behavior.* New York: Wiley.

Jaremka, L. M., Fagundes, C. P., Peng, J., Bennett, J. M., Glaser, R., Malarkey, W. B., & Kiecolt-Glaser, J. K. (2013). Loneliness promotes inflammation during acute stress. *Psychological Science, 24*(7), 1089–1097.

Jaremka, L. M., Glaser, R., Malarkey, W. B., & Kiecolt-Glaser, J. K. (2013). Marital distress prospectively predicts poorer cellular immune function. *Psychoneuroendocrinology, 38*(11), 10.

Jarlenski, M., Barry, C. L., Gollust, S., Graves, A. J., Kennedy-Hendricks, A., & Kozhimannil, K. (2017). Polysubstance use among U.S. women of reproductive age who use opioid for nonmedical reasons. *American Journal of Public Health, 107,* 1308–1310.

Jarrett, R. B., & Vittengl, J. (2016, October 21). Unipolar depression in adults: Continuation and maintenance treatment. *UpToDate.* Retrieved from www.uptodate.com.

Jarrett, M. A., Wolff, J. C., Davis, T. E., Cowart, M. J., & Ollendick, T. H. (2016). Characteristics of children with ADHD and co-morbid anxiety. *Journal of Attention Disorders, 20,* 636–644.

Jaschek, G., Carater-Pokras, O., He, X., Lee, S., & Canino, G. (2016). Association of child maltreatment and depressive symptoms among Puerto Rican youth. *Child Abuse & Neglect, 58,* 63–71.

Javier, S. J., Moore, M. P., & Belgrave, F. Z. (2016). Racial comparisons in perceptions of maternal and peer attitudes, body dissatisfaction, and eating disorders among African American and White women. *Women's Health, 56*(6), 615–633.

Jennings, J. R., Pardini, D. A., & Matthews, K. A. (2017). Heart rate, health, and hurtful behavior. *Psychophysiology, 54*(3), 399–408.

Jensen, M. P., Day, M. A., & Miró, J. (2014). Neuromodulatory treatments for chronic pain: Efficacy and mechanisms. *Nature Reviews Neurology, 10*(3), 167–178.

Jensen, M. P., Ehde, D. M.,. Gertz, K. J., Stoelb, B. L., Dillworth, T. M., Hirsh, A. T., Molton, I. R., & Kraft, G. H. (2011). Effects of self-hypnosis training and cognitive restructuring on daily pain intensity and catastrophizing in individuals with multiple sclerosis and chronic pain. *International Journal of Clinical and Experimental Hypnosis, 59*(1), 45–63.

Jessen, F. (2014). Therapy for patients with dementia: Treatment strategies in the elderly. *Der Internist, 55*(7), 769–774.

Jewell, T., Blessitt, E., Stewart, C., Simic, M., & Eisler, I. (2016). Family therapy for child and adolescent eating disorders: A critical review. *Family Process, 55*(3), 577–594.

Jhanjee, S. (2014). Evidence-based psychosocial interventions in substance use. *Indian Journal of Psychological Medicine, 36*(2), 112–118.

Jiang, W., Krishnan, R., Kuchibhatla, M., Cuffe, M. S., Martsberger, C., Arias, R. M., & O'Connor, C. M. (2011). Characteristics of depression remission and its relation with cardiovascular outcome among patients with chronic heart failure (from the SAD-HART-CHF Study). *American Journal of Cardiology, 107*(4), 545–551.

Jiann, B-P., Su, C-C., & Tsai, J-Y. (2013). Is female sexual function related to the male partners' erectile function? *Journal of Sexual Medicine, 10,* 420–429.

Jibson, M. D. (2017, March 6). First-generation antipsychotic medications: Pharmacology, administration, and comprehensive side effects. *UpToDate.* Retrieved from http://www.uptodate.com.

Joe, S., Ford, B. C., Taylor, R. J., & Chatters, L. M. (2014). Prevalence of suicide ideation and attempts among Black Americans in later life. *Transcultural Psychiatry, 51*(2), 190–208.

Joffe, A. R., Bara, M., Anton, N., & Nobis, N. (2016). The ethics of animal research: A survey of the public and scientists in North America. *BMC Medical Ethics, 17,* 17.

John, A. P., Yeak, K., Ayres, H., Dragovic, M. (2017). Successful implementation of a cognitive remediation program in everyday clinical practice for individuals living with schizophrenia. *Psychiatric Rehabilitation Journal, 40*(1), 87–93.

John, L. K., Loewenstein, G., & Prelec, D. (2012). Measuring the prevalence of questionable research practices with incentives for truth telling. *Psychological Science, 23*(5), 524–532.

John, S. E., Gurnani, A. S., Bussell, C., Saurman, J. L., Griffin, J. W., & Gavett, B. E. (2016). The effectiveness and unique contribution of neuropsychological tests and the δ latent phenotype in the differential diagnosis of dementia in the uniform data set. *Neuropsychology, 30*(8), 946–960.

Johnson, L. A. (2005, July 21). Lobotomy back in spotlight after 30 years. *Netscape News.*

Johnson, S. (2017). An emotionally focused approach to sex therapy. In Z. D. Peterson (Ed.), *The Wiley-Blackwell handbook of sex therapy* (Chap. 16, pp. 250–266). Hoboken, NJ: Wiley-Blackwell.

Johnson, S., Sathyaseelan, M., Charles, H., & Jacob, K. S. (2014). Predictors of disability: A 5-year cohort study of first-episode schizophrenia. *Asian Journal of Psychiatry, 9,* 45–50.

Johnson, T. D. (2011, December). Online-only: Report: Teens who often eat dinner with family less likely to drink, smoke, or use drugs. *The Nation's Health, 41*(9), E46.

Johnson, V. C., Kryski, K. R., Sheikh, H. I., Smith, H. J., Singh, S. M., & Hayden, E. P. (2016). The serotonin-transporter promoter polymorphism moderates the continuity of behavioral inhibition in early childhood. *Development and Psychopathology, 28,* 1103–1116.

Johnston, J. E. (2017, January 19). Serial killers in 2016. *Psychology Today.*

Johnston, L. D., O'Malley, P. M., Miech, R. A., Bachman, J. G., & Schulenberg, J. E. (2017). *Monitoring the Future national survey results on drug use, 1975–2016: Overview, key findings on adolescent drug use.* Ann Arbor: Institute for Social Research, The University of Michigan.

Joiner, T. E., Jr. (2002). Depression in its interpersonal context. In I. H. Gotlib & C. L. Hammen (Eds.), *Handbook of depression* (pp. 295–313). New York: Guilford Press.

Joiner, T. E. (2005). *Why people die by suicide.* Cambridge, MA: Harvard University Press.

Joiner, T. E. (2009). The interpersonal-psychological theory of suicidal behavior: Current empirical status. *American Psychological Association.* Retrieved from http://www.apa.org/science/about/psa/2009/06/sci-brief.aspx.

Joiner, T. E., Buchman-Schmitt, J. M., Chu, C., & Horn, M. A. (2017). A sociobiological extension of the interpersonal theory of suicide. *Crisis, 38*(2), 69–72.

Jonason, P. K., Foster, J. D., Egorova, M. S., Parshikova, O., Csathó, Á., Oshio, A., & Gouveia, V. V. (2017). The Dark Triad traits from a life history perspective in six countries. *Frontiers in Psychology, 8,* 1476.

Jonason, P. K., Girgis, M., & Milne-Home, J. (2017). The exploitive mating strategy of the Dark Triad traits: Tests of rape-enabling attitudes. *Archives of Sexual Behavior, 46*(3), 697–706.

Jonason, P. K., Li, N. P., & Buss, D. M. (2010). The costs and benefits of the Dark Triad: Implications for mate poaching and mate retention tactics. *Personality and Individual Differences, 48*(4), 373–378.

Jonason, P. K., Li, N. P., Webster, G. D., & Schmitt, D. P. (2009). The Dark Triad: Facilitating a short-term mating strategy in men. *European Journal of Personality, 23,* 5–18.

Jonason, P. K., Valentine, K. A., Li, N. P., & Harbeson, C. L. (2011). Mate-selection and the Dark Triad: Facilitating a short-term mating strategy and creating a volatile environment. *Personality and Individual Differences, 51,* 759–763.

Jones, D. N., & Paulhus, D. L. (2017). Duplicity among the Dark Triad: Three faces of deceit. *Journal of Personality and Social Psychology, 113*(2), 329–342.

Jones, D. W. (2017). Moral insanity and psychological disorder: The hybrid roots of psychiatry. *History of Psychiatry, 28,* 263–279.

Jones, I., Chandra, P. S., Dazzan, P., & Howard, L. M. (2014). Bipolar disorder, affective psychosis, and schizophrenia in pregnancy and the post-partum period. *Lancet, 384*(9956), 1789.

Jones, M. C. (1968). Personality correlates and antecedents of drinking patterns in males. *Journal of Consulting and Clinical Psychology, 32,* 2–12.

Jones, M. C. (1971). Personality antecedents and correlates of drinking patterns in women. *Journal of Consulting and Clinical Psychology, 36,* 61–69.

Jørgensen, T. S., Wium-Andersen, I. K., Wium-Andersen, M. K., Jørgensen, M. B., Prescott, E., Maartensson, S., . . . Osler, M. (2016). Incidence of depression after stroke, and associated risk factors and mortality outcomes, in a large cohort of Danish patients. *JAMA Psychiatry, 73*(10), 1032.

Joshi, S., Mooney, S. J., Rundle, A. G., Quinn, J. W., Beard, J. R., & Cerdá, M. (2016). Pathways from neighborhood poverty to depression among older adults. *Health & Place, 43,* 138–143.

Joshi, S. V., Hartley, S. N., Kessler, M., & Barstead, M. (2015). School-based suicide prevention: Content, process, and the role of trusted adults and peers. *Child and Adolescent Psychiatric Clinics of North America, 24*(2), 353–370.

Jovanovic, T., Nylocks, K. M., Gamwell, K. L., Smith, A., Davis, T. A., Norrholm, S. D., & Bradley, B. (2014). Development of fear acquisition and extinction in children: Effects of age and anxiety. *Neurobiology of Learning and Memory, 113,* 135–142.

Joyal, C. C. (2015). Defining "normophilic" and "paraphilic" sexual fantasies in a population-based sample: On the importance of considering subgroups. *Sexual Medicine, 3*(4), 321–330.

Juan, W., Ziao-Juan, D., Jia-Ji, W., Xin-Wang, W., & Liang, X. (2011). How do risk-taking behaviors relate to suicide ideation and attempts in adolescents? *Clinician's Research Digest, 29*(1).

Juckel, G. (2014). Serotonin: From sensory processing to schizophrenia using an electrophysiological method. *Behavioural Brain Research.* [Advance electronic publication]

Juel-Nielsen, N., & Videbech, T. (1970). A twin study of suicide. *Acta Geneticae Medicae et Gemellologiae, 19,* 307–310.

Juliano, L. M., Anderson, B. L., & Griffiths, R. R. (2011). Caffeine. In J. H. Lowinson & P. Ruiz (Eds.), *Substance abuse: A comprehensive textbook* (5th ed.). Philadelphia, PA: Lippincott Williams & Wilkins.

Juliano, L. M., & Griffiths, R. R. (2004). A critical review of caffeine withdrawal: Empirical validation of symptoms and signs, incidence, severity, and associated features. *Psychopharmacology, 176*(1), 1.

Juvonen, J., & Ho, A. Y. (2008). Social motives underlying antisocial behavior across middle school grades. *Journal of Youth and Adolescence, 37*, 747.

Kabat-Zinn, J. (2005). *Wherever you go, there you are: Mindfulness meditation in everyday life.* New York: Hyperion.

Kagan, J. (2007). The limitations of concepts in developmental psychology. In G. W. Ladd (Ed.), *Appraising the human developmental sciences: Essays in honor of Merrill-Palmer Quarterly* (pp. 30–37). Detroit, MI: Wayne State University Press.

Kahn, A. P., & Fawcett, J. (1993). *The encyclopedia of mental health.* New York: Facts on File.

Kaipainen, K., Välkkynen, P., & Kilkku, N. (2016, November 28). Applicability of acceptance and commitment therapy-based mobile app in depression nursing. *Translational Behavioral Medicine.* [Epub ahead of print]

Kalibatseva, Z., & Leong, F. T. L. (2014). A critical review of culturally sensitive treatments for depression: Recommendations for intervention and research. *Psychological Services, 1*(4), 433–450.

Kamenov, K., Twomey, C., Cabello, M., Prina, A. M., & Ayuso-Mateos, J. L. (2017). The efficacy of psychotherapy, pharmacotherapy and their combination on functioning and quality of life in depression: A meta-analysis. *Psychological Medicine, 47*(3), 414–425.

Kaminski, J. W., & Claussen, A. H. (2017). Evidence-base update for psychosocial treatments for disruptive behaviors in children. *Journal of Clinical Child and Adolescent Psychology, 46*, 477–499.

Kampman, K. (2017, May 15). Approach to treatment of stimulant use disorder in adults. *UpToDate.* Retrieved from http://www.uptodate.com.

Kampmann, I. L., Emmelkamp, P. M., Hartanto, D., Brinkman, W. P., Zijlstra, B. J., & Morina, N. (2016). Exposure to virtual social interactions in the treatment of social anxiety disorder: A randomized controlled trial. *Behaviour Research and Therapy, 77*, 147–156.

Kan, K. J., Dolan, C. V., Nivard, M. G., Middeldorp, C. M., van Beijsterveldt, C. E., Willemsen, G., & Boomsma, D. I. (2013). Genetic and environmental stability in attention problems across the lifespan: Evidence from the Netherlands twin register. *Journal of the American Academy of Child and Adolescent Psychiatry, 52*, 12–25.

Kane, J. M., Robinson, D. G., Schooler, N. R., Mueser, K. T., Penn, D. L., Rosenheck, R. A., . . . Heinssen, R. K. (2016). Comprehensive versus usual community care for first-episode psychosis: 2-year outcomes from the NIMH RAISE Early Treatment Program. *American Journal of Psychiatry, 173*(4), 362.

Kanehisa, M., Kawashima, C., Nakanishi, M., Okamoto, K., Oshita, H., Masuda, K., . . . Akiyoshi, J. (2017). Gender differences in automatic thoughts and cortisol and alpha-amylase responses to acute psychosocial stress in patients with obsessive-compulsive personality disorder. *Journal of Affective Disorders, 217*, 1–7.

Kang, H. S., Myung, W., Na, D. L., Kim, S. Y., Lee, J., Han, S., . . . Kim, D. K. (2014). Factors associated with caregiver burden in patients with Alzheimer's disease. *Psychiatry Investigation, 11*(2), 152–159.

Kang, S. G., Na, K. S., Choi, J. W., Kim, J. H., Son, Y. D., & Lee, Y. J. (2016). Resting-state functional connectivity of the amygdala in suicide attempters with major depressive disorder. *Progress in Neuro-Psychopharmacology & Biological Psychiatry, 77*, 222–227.

Kangelaris, K. N., Vittinghoff, E., Otte, C., Na, B., Auerbach, A. D., & Whooley, M. A. (2010). Association between a serotonin transporter gene variant and hopelessness among men in the Heart and Soul Study. *Journal of General Internal Medicine, 25*(10), 1030–1037.

Kanner, B. (1995). *Are you normal? Do you behave like everyone else?* New York: St. Martin's Press.

Kanner, B. (1998, February). Are you normal? Turning the other cheek. *American Demographics.*

Kanner, B. (2005). *Are you normal about sex, love, and relationships?* New York: St. Martin's Press.

Kanner, L. (1943). Autistic disturbances of affective contact. *Nervous Child, 2*, 217.

Kanner, L. (1954). To what extent is early infantile autism determined by constitutional inadequacies? In *Genetics and the inheritance of integrated neurological and psychiatric patterns.* Baltimore: Williams and Wilkins.

Kantor, E. D., Rehm, C. D., Haas, J. S., Chan, A. T., & Giovannucci, E. L. (2015). Trends in prescription drug use among adults in the United States from 1999–2012. *Journal of the American Medical Association, 314*(17), 1818–1831.

Kantor, M. (2010). *The essential guide to overcoming avoidant personality disorder.* Santa Barbara, CA: Praeger/ABC-CLIO.

Kantrowitz, B., & Springen, K. (2004, August 9). What dreams are made of. *Newsweek, 144*(6), 40–47.

Kapardis, A. (2017). Offender-profiling today: An overview. In C. D. Spinellis, N. Theodorakis, E. Billis, & G. Papadimitrakopoulos (Eds.), *Europe in crisis: Crime, criminal justice, and the way forward* (pp. 739–754). Greece: Ant. N. Sakkoulas Publishers. Retrieved from http://www.crime-in-crisis.com.

Kapfhammer, H. P. (2017). Factitious disorders. *Nervenarzt, 88*(5), 549–570. [German]

Kaplan, H. S. (1974). *The new sex therapy: Active treatment of sexual dysfunction.* New York: Brunner/Mazel.

Kaplan, M. (2016). Clinical considerations regarding regression in psychotherapy with patients with conversion disorder. *Psychodynamic Psychiatry, 44*(3), 367–384.

Karam, S. M., Barros, A. J., Matijasevich, A., Dos Santos, I. S., Anselmi, L., Barros, F., . . . Black, M. M. (2016). Intellectual disability in a birth cohort: Prevalence, etiology, and determinants at the age of 4 years. *Public Health Genomics, 19*(5), 290–297.

Karch, C. M., Jeng, A. T., & Goate, A. M. (2013). Calcium phosphatase calcineurin influences tau metabolism. *Neurobiology of Aging, 34*(2), 374–386.

Karim, A. K., & Begum, T. (2017). The parental bonding instrument: A psychometric measure to assess parenting practices in the homes in Bangladesh. *Asian Journal of Psychiatry, 25*, 231–239.

Karlsson, E. (2017). How anti-psychiatry researchers attack antidepressants with faulty statistics. *Debunking Denialism*, February 21.

Karmiloff-Smith, A., Doherty, B., Cornish, K., & Scerif, G. (2016). Fragile X syndrome as a multilevel model for understanding behaviorally defined disorders. In D. Cicchetti (ed.), *Developmental psychopathology, Vol. 3: Maladaptation and psychopathology* (3rd ed.). New York: Wiley.

Karon, B. P. (1985). Omission in review of treatment interactions. *Schizophrenia Bulletin, 11*(1), 16–17.

Karsoho, H., Fishman, J. R., Wright, D. K., & Macdonald, M. E. (2016). Suffering and medicalization at the end of life: The case of physician-assisted dying. *Social Science & Medicine, 170*, 188–196.

Kashdan, T. B., Adams, L., Savostyanova, A., Ferssizidis, P., McKnight, P. E., & Nezlek, J. B. (2011). Effects of social anxiety and depressive symptoms on the frequency and quality of sexual activity: A daily process approach. *Behaviour Research and Therapy, 49*(5), 352–360.

Kaslow, N. J. (2014, December 23). The psychology of torture. *American Psychological Association.*

Kassel, J. D., Wardle, M. C., Heinz, A. J., & Greenstein, J. E. (2010). Cognitive theories of drug effects on emotion. In J. D. Kassel (Ed.), *Substance abuse and emotion* (pp. 61–82). Washington, DC: American Psychological Association.

Katz, J. (2017, June 5). Drug deaths in America are rising faster than ever. *New York Times,* Section: The Upshot.

Katz, L. Y., Kozyrskyj, A. L., Prior, H. J., Enns, M. W., Cox, B. J., & Sareen, J. (2008). Effect of regulatory warnings on antidepressant prescription rates, use of health services and outcomes among children, adolescents and young adults. *Canadian Medical Association Journal, 178*(8), 1005–1011.

Kauders, A. D. (2017). The social before sociocognitive theory: Explaining hypnotic suggestion in German-speaking Europe, 1900–1960. *American Journal of Clinical Hypnosis, 59*(4).

Kaufman, L. (2014, February 4). In texting era, crisis hotlines put help at youths' fingertips. *New York Times.*

Kaufman, S. B. (2013, October 3). The real link between creativity and mental illness. *Scientific American.*

Kaye, W. H., Wierenga, C. E., Bailer, U. F., Simmons, A. N., & Bischoff-Grethe, A. (2013). Nothing tastes as good as skinny feels: The neurobiology of anorexia nervosa. *Trends in Neurosciences, 36*(2), 110–120.

Kayhan, F., Küçük, A., Satan, Y., Ilgün, E., Arslan, S., & Ilik, F. (2016). Sexual dysfunction, mood, anxiety, and personality disorders in female patients with fibromyalgia. *Neuropsychiatric Disease and Treatment, 12*, 349–355.

Kazano, H. (2012). Asylum: The huge psychiatric hospital in the 19th century U.S. *Seishin*

Shinkeigaku Zasshi = Psychiatria Et Neurologia Japonica, 114(10), 1194–1200.

Kazdin, A. E. (2002). Psychosocial treatments for conduct disorder in children and adolescents. In P. E. Nathan & J. M. Gorman (Eds.), *A guide to treatments that work* (2nd ed., pp. 57–85). London: Oxford University Press.

Kazdin, A. E. (2005). *Parent management training: Treatment for oppositional, aggressive, and antisocial behavior in children and adolescents.* New York: Oxford University Press.

Kazdin, A. E. (2010). Problem-solving skills training and parent management training for oppositional defiant disorder and conduct disorder. In J. R. Weisz, & A. E. Kazdin (Eds.), *Evidence-based psychotherapies for children and adolescents* (2nd ed., pp. 211–226) New York: Guilford Press.

Kazdin, A. E. (2012). *Behavior modification in applied settings* (7th ed.). Long Grove, IL: Waveland Press.

Kazdin, A. E. (2015). Clinical dysfunction and psychosocial interventions: The interplay of research, methods, and conceptualization of challenges. *Annual Review of Clinical Psychology, 11*, 25–52.

Kazdin, A. E. (2017). *Research design in clinical psychology* (4th ed.). New York: Pearson.

Kearney, C. A. (2013). *Casebook in child behavior disorders* (5th ed.). Independence, KY: Cengage Publications.

Kedmey, D. (2013, June 5). Avatar therapy may silence schizophrenia sufferers' demons. *Time.*

Keefer, A. (2015, January 28). Elderly living with family. *Livestrong.com.* Retrieved from Live Strong website: http://www.livestrong.com/article/95828.

Keen, E. (1970). *Three faces of being: Toward an existential clinical psychology.* New York: Appleton-Century-Crofts.

Keene, C. D., Montine, T. J., & Kuller, L. H. (2017, May 30). Epidemiology, pathology, and pathogenesis of Alzheimer disease. *UpToDate.* Retrieved from http://www.uptodate.com.

Keeshin, B. R., Strawn, J. R., Luebbe, A. M., Saddaña, S. N., Wehry, A. M., DelBello, M. P., & Putnam, F. W. (2014). Hospitalized youth and child abuse: A systematic examination of psychiatric morbidity and clinical severity. *Child Abuse and Neglect, 38*(1), 76–83.

Keitner, G. (2017, March 30). Family and couples therapy for treating depressed adults. *UpToDate.* Retrieved from https://uptodate.com.

Keller, W. R., Fischer, B. A., McMahon, R., Meyer, W., Blake, M., & Buchanan, R. W. (2014). Community adherence to schizophrenia treatment and safety monitoring guidelines. *Journal of Nervous and Mental Disease, 202*(1), 6–12.

Kellett, S., & Hardy, G. (2014). Treatment of paranoid personality disorder with cognitive analytic therapy: A mixed methods single case experimental design. *Clinical Psychology and Psychotherapy, 21*(5), 452–464.

Kelley, M. L., Linden, A. N., Milletich, R. J., Lau-Barraco, C., Kurtz, E. D., D'Lima, G. M., . . . Sheehan, B. E. (2014). Self and partner alcohol-related problems among ACOAs and non-ACOAs: Associations with depressive symptoms and motivations for alcohol use. *Addictive Behaviors, 39*(1), 211–218.

Kellner, C. (2016, August 23). Unipolar major depression in adults: Indications for and efficacy of electroconvulsive therapy (ECT). *UpToDate.* Retrieved from www.uptodate.com.

Kellner, C. (2016, October 4). Bipolar disorder in adults: Indications for and efficacy of electroconvulsive therapy (ECT). *UpToDate.* Retrieved from www.uptodate.com.

Kellner, C. (2017, January 12). Technique for performing electroconvulsive therapy (ECT) in adults. *UpToDate.* Retrieved from www.uptodate.com.

Kellner, C. H., Husain, M. M., Knapp, R. G., McCall, W. V., Petrides, G., Rudorfer, M. V., . . . CORE/PRIDE Work Group. (2016). Right unilateral ultrabrief pulse ECT in geriatric depression: Phase 1 of the PRIDE Study. *American Journal of Psychiatry, 173*(11), 1101–1109.

Kelly, J. F. (2017). Is Alcoholics Anonymous religious, spiritual, neither? Findings from 25 years of mechanisms of behavior change research. *Addiction, 112*(6), 929–936.

Kelly, K. M., & Mezuk, B. (2017). Predictors of remission from generalized anxiety disorder and major depressive disorder. *Journal of Affective Disorders, 208*, 467–474.

Kendall, J., & Hatton, D. (2002). Racism as a source of health disparity in families with children with attention deficit hyperactivity disorder. *Advances in Nursing Science, 25*(2), 22–39.

Kendall-Tackett, K. A. (2010). *Depression in new mothers: Causes, consequences, and treatment alternatives* (2nd ed.). New York: Routledge/Taylor & Francis Group.

Kendig, S., Keats, J. P., Hoffman, M. C., Kay, L. B., Miller, E. S., Simas, T. A., . . . Lemieux, L. A. (2017). Consensus bundle on maternal mental health: Perinatal depression and anxiety. *Journal of Midwifery & Women's Health, 129*, 422–430.

Kendler, K. S., Aggen, S. H., Czajkowski, N., Reysamb, E., Tambs, K., Torgersen, S., . . . Reichborn-Kjennerud, T. (2008). The structure of genetic and environmental risk factors for DSM-IV personality disorders: A multivariate twin study. *Archives of General Psychiatry, 65*(12), 1438.

Kendler, K. S., & Engstrom, E. J. (2016). Kahlbaum, Hecker, and Kraepelin and the transition from psychiatric symptom complexes to empirical disease forms. *American Journal of Psychiatry.* [Advance online publication.]

Kendler, K. S., Heath, A., & Martin, N. G. (1987). A genetic epidemiologic study of self-report suspiciousness. *Comprehensive Psychiatry, 28*(3), 187–196.

Kendler, K. S., Neale, M. C., Kessler, R. C., Heath, A. C., & Eaves, L. J. (1993). Panic disorder in women: A population-based twin study. *Psychological Medicine, 23*, 397–406.

Kendler, K. S., Ohlsson, H., Keefe, R. S. E., Sundquist, K., & Sundquist, J. (2018). The joint impact of cognitive performance in adolescence and familial cognitive aptitude on risk for major psychiatric disorders: A delineation of four potential pathways to illness. *Molecular Psychiatry.* [Manuscript in press]

Kendler, K. S., Ochs, A. L., Gorman, A. M., Hewitt, J. K., Ross, D. E., & Mirsky, A. F. (1991). The structure of schizotypy: A pilot multitrait twin study. *Psychiatry Research, 36*(1), 19–36.

Kendler, K. S., Walters, E. E., Neale, M. C., Kessler, R. C., Heath, A. C., & Eaves, L. J. (1995). The structure of the genetic and environmental risk factors for six major psychiatric disorders in women: Phobia, generalized anxiety disorder, panic disorder, bulimia, major depression, and alcoholism. *Archives of General Psychiatry, 52*(5), 374–383.

Kenneback, S., & Bonin, L. (2016, October 4). Suicidal behavior in children and adolescents: Epidemiology and risk factors. *UpToDate.* Retrieved from www.uptodate.com.

Kennebeck, S., & Bonin, L. (2017, April 7). Suicidal ideation and behavior in children and adolescents: Evaluation and management. *UpToDate.* Retrieved from www.uptodate.com.

Kerber, K., Taylor, K., & Riba, M. B. (2011). Treatment resistant depression and comorbid medical problems: Cardiovascular disease and cancer. In J. F. Greden, M. B. Riba, & M. G. McInnis (Eds.), *Treatment resistant depression: A roadmap for effective care* (pp. 137–156). Arlington, VA: American Psychiatric Publishing.

Kernberg, O. F. (1989). Narcissistic personality disorder in childhood. *Psychiatric Clinics of North America, 12*(3), 671–694.

Kernberg, O. F. (1992). *Aggression in personality disorders and its perversions.* New Haven, CT: Yale University Press.

Kernberg, O. F. (1997). Convergences and divergences in contemporary psychoanalytic technique and psychoanalytic psychotherapy. In J. K. Zeig (Ed.), *The evolution of psychotherapy: The third conference.* New York: Brunner/Mazel.

Kernberg, O. F. (2001). The concept of libido in the light of contemporary psychoanalytic theorizing. In P. Hartocollis (Ed.), *Mankind's Oedipal destiny: Libidinal and aggressive aspects of sexuality* (pp. 95–111). Madison, CT: International Universities Press.

Kernberg, O. F. (2005). Object relations theories and technique. In E. S. Person, A. M. Cooper, & G. O. Gabbard (Eds.), *The American Psychiatric Publishing textbook of psychoanalysis* (pp. 57–75). Washington, DC: American Psychiatric Publishing.

Kernberg, O. F. (2010). Narcissistic personality disorder. In J. F. Clarkin, P. Fonagy, & G. O. Gabbard (Eds.), *Psychodynamic psychotherapy for personality disorders: A clinical handbook* (pp. 257–287). Arlington, VA: American Psychiatric Publishing.

Kerns, C. E., Elkins, R. M., Carpenter, A. L., Chou, T., Green, J. G., & Comer, J. S. (2014). Caregiver distress, shared traumatic exposure, and child adjustment among area youth following the 2013 Boston Marathon bombing. *Journal of Affective Disorders, 167*, 50–55.

Kerns, C., Pincus, D. B., McLaughlin, K., & Comer, J. S. (2017). Maternal emotion regulation during child distress, child anxiety accommodation, and links between maternal and child anxiety. *Journal of Anxiety Disorders, 50*, 52–59.

Kerr, J. H., Lindner, K. J., & Blaydon, M. (2007). *Exercise dependence.* London: Routledge.

Kerridge, B. T., Pickering, R., Chou, P., Saha, T. D., & Hasin, D. S. (2018). DSM-5 cannabis use disorder in the National Epidemiologic Survey on Alcohol and Related Conditions-III: Gender-specific profiles. *Addictive Behaviors, 76*, 52–60.

Kessler, R. C., Adler, L. A., Barkley, R., Biederman, J., Conners, C. K., Faraone, S. V., . . . Zaslavsky, A. M. (2005). Patterns and predictors of attention-deficit/hyperactivity disorder persistence into adulthood: Results from the National Comorbidity Survey Replication. *Biological Psychiatry, 57*(11), 1442–1451.

Kessler, R. C., Adler, L. A., Berglund, P., Green, J. G., McLaughlin, K. A., Fayyad, J., Russo, L. J., Sampson, N. A., Shahly, V., & Zaslavsky, A. M. (2014). The effects of temporally secondary co-morbid mental disorders on the associations of DSM-IV ADHD with adverse outcomes in the U.S. National Comorbidity Survey Replication Adolescent Supplement (NCS-A). *Psychological Medicine, 44*(8), 1779–1792.

Kessler, R. C., Avenevoli, S., Green, J., Gruber, M. J., Guyer, M., He, Y., . . . Merikangas, K. R. (2009). National comorbidity survey replication adolescent supplement (NCS-A): III. Concordance of DSM-IV/CIDI diagnoses with clinical reassessments. *Journal of the American Academy of Child and Adolescent Psychiatry, 48*(4), 386–399.

Kessler, R. C., Demier, O., Frank, R. G., Olfson, M., Pincus, H. A., Walters, E. E., . . . Zaslavsky, A. M. (2005). Prevalence and treatment of mental disorders, 1990 to 2003. *The New England Journal of Medicine, 352*(24), 2515–2523.

Kessler, R. C., DuPont, R. L., Berglund, P., & Wittchen, H. U. (1999). Impairment in pure and comorbid generalized anxiety disorder and major depression at 12 months in two national surveys. *American Journal of Psychiatry, 156*(12), 1915–1923.

Kessler, R. C., Gruber, M., Hettema, J. M., Hwang, I., Sampson, N., & Yonkers, K. A. (2010). Major depression and generalized anxiety disorder in the National Comorbidity Survey follow-up survey. In D. Goldberg, K. S. Kendler, P. J. Sirovatka, & D. A. Regier (Eds.), *Diagnostic issues in depression and generalized anxiety disorder: Refining the research agenda for DSM-V* (pp. 139–170). Washington, DC: American Psychiatric Association.

Kessler, R. C., McGonagle, K. A., Zhao, S., Nelson, C. B., Hughes, M., Eshleman, S., . . . Kendler, K. S. (1994). Lifetime and 12-month prevalence of DSM-III-R psychiatric disorders among persons aged 15–54 in the United States: Results from the National Comorbidity Survey. *Archives of General Psychiatry, 51*(1), 8–19.

Kessler, R. C., Petukhova, M., Sampson, N. A., Zaslavsky, A. M., & Wittchen, H. (2012). Twelve-month and lifetime prevalence and lifetime morbid risk of anxiety and mood disorders in the United States. *International Journal of Methods In Psychiatric Research, 21*(3), 169–184.

Kessler, R. C., Ruscio, A. M., Shear, K., & Wittchen, H-U. (2010). Epidemiology of anxiety disorders. In M. B. Stein & T. Steckler (Eds.), *Behavioral neurobiology of anxiety and its treatment. Current topics in behavioral neurosciences* (pp. 21–35). New York: Springer Science + Business Media.

Kessler, R. C., Sampson, N. A., Berglund, P., Gruber, M. J., Al-Hamzawi, A., Andrade, L., . . . Wilcox, M. A. (2015). Anxious and non-anxious major depressive disorder in the World Health Organization Mental Health Surveys. *Epidemiology and Psychiatry Sciences, 24*(3), 210–226.

Kety, S. S. (1988). Schizophrenic illness in the families of schizophrenic adoptees: Findings from the Danish national sample. *Schizophrenia Bulletin, 14*(2), 217–222.

Kety, S. S., Rosenthal, D., Wender, P. H., & Schulsinger, F. (1968). The types and prevalence of mental illness in the biological and adoptive families of schizophrenics. *Journal of Psychiatric Research, 6,* 345–362.

Keuthen, N. J., Siev, J., & Reese, H. (2012). Assessment of trichotillomania, pathological skin picking, and stereotypic movement disorder. In J. E. Grant, D. J. Stein, D. W. Woods, N. J. Keuthen (Eds.), *Trichotillomania, skin picking, and other body-focused repetitive behaviors* (pp. 129–150). Arlington, VA: American Psychiatric Publishing.

Keys, A., Brozek, J., Henschel, A., Mickelson, O., & Taylor, H. L. (1950). *The biology of human starvation.* Minneapolis: University of Minnesota Press.

KFF (Kaiser Family Foundation). (2016). *Population distribution by race/ethnicity.* Retrieved from http://kff.org/other/state-indicator/distribution-by-race/ethnicity.

Khan, A. (2015). The amyloid hypothesis and potential treatments for Alzheimer's disease. *Journal of Quality Research in Dementia, 4.* Retrieved from Alzheimers website: http://www.alzheimers.org.uk.

Khan, M. Z. (2016). A possible significant role of zinc and GPR39 zinc sensing receptor in Alzheimer disease and epilepsy. *Biomedicine & Pharmacotherapy, 79,* 263–272.

Khandaker, G., Jung, J., Britton, P. N., King, C., Yin, J. K., & Jones, C. A. (2016). Long-term outcomes of infective encephalitis in children: A systematic review and meta-analysis. *Developmental Medicine and Child Neurology, 58,* 1108–1115.

Kharasch, E. D. (2017). Current concepts in methadone metabolism and transport. *Clinical Pharmacology in Drug Development, 6*(2), 125–134.

Khazan, O. (2015, April 7). Most prisoners are mentally ill. *The Atlantic.*

Khazan, O. (2017, April 18). The link between opioids and unemployment. *The Atlantic.*

Kibria, A. A., & Metcalfe, N. H. (2016). A biography of William Tuke (1732–1822): Founder of the modern mental asylum. *Journal of Medical Biography, 24*(3), 384–388.

Kiecolt-Glaser, J. K., Garner, W., Speicher, C., Penn, G. M., Holliday, J., & Glaser, R. (1984). Psychosocial modifiers of immunocompetence in medical students. *Psychosomatic Medicine, 46,* 7–14.

Kiecolt-Glaser, J. K., Glaser, R., Gravenstein, S., Malarkey, W. B., & Sheridan, J. (1996). Chronic stress alters the immune response to influenza virus vaccine in older adults. *Proceedings of the National Academy of Science, 93,* 3043–3047.

Kienast, T., Stoffers, J., Bermpohl, F., & Lieb, K. (2014). Borderline personality disorder and comorbid addiction: Epidemiology and treatment. *Deutsches Ärzteblatt International, 111*(16), 280–286.

Kiernan, W. (2000). Where we are now: Perspectives on employment of persons with mental retardation. *Focus on Autism and Other Developmental Disabilities, 15*(2), 90–96.

Kiesler, D. J. (1966). Some myths of psychotherapy research and the search for a paradigm. *Psychological Bulletin, 65,* 110–136.

Kiesler, D. J. (1995). Research classic: Some myths of psychotherapy research and the search for a paradigm: Revisited. *Psychotherapy Research, 5*(2), 91–101.

Kiev, A. (1989). Suicide in adults. In J. G. Howells (Ed.), *Modern perspectives in the psychiatry of the affective disorders.* New York: Brunner/Mazel.

Kikkert, M. J., Driessen, E., Peen, J., Barber, J. P., Bockting, C., Schalkwijk, F., . . . Dekker, J. J. (2016). The role of avoidant and obsessive-compulsive personality disorder traits in matching patients with major depression to cognitive behavioral and psychodynamic therapy: A replication study. *Journal of Affective Disorders, 205,* 400–405.

Kikuchi, H., Fujii, T., Abe, N., Suzuki, M., Takagi, M., Mugikura, S., Takahashi, S., & Mori, E. (2010). Memory repression: Brain mechanisms underlying dissociative amnesia. *Journal of Cognitive Neuroscience, 22*(3), 602–613.

Killingsworth, M. (2013, July 16). Does mind-wandering make you unhappy? *Greater Good.* Retrieved from http://greatergood.berkeley.edu.

Killingsworth, M. A., & Gilbert, D. T. (2010). A wandering mind is an unhappy mind. *Science, 330*(6006), 932.

Kim, C., & Cho, Y. (2017). Does unstable employment have an association with suicide rates among the young? *International Journal of Environmental Research and Public Health, 14*(5).

Kim, D. R., Epperson, C. N., Weiss, A. R., & Wisner, K. L. (2014). Pharmacotherapy of postpartum depression: An update. *Expert Opinion on Pharmacotherapy, 15*(9), 1223–1234.

Kim, E., Lee, J-A., Sung, Y., & Choi, S. M. (2016). Predicting self-posting behavior on social networking sites: An extension of theory of planned behavior. *Computers in Human Behavior, 62,* 116–123.

Kim, E. S., Chopik, W. J., & Smith, J. (2014). Are people healthier if their partners are more optimistic? The dyadic effect of optimism on health among older adults. *Journal of Psychosomatic Research, 76*(6), 447–453.

Kim, H., Lim, C-S., & Kaang, B-K. (2016). Neuronal mechanisms and circuits underlying repetitive behaviors in mouse models of autism spectrum disorder. *Behavioral and Brain Functions, 12,* 3.

Kim, J. M., Park, J. W., & Lee, C. S. (2014). Evaluation of nocturnal bladder capacity and nocturnal urine volume in nocturnal enuresis. *Journal of Pediatric Urology, 10*(3), 559–563.

Kim, J. S., Lee, E. J., Chang, D. I., Park, J. H., Ahn, S. H., Cha, J. K., . . . Choi-Kwon, S. (2017). Efficacy of early administration of escitalopram on depressive and emotional symptoms and neurological dysfunction after stroke: A multicentre, double-blind, randomised, placebo-controlled study. *Lancet Psychiatry, 4*(1), 33–41.

Kim, J. W., & Chock, T. M. (2015, July). Body image 2.0: Associations between social grooming on Facebook and body image concerns.

Computers in Human Behavior, 48(2015), 331–339.

Kim, J. Y., Yang, S. H., Kwon, J., Lee, H. W., & Kim, H. (2017). Mice subjected to uncontrollable electric shocks show depression-like behaviors irrespective of their state of helplessness. *Behavioural Brain Research, 322*(Pt. A), 138–144.

Kim, K-H., Lee, S-M., Paik, J-W., & Kim, N-S. (2011). The effects of continuous antidepressant treatment during the first 6 months on relapse or recurrence of depression. *Journal of Affective Disorders, 132*(1), 121–129.

Kim, K. J., Na, Y. K., & Hong, H. S. (2016). Effects of progressive muscle relaxation therapy in colorectal cancer patients. *Western Journal of Nursing Research, 38*(7), 959–973.

Kim, M. K., Kim, B., Kiu Choi, T., & Lee, S. H. (2017). White matter correlates of anxiety sensitivity in panic disorder. *Journal of Affective Disorders, 207*, 148–156.

Kim, M. K., Lee, K. S., Kim, B., Choi, T. K., & Lee, S. H. (2016). Impact of mindfulness-based cognitive therapy on intolerance of uncertainty in patients with panic disorder. *Psychiatry Investigation, 13*(2), 196–202.

Kim, S., Colwell, S. R., Kata, A., Boyle, M. H., Georgiades, K. (2018). Cyberbullying victimization and adolescent mental health: Evidence of differential effects by sex and mental health problem type. *Journal of Youth and Adolescence.* [Manuscript in press]

Kim, S., Ha, J. H., Yu, J., Park, D., & Ryu, S. (2014). Path analysis of suicide ideation in older people. *International Psychogeriatrics / IPA, 26*(3), 509–515.

Kim, S. M., Baek, J. H., Han, D. H., Lee, Y. S., & Yurgelun-Todd, D. A. (2015). Psychosocial environmental risk factors for suicide attempts in adolescents with suicide ideation: Findings from a sample of 73,238 adolescents. *Suicide & Life-Threatening Behavior, 45*(4), 477–487.

Kimball, A. (1993). Nipping and tucking. In Skin deep: Our national obsession with looks. *Psychology Today, 26*(3), 96.

King, L. (2002, March 19). Interview with Russell Yates. *Larry King Live, CNN.*

King, M., Lodwick, R., Jones, R., Whitaker, H., & Petersen, I. (2017). Death following partner bereavement: A self-controlled case series analysis. *PLoS ONE, 12*(3), e0173870.

King, R. A. (2003). Psychodynamic approaches to youth suicide. In R. A. King & A. Apter (Eds.), *Suicide in children and adolescents* (pp. 150–169). New York: Cambridge University Press.

King, S. M., Iacono, W. G., & McGue, M. (2004). Childhood externalizing and internalizing psychopathology in the prediction of early substance use. *Addiction, 99*(12), 1548–1559.

Kingsberg, S. A., Tkachenko, N., Lucas, J., Burbrink, A., Kreppner, W., & Dickstein, J. B. (2013). Characterization of orgasmic difficulties by women: Focus group evaluation. *Journal of Sexual Medicine, 10*, 2242–2250.

Kiosses, D. N., Gross, J. J., Banerjee, S., Duberstein, P. R., Putrino, D., & Alexopoulos, G. S. (2017). Negative emotions and suicidal ideation during psychosocial treatments in older adults with major depression and cognitive impairment. *American Journal of Geriatric Psychiatry, 25*, 620–629.

Kirkham, F. J. (2017). Neurocognitive outcomes for acute global acquired brain injury in children. *Current Opinion in Neurology, 30,* 148–155.

Kirmayer, L. J. (2001). Cultural variations in the clinical presentation of depression and anxiety: Implications for diagnosis and treatment. *Journal of Clinical Psychiatry, 62*(Suppl. 13), 22–28.

Kirmayer, L. J. (2002). The refugee's predicament. *Evolution Psychiatrique, 67*(4), 724–742.

Kirmayer, L. J. (2003). Failures of imagination: The refugee's narrative in psychiatry. *Anthropology and Medicine, 10*(2), 167–185.

Kirsch, I. (2014). Antidepressants and the placebo effect. *Zeitschrift für Psychologie, 222*(3), 128–134.

Kishita, N., & Laidlaw, K. (2017). Cognitive behaviour therapy for generalized anxiety disorder: Is CBT equally efficacious in adults of working age and older adults? *Clinical Psychology Review, 52*, 124–136.

Klan, T., Jasper, F., & Hiller, W. (2017). Predictors of the application of exposure in vivo in the treatment of agoraphobia in an outpatient clinic: An exploratory approach. *Psychotherapy Research, 27*(1), 64–73.

Klein, D., & Attia, E. (2017, February 15). Anorexia nervosa in adults: Clinical features, course of illness, assessment, and diagnosis. *UpToDate.* Retrieved from www.uptodate.com.

Klein, D. F. (1964). Delineation of two drug-responsive anxiety syndromes. *Psychopharmacologia, 5*, 397–408.

Klein, D. F. (2016). RDoC is adverse to scientific creativity. *Acta Psychiatrica Scandinavica, 134*(5), 452–454.

Klein, D. F., & Fink, M. (1962). Psychiatric reaction patterns to imipramine. *American Journal of Psychiatry, 119*, 432–438.

Klein, E. R., Armstrong, S. L., & Shipon-Blum, E. (2013). Assessing spoken language competence in children with selective mutism: Using parents as test presenters. *Communication Disorders Quarterly, 34*, 184–195.

Klein, J. (2015). Chronic pain, psychopathology, and DSM-5 somatic symptom disorder. *Canadian Journal of Psychiatry, 60*(11), 528.

Kleinman, A. (2004). Culture and depression. *New England Journal of Medicine, 351*(10), 951–953.

Kleinplatz, P. J. (2010). "Desire disorders" or opportunities for optimal erotic intimacy? In S. R. Leiblum (Ed.), *Treating sexual desire disorders: A clinical casebook* (pp. 92–113). New York: Guilford Press.

Kline, N. S. (1958). Clinical experience with iproniazid (Marsilid). *Journal of Clinical and Experimental Psychopathology, 19*(1, Suppl.), 72–78.

Kluft, R. P. (1985). Hypnotherapy of childhood multiple personality disorder. *American Journal of Clinical Hypnosis, 27*(4), 201–210.

Kluft, R. P. (1987). The simulation and dissimulation of multiple personality disorder. *American Journal of Clinical Hypnosis, 30*(2), 104–118.

Kluft, R. P. (1988). The dissociative disorders. In J. Talbott, R. Hales, & S. Yudofsky (Eds.), *Textbook of psychiatry.* Washington, DC: American Psychiatric Press.

Kluft, R. P. (1991). Multiple personality disorder. In A. Tasman & S. M. Goldfinger (Eds.), *American Psychiatric Press review of psychiatry* (Vol. 10). Washington, DC: American Psychiatric Press.

Kluft, R. P. (2000). The psychoanalytic psychotherapy of dissociative identity disorder in the context of trauma therapy. *Psychoanalytical Inquiry, 20*(2), 259–286.

Kluft, R. P. (2001). Dissociative disorders. In H. S. Friedman (Ed.), *Specialty articles from the encyclopedia of mental health.* San Diego: Academic Press.

Knatz, S., Murray, S. B., Matheson, B., Boutelle, K. N., Rockwell, R., Eisler, I., & Kaye, W. H. (2015) A brief, intensive application of multi-family-based treatment for eating disorders. *Eating Disorders, 23*(4), 315–324.

Knecht, T. (2014). "Biastophilia"—rape as a form of paraphilia? *Archiv Für Kriminologie, 233*(3-4), 130–135.

Knezevic, D., & Mizrahi, R. (2018). Molecular imaging of neuroinflammation in Alzheimer's disease and mild cognitive impairment. *Progress in Neuro-Psychopharmacology and Biological Psychiatry, 80*(Pt. B), 123–131.

Knoll, J. L. (2010). The "pseudocommando" mass murderer: Part I, the psychology of revenge and obliteration. *Journal of the American Academy of Psychiatry and the Law. 38,* 87–94.

Knoll, J. L. (2015). The psychiatrist's duty to protect. *CNS Spectrums, 20*(3), 215–222.

Knott, L. (2011). Delusions and hallucinations. *Patient.co.uk.* Retrieved from http://www.patient.co.uk/print/1715.

Knott, L. (2011). Hypnagogic hallucinations. *Patient.co.uk.* Retrieved from http://www.patient.co.uk/print/2297.

Knowles, M. M., Foden, P., El-Deredy, W., & Wells, A. (2016). A systematic review of efficacy of the attention training technique in clinical and nonclinical samples. *Journal of Clinical Psychology, 72*(10), 999–1025.

Knowthenet. (2013). Nineteen year old males revealed as top trolling target. Retrieved from http://www.knowthenet.org.uk/articles/nineteen-year-old-males.

Knudson, R. M. (2006). Anorexia dreaming: A case study. *Dreaming, 16*(1), 43–52.

Ko, J. Y., Rockhill, K. M., Tong, V. T., Morrow, B., & Farr, S. L. (2017 February 17). Trends in postpartum depressive symptoms—27 states, 2004, 2008, and 2012. *Morbidity and Mortality Weekly Report/CDC, 66*(6), 153–158.

Kocsis, R. N. (2008). *Serial murder and the psychology of violent crimes.* Totowa, NJ: Humana Press.

Kocsis, R. N., & Palermo, G. B. (2013). Disentangling criminal profiling: Accuracy, homology, and the myth of trait-based profiling. *International Journal of Offender Therapy and Comparative Criminology,* December 12, 2013.

Kocsis, R. N., & Palermo, G. B. (2016. Criminal profiling as expert witness evidence: The implications of the profiler validity research. *International Journal of Law and Psychiatry, 49*(Pt. A), 55–65.

Koegel, L. K., Koegel, R. L., & Brookman, L. I. (2005). Child-initiated interactions that are pivotal in intervention for children with autism. In E. D. Hibbs & P. S. Jensen (Eds.), *Psychosocial treatments for child and adolescent disorders: Empirically based strategies for clinical practice* (2nd ed., pp. 633–657). Washington, DC: American Psychological Association.

Koegel, R. L., Koegel, L. K., Vernon, T. W., & Brookman-Frazee, L. (2010). Empirically supported pivotal response treatment for children with autism spectrum disorders. In J. R. Weisz, & A. E. Kazdin (Eds.), *Evidence-based psychotherapies for children and adolescents* (2nd ed., pp. 327–344) New York: Guilford Press.

Koenen, K. C., Lyons, M. J., Goldberg, J., Simpson, J., Williams, W. M., Toomey, R., et al. (2003). Co-twin control study of relationships among combat exposure, combat-related PTSD, and other mental disorders. *Journal of Traumatic Stress, 16*(5), 433–438.

Koenig, H. G. (2015). Religion, spirituality, and health: A review and update. *Advances in Mind-Body Medicine, 29*(3), 19–26.

Koenigsberg, H. W., Harvey, P., Mitropoulou, V., New, A. Goodman, M., Silverman, J., . . . Siever, L. J. (2001). Are the interpersonal and identity disturbances in the borderline personality disorder criteria linked to the traits of affectivity and impulsivity? *Journal of Personality Disorders, 15*, 358–370.

Koerner, B. I. (2007). Drug makers find new markets by publicizing "hidden epidemics" of mental illness. In A. Quigley (Ed.), *Current controversies: Mental health*. Detroit: Greenhaven Press/Thomson Gale.

Koerner, N., Mejia, T., & Kusec, A. (2017). What's in a name? Intolerance of uncertainty, other uncertainty-relevant constructs, and their differential relations to worry and generalized anxiety disorder. *Journal of Clinical Psychiatry, 46*(2), 141–161.

Koetting, C. (2015). Caregiver-fabricated illness in a child. *Journal of Forensic Nursing, 11*(2), 114–117.

Koh, M., Nishimatsu, Y., & Endo, S. (2000). Dissociative disorder. *Journal of International Society of Life Information Science, 18*(2), 495–498.

Koh, Y. W., Chui, C. Y., Tang, C. K., & Lee, A. M. (2014). The prevalence and risk factors of paternal depression from the antenatal to the postpartum period and the relationships between antenatal and postpartum depression among fathers in Hong Kong. *Depression Research and Treatment, 2014,* 127632.

Kohen, D. P., & Olness, K. (2011). *Hypnosis and hypnotherapy with children* (4th ed.). New York: Routledge/Taylor & Francis Group.

Kohut, H. (1977). *The restoration of the self*. New York: International Universities Press.

Kohut, H. (2001). On empathy. *European Journal for Psychoanalytic Therapy and Research, 2*(2), 139–146.

Kok, R., Avendano, M., Bago d'Uva, T., & Mackenbach, J. (2012). Can reporting heterogeneity explain differences in depressive symptoms across Europe? *Social Indicators Research, 105*(2), 191–210.

Kolar, D. (2017). Current status of electroconvulsive therapy for mood disorders: A clinical review. *Evidence-Based Mental Health, 20*, 12–14.

Kolata, G. (2016, October 1). The shame of fat shaming. *New York Times*.

Kolko, D. J., & Berkout, O. V. (2017, April). Child physical abuse. In S. N. Gold (Ed.), *APA handbook of trauma psychology* (Vol. 1, Chap. 17, pp. 99–115). Washington, DC: APA.

Konrad, N., Welke, J., & Opitz-Welke, A. (2015). Paraphilias. *Current Opinion in Psychiatry, 28*(6), 440–444.

Koo, K. H., Nguyen, H. V., Gilmore, A. K., Blayney, J. A., & Kaysen, D. L. (2014). Post-traumatic cognitions, somatization, and PTSD severity among Asian American and white college women in sexual trauma histories. *Psychological Trauma: Theory, Research, Practice and Policy, 6*(4), 337–344.

Kooyman, I., & Walsh, E. (2011). Societal outcomes in schizophrenia. In D. R. Weinberg & P. Harrison (Eds.), *Schizophrenia* (pp. 644–665). Hoboken, NJ: Wiley-Blackwell.

Kopelowicz, A., Liberman, R. P., & Zarate, R. (2007). Psychosocial treatments for schizophrenia. In P. E. Nathan & J. M. Gorman (Eds.), *A guide to treatments that work* (3rd ed., pp. 243–269). New York: Oxford University Press.

Kopelowicz, A., Liberman, R. P., & Zarate, R. (2008). Psychosocial treatments for schizophrenia. In K. T. Mueser & D. V. Jeste (Eds.), *Clinical handbook of schizophrenia* (pp. 243–269). New York: Guilford Press.

Korda, J. B., Goldstein, S. W., & Goldstein, I. (2010). The role of androgens in the treatment of hypoactive sexual desire disorder in women. In S. R. Leiblum (Ed.), *Treating sexual desire disorders: A clinical casebook* (pp. 201–218). New York: Guilford Press.

Korda, J. B., & Sommer, F. (2010). Anti-androgen treatment of paraphilias from the urologist's perspective. *Forensische Psychiatrie, Psychologie, Kriminologie, 4*(Suppl. 1), S17–S21.

Korte, K. J., Bountress, K. E., Tomko, R. L., Killeen, T., Moran-Santa Maria, M., & Back, S. E. (2017). Integrated treatment of PTSD and substance use disorders: The mediating role of PTSD improvement in the reduction of depression. *Journal of Clinical Medicine, 6*(1), 9.

Kosinski, M., Stillwell, D., & Graepel, T. (2013). Private traits and attributes are predictable from digital records of human behavior. *Proceedings of the National Academy of Sciences of the United States of America, 110*(15), 5802–5805.

Koss, M. P. (1993). Rape: Scope, impact, interventions, and public policy responses. *American Psychologist, 48*(10), 1062–1069.

Koss, M. P. (2005). Empirically enhanced reflections on 20 years of rape research. *Journal of Interpersonal Violence, 20*(1), 100–107.

Koss, M. P., Abbey, A., Campbell, R., Cook, S., Norris, J., Testa, M., . . . White, J. (2008). Revising the SES: A collaborative process to improve assessment of sexual aggression and victimization: Erratum. *Psychology of Women Quarterly, 32*(4), 493.

Koss, M. P., & Heslet, L. (1992). Somatic consequences of violence against women. *Archives of Family Medicine, 1*(1), 53–59.

Koss, M. P., Swartout, K. M., White, J. W., Thompson, M. P., Abbey, A., & Bellis, A. L. (2015). Trajectory analysis of the campus serial rapist assumption. *JAMA Pediatrics, 169*, 1148–1154.

Koss, M. P., White, J. W., & Kazdin, A. E. (2011). Violence against women and children: Perspectives and next steps. In M. P. Koss, J. W. White, & A. E. Kazdin (Eds.), *Violence against women and children, Vol. 2: Navigating solutions* (pp. 261–305). Washington, DC: American Psychological Association.

Koss, M. P., White, J. W., & Kazdin, A. E. (Eds.). (2011). *Violence against women and children, Vol. 2: Navigating solutions*. Washington, DC: American Psychological Association.

Kosten, T. R., George, T. P., & Kleber, H. D. (2005). The neurobiology of substance dependence: Implications for treatment. In R. J. Frances, A. H. Mack, & S. I. Miller (Eds.), *Clinical textbook of addictive disorders* (3rd ed., pp. 3–15). New York: Guilford Press.

Kosten, T. R., George, T. P., & Kleber, H. D. (2011). The neurobiology of substance dependence: Implications for treatment. In R. J. Frances, S. I. Miller, & A. H. Mack (Eds.), *Clinical textbook of addictive disorders* (3rd ed., Chap. 1). New York: Guilford Press.

Kösters, G., Steinberg, H., Kirkby, K. C., & Himmerich, H. (2015). Ernst Rüdin's unpublished 1922–1925 study "Inheritance of manic-depressive insanity": Genetic research findings subordinated to eugenic ideology. *PLoS Genetics, 11*(11), e1005524.

Koutra, K., Triliva, S., Roumeliotaki, T., Basta, M., Simos, P., Lionis, C., & Vgontzas, A. N. (2015). Impaired family functioning in psychosis and its relevance to relapse: A two-year follow-up study. *Comprehensive Psychiatry, 62,* 1–12.

Kposowa, A. J., McElvain, J. P., & Breault, K. D. (2008). Immigration and suicide: The role of marital status, duration of residence, and social integration. *Archives of Suicide Research, 12*(1), 82–92.

Kraan, T. C., Velthorst, E., Themmen, M., Valmaggia, L., Kempton, M. J., McGire, P., . . . EGEI High Risk Study. (2018). Child maltreatment and clinical outcome in individuals at ultra-high risk for psychosis in the EU-GEI High Risk Study. *Schizophrenia Bulletin*. [Manuscript in press]

Krack, P., Hariz, M. I., Baunez, C., Guridi, J., & Obeso, J. A. (2010). Deep brain stimulation: From neurology to psychiatry? *Trends in Neurosciences, 33*(10), 474–484.

Kralovec, K., Kunrath, S., Fartacek, C., Pichler, E. M., & Plöderl, M. (2018). The gender-specific associations between religion/spirituality and suicide risk in a sample of Austrian psychiatric inpatients. *Suicide and Life-Threatening Behavior*. [Manuscript in press]

Kramer, A. D. I., Guillory, J. E., & Hancock, J. T. (2014). Experimental evidence of massive-scale emotional contagion through social networks. *PNAS, 111*(24), 8788–8790.

Kramer, U. (2017). The role of coping change in borderline personality disorder: A process-outcome analysis on dialectical-behaviour skills training. *Clinical Psychology & Psychotherapy, 24*(2), 302–311.

Kramer, U., & Meystre, C. (2010). Assimilation process in a psychotherapy with a client presenting schizoid personality disorder. *Schweizer Archiv für Neurologie und Psychiatrie, 161*(4), 128–134.

Krasnova, H., Wenninger, H., Widjaja, T., & Buxmann, P. (2013). Envy on Facebook: A hidden threat to users' life satisfaction? *Internationale Tagung Wirtschaftsinformatik, 27.02.* Retrieved from http://www.AISEL.SIDNRT.ORG/WI2013.

Krause, N., & Hayward, R. D. (2015). Race, religion, and virtues. *International Journal for the Psychology of Religion, 25*(2), 152–169.

Krause-Utz, A., Frost, R., Winter, D., & Elzinga, B. M. (2017). Dissociation and alterations in brain function and structure: Implications for borderline personality disorder. *Current Psychiatry Reports, 19*(1), 6.

Kravitz, R. L., Epstein, R. M., Feldman, M. D., Franz, C. E., Azari, R., Wilkes, M. S., . . . Franks, P. (2005). Influence of patients' requests for direct-to-consumer advertised antidepressants. *Journal of the American Medical Association, 293*(16), 1905–2002.

Krebs, G., de la Cruz, L. F., Monzani, B., Bowyer, L., Anson, M., Cadman, J., . . . Mataix-Cols, D. (2017). Long-term outcomes of cognitive-behavior therapy for adolescent body dysmorphic disorder. *Behavior Therapy.*

Kreukels, B. P. (2016). Quote cited in Russo, F. (2016, January 1). Is there something unique about the transgender brain? *Scientific American.*

Kring, A. M., & Neale, J. M. (1996). Do schizophrenic patients show a disjunctive relationship among expressive, experiential, and psychophysiological components of emotion? *Journal of Abnormal Psychology, 105*(2), 249–257.

Krippner, S., & Paulson, C. M. (2006). Post-traumatic stress disorder among U.S. combat veterans. In T. G. Plante (Ed.), *Mental disorders of the new millennium, Vol. 2: Public and social problems.* Westport, CT: Praeger Publishers.

Krisberg, B. A. (2018). *Juvenile justice and delinquency.* Thousand Oaks, CA: Sage.

Krishnan, R. (2017, March 7). Unipolar depression in adults: Epidemiology, pathogenesis, and neurobiology. *UpToDate.* Retrieved from http://www.uptodate.com.

Kroemer, N. B., Guevara, A., Vollstädt-Klein, S., & Smolka, M. N. (2013). Nicotine alters food-cue reactivity via networks extending from the hypothalamus. *Neuropsychopharmacology, 38*(11), 2307–2314.

Kroon Van Diest, A. M., Tartakovsky, M., Stachon, C., Pettit, J. W., & Perez, M. (2014). The relationship between acculturative stress and eating disorder symptoms: Is it unique from general life stress? *Journal of Behavioral Medicine, 37*(3), 445–457.

Krueger, R. B. (2010). The DSM diagnostic criteria for sexual masochism. *Archives of Sexual Behavior, 39*(2), 346–356.

Krug, O. (2016). Existential, humanistic, experiential psychotherapies in historical perspective. In A. J. Consoli, L. E. Beutler, & B. Bongar (Eds.), *Comprehensive textbook of psychotherapy: Theory and practice* (2nd ed., pp. 91–105). New York: Oxford University Press.

Krull, K. R. (2017, January 4). Attention deficit hyperactivity disorder in children and adolescents: Clinical features and diagnosis. *UpToDate.* Retrieved from http://www.uptodate.com.

Krull, K. R. (2017, June 14). Attention deficit hyperactivity disorder in children and adolescents: Overview of treatment and prognosis. *UpToDate.* Retrieved from http://www.uptodate.com.

Krull, K. R. (2017, March 28). Attention deficit hyperactivity disorder in children and adolescents: Epidemiology and pathogenesis. *UpToDate.* Retrieved from http://www.uptodate.com.

Krupnick, J. L., Green, B. L., Amdur, R., Alaoui, A., Belouali, A., Roberge, E., . . . Dutton, M. A. (2016, September 8). An Internet-based writing intervention for PTSD

in veterans: A feasibility and pilot effectiveness trial. *Psychological Trauma.* [Epub ahead of print]

Kuehner, C. (2017). Why is depression more common among women than among men? *Lancet Psychiatry, 4*(2), 146–158.

Kuhn, R. (1958). The treatment of depressive states with G-22355 (imipramine hydrochloride). *American Journal of Psychiatry, 115,* 459–464.

Kuhn, T. S. (1962). *The structure of scientific revolutions.* Chicago: University of Chicago Press.

Kukla, L., Selesova, P., Okrajek, P., & Tulak, J. (2010). Somatoform dissociation and symptoms of traumatic stress in adolescents. *Activitas Nervosa Superior, 52*(1), 29–31.

Kulkarni, J. (2017). Complex PTSD — A better description for borderline personality disorder? *Australasian Psychiatry, 25*(4), 333–335.

Kumari, V., Uddin, S., Premkumar, P., Young, S., Gudjonsson, G. H., Raghuvanshi, S., . . . Das, M. (2014). Lower anterior cingulate volume in seriously violent men with antisocial personality disorder or schizophrenia and a history of childhood abuse. *Australian and New Zealand Journal of Psychiatry, 48*(2), 153–161.

Kunst, J. (2014, February 7). A headshrinker's guide to the galaxy: Psychoanalysis wisdom for everyday life. *Psychology Today.*

Kunst, M. J. J. (2011). Affective personality type, post-traumatic stress disorder symptom severity and post-traumatic growth in victims of violence. *Stress and Health: Journal of the International Society for the Investigation of Stress, 27*(1), 42–51.

Kuo, W., Gallo, J. J., & Eaton, W. W. (2004). Hopelessness, depression, substance disorder, and suicidality. *Social Psychiatry and Psychiatric Epidemiology, 39,* 497–501.

Kurlansik, S. L., & Maffei, M. S. (2016). Somatic symptom disorder. *American Family Physician, 93*(1), 49–54.

Kyaga, S., Landén, M., Boman, M., Hultman, C. M., Långström, N., & Lichtenstein, P. (2013). Mental illness, suicide and creativity: 40-year prospective total population study. *Journal of Psychiatric Research, 47*(1), 83–90.

Kyaga, S., Lichtenstein, P., Boman, M., Hultman, C., Långström, N., & Landén, M. (2011). Creativity and mental disorder: Family study of 300,000 people with severe mental disorder. *British Journal of Psychiatry, 199*(5), 373–379.

Laan, E., Rellini, A. H., & Barnes, T. (2013). Standard operating procedures for female orgasmic disorder: Consensus of the International Society for Sexual Medicine. *Journal of Sexual Medicine, 10,* 74–82.

La Greca, A. M., Comer, J. S., & Lai, B. (2016). Trauma and child health: An introduction to the Special Issue. *Journal of Pediatric Psychology, 41,* 1–4.

Lahey, B. B. (2008). Oppositional defiant disorder, conduct disorder, and juvenile delinquency. In S. P. Hinshaw & T. P. Beauchaine (Eds.), *Child and adolescent psychopathology* (pp. 335–369). Hoboken, NJ: Wiley.

Lahmann, C., Henningsen, P., & Noll-Hussong, M. (2010). Somatoform pain disorder—Overview. *Psychiatria Danubina, 22*(3), 453–458.

Lai, C. Y., Zauszniewski, J. A., Tang, T., Hou, S. Y., Su, S. F., & Lai, P. Y. (2014). Personal beliefs, learned resourcefulness, and adaptive functioning in depressed adults. *Journal of Psychiatric and Mental Health Nursing, 21*(3), 280–287.

Lai, M. H., Maniam, T., Chan, L. F., & Ravindran, A. V. (2014). Caught in the web: A review of web-based suicide prevention. *Journal of Medical Internet Research, 16*(1), e30.

Laidlaw, C., & Howcroft, G. (2015). Encountering a cartwheeling princess: Relational psychoanalytic therapy of a child with attachment difficulties and ADHD. *Journal of Child & Adolescent Mental Health, 27*(3), 227–245.

Lake, C. R. (2012). *Schizophrenia is a misdiagnosis: Implications for the DSM-5 and ICD-11.* New York: Springer Science & Business Media.

Lake, N. (2014). *The caregivers: A support group's stories of slow loss, courage, and love.* New York: Scribner.

Lakhan, S. E., & Vieira, K. F. (2008). Nutritional therapies for mental disorders. *Nutrition Journal, 7,* 2.

Lamar, M., Foy, C. M. L., Beacher, F., Daly, E., Poppe, M., Archer, N., . . . & Murphy, D. G. M. (2011). Down syndrome with and without dementia: An in vivo proton Magnetic Resonance Spectroscope study with implications for Alzheimer's disease. *NeuroImage, 57*(1), 63–68.

Lambdin, B. H., Masao, F., Chang, O., Kaduri, P., Mbwambo, J., Magimba, A., . . . Bruce, R. D. (2014). Methadone treatment for HIV prevention-feasibility, retention, and predictors of attrition in Dar es Salaam, Tanzania: A retrospective cohort study. *Clinical Infectious Diseases, 59*(5), 735–742.

Lambert, K. G., & Kinsley, C. H. (2010). *Clinical neuroscience: Psychopathology and the brain.* New York: Oxford University Press.

Lambert, M. J. (2010). Using outcome data to improve the effects of psychotherapy: Some illustrations. In M. J. Lambert, *Prevention of treatment failure: The use of measuring, monitoring, and feedback in clinical practice* (pp. 203–242). Washington, DC: American Psychological Association.

Lambert, M. J. (2015). Progress feedback and the OQ-system: The past and the future. *Psychotherapy (Chicago), 52*(4), 381–390.

Lambert, M. J., Shapiro, D. A., & Bergin, A. E. (1986). The effectiveness of psychotherapy. In S. L. Garfield & A. E. Bergin (Eds.), *Handbook of psychotherapy and behavioral change* (3rd ed.). New York: Wiley.

Lampe, L. (2015). Social anxiety disorders in clinical practice: Differentiating social phobia from avoidant personality disorder. *Australasian Psychiatry, 23*(4), 343–346.

Lampe, L. (2016). Avoidant personality disorder as a social anxiety phenotype: Risk factors, associations and treatment. *Current Opinion in Psychiatry, 29*(1), 64–69.

Lamprecht, F., Kohnke, C., Lempa, W., Sack, M., Matzke, M., & Munte, T. F. (2004). Event-related potentials and EMDR treatment of posttraumatic stress disorder. *Neuroscience Research, 49*(2), 267–272.

Lanas, A., & Chan, F. K. L. (2017, February 24). Peptic ulcer disease. *The Lancet.* Retrieved from http://dx.doi.org/10.1016/S0140-6736(16)32404-7.

Lancet. (2010, February 2). Retraction—Ileal-lymphoid-nodular hyperplasia, non-specific colitis, and pervasive developmental disorder in children. *The Lancet.*

Lancioni, G. E., Singh, N. N., O'Reilly, M. F., Sigafoos, J., Bosco, A., Zonno, N., & Badagliacca, F. (2011). Persons with mild or moderate Alzheimer's disease learn to use urine alarms and prompts to avoid large urinary accidents. *Research in Developmental Disabilities, 32*(5), 1998–2004.

Landrigan, P. J. (2011). Environment and autism. In E. Hollander, A. Kolevzon, & J. T. Coyle (Eds.), *Textbook of autism spectrum disorders* (pp. 247–264). Arlington, VA: American Psychiatric Publishing, Inc.

Landry, M. J. (1994). *Understanding drugs of abuse: The processes of addiction, treatment, and recovery.* Washington, DC: American Psychiatric Press.

Lane, C. (2013, May 4). The NIMH withdraws support for DSM-5. *Psychology Today.*

Lane, H., Rose, L. E., Woodbrey, M., Arghavani, D., Lawrence, M., & Cavanaugh, J. T. (2017). Exploring the effects of using an oral appliance to reduce movement dysfunction in an individual with Parkinson disease: A single-subject design study. *Journal of Neurologic Physical Therapy, 41*(1), 52–58.

Lang, F. U., Otte, S., Vasic, N., Jäger, M., & Dudeck, M. (2015). Impulsiveness among short-term prisoners with antisocial personality disorder. *Psychiatrische Praxis, 42*(5), 274–277.

Lang, J. (1999, April 16). Local jails dumping grounds for mentally ill. *Detroit News.*

Lang, P. J., McTeague, L. M., & Bradley, M. M. (2014). Pathological anxiety and function/dysfunction in the brain's fear/defense circuitry. *Restorative Neurology and Neuroscience, 32*(1), 63–77.

Lange, C., Deutschenbaur, L., Borgwardt, S., Lang, U. E., Walter, M., & Huber, C. G. (2017). Experimentally induced psychosocial stress in schizophrenia spectrum disorders: A systematic review. *Schizophrenia Research, 182,* 4–12.

Langleben, D. D., Hakun, J. G., Seelig, D., Wang, A. L., Ruparel, K., Bilker, W. B., & Gur R. C. (2016). Polygraphy and functional magnetic resonance imaging in lie detection: A controlled blind comparison using the concealed information test. *Journal of Clinical Psychiatry. 77*(10), 1372–1380.

Langleben, D. D., & Moriarty, J. C. (2013). Using brain imaging for lie detection: Where science, law and research policy collide. *Psychology, Public Policy, and Law, 19*(2), 222–234.

Långström, N., & Seto, M. C. (2006). Exhibitionist and voyeuristic behavior in a Swedish national population survey. *Archives of Sexual Behavior, 35,* 427–435.

Lanier, C. (2010). Structure, culture, and lethality: An integrated model approach to American Indian suicide and homicide. *Homicide Studies: An Interdisciplinary & International Journal, 14*(1), 72–78.

Lanius, R., Frewen, P. A., & Brand, B. (2016, June 28). Dissociative aspects of posttraumatic stress disorder: Epidemiology, clinical manifestations, assessment, and diagnosis. Retrieved from https://www.uptodate.com.

Lankford, A. (2013). *The myth of martyrdom.* New York: St. Martin's Press.

Lankford, A., & Tomek, S. (2018). Mass killings in the United States from 2006 to 2013: Social contagion or random clusters? *Suicide and Life-Threatening Behavior.* [Manuscript in press]

Lapidus, K. B., Kopell, B. H., Ben-Haim, S., Rezai, A. R., & Goodman, W. K. (2013). History of psychosurgery: A psychiatrist's perspective. *World Neurosurgery, 80*(3-4), S27.e1–16.

Large, M., Mullin, K., Gupta, P., Harris, A., & Nielssen, O. (2014). Systematic meta-analysis of outcomes associated with psychosis and co-morbid substance use. *Australian and New Zealand Journal of Psychiatry, 48*(5), 418–432.

Larson, E. B. (2017, June 19). Risk factors for cognitive decline and dementia. *UpToDate.* Retrieved from http://www.uptodate.com.

Lasker Foundation. (2000). Exceptional returns: The economic value of America's investment in biomedical research, 2000. Retrieved from http://www.laskerfoundation.org/reports/pdf/exceptional.pdf.

Latzer, Y., Katz, R., & Spivak, Z. (2011). Facebook users more prone to eating disorders. University of Haifa, Israel. [Unpublished manuscript]

Lau, J. Y., Belli, S. R., Gregory, A. M., & Eley, T. C. (2014). Interpersonal cognitive biases as genetic markers for pediatric depressive symptoms: Twin data from the Emotions, Cognitions, Heredity and Outcome (ECHO) study. *Development and Psychopathology, 26,* 1267–1276.

Laumann, E. O., Gagnon, J. H., Michael, R. T., & Michaels, S. (1994). *The social organization of sexuality.* Chicago: University of Chicago Press.

Laumann, E. O., Nicolosi, A., Glasser, D. B., Paik, A., Gingell, C., Moreira, E., & Wang, T. (2005). Sexual problems among women and men aged 40–80 years: Prevalence and correlates identified in the Global Study of Sexual Attitudes and Behaviors. *International Journal of Impotence Research, 17,* 39–57.

Laumann, E. O., Paik, A., & Rosen, R. C. (1999). Sexual dysfunction in the United States: Prevalence and predictors. *Journal of the American Medical Association, 281*(13), 1174.

Laursen, T. M., Nordentoft, M., & Mortensen, P. B. (2014). Excess early mortality in schizophrenia. *Annual Review of Clinical Psychology, 10,* 425–448.

Lavender, J. M., Brown, T. A., & Murray, S. B. (2017). Men, muscles, and eating disorders: An overview of traditional and muscularity-oriented disordered eating. *Current Psychiatry Reports, 19*(6), 32.

Lavender, J. M., Wonderlich, S. A., Peterson, C. B., Crosby, R. D., Engel, S. G., Mitchell, J. E., . . . Berg, K. C. (2014). Dimensions of emotion dysregulation in bulimia nervosa. *European Eating Disorders Review, 22*(3), 212–216.

Lavin, M. (2008). Voyeurism: Psychopathology and theory. In D. R. Laws & W. T. O'Donohue (Eds.), *Sexual deviance: Theory, assessment, and treatment* (2nd ed., pp. 305–319). New York: Guilford Press.

Lavonas, E. J. (2016, September 19). First generation (typical) antipsychotic medication poisoning. *UpToDate.* Retrieved from http://www.uptodate.com.

Law, E., Yang, J. H., Coit, M. H., & Chan, E. (2016). Toilet school for children with failure to toilet train: Comparing a group therapy model with individual treatment. *Journal of Developmental & Behavioral Pediatrics. 37*(3), 223–230.

Lawlor, P. G., & Bush, S. H. (2014). Delirium diagnosis, screening and management. *Current Opinion in Supportive and Palliative Care, 8*(3), 286–295.

Laws, R. (2016). The rise and fall of relapse prevention: An update. In D. P. Boer, *The Wiley handbook on the theories, assessment and treatment of sexual offending* (Vol. 3, Chap. 60, pp. 1299–1312). Hoboken, NJ: Wiley-Blackwell.

Lawson, E. A., & Miller, K. K. (2016, February 24). Anorexia nervosa: Endocrine complications and their management. *UpToDate.* Retrieved from www.uptodate.com.

Lawton, E. M., Shields, A. J., & Oltmanns, T. F. (2011). Five-factor model personality disorder prototypes in a community sample: Self- and informant-reports predicting interview-based DSM diagnoses. *Personality Disorders, 2*(4), 279–292.

Lazarou, D., Richiem, J. P., & Chen, W. (2016, September 23). Surgical treatment of erectile dysfunction. *UpToDate.* Retrieved from http://www.uptodate.com.

Lazarov, O., Robinson, J., Tang, Y. P., Hairston, I. S., Korade-Mirnics, Z., Lee, V. M., . . . Sisodia, S. S. (2005). Environmental enrichment reduces A-beta levels and amyloid deposition in transgenic mice. *Cell, 120*(5), 572–574.

Lazarus, A. A. (1965). The treatment of a sexually inadequate man. In L. P. Ullman & L. Krasner (Eds.), *Case studies in behavior modification.* New York: Holt, Rinehart & Winston.

Lazarus, R. S., & Folkman, S. (1984). *Stress, appraisal, and coping.* New York: Springer Publishing.

Lazarus, S. A., Cheavens, J. S., Festa, F., & Zachary Rosenthal, M. (2014). Interpersonal functioning in borderline personality disorder: A systematic review of behavioral and laboratory-based assessments. *Clinical Psychology Review, 34*(3), 193–205.

Lazzari, C., Shoka, A., & Kulkarni, K. (2017, March). Are psychiatric hospitals and psychopharmacology the ultimate remedies for social problems? A narrative approach to aid socio-psychopharmacological assessment and treatment. *International Journal of Medical Research and Pharmaceutical Sciences, 4*(3).

Leavy, P. (2017). *Research design: Quantitative, qualitative, mixed methods, arts-based, and community-based participatory research approaches.* New York: Guilford Press.

Lebedeva, A., Westman, E., Lebedev, A. V., Li, X., Winblad, B., Simmons, A., . . . Aarsland, D. (2014). Structural brain changes associated with depressive symptoms in the elderly with Alzheimer's disease. *Journal of Neurology, Neurosurgery, and Psychiatry, 85*(8), 930–935.

LeBlanc, S. (2017, April 25). Baker proposal targets revenge porn, teenagers' sexting. *US News.*

Lebow, J. L., & Uliaszek, A. A. (2010). Couples and family therapy for personality disorders. In J. J. Magnavita (Ed.), *Evidence-based treatment of personality dysfunction: Principles, methods, and processes.* (pp. 193–221).

Washington, DC: American Psychological Association.

Lebow, J. L., Chambers, A. L., Christensen, A., & Johnson, S. M. (2012). Research on the treatment of couple distress. *Journal of Marital and Family Therapy, 38*(1), 145–168.

Lebow, M. A., & Chen, A. (2016). Overshadowed by the amygdala: The bed nucleus of the stria terminalis emerges as key to psychiatric disorders. *Molecular Psychiatry, 21*, 450–463.

Lebowitz, E. R., Scharfstein, L., & Jones, J. (2015). Child-report of family accommodation in pediatric anxiety disorders: Comparison and integration with mother-report. *Child Psychiatry and Human Development, 46*, 501–511.

LeCroy, C. W., & Holschuh, J. (Eds.). (2012). *First person accounts of mental illness and recovery.* Hoboken, NJ: Wiley.

LeDoux, J. E. (2000). Emotion circuits in the brain. *Annual Review of Neuroscience, 23*, 155–184.

LeDoux, J. E., & Pine, D. S. (2016). Using neuroscience to help understand fear and anxiety: A two-system framework. *American Journal of Psychiatry, 173*(11), 1083–1093.

Ledoux, S., Miller, P., Choquet, M., & Plant, M. (2002). Family structure, parent-child relationships, and alcohol and other drug use among teenagers in France and the United Kingdom. *Alcohol and Alcoholism, 37*(1), 52–60.

Lee, D. J., Weathers, F. W., Sloan, D. M., Davis, M. T., & Domino, J. L. (2017). Development and initial psychometric evaluation of the Semi-Structured Emotion Regulation Interview. *Journal of Personality Assessment, 99*(1), 56–66.

Lee, E. B., An, W., Levin, M. E., & Twohig, M. P. (2015). An initial meta-analysis of Acceptance and Commitment Therapy for treating substance use disorders. *Drug and Alcohol Dependence, 155*, 1–7.

Lee, G., & Bae, H. (2017). Therapeutic effects of phytochemicals and medicinal herbs on depression. *BioMed Research International, 207*, article 6596241.

Lee, J., & Freeman, J. L. (2014). Zebrafish as a model for investigating developmental lead (Pb) neurotoxicity as a risk factor in adult neurodegenerative disease: A mini-review. *Neurotoxicology, 43*, 57–64.

Lee, J., & Freeman, J. L. (2016). Embryonic exposure to 10 ug L(-1) lead results in female-specific expression changes in genes associated with nervous system development and function and Alzheimer's disease in aged adult zebrafish brain. *Metallomics, 8*(6), 589–596.

Lee, J. E., Bisht, B., Hall, M. J., Rubenstein, L. M., Louison, R., Klein, D. T., & Wahls, T. L. (2017). A multimodal, nonpharmacologic intervention improves mood and cognitive function in people with multiple sclerosis. *Journal of the American College of Nutrition, 36*(3), 150–168.

Lee, K. S. (2015). History of chronic subdural hematoma. *Korean Journal of Neurotrauma, 11*(2), 27–34.

Lee, S., Yoon, S., Kim, J., Jin, S., & Chung, C. K. (2014). Functional connectivity of resting state EEG and symptom severity in patients with post-traumatic stress disorder. *Progress in Neuro-Psychopharmacology and Biological Psychiatry, 51*, 51–57.

Lee, S. E., & Miller, B. L. (2016, January 6). Frontotemporal dementia: Clinical features and diagnosis. *UpToDate.* Retrieved from http://www.uptodate.com.

Leeman, R. F., Hoff, R. A., Krishnan-Sarin, S., Patock-Peckham, J. A., & Potenza, M. N. (2014). Impulsivity, sensation-seeking, and part-time job status in relation to substance use and gambling in adolescents. *Journal of Adolescent Health, 54*(4), 460–466.

Leemans, C., & Loas, S. (2016). On the relationship between emotional dependency and abuse [French]. *Revue Médicale de Bruxelles, 37*(2), 79–86.

Leenaars, A. A. (2004). Altruistic suicide: A few reflections. *Archives of Suicide Research, 8*(1), 1–7.

Leenaars, A. A. (2007). Gun-control legislation and the impact of suicide. *Journal of Crisis Intervention and Suicide Prevention, 28*(Suppl. 1), 50–57.

Leenaars, A. A., & Lester, D. (2004). The impact of suicide prevention centers on the suicide rate in the Canadian provinces. *Crisis, 25*(2), 65–68.

Leff, J., Williams, G., Huckvale, M., Arbuthnot, M., & Leff, A. (2013). Computer-assisted therapy for medication-resistant auditory hallucinations: Proof-of-concept study. *British Journal of Psychiatry, 202*, 428–433.

Leff, J., Williams, G., Huckvale, M., Arbuthnot, M., & Leff, A. P. (2014). Avatar therapy for persecutory auditory hallucinations: What is it and how does it work? *Psychosis, 6*(2), 166–176.

Lehman, S. (2016, March 8). Kids who skip lunch are missing out on essential nutrients. *Health News.*

Lehrer, S., & Rheinstein, P. H. (2015). Is Alzheimer's disease autoimmune inflammation of the brain that can be treated with nasal nonsteroidal anti-inflammatory drugs? *American Journal of Alzheimer's Disease and Other Dementias, 30*(3), 225–227.

Leiblum, S. R. (2007). Sex therapy today: Current issues and future perspectives. In S. R. Leiblum (Ed.), *Principles and practice of sex therapy* (4th ed., pp. 3–22). New York: Guilford Press.

Leiblum, S. R. (2010). Introduction and overview: Clinical perspectives on and treatment for sexual desire disorders. In S. R. Leiblum (Ed.), *Treating sexual desire disorders: A clinical casebook* (pp. 1–22). New York: Guilford Press.

Leibold, N. K., van den Hove, D., Viechtbauer, W., Kenis, G., Goossens, L., Lange, I., . . . Schruers, K. R. (2017). Amiloride-sensitive cation channel 2 genotype affects the response to a carbon dioxide panic challenge. *Journal of Psychopharmacology, 31*, 1294–1301.

Leibowitz, S., & de Vries, A. L. (2016). Gender dysphoria in adolescence. *International Review of Psychiatry, 28*(1), 21–35.

Leichsenring, F., & Salzer, S. (2014). A unified protocol for the transdiagnostic psychodynamic treatment of anxiety disorders: An evidence-based approach. *Psychotherapy, 51*(2), 224–245.

Lembke, A., & Humphreys, K. (2016). Self-help organizations for substance use disorders. In K. J. Sher (Ed.). *Oxford handbook of substance use and substance use disorders* (Vol. 2, Chap. 20, pp. 582–593). New York: Oxford University Press.

Lenhard, F., Andersson, E., Mataix-Cols, D., Ruck, C., Vigerland, S., Högström, J., . . . Serlachius, E. (2017). Therapist-guided, Internet-delivered cognitive-behavioral therapy for adolescents with obsessive-compulsive disorder: A randomized controlled trial. *Journal of the American Academy of Child and Adolescent Psychiatry, 56*(1), 10–19.

Lenzenweger, M. F., & Depue, R. A. (2016). Toward a developmental psychopathology of personality disturbance: A neurobehavioral dimensional model incorporating genetic, environmental, and epigenetic factors. In D. Cicchetti (Ed.), *Developmental psychopathology* (3rd ed., Vol. 3, Chap. 24, pp. 1079–1110). New York: Wiley.

Lenzenweger, M. F., Lane, M. C., Loranger, A. W., & Kessler, R. C. (2007). DSM-IV personality disorders in the National Comorbidity Survey Replication. *Biological Psychiatry, 62*(6), 553.

Lepiéce, B., Reynaert, C., Jacques, D., & Zdanowicz, N. (2015). Poverty and mental health: What should we know as mental health professionals? *Psychiatria Danubina, 27*(Suppl. 1), S92–S96.

Lepp, A., Barkley, J. E., & Karpinski, A. C. (2014). The relationship between cell phone use, academic performance, anxiety, and satisfaction with life in college students. *Computers in Human Behavior, 31*, 343–350.

Lepping, P., & Raveesh, B. N. (2014). Overvaluing autonomous decision-making. *British Journal of Psychiatry, 204*(1), 1–2.

Lerner, J. S., Li, Y., & Weber, E. U. (2013). The financial costs of sadness. *Psychological Sciences, 24*(1), 72–79.

Lester, D. (1985). The quality of life in modern America and suicide and homicide rates. *Journal of Social Psychology, 125*(6), 779–780.

Lester, D. (2000). Why people kill themselves: A 2000 summary of research on suicide. Springfield, IL: Charles C. Thomas.

Lester, D. (2011). Evidence-based suicide prevention by helplines: A meta-analysis. In M. Pompili & R. Tatarelli (Eds.), *Evidence-based practice in suicidology: A source book* (pp. 139–151). Cambridge MA: Hogrefe Publishing.

Lester, D. (2011). Evidence-based suicide prevention by lethal methods restriction. In M. Pompili & R. Tatarelli (Eds.), *Evidence-based practice in suicidology: A source book* (pp. 233–241). Cambridge MA: Hogrefe Publishing.

Lester, D., Innamorati, M., & Pompili, M. (2007). Psychotherapy for preventing suicide. In R. Tatarelli, M. Pompili, & P. Girardi (Eds.), *Suicide in psychiatric disorders.* New York: Nova Science Publishers.

Leung, G. M., Leung, T. K., & Ng, M. T. (2013). An outcome study of gestalt-oriented growth workshops. *International Journal of Group Psychotherapy, 63*(1), 117–125.

Leutwyler, K. (1996). Paying attention: The controversy over ADHD and the drug Ritalin is obscuring a real look at the disorder and its underpinnings. *Scientific American, 272*(2), 12–13.

Leve, L. D., & Cicchetti, D. (2016). Longitudinal transactional models of development and psychopathology. *Development and Psychopathology, 28*, 621–622.

Levenson, J. L. (2015, December 15). Illness anxiety disorder: Treatment and prognosis. *UpToDate*. Retrieved from www.uptodate.com.

Levenson, J. L. (2015, November 25). Illness anxiety disorder: Epidemiology, clinical presentation, assessment, and diagnosis. *UpToDate*. Retrieved from www.uptodate.com.

Levenson, J. L. (2016, November 10). Psychological factors affecting other medical conditions: Clinical features, assessment, and diagnosis. *UpToDate*. Retrieved from www.uptodate.com.

Levi, O., Shoval-Zuckerman, Y., Fruchter, E., Bibi, A., Bar-Haim, Y., & Wald, I. (2017). Benefits of a psychodynamic group therapy (PGT) model for treating veterans with PTSD. *Journal of Clinical Psychology, 73,* 1247–1258.

Levin, M. E., Pistorello, J., Hayes, S. C., Seeley, J. R., & Levin, C. (2015). Feasibility of an acceptance and commitment therapy adjunctive web-based program for counseling centers. *Journal of Counseling Psychology, 62*(3), 529–536.

Levine, D. (2017, June 6). The many ways exercise fights depression. *U.S. News & World Report.*

Levine M. P. (2016) Universal prevention of eating disorders: A concept analysis. *Eating Behaviors*. pii: S1471-0153(16)30319-1. [Epub ahead of print]

Levine, S. B. (2017). Ethical concerns about emerging treatment paradigms for gender dysphoria. *Journal of Sex & Marital Therapy, 23,* 1–16.

Levinson, D. F., & Nichols, W. E. (2014). *Major depression and genetics*. Stanford, CA: Stanford, School of Medicine.

Levinson, H. (2011, November 8). The strange and curious history of lobotomy. *BBC News Magazine.*

Levy, J., & Finnegan, P. (2016). A clinical case presentation: Understanding and interpreting dreams while working through developmental trauma. *Journal of the American Psychoanalytic Association, 64*(1), 13–45.

Levy, R. A., Ablon, J. S., & Kächele, H. (2011). *Psychodynamic psychotherapy research: Evidence-based practice and practice-based evidence (Current Clinical Psychiatry)*. Totowa, NJ: Humana Press.

Levy, T., & Bloch, T. (2012). Pharmacotherapy for conduct disorder in children and adolescents. *Harefuah, 151*(7), 421–426, 434, 435.

Levy, T. B., Barak, Y., Sigler, M., & Aizenberg, D. (2011). Suicide attempts and burden of physical illness among depressed elderly inpatients. *Archives of Gerontology and Geriatrics, 52*(1), 115–117.

Leweke, F. M., Gerth, C. W., Koethe, D., Klosterkotter, J., Ruslanova, I., Krivogorsky, B., . . . Yolken, R. H. (2004). Antibodies to infectious agents in individuals with recent onset schizophrenia. *European Archives of Psychiatry and Clinical Neuroscience, 254*(1), 4–8.

Lewinsohn, P. M., Antonuccio, D. O., Steinmetz, J. L., & Teri, L. (1984). *The coping with depression course*. Eugene, OR: Castalia.

Lewinsohn, P. M., Clarke, G. N., Hops, H., & Andrews, J. (1990). Cognitive-behavioral treatment for depressed adolescents. *Behavior Therapist, 21,* 385–401.

Lewis, C. M. (2016). Polygenic interactions with environmental adversity in the aetiology of major depressive disorder. *Psychological Medicine, 46,* 759–770.

Lewis, R. W., Fugl-Meyer, K. S., Corona, G., Hayes, R. D., Laumann, E. O., Moreira, E. D., Jr., . . . Segraves, T. (2010). Definitions/epidemiology/risk factors for sexual dysfunction. *Journal of Sexual Medicine, 7,* 1598–1607.

Li, B. Y., Wang, Y., Tang, H. D., & Chen, S. D. (2017). The role of cognitive activity in cognition protection: From bedside to bench. *Translational Neurodegeneration, 6,* 7.

Li, C-Y., Larsen, S., & Yap, T. (2017). Nocturnal penile tumescence study. In S. Minhas & J. Mulhall (Eds.), *Male sexual dysfunction: A clinical guide* (Chap. 15, pp. 129–132). UK: John Wiley & Sons.

Li, H., Lu, Q., Xiao, E., Li, Q., He, Z., & Mei, X. (2014). Methamphetamine enhances the development of schizophrenia in first-degree relatives of patients with schizophrenia. *Canadian Journal of Psychiatry, 59*(2), 107–113.

Li, L., Wu, M., Liao, Y., Ouyang, L., Du, M., Lei, D., . . . Gong, Q. (2014). Grey matter reduction associated with posttraumatic stress disorder and traumatic stress. *Neuroscience and Biobehavioral Reviews, 43,* 163–172.

Li, L., Xue, Z., Chen, L., Chen, X., Wang, H., & Wang, X. (2017). Puerarin suppression of Aβ$_{1-42}$-induced primary cortical neuron death is largely dependent on ERβ. *Brain Research, 1657,* 87–94.

Li, Q., Xiang, Y., Su, Y., Shu, L., Yu, X., Chiu, H. F., . . . Si, T. (2014). Antipsychotic polypharmacy in schizophrenia patients in China and its association with treatment satisfaction and quality of life: Findings of the third national survey on use of psychotropic medications in China. *Australian and New Zealand Journal of Psychiatry*. [Electronic publication]

Li, R., & El-Mallakh, R. S. (2004). Differential response of bipolar and normal control lymphoblastoid cell sodium pump to ethacrynic acid. *Journal of Affective Disorders, 80*(1), 1–17.

Li, R., Cui, J., & Shen, Y. (2014). Brain sex matters: Estrogen in cognition and Alzheimer's disease. *Molecular and Cellular Endocrinology, 389*(1-2), 13–21.

Li, W., & Caltabiano, N. (2017). Prevalence of substance abuse and socio-economic differences in substance abuse in an Australian community-dwelling elderly sample. *Health Psychology Open, 4*(1). doi:10.1177/2055102917708136

Li, Y., Tsui, W., Rusinek, H., Butler, T., Mosconi, L., Pirraglia, E., . . . de Leon, M. J. (2015). Cortical laminar binding of PET amyloid and tau tracers in Alzheimer disease. *Journal of Nuclear Medicine, 56*(2), 270–273.

Liang, K. Y., Wang, Y., Shugart, Y. Y., et al. (2008). Evidence for potential relationship between SLC1A1 and a putative genetic linkage region on chromosome 14q to obsessive-compulsive disorder with compulsive hoarding. *American Journal of Medical Genetics, Part B, 147B,* 1000–1002.

Libman, H., Melin, J. A., Sullivan, D. J., & Sokol, H. N. (2017, July 7). What's new in geriatrics. *UpToDate*. Retrieved from http://www.uptodate.com.

Lieberman, A. F., & Chu, A. T. (2016). Childhood exposure to interpersonal trauma. In D. Cicchetti, *Developmental psychopathology, Vol. 3: Maladaptation and psychopathology* (3rd ed., Chap. 10). New York: Wiley.

Lieberman, L., Gorka, S. M., Shankman, S. A., & Phan, K. L. (2017). Impact of panic on psychophysiological and neural reactivity to unpredictable threat in depression and anxiety. *Clinical Psychological Science, 5*(1), 52–63.

Liebman, J. I., McKinley-Pace, M. J., Leonard, A. M., Sheesley, L. A., Gallant, C. L., Renkey, M. E., & Lehman, E. B. (2002). Cognitive and psychosocial correlates of adults' eyewitness accuracy and suggestibility. *Personality and Individual Differences, 33*(1), 49–66.

Liera, S. J., & Newman, M. G. (2014). Rethinking the role of worry in generalized anxiety disorder: Evidence supporting a model of emotional contrast avoidance. *Behavior Therapy, 45*(3), 283–299.

Liersch-Sumskis, S., Moxham, L., & Curtis, J. (2014). Choosing to use compared to taking medication: The meaning of medication as described by people who experience schizophrenia. *Perspectives in Psychiatric Care*. [Electronic publication]

Liese, B. S., & Reis, D. J. (2016). Failing to diagnose and failing to treat an addicted client: Two potentially life-threatening clinical errors. *Psychotherapy (Chicago), 53*(3), 342–346.

Lightdale, H. A., Mack, A. H., & Frances, R. J. (2008). Psychodynamics. In H. D. Kleber & M. Galanter (Eds.), *The American Psychiatric Publishing textbook of substance abuse treatment* (4th ed., pp. 333–347). Arlington, VA: American Psychiatric Publishing.

Lightdale, H. A., Mack, A. H., & Frances, R. J. (2011). Psychodynamic psychotherapy. In M. Galanter & H. D. Kleber (Eds.), *Psychotherapy for the treatment of substance abuse* (pp. 219–247). Arlington, VA: American Psychiatric Publishing.

Lilenfeld, L. R. R. (2011). Personality and temperament. In R. A. H. Adan & W. H. Kaye (Eds.), *Behavioral neurobiology of eating disorders. Current topics in behavioral neurosciences* (pp. 3–16). New York: Springer-Verlag Publishing.

Lilienfeld, S. O., Watts, A. L., & Smith, S. F. (2015). Successful psychopathy: A scientific status report. *Current Directions in Psychological Science, 24,* 298–303.

Lim, A., Hoek, H. W., Deen, M. L., Blom, J. D., & GROUP Investigators. (2016). Prevalence and classification of hallucinations in multiple sensory modalities in schizophrenia spectrum disorders. *Schizophrenia Research, 176,* 493–499.

Lin, L., Zhang, J., Zhou, L., & Jiang, C. (2016). The relationship between impulsivity and suicide among rural youths aged 15–35 years: A case-control psychological autopsy study. *Psychology, Health & Medicine, 21*(3), 330–337.

Lin, L. Y., Sidani, J. E., Shensa, A., Radovic, A., Miller, E., Colditz, J. B., . . . Primack, B. A. (2016). Association between social media use and depression among U.S. young adults. *Depression and Anxiety, 33*(4), 323–331.

Lindau, S. T., Schumm, L. P., Lamann, E. O., Levinson, W., O'Muircheartaigh, C. A., & Waite, L. J. (2007). A study of sexuality and health among older adults in the United States. *New England Journal of Medicine, 357,* 762–774.

Lindblom, J., Vänskä, M., Flykt, M., Tolvanen, A., Tiitinen, A., Tulppala, M., & Punamäki, R. L. (2016, November 17). From early family systems to internalizing symptoms: The role of emotion regulation and peer relations. *Journal of Family Psychology*. [Epub ahead of print]

Lindqvist, E. K., Sigurjonsson, H., Möller-mark, C., Rinder, J., Farnebo, F., & Lundgren, T. K. (2017). Quality of life improves early after gender reassignment surgery in transgender women. *European Journal of Plastic Surgery, 40*(3), 223–226.

Lindsley, C. W. (2017). Chronic traumatic encephalopathy (CTE): A brief historical overview and recent focus on NFL players. *ACS Chemical Neuroscience, 8*(8), 1629–1631.

Linehan, M. M. (2014). *DBT skills training manual* (2nd ed.). New York: Guilford Press.

Linehan, M. M., Cochran, B. N., & Kehrer, C. A. (2001). Dialectical behavior therapy for borderline personality disorder. In D. H. Barlow (Ed.), *Clinical handbook of psychological disorders* (3rd ed., pp. 470–522). New York: Guilford Press.

Linehan, M. M., Dimeff, L. A., Reynolds, S. K., Comtois, K. A., Welch, S. S., Heagerty, P., & Kivlahan, D. R. (2002). Dialectical behavior therapy versus comprehensive validation therapy plus 12-step for the treatment of opioid dependent women meeting criteria for borderline personality disorder. *Drug and Alcohol Dependence, 67*(1), 13–26.

Linehan, M. M., Korslund, K. E., Harned, M. S., Gallop, R. J., Lungu, A., Neacsiu, A. D., . . . Murray-Gregory, A. M. (2015). Dialectical behavior therapy for high suicide risk in individuals with borderline personality disorder: A randomized clinical trial and component analysis. *JAMA Psychiatry, 72*(5), 475–482.

Lines, L. M., & Wiener, J. M. (2014, February). *Racial and ethnic disparities in Alzheimer's disease: A literature review.* Research Triangle Park, NC: RTI International. Retrieved from https//aspe.hhs.gov.

Ling, H. (2018). Untangling the tauopathies: Current concepts of tau pathology and neurodegeneration. *Parkinsonism & Related Disorders.* [Manuscript in press]

Linz, S. J., & Sturm, B. A. (2016). Facilitating social integration for people with severe mental illness served by Assertive Community Treatment. *Archives of Psychiatric Nursing, 30*(6), 692–699.

Lipkin, P. H., Cozen, M. A., Thompson, R. E., & Mostofsky, S. H. (2005). Stimulant dosage and age, race, and insurance type in a sample of children with attention-deficit/hyperactivity disorder. *Journal of Child and Adolescent Psychopharmacology, 15*(2), 240–248.

Lippy, C., & DeGue, S. (2016). Exploring alcohol policy approaches to prevent sexual violence perpetration. *Trauma, Violence, & Abuse, 17*(1), 26–42.

Lipton, A. A., & Simon, F. S. (1985). Psychiatric diagnosis in a state hospital: Manhattan State revisited. *Hospital Community Psychiatry, 36*(4), 368–373.

Litjens, R. W., Brunt, T. M., Alderliefste, G., & Westerink, R. S. (2014). Hallucinogen persisting perception disorder and the serotonergic system: A comprehensive review including new MDMA-related clinical cases. *European Neuropsychopharmacology, 24*(8), 1309–1323.

Littlefield, A. K., & Sher, J. K. (2010). The multiple, distinct ways that personality contributes to alcohol use disorders. *Social and Personality Psychology Compass, 4*(9), 767–782.

Liu, A. (2007). *Gaining: The truth about life after eating disorders.* New York: Warner Books.

Liu, H., Liao, J., Jiang, W., & Wang, W. (2014). Changes in low-frequency fluctuations in patients with antisocial personality disorder revealed by resting-state functional MRI. *PLoS One, 9*(3), e89790.

Liu, R. T., Kleiman, E. M., Nestor, B. A., & Cheek, S. M. (2015). The hopelessness theory of depression: A quarter century in review. *Clinical Psychology, 22*(4), 345–365.

Liu, W., Fang, F., Zhang, C., & Storch, E. A. (2017). Cognitive behavioral therapy practices in the treatment of obsessive-compulsive disorder in China. *Annals of Translational Medicine, 5*(1), 8.

Liu, Y., Yu, X., Yang, B., Zhang, F., Zou, W., Na, A., . . . Yin, G. (2017). Rumination mediates the relationship between overgeneral autobiographical memory and depression in patients with major depressive disorder. *BMC Psychiatry, 17*(1), 103.

Livesley, W. J. (2017). *Integrated modular treatment for borderline personality disorder: A practical guide to combining effective treatment methods.* New York: Cambridge University Press.

Livesley, W. J., & Larstone, R. (Eds.). (2018). *Handbook of personality disorders: Theory, research, and treatment* (2nd ed.). New York: Guilford Press.

Lizarraga, L. E., Phan, A. V., Cholanians, A. B., Herndon, J. M., Lau, S. S., & Monks, T. J. (2014). Serotonin reuptake transporter deficiency modulates the acute thermoregulatory and locomotor activity response to 3,4-(±)-methylenedioxymethamphetamine, and attenuates depletions in serotonin levels in SERT-KO rats. *Toxicological Sciences, 139*(2), 421–431.

Loas, G., Baelde, O., & Verrier, A. (2015). Relationship between alexithymia and dependent personality disorder: A dimensional analysis. *Psychiatry Research, 225*(3), 484–488.

Loas, G., Cormier, J., & Perez-Dias, F. (2011). Dependent personality disorder and physical abuse. *Psychiatry Research, 185*(1-2), 167–170.

Lochman, J. E., Barry, T., Powell, N., & Young, L. (2010). Anger and aggression. In D. W. Nangle, D. J. Hansen, C. A. Erdley & P. J. Norton (Eds.), *Practitioner's guide to empirically based measures of social skills* (pp. 155–166). New York: Springer Publishing.

Lochman, J. E., Boxmeyer, C. L., Powell, N. P., Barry, T. D., & Pardini, D. A. (2010). Anger control training for aggressive youths. In J. R. Weisz & A. E. Kazdin (Eds.), *Evidence-based psychotherapies for children and adolescents* (2nd ed., pp. 227–242). New York: Guilford Press.

Lochman, J. E., Powell, N. P., Boxmeyer, C. L., & Jimenez-Camargo, L. (2011). Cognitive-behavioral therapy for externalizing disorders in children and adolescents. *Child and Adolescent Psychiatric Clinics of North America, 20*(2), 3095–318.

Loewenstein, R. J. (2014, February 24). Dissociative amnesia. *UpToDate.* Retrieved from http://www.uptodate.com

Loftus, E. F. (1993). The reality of repressed memories. *American Psychologist, 48,* 518–537.

Loftus, E. F. (2001). Imagining the past. *Psychologist, 14*(11), 584–587.

Loftus, E. F. (2003). Make-believe memories. *American Psychologist, 58*(11), 867–873.

Loftus, E. F. (2017). Eavesdropping on memory. *Annual Review of Psychology, 68,* 1–18.

Loftus, E. F., & Cahill, L. (2007). Memory distortion: From misinformation to rich false memory. In J. S. Nairne (Ed.), *The foundations of remembering: Essays in honor of Henry L. Roediger, III.* New York: Psychology Press.

Loftus, E. F., & Greenspan, R. L. (2017). If I'm certain, is it true? Accuracy and confidence in eyewitness memory. *Psychological Science in the Public Interest, 18*(1), 1–2.

Logie, C. H., Lacombe-Duncan, A., Lee-Foon, N., Ryan, S., & Ramsay, H. (2016). "It's for us newcomers, LGBTQ persons, and HIV-positive persons. You feel free to be": A qualitative study exploring social support group participation among African and Caribbean lesbian, gay, bisexual and transgender newcomers and refugees in Toronto, Canada. *BMC International Health and Human Rights, 16*(1), 18.

Lohani, S., Poplawsky, A. J., Kim, S. G., & Moghaddam, B. (2017). Unexpected global impact of VTA dopamine neuron activation as measured by opto-fMRI. *Molecular Psychiatry, 22*(1), 585–591.

Lohse, T., Rohrmann, S., Richard, A., Bopp, M., Faeh, D., & Swiss National Cohort Study Group. (2017). Type A personality and mortality: Competitiveness but not speed is associated with increased risk. *Atherosclerosis, 262,* 19–24.

Loo, C. M. (2016). *PTSD among ethnic minority veterans.* Washington, DC: National Center for PTSD. Retrieved from http://www.ptsd.va.gov.

Loomer, H. P., Saunders, J. C., & Kline, N. S. (1957). A clinical and pharmacodynamic evaluation of iproniazid as a psychic energizer. *America Psychiatric Association Research Report, 8,* 129.

Lopes, B., & Yu, Y. (2017). Who do you troll and why: An investigation into the relationship between the Dark Triad personalities and online trolling behaviours towards popular and less popular Facebook profiles. *Computers in Human Behavior, 77,* 69–76.

López, I., Rivera, F., Ramirez, R., Guarnaccia, P., Canino, G., & Bird, H. (2011). Ataques de nervous and somatic complaints among Island and mainland Puerto Rican children, *CNS Neuroscience & Therapeutics, 17,* 158–166.

López, S. R., & Guarnaccia, P. J. (2000). Cultural psychopathology: Uncovering the social world of mental illness. *Annual Review of Psychology, 51,* 571–598.

López, S. R., & Guarnaccia, P. J. (2005). Cultural dimensions of psychopathology: The social world's impact on mental illness. In B. A. Winstead & J. E. Maddux, *Psychopathology: Foundations for a contemporary understanding* (pp. 19–37). Mahwah, NJ: Lawrence Erlbaum.

Lopez-Vergara, H. I., Colder, C. R., Hawk, L. W., Jr., Wieczorek, W. F. Eiden, R. D., Lengua, L. J., & Read, J. P. (2012). Reinforcement sensitivity theory and alcohol outcome expectancies in early adolescence. *American Journal of Drug and Alcohol Abuse, 38*(2), 130–134.

LoPiccolo, J. (1991). Post-modern sex therapy for erectile failure. In R. C. Rosen & S. R. Leiblum (Eds.), *Erectile failure: Diagnosis and treatment.* New York: Guilford Press.

LoPiccolo, J. (2002). Postmodern sex therapy. In F. W. Kaslow (Ed.), *Comprehensive handbook of psychotherapy: Integrative/eclectic* (Vol. 4, pp. 411–435). New York: Wiley.

LoPiccolo, J. (2004). Sexual disorders affecting men. In L. J. Haas (Ed.), *Handbook of primary care psychology* (pp. 485–494). New York: Oxford University Press.

LoPiccolo, J., & Van Male, L. M. (2000). Sexual dysfunction. In A. E. Kazdin (Ed.), *Encyclopedia of psychology* (Vol. 7, pp. 246–251). Washington, DC: Oxford University Press/American Psychological Association.

Lorand, S. (1968). Dynamics and therapy of depressive states. In W. Gaylin (Ed.), *The meaning of despair.* New York: Jason Aronson.

Loukusa, S., Mäkinen, L., Kuusikko-Gauffin, S., Ebeling, H., & Moilanen, I. (2014). Theory of mind and emotion recognition skills in children with specific language impairment, autism spectrum disorder and typical development: Group differences and connection to knowledge of grammatical morphology, word-finding abilities and verbal working memory. *International Journal of Language and Communication Disorders,* May 29, 2014.

Lovaas, O. I. (1987). Behavioral treatment and normal educational/intellectual functioning in young autistic children. *Journal of Consulting and Clinical Psychology, 55,* 3–9.

Lovaas, O. I. (2003). *Teaching individuals with developmental delays: Basic intervention techniques.* Austin, TX: Pro-Ed.

Love, S. (2016, July 29). Transgender identity is considered a mental illness by WHO. But that may soon change. *Chicago Tribune.*

Lovejoy, M. (1982). Expectations and the recovery process. *Schizophrenia Bulletin, 8*(4), 605–609.

Lovejoy, M. (2001). Disturbances in the social body: Differences in body image and eating problems among African-American and white women. *Gender and Society, 15*(2), 239–261.

Lovett, E. (2012, January 12). Most models meet criteria for anorexia, size 6 is Plus Size: Magazine. *Good Morning, America, World News.*

Lowes, R. (2016, December 29). Assisted death: Physician support continues to grow. *Medscape.*

Luber, B. M., Davis, S., Bernhardt, E., Neacsiu, A., Kwapil, L., Lisanby, S. H., & Strauman, T. J. (2017). Using neuroimaging to individualize TMS treatment for depression: Toward a new paradigm for imaging-guided intervention. *Neuroimage, 148,* 1–7.

Lublin, N. (2014, February 4). Cited in L. Kaufman, In texting era, crisis hotlines put help at youths' fingertips. *New York Times.*

Luborsky, L. (1973). Forgetting and remembering (momentary forgetting) during psychotherapy. In M. Mayman (Ed.), *Psychoanalytic research and psychological issues* (Monograph 30). New York: International Universities Press.

Luborsky, L. B., Barrett, M. S., Antonuccio, D. O., Shoenberger, D., & Stricker, G. (2006). What else materially influences what is represented and published as evidence? In J. C. Norcross, L. E. Beutler, & R. F. Levant (Eds.), *Evidence-based practices in mental health: Debate and dialogue on the fundamental questions* (pp. 257–298). Washington, DC: American Psychological Association.

Luborsky, L., Rosenthal, R., Diguer, L., Andrusyna, T. P., Berman, J. S., Levitt, J. T., . . . Krause, E. D. (2002). The dodo bird verdict is alive and well—mostly. *Clinical Psychology: Science and Practice, 9*(1), 2–12.

Luborsky, L., Singer, B., & Luborsky, L. (1975). Comparative studies of psychotherapies. *Biological Psychiatry, 32,* 995–1008.

Lucas, G. (2006). Object relations and child psychoanalysis. [French]. *Revue Française de Psychanalyse, 70*(5), 1435–1473.

Lucas, L. (2016, September 28). Changing the way police respond to mental illness. *CNN.*

Łucka, I., & Dziemian, A. (2014). Pedophilia—a review of literature, casuistics, doubts. *Psychiatria Polska, 48*(1), 121–134.

Luders, E., Sánchez, F. J., Tosun, D., Shattuck, D. W., Gaser, C., Vilain, E., & Toga, A. W. (2012). Increased cortical thickness in male-to-female transsexualism. *Journal of Behavioral and Brain Science, 2*(3), 357–362.

Ludwig, A. M. (1995). *The price of greatness: Resolving the creativity and madness controversy.* New York: Guilford Press.

Luftman, K., Aydelotte, J., Rix, K., Ali, S., Houck, K., Coopwood T. B., Teixeira, P., Eastman, A., Eastridge, B., Brown, C. V., & Davis, M. (2017). PTSD in those who care for the injured. *Injury, 48*(2), 293–296.

Lundberg, U. (2011). Neuroendocrine measures. In R. J. Contrada & A. Baum (Eds.), *The handbook of stress science: Biology, psychology, and health* (pp. 531–542). New York: Springer Publishing.

Lusk, J., Brenner, L. A., Betthauser, L. M., Terrio, H., Scher, A. I., Schwab, K., & Poczwardowski, A. (2015). A qualitative study of potential suicide risk factors among Operation Iraqi Freedom/Operation Enduring Freedom soldiers returning to the Continental United States (CONUS). *Journal of Clinical Psychology, 71*(9), 843–855.

Lustig, S. L., Blank, A. R., Cirelli, R. J., Friedman, S. R., Green, F. C., Lopez, W. M., . . . Shampaine, V. C. (2013). Optimizing managed care peer reviews: Turning a "Doc to Doc" talk into better advocacy for psychiatric inpatients. *Psychiatric Services* (Washington, D.C.), *64*(8), 800–803.

Lutz, W., Schiefele, A. K., Wucherpfennig, F., Rubel, J., & Stulz, N. (2016). Clinical effectiveness of cognitive behavioral therapy for depression in routine care: A propensity score based comparison between randomized controlled trials and clinical practice. *Journal of Affective Disorders, 189,* 150–158.

Lyman, B. (1982). The nutritional values and food group characteristics of foods preferred during various emotions. *Journal of Psychology, 112,* 121–127.

Lyness, J. M. (2016, September 13). Unipolar depression in adults: Assessment and diagnosis. *UpToDate.* Retrieved from https://uptodate.com.

Lyness, J. M. (2017, January 14). Unipolar depression in adults: Clinical features. *UpToDate.* Retrieved from http://www.uptodate.com.

Lynn, S. J., & Deming, A. (2010). The "Sybil tapes": Exposing the myth of dissociative identity disorder. *Theory & Psychology, 20*(2), 289–291.

Lyons, L. (2015). *Using hypnosis with children: Creating and delivering effective interventions* (1st ed.). New York: Norton.

Lysaker, P. H., & Hermans, H. J. M. (2007). The dialogical self in psychotherapy for persons with schizophrenia: A case study. *Journal of Clinical Psychology, 63*(2), 129–139.

Lysaker, P. H., Leonhardt, B. L., Brüne, M., Buck, K. D., James, A., Vohs, J., . . . Dimaggio, G. (2014). Capacities for theory of mind, metacognition, and neurocognitive function are independently related to emotional recognition in schizophrenia. *Psychiatry Research, 219*(1), 79–85.

Lysaker, P. H., Vohs, J., Hamm, J. A., Kukla, M., Minor, K. S., de Jong, S., . . . Dimaggio, G. (2014). Deficits in metacognitive capacity distinguish patients with schizophrenia from those with prolonged medical adversity. *Journal of Psychiatric Research, 55,* 126–132.

Ma, J., Batterham, P. J., Calear, A. L., & Han, J. (2016). A systematic review of the predictions of the Interpersonal-Psychological Theory of Suicide behavior. *Clinical Psychology Review, 46,* 34–45.

MacDonald, W. L. (1998). The difference between blacks' and whites' attitudes toward voluntary euthanasia. *Journal for the Scientific Study of Religion, 37*(3), 411–426.

MacIntosh, H. B., Fletcher, K., & Collin-Vézina, D. (2016) "As time went on, I just forgot about it": Thematic analysis of spontaneous disclosures of recovered memories of childhood sexual abuse. *Journal of Child Sexual Abuse, 25*(1), 56–72.

MacIsaac, T. (2014, January 30). Life beyond Earth: Space aliens live quietly among us, say some scientists and officials. *Epoch Times.* Retrieved from http://www.theepochtimes.com.

MacLaren, V. V. (2001). A qualitative review of the Guilty Knowledge Test. *Journal of Applied Psychology, 86*(4), 674–683.

Macleod, S. H., Elliott, L., & Brown, R. (2011). What support can community mental health nurses deliver to carers of people diagnosed with schizophrenia? Findings from a review of the literature. *International Journal of Nursing Studies, 48*(1), 100–120.

MacNeill, L. P., & Best, L. A. (2015). Perceived current and ideal body size in female undergraduates. *Eating Behaviors, 18,* 71–75.

Mader, J. (2017, March 1). How teacher training hinders special-needs students. *The Atlantic.*

Madsen, T., Erlangsen, A., & Nordentoft, M. (2017, March 2). Risk estimates and risk factors related to psychiatric inpatient suicide: An overview. *International Journal of Environmental Research and Public Health, 14*(3).

Maheu, M. M., Drude, K. P., & Wright, S. D. (2017). *Career paths in telemental health.* New York: Springer Science + Business Media.

Maier, S. F., & Seligman, M. E. (2016). Learned helplessness at fifty: Insights from neuroscience. *Psychological Review, 123*(4), 349–367.

Mainwaring, D. (2017, May 25). More people are getting "sex change" surgeries than ever before . . . but it's not what you think. *LifeSite News.*

Maj, M. (2016). Narrowing the gap between ICD/DSM and RDoC constructs: Possible steps and caveats. *World Psychiatry, 15*(3), 193–194.

Majumder, A., & Sanyal, D. (2016). Outcome and preferences in female--to-male subjects with gender dysphoria: Experience from Eastern India. *Indian Journal of Endocrinology and Metabolism, 20*(3), 3308–3311.

Majumder, A., & Sanyal, D. (2017). Outcome and preferences in male-to-female subjects with gender dysphoria: Experience from Eastern India. *Indian Journal of Endocrinology and Metabolism, 21*(1), 21–25.

Mäkinen, M., Lindberg, N., Komulainen, E., Puukko-Viertomies, L. R., Aalberg, V., & Marttunen, M. (2015). Psychological well-being in adolescents with excess weight. *Nordic Journal of Psychiatry, 69*(5), 354–363.

Mäkinen, M., Marttunen, M., Komulainen, E., Terevnikov, V., Puukko-Birtyomird, L-R., Aalberg, V., & Lindberg, N. (2015). Development of self-image and its components during a one-year follow-up in non-referred adolescents with excess and normal weight. *Child and Adolescent Psychiatry and Mental Health, 9,* 5.

Mäkinen, M., Puukko-Viertomies, L-R., Lindberg, N., Siirnes, M. A., & Aalberg, V. (2012). Body dissatisfaction and body mass in girls and boys transitioning from early to mid-adolescence: Additional role of self-esteem and eating habits. *BMC Psychiatry, 12,* 35.

Makovac, E., Meeten, F., Watson, D. R., Herman, A., Garfinkel, S. N., Critchley, H. D., & Ottaviani, C. (2016). Alterations in amygdala-prefrontal functional connectivity account for excessive worry and autonomic dysregulation in generalized anxiety disorder. *Biological Psychiatry, 80,* 786–795.

Malhi, G. S., Tanious, M., Das, P., Coulston, C. M., & Berk, M. (2013). Potential mechanisms of action of lithium in bipolar disorder. Current understanding. *CNS Drugs, 27*(2), 135–153.

Malki, S., & Einat, T. (2017, May 24). To include or not to include—This is the question: Attitudes of inclusive teachers toward the inclusion of pupils with intellectual disabilities in elementary schools. *Education, Citizenship and Social Justice.*

Maller, R. G., & Reiss, S. (1992). Anxiety sensitivity in 1984 and panic attacks in 1987. *Journal of Anxiety Disorders, 6*(3), 241–247.

Malm, U. I., Ivarsson, B. R., & Allebeck, P. (2014). Durability of the efficacy of integrated care in schizophrenia: A five-year randomized controlled study. *Psychiatric Services* (Washington, D.C.), 65(8), 1054–1057.

Maloney, J., & Chaudhuri, S. (2017, April 23). Against all odds, the U.S. tobacco industry is rolling in money. *The Wall Street Journal.*

Mamarde, A., Navkhare, P., Singam, A., & Kanoje, A. (2013). Recurrent dissociative fugue. *Indian Journal of Psychological Medicine, 35*(4), 400–401.

Manchanda, S. C., & Madan, K. (2014). Yoga and meditation in cardiovascular disease. *Clinical Research in Cardiology, 103*(9), 675–680.

Mandal, A. (2014). Hallucination types. *News-Medical.* Retrieved from http://www.news-medical.net/health/hallucination-types.aspx.

Mandell, D. S., Barry, C. L., Marcus, S. C., Xie, M., Shea, K., Mullan, K., & Epstein, A. J. (2016). Effects of autism spectrum disorder insurance mandates on the treated prevalence of autism spectrum disorder. *JAMA Pediatrics, 170*(9), 887–893.

Manfredi, C., Caselli, G., Rovetto, F., Rebecchi, D., Ruggiero, G. M., Sassaroli, S., & Spada, M. M. (2011). Temperament and parental styles as predictors of ruminative brooding and worry. *Personality and Individual Differences, 50*(2), 186–191.

Mann, J. J., & Currier, D. (2007). Neurobiology of suicidal behavior. In R. Tatarelli, M. Pompili, & P. Girardi (Eds.), *Suicide in psychiatric disorders.* New York: Nova Science Publishers.

Mann, M. (2009). The secrets behind the ten happiest jobs. *Excelle.* Retrieved from http://www.excelle.monster.com/benefits/articles/4033.

Mann, R. E., Ainsworth, F., Al-Attar, Z., & Davies, M. (2008). Voyeurism: Assessment and treatment. In D. R. Laws & W. T. O'Donohue (Eds.), *Sexual deviance: Theory, assessment, and treatment* (2nd ed., pp. 320–335). New York: Guilford Press.

Manschreck, T. (2015, November 12). Delusional disorder. *UpToDate.* Retrieved from http://www.uptodate.com.

Maples-Keller, J. L., Price, M., Rauch, S., Gerardi, M., & Rothbaum, B. O. (2017). Investigating relationships between PTSD symptom clusters within virtual reality exposure therapy for OEF/OIF Veterans, *Behavior Therapy, 48*(2), 147–155.

Marceaux, J. C., & Melville, C. L. (2011). Twelve-step facilitated versus mapping-enhanced cognitive-behavioral therapy for pathological gambling: A controlled study. *Journal of Gambling Studies, 27*(1), 171–190.

Marchand, W. R. (2014). Neural mechanisms of mindfulness and meditation: Evidence from neuroimaging studies. *World Journal of Radiology, 6*(7), 471–479.

Marcoux, L., Michon, P., Lemelin, S., Voisin, J. A., Vachon-Presseau, E., & Jackson, P. L. (2014). Feeling but not caring: Empathic alteration in narcissistic men with high psychopathic traits. *Psychiatry Research, 224*(3), 341–348.

Marden, J. R., Walter, S., Kaufman, J. S., & Glymour, M. M. (2016). African ancestry, social factors, and hypertension among non-Hispanic blacks in the health and retirement study. *Biodemography and Social Biology, 62*(1), 19–35.

Marder, S. (2016, November 17). Treatment of postpartum psychosis. *UpToDate.* Retrieved from http://www.uptodate.com.

Marder, S., & Davis, M. (2016, May 31). Clinical manifestations, differential diagnosis, and initial management of psychosis in adults. *UpToDate.* Retrieved from http://www.uptodate.com.

Marder, S., & Stroup, T. C. (2016, December 1). Pharmacotherapy for schizophrenia: Side effect management. *UpToDate.* Retrieved from http://www.uptodate.com.

Margo, J. L. (1985). Anorexia nervosa in adolescents. *British Journal of Medical Psychology, 58*(2), 193–195.

Maris, R. W. (2001). Suicide. In H. S. Friedman (Ed.), *Specialty articles from the encyclopedia of mental health.* San Diego: Academic Press.

MarketWatch. (2014). Packaging for an aging population. *MarketWatch* press release, July 10, 2014.

Markowitz, F. E. (2015). Involvement in mental health self-help groups and recovery. *Health Sociology Review, 24*(2), 199–212.

Marks, B., Sisirak, J., Heller, T., & Wagner, M. (2010). Evaluation of community-based health promotion programs for Special Olympics athletes. *Journal of Policy and Practice in Intellectual Disabilities, 7*(2), 119–129.

Marks, I. M. (1977). Phobias and obsessions: Clinical phenomena in search of a laboratory model. In J. Maser and M. Seligman (Eds.), *Psychopathology: Experimental models.* San Francisco: Freeman.

Marks, I. M. (1987). *Fears, phobias and rituals: Panic, anxiety and their disorders.* New York: Oxford University Press.

Marks, I. M., & Gelder, M. G. (1967). Transvestism and fetishism: Clinical and psychological changes during faradic aversion. *British Journal of Psychiatry, 113,* 711–730.

Marks, J. W. (2014). *Peptic ulcer disease.* Retrieved from MedicineNet website: http://www.medicinenet.com/peptic_ulcer/article.

Marlatt, G. A., Kosturn, C. F., & Lang, A. R. (1975). Provocation to anger and opportunity for retaliation as determinants of alcohol consumption in social drinkers. *Journal of Abnormal Psychology, 84*(6), 652–659.

Marques, F. de A., Legal, E-J., & Hofelmann, D. A. (2012). Body dissatisfaction and common mental disorders in adolescents. *Revista Paulista de Pediatria, 30*(4), 553–561.

Marmar, C. R., Schlenger, W., Henn-Haase, C., Qian, M., Purchia, E., Li, M., . . . Kulka, R. A. (2015). Course of posttraumatic stress disorder 40 years after the Vietnam War: Findings from the National Vietnam Veterans Longitudinal Study. *JAMA Psychiatry, 72*(9), 875–881.

Mars, B., Heron, J., Biddle, L., Donovan, J. L., Holley, R., Piper, M., . . . Gunnell, D. (2015). Exposure to, and searching for, information about suicide and self-harm on the Internet: Prevalence and predictors in a population based cohort of young adults. *Journal of Affective Disorders, 185,* 239–245.

Marsh, R., Stefan, M., Bansal, R., Hao, X., Walsh, B. T., & Peterson, B. S. (2015). Anatomical characteristics of the cerebral surface in bulimia nervosa. *Biological Psychiatry, 77*(7), 616–623.

Marshall, J. J. (1997). Personal communication.

Marshall, T., Jones, D. P. H., Ramchandani, P. G., Stein, A., & Bass, C. (2007). Intergenerational transmission of health benefits in somatoform disorders. *British Journal of Psychiatry, 191*(4), 449–450.

Marshall, W. L., Hucker, S. J., Nitschke, J., & Mokro, A. (2016). Assessment of sexual sadism. In D. P. Boer, *The Wiley handbook on the theories, assessment and treatment of sexual offending* (Vol. 2, Chap. 13). Hoboken, NJ: Wiley-Blackwell.

Marshall, W. L., & Marshall, L. E. (2015). Psychological treatment of the paraphilias: A review and an appraisal of effectiveness. *Current Psychiatry Reports, 17,* 47.

Marshall, W. L., & Marshall, L. E. (2016). The treatment of adult male sexual offenders. In D. P. Boer, *The Wiley handbook on the theories, assessment and treatment of sexual offending* (Vol. 3, Chap. 1). Hoboken, NJ: Wiley-Blackwell.

Marshall, W. L., Marshall, L. E., Serran, G. A., & O'Brien, M. D. (2011). *Rehabilitating sexual offenders: A strength-based approach.* Washington, DC: American Psychological Association.

Marshall, W. L., Serran, G. A., Marshall, L. E., & O'Brien, M. D. (2008). Sexual deviation. In M. Hersen & J. Rosqvist (Eds.), *Handbook of psychological assessment, case conceptualization and treatment, Vol. 1: Adults.* Hoboken, NJ: John Wiley & Sons.

Marsiglia, F. F., & Smith, S. J. (2010). An exploration of ethnicity and race in the etiology of substance use: A health disparities approach. In L. Scheier (Ed.), *Handbook of drug use etiology: Theory, methods, and empirical findings* (pp. 289–304). Washington, DC: American Psychological Association.

Marston, W. M. (1917). Systolic blood pressure changes in deception. *Journal of Experimental Psychology, 2,* 117–163.

Martell, C. R., Dimidjian, S., & Herman-Dunn, R. (2010). *Behavioral activation for depression: A clinician's guide.* New York: Guilford Press.

Martell, C. R., Dimidjian, S., & Herman-Dunn, R. (2013). *Behavioral activation for depression: A clinician's guide.* New York: Guilford Press.

Martin, A. K., Gibson, E. C., Mowry, B., & Robinson, G. A. (2016). Verbal initiation, suppression, and strategy use and the relationship with clinical symptoms in schizophrenia. *Journal of the International Neuropsychological Society, 22*(7), 735–743.

Martin, A. L., Huelin, R., Wilson, D., Foster, T. S., & Mould, F. J. (2013). A systematic review assessing the economic impact of sildenafil citrate (Viagra) in the treatment of erectile dysfunction. *Journal of Sexual Medicine, 10,* 1389–1400.

Martin, D. M., Gálvez, V., & Loo, C. K. (2015). Predicting retrograde autobiographical memory changes following electroconvulsive therapy: Relationships between individual, treatment, and early clinical factors. *The International Journal of Neuropsychopharmacology* 1–8. [Advance publication]

Martin, L. A., Neighbors, H. W., & Griffith, D. M. (2013). The experience of symptoms of depression in men vs women: Analysis of the National Comorbidity Survey Replication. *JAMA Psychiatry, 70*(10), 1100–1106.

Martin, S. A., Atlantis, E., Lange, K., Taylor, A. W., O'Loughlin, P., Wittert, G. A., and members of the Florey Adelaide Male Ageing Study (FAMAS). (2014). Predictors of sexual dysfunction incidence and remission in men. *Journal of Sexual Medicine, 11,* 1136–1147.

Martin, S. F., & Levine, S. B. (2016, December 13). Fetishistic disorders. *UpToDate.* Retrieved from http://www.uptodate.com.

Martín-Blanco, A., Soler, J., Villalta, L., Feliu-Soler, A., Elices, M., Pérez, V., . . . Pascual, J. C. (2014). Exploring the interaction between childhood maltreatment and temperamental traits on the severity of borderline personality disorder. *Comprehensive Psychiatry, 55*(2), 311–318.

Martino, F., Caselli, G., Berardi, D., Fiore, F., Marino, E., Menchetti, M., . . . Sassaroli, S. (2015). Anger rumination and aggressive behavior in borderline personality disorder. *Personality and Mental Health.* [Electronic publication]

Martino, F., Spada, M. M., Menchetti, M., Lo Sterzo, E., Sanza, M., Tedesco, P., . . . Berardi, D. (2017, February 14). Substance-related and addictive disorders as mediators between borderline personality disorder and aggressive behavior. *Clinical Psychologist.* [Epub ahead of print]

Martino, M., Magioncalda, P., Yu, H., Li, X., Wang, Q., Meng, Y., . . . Li, T. (2018). Abnormal resting-state connectivity in a substantia nigra-related striato-thalamo-cortical network in a large sample of first-episode drug-naïve patients with schizophrenia. *Schizophrenia Bulletin.* [Manuscript in press]

Martins, M. V., Peterson, B. D., Almeida, V., Mesquita-Guimarães, J., & Costa, M. E. (2014). Dyadic dynamics of perceived social support in couples facing infertility. *Human Reproduction* (Oxford, England), *29*(1), 83–89.

Mash, E. J., & Wolfe, D. A. (2015). *Abnormal Child Psychology.* New York: Wadsworth.

Mash, E. J., & Wolfe, D. A. (2018). *Abnormal Child Psychology.* Boston, MA: Cengage Learning.

Maslow, A. H. (1970). *Motivation and personality* (2nd ed.). New York: Harper & Row.

Masse, J. J., McNeil, C. B., Wagner, S., & Quetsch, L. B. (2016). Examining the efficacy of Parent-Child Interaction Therapy with children on the autism spectrum. *Journal of Child and Family Studies, 25,* 2508–2525.

Masten, A. S., & Cicchetti, D. (2016). Resilience in development: Progress and transformation. In D. Cicchetti (Ed.), *Developmental psychopathology: Vol. 4, Risk, resilience, and intervention* (3rd ed., Chap. 6, pp. 271–333). New York: Wiley

Masters, W. H., & Johnson, V. E. (1966). *Human sexual response.* Boston: Little, Brown.

Masters, W. H., & Johnson, V. E. (1970). *Human sexual inadequacy.* Boston: Little, Brown.

Mataix-Cols, D., & de la Cruz, L. F. (2016, June 27). Hoarding disorder in adults: Epidemiology, pathogenesis, clinical manifestations, course, assessment, and diagnosis. *UpToDate.* Retrieved from http://www.uptodate.com.

Mataix-Cols, D., & de la Cruz, L. F. (2016, December 7). Treatment of hoarding disorder in adults. *UpToDate.* Retrieved from http://www.uptodate.com.

Mather, M. (2016). *Fact sheet: Aging in the United States.* Washington, DC: PRB.

Mather, M., Jacobsen, L. A., & Pollard, K. M. (2015, December). Aging in the United States. Washington, DC: PRB.

Mathes, B. M., Oglesby, M. E., Short, N. A., Portero, A. K., Raines, A. M., & Schmidt, N. B. (2017). An examination of the role of intolerance of distress and uncertainty in hoarding symptoms. *Comprehensive Psychiatry, 72,* 121–129.

Mathew, J., & McGrath, J. (2002). Readability of consent forms in schizophrenia research. *Australian and New Zealand Journal of Psychiatry, 36*(4), 564–565.

Matsumoto, D., & Juang, L. (2016). *Culture and psychology* (6th ed.). Stanford, CT: Wadsworth Publishing.

Matsunaga, H., & Seedat, S. (2011). Obsessive-compulsive spectrum disorders: Crossnational and ethnic issues. In E. Hollander, J. Zohar, P. J. Sirovatka, & D. A. Regier (Eds.), *Obsessive-compulsive spectrum disorders: Refining the research agenda for DSM-V* (pp. 205–221). Washington, DC: American Psychiatric Publishing.

Mattheisen, M., Samuels, J. F., Wang, Y., Greenberg, B. D., Fyer, A. J., McCracken, J. T., . . . Nestadt, G. (2015). Genome-wide association study in obsessive-compulsive disorder: Results from the OCGAS. *Molecular Psychiatry, 20,* 337–344.

Matthys, W., & Lochman, J. E. (2017). *Oppositional defiant disorder and conduct disorder in childhood* (2nd ed.). New York: Wiley.

Mattison, M. (2016, August 17). Hospital management of older adults. *UpToDate.* Retrieved from http://www.uptodate.com.

Mauthner, N. S. (2010). "I wasn't being true to myself": Women's narratives of postpartum depression. In D. C. Jack & A. Ali (Eds.), *Silencing the self across cultures: Depression and gender in the social world* (pp. 459–484). New York: Oxford University Press.

Mayberg, H. S., Brannan, S. K., Mahurin, R. K., Jerabek, P. A., Brickman, J. S., Tekell, J. L., . . . Fox, P. T. (1997). Cingulate function in depression: A potential predictor of treatment response. *Neuroreport, 8,* 1057–1061.

Mayberg, H. S., Brannan, S. K., Mahurin, R. K., & McGinnin, S. (2000). Regional metabolic effects of fluoxetine in major depression: Serial changes and relationship to clinical response. *Biological Psychiatry, 48,* 830–84.

Mayberg, H. S., Lozano, A. M., Voon, V., McNeely, H. E., Seminowicz, D., Hamani, C., . . . Kennedy, S. H. (2005). Deep brain stimulation for treatment-resistant depression. *Neuron, 45,* 651–660.

Mayes, S. D., Waxmonsky, J. D., Calhoun, S. L., & Bixler, E. O. (2016). Disruptive mood dysregulation disorder symptoms and association with oppositional defiant and other disorders in a general population child sample. *Journal of Child and Adolescent Psychopharmacology, 26,* 101–106.

Mayo, C., & George, V. (2014). Eating disorder risk and body dissatisfaction based on muscularity and body fat in male university students. *Journal of American College Health, 62*(6), 407–415.

Mayo, D., Corey, S., Kelly, L. H., Yohannes, S., Youngquist, A. L., Stuart, B. K., . . . Loewy, R. L. (2017). The role of trauma and stressful life events among individuals at clinical high risk for psychosis: A review. *Frontiers in Psychiatry, 8,* 55.

Mayo Clinic. (2016, January 16). Depression in women: Understanding the gender gap. Retrieved from http://mayoclinic.org/diseases-conditions/depression/in-depth/depression/art-20047725.

Maza, C. (2015, April 13). Tribes battle high teen suicide rates on Native American reservations. *CSMonitor.* Retrieved from CS Monitor website: http://www.csmonitor.com/USA/USA-update/2015/0413.

Mazza, M., Mariano, M., Peretti, S., Masedu, F., Pino, M. C., & Valenti, M. (2017). The role of theory of mind on social information processing in children with autism spectrum disorders:

A mediation analysis. *Journal of Autism and Developmental Disorders, 47,* 1369–1379.

McAfee. (2014). *Study reveals majority of adults share intimate details via unsecured digital devices.* Santa Clara, CA: Author.

McAnulty, R. D. (2006). Pedophilia. In R. D. McAnulty & M. M. Burnette (Eds.), *Sex and sexuality, Vol. 3: Sexual deviation and sexual offenses* (Chap. 4, pp. 81–91). Westport, CT: Praeger Publishers.

McArthur, G., Castles, A., Kohnen, S., Larsen, L., Jones, K., Anandakumar, T., & Banales, E. (2013, October 13). Sight word and phonics training in children with dyslexia. *Journal of Learning Disabilities.*

McCabe, R. E. (2016, June 27). Agoraphobia in adults: Epidemiology, pathogenesis, clinical manifestations, course, and diagnosis. *UpToDate.* Retrieved from http://www.uptodate.com.

McCabe, R. E. (2017, February 17). Specific phobia in adults: Epidemiology, clinical manifestations, course and diagnosis. *UpToDate.* Retrieved from http://www.uptodate.com.

McCabe, R. E., & Swinson, R. (2015, November 6). Psychotherapy for specific phobia in adults. *UpToDate.* Retrieved from http://www.uptodate.com.

McCance-Katz, E. F., & Kosten, T. R. (2005). Psychopharmacological treatments. In R. J. Frances, A. H. Mack, & S. I. Miller (Eds.), *Clinical textbook of addictive disorders* (3rd ed., pp. 688–614). New York: Guilford Press.

McCarthy, B., & McCarthy, E. (2012). *Sexual awareness: Your guide to healthy couple sexuality* (5th ed.). New York: Routledge/Taylor & Francis Group.

McCarthy, B., & Wald, L. M. (2017). A psychobiosocial approach to sex therapy. In Z. D. Peterson (Ed.), *The Wiley-Blackwell handbook of sex therapy* (Chap. 12, pp. 190–202). Hoboken, NJ: Wiley-Blackwell.

McClintock, A. S., Perlman, M. R., McCarrick, S. M., Anderson, T., & Himawan, L. (2017). Enhancing psychotherapy process with common factors feedback: A randomized, clinical trial. *Journal of Counseling Psychology, 64*(3), 247–260.

McClintock, C. H., Lau, E., & Miller, L. (2016). Phenotypic dimensions of spirituality: Implications for mental health in China, India, and the United States. *Frontiers in Psychology, 7,* 1600.

McCloud, A., Barnaby, B., Omu, N., Drummond, C., & Aboud, A. (2004). Relationship between alcohol use disorders and suicidality in a psychiatric population: In-patient prevalence study. *British Journal of Psychiatry, 184*(5), 439–445.

McConnaughey, J. (2007, May 31). NFL study links concussions, depression. *San Francisco Chronicle.* Retrieved from http://www.sfgate.com/cgi-bin/article.cgi?f=/n/a/2007/05/31/sports/s135640D10.DTL.

McConnaughey, J. (2014, May 17). Alcohol use may worsen in nursing homes. *ABC News.* Retrieved from ABC News website: http://abcnews.go.com/health.

McConnell, D., Feldman, M., & Aunos, M. (2017). Parents and parenting with intellectual disabilities: An expanding field of research. *Journal of Applied Research in Intellectual Disabilities, 30,* 419–422.

McConnell, E. A., Birkett, M., & Mustanski, B. (2016). Families matter: Social support and mental health trajectories among lesbian, gay, bisexual, and transgender youth. *Journal of Adolescent Health, 59*(6), 674–680.

McCrady, B. S. (2014). Alcohol use disorders. In D. H. Barlow, *Clinical handbook of psychological disorders* (5th ed., Chap. 13). New York: Guilford Press.

McCrady, B. S., Owens, M. D., Borders, A. Z., & Brovko, J. M. (2014). Psychosocial approaches to alcohol use disorders since 1940: A review. *Journal of Studies on Alcohol and Drugs, 75*(Suppl. 75), 68–78.

McDaniel, B. T., Drouin, M. (2015). Sexting among married couples: Who is doing it, and are they more satisfied? *Cyberpsychology, Behavior, and Social Networking, 18*(11), 826–834.

McDermott, B. E., Leamon, M. H., Feldman, M. D., & Scott, C. L. (2012). Factitious disorder and malingering. In J. A. Bourgeois, U. Parthasarathi, & A. Hategan (Eds.), *Psychiatry review and Canadian certification exam preparation guide* (pp. 267–276). Arlington, VA: American Psychiatric Publishing.

McDermott, B. M., & Jaffa, T. (2005). Eating disorders in children and adolescents: An update. *Current Opinions in Psychiatry, 18*(4), 407–410.

McDowell, D. (2005). Marijuana, hallucinogens, and club drugs. In R. J. Frances, A. H. Mack, & S. I. Miller (Eds.), *Clinical textbook of addictive disorders* (3rd ed., pp. 157–183). New York: Guilford Press.

McDowell, D. (2011). Marijuana, hallucinogens, and club drugs. In R. J. Frances, S. I. Miller, & A. H. Mack (Eds.), *Clinical textbook of addictive disorders* (3rd ed., Chap. 8). New York: Guilford Press.

McEachin, J. J., Smith, T., & Lovaas, O. I. (1993). Long-term outcome for children with autism who received early intensive behavioral treatment. *American Journal of Mental Retardation, 97*(4), 359–372.

McFarlane, W. R. (2011). Integrating the family in the treatment of psychotic disorders. In R. Hagen, D. Turkington, T. Berge, & R. W. Gråwe (Eds.), *CBT for psychosis: A symptom-based approach (The International Society for Psychological and Social Approaches to Psychosis Book Series)* (pp. 193–209). New York: Routledge/Taylor & Francis Group.

McFarlane, W. R. (2016). Family interventions for schizophrenia and the psychoses: A review. *Family Process, 55*(3), 460–482.

McFeeters, D., Boyda, D., & O'Neill, S. (2015). Patterns of stressful life events: Distinguishing suicide ideators from suicide attempters. *Journal of Affective Disorders, 175,* 192–198.

McGauran, D. (2016, January 7). The 10 most common fear motivators. *Active Beat.*

McGhie, A., & Chapman, J. S. (1961). Disorders of attention and perception in early schizophrenia. *British Journal of Medical Psychology, 34,* 103–116.

McGlothlin, J. M. (2008). *Developing clinical skills in suicide assessment, prevention, and treatment.* Alexandria, VA: American Counseling Association.

McGoldrick, M., Loonan, R., & Wohlsifer, D. (2007). Sexuality and culture. In S. R. Leiblum (Ed.), *Principles and practice of sex therapy* (4th ed., pp. 416–441). New York: Guilford Press.

McGrath, R. E., & Carroll, E. J. (2012). The current status of "projective" "tests". In H.

Cooper, P. M. Camic, D. L. Long, A. T. Panter, D. Rindskopf, & K. J. Sher (Eds.), *APA handbook of research methods in psychology. Vol. 1: Foundations, planning, measures, and psychometrics* (pp. 329–348). Washington, DC: American Psychological Association.

McGuffin, P., Katz, R., Watkins, S., & Rutherford, J. (1996). A hospital-based twin register of the heritability of DSM-IV unipolar depression. *Archives of General Psychiatry, 53,* 129–136.

McGuire, P. K., Silbersweig, D. A., Wright, I., Murray, R. M., Frackowiak, R. S., & Frith, C. D. (1996). The neural correlates of inner speech and auditory verbal imagery in schizophrenia: Relationship to auditory verbal hallucinations. *British Journal of Psychiatry, 169*(2), 148–159.

McGuire, T. G. (2016). Achieving mental health care parity might require changes in payments and competition. *Health Affairs, 35*(6), 1029–1377.

McGurk, S. R., Mueser, K. T., Mischel, R., Adams, R., Harvey, P. D., McClure, M. M., . . . Siever, L. J. (2013). Vocational functioning in schizotypal and paranoid personality disorders. *Psychiatry Research, 210*(2), 498–504.

McIlvaine, R. (2011, January 25). 3-D software becoming safeware to returning soldiers with PTSD. *Army News Service.*

McIngvale, E., Rufino, K., Ehlers, M., & Hart, J. (2017, March 1). An in-depth look at the scrupulosity dimension of obsessive-compulsive disorder. *Journal of Spirituality in Mental Health.* [Published online]

McKee, A. C., Stern, R. A., Nowinski, C. J., Stein, T. D., Alvarez, V. E., Daneshvar, D. H., . . . Cantu, R. C. (2013). The spectrum of disease in chronic traumatic encephalopathy. *Brain, 136*(Pt 1), 43–64.

McKenna, K., Gallagher, K. S., Forbes, P. W., & Ibeziako, P. (2015). Ready, set, relax: Biofeedback-assisted relaxation training (BART) in a pediatric psychiatry consultation service. *Psychosomatics, 56*(4), 381–389.

McKenzie, J. A., McConkey, R., & Adnams, C. (2013). Intellectual disability in Africa: Implications for research and service development. *Disability and Rehabilitation, 35*(20), 1750–1755.

Mckew, M. (2017). Study finds risk of suicide higher for female nurses. *Nursing Standard, 31*(30), 10.

McKinney, C., & Caetano, R. (2016). Substance use and race and ethnicity. In K. J. Sher (Ed.). *Oxford handbook of substance use and substance use disorders* (Vol. 1, Chap. 14, pp. 483–525). New York: Oxford University Press.

McLay, R. N. (2013). How does virtual-reality therapy for PTSD work? *Scientific American, 24*(5).

McLay, R. N., Daylo, A. A., & Hammer, P. S. (2006). No effect of lunar cycle on psychiatric admissions or emergency evaluations. *Military Medicine, 17*(12), 1239–1242.

McLean, B. (2014). *The hope for mental illness: Research.* Arlington, VA: NAMI (National Alliance on Mental Illness).

McLean, C. P., & Foa, E. B. (2017). Emotions and emotion regulation in posttraumatic stress disorder. *Current Opinion in Psychology, 14,* 72–77.

McLean, D., Thara, R., John, S., Barrett, R., Loa, P., McGrath, J., & Mowry, B. (2014). DSM-IV "Criterion A" schizophrenia symptoms across ethnically different populations: Evidence for differing psychotic symptom content or structural organization? *Culture, Medicine and Psychiatry, 38*(3), 408–426.

McLellan, T. M., Caldwell, J. A., & Lieberman, H. R. (2016). A review of caffeine's effects on cognitive, physical and occupational performance. *ScienceDirect, 71,* 294–312.

McMahon, C. G., Jannini, E., Waldinger, M., & Rowland, D. (2013). Standard operating procedures in the disorders of orgasm and ejaculation. *Journal of Sexual Medicine, 1,* 204–229.

McMahon, R. J., & Frick, P. J. (2005). Evidence-based assessment of conduct problems in children and adolescents. *Journal of Clinical Child and Adolescent Psychology, 34,* 477–505.

McMahon, R. J., & Frick, P. J. (2007). Conduct and oppositional disorders. In E. J. Mash & R. A. Barkley (Eds.), *Assessment of childhood disorders* (4th ed., pp. 132–183) New York: Guilford Press.

McMahon, R. J., Witkiewitz, K., & Kotler, J. S. (2010). Predictive validity of callous-unemotional traits measured in early adolescence with respect to multiple antisocial outcomes. *Journal of Abnormal Psychology, 119*(4), 752–763.

McMain, S. F. (2015). Advances in the treatment of borderline personality disorder: An introduction to the special issue. *Journal of Clinical Psychology, 71*(8), 741–746.

McManus, M. A., Hargreaves, P., Rainbow, L., & Alison, L. J. (2013). Paraphilias: Definition, diagnosis and treatment. *F1000prime Reports, 536.*

McNally, R. J. (2004, April 1). Psychological debriefing does not prevent posttraumatic stress disorder. *Psychiatric Times,* p. 71.

McNally, R. J. (2016). The legacy of Seligman's "Phobias and Preparedness" (1971). *Behavior Therapy, 47*(5), 585–594.

McNally, R. J. (2017) False memories in the laboratory and in life: Commentary on Brewin and Andrews, 2016. *Wiley Online Library.* Retrieved from http://wileyonlinelibrary.com.

McNally, R. J., Clancy, S. A., Barrett, H. M., & Parker, H. A. (2005). Reality monitoring in adults reporting repressed, recovered, or continuous memories of childhood sexual abuse. *Journal of Abnormal Psychology, 114*(1), 147–152.

McNally, R. J., & Geraerts, E. (2009). A new solution to the recovered memory debate. *Perspectives on Psychological Science, 4*(2), 126–134.

McNeil, E. B. (1967). *The quiet furies.* Englewood Cliffs, NJ: Prentice Hall.

McNicol, M. L., & Thorsteinsson, E. B. (2017). Internet addiction, psychological distress, and coping responses among adolescents and adults. *Cyberpsychology, Behavior, and Social Networking, 20*(5), 296–304.

McPhail, D., Rountree-James, M., & Whetter, I. (2016). Addressing gaps in physician knowledge regarding transgender health and healthcare through medical education. *Canadian Medical Education Journal, 7*(2), e70–e78.

McPherson, M., Smith-Lovin, L., & Brashears, M. (2006). Social isolation in America: Changes in core discussion networks over two decades. *American Sociological Review, 71,* 353–375.

McPhillips, D. (2016, September 14). U.S. among most depressed countries in the world. Mental health issues cut the most years off of life in Asia and the U.S. Washington, D.C.: *U.S. News & World Report.*

McSherry, B., & Weller, P. (2010). *Rethinking rights-based mental health law.* Portland, OR: Hart Publishing.

Meana, M. (2012). *Sexual dysfunction in women. Advances in psychotherapy—Evidence-based practice.* Cambridge, MA: Hogrefe Publishing.

Meana, M., Fertel, E., & Maykut, C. (2017). Treating genital pain associated with sexual intercourse. In Z. D. Peterson (Ed.), *The Wiley-Blackwell handbook of sex therapy* (Chap. 7, pp. 98–114). Hoboken, NJ: Wiley-Blackwell.

Meaney, R., Hasking, P., & Reupert, A. (2016, May 12). Prevalence of borderline personality disorder in university samples: Systematic review, meta-analysis and meta-regression. *PLoS ONE.*

Mechem, C. C. (2016, April 13). Pulmonary complications of cocaine abuse. *UpToDate.* Retrieved from http://www.uptodate.com.

Meehl, P. E. (1960). The cognitive activity of the clinician. *American Psychologist, 15,* 19–27.

Meehl, P. E. (1996). *Clinical versus statistical prediction: A theoretical analysis and a review of the evidence.* Northvale, NJ: Jason Aronson.

Meersand, P. (2011). Psychological testing and the analytically trained child psychologist. *Psychoanalytic Psychology, 28*(1), 117–131.

Mehler, P. (2016, August 2). Anorexia nervosa in adults and adolescents: Medical complications and their management. *UpToDate.* Retrieved from www.uptodate.com.

Mehler, P. (2017, April 29). Anorexia nervosa in adults and adolescents: The refeeding syndrome. *UpToDate.* Retrieved from www.uptodate.com.

Mehler, P. (2017, April 5). Anorexia nervosa in adults: Evaluation for medical complications and criteria for hospitalization to manage these complications. *UpToDate.* Retrieved from www.uptodate.com.

Mehta, D., Newport, D. J., Frishman, G., Kraus, L., Rex-Haffner, M., Ritchie, J. C., . . . Binder, E. B. (2014). Early predictive biomarkers for postpartum depression point to a role for estrogen receptor signaling. *Psychological Medicine,* 1–14.

Meichenbaum, D. (2017). *The evolution of CBT: A personal and professional journey with Don Meichenbaum.* New York: Routledge.

Meichenbaum, D. H. (1975). A self-instructional approach to stress management: A proposal for stress inoculation training. In I. Sarason & C. D. Spielberger (Eds.), *Stress and anxiety* (Vol. 2). New York: Wiley.

Meichenbaum, D. H. (1993). Stress inoculation training: A 20-year update. In P. M. Lehrer & R. L. Woolfolk (Eds.), *Principles and practice of stress management* (2nd ed.). New York: Guilford Press.

Meijer, E. H., & Verschuere, B. (2010). The polygraph and the detection of deception. *Journal of Forensic Psychology Practice, 10*(4), 325–338.

Meinhard, N., Kessing, L. V., & Vinberg, M. (2014). The role of estrogen in bipolar disorder, a review. *Nordic Journal of Psychiatry, 68*(2), 81–87.

Melechi, A. (2016, September 29). Bodies of evidence: Psychologists and the CIA torture scandal. *Times Higher Education.*

Meloy, J. R., & Yakeley, J. (2010). Psychodynamic treatment of antisocial personality disorder: Psychodynamic psychotherapy for personality disorders: A clinical handbook. In J. F. Clarkin, P. Fonagy, & G. O. Gabbard (Eds.), *Psychodynamic psychotherapy for personality disorders: A clinical handbook* (pp. 311–336). Arlington, VA: American Psychiatric Publishing.

Melton, G. B., Petrila, J., Poythress, N. G., & Slobogin, C. (2007). *Psychological evaluations for the courts: A handbook for mental health professionals and lawyers* (3rd ed.). New York: Guilford Press.

Melton, G. B., Petrila, J., Poythress, N. G., Slobogin, C., Otto, R. K., Mossman, D., & Condie, L. O. (2017). *Psychological evaluations for the courts: A handbook for mental health professionals and lawyers* (4th ed.). New York: Guilford Press.

Meltzer, H. Y. (2011). Evidence-based treatment for reducing suicide risk in schizophrenia. In M. Pompili & R. Tatarelli (Eds.), *Evidence-based practice in suicidology: A source book* (pp. 317–328). Cambridge MA: Hogrefe Publishing.

Melville, J. (1978). *Phobias and obsessions.* New York: Penguin.

Membride, H. (2016). Mental health: Early intervention and prevention in children and young people. *British Journal of Nursing, 25*(10), 552–554.

Mendels, J. (1970). *Concepts of depression.* New York: Wiley.

Mendoza, M. E., Capafons, A., Gralow, J. R., Syriala, K. L., Suárez-Rodrigues, J. M., Fann, J. R., & Jensen, M. P. (2016, July 28). Randomized controlled trial of the Valencia model of waking hypnosis plus CBT for pain, fatigue, and sleep management in patients with cancer and cancer survivors. *Psycho-Oncology.* [Epub ahead of print]

Meng, L., Chen, Y., Xu, X., Chen, T., Lui, S., Huang, X., Sweeney, J. A., Li, K., & Gong, Q. (2018). *The neurobiology of brain recovery from traumatic stress: A longitudinal DTI study. Journal of Affective Disorders, 225,* 577–584.

Mercer, L. D., Higgins, G. C., Lau, C. L., Lawrence, A. J., & Beart, P. M. (2017). MDMA-induced neurotoxicity of serotonin neurons involves autophagy and rilmenidine is protective against its pathobiology. *Neurochemistry International, 105,* 80–90.

Merenda, R. R. (2008). The posttraumatic and sociocognitive etiologies of dissociative identity disorder: A survey of clinical psychologists. *Dissertation Abstracts International: Section B: The Sciences and Engineering, 68*(8-B), 55–84.

Merikangas, K. R., & Swanson, S. A. (2010). Comorbidity in anxiety disorders. In M. B. Stein & T. Steckler (Eds.), *Behavioral neurobiology of anxiety and its treatment. Current topics in behavioral neurosciences* (pp. 37–59). New York: Springer Science + Business Media.

Merikangas, K. R., He, J-P., Burstein, M., Swanson, S. A., Avenevoli, S., Cui, L., & Benjet, C. (2010). Lifetime prevalence of mental disorders in U.S. adolescents: Results from the National Comorbidity Survey Replication-Adolescent Supplement. *Journal of the American Academy of Child and Adolescent Psychiatry, 49*, 980–989.

Merikangas, K. R., He, J., Rapoport, J., Vitiello, B., & Olfson, M. (2013). Medication use in U.S. youth with mental disorders. *JAMA Pediatrics, 167*(2), 141–148.

Merrick, J., Uldall, P., & Volther, J. (2014). Intellectual and developmental disabilities: Denmark, normalization, and de-institutionalization. *Frontiers in Public Health, 2*, 161.

Mesri, B., Niles, A. N., Pittig, A., LeBeau, R. T., Haik, E., & Craske, M. G. (2017). Public speaking avoidance as a treatment moderator for social anxiety disorder. *Journal of Behavior Therapy and Experimental Psychiatry, 55*, 66–72.

Metsälä, E., & Vaherkoski, U. (2014). Medication errors in elderly acute care: A systematic review. *Scandinavian Journal of Caring Sciences, 28*(1), 12–28.

Metzl, J. M. (2004). Voyeur nation? Changing definitions of voyeurism, 1950–2004. *Harvard Review of Psychiatry, 12*(q), 127–131.

Meuret, A. E., Rosenfield, D., Bhaskara, L., Auchus, R., Liberzon, I., Ritz, T., & Abelson, J. L. (2016). Timing matters: Endogenous cortisol mediates benefits from early-day psychotherapy. *Psychoneuroendocrinology, 74*, 197–202.

Meyer, J. D., Koltyn, K. F., Stegner, A. J., Kim, J. S., & Cook, D. B. (2016). Influence of exercise intensity for improving depressed mood in depression: A dose-response study. *Behavior Therapy, 47*(4), 527–537.

Meyer, V. (1966). Modification of expectations in cases with obsessional rituals. *Behavioral Research and Therapy, 4*, 273–280.

Meyers, E., DeSerisy, M., & Roy, A. K. (2017). Disruptive mood dysregulation disorder (DMDD): An RDoC perspective. *Journal of Affective Disorders.*

Mez, J., Daneshvar, D. H., Kiernan, P. T., Abdolmohammadi, B., Alvarez, V. E., Huber, B. R., . . . McKee, A. C. (2017). Clinicopathological evaluation of chronic traumatic encephalopathy in players of American football. *JAMA, 318*(4), 360–370.

MHA (Mental Health America). (2008). *Americans reveal top stressors, how they cope.* Alexandria, VA: Author.

MHA (Mental Health America). (2017). *Housing.* Alexandria, VA: MHA.

MHA (Mental Health America). (2017). Position Statement 55: Confining sexual predators in the mental health system. Alexandria, VA: MHA.

MHA (Mental Health America). (2017). *Self-injury (cutting, self-harm or self-mutilation).* Alexandria, VA: MHA.

MHF (Mental Health of the Future). (2014). *Suicide statistics and facts.* Retrieved from http://www.genpsych.com/suicide-statistics-and-facts.

MHFA (Mental Health Foundation of Australia). (2014). *Sadness and depression.* Richmond, Canada: MHFA.

Mian, N. D. (2014). Little children with big worries: Addressing the needs of young, anxious children and the problem of parent engagement. *Clinical Child and Family Psychology Review, 17*(1), 85–96.

Miano, A., Grosselli, L., Roepke, S., & Dziobek, I. (2017). Emotional dysregulation in borderline personality disorder and its influence on communication behavior and feelings in romantic relationships. *Behaviour Research and Therapy, 95*, 148–157.

Michaelis, D. (2017). Please. It's just a phone. Read these crazy Smartphone addiction stats. *aNewDomain.* Retrieved from http://anewdomain.net.

Michal, M. (2011). Review of depersonalization: A new look at a neglected syndrome. *Journal of Psychosomatic Research, 70*(2), 199.

Middleman, A. B., & Olson, K. A. (2017, March 16). Confidentiality in adolescent health care. *UpToDate.* Retrieved from http://www.uptodate.com.

Miguel, E. M., Chou, T., Golik, A., Cornacchio, D., Sanchez, A. L., DeSerisy, M., & Comer, J. S. (2017). Examining the scope and patterns of deliberate self-injurious cutting content in popular social media. *Depression and Anxiety, 34*, 786–793.

Mihura, J. L., Meyer, G. J., Dumitrascu, N., & Bombel, G. (2016). On conducting construct validity meta-analyses for the Rorschach: A reply to Tibon Czopp and Zeligman (2016). *Journal of Personality Assessment, 98*(4), 343–350.

Millan, M. J., Fone, K., Steckler, T., & Horan, W. P. (2014). Negative symptoms of schizophrenia: Clinical characteristics, pathophysiological substrates, experimental models and prospects for improved treatment. *European Neuropsychopharmacologyy, 24*(5), 645–692.

Miller, A. (2015). The purpose of a clinical interview in a psychological assessment. *Chron.com.* Retrieved from http://work.chron.com/purpose-clinical-interview-psychological.

Miller, A. (2017). Dissociation in families experiencing intimate partner violence. *Journal of Trauma & Dissociation.* February 16, 1–14. [Epub ahead of print]

Miller, A. (2017, July 5). Examples of why you want to be a counselor. *Career Trend.* Retrieved from https://careertrend.com.

Miller, A. L., McEvoy, J. P., Jeste, D. V., & Marder, S. R. (2012). Treatment of chronic schizophrenia. In J. A. Lieberman, T. S. Stroup, & D. O Perkins (Eds.), *Essentials of schizophrenia* (pp. 225–243). Arlington, VA: American Psychiatric Publishing.

Miller, C. M., & Burch, A. D. S. (2017, March 15). Before suicide by hanging, girl pleaded in vain for mom's acceptance. *Miami Herald.* Retrieved from http://www.miamiherald.com.

Miller, D. (2014, February 4). Defining who we mean by "the mentally ill." *Psychology Today.*

Miller, D., & Hanson, A. (2016, October 16). *Committed: The battle over involuntary psychiatric care.* Baltimore, MD: JHU Press.

Miller, D. C. (Ed.). (2010). *Best practices in school neuropsychology: Guidelines for effective practice, assessment, and evidence-based intervention.* Hoboken, NJ: John Wiley & Sons.

Miller, D. N. (2011). *Child and adolescent suicidal behavior: School-based prevention, assessment, and intervention. The Guilford practical intervention in the schools series.* New York: Guilford Press.

Miller, G. (2012). Neuropathology. Blast injuries linked to neurodegeneration in veterans. *Science, 336*(6083), 790–791.

Miller, J. D., Lynam, D. R., Hyatt, C. S., & Campbell, W. K. (2017). Controversies in narcissism. *Annual Review of Clinical Psychology, 13*, 291–315.

Miller, K. (2016, January 4). The shocking results of Yahoo Health's body-positivity survey. *Yahoo.com.*

Miller, K. L., Dove, M. K., & Miller, S. M. (2007). *A counselor's guide to child sexual abuse: Prevention, reporting and treatment strategies.* Paper based on a program presented at the Association for Counselor Education and Supervision Conference, Columbus, OH.

Miller, M., & Kantrowitz, B. (1999, January 25). Unmasking Sybil: A re-examination of the most famous psychiatric patient in history. *Newsweek*, pp. 66–68.

Miller, N. E. (1948). Studies of fear as an acquirable drive: I. Fear as motivation and fear-reduction as reinforcement in the learning of new responses. *Journal of Experimental Psychology, 38*, 89–101.

Miller, P. M., Ingham, J. G., & Davidson, S. (1976). Life events, symptoms, and social support. *Journal of Psychiatric Research, 20*(6), 514–522.

Miller, R., & Hilsenroth, M. (2016, December 12). Assessing anaclitic and introjective characteristics using the SWAP-200 Q-sort: Concurrent validity with the Inventory of Interpersonal Problems Circumplex Scales. *Clinical Psychology & Psychotherapy.* [Epub ahead of print]

Miller, S. G. (1994). Borderline personality disorder from the patient's perspective. *Hospital Community Psychiatry, 45*(12), 1215–1219.

Miller, S. G. (1999). Borderline personality disorder in cultural context: Commentary on Paris. *Psychiatry, 59*(2), 193–195.

Miller, T. (2013, August 12). Too many selfies on Facebook can damage relationships: Study. *New York Daily News.*

Millichap, J. G. (2010). *Attention deficit hyperactivity disorder handbook: A physician's guide to ADHD* (2nd ed.). New York: Springer Science + Business Media.

Millon, T. (1969). *Modern psychopathology: A biosocial approach to maladaptive learning and functioning.* Philadelphia: Saunders.

Millon, T. (2011). *Disorders of personality: Introducing a DSM/ICD spectrum from normal to abnormal* (3rd ed.). Hoboken, NJ: John Wiley Sons.

Mills, J. F., Kroner, D. F., & Morgan, R. D. (2011). *Clinician's guide to violence risk assessment.* New York: Guilford Press.

Milner, A., Page, A., Morrell, S., Hobbs, C., Carter, G., Dudley, M., . . . Taylor, R. (2014). The effects of involuntary job loss on suicide and suicide attempts among young adults: Evidence from a matched case-control study. *The Australian and New Zealand Journal of Psychiatry, 48*(4), 333–340.

Milner, A., Spittal, M. H., Pirkis, J., & LaMontagne, A. D. (2013). Suicide by occupation: Systematic review and meta-analysis. *British Journal of Psychiatry: The Journal of Mental Science, 203*(6), 409–416.

Minkkinen, J., Oksanen, A., Kaakinen, M., Keipi, T., & Räsänen, P. (2017). Victimization and exposure to pro-self-harm and pro-suicide websites: A cross-national study. *Suicide and Life-Threatening Behavior, 47*(1), 14–26.

Minkkinen, J., Oksanen, A., Nasi, M., Keipi, T., Kaakinen, M., & Rasanen, P. (2016). Does social belonging to primary groups protect young people from the effects of pro-suicide sites? *Crisis, 37*(1), 31–41.

Minnes, S., Singer, L., Min, M. O., Wu, M., Lang, A., & Yoon, S. (2014). Effects of pre-natal cocaine/polydrug exposure on substance use by age 15. *Drug and Alcohol Dependence, 134,* 201–210.

Mintem, G. C., Horta, B. L., Domingues, M. R., & Gigante, D. P. (2014). Body size dissatisfaction among young adults from the 1982 Pelotas birth cohort. *European Journal of Clinical Nutrition, (7),* 1–7.

Mintz, L. B., Sanchez, J., & Heatherly, R. P. (2017). Treating lack of sexual passion in relationships. In Z. D. Peterson (Ed.), *The Wiley-Blackwell handbook of sex therapy* (Chap. 10, pp. 143–162). Hoboken, NJ: Wiley-Blackwell.

Minuchin, S. (1974). *Families and family therapy.* Cambridge, MA: Harvard University Press.

Minuchin, S. (1987). My many voices. In J. K. Zeig (Ed.), *The evolution of psychotherapy.* New York: Brunner/Mazel.

Minuchin, S. (2007). Jay Haley: My teacher. *Family Process, 46*(3), 413–414.

Minuchin, S., Lee, W-Y., & Simon, G. M. (2006). *Mastering family therapy: Journeys of growth and transformation* (2nd ed.). Hoboken, NJ: John Wiley & Sons.

Minuchin, S., Zeig, J., & Johnson, S. (2017). *A dialogue with Salvador Minuchin.* Presented at the 2017 Psychotherapy Networker Symposium in Washington, D.C.

MIP (Mental Illness Policy). (2017). 250,000 mentally ill are homeless. 150,000 seriously mentally ill are homeless. New York: MIP. Retrieved from https://www.mentalillnesspolicy.org.

MIP (Mental Illness Policy). (2017). *Victimization of people with mental illness* (two articles). New York: MIP. Retrieved from https://www.mentalillnesspolicy.org.

Miranda, J., Siddique, J., Belin, T. R., & Kohn-Wood, L. P. (2005). Depression prevalence in disadvantaged young black women: African and Caribbean immigrants compared to U.S.-born African Americans. *Social Psychiatry and Psychiatric Epidemiology 40*(4), 253–258.

Miret, M., Nuevo, R., Morant, C., Sainz-Cortón, E., Jiménez-Arriero, M. A., López-Ibor, J. J., et al. (2011). The role of suicide risk in the decision for psychiatric hospitalization after a suicide attempt. *Crisis: Journal of Crisis Intervention and Suicide Prevention, 32*(2), 65–73.

Mitchell, A. E., Dickens, G. L., & Picchioni, M. M. (2014). Facial emotion processing in borderline personality disorder: A systematic review and meta-analysis. *Neuropsychology Review, 24*(2), 166–184.

Mitchell, A. J., Rao, S., & Vaze, A. (2011). Can general practitioners identify people with distress and mild depression? A meta-analysis of clinical accuracy. *Journal of Affective Disorders, 130*(1-2), 26–36.

Mitchell, J. E. (2016, July 28). Bulimia nervosa in adults: Cognitive-behavioral therapy (CBT). *UpToDate.* Retrieved from www.uptodate.com.

Mitchell, J. E., & Zunker, C. (2016, July 27). Bulimia nervosa and binge eating disorder in adults: Medical complications and their management. *UpToDate.* Retrieved from www.uptodate.com.

Mitchell, J. T. (1983). When disaster strikes. . . the critical incident stress debriefing process. *Journal of Emergency Medical Services, 8,* 36–39.

Mitchell, J. T. (2003). Crisis intervention & CISM: A research summary. Retrieved from http://www.icisf.org/articles/cism_research_ summary. pdf.

Mitchell, S. L. (2017, March 1). Palliative care of patients with advanced dementia. *UpToDate.* Retrieved from http://www.uptodate.com.

Mitra, S., Mahintamani, T., Kavoor, A. R., & Nizamie, S. H. (2016). Negative symptoms in schizophrenia. *Industrial Psychiatry Journal, 25*(2), 135–144.

Mittal, V. A., Kalus, O., Bernstein, D. P., & Siever, L. J. (2007). Schizoid personality disorder. In W. O'Donohue, K. A. Fowler, & S. O. Lilienfeld (Eds.), *Personality disorders: Toward the DSM-V.* Los Angeles: Sage Publications.

Mittelman, M. S., & Bartels, S. J. (2014). Translating research into practice: Case study of a community-based dementia caregiver intervention. *Health Affairs (Project Hope), 33*(4), 587–595.

Miura, H., & Itoh, Y. (2016). The effect of suggestibility on eyewitness identifications: A comparison between showups and lineups. [Article in Japanese] *Shinrigaku Kenkyu, 87*(1), 32–39.

Moberg, T., Nordström, P., Forslund, K., Kristiansson, M., Asberg, M., & Jokinen, J. (2011). Csf 5-hiaa and exposure to and expression of interpersonal violence in suicide attempters. *Journal of Affective Disorders, 125*(1-3), 388–392.

Modrow, J. (1992). *How to become a schizophrenic: The case against biological psychiatry.* Everett, WA: Apollyon Press.

Moeller, S. J., & Paulus, M. P. (2018). Toward biomarkers of the addicted human brain: Using neuroimaging to predict relapse and sustained abstinence in substance use disorder. *Progress in Neuro-Psychopharmacology and Biological Psychiatry, 80*(Pt. B), 143–154.

Mohamed, S., Rosenheck, R., He, H., & Yuping, N. (2014). Insight and attitudes towards medication among inpatients with chronic schizophrenia in the U.S. and China. *Social Psychiatry and Psychiatric Epidemiology, 49*(7), 1063–1070.

Mohler, H., & Okada, T. (1977). Benzodiazepine receptor: Demonstration in the central nervous system. *Science, 198*(4319), 849–851.

Mok, K., Jorm, A. F., & Pirkis, J. (2015). Suicide-related Internet use: A review. *Australian & New Zealand Journal of Psychiatry, 49*(8), 697–705.

Mokros, A., Schilling, F., Weiss, K., Nitschke, J., & Eher, R. (2014). Sadism in sexual offenders: Evidence for dimensionality. *Psychological Assessment, 26*(1), 138–147.

Moldavsky, D. (2004, June 1). Transcultural psychiatry for clinical practice. *Psychiatric Times, XXI*(7), p. 36.

Molina, A. (2017, June 23). 11 healthy habits for fighting depression. *Huffington Post.*

Monahan, K. C., Guyer, A. E., Silk, J., Fitzwater, T., & Steinberg, L. (2016). Integration of developmental neuroscience and contextual approaches to the study of adolescent psychopathology. In D. Cicchetti (Ed.), *Developmental psychopathology, Vol. 2: Developmental neuroscience* (3rd ed.). New York: Wiley.

Monson, C. M., Resick, P. A., & Rizvi, S. L. (2014). Posttraumatic stress disorder. In D. H. Barlow (Ed.), (2014). *Clinical handbook of psychological disorders: A step-by-step treatment manual* (5th ed., pp. 62–113). New York: Guilford Press.

Monteith, L. L., Bahraini, N. H., & Menefee, D. S. (2018). Perceived burdensomeness: Thwarted belongingness, and fearlessness about death: Associations with suicidal ideation among female veterans exposed to military sexual trauma. *Journal of Clinical Psychology.* [Manuscript in press]

Montejo, A-L., Perahia, D. G. S., Spann, M. E., Wang, F., Walker, D. J., Yang, C. R., & Detke, M. J. (2011). Sexual function during long-term duloxetine treatment in patients with recurrent major depressive disorder. *Journal of Sexual Medicine, 8*(3), 773–782.

Monteleone, A. M., Castellini, G., Volpe, U., Ricca, V., Lelli, L., Monteleone, P., & Maj, M. (2018). Neuroendocrinology and brain imaging of reward in eating disorders: A possible key to the treatment of anorexia nervosa and bulimia nervosa. *Progress in Neuro-Psychopharmacology and Biological Psychiatry, 80*(Pt. B), 132–142.

Montes, K. S., Witkiewitz, K., Andersson, C., Fossos-Wong, N., Pace, T., Berglund, M., & Marimer, M. E. (2017). Trajectories of positive alcohol expectancies and drinking: An examination of young adults in the U.S. and Sweden. *Addictive Behaviors, 73,* 74–80.

Monti, F., Agostini, F., & Martini, A. (2004). Postpartum depression and mother-infant interaction. *Eta Evolutiva, 78,* 77–84.

Moon, J. R., Glymour, M. M., Vable, A. M., Liu, S. Y., & Subramanian, S. V. (2014). Short- and long-term associations between widowhood and mortality in the United States: Longitudinal analyses. *Journal of Public Health (Oxford, England), 36*(3), 382–389.

Moore, G., & Pfaff, J. A. (2017, May 23). Assessment and emergency management of the acutely agitated or violent adult. *UpToDate.* Retrieved from http://www.uptodate.com.

Moraes, F., & Góes, A. (2016). A decade of human genome project conclusion: Scientific diffusion about our genome knowledge. *Biochemistry and Molecular Biology Education, 44*(3), 215–223,

Moreland, C. S., & Bonin, L. (2016, August 24). Effect of antidepressants on suicide risk in children and adolescents. *UpToDate.* Retrieved from www.uptodate.com.

Moreno, C., Laje, G., Blanco, C., Jiang, H., Schmidt, A. B., & Olfson, M. (2007). National trends in the outpatient diagnosis and treatment of bipolar disorder in youth. *Archives of General Psychiatry, 64*(9), 1032–1039.

Morgan, C. A., Southwick, S., Steffian, G., Hazlett, G. A., & Loftus, E. F. (2013). Misinformation can influence memory for recently experienced, highly stressful events. *International Journal of Law and Psychiatry, 36*(1), 11–17.

Morgan, C. A., III, Wang, S., Rasmusson, A., Hazlett, G., Anderson, G., & Charney, D. S. (2001). Relationship among plasma cortisol, catecholamines, neuropeptide Y, and human performance during exposure to uncontrollable stress. *Psychosomatic Medicine, 63*(3), 412–422.

Morgan, C. D., & Murray, H. A. (1935). A method of investigating fantasies: The Thematic Apperception Test. *Archives of Neurological Psychiatry, 34,* 289–306.

Morgan, J., & Shoop, S. A. (2004, January 3). Terry Bradshaw's winning drive against depression. *USA Today.*

Morgan, J. F. (2012). Male eating disorders. In J. Alexander and J. Treasure (Eds.), *A collaborative approach to eating disorders* (pp. 272–278). New York: Routledge/Taylor & Francis Group.

Morgan, J. P. (2015, September 14). Evaluation and management of the cardiovascular complications of cocaine abuse. *UpToDate.* Retrieved from http://www.uptodate.com.

Morgan, L., Brittain, B., & Welch, J. (2015). Medical care following multiple perpetrator sexual assault: A retrospective review. *International Journal of STD and AIDS, 26*(2), 86–92.

Morgan, P. L., & Farkas, G. (2016). Evidence and implications of racial and ethnic disparities in emotional and behavioral disorders identification and treatment. *Behavioral Disorders, 41,* 122–131.

Moroni, F., Procacci, M., Pellecchina, G., Semerari, A., Nicolo, G., Carcione, A., . . . Colle, L. (2016). Mindreading dysfunction in avoidant personality disorder compared with other personality disorders. *Journal of Nervous and Mental Disease, 204*(10), 752–757.

Morris, A. (2017, March 6). NH struggling to solve psychiatric problem. *U.S. News & World Report.*

Morris, M. C., Kouros, C. D., Hellman, N., Rao, U., & Garber, J. (2014). Two prospective studies of changes in stress generation across depressive episodes in adolescents and emerging adults. *Development and Psychopathology, 26,* 1385–1400.

Morris, N. P. (2017, April 24). "Pro-suicide" websites lure too many people. *Chicago Tribune.* Retrieved from http://www.chicagotribune.com.

Morris, S. (2012). Shakespeare's minds diseased: Mental illness and its treatment. Retrieved from theshakespeareblog.com.

Morrison, A. P., Pyle, M., Chapman, N., French, P., Parker, S. K., & Wells, A. (2014). Metacognitive therapy in people with a schizophrenia spectrum diagnosis and medication resistant symptoms: A feasibility study. *Journal of Behavior Therapy and Experimental Psychiatry, 45*(2), 280–284.

Morrison, A. P., Turkington, D., Pyle, M., Spencer, H., Brabban, A., Dunn, G., . . . Hutton, P. (2014). Cognitive therapy for people with schizophrenia spectrum disorders not taking antipsychotic drugs: A single-blind randomised controlled trial. *Lancet, 383*(9926), 1395–1403.

Morrison, S. D., Dy, G. W., Chong, H. J., Holt, S. K., Vedder, N. B., Sorensen, M. D., . . . Fiedrich, J. B. (2017). Transgender-related education in plastic surgery and urology residency programs. *Journal of Graduate Medical Education, 9*(2), 178–183.

Morrissey, J. P., & Cuddeback, G. S. (2008). Jail diversion. In K. T. Mueser & D. V. Jeste (Eds.), *Clinical handbook of schizophrenia* (pp. 524–532). New York: Guilford Press.

Mort, J. R., Sailor, R., & Hintz, L. (2014). Partnership to decrease antipsychotic medication use in nursing homes: Impact at the state level. *South Dakota Medicine, 67*(2), 67–69.

Morton, P. M., Turiano, N. A., Mroczek, D. K., & Ferraro, K. F. (2016, March 12). Childhood misfortune, personality, and heart attack: Does personality mediate risk of myocardial infarction? *Journals of Gerontology. Series B, Psychological Sciences and Social Sciences.* [Epub ahead of print]

Mosca, N. W., & Schatz, M. L. (2013). Encopresis: Not just an accident. *NASN School Nurse, 28*(3), 218–221.

Mosconi, L., Berti, V., Glodzik, L., Pupi, A., De Santi, S., & de Leon, M. J. (2010). Pre-clinical detection of Alzheimer's disease using FDG-PET, with or without amyloid imaging. *Journal of Alzheimer's Disease, 20*(3), 843–854.

Mosconi, L., De Santi, S., Li, J., Tsui, W. H., Li, Y., Boppana, M., . . . de Leon, M. J. (2008). Hippocampal hypometabolism predicts cognitive decline from normal aging. *Neurobiology of Aging, 29*(5), 676–692.

Mosconi, L., Murray, J., Davies, M., Williams, S., Pirraglia, E., Spector, N., . . . de Leon, M. J. (2014). Nutrient intake and brain biomarkers of Alzheimer's disease in at-risk cognitively normal individuals: A cross-sectional neuroimaging pilot study. *BMJ Open, 4*(6), E004850.

Mosconi, M. W., Mohanty, S., Greene, R. K., Cook, E. H., Vaillancourt, D. E., & Sweeney, J. A. (2015). Feedforward and feedback motor control abnormalities implicate cerebellar dysfunctions in autism spectrum disorder. *Journal of Neuroscience, 35,* 2015–2025.

Moscovitch, D. A., Rowa, K., Paulitzki, J. R., Ierullo, M. D., Chiang, B., Antony, M. M., & McCabe, R. E. (2013). Self-portrayal concerns and their relation to safety behaviors and negative affect in social anxiety disorder. *Behaviour Research and Therapy, 51*(8), 476–486.

Moszczynska, A., & Callan, S. P. (2017, June 19). Molecular, behavioral and physiological consequences methamphetamine neurotoxicity: Implications for treatment. *Journal of Pharmacology and Experimental Therapeutics,* jpet.116.238501.

Mojtabai, R. (2016, October 26). Brief psychotic disorder. *UpToDate.* Retrieved from http://www.uptodate.com.

Mott, J. M., Barrera, T. L., Hernandez, C., Graham, D. P., & Teng, E. J. (2014). Rates and predictors of referral for individual psychotherapy, group psychotherapy, and medications among Iraq and Afghanistan veterans with PTSD. *The Journal of Behavioral Health Services & Research, 41*(2), 99–109.

Mott, J. M., Hundt, N. E., Sansgiry, S., Mignogna, J., & Cully, J. A. (2014). Changes in psychotherapy utilization among veterans with depression, anxiety, and PTSD. *Psychiatric Services, 65*(1), 106–112.

Moultrie, J. K., & Engel, R. R. (2016, December 5). Empirical correlates for the Minnesota Multiphasic Personality Inventory-2-Restructured Form in a German inpatient sample. *Psychological Assessment.* [Epub ahead of print]

Mowrer, O. H. (1939). A stimulus-response analysis of anxiety and its role as a reinforcing agent. *Psychological Review, 46,* 553–566.

Mowrer, O. H. (1947). On the dual nature of learning: A reinterpretation of "conditioning" and "problem-solving." *Harvard Education Review, 17,* 102–148.

Mowrer, O. H., & Mowrer, W. M. (1938). Enuresis: A method for its study and treatment. *American Journal of Orthopsychiatry, 8,* 436–459.

MRS (Market Research Store). (2016). Global depression drug market poised to surge from USD 14.51 billion in 2014 to USD 16.80 billion by 2020. *Market ResearchStore.com,* May 10.

Mu, S. H., Xu, M., Duan, J. X., Zhang, J., & Tan, L. H. (2017). Localizing age-related changes in brain structure using voxel-based morphometry. *Neural Plasticity, 2017,* 6303512.

Mukamal, K. J. (2016, February 16). Overview of the risks and benefits of alcohol consumption. *UpToDate.* Retrieved from ww.uptodate.com.

Mulder, R. T. (2010). Antidepressants and suicide: Population benefit vs. individual risk. *Acta Psychiatrica Scandinavica, 122*(6), 442–443.

Muller, H. A., Benke, D., Ralvenius, W. T., Mu, L., Schibli, R., Zeilhofer, H. U., & Krämer, S. D. (2017). GABAA receptor subtypes in the mouse brain: Regional mapping and diazepam receptor occupancy by in vivo [18F] flumazenil PET. *Neuroimage, 150,* 279–291.

Müller, N., Weidinger, E., Leitner, B., & Schwarz, M. J. (2015). The role of inflammation in schizophrenia. *Frontiers in Neuroscience, 9,* 372.

Mullins, N., Power, R. A., Fisher, H. L., Hanscombe, K. B., Euesden, J., Iniesta, R., . . . Lewis, C. M. (2016). Polygenic interactions with environmental adversity in the aetiology of major depressive disorder. *Psychological Medicine, 46*(4), 759–770.

Munsey, C. (2010). The kids aren't all right. *Monitor on Psychology, 41*(1), 22–25.

Muntner, P., Adballa, M., Correa, A., Griswold, M., Hall, J. E., Jones, D. W., . . . Appel, L. J. (2017). Hypertension in blacks: Unanswered questions and future directions for the JHS (Jackson Heart Study). *Hypertension, 69*(5), 761–769.

Murad, M. H., Elamin, M. B., Garcia, M. Z., Mullan, R. J., Murad, A., Erwin, P. J., & Montori, V. M. (2010). Hormonal therapy and sex reassignment: A systematic review and meta-analysis of quality of life and psychosocial outcomes. *Clinical Endocrinology, 72*(2), 214.

Murayama, Y., Ohba, H., Yasunaga, M., Nonaka, K., Takeuchi, R., Nishi, M., . . . Fujiwara, Y. (2014). The effect of intergenerational programs on the mental health of elderly adults. *Aging and Mental Health,* 1–9.

Murdock, K. K. (2013). Texting while stressed: Implications for students' burnout, sleep, and well-being. *Psychology of Popular Media Culture, 2,* 207–221.

Muris, P., Merckelbach, H., Otgaar, H., & Meijer, E. (2017). The malevolent side of human nature: A meta-analysis and critical review of the literature on the Dark Triad (narcissism, Machiavellianism, and psychopathy). *Perspectives on Psychological Science, 12,* 183–204.

Muris, P., & Ollendick, T. H. (2015). Children who are anxious in silence: A review on selective mutism, the new anxiety disorder in DSM-5. *Clinical Child and Family Psychology Review, 18,* 151–169.

Murphy, W. D., & Page, I. J. (2006). Exhibitionism. In R. D. McAnulty & M. M. Burnette (Eds.), *Sex and sexuality, Vol. 3: Sexual deviation and sexual offenses.* Westport, CT: Praeger Publishers.

Murray, A. L., Eisner, M., & Ribeaud, D. (2016, September 1). Development and validation of a brief measure of violent thoughts: The Violent Ideations Scale (VIS). *Assessment.* [Epub ahead of print]

Murray, L. K., Nguyen, A., & Cohen, J. A. (2014). Child sexual abuse. *Child and Adolescent Psychiatric Clinics of North America, 23*(2), 321–337.

Murray-Close, D., Nelson, D. A., Ostrov, J. M., Casas, J. F., & Crick, N. R. (2016). Relational aggression: A developmental psychopathology perspective. In D. Cicchetti (Ed.), *Developmental psychopathology, Vol. 4: Risk, resilience, and intervention* (3rd ed.). New York: Wiley.

Muscatell, K. A., Eisenberger, N. I., Dutcher, J. M., Cole, S. W., & Bower, J. E. (2016). Links between inflammation, amygdala reactivity, and social support in breast cancer survivors. *Brain, Behavior, and Immunity, 53,* 34–38.

Musser, E. D., & Nigg, J. T. (2018). Emotion dysregulation across emotion systems in attention deficit/hyperactivity disorder. *Journal of Clinical Child and Adolescent Psychology.* [Manuscript in press]

Myers, C. E., Radell, M. L., Shind, C., Ebanks-Williams, Y., Beck, K. D., & Gilbertson, M. W. (2016). Beyond symptom self-report: Use of a computer "avatar" to assess post-traumatic stress disorder (PTSD) symptoms. *Stress, 19*(6), 593–598.

MyPlan.com. (2016). Top ten lists/Highest job satisfaction. Retrieved from www.myplan.com/careers/top_ten/highest-job-satisfaction.php.

Mysko, C. (2016, November 17). Interview. In C. Abate, Body shaming in an age of social media. *Healthline News.*

Nace, E. P. (2005). Alcohol. In R. J. Frances, A. H. Mack, & S. I. Miller (Eds.), *Clinical textbook of addictive disorders* (3rd ed., pp. 75–104). New York: Guilford Press.

Nace, E. P. (2011). Alcohol. In R. J. Frances, S. I. Miller, & A. H. Mack (Eds.), *Clinical textbook of addictive disorders* (3rd ed., Chap. 5). New York: Guilford Press.

NAELA (National Academy of Elder Law Attorneys). (2014). Aging and special needs statistics. Retrieved from http://www.naela.org/public/about_NAELA/Media/.

NAELA (National Academy of Elder Law Attorneys). (2016). *Aging and special needs statistics.* Vienna, VA: NAELA.

Nahata, L., Chelvakumar, G., & Leibowitz, S. (2017). Gender-affirming pharmacological interventions for youth with gender dysphoria: When treatment guidelines are not enough. *Annals of Pharmacotherapy, 51,* 1023–1032.

Naidoo, S., & Mkize, D. L. (2012). Prevalence of mental disorders in a prison population in Durban, South Africa. *African Journal of Psychiatry, 15*(1), 30–35.

Naik, G. (2017). Peer-review activists push psychology journals towards open data. *Nature, 543*(7644), 161.

Nair, G., Evans, A., Bear, R. E., Velakoulis, D., & Bittar, R. G. (2014). The anteromedial GPi as a new target for deep brain stimulation in obsessive compulsive disorder. *Journal of Clinical Neuroscience, 21*(5), 815–821.

NAMI (National Alliance on Mental Illness). (2009, December 10). *Depression survey: Implications for diverse communities.* Arlington, VA: NAMI.

NAMI (National Alliance on Mental Illness). (2009). *Depression survey initiative.* Arlington, VA: NAMI.

NAMI (National Alliance on Mental Illness). (2014). *Find your local NAMI.* Arlington, VA: NAMI.

NAMI (National Alliance on Mental Illness). (2016). *Mental health by the numbers.* Arlington, VA: NAMI.

NAMI (National Alliance on Mental Illness). (2017). Act 4 Mental Health! Join NAMI's Virtual Hill Day. Arlington, VA: NAMI.

NAN (National Autism Network). (2017). *Autism facts and statistics.* Retrieved from http://nationalautismnetwork.com.

Naoi, M., Maruyama, W., & Shamoto-Nagai, M. (2018). Type A monoamine oxidase and serotonin are coordinately involved in depressive disorders: From neurotransmitter imbalance to impaired neurogenesis. *Journal of Neural Transmission (Vienna),* [Manuscript in press]

Naragon-Gainey, K., Prenoveau, J. M., Brown, T. A., & Zinbarg, R. E. (2016). A comparison and integration of structural models of depression and anxiety in a clinical sample: Support for and validation of the tri-level model. *Journal of Abnormal Psychology, 125,* 853-867.

Narang, P., Retzlaff, A., Brar, K., & Lippmann, S. (2016). Deep brain stimulation for treatment-refractory depression. *Southern Medical Journal, 109*(11), 700–703.

Nardi, B., Francesconi, G., Catena-Dell'osso, M., & Bellantuono, C. (2013). Adolescent depression: Clinical features and therapeutic strategies. *European Review for Medical and Pharmacological Sciences, 17*(11), 1546–1551.

Nathan, D. (2011). *Sybil exposed: The extraordinary story behind the famous multiple personality case.* New York: Free Press.

National Center for PTSD. (2008). Appendix A. Case examples from Operation Iraqi Freedom. *Iraq War Clinician Guide.* Washington, DC: Department of Veterans Affairs.

Nauert, R. (2014. May 7). Virtual reality therapy may reduce PTSD symptoms. *Psych Central.*

Nauert, R. (2016). Psychotherapy for anxiety may be most effective in the morning. *Psychcentral.com.* Retrieved from https://psychcentral.com.

Nauert, R. (2016, July 12). Insurance mandates improved care of autism, but many still uncovered. *Psych Central News.*

Nauert, R. (2016, July 14). Suicide prevention hotlines can be improved. *Psych Central News.*

Nauert, R. (2016, September 12). Myriad health & other problems linger 15 years after 9/11. *Psych Central News.* Retrieved from http://psychcentral.com.

Nautiyal, K. M., Okuda, M., Hen, R., & Blanco, C. (2017). Gambling disorder: An integrative review of animal and human studies. *Annals of the New York Academy of Sciences, 1394*(1), 106–127.

Nawata, H., Ogomori, K., Tanaka, M., Nishimura, R., Urashima, H., Yano, R., . . . Kuwabara, Y. (2010). Regional cerebral blood flow changes in female to male gender identity disorder. *Psychiatry and Clinical Neurosciences, 64*(2), 157–161.

NB (No Bullying). (2016, September 30). *How many kids get bullied a year.* (In Bullying Facts, Bullying Resources). Retrieved from https://nobullying.com.

NB (No Bullying). (2017, April 10). *Bullying statistics: The ultimate guide!* Retrieved from https://nobullying.com.

NBC (National Broadcasting Company). (2012, February 2). *Mystery teen illness grows in upstate New York. NBC Nightly News.*

NBPC (National Bullying Prevention Center). (2016, December 8). *Bullying statistics.* Retrieved from http://www.pacer.org/bullying/resources.

NCBH (National Council for Behavioral Health). (2015, August 31). *Is the problem cultural incompetence or racism?* Washington, DC: Author.

NCBH (National Council for Behavioral Health). (2017, March 28). *The psychiatric shortage: Causes and solutions.* Washington, DC: Author.

NCES (National Center for Education Statistics). (2016). *Table 318.30. Bachelor's, master's, and doctor's degrees conferred by postsecondary institutions, by sex of student and discipline division: 2013–2014.* Washington, DC: National Center for Education Statistics.

NCES (National Center for Education Statistics). (2016). *Table 322.50. Bachelor's degrees conferred to females by postsecondary institutions, by race/ethnicity and field of study: 2012–13 and 2013–14.* Washington, DC: National Center for Education Statistics.

NCES (National Center for Education Statistics). (2016). *Table 322.40. Bachelor's degrees conferred to males by postsecondary institutions, by race/ethnicity and field of study: 2012–13 and 2013–14.* Washington, DC: National Center for Education Statistics.

NCHS (National Center for Health Statistics). (2016). *Health, United States, 2016, with chartbook on long-term trends in health.* Hyattsville, MD: NCHS.

NCPTSD (National Center for PTSD). (2016, July 17). Facts about PTSD. *PsychCentral.*

NCSL (National Conference of State Legislatures). (2017, April 21). *State medical marijuana laws. NCSL.* Retrieved from http://www.ncsl.org.

NCVS (National Crime Victimization Survey). (2014). *National Crime Victimization Survey, 2013.* Washington, DC: Bureau of Justice Statistics.

NCVS (National Crime Victimization Survey). (2014). *Rape trauma syndrome.* Washington, DC: Bureau of Justice Statistics.

NCVS (National Crime Victimization Survey). (2017). *Data collection.* Retrieved from http://bjs.ojp.usdoj.gov/index.

Neacsiu, A. D., & Linehan, M. M. (2014). Dialectical behavior therapy for borderline personality disorder. In D. H. Barlow (Ed.), *Clinical handbook of psychological disorders* (5th ed., pp. 394–461). New York: Guilford Press.

Negele, A., Kaufhold, J., Kallenbach, L., & Leuzinger-Bohleber, M. (2015, November

29). Childhood trauma and its relation to chronic depression in adulthood. *Depression Research and Treatment.* Retrieved from http://dx.doi.org/10.1155/2015/650804.

Nelson, L., & Odujebe, O. (2017, June 21). Cocaine: Acute intoxication. *UpToDate.* Retrieved from http://www.uptodate.com.

Nelson, R. (2016). As spending skyrockets for direct-to-consumer prescription drug ads, so does pushback. *American Journal of Nursing, 116*(12), 20–21.

Nenadić-Šviglin, K., Nedic, G., Nikolac, M., Kozarić-Kovačić, D., Stipcevic, T., Šeler, D. M., & Pivac, N. (2011). Suicide attempt, smoking, comorbid depression, and platelet serotonin in alcohol dependence. *Alcohol, 45*(3), 209–216.

Nesi, J., & Prinstein, M. J. (2015). Using social media for social comparison and feedback-seeking: Gender and popularity moderate associations with depressive symptoms. *Journal of Abnormal Child Psychology, 43,* 1427–1438.

Netz, Y. (2017). Is the comparison between exercise and pharmacologic treatment of depression in the clinical practice guideline of the American College of Physicians evidence-based? *Frontiers in Pharmacology, 8,* 257.

Neumaier, F., Paterno, M., Alpdogan, S., Tevoufouet, E. E., Schneider, T., Hescheler, J., & Albanna, W. (2016, October 13). Surgical approaches in psychiatry: A survey of the world literature on psychosurgery. *World Neurosurgery,* S1878-8750(16)30995-0. [Epub ahead of print]

Neumaier, F., Paterno, M., Alpdogan, S., Tevoufouet, E. E., Schneider, T., Hescheler, J., & Albanna, W. (2017). Surgical approaches in psychiatry: A survey of the world literature on psychosurgery. *World Neurosurgery, 97,* 603–634.

Neumark-Sztainer, D. R., Wall, M. M., Haines, J. I., Story, M. T., Sherwood, N. E., & van den Berg, P. A. (2007). Shared risk and protective factors for overweight and disordered eating in adolescents. *American Journal of Preventative Medicine, 33*(5), 359–369.

Newcomer, J. W., & Leucht, S. (2011). Metabolic adverse effects associated with antipsychotic medications. In D. R. Weinberg & P. Harrison (Eds.), *Schizophrenia* (pp. 577–597). Hoboken, NJ: Wiley-Blackwell.

Newman, B. M., Bauer, I. E., Soares, J. C., & Sheline, Y. I. (2017). Neural structure and organization of mood pathology. In R. J. DeRubeis & D. R. Strunk (Eds.), *The Oxford handbook of mood disorders* (Chapter 19). New York: Oxford University Press.

Newman, F. (2013, May 1). Determining what is normal behavior and what is not. *Psychology Today.*

Newman, M., LaFreniere, L. S., & Shin, K. E. (2016). Cognitive-behavioral therapies in historical perspective. In A. J. Consoli, L. E. Beutler, & B. Bongar (Eds.), *Comprehensive textbook of psychotherapy: Theory and practice* (2nd ed., pp. 61–75). New York: Oxford University Press.

Newman, M. G. (2016). Honoring the past and looking to the future: Updates on seminal behavior therapy publications on current therapies and future directions. *Behavior Therapy, 47*(6), 773–775.

Newnham, E. A., & Janca, A. (2014). Childhood adversity and borderline personality disorder: A focus on adolescence. *Current Opinion in Psychiatry, 27*(1), 68–72.

Neziroglu, F., McKay, D., Todaro, J., & Yaryura-Tobias, J. A. (1996). Effect of cognitive behavior therapy on persons with body dysmorphic disorder and comorbid Axis II diagnoses. *Behavior Therapist, 27,* 67–77.

Neziroglu, F., Roberts, M., & Yaryura-Tobias, J. A. (2004). A behavioral model for body dysmorphic disorder. *Psychiatric Annals, 34*(12), 915–920.

NFER (National Foundation for Educational Research). (2010). Tellus4 national report (DCSF Research Report 218). Retrieved from http://www.nfer.ac.uk/publications/TEL01/.

Ng, T. S., Lin, A. P., Koerte, I. K., Pasternak, O., Liao, H., Merugumala, S., . . . Shenton, M. E. (2014). Neuroimaging in repetitive brain trauma. *Alzheimer's Research and Therapy, 6*(1), 10.

NGA (National Governors Association). (2016). A compact to fight opioid addiction. *NGA.* Retrieved from https://www.nga.org.

NIAAA (National Institute on Alcohol Abuse and Alcoholism). (2017, February). *Alcohol facts and statistics.* NIAAA. Retrieved from http://www.niaaa.nih.gov.

NIAAA (National Institute on Alcohol Abuse and Alcoholism). (2017). *College drinking.* NIAAA. Retrieved from http://www.niaaa.nih.gov.

NICHD (National Institute of Child Health and Human Development). (2015). *What causes Down syndrome?* Washington, DC: NICHD.

NICHD (National Institute of Child Health and Human Development). (2015). *What causes phenylketonuria (PKU)?* Washington, DC: NICHD.

Nichols, M. P. (2013). *The essentials of family therapy* (6th ed.). Boston: Pearson.

Nichols, W. C. (2004). Integrative marital and family treatment of dependent personality disorders. In M. M. MacFarlane (Ed.), *Family treatment of personality disorders: Advances in clinical practice* (pp. 173–204). Binghamton, NY: Haworth Clinical Practice Press.

Nicholson, A. A., Rabellino, D., Densmore, M., Frewen, P. A., Paret, C., Kluetsch, R., . . . Lanius, R. A. (2017). The neurobiology of emotion regulation in posttraumatic stress disorder: Amygdala downregulation via real-time fMRI neurofeedback. *Human Brain Mapping, 38,* 541–560.

Nicholson, T. R., Aybek, S., Craig, T., Harris, T., Wojcik, W., David, A. S., & Kanaan, R. A. (2016). Life events and escape in conversion disorder. *Psychological Medicine, 46*(12), 2617–2626.

Nicolini, H., Arnold, P., Nestadt, G., Lanzagorta, N., & Kennedy, J. L. (2011). Overview of genetics and obsessive-compulsive disorder. In E. Hollander, J. Zohar, P. J. Sirovatka, & D. A. Regier (Eds.), *Obsessive-compulsive spectrum disorders: Refining the research agenda for DSM-V* (pp. 141–159). Washington, DC: American Psychiatric Association.

NIDA (National Institute on Drug Abuse). (2014). America's addiction to opioids: Heroin and prescription drug abuse. *NIDA.* (Retrieved from https://www.drugabuse.gov.

NIDA (National Institute on Drug Abuse). (2016). Cocaine. *NIDA.* Retrieved from https://www.drugabuse.gov.

NIDA (National Institute on Drug Abuse). (2016). *Misuse of prescription drugs: Older adults.* Bethesda, MD: NIH.

NIDA (National Institute on Drug Abuse). (2016). Monitoring the Future study: Trends in prevalence of various drugs. *NIDA.* Retrieved from https://www.drugabuse.gov.

NIDA (National Institute on Drug Abuse). (2016). Monitoring the Future 2016 survey results. *NIDA.* Retrieved from https://www.drugabuse.gov.

NIDA (National Institute on Drug Abuse). (2017, April 21). Trends & statistics. *NIDA.* Retrieved from https://www.drugabuse.gov.

Nigg, J. T. (2016). Attention and impulsivity. In D. Cicchetti (Ed.), *Developmental psychology, Vol. 3: Maladaptation and psychopathology* (3rd ed.). New York: Wiley.

NIH (National Center for Complementary and Integrative Health). (2016). Use of complementary health approaches in the U.S.: Most used mind & body practices. *NCCIH.* Retrieved from https://nccih.nih.gov.

NIH (National Institute on Deafness and Other Communication Disorders). (2016, May 19). Quick statistics on voice, speech, language. Retrieved from https://www.nidcd.nih.gov.

Nijinsky, V. (1936). *The diary of Vaslav Nijinsky.* New York: Simon & Schuster.

Nillni, Y. I., Rohan, K. J., & Zvolensky, M. J. (2012). The role of menstrual cycle phase and anxiety sensitivity in catastrophic misinterpretation of physical symptoms during a CO2 challenge. *Archives of Women's Mental Health, 15*(6), 413–422.

NIMH (National Institute of Mental Health). (2004). *Depression and cancer.* Bethesda, MD: Author.

NIMH (National Institute of Mental Health). (2004). *Depression and heart disease.* Bethesda, MD: Author.

NIMH (National Institute of Mental Health). (2004). *Depression and stroke.* Bethesda, MD: Author.

NIMH (National Institute of Mental Health). (2010). *Questions and answers about the NIMH Treatment for Adolescents with Depression Study (TADS).* Retrieved from http://www.nimh.nih.gov/trials/practical/tads/questions-and-answers.shtml.

NIMH (National Institute of Mental Health). (2010). *Schizophrenia.* Retrieved from http://www.nimh.nih/gov/statistics/1SCHIZ.shtml.

NIMH (National Institute of Mental Health). (2010). Use of mental health services and treatment among adults. Retrieved from http://www.nimh.nih.gov/statistics/3USE_MT_ADULT.shtml.

NIMH (National Institute of Mental Health). (2012). *Percentage of Americans with phobias.* Bethesda: MD: NIMH.

NIMH (National Institute of Mental Health). (2014). *Bipolar disorder among adults.* Retrieved from NIMH website: http://www.nimh.nih.gov/statistics/1bipolar_adult.shtml.

NIMH (National Institute of Mental Health). (2014). *Panic disorder among adults.* Bethesda, MD: NIMH.

NIMH (National Institute of Mental Health). (2014). *Social phobia among adults.* Bethesda, MD: NIMH.

NIMH (National Institute of Mental Health). (2014). *Specific phobia among adults.* Bethesda, MD: NIMH.

NIMH (National Institute of Mental Health). (2015). *Any disorder among children.* Retrieved from http://www.nimh.nih.gov/health/statistics/prevalence/_148474.pdf.

NIMH (National Institute of Mental Health). (2015). *Women and depression.* Retrieved from http://psychcentral.com/lib/women-and-depression.

NIMH (National Institute of Mental Health). (2016). *Major depression with severe impairment among adolescents.* Bethesda, MD: Author.

NIMH (National Institute of Mental Health). (2017). *Agoraphobia among adults.* Bethesda, MD: Author.

NIMH (National Institute of Mental Health). (2017). *Any anxiety disorder among adults.* Bethesda, MD: Author.

NIMH (National Institute of Mental Health). (2017). *Any personality disorder.* Bethesda, MD: Author.

NIMH (National Institute of Mental Health). (2017). *Attention-deficit/hyperactivity disorder among adults.* Bethesda, MD: Author.

NIMH (National Institute of Mental Health). (2017). *Avoidant personality disorder.* Bethesda, MD: Author.

NIMH (National Institute of Mental Health). (2017). *Bipolar disorder among adults.* Bethesda, MD: Author.

NIMH (National Institute of Mental Health). (2017). *Eating disorders among adults – Anorexia nervosa.* Bethesda, MD: NIMH.

NIMH (National Institute of Mental Health). (2017). *Eating disorders among adults – Bulimia nervosa.* Bethesda, MD: NIMH.

NIMH (National Institute of Mental Health). (2017). *Generalized anxiety disorder among adults.* Bethesda, MD: Author.

NIMH (National Institute of Mental Health). (2017). *Panic disorder among adults.* Bethesda, MD: Author.

NIMH (National Institute of Mental Health). (2017). *Post-traumatic stress disorder among adults.* Bethesda, MD: Author.

NIMH (National Institute of Mental Health). (2017). *Schizophrenia.* Bethesda, MD: Author.

NIMH (National Institute of Mental Health). (2017). *Social phobia among adults.* Bethesda, MD: Author.

NIMH (National Institute of Mental Health). (2017). *Specific phobia among adults.* Bethesda, MD: Author.

NIMH (National Institute of Mental Health). (2017). *Use of mental health services and treatment among adults.* Bethesda, MD: Author.

Nisenblat, V., & Norman, R. J. (2016, August 24). The effects of caffeine on reproductive outcomes in women. *UpToDate.* Retrieved from http://www.uptodate.com.

Nitschke, J., Mokros, A., Osterheider, M., & Marshall, W. L. (2013). Sexual sadism: Current diagnostic vagueness and the benefit of behavioral definitions. *International Journal of Offender Therapy and Comparative Criminology, 57*(12), 1441–1453.

Nivard, M. G., Gage, S. H., Hottenga, J. J., van Beijsterveldt, C. E., Abdellaoui, A., Bartels, M., . . . Middeldorp, C. M. (2018). Genetic overlap between schizophrenia and developmental psychopathology: Longitudinal and multivariate polygenic risk predictions of common psychiatric traits during development. *Schizophrenia Bulletin.* [Manuscript in press]

NLM (National Library of Medicine). (2015). *Encopresis.* Retrieved from MedlinePlus website: https://www.nlm.nih.gov/medlineplus/ency/article/001570.htm.

NLM (National Library of Medicine). (2015). *Intellectual disability.* Retrieved from MedlinePlus website: https://www.nlm.nih.gov/medlineplus/ency/article/001523.htm.

NMHA (National Mental Health Association). (1999, June 5). Poll. *U.S. Newswire.*

Nobis, N. (2016). *Animals and ethics 101: Thinking critically about animal rights.* Open Philosophy Press.

Nobles, C. J., Valentine, S. E., Borba, C. P., Gerber, M. W., Shtasel, D. L., & Marques, L. (2016). Black-white disparities in the association between posttraumatic stress disorder and chronic illness. *Journal of Psychosomatic Research, 85,* 19–25.

Nobre, P. J. (2017). Treating men's erectile problems. In Z. D. Peterson (Ed.), *The Wiley-Blackwell handbook of sex therapy* (Chap. 4, pp. 40–56). Hoboken, NJ: Wiley-Blackwell.

Nock, M. K., Deming, C. A., Fullerton, C. S., Gilman, S. E., Goldenberg, M., Kessler, R. C. . . . Ursano, R. J. (2013). Suicide among soldiers: A review of psychosocial risk and protective factors. *Psychiatry: Interpersonal and Biological Processes, 76,* 97–125.

Nock, M. K., Dempsey, C. L., Aliaga, P. A., Brent, D. A., Heeringa, S. G., Kessler, R. C., . . . Benedek, D. (2017, May 15). Psychological autopsy study comparing suicide decedents, suicide ideators, and propensity score matched controls: Results from the study to assess risk and resilience in service members (Army STARRS). *Psychological Medicine, 47,* 2663–2674.

Nock, M. K., Green, J. G., Hwang, I., McLaughlin, K. A., Sampson, N. A., Zaslavsky, A. M., & Kessler, R. C. (2013). Prevalence, correlates, and treatment of lifetime suicidal behavior among adolescents: Results from the National Comorbidity Survey Replication Adolescent Supplement. *JAMA Psychiatry, 70*(3), 300–310.

Nock, M. K., Park, J. M., Finn, C. T., Deliberto, T. L., Dour, H. J., & Banaji, M. R. (2010). Measuring the suicidal mind: Implicit cognition predicts suicidal behavior. *Psychological Science, 21*(4), 511–517.

Nock, M. K., Stein, M. B., Heeringa, S. G., Ursano, R. J., Colpe, L. J., Fullerton, C. S., . . . Kessler, R. C. (2014). Prevalence and correlates of suicidal behavior among soldiers: Results from the army study to assess risk and resilience in service members (Army STARRS). *JAMA Psychiatry, 71*(5), 514–522.

Noeker, M. (2004). Factitious disorder and factitious disorder by proxy. *Praxis der Kinderpsychologie und Kinderpsychiatrie, 53*(7), 449–467.

Noh, Y. (2009). Does unemployment increase suicide rates? The OECD panel evidence. *Journal of Economic Psychology, 30*(4), 575–582.

Nolan, D., & Amico, C. (2016, February 23). How bad is the opioid epidemic? *Frontline.* Retrieved from http://www.pbs.org/WGBH/frontline.

Nolen-Hoeksema, S. (1990). *Sex differences in depression.* Stanford, CA: Stanford University Press.

Nolen-Hoeksema, S. (2002). Gender differences in depression. In I. H. Gotlib & C. L. Hammen (Eds.), *Handbook of depression* (pp. 492–509). New York: Guilford Press.

Nolen-Hoeksema, S. (2012). Emotion regulation and psychopathology: The role of gender. *Annual Review of Clinical Psychology, 8,* 161–187.

Noll-Hussong, M., Herberger, S., Grauer, M., Otti, A., & Gündel, H. (2013). Aspects of post-traumatic stress disorder after a traffic accident. *Versicherungsmedizin/Herausgegeben Von Verband Der Lebensversicherung-Unternehmen, 65*(3), 132–135.

Nomi, J. S., Bolt, T. S., Ezie, C. E. C., Uddin, L. Q., & Heller, A. S. (2017). Moment-to-moment BOLD signal variability reflects regional changes in neural flexibility across the lifespan. *Journal of Neuroscience, 37*(22), 5539–5548.

Noonan, D. (2003, June 16). A healthy heart. *Newsweek, 141*(24), 48–52.

Noonan, S. (2014). Veterinary wellness: Mindfulness-based stress reduction. *Canadian Veterinary Journal, 55,* 134–135.

Norcross, J. C., & Beutler, L. E. (2014). Integrative psychotherapies. In D. Wedding & R. J. Corsini (Eds.), *Current psychotherapies* (10th ed., pp. 499–532). Independence, KY: Cengage Publications.

Norcross, J. C., Bike, D. H., & Evans, K. L. (2009). The therapist's therapist: A replication and extension 20 years later. *Psychotherapy Theory, Research, Practice, Training, 46*(1), 32–41.

Norcross, J. C., & Farber, B. A. (2005). Choosing psychotherapy as a career: Beyond "I want to help people." *Journal of Clinical Psychology, 61*(8), 939–943.

Norcross, J. C., Goldfried, M. R., & Zimmerman, B. E. (2016). Integrative therapies in historical perspective. In A. J. Consoli, L. E. Beutler, & B. Bongar (Eds.), *Comprehensive textbook of psychotherapy: Theory and practice* (2nd ed., pp. 188–204). New York: Oxford University Press.

Norcross, J. C., Hogan, T. P., Koocher, G. P., & Maggio, L. A. (2016). *Clinician's guide to evidence-based practices: Behavioral health and addictions* (2nd ed.). New York: Oxford University Press.

Norcross, J. C., Karpiak, C. P., & Santoro, S. O. (2005). Clinical psychologists across the years: The division of clinical psychology from 1960 to 2003. *Journal of Clinical Psychology, 61*(12), 1467–1483.

Norcross, J. C., & Lambert, M. J. (2011). Psychotherapy relationships that work II. *Psychotherapy, 48*(1), 4–8.

Nord, M., & Farde, L. (2011). Antipsychotic occupancy of dopamine receptors in schizophrenia. *CNS Neuroscience & Therapeutics, 17*(2), 97–103.

Nordahl, H. M., Vogel, P. A., Morken, G., Stiles, T. C., Sandvik, P., & Wells, A. (2016). Paroxetine, cognitive therapy or their combination in the treatment of social anxiety disorder with and without avoidant personality disorder: A randomized clinical trial. *Psychotherapy and Psychosomatics, 85*(6), 346–356.

Nordqvist, C. (2016, April 20). Crystal meth: Facts, effects and addiction. *Medical News Today.* Retrieved from http://www.medicalnewstoday.com.

Norko, M. A., Wasser, T., Magro, H., Leavitt-Smith, E., Morton, F. J., & Hollis, T. (2016). Assessing insanity acquittee recidivism in Connecticut. *Behavioral Sciences & the Law. 34*(2-3), 423–443.

Norman, G. R., Monteiro, S. D., Sherbino, J., Ilgen, J. S., Schmidt, H. G., & Mamede, S. (2017). The causes of errors in clinical reasoning: Cognitive biases, knowledge deficits, and dual process thinking. *Academic Medicine, 92*(1), 23–30.

North, C. S. (2005). Somatoform disorders. In E. H. Rubin & C. F. Zorumski (Eds.), *Adult psychiatry* (2nd ed., pp. 261–274). Oxford, England: Blackwell Publishing.

North, C. S., & Pfefferbaum, B. (2013). Mental health response to community disasters: A systematic review. *Journal of the American Medical Association, 310*(5), 507–518.

Norton, A. (2011). Imagined smells can precede migraines. Retrieved from http://www.reuters.com/assets/print?aid=USTRE79D4L120111014.

Norton, P. J., & Paulus, D. J. (2016). Toward a unified treatment for emotional disorders: Update on the science and practice. *Behavior Therapy, 47*(6), 854–868.

Nosek, B. A., Alter, G., Banks, G. C., Borsboom, D., Bowman, S. D., Breckler, S. J., . . . Yarkoni, T. (2015). Promoting an open research culture. *Science, 348*(6242), 1422–425.

Nourse, R., Adamshick, P., & Stoltzfus, J. (2017). College binge drinking and its association with depression and anxiety: A prospective observational study. *East Asian Archives of Psychiatry, 24*(1), 18–25.

Novais, F., Araujo, A., & Godinho, P. (2015). Historical roots of histrionic personality disorder. *Frontiers in Psychology, 6*, 1463.

Nowak, D. E., & Aloe, A. M. (2014). The prevalence of pathological gambling among college students: A meta-analytic synthesis, 2005–2013. *Journal of Gambling Studies, 30*(4), 819–843.

NPD Group. (2008). Entertainment Trends Report. Cited by Mike Antonucci in *San Jose Mercury News,* April 3, 2008.

NPT (Network of Philanthropic Trust). (2017). *Charitable giving statistics.* Retrieved from https://www.nptrust.org/philanthropic-resources/charitable-giving-statistics/.

NSDUH (National Survey on Drug Use and Health). (2013). Results from the 2012 National Survey on Drug Use and Health: Mental health findings, NSDUH Series H-47, HHS Publication No. (SMA) 13-4805. Rockville, MD: Substance Abuse and Mental Health Services Administration.

NSDUH (National Survey on Drug Use and Health). (2016, September 8). *Results from the 2015 National Survey on Drug Use and Health: Detailed Tables. Prevalence estimates, standard errors, P values, and sample sizes.* Rockville, MD: Abuse and Mental Health Services Administration.

NSDUH (National Survey on Drug Use and Health). (2017). *Results from the 2016 National Survey on Drug Use and Health: Detailed tables.*

Rockville, MD: Substance Abuse and Mental Health Services Administration.

NSF (National Sleep Foundation). (2017). *Healthy sleep tips.* Arlington, VA: NSF.

NSPCC (National Society for the Prevention of Cruelty to Children). (2013). Reported in *BBC News,* One in five children bullied online, says NSPCC survey (August 11, 2013).

Nugent, A. C., Bain, E. E., Carlson, P. J., Neumeister, A., Bonne, O., Carson, R. E., . . . Drevets, W. C. (2013). Reduced post-synaptic serotonin type 1A receptor binding in bipolar depression. *European Neuropsychopharmacology, 23*(8), 822–829.

Numan, T., van den Boogaard, M., Kamper, A. M., Rood, P. J. T., Peelen, L. M., Slooter, A. J. C., & Dutch Delirium Detection Study Group. (2017, May 12). Recognition of delirium in postoperative elderly patients: A multicenter study. *Journal of the American Geriatrics Society.* [Epub ahead of print]

Nunes, K. L., Hermann, C. A., Renee Malcom, J., & Lavoie, K. (2013). Childhood sexual victimization, pedophilic interest, and sexual recidivism. *Child Abuse and Neglect, 37*(9), 703–711.

Nurkkala, M., Keränen, A. M., Koivumaa-Honkanen, H., Ikäheimo, T. M., Ahola, R., Pyky, R., . . . Korpelainen, R. (2016). Disordered eating behavior, health and motives to exercise in young men: Cross-sectional population-based MOPO study. *BMC Public Health, 16*, 483.

Nuss, P. (2015). Anxiety disorders and GABA neurotransmission: A disturbance of modulation. *Neuropsychiatric Disease and Treatment, 11*, 165–175.

NVSR (National Vital Statistics Reports). (2010, August 9). Births: Final data for 2007. National vital statistics reports, *58*(24). Hyattsville, MD: National Center for Health Statistics.

NVSR (National Vital Statistics Reports). (2016, June 2). *Births: Preliminary data for 2015.* Volume *65*(3). Hyattsville, MD: National Center for Health Statistics.

NVSR (National Vital Statistics Reports). (2016, June 30). Deaths: Final data for 2014. *NVSS, 65*(4).

Nygaard, E., Hussain, A., Sigveland, J., & Heir, T. (2016). General self-efficacy and post-traumatic stress after a natural disaster: A longitudinal study. *BMC Psychology, 4*, 15.

Nyström, M. B., Stenling, A., Sjöström, E., Neely, G., Lindner, P., Hassmén, P., . . . Carlbring, P. (2017). Behavioral activation versus physical activity via the Internet: A randomized controlled trial. *Journal of Affective Disorders, 215*, 85–93.

OA (Opportunity Agenda). (2017). *A review of public opinion research related to black male achievement.* New York: OA.

Oar, E. L., Farrell, L. J., Waters, A. M., & Ollendick, T. H. (2016). Blood-injection-injury phobia and dog phobia in youth: Psychological characteristics and associated features in a clinical sample. *Behavior Therapy, 47*, 312–324.

Oates, G. L. (2016). Effects of religiosity dimensions on physical health across non-elderly Black and White American panels. *Review of Religious Research, 58*(2), 249–270.

O'Brien, C. P. (2013). Cited in NPR Staff, With addiction, breaking a habit means resisting a reflex. *Weekend Edition Sunday.* Retrieved from http://www.npr.org/2013/10/20/238297311/with-addiction-breaking.

O'Brien, C. P., O'Brien, T. J., Mintz, J., & Brady, J. P. (1975). Conditioning of narcotic abstinence symptoms in human subjects. *Drug and Alcohol Dependence, 1*, 115–123.

O'Brien, S. A. (2017, March 1). Facebook wants to get smarter about suicide prevention. *CNN Money.* Retrieved from http://money.cnn.com.

O'Brien, W. B., Piedrahita, J. G., & Bacatan, F. P., Jr. (2011). The therapeutic community. In J. H. Lowinson & P. Ruiz (Eds.), *Substance abuse: A comprehensive textbook* (5th ed.). Philadelphia, PA: Lippincott Williams & Wilkins.

O Ciardha, C., Gannon, T. A., & Ward, T. (2016). The cognitive distortions of child sexual abusers: Evaluating key theories. In D. P. Boer, *The Wiley handbook on the theories, assessment and treatment of sexual offending* (Vol. 1, Chap. 10, pp. 207–222). Hoboken, NJ: Wiley-Blackwell.

Odagaki, Y. (2017). A case of persistent generalized retrograde autobiographical amnesia subsequent to the Great East Japan Earthquake in 2011. *Case Reports in Psychiatry,* article 5173605.

O'Dea, B., Larsen, M. E., Batterham, P. J., Calear, A. L., & Christensen, H. (2018). A linguistic analysis of suicide-related Twitter posts. *Crisis.* [Manuscript in press]

O'Donohue, W., Fowler, K. A., & Lilienfeld, S. O. (Eds.). (2007). *Personality disorders: Toward the DSM-V.* Los Angeles: Sage Publications.

Ogawa, Y., Niizuma, K., & Tominaga, T. (2017). Fine morphological evaluation of hypothalamus in patients with hyperphagia. *Acta Neurochirurgica, 159*(5), 865–871.

Ogle, C. M., Rubin, D. C., & Siegler, I. C. (2014). Cumulative exposure to traumatic events in older adults. *Aging & Mental Health, 18*(3), 316–325.

O'Hara, M. W., & Wisner, K. L. (2014). Perinatal mental illness: Definition, description and aetiology. *Best Practice & Research. Clinical Obstetrics and Gynaecology, 28*(1), 3–12.

Ohman, A., & Mineka, S. (2003). The malicious serpent: Snakes as a prototypical stimulus for an evolved module of fear. *Current Directions in Psychological Science, 12*(1), 5–9.

Ohring, R., Graber, J. A., & Brooks-Gunn, J. (2002). Girls' recurrent and concurrent body dissatisfaction: Correlates and consequences over 8 years. *International Journal of Eating Disorders, 31*(4), 404–415.

Olnas-Kukkonen, H., & Mantila, L. (2010). Lisa, Lisa the machine says I have performed an illegal action. Should I tell the police? A survey and observations of inexperienced elderly Internet users. Paper submitted to *Journal of the Southern Association for Information Systems.*

OJJDP (Office of Juvenile Justice and Delinquency Prevention). (2010, February). In Focus: Girls' delinquency. NCJ228414. Washington, DC: OJJDP.

Okawa, J. B., & Hauss, R. B. (2007). The trauma of politically motivated torture. In E. K. Carll (Ed.), *Trauma psychology: Issues in violence, disaster, health, and illness* (Vol. 1). Westport, CT: Praeger Publishers.

Okpokoro, U., Adams, C. E., & Sampson, S. (2014). Family intervention (brief) for schizophrenia. *Cochrane Database of Systematic Reviews, 3,* CD009802.

Oldehinkel, A. J., Ormel, J., Verhulst, F. C., & Nederhof, E. (2014). Childhood adversities and adolescent depression: A matter of both risk and resilience. *Development and Psychopathology, 26*(4, Pt. 1), 1067–1075.

Olfson, M., King, M., & Schoenbaum, M. (2016). Stimulant treatment of young people in the United States. *Journal of Child and Adolescent Psychopharmacology, 26,* 520–526.

Olfson, M., Marcus, S. C., Tedeschi, M., & Wan, G. J. (2006). Continuity of antidepressant treatment for adults with depression in the United States. *American Journal of Psychiatry, 163,* 101.

Olfson, M., Wall, M., Wang, S., Crystal, S., Gerhard, T., & Blanco, C. (2017). Suicide following deliberate self-harm. *American Journal of Psychiatry, 174,* 765–774.

Oliver, C., Licence, L., & Richards, C. (2017). Self-injurious behavior in people with intellectual disability and autism spectrum disorder. *Current Opinion in Psychiatry, 30,* 97–101.

Ollendick, T. H. (2014). Advances toward evidence-based practice: Where to from here? *Behavior Therapy, 45*(1), 51–55.

Ollove, M. (2017). Getting the mentally ill out of jails. *Pew Charitable Trusts.* Retrieved from http://www.pewtrusts.org.

Olmsted, M. P., MacDonald, D. E., McFarlane, T., Trottier, K., & Colton, P. (2015). Predictors of rapid relapse in bulimia nervosa. *International Journal of Eating Disorders, 48*(3), 337–340.

Olson, K. R., Durwood, L., DeMeules, M., & McLaughlin, K. A. (2016). Mental health of transgender children who are supported in their identities. *Pediatrics, 137,* e20153223.

Olson, L. A., & Patrick, C. J. (2018). Clinical aspects of antisocial personality disorder and psychopathy. In W. J. Livesley & R. Larstone (Eds.), *Handbook of personality disorders: Theory, research, and treatment* (2nd ed.). New York: Guilford Press.

Olson-Kennedy, J., & Forcier, M. (2017, June 14). Management of gender nonconformity in children and adolescents. *UpToDate.* Retrieved from http://www.uptodate.com.

Oltean, H. R., Hyland, P., Vallières, F., & David, D. O. (2018). An empirical assessment of REBT models of psychopathology and psychological health in the prediction of anxiety and depression symptoms. *Behavioural and Cognitive Psychotherapy, 45,* 600–615.

O'Malley, S. S., Jaffe, A. J., Chang, G., Schottenfeld, R., Meyer, R., & Rounsaville, B. (1992). Naltrexone and coping skills therapy for alcohol dependence. *Archives of General Psychiatry, 49,* 881–888.

O'Malley, S. S., Jaffe, A. J., Rode, S., & Rounsaville, B. J. (1996). Experience of a "slip" among alcoholics treated with naltrexone or placebo. *American Journal of Psychiatry, 153,* 281–283.

O'Malley, S. S., Krishnan-Sarin, S., Farren, C., & O'Connor, P. G. (2000). Naltrexone-induced nausea in patients treated for alcohol dependence: Clinical predictors and evidence for opioid-mediated effects. *Journal of Clinical Psychopharmacology, 20*(1), 69–76.

Omar, H., Tejerina-Arreal, M., & Crawford, M. J. (2014). Are recommendations for psychological treatment of borderline personality disorder in current U.K. guidelines justified? Systematic review and subgroup analysis. *Personality and Mental Health, 8*(3), 228–237.

Öncü, F., Türkcan, S., Canbek, Ö., Yesilbursa, D., & Uygur, N. (2009). Fetishism and kleptomania: A case report in forensic psychiatry. *Nöropsikiyatri Arşivi/Archives of Neuropsychiatry, 46*(3), 125–128.

Ong, C., Pang, S., Sagayadevan, V., Chong, S. A., & Subramaniam, M. (2015). Functioning and quality of life in hoarding: A systemic review. *Journal of Anxiety Disorders, 32,* 17–30.

Onoue, T., Toda, H., & Nakai, Y. (2013). Childhood stress and depression. *Nihon Shinkei Seishin Yakurigaku Zasshi, 33*(3), 105–110.

ONS (Office for National Statistics). (2017, March 9). *Sickness absence in the labour market: 2016.* London, UK: Author.

Onwuteaka-Philipsen, B. D., Brinkman-Stoppelenburg, A., Penning, C., de Jong-Krul, G. J. F., van Delden, J. J. M., & van der Heide, A. (2012, July 11). Trends in end-of-life practices before and after the enactment of the euthanasia law in the Netherlands from 1990 to 2010: A repeated cross-sectional survey. *The Lancet.* Retrieved from http://dx/doi.org/10.1016/S0140-6736(12)61034-4.

OPA (Office of Protection and Advocacy for Persons with Disabilities). (2016). *"Your rights in a psychiatric facility," A P&A self-help publication.* CT: Author.

Opinion Research Corporation. (2004). National Survey Press Release. May 17, 2004.

Opinion Research Corporation Poll/CNN. (2011, March 18-20). Disaster preparedness and relief. *PollingReport.com.*

Oquendo, M. A., Dragatsi, D., Harkavy-Friedman, J., Dervic, K., Currier, D., Burke, A. K., . . . Mann, J. J. (2005). Protective factors against suicidal behavior in Latinos. *Journal of Nervous and Mental Disease, 193*(7), 438–443.

Oquendo, M. A., Lizardi, D., Greenwald. S., Weissman, M. M., & Mann, J. J. (2004). Rates of lifetime suicide attempt and rates of lifetime major depression in different ethnic groups in the United States. *Acta Psychiatrica Scandinavica, 110*(6), 446–451.

Oquendo, M. A., Russo, S. A., Underwood, M. D., Kassir, S. A., Ellis, S. P., Mann, J. J., & Arango, V. (2006). Higher postmortem prefrontal 5-HT2A receptor binding correlates with lifetime aggression in suicide. *Biological Psychiatry, 59,* 235–243.

Ordemann, G. J., Opper, J., & Davalos, D. (2014). Prospective memory in schizophrenia: A review. *Schizophrenia Research, 155*(1-3), 77–89.

O'Riley, A. A., Van Orden, K. A., He, H., Richardson, T. M., Podgorski, C., & Conwell, Y. (2014). Suicide and death ideation in older adults obtaining aging services. *The American Journal of Geriatric Psychiatry, 22*(6), 614–622.

Orri, M., Paduanello, M., Lachal, J., Falissard, B., Sibeoni, J., & Revah-Levy, A. (2014). Qualitative approach to attempted suicide by adolescents and young adults: The (neglected) role of revenge. *PLoS One, 9*(5), e96716.

Orwelius, L., Kristenson, M., Fredrikson, M., Walther, S., & Sjöberg, F. (2017). Hopelessness: Independent associations with health-related quality of life and short-term mortality after critical illness: A prospective, multicentre trial. *Journal of Critical Care, 41,* 58–63.

O'Shea, L. E., & Dickens, G. L. (2016). Role of assessment components and recent adverse outcomes in risk estimation and prediction: Use of the Short Term Assessment of Risk and Treatability (START) in an adult secure inpatient mental health service. *Psychiatry Research, 240,* 398–405.

Oshima, I., Mino, Y., & Inomata, Y. (2005). Effects of environmental deprivation on negative symptoms of schizophrenia: A nationwide survey in Japan's psychiatric hospitals. *Psychiatry Research, 136*(2–3), 163–171.

Osmanağaoğlu, N., Creswell, C., & Dodd, H. F. (2018). Intolerance of uncertainty, anxiety, and worry in children and adolescents: A meta-analysis. *Journal of Affective Disorders, 225,* 80–90.

Öst, L. G., Havnen, A., Hansen, B., & Kvale, G. (2015). Cognitive behavioral treatments of obsessive-compulsive disorder: A systematic review and meta-analysis of studies published 1993–2014. *Clinical Psychology Review, 40,* 156–169.

Öst, L. G., Riise, E. N., Wergeland, G. J., Hansen, B., & Kvale, G. (2016). Cognitive behavioral and pharmacological treatments of OCD in children: A systematic review and meta-analysis. *Journal of Anxiety Disorders, 43,* 58–69.

O'Sullivan, L. F., Brotto, L. A., Byers, S., Majerovich, J. A., & Wuest, J. A. (2014). Prevalence and characteristics of sexual functioning among sexually experienced middle to late adolescents. *Journal of Sexual Medicine, 11,* 630–641.

Otani, K., Suzuki, A., Matsumoto, Y., Enokido, M., & Shirata, T. (2016). Effects of perceived affectionless control parenting on working models of the self and others. *Psychiatry Research, 242,* 315–318.

Otowa, T., Hek, K., Lee, M., Byrne, E. M., Mirza, S. S., Nivard, M. G., . . . Hettema, J. M. (2016). Meta-analysis of genome-wide association studies of anxiety disorders. *Molecular Psychiatry, 21*(10), 1391–1399.

Oudgenoeg-Paz, O., Mulder, H., Jongmans, M. J., van der Ham, J. M., & Van der Stigchel, S. (2017). The link between motor and cognitive development in children born preterm and/or with low birth weight: A review of current evidence. *Neuroscience and Biobehavioral Reviews, 80,* 382–393.

Overdorf, V., Kollia, B., Makarec, K., & Alleva Szeles, C. (2016). The relationship between physical activity and depressive symptoms in healthy older women. *Gerontology and Geriatric Medicine, 2,* 2333721415626859.

Overton, D. (1964). State-dependent or "dissociated" learning produced with pentobarbital. *Journal of Comparative Physiology and Psychology, 57,* 3–12.

Overton, D. (1966). State-dependent learning produced by depressant and atropine-like drugs. *Psychopharmacologia, 10,* 6–31.

Owen, R., Dempsey, R., Jones, S., & Gooding, P. (2018). Defeat and entrapment in bipolar disorder: Exploring the relationship with suicidal ideation from a psychological theoretical perspective. *Suicide and Life-Threatening Behavior.* [Manuscript in press]

Owen-Howard, M. (2001). Pharmacological aversion treatment of alcohol dependence. I. Production and prediction of conditioned alcohol aversion. *American Journal of Drug and Alcohol Abuse, 27*(3), 561–585.

Owens, G. P., Held, P., Blackburn, L., Auerbach, J. S., Clark, A. A., Herrera, C. J., . . . Stuart, G. L. (2014). Differences in relationship conflict, attachment, and depression in treatment-seeking veterans with hazardous substance use, PTSD, or PTSD and hazardous substance use. *Journal of Interpersonal Violence, 29*(7), 1318–1337.

Özdel, K., Taymur, I., Guriz, S. O., Tulaci, R. G., Kuru, E., Turkcapar, M. H. (2014, August 29). Measuring cognitive errors using the Cognitive Distortions Scale (CDS): Psychometric properties in clinical and non-clinical samples. *PLOS One.* Retrieved from https://doi.org/10.137/journal.pone.0105956.

PA (Parents Anonymous). (2017). Website. Claremont, CA: Parents Anonymous. Retrieved from http://parentsanonymous.org.

Paast, N., Khosravi, Z., Memari, A. H., Shayestehfar, M., & Arbabi, M. (2016). Comparison of cognitive flexibility and planning ability in patients with obsessive compulsive disorder, patients with obsessive compulsive personality disorder, and healthy controls. *Shanghai Archives of Psychiatry, 28*(1), 28–34.

Padwa, L. (1996). *Everything you pretend to know and are afraid someone will ask.* New York: Penguin.

Page, T. F., Pelham, W. E., Fabiano, G. A., Greiner, A. R., Gnagy, E. M., Hart, K. C., Coxe, S., Waxmonsky, J. G., Foster, E. M., & Pelham, W. E. (2016). Comparative cost analysis of sequential, adaptive, behavioral, pharmacological, and combined treatments for childhood ADHD. *Journal of Clinical Child and Adolescent Psychology, 45,* 416–427.

Palamar, J. J., Acosta, P., Ompad, D. C., & Cleland, C. M. (2017). Self-reported Ecstasy/MDMA/"Molly" use in a sample of nightclub and dance festival attendees in New York City. *Substance Use & Misuse. 52*(1), 82–91.

Pallardy, C. (2015, February 15). Male & female active physicians: 70 statistics by specialty. *Becker's GI & Endoscopy.* Retrieved from http://www.beckersasc.com/gastroenterology-and-endoscopy/male-female.html.

Palley, W. (2014). Data point: Digital distractions help drive Millennials to mindfulness. *JWT Intelligence,* February 7, 2014.

Pandey, D., & Shrivastava, P. (2017). Mediation effect of social support on the association between hardiness and immune response. *Asian Journal of Psychiatry, 26,* 52–55.

Pankevich, D. E., Teegarden, S. L., Hedin, A. D., Jensen, C. L., & Bale, T. L. (2010). Caloric restriction experience reprograms stress and orexigenic pathways and promotes binge eating. *Journal of Neuroscience, 30*(48), 16399–16407.

Papolos, D., Hennen, J., & Cockerham, M. S. (2005). Factors associated with parent-reported suicide threats by children and adolescents with community-diagnosed bipolar disorder. *Journal of Affective Disorders, 86*(2–3), 267–275.

Parikh, S. V., Quilty, L., Ravitz, P., Rosenbluth, M., Pavlova, B., Grigoriadis, S., . . . Ravindran, A. V. (2017). Rating short-term psychodynamic therapy for the Canadian Network for Mood and Anxiety Treatments Depression Guidelines. *The Canadian Journal of Psychiatry, 62*(10), 77–78.

Paris, J. (2005). Borderline personality disorder. *Canadian Medical Association Journal, 172*(12), 1579–1583.

Paris, J. (2010). Estimating the prevalence of personality disorders in the community. *Journal of Personality Disorders, 24*(4), 405–411.

Paris, J. (2012). The rise and fall of dissociative identity disorder. *Journal of Nervous and Mental Disease, 200*(12), 1076–1079.

Paris, J. (2014). Modernity and narcissistic personality disorder. *Personality Disorders, 5*(2), 220–226.

Paris, J. (2018). Borderline personality disorder. In W. J. Livesley & R. Larstone (Eds.), *Handbook of personality disorder: Theory, research, and treatment* (2nd ed.). New York: Guilford Press.

Park, C. H. K., Yoo, S. H., Lee, J., Cho, S. J., Shin, M. S., Kim, E. Y., . . . Ahn, Y. M. (2017). Impact of acute alcohol consumption on lethality of suicide methods. *Comprehensive Psychiatry, 75,* 27–34.

Park, E. R. (2010, April 25). Behavioral approaches to smoking cessation. *UpToDate.* Retrieved from http://www.uptodate.com.

Park, M. (2016, July 1). Crisis text line takes suicide prevention into the age of texting. *USA Today.*

Park, S. H., & Han, K. S. (2017, April 6). Blood pressure response to meditation and yoga: A systematic review and meta-analysis. *Journal of Alternative and Complementary Medicine.* [Epub ahead of print]

Park, S. Y., Cervesi, C., Galing, B., Molteni, S., Walyzada, F., Ameis, S. H., Gerhard, T., & Olfson, M. (2016). Antipsychotic use trends in youth with autism spectrum disorder and/or intellectual disability: A meta-analysis. *Journal of the American Academy of Child and Adolescent Psychiatry, 55,* 456–468.

Parker, G. E. (2016). A framework for navigating Institutional Review Board (IRB) oversight in the complicated zone of research. *Cureus, 8*(10), e844.

Parker, S., Nichter, M., Vuckovic, N., Sims, C., & Ritenbaugh, C. (1995). Body image and weight concerns among African American and white adolescent females: Differences that make a difference. *Human Organization, 54*(2), 103–114.

Parker, T. S., Blackburn, K. M., Perry, M. S., & Hawks, J. M. (2012). Sexting as an intervention: Relationship satisfaction and motivational considerations. *American Journal of Family Therapy, 41*(1), 1–12.

Parmar, A., & Sarkar, S. (2016). Neuroimaging studies in obsessive compulsive disorder: A narrative review. *Indian Journal of Psychological Medicine, 38*(5), 386–394.

Parrott, A. C., Montgomery, C., Wetherell, M. A., Downey, L. A., Stough, C., & Scholey, A. B. (2014). MDMA, cortisol, and heightened stress in recreational ecstasy users. *Behavioural Pharmacology, 25*(5-6), 458–472.

Parsons, E. M., Straub, K. T., Smith, A. R., & Clerkin, E. M. (2017). Body dysmorphic, obsessive-compulsive, and social anxiety disorder beliefs as predictors of in vivo stressor responding. *Journal of Nervous and Mental Disease, 205,* 471–479.

Pasalich, D. S., Witkiewitz, K., McMahon, R. J., Pinderhughes, E. E., & the Conduct Problems Prevention Research Group. (2016). Indirect effects of the Fast Track Intervention on conduct disorder symptoms and callous-unemotional traits: Distinct pathways involving discipline and warmth. *Journal of Abnormal Child Psychology, 44,* 587–597.

Paslakis, G., Graap, H., & Erim, Y. (2015). Media exposure and posttraumatic stress disorder: Review and implications for psychotherapy. [German] *Psychotherapie, Psychosomatik, Medizinische Psychologie, 65*(11):405–11.

Patel, N. A., & Elkin, G. D. (2015). Professionalism and conflicting interests: The American Psychological Association's involvement in torture. *AMA Journal of Ethics, 17*(10), 924–930.

Patel, S. R., Humensky, J. L., Olfson, M., Simpson, H. B., Myers, R., & Dixon, L. B. (2014). Treatment of obsessive-compulsive disorder in a nationwide survey of office-based physician practice. *Psychiatric Services (Washington, D.C.), 65*(5), 681–684.

Paterniti, S., Sterner, I., Caldwell, C., & Bisserbe, J. C. (2017). Childhood neglect predicts the course of major depression in a tertiary care sample: A follow-up study. *BMC Psychiatry, 17*(1), 113.

Paton, C., & Beer, D. (2001). Caffeine: The forgotten variable. *International Journal of Psychiatry in Clinical Practice, 5*(4), 231–236.

Patrick, C. J. (2007). Antisocial personality disorder and psychopathy. In W. O'Donohue, K. A. Fowler, & S. O. Lilienfeld (Eds.). *Personality disorders: Toward the DSM-V.* Los Angeles: Sage Publications.

Patrick, M. E., Fairlie, A. M., & Lee, C. M. (2018). Motives for simultaneous alcohol and marijuana use among young adults. *Addictive Behaviors, 76,* 363–369.

Patrick, M. E., & Terry-McElrath, Y. M. (2017). High intensity drinking by underage young adults in the United States. *Addiction, 112*(1), 82–93.

Patriquin, M. A., Hamon, S. C., Harding, M. J., Nielsen, E. M., Newton, T. F., De La Garza, R., 2nd, & Nielsen, D. A. (2017). Genetic moderation of cocaine subjective effects by variation in the TPH1, TPH2, and SLC6A4 serotonin genes. *Psychiatric Genetics, 27,* 178–186.

Patterson, D. (2011). The linkage between secondary victimization by law enforcement and rape case outcomes. *Journal of Interpersonal Violence, 26*(2), 328–347.

Patterson, P. H. (2012). Animal models of the maternal infection risk factor for schizophrenia. In A. S. Brown & P. H. Patterson (Eds.), *The origins of schizophrenia* (pp. 255–281). New York: Columbia University Press.

Paul, G. L. (1967). The strategy of outcome research in psychotherapy. *Journal of Counseling Psychology, 31,* 109–118.

Paul, G. L. (2000). Milieu therapy. In A. E. Kazdin (Ed.), *Encyclopedia of psychology* (Vol. 5, pp. 250–252). New York: Oxford University Press.

Paul, G. L., & Lentz, R. (1977). *Psychosocial treatment of the chronic mental patient.* Cambridge, MA: Harvard University Press.

Paul, R., & Gilbert, K. (2011). Development of language and communication. In E. Hollander, A. Kolevzon & J. T. Coyle (Eds.), *Textbook of autism spectrum disorders* (pp. 147–157). Arlington, VA: American Psychiatric Publishing, Inc.

Paulhus, D. L., & Williams, K. M. (2002). The Dark Triad of personality: Narcissism, Machiavellianism and psychopathy. *Journal of Research in Personality, 36,* 556–563.

Paulk, A., Dowd, D. A., Zayac, R., Eklund, A., & Kildare, C. (2014). The relationship between culture, geographic region, and gender on body image: A comparison of college students in the Southeast and Pacific Northwest regions of the United States. *Sociological Spectrum, 34*(5), 442–452.

Paulo, M., Scruth, E. A., & Jacoby, S. R. (2017). Dementia and delirium in the elderly hospitalized patient: Delirium is a medical emergency. *Clinical Nurse Specialist, 31*(2), 66–69.

Paulus, M. (2017, January 15). Methamphetamine use disorder: Epidemiology, clinical manifestations, course, assessment, and diagnosis. *UpToDate.* Retrieved from http://www.uptodate.com.

Payne, A. F. (1928). *Sentence completion.* New York: New York Guidance Clinics.

Payne, J. (2016, September 13). Postpartum psychosis: Epidemiology, pathogenesis, clinical manifestations, course, assessment, and diagnosis. *UpToDate.* Retrieved from http://www.uptodate.com.

Pazzanese, C. (2016, July 12). The high price of workplace stress. *Harvard Gazette.* Retrieved from http://news.harvard.edu/gazette.

Pear, R. (2013, December 11). Fewer psychiatrists seen taking health insurance. *New York Times.*

Pearson, C. (2013, May 21). Oklahoma tornado PTSD: How survivors are coping. *Huffington Post.*

Peavy, M. (2017, May 26). Psychosocial interventions for opioid use disorder. *UpToDate.* Retrieved from http://www.uptodate.com.

Pedersen, C. G., Jensen, S. W., Gradus, J., Johnsen, S. P., & Mainz, J. (2014). Systematic suicide risk assessment for patients with schizophrenia: A national population-based study. *Psychiatric Services* (Washington, D.C.), *65*(2), 226–231.

Pedersen, T. (2016, July 6). How a child's brain adapts to handle adversity. *Psych Central News.* Retrieved from http://psychcentral.com.

Pedersen, T. (2016, October 31). Childhood PTSD may alter structure of brain networks. *Psych Central News.* Retrieved from http://psychcentral.com.

Pekkanen, J. (2002, July 2). Dangerous minds. *Washingtonian.*

Pekkanen, J. (2007). Involuntary commitment is essential. In A. Quigley (Ed.), *Current controversies: Mental health.* Detroit: Greenhaven Press/Thomson Gale.

Pelak, V. S. (2016, August 22). Approach to the patient with visual hallucinations. *UpToDate.* Retrieved from http://www.uptodate.com.

Pelham, W. E., Fabiano, G. A., & Massetti, G. M. (2005). Evidence-based assessment of attention deficit hyperactivity disorder in children and adolescents. *Journal of Clinical Child and Adolescent Psychology, 34,* 449–476.

Pelham, W. E., Fabiano, G. A., Waxmonsky, J. G., Greiner, A. R., Gnagy, E. M., Pelham, W. E., . . . Murphy, S. A. (2016). Treatment sequencing for childhood ADHD: A multiple-randomization study of adaptive medication and behavioral interventions. *Journal of Clinical Child and Adolescent Psychology, 45,* 396–415.

Pelletier, J. F., & Davidson, L. (2015). At the very roots of psychiatry as a new medical specialty: The Pinel–Pussin partnership. {French.} *Santé Mentale au Québec, 40*(1), 19–33.

Pendery, M. L., Maltzman, I. M., & West, L. J. (1982). Controlled drinking by alcoholics? New findings and a reevaluation of a major affirmative study. *Science, 217*(4555), 169–175.

Pennoyer, T. (2017, May 5). Quoted in T. Wayne, Social insecurity? Internet turns boomers into twits. *New York Times.* Retrieved from https://www.nytimes.com.

Perdeci, Z., Gulsun, M., Celik, C., Erdem, M., Ozdemir, B., Ozdag, F., & Kilic, S. (2010). Aggression and the event-related potentials in antisocial personality disorder. *Bulletin of Clinical Psychopharmacology, 20*(4), 300–306.

Perez, M., Ohrt, T. K., & Hoek, H. W. (2016). Prevalence and treatment of eating disorders among Hispanics/Latino Americans in the United States. *Current Opinion in Psychiatry, 29*(6), 378–382.

Perillo, A. D., Spada, A. H., Calkins, C., & Jeglic, E. L. (2014). Examining the scope of questionable diagnostic reliability in sexually violent predator (SVP) evaluations. *International Journal of Law and Psychiatry, 37*(2), 190–197.

Perkins, H. W. (2002). Surveying the damage: A review of research on consequences of alcohol misuse in college populations. *Journal of Alcohol Studies,* Suppl. 14, 91–100.

Perlin, M. L. (2017). The insanity defense: Nine myths that will not go away. In M. D. White (Ed.), *The insanity defense: Multidisciplinary views on its history, trends, and controversies* (Chap. 1, pp. 3–22). Westport, CT: Praeger.

Perna, G., Alciati, A., Riva, A., Micieli, W., & Caldirola, D. (2016). Long-term pharmacological treatments of anxiety disorders: An updated systematic review. *Current Psychiatry Reports, 18*(3), 23.

Perpetuini, D., Bucco, R., Zito, M., & Merla, A. (2018). Study of memory deficit in Alzheimer's disease by means of complexity analysis of fNIRS signal. *Neurophotonics, 5*(1), 011010.

Perrault, E. K., & Nazione, S. A. (2016). Informed consent–uninformed participants: Shortcomings of online social science consent forms and recommendations for improvement. *Journal of Empirical Research on Human Research Ethics, 11*(3), 274–280.

Perrin, M., Vandeleur, C. L., Castelao, E., Rothen, S., Glaus, J., Vollenweider, P., & Preisig, M. (2014). Determinants of the development of post-traumatic stress disorder, in the general population. *Social Psychiatry and Psychiatric Epidemiology, 49*(3), 447–457.

Perrone, J., & Chatterjee, P. (2016, September 29). Lithium poisoning. *UpToDate.* Retrieved from www.uptodate.com.

Perry, J. C. (2005). Dependent personality disorder. In G. O. Gabbard, J. S. Beck, & J. Holmes (Eds.), *Oxford textbook of psychotherapy* (pp. 321–328). New York: Oxford University Press.

Perry, K. (2017, March 8). Franklin County coroner spars with politicians over heroin fight. *The Columbus Dispatch.*

Perry, K. J., & Ostrov, J. M. (2018). Testing a higher order model of internalizing and externalizing behavior: The role of aggression subtypes. *Child Psychiatry and Human Development.* [Manuscript in press]

Perugi, G., Medda, P., Zanello, S., Toni, C., & Cassano, G. B. (2011, March 21). Episode length and mixed features as predictors of ECT nonresponse in patients with medication-resistant major depression. *Brain Stimulation, 5*(1), 18–24.

Peteet, J. R., Lu, F. G., & Narrow, W. E. (Eds.). (2011). *Religious and spiritual issues in psychiatric diagnosis: A research agenda for DSM-V.* Washington, DC: American Psychiatric Association.

Peters, E. M. J., Müller, Y., Snaga, W., Fliege, H., Reisshauer, A., Schmidt-Rose, T., . . . Kruse, J. (2017). Hair and stress: A pilot study of hair and cytokine balance alteration in healthy young women under major exam stress. *PLoS One, 12*(4), e0175904.

Petersen, J. L., & Hyde, J. S. (2011). Gender differences in sexual attitudes and behaviors: A review of meta-analytic results and large datasets. *Journal of Sex Research, 48*(2-3), 149–165.

Petersen, L., Mortensen, P. B., & Pedersen, C. B. (2011). Paternal age at birth of first child and risk of schizophrenia. *American Journal of Psychiatry, 168*(1), 82–88.

Petersen, L., Sørensen, T. A., Kragh Andersen, P., Mortensen, P. B., & Hawton, K. (2014). Genetic and familial environmental effects on suicide attempts: A study of Danish adoptees and their biological and adoptive siblings. *Journal of Affective Disorders, 155,* 273–277.

Peterson, D., Munger, C., Crowley, J., Corcoran, C., Cruchaga, C., Goate, A. M., . . . Kauwe, J. K. (2014). Variants in PPP3R1 and MAPT are associated with more rapid functional decline in Alzheimer's disease: The Cache County Dementia Progression Study. *Alzheimer's and Dementia, 10*(3), 366–371.

Peterson, Z. D. (Ed.). (2017). *The Wiley-Blackwell handbook of sex therapy.* Hoboken, NJ: Wiley-Blackwell.

Pettypiece, S. (2015, April 10). How psychiatrists are failing the patients who need them most. *Bloomberg.com.*

Pew Research Center. (2010). *8% of online Americans use Twitter.* Washington, DC: Author.

Pew Research Center. (2011). Twitter, launched five years ago, delivers 350 billion tweets a day. *Media Mentions.* Washington, DC: Pew Internet & American Life Project.

Pew Research Center. (2013). 50 years after the march on Washington, many racial divides remain: Personal experiences with discrimination. *Pew Social Trends.* Retrieved from http://www.pewsocialtrends.org/2013/08/22.

Pew Research Center. (2013). 10 findings about women in the workplace. *Pew Social Trends.* Retrieved from http://www.pewsocialtrends.org/2013/12/11.

Pew Research Center. (2013). *Majority now supports legalizing marijuana.* Washington, DC: Pew Research Center for the People & the Press.

Pew Research Center. (2013). Modern parenthood. *Pew Social Trends.* Retrieved from http://www.pewsocialtrends.org/2013/03/14.

Pew Research Center. (2013). *Social networking fact sheet.* Washington, DC: Pew Internet & American Life Project.

Pew Research Center. (2014, November 14). *Chapter 2: The demographics of remarriage.* Washington, DC: Author. Retrieved from http://www.pewsocialtrends.org.

Pew Research Center. (2014). *Social media update 2013: Main findings.* Washington, DC: Pew. Retrieved from Pew Internet website: http://www.pewinternet.org/2013/12/30/social-media-update-2013.

Pew Research Center. (2015, August 4). *Texting is most common way teens get in touch with closest friend.* Retrieved from Pew Internet website: http://www.pewinternet.org.

Pew Research Center. (2015, August 16). Americans' views on mobile etiquette. *Pew Research Center.* Retrieved from http://www.pewinternet.org.

Pew Research Center. (2015, October 5). California legalizes assisted suicide amid growing support for such laws. *Pew Research.* Retrieved from http://www.pewresearch.org/fact-tank/2015/10/05.

Pew Research Center. (2015). *Raising kids and running a household: How working parents share the load.* Washington, DC: Pew Research Center.

Pew Research Center. (2016, May 4). *5 facts about prayer.* Washington, DC: Author.

Pew Research Center. (2016, July 6). Few have a lot of confidence in information from professional news outlets or friends and family, though majorities show at least some trust in both, but social media garners less trust than either. *Pew Research Center Journalism & Media.* Retrieved from http://www.pewinternet.org.

Pew Research Center. (2016, October 12). Support for marijuana legalization continues to rise. *Pew.*

Pew Research Center. (2016, November 11). *Social media update 2016.* Washington, DC: Author.

Pew Research Center. (2016). *Racial, gender wage gaps persist in U.S. despite some progress.* Washington, DC: Pew Research Center.

Pew Research Center. (2016). *Research in the crowdsourcing age, a case study.* Washington, DC: Pew Research Center.

Pew Research Center. (2016). *Roughly half of Hispanics have experienced discrimination.* Washington, DC: Pew Research Center.

Pew Research Center. (2017, May 17). *1. Technology use among seniors.* Washington, DC: Author. Retrieved from http://www.pewinternet.org.

Pew Research Center. (2017, June 27). U.S. public trust in science and scientists. *Pew Research Center: Internet & Technology.* Retrieved from http://www.pewinternet.org.

Pew Research Center. (2017, July 11). Online harassment 2017. *Pew Research Center: Internet & Technology.* Retrieved from http://www.pewinternet.org.

Pew Research Center. (2017). *2. Living arrangements of older Americans by gender.* Washington, DC: Author.

Pfäfflin, F. (2016). Psychoanalytic treatment of sex offenders: A short historical sketch. In B. P. Boer, *The Wiley handbook on the theories, assessment and treatment of sexual offending* (Vol. 3, Chap. 8). Hoboken, NJ: Wiley-Blackwell.

Pfeffer, C. R. (1986). *The suicidal child.* New York: Guilford Press.

Pfeffer, C. R. (2003). Assessing suicidal behavior in children and adolescents. In R. A. King & A. Apter (Eds.), *Suicide in children and adolescents* (pp. 211–226). Cambridge, England: Cambridge University Press.

Pfefferbaum, B., Newman, E., & Nelson, S. D. (2014). Mental health interventions for children exposed to disasters and terrorism. *Journal of Child and Adolescent Psychopharmacology, 24*(1), 24–31.

Pham, A. V., Carlson, J. S., & Koschiulek, J. F. (2010). Ethnic differences in parental beliefs of attention-deficit/hyperactivity disorder and treatment. *Journal of Attention Disorders, 13*(6), 584–591.

Philippi, C. L., Motzkin, J. C., Pujara, M. S., & Koenigs, M. (2015). Subclinical depression severity is associated with distinct patterns of functional connectivity for subregions of anterior cingulate cortex. *Journal of Psychiatric Research, 71,* 103–111.

Phillips, D. P. (1974). The influence of suggestion on suicide: Substantive and theoretical implications of the *Werther* effect. *American Sociological Review, 39,* 340–354.

Phillips, D. P., & Ruth, T. E. (1993). Adequacy of official suicide statistics for scientific research and public policy. *Suicide and Life-Threatening Behavior, 23*(4), 307–319.

Phillips, K. (2015). Obsessive-compulsive and related disorders. In A. Tasman, J. Kay, J. A. Lieberman, M. B. First, & M. Riba (Eds.). *Psychiatry* (2 vol. set, 4th edition, pp. 1093–1128). Hoboken, NJ: Wiley-Blackwell.

Phillips, K., Keane, K., & Wolfe, B. E. (2014). Peripheral brain derived neurotrophic factor (BDNF) in bulimia nervosa: A systematic review. *Archives of Psychiatric Nursing, 28*(2), 108–113.

Phillips, K. A. (2016, May 24). Body dysmorphic disorder: Epidemiology, pathogenesis, and clinical features. *UpToDate.* Retrieved from http://www.uptodate.com.

Phillips, K. A. (2017, January 15). Body dysmorphic disorder: Treatment and prognosis. *UpToDate.* Retrieved from http://www.uptodate.com.

Philo, C., & Andrews, J. (2016). Introduction: Histories of asylums, insanity and psychiatry in Scotland. *History of Psychiatry.* [Advance online publication, PMID: 27956649]

Piacentini, J., Bennett, S., Compton, S. N., Kendall, P. C., Birmaher, B., Albano, A. M., . . . & Walkup, J. (2014). 24- and 36-week outcomes for the Child/Adolescent Anxiety Multimodal Study (CAMS). *Journal of the American Academy of Child and Adolescent Psychiatry, 53,* 297–310.

Planta, R. C. (2016). Classroom processes and teacher-student interaction: Integrations with a developmental psychopathology perspective.

In D. Cicchetti (Ed.), *Developmental psychopathology, Vol. 4: Risk, resilience, and intervention* (3rd ed.). New York: Wiley.

Piatt, A. (2013). Facebook may improve working memory, cognition in elderly. *Neuropsychology.* Retrieved from http://www.neuropsychology.co/2013/03/03/working-memory.

Piccirillo, M. L., Taylor Dryman, M., & Heimberg, R. G. (2016). Safety behaviors in adults with social anxiety: Review and future directions. *Behavior Therapy, 47*(5), 675–687.

Pickert, K. (2014, February 3). The art of being mindful, *Time.*

Pierce, K., & Courchesne, E. (2001). Evidence for a cerebellar role in reduced exploration and stereotyped behavior in autism. *Biological Psychiatry, 49*(8), 655–664.

Pierce, K., & Courchesne, E. (2002). "A further support to the hypothesis of a link between serotonin, autism and the cerebellum": Reply. *Biological Psychiatry, 52*(2), 143.

Pieters, S., Van Der Zwaluw, C. S., Van Der Vorst, H., Wiers, R. W., Smeets, H., Lambrichs, E., . . . Engels, R. E. (2012). The moderating effect of alcohol-specific parental rule-setting on the relation between the dopamine D2 receptor gene (DRD2), the m-opioid receptor gene (OPRM1) and alcohol use in young adolescents. *Alcohol and Alcoholism* (Oxford, England), *47*(6), 663–670.

Pietrzak, R. H., el-Gabalawy, R., Tsai, J., Sareen, J., Neumeister, A., & Southwick, S. M. (2014). Typologies of posttraumatic stress disorder in the U.S. adult population. *Journal of Affective Disorders, 162,* 102–106.

Pigott, H. E., Leventhal, A. M., Alter, G. S., & Boren, J. J. (2010). Efficacy and effectiveness of antidepressants: Current status of research. *Psychotherapy and Psychosomatics, 79*(5), 267–279.

Pike, K. (2017, March 17). Anorexia nervosa in adults: Cognitive-behavioral therapy (CBT). *UpToDate.* Retrieved from www.uptodate.com.

Pike, K. M., Dunne, P. E., & Addai, E. (2013). Expanding the boundaries: Reconfiguring the demographics of the "typical" eating disordered patient. *Current Psychiatry Reports, 15*(11), 411.

Pilecki, B., & McKay, D. (2016). Evidence-based therapies, evidence-based practice, and the intersection of nomothetic and idiographic foundations of psychotherapy research and application: A reply to Shean. *Psychodynamic Psychiatry, 44*(1), 25–38.

Pillay, B., Lee, S. J., Katona, L., Burney, S., & Avery, S. (2014). Psychosocial factors predicting survival after allogeneic stem cell transplant. *Supportive Care in Cancer, 22*(9), 2547–2555.

Pinals, D. A., Packer, I., Fisher, B., & Roy, K. (2004). Relationship between race and ethnicity and forensic clinical triage dispositions. *Psychiatric Services 55,* 873–878.

Pinkham, A. E. (2014). Social cognition in schizophrenia. *Journal of Clinical Psychiatry, 75*(Suppl 2), 14–19.

Pinto, A., Eisen, J. L., Mancebo, M. C., & Rasmussen, S. A. (2008). Obsessive-compulsive personality disorder. In J. S. Abramowitz, D. McKay, & S. Taylor (Eds.), *Obsessive-compulsive disorder: Subtypes and spectrum conditions.* Oxford, England: Elsevier.

Piper, W. E., & Joyce, A. S. (2001). Psychosocial treatment outcome. In W. J. Livesley (Ed.), *Handbook of personality disorders: Theory, research, and treatment* (pp. 323–343). New York: Guilford Press.

Pirutinsky, S., Carp, S., & Rosmarin, D. H. (2016, September 8). A paradigm to assess implicit attitudes towards God: The positive/negative God associations task. *Journal of Religion & Health.* [Epub ahead of print]

Pivalizza, P. (2016, May 26). Intellectual disability in children: Evaluation for a cause. *UpToDate.* Retrieved from http://www.uptodate.com.

Pivalizza, P. (2016, October 31). Intellectual disability in children: Management, outcomes, and prevention. *UpToDate.* Retrieved from http://www.uptodate.com.

Pizzagalli, D. A. (2017). Frontocingulate dysfunction in depression: Toward biomarkers of treatment response. *Nature.* Retrieved from http://www.nature.com.

Plante, T. G. (2016). Is Facebook the new Rorschach? *Psychology Today.*

Planty, M., Hussar, W., Snyder, T., Provasnik, S., Kena, G., Dinkes, R., . . . Kemp, J. (2008). *The condition of education 2008.* Washington, DC: National Center for Education Statistics.

Plaud, J. J. (2007). Sexual disorders. In P. Sturmey (Ed.), *Functional analysis in clinical treatment. Practical resources for the mental health professional* (pp. 357–377). San Diego, CA: Elsevier Academic Press.

Plener, P. L., Allroggen, M., Kapusta, N. D., Brähler, E., Fegert, J. M., & Groschwitz, R. C. (2016). The prevalence of nonsuicidal self-injury (NSSI) in a representative sample of the German population. *BMC Psychiatry, 16*(1), 353.

Pletcher, M. J., Vittinghoff, E., Kalhan, R., Richman, J., Safford, M., Sidney, S., . . . Kertesz, S. (2012). Association between marijuana exposure and pulmonary function over 20 years. *Journal of the American Medical Association, 307*(2), 173–181.

PMH (PubMed Health). (2017, January 12). *Depression: Can St. John's wort products help?* Retrieved from https://www.ncbi.nlm.nih.gov.

Polderman, T. J., Benyamin, B., de Leeuw, C. A., Sullivan, P. F., van Bochoven, A., Visscher, P. M., & Posthuma, D. (2015). Meta-analysis of the heritability of human traits based on fifty years of twin studies. *Nature Genetics, 47*(7), 702–709.

Polo, A. J., Alegria, M., Chen, C.-N., & Blanco, C. (2011). The prevalence and comorbidity of social anxiety disorder among United States Latinos: A retrospective analysis of data from 2 national surveys. *Journal of Clinical Psychiatry, 72*(8), 1096–1105.

Pompili, M., Innamorati, M., Girardi, P., Tatarelli, R., & Lester, D. (2011). Evidence-based interventions for preventing suicide in youths. In M. Pompili & R. Tatarelli (Eds.), *Evidence-based practice in suicidology: A source book* (pp. 171–209). Cambridge, MA: Hogrefe Publishing.

Pompili, M., Lester, D., Leenaars, A. A., Tatarelli, R., & Girardi, P. (2008). Psychache and suicide: A preliminary investigation. *Suicide and Life-Threatening Behavior, 38*(1), 116–121.

Pompili, M., Venturini, P., Palermo, M., Stefani, H., Seretti, M. E., Lamis, D. A. (2013). Mood disorders medications: Predictors of nonadherence—Review of the current literature. *Expert Review of Neurotherapeutics, 13,* 809.

Pondé, M. P., Caron, J., Mendonça, M. S., Freire, A. C., & Moreau, N. (2014). The relationship between mental disorders and types of crime in inmates in a Brazilian prison. *Journal of Forensic Sciences, 59*(5), 1307–1314.

Pongan, É., Padovan, C., Coste, M., Krolak-Salmon, P., & Rouch, I. (2012). Caring for young patients with Alzheimer's disease or associated disorders in day care centers of the Rhône-Alpes region. *Gériatrie Et Psychologie Neuropsychiatrie Du Vieillissement, 10*(3), 343–348.

Pop, C. (2016). Self-esteem and body image perception in a sample of university students. *Eurasian Journal of Educational Research, 64,* 31–44.

Pope, K. S. (1988). How clients are harmed by sexual contact with mental health professionals. *Journal of Counseling and Development, 67,* 222–226.

Pope, K. S. (1994). *Sexual involvement with therapists: Patient assessment, subsequent therapy, forensics.* Washington, DC: APA.

Pope, K. S., & Tabachnick, B. G. (1993). Therapists' anger, hate, fear and sexual feelings: National survey of therapists' responses, client characteristics, critical events, formal complaints and training. *Professional Psychology: Research and Practice, 24,* 142–152.

Pope, K. S., & Tabachnick, B. G. (1994). Therapists as patients: A national survey of psychologists' experience, problems, and beliefs. *Professional Psychology: Research and Practice, 25,* 247–258.

Pope, K. S., Tabachnick, B. G., & Keith-Spiegel, P. (1987). Ethics of practice: The beliefs and behaviors of psychologists as therapists. *American Psychologist, 42,* 993–1006.

Pope, K. S., & Vasquez, M. J. T. (2011). *Ethics in psychotherapy and counseling: A practical guide* (4th ed.). Hoboken, NJ: John Wiley & Sons.

Pope, K. S., & Vasquez, M. J. T. (2016). *Ethics in psychotherapy and counseling: A practical guide* (5th edition). New York: Wiley.

Pope, K. S., & Wedding, D. (2014). Contemporary challenges and controversies. In D. Wedding & R. J. Corsini (Eds.), *Current psychotherapies* (10th ed., pp. 569–604). Independence, KY: Cengage Publications.

Popov, S. P., Mateva, N. G., Iliev, Y. T., Dechev, I. D., & Karalilova, R. V. (2015). Sexual fears and avoidant sexual behavior in medical students. *Folia Medica, 57*(2), 144–148.

Popova, S., Lange, S., Probst, C., Gmel, G., & Rehm, J. (2017, March). Estimation of national, regional, and global prevalence of alcohol use during pregnancy and fetal alcohol syndrome: A systematic review and meta-analysis. *Lancet Global Health, 5,* e290–e299.

Poppelaars, M., Tak, Y. R., Lichtwarck-Aschoff, A., Engels, R. C., Lobel, A., Merry, S. N., . . . Granic, I. (2016). A randomized controlled trial comparing two cognitive-behavioral programs for adolescent girls with subclinical depression: A school-based program (Op Volle Kracht) and a computerized program (SPARX). *Behavior Research and Therapy, 80,* 33–42.

Poretz, M., & Sinrod, B. (1991). *Do you do it with the lights on?* New York: Ballantine Books.

Portugal, F. B., Campos, M. R., Correia, C. R., Gonçalves, D. A., Ballester, D., Tófoli, L. F., . . . Fortes, S. (2016). Social support network, mental health and quality of life: A cross-sectional study in primary care. *Cadernos de Saúde Pública, 32*(12), e00165115.

Posmontier, B. (2010). The role of midwives in facilitating recovery in postpartum psychosis. *Journal of Midwifery & Women's Health, 55*(5), 430–437.

Post, R. M. (2017, February 16). Bipolar disorder in adults: Choosing maintenance treatment. *UpToDate.* Retrieved from http://www.uptodate.com.

Post, R. M., Ballenger, J. C., & Goodwin, F. K. (1980). Cerebrospinal fluid studies of neurotransmitter function in manic and depressive illness. In J. H. Wood (Ed.), *The neurobiology of cerebrospinal fluid* (Vol. 1). New York: Plenum Press.

Post, R. M., Lake, C. R., Jimerson, D. C., Bunney, J. H., Ziegler, M. G., & Goodwin, F. K. (1978). Cerebrospinal fluid norepinephrine in affective illness. *American Journal of Psychiatry, 135*(8), 907–912.

Poulsen, S., Lunn, S., Daniel, S. F., Folke, S., Mathiesen, B. B., Katznelson, H., & Fairburn, C. G. (2014). A randomized controlled trial of psychoanalytic psychotherapy or cognitive-behavioral therapy for bulimia nervosa. *American Journal of Psychiatry, 171*(1), 109–116.

Pouncey, C. L., & Lukens, J. M. (2010). Madness versus badness: The ethical tension between the recovery movement and forensic psychiatry. *Theoretical Medicine and Bioethics, 31*(1), 93–105.

Powell, D., Caban-Holt, A., Jicha, G., Robertson, W., Davis, R., Gold, B. T., . . . Head, E. (2014). Frontal white matter integrity in adults with Down syndrome with and without dementia. *Neurobiology of Aging, 35*(7), 1562–1569.

Powell, M. P., Lochman, J. E., Boxmeyer, C. L., Barry, T. D., & Pardini, D. A. (2017). The Coping Power Program for aggressive behavior in children. In J. R. Weisz & A. E. Kazdin (Eds.), *Evidence-based psychotherapies for children and adolescents* (3rd ed.). New York: Guilford.

Pozzi, M., Radice, S., Clementi, E., Molteni, M., & Nobile, M. (2016). Antidepressants and suicide and self-injury: Causal or casual association? *International Journal of Psychiatry in Clinical Practice, 20*(1), 47–51.

PRB (Population Reference Bureau). (2015, December). Population bulletin: Aging in the United States. *PRB, 70*(2).

Predmore, Z., Ramchand, R., Ayer, L., Kotzias, V., Engel, C., Ebener, P., . . . Haas, G. L. (2017). Expanding suicide crisis services to text and chat. *Crisis, 38,* 255–260.

Press, D., & Alexander, M. (2017, February 9). Safety and societal issues related to dementia. *UpToDate.* Retrieved from http://www.uptodate.com.

Press, D., & Alexander, M. (2017, March 14). Treatment of dementia. *UpToDate.* Retrieved from http://www.uptodate.com.

Press, D., & Alexander, M. (2017, May 10). Prevention of dementia. *UpToDate.* Retrieved from http://www.uptodate.com.

Preti, A. (2011). Animal model and neurobiology of suicide. *Progress in Neuro-Psychopharmacology & Biological Psychiatry, 35*(4), 818–830.

Preti, A. (2011). Do animals commit suicide? Does it matter? *Crisis: Journal of Crisis Intervention and Suicide Prevention, 32*(1), 1–4.

Price, M. (2011). Upfront: Marijuana addiction a growing risk as society grows more tolerant. *Monitor on Psychology, 42*(5), 13.

Priday, L. J., Byrne, C., & Totsika, V. (2017). Behavioural interventions for sleep problems in people with an intellectual disability: A systematic review and meta-analysis of single case and group studies. *Journal of Intellectual Disability Research, 61*(1), 1–15.

Princeton Survey Research Associates. (1996). Healthy steps for young children: Survey of parents. Princeton: Author.

Privitera, G. J. (2016). *Research methods for the behavioral sciences* (2nd ed.). Thousand Oaks, CA: Sage Publications.

Prizant-Passal, S., Shechner, T., & Aderka, A. (2015). Social anxiety and internet use—A meta-analysis: What do we know? What are we missing? *Computers in Human Behavior, 62,* 221–229.

Prochaska, J. O., & Norcross, J. C. (2003). *Systems of psychotherapy: A transtheoretical analysis* (5th ed.). Pacific Grove, CA: Brooks/Cole.

Prochaska, J. O., & Norcross, J. C. (2006). *Systems of psychotherapy: A transtheoretical analysis* (6th ed.). Pacific Grove, CA: Brooks/Cole.

Prochaska, J. O., & Norcross, J. C. (2010). *Systems of psychotherapy: A transtheoretical analysis* (7th ed.). Pacific Grove, CA: Brooks/Cole.

Prochaska, J. O., & Norcross, J. C. (2013). *Systems of psychotherapy: Transtheoretical analysis* (8th ed.). Independence, KY: Cengage Learning.

ProCon. (2016). *Should prescription drugs be advertised directly to consumers?* Santa Monica, CA: ProCon.

Proud2Bme. (2012, March 26). *Overall, do social networking sites like Facebook and Twitter help or hurt your body confidence?* Retrieved from http://proud2bme.org.

Pruchno, R. (2014). All in the family: Prison or treatment for people with mental illness? *Psychology Today.* Retrieved from *Psychology Today* website: http://www.psychologytoday.com/blog/all-in-the-family/201402/prison-or-treatment-people-mental-illness.

Pruessner, M., Cullen, A. E., Aas, M., & Walker, E. F. (2017). The neural diathesis-stress model of schizophrenia revisited: An update on recent findings considering illness stage and neurobiological and methodological complexities. *Neuroscience & Biobehavioral Reviews, 73,* 191–218.

Puhl, R. M., Latner, J. D., O'Brien, K., Luedicke, J., Danielsdottir, S., & Forhan, M. (2015). A multinational examination of weight bias: Predictors of anti-fat attitudes across four countries. *International Journal of Obesity, 39*(7), 1166–1173.

Purcell, M. (2017). Beating the holiday blues. *Psych Central.*

Putnam, F. W. (1984). The psychophysiologic investigation of multiple personality disorder. *Psychiatric Clinics of North America, 7,* 31–40.

Putnam, F. W. (2000). Dissociative disorders. In A. J. Sameroff, M. Lewis et al. (Eds.), *Handbook of developmental psychopathology* (2nd ed., pp. 739–754). New York: Kluwer Academic/Plenum Press.

Putnam, F. W. (2006). Dissociative disorders. In D. Cicchetti & D. J. Cohen (Eds.), *Developmental psychopathology, Vol. 3: Risk, disorder, and adaptation* (2nd ed., pp. 657–695). Hoboken, NJ: John Wiley & Sons.

Putnam, F. W., Zahn, T. P., & Post, R. M. (1990). Differential autonomic nervous system activity in multiple personality disorder. *Journal of Psychiatric Research, 31*(3), 251–260.

Quah, S. (2014). Caring for persons with schizophrenia at home: Examining the link between family caregivers' role distress and quality of life. *Sociology of Health and Illness, 36*(4), 596–612.

Quas, J. A., Malloy, L. C., Melinder, A., Goodman, G. S., D'Mello, M., & Schaaf, J. (2007). Developmental differences in the effects of repeated interviews and interviewer bias on young children's event memory and false reports. *Developmental Psychology, 43*(4), 823–837.

Queinec, R., Beitz, C., Contrad, B., Jougla, E., Leffondré, K., Lagarde, E., & Encrenaz, G. (2011). Copycat effect after celebrity suicides: Results from the French national death register. *Psychological Medicine: Journal of Research in Psychiatry and the Allied Sciences, 41*(3), 668–671.

Quek, J., Newman, L. K., Bennett, C., Gordon, M. S., Saeedi, N., & Melvin, G. A. (2017). Reflective function mediates the relationship between emotional maltreatment and borderline pathology in adolescents: A preliminary investigation. *Child Abuse & Neglect, 72,* 215–226.

Quill, T. E., & Battin, M. P. (2017, June 2). Physician-assisted dying: Understanding, evaluating, and responding to requests for medical aid in dying. *UpToDate.* Retrieved from http://www.uptodate.com.

Quillian, L., & Pager, D. (2010). Estimating risk: Stereotype amplification and the perceived risk of criminal victimization. *Social Psychology Quarterly, 73*(1), 79–104.

Quirk, S. E., Berk, M., Chanen, A. M., Koivumaa-Honkanen, H., Brennan-Olsen, S. L., Pasco, J. A., & Williams, L. J. (2016). Population prevalence of personality disorder and associations with physical health comorbidities and health care service utilization: A review. *Personality Disorders, 7*(2), 136–146.

Quirk, S. E., Berk, M., Pasco, J. A., Brennan-Olsen, S. L., Chanen, A. M., Koivumaa-Honkanen, H., . . . Williams, L. J. (2017). The prevalence, age distribution and comorbidity of personality disorders in Australian women. *Australian & New Zealand Journal of Psychiatry, 51*(2), 141–150.

Qureshi, N. A., & Al-Bedah, A. M. (2013). Mood disorders and complementary and alternative medicine: A literature review. *Neuropsychiatric Disease and Treatment, 9,* 639–658.

Rabella, M., Grasa, E., Corripio, I., Romero, S., Mananas, M. A., Antonijoan, R. M., . . . Riba, J. (2016). Neurophysiological

evidence impaired self-monitoring in schizotypal personality disorder and its reversal by dopaminergic antagonism. *NeuroImage: Clinical, 11,* 770–779.

Rabin, R. C. (2013, July 29). Concerns about dementia screening. *New York Times,* D4

Rabinovici, G. D. (2017). Advances and gaps in understanding chronic traumatic encephalopathy: From pugilists to American football players. *JAMA, 318*(4), 338–340.

Rabinowitz, J., Werbeloff, N., Caers, I., Mandel, F. S., Stauffer, V., Ménard, F., . . . Kapur, S. (2014). Determinants of antipsychotic response in schizophrenia: Implications for practice and future clinical trials. *Journal of Clinical Psychiatry, 75*(4), e308–e316.

Raboch, J., Jr., & Raboch, J. (1992). Infrequent orgasm in women. *Journal of Sex and Marital Therapy, 18*(2), 114–120.

Rachman, S. (1966). Sexual fetishism: An experimental analog. *Psychological Record, 18,* 25–27.

Radcliff, N. (2017, May 12). Laugh, giggle, be joyful for lol. *Washington Times.* Retrieved from http://www.washingtontimes.com.

Radulovic, J., Jovasevic, V., & Meyer, M. A. (2017). Neurobiological mechanisms of state-dependent learning. *Current Opinion in Neurobiology, 45,* 92–98.

Ragland, J. D., Ranganath, C., Harms, M. P., Barch, D. M., Gold, J. M., Layher, E., . . . Carter, C. S. (2015). Functional and neuroanatomic specificity of episodic memory dysfunction in schizophrenia: A functional magnetic resonance imaging study of the relational and item-specific encoding task. *JAMA Psychiatry, 72*(9), 909–916.

Rahim, Z. (2017, March 20). Norway is happiest country in the world. What's the secret? *Time.com.*

Raiker, J. S., Freeman, A. J., Perez-Algorta, G., Frazier, T. W., Findling, R. L., & Youngstrom, E. A. (2017). Accuracy of Achenbach scales in the screening of attention-deficit/hyperactivity disorder in a community mental health clinic. *Journal of the American Academy of Child and Adolescent Psychiatry, 56,* 401–409.

Rainie, L., Purcell, K., & Smith, A. (2011). The social side of the internet. *Report: Communities, religion, social networking.* Washington, DC: Pew Internet & American Life Project.

RAINN (Rape, Abuse & Incest National Network). (2009). *Campus safety.* Retrieved from RAINN website: https://www.rainn.org/public-policy/campus-safety.

RAINN (Rape, Abuse & Incest National Network). (2016). *Campus sexual violence: Statistics.* Retrieved from https://www.rainn.org/statistics.

RAINN (Rape, Abuse & Incest National Network). (2016). *The Criminal Justice System: Statistics.* Retrieved from https://www.rainn.org/statistics.

RAINN (Rape, Abuse & Incest National Network). (2016). *Perpetrators of sexual violence: Statistics.* Retrieved from https://www.rainn.org/statistics.

RAINN (Rape, Abuse & Incest National Network). (2016). *Victims of sexual violence: Statistics.* Retrieved from https://www.rainn.org/statistics.

Raj, V., Rowe, A. A., Fleisch, S. B., Paranjape, S. Y., Arain, A. M., & Nicolson, S. E. (2014). Psychogenic pseudosyncope: Diagnosis and management. *Autonomic Neuroscience: Basic and Clinical, 184,* 66–72.

Rametti, G., Carrillo, B., Gómez-Gil, E., Jungue, C., Segovia, S., Gomez, A., & Guillamon, A. (2011). White matter microstructure in female to male transsexuals before cross-sex hormonal treatment. A diffusion tensor imaging study. *Journal of Psychiatric Research, 45*(2), 199–204.

Ramey, C. T., & Ramey, S. L. (2004). Early learning and school readiness: Can early intervention make a difference? *Merrill-Palmer Quarterly, 50*(4), 471–491.

Ramey, C. T., & Ramey, S. L. (2007). Early learning and school readiness: Can early intervention make a difference? In G. W. Ladd, (Ed.), *Appraising the human developmental sciences: Essays in honor of* Merrill-Palmer Quarterly, *Landscapes of childhood* (pp. 329–350). Detroit, MI: Wayne State University Press.

Ramey, C. T., Sparling, J., & Ramey, S. (2012). *Abecedarian: The ideas, the approach, and the findings.* Los Altos, CA: Sociometrics.

Rampell, C. (2013, July 2). Most U.S. health spending is exploding—but not for mental health. *New York Times.*

Ramsey, C. M., Spira, A. P., Mojtabai, R., Eaton, W. W., Roth, K., & Lee, H. B. (2013). Lifetime manic spectrum episodes and all-cause mortality: 26-year follow-up of the NIMH Epidemiologic Catchment Area Study. *Journal of Affective Disorders, 151*(1), 337–342.

Rao, N. P., & Remington, G. (2014). Targeting the dopamine receptor in schizophrenia: Investigational drugs in Phase III trials. *Expert Opinion on Pharmacotherapy, 15*(3), 373–383.

Rappaport, L. M., Moskowitz, D. S., Galynker, I., & Yaseen, Z. S. (2014). Panic symptom clusters differentially predict suicide ideation and attempt. *Comprehensive Psychiatry, 55*(4), 762–769.

Rapport, M. D., Kofler, M. J., Alderson, R. M., & Raiker, J. S. (2008). Attention-deficit/hyperactivity disorder. In D. Reitman (Ed.), *Handbook of psychological assessment, case conceptualization, and treatment, Vol. 2: Children and adolescents.* Hoboken, NJ: John Wiley & Sons.

Rash, C. J., Stitzer, M., & Weinstock, J. (2017). Contingency management: New directions and remaining challenges for an evidence-based intervention. *Journal of Substance Abuse Treatment, 72,* 10–18.

Rasic, D., Hajek, T., Alda, M., & Uher, R. (2014). Risk of mental illness in offspring of parents with schizophrenia, bipolar disorder, and major depressive disorder: A meta-analysis of family high-risk studies. *Schizophrenia Bulletin, 40*(1), 28–38.

Raskin, N. J., Rogers, C. R., & Witty, M. C. (2014). Client-centered therapy. In D. Wedding & R. J. Corsini (Eds.), *Current psychotherapies* (10th ed., pp. 95–150). Independence, KY: Cengage Publications.

Rasmussen Reports. (2014, March 5). 22% expect a cure for Alzheimer's in next 10 years. *Rasmussen Reports.*

Rasmusson, A. M., & Shalev, A. Y. (2014). Integrating the neuroendocrinology, neurochemistry, and neuroimmunology of PTSD to date and the challenges ahead. In M. J. Friedman, T. M. Keane, & P. A. Resick (Eds.). *Handbook of PTSD: Science and practice* (pp. 275–299) (2nd ed.). New York: Guilford Press.

Rastad, C., Wetterberg, L., & Martin, C. (2017, January). Patients' experience of winter depression and light room treatment. *Psychiatry Journal.* [Epub ahead of print]

Ratcliffe, R. (2014). How do other countries tackle bullying? *The Guardian.* Retrieved from http://www.theguardian/teacher-network/teacher-blog/2013.

Rathbone, C. J., Ellis, J. A., Baker, I., & Butler, C. R. (2014). Self, memory, and imagining the future in a case of psychogenic amnesia. *Neurocase, 21*(6), 727–737.

Rauscher, L., & Wilson, B. D. (2017). Super heroes and lucky duckies: Racialized stressors among teachers. *Cultural Diversity & Ethnic Minority Psychology, 23*(2), 220–229.

Raveneau, G., Feinstein, R., Rosen, L. M., & Fisher, M. (2014). Attitudes and knowledge levels of nurses and residents caring for adolescents with an eating disorder. *International Journal of Adolescent Medicine and Health, 26*(1), 131–136.

Ravitz, P., Watson, P., & Grigoriadis, S. (2013). *Psychotherapy essentials to-go: Interpersonal therapy for depression.* New York: W. W. Norton.

Raviv, S. (2010). *Being Ana.* Bloomington, IN: iUniverse.

Raymond, K. B. (1997). The effect of race and gender on the identification of children with attention deficit hyperactivity disorder. *Dissertation Abstracts International: Section A: Humanities and Social Sciences, 57*(12-A), 5052.

Raz, M. (2013). *The lobotomy letters: The making of American psychosurgery (Rochester studies in medical history).* New York: University of Rochester Press.

Razali, S. M., & Yusoff, M. M. (2014). Medication adherence in schizophrenia: A comparison between outpatients and relapse cases. *East Asian Archives of Psychiatry, 24*(2), 68–74.

Rea, I. M. (2017, June 17). Towards ageing well: Use it or lose it: Exercise, epigenetics and cognition. *Biogerontology.* [Epub ahead of print]

Read, J. (2016, October 24). Why auditory hallucinations are commonplace and have meaning. *Newsweek.*

Reamer, F. G. (2013). Social work in a digital age: Ethical and risk management challenges. *Social Work, 58*(2), 163–172.

Recupero, P. R. (2016). New technologies, new problems, new laws. *Journal of the American Academy of Psychiatry and the Law, 44*(3), 322–327.

Redmond, D. E. (1977). Alterations in the function of the nucleus locus coeruleus: A possible model for studies of anxiety. In I. Hanin & E. Usdin (Eds.), *Animal models in psychiatry and neurology.* New York: Pergamon Press.

Redmond, D. E. (1979). New and old evidence for the involvement of a brain norepinephrine system in anxiety. In W. E. Fann, I. Karacan, A. D. Pokorny, & R. L. Williams (Eds.), *Phemenology and treatment of anxiety.* New York: Spectrum.

Redmond, D. E. (1981). Clonidine and the primate locus coeruleus: Evidence suggesting anxiolytic and anti-withdrawal effects. In H. Lal & S. Fielding (Eds.), *Psychopharmacology of clonidine.* New York: Alan R. Liss.

Reed, P., Sejunaite, K., & Osborne, L. A. (2016). Relationship between self-reported health and stress in mothers of children with autism spectrum disorders. *Journal of Autism and Developmental Disorders, 46*(3), 934–941.

Rees, C. S., & Pritchard, R. (2013). Brief cognitive therapy for avoidant personality disorder. *Psychotherapy.* [Advance online publication]

Regier, D. A., Narrow, W. E., Kuhl, E. A., & Kupfer, D. J. (Eds.) (2011). *The conceptual evolution of DSM-5.* Arlington, VA: American Psychiatric Publishing.

Regier, P. (2016). Drug epidemics: Now and then. *Addiction Unscripted.*

Rehm, I. C., Foenander, E., Wallace, K., Abbott, J. M., Kyrios, M., & Thomas, N. (2016). What role can avatars play in e-mental health interventions? Exploring new models of client-therapist interaction. *Frontiers in Psychiatry, 7,* 186.

Rehm, L. P. (2010). *Depression. Advances in psychotherapy—Evidence-based practice.* Cambridge, MA: Hogrefe Publishing.

Rehm, L. P. (2015). Cognitive and behavioral theories of depression. In B. Wolberg & G. Stricker (Eds.), *Depressive disorders.* Retrieved from http://freepsychotherapy books.org.

Reich, J., & Schatzberg, A. (2014). An empirical data comparison of regulatory agency and malpractice legal problems for psychiatrists. *Annals of Clinical Psychiatry, 26*(2), 91–96.

Reichenberg, A., Cederlof, M., McMillan, A., Trzaskowski, M., Kapara, O., Fruchter, E., . . . Lichtenstein, P. (2016). Discontinuity in the genetic and environmental causes of the intellectual disability spectrum. *Proceedings of the National Academy of Sciences, 113,* 1098–1103.

Reichenberg, A., Gross, R., Kolevzon, A., & Susser, E. S. (2011). Parental and perinatal risk factors for autism. In E. Hollander, A. Kolevzon & J. T. Coyle (Eds.), *Textbook of autism spectrum disorders* (pp. 239–246). Arlington, VA: American Psychiatric Publishing, Inc.

Reichle, J., Ganz, J., Drager, K., Parker-McGowan, Q. (2016). Augmentative and alternative communication applications for persons with ASD and complex communication needs. In D. Keen, H. Meadan, N. C. Brady, & J. W. Halle (Eds.), *Prelinguistic and minimally verbal communicators on the autism spectrum.* New York: Springer.

Reid, T. (2017, February 13). UA students take stance against campus sexual assault with "It's On Us" campaign. Tuscaloosa, AL: *WIAT.* Retrieved from http://wiat.com.

Reidenberg, D. (2017). Facebook takes steps to stop suicides on Live. Interviewed in Guynn, J. (2017, March 1). *USA Today.*

Reinders, A. A., Willemsen, A. T., Vissia, E. M., Vos, H. P., den Boer, J. A., & Nijenhuis, E. R. (2016). The psychobiology of authentic and simulated dissociative personality states: The full monty. *Journal of Nervous and Mental Disease, 204*(6), 445–457.

Reinfjell, T., Karstad, S. B., Berg-Nielsen, T. S., Luby, J. L., & Wichstrøm, L. (2016). Predictors of change in depressive symptoms from preschool to first grade. *Development and Psychopathology, 28,* 1517–1530.

Reisch, T., Seifritz, E., Esposito, F., Wiest, R., Valach, L., & Michel, K. (2010). An fMRI study on mental pain and suicidal behavior. *Journal of Affective Disorders, 126*(1–2), 321–325.

Reisner, A. D., Piel, J., & Makey, M., Jr. (2013). Competency to stand trial and defendants who lack insight into their mental illness. *Journal of the American Academy of Psychiatry and the Law, 41*(1), 85–91.

Reisner, S. L., Conron, K. J., Tardiff, L. A., Jarvi, S., Gordon, A. R., & Austin, S. B. (2014). Monitoring the health of transgender and other gender minority populations: Validity of natal sex and gender identity survey items in a U.S. national cohort of young adults. *BMC Public Health, 14*, 1224.

Reitan, R. M., & Wolfson, D. (1996). Theoretical, methodological, and validational bases of the Halstead-Reitan neuropsychological test battery. In I. Grant & K. M. Adams (Eds.), *Neuropsychological assessment of neuropsychiatric disorders* (2nd ed., pp. 3–42). New York: Oxford University Press.

Reitan, R. M., & Wolfson, D. (2005). The effect of age and education transformations on neuropsychological test scores of persons with diffuse or bilateral brain damage. *Applied Neuropsychology, 12*(4), 181–189.

Relkin, N. (2015, May 28). Neuroimaging studies in the evaluation of dementia. *UpToDate.* Retrieved from http://www.uptodate.com.

Remberk, B., Bażyńska, A. K., Bronowska, Z., Potocki, P., Krempa-Kowalewska, A., Niwiński, P., & Rybakowski, F. (2014). Which aspects of long-term outcome are predicted by positive and negative symptoms in early-onset psychosis? An exploratory eight-year follow-up study. *Psychopathology.* [Advance online publication]

Remes, O., Brayne, C., van der Linde, R., & Lafortune, L. (2016). A systematic review of reviews on the prevalence of anxiety disorders in adult populations. *Brain and Behavior, 6*(7), e00497.

Remick, R. A., Evans, A., & Bates, A. T. (2017). Exercise as medicine: An evidence-based treatment for depression. *BC Medical Journal, 59*(2), 83–84.

Remington, G., Foussias, G., Fervaha, G., & Agid, O. (2014). Schizophrenia, cognition, and psychosis. *JAMA Psychiatry, 71*(3), 336–337.

Renaud, J., Berlim, M. T., McGirr, A., Tousignant, M., & Turecki, G. (2008). Current psychiatric morbidity, aggression/impulsivity, and personality dimensions in child and adolescent suicide: A case-control study. *Journal of Affective Disorders, 105*(1–3), 221–228.

Reuters. (2010, April 8). *They walk among us: 1 in 5 believe in aliens?* Retrieved from http://www.reuters.com/assets/print?aid.

Reynolds, G., Field, A. P., & Askew, C. (2017). Reductions in children's vicariously learnt avoidance and heart rate responses using positive modeling. *Journal of Clinical Child and Adolescent Psychology.* DOI: 10.1080/15374416.2016.1138410.

Rezaee, R., Kingsberg, S., & Spadt, S. K. (2016, November 10). Approach to the woman with sexual pain. *UpToDate.* Retrieved from http://www.uptodate.com.

Rezaei, M., Khalighinasab, M. R., & Saadat, M. (2017). Association between genetic polymorphisms at promoter region of the catalase gene and risk of dependency to heroin. *Psychiatry Research, 251*, 235–236.

Rhéaume, C., Arsenault, B. J., Després, J., Faha, Boekholdt, S. M., Wareham, N. J., . . . Chir, M. (2014). Impact of abdominal obesity and systemic hypertension on risk of coronary heart disease in men and women: The EPICNorfolk Population Study. *Journal of Hypertension, 32*(11), 2224–2230.

Rhebergen, D., & Graham, R. (2014). The re-labelling of dysthymic disorder to persistent depressive disorder in DSM-5: Old wine in new bottles? *Current Opinion in Psychiatry, 27*(1), 27–31.

Ribeiro, J. D., Gutierrez, P. M., Joiner, T. E., Kessler, R. C., Petukhova, M. V., Sampson, N. A., . . . Nock, M. K. (2017). Health care contact and suicide risk documentation prior to suicide death: Results from the Army Study to Assess Risk and Resilience in Servicemembers (Army STARRS). *Journal of Consulting and Clinical Psychology, 85*(4), 403–408.

Ribeiro, J. D., & Joiner, T. E. (2009). The interpersonal-psychological theory of suicidal behavior: Current status and future directions. *Journal of Clinical Psychology. 65*(12), 1291–1299.

Richardson, J. R., Roy, A., Shalat, S. L., von Stein, R. T., Hossain, M. M., Buckley, B., . . . German, D. C. (2014). Elevated serum pesticide levels and risk for Alzheimer disease. *JAMA Neurology, 71*(3), 284–290.

Richmond, M. K., Pampel, F. C., Wood, R. C., & Nunes, A. P. (2016). Impact of employee assistance services on depression, anxiety, and risky alcohol use: A quasi-experimental study. *Journal of Occupational and Environmental Medicine, 58*(7), 641–650.

Rickard, N., Arjmand, H. A., Bakker, D., & Seabrook, E. (2016). Development of a mobile phone app to support self-monitoring of emotional well-being: A mental health digital innovation. *JMIR Mental Health, 3*(4), e49.

Riddle, M. A., Maher, B. S., Wang, Y., Grados, M., Bienvenu, O. J., Goes, F. S., . . . Samuels, J. (2016). Obsessive-compulsive personality disorder: Evidence for two dimensions. *Depression and Anxiety, 33*(2), 128–135.

Rieber, R. W. (1999, March). Hypnosis, false memory, and multiple personality: A trinity of affinity. *History of Psychiatry, 10*(37), 3–11.

Rieber, R. W. (2002). The duality of the brain and the multiplicity of minds: Can you have it both ways? *History of Psychiatry 13*(49, pt1), 3–18.

Rieber, R. W. (2006). *The bifurcation of the self: The history and theory of dissociation and its disorders.* New York: Springer Science + Business Media.

Riesch, S. K., Jacobson, G., Sawdey, L., Anderson, J., & Henriques, J. (2008). Suicide ideation among later elementary school-aged youth. *Journal of Psychiatric and Mental Health Nursing, 15*(4), 263–277.

Rigotti, N. A. (2017, February 17). Overview of smoking cessation management in adults. *UpToDate.* Retrieved from http://www.uptodate.com.

Rigotti, N. A. (2017, September 7). Pharmacotherapy for smoking cessation in adults. *UpToDate.* Retrieved from http://www.uptodate.com.

Rigotti, N. A., & Kalkhoran, S. (2017, August 22). E-cigarettes. *UpToDate.* Retrieved from http://www.uptodate.com.

Rindal, E. J., Chrobak, Q. M., Zaragoza, M. S., & Weihing, C. A. (2017, February 7). Mechanisms of eyewitness suggestibility: Tests of the explanatory role hypothesis. *Psychonomic Bulletin and Review.* [Epub ahead of press]

Rinker, D. V. (2016). *Examining the association between "drunkorexia, perceived norms, and drinking to cope.* New Orleans: Presentation, Research society on alcoholism.

Risch, N., Hoffmann, T. J., Anderson, M., Croen, L. A., Grether, J. K., & Windham, G. C. (2014). Familial recurrence of autism spectrum disorder: Evaluating genetic and environmental contributions. *American Journal of Psychiatry* [Electronic publication], 591.

Ristow, A., Westphal, A., & Scahill, L. (2011). Treating hyperactivity in children with pervasive developmental disorders. In E. Hollander, A. Kolevzon, & J. T. Coyle (Eds.), *Textbook of autism spectrum disorders* (pp. 479–486). Arlington, VA: American Psychiatric Publishing.

Ritsner, M. S., Gottesman, I. I. (2011). The schizophrenia construct after 100 years of challenges. In M. S. Ritsner (Ed.), *Handbook of schizophrenia spectrum disorders, conceptual issues and neurobiological advances* (Vol. 1, pp. 1–44). New York: Springer.

Ritter, K., Vater, A., Rüsch, N., Schröder-Abé, M., Schütz, A., Fydrich, T., . . . Roepke, S. (2014). Shame in patients with narcissistic personality disorder. *Psychiatry Research, 215*(2), 429–437.

Ritter, M. (2008, January 27). Lead linked to aging in older brains. *YAHOO! News.*

Ritter, M. R., Blackmore, M. A., & Heimberg, R. G. (2010). Generalized anxiety disorder. In D. McKay, J. S. Abramowitz, & S. Taylor (Eds.), *Cognitive-behavioral therapy for refractory cases: Turning failure into success* (pp. 111–137). Washington, DC: American Psychological Association.

Riva-Posse, P., Choi, K. S., Holtzheimer, P. E., Crowell, A. L., Garlow, S. J., Rajendra, J. K., . . . Mayberg, H. S. (2018). A connectomic approach for subcallosal cingulate deep brain stimulation surgery: Prospective targeting in treatment-resistant depression. *Molecular Psychiatry.* [Manuscript in press]

Rizvi, S. L., Dimeff, L. A., Skutch, J., Carroll, D., & Linehan, M. M. (2011). A pilot study of the DBT coach: An interactive mobile phone application for individuals with borderline personality disorder and substance use disorder. *Behavior Therapy, 42*, 589–600.

Rizzi, M., & Marras, C. E. (2017). Deep brain stimulation for the treatment of aggressive behaviour: Considerations on pathophysiology and target choice. *Stereotactic and Functional Neurosurgery, 95*(2), 114–116.

Robert, G., & Zadra, A. (2014). Thematic and content analysis of idiopathic nightmares and bad dreams. *Sleep, 37*(2), 409–417.

Robertson, A. G., Swanson, J. W., Frisman, L. K., Lin, H., & Swartz, M. S. (2014). Patterns of justice involvement among adults with schizophrenia and bipolar disorder: Key risk factors. *Psychiatric Services* (Washington, D.C.), [Manuscript submitted for publication], 468.

Robertson, C. A., & Knight, R. A. (2014). Relating sexual sadism and psychopathy to one another, non-sexual violence, and sexual crime behaviors. *Aggressive Behavior, 40*(1), 12–23.

Robins, C. J., Zerubavel, N., Ivanoff, A. M., & Linehan, M. M. (2018). Dialectical behavior therapy. In W. J. Livesley & R. Larstone (Eds.), *Handbook of personality disorders: Theory, research, and treatment* (2nd ed.). New York: Guilford Press.

Robinson, M. (2017, January 8). It's 2017: Here's where you can legally smoke weed now. *Business Insider*.

Robinson-Papp, J., Sharma, S. K., George, M. C., & Simpson, D. M. (2017). Assessment of autonomic symptoms in a medically complex, urban patient population. *Clinical Autonomic Research, 27*(1), 25–29.

Robles, R., Fresán, A., Vega-Ramirez, H., Cruz-Islas, J., Rodriguez-Pérez, V., Dominguez-Martinez, T., & Reed, G. M. (2016). Removing transgender identity from the classification of mental disorders: A Mexican field study for ICD-11. *Lancet Psychiatry, 3*(9), 850–859.

Robson, D. (2017, January 19). How East and West think in profoundly different ways. *BBC-Future*. Retrieved from http://www.bbc.com/future/story/20170118-how-east-and-west-think-in-profoundly-different-ways.

Rocca, P., Montemagni, C., Zappia, S., Pierà, R., Sigaudo, M., & Bogetto, F. (2014). Negative symptoms and everyday functioning in schizophrenia: A cross-sectional study in a real world-setting. *Psychiatry Research, 218*(3), 284–289.

Roche, B., & Quayle, E. (2007). Sexual disorders. In D. W. Woods & J. W. Kanter (Eds.), *Understanding behavior disorders: A contemporary behavioral perspective*. Reno, NV: Context Press.

Roche, T. (2002, January 20). The Yates odyssey. *TIME.com: Nation*.

Rochon, P. A. (2017, May 26). Drug prescribing for older adults. *UpToDate*. Retrieved from http://www.uptodate.com.

Rocks, T., Pelly, F., & Wilkinson, P. (2014). Nutrition therapy during initiation of refeeding in underweight children and adolescent inpatients with anorexia nervosa: A systematic review of the evidence. *Journal of the Academy of Nutrition and Dietetics, 114*(6), 897–907.

Rodav, O., Levy, S., & Hamdan, S. (2014). Clinical characteristics and functions of non-suicide self-injury in youth. *European Psychiatry, 29*(8), 503–508.

Rodebaugh, T. L., Levinson, C. A., Langer, J. K., Weeks, J. W., Heimberg, R. G., Brown, P. J., . . . Liebowitz, M. R. (2017). The structure of vulnerabilities for social anxiety disorder. *Psychiatry Research, 250,* 297–301.

Rodgers, R. F., Lowy, A. S., Halperin, D. M., & Franko, D. L. (2016). A meta-analysis examining the influence of pro-eating disorder websites on body image and eating pathology. *European Eating Disorders Review, 24*(1), 3–8.

Rodnitzky, R. (2017, January 25). Cognitive impairment and dementia in Parkinson disease. *UpToDate*. Retrieved from http://www.uptodate.com.

Roelofs, K., Hoogduin, K. A. L., Keijsers, G. P. J., Naering, G. W. B., Moene, F. C., & Sandijck, P. (2002). Hypnotic susceptibility in patients with conversion disorder. *Journal of Abnormal Psychology, 111*(2), 390–395.

Roepke, S., & Vater, A. (2014). Narcissistic personality disorder: An integrative review of recent empirical data and current definitions. *Current Psychiatry Reports, 16,* 445.

Roesch, R. (1991). *The encyclopedia of depression*. New York: Facts on File.

Roesch, R. (2016, December). Competency to stand trial in the American legal system. *Oxford Research Encyclopedia of Psychology*. Retrieved from http://psychology.oxfordre.com.

Roesch, R., Zapf, P. A., & Hart, S. D. (2010). *Forensic psychology and law*. Hoboken, NJ: John Wiley & Sons.

Roesler, T. A., & Jenny, C. (2016, August 11). Medical child abuse (Munchausen syndrome by proxy). *UpToDate*. Retrieved from www.uptodate.com.

Roesler, T. A., & McKenzie, N. (1994). Effects of childhood trauma on psychological functioning of adults sexually abused as children. *Journal of Nervous and Mental Disease, 182*(3), 145–150.

Rogers, C. R. (1951). *Client-centered therapy*. Boston: Houghton Mifflin.

Rogers, C. R. (1954). The case of Mrs. Oak: A research analysis. In C. R. Rogers & R. F. Dymond (Eds.), *Psychotherapy and personality change* (pp. 259–269). Chicago: University of Chicago Press.

Rogers, C. R. (1987). Rogers, Kohut, and Erickson: A personal perspective on some similarities and differences. In J. K. Zeig (Ed.), *The evolution of psychotherapy*. New York: Brunner/Mazel.

Rogers, M. L., Kelliher-Rabon, J., Hagen, C. R., Hirsch, J. K., & Joiner, T. E. (2017). Negative emotions in veterans relate to suicide risk through feelings of perceived burdensomeness and thwarted belongingness. *Journal of Affective Disorders, 208,* 15–21.

Rogers, R. (2008). Insanity evaluations. In R. Jackson (Ed.), *Learning forensic assessment* (pp. 109–128). New York: Routledge/Taylor & Francis Group.

Rogler, L. H., Malgady, R. G., & Rodriguez, O. (1989). *Hispanics and mental health: A frame-work for research*. Malabar, FL: Krieger Publishing.

Roh, D., Chang, J., Kim, C., Cho, H., An, S. K., & Jung, Y. (2014). Antipsychotic polypharmacy and high-dose prescription in schizophrenia: A 5-year comparison. *Australian and New Zealand Journal of Psychiatry, 48*(1), 52–60.

Rohn, T. T., McCarty, K. L., Love, J. E., & Head, E. (2014). Is apolipoprotein E4 an important risk factor for dementia in persons with Down Syndrome? *Journal of Parkinson's Disease and Alzheimer's Disease, 1*(1), 7.

Rojas, S. L., & Widiger, T. A. (2016, September 12). Coverage of the DSM-IV-TR/DSM-5 Section II personality disorders with the DSM-5 dimensional trait model. *Journal of Personality Disorders*. [Epub ahead of print]

Rollin, H. R. (1980). *Coping with schizophrenia*. London: Burnett.

Rolls, E. T. (2017). The roles of the orbitofrontal cortex via the habenula in non-reward and depression, and in the responses of serotonin and dopamine neurons. *Neuroscience & Biobehavioral Reviews, 75,* 331–334.

Romanelli, R. J., Wu, F. M., Gamba, R., Mojtabai, R., & Segal, J. B. (2014). Behavioral therapy and serotonin reuptake inhibitor pharmacotherapy in the treatment of obsessive-compulsive disorder: A systematic review and meta-analysis of head-to-head randomized controlled trials. *Depression and Anxiety, 31*(8), 641–652.

Romero-Martínez, A., Figueiredo, B., & Moya-Albiol, L. (2014). Childhood history of abuse and child abuse potential: The role of parent's gender and timing of childhood abuse. *Child Abuse and Neglect, 38*(3), 510–516.

Roney, T., & Cannon, J. (2014). Dialectical behavior group therapy for borderline personality disorder. *International Journal of Group Psychotherapy, 64*(3), 400–408.

Ronningstam, E. (2011). Narcissistic personality disorder: A clinical perspective. *Journal of Psychiatric Practice, 17*(2), 89–99.

Ronningstam, E. (2017). Intersect between self-esteem and emotion regulation in narcissistic personality disorder: Implications for alliance building and treatment. *Borderline Personality Disorder and Emotion Dysregulation, 4,* 3.

Rook, K. S., August, K. J., & Sorkin, D. H. (2011). Social network functions and health. In R. J. Contrada & A. Baum (Eds.), *The handbook of stress science: Biology, psychology, and health* (pp. 123–135). New York: Springer Publishing.

Roper. (2017). *Public attitudes about mental health*. Ithaca, NY: Roper Center for Public Opinion Research, Cornell University.

Ros, R., & Graziano, P. (2018). Social functioning in children with or at risk for attention deficit/hyperactivity disorder. *Journal of Clinical Child and Adolescent Psychology*. [Manuscript in press]

Rosa, M. H. (2015). Love at a distance: Aggression and hatred in a schizoid personality. *Psychoanalytic Review, 102*(4), 503–530.

Rosalyn, H., Hamburg, S., Knight, B., & Strydom, A. (2017). Cognitive decline and dementia in Down syndrome. *Current Opinion in Psychiatry, 30,* 102–107.

Rosch, P. J. (2016). Why do women suffer more from depression and stress? *American Institute of Stress*. Retrieved from https://www.stress.org.

Rose, T., Joe, S., & Lindsey, M. (2011). Perceived stigma and depression among black adolescents in outpatient treatment. *Children and Youth Services Review, 33*(1), 161–166.

Rosell, D. R. (2017, June 14). Schizotypal personality disorder: Epidemiology, pathogenesis, clinical manifestations, course, and diagnosis. *UpToDate*. Retrieved from http://www.uptodate.com.

Rosellini, A. J., & Bagge, C. L. (2014). Temperament, hopelessness, and attempted suicide: Direct and indirect effects. *Suicide and Life-Threatening Behavior, 44*(4), 353–361.

Rosen, E. F., Anthony, D. L., Booker, K. M., Brown, T. L., Christian, E., Crews, R. C., . . . Petty, L. C. (1991). A comparison of eating disorder scores among African American and white college females. *Bulletin of Psychosomatic Society, 29*(1), 65–66.

Rosen, R. C. (2007). Erectile dysfunction: Integration of medical and psychological approaches. In S. R. Leiblum (Ed.), *Principles and practice of sex therapy* (4th ed., pp. 277–310). New York: Guilford Press.

Rosen, R. C., & Rosen, L. R. (1981). *Human sexuality.* New York: Knopf.

Rosenblum, G. D., & Lewis, M. (1999). The relations among body image, physical attractiveness, and body mass in adolescence. *Child Development, 70*(1), 50–64.

Rosenhan, D. L. (1973). On being sane in insane places. *Science, 179*(4070), 250–258.

Rosenthal, R. (1966). *Experimenter effects in behavioral research.* New York: Appleton-Century-Crofts.

Rosenthal, R. N. (2011). Alcohol abstinence management. In J. H. Lowinson & P. Ruiz (Eds.), *Substance abuse: A comprehensive textbook* (5th ed.). Philadelphia, PA: Lippincott Williams & Wilkins.

Rosenthal, R. N., & Levounis, P. (2005). Polysubstance use, abuse, and dependence. In R. J. Frances, A. H. Mack, & S. I. Miller (Eds.), *Clinical textbook of addictive disorders* (3rd ed., pp. 245–270). New York: Guilford Press.

Rosenthal, R. N., & Levounis, P. (2011). Polysubstance use, abuse, and dependence. In R. Frances, S. Miller, & A. Mack (Eds.), *Clinical textbook of addictive disorders* (3rd ed., Chap. 11, pp. 245–270). New York: Guilford Press.

Roslan, N. S., Jaafar, N. R. N., Sidi, H., Baharuddin, N., Kumar, J., Das, S., & Hussein, N. H. N. (2017, June 21). The bio-psycho-social dimension in women's sexual desire: "Argumentum ad novitatem." *Current Drug Targets.* [Epub ahead of print]

Roskar, S., Podlesek, A., Kuzmanic, M., Demsar, L. O., Zaletel, M., & Marusic, A. (2011). Suicide risk and its relationship to change in marital status. *Crisis: Journal of Crisis Intervention and Suicide Prevention, 32*(1), 24–30.

Rosky, J. W. (2013). The (f)utility of post-conviction polygraph testing. *Sexual Abuse: A Journal of Research and Treatment, 25*(3), 259–281.

Rosky, J. W. (2015). More polygraph futility: A comment on Jensen, Shafer, Roby, and Roby (2015). *Journal of Interpersonal Violence, 31*(10) 1956–1970.

Rosky, J. W. (2016). More polygraph futility: A comment on Jensen, Shafer, Roby, and Roby (2015). *Journal of Interpersonal Violence, 31*(10), 1956–1970.

Ross, C. A., & Gahan, P. (1988). Techniques in the treatment of multiple personality disorder. *American Journal of Psychotherapy, 42*(1), 40–52.

Ross, C. A., & Ness, L. (2010). Symptom patterns in dissociative identity disorder patients and the general population. *Journal of Trauma & Dissociation, 11*(4), 458–468.

Ross, D. A., Arbuckle, M. R., Travis, M. J., Dwyer, J. B., van Schalkwyk, G. I., & Ressler, K. J. (2017). An integrated neuroscience perspective on formulation and treatment planning for posttraumatic stress disorder: An educational review. *JAMA Psychiatry, 74,* 407–415.

Ross, S. (2014, October 20). Alcohol use disorders in the elderly. *Psychiatry Weekly.*

Rossi-Arnaud, C., Spataro, P., Saraulli, D., Mulligan, N. W., Sciarretta, A., Marques, V. S., & Cestari, V. (2014). The attentional boost effect in schizophrenia. *Journal of Abnormal Psychology, 123*(3), 588–597.

Rotenberg, K. J., Costa, P., Trueman, M., & Lattimore, P. (2012). An interactional test of the reformulated helplessness theory of depression in women receiving clinical treatment for eating disorders. *Eating Behaviors, 13*(3), 264–266.

Roth, D. L., Usher, T., Clark, E. M., & Holt, C. L. (2016). Religious involvement and health over time: Predictive effects in a national sample of African Americans. *Journal for the Scientific Study of Religion, 55*(2), 417–424.

Rothbaum, B. O. (2017, February 3). Psychotherapy for posttraumatic stress disorder in adults. *UpToDate.* Retrieved from https://www.uptodate.com.

Rothbaum, B. O., Foa, E. B., Riggs, D. S., Murdock, T., & Walsh, W. (1992). A prospective examination of posttraumatic stress disorder in rape victims. *Journal of Traumatic Stress, 5*(3), 455–475.

Rothbaum, B. O., Price, M., Jovanovic, T., Norrholm, S. D., Gerardi, M., Dunlop, B., . . . Ressler, K. J. (2014). A randomized, double-blind evaluation of D-cycloserine or alprazolam combined with virtual reality exposure therapy for posttraumatic stress disorder in Iraq and Afghanistan War veterans. *American Journal of Psychiatry, 171*(6), 640–648.

Rothenberg, A. (2015, March 8). Creativity and mental illness. Creativity is highly adaptive and the actual processes involved are all healthy. *Psychology Today.* Retrieved from https://www.psychologytoday.com/blog/creativity-exploratiions-in-art-literature-science-and-the-everyday/201503/creativity-and-mental.

Rothschild, A. J. (2016, June 6). Unipolar major depression with psychotic features: Acute treatment. *UpToDate.* Retrieved from http://www.uptodate.com.

Rothschild, A. J. (2017, March 23). Unipolar major depression with psychotic features: Maintenance treatment and course of illness. *UpToDate.* Retrieved from www.uptodate.com.

Rotter, M. (2011). Embitterment and personality disorder. In M. Linden & A. Maercker (Eds.), *Embitterment: Societal, psychological, and clinical perspectives* (pp. 177–186). New York: Springer-Verlag Publishing.

Rouse, A. (2017). Sinead O'Connor and her misdiagnosis of bipolar disorder. *Verywell.com* (January 23).

Rowan, P. (2005, July 31). Cited in J. Thompson, "Hungry for love": Why 11 million of us have serious issues with food. *Independent on Sunday.*

Rowland, D. L. (2012). *Sexual dysfunction in men. Advances in psychotherapy—Evidence-based practice.* Cambridge, MA: Hogrefe Publishing.

Rowland, D. I., & Cooper, S. E. (2017). Treating men's orgasmic difficulties. In Z. D. Peterson, *The Wiley-Blackwell handbook of sex therapy* (Ch. 6, pp. 72–97). Hoboken, NJ: Wiley-Blackwell.

Rowland, D. L., Georgoff, V. L., & Burnett, A. L. (2011). Psychoaffective differences between sexually functioning and dysfunctional men in response to a sexual experience. *Journal of Sexual Medicine, 8*(1), 132–139.

Roy, A. (1992). Genetics, biology, and suicide in the family. In R. W. Maris, A. L. Berman, J. T. Maltsberger, & R. I. Yufitet (Eds.), *Assessment and prediction of suicide* (pp. xxii, 697). New York: Guilford Press.

Roy, A. (2011). Combination of family history of suicidal behavior and childhood trauma may represent correlate of increased suicide risk. *Journal of Affective Disorders, 130*(1-2), 205–208.

Roy, A., Hechtman, L., Arnold, L., Sibley, M. H., et al. (2016). Childhood factors affecting persistence and desistence of attention-deficit/hyperactivity disorder symptoms in adulthood: Results from the MTA. *Journal of the American Academy of Child and Adolescent Psychiatry, 55,* 937–944.

Roy, A. K., Klein, R. G., Angelosante, A., Bar-Haim, Y., Leibenluft, E., Hulvershorn, L., . . . Spindel, C. (2013). Clinical features of young children referred for impairing temper outbursts. *Journal of Child and Adolescent Psychopharmacology, 23*(9), 588–596.

Roy, M. (2016). Sexuality and people with intellectual disabilities. In A. Roy, M. Roy, & D. Clarke (Eds.), *The psychiatry of intellectual disability.* Seattle: Radcliff Publishing.

Roy-Byrne, P. P. (2016, May 26). Panic disorder in adults: Epidemiology, pathogenesis, clinical manifestations, course, assessment, and diagnosis. *UpToDate.* Retrieved from http://www.uptodate.com.

Roy-Byrne, P. P. (2016, October 20). Pharmacotherapy for panic disorder in adults. *UpToDate.* Retrieved from http://www.uptodate.com.

Roy-Byrne, P. P., Arguelles, L., Vitek, M. E., Goldberg, J., Keane, T. M., True, W. R., et al. (2004). Persistence and change of PTSD symptomatology: A longitudinal co-twin control analysis of the Vietnam Era Twin Registry. *Social Psychiatry and Psychiatric Epidemiology, 39*(9), 681–685.

Rubens, S. L., Gudiño, O. G., Fite, P. J., & Grande, J. M. (2016, December 15). Individual and neighborhood stressors, sleep problems, and symptoms of anxiety and depression among Latino youth. *American Journal of Orthopsychiatry.* [Epub ahead of print]

Rubenstein, L. M., Freed, R. D., Shapero, B. G., Fauber, R. L., & Alloy, L. B. (2016). Cognitive attributions in depression: Bridging the gap between research and clinical practice. *Journal of Psychotherapy Integration, 26*(2), 103–115.

Rubin, D. M., Curtis, M. L., & Matone, M. (2014). Child abuse prevention and child home visitation: Making sure we get it right. *JAMA Pediatrics, 168*(1), 5–6.

Rubinstein, S., & Caballero, B. (2000). Is Miss America an undernourished role model? *Journal of the American Medical Association, 283*(12), 1569.

Rubio-Aurioloes, E., & Bivalacqua, T. J. (2013). Standard operational procedures for low sexual desire in men. *Journal of Sexual Medicine, 10,* 94–107.

Rudd, M. D., Berman, L., Joiner, T. E., Nock, M., Mandrusiak, M., Van Orden, K., . . . Witte, T. (2006). Warning signs for suicide: Theory, research, and clinical application. *Suicide and Life-Threatening Behavior, 36,* 255–262.

Rudd, M. D., & Brown, G. K. (2011). A cognitive theory of suicide: Building hope in treatment and strengthening the therapeutic relationship. In K. Michel & D. A. Jobes (Eds.), *Building a therapeutic alliance with the suicidal patient* (pp. 169–181). Washington, DC: American Psychological Association.

Rudd, M. D., Bryan, C. J., Wertenberger, E. G., Peterson, A. L., Young-McCaughan, S., Mintz, J., . . . Bruce, T. O. (2015). Brief cognitive-behavioral therapy effects on post-treatment suicide attempts in a military sample: Results of a randomized clinical trial with 2-year follow-up. *The American Journal of Psychiatry, 172*(5), 441–449.

Rudge, S., Feigenbaum, J. D., & Fonagy, P. (2018). Mechanisms of change in dialectical behaviour therapy and cognitive behaviour therapy for borderline personality disorder: A critical review of the literature. *Journal of Mental Health.* [Manuscript in press]

Ruggero, C. J., Kotov, R., Callahan, J. L., Kilmer, J. N., Luft, B. J., & Bromet, E. J. (2013). PTSD symptom dimensions and their relationship to functioning in World Trade Center responders. *Psychiatry Research, 210*(3), 1049–1055.

Ruocco, A. C., & Carcone, D. (2016). A neurobiological model of borderline personality disorder. *Harvard Review of Psychiatry, 24*(5), 311.

Rupert, P. A., Miller, A. O., Tuminello Hartman, E. R., & Bryant, F. B. (2012). Predictors of career satisfaction among practicing psychologists. *Professional Psychology: Research and Practice, 43*(5), 495–502.

Rus-Calafell, M., Garety, P., Ward, T., Williams, G., Huckvale, M., Leff, J., & Craig, T. K. (2015). Confronting auditory hallucinations using virtual reality: The avatar therapy. *Studies in Health Technology and Informatics, 219*, 192–196.

Rüsch, N., Corrigan, P. W., Heekeren, K., Theodoridou, A., Dvorsky, D., Metzler, S., . . . Rössler, W. (2014). Well-being among persons at risk of psychosis: The role of self-labeling, shame, and stigma stress. *Psychiatric Services, 65*(4), 483–489.

Ruscio, J. (2015). Labeling theory. In R. L. Cautin & S. O. Lilienfeld, *The encyclopedia of clinical psychology* (1st ed.). Hoboken, NJ: John Wiley & Sons.

Rusconi, E., & Mitchener-Nissen, T. (2013). Prospects of functional magnetic resonance imaging as lie detector. *Frontiers in Human Neuroscience, 7*594.

Russell, J. E. A. (2014, July 10). Practice mindfulness for better, and quite possibly longer, life. *Tampa Bay Times.*

Russo, F. (2016, January 1). Is there something unique about the transgender brain? *Scientific American.*

Russo, F. (2016, January 1). Transgender kids: What does it take to help them thrive? *Scientific American.*

Russo, F. (2017, January 6). Where transgender is no longer a diagnosis. *Scientific American.*

Russo, N. F., & Tartaro, J. (2008). Women and mental health. In F. L. Denmark & M. A. Paludi (Eds.), *Psychology of women: A handbook of issues and theories* (2nd ed., pp. 440–483). Westport, CT: Praeger Publishers.

Rutan, J. S., & Shay, J. J. (2016). Group therapy: Theory and practice. In A. J. Consoli, L. E. Beutler, & B. Bongar (Eds.), *Comprehensive textbook of psychotherapy: Theory and practice* (2nd ed., pp. 223–238). New York: Oxford University Press.

Rutledge, P. (2013, October 20). Positively media: How we connect and thrive through emerging technologies. *Psychology Today.*

Ruzek, J. I., & Batten, S. V. (2011). Enhancing systems of care for posttraumatic stress disorder: From private practice to large health care systems. In J. I. Ruzek, P. P. Schnurr, J. J. Vasterling, & M. J. Friedman (Eds.), *Caring for veterans with deployment-related stress disorders* (pp. 261–282). Washington, DC: American Psychological Association.

Ruzek, J. I., Schnurr, P. P., Vasterling, J. J., & Friedman, J. (Eds.). (2011). *Caring for veterans with deployment-related stress disorders.* Washington, DC: American Psychological Association.

Ryan, S. M., Strege, M. V., Oar, E. L., & Ollendick, T. H. (2017). One session therapy for specific phobias in children: Comorbid anxiety disorders and treatment outcome. *Journal of Behavior Therapy and Experimental Psychiatry, 54*, 128–134.

Rynn, M. A., Walkup, J. T., Compton, S. N., Sakolsky, D. J., Sherrill, J. T., et al. (2015). Child/adolescent anxiety multimodal study: Evaluating safety. *Journal of the American Academy of Child and Adolescent Psychiatry, 54*, 180–190.

Ryan, W. J. (2016). The handbook of forensic psychology. *Journal of Personality Assessment, 98*(5), 553–554.

Saba, L. M., Flink, S. C., Vanderlinden, L. A., Israel, Y., Tampier, L., Colombo, G., . . . Tabakoff, B. (2015). The sequenced rat brain transcriptome—its use in identifying networks predisposing alcohol consumption. *The FEBS Journal.* [Electronic publication]

Sabouri, S., Gerber, M., Lemola, S., Becker, S. P., Shamsi, M., Shakouri, Z., . . . Brand, S. (2016). Examining Dark Triad traits in relation to sleep disturbances, anxiety sensitivity and intolerance of uncertainty in young adults. *Comprehensive Psychiatry, 68*, 103–110.

Sabouri, S., Gerber, M., Sadeghi Bahmani, D., Lemola, S., Clough, P. J., Kalak, N., . . . Brand, S. (2016). Examining Dark Triad traits in relation to mental toughness and physical activity in young adults. *Neuropsychiatric Disease and Treatment, 27*(12), 229–235.

Sacks, O. (2012). *Hallucinations.* New York: Vintage Books.

Sacks, O. (2012, November 3). Seeing things? Hearing things? Many of us do. *New York Times.*

Sadeghi, K., Ahmadi, S. M., Moghadam, A. P., & Parvizifard, A. (2017). The study of cognitive change process on depression during aerobic exercises. *Journal of Clinical and Diagnostic Research, 11*(4), IC01–IC05.

Sadeghi, K., Ahmadi, S. M., Rezaei, M., Miri, J., Abdi, A., Khamoushi, F., . . . Jamshidi, K. (2016). A comparative study of the efficacy of cognitive group therapy and aerobic exercise in the treatment of depression among the students. *Global Journal of Health Science, 8*(10), 54171.

Sadeh, N., Londahl-Shaller, E. A., Piatigorsky, A., Fordwood, S., Stuart, B. K., McNiel, D. E., . . . Yaeger, A. M. (2014). Functions of non-suicidal self-injury in adolescents and young adults with borderline personality disorder symptoms. *Psychiatry Research, 216*(2), 217–222.

Sadiq, S., Suhail, K., Gleeson, J., & Alvarez-Jimenez, M. (2017). Expressed emotion and the course of schizophrenia in Pakistan. *Social Psychiatry and Psychiatric Epidemiology, 52*(5), 587–593.

Safer, D. (1994). The impact of recent lawsuits on methylphenidates sales. *Clinical Pediatrics, 33*(3), 166–168.

Safer, D. J. (2016). Recent trends in stimulant usage. *Journal of Attention Disorders, 20*, 471–477.

Safer, M. A., Murphy, R. P., Wise, R. A., Bussey, L., Millett, C., & Holfeld, B. (2016). Educating jurors about eyewitness testimony in criminal cases with circumstantial and forensic evidence. *International Journal of Law and Psychiatry, 47*, 86–92.

Sagan, A. (2015, February 24). Pro-anorexia, bulimia communities thriving online. *CBC News.* Retrieved from http://www.cbc.ca/news.

Sajatovic, M., & Chen, P. (2017, July 6). Geriatric bipolar disorder: Epidemiology, clinical features, assessment, and diagnosis. *UpToDate.* Retrieved from http://www.uptodate.com.

Sajatovic, M., & Chen, P. (2017, July 6). Geriatric bipolar disorder: General principles of treatment. *UpToDate.* Retrieved from http://www.uptodate.com.

Sakinofsky, I. (2011). Evidence-based approaches for reducing suicide risk in major affective disorders. In M. Pompili & R. Tatarelli (Eds.), *Evidence-based practice in suicidology: A source book* (pp. 275–315). Cambridge, MA: Hogrefe Publishing.

Salari, A., Bakhtiari, A., & Homberg, J. R. (2015). Activation of GABA-A receptors during postnatal brain development increases anxiety- and depression-related behaviors in a time- and dose-dependent manner in adult mice. *European Neuropsychopharmacy: The Journal of the European College of Neuropsychopharmacology, 25*(8), 1260–1274.

Salary.com. (2016). Psychologist salaries. Retrieved from www1.salary.com/psychologist-salary.html.

Salcioglu, E., Urhan, S., Pirinccioglu, T., & Aydin, S. (2017). Anticipatory fear and helplessness predict PTSD and depression in domestic violence survivors. *Psychological Trauma, 9*(1), 117–125.

Salk, R. H., Petersen, J. L., Abramson, L. Y., & Hyde, J. S. (2016). The contemporary face of gender differences and similarities in depression throughout adolescence: Development and chronicity. *Journal of Affective Disorders, 205*, 28–35.

Salkind, N. J. (2017). *Research design: Quantitative, qualitative, mixed methods, arts-based, and community-based participatory research approaches.* New York: Guilford Press.

Salkovskis, P. M. (1985). Obsessional-compulsive problems: A cognitive-behavioural analysis. *Behavioral Research and Therapy, 23*, 571–584.

Salkovskis, P. M. (1999). Understanding and treating obsessive-compulsive disorder. *Behavioral Research and Therapy, 37*(Suppl. 1), S29–S52.

Salkovskis, P. M., Thorpe, S. J., Wahl, K., Wroe, A. L., & Forrester, E. (2003). Neutralizing increases discomfort associated with obsessional thoughts: An experimental study with obsessional patients. *Journal of Abnormal Psychology, 112*(4), 709–715.

Saltzman, J. A., & Liechty, J. M. (2016, August 22). Family correlates of childhood binge eating: A systematic review. *Eating Behaviors*. [Epub ahead of print]

Sam, F. E. (2016, October 8). Reasons why fear is actually a good thing. *The Blog*. Retrieved from http://www.huffingtonpost.com.

Samek, D. R., Keyes, M. A., Hicks, B. M., Bailey, J., McGue, M., & Iacono, W. G. (2014). General and specific predictors of nicotine and alcohol dependence in early adulthood: Genetic and environmental influences. *Journal of Studies on Alcohol and Drugs, 75*(4), 623–634.

SAMHSA (Substance Abuse and Mental Health Services Administration). (2012). Cited in NAMI, *Survey finds many living with mental illness go without treatment*. Arlington, VA: NAMI.

SAMHSA (Substance Abuse and Mental Health Services Administration). (2012). *Mental health, United States, 2010*. (HHS Publication 12-4682). Rockville, MD: SAMHSA.

SAMHSA (Substance Abuse and Mental Health Services Administration). (2014). *Projections of national expenditures for treatment of mental and substance use disorders. 2010–2020*. Rockville, MD: SAMHSA.

SAMHSA (Substance Abuse and Mental Health Services Administration). (2015, October 29). *Suicide prevention*. Rockville, MD: SAMHSA.

SAMHSA (Substance Abuse and Mental Health Services Administration). (2016, August 9). *Treatments for substance use disorders*. Rockville, MD: SAMHSA.

SAMHSA (Substance Abuse and Mental Health Services Administration). (2016). *National Mental Health Services Survey (N-MHSS): 2014. Data on mental health treatment facilities*. BHSIS Series S-87, HHS Publ. No. (SMA) 16-5000. Rockville, MD: SAMHSA.

SAMHSA (Substance Abuse and Mental Health Services Administration). (2017). *Buprenorphine*. Retrieved from https://www.samhsa.gov/medication-assisted-treatment/treatment/buprenorphine.

SAMHSA (Substance Abuse and Mental Health Services Administration). (2017). *Data, outcomes, and quality*. Rockville, MD: SAMHSA.

SAMHSA (Substance Abuse and Mental Health Services Administration). (2017, February 15). *Services grant program for residential treatment for pregnant and postpartum women*. SAMHSA. Retrieved from https://www.samhsa.gov.

Samorodnitzky-Naveh, G., Geiger, S. B., & Levin, L. (2007). Patients' satisfaction with dental esthetics. *Journal of the American Dental Association, 138*(6), 805–808.

Samos, L. F., Aguilar, E., & Ouslander, J. G. (2010). Institutional long-term care in the United States. In H. M. Fillit, K. Rockwood, & K. Woodhouse (Eds.), *Brocklehurst's textbook of geriatric medicine and gerontology* (7th ed.). Philadelphia, PA: Saunders Publishers.

Sampath, G., Shah, A., Kraska, J., & Soni, S. D. (1992). Neuroleptic discontinuation in the very stable schizophrenic patient: Relapse rates and serum neuroleptic levels. *Human Psychopharmacology: Clinical and Experimental, 7*(4), 255–264.

Sample, I. (2015, November 14). Was Ripon school gripped by mass psychogenic illness? *The Guardian*. Retrieved from https://www.theguardian.com/science/2015/nov/14.

Samuels, J., Wang, Y., Riddle, M. A., Greenberg, B. D., Fyer, A. J., McCracken, J. T., . . . Nestadt, G. (2011). Comprehensive family-based association study of the glutamate transporter gene SLC1A1 in obsessive-compulsive disorder. *American Journal of Medical Genetics Part B, 156*, 472–477.

Sanburn, J. (2013, September 13). Inside the National Suicide Hotline: Preventing the next tragedy. *Time.com*.

Sanchez, A. L., Cornacchio, D., Chou, T., Leyfer, O., Coxe, S., Pincus, D. B., & Comer, J. S. (2017). Development of a scale to evaluate young children's responses to uncertainty and low environmental structure. *Journal of Anxiety Disorders, 45*, 17–23.

Sanchez, A. L., Kendall, P. C., & Comer, J. S. (2016). Evaluating the intergenerational link between maternal and child intolerance of uncertainty: A preliminary cross-sectional examination. *Cognitive Therapy and Research, 40*, 532–539.

Sanders, T. (2016, December 1). *The Oxford handbook of sex offences and sex offenders* (1st edition). New York: Oxford University Press.

Sandler, C. X., Goldstein, D., Horsfield, S., Bennett, B. K., Friedlander, M., Bastick, P. A., . . . Lloyd, A. R. (2017, May 11). Randomized evaluation of cognitive-behavioral therapy and graded exercise therapy for post-cancer fatigue. *Journal of Pain and Symptom Management*. [Epub ahead of print]

Sandler, I., Wolchik, S. A., Cruden, G., Mahrer, N. E., Ahn, S., Brincks, A., & Brown, C. H. (2014). Overview of meta-analyses of the prevention of mental health, substance use, and conduct problems. *Annual Review of Clinical Psychology, 10*, 243–273.

Sandler, I. N., Wolchik, S. A., & Ayers, T. S. (2008). Resilience rather than recovery: A contextual framework on adaptation following bereavement. *Death Studies, 32*, 59–73.

Sandler, M. (1990). Monoamine oxidase inhibitors in depression: History and mythology. *Journal of Psychopharmacology, 4*(3), 136–139.

Sanftner, J. L., & Tantillo, M. (2011). Body image and eating disorders: A compelling source of shame for women. In R. L. Dearing & J. P. Tangney (Eds.), *Shame in the therapy hour* (pp. 277–303). Washington, DC: American Psychological Association.

Sanger-Katz, M. (2014, August 13). The science behind suicide contagion. *The New York Times*.

Sansone, R. A., & Sansone, L. A. (2011). Personality disorders: A nation-based perspective on prevalence. *Innovations in Clinical Neuroscience, 8*(4), 13–18.

Sareen, J. (2015, December 15). Posttraumatic stress disorder in adults: Epidemiology, pathophysiology, clinical manifestations, course, assessment, and diagnosis. *UpToDate*. Retrieved from http://www.uptodate.com.

Sareen, J., Afifi, T. O., McMillan, K. A., & Asmundson, G. J. G. (2011). Relationship between household income and mental disorders: Findings from a population-based longitudinal study. *Archives of General Psychiatry, 68*(4), 419–426.

Sarin, F., & Wallin, L. (2014). Cognitive model and cognitive behavior therapy for schizophrenia: An overview. *Nordic Journal of Psychiatry, 68*(3), 145–153.

Savino, A. C., & Fordtran, J. S. (2006). Factitious disease: Clinical lessons from case studies at Baylor University Medical Center. *Proceedings (Baylor University Medical Center), 19*(3), 195–208.

Savitz, J., & Drevets, W. C. (2011). Neuroimaging and neuropathological findings in bipolar disorder. In C. A. Zarate, Jr. & H. K. Manji (Eds.), *Bipolar depression. Molecular neurobiology, clinical diagnosis and pharmacotherapy. Milestones in drug therapy* (pp. 201–225). Cambridge, MA: Birkhäuser.

Sawni, A., & Breuner, C. C. (2017, March 24). Clinical hypnosis, an effective mind-body modality for adolescents with behavioral and physical complaints. *Children (Basel), 4*(4).

Scheuerman, O., Grinbaum, I., & Garty, B. Z. (2013). Münchausen syndrome by proxy. *Harefuah, 152*(11), 639.

Scheuermann, B., Webber, J., Boutot, E. A., & Goodwin, M. (2003). Problems with personnel preparation in autism spectrum disorders. *Focus on Autism and Other Developmental Disabilities, 18*, 197–206.

Schienle, A., Hettema, J. M., Cáceda, R., & Nemeroff, C. B. (2011). Neurobiology and genetics of generalized anxiety disorder. *Psychiatric Annals, 41*(2), 111–123.

Schildkraut, J. J. (1965). The catecholamine hypothesis of affective disorders: A review of supporting evidence. *American Journal of Psychiatry, 122*(5), 509–522.

Schiller, B. (2014). *Hiding GPS inside shoes to keep track of wandering Alzheimer's patients*. New York: Co.Exist. Retrieved from http://www.fastcoexist.com/30225268.

Schlarb, A. A., Jaeger, S., Schneider, S., In-Ablon, T., & Hautzinger, M. (2016). Sleep problems and separation anxiety in preschool-aged children: A path analysis. *Journal of Child and Family Studies, 25*, 902–910.

Schmidt, A. F., Gykiere, K., Vanhoeck, K., Mann, R. E., & Banse, R. (2014). Direct and indirect measures of sexual maturity preferences differentiate subtypes of child sexual abusers. *Sexual Abuse, 26*(2), 107–128.

Schmidt, A. F., Mokros, A., & Banse, R. (2013). Is pedophilic sexual preference continuous? A taxometric analysis based on direct and indirect measures. *Psychological Assessment, 25*(4), 1146–1153.

Schmidt, H. M., Munder, T., Gerger, H., Frühauf, S., & Barth, J. (2014). Combination of psychological interventions and phosphodiesterase-5 inhibitors for erectile dysfunction: A narrative review and meta-analysis. *Journal of Sexual Medicine, 11*, 1376–1391.

Schmidtman, E. A., Hurley, R. A., & Taber, K. H. (2017). Secular mindfulness-based interventions: Efficacy and neurobiology. *Journal of Neuropsychiatry and Clinical Neurosciences, 29*(2), A6–A83.

Schneider, K. J., & Krug, O. T. (2010). *Existential–humanistic therapy. Theories of psychotherapy*. Washington, DC: American Psychological Association.

Schneider, K. L., & Shenassa, E. (2008). Correlates of suicide ideation in a population-based sample of cancer patients. *Journal of Psychosocial Oncology, 26*(2) 49–62.

Schneier, F. R. (2016, April 13). Social anxiety disorder in adults: Epidemiology, clinical manifestations, and diagnosis. *UpToDate*. Retrieved from http://www.uptodate.com.

Schoonover, K. E., McCollum, L. A., & Roberts, R. C. (2017). Protein markers of neurotransmitter synthesis and release in post-mortem schizophrenia substantia nigra. *Neuropsychopharmacology, 42*(2), 540–550.

Schrag, M., Mueller, C., Oyoyo, U., Smith, M. A., & Kirsch, W. M. (2011). Iron, zinc and copper in the Alzheimer's disease brain: A quantitative meta-analysis. Some insight on the influence of citation bias on scientific opinion. *Progress in Neurobiology, 94*(3), 296–306.

Schreiber, F. R. (1973). *Sybil*. Chicago: Regnery.

Schreiber, J., & Culpepper, L. (2016, August 8). Suicidal ideation and behavior in adults. *UpToDate*. Retrieved from http://www.uptodate.com.

Schreier, H. A., Ayoub, C. C., & Bursch, B. (2010). Forensic issues in Munchausen by Proxy. In E. P. Benedek, P. Ash, & C. L. Scott (Eds.), *Principles and practice of child and adolescent forensic mental health* (pp. 241–252). Arlington, VA: American Psychiatric Publishing.

Schuch, F. B., Morres, I. D., Ekkekakis, P., & Rosenbaum, S. (2017, April). Exercise works for depression: Bridging the implementation gap and making exercise a core component of treatment. *Acta Neuropsychiatrica, 29*(2), 124–126.

Schulman, J. K., & Erickson-Schroth, L. (2017). Mental health in sexual minority and transgender women. *Psychiatric Clinics of North America, 40*(2), 309–319.

Schultz, D. S., & Brabender, V. M. (2012). More challenges since Wikipedia: The effects of exposure to internet information about the Rorschach on selected comprehensive system variables. *Journal of Personality Assessment, 95*(2), 149–158.

Schultz, L. T., Heimberg, R. G., & Rodebaugh, T. L. (2008). Social anxiety disorder. In M. Hersen & J. Rosqvist (Eds.), *Handbook of psychological assessment, case conceptualization, and treatment, Vol. 1: Adults* (pp. 204–236). Hoboken, NJ: John Wiley & Sons.

Schulz, S., & Laessle, R. G. (2012). Stress-induced laboratory eating behavior in obese women with binge eating disorder. *Appetite, 58*(2), 457–461.

Schumm, J. A., Koucky, E. M., & Bartel, A. (2014). Associations between perceived social reactions to trauma-related experiences with PTSD and depression among veterans seeking PTSD treatment. *Journal of Traumatic Stress, 27*(1), 50–57.

Schumm, J. A., Walter, K. H., Bartone, A. S., & Chard, K. M. (2015). Veteran satisfaction and treatment preferences in response to a posttraumatic stress disorder specialty clinic orientation group. *Behaviour Research and Therapy, 69*, 75–82.

Schuster, S. (2016, April 6). Facebook creates new support tool to help people who are suicidal. *The Mighty*. Retrieved from http://www.themighty.com.

Schwartz, M. (2011). The retrospective profile and the facilitated family retreat. In J. R. Jordan & J. L. McIntosh (Eds.), *Grief after suicide: Understanding the consequences and caring for the survivors. Series in death, dying and bereavement* (pp. 371–379). New York: Routledge/Taylor & Francis Group.

Schwartz, R. C., & Blankenship, D. M. (2014). Racial disparities in psychotic disorder diagnosis: A review of empirical literature. *World Journal of Psychiatry, 4*(4), 133–140.

Schwartz, R. J., Sison, C., Kerath, S. M., Murphy, L., Breil, T., Sikavi, D., & Taioli, E. (2015). The impact of Hurricane Sandy on the mental health of New York area residents. *American Journal of Disaster Medicine, 10*(4), 339–346.

Schwartz, S. (1993). *Classic studies in abnormal psychology*. Mountain View, CA: Mayfield Publishing.

Schwartzman, C. M., Boisseau, C. L., Sibrava, N. J., Mancebo, M. C., Eisen, J. L., & Rasmussen, S. A. (2017). Symptom subtype and quality of life in obsessive-compulsive disorder. *Psychiatry Research, 249*, 307–310.

Schwarz, A. (2010, October 20). As injuries rise, scant oversight of helmet safety. *New York Times*.

Schwarz, A., & Cohen, S. (2013, March 31). ADHD seen in 11% of U.S. children as diagnoses rise. *New York Times*.

Scimeca, G., Alborghetti, A., Bruno, A., Troili, G. M., Pandolfo, G., Muscatello, M. R., & Zoccali, R. A. (2016). Self-worth and psychological adjustment of obese children: An analysis through the Draw-A-Person. *World Journal of Psychiatry, 6*(3), 329–338.

Seaward, B. L. (2013). *Essentials of managing stress*. (3rd ed.). Burlington, MA: Jones & Bartlett Learning.

Sebastian, R. S., Goldman, J. D., & Enns, C. W. (2010, September). *Snacking patterns of U.S. adolescents. Food Surveys Research Group, Dietary Data Brief No. 2*. Retrieved from www.ars.usda.gov/ba/bhnrc/fsrg.

Sebert, K. R. (2014, July 17). Kesha reborn. *Elle Magazine* (UK edition).

Sedghi, A. (2013). 10 years of bullying data: What does it tell us? *The Guardian*. Retrieved from http://www.theguardian.com/news/datablog/2013/may/23/.

Seeman, P. (2011). Schizophrenia diagnosis and treatment. *CNS Neuroscience & Therapeutics, 17*(2), 81–82.

Seery, M. D., Holman, E. A., & Silver, R. C. (2010). Whatever does not kill us: Cumulative lifetime adversity, vulnerability, and resilience. *Journal of Personality and Social Psychology, 99*, 1025–1041.

Segal, R. (2008). *The national association for retarded citizens*. Silver Spring, MD: The Arc.

Segal, Z. (2017, January 10). Mindfulness based cognitive therapy as maintenance treatment for unipolar major depression. *UpToDate*. Retrieved from http://www.uptodate.com.

Seiden, R. H. (1981). Mellowing with age: Factors influencing the nonwhite suicide rate. *International Journal of Aging and Human Development, 13*, 265–284.

Seidman, L. J., & Nordentoft, M. (2015). New targets for prevention of schizophrenia: Is it time for interventions in the premorbid phase? *Schizophrenia Bulletin, 41*(4), 795–800.

Seitz, D., Purandare, N., & Conn, D. (2010). Prevalence of psychiatric disorders among older adults in long-term care homes: A systematic review. *International Psychogeriatrics, 22*(7), 1025–1039.

Seligman, M. E. P. (1971). Phobias and preparedness. *Behavior Therapist, 2*, 307–320.

Seligman, M. E. P. (1975). *Helplessness*. San Francisco: Freeman.

Seligman, M. E. P. (2002). *Authentic happiness: Using the new positive psychology to realize your potential for lasting fulfillment*. New York: Free Press.

Seligman, M. E. P. (2012, paperback). *Flourish: A visionary new understanding of happiness and well-being*. New York: Atria Books.

Seligman, M. E. P., & Fowler, R. D. (2011). Comprehensive soldier fitness and the future of psychology. *American Psychologist, 66*(1), 82–86.

Selkoe, D. J. (1992). Alzheimer's disease: New insights into an emerging epidemic. *Journal of Geriatric Psychiatry, 25*(2), 211–227.

Selkoe, D. J. (2011). Alzheimer's disease. *Cold Spring Harbor Perspectives in Biology, 3*(7).

Selle, V., Schalkwijk, S., Vázquez, G. H., & Baldessarini, R. J. (2014). Treatments for acute bipolar depression: Meta-analyses of placebo-controlled, monotherapy trials of anticonvulsants, lithium and antipsychotics. *Pharmacopsychiatry, 47*(2), 43–52.

Selling, L. S. (1940). *Men against madness*. New York: Greenberg.

Sergeant, S., & Mongrain, M. (2014). An online optimism intervention reduces depression in pessimistic individuals. *Journal of Consulting and Clinical Psychology, 82*(2), 263–274.

Seto, M. C. (2008). *Pedophilia and sexual offending against children: Theory, assessment, and intervention*. Washington, DC: American Psychological Association.

Seto, M. C., Kingston, D. A., & Bourget, D. (2014). Assessment of the paraphilias. *Psychiatric Clinics of North America, 37*(2), 149–161.

Sevarino, K. (2016, August 29). Medically supervised opioid withdrawal during treatment for addiction. *UpToDate*. Retrieved from http://www.uptodate.com.

Shaffer, J. J., Peterson, M. J., McMahon, M. A., Bizzell, J., Calhoun, V., van Erp, T. G., . . . Belger, A. (2015). Neural correlates of schizophrenia negative symptoms: Distinct subtypes impact dissociable brain circuits. *Molecular Neuropsychiatry, 1*(4), 191–200.

Shafi, A. M. A., & Shafi, R. M. A. (2014). Cultural influences on the presentation of depression. *Open Journal of Psychiatry, 4*, 390–395.

Shain, M., & AAP Committee on Adolescence. (2016). Suicide and suicide attempts in adolescents. *Pediatrics, 138*(1).

Shapiro, E. R. (2004). Discussion of Ernst Prelinger's "Thoughts on hate and aggression." *Psychoanalytic Study of the Child, 39*, 44–51.

Shapiro, F., & Forrest, M. S. (2016). *EMDR: The breakthrough therapy for overcoming anxiety, stress, and trauma*. New York: Hachette Book Group.

Shapiro, J. R., Bauer, S., Andrews, E., Pisetsky, E., Bulik-Sullivan, B., Hamer, R. M., & Bulik, C. M. (2010). Text messaging in the treatment of bulimia nervosa. *Clinician's Research Digest, 28*(12).

Sharf, R. S. (2015). *Theories of psychotherapy & counseling: Concepts and cases* (6th edition). Belmont, CA: Brooks Cole.

Sharif, F., Mahmoudi, A., Shooshtari, A. A., & Vossoughi, M. (2016). The effect of family-centered psycho-education on mental health and quality of life of families of adolescents with bipolar mood disorder: A randomized controlled clinical trial. *International Journal of Community Based Nursing and Midwifery, 4*(3), 229–238.

Sharma, A., Madaan, V., & Petty, F. D. (2006). Exercise for mental health. *Primary Care Companion, Journal of Clinical Psychiatry.* (2), 106.

Sharpe, K. (2012). *Coming of age on Zoloft: How antidepressants cheered us up, let us down, and changed who we are.* New York: HarperCollins.

Shaw, K. (2004). *Oddballs and eccentrics.* Edison, NJ: Castle Books.

Shaw, R. J., Spratt, E. G., Bernard, R. S., & DeMaso, D. R. (2010). Somatoform disorders. In R. J. Shaw & D. R. DeMaso (Eds.), *Textbook of pediatric psychosomatic medicine* (pp. 121–139). Arlington, VA: American Psychiatric Publishing.

Shean, G. (2016). Psychotherapy outcome research: Issues and questions. *Psychodynamic Psychiatry, 44*(1), 1–24.

Sheerin, C. M., Lind, M. J., Bountress, K., Nugent, N. R., & Amstadter, A. B. (2017). The genetics and epigenetics of PTSD: Overview, recent advances, and future directions. *Current Opinion in Psychology, 14,* 5–11.

Shehab, N., Lovegrove, M. C., Geller, A. I., Rose, K. O., Weidle, N. J., & Budnitz, D. S. (2016). US emergency department visits for outpatient adverse drug events, 2013–2014. *JAMA, 316*(20), 2115–2125.

Sheikh, K. (2017, August 10). Do you hear what I hear? Auditory hallucinations yield clues to perception. *Scientific American.*

Sheldon, P. (2008). The relationship between unwillingness-to-communicate and student's Facebook use. *Journal of Media Psychology, 20*(2), 67–75.

Sheng, C., Huang, Y., & Han, Y. (2018). Dissection of prodromal Alzheimer's disease. *Frontiers in Bioscience (Landmark Edition), 23,* 1272–1291.

Shengchao, Y., Brackbill, R. M., Locke, S., Stellman, S. D., & Gargano, L. M. (2016). Impact of 9/11-related chronic conditions and PTSD comorbidity on early retirement and job loss among World Trade Center disaster rescue and recovery workers. *American Journal of Industrial Medicine, 59*(9), 731–741.

Shenk, D. (2001). *The forgetting: Alzheimer's: Portrait of an epidemic.* New York: Doubleday.

Shepherd, J. (2016). "I am very glad and cheered when I hear the flute": The treatment of criminal lunatics in late Victorian Broadmoor. *Medical History, 60*(4), 473–491.

Shepphird, S. (2016, January 4). Interview. In K. Miller, The shocking results of Yahoo Health's Body Positivity Survey. *Yahoo.com.*

Sher, K. J. (Ed.). (2016). *Oxford handbook of substance use and substance use disorders* (Volumes 1 & 2). New York, NY: Oxford University Press.

Sher, L. (2015). Suicide medical malpractice: An educational overview. *International Journal of Adolescent Medicine and Health, 27*(2), 203–206.

Sher, L., Fisher, A. M., Kelliher, C. H., Penner, J. D., Goodman, M., Koenigsberg, H. W., . . . Hazlett, E. A. (2016). Clinical features and psychiatric comorbidities of borderline personality disorder patients with versus without a history of suicide attempt. *Psychiatry Research, 246,* 261–266.

Sheras, P., & Worchel, S. (1979). *Clinical psychology: A social psychological approach.* New York: Van Nostrand.

Shergill, S. S., Brammer, M. J., Williams, S. R., Murray, R. M., & McGuire, P. K. (2000). Mapping auditory hallucinations in schizophrenia using functional magnetic resonance imaging. *Archives of General Psychiatry, 57*(11), 1033–1038.

Sherry, A., & Whilde, M. R. (2008). Borderline personality disorder. In M. Hersen & J. Rosqvist (Eds.), *Handbook of psychological assessment, case conceptualization and treatment, Vol. 1: Adults* (pp. 403–437). Hoboken, NJ: John Wiley & Sons.

Sherva, R., & Kowall, N. W. (2016, November 11). Genetics of Alzheimer disease. *UpToDate.* Retrieved from http://www.uptodate.com.

Shields, B. (2010). The advantages of animal testing. *eHOW.* Retrieved from www.ehow.com/print/list_5996753_advantages-animal-testing.html.

Shifren, J. L. (2016, April 4). Sexual dysfunction in women: Epidemiology, risk factors, and evaluation. *UpToDate.* Retrieved from http://www.uptodate.com.

Shifren, J. L. (2017, April 14). Sexual dysfunction in women: Management. *UpToDate.* Retrieved from http://www.uptodate.com.

Shin, Y. C., Lee, D., Seol, J., & Lim, S. W. (2017). What kind of stress is associated with depression, anxiety and suicidal ideation in Korean employees? *Journal of Korean Medical Science, 32*(5), 843–849.

Shinba, T. (2017). Major depressive disorder and generalized anxiety disorder show different autonomic dysregulations revealed by heart-rate variability analysis in first-onset drug-naive patients without comorbidity. *Psychiatry and Clinical Neurosciences, 71*(2), 135–145.

Shipherd, J. C., Salters-Pedneault, K., & Matza, A. (2016). Intrusive cognitive content and postdeployment distress. *Journal of Traumatic Stress, 29,* 301–308.

Shiratori, Y., Tachikawa, H., Nemoto, K., Endo, G., Aiba, M., Matsui, Y., & Asada, T. (2014). Network analysis for motives in suicide cases: A cross-sectional study. *Psychiatry and Clinical Neurosciences, 68*(4), 299–307.

Shire, S. Y., Chang, Y. C., Shih, W., Bracaglia, S., Kodjoe, M., & Kasari, C. (2017). Hybrid implementation model of community-partnered early intervention for toddlers with autism: A randomized trial. *Journal of Child Psychology and Psychiatry, 58,* 612–622.

Shnaider, P., Pukay-Martin, N. D., Fredman, S. J., Macdonald, A., & Monson, C. M. (2014). Effects of cognitive-behavioral conjoint therapy for PTSD on partners' psychological functioning. *Journal of Traumatic Stress, 27*(2), 129–136.

Shneidman, E. S. (1963). Orientations toward death: Subintentioned death and indirect suicide. In R. W. White (Ed.), *The study of lives.* New York: Atherton.

Shneidman, E. S. (1979). An overview: Personality, motivation, and behavior theories. In L. D. Hankoff & B. Einsidler (Eds.), *Suicide: Theory and clinical aspects.* Littleton, MA: PSG Publishing.

Shneidman, E. S. (1981). Suicide. *Suicide and Life-Threatening Behavior, 11*(4), 198–220.

Shneidman, E. S. (1985). *Definition of suicide.* New York: Wiley.

Shneidman, E. S. (1987, March). At the point of no return. *Psychology Today.*

Shneidman, E. S. (1993). *Suicide as psychache: A clinical approach to self-destructive behavior.* Northvale, NJ: Jason Aronson.

Shneidman, E. S. (2001). *Comprehending suicide: Landmarks in 20th-century suicidology.* Washington, DC: American Psychological Association.

Shneidman, E. S. (2005). Anodyne psychotherapy for suicide: A psychological view of suicide. *Clinical Neuropsychiatry, 2*(1), 7–12.

Shneidman, E. S., & Farberow, N. (1968). The Suicide Prevention Center of Los Angeles. In H. L. P. Resnick (Ed.), *Suicidal behaviors: Diagnosis and management.* Boston: Little, Brown.

Shou, H., Yang, Z., Satterthwaite, T. D., Cook, P. A., Bruce, S. E., Shinohara, R. T., . . . Sheline, Y. I. (2017). Cognitive behavioral therapy increases amygdala connectivity with the cognitive control network in both MDD and PTSD. *NeuroImage: Clinical, 14,* 464–470.

Shuttleworth-Edwards, A. B. (2016). Generally representative is representative of none: Commentary on the pitfalls of IQ test standardization in multicultural settings. *Clinical Neuropsychologist, 30*(7), 975–998.

Sibley, M. H., Campez, M., & Ralker, J. S. (2018). Reexamining ADHD-related self-reporting problems using polynomial regression. *Assessment.* [Manuscript in press]

Sibley, M. H., Kuriyan, A. B., Evans, S. W., Waxmonsky, J. G., & Smith, B. H. (2014). Pharmacological and psychosocial treatments for adolescents with ADHD: An updated systematic review of the literature. *Clinical Psychology Review, 34*(3), 218–232.

Sicile-Kira, C. (2014). *Autism spectrum disorder (revised): The complete guide to understanding autism.* New York: Perigee Trade.

Sidran Institute. (2016). *Post traumatic stress disorder fact sheet.* Retrieved from https://www.sidran.org.

Siemaszko, C. (2006, February 2). Cybersplit online affair spurs off-line divorce. *New York Daily News.*

Siemens Healthcare. (2013, May 6). *Survey: The value of knowing.* Press Release.

Sifferlin, A. (2013, April 10). Doctors not informed of drug side effects during sales visits. *Time.*

Sifferlin, A. (2013, May 15). Looking good on Facebook: Social media leads to spikes in plastic surgery requests. *Time.*

Sifferlin, A. (2013, September 6). Social media: Why selfies matter. *Time.*

Sifferlin, A. (2013, October 31). Bad news about your favorite health apps: They don't work. *Time.*

Sifferlin, A. (2013, December 5). Dementia cases expected to triple in coming decades. *Time.*

Sifferlin, A. (2014, January 15). Mashed up memory: How alcohol speeds memory loss in men. *Time.*

Sifferlin, A. (2017, May 22). Gender confirmation surgery is on the rise in the U.S. *TIME Health.*

Sigerist, H. E. (1943). *Civilization and disease.* Ithaca, NY: Cornell University Press.

Sigurdsson, T. (2016). Neural circuit dysfunction in schizophrenia: Insights from animal models. *Neuroscience, 321,* 42–65.

Silbersweig, D. A., Stern, E., Frith, C., Cahill, C., Holmes, A., Grootoonk, S, . . . Frackowiak, R. S. J. (1995). A functional neuroanatomy of hallucinations in schizophrenia. *Nature, 378*, 176–179.

Silk, J. S., Tan, P. Z., Ladouceur, C. D., Meller, S., Siegle, G. J., McMakin, D. L., . . . Ryan, N. D. (2018). A randomized clinical trial comparing individual cognitive behavioral therapy and child-centered therapy for child anxiety disorders. *Journal of Clinical Child and Adolescent Psychology.* [Manuscript in press]

Silk, K. R., & Jibson, M. D. (2010). Personality disorders. In M. D. Rothschild & J. Anthony (Eds.), *The evidence-based guide to antipsychotic medications* (pp. 101–124). Arlington, VA: American Psychiatric Publishing.

Silva, C., Hagan, C. R., Rogers, M. L., Chiurliza, B., Podlogar, M. C., Horn, M. A., . . . Joiner, T. E. (2017). Evidence for the propositions of the interpersonal theory of suicide among a military sample. *Journal of Clinical Psychology. 73*(6), 669–680.

Silverman, K., Evans, S. M., Strain, E. C., & Griffiths, R. R. (1992). Withdrawal syndrome after the double-blind cessation of caffeine consumption. *New England Journal of Medicine, 327*(16), 1109–1114.

Silverstein, M. L. (2007). Descriptive psychopathology and theoretical viewpoints: Paranoid, obsessive-compulsive, and borderline personality disorders. In M. L. Silverstein, *Disorders of the self: A personality-guided approach* (pp. 97–113). Washington, DC: American Psychological Association.

Simard, V., Nielsen, T. A., Tremblay, R. E., Boivin, M., & Montplaisir, J. Y. (2008). Longitudinal study of bad dreams in preschool-aged children: Prevalence, demographic correlates, risk and protective factors. *Sleep, 31*(1), 62–70.

Simeon, D. (2015, August 27). Depersonalization/derealization disorder: Epidemiology, pathogenesis, clinical manifestations, course, and diagnosis. *UpToDate.* Retrieved from http://www.uptodate.com.

Simeon, D. (2017, April 4). Psychotherapy of depersonalization/derealization disorder. *UpToDate.* Retrieved from http://www.uptodate.com.

Simmon, J. (1990). Media and market study. In skin deep: Our national obsession with looks. *Psychology Today, 26*(3), 96.

Simon, G., & Ciechanowski, P. (2015, December 23). Unipolar major depression in adults: Choosing initial treatment. *UpToDate.* Retrieved from http://www.uptodate.com.

Simon, G., & Ciechanowski, P. (2017, March 17). Unipolar depression in adults and initial treatment: General principles and prognosis. *UpToDate.* Retrieved from http://www.uptodate.com.

Simon, H. (2013, August 29). In-depth report: Complications of peptic ulcer. *New York Times.*

Simon, R. (Ed.) (2011). *Psychotherapy Networker.* Retrieved from www.psychotherapynetworker.org.

Simon, V. A., Feiring, C., & Cleland, C. M. (2016). Early stigmatization, PTSD, and perceived negative reactions of others predict subsequent strategies for processing child sexual abuse. *Psychology of Violence, 6*(1), 112–123.

Simonton, D. K. (2010). So you want to become a creative genius? You must be crazy! In

D. H. Cropley, A. J. Cropley, J. C. Kaufman, & M. A. Runco (Eds.), *The dark side of creativity* (pp. 218–234). New York: Cambridge University Press.

Simpson, H. B. (2015, January 21). Pharmacotherapy for obsessive-compulsive disorder in adults. *UpToDate.* Retrieved from http://www.uptodate.com.

Simpson, H. B. (2016, March 6). Obsessive-compulsive disorder in adults: Epidemiology, pathogenesis, clinical manifestations, course, and diagnosis. *UpToDate.* Retrieved from http://www.uptodate.com.

Simpson, J. R. (2008). Functional MRI lie detection: Too good to be true? *Journal of the American Academy of Psychiatry and the Law, 36*(4), 491–498.

Singal, J. (2017, May 12). Psychologists: Stop blaming mass shootings on video games. *New York Magazine.*

Singh, A. (2013, July 16). Dementia rate in the elderly has dropped 24% in past 20 years: What this means for coming generations. *Medical Daily.com.*

Singh, G. K., & Siahpush, M. (2014). Widening rural-urban disparities in all-cause mortality and mortality from major causes of death in the USA, 1969–2009. *Journal of Urban Health, 91*(2), 272–292.

Singh, S., Kumar, A., Agarwal, S., Phadke, S. R., & Jaiswal, Y. (2014). Genetic insight of schizophrenia: Past and future perspectives. *Gene, 535*(2), 97–100.

Sipe, T. A., Finnie, R. C., Knopf, J. A., Qu, S., Reynolds, J. A., Thota, A. B., . . . Nease, D. J. (2015). Effects of mental health benefits legislation: A community guide systematic review. *American Journal of Preventive Medicine, 48*(6), 755–766.

Sirey, J. A., Franklin, A. J., McKenzie, S. E., Ghosh, S., & Raue, P. J. (2014). Race, stigma, and mental health referrals among clients of aging services who screened positive for depression. *Psychiatric Services, 65*(4), 537–540.

Siris, S. G., & Braga, R. J. (2016, September 22). Depression in schizophrenia. *UpToDate.* Retrieved from http://www.uptodate.com.

Siris, S. G., & Braga, R. J. (2017, March 13). Anxiety in schizophrenia. *UpToDate.* Retrieved from http://www.uptodate.com.

Sitt, D. (2013, June 18). Dear Technology . . . Signed Mindfully. *Psychology Today.*

Sizemore, C. C. (1991). *A mind of my own: The woman who was known as "Eve" tells the story of her triumph over multiple personality disorder.* New York: William Morrow.

Sizemore, C. C., & Pitillo, E. S. (1977). *I'm Eve.* Garden City, NY: Doubleday.

Skinner, B. F. (1957). *Verbal behavior.* Englewood Cliffs, NJ: Prentice-Hall.

Skinner, B. F. (1958). Diagramming schedules of reinforcement. *Journal of the Experimental Analysis of Behavior, 1*, 67–68.

Skodol, A. (2016, February 18). Personality disorders. *UpToDate.* Retrieved from http://www.uptodate.com.

Skodol, A. (2016, February 23). Treatment of borderline personality disorder. *UpToDate.* Retrieved from http://www.uptodate.com.

Skodol, A. (2017, April 27). Borderline personality disorder: Epidemiology, clinical features, course, assessment, and diagnosis. *UpToDate.* Retrieved from http://www.uptodate.com.

Skodol, A., & Bender, D. (2016, September 2). Approaches to the therapeutic relationship in patients with personality disorders. *UpToDate.* Retrieved from http://www.uptodate.com.

Skodol, A., & Bender, D. (2016, September 26). Establishing and maintaining a therapeutic relationship in psychiatric practice. *UpToDate.* Retrieved from http://www.uptodate.com.

Slater, M. D., Kelly, K. J., Lawrence, F. R., Stanley, L. R., & Comello, M. L. G. (2011). Assessing media campaigns linking marijuana non-use with autonomy and aspirations: "Be under your own influence" and ONDCP's "above the influence." *Prevention Science, 12*(1), 12–22.

Slavich, G. M., & Irwin, M. R. (2014). From stress to inflammation and major depressive disorder: A social signal transduction theory of depression. *Psychological Bulletin, 140*(3), 774–815.

Slesnick N., & Zhang, J. (2016). Family systems therapy for substance-using mothers and their 8- to 16-year-old children. *Psychology of Addictive Behaviors, 30*(6), 619–629.

Sloan, D. M. (2002). Does warm weather climate affect eating disorder pathology? *International Journal of Eating Disorders, 32*, 240–244.

Slovenko, R. (2004). A history of the intermix of psychiatry and law. *Journal of Psychiatry and Law, 32*(4), 561–592.

Slovenko, R. (2009). *Psychiatry in law/Law in psychiatry* (2nd ed.). New York: Routledge/Taylor & Francis Group.

Slovenko, R. (2011). Psychotherapy testimonial privilege in criminal cases. Presentation at American College of Forensic Psychiatry conference, San Diego, CA. March 23, 2011.

Sluhovsky, M. (2007). *Believe not every spirit: Possession, mysticism, & discernment in early modern Catholicism.* Chicago: University of Chicago Press.

Sluhovsky, M. (2011). Spirit possession and other alterations of consciousness in the Christian Western tradition. In E. Cardeña & M. Winkelman (Eds.), *Altering consciousness: Multidisciplinary perspectives (Vols. 1 and 2): History, culture, and the humanities: Biological and psychological perspectives* (pp. 73–88). Santa Barbara, CA: Praeger/ABC-CLIO.

SMA (SurveyMonkey Audience). (2017, June 21). Study: Feeling selfie-ish? You're not alone. *SurveyMonkey.* Retrieved from https://www.surveymonkey.com/blog.

Smallwood, R. F., Potter, J. S., & Robin, D. A. (2016). Neurophysiological mechanisms in acceptance and commitment therapy in opioid-addicted patients with chronic pain. *Psychiatry Research, 250*, 12–14.

Smart-Richman, L., Pek, J., Pascoe, E., & Bauer, D. J. (2010). Discrimination is bad for your health. *Clinician's Research Digest, 28*(11).

Smietana, B. (2016, December 6). Most Americans say assisted suicide is morally acceptable. *Lifeway Research.*

Smith, A. (2014). *6 new facts about Facebook.* Washington, DC: Pew Research Center.

Smith, A. B., Butow, P., Olver, I., Luckett, T., Grimison, P., Toner, G. C., . . . King, M. T. (2016). The prevalence, severity, and correlates of psychological distress and impaired health-related quality of life following treatment for testicular cancer: A survivorship study. *Journal of Cancer Survivorship, 10*(2), 223–233.

Smith, A. J., & Hughes, M. (2016). Challenges to the empirical investigation of mass shootings. In L. C. Wilson (Ed.). *The Wiley handbook of the psychology of mass shootings* (Ch. 1, pp. 3–19). Hoboken, NJ: Wiley-Blackwell.

Smith, A. J., & Smith, L. A. (2016). Viral carcinogenesis. *Progress in Molecular Biology and Translational Science, 144,* 121–168.

Smith, B. L., Lyons, C. E., Correa, F. G., Benoit, S. C., Myers, B., Solomon, M. B., & Herman, J. P. (2017). Behavioral and physiological consequences of enrichment loss in rats. *Psychoneuroendocrinology, 77,* 37–46.

Smith, K., & Milazzo-Sayre, L. (2014, August 7). *Highlights of the National Mental Health Services Survey, 2010.* Rockville, MD: NCBI Bookshelf, The CBHSQ Report.

Smith, M., Segal, R., & Segal, J. (2017). Phobias and irrational fears. *Helpguide.org.*

Smith, M. L., & Glass, G. V. (1977). Meta-analysis of psychotherapy outcome studies. *American Psychologist, 32*(9), 752–760.

Smith, M. L., Glass, G. V., & Miller, T. I. (1980). *The benefits of psychotherapy.* Baltimore: Johns Hopkins University Press.

Smith, R., Shepard, C., Wiltgen, A., Rufino, K., & Fowler, J. C. (2017). Treatment outcomes for inpatients with obsessive-compulsive personality disorder: An open comparison trial. *Journal of Affective Disorders, 209,* 273–278.

Smith, T. (2008, January 29). Real-life fears faced in online world: Helping alter-egos in "second life" helps people cope. *CBS News.* Retrieved from http:www.cbsnews.com/video/watch/?id=3764862.

Smith, T., & Iadarola, S. (2015). Evidence base update for autism spectrum disorder. *Journal of Clinical Child and Adolescent Psychology, 44,* 897–922.

Smith, T. W. (2007). *Job satisfaction in the United States.* Chicago, IL: University of Chicago.

Smith, Y., & Spitzmueller, M. C. (2016). Worker perspectives on contemporary milieu therapy: A cross-site ethnographic study. *Social Work Research, 40*(2), 105–116.

Smyth, J. M., & Pennebaker, J. W. (2001). What are the health effects of disclosure? In A. Baum, T. A. Revenson, & J. E. Singer (Eds.), *Handbook of health psychology* (pp. 339–348). Mahwah, NJ: Lawrence Erlbaum.

Snoeren, E. M. S., Chan, J. S. W., de Jong, T. R., Waldinger, M. D., Olivier, B., & Oosting, R. S. (2011). A new female rat animal model for hypoactive sexual desire disorder: Behavioral and pharmacological evidence. *Journal of Sexual Medicine, 8*(1), 44–56.

Snyder, S. (1980). *Biological aspects of mental disorder.* New York: Oxford University Press.

Snyder, W. V. (1947). *Casebook of non-directive counseling.* Boston: Houghton Mifflin.

Soares, W. B., Dos Santos, E. B., Bottino, C. M. C., & Elkis, H. (2017). Psychotic symptoms in older people without dementia from a Brazilian community-based sample: A seven years' follow-up. *PLoS One, 12*(6), e0178471.

Sobell, M. B., & Sobell, L. C. (1973). Individualized behavior therapy for alcoholics. *Behavior Therapist, 4*(1), 49–72.

Sobell, M. B., & Sobell, L. C. (1984). The after-math of heresy: A response to Pendery

et al.'s (1982) critique of "Individualized Behavior Therapy for Alcoholics." *Behavioral Research and Therapy, 22*(4), 413–440.

Sobhani, M., Baker, L., Martins, B., Tuvblad, C., & Aziz-Zadeh, L. (2015). Psychopathic traits modulate microstructural integrity of right uncinate fasciculus in a community population. *NeuroImage: Clinical, 8,* 32–38.

Sofin, Y., Danker-Hopfe, H., Gooren, T., & Neu, P. (2017). Predicting inpatient detoxification outcome of alcohol and drug dependent patients: The influence of sociodemographic environment, motivation, impulsivity, and medical comorbidities. *Journal of Addiction,* ID 6415831. Retrieved from https://www.hindawi.com.

Solar, A. (2014). A supported employment linkage intervention for people with schizophrenia who want a chance to work. *Australasian Psychiatry, 22*(3), 245–247.

Soler, J., Elices, M., Pascual, J. C., Martin-Blanco, A., Feliu-Soler, A., Carmona, C., & Portelia, M. J. (2016, January 11). Effects of mindfulness training on different components of impulsivity in borderline personality disorder: Results from a pilot randomized study. *Borderline Personality Disorder and Emotion Dysregulation, 3,* 1.

Soliman, M., Santos, A. M., & Lohr, J. B. (2008). Emergency, inpatient, and residential treatment. In K. T. Mueser & D. V. Jeste (Eds.), *Clinical handbook of schizophrenia* (pp. 339–353). New York: Guilford Press.

Soloff, P. H., & Chiappetta, L. (2018). Suicidal behavior and psychosocial outcome in borderline personality disorder at 8-year follow-up. *Journal of Personality Disorders.* [Manuscript in press]

Soloff, P. H., Chiappetta, L., Mason, N. S., Becker, C., & Price, J. C. (2014). Effects of serotonin-2A receptor binding and gender on personality traits and suicidal behavior in borderline personality disorder. *Psychiatry Research, 222*(3), 140–148.

Solso, S., Xu, R., Proudfoot, J., Hagler, D. J., Campbell, K., Venkatraman, V., . . . Courchesne, E. (2016). Diffusion tensor imaging provides evidence of possible axonal overconnectivity in frontal lobes in autism spectrum disorder in toddlers. *Biological Psychiatry, 79,* 676–684.

Sommers-Flanagan, J., & Sommers-Flanagan, R. (2017). *Clinical interviewing* (6th edition). Hoboken, NJ: Wiley.

Song, G. M., Tian, X., Shuai, T., Yi, L. J., Zeng, Z., Liu, S., . . . Wang, Y. (2015, July). Treatment of adults with treatment-resistant depression: Electroconvulsive therapy plus antidepressant or electroconvulsive therapy alone? Evidence from an indirect comparison meta-analysis. *Medicine, 94*(26), e1052.

Song, Y., & Shi, M. (2017). Associations between empathy and big five personality traits among Chinese undergraduate medical students. *PLoS ONE, 12*(2), e0171665.

Sood, M. R. (2016, December 21). Functional fecal incontinence in infants and children: Definition, clinical manifestations and evaluation. *UpToDate.* Retrieved from http://www.uptodate.com.

Sood, M. R. (2017, February 10). Chronic functional constipation and fecal incontinence in

infants and children: Treatment. *UpToDate.* Retrieved from http://www.uptodate.com.

Soole, R., Kölves, K., & De Leo, D. (2015). Suicide in children: A systematic review. *Archives of Suicide Research, 19*(3), 285–304.

Sotgiu, I. (2016). How do we remember happy life events? A comparison between eudaimonic and hedonic autobiographical memories. *Journal of Psychology, 150*(6), 685–703.

Southwick, S. M., & Charney, D. S. (2012). *Resilience: The science of mastering life's greatest challenges.* New York: Cambridge University Press.

Soyka, M. (2017). Treatment of benzodiazepine dependence. *New England Journal of Medicine, 376*(24), 2399–2400.

Spanton, T. (2008, July 28). UFOs: We believe. *The Sun.* Retrieved from http://www.thesun.co.uk/sol/homepage/news/ufos/article1477122.ece.

Sparta, D. R., & Stuber, G. D. (2014). Cartography of serotonergic circuits. *Neuron, 83*(3), 513–515.

Spaulding, W., & Sullivan, M. (2016). Psychotherapy and the schizophrenia spectrum: Theory and practice. In A. J. Consoli, L. E. Beutler, & B. Bongar (Editors). (2016). *Comprehensive textbook of psychotherapy* (2nd edition), (Ch. 25, pp. 378–393). New York: Oxford University Press.

Sperry, L. (2003). *Handbook of diagnosis and treatment of DSM-IV-TR personality disorders* (2nd ed.). New York: Brunner Routledge.

Spiegel, D. (2009). Coming apart: Trauma and the fragmentation of the self. In D. Gordon (Ed.), *Cerebrum 2009: Emerging ideas in brain science* (pp. 1–11). Washington, DC: Dana Press.

Spiegler, M. D., & Guevremontt, D. C. (2015). *Contemporary behavior therapy* (6th edition). Independence, KY: Cengage Learning.

Spirito, A., Simon, V., Cancilliere, M. K., Stein, R., Norcott, C., Loranger, K., & Prinstein, M. J. (2011). Outpatient psychotherapy practice with adolescents following psychiatric hospitalization for suicide ideation or a suicide attempt. *Clinical Child Psychology and Psychiatry, 16*(1), 53–64.

Spitzer, R. L., Gibbon, M., Skodol, A. E., Williams, J. B. W., & First, M. B. (Eds.). (1994). *DSM-IV casebook: A learning companion to the diagnostic and statistical manual of mental disorders* (4th ed.). Washington, DC: American Psychiatric Press.

Spitzer, R. L., Skodol, A., Gibbon, M., & Williams, J. B. W. (1981). *DSM-III case book* (1st ed.). Washington, DC: American Psychiatric Press.

Spitzer, R. L., Skodol, A., Gibbon, M., & Williams, J. B. W. (1983). *Psychopathology: A case book.* New York: McGraw-Hill.

Spoelder, M., Dourojeanni, J. P. F., de Git, K. C. G., Baars, A. M., Lesscher, H. M. B., & Vanderschuren, L. J. M. J. (2017). Individual differences in voluntary alcohol intake in rats: Relationship with impulsivity, decision making and Pavlovian conditioned approach. *Psychopharmacology, 234*(14), 2177–2196.

SPRC (Suicide Prevention Resource Center). (2013). *Suicide among racial/ethnic populations in the U.S.: American Indians/Alaska Natives.* Waltham, MA: Education Development Center, Inc.

Springman, R. E., Wherry, J. N., & Notaro, P. C. (2006). The effects of interviewer race and child race on sexual abuse disclosures in forensic interviews. *Journal of Child Sexual Abuse, 15*(3), 99–116.

Springsteen, B. (2016). *Born to run.* New York: Simon & Schuster.

Spurk, D., Keller, A. C., & Hirschi, A. (2015). Do bad guys get ahead or fall behind? Relationships of the dark triad of personality with objective and subjective career success. *Social Psychological and Personality Science, 7*(2), 113–121.

SR (Speaking of Research). (2016, June 9). *USDA publishes 2015 animal research statistics.* Retrieved from https://speakingofresearch.com./2016/06/09.

Sroufe, A., Egeland, B., Carlson, W., & Collins, A. (2005). *The development of the person: The Minnesota study of risk and adaptation from birth to adulthood.* New York: Guilford Press.

Stack, S. (2004). Emile Durkheim and altruistic suicide. *Archives of Suicide Research, 8*(1), 9–22.

Stack, S., & Rockett, I. R. H. (2016, December 16). Are suicide note writers representative of all suicides? Analysis of the National Violent Death Reporting System. *Suicide and Life-Threatening Behavior.* [Epub ahead of print]

Stafford, M. R., Jackson, H., Mayo-Wilson, E., Morrison, A. P., & Kendall, T. (2013). Early interventions to prevent psychosis: Systematic review and meta-analysis. *BMJ, 346,* f185.

Stahl, S. M. (2014). *Prescriber's guide: Stahl's essential psychopharmacology.* New York: Cambridge University Press.

Stahlberg, O., Anckarsater, H., & Nilsson, T. (2010). Mental health problems in youths committed to juvenile institutions: Prevalences and treatment needs. *European Child & Adolescent Psychiatry, 19*(12), 893–903.

Staller, K. M., & Faller, K. C. (Eds.). (2010). *Seeking justice in child sexual abuse: Shifting burdens and sharing responsibilities.* New York: Columbia University Press.

Stange, J. P., Alloy, L. B., Flynn, M., & Abramson, L. Y. (2013) Negative inferential style, emotional clarity, and life stress: integrating vulnerabilities to depression in adolescence. *Journal of Clinical Child and Adolescent Psychology, 42*(4), 508–518.

Stänicke, E., Strømme, H., Killingmo, B., & Gullestad, S. E. (2015). Analytic change: Assessing ways of being in a psychoanalytic follow-up interview. *International Journal of Psychoanalysis, 96*(3), 797–815.

Stanley, I. H., Horn, M. A., & Joiner, T. E. (2015). Mental health service use among adults with suicide ideation, plans, or attempts: Results from a national survey. *Psychiatric Services* (Washington, D.C.), app.ips 201400593. [Electronic publication]

Stanos, S. P. (2017). Stemming the tide of the pain and opioid crisis: AAPM reaffirms its commitment to multidisciplinary biopsychosocial care and training. *Pain Medicine, 18*(6), 1005–1006.

Starcevic, V. (2015). Trichotillomania: Impulsive, compulsive or both? *Australian and New Zealand Journal of Psychiatry, 49*(7), 660–661.

Starcevic, V., & Brakoulias, V. (2014). New diagnostic perspectives on obsessive-compulsive personality disorder and its links with other conditions. *Current Opinion in Psychiatry, 27*(1), 62–67.

Starcevic, V., & Brakoulias, V. (2017). Current understanding of the relationships between obsessive-compulsive disorder and personality disturbance. *Current Opinion in Psychiatry, 30*(1), 50–55.

Starr, L. R., Hammen, C., Conway, C. C., Raposa, E., & Brennan, P. A. (2014). Sensitizing effect of early adversity on depressive reactions to later proximal stress: Moderation by polymorphisms in serotonin transporter and corticotropin releasing hormone receptor genes in a 20-year longitudinal study. *Development and Psychopathology, 26,* 1241–1254.

Starr, T. B., & Kreipe, R. E. (2014). Anorexia nervosa and bulimia nervosa: Brains, bones and breeding. *Current Psychiatry Reports, 16*(5), 441.

STAT. (2016, April 5). 'Truly terrifying': Chinese suppliers flood US and Canada with deadly fentanyl. *STAT.* Retrieved from https://www.statnews.com.

Statista. (2017). *Number of reported forcible rape cases in the United States from 1990 to 2015.* Retrieved from https://www.statista.com/statistics.

Steadman, H. J., Monahan, J., Robbins, P. C., Appelbaum, P., Grisso, T., Klassen, D., . . . Roth, L. (1993). From dangerousness to risk assessment: Implications for appropriate research strategies. In S. Hodgins (Ed.), *Mental disorder and crime.* New York: Sage.

Steffen, P. R., Masters, K. S., & Baldwin, S. (2016, February 19). What mediates the relationship between religious service attendance and aspects of well-being? *Journal of Religion & Health.* [Epub ahead of print]

Stein, C. H., Leith, J. E., Osborn, L. A., Greenberg, S., Petrowski, C. E., Jesse, S., . . . May, M. C. (2015). Mental health system historians: Adults with schizophrenia describe changes in community mental health care over time. *The Psychiatric Quarterly, 86*(1), 33–48.

Stein, J. (2003, August 4). Just say Om. *Time, 162*(5), pp. 48–56.

Stein, M. B. (2016, July 7). Pharmacotherapy for social anxiety disorder in adults. *UpToDate.* Retrieved from http://www.uptodate.com.

Stein, M. B. (2017, February 3). Pharmacotherapy for posttraumatic stress disorder in adults. *UpToDate.* Retrieved from http://www.uptodate.com.

Steinglass, J. (2016, September 28). Anorexia nervosa in adults and adolescents: Nutritional rehabilitation (nutritional support). *UpToDate.* Retrieved from www.uptodate.com.

Steinmetz, K. (2014, June 9). America's transition. *Time Magazine.*

Stekel, W. (2010). *Sadism and masochism: The psychopathology of sexual cruelty.* Chicago, IL: Solar Books/Solar Asylum.

Stene, L. S., Wentzel-Larsen, T., & Dyb, G. (2016). Healthcare needs, experiences and satisfaction after terrorism: A longitudinal study of survivors from the Utoya attack. *Frontiers in Psychology, 7*(1809).

Stephan, B. C., & Parsa, F. D. (2016). Avoiding opioids and their harmful side effects in the postoperative patient: Exogenous opioid, endogenous endorphins, wellness, mood, and their relation to postoperative pain. *Hawaii Journal of Medicine & Public Health, 75*(3), 63–67.

Stephens, R., Atkins, J., & Kingston, A. (2009). Swearing as a response to pain. *Neuro-Report, 20*(12). 1056–1060.

Stern, A. (1938). Psychoanalytic investigation and therapy in the borderline group of neuroses. *Psychoanalytical Quarterly, 7,* 467–489.

Sternberg, R. J., Grigorenko, E. L., & Bundy, D. A. (2001). The predictive value of IQ. *Merrill-Palmer Quarterly, 47*(1), 1–41.

Stevens, J., Harman, J. S., & Kelleher, K. J. (2005). Race/ethnicity and insurance status as factors associated with ADHD treatment patterns. *Journal of Child and Adolescent Psychopharmacology, 15*(1), 88–96.

Stevens, J. P., Wall, M. J., Novack, L., Hsu, D. J., & Howell, M. D. (2018). The critical care crisis of opioid overdoses in the United States. *Annals of the American Thoracic Society.* [Manuscript in press]

Stevenson, R. W. D., & Elliott, S. L. (2007). Sexuality and illness. In S. R. Leiblum (Ed.), *Principles and practice of sex therapy* (4th ed., pp. 313–349). New York: Guilford Press.

Stewart, E. G. (2015, November 18). Differential diagnosis of sexual pain in women. *UpToDate.* Retrieved from http://www.uptodate.com.

Stewart, J. G., Valeri, L., Esposito, E. C., & Auerbach, R. P. (2017, April 25). Peer victimization and suicidal thoughts and behaviors in depressed adolescents. *Journal of Abnormal Child Psychology.* [Epub ahead of print]

Stewart, R. E., & Chambless, D. L. (2007). Does psychotherapy research inform treatment decisions in private practice? *Journal of Clinical Psychology, 63*(3), 267–281.

Stewart, T. M., & Williamson, D. A. (2008). Bulimia nervosa. In M. Hersen & J. Rosqvist (Eds.), *Handbook of psychological assessment, case conceptualization and treatment, Vol. 1: Adults.* Hoboken, NJ: John Wiley & Sons.

Stibich, M. (2017, March 16). Sexual activity among older populations. *Verywell.*

Stice, E. (2016). Interactive and mediational etiologic models of eating disorder onset: Evidence from prospective studies. *Annual Review of Clinical Psychology, 12,* 359–381.

Stice, E., Becker, C. B., & Yokum, S. (2014). Eating disorder prevention: Current evidence-base and future directions. *International Journal of Eating Disorders, 46*(5), 478–485.

Stice, E., Gau, J. M., Rohde, P., & Shaw, H. (2017). Risk factors that predict future onset of each DSM-5 eating disorder: Predictive specificity in high-risk adolescent females. *Journal of Abnormal Psychology, 126*(1), 38–51.

Stice, E., Hayward, C., Cameron, R. P., Killen, J. D., & Taylor, C. B. (2000). Body-image and eating disturbances predict onset of depression among female adolescents: A longitudinal study. *Journal of Abnormal Psychology, 109*(3), 438–444.

Stice, E., Marti, C. N., & Rohde, P. (2013). Prevalence, incidence, impairment, and course of the proposed DSM-5 eating disorder diagnoses in an 8-year prospective community study of young women. *Journal of Abnormal Psychology, 122*(2), 445–457.

Stice, E., & Presnell, K. (2010). Dieting and the eating disorders. In W. S. Agras (Ed.),

The Oxford handbook of eating disorders (pp. 148–179). New York: Oxford University Press.

Stice, E., Rohde, P., Shaw, H., & Gau, J. M. (2017). Clinical-led, peer-led, and internet-delivered dissonance-based eating disorder prevention programs: Acute effectiveness of these delivery modalities. *Journal of Consulting and Clinical Psychology, 85*, 883–895.

Stice, E., Yokum, S., & Waters, A. (2015, December 7). Dissonance-based eating disorder prevention program reduces reward region response to thin models: How actions shape valuation. *PLOS ONE*. Retrieved from https://doi.org/10.1371/journal.pone.0144530.

Stickel, F., Moreno, C., Hampe, J., & Morgan, M. Y. (2017). The genetics of alcohol dependence and alcohol-related liver disease. *Journal of Hepatology, 66*, 195–211.

Stickley, A., Ng, C. F. S., Inoue, Y., Yazawa, A., Koyanagi, A., Kodaka, M., . . . Wantanabe, C. (2016). Birthdays are associated with an increased risk of suicide in Japan: Evidence from 27,007 deaths in Tokyo in 2001–2010. *Journal of Affective Disorders, 200*, 259–265.

Stifter, C., & Dollar, J. (2016). Temperament and developmental psychopathology. In D. Cicchetti (Ed.), *Developmental Psychopathology Volume 4, Risk, Resilience, and Intervention* (3rd ed.). New York: Wiley.

Stinchfield, R., McCready, J., Turner, N. E., Jimenez-Murcia, S., Petry, N. M., Grant, J., . . . Chapman, H. (2016). Reliability, validity, and classification accuracy of the DSM-5 diagnostic criteria for gambling disorder and comparison to DSM-IV. *Journal of Gambling Studies, 32*(3), 905–922.

Stitzer, M., & Cunningham, C. S. (2015, August 28). Contingency management for substance use disorders: Theoretical foundation, principles, assessment, and components. *UpToDate*. Retrieved from http://www.uptodate.com.

Stitzer, M., & Cunningham, C. S. (2016, December 6). Contingency management for substance use disorders: Efficacy, implementation, and training. *UpToDate*. Retrieved from http://www.uptodate.com.

Stolbach, A., & Hoffman, R. S. (2017, May 8). Acute opioid intoxication in adults. *UpToDate*. Retrieved from http://www.uptodate.com.

Stolberg, R. A., Clark, D. C., & Bongar, B. (2002). Epidemiology, assessment, and management of suicide in depressed patients. In I. H. Gotlib & C. L. Hammen (Eds.), *Handbook of depression* (pp. 581–601). New York: Guilford Press.

Stone, J., & Sharpe, M. (2015, November 24). Conversion disorder in adults: Terminology, diagnosis, and differential diagnosis. *UpToDate*. Retrieved from http://www.uptodate.com.

Stone, J., & Sharpe, M. (2015, November 24). Conversion disorder in adults: Epidemiology, pathogenesis, and prognosis. *UpToDate*. Retrieved from http://www.uptodate.com.

Stone, J., & Sharpe, M. (2016, January 28). Conversion disorder in adults: Treatment. *UpToDate*. Retrieved from http://www.uptodate.com.

Stone, J., & Sharpe, M. (2016, July 26). Conversion disorder in adults: Clinical features, assessment, and comorbidity. *UpToDate*. Retrieved from http://www.uptodate.com.

Stone, K. (2016, October 13). The most prescribed medications by drug class: Prescriptions being filled at an all-time high. *The Balance*. Retrieved from https://www.thebalance.com/the-most-prescribed-medications-by-drug-class-2663215.

Stone, M. H. (2010). Sexual sadism: A portrait of evil. *Journal of the American Academy of Psychoanalysis and Dynamic Psychiatry, 38*(1), 133–157.

Stoppler, M. C. (2014). Holiday depression and stress. *MedicineNet.com*.

Stotland, N. (2010). DSM5: The debate continues. *Psychiatric Times*. Retrieved from http://www.psychiatrictimes.com/bipolar-ii-disorder/content/article/10168/1583072.

Stovall, J. (2016, March 14). Bipolar disorder in adults: Epidemiology and pathogenesis. *UpToDate*. Retrieved from http://www.uptodate.com.

Stovall, J. (2016, May 17). Bipolar disorder in adults: Pharmacotherapy for acute mania and hypomania. *UpToDate*. Retrieved from www.uptodate.com.

Stovall, J. (2017, March 20). Bipolar disorder in adults: Pharmacotherapy for acute depression. *UpToDate*. Retrieved from www.uptodate.com.

Strachan, E. (2008). Civil commitment evaluations. In R. Jackson (Ed.), *Learning forensic assessment* (pp. 509–535). New York: Routledge/Taylor & Francis Group.

Strain, E. (2017, January 13). Pharmacotherapy for opioid use disorder. *UpToDate*. Retrieved from http://www.uptodate.com.

Strain, E. (2017, April 10). Opioid use disorder: Epidemiology, pharmacology, clinical manifestations, course, screening, assessment, and diagnosis. *UpToDate*. Retrieved from http://www.uptodate.com.

Strassberg, D. S., Cann, D., & Velarde, V. (2017). Sexting by high school students. *Archives of Sexual Behavior, 46*, 1667–1672.

Strassberg, D. S., McKinnon, R. K., Sustaíta, M. A., & Rullo, J. (2013). Sexting by high school students: An exploratory and descriptive study. *Archives of Sexual Behavior, 42*(1), 15–21.

Stratemeier, M. W., & Vignogna, L. (2014). Peptic ulcers. *eMedicineHealth*. Retrieved from http://www.emedicinehealth.com.

Strawn, J. R., Dobson, E. T., & Giles, L. L. (2017). Primary pediatric care psychopharmacology: Focus on medications for ADHD, depression, and anxiety. *Current Problems in Pediatric and Adolescent Health Care, 47*(1), 3–14.

Street, A. E., Bell, M. E., & Ready, C. B. (2011). Sexual assault. In D. M. Benedek, & G. H. Wynn (Eds.), *Clinical manual for management of PTSD* (pp. 325–348). Arlington, VA: American Psychiatric Publishing.

Strickland, B. R., Hale, W. D., & Anderson, L. K. (1975). Effect of induced mood states on activity and self-reported affect. *Journal of Consulting and Clinical Psychology, 43*(4), 587.

Strober, M., & Yager, J. (1985). A developmental perspective on the treatment of anorexia nervosa in adolescents. In D. M. Garner & P. E. Garfinkel (Eds.), *Handbook of psychotherapy for anorexia nervosa and bulimia*. New York: Guilford Press.

Strohl, K. P. (2016, June 24). Overview of obstructive sleep apnea in adults. *UpToDate*. Retrieved from http://www.uptodate.com.

Stroup, T. S., & Marder, S. (2017, May 23). Pharmacotherapy for schizophrenia: Acute and maintenance phase treatment. *UpToDate*. Retrieved from http://www.uptodate.com.

Strümpfel, U. (2006). *Therapie der gefüble: For-schungsbefunde zur gestalttherapie.* Cologne, Germany: Edition Huanistiche Psychologie.

Stuart, S., Noyes, R., Jr., Starcevic, V., & Barsky, A. (2008). An integrative approach to somatoform disorders combining interpersonal and cognitive-behavioral theory and techniques. *Journal of Contemporary Psychotherapy, 38*(1), 45–53.

Stubbs, B., Vancampfort, D., Rosenbaum, S., Ward, P. B., Richards, J., Soundy, A., . . . Schuch, F. B. (2016). Dropout from exercise randomized controlled trials among people with depression: A meta-analysis and meta regression. *Journal of Affective Disorders, 190*, 457–466.

Stuber, J. P., Rocha, A., Christian, A., & Link, B. G. (2014). Conceptions of mental illness: Attitudes of mental health professionals and the general public. *Psychiatric Services, 65*(4), 490–497.

Štulhofer, A., Træen, B., & Carvalheira, A. (2013). Job-related strain and sexual health difficulties among heterosexual men from three European countries: The role of culture and emotional support. *Journal of Sexual Medicine, 10*, 747–756.

Stunkard, A. J. (1959). Eating patterns and obesity. *Psychiatric Quarterly, 33*, 284–295.

Sturmey, P. (2008). Adults with intellectual disabilities. In M. Hersen & J. Rosqvist (Eds.), *Handbook of psychological assessment, case conceptualization, and treatment, Vol. 1: Adults.* Hoboken, NJ: John Wiley & Sons.

Sturmey, P., & Didden, R. (2014). *Evidence-based practice and intellectual disabilities.* Hoboken, NJ: Wiley.

Su, S., Wang, X., Kapuku, G. K., Treiber, F. A., Pollock, D. M., Harshfield, G. A., . . . Pollock, J. S. (2014). Adverse childhood experiences are associated with detrimental hemodynamics and elevated circulating endothelin-1 in adolescents and young adults. *Hypertension, 64*(1), 201–207.

Sujan, A. C., Humphreys, K. L., Ray, L. A., & Lee, S. S. (2014, July 16). Differential association of child abuse with self-reported versus laboratory-based impulsivity and risk-taking in young adulthood. *Child Maltreatment*. [Electronic publication]

Sukel, K. (2016). *How are direct-to-consumer-advertisments changing psychiatric drug use?* The Dana Foundation.

Suler, J. (2004). The online disinhibition effect. *Cyber Psychology and Behavior, 7*(3), 321–326.

Suler, J. (2016). *The online disinhibition effect, 20 years later.* Fifteen Eighty Four: Cambridge University Press.

Sullivan, E. L., Smith, M. S., & Grove, K. L. (2011). Perinatal exposure to high-fat diet programs energy balance, metabolism and behavior in adulthood. *Neuroendocrinology, 93*(1), 1–8.

Sullivan, E. M., Annest, J. L., Simon, T. R., Luo, F., & Dahlberg, L. L. (2015). Suicide trends among persons aged 10–24 years—United States, 1994–2012. *Morbidity and Mortality Weekly Report, 64*(8), 201–205.

Sullivan, H. S. (1953). *The interpersonal theory of psychiatry.* New York: Norton.

Sullivan, H. S. (1962). *Schizophrenia as a human process.* New York: Norton.

Sun, F. K., Lu, C. Y., Tseng, Y. S., & Chiang, C. Y. (2018). Factors predicting recovery from suicide in attempted suicide patients. *Journal of Clinical Nursing.* [Manuscript in press]

Sun, Y. R., Herrmann, N., Scott, C. J. M., Black, S. E., Khan, M. M., & Lanctôt, K. L. (2018). Global grey matter volume in adult bipolar patients with and without lithium treatment: A meta-analysis. *Journal of Affective Disorders, 225,* 599–606.

Sungur, M. Z., & Gündüz, A. (2014). A comparison of DSM-IV-TR and DSM-5 definitions for sexual dysfunctions: Critiques and challenges. *Journal of Sexual Medicine, 11,* 364–373.

Suo, X., Lei, D., Chen, D., Wu, M., Lei, L., Sun, L., . . . Gong, Q. (2017, March). Anatomic insights into disrupted small-world networks in pediatric posttraumatic stress disorder. *RSNA Radiology, 28*(3). Online publication.

Suor, J. H., Sturge-Apple, M. L., Davies, P. T., Cicchetti, D., & Manning, L. G. (2016). Tracing differential pathways of risk: Associations among family adversity, cortisol, and cognitive functioning in childhood. *Child Development, 86,* 1142–1158.

Suppes, T., Baldessarini, R. J., Faedda, G. L., & Tohen, M. (1991). Risk of recurrence following discontinuation of lithium treatment in bipolar disorder. *Archives of General Psychiatry, 48*(12), 1082–1088.

Suppes, T., & Cosgrove, V. E. (2016, January 4). Bipolar disorder in adults: Clinical features. *UpToDate.* Retrieved from http://www.uptodate.com.

Surawy, C., McManus, F., Muse, K., & Williams, J. M. (2015). Mindfulness-based cognitive therapy (MBCT) for health anxiety (hypochondiasis): Rationale, implementation and case illustration. *Mindfulness, 6*(2), 382–392.

Svartberg, M., & McCullough, L. (2010). Cluster C personality disorders: Prevalence, phenomenology, treatment effects, and principles of treatment. In J. F. Clarkin, P. Fonagy, & G. O. Gabbard (Eds.), *Psychodynamic psychotherapy for personality disorders: A clinical handbook* (pp. 337–367). Arlington, VA: American Psychiatric Publishing.

Svartberg, M., & Stiles, T. C. (1991). Comparative effects of short-term psychodynamic psychotherapy: A meta-analysis. *Journal of Consulting and Clinical Psychology, 59,* 704–714.

Swain, S. P., Behura, S. S., Dash, M. K., Nayak, A. K., & Pati, S. S. (2017). The influence of psychosocial dysfunctions in chronic schizophrenia patients in remission: A hospital-based study. *Indian Journal of Psychological Medicine, 39*(2), 157–163.

Swami, V., Barron, D., Weis, L., & Furnham, A. (2016). Bodies in nature: Associations between exposure to nature, connectedness to nature, and body image in U.S. adults. *Body Image, 18,* 153–161.

Swanson, J., & Cooper, A. (2016). *The relapse prevention program: An evidence-based approach.* Center City, MN: Hazelden Publishing.

Swanson, J., Swartz, M., Van Dorn, R. A., Monahan, J., McGuire, T. G., Steadman, H. J., & Robbins, P. C. (2009). Racial disparities in involuntary outpatient commitment: Are they real? *Health Affairs, 28*(3), 816–826.

Swanson, J. M., Arnold, L. E., Molina, B. S. G., Sibley, M. H., Hechtman, L. T., et al. (2017). Young adult outcomes in the follow-up of the Multimodal Treatment Study of Attention-deficit/hyperactivity disorder. *Journal of Child Psychology and Psychiatry, 58,* 663–678.

Swanson, J. W. (2010). Cited by Tony Leys, "Crimes distort reality of schizophrenia." *Des Moines Register,* March 6, 2010.

Swanson, S. A., & Colman, I. (2013). Association between exposure to suicide and suicidality outcomes in youth. *Canadian Medical Association Journal, 185*(10), 870–877.

Swartz, H. A. (2015, October 26). Interpersonal psychotherapy (IPT) for depressed adults: Specific interventions and techniques. *UpToDate.* Retrieved from http://www.uptodate.com.

Swartz, H. A. (2016, November 14). Interpersonal psychotherapy (IPT) for depressed adults: Indications, theoretical foundation, general concepts, and efficacy. *UpToDate.* Retrieved from http://www.uptodate.com.

Swartz, M. S., Frohberg, N. R., Drake, R. E., & Lauriello, J. (2012). Psychosocial therapies. In J. A. Lieberman, T. S. Stroup, & D. O Perkins (Eds.), *Essentials of schizophrenia* (pp. 207–224). Arlington, VA: American Psychiatric Publishing.

Swift, A. (2016, September 14). Americans' trust in mass media sinks to new low. *Gallup.* Retrieved from http://www.gallup.com/poll/195542.

Swift, R. M. (2016). Pharmacotherapy for substance use, craving, and acute abstinence syndromes. In K. J. Sher (Ed.), *Oxford handbook of substance use and substance use disorders* (Vol. 2, Ch. 21, pp. 594–620). New York: Oxford University Press.

Sylvester, C. & Pine, D. (2016). Anxiety disorders. In J. L. Luby (Ed.), *Handbook of preschool mental health: Development, disorders, and treatment.* New York: Guilford.

Sysko, R., & Devlin, M. (2016, July 4). Binge eating disorder: Cognitive-behavioral therapy (CBT). *UpToDate.* Retrieved from http://www.uptodate.com.

Sysko, R., & Devlin, M. (2016, July 12). Binge eating disorder in adults: Overview of treatment. *UpToDate.* Retrieved from http://www.uptodate.com.

Szabo, M., & Lovibond, P. F. (2004). The cognitive content of thought-listed worry episodes in clinic-referred anxious and nonreferred children. *Journal of Clinical Child and Adolescent Psychology, 33*(3), 613–622.

Szalavitz, M. (2013, March 1). How Facebook improves memory. *Time.* Retrieved from http://healthland.time.com/2013/03/01.

Szalavitz, M. (2013, July 18). Apps for mastering your mood. *Time.*

Szasz, T. S. (1960). The myth of mental illness. *American Psychologist, 15,* 113–118.

Szasz, T. S. (1963). *The manufacture of madness.* New York: Harper & Row.

Szasz, T. S. (2011). The myth of mental illness: 50 years later. *The Psychiatrist, 35*(5), 179–182.

TAC (Treatment Advocacy Center). (2017). *Assisted outpatient treatment: Frequently asked questions.* Arlington, VA: Author.

TACA (Talking About Curing Autism). (2017, January 29). *Latest autism statistics.* Retrieved from https://www.tacanow.org.

Tackett, J. L., Herzhoff, K., Balsis, S., & Cooper, L. (2016). Toward a unifying perspective on personality pathology across the lifespan. In D. Cicchetti (Ed.), *Developmental psychopathology Vol. 3: Developmental neuroscience* (3rd ed., pp. 1039–1078). New York: Wiley.

TADS (Treatment for Adolescents with Depression Study Team, U.S.). (2004). Fluoxetine, cognitive behavioral therapy, and their combination for adolescents with depression: Treatment for Adolescents with Depression Study (TADS) randomized controlled trial. *Journal of the American Medical Association, 292*(7), 807–820.

TADS (Treatment for Adolescents with Depression Study Team, U.S.). (2007). The Treatment for Adolescents with Depression Study (TADS): Long-term effectiveness and safety outcomes. *Archives of General Psychiatry, 64*(10), 1132–1144.

TADS (Treatment for Adolescents with Depression Study Team, U.S.). (2010). *Treatment for Adolescents with Depression Study.* Retrieved from NIMH website: http://www.nimh.nih.gov/trials/practical/tads/index.shtml.

Takano, A., Miyamoto, Y., Kawakami, N., Matsumoto, T., Shinozaki, T., & Sugimoto, T. (2016). Web-based cognitive behavioral relapse prevention program with tailored feedback for people with methamphetamine and other drug use problems: Protocol for a multicenter randomized controlled trial in Japan. *BMC Psychiatry, 16,* 87.

Takeda, A. (2015, April 13). Zoe Kravitz gets real about past struggles with eating disorders: New film The Road Within "triggered some old stuff." *Us Weekly.*

Takenaka, M. C., Araujo, L. P., Maricato, J. T., Nascimento, V. M., Guereschi, M. G., Rezende, R. M., . . . Basso, A. S. (2016). Norepinephrine controls effector T cell differentiation through β2-adrenergic receptor-mediated inhibition of NF-κB and AP-1 in dendritic cells. *Journal of Immunology, 196*(2), 637–644.

Takizawa, R., Maughan, B., & Arseneault, L. (2014). Adult health outcomes of childhood bullying victimization: Evidence from a five-decade longitudinal British birth cohort. *American Journal of Psychiatry, 171,* 777–784.

Talaue, C. (2015, April 15). Madness in Shakespeare: William Shakespeare uses the concept of madness in his tragedies to show the effects of a character's external environment on their mental state. Retrieved from *Prezi.com.*

Tallis, F. (2014, January 23). *How to stop worrying: New edition (Overcoming common problems).* Sheldon Press. [Kindle]

Tallis, F. (2015, October 22). *The Sheldon short guide to worry and anxiety.* Sheldon Press. [Kindle]

Tallis, F., Davey, G., & Capuzzo, N. (1994). The phenomenology of non-pathological worry: A preliminary investigation. In G. Davey & F. Tallis (Eds.), *Worrying: Perspectives on theory, assessment and treatment* (pp. 61–89). Chichester, England: John Wiley.

Tandon, S., Keefe, K. A., & Taha, S. A. (2017). Mu opioid receptor signaling in the nucleus accumbens shell increases responsiveness of satiety-modulated lateral hypothalamus neurons. *European Journal of Neuroscience, 45,* 1418–1430.

Tang, W., Zhu, Q., Gong, X., Zhu, C., Wang, Y., & Chen, S. (2016). Cortico-striato-thalamo-cortical circuit abnormalities in obsessive-compulsive disorder: A voxel-based morphometric and fMRI study of the whole brain. *Behavioural Brain Research, 313,* 17–22.

Tang, Y. Y., & Bruya, B. (2017, May 9). Mechanisms of mind-body interaction and optimal performance. *Frontiers in Psychology, 8,* 647.

Tangpricha, V., & Safer, J. D. (2016, September 19). Transgender men: Evaluation and management. *UpToDate.* Retrieved from http://www.uptodate.com.

Tangpricha, V., & Safer, J. D. (2017, May 16). Transgender women: Evaluation and management. *UpToDate.* Retrieved from http://www.uptodate.com.

Tanzilli, A., Muzi, L., Ronningstam, E., & Lingiardi, V. (2017). Countertransference when working with narcissistic personality disorder: An empirical investigation. *Psychotherapy, 54*(2), 184–194.

Tarquinio, C., Rotonda, C., Houllé, W.A., Montel, S., Rydberg, J.A., Minary, L., . . . Alla, F. (2016). Early psychological preventive intervention for workplace violence: A randomized controlled explorative and comparative study between EMDR-recent event and critical incident stress debriefing. *Issues in Mental Health Nursing, 37*(11), 787–799.

Tarsy, D. (2016, December 14). Tardive dyskinesia: Clinical features and diagnosis. *UpToDate.* Retrieved from http://www.uptodate.com.

Tarsy, D. (2016, December 14). Tardive dyskinesia: Etiology and epidemiology. *UpToDate.* Retrieved from http://www.uptodate.com.

Tarsy, D. (2017, May 4). Tardive dyskinesia: Prevention and treatment. *UpToDate.* Retrieved from http://www.uptodate.com.

Tartakovsky, M. (2016). Schizophrenia and genetics: Research update. *Psych Central.* Retrieved from https://psychcentral.com.

Tarter, R. E., Alterman, A. I., & Edwards, K. L. (1985). Vulnerability to alcoholism in men: A behavior-genetic perspective. *Journal of Studies on Alcohol, 46*(4), 329–356.

Tashakova, O. (2011, March 25). Am I too fat? *Khaleej Times.*

Taube-Schiff, M., & Lau, M. A. (2008). Major depressive disorder. In M. Hersen & J. Rosqvist (Eds.), *Handbook of psychological assessment, case conceptualization, and treatment, Vol. 1: Adults* (pp. 319–351). Hoboken, NJ: John Wiley & Sons.

Taylor, A., & Kim-Cohen, J. (2007). Meta-analysis of gene-environment interactions in developmental psychopathology. *Development and Psychopathology, 19,* 1029–1037.

Taylor, B., Carswell, K., & Williams, A. C. (2013). The interaction of persistent pain and post-traumatic re-experiencing: A qualitative study in torture survivors. *Journal of Pain and Symptom Management, 46*(4), 546–555.

Taylor, E. A., Ward, R. M., & Hardin, R. (2017, Spring). Examination of drinking habits and motives of collegiate student-athletes. *Journal of Applied Sport Management, 9*(1), 56.

Taylor, F. R. (2016, October 13). Tension-type headache in adults: Pathophysiology, clinical features, and diagnosis. *UpToDate.* Retrieved from http://www.uptodate.com.

Taylor, L. E., Swerdfeger, A. L., & Eslick, G. D. (2014). Vaccines are not associated with autism: An evidence-based meta-analysis of case-control and cohort studies. *Vaccine, 32*(29), 3623–3629.

Taylor, M. J., Doesburg, S. M., & Pang, E. W. (2014). Neuromagnetic vistas into typical and atypical development of frontal lobe functions. *Frontiers in Human Neuroscience, 18*(8), 453.

Taylor, W. D. (2014). Depression in the elderly. *New England Journal of Medicine, 371,* 1228–1236.

Ten Have, M., Nuyen, J., Beekman, A., & de Graaf, R. (2013). Common mental disorder severity and its association with treatment contact and treatment intensity for mental health problems. *Psychological Medicine, 43*(10), 2203–2213.

Tenke, C. E., Kayser, J., Pechtel, P., Webb, C. A., Dillon, D. G., Goer, F., . . . Bruder, G. E. (2017). Demonstrating tests-retest reliability of electrophysiological measures for healthy adults in a multisite study of biomarkers of antidepressant treatment response. *Psychophysiology, 54*(1), 34–50.

Terry-McElrath, Y. M., O'Malley, P. M., & Johnston, L. D. (2014). Energy drinks, soft drinks, and substance use among United States secondary school students. *Journal of Addiction Medicine, 8*(1), 6–13.

Testa, M., & Cleveland, M. J. (2017). Does alcohol contribute to college men's sexual assault perpetration? Between- and within-person effects over five semesters. *Journal of Studies on Alcohol and Drugs, 78*(1), 5–13.

Tetrault, J. M., & O'Connor, P. G. (2017, May). Risky drinking and alcohol use disorder: Epidemiology, pathogenesis, clinical manifestations, course, assessment, and diagnosis. *UpToDate.* Retrieved from http://www.uptodate.com.

Thackray, A. E., Deighton, K., King, J. A., & Stensel, D. J. (2016, September 21). Exercise, appetite and weight control: Are their differences between men and women? *Nutrients, 8*(9), 583.

Thase, M., & Connolly, K. R. (2016, July 20). Unipolar depression in adults: Treatment of resistant depression. *UpToDate.* Retrieved from http://www.uptodate.com.

Thase, M. E. (2012). Social skills training for depression and comparative efficacy research: A 30-year retrospective. *Behavior Modification, 36*(4), 545–557.

Thase, M. E., Mahableshwarkar, A. R., Dragheim, M., Loft, H., & Vieta, E. (2016). A meta-analysis of randomized, placebo-controlled trials of vortioxetine for the treatment of major depressive disorder in adults. *European Neuropsychopharmacology, 26*(6), 979–993.

Thase, M. E., Trivedi, M. H., & Rush, A. J. (1995). MAOIs in the contemporary treatment of depression. *Neuropsychopharmacology, 12*(3), 185–219.

Thibaut, F., Bradford, J. M., Briken, P., De La Barra, F., Hassler, F., Cosyns, P., & WFSBP Task Force on Sexual Disorders. (2016). The World Federation of Societies of Biological Psychiatry (WFSBP) guidelines for the treatment of adolescent sexual offenders with paraphilic disorders. *World Journal of Biological Psychiatry, 17*(1), 2–38.

Thibaut, F., De LaBarra, F., Gordon, H., Cosyns, P., Bradford, J. M. W. (2010). The World Federation of Societies of Biological Psychiatry (WRSBP) guidelines for the biological treatment of paraphilias. *World Journal of Biological Psychiatry, 11*(3-4), 604–655.

Thigpen, C. H., & Cleckley, H. M. (1957). *The three faces of Eve.* New York: McGraw-Hill.

Thimm, J. C., Jordan, S., & Bach, B. (2016). The Personality Inventory for DSM-5 Short Form (PID-5-SF): Psychometric properties and association with big five traits and pathological beliefs in a Norwegian population. *BMC Psychology, 4*(1), 61.

Thomas, C., & Haushofer, J. (2015, April 21). Get happy, get rich: The relationship between depression and poverty. *StrongMinds.* Retrieved from https://strongminds.org.

Thomas, C. P., Fullerton, C. A., Kim, M., Montejano, L., Lyman, D. R., Daniels, A. S., . . . Delphin-Rittmon, M. E. (2014). Medication-assisted treatment with buprenorphine: Assessing the evidence. *Psychiatry Services, 65*(2), 158–170.

Thomas, J. (2014, January/February). Most psychologists misinformed on "duty to warn." *The National Psychologist,* pp. 3–4.

Thomas, J., & Altareb, B. (2012). Cognitive vulnerability to depression: An exploration of dysfunctional attitudes and ruminative response styles in the United Arab Emirates. *Psychology and Psychotherapy, 85*(1), 117–121.

Thomas, K., & Gunnell, D. (2010). Suicide in England and Wales 1871–2007: A time-trends analysis. *International Journal of Epidemiology, 39*(6), 1464–1475.

Thomasson, E. (2012, June 12). Right-to-die movement sees gain as world ages. *Reuters.*

Thompson, A. B., Goodman, M. S., & Kwate, N. O. (2016). Does learning about race prevent substance abuse? Racial discrimination, racial socialization and substance use among African Americans. *Addictive Behaviors, 61,* 1–7.

Thompson, D. F., Ramos, C. L., & Willett, J. K. (2014). Psychopathy: Clinical features, developmental basis and therapeutic challenges. *Journal of Clinical Pharmacy and Therapeutics, 39*(5), 485–495.

Thompson, L. (2016, March 30). FOMO: It's your life you're missing out on. *Science Daily.*

Thompson, N. J., Fiorillo, D., Rothbaum, B. O., Ressler, K. J., & Michopoulos, V. (2018). Coping strategies as mediators in relation to resilience and posttraumatic stress disorder. *Journal of Affective Disorders, 225,* 153–159.

Thompson, R. A., & Sherman, R. T. (2010). *Eating disorders in sport.* New York: Routledge/Taylor & Francis Group.

Thompson, S. (2016, October 27). The 13 highest-grossing horror film franchises of all time at the U.S. box office. *Forbes.* Retrieved from http://www.forbes.com.

Thompson, S. (2017, August). 3 exercise tips to prevent and treat depression. *FastTwitchGrandma.* Retrieved from https://fasttwitchgrandma.com.

Thompson-Brenner, H. (2016). Relationship-focused therapy for bulimia and binge eating: Introduction to the special section. *Psychotherapy, 53*(2), 185–187.

Thompson-Hollands, J., Kerns, C. E., Pincus, D. B., & Comer, J. S. (2014). Parental accommodation of child anxiety and related symptoms: Range, impact, and correlates. *Journal of Anxiety Disorders, 28,* 765–773.

Thornton, L., Handley, T., Kay-Lambkin, F., & Baker, A. (2017). Is a person thinking about suicide likely to find help on the internet? An evaluation of Google search results. *Suicide and Life-Threatening Behavior, 47*(1), 48–53.

Thornton, L. M., Mazzeo, S. E., & Bulik, C. M. (2011). The heritability of eating disorders: Methods and current findings. In R. A. H. Adan & W. H. Kaye (Eds.), *Behavioral neurobiology of eating disorders. Current topics in behavioral neurosciences* (pp. 141–156). New York: Springer-Verlag Publishing.

Thurston, M. D., Goldin, P., Heimberg, R., & Gross, J. J. (2017). Self-views in social anxiety disorder: The impact of CBT versus MBSR. *Journal of Anxiety Disorders, 47*, 83–90.

Tietze, K. J., & Fuchs, B. (2017, June 15). Sedative-analgesic medications in critically ill adults: Properties, dosage regimens, and adverse effects. *UpToDate.* Retrieved from http://www.uptodate.com.

Tiggemann, M., & Slater, A. (2013, September 5). NetTweens: The Internet and body image concerns in preteenage girls. *Journal of Early Adolescence.* [Online publication]

Tight, M. (2017). *Understanding case study research: Small-scale research with meaning* (1st ed.). Los Angeles: Sage Publications.

Tindall, L., Mikocka-Walus, A., McMillan, D., Wright, B., Hewitt, C., & Gascoyne, S. (2017, March 16). Is behavioural activation effective in the treatment of depression in young people? A systematic review and meta-analysis. *Psychology and Psychotherapy.* [Epub ahead of print].

Tint, A., Thomson, K., & Weiss, J. A. (2017). A systematic literature review of the physical and psychosocial correlates of Special Olympics participation among individuals with intellectual disability. *Journal of Intellectual Disability Research, 61*(4), 301–324.

Tolan, P., Gorman-Smith, D., & Henry, D. (2006). Family violence. *Annual Review of Psychology, 57*, 557–583.

Tolan, P. H. (2016). Community violence exposure and developmental psychopathology. In D. Cicchetti (Ed.), *Developmental psychopathology, Vol. 4: Risk, resilience, and intervention* (3rd ed.). New York: Wiley.

Tompson, M. C., Sugar, C. A., Langer, D. A., & Asarnow, J. R. (2017). A randomized clinical trial comparing family-focused treatment and individual supportive therapy for depression in childhood and early adolescence. *Journal of the American Academy of Child and Adolescent Psychiatry, 56*, 515–523.

Tondo, L., Vázquez, G. H., Baethge, C., Baronessa, C., Bolzani, L., Koukopoulos, A., . . . Baldessarini R. J. (2015). Comparison of psychotic bipolar disorder, schizoaffective disorder, and schizophrenia: An international, multisite study. *Acta Psychiatrica Scandinavica.* [Electronic publication]

Tone, E. B., Garn, C. L., & Pine, D. S. (2016). Anxiety regulation: A developmental psychopathology perspective. In D. Cicchetti (ed.), *Developmental psychopathology, Vol. 2: Developmental neuroscience* (3rd ed.). New York: Wiley.

Tone, E. B., Garn, C. L., & Pine, D. S. (2016). Anxiety regulation: A developmental psychopathology perspective. In D. Cicchetti (Ed.), *Developmental psychopathology, Vol. 3:*

Developmental neuroscience (3rd ed.). New York: Wiley.

Topper, M., Emmelkamp, P. M., Watkins, E., & Ehring, T. (2017). Prevention of anxiety disorders and depression by targeting excessive worry and rumination in adolescents and young adults: A randomized controlled trial. *Behaviour Research and Therapy, 90*, 123–136.

Torales, J., Barrios, I., & Villalba, J. (2017). Alternative therapies for excoriation (skin picking) disorder: A brief update. *Advances in Mind/Body Medicine, 31*(1), 10–13.

Torgersen, S., Lygren, S., Oien, P. A., Skre, I., Onstad, S., Edvardsen, J., . . . Kringlen, E. (2000). A twin study of personality disorders. *Comprehensive Psychiatry, 41*(6), 416.

Torres, A. R., Shavitt, R. G., Torresan, R. C., Ferrão, Y. A., Miguel, E. C., & Fontenelle, L. F. (2013). Clinical features of pure obsessive-compulsive disorder. *Comprehensive Psychiatry, 54*(7), 1042–1052.

Torrey, E. F. (2001). *Surviving schizophrenia: A manual for families, consumers, and providers* (4th ed.). New York: HarperCollins.

Torrey, E. F. (2014). *Surviving schizophrenia: A family manual* (6th edition). New York: Harper Paperbacks.

Toteja, N., Gallego, J. A., Saito, E., Gerhard, T., Winterstein, A., Olfson, M., & Correll, C. U. (2014). Prevalence and correlates of antipsychotic polypharmacy in children and adolescents receiving antipsychotic treatment. *International Journal of Neuropsychopharmacy, 17*(7), 1095–1105.

Toth, S. L., Petrenko, C. L. M., Gravener-Davis, J. A., & Handley, E. D. (2016). Advances in prevention science: A developmental psychopathology perspective. In D. Cicchetti (Ed.), *Developmental psychopathology, Vol. 4: Risk, resilience, and intervention* (3rd ed.). New York: Wiley.

Town, J. M., Abbass, A., Driessen, E., Luyten, P., & Weerasekera, P. (2017). Updating the evidence and recommendations for short-term psychodynamic psychotherapy in the treatment of major depressive disorder in adults. *The Canadian Journal of Psychiatry, 62*(1), 73–74.

Trapp, M., Trapp, E., Egger, J. W., Domej, W., Schillaci, G., Avian, A., . . . Baulmann, J. (2014). Impact of mental and physical stress on blood pressure and pulse pressure under normobaric versus hypoxic conditions. *Plos One, 9*(5), e89005.

Trauer, J. M., Qian, M. Y., Doyle, J. S., Rajaratnam, S. W., & Cunnington, D. (2015). Cognitive behavioral therapy for chronic insomnia: A systematic review and meta-analysis. *Annals of Internal Medicine, 163*(3), 191–204.

Travis, C. B., & Meltzer, A. L. (2008). Women's health: Biological and social systems. In F. L. Denmark & M. A. Paludi (Eds.), *Psychology of women: A handbook of issues and theories* (2nd ed., pp. 353–399). Westport, CT: Praeger Publishers.

Traynor, V., Cordato, N., Burns, P., Xu, Y., Britten, N., Duncan, K., . . . McKinnon, C. (2015). Is delirium being detected in emergency? *Australasian Journal on Ageing.* [Electronic publication]

Treasure, J., & Cardi, V. (2017). Anorexia nervosa, theory and treatment: Where are we 35

years on from Hilde Bruch's foundation lecture? *European Eating Disorders Review, 25*(3), 139–147.

Treatment Advocacy Center. (2007). *Briefing paper: Criminalization of individuals with severe psychiatric disorders.* Retrieved from www.Treatmentadvocacycenter.org.

Treece, D., Rangarajan, H. P., & Thompson, J. (2011, April). Past, present, and future of the asylum. *Inovation Incubator*, 1–20.

Trevisan, L. A. (2014, May 9). Elderly alcohol use disorders: Epidemiology, screening, and assessment issues. *Psychiatric Times.*

Triebwasser, J., Chemerinski, E., Roussos, P., & Siever, L. J. (2013). Paranoid personality disorder. *Journal of Personality Disorders, 27*(6), 795–805.

Tripoli, T. M., Sato, H., Sartori, M. G., de Arauio, F. F., Girao, M. J. B. C., & Schor, E. (2011). Evaluation of quality of life and sexual satisfaction in women suffering from chronic pelvic pain with or without endometriosis. *Journal of Sexual Medicine, 8*(2), 497–503.

Trotter, D. M., Bateman, B., & Avorn, J. (2017). Educational outreach to opioid prescribers: The case for academic detailing. *Pain Physician, 20*(2S), S147–S151.

True, W. R., & Lyons, M. J. (1999). Genetic risk factors for PTSD: A twin study. In R. Yehuda (Ed.), *Risk factors for posttraumatic stress disorder.* Washington, DC: American Psychiatric Press.

Trull, T. J., Jahng, S., Tomko, R. L., Wood, P. K., & Sher, K. J. (2010). Revised NESARC personality disorder diagnoses: Gender, prevalence, and comorbidity with substance dependence disorders. *Journal of Personality Disorders, 24*(4), 412–426.

Trull, T. J., & Prinstein, M. (2012). *Clinical psychology.* Independence, KY: Cengage Learning.

Trull, T. J., & Widiger, T. A. (2003). Personality disorders. In G. Stricker, T. A. Widiger, & I. B. Wiener (Eds.), *Handbook of psychology: Clinical psychology.* New York: Wiley.

Tsanas, A., Saunders, K. E., Bilderbeck, A. C., Palmius, N., Osipov, M., Clifford, G. D., . . . De Vos, M. (2016). Daily longitudinal self-monitoring of mood variability in bipolar disorder and borderline personality disorder. *Journal of Affective Disorders, 205*, 225–233.

Tsay-Vogel, M., Shanahan, J., & Signorielli, N. (2016) Social media cultivating perceptions of privacy: A 5-year analysis of privacy attitudes and self-disclosure behaviors among Facebook users. *New Media & Society.*

Tsuang, M., Domschke, K., Jerkey, B. A., & Lyons, M. J. (2004). Agoraphobic behavior and panic attack: A study of male twins. *Journal of Anxiety Disorders, 18*(6), 799–807.

Tsui, P., Deptula, A., & Yuan, D. Y. (2017). Conversion disorder, functional neurological symptom disorder, and chronic pain: Comorbidity, assessment, and treatment. *Current Pain and Headache Reports, 21*(6), 29.

Tu, N. D., & Baskin, L. S. (2017, June 14). Nocturnal enuresis in children: Management. *UpToDate.* Retrieved from http://www.uptodate.com.

Tu, N. D., Baskin, L. S., & Arnhym, A. M. (2017, July 12). Nocturnal enuresis in children: Etiology and evaluation. *UpToDate.* Retrieved from http://www.uptodate.com.

Tuckey, M. R., & Scott, J. E. (2014). Group critical incident stress debriefing with emergency services personnel: A randomized controlled trial. *Anxiety, Stress, and Coping, 27*(1), 38–54.

Tull, M. (2017, February 15). Are some racial groups more likely to develop PTSD? *Verywell*. Retrieved from https://www.verywell.com.

Tune, L. E., & DeWitt, M. A. (2011). Delirium. In E. Coffey, J. L. Cummings, M. S. George, & D. Weintraub (Eds.), *The American Psychiatric Publishing textbook of geriatric neuropsychiatry*. Arlington, VA: American Psychiatric Publishing, Inc.

Turkat, I. D., Keane, S. P., & Thompson-Pope, S. K. (1990). Social processing errors among paranoid personalities. *Journal of Psychopathology and Behavioral Assessment, 12*(3), 263–269.

Turkle, S. (2012). *Alone together: Why we expect more from technology and less from each other*. New York: Basic Books.

Turkle, S. (2013, October 10). "We need to talk": Missed connections with hyperconnectivity. Cited in *NPR*. Retrieved from http://www.npr.org/2013/02/10/171490660.

Turkle, S. (2013, December 21). Cited in K. Eisold, Hidden motives: A look at the hidden factors that really drive our social interactions. *Psychology Today*.

Turkle, S. (2015). *Reclaiming conversation: The power of talk in a digital age*. New York: Penguin Press.

Turner, B. H., Dixon-Gordon, K. L., Austin, S. B., Rodriguez, M. A., Rosenthal, M. Z., & Chapman, A. L. (2015). Non-suicidal self-injury with and without borderline personality disorder: Differences in self-injury and diagnostic comorbidity. *Psychiatry Research 230*(1), 28–35.

Turner, D. S. (2017). Crack epidemic: United States history (1980s). *Encyclopaedia Britannica*. Retrieved from https://www.britannica.com.

Turner, E. H., Matthews, A. M., Linardatos, E., Tell, R. A., & Rosenthal, R. (2008). Selective publication of antidepressant trials and its influence on apparent efficacy. *New England Journal of Medicine, 358*, 252–260.

Turner, S. M., Beidel, D. C., & Frueh, B. C. (2005). Multicomponent behavioral treatment of chronic combat-related posttraumatic stress disorder: Trauma management therapy. *Behavior Modification, 29*(1), 39–69.

Turton, M. D., O'Shea, D., Gunn, I., Beak, S. A., Meeran, E. K., Choi, S. J. . . . Bloom, S. R. (1996, January 4). A role for glucagon-like peptide-1 in the central regulation of feeding. *Nature, 379*, 69–72.

Twain, M. (1885). *The Adventures of Huckleberry Finn*.

Twenge, J. M., & Foster, J. D. (2008). Mapping the scale of the narcissism epidemic: Increases in narcissism 2002–2007 within ethnic groups. *Journal of Research in Personality, 42*, 1619–1622.

Twining, R. C., Vantrease, J. E., Love, S., Padival, M., & Rosenkranz, J. A. (2017). An intra-amygdala circuit specifically regulates social fear learning. *Nature Neuroscience, 20*, 459–469.

Uchiyama, T., Kurosawa, M., & Inaba, Y. (2007). MMR-vaccine and regression in autism spectrum disorders: Negative results presented from Japan. *Journal of Autism and Developmental Disorders, 3*(2), 210–217.

Udesky, L. (2014). Stroke and depression. *HealthDay*. Retrieved from http://consumer.healthday.com/encyclopedia.

Uher, R., & Zwicker, A. (2017). Etiology in psychiatry: Embracing the reality of poly-gene-environmental causation of mental illness. *World Psychiatry, 16*(2), 121–129.

Ulrich, R. S. (1984). View from a window may influence recovery from surgery. *Science, 224*, 420–421.

UNESCO (United Nations Educational, Scientific and Cultural Organization). (2017). *School violence and bullying: Global status Report*. Paris: UNESCO.

Ungar, W. J., Mirabelli, C., Cousins, M., & Boydell, K. M. (2006). A qualitative analysis of a dyad approach to health-related quality of life measurement in children with asthma. *Social Science and Medicine, 63*(9), 2354–2366.

United Nations. (2013). *World population ageing 2013*. Geneva: UN, Department of Economic and Social Affairs, Population Division.

United Nations. (2016). *Human Development Reports: Table I: Human Development Index and its components*. New York: UN Development Programme.

United Nations. (2017). *World population aging 1950–2050: III. Changing balance between age groups*. New York: UN, DESA, Population Division.

Urcuyo, K. R., Boyers, A. E., Carver, C. S., & Antoni, M. H. (2005). Finding benefit in breast cancer: Relations with personality, coping, and concurrent well-being. *Psychology and Health, 20*(2), 175–192.

Urošević, S., Collins, P., Muetzel, R., Schissel, A., Lim, K. O., & Luciana, M. (2014). Effects of reward sensitivity and regional brain volumes on substance use initiation in adolescence. *Social Cognitive and Affective Neuroscience*. [Manuscript submitted for publication]

Ursano, R. J., Boydstun, J. A., & Wheatley, R. D. (1981). Psychiatric illness in U.S. Air Force Vietnam prisoners of war: A five-year follow-up. *American Journal of Psychiatry, 138*(3), 310–314.

Ursano, R. J., McCarroll, J. E., & Fullerton, C. S. (2003). Traumatic death in terrorism and disasters: The effects of posttraumatic stress and behavior. In R. J. Ursano, C. S. Fullerton, & A. E. Norwood (Eds.), *Terrorism and disaster: Individual and community mental health interventions* (pp. 308–332). New York: Cambridge University Press.

Usami, M., Iwadare, Y., Watanabe, K., Kodaira, M., Ushijima, H., Tanaka, T., & Saito, K. (2016). Long-term fluctuations in traumatic symptoms of high school girls who survived from the 2011 Japan tsunami: Series of questionnaire-based cross-sectional surveys. *Child Psychiatry & Human Development, 47*(6), 1002–1008.

U.S. Census Bureau. (2010). Race and ethnicity. *American FactFinder*. Retrieved from http://factfinder.census.gov/serviet/ACSSAFFPeople?.

U.S. Census Bureau. (2015, March 3). *New Census Bureau report analyzes U.S. population projections*. Retrieved from http://www.census.gov/newsroom/press-release/CB15-TPS.16.html.

U.S. Census Bureau. (2016). International populations reports, P95/16-1, *An Aging World: 2015*. Washington, DC: U.S. Government Publishing Office.

U.S. Census Bureau. (2016, March). *An aging world: 2015: International population reports*. Retrieved from https://www.census.gov/.

U.S. Census Bureau. (2016, April 15). *FFF: Older Americans Month: May 2016*. Release no. CB16-FF.08. Washington, DC: U.S. Census Bureau.

U.S. Census Bureau. (2016, September 13). *Income and poverty in the United States: 2015*. Report #P60-256. Washington, DC: U.S. Government Publishing Office.

U.S. Census Bureau. (2016, November 17). *The majority of children live with two parents, Census Bureau reports*. Retrieved from http://www.census.gov/newsroom/press-releases/2016/CB16-192.html.

U.S. Census Bureau. (2017, April 10). *Facts for features: Older Americans Month: May 2017*. Release no. CB17-FF.08. Washington, DC: U.S. Census Bureau.

USDA (U.S. Department of Agriculture). (2016, June 1). Annual report animal usage by fiscal year. Retrieved from https://www.aphis.usda.gov/animal_welfare/downloads/7023/Anjual-Reeports-FY2015.

USDHHS (U.S. Department of Health and Human Services). (2017). *Facts about bullying*. Retrieved from https://www.stopbullying.gov/media/facts.

USDVA (U.S. Department of Veteran Affairs). (2015, August 13). *PTSD: National Center for PTSD: Women, trauma, and PTSD*. Retrieved from https://www.ptsd.va.gov.

USDVA (U.S. Department of Veteran Affairs). (2016, February 23). *PTSD: National Center for PTSD: Types of debriefing following disasters*. Retrieved from https://www.ptsd.va.gov.

USDVA (U.S. Department of Veteran Affairs). (2016, July 6). *VA Suicide Program: Facts about veteran suicide, July 2016*. Retrieved from https://www.va.gov/publications/factsheets/suicide_prevention_factsheet_New_VA_Stats_070616_1400.pdf.

USGS (U.S. Geological Survey). (2011, April 14). Earthquakes with 1000 or more deaths since 1900. Retrieved from http://earthquake.usgs/gov/earthquakes/world/world_deaths.php.

U.S. Surgeon General. (2016, November). Facing addiction in America. *U.S. DHHS*. Retrieved from https://addiction.surgeongeneral.gov.

Vadini, F., Calella, G., Pieri, A., Ricci, E., Fulcheri, M., Verrocchio, M. C., . . . Parruti, G. (2018). Neurocognitive impairment and suicide risk among prison inmates. *Journal of Affective Disorders, 225*, 273–277.

Vahia, V. N., & Vahia, I. V. (2008). Schizophrenia in developing countries. In K. T. Mueser & D. V. Jeste (Eds.), *Clinical handbook of schizophrenia* (pp. 549–555). New York: Guilford Press.

Vakil, N. B. (2015, March 12). Peptic ulcer disease: Genetic, environmental, and psychological risk factors and pathogenesis. *UpToDate*. Retrieved from http://www.uptodate.com.

Vaknin S. (2015, June 30). *Malignant self-love: Narcissism revisited* (10th ed.). *Amazon Digital Services.*

Vaknin, S. (2016). The borderline patient: A case study. *HealthyPlace.* Retrieved from https://www.healthyplace.com/personality-disorders.

Valbak, K. (2001). Good outcome for bulimic patients in long-term group analysis: A single-group study. *European Eating Disorders Review, 9*(1), 19–32.

Valenstein, E. S. (1986). *Great and desperate cures.* New York: Basic Books.

Vall, E., & Wade, T. D. (2015). Predictors of treatment outcome in individuals with eating disorders: A systematic review and meta-analysis. *International Journal of Eating Disorders.* [Electronic publication]

Vallarino, M., Henry, C., Etain, B., Gehue, L. J., Macneil, C., Scott, E. M., . . . Scott, J. (2015). An evidence map of psychosocial interventions for the earliest stages of bipolar disorder. *Lancet Psychiatry, 2,* 548–563.

Vallejos, M., Cesoni, O. M., Farinola, R., & Prokopez, C. R. (2017, March 17). Childhood adversities in men with schizophrenia: Dose-response vs. trauma specific hypothesis. *Archives of Paediatrics and Developmental Pathology, 1*(1), 1002.

van de Grift, T. C., Elaut, E., Cerwenka, S. C., Cohen-Kettenis, P. T., De Cuypere, G., Richter-Appelt, H., & Kreukels, B. P. (2017). Effects of medical interventions on gender dysphoria and body image: A follow-up study. *Psychosomatic Medicine, 79,* 815–823.

van den Noort, M., Lim, S., Litscher, G., & Bosch, P. (2018). Transcranial magnetic stimulation for treating older patients with treatment-resistant depression. *Journal of Affective Disorders, 225,* 278–279.

van der Kruijs, S. M., Bodde, N. G., Carrette, E., Lazeron, R. C., Vonck, K. J., Boon, P. M., . . . Aldenkamp, A. P. (2014). Neurophysiological correlates of dissociative symptoms. *Journal of Neurology, Neurosurgery, and Psychiatry, 85*(2), 174–179.

van der Stouwe, T., Asscher, J. J., Stams, G. J. J. M., Deković, M., & van der Laan, P. H. (2014). The effectiveness of Multisystemic Therapy (MST): A meta-analysis. *Clinical Psychology Review, 34,* 468–481.

van Duijl, M., Nijenhuis, E., Komproe, I. H., Gernaat, H. B. P. E., & de Jong, J. T. (2010). Dissociative symptoms and reported trauma among patients with spirit possession and matched healthy controls in Uganda. *Culture, Medicine and Psychiatry, 34*(2), 380–400.

Van Durme, K., Goossens, L., & Braet, C. (2012). Adolescent aesthetic athletes: A group at risk for eating pathology? *Eating Behaviors, 13*(2), 119–122.

van Geel, M., Vedder, P., & Tanilon, J. (2014). Relationship between peer victimization, cyberbullying, and suicide in children and adolescents: A meta-analysis. *JAMA Pediatrics, 168*(5), 435–442.

Van Hecke, A. V., Oswald, T., & Mundy, P. (2016). Joint attention and the social phenotype of autism spectrum disorder: A perspective from developmental psychopathology. In D. Cicchetti (ed.), *Developmental psychopathology, Vol. 3: Maladaptation and psychopathology* (3rd ed.). New York: Wiley.

van Holst, R. J., van Timmeren, T., & Goudriaan, A. E. (2017). Are there differences in disruptions of reward processing between substance use disorder and gambling disorder? *JAMA Psychiatry, 74,* 759–760.

van Lankveld, J. J. D. M. (2017). Self-help and biblio-sex therapy. In Z. D. Peterson (Ed.), *The Wiley handbook of sex therapy* (Part IV, Ch. 29, pp. 468–482). Chichester, UK: John Wiley & Sons.

Van Meter, A. R., Burke, C., Kowatch, R. A., Findling, R. L., & Youngstrom, E. A. (2016). Ten-year updated meta-analysis of the clinical characteristics of pediatric mania and hypomania. *Bipolar Disorder, 18,* 19–32.

Van Orden, K. A., Witte, T. K., Selby, E. A., Bender, T. W., & Joiner, T. E., Jr. (2008). Suicidal behavior in youth. In J. R. Z. Abela & B. L. Hankin (Eds.), *Handbook of depression in children and adolescents.* New York: Guilford Press.

Van Schrojenstein Lantman, M., Mackus, M., Otten, L. S., de Kruijff, D., van de Loo, A. J., Kraneveld, A. D., . . . Verster, J. C. (2017). Mental resilience, perceived immune functioning, and health. *Journal of Multidisciplinary Healthcare, 10,* 107–112.

Van Spronsen, F. J., van Wegberg, A. M. J., Ahring, K., Belanger-Quintana, A., Blau, N., Bosch, A. M., et al. (2017). Key European guidelines for the diagnosis and management of patients with phenylketonuria. *Lancet: Diabetes and Epidemiology, 5,* 743–756.

Van Vonderen, K. E., & Kinnally, W. (2012). Media effects on body image: Examining media exposure in the broader context of internal and other social factors. *American Communication Journal, 14*(2), 41–57.

Vaquero, L., Cámara, E., Sampedro, F., Perez de Los Cobos, J., Batile, F., Fabregas, J. M., . . . Riba, J. (2017). Cocaine addiction is associated with abnormal prefrontal function, increased striatal connectivity and sensitivity to monetary incentives, and decreased connectivity outside the human reward circuit. *Addiction Biology, 22*(3), 844–856.

Vasquez, M. J. T., & Vasquez, E. M. (2016). Psychotherapy with women: theory and practice. In A. J. Consoli, L. E. Beutler, & B. Bongar (Eds.), *Comprehensive textbook of psychotherapy: Theory and practice* (2nd ed. pp. 299–314). New York: Oxford University Press.

Vasterling, J. J., Asian, M., Proctor, S. P., Ko, J., Marx, B. P., Jakupcak, M., . . . Concato, J. (2016). Longitudinal examination of posttraumatic stress disorder as a long-term outcome of Iraq War deployment. *American Journal of Epidemiology, 184,* 796–805.

Vaz, S., Parsons, R., Passmore, A. E., Andreou, P., & Falkmer, T. (2013). Internal consistency, test-retest reliability and measurement error of the self-report version of the social skills rating system in a sample of Australian adolescents. *Plos One, 8*(9), e73924.

Vazquez, K., Sandler, J., Interian, A., & Feldman, J. M. (2017). Emotionally triggered asthma and its relationship to panic disorder, *ataques de nervois,* and asthma-related death of a loved one in Latino adults. *Journal of Psychosomatic Research, 93,* 76–82.

Vedel, A., & Thomsen, D. K. (2017). The Dark Triad across academic majors. *Personality and Individual Differences, 116,* 86–91.

Veiga-Martínez, C., Perez-Alvarez, M., & Garcia-Montes, J. M. (2008). Acceptance and commitment therapy applied to treatment of auditory hallucinations. *Clinical Case Studies, 7,* 118–135.

Veale, D., & Bewley, A. (2015). Body dysmorphic disorder. *BMJ (Clinical Research Ed.), 240,* h2278.

Ventura, J., Subotnik, K. L., Ered, A., Hellemann, G. S., & Nuechterlein, K. H. (2016). Cognitive Assessment Interview (CAI): Validity as a co-primary measure of cognition across phases of schizophrenia. *Schizophrenia Research, 172*(1–3), 137–142.

Vermote, R., Lowyck, B., Luyten, P., Vertommen, H., Corveleyn, J., Verhaest, Y., . . . Peuskens, J. (2010). Process and outcome in psychodynamic hospitalization-based treatment for patients with a personality disorder. *Journal of Nervous and Mental Disease, 198*(2), 110–115.

Vetter, H. J. (1969). *Language behavior and psychopathology.* Chicago: Rand McNally.

Vicianova, M. (2015). Historical techniques in lie detection. *European Journal of Psychology, 11*(3): 522–534.

Vickrey, B. G., Samuels, M. A., & Ropper, A. H. (2010). How neurologists think: A cognitive psychology perspective on missed diagnoses. *Annals of Neurology, 67*(4), 425–433.

Victor, S. E., & Klonsky, E. D. (2014). Correlates of suicide attempts among self-injurers: A meta-analysis. *Clinical Psychology Review, 34*(4), 282–297.

Vidal-Ribas, P., Brotman, M. A., Valdivieso, I., Leibenluft, E., & Stringaris, A. (2016). The status of irritability in psychiatry: A conceptual and qualitative review. *Journal of the American Academy of Child and Adolescent Psychiatry, 55,* 556–570.

Vierck, E., & Silverman, J. M. (2011). Family studies of autism. In E. Hollander, A. Kolevzon, & J. T. Coyle (Eds.), *Textbook of autism spectrum disorders* (pp. 299–312). Arlington, VA: American Psychiatric Publishing, Inc.

Vieta, E., & Colom, F. (2017, March 22). Bipolar disorder in adults: Managing poor adherence to maintenance pharmacotherapy. *UpToDate.* Retrieved from http://www.uptodate.com.

Viguera, A. (2016, November 9). Postpartum unipolar major depression: Epidemiology, clinical features, assessment, and diagnosis. *UpToDate.* Retrieved from http://www.uptodate.com.

Viguera, A. (2017, January 12). Severe postpartum unipolar major depression: Treatment. *UpToDate.* Retrieved from http://www.uptodate.com.

Vinogradov, S., Fisher, M., & de Villers-Sidani, E. (2012). Cognitive training for impaired neural systems in neuropsychiatric illness. *Neuropsychopharmacology, 37*(1), 43–76.

Vissia, E. M., Giesen, M. E., Chalavi, S., Nijenhuis, E. R. S., Draijer, N., Brand, B. L., & Reinders, A. A. T. S. (2016, May). Is it trauma- or fantasy-based? Comparing dissociative identity disorder, post-traumatic stress disorder, simulators, and controls. *Acta Psychiatrica Scandinavica, 134.*

Vitelli, R. (2013). Can social media spread epidemics? *Psychology Today.* Retrieved from http://www.psychologyto-day.com/blog/media-spotlight/201309/cann-social-media-spread-epidemics.

Vitelli, R. (2016, May 4). Can celebrity suicides lead to copycat deaths? *Psychology Today.*

Vogel, J., & Baran, M. (2016). Inconclusive: The truth about lie detector tests. *APM (American Public Media) Reports.*

Vogt, D., Smith, B. N., Fox, A. B., Amoroso, T., Taverna, E., & Schnurr, P. P. (2017). Consequences of PTSD for the work and family quality of life of female and male U.S. Afghanistan and Iraq War veterans. *Social Psychiatry and Psychiatric Epidemiology, 52*(3), 341–352.

Vogt, L., Reichlin, T. S., Nathues, C., & Würbel, H. (2016). Authorization of animal experiments is based on confidence rather than evidence of scientific rigor. *PLoS Biology, 14*(12), e200598.

Volk, D. W., Sampson, A. R., Zhang, Y., Edelson, J. R., & Lewis, D. A. (2016). Cortical GAMA markers identify a molecular subtype of psychotic and bipolar disorders. *Psychological Medicine, 46*(12), 2501–2512.

Volkert, J., Schulz, H., Härter, M., Wlodarczyk, O., & Andreas, S. (2013). The prevalence of mental disorders in older people in Western countries: A meta-analysis. *Ageing Research Reviews, 12,* 339–353.

Volkow, N. D., & Collins, F. S. (2017). The role of science in addressing the opioid crisis. *New England Journal of Medicine, 377*(4), 391–394.

Volkow, N. D., Fowler, J. S., & Wang, G. J. (2002). Role of dopamine in drug reinforcement and addiction in humans: Results from imaging studies. *Behavioral Pharmacology, 13,* 355–366.

Volkow, N. D., Fowler, J. S., & Wang, G. J. (2004). The addicted human brain viewed in the light of imaging studies: Brain circuits and treatment strategies. *Neuropharmacology, 47*(Suppl. 1), 3–13.

Volkow, N. D., Koob, G. F., & McLellan, T. (2016). Neurobiologic advances from the brain disease model of addiction. *New England Journal of Medicine, 374,* 363–371.

Volman, I., von Borries, A. K. L., Bulten, B. H., Verkes, R. J., Toni, I., & Roelofs, K. (2016). Testosterone modulates altered prefrontal control of emotional actions in psychopathic offenders(1,2,3). *eNeuro, 3*(1), Jan-Feb.

Volmer, J., Koch, I. K., & Göritz, A. S. (2016). The bright and dark sides of leaders' Dark Triad traits: Effects on subordinates' career success and well-being. *Personality and Individual Differences, 101,* 413–418.

Volz, K., Leonhart, R., Stark, R., Vaitl, D., & Ambach, W. (2017). Psychophysiological correlates of the misinformation effect. *International Journal of Psychophysiology,* April 8, *117,* 1–9. [Epub ahead of print]

von Hahn, L. E. (2016, September 29). Specific learning disabilities in children: Clinical features. *UpToDate.* Retrieved from http://www.uptodate.com.

von Hahn, L. E. (2016, November 9). Specific learning disabilities in children: Evaluation. *UpToDate.* Retrieved from http://www.uptodate.com.

von Hahn, L. E. (2017, April 28). Specific learning disabilities in children: Role of the primary care provider. *UpToDate.* Retrieved from http://www.uptodate.com.

Voon, P., Karamouzian, M., & Kerr, T. (2017). Chronic pain and opioid misuse: A review of reviews. *Substance Abuse Treatment, Prevention, and Policy, 12*(1), 36.

Vos, J., Craig, M., & Cooper, M. (2015). Existential therapies: A meta-analysis of their effects on psychological outcomes. *Journal of Consulting and Clinical Psychology, 83*(1), 115–128.

Waddington, J. L., O'Tuathaigh, C. M. P., & Remington, G. J. (2011). Pharmacology and neuroscience of antipsychotic drugs. In D. R. Weinberg & P. Harrison (Eds.), *Schizophrenia* (pp. 483–514). Hoboken, NJ: Wiley-Blackwell.

Wade, T. D., & Watson, H. J. (2012). Psychotherapies in eating disorders. In J. Alexander & J. Treasure (Eds.), *A collaborative approach to eating disorders* (pp. 125–135). New York: Taylor & Francis.

Wadsworth, M. E., Evans, G. W., Grant, K., Carter, J. S., & Duffy, S. (2016). Poverty and the development of psychopathology. In D. Cicchetti (Ed.), *Developmental psychopathology (Third Edition): Volume 4, Risk, resilience, and intervention.* New York: Wiley.

Waehrer, G. M., Miller, T. R., Hendrie, D., & Galvin, D. M. (2016). Employee assistance programs, drug testing, and workplace injury. *Journal of Safety Research, 57,* 53–60.

Wagstaff, K. (2015, December 15). Pew study finds half of Americans play video games. *NBCNEWS.*

Waisbren, S. E. (2011). Phenylketonuria. In S. Goldstein, & C. R. Reynolds (Eds.), *Handbook of neurodevelopmental and genetic disorders in children* (2nd ed., pp. 398–424) New York: Guilford Press.

Wakefield, A. J., Murch, S. H., Anthony, A., Linnell, J., Casson, D. M., Malik, M., . . . Walker-Smith, J. A. (1998). Retracted: Ileal-lymphoid-nodular hyperplasia, non-specific colitis, and pervasive developmental disorder in children. *The Lancet, 351*(9103), 637–641.

Wakefield, J. C. (2015). DSM-5, psychiatric epidemiology and the false positives problem. *Epidemiology and Psychiatric Sciences, 24*(3), 188–196.

Walentynowicz, M., Raes, F., Van Diest, I., & Van den Bergh, O. (2017). The specificity of health-related autobiographical memories in patients with somatic symptom disorder. *Psychological Medicine, 79*(1), 43–49.

Walkup, J. T., Albano, A. M., Piacentini, J., Boris, B., Compton, S. N., Sherrill, J., et al. (2008). Cognitive behavioral therapy, sertraline, or a combination in childhood anxiety. *New England Journal of Medicine, 359,* 2753–2766.

Wallace, G. L., White, S. F., Robustelli, B., Sinclair, S., Hwang, S., Martin, A., & Blair, R. J. (2014). Cortical and subcortical abnormalities in youths with conduct disorder and elevated callous-unemotional traits. *Journal of the American Academy of Child and Adolescent Psychiatry, 53*(4), 456–465.

Walker, E. F., Brennan, P. A., Esterrberg, M., Brasfield, J. L., Pearce, B., & Compton, M. T. (2010). Longitudinal changes in cortisol secretion and conversion to psychosis in at-risk youth. *Journal of Abnormal Psychology, 119*(2), 401–408.

Walker, E. F., Mittal, V., & Tessner, K. (2008). Stress and the hypothalamic pituitary adrenal axis in the developmental course of schizophrenia. *Annual Review of Clinical Psychology, 4,* 189–216.

Walker, E. F., Ryan, A. T., Bridgman Goines, K. C., Novacek, D. M., Goulding, S. M., . . . Trotman, H. D. (2016). Multilevel approaches to schizophrenia and other psychotic disorders: The biobehavioral interface. In D. Cicchetti (Ed.), *Developmental psychopathology* (Vol. 3, Maladaptation and psychopathology, Ch. 22, pp. 997–1038). Hoboken, NJ: John Wiley & Sons.

Walker, E. R., & Druss, B. G. (2016). Cumulative burden of comorbid mental disorders, substance use disorders, chronic medical conditions, and poverty on health among adults in the U.S.A. *Psychology, Health & Medicine.* Published online.

Waller, G., Gray, E., Hinrichsen, H., Mountford, V., Lawson, R., & Patient, E. (2014). Cognitive-behavioral therapy for bulimia nervosa and atypical bulimic nervosa: Effectiveness in clinical settings. *International Journal of Eating Disorders, 47*(1), 13–17.

Waller, B. M. (2013). Facial expression in nonhuman animals. *Emotion Review, 5*(1), 54–59.

Waller, B. M., Whitehouse, J., & Micheletta, J. (2016). Macaques can predict social outcomes from facial expressions. *Animal Cognition, 19*(5), 1031–1036.

Walser, R. D., Garvert, D. W., Karlin, B. E., Trockel, M., Ryu, D. M., & Taylor, C. B. (2015). Effectiveness of acceptance and commitment therapy in treating depression and suicidal ideation in veterans. *Behaviour Research and Therapy, 74,* 25–31.

Walsh, B. T. (2017, January 9). Anorexia nervosa in adults: Pharmacotherapy. *UpToDate.* Retrieved from http://www.uptodate.com.

Walsh, K., Resnick, H. S., Danielson, C. K., McCauley, J. L., Saunders, B. E., & Kilpatrick, D. G. (2014). Patterns of drug and alcohol use associated with lifetime sexual revictimization and current posttraumatic stress disorder among three national samples of adolescent, college, and household–residing women. *Addictive Behaviors, 39*(3), 684–689.

Walter, E. E., Fernandez, F., Snelling, M., & Barkus, E. (2016). Genetic consideration of schizotypal traits: A review. *Frontiers in Psychology, 7,* 1769.

Walters, M., Hackett, K., Caesar, E., Isaacson, R., & Mosconi, L. (2017). Role of nutrition to promote healthy brain aging and reduce risk of Alzheimer's disease. *Current Nutrition Reports, 6*(2), 63–71.

Wampold, B. E. (2015). How important are the common factors in psychotherapy? An update. *World Psychiatry, 14*(3), 270–277.

Wang, G. S. (2016, October 13). Cannabis (marijuana): Acute intoxication. *UpToDate.* Retrieved from http://www.uptodate.com.

Wang, J., Wei, Q., Yuan, X., Jiang, X., Xu, J., Zhou, X., . . . Wang, K. (2018). Local functional connectivity density is closely associated with the response of electroconvulsive therapy in major depressive disorder. *Journal of Affective Disorders, 225,* 658–664.

Wang, M., & Jiang, G.-R. (2007). Psychopathological mechanisms and clinical assessment of dissociative identity disorder. *Chinese Journal of Clinical Psychology, 15*(4), 426–429.

Wang, M., Wang, X., & Liu, L. (2016). Paternal and maternal psychological and physical aggression and children's anxiety in China. *Child Abuse & Neglect, 51,* 12–20.

Wang, P. S., Berglund, P., Olfson, M., Pincus, H. A., Wells, K. B., & Kessler, R. C. (2005). Failure and delay in initial treatment contact after first onset of mental disorders in the National Comorbidity Survey Replication. *Archives of General Psychiatry, 62,* 603–613.

Wang, P. S., Lane, M., Olfson, M., Pincus, H. A., Wells, K. B., & Kessler, R. C. (2005). Twelve-month use of mental health services in the United States. *Archives of General Psychiatry, 62,* 629–640.

Wang, Q., Shelton, R. C., & Dwivedi, Y. (2018). Interaction between early-life stress and FKBP5 gene variants in major depressive disorder and post-traumatic stress disorder: A systematic review and meta-analysis. *Journal of Affective Disorders, 225,* 422–428.

Wang, S. S. (2007, December 4). The graying of shock therapy. *Wall Street Journal Online.* Retrieved from http://online.wsg.com/public/article_print/SB119673737406312767.html.

Wang, S. W., & Repetti, R. L. (2016). Who gives to whom? Testing the support gap hypothesis with naturalistic observations of couple interactions. *Journal of Family Psychology, 30*(4), 492–502.

Wang, Y., & Gorenstein, C. (2013). Psychometric properties of the Beck Depression Inventory-II: A comprehensive review. *Revista Brasileira De Psiquiatria, 35*(4), 416–431.

Wang, Y., Hung, K. S. Y., Deng, M. Y., Lui, S. S. Y., Lee, J. C. Y., Mak, H. K. F., . . . Chan, R. C. K. (2017). Altered resting-state functional connectivity of striatum in first-episode schizophrenia. *Schizophrenia Bulletin, 43*(Suppl.1), S197–S198.

Wang, Y., Tang, J., Zhou, F., Yang, L. & Wu, J. (2017). Comprehensive geriatric care reduces acute perioperative delirium in elderly patients with hip fractures: A meta-analysis. *Medicine, 96*(26), e7361.

Wang, Y., Wang, X., Liu, F., Jiang, X., Xiao, Y., Dong, X., . . . Qu, Z. (2016, December 15). Negative life events and antenatal depression among pregnant women in rural China: The role of negative automatic thoughts. *PLOS ONE, 11*(12), e0167597.

Wang, Y. Y., Liao, Y. L., Gao, L. L., Hu, X. Y., & Yue, J. R. (2017). Localization establishment of an interdisciplinary intervention model to prevent post-operative delirium in older patients based on "Hospital Elder Life Program" [article in Chinese; abstract in English]. *Hu Li Za Zhi, 64*(3), 33–42.

Warner, C. M., Colognori, D., Brice, C., Herzig, K., Mufson, L., Lynch, C., . . . Klein, R. G. (2016). Can school counselors deliver cognitive-behavioral treatment for social anxiety effectively? A randomized controlled trial. *Journal of Child Psychology and Psychiatry, 57,* 1229–1238.

Washburn, I. J., Capaldi, D. M., Kim, H. K., & Feingold, A. (2014). Alcohol and marijuana use in early adulthood for at-risk men: Time-varying associations with peer and partner substance use. *Drug and Alcohol Dependence, 140,* 112–117.

Waters, B. (2015, June 24). 23 mental health professionals interviewed about their jobs. *Psychology Today.*

Waters, F., & Fernyhough, C. (2017). Hallucinations: A systematic review of points of similarity and difference across diagnostic classes. *Schizophrenia Bulletin, 43*(1), 32–43.

Watkins, E. R., & Nolen-Hoeksema, S. (2014). A habit-goal framework of depressive rumination. *Journal of Abnormal Psychology, 123*(1), 24–34.

Watson, J. B., & Rayner, R. (1920). Conditioned emotional reaction. *Journal of Experimental Psychology, 3,* 1–14.

Watson, P. J., & Shalev, A. Y. (2005). Assessment and treatment of adult acute responses to traumatic stress following mass traumatic events. *CNS Spectrums, 10*(2), 123–131.

Watson, T. S., Watson, T. S., & Ret, J. (2008). Learning, motor, and communication disorders. In D. Reitman (Ed.), *Handbook of psychological assessment, case conceptualization, and treatment, Vol. 2: Children and adolescents.* Hoboken, NJ: John Wiley & Sons.

Watterson, R. A., Williams, J. V., Lavorato, D. H., & Patten, S. B. (2017). Descriptive epidemiology of generalized anxiety disorder in Canada. *Canadian Journal of Psychiatry, 62*(1), 24–29.

Waugh, J. L. (2013). Acute dyskinetic reaction in a healthy toddler following methylphenidate ingestion. *Pediatric Neurology, 49*(1), 58–60.

Way, M. J., Ali, M. A., McQuillin, A., & Morgan, M. Y. (2017). Genetic variants in ALDH1B1 and alcohol dependence risk in a British and Irish population: A bioinformatic and genetic study. *PLOS ONE, 12*(6), e0177009.

Wayne, J. G., & Hellstrom, M. D. (2017, June 27). Male dyspareunia. *UpToDate.* Retrieved from http://www.uptodate.com.

Wayne, T. (2017, May 5). Social insecurity: Internet turns boomers into twits. *New York Times.*

WCSAP (Washington Coalition of Sexual Assault Programs). (2016, December 6). *The effects of sexual assault.* Olympia, WA: WCSAP.

Webb, J. B., Fiery, M. F., & Jafari, N. (2016). "You better not leave me shaming!": Conditional indirect effect analyses of anti-fat attitudes, body shame, and fat talk as a function of self-compassion in college women. *Body Image, 18,* 5–13.

Weber, B. (2016, August 5). Chris Costner Sizemore, patient behind "The Three Faces of Eve," dies at 90. *New York Times.*

Weber, S. R., Wehr, A. M., & Duchemin, A. M. (2016). Prevalence of antipsychotic prescriptions among patients with anxiety disorders treated in inpatient and outpatient psychiatric settings. *Journal of Affective Disorders, 191,* 292–299.

Weber, T., & Ornstein, C. (2013). Half of drug company payoffs go to one "specialty"—psychiatry. *ProPublica.* Retrieved from http://www.psychsearch.net.

Webster-Stratton, C. (2016). The incredible years: Use of play interventions and coaching for children with externalizing difficulties. In T. M. Reddy, T. Files-Hall, & C. E. Schaefer (Eds.), *Empirically based play interventions for children* (2nd ed). Washington, D.C.: American Psychological Association.

Wechsler, H., Davenport, A., Dowdall, G., Moeykens, B., & Castillo, S. (1994). Health and behavioral consequences of binge drinking in college. *Journal of the American Medical Association, 272*(21), 1672–1677.

Wechsler, H., Dowdell, G. W., Davenport, A., & Castillo, S. (1995). Correlates of college student binge drinking. *American Journal of Public Health, 85*(7), 921–926.

Wechsler, H., Lee, J. E., Kuo, M., Seibring, M., Nelson, T. F., & Lee, H. (2002). Trends in alcohol use, related problems and experience of prevention efforts among US college students 1993 to 2001: Results from the 2001 Harvard School of Public Health College Alcohol Study. *Journal of American College Health, 50,* 203–217.

Wechsler, H., Seibring, M., Liu, I. C., & Ahl, M. (2004). Colleges respond to student binge drinking: Reducing student demand or limiting access. *Journal of American College Health, 52*(4), 159–168.

Weck, F., Grikscheit, F., Höfling, V., Kordt, A., Hamm, A. O., Gerlach, A. L., . . . Lang, T. (2016). The role of treatment delivery factors in exposure-based cognitive behavioral therapy for panic disorder with agoraphobia. *Journal of Anxiety Disorders, 42,* 10–18.

Weck, F., Neng, J. B., Richtberg, S., Jakob, M., & Stangier, U. (2015). Cognitive therapy versus exposure therapy for hypochondriasis (health anxiety): A randomized controlled trial. *Journal of Consulting and Clinical Psychology, 83*(4), 665–676.

Weeks, D., & James, J. (1995). *Eccentrics: A study of sanity and strangeness.* New York: Villard.

Weeks, D. J. (2015). *The gifts of eccentrics: Imagination in reality.* CreateSpace Publishing Platform.

Weersing, V. R., Jeffreys, M., Do, M. T., Schwartz, K. T., & Bolanco, C. (2017). Evidence base update of psychosocial treatments for child and adolescent depression. *Journal of Clinical Child and Adolescent Psychology, 46,* 11–43.

Wei, Y., Szumilas, M., & Kutcheer, S. (2010). Effectiveness on mental health of psychological debriefing for crisis intervention in schools. *Educational Psychology Review, 22*(3), 339–347.

Weiner, R. (2014, September 13). Colleges ramp up efforts to prevent sex assaults. *USA Today.* Retrieved from http://www.usatoday.com/story/news/nation/2014/09/13/.

Weinshenker, N. (2014). *Teenagers and body image: What's typical and what's not?* New York: NYU Child Study Center. Retrieved from http://www.education.com.

Weis, J., Gully, J., & Marks, S. (2016). The interplay of factitious disorder and palliative care encounters: A case series. *Journal of Palliative Medicine, 19*(2), 238–243.

Weishaar, M. E., & Beck, A. T. (2006). Cognitive theory of personality and personality disorders. In S. Strack (Ed.), *Differentiating normal and abnormal personality* (2nd ed., pp. 113–135). New York: Springer Publishing Co.

Weiss, D. E. (1991). *The great divide.* New York: Poseidon Press/Simon & Schuster.

Weiss, F. (2011). Alcohol self-administration. In M. C. Olmstead (Ed.), *Animal models of drug addiction. Springer protocols: Neuromethods* (pp. 133–165). Totowa, NJ: Humana Press.

Weisskirch, R. S., Drouin, M., & Delevi, R. (2017). Relational anxiety and sexting. *Journal of Sex Research, 54*(6), 685–693.

Weissman, L., & Bridgemohan, C. (2017, June 14). Autism spectrum disorder in children and adolescents: Behavioral and educational interventions. *UpToDate.* Retrieved from http://www.uptodate.com.

Weissman, L., & Bridgemohan, C. (2017, July 12). Autism spectrum disorder in children and adolescents: Pharmacologic interventions. *UpToDate.* Retrieved from http://www.uptodate.com.

Weissman, M. M., Berry, O. O., Warner, V., Gameroff, M. J., Skipper, J., Talati, A., . . . Wickramaratne, P. (2016). A 30-year study of 3 generations at high risk and low risk for depression. *JAMA Psychiatry, 73*(9), 970–977.

Weissman, M. M., Wickramaratne, P., Gameroff, M. J., Warner, V., Pilowsky, D., Kohad, R. G., . . . Talati, A. (2016). Offspring of depressed parents: 30 years later. *American Journal of Psychiatry, 173*, 1024–1032.

Wells, A. (2005). The metacognitive model of GAD: Assessment of meta-worry and relationship with DSM-IV generalized anxiety disorder. *Cognitive Therapy and Research, 29*(1), 107–121.

Wells, A. (2010). Metacognitive therapy: Application to generalized anxiety disorder. In D. Sookman & R. L. Leahy (Eds.), *Treatment resistant anxiety disorders: Resolving impasses to symptom remission* (pp. 1–29). New York: Routledge/Taylor & Francis Group.

Wells, A. (2011). Metacognitive therapy. In J. D. Herbert & E. M. Forman (Eds.), *Acceptance and mindfulness in cognitive behavior therapy: Understanding and applying the new therapies* (pp. 83–108). Hoboken, NJ: John Wiley & Sons Inc.

Wells, A. (2014). *Cognitive therapy of anxiety disorders: A practical guide* (2nd ed.). Hoboken, NJ: Wiley-Blackwell.

Wells, G. L., Steblay, N. K., & Dysart, J. E. (2011). *A test of the simultaneous vs. sequential lineup methods: An initial report of the AJS National Eyewitness Identification Field Studies.* Des Moines, Iowa: American Judicature Society.

Wells, G. L., Steblay, N. K., & Dysart, J. E. (2015). Double-blind photo lineups using actual eyewitnesses: An experimental test of a sequential versus simultaneous lineup procedure. *Law and Human Behavior, 39*(1), 1–14.

Wen, T. (2016). Can you beat a lie detector test? *BBC Future.*

Werth, J. L., Jr. (2004). The relationships among clinical depression, suicide, and other actions that may hasten death. *Behavioral Sciences and the Law, 22*(5), 627–649.

Wertheimer, A. (2001). *A special scar: The experiences of people bereaved by suicide* (2nd ed.). East Sussex, England: Brunner-Routledge.

Wesselhoeft, R., Heiervang, E. R., Kragh-Sorensen, P., Sorensen, M. J., & Bilenberg, N. (2016). Major depressive disorder and subthreshold depression in prepubertal children from the Danish National Birth Cohort. *Comprehensive Psychiatry, 70*, 65–76.

West, R. (2016, April 14). *Yes, America can afford to dramatically reduce poverty and increase opportunity.* Washington, DC: Center for American Progress.

Westermeyer, J. (1993). Substance use disorders among young minority refugees: Common themes in a clinical sample. *NIDA Research Monograph 130*, 308–320.

Westermeyer, J. (2001). Alcoholism and co-morbid psychiatric disorders among American Indians. *American Indian and Alaska Native Mental Health Research, 10*, 27–51.

Westermeyer, J. (2004). Acculturation: Advances in theory, measurement, and applied research. *Journal of Nervous and Mental Disease, 192*(5), 391–392.

Weyandt, L. L., Verdi, G., & Swentosky, A. (2011). Oppositional, conduct, and aggressive disorders. In S. Goldstein, & C. R. Reynolds (Eds.), *Handbook of neurodevelopmental and genetic disorders in children* (2nd ed., pp. 151–170). New York: Guilford Press.

Whalen, D. J., Sylvester, C. M., & Luby, J. (2017). Depression and anxiety in preschoolers: A review of the past 7 years. *Child and Adolescent Psychiatric Clinics of North America, 26*, 503–522.

Wheaton, M. G., & Pinto, A. (2017). The role of experimental avoidance in obsessive-compulsive personality disorder traits. *Personality Disorders, 8*, 383–388.

Wheeler, B. W., Gunnell, D., Metcalfe, C., Stephens, P., & Martin, R. M. (2008). The population impact on incidence of suicide and non-fatal self harm of regulatory action against the use of selective serotonin reuptake inhibitors in under 18s in the United Kingdom: Ecological study. *British Medical Journal, 336*(7643), 542.

WHF (Women's Heart Foundation). (2011). *Women and heart disease facts.* Retrieved from www.womensheart.org/content/heartdisease/heart_disease_facts.asp.

Whisman, M. A. (2001). The association between depression and marital dissatisfaction. In S. R. H. Beach (Ed.), *Marital and family processes in depression: A scientific foundation for clinical practice* (pp. 3–24). Washington, DC: American Psychological Association.

Whisman, M. A., & Baucom, D. H. (2012). Intimate relationships and psychopathology. *Clinical Child and Family Psychology Review, 15*(1), 4–13.

Whisman, M. A., & Beach, S. H. (2012). Couple therapy for depression. *Journal of Clinical Psychology, 68*(5), 526–535.

Whitaker, R. (2002). *Mad in America: Bad science, bad medicine, and the enduring mistreatment of the mentally ill.* Cambridge, MA: Perseus.

Whitaker, R. (2010). *Anatomy of an epidemic: Magic bullets, psychiatric drugs, and the astonishing rise of mental illness in America.* Norwalk, CT: Crown House Publishing Limited.

Whitbourne, S. K. (2013). Shedding light on psychology's Dark Triad. *Psychology Today, 1*, 1–7.

Whitbourne, S. K. (2016, August 27). Are selfie-takers really narcissists? *Psychology Today.*

White, G. B. (2015, February 12). The alarming, long-term consequences of workplace stress. *The Atlantic.*

White, M. D. (Ed.). (2017). *The insanity defense: Multidisciplinary views on its history, trends, and controversies.* Westport, CT: Praeger.

White, M. P., Alcock, I., Wheeler, B. W., & Depledge, M. H. (2013). Would you be happier living in a greener urban area? A fixed-effects analysis of panel data. *Psychological Science, 24*(6), 920–928.

The White House. (2017, January 5). *Fact Sheet: Final It's on Us Summit and Report of the White House Task Force to Protect Students from Sexual Assault.* Retrieved from https://obamawhitehouse.archives.gov/the-press-office.

Whitney, S. D., Renner, L. M., Pate, C. M., & Jacobs, K. A. (2011). Principals' perceptions of benefits and barriers to school-based suicide prevention programs. *Children and Youth Services Review, 33*(6), 869–877.

Whitton, A., Henry, J., & Grisham, J. (2014). Moral rigidity in obsessive-compulsive disorder: Do abnormalities in inhibitory control, cognitive flexibility and disgust play a role? *Journal of Behavior Therapy and Experimental Psychiatry, 45*(1), 152–159.

WHO (World Health Organization). (2012). *10 facts on ageing and the life course.* Retrieved from http://www.who.int/features/factfiles/.

WHO (World Health Organization). (2012). *About ageing and life course.* Retrieved from http://www.who.int/ageing/about/ageing_life_course/en/.

WHO (World Health Organization). (2014). *7. Addiction to nicotine.* Retrieved from http://www.who.int/tobacco/publications/gender/women_tob_epidemic/en/.

WHO (World Health Organization). (2014). *Tobacco.* (Fact Sheet 339). Retrieved from http://www.who.int/mediacentre/factsheets/fs339/en/.

WHO (World Health Organization). (2016). *Depression.* Retrieved from http://www.who.int/mediacentre/factsheets/fs369/en/.

WHO (World Health Organization). (2016). Media centre: *Depression: Let's talk.* Retrieved from http://who.int/memdiacentre/factsheets/fs369/en/.

WHO (World Health Organization). (2016). Mental health: *Depression: Let's talk.* Retrieved from http://who.int/mental_health/management/depression/en/

WHO (World Health Organization). (2016, April). *Schizophrenia.* Retrieved from http://www.who.int/mediacentre/factsheets/fs397.

WHO (World Health Organization). (2017). *Chronic respiratory diseases.* Retrieved from http://www.who.int/respiratory/asthma/en.

WHO (World Health Organization). (2017). *Depression.* Retrieved from http://www.who.int/mediacentre/factsheets/fs369/en/.

WHO (World Health Organization). (2017). *Gender and women's mental health.* Retrieved from http://www.who.int/mental_health/prevention/genderwomen/en/.

WHO (World Health Organization). (2017, April 4). *Age-standardized suicide rates (per 100,000 population).* Retrieved from WHO/Global Health Observer data repository, http://apps.who.int/gho.

WHO (World Health Organization). (2017). *Tobacco Free Initiative (TFI): WHO report on the global tobacco epidemic 2017.* Retrieved from http://www.who.int/tobacco/global_report/2017/en/.

WHO (World Health Organization). (2017, May). *Tobacco.* Retrieved from http://www.who.int/mediacentre/factsheets/fs339/en/.

Wicherts, J. M., Bakker, M., & Molenaar, D. (2011). Willingness to share research data is related to the strength of the evidence and the quality of reporting of statistical results. *PLoS ONE*, article e0026828.

Wicherts, J. M., Borsboom, D., Kats, J., & Molenaar, D. (2006). The poor availability of psychological research data for reanalysis. *American Psychologist, 61*(7), 726–728.

Wichstrom, L., Belsky, J., & Steinsbekk, S. (2017). Homotypic and heterotypic continuity of symptoms of psychiatric disorders from age 4 to 10 years: A dynamic panel model. *Journal of Child Psychology and Psychiatry.*

Wiebking, C., & Northoff, G. (2013). Neuroimaging in pedophilia. *Current Psychiatry Reports, 15*(4), 351.

Wieczner, J. (2016). Meditation has become a billion-dollar business. *Fortune.* Retrieved from http://fortune.com.

Wiederhold, B. K. (2015). Does sexting improve adult sexual relationships? *Cyberpsychology, Behavior, and Social Networking, 18*(11), 627.

Wiederman, M. W. (2001). "Don't look now": The role of self-focus in sexual dysfunction. *Family Journal: Counseling and Therapy for Couples and Families, 9*(2), 210–214.

Wiegand, T., Thai, D., & Benowitz, N. (2008). Medical consequences of the use of hallucinogens: LSD, mescaline, PCP, and MDM ("ecstasy"). In J. Brick (Ed.), *Handbook of the medical consequences of alcohol and drug abuse* (2nd ed., pp. 461–490). New York: Haworth Press/Taylor & Francis Group.

Wierckx, K., Van Caenegem, E., Schreiner, T., Haraldsen, I., Fisher, A., Toye, K., . . . T'Sjoen, G. (2014). Cross-sex hormone therapy in trans persons is safe and effective at short-time follow-up: Results from the European network for the investigation of gender incongruence. *Journal of Sexual Medicine, 11*(8), 1999–2011.

Wilens, T. E., Yule, A., Martelon, M., Zulauf, C., & Faraone, S. V. (2014). Parental history of substance use disorders (SUD) and SUD in offspring: A controlled family study of bipolar disorder. *American Journal on Addictions, 23*(5), 440–446.

Wiley-Exley, E. (2007). Evaluations of community mental health care in low- and middle-income countries: A 10-year review of the literature. *Social Science and Medicine, 64*(6), 1231–1241.

Will, O. A. (1961). Paranoid development and the concept of self: Psychotherapeutic intervention. *Psychiatry, 24*(2), 516–530.

Will, O. A. (1967). Psychological treatment of schizophrenia. In A. M. Freedman & H. I. Kaplan (Eds.), *Comprehensive textbook of psychiatry*. Baltimore: Williams & Wilkins.

Williams, J., & Nieuwsma, J. (2016, July 19). Screening for depression in adults. *UpToDate*. Retrieved from http://www.uptodate.com.

Williams L. M. (2017). Defining biotypes for depression and anxiety based on large-scale circuit dysfunction: A theoretical review of the evidence and future directions for clinical translation. *Depress Anxiety, 34*(1), 9–24.

Williams, P. (2010). Psychotherapeutic treatment of Cluster A personality disorders. In J. F. Clarkin, P. Fonagy, & G. O. Gabbard (Eds.), *Psychodynamic psychotherapy for personality disorders: A clinical handbook*. Arlington, VA: American Psychiatric Publishing, Inc.

Williams, T. M. (2008). *Black pain: It just looks like we're not hurting*. New York: Scribner.

Willick, M. S. (2001). Psychoanalysis and schizophrenia: A cautionary tale. *Journal of the American Psychoanalytical Association, 49*(1), 27–56.

Wills, T. A., & Ainette, M. G. (2010). Temperament, self-control, and adolescent substance use: A two-factor model of etiological processes. In L. Scheier (Ed.), *Handbook of drug use etiology: Theory, methods, and empirical findings* (pp. 127–146). Washington, DC: American Psychological Association.

Wilson, G. T. (2005). Psychological treatment of eating disorders. *Annual Review of Clinical Psychology, 1*(1), 439–465.

Wilson, G. T. (2010). Cognitive behavioral therapy for eating disorders. In W. S. Agras (Ed.), *The Oxford handbook of eating disorders. Oxford library of psychology* (pp. 331–347). New York: Oxford University Press.

Wilson, G. T. (2010). What treatment research is needed for bulimia nervosa? In C. M. Grilo & J. E. Mitchell (Eds.), *The treatment of eating disorders: A clinical handbook* (pp. 544–553). New York: Guilford Press.

Wilson, G. T., Becker, C. B., & Heffernan, K. (2003). Eating disorders. In E. J. Mash & R. A. Barkley (Eds.), *Child psychopathology* (2nd ed., pp. 687–715). New York: Guilford Press.

Wilson, J. (2017). Biological, genetic and environmental causes of oppositional defiant disorder. *News-Medical*. Retrieved from https://www.news-medical.net.

Wilson, K. R., Jordan, J. A., Kras, A. M., Tavkar, P., Bruhn, S., Asawa, L. E., . . . Trask, E. (2010). Adolescent measures: Practitioner's guide to empirically based measure of social skills. In D. W. Nangle, D. J. Hansen, C. A. Erdley, & P. J. Norton (Eds.), *Practitioner's guide to empirically based measures of social skills* (pp. 327–381). New York: Springer Publishing.

Wilson, L. C. (2016). *The Wiley handbook of the psychology of mass shootings*. Hoboken, NJ: Wiley-Blackwell.

Wilson, P. W. F., & Douglas, P. S. (2017, April 6). Epidemiology of coronary heart disease. *UpToDate*. Retrieved from http://www.uptodate.com.

Wilson, R. S., Scherr, P. A., Schneider, J. A., Tang, Y., & Bennett, D. A. (2007). Relation of cognitive activity to risk of developing Alzheimer disease. *Neurology, 69*(20), 1911–1920.

Wilson, R. S., Segawa, E., Boyle, P. A., & Bennett, D. A. (2012). Influence of late-life cognitive activity on cognitive health. *Neurology, 78*(15), 1123–1129.

Winch, G. (2015, October 2). The important difference between sadness and depression . . . and why so many get it wrong. *Psychology Today*.

Winchester, C. L., Pratt, J. A., & Morris, B. J. (2014). Risk genes for schizophrenia: Translational opportunities for drug discovery. *Pharmacology and Therapeutics, 143*(1), 34–50.

Wincze, J. P., Bach, A. K., & Barlow, D. H. (2008). Sexual dysfunction. In D. H. Barlow (Ed.), *Clinical handbook of psychological disorders: A step-by-step treatment manual* (4th ed.). New York: Guilford Press.

Winegard, B., & Ferguson, C. J. (2016). The development of rampage shooters: Myths and uncertainty in the search for causes. In L. C. Wilson (Ed.). *The Wiley handbook of the psychology of mass shootings* (Ch. 4, pp. 59–76). Hoboken, NJ: Wiley-Blackwell.

Winick, B. J. (2008). A therapeutic jurisprudence approach to dealing with coercion in the mental health system. *Psychiatric and Psychological Law, 15*(1), 25–39.

Winslade, W. J., & Ross, J. (1983). *The insanity plea*. New York: Scribner's.

Winston, D. (2016, February 26). A 5-minute breathing meditation to cultivate mindfulness. *Mindful*. Retrieved from https://www.mindful.org.

Winter, E. C., & Bienvenu, O. J. (2011). Temperament and anxiety disorders. In D. McKay & E. A. Storch (Eds.), *Handbook of child and adolescent anxiety disorders* (pp. 203–212). New York: Springer Science & Business Media.

Winter, S., Diamond, M., Green, J., Karasic, D., Reed, T., Whittle, S., & Wylie, K. (2016).

Transgender people: Health at the margins of society. *Lancet, 23*, 388, 390–400.

Wise, R. A., Sartori, G., Magnussen, S., & Safer, M. A. (2014). An examination of the causes and solutions to eyewitness error. *Frontiers in Psychiatry, 5*, 102.

Wisehart, D. (2015, March 9). 9 fundamental fears that motivate your characters. *Characterchange*.

Wiste, A., Robinson, E. B., Milaneschi, Y., Meier, S., Ripke, S., Clements, C. C., . . . Perlis, R. H. (2014). Bipolar polygenic loading and bipolar spectrum features in major depressive disorder. *Bipolar Disorders, 16*(6), 608–616.

Witkiewitz, K. A., & Marlatt, G. A. (2004). Relapse prevention for alcohol and drug problems: That was zen, this is tao. *American Psychologist, 59*(4), 224–235.

Witkiewitz, K. A., & Marlatt, G. A. (Eds.). (2007). *Therapist's guide to evidence-based relapse prevention*. San Diego, CA: Elsevier.

Witt, K., Milner, A., Allisey, A., Davenport, L., & LaMontagne, A. D. (2017). Effectiveness of suicide prevention programs for emergency and protective services employees: A systematic review and meta-analysis. *American Journal of Industrial Medicine, 60*(4), 394–407.

Witthöft, M., & Hiller, W. (2010). Psychological approaches to origins and treatments of somatoform disorders. *Annual Review of Clinical Psychology, 6*, 257–283.

Wittkowski, H., Hinze, C., Häfner-Harms, S., Oji, V., Masjosthusmann, K., Mooninger, M., . . . Foell, D. (2017). Munchausen by proxy syndrome mimicking systemic autoinflammatory disease: Case report and review of the literature. *Pediatric Rheumatology Online Journal, 15*(1), 19.

Wixted, J. T., Mickes, L., Dunn, J. C., Clark, S. E., & Wells, W. (2016). Estimating the reliability of eyewitness identifications from police lineups. *Proceedings of the National Academy of Sciences USA, 113*(2), 304–309.

Wixted, J. T., & Wells, G. L. (2017). The relationship between eyewitness confidence and identification accuracy: A new synthesis. *Psychological Science in the Public Interest, 18*(1), 10–65.

Wohltmann, J. (2013). *Should grandma join Facebook?* Presentation at International Neuropsychological Society Annual Meeting. Hawaii.

Wolberg, L. R. (1967). *The technique of psychotherapy*. New York: Grune & Stratton.

Wolberg, L. R. (2005). *The technique of psychotherapy*. Lanham, MD: Jason Aronson.

Wolf, M. R., & Nochajski, T. H. (2013). Child sexual abuse survivors with dissociative amnesia: What's the difference? *Journal of Child Sexual Abuse, 22*(4), 462–480.

Wolk, C. B., Carper, M. M., Kendall, P. C., Olino, T. M., Marcus, S. C., & Beidas, R. S. (2016). Pathways to anxiety-depression comorbidity: A longitudinal examination of childhood anxiety disorders. *Depression and Anxiety, 33*, 978–986.

Wolk, D. A., & Dickerson, B. C. (2017, May 12). Clinical features and diagnosis of Alzheimer disease. *UpToDate*. Retrieved from http://www.uptodate.com.

Wolpe, J. (1958). *Psychotherapy by reciprocal inhibition*. Stanford, CA: Stanford University Press.

Wolpe, J. (1969). *The practice of behavior therapy*. Oxford, England: Pergamon Press.

Wolpe, J. (1987). The promotion of scientific psychotherapy: A long voyage. In J. K. Zeig (Ed.), *The evolution of psychotherapy*. New York: Brunner/Mazel.

Wonderlich, S. A., Peterson, C. B., Crosby, R. D., Smith, T. L., Klein, M. H., Mitchell, J. E., & Crow, S. J. (2014). A randomized controlled comparison of integrative cognitive-affective therapy (ICAT) and enhanced cognitive-behavioral therapy (CBT-E) for bulimia nervosa. *Psychological Medicine, 44*(3), 543–553.

Wong, E. C., & Miles, J. N. (2014). Prevalence and correlates of depression among new U.S. immigrants. *Journal of Immigrant and Minority Health, 16*(3), 422–428.

Wong, J. P. S., Stewart, S. M., Claassen, C., Lee, P. W. H., Rao, U., & Lam, T. H. (2008). Repeat suicide attempts in Hong Kong community adolescents. *Social Science and Medicine, 66*(2), 232–241.

Wong, M. M., Brower, K. J., & Zucker, R. A. (2011). Sleep problems, suicidal ideation, and self-harm behaviors in adolescence. *Journal of Psychiatric Research, 45*(4), 505–511.

Wood, J. (2016, May 27). Multiple personality disorder rooted in traumatic experiences. *Psych Central*. Retrieved from http://psychcentral.com.

Wood, J. (2016, November 5). Brain scan can beat polygraph at detecting lies. *Psych Central News*.

Woodside, D. B., Bulik, C. M., Halmi, K. A., Fichter, M. M., Kaplan, A., Berrettini, W. H., . . . Kaye, W. H. (2002). Personality, perfectionism, and attitudes towards eating in parent of individuals with eating disorders. *International Journal of Eating Disorders, 31*(3), 290–299.

Worthen, M. (2016). *Sexual deviance and society*. New York: Routledge.

Worthen, M., Rathod, S. D., Cohen, G., Sampson, L., Ursano, R., Gifford, R., . . . Ahern, J. (2014). Anger problems and post-traumatic stress disorder in male and female National Guard and Reserve Service members. *Journal of Psychiatric Research, 5552–5558.*

Wright, C. B. (2017, May 2). Etiology, clinical manifestations, and diagnosis of vascular dementia. *UpToDate*. Retrieved from http://www.uptodate.com.

Wright, J. (2017, February 7). *Get well soon: History's worst plagues and the heroes who fought them*. New York: Harry Holt & Co.

Wright, L. W., Jr., Hatcher, A. P., & Willerick, M. S. (2006). Violent sex crimes. In R. D. McAnulty & M. M. Burnette (Eds.), *Sex and sexuality, Vol. 3: Sexual deviation and sexual offenses*. Westport, CT: Praeger Publishers.

Wyatt, G. W., & Parham, W. D. (2007). The inclusion of culturally sensitive course materials in graduate school and training programs. *Psychotherapy: Theory, Research, Practice, Training, 22*(2, Suppl.) Sum. 1985, 461–468.

Wykes, T., Huddy, V., Cellard, C., McGurk, S. R., & Czobor, P. (2011). A meta-analysis of cognitive remediation for schizophrenia: Methodology and effect sizes. *American Journal of Psychiatry, 168*(5), 472.

Wymbs, B. T., McCarthy, C. A., Mason, W. A., King, K. M., Baer, J. S., Vander Stoep, A., & McCauley, E. (2014). Early adolescent substance use as a risk factor for developing conduct disorder and depression symptoms. *Journal of Studies on Alcohol and Drugs, 75*(2), 279–289.

Wynn, S. T. (2017). Natural disasters: Planning for psychological first aid. *Journal of Christian Nursing, 34*(1), 24–28.

Xu, W., Liu, Y., Chen, J., Guo, Q., Liu, K., Wen, Z., . . . Shi, Y. (2017). Genetic risk between the CACNA1I gene and schizophrenia in Chinese Uygur population. *Hereditas, 155*, 5.

Xue, L., Shi, Y. W., Knoll, J. L., & Zhao, H. (2015). Chinese forensic psychiatry: History, development and challenges. *Journal of Forensic Science and Medicine, 1*, 61–67.

Yaghoubi-Doust, M. (2013). Reviewing the association between the history of parental substance abuse and the rate of child abuse. *Addiction & Health, 5*(3–4), 126–133.

Yalof, J. (2015). Discussion of difficult assessment cases: Psychodynamic perspectives. *Journal of Personality Assessment, 97*(3), 250–251.

Yalom, I. D. (2014). Existential psychotherapy. In D. Wedding & R. J. Corsini (Eds.), *Current psychotherapies* (10th ed., pp. 299–338). Independence, KY: Cengage Publications.

Yan, Z. (2017). Child and adolescent use of mobile phones: An unparalleled complex developmental phenomenon. *Child Development*.

Yang, H., Brand, J. S., Fang, F., Chiesa, F., Johansson, A. L., Hall, P., & Czene, K. (2017). Time-dependent risk of depression, anxiety, and stress-related disorders in patients with invasive and in situ breast cancer. *International Journal of Cancer, 140*(4), 841–852.

Yang, W., & Zhang, X. (2017, January 17). Common factors vs. specific ingredients in psychotherapy: Controversy and integration. *Advances in Psychological Science, 25*(2), 253–264.

Yaser, A., Slewa-Younan, S., Smith, C. A., Olson, R. E., Guajardo, M. G. U., & Mond, J. (2016). Beliefs and knowledge about post-traumatic stress disorder amongst resettled Afghan refugees in Australia. *International Journal of Mental Health Systems, 10*, 31.

Yates, G. P., & Feldman, M. D. (2017). Factitious disorder: A systematic review of 455 cases in the professional literature. *General Hospital Psychiatry, 41*, 20–28.

Yehuda, R., & Bierer, L. M. (2007). Transgenerational transmission of cortisol and PTSD risk. *Progress in Brain Research, 167*, 121–135.

Yehuda, R., Flory, J. D., Bierer, L. M., Henn-Haase, C., Lehrner, A., Desarnaud, F., . . . Meaney, M. J. (2015). Lower methylation of glucocorticoid receptor gene promoter 1F in peripheral blood of veterans with posttraumatic stress disorder. *Biological Psychiatry, 77*(4), 356–364.

Yehuda, R., Southwick, S. M., Krystal, J. H., Bremner, D., Charney, D. S., & Mason, J. W. (1993). Enhanced suppression of cortisol following dexamethasone administration in posttraumatic stress disorder. *American Journal of Psychiatry, 150*(1), 83–86.

Yin, S. (2016, July 25). Opioid withdrawal in adolescents. *UpToDate*. Retrieved from http://www.uptodate.com.

Yom-Tov, E. (2016). *Crowd-sourced health: How what you do on the internet will improve medicine*. Cambridge, MA: MIT Press.

Yom-Tov, E., Brunstein-Klomek, A., Hadas, A., Tamir, O., & Fennig, S. (2016). Differences in physical status, mental state and online behavior of people in pro-anorexia web communities. *Eating Behaviors, 22*, 109–112.

Yong, E. (2012, May 16). Replication studies: Bad copy. *Nature.com*.

Yontef, G., & Jacobs, L. (2014). Gestalt therapy. In D. Wedding & R. J. Corsini (Eds.), *Current psychotherapies* (10th ed., pp. 299–338). Independence, KY: Cengage Publications.

Yoo, Y., Cho, O., & Cha, K. (2014). Associations between overuse of the internet and mental health in adolescents. *Nursing and Health Sciences, 16*(2), 193–200.

Yoon, J. H., Minzenberg, M. J., Raouf, S., D'Esposito, M., & Carter, C. S. (2013). Impaired prefrontal-basal ganglia functional connectivity and substantia nigra hyperactivity in schizophrenia. *Biological Psychiatry, 74*(2), 122–129.

Yoon, J. H., Westphal, A. J., Minzenberg, M. J., Niendam, T., Ragland, J. D., Lesh, T., . . . Carter, C. S. (2014). Task-evoked substantia nigra hyperactivity associated with prefrontal hypofunction, prefrontonigral disconnectivity, and nigrostriatal connectivity predicting psychosis severity in medication naïve first episode schizophrenia. *Schizophrenia Research, 159*(2–3), 521–526.

Yorifuji, T., Kato, T., Ohta, H., Bellinger, D. C., Matsuoka, K., & Grandjean, P. (2016). Neurological and neuropsychological functions in adults with a history of developmental arsenic poisoning from contaminated milk powder. *Neurotoxicology and Teratology, 53*, 75–80.

Yoshida, K., Bies, R. R., Suzuki, T., Remington, G., Pollock, B. G., Mizuno, Y., . . . Uchida, H. (2014). Tardive dyskinesia in relation to estimated dopamine D2 receptor occupancy in patients with schizophrenia: Analysis of the CATIE data. *Schizophrenia Research, 153*(1–3), 184–188.

Yoshida, K., Orita, M., Goto, A., Kumagai, A., Yasui, K., Ohtsuru, A., . . . Takamura, N. (2016). Radiation-related anxiety among public health nurses in the Fukushima Prefecture after the accident at the Fukushima Daiichi Nuclear Power Station: A cross-sectional study. *BMJ Open, 6*(10), e013564.

You, S., Van Orden, K. A., & Conner, K. R. (2011). Social connections and suicidal thoughts and behavior. *Psychology of Addictive Behaviors, 25*(1), 180–184.

Young, G. (2017). PTSD in court II: Risk factors, endophenotypes, and biological underpinnings in PTSD. *International Journal of Law and Psychiatry, 51*, 1–21.

Young, J. E., Rygh, J. L., Weinberger, A. D., & Beck, A. T. (2014). Cognitive therapy for depression. In D. H. Barlow, *Clinical handbook of psychological disorders* (5th ed., Ch. 7). New York: Guilford Press.

Young, K. S. (2017). The evolution of internet addiction. *Addictive Behaviors, 64*, 229–230.

Young, L., & Kemper, K. J. (2013). Integrative care for pediatric patients with pain. *Journal of Alternative and Complementary Medicine, 19*(7), 627–632.

Young, M. E., Bell, Z. E., & Fristad, M. A. (2016). Validation of a brief structured interview: The Children's Interview for Psychiatric Syndromes (ChIPS). *Journal of Clinical Psychology in Medical Settings, 23*(4), 327–340.

Ystrom, E., Reichborn-Kjennerud, T., Neale, M. C., & Kendler, K. S. (2014). Genetic and environmental risk factors for illicit substance use and use disorders: Joint analysis of self and co-twin ratings. *Behavior Genetics, 44*(1), 1–13.

Yu, S., Brackbill, R. M., Locke, S., Stellman, S. D., & Gargano, L. M. (2016). Impact of 9/11-related chronic conditions and PTSD comorbidity on early retirement and job loss among World Trade Center disaster rescue and recovery workers. *American Journal of Industrial Medicine, 59*(9), 731–741.

Yu, Y. H. (2017). Making sense of metabolic obesity and hedonic obesity. *Journal of Diabetes, 9*, 656–666.

Yuan, T. F., Li, A., Sun, X., Arias-Carrión, O., & Machado S. (2016). Vagus nerve stimulation in treating depression: A tale of two stories. *Current Molecular Medicine, 16*(1), 33–39.

Yusko, D. (2008). At home, but locked in war. Retrieved from *Times-Union (Albany) Online.*

Zaejian, J. (2014, February 18). Current research on outpatient commitment laws ("Laura's Law" in California). *Mad in America.* Retrieved from https://www.madinamerica.com.

Zafar, S., Shafiq, M., Younas, N., Schmitz, M., Ferrer, I., & Zerr, I. (2017). Prion protein interactome: Identifying novel targets in slowly and rapidly progressive forms of Alzheimer's disease. *Journal of Alzheimer's Disease, 59*(1), 265–275.

Zahn, R., Lythe, K. E., Gethin, J. A., Green, S., Deakin, J. F., Young, A. H., & Moll, J. (2015). The role of self-blame and worthlessness in the psychopathology of major depressive disorder. *Journal of Affective Disorders, 186*, 337–341.

Zalsman, G., Hawton, K., Wasserman, D., van Heeringen, K., Arensman, E., Sarchiapone, M., . . . Zohar, J. (2016). Suicide prevention strategies revisited: 10-year systematic review. *Lancet Psychiatry, 3*(7), 646–659.

Zanarini, M. C., Frankenburg, F. R., Dubo, E. D., Sickel, A. E., Trikha, A., Levin, A., & Reynolds, V. (1998). Axis I comorbidity of borderline personality disorder. *American Journal of Psychiatry, 155*(12), 1733–1739.

Zanarini, M. C., Frankenburg, F. R., Reich, D. B., & Fitzmaurice, G. M. (2016). Fluidity of the subsyndromal phenomenology of borderline personality disorder over 16 years of prospective follow-up. *American Journal of Psychiatry, 173*(7), 688–694.

Zanarini, M. C., Horwood, J., Wolke, D., Waylen, A., Fitzmaurice, G., & Grant, B. F. (2011). Prevalence of DSM-IV borderline personality disorder in two community samples: 6,330 English 11-year-olds and 34,653 American adults. *Journal of Personality Disorders, 25*(5), 607–619.

Zannas, A. (2014, October 18). Why depression and aging are linked to increased disease risk. *European College of Neuropsychopharmacology.*

Zannas, A. S., & West, A. E. (2014). Epigenetics and the regulation of stress vulnerability and resilience. *Neuroscience, 264*, 157–170.

Zarbo, C., Tasca, G. A., Cattafi, F., & Compare, A. (2015). Integrative psychotherapy works. *Frontiers in Psychology, 6*, 2021.

Zarzar, T., Sheitman, B., Cook, A., & Robbins, B. (2018). Reducing length of acute inpatient hospitalization using a residential step down model for patients with serious mental illness. *Community Mental Health Journal.* [Manuscript in press]

Zeigler-Hill, V., Besser, A., Morag, J., & Campbell, W. K. (2016). The Dark Triad and sexual harassment proclivity. *Personality and Individual Differences, 89*, 47–54.

Zeliadt, N. (2015, October 22). Three autism mouse models marked by defects in same circuit. *Autism Research News.* Retrieved from https://spectrumnews.org.

Zelkowitz, P., Paris, J., Guzder, J., & Feldman, R. (2001). Diathesis and stressors in borderline pathology of childhood: The role of neuropsychological risk and trauma. *Journal of the American Academy of Child and Adolescent Psychiatry, 40*, 100–105.

Zemore, S. E. (2017). Implications for future research on drivers of change and alternatives to Alcoholics Anonymous. *Addiction, 112*(6), 940–942.

Zerbe, K. J. (2008). *Integrated treatment of eating disorders beyond the body betrayed.* New York: W. W. Norton.

Zerbe, K. J. (2010). Psycodynamic therapy for eating disorders. In C. M. Grilo & J. E. Mitchell (Eds.), *The treatment of eating disorders: A clinical handbook* (pp. 339–358). New York: Guilford Press.

Zerwas, S., Lund, B C., Von Holle, A., Thornton, L. M., Berrettini, W. H., Brandt, H., . . . Bulik. C. M. (2013). Factors associated with recovery from anorexia nervosa. *Journal of Psychiatric Research, 47*(7), 972–979.

Zeschel, E., Bingmann, T., Bechdolf, A., Krüger-Oezguerdal, S., Correll, C. U., Leopold, K., . . . Juckel, G. (2015). Temperament and prodromal symptoms prior to first manic/hypomanic episodes: Results from a pilot study. *Journal of Affective Disorders, 173*, 339–344.

Zhang, X. (2016). *Generalized anxiety disorder in the elderly: Role of bio-environmental factors and genetic vulnerability.* Universite Montpellier.

Zhang, X., Norton, J., Carriere, I., Ritchie, K., Chaudieu, I., & Ancelin, M. L. (2015). Generalized anxiety in community-dwelling elderly: Prevalence and clinical characteristics. *Journal of Affective Disorders, 172*, 24–29.

Zhang, X., Zhang, J., Procter, N., Chen, X., Su, Y., Lou, F., & Cao, F. (2017). Suicidal ideation and psychological strain among patients diagnosed with stomach cancer: The mediation of psychopathological factors. *Journal of Nervous and Mental Disease, 205*, 550–557.

Zhao, L. N., Lu, L., Chew, L. Y., & Mu, Y. (2014). Alzheimer's disease: A panorama glimpse. *International Journal of Molecular Sciences, 15*, 12631–12650.

Zhao, Y., He, A., Zhu, F., Ding, M., Hao, J., Fan, Q., . . . Ma, X. (2018). Integrating genome-wide association study and expression quantitative trait locus study identifies multiple genes and gene sets associated with schizophrenia. *Progress in Neuro-Psychopharmacology and Biological Psychiatry, 81*, 50–54.

Zheng, Z., Li, R., Xiao, F., He, R., Zhang, S., & Li, J. (2017). Sex matters: Hippocampal volume predicts individual differences in associative memory in cognitively normal older women but not men. *Frontiers in Human Neuroscience, 11*, 93.

Zhou, E. S., & Bober, S. L. (2017). Treating sexual problems in cancer patients and survivors. In Z. D. Peterson, *The Wiley-Blackwell handbook of sex therapy* (Ch. 23, pp. 369–388). Hoboken, NJ: Wiley-Blackwell.

Zhou, J. N., Hofman, M. A., Gooren, L. J. G., & Swaab, D. F. (1995). A sex difference in the human brain and its relation to transsexuality. *Nature, 378*, 68–70.

Zhou, J. N., Hofman, M. A., Gooren, L. J. G., & Swaab, D. F. (1997). A sex difference in the human brain and its relation to transsexuality. *International Journal of Transgenderism, 1*(1), http://www.symposion.com/ijt/ijtc0106.htm.

Zhou, X., Liu, L., Zhang, Y., Pu, J., Yang, L., Zhou, C., . . . Xie, P. (2017). Metabolomics identifies perturbations in amino acid metabolism in the prefrontal cortex of the learned helplessness rat model of depression. *Neuroscience, 343*, 1–9.

Zhou, X., Min, S., Sun, J., Kim, S. J., Ahn, J., Peng, Y., . . . Ryder, A. G. (2015). Extending a structural model of somatization to South Koreans: Culture values, somatization tendency, and the presentation of depressive symptoms. *Journal of Affective Disorders, 176*, 151–154.

Zhou, X., Peng, Y., Zhu, X., Yao, S., Dere, J., Chentsova-Dutton, Y. E., & Ryder, A. G. (2015). From culture to symptom: Testing a structural model of "Chinese somatization." *Transcultural Psychiatry.*

Zhu, Y., Tang, Y., Zhang, T., Li, H., Tang, Y., Li, C., . . . Wang, J. (2017). Reduced functional connectivity between bilateral precuneus and contralateral parahippocampus in schizotypal personality disorder. *BMC Psychiatry, 17*(1), 48.

Zilber, C. (2016, November 29). Ethics considerations of involuntary outpatient treatment. *Psychiatric News.* Retrieved from http://psychnews.psychiatryonline.org.

Zilboorg, G., & Henry, G. W. (1941). *A history of medical psychology.* New York: Norton.

Zimbardo, P. (1976). *Rational paths to madness.* Presentation at Princeton University, Princeton, NJ.

Zipursky, R. B. (2014). Why are the outcomes in patients with schizophrenia so poor? *Journal of Clinical Psychiatry, 75*(Suppl. 2), 20–24.

Zoroya, G. (2013, December 10). PTSD hits civilians serving on war fronts, study finds. *USA Today.*

Zoroya, G. (2016, May 4). U.S. military suicides remain high for 7th year. *USA Today.* Retrieved from https://www.usatoday.com.

Zucker, K. J. (2010). Gender identity and sexual orientation. In M. K. Dulcan (Ed.), *Dulcan's textbook of child and adolescent psychiatry* (pp. 543–552). Arlington, VA: American Psychiatric Publishing.

Zucker, K. J., & Bradley, S. J. (1995). *Gender identity disorder and psychosexual problems in children and adolescents.* New York: Guilford Press.

Zucker, K. J., Bradley, S. J., Owen-Anderson, A., Kibblewhite, S. J., Wood, H., Singh, D., & Choi, K. (2012). Demographics, behavior problems, and psychosexual characteristics of adolescents with gender identity disorder or transvestic fetishism. *Journal of Sex and Marital Therapy, 38*(2), 151–189.

Zucker, K. J., Lawrence, A. A., & Kreukels, B. P. (2016). Gender dysphoria in adults. *Annual Review of Clinical Psychology, 12,* 217–247.

Zucker, R. A., Ellis, D. A., Bingham, C. R., & Fitzgerald, H. E. (1996). The development of alcoholic subtypes: Risk variation among alcoholic families during early childhood. *Alcohol Health and Research World, 20,* 46–54.

Zucker, R. A., Hicks, B. M., & Heitzeg, M. M. (2016). Alcohol use and the alcohol use disorders over the life course: A cross-level developmental review. In D. Cicchetti (Ed.), *Developmental psychopathology* (Vol. 3, Maladaptation and psychopathology, Ch. 18, pp. 793–832). Hoboken, NJ: John Wiley Sons.

Zurolo, A., & Napolitano, S. (2008). Il feticcio e la maschera. [The fetishism and the mask.] *Psicoterapia Psicoanalitica, 15*(2), 179–196.

Zvolensky, M. J., Forsyth, J. P., & Johnson, K. (2014). Laboratory methods in experimental psychopathology. In J. S. Comer & P. C. Kendall (Eds.), *Oxford handbook of research strategies for clinical psychology.* New York: Oxford University Press.

Credits

Permission has been given to republish excerpts on the pages listed from the following sources (**bold** page numbers indicate the locations of the excerpts in this text):

Chapter 1

page 6: Frank, Jerome D., M.D., Ph.D. *Persuasion and healing: A comparative study of psychotherapy.* pp. 2–3. © 1961, 1973 The Johns Hopkins University Press. Reprinted with permission of Johns Hopkins University Press.

Chapter 2

page 26: Freud, S. (1909). Analysis of a phobia in a five-year-old boy ["Little Hans"]. In *Sigmund Freud: Collected Papers, Vol. 3: Case Histories,* translated by Alix and James Strachey. New York: Basic Books, 1959. Copyright © 1959. Reprinted by permission of Basic Books, an imprint of Hachette Book Group, and by permission of The Marsh Agency Ltd. on behalf of Sigmund Freud Copyrights. Also from *The Standard Edition of the Complete Psychological Works of Sigmund Freud, Vol. X,* translated and edited by James Strachey. Published by Hogarth Press. Reprinted by permission of The Random House Group Limited.

Chapter 3

page 46: Spitzer, R. L., Skodol, A., Gibbon, M., & Williams, J. B. W. (1983). *Psychopathology: A case book.* New York: McGraw-Hill; **page 56**: Wolberg, L. R. (1967). *The technique of psychotherapy.* WB Saunders Co. Elsevier Health Science Books, p. 662; **page 62**: Republished with permission of Guilford Publications from Beck, A. T., Rush, A. J., Shaw, B. F., & Emery, G., *Cognitive therapy of depression* (1979). Copyright © 1979 Guilford Publications; permission conveyed through Copyright Clearance Center, Inc.; **page 68**: Snyder, W. V. (1947). *Casebook of non-directive counseling.* Boston: Houghton Mifflin, pp. 2–24; **page 70**: Keen, E. (1970). *Three faces of being: Toward an existential clinical psychology.* New York: Meredith Corp, p. 200. (Reprinted by permission of Irvington Publishers); **page 75**: Sheras, P., & Worchel, S. (1979). *Clinical psychology: A social psychological approach.* New York: Van Nostrand, pp. 108–110.

Chapter 4

page 90: Aiken, L. R. (1985). *Psychological testing and assessment* (5th ed.). Boston: Allyn & Bacon, p. 372.

Chapter 5

page 119: Ellis, Albert. (1962). *Reason and emotion in psychotherapy.* Secaucus, NJ: Lyle Stuart. Copyright © 1962. All rights reserved. Reprinted by arrangement with Kensington Publishing Corp, www .kensingtonbooks.com; **page 121**: Ellis, A. (1962). *Reason and emotion in psychotherapy.* Secaucus, NJ: Lyle Stuart; **page 125**: Melville, J. (1978). *Phobias and obsessions.* New York: Penguin, p. 59; **page 129**: Marks, I. M. (1977). Phobias and obsessions: Clinical phenomena in search of a laboratory model. In J. Maser & M. Seligman (Eds.), *Psychopathology: Experimental models.* New York: Worth Publishers, p. 192; **page 130**: Hogan, R. A. "The implosive technique." *Behaviour Research and Therapy* 6 (1968), pp. 423–431. Copyright © 1968. Republished with permission of Elsevier Science and Technology Journals; permission conveyed through Copyright Clearance Center, Inc.; **page 131**: Agras, W. S. (1985). *Panic: Facing fears, phobias, and anxiety.* New York: Worth Publishers. Reprinted with permission; **page 136**: LeCroy, C. W., & Holschuch, J. (2012). *First person accounts of mental illness and recovery.* Hoboken, NJ: Wiley; **page 141**: Spitzer, R. L., Skodol, A., Gibbon, M., & Williams, J. B. W. (1981). *DSM-III case book* (1st ed.). Washington, DC: American Psychiatric Press; **page 144**: Emmelkamp, P. M. (1982). Exposure in vivo treatments. In A. Goldstein & D. Chambless (Eds.), *Agoraphobia: Multiple perspectives on theory and treatment.* New York: Wiley; **page 148**: Marks, I. M. (1987). *Fears, phobias and rituals: Panic, anxiety and their disorders.* New York: Oxford University Press, p. 371.

Chapter 6

page 153: National Center for PTSD 2008, Appendix A: Case examples from Operation Iraqi Freedom. *Iraq War Clinician Guide.* Washington,

DC: Department of Veteran Affairs, http://www.ptsd.va.gov/professional/materials/manuals/iraq-war-clinician-guide.asp; **page 174**: James, W. (1890). *Principles of psychology* (Vol. 1). New York: Holt, Rinehart & Winston, pp. 391–393; **page 178**: Schreiber, F. R. (1973). *Sybil.* Chicago: Regnery, p. 160; **page 185**: Kluft, R. P. (1988). The dissociative disorders. In J. A. Talbott, R. E. Hales, & S. C. Yudofsky (Eds.), *Textbook of psychiatry.* Washington, DC: American Psychiatric Press, p. 580.

Chapter 7

page 189: From *Willow weep for me: A black woman's journey through depression* by Meri Nana-Ama Danquah. Copyright © 1998 by Meri Nana-Ama Danquah. Used by permission of W. W. Norton & Company, Inc., and by permission of Anne Edelstein Literary Agency. All rights reserved; **pages 191, 192**: Williams, T. M. (2008). *Black pain: It just looks like we're not hurting.* New York: Scribner, p. 9; **page 199**: Arieti, S., & Bemporad, J. R. (1978). *Severe and mild depression: The psychotherapeutic approach.* New York: Basic Books, pp. 275–284; **page 202**: Fieve, R. R. (1975). *Moodswing.* New York: Morrow; **page 204**: Spitzer, R. L., Skodol, A., Gibbon, M., & Williams, J. B. W. (1983). *Psychopathology: A case book.* New York: McGraw-Hill; **pages 213–214**: *British Journal of General Practice.* Sep 1, 2006; 56(530): 726–728. On madness: a personal account of rapid cycling bipolar disorder. By Anonymous.

Chapter 8

page 222: National Alliance on Mental Illness. (2009). Depression Survey Initiative, November 9; **page 223**: Republished with permission of Guilford Publications from Lorand, S., Dynamics and therapy of depressive states. *Psychoanalytic Review* XXIV, 1937, pp. 337–349. Copyright © 1937 Guilford Press. Permission conveyed through Copyright Clearance Center, Inc; **page 224**: Martell, Christopher R.; Dimidjian, Sona; Herman-Dunn, Ruth. (2010-01-04). *Behavioral activation for depression: A clinician's guide* (Kindle Locations 1811–1817). Guilford Publications. Kindle Edition; **pages 226, 227**: Republished with permission of Guilford Publications from Beck, A. T., Rush, A. J., Shaw, B. F., & Emery, G., *Cognitive therapy of depression* (1979). Copyright © 1979 Guilford Publications; permission conveyed through Copyright Clearance Center, Inc; **page 229**: Republished with permission of Transaction Aldine, from *The silent language of psychotherapy: Social reinforcement of unconscious processes,* Beier & Young, second edition, 1984; permission conveyed through Copyright Clearance Center, Inc.; **page 234**: Sharpe, Katherine. (2012-06-05). *Coming of age on Zoloft: How antidepressants cheered us up, let us down, and changed who we are* (p. 12). HarperCollins. Kindle Edition; **page 234**: Excerpt from "An episodic illness turns chronic," in *Anatomy of an epidemic: Magic bullets, psychiatric drugs, and the astonishing rise of mental illness in America,* by Robert Whitaker, copyright © 2010 by Robert Whitaker. Used by permission of Crown Books, an imprint of the Crown Publishing Group, a division of Random House LLC. All rights reserved. Any third party use of this material, outside of this publication, is prohibited. Interested parties must apply directly to Penguin Random House LLC for permission; **page 237**: With permission of Dr. Robert Palmer and the estate of Dr. Sydney Brandon; **page 242**: Excerpt from *An unquiet mind,* by Kay Redfield Jamison, copyright © 1995 by Kay Redfield Jamison. Used by permission of Alfred A. Knopf, an imprint of the Knopf Doubleday Publishing Group, a division of Random House LLC. All rights reserved.

Chapter 9

page 249: Yusko, D. (2008). At home, but locked in war. Retrieved from: *Times Union (Albany) Online.* Copyright © 2008. Reprinted by permission of the Times Union; **page 250**: Shneidman, E. S. (1985). *Definition of suicide.* New York: Wiley; **page 257**: Shneidman, E. S. (1987, March). At the point of no return. *Psychology Today,* p. 56; **page 262**: Gill, A. D. (1982). Vulnerability to suicide. In E. L. Bassuk, S. C. Schoonover, & A. D. Gill (Eds.), *Lifelines: Clinical perspectives on suicide.* New York: Plenum Press, p. 15; **page 267**: Pfeffer, C. R. (1986). *The suicidal child.* New York: Guilford Press; **page 267**: French, A. P., & Berlin, I. N. (1979). *Depression in children and adolescents.* New York: Human Sciences Press, p. 144; **page 268**: Berman, A. L. (1986). Helping suicidal adolescents: Needs and responses. In C. A. Corr & J. N. McNeil (Eds.), *Adolescence and death*. New York: Springer; **page 273**: Gernsbacher, L. M. (1985). *The suicide syndrome*. New York: Human Sciences Press, pp. 227–28. Copyright © 1985. Reprinted by permission of Dr. M. Willson Williams.

Chapter 10

page 284: Excerpt from Savino, Adria C., & Fordtran, John S., "Factitious disease: Clinical lessons from case studies at Baylor University Medical Center," in *Baylor University Medical Center Proceedings 19.3* (July 2006). Copyright © 2006, Baylor University Medical Center. Reprinted by permission; **page 290**: Spitzer, R. L., Skodol, A., Gibbon, M., & Williams, J. B. W. (1981). *DSM-III case book: A learning companion to the diagnostic and statistical manual of mental disorders* (1st ed.). Washington, DC: American Psychiatric Press; **page 291**: Green, S. A. (1985). *Mind and body: The psychology of physical illness*. Washington, DC: American Psychiatric Press; **page 303**: Holmes, T. H., & Rahe, R. H., "The Social Readjustment Rating Scale," in *Journal of Psychosomatic Research 11*, pp. 213–218. Copyright 1967. Reprinted with permission from Elsevier.

Chapter 11

pages 313, 316: Raviv, S. (2010). *Being Ana: A memoir of anorexia nervosa*. Bloomington: iUniverse; **page 315**: Bruch, H. (1973). *Eating disorders: Obesity, anorexia nervosa and the person within*. New York: Basic Books; **pages 316, 319**: Hall, L., with Cohn, L. (1980). *Eat without fear*. Santa Barbara, CA: Gürze; **page 323**: Bruch, H. (1978). *The golden cage: The enigma of anorexia nervosa*. Cambridge, MA: Harvard University Press; **page 329**: Zerbe, K. J. (2008). *Integrated treatment of eating disorders beyond the body betrayed*. New York: W. W. Norton; **pages 333, 334**: Republished with permission of Guilford Publications, from Strober, M., & Yager, J., A developmental perspective on the treatment of anorexia nervosa in adolescents. In D. M. Garner & P. E. Garfinkel (Eds.), *Handbook of Psychotherapy for anorexia nervosa and bulimia* (1985). Copyright © 1985 Guilford Publications; permission conveyed through Copyright Clearance Center, Inc.

Chapter 12

page 343: Spitzer, R. L., Skodol, A., Gibbon, M., & Williams, J. B. W. (1983). *Psychopathology: A case book*. New York: McGraw-Hill; **page 353**: Hart, C., & Ksir, C. (2013). *Drugs, society, and human behavior*. New York: McGraw-Hill Education.

Chapter 13

pages 388, 397: Spitzer, R. L., Skodol, A., Gibbon, M., & Williams, J. B. W. (1983). *Psychopathology: A case book*. New York: McGraw-Hill; **page 391**: This material was published in *Human sexuality and its problems*, ISBN 978-0443034558, Bancroft, J., 1989. Copyright Elsevier; **page 392**: Rosen, R. C., & Rosen, L. R. (1981). *Human sexuality*. New York: Knopf; **page 405**: Coskun, M., & Ozturk, M. (2013). Excerpt from p. 200 in "Sexual fetishism in adolescence: Report of two cases." *Düşünen Adam: The Journal of Psychiatry and Neurological Sciences 26.2*, pp. 199–205. Copyright © 2013. Reprinted by permission; **page 406**: Janus, S. S., & Janus, C. L. (1993). *The Janus report on sexual behavior*. New York: Wiley. Reprinted with permission of the Janus estate.

Chapter 14

page 421: Arieti, S. (1974). *Interpretation of schizophrenia*. New York: Basic Books; **page 424**: Rollin, H. R. (1980). *Coping with schizophrenia*. London: Burnett; **page 426**: Bateson, G. (1974). *Perceval's narrative: A patient's account of his psychosis*. New York: William Morrow; **page 426**: McGhie, A., & Chapman, J. (1961). Disorders of attention and perception in early schizophrenia. *British Journal of Medical Psychology, 34*: 103–116; **page 428**: Anonymous, "First person account: Social, economic, and medical effects of schizophrenia." Republished with permission of Oxford University Press from *Schizophrenia Bulletin 22.1* (1996), pp. 183–85; permission conveyed through Copyright Clearance Center, Inc.; **page 429**: Nijinsky, V. (1936). *The diary of Vaslav Nijinsky*. New York: Simon & Schuster; **page 441**: Modrow, J. (1992). *How to become a schizophrenic: The case against biological psychiatry*. Everett, WA: Apollyon Press. Reprinted by permission of the author.

Chapter 15

page 447: Excerpt from "Anecdotal Thoughts" in *Anatomy of an epidemic: Magic bullets, psychiatric drugs, and the astonishing rise of mental illness in America* by Robert Whitaker, copyright © 2010 by Robert Whitaker. Used by permission of Crown Books, an imprint of the Crown Publishing Group, a division of Random House LLC. All rights reserved. Any third party use of this material, outside of this publication, is prohibited. Interested parties must apply directly to Penguin Random House LLC for permission; **page 454**: Comer, R. (1973). Therapy interviews with a schizophrenic patient. Unpublished manuscript; **page 459**: Republished with permission of Springer Science and Business Media B.V., from Hayward, M. D., & Taylor, J. E. (1956). A schizophrenic patient describes the action of intensive psychotherapy. *Psychiatric Quarterly, 30*. Copyright © 1956 Springer Science and Business Media B.V.; permission conveyed through Copyright Clearance Center, Inc.; **page 463**: Republished with permission of Guilford Publications from Heinrichs, D. W., & Carpenter, W. T., Jr., The coordination of family therapy with other treatment modalities for schizophrenia. In W. McFarlane (Ed.), *Family therapy in schizophrenia* (1983); permission conveyed through Copyright Clearance Center, Inc.

Chapter 16

pages 478, 479 499, 504: Millon, T. (2011). *Disorders of personality: Introducing a DSM/ICD spectrum from normal to abnormal* (3rd ed.). Hoboken, NJ: John Wiley & Sons. Copyright © 2011. Reproduced with permission of John Wiley & Sons, Inc. (ISBN: 9780470040935); **page 482**: Hare, R. D. (1993). *Without conscience: The disturbing world of the psychopaths among us*. New York: Pocket Books. Copyright Guilford Press. Reprinted with permission of The Guilford Press; **page 487**: Sam Vaknin, *Malignant self-love* (Narcissus Publications, 2015). Copyright © 1999–2013 by Lidija Rangelovska.

Chapter 17

pages 513, 523, 534: Republished with permission of South-Western College Publishing, a division of Cengage Learning, from *Casebook in child behavior disorders*, Kearney, C. A., 5th ed. (2013); permission conveyed through Copyright Clearance Center, Inc.; **page 529**: Gelfand, D. M., Jenson, W. R., & Drew, C. J. (1982). *Understanding child behavior disorders*. New York: Holt, Rinehart & Winston; **page 531**: Leutwyler, Kristin. (August 1996). Paying attention: The controversy over ADHD and the drug Ritalin is obscuring a real look at the disorder and its underpinnings. *Scientific American, 272*(2), 12–13. Copyright © 1996 by Scientific American, a division of Nature, Inc. All rights reserved. Reproduced with permission; **page 541**: Bogdan, R., & Taylor, S. (1976, January). The judged, not the judges: An insider's view of mental retardation. *American Psychologist, 31*(91), 47–52.

Chapter 18

page 553: Heston, Leonard L. (1992). Excerpts from the book *Mending minds: A guide to the new psychiatry of depression, anxiety, and other serious mental disorders* by Leonard L. Heston. Copyright © 1991 by Leonard L. Heston. Used by permission of Henry Holt and Company. All rights reserved; **page 556**: Hinrichsen, G. A. (1999). Interpersonal psychotherapy for late-life depression. In M. Duffy (Ed.), *Handbook of counseling and psychotherapy with older adults*. New York: Wiley; **pages 564, 565, 573**: Excerpt from *The forgetting: Alzheimer's: Portrait of an epidemic* by David Shenk, copyright © 2001, 2002 by David Shenk. Used by permission of ICM Partners and by permission of Doubleday, an imprint of the Knopf Doubleday Publishing Group, a division of Penguin Random House LLC. All rights reserved. Any third party use of this material, outside of this publication, is prohibited. Interested parties must apply directly to Penguin Random House LLC for permission.

Chapter 19

page 584: Coleman, L. (1984). *The reign of error: Psychiatry, authority, and law*. Boston: Beacon. Copyright 1984, Lee Coleman. Used by permission.

Name Index

Subject Index

~
6/05

DATE DUE

MAR 2 8 2005			
APR 0 6 2005			
APR 2 5 2005			
JUN 13 2005			
JUL 19 2005			
OCT 25			
11-14-05			
12-05-05			
Jan 17 2006			
GAYLORD			PRINTED IN U.S.A.

About the Author

ebbie Stoller was born in Brooklyn, New York, to an American father and a Dutch mother. She spent many summers in Holland, surrounded by knitters, including her mother, her aunt, her grandmother, and many great-aunts. In high school, Debbie was the geek who sewed all the costumes for the school play, and secretly enjoyed an even geekier hobby: counted cross-stitch. But knitting was not a passion—in fact, for many years she pretty much hated it. Following two and a half miserable years at a state college that shall remain unnamed, Debbie lived in Holland for six months, then started graduate school at Yale University, where she spent the next six years studying the psychology of women, earning her Ph.D., and not knitting at all. Upon graduation she did what many Ph.D.s do—she became a secretary, and after a number of directionless years as a low-level cubicle slave, Debbie started the third-wave feminist 'zine *BUST* with a couple of girl-friends. Soon the magazine grew and spawned a book: *The BUST Guide to the New Girl Order* (1999, Penguin), of which she is co-editor. It was while promoting this book that Debbie tried knitting again, and actually ended up liking it. Today Debbie is the co-publisher of *BUST,* together with Laurie Henzel, and serves as its editor-in-chief. She is also the author of *Stitch 'n Bitch: The Knitter's Handbook* (2003, Workman Publishing). She lives in Brooklyn with her dog, Shadow, and a giant yarn collection. In addition to knitting and publishing her magazine, she enjoys bird-watching, gardening, and other nerdy pastimes.

stitcH 'N bitcH
Nation

BY DEBBIE STOLLER

Fashion Photography by Karen Pearson   *Illustrations by Adrienne Yan*

WORKMAN PUBLISHING · NEW YORK

Dedication

For Shadow, my little bear

Art direction and design: Janet Vicario

Cover photography: Karen Pearson

Workman books are available at special discounts when purchased in bulk for premiums and sales promotions as well as for fund-raising or educational use. Special editions or book excerpts can also be created to specification. For details, contact the Special Sales Director at the address below.

Workman Publishing Company, Inc.

708 Broadway

New York, NY 10003-9555

www.workman.com

Printed in the United States of America

First printing: October 2004

10 9 8 7 6 5 4 3 2 1

Acknowledgments

More than a hundred people were involved in the production of this book—from those who reviewed their favorite yarn stores, to the folks who contributed their favorite knitting tips, to the Stitch 'n Bitch members who sent in profiles of their groups—and I am deeply indebted to them all. But I owe my greatest appreciation to the amazing knitters whose innovative designs are included here, and who deserve the most credit for making this book what it is.

The past six months have been a whirlwind of late nights and working weekends as I raced to meet a series of tight deadlines. I never would have survived it, and this book wouldn't have come together, if it hadn't been for the hard work, support, and love of the following people and one dog.

At Workman Publishing, I'd like to thank Ruth Sullivan, my meticulous and tireless editor, and designer Janet Vicario, for putting so much time and care into this book, and, of course, Peter Workman, for giving me the opportunity to continue stitchin' and bitchin'.

I am grateful to Leora Kahn for organizing such a fabulous photo shoot, as well as Ellen Silverstein for picking such stylin' clothes and Amy Schiappa for creating such purty hair and makeup, as well as photographer Karen Pearson for taking the beautiful shots. The super-cute models—Kelly Alpin, Melinda Ball, Kate Edwards, Brian McCormack, Joy Merrifield, and Aja Spears— also played a big part in making these projects look their best. I am so glad that Adrienne Yan was available to make such awesome illustrations for the book once again. If you ever want to know what Adrienne looks like, just look at the girls she draws: most of them look just like her!

I'd like to thank technical editors Kate Watson and Kiki Wolfson for plodding through the jungle of numbers in these patterns and weeding out errors. Their fastidious attention to detail on these patterns was remarkable. Many thanks go out to production editor Anne Cherry, to copyeditor Judit Bodnar, and to Jarrod Dyer, Michael Fusco, and Philip Hoffhines for technical support. I am very thankful for the great job that Colleen Kane did on editing the Stitch 'n Bitch group descriptions and Local Yarn Store reviews, and I also want to give a shout-out to my brother, Peter

Stoller, the Linus to my Lucy, who helped me in the early stages of this book by sending out contracts and contacting yarn companies on my behalf.

I am, once again, so very appreciative of the members of the NYC Stitch 'n Bitch who were willing to lend a helping hand to get some of these projects knit, including Jill Astmann, Jackie Broner, Kimberli MacKay, Claudine Monique, Katy Moore, Diana Parrington, Karola Wright, and especially my speed-knitters, Eileene Coscolluela and Marney Andersen. Y'all's willingness to help out a knitting sister in need is so moving to me.

Big sloppy kisses go out to the lovely ladies of *BUST* magazine for cutting me some slack when this book pulled me away from my responsibilities at the mag, and especially to my co-publisher, Laurie Henzel, for being the best business partner a girl could ever hope for.

I want to thank Johanna and Bernard Stoller for their unwavering confidence in me, and especially Michael Uman for always helping me to step away from the cliff, even when the knit hits the fan. His love and support have kept me sane for the past nine years and three books, and I am grateful.

Finally, I wish to thank my seventeen-year-old blind dog, Shadow, one of the sweetest creatures ever to walk the planet, for teaching me more about unconditional love and trust than I ever thought possible. He's brought so much joy to my life in the twelve years while he's been my roommate and companion, and there hasn't been a thing I've knit that didn't have a little bit of him woven into it. As he battles cancer and nears his final days, I know I'll miss him forever.

CONTENTS

PART I

I Knit It My Way /1

HOW TO MAKE ANY KNITTING PATTERN WORK WITH YOUR YARN, YOUR GAUGE, YOUR BODY, AND YOUR STYLE

PART II

The Patterns /31

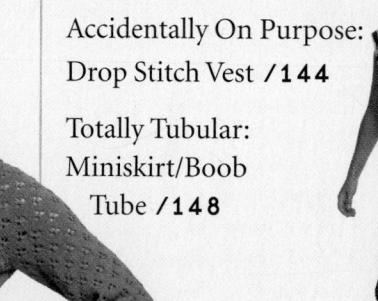

The Patterns (CONTINUED)

PART III
The Knitty-Gritty
A REFRESHER COURSE /253

PART IV
Resources

I Knit It My Way

HOW TO MAKE ANY KNITTING PATTERN WORK WITH YOUR YARN, YOUR GAUGE, YOUR BODY, AND YOUR STYLE

When *Stitch 'n Bitch: The Knitter's Handbook* was published last year, I was both proud and relieved. I and so many others had put so much work into it, and now, finally, it was out there in the world. Seeing it displayed in bookstores across the country was exhilarating, but it was even more exciting the first time I saw a project made from the book posted on the Internet. Soon I began spotting all sorts of projects from *Stitch 'n Bitch*: knit wrist cuffs, baby hats, baby blankets, kitty hats, and Skully sweaters. People were even showing up at my book signings wearing items they'd made from the book. It was amazing!

Of course, many of these knitters chose their own colors for their projects, and others used entirely different yarn than the pattern called for. Still other brave souls made more extensive alterations to the patterns—from replacing the star motif on the wrist cuffs with little Pacman figures to lengthening the Under the Hoodie sweater so that it was less cropped, making a mini version of Meema's Felted Marsupial Tote for a toddler, shortening the extra-long sleeves on To Dye For, and adding shaping to the loose, oversized Skully sweater.

I pull out my handy-dandy calculator (no old-school long division for me), divide 28 by 4, and get 7. Okay, so that's my stitches-per-inch gauge: 7.

Next, I figure out my row gauge.

ROWS PER INCH = NUMBER OF ROWS DIVIDED BY SWATCH LENGTH

Here, the designer tells me she has to knit 15 rows to get 4" of fabric.

So, I divide 15 by 4 and get 3.75. I like to keep only one digit after the decimal, so I'll round this up to 3.8. Okay, so 3.8 is my row gauge.

Now, back to that pattern. The designer tells me to start by casting on 36 stitches. I already know that every 7 stitches equals an inch, but just how many inches does that number 36 represent? In other words, how many times does 7 (the stitches per single inch) go into 36? That's easy: just divide 36 by 7, and you get 5.1428571429. This is a bit unwieldy, so let's just say the scarf is gonna be about 5" wide—a nice size for a scarf.

Next, the pattern says to work 18 rows of color A. How long is that? Easy, peasy: Take 18 and divide it by the row gauge, which was 3.8. 18 ÷ 3.8 = 4.73. So each stripe is about 5" long. The pattern tells me to make this two-stripe color pattern once, and then 5 times more; in other words, I have to do it 6 times altogether. One stripe is 5", so two stripes are 10". Knitting those two stripes 6 times would result in a scarf that's 60" (or 5 feet) long. I will definitely be able to wrap this cute stripy scarf around my neck and have both ends hanging down to keep me warm.

We've used our decoder ring—the stitches per inch and rows per inch—and figured out what's going on in this pattern. It's all a bit like dissecting a frog: kinda gross, kinda nauseating, but extremely informative. It's super important to understand how things are put together if you ever want to change them.

CONTESTANT NUMBER 2
A Straightforward Sweater

If you want to add a room to a house or remodel the kitchen, you need to be able to understand the blueprints. It's the same thing with altering a sweater: To lengthen a sleeve, change a neckline, or shorten the body, you need to understand the pattern. Sweater patterns often include what's called a "schematic"—a blueprint-like line drawing that gives you the exact measurements, in inches, of the completed pieces of knit fabric. So, unlike with the "White Stripes Scarf," you don't need the stitch and row gauge to picture what you're making: It's all laid out for you. But you'll still need your decoder ring—that business about the stitches and rows per inch that you just learned—to help you understand what's really going on in each of those pieces, and it will be the key to changing anything in the pattern.

Let's take a quick stroll through a typical sweater pattern just to see how this works. But I have to warn you: The following section contains plenty of twists and turns, so hang on tight. When we come out on the other side, you might be a bit dizzy, but you'll be a changed knitter. Never again will you blindly increase, decrease, and cast on stitches just because someone told you to; you'll actually understand why you're doing those things, and that knowledge will allow you to do things differently. May the force be with you.

Here is a pattern for a baby sweater:

Li'l Dumplin' Baby Sweater

DIRECTIONS

BACK

Ⓐ CO 42 sts.

K 2 rows in seed st.

K in St st until piece measures 9½" from beg, ending with a WS row.

Ⓑ Next row: K16, BO 10 sts, k16.

Working both sides at the same time, BO 1 st each neck edge EOR 4 times.

BO remaining 12 sts.

FRONT

Work same as for back.

Ⓒ SLEEVES (MAKE 2)

CO 21 sts.

K 2 rows in seed st.

Cont in St st, inc1 st each side EOR 2 times, then every 4th row 5 times (35 sts).

Cont in St st until sleeve measures 5½".

FINISHING

Sew shoulder seams.

Sew sleeves to front and back, beg and ending 5" down from shoulder seam on each side.

Sew side and sleeve seam.

Size

12 months

Finished chest = 24"

Materials

3 skeins Funky Monkey Chunky Yarn (80% merino wool/20% acrylic; 1.75 oz/137 yds)

US 9 (5.5 mm) straight needles

Gauge

14 sts and 20 rows = 4" in St st

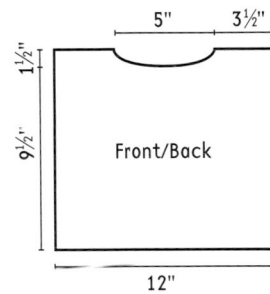

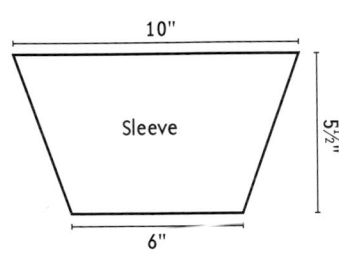

List of abbreviations appears on page 32.

According to the pattern, the gauge for the sweater is 14 stitches and 20 rows per 4".

Before we do anything else, we need to get out that decoder ring. In this case, the stitches per inch = 3.5 (14 stitches ÷ 4" swatch). And the rows per inch = 5 (20 rows ÷ 4" swatch).

Now, let's take on this sweater piece by piece.

Ⓐ THE BACK

The pattern says that to knit the back of this sweater, you start by casting on 42 stitches. If you take that and divide it by your stitches per inch, you should get the width of half of the sweater. Sure enough, 42 ÷ 3.5 = 12.

Next, the pattern says to knit 2 rows in seed stitch, and then to continue in stockinette stitch until the back measures 9½" from the beginning. It does not tell you how many rows to knit to get there, and that's one of the truths about most patterns: row gauge is not as important as stitch gauge.

Ⓑ THE NECK

After you have a 9½"-long piece of fabric, the pattern tells you to knit 16 stitches, bind off the center 10 stitches, and then knit another 16 stitches. Next, you have to bind off 1 stitch at each neck edge on every other row 4 times—that eliminates 8 stitches altogether. Thus, the neck, which you created by binding off 10 stitches and then decreasing another 8 stitches, is 18 stitches wide. According to the stitch gauge, that makes it 18 ÷ 3.5, or 5.14" wide. Sounds kinda like 5" to me.

In fact, all those numbers check out with the schematic. It's right, we're right, and all's right with the world (or at least with the pattern).

The back of the sweater is done. For the front, knit another piece just like it.

Ⓒ THE SLEEVES

Now that we're at the sleeves, things are about to diverge from the straight and narrow. I just said that row gauge was less important than stitch gauge in most patterns, but that's not to say that row gauge doesn't matter to the pattern designer—especially when it comes to sleeves or other areas with a good number of increases or decreases. She cares about row gauge truly, madly, and deeply, and she's very carefully worked out just how many stitches you need to increase, and over how many rows, so those sleeves don't wind up so long that you can't find the baby's hands. These numbers have been calculated with the beady-eyed precision of a child who is being forced to share half her candy with her brother.

You can see from the schematic that this sleeve gets quite a bit wider between the wrist, where it begins, and the shoulder, where it will be attached to the body of the sweater. Let's see how this is done.

The instructions for the sleeves say "CO 21 stitches."

Okay, that's easy: 21 stitches ÷ 3.5 stitches per inch = 6". The bottom of the sleeve is going to be 6" wide, and that checks out with the schematic.

Next, the directions say to knit 2 rows in seed stitch, and then to continue in stockinette stitch, increasing 1 stitch at each side every other row 2 times, and every 4th row 5 times (35 sts)—so you'll end up with 35 stitches. Then it says to continue in stockinette until the piece measures 5½".

So what's going on with those increases? Why is it written so enigmatically, with all the "every other row

2 times and every 4th row 5 times"? If I keep saying "there's no place like home" while I'm doing them, will I end up in Kansas?

Well, actually, there is something a bit like magic going on there, and I'll explain. First off, the designer wants a sleeve that starts off 6" (21 stitches) wide, and ends up 10" (35 stitches) wide. She also wants that sleeve to be exactly 5½" long, so it can fit that tiny arm correctly. But how does she get from the 21 stitches, at the wrist, to the 35 stitches, at the shoulder, in only 5"? (Remember she doesn't start increasing the sleeves until after about ½ inch of seed stitch rows.) Since we know the row gauge, we know she has only 25 rows over which to add on those 14 stitches (5" × 5 rows per inch = 25 rows). And, if she is a nice designer, she probably wants to make the increases symmetrically: 1 on each side of the sleeve. She also wants to place them so all the increases are made on the right-side rows, because it's easier to make them on knitted stitches than on purled stitches.

This is where the "every other row 2 times and every 4th row 5 times" mumbo-jumbo comes in. The designer has done some fancy-ass math, and figured out that this is the prettiest way to make those increases work out evenly along the sleeve. She may have used trial and error till she got to these numbers, working out the sleeves on graph paper till the numbers worked. She may have used something called "the magic formula" to work out the nice increases (there is such a thing, really, see page 18). Hell, she may have just punched the numbers into some knitting software she had. Whatever the case, she's sharing the fruits of her calculations with you in her pattern.

I'm just pointing out the fancy footwork that goes into placing increases or decreases in a knitting pattern, because this is one of the places where altering a pattern can get a little hairy. In the next few sections I'll show you a number of ways to deal with this when making changes, and if you can keep your eyes on the prize and your finger on the calculator, you'll be sure to get through it.

The Li'l Dumplin' Baby Sweater is simpler than many patterns you may knit, but not by much. All patterns are based on this business of gauge, from the cast-on to the bind-off and all the increasing and decreasing in between. And now that you understand the real knitty-gritty of all knitting patterns, the power is yours. You can change the gauge. You can change the shape. You can do whatever you want.

The Gauge of Reason
REPLACING ONE YARN WITH ANOTHER OF THE SAME GAUGE

the most common alteration to any pattern, and one you may already have done, is to replace the yarn the pattern calls for with a yarn of your own choosing. Now that you know how absolutely dependent each line of a pattern is on that decoder ring—the gauge—you can also understand why replacing yarn with another *of the same gauge* means that you'll be able to follow the pattern exactly as written. But figuring out what yarn to use as a replacement can be a little tricky.

The first challenge is to find yourself some yarn that knits up to the same gauge as called for in the pattern. But where do you begin? There are thousands of

yarns out there; do you just choose one willy-nilly and start swatching like mad?

Well, of course not. The first thing to do is figure out what weight the yarn in the pattern is, then try replacing it with a *yarn of the same weight*. The problem is, most patterns don't tell you what weight yarn was used. They do give you the gauge, though, from which you can probably figure this out.

For instance, a pattern may state at the top:

Materials

Loonyland Quikstuff (70% wool, 30% acrylic; 3 oz/135 yds)

8 skeins Flamin' Flamingo

Gauge

12 sts and 17 rows = 4" in St st using size 10½ needles

Just look up that gauge on the Craft Yarn Council's table on the next page, which gives yarn weight standards and categorizes yarn into six weights.

As you can see, there is quite a bit of variety here. "Superfine," for instance, is any yarn whose recommended gauge is between 27 and 32 stitches per 4", knit on size 1, 2, or 3 needles. Although it's awfully nice of the Craft Yarn Council to have come up with these categories, it doesn't do us much good if the yarn companies don't label their stuff with this information—and most of them don't.

Still, with a bit of detective work, you can figure out the weight of the yarn in the pattern. We'll start by looking at our gauge again. In this case, the gauge is 12 stitches per 4", which would place this yarn right into category 5: bulky-weight yarn. We're lucky that this gauge is given over stockinette stitch; if it had been given over a pattern stitch—especially ribbing, which pulls the stitches closer together—the gauge would not be so useful. The bulky yarn in this pattern might very well knit up to 16 stitches over 4" when it's knit in a k1, p1 rib, but that certainly doesn't mean that it's suddenly transformed itself into a category 4, medium-weight yarn.

But all is not lost. If the gauge is given over a pattern stitch, just look at the needle sizes suggested in the pattern to get a sense of the yarn's weight. In this case, the needle is 10½, which is again consistent with this yarn falling into category 5, bulky.

When determining a yarn's weight by looking at gauge and needle size, you also need to be aware of the texture of the finished piece. Take a close look at the completed project, or as good a look as you can get from a photo. Does the yarn seem like it's been knit to the recommended gauge, yielding a nice, solid fabric that you can't see through? Or does it look almost netlike, similar to a mesh, so that if the model hadn't worn a T-shirt under that sweater you'd see her bra? If it's loose, then the yarn was likely knit at a larger gauge than is recommended for that yarn, meaning that the designer used needles quite a bit thicker than would normally be used with this weight of yarn so that she could achieve an open, airy texture. Thus, neither the gauge nor the needle size given will help you in your quest to figure out this yarn's weight. What's a knitter to do?

Well, you could head over to your LYS, find the yarn in question (assuming that they carry it), and read the

Standard Yarn Weight System

Yarn Weight Symbol & Category Names	1 SUPER FINE	2 FINE	3 LIGHT	4 MEDIUM	5 BULKY	6 SUPER BULKY
Type of Yarns in Category	Sock, Fingering, Baby	Sport, Baby	DK, Light Worsted	Worsted, Afghan, Aran	Chunky, Craft, Rug	Bulky, Roving
Knit Gauge Range in Stockinette Stitch to 4 inches	27–32 sts	23–26 sts	21–24 sts	16–20 sts	12–15 sts	6–11 sts
Recommended Needle in Metric Size Range	2.25–3.25mm	3.25–3.75mm	3.75–4.5mm	4.5–5.5mm	5.5–8mm	8mm and larger
Recommended Needle U.S. Size Range	1 to 3	3 to 5	5 to 7	7 to 9	9 to 11	11 and larger

ball band to find the recommended gauge and needle size, and thereby figure out its weight. But, of course, you don't have to actually leave the house to find info about a ball of yarn. Today we have the Internet, and if you can track down information about old classmates and ex-boyfriends on the Web, you can certainly get the lowdown on some yarn. Just enter the full name of the yarn you want to know about in your favorite search engine. Yarn stores that carry the yarn will pop up (possibly even the company that makes the yarn), and at least one of them will list the recommended gauge and needle size. With that info in hand, you can finally figure out the weight of that darn yarn.

SWATCH WATCH
What a Gauge Swatch Can Tell You About Your Yarn (Besides Its Gauge)

Of course, the main way to figure out what's going on with your yarn, and whether it will make a good replacement, is to really get to know it. And you do that by making a swatch. After all, yarn can look just so cute in its balled-up state, but you really don't know what it can grow up to be unless you knit up a bit of it and find out. Some yarn shops even have sample skeins of the yarn they carry so you can swatch some up in a corner of the store and get an idea of what the yarn does before you take it home and marry it.

To make a nice swatch, begin with the needle size suggested on the ball band and cast on one and a half times the number of stitches suggested for a 4" swatch. You need to make a sizable swatch at least 6" wide if you really want to get a sense of the yarn. Knit a couple of rows in garter stitch, then continue in stockinette till you have about 3" of fabric. Stop. Count how many stitches are in a 2"-wide area smack in the center of the swatch. If all you get is one leg of the stitch at the end, count it as half a stitch. Measure another 2" spot; count again. If you keep getting different numbers, take an

average. Then double that to get the gauge for 4". If you have fewer stitches in that 4" swatch than the pattern requires, go up a needle size and swatch some more. If you have too many stitches, go down a size. Work another row of garter stitch before you start the new section, so you can keep them separated. Knit another 3" of stockinette and measure again.

Now you can begin learning about your yarn's personality. What is its "hand"? Meaning, how does it feel in your hand? Lay it over your fist or a can of soda. How does it drape? Will a sweater made out of it hang nicely on your body or is it so stiff that it will stand away from you like a cardboard box? Feel up your swatch. Does it have some "body" or is it completely spineless and loose? How much elasticity does it seem to have? Is the yarn so slippery and drapey that the lovely poncho you want to make will hang on you like so much wet hair? If it's very colorful or slubby or furry, you may realize that the busyness of the colors will obscure all those interesting (and time-consuming) knit-and-purl patterns or cables that are the coolest thing about the sweater, and you may decide to save this yarn for something knit in plain stockinette. Or maybe, hopefully, you'll think, Hot damn, I love this yarn and I can't wait to make this sweater out of it—it's perfect.

GOODNESS GRACIOUS, GREAT BALLS OF FIBER
How Much Yarn Do You Need?

Once you've decided on your replacement yarn, it's time to figure out how much of the stuff you'll need to make the sweater (or, if it's yarn you already have on hand, whether you have enough of it). This is super easy to do. Just look at the number of yards of yarn the original pattern calls for, and figure out how many balls of your replacement yarn would be required to yield that many yards of yarn. In the Loonyland example, every 3-ounce ball of Quikstuff contains 135 yards, and for your size, the pattern says you'll need 8 balls of it. That means you need at least 1,080 yards of Quikstuff to make this sweater (135 yards per ball × 8 balls = 1,080 yards).

Now let's say the yarn you want to use, Marvelous Munchkin, is sold in 50-gram balls that contain only 60 yards of yarn apiece. If you're in a car traveling at 60 miles an hour on your way to your LYS, how many balls of Marvelous Munchkin will you need to buy when you get there? Well, this math problem is no problem at all: You just divide the total number of yards of yarn needed by the yards per ball of the replacement yarn. In this case, that's 1,080 ÷ 60 = 18. So, you whip out your credit card, take home 18 balls of the Munchkin yarn, and get down to the business of making your new dream sweater.

Gauging a Reaction
KNITTING A PATTERN USING A DIFFERENT GAUGE YARN

Knitting a sweater out of a different yarn of the same gauge is easy because you can use the pattern exactly as written. But sometimes you really want to use a yarn that's just not going to work at that gauge. You may have chosen a yarn that you thought would knit up to the same gauge as the one called for in the pattern, but it turns out that in order to get that gauge, you have to knit it on such small needles, it makes the fabric really tight. You quickly realize that if you knit the sweater at this gauge, you'll end up with a

garment that could stand up by itself. You've tried larger needles and found that this gives you a much nicer, drapier fabric, but, of course, that also gives you an entirely different gauge.

Or maybe there's a sweater you want to knit that calls for such lightweight yarn you just know it will take too long for you to knit it. You want to knit it in a bit heavier yarn, say a worsted rather than a sport-weight, and you've already swatched up the yarn and know that your sweater would hang just as nicely using this yarn.

Since you know how important gauge is to any pattern, you already know that changing the gauge is gonna require a good number of changes to the pattern. You also know you can do it. With some time, and a calculator, you can knit whatever you want in whichever yarn you want.

Let's start with a simple alteration, by considering a super easy scarf pattern:

SCARF FACE

Materials

3 skeins Free Woolly (100% wool; 4 oz/350 yds)

Gauge

24 sts and 28 rows = 4" in garter st

DIRECTIONS

CO 42 st, k in garter st till piece measures 50", BO.

Like most scarf patterns, this one doesn't give you a schematic, but you can tell that this pattern is going to make a scarf that's exactly 7" wide by 50". (You know it's 7" because the designer tells you she gets 4" to every 24 stitches, which is a gauge of 6 stitches to the inch; since she's casting on 42 stitches, and $42 \div 6 = 7$".)

Now, let's say you want to knit this in some yarn that's got a different gauge—say, an acrylic yarn that gives you 18 stitches and 24 rows per 4" in garter stitch.

First you need to get your decoder ring: In this case, for the acrylic yarn, that's 4.5 stitches per inch ($18 \div 4 = 4.5$) and 6 rows per inch ($24 \div 4 = 6$). Since you want a scarf that's 7" wide, you just multiply your stitches per inch by the number of inches for the width of the scarf: $4.5 \times 7 = 31.5$. Since you can't cast on 31.5 stitches, you'll round it up to 32 stitches and call it a day.

For the next part, the pattern tells you to knit in garter stitch till the scarf measures 50". Well, guess what? That's just what you're gonna do. There's no decreasing, no increasing, nothing special that happens in this pattern on any special row, so you can just knit the light fantastic and put your dang calculator away for the time being. That's that: You've recalculated your first pattern. Good times.

THE GAUGE OF CONSENT
Dealing with Pattern Repeats

Now let's take a look at that White Stripes ribbed scarf pattern we dissected awhile ago (p. 6). This scarf was knit in a k3, p3 rib that had a gauge of 28 stitches and 15 rows per 4". Once we decoded the pattern, we discovered that the scarf was 5" wide and 60" long, with 5" stripes of alternating colors.

Let's say you want to do it in a thinner yarn that gives you 32 stitches and 24 rows to 4". Your decoder ring tells you that means you get 8 stitches to the inch

and 6 rows per inch. You might think you just multiply 8 (the stitches per inch) by 5 (the width of the scarf), get the answer 40, and cast on 40 stitches and start knitting.

But you'd run into a problem, because that ribbing pattern (k3, p3) is based on a 6-stitch repeat, and that's why the pattern designer so thoughtfully told you to cast on 36 stitches—36 is a multiple of 6.

If you cast on 40, you'll innocently knit and purl along 6 times, and then, after knitting 36 stitches, you'll go knit, knit, knit, purl, OH NO! You'll have run out of stitches, and you won't have finished off your purty ribbing pattern!

Don't panic. You have options. One of them is to say, "Screw the ribbing pattern." So what if you have one lone stitch at the end that doesn't get to make a whole rib? Don't worry about it, just knit away.

Another option is to split the difference: Instead of leaving those 4 stitches at the end of your row, where they'll be hanging out possibly looking all kinds of wrong, why don't you stick 2 of them at the beginning of your row and 2 at the end?

Or you could just add another 2 stitches to your cast-on, making it 42, then do your k3, p3 rib according to the pattern. The scarf may be a bit wider than the one the designer envisioned, but what the hey.

Of course, which options you choose will depend on your own taste and on what it is you're knitting. Adding or subtracting a couple of stitches on a scarf might not matter so much, but doing it on a snug-fitting hat may mean you'll have to give it to your friend's small-headed baby, or, if it's too big, to someone with a Charlie Brown head. In sweater knitting, things can also get sketchy if you're adding extra stitches or taking them away willy-nilly. In those instances, evaluate your options and do what you think is best. It might not matter if your sweater is ½" wider in the front and the back, making it 1" wider all around. On the other hand, you might prefer to have some stitches on either side of your work that don't quite make up an entire pattern repeat, but at least the thing fits right.

GAUGE AGAINST THE MACHINE
Knitting a Sweater in a Different Gauge

Of course, you can also rewrite a pattern for something more complicated than a scarf, using a different gauge. Let's try the baby sweater (p. 8). It was designed using yarn that has a gauge of 14 stitches and 20 rows per 4". But say you've got something really lovely and soft you'd like to use for it that's a bit thinner, and it knits up at 18 stitches and 26 rows per 4".

Now, there are two ways to go about this. One would be to take all the measurements from the schematic—the width of the bottom of the sweater, the length of the sweater, the width and length of the sleeves, the width of the neck—and calculate the number of stitches and rows you'll need in order to knit all those dimensions and shapes. Luckily, there is an easier way to do this: You can just take the numbers in the existing pattern and resize them up or down in the same proportion that your yarn's gauge differs from the pattern's gauge.

The first thing to do is to get your stitch ratio; meaning, the ratio of the stitches per inch of your yarn to the stitches per inch of the pattern's yarn. Here's the formula:

STITCH RATIO = YOUR STITCH GAUGE DIVIDED BY THE PATTERN'S STITCH GAUGE

In this case, the stitch ratio is $18 \div 14 = 1.29$, which you'll round up to 1.3.

One nice thing about the above formula is that it doesn't matter if you're plugging in your gauge per 4" or per 1" or per 6½", as long as the pattern gauge is for the same measurement.

There are a couple of things to notice about the number 1.3. For one thing, it's greater than 1, meaning that you will have to knit all the stitches PLUS MORE to get the same measurement your pattern is calling for. Actually, you already know that, because you had to knit 18 whole tiresome stitches just to get the same 4" that the pattern designer whipped out in a mere 14 stitches.

Seeing what the ratio turns out to be, and whether it makes sense to you, is one way to remember how to calculate this figure. But if you ever have a hard time remembering the order of the numbers, just remember this: As in everything else in life, YOU COME FIRST! It's always YOUR number on the top of the division line, and the pattern designer's gauge at the bottom. YOU COME FIRST, she comes last. You're on top, she's on the bottom. (I mean, who the hell is she, anyway?)

Once you have your stitch ratio, you'll also need to figure out your row ratio. You're a pro at this by now, so I bet you already figured out that:

ROW RATIO = YOUR ROW GAUGE DIVIDED BY THE PATTERN'S ROW GAUGE

Once again, you come first!

In the example above, the original Li'l Dumplin' pattern called for 20 rows per 4", and your lighter-weight yarn is giving you 30 rows per 4".

So what's your row ratio? It's 30 (your row gauge) divided by 20 (the pattern's row gauge). And here ya go: it's 1.5.

Now, to really get down to modifying that pattern for this new yarn, all you need to do is take your stitch ratio and multiply all the stitches in the pattern to get the new stitch numbers, and take your row ratio and multiply all the rows in the pattern to get the new row numbers. Basically, you're adjusting the horizontal measurements on the pattern using your stitch ratio, and the vertical measurements using your row ratio.

Ⓐ FRONT AND BACK

For the front and back, where it says to CO 42 stitches, multiply that by your stitch ratio. So, you'll cast on $42 \times 1.3 = 54.6$ stitches, which you'll round up to 55 stitches.

Next, you'll knit for 9½", just as the pattern says, in however many rows it takes you to get there, and you'll end on a wrong-side row.

Ⓑ THE NECK

Next, the pattern says to knit 16 stitches, bind off 10 stitches, and knit 16 stitches.

You'll multiply each number by the stitch ratio:
$16 \times 1.3 = 20.8$, round up to 21
$10 \times 1.3 = 13$
$16 \times 1.3 = 20.8$, round up to 21

This means you should knit 21 stitches, BO 13, then knit another 21. Just to check your math, these numbers should add up to all the stitches you have on the needle. And, indeed, $21 + 13 + 21 = 55$, which is how many stitches you cast on to begin with.

Now things get a bit tricky. The pattern says to BO 1 stitch each neck edge every other row 4 times.

We already figured out that this means you have to knit 8 rows, over which you'll be decreasing 8 stitches. Now, let's multiply both of these by your row and stitch ratios:

8 rows (for decreasing) $\times$ 1.5 (row ratio) = 12 rows

and

8 stitches (to be decreased) $\times$ 1.3 (stitch ratio) = 10.4, round down to 10.

So where the original pattern told you to decrease 8 stitches over 8 rows, you'll need to decrease 10 stitches over 12 rows. How can you do that? Again, it's easy: You'll just bind off 1 stitch each side every other row 5 times, which will use up 10 of those rows, and then knit 2 more rows plain. Done deal.

C THE SLEEVES

The pattern says to cast on 21 sleeve stitches. Multiplying that by your stitch ratio gives you 21 $\times$ 1.3 = 27.3, so you'll cast on 27 stitches.

Then you'll knit 2 rows in seed stitch before continuing with stockinette stitch.

Now, you need to end up with 35 stitches $\times$ 1.3, or 45.5, which you can round *down* to 45 (you'll see why in a second). This means you need to go from 21 stitches to 45 stitches—giving you 18

stitches to increase. Since this is an even number, you can make these increases in pairs. (Now you know why we rounded down, instead of up.) But how? You can increase 2 stitches at a time, 9 times.

To figure out how many rows you need to make those increases over, let's go back to the original pattern. It says to increase every other row 2 times, and every 4th row 5 times. In other words, increase 7 times altogether, adding 2 stitches each time, for a total of 14 stitches increased. And it says to make them over 24 rows $(2 \times 2) + (4 \times 5)$.

Multiplying that 24 by your row ratio (24×1.5) gives you 36. Next, take these rows (36) and divide them by the number of increase rows you need to make (9). Or 36 ÷ 9 = 4. So, you'll increase 1 stitch on each side of the sleeve every 4 rows, and you'll do it 9 times total.

Unfortunately, many times the division won't work out so neatly. When that happens, just tuck those increase rows here and there as evenly as you can. I told you there was magic involved in getting those numbers in the first place—and if we're gonna muck with magic, we need to use a little fudge. So, let's say you had 10 decrease rows instead of 9 to fit into those 36 rows above. 3 divided by 10 gives you 3.6. Why not just make half of those decreases—5 of them— every 4th row, to use up 20 rows,

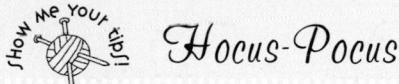

Hocus-Pocus

USING THE MAGIC FORMULA TO SPACE INCREASES AND DECREASES EVENLY ALONG A DIAGONAL

A long time ago, during the time of the Greeks, some mathematician with a lot of time on his hands came up with a formula that, thousands of years later, is frequently used by knitters to calculate nice increases and decreases along a diagonal.

I've seen this formula explained in a number of ways, but the one I like best is Maggie Righetti's version, in her wonderful book, *Sweater Design in Plain English.*

Here's my variation on her theme:

Say you have to increase 28 stitches over 91 rows for a sleeve. First, reduce the rows you're working with to the next even number down. So, here we'll make that 91 into 90 rows. Next, realize that since you'll be making one increase at each side of the sleeve, you really only need 14 spaces in the sleeve to make your 28 increases (28 ÷ 2 = 14). Now, divide the number of increases you need to make by the number of rows you have available to you: 90 ÷ 14 = 6.42

Obviously, you can't make those increases every 6.42 rows. You probably would, however, like to make your increases only on your right-side rows, or on the knit side in stockinette stitch. To make that happen, you need to find the first even number that's less than your result, and the first even number that's greater.

In this case, that's 6 and 8. These two numbers are now the number of rows between your increases.

Next, pretend you were going to make all the increases using the lower of these two numbers, and figure out how many rows that would use up. In our case, that would be 6 (the lower even number) × 14 (the number of increase rows we need to make), and the result is 84.

Now, figure out how many rows are left, divide that number by 2, and you'll get the number of times you need to do the larger increase. So, 90 rows − 84 = 6, and 6 divided by 2 is 3. You'll have to increase every 8 rows 3 times.

The number of increases you have left to make is how many times you'll need to increase by the lower number: So, we had 14 increases altogether, and we're doing 3 increases every 8 rows, which leaves us 11 more increases left to do. We'll be doing those 11 increases every 6th row.

Does it all check out? Indeed it does: 11 increases every 6th row = 66 rows, 3 increases every 8th row = 24 rows. That's 14 increases over 90 rows.

I told you it was magic!

and then make the other 5 every 3 rows, to use up another 15. Sure, it only adds up to 35 rows instead of 36, but that's what makes fudge so delicious: You don't need to worry about it. Or, if you have a really strong stomach, you can take a spin on the Magic Formula (above) to figure out the perfect spacing of increases over the rows you have.

Having a Knit Fit

HOW TO GET GREAT-FITTING KNITTING

few things are more frustrating than spending weeks or months on a sweater only to discover, once it's done, that it pulls too tightly across your chest or that the sleeves are so long you have to

roll them back just to find your fingers. In this next section, I'm going to show you how you can figure out how well a pattern for a sweater is going to fit *before* you make it, and then alter it, if necessary, so it fits you the way you want it to.

First you need to understand some basics about how knitwear is sized. Designers work up their sweaters around certain well-proportioned body standards, and, for the most part, they think of you as nothing more than a pair of boobs. (Or, for gents, a set of pecs). You may be tall, you may be thin, you may be short, you may be chubby. But if you have a 38" bust, as far as the designer is concerned, you're gonna wear a sweater sized for that 38" chest. Based on that one measurement, she's gonna make assumptions about your arm length, your shoulder width—hell, even your hip size. She's going to get this information, not by coming over to your house and measuring you, but by looking up your measurements on a table.

For a long time there were no real knitting size standards, so designers were free to refer to their own standard sizing charts, but now the Craft Yarn Council has come up with a set of measurements that's based on figures averaged from a whole lot of people (see the chart on page 20). Designers are supposed to refer to these when they are making their sweaters for a variety of sizes of imaginary people (we used them for the sizes in this book). In the real world, however, we know that people don't come in standard sizes. I mean, Pam Anderson and Kathy Bates may very well measure the same size around the chest (I'm just guessing here), but I don't think they're going to be sharing clothing anytime soon, least of all sweaters.

EASE ON DOWN THE ROAD
Understanding Ease

even if you're built exactly like a store mannequin, deciding which size sweater to make can be less than simple. That's because, for one thing, many patterns don't tell you what size person they're made for; they just give you the finished measurements, and usually only the finished circumference at the bust. But just take a look at any book of patterns, and you'll see that a woman's medium-size sweater can have a finished bust measurement anywhere from 30" to 42". So, what's going on here? Certainly the designers aren't so far out of synch that one considers medium to be a 30" pair of knockers while another thinks medium is a 42" rack?

No, that's not the problem. The difference in the bust measurements here has to do with the amount of ease that's added to the sweater. Ease is simply the additional number of inches the designer added (or subtracted) from the wearer's bust measurement to design a sweater that would fit in a certain way. Lana Turner and Kurt Cobain were both known to be sweater wearers, but the way Lana wore hers definitely differed from how Kurt wore his. Whereas Lana's sweaters were stretched taut across her bosom to achieve that much-coveted "sweater girl" look, Kurt's mohair cardigans were baggy and slouchy, hiding the outlines of his body and giving him the quintessential grunge silhouette. These variations in sweater styles are due to variations in the amount of ease in their sweaters: Lana's were probably about 1" to 2" narrower than her actual body size (a 36" sweater stretched across a 38" chest), whereas Kurt's were probably 4" to 6" wider than his body (a 44" sweater around a 38" chest).

Craft Yarn Council Standard Body Measurements*

Woman's Size	X-SMALL	SMALL	MEDIUM	LARGE	1X	2X	3X
Bust (inches)	28–30	32–34	36–38	40–42	44–46	48–50	52–54
Center Back (Neck to Cuff)	27–27½	28–28½	29–29½	30–30½	31–31½	31½–32	32½–33
Back Waist Length	16½	17	17¼	17½	17¾	18	18
Cross Back (Shoulder to Shoulder)	14–14½	14½–15	16–16½	17–17½	17½	18	18
Sleeve Length to Underarm	16	17	17	17½	17	18	18

*For more sizes, including men and children, go to www.yarnstandards.com.

In fact, designers usually design to one of the following **ease dimensions**:

● **Very close fitting:** 1"– 2" narrower than your actual measurements. Hello, Lana Turner!

● **Close fitting:** Snug but not tight, your exact size. Works best with lighter-weight yarns. Knit summer tanks are often sized this way.

● **Standard-fitting:** 2"– 4" more than your body measurements. You can easily wear this over a T-shirt or other top; it will still show your curves quite nicely. This is the basic fit of most pullover sweaters.

● **Loose fitting:** 4"– 6" wider than your body. Nice, comfy, sweatshirty or almost baggy sweater; it will hang straight on your body rather than hug your curves. Cardigans that are meant to be worn over other shirts and sweaters are often made with this much ease.

● **Oversized:** 6" or more of ease. Something you want to cuddle up in. An oversized sweater is so loose, you could probably even fit something else—a cocker spaniel, a baby, your own folded-up legs—in the sweater along with you.

Armed with this knowledge, you can now begin to get a feel for how that size medium sweater with a finished bust measurement of 40" is going to fit your 38" bust.

SWEATIN' TO THE OLDIES
Getting Measurements from Your Fave Sweaters

Now that you understand fit, the real question is how you want your sweater to fit you. Perhaps you're the kind of gal on whom standard-fitting sweaters show not only the luscious curves of your bust but also those of

your beer belly, and you really only like to wear much baggier sweaters. Alternately, maybe you are so petite that wearing anything but a close-fitting garment gives you such a shapeless form that you look like you left the house wearing your boyfriend's clothes. The best way to know how you'd like a sweater to fit is not to measure your own body and compare it to the pattern, but to measure one of your favorite sweaters. Simply lay the sweater down flat and measure it across the chest, right below the armpit. Double that, and you have the finished chest measurement you want to go for. Or try measuring a number of your favorite sweaters and comparing them to your own chest measurement (measured around your back and across the pointiest part of your bust, while you're wearing a bra. Boys don't have to wear a bra while measuring but should feel free to do so). Not only will this give you a good idea of the sweater sizes you should be knitting, but also how these variations in fit—very close fitting, close fitting, standard, and oversized—look and feel in relation to your body. And, hell, if you don't have a large enough sweater wardrobe to do this, pop into a store and take a stack of sweaters and your handy-dandy measuring tape into the dressing room. There's no law against it!

While you're trying them on, measure how long they are from the top of your shoulder to the bottom of the sweater. The length of a sweater also makes a big difference in how it fits and feels. A sweater may be just long enough to primly reach one woman's waist, but may give another an inadvertent Britney Spears, belly-baring look. And while most patterns won't give you a finished length measurement, you can usually see what that is from the pattern's schematic. Hip-length sweaters are also nice; how long you want yours to be is another thing to check out during your sweater-measuring expedition.

Now you have a better idea of the right size sweater to knit for your size and your tastes. If you have a 36" chest and your very favorite sweater is 19" across when you measure it flat (38" around), then by all means choose the sweater that has a 38" finished measurement, no matter what size it's intended for. But be aware of something: A sweater that's designed to be big and boxy will never give you a sweater-girl shape even if you knit it 2" smaller than your bust size; that boxiness is in the shape of the sweater itself. So play with the ease and your selected size just a bit, but don't try to force a style or design to be a completely different one. If it's body hugging you want, choose a sweater that hugs the body of the model in the picture; if you like boxy, choose one that looks like that in the picture. Use the ease and size measurements here to help you select which size instructions you should follow. Finally, consider the material you're using in your sweater when determining the amount of ease you want. Close-fitting garments work best in knits made of thinner yarn. Thicker yarns are better suited to projects with more ease, because the width of the yarn itself will use up some of that ease.

THE SHAPE OF THINGS TO COME
Basic Sweater Shapes

there's one more thing that will affect how a sweater fits, and that's the shape of the sweater itself. At first glance, most sweaters seem to be pretty similar: They're basically a torso with sleeves. But take a closer look and you'll see that a sweater is really a body tube connected

to two sleeve tubes. How those sleeve tubes connect to the body determines the three basic sweater shapes.

First, and simplest, is the **drop shoulder sweater.** The body is a straight rectangle, and the sleeves grow at an angle and then are bound off all at once, in a straight line, across the top. Those sleeves are knit shorter than a person's arms, because when you wear a sweater like this, the shoulders of the sweater hang down over your own shoulders, and cover part of your arms. The sleeves drop down from that. A drop shoulder sweater is the quintessential slouchy sweater shape—they were a huge hit in the '80s. Because this type of sweater will always hang over your shoulder, it will not work well for a sweater that you want to hug your body.

A raglan sweater has a body that angles inward toward the neck a bit below the armhole point, and the tops of the sleeves also angle toward each other. The very top of the sleeves becomes part of the shoulder and neckline. Raglan sweaters are shaped like baseball jerseys; they have a nice, classic fit, and while they should be rather roomy in the armpit area, the body can fit quite closely if you want it to.

A sweater with fitted sleeves has a little bite taken out of each side where the sleeves will go, and then the sleeve has a matching sleeve cap that fits perfectly into that hole on the sweater. A fitted sleeve is what most sewn shirts have: Blouses and T-shirts are fitted this way. As their name suggests, fitted sleeves are the nicest style to use if you want a sweater or tank that will really hug your body and arms, but this style of sleeve can easily be used on a roomier sweater as well.

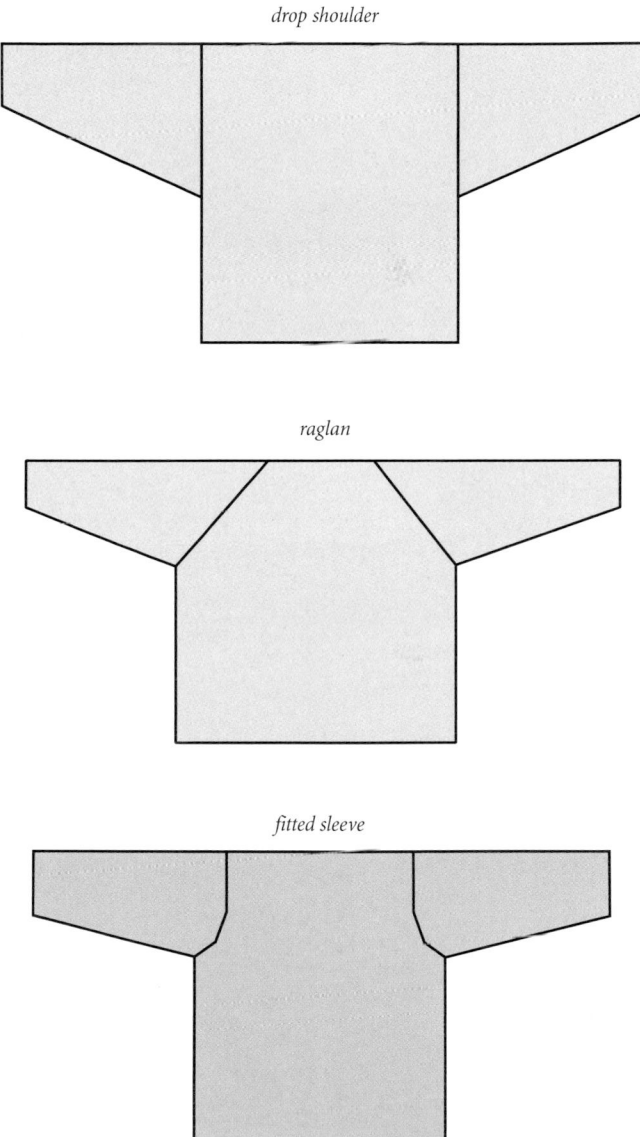

drop shoulder

raglan

fitted sleeve

MEASURING UP

Taking Your Own Measurements

If you want to guarantee a great-fitting garment, you should also quickly take your own (or the intended wearer's) measurements. Although these will not tell you how a sweater is likely to fit, they can tell you how much you follow or deviate from the standard measurements used by pattern designers. In other books and on some Web sites, I've read this procedure given in such intense and complicated detail that it makes taking your measurements sound only slightly less exacting and time-consuming than an MRI. It doesn't need to be. Just whip out a tape measure, and measure yourself this way:

CENTER BACK, NECK TO CUFF: Hold one arm straight out to your side, then measure from the bump at the top of your spine to the bump at the side of your wrist.

BACK WAIST LENGTH: Measure from the bump at the top of your spine down to your waist—the part where your body is most indented.

CROSS BACK, SHOULDER TO SHOULDER: Measure from the bump at the top of your shoulder across to the bump on your other shoulder.

SLEEVE LENGTH: Measure from your armpit, down your slightly bent arm, to the bump on the outside of your wrist.

BUST: Measure around those two bumps on your front. Hold the tape measure across the fullest part of your chest, right across your nipples, and if you're a 36L (long!), be sure to wear a bra when you're measuring.

You'll need someone to help you get your back-to-waist measurement and your shoulder-to-shoulder measurement, but as long as you don't mind said person seeing you in your bra, it could be just about anyone. Also, although the standard measurements don't call for it, measure your waist at its most indented place as well (useful with a pattern that has waist shaping or if you decide to add your own; see pages 25, 27).

Now, compare your measurements to those of the Craft Yarn Council's table on page 20. There's enough leeway in those measurements, so maybe you're lucky to fit pretty comfortably into a standard size. But you might not fit into them so well, because these standards assume that if one part of you is bigger, all the other parts will be bigger, too. Larger boobs go with longer arms, smaller boobs with shorter ones. Of course, a lady who gets breast implants and goes from a size 32B to a size 32D doesn't all of a sudden get longer arms, too. An extra-small sweater will pull tightly across her bodacious frame, while a large might give her sleeves that hang below her fingertips.

Let's say you're tall, slender, and somewhat flat-chested: A large sweater will bag across your chest, although the sleeves may fit you nicely, and a small one will fit your chest nicely, but the sleeves will always look pulled up. Or your boobs and arms may be a designer's dream and fit the chart exactly, but if you've got a long torso (your neck-to-waist measurement deviates from the standard), you're probably mighty tired of wearing sweaters that always ride up on you. All of you should choose the size that fits best across your chest, and then shorten or lengthen the sleeves to fit your arms, if necessary, and shorten or lengthen the sweater so that it lands in the right place on your torso. In the next section, I'll show you how to do that.

Ch-Ch-Ch-Changes

HOW TO MAKE ADJUSTMENTS TO A PATTERN TO FIT YOUR BODY AND YOUR STYLE

Here's where you'll learn to make adjustments to sweaters to accommodate your real-life body. But even if your measurements are a designer's dream, you may still want to alter a pattern. You may be drooling over a cropped sweater, but your belly hasn't seen the sun since 1975 and you don't want to reintroduce the two of them now; instead, you'd like to lengthen the sweater to hip length. Or the sleeves of a sweater you're interested in making are primly wrist length, and you'd like them to hang a bit over your hands for a nice punky or matchstick girl look. You might like to show off your neck by swapping a turtleneck with a scoop neck, or make the sweater more femme-y by replacing a roll bottom with a picot edge hem. Using your pattern as a guide, and a trusty little calculator, each of these things can be accomplished.

GET SHORTY

Making a Sweater Longer or Shorter

This one's the easiest to do. If you have a long torso and would prefer to add a few inches to your sweater, just go ahead and add them. To make it shorter, do the reverse: Subtract a couple of inches. Look for the beginning of the armhole shaping instructions—most often, they start with having you bind off about 1" worth of stitches on each side of your sweater—and make sure you add or subtract the extra stitches *before* that point, and *after* the bottom ribbing (or whatever the bottom edge is).

AT ARM'S LENGTH

Making Sleeves Longer (or Shorter)

Adding or subtracting length from sleeves is a bit more challenging, as they often get wider from the wrist to the shoulder, and thus there are increases involved. You want to try to make your length changes evenly between those increases. So, first get your row gauge, figure out how many inches of fabric you're adding and how many extra rows that means you are going to knit. To make things easy on yourself, round that up or down to the closest even number. Then take that number of rows and distribute them as evenly as possible among your increases, in sets of 2 rows at a time.

Let's try this out with our old pal, the Li'l Dumplin' sweater. Suppose you want to knit this for a baby who has exceptionally long arms (perhaps Mommy or Daddy hadn't quite finished evolving), and you now want to add 2 whole inches to each sleeve. Here are the original instructions for the sleeve:

SLEEVES

K 2 rows in seed st.

Cont in St st, inc1 st each side EOR 2 times, then every 4th row 5 times (35 sts).

Cont in St st until sleeve measures 5½".

The row gauge on that sweater is 5 per inch, so you'll have to add 10 rows to the sleeves.

Since you'll be adding those 10 rows 2 at a time, you'll need 5 places in the pattern where you can slip in your extra rows. This pattern has 7 places for increases already built in (every other row 2 times, every 4th row 5 times).

Waist Management

ADDING WAIST SHAPING TO A SWEATER

Most sweater patterns have a simple, straight shape that can be unflattering to many women. Waist shaping is easy to add, and this method will work well on a sweater that is hip length or below and has a raglan or set-in sleeve. Here's how.

When you knit a sweater, you typically work between 1" and 3" of edging (ribbing, seed, garter, etc.), followed by 10" to 14" of body before the armhole shaping. With this method, you'll decrease stitches between the ribbing and the waist, knit for about an inch, then increase till you reach about 3" before the armhole shaping. The beauty part is, you'll have the exact same number of stitches at this point as if you hadn't done any shaping at all. Waist not, want not!

Know your measurements and know your pattern: Take your bust and waist measurements, be honest with yourself, and write them down. You'll figure out the amount of decreasing you need to make at the waist by subtracting your waist from your bust measurement. You don't need a sweater to be waist-hugging in order to be flattering; often, decreasing about 4" at the waist is enough.

Next, measure yourself from your armpit to the most indented part of your side, where your waist is. Then look at your pattern and calculate how many inches you are supposed to knit before you get to the armhole shaping.

Finally, check your gauge. Figure out how many stitches per inch and how many rows per inch you're knitting.

Calculate: Start with the number of inches you are going to decrease; multiply that by your stitches per inch; divide that number by 4. This gives you your total number of decrease and increase rows (X). Take your length from armpit to waist (A) and

subtract 3½". Multiply your result by your rows-per-inch gauge. This is the number of rows over which you will be increasing after the waist (Y).

Take the length of the sweater from armpit to lower edge (B), subtract A, and subtract 3½". Multiply the result by your rows-per-inch gauge. This is the number of rows over which you will be decreasing to the waist (Z).

Divide Y by X. This is the number of rows you will be making between increase rounds.

Divide Z by X. This is the number of rows you will be making between decrease rounds.

On your mark, get set, knit:

Begin by knitting 3" according to the pattern directions.

Next, decrease 1 stitch each edge every (Z ÷ X) rows. If you're knitting flat, that means decrease 1 stitch at each side of the front and back pieces. If you're knitting in the round, place a marker at the points that would be the left and right side edges; then decrease 1, knit 1 before marker and knit 1, decrease 1 after marker.

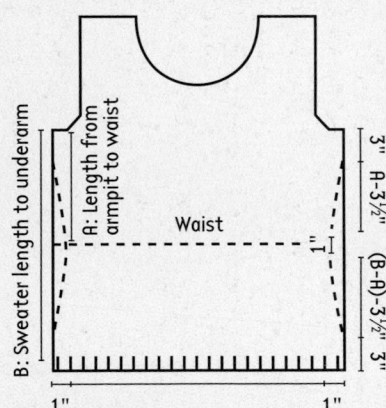

Knit straight for 1".

Next, increase 1 stitch each edge every (Y ÷ X) rows.

Knit straight for 3". You should now be at the correct length for the underarm shaping.

Christina McNamee, Arlington, VA

Lucky you, you can just slip the 2 extra rows between the last 5 increases every 4th row and be done with your 10 extra rows. So, after the ribbing, you'll increase 1 stitch each side every other row 2 times, and every 6th row 5 times, instead of every 2nd and every 4th row, as the pattern was written. And, of course, you continue in stockinette stitch until the sleeves for the baby with the monkey arms measure 7½". Obviously, if you're trying to shorten the sleeves, you do the same thing in reverse: you subtract pairs of rows from between your increases.

PRIMARY COLLARS
Choosing Your Own Neckline

If you don't like the turtleneck called for on a sweater, and would prefer a roll neck, or you want to raise the scoop neck that's on a woman's sweater and add a nice little crew neck when you knit it for a guy, you can. Here's how:

● For a **crew neck,** you want the neckline to be only about 2" deep. If you're working on a design with a neckline lower than that, you'll have to adjust where you start your neckline. Figure out how many stitches are cast off for the neckline in the original pattern, and don't start binding them off until you are about 2" from the top. You'll want to bind off at least half of the neckline stitches in that first step, then bind off 1 or 2 stitches at each end of every row till you get through them all. Figure out how many rows you have in that 2", and if you need to add a few more stitches to that first bind off, go ahead and do so.

Next, sew one or both of the shoulder seams. Then, using straight needles if you sewed up one shoulder, or

crew neck   turtleneck   roll neck   scoop neck   V-neck

circulars if you seamed them both, pick up one stitch for every stitch bound off, all around the front and the back of the neckline. Now just knit a k1, p1 rib for about an inch, then bind off *very loosely.* In fact, to make sure that the sweater will go over anyone's head, and not just a pinhead, you might want to bind off using needles one or two sizes larger.

- For a **turtleneck,** follow the directions for a crew neck but keep knitting for about 3" of rib, then switch to larger needles and knit another 3", then bind off. The last bit of ribbing knit on larger needles will fold nicely over the ribbing knit on smaller needles.

- For a **roll neck,** follow the directions for crew neck but instead of knitting ribbing on your picked-up stitches, just knit straight stockinette for about 1½". It will roll over onto itself, just as God intended stockinette stitch to do.

- For a **scoop neck,** make the neckline a bit deeper—at least 3" deep. The simplest way to finish off a scoop neck is to crochet the edge in crab stitch (see page 268).

- For a **V-neck,** things get a little more complicated. Begin shaping the V-neck at the same point as where the armhole shaping begins. You'll want to bind off the V-neck stitches on each side in a nice diagonal line from here to the shoulder. Use the Magic Formula (page 18), or trial and error, to calculate the diagonal decreases so that you can bind off all of the neckline stitches evenly—it should be

It's a Cinch

ADDING RIBBING TO MAKE A SWEATER MORE SHAPED

I love big, warm, bulky sweaters, but sometimes you need a sweater that shows off what you've got. Adding ribbing to the sides of a garment is a great way to make it form-fitting without the complication of increasing and decreasing. All you need are two measurements: how much narrower you'd like the sweater to be (in inches), and the number of stitches per inch of your gauge. The first measurement tells you how much ribbing you want on each side of the sweater, and the second tells you approximately how many stitches to rib.

If the sweater circumference is 35" and you want it to fit your waist at 30", you will need to knit 5" of ribbing on each side of the sweater body, from bottom ribbing to armpit. That's because an equal rib (1 × 1, 2 × 2, 3 × 3, etc.) contracts to about half the width of even knitting, so 10" of ribbing (5" on each side) will pull the sweater in about 5". If your gauge is 4 stitches per inch, for example, that means you'll need to rib about 20 stitches on each side to get 5" less overall. If you're knitting the sweater flat in two pieces (back and front), divide that number in half and rib that number of stitches at each side of the front and the back. For the example above, you'll rib 10 stitches at the left and right sides of the front and do the same on the back. If you're knitting in the round, just rib 20 stitches on each side. If the sweater has a ribbed collar or cuffs, use that as a guide for your side ribbing. Fortunately, ribs are very forgiving, so the same stretch that allows them to hug your curves will also hide any mishaps while you experiment with this technique.
Susan Kelley,
Portland, OR

about a third of the stitches you have left after binding off for the armholes. Now sew both shoulder seams, and pick up stitches evenly around the back and front of the neckline, being sure to pick up one stitch right smack in the center of the lowest point of your V. Knit in k1, p1 rib till you get to two stitches before that middle stitch; ssk, then knit the center stitch, then k2 together, and carry on in the k1, p1 rib from before. Do that every row for about an inch, then bind off all stitches loosely.

EDGING OUT THE COMPETITION
Changing the Edging at the Bottom of Sweaters and Sleeves

Sweaters and tanks are almost always knit with some kind of edging at the bottom. That's either to make the sweater hold closer to the body at those points, which is what ribbing does very well, or just to keep the dang stockinette fabric from rolling up, which may be accomplished with a number of seed stitch or garter stitch rows.

What if you really hate the way ribbing at the bottom of a sweater looks, and you'd prefer to let it just all hang out? Ribbing pulls in at the bottom of a sweater, while a garter-edge border hangs straight. Beware, though, that while ribbing is narrower than stockinette, garter stitch is wider (and also stiffer), so if you don't want your sweater to look like a hoop skirt, you'll want to knit your garter-stitch border using needles one or two sizes smaller than the needles you use for the rest of the sweater. Also, you'll only need to knit a few rows of garter stitch—about ½" worth—to make a nice straight edge.

You might like the look of a rolled stockinette stitch edge, and if so, more power to you! This is a very cool look. Just be sure to add a good number of extra rows at the bottom of your piece, so that it can roll up and still be the right length. Otherwise, you might look like someone accidentally yanked on the shade-pull of your sweater: it could roll up and let your belly stick out.

If you like ribbing at the bottom of your sweater but don't want it to pull in so much, just make the ribbing shorter: say, 1" or ½" ribbing. You could also try knitting the ribbing on needles a size or two larger than you plan on using for the rest of the pattern.

Last but not least, if you'd like an edge that's completely straight and hemmed (and this works best with thinner yarn) begin by knitting for about ½" to 1" in stockinette stitch. Then do one purl row, and continue in stockinette or whatever stitch pattern your sweater calls for. When the front and back pieces are done, fold the lower edge along that purl row—sometimes called a "turning row"—and sew the edge of the hem to the

Earnestly Hemming Away
HOW TO KEEP A HEM FROM FLIPPING OUT

To keep stockinette stitch hems from rolling up or flipping out, try the following: Cast on with needles one size smaller than the rest of your work, then knit for the number of stockinette stitch rows you would like for your hem, usually at least ½" of knitting (this part will be folded under). Make one purl row, then switch to regular-size needles and knit two extra stockinette stitch rows before you start on the pattern. This will cause the hem to roll under slightly. Without those two extra stockinette stitch rows, my hems start to flip out after a couple of minutes. *Tina Hsu, Washington, D.C.*

inside. For an even fancier finish, make a picot edge, something my mom says they called "mouse teeth" in her day: Follow the directions above, but instead of knitting a purl row, you'll yarn over, knit 2 together, all the way across the row, then continue on in stockinette stitch. When you fold up the hem on this row, you'll have super-cute little "mouse teeth" across the bottom of your sweater.

Try making a swatch of your intended edging, followed by a couple of inches in stockinette stitch, just to see how it behaves with your yarn. If worse comes to worst and you hate the way your new edging experiment turned out, don't fret. It's not too hard to unravel the sweater from the bottom up, then knit back down using an edging that works better.

DIG IF YOU WILL, A PICTURE
Adding or Changing Color Designs

Just because your pattern calls for stripes or features giant, corny reindeer heads doesn't mean you can't replace them with something else. If squirrels are your thing, knit an army of them along the yoke of a sweater, or add a tribal tattoo design around the sleeves. If you're into old-school video games, decorate the front of your piece with a realistic Space Invaders motif, or knit a Rubik's cube and be part of the '80s revival.

Start, as always, by working out your gauge, then sketch out how many stitches wide and how many rows tall your design should be. For a Fair Isle pattern, try not to let your color stitches be more than 4 or 5 stitches apart from each other, and for an intarsia design, remember that large blocks of color work best; if you have lots of little details in your image, you might want to add them on at the end with duplicate stitch.

The most important thing when working out a picture to knit into your work, however, is to remember to draw it on knitter's graph paper (see page 30). Unlike regular graph paper, where each box is a square, knitter's graph paper has boxes that are wider than they are tall. That's because knit stitches are not shaped like squares; in fact, each knit stitch is only about $\frac{2}{3}$ as tall as it is wide. If you use graph paper that is not made to these proportions, you'll end up with knit images that are squashed flat, and your squirrels may look like they've been run over by a car. And that would be very sad.

Looks Like You Made It
TAKING THE PLUNGE AND LEARNING FROM YOUR MISTAKES

If I had a Girl Scout–type badge to give you for making it through this chapter I would—you've certainly earned it. Once you peel back the skin of a knitting pattern, you see that the guts can be pretty gnarly. Still, it's the only way to really get a handle on what you're knitting and, best of all, knit things the way you truly want them to be. And, as you may have guessed by now, once you master making major and minor alterations to knitting patterns, you're just a hop, knit, and a purl away from designing your own.

There is one cautionary word I want to leave you with, and that is to expect failure. You may add a crew neck to a sweater, thinking it will look great, and decide that you hate it when it's done. You may try shortening

the sleeves and find that you made too many decreases and the thing now makes your arms look like sausages. You may have changed the gauge of a sweater successfully, and even checked your little swatch, but now that it's all done you decide that the bulky cotton you used doesn't wear nicely after all.

What I want you to know is that in knitting, as in life, sometimes making mistakes is the best way to learn something. It's like when you were first learning to knit: It wasn't until you made a ribbing that went all wrong that you figured out what needed to be done for it to go right, and now you'll never make a ribbing the wrong way again. It's the same with mucking about with sweater patterns. I've learned the very most when things have gone wrong as I tried to execute an idea.

The good news is, you can afford to make mistakes in knitting. Unlike in woodworking—where the rule is to measure twice, cut once, because once the wood is cut you can't put it back together—in knitting, if you don't like the way something has turned out, you can always unravel it and do it over. In fact, I'm willing to venture a guess that there isn't a single thing you'll try from this chapter that *will* go according to plan the first time. It may take a second or even a third attempt. But then, once you get it, you *really* get it, in a way that no book or class alone can ever teach you.

So go out there. Get some yarn and some needles, and a pattern. Make some changes. Small ones at first, then bigger ones. Make mistakes. Unravel your work. Do it again. The exhilaration you'll get out of completing a project that is really and truly as unique as you are will give you the kind of pride known only to first-time mothers. And if that's not worth a few late nights and curse words, what is?

Graphic Design

MAKING YOUR OWN KNITTING GRIDS

I have made my own patterns from day one, but I'm a perfectionist and always want the flexibility to try a few different ideas. Instead of using grid paper, a pencil, and a *large* eraser, I use Excel to create custom knitting-stitch-size graph paper on my computer. I format the cells into squares and use the background color to fill them in. Then I put a P in the square to indicate a purl, etc. I used this format to make a chart from an illustration of a piece of sushi that will some day be knitted into the side of a purse. It works great for any intarsia-type color combo. Then I thicken the left border on every 5th cell, and those lines are where I place my stitch markers. Makes it easy to keep track of complicated designs. *Sharon Silverman, Portland, OR*

● To make knitting graph paper in Excel, open a new worksheet and select the entire sheet (click in the box that's to the left of column A and above row 1). Format all your rows to have a height of 10, and the columns to have a width of 1.2. Finally, with all the cells selected, apply borders around each cell by choosing the All Borders option from the borders pull-down button.

To make knitting graph paper in Word, open a new document. From the menu bar at top, choose Table and then Insert Table. Create a table with 31 columns and 67 rows. Then select the entire table by choosing Select All in the Edit menu. With the table selected, go to Table and then Cell Height and Width. Set the width of the columns to be .2", then click on the Rows tab. Here, set the width to be "Exactly" and enter the number 9.6. Click OK. *DS*

i love you ♥
now change!
3/4 sleeves
turtleneck to V-neck
FATTER yarn (yum!)
STRIPES
shorten to waist
lose Ribbing... Rollbottom!
KNIT
KNIT

It was clear that at least a few knitters were ready to look at patterns, not as a be-all and end-all to their knitting projects, but rather as a starting point from which to make their knitting dreams come true. And from the questions and enthusiastic comments about these revised SnB projects that were being posted on knitters' blogs, it seemed that many other Stitch 'n Bitchers were hungry to do the same, if only they knew how.

I also found, unfortunately, that some folks who had completed projects from that first book were less than pleased with their results. One knitter discovered that the Skully sweater was much too loose and oversized for her to wear; yet another, posing in her newly completed Skully, proved that the sweater fit her just fine. So why did one knitter get such unhappy results, while another knitter didn't? I realized that if knitters could figure out from a pattern how a sweater might fit them before they made it, they'd encounter less frustration. Better yet, they'd know how to pick the right size to knit from the list of available sizes.

In fact, it seemed that all across the country, a nation of knitters—both brand new and more seasoned—were beginning to get restless. They were crying out for knowledge. They wanted to have the power to really understand what it was they were making, so that they could take their knitting to the next level, and make changes if they wanted to. They yearned to be free to use a yarn of their own choosing, whether or not it matched the gauge stipulated in the pattern. They longed to be able to make simple alterations to patterns—lengthening a body here, shortening a sleeve there. And they were itching to make projects that would fit and flatter their bodies. They didn't want to spend countless hours working on sweaters only to have them be more appropriate for an elephant or an Olson twin than themselves.

In this chapter I'll try to arm you with some of that knowledge. I'll help you understand the secret language of knitting patterns and tell you a few things you need to think about when you're choosing a different yarn for a project. I'll show you how—with the miracle of math—you can rewrite a pattern to use thicker or thinner yarn than the pattern calls for or make simple alterations so that it will fit you better. I'll even explain the mystery of pattern fit and sizing, so that you can choose the correct size to knit from the get-go. Finally, I'll teach you how to change particular details of a sweater—like switch a turtleneck to a V-neck or replace a ribbed edge with a rolled one. Eventually, you'll be changing so many things about a pattern—using thicker yarn, shortening the sleeves, popping on a crew neck, lengthening the body, adding a different edging, replacing a picture of a rock star with a picture of your doggie—that it may become an entirely different project altogether. In fact, you may have changed it so much that you will have practically designed your *own* sweater. With a bit more practice, and a bit more willingness to take the leap and depart from following patterns to the letter, you'll be ready to do just that.

Very few of the patterns in this book were made by folks who are knitwear designers by trade. Most of them were contributed by knitters who were just brave (or stubborn) enough to get an idea into their head for a project and not let go until they had figured out how to make it. Soon you'll be one of them too, or maybe you already are. And perhaps it will be one of your patterns that will appear in a future *Stitch 'n Bitch* book, for others to knit, and, of course, change completely to suit their whim and fantasy.

So what are you waiting for? It's time to get your knit on.

Decode the Code
HOW TO UNDERSTAND A KNITTING PATTERN

When you first start knitting, a pattern can seem a lot like a pirate's map pointing the way to buried treasure. It promises to give you every bit of information you need—from the brand, color, and quantity of yarn to buy to specific step-by-step knitting directions, which, if followed exactly, will lead you to the treasure: that sweater you've been drooling over in the book or magazine. And it may also seem that unless you follow the directions exactly, you run the risk of landing in quicksand or at least winding up with something other than that longed-for garment.

But after you've knit enough patterns, you discover something else: Following the directions doesn't always take you to the treasure. You may very well end up with the same sweater the model is wearing, but you didn't realize it would look baggy on you. Or you may decide that the fitted cropped sweater which made the model look so cute and sassy makes you look short and dumpy. How much nicer would it be to foresee these problems and knit the sweater into the exact, flattering shape you actually want?

Alternately, maybe you really like the shape of the mohair hoodie the model is wearing, but you already have a large bag of ribbony rayon you'd like to use. Or perhaps you're a vegan, and would prefer to knit something out of acrylic instead of wool. Finally, suppose you just bought a giant load of gorgeous sport-weight cashmere blend yarn on eBay, and you want to use it to knit up a sweater that calls for worsted-weight yarn. What you really want to do is change the pattern so it will work with *your* yarn. Is that so wrong?

I'm here to tell you that any and all of these things can be done. That's because a pattern is not at all like a cryptic pirate's map. Instead, in every pattern the designers have laid bare, for all to see, exactly how the fabric for the sweater is to be made. They have included explicit details about every tiny curve and inch-by-inch information about the exact size it will turn out to be. And they won't mind a bit if you use their instructions as a guideline for working out a sweater that will fit you a bit better, or be a bit longer, or narrower, or in an entirely different gauge yarn than they call for. In fact, they would probably be thrilled to have you do that. Once you understand how to read all the clues that are written out for you in each and every pattern, you'll realize that it's much more than just a way to get to the buried treasure: It offers you the keys to the entire friggin' city!

In order to make changes to a pattern, you need to really understand it—not just the stitches or the instructions, but what makes it tick. Every pattern is jam-packed with numbers: measurements in inches, numbers of stitches to cast on and decrease or increase, and how many rows to knit. But why are those numbers there? What do they mean? How does the jumble of numbers in your pattern relate to the finely detailed pullover in the photo? In this next section, I'm going to walk you through a few simple patterns so that you can get

to know them from the inside out. Before we begin, though, you might want to put on your propeller beanie: There's lots of math involved here. It's simple math, for the most part, but there's plenty of it. I believe it was talking Barbie who so famously said, "Math is hard," but pay her no mind. Women have been relying on math in their knitting for centuries, and these days, knitting is even used in certain elementary school programs to help kids understand arithmetic. If you were born with the math gene, have fun with the next section. And if you were born without it, just remember that math is your friend. It's the secret code of all knitting, and it is the shared language that all knitters speak. In fact, math is as powerful and magical as any kind of witchcraft.

CONTESTANT NUMBER ONE
A Simple Scarf

Let's take a look at the pattern below for a knit scarf. How can you know what this scarf will look like before you go ahead and knit it? Is it a skinny, '80s-style scarf, or is it wide? Will it be long enough to wrap around your neck twice or does it fit like an ascot? You can tell it has stripes—the name gives that away—but are they narrow or wide? The answers to all these questions lie in the pattern itself.

The key piece of information in any knitting pattern is the **gauge**. Most patterns will give a gauge over 4 inches. The first thing you want to do when reading a pattern is to calculate the gauge of stitches and rows per *inch*. This information can work like a decoder ring to help you understand everything else that's going on in a pattern. Here's how:

STITCHES PER INCH = NUMBER OF STITCHES DIVIDED BY SWATCH WIDTH

For example, in this scarf pattern, the designer tells me she has to knit 28 stitches in the pattern to get a swatch of fabric 4" wide.

WHITE STRIPES SCARF

Materials

Cuddly Wuddly Cotton (100% cotton)

Color A: 3 skeins Rock Red

Color B: 3 skeins "Meg White"

US 9 (5.5 mm) straight needles

Gauge

28 sts and 15 rows = 4" in st patt

STITCH PATTERN
K3, p3.

DIRECTIONS

With color A, CO 36 sts.

*K with color A in st pattern for 18 rows.

K with color B in st pattern for 18 rows*.

Rep from * to * 5 times more.

List of abbreviations appears on page 32.

The Patterns

Knit Happens
PATTERNS FROM THE EDGE

Welcome to the creamy chocolate filling of this book: the patterns. To find them, I put out a call for submissions to Stitch 'n Bitch groups all across the country and beyond. I was overwhelmed by the response; there was so much great stuff, it was really difficult to choose. In the end, I selected the fifty fun, fierce projects you see here. They were designed by knitters who hail from all corners of the country: from Philadelphia to Phoenix, San Diego to St. Paul, Los Angeles to Lexington, and everywhere in between. These ladies and gents vary in experience from impassioned newbie knitters to those who have knit their way around the block a few times. The one thing they share is the ability to think of something cool to knit, then work out an interesting way to make it. The energy, inspiration—and, of course, frustration—that went into designing these projects and writing up these patterns just about explode off these pages, and I hope you'll dig them all as much as I do. I am truly awestruck at the talent, creativity, and balls-out bravery of our nation of knitters.

ABBREVIATIONS

beg	begin(ning)(s)	dpn	double-pointed needle	pm	place marker	ssk	slip next st knitwise twice, k sts tog tbl
BO	bind off	EOR	every other row	psso	pass slipped stitch over		
C4B	sl 2 sts to cn and hold to back, k 2, k 2 from cn	ER	every row	pu	pick up	ssp	slip 2 stitches from left needle to the right, then slide the left needle through them from the left to right through the back legs, and purl them
		est	established	pwise	purlwise: insert needle into the next stitch as if to purl		
C4F	same as above, but hold cn to front of work	f&b	front and back				
		foll	follow(ing)	rem	remain(s)(ing)		
		inc	increase	rep	repeat(ed)(ing)(s)		
C6B	sl 3 sts to cn and hold to back, k3, k3 from cn	k	knit	rev St st	reverse stockinette stitch	sssk	slip next st knitwise 3 times, k all sts tog tbl
		k2tog	insert needle through next 2 sts knitwise, knit them as one	RH	right hand		
C6F	same as above, but hold cn to front of work			rnd(s)	round(s)	st(s)	stitch(es)
		kwise	knitwise: insert needle into the next stitch as if to knit	RS	right side(s)	St st	stockinette stitch
CC	contrasting color			sc	single crochet	tbl	through back loop
ch	chain	LH	left hand	skp	slip 1 st, k next st, pass slipped st over k st	tog	together
cn	cable needle	M1	make 1 increase			yo	yarn over
CO	cast on	MC	main color			W&T	wrap and turn
cont	continu(e)(ed)(es)(ing)	meas	measures	sl	slip	WS	wrong side(s)
		p	purl	sm	slip marker	yd(s)	yard(s)
dec	decrease	patt	pattern				

In addition to the patterns, the next section contains profiles of a number of Stitch 'n Bitch groups (by region) that have sprung up all across America—as well as a few that have popped up beyond our borders. So many new SnB groups have been started in the years since I began one in New York City five years ago, and since the publication of *Stitch 'n Bitch: The Knitter's Handbook* that number has mushroomed. Today, thousands of knitterati are enjoying getting together to work on projects and to shoot the knit. Contact info for most of these groups is listed on Brenda Janish's amazing Web site: www.stitchnbitch.org. If you're looking to hook up with an SnB in your neighborhood, her site is the first place to go. If there doesn't seem to be a group in your area, do what I and everyone else in this book did: Start your own. The success stories on these pages prove how easy—and satisfying—that is to do.

I've also collected tried-and-true tips from knitters all across the land. You may already be familiar with some of these, but others are sure to be a useful surprise. One of the best things about having a Stitch 'n Bitch is the ability to share knitting knowledge with one another, just as women have done for centuries: handing down the craft from generation to generation. Now we have the chance to do the same. So slip one, knit one, pass slipped stitch over—and don't forget to pass along your knitting know-how to the next gal. Knitting is not a craft that belongs to an inner circle of people in the know—there's no room for elitism here. Share the joy, share your skills, and welcome every new knitter into the fold. Our Stitch 'n Bitch nation is always happy to have new citizens.

Some of the projects that follow are quite simple; others are more challenging. The directions to make each one are explained, step by step, in each pattern. On the opposite page is a glossary of all the abbreviations used in the book, in the sidebar, right, are reminders about how to read the patterns. If you can't remember how to make a certain stitch, be sure to check out the knitter's cheat sheets that appear at the end of the patterns section, page 253.

Pattern Recognition

HOW TO FOLLOW A KNITTING PATTERN

Most patterns are written the way we present them here. First, the pattern will give you the finished measurements of the garment, followed by the materials you'll need to make the project, including the brand and amount of yarn; the size and type of needles; and any additional notions or tools.

Next, and perhaps most crucial, is the gauge information. Here's an example: 15 sts and 17 rows to 4"/10cm over k2, p2 rib using size 11 needles. This means with your size 11 needles you knit up a swatch that's a little bigger than the 15 stitches—say, 20 stitches—in the stitch pattern requested (here it's knit 2, purl 2 ribbing). Knit a piece a little longer than 4", then bind off, lay the swatch down flat, and measure it to see if 15 stitches do in fact make up 4". If your swatch comes out bigger, reknit another swatch using knitting needles one size smaller. (If it comes out smaller, go up one needle size and reknit.)

Then come the instructions. When knitting patterns give directions for more than one size, the first number given refers to the smallest size, and the instructions for the remaining sizes are presented, from smallest to largest, in parentheses, separated by commas. For example, if a pattern says: S (M, L), the first line of that pattern might read: CO 24 (30, 38) st.

Last, but not least, is the shorthand of asterisks for repeating something in a pattern. For example, "K2, *k2, p1; rep from * 6 times, k4" translates as: Start your row by knitting 2 stitches (k2). Then repeat what comes between the asterisks the number of times given. In this case, you'd knit 2 and purl 1 six times. Then you finish the row with 4 knit stitches. Finally, patterns that involve knitting pieces into somewhat complicated shapes will often give you schematics, or diagrams, of all the pieces you'll be making, which can help you visualize what it is that you're doing.

Scarf It Up

You can never make too many scarves. Yet scarves are deceptively demanding: They have to be made in a stitch that will lie flat, they should look good from both sides (since both sides show when folks wear them) and they should be simple to make, as you often find yourself cranking out a whole bunch of them come the holidays. Here, then, are four scarf patterns that meet all these criteria and more: They're complicated-looking but easy to do, they're cool and a bit different, and they're ready, willing, and able to decorate the necks of all your friends and family.

ELLEN R. MARGULIES

Yo, Drop It!

I've made several scarves from ribbon, but never felt that the ribbon's texture was properly highlighted. Every stitch combination fell short, until I discovered the magic of drop stitches, which expose the ribbon's character. I love the "danger" of dropping the stitches off the needle. Usually drop stitch causes knitters grief, but in this case it's a fun way to make a cool design.

Size

Finished length: 88"

Finished width: 3½"

Materials

Trendsetter Aquarius (78% polyester, 22% cotton; 50g/96 yds), 2 skeins #810 Abalone

US 11 (8 mm) straight needles, or size needed to obtain gauge

Gauge

16 sts and 20 rows = 4" in garter st

STITCH PATTERN

DROP STITCH PATTERN

Row 1: *K1, yo; rep from * to last st, k1.

Row 2: *K1, drop the yo by slipping it off the needle; rep from * to last st, k1.

Rows 3 & 4: K.

DIRECTIONS

CO 17 sts.

Work 6 rows in garter st.

Work in drop st patt until piece measures 86½" from beg, ending with a Row 2.

Work 6 rows in garter st.

BO.

RACHAEL RUSS
Wavy Gravy

the idea for this pattern came to me while flying on an airplane. As I was looking out the window at the amazing patterns in the landscape, I started playing around with knitting wavy shapes and ended up with one of my favorite scarves. It's pretty simple, and it's a great way to practice increasing and decreasing stitches. You can have lots of fun playing around with color combinations and different sizes of "waves."

About Ellen

When I was a teenager, I found a miraculous little book in the library that was illustrated with fluid line drawings of yarn looping and twisting over itself. I kept renewing it, reading it again and again, mentally rehearsing the process, until all of a sudden it clicked—and I was knitting. Although I'm originally from Sheepshead Bay, Brooklyn, I now live with my husband and daughter in the beach community of Pacific Palisades, California.

Size

Finished length: 58"

Finished width: 5"

Materials

Brown Sheep Lamb's Pride Worsted (85% wool, 15% mohair; 113g/190 yds)

A: 1 skein #M51 Winter Blue

B: 1 skein #M16 Sea Foam

US 11 (8mm) straight needles, or size needed to obtain gauge

Gauge

14 sts and 21 rows = 4" in garter st

DIRECTIONS

With one strand of A and B held tog, CO 6 sts.

**K 1 row even.

Next row: K1, inc 1, k to last st, inc 1, k1.** Pm at end of row to mark RS.

Rep from ** to ** until there are 16 sts.

Work 3 rows in garter st.

**K1, k2tog, k to last 3 sts, k2tog, k1.

Next row: K.**

Rep from ** to ** until there are 8 sts.

Work 3 rows in garter st.

Rep from ** until piece measures 58" from beg, ending with 8 sts after decs. K 1 row even.

Next row: K1, k2tog, k2, k2tog, k1.

BO and weave in ends.

NICHOLAS CARATZAS

Mom's Sophisticated Scarf

I made the mistake of letting my mother know about my new hobby about three weeks after I'd started knitting. That's when she conscripted me: "That's great! I want a scarf for my birthday to go with my new red jacket." You don't say no to my mother, so I got to work. This scarf is made in a merino yarn that's soft on the skin but twisted more tightly than most wool, which helped to keep my clumsy

About Rachael

My childhood was filled with all kinds of crafty projects inspired by my mom—everything from bags made out of old blue jeans to the many uses for the Be-Dazzler! My love of crafts took me all the way to an M.F.A. in metalsmithing, and now I work in sculpture and installation using various kinds of materials. I'm part of a small crafts circle here in Chicago called the Crafty Beavers (they rock!), and I especially love knitting booties for my new nephew, Zev.

Size

Finished length: 70"

Finished width: 7½"

Materials

Karabella Aurora 8
(100% merino wool; 50g/98 yds),
5 skeins #22 Charcoal

US 8 (5mm) straight needles,
or size needed to obtain gauge

Gauge

20 sts and 28 rows = 4" in basketweave patt

beginner's fingers from splitting loops. The basketweave stitch is so easy to knit up, it almost seems like cheating to be making such an interesting pattern using nothing more than knits and purls. Now Mom wants me to teach her to knit.

STITCH PATTERNS

SEED STITCH

Row 1: *K1, p1; rep from * to end.

Row 2: *P1, k1; rep from * to end.

BASKETWEAVE PATTERN

Rows 1, 3, 6, 8: K1, p1, k1, *k2, p4; rep from * to last 5 sts, k3, p1, k1.

Rows 2, 4, 7, 9: K1, p1, k1, *p2, k4; rep from * to last 5 sts, p2, k1, p1, k1.

Row 5: K1, p1, k1, p to last 3 sts, k1, p1, k1.

Row 10: K1, p1, k to last 2 sts, p1, k1.

DIRECTIONS

CO 38 sts.

Work 6 rows in seed st.

Work in basketweave patt until scarf measures 68" from beg, ending with a patt row 9.

Work 6 rows in seed st.

BO and weave in ends.

About Nick

Besides being a financial analyst I'm a nerd with a natural interest in technology, so when my girlfriend, Karen, bought the first *Stitch 'n Bitch* book I absolutely had to learn the theory behind her mysterious new hobby. She got me started right after Christmas 2003, and by the time New Year's rolled around I was hooked. My approach to knitting is heavily influenced by my analytical background; I use Excel, experiments, and equations as much as pencil and paper when planning a piece. Since then, Karen has organized a Stitch 'n Bitch that meets weekly in New Haven, Connecticut, and our mutual hobby has become an excuse to go on weekend yarn-store road trips.

AILEEN ARRIETA
Warm Fuzzies

Initially I designed this remarkably soft and fuzzy scarf for my niece, who loves all things pink. But when I finished, I couldn't bear to part with it. It's a perfect project for anyone just beginning to learn about cables—you don't even need to use a cable needle. When you're done, one side of the scarf will show the cable pattern; the other side will be ribbing.

STITCH PATTERN

MOCK-CABLE RIB PATTERN

Row 1: *P1, k the second st on the left needle, leave this st on the needle and k the first st on the left needle; drop both sts off needle; rep from * to last st, p1.

Row 2: *K1, p2; rep from * to last st, k1.

DIRECTIONS

With one strand of each yarn held tog, CO 22 sts.

Work in mock-cable rib pattern until piece measures 54" from beg.

BO and weave in ends.

Size

Finished length: 54"

Finished width: 4½"

Materials

Anny Blatt Angora Super
(70% angora, 30% wool; 25g/116 yds)

2 skeins #164 Dragee

2 skeins #50 Blanc

US 11 (8mm) straight needles,
or size needed to obtain gauge

Gauge

19 sts and 15 rows = 4" in mock-cable rib patt

About Aileen

When I was seven, a neighbor from Germany taught my mother, sister, and me to knit. I picked it up again when living in Sweden as a foreign exchange student (the coldest winter in Sweden since 1898). My best friends at school sat in the back row so that they could knit sweaters during class—without looking and without patterns! I let my knitting drop when I became a securities litigation partner in a large law firm. When I was forced into early retirement, I turned to knitting again. Now I knit for relaxation—and to enjoy the finished product. When I'm not knitting, I'm busy remodeling my 1907 San Francisco Victorian, which I share with my two standard poodles, Fiona and Gracie.

ADINA ALEXANDER

Butterflies Are Free

With all the floral embellishments around, I'd never seen a knitted butterfly, so I invented one. Butterflies fascinated me long before they became part of the current fashion trend, and this was a fun way to combine that interest with my knitting. The loop underneath the butterfly keeps the scarf from slipping out of place while you wear it and requires no sewing—you just pick up stitches from the scarf and bind them back to the scarf after a few rows. Since the butterfly is attached to the loop, it's always sitting in the right spot, no matter how you adjust the fit. I've based the colors of my butterflies on actual species, but of course you're free to make them whatever color you like.

DIRECTIONS

SCARF

With MC and straight needles, CO 12 sts.

Work in 1 × 1 rib until piece measures 48" from beg.

BO.

SCARF LOOP

Pu 7 sts from the center of the scarf 14" from the CO edge.

Size

Finished length: 48"

Finished width: 2"

Materials

Crystal Palace Cotton Chenille
(100% mercerized cotton; 50g/98 yds)

MONARCH BUTTERFLY

MC: 1 skein #4043 Cypress

CC1: 1 skein #2230 Mango

CC2: 1 skein #3433 Rosewood

MORPHO BUTTERFLY

MC: 1 skein #1015 Natural

CC1: 1 skein #2214 Bluebell

CC2: 1 skein #9292 Charcoal

US 6 (4mm) straight needles,
or size needed to obtain gauge

US 6 (4mm) double-pointed needles
(set of 2)

US G (4.25mm) crochet hook

Stitch holder

Gauge

16 sts and 20 rows = 4" in St st

Special Skill

SINGLE CROCHET

Work in garter st until loop measures 3" from beg.

BO and secure loop 17" from the CO edge.

BUTTERFLY
WING SET 1 (MONARCH)

With CC1 and straight needles, CO 7 sts.

Row 1: K4, turn, placing rem 3 sts on holder.

Row 2: P2, m1, p2.

Row 3: K.

Row 4: P.

Row 5: K2, m1, k1, m1, k2.

Row 6: P.

Row 7: K.

Row 8: P.

Row 9: K2tog, k3, k2tog.

Row 10: P2tog, p1, p2tog.

BO and, with RS facing, rejoin CC1 to sts on holder.

Row 1: K.

Row 2: P.

Row 3: K1, inc1, k1.

Row 4: P.

Row 5: K2, m1, k2.

Row 6: P.

BO.

WING SET 2 (MORPHO)

With CC1 and straight needles, CO 7 sts.

Row 1: K3, turn, placing rem 4 sts on holder.

Row 2: P.

Row 3: K1, inc1, k1.

Row 4: P.

Row 5: K2, m1, k2.

Row 6: P.

BO and, with RS facing, rejoin CC1 to sts on holder.

Row 1: K.

Row 2: P2, m1, p2.

Row 3: K.

Row 4: P.

Row 5: K2, m1, k1, m1, k2.

Row 6: P.

Row 7: K.

Row 8: P.

Row 9: K2tog, k3, k2tog.

Row 10: P2tog, p1, p2tog.

BO.

BODY

With CC2 and dpns, CO 5 sts. Work in I-cord for 2½".

Next row: K2, ssk, k1, turn; place
last 2 sts on holder.

Work in garter st for 4 rows.

BO and rejoin CC2 to sts on holder.

Work in garter st for 4 rows.

BO.

FINISHING

With crochet hook and CC2, beg between forewing and hind-wing, SC around outer edges of both sets of wings. Break yarn, leaving a 12" tail.

Using the 12" tail from one of the wings, sew both wings to body.

Using the 12" tail from the other wing, sew butterfly to center of scarf loop.

Weave in ends.

About Adina

I was born and raised in Hamden, Connecticut, and I am a Web designer, photographer, sewer, costumer, and theatrical swordfighter. At age fifteen I was taught to knit by my mother, who had learned from *her* mother, but my interest didn't resurface for almost another decade. My primary reinspiration was my great-aunt Adele, who was an extremely talented and experienced knitter. As a "picker" rather than a "thrower," I am a firm believer that there is no wrong way to knit as long as you get the results you want.

Organizing Principles

KEEPING YOUR YARN, NEEDLES, AND PATTERNS IN ORDER

If you want a nice holder for your beautiful bamboo needles, check out an art supply store for the pretty roll-up cases that are designed to carry calligraphy brushes. These look like sushi mats on the outside and are lined with canvas and have multiple pockets. They tie with a canvas strip and match your wooden needles perfectly. *Christina Berdoulay, San Mateo, CA*

● Keeping my patterns organized was becoming overwhelming until I bought some large three-ring binders, dividers, and sheet protectors. Now I keep each pattern in its own sleeve in the appropriate binder for babies, kids, men, and women. I use the dividers to organize each binder by type of project. For instance, in my Babies binder I have sections for blankets, booties, hats, cardigans, pullovers, and other. This keeps me from going bonkers trying to find a particular pattern. *CB*

● Removing one of the inside dividers from a laptop computer bag turns it into a great carry-all for knitting supplies. It has a lot of pockets for small stuff and zipper compartments for patterns. *Lou Simon, Atlanta, GA*

● The best bags to hold your stitch markers, tape, notebook, and other knitting accessories are the ones you get at bonus time from Clinique. Everyone in my Stitch 'n Bitch group seems to be using one. They come in great colors, are made of sturdy plastic, and are just the right size. *Sara Daily, Chapel Hill, NC*

● Here's a good way to keep your circular needles organized: Simply write both the gauge and length on the needle with a fine permanent marker, then cover with a thin layer of clear nail polish to keep it from rubbing off. *Mary Goodman, New Canaan, CT*

ANNE WOLFE

Bzzz Hat for Queen Bees

My roommate likes homemade presents, and before Christmas she was debating taking a class in beekeeping, so I had bees on the brain while trying to come up with a present for her. I'd never even knit a hat before, so getting my first one published is amazing. A friend of mine said, "Your beehive hat is inspired!" to which I replied, "No, I just copied a beehive." The hat has since turned into a group effort. I had help from my friend Lora Power, whose synesthesia dictated the final number of buttons (to her, seven is the same color as the hat). Joe Blair suggested doing the hats in different "funky" colors and getting more stylized buttons so that men would wear them too instead of just buying them for their girlfriends. And Catherine Chang (age four) gave them the name "Bzzz."

Size

Finished circumference: 20"

Materials

Harrisville New England Highland (100% wool; 100g/200 yds), 1 skein #4 Gold or #22 Plum

US 8 (5mm) 16" circular needle, or size needed to obtain gauge

US 8 (5mm) double-pointed needles (set of 5)

7 bee buttons from Incomparable Buttons, www.buttonmad.com

Tapestry needle

Gauge

20 sts and 36 rows = 4" in patt st on larger needles

DIRECTIONS

With circular needle, CO 100 sts. Pm, join, and K 1 rnd tbl.

Work in rev St st for 4 rnds. Work in St st for 2 rnds. Rep from * to * 6 times.

Work in rev St st for 4 rnds.

Next rnd: *K8, k2tog; rep from * to end.

K 1 rnd.

Work in rev St st for 4 rnds.

Next rnd: *K7, k2tog; rep from * to end.

K 1 rnd.

Change to dpns.

Cont as est, alternating 4 rnds of rev St st with 2 rnds of St st and working 1 st less between decs per dec row until 40 sts rem.

Work 4 rnds in rev St st.

Break yarn, leaving a 12" tail. Draw tail through rem sts and secure on the inside of the hat.

FINISHING

Sew on bee buttons to correspond with picture.

Weave in ends.

Show Me Your Knits! The Itchy and Scratchy Show

TESTING ITCHY YARN AND DEALING WITH A SCRATCHY HAT

To find out if a yarn is itchy and whether it will fuzz or pill under agitation, try the following: Thread a couple of strands of the yarn you want to test through a pendant and wear it around your neck for a few days. Move it around your neck often. Then you can decide if you want to use it.

If you don't have a chance to do this and end up knitting a hat that's too scratchy, here's how to fix it: Pick up all the stitches at the bottom edge of the hat, using a smaller needle than you used for the original hat, and knit a hat liner out of a yarn that doesn't make you itch.

Michelle Ciccariello, Yermo, CA

About Anne

After my third law degree, I ran away for a year to travel the world. To be practical, I learned to knit to while away hours on buses and trains. On the eve of a three-week trip on the Trans-Mongolian Express, I bought a lot of yarn in China, then knit my way across Asia and Europe. Much to my surprise, it turned into a big bonding experience, with everyone—the older women in my group and even Russian soldiers—working on my project. Now I'm back in the United States and knitting on my lunch hour from work, and to avoid doing my homework for an L.L.M. in global technology law. In my nonknitting time, I row, cycle, and blog at www.goannego.com.

STITCH 'N BITCH ACROSS THE NATION
New England

BOSTON, MASSACHUSETTS, SnB

I founded Stitch 'n Bitch Boston in the spring of 2002, when I was a newly-wed who knew few young knitters. After asking around my office to see if anyone wanted to learn to knit, I ended up teaching a packed class of twenty eager young women on their lunch hour. When the class was over, a large group wanted to continue getting together to knit. So when a friend told me about the Stitch 'n Bitch phenomenon, I started a group here through flyers left at a local yarn shop and word of mouth. When I moved that fall, I passed on my leadership role to Martha Spizziri.

Fueled by items in local papers, including the *Boston Globe*'s November 2003 story on knitting, which featured our group, SnB Boston's membership sky-rocketed, expanding from a single weekly meeting in Cambridge to about a dozen in greater Boston and beyond. The Yahoo group has snowballed to around 900 members, and today you can go to a Stitch 'n Bitch somewhere around Boston pretty much any day of the week.

We've also organized charity knitting and held group dinners and parties, and were involved in Boston's Knit-Out & Crochet, where we came out to teach people to knit on the Boston Common.

Laura Erickson and Martha Spizziri

HARTFORD, CONNECTICUT, SnB

Here in Hartford, the knitting craze hit in Christmas 2003—suddenly, the scarf was the new black. That's what prompted a bunch of us to learn to knit last winter. Being the punk rock, crafty fashionista that I am, I was drawn to the Stitch 'n Bitch phenomenon as something that would allow me to let my inner grandma out. It was a loophole for cool people to do something ol' fogie and be damn proud of it! Before I set up the Yahoo group for Hartford, I took a trip to the New Haven SnB and learned the magic combination: coffee, talk, and knit. Pretty simple!

By the second Hartford SnB meeting, twelve people were squished around a few tables at the local Borders. Since then, about eight regulars meet every Wednesday

Hartford, Connecticut

Boston, Massachusetts

evening, and it's a fight to find table space. We'll often sit like vultures around a little square table until we see someone leaving another table. Then we'll spring up and grab it and drag it across the café. We look a little crazy and territorial, but hey, we love it.

This summer we've been working on bags and beach totes, bikinis, tanks, baby clothes . . . and did someone mention strippers' tassels?

Erica Chandler

NEW HAVEN, CONNECTICUT, SNB

I started knitting back in December 2003, after I bought myself a knitting kit and the *Stitch 'n Bitch* book. My mom (who died 10 years ago) had taught me to knit and purl when I was little, but I hadn't touched a needle in almost 25 years.

After reading the book, I sought in vain for a local SnB. So I made a New Year's resolution to start my own group, and in January a friend and I began meeting at a local coffeehouse. Now we have close to seventy members, thanks to my pimping the group on the SnB site, in the *New Haven Advocate,* in the Yale bulletin and calendar, and on various Web sites. Among our members are undergrads at Yale and Southern Connecticut State College, grad students and their spouses, and Yale employees and townies. Ages range from freshmen to "ladies of a certain age," and there are two guys. Knit, crochet, embroider, or sew; we're open to men and women of all ages and skill levels who like to partake of portable crafts.

Karen Unger

PEAKS ISLAND, MAINE, CHICKS WITH STICKS

We are a tight-knit group of women who live on beautiful Peaks Island, Maine, about two miles out to sea. Our group emerged one evening in the fall of 2003 as we gathered at the community center to watch a movie, and several women brought their knitting, which piqued the interest of others.

We now get together one afternoon a week to knit a little, eat a little, laugh a lot, and spin a few yarns. Sometimes we gather in front of a fire, sometimes on a deck, sometimes on the rocks, but wherever we choose to click our sticks, the ocean is always our backdrop and inspiration. We also draw inspiration from the artists who live and work on Peaks Island, some of whom have joined our group, bringing their color and design savvy to original fabric creations. Watching them has inspired many of us to "stitch outside the lines" by changing a pattern to make it our own.

Our group shrinks in winter as summer residents depart for warmer climes. One of them, Claire, had become so obsessed that when she went back to South Carolina for the winter, she started her own group there. We call her our knitomaniac; we got her started knitting, and now we can't get her to stop.

Knitting together has itself become a pattern for us, as much a part of the

New Haven, Connecticut

rhythm of our days as the tides and the ferry schedule. Yes, we take great collective satisfaction in the completion of each project. But the greatest boon of our weekly group is that it gives good friends another good reason to get together.

Roxanne Marks

PORTLAND, MAINE, KNITTERS OUT ON THE TOWN

It started simply enough—just a few friends getting together at my house for a night of knitting, snacking, and a little reality TV. My dog was happy to have the extra company, and I enjoyed getting to share my passion with some wonderful women friends. But as the knitting wave rose, I thought, "This isn't just a stay-at-home kind of craft anymore." So in January of 2004 we decided to scout out a place and take our knitting "out on the town." Since then, about seventeen of us have gotten together to knit in Portland's coffee shops, bookstores, wine bars, and an Irish

Portland, Maine

Peaks Island, Maine

pub. We've recruited interested comrades through friends, at work, and through the Maine Stitch 'n Bitch online group.

We've got a great mix of styles—one knitter has been working on the same afghan for months; another only does scarves, but never uses a pattern, coming up with her own fabulous combinations of yarns and beads. She even makes up her own stitches. And for three members, Knitters Out on the Town has become an extension of their divorced women's support group.

As our first official summer together approaches, we look forward to really taking our knitting outdoors—to patios, the beach, maybe even a boat.

Tina Curcuru

KATHY BATEMAN

Russian Winter

Size
Adult

Materials
A: GGH Lara
(90% wool, 10% nylon; 50g/55 yds)

Plain: 3 skeins #2 White

Bear: 3 skeins #12 Coffee

B: GGH Davos (60% merino wool, 40% acrylic; 50g/95 yds)

Plain: 1 skein #9 White

Bear: 1 skein #6 Dark Brown

CC (Bear only): GGH Maxima
(100% merino wool; 50g/120 yds),
1 skein #34 Rose

US 8 (5mm) straight needles

US 10½ (6.5mm) straight needles,
or size needed to obtain gauge

US 10½ (6.5mm) 24" circular needle

US 15 (10mm) 24" circular needle,
or size needed to obtain gauge

Tapestry needle

4 safety pins

2" pom-pom maker or template

Gauge
10 sts and 14 rows = 4" in St st with
2 strands of MC held tog and larger
needles

've always loved hats. Even as a kid, when I helped my mom cook, I wore a metal colander upside down on my head as a "cooking hat." My fashion sense has improved since then, but I still enjoy unique hats. These bonnets, as with many of the hats I make, were inspired by the vast array of lovely eyelash yarn available these days. I'm amazed by how similar to real animal fur the knit yarn looks. Using circular needles for this pattern isn't strictly necessary, but it will make it significantly easier to knit, because of the tight curve of the bonnet shape. And because they're made of wool, these hats will actually keep your head warm, even in Siberia.

DIRECTIONS
BONNET
With 2 strands of A held tog, using size 10½ circular needle, CO 8 sts.

Row 1: K.

Row 2: P.

Row 3: K2, inc L, k to last 2 sts, inc R, k2.

Row 4: P.

Rep these 4 rows 3 times more—16 sts.

Rows 17, 21, and 23: K.

Rows 18 and 20: P.

Row 19: K1, ssk, k to last 3 sts, k2tog, k1.

Rows 22 and 24: P1, p2tog, p to last 3 sts, ssp, p1.

Row 25: Rep Row 19—8 sts.

Abbreviations
Inc R: Insert right needle into top of the loop below the next st. K the loop.

Inc L: Insert left needle into top of the loop below the st. K into front of loop.

Break yarn, leaving sts on needle.

With RS facing, pu 20 sts between right side of CO edge and sts on needle. K sts from needle. Pu 20 sts down left side to CO edge—48 sts.

Beg with a WS row, work in St st until piece measures 7" from picked up sts.

Using size 15 needle, BO very loosely.

EARS (BEAR ONLY; MAKE 2)

Back side:

With 2 strands of A held tog and size 10½ straight needles, CO 10 sts, leaving a 24" tail.

Rows 1, 3, and 5: P.

Rows 2 and 6: K.

Row 4: K2tog, k6, ssk.

Row 7: Ssp, p4, p2tog.

Row 8: K2tog, k2, ssk—4 sts.

Break yarn, leaving a 48" tail. Leave sts on needle.

Front side:

With CC and size 8 needles, CO 12 sts, leaving a 24" tail.

Rows 1, 3, and 5: P.

Row 2: K.

Rows 4 and 6: K2tog, k to last 2 sts, ssk.

Row 7: Ssp, p4, p2tog.

Row 8: K2tog, k2, ssk—4 sts.

Break yarn, leaving an 8" tail. Leave sts on needle.

FINISHING

Ear assembly:

Holding front and back with WS tog, use top MC tail to whipstitch the live sts tog. Whipstitch from top down on both edges. Slip tapestry needle under whipstitches. Pull gently on the yarn until ear curves forward and arcs, resembling a D if turned. Weave in ends, leaving the 48" tails loose.

Make 2nd ear as first.

Ear placement:

With safety pins, arrange ears on hat 5" from the front edge of the bonnet. The inner corners should be placed 4" from each other. The outer corners should each be 6" from the lower edge of the bonnet.

Use corresponding tails to sew back and front of ears to bonnet.

TIES (MAKE 2)

With B, size 8 needles, and a double CO, CO 50 sts.

BO.

Attach one end of each tie to front corners of bonnet.

Use A to make two 2" pom-poms.

Attach one pom-pom to end of each tie.

Weave in ends.

Optional finishing:

Gently brush bonnet with a cat slicker brush to bring more of the fur to the outside.

About Kathy

As a child I was taught how to knit using sharpened pencils. After finishing a few inches I put it away and forgot it. Years later, after a friend reintroduced me to knitting, I quickly became caught up and absorbed in it. Now, whenever I'm not doing something technical or artsy on my computer, I spend my time knitting. I enjoy the meditative quality of it and the challenge of developing new patterns. Many of my hats can be seen on my Web site, www.PlatypusDreams.com, along with the various knitwear creations I sell through my company, Platypus Dreams. I live in Austin, Texas, in a house full of people, rabbits, and yarn.

It All Adds Up

COUNTING YOUR STITCHES

When casting on a large number of stitches, I usually put a plastic ring every 25 or 30 stitches. It saves on counting and recounting! *Debbie Brown, Evanston, IL*

● When I picked up knitting again, I remembered one thing my grandma Mitchell had taught me: When counting your stitches, count by twos and then by threes. So count 2 stitches, then 5, then 7, then 10, then 12, then 15, and so on. It takes a little bit of time to get the flow, but once you do it's quick and I find that I lose count less often. *Sue Mitchell, Raleigh, NC*

HEATHER DIXON
Valentine's Hat & Mittens

My city is frigid in February, so when Valentine's Day rolls around I don't want to be left out in the cold—not without something bright and cheerful to snuggle up in. That was the impetus behind this hat and mitten set, and I've loved it ever since! The hat keeps my ears from freezing and the flip-top mittens solve the problem of swiping my subway card without having to take them off.

You can change the colors and motif if pink hearts aren't your thing. Customize by adding tassels or pom-poms to the hat or a long I-cord to the mittens for times when just flipping the tops off isn't enough.

Enjoy, and stay warm!

STITCH PATTERN
STRIPE SEQUENCE FOR HAT
7 rnds CC, 2 rnds MC, 2 rnds CC, 2 rnds MC, 2 rnds CC, 2 rnds MC, 2 rnds CC, cont even in MC.

DIRECTIONS
MITTENS
With MC, CO 20 sts. Divide sts among 4 dpns, 5 sts on each.

Join and, working in k2, p2 rib, work 2 rnds in MC, then 2 rnds in CC. Rep these 4 rnds twice. Change to MC and work 1 rnd even in rib.

Next rnd: K2, p2, inc1, k1, p2, k1, inc1, p2, k2, inc1, p1, k2, p1, inc1—24 sts.

Work even in St st for 2".

Size
Women's M

MITTENS
Finished length: 10½"

Finished circumference: 7½"

HAT
Finished circumference: 19½"

Materials
Brown Sheep Lamb's Pride Bulky (85% wool, 15% mohair; 113g/125 yds)

MC: 2 skeins #M81 Red Baron

CC: 1 skein #M105 RPM Pink

US 10½ (6.5mm) double-pointed needles, or size needed to obtain gauge (set of 5)

Stitch holder

Tapestry needle

Gauge
13 sts and 20 rows = 4" in St st

Special Skill
DUPLICATE STITCH

Next rnd:

Right mitten: K12, place 4 sts on st holder, k8.

Left mitten: K8, place 4 sts on st holder, k12.

Next rnd:

Right mitten: K12, CO 4, k8.

Left mitten: K8, CO 4, k12.

Next rnd:

Right mitten: K5, k1 pm through this st, k14.

Left mitten: K14, k1 pm through this st, k5.

Work even in St st for 2".

Change to CC and BO tightly.

THUMB

With CC, k 4 sts from holder. Pu 4 sts over those that were CO over the held sts.

Divide sts among dpns and work in St st for 2".

Next rnd: K3tog twice, k2tog.

Next rnd: K3tog.

Break yarn and draw tail through rem st to secure.

FLIP TOP

With MC, tightly CO 12 sts.

Beg with a RS row, work in St st for 5 rows. Place sts on holder.

With MC, RS of mitten facing and working 5 rows down from mitten BO, pu 12 sts. K 12 sts from holder.

Divide sts among dpns and work in St st for 2".

Change to CC.

					9
					8
					7
					6
					5
					4
					3
					2
					1

■ MC

■ CC

About Heather

Born and bred near Nottingham, England, I needed more excitement in my life, so I headed for the bright lights and high rents of New York City. There I fulfilled my dreams of becoming a successful fashion designer and underground rock 'n' roll goddess. I taught myself to knit at age six and haven't put my needles down since. I also design the contemporary ladies' sweater line called Relais. The small amount of spare time I have is spent enjoying my crazy adopted city and dreaming of travels to faraway places—taking my knitting with me, of course! My latest creations can be seen on my Web site, www.armyofknitters.com.

Next rnd: K2tog, k8, k2tog tbl, k2tog, k8, k2tog tbl.

Work 1 rnd even.

Next rnd: K2tog, k6, k2tog tbl, k2tog, k6, k2tog tbl.

Work 1 rnd even.

Next rnd: K2tog, k4, k2tog tbl, k2tog, k4, k2tog tbl.

Work 1 rnd even.

Next rnd: K2tog, k2, k2tog tbl, k2tog, k2, k2tog tbl—8 sts.

Break yarn, leaving a 6" tail. Draw tail through rem sts, pull tightly to the inside, and secure.

FINISHING

With CC, duplicate stitch motif from chart to top of each mitten, beg with marked st as the bottom point of the heart.

Weave in ends.

HAT

With CC, CO 9 sts. Divide sts among dpns, 2 sts on the first 3 and 3 sts on the fourth. Join and work 3 rnds in St st.

Working in stripe sequence, inc as follows:

Next row: Inc1, k1, (inc1, inc1, k1) twice, inc1—15 sts.

Work 2 rnds even.

Next row: Inc1, k3, (inc1, inc1, k3) twice, inc1—21 sts.

Work 2 rnds even.

Cont as est, working 2 extra sts per rnd between incs and 2 rows even between inc rnds, to 63 sts.

Work 13 rnds even.

Next row: With MC, k24; with CC, BO 15; with MC, k48 (24 sts past beg of rnd).

EAR FLAPS

Turn work and, beg with a P row, work 7 rows back and forth in St st.

Change to CC. K15 and place these sts on a holder, BO 18, k15.

Next row: P2tog, p11, p2tog.

Alternating 2 rows of MC and 2 rows of CC, dec 1 st from each edge on every row to 5 sts.

Work rem 5 sts in I-cord, cont to alternate colors as est, until cord measures 9½".

Break yarn and draw tail through sts to secure.

Rep for second flap with holder sts.

FINISHING

With CC, duplicate stitch motif from chart, centering bottom st of heart over center front, 7 rows up from CC BO.

Weave in ends.

Left Holding the Bag

A NEW USE FOR BAG SEALERS

*U*se the sealers that come on plastic bread or potato bags to hold the leftover yarn from a long-tail cast on, or as smaller bobbins for intarsia work. *Lindsay Woodel, Providence, RI*

M. K. CARROLL

Head Huggers

NECKWARMER & EARWARMER

Size

Finished measurements, neckwarmer:
11" long (+ ties), 1½" wide

Finished measurements, earwarmer:
17" long (+ ties), 3¼" wide

Materials

MC: Debbie Bliss Cashmerino Aran
(55% merino wool, 33% microfiber,
12% cashmere; 50g/98 yds)

Neckwarmer: 1 skein #101 Ivory

Earwarmer: 1 skein #300 Black

CC1: Debbie Bliss Merino Chunky
(100% merino wool; 50g/55 yds),
1 skein 700 Red

CC2: Debbie Bliss Merino DK
(100% merino wool; 50g/102 yds),
1 skein 501 Lime

Flowers: DMC embroidery floss,
turquoise 3845, 1 skein

Optional: beads, bead needle, thread
to match flower

US 8 (5mm) straight needles (optional)

US 8 (5mm) double-pointed needles, or
size needed to obtain gauge (set of 2)

Stitch markers

Tapestry needle

Gauge

20 sts and 28 rows = 4" in St st

I was growing out a pixie cut and having a bad hair year. That autumn, I knit a little hair band to help keep it in check and, when the weather got colder, a wider one that would cover my ears, too. This project uses a single skein of a luscious yarn, making it a small, luxurious gift or a nice treat for yourself. The shorter band doubles as a neckwarmer, a sweet addition on days when you need a sweater but don't want a long, bulky scarf. The entire piece can be worked on double-pointed needles, especially if you use point protectors to convert them temporarily to straights (thereby giving the work only one end to leap off), or use straight needles if you prefer.

DIRECTIONS
NECKWARMER

With MC and dpns, CO 2 sts. Work in I-cord for 9".

Change to straight needles, or place point protectors at the ends of the dpns to convert them to straights.

Inc row 1: K1, m1, k1.

Row 2: Sl1, p to end.

Row 3: Sl1, m1f, k1, m1b, k1.

Row 4: Sl1, p to end.

Row 5: K1, m1f, k3, m1b, k1.

Row 6: Sl1, work in 1 × 1 rib to last 2 sts, p2.

Abbreviations

M1f: Make 1, front (left slanting). Pick up as for m1 from front to back. Knit the strand through the back loop.

M1b: Make 1, back (right slanting). Pick up as for m1 from back to front. Knit the strand through the front loop.

Row 7: Sl1, m1f, rib to last 2 sts, k1, m1b, k1.

Row 8: Sl1, p2, rib to last 2 sts, p2.

Row 9: Sl1, m1f, rib to last st, m1b, k1.

Row 10: Sl1, rib to end.

Row 11: Sl1, m1f, rib to last st, m1b, k1.

Pm on RS of work. Work in 1 × 1 rib, slipping first st of every row pwise, until piece measures 9½" from beg, ending with RS facing.

Dec row 1: Sl1, k2tog tbl, rib to last 3 sts, k2tog, k1.

Row 2: Sl1, rib to last 2 sts, p2.

Row 3: Sl1, k2tog tbl, rib to last 3 sts, k2tog, k1.

Row 4: Sl1, p2, rib to end.

Row 5: Sl1, k2tog tbl, p1, k1, p1, k2tog, k1.

Row 6: Sl1, rib to last 2 sts, p2.

Row 7: Sl1, k2tog tbl, k1, k2tog, k1.

Row 8: Sl1, p to end.

Row 9: Sl1, k2tog tbl, k2tog.

Row 10: Sl1, p2tog.

Row 11: K.

Change to dpns.

With RS facing, work in I-cord on rem 2 sts for 9".

Next row: K2tog, break yarn, and draw tail through st to secure.

EARWARMER

Using dpns, CO 2 sts. Work in I-cord for 11".

Change to straight needles.

Inc row 1: K1, m1, k1.

Row 2: Sl1, p to end.

Row 3: Sl1, m1f, k1, m1b, k1.

Row 4: Sl1, work in 1 × 1 rib to end.

Row 5: Sl1, m1f, rib to last st, m1b, k1.

Row 6: Sl1, rib to last 2 sts, p2.

Row 7: Sl1, m1f, rib to last st, m1b, k1.

Row 8: Sl1, p2, rib to last 2 sts, p2.

Rep rows 5 to 8 four times more.

Rep rows 5 to 6 once more.

Pm on RS of work. Work in 1 × 1 rib, slipping first st of every row pwise, until piece measures 13" from beg, ending with RS facing.

Dec row 1: Sl1, k2tog tbl, rib to last 4 sts, k1, k2tog, p1.

Row 2: Sl1, p2, rib to end.

Row 3: Sl1, k2tog tbl, rib to last 4 sts, p1, k2tog, p1.

Tie one on: Earwarmer may be fastened beneath chin or under hair.

Row 4: Sl1, rib to end.

Rep dec rows 1 to 4 four times.

Row 21: Sl1, k2tog tbl, k1, k2tog, p1.

Row 22: Sl1, p to end.

Row 23: Sl1, k2tog tbl, k2tog.

Row 24: Sl1, p2tog.

Row 25: K.

Change to dpns. With WS facing, work in I-cord on rem 2 sts for 11".

Next row: K2tog, break yarn, and draw tail through st to secure.

5-PETAL FLOWER
(MAKE 1 FOR EARWARMER)

With CC1 and straight needles, CO 42 sts.

Row 1: K.

Row 2: K2, *k1, slip st to left needle, lift next 5 sts over and off end of needle, k slipped st again, k2; rep from * to end.

Rows 3 and 5: P

Rows 4 and 6: K1, *k2tog; rep from * to end.

Break yarn and thread tail through rem sts.

6-PETAL FLOWER (MAKE 1 EACH FOR NECKWARMER
AND EARWARMER)

With CC1 and straight needles, CO 50 sts.

Row 1: K.

Row 2: K2, *k1, slip st to left needle, lift next 5 sts over and off end of needle, k slipped st again, k2; rep from * to end.

Row 3: K.

Row 4: *P2tog; rep from * to end.

Row 5: *K2tog, rep from * to end.

Break yarn and thread tail through rem sts.

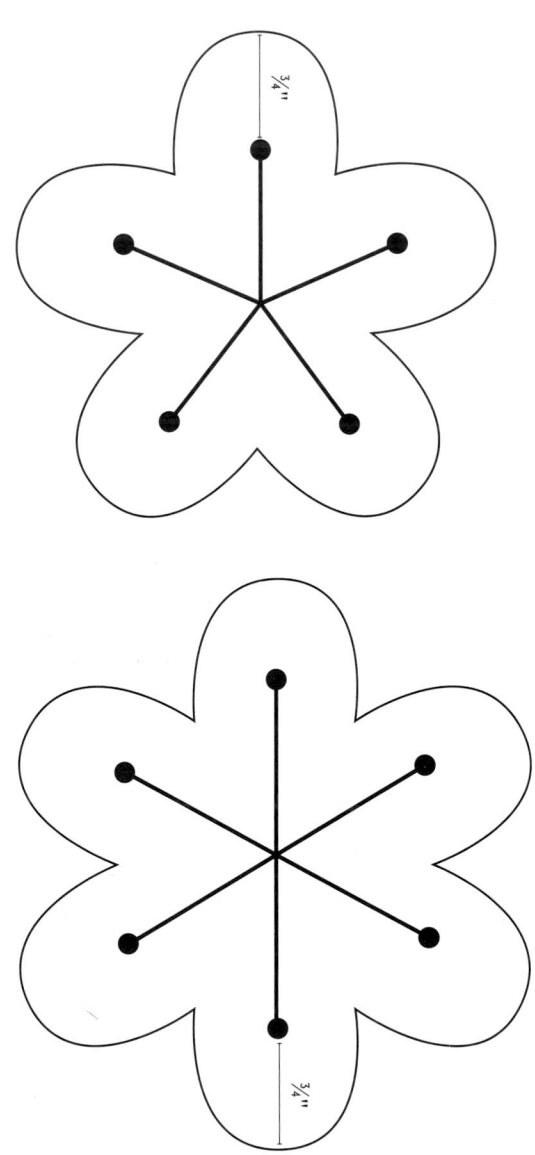

SMALL LEAF (MAKE 1 EACH FOR NECKWARMER AND EARWARMER)

With straight needles, CO 3 sts.

Row 1: P.

Row 2: (K1, m1) twice, k1.

WS rows 3 to 11: P.

Row 4: (K1, m1) to last st, k1.

Row 6: K.

Row 8: (K2, m1) twice, k1 (m1, k2) twice, k2.

Row 10: Sl1, *k2tog; rep from * to end.

Row 12: Sl1, *k2tog; rep from * to end.

Row 13: (Sl1, p1, psso) twice.

Row 14: K.

Change to dpns. With RS facing, work I-cord to desired length.

Next row: K2tog.

Break yarn, leaving a 6" tail, and draw tail through rem sts.

LARGE LEAF (MAKE 1 EACH FOR NECKWARMER AND EARWARMER)

Work as for small leaf to row 9. Work rows 6–7 twice. Work as for small leaf from row 10 to end.

FINISHING

Block all pieces. Whipstitch flower ends tog. Use a double strand of embroidery thread to make stamens in the center of the flowers with either beads or French knots. Attach flowers and leaves to warmers to correspond with picture. Weave in all ends.

Neckwarmer doubles as a vintage-style hairband!

About M. K.

My mother says that I insisted I knew how to sew at the age of four and that I demanded she teach me to knit when I was five. After learning to purl, I chucked knitting for crocheting and started telling grown-ups the same thing I tell people today when they ask me what I'm making: "I don't know." It took nearly twenty years for me to get back to it, but I haven't traveled without needles and yarn since. I've recently moved back to my hometown in Hawaii, where I'm exploring the knitting possibilities for subtropical conditions. When I'm not roaming around the United States, I'm working in natural-food cooperatives.

STITCH 'N BITCH ACROSS THE NATION
New York

ALBANY, NEW YORK, KNITWITS

Albany's KnitWits was born when two chicks—Renee McAllister and Melissa Mansfield—met at a party and decided to get together for a knit. Renee had worked at most of the cafes in town and didn't care to return, and Melissa had enough energy that she didn't need a caffeine boost, so they decided to go the bar route. Dozens of knitters were invited to knit at Albany's infamous dive bar, the Palais Royale. Unfortunately, no one showed, so Renee and Melissa sat there alone. Renee taught Melissa how to purl and Melissa encouraged Renee to finish that pesky scarf, and they decided to keep meeting.

As they knit their way through trendy Center Square neighborhood watering-holes, the two became five, and they now

Bushwick, Brooklyn

have a rotating group of around twenty who meet regularly at the Wine Bar. Among their members is craftivist Cat Mazza, who knits corporate logos to raise sweatshop awareness and is responsible for the group's blog at www.microrevolt.org.

The Albany KnitWits are dedicated to teaching strangers and each other fiber arts while talking about needle preferences, boyfriends, and feminist porn within a bar scene. And it's working.

Melissa Mansfield

BUSHWICK, BROOKLYN, NEW YORK, HARBOR SCHOOL KNITTING CLUB

I'm a guidance counselor at the New York Harbor School, a themed high school in an impoverished section of Brooklyn where many students are recent immigrants and many have special needs. The intention behind the theme is to keep kids interested, and the after-school programs, such as the rowing team and the boat-building club, generally tie into it.

And then there's Stitch 'n Bitch. It started when a few students wandered into my office while I was knitting, asked me what I was doing, and said they wanted to learn how. I couldn't believe they wanted to

learn to knit—I was so excited. I got donations of fifteen beginner knitting kits, and the Harbor School Knitting Club (aka Stitch 'n Bitch) was officially formed. The fifteen spots were filled before I could finish stapling the sign-up sheet to the bulletin board. When I looked at the names on the list, I did a double take: Ten of the fifteen kids who signed up were boys.

The first meeting was spent teaching the students the basics of casting on and knitting. The next day, I spotted my proud new knitters in the cafeteria finishing their lunch in a hurry so they could get back to their knitting! Soon enough, word spread and SnB Bushwick now has thirty new knitters (in a school of only 125) and

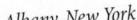

Albany, New York

twenty-five more kids on a waiting list. Lunch has become a knitting clinic, and the SnB meets every morning before school. Everyone's knitting: boys, girls, popular kids, not-so-popular kids, jocks, and bookworms. Knitting is the hottest thing to hit the Harbor School since Timberland boots and do-rags!

Ali Newman

HARLEM, NEW YORK, HARLEM KNITTING CIRCLE

After a workplace accident left me disabled, financially compromised, and temporarily discouraged, I took a knitting class in the spring of 2003. As I struggled with the technique the teacher was forcing on me, I suddenly remembered knitting as my grandmother had taught me at age eight. I left the class

Harlem, New York

and began knitting like a demon.

My knitting jones drove me to create the Harlem Knitting Circle, where no one is excluded, regardless of identity or income. The NYC Parks Department granted us a space for a few weeks, but then asked that we pay membership fees. This went against my premise that everyone should be included, so we found a new home in January 2004 at the George Bruce Library. The auditorium is beautiful and elevator accessible, which is very important to me.

Our diverse multicultural group reflects the changing landscape of Harlem. In HKC's core of about thirty knitters, crocheters, crafters, designers, and artists, the youngest participant is five years old and the senior member is eighty.

We recently completed our first charity project of chemotherapy hats and lap covers for Harlem Hospital's cancer unit. We welcome everyone and hope to see you soon!

Anntoinette Njoya Angrum

ITHACA, NEW YORK, SNB

After completing our first knitting class in the fall of 2003 at Homespun, our LYS, my friend and I couldn't bear for it to be over and launched the Ithaca SnB at Wownet Digital Café.

Ithaca, New York

With about five core members, Ithaca SnB sees a lot of folks cycle in and out—the largest crew so far is ten people plus two dogs. We've got folks working on everything from the ever-popular scarves to children's sweaters to yoga pants, and we're considering starting a "sweater support group" to encourage folks to branch out a bit. Our conversation topics range from politics to drug culture to parenting (although few of us are parents). A male knitting genius once made a cameo appearance, and at some meetings three generations of the same family show up—they're a total blast! I'm glad we took the plunge and started the group. It's helped me develop my knitting skills, and most of all, it's given me the opportunity to meet some amazing people who share a passion for creating.

Natasha Ribeiro

LONG ISLAND CITY, NEW YORK, SNB

Our meetings are about more than knitting and companionship. They're a comforting, familiar highlight to a

stressful week—a refuge and a support group. Since we first formed, at Café Ten63, our members devoutly show up every week, rain or shine, and whoever doesn't attend hears about it. Like when our boy knitter, Dave, passed up an evening of knitting to sit outside his school classroom to catch a glimpse of P. Diddy—that stuff just doesn't float. And trying to avoid knitting a gauge swatch doesn't sit well with our resident Gauge-Swatch Patrol Woman, Melissa.

In the time our group has been in existence, all of us have come to know one another, our creativity, and our individuality, which we spend three hours every week turning into knitted objects in each other's company. We get excited about hearing the reactions of a mom or a brother when one of us gives away something she or he has just finished knitting, something we were privileged to watch grow stitch by stitch. We are the audience and the orators of countless stories of the trials and tribulations, pitfalls and triumphs of every waking hour that is our life. What more could I hope for? Well, maybe that P. Diddy could start knitting with us.

Anja Shutz

New York, New York, SnB

Back in 1999 I became obsessed (obsessed!) with knitting and soon didn't want to do much else. I'd go to rock concerts or bars or parties, only to find myself standing there bored, wishing I were at home making progress on one of my knitting projects. At the same time, more and more people were asking me to teach them to knit. So I decided to combine two activities—knitting and socializing—and started NYC Stitch 'n Bitch. I invited anyone who knew how to knit or wanted to learn, and we began meeting in a small coffeeshop in the East Village. Over the years, we've moved locales many times, sometimes being welcomed into our new homes; other times not, like at one cafe where disgruntled baristas tried to blast us out by playing the most annoying heavy metal music they could find. It didn't work.

Our membership, too, is ever-changing, with very few folks from the early years still attending meetings today. In fact, every year or so there seems to be a complete turnover, as people move out of town, schedule something else for that weeknight, simply decide to give up knitting or suddenly take it up. Even I have barely had time to attend the group since I moved to Brooklyn. But that doesn't matter; the group doesn't need me, or any leader—it just needs a day of the week, a place to meet, and folks who want to knit. Though not many of us socialize outside our SnB meetings, our connection is significant. Knitting somehow frees up your mind to listen more intently to someone who's speaking. As a result, like the strands of yarn that we weave together with the click-click-click of our knitting needles, we can't help but become entwined in each other's lives as we meet for a few hours each week to share stories, share laughs, and share skills.

Debbie Stoller

New York, New York

Long Island City, New York

SHANNITA WILLIAMS-ALLEYNE

Headline News

CABLED NEWSBOY CAP

n my quest for the perfect Rasta hat for my dredlocked huz, I found that almost any hat I could buy looked great on him. But when *I* tried them on, they looked awful. I decided to take matters into my own hands and make a funky newsboy-styled cap that could double as a Rasta cap with a few minor tweaks. I wanted the hat to be both funky and feminine, and flatter everyone from conservative grrls to sisters with attitude.

STITCH PATTERN
CABLE PATTERN
Rnds 1–3: *P2, k9, p2, k6; rep from * to end.

Rnd 4: *P2, k9, p2, c6b; rep from * to end.

DIRECTIONS
With shorter, smaller circular needle, CO 76 sts. Pm, join in the rnd, and work in 1 × 1 rib for 1". (Optional: To make rib tighter, carry a thin strand of matching elastic along with yarn in ribbing.)

Change to larger circular needle.

Next rnd: *K2, m1; rep from * to end—114 sts.

Work 1 rnd even in St st.

Work cable patt 3 times or, to make hat larger to accommodate dredlocks, braids, or big hair, rep cable patt until piece is 5 to 7" long.

Size
Women's M

Materials
Blue Sky Worsted Hand Dyes (50% alpaca, 50% merino; 100g/ 100 yds), 2 skeins #2004 purple

US 8 (5mm) 16" circular needle

US 8 (5mm) 24" circular needle

US 10½ (6.5mm) 16" circular needle, or size needed to obtain gauge

US 10½ (6.5mm) double-pointed needles (set of 4)

Cable needle

Tapestry needle

1 sheet plastic mesh

Optional: 1 card Rainbow Elastic in color to match

Gauge
16 sts and 22 rows = 4" in St st on larger needles

Special Skill
CABLES

SHAPE TOP

(Change to dpns when necessary.)

Rnd 1: Working in St st, *P2, k2tog, k7, p2, k6; rep from * to end.

Rnd 2: *P2, k8, p2, k6; rep from * to end.

Rnd 3: *P2, k6, k2tog, p2, k6; rep from * to end.

Rnd 4: *P2, k7, p2, c6b; rep from * to end.

Cont as est, working 1 less st before/after decs and maintaining cable every 4th rnd to 72 sts, ending with a rnd 4.

Next rnd: *P2tog, k2tog, p2tog, k6; rep from * to end.

Next rnd: *K1, p2, k6; rep from * to end.

Next rnd: *P2tog, p1, c6b; rep from * to end.

Next rnd: *K2tog; rep from * to end.

Next rnd: *K2tog; rep from * to end.

Next rnd: *K2tog; rep from * to end—6 sts.

Break yarn, leaving a 6" tail. Draw tail through rem sts, pull to inside, and secure.

BRIM

With longer, smaller circular needle,
pu 7 sts before and 7 sts after hat CO join.

P 1 row.

Next row: K2, m1, pm, k10, pm, m1, k2. Pu 2 sts from hat CO edge.

Next row: P to end, pu 2 sts from hat CO edge.

Next row: K to marker, m1, sm, k10, sm, m1, k to end, pu 2 sts from hat CO edge.

Next row: P to end, pu 2 sts from hat CO edge.

Rep last 2 rows until brim measures 2" (measured from center), ending with RS facing.

Turning ridge (RS): P 1 row.

Brim Template
(actual size)

Scarves, Hats, and Mittens

**Next row: BO2, slipping first st before binding off rather than purling it, p to end.

Next row: BO2, slipping first st before binding off rather than knitting it, k to 2 sts before marker, ssk, sm, k10, sm, k2tog, k to end.**

Rep from ** to ** to 14 sts, ending with RS facing.

BO.

Using brim template, cut plastic mesh for brim. Slip into brim pocket and stitch edge closed.

Optional: To make hat more "Rasta," stitch edge closed without plastic mesh.

About Shannita

Once a devout crocheter, I'm a former marketing executive who learned to knit in the aftermath of the Great Dot-com Crash of 2001. With a severance package and too much time on my hands, I picked up two sticks and some string and never looked back. I now work at the Los Angeles knit shop Jennifer Knits and sell my own designs through my company, Craftydiva Handmade Wears.

Purl Jams

MAKING TIGHTER PURL STITCHES

If the last knit stitch of your cable or wide rib tends to be loose, try this: On the wrong side of the fabric, when you come to purl the stitch that would otherwise be loose, instead of wrapping the yarn over the needle counterclockwise (from top right) to purl it, try wrapping it the other way (clockwise from bottom right). This takes less yarn, so it creates a tighter purl stitch (and thus a tighter knit stitch on the right side of your work). Then, when you come to knitting that stitch on the right side, you will have to *knit it through the back loop*. If you purl much looser than you knit, this could be a permanent way for you to deal with that problem. Or you could just use a size smaller needle on the purl rows in stockinette stitch. Or you could change your name to Elizabeth Zimmermann and work everything in the round and never purl again.

Darrow Wendoloski, Victoria, Australia

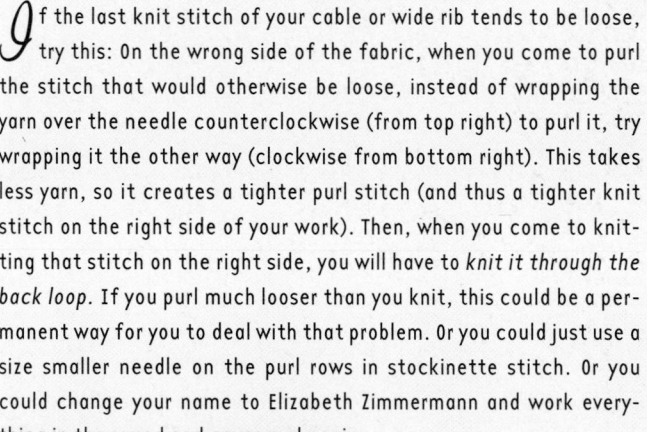

LAURA GRUTZECK

Later 'Gator Mitts

Sizes

Child's 2–6 (Child's 8–12, Women's S/M)

Finished length: 6½ (8, 10¼)"

Finished circumference: 4¾ (6¼, 8)"

Materials

Cascade 220 (100% wool; 100g/220 yds)

MC: 1 skein #7814 Chartreuse

CC1: 1 skein #8895 Christmas Red

CC2: 1 skein #8505 White

US 5 (3.75mm) double-pointed needles (set of 5)

US 7 (4.5mm) double-pointed needles, or size needed to obtain gauge (set of 5)

Two pairs sew-on wiggly eyes, 12 (12, 15)mm

Tapestry needle

Stitch holder

Gauge

20 sts and 26 rows = 4" in St st on larger needles

22 sts and 44 rows = 4" in garter st on smaller needles

t his design is dedicated to my coworker Erin, because without her I would never have realized that I needed a pair of alligator mittens. Erin came in to work one day with a pair of child-size alligator mittens that her great-grandmother had knit more than twenty years ago. The mittens were really cute, but so small that Erin couldn't wear them without stretching the heck out of them. Everyone at work wanted a pair, so I told them I would try to create my own version of the mittens, for children *and* adults. This pattern is the result. One warning: Wearing these mittens may lead to impromptu puppet shows!

DIRECTIONS
(MAKE 2)

With smaller needles and MC, CO 24 (30, 38) sts. Divide sts among dpns, 6 (7, 9) sts on first 3 needles and 6 (9, 11) sts on 4th.

Join and work in k1, p1 rib for 13 (16, 20) rnds.

Change to larger needles and work 10 (13, 16) rnds in St st.

Next rnd: Inc1, k12 (16, 18), inc1 into next 2 sts, k8 (14, 16), inc1—28 (34, 42) sts.

Remainder of mitt is worked flat, using 2 of the dpns.

BOTTOM

Next row: Turn (WS facing) and p12 (16, 20) sts onto 1 needle, placing rem sts on a holder.

Work even in St st for 4 (6, 10) rows.

Next row (RS): K1, ssk, k to last 3 sts, k2tog, k1.

Next row: P.

Rep these 2 rows 2 (3, 4) times more—6 (8, 10) sts.

P 1 row even. BO and break yarn.

TOP

With WS facing, using MC, p16 (18, 22) sts from holder onto 1 dpn.

Work even in St st for 9 (13, 19) rows.

Next row (RS): K1, ssk, k to last 3 sts, k2tog, k1.

Next row: P.

Rep these 2 rows 4 (4, 5) times more—6 (8, 10) sts.

P 1 row even. BO.

MOUTH

With 2 of the smaller needles and CC1, CO 4 (6, 8) sts.

*Row 1: K even.

Row 2: K1, inc1, k to last 2 sts, inc1, k1.

Rows 3–4: K.*

Rep from * to * 4 (4, 5) times—14 (16, 20) sts.

Work even in garter st for 30 (40, 50) rows.

Next row (WS): P1, p2tog, p to last 3 sts, p2tog, p1.

Next row: K1, ssk, k to last 3 sts, k2tog, k1—10 (12, 16) sts.

Work 9 (13, 19) rows even in garter st.

*Next row (RS): K1, ssk, k to last 3 sts, k2tog, k1.

Next 3 rows: K.*

Rep from * to * 2 (2, 3) times—
4 (6, 8) sts.

K 1 row even. BO.

About Laura

My mother taught me to knit when I was about ten, but, for reasons I can't remember, my lessons never progressed past the garter stitch strip. Many years later something inspired me to knit mittens for Christmas gifts, so I bought yarn and a how-to book and taught myself to knit on double-pointed needles. Although the mittens came out looking like giant misshapen potholders, that didn't discourage me, oddly enough, and I have been knitting ever since. For the past two years I have worked part-time at Rosie's Yarn Cellar in Philadelphia, which has given me the opportunity to mingle with many talented and creative knitters. I plan to retire someday to a large house in the country, where I will have room for all my dogs and my embarrassingly large yarn stash.

FINISHING

Steam-block all pieces.

Using French knots and CC2, embroider teeth inside top and bottom of mouth as follows: Thread a tapestry needle with a length of CC2. Attach the yarn to the WS of the mouth and bring the yarn through to the front of the work. Hold the needle close to your work and wrap the yarn around the needle 3 times. Put the needle half a st away from where you originally pulled the yarn through and pull it to the back of your work. Carefully pull the yarn through until it tightens into a knot, holding the wraps against your work while you pull the yarn through. Be careful not to pull too hard, or the knot could be pulled through to the back.

Holding the WSs of the work tog and matching the wider part of the mouth to the wider part of the head, use mattress st to sew the pieces tog. Weave in all ends and sew the eyes to the top of the wider part of the head.

Lift and Separate

MAKING YOUR OWN YARN BRAS

I'm sure you've seen those plastic-netting "yarn bras" used to keep yarn from unraveling. Recently, while working on a pair of particularly fine-gauge socks, I found my ball of yarn unraveling. I improvised with the red netting that baby gouda cheese comes in. (It looks just like the yarn bras you see in yarn stores and magazines!) You can find those plastic nets holding little cheeses, potatoes, garlic, and so on in the produce aisle. Simply cut off one end and you have an instant homemade yarn bra. *Jamie Henderson, Chicago, IL*

● At any given time, I usually have several pairs of stockings that are too holey to wear (I don't know why I keep them, other than that I'm a third-generation pack rat). I've started recycling them to contain unruly balls of yarn in my WIP bag. Cut the foot off about 3 inches above the heel and stuff your yarn in the foot. It will hold your ball together nicely, keep it from tangling with other balls, and make it easy to "spin out" twisted yarn—just hold the yarn at one end, let the ball of yarn in the stocking toe dangle freely, and allow it to untwist itself. Should you need to knit with yarn from the inside and outside of the ball, there's enough give in the nylon to allow for a double feed. Simply cut the toe off and pull the other end of the yarn from there. *Mindy Weisberger, Union City, NJ*

● I've found that I can reduce tangles coming from the center of large skeins of yarn if I remove the label, then place 2 or 3 rubber bands loosely around the outside of the skein. This seems to keep the tension constant as I pull yarn from the center, which is how I prefer to work. A few rubber bands work just as well as the "yarn bras" sold for this purpose. *Shauna Armstrong, Austin, TX*

SHOW ME YOUR TIPS!

CHRISTINE QUIRION

Basic Cable

Size
Finished circumference: 21½"

Materials

JELLYBEAN HAT
Brown Sheep Lamb's Pride Worsted
(85% wool, 15% mohair; 113g/190 yds)

A: 1 skein #M69 Old Sage

B: 1 skein #M105 RPM Pink

C: 1 skein #M155 Lemon Drop

D: 1 skein #M110 Orange You Glad

BLACK LICORICE HAT
Brown Sheep Prairie Silk (72% wool,
18% mohair, 10% silk; 50g/88 yds),
2 skeins #PS150 Obsidian

US 7 (4.5mm) 16" circular needle

US 8 (5mm) 16" circular needle,
or size needed to obtain gauge

US 8 (5mm) double-pointed needles
(set of 4)

Cable needle

1 stitch marker

Jellybean hat only: 3" pom-pom maker
or template

Gauge
18 sts and 24 rows = 4" in 2 × 2 rib on
larger needles

Special Skill
CABLES

I n the dead of winter, I had trekked north from Boston to Vermont, armed with a cable needle and some really wonderful yarn. Mittens were the original plan, but things weren't working out. My inner Girl Scout encouraged me to be experimental and try something else with my circular needles. I'd seen a few smartly cabled hats on the morning T train, and I thought I might be able to come up with a design of my own. I wanted a hat that would fit me snugly, without riding up my hair to the top of my head or stretching out to the size of a purse. Even on my very round head, this hat has stayed true to its shape, thanks to the cables and ribbing. The pattern is very versatile and with a change of colors looks great on both sexes.

STITCH PATTERN
JELLYBEAN COLOR SEQUENCE
*4 rnds A, 4 rnds B, 4 rnds C, 4 rnds D; rep from *.

DIRECTIONS
With smaller circular needle, CO 96 sts.

(For Jellybean colorway, follow stripe sequence for entire hat.)

Join and work in k1, p2 ribbing for 6 rnds.

Change to larger circular needle.

**Rnds 1, 2, 3, 4, and 5: *K2, p2, k6, p2; rep from * to end of round.

Rnd 6: *K2, p2, c6f, p2; rep from * to end of round.**

Rep from ** to ** 3 times.

Rep rnds 1 and 2 again.

Divide sts between 3 dpns, 32 sts on each.

Dec rnd 1: *K2, p2, k1, k2tog, k2tog, k1, p2; rep from * to end of rnd—80 sts.

Rnds 2, 3, and 5: *K2, p2, k4, p2; rep from * to end of rnd.

Rnd 4: *K2, p2, c4f, p2; rep from * to end of rnd.

Rnd 6: *K2, p2, k1, k2tog, k1, p2; rep from * to end of rnd—72 sts.

Rnd 7: *K2, p2, k3, p2; rep from * to end of rnd.

Rnd 8: *K2tog, p2tog, ssk, k1, p2tog; rep from * to end of rnd—40 sts.

Rnd 9: *K1, p1, k2tog, p1; rep from * to end of rnd—32 sts.

Rnd 10: *K1, p1, k1, p1; rep from * to end of rnd.

Rnd 11: *K2tog; rep from * to end of rnd—16 sts.

Rnd 12: K.

Rnd 13: *K2tog; rep from * to end of rnd—8sts.

Break yarn, leaving a 12" tail. Draw tail through rem sts to the inside and secure.

FINISHING

For Jellybean hat: Make pom-pom from colors A, B, C, D and attach to center top of hat.

Weave in ends.

About Christine

I started knitting while I was finishing up grad school for library science. I bartered a lesson in computer graphics for a knitting lesson from a classmate. Since learning to knit, it's been the "knitting with others" experience that inspires me to take on new projects and try out new yarns. Each week, I look forward to seeing my knitting cohorts at Peet's in Harvard Square. Knitting and crafting have added a dimension to my life that I didn't even know was missing, and introduced me to intelligent, creative, and quirky people. I work as a librarian at an academic library in Boston, and when I'm not knitting or searching out new craft ideas on the Web, I spend time singing badly at karaoke, watching bad TV, going bowling, or hanging out with my favorite people and animals.

Licorice basic cable

Pick Your Nostepinne

TWO WAYS TO MAKE YOUR OWN YARN WINDING TOOL

A nostepinne is an old Swedish knitting tool used to wind yarn into a beautiful center-pull ball by hand. To use one, begin by wrapping the end of your yarn a few times around the neck of the nostepinne, a few inches up from the bottom of it. Hold the nostepinne with your left hand, and, with your right, begin winding the yarn a few inches down from the top, laying each wrap of yarn next to another until you have about a 1½" width of wraps. Wind your yarn diagonally across these wraps while turning the nostepinne slowly with your left hand until all of the yarn is wound. When you're done, slip the ball of yarn off the nostepinne, and begin knitting with the yarn end that is hanging out of the center. *DS*

● Empty M & M tubes can be used as nostepinnes. I know people use empty medicine bottles and toilet paper tubes, but I find the large M & M tubes easier to hold on to. Plus, since it's about an inch wide, if the ball is wound tightly, there is usually enough give once the tube is removed from the ball that the ball will soften up and be perfect to knit from. *Helen Keier, Bronx, NY*

● You know those beautiful nostepinnes you see at craft sales? The ones for $25 and more? They look like they've been handmade on Grandfather's lathe. I come from a long line of women who see something they want (a dress, a sweater, a nostepinne) and decide that they can make it cheaper. So, I went to Lowes and bought an unfinished ash table leg (12" long). One end has a screw for attaching the leg to a table. The other is rounded. I sawed off the rounded end, drilled a hole in it, and screwed it into the other end, so it would have a narrow end for sliding off the finished ball and a nice pattern of grooves for anchoring the inside strand of yarn. I sanded and then finished it with Danish oil. Tada! A nostepinne for around $6.00! *Pamela Potter, Seattle, WA*

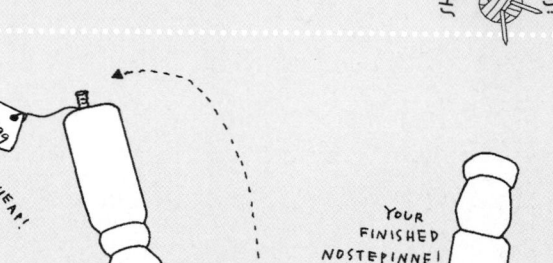

$5.99
← CHEAP!

THE BOTTOM GOES ON TOP!

YOUR FINISHED NOSTEPINNE!

Show me your tips!

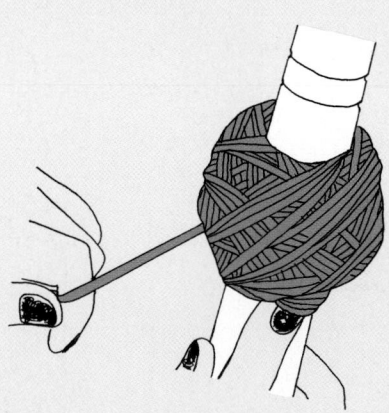

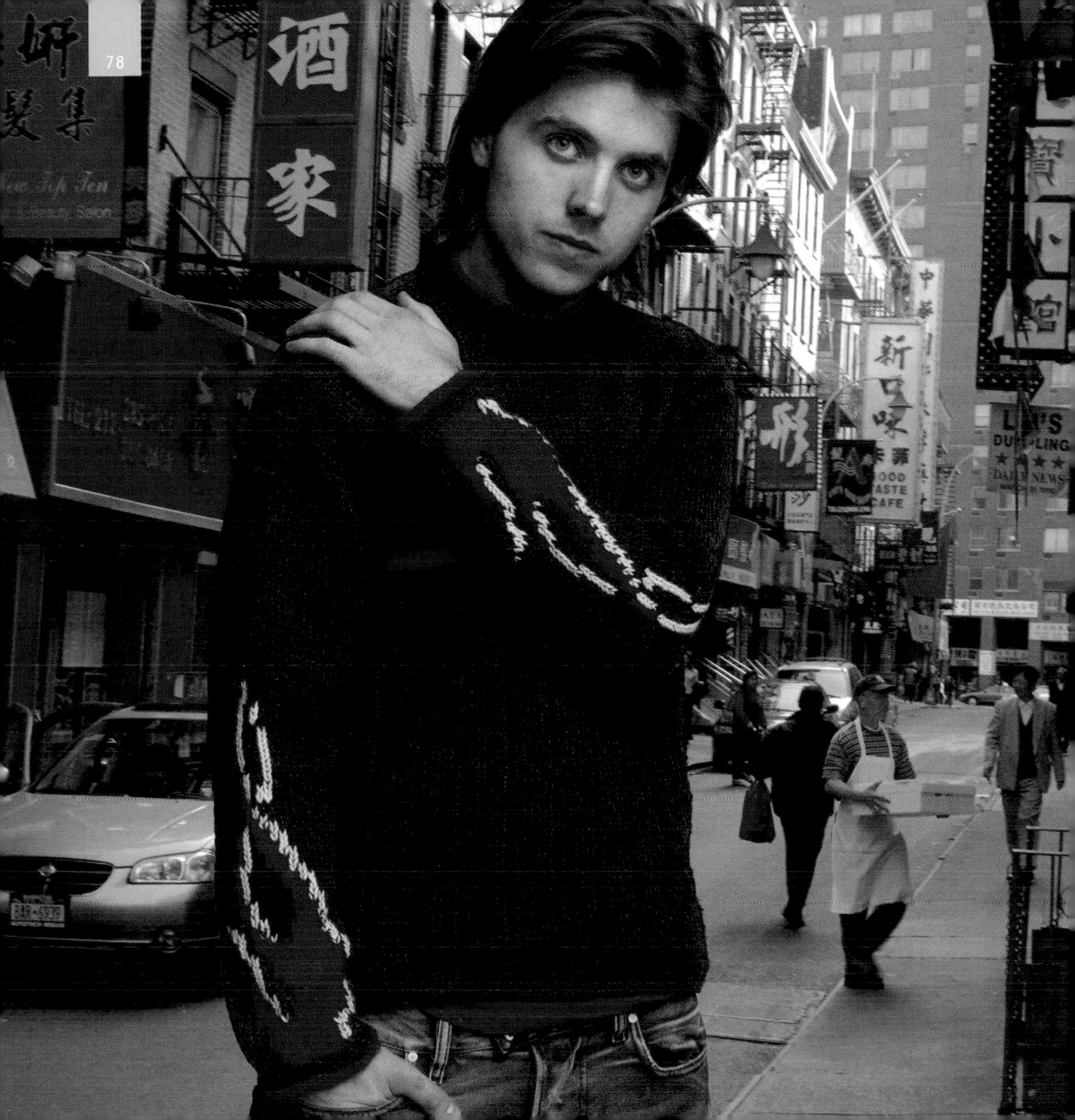

APRIL FISCHER

Jesse's Flames

t he idea for this sweater came to me one night from an episode of *Monster Garage*. I was knitting a sweater for one of my kids and watching the show when Jesse James made a comment about projects and designs, saying, "everything looks cooler with flames." And a sweater pattern was born. Of course, Jesse was referring to the detailed, freestyle flames that adorn his Monster Garage projects and custom motorcycles, but I spent many nights trying to come up with a flame design that would look cool, be fun to knit, *and* stand out in a crowd. I think this sweater does just that.

Size
Men's S (M, L, XL)

Finished chest: 36 (41, 44, 47)"

Finished length: 25½ (26½, 27, 27½)"

Materials
Lion Brand Wool-Ease
(80% acrylic, 20% wool; 85g/197 yds)

MC: 7 (7, 8, 9) skeins #153 Black

CC1: 1 skein #102 Ranch

CC2: 1 skein #158 Buttercup

US 8 (5mm) straight needles,
or size needed to obtain gauge

US 7 (4.5mm) straight needles

Gauge
18 sts and 24 rows = 4" in St st

Special Skills
INTARSIA/DUPLICATE STITCH

DIRECTIONS
FRONT
**With MC and larger needles, CO 85 (92, 99, 106) sts.

Row 1: P1, *K6, p1; rep from * to end.

Next row: P.

Rep these 2 rows until work measures 15½ (16, 16, 16½)" from beg, ending with RS facing.

Shape raglan:

Change to CC1.

Dec row: K1, ssk, k to last 3 sts, k2tog, k1.

Next row: P.

Rep these 2 rows once.**

Change to MC and work dec row, then EOR 18 (19, 20, 20) times more—43 (48, 53, 60) sts.

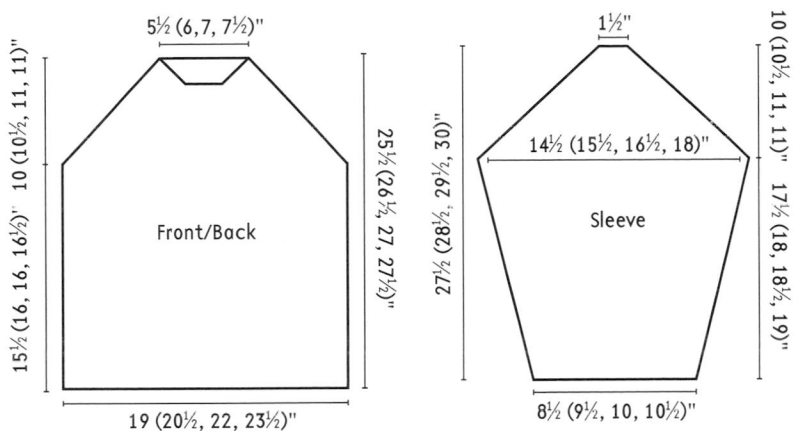

Work 1 row even.

Next row (RS): K1, ssk, k13 (14, 16, 18), BO 11 (14, 15, 18), k13 (14, 16, 18), k2tog, k1—30 (32, 36, 40) sts.

Joining a new ball of MC to left front, work both sides of neck at once and cont to dec one st at each shoulder edge EOR and, at the same time, BO 1 st from each neck edge EOR until there is 1 st on each side.

Break yarn. Draw tail through rem st to secure.

BACK

Work as for front from ** to **.

Change to MC.

Rep dec row as est 28 (30, 32, 34) times—25 (28, 31, 34) sts.

Next row (WS): P.

BO.

SLEEVES

With CC1 and smaller needles, CO 38 (42, 44, 48) sts.

Work 3 rows in garter st.

Change to MC and larger needles.

Next row (RS): K1, m1, k8 (10, 11, 13), pm, k20, pm, k8 (10, 11, 13), m1, k1.

MC ■
CC1 ■
CC2 ▢

Left Sleeve

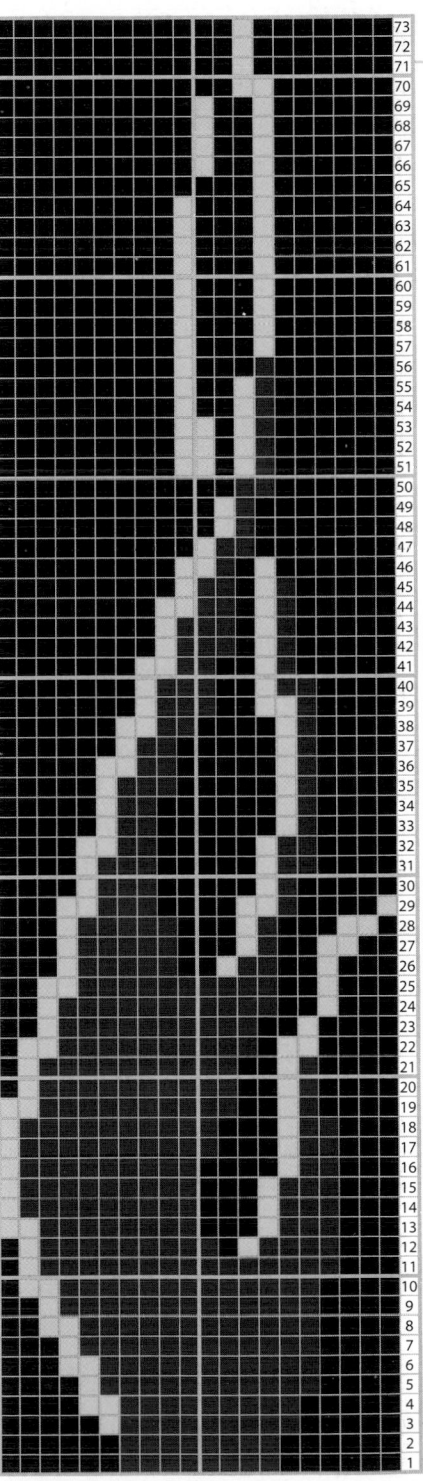

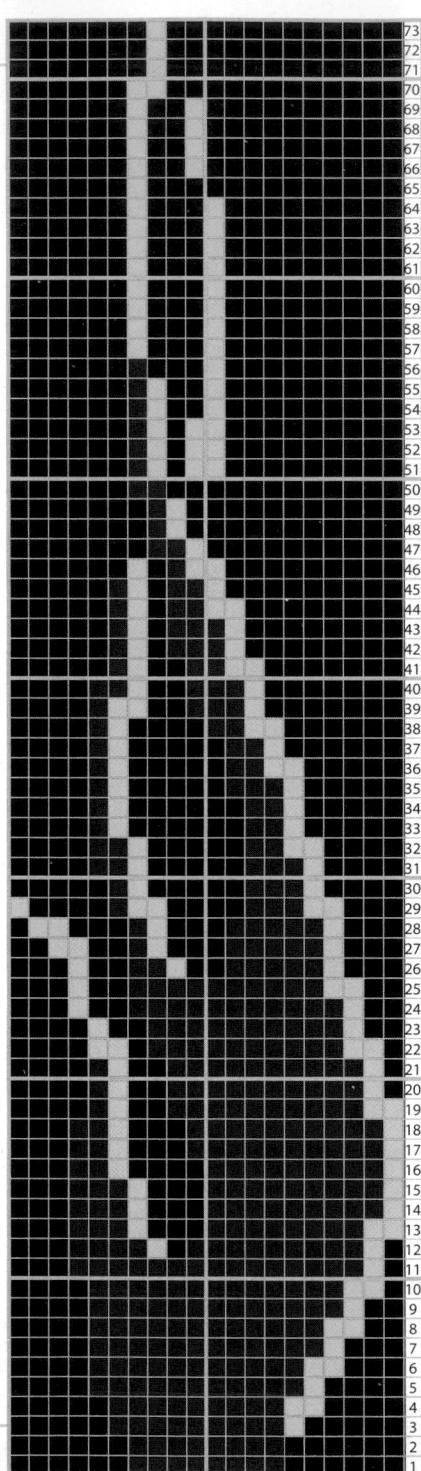

Right Sleeve

Working in St st, inc 1 st at each edge of every foll 7th row to 66 (70, 74, 80) sts.

At the same time, when work measures 1" from beg, foll chart between markers, working all CC2 sts in MC. (These will be duplicate-stitched on at end.)

When chart and all incs have been worked, work even until piece measures 17½ (18, 18½, 19)" from beg.

Shape caps:

Next row: K1, ssk, k to last 3 sts, k2tog, k1.

Next row: P.

Rep these 2 rows 28 (30, 32, 34) times—8 (8, 8, 10) sts.

BO.

FINISHING

Duplicate st CC2 between markers, beg 1" from CO edge on sleeves, following chart.

Mattress st both sleeves to front of body and right sleeve to back of body.

COLLAR

With MC and larger needles, pu 68 (76, 80, 88) sts around neckline.

Work in 2 × 2 rib until collar measures 1½" from beg, ending with WS facing.

Change to CC1 and p 1 row.

BO in rib patt.

Mattress st left sleeve to back of body and stitch collar edges together.

Mattress st side and sleeve seams.

Weave in all ends.

About April

I began knitting three years ago, when I decided I wanted to make my own sweaters. I went to the local crafts store, bought some yarn, needles, and a how-to book, and slowly taught myself to knit. Within a few months, I completed my first sweater, joined the local knitting guild, and began improving my craft. I finally became confident enough to put my first sketches on my knitting Blog, www.knittingiscool.type-pad.com/knit_kitty, and the response was very positive. Those sketches eventually became the sweater in this book. I live in Cary, Illinois, with my husband, our three amazing kids, and a very mischievous Labrador retriever.

KATE WATSON

Fairly Easy Fair Isle

frightened of Fair Isle? Why not cut your colorwork teeth on this super-simple cardigan? The basic motifs, flat construction, and bulky yarn combine into a sweater that's as easy to knit as a single-colored version would be.

DIRECTIONS

BODY

With MC and longer circular needle, CO 105 (116, 128, 140, 152) sts.

Beg with a WS row, work 3 rows in garter st.

Work in St st until piece measures 13 (14, 14, 15, 15)" from beg.

Place all sts on scrap yarn.

SLEEVES (MAKE 2)

With MC and straight needles, CO 27 (32, 32, 42, 42) sts.

K 1 row (WS).

Work 2 rows in St st.

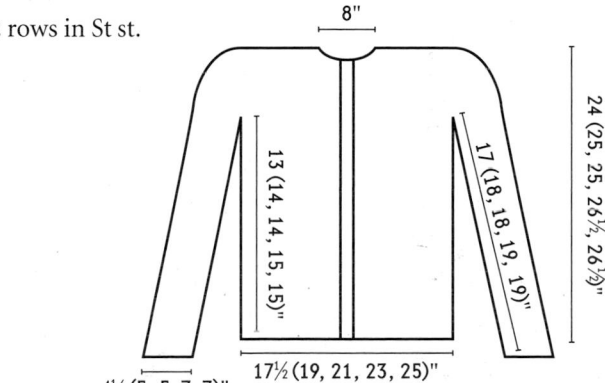

8"

13 (14, 14, 15, 15)"

17 (18, 18, 19, 19)"

24 (25, 25, 26½, 26½)"

4½ (5, 5, 7, 7)"

17½ (19, 21, 23, 25)"

Size

Women's XS (S, M, L, XL)

Finished bust: 35 (38, 42, 46, 50)"

Finished length: 24 (25, 25, 26½, 26½)"

Materials

Brown Sheep Lamb's Pride Bulky
(85% wool, 15% mohair; 113g/125 yds)

DARK
MC: 5 (5, 6, 6, 7) skeins #M05 Onyx

CC1: 1 skein #M83 Raspberry

CC2: 1 skein #M38 Lotus Pink

CC3: 1 skein #M34 Victorian Pink

FAIR
MC: 5 (5, 6, 6, 7) skeins #M10 Crème

CC1: 1 skein #M160 Dynamite Blue

CC2: 1 skein #M120 Limeade

CC3: 1 skein #M59 Periwinkle

US 10½ (6.5mm) straight needles
(third needle optional), or size needed
to obtain gauge

US 10½ (6.5mm) 30" circular needle, or
size needed to obtain gauge

US 10½ (6.5mm) 16" circular needle

Six 1" buttons

Tapestry needle

Stitch holders

Gauge

12 sts and 16 rows = 4" in St st

Special Skill

FAIR ISLE

Work from sleeve chart for 11 rows.

Work 1 row in St st.

Next row (RS): Dec 6 (9, 7, 5, 5) sts evenly across—21 (23, 25, 37, 37) sts.

Work 1 row even.

Inc 1 st at each edge on next row, then every foll 6 (5, 4, 5, 4)th row 8 (10, 12, 9, 12) times more—39 (45, 51, 57, 63) sts.

Work even until piece measures 17 (18, 18, 19, 19)" from beg.

Place all sts on scrap yarn.

Join:

With RS facing and MC, using longer circular needle and beg at right front of body, work across 20 (23, 26, 28, 31) sts.

**Place 9 (11, 12, 13, 14) sts on holder.

Place 4 (5, 6, 6, 7) sleeve sts on holder.

Work across 30 (34, 39, 44, 49) sts from sleeve.

Place rem 5 (6, 6, 7, 7) sleeve sts on holder.**

Work across 42 (48, 52, 58, 62) sts from body back.

Rep from ** to ** once.

Work across 20 (23, 26, 28, 31) sts from left front—142 (162, 182, 202, 222) sts on needle.

YOKE

Work 3 rows even in MC.

Work from yoke chart for 4 rows.

Next row (chart row 5): K6 (11, 0, 11, 6), *k7 (5, 5, 4, 4), k2tog; rep from * 14 (19, 24, 29, 34) times, k6 (11, 7, 11, 6)—127 (142, 157, 172, 187) sts.

Work from yoke chart for 9 rows.

Next row (chart row 15): K6 (11, 0, 11, 6), *k6 (4, 4, 3, 3), k2tog; rep from * 14 (19, 24, 29, 34) times, k6 (11, 7, 11, 6)—112 (122, 132, 142, 152) sts.

Work from yoke chart for 5 rows.

Next row (chart row 21): K6 (11, 0, 11, 6), *k5 (3, 3, 2, 2), k2tog; rep from * 14 (19, 24, 29, 34) times, k6 (11, 7, 11, 6)—97 (102, 107, 112, 117) sts.

Work from yoke chart for 5 rows.

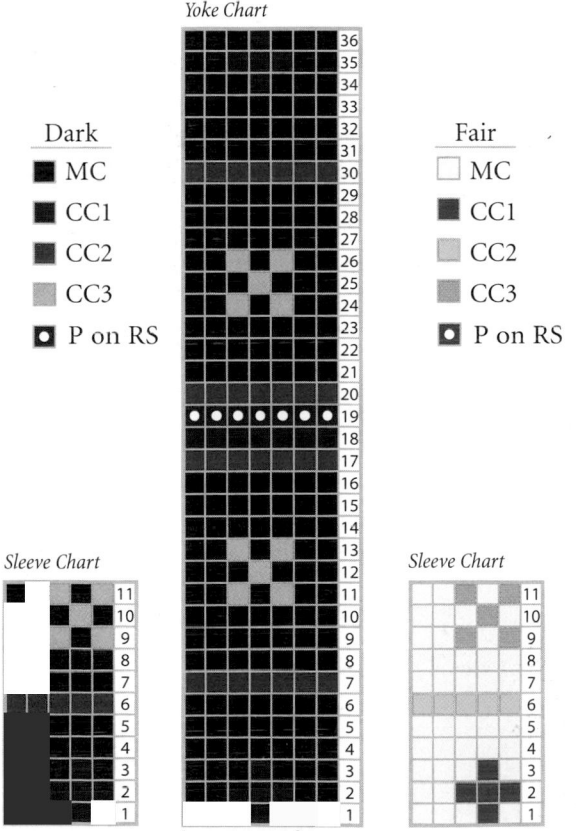

Dark
- ■ MC
- ■ CC1
- ■ CC2
- ■ CC3
- ◙ P on RS

Fair
- □ MC
- ■ CC1
- ■ CC2
- ■ CC3
- ◙ P on RS

Yoke Chart

Sleeve Chart

└ 5 st rep ┘

Next row (chart row 27): K6 (11, 0, 11, 6), *k4 (2, 2, 1, 1), k2tog; rep from * 14 (19, 24, 29, 34) times, k6 (11, 7, 11, 6)—82 sts.

Work from yoke chart for 5 rows.

Next row (chart row 33): K3, (K1, k2tog) 25 times, K4—57 sts.

Work remainder of yoke chart.

After all chart rows are complete, with MC only, work 2 (2, 2, 4, 4) rows in St st.

Work in garter st for 3 rows.

BO.

FINISHING

Button band:

Pu 56 (60, 60, 64, 64) sts from left side edge.

Work in garter st for 4 rows.

BO.

Buttonhole band:

Pu 56 (60, 60, 64, 64) sts from right side edge.

Row 1: K.

Row 2: K2 (4, 4, 6, 6), BO2, *k8, BO2; rep from * 5 times, k2 (4, 4, 6, 6).

Row 3: K2 (4, 4, 6, 6), CO2, *k8, CO2; rep from * 5 times, k2 (4, 4, 6, 6).

Row 4: K.

BO.

Transfer 11 holder sts from each armhole edge to straight needles. Use 3-needle BO or kitchener st to seam armholes.

Mattress st sleeve seams.

Attach buttons along button band to correspond with buttonholes.

Two's Company:

KNITTING TWO PIECES AT THE SAME TIME

*W*hen knitting two pieces that have to be even (sleeves or sweater fronts, for instance, as for a cardigan), knit them at the same time. Just cast them both onto the same needle, one after the other, using two separate balls of yarn. That way your pieces will always end up the same length, and your increases and decreases will be on the same row on each piece. The only tricky part is remembering which way you were going if you happen to stop with one piece on each needle. I always knit at least 2 or 3 stitches into the next piece before putting my project away. The other benefit to knitting two pieces at once is that when you're finished, you've got *both* sleeves or sweater fronts done! *Debbie Brown, Evanston, IL*

About Kate

*K*ate is fighting a losing battle in Toronto, Ontario, trying to maintain her sanity as a single mother of two boys. When not pulling out her hair (figuratively, since she shaves her head), she does technical editing for *Knitty.com* quarterly and writes sweater patterns on napkins, matchbooks, and anything else that doesn't move fast enough to get away.

NILDA MESA

Razor's Edge

I conceived this project because I wanted a hands-free shawl that I wouldn't have to clutch to keep from falling off (which is a drag when you're chasing after kids). In my art and in my knitting, I like working with light and shadow and using materials in unexpected ways, so I hit on the idea of making lace with bulky yarn. After a lot of swatching, the razor shell lace pattern rose to the top. The shape was inspired by a glorious cape worn by Donna Murphy in the Broadway show *Wonderful Town*. Even though the sides of this version don't sweep the floor, you can still fling it insouciantly when you enter a room, or just let it drape beguilingly.

STITCH PATTERN
MAIN LACE PATTERN
Row 1 (WS): P.

Row 2: K1, *yo, k2, sl1, k2tog, psso, k2, yo, k1, yo, k2; rep from * to last 7 sts, sl1, k2tog, psso, k2, yo, k2.

DIRECTIONS
With larger needles, CO 78 sts.

Work in garter st for 4 rows.

Work in main lace patt until piece measures 21" from beg, ending with WS facing.

Next row: P39, join 2nd skein of yarn and P to end. Cont in pattern as est, working both sides at same time with separate skeins of yarn for 10½", ending with WS facing.

Size
Finished width: 32"

Finished length: 53"

Materials
Brown Sheep Lamb's Pride Bulky (85% wool, 15% mohair; 113g/125 yds), 5 skeins #M05 Onyx

US 17 (12.75mm) 29" circular needle, or size needed to obtain gauge

US 15 (10mm) 16" circular needle

3" × 5" card stock

Crochet hook

Tapestry needle

Gauge
9 sts and 11 rows = 4" in St st on larger needles

Special Skill
LACE

With first skein of yarn, p across all sts. Break yarn from second skein, leaving a 6" tail.

Work in main lace patt until piece measures 53" from beg.

Work 4 rows in garter st.

BO.

FINISHING

Collar:

With smaller needle, pu 42 sts evenly around neck. Join and work in 1 × 1 rib for 3 rounds.

BO in rib.

Fringe:

Wrap yarn around 3" side of 3" × 5" card. Cut along one edge to make 6" lengths. Fold 6" lengths in half. Using 1 strand, pull loop through edge stitch with crochet hook and bring tail ends through loop to make fringe. Rep around bottom edge of poncho, working 1 fringe in each edge st. Trim ends to uniform length.

Weave in ends.

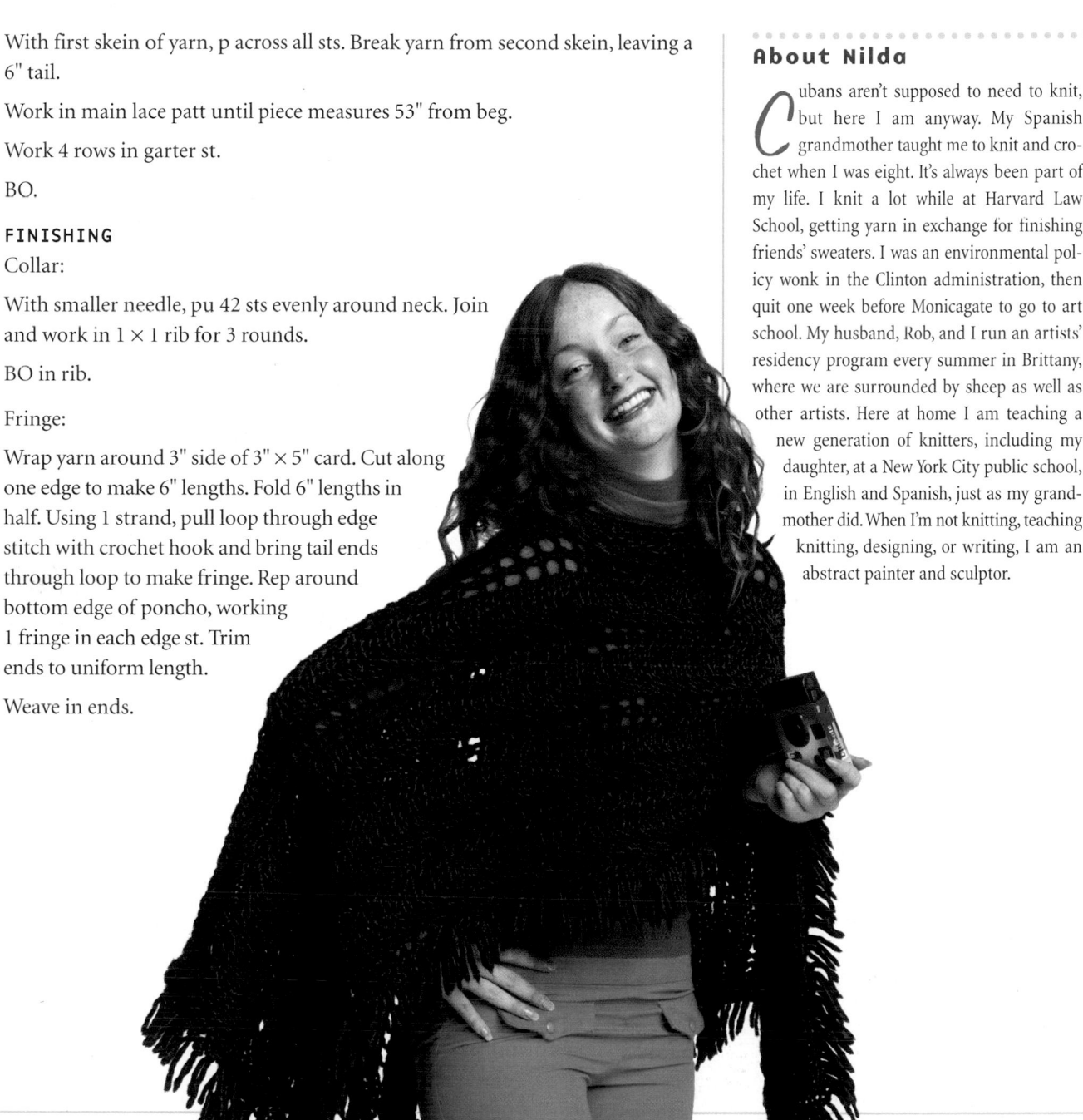

About Nilda

Cubans aren't supposed to need to knit, but here I am anyway. My Spanish grandmother taught me to knit and crochet when I was eight. It's always been part of my life. I knit a lot while at Harvard Law School, getting yarn in exchange for finishing friends' sweaters. I was an environmental policy wonk in the Clinton administration, then quit one week before Monicagate to go to art school. My husband, Rob, and I run an artists' residency program every summer in Brittany, where we are surrounded by sheep as well as other artists. Here at home I am teaching a new generation of knitters, including my daughter, at a New York City public school, in English and Spanish, just as my grandmother did. When I'm not knitting, teaching knitting, designing, or writing, I am an abstract painter and sculptor.

STITCH 'N BITCH ACROSS THE NATION
Mid-Atlantic

ARLINGTON, VIRGINIA, SnB

Our group attracted more than one hundred members in its first few months of existence this year, with about twenty terrific women showing up every week at Greenberry's, the neighborhood coffee place. At times, we have worried we would get kicked out for being too boisterous or scaring men away with our pointy objects! So far, though, we have been able to control ourselves.

We are lucky to have such a diverse group, with members of all different ages and levels of experience. At every meeting, there is lots of inspiration and support, knitting-related and otherwise. One of our recent hot topics was copyright as it applies to pattern design, and we gathered input from all sides, including straight from the U.S. Patent and Trademark Office. I look forward to our meetings every week; I absolutely love being around other people who "get it" and seeing what they're doing.

Brittany Martin

BALTIMORE, MARYLAND, CAST-OFF

Cast-Off is a continuation of a Stitch 'n Bitch that was started by Laura Cherry in 2001. It was held in the upstairs of a bar and was very popular—until the bar owners no longer wanted to be associated with something as feminine/feminist as a sewing circle, opting for Monday-night football instead.

Baltimore, Maryland, Cast-Off

In November of 2003, we began using the convenient, comfortable, and well-lit university lounges at Johns Hopkins to start a university-affiliated Stitch 'n Bitch for students, staff, and members of the community. Three weeks later, we were told that if we were to continue to use university Web space and claim affiliation, "bitch" was not allowed in the name. So we decided on "Cast-Off" to reflect the loss of the name, as well as the attitude of some university administrators toward the group. The controversy may have actually benefited us, since the graduate-student newspaper ran a conspicuous blurb with "bitch"

Arlington, Virginia

written 100 times next to an article introducing Cast-Off.

Group attendance varies from five to twenty people and interest keeps growing. In March 2004 we organized a yarn swap and gave extra skeins of yarn to the Indiana Women's Prison knitting charity. We also plan to attend the Maryland Sheep and Wool Festival—a knitter's and spinner's dream/nightmare, depending on how much money and space you have for the amazing variety of beautiful yarns, wool, and fiber-art supplies sold there.

Sarah Carmichael

BALTIMORE, MARYLAND, SNB

Our group was founded in 1999 when knit-mistress Sarah Landon and some friends took a class at a local yarn shop. Their newfound passion for fiber led to countless questions, and they invited a friend and master knitter to join the group

Baltimore, Maryland

to give lessons and soon found that they had created a new community of folks who just loved to bitch and knit.

Politics and education tend to dominate the conversations among our group of artists, professors, graduate students, moms, and professionals. We are unabashed liberals who passionately debate topics that range from regime change in Washington, D.C., to giving our kids a progressive and rigorous education. An April 2004 knitting group was devoted to attending, with our children, the March for Women's Lives in D.C.

The most rewarding aspect of our Stitch 'n Bitch is the community we offer one another. The group is a place where we can complain, debate, and share ideas or problems without passing judgment. We look forward to meeting twice a month free from beckoning families, laundry, and dust balls in the house or weeds in the garden. We get to chat about whatever is bugging us as our needles click away in the comfort of one another's company.

Sarah Landon

JERSEY CITY, NEW JERSEY, SNB

Only one person showed up for the first Jersey City Stitch 'n Bitch meeting in the fall of 2003. Now more than

Jersey City, New Jersey

fifty people are on our e-mail list, and newcomers arrive at every session. Most of our members live in the neighborhood and walk over to Basic, the great local café where we get together. The group has all levels of knitters—from people who are just learning to those who've been knitting all their lives. There's always someone to help a person out when she is stuck, or who has a pattern for a project someone else wants to make. One of our members, a librarian, can always be counted on to bring the newest knitting books to check out. We do have a guy on our e-mail list, but so far only women have showed up to stitch and bitch. What do we usually end up talking about? Surprise—knitting!

It's always inspiring to see what other people are making, and we learn so much from one another. Last fall we took a trip upstate to Woodstock, N.Y., to check out

its gorgeous knitting shop, and we're planning a trip this year to attend the Sheep and Wool festival. The group is a terrific way to meet people with whom you automatically have one thing in common—and often much more.

Christy Sayre and Barbara Landes

PITTSBURGH, PENNSYLVANIA, KNITTINESS

In December of 2002, when the owner of the Quiet Storm coffeehouse complained that people always mentioned using his space to do projects but never got around to doing them there, artist Jude Vachon grabbed a piece of paper and wrote up a contract to start Pittsburgh's Knittiness group. The former nuisance bar in a distressed neighborhood is now a welcoming coffeehouse and showcase for local artists, with great vegetarian food and comfy seating. A toy area and pinball machine keep children entertained while mamas knit, and one never knows what else might be going on in the shared space—shiatsu massage therapy, a band performance, or screenings of locally made films.

Jude (pictured right) recently demonstrated her new technique of knitting large,

Pittsburgh, Pennsylvania

webby fabric using her own arms as knitting needles and yarn she made of torn-up T-shirts.

"Age? What's that?" has become one of this multigenerational group's mottos. Being wacky, creative freethinkers, they know their different ages have nothing to do with the fun times, great conversation, and sharing of knitting tips that take place each week.

Kristilee Helmick

WASHINGTON, D.C., SnB

Our group began as just a few lonesome knitters at a Logan Circle coffee shop, but now we are part of nothing less than a Washington, D.C., knitting empire! When I moved to D.C. I was inspired by the SnB group I'd left behind in Chapel Hill, N.C., to begin a new group in my new town. We started out modestly, but when *Stitch 'n Bitch* was published, knitters and crocheters joined in droves, with membership in excess of 160 and three weekly meetings.

Sunday afternoon at Sparky's is our core knitting time. Here large groups of SnBers battle for seats with students and readers who are hoping

Washington, D.C.

for some peace and quiet to read (they soon leave). The more intimate Thursday night SnBers gather at a stitcher's house for cheap wine, cheese, and a wind-down from the week. These girls plan group events and craft nights. The talk gets a bit racy and they share the horror stories of the week as well as the triumphs. Popular demand for weeknight knitting has spawned Stitch 'n Belch, featuring half-off Belgian ales at a local bar in hopes of attracting more male knitters.

With the sheer creative force that comes with so many diverse talents and causes, SnB D.C. is a force to be reckoned with. Community is difficult to find in an urban setting of apartment buildings and inhabitants with long workdays, but Stitch 'n Bitch creates that community by bringing people who live close to each other into a place where they can meet, knit, and network.

Gwen Shlichta

Size

Women's S/M (L/XL)

Finished chest: 33 (41)" (see note)

Finished length: 23 (24)"

Materials

GGH Soft Kid (70% kid mohair, 25% nylon, 5% wool; 25g/154 yds)

MC: 7 (8) skeins #26 Blue

CC1: 2 skeins #2 White

CC2: 2 (3) skeins #30 Bright Red

US 10½ (6.5mm) straight needles

US 13 (9mm) straight needles

Optional: US I (5.5mm) crochet hook

Gauge

14 sts and 19 rows = 4" in St st

Special Skill

INTARSIA

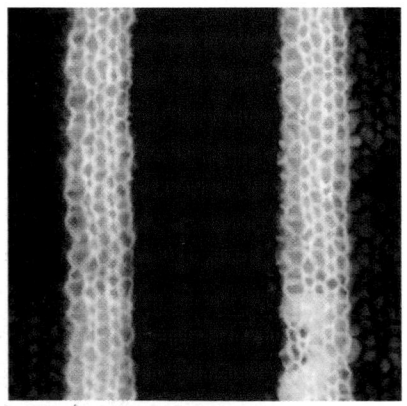

HANNAH HOWARD
London Calling

I grew up in Virginia Beach, Virginia, a town better known for its conservative leanings than its music scene. You could find a 7-Eleven and a church on any corner, making it the only place I know where you can self-medicate with Jesus and a Slurpee at any time of day. Nevertheless, my fondest memory is of moshing underage at the Boathouse. The musicians were gods to a suburban church girl turned punk rock acolyte, and salvation was a baptism in angry guitar riffs and cigarette smoke.

This sweater is inspired by all things punk rock and by my friend Christopher, closet rock star and Anglophile. **Note:** This very fine, almost diaphanous sweater is very stretchy. That's why the finished measurements are smaller than actual bust size, to achieve a nice fit.

DIRECTIONS

BACK

With MC, CO 66 (80) sts using larger needles.

Change to smaller needles and, beg with a RS row, work 4 (8) rows in St st.

Next (dec) row: K1, ssk, k to last 3 sts, k2tog, k1.

Rep dec row every 14th row 3 times—58 (72) sts.

Work even in St st until piece measures 14½ (15)" from beg.

Armhole shaping:

BO 2 sts at beg of next 2 rows.

BO 1 st at beg of next 4 rows 50 (64) sts.

Work even in St st until piece measures 21 (22)" from beg, ending with RS facing.

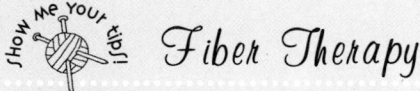

Fiber Therapy

UNDERSTANDING YARN BEHAVIOR

Very fluffy yarns such as mohair or angora can be made to behave (before knitting or wearing) if you stick them in the Naughty Corner of your freezer for about an hour or so. This is a handy trick too if you need to frog them and they just won't rip back. If you're using a less resilient yarn such as silk or alpaca and you're working bands (around the cuffs, waist, or neck), they'll sag less if, on the wrong side, you knit through the back of all the knit stitches. You can also do this when you're picking up stitches for neckbands or armholes. Finally, cotton is going to expand, and there's nothing you can do about it, so plan ahead. *Darrow Wendoloski, Victoria, Australia*

Shape neck:

K18 (23), place these sts on holder, BO 16 (18), k to end.

P 1 row.

BO 2 sts from beg of next row, then EOR 1 (2) times— 12 (17) sts.

BO rem sts.

Transfer holder sts to needle and work left shoulder as for right shoulder, reversing shaping.

FRONT

Using larger needles, with MC, CO 66 (80) sts.

Change to smaller needles and, beg with a RS row, beg working from chart; *at the same time,* work shaping as for back.

SLEEVES (MAKE 2)

Using larger needles, with MC, CO 32 (36) sts.

Change to smaller needles and, beg with a RS row, work 4 rows in St st.

Inc 1 st at each edge of next row, then every 8th row 10 times—54 (58) sts.

Work even in St st until piece measures 20" from beg, ending with RS facing.

BO 2 sts at beg of next 2 rows.

Dec 1 st at each edge of next 2 (4) rows.

Work 2 rows even in St st.

BO very loosely, using larger needles.

FINISHING

Seam shoulders.

Sew sleeve caps into armholes.

Seam sleeves and sides.

Optional: Crab st around neckline.

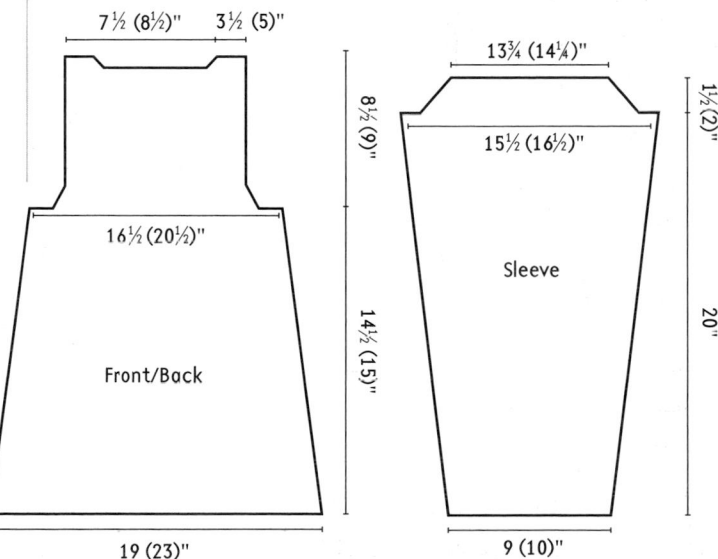

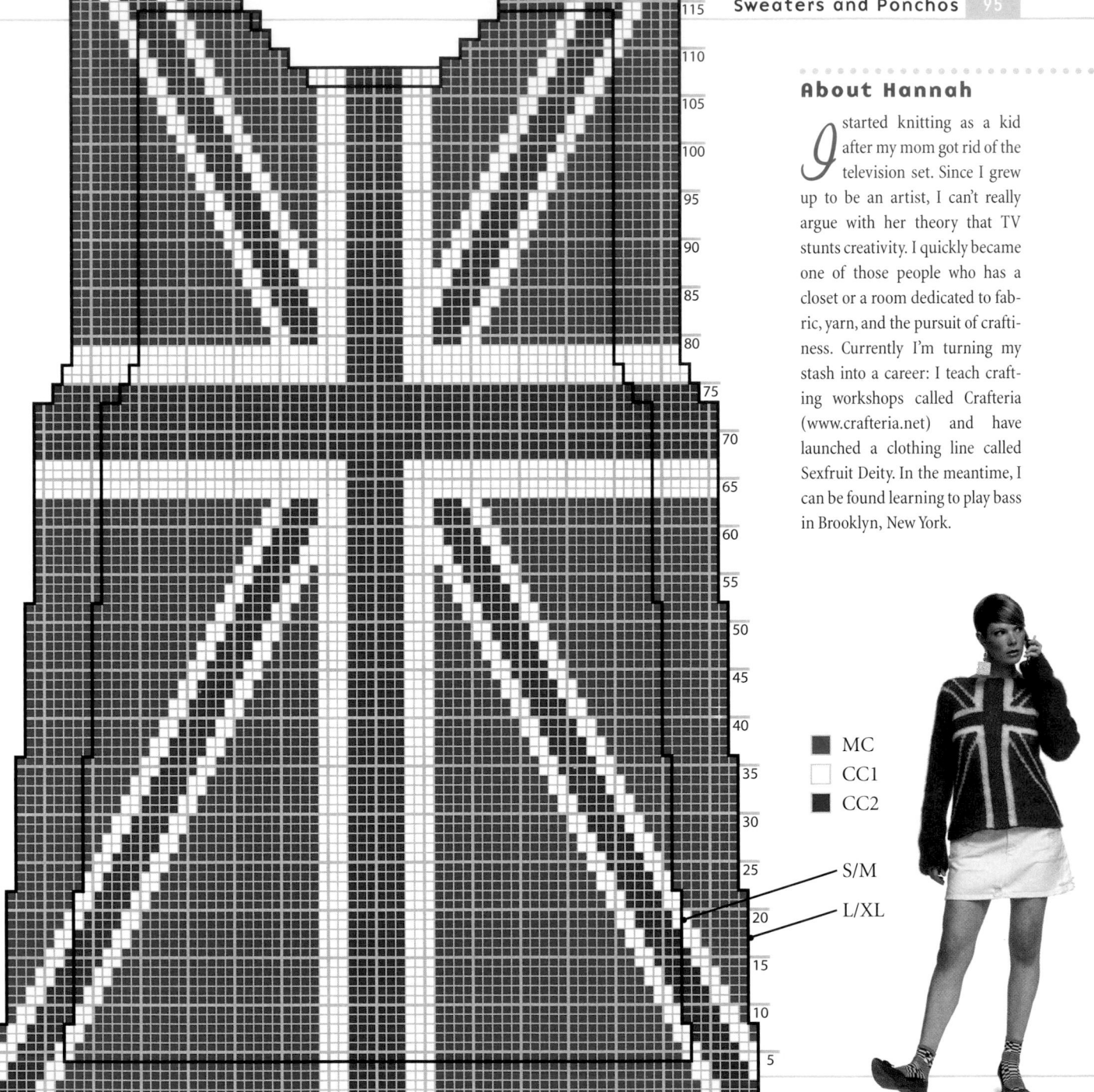

About Hannah

I started knitting as a kid after my mom got rid of the television set. Since I grew up to be an artist, I can't really argue with her theory that TV stunts creativity. I quickly became one of those people who has a closet or a room dedicated to fabric, yarn, and the pursuit of craftiness. Currently I'm turning my stash into a career: I teach crafting workshops called Crafteria (www.crafteria.net) and have launched a clothing line called Sexfruit Deity. In the meantime, I can be found learning to play bass in Brooklyn, New York.

■ MC
□ CC1
■ CC2

S/M
L/XL

LAURA-JEAN, THE KNITTING QUEEN

Flower Power

I came up with this project after accidentally shrinking and felting a mohair sweater that made its way into the wash. I loved the texture of the fabric, so I cut it into patches for appliqués. When I was trimming the loose threads from the sewing, I realized I liked that extra bit of green mohair hanging—it actually looked like roots. Everyone who tries this loves the roots, so that's another cool part of this sweater that just happened. The shape of this sweater is a bit fitted and it has longer-than-average sleeves. It's the kind of thing you can just throw on with jeans or a skirt and go! It's comfy and cozy and fun—what more could you want in a sweater?

DIRECTIONS

BACK

With MC, CO 81 (86, 90, 95) sts. Work in St st until piece measures 2¾ (3½, 4½, 5½)" from beg, ending with RS facing.

Dec 1 st at each edge of next row, then foll 4th and 8th rows—75 (80, 84, 89) sts.

Work 1 row even.

Inc 1 st at each edge of next row, then every 10 (10, 9, 9)th row 9 times—85 (90, 94, 99) sts.

Shape armholes:

BO 3 (4, 4, 6) sts at beg of next 2 rows.

Dec 1 st from each edge of every row 3 (3, 4, 4) times, then EOR 3 (3, 4, 4) times—67 (70, 70, 71) sts.**

Size

Women's XS (S, M, L)

Finished bust: 34 (36, 38, 40)"

Finished length: 21 (22, 23, 25)"

Materials

MC: Brown Sheep Nature Spun Worsted (100% wool; 100g/245 yds), 5 (6, 7, 7) skeins #N46 Red Fox

Katia Ingenua Mohair (78% mohair, 13% nylon, 9% wool; 50g/153 yds)

CC1: 1 skein #20 Hot Pink

CC2: 1 skein #21 Light Pink

CC3: 1 skein #14 Olive Green

US 6 (4mm) straight needles, or size needed to obtain gauge

Sewing machine

Stitch-N-Tear stabilizing backing

Sewing thread complementary to CC1, CC2, and CC3

Gauge

19 sts and 26 rows = 4" in St st with MC

18 sts and 22 rows = 4" in St st with CC1

Work even in St st until piece measures 21 (22, 23, 24)" from beg.

BO.

FRONT

Work as for back to **.

Work even in St st until piece measures 19½ (20½, 21½, 22½)", ending with RS facing.

K13 (14, 14, 14), place these sts on a holder, BO 41 (42, 42, 43), k13 (14, 14, 14).

Dec 1 st from neck edge on this row, then EOR 3 (4, 4, 4) times. BO.

Transfer holder sts to needle and work as for left side, reversing shaping.

SLEEVES (MAKE 2)

CO 48 (48, 50, 52).

Working in St st, dec 1 st at each side of every 3rd row 4 times—40 (40, 42, 44) sts.

Work even in St st until piece measures 3½" from beg, ending with RS facing.

Inc 1 st at each side of next row, then every 6 (5, 5, 6)th row 15 (19, 20, 17) times—72 (76, 82, 86) sts.

Shape cap:

Working in St st, BO 3 (4, 4, 6) sts at beg of next 2 rows.

Dec 1 st from each edge of every row 4 (4, 6, 6) times, then EOR 14 times.

BO 2 sts at beg of next 4 rows.

BO rem 22 (24, 26, 26) sts.

FELTED SWATCHES

For petals, CO 48 stitches with CC1 and work for 10".

For flower center, CO 18 stitches with CC1 and work for 4".

For leaf, CO 24 stitches with CC2 and work for 3".

To felt, toss the swatches in the washer on hot until they are approximately two thirds their original size. (Petals swatch should be approximately 7" × 6½", flower center swatch should be approximately 2½" × 2½", and leaf swatch should be approximately 3½" × 2").

Using the templates on the following page, cut out petals, flower center, and leaves from the appropriate swatches. Pin them in the correct locations to front of sweater.

Twist 3 strands of CC3 tog and pin stem in place, leaving a bit hanging off the bottom for roots. The secret to sewing all this on is to back it with Stitch-N-Tear (a tear-away stabilizer). Make sure every edge, including stem, has Stitch-N-Tear behind it.

Set stitching on your sewing machine to a midlength stitch and wide zigzag; stitch down all edges of felt appliqués. Lift presser foot often and rearrange what you're sewing so it doesn't stretch strangely.

About Laura-Jean

I spent the first seventeen years of my life in Saskatoon, Saskatchewan, where it is seriously cold most of the year and access to fashion is painfully limited. So, of course, I learned to make my own cute clothes and sweaters. I've been sewing since age twelve and knitting since I was sixteen. I got serious about fashion when I moved to Toronto and needed a career. A basic "how to use a knitting machine" course got me started, and pretty soon my company Fresh Baked Goods (and my royal title, the Knitting Queen) was born. I now sell tons of sweaters (and other clothing and accessories) in my two Toronto stores and on my Web site, www.freshbakedgoods.com. I can't believe I make a living having so much fun!

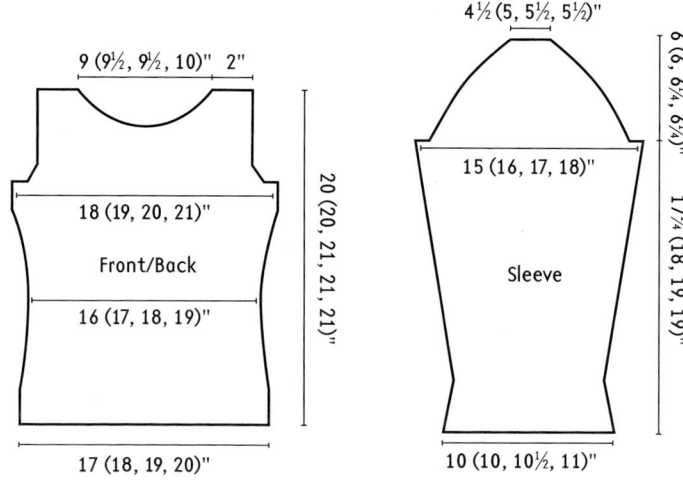

Copy these flower and leaf templates, then use them to cut pieces from felt.

You Spin Me Right Round, Baby

CHANGING A PATTERN FROM STRAIGHT KNITTING TO KNITTING IN THE ROUND

*I*f you are a circular knitting fanatic, there's nothing to stop you from knitting most of a sweater in the round even if a pattern tells you to knit it flat. You just need to make a few simple adjustments. Start with the front, casting on the total number of stitches minus 2, and place a stitch marker. Then cast on the total number of stitches for the back minus 2 stitches, place another stitch marker, and join your round. This reduction of 4 stitches—1 per side per piece—is what would have been taken up by the seams. Since you're knitting in the round, you won't need to make side seams (yay!) so you can lose those stitches.

Then just knit in the round until you get to the armhole shaping. Here you'll have to accommodate your changes in the pattern for the missing seam once again, and the number of bound-off stitches to start the armhole shaping will have to be reduced by 2 on each side. So, if the bind-off for each side is 5 stitches, meaning 10 stitches for the entire armhole (front and back combined), knit to 4 stitches before the stitch marker, remove the marker and bind off 8 stitches, then knit to 4 stitches before the next stitch marker, bind off 8 stitches again, and remove the second stitch marker.

Knit the remainder of the sweater back and forth in the usual way. Just put all the stitches for the first side on a spare circular needle or scrap yarn and work the front and the back of the sweater separately.

● There are a few important things to take into account when altering a flat-knit pattern for knitting in the round. First, your gauge for knitting in the round may be tighter than for knitting back and forth. If this is true for you, knit the back-and-forth parts on a smaller needle so that your gauge is consistent. Second, if you're working with a stitch pattern other than stockinette, you'll have to make sure that the pattern works all the way around. There is some leeway in the number of stitches you can decrease, as long as you make sure you take that into consideration when you bind off for the armholes. Finally, any shaping that is done in the body of the sweater has to be done at least a couple of stitches in from the stitch marker on either side to make the sides flow smoothly. *Marney Anderson, New York, NY*

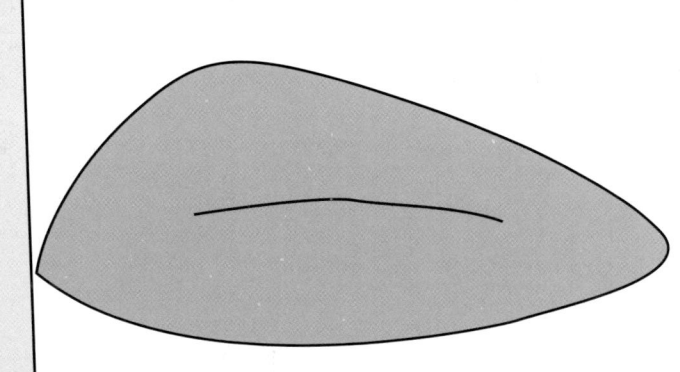

MELISSA WHERLE

Lucky

CLOVER LACE WRAP

his wrap cardigan was inspired by fashion's return to femininity. In my daily uniform of T-shirt, jeans, and Chuck Taylors, I am not much of a spokesperson for girliness, so it might seem strange that I enjoy designing and knitting lacy, femme sweaters. This is the perfect sweater to throw on over a little slip dress, or you can keep it casual with a T-shirt and jeans. It's knit out of cotton, my favorite fiber, and it is light enough for warmer spring days, which ensures a long season of wear.

Size

Women's XS (S, M, L, XL)

Finished bust: 32 (36, 40, 44, 48)"

Finished length: 19 (19½, 20, 20½, 22)"

Materials

Rowan 4-Ply Cotton
(100% Cotton; 50g/186 yds), 8 (8, 10, 10, 11) skeins #129 Aegean

US 2 (2.5mm) straight needles

US 3 (3mm) straight needles,
or size needed to obtain gauge

Tapestry needle

2 yds 1" ribbon in complementary color

Gauge

26 sts and 32 rows = 4" in clover lace st

Special Skill

LACE

STITCH PATTERN
CLOVER LACE

Rows 1 and 7: K.

Row 2 and all WS rows: P.

Row 3: K2, yo, sl1, k2tog, psso, yo, *k5, yo, sl1, k2tog, psso, yo*; rep from * to * to last 2 sts, k2.

Row 5: K3, yo, ssk, *k6, yo, ssk*; rep from * to * to last 2 sts, k2.

Row 9: K1, *k5, yo, sl1, k2tog, psso, yo*; rep from * to * to last 6 sts, k6.

Row 11: K7, *yo, ssk, k6*; rep from * to * to end.

Row 12: P

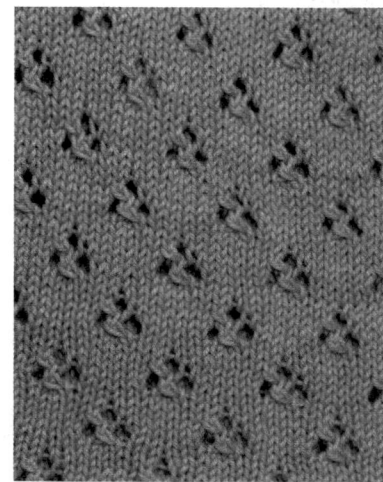

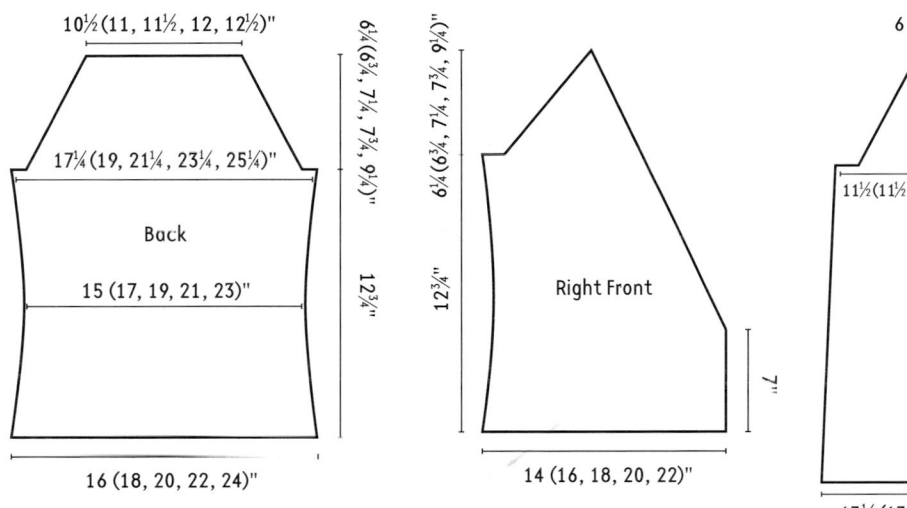

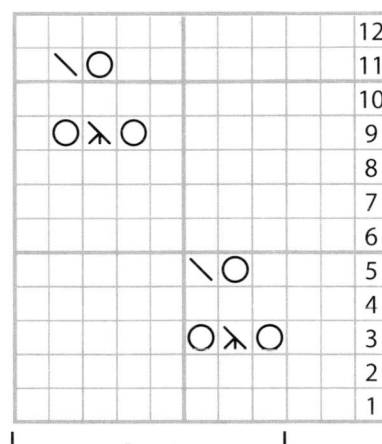

							12
	╲	O					11
							10
O	⅄	O					9
							8
							7
							6
				╲	O		5
							4
			O	⅄	O		3
							2
							1

Clover lace

☐ k on RS; p on WS

O yo

⅄ sl1 kwise, k2tog, psso

╲ ssk

DIRECTIONS

BACK

With smaller needles, CO 106 (119, 132, 145, 158) sts.

Work 4 rows in 1 × 1 rib. Change to larger needles. P next row on WS. Work 2 rows in clover lace st.

Maint cont of st patt, dec 1 st at each edge of next row, then every foll 9th row 3 times more—98 (111, 124, 137, 150) sts.

Work even in st patt for 1".

Inc 1 st at each edge of next row, then every foll 7th row 6 times more—112 (125, 138, 151, 164) sts.

Work even in patt until piece measures 12¾" from beg.

Shape raglan:

BO 7 sts at beg of next 2 rows.

Dec 1 st each edge of every 2nd row 6 (14, 22, 30, 34) times, then every 4 (4, 4, 0, 4)th row 9 (6, 3, 0, 1) times—68 (71, 74, 77, 80) sts.

BO.

RIGHT FRONT

With smaller needles, CO 91 (104, 117, 130, 143) sts.

Work 4 rows in 1 × 1 rib. Change to larger needles. Working 4 sts in 1 × 1 rib at right edge (RS facing) of every row, p next row on WS. Work 2 rows in clover lace st. Shape waist as foll:

Dec 1 st at waist edge of next row, then every foll 9th row 3 times more—87 (100, 113, 126, 139) sts.

Work even in st patt for 1".

Inc 1 st at waist edge of next row, then every foll 7th row 6 times more—94 (107, 120, 133, 146) sts.

At the same time, when piece measures 7" from beg, shape neckline:

BO 4 sts at neck edge of next row.

Dec 1 st at neck edge every row 22 (34, 46, 58, 64) times.

Then dec 1 st at neck edge every other row 46 (42, 38, 34, 36) times.

At the same time, when piece measures 12¾" from beg, shape raglan:

BO 7 sts at beg of next row.

Dec 1 st at armhole edge every 2nd row 6 (14, 22, 30, 34) times, then every 4 (4, 4, 0, 4)th row 9 (6, 3, 0, 1) times.

LEFT FRONT

Work as for right front, reversing shaping.

SLEEVES (MAKE 2)

With smaller needles, CO 86 (86, 86, 92, 92) sts.

Work 6 rows in 1 × 1 rib.

Change to larger needles and working in clover lace patt, dec 1 st at each edge of every 21st row 3 times, then every 22nd row twice—76 (76, 76, 82, 82) sts.

Work even in patt until piece measures 17½" from beg.

Seams Sew Right

MAKING PERFECT SIDE-TO-SIDE SEAMS

My seams used to look terrible, but now they're scarily perfect, and yours can be too. When preparing to sew seams together, just run a smaller-gauge circular needle through the line of stitches you're using for each seam edge (figure 1) (this means two seam edges need two circular needles), and then sew back and forth between the two edges (figure 2). When you've finished the seam, all you have to do is pull out the two circulars, pull the sewing yarn tight, and weave in the ends. I find this makes it easier for me to pick up and sew the stitches with my yarn needle and allows me to connect them row to row more evenly. In a pinch (if you don't have two spare circulars kicking around, for instance), you can use a smooth cotton or rayon contrasting yarn instead. *David Demchuk, Toronto, Canada*

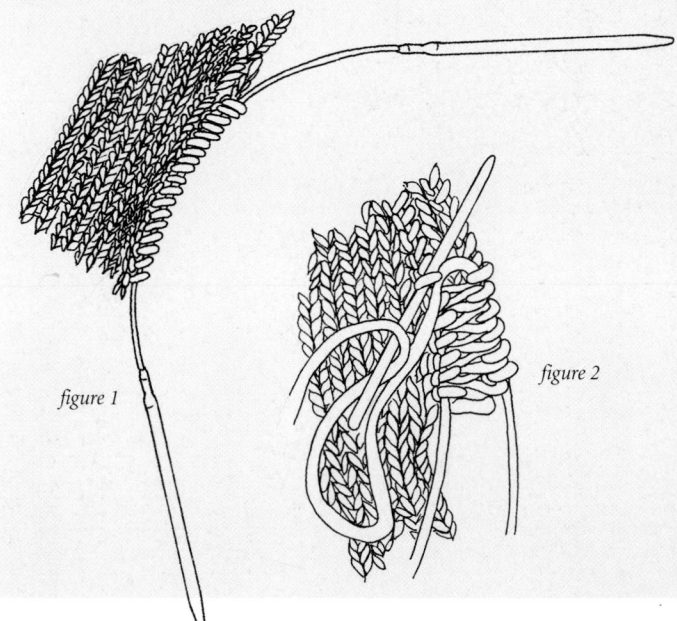

figure 1

figure 2

Shape raglan cap:

BO 7 sts at beg of next 2 rows.

Dec 1 st at each edge of every 4 (4, 4, 4, 6)th row 9 (7, 5, 3, 8) times, then every 6 (6, 6, 6, 8)th row 2 (4, 6, 8, 3) times. BO rem sts.

NECK BAND

With smaller needles, CO 13 sts.

Work in 1 × 1 rib until band measures 62½" from beg.

SIDE TIE

With smaller needles, CO 13 sts.

Work in 1 × 1 rib until tie measures 18" from beg.

FINISHING

Block all pieces.

Sew sleeves to fronts and back along raglan armhole seams.

Sew neck band to neck beg at left front edge, leaving 17" at right front edge for tie.

Sew side and underarm seams.

On left side of garment, 5½" up from hem, sew side tie into side seam.

On left front at edge on inside and on right side seam inside, sew in ribbon for tie.

Weave in ends.

About Melissa

I'm originally from southern New Jersey and moved to New York City to study at the Fashion Institute of Technology, where I majored in fashion design and specialized in knitwear. Today I am a sweater designer for a women's fashion company. My grandmother taught me how to knit when I was eight years old, but after knitting tons of Barbie tube dresses, I got a little bored. I revived my relationship with needles again during my first year of knitwear specialization in college, and the weekly meetings of my Long Island City Stitch 'n Bitch group keep me inspired and challenged. My only problem now is so many projects, so little time!

STITCH 'N BITCH ACROSS THE NATION
The South

AUSTIN, TEXAS, SNB

Before moving to Austin, I had started an L.A. chapter of SnB, where I was thrilled to have a group of intelligent, funky, fantastically crafty women working on projects and discussing everything from careers to birth control. We were gloriously open to one another's differences, so the offense some took to our group was surprising. One incident involved a gal leaving the coffee shop, refusing to share space with women who would actually be seen knitting. Another time, we were assailed by a young man who asked, "Why can't you call yourselves a more acceptable name like 'Stitch and Discourse'?"

In my new hometown, the term Stitch 'n Bitch and all it embodies are totally embraced. The Austin SnB is thriving and we've already outgrown two different venues. Onlookers often give us a thumbs-up and a smile when they see the strange mélange of coeds in cat's-eye glasses mingling with middle-aged professionals, Gen-X hipsters, and kindly grandmothers. We've become not only a knitting informational support system for each other, but also an invaluable social outlet. Stitch 'n Bitch has become an institution for those teetering on the line between social acceptance and creative anarchy.

Although the purpose may vary slightly, the result is the same: the coming together of diverse, kick-ass people to relate, shatter stereotypes, and revel in our craftiness.

Vickie Howell

CHAPEL HILL, NORTH CAROLINA, SNB

The savvy stitchers of SnB Chapel Hill came together in the summer of 2002 after founding member Gwen Schlicta read the article in *BUST* about the joys of stitching and bitching. She and four friends KIPed (knitted in public) in local coffee shops to encourage other knitters to join in. Word of mouth spread quickly, and the small Sunday afternoon knitting circle blossomed into a group with 127 members and three knitting circles a week.

In addition to the lovely moral support our group provides whenever someone has to completely frog a sweater-in-progress, SnB has become an incredible social network for its members. The women, few of whom knew each other before joining, have formed fast and lasting friendships. When we're not obsessing over the latest Rowan yarn, our conversations range from relationships to theses, pink shoes to politics. In fact, the political performance art group Keys of Resistance was formed by four Stitch 'n Bitchers after knitting chats revealed a common interest in helping people express their political views to government officials. Wearing

Austin, Texas

Chapel Hill, North Carolina

thirteen knitters show up for the twice-monthly gatherings, filling the community room at Central Market with knitting and crocheting, laughter and fun. SnB Dallas knitters range in age from twenty to fifty-something. Some have been knitting for years, while others come to learn how to start knitting and purling. When in the Dallas area, drop in and cast one on!

Chris Ingle

LEXINGTON, KENTUCKY, SNB

I wanted my granny to teach me to knit, but granny was not a knitter. So I used the money she gave me for Christmas of 2002 to buy some acrylic yarn, a pair of needles, and a hideous book titled *I Can't Believe I'm Knitting*. After a few torturous months, I more or less had the hang of knit and purl, but I wanted to learn more. Being the geek girl I am, I started posting messages on the Internet, looking for other Lexington knitters. Enter Renee Rigdon.

1940s secretarial dress and using antique typewriters, they set up temporary "offices" in public spaces (such as the March for Women's Lives in Washington, D.C.) and take dictation from anyone wishing to write a letter to an elected official. Another spinoff group was formed by SnBers' nonknitting male partners who frequently found themselves home alone. The guys go to their Kitsch 'n Bitch to watch terrible movies, gnaw on beef jerky, and drink orange soda.

Despite these extracurriculars, for us it always comes back to the simple joy of the click of needles, the pull of yarn through our fingers, and the company of women. The wine, cheese, coffee, happy hours, and political action groups are just the pom-pom on the hat.

Sara Daily

DALLAS, TEXAS, SNB

Stitch 'n Bitch Dallas may very well be the first knitting circle ever to count both a research scientist and a professional wrestler among its ranks, along with a few less surprising professionals: a technical writer, a restaurant owner, a teacher, a university fund-raiser, and a librarian. Our organization was formed in March 2004 with a posting on a Web site looking for kindred knitting spirits in the north Texas area, since amazingly, there was no Stitch 'n Bitch group. We figured that in a city as big as Dallas, surely there must be other knitters out there—we just needed to find them! Since then, the group has grown to more than thirty members. On average, seven to

Dallas, Texas

Unlike me, Renee was a total craft-whore crunchy goddess who had been knitting on and off for years, along with dressmaking, bag sewing, and cloth diapering. The first SnB book had inspired her to seek out other knitters who could appreciate her wacky DIY drive. Renee and I joined forces through the Knitting Meetup Web site, and when Debbie Stoller came to town for a book signing, we showed up with fliers advertising our brand-new Stitch 'n Bitch group.

As press about the national knitting phenomenon grew, many people joined in to make the SnB Lexington group a fabulous fifty-member forum for knitters in the Bluegrass State. To counterbalance the hedonism of knitting for ourselves, we started quarterly charity projects that focus on the principle of thinking globally and acting locally.

Zabet Stewart

RALEIGH, NORTH CAROLINA, SnB

Our Stitch 'n Bitch was started following the "if you knit it, they will come" philosophy—two or three of us would sit in a popular coffee shop and KIP (knit in public), trawling for new members. Unfortunately, that didn't work, so we put fliers in the LYS and hipped the staff to our group. The store sent some very bitchin' members our way, and we moved to a more popular café with a spectacular DJ. We have now grown to more than fifty members.

We range in age from twelve to forty-nine, with about a dozen of us—professional women, grad students, feminists, and environmental activists—meeting every Wednesday night at Helios Coffee Company in downtown Raleigh. Many of us participated in a knitathon to benefit a local women's shelter, others donate knit items for fund-raisers for causes such as the NC Conservation Network and the Student Action with Farmworkers, and we hope to collaborate on much more "craftivism."

Our turn-ons include red wine, handbags, world-beat remixes, easy shawl patterns, and cute baristas. Our turn-offs include bad art shows that stay on exhibit for months on end, double-pointed needles, and mood lighting.

Raleigh, North Carolina

SnB Raleigh is proudest of member Nicole, who engineered a hands-free tea-sipping knitting helmet with her genius boyfriend, Les. Next, we plan to invent a DJ cozy to keep DJ Keith toasty warm while he spins down-tempo rhythms in synch with our knitting.

Fawn Pattison

Lexington, Kentucky

ERIN WECKERLE

Spiderweb Capelet

I design a lot of knitted items, and most of my patterns come from trial and error, with one project leading organically to the next. This capelet pattern came about when I wanted to make something that was more airy and delicate than the sweaters and ponchos I had been knitting all winter. The design is a combination of a simple scarf and a circular poncho. Simple shaping at the shoulders keeps it relaxed and drapey enough to fit anyone, but the lace stitch and the pom-pom ties make it a fancy, girly, vintage-inspired accessory. Purldrop, the name of my knitwear line, comes from practicing the "purl, drop" row for the spiderweb lace used in this capelet. After muttering that to myself over and over, it just clicked.

DIRECTIONS

CO 92 sts.

Row 1: K.

Rows 2 and 6: K2, *yo, k1; rep from * to last 2 sts, k2.

Rows 3 and 7: P3, *drop 1, p1; rep from * to last 2 sts, p2.

Row 4: K1, *sl2 pwise, k2tog, pass 2 slipped sts over, k1 without dropping st off needle, yo, p1 without dropping st off needle, yo, k1 without dropping st off needle, yo, p1 and drop st off needle; rep from * to last st, k1.

Rows 5, 9, and 19: P.

Size
Adult

Materials
Crystal Palace Merino Frappe (80% merino wool, 20% nylon; 50g/140 yds), 2 skeins #020B New Sage OR #145 Hibiscus

US 15 (10mm) straight needles

US F/5 (4mm) crochet hook

2" pom-pom maker or template

Gauge
10 st and 10 rows = 4" in St st

Special Skill
Lace

Row 8: K1, *k1 without dropping st off needle, yo, p1 without dropping st off needle, yo, k1 without dropping st off needle, yo, p1 and drop st off needle, sl2 pwise, k2tog, pass 2 slipped sts over; rep from * to last st, k1.

Rows 10–17: Rep rows 2–9.

Row 18: *K3, k2tog; rep from * to last 2 sts, k2—74 sts.

Row 20: K1, *yo, k2tog, k2tog; rep from * to last st, k1—56 sts.

Row 21: P.

BO.

FINISHING

With crochet hook, chain two 10" lengths of cord.

Attach one cord to each of the top corners.

Make two 2" pom-poms and secure one to each of the cord ends.

Weave in ends.

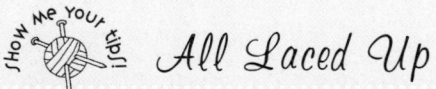

All Laced Up

KEEPING TRACK OF YOUR LACE WORK

When working in a complicated lace pattern, place markers between every pattern repeat. It makes finding mistakes easier. Also, if you are having real trouble and need to unravel a lace pattern periodically, knit in a piece of nylon or mercerized cotton yarn (it is important that it be slippery) every ten rows or so. If you need to unravel, you can put your needle in along this piece of yarn before unraveling to that spot. It will keep you from dropping yarnovers. If you get past the ten rows with no problem, simply pull the guide yarn out and knit it in again on the next row.

Lucy Lee, Cambridge, MA

About Erin

I grew up in Pittsburgh, moved to Philadelphia to attend Tyler School of Art, then moved to New Haven to get my M.F.A. at Yale. While there, my best friend, who was studying photography, taught me how to knit, both as an alternative to the stress of the studio and as a complement to our art practice. I made scarves for all my friends that Christmas but it wasn't until I moved back to Philly and was working at a record store that I had time to practice my new skill. I would just listen to music and knit all day. Soon I started selling my stuff at local shops. In October 2002 my friend Rebekah Maysles and I opened a hand-made and vintage clothing shop in the back room of another store in Philly. I launched www.purldrop.com this year and we moved the shop, Sodafine, to Brooklyn, New York, in February.

In a Bind

BINDING OFF WITH A CROCHET HOOK

Here's my unconventional way of binding off. I find it easier than passing stitches over each other with two needles, and it produces a neatly finished edge. If the piece is knit with straight needles, when you come to the row to be bound off, just knit it onto a circular needle of the same size (or larger if you want to be sure to bind off loosely). Don't actually bind off the stitches. Push all the stitches to the right. Holding the knitting needle in your left hand and an appropriate-size crochet hook in your right, insert the hook into the first stitch purlwise and take the stitch off the needle. Then use the hook to pull the second stitch off the needle and through the first one (as if you are making a crochet chain). Continue with all stitches until you get to the end, then pull the yarn end through the last loop. Done! *Edina Tien, Vancouver, WA*

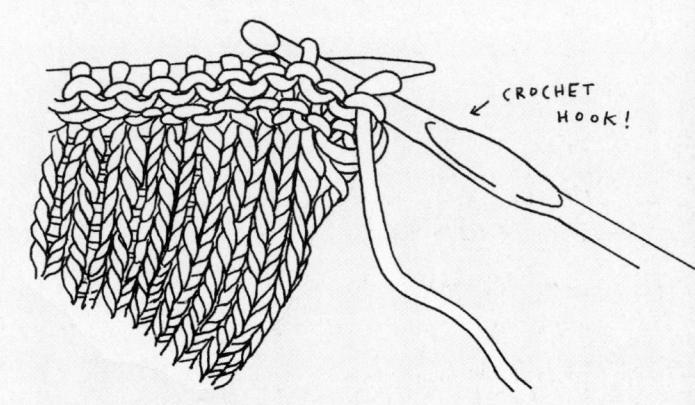

← CROCHET HOOK!

Loosen Up

HOW TO BIND OFF AND CAST ON MORE LOOSELY

As a new knitter I cast on and bind off *way* too tightly. But casting on over two needles, as is often suggested, results in stitches that are too loose for my taste. I compromise and cast on and bind off with a needle a few sizes larger than the one I knit with. Problem solved. *Crissy Hatfield, Winetka, CA*

MELANIE SCOLES

That Seventies Poncho

A n eye-catching color combination adds interest to this otherwise simple poncho. It is worked from the neck down: The first 17 rows are worked flat to form a split neckline, then the piece is joined and worked in the round. Switch to longer needles when needed as the piece increases in diameter. For texture, random rounds are purled. New colors should be started in the front center. It's helpful to use different-colored markers to identify the front once the piece is joined. An I-cord laced through the eyelets completes the neckline.

STITCH PATTERN
COLOR SEQUENCE
8 rows A, 4 rows D, 10 rows/rnds B, 16 rnds C, 10 rnds A, 6 rnds E, 18 rnds B, 12 rnds A, 10 rnds C, 6 rnds D, 4 rnds A, 8 rnds B, 4 rnds E, 1 rnd A.

Size
Adult

Finished neck circumference: 27"

Finished length: 25½"

Materials
Lion Brand Cotton-Ease (50% cotton, 50% acrylic; 100g/207 yds)

A: 3 skeins #113 Cherry Red

B: 3 skeins #102 Bubblegum

C: 2 skeins #133 Orangeade

D: 1 skein #153 Licorice

E: 1 skein #100 Vanilla

US 10 (6mm) circular needle with interchangeable cords OR 1 each 16", 24", and 36", or size needed to obtain gauge

US 4 (3.25mm) double-pointed needles (set of 2)

Stitch markers

Gauge
17 sts and 19 rows = 4" in St st

DIRECTIONS

With shortest circular needle and A, CO 115 sts. Working in color sequence, cont as follows:

Work flat in St st for 2 rows.

Row 3: K1, pm, yo, k56, yo, pm, k1, pm, yo, k56, yo, pm, k1.

Row 4: P.

Row 5: K1, sm, yo, k to next marker, yo, sm, k1, sm, yo, k to next marker, yo, sm, k1.

Rep rows 4 and 5 six times, maintaining color sequence.

Join into round, working first and last st tog.

Rnd 1: K.

Rnd 2: K1, sm, yo, k to next marker, yo, sm, k1, sm, yo, k to next marker, yo, sm.

Rep rnds 1 and 2, maintaining stripe sequence, to end of color patt—35 sts.

Optional: Randomly p a few of the k rnds to create texture.

With A, BO pwise.

Extreme Measures

IMPROMPTU RULERS

*I*f you find yourself without a ruler while knitting, you can do pretty well with a standard 8½" × 11" piece of paper, index cards (3" × 5" or 4" × 6"), or a dollar bill (approximately 2" × 6"). Fold them in halves, thirds, or quarters to get smaller measurements.
Evelyn Rowe, Washington, D.C.

● When casting on the first row of a sweater or any other knit item, make sure you leave a tail of yarn long enough to cut to the length of the piece that you are knitting. For example, if the sweater is to be knit to 24", make the tail 24" long. That way, if you are out or are not near your tape measure, you have a way of measuring how much more you need to knit.
Cindy Kuo, Northbrook, IL

● Measure your hand. That's right, your hand. There may be some portions of it that can be measured in even increments of centimeters or inches. If you know what these measurements are, you can measure your knitting whenever you want, whether or not you remembered to bring a tape measure.

For instance, I know that my hand (either one—mine are both the same) is 4" from wrist to end of palm; my middle finger is 3" long; my little finger is 2" long. From my wrist to the end of the first joint of my middle finger is roughly 5", and to the end of the second joint is roughly 6". From wrist to end of middle finger is 7". With these measurements, I can do almost anything, adding them together when necessary. When instructions get very precise and it's down to half inches, of course, I do use a tape measure. *Luanne Redmond, Chicago, IL*

TIES

With dpns and A, CO 2 sts. Work in I-cord with A for 10", then in D for 1½", then in B for 2¼", then in D for 1½", and then in A for 10".

Break yarn and draw tail through sts.

FINISHING

Weave in ends on poncho and ties.

Thread ties through every other eyelet at the neck opening in the front.

SHARE ROSS

Bam 13

S hortly after I learned to knit, I made a beautiful cashmere scarf for my husband, Bam, and we both agreed it was just too "nice" for him. That's when he said the magic words. "Why don't you knit things that you'd never find in a shop? Scarves that look like rags instead of looking perfect. Sweaters that appear torn instead of flawless." I thought he'd hit on something interesting, and I set out to find the best yarn combination for this new concept. I started with a loosely knit scarf using a combination of a rag and chenille yarn, and that led to this sweater. I struggled a lot with the design and worked hard to figure out how to write the pattern, especially with such a big gauge. In fact, knitting these two yarns together is a little bit like wrestling, and it requires a good bit of man-handling to get it. Every few rows, you should give the whole piece a good tug downward to get the stitches a little more settled. But be prepared: No matter what you do, the rows *will* look uneven. That's why it's punk!

STITCHES
W&T (WRAP AND TURN)
Sl the next st pwise, bring the yarn between the needles to the front of the work, and sl the st back to the left-hand needle. Turn the work, and begin working in the opposite direction. When you get to the wrapped st on the next row, sl the needle through both the wrap and the wrapped st kwise, and k them tog.

Size
Men's S (M, L, XL)

Finished chest circumference: 36 (40, 44, 48)"

Finished length: 24 (25, 26, 27)"

Materials
A: Colinette Tagliatelli (90% merino wool, 10% nylon; 100g/175 yds), 3 skeins #141 Zebra

B: Sirdar Snowflake Chunky (100% polyester; 50g/137 yds), 3 skeins #380 Black

US 35 (20mm) 32" circular needle, or size needed to obtain gauge

Gauge
6 sts and 8 rows = 4" in garter st

Special Skill
SHORT ROW SHAPING

Pre-Knitual Agreement

AVOIDING THE CASE OF THE LOVE SWEATER

I'd heard so many horror stories about the curse of the love sweater that I asked my fiancé to sign a pre-knitual agreement. Prior to casting on for his sweater, I had him promise to:

1. Appreciate all the work I put into the sweater by lavishing much praise on my knitting skills

2. *Not* pretend to like the finished product if he doesn't (I don't want "pity" wear)

3. Give the sweater back to me if, God forbid, we ever break up

I am hoping that this will take some of the pressure off of us both, so I can happily knit away without fear that I am inadvertently bringing about the end of our relationship.
Chelsea Fowler-Biondolillo, Rockville, MD

DIRECTIONS
BACK

**With 1 strand of A and B held tog, CO 27 (30, 33, 36) sts.

K 1 row.

Next 2 rows: K to last 2 sts, W&T. (Tip: You may want to tie a piece of waste yarn onto the wrapped yarn. It's much easier to figure out which yarn is the wrap later when you need to knit it.)

Next 2 rows: K to last 3 sts, W&T.

Next 2 rows: K to last 4 sts, W&T.

Next 2 rows: K across, working wrap sts tog with sts as you pass them.

Work in garter st until piece measures 16 (17, 17½, 18)" from beg.

Shape armholes:

BO 2 (2, 3, 3) sts at beg of next 2 rows.

BO 1 st at beg of next 2 rows—21 (24, 25, 28) sts.**

Work in garter st until piece measures 6 (6, 6½, 7)" from beg of armhole shaping.

Shape shoulders:

BO 3 (3, 3, 4) sts at beg of next 2 rows.

BO 4 sts at beg of 2 next rows.

BO rem 7 (10, 11, 12) sts.

FRONT

Work as for back from ** to **.

Work in garter st until piece measures 3 (3, 3½, 4)" from beg of armhole shaping.

Next row: K8 (9, 9, 10), join a second ball of yarn (1 strand of each), BO 5 (6, 7, 8), k to end.

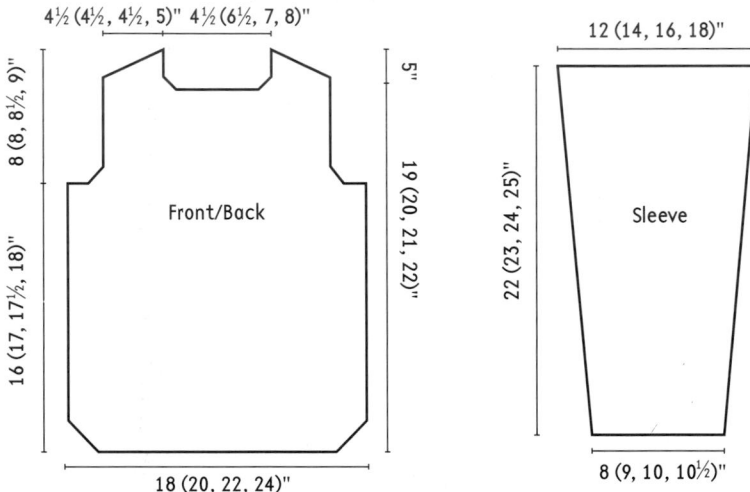

Working both sides at the same time, dec 1 st from neck edges EOR 1 (2, 2, 2) times.

BO 3 (3, 3, 4) sts at beg of next 2 rows.

BO 4 sts at beg of next 2 rows.

Mattress st shoulders of front and back tog.

SLEEVES

With 1 strand of each yarn and body laid flat with RS facing, pu 18 (22, 24, 28) sts around armhole.

Work in garter st for 3 rows.

Dec 1 st at each edge on next row, then every foll 10th row 2 (3, 3, 4) times— 12 (14, 16, 18) sts.

Work in garter st until piece measures 22 (23, 24, 25)" from beg.

BO.

FINISHING

Mattress st sleeve and side seams.

Wet-block to measurements.

About Share

My entire life has revolved around music, so when I announced to my family and friends that I had discovered knitting, they were surprised because it had nothing to do with rock 'n' roll. I started knitting in November 2003 when a friend came to our house in L.A. wearing a scarf she had knit for herself. She didn't have time to teach me the basics, so I sat at my computer, ordered yarn and needles, and then learned to cast on and knit from an Internet video! From there, it became apparent that I was addicted, and I started a blog to keep track of my ideas and thoughts about knitting: bubblebabble.typepad.com/knitaddictions. In addition to knitting, I've been lucky enough to tour the globe while playing guitar and singing for my band, Bubble, along with building Web sites and recording other bands in our studio. But I always manage to find time to knit and enjoy giving my family, friends, and fellow musicians loads of cool wristbands, sweaters, fingerless gloves, and scarves.

JENNA ADORNO
Ultra Femme

Size

Women's XS (S, M, L, XL)

Finished bust: 30 (33, 35½, 38½, 41)"

Finished length: 20 (21, 22, 23, 24)"

Materials

A: Rowan All Seasons Cotton
(60% cotton, 40% acrylic; 50g/98 yds),
2 (3, 3, 4, 4) skeins #202 Light Pink

B: GGH Soft Kid (70% kid mohair,
25% nylon, 5% wool; 25g/154 yds),
2 (2, 2, 3, 3) skeins #005 Light Pink

US 5 (3.75mm) double-pointed needles
(set of 5)

US 7 (4.5mm) double-pointed needles, or
size needed to obtain gauge (set of 2)

US 5 (3.75mm) 16" circular needle

US 7 (4.5mm) 16" circular needle,
or size needed to obtain gauge

2 yds 2"-wide ribbon, black

Stitch holders

Gauge

16 sts and 22 rows = 4" in St st with A
and larger needles

28 sts and 34 rows = 4" in St st with B
and smaller needles

At 5 feet, 100 pounds, I rarely find clothes that fit. Likewise, clothes knit from patterns often drape poorly or fall off my tiny frame. So when I was shopping recently in a trendy boutique and noticed the body-skimming fuzzy sweaters, I knew my only hope of having one that fit was to design it myself. Several swatches and attempts at the perfect belt loop later, I had created my favorite sweater to date. A sweater that makes people ask "Where did you buy that?" instead of "Did you make that yourself?"

This sweater, knit totally in the round, has a simple, seamless construction that requires minimal finishing. And for petite women everywhere, I have included my original extra-small pattern, a size that (I know from experience) is rarely included in knitting books.

DIRECTIONS

With A and larger circular needle, CO 120 (132, 142, 154, 164) sts.

Pm, join, and work 2 rnds in St st.

Next rnd: *Yo, k2tog; rep from * to end.

Work 2 rnds in St st.

Next rnd: Fold hem in half at the eyelet row and *pu 1 st from the CO edge and k tog with 1 st from the needle; rep from * to end.

Next rnd: *Work 10 (11, 10, 11, 10) sts, m1; rep from * 12 (12, 14, 14, 16) times, work 0 (0, 2, 0, 4) sts—132 (144, 156, 168, 180) sts.

Work even in k2, p2 rib for 9 (9½, 10, 10½, 11)".

Swatch Watch

GETTING AN ACCURATE GAUGE FOR CIRCULAR KNITTING

Your gauge in stockinette stitch on circular needles (knit every row) can be significantly different from your gauge on straight needles (knit one row, purl one row), because many of us make our knit stitches tighter than our purl stitches. Usually, trying to figure out what your gauge is in circular knitting requires that you knit something in the round, which will need many more stitches than a flat-knit swatch and can take up considerable time. Some people say to just start knitting the first sleeve of your project and measure to see if you're getting the right gauge; if you are, at least you already have some work done on the sweater.

But if you're picking up and knitting the sleeves from the top down or knitting a tank top, you won't be able to do this. Instead, you can make what I call a "pseudocircular swatch." To do this, cast on the number of stitches you'd use for knitting a flat swatch (usually 20 or so), and then cast on several extra. (The stitches at the edges will be too sloppy to get a realistic gauge, so you want to cast on enough stitches to avoid getting anywhere near those edge stitches when you're measuring the swatch.)

Next, knit across your swatch. At the end of the row, do *not* turn your work. Instead, keep your work facing you and go back to the right edge, leaving a long strand of the yarn hanging loose across the back of your swatch. You want enough "free" working yarn across the back so that you'll be able to flatten your swatch to measure it, without having these "floats" across the back pulling or distorting the swatch. This is sort of like making I-cord, only you're not pulling the working yarn tight. Continue knitting in this manner until you have a swatch you can live with, then check your gauge, keeping well away from the edges. You've just made a stockinette swatch using only knit stitches, without having to knit it in the round!
Chris Silker, Minneapolis, MN

BELT LOOPS

Next rnd: *With larger dpns, inc1 into the next 2 sts—4 sts. With these 4 sts, work in I-cord for 11 rows. BO and break yarn, leaving a 6" tail.

Join yarn to the sts on the circular needle, work 10 sts in est patt. Rep from * to end of round—11 (12, 13, 14, 15) belt loops.

TOP OF BODY

With B and smaller circular needle *k1, inc1 in next st; rep from * to end of round, pu sts along back of each belt loop and working them in inc patt as est as you pass them—198 (216, 234, 252, 270) sts.

Work even in St st for 5 (5½, 6, 6½, 7)".

K42 (45, 49, 53, 56); place next 15 (18, 19, 20, 23) sts on holder for underarm.

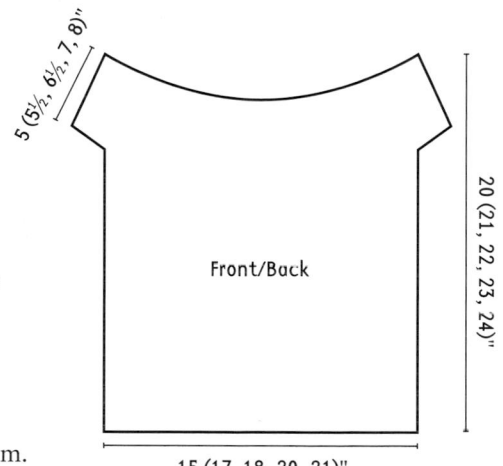

5 (5½, 6½, 7, 8)"

20 (21, 22, 23, 24)"

Front/Back

15 (17, 18, 20, 21)"

LEFT SLEEVE

With a new ball of CC and smaller dpns, CO 70 (78, 82, 89, 96) sts and divide among needles.

Join and work in St st for 1½ (2, 2½, 3, 3½)". Place first 15 (18, 19, 20, 23) sts of rnd on holder for underarm.

JOIN SLEEVE TO BODY

With smaller circular needle holding body sts, k55 (60, 63, 69, 73) sts of the sleeve from dpns. K84 (90, 98, 106, 112) body sts. Place rem 15 (18, 19, 20, 23) sts on holder for underarm.

RIGHT SLEEVE

Work as for left sleeve, place first 15 (18, 19, 20, 23) sts of rnd on holder, and join sleeve to body by knitting across sleeve sts with smaller circular needle holding body sts.

Work rem 42 (45, 49, 53, 56) body sts to complete round— 278 (300, 322, 350, 370) sts.

Work even in St st for 3½ (3½, 4, 4, 4½)".

Next rnd: *K1, k2tog; rep from * to end of rnd.

BO.

FINISHING

Stitch belt loops to body.

Graft underarms with kitchener st.

Weave in ends.

Thread ribbon through belt loops and tie. Trim ends if desired.

About Jenna

I learned to knit from my grandmother when I was eighteen, although it did not turn into an obsession until I was twenty-six, when my partner and I were trying unsuccessfully to conceive. In need of an outlet for my unquenched maternal urge, I knit baby clothes with a passion. Today my long-awaited four-year-old son and my partner are regular recipients of my knitting. With a degree in sociology and women's studies, I have a love of and interest in traditional female crafts. You can find me (and all of my knitting) online at www.thisgirlknits.com. I work in the software industry in Seattle, but dream of being paid fabulously to design knit garments full-time.

KIMBERLY FAIRCHILD

Sexie

Size

XS (S, M, L, XL)

Finished bust: 19 (23, 27, 31, 35)"
(see Note)

Finished length: 15 (16, 16½, 18½, 20)"

Materials

Berroco Glacé (100% rayon; 50g/75 yds)

MC: 5 (6, 8, 10, 11) skeins #2562
Emulsion (#2655 Cool Red)

CC: 1 skein #2422 Plum (#2012 Black)

US 7 (4.5mm) straight needles,
or size needed to obtain gauge

US 7 (4.5mm) double-pointed needles
(set of 2)

US G/6 (4mm) crochet hook

Stitch holders

Gauge

20 sts and 28 rows = 4" in St st

Note: The Berroco Glacé knits up to a very
silky, stretchy material, and the eyelets in
back also stretch out, meaning that this
halter can comfortably fit a chest that is
10" larger than the finished measurements
above.

Who thought the inspiration for a halter top could come from a male comedian? This halter's original design was created while watching the very sexy Eddie Izzard perform his standup show "Sexie." After some experimenting and tweaking, the final product is a hot little number that can be dressed up or down, but will always inspire that sexy, sassy self-confidence that Eddie displays onstage.

This halter is a quick one-piece knit with little finishing needed. The lace is created by a simple yarn-over pattern, and the center eyelets line up in a column thanks to a clever p2tog on the wrong side. The ribbon yarn adds a nice shine. Experiment with your own color combinations to create something unique. The back tie can be tightened or loosened to give a perfect fit and an open or closed look.

DIRECTIONS

With MC, CO 90 (110, 130, 150, 170) sts.

Row 1 (RS): K2, yo, p2tog, *k2, p2; rep from * to last 4 sts, p2tog, yo, k2.

Row 2: P2, *k2, p2; rep from * to end.

Row 3: K1, *yo, k2tog; rep from * 6 (6, 6, 9, 9) times; k30 (40, 50, 54, 64), yo, k30 (40, 50, 54, 64), **ssk, yo; rep from ** 6 (6, 6, 9, 9) times, k1.

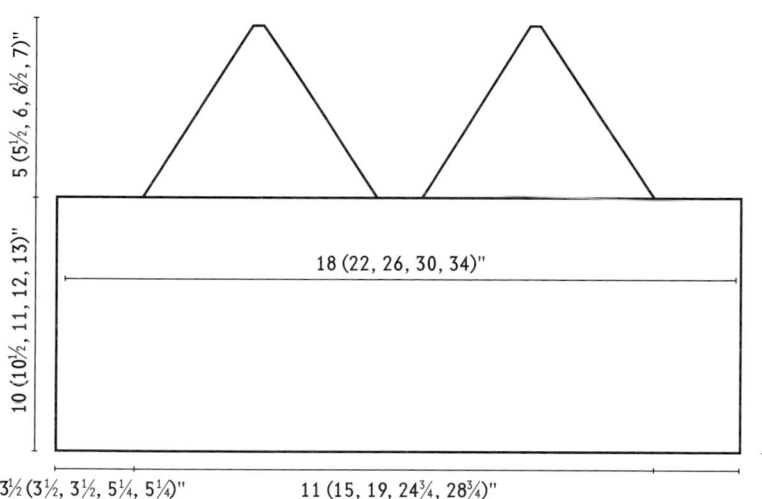

5 (5½, 6, 6½, 7)"

10 (10½, 11, 12, 13)"

18 (22, 26, 30, 34)"

15 (16, 17, 18½, 20)"

3½ (3½, 3½, 5¼, 5¼)"   11 (15, 19, 24¾, 28¾)"

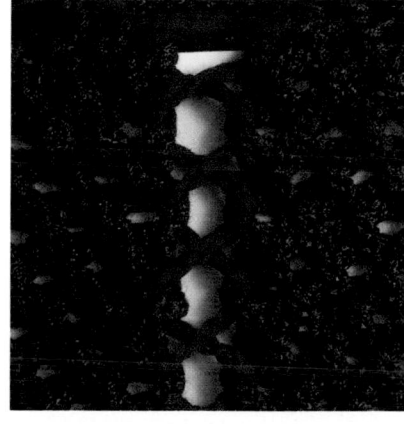

Lace up the back as tightly or as loosely as you want.

Rows 4 and 8: P44 (54, 64, 74, 84), p2tog, p to end.

Rows 5 and 9: K.

Row 6: P.

Row 7: K2, *yo, k2tog; rep from * 6 (6, 6, 9, 9) times; k29 (39, 49, 53, 63), yo, k29 (39, 49, 53, 63), **ssk, yo; rep from ** to last 2 sts, k2.

Row 10: P.

Rep rows 3–10 until work measures 10 (10½, 11, 12, 13)" from beg (measured over St st center panel) and end with a row 6 or 10.

Next row: K2, yo, p2tog, *k2, p2; rep from * 2 (2, 2, 3, 3) times; k29 (39, 49, 55, 65), yo, k29 (39, 49, 55, 65), **p2, k2; rep from ** 2 (2, 2, 3, 3) times, p2tog, yo, k2.

Next row: *P2, k2; rep from * 3 (3, 3, 4, 4) times; k1, p27 (37, 47, 53, 63), p2tog, p27 (37, 47, 53, 63), k1, **k2, p2; rep from ** to end.

Next row: BO 17 (17, 17, 23, 23) sts in 1 × 1 rib, k27 (37, 47, 53, 63), BO 2, k27 (37, 47, 53, 63), p1, work in 1 × 1 rib to end.

Next row: BO 17 (17, 17, 23, 23) sts in 1 × 1 rib, p27 (37, 47, 53, 63), join new yarn to left side and p27 (37, 47, 53, 63).

Next row (RS, working both sides at the same time): K1, k2tog, k to last 3 sts, ssk, k1.

Next row: P.

Rep last 2 rows until 5 (5, 7, 9, 11) sts rem.

Next row: K1 (1, 2, 3, 4), k2tog, k2 (2, 3, 4, 5).

Next row: P.

Next row: K1 (1, 1, 2, 3), k2tog, k1 (1, 2, 3, 4).

Next row: P.

Place rem sts on holders.

FINISHING

With CC, RS facing, and beg to the right of the live stitches of the right side, SC around neck from the right side to the live sts of the left side. *Make 1 extra sc loop and transfer this and the live sts to a dpn.

Next row: K1, k2tog 1 (1, 2, 2, 3) times, k1 (1, 1, 2, 2).

Work in I-cord on rem sts until cord is long enough to comfortably tie around your neck (approx. 10").*

With RS live sts, rep from * to *.

With CC, crochet a chain 60" long.

Lace the tie up the back, starting with rib hole at bottom and lacing into each side hole from the k2 yo rows (skip the k1 yo rows).

Weave in ends.

About Kimberly

To reduce my boredom in graduate school, I got my grandmom to teach me to knit. Since then, I've created sweaters, scarves, and bags and developed a strong addiction to yarn, needles, and knitting magazines and books. When I'm not satisfying my knitting jones, I'm taking classes and conducting research on my way to a Ph.D. in social psychology from Rutgers University. I've been lucky enough to teach my own classes, my favorite of which is the psychology of women. Next semester I'll even be teaching a knitting class! Now if only I could find a way to do the psychology of knitting. . . . You can keep up with my knitting adventures at www.eden.rutgers.edu/~kfairchi/knitting.html.

Don't Get Your Knitters in a Twist

WORDS TO KNIT BY

There are no mistakes, only unique variations in the design.

Design something. Even if it's just a coaster.

Patterns are guidelines, not absolute rules.

Knit at lunchtime; it'll calm you for the afternoon.

Ali Hawke, St. Louis, MO

● If you can't decide whether an error in your knitting needs to be frogged or can be ignored, just remember what we say in my knitting group: "If you couldn't spot it from a prancing pony, it isn't that big a deal." It is unclear, however, if you are viewing the object from the prancing pony or if you are watching it go by on said prancing pony. *Lucy Lee, Cambridge, MA*

● My tip, as a beginner, is to have a glass of wine to sip on while you knit. Your stitches might not be perfect but you'll be feeling relaxed, and, hey, isn't relaxation one of the major benefits of knitting? *Andrea Nold, St. Louis, MO*

STITCH 'N BITCH ACROSS THE NATION
The Southwest

Boulder, Colorado

BOULDER, COLORADO, SNB

Set in the shadow of the breathtaking flagstone peaks of the Flatirons, the Boulder Stitch 'n Bitch group mirrors its eclectic, laid-back town. After moving here, I knit my first hat on Thanksgiving Day of 2002. A year later, I started a Stitch 'n Bitch group with a handful of knitters, and within six months we had grown to nearly fifty. We meet three times a month at a trendy teahouse or an Irish pub, which kind of sums up our group—we're a tea and Guinness crowd. Among our members are teachers, college students, obsessive knitters, free-form ("What's a gauge, anyway?") knitters, pattern knitters, sparkly-yarn knitters, and knitters who can't believe there will ever be a day when they can knit without looking. We make even our lone crocheter feel at home. Tara Jon Manning, who authored *Men in Knits,* is an inspiring member of our group. Many of us have completed projects from her book, and we enjoy having her around to hit up for tips and suggestions. We urge all visiting knitters to join in the stitching and bitching when they're in town.

Brenda Payne

DENVER, COLORADO, SNB

Our group is relatively new, having started in March 2004, but Denver Stitch 'n Bitch has more than fifty members, with a core group of six and some out-of-state knitters who just want to connect with a sisterhood. When we started the group we didn't know what we were getting into, who would be interested, or how much fun it would be. We tend to draw comments wherever we go. Our favorite reaction was from a woman

Denver, Colorado

who frantically knocked on the window of the coffee shop to get our attention and ran inside to tell us how cool she thought the meeting was.

We've gone on field trips to visit local yarn stores, and we get regular updates on one member's ex-husband. We call him "H," and because of his ever-present personality, we've thought of changing the group name to Stitch 'n H. Another bonding activity is hating on our LYS yarn Nazi.

We've been amazed by the immediate bond we've formed with one another, how big needles can be, our members' willingness to explore and share secrets, why felted bags shrink one way and not the other, and how many male knitters there are. Our favorite meeting place is Lisa Marie's Coffee and Tea House, but for summer gatherings, we are looking for a great margarita-with-a-patio spot.

Amber Bell

PHOENIX, ARIZONA, SNB

I got the urge to knit when my mother-in-law, who hails from Northern Ireland, knit a roll-neck sweater for my daughter. About that time, I moved to Portland, Oregon, for six months, took classes at Northwest Wools, and fell in love with knitting. I was sad to have to leave such a knitter-friendly city, and I was concerned that in the Arizona climate there would be little interest in knitting.

Phoenix, Arizona

I needn't have worried—Phoenix Stitchin' and Bitchin's first meeting, at the end of 2003, drew about thirty very enthusiastic knitters and crocheters, and we now have a growing e-mail list of more than one hundred. Our members span an incredible range of ages from eighteen-year-old newbies to experienced grandmas. We have a loose requirement that members knit one item a year for charity. The first beneficiary was Banner Desert Hospital in Mesa. We knit lap robes, blankets, hats, and booties for preemie babies and cancer patients, then collected the items in early December and delivered them for Christmas.

Kim Dallas

SALT LAKE CITY, UTAH, SNB

Salt Lake City is such a conservative place that just meeting in a coffee shop can peg you as some sort of revolutionary. But that's cool with SLC SnB. Our nearly forty members are outspoken,

witty, blatant, daring, kind, and supportive. Our ages span thirty-plus years, and we are married, single, straight, bi, young, young at heart, mothers, grandmothers, teachers, midwives, stand-up comedians, Web-site developers, librarians, feminists, thinkers, as well as knitters.

Some of us travel more than forty miles for the Tuesday knit nights—it's that much fun! Sometimes I don't get much knitting of my own done because I'm too busy admiring someone else's project, teaching a newbie the basics, or knitting a few rows for another knitter, but I always enjoy the experience. We all do. The warmth, the sharing, the openness, the raucous laughter . . . It's all there and it's all good. We're having a ball.

Laurie Oberg Hadden

Salt Lake City, Utah

JENNA ADORNO

Mud Flap Girl Tank Top

emember when Thelma and Louise first tackled the mud flap girl in that great chick flick? When they lured an offensive truck driver with a girl-clad truck off the road, women everywhere cheered. But in the end our unfortunate heroines died. On *Sex in the City,* liberated Samantha sported a mud flap girl necklace. She went on to stay happily single, remaining carefree and proudly alive. Now, *that's* worth commemorating on a mud flap.

This tank was designed for all the strong, sassy, female-positive women everywhere. What's better than a sexy girl sporting a sexy girl image and taking it as her own?

DIRECTIONS

BACK

With MC, CO 80 (90, 100, 110, 120) sts.

Next row (RS): P 1 row.

Beg with a p row, work in St st until piece measures 2" from beg, ending with RS facing.

Next (dec) row: K1, k2tog, k to last 3 sts, ssk, k1.

Working in St st, rep dec row every foll 4th row to 64 (74, 84, 94, 104) sts.

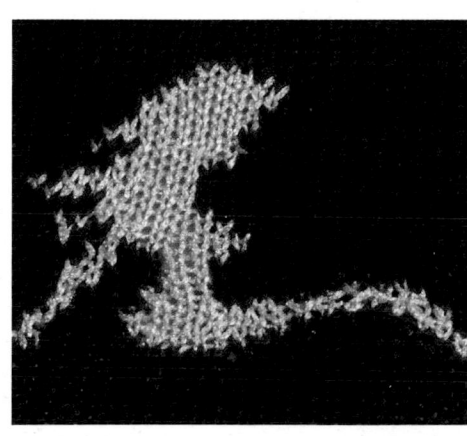

Size

Women's XS (S, M, l, Xl)

Finished bust: 32 (36, 40, 44, 48)"

Finished length: 20 (20, 21, 21, 22½)"

Materials

MC: Brown Sheep Cotton Fleece (80% cotton, 20% wool; 100g/215 yds), 3 (4, 4, 5, 5) skeins #CW005 Cavern

CC: Berroco Metallic FX (85% rayon, 15% metallic; 25g/85 yds), 1 skein #1002 Silver

US 6 (4mm) straight needles, or size needed to obtain gauge

US G/6 (4mm) crochet hook

Stitch holders

Tapestry needle

Gauge

20 sts and 28 rows = 4" in St st using MC

Special Skill

INTARSIA

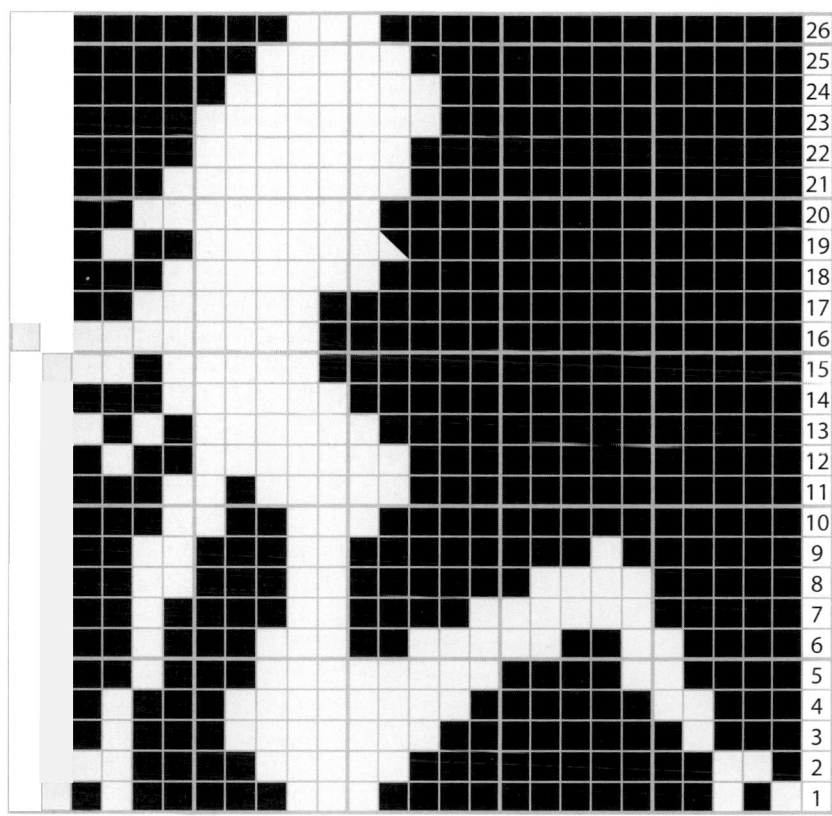

About Jenna
See Ultra Femme, page 125 for Jenna's bio.

■ MC □ CC

◣ CC half duplicate stitch

Work even in St st until piece measures 7" from beg, ending with RS facing.**

Next (inc) row: K1, m1, k to last 2 sts, m1, k1.

Working in St st, rep inc row every foll 4th row to 80 (90, 100, 110, 120) sts.

Work even in St st until piece measures 12½" from beg.

Shape armholes:

BO 4 (4, 5, 6, 6) sts at beg of next 2 (4, 4, 2, 4) rows, 3 (3, 3, 5, 5) sts at beg of next 2 (2, 4, 2, 4) rows, 2 (2, 0, 4, 0) sts at beg of next 4 (2, 0, 4, 0) rows. Dec 1 st at each edge of EOR to 44 (48, 50, 52, 54) sts.

Shape neck:

K16 (18, 19, 19, 20), place these sts on a holder, BO 12 (12, 12, 14, 14), k to end.

Next row: P to end.

Next row: BO3, k to end.

Next row: P to end.

Next row: BO2, k to end.

Next row: P to end.

Dec 1 st from neck edge every row 3 (5, 5, 5, 5) times—8 (8, 9, 9, 10) sts.

Work even in St st until piece measures 7½ (7½, 8, 8, 8½)" from beg of armhole shaping.

Place sts on st holder.

Transfer left strap sts to needles and work as for right strap, reversing shaping.

FRONT

Work as for back to **.

Next (inc) row: K1, m1, k to last 2 sts, m1, k1.

Working in St st, rep inc row every foll 4th row to 80 (90, 100, 110, 120) sts; *at the same time,* when piece has been increased to 76 (86, 96, 106, 116) sts, beg working from chart as foll with RS facing.

Next row: K25 (30, 35, 40, 45), work 26 chart sts, k25 (30, 35, 40, 45).

Cont as est for back, working from chart while shaping.

FINISHING

Join front and back straps with kitchener st.

Sew side seams.

Crab st around armholes and neckline.

Add single half duplicate stitch for nose.

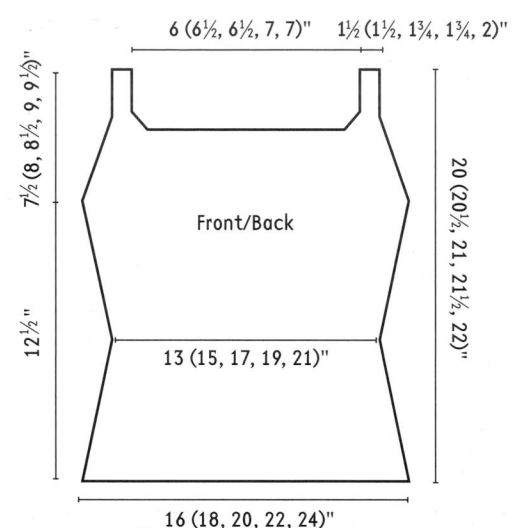

6 (6½, 6½, 7, 7)"   1½ (1½, 1¾, 1¾, 2)"

7½ (8, 8½, 9, 9½)"

20 (20½, 21, 21½, 22)"

Front/Back

12½"

13 (15, 17, 19, 21)"

16 (18, 20, 22, 24)"

Slip Up

MAKING A NICER DECREASE

The next time a pattern calls for an ssk decrease (slip as to knit, slip as to knit, then knit both together), try making a spk instead: Slip as to knit, slip as to purl, then knit both together. It seems to make a smoother-lying decrease. *Margene Merrill Smith, Salt Lake City, UT*

JOAN MCGOWAN-MICHAEL

Quick and Dirty
2-NEEDLE FISHNET STOCKINGS

Size
One size

Materials
Cascade Fixation (98.3% cotton, 1.7% elastic; 50g/100 yds relaxed, 186 yds stretched), 2 balls #6185 Hot Pink OR #8990 Black

US 6 (4mm) straight needles, or size needed to obtain gauge

US 8 (5mm) straight needles

Tapestry needle

Stitch markers

Elastic thread (optional)

Gauge
20 sts and 32 rows = 4" in St st on smaller needles.

e ven the knitter who is double-pointed-needle- or lace-impaired can bang out these sexy, seamed, lacy stockings in a weekend. They're worked from the toe up, so simply stop knitting and add some ribbing when they're the length you want. Then, to keep these thigh-highs from falling down, wear them with garters (sexy!).

When asked if this stitch had a name, I had to think for a moment, and realized that this was a pattern that I'd used to make windowpane vests for my Barbie doll in the late '60s. Since I don't recall seeing it in any stitch dictionaries, it may very well be the product of a seven-year-old mind. In any event, when stretched over a shapely leg it becomes an attractive openwork stocking pattern.

STITCH PATTERN
WINDOWPANE STITCH
*K1, return same st to left-hand needle, k same st again, return same st to left-hand needle, k same st again for total k3 times each st; rep from * across row.

DIRECTIONS
TOE
With smaller needles, CO 12 sts.

P 1 row.

Next row: K3, pm, k6, pm, k3.

Work in St st, increasing 1 st before first and after second marker on every RS row 4 times—20 sts.

P 1 row.

Work in windowpane st until piece measures 4" from beg, ending with RS facing.

Next 2 RS rows: K1, m1, work in windowpane st to last st, m1, k1—24 sts.

Work 1 row even in windowpane st.

Dec 1 st at each edge on next, then EOR 3 times—16 sts.

Work in windowpane st for 5", ending with RS facing.

Change to larger needles.

Next (inc) row: K1, m1, work in windowpane st to last st, m1, k1—18 sts.

Work in windowpane st for 3", ending with RS facing.

Rep inc row next, then every 4th row 2 times—24 sts.

Work in windowpane st until piece measures 27" from beg (or to desired length), ending with RS facing.

Next row: K, picking up 1 st between each st—47 sts.

Change to smaller needles.

Work in 2 × 2 rib for 1½".

BO in rib patt.

FINISHING

Fold stocking so that seam is centered in back; seam across toe. Loosely seam back leg.

Lightly press with cool iron.

Optional: Sew elastic thread invisibly through WS of ribbing.

About Joan

I like to knit and I like to make clothes. Thankfully, I can do both from my recliner. For the past twenty years, I've been designing clothing professionally, including a lengthy stint at Frederick's of Hollywood. My company, White Lies Designs, specializes in romantic (and provocative!) knitting patterns for a wide range of sizes. I've had designs and articles published in *Vogue Knitting, Interweave Knits, Knitters, Cast On,* and other knitting publications, and keep a Web site at www.whitelies designs.com.

Block Out with Your Sock Out

HOW TO MAKE A SOCK BLOCKER FROM A WIRE HANGER

Start with your average triangle-shape wire hanger. Imagine that the hook is point A, the left-hand corner is B, and right-hand corner is C. Place your index finger halfway between B and C and pull away from A, creating a diamond shape. Now push B in toward C, so that the point is concave instead of convex, and voilà—you have a sock shape. These hangers are great when you don't have the space for all those wool socks you've knit to lie flat to dry; just hang them up on a shower rod or anywhere else that's easy. *Amanda White Berka, Fort Collins, CO*

Show me your tips!

A

C

B

push! B

A

C

;pull! & down

ZOE SARGENT

Itsy-Bitsy Teeny-Weeny Purple Polka-Dot Tankini

Last winter I made the bikini from the first *Stitch 'n Bitch* book and added my own polka-dot pattern. I liked it a lot, but wanted something a little different, and even more dots. Several revisions and a billion polka dots later, this tankini was born. The top can work with shorts or a skirt off the beach, too.

The yarn I used has a bit of elastic for a nice snug fit. I modeled the bottoms on my favorite, best-fitting underwear. They have a good amount of coverage but won't make you look like you're wearing granny panties. It's perfect for sunbathing and frolicking on the beach. Have fun, and don't forget your sunscreen!

DIRECTIONS

TOP FRONT

With MC, CO 90 (98, 106) sts.

Rows 1–3: Work in 1 × 1 rib.

Row 4: P.

Rows 5–17: Work from chart for 12 rows, working first and last st of every row in MC.

Next (dec) row: K2, k2tog, k to last 4 sts, ssk, k2.

Rep dec row every 10th row twice more—84 (92, 100) sts.

Work even in St st until piece measures 6 (6½, 7)" from beg, ending with RS facing.

Size

Women's S (M, L)

Finished bust: 28 (31, 33)"

Finished hip: 28½ (30, 32½)"

To fit bust: 34 (36, 38)"

To fit hips: 36 (38, 40)"

Materials

Cascade Fixation (98.3% cotton, 1.7% elastic; 50g/186 yds)

MC: 4 (5, 6) skeins #2406 Light Purple

CC: 1 skein #6388 Dark Purple

US 3 (3.25mm) straight needles, or size needed to obtain gauge

Stitch holder

2 yards ¼" elastic

Sewing needle and thread

Gauge

24 sts and 40 rows = 4" in St st

Special Skill

FAIR ISLE

Next (inc) row: K2, inc1, K to last 3 sts, inc1, k2.

Rep inc row every 9th row twice more—90 (98, 106) sts.

Work from chart 2 for 5 rows, working first and last st of every row in MC.**

Knitting the first and last sts of every row, shape left side of halter as follows, while maintaining the integrity of the chart:

Next row (RS facing): K45 (49, 53), place rem sts on holder.

Next row: K3, p2tog tbl, p to last 3 sts, k3.

Setup row: K4 (6, 8), work from chart, k3 (5, 7).

Cont to work garter edges in MC and center sts from chart as est, shape left side of halter:

Rows 1, 3, 15, 17, 19, 29, 31, 37, and 39: P.

Rows 2, 14, 16, 18, 20, and 22: K to last 5 sts, ssk, k3.

Rows 4, 6, 8, 10, 12, 24, 26, and 34: K.

Rows 5, 7, 9, 11, 13, and 21: K3, p2tog tbl, p to last 3 sts, k3.

Rows 23, 25, 27, 33, and 35: K3, p2tog tbl, p to last 5 sts, p2tog, k3.

Rows 28, 30, 32, 36, 38, and 40: K3, k2tog, k to last 5 sts, ssk, k3.

Row 41: K3, p2tog tbl, p to last 5 sts, p2tog, k3.

Medium and large only:

Next row: K3, k2tog, k to last 5 sts, ssk, k3. Next row: K3, p2tog tbl, p to last 5 sts, p2tog, k3.

Large only:

Rep last 2 rows once.

All sizes:

Next row: K2, k2tog, ssk, k2—6 sts.

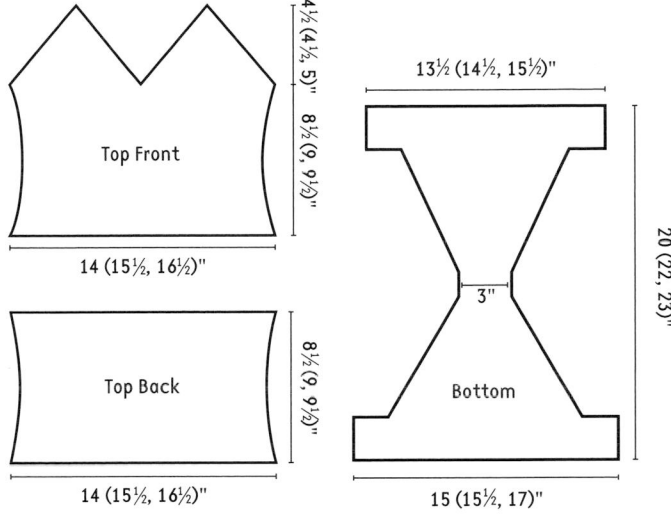

Strap:

Work in garter st on rem 6 sts for 16" or to a length that will tie comfortably around the neck. BO.

Right side of halter:

Work as for left side, reversing shaping and chart.

TOP BACK

Work as for front to **.

Work in 1 × 1 rib for 3 rows.

BO.

BIKINI BOTTOM

With MC, CO 82 (88, 94) sts.

Rows 1–3: Work in 1 × 1 rib.

Row 4: P.

Rows 5–17: Work from chart for 12 rows.

Work in St st for 2 (2½, 3)", ending with RS facing.

Next row: K52 (55, 59) beg with a k st, work in 1 × 1 rib to end.

Next row: Work in 1 × 1 rib for 30 (33, 35) sts, k22 (22, 24), rib to end.

Rep last row once.

Next row: BO 27 (30, 32), rib 2 sts, k24 (24, 26), rib to end.

Next row: BO 27 (30, 32), rib 2 sts, p to end.

P the first and last st of every row, cont as follows:

Next (dec) row: P3, k2tog, k to last 5 sts, ssk, p3. Rep dec row every 6th row 4 (4, 5) times more.

Work even in St st for 2 (2, 3)".

P 1 row.

Inc 1 st on each edge, 3 sts in from edge of next row, then EOR 25 (27, 29) times more, then EOR 10 (10, 12) times more—90 (94, 102) sts.

Next row: K1, p1, k to last 2 sts, p1, k1.

Next row: P1, k1, p to last 2 sts, k1, p1.

Next row: K1, p1, k to last 2 sts, p1, k1.

Work even in St st for 2 (2½, 3)".

Work from chart 1 for 12 rows.

Work in 1 × 1 rib for 3 rows.

BO.

FINISHING

Seam top sides.

Seam bottom sides.

Weave in ends.

Attach elastic:

Turn the bottom inside out. On the inside top edge along the ribbing, attach one end of the elastic to a side seam with a safety pin. Thread tapestry needle with several feet of doubled MC and secure end underneath elastic. Work in herringbone st over elastic around entire waistband.

Try the bottom on and adjust elastic to fit. Sew elastic ends tog with thread.

MC ▮   CC ▮

— Repeat —

Chart rows: 14, 13, 12, 11, 10, 9, 8, 7, 6, 5, 4, 3, 2, 1

About Zoe

I started knitting at age seven at a Waldorf School, and all the scarves, socks, and swimsuits I've knitted since then could probably reach around the globe—or at least around the block a couple of times (but it's a large block). The tankini is my ultimate creation so far. Tentative future plans include knitting sweaters for my pet chickens to protect them from the frigid Boston winters. I'm a recent graduate of the Sudbury Valley School and hope to pursue a career that involves my passion for all things crafty and to continue my other interests—gardening, yoga, and belly dancing.

JAMIE CHUPICK

Accidentally on Purpose

DROP STITCH VEST

Size

Women's S (M, L)

Finished bust: 30 (39, 48)"

Finished length: 23 (24, 25)"

Materials

Patons Grace
(100% mercerized cotton; 50g/136
yds), 5 (7, 9) skeins #438 Fuchsia

US 5 (3.5mm) straight needles,
or size needed to obtain gauge

Stitch holder

Tapestry needle

Gauge

24 sts and 26 rows = 4" in St st

16 sts and 26 rows = 4" in drop st patt

Abbreviations

DBO2: Drop next st, lift up resulting
ladder, k into front of ladder, k into back
of ladder, BO first st, BO next st.

On WS, work as for RS but p into front
and then back of ladder.

this vest was originally designed to be machine knit with much finer yarn. But it's so versatile that any weight of yarn may be used, and it can be worn in various ways. It's casual and funky worn with a long- or short-sleeved T-shirt underneath, and totally sexy with just a camisole. The smooth and silky cotton yarn makes a sleek, stretchy fabric, and it's fun to knit, too. The stitch pattern only happens as you are binding off stitches at the very end. It's a lot like turning a hole in your stocking into a "ladder," except the stitches will "run" down from the neck instead of upward.

There's no shaping needed for the armholes or the back (even at the neck). So, even though the directions look complicated, it's a breeze. You get to drop stitches all the way down to the bottom—on purpose!

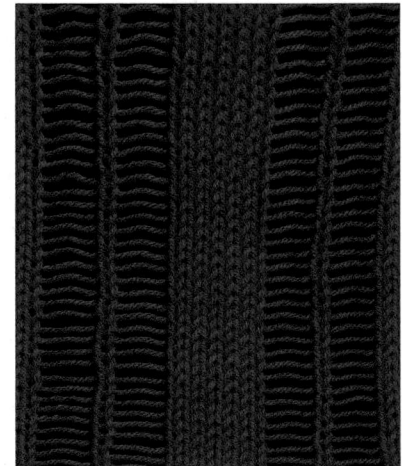

DIRECTIONS

FRONT

CO 60 (78, 96) sts.

Work even in St st until piece measures 21 (22, 23)"
from beg, ending with RS facing.

Little Miss Marker

IDEAS FOR IMPROVISED STITCH MARKERS

I have a large collection of unused earrings. Some I grew out of, others were fashion no-nos, and some became single after their buddy was lost. I've been able to give those abandoned and orphaned earrings new life. You see, like Wonder Woman, they have a secret identity—they're not just earrings, they're stitch markers! Those with a hook or post can be used as row markers by simply slipping them gently through stitches in your work, while hoops or those with kidney-style findings can be used to mark stitches on your needles.
Marie Irshad, Cardiff, Wales

● Plastic-coated paper clips (not to be confused with all-plastic paper clips) make dandy markers and can be purchased in large quantities at any office supply store.
Evelyn Rowe

● You can always use one of your old rings that doesn't fit anymore as a stitch marker. It's a great way to see it every day and get some joy out of it—rather than keeping it tucked away in a drawer. *Catherine Clift, Melbourne, Australia*

● I use the very small "ouchless" hair elastics—those elasticky circles, about ¾" across, and sold in a bag of a hundred—as stitch markers. They come in many colors, which makes it easy to keep track of which part you're marking.
Anne Leonard

Shape neck, right side:

Small:
Next row: K26 and place these sts on a holder, DBO2, BO6, DBO2, k26.

Next and all WS rows: P.

Next row: BO1, DBO2, BO1, k to end.

Next RS row: BO4, k to end.

Next RS row: BO1, DBO2, BO1, k to end.

Next RS row: DBO2, BO2, k to end.

Next RS row: BO4, k to end.

Next RS row: DBO2, BO1, DBO2, BO6.

Medium:
Next row: K33 and place these sts on a holder, DBO2, BO1, DBO2, BO6, DBO2, BO1, DBO2, k33.

Next and all WS rows: P.

Next RS row: BO4, k to end. Next RS row: BO2, DBO2, BO1, k to end.

Next RS row: DBO2, BO3, k to end. Next RS row: BO3, DBO2, k to end.

Next RS row: BO1, DBO2, BO1, k to end.

Next RS row: BO3, k to end.

Next RS row: BO2, DBO2, BO1, DBO2, BO6.

Large:
Next row: K41 and place these sts on a holder, BO1, DBO2, BO1, DBO2, BO6, DBO2, BO1, DBO2, BO1, k41.

Next and all WS rows: P.

Next RS row: BO3, k to end.

Next RS row: BO2, DBO2, k to end.

Next RS row: BO1, DBO2, BO1, k to end.

Next RS row: BO3, k to end.

Next RS row: BO2, DBO2, k to end.

Next RS row: BO1, DBO2, BO1, k to end.

Next RS row: BO3, k to end.

Next RS row: BO2, DBO2, BO1, k to end.

Next RS row: DBO2, BO3, k to end.

Next RS row: BO3, DBO2, BO1, DBO2, BO6.

Shape neck, left side:

Transfer holder sts to needle and work as for right side, connecting yarn at neck edge and beg with a WS (p) row, reversing shaping.

BACK

CO 60 (78, 96) sts.

Work even in St st until piece measures 23 (24, 25)" from beg, ending with RS facing.

Next row: *BO 6, DBO2, BO1, DBO2; rep from * 5 (7, 9) times, BO 6.

FINISHING

Seam shoulders.

Seam sides from CO edge to 7 (8, 8½)" below beg of shoulder BO.

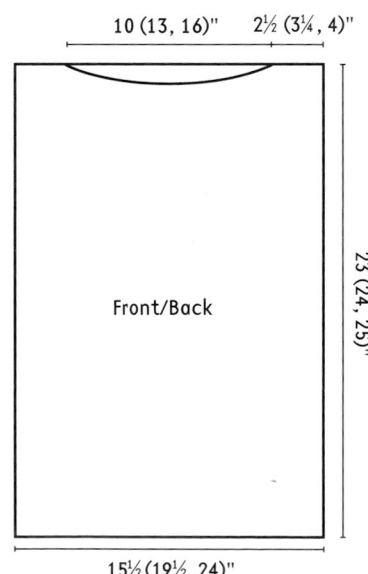

10 (13, 16)"   2½ (3¼, 4)"

Front/Back

23 (24, 25)"

15½ (19½, 24)"

About Jamie

My grandmother taught me how to knit and crochet when I was seven, but I never imagined I would be pursuing it as a career. In fact, it wasn't until I was eighteen and moved from Dallas to Los Angeles to study textile design that I discovered my passion for knitting. I am currently developing Little Ditties, a line of sweaters, ponchos, wristbands, legwarmers, and other accessories. They are available at chocosho.com, a forum where designers and artists sell their creations. When I'm not busy knitting, I work as a designer of quilting fabrics.

STEFANIE JAPEL

Totally Tubular
MINISKIRT/BOOB TUBE

t he idea for this pattern came to me while packing for a trip last spring. I travel a lot and was thinking that if one piece of clothing could have multiple uses, it would cut down on the number of things I'd have to take in my suitcase. Then I remembered the "modular clothing" of the mid-'80s: simple tubes, rectangles, and squares and combined in an infinite number of ways. A shirt could be a skirt or be scrunched up into a belt. Here's my take on that concept—a multifunctional piece of clothing that can go from boob tube to miniskirt. On a cool evening, it can be a shoulder warmer. On a hot day, you can wear it as a skirt.

STITCH PATTERNS
LACE PATTERN (TUBE 1 ONLY)
Rnd 1: *K2tog, yo; rep from * 9 times.

Rnds 2 and 4: K.

Rnd 3: *Yo, k2tog; rep from * 9 times.

BOBBLE STITCH (TUBE 1 ONLY)
K3 into next stitch, turn, p3, turn, k3, turn, sl1, k2tog, psso.

LACE PATTERN (TUBE 2 ONLY)
Rnds 1, 3, 5, and 7: Yo, k2tog, yo.

Rnds 2, 4, 6, and 8: K.

Rnd 9: yo, k2tog.

Size
Finished waist or shoulder: 27 (31, 35, 39)"

Finished length: 18 (18, 19, 19)"

Materials
Berroco Cotton Twist (70% mercerized cotton, 30% rayon; 50g/85 yds)

Tube 1
7 (7, 8, 9) skeins #8311 True Red

Tube 2
7 (7, 8, 9) skeins #8387 Soul

US 5 (3.5mm) 24" circular needle

US 8 (5mm) 24" circular needle, or size needed to obtain gauge

Gauge
20 sts and 24 rows = 4" in St st with larger needle

24 sts and 36 rows = 4" in St st with smaller needle

Special Skill
LACE

VEGAS OR BUST

DIRECTIONS, TUBE 1

With smaller needle, CO 160 (180, 200, 220) sts.

Join and pm to mark beg of rnds, work 5 rnds in garter st.

Work in St st until piece measures 4½ (4½, 5½, 5½)" from beg.

Change to larger needle and K 1 rnd.

Next rnd: Work in lace patt for 20 sts, pm, k40 (50, 60, 70), pm, work in lace patt for Tube 1 for 20 sts, pm, k80 (90, 100, 110).

Circular Logic

TIPS FOR WORKING WITH CIRCULAR NEEDLES

To alleviate the "crazed serpentine" nature of circular needles, dip the plastic cords that connect the needle points into boiling water for just a second to release them and soften them up. I pull them straight while they cool, and it seems to make them less twisty and much easier to work with. *Katy Burns, Chicago, IL*

● With circular needles, the place where the plastic cable joins the needle is often smoother on one side than it is on the other. Reserve the smoother join for the needle you are knitting *from*, since this is the end where you'll be pushing stitches from the cable onto the needle, and any imperfections in the join will snag your stitches. The end you are knitting *to* has stitches just worked sliding from the needle to the (smaller) cable, so it usually doesn't matter much if this join isn't as nice. *Joan Dyer, New York, NY*

● When starting a piece of circular knitting, cast on one more stitch than is required for the pattern. When getting ready to join (on the first row of knitting), slip the extra stitch from the right needle to the left, then knit these first two stitches together (the first cast-on and the last cast-on "extra stitch"). This will leave the correct number of stitches on your needles and will give a great, almost invisible join at the beginning of the work. *Catherine Clift, Melbourne, Australia*

Cont as est, working lace patt at sides and St st between, until piece measures 16 (16, 17, 17)" from beg.

TRIM

Work 5 rnds in garter st.

Work 2 rnds in St st.

Next rnd: *K4, make bobble; rep from * to end of round.

Work 2 rnds in St st.

Work 5 rnds in garter st.

BO.

DIRECTIONS, TUBE 2

With smaller needle, CO 160 (180, 200, 220) sts.

Join and work 5 rnds in garter st.

Work in St st until piece measures 3 (4, 4, 4½)" from beg.

Change to larger needle and work 5 rnds in St st.

Next 9 rnds: K10, work lace patt for Tube 2, k to end.

Work 5 rnds in St st.

Next 9 rnds: K15, work lace patt, k to end.

Work 5 rnds in St st.

Cont as est, working 5 more sts before lace patt with every rep until 30 sts have been worked before lace patt.

Work 5 rnds in St st.

Work 5 rnds in garter st.

BO.

About Stefanie

I was born in Wichita, Kansas, and lived in eight different towns before my parents settled in Pleasant Hill, Iowa, when I was in third grade. I've got two postgraduate degrees in geology and currently live in Mainz, Germany, where I'm a research scientist in high-pressure mineral physics. I was first taught to knit when I was eight by my grandmother but I didn't become completely obsessed until I was twenty and playing drums in an all-girl punk band (called Period). I had to have cool stuff to wear at our performances so people would see me way back there behind three hot guitar players! Even though I'm older now (thirty-three), I still knit with that punk aesthetic in mind. Individuality is the key to happiness. I have a knitting weblog at www.glampyre.com.

HEATHER DIXON

Candy Stripers
MESSENGER AND LAPTOP BAGS

L ike a lot of women I know, I carry a ton of completely necessary stuff around with me every day, so last year, when my favorite multicolored leather patchwork shoulder bag bit the dust, I decided to try my hand at designing a felted knit replacement. I had seen patterns for felted bags around, but I needed something a little more substantial that I could throw over my shoulder to leave both hands free. Now this stripy orange and pink messenger bag, my new favorite, goes everywhere I go. The laptop version is made in the same way, just altering the measurements, and it looks so pretty in springtime colors!

Proportions are based on my leather shoulder bag. Directions for messenger bag are followed by directions for laptop bag in parentheses; italic type indicates directions for messenger bag only. Where there is only one direction, it applies to both.

STITCH PATTERN
HORIZONTAL HERRINGBONE STITCH
Row 1: K1, *s1, k1, raise sl st with left-hand needle but do not drop it, k into back of raised st, drop from needle; rep from * to last st, k1.

Row 2: *P2tog, then purl first st again, slipping both sts off needle tog; rep from * to end.

Size
Finished measurements:

Messenger bag: 10" × 6½" × 4½"

Laptop bag: 16" × 10½" × 2¼"

Materials
Brown Sheep Lamb's Pride Bulky (85% wool, 15% mohair; 113g/125 yds)

MESSENGER BAG

MC: 2 skeins M22 Autumn Harvest

CC1: 1 skein M38 Lotus Pink

CC2: 1 skein M105 RPM Pink

CC3: 1 skein M155 Lemon Drop

LAPTOP BAG

MC: 2 skeins M120 Limeade

CC1: 2 skeins M52 Spruce

CC2: 1 skein M155 Lemon Drop

CC3: 1 skein M10 Crème

US 15 (10mm) straight needles, or size needed to obtain gauge

10 (16)" zipper to match CC1

One 2" metal ring

Stitch markers

Tapestry needle

Gauge
10 sts and 15 rows = 4" in St st

STRIPE SEQUENCES

Front panel:

8 rows MC, 6 rows CC1, 2 rows CC2, 2 rows CC3, 2 rows CC2, 4 rows CC1, 8 rows MC (8 rows MC, 4 rows CC1, 2 rows CC2, 2 rows CC3, 2 rows MC, 2 rows CC2, 2 rows CC3, 4 rows CC1, 2 rows CC2, 6 rows MC, 4 rows CC1, 2 rows CC2, 2 rows CC3, 2 rows MC, 2 rows CC2, 2 rows CC3, 4 rows CC1, 2 rows CC2, 4 rows MC).

Back panel:

6 rows MC, 4 rows CC1, 2 rows CC2, 2 rows CC3, 2 rows MC, 2 rows CC2, 2 rows CC3, 4 rows CC1, 2 rows CC2, 6 rows MC (10 rows MC, 6 rows CC1, 2 rows CC2, 2 rows CC3, 2 rows CC2, 4 rows CC1, 8 rows MC, 6 rows CC1, 2 rows CC2, 2 rows CC3, 2 rows CC2, 4 rows CC1, 8 rows MC).

To adjust the pattern to fit your laptop, just add or subtract CO stitches from the front and back panels.

DIRECTIONS

BASE

With MC, CO 20 (12)sts. Work in horizontal herringbone st, alternating 2 rows MC and 2 rows CC1 for 30 (50) rows.

BO.

FRONT PANEL

With RS of base facing and MC, pick up 30 (50) sts from one long base edge. Beg with a RS row, work in St st foll stripe sequence for front panel.

Change to CC1 and BO.

BACK PANEL

Work as for front panel, foll stripe sequence for back panel.

FIRST SIDE PANEL

Messenger bag only:

Stripe sequence: 4 rows MC, 4 rows CC1, 2 rows CC2, 2 rows CC3, 2 rows CC2, 2 rows CC1, 6 rows MC.

With RS of base facing and MC, pick up 20 (10) sts from base CO edge.

Working in horizontal herringbone st, foll stripe sequence above (***alternate 2 rows of MC and 2 rows of CC1 for 158 rows, pm at each edge of row 36; BO).

Messenger bag only:

Next row: With CC1, k2tog, then work horizontal herringbone st to last 3 sts, k1, k2tog.

Next row: P1, then work horizontal herringbone st to last st, p1.

Rep these 2 rows, alternating 2 rows of MC with

2 rows of CC1 until 8 sts rem, and pm at each edge of second row of MC stripe in dec patt.**

Cont in stripe sequence as est, working even in horizontal herringbone st for 20 more rows.

BO.

SECOND SIDE PANEL

Messenger bag only:

Stripe sequence: 2 rows MC, 2 rows CC1, 2 rows CC2, 2 rows CC3, 2 rows CC2, 6 rows CC1, 6 rows MC.

Work as for first side panel to **, foll stripe sequence above. Cont in stripe sequence as est, work even in horizontal herringbone st for 80 more rows (work as for first side panel to ***, alternating 2 rows of MC and 2 rows of CC1 for 58 rows). BO.

With WS tog (so that the seams are on the outside), pin front and back to side panels so that top of front and back line up with the markers on side panels.

Back st these 4 seams.

TOP

Wind off about a small apple-sized ball of MC (piece requires working 2 sections at the same time).

With MC, pu 8 (10) sts from wrong side of shorter side panel at top of dec shaping (6 rows up from markers).

Work 2 (4) rows even in St st.

Messenger bag only:

Cont in St st, inc 1 st at each edge of next row, then EOR to 14 sts, ending with RS facing.

Divide for bag opening:

K7 (5), join new ball of MC and use to k7 (5).

Next row: With new ball of MC, p7 (5); with first ball of MC, p7 (5).

A Very Kinky Girl

WHEN TO SHOWER WITH YOUR YARN

*I*f you've unraveled yarn from a project and would like to reuse it, here's one way to remove the kinks. Wrap the yarn loosely around a wide piece of cardboard, then take this giant loop off the cardboard and hang it over a plastic coat hanger. Hang the yarn in the bathroom the next time you take a shower. The bathroom will fill up with steam, and by the time you finish your shower, all the kinks in the yarn will have loosened up and it will be nice and workable again. *Amy Singleton, Galveston, TX*

Rep these 2 rows 18 (39) times.

Join bag opening:

With first ball of MC, k all 14 (10) sts. Break 2nd ball of yarn.

Work 1 (3) rows even in St st.

BO.

Messenger bag only:

Dec 1 st at each edge of next row, then EOR to 8 sts, ending with RS facing.

Work 2 rows even in St st.

BO.

FINISHING

WS tog, pin top section to top of bag so that BO edge matches CO edge at opposite side panel and top edges of front and back are neatly in place. Backstitch tog.

Weave in ends.

To felt, place bag in a zippered pillow case and run through a hot wash cycle. Wash until desired felting has occurred (this may take 2 to 3 washes). Optional: Add a few pairs of jeans to the cycle to help with agitation.

Once your bag is the size you like, pull corners and squeeze seams to form a boxy bag shape and leave in warm and airy place to dry fully.

Pin one side of zipper into opening so that only the teeth will show from the outside.

Sew zipper in place close to edge of bag opening and again at outer edge of zipper tape.

Repeat on other side of bag opening, being careful not to stretch edges.

Thread metal ring over shorter strap, fold strap to inside, and firmly sew down BO edge to start of top section.

Take longer strap and thread it through metal ring. Fold end of strap to length required and sew firmly, close to ring and at BO edge.

About Heather

See Valentine's Hat and Mittens pattern, page 54, for Heather's bio.

That Felt Great

A FEW GOOD FELTING IDEAS

A member of Chicago Stitch 'n Bitch once told me that using Dawn dish detergent for felting works best. When I tried it on a felted purse, it worked like a charm. *Jen Mindel, Chicago, IL*

● I have a washing machine in my rented Brooklyn apartment, but I'm wary of clogging the pipes with all the little bits of fuzz that come off when you felt. I've found that placing the article in an old pillow case and then folding over and pinning the edge closed with safety pins keeps the little fuzzies inside. Tossed in the washer with a couple pairs of old jeans, it still provides enough agitation for felting. *Jen Greely, Jersey City, NJ*

● All the felting instructions I've come across are for home, top-loader machines, where they tell you to check on the progress every ten minutes. But there's no reason why we laundromat-dependent people can't felt too. Just stick your finished product into the machine (in a pillow case or some such), along with something to create friction (jeans), put your quarters in, and relax. It'll take a couple of runs. Keep washing until you're happy with the result. *Valentina, Nakic, NY*

● Long, skinny items felt more evenly if you put them in a small-ish bag, a bit smaller than a pillowcase. That way they won't get wrapped around the agitator or pulled out of whack from the water they're holding, and end up longer than before felting. *Kate Pickering Antonova, New York, NY*

● When choosing yarn for a felted project, beware of using very light colors, especially white. White and very pale yarns have often been bleached, which damages the fibers too much for them to felt well. *KPA*

● Felting by hand can get pretty boring and definitely splashy. I prefer to combine it with another favorite evening activity—a soak in the tub. I take in with me a short tub on a tray (for small items), or a big bucket (for larger projects). Make sure it's a clean bucket, obviously, and put in your soap, vinegar, and any other tools you might need (such as a wooden spoon for agitating). Hot and cold water are as convenient as can be, and I use a nice-smelling, gentle soap for both the tub and the felting bucket, so I don't mind all the splashing around. *KPA*

● In my experience, it doesn't make anything felt faster or better to use painfully hot water, or to agitate so vigorously that it either tires your hands or—if you're rubbing against something, like a cookie rack—unnecessarily rips the wool. Simply kneading the wool like bread dough, in comfortably hot water with plenty of soap, works just as fast and never does any damage. *KPA*

● Felted slippers can be slippery to walk in. An alternative to buying expensive slipper bottoms is to paint a pattern on the bottom of the slippers with puffy fabric paint (found in any crafts store for about 99¢ per bottle). Try painting concentric circles or flowers on the heels and toes. For my grandpa, who lives in the Alzheimer's ward of a nursing home, I painted his name and washing instructions on the bottom of each slipper. *KPA*

● If you accidentally felt too much, it's remarkably easy to stretch the item back to where you want it as long as it's still warm and wet. If you've already let it dry, try dipping it back in warm, slightly soapy water until it's soaked (but don't agitate). Then stretch it, fix it onto some object, and let it dry. *KPA*

Size

Finished height: 6 (8)" + handles

Finished width: 10 (14)"

Finished depth: 3½ (5)"

Materials

SMALL BAG

Cascade 220 (100% wool; 100g/220 yds)

MC: 2 skeins #7919 Turquoise

CC: 1 skein #8505 White

US 8 (5mm) straight needles,
or size needed to obtain gauge

US 8 (5mm) double-pointed needles
(set of 2)

7" white zipper

LARGE BAG

Brown Sheep Lamb's Pride Worsted
(85% wool, 15% mohair; 113g/190 yds)

MC: 2 skeins #M-38 Lotus Pink

CC: 1 skein #M-05 Onyx

US 11 (8mm) straight needles,
or size needed to obtain gauge

US 11 (8mm) double-pointed needles
(set of 2)

12" black zipper

BOTH BAGS

2 stitch holders

Sewing needle

Thread to match MC

Gauge

Small bag: 17 sts and 22 rows = 4" in St st

Large bag: 12 sts and 16 rows = 4" in St st

GEORGIA A. COLEMAN

Letter Have It

'm crazy about the new initial craze! I want one of everything with a big ole G right smack in the middle. Only, I've encountered a little problem: Nobody sells anything with a G on it. I've found plenty of Ks and a ton of Js. But c'mon, we aren't all Kimberly or Jessica! This bag is my tribute to all the unpopular initials out there, and its shape is inspired by my love of 1950s bowling bags. Best of all, by simply changing the needle size, you can make the bag big or little. The bigger bag is perfect for toting around knitting projects, and the little one is just the right size for your wallet and keys. It makes a perfect personalized gift.

DIRECTIONS

FRONT

With MC and straight needles, CO 48 sts.

Beg with a RS row, work in St st for 10 rows.

Row 11: K14, work row 1 of chart, k14.

Row 12: P14, work row 2 of chart, p14.

Cont as est until row 12 of chart has been completed.

Next row: K2, k2tog, k10, work row 13 of chart, k10, k2tog, k2.

Next row: P13, work row 14 of chart, p13.

Cont as est, working decs on RS rows, until all rows of chart have been completed.

Next row: K2, k2tog, k to last 4 sts, k2tog, k2.

Next row: P.

Rep last 2 rows once—30 sts.

BO loosely.

BACK

With MC and straight needles, CO 48 sts.

Beg with a RS row, work in St st for 22 rows.

Next row: K2, k2tog, k to last 4 sts, k2tog, k2.

Next row: P.

Rep last 2 rows 8 times more—30 sts.

BO loosely.

CENTER PANEL

With MC and straight needles, CO 16 sts.

Work in garter st for 38½ (42)".

Next row: K8, place rem sts on holder.

Work in garter st on these 8 sts for 9 (10½)". Place sts on 2nd holder. Break yarn, leaving a 6" tail.

Join yarn to sts on 1st holder. Work in garter st on these 8 sts for 9 (10½)".

Next row: K8 from left-hand needle, then k8 from holder. Work in garter st on all 16 sts for 1½".

BO loosely.

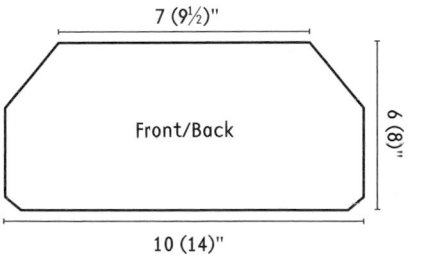

Smaller needles make a smaller bag; larger needles make a bigger one!

About Georgia

I can't remember a time when I didn't want to knit. The only problem was that I didn't know how. Around three years ago I finally got the chance to learn—a woman I was working with showed me how to cast on and how to make the knit stitch. After about a hundred garter stitch items I decided it was time to learn the rest, and I have been knitting everything from lace to Fair Isle ever since. About a year ago I started a blog, www.onmymind.blogdrive.com, to chronicle my knitting journeys. In my real life I am a full-blooded Chicagoan and a third-year college student. Although crazy school schedules often keep me from attending the Chicago Stitch 'n Bitch, I have unofficial knitting get-togethers all the time.

HANDLES (MAKE 2)

With MC and straight needles, CO on 7 sts.

Work in garter st until piece measures 8 (9½)" from beg.

BO loosely.

PIPING (MAKE 2)

With CC1 and dpns, CO on 3 sts.

Work in I-cord for 41 (54)".

Place sts on a holder. Break yarn, leaving a 9" tail.

FINISHING

With MC, sew the CO and BO edges of the center panel tog.

Sew the front and back to the center panel, ensuring that the zipper opening is centered along the top.

With CC1, sew I-cord along the outer edges of the front and back.

If necessary, adjust length of piping by taking sts off holder and working in I-cord or ripping back to appropriate length. Draw tail through sts and secure ends of piping tog.

Sew handles right next to piping on the center panel, placed at the beginning and end of the BO edge.

Weave in ends.

FELTING

Place the bag in a zippered pillow or laundry bag, then in the washer on the hot cycle with a tablespoon of dish soap or laundry detergent. Stop occasionally to check the bag. If it is not completely dense after one cycle, run it through again until it is.

When felted, remove excess water by letting the bag go through the spin cycle.

Remove the bag from the washer, shape, and stuff with plastic bags. Set the bag on a towel and allow it to dry completely.

Pin the zipper in place and sew it in by hand.

We All Cord for I-cord *Show Me Your Tips!*

MAKING I-CORD ON CIRCULAR NEEDLES

*F*or my current project, I desperately needed to make an I-cord. After getting directions from a friend, I set out to look for double-pointed needles. Despite the number of craft stores in Austin, I was unable to find the right size. That's when I realized that if the right circular needle is used, you can create I-cord with only one needle. Simply move the I-cord from one side of the needle to the other as you knit. I call it "I-cord for the desperate."

Jennifer Mailloux, Austin, TX

Initial charts continued on next page ⟶

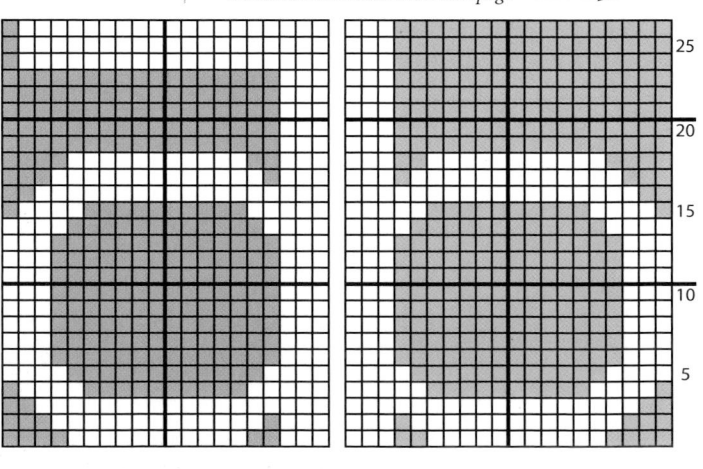

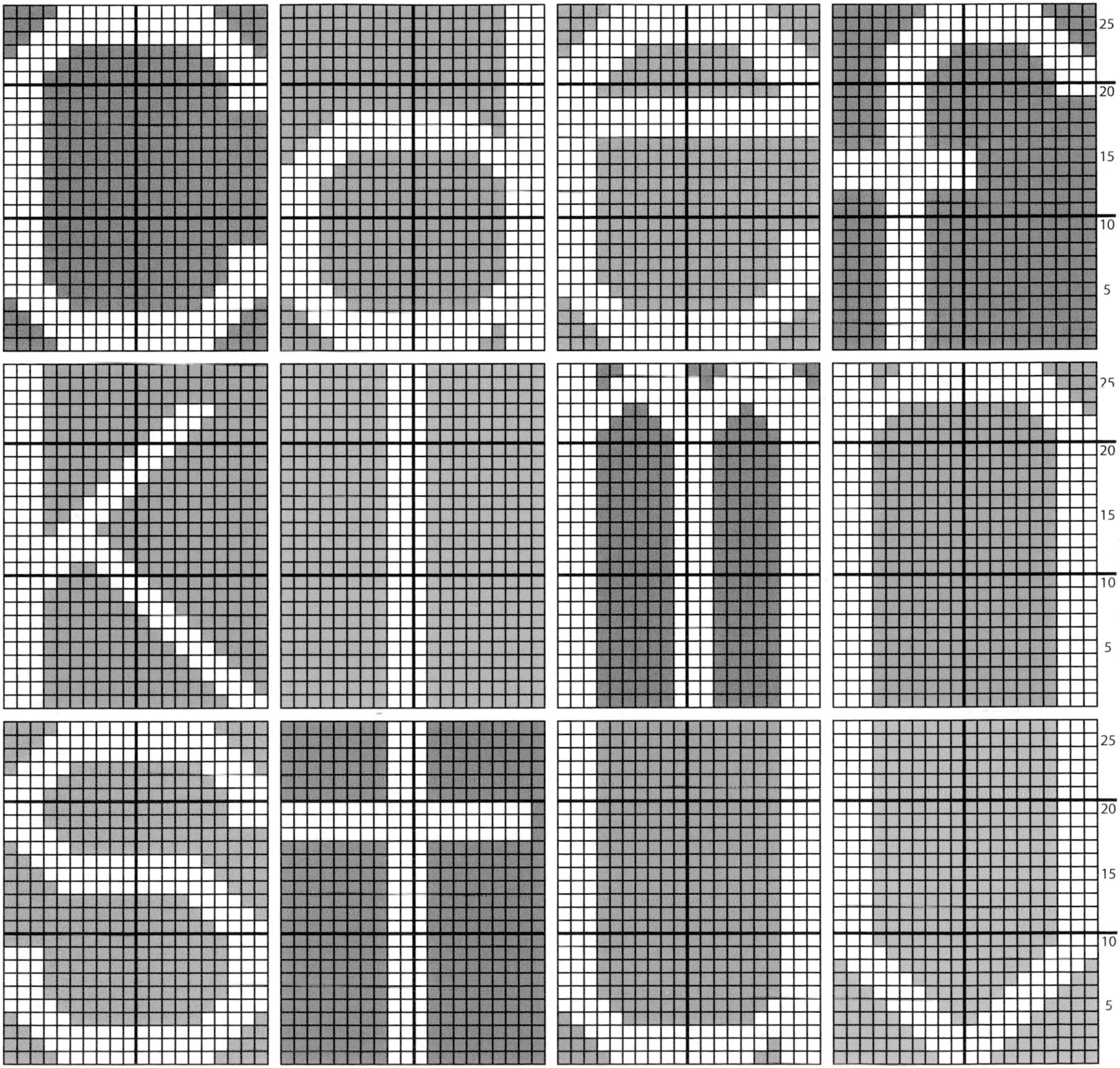

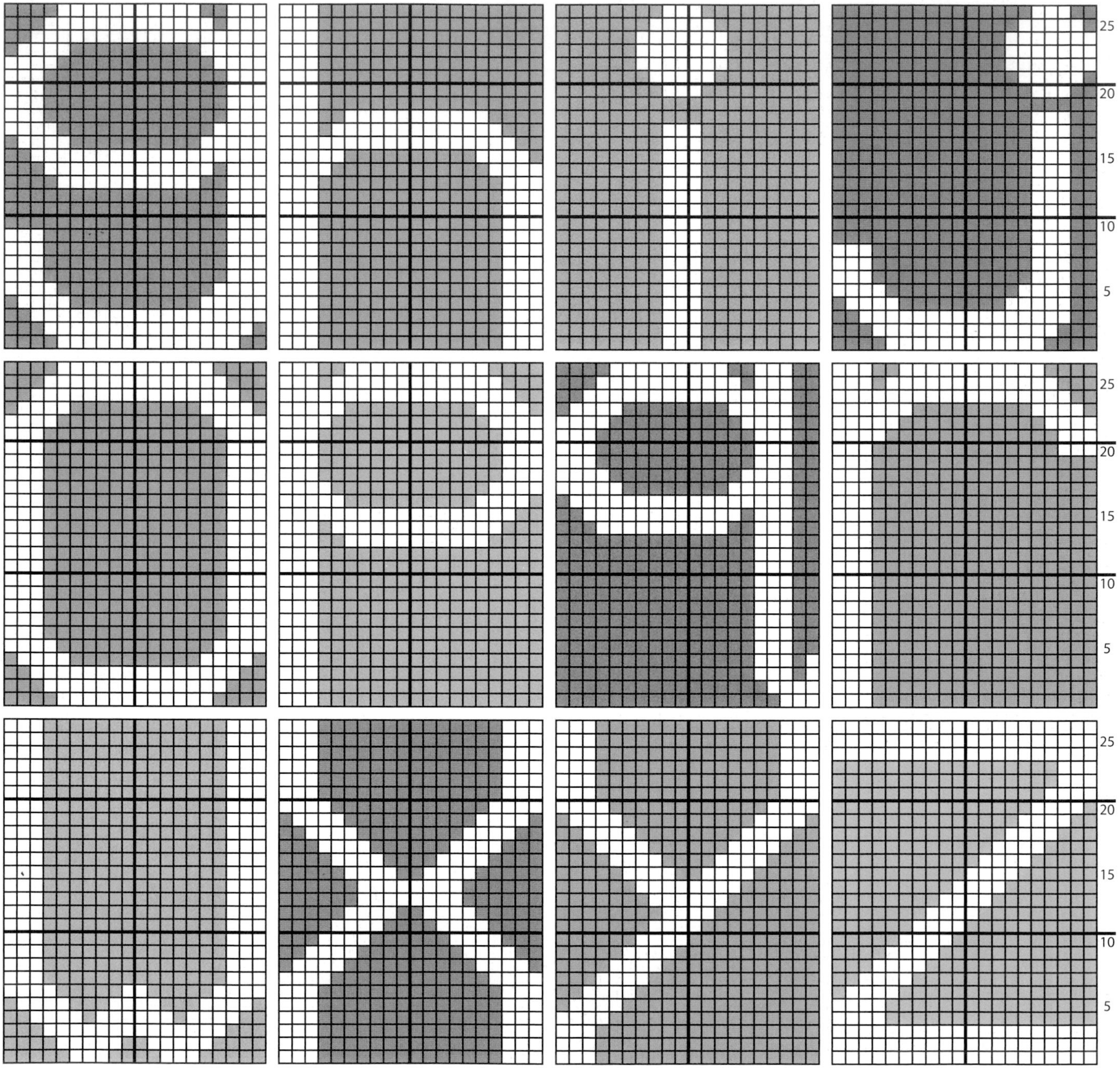
25
20
15
10
5
25
20
15
10
5
25
20
15
10
5

DEBBIE STOLLER

Poster Boy

these days, everyone's carrying interesting little tote bags with images screenprinted onto them. Poster boy came about when I was trying to figure out if there was a way to make a similar image in knitting. I wanted to make a two-color image that was not as regular as the kind usually done in Fair Isle patterns, yet not as simple as those often made using the intarsia method.

Poster Boy is knit using the Fair Isle method, where the color not in use is carried along behind the working color, but is twisted with the other yarn about every five stitches so as to avoid long strands hanging at the back of your work. Just about any black-and-white image that isn't too complicated can be knit this way. Start by taking an image into Photoshop and making it 11" wide, with a resolution of only 6 pixels per inch. Play around with the brightness and contrast so that the image is reduced to black and white but is still recognizable. Print out the image, get yourself some knitter's graph paper, and lay the pixelated image underneath it on a lightbox. Color in your chart with a pencil. Then grab your needles and make that poster boy come to life!

DIRECTIONS

BAG

With CC and circular needle, CO 112 sts.

Join and work in the round as follows:

Row 1: P1, pm, k55, p1, pm, k55.

Work 3 more rows in St st, with 1 p st before markers as est.

Size

Finished width: 11"

Finished length: 12"

Materials

Brown Sheep Lamb's Pride Worsted (85% wool, 15% mohair; 113g/125 yds)

MC: 1 skein M81 Red Baron

CC: 1 skein M105 Black

US 8 (5mm) 16" circular needle, or size needed to obtain gauge

US 7 (4.5mm) straight needles

1 yd lining fabric

Sewing thread to match lining

Gauge

18 sts and 26 rows = 4"

Special Skill

FAIR ISLE

Row 5: Beg working from chart, 1 rep on each side of the markers. Carry color not in use loosely behind work, catching it in place with working yarn every 5 sts. Vary the placement of yarn twists on each rnd.

Working from chart, cont in St st, maintaining p sts as est, until all chart rows have been worked.

Break CC and cont in MC, working 3 rnds in St st.

P 1 rnd.

K 3 more rounds in St st.

BO loosely.

STRAPS (MAKE 2)

With MC and straight needles, CO 13 sts.

Work in St st until piece measures 27" from beg.

BO.

FINISHING

Fold straps in half, WS tog, and mattress st tog along lengthwise edge.

Seam bottom of bag closed.

Fold top of bag toward WS at purl row; stitch down hem.

Fold straps so that the seams are centered on the back side of straps. Attach one strap to the front of the bag and the other strap to the back of the bag, with the ends of the straps $1\frac{1}{2}$" in the outer edge of the bag.

Cut the lining fabric into two 12" × 13" pieces. With RS tog, sew seam across bottom and sides, $\frac{1}{2}$" from edge.

Press top $\frac{1}{2}$" of lining to outside (WS).

Place lining bag inside knit bag and, with sewing thread, sew the top of the lining to the hem of the knit bag.

About Debbie

My mother taught me to knit when I was six. When I was twenty, I was retaught by my grandmother—a woman who knit for ninety of her 103 years. But I didn't enjoy the process and quickly gave up the hobby. Then, about fifteen years later—in 1999—I picked up an unfinished sweater and worked on it during a three-day, cross-country train trip, and finally it all clicked. Suddenly I was hooked, and couldn't get enough of the craft, reading about it, studying it, and, of course, practicing it. I also quickly became aware of knitting's relatively low regard in our culture and went on a mission to "Take Back the Knit"—writing about knitting in my magazine, *BUST,* and starting a Stitch 'n Bitch group in NYC to teach as many people as I could the myriad joys of knitting. When I'm not knitting, working on my magazine, or writing knitting books—I'm sleeping!

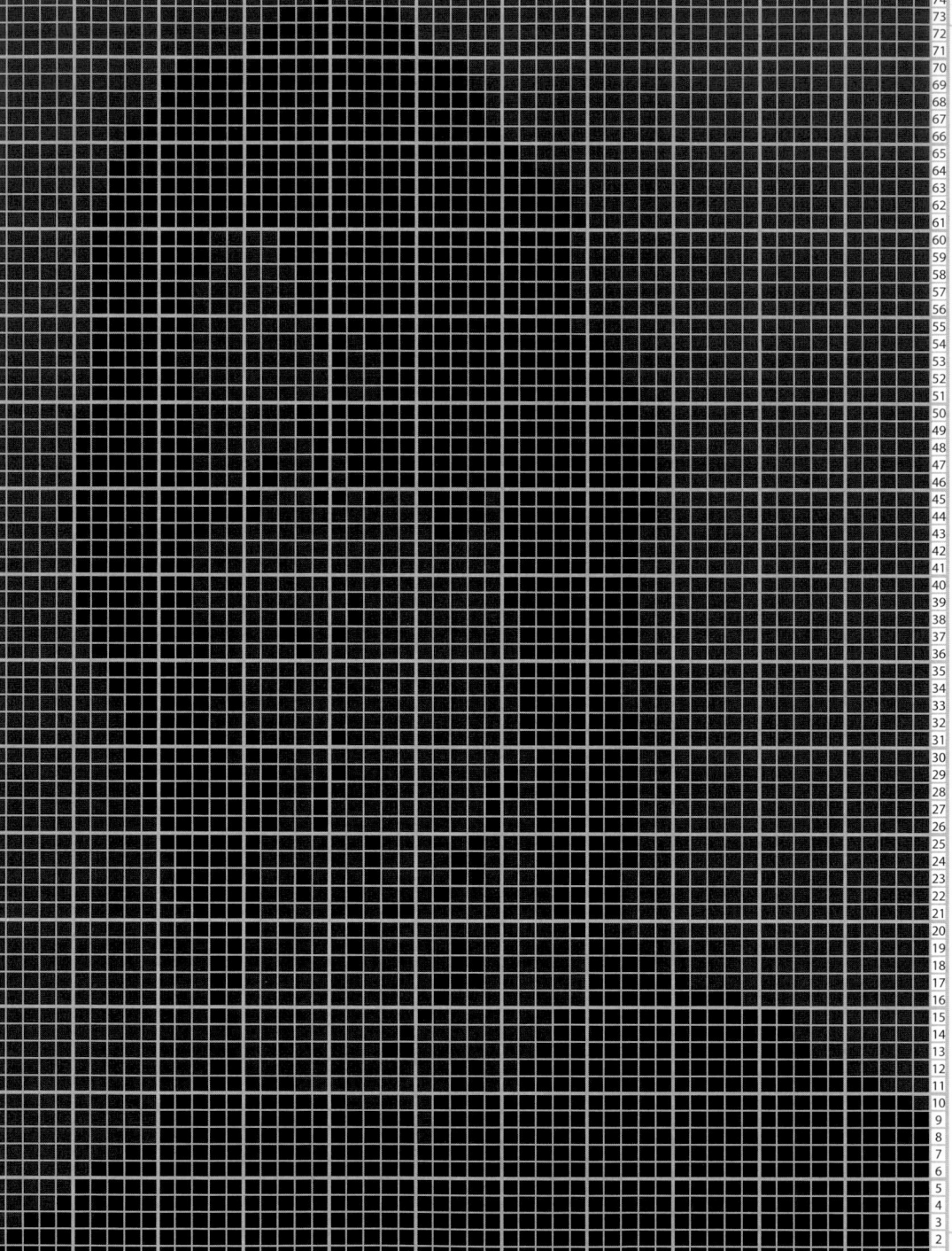

MC
CC

74
73
72
71
70
69
68
67
66
65
64
63
62
61
60
59
58
57
56
55
54
53
52
51
50
49
48
47
46
45
44
43
42
41
40
39
38
37
36
35
34
33
32
31
30
29
28
27
26
25
24
23
22
21
20
19
18
17
16
15
14
13
12
11
10
9
8
7
6
5
4
3
2
1

STEPHANIE MRSE

Om Yoga Mat Bag

came up with the idea for this bag while looking at patterns for knit mesh shopping bags. At the same time, I was getting back into yoga and noticing that you can buy yoga mat bags online for outrageous amounts of money!

This lace pattern looks impressive, but it is easy to memorize and knit. The sturdy cotton yarn can be purchased inexpensively at almost any craft store.

Size
22" long × 11" in diameter

Materials
Lion Brand Lion Cotton
(100% cotton; 142g/236 yds),
2 skeins #148 Turquoise

US 9 (5.5mm) straight needles

US 8 (5mm) straight needles,
or size needed to obtain gauge

1 yd white drawstring cord

Gauge
16 sts and 22 rows = 4" in diagonal lace st, slightly stretched, on smaller needles

Special Skill
LACE

STITCH PATTERN
DIAGONAL LACE STITCH
Rows 1, 3, 5, and 7: P.

Row 2: K2, *yo, sl1, k2tog, psso, yo, k1; rep from * to last 2 sts, k2.

Row 4: K2, *k1, yo, sl1, k2tog, psso, yo; rep from * to last 2 sts, k2.

Row 6: K1, k2tog, *yo, k1, yo, sl1, k2tog, psso; rep from * to last 5 sts, yo, k1, yo, ssk, k2.

Row 8: K2, k2tog, *yo, k1, yo, sl1, k2tog, psso; rep from * to last 4 sts, yo, k1, yo, ssk, k1.

DIRECTIONS
STRAP
With larger needles and 2 strands of yarn held tog, CO 6 sts.

Work in 1 × 1 rib, slipping the 1st st of every row kwise, until piece measures 29" from beg.

BO.

BAG

With smaller needles, CO 80 sts.

Work in diagonal lace st until piece measures 13½" from beg.

BO kwise.

FINISHING

Mattress st CO edge to BO edge.

Thread yarn in and out through the bottom, pull tails tight to the inside, and secure.

Sew CO edge of strap to the top end of the bag, along the seam line. Sew BO edge of strap 3 inches from the bottom of the bag, along the seam line.

Weave in all ends.

Thread drawstring in and out through the lace patt along the top edge of the bag. Tie overhand knots at each end of the drawstring.

About Stephanie

My grandmother taught me to knit when I was a child. I loved spending the night at her house because she always had something crafty to keep me occupied. I started knitting seriously again when I was in graduate school and decided I wanted to learn to knit socks. In real life I am a chemist and live in San Diego with my wonderful husband and cute dog. When I'm not knitting, I'm usually sewing, cross-stitching, or watching sports.

Knowing Right from Wrong

HOW TO REMEMBER WHICH SIDE OF YOUR WORK IS WHICH

Having different-colored same-size needles—say, a pair of blue and a pair of red US 9s—makes working with every-other-row-type patterns easier. Using one red and one blue needle, I just keep in mind which one works the second row of a pattern, and then when that needle is in my right hand, I know to work the second row. Or I remember that red equals the right side, blue equals the back. This has helped me loads when I pick up my knitting in the middle of a row and am not sure which row of my pattern to start working again. *Tricia Mitchell, Johnston, PA*

STITCH 'N BITCH ACROSS THE NATION
The Midwest

Akron, Ohio

Cedar Rapids, Iowa

AKRON, OHIO, SNB

We like to say "If you can do it sitting in a chair, bring it and come hang out." Launched in January 2004, the Akron Stitch 'n Bitch grew quickly, due largely to a newspaper article that was written by one of our knitters. We meet weekly at Square Records to share knitting projects and skills, as well as donated homemade treats and coffee. Although shoppers sometimes give us surprised looks, Square Records is a great environment for our meetings, with exhibits of local artists' work and great music playing. Being surrounded by so many art forms encourages our creativity. A lot of nights we go home having made progress on our projects—and with a few new records, too!

Our knitters are mostly in their twenties and thirties, but Akron SnB has drawn all ages and skill levels, as well as crocheters, spinners, cross-stitchers, and sewers. We've taught a few dozen people to knit (including at least five guys), and even if we don't see these new knitters every week, we know that they carry their knitting skills with them.

Moving beyond Wednesday-night meetings, we took a summertime trip to shear alpacas and spin the donated fleece, which we used to knit clothing for local shelters for the upcoming winter. We've also spawned two other Stitch 'n Bitch groups in nearby Canton and Barberton.

Megan Marucco, Rae Nester, and
Juniper Sage

CEDAR RAPIDS, IOWA, SNB

The Cedar Rapids Stitch 'n Bitch may be one of the smallest groups around—there are only three of us—but we're probably one of the most loyal. We first met around fall of 2003 at Coffeesmiths, a place where we can spread out on comfy chairs in front of a burning log fire. Although we're stymied by the lack of local yarn shops here in the heartland,

Chicago, Illinois

the Cedar Rapids SnB trio keeps up on the latest yarn and pattern trends through visits to the excellent yarn shops within a few hours' drive and by checking out Internet sites and knitting blogs.

The biggest challenge for us is just making the time for knitting. We've found our gatherings a haven, a wonderful time to deepen friendships while sharing our precious projects. We're planning knitting weekends away from our kids and husbands, and knit-along ventures as well.

Ann Rushton

CHICAGO SnB

The Chicago Stitch 'n Bitch wasn't the first SnB chapter, but if you look at mailing list numbers, we're definitely the largest, with more than one thousand subscribers. Luckily, we draw only about fifteen or twenty people a week, and it's not always the same twenty people, which keeps things fresh. My guess is that many of the list members don't even live in Chicago, but in cities without SnBs, so they sign up for the feeling of being a part of a like-minded group, a community that shares their love of the craft. I felt that way myself until I ventured out of my comfort zone (I'm more of a wallflower than a social diva) and organized my own group, which turned out surprisingly well.

I'm constantly amazed at the life force of the Chicago group and at the quality, generosity, and passion of the people it has attracted. I want to encourage the non-Chicagoans lurking on the list (you know who you are) to take the next step and start a group of your own. Don't be daunted by it, don't overthink it, don't be afraid to be a leader; just pick a place to meet and tell a few friends who will tell a few other friends. You'll be amazed at how many people there are just like you, waiting for a group to join, and who will jump at the chance to hang with you. Once the group starts meeting regularly, you'll see that it will take on a personality and direction all its own—and that's when the real fun begins.

In our first four years, Chicago members taught beginners at Ladyfest Midwest, knitted afghans for fire stations, were featured on a local TV show and in various publications, and even produced a one-hour cable access show of our own. But the coolest thing we've done is pass on our love and knowledge of the craft to others: curious nonknitters who walked by our meeting one week and joined the group the next; beginners who are now teaching their own classes; people who read about our group and bought a book to teach themselves. That's the power of groups like ours, and like the one you're going to start in your own town. Once you get the ball rolling and watch the group take on a life of its own, I'm sure you'll discover—as I have in the years I've been part of this phenomenal group of Chicago people—that there's nothing knitters can't do.

Brenda Janish

CLEVELAND, OHIO, SnB

With the help of *Stitch 'n Bitch: The Knitter's Handbook*, I taught my friend how to knit (and she taught me how to crochet). Then, with our newfound skills and needles in hand, we began enlisting others in our crafting crusade. We meet at Capsule, an Internet "cybar" that provides the architecture and atmosphere of a 1970s sci-fi TV series: orange circular couches, cosmic backdrops, blue drinks, and moody lighting. (No rocking chairs, please!) Metal, punk, and indie-rock DJs provide the necessary rhythm for knitting the night away.

Our group was soon joined by crocheters who were already making loads of products for local craft shows. There's a rumor out there about an age-old grudge between knitters and crocheters, but it's not so with the Cleveland SnB, who strive for a mutually respectful atmosphere. We knitters have learned to appreciate the speed of crocheting and the look of different projects. (In the wild, crotcheters and knitters are natural enemies, but if you raise 'em together as pups . . .)

We've also attracted nonknitting writers and artists, who have been put to use making center-pulled balls of yarn. We've taught several beginners some basics and were surprised by how few people knew how to tie square knots.

Teachers, small-business owners, Ph.D. candidates, financial advisers, graphic designers, and advertising reps all unite for the love of yarn and yarns, and we encourage quiet people to get loud by frequently interrupting meetings with the chant "Less stitching, more bitching."

In addition to a group Web site and a Yahoo group, our members sell their handiwork on our merchandise site, www.there-she-goes.com. We offer quality handmade bags and accessories. Schemes in the works include visits to the Akron and Chicago SnBs and attracting a cross-dressing cross-stitcher to the group.

Susan Ensor

Cleveland, Ohio

LESLIE BARBAZETTE
Saucy Tote

Size

Finished height: 9" (+ straps)

Finished width: 12"

Materials

Caron Craft & Rug 3 Ply
(100% polyester; 39.7g/60 yds)

MC: 3 skeins #105 Medium Pink

CC: 1 skein #658 Christmas Green

US 11 (8mm) 24" circular needle,
or size needed to obtain gauge

Clear plastic canvas: two 9" × 11½"
pieces, two 4¼" × 9" pieces, one
4¼" × 11½" piece

Cotton fabric: one 35" × 12" piece,
one 6" × 14" piece

2 yds string or embroidery floss

Tapestry needle

Pointed large-eyed needle

12 large paper clips

One 2" button

Gauge

12 sts and 16 rows = 4" in St st

originally made this bag for my friend Melissa's twenty-seventh birthday. Mel's mom calls her saucy, hence the name. I wanted a knit bag that had a clean and defined shape (no sagging allowed). After trying to shape it with cardboard and foam from craft stores, I finally figured out that by using plastic canvas I could keep the shape of the bag and have it still be washable. Kits for making this bag are available at my Web site, www.citizenbags.com.

DIRECTIONS
BODY
With MC, CO 100 sts.

Pm and join, work in St st until piece measures 8½" from beg.

BO and break yarn, leaving a 36" tail.

STRAP (MAKE 2)
With MC, CO 8 sts, leaving a 12" tail.

Work in St st until piece measures 15" from beg.

BO and break yarn, leaving a 12" tail.

BUTTON FLAP

With MC, CO 11 sts, leaving a 20" tail.

Work in St st until piece measures 4" from beg, ending with RS facing.

Next row: K4, BO 3, k4.

Next row: P4, CO 3, p4.

Work in St st until piece measures 5½" from beg.

BO.

BOTTOM

With CC, CO 34 sts.

Work in St st until piece measures 4½" from beg.

BO and break yarn, leaving a 36" tail.

FINISHING

Body assembly:

With 24" lengths of white string and leaving at least a 6" tail, whipstitch the 9" sides of the plastic canvas tog. Tie the top and bottom of the strings tog to secure (**figure 1**).

Place the large piece of fabric WS up under the canvas and lay the plastic canvas flat on top of it. Fold the ends of the fabric over the canvas and use paperclips to hold everything tog.

Fold this in half with RS facing. With the sharp needle and 1 yd of MC, whipstitch the 2 ends of the bag tog through both the layers of fabric and plastic canvas (**figure 2**).

Slip the knitted body of the bag over the interior, with the BO being the top of the bag. Rearrange the paper clips to hold the knit piece to the interior. Beg with the top, using the BO tail, whipstitch the top edge of the bag through both the knit piece and the plastic canvas. Rep on the bottom edge.

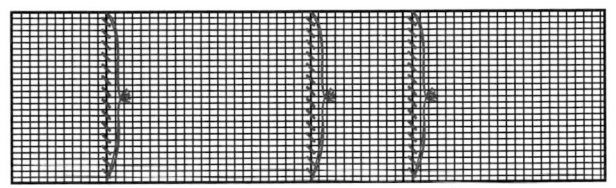

figure 1

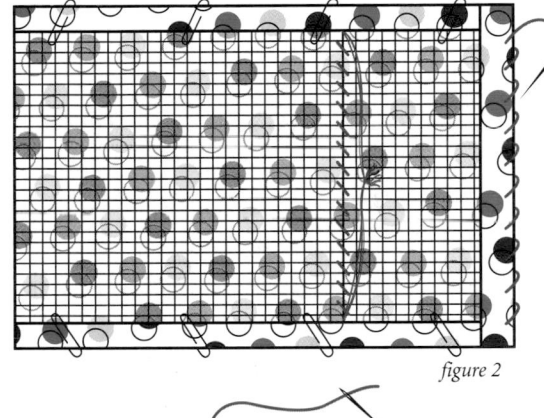

figure 2

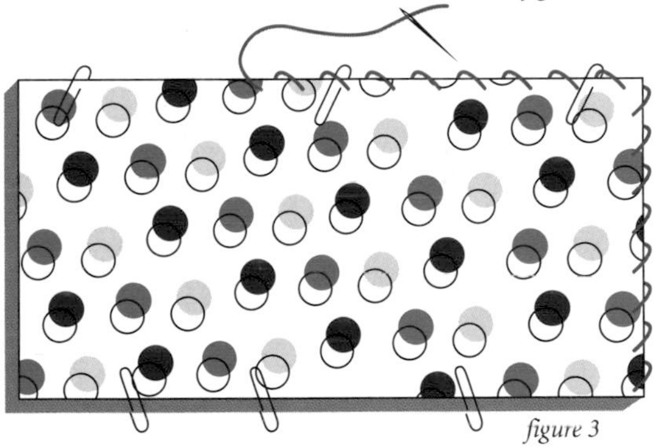

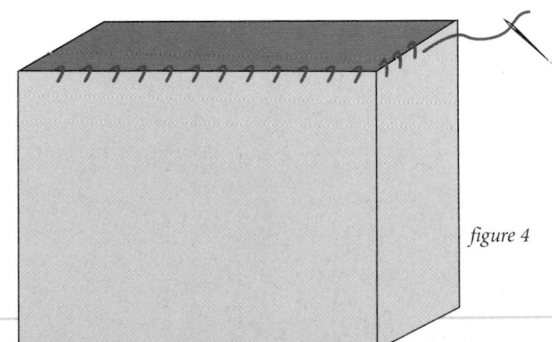

figure 3

figure 4

Bottom assembly:

Place the 6" × 14" fabric WS up and lay the 4¼" × 11½" plastic canvas on top of it, then fold the ends of the fabric over the plastic canvas, using paper clips to hold the pieces tog. Then lie the knit bottom WS up, place the fabric-covered mesh bottom on top of it with the fabric facing up, and adjust the paper clips to hold all 3 layers tog. Using the long tail and the sharp needle, whipstitch along the edges (**figure 3**).

With MC, whipstitch the knit bottom of the bag to the knit body of the bag (**figure 4**).

Mattress st the strap to the top of the bag 1" from each end. Rep on other side.

Mattress st the flap to the top center of the back.

Sew button to correspond with buttonhole on flap, sewing through the plastic canvas but not the fabric interior.

Weave in ends.

About Leslie

I taught myself how to knit in the back of my parents' olive-green Volkswagen bus during a road trip to Truckee, California, when I was eight. I've had some really clever moments since then, like when I believed one ball of yarn would make me a whole sweater. The sadness that ensued when I ran out of yarn and couldn't find more of the same color made me stop knitting for a few years. I caught the knitting bug again upon returning to the Bay Area after living in London for five years. This bug grew into a small handbag company called Citizen Bags. I live in Oakland, California, with my husband, who feeds every cat in the neighborhood. My first book, *Viva Poncho*, which includes poncho and capelet patterns, comes out in spring 2005.

Have Yarn, Will Travel

MAKING A STASH SAMPLE CARD

I made a card that has a strand of yarn from each of my "on hand" skeins that I keep tucked away in my purse (you never know when you'll be able to pop into the yarn shop). Take a 3" × 5" piece of white, sturdy cardboard, and make notches every ½" on the 5" edge. Then wind about 12" of each yarn around it by color, leaving some open spaces. Now you have the ability to pick up additional yarns to add into projects for pizzazz or to find that complementary yarn you need without having to carry your entire supply along. *Lili Brandt, San José, CA*

TRINITY MULLER

Going Out with a Bag

Swinging insouciantly from the wrist, this bag is the perfect size to hold your essentials when you're out for a night on the town or tearing it up on the dance floor. The pattern I give here can be varied endlessly. You can change the size or shape, use the leftover yarn in your stash, pick funky colored zippers, string buttons on it instead of beads, use ribbon for the wrist strap, add a fabric lining, or any other variation you can think of. Really, make this project yours! It knits up quickly and makes a great gift. And you never have to worry about the fit.

Instructions for the pink colorway are followed by instructions for the black colorway in parentheses. Where there is only one number, it applies to both bags.

Sparkly crystal beads and soft, fuzzy yarn make this bag glamour-rific!

SPECIAL INSTRUCTIONS

To string beads with a helper thread: Thread the needle with thread as normal, then thread the needle from the opposite direction to create a loop of thread. Thread B yarn through the thread loop and string the beads using the needle and thread to get the beads on the B yarn. Once the beads are on the B yarn, separate the yarn from the thread.

Size

Finished width: 5"

Finished length: 4"

Materials

A: Katia Danubio
(76% wool, 24% nylon; 50g/100 yds),
1 skein #10 Light Pink (#2 Black)

B: Jaeger Siena (100% mercerized cotton; 50g/153 yds), 1 skein #403 Marshmallow (#418 Black)

US 6 (4mm) straight needles,
or size needed to obtain gauge

37 8mm Swarovski crystal beads,
Clear (Amethyst), from Bead Diner,
www.beaddiner.com

4" (10 cm) zipper, Pink (Black)

Sewing thread to match B

Sewing needle

Tapestry needle

Gauge

20 sts and 28 rows = 4" in St st

Abbreviation

Pb: Place bead. Slide 1 bead up B and place tightly next to last k st.

DIRECTIONS

BAG

String 31 beads onto B using a helper thread.

Slide beads down and CO 24 sts with 1 strand of A and B held tog, leaving a 12" tail.

Beg with a RS row, work in St st for 6 rows.

Row 7: K6, pb, sl next st pwise, *k5, pb, sl1 st pwise; rep from * once, k5.

Row 8: P.

Row 9: K3, pb, sl1 pwise, *k5, pb, sl1 pwise; rep from * twice, k2.

Row 10: P.

Rep rows 7 to 10 until all beads have been worked, ending with row 8.

Work in St st until piece measures 8" from beg, ending with RS facing.

BO, leaving a 12" tail.

WRIST STRAP

Cut three 30" strands of B. Beg 6" from ends, braid strands tog until braid measures 14" from beg.

FINISHING

Fold the piece in half lengthwise with WS tog. With CO and BO tails, mattress st sides tog. Weave in ends.

Sew zipper into bag using back st.

Attach strap to bag by threading one end of the braid through zipper pull hole. Knot the loose strands from either side of the braid tog. With a helper thread, thread one bead onto each loose strand. Tie the yarn off below the beads, varying the lengths of the yarn that the beads hang from. Cut off any extra yarn.

About Trinity

My knitting addiction began in Minneapolis and moved with me to Boston. I'm a self-taught knitter who thought she'd never grow tired of small projects. Though I recently completed my first poncho and have moved on to designing a queen-size knitted blanket, I still love the satisfaction of a quickly knit-up project like this one. I also make beaded jewelry, thanks to my friend Jamie, who got me hooked on beads in return for my teaching her to knit. Using both crafts doubles the pleasure and the design possibilities.

The Mile-High (Knitting) Club

TIPS FOR FREQUENT FLIERS

In the wake of September 11, 2001, the question of whether one can bring one's knitting needles aboard an airplane has become the most frequently asked question on knitting e-mail lists and bulletin boards. The answer is that today you should have no problem knitting your way past airport security checkpoints, but not all your knitting supplies may pass muster. According to the Transportation Security Administration (TSA), as of June 23, 2004, knitting needles and crochet hooks are allowed on planes in carry-on luggage as well as checked luggage. It recommends that needles in carry-on be less than 31 inches in total length and that they be made of bamboo or plastic (take metal needles in your checked luggage). Just in case the screener still won't let your needles through, the TSA suggests that you take along a self-addressed stamped envelope so you can have them mail your supplies to you, and that you carry a crochet hook so you can quickly bind off the project if your needles are confiscated. Finally, metal scissors with pointed tips—most embroidery scissors would fall into this category—are not allowed in hand luggage, but you can take them in your checked luggage. Even those cute little circular yarn cutters with a blade inside are a no-no in your carry-on bag.

For the latest info, check the TSA's Web site at www.tsa.gov and be sure to look at the "Special Considerations" page, where the topic of knitting supplies is specifically addressed, or call them at 866-289-9673. *DS*

● Even though my size 15 Brittany wooden needles made it past security on my last flight, I received evil looks from other passengers and a flight attendant accused me of being Buffy the Vampire Slayer. When I travel next, I'm going to take only small projects (on small needles) to avoid attention. Knitting keeps me sane on long flights! *Amy Secrest, Chandler, AZ*

● When flying, I always carry a pack of dental floss with my knitting. You can cut even thick wooly yarn under the floss cutter, and it's 100% airline friendly! *AS*

● I travel a lot and usually need a scissors in the middle of a flight. So I always take along my nail clippers, which are allowed on planes. If I need to break my yarn, I just clip it! I haven't met a yarn it hasn't worked on. *Jamie Kennealy, Austin, TX*

RENEE LADD

The Bead Goes On
BEADED WRIST CUFFS

love knitting with beads and am always looking for new ways to combine beads and yarn. I took a class at Arnhild Hillesland's knitting studio in 2001 and learned about traditional Norwegian pulse warmers (more commonly known as wrist warmers). I made a pair to warm my hands in my very cold office (they really do work!), then decided my sixteen-year-old niece would love a pair. After seeing the Skully sweater in *Stitch 'n Bitch,* I knew the combination of girly pearls and edgy skulls would be perfect for her. I've also included an alternative broken heart design for the sixteen-year-old in all of us.

STITCH PATTERN
KNITTING WITH BEADS
Sl a bead before each st marked in black on the chart by pushing a bead as close to the right needle as possible. K the next st as normal, securing the bead between two k sts. The bead will be on the RS of the work as you are working the WS. The following row (the RS row) will be knit without beads.

DIRECTIONS
With beading needle, thread 172 beads for the skull (283 for the heart) onto your yarn. Push the beads down on the yarn and CO 25 sts.

Work in garter st, without beads, until piece measures 1½" from beg. Work in garter st, k with beads, foll chart, until all chart rows have been completed.

Size

Adult

Finished circumference: 6½"

Finished width: 3"

Materials

Sandnes Lanett
(100% merino wool; 50gr/213 yds),
1 skein #1099 Black

3 US 0 (2mm) straight needles,
or size needed to obtain gauge

172 silver (283 red) size 8 seed beads

Twisted wire collapsible-eye beading needle

Gauge

24 sts and 66 rows = 4" in beaded garter st

Work in garter st until piece measures 6½" from beg.

Break yarn, leaving an 18" tail, and keep sts on needle.

FINISHING

Pu all 25 sts from CO edge with a third needle. With RS together, join the picked-up sts to the final row using a 3-needle BO.

Weave in ends and turn RS out.

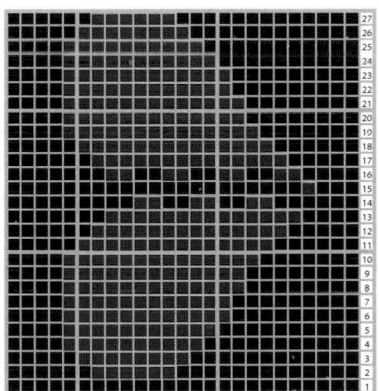 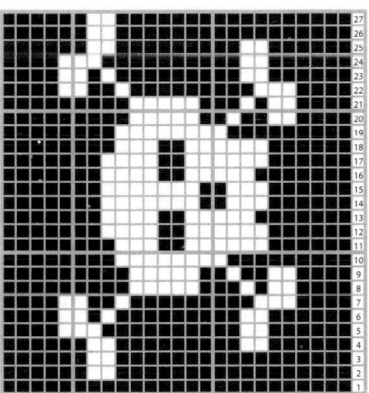

Note: The chart shows only the RS (beaded) rows.

About Renee

I am a thirty-five-year-old attorney living in St. Paul, Minnesota. When I was in college, I lived across the street from a yarn store and was drawn to the beautiful yarns and creativity of knitting, but it all seemed too expensive for my student budget. After jealously watching a fellow student knit during our law school classes, I finally took a community ed class. A great and unending love was born. I've dabbled in quilting, scrapbooking, beading, needlework, and other crafts, but I always return to the magic of two sticks and a string. When I'm not working or knitting, I am cheering on the Minnesota sports teams or indulging my love of good food, great conversation, books, and movies.

Point Taken

HOW TO MAKE YARN INTO A BEADING NEEDLE

W hen knitting with beads it can be really hard to find a needle that is both small enough to go through the bead and has an eye large enough to thread the yarn through. Try putting clear nail polish on the end of the yarn where you'll be threading the beads and, as it dries, shape it into a point. It can take a few applications to get it stiff enough, but it's much easier than trying to find a needle that fits the bill. *Vanessa Hays, Durham, NC*

Good Wool Hunting

RECYCLING YARN FROM THRIFT-STORE SWEATERS

Good-quality yarns, especially those that contain luxury fibers such as mohair, cashmere, or silk, can cost you an arm and a leg. But there are bargains to be had at your local thrift store if you're willing to recycle old yarn from a second-hand sweater instead of buying brand-new yarn. Begin by visiting your favorite thrift store and looking through the sweater rack for something made in a yarn you like. I find that mohair, wool, and various novelty yarns (fuzzy, sparkly, what have you) are pretty easy to come by; I've also found nice cotton yarns and interesting ribbon yarns. Before you lay down your $3 for the sweater, check the seams! Some cheap sweaters are made by cutting pieces out of machine-knit cloth; these pieces are then serged together with what looks like a zigzag stitch. If you took apart a sweater like that, you'd just have lots of little lengths of yarn. So make sure that the inside seams of the sweater look like knit edges, sewn together. This means that each piece of the sweater was individually knit (by hand or machine) and should come apart into one or two lengths of yarn.

To take the sweater apart:

Most sweaters come apart into four pieces: front, back, and two sleeves. Some have a collar or other elements. You're going to reduce the sweater to these component parts by undoing all the seams. Turn the sweater inside out and start with a side seam because it's the easiest. Find the thread that's holding the seam together. It will be a different type of thread from the yarn (a bit like embroidery floss, but thinner) and will show up *on one side of the seam* as a row of little Vs. Follow the *tops* of those Vs to one end of the seam. Then use small, pointed scissors to cut through one side of one of the Vs, as close to the end of the seam as you can. Then, with the scissors' point or a knitting needle, pull up on the same side of the next V down; that should pull up the end of the thread you just cut. Grab that loose end with your fingers and pull. It should undo all of the Vs (which turn out to be little loops) down the entire seam. If it catches and stops, just pull the two sides of the seam apart with a sharp but gentle tug, and things should loosen up. If you get really stuck, you can always pick another V and start again with a new loose end. Repeat this process with all the seams until you have four (or more) flat pieces of knit fabric. (*Note:* Sometimes a shoulder or neck-edge seam will be bound with some kind of stitching or is especially difficult to undo. You can, in a pinch, cut along the top of a knit piece and take that seam off; you'll only lose a few yards of the yarn that way. But *never, ever cut along a side seam!*)

Pick one piece and start unraveling:

If you can, find the loose end at one top corner of the piece and undo it; otherwise you can just cut into the top row somewhere and start pulling it apart. If the yarn catches a bit at the end of a row, a gentle tug should loosen it. As you unravel, wind the yarn into a ball. The yarn will be kinky, but this won't affect the ease of knitting with it or the way it looks once it's reknit. And you've got yourself three or four or five balls of some really cool yarn for the price of one skein of cheap acrylic! *Miranda Hassett, Carrboro, NC*

TRACI TRUESDALE
Roller Girl Legwarmers

t en years ago, when I was in college, I worked at a coffee shop con-nected to *the* music venue in town. I frequently wore my roller skates to work, hoping my moves would encourage better tips. Wanting to celebrate my former love for everything rollerskates and the resur-gence of '80s fashion, I made myself a pair of these legwarmers. I even brought out the old skates for a test drive. This pattern is perfect for beginners who are yearning to flex their creative muscles on a project that is a little more challeng-ing than a basic scarf. So knit up these legwarmers, find an old pair of skates, and shake your groove thang.

STITCH PATTERN
STRIPE SEQUENCE
7 rows MC, 4 rows CC, 4 rows MC, 4 rows CC, 7 rows MC.

Size
Women's S (M, L)

Finished circumference (upper calf): 12 (14½, 17½)"

Finished length: 16 (17, 18)"

Materials
Cascade 220 (100% wool; 100g/220 yds)

MC: 2 (2, 3) skeins #2410 Purple

CC: 1 skein #7814 Chartreuse

US 8 (5mm) double-pointed needles (set of 5) or US 8 (5mm) 16" circular needle, or size needed to obtain gauge

Gauge
20 sts and 28 rows = 4" in St st

DIRECTIONS (MAKE 2)

With MC, CO 60 (72, 88) sts. If using dpns, divide sts among 4 dpns, 15 (18, 22) sts on each.

Join and, foll stripe sequence, work 26 rnds in 2 × 2 rib.

With MC, work in St st until piece measures 16 (17, 18)" from beg.

BO.

FINISHING

Weave in ends.

Show me your tips! *Get a Hold of Yourself*

USING DPNS AND CIRCULARS TO HOLD LIVE STITCHES

Use circular and double-pointed needles instead of stitch holders. Since they operate from both ends, these needles eliminate the tedious slipping back and forth of stitches from traditional stitch holders. This is particularly useful when you intend to use the three-needle bind-off at the shoulders and when you are picking up stitches around the neck. I use short-row shaping for the shoulders if it's needed, instead of binding off to shape them, and put them on double-pointed needles when they're done so I can use the three-needle bind-off to connect them. The same works for the neck edge: Put the stitches for the front of the neck on double-pointed needles rather than binding them off and picking them up again later. Wrap a rubber band around each end of the double-pointed needles to keep the stitches from falling off. *Lindsay Woodel, Providence, RI*

About Traci

I live in Chicago with my husband and daughter. I started knitting several years ago when a coworker's mother dropped by the office while our boss was out of town. Knowing that she had an eager pupil, she brought me my first pair of bamboo needles and some delicious fluffy green yarn. I caught on pretty quickly and was immediately impressed with how easily my scarf grew. After I knit diligently all afternoon under the close supervision of my teacher, I then forgot all that I had just learned while trying to knit on the train ride home. An emergency trip to the knitting section at the library put me back on course. Today, with my habit fully in control of my life, I fantasize about knitting professionally someday and continue to try out my designs on unsuspecting friends and family.

STITCH 'N BITCH ACROSS THE NATION
California

Berkeley, California

BERKELEY, CALIFORNIA, SnB

On a Friday night in January of 2004, five friends and I gathered in my living room to remember or learn how to knit. We were armed with a copy of *Stitch 'n Bitch,* several skeins of yarn, and some old needles—the only situation in which it's okay to share them. Little did we know that in less than six weeks we'd outgrow the living room with more than one hundred members in our SnB group.

Most of our group's early members were seminary students and staff from the Pacific School of Religion and the Graduate Theological Union, both in Berkeley, who were drawn to the craft for its meditative nature. Then UC Berkeley students showed up and brought friends,

and it became an eclectic group of stitchers from all over the East Bay.

We've knit for charities such as Afghans for Afghans (crafting to assist the people of Afghanistan), the Knitter Critters Knitathon (making blankets for shelter animals), and a prayer shawl ministry (creating special shawls that the knitter infuses with prayers). Right now, we're planning a stitcher's retreat to explore knitting and other handwork as spiritual practice. For us, knitting is stress release and community-building. It develops patience, awareness, and much more.
Miss JoJo St. Purl

LOS ANGELES, CALIFORNIA, SnB

When *Stitch 'n Bitch* was published last year, the *LA Times* covered the LA SnB, and our membership soared. What started with seven girls knitting at a coffeehouse in Santa Monica in 2002 has since grown to four hundred girls and boys throughout the greater Los Angeles region. Six other branches of SnB L.A. have cropped up in the far-flung corners of the city, and our calendar now shows events just about daily.

If you're a member of a Stitch 'n Bitch in Los Angeles, you basically have to agree

to pretend there is winter. We send wooly scarves and sweaters to friends in Vermont and Seattle, and make ourselves felted slippers and afghans for the few really cool nights a year here. We use summer cottons and light acrylics all year long. Our natives have thin blood and wear knitted hats in 68-degree weather. And most of our SnB crew is so hard core, we continue knitting and crocheting through the 110-degree days of mid-September.

Because so many group members are designers, our talk often revolves around the licensing, copyrighting, and pricing of our products, as well as where to get labels and dress forms. Also, L.A. has more than

Los Angeles, California

thirty LYSs, so a lot of our bitching tends to be about the best and worst yarn stores around. Mostly, we are a bunch of like-minded girls and boys making new friends and getting caffeinated. Many of us don't have other friends who do what we do. But we're Stitch 'n Bitch—and we recruit.

Faith Landsman

San Francisco, California

SAN FRANCISCO, CALIFORNIA, CHICKS WITH STICKS

San Francisco Chicks with Sticks was born in the fall of 2002 when room-mates Gabrielle Pope and Kathy Barobs invited a few women over to their apartment for a night of knitting. After they spent more time watching *The Bache-lorette* and drinking wine than knitting, they decided to look for a place without a TV. They chose Bliss Bar, in Noe Valley. Happily, the owner offered them the use of the back room, on one condition: They had to share the room on the last Monday of every month with a group called Munch,

which meant that the SnB chicks found themselves knitting once a month surrounded by a group of S&M enthusiasts. Surprisingly enough, it was the knitters who got the odd-est looks!

Typically, twenty to thirty members show up for a good three hours of knitting and chatting, and, if they're lucky, Cabaret Chocolates contributes gourmet goodies for knitting energy. Though some members have been knitting for years, quite a few show up with no experience at all. Now people who have learned how to cast on at SFCWS are teaching the next set of knitters. The members inspire one another to try harder projects—and not to fear their favorite cheer: "Rip it out! Rip it out!" As one member put it, "I used to hate Mondays, and now they're my favorite night of the week!"

Kathy Barobs

SAN FRANCISCO PENINSULA, CALIFORNIA, SnB

If you're having trouble recruiting knitters to your SnB group, follow our example: Schedule meetings in the lounge of a local restaurant or bar, don't require an RSVP, and they will come. We have more than fifty members and two weekly meet-ings of newcomers and lifelong knitters alike. We have fun trying to recruit the curious men who ask what we're doing; no luck yet, but we'll keep trying.

San Francisco Peninsula, California

We relish seeing the completed proj-ects of our fellow knitters, since being involved from the beginning makes us feel as if we gave birth to ten projects instead of just one. And projects tend to catch on like wildfire: First it was felted bags, then scribble scarves, then "poncho-palooza." Who knows what next season will bring?

Knitting with the group has given each of our members the confidence to do more than she'd do on her own. Together we've learned:

1. There is always someone out there with a larger stash than yours.
2. If you know how to knit a scarf, you are absolutely ready for a sweater.
3. Knitting without a pattern isn't as scary as you think (some people prefer it).
4. Weaving in your ends is overrated—if you're the only one who sees them, let 'em hang!

Leslie Harrison

SAN JOSÉ, CALIFORNIA, SNB

If you've read anything about Silicon Valley, then you must know that life has been a roller coaster for us. Watching as friends and family lose their jobs, businesses, and sometimes their homes is devastating. But it seems that the more we are challenged, the more we strive to achieve, and many of us find ourselves doing things we never thought possible. Take me, for instance. I wanted to start a knitting group in September 2003, and even in the midst of schoolwork, charity knitting, and selling my line of knitting handbags to yarn stores, I did it.

Not much happens on a Sunday afternoon in the valley, but if you take a closer look, you'll see a cluster of tables, bobbing heads, and clicking needles—it's the Stitch 'n Bitch, that odd mix of ladies talking nonstop and knitting. The ones discovering talent that some of them never knew they had. The ones giving advice to those who ask for it (move over, Dr. Laura), swapping tried-and-true patterns and making up new ones, planning group projects, and giggling. The members of our little group are as varied as the stitches on your granny's afghan, but they do have a common thread—the art of knitting. We ooh and aah over every newly completed scarf, sweater, blanket, felted purse and hat, and even fish for compliments the way a mother does over photos of her new baby.

Jordana Paige

SANTA CRUZ, CALIFORNIA, SNB

The Santa Cruz Stitch 'n Bitch was born in September 2003, when best friends Gunilla and Babs pored over their regular knitting schedules and couldn't come up with a single day that week on which they could get together and have coffee and knit. "We should set a specific time and just do it—have a Stitch 'n Bitch like every Saturday afternoon," said Gunilla. "That's a damn good idea!" said Babs. Today they hold regular knitting sessions with about ten regulars every Saturday afternoon at their usual hangout, the 120 Union coffee shop. They all cheer one another on, no matter how crazy the project. Help is always readily available, and they welcome visitors and beginners into the flock. The first hit's always free. (No—wait! That didn't sound right. . . .)

One newcomer, a young, male UCSC student, showed up wanting to knit a hat with a ball of brown sheep wool worsted and size 10 circulars at the ready. Gunilla showed him how to cast on and how to knit Continental style (she's from Sweden, after all). He quickly got the hang of it, and under Gunilla's direction, he finished the hat the next day. He hasn't returned to SnB, but he was spotted at a yarn shop where he was getting materials for his next project, a felted hat. Future plans for Santa Cruz SnB include a Purl 'n Hurl—knitting's response to the pub crawl.

Gunilla Leavitt

Santa Cruz, Califonia

San José, California

AMY SWENSON

Felted Furry Foot Warmers

Finished size
Women's M

Materials
MONSTER
A: Brown Sheep Lamb's Pride Bulky (85% wool, 15% mohair; 113g/125 yds), 3 skeins #M110 Orange You Glad

B: Lion Brand Fun Fur (100% polyester; 50g/60 yds), 2 skeins #195 Hot Pink

US 13 (9mm) 24" circular needle

1 sheet red craft felt

1 sheet white craft foam

Four 1½" (40mm) wiggle eyes

Glue

PLAIN
A: Brown Sheep Lamb's Pride Bulky (85% wool, 15% mohair; 113g/125 yds), 3 skeins #M38 Lotus Pink

B: Lion Brand Fun Fur (100% polyester; 50g/60 yds), 2 skeins #191 Violet

US 13 (9mm) 24" circular needle

US 13 (9mm) double-pointed needle (1 needle)

Gauge
12 sts and 16 rows = 4" with A, but exact gauge is unimportant for this project

Special Skill
SHORT-ROW SHAPING

these fun slippers are great for keeping your toes toasty while appealing to your inner child. Knit a pair of happy monsters with gaping mouths, pointy felt teeth, and giant googly eyes. Or knit a pair that's plain (but far from boring). Knit with bulky wool and fun fur and then felted, the slippers are thick and fluffy and perfect for shuffling around in on a lazy weekend morning. They're also a great quick-to-knit gift.

STITCH
W&T (WRAP AND TURN)
Sl the next st pwise, bring the yarn between the needles to the front of the work, and sl the st back to the left-hand needle. Turn the work, and begin working in the opposite direction. When you get to the wrapped st on the next row, sl the needle through both the wrap and the wrapped st kwise, and k them tog.

Violet variation

 **The Long and Winding Yarn**

KEEPING YOUR YARN STILL WHILE YOU WIND IT UP

*I*f you buy a skein of yarn that is center-pulled, but no matter how much you search you can't find the inside end, you may want to rewind it. To work quickly without the yarn flying all over the place while you're winding, just put the yarn into a wide and deep plastic hamper. Or try an empty CD holder: Packs of blank CDs come stacked in a plastic container, with a bar sticking up in the center. Simply place your yarn on the bar as if it were a spool and wind away. *Diana Camden, Costa Mesa, CA*

DIRECTIONS
SOLE
With A, CO 9 sts.

Working in St st, shape sole:

Row 1: K.

Rows 2–3: Inc 1 st at each edge.

Row 4: P.

Row 5: Inc 1 st at each edge.

Rows 6–8: Work even in St st.

Row 9: Inc 1 st at each edge.

Work even in St st until piece measures 14" from beg, ending with RS facing.

Dec 1 st from each edge of next row, then EOR once.

Next (turning) row (WS): K.

Inc 1 st from each edge of next row, then EOR once.

Work in St st until piece measures 13½" from turning row, ending with RS facing.

Next row: Ssk, k to last 2 sts, k2tog.

Work 3 rows even.

Dec 1 st from each edge of next row, then EOR once— 9 sts.

BO; do not break yarn.

Fold sole with WS tog (the turning row becomes the heel edge). Beg at toe end, pu sts through each half of the sole as foll:

Pu 53 sts along left edge of sole, 13 sts along heel edge, 53 sts along right edge, and 9 sts along toe edge—128 sts.

Join B, and with 1 strand of each yarn held tog, k 1 rnd even.

Next rnd and cont with both yarns tog: K30, BO 59, working 2 sts tog 5 times evenly across BO, k39—69 sts.

MONSTER ONLY
K 1 row, turn.

Shape as follows:

K34, w&t, sl1, k34. Turn work.

K28, w&t, sl1, k40, turn.

K34, w&t, sl1, k34, turn.

K28, w&t, sl1, k40, w&t.

Next row: Sl1, k11, k2tog, w&t.

Rep last row 9 times more—59 sts.

Next row: Sl1 st, k4, k2tog, k5, k2tog, w&t.

Next row: Sl1, k10, k2tog, w&t.

Rep last row 4 times more—52 sts.

Next row: Sl1, k4, k2tog, k4, k2tog, w&t.

Next row: Sl1, k9, k2tog, w&t.

Rep last row 4 times more—45 sts.

Next row: Sl1, k3, k2tog, k4, k2tog, w&t.

Next row: Sl1, k8, k2tog, w&t.

Rep last row 3 times more—39 sts.

Next row: Sl1, k3, k2tog, k3, k2tog, w&t.

Next row: Sl1, k7, k2tog, w&t.

Rep last row 5 times more—31 sts.

Next row: Sl1, k2, k2tog, k3, k2tog, w&t.

Next row: Sl1, k6, k2tog, w&t.

Rep last row 4 times more—24 sts.

Next row: Sl1, k2, k2tog, k2, k2tog, w&t.

Next row: Sl1, k5, k2tog, w&t.

Rep last row 13 times more—8 sts.

Next row: Sl1, k5, k2tog, pu 5 sts along side of top and 1 st on sole edge. Turn work.

Next row: Sl1, k10, k2tog, pu 5 sts along side and 1 st on sole edge. Turn work.

BO.

PLAIN ONLY

K 2 rows even.

Next row: K30, place rem sts on spare needle.

Work in garter st on first 30 sts until slipper top is 6" from sole edge.

Use 3-needle BO to attach 30 live sts to 30 sts on spare needle.

Graft the 9 rem live sts to toe edge of slipper top.

FINISHING

Loosely tack any yarn ends to prevent unraveling, then felt slippers to desired size.

Monster only:

The still wet felted slipper will have an extra bulge of fabric at the top of the toe. Push this in to form a mouth and let dry. Cut out tongue and teeth as desired from felt and craft foam, and glue in place. Glue on eyes where desired.

About Amy

Although I grew up in Chicago, I now live in Calgary, Alberta, where warm slippers are useful practically year-round. I finance my overwhelming addiction to yarn through my work as a business requirements analyst for a leading interactive services agency. More information about my line of original knitting patterns can be found at www.indiknits.com.

RENEE RIGDON

Hurry Up Spring Armwarmers

Snow on the ground; ice on my sidewalk—I'd had enough of winter and it was only January. In need of a pick-me-up, I headed off to my friendly LYS for my favorite drug, Noro Kureyon. While I fondled its woolly goodness, I tried to envision vines and leaves sprouting, banishing the snow for another year. These armwarmers are as close as I could get to changing the seasons with a wave of my hand. They are a little bit earth goddess and a whole lot of sass on a brisk day, with just enough coverage to keep your hands toasty, but still leave you use of your fingers.

Because everything but the thumb gusset and the section that's knit from the chart is ribbed, shaping is unnecessary and these armwarmers fit just about anyone. They kept me warm while I dreamed of spring and will do the same for you.

DIRECTIONS
RIGHT ARMWARMER
CO 32 sts.

Divide sts among 3 dpns with 11 sts on 1st needle, 10 sts on 2nd, and 11 sts on 3rd.

Join and, beg and ending with k1, work in 2 × 2 rib until piece measures 1½" from beg.

Cont rib on 1st and 3rd needles, work from chart on 2nd needle until 30 chart rows have been worked.

Size

Women's M

Finished circumference: 6½"

To fit: Up to 10½" circumference

Materials

Noro Kureyon (100% wool; 50g/110 yds), 2 skeins #88 (green/brown/orange/yellow) OR #130 (pink/purple/yellow/red)

US 7 (4.5mm) double-pointed needles, or size needed to obtain gauge (set of 4)

Cable needle

Stitch markers

Stitch holder

Gauge

16 sts and 24 rows = 4" in St st

Maintaining rib and chart patt as est, beg thumb gusset on 3rd needle:

Rnd 1, needle 3: P2, k1, pm, m1, pm, cont in patt as est.

Rnd 2, needle 3: Sm, m1, k1, m1, sm, cont in patt as est.

Cont to work gusset by k into the back and front of the first and last sts between the markers on each rnd to 13 sts between markers.

Place gusset sts on holder.

Cont in the round, work in patt until all chart rows have been completed.

Work in 2 × 2 rib for 1".

BO.

Use color #130 to make these sunset-colored warmers.

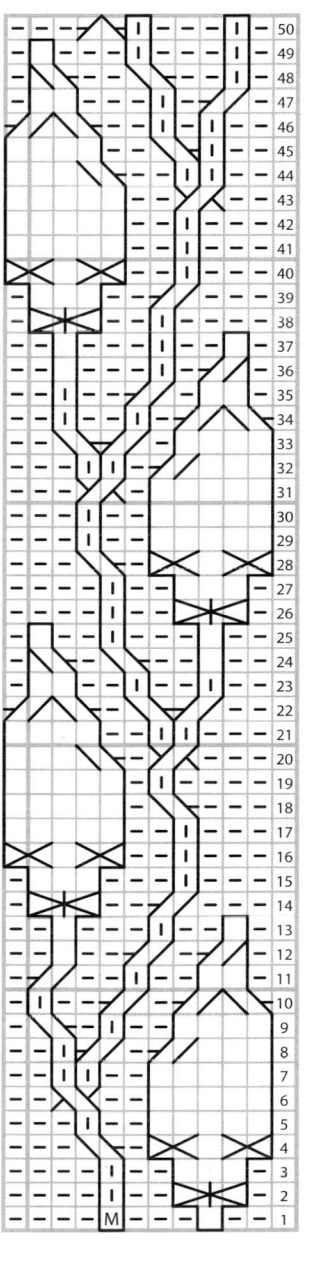

- = p

□ = k

I = ktbl

M = m1

= sl1 st to cn, hold in front, p1, k1 from cn

= sl1 st to cn, hold to back, k1, p1 from cn

= sl1 st to cn, hold to front, k1, k1 from cn

= sl1 st to cn, hold to back, k1, k1 from cn

= sl right needle through next 3 sts as if to k, k through the front, back, and front of all 3 sts

= sl right needle through next 2 sts as if to k through the back, k through the back and front of both sts

= p2tog

Thumb:

Divide holder sts between 3 dpns.

Join new yarn and k first and last gusset sts tog.

Work in St st for 2 rnds, then in 2 × 2 rib for 2 rnds.

BO.

LEFT ARMWARMER

Work as for right armwarmer, reversing chart.

Reverse placement of thumb gusset as follows:

Rnd 30, needle 1: K1, p2, k2, p2, k1, pm, m1, pm, k1, p2, work to row 30 of chart. Cont left armwarmer as for right armwarmer.

FINISHING

Weave in ends, using tail from thumb BO to seam the hole between the thumb gusset and the palm.

About Renee

When I was five years old, my nana taught me how to crochet. I'm sure that my snakelike chains, some extending the length of my yard, were a portent of the fiber addiction that would take hold when I taught myself to knit thirteen years later. Now I balance knitting time with caring for my seventeen-month-old, "Monkey Boy" Cayden, and his sidekick, Dog Wonder, and thwarting my husband's evil plans. I helped start the Lexington, Kentucky, Stitch 'n Bitch and intend to own a kickass yarn shop within ten years.

Wet It and Forget It

JOINING YARN WITH THE SPIT-SPLICE METHOD

When you need to start a new ball of wool, rather than tying the old and new ends together, you can attach them to each other almost invisibly by using your own God-given saliva. This method works only with 100% wool yarns. First, fray the two ends of the yarn to be joined, then use a pair of scissors or your hands to remove a little bit of yarn from each end. Suck on the ends (this is the "spit" part). Lay the ends across each other so that they overlap slightly. Then rub them rapidly back and forth with the palm of your hand against a fabric that has a little texture to it, like your jeans. The friction and heat will make the fibers stick together (it can take a couple of minutes). Then just go right on knitting!

Meg Poehler, Portland, OR

CARRIE COLLINS

Belt de Jour

during a monthlong job hiatus last winter, I did nothing but knit for three weeks straight. I had acquired a hefty stash of yarn and had to come up with dozens of ways to use it. It wasn't hard, until I came across a beautiful sweater pattern with a cable pattern running down the front. I didn't have enough yarn for the sweater and had already spent my entire yarn budget for the year. But as I started knitting the cable pattern, just to try it out, I discovered that it was the perfect width for a belt. It's a great cheap project and an easy introduction to cables.

Size

Length: To fit

Width: 1¾"

Materials

Lamb's Pride Worsted (85% wool, 15% mohair; 113g/190 yds), 1 skein M78 Aztec Turquoise OR M120 Limeade

US 7 (4.5mm) straight needles, or size needed to obtain gauge

Cable needle

Belt buckle: One ¾" rhinestone buckle #19830 for Aztec Turquoise belt; one ¾" metal buckle #31091 for Limeade belt, both from M & J Trimming, www.mjtrim.com

Gauge

18 stitches and 22 rows = 4" in St st

STITCH PATTERN
CABLE PATTERN

Row 1: K8.

Row 2: P8.

Row 3: C4b, c4f

Row 4: P8.

Row 5: K8.

Row 6: P8.

DIRECTIONS

BELT

CO 12 sts.

Row 1: Sl1 pwise, p1, cable patt row 1, p2.

Row 2: Sl1 kwise, k1, cable patt row 2, k2.

Row 3: Sl1 pwise, p1, cable patt row 3, p2.

Row 4: Sl1 kwise, k1, cable patt row 4, k2.

Row 5: Sl1 pwise, p1, cable patt row 5, p2.

Row 6: Sl1 kwise, k1, cable patt row 6, k2.

Rep rows 1 to 6 until belt is 1" longer than desired length.

BO.

BELT LOOP (OPTIONAL)

CO 4 sts.

Work in garter st for 1½" from beg.

BO.

FINISHING

Block pieces.

Sew belt loop onto belt 5" from CO edge.

Attach belt buckle to CO end of belt.

Fold corners of BO end into a triangle and sew tog.

About Carrie

I recently moved to Chicago from San Francisco, where I teach knitting and piano. I started knitting when I was eleven or twelve years old, but then started focusing on music in my "spare" time. After my last recital, I wanted to do something completely different from playing the piano, so I picked up knitting again. My boyfriend gladly accepted my first "punk rock" scarf—aptly named for the many accidental holes and wavy sides. I've been a compulsive knitter ever since.

Ancient Chinese Secret

MAKING KNITTING NEEDLES FROM CHOPSTICKS

I came up with the idea of making chopstick knitting needles after many late nights at the China Buffet. It is a great way to save money and fill in your needle collection. To make them, you'll need:

- A pair of chopsticks (of course)
- A pencil sharpener
- Medium- and fine-grain sandpaper
- Old rag or fabric scrap
- Small amount of polymer clay
- Craft glue
- Clear polyurethane (optional)

(1) Sharpen the "food" tip of each chopstick with a pencil sharpener.

(2) Sand down the entire needle (with the grain) using the medium-grain sandpaper and then the fine-grain sandpaper. Be sure to make the tip rounded, not pointed—we don't want any knitting-related injuries, do we?

(3) When both needles have been fully sanded, rub them with your cloth until they are silky smooth.

(4) To make the ends of the needles, take a small amount of polymer clay and wrap it around each end in any fashion your heart desires. Bake the needles and clay according to the instructions on the package. Polymer clay shrinks when it cooks, so the ends should be stuck to the needles after baking. If an end falls off, simply glue it back in place with craft glue.

(5) You have a few options when it comes to finishing the needles. By far the most durable method is to coat the needles with a layer of clear polyurethane. Another way is to alternate rubbing the needle with waxed paper (until hot) and then a fabric scrap. This will make the wood satiny, and it will help fill in any spaces left by sanding. *Cassie Christenson, Oshkosh and Dodgeville, WI*

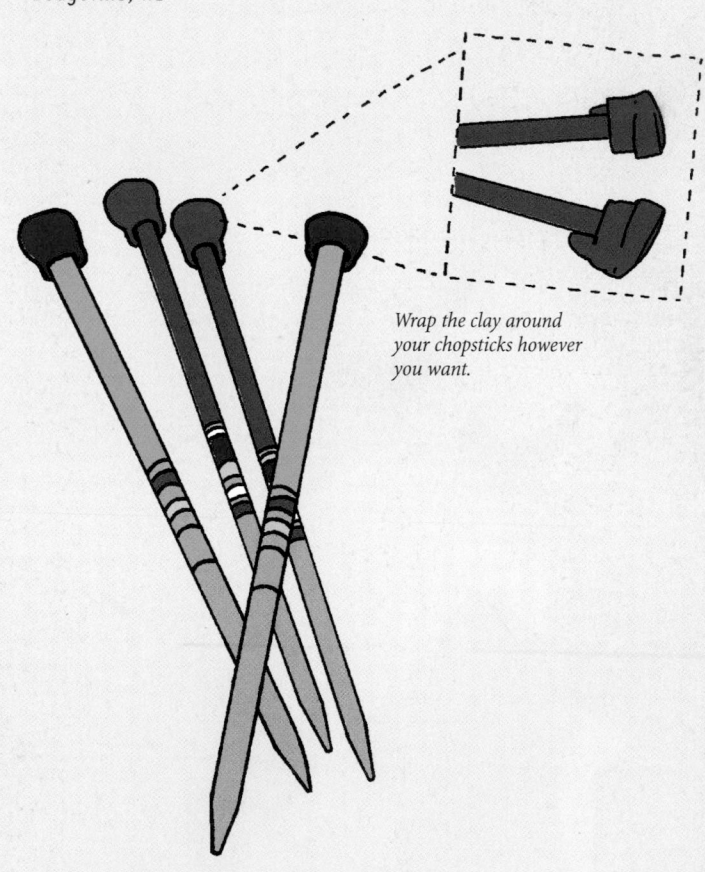

Wrap the clay around your chopsticks however you want.

MARCY NETH

Li'l Devil Pants

these pants are based on a pair of knitted baby pants my husband and I borrowed from friends for our first son. We used to call them his Mussolini pants because they looked like a pair of ski pants Mussolini had worn and made the baby resemble a tiny fascist dictator. When our second son was born I wanted similar pants, and came up with these. They are soft and easy to put on. The devil tail is in keeping with the dictator theme. (Life with my sons is not easy.) The little garter stitch devil point at the end of the tail can be reversed to be a heart shape for good, sweet babies, if any such babies exist.

DIRECTIONS

PANTS

Waist hem:

With straight needles, CO 70 (74, 78) sts.

Work in St st until piece measures 1" from beg, ending with WS facing.

Turning ridge (WS): K.

Work next 3 rows in St st, beg with a K row.

Drawstring hole:

Next row: *K8, turn.

Next row: P8, turn.

Rep from * 1 time.

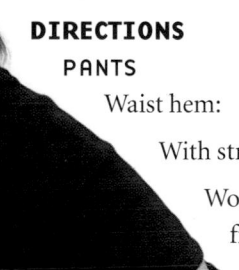

Size

6 (12, 18) months

Finished waist: 17 (18, 19)"

Finished length: 15 (16½, 18)"

Materials

Sandnes Lanett Superwash (100% merino wool; 50g/213 yds), 3 (4, 4) skeins #4128 Cherry Red

US 3 (3.25mm) straight needles, or size needed to obtain gauge

US 3 (3.25mm) double-pointed needles (set of 2)

One ¾" button

Gauge

32 sts and 42 rows = 4" in St st

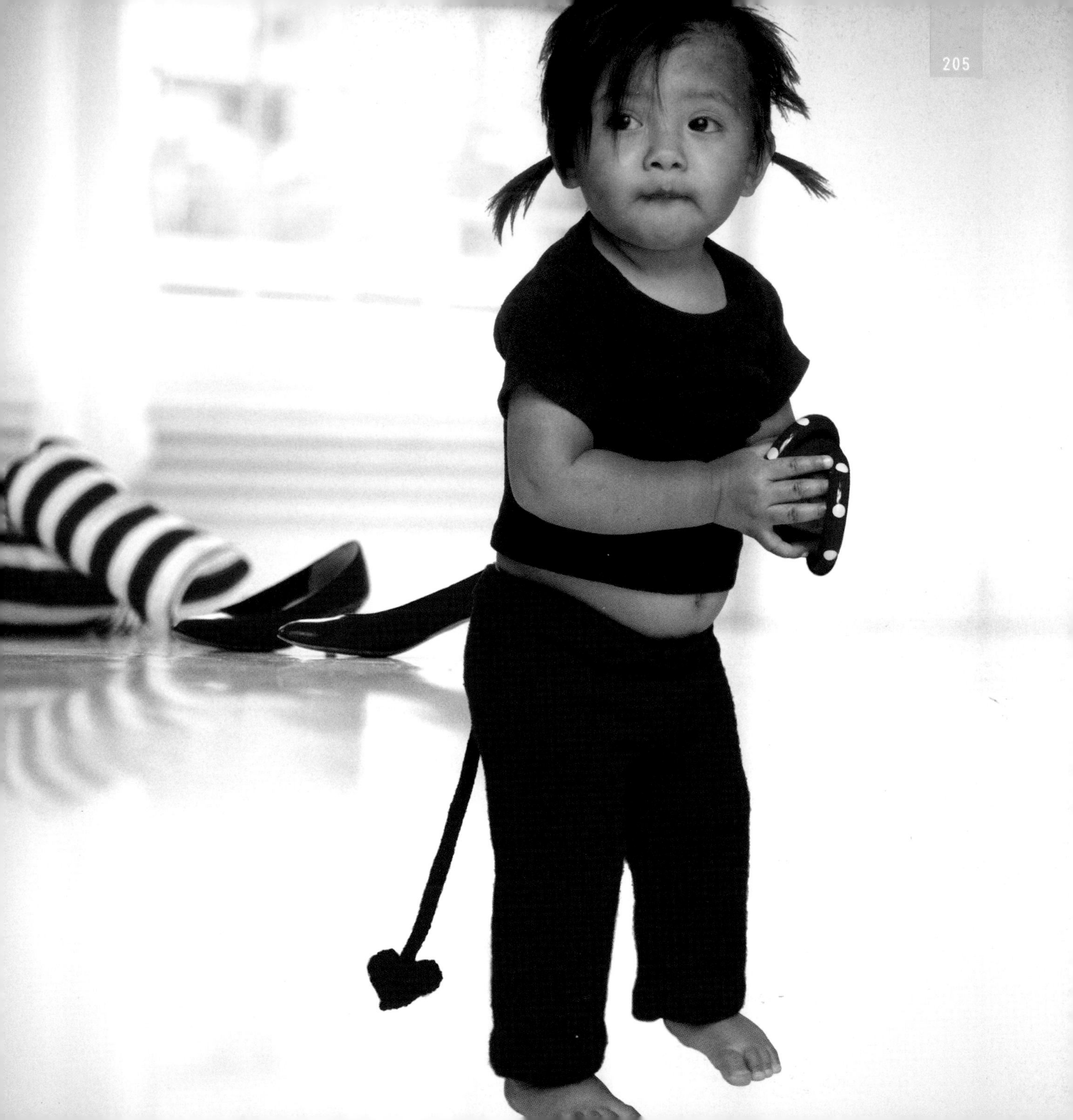

Next row: K8 and place these sts on a holder. Break yarn, leaving a 4" tail.

Join yarn to sts on left-hand needle and k 62 (66, 70) sts.

Work in St st on these 62 (66, 70) sts for 4 more rows.

Next row: P 70 (74, 78) sts, including sts from holder.

Top:

Work in St st until piece measures 6 (6½, 7)" from beg, ending with RS facing.

Inc 1 st at each edge of next row, then EOR 3 times, then ER 8 times—94 (98, 102) sts.

Work in St st until piece measures 7½ (8, 8½)" from beg, ending with RS facing.

Leg:

Dec 1 st at each edge of next row, then every foll 12 (14, 14)th row 6 times—80 (84, 88) sts.

Work in St st until piece measures 16 (17½, 19)" from beg, ending with WS facing.

Turning ridge (WS): K.

Work next 3 rows in St st, beg with a K row.

BO.

Make a second piece as for the first, reversing drawstring hole shaping as follows:

Next row: *K62 (66, 70), turn.

Next row: P62 (66, 70), turn.

Rep from * 1 time.

Next row: K62 (66, 70) and place these sts on a holder. Break yarn, leaving a 4" tail.

Join yarn to sts on left-hand needle and k8.

Work in St st on these 8 sts for 4 more rows.

Next row: P70 (74, 78) sts, inc 1 st from holder.

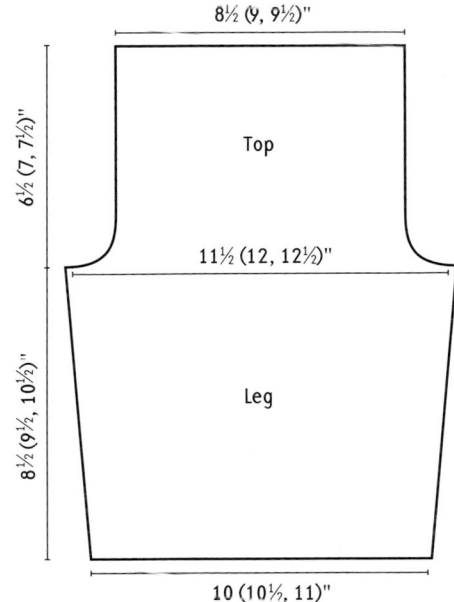

TAIL

With straight needles, CO 3 sts.

P 1 row.

Inc 1 st at each edge of next row, then EOR 2 times more—9 sts.

Work in St st until piece measures 10" from beg, ending with RS facing.

Dec 1 st at each edge of next row, then EOR 2 times more—3 sts.

BO.

DEVIL POINT (MAKE 2)

With straight needles, CO 1 st.

K 1 row.

Next row: Inc1—2 sts.

K 1 row.

Next row: Inc1 twice—4 sts.

K 2 rows.

Next row: *Inc1, k to last st, inc1.
K 1 row.* Rep from * to * once more.

Next row: *Inc1, k to last st, inc1.
K 2 rows.* Rep from * to * three times more—16 sts.

Next row: K6, k2tog, turn, placing rem sts on holder.

**K 1 row.

Next row: K2tog, k3, k2tog, turn.

K 1 row.

Next row: K2tog, k1, k2tog, turn.

BO.**

Transfer holder sts to needle. Join yarn and k2tog, k6.

Rep from ** to **.

DRAWSTRING
With dpns, CO 3 sts.

Work in I-cord for 25 (27, 29)".

Break yarn, leaving a 4" tail. Draw tail through sts and secure.

FINISHING
Mattress st body and inseam of pants, leaving a ½" space open 2" down from the garter ridge at the top of the back.

Reinforce drawstring holes and back tail hole with blanket st.

Fold body hem to the inside at the turning ridge and whipstitch in place, leaving drawstring holes open.

Thread drawstring through holes.

Fold leg hems to the inside at the turning ridge and whipstitch in place.

Sew button to the tail at CO end.

Tack devil points onto either side of the rem end of the tail and sew tog.

Weave in all ends.

About Marcy

I am a lapsed librarian who is currently a stay-at-home mom. A friend taught me to knit in the 1980s when I wanted a plain black sweater and could not find one anywhere. (One day I will make that black sweater.) A long stint at the Art Institute of Chicago taught me that almost anything can be knit out of any material. As much as I love wool, I know that strings and sticks can be combined in limitless ways.

DELIA LAM

Baby's First Tattoo

Lately there has been a spate of new babies among my friends, and that means a never-ending need for baby gifts. This little sweater was developed in response to looking for something classic but contemporary and still a bit saucy to fit modern mommy tastes. It's a twist on a simple piece that offers an opportunity for a fine gauge and intarsia in a smaller project.

Classic tattoos and vintage textiles inspired the swallows, but if you omit these motifs and knit in a solid color, the cardi is still absolutely elegant due to its fine gauge. Add the motifs and the contrasting trim and the variations are endless for customizing. The directions are written for mirrored motifs on the chest, but this cardi really invites experimentation and is a great baby shower standard.

DIRECTIONS

BACK

With CC, CO 70 (76, 84, 90) sts. Work in seed st for 6 rows. Change to MC and work in St st until piece measures 4½ (5, 5½, 6)" from beg, ending with a WS row.

Size

3 (6, 12, 18) months

Finished chest: 20 (22, 24, 26)"

Finished length: 8¾ (9¾, 10¾, 11¾)"

Materials

Rowan 4-Ply Soft
(100% merino wool; 50g/162 yds)

MC: 2 (3, 3, 4, 4) skeins #377 Wink

CC: 1 skein #389 Expresso

US 3 (3mm) straight needles,
or size needed to obtain gauge

4 small snaps

Tapestry needle

Stitch holders

Gauge

28 sts and 36 rows = 4" in St st

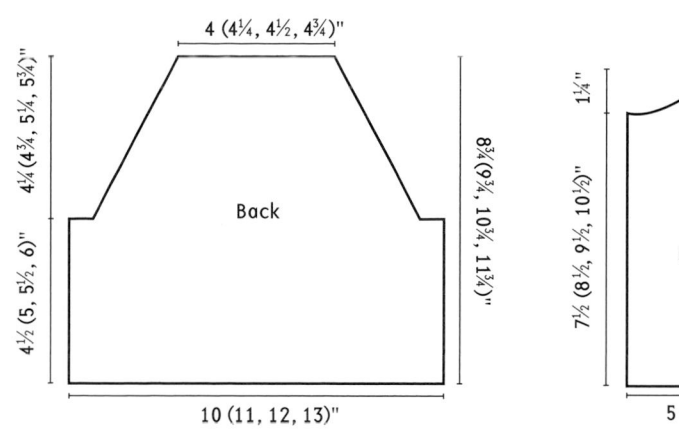

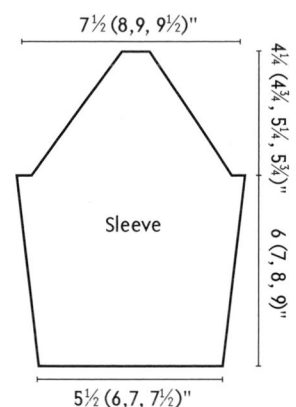

Shape raglan:

BO 3 sts at beg of next 2 rows.

Next row (RS): Sl1 kwise, k1, ssk, k to last 4 sts, k2tog, k2.

Next row: Sl1 kwise, p to end.

Rep last 2 rows until 28 (30, 32, 34) sts rem.

Place rem sts on holder.

LEFT FRONT

With CC, CO 35 (38, 42, 45) sts. Work in seed st for 6 rows.

Change to MC and work in St st last 4 sts.

With CC, work in seed st for front band to end.

Keeping in patt as established, work until piece measures 4½ (5, 5½, 6)" from beg, end with a WS row.

Work raglan shaping at side edge as for back, *at the same time,* when piece measures 7½ (8½, 9½, 10½)" from beg, end with a RS row and shape neck as foll:

BO 4 (5, 6, 7) sts and cont to dec 1 st at neck edge every row 10 times more.

RIGHT FRONT

Work as for left front, reversing all shaping.

SLEEVE (MAKE 2)

With CC, CO 38 (42, 48, 52) sts. Work in seed st for 6 rows.

Change to MC and work in St st, inc 1 st each side every 4th row 8 times—54 (58, 64, 68) sts.

Work until piece measures 6 (7, 8, 9)" from beg.

Shape raglan cap:

BO 3 sts at beg of next 2 rows.

Next row (RS): Sl1 kwise, k1, ssk, k to last 4 sts, k2tog, k2.

Next row: Sl1 kwise, p to end.

Rep last 2 rows until 12 sts rem.

Place rem sts on holder.

FINISHING

Sew raglan sleeves to back and fronts. Sew side and sleeve seams.

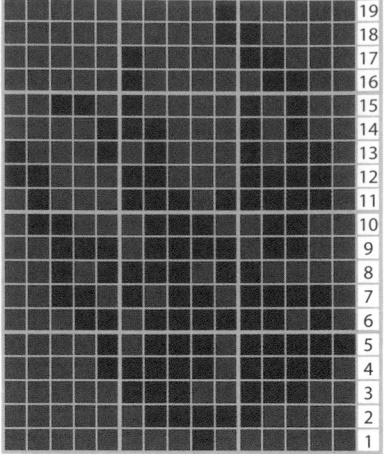

swallow for left side

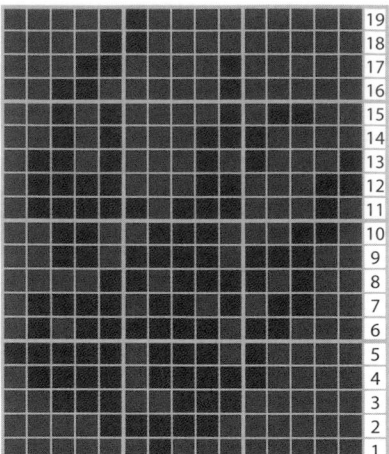

swallow for right side

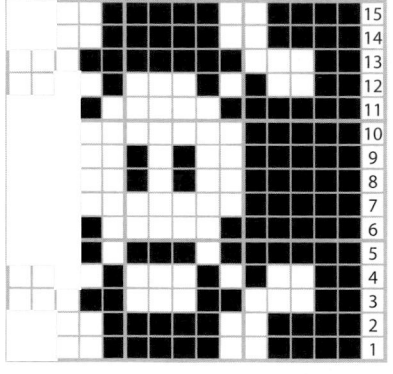

skull motif

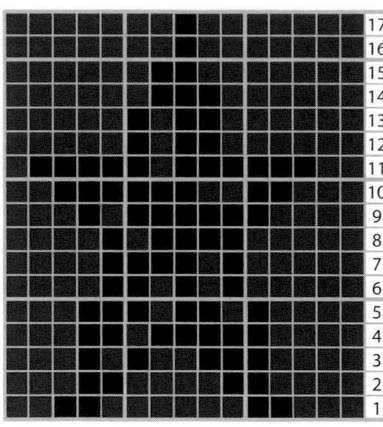

star motif

About Delia

I've been knitting since I was five, thanks to my grandmother. I shared a room with her when I was little and every night I fell asleep to the sound of her needles clacking away, soothing and lulling me with their rhythm. These days, I love how many people knit—the bouncer at the bar, the hipster at the show, the student at the library, the friend, the neighbor, the boss. As a lifelong yarn junkie as well as crafting fiend, I haunt yarn shops, buy and stash more than I can sensibly knit, dream of patterns, and think of my grandmother. When not knitting, I can be found getting a late start learning how to drive a stick shift on the streets of Minneapolis and St. Paul.

Neck band:

With CC and RS facing, pu and k15 sts up right front neck, transfer sts from holders to needle, pu and k15 sts down left front neck—82 (84, 86, 88) sts. Work in seed st for 6 rows.

BO.

St chosen motif onto left and right fronts of cardigan, beg lower right hand corner of chosen chart so that chart is centered on front and bottom edge of motif is in line with beg of raglan shaping.

JENNIFER SMALL

Bunny Hat

I originally started making baby hats as gifts because they were a great return on my investment—they don't take long, and you can add lots of cute details for maximum oohs and aahs when you give them at a baby shower. I made this hat for my friend Eric's new baby girl. He is a very hip Gen-X guy, and I wanted to make something embarrassingly cute to welcome him into fatherhood. The wool in this wool- and cotton-blend yarn makes it stretchy and easy to work with, and the cotton makes it soft and light for comfort. I use short-row shaping for the ear flaps so they're extra stretchy. The hat is designed in pink with white inner ears for a girl, but you could make it in light blue or even in tan with pink inner ears for a Peter Rabbit vibe.

STITCH

W&T (WRAP AND TURN)

Sl the next st pwise, bring the yarn between the needles to the front of the work, and sl the st back to the left-hand needle. Turn the work, and begin working in the opposite direction. When you get to the wrapped st on the next row, sl the needle through both the wrap and the wrapped st kwise, and k them tog.

DIRECTIONS

HAT

With MC and dpn or circular needles, cast on 44 (56) sts.

Size

3–12 (18–36) months

Finished circumference: 14 (16)"

Materials

Rowan Wool Cotton (50% merino wool, 50% cotton; 50g/123 yds)

MC: 2 balls #951 Tender

CC1: 1 ball #900 Antique

CC2: 1 ball #908 Inky

US 5 (3.5mm) 16" circular needle, or size needed to obtain gauge

US 5 (3.5mm) double-pointed needles (set of 5)

Stitch marker

Tapestry needle

Gauge

22 sts and 32 rows = 4" in St st

Special Skill

SHORT-ROW SHAPING

Ear flaps:

Working back and forth, work 9 rows in garter st.

**Next row: K21 (27), w&t.

Next row: K.

Rep these 2 rows, working 1 less st before each wrap, until 8 live sts rem.

Turn and work to end.

Next row: K all sts, picking up wraps and working them tog with sts as you work across.**

Rep from ** to ** for second ear flap.

Body of hat:

Next row (back of hat): K19 (27), *m1, k1; rep from * 6 (2) times, k19 (27).

Without turning, pm (first marker) and CO 30 sts (front of hat)—80 (88) sts.

Pm (second marker and beg of rnd) and join, being careful not to twist sts.

Next rnd: P5, k40, p5, sl marker, p to end of rnd.

Work 6 rnds more as established, working 1 less p st every other row before first marker and after 2nd marker.

Remove first marker and work in St st until piece measures 3½ (4)" from CO edge.

Next rnd: *K6, k2tog; rep from * to end. K 1 rnd.

Rep these 2 rnds, working 1 less st bet decs until 20 (22) sts rem.

Next rnd: K2tog around—10 (11) sts.

Next rnd: K0 (1), k2tog around—5 (6) sts.

Break yarn, draw tail through rem sts and secure.

Embroidery chart

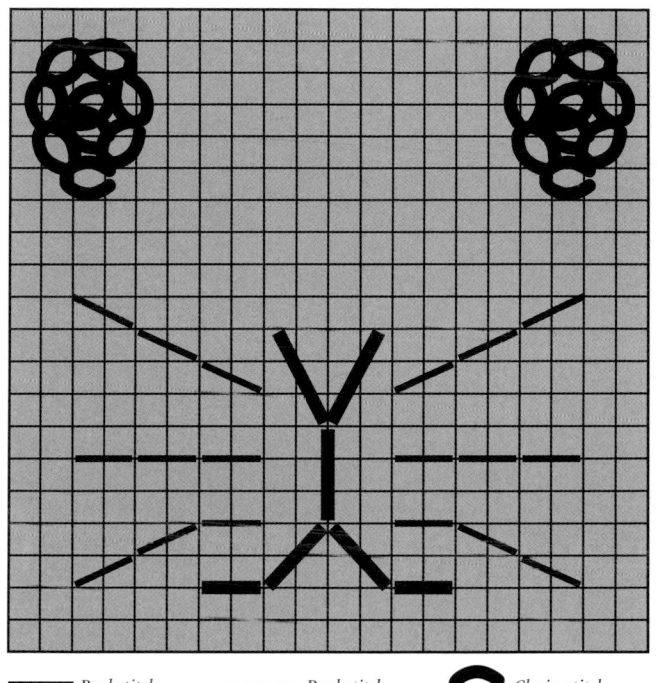

▬▬▬ Backstitch (black yarn)   ▬▬▬ Backstitch (split black yarn in half)   ◖ Chain stitch (black yarn)

TIES
With dpn, pu 3 sts from bottom corner of ear flap. Work in I-cord for 10".

Repeat on second ear flap.

OUTER EAR (MAKE 2)
With MC, CO 13 sts.

Work in St st for 20 rows.

Next row: Ssk, k9, k2tog.

**Work in St st for 5 rows.

Next row: Ssk, k7, k2tog.

Work in St st for 3 rows.

Next row: Ssk, k5, k2tog.**

Rep from ** to **, working 2 less sts bet decs, until 5 sts rem.

Work in St st for 3 rows.

BO.

INNER EAR (MAKE 2)

With CC1, CO 9 sts.

Work in St st for 20 rows.

Next row: Ssk, k5, k2tog.

Work in St st for 5 rows.

Rep these 6 rows, working 2 less sts bet decs, until 3 sts rem.

Work in St st for 3 rows.

BO.

FINISHING

Steam-block earpieces.

With MC, blanket st inner ear to outer ear: Beg at the bottom of one edge, sew up to the top. At the top, there will be a few more rows of the outer ear. Seam the two tips together. Sew down the inner ear to the other outer ear edge.

Steam-block the ears flat and sew them to hat to correspond with picture.

With CC2 and tapestry needle, embroider face on front of hat to correspond with diagram.

About Jennifer

Chicago's my town, where I work as a software designer. Knitting is a great way for me to be creative with my hands and not just my brain. I've always loved fiber arts, and even have an art degree in it. I only began knitting about three years ago, and I'm delighted with its potential. I especially love shaping with knitting; it's magical that a 3-D shape can appear from my needles. I've been knitting for all of my friends' babies for the last few years, and now am eagerly expecting a baby of my own to adorn with all sorts of silly and cute items!

Presto Chango

MAKING NICER COLOR CHANGES IN RIBBING

When changing colors in a rib, knit the entire first row (even the purl stitches) of the new color. Knit the next row with the same color in the normal way for ribbing: Knit the knits and purl the purls. You will avoid that funny jog you get on the purl stitches and make a smooth color transition, and that knit row will essentially disappear. Magic!

Lucy Lee, Cambridge, MA

HEIDI NEURAUTER

One-Hour Baby Booties

Size
Newborn (3–6 months)

Materials
Lamb's Pride Bulky
(85% wool, 15% mohair; 113g/125 yds),
1 skein M115 Oatmeal

For newborn: US 8 (5mm) straight
needles

For 3–6 months: US 9 (5.5mm) straight
needles

US I/9 (5.5mm) crochet hook

Two ½" buttons

1 packet blue Kool-Aid w/ a pinch of
cherry (to mute the blue)

Gauge
13 sts and 22 rows = 4" garter st
on size 8 needles

12 sts and 20 rows = 4" on size
9 needles

Abbreviation
Inc1: K and p into the same st.

before my daughter was born, I spent much of my then underappreciated free time knitting her a bunch of teensy socks and booties. The footwear in question was knit on size 0 needles using very soft, very expensive, very dry-clean-only cashmere. They were delicate, and looked so sweet stacked neatly in her dresser drawer. Of course, I birthed a guileless free spirit who couldn't be bothered with socks. Or booties. Or cashmere. Did I mention the socks were bland and slippery? How could I blame my discerning baby for rejecting them? I can only blame myself. Who in her right mind would knit something with a 2- or 3-month shelf life using size 0 needles?

Today, as a mom, I am a lot more practical, and into saving precious time and energy whenever possible. I designed these booties, which can be knit in one hour or less, to appeal to both the knitter and the infant geniuses who will wear them with pride and adulation.

DIRECTIONS
BOOTY (MAKE 2)
CO 9 sts.

Row 1: K1, inc1, k1, inc1, inc1, inc1, k1, inc1,
k1—14 sts.

Rows 2, 4, 6, 8, and 9: K.

Row 3: K2, inc1, k2, inc1, k1, m1, k1, inc1, k2, inc1,
k2—19 sts.

Row 5: K3, inc1, k2, inc1, k2, inc1, k2, inc1, k2, inc1, k3—24 sts.

Row 7: K8, inc1, k3, m1, k3, inc1, k8—27 sts.

Row 10: K15, skp, turn.

Row 11: K4, k2tog, turn.

Rows 12 and 14: Sl1 pwise, p3, skp, turn.

Rows 13 and 15: Sl1 kwise, k3, k2tog, turn.

Row 16: Sl1 pwise, p4, k8.

Row 17: K.

BO.

FINISHING

Mattress st sole and heel.

STRAP

Use Kool-Aid to dye 1 oz of main yarn as directed on opposite page.

With crochet hook and dyed yarn, insert into inside instep of bootie and chain 20.

Join last 6 sts tog into a loop.

Sew button to other side of bootie to correspond with strap loop.

Rep for second bootie.

Block by wetting thoroughly with warm water and squaring the toes by inserting tissue into the front.

About Heidi

I was raised by a mother who knit, and I believe I "osmosed" the process from her. I don't remember learning how to knit or purl, but I do remember, vividly, using hideous acrylic yarn to knit various long strips that could fit the general description of a "scarf."

In 1993 I moved to New York City and discovered, among other things, a local yarn store that seduced me with its warm, fuzzy, and (most important) nonsynthetic embrace. I began knitting again as a way to minimize my erupting yarn stash. In 2002 I started a small business selling baby-related hand knits and odds and ends (www.amobaby.com). When I'm not expending all of my energy learning the ways of the world from my toddler, I sometimes act, I sometimes write, and I almost always knit.

DIY Dye

HOW TO DYE YARN WITH KOOL-AID

Kool-Aid will work only with animal fibers, so wool, mohair, angora, and silk work well, but cotton, linen, and rayon won't hold the color.

The suggested starting point for mixing the colors is 1 packet unsweetened Kool-Aid mixed with 1 cup (8 oz) of luke-warm water. (You'll probably end up using about 3 packets of each color.)

You can add 1 oz. white vinegar to help with colorfastness, although some people feel this isn't necessary, as the Kool-Aid contains citric acid. I suggest using clear measuring cups, so you'll be able to see the color clearly.

You can mix different Kool-Aid colors like watercolors; add more water to make lighter colors, or more Kool-Aid for more saturated colors. The grape color is very intense and acts like a black. When you add a very diluted solution of grape to a primary red, you'll get a raspberry color. Play around with the colors; perhaps even knit a swatch to see how the dyed yarn looks knit. If you are going to use more than 1 skein for a project, take notes about your color mixtures and dilutions so you can dupli-cate them.

1. Wind your yarn into hanks if it doesn't already come that way. Don't try to dye a ball of yarn, because the middle won't get the color. Try to make the hanks consistent if you are dyeing multiple skeins for a project.

2. Loosely tie the hanks in at least 4 places so they don't unwind and get tangled.

3. Soak the hanks in room-temperature water for at least 20 minutes. Don't stir your yarn or make temperature changes, as this can result in felted fibers, which you won't be able to use.

4. When you are ready to dye your yarn, carefully lift one hank at a time out of the water. Let as much water drain as pos-sible. You can gently squeeze the bottom of the hank to get excess water out.

If you are dyeing your yarn more than one color:

1. Lay your hank(s) out on a plastic-covered surface, because Kool-Aid dyes more than just yarn.

2. Pour the Kool-Aid liquid onto your hank a little at a time. You can leave space between the colors, or let them bleed into each other.

3. Place the hank in a medium-size microwaveable casse-role dish. Cover with plastic wrap that has a few holes punched in it.

4. Microwave on high for 2–4 minutes, or until the water in the dish is clear.

5. Put the yarn in your sink or bathtub and let cool. Fill the basin with lukewarm water to rinse the yarn, but don't let the force of the water hit the yarn directly.

6. Hang the yarn in the shower to dry overnight.

If you are dyeing your yarn one solid color:

1. Place the hank of yarn in a medium-size microwaveable casserole dish. Pour in the Kool-Aid, making sure to coat the yarn evenly. You can use your gloved hands to gently push the yarn down into the liquid to make sure it is evenly dyed.

2. Follow steps 4–6 above.

Martha Lazar, Brooklyn, NY

STITCH 'N BITCH ACROSS THE NATION
The Northwest

OCEAN SHORES, WASHINGTON, SIT 'N KNIT

A Group for Kids

For my thirteenth birthday, I asked my parents for a knitting lesson. I had just gotten a new dog and wanted to make him a sweater. Then in February 2004 I moved to Ocean Shores, Washington. Inspired by *Stitch 'n Bitch*, I contacted Debbie Stoller to ask if I could join the Seattle Stitch 'n Bitch. Debbie explained that the group consisted of adults who met at night in bars and that perhaps I should start a group for kids my age.

On my first day at my new school, I sat down at a table in the lunchroom and took out my knitting. Some people said, "That's for grandmas," but I told them, "I knit and I'm not a grandma." Other kids were definitely interested, and many already knew how to crochet. Our group, Sit 'n Knit, is very small, with about four members ranging in age from ten to thirteen, plus my cousin, who goes to a different school. The meetings are not always on the same day, but wherever we go, there's lots of knitting to be found. We meet at lunchtime in the library, in art class, or in people's homes. We talk about yarns, what's going on in the school, and politics. Now we're starting to recognize how things are put together. We stare at other people's sweaters and say, "I could make that."

My advice to kids who want to start a knitting group is "Just do it." I started teaching my friends to knit so they wouldn't be bored when I talked obsessively about it, and the guys are more excited than the girls. When kids get frustrated, I tell them something I read in

Portland, Oregon

Maggie Righetti's knitting book: "It's not a mistake if you know how you made it."

Joceyln Caven

PORTLAND, OREGON, SnB

You could call me the "queen bee" of the PDX Stitch 'n Bitch group (I founded it), but in reality I'm not the most knowledgeable member. In fact, I started the group for the purely selfish goal of getting master knitters into my network to teach me the knitty gritty. For some crazy reason, people liked the idea enough to join!

SnB Portland is an outlet for knitters and crocheters to meet up, vent, teach,

Ocean Shores, Washington

learn, make new friends, and best of all, create and be creative. Crocheters play well in the group too. There's always the ongoing debate between crocheters ("One stick is better than two!") and knitters ("Knitting is a science built on the foundations of counting, and crocheting is for lazy people"), but both share the addiction to yarn, so what's all the fuss is about? Plus, there are the memorable teaching lessons where you hear stuff like, "Take the hook and poke it in the part that looks like a butt!" or "Wrap the string this way, then stab it here!" In the end, we're all having fun, and in the process, we're doing a little good for the community by donating blankets and our other handmade crafts to neighbors in need.

Malia Smith

SEATTLE, WASHINGTON, PURLYGIRLS

Seattle PurlyGirls was started in January 2004 by PurlyGirl extraordinaire Nichole, whose infectious enthusiasm brought membership to 130 knitters in three months. About thirty PurlyGirls show up weekly in a private room at a swanky Seattle club, where the owners know their names and favorite drinks.

The group holds regular special events, including knitting slumber parties and tea parties, bringing in massage therapists to soothe sore knitting hands, and organizing field trips to wool festivals and yarn sales. With members from the local yarn shops, they have the inside scoop on upcoming sales and events, as well as the lowdown on the newest yarns to hit the market. Although there's a "no kids allowed" rule for the regular weekly meet-ups, the PurlyGirls have an additional Saturday group at a local playground where the kids run freely and the moms knit in peace.

One of the PurlyGirls' favorite yarn stores, Churchmouse Yarns and Teas, is a short ferry ride across Puget Sound. PGirls often gather to make the day trip together, and the store owners reserve a table in the shop and hang out the welcome sign (literally) for their arrival. The girls are always open to impromptu gatherings: small groups at coffee shops, or knitting picnics in the park on the rare sunny Seattle day.

The PurlyGirls vary in age, culture, and skill level, but no problem—from perfecting the kitchener stitch to Fair Isle to socks on circular needles—is too hard for someone in the group to solve.

Jenna Adorno

Seattle, Washington

PEGGY DEPUE

Casey's Coat

Size

S (M, L)

Finished length: 12 (16, 21)"

Finished circumference: 15 (18, 22)"

Materials

Brown Sheep Lamb's Pride Worsted
(85% wool, 15% mohair; 113g/190 yds)

MC: 1 (2, 2) skeins #M38 Lotus Pink
(#M78 Aztec Turquoise)

CC: 1 (1, 2) skeins #M110 Orange You
Glad (#M120 Limeade)

US 7 (4.5mm) straight needles

US 8 (5mm) straight needles,
or size needed to obtain gauge

US 7 (4.5mm) double-pointed needles
(set of 4)

Tapestry needle

Gauge

4.5 sts and 6 rows = 4" in St st with
larger needles

L ast winter my grandmother was in the hospital on and off over several weeks. When I went to Ohio to visit her, I offered to take her little white terrier, Casey, home to New Jersey with me until Grandmother was in better health. Casey came to me wearing an orange acrylic sweater (it helped my grandmother, whose eyesight is poor, see her against her pale carpet). After a romp in the snow, Casey's sweater was soaked and I decided to make her a new-and-improved one out of wool.

This sweater was meant for a small dog, but I've resized it to fit medium-size and larger breeds as well. Measure your dog before you start to make sure the sweater will fit when it's finished. Even better, knit the sweater on circular needles and try it on the dog from time to time, adding more or fewer rows of stockinette stitch to ensure a proper fit.

At its core, this is a simple stockinette stitch dog sweater. You can make the stripe sequence as complicated or as easy as you like. Switching colors on RS rows and carrying CC behind the RS reduces the number of yarn ends to weave in.

Left Hanging

HOW TO KEEP YOUR KNITTING ON THE NEEDLES

To keep your work from falling off the needles when you are taking a break or storing your knitting, use an empty film canister. With pointy scissors, poke a small hole in the bottom of the canister. Insert the needle holding your knitting into the hole (it should fit tightly). This will keep the stitches from falling off the needle. *Wendy Robinette, Burlingame, CA*

STITCH PATTERNS

STRIPE SEQUENCE (SMALL)

4 rows MC, 4 rows CC, 18 rows MC, 2 rows CC, 4 rows MC, 2 rows CC, 2 rows MC, 6 rows CC, 4 rows MC, 2 rows CC, 6 rows MC, 2 rows CC, 2 rows MC, 2 rows CC, 2 rows MC, 2 rows CC, 2 rows MC.

STRIPE SEQUENCE (MEDIUM)

4 rows MC, 4 rows CC, 2 rows MC, 2 rows CC, 18 rows MC, 4 rows CC, 4 rows MC, 2 rows CC, 2 rows MC, 2 rows CC, 10 rows MC, 2 rows CC, 4 rows MC, 2 rows CC, 4 rows MC, 4 rows CC, 2 rows MC, 2 rows CC, 10 rows MC.

STRIPE SEQUENCE (LARGE)

4 rows MC, 4 rows CC, 2 rows MC, 2 rows CC, 28 rows MC, 2 rows CC, 2 rows MC, 6 rows CC, 2 rows MC, 6 rows CC, 6 rows MC, 2 rows CC, 2 rows MC, 2 rows CC, 24 rows MC, 2 rows CC, 4 rows MC, 2 rows CC, 4 rows MC, 4 rows CC, 2 rows MC, 2 rows CC, 11 rows MC.

DIRECTIONS

With smaller needles and CC, CO 44 (70, 80) sts.

Work in 1 × 1 rib for 2 rows.

Change to MC and work in 1 × 1 rib until collar measures 3 (3, 4)" from beg, ending with RS facing.

Beg stripe sequence and shape sweater as follows:

Next row: Inc 16 (18, 20) sts evenly across row.

Change to larger needles and work in St st until piece measures 4 (5, 7)" from beg, ending with RS facing.

Next row: K9 (12, 15), join new yarn, BO 6 (8, 10), k to last 15 (20, 25) sts, join new yarn, BO 6 (8, 10), k9 (12, 15).

Work even in St st, working the 3 pieces with separate yarn, until piece measures 2½ (3, 4)" from new yarn join, ending with RS facing.

Next row: With first ball of yarn, k9 (12, 15), CO 6 (8, 10), k to last 15 (20, 25) sts, CO 6 (8, 10), 9 (12, 15).

Break 2nd and 3rd ball of yarn.

Work even in St st until piece measures 9 (12, 15½)" from beg, ending with RS facing.

BO 6 (9, 13) sts at beg of next 2 rows.

BO 4 (3, 3) sts at beg of next 2 (4, 4) rows—40 (58, 62) sts.

Dec 1 st from each edge of next row then EOR 9 (13, 14) times—20 (30, 32) sts.

BO 4 (3, 2) sts at beg of next 2 (4, 5) rows.

BO rem sts and weave in yarn ends.

SLEEVES

With dpns and MC, pu 22 (28, 36) sts around leg opening. Work in 1 × 1 rib for 2 (3, 3)". Change to CC and work 1 row in rib.

BO.

Work second sleeve as for first, reversing colors.

FINISHING

With smaller needles and CC, pu 144 (192, 242) sts around bottom edge. Work in 1 × 1 rib for 1". BO.

Sew center seam.

Weave in ends.

About Peggy

A couple of years ago I was reading *Martha Stewart Living* and came across an article about knitting that had step-by-step instructions. I hadn't touched knitting needles since I was a five-year-old sitting on the porch with Hazel, the little old lady next door, but the steps felt familiar and I caught on again quickly. I've been addicted to knitting and buying (way too much) yarn ever since. I'm an art student living with my husband, three-year-old daughter, and eleven-month-old chocolate Lab, Lily, in a condo nestled in the mountains of northern New Jersey. I spend most of my time (what I don't spend chasing my daughter around, that is) being arty: drawing, painting, making soap, and of course, knitting and designing my own patterns. I also have a Web site, www.my-daydream.com, where I chronicle my adventures in knitting, motherhood, soapmaking, and life.

Ball of Confusion

HOW TO KEEP YOUR YARN UNDER CONTROL

Clean out your cottage cheese containers and insert a grommet in the lid to make a tidy hole for yarn to travel through. Put the ball inside, thread the yarn through the hole, and close the lid. *Amanda White Berka, Fort Collins, CO*

● Try toting cone yarns in a shoe box. Select a sturdy shoe box that is deep enough for the cone to be laid on its side. Cut a hole in each of the shorter sides of the box to accommodate a dowel. Thread the dowel through one hole, then through the cone and the opposite hole in the shoebox. The cone will be suspended and spin easily as you knit. If you don't have a dowel, use a long metal knitting needle. *AWB*

● To keep your yarn from rolling away, try using one of those 32- or 44-ounce hard plastic soda cups with a straw hole in the lid. Put the yarn inside, feed the end through the hole, and screw on the top. It works great for large skeins of yarn that unwind from the center. *Diana Camden, Huntington Beach, CA*

● When working on projects involving multiple colors of yarn, take a sandwich-size zippered plastic bag, snip off a small corner, and place each ball in its own bag. Thread the yarn end through the hole in the corner and seal the top. This can also help you keep your sanity when working with strandy and hairy novelty yarns that love to tangle upon themselves or each other. *Christina Berdoulay, San Mateo, CA*

MICHELLE AMERON

Catwarming Set

A fter seeing my cat promptly and viciously destroy the store-bought mouse toys that she loves so, I wondered if a more durable one might be made. I also wanted to design a gift set to welcome new baby kitties to their home—a "catwarming" set. The swishy string can be swung about or draped over a doorknob or claw-safe furniture for lots of super-fun kitty times, and the three blind mice . . . well, the possibilities are endless! While my cat doesn't really "get" catnip, I know many cats do, so instructions for adding it as part of the stuffing are included.

DIRECTIONS

MOUSE (MAKE 3, ALTERNATING WHICH COLORS ARE MC AND CC AS SHOWN)

With MC and straight needles, CO 3 sts.

Row 1: Inc1 into each st.

Row 2 and all even rows: P.

Row 3: (K1, inc1) twice, k2 (inc1, k1) twice.

Row 5: K2 (m1, k2) 4 times.

Row 7: (K3, m1) twice, k2, (m1, k3) twice.

Row 9: (K4, m1) twice, k2 (m1, k4) twice.

Rows 10–16: Work even.

Change to CC and work 2 rows.

Change to MC and work 5 rows.

Next row: (K3, k2tog) twice, k2 (k2tog, k3) twice.

Sizes

MOUSE

Finished length: 3" + tail

Finished circumference: 3¾"

STRING TOY

Finished length: 44"

Materials

Red Heart Sport
(100% acrylic; 70g/250 yds)

A: 1 skein #414 Charcoal

B: 1 skein #755 Pale Rose

C: 1 skein #918 Vermillion

US 4 (3.5mm) straight needles, or size needed to obtain gauge

US 4 (3.5mm) double-pointed needles (set of 2)

Tapestry needle

Polyester stuffing

Catnip (optional)

¼ yd muslin (optional)

Gauge

24 sts and 32 rows = 4" in St st

P 1 row.

Next row: *K1, k2tog; rep from * to end.

P 1 row.

Next row: K2tog; rep to end.

Break yarn, leaving a 12" tail. Draw tail through rem sts, pull tightly to the inside, and secure.

Ears (Make 6, two in each body color):

With MC and straight needles, CO 6 sts.

Work 2 rows in St st.

Next row: K2tog; rep to end.

Break yarn, leaving a 6" tail. Draw tail through rem sts and secure.

Tails (Make 3, one in each body color):

With MC and dpns, CO 2 sts. Work in I-cord until 3½" from beg.

Break yarn, leaving a 6" tail. Draw tail through rem sts and secure.

FINISHING

Using tail of body yarn, mattress st body, leaving 1" open at end.

Stuff body with polyester filling, adding optional packet of catnip (see below) and taking care not to add too much filling, just enough to retain desired shape.

Mattress st opening closed.

Optional:

Cut two 5" × 5" squares of muslin diagonally in half. Fold 3 pieces in half, with shorter ends meeting, and seam along each short end, forming a cone. Fill with catnip. Fold sides of open end in toward middle and sew shut. Machine sewing is recommended to keep the catnip secure. Trim excess fabric. Add to mouse when stuffing, with pointed end toward the nose, and mattress st seam.

Sew ears to top of mouse heads about halfway between the nose and the contrast stripe with RS of ears facing forward. Pull the string that was threaded through the last 3 sts of ears to make them curve slightly to the front.

Attach tail, using yarn tail to secure.

Stitch eyes and nose in contrasting color.

Weave in ends.

STRING TOY

(When alternating colors, carry yarn up to next stripe rather than breaking yarn after each color change.)

Ball (Make 2):

With A and straight needles, CO 9 sts.

Alternating 2 rows A, 2 rows B, 2 rows C, shape ball as follows:

Row 1 and every odd row: P.

Row 2: *K1, m1; rep from * to end.

Row 4: *K2, m1; rep from * to end.

Row 6: K3, m1, (k5, m1) 4 times, k4.

Work 9 rows even in St st, cont to alt colors as est.

Row 16: K2, *k2tog, k4; rep from * to end.

Row 18: *K1, k2tog; rep from * to end.

Row 20: K2tog, rep to end.

Break yarn, leaving a 12" tail. Draw tail through rem sts and secure. Use tail to mattress st seam closed, leaving 1" open. Stuff with polyester filling, adding optional packet of catnip (see below), and finish seam.

Optional:

Fold 2" × 4" piece of muslin in half with right sides tog and sew sides. Turn right side out, fill with catnip, and sew top closed. Machine sewing is recommended to keep the catnip secure. Add to ball before sewing seam, making sure to mold it to round shape, and mattress st seam.

Cord:

With A and dpns, CO 3 sts, leaving a 10" tail.

Alternating 2½" of color A, then B, then C, work in I-cord until piece measures 40" from beg, ending with A.

Leaving a 10" tail, break yarn and draw tail through sts to secure.

FINISHING
Sew cord to balls, using 10" tails to secure. Weave in ends.

About Michelle

I started knitting properly about two years ago, after many years of sporadic, failed attempts. Apparently my mother used to knit many moons ago and, while it's hard to believe, there is one scarf in the family to substantiate that claim. Needless to say, the skill wasn't passed down, and it took awhile before I finally got the hang of it. But I've had projects on the go ever since—way too many scarves, grand plans, and works in progress. The result of my endeavors (sewing, knitting, and otherwise) will be housed at orangeplush.com. I work as a graphic designer in Toronto, Ontario, which, happily, is also home to an active, creative, and inspiring knitting and crafting community.

I'm with the Band

SHOW ME YOUR TIPS!

THINGS TO DO WITH YOUR BALL BAND

*T*he most helpful tip my mom gave me was to use the paper band around the yarn to start winding the ball. That way, when you run out of yarn, you've got the color and dye lot right there to buy more! *Kate Lew, Napa, CA*

● I learned the hard way that when a pattern calls for a particular type of yarn, it makes sense to staple the ball band or write the yardage and weight of the yarn on the pattern. That way, if the yarn is discontinued or if you want to use a different yarn, you've got the info you need to make a good substitution. *Susan Smith Crawson, Tewksbury, MA*

M. K. CARROLL

Mobile Monsters

You might be wondering why I call these Bunny and Piggy cell phone cozies "monsters," but don't be fooled by their squishy fluffiness. These are in fact criminal masterminds, hellbent on taking over the world, which is why they want your mobile phone (and have also been known to snack on PDAs and mp3 players). Don't believe me? You won't see a pattern here for a kitty, because the one I knitted stole my phone and drove off in my car, never to be seen again.

You can get two monsters out of one skein, as I discovered when I showed the first monster to my anime-crazed teenage sister, who immediately claimed it as her own, and the sizes here should accommodate most styles. Piggy can hold most folding phones with slot-shape plug-ins, and Bunny can hold longer phones with pin-shape plug-ins. The pocket is the right size for the hands-free headset and cord that I use, and the openings at the bottom let me plug in the headset and look like I'm talking to a small fluffy toy. Whether you put the pocket on the front or the back of the cozy is up to you; some of us carry our junk in the trunk and some of us keep the junk up front.

Trying to measure a gauge swatch made with this yarn can make you cry, which is why I listed black thread in the notions. Knitted together with the Plush, it makes counting stitches and rows much easier.

Sizes

Finished measurements:

Bunny: 5" high, 2¾" wide, 1" deep

Piggy: 4" high, 3" wide, ½" deep

Materials

Berroco Plush (100% nylon; 50g/90 yds)

BUNNY

1 skein #1934 Black Out or #1924 Jazzy Turquoise

Small piece of white felt

Two ¼" round beads

PIGGY

1 skein #1932 Precious Pink

Small piece of pink felt

Two ⁷/₁₆" domed shank buttons

One 1" pink 4-hole coat button

US 5 (3.75mm) straight needles, or size needed to obtain gauge

Stitch markers

Tapestry needle

Sewing needle

Black sewing thread and thread to match yarn

Gauge

20 sts and 19 rows = 4" in garter st

DIRECTIONS

BUNNY BODY

CO 27 sts. Work in garter st until piece measures 5" from beg.

Next row: BO 19, k8.

Work 2 rows in garter st.

Next row: K1, *yo, k2tog; rep from * to last st, k1.

Work 2 rows in garter st.

BO.

Sew base (see diagram) and side seam.

PIGGY BODY

CO 32 sts. Work in garter st until piece measures 4" from beg.

BO and break yarn, leaving a 15" tail.

Use tail to sew side seam. With phone inside, whipstitch bottom seam closed, leaving space open so that slot is accessible.

FACE (FOR BOTH)

Select which side will be the back. Pu 10 sts along the top edge of the back, centered on the body.

Work 5 rows in garter st.

Next row: K1, inc1, k to last 2 sts, inc1, k1.

Next row: K all sts.

Rep these 2 rows twice more—16 sts.

Work 4 rows in garter st.

Next row: K1, skp, k to last 3 sts, k2tog, k1.

Next row: K all sts.

Rep these 2 rows 3 times more.

Next row: K1, skp, k2, k2tog, k1—6 sts.

BO.

BUNNY EAR (MAKE 2)

Pu 5 sts from top edge of face to correspond with picture.

Work 2 rows in garter st.

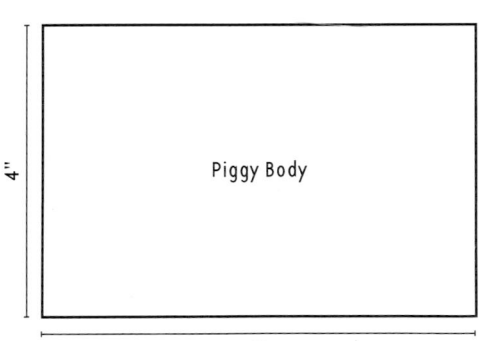

Bunny Body

Sew side A to side B, then side C to what remains of side B.

6"
5¼"
5"
C
A
B
3¾"

Piggy Body

4"
6"

Next row: K1, inc1, k1, inc1, k1

Work in garter st until ear measures 2½" from beg.

Next row: K1, skp, k1, k2tog, k1

Next row: K all sts.

BO.

PIGGY EAR (MAKE 2)

Pick up 5 sts to correspond with picture.

Work 2 rows in garter st.

Next row: Skp, k1, k2tog.

Next row: Skp, k1.

Next row: K2tog.

Break yarn and pull tail through rem st to secure.

POCKET (FOR BOTH)

CO 12 sts.

Work in garter st until piece measures 2½" from beg.

BO, leaving a 20" tail.

FINISHING

Bunny:

Sew on beads for eyes. Cut out felt shapes for teeth and the tongue, using the templates given below, and sew in place. Use very small stitches on the face side. Trim teeth to desired size, if necessary. Sew pocket on desired location. Weave in all ends.

Piggy:

Sew on eye buttons and nose button. Cut out a felt shape for the tongue, using the template given, and sew in place. Use very small stitches on the face side. Sew pocket in desired location. Weave in all ends.

About M.K.

See the Head Huggers pattern, page 59, for M. K.'s bio.

Ears: 1" x ½"

Ears: 1½" x 3¾"
Neck and Face: 3" x 3"

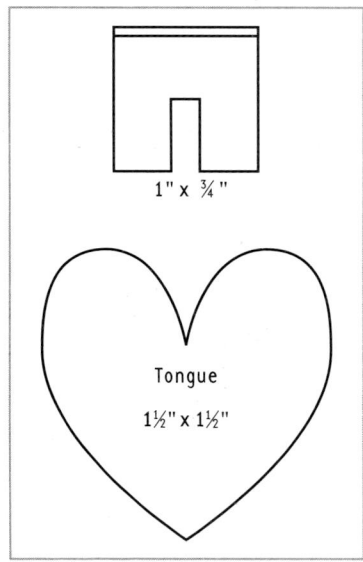

1" x ¾"

Tongue
1½" x 1½"

ANGELA HACKNER

Knit Your Own Rock Star

JOEY RAMONE, HENRY ROLLINS, AND JOAN JETT

After abandoning my dream writing project, "Knitting with Rollins," I decided that the world desperately needed a punk rock doll. So with furrowed brow and a tangle of yarn, I set out to knit my own Henry Rollins doll, complete with tattoos and self-deprecating wit. With his angst channeling through me, I began knitting his doll lookalike. I kept clicking away, and next came Joey Ramone, then Joan Jett. Make up your own dolls. Take this pattern and mix it up. Shred it to pieces. Set it on fire. Destroy it. Then start knitting and see who comes screaming off the needles.

DIRECTIONS

UPPER BODY—*JOEY RAMONE AND HENRY ROLLINS DOLLS* (MAKE 2)

With red (black) yarn, CO 22 (24) sts.

For Joey, alt 2 rows of red with 2 rows of blue yarn; for both dolls, work in St st for 30 (20) rows, ending with RS facing.

BO 1 st at beg of next 2 rows.

Size

Finished height: Joey: 16 (Henry: 13, Joan: 13)"

Materials

Tahki Cotton Classic
(100% mercerized cotton; 50g/108 yds)

JOEY RAMONE

1 skein #3001 White

1 skein #3002 Black

1 skein #3003 Off White

1 skein #3997 True Red

1 skein #3874 Blue

HENRY ROLLINS

1 skein #3001 White

1 skein #3002 Black

1 skein #3003 Off White

1 skein #3336 Dark Brown

JOAN JETT

1 skein #3001 White

1 skein #3002 Black

1 skein #3003 Off White

1 skein #3997 True Red

Note: *Main pattern instructions are written for the Joey Ramone doll. Any specific changes for the other dolls are in parentheses (Henry Rollins followed by Joan Jett).*

(continued)

*Next row (RS): K1, sl1, k1, psso, k to last 3 sts, k2tog, k1.

Work 1 row even.*

Rep from * to * 5 times more.

BO.

UPPER BODY FRONT: JOAN JETT

With black yarn, CO 21 sts.

Work even in St st for 10 rows.

*Next row: K1, sl1, k1, psso, k to last 3 sts, k2tog, k1.

Work 1 row even.*

Rep from * to * 1 time.

Work even in St st for 4 rows.

Next row: K2, m1, k to last 2 stitches, m1, k2.

Work 1 row even.

Work even in St st for 2 rows.**

Next row: K1, sl1, k1, psso, k6, work 7 chart sts, k6, k2tog, k1.

Work 1 row even.

Cont as est, working 1 less st before and after chart on RS rows for 6 rows.

BO.

UPPER BODY BACK: JOAN JETT

Work as for front to **.

*Next row: K1, sl1, k1, psso, k to last 3 sts, k2tog, k1.

Work 1 row even.*

Rep from * to * twice.

Work even in St st for 2 rows.

BO.

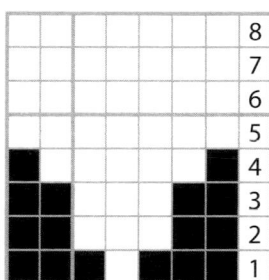

□ Off White   ■ Black

Materials (*continued*)

Fonty Serpentine
(100% polyamide; 50g/145 yds)

JOEY RAMONE

1 skein #825 Black (for optional jacket)

Katia Danubio
(76% wool, 24% nylon; 50g/100 yds),
1 skein #2 Black (for hair)

US 6 (4mm) straight needles,
or size needed to obtain gauge

US 6 (4mm) double-pointed needles
(set of 5)

Tapestry needle

Fiber fill

Gauge

20 sts and 28 rows = 4" in St st with
Tahki Cotton Classic

ARM (MAKE 2 EACH)

With off-white yarn, CO 10 (10, 7) sts.

Working in St st, inc 1 st at each edge of EOR 2 (2, 4) times, then every foll 4th row 3 (3, 0) times.

Work even in St st for 13 (15, 16) rows.

Change to blue (black) yarn.

Work even in St st for 2 rows.

For Joey Ramone:

Change to red yarn and work in St st for 2 rows. Alternating 2 rows blue and 2 rows red, cont as follows:

BO 1 st at beg of next 2 rows.

For Joey Ramone and Joan Jett:

*Next row: K1, sl1, k1, psso, k to last 3 sts, k2tog, k1.

Work 1 row even.*

Rep from * to * 5 (3) times.

For all dolls:

BO.

LEG (MAKE 2 EACH)

With black (brown, black) yarn, CO 18 (20, 18) sts.

*Work even in St st for 16 (14, 14) rows.

Next (dec) row: K1, sl1, k1, psso, k to last 3 sts, k2tog, k1.

Work 1 row even.*

For Joey Ramone and Henry Rollins:

Rep from * to * once more, changing to off-white yarn on row 17 for Henry.

Work even in St st for 8 (8, 10) rows.

For Joan Jett:

Change to white yarn and work 1 row even.

Change to red yarn and work 1 row even.

Enough Is Enough

THE RIGHT YARN LENGTH FOR COLOR WORK AND TO FINISH A ROW

When working intarsia, I like to pull out a strand of color the length of my extended arms (from palm to palm, about 3 feet). I can always undo the tangles in that length or a bit shorter. *Skippy Kaufman, N. Versailles, PA*

● When you're nearing the end of a ball of yarn, fold the tail in half and tie a loose slip knot at the center point. If you come to the halfway knot while knitting the next row, you don't have enough yarn to complete another row. *Nikki Myers, New York, NY*

Rep dec row.

Work even in St st for 5 rows.

Change to white yarn and *rep dec row.

Work 1 row even.*

Rep from * to * once.

For Joey Ramone:

Change to white yarn and work in St st for 2 rows.

Change to black yarn.

Rep dec row.

Work even in St st for 6 rows.

Change to white yarn and *work 1 row even.

Rep dec row.*

Rep from * to * once

For Henry Rollins:

Rep dec row.

For all dolls:

Break yarn and draw tail through rem sts, pull tight, and secure.

FINISHING BODY

Mattress st sleeve edges to front and back armholes. Seam sleeves and side seams.

HEADS

With off-white yarn and dpns, pick up 24 (24, 32) sts around neck opening.

Work 5 (5, 1) rnds in St st.

For Joey Ramone and Henry Rollins:

*Next rnd: Inc 2 sts evenly around.

Work 2 rnds even.*

Rep from * to * 3 times.

Work 2 rnds even.

Joey's face

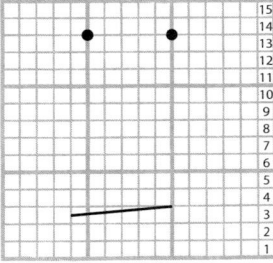

Joan's face

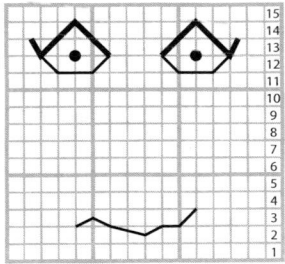

Henry's face

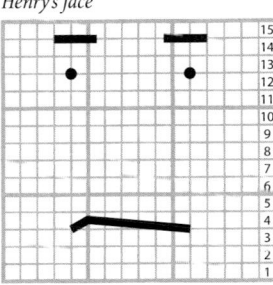

Henry's tattoos

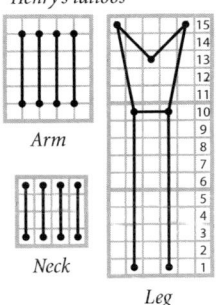

Arm

Neck

Leg

── *Cotton Classic*

── *Cotton Classic, go over the same stitches 3 times*

● *French knots*

── *Cotton Classic, split*

For all dolls:

Next rnd: *K6, k2tog*; rep from * to * to end of rnd.

Work 1 rnd even.

Rep last 2 rows, working 1 less st between decs on every other rnd, to 16 (16, 20) sts.

Work 1 (1, 3) rnd even in St st.

For Joan Jett:

Work 2 rnds in St st, increasing 2 sts evenly on each rnd.

*Work 1 rnd even.

Work 1 rnd, increasing 2 sts evenly around.*

Rep from * to * once.

Work 4 rnds even.

Next rnd: K5, k2tog.

Work 1 rnd even.

Rep last 2 rnds, working 1 less st between decs on every other rnd, to 16 sts.

For all dolls:

*K2tog; rep from * to end of rnd.

Break yarn and draw tail through rem sts. Pull tight and secure.

FINISHING DOLLS

Seam back of legs.

Embroider facial features and tattoos on dolls to correspond with templates given.

Stitch laces onto Joey's and Joan's sneakers. For Joey's hair, attach strands of Katia Danubio to head. For Henry, duplicate stitch hair onto head. For Joan's hair, attach strands of black yarn to head and cut into a mullet.

Stuff all body parts with fiber fill and mattress st rem seams. Sew upper body to lower body.

About Angela

For me, knitting was an acquired taste. After learning the basics from my mom, I crept along for six months on my first project—a potholder that I gave to my boyfriend. Luckily, I was ignorant of the boyfriend potholder curse (and its variations); otherwise he and I might not be married today. The experience underwhelmed me, but after I moved from dusty Texas to sunny Los Angeles, where all knitters are beautiful, I gave it another chance. This time something was different, and I dove right in and knit my way through a novelty scarf and a baby hat that, upon completion, resembled a giant square of Shredded Wheat cereal. I spend my sunshiny days tangled in a mess of audio wires, making sound for film and television. I spend each night at home tangled in a mess of yarn, knitting punk rock dolls and chronicling my crafting adventures at www.yarngirls.com.

The Binds that Tie

BEEFING UP THE LAST BOUND-OFF STITCH

Here's a trick to neaten the last stitch of a bind-off: Cast off your row until only one stitch remains on the left needle and one on the right. Slip the stitch from the left needle onto the right so there are now two loops on the right needle. With the tip of the left needle pick up the left side of the loop of the stitch *below* the slipped stitch from front to back. Slip the slipped stitch back onto the left needle (there are now two loops on the left needle) and knit both loops together. Slip the next-to-last stitch over this knitted stitch, and then pull yarn through last remaining stitch. Altogether tidier! Susan Hoover, Mount Vernon, NY

REBECCA DEWEY

Knit My Ride

FUZZY DICE & STEERING WHEEL COVER

Size

Finished measurements:
Dice: 3½" × 3½" × 3½"

Finished measurements:
Steering wheel cover: to fit

Materials

DICE

MC: Paton's Allure (100% nylon; 50g/47 yds), 2 skeins #4532 Garnet

Embroidery floss to match MC

CC: 2 yds black scrap yarn

Two 3" foam cubes

42 black felt dots with sticky backing

STEERING WHEEL COVER

Paton's Allure (100% nylon; 50g/47 yds), 2 skeins #4532 Garnet

Nonslip drawer padding OR glue gun

BOTH

US 8 (5mm) straight needles, or size needed to obtain gauge

DMC rayon floss in Red

Sewing needle

Gauge

16 sts and 20 rows = 4" in garter st

his dice pattern came about as a joke for a friend. I had recently gotten back into knitting and kept saying that I would knit her seat covers for her new car. That never happened, but one day I thought, What about fuzzy dice? And they came about by themselves. As for why the steering wheel cover, I live in Arizona, where it can get to 125 degrees in the summer, and you need something to protect your hands from getting scalded on the steering wheel. A matching steering wheel cover just seemed like a perfect fit for the fuzzy dice.

DIRECTIONS

DICE (MAKE 2)

With MC, CO 12 sts.

Work in garter st until piece measures 3" from beg.

CO 12 sts at beg of next 2 rows—36 sts.

Work in garter st until piece measures 6" from beg.

BO 12 sts at beg of next 2 rows—12 sts.

Work in garter st until piece measures 12" from beg.

BO.

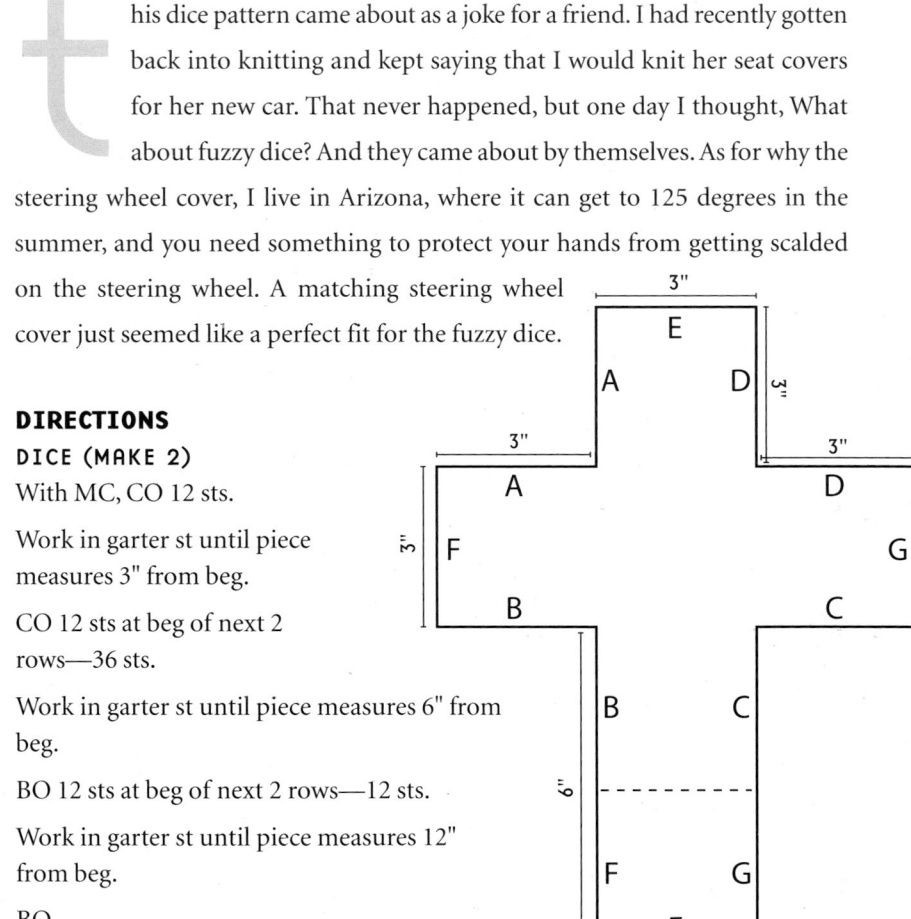

CORD

With CC, CO 40 sts.

BO.

FINISHING

With red floss, seam adjoining sides A, B, C, and D to form a cube shape, leaving 2 sides of the top flap open. Place foam cube inside and sew one side shut. Place one end of the cord into the corner and continue the seam through both the fabric and the cord. Rep for second die using the other end of the cord.

Stick felt dots on the dice to correspond with a real die.

STEERING WHEEL COVER

To determine the number of sts to CO (X), measure around the outside of the wheel and add ½". Multiply this number by 4 and round off to the closest whole number, if necessary.

To determine the length you should knit to (Y"), measure the diameter of your steering wheel (from edge to edge across the center). Multiply this number by 3.14. Then subtract 6 and round off to the closest whole or half number, if necessary.

CO X sts.

Work in garter st until piece measures Y" from beg.

BO.

FINISHING

Either cut 7 pieces of nonslip drawer padding 3" × 2" and sew them to WS of fabric with red DMC floss every six inches *or* use a hot glue gun to evenly space rows of glue every 6" on WS of fabric and allow to cool. This will help keep the cover from slipping off.

Sew CO row to BO row, turn RS out, and pull it onto steering wheel.

About Becky

I am a twenty-four-year-old hair stylist and Arizona native. My mom taught me to knit and would always cast on and bind off for me. I did about five scarves and left it at that. I got back into knitting about three years ago, I guess as a way to stay connected with my mom after her death. I took a class at my LYS to relearn the basics and have kept on knitting since then. When I'm not knitting, I spend time playing with my cats, Pepper Ann and Moose, and my Chihuahua, Maggie, and learning to spin with a drop spindle.

STITCH 'N BITCH GROUPS
Beyond the Borders

Aberdeen, Scotland

Taiwan, as close as Ireland and England, and include a resident Scottish "pit-knitter" (aye, many lasses in Scotland do knit with a needle in their armpit!). Our knitting styles are as unique and interesting as the members. Somehow, nobody ever looks as if we are doing the same thing, and yet we are all knitting.

Helen Ralph

BRISTOL, ENGLAND, SnB

Stitch 'n Bitch Bristol arose when a gang from Ladyfest Bristol took a trip to offer support, sell 'zines, and have fun

Bristol, England

ABERDEEN, SCOTLAND, SnB

While knitting in a pub during the local playgroup's "mums' night out," I met a few fellow knitting moms who fancied having a real Stitch 'n Bitch session. As a Cincinnati expat, I used just the initials "SnB," fearing British knitters might hesitate to join a "Bitch" group, but this was completely unnecessary, as all the knitters have enthusiastically embraced the name. In February 2003, the Aberdeen Stitch 'n Bitch was formed, and it became the first UK group to be listed on the SnB Web site.

Since then, things have really taken off, and the group's gotten media coverage from *The Sunday Times, The Sun,* and BBC Radio Scotland. We meet at a cafe that's inside a movie theater. It's got good lighting, it's comfortable, and it's not too smoky. It's the ideal place to knit, chat, and drink vodka and tonic.

Our two dozen members hail from as far away as Canada, Germany, Estonia, and

with the kids from Ladyfest Devon. But when we arrived at the venue, we discovered that nearly every person in the building was knitting. At first we were totally put off by this, but slowly we got drawn into the knitting frenzy and by the end of the night many of us were totally hooked—although our first stumbling knitting efforts were done under the influence of girl bands and too much booze.

Cardiff, Wales

Upon our return home, we were determined to continue to knit together, so in November 2003 we held our first official Stitch 'n Bitch at our organization's Here shop and gallery. We meet online under the banner "the post-ironic spinsterhood" and gather at the shop for stitchin' 'n bitchin', sewing, crocheting, puppet making, storytelling, and drawing. I'm not sure any of us are what you would call accomplished knitters—it's all about getting together, reviving an old craft, and sharing skills and passing on knowledge. And it's more than just knitting; it's networking for women who have skills and talents and don't know where to go with them. It's a safe space to try stuff out.

Camilla Stacey

CARDIFF, WALES, SNB

I started knitting in 2001 and used to feel so jealous when I read about the exciting Stitch 'n Bitch groups springing up all over the U.S. I wanted a group like that near me! So I found A Shot in the Dark, a good café with organic, fair-trade coffee and tea, comfy seats, and nice big tables where people could spread out their projects.

A few of my friends attended the first meeting, and since then we've met up every month at the coffee shop and sometimes we have special sessions at one another's homes. Among those who've joined is one member who got *Stitch 'n Bitch* as a Christmas present, went to stitchnbitch.org like the book advises to see if there were any meetings near her, and found us. She couldn't believe there was a group in Cardiff.

We usually meet on a Saturday afternoon. We used to joke that one end of the table was for stitching, the other for bitching, but even the nonknitters have been inspired to pick up needles. Cardiff SnB is the only chapter in Wales and one of only four in the United Kingdom. We hope that will soon change.

Marie Irshad

MELBOURNE, AUSTRALIA, SNB

Despite not having knit since age five, when I was thirty six I decided that I could make my own lace sweaters. I began devouring knitting books and while scouring the Internet for inspiration discovered the phenomenon of Stitch 'n Bitch groups. Stitch 'n Bitch Melbourne held its first official meeting in January

Melbourne, Australia

2003 in a coffee shop on trendy Chapel Street, and since then the group has expanded to more than one hundred. Thirty regulars begin meetings by showing off knit projects to rounds of applause, and then quickly mess up the café tables with vintage patterns, the latest books, and yarn. We've even pulled out ball winders and swifts and set up a whole production number in the window, becoming quite the spectacle and attracting new members in the process. Online we share Web links and book titles, give technical assistance and advice on pattern choices, and arrange ad hoc SEX (stash-enhancing excursions) and trips to yarn events.

The group remains united through the simplicity of yarn, needles, conversation, and real friendships that feed the soul. When one member's father died in April, the group rallied 'round, and knitting became a way to pick up the pieces and knit herself back together.

Sharon Steer-Courtenay

MONTREAL, CANADA, KNITTING BEE

When the Montreal Knitting Bee members became the Revolutionary Knitting Circle and held a knit-in at a tent city to highlight a housing crisis, some of our supplies and projects were confiscated by riot police. It's not always this political for the group, who formed in the fall of 2002 as part of the Montreal Church of Craft. About ten of us (out of eighty) meet once a week in a member's home to knit or create other fiber arts, chat, and sample homemade vegan deserts. There are a few male members, and all ages from two on up are represented. Projects in the works include a knitting sound art project with a record label and a knitting fashion show. We've been the subject of a documentary and an anthropological study and are looking for more opportunities to go out into the community and spread the word.

Alanna Lynch

Montreal, Canada

TOKYO, JAPAN, SNB

I started the Tokyo Stitch 'n Bitch with American expat Jennifer Okano in January 2004. It wasn't very hard to drum up interest. Unlike in the U.S., there have always been books and magazines in Japan that cater to the younger knitter. It is really common for teenage girls and young women to knit a scarf or sweater for their boyfriend; it is a sign of love. The magazines geared to them focus on the bulkier yarns and on patterns for small accessory items in fun colors, and they're big on layering.

Several members of Tokyo SnB are bilingual, so our meetings are carried out in a mixture of Japanese and English. We find that our love for all things crafty helps us overcome any language barriers.

The big differences between American and Japanese knitters are that most Japanese work in Continental style and Japanese patterns consist mostly of diagrams, rather than words and abbreviations. It really helps the knitter visualize the project, rather than just following directions and knitting blindly. We also have access to local Avril yarns, which are gaining notoriety Stateside.

Tokyo can sometimes be a big, faceless city, but our Stitch 'n Bitch has provided many of us with a warm, cozy environment where we can talk about the latest in knitting magazines and craft ideas, as well as the problems and joys of living in a foreign city.

Kat Mok

KAREN BAUMER
Chill Pillows

the design of these pillows was inspired by the groovy 1970s-era house my friends bought on the side of a hill near Los Angeles. They built a cushioned sofalike platform along two sides of their living room, and suddenly they needed pillows—lots of pillows—to pad the "back" of the sofa, which was simply a wall. This was just the excuse I needed to play with some funky stitch patterns (loop and nubble) that would mesh well with the overall look of the house.

Tip: If you prefer, you can use fabric for the backs of the pillows instead of knitting them. This is especially handy if you want to use up leftover yarn and don't have enough to make both a front and a back panel.

STITCH PATTERN
LOOP STITCH
Row 1 (WS): K.

Row 2 (RS): K1, *ML; rep from * to last st, k1.

Note: Directions for nubbly pillow on page 249.

Size
14" square

Materials
LOOP PILLOW
Brown Sheep Lamb's Pride Worsted (85% wool, 15% mohair; 113g/190 yds), 3 skeins #78 Aztec Turquoise

US 8 (5mm) straight needles, or size needed to obtain gauge

Tapestry needle

14" square pillow form

Gauge
12 sts and 16 rows = 4" in loop st

16 sts and 32 rows = 4" in garter st

Abbreviations
ML (MAKE LOOP)
K1 without slipping st off left needle. Bring yarn to front between needles. Wrap yarn around left thumb to form a loop. Bring yarn to back, between the needles, and k the same st again, this time slipping to right needle (2 sts now on right needle). Lift first st over second st and drop it off the needle.

DIRECTIONS

LOOPY PILLOW

Front:

CO 42 sts.

Work in loop st patt until piece measures 14" from beg, ending with RS facing.

BO.

Back:

CO 2 sts.

Next row: Inc1, k to end.

Rep inc row until the side measures 14".

Next row: Skp, k to end.

Rep dec row until 2 stitches rem.

BO.

FINISHING

Mattress st back to front along 3 sides, being careful not to catch loops into seam. Insert pillow form and seam last side closed.

Wrap Star

A NEW WAY TO HOLD YOUR YARN

I've been knitting for about five years, but only recently started knitting like a madwoman. The reason? I finally found a comfortable way to hold the yarn. When I began experimenting, I found that I knit best when I wrap the yarn twice around both my middle and ring fingers held together. It helps me maintain an even tension, feels more secure on my fingers yet is easy to take off, and I can just slide my fingers down the yarn to adjust the amount I need without having to drop it off my fingers and pick it up again. *Amanda Schehr, St. Louis, MO*

About Karen

I have been knitting and designing since I was a young teen and my mother taught me the basics of knitting. A couple of years ago, as knitting started to take off and suddenly more books and magazines appeared, I decided to submit designs for publication. I make my "real" living as a linguist, primarily in the field of verbal skills test development for graduate school entrance examinations. I live in Sunnyvale, California, the heart of Silicon Valley, where I have to be careful not to impale an engineer every time I pull out my knitting needles in public.

STITCH PATTERN

NUBBLE

Row 1 (WS): K.

Row 2 (RS): K1, *MN, k1; rep from * to end.

Row 3: K1, *p1, k1; rep from * to end.

Rows 4 and 5: K.

Row 6: K1, *k1, MN; rep from * to last 2 sts, k2.

Row 7: K2, *p1, k1; rep from * to last st, k1.

Row 8: K.

DIRECTIONS

NUBBLY PILLOW

CO 55 sts.

Work in nubble patt until piece measures 14" from beg, ending with a row 3 or row 7. Change to garter st and work even until piece measures 28" from beg.

BO.

FINISHING

Fold piece in half with wrong sides tog. Mattress st back to front along 2 sides. Turn RS out. Insert pillow form and seam last side closed.

Size

14" square

Materials

NUBBLY PILLOW
Brown Sheep Lamb's Pride Worsted (85% wool, 15% mohair; 113g/190yds)

3 skeins #140 Aran

US 8 (5mm) straight needles, or size needed to obtain gauge

Tapestry needle

14" square pillow form

Gauge

16 sts and 24 rows = 4" in nubble st

16 sts and 32 rows = 4" in garter st

Abbreviation

MN (MAKE NUBBLE)
Pull loop through next st as if to k, then place this loop on left needle next to original st—2 sts. Pull new loop through second st as if to k, then place loop on left needle next to second st—3 sts. Repeat twice—5 sts. BO 4 kwise. The fifth stitch is now on the right needle.

AMY BARKER

Two for Tea

Size

Fits a classic 4-cup teapot

Finished width: 7½"

Finished height: 7½"

Materials

Brown Sheep Nature Spun Worsted
(100% wool, 100g/245 yds)

8 BALL
MC: 1 skein #601 Pepper

CC: 1 skein #740 Snow

COFFEE, TEA, OR ME? (CTOM)
MC: 1 skein #115 Bit of Blue

CC1: 1 skein #N54 Orange You Glad

CC2: 1 skein #108 Cherry Delight

US 6 (4mm) straight needles,
or size needed to obtain gauge

US G/6 (4mm) crochet hook

Tapestry needle

Safety pins

Gauge

17 sts and 26 rows = 4" in St st

Special Skills

INTARSIA/DUPLICATE STITCH

there was a time when no self-respecting hostess would serve her guests from a (gasp!) naked teapot. Today we are a little more open-minded about these matters, but maybe those ladies were on to something—a knitted cozy does keep your brew toasty warm.

I'm a three-cup-a-day tea drinker (Earl Grey, black, two sugars) and a knitter as well, so putting together a tea cozy seemed logical. But the frilly patterns out there left me cold. I wanted something with a sense of humor to fit in with my retro kitchen (emphasis on kitsch), and this is the result. These 8-ball and Coffee, Tea, or Me? cozies fit a classic four-cup teapot and will keep your tea hot, hot, hot!

DIRECTIONS

BACK

(Instructions are for 8-ball, with CTOM directions in parentheses.)

With MC (CC2), CO 44 sts.

Work 8 rows (2 rows of MC and 2 rows of CC)
in 1 × 1 ribbing.

With MC, work in St st for 24 rows.

**Next row: K2tog, k to last 2 sts,
k2tog.

P 1 row.**

Rep from ** to ** to 36 sts.

Next row: K2tog, k8, k2tog, pm, k10,
k2tog, pm, k10, k2tog.

P 1 row.

Next row: K2tog, *k to 2 sts before marker, k2tog, sm; rep from * once, k to last 2 sts, k2tog.

P 1 row.

Rep last 2 rows to 16 sts.

Next row: K2tog across row.

BO.

FRONT

Work as for back, beg chart on 5th row of St st as foll:

K14 (6), k16 (32) sts from chart, k14 (6). Cont shaping as for back and working chart at the same time.

Optional: The "8" of the 8-ball cozy can be knit when working from the chart or those sts can be worked in CC and embroidered on with MC and duplicate st.

FINISHING

Duplicate st "8" on 8-ball cozy motif if necessary.

With RS tog, use safety pins to temporarily join, marking openings for spout and handle. Turn cozy RS out before you seam to make sure the design is on the side that will be seen while the tea is being poured (you may want to make one of these for a left-handed tea drinker). Turn wrong side out and use MC and crocheted slip st to join.

About Amy

I am an American expat living in Sydney, Australia, with my husband and one very spoiled cat. My mother-in-law taught me to knit a few years ago while we were visiting her in Florida, and I've been hooked ever since. I consider myself a "short attention span knitter" and favor projects that can be completed in a sitting or two. Of course, in that warm Sydney sun we can only use so many hats and scarves, so I knit lots of cat toys and home accessories. A few years ago I was a featured knitter in the Australian book *It's My Party and I'll Knit if I Want To,* by Sharon Aris. Sharon and I met at a local SnB while dropping stitches over beer.

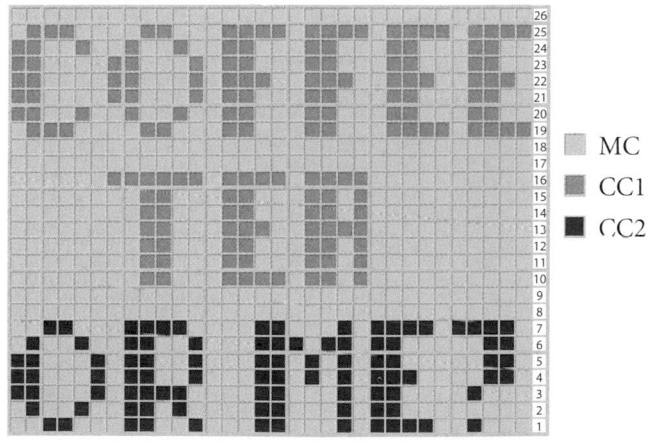

MC
CC1
CC2

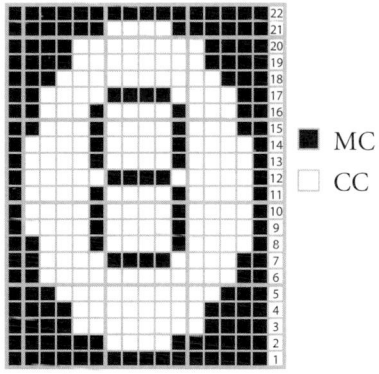

MC
CC

The Knitty-Gritty

A REFRESHER COURSE

Slip Knot

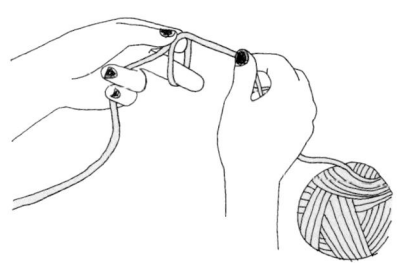 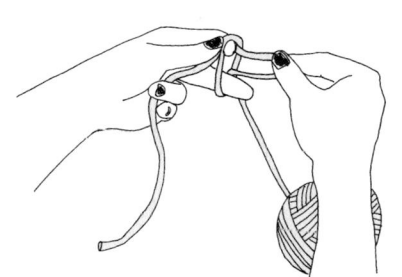 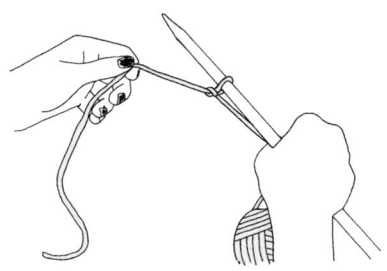

1 Wrap the ball end of the yarn clockwise around your forefinger and middle finger, with your fingers spread approximately 1 inch apart.

2 Pull a loop of the ball end of the yarn through the loop of yarn around your fingers.

3 Slide that loop onto a knitting needle, and pull on the tail and ball ends to tighten it.

Double Cast-on (CO)

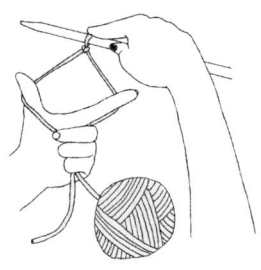 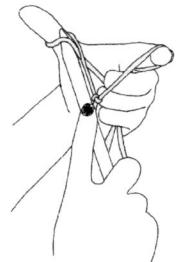 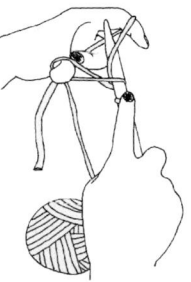 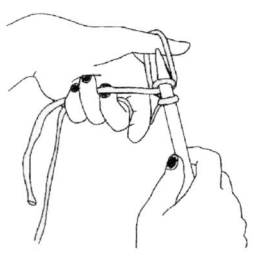

1 Make a slip knot, leaving a tail that's at least three times the width of the piece you want to knit. Hold the needle with your right hand, with the long tail end hanging to the left and the ball end hanging to the right. Close the bottom three fingers of your left hand

around the yarn and, with your thumb and forefinger, spread apart the two strands of yarn.

2 Scoop up the strand of yarn that runs across your palm to the bottom of your thumb.

3 Wrap the yarn on your left forefinger around the front of your knitting needle, counter-clockwise.

4 Bring the loop of yarn that's on your left thumb over the tip of your knitting needle. Pull your thumb outta there and

tighten the cast-on stitch, returning your left hand to the same position as in step 1. Continue steps 2–4 until you've cast on the desired number of stitches.

Single Cast-on (CO)

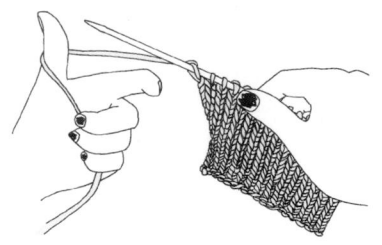 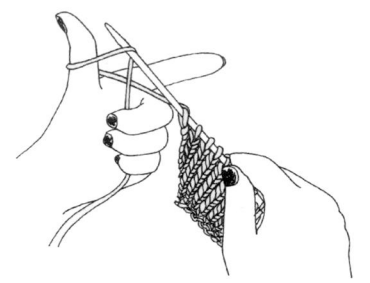 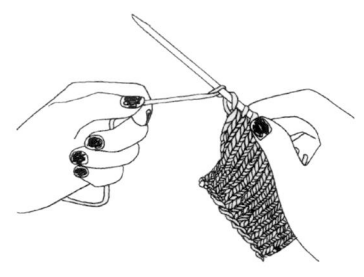

1 Take the needle with the stitches on it in your *right hand,* and close the bottom three fingers of your left hand around the ball end of the yarn. Then, let the yarn run across your palm and over your thumb.

2 Scoop up the yarn strand that runs from your three fingers to the base of your thumb from underneath.

3 Drop that loop off your thumb, and tighten the stitch.

Cable Cast-on (CO)

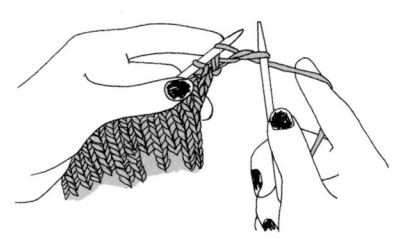 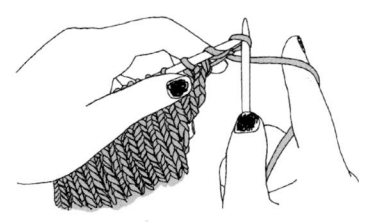 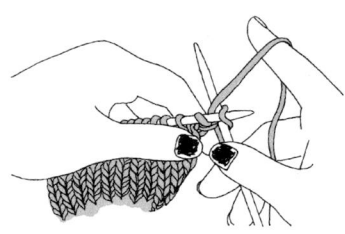

1 Knit a stitch, but do not drop the old stitch off the left needle.

2 Transfer the new stitch to the left-hand needle by inserting the left needle into the front leg of this loop from *right to left* (and from front to back) and pulling it off the right needle.

3 To continue casting on, stick your right needle *in between* the first two stitches on the left needle and knit a stitch (wrap the yarn around the needle, and pull it through to the front), but do not drop the old stitch off the left needle. Transfer the new stitch to the left needle in the same manner as you did in step 2.

Knit Stitch (K)

THE ENGLISH (RIGHT-HAND) WAY

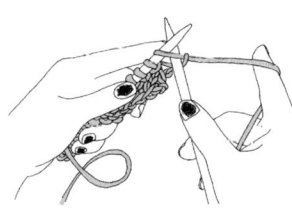 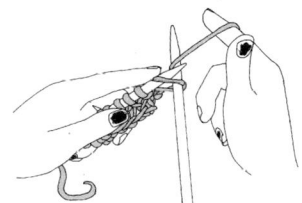 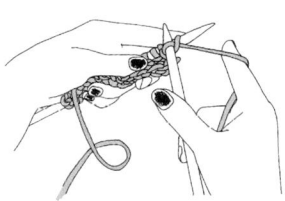 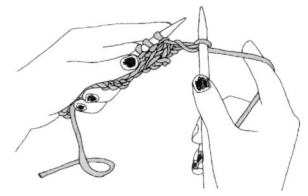

1 Take the needle with the stitches on it in your left hand. Hold the yarn in your right hand, over your right forefinger. Slide the point of the right needle through the first loop on the left needle from front to

back so that the two needles make an X.

2 With your right hand, wrap the yarn around the tip of the right needle counterclockwise (from back to front).

3 Pull the yarn taut (not tight!) with your forefinger, and slide the point of your right needle down and back out of the loop the opposite of the way you came in: *from the back to the front.* Make sure you bring the new loop along!

4 Once you're back out, slide the right needle up again so that the new loop is about 1½ inches from the tip, and push the old loop off the tip of the left needle.

THE CONTINENTAL (LEFT-HAND) WAY

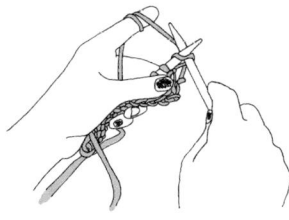 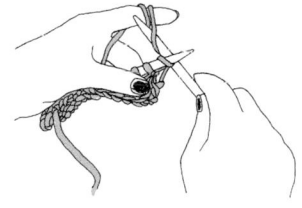 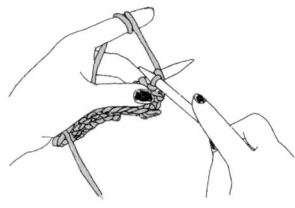 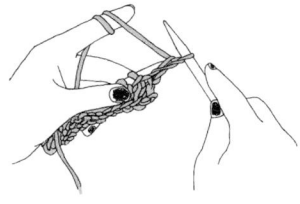

1 Hold the yarn with your left hand, with the yarn wrapped around your left forefinger, and use your bottom two fingers to hold the needle. Slide the point of the right needle through the first loop on the left needle

from front to back so that the two needles make an X.

2 With the tip of the right needle, grab that strand of yarn that's coming from your forefinger so that it wraps counterclockwise around the right needle.

3 Pull this new loop back out the loop you came in from.

4 Once you're back out, slide the right needle up again so that the new loop is about 1½ inches from the tip, and push the old loop off the left needle.

Purl Stitch (P)

THE ENGLISH (RIGHT-HAND) WAY

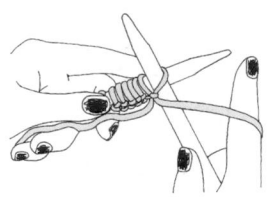 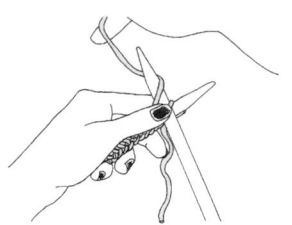 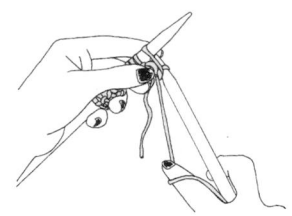 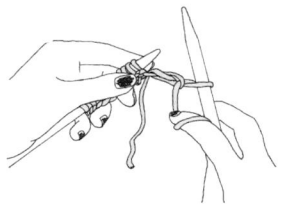

1 Hold your yarn and needles the same way you would to make a knit stitch, but bring the yarn between the tips of your needles so that it is *in front* of your right needle. Insert the right needle from

back to front through the first stitch on the left needle. Your needles are now in an X shape.

2 Take the yarn in your right hand, and loop it around the point of your right needle counterclockwise.

3 Carefully slide your right needle down along the base of the left needle, pushing the point of the right needle—and your new loop—out through the back of the stitch you came in through.

4 Push the right needle back up again and slide the old loop up and off the left needle.

THE CONTINENTAL (LEFT-HAND) WAY

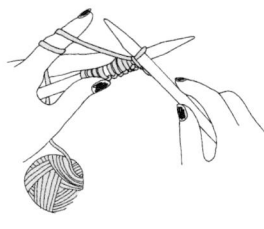 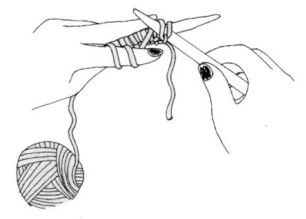 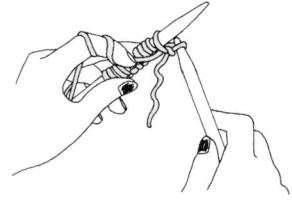 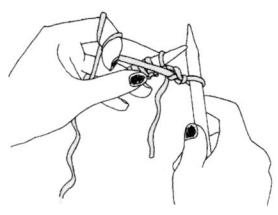

1 Hold your yarn and needles the same way you would to make a knit stitch, but bring the yarn between the tips of your needles so that it is *in front* of your left needle. Insert your right needle from back to front through the loop on the first stitch on the left needle.

Your needles are now in an X shape.

2 Bring the yarn in your left hand around the point of your right needle counterclockwise, then bring your left pointer finger (the one with the yarn around it), down below the center of the X.

3 Carefully slide your right needle down along the base of the left needle, pushing the point of the right needle out through the back of the stitch you came in through.

4 Slide the right needle back up again and push the old loop up and off the left needle.

Binding Off (BO)

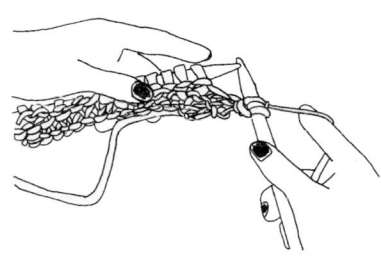

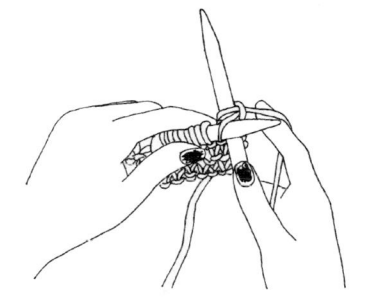

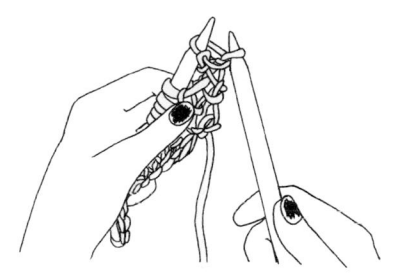

1 Starting at the beginning of a row, knit two stitches.

2 Slide the tip of the left needle under the front leg of the first stitch you knit.

3 Then lift that stitch up and over the second stitch and let it drop off the tip of the right needle.

Binding Off *(continued)*

Bar Increase (INC 1)

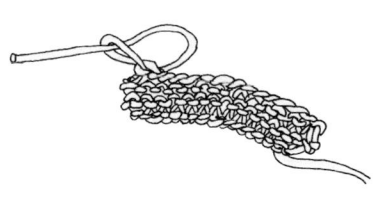

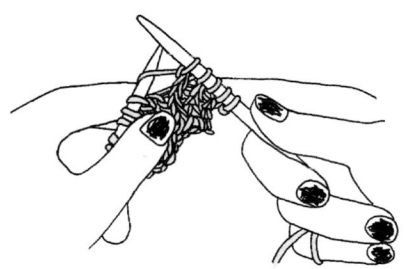

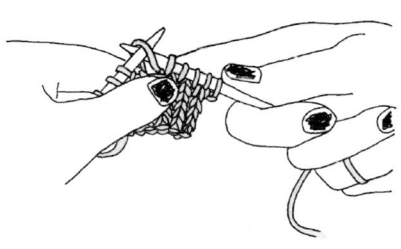

4 Repeat until all of your stitches have been bound off, and you're left with only one stitch. Cut the yarn about 6 inches from the end and pull it through that last stitch, tightening gently.

1 Knit into the next stitch on the needle, *but don't drop it off the left needle.*

2 Now, knit into the *back leg* of that same stitch. This time drop it off the needle; you should now have an extra stitch on your right needle.

Make One Increase (M1)

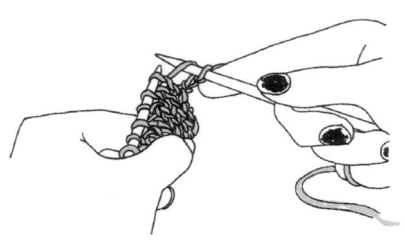 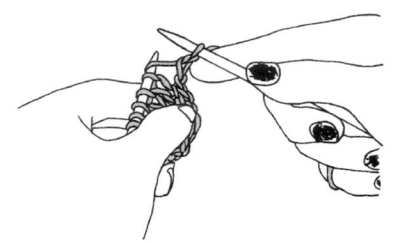 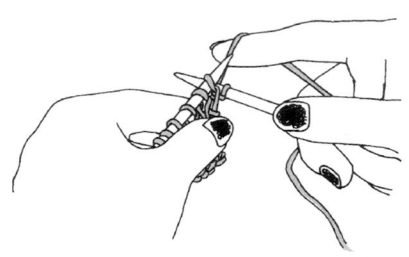

1 With the right needle, pick up the strand of yarn that lies between the stitch you just knit and the next stitch on the needle. Pick up this strand by inserting the needle under it *from front to back*.

2 Lift this strand off the right needle and onto the left by inserting the left needle under it *from front to back* and dropping it off the right needle.

3 Knit into the *back* of this stitch.

Yarn Over (YO)

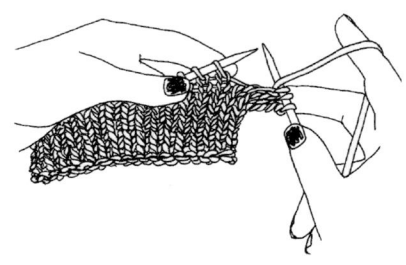 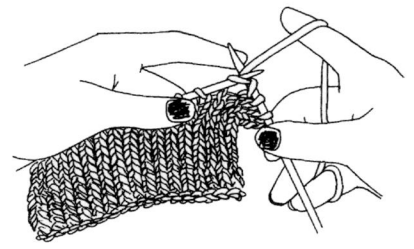

1 Knit the first stitch, then bring your yarn to the front between the two points of your needles.

2 With the yarn still in front, knit the next stitch. Knitting a stitch this way will leave an extra strand of yarn lying across your needle.

Knit Two Together (K2TOG)

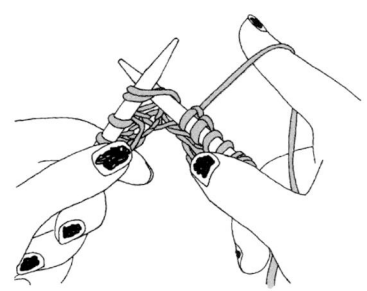

1 Stick the right needle into the next two stitches on the left needle knitwise. Knit these stitches together as one.

Piece of cake, right? And, just as you can knit two knit stitches together, you can also purl two purl stitches together.

Slip. Slip. Knit (SSK)

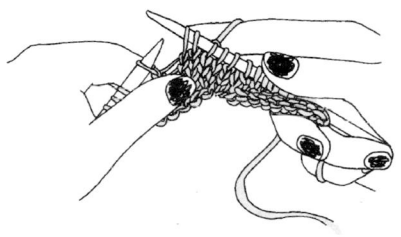 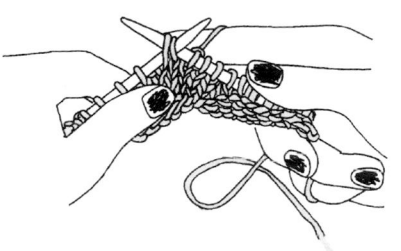 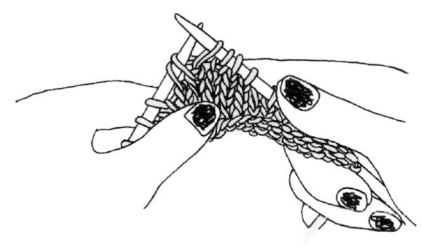

1 Stick your right needle into the next stitch as if you were going to knit it, but then slide it off the left needle and onto the right. Slip the next stitch knitwise too.

2 Take your left needle and slip it through the front legs of those two stitches, from left to right.

3 With the needles in that position, make a knit stitch by wrapping the yarn around, pulling the loop through to the front, then dropping the old loops off the left-hand needle.

Slip. Knit. Pass Slipped Stitch Over (SKP)

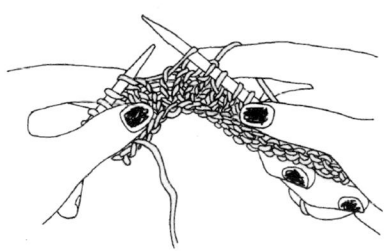 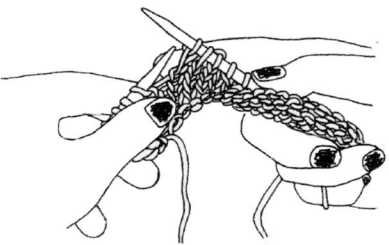 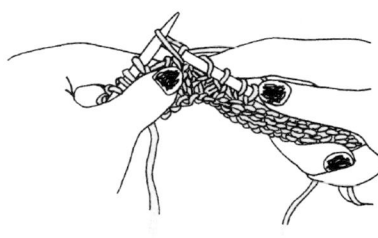

1 Slip one stitch knitwise.

2 Knit the next stitch.

3 Insert the left needle into the front leg of the slipped stitch and lift it over the stitch you just knit and off the needle—just like when you're binding off.

Sewing Side Seams

1. Before sewing two knit pieces together, you'll need to tack the yarn in place. Begin by threading a yarn needle with a length of yarn long enough to sew the entire seam, and at least another 12" left over. Then tack the yarn in place by pulling the needle up through the rightmost corner stitch at the bottom of the left-hand piece.

2. Secure the yarn by inserting the needle back up through the same hole.

3. Now bring the needle up through the leftmost corner stitch at the bottom of the right-hand piece, and then up through the same hole in the left-hand piece. Pull taut. You've made a little figure eight, and the two corners of your fabric should be right up close together. Continue with the mattress stitch, below.

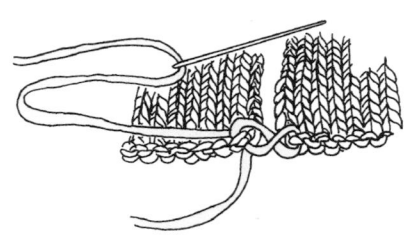

Mattress Stitch

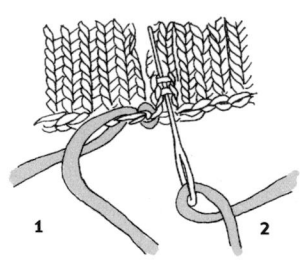
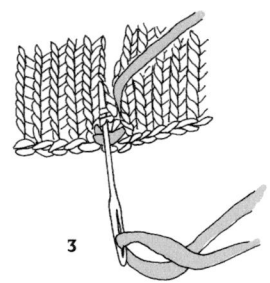
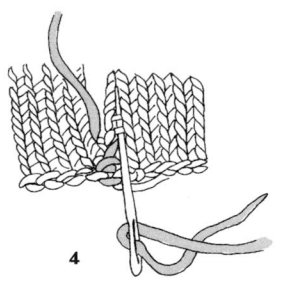

1 Take a close look at the side edge of a piece of stockinette fabric. If you carefully pull apart the edge stitch and the first real row of knit V stitches, you will see the running bars, something like a ladder of yarn. You'll be sewing the two sides together by stitching around these bars. Start by pinning your pieces together, right sides up, and tacking the yarn in place.

2 Pass the needle under the first two running bars of the right-hand piece of fabric, from the bottom to the top.

3 Now pass the needle under the first two running bars of the left-hand piece of fabric the same way.

4 Insert the needle down into the same point where it came out on the right-hand piece of fabric, and carry it under the next two running bars.

5 Insert the needle back into the same point where it came out on the left-hand piece of fabric, and come up two bars later. Repeat those last two steps until you have 2 or 3 inches done, then pull the yarn taut so that the seam becomes invisible.

Two Ways to Sew Tops of Pieces Together

FAKE GRAFTING

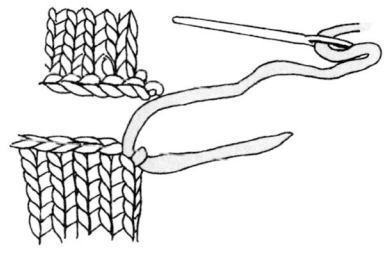
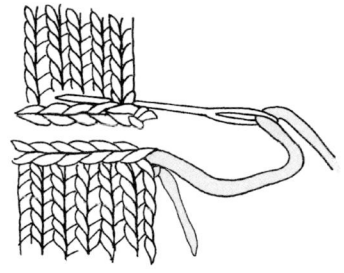
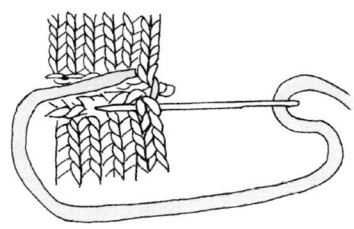

1 Tack a length of yarn to your work by bringing your needle up through the center of the right-most V on the bottom piece, just below the bound-off edge (leave a 6-inch tail). Now come back up through the center of this V again (the yarn can go around the outside edge of the piece).

2 Bring your yarn down to the right of the bottom of the right-most V on the top piece, and back up to the left of that V.

3 Insert the needle back down into the center of the same V in the bottom piece of fabric where your yarn originated, and come up in the center of the next V to the left. Repeat across.

KITCHENER STITCH

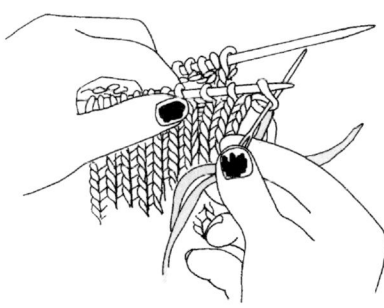
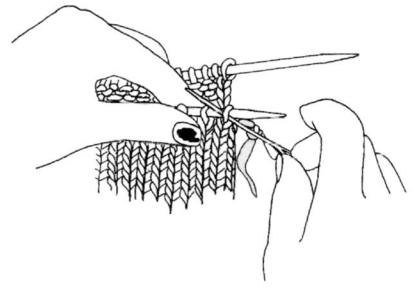
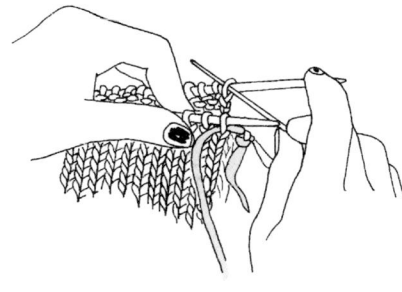

1 Slide the yarn needle through the first stitch on the front needle *as if to knit.* Pull the yarn through and drop that stitch off the needle.

2 Pass the yarn needle through the second stitch on the front needle as if to purl. Don't drop the stitch off the needle.

3 Pass the yarn needle through the first stitch on the back needle *as if to purl.* Drop the stitch off the needle.

Picking Up Stitches

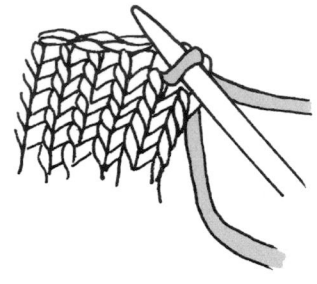

1 With the front of the piece facing you, insert your knitting needle through the center of a stitch.

2 Wrap your yarn around it.

3 Draw this new loop from the back of the fabric to the front.

Three-Needle Bind-off

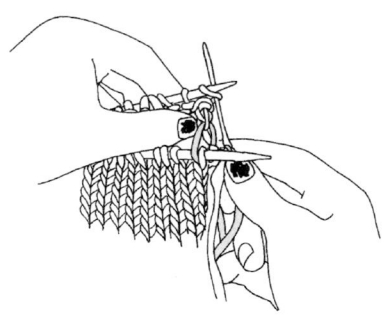

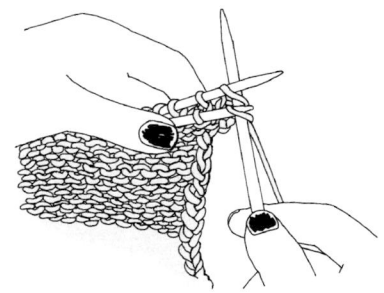

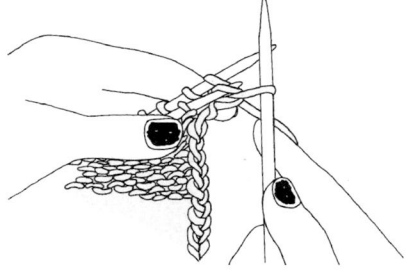

4 Pass the needle through the second stitch on the back needle *as if to knit*. Leave that stitch on the needle. Repeat steps 1–4 until all the stitches are grafted together.

1 With the right sides of your work facing each other, hold the two knitting needles in your left hand with their points facing to the right. Then, take a third needle and insert it, knitwise, through the first stitch on the front needle and knitwise through the first stitch on the back needle.

2 Knit the two stitches together. Do the same on the next stitch, then leapfrog the first stitch over this second one. Repeat to the end.

Fringe

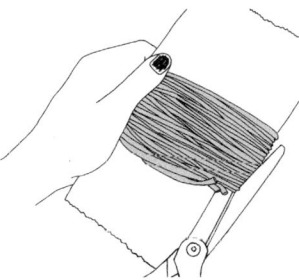

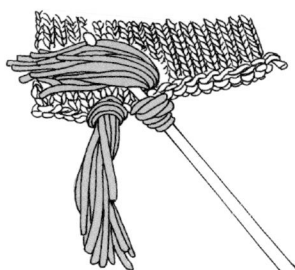

1 Wrap yarn around a sturdy rectangular thing that's a bit longer than the length you want your fringe to be, then cut it at one end.

2 Grab a few strands and fold them in half. Stick a crochet hook *from back to front* through the space in your knitting where you want to add fringe. Hang your folded yarn over the hook and pull it through to the back of the fabric. With a crochet hook or with your fingers, pull the tails of the yarn through the loop.

3 Keep hanging fringe until your piece is all fringed up. Then trim the bottoms so they line up like little toy soldiers.

I-Cord

Blanket Stitch

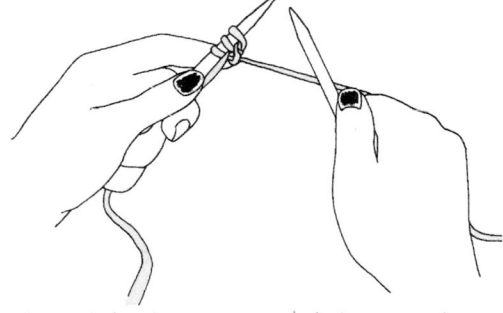

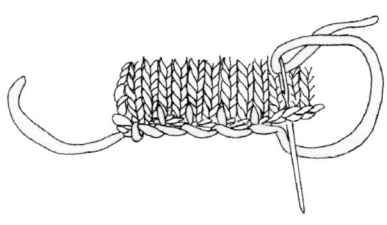

Start by casting three stitches (or as many as your knitting pattern tells you to) onto a double-pointed needle. Knit those stitches. Switch the needles in your hands without turning your work, and slide the stitches to the other side of the needle. With the yarn still hanging from the left,

knit across using another double-pointed needle. Be sure to pull the yarn tight when you make your first stitch so that the fabric rolls in on itself.

Tack the yarn at the left-hand edge of fabric. Insert the needle into the fabric about ½" to the right of this, and ½" above the edge. Hold the yarn tail down and slip the point of the needle over it. Pull through. Continue around the edge of your work.

Pom-Poms

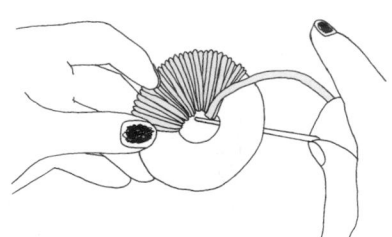
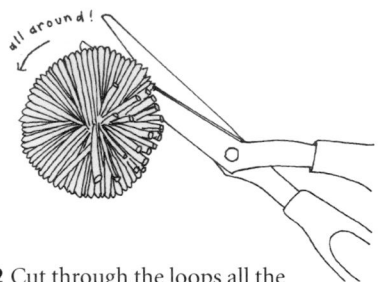
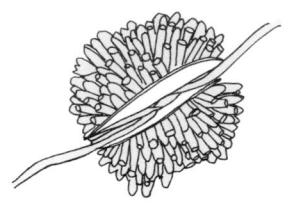

1 First, create a little pom-pom maker with two doughnut-shaped pieces of cardboard or plastic. The hole in the center should be about half the size of the circle itself. Then take your yarn, either threaded on a needle or with your fingers, and wind it around the two stacked doughnut shapes, until the center hole is filled with yarn.

2 Cut through the loops all the way around the outside of the doughnut.

3 Pull a length of yarn up between the two halves of the pom-pom, wrap it tightly around the core of the pom-pom, and make a sturdy square knot to hold it together. Cut out the cardboard rings, fluff up your pom-pom, and trim it as necessary to even up the ends.

Duplicate Stitch

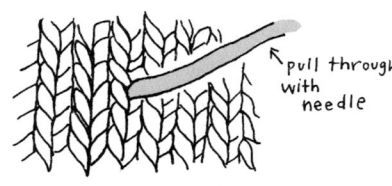
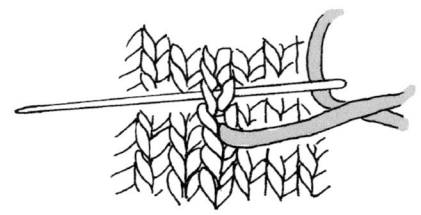
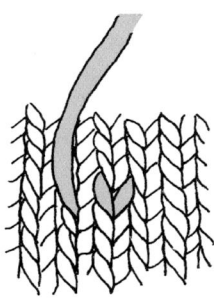

1 Thread a length of yarn through a yarn needle, and come up from the back to the front of your work through the bottom point of one of your knit Vs. Pull the yarn up and through to the right, leaving a nice 6-inch tail at the back that you can work away later.

2 Now pass the needle under the bottom two legs of the stitch above the one you are duplicating, from *right to left*. Pull the yarn through, gently.

3 Insert the needle back down into the first hole you came up through. Come back up at the base of the next stitch you need to duplicate. Continue to do this with all the stitches you want to color in, pulling the yarn through so that the new stitch just sits on top of the original stitch.

Cables

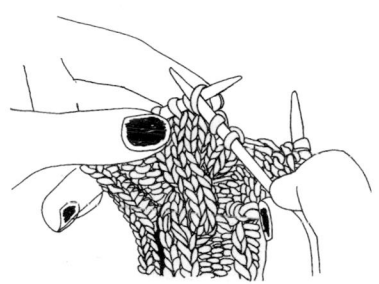
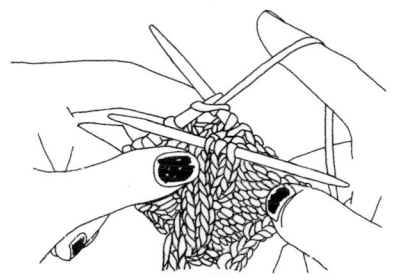
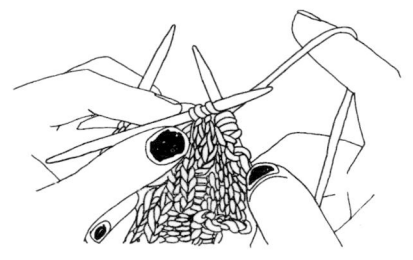

1 To make a cable, slip the required number of stitches purlwise onto a cable needle. For a front-crossed cable, let the cable needle with the stitches dangle to the front of your work. For a back-crossed cable, hang the stitches to the back of your work.

2 Knit the next stitch on the needle, pull the yarn tight, and knit the remaining number of required stitches.

3 Now knit the first stitch off the cable needle, pull the yarn tight, and knit the remaining stitches.

Fair Isle

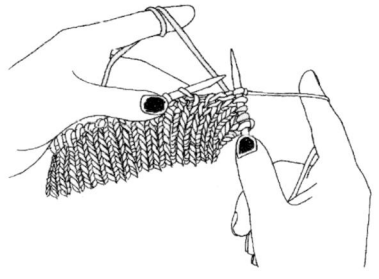
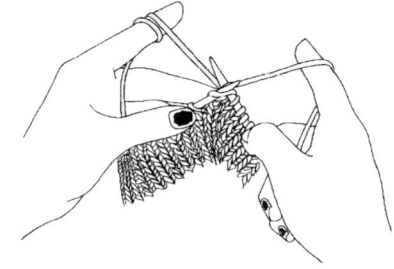

1 Take the main color of yarn in your right hand and hold it as you would for English knitting (see page 256). Take the other color in your left hand and hold it as you would for Continental knitting (see page 256).

2 As each color is needed, knit it with the hand that is holding that color yarn. Be careful not to pull the yarn too tightly. It is very important, when carrying yarn at the back of your work, that you leave enough of it between stitches so that it lies flat but still allows the fabric to stretch.

Intarsia

TO ADD A SECOND COLOR OF YARN IN A ROW:

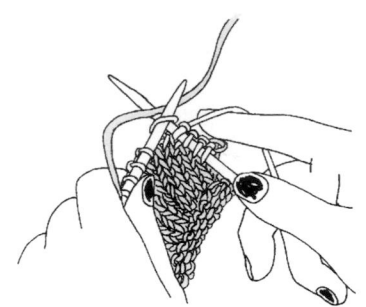

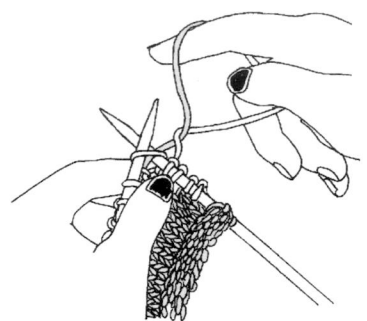

1 Slide your right needle into the first stitch as if to knit (or purl if that's what you're doing), but don't make the new stitch. Instead, lay the *new* color of yarn across the tip of the needle, leaving about a 6-inch tail hanging to the left and the ball end of the yarn to the right.

2 Bring the ball end of the yarn *around and underneath* the old color, then wrap it around the needle to make a knit (or purl) stitch. Finish the stitch in the usual way, dropping both the old loop and the tail of the new yarn over the newly formed stitch.

TO CHANGE FROM ONE COLOR TO THE NEXT IN A ROW:

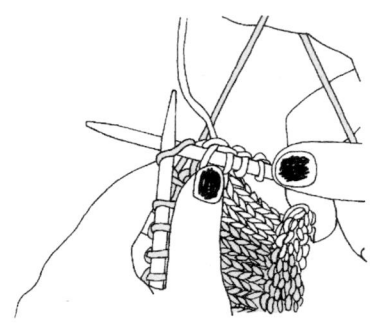

1 Bring the old color up and to the left, then bring the new color up *from under* the old color, and make the new stitch, linking the two stitches together.

Chain Stitch

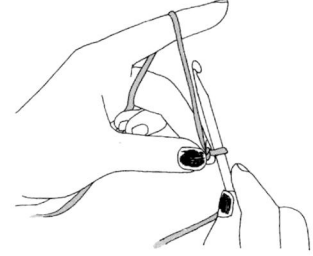

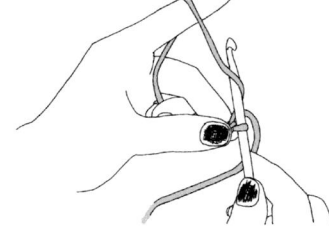

1 Make a slip knot about 6 inches from the end of your yarn and tighten it at the neck of the crochet hook. Hold the crochet hook in your right hand and the ball end of the yarn in your left.

2 With the hook facing up, wrap the yarn over the front of the needle clockwise, from right to left.

3 Twist the crochet hook so that the hook faces down and toward the knot, and pull the yarn through the loop.

4 Twist the hook so that the hook part is facing up again, wrap the yarn as in step 2, and pull another loop through.

Crab Stitch

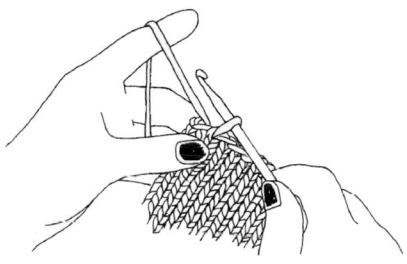

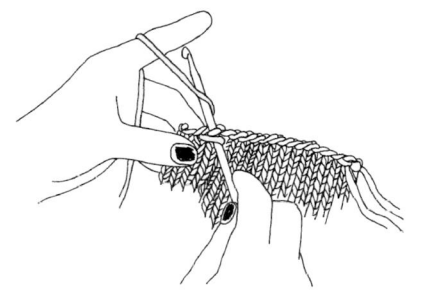

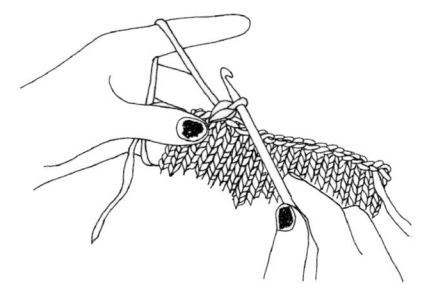

1 Insert a crochet hook into the edge of your knitting. Wrap the yarn around your hook clockwise, and pull a loop through.

2 Slide your crochet hook back into the fabric, in a space to the right of your last crab stitch. Wrap the ball end of the yarn clockwise around your crochet hook.

3 Pull the yarn through, so that you now have two loops on your crochet hook. Wrap your yarn one last time around the crochet hook, clockwise, then pull it through both loops.

Single Crochet (sc)

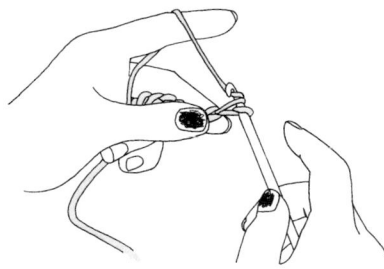

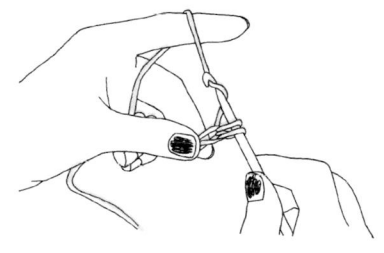

1 Slip your crochet hook through the second chain stitch from the hook, wrap the yarn around it clockwise, from right to left, and pull the loop through one loop. You now have two loops on your crochet hook.

2 Wrap the yarn around the crochet hook again, and this time pull it through *both* the loops on the hook.

Reminder:

Crocheting requires you to constantly pull loops of yarn through your previously formed loops. So you want to leave enough space in those loops to pass a crochet hook through. You might even try leaving them purposely loose until you get the hang of how small they can go and still allow your hook to fit.

Also, when you make a chain stitch or a single crochet, you are always working from right to left—like reading Hebrew. The crab stitch is the exception: It is made from left to right.

Resources

Yarn Store Nation

A STITCH 'N BITCH GUIDE TO LOCAL YARN STORES

Arizona

MESA

Fiber Factory
150 West Main Street
Mesa, AZ 85201
480-969-4346
888-969-9276
www.fiberfactory.com
I always make a point to visit the Fiber Factory when I'm in town. The employees are very helpful to beginners. They also teach kids and offer a wealth of classes in spinning, socks, crochet, tatting and bobbin lace, and dying and weaving.
Sandra Harper

SCOTTSDALE

Knitting in Scottsdale
7116 East Mercer Lane
Scottsdale, AZ 85254
480-951-9942
The owner, Roberta, carries mostly natural fibers, including a number of good ole standards. She really takes time to work with you on projects and provides a fun atmosphere for knitting. Every time I drop in, I feel like I'm catching up with an old friend.   *Onida Perkel*

California

LONG BEACH

Alamitos Bay Yarn Company
174 Marina Drive
Long Beach, CA 90803
562-799-8484
www.yarncompany.com
This store has a very helpful staff, a beautiful selection, and even a birthday club.
Tina Paredes

LOS ANGELES AREA

Jennifer Knits
108 Barrington Walk
Los Angeles, CA 90049
310-471-8733
www.jenniferknits.com
Jennifer is awesome. She creates custom designs and helps everyone pick out the perfect yarn for their project. Many west side knitters consider this small Brentwood haven their home away from home.
Faith Landsman

Knit Cafe
8441 Melrose Avenue
Los Angeles, CA 90069
323-658-5648
www.knitcafe.com
If you're looking for a cute chick with cat-eye glasses to teach you to purl, Mary Heather's your girl. They have inspiring and original knit and crocheted artwork throughout, including Ellen Bloom's famous (and oft stolen) crocheted Oreo cookies.
Faith Landsman

Stitch Cafe
12443 Magnolia Boulevard
Valley Village, CA 91607
818-980-1234
www.stitchcafe.com
Not content to have wonderful staffers, serve yummy sandwiches, and offer comfy couches, they sometimes stay open until midnight. Who could ask for more?
Faith Landsman

Stitches from the Heart
3306 West Pico Boulevard
Santa Monica, CA 90405
310-452-5151
www.stitchesfromtheheart.org
This shop has high-end and lower-end yarn, classes, and a cheerful volunteer staff. Purchases are tax-deductible donations to the Stitches from the Heart nonprofit organization, which donates knitted and crocheted items to premature babies at hospitals.
Ellen Bloom

Suss Design
7350 Beverly Boulevard
Los Angeles, CA 90036
323-954-9637
www.sussdesign.com
Their selection is yummy and still competitively priced, and all the yarns are swatched (which really gives you a taste of what these yarns will do). The finished articles around the store are incredibly inspiring. Suss also has her own line of easy and hip patterns.
Hilda Erb

Unwind
818 N. Hollywood Way
Burbank, CA 91505
818-840-0800
www.unwindyarn.com
This centrally located store has luscious yarns that will make any knitter drool. Plus, owner Stephanie Steinhaus holds Atwater Stitch 'n Bitch meetings at her store.
Karen Cahall

MONTEREY AREA

Monarch Knitting and Quilts
529 Central Avenue, Suite 3
Pacific Grove, CA 93950
888-575-YARN
www.monarchknitting.com
This place exemplifies why the term "stuffed to the gills" was invented. You can find sale

yarns in the back, and balls of remnants for 50 cents each, and they frequently have good bag deals. Monarch has a very friendly staff—and a huge white dog.   *Gunilla Leavitt*

ORANGE COUNTY AREA
Micki's California Yarn Sales
9542 Hamilton Avenue
Huntington Beach, CA 92646
714-965-0018
This small tucked-away shop is owned by Micki, an amazing Japanese lady who is always helpful with knitting, crochet, and anything to do with yarn. She'll also help match yarns to your specifications and quickly order whatever you need.
Diana Camden

Strands and Stitches
1516 South Coast Highway
Laguna Beach, CA 92651
949-497-5648
Strands and Stitches is great, and, unlike another area store that pulled the first *Stitch 'n Bitch* book from the shelves because of "vulgar" language, they sell it and recommend it!
Melissa Sheppard

PARADISE
Knitwits
6433 Skyway
Paradise, CA 95969
530-877-YARN
My knitting group meets here weekly, and Devvy has been great at finding any yarn we request.   *Heatherly Walker*

SAN FRANCISCO AREA
Artfibers
124 Sutter Street
San Francisco, CA 94104
415-956-6319
888-326-1112
www.artfibers.com
Hidden away on the second floor of a small building in San Francisco's financial district, Artfibers might seem to be an intimidating lair, but beginning knitters are most welcome. They sell only their own brand of yarn, which is created especially for them all over the world, and knitted samples hang by the shelves of lustrous yarns with informational cards describing the yarns in detail, from content to gauge to suggested quantities for various types of projects. The store has a circle of comfortable chairs, all sizes of needles, and, amazingly, balls of sample yarns so any interested buyer can knit a swatch for him- or herself before buying.
Karen Hudson

Article Pract
5010 Telegraph Avenue
Oakland, CA 94609
510-652-7435
This is the coolest, hippest, most happening yarn store in the East Bay. Everything about it inspires creativity and gets the juices flowing—from the always encouraging owner, Christina, to the yarns, which are luscious, vibrant, and begging to

be fondled, to the supportive clientele, from whom I have received many a tip as well as hands-on help. The store itself, located in a bustling Oakland neighborhood, calls you in with the ever-changing window displays. If someone asked me where to go for knitting and crafty adventure and fun, I'd send them straight to Article Pract.   *Lucretia Ausse*

ImagiKnit
3897 18th Street
San Francisco, CA 94114
415-621-6642
www.imagiknit.com
A cozy, well-stocked, and very inviting shop, ImagiKnit is the kind of place that you want to visit just because the atmosphere is so nice. One can get lost just handling the yarns, flipping through the books and patterns, or sitting in the back and working out the latest trouble spot with a friendly staff member.   *Michael Cooper*

Knitting Arts
14554 Big Basin Way
Saratoga, CA 95070
408-867-5010
www.goknit.com
This shop's energetic and knowledgeable employees won't leave you high and dry. They carry most of the higher-end yarns, as well as Brown Sheep and Sirdar yarns for budget-minded knitters. Having a computerized inventory means they

can tell you exactly how many balls in each color are in stock, and they also offer dozens of classes and free in-house patterns.   *Mary Wisnewski*

Lacis
3163 Adeline Street
Berkeley, CA 94703
tel: 510-843-7178
fax: 510-843-5018
www.lacis.com
This shop is a lacemaker's dream. In their huge space, they carry supplies for making crocheted, tatted, and knitted lace, lace panels, and a wide variety of old and out-of-print books on all sorts of needlecrafts. They also have a large amount of vintage and antique lace for sale, as well as antique clothing on display. It's really more than a store—it's almost a museum. After five minutes in there I understood why my pen pal in Germany orders all of her supplies from Lacis.
Marizel Pelayo

Urban Knitting Studio
320 Fell Street
San Francisco, CA 94102
415-552-5333
www.urbanknitting.com
Urban Knitting Studio is airy and modern, with a lounge in the front next to large windows, so it's perfect for my two favorite activities: knitting and people-watching. They have a great selection and a friendly, helpful staff that doesn't watch

you like a hawk when you're using their skein winder in the back of the store.   *Jen Tanner*

SAN JOSÉ AREA
The Golden Fleece
303 Potrero Street
Number 29-101
Santa Cruz, CA 95060
831-426-1425
www.thegoldenfleece.com
This beautiful store has wonderful yarns (some on the expensive side), a friendly, helpful staff, and a very nice classroom. Sale yarns (30 percent off) are out front in baskets.
    Gunilla Leavitt

The Rug and Yarn Hut
350 East Campbell Avenue
Campbell, CA 95008
408-871-0411
www.rughut.com
This yarn store has comfy chairs to just sit and knit in. They offer classes and instruction and are right across the street from the San Jose Stitch 'n Bitch site. In the back is an inflatable kiddie pool full of sale yarns, and they're not kidding, either—"sale" here means 50 percent off!
    Gunilla Leavitt

The Yarn Place
625 Capitola Avenue
Capitola, CA 95010
831-476-6480
www.theyarnplace.com
This is a smallish three-room store with a huge selection of

yarns; make sure you go over each room thoroughly at least twice. Their prices are reasonable (I've seen the same yarns in other places for more money) and there's a sale nook in the back room.   *Gunilla Leavitt*

Colorado
BOULDER
Shuttles, Spindles, and Skeins
635 South Broadway, Unit E
Boulder, CO 80305
303-494-1071
800-283-4163
www.shuttlesspindlesand
    skeins.com
They have a terrific selection of classic and trendy yarns, patterns, and other essentials for knitting, weaving, and spinning. Their classes are known throughout the area. One of the owners has a bearded collie who is as much a fixture in the store as the yarn is!
    Karen Scappini

COLORADO SPRINGS
Green Valley Weavers & Knitters Supply
2115 West Colorado Avenue
Colorado Springs, CO 80904
719-448-9963
800-457-8559
This store is absolutely fabulous! It's not big, but very cozy. The class schedule is excellent, and the owners are kind and down-to-earth. They even have a shop dog and shop-dog-in-training.   *Melanie Wallace*

DENVER AREA
A Knitted Peace
5654-C South Prince Street
Littleton, CO 80120
303-730-0366
www.aknittedpeace.com
You'll find plenty of Brown Sheep, Rowan, Interlacements, Mission Falls, and Noro yarns, alongside books, kits, and needles. Owner Peggy Anderson has been known to set up one-of-a-kind private classes for small groups. Although this store is not as fully stocked as some of the other well-known Colorado shops, they more than make up for it in ambiance and friendliness.   *Amanda Berka*

Lambspun of Colorado
1101 East Lincoln Avenue
Fort Collins, CO 80524
970-484-1998
800-558-5262
www.lambspun.com
Family owned for more than a decade, this is a shop with a very sweet staff. They have classes, selection, and prices. They're the leading source for fine fiber arts and are committed to finding the best yarns nature has to offer in to-die-for colors.   *Amber Bell*

La Ti Da
1551 South Pearl Street
Denver, CO 80210
303-715-1414
www.latidadenver.com
La Ti Da is the best yarn store in Denver! Rita and Zack are

always generous with tips and suggestions. Their Pajama midnight sale is an event not to be missed. The store has a coffee shop complete with treats from a local bakery, a gift shop, and a live music series in the spring and summer months.
    Amber Bell

LAKEWOOD
The Recycled Lamb
2010 Youngfield Street
Lakewood, CO 80215
303-234-9337
www.recycledlamb.com
The staff couldn't be friendlier or more helpful, and they offer great classes in knitting, crocheting, spinning, and weaving. Their outstanding newsletter celebrates the joy of knitting in light of holidays and seasonal weather changes.
    Danielle Fay

Connecticut
DEEP RIVER
Yarns Down Under
37C Hillside Terrace
Deep River, CT 06417
860-526-9986
www.yarnsdownunder.com
This peaceful and welcoming shop is on a golf course near a pond. They recently put in an addition that is now chock-full of yarn. The combination of helpful owners, atmosphere, and surroundings make it a nice place to spend a few hours.   *Suzanne Barnes*

TORRINGTON

Hither and Yarn
835 New Harwinton Road
Torrington, CT 06790
860-489-9276
Hither and Yarn's owner is a prolific designer and a very sweet woman. She stocks a bounty of rare treasures, including unusual choices from Europe and hand-painted yarns produced by local farmers. You can even pick up fabric for lining your latest knitted handbag. When you're here, be sure to say hi to Phoebe, the poodle, who is always dressed to the nines.
Rebecca Lovelace

District of Columbia

WASHINGTON AREA

Knit and Stitch = Bliss
4706 Bethesda Avenue
Bethesda, MD 20814
301-652-7194
866-5NEEDLE
www.knitandstitch.com
Just when you think you'll never fall in love with another yarn, you discover ten more at this store! This place has the widest variety of yarns in the area and stocks everything from the finest hand-dyed fibers from New Adirondack to those irresistible novelty scarf yarns. The staff is new-and-improved and they all know and love the craft of knitting.
Ricki Seidman

Springwater Fiber Workshop
808 North Fairfax Street
Alexandria, VA 22314
703-549-3634
www.springwaterfiber.org
Springwater Fiber has a wide range of yarns, from exotic handspun and dyed yarns to easy-care, less expensive yarns (perfect for knitting baby clothes that can be worn for more than just a studio picture). They carry a lot of knitting notions and offer a very wide range of fiber art classes.
Tina Hsu

Stitch DC
731 8th Street SE
Washington, DC 20003
202-544-8900
www.stitchdc.com
The shop just opened this summer and is shaping up to be pretty great. There's a good selection of yarn and more arriving every day. The owner, Marie Connolly, is super nice and friendly, very helpful, and loves to let you browse. She has an outdoor courtyard in the middle of the shop, with a few tables and chairs for people to sit and knit with friends, as well as a couch and couple of chairs inside for those muggy D.C. summer days. She also has a back room with a large table for classes. She's happy to host Stitch 'n Bitch groups and is also happy to let random knitters hang out and knit away.
Anna Pohl

Woolwinders
404 King Farm Boulevard
Rockville, MD 20850
240-632-YARN
www.woolwinders.com
I go to the suburbs only for necessities, and Woolwinders is tops on my list of must visits. You can find what you need for projects at any price or skill level, and their excellent return policy allows you to buy that one skein extra so you won't have to finish with the wrong dye lot.
Ricki Seidman

Yarns International
5110 Ridgefield Road
Suite 200
Bethesda, MD 20816
301-913-2980
www.yarnsinternational.com
With high-quality natural fibers at the right price and an inspirational staff, you'll probably find exactly what you're looking for at Yarns International. It's a paradise for Fair Isle knitters; they've even developed their own line of yarn.
Ricki Seidman

Georgia

ATLANTA

Neases Needlework
345 West Ponce de Leon Avenue
Decatur, GA 30030
404-377-6875
www.neasesneedlework.com
The woman who owns and runs Neases will sit down and help anyone with his or her knitting needs, and she carries a great selection of yarn including Manos del Uruguay (my favorite), which is made by a collective of women abroad. Neases also holds silent auctions to raise money for charity.
Mahsa Yazdy

Illinois

CHICAGO AREA

Arcadia Knitting
1211 Balmoral
Chicago, IL 60640
773-293-1211
www.arcadiaknitting.com
Two stylin' sisters take the fear out of knitting in their North Chicago store. Featuring shelves full of yarn in glorious textures and colors, this small store has every kind of yarn you never knew you wanted—and best of all, it's organized by color! The always welcoming Arcadia gals are ready to help you check your gauge, figure out the Greek that is your pattern, or just let you sit on one of the front sofas and knit. Their classes offer something for every level of knitter, and their passion for passing on the knitting bug abounds.
Sarah Stray

CloseKnit, Inc.
622 Grove Street
Evanston, IL 60201
847-328-6760
A cozy yarn shop near the campus of Northwestern University, CloseKnit offers

an assortment of designer yarns, lots of patterns, buttons, and handmade gifts.

Claire Buenaflor

Have Ewe Any Wool
120 North York Road, Suite 220
Elmhurst, IL 60126
630-941-YARN
www.haveeweanywool.com
This shop's staff is helpful without being pushy, and classes are wonderfully instructive and full of interesting people. The yarn is of the highest quality, some with prices to match. Saturday mornings can be hectic, with several classes going on at the same time, but Peggy keeps things fun by serenading everyone with tunes on her Barbie karaoke machine.

Kerri Skrudland

Knitters Niche
3206 North Southport Avenue
Chicago, IL 60657
773-472-9276
Lots of people are afraid of this yarn shop, but I think it's the best one in Chicago. The owner, MaryAnn, is kind of gruff and doesn't like dealing with people who want her to cast on for them, but she has a heart of gold. Her classes are awesome, and they're much cheaper and longer than others in the city.

Lena Parsons

Knitting Etc., Inc.
9980 West 151st Street
Orland Park, IL 60462
708-349-7941
This store, converted from a big, old home, is my favorite in the area. The ladies who work here are extremely knowledgeable and helped me go from fledgling knitter to designer. And unlike some craft stores, the yarn here is displayed neatly according to yarn type and color in the front room.

Kim Fermoyle

Knitting Workshop
2218 North Lincoln Avenue
Chicago, IL 60614
773-929-5776
www.knittingworkshop.com
Knitting Workshop carries lots of designer yarns as well as good old standards. This shop has more books than other city shops and displays projects that inspire you to knit. Shop owner Mary offers classes as well as a weekly knit night.

Michele Cullom

Mosaic Yarn Studio, Ltd.
1585 Ellinwood Street #101
Des Plaines, IL 60016
847-390-1013
www.mosaicyarnstudio.com
Mosaic Yarn Studio carries many designer yarns, books, and a full supply of knitting needles and notions. The staff is extremely helpful, and the store is roomy, so you don't

feel crowded while browsing. They also offer classes and a frequent buyer card.

Claire Buenaflor

Pearl Art & Craft Supplies
225 West Chicago Avenue
Chicago, IL 60610
312-915-0200
Pearl sells some knitting supplies, such as needles and yarns from Lion Brand. They don't have much of a selection, but their prices are great!

Cindy Iglesias

We'll Keep You in Stitches
67 East Oak Street, 4th Floor
Chicago, IL 60611
312-642-2540
This shop, located just off of the Magnificent Mile, stocks an assortment of designer yarns and some knitting needles and accessories in a small space. The staff is knowledgeable and helpful. It's a nice change of pace if you feel the yarn yen while shopping in downtown Chicago.

Claire Buenaflor

Indiana

BOONVILLE

The Village Knitter
8A West Jennings
Newburgh, IN 47630
812-842-2360
www.thevillageknitter.com
Docia, the owner, is very knowledgeable, is always willing to help, will order anything

she can get from suppliers, and will even carry lines that you suggest.

Chris Behme

Iowa

MUSCATINE

Crazy Girl Yarn Shop
208 West 2nd Street
Muscatine, IA 52761
563-263-YARN
www.crazygirlyarnshop.com
This oasis for knitters from eastern Iowa and western Illinois is set in the corner of a refurbished button factory overlooking the Mississippi. With unique displays (bamboo knitting needles stuck into a vat of popcorn kernels), the shop sells well-known yarns, including Brown Sheep and Mission Falls, as well as locally produced yarns. The Crazy Girls hand-dye yarn, hold regular Knit and Whine nights, and have a growing button line.

Ann Rushton

Kansas

LAWRENCE

Yarn Barn
930 Massachusetts
Lawrence, KS 66044
785-842-4333
www.yarnbarn-ks.com
Yarn Barn has a great selection, and the staff are quick to adopt new things. They also stock weaving yarns, fleece, looms, and spinning wheels. I am

glad it's such a ways away from me, or I'd be spending more money there than I already do.   *Roberta Bragg*

Maryland

BALTIMORE

A Good Yarn
1738 Aliceanna Street
Baltimore, MD 21231
410-327-3884
www.agoodyarn.com
A Good Yarn is located on a tree-lined street in the historic Fell's Point neighborhood and has become a warm and welcoming meeting point for the local knitting community. The store carries mostly natural fibers, including some hand-spun yarns. Owner Lorraine Gaudet invites you to come in to drink a cup of tea, chat a while, and get inspired!

Beth Demko

FUNKSTOWN

Y2Knit
100 East Baltimore Street
Funkstown, MD 21734
301-766-4543
www.y2knit.net
Located in a building that's more than two hundred years old, in the lovely village of Funkstown, Y2Knit has character to spare. The staffers at Y2Knit are friendly and helpful, and the yarn is carefully laid out in colorful displays.

Emma K. Williams

Massachusetts

BOSTON AREA

A Good Yarn
4 Station Street
Brookline, MA 02445
617-731-4900
www.agoodyarn.biz
A colorful shop with reasonably priced yarns and a welcoming feel. The owner, Beverly, really takes the time to help you with projects and has a big table where people are always working on things.   *Amy Corveleyn*

Black Sheep Knitting Co.
1500 Highland Avenue
Needham, MA 02492
781-444-0694
The Black Sheep Knitting Co. is an unpretentious, bright, and very well organized store with a fabulous selection of yarns. The staff is always helpful without being pushy. It has a very friendly and relaxing atmosphere, complete with classical music and M&Ms.

Hannah Loughlin

Circles: A Knitting Salon
555 Amory Street
Jamaica Plain, MA 02130
617-524-5500
www.circles-salon.com
Circles's knowledgeable and kind owner Allison will help you with any problem and has an uncanny knack for locating patterns based on almost no description. She selects her spectacular yarns

with supporting artists and sustainability in mind. The store has a knitting room and a children's playroom.

Karen Noyes

The Knitting Room
2 Lake Street
Arlington, MA 02474
781-483-3442
www.knitroomboston.com
The very helpful staff of the Knitting Room is always willing to take time out to answer your questions. They offer a wide selection of yarns and a great variety of courses on knitting and crocheting.   *Crystal Smith*

Mind's Eye Yarns
22 White Street
Cambridge, MA 02140
617-354-7253
www.mindseyeyarns.com
The owner, Lucy, carries mostly natural-fiber yarns. She even stocks some of her own hand-spun yarns, and she spins in the store. The atmosphere is cozy, and even though the shop is small, it never feels overcrowded. Lucy's a good teacher and a fabulous enabler!

Dyana Fine

Putting on the Knitz
1282 Washington Street
West Newton, MA 02465
617-969-8070
Although there are no official classes here, newbies and experienced knitters alike are welcome to—and do!—stop by at

any time and get help with their projects free of charge. The store's friendly owners stock a wide variety of imported and domestic yarns and patterns and more than twenty major brands for one-stop stash enrichment at its best.

Beth Demko

Wild & Woolly Studio
7A Meriam Street
Lexington, MA 02420
781-861-7717
I like this suburban store because it is a good size with a correspondingly large selection of yarns. I also like the selection of books, which seems larger than what most other stores offer.   *Martha Spizziri*

Windsor Button
35 Temple Place
Boston, MA 02111
617-482-4969
www.windsorbutton.com
Charming in a quirky, anti-yuppie way, Windsor Button has an interesting vibe, and it's located right off the Common in a forgotten block near wig shops and an antique book-seller. It's an old button and sewing shop that has expanded its yarn selection by leaps and bounds.   *Aimee Dawson*

Woolcott and Company
61 JFK Street
Cambridge, MA 02138
617-547-2837
www.woolcottandco.com

Next door to the Redline Bar (where a Stitch 'n Bitch is held weekly), Woolcott and Company focuses on natural fibers but also carries some novelty yarns. The people who work there are obsessive about knitting, and the wool overflows from the shelves. Knitters like to stop by and show off what they've made.

Jessica Marcus

LENOX
Colorful Stitches
48 Main Street
Lenox, MA 01240
413-637-8206
www.colorful-stitches.com
This store is well worth a visit if you're in western Massachusetts. They have two floors full of mostly high-end yarns, patterns, and notions, and a sitting area where you can look at patterns or knit. You can also shop on-line.

Martha Spizziri

Minnesota

TWIN CITIES
Borealis Yarns
1340 Thomas Avenue
St. Paul, MN 55104
651-646-2488
www.borealisyarns.com
The Twin Cities' newest yarn store has a great mixture of the fancy and the classic. There's a big table up in front by the windows where knitters are always

welcome to sit and chat or ask questions. The store hosts a weekly community and charity knitting group in addition to its weekly knit night.   *Chris Silker*

Crafty Planet
2318 Lowry Avenue NE
Minneapolis, MN 55418
612-788-1180
www.craftyplanet.com
Crafty Planet is the place for the renegade crafter, with ever expanding hours and selection and unique classes. They are always on the lookout for new knitting, crocheting, sewing, and needlework supplies, so bring suggestions. Don't miss CCCP (Craft 'n Chat @ Crafty Planet), and look for owners Matt and Trish's vintage Vespas outside.   *Meghan McInerny*

Depth of Field Yarn
405 Cedar Avenue
Minneapolis, MN 55454
612-340-0529 x3
www.depthoffieldyarn.com
You can't go wrong with this store; it has classes in the basement, an amazing array of yarns on the main floor, and a great sale loft. There is so much yarn, it's astounding!

Chris Silker

Needlework Unlimited
4420 Drew Avenue South
Minneapolis, MN 55410
612-925-2454
888-925-2454
www.needleworkunlimited.com

Needlework Unlimited recently became more working-girl friendly with the addition of later weeknight hours. They offer a variety of classes, books, and patterns, and the staff has rescued me from disaster on more than one occasion with patience and good humor. Their monthly Karen's Knit Knite is a fun way to socialize and compare projects with knitters of all levels.

Meghan McInerny

Missouri

ROLLA
Uniquely Yours
404 East Highway 72
Rolla, MO 65401
573-364-2070
www.rollanet.org/~uniquely
Uniquely Yours is a fiber and quilt shop that carries crafting supplies and yarn and also offers classes. They offer a nice range of mid-priced yarns in a fabulous selection of colors and weights. Other perks are the monthly potluck and the cozy back room for classes and gatherings.

Catherine Popalisky

ST. LOUIS AREA
Weaving Department
The Historic Myers House
180 West Dunn Road
Florissant, MO 63031
314-921-7800
Located on the second floor of a historic building (above a

quilting store), this shop is set up in several yarn-filled rooms. Owner Nancy Quade offers classes in knitting, weaving, spinning, and machine knitting. This fantastic find draws customers from other states.

Sharron Miller

New Jersey

PRINCETON
Glenmarle Woolworks
301 North Harrison Street
Princeton, NJ 08559
609-921-3022
www.glenmarlewoolworks.com
The entire Rowan line, Koigu, and Manos del Uruguay are only part of the yummy natural-fiber feast available at Glenmarle. A separate section of the store is devoted to novelty yarns, another to felting. Hand-sewn and hand-blown glass buttons and hand-painted needles round out the selection at this upscale shop.   *Beth Demko*

New York

IRVINGTON
Flying Fingers Yarn Shop
19 Main Street
Irvington, NY 10533
914-591-4113
www.flyingfingersyarnshop.com
Elise, the friendly owner, offers innovative classes—"Beyond Scarves," for instance—to calm first-sweater fears and a seasonal introductory course for

college students on winter break. "Fine and unusual yarns from unique sources" is more than just a motto—Elise will honor special orders to far-away lands such as Australia.
Jane Murray-Stringer

NEW YORK CITY
Brooklyn General
135 Union Street
Brooklyn, NY 11231
718-855-8885
I'm really lucky that Brooklyn has so many cool stores, like the fairly new Brooklyn General. It's a very cute store with a small selection of high-quality, interesting stuff, and the staff gives lessons.
Dalton Rooney

Downtown Yarns
45 Avenue A
New York, NY 10009
212-995-5991
This shop is like a little piece of western Massachusetts snuggled up in the East Village. They don't have a compost heap out back, but they do have a terrific selection of yarns in different price ranges and an adorable dog who will wag his tail for free.
Susanna Goldfinger

Knit-A-Way
398 Atlantic Avenue
Brooklyn, NY 11217
718-797-3305
This place rocks! It's one of the many reasons to go to Brooklyn. They have both high-

and low-end yarns—and good karma.
Kathleen Woodberry

Knit New York
307 East 14th Street
New York, NY 10003
212-387-0707
www.knitnewyork.com
When I first started knitting, Jill at Knit New York set me straight with advice on yarn, needles, reading patterns, and general techniques. The store has very snazzy yarns and delicious teas, too. It might be a bit pricey, but I like supporting independents, and everyone is so darn nice there. Plus they're open later than most stores in the city.
Lynn Andriani

P&S Fabrics
355 Broadway
New York, NY 10013
212-226-1534
www.psfabrics.com
Not just a knitting store, but a cheap-yarn bonanza. Lots of Lion Brand (some of the best prices around), Red Heart, and other brands. They also stock Patons booklets, books, needles, and supplies.
Olugbemisola Amusashonubi-Perkovich

Purl
137 Sullivan Street
New York, NY 10012
212-420-8796
www.purlsoho.com
The walls are painted a soothing mint green and the floor-

to-ceiling shelves hold a rainbow assortment of mostly luxury yarns. Purl's SoHo location makes it the prime destination for crafty fashionistas, and the women who work there are hip and friendly.
Susanna Goldfinger

School Products Co., Inc.
1201 Broadway
New York, NY 10001
212-679-3516
www.schoolproducts.com
If you're from out of town, this should be the first yarn store you visit in NYC. In addition to some of the usual suspects, you'll find cheap cones of mohair, angora, cashmere, and other specialty yarns left over from designer knitwear factories. Only in New York, kids, only in New York.
DS

Seaport Yarn
135 William Street,
near Fulton, 5th floor
New York, NY 10038
212-608-3100
www.seaportyarn.com
It might not look like much from the outside, but once inside the store, you won't be disappointed. There are several rooms of yarn, everything from Artful Yarns to Adrienne Vittadini, and the prices are the lowest in the city.
Elaine Hamilton

The Yarn Company
2274 Broadway, 2nd floor
New York, NY 10024
212-787-7878
888-YARNCO1
www.theyarnco.com
The Yarn Company carries a wide selection of imported and hand-dyed yarns and a large variety of patterns. The staff are very helpful and welcome you to come in, take a seat, and knit, knit, knit.
Kathleen Woodberry

Unique Knitkraft
257 West 39th Street
New York, NY 10018
212-840-6950
www.uniqueknitkraft.com
Unique Knitkraft carries lots of European and Asian yarns and some Patons at great prices. You'll be able to pick up a nice surprise every time you visit.
Olugbemisola Amusashonubi-Perkovich

PELHAM
Wool Works
214 Fifth Avenue
Pelham, NY 10803
914-738-0104
Situated in the center of Pelham, Wool Works has a small but very nice selection of yarn, groovy patterns, a mellow vibe, and two cordial owners. They gave me a free tape measure, which makes me a fan for life!
Neela Banerjee

North Carolina

HILLSBOROUGH

Wal-Mart Supercenter
501 Hampton Pointe
Boulevard
Hillsborough, NC 27278
919-732-9172
I have been to plenty of knitting boutiques and online stores, as well as many Wal-Marts, but Store #1191 is a standout! They have an awesome stock of Red Heart, Caron, and Bernat, and a selection of eyelash and boa yarns. If you are in the area, be sure to stop by and stock up.
Samantha List

Ohio

COLUMBUS

Wolfe Fiber Arts
1188 West 5th Avenue
Columbus, OH 43212
614-487-9980
www.wolfefiberarts.com
Wolfe Fiber Arts is a cool store with an independent spirit. They offer plenty of unusual classes, including courses in dying, spinning, and Japanese braiding. Best of all, they have a trunk that's full of chocolate—perfect for convincing spouses and children to be patient while you browse! *Rebecca Pavia*

WOODMERE

The Knitting Room
28450 Chagrin Boulevard
Woodmere, OH 44122
216-464-8450

The selection here is fabulous; you can find delicious yarn at any price, the women are wonderful and helpful, and the samples on display make you want to knit. *Marne Loveman*

Oregon

EUGENE

dyelots!
676 Polk Street
Eugene, OR 97402
541-485-1880
This downtown cottage is chock-full of hand-painted yarns (some from local shepherdesses), loose fiber for spinning and felting, soy silk yarns, and hand-painted alpaca yarn. It's a riot of color in yarn, fiber, and accessories for knitters, spinners, weavers, felters, and surface design junkies. There's even a dye kitchen on site for those who are daring enough to color their own.
Janis Thompson

PORTLAND

Yarn Garden
1413 SE Hawthorne Boulevard
Portland, OR 97214
503-239-7950
www.yarngarden.net
My favorite of Portland's many yarn emporiums is the comfy and often charmingly jumbled Yarn Garden. The wacky chicks and fellas who work there are hilarious, helpful, and willing to correct your mistakes so that you can get your WIP under

control. Despite the siren song of some of the newer boutiquey yarn shops, this place keeps me coming back. *Amanda Valley*

Pennsylvania

PHILADELPHIA

Sophie's Yarns
918 Pine Street
Philadelphia, PA 19107
215-925-KNIT
www.sophiesyarns.com
Sophie's Yarns recently moved to a sunny, roomy shop with gorgeous yarns and books, all beautifully displayed. They host regular classes and knitting circles. I always feel welcome, even if I'm just browsing.
Kitty Schmidt

Rhode Island

MIDDLETOWN

Knitting Traditions and More
1077 Aquidneck Avenue
Middletown, RI 02842
401-847-2373
Recently redesigned, with a big sign boasting "the largest scarf bar in New England," this yarn and bead shop is owned by a handful of women who really love to knit. They encourage you to come in and touch everything. *Rubi McGrory*

PROVIDENCE

Bella Yarns
508 Main Street
Warren, RI 02885
401-247-7243

What Bella Yarns lacks in size, it makes up for in character. Owner Kim Conterio will order whatever you desire, be it felting, eyelash, or a rare sweater yarn. *Dana Eltringham*

WICKFORD

And the Beadz Go On
1 West Main Stret
Wickford, RI 02852
401-268-3899
Set in an older storefront on the main street of a charming old port town, this store is expensive but on the cutting edge of yarn trends.
Lindsay Woodel

Texas

AUSTIN

Hill Country Weavers
1701 South Congress
Austin, TX 78704
512-707-7396
www.hillcountryweavers.com
Don't let the country-folk-sounding name scare you off. This is actually a fairly hip little cottage with a decent variety of yarns. I'm from L.A., where there tends to be a little bit of knitting snobbery in some of the shops. You won't find that here! *Vickie Howell*

DALLAS AREA

The Woolie Ewe
1301 Custer Road #328
Plano, TX 75075
972-424-3163
800-460-YARN

www.woolieewe.com
This inviting store is owned and run by a sweet and helpful mother-daughter team. They stock mostly high-end yarns, but offer a little something for every price range. There are always people knitting away at a table with one of the owners helping them out. It's like a slice of heaven in there!

Adelle Locatelli

HOUSTON
Yarns 2 Ewe, Inc.
603 West 19th Street
Houston, TX 77008
713-880-KNIT
This store is a great asset to the Houston knitting scene. Owner Wendy Moses learns every customer's name immediately. She has a great selection of yarns, several class offerings, and even throws a pizza-and-knitting party every Friday night. The shop has a little living room area where you can always find several knitters enjoying one another's company.

Sharron Miller

Vermont
BURLINGTON
Kaleidoscope Yarns
15 Pearl Street
Essex Junction, VT 05452
802-288-9200
www.kaleidoscopeyarns.com
www.kyarns.com
Just outside Burlington, this store is an embarrassment of riches. Beautiful custom yarns and a huge selection of knitting supplies make this a favorite in the area.

Rebecca Schiff

Virginia
ALEXANDRIA
Knit Happens
127A North Washington Street
Alexandria, VA 22314
703-836-0039
Knit Happens is a lovely pink store with huge armchairs, lots of fun novelty yarns, and an excellent selection of mainstream yarns. Liz and Kristine are really helpful—they even got down on their hands and knees to help me find the pattern I was looking for.

Amelia Jones

RICHMOND AREA
Got Yarn
13211 Midlothian Turnpike
Midlothian, VA 23113
804-594-0323
www.gotyarn.com
Got Yarn has a full supply of novelty and sock yarns. The staff is attentive without being overbearing. It's close to three different interstates, making it easily accessible.

Evelyn Rowe

Washington
BAINBRIDGE ISLAND
Churchmouse Yarns & Teas
118 Madrone Lane
Bainbridge Island, WA 98110
206-780-2686
www.churchmouseyarns.com
Churchmouse, located a ferry ride away from Seattle, is a delightful find! It's adorable and a knitter's dream. They offer a beautiful selection of fiber, a charming staff, and tea.

Jill Woolcock

KENT
Pastimes Yarn & Sitting Room
321 West Smith Street
Kent, WA 98032
877-520-YARN
253-520-YARN
www.pastimesyarn.com
Beautiful fiber is everywhere you look at Pastimes: displayed in gorgeous wooden cabinets, stacked up along the walls, or hanging just so. The shop is bright and welcoming, and the staffers are all excellent knitters. It's worth the drive south of the city.

Jill Woolcock

SEATTLE
Acorn Street Shop
2818 NE 55th Street
Seattle, WA. 98105
206-525-1726
www.acornstreet.com
Acorn Street Shop is one of those little treasures that lure lifelong knitters time and again through the front door into a welcoming librarylike maze of floor-to-ceiling shelves jammed with rich and vibrant yarns. Textured swatches and handmade garments sporting a mix of domestic and international yarns and an entire wall of pattern books and magazines complete a cozy and inviting atmosphere that will delight both the novice and seasoned knitter. This shop is not to be missed!

Sharon Holt Gann

Hilltop Yarn and Needlepoint
2224 Queen Anne Avenue
   North
Seattle, WA 98109
206-282-1332
www.hilltopyarn.com
Beautiful yarn, personal service, and expert instruction and advice can be found in this warm, elegantly restored Craftsman-style home in the Queen Anne shopping district.

Jennifer Hill

Wisconsin
DELAVAN
Needles 'n Pins Yarn Shoppe
W9034 County Road A
Delavan, WI 53115
608-883-9922
www.needlesnpinsyarnshoppe.
   com
Needles 'n Pins is the largest knitter's and crocheter's shop in the area, with a lot of high-quality yarns, books, patterns, and needles. It's well organized, bright, and spacious. Funny and always willing to help, owner Doreen makes you feel right at home.

Cinda Collins

EAU CLAIRE

Yellow Dog Knitting
420 South Barstow Street
Eau Claire, WI 54701
715-839-7272
www.yellowdogknitting.com
This is a great little knitting
shop with a huge selection of
interesting yarns of all sorts.
Another perk is the friendly
staffers who will gladly help
you out. If stopping in small
towns to hunt for yarn while
road tripping through the
Midwest is your thing, this is
one place not to miss.
Jessica Brooke Rodenwald

AUSTRALIA

Victoria

MELBOURNE AREA

AK Traditions
524 Malvern Road
Prahan VIC 3181
03-9533-7576
www.aktraditions.com
AK supports a community in
Kirgizstan who make felt and
felted products for the store
(not slave-labor style), have
their own doll designs that
you can get kits and patterns
to knit clothes for, and also
stock Rowan, Jo Sharp, and a
few knitting accessories.
Sharon Steer-Courtenay

Craftee Cottage
Shop 40-41
Oakleigh Central Shopping
Centre
Portman Street
Oakleigh VIC 3166
03-9567-0311
www.crafteecottage.com.au
Craftee Cottage carries a wide
range of (Australian) Patons
yarns, along with Cleckheaton,
Heirloom, JJ's hand-dyed
mohair, Panda yarns, Shepherd,
Sirdar, and Wendy, plus pat-
terns. They also do mail orders.
Lynne Shandley

Knit 'n Purl
179 Lonsdale Street
Dandenong VIC 3175
03-9793-3530
Knit 'n Purl has the best range
of eight-ply (DK or worsted
weight) yarns that I have ever
seen. They also carry a range
of Anny Blatt yarns and Italian
novelty yarns.   *Lynne Shandley*

Mansfield Craft Den
21 High Street
Mansfield VIC 3724
03-5775-2044
www.craftden.com.au
Gina carries a range of
Naturally NZ wools, plus
Heirloom and Noro, Opal
sock yarns, Cleckheaton and
Paton's wools, alpaca blends,
and a few U.S. imports. It's
always worth popping in.
Lynne Shandley

Marta's Yarns
33 Waverley Road
East Malvern VIC 3145
03-9572-0319
www.martasyarns.com
Marta's Yarns is just gobsmack-
ing. Marta hand dyes her rainbow of mohair and wool yarns.
There are walls full of beautiful colors, including a wide
range of mostly novelty yarns,
including yarns from On Line.
This is glitzy knitting in spades!
Lynne Shandley

Sunspun
185 Canterbury Road
Canterbury VIC 3126
03-9830-1609
www.sunspun.com.au
Sunspun is an "olde worlde-
style" shop stuffed to the brim
with yummy European yarns
and inspirational contemporary and traditional samples.
I got addicted to Rowan yarns
here, but they run a discount
program and are happy to
hold yarns if you are on a
budget.
Sharon Steer-Courtenay

Wool Baa
124 Bridport Street
Albert Park VIC 3206
03-9690-6633
www.woolbaa.com.au
Owner Leonie has used her
keen eye and attention to
detail to create a light and
bright shop with carefully

displayed pattern books
along the wall, pattern leaflets
arranged in plastic sleeves in
categorized folders, and interesting buttons in natty little
jars.   *Trish Blackman*

Wool Village
Brandon Park Shopping
Centre
Springvale Road
Mulgrave VIC 3170
03-9560-5869
The Wool Village's amazing
range of new and old yarns
attests to their many years in
business. Most of the yarns are
packed in boxes and bags, and
it is preferred that you don't
paw them before taking them
to the counter. *Lynne Shandley*

Queensland

Threads and More
141 Boundary Road
Bardon QLD 4065
www.threadsandmore.com.au
Sue and her team carry a range
of totally droolsome European
and American yarns like Debbie
Bliss, Jo Sharp, Noro, On Line,
Touch, and Trendsetter. They
also have an on-site cafe and
run regular classes.
Lynne Shandley

CANADA

Alberta

EDMONTON

Knit & Purl
10412 124th Street
Edmonton, Alberta T5N 1R5
780-482-2150
Knit & Purl carries a wide variety of domestic and international yarns in all price ranges and has great novelty yarns. The staff will help you customize your garment so that it is a "one-of-a-kind" piece. Or if a pattern doesn't fit, they will adjust it for your body type.
Penny Erickson

Manitoba

WINNIPEG

Camille's Elegant Yarn
935 Nairn Avenue
Winnipeg, Manitoba R3T 5A1
204-667-6265

Camille carries an assortment of yarns that ranges from utilitarian to exotic, and her prices are often lower than other stores'. She also carries an excellent array of buttons and closures as well as patterns (commercial and her own creations).
Leslie Hancock

Ontario

OTTAWA

Yarn Forward and Sew On
581 Bank Street
Glebe, Ottawa
Ontario K1S 3T4
613-237-8008
www.yarnforward.com
Yarn Forward has a good selection of kits and needles and different kinds of yarn from the exotic to the everyday. They offer lots of great advice for a seminovice like me, like telling me to use smaller-size needles for socks when I would have bought the size listed on the yarn label.
Jennifer Amey

TORONTO

Lettuce Knit
66½ Nassau Street
Kensington Market
Toronto, Ontario M5T 1M5
416-203-9970
www.lettuceknit.com
Located in vibrant Kensington Market, Lettuce Knit's shelves burst with hand-picked yarn. The shop is home to weekly Stitch 'n Bitch meetings and at least one Church of Craft craft-on. Owner Meagan is helpful with those pesky knitting questions and offers great workshops and one-on-one lessons. She even served champagne and cupcakes on Valentine's Day!
Carla Agnesi

UNIONVILLE

Mary's Yarns
136 Main Street
Unionville, Ontario L3R 2G5
905-479-7833
Mary and her associate, Christine, made me feel completely at home when I was a shy new knitter. Now they know me and ask about my projects, and I always appreciate feeling part of a friendly community. Oh, and they have a great selection of yarns, too.
Maggie Simser

Quebec

MONTREAL

Magasin de Fibre L. B. Inc.
La Bobineuse de Laine
2270 Mont-Royal East
Montreal, Quebec H2H 1K6
514-521-9000
Here they sell yarn by the pound and they'll spool together a selection of different fibers from their vast assortment for you. The staff is really warm and the prices are super-cheap.
Alanna Lynch

Yarn Suppliers

ANNY BLATT

Rue de la Concorde
84107 ORANGE
Cedex FRANCE
+33 4 90 11 80 88
www.annyblatt.com

AUSTERMANN VERTRIEBS-GMBH

(Distributes Austermann)
Bühlstrasse 14
D-73079 Süssen
Germany
Tel: +49 7162 9603 0
Fax: +49 7162 9603 10
www.austermann-wolle.de

BERROCO, INC.

P.O. Box 367
14 Elmdale Road
Uxbridge, MA 01569-0367
508-278-2527
www.berroco.com

BLUE SKY ALPACAS, INC.

P.O. Box 387
St. Francis, MN 55070
888-460-8862
www.blueskyalpacas.com

BROWN SHEEP YARN COMPANY

100662 County Road 16
Mitchell, NE 69357
www.brownsheep.com

CARON INTERNATIONAL

P.O. Box 222
Washington, NC 27889
www.caron.com

CASCADE

P.O. Box 58168
Tukwila, WA 98138
800-548-1048
www.cascadeyarns.com

COATS & CLARK

(Distributes Red Heart)
P.O. Box 12229
Greenville, SC 29612-0229
800-648-1479
www.coatsandclark.com

CRYSTAL PALACE

2320 Bissell Avenue
Richmond, CA 94804
510-237-9988

HARRISVILLE DESIGNS

Center Village
P.O. Box 806
Harrisville, NH 03450
603-827-3333
800-338-9415
www.harrisville.com

KARABELLA YARNS

1201 Broadway
New York, NY 10001
800-550-0898
www.karabellayarns.com

KNITTING FEVER, INC.

(Distributes Katia, Noro,
Debbie Bliss)
35 Debevoise Avenue
Roosevelt, NY 11575
www.knittingfever.com

LION BRAND YARN

34 West 15th Street
New York, NY 10011
800-258-YARN
www.lionbrand.com

MUENCH YARNS, INC.

(Distributes GGH)
285 Bel Marin Keys
Boulevard #8
Novato, CA 94949
www.muenchyarns.com

PATONS

P.O. Box 40
Listowel, ON N4W 3H3
Canada
www.patonsyarns.com

TAHKI STACY CHARLES, INC.

8000 Cooper Avenue
Building 1
Glendale, NY 11385
800-338-YARN

TRENDSETTER YARNS

16745 Saticoy Street #101
Van Nuys, CA 91406
818-780-5497

UNIQUE KOLOURS

(Distributes Colinette)
1428 Oak Lane
Downington, PA 19335
800-25-2DYE4

WESTMINSTER FIBERS

(Distributes Rowan)
4 Townsend West, Unit 8
Nashua, NH 03063
www.knitrowan.com

NOTIONS, ETC.

BEAD DINER

www.beaddiner.com

INCOMPARABLE BUTTONS

1307 Commonwealth
Avenue, #8
Allston, MA 02134
617-787-6099
www.buttonmad.com

M & J TRIMMING AND M & J BUTTONS

1000 and 1008 Avenue of
   the Americas
New York, NY 10018
1-800-9MJ-TRIM
www.mjtrim.com

Index

Credits

Fashion photography: Karen Pearson

Styling: Ellen Silverstein

Hair and makeup: Amy Schiappa

Cover photograph: Karen Pearson

Cowgirl cover art: Enoch Bolles

Miscellaneous spot photography: Michael Fusco

Additional photos, pages 209, 217: Dietrich Gehring

FASHION CREDITS Page 40: dress and jacket—Screaming Mimi's; pages 50 and 52: jackets—Free People; pages 55 and 56: jacket—Paul & Joe for Simon; pages 58–60: dresses—courtesy Victoria Escalle; page 74: sweater—courtesy Victoria Escalle; pages 87 and 88: turtleneck—Twinkle for Steven Alan; page 102: hat—Lola, skirt—courtesy Victoria Escalle, tank top—Free People; page 106: skirt—Free People; page 148: left, socks—Ralph Lauren, right, skirt and tank top—Free People; page 150: skirt and tank top—Free People; page 160: chevron sweater—Twinkle for Steven Alan; page 164: suit—Free People, shoes—courtesy Victoria Escalle; page 174: dress—courtesy Victoria Escalle; pages 179 and 180: left, dress—Twinkle for Steven Alan; pages 186–188: dress and shoes—courtesy Victoria Escalle; page 192: pajamas—Tepper Johnson; page 197: shirt—Free People; pages 200 and 202: green sweater—Paul & Joe for Simon, green plaid skirt—Free People, multicolored striped skirts—Screaming Mimi's; pages 204–205: shirt—Space kiddets; page 215: jacket and sweater—Natalie & Friends; page 232: dresses—courtesy Victoria Escalle.

Author's Note

Each of the patterns in *Stitch 'n Bitch Nation* has been checked by not one but two technical editors. However, despite our best efforts, sometimes errors will occur. Please check my Web site, www.knithappens.com, for the most current list of corrections. Should you have a question about a pattern or discover a mistake, please e-mail me at stitchnbitch@bust.com, and let me know.

Knitting Notes

Knitting Notes

Knitting Notes

Knitting Notes

Knitting Notes

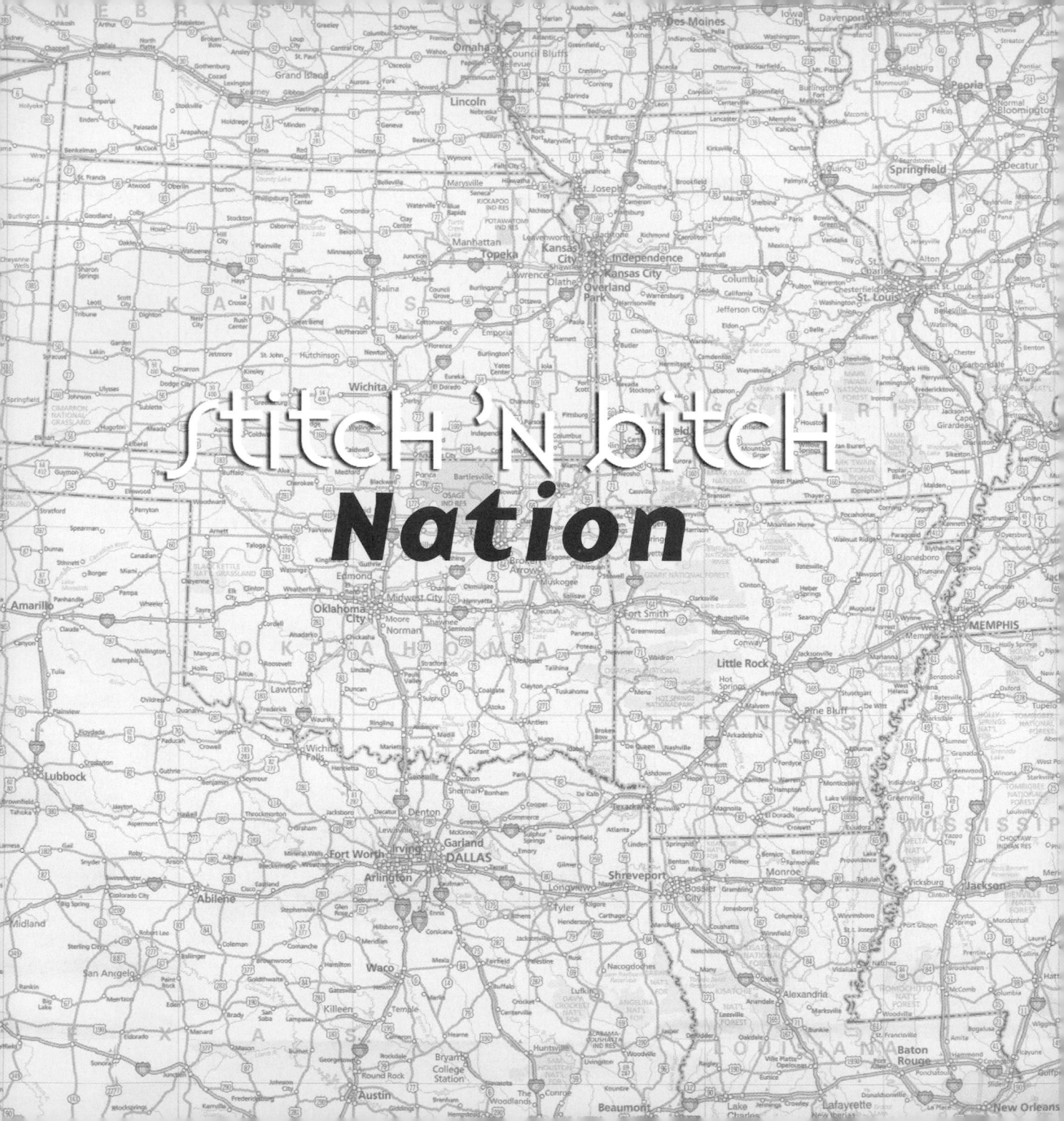

On Friday morning Julius called her into his office. 'How are you getting on with Tree Park?'

'There's a factory near Heathrow which could produce goods under licence, but I'm not sure they're upmarket enough. It might be better to buy them out. The problem is the owner. He's some old dodderer of ninety who . . .' She remembered Sir Larry and went scarlet.

Julius ignored her discomfiture. 'Sport is going to be the big money-spinner of the next decade. The trend is away from processed food and plastic. Look at women's clothing. Natural fibres and ethnic designs. Look at all these health food shops springing up like mushrooms. The obvious progression is fitness, and people who keep fit do so to feel good and to look attractive to the opposite sex – or their own if that's their tipple – and they want glamorous sportswear in which to show off their improved bodies. You have to pinpoint the logic. The members of a club like Tree Park want to be seen to have spent money, so design and quality are essential. Hence our recommendation is for the club to buy the factory. Next, we advise them how much to offer and how to raise the finance.'

'Supposing the owner won't sell?'

Find out more about him. If he drinks, gambles, or keeps a mistress, he's going to be more inclined to sell than if he's a recluse with one beloved grandchild doing fashion at the Royal College to whom he has promised to leave the business. You have to know what make's your opponent tick in order to understand the rules of his game.'

Jonathan was waiting in their office. 'Come on, we're going to the pub, we always go on Fridays.'

'What about Colin?'

'He's gone ahead . . . to keep a seat for you. Love's young dream.'

'Don't be silly.'

'I'm not. He can't keep his eyes off you. It's bad luck on Colin – he's by far the cleverest of us six but he will never be frontline material, and it's not just because he's . . .'

'Not an old Etonian?'

'I didn't mean that.'

11

'I didn't go to Eton either, Jonathan.'

'It's different for girls.'

'You sound like my mother. My parents couldn't afford to send us to public school. My father is an unambitious country solicitor. He spends hours helping old ladies sort out their garden fence problems, and then doesn't charge them. Needless to say, his firm pays him accordingly. But because my mother refused to have to admit to her friends that we weren't being educated privately, we were packed off to the worst kind of girls' day school – small and genteel, with mistresses who'd been sacked from everywhere else. The kind of place where it didn't matter what you wrote so long as your handwriting was pretty!' She tried to keep her voice light, but resentment showed through.

'If it was that bad, how on earth did you manage to get into Oxford?'

'I did my A levels at a polytechnic. Mother always referred to it as a college.'

The pub was low and old and crowded, and they had to fight their way through to find Colin, who was sitting at a corner table, deep in conversation with a girl who looked like the sort of French mistress men don't fantasise about. She was small and skinny with fair hair scraped into a pony tail and a dead white, haughty face.

Colin glanced up and smiled. 'Olivia, I meant to save you a seat but . . . have you met Bernadette?'

'Hello.'

'Hello.' Bernadette had a slight accent. 'As I was saying, Colin, I'm sure Roland will want me to stay in International. I'm so useful. After all, I do speak French, Parisian French.' She nibbled intensely on a cress sandwich.

Jonathan nudged Olivia. 'See what I mean?'

An arm encircled her and a cheerful urchin face appeared next to hers. 'So this is the lovely Olivia. What a pity I got married last month! If only I'd known . . . Mike the money-broker at your service, madam.'

Jonathan gave him a friendly nudge. 'I'll tell Katie if you misbehave.' 'Misbehave!' He held out his hands on which there were traces of white paint. I spent all weekend decorating the kitchen so that when my mother-in-law comes to lunch

12

next Sunday, she doesn't purse her fat little lips and recall the much nicer boyfriend Katie had before me. But in spite of that, I wouldn't swop my wife for anyone in the world – not even for Roland Culross's most gorgeous girlfriend.

Bernadette stood up. 'I must hurry.' She pushed past Mike.

'Tactless!' said Jonathan.

'Bloody hell, she's got to face reality.'

'She wasn't nearly so aggressive at Harvard,' said Hamish, joining them.

'She wasn't in love with power and money then.'

Later that afternoon Olivia took a good look at herself in the cloakroom mirror. She lifted up her hair, pulling her layered fringe back from her eyes – her best feature, or so everyone said. Teddy-bear eyes was what her father called them, for they were big and brown and slightly flecked. She wondered if she should pluck her eyebrows, she'd tried once but it was so painful ... still ... other girls did it and looked better – presumably. She twisted her head sideways. Her chin was a little too determined for the rest of her face, but her neck was long and graceful and her ears were small and feminine. The trouble was her hair covered them. Perhaps I should tie it back like Bernadette ... no, perhaps not. I could do with a bit more bust. She breathed in and straightened her shoulders. At least I don't have a weight problem. She thought of poor Jane subsisting on a diet of cottage cheese and calorie-reduced biscuits.

Suddenly she heard a noise in the corridor. Quickly she pretended to wash her hands. What on earth would Culross say if their newest fast-tracker was found preening herself in the ladies loo in the middle of the afternoon?

She spent that weekend with her parents who lived on the outskirts of Newbury.

'Glad the new job's going well.' Her father crunched across the gravel as she halted her old mini before the black-beamed Tudor house – actually it was mock Tudor but her mother refused to admit it. She got out and he hugged her, his tired periwinkle eyes misting over. Olivia was his bright treasure. Fiona was her mother's favourite, and Marjorie Steele, now

13

standing on the doorstep and giving them the benefit of her bright blonde smile, her doll-like look, was glad she had a daughter like Fiona, a girl who had wanted no more than to find a man like Hugo and settle down to a nice house, two children and no wild moonbeams to go chasing. Of course Simon hadn't been as . . . suitable as Hugo, being the son of a garage owner not of a brigadier, even a dead one, and unlike Hugo there had been no large house to come his way, but he had been nice and Olivia wasn't easy. She was so restless, always convinced the grass was greener on the other side.

'Tim, darling, do leave Olivia alone and make me a gin and tonic, just a teeny-weeny one.'

'Drinks all round? Ah, here come Hugo and Fiona but no Charlie and Phoebe. Whay a pity! I suppose Hugo's mother insisted on keeping the children again?

As usual Olivia was struck by her sister's prettiness. Fiona has always been the prettier of the two. With her golden hair held in place by an Alice band and her sweet pansy face dotted with golden freckles, the child who had played with Virgin Mary had grown into the young woman of whom her mother-in-law said, 'Fiona's the ideal wife for Hugo. I couldn't be more pleased.' When Olivia had been ten and Fiona thirteen she had compared their reflections in the bathroom mirror and known unfairness – her own tangled brown curls to Fiona's golden smoothness, her lanky boyish frame to Fiona's daintiness, her knee-socks which rumpled round her ankles: even her feet were two sizes larger.

Five years later, Fiona, living in London and working as a secretary to an advertising agency, had gone off on a skiing holiday and come back with Hugo. Olivia, gangling and scruffy, had watched miserably as Fiona, prettier still in love, had brought Hugo down for the weekend. She was jealous, envious, unhappy – but never for one moment did she think that she and not Fiona deserved such a prize, for it was obvious that someone as eligible as Hugo would want a neat, tidy, kind girl like Fiona. Olivia's bleakest moment had come during the wedding reception when, ridiculous in a frothy pink bridesmaid's dress, she overheard her mother's elder sister Flora, known throughout the family as an ugly duckling, say 'Poor Olivia, I know just how she feels.'

But Olivia had grown up. She'd stopped trying to look like a dark-haired version of Fiona and had developed her own style of bright colours which suited her high colouring, and bold almost masculine designs which looked so ultra-feminine when she strode along, legs swinging, unconsciously using her body well, her teddy-bear eyes soft and slightly bruised, her smile tentative but friendly, her hair, the bugbear of childhood, suddenly deemed attractive and gypsyish. She had gained a sensuality which eclipsed Fiona, who remained merely pretty, still the prettier, but now Olivia was something else; and part of her charm was that she still saw herself as an almost-ugly duckling.

In the sitting-room her mother produced the *Daily Mail*. 'There's a picture of your boss here. "Roland Culross dancing cheek to cheek with his latest blonde." Is he the future baronet, dear?'

'No, that's Lawrence and he's married, mother.'

'Don't snap, darling. You always complain I'm not interested in your jobs.' Her eyes fell on the column next to Roland's picture. 'Poor Drucilla – Jeremy's left her for a twenty year old. He always was a rotter. I could have told her that.' She smoothed the golden sausage of her curl and gave a tiny laugh, her 'brightest hours' laugh, making sure they hadn't forgotten that although she was now a country solicitor's wife she'd once known greater things. 'Of course, their's was the wedding of the year. St Margaret's, Westminster.'

'Did you go?' Fiona gave her mother an encouraging smile.

'I really can't remember, darling, I went to so many things in those days.'

Olivia cringed into her armchair. The wedding would have been wonderful but her mother would not have been invited. 'Poor Drucilla' probably hadn't the faintest idea who her mother was and never had. At most they'd exchanged the sort of vague smiles women give each other in ladies' cloakrooms when they stand next to each other at the mirror.

Tree Park bought their factory. 'We did a good job,' said Julius. 'Not a six-figure, of course, but . . .'

'A six-figure?'

'A fee of a hundred thousand. Our fees are roughly two per cent, so to get a six figure deal has to be worth five million. Peanuts by American standards and soon to be peanuts over here if inflation carries on. But in England, in 1971, a hundred thousand is a lot of money – and we haven't had one yet. However,' he smiled his closed smile, 'we may do so on the next deal. The Saltridge Property Company want to go public next autumn. Property's beginning to boom and they've been doing very well. Have a look at their file.' He waited till she reached the door, then he said, 'You have good instincts. No wonder Bill was sorry to lose you.'

Olivia spent the following weeks working on the Saltridge deal. She drafted letters which Julius criticised, and wrote reports which came back covered in red lines. It was hard work. He was a tough taskmaster. Each evening she arrived home exhausted, and each evening Jane went out. Not once in the four months since Olivia had parted from Simon had Jane suggested that she join her to meet some new people.

'You're looking a bit glum,' said Jonathan as they walked back from the pub one Friday. 'Having boyfriend trouble?'

'No, not any more. We split up last November.'

'It's hard getting back into the swing of things isn't it? Do you know many people in London?'

'No, but that's my fault. Simon didn't like groups. He always refused to go to parties. Of course, I should have made an effort to meet people myself, but I didn't.'

'Come to a party tomorrow night.'

'Well ... er ... all right.' She brightened. 'Thanks.'

'Next morning she tried on all her clothes and realised that everything she possessed had been bought according to Simon's conservative taste. Each dress and skirt held memories. She set off for Chelsea and the Kings Road. By lunchtime she had been into every boutique from Sloane Square to the Town Hall without success. Finally, she plucked up the courage to try on some deep purple crushed velvet hot pants, a fashion of which Simon thoroughly disapproved. She matched them with knee-high purple boots. Her legs looked longer and shaplier, her hips undulated as she moved. She wished she had the nerve to ask the opinion of the two assistants gossiping by the till, but she didn't, so she added a ruffled shirt and several

16

pairs of plum coloured tights, took a deep breath and opened her cheque book.

'You look amazing!' gasped Jane when she arrived home to find Olivia hovering in the hall, dressed in her finery.

'Do you really think so? I was about to take it all off and put on my black velvet skirt.'

'Oh, no, you don't! So . . . who's the lucky man? Not old Simon, I presume?'

'Can you imagine what he'd say!' Olivia shook a plum-coloured leg and giggled nervously. 'No, I'm just going to a party with someone from work. I was telling him about Simon and he invited me along, I think he felt sorry for me.'

'I bet he did.'

The bell rang.

Jane pressed the intercom button. 'Olivia Steele? Yes, she lives here. Hey, he sounds a bit of all right.' She opened the door. 'Ask him in for a drink.'

'Not tonight.' Olivia picked up her bag. 'Anyhow, there isn't any, only your pony's cough mixture.'

'Wow!' Jonathan grinned at Olivia. 'If Roland Culross could see you now.'

The party was in a mews flat just off the Fulham Road, in one of those narrow cobbled streets guarded by tubs of geraniums. The house had a bright pink front door and a steep flight of stairs leading to a bright white sitting-room, decorated with pot plants and Aubrey Beardsley posters. It was the kind of place Olivia longed to own, so different from the depressing flat in Earl's Court, and Fenella, her hostess, who was wafting towards them in an orange kaftan and a geometric Vidal Sassoon haircut had just the sort of confidence and panache which she envied.

'Come in! Come in!' Fenella hugged Jonathan. 'Glad you could make it, Olivia. Wine? Red or white?' She handed them both red. 'Olivia, come and meet some men. Johnny, I meant to warn you – Cleo's here.'

'Oh, that's all right.' He pretended to be casual but his eyes were fixed on a tall thin girl with a mass of coppery renaissance curls.

Fenella propelled Olivia towards a circle of people. 'Poor Jonathan, he's pretty cut up. I expect he told you . . . he and

Cleo. Now then, you men, here's Olivia. She works with Jonathan at Culross. A lady banker! She's clever.'

They laughed and glanced at Olivia's plum-coloured legs, so well displayed between the tops of her knee-high suede boots and the cuffs of her hot pants.

James, the nicest looking, who turned out to be Jonathan's flat mate, put an arm round her shoulder, 'I've always wanted someone to explain to me the difference between . . .'

'James, out with it! You want to see her figures.'

She had forgotten what it was like to go to a party and find herself, if not the centre of attention, then one of its centres. At midnight Jonathan came to find her, 'I'm going. Do you want a lift now or . . .?'

'I'll see she gets home,' said James.

Olivia noticed that the coppery girl was also saying her goodbyes.

It was after three when she tottered up the steps to her front door, calling her thanks to James and waving to him; she couldn't remember when she'd had so much fun.

3

That summer was the beginning of the boom in the City. The stockmarket rose, the pound appeared strong against the dollar, and a new breed of clever young financiers like Jim Slater of Slater Walker, the best known of the asset-strippers, were heroes to Jonathan and Olivia – and envied by Roland who could not hope to emulate them so long as Sir Larry held Culross in his grip. Of course, there were still gloom and doom merchants who reminded people that bull markets can turn into bears and borrowers sometimes default: they recalled that Barings had once nearly come unstuck through loans to Argentina. But that had been almost a century before these heady days of 1971, when the pound stood at $2.50, property was up thirty per cent a year, and everyone knew someone who was making a killing.

To Olivia this feeling that things could only go from strength to strength was part and parcel of her new outlook on life. She enjoyed the work and the challenge of Culross. She also began to enjoy her freedom, not that she was often alone. Jonathan and James took her under their wing and included her in their social arrangements. It was always, 'Let's phone Olivia. Let's see what Olivia is up to.' The mantelpiece of her bedroom had its share of invitations, to Pimms parties, to fancy dress parties, to birthday parties on boats on the Thames, and on those evenings when she would cry off and stay at home, the phone which had once rung solely for Jane now also rang for her.

'Not going out tonight?' asked Jane one evening, see-ing Olivia stretched out on the sofa with her eyes closed and the television burbling in the background.

'Uhhhu.'

'Want to come to a party?'

'No, thanks.'

Jane left. Olivia listened to her retreating footsteps with relief.

An hour later Jonathan telephoned. 'Fenella's furious. The buyer on the mews has dropped out at the last minute and she's desperate to be in Paris by the end of the month. Why don't you buy it? You've always said it's your dream flat.'

'I don't think I could afford it,' she picked a loose thread from the shabby sofa.

'She'd lower the price for a quick, private sale. Meet me there.'

Half an hour later Olivia was being poured a large Pimms by a furious Fenella in a bright turquoise kaftan. 'So this jerk rings me this morning, the day when he's meant to be signing the contract, to say that he's changed his mind. Changed his mind!' She slumped to the ground. 'What am I going to do?'

'I might be interested. It's a question of price.'

'I'd drop to twenty-five thousand, including furniture, for an immediate sale – without any estate agency involved.'

'Let me have another look round. 'Olivia went into the bedroom which was exotic and red, and dominated by a double bed covered in red and black cushions, then into the jazzy, black and white bathroom and finally to the minuscule kitchen. 'I have to work out my finances,' she said. 'I'll let you know tomorrow, by midday.'

When Jonathan drove her home, he said, 'Buy it if you can. It'll be worth twice as much in three years, and you'll get a cheap loan from Culross.

Next morning Olivia woke to her dreary bedroom. With the money she'd saved, the thousand pounds her grandmother had left her, a loan from Culross, and less extravagance, she could just afford to buy the mews.

At eight she telephoned her father. 'Don't worry about the legal side,' he told her.

At nine she spoke to Julius. He listened impassively, then said, 'It sounds sensible if the survey's good and you can meet the repayments.'

At eleven she called Fenella.

After that she had to force her attention to the sale of shares in Saltridge, and away from the mews with its bright pink front door.

She was on the phone to Saltridge's accountant when Jonathan called from the doorway. 'Come on, houseowner! Time for lunch.'

That afternoon Julius asked her into his office, 'You spoke to Saltridge this morning?'

'Yes.'

'But you failed to note your call in their file.'

'Oh, I'm sorry, I went out for lunch and . . .'

'You're not the only one working on this deal, Olivia.'

'I know. I'm terribly sorry.'

'Do you know who Dean Acheson was?'

'Er . . .'

'He was an American statesman and the man who said "A memorandum is written not to inform the reader but to protect the writer." '

She slunk back to her desk and rechecked her draft proposal, finding three errors in it. She thought of her new life, her new friends, the mews, the new car she hoped to buy – what would she do if she lost them?

Six weeks later the mews became hers, and she moved in with help from Jonathan and James, who heaved her suitcase up the narrow stairs whilst she plied them with champagne in plastic cups: Fenella had removed the glasses. It was late when they finally left. Olivia watched from her kitchen window as they wove their way among the geranium tubs and disappeared into the night. The air smelled of flowers and dampness, from somewhere nearby came the strumming of a guitar, she turned and surveyed her home – and hugged herself.

In October, Saltridge gave Culross their first six-figure. The company was floated at just over five million, and at a two per cent management fee the bank made their hundred thousand. The evening before the shares opened on the market, Julius produced a crate of champagne, saying 'You're shaping up

21

into a good team. We did a good job. Olivia, we're lunching Saltridge in the dining-room on Friday. I think you will remember I once quoted Dean Acheson's remark about memos?'

'Yes.' Why did he have to bring that up now?

'Another rule of a banker is that you never meet your client alone. You work as a team, then your team-mate can vouch for what you say – or don't say. This isn't true of tomorrow. I'm including you because you've done a good job, I already had my back-up – my brother Roland will be present.'

The admiring glances Olivia received almost justified the expense of her new black velvet suit. Determined to look smart for her first important lunch she had rushed up to Bond Street and pounded the pavements of Mayfair until she had seen this in the window of a new boutique called Browns. The jacket was collarless, the skirt the new fashionable midi length and the shirt a delicious shade of cream.

'Another sherry, Olivia?'

'No, thank you.' It wouldn't do to be seen to drink much. The butler came to the door. 'Lunch is served.'

They rose. The men stepped aside to let her pass. She led the way into the magnificent dining-room, with its two Waterford chandeliers and a perfect mahogany table. When the Culross family had lived in Lombard Street they had used this as their drawing-room. In 1860 Queen Victoria and Prince Albert had attended a reception here to celebrate Lawrence Culross receiving his baronetcy. A year later both Prince Albert and Sir Lawrence were dead.

Olivia was placed on Roland's left, the managing director of Saltridge on his right. The conversation centred on property. She listened intently. It then swung around to old Sir Larry.

'What's really holding us back is the old man,' said Roland.

'No chance of him giving up?'

'Not a hope. Trouble is, he terrifies most of the staff – isn't that so, Olivia?'

'Ummm . . . yes.' She was astonished that Roland spoke so openly. When she and Jonathan discussed Culross in a public place they did so in lowered voices, conscious of their responbility.

'Of course, the old boy used to be brilliant.' Roland passed
the port as the phone on the sideboard behind him gave a sharp
trill. He reached for it.

'Vicky? Can't it wait, I'm in the middle of . . . What? A heart
attack!'

On a freezing December morning, the memorial service for Sir
Larry was held at St Paul's Cathedral. As the congregation
stood to sing the final hymn, and deep male voices sent the
words of 'Fight the Good Fight' up into the whispering gallery,
Lawrence, Roland and Julius presented a united front. When
the service ended they escorted Lady Vicky down the aisle. She
was dressed in black and heavily veiled. The congregation
shuffled after them.

Jonathan nudged Olivia and pointed to the side aisle. 'Come
on or we'll be here all day.'

They talked in lowered voices until they reached the main
door, where they joined the mass of people cascading down
the long flight of stone steps, clutching their coats against the
bitter wind. At the bottom of the steps, in the area where at
state funerals or royal weddings the carriages draw up, a chaos
of television cameras and determined reporters pushed forward to capture the occasion for the lunchtime news.

'I've got to dash,' said Jonathan. 'I'm meeting my father for
lunch. Hamish is just behind us. Will you be all right?'

'Don't worry. I'll wait for him.' She hovered from frozen
foot to frozen foot. Up by the great door she could see the
Culross brothers talking to Lady Vicky. They were joined by a
fourth man. Julius and Lady Vicky turned to welcome him, but
Lawrence moved off. So did Roland. Then they came down
the steps and Olivia saw that the newcomer had that kind of
rangy tawniness which suggested he would be as at home
sleeping out under the stars as he was in his city suit on the
steps of St Paul's Cathedral. He reached the bottom step,
swept the crowd with his slightly hooded eyes, said something to Julius, kissed Lady Vicky on the cheek — and than he
was gone.

'Olivia!' Roland touched her shoulder. 'Would you like a lift?'

'Oh, thank you.'

He ushered her to a black Rolls Royce. Julius was already ensconced in the back.

'Are you sure?' she asked, 'I mean, I don't want to intrude.'

Julius gave her a brief smile. 'You're not intruding.'

'Mark not coming to the lunch?' asked Roland as they set off.

'He has to be back in court.'

'He must be pretty sore about the will.'

Julius glanced at Olivia, who looked out of the window. 'If Mark had wanted to be part of Culross he had plenty of opportunities whilst grandfather was alive.'

'Better for us he didn't. The old boy would probably have left him the lot. As it is, Mark's to get the most valuable picture in the estate, because his black sheep father loved it. Who wouldn't love a Turner!'

'I don't think this is a subject for . . .'

'Oh, stop looking so pious. The whole bank will know of Mark's existence soon.'

'I'm sorry, Olivia, this is very tedious for you.'

'Of course, what really annoyed grandfather was that Mark did so well in spite of his chorus-girl mother and his penniless childhood in the back streets of Leeds.'

'Or maybe,' said Julius softly, 'because of it.'

A fortnight later the directors of Culross called a meeting of all staff. It was held in the boardroom, a replica of the dining-room, except that folding doors opened on to an inner room where the employees sat on rows of hardback chairs facing the boardroom table and the directors.

Lawrence spoke first. He thanked the staff for their support and sympathy, gabbled on for ten minutes assuring everyone that Culross would not change, and ended by saying, 'With the death of my grandfather I inherit the chairmanship but . . . er . . . it has been decided that the position of chairman of the executive committee will be held by my brother Roland.'

'Thank God for that!' whispered Jonathan.

Julius spoke next. 'We intend to go public by the end of 1974.'

There were murmurs of excitement and approval.

'Maybe even earlier. In the meantime we shall do a private placing of a certain number of our shares in order to raise the capital.' He paused and looked at their upturned faces. 'It's no secret that Culross has not done well recently. That has to change. Unpunctuality and inefficiency will no longer be tolerated. Every one of you has to earn your keep. Those who don't will not be carried by the rest of us. We can get back on top – but we need you to help us.'

Jonathan began to clap, and soon the whole room was clapping.

Roland took over. 'I have some promotions. Jonathan Burlington, Hamish Wells and Olivia Steele are promoted to manager. Olivia you are transferring to International. Now, back to work all of you, and remember – we can do it if we try.'

'Watch out for Bernadette,' murmured Jonathan as they went downstairs. 'Cyanide in your tea, strychnine in your coffee.'

In the hall the old porter was emptying the ashtrays whilst the young porter polished the leaves of the enormous rubber plant. Above them the dead bulbs in the chandelier had already been replaced. News travelled fast.

On Olivia's first morning in the International Division, Roland instructed Bernadette to explain the Euromarket to her. 'Olivia's to work with you,' he said. 'Then she'll see what's going on.'

For the next three days Olivia sat at her desk doing nothing. On Thursday morning, she said, 'Bernadette, Rolex said . . .'

'Do you mean Mr Roland Culross, Olivia?'

'Well . . . yes, of course I do, everyone calls him Rolex. He said that I was to work on the next Eurodollar loan.'

'I can't think why. I always work on the Euromarket.'

She gave it another day before saying. 'Look, Bernadette, I know you resent my presence but . . .'

'Olivia, I am doing an urgent translation. Can't you see how busy I am?'

That evening, as she was leaving, Roland called her to his office. 'How are you getting on?' he asked.

'Well . . . I . . .'

'Bernadette?'

'Frankly, yes.'

'I'm afraid she's jealous of your ability,' he leaned back in his chair, and gave her his smooth smile. 'Don't worry, I'm having her transferred to Banking. We're acquiring Colin.' He glanced at his watch. 'It's been a long day. We deserve a drink.'

The doorman of the Carlton Towers leapt to open Olivia's door as the Culross Rolls drew up outside the hotel. The security guard who checked Olivia's handbag, as was the custom in most hotels, said, 'Terrible news at Aldershot, madam. Another bomb. Seven killed.'

'Awful, isn't it,' she said to Roland as they crossed the foyer.

'What's awful?'

'About the bomb.'

'My dear Olivia, I was much too busy admiring you to think of bombs. There's nothing so sexy as a woman in a man's shirt. Masculine lines against a feminine body, the ultimate dichotomy.'

They went down a short flight of stairs and into a large, warmly lit room with a bar on the left and round tables dotted across a plush carpet to a piano and long windows on the far side. It was crowded, and well-bred, well-oiled voices rose above the tinkling of the pianist. Roland led her to a table near the window.

'Champagne?' He raised his hand and a waitress materialised. 'A bottle of Veuve Cliquot '61.'

It's the way he does things, Olivia decided. There were plenty of other people waiting but the waitress had instinctively come to Roland. She leaned back in her chair and crossed her legs. She was wearing a black straight skirt and smart black and white houndstooth jacket, her first extravagance for months but she had fallen in love with the skirt which clung in all the right places and swivelled in the wrong ones, and had slits up each side to reveal the most flattering angle of her long legs.

Roland laid his hand on her arm, 'Bernadette's transfer is strictly between you and me for the moment.'

'Of course.' She was very conscious of his touch on her sleeve.

'You're in a class of your own. Olivia?' His fingers moved in a soft circle.

'Thank you.' She raised her glass – her third – to her lips.

'I mean it.' He withdrew his hand and began to talk of Wall Street.

She noticed that they had finished the champagne. He did not order any more. She allowed her eyes to drift casually over the neighbouring tables whilst acknowledging to herself the power of Roland Culross. Was it simply that – power? The sexuality of power. He was still talking about New York. Her thoughts turned to tomorrow and the office – and the inevitable humiliation. She leaned forward. 'Eight-thirty! Oh, no! I'm expected at dinner.'

'What a pity, I'd hoped . . .'

'Thank you so much – it was a lovely treat.'

'I'll ask the porter to find you a taxi.'

'Don't worry.'

She had to keep up the pretence of dinner by giving a false address, but as soon as the taxi turned in Sloane Street she called to the driver.

He chuckled. 'Don't blame you, miss, not wanting him to know where you live. Just the sort of smooth-talker a girl like you can do without.'

She went to bed early and thought of Roland as she lay propped against the cushions flicking the television from channel to channel. She pictured him lying beside her, on the bed, close, and wondered what *it* would be like. He would be expert and sophisticated. She wriggled her toes. He would be daring. She stretched her legs. Then she remembered a friend of Jane's who'd had a brief affair with a man who liked her to dress up in an orange plastic raincoat. Surely Roland wouldn't be like that! No, he'd be . . . adventurous. She giggled, then stopped, remembering the reason for her hurried departure from the Carlton Towers – she had pictured herself sitting at her desk, with Roland walking past, ignoring her.

Nevertheless, in the days which followed she was intensely aware of him. When he called her into his office there was a delicious frisson between them, when they passed in the corridor she did not need to look at him to know that he was watching her. On Friday afternoon he asked them all to his office. 'I have to relinquish some of you to other sections,' he said. 'You're a good team but I can't keep you all to myself – also, frankly, some of you need to widen your experience.' He read out the names of three people moving to Banking, paused and added, 'You too, Bernadette.'

'Why?'

'I've just told you.'

'You need me here.'

The others hurried out, but before they had gone far Bernadette grabbed Olivia by the arm. 'I suppose this is you're doing?'

'I don't know what you're talking about.'

'Look, Bernadette,' Colin intervened diplomatically, 'I'm sure . . .'

'Oh, shut up!'

'Bernadette!' shouted Roland from the doorway of his office.

'It's true. Until she came you . . .'

'Get out or I'll call security.'

'I'm going.' Bernadette picked up her bag and coat. 'I'm going and I'm never coming back. That's what you want, isn't it, you bastard!'

Olivia bent her head to her work. Had it been so obvious that she found Roland attractive? Was everyone gossiping and sniggering behind her back. She glanced around the office. Each head was studiously turned to its task. Thank God she hadn't succumbed to him. To have been his girlfriend would have been bad enough, to be his bit on the side – or one of his many bits on the side – would have been humiliating beyond words. Her dislike of Bernadette did not prevent her from feeling a tiny bit sorry for the French girl.

A week later Roland stopped her in the corridor. 'I think we deserve another bottle of Veuve Cliquot this evening, don't you?'

'Oh . . . er . . . thank you, but I have a prior engagement.'

'What a pity.'

That afternoon she overheard him talking on the telephone. He was saying, 'Darling, you know I miss you. Didn't you feel it . . . last night?' and she muttered another prayer of thanksgiving.

Being in International meant mastering a whole new field. She learned that Eurodollars are dollars domiciled outside America and therefore not restricted by that country's laws and that Eurobonds are long-term bearer bonds denominated in Eurodollars and desirable for their anonymity. She also spent days analysing data for deals which frequently came to nothing or gathering information on loans which never saw the light of day. It was frustrating hard graft but, as she told herself, everyone has to start at the beginning.

One morning in May Jonathan burst into their office. 'Hey, you lot, have you heard? Shares are going through the roof. The stock market's up to 543!'

'No!'

'You're joking!'

'543!'

It was half an hour before the uproar subsided. 'What about the rail strike?' Colin asked into the lull. 'Is it still on for this weekend?'

'Haven't a clue.' Jonathan was perched on the corner of Olivia's desk, swinging his legs. 'Come on! Lunch! Let's celebrate. Colin?'

'No thanks. You know,' a frown creased his pallid brow, 'I'm sure it's all wrong. We import far more than we export. Money is pouring out of the country. Look at the deficit in the trade balance.'

Jonathan groaned. 'Colin you're a doom and gloom merchant. The City's booming and there you are, moaning away. The only problem is that the pound's too high. It's up to $2.60 and it should be $2.40. Once it drops our goods will become more attractive.'

'We still have to purchase raw materials,' said Olivia. 'If the pound falls, they'll be more expensive.'

'Then we'd better hurry up and buy that bottle of champagne!'

That afternoon Roland arrived back from New York, looking very pleased with himself. 'We've got a chance at being in on a highly lucrative deal,' he told Olivia. 'I met that Italian, Sindona.

'I thought he was meant to be shady.'

'Oh, that's rumour. Sindona's sharp but at least he's no

icecream salesman. We've got to get in on the international scene. Chase Manhattan are into Iran in a big way. They're making huge loans.'

'Chase are an enormous commercial bank.'

'And we're a little merchant bank? Think big, Olivia! The giants may take the steak, but that doesn't mean there aren't any drops of gravy for Culross. If we could manage one of these huge loans, say, to Brazil.'

'Their current account balance is completely up the shoot. How will they ever repay us?'

'Have you ever heard of a country going broke?'

'Well . . . um . . .'

'Exactly! They will pay up eventually, and it's time we began to put our money where our mouth is. It's all very well to say a merchant bank is only a procurer, but there's no harm in providing a bit too. The private placing of our shares – twenty-four per cent between six institutions – will generate some capital. We should use it. Invest it. Buy a yacht for entertaining clients. We must think big. Bill your old boss at Maxifunds is one of the six taking shares. Seen him lately?'

'Not for some time.'

'He'll be at the share placement party. Arrange to have lunch with him. This is a people business, Olivia, and Bill is some person.' He smiled at her. Typically, since she was no longer responsive he treated her with more respect. 'You know, we're very lucky to be here now. This must be the most exciting time in the City. We're all going to be rich. He laughed, 'Very, very rich.'

A fortnight later the pound began its downward float on the world money markets whilst in Washington five intruders were answering questions as to what they were doing in the Watergate building.

4

Olivia slithered into her red silk jersey dress, bought specially for the Culross private share placement party, and wondered why, although she met a lot of men, she so rarely met any she found attractive. It's over a year and a half since Simon and I split up, since . . . she thought, adding gloss to her lips and slipping her feet into her new platform-heeled shoes. They didn't do much for her legs – for anyone's legs – but they were the height of fashion. At this rate I'm going to turn into a nun. She sprayed Diorella on her wrists and neck – then up her skirt for good measure.

The reception was held in the boardroom, where so many glittering occasions had been held before. The double doors had been thrown open to include the surrounding rooms, and guests circulated beneath the magnificent chandeliers, sipping champagne and eating caviar canapés.

The first person Olivia saw was Bill. He introduced her to a circle of people, saying 'Culross pinched my best girl, but we're getting our own back by taking their shares.'

They were middle-aged men with families of her age, and they made her the centre of attention. 'If you ever decide to leave Culross, Stephendale Bank could do with someone like you.'

'Oh, don't listen to him, Olivia. Stephendale's a dump. Come to me at Childeberts.'

'Don't listen to either of them,' Bill put a fatherly arm about her shoulders. 'You come back to Maxifunds.'

She laughed and parried their offers, saying, 'I'm very happy where I am, thank you.'

She went in search of Jonathan, finding him with the exquisite magenta-gowned figure of Lady Vicky.

'I remember you,' said Lady Vicky. 'My father saw you with poor old Burns and shouted at him.

'Lady Vicky's husband was a great friend of my grandfather's,' said Jonathan. 'My great uncle bought his best stallion from her stud farm.'

'You make me sound ancient, and I am – but not so ancient. You see, my husband was twenty years older than me. Marry an older man, dear, it's so good for the morale. You're always a youngster to him.' She laid her hand on Olivia's arm and lowered her voice. 'I do hope there wasn't a frightful scandal over the French girl. I've told Roland before to stay away from the girls at the bank. There are thousands of others in the world. Oh, I probably shouldn't mention it.' Lady Vicky had the air of one who frequently said what she shouldn't, on purpose. 'Oh, here comes Julius with his nice new girlfriend . . . what is her name . . . Sarah. I hope he marries her. She loosens him up.'

Shortly afterwards Olivia found herself face to face with Roland. 'I've been looking for you.' He took her arm. 'I want you to meet someone who's convinced that all lady bankers are sexless harridans. I promised to prove him wrong.' He led her across the room, to a large man who had something of Oscar Wilde about him – a silver-haired, velvet-jacketed mixture of sophistication and dissipation with magnetic blue eyes and a mocking intelligence.

'At least I am selective in my women.' The man lifted Olivia's hand to his full lips. 'Unlike you, Roland.'

'That's enough, Gerald.'

'Nothing is hidden from the press. You forget we are the devil's advocate.'

'You're a vulture.'

'And my beak is sealed.'

'It's not your beak I'm worried about, it's your pen.'

Gerald laughed and lit a small cigar. 'Tell me, has Culross rid itself of its famous four reverse gears?' His eyes had settled on the portly form of Lawrence.

'You're impossible! Be careful of him, Olivia.'

As soon as they were alone, Gerald said to Olivia. 'Now,

who shall we talk about? Oh, I know. Look, that tall man by the door, the one with the suntan. What a romance to tear at the heart-strings: Mother a chorus girl, marries Piers Culross, the favourite son. A black sheep, of course – got to get in the prodigal son element, except unfortunately he was killed before he had time to beg forgiveness, not that I think he'd have done so. The old boy rejects unsuitable daughter-in-law. A starving widow, she's left to bring up her son in a back-street slum. Then remorse sets in, though not till common daughter-in-law has snuffed it. Old man begs to see grandson but grandson, honouring mother's memory, refuses to accept any part of grandfather's fortune. Off-stage violins strike up haunting melody as spotlight focuses on mother's grave.' He finished his glass of champagne in one gulp.

Olivia laughed. 'You tell it brilliantly, and I know who it is, it's Mark Culross.'

'Not Culross! The chorus girl had her pride. When the old boy told her not to darken his door, she upped and changed her name back to Denholm. It's Mark Denholm. Mind you, Denholm was a stage name, the dear creature had been born Mabel Watts – so who could blame her for preferring Lily Denholm?'

Olivia watched. Mark Denholm was shaking his head politely but firmly, the way people do when refusing an invitation.

'You notice that it's Julius and old Lady Vicky who want him to join them for dinner, not Lawrence and not Roland.' He glanced at his watch. 'I'd love to ask you to dinner but I have to write my piece by midnight.' He raised her hand to his lips for the second time. 'You've restored my faith in lady bankers. I hope we meet again.'

'I bet you had an interesting conversation,' said Hamish as Gerald disappeared.

'Why do you say that?'

'Gerald Quentin's brilliant. I always read his article in the *London Evening Echo*. He used to be City editor of the *London Chronicle*. I never buy it since he left.

'Of course! Gerald Quentin. I didn't catch his surname. Funny, I'd always imagined him to be more . . . serious.'

Next morning Olivia met Roland in the corridor.

'You seem to get on well with Gerald Quentin,' he said.

'He's most amusing.'

'At other people's expense. Be careful what you say to him. Journalists can never be trusted.'

Whatever it was that Roland had been trying to achieve in the States ended with him storming into the office and shouting down the telephone. 'Julius! What the hell's the point in me working my butt off to put together a deal if you all vote against it? . . . Of course I knew I had to have boardroom approval . . . No, I'm not overstepping my powers as chairman of the executive committee . . . Well, I didn't stand a chance once you voted against it. They all followed like bloody lambs. Damn Bill, I don't care who says he's one of the best financial brains in the City. I thought we were trying to make money.' He slammed down the receiver.

Five minutes later Olivia's phone rang.

'Olivia Steele?'

'Yes.'

'It's the harridan-hater here. I've been invited to a reception at Goldsmiths' Hall tomorrow and I thought you might like to brighten up my evening.'

'I'd love to.'

'Good. I'm notoriously unpunctual so if I say I'll pick you up at six thirty you can expect me at seven.' He paused. 'I gather the storm clouds have broken at Culross.'

'How on earth . . .'

He was laughing as he said goodbye.

He was nearly an hour late but completely unflustered by it. 'When we leave,' he told her as they went up the great double staircase of Goldsmith's Hall, 'we will compare notes and give it a vote of one to ten on the boredom scale.'

'Supposing it's minus?'

'My dear Olivia, that only happens when one has the misfortune to be cornered by Lawrence Culross.' He took her arm and ushered her into the reception with all the wickedness of a small boy bent on wrecking a nice little girl's birthday party.

Gerald seemed to know everyone, at least that's how it

appeared to Olivia, and whatever he might say behind their backs he revelled in their attention. 'The press are the opposition,' he told one pompous young banker. 'Ours is to question, probe, criticise but never to govern.'

'Don't you think you overdo it?'

'Not at all. We are vultures feasting on the carrion of sins. It's your fault for committing them.'

As they moved on, Gerald whispered. 'You'd never think it but they say he wears latex rubber vests and is heavily into sado-masochism.'

She choked on her drink. 'How do you know?'

'Takes one to know one.' He grinned, enjoying her discomfort. 'No, I'm only joking — anyhow, I never indulge on Thursdays. Andrew,' he introduced a small bespectacled man, 'Andrew, tell Olivia that you are my greatest friend, sometimes my only friend, and that I'm really an angel.'

Gerald judged the reception as three out of ten on his boredom scale, Olivia said it was six — she'd enjoyed it. Being with him was a challenge. One mistake and he mocked, a clever comment and you were his confidante, the recipient of his gossip, the one person he really wanted to talk to.

He took her to dinner at a small Italian restaurant in Soho where the proprietor hurried towards them, 'Ah, Geraldo, we thought you had forgotten us, but I see you have found a beautiful young lady.'

'She's my niece, Gino, and I'm looking after her. Aren't I, dear?'

'Yes, Uncle Gerald. You promised to take me to the zoo.'

'Only if you're a good girl.' He squeezed her hand. 'Gino bring us a bottle of your best chianti and tell us what you recommend us to eat.'

It was raining when they left the restaurant and they had to walk right down to Shaftesbury Avenue before they found a taxi.

'Don't you drive?' she asked, casually, as it drew into the curb.

'No.'

'How strange!'

'How strange! How strange! How dare you make that type of comment. Who the hell do you think you are?'

'I'm terribly sorry I didn't mean to . . .'

'Get in!'

'Gerald, please, I'm . . .'

He pushed her into the back seat, slammed the door, then turned and walked back up into Soho.

'Gentleman not coming, luv?'

'So it seems.'

She heard nothing from him for six months, by which time Richard Nixon had been re-elected President of the United States, Britain had joined the Common Market, the last American soldier had left Vietnam, Jane had married someone in the army, James had fallen in love, and Jonathan was back with the haughty Cleo.

Had Gerald been anyone else Olivia would probably have forgotten him, but his name jumped out at her from newspapers and magazines. His photograph mocked those who read his column. When he was interviewed on one of the television money programmes he spoke in such a caressing way that it seemed as though his confidences were for a select few.

Finally, after six months, he telephoned her with no explanation, just 'I'm meeting Andrew for a drink in the Wig and Pen on Thursday. Do join us?'

She accepted. Why not?

The Wig and Pen is a quaint-looking timbered dining and drinking club at the top end of Fleet Street. Before entering Olivia pretended to study the old Vanity Fair prints in the window, whilst in reality straightening the collar of her shirt. Then she went in, to a small hall of heavy carved wood and signed photos of members and eminent guests.

'Can I help you, madam?'

'I'm meeting someone. Gerald Quentin.'

'He's not here yet. Why don't you use a waiter – that's what we call it when a lady arrives on her own. He'll find you a seat and . . .'

'There you are.' Gerald burst through the door and kissed her warmly on the cheek. 'Seen Andrew? Oh, there he is. Come on.'

They eased their way through a crowded bar room to where

Andrew sat at a table.

'You two still . . .?' He looked at Olivia with surprise.

'Yes. Isn't she lovely?' Gerald put an arm around her waist and leaned proprietorially against her. 'Andrew, do you see who's come in? That tall, very thin man by the door. I bet he's scouting for another job.'

'Gerald, he's a director of . . .'

'Not for much longer.'

'Inside information?' asked Olivia.

He patted her hand. 'I never reveal my sources.'

At that moment a fresh-faced boy pushed his way through to them. 'The editor can't find your piece, Gerald. He's turned the office upside down but . . .'

'I left it on his desk, the idiot. But I'm not surprised. Our City editor can barely read. Oh, well, I'd better go. Wait for me. I'll be back in ten minutes.'

Half an hour later he had not returned, and when Andrew left to catch his train home to Sutton, she had no alternative but to leave as well. 'Typical Gerald,' said Andrew, as they walked together to Temple underground station, 'but I'm sure you don't need me to tell you that.'

She was furious – but less so next morning when two dozen roses arrived at Culross. Inside was a note.

Sorry.
Gerald.

She rang to thank him. They met again. This time his attention was all hers, his confidences all for her, and if he seemed to drink a lot she put it down to his profession. Didn't all journalists drink heavily? When he dropped her home by taxi, he kissed her on both cheeks and said, 'What I like best about you, Olivia, is that you're a real winner.'

Next morning she read in the *Financial Times* that the very thin man she'd seen in the Wig and Pen had been ousted from his directorship. Gerald had been right – and she felt that curious glow of knowing someone in the know.

She saw Gerald four times in the next ten days and in between he telephoned frequently, usually late at night as she was dropping off to sleep. Then suddenly she heard nothing from him. A week passed. She went down to Dorking to stay with Fiona and Hugo and lay in the sun – and brooded. Another week. She went to a Sunday lunchtime barbeque with Jonathan and James but made her excuses and left early. As she parked her mini in the news her phone began to ring.

'Olivia, it's Gerald.'

'Oh . . . hello.'

'I want to see you.'

'I'm free on Tuesday.'

'Tonight.'

'Gerald, I'm rather busy, I have to . . .'

'Please! He lowered his voice, 'I need you.'

She wore a white silk shirt with red and black Aztec embroidery, knotted at the waist to reveal slim bare suntanned stomach, and a pair of the tightest white jeans and high-heeled red sandals, slightly tarty shoes. For the first time she was conscious of dressing for Gerald.

'You should wear white more often,' he said, kissing her suntanned cheek. 'It suits you. White on top and black underneath.'

'Black bras under white shirts look dreadful.'

'No, deliciously vulgar.'

She pulled a face and he laughed, taking her hand and playing with her fingers. 'Why are most women so boring?'

'What about most men?'

'So much the better for me if they're boring. Less competition.' He ran his forefinger up the back of her hand, studying her reaction to his next words. 'I'm too old for you.'

'You're not.'

'I'm forty-three.'

She'd presumed him nearer fifty. 'I'm twenty-six.'

He ruffled her hair. 'A mere baby.'

She met his gaze, and felt that tingling up and down her arms, underneath her skin, not exactly inside her, more like a prelude, a beginning. 'Not such a baby.'

'No?'

'No.'

They ate – though she was hardly aware of what – and left the restaurant early, walking down through Soho, into the Haymarket and along Pall Mall till they came to St James's Palace. There they turned down towards the park.

'This is my favourite park,' said Gerald, glancing first down at Admiralty Arch then turning to look at Buckingham Palace. 'Isn't it odd to think of all those people who cram in here whenever there's a coronation or royal wedding, and now . . . but I prefer it at night, when there's no one around.' He put his arms around her and pulled her to him. She was surprised by his strength. He was a big man but somehow she had not expected him to be muscular. 'I'm not going to take you home,' he said, looking down into her shiny brown eyes. 'I'd want to come in and make love to you and be with you till the morning – and tomorrow I have to catch an early plane to New York.'

'How . . . how long are you going for?'

'A week. I'm doing a piece of the New York City debt. Do you know, that city owes so much money that if it were one of the so-called less developed countries its bankers would be threatening to foreclose.' He kissed her nose. 'I didn't tell you I was going away because I didn't want to spoil the evening, but now I'm going to put you in a taxi and send you off.' He lifted her chin. 'I don't want us to begin with a few hours, then me to hurry away from you. I want it to be different. We're different.' He took her by the shoulders and kissed her hard on the mouth, almost brutally, as if she were to blame. Then he released her, hailed a taxi, and bundled her inside as though afraid that temptation might get the better of him.

A week later Olivia received a postcard, a picture of the Statue of Liberty:

A poor substitute for you,
Gerald

It seemed incredible to Olivia that when she had first met Gerald she had not thought of him sexually and now she could hardly concentrate on anything else. He came into her thoughts, so that she would find herself gazing at a page without reading a word, he came into the veins of her body, warm, tingling and wicked. She pictured him as he had been when they'd kissed in the park, his head dark against the orange city night. That hint of decadence. Brutality. If Simon had seemed childish compared to Roland, how much more so did he seem in comparison to Gerald.

39

She wondered if they would make love at her flat or at his. He lived in one of those red-brick blocks of flats off the Finchley Road where the names beside the intercom read like an Eastern European telephone directory and elderly Jews walk their memories on summer Sunday evenings. She hadn't been there. He'd told her, 'It's just somewhere I go to bath and sleep,' so she suspected they would go to her mews and she tidied it each morning, kept a couple of bottles of wine chilling in the fridge, bought proper coffee and expensive Fortnum and Mason marmalade-with-brandy for the breakfast they would share. And it wasn't just the flat which received attention: she rose early every morning, had a long scented bath instead of her usual quick dip, shaved her legs every day instead of every two, and washed her hair even when it didn't need to.

The *London Evening Echo* carried Gerald's article under the heading 'Orchids on a Dung Heap'. It was a seering description of the glorious gleaming skyscrapers of Wall Street rising out of a ground tunnelled by stinking rotten subways. Olivia read it avidly – then waited for his call.

A week passed.

And another.

Olivia told herself she didn't care, that she'd never cared.

On Friday afternoon, the twenty-fifth day since his departure, he rang from the Wig and Pen. 'I need to see you. I'm in the most frightful mood and I need a friend – I need you. Don't say no . . . please!'

Against her better judgment she agreed and an hour later she arrived to find him morosely contemplating an empty bottle of wine. 'What's wrong?' she asked, sitting down beside him.

'I got back to find that the City editor had cut so much out of my New York piece that it sounded like an article on gardening.'

'I thought it was good.'

'For gardeners.' He ordered another bottle. 'On top of that my mother spent an hour on the phone, bitching at me because I didn't send her a postcard. A postcard! I'm researching the best piece the *Echo* has ever published and all my mother can think about is a postcard.'

'Don't you get on with her?'

'I used to – till I realised what she was like. My father died when I was two and for the next ten years mother and I did everything together. She was wonderful. I was her world. Then she met my stepfather, and I was packed off to boarding school. Now he's dead, she thinks she can come running back to me.'

'I suppose it was only natural that when she remarried . . .'

'Natural!' He dug his fingers into her arm. 'Natural!'

'Hello, you two.' Andrew beamed down on them. 'Still with this rogue, Olivia? You must be a glutton for punishment.'

'Don't go putting her off me.' Gerald released her arm and kissed her on the cheek. 'Sit down. Andrew. Have a drink!'

So much for *our* evening, thought Olivia, listening as the two men discussed a third. But Gerald was at his most amusing and by the time they sat down to dinner her resentment had passed.

'Well . . .' he said as they walked out into the warm night of an almost deserted Fleet Street.

'Well what?' She smiled up at him.

He drew her close. 'I got up early this morning, something against my nature, to finish this week's article so that I don't have to do it tonight. In fact, I nearly phoned you at dawn to tell you what I was doing, then I decided that was tempting providence.' He kissed her gently on the lips. 'I want you – I want you very much. If you don't take me home with you I shall make love to you here.'

'In the street?'

'Under a lamp post.' He undid the top button of her silk shirt.

They took a taxi to the mews. She waited nervously whilst he paid.

'Aren't you going to open the front door?' he asked, hugging her from behind.

She took out her key. His hand closed over hers. With his help, she turned it in the lock . . .

They went inside, she ahead of him, climbing the narrow stairs. When they were halfway up, she felt his hand on the back of her leg. She chuckled. His hand moved up. He pinched the inside of her thigh.

'Gerald!'

'What's the matter?' His voice was slurred. He clamped his

hand around her leg and pulled her backwards, almost on top of him.

'The bedroom's only another six steps,' she said, trying to disentangle herself. 'Can't you wait?'

'No.' He pushed her forward, so hard and so suddenly that she stumbled and fell to her knees, banging her cheek on the top step. Then, whilst she was still dazed, she felt him pushing her skirt up to her waist and grabbing at the thin satin strip of her pants.

'Gerald, please!'

'Shut up!'

He was brutal, angry, thrusting. She was miserable and confused. When it was over he stepped back, letting her go so suddenly that she fell again, this time landing on her shoulder. She stood up slowly but did not look at him, expecting him to turn and walk back down the stairs. But he didn't. He came to her and hugged her, kissing her bruised cheek. 'Darling, you were wonderful, I knew you would be,' he eased past her into the flat, 'and your home is lovely. I can't bear women who live in ugly places, they always have tights dripping in the bathroom. Now, for the fridge. White wine. Good girl!'

She reached for two glasses, still unable to think of what to say.

He put back one of the glasses. 'One's enough. We'll share.' He led her to the sofa, poured the wine and kissed her gently. He was tender and loving, all the things he hadn't been on the stairs – and gradually Olivia relaxed. She told herself that the first time was always difficult, at least that's what women's magazines said; she was no judge, because Simon was her only other lover and the first time with him had been the first time ever, and she hadn't enjoyed it at all. She smiled at Gerald. He was probably just as nervous as she was.

He undressed whilst she was in the bathroom, so that by the time she came back he was already in bed, the small soft lights glowing, the wine on the bedside table. For a moment Olivia wondered if he didn't like being seen naked because he was a bit overweight, then she decided he was modest and she warmed to him. Being unashamed of nakedness herself, it made her feel less unsophisticated. As soon as she was in bed he drew her to him, and they made love, slowly and sensuously, exactly as they had in her fantasies – or almost exactly, for there was one thing missing.

'It takes time, she told herself later, listening to his deep breathing. 'After all, it took over a year with Simon before anything . . . happened. Mind you,' she rolled over on her back, 'I didn't know what I was missing before that.'

Gerald stayed with her all Saturday. He seemed content to lie in bed watching television, getting up only when she cooked supper. They watched the late night movie, made love, and in the small hours made love again; and again she told herself it took time.

On Sunday morning he went to buy the newspapers whilst she cooked breakfast.

'Nixon's denied all knowledge of Watergate,' he said, dropping fried egg on the front page of the *Sunday Times*.

She was in the kitchen, making a second pot of coffee. 'What do you think?'

'He's guilty.'

'He's the President. Surely . . .'

'What's that got to do with it? How do you think people get into power? By remembering to say thank you?'

'There's a big difference between fighting your way up and being dishonest.'

'Really? You should meet my City editor.'

'Is he dishonest?'

'No, he's a fool – but then the powers-that-be would rather have a yes-man than someone with flair.'

'They should give you the job. You were a City editor once – and you write brilliantly.' She sat down and began to eat her eggs and bacon, now slightly cold.

'I'm not even on the regular payroll.'

'But you have a weekly column.'

'I write an article once a week and they print it because it's bloody good, but they won't take me on permanently.' He turned back to the newspaper. 'Not that I care. Only small-minded people need paid holidays and pensions. Those with talent don't need security. They're always in demand.' He read the paper in silence for half an hour, then suddenly his mood lifted and he looked at her, smiling, 'I'm going to buy you a present next week.'

'What?'

'A surprise – but only if you're a good girl!'

Two days later he bought her a bright red suspender belt with black ribbons, a black bra scooped low, and a pair of black pants with red tassles.

'Put them on,' he said. 'And the stockings. That's right, straighten out the seams. Now, walk up and down.'

She did, trying not to show she was embarrassed by the vulgarity of what he had bought her.

'You must never wear tights,' he said, 'not when you're with me. And you should wear high heels, black patent stilettos, not those horrid clumsy shoes.'

'Gerald, they're the height of fashion.'

'Fashionable does not mean attractive.' He grabbed the back of her thigh and pinched her till she cried out. 'Don't you like it when I hurt you?' he asked.

'No . . . yes . . . but not when you hurt me like that.'

'All women want to be hurt,' he said defensively.

'Do they?'

'Of course.' He poured himself another glass of wine. She watched him, feeling stupid and inadequate. 'Get dressed,' he said. 'Put on something sexy. I'm taking you out to dinner and I want other men to envy me. I want to hear them whisper "How does he do it? A girl like that! He must be a fantastic lover." '

During the rest of that summer Olivia saw Gerald frequently, at least it seemed so from her diary, although she spent much of the time hanging around waiting for him to phone or waiting for him to arrive. But once she was with him, she forgot about the bad times, the waiting, his moods, his sudden vicious outbursts – until they happened again. Even then, she did not stop seeing him. She couldn't. Though if anyone had asked her why, she could not have explained. She did not love him, at least she seemed to spend more time hating him. She never relaxed with him. She was afraid of him. And yet he obsessed her every moment.

She bought a bright red sportscar with the help of a loan from Culross. It had a soft top and when the sun shone Gerald liked her to drive him around in it. At the traffic lights he would make a great show of affection, so that to all appearances he was a wealthy man indulging his pretty young mistress.

Once when she was driving slowly up Sloane Street in heavy traffic on her way to meet Gerald, a man walking past the car met her eyes. He was young, goodlooking. He smiled. She smiled. A moment later when she looked in the wing mirror she saw that he was writing down her registration number.

A week later Fiona phoned. 'Have you seen *The Times* today?'

'No. Why?'

'There's an ad. in the personal column. Listen, I'll read it:

'Will the beautiful dark-haired lady driving a red Spitfire number . . . up Sloane Street last Saturday please write to an admirer. Box number . . .

She told Fiona about the man, and they laughed.

She told Gerald, but he was furious. 'Invite him round and we'll have a threesome – that is, unless you intended to see him on his own.'

'Gerald, I never said I meant to reply.'

'Women never do.'

'Would you rather I hadn't told you?'

'No, I'd rather it hadn't happened.' He dug his fingers into her shoulders. 'What man goes to the trouble of putting a message in *The Times* for a strange woman unless he has a good idea that she'll reply. I can just imagine it – pretty little Olivia in her red sportscar grinning inanely at some fool. But so long as you're with me, sweetie, perhaps you'd resist the urge to pick up every Tom, Dick and Harry, because I don't want to pick up any so-called unmentionable diseases.'

'I don't pick up people.' She pulled away from him. 'You're jealous but you've no reason to be.'

There was silence, then he drew her gently to him and kissed her.

Several mornings later Jonathan stopped her in the corridor. 'Cleo's having a party on Saturday. Do come!'

'It's kind of you but . . .'

'Bring him if you like.'

'Him?'

'The secret lover who occupies all your spare time, the one who's put the sparkle into your eyes. Oh, you can't hide anything from Uncle Jonathan.'

She waited till Friday to tell Gerald, knowing how he hated anything which smacked of couples or 'we' (unless it was his idea), but to her surprise he said he'd like to go.

On Saturday morning they were lying in bed listening to the news on the radio when the phone rang. It was her mother. 'I'm in Knightsbridge underground station . . . yes, in a call box . . . and I though I'd come round and have coffee with you. I've been staying with Fiona. Oh, you haven't spoken to her this week? No, it has to be now because I'm catching the lunchtime train home. No, there's nothing wrong. I just want to make sure you're still alive, since you don't come down to see us any more.'

'Who is it?' asked Gerald.

She covered the mouthpiece. 'My mother.'

'So I'll take the number 14 bus and . . .'

'Tell her it's too early.'

'Sssssh . . . er . . . Mummy, why don't I meet you in Harrods in half an hour – so much easier for you.'

'Don't be silly! I'd much rather come to your flat. I'll be there in twenty minutes at the most.'

'Oh, God! Gerald, she's coming. Quick!' Olivia rushed into the bathroom, turned on the bath, ran naked through the sitting-room, picking up glasses and ashtrays and depositing them in the sink. 'You must get up!' she called as she ran back into the bathroom.

'Why?'

'What?' She hopped into the bath and hurriedly soaped herself. In a minute she was out, frantically rubbing herself dry.

'Why should I get up?'

'Because my mother would have a fit.'

'Because I'm too old for you?'

'No, because I've got a man in my bed.'

'Surely she doesn't think you're a virgin?'

'No, but she doesn't want to be confronted with the evidence.' She came to the bedroom door and looked at him, propped against the pillows, smoking his first cigarette of the morning, and in spite of her obsession she saw him through her mother's eyes, a dissipated overweight roué. Then she pictured her mother as Gerald would see her, a tinsel blonde steeped in small town snobbery.

'Oh, all right.' He got up and dressed, without bothering to wash.

She dressed in the bathroom, in a big white sloppy jumper and a pair of jeans, and by the time Gerald came through she was in the kitchen washing up. 'Would you like some coffee?' she asked with an anxious smile.

'Don't bother. Save it for Mother.' He walked out and slammed the door behind him.

She opened the kitchen window. 'Gerald! Gerald! What about Jonathan's party?'

He walked on.

That evening, as Olivia dressed for the party in a bright yellow satin jumpsuit, she told herself he'd come back. As time ticked by – eight o'clock – nine o'clock – she told herself he'd been unavoidably delayed. Once, a taxi turned into the mews and she leaped up only to hear it pass on. At eleven the phone rang. It was a wrong number. At midnight she undressed and went to bed.

It was Sunday evening before Gerald came back. He handed her one red rose beautifully wrapped in cellophane and nestling among ferns.

She should have thrown him out, of course she should, she knew she should, she would have with anyone else, with Simon – but then with Simon she had been the cat, with Gerald she was the mouse.

47

5

Roland spent much of that summer flitting between New York and Italy. 'You're doing well at Culross,' he told Olivia on his return from one trip. 'We've never had a lady above the level of manager before, I shouldn't think many other banks have either, but if you carry on as you are . . .' He leaned back in his chair and tapped his fingers on the edge of the desk, she sat opposite him, waiting. 'Would you like to be an assistant director?'

She went pink. 'Of course. Thank you.'

'You deserve it.' He gave her his most dazzling smile. 'In future when I'm away you will be senior manager. I shall advise the others. Now, more good news. We've had an application for a major shipping loan. Linea Pan Liguria, a Panamanian shipping company, have a charter to ship agricultural equipment from Genoa to South America. They already own one vessel and want to borrow funds to buy a second. Just the sort of business Culross needs.'

She took her notepad. 'How much is the loan?'

'Ten million – and this time I'm going to see we get a decent share of the profits. If we put in two million of our own and syndicate the rest, we'll not only pick up the management fee but we'll get a healthy return on our investment. You'll be working on this one with me, Olivia. Frankly, you're the only one up to it.'

'Thank you.' She went pink for the second time.

'Here's the company's address. It's privately owned and the managing director lives in Genoa. I'll give you his name later. The ship is a roll-on, roll-off called the *Ariosto*. It's currently docked at Genoa. The owner is a Dutchman. Here's his name. The charter party – the contract to ship the equipment – is from the Conduit Truck Company. Very respectable and therefore very bankable.

'How long is the loan for?'

'Two years.'

'To pay back ten million!'

'They'll easily do it. I've checked the figures!'

'How much is the deposit?'

'Twenty per cent – two million dollars. Seller insists because Linea Pan Liguria are a new company – it is not unusual. The deposit to be paid in March, balance in May.'

'So we're lending the total price of the ship, surely that's . . .'

'I know we don't normally lend more than seventy per cent but this is a low risk venture and we've got to break into this market. Property's all very well but one has to spread one's interests.'

This was exactly what Gerald kept saying. 'Do you think there might be a problem about the timing?'

'Because we're going public in May and this will be a big loan? Oh, the accountants will moan, so will Lawrence, but we can't stop doing business just because the bank's being floated. A loan counts as an asset. It is an asset.'

She nodded. Roland was her boss, the chairman of the executive committee, and if he saw no problem then why should she?

The phone rang. He answered. 'Julius . . . yes, I flew in this morning . . . yes, from New York. Lunch today . . . good idea. With Jonathan and Hamish? Then I'll bring Olivia, if she's free. Yes, it's time we gave our fast-trackers a few treats.' He smiled at Olivia, and for the third time that morning she went pink.

On October 6th the Arab-Israeli War broke out. Egypt and Syria attacked Israel, who retaliated by crossing the Suez Canal. Britain – and others – stopped supplying arms to the Middle East. The Arabs cut oil supplies to the West. North Sea Oil was still four years away and the West needed oil – even at a price.

Mike came dashing down from the foreign exchange desk, almost knocking Ma Patent and her coffee tray to the floor. 'Hey, you guys, have you heard about the London and County Bank?'

Eight pairs of eyes looked up. 'What?'

'They're in trouble.'

Olivia dropped her pen. 'I don't believe it!'

'What about the stockmarket?'

'Plummeting.'

'Jesus!'

'Another depression!'

'Worse than the thirties!'

Roland came in looking tense. 'So you've all heard,' he said, resting his briefcase on Olivia's desk. 'It's true that London and County are in trouble, and so are a number of other secondary banks who lent heavily in the property market – luckily we didn't – but there's no suggestion of any going bankrupt, so let's not over-react. If we start to panic, can you imagine what the man in the street will do?'

'Do you think things will get worse?' asked Olivia.

'Oh, no, it's just a scare.'

'Will this effect Culross going public?'

'Why should it? People have to invest their money somewhere, and banking shares have always been healthy.'

Gerald rang. 'I can't meet you this evening, there's a panic on.'

'I know. Everyone's stunned. Do you think it's just a scare?'

'No, this is just the beginning. If you have any shares, sell them.'

At lunchtime they all met in a pub, in an atmosphere of wild speculation. Everyone, from the lowliest bank clerk to those like Olivia, supposedly in the know, had an opinion.

'Of course, it's all the Arabs' fault for cutting the oil supplies,' said Hamish.

'That's ridiculous,' snorted Jonathan. 'You might as well blame it on the Israelis for refusing to withdraw their tanks.'

'Perhaps it's our fault for being too dependent.' Olivia repeated one of Gerald's pet phrases.

'We're a manufacturing nation, of course we're dependent on other countries for raw materials, just as they depend on us to buy them.'

They waited for her reply but the trouble with using someone else's opinions is that the tape records, it does not create.

'The City is based on confidence,' Olivia overheard Julius tell Roland some days later, 'and confidence has been badly shaken.'

'Oh, don't be so gloomy? The Old Lady's lifeboat won't let anyone drown.'

That evening Olivia asked Gerald what the lifeboat meant.

'How on earth do you know about that?' he said.

'I . . . er . . . overheard a conversation.'

He laughed. 'Eavesdropper! You should be a journalist. The Old Lady, as you know, is the Bank of England, and the lifeboat is its plan to prop up the fringe banks so that depositors don't panic and demand all their money back, as they do in cowboy films when the bank is held up and the townspeople rush in to demand their gold.'

'And the hero calms them down, kills the villains, marries the sheriff's daughter, and becomes President of the United States.'

'Exactly!' He ruffled her brown curls.

'Are there others in trouble, real trouble, apart from London and County?'

'Yes, and there'll be more. Slater Walker's in for a rough ride and Burmah Oil has got itself into a mess over tankers: no one needs large tankers when there's an oil embargo. We're in for a worldwide slump. There are going to be people shooting themselves before it's over, just as they did in 1929 when Wall Street crashed.' He was excited. Catastrophes were his bread and butter.

Over the next weeks there were rumblings and rumours. The stockmarket dropped slightly. So did house prices. But there was nothing like the mad panic Gerald had predicted, at least not outwardly, and Olivia like most people in the City came to the conclusion that the worst was over.

'How are you getting on with the shipping loan?' Roland asked her one evening.

'I've revised the first draft from the lawyers.'

'Good. I'll take it home to read. How about a drink?'

'It's very kind of you but . . .'

'Ah, some lucky man!'

She blushed but said nothing. She never talked of Gerald at work and to the best of her knowledge no one was aware of her relationship with him. If he rang when she was out, he left his number, never his name. When they met, it was at the Wig and Pen or at the mews. Only on the very first occasion had he collected her from the bank.

Gerald was in an excellent mood. He hugged and kissed her, told her she grew more attractive each day, and said he lived in fear of her falling for a younger man. She laughed and nestled against him, and assured him she wanted no one else. That night when they were lying in bed cuddled together in the aftermath of their lovemaking, he said suddenly, 'The trouble with you is that you try too hard.'

She felt as if she had been kicked in the stomach.

'After all,' he went on, 'Culross is just a tinpot merchant bank.'

'That . . . that doesn't mean I don't want to do well there.'

'They've got a pathetic reputation.'

'I like Culross. Anyhow, they're doing much better than they were – and I can't see the point in not trying.'

'Oh, so you think I'm a failure because I'm not a City editor?'

'I never said that.'

'You intimated it.'

'I didn't!'

'Forget it, Olivia, I'm tired.' He turned his back on her.

She lay in the darkness, wondering what she had done to make him turn on her. 'You could easily be a City editor if you wanted to,' she said quietly. 'Everyone says you're the best financial journalist around.'

'Do they?' He sounded like a small boy with a new present.

'Yes.'

'Who?'

'Oh, everyone . . . people at work.'

He fell asleep, but she didn't. She couldn't forget how he'd taken her words and twisted them, how he'd attacked her for no reason.

Was Olivia in love with Gerald? She did not know, she only knew that he obsessed her, magnetised her, swept her along with his wit, his charm — and his cruelty. When she sat at home, waiting for the telephone to ring, picking up the receiver to see if it were still in working order, replacing it hurriedly in case he chose that moment to call, then she hated him — and herself.

It seemed too (as it does when you are obsessed with something) that every newspaper and magazine carried articles relating to her situation. 'Sex and the Older Man', 'How to Satisfy a Sophisticated Lover', 'If your Man Drinks . . .' She read them avidly.

Occasionally, when Gerald was abroad and there was no point in hovering over the telephone, Olivia would call up everyone — Fiona and Hugo, her parents, Jonathan, James, Jane — in a sudden burst of energy and a desperate desire not to lose contact.

Once, when she had waited all evening for him to call she went into the bathroom and examined herself in the mirror, listing out loud her good points. 'I've got a good figure, I've got nice hair, I'm not a financial drain, I've got nice clothes — I mean, I dress in the way he likes. How dare he treat me like this!' But even as she stood looking at herself, one ear listening for the phone, her shoulders began to droop and the skin around her eyes took on a dark, bruised look, and a little inner voice whispered, 'Why should you expect any more?'

Another time when he went to Birmingham to cover a trade fair, she heard on the news that the body of a small girl had been discovered in the area, sexually assaulted and strangled, and she was appalled to find herself considering that Gerald might have done it. Over the next twenty-four hours she kept remembering the way he had taken her on the stairs. His brutality. The pleasure he took in hurting her. It was with great relief she heard the police had caught the murderer — a young man in his early twenties. How could she have suspected Gerald!

On December 23rd 1973 Iran doubled the price of oil — and Britain began a three-day working week to conserve fuel as inflation galloped towards twenty-five per cent.

I'll be in a board meeting all morning,' Roland told Olivia in early January. 'We're scheduled to discuss the shipping loan – so long as Lawrence doesn't waste bloody hours talking about the share issue. I can't seem to make them understand that we'll lose this deal if we keep Linea Pan Liguria hanging around much longer.'

'Good luck!' She gave him an encouraging smile. It was not the moment to say that considering the loan was for a hundred per cent of the purchase price it was hardly surprising the other directors were being cautious.

Two hours later Roland was back. 'They've agreed! We've won! The property slump's worked in our favour. Even old Lawrence understands that everyone will be trying to diversify. Thank God for falling house prices!' He left and did not return till the late afternoon, when he handed her the file saying, 'Draft the formal offer to Linea Pan Liguria as soon as possible.'

'Have they been advised?'

'Of course.' He went into his office and closed the door.

She opened the file, but there was no mention in it of Roland having spoken to the shipping company. Dean Acheson's words came into her mind. She knocked on Roland's door.

He was sitting at his desk, smoking a large cigar. 'Yes?'

'I think you forgot to note down that you'd informed . . .'

'Good God, Olivia, do you have to bother me with every petty detail!' He snatched the file from her and wrote 'Advised by phone.'

But he hadn't made a telephone call, not from the office.

The energy crisis was in full swing and the measures to combat it affected everyone. The times of power cuts for each district were published in the papers, and people watching television in one area rushed to friends in another in order to see the second half of the programme. Those who had lived through wartime blackouts were reminded of the past when they woke to the dark and cold, and hurried to work through unlit streets.

Sales of candles rose sharply. So did the price. Dickensian streets became Dickensian again as candlelight flickered behind drawn curtains.

In the cold and frequently unlit bank, Roland and Olivia finalised the details of the shipping loan.

'Payment of the deposit of two million dollars to be made on March 9th,' he instructed. 'As paying agent, Olivia, you will authorise the transfer of funds to his account.' He handed her a piece of paper on which was typed a number and the name of a bank in Switzerland.

'A Swiss bank?'

'It's perfectly normal.'

'Yes . . . of course. When is the balance of the money due?'

'May 16th.'

'Ten days after the share issue. Isn't that . . .'

'Do you have to question every instruction I give you?' he snapped.

'No.'

'Do you think we should stop the deal because of the share issue?'

Her face was burning. 'Of course not.'

'Then kindly obey my instructions! When I chose you to work on this deal I did so because I thought you were smart. Now I'm beginning to wonder – and about your promotion.'

She slunk from his office.

That evening Gerald said, 'You're very quiet. What's the matter?'

'Oh, something that happened at work today.'

'What?'

'Nothing . . . nothing much.'

'Not going to tell me?'

'It's nothing.' She forced a smile and tried to put Roland from her mind.

On March 9th Britain returned to a five day working week and Olivia transferred two million dollars to a numbered Swiss bank account.

'No champagne lunch to celebrate the deal of the decade?' asked Hamish when he next came up to their office.

Olivia shook her head.

'Don't tell me you're not Rolex's blue-eyed girl any more.'

'There's the share issue party at the beginning of May,' Colin gave her an encouraging smile. 'One celebration's enough.'

She returned his smile with gratitude. He always stood up for her. If only Gerald could be like that. 'I wonder what price the shares will be pitched at,' she said, switching to the subject which was a constant source of speculation at the bank.

Hamish took the bait. 'Well, with the private placement taking twenty-four per cent and the Culross family taking fifty-one per cent, I'd say that the remaining twenty-five per cent are a pretty attractive buy. At Harvard we had a very interesting discussion . . .

Olivia caught Colin's eye and giggled.

Next time she met Gerald in the Wig and Pen, he said, 'Culross are mad to go public now. Look how the market's dropping. Who's going to put their money into some second-rate merchant bank?'

'Don't take it to heart,' Andrew said to Olivia when Gerald went to the telephone. 'He's in an evil mood because the City editor is leaving the *Echo* and he assumed he'd be offered the post but they're considering other people.'

'Why? Gerald's a brilliant writer.'

'Yes, but he's unreliable. That's why he got the sack from the *Chronicle*. You know Gerald, he never rings when he says he will, never is where he says he'll be. A City editor has to be contactable.' He paused. 'On top of that, Gerald drinks.'

'Don't all journalists?'

'There's a difference between drinking heavily and drinking with a capital D.'

'Andrew, why doesn't he drive? I asked him once and he blew his top.'

'Because ten years ago he had a crash when he was drunk and his passenger has been in a wheelchair ever since.' He paused. 'Haven't you met Gerald's mother?'

'His mother? You mean . . . how dreadful! I had no idea.' It explained so much – his moods, his guilt, his hatred – and with this rational explanation Olivia was able to forgive Gerald even more than she had before.

Excitement built up at Culross. The share issue was published in the *Financial Times*, at a starting price of seventy pence – it would have been higher had times not been so uncertain. There was a flurry of preparations in advance of the share issue party which was to be held on the Friday before they went public and, weather permitting, on the lawns in front of the bank. Every employee right down the pecking order to Ma Patent was invited, and after lunch each day the ladies' cloakrooms were full of half-dressed women trying on outfits purchased during the lunch hour.

But not everyone was to be invited to the buffet supper at the Dorchester after the party. Once it was known that Culross had booked the rooftop Pavilion and Penthouse, which rumour had it took eighty at the most, speculation abounded as to who would be included – and who would be left out. Between the Culross family, the directors, and various senior members of staff, most of whom would bring their wives, it was calculated that no more than three managers could be invited – and there were twenty scattered throughout the bank.

'Now we'll see who's for the fast track,' said Jonathan.

Olivia nodded. Jonathan would be invited. So would Hamish. But not her. Not after what Roland had said.

But to her astonishment Roland did a complete volte-face. She not only received the stiff white invitation with the Ross lions' crest, but he said, 'If you want to slip off early to buy a new dress, feel free. Can't have the typists upstaging you – not that they stand a chance, of course.'

She was so relieved to be invited – she realised now how mortified she would have been to be left out – that although she did not need to buy something new, she did: a midi-length dress of clinging crêpe de chine in the most vivid blue, the kind of singing blue which makes all other blues look tired.

The application list for shares closed on the Tuesday. Demand had been high. The issue was oversubscribed. Next Monday when dealing opened, the price was expected to rise by ten to fifteen per cent.

'So you're all wagging your tails, are you?' Gerald mocked over the telephone.

'And why not?'

'You think I was wrong?'

She chuckled.

'Too busy to have dinner with me later?'

'I am very busy.'

'Busy – or cross because I haven't phoned you for five days?'

'Busy.'

'I had to see my mother and I only got back today. I missed you. I'll be in the Wig and Pen between seven fifteen and a quarter to eight. Try to make it.'

She began by telling herself she wouldn't go, but as time ticked by she couldn't keep away.

'Working late?' Roland asked, as he came out of his office.

'Just tidying up a few things.'

'Goodnight.'

'Goodnight.'

She waited till the office door swung shut behind him, then she took a bottle of nail varnish from her desk drawer and began to paint her nails. Finished, she went to the ladies' cloakroom, redid her make-up, plucked out a rogue eyebrow hair and adjusted her stockings. It was seven o'clock but Gerald would be late – of course – and she could not bear another evening of sitting over a solitary drink, pretending to read the newspaper, whilst in her mind's eye she saw people sniggering quietly, so she repainted her nails, added more mascara, readjusted her stocking; but like everything else which comes to a pitch, that state cannot be maintained, it regresses, so that by the time she finally went to meet Gerald she had lost that fresh glow. Too much mascara had clogged her lashes, her second coat of nail varnish sat thickly on the first: Gerald put everything against her.

She arrived at eight o'clock and met Andrew who was just leaving. 'Gerald's been and gone,' he told her.

'Did he say if he's coming back?'

He patted her arm. 'You know how cross the unpunctual become when they themselves are kept waiting.'

For once she would not allow herself to wait. She decided to walk home, to fill the gap of having nothing else to do, and made her way along the Strand, with the buses lumbering past, and the endless cheap shoe shops and kiosks selling nodding guardsmen or plastic replicas of Buckingham Palace. In Trafalgar Square a coachload of Japanese students were dutifully photographing Nelson's Column. She cut through them and headed up the Mall, along the tree-lined pavement which runs beside St James's Park – Gerald's favourite park. 'I've got to stop seeing him,' she told herself. 'He's destroying me.'

A taxi stopped. 'Olivia! Olivia!' Gerald climbed out and paid the driver. 'That was a bit of luck. I was coming to the mews when I saw this lonely figure wandering along between the trees.' He kissed her flamboyantly and she tasted whisky in his mouth.

'You've let the taxi go.'

'Yes, let's walk.' They set off across the grass towards the lake, his arm around her shoulders. 'I really thought I'd missed you that time. Why didn't you wait?'

'Gerald, I'm always waiting – and if I'm going to wait, I'd rather do it at home.'

'Poor darling. Let's sit down, here on this bench.' His arms were strong and he was drunk, but not obnoxiously so. He ran his hand down her throat until it reached the buttons of her blouse. He undid one, and slid his hand inside.

'Gerald, someone will see us.'

He took her hand. 'No, they won't.'

'Gerald, please, we'll get arrested.'

'Come on, darling.'

'Let's go home.'

'No, no, do it to me . . . Now! Now!'

Not far away a couple were sauntering along a path, arms entwined, chatting happily, smiling into each other's eyes, whilst Gerald was subjecting her to his will, humiliating her because that gave him as much pleasure as did her touch.

On the way home they bought a Chinese take-away and a bottle of wine. They ate in front of the television. He was tender and loving, as he always was when he had abused her.

The phone rang. 'It'll be for me,' he said. 'Keep your fingers crossed that I've finally made it to editor.' He stretched for the 'phone. 'Hello . . . yes . . . what! What do you mean they're keeping an open mind? . . . A scoop? Well, is it my fault that I get sent to dumps like Birmingham?' He slammed down the receiver, 'Bastards! Fucking bastards!'

Olivia froze.

He helped himself to more wine. 'So Culross shares are being floated at seventy pence. Can't think why. You haven't had a decent deal in fifteen years.'

'We've had the odd one.'

Tell me!'

She shrugged. She must not let him rile her.

'What? Property? I bet you got stung.'

'No, not property – and we didn't get stung.'

'You mean you have other deals? What? Lending a thousand pounds here and two thousand there? Come on, Olivia, everyone knows that Culross does no business.

'We manage big loans, just like other banks.'

He punched her arm with his clenched fist. 'Don't talk crap!'

'I'm not talking crap. We're involved in a big shipping loan.'

'The nearest Culross ever got to a ship is a dinghy.'

'That's not true!'

'Then it's a supertanker.' He chuckled. 'And just when there's a shortage of oil. Trust Culross!'

'It's not a supertanker. It's roll-on, roll-off, and it's going to take agricultural equipment to South America.'

'I bet you no ship exists. It'll be a brassplate company – Panamanian – and they'll be taking Culross for an almighty ride.'

'There is a ship.'

'OK – so where is it and what's its name?'

'You know I'm not allowed to give details of . . .'

He laughed triumphantly, his eyes narrowing to slits. Once again he'd beaten this clever, attractive, young girl who had all her life – and hopes – before her.

She stood up. 'You're wrong. I know you hate to be wrong, but this time you are. The ship is called the *Ariosto*, it's in Genoa, and there's a perfectly respectable charter party from the Conduit Truck Company to ship agricultural equipment to South America.' She marched into her bedroom and slammed the door.

There was a silence. She sat on the side of the bed. A few minutes passed, then Gerald came in. 'Olivia.' He took her hands. 'Olivia, darling, we mustn't fight.' He smiled as he drew her to him and kissed her hot angry face.

Olivia woke next morning to find Gerald gone and a note propped on the bedside table.

Had to leave at dawn so I didn't wake you. G.

She got up and pulled back the curtains on to a glorious sunny morning. It was Friday, the day of the Culross party, the day when summer suddenly came to the streets and parks of London, and Olivia like every other city dweller with limited space dragged out her suitcases and emptied her summer clothes on to her bed. She selected a cream safari suit. Then began her dash between the bath, the iron, breakfast and the hairdryer. Finally she folded the blue silk dress carefully into its bag – there'd be no time to come home to change – packed a vanity case, remembered her black patent shoes, and hurried down to a waiting minicab.

Only once she was in the car did her thoughts have time to return to Gerald. He might have put 'Love Gerald', or even 'See you soon'. She sighed.

Culross was in a turmoil of festive activity. Glasses were being polished, trestle tables carried out to the lawn, and people who were normally too busy to talk perched on desks and gossiped. Gossip! Olivia felt a slight twinge of conscience, that I-wish-I-hadn't-said-that-feeling, as she tried to remember exactly what she had told Gerald about the *Ariosto*. The twenty per cent deposit? No, she definitely hadn't mentioned that. A Panamanian brassplace company? That had been spoken of, but by Gerald – surely? At lunchtime she dialled his number and steeled herself for his mocking, 'Of course I won't repeat what you told me.' There was no answer. In the late afternoon she rang the *Echo*. He wasn't expected back till Monday. She tried his home again. No answer. With studied casualness she took the heavy Culross Employee Manual from the bottom drawer of her desk and flicked through it until she came to clause eighteen:

. . . no employee shall communicate confidential information to a third person without authority . . .

She felt sick – then she told herself not to be so silly.

6

Culross had never looked more magnificent than on that early May evening when the sinking sun fired the great glass windows of the new buildings and threw down a lake of gold on the guests gathered on the lawned courtyard below, enhancing the bright white shirts of the men and the almost iridescent summer dresses of the women. It seemed incredible that this scene should be taking place in the centre of London and that Lombard Street, fast emptying of its office workers, was not the drive to some large country house.

Olivia's blue dress was an unqualified success. The silk lay soft against her skin, the blue enhanced the pink of her cheeks and the glossy brownness of her hair. It's funny how one never really knows with clothes until their first outing, she thought, as she accepted a glass of champagne and made her way towards Jonathan.

'Olivia, you look fantastic.' He kissed her on both cheeks and lowered his voice. 'You know it's only you, Hamish and me for the Dorchester.'

'Poor Colin!'

'Yes, poor chap!'

'Let's go and talk to him, shall . . .'

'It's quite terrifying to think of the secrets these little girls know,' Lawrence's voice boomed out. 'Of course they sign a form and promise not to discuss bank affairs, but we have no way of knowing if they do.'

Jonathan touched her arm. 'What were you saying?'

'Oh . . . er . . . nothing.'

From somewhere – it was obviously in the same group as

Lawrence but it felt as though it were coming through the back of her head – she heard a man's voice. He did not have an Etonian accent like Jonathan nor cockney like Mike, but it was the voice of someone who in childhood had had the soft burr of the North and since then, unintentionally and merely through circumstances, had lost the identifying region but kept the burr. The voice was gravelly, forceful, attractive, as it said, 'Gossip is an occupational hazard of all businesses, Lawrence, but you can console yourself that the intelligent employees know better than to be careless and the others are more interested in talking about clothes or boyfriends.'

Olivia's skin felt cold and prickly. Her glass slithered in her wet palms. She almost dropped it. Jonathan was talking to her but she could not concentrate. She accepted a cigarette although she seldom smoked – she needed to occupy her hands – but her fingers were so wet with nerves and the dripping glass, that the cigarette paper turned soggy. It disintegrated. The tobacco burst out. The clean and pure fell apart. She crushed it with her heel.

'Have another.' The gravelly voice belonged to the elusive Culross cousin, Mark Denholm.

'Thanks.' She took one.

'I'm Mark Denholm – and you're Olivia Steele.'

She inhaled and choked.

'Don't you smoke?'

'No . . . well . . . occasionally.'

'And this is one of those occasions?'

She felt sick.

'I believe we're both going on to the Dorchester. Can I offer you a lift?'

'No . . . No . . . thanks. I have to see someone on the way. I have to do something.' She sounded ungrateful and cross but it was only nerves. He kept looking at her from under his cobra-like hooded eyelids as if he were about to strike. She couldn't think of anything to say, she wished he'd leave her alone.

Mark was disappointed in Olivia. He'd liked her mixture of elegance and earthiness, her glossy brown hair, her slightly bruised look, but talking to her was an uphill battle with him doing all the climbing. He concluded that she was the sort of girl who had never had to try, just like Erica his girlfriend – no, as of six weeks his ex-girlfriend. Erica had been charming so long as she was the centre of attention, pure hell if she wasn't. It had taken him nearly a year to end the affair and the last thing he wanted was another Erica.

Olivia slipped away from the party at half past seven and made her way along Lombard Street praying that no one would notice her absence. By Bank underground station she grabbed a taxi. 'Fleet Street. The Wig and Pen.'

Andrew was talking to the porter. 'Hello, there, you're looking very glamorous.'

'Thanks.' She forced a smile. 'Have you seen Gerald?'

'Didn't you see him last night?'

'Yes, yes I did. I meant this evening.'

'No, he hasn't been in.'

She went out into a hot dusty Fleet Street and started walking down, past the bottom of Chancery Lane, trying to remember Gerald's other watering holes. She walked as fast as she could, in her clinging silk skirt and high heels. Ten to eight. It would take at least fifteen minutes to reach Park Lane. A bus roared past, blowing hot exhaust fumes in her face. She pushed back her hair and tried to ignore her aching feet and the blister on one heel. Damn Gerald for making her buy these shoes.

At El Vino's she hesitated. Women were still not allowed inside – but she had to find Gerald.

As she crossed the threshold, the barman called out. 'Sorry. No ladies.'

'I'm looking for Gerald Quentin.'

A dozen men turned to stare, and one grumbled loudly, 'Bloody women! Can't a man drink in peace.'

'Gerald Quentin!' shouted the barman.

'Not here today.' Came a reply from the back.

She went on and crossed the road, to the narrow alleyway leading to the Cheshire Cheese.

The barman shook his head. 'Haven't seen him in weeks.'

It was eight twelve. She told herself that she was being neurotic. Of course Gerald wouldn't repeat what she'd told him, why should he? But why then was there a hard knot in the pit of her stomach? And why too were her nostrils, her hair, her every sense filled with the sickening smell of inpending betrayal?

At eight twenty-seven her taxi drew up outside the Dorchester. A moment later she was in the ladies' cloakroom washing the City grime from her face and hands and brushing its dust from her hair. She repaired her smudged make-up, patted some Diorella about her throat and wrists, then took the lift to the roof.

The green Pavilion Room was packed. Lawrence was talking loudly in one corner, Roland was telling smart jokes in another. A few people had already started on the cold buffet. Olivia moved on to the Penthouse Suite, the room which Oliver Messel, the theatrical designer, had transformed into an intimate arbour of carved leaves, mirrors and sweeping rose curtains. She caught sight of herself in one of the mirrors: she looked terrible. Nodding and smiling at various people, and telling herself to relax, she went out into the warm night of the terrace, where the statue of Leda and the Swan reclined above a small pool and the rooftops of Mayfair stretched into the beyond.

'Olivia.' Julius called her to his group. 'I don't think you've met Sarah.' He put his arm around the same pretty blonde who had been with him at the previous party. 'Or my cousin Mark.'

'We have met,' said Mark. 'I offered Olivia a lift.'

'Yes. But I had to go somewhere.'

Julius moved away. Sarah followed. Olivia hovered on the edge of the group. A man was telling a long and complicated story. She could not see any point to it but she nodded at intervals as people do when not wanting to appear rude.

Mark watched Olivia. She seemed nervous. He was surprised. Erica would have pushed herself forward, taken over the conversation, charmed everyone, flirted outrageously – and later accused him of ignoring her. He moved closer. 'You're not paying attention, Miss Steele,' he murmured down her neck as the man paused for breath.

She giggled – mainly with nervous exhaustion.

'Unless you wish to hear the continuing saga you'd better start talking to me.'

'What shall I say? That you've grown so much since I last saw you?'

'No, tell me I don't look a day over thirty.'

'How old are you?'

'Thirty.' He lowered one hooded eyelid in a half wink. 'In my prime.'

'Not according to women's magazines.'

'I wasn't talking about that sort of prime.'

Suddenly she felt light-hearted, punchdrunk. Everything was going to be all right, of course it was. She looked up at Mark. He was really very attractive in his way, a bit of a rough diamond in a semi-smooth setting, but with a lovely lazy smile. She accepted another glass of champagne. Hamish beckoned her to another group, she went, smiling, and suddenly everything seemed wonderful and everyone amusing.

'What on earth was Lawrence saying to make you laugh?' asked Jonathan. 'He's never made anyone laugh.' They were sitting on the low wall around the pond, facing inwards, with their backs to the view.

'I can't remember.' She squashed a strawberry into the residue of lemon and sugar.

'Oh, damn, I've left my cigarettes on the table. Coming in?'

'I like it out here.' She watched a car cruise through the streets of Mayfair, its headlights flicking from side to side.

Mark came over to her. 'Beautiful isn't it?'

'Yes.'

'One should be able to capture moments like this.'

'Yes.' She swallowed hard. Her euphoria was gone and her fears returned, multiplied by the night and the champagne. For a moment she wished she could confide in Mark Denholm, to say, I told someone something, nothing important, but it's on my mind . . . and for him to say, Oh, that's nothing. Don't worry. Or even, just supposing, he told her she'd committed the greatest crime imaginable, at least the waiting would be over and she would know her punishment.

But would it be over? And why should she confess to something which was far less than Roland did every day, than many people did every day – and got away with.

'The party appears to be ending,' said Mark. 'Can I give you a lift home?'

She hesitated, then answered firmly, almost rudely, 'No thank you,' because she knew that had she accepted, somewhere between Park Lane and Chelsea she would have burst into tears and told him about Gerald.

Saturday was a nightmare. Olivia was obliged to go to her parents because her mother's elder sister Flora, the one with whom she'd been compared as an ugly duckling, was over from South Africa with her husband. She tried Gerald's number before leaving London and again from a service station just off the motorway, building up into a crescendo of nerves as she dialled, then telling herself not to be so stupid.

The English countryside was at its most beautiful that early summer morning and the delicate white petals of wild cherry blossom dropped on to the shiny red bonnet of her car as she roared down country lanes. But Olivia did not notice beauty or petals.

'So how's my clever little niece?' asked her uncle Luke, enfolding her in his enormous arms and his harsh Afrikaans accent. 'Not found yourself a husband yet? Shame of the English!'

'Luke, stop trying to pair her off,' chided Flora.

'Ach, I just want her to be happy like us.' He squeezed his wife's thin hand in his massive paw.

Flora had emigrated to South Africa in her late forties to teach in an English school and to devote herself to innumerable charities because, according to Olivia's mother, she realised she'd never find a husband. This was said with a kind of smug pity, for it was acknowledged that although Flora had brains she was no beauty. Tall, thin and beaky she was in complete contrast to Marjorie Steele's flirtatious femininity. So when she married Luke van Rooyen, a widower with four grown-up daughters, the family had been convinced that she'd done so as a last resort. Why else would a cultured English lady marry a burly Afrikaans farmer from the Orange Free State who, by his own admission, was as big and rough as the Kimberley diamond – a man whose mother had been born in a British concentration camp during the Boer War and who was still so fervently anti-British that she refused to speak anything but Afrikaans, and until recently had refused to speak to Flora at all. But there was nothing last resort about Flora and Luke.

They loved each other. The dry spinster bloomed on the hot sprawling farm. She learned Afrikaans, overcame her mother-in-law's hostility, and acquired the sort of glow which prompted Olivia's mother to say, 'The most unlikely people turn out to be sex-mad.'

'Mind you, I did find it a bit . . . odd when Flora married Luke,' Olivia's father confided when they were alone. 'It's not that I don't like him, I do, it's just that her early letters were so full of the wrongs of apartheid that I used to be afraid she'd get arrested – then she ups and marries an Afrikaaner! Oh, I'm sure she's kind to her . . . blacks, but . . . Don't tell you mother what I've said, Livvi, she wouldn't understand.' He paused. 'You're very pale. Everything all right?'

'She looks tired,' said her mother, coming into the dining-room. 'That's what comes of having a career. Women aren't meant to compete, it's not in our nature.'

Driving back to London on Sunday evening Olivia told herself she was a fool to worry. Life went on, it did not change its course because of one five minute indiscretion. People made mistakes far worse than hers and got away with it, of course they did. Shadows lengthened, the air turned sharp, black and white Friesian cows browsed among buttercups, and church bells rang from grey stone spires. She felt calm but sad – for there is an eternity about summer Sunday evenings, in that the sun will set again and the shadows will return, as they have always done, and yet there is sadness – because eternity is not ours.

7

At 9.30 am. the London Stock Exchange opened and trading began on Culross shares. Interest was brisk. Within an hour the price was up by ten per cent.

At 11.30 am. the lunchtime edition of the *London Evening Echo* hit the streets. Within five minutes Culross dropped back to 70p – then 65p – then 60p – then 50p, as brokers tried to offload shares in panic selling. At midday it was announced that over six million pounds had been knocked off the value of the shares in less than half an hour. A minute later dealing was suspended.

Olivia was sitting at her desk when Jonathan burst in waving a copy of *The Echo*. 'They've had to pull the issue,' he cried. 'The price fell through the floor because of . . . look!' He pointed to the lead article.

THE FOOLISH DEBUTANTES OF LOMBARD STREET
by Gerald Quentin

The eminently respectable merchant bank of Culross, making its public debut this morning with share price starting at 70p, has, like many debutantes, been seduced by honeyed words and false intent. A ten million dollar loan to buy the *Ariosto*, a roll-on, roll-off ship at present docked at Genoa, was granted to Linea Pan Liguria, a Panamanian brassplate company, on the strength of a charter party from the highly respectable and bankable Conduit Truck Company:

69

the charter is to ship agricultural equipment to South America. What could be safer for a merchant bank in these uncertain times, I ask you? How proudly once-beleaguered Culross are managing the loan and syndicating it out to others of their ilk.

So what is wrong?

When I visited Mr Stead, the managing director of the Conduit Truck Company, in his office late on Friday afternoon he told me he had never heard of Linea Pan Liguria and has no charters to ship anything to South America at present. What is more, he willingly confirmed this by telex to the editor of this newspaper.

So why are Culross lending the money — and for what reason does Linea Pan Liguria require it? The ship exists. I saw her myself on Saturday. She's an ordinary roll-on, roll-off, suitable for tractors — or tanks. The moral of this strange tale, which doubtless will have buyers of Culross hurrying to consult their brokers, is that debutantes should take precautions — or say no.

Olivia went to the cloakroom and was violently sick — but even when she could be sick no more, when the muscles of her stomach ached and her face dripped cold sweat, she could not get rid of the smell of betrayal.

'Olivia!' Jonathan shouted from the corridor. 'Meeting in the boardroom. Now! I'll keep you a seat!'

She straightened up, pushed back her hair. 'I won't be a moment.'

Jonathan was sitting in the front row. He would be, thought Olivia, as she slipped in beside him. Barely five yards away, Julius, Roland and Lawrence sat at the boardroom table.

Roland spoke first. 'I'll come straight to the point. We've had to suspend the share issue because an article appeared in the *London Evening Echo* to the effect that a loan managed by us is not properly secured. That is still being verified, but we had to pull the issue or the price would have dropped to nothing. Dealing will remain suspended until the matter is cleared up. I need hardly say that for such a thing to have happened to a bank is disastrous. A number of people were privy to information concerning the loan. Our accountants. Our lawyers. Those in the syndication. But it was confidential.' He paused. 'Someone must have talked to the press.'

There was a brief silence. Then Olivia stood up. 'It's . . . my fault.'

70

'Your fault!' Roland looked astonished, then he remembered. 'Of course! You and Gerald Quentin! OK, the rest of you. Back to work.'

They slipped from their chairs, hurrying away, ignoring Olivia, except for Jonathan who gave her hand an encouraging squeeze.

As the door closed behind them, Roland burst out. 'Don't tell me you've been seeing Gerald Quentin ever since ... Olivia, I warned you about him.'

She said nothing.

'Have you been having an affair with Gerald Quentin?' asked Julius.

'Of course she has! He's been screwing her stupid for months. She's told him everything. No wonder his articles are so apt. My God, I could kill you.'

'Olivia, is it true?'

She forced herself to look at Julius. 'Yes, but I didn't tell him anything about the bank.'

'Balls!' Roland thumped the table.

'It's the truth.'

'What about this article?'

'That was a mistake. I didn't mean to tell him, it came out unintentionally. It just sort of ... came out.'

'We lose five million off our share value because it "sort of came out"?' Roland thumped the table. 'I don't believe it "came out". What I want to know is, how much he paid you for this latest gem.'

'He didn't pay me.'

'I don't believe you.'

'It's true.'

'I was right,' interposed Lawrence. 'I was only telling Mark the other day that we run a terrible risk with all these gossiping ...'

Julius cut across him. 'Olivia, what exactly did you tell Gerald Quentin?'

Fists clenched at her sides, words choking in her throat, Olivia repeated as best she could her conversation with Gerald, ending with, 'Ever since that night I have had this terrible sinking feeling. I tried to contact him to ask him not to repeat what I said. I am so sorry,' she swallowed hard, 'so terribly sorry.'

'Why didn't you warn us?'

'I never imagined he'd use it in an article. I only wanted to ask him to keep it to himself.'

'A journalist keep something to himself! Are you stupid?'

'I know, but . . .'

'He was your lover so you thought he cared?' sneered Roland.

'Yes,' her voice broke, 'yes, of course I did.'

'But you were wrong, weren't you?'

'Yes.'

'What other bank affairs have you discussed with him?' asked Julius.

'None. I've always been so careful, that's why . . .' she wanted to say that's why it seems so unfair.

'Wait in the dining-room,' said Julius. 'We shall want to speak to you when we have consulted the bank's solicitor.'

She sat at the dining-room table, shivering in her cotton safari suit and biting the inside of her lower lip till she tasted blood.

Half an hour passed.

An hour passed.

Roland opened the door. 'Come here!'

She stood up and walked unsteadily towards him – and as she reached him he hissed into her face, 'I know he paid you, you little bitch. Don't think you're going to get away with this.' Before she had time to protect herself, he slapped her face with the back of his hand, not hard enough to knock her off her feet but enough to send her tottering sideways and to bring tears to her eyes. Then he let her pass, confident that she wouldn't complain, knowing she had no one to complain to.

Mark Denholm was sitting at the far end of the boardroom table, between Julius and Culross's solicitor. He looked up as Olivia entered, his face impassive even when his eyes rested on her reddening cheek.

'Sit down, Olivia.' Julius pointed to a chair.

Roland took his place next to Lawrence.

'Miss Steele,' the solicitor began,' the directors of Culross have asked Mr Denholm and myself to advise them on this most serious matter. As you know, when commencing employment with Culross you signed this.' He held up the confidentiality form with her signature. 'Your breaking of this agreement means your instant dismissal.'

She nodded miserably.

'But your indiscretion has led to considerable financial loss . . .'

'Not to mention damage to our reputation,' interrupted Lawrence.

'We are still verifying the *Echo*'s claim concerning the loan. I should like to hear exactly what happened.

She repeated her story yet again.

'So you and Mr Quentin were . . .'

'They were lovers,' snapped Roland.

'Yes, he was my lover.'

'How long had the relationship been going on?'

'About a year. We met at the Culross party, the one for the private placement.'

'I warned her about him, the very next day,' said Roland. 'I told her he was untrustworthy and to be careful. My God, I never thought she'd go on seeing him.'

'All women are fools,' said Lawrence. He was hungry and it was well past one o'clock.

'Didn't it occur to you, Miss Steele, that as a financial journalist and one with a reputation for sensational scoops Mr Quentin might try to extract information from you?'

'She sold it to him,' said Roland. 'I've told you that already. It's obvious.'

Mark spoke for the first time. 'I have been asked to join as counsel for Culross. Roland suggests you obtained financial gain from divulging this and other pieces of information. Is this true?'

'No, no, it isn't!' Olivia stood up. 'I never told him anything until last Thursday, I've always been so careful, and I didn't mean to then. It was only because he was mocking Culross, saying our shares weren't worth seventy pence and we never did any decent deals, that I mentioned the shipping loan. I was wrong. I shouldn't have let myself be provoked. But I swear I had no idea he intended to use it in an article – and that it would lead to this.' She pushed her hair back from her face. One strand stuck to her wet cheeks. 'I'm sorry. Terribly sorry. I've let you down. I've lost the job I loved. I'll lose my friends at

73

Culross – my workmates. Do you really think I would deliberately risk these things which mean so much? Do you think money could compensate? She looked around the table, at each of them in turn, 'Don't you think that if it were possible I would turn back the clock?'

In the silence which followed she left the room and went down the main stairs to the hall where the old porter handed her a carrier bag containing her possessions.

She thanked him.

He said nothing.

But as she went out into the warm afternoon air she heard the young one say. 'That Olivia Steele thought she was top dog,' and the old one reply, 'So do all over-confident puppies.'

It could have happened to anyone, for we are all indiscreet and we have all at some time repeated something we shouldn't – but it had happened to Olivia.

She walked through the deadness of a hot afternoon which comes over certain parts of the City, those streets where there are no pubs and wine bars to spill their life across pavements. The few people she saw were hurrying to join others, clerks with their shirt sleeves rolled up to reveal pallid arms, girls in cotton dresses rapidly losing that morning's crispness, men with their noses pressed against the window of a television rental shop watching for the test match score before moving on. No one took any notice of the brown-haired girl in a safari suit.

To avoid Fleet Street and the possibility of meeting Gerald or any of his cronies, she cut down to the river and made her way along the Embankment. Walking gave her a sense of being nowhere, like the impersonality of airport departure lounges; so long as she was walking she did not belong to the present and she did not have to face the future.

The humiliation of Gerald's betrayal came over her in waves. The emotional betrayal. The physical betrayal: that someone with whom she had lain naked, who had penetrated her physically and mentally, could have done this to her. She sought excuses, reasons. She could not believe that he had risen from her bed, written the note, propped it beside her as she lay sleeping – then hurried off to betray her. Or worse still, that the night before, as they made love, he had known he would betray her. She could not bring herself to accept it – and yet, that is what he had done.

When she reached the mews she went straight to the bathroom. But she could not be sick again, there was nothing left inside her. She slid slowly to the floor and buried her face in her towel, still damp from her morning bath. At six o'clock she turned on the television news. The first story was the resignation of Willy Brandt, the second was Culross.

And now to our financial correspondent for the latest on Culross. (Cut to a man standing at the entrance to Culross.) Panic selling of the shares of Culross, the merchant bank, caused the issue to be suspended within hours of flotation. The reason for the scare was an article in the . . . (cut to front page of the *Echo*) which claims that Culross have an unsecured shipping loan. (Cut to aerial view of iron hulk of the *Ariosto*.) This evening Mr Gerald Quentin, the journalist concerned, admitted that his original source of information was a Culross employee, Miss Olivia Steele.

The phone rang. It was her father. He listened to her story, abridged – for what was the point of telling him that Gerald had been her lover – tried to persuade her to leave London, and ended with, 'If there's anything you need, Livvi, we are your parents.'

She was crying when Fiona rang. 'Olivia, listen, come and stay with us. Come tomorrow . . . All right, then come next week. On Tuesday. We're having a dinner party on Saturday evening. You'll enjoy it.'

'Fiona, I couldn't.'

'Don't be silly!'

'Fiona, you don't understand.'

'We think its rotten of Culross to sack you just because some horrid sneaky journalist uses something you let slip at a cocktail party.'

'Fiona, it wasn't like that, he was my . . .'

'Well if he did that to you, you're well shot of him. I expect you on Tuesday – and if you don't turn up Hugo will come and fetch you.'

Jonathan phoned. 'You OK?'

'Yes . . . thanks.'

'We're all very sorry. I'm sure you didn't mean to do it.'

'I didn't.'

'Bad luck. It could have happened to any of us. I can't tell you the times I've said something then thought whoops!'

'Yes.'

'You will keep in touch . . . Olivia, would you like me to come around?'

'No, I'm better on my own. Thanks.'

She lay down on her bed, exhausted but unable to sleep, images chases images around her mind, over and over again she thought, if only . . . until, as the midnight hour approached, she persuaded herself that Gerald must have had some desperate reason to betray her.

She dialled his number. 'Gerald . . .'

He slammed down the receiver.

She rang again.

He did not answer.

She picked up the pillow where he had laid his head and hurled it across the room.

The doorbell interrupted her fitful sleep. She looked at her clock. It was half past seven. Putting on a dressing gown she went downstairs to open it.

A strange man was standing on her doorstep. 'Miss Steele?'

'Yes.'

'Have you anything to say about the cartoon in the *Daily Mail*?'

'What cartoon?'

'This one.' Triumphantly he produced the newspaper, open at a page which depicted her in an outrageously sexy suit offering an envelope to Gerald who looked fat and depraved. The caption read, 'Would you like a loan or some information, darling?' For a moment Olivia could not think what to do. Then she jumped back into the house and slammed the door – but already the phone was ringing.

She was besieged. She sat inside, trapped, listening with mounting fury to the chatter and laughter of the reporters on her doorstep. The home she loved had become a prison. She was isolated. Neither friends nor family could reach her, because each time she replaced the receiver another journalist rang to ask, 'How does it feel to be betrayed by your lover?'

Gerald appeared on the lunchtime news.

'Mr Quentin, is it true that Miss Steele gave you this information in the form of a private conversation?'

'How else do most journalists get their leads? You're in the same business. You know.'

'You haven't denied that you and Miss Steele had a personal relationship. Don't you think that in the circumstances . . .'

'I'm a journalist first and a lover second.'

She kicked the television. It fell backwards off its table, spluttered and went blank. She threw herself down on her bed. Someone nearby was playing Carole King:

When you're down and troubled
And you need some loving care . . .

She got up and closed the window.

Over the next few days Olivia alternated between rage and despair. During the daytime, the chattering of the reporters drove her to fury. At night, when only a couple remained and they whispered – the other residents had complained – she would wander listlessly around her prison, eventually throwing herself on her bed fully clothed, looking up into the dark – and remembering Gerald. Less than a week ago he'd been with her, beside her, inside her. How she wished she could claw out his eyes, pummel his face till he could speak no more, stamp on his fingers so that he could never write again. God, how she hated him!

On the Friday Culross issued a press release. They acknowledged that enquiries had proved the charter party to be false, they referred to 'various persons who had provided misleading information', and announced that no further monies would be paid against the loan and that, in the interests of goodwill, they would repay out-of-pocket expenses to all those in the syndication.

An hour later the seller of the *Ariosto*, a tubby Dutchman, flashed his beringed fingers at the television cameras and said, 'If your Engleesh bank think I vill pay back ze deposit zen zey are mad.'

'How much was the deposit, sir?'

'One million dollars.'

Olivia sat up with a jolt. It had been two million. She reached for the telephone, then sank back. Who was she going to tell? Perhaps she had misunderstood or the Dutchman had made an error in his English.

But there was no mistake. Culross was back in the hot seat:

Further controversy surrounds the Culross shipping loan. In an interview today the Dutch owner of the *Ariosto* spoke of a one million dollar deposit but a spokesman for Culross had earlier referred to two million dollars. Mr Roland Culross, head of the International Division where this loan was sanctioned, and where Olivia Steele worked, refused to comment.

The seige continued throughout Saturday – then suddenly on Sunday it was over. The street was empty. She ventured out, half-expecting the reporters to rush around the corner but there was no one. She bought a newspaper and a carton of orange juice. No one paid any attention to her. She walked up to Hyde Park and sat on a bench in the sun. People passed without so much as a glance. She opened the newspaper, skimming over articles about Italy's referendum on divorce, until a heading caught her eye.

Intelligence is No Protection Against Infatuation
The news that an attractive young lady banker . . .

She refolded the paper. Why should she be hounded and pilloried whilst Gerald got away scot free?

She waited till the evening before driving up to North London, to Gerald's address, a large red-brick apartment block some way north of Swiss Cottage. It was eight o'clock. She rang the bell to flat ten. There was no answer. She went back to the car, and reversed some twenty yards down the road so that he wouldn't see it and run off. Then she waited. By ten she was stiff and cold. By eleven she was about to give up. At eleven thirty she reached for the ignition. At that moment she heard the rumble of an approaching taxi. It stopped, and Gerald staggered out.

Stealthily – she did not want to warn him – she crossed the twenty yards between them. 'Gerald!'

He spun around. 'What the . . .'

'I want to talk to you.'

78

'Well, I don't want to talk to you.'

'You've got to.' She planted herself between him and his front door. 'It's the least you can do.'

'I don't owe you anything.'

'I lost my job because of you. Did you know that? Did you?'

'I always said you should leave Culross.'

'You bastard!' She slapped his face so hard that her hand ached. 'You . . .'

'Shut up!' He lunged at her but missed.

'Why did you do it, Gerald? For promotion? Was that it? Did you sell me down the line because you're nothing but a fucking failure?' She raised her arm to hit him again, but he parried her blow with one hand and punched her in the stomach with the other, so hard that he sent her careering backwards into a nearby hedge. By the time she was on her feet, he was inside the door slamming it behind him. But Olivia would not give up. She leaned against his doorbell, letting it ring long and hard.

'Go away!' His voice crackled down the intercom.

'No. You've put me through hell.'

'If you don't go away I'll call the police.

'Call them, I don't care.' She leaned against the bell.

Within five minutes a police car screeched to a halt and two policemen got out. 'Now then, young lady, what's going on? A lover's tiff, is it? Come along.' One of them took her gently by the arm. 'Which is your car? The red one. Not been drinking, have you?'

'I wish I had.'

'Won't seem half as bad in the morning.'

'Won't it?'

She arrived home to the ringing of her telephone.

'If you ever trouble me again I shall call the police immediately. Do you understand?'

She did not reply.

There was a slight chuckle. 'It's a pity you've taken it so hard, Olivia, because you're the best fuck I've ever known.'

'It's a pity you betrayed me, Gerald, because one day you're going to wish you hadn't known me.'

8

To threaten revenge is not the same as exacting it. That needed power and opportunity, neither of which Olivia possessed. But she felt better. The victim had protested. It was a start.

On Tuesday she drove down to Fiona and Hugo's pretty, mellow house on the outskirts of Dorking. She found her sister sitting in a deckchair outside the French windows, contemplating her pride and joy – the garden – as she swung her long freckled legs backwards and forwards in the late afternoon sun, the skirt of her thin cotton dress pushed up above her knees, its floral pattern in muted colours like small dead flowers floating on a muddy puddle. Fiona looked up as Olivia approached. 'I didn't hear your car. I must have been asleep. The children have gone to a birthday party, so I've had a peaceful afternoon. Had a good drive down?'

'Yes, thanks.' Olivia sank to the grass.

'Want a cup of tea?'

'Not at the moment.'

'Drink?'

'Later . . . thanks.'

'Hugo will be back at seven. He'll get us one. You all right . . . Livvi?'

'Yes, thanks . . . Fee.' She swallowed hard. They had not been Fee and Livvi since childhood.

'The garden always looks its best in May.'

'Yes.' Olivia waited for Fiona to ask her some questions about Gerald, but there were none. What had happened was so far outside Fiona's sphere that she did not know what to say, so they sat there in the garden with *it* hanging between them, like death between two people when one is bereaved and the other doesn't know whether to say 'I'm sorry' or to say nothing. Olivia ran her fingers through the warm damp grass and wished she hadn't come.

That night as Olivia lay in bed, watching the pink ruched curtains dancing in the breeze like knickers on a washing line and wondering if Hugo ever got fed up with the endless little flowers and frills which decorated his house and his wife, she heard them talking on the landing.

Hugo. 'She looks jolly peaky, did she talk about it?'

'No, nor did I.'

'Best thing. She's got to get over it. That man sounds frightful. Do you think she and Basil . . . you did invite him for Saturday, didn't you?'

In the darkness of the spare room tears of mortification filled Olivia's eyes. It might have been, 'Olivia's dog's been run over. Never mind, I'll get her another. One dog's as good as another.'

They meant it kindly, that was what was so mortifying.

Each group of people has its pecking order, each family its roles. Since Olivia had emerged from her gawky chrysalis she had been the outgoing adventurer to Fiona's orderly femininity. Now their roles changed and Olivia became a surrogate child, trailing up and down supermarket aisles after her elder sister, helping put the dried plates away, or sent out to sunbathe in the garden whilst Fiona whisked up a soufflé. Gerald was another world.

Basil was tall, thin and sexless like an unkempt neutered greyhound. He worked for a local estate agency and had clammy hands. Olivia fled to the dining-room. 'Can I do anything to help?' she asked Fiona who was adjusting the flowers in the centre of a perfectly laid table.

'No thanks, I prefer to do everything myself. Oh, I am glad you wore the yellow dress.' It was on the tip of her tongue to ask Olivia what she thought of Basil, but she didn't.

Dinner seemed to last for ever. Of the eight people, all but Olivia lived in the area and as they had been primed not to mention London/banks/ jobs or journalists there was little for them to talk about to Olivia, so they soon relapsed into local gossip.

81

That night she heard Fiona say, 'I don't think Basil and Olivia . . .'

'We must think of someone else.'

(Oh, dear, that dog's no good, we'll have to buy another.)

When Olivia arrived back in London she found a letter on her doorstep, its envelope bearing the familiar Ross lions' crest. For one wild moment she thought – hoped – she'd been given a second chance. As she ripped open the envelope she imagined the words, 'after consideration the directors are prepared to give you . . .' But it was one crisply folded page.

. . . our enquiries reveal that certain discrepancies occurred in the division where you were employed. This letter does not preclude us from taking legal action against you.

She sank on to the sofa.

As an employee you benefited from reduced interest rate loans which enabled you to purchase your flat and your car. We should be grateful if you would make the necessary arrangements to repay these loans within sixty days. Failure to do so will oblige us to exercise our first charge on the relevant properties.

Of course, a firm which granted cheap loans as a perk expected to be repaid if its employees left. In normal circumstances the next employer would take over the loan – but these weren't normal circumstances. Olivia had no new employer and no bank or building society would lend her the money to pay back Culross until she had a job. She looked down on her shiny red sportscar. It was the symbol of her success. To lose it would be to acknowledge failure.

Settling down with a mug of coffee, she made a list of all the people who had ever tried to headhunt her, banks like Childeberts and Stephendales, but not Maxifunds. Of course Bill would give her a job, but Maxifunds would be a step backwards.

She rang Childeberts and asked for Jim Hazelbury.

His secretary came on the line. 'Who's calling please?'

'Olivia Steele.'

'One moment.' A long pause, a click, then a cautious, 'Hello, Olivia.'

'Jim, you remember that you asked me if I was interesting in working for Childeberts . . .'

'Yes, but we don't need anyone at the moment.'

'Oh . . . umm . . . shall I give you my number just in case?'

'Very well.'

She had an odd feeling that he did not bother to write it down.

She made three more calls. The first was busy, the second pretended he didn't know who she was, and the third was away on holiday. Refusing to be disheartened, she made herself another mug of coffee and phoned Henry Furness, the financier friend of Bill's. He sounded genuinely pleased to hear from her. 'I'll see what I can do, Olivia. I'm away for the next few days but I'll call you when I get back. Give me your number.'

Her spirits lifted. She ate the last raspberry yoghurt.

Next morning the phone rang. 'Olivia, it's Bill. How are you?'

'Oh, fine . . . considering.'

'Meet me for lunch, Simpsons.'

'Bill I'd love to but I'm meant to be looking for a job.'

'One o'clock. It's important.'

Bill sounded so tense that she wondered if he'd heard she was looking for work and was annoyed she hadn't approached him first. Still . . . she thought as she gave the mews a much needed tidy up, it would be no bad thing to have a back-up offer from Maxifunds when I come to negotiate salary with Henry Furness. She emptied the rubbish bin. But I wouldn't want to go back to Maxifunds. Three hours until lunch. She went to the bank and withdrew twenty pounds – she had to be economical now. Two hours, she dug out her typewriter and began to revamp her *curriculum vitae*. One hour, she had a bath, washed her hair, dressed in a smart black and white print silk dress and set off, her red shoes shining in the sunlight. On the Fulham Road she hesitated . . . Taxi or Bus? Bus. No, to hell with it, taxi.

Bill chatted idly about his recent holiday in Provence, with no mention of Culross or Olivia, until the waiter brought their asparagus. 'Why didn't you contact me before you rang the others?' he asked.

'You mean, about a job?'

'Yes.'

'Did Henry Furness tell you?'

'Yes, and I saw Tim Hazelbury from Childeberts last night. Olivia, they'd like to help you but . . .'

'Have they been complaining?'

'Not complaining, just embarrassed.'

'Henry said he was going to call me back. I thought . . . He even asked for my number.'

'Because he knew I'd been trying to find you. I went to your old address in Earls Court but you'd moved.'

She pushed the tip of an asparagus round and round in the butter. 'So Henry isn't going to offer me a job?'

'No.'

'I see.'

'Olivia, do you trust me?'

'She didn't look at him, there was a lump in her throat and tears in her eyes. 'Yes.'

'I'll give you some advice which will hurt but it will save you from a lot of wasted time and heartache. You are not going to get a job in the City. No financial institution can afford to take on someone whom their clients might consider untrustworthy.'

'I'm not untrustworthy,' she said in a small, strangled voice.

'I know that – but they don't.' You were stupid, and I'm not saying that Culross should have kept you but there was obviously negligence at a higher level. There's this business of the deposit. Roland was your boss. I suspect you've been made a scapegoat for his mistakes as well as your own. I think you should know he's putting it about that you were dishonest.'

'No! Bill, I've got to stop him.'

'You can't. He'd deny it.'

'But I have to stop him. If I don't, I'm finished.'

He said nothing.

'You mean I'm finished already?'

He smiled sadly.

'I admit I made a mistake. I was a fool. I know that now. But I was never dishonest. If anyone at Culross is dishonest, it's Roland.'

'Why do you say that?'

'Because every time I queried something on the loan, like the twenty per cent deposit, he bit my head off and threatened to block my promotion.'

'Can you substantiate that?'

'No, of course not.'

'Then don't say it or you'll be in even worse trouble.'

'Give a dog a bad name.'

'No, find a dog with a bad name and blame it for everything else.'

The waiter took away her asparagus, uneaten. The steak she'd been looking forward to arrived. She picked at the garnish.

'How are you off . . . financially?'

'All right.'

'You bought a flat? Presumably with money from Culross?'

'Yes. And a car. They're going to repossess if I can't transfer the loan elsewhere. Oh, God!' She seemed to grow smaller before his eyes.

'I'll give you some more advice,' he said. 'Buy yourself time with Culross by acknowledging their letter. Say you're looking for a job and will write again at the end of the month. If you haven't found something in a fortnight, sell the car and repay that money. Try jobs in a different field, say, advertising. Forget the City. Finally, don't let them repossess the flat if possible because you'll lose what you've paid. If necessary, sell it and buy something cheaper – or rent till you sort yourself out.'

She nodded miserably.

They parted outside the restaurant, just as she had parted from Roland Culross on this very spot three years earlier. 'Call me if you need anything,' he said. 'I may not be able to give you a job but at least I can buy you lunch – only next time, please eat it.'

Two days later Culross was back in the news.

Merchant Bank offers to buy back shares.

Ten days later a man rang Olivia's doorbell. 'Miss Olivia Steele?'

'Yes.'

He handed her a long brown envelope and walked away.
She opened it.

IN THE HIGH COURT OF JUSTICE

QUEEN'S BENCH DIVISION   1974 C. no.

CULROSS   **Plaintiff**

and

OLIVIA STEELE   **Defendant**

The Plaintiff claims an injunction and aggravated damages for wilful
and malicious breach by the Defendant of her contract of employment . . .

They had kicked her when she was down. Now they were
trampling her into the ground.

9

Her taxi stopped by the entrance to the High Court, that castle to British justice whose turreted façade reaches up to grey slated pinnacles and whose stone, no longer virginal white, is somehow the better for it.

'Here she comes.' A tide of newsmen swept forward. 'Miss Steele, do you agree that you have been made a scapegoat?'

She did not reply.

'Don't you think it's unusual for a bank to sue an employee?'

'What do you have to say about the rumour that dishonesty . . .'

'Do you regret what you . . .'

'Have you seen Mr Quentin?'

She pushed through them, her face flushed, and hurried up the steps to the main door, submitting her handbag to the security guard's inspection before setting off across the great hall, her high heels clattering conspicuously on the grey, greyish-white and pinkish-grey mosaic floor. From huddled corners black-robed barristers gave her irritated glances and from the walls the portraits of long dead judges, stiff in their wigs, watched her with disapproval. Just one more day, she told herself, straightening her shoulders inside her cream linen jacket, just one more day and it will be all over.

The porters had told her to go to the notice boards on the first floor. As she went up the carved stone staircase two barristers hurried down, one old and grey, his wig old and grey, the other young with dark hair, his wig bright novice white. They passed, and their gowns moved the air as lorries do when overtaking on the motorway, and she wondered if she would ever again be carefree and drive down the motorway in her open top red sportscar, the wind and the sun in her hair.

The injunction hearing of *Culross versus Olivia Steele* was to be heard in the Queen's Bench Division. She found it — eventually — with the help of a kindly old barrister whom she had discovered fossilised on to a stone bench, papers spread on his bony knees. Mark was sitting in the front of the courtroom. It took her a moment to recognise him, for he was wearing his wig and gown, the uniform of his profession designed to remove all individuality and allow a barrister to argue passionately and anonymously on behalf of things and people whom tomorrow he will have forgotten, because tomorrow he will be working on another case.

But Mark could not be anonymous. The uniform failed. His individuality came from his face, his slightly hooded eyes, the way his cheekbones were high but in a funny way flat. His eyes met Olivia's, then he looked away and carried on talking to the Culross solicitor, his words listened to intently by Lawrence and Roland: Julius sat and frowned.

'Where do I sit?' Olivia asked a black-gowned usher at the back of the court.

'Who are you?'

'The . . . er . . . defendant.'

'Front left. Where's your counsel?'

'I'm defending myself.'

With her eyes fixed straight ahead Olivia walked down beside the rows of benches, the back two containing the press sucking pencils and fiddling with notepads, and crossed the room between Mark and the judge's empty bench. The floorboards creaked. Her high heels clattered. Everyone watched her. She sat down, laid her briefcase on the bench and took out her carefully prepared papers — lists of times and dates: the date when Roland had first mentioned the loan, his instructions, his exact words when he had threatened to block her promotion — and the catalogue of her affair with Gerald.

Of course, none of this would make any difference if they stuck to the breach of contract. Olivia might not have practised law and it was more than six years since she'd left Oxford, but she remembered enough to know that all her preparation was possibly for nothing. On the other hand, if the case touched on the question of dishonesty – and she prayed it would so as to give her the opportunity to defend herself publicly – then she needed to be prepared. Nobody, she thought ruefully, gets a second chance in this life.

The usher called. 'Silence. All rise.'

The judge entered, bowed, and took his place on the bench. The court sat.

'Culross against Olivia Steele,' called the Clerk.

The judge looked from the Culross brothers, with their counsel and solicitor, to Olivia sitting alone at the other end of the front bench.

'You are the defendant, Olivia Steele?'

'Yes, my lord.'

'Are you intending to conduct your own defence?'

'Yes, my lord.'

'I do not think that the plaintiffs will mind my pointing out that it is not always wise to do so.'

'I am aware of that.' What was the point of wasting money on legal fees when the odds were stacked against her?

'Very well. Let us proceed.'

Mark spoke first – deliberately, slowly, his gravelly voice resounding through the room. He referred to the 'position of trust' which Olivia had enjoyed at Culross and the 'confidential information to which all bankers are privy'.

The usher stifled a yawn. The press listened with half an ear. The judge frowned.

Mark spoke a little faster. He drew their attention to the contract of employment signed by Olivia, and in particular clause eighteen: 'no employee shall communicate . . .' When he read the word 'without authority' he paused for so long that Olivia wondered if he'd finished. 'So I put it to your Lordship,' his voice rose, 'that the defendant having formed a sexual relationship with the journalist Gerald Quentin . . .'

At the word sexual the courtroom woke up. Pencils sped over notepads, noting Olivia's 'flushed face', 'clenched hands' and 'trembling lower lip'.

Mark proceeded. 'She did wilfully and maliciously communicate information to him concerning the loan to Linea Pan Liguria knowing that he would use it in a manner detrimental to her employers. This he did. As proof, I invite your Lordship to look at schedule B, a copy of the *London Evening Echo*.' He paused. 'It is now common knowledge that the loan was granted against a false charter party but that fact does not form part of this claim. This case rests on the defendant's communication of information in breach of her contract and I will prove to the court that she was not the meek, serious employee whom she endeavours to portray but someone who constantly flouted authority and thereby had little respect for it. I request permission to call my first witness, Mr Roland Culross.'

Step by step Mark took Roland through Olivia's employment, asking simple questions to which the answer was obvious. At the back the reporters surreptitiously sucked sweets as the somnolent hunger for approaching lunch pervaded the courtroom. Finally, Mark continued, 'You said in your statement that the defendant challenged your authority to the extent that you threatened not to recommend her for promotion. Please tell the court of this instance.'

Roland smoothed down his cuff. 'When I informed Miss Steele that the loan had been granted she queried the amount of the deposit and later when I instructed her to pay it she became very argumentative.'

'And I was right.' Olivia was on her feet. 'The charter party was false, I knew something was wrong, I sensed it.'

'Miss Steele!' The judge rapped his bench.

'It's true.'

'Sit down! The security of the loan is not a question for this court. If you interrupt again I shall have you removed.'

At the back the reporters scribbled avidly.

'What happened then?' Mark was asking Roland.

'I told her that if she didn't stop questioning my authority she would not be promoted.'

'Would you say that promotion was important to her?'

'Very.'

'What was her attitude to you after you had admonished her?'

'She sulked.'

'Did she question your authority again?'

'No, she obeyed with bad grace.'

'How long was this before the article appeared in the *London Evening Echo*?'

'Two months.'

'Were you aware that she was having an affair with Gerald Quentin during this time?'

'No. I knew she had met him, but that was eighteen months ago. I warned her about him at the time – and about journalists in general.'

'Why did you warn her?'

'Because I saw that they hit it off.'

'Did you think she had taken your advice?'

'I never saw them together again so I thought no more about it.'

'Thank you, Mr Culross.'

The judge turned to Olivia. 'Do you wish to question the witness?'

She nodded and approached Roland. 'Would you or would you not agree' – she was careful not to put words into the witness's mouth – 'that I was right to query the shipping loan?'

Mark was on his feet. 'My Lord, the validity of the shipping loan is not a matter for this court.'

The judge nodded. 'Objection sustained. Miss Steele confine yourself to the case in question.'

She began again. 'Do you think that an employee is right to question an action if she thinks that it might be detrimental to her employer?'

'Yes.'

'Isn't that just what I was doing?'

Roland said nothing.

The judge leaned forward. 'Mr Culross, you must answer the question.'

Roland frowned. 'Yes, but . . .'

She knew she mustn't lose her advantage, so she cut in quickly. 'Thank you, Mr Culross. No more questions.'

The court recessed for lunch. The reporters rushed for the telephones and the nearest bar. Mark and the Culross brothers left together. Olivia hung back until she was sure of not being obliged to share a lift with any of them. She had an hour, and no one to be with. She walked out through the back of the building and into Carey Street, bought some sandwiches and a carton of orange juice, and went into Lincoln's Inn, one of the four Inns of Court to which all barristers belong, picking her way across the uneven flagstones beside the arched base of the chapel to the expanse of grass and trees near the library. It was hot and sunny, and strewn across the velvety lawn were groups of typists in scuffed white shoes and cheap cotton jackets from the Leather Lane Market gossiping about boyfriends or exchanging recipes, whilst in the shade solicitors' clerks rolled up their sleeves and argued about the test match.

Olivia found an empty patch of grass and sank to the ground, wishing that she could stretch out and close her eyes and never have to leave this quiet oasis of trees and flowers amid bustling central London.

At twenty to two she started back. Barristers in two and threes passed her, deep in conversation, their tread ponderous and Victorian. There was a feeling of continuity about the Inn which struck Olivia as both reassuring and horrifying — horrifying because it meant that human beings are continually in dispute. Other people had walked back to court to verdicts which would go against them, other people had become infatuated, made mistakes, been indiscreet, and had woken up to regret it — and would do so again. But why them? Why me?

It was Olivia's turn to present her case. In a voice more confident than she felt she took the oath. 'I promise to tell the truth, the whole truth and nothing but the truth'. On the word 'truth' she straightened her shoulders and lifted her chin. 'I do not deny that I spoke to Gerald Quentin about the Linea Pan Liguria loan, and that by doing so I was in breach of contract, but I do deny that I did so wilfully and maliciously.' She took a deep breath. 'I had known Mr Quentin for just over a year and had never previously divulged confidential information. I was most careful not to do so – either to him or to anyone else. On the occasion when I spoke to him of this shipping loan I did so because he was criticising Culross, saying we . . . they . . . never did any decent business. I was defending us . . . them. I cited the loan as an example. I said more than I meant to. I made a mistake. A mistake!'

There was a brief silence. The judge looked at Olivia. 'Have you finished Miss Steele?'

'Er . . . yes.' Perhaps she should have employed a solicitor after all.

Mark stood to cross-examine. He began slowly, maddeningly slowly. 'Did you enjoy a position of trust at Culross?'

'Yes.'

'Is it not a fact that you signed a contract agreeing not to divulge information about the bank to third parties without authorisation?'

'Yes.' Why did he have to keep going over the same ground?

'Would you not agree that by divulging information to Mr Quentin you were in breach of that contract?'

'I've already admitted that.'

'Yes or no?'

'Yes!'

Mark had learned from experience that unintelligent people plod through simple questions, relieved not to be asked anything difficult, but clever people like Olivia became frustrated: they start to answer the question they think they should have been asked, become annoyed when reprimanded – they're not used to looking stupid – and in that lies their downfall. 'Is it not true,' he asked ponderously, 'that Mr Quentin having been dismissed from his previous post as a City editor was anxious to obtain such a position again?'

'Yes, but that doesn't mean that I would . . .'

'And that he was on the look out for some means of proving himself?'

'I don't know.'

'How long had you known him?'

'Over a year.'

'And in a year he did not discuss his hopes with you?'

'Of course.'

'Would it not be true to say that a journalistic scoop such as the Culross shipping loan would help his career?'

She looked down at her hands.

'Miss Steele, answer the question.'

'I suppose so.'

Mark altered course. 'How long were you and Mr Quentin lovers?'

'Since last summer.'

'What were your feelings for him?'

'I was . . .' she straightened her shoulders, 'I was infatuated with him.'

The press scribbled, 'High-Flyer Admits Infatuation.'

'What were his feelings for you?'

'I . . . er . . . thought he was fond of me.'

'What were your feelings for Mr Roland Culross after he had admonished you for questioning his authority?'

'I was upset. I was only doing my duty when I queried the loan and I was right to do . . .'

'We are not discussing the validity of the loan. Did you think you had lost your chance of promotion?'

'Yes, I was afraid I might have.'

'Did Mr Quentin already know about the shipping loan before you mentioned it?'

'No.'

'So you volunteered the information?'

'No . . . yes . . . He was running down Culross, saying their shares weren't worth anything because they never did any decent business and I . . . defended them. I suppose,' she added in a small voice, 'I rose to the bait.'

'Were you aware afterwards that you had been indiscreet?'

'Yes. I tried to contact him, but he was away.'

'Researching his article?'

'Yes – but I didn't know that then.'

'Did you warn your employers that you had been indiscreet?'

'No.'

'Why not?'

'I hoped for the best.'

'When did you finally tell them?'

'After the article appeared. Mr Roland Culross said someone must have talked to the press and I admitted it was me.'

'Have you spoken to Mr Quentin since your dismissal from Culross?'

'No . . . yes.'

Quick as a flash he was on her. 'Then I put it to you Miss Steele that thinking you had lost all chance of promotion at Culross and being infatuated with a man whom in your own words you only *thought* was fond of you, you decided to try to win his love at the expense of your employer by giving him the scoop he needed.'

'No! That's not true. I never meant to harm Culross. I loved my job. I only told Gerald about the loan because he was being so insulting. I shouldn't have done it, I know that now, I knew it the next day. I made a mistake. I admit it. Don't you think I regret it?'

'Miss Steele!'

But no judge could stop her now.

'I've lost my job,' she went on. 'No one else will employ me. I've upset my parents, I've alienated my friends, I've been hounded by the press, the man I loved . . . thought I loved . . . has publicly humiliated me. Don't you think I'm paying for my mistake? Don't you imagine I'm ashamed? Don't you think I regret the day that I laid eyes on Gerald Quentin? Haven't I gone through enough without you dragging me in here, accusing me of . . .'

'Miss Steele, you are in contempt of my court.'

'It's true. I've paid for what I did. I made a mistake, I was stupid, and I've been punished. I did wrong.' Her voice quavered, 'but don't tell me that there is anyone in this room who has never repeated what they shouldn't. We all have.' She looked across at Mark. 'We've all woken up to that feeling of "I wish I hadn't said that." The only different is that I didn't get away with it.'

There was silence, then the judge said, 'The defendant will remain behind after the trial. Now let us proceed in an orderly manner. Miss Steele, if you have no witnesses do you wish to address me further?'

'I have nothing else to say.'

'Mr Denholm?'

Mark went through it all again, step by step, ending with, '. . . and so the defendant's volatile temperament turned against her employer and mindless of her contract, she wilfully and maliciously divulged the information.'

The court adjourned for the judge to consider his verdict. Olivia remained at her end of the bench, at the other Mark talked to Roland.

The judge returned.

They rose.

The judge spoke. 'In an action for damages the onus of proof lies with the plaintiffs, Culross, to prove cause or connection between the defendant, Olivia Steele, and their loss. It is well known that, following the article in the *Echo*, Culross were obliged to withdraw their share issue and thus suffered financial loss, but that loss was as a result of the shipping loan being unsecured, brought to light by the defendant's breach of contract but not as a result of that breach.' He leaned forward and rested his elbows on the bench. 'Miss Steele, I do not believe you acted maliciously. I believe you are a clever, ambitious young girl who stupidly allowed your infatuation for a man who did not love you to impair your common sense. In other circumstances you would simply have been dismissed from your post. However, the plaintiffs for their reasons – and they are within their rights – have taken action against you. I find that you are guilty of breach of contract, no more, and that the plaintiffs are entitled to an injunction restraining you from imparting further confidential information. In view of my finding I see no need for a full trial and I award nominal damages of fifty pounds.' There was an audible gasp of annoyance from Roland before the judge went on, 'I have taken into account that Culross will call in the loans on your house and car and that you are likely to be dispossessed of them. I also do not intend to let this matter hang over you for years to come by insisting that you pay the plaintiffs' considerable costs.'

He rose.

The Court rose.

He left.

On the other side of the courtroom Roland said as loudly as he dared, 'The old fool fancies her. It's a disgrace. We're going to appeal.'

'Don't be ridiculous,' said Mark. 'You've gone far enough, and against my better judgment as it is, but you and Lawrence were determined to have your pound of flesh.'

'Yes, and I'm still going to get it.'

'If you want to appeal, tell your solicitor to instruct other counsel.'

'If you back out I'll report you to the Bar Council.'

'Don't you threaten me! I took this case on for Julius's sake, to save him – not you or Culross – from an even worse fiasco, and I have every right to withdraw from an appeal.' He handed his papers to his pupil and swept up the aisle.

At the door Julius touched his arm. 'Lunch?'

'Thanks.'

'We had to go along with Roland. If we'd refused to sue her he might have suspected we were on to him.'

'Oh, I know, and she deserved it. Or some of it – though not all of it.' He looked across at the lone and rigid figure of Olivia Steele.

When Mark had heard that it was Olivia who'd talked to the press he'd thought, how typical, how like Erica; the rules of the common herd apply to everyone but the Ericas and Olivias of this world. Olivia opting to conduct her own defence was also typical, or so he'd thought. At that moment he'd been almost glad to be involved. She deserved to get her come-uppance. He had enjoyed seeing her reprimanded by the judge and frustrated by his own pedantic questioning, but when she had stood in the dock and made her impassioned speech, mindless of the judge's intervention, admitting that she'd been wrong, then he knew he'd been wrong to equate her with Erica. She had shown courage as the rug was pulled from under her feet. She had made, as she said, a very human error for which she was paying an inhuman price. He remembered the time when as a very green pupil-barrister he was talking . . . no, boasting . . . to a friend about a case when to his horror the friend had said, 'My sister used to be married to your client.' The friend had been discreet. Mark had got away with it. He'd been lucky.

The judge returned. He beckoned Olivia to the bench. 'You were in contempt of my court.'

'Yes, I'm very sorry but I just had to say . . .'

'Not in my court, you didn't. You're lucky that I've decided not to punish you. Now, young lady, put all this behind you, stay away from disreputable men, and start rebuilding your life. It won't be easy. It never is.'

She went out into the warm summer streets where the late editions were selling fast. Two stories fought for front page prominence. '**The High-Flyer Who Came a Cropper**' and '**Watergate Tapes Subpoenaed.**'

10

In London people live north or south – of Hyde Park. They may move house many times but they tend to remain in their half, which all depends on where they lived when they first came to London, which in turn depends on where their friends lived if they had any before coming to the capital – or if they didn't know anyone, where they were first happy. (Like most capitals London is largely inhabited by people who weren't born there.)

Olivia had always lived south. Now she moved north to Islington, where she knew no one, to that area of dilapidated Victoriana beyond the Balls Pond Road and the railway line which just manages not to be called Hackney. The houses, three storey, narrow and painted white, were built during the last century after the opening of the Regent Canal. They are Victorian in date but more Georgian in style and their early occupants worked in the City, men of respectability with ink-stained fingers and eyesight weak from badly lit offices who hurried home through gas-lit Dickensian streets perhaps fearing that Jack the Ripper, not all that far away in Whitechapel, might decide to widen his net.

If Hampstead is the Chelsea of North London then Islington is perhaps its Fulham, a less expensive hotchpotch of large houses in elegant streets, artisans' cottages rapidly being bought by the young successful, and sprawling council estates covered in graffiti. Canonbury Square in Islington is highly desirable: the area to which Olivia moved had yet to be so. It was inhabited by the descendants of those early clerks, by young people on low salaries, by artists and musicians awaiting the big break, and by the odd professional couple who saw potential and spent their weekends scraping off layers of fifties wallpaper and replacing it with small prints from Laura Ashley or wide stripes from Habitat.

Olivia had answered an advertisement in the *Evening Standard* and paid a deposit on a top floor room 'with use of bathroom and kitchen' in a house owned by an elderly Hungarian lady who lived on the ground floor. It was depressingly basic, and seemed like the end of the world to Olivia as she paid off the taxi and began to lug her belongings up the steps into the hall where the communal telephone sat on a pile of well-thumbed directories.

'You have the rent?' Old Maria lumbered forward, her hand outstretched.

'Of course.' She dropped her suitcases, her duvet, and endless carrier bags to the floor. 'Forty pounds. I gave you ten yesterday, so I'm paid up till the end of the month.'

Fifty pounds a month for a semi-bare room! She thought longingly of her mews, now the property of an Arab playboy's mistress, as she set off up the stairs, to a faded pink candlewick bedspread on a narrow single bed, a threadbare carpet and a rickety table with one even more rickety chair.

'Want a hand?'

'Oh?' She spun around to find a young Indian standing in the opposite doorway.

'I'm Sanjiv.' He gave her a friendly smile, a flash of white teeth against his brown skin. 'Here, let me help. More downstairs? Don't worry, I'll fetch them.'

'Thanks.' She'd forgotten about neighbours. She'd imagined herself living a solitary existence, almost as though she did not deserve human contact.

Sanjiv pounded up the stairs carrying Olivia's duvet and old television, the one she'd once kicked: it now only worked on black and white. 'I'm studying to be an accountant but I also work in my uncle's shop,' he told her. 'It's on the corner. We stay open till midnight so if you ever need anything . . . This is horrible! He yanked the faded pink bedspread off the bed and replaced it with Olivia's duvet which hung down to the floor: it was meant for a double bed. 'That's better.' He turned with a pleased smile but when he saw her face the smile disappeared. 'You look very miserable.'

She shrugged.

'Just moved to London?'

'No.'

'Broken up with your boyfriend?'

She shook her head.

'OK, you don't want to talk. A lady of mystery! How about a nice hot mug of tea? Make you feel better. Come on.' He led the way to his room, which was littered with books and magazines, and had a large table by the window bearing an ancient typewriter with yellowed keys. 'You have to remember to keep a supply of ten pence pieces,' he said, slotting one into the meter. 'This contraption eats them. So does the gas meter in the bathroom. Actually,' he plugged in the kettle, 'I wouldn't be surprised if Maria doctors them so as to make more out of us.'

'She does seem very . . . money-minded.'

'She's as mean as hell.'

'I was hardly inside the front door before she was hassling me for the balance of the rent.'

'You're lucky she let you get that far.' He cleared a chair of its books. 'Sit down.'

She sat, and wondered what she was doing following a strange man into his bedroom. 'Have you lived here long?'

'Since June. Before that I lived with my uncle above his shop. And before that we were in Uganda – till Amin kicked us out.'

'Do you like living in England?' she ventured. She was afraid to offend. The question implied race – who had and who did not have the right to live here. Or who, in the eyes of some white people, had lesser rights.

'Oh, the weather's dreadful. My parents couldn't stand the cold so they've gone to India.' He poured the boiling water into two mugs. 'But I like the freedom – and there are better opportunities for me here. Of course I'm lucky. I have lots of relatives in London.' He pulled a face. 'That's why I moved into this house. You see, I failed my exams in June and I have to resit them in the autumn, and my uncle's house is always full of people so I didn't study properly. You mustn't let me talk too much . . . er . . .'

'Olivia.'

He offered her a biscuit. 'I'll tell you about the other people in the house. There's Barry on the first floor in the back room. He keeps to himself and I think he's gay but hasn't come out yet. Harriet's in the first floor front, the room below yours. She works for a women's organisation and she hasn't spoken to me since I told her I'd been engaged to my third cousin since she was fourteen.'

'Is it an . . .' She stopped.

'Arranged marriage? By your standards, yes, but that doesn't mean Lalita will be dragged sobbing to the temple and handed over against her will. I was introduced to about twenty girls and Lalita to as many boys — but I chose her.' He smiled bashfully. 'She was the twentieth and I liked her immediately — and she liked me.'

'Were your parents pleased?'

'Of course! They had arranged for us to meet.'

His life sounded so simple. She felt a stab of envy for its determined order. 'I must leave you to your studies.' She stood up. 'Thanks for the tea.'

She went to bed early and lay on the lumpy narrow mattress listening to the trains rattling along the nearby cutting. She felt terribly lonely.

On Sunday she explored the area, wandering through the elegantly restored Canonbury Square, cutting east across the dusty, dirty Essex Road, then making her way home down streets which had seen better days (and within a decade would see better days again). Men repaired cars. Children played in the street. Couples walked arm in arm. It was London, and yet to Olivia it seemed as though she were in another city.

She stopped at Sanjiv's uncle's shop. It was no different from the hundreds of other Indian shops which she had hurried into, often late at night, bought from, and left, without ever thinking about the people who owned them. Sanjiv was alone behind the till. 'Hello there. What can I do for you?'

'Coffee, tea, milk, cornflakes, bread, sugar, soap. Everything.'

'When she came to pay he gave her the change in ten pence pieces, saying, 'You'll need them for the meter.'

It was her daytime family at Culross which Olivia missed more than anything next morning, when she stood in the

101

dreary hall, telephoning from the communal payphone, answering jobs advertised in *The Times*, whilst old Maria pretended to polish the front door knob. 'No, I'm afraid I can't do shorthand . . . Yes, I can type but not very fast . . . No, I don't have any experience.'

She did manage to arrange one interview, with an advertising company, for which she wore her cream linen suit. Her interviewer wore designer jeans. The phone rang incessantly. Between calls she was asked, 'Any media experience? A bank! Wait a minute, aren't you that girl who . . . Sorry, luv, we couldn't risk it. Our clients wouldn't like it.'

She had promised to call her parents when she moved. Her mother answered. 'Where? A rented room in Islington! But Olivia, darling, what about all your nice friends? Surely you could have found someone to share with?'

Half an hour later Fiona rang. 'Mummy's having a fit. She says you're living in a boarding house.'

'It's not exactly a boarding house.' She was aware that Maria was polishing the front door knob yet again. 'I've rented a room. I had to get out of the mews.'

'I know, but why Islington when all your friends live round Chelsea?'

'I wanted to get away.'

'Have you got a job?'

'Not yet.' Maria was picking specks of dust off the letter box.

'Perhaps you should try something less ambitious, like a secretary.'

'A secretary!'

'There's nothing wrong with being a secretary, Olivia. I was one. So are many many girls and they have perfectly interesting, satisfying jobs. It's you – you've always believed you can go one better than the rest of us.'

'Fiona, please not now.'

'It's Daddy's fault, he encouraged you.'

'Fiona, it isn't Daddy's fault. I wanted that life – I still want it.'

For three weeks Olivia trudged the tired August streets, climbed narrow stairs, filled in application forms, and was interviewed by confident gossipy girls, not one of whom had anything to offer a high-flying banker no longer acceptable in banking circles.

After four weeks and twenty-two unsuccessful interviews she signed on with a temporary secretarial agency.

On September 8th, Richard Nixon was granted a full pardon for his part in the Watergate scandal and Olivia Steele started work as a temporary clerk-typist with an insurance company in Holborn.

She thought she would die of boredom. Every fifteen minutes she looked at her watch convinced that at least an hour must have passed – but it hadn't. In front of her was a pile of invoices with figures pencilled in. Her job was to type them, hand them to the next girl who did the envelopes, who in turn handed them to the vacant looking supervisor surreptitiously knitting beneath her desk. Every hour the supervisor slid her knitting into a drawer and checked the typed invoices. Only then were the pencilled figures rubbed out by a junior clerk. This went on all day. At the end the supervisor called Olivia to her desk.

'Miss Steele, is this all you've done today?'

'Yes, but I will get quicker.'

'I hope so, I do indeed.'

She did get quicker but the monotony did not change, and as the strangeness of living in a new place wore off she was left with long lonely evenings eating takeaway fish and chips in front of her flickering black and white television. Now Olivia understood why the clerks at Culross had longed so desperately for Fridays.

One evening she came back to find Sanjiv standing in the middle of her room holding an envelope which her mother had forwarded to her.

'What are you doing?' She demanded, taking it from him.

'I came to see you.'

'I mean with this.'

'I'm sorry, it was lying on the table and I picked it up – I just wanted to see what your surname was.'

'Now you know.'

'Yes. I knew I'd seen your face somewhere. Why the secret?'

'I don't want to talk about it.' She walked to the window and looked down on the decaying houses opposite.

'It might help.'

'Sanjiv, leave me alone . . . please!'

He went. But half an hour later he was back. 'Lalita and I are going to the cinema. Come with us.'

'No . . . thank you.'

'You're still cross with me?'

'No. Really. I'd love to come another time but I don't want to go out tonight.'

'Another time then.' He smiled.

She smiled back. But there would be no other time, not at the moment. She had so little self-confidence that she could not even face a darkened cinema.

The days ground past in a relentless succession of wet bus queues and takeways. She was putting on weight, she could no longer fit into her jeans, her hair needed cutting and her skin was sallow. One evening Harriet met her on the steps. 'What's that? Fish and chips? I do wish you'd come to talk to our group, Olivia.'

'What about?'

'Being turned into a victim by men.'

'I'm not a victim!'

'You are. Look at you! Stuffing yourself. Making yourself fat and ugly. Because men said you were bad, you're finishing the job for them and turning yourself into the wreck they wanted. Will you come?'

'No. No.' She ran up the stairs, pushing past old Maria who was eavesdropping as usual, and into her room. There she took off her coat and studied herself in the mirror. Her waist had thickened, her stomach bulged beneath her belt, her face was greasy and her eyes had a haunted, hunted look. She went into the kitchen and threw away the chips.

'You're crying,' said Sanjiv, coming out of his room as he always did when she returned from work.

'I'm fat and revolting and . . .'

'Go on a diet.'

'Oh, it's not just being fat, it's . . .' The words stuck in her throat.

He laid his brown hand on her white arm. His skin glowed,

104

hers was lifeless. 'In Hinduism we believe in the law of Karma – that each person is responsible for his situation. When things went well for you, didn't you believe it was as a result of your efforts?'

'Yes, I suppose I did.'

'Try again to make them go well.'

'I'm so tired of trying.'

He touched her cheek and for a moment she wondered if he were about to make love to her and what she would do if he did. She wanted to believe she would refuse him, she knew he pitied her, but she was starved of human contact – of warmth and affection.

He stepped back. 'I must go. I have my exam the day after tomorrow.'

Olivia had always despised women who were fat – all they needed was a little self-control, she used to say. Now she discovered how hard it was to lose those excess pounds, how boring the endless round of rabbit food, how revolting the cottage cheese on calorie-reduced crisp breads, but she also discovered the sistership of dieters. From the moment when her neighbour at work offered her a sweet and she replied, 'No, thanks, I'm on a diet,' she was welcomed to the circle: they now had something in common with the good-looking but sad-eyed girl who had kept very much to herself. The diet broke the ice and Olivia became part of the 'How much have you lost? . . . You do look thinner . . . Do I look thinner?'

After ten days of semi-starvation and only minimal cheating Olivia lost eight pounds.

A month later Sanjiv heard that he had passed his exams. 'I only just got through,' he told Olivia. 'I have another part to do next year. Here's your invitation to our wedding. You will come, won't you?'

Three days before the wedding her mother telephoned. 'Darling, you haven't been here since . . . well . . . and I do understand, but Fiona and Hugo are coming this weekend and I thought . . . Why not? An Indian wedding! Surely you don't *have* to go? You want to go!' A slight pause. 'I suppose you saw Simon's engagement in *The Times*. You didn't? How odd, I thought you always read *The Times*.'

Replacing the receiver, Olivia felt one of those totally unreasonable but utterly human pangs of selfishness. Simon had been hers. Now he wasn't.

Sanjiv and Lalita's wedding was on one of those late autumn days when the sun shines crisp on golden leaves and the air is rarified – pure – and there is an exquisite pain in the knowledge that soon the branches will be bared and the pavements black with cold: it is the sort of pain which comes only because something precious is about to end.

Olivia wore her black velvet suit she had bought for her first business lunch at Culross. Conspicuously Western among the bright saris of the Indian women, she sat at the back of the temple listening to the never-ending chant of the Brahmin. At the front Sanjiv sat alone. He'd been there for over an hour but there was no sign of Lalita. Olivia studied the other guests. She wasn't the only European. There were two middle-aged couples, business friends of Sanjiv's uncle, a couple of Sanjiv's friends from college, and a pretty but blowsy blonde whispering fiercely to an embarrassed Indian man. Olivia speculated on their relationship. Lovers? No, he wouldn't have brought her. Married. But what was the girl hissing about? Some slight from her Indian mother-in-law?

Suddenly there was a commotion at the back as the doors were flung open and Lalita's uncle marched in, carrying the bride in his arms as if she were a beautiful butterfly too precious to touch the ground, and as he walked the ritual golden coins on her forehead tinkled in expectation.

Olivia left the reception as soon as was decently possible. She hadn't known anyone and had found the strain of forced conversation over soft drinks and sticky, sweet cakes more than she could bear. Sanjiv, her friend, her neighbour, was no longer hers, he was part of these very different people for whom she was an outsider. Everyone goes back to their own in the end, she thought – except for me.

She could not bear to go back to the house, so she went to a cinema where they were showing an old black and white movie, *Now Voyager*, biting her lip at the end when Bette Davis looks up at the sky and says, 'Oh, Jerry, don't let's ask for the moon. We have the stars,' because Olivia had wanted the stars and the moon – and she'd ended up with nothing.

11

Cars crawled up Grays Inn Road, their wipers helpless against the driving rain, their windscreens fugged up by the condensation inside. Olivia shivered by the bus stop, her shoulders hunched, her fingers freezing inside her wet woollen gloves.

A long, low black MGB GT sportscar drew level. Its unseen driver gave a sharp toot on the horn. Lucky person getting a lift, she thought. The driver tooted again. No one stepped forward. The driver lowered the passenger window.

'Olivia Steele?'

She bent to the open window.

'Would you like a lift?'

'No.' She drew back.

'Olivia!'

'Please leave me alone, Mr Denholm.'

'Come on, I'll drive you home.'

'No.' Drops of rain rolled down her hair and chin.

'Why not?'

'I'd rather take the bus.'

'Don't be silly.'

'How dare you call me silly! I'm not at Culross any more nor are we in the High Court.' She turned her back on the car.

The bus arrived. The queue moved forward.

'Sorry, luv.' The conductor barred her way. 'Full up.'

'But I've been waiting for ages.'

'Regulations. No more than five standing. Can't risk my job, luv. There'll be another bus along in a few minutes.'

Mark got out of his car and opened the passenger door. 'Please!'

If there had been a bus in sight . . . if it hadn't been raining . . . if she could have afforded a taxi, then she'd have refused, but . . . she settled into the comfortable leather seat and stretched her legs out into the warmth under the dashboard.

'Where do you live?' he asked.

'Islington.'

Mark drove well. She glanced at his hands on the steering wheel, his skin was lightly tanned against the white cotton of his cuffs. She wondered where he'd been, picturing him on some Caribbean beach with other successful people, and somewhere there would be a girl, perhaps stalking out of the sea in a white bikini, as Ursula Andress had done in *Dr No*. She looked down at her own hands, hidden in cheap woollen gloves – two pairs for a pound in the Leather Lane Market.

They passed a pub.

'How about a drink?' he said.

'Well, I should be . . .' She was weak, but she couldn't help it, all that awaited her was solitude and the television.

They went into the warmth where cheerful young men crowded around the bar and couples sat on red velvet chairs, leaning their elbows on small round tables. Mark settled her at a table by the fire. 'What would you like?'

'Gin and tonic . . . thanks.'

He brought it to her, the ice tinkling against the glass. 'I used to come here when I first lived in London,' he said. 'During my first year at the Bar I had a room behind King's Cross and this was about the only decent pub nearby to which I could bring . . . young ladies.'

'You lived around here! It's almost as bad as Soho!'

'I wanted to be central and it was the only place I could afford. Anyhow,' he smiled ruefully, 'I was brought up to be streetwise. Where are you working?'

She had her answer prepared. 'Various places, mainly short term assignments.'

'In banking?'

She thought of the piles of invoices she had typed that day. 'Related.'

'But you're not properly fixed up?'

'Oh, yes. I have just been offered an excellent job, exactly what I've been looking for.'

'Where?'

'I don't think that's anything to do with you.'

He raised an eyebrow but made no comment. A moment later he said, 'I have an old Venetian tower on Anataxos, an island north of Corfu. You could go there for the winter.'

'Why should I want to go away when I've just found a good job.'

'Bear it in mind.'

'Why should you want me to live in your tower?'

'It's merely a suggestion. I thought you might like a break — and I'd be glad of someone to oversee the renovations. I'm having the place done up.' He took a card from his inside jacket pocket and dropped it into her open handbag, saying, 'If you change your mind, you've got my number.'

'Don't tell me Culross have a conscience.' She rummaged for the card, she wanted to give it back, but all she got was a handful of used bus tickets and a half-eaten polo mint.

'It has nothing to do with Culross. The tower is mine.'

'So it's you. Isn't it a bit late for feeling guilty?'

'I'm not feeling remotely guilty. I prosecuted you because I was instructed to do so.'

'Just like that!'

'You don't imagine I did it for personal reasons?'

'You're immoral. You're just like Roland.' She stood up and pushed back her chair with such force that it crashed backwards. 'I can't imagine why you refused your cut of Culross. Think how much you could have screwed out of old Sir Larry's conscience.

His jaw tightened. They glared at each other. Then she picked up her coat and hurried out into the night.

Every time Olivia remembered that evening she gritted her teeth. She'd stormed out of the pub and up the street, then realised that she hadn't a clue where she was, so she'd begun to walk slowly, expecting Mark to catch up with her and insist on seeing her home as any other man would have done, any decent man: but he hadn't. He'd come out, got into his car, and driven off at high speed, leaving her to battle through the rain and the badly lit streets until, finally, she'd come out in the murky depths of the Caledonian Road – and been forced to take a taxi home, using up ten days' worth of bus money.

Christmas was six weeks away and Olivia dreaded it. The unasked questions in her parents' eyes, the fended enquiries from her mother's friends, 'And what is dear Olivia doing now?', the frightful men Fiona and Hugo would dredge up for her.

One morning at the beginning of December, after her fire refused to light, her milk was frozen, and old Maria told her that the rent was going up, she stood by the bus stop watching an aeroplane cut across the grey sky and thought of Greece. Why shouldn't she take advantage of Mark's offer? Why shouldn't she use him – them – as they had used her? She dawdled past a travel agency offering cheap flights. During her lunch hour she calculated her finances and later that afternoon she telephoned her agency.

'You want to work weekends and evenings, Olivia? That's marvellous! One of our best clients . . . an engineering firm moving offices . . . not interesting but they'll pay double time . . . you'll take it? I always said you'd turn out to be one of our best girls. Take my advice, dear, and do a shorthand course. Then we can send you out as a shorthand typist!'

One Saturday morning, ten days before Christmas, Olivia telephoned Mark at his home. A motherly-sounding woman who reminded her immediately of Ma Patent answered, 'No dear, 'e's gone out. I expect 'e'll be gone all day, 'e usually is when 'e goes pistol shooting.'

'Could you tell me where he goes shooting?'

'I don't think I should.'

'Oh, please, I'm a very old friend and I'm only in England for today. We haven't seen each other for years. I've known him since . . . playschool.'

'I dunno.'

'Please.'

'All right but I 'ope 'e isn't cross.'

'He won't be, I promise you.'

Olivia wrote down the address of the pistol club on the outskirts of Henley and hoped that God would be kind and understanding about her lies and not send her more bad luck.

It was cold and raining when Olivia boarded the train at Paddington, but by the time she arrived at Henley, an hour later, the sun was pushing its way through. She asked directions and crossed the old stone bridge spanning the Thames, which would be thronged with people and boats at the time of the summer regatta but was now deserted, with the water rippling grey.

The pistol club was in the grounds of a large Queen Anne house. It had been founded by an eccentric and lonely field marshal. In his will he bequeathed the shooting gullies to the club but the house to a society which cared for aged officers. Both sides had contested. The club had claimed that it would not be long before some old buffer wandered into the firing line, the society that the inmates required peace and not the constant rattle of pistol fire. But their benefactor knew what he was doing. Most of the old men were too deaf to mind the firing and too lame to reach the gullies. Furthermore, they didn't want to be shut away to die. The club was the highlight of their waning existence. They loved the coming and going of men who knew about guns. Didn't they too know about guns?

As Olivia came up the drive she saw Mark's car parked beside a glossy-leaved rhododendron bush. Beyond it were a dozen or so other cars. She found two old men gossiping by the entrance. 'Excuse me, I'm looking for Mark Denholm.'

'Denholm!'

'Shoots with a Colt 45 automatic.'

'Prefer a Webley Mark VI myself – I like to see the chamber turn.'

'Young Denholm's a damned good shot. He won the cup last year. Two bull's eyes in a row. What a marksman!'

'Could you . . . er . . . tell me where he is?'

'Oh, yes, sorry, my dear, he's in the far gully. That way. But stick to the path or you'll get that pretty head of yours blown off.'

Mark was alone. He was standing at one end of a deep gully, just in front of a wooden shed, his right arm outstretched to hold the sort of vicious pistol with which Mafia bosses massacre each other over plates of spaghetti. He was wearing earmuffs to protect his eardrums and his eyes were fixed on the targets – seven cardboard Hitlers turning on pivots. Watching him Olivia sensed the tension in his body. The concentration. The cold precision.

Somehow he knew she was there, or knew someone was there, because he glanced around. She expected him to speak. He didn't. He took aim – and fired. There was a deafening report as the pistol kicked in his hand, and almost simultaneously one of the Hitlers fell back. Six more shots followed in quick succession. Each one of the Hitlers fell back. Still not speaking, Mark lowered his arm and, keeping the barrel pointed at the ground, he checked the empty magazine. Satisfied he walked to the shed and laid the gun on a wooden ledge, the breech open. Then he turned to Olivia.

'How did you know I was here?'

'Your ... er ... a lady at your house ...'

'My cleaning lady gave you this address?'

'Yes, but you mustn't blame her. I'm afraid I told her a lie. I said we were friends from childhood and I was only in England for today.'

'Are you in the habit of telling lies?'

'Of course not.'

He gave her a questioning look.

'I want to take up your offer to go to Greece.'

'Couldn't it wait till I got back to London?'

'I have to sort it out today.'

'The excellent job?'

She said nothing.

He held out a spare pair of earmuffs. 'Put these on or you'll be deafened – and for God's sake keep well behind me.'

She watched as he loaded the bullets into the magazine. Surely he wasn't going to keep her hanging around all day whilst he played with guns? He took aim, fired, fired again. Her eyes drifted down his body to his hips, to his jeans stretched tight over the hip-bone. Hurriedly she looked away, but her mind did not leave him; she kept imagining his skin, cool and flat beneath the tough denim, and she kept thinking that if she touched him she would feel that coolness and that flat hardness.

'Would you like to try?' he asked.

'Yes.'

112

'Have you fired a gun?'

'No.'

He gave a half-smile but made no comment as he slotted the loaded magazine into the grip and handed the pistol to her, the barrel pointing at the ground. 'Feet slightly apart. That's right.' He stood behind her and took her by the shoulders. 'Arm outstretched. Level up the sights till you see the target. You'll feel a kick when you fire so don't steel yourself, allow your arm to rise slightly. All right?'

'Yes.'

He stepped back. 'Squeeze the trigger . . . gently.'

Her finger was hooked around the trigger. She looked down the barrel to line up the sights again, only by now her arm was tired and the weapon weighed heavier by the second, and the tension in her arms made it waver.

'Don't hesitate, Olivia. Take aim and fire. Go on!'

She did – with her eyes tightly closed – and the kick nearly sent her over backwards. She turned. 'Sorry, I wasn't very . . .'

'Don't point the gun at me!'

'Oh . . . sorry.'

'Take aim.'

She did, and this time she was prepared for the kick – but not one of her shots hit a target. It was mortifying.

'Want to try again?'

'Yes.'

He reloaded the pistol.

She took aim and fired, attempting to copy his stance, shooting quickly, one after the other – and by some fluke she hit two of the Hitlers.

'Beginner's luck,' said Mark.

'No. Consummate skill.'

He laughed. 'Come on, I'll show you the club house and you can liven up some old colonel's day.'

They set off across the lawn, their feet leaving silvery imprints in the wet grass. 'When do you want to leave for Anataxos?' he asked.

'As soon as possible.'

'The tower's pretty basic.'

'I don't mind.'

'Things must be tough.'

113

She didn't reply.

'It's Venetian,' he said. 'The Venetians ruled that part of the Med. until the eighteenth century. It's built on a headland overlooking the only village. Fantastic views, but very isolated. I bought it two years ago and have only used it in summer, when it's hot and I don't mind roughing it, but I'd like to be able to go there at other times – and to lend it to friends. There's an old Greek called Vasili who keeps an eye on the place. He was meant to organise the retiling but he's not up to it. I'll show you the sort of thing I like, but it will depend on the materials available. Vasili will pay. I've always transferred money to him for repairs and he'd be offended if I stopped. All it really needs is for someone to choose the tiles and get things moving.'

'Just show me what you want done.'

'Do you speak Greek?'

'No – but then I hadn't fired a gun before today either.'

He stopped. The pale sun caught his face, softening its harder lines. The wind ruffled his hair, lifting the blonder top hairs so that they too caught the sun. He looked fit and tough, but no longer so detached. 'You're quite a little fighter, aren't you?'

She swallowed hard and looked determinedly across the lawn, to the house and a group of old colonels standing outside it. The lonely evenings in front of the television, the relentless tedium of her job, the shame, the disgrace, she couldn't speak of them to him because he was one of *them*. Pride stopped her – pride, and the fear that her confidences would again be used against her.

114

12

Greece

The white light of Greece hit Olivia as she stepped out on deck.
The white light. The sharpness of the colours – the sea – the
sky – which threw back brightness in her eyes.

'Anataxos!' A sailor shouted to her.

She nodded, but she could see nothing except the wall of
grey-green water until the ferry rose on the next wave, and
there it was, straight ahead, a jewel of an island basking in the
bitter sun, its great emerald mountain rising up into the sky.

Since that Saturday with Mark, Olivia had felt confident
and excited. She'd counted the days until she could leave her
job, leave Islington, leave England, but now as they
approached her destination her confidence ebbed away. She
was going to a place where she knew no one, to an island in a
country whose language she didn't understand, to a house
practically unlived in for two hundred years: she tried not to
think of her parents settling into an evening of television
before a roaring fire.

Night falls quickly in the Mediterranean and by the time the
ferry drew into the small harbour the white light had been lost
to a fiery sinking sun. Olivia studied the village, a cluster of
flat-roofed whitewashed houses, and wondered what on earth
she would find to do here. She watched people hurrying down
to the ferry and hoped fervently that Vasili was among them.
Mark had said he would meet her.

Ten minutes later she was standing on the jetty, trying not to
panic. The other passengers were fast disappearing up narrow
streets and into houses shuttered against the night. In front of

115

her was a small square surrounding an ancient gnarled tree. It was deserted. Five more minutes passed. A door opened, throwing a shaft of light to the base of the tree, and two figures came out, one old and one young.

'Olivia! Friend of Mark!' shouted the old man. 'I am Vasili. Good morning. Goodbye.' He came to her smiling his tooth-less smile. 'Good afternoon.'

'Good evening. Oh, I'm so glad to see you. I'm afraid I was beginning to think that . . .'

'My grandfather not understand English,' said the boy. 'He only speak ten words. I am Nikos. My English is good?'

'Very good.' She would have gladly told him he was word-perfect.

They took Olivia to the bar, ordered her a glass of ouzo and a small cup of acrid black coffee, offered her a vile-smelling cigarette, laughing when she wrinkled up her nose – and there she sat for the next two hours with Vasili proudly beside her, chattering to two old fishermen. From time to time he would pat her arm and say something about Mark, though she had no idea what because Nikos had disappeared.

Mark had given her some money to buy Vasili a large bottle of Glenfiddich at the airport. She wondered whether to give it to him now or later, then decided he would like it now, in front of his friends. She dug into her bag and produced it, saying 'From Mark.'

There were cheers. Vasili shook her hand. More talk of Mark. Fresh glasses appeared. Whisky was poured. Toasts drunk to Greece, to England, to Mark. Olivia began to feel lightheaded. In the past thirty-six hours she'd flown to Athens, caught a ferry to Corfu, taken a bus across the island, boarded the ferry for Anataxos – and all she had eaten was a plastic in-flight meal and a series of stale sandwiches. She was tired and hungry and she longed to go to bed.

By the time Nikos returned it was too late to go to the tower, so she had to spend the night as Vasili's house where his wife, a rotund woman with a face like the Cheshire cat in *Alice in Wonderland*, insisted that she ate some greasy dish of rice and mutton before leading her down a stone passage to a small and hastily vacated bedroom. It was Nikos's room, and as she lay down on top of the bed, fully clothed, she was aware that she ought to have protested and offered to sleep elsewhere – but she was too tired to offer anything.

The braying of a donkey outside the window woke her. She looked at her watch. Eight o'clock. She was stiff and cold. She closed her eyes, but she could not go back to sleep because Vasili began to shout at Nikos who was shouting at a dog which began to bark furiously.

After a wash in cold water, she breakfasted on sweet black coffee and a pink sugary cake.

'Ready?' asked Nikos.

'Yes. Please thank your grandmother for me.'

'He said something in Greek. The old woman smiled and nodded. 'We go! Come!'

She went out into the white light which had returned with the morning and sniffed the air, which smelt of damp earth, salt and lemons. Vasili strapped her case to the donkey's back and set off, leading the animal. Nikos followed with Olivia. As they crossed the village square, where the bar was already open, she was struck by the prosperity of the island. The houses were freshly whitewashed. The green shutters were glossy. Even the street was painted white. Two women, probably in their early fifties and obviously Northern European and wealthy, were buying vegetables from an elderly Greek lady. One of the women was bubbly and redhaired, the other grey-blonde with a lean, leathery elegance. The contrast between their smart trousers and designer jackets and the shapeless black of the Greek lady seemed almost obscene. But was it? For surely it was these escapees from northern inland revenues who had brought prosperity to Anataxos.

They reached the harbour wall and turned along the sea front. To their left was the sparkling Mediterranean, to their right a boutique, closed for the winter, in whose window was a scarf with the inimitable initials YSL.

'Look! The tower!' Nikos touched her arm.

On a rocky headland jutting out into the sea stood a round white tower, just like a lighthouse guarding the bay. Behind it the trees, now devoid of leaves, came down the hill. Below it the land fell to rocks and waves. It was magnificent, isolated, brilliant white against a brilliant blue sky. No wonder Mark had bought it.

The road followed the bay to the beginning of the headland, then it wound inland, through olive groves. At this point Vasili turned up a rough track which twisted through the trees along the side of the headland, coming out at the foot of a flight of wide stone steps leading up to a huge mulberry tree beside the tower.

Vasili said something in Greek, and Nikos translated. 'My grandmother came yesterday.' He pointed out the freshly washed floor, and the sheets and blankets draped over chairs to air.

'Thank you – and please thank her.' She put her bag down on a long wooden table. The tower had been opened up with arches, the back leading to a kitchen and bathroom, the sides to magnificent views of the island, the front to the terrace and the glittering sea. There was hardly any furniture, just the table, six chairs and a long low window seat covered in blue and white striped hessian.

Nikos carried her case up the stone stairs which encircled the inside of the tower. He put it down in the first floor bedroom, a small room with two single beds and a wicker chair. The bedspread and the curtains were of the same rough woven blue and white striped material. 'Mark sleep above,' he said. 'You want to see?'

'Yes. Why not?'

They went on up the circular stairs to a completely circular room which filled the entire top of the tower, reaching up in a peak to wooden rafters. Here the stripes were red and white, again of that rough natural weave, but this room had a more lived in feeling. There was a bookshelf crammed with holiday paperbacks, a wooden cupboard, a poster which Olivia recognised as Matisse, and a double bed.

Downstairs, Nikos showed her a shed full of more chopped firewood. 'We bring yesterday,' he smiled proudly. 'And the gas.' He showed her a spare cylinder for the stove, saying, when she pulled a face, 'You are afraid to change the cylinder?'

'Terrified.'

'It's easy.' He translated to Vasili and they both laughed. Finally, and even more proudly, they showed her the stock of provisions – eggs, olive oil, potatoes, onions and a barrel of wine.

'Oh, thank you. Thank you very much. She fished in her bag. 'Er . . . how much do I . . .?'

'Nothing. Mark pay.'

'What about the cleaning?'

'Mark pay.'

Vasili patted her on the shoulder. 'Good afternoon. Made in England. Goodbye.' He went off, massaging his empty gums with the end of a match.

She listened to their diminishing voices as they made their way back along the headland. Should she unpack? Light a fire? Have a glass of wine? She found a glass and tipped the barrel. A strange brackenish liquid appeared. She took her glass out on the terrace, where the wind caught her hair and blew it across her face. The air was cold but the sun surprisingly strong. She sipped at the wine, grimacing at its musky roughness. Over by the jetty the ferry hooted and pulled up its drawbridge. Moments later it departed for Corfu. A helicopter clattered overhead, climbed a little way up the mountain, hovered, then dropped from sight behind a ridge. Olivia waited for it to reappear but it didn't. Silence. She looked up at the tower. Mark was right, it had a spartan beauty. She finished the glass of wine. The taste wasn't so bad after all, in fact . . . she pondered having another, then thought why not? After all, it was Christmas Day.

It rained for three solid days. Olivia stood at the window and watched sheets of water sweep over the sea to engulf the island. Three times she lit the fire, only to have it reduced to a hissing pile as rain found its way down the chimney. Twice the electricity failed. The first time she was left scrabbling in darkness, the second time she was prepared: she had found a paraffin lamp. The stock of food proved invaluable. She had intended to go down to the village on her second day, to change money and buy more food, but she put off the expedition, existing on a diet of potato omelettes and the musky white wine whilst she spent her days snuggled under the blankets reading paperbacks from Mark's room. One was stamped 'Henley Public Library'. She wondered if he had lent the tower to someone at the pistol club. It was a strange limbo existence. She might have been entirely alone on the island.

On the fourth day she woke to shafts of sunshine dissecting the room. Afraid that the bad weather might return, she washed her dirty clothes, dressed in her only remaining clean jeans and only clean jersey, and set out for the village, slithering down the rough path until she came to the road. It took less than an hour to explore the village and do her shopping. As she was leaving the bank, the leathery grey-blonde tapped her on the shoulder. I'm Gwen. You must be Mark's friend.'

'Oh . . . yes.' She wasn't his friend but she had no intention of explaining their relationship. 'I'm Olivia.'

'Join me for a coffee.' Gwen led the way to the square where a table and some chairs had been put out in the sun. 'We're dying to meet you.'

'Oh. Why?'

'A new face, of course.' Gwen relaxed her long lean body into a chair, flicked open her bag, and took out a gold cigarette case. 'Smoke?'

'No, thanks. I do occasionally but . . . I want to stop.'

The gold cigarette case was followed by a gold Cartier lighter. Gwen's hands shook very slightly until she had inhaled the first draught.

'Gwen!' The other woman, the bubbly redhead bounced over and Olivia saw that her hair colour owed more to a bottle than nature. 'Hello. I'm Monica. Welcome to Anataxos! I hope I haven't missed any gossip. What are you doing here in the middle of winter?'

'I'm having a few months' break from London.'

'How's Mark?'

'Very well.'

'You're not his new girlfriend, are you?'

'No.'

'Has he still got that neurotic creature . . . what's her name . . . Erica? Oh God, don't tell me she's your best friend.'

'No, she's not, I've never met her. I don't know Mark very well either.'

The two women chatted. Olivia listened. The sun was warm. Along the harbour wall the fishermen were mending their nets. An old Greek widow wrapped in black crossed the square. From inside the bar came the rattle of backgammon dice.

The peace was ruptured by the arrival of a red jeep driven by an over-sleek, almost-young man. He swaggered over and, to Olivia's astonishment, ruffled Monica's hair.

'Gianni,' said Gwen. 'This is Olivia.'

'Darling.' Monica reached up for his hand. 'I thought you were working on your play.'

'I was. I'm bored.'

'Then I'll come home and keep you company.' She stood up and patted her red curls with a girlish gesture which reminded Olivia of her mother.

'I wish Monica would get rid of him' said Gwen as soon as they were out of earshot. 'She's a lovely person, and he's using her. Playwright! Jim couldn't stand him. Jim was my husband. He died last year. Cancer.' A shaft of pain crossed her face and she rose abruptly. 'Come to my New Year's Eve party. Everyone comes − except for Jake.

'Who's Jake?'

'Jake Hammond, the world famous sculptor. The King of Anataxos.'

'Jim and Gwen's New Year's Eve party has always been *the* evening of the winter,' Monica told Olivia when they met in the bread shop. 'Everyone dresses up. Didn't Mark warn you that Anataxos is like that? Typical man! I'll send over some of Maggie's clothes . . . Maggie's my daughter.'

'Don't worry. I . . . er . . . haven't been very well lately and I'm not really up to a party.'

'You can't be on your own on New Year's Eve!'

'But your daughter might not like me to have her clothes.'

'Maggie's a backing singer with a rock group called Black Masco − I expect you've heard of them. She only wears black leather. Anyhow, I haven't heard from her in two years − since she swore she'd never speak to me again.'

That afternoon Olivia went for a walk along the beach and wondered how she could get out of the party. She wanted to be on her own, to think out her life, her future, and not get sucked into the goldfish bowl of expatriate life. I could pretend to be ill. She kicked at the wet sand. Of course, it's very kind of Gwen to invite me. She hurled a pebble into the sea, and seemed to hear her mother saying, 'You should accept every invitation, dear, you never know who you might meet'. But I don't want to meet anyone! She hurled a second pebble into the sea.

On her return she found a pile of clothes on the terrace: an exquisite pink silk dress of floating scarves by Zandra Rhodes – with an enormous rip down the back: an Inca-type dress of white cotton embroidered with red and black – with a red wine stain down the front: a couple of mini skirts: and a pair of red suede boots, the only item not either ripped, marked or outdated.

Gwen's house was set on the hillside above the village. It was a modern villa with a cascading garden and a lavishly furnished interior. There were some thirty people at the party by the time Olivia arrived. Half a dozen lived on the island, the rest were house guests out from England or over from the States. They all seemed to know each other. She stood on the edge of the circle and wondered if anyone would notice if she slipped away.

'How clever of you to think of cutting off the wine stain!' said Monica, catching sight of the Inca dress, belted at the waist over black trousers tucked into the red boots. You look like a Cossack. Oh, Gianni, darling, I spend a fortune on clothes and I'm sure no one can tell.' She put an arm round Olivia and ushered her forward, whilst smoothing down the clinging black skirt of her Yves St Laurent cocktail dress with the other hand.

'I see Jake isn't here.' Gianni offered Olivia a cigarette.

'He never comes.'

'There was an exhibition of his work in London two years ago,' said Olivia. 'I remember seeing pictures of the crowds trying to get in. What is he like?'

'He's charming when he wants to be – and an evil-tempered old devil when he doesn't, which is most of the time.'

'But he does give the most magnificent party every July,' said Gianni. 'Everything is flown in. Caviar. Champagne. A steel band. The cabaret. The yachts. And you should see the guests. All famous society people.'

Monica gave him an indulgent smile. 'You're too easily impressed. Why, you think this house is perfect when even Gwen admits that Jim could never understand bigger, bolder and shinier did not mean better.'

'You have always been rich,' said Gianni, with an edge to his voice.

'I know, I'm lucky. Dear Jim started with nothing and he made his fortune. So did Jake, of course, but you could not meet two men more different. It was all most unpleasant, Olivia. Jake would not invite Jim to his summer party. Jim and Gwen were the only people not to go, and all because Jim insisted that McCarthy had been right – even after he knew Jake had suffered from McCarthy's witch hunts. It's all so stupid, isn't it. That reds-under-the-bed stuff happened twenty years ago. People should forget and forgive. They shouldn't bear grudges. Don't you agree, Olivia?'

'No, I'm afraid I don't.'

'Then you'll get on very well with Jake – and with my daughter.'

They went into dinner, in the glass dining-room which overlooked a floodlit kidney-shaped pool, half-empty and sad as swimming pools are unless filled with blue water. Olivia was placed between Gianni and a taciturn German. Afterwards they moved back to the drawing-room, and as she was wondering again if she could escape, Gwen marshalled them into a circle. As Big Ben struck twelve, they joined hands and sang 'Auld Lang Syne'. Suddenly the door was opened by a skinny girl with blonde spiky hair and a white but not unpretty face. She was wearing black leather trousers, a studded black leather jacket and the highest of high heels. 'Hello, Mummy.'

'Maggie!' Monica rushed forward, then stopped, her outstretched arms falling to her sides. 'What a lovely surprise! Look, everyone, it's my daughter, Maggie. How long are you staying, darling? I mean, I hope you are . . .'

'Two nights. We're doing a gig in Athens on Saturday.'

Maggie's kohl-rimmed eyes drifted around the room till they came to Olivia. 'My dress?'

'I hope you don't mind.'

'I couldn't give a fuck!'

Olivia was thankful to get back to the tower: it was all very well for Gwen to say 'Maggie doesn't mean it'. Next morning she sat on the terrace, her back to the village: she had no intention of returning to it until after the holiday, until all the people who had witnessed her embarrassment had left Anataxos. She closed her eyes and lifted her face to the sun.

'Hi.'

She turned to find Maggie hovering at the top of the terrace steps. 'Please go away.'

'Look, I'm sorry about last night.'

'This is private property and you are trespassing.'

'I want to explain. The last time I saw my mother I was wearing the Inca dress and she threw a glass of red wine over me. You must have cut off the stain. When I saw you in it last night I thought she'd stage-managed the whole thing.'

Olivia shrugged.

'Mind if I sit down?' Maggie didn't wait for an answer but perched her thin bottom on the wall, opened a small leather pouch and proceeded to roll a joint. 'Smoke?'

'No.'

'You're still cross.' She drew deeply on the smoke. 'I don't blame you. You see, mother left father four years ago. He was heartbroken and I thought she missed him. I suppose like many kids whose parents split up, I hoped mine would get back together again. So I planned their reconciliation. I arranged to come out here two years ago, for Christmas, and I pretended to him that she was in New York, but I didn't tell Mummy that Daddy was coming. The trouble was,' she pulled a face, 'I didn't know about Gianni. There was a terrible row. Father took the next ferry home. I slapped mother – and she threw a glass of red wine over me.' Maggie gave Olivia a tentative smile. 'I'm very sorry about last night.' She stood up and her ridiculously high heels clattered as she crossed the terrace to retrieve a plastic bag from behind one of the stone flower tubs. 'I've brought you some more clothes. Less tatty ones. They're summer clothes, tee shirts and jeans.'

'Thanks – but I don't need them.

'Please take them. It'll make me feel better.'

'Oh, all right.'

'I wish I had shiny hair like yours. No wonder Gianni fancies you.'

'He doesn't!'

'He told Gwen he did.'

'Well, his luck's out.'

'I don't blame you. He's a jerk. But I can highly recommend Nikos.'

'What!'

'I was his first lover,' Maggie gave an impish grin, 'and he was my fifty-ninth.'

Unable to contain her curiosity, Olivia asked, 'Do you keep a record?'

'In my address book, but I've stopped allotting them marks out of ten. It was too depressing. That's what comes of being on the road.' She gave a small sad smile to hotel rooms, to half-empty glasses, and to men she'd met at all night parties. 'I'm the queen of the two-night-stand – and I'm lonely.' She set off down the steps, her high heels making her ungainly on the slope. 'Perhaps if I looked healthy like you some nice man would go for me?'

'It's no guarantee,' said Olivia cautiously.

'No?'

'No.' She did not elaborate.

A week later Olivia received a postcard – a picture of a gorilla.

My

new man

love Maggie

She stared at the writing and wondered if she could ever be as forthcoming as Maggie or if Gerald and Culross had scarred her permanently.

After Gwen's party Olivia kept to herself. She liked Gwen – and she even quite like Monica – but she could not bear the four-hour lunches where ageing house guests drank themselves under the table and talked of people she did not know. Instead, she explored the island. One morning she followed the road beyond the tower, turning inland up the valley, walking between gnarled olive trees which rose out of a badly furrowed soil, their trunks twisted and grey. At a certain point, she wasn't sure when, she became aware of a man singing. She stopped, listened, then walked on. The road came out below a terraced wall, so long that it spanned the entire head of the valley like the outer ramparts of some mountain fortress. Above her, was a huge white-haired man, his head lifted to the sky, his voice booming out: 'Bella ciao, bella ciao, bella ciao, ciao, ciao.'

'Ah, there you are,' he said. 'Knew you'd be up sooner or later.'

'How?'

'They all come.'

'Oh.'

'Haven't brought any of those old cats, have you?'

'No.'

'Then come up and have some wine – and you can admire my latest work.'

'What is it?'

'The copulation of the big cats.'

'Human or feline?'

'For that you can stay to lunch. Aphrodisia!' The ugliest woman Olivia had ever seen appeared at the far end of the terrace. 'This young lady's staying to lunch.'

'Is her name really Aphrodisia?'

'How should I know?' He led the way into the house. On a mobile stand beside a beautiful Persian carpet stood a half-finished white marble sculpture some two feet high. The forms of the two cats, twisting into each other turning on a central pivot, as if it were not just their feline desire which brought them together but some magnetic force. Jake picked up a chisel, placed it by one cat's front paw, and began to tap the other end with a wooden mallet, sending slivers of white marble scattering over the silky red and blue carpet.

'Do you always work in here?' she asked.

'I've got a studio in the garden but sometimes I need a change of scenery.'

He picked up a pair of callipers. Only then did Olivia realise that he was scaling up from a much smaller model.

'Do you do all the work yourself?' she asked.

'You mean, do I leave the hard graft to others whilst reaping

126

all the glory and the rewards?'

'I didn't mean it like that.'

He wiped the marble dust from his face. 'The art of sculptor, young lady, is one of participation. Marble contains everything – every form, design, and line – it's up to the sculptor with his ideas to bring forth the beauty.' He picked up the chisel. 'But he can't do it alone. He may go up to the mountain face to choose his block but he is dependent on others to quarry it, on lorry drivers to transport it down the hillside, on foundry works to cut it into a manageable block, and on artisans to help him scale up the model. A sculptor may be the toast of London, Paris, Tokyo and New York but he's a fool if he gives himself airs and graces in the foundry.' He patted the haunches of the female cat. 'Ah, that's better.'

'Where does the marble come from?'

'Monte Altissimo.' He walked out of the room and banged the door viciously.

Olivia was left wondering what she'd done wrong. She hovered by the sofa, then sat down on one end and pretended to be fascinated by the room, which was large and airy and decorated in shades of cream and blue, which managed to compliment the Persian carpet without being overpowered by it. On the table were two photographs in silver frames, one of a white-blonde girl with the glacial geometric beauty of certain fashion models, the other of a clean cut boy, a sort of unrebellious James Dean.

Jake returned carrying two glasses of wine. For the first time she noticed he had a slight limp.

'Are those your children?' she asked.

'Yes.'

'They're very goodlooking.'

'They were. Billy's dead and Dee drinks.'

At lunch Olivia was rigid with the awkward knowledge that he could not wait to get rid of her and she hated him for the humiliation of it.

Three days later, very early in the morning, she woke to banging at the terrace door and Jake's voice yelling. 'Olivia! Olivia!'

She scrambled out of bed, wrapped herself in a blanket and ran downstairs.

'I've come to make amends,' he said, as she opened the door. 'I'm taking you to lunch.'

'Now? But it's not even eight o'clock.'

'Bring your passport. We're going to Amalfi.'

'Lunch in Italy?' She laughed, infected by his enthusiasm.

'You've got fifteen minutes to get ready. Aphrodisia's making us breakfast. She's not a pretty sight at the best of times, but she's a hell of a lot worse when she's cross.'

Olivia rushed to the bathroom, climbed into a tepid bath, out again in two minutes rubbing her goosepimples with a rough towel, ran upstairs, pulled on her least worn pair of jeans and a red jumper, her mother's Christmas present, forcing her feet into Maggie's suede boots as she simultaneously brushed her hair. Scent. Make-up – no, not much. Passport. Money. Sixteen minutes later she was ready. Jake was already heading for the jeep as she closed the terrace door.

Half an hour later he was strapping her into the passenger seat of the gleaming white helicopter. 'Ever been in one before?'

'No, never.'

'Life jackets under the seats.'

'You're joking!' The helicopter suddenly seemed horribly fragile. She turned: behind her were seven empty seats. She looked ahead: in front was glass – thick glass, but still just glass.

'Don't worry!' He chuckled. 'Only the good die young.'

'Thanks.'

With a roar the engine came to life, rotating the blades above them. On either side the grass was flattened by the force of air. Olivia gritted her teeth as they rose vertically from the concrete landing pad. For a moment they hovered. Then they crossed the house and the swimming pool, hewn out of the side of the mountain, and swooped off down the valley, past the tower, and out to sea. There they turned and came in over the village, climbing the far ridge of the mountain, and as they did so Olivia looked down. She could see the entire island. It was just like an emerald.

'Enjoying yourself?'

'Yes.'

'Frightened?'

'Getting used to it.' The sea stretched into a hazy horizon. 'Where's Italy?'

'Not long now.'

The heel of Italy came into sight. It was dotted with small villages, and just one large road running down the centre. A train was chugging north. Beside the railway, the road carried a car. At first the car was ahead, then the train, then the car again.

'Italian drivers!' Shouted Jake, laughing. He flicked on the radio. 'Taranto?' A stream of Italian followed, to which Jake replied, just as quickly. Then he tapped Olivia's arm. 'Italian Navy base.' He pointed to ships bathed in the morning sun.

They crossed the coast. The land was flat. A river wound its way down to the sea. Suddenly she saw mountains, straight ahead. She held her breath as they rose with the land. Higher. Higher. She closed her eyes. Jake laughed. She peered out. They were flying up a valley, the river faint below them. They crossed a town, turned slightly west and suddenly she could see the great glittering sweep of the Gulf of Salerno before her – and at that moment the radio crackled into life, 'Salerno! Salerno! Jake? Jake?' – and Jake and the radio operator joined in a joyous rendering of: '*Bella ciao, bella ciao, bella ciao, ciao, ciao.*'

He was greeted like a long lost friend by the men in the customs office. His passport was waved aside. Olivia's was given a perfunctory glance.

'Signor Jake!' A young taxi driver ran over from his yellow cab.

'Olivia, this is Alfredo – he always drives for me.'

'Hel . . . lo.' She forced herself not to flinch as Alfredo turned to her and the full horror of his appallingly burned face was revealed. 'Hello.' She held out her hand.

He smiled – and the white triangle of skin stretching from his cheekbone to his jaw grew taut and shiny.

They set off at an unbelievable speed through the suburbs of Salerno until they reached the centre. There Olivia caught glimpses of elegant palaces in narrow streets strung with washing. It looked fascinating. She wished they could slow down, but Alfredo had turned along the seafront and had his hand hard on the horn as they raced around the bay and up the long hill, away from the city. They turned the corner. Now the road clung to the mountainside, twisting between luxury villas and hotels, all closed for the winter, whilst down in the rocky coves the sea beat a relentless tattoo.

She wondered how old Jake was. Sixty? Sixty-five? It was hard to tell. He was handsome in a craggy way, distinguished with his mane of white hair, bubbling with enthusiasm as his hands tapped a tune on his big knees. She stared at the back of Alfredo's neck. From this angle she couldn't see his face, so he was just another young man driving a car. She glanced at Jake. His daughter was beautiful, his son was goodlooking, he lived in a house where every item enhanced the beauty of the next. The food he ate, the wine he drank, were simple – simply the best. From blocks of marble he created beauty. And yet, he employed Aphrodisia who was hideous beyond description and he made a point of hiring a driver whose face must make many prospective passengers turn away.

Alfredo dropped them in Amalfi, at a bar where Jake ordered coffee and brandy and Olivia bought postcards. He read a newspaper. She wrote, to her parents, to Fiona and Hugo, to Sanjiv and Lalita.

'Postcards!' he said contemptuously. 'The perfect means of communication for those who wish to say nothing. "Having a lovely time. Wish you were here – but glad you're not!".'

'Cynic!'

'No. Realist.'

They lunched in a tiny restaurant high above the town, sitting in the window so that they could see the dramatic coastline.

'It's odd that Italy is so different from Greece,' she said. 'The light is warmer, more terracotta.'

'Why is it odd? England is only twenty-one miles from France and look how different they are.'

'Yes, but somehow one expects Greece and Italy to be more alike.'

'You do. They don't.' He glanced around. At a secluded table a silky woman in her late forties was murmuring to a well-dressed man. 'Greece purifies the mind but ruins the digestion. Italy is a gourmet's paradise and a conman's heaven. Greece is one's best friend – Italy is one's mistress.'

She wanted to ask him which he preferred, but something stopped her.

The post was not delivered to the tower so every couple of days Olivia would check at the post office. On the morning after the trip to Italy she received a typed letter from Mark.

Dear Olivia,
I have today transferred funds to Vasili for the tiles. Nikos seems to think the tile merchant is short on square tiles. If that is so, you can see if he has hexagonal ones. But not those curly ones. I want the whole ground floor and terrace done, and a seating ledge added to the terrace wall. Make sure this is built first. If you have problems, ask Gwen — you must have met her by now. Tell her I want the simplicity of Jake's house. She'll understand.

I had expected to be out for Easter but have a big case on so it will be more like the end of June.

I hope you are enjoying the island.

Mark

So he didn't even think she was capable of choosing a large plain tile. His attitude took her back to the lonely room in Islington and the relentless tedium of her job with the insurance firm — a boring job, because she's been incapable of doing anything else, or believed herself to be incapable, which all came down to the same thing.

They were roasting chestnuts over the open fire, a bottle of demestica between them, when Olivia told Jake about Mark's letter, ending, 'I don't really want to involve Gwen, she's very nice but . . .'

'She's a gutsy lady but she's a bad judge of character. I'm sure they must have told you how unforgiving I was to "poor Jim".'

'Yes, they have.'

'Do you think I was wrong?'

'Tell me what happened.'

He looked at her face, flushed in the warmth and the light from the open fire. 'You remind me so much of her.'

'Her?'

'Gisella. She's part of the story — she is the story. You see, in December 1941 when the Japs attacked Pearl Harbor I was a

131

twenty-six-year-old blue-eyed American boy who believed he lived in the greatest country in the world. OK, so I hadn't done much to help it be great. By day I was working in a hardware store of New York's Upper West Side, by night I was driving cars – not always my own – but I had a dream, many dreams, and I was proud to be an American. As soon as the war was declared I signed up. I couldn't wait to go. From being nothing but a boy in a hardware store I was suddenly doing something worthwhile.' He grinned and shook his great white head. 'Girls were impressed. I met Mary Jo, and a week later we were married. One of those war whirlwinds. But why wait? There might not be a tomorrow . . . By the time I left for England she was expecting the twins.' He watched a long orange flame curl up the chimney. 'In one way I loved the war. That sounds terrible but it's true. It gave me a chance. It brought out something in me, I proved myself – to others – to myself. I longed to be a pilot. I succeeded.' He emptied the bottle of wine into their glasses. 'At the same time I hated war. I loathed the destruction. You saw Alfredo? When we landed at Salerno in 1943 I found him huddled in a ruin. He was three years old, his family was dead, and one side of his face had been destroyed by a burning rafter.'

'Did you take him back to the States?'

'Oh, no. You see, I didn't go back, not to live. No, I took him to a convent and left him with the nuns. Later, when I became successful, I paid for him to go to Switzerland to have his face remoulded. Poor Alfredo – but he was one of so many killed or injured. A friend of mine was killed at Salerno, a very close friend. I was distraught. But next time a close friend was killed, I was less distraught; I had learned to accept death. I hated that in myself, but it was necessary to survive.'

He was silent for a while, before continuing. 'When we arrived in Salerno, Mussolini had already been overthrown and Italy was on the side of the Allies. In fact,' he laughed, 'it was almost impossible to find an Italian who would admit to ever having sided with the Germans – but they had, many of them, though they prefer to forget it. Oh, I love Italians, they're so wonderfully amoral.' He lit a cigar, he didn't often smoke, just occasionally. 'The Italian partisans were growing in strength, but most were north of Rome and behind the

German lines. They were desperate for arms and medicines. The way they harrassed the Germans was brilliant but the reprisals against the civilian population were terrible. There is a village called Sant'Anna di Stazzema in the hills south of Carrara. Five hundred and sixty women and children were butchered. I know. I heard. But I could do nothing, because I was lying in a cave with my leg broken in two places.' He tapped his lame leg. 'Even now, after over thirty years, I can't forget. My hands tremble.' He held them out before him. 'The hairs on my arms stand up.' He stretched out his arms. 'And I feel sick with impotent rage.

'I had begged to be allowed to do a "drop" – to drop supplies to the partisans. I remember it was a dangerously clear night, a summer night, the summer of '44, nearly a year since Salerno but the Germans still held much of Northern Italy. We had been waiting for clouds but the partisans were desperate, so we decided to risk it. At midnight we flew across the Gothic Line, the German defence line which ran from Pisa to Rimini. The Germans saw us – hell, they'd have been blind not to – and they turned their anti-aircraft guns on us. I thought we'd got away with it. Twenty minutes later we were over the dropping zone. The partisans knew we were coming because there was this girl, Rosa, who broadcast in secret. They called it Radio Rosa. She was decorated after the war. She deserved it. When we were coming in to do a drop they'd say "*Arriva Pepe.*" Pepe was me – all Americans. I suppose it comes from Giuseppe, meaning Joseph, you know, good old American Joe. Well, my co-pilot pushed out the supplies and gave me the thumbs up, so I turned towards the sea – only I couldn't turn. The plane kept swerving to the right, towards the mountains. We were losing height. I was afraid we would go into a spin. I shouted "Jump! Jump!" He went. I saw his 'chute open. Then, as I was about to follow, the nose came up and I thought I could save the plane – we were so short of them.' He grinned. 'And I was scared to jump. I'd practised off a wall, head tucked in, knees bent, feet together – but that was from four feet, this was different. A moment later the control went and I had to go. I think I must have blacked out with fear because the next thing I remember was the plane exploding against the hillside and me floating down towards this white mountain. I remember thinking, snow, good, soft landing, no need to bend my knees.' He chuckled. 'But it wasn't snow, I realised that too late, it was marble. That's how I broke my leg.'

'Was Jim your co-pilot?'

'Oh, no, I didn't meet Jim till I came to Anataxos. My co-pilot was a guy named Ted. Poor Ted. It was months before I heard what had happened to him. He landed in Lake Massaciuccoli, by Puccini's house. I suppose he must have panicked as he hit the water because they found him still in his harness, still struggling. You see, if you land in water the 'chute settles and you're trapped unless you undo the harness and swim out. You know the really ironic part? He hated classical music and the poor bastard has to damned well go and die in Puccini's lake – and I had to damn well go and tell him to jump when I did.'

She touched his gnarled hand. 'You weren't to know.'

'Another minute and he'd have cleared the lake.'

'But he might have landed in the arms of a German patrol. It wasn't your fault that he died.'

'That's what I've been telling myself all these years.'

Aphrodisia brought them each a cheese sandwich. She said something to Jake who gave her a smile of deep affection. Then he went on with his story, as though desperate to purge himself of it. 'It's odd how when you scratch yourself the pain comes immediately but if you are badly injured it takes time. I remember lying on the side of the marble mountain, with my shattered leg underneath me, making perfectly lucid decisions. I was at the top of a cascade of marble stones, the result of dynamiting above, but further down I could see trees. I pulled in my 'chute – we'd been taught to hide them – and made a bundle of it. Then I started to crawl diagonally across the loose stones. I remember planning how I would tear up my canopy to tie a splint to my leg and wondering how long it would be before I could play baseball, when I slipped – or the stones did – and I rolled down the hillside.

'It was three days before Gisella found me, by which time I was delirious. I don't remember much of that time, except the agony of my leg and the agonising thirst made worse by the heat of the summer and the sound of trickling water. I had fallen into the undergrowth beside the River Serra which runs down from Monte Altissimo in the Apuan Alps. For a brief period in spring and autumn it is full, but that midsummer it was a vast expanse of marble river bed, too wide for me to crawl to the water in the middle. But I do recall the blinding light as the sun hit the white marble pebbles and that sometimes I thought I heard women's voices – I was told later that they collect the stones to sell. Then I remember looking up into the face of a beautiful young madonna, and I was convinced I was in heaven. I remember feeling relieved.'

Aphrodisia called to Jake. He answered, then turned to Olivia.

'She says it's raining hard and it's after midnight, so she's made up Dee's bed for you.'

Neither of them had noticed the rain till then.

Jake returned to his story. 'But I wasn't in heaven. My madonna was a fifteen-year-old Italian girl called Gisella. She lived with her mother on the other side of the valley. Her father was dead. Her brother was with the partisans. He and his friends carried me up to a cave. They set my leg as best they could, gave me blankets and a gun – and every couple of nights Gisella would bring me food and water. She would creep out of her house, down through the woods and across the river bed – that was the most dangerous part, for it was white and she was a dark figure. I fell in love with her. I never stopped loving her. I could just see the roof of their little stone house and I used to spend hours watching it, thinking of her, wondering what she was doing. My leg healed quickly but it was impossible for me to slip back through the German lines, so I spent the winter in the cave. That is when I began sculpting. I used to select a lump of marble and take it to the back of the cave where I could not be heard, and chip away.' He chuckled. 'They say that Michelangelo got his marble from Monte Altissimo. Perhaps I was handling the pieces he had rejected. What a pity that marble can tell no tales!'

They watched the fire.

'War ended the following year but I couldn't bear to leave Gisella, or the valley, or the river – or the great white marble mountain. I bought a house, Pietra Alta – the high stone – right up the valley. Houses there cost little after the war. Gisella came to live with me. Mary Jo divorced me. Dee would not speak to me till she was fourteen – till I was rich and famous, I'm afraid to say.'

'And your son?'

'Poor Billy!' He was one of the unlucky ones. Another couple of years and we'd have pulled out of Vietnam – I mean been driven out. The worst part is I knew he couldn't come back, it was the way he wrote, "I wish I didn't have to go, Dad, but someone has to show these people that the free world means business." Jesus! We'd gone into Vietnam to support a régime so corrupt that it was like shielding yourself with a rotten apple. Billy never saw a Vietcong. He was napalmed by his own side. "This tragic error" was how they called it. You know, it happens often in war, a patrol gets lost and ends up being shot at by its own side. "This tragic error" – and my kid died screaming, burning, his skin peeling off in chunks.'

'Jake, you can't blame yourself for Billy.'

'That's what Gisella said, but she felt guilty too, for taking me away from them.'

'Did you marry Gisella?'

'She refused. I was a divorced man and she a strict Catholic. She would not marry me, and yet she loved me enough to live with me and her brother did not speak to her for seven years. I think he would have killed me – he would think nothing of sticking a knife into someone – if he had thought it was I who refused marriage. Oh, I felt bad for his sake and for her family's sake, but I loved her and love is many things, including selfish. I could not give up Gisella. It took them a long time to accept our situation. She suffered for it. I suffered for her suffering.'

'Why didn't you move away, to another part of Italy?'

'Because we loved that valley. Pietra Alta became our kingdom – a kingdom for two.'

That was what Olivia wanted: to be in a kingdom for two. How could she have confused her infatuation with Gerald for the real thing?

'Gisella died five years ago,' said Jake. 'She'd never been to London or Paris. She did not want to go. I always went alone, hurrying home as soon as each exhibition was over, home to Pietra Alta – and Gisella. I haven't been back there since . . .

since she died. One day I'll go, but not yet, not till . . .' He stood up. 'It's after five. Let's make some coffee and watch the dawn.'

Out on the terrace it was dark. But in the East, beyond the village of Anataxos, there was a faint streak of light across the horizon.

Funny to think we share the same sun as Albania and all those Communist countries,' said Olivia.

'Now I remember how we began this talk. You asked me about Jim.'

'Was he a Communist?'

'Hell, no! The opposite.' He dunked a piece of bread into his milky coffee. 'For someone who did not know America in the early fifties the atmosphere which nurtured McCarthyism is inconceivable. But it happened. It began with a list of organisations, like the Communist Party, to which people applying for federal positions must not belong – or have belonged, and it spread like wildfire so that anyone who knew or had met or had spoken to a suspect was himself suspect. It was guilt by association. People were terrified, and fear makes decent men and women point the finger to save their own skins. What your generation find hard to understand is that in the thirties most intelligent young people had left-wing views. In fact there was something the matter with those who didn't. The previous decade had seen the Wall Street crash, German currency used as wallpaper, and the general strike in England. Was it surprising that many people wondered if maybe Karl Marx had a point? Oh, I don't mean that we were Communists as we think of the Soviet Union today, but more like socialists. Later, rumours of Stalin's purges slipped through, and when those rumours were proved a horrific fact most people said, if that's communism, it's not for me. They had listened, considered, and decided against. For Joe McCarthy the mere fact of them having listened was enough. They were doomed to the witch hunt.'

'Was Jim a hunter?'

'He was typical of a certain kind of self-made millionaire who is terrified that liberals will take away his fortune. He thought McCarthy hadn't gone far enough, and he was still saying so twenty years later. He said it to me. In 1952, just as my work was beginning to gain recognition, I made a short trip to New York. On my last day my passport was taken away, because some of the Italian partisans I had known – and still knew – were now members of the Communist Party. They may have been communists all along, I don't know, our concern had been to fight the Nazis. But I was suspect through guilty association. I went to gaol for six months.

'Gisella?'

'That was when her brother finally spoke to her.'

'I still don't understand why you blamed Jim.'

'It was what he stood for – had stood for. The monstrous inquisition: it turned on so many. Writers like Dashell Hammett. Many never recovered. I haven't been back to the States since the day I left prison. Why should I have been nice to poor Jim, a man who said openly that I deserved to go to gaol?' He took her by the shoulders and turned her to face him. 'I was in London last summer. Will you ever forgive Gerald Quentin?'

'Never! Never!'

It was a cold winter for Greece. The mornings were white with frost and there was snow on the mountain peak, but for Olivia those months were a time of beauty, of daytimes spent alone – walking or reading or merely thinking – of evenings with Jake, listening to him talk as they roasted chestnuts: but most of all it was a time when she regained her strength.

Once, not thinking about what she was saying, she told Jake, 'Next winter I'm going to get some thermal underwear.'

'You won't be here next winter, at least you shouldn't be.' His voice was extraordinarily gentle.

Another day, on a bright cold afternoon when she was lying on the studio couch reading a trashy novel, he said, 'Stop wriggling!'

'Why?'

'Because I say so.' He chipped at a piece of marble, looked at her, measured her length with his callipers, then chipped again.

She got up. 'Oh, Jake, you've made me look like a snake.'

'You are a snake, you're a snake waiting to strike. I shall call this piece The Snake Girl. Now, lie down and keep still.'

She watched him work. 'Are you ever afraid that people won't like what you do?'

'Yes. Every time I have an exhibition I feel sick with fear. I once had a really bad review, a critic wrote that it was a pity I didn't work in plastic because then there'd be more chance of my pieces disintegrating.'

'It didn't stop you?'

'No, but a bad review is like the death of someone close. It makes you realise you aren't immortal.'

The spring came and the island turned to a carpet of flowers – red poppies, white daisies, and yellow flowers whose name Olivia did not know. At the beginning of May the tiles finally arrived, and each morning when the workmen came to lay them she took herself off to the secluded bay, where she sunbathed nude behind a large rock.

'I approve,' said Jake, when she showed him the tiled floor. 'When does Mark arrive?'

'Not till the beginning of July.'

'In time for my party, I hope. How long's he staying?'

'A month, at least.' She paused. 'He says I can stay here all summer but . . . well . . . I'm not sure if he expects me to move out when he comes.'

'You can stay with me. Dee's coming in a fortnight. She'll be here till August but I've plenty of room. Try to like her for me, won't you. Not many people do I'm afraid. I don't think I do. I give her all she needs – probably too much – but I don't . . . like her. She's not one of us, not like you and Gisella and me – and Mark.'

13

The summer came – and so did the visitors. Not droves of package holiday makers, but people who shopped for designer suntan oil in the smart boutiques and overburdened the telephone system by calling their friends in Long Island's The Hamptons. When the ferry arrived it disgorged a Lamborghini and a Range Rover, from the terrace Olivia could hear the squeals of water skiers as they lost their balance, when she went to the secluded bay it was no longer hers alone, and at night the evening laughter drifted to her from yachts moored along the jetty. She resented the invasion and at the same time she longed to be a part of it.

One afternoon she returned from the beach to find a note: 'Dee arrived. Come to dinner. Love Jake'

'Hi, you must be Olivia.' A geometric blonde in black silk pyjamas was lounging on a sunbed.

'Yes. Hello.'

'This is Toby.'

'Hi.' He was fair, bronzed, ten years younger than Dee, and rolling a joint.

'Dad's fixing the drinks.' Dee sat up and the evening sun caught the puffiness of her eyes. She seemed to realise, because she sank back quickly and lit a cigarette.

Jake appeared, only he wasn't the usual Jake but a bluff nervous father. 'During the winter I kept saying to Olivia that I had to get on with my work so as to be free if you arrived,' he told Dee. 'Pity you can only stay a few weeks. It would do you good to spend the summer here.'

'Then you'd be as suntanned as Olivia,' said Toby, smirking. 'Tell me, Olivia, are you tanned all over?'

Jake came to the tower next morning. 'I'm sorry about last night. You did your best. I did my best. Hell!' He slumped into a deckchair.

'Did you know Toby was coming?'

'No, and I don't like him. He's using Dee. She asked me for ten thousand bucks yesterday morning. I set up a trust when she was twenty-one which gives her forty thousand dollars a year. I bought her an apartment in Manhattan so she doesn't pay rent, I pay her flight whenever she deigns to visit me. Then she tells me she's in debt and she's got to have ten thousand bucks – immediately.'

'Are you going to give it to her?'

'No.' He clenched his fists. 'No.'

'Didn't you say she's a fashion editor with a magazine? Surely she has a salary?

She was fired – though she doesn't know that I know. She's an alcoholic – that and drugs. Oh, I'm aware that life hasn't been easy for her. You see, she was a very successful model in the sixties. Vogue, Elle, Harpers. They all wanted her. She used to be so beautiful.'

'She still is.'

'Olivia, she's only thirty-three! Oh, I know it was distressing for her when her agency stopped calling and younger models took her place. That's when she started taking slimming pills. Ridiculous! She wasn't fat. But she got hooked on the pills, and now she takes them to counteract the drink.' He studied the healthy curve of Olivia's body.

'I was fat too,' she said. 'When things went wrong for me in London I stuffed myself with junk food and I'm sure if I could have got hold of slimming pills I would have taken them. I was so . . . desperate. Luckily I was also so poor I could only afford willpower.'

He smiled. 'I know I shouldn't say it, but I wish you were my daughter.'

'That's only because I'm not.'

That night Olivia wrote to her parents.

Jake was working. Dee was helping to organise the party. Olivia had nothing to do. Laughter reached her from a nearby boat. On the beach couples oiled each other's bodies. She watched them, envious. She set off for the village, and found Monica and Gwen at the beach taverna sharing a large Greek salad of tomatoes, cucumber and goat's cheese. They invited her to join them, and she sensed they felt sorry for her because Dee had ousted her from Jake's attention. After two glasses of wine she left them, and went down to the beach, stretching out on the sand to dream the sort of odd dreams which come with wine and sun. She woke with a start, hot and sticky and her mouth dry. Staggering across the burning sand to the taverna she discovered that Monica and Gwen had left, so she ordered a yogurt and some orange juice and sat down, stretching out her legs to the roasting sun.

'Some boat!' exclaimed an English voice nearby.

She looked up to see a large white yacht come out of the western sky, its curved prow slicing through the blue water. It was called the *Belladonna*. On board were some dozen people, all with sultry Italian elegance. The sun glinting off their designer sunglasses, white bikinis against brown bodies, gold bracelets tinkling, golden laughter. Somewhere a champagne bottle was being uncorked. Olivia watched and listened. The yacht turned for the harbour, and as it did she noticed a man standing alone on the forward deck, leaning on the rail. He was not particularly tall, almost stocky, with a face like a decadent angel and the dark glamour of suspect wealth.

In the early evening she went down to the village. The square was packed and the three small restaurants overflowed to the harbour wall. She wandered in and out of the boutiques, wishing she could afford to buy something new. In one she saw a ravishingly simple white shift of purest silk with nothing but thin gold chains for shoulder straps, and a pair of gold slave sandals for footwear.

'Olivia!'

She turned to find Gianni grinning inanely. 'Oh, I thought you and Monica were in London.'

'We came back for Jake's party. Monica's resting. Let me offer you a drink.'

'Oh . . . er . . . Thanks.' They sat down on the square. Over Gianni's shoulder Olivia could see dinner in progress aboard the *Belladonna*. Four elegant women raised champagne glasses in their polished mouths. Four men, casually wealthy.

'I care for Monica,' Gianni was saying. 'It's not just her money. You believe me, don't you?'

The Italian beckoned to his servant.

'. . . and of course a woman is still beautiful at fifty-five, but . . .'

The Italian murmured to his servant.

'. . . and I am still young, twenty-seven . . .'

Olivia knew he was thirty-five.

The servant lit the fire. A flame leaped up into the black-blue sky.

'. . . a young man needs a younger woman . . .'

The servant tossed the crêpe suzette.

'I never realised you were so . . . sympathetic, Olivia.'

She stood up, 'Thanks for the drink, Gianni. Goodnight.'

That night she dreamed of courtrooms – only this time it was Gerald and the Italian in the dock.

The next morning the *Belladonna* had gone.

The excitement built up as the day of Jake's party approached. A steel band arrived. More yachts docked. More yachts – but not the *Belladonna*. Mark was arriving in four days. Olivia cleaned the tower from top to bottom, hosed down the terrace, gave the red geraniums a double watering, and ordered another barrel of wine although she could hardly afford it – she only had eighty pounds to her name.

On the day before the party she went to the secluded bay. Three times Jake flew over with the chopper, collecting crates of champagne or smoked salmon and caviar, all sent out specially to Corfu. On the last trip he came in very low. She raised her hand to wave, but quickly turned it to a shield as he lowered the machine on to the sand, whipping up a whirlwind as he did so.

'That's got rid of them' he shouted, pointing at a family who had taken to using the bay. 'Damned tourists! It's our beach. Come on, we're going for a ride.'

She pulled on her tee shirt. 'Shouldn't you be organising your helpers?'

'House is full of women. Chatter. Chatter. Drives me mad. Can't wait for them all to go.'

'How's Dee?'

'Don't ask.'

She climbed into the chopper beside him.

'Want to fly her?'

'Umm . . . all right.'

'That's my girl.' He reached under the instrument panel. 'I had duel controls fitted in case Dee wanted to learn, but she didn't. It's easy. Stick forward, and you go forward and down. Stick back, and you go backwards and up. Pedals on floor.' He pointed to two pedals. 'The right one turns you to the right, and left turns you to the left. Now, I'll get her up.' The engine roared. 'Then you can take over.'

'Surely it's not allowed,' Olivia shouted over the din. 'I mean, don't I need a licence?'

'Rules are for little people – not for us.'

They went up, and out over the sea. 'Keep your eyes on the altimeter. Don't look over the side at the sea, it's misleading. Take the stick! Go on?'

Nervously Olivia pushed it forward. The nose went down and they moved forward.

'You need to counteract.' He pulled a lever between them and their altitude increased. 'Go on!' They went on, further out to sea. She was frightened but excited. 'Turn right! Right! OK, we've turned left. Why can't women ever tell the difference!'

Ahead was Anataxos – the tower and the beach. Her eyes fluttered between the island and the altimeter. It hovered around five hundred feet. She looked at the tower. How beautiful it was! Then suddenly she noticed a figure standing on the terrace, shielding his eyes against the sun as he watched them approach. Behind him, half-hidden by the terrace door was someone else whose pink skirt caught the afternoon breeze. Unaware of what she was doing Olivia pulled the stick back. They shot backwards, out to sea. Panicking, she pushed the stick forward, and a second later they were heading for the water.

144

Jake grabbed his stick as she screamed. He counteracted just as the spray hit the windscreen. 'What the devil . . .!'

'I'm . . . I'm sorry.'

He brought them down on the beach. A man was roaring down the path towards them on an enormous black shiny motorcycle. 'It's Mark!' yelled Jake. 'Hey, you young bastard, what do you mean by upsetting Olivia?'

Mark parked the bike and crossed the sand with easy strides. He looked up at Olivia, who was still in her seat. 'I didn't know you were training to be a kamikaze pilot,' he said.

She smiled, at least she tried to, opened the door, stepped out – and collapsed on the sand as her legs buckled under her.

She was up before they could reach her, wobbly inside and out, wanting to cry but determined not to.

Mark took one arm. 'You've had a bad fright.'

Jake took the other arm. 'Poor Livvi.' Her father's nickname, he'd never used it before. Again she wanted to cry.

'I'll take you home,' said Mark. 'Can you make it to the bike?'

She was about to say, 'Yes,' when she remembered the pink skirt. 'It's all right, I'm staying with Jake.'

'I see.'

She wanted to ask him what he saw, but couldn't. When they helped her back into the chopper she wanted to say she was afraid to go up again, but couldn't.

'We weren't expecting you till tomorrow,' Jake was saying to Mark.

'Oh, I went to Athens to buy the bike then drove it up here. What roads! I was nearly shaken to pieces.'

She wondered if the pink skirt had braved the uneven road, doubtless without a single word of complaint, and now she would be in the kitchen, rifling through Olivia's provisions as she knocked up a five course candlelit dinner.

Dee had left a note for Jake, 'Gone to Monica's', so he and Olivia had a quiet supper on the terrace. It was almost like old times.

'We should have asked Mark to join us,' he said.

'Oh, I'm sure he's busy.' She did not feel up to the certain glamour of the pink skirt, not tonight.'

'You don't like him?'

'No . . . yes . . . I don't know.'

'How come you borrowed his tower then?'

She gave him a tough look. 'Why shouldn't I? He offered it.'

They went to bed early, Olivia to a small guest bedroom across the corridor from Dee. She slept fitfully. She felt disconnected. The tower had been her home – it was hers no longer. Jake had been her friend – he now had other commitments. Anataxos, where she had felt safe, though sometimes bored, was no longer safe. She thought of the Italian. Tomorrow she would ask Jake about him. She thought of Mark, and imagined the pink skirt saying, 'Did you get rid of her, darling?' and Mark replying 'Yes, thank God!'

It was still dark when she was woken by Dee crying, 'I saw you with Monica you bastard!'

'You're drunk.'

'I'm not, I only had . . .'

'Only? What about those little pills, eh? "Hey, doctor, give me pills to make me young and slim again." '

'Toby, I love you. Toby, please don't go.'

A door opened. Olivia strained her ears into the silence. Then she heard her own door open and Toby slipped inside. 'Olivia!'

She didn't answer. She closed her eyes – almost – but not so tight that she could not watch him through the furriness of her lashes. His chest was bare. His jeans undone, resting on his hip bones. He moved forward. She steeled herself. He hesitated. She gripped the top sheet. He leaned down and grabbed at it.

'Get out!' she hissed.

He pulled at the sheet.

She pulled back.

The light was turned on. Dee stood in the doorway, swaying naked, her face streaked with tears, her eyes unnaturally dilated. 'Toby! Toby, no, I love you.'

'What the devil's going on?' Jake pushed past his daughter, grabbed hold of Toby and threw him across the room, shouting, 'Don't you act like this in my house, boy! If it wasn't for Dee you'd be out on your ear, in the middle of the night. Now, get out of this room – both of you!'

'I'm sorry,' he told Olivia once they were alone.

'It's not your fault.'

'As soon as the party's over he's going – even if Dee goes with him. You'd better sleep in my dressing-room.'

Olivia spent the next day helping Jake with the party. Dee spent it in bed. Toby disappeared. In the later afternoon Jake told her, 'I have to go to the village. Do you need anything from the tower? She gave him a list: her scent, make-up, shoes, clean clothes, and Maggie's pink silk scarf dress, the one with the tear which she had painstakingly though not very successfully mended.

He came back as she was drying her hair and handed her a large white box. Inside, carefully wrapped in tissue paper, was the white silk dress with the gold slave sandals.

'Oh, Jake!' She hugged him. 'Thank you. Thank you. But how did you know I wanted them?'

'Gwen.' He produced two glasses of champagne. 'Our private toast. To us!'

'To us!' The bubbles hit her nose and she giggled. 'Oh, I've been meaning to ask you. I saw this fantastic yacht called the *Belladonna* with a mysterious-looking Al Capone type on board. Is he coming tonight?'

'Yes.'

'Who is he?'

'Don't you know?'

She shook her head.

'Oh, no, don't involve me!'

'What do you mean, Jake? Why the secret? Come on, you know I can't bear ambiguous conversations.'

'Ask Mark – but stay away from Lorenzo.'

'If you don't like him how come you've invited him?'

'Because he is Gisella's brother and she would want it.' He walked away, leaving Olivia feeling foolish but no less curious.

An hour later, with the steel band playing and the first guests already arrived, Olivia walked out on to the long terrace – and made every other woman look overdressed. Her hair gleamed glossy brown in the fairy lights, the white silk of her dress enhanced the golden tan of her arms, the simple shift with shoulders held together by a whisper of gold chain gave her the appearance of a sensuous but untameable slave.

The Italian was standing at the far end of the terrace. He gave her a half-bow. 'The lady from the village square.'

147

She raised her glass to him. 'The gentleman from the *Bella-donna*.'

He moved closer. 'I'd have invited you aboard but I was afraid you might bring your aging toy boy with you.'

'Gianni is nothing to do with me.'

'You have answered my question.'

'You could have asked me outright.'

'I never do – that's the secret of my success. Let us dance.' He led her through the chattering crowd to the garden, where a wooden dance floor had been laid beneath the stars. She longed to ask him how he had acquired the trappings of wealth when Jake has spoken of Gisella coming from a little stone house across the valley. But she kept her questions to herself: she remembered Jake saying that Gisella's brother would think nothing of sticking a knife into someone. Of course Jake was exaggerating, he always did. Nevertheless, there was a brooding violence about the Italian which made her uneasy. At one point she caught sight of Mark. He was standing near the pool, looking annoyingly at home in this very unEnglish, unCity, unlegal atmosphere. His hair had been tipped blonde by the sun and his face and neck were a golden tan against the white of his open-neck shirt. If I didn't know what he was like I could almost find him very attractive, she thought. A pretty blonde in a red dress was hurrying towards Mark. The pink skirt? Over the sleek blonde head she met Mark's gaze, then she turned away and pretended to laugh at something the Italian had said.

Jake came between them as they left the dance floor. 'So you have met Olivia?'

'Yes – and she reminds me of her too.'

'I wondered if you'd see that.'

'Remind you of whom?' asked Olivia.

'Of Gisella.' Jake beckoned to Mark. 'Lorenzo, I don't think you know Mark Denholm. Mark, this is . . .'

'We haven't met, but I believe you know my cousin, Roland Culross.'

'Oh, so I do!' Lorenzo gave an unfriendly chuckle, and at that moment two of the silky Italian women claimed him. 'Safety in numbers,' he said, as they linked their arms through his.

Until the moment when Mark had mentioned Roland, Olivia had felt good. Now she didn't. Jake was talking to Gwen, Toby was dancing with Monica, Gianni was sulking in a corner, Dee had disappeared. Olivia was left with Mark. They stood side by side, silent and awkward. The word Culross hung between them. On the floor a hundred people girated to a samba, but Mark did not ask her to dance, and she felt as she had when she was in her ugly duckling stage, packed off to teenage dances in fluffy dresses, which had looked so pretty on Fiona, to stand miserably next to some boy who made it plain he would rather be with another girl or quaffing cider cup with the boys. Without a word, she walked away. When she reached the other side of the terrace, she turned to see him take to the floor with the blonde in red.

The party went on into the balmy night. The band played. Champagne flowed. Caviar dripped from slivers of brown toast. And people threw themselves into the swimming pool. In the small hours breakfast was served — buck's fizz and scrambled eggs — and, finally, as dawn broke the guests began to leave. They all agreed it was the best party Jake had ever given.

'Dee's disappeared,' he whispered to Olivia as people crowded around to thank him. 'Aphrodisia says she had a row with Toby . . . goodbye, so glad you could come . . . and she ran down the garden . . . goodnight, thank you for coming . . . Gwen thinks Toby's about to latch on to Monica . . . Jesus, I wish they would hurry up and leave.'

Olivia waited for a lull. 'I'll go and look for her.'

'Try the beach.' He forced a smile.

Mark joined them. 'Is anything wrong?'

'It's Dee. She's had a row with Toby and she's run off, probably down to the beach. Olivia's offered to . . . however many more people?'

'I'll help. Don't worry, we'll find her.'

They slipped away, down the steps and into the garden, Olivia leading him along the narrow rocky path, weaving in and out of wild, beautiful but poisonous oleanders, their pink and white flowers closed against the night. It was dark among the bushes.

'How far is it?' he asked.

'Three hundred yards.' As she turned to reply, her foot slipped and she grabbed his arm. 'Ouch! Sorry, it's these shoes. I'd take them off but I'm afraid of snakes.'

'Let me go first.' He squeezed past. 'I'll frighten them away.'

They went on quickly, in Indian file, silent, their eyes searching the rocky terrain between the bushes until they came to the beach.

'Let's check the sea first,' he said. 'You take the left side. I'll take the right. We'll meet in the middle.'

She kicked off her gold sandals and raced across the sand to where the sea pounded on the rocks below the tower. Then she came back along the water's edge, searching out to sea and up the beach. Suddenly she stopped. 'Mark! Mark!' She ran into the water towards a floating human bundle. In a moment Mark was beside her. He lifted the unconscious Dee by the shoulders and with her head lolling to one side, pulled her up the beach. There he threw her down on her back and began to work her arms as he pumped her chest. Nothing happened.

'Is she dead?'

'I don't know.' He pumped harder.

There was a gurgle – then another – and Dee rolled over, sicking up sea water and crying. 'Oh, God! Oh God! Let me die.'

'Dee.' Mark slapped her face. 'Dee, stop it.'

'I love him. I want to die. Oh . . .' She was sick again.

'Mark! Olivia.' Jake ran down the beach. 'You've found her. Is she . . .? Oh, thank God.'

They carried Dee up to the tower – it was nearer than Jake's house – and put her to bed in Olivia's room. Meanwhile, Jake called the doctor, who came immediately and without questions: after all, he had been a guest at the party. An unwise swim after a little too much alcohol would be the official explanation. He gave Dee something which made her sick again, then when she began to cry and scream hysterically he ministered a mild sedative and told them to keep her in bed for twenty-four hours. He left as the sun was rising. Olivia made coffee, and they sat on the terrace, talking quietly.

'I have to get her into a clinic,' said Jake. 'I know she has to want to be cured for it to work but I can't stand by and watch my daughter kill herself. Alcohol. Slimming pills. Coke – she's been getting it from Toby. I had him checked out and he's a well-known supplier. That's why she needed ten thousand bucks. I told Gwen to warn Monica about him.' He sighed. 'If only I could give Dee the will to live, if only I could give her a reason for living.'

'You can't, said Olivia gently. 'She has to find it for herself. You can only help – and you are helping. We'll all help.'

'Yes, we will.' Mark gave her a genuinely nice smile.

'I think we'd better watch her to make sure she doesn't try again,' said Olivia. 'I'll sleep out here on the terrace, across the doorway.'

'No you won't,' said Mark, 'I will.'

Jake stood up. 'I will. She's my daughter.'

'But I often sleep out here.' Olivia dragged a sunbed across the terrace. 'Jake, you've got the remains of your party to sort out and Mark has hardly had any sleep since arriving here.'

There was silence, then Jake hugged her. 'You are right – if you don't mind.' He looked over at Mark. 'This young lady's brought light into my life, she's a very special person.'

Olivia woke with a start. Mark was standing beside her, dressed in nothing but a pair of faded jeans. For a moment she couldn't think what was happening, then she gasped. 'Has something . . . did I miss her?'

'No, she's still asleep. I meant to take over from you earlier but I only woke up when Jake arrived. I'm sorry. I hope you haven't got too burned.' He looked down at her long brown legs and her once lovely dress, now stiff with sand and seawater and ruckled up about her thighs. 'Would you like some orange juice?'

'Yes. Thanks. What time is it?'

'Six. We've been asleep for nearly twelve hours.' He sat down on the recently built terrace ledge, laying his arms out on either side along the top of the wall, stretching his legs out before him, his feet casually crossed at the ankles. 'Jake's gone to buy some steaks and salads. We thought we'd eat here this evening – unless you're busy.'

'That would be lovely.' Where on earth did he think she might be going!

'I haven't told you how much I like what you've done to the tower.'

'There hasn't been much time.'

'I'm very grateful.'

'It was kind of you to let me stay here.'

'That sounds like Jake's jeep. Shall we go for a swim when he arrives?'

They went down to the beach as the sun dipped into the sea. The sand was warm and the air heavy with that mixture of earth and salt and lemons so typical of Greece. At the water's edge they stopped. Olivia had pulled on her white bikini bottom under her dress but not the top; she'd forgotten it. She lifted the hem of her dress, then hesitated. She who thought nothing of sunbathing completely naked in front of strangers suddenly felt embarrassed to undress before this one man.

'Are you going to swim in your dress?' he asked with amusement and – yes, there was understanding.

'I . . . er . . . left my sandals on the beach last night. I'm going to find them.'

By the time she returned, her gold sandals in hand, Mark was swimming far out to sea. She undressed and plunged into the water, swimming out, but not to where Mark trod water to the other side. Nevertheless, she was intensely aware of him, of his shoulders glistening in the water and his wet hair catching the sun. She intended to be dressed by the time he returned to the shore, but the water was so wonderfully refreshing that she missed her chance and he reached the beach first, so she was obliged to walk straight out of the sea, to where he stood almost on top of her dress. It would have been ridiculous to cover her breasts with her hands. She made a supreme effort to appear casual.

Jake was cooking three huge steaks on the barbecue. On the table was a freshly chopped salad in a wooden bowl, a loaf of bread, cheese, and two bottles of white wine, so cold that condensation dripped down their sides. He looked up as Mark and Olivia appeared, smiled, and went on with the cooking.

'How's Dee?' asked Olivia.

'Asleep. I gave her a glass of milk but she only drank half. Supper's in ten minutes. Time for a quick shower.'

Olivia showered first. When she came out, wrapped in a towel, Mark was waiting. He stepped aside to let her pass. She stepped in the same direction. They stepped back, laughed sheepishly, then he waited till she passed.

Up in her room she dressed with care whilst telling herself that she wasn't. Didn't she often wear her white jeans and a tight white tee shirt? Didn't lots of people wear gold chains around their necks? She touched her lips with a pinkish gloss, purely to stop them drying, and patted some scent on her wrists and behind her ears, such a waste to let it evaporate! Then she looked at herself in the mirror and giggled, and wondered if there was any action for which she could not, with a bit of imagination, find a perfectly valid excuse.

They sat on the terrace, the paraffin lamps throwing warm shadows across their faces. Jake and Mark did most of the talking. Olivia listened. She looked up at the white tower cut into the dark blue sky, she heard the cicadas rubbing their legs together, that sound of Mediterranean nights which is impossible to describe. A frog croaked. An owl hooted. The air was warm and dark around them. She was so tired that she could barely keep her eyes open, and yet she did not want to go to bed because she did not want to break the spell.

Eventually Jake stood up. 'Can you cope with Dee for another night? I really hate to impose on you, Mark, but . . .'

'It's no imposition. Only tonight,' he leaned across and ruffled Olivia's sleepy head, 'I insist on sleeping downstairs.'

Jake left them to the intimacy of the terrace.

'More coffee?' Mark picked up the jug.

'Thanks. Half a cup.'

'Poor Jake.'

'He blames himself.'

'Dee's mother drank, he told me so today, it's what killed her in the end. Mind you, it's not easy for a woman on her own to bring up children. What kept my mother going was the loving memory of my father – and her intense hatred of the Culross family.'

He'd said Culross so casually but for Olivia it hung between them, an unmentionable subject, in the same way as it had hung between Fiona and herself in the garden at Dorking. She sat rigidly on the edge of her sun-lounger and as soon as she had drunk her coffee she went to bed – to Mark's room, where his possessions were scattered in friendly chaos and his sheets had a fresh masculine smell which made her aware of her own body as she lay between them, almost as though it were no part of her but an extraneous thing with a will and confusions of its own.

They had breakfast on the terrace. Coffee and croissants.

'It's the white light of Greece which I remember when I'm in England,' he said.

'Yes, and the smell.'

'Earth and lemons.'

'With a touch of salt.' They smiled at each other.

She broke off by saying, 'I'd better go and see if Dee wants anything.'

Olivia gave Dee a glass of milk and some toast. She ate slowly, staring at her hands, then fell asleep again.

When Olivia came down, Mark said, 'We seem to have become surrogate parents. Would you like the last croissant, Mummy?'

'No, you have it Daddy dear.'

He laughed, it was the first time she'd made him laugh. 'We'll share it.' He tore it in two and handed her one half. 'When I was young I longed to dunk things in my hot milk but my mother wouldn't let me. Now when I do it I seem to hear her voice saying, "Mark, eat properly! What would your father say!" '

When Jake arrived they went down to the beach, just the two of them. This time Olivia was even more aware of Mark. Whilst he swam she stretched out between the rocks, her feet in a rock pool, her eyes closed. Suddenly cold water hit her sizzling stomach and she squealed.

'I couldn't resist it.'

'Beast!' She scooped up a handful of sand and threw it at him.

He dodged, and lay down a few yards from her, picked up a book and began to read. She lay on her back, the now warm water sliding in rivulets down her oiled stomach. Through the fuzz of her eyelashes she studied him, telling herself that it was their situation — the tower, the beach, the heat.

He turned and caught her watching him. He closed his book.

She jumped up. 'I'm . . . going for a swim.' She was running away but she was afraid of having pain dished out to her at some vulnerable moment.

When she came back Mark had gone.

Again Jake cooked supper and again they sat on the terrace with the night so thick around them it felt like a wall of blackness. If Olivia had had to face Mark alone that evening she would have retreated into her shell, but with Jake between them, joking and laughing, the closeness returned.

'Hi!' Dee stood in the doorway, dishevelled, pale and pathetic.

They jumped up to make room for her, offering her food which she declined. 'I'm so sorry.' She flopped down into Olivia's chair, the one in the middle. 'I'm so . . .' she leaned towards Mark and burst into tears.

He put a comforting arm around her.

He has to, thought Olivia.

'You've been so kind.' Dee turned her tearstained face to him. 'I'm sorry . . . I didn't mean to drown myself. You believe me, don't you Mark? I was just upset about Toby. Oh, how could he?' She started to cry again, then stopped suddenly. 'But I don't care. He's no good for me, and I'm not going to let a bastard like that finish me off. I'm going to get better. Mark . . . Dad . . . I'm going to stop drinking. I can, I know I can.'

'Of course you can,' said Mark gently.

'You'll help me, won't you?'

'Of course I will.'

Olivia felt sick – with jealousy and with herself for being jealous, but she could not help comparing Mark with Dee to Mark in the High Court. There had been no consoling arm for Olivia.

Jake stood up. 'It's very late and I must go to bed . . . and you should too, Dee.'

Fresh tears. 'I can't come back yet, Dad, not till Toby . . .'

'I threw him out. He's left the island.'

'Let me stay here one more night. I feel so peaceful in that little room. You don't mind going with Dad, do you, Olivia?'

What could she say but, 'Of course not, Dee.'

Before she fell asleep she remembered that she still did not know the identity of the pink skirt but somehow it didn't matter any more: now there was Dee. Then she told herself, crossly, I'm not after Mark, it's just that . . . but she couldn't quite work out what.

Dee's powers of recovery were remarkable. One day she was a pale sobbing wreck, the next she was sparkling over dinner at a harbourside restaurant – and she sparkled for Mark, sitting next to him, touching his arm, giving him her peculiarly vulnerable smile one moment and her New York model profile the next. Olivia watched in silence.

She stayed away from the tower for two whole days. If Mark and Dee were lovers she did not want to know, and she certainly did not want to catch them making love. Eventually lack of clean clothes forced her to return. She found Jake, Dee and Gwen on the terrace. Mark was nowhere to be seen.

'I'm determined to give up drink,' Dee was saying. 'Mark says they have really good clinics in England . . . Oh, hi, Olivia . . . so I'll check into one of them – one not far from London so we can see each other.'

Olivia went inside, had a cooling shower and dressed in one of Maggie's more feminine outfits, a pale apricot cotton skirt with a short sleeved shirt which knotted at the waist, leaving her stomach bare. In the kitchen she helped herself to some orange juice, drinking it there, her bare feet cool on the tiled floor. From the terrace came the murmur of voices, from the hillside the wonderfully hideous braying of a donkey.

Mark appeared on the stairs. 'You're back.'

'Yes.'

'You look very pretty.'

'Thank you.'

'I wanted to ask you something.'

'Yes?' She waited for him to say 'Would you mind staying up at Jake's until . . .'

'Are you and . . .'

'Mark!' Dee rushed in. 'Dad says you're going out tonight. Why didn't you tell me?'

'I'm going to have dinner with a friend.'

'Can I come?'

Olivia slipped away. She went up to her room. On the terrace Mark was offering Gwen a lift on his motorbike. She watched them leave. A few minutes later a protesting voice rose from below. 'But I want to stay here, Dad. Mark said he'd

156

help me. I need help, Dad. You don't want me to start drinking again, do you?'

'I don't, but it's not fair on Mark.'

'What do you mean "not fair"?'

'I mean that he wants his freedom. He's a young man on holiday and . . .'

'He likes me. He said he did. If you make me leave I'll start drinking again. I might kill myself – and it will be all your fault.'

Olivia felt sick at heart for Jake. She fully expected him to back down, but he answered gently and firmly, 'You're wrong. It will be your own fault – and it will show Mark that you don't really want to be cured.'

Next morning Dee sulked, Jake worked and Olivia escaped to the beach. Some time later she heard the roar of Mark's bike as he headed for town. Not long afterwards it roared back – but he did not stop where the track to the tower turned off the road, he came on down to the beach and parked the machine under a tree. Olivia saw him coming, striding across the sand, barechested in his jeans – but she pretended not to until his shadow fell across her.

'I didn't finish asking my question,' he said.

'Yes?'

'Are you and Jake lovers?'

'No.'

'I didn't think so.'

'Then why ask me?'

'I needed to be sure.' He picked up her shorts and her bikini and handed them to her. 'Get dressed.'

'Why?'

'Because I want you to . . . please.'

She slipped on her bikini bottom, then the top, then pulled on her shorts. He took her hand and led her up the beach, to the shiny black motorbike.

'Where are we going?' she asked, as he was about to kick start the machine.

He turned and looked at her, at her face, into her eyes. 'I'm going to make love to you.' His foot came down, the engine sprang into life, his powerful hands twisting, revving.

She swallowed, hesitated, then swung her bare legs over the

157

seat behind him, linking her arms around his waist, her knees tucked under his thighs, her chest bare except for her bikini top, touching his bare back — and they roared up the path, away from the beach and the tower and the town and the people.

14

They rode towards the sun, to where the road ended and beyond, skidding over the rough track, stones flying beneath the tyres. To their left was the sea, to their right olive trees clinging to the hillside. Then the olives gave way to bare rocky mountain and the beach to steep rocky cliffs. They stopped just short of a small whitewashed Byzantine church perched above the glittering sea. The island went no further. This was the western tip of the emerald.

He took her hand and led her towards the church, saying, 'Did you know that each of these little churches dotted around the island is named after a saint and that the priest only comes on that saint's day. During the rest of the year the people look after it. They bring flowers, wild flowers.' He opened the ancient wooden door. A golden cross stood on a rough altar and an offering of wild flowers lay by it, drooping in the heat of the airless interior. Olivia hung back. Surely he didn't mean to make love to her in a church! She wasn't religious, well . . . not very . . . at least, she didn't go to church although she did believe in God, or she thought she did – though recently she'd wondered if she'd been misled – but that did not stop her from feeling horrified at the idea of making love in a church.

To her relief they left the church and went beyond the low church wall to a niche in the cliff, a large flat rock shaped like an enormous chair looking out over the sea. He sat down. She sat down.

'I love this place.' He leaned back, stretching out his legs, his fingers loosely entwined with Olivia's.

'I've never been this far before.' She leaned back beside him and wondered with whom he had come.

'No?' He squeezed her hand. 'You seem to have got to know everyone and every place on Anataxos.'

'It's a small island.'

'Did you enjoy being here in the winter?'

'Yes – but one can't lie on a beach forever.'

'That's true.' He linked his arm over her bare leg.

She waited. Nothing happened. They watched the sun turn red and dip into the sea. Still nothing happened. Olivia tried not to look at Mark in case he read the query in her eyes. She tried not to think about him . . . about *it* . . . but how could she do otherwise? His arm was warm against her leg, his hand strong, his fingers involved with hers – and he had said they were going to make love. He'd brought her to this remote, romantic though uncomfortable spot – and now nothing. She watched the sea. Perhaps he'd changed his mind. Perhaps he didn't fancy her after all.

Mark was talking about Jake. 'I admire him probably more than I've ever admired anyone.'

This was her lead in. 'Why did you ask if he and I were lovers?'

He ran his thumb down the soft inside of her leg. 'Dee said you were. I didn't believe her at first but when you went off so happily to spend the night at his house and the next day you were very detached, I thought maybe she was right. I had to be sure.' He shrugged, smiled, and kissed her on the cheek, then he looked at his watch. 'I'm starving. Vasili's cousin opened a new restaurant on the other side of town. Let's try it.' He helped her to her feet – but nothing else.

Olivia was convinced he would make a move as soon as they reached the tower, and on the journey back she held him tight, tighter than necessary, to encourage him without openly encouraging him just in case he'd changed his mind or she'd misheard him or whatever else could be the reason.

'You have first shower,' he said.

She used her sweetest smelling soap, scrubbed herself all over, washed her hair and rubbed it half dry, and came out wrapped seductively in a towel, expecting to find Mark waiting – but he wasn't. So she scampered upstairs, she had no intention of being caught hanging around like an open invitation.

160

Mark had liked the apricot skirt so she wore that, with her prettiest white lace knickers and no bra, tying the matching top so tightly under her breasts that she exposed maximum cleavage and the full length of her bare brown stomach. Then she brushed her hair, glossed her lips, and slopped enough scent over her wrists and chest to make her intentions obvious to anyone within a radius of fifty yards.

By the time she came downstairs Mark was showered and dressed and on the terrace. Walking towards him Olivia could not imagine how she had not been immediately attracted to him. How was it possible that she had been so blind? Then she remembered the pink skirt, and all those self-protective warnings were amplified in her mind . . . don't risk it . . . he'll only hurt you . . . what about tomorrow . . . so that by the time she reached him her smile was wary and when he took her hand she almost flinched. But two hours later, over a lingering dinner table and Mark's gravelly voice, self-protection took a back seat. She wanted him. She couldn't wait to touch him. To feel him. To be a part of him. She tried not to think about the tomorrows.

'I came to Anataxos by chance,' he was saying. 'I was with a friend, a fellow student from the bar, and we'd been backpacking round the islands. We were on our way home when we stopped off in Corfu and someone mentioned Anataxos. So we caught the next ferry over and slept on the beach – on our beach. Nowadays there'd be an uproar but in those days there were no smart boutiques or smart visitors. I remember waking up very early and seeing the tower. I climbed up to it. There was no terrace, no windows, the whole place was in a terrible state – but I decided then that one day it would be mine.'

'Did you buy it immediately?'

'Hardly. I was an impoverished student struggling on a grant. It took me nine years. Well, eight years to save the money and a further year to acquire it. Things move slowly in Greece.

She stretched out her legs so that they could not help but touch his. He put his hand on her knee and gently ran his fingers up and down the inside, down a little, up a little – but not high, not where Olivia longed for him to touch her. Then he patted her on the leg and pulled her skirt down to cover her knees – and all this without a flicker in his hooded eyes. She could have kicked him. Somehow he'd turned the tables so that she was chasing and he was merely responding – or not. She was furious. Had he said he wanted to make love to her just to tease – to see if she would go with him, and her having gone was enough, because now he knew he could have had her if he'd wanted to? Well, he could stuff it as far as she was concerned.

Olivia was pointedly detached when they returned to the tower, saying that she did not want coffee or brandy – not that he suggested either. 'I'm going to bed,' she told him. 'Thank you *so* much for a *delicious* dinner.' There was no harm in ladling on the saccharine.

He yawned and stretched. 'It was my pleasure. Goodnight.' And he started up the stairs ahead of her.

She wasn't going to hang around looking spare, on the other hand she had no intention of pounding eagerly at his heels, so she waited till he was nearly at the first floor, picked up a book as though intending to read, and followed. When she reached the first floor he was already with one foot on the next flight. She gave him a formal smile and firmly opened her bedroom door.

Mark took two steps backwards, stretched out his arm behind him and clamped it round her wrist. 'Where are you going?'

'To bed.'

He studied her face. She was thinking of the pink skirt and the tomorrows. Releasing her, he carried on up the stairs.

Olivia went into her room and closed the door. He obviously wasn't that interested, she thought, so I'm glad I didn't . . . give in to him. Give in to him! I sound like mother: 'a man doesn't respect a woman who gives in to him because he'll never believe she doesn't do it with everyone else. She stared at the bed. It wouldn't have been giving in. She wanted him.

'Olivia!'

She shot out of her room. 'Yes?'

He was on the landing. 'Would you like to see my etchings?'

She shook her head.

'What about my collection of butterflies?'

She giggled. 'No thank you.'

'You don't know what you're missing.'

She shook her head again. This was not at all what she had imagined. Simon had been fumbling and intense, Gerald had been brutal – but Mark? She could not make him out.

'Oh, well, rejected again,' He walked up stairs, opened his bedroom door, shut it – then there was silence.

Olivia stood in the doorway to her room listening. She thought of the care she had taken with her appearance, the anticipation, the excitement – and for what? To lie in her solitary bed wishing she were one floor up but afraid to mount the stairs because Gerald had left her a legacy of fear of rejection. But Gerald's not going to get the better of me! She straightened her shoulders – and walked up the stairs, quickly before she lost her nerve.

Mark was leaning against the outer doorpost. Without a word he came down, took her hand, and led her into his room, turning to her in the warm light of the bedside lamp, pulling her gently to him, his arms linked behind her neck so that she could not escape even if she wanted to. 'You're like the deer in Richmond Park,' he said, looking into her button brown eyes. 'You only approach if one pretends one isn't interested.'

'I came with you on the bike.'

'And backed off every time I made a move in your direction.' His fingers entwined in her hair. A tremor ran through her body. She moved against him, the bare length of her stomach against his belt, her legs pressed to him, feeling him, how much he wanted her, as his mouth came down on hers.

'You're not going to escape again,' he murmured.

'Do you think I want to.' She ran her hands up and down his back.

He did not answer. He undressed her slowly – the blouse – the skirt – the wisp of white lace. She undressed him, her hands trembling on the buckle of his belt. His mouth was on her face and neck, his arms around her. She felt herself melting into him. She pulled him down to her as they fell back naked on the bed. She wanted him to pierce her, to hurt her – and yet not to hurt her. He took her, at first gently, holding back so that she was always one step ahead, wanting more . . . He titillated so that her skin shivered and her little white teeth bit into his neck. He pushed her hands above her head, holding them there, looking down into her eyes as he made love to her – and when he increased his rhythm she went with him, wanting him to penetrate every corner of her body, digging her finger-nails into his back, as he ground her into the bed, crying out but unaware of doing so as his body broke in spasms. But she was aware of one thing – acutely: neither with Simon nor with Gerald – especially with Gerald – had it ever been like this. With them she had been left wanting.

He was breathing quietly into her neck, stroking her arm. 'You can't go back to Richmond Park now,' he said, 'the other deer wouldn't want you.'

She nuzzled up to him. 'They'd say I was a traitor to the herd allowing myself to be seduced by a human.'

He smoothed her hair back from her face. 'I might have to fight the stag for you.'

'Antlers at dawn!'

He chuckled and rolled over on his back, drawing her with him so that her head nestled on his chest. 'You didn't really think I was going to make love to you in the church, did you?'

'Well, I . . .'

They made love again – and again she cried out, clinging to him, enveloped by him. Afterwards he slept, his arms loosely about her shoulders, but the heat of the summer night and of their love kept Olivia awake. Her last thought was that she had reached twenty-eight before really knowing what it was all about – then she too fell asleep.

Jake arrived as they were having a late breakfast. He made no comment. Olivia was glad. But when Mark went to the village to telephone London, he said, 'I'm pleased for you both.'

'Is it that . . . obvious?'

'Yes. You're pink. No, don't glare at me, it's beautiful!'

'How is Dee?'

'Drinking.'

'It's not your fault!' She touched his hand.

'Isn't it?'

Later that day Mark said, 'Let's go to the church again, you didn't appreciate it yesterday.'

'That's because I was living in dread of rape and pillage.'

'Dread?'

'Well . . . sort of dread.'

He hugged her and kissed the tip of her nose, saying, 'You are funny, that's one of the things I like best about you,' and she longed to tell him that no other man had made her feel like this but she didn't, she was afraid of making him feel possessed.

For three days they were enveloped in themselves, seeing no one, not even Jake. On the fourth evening they went to Vasili's cousin's restaurant and sat where they had sat before, at a secluded table at the far corner of the terrace; only it wasn't as before, because now they were together. They had finished their meal and were looking down on the harbour, smiling, touching, laughing at nothing in particular, when Jake's white jeep roared up the narrow street, sending the people leaping for their lives, and crashed into the restaurant steps. Dee got out. She was wearing the pink skirt.

'Oh, God!' exclaimed Mark.

Oh, no, thought Olivia as Dee staggered up the steps, screaming, 'Mark! Mark! Where are you, you bastard?'

The restaurant fell silent. Dee swayed. Olivia looked at the pink skirt but that was unimportant now — what did matter was her sickening apprehension.

Mark tossed his wallet at her with a quick, 'Settle up!' and hurried to Dee's side, scooping her up in his arms and carrying her down the steps as if she were a rag doll. Behind him, Olivia paid the bill. In the street Dee was crying, 'I want you, you like me, you said you did. She doesn't want you, she's with Dad.' Somehow he managed to open the jeep's buckled door and push Dee into the passenger seat. Then she caught sight of Olivia. 'Go away!' she screamed, hurling her cigarettes and lighter at Olivia, who jumped back, shaken and scarlet.

'Get into the restaurant!' snapped Mark. 'Can't you see you're making her worse?'

She slunk back. A man handed her Dee's lighter and cigarettes. She put them in her pocket, and tried not to think that this had been inevitable — that her tomorrow had come.

Dee was crying quietly now, her head on the dashboard, Mark's hand clutched against her face. 'Poor butterfly,' he straightened out her skirt, 'you have been caught in a storm.'

Olivia looked away. She was enraged by his compassion, and with herself for being jealous of a washed-out woman in a pink skirt.

'I'll have to drive her home,' he said.

'Of course.'

'What's the matter?'

'Nothing.' She nearly added, 'I enjoy walking home, alone, in the dark,' but she didn't. She watched as he reversed the jeep off the steps.

He had not gone ten yards before Jake arrived on the back of Nikos's scooter. 'Vasili sent for me. Is Dee all right? She hasn't injured anyone? Oh, thank God for that! She'd been drinking all day but I thought she'd fallen asleep, then I heard the jeep start up.' He climbed in behind the steering wheel, declining Mark's offer of further help. 'No, Aphrodisia will help me. She's used to Dee. But thanks again. I'm so grateful to you . . . both.' He gave Olivia an understanding smile.

'I'm going back to the tower,' Mark told Olivia as Jake drove off. He began to walk down the narrow street towards the motorbike, which was parked in the square.

'May I have a lift – or do I walk?'

'If you sulk, you walk.'

'I am not sulking!'

He kicked the bike into life. 'Then why the long face?'

'Because I have feelings.' She swung her leg over the back-seat, 'and if you showed me one iota of the understanding you lavish on Dee . . .'

They roared along the seafront. 'Why should I be sympathetic towards you?'

'Because . . .' The wind brought tears to her eyes. '. . . Because I've had just as hard a time as she has.'

They skidded to a halt in a shower of stones. 'When?'

'When! What do you think it was like for me when I was booted out of Culross and hounded by the press, when I lost my house and couldn't get a decent job.' She pummelled his back with her clenched fists. 'When nobody wanted me. Don't I deserve sympathy?'

'No.' He pushed her with his arm, harder than he intended, and she toppled backwards off the bike into the side of the road.

She was up in a flash, her arm raised. 'Don't you push me into the gutter!'

He parried her arm. 'From the way you regard yourself you wouldn't have far to fall.'

'If that's true, it's you, the Culrosses, who've put me there.'

'Don't accuse me,' he swung off the bike and made a grab for her, 'I'm nothing to do with Culross.'

She jumped back, on the beach. 'Of course *you* are the one who struggled up *from* the gutter. No wonder you want to push the rest of us into it.'

He came towards her. 'And you are the snotty little girl who had every opportunity in life and threw it all away over some dissolute drunken penpusher.'

She held her ground. 'Obviously I'm a bad judge of lovers.'

'Don't couple me with that . . .'

'Penpusher? And what are you? A wordpusher! A defender of causes you don't believe in, an accuser of persons whose fate you don't give a damn about. What was it you told me? That it was just part of the job? But I don't expect you'll need a job for much longer because you'll talk your way into Culross and take what old Sir Larry would have given you and more – I suppose he couldn't meet your price. Yes, and I expect you'll even change your name to Culross.'

'At least I'm not an unemployable banker who couldn't keep her trap shut.'

'You bastard! That hurt!'

'It was meant to.'

She was speechless that he had purposefully set out to wound her in the way he knew would hurt most. She turned and walked away, down the beach. But Mark came after her, caught her, pushed her down on to the sand. 'You vicious hellcat, don't you walk off like that! How dare you suggest I'd sell myself to Culross. If you want a roof over your head tonight, you'd better apologise.'

'I'd rather sleep on the beach.'

'Sleep on the beach then!'

'I will! I'd prefer to sleep anywhere than in your bed.'

He looked at her, then he turned and walked back to the bike, mounted it, and headed for the tower, the headlight weaving in and out of the trees as he rode along the headland.

Then the light went out. A moment later Mark appeared on the terrace. He marched into the house, without once looking down at the beach, and slammed the door so hard that the sound echoed right across the bay.

Olivia walked up the beach and along the road to the secluded bay – if she were going to sleep in the open, she preferred to do so in her special place, and there was no way, absolutely no way, that she was going back to the tower. She kicked at the sand. To think that she had clung to him in moments of ecstasy. She hurled a pebble into the sea. To think that she had allowed him to invade her body. She settled down on her favourite rock. Heaven knows why she'd been so afraid of losing him.

By midnight the temperature had dropped. By two it was freezing. The damp crept right through her thin cotton tee shirt. She huddled against the rock, trying not to think of Mark stretched out on their soft warm bed, damn him! She dug in her pocket and found Dee's cigarettes and lighter, lit one, and smoked it fiercely. Other people found solace in nicotine, so why shouldn't she? The first drag made her cough but she persevered, finished the cigarette, and lit another – and another, curled up on the rock, puffing furiously.

She must have fallen asleep because she did not hear Mark approach until he was almost on top of her. Then she sat up sharply and hissed, 'Go away!'

'No, I won't.' He pulled her to her feet and kissed her hard on the mouth.

She knew she was meant to kick him where it hurts but she didn't, she clung to him, tears rolling down her cheeks, so glad that he had come for her. He took her face in his hands and wiped away her tears. 'Tomorrow I will tell you exactly why I was so angry and you can tell me exactly why you were so angry, but now I think we should both say we're sorry.' Against her lips he whispered, 'I'm sorry,' and simultaneously she replied, 'I'm sorry.'

'Oh, look,' he said, hugging her, 'some disgusting neurotic person has been sitting on the beach smoking cigarettes.'

'My goodness!' exclaimed Olivia, as they crossed the terrace and entered the tower. 'We've had an intruder. He's drunk half a bottle of brandy. How revolting.'

Later, as Olivia was drifting off into a blissful warm sleep Mark said, 'The only thing I really hate about your past is what that man did to your confidence. You're frightened to take a chance on us in case it doesn't work.'

'Is that why you aren't sympathetic to me?'

'But I am to Dee? No, it's because she's a loser and you're not, and it you had more faith in yourself you'd see that.'

'I used to have faith.'

'Then get it back.' He ruffled her hair. 'You didn't really imagine I was interested in Dee, did you? I may have odd taste . . .' He ran his hand down her bare back.

'Thanks.'

'Umm, I thought you said you'd rather sleep anywhere than in my bed.'

'I'm not asleep.'

'You should be. Olivia! Stop it! Take your hands off my body, it's the only one I've got . . .'

Morning brought the realisation that Mark was exactly half way through his holiday. From now on the days would descend into the moment when he left.

'I've got a headache.'

'I've got a sore throat.'

'Nicotine addict!'

'Drunkard!'

'If I drank like Dee I'd be dead within a week.'

'If I smoked like Dee I'd lose my voice.'

'Oh, for a silent woman . . . have another cigarette.'

'Beast . . . Mark? Go away! I thought you said you'd got a headache.'

'Not *that* sort of headache!'

They stayed in bed until the late afternoon and when they finally went downstairs there was a note from Jake on the table:

Am taking Dee to Geneva. Gwen has heard of a clinic there so keep your fingers crossed. Will be back in a couple of days once Dee is settled. Come to dinner on Thursday. Just us – at last!

Jake.

Olivia was glad for Jake, glad for Dee – and glad for herself because although she loved Jake she wanted Mark entirely to herself.

That evening he talked about his mother, saying, 'She loved my father and he loved her, but that wasn't good enough for Sir Larry because my mother was from a very ordinary background. She was born in Yorkshire but when her mother died and her father remarried, they came south. He bought a greengrocer's in Streatham. It doesn't exist now, it was bombed during the war. My mother was very pretty and loved dancing. With a friend she applied for a job as a chorus girl with a touring company. They were accepted. But the night before they were due to leave, the other girl lost her nerve – so mother went on her own. She had only been with the company for two months when my father saw her on the stage. I believe he went straight round to the dressing-rooms and pushed his way through all the half-naked ladies till he found her.'

'How romantic!'

'Yes, it was – until he introduced her to his family. Sir Larry took one look at my mother and demanded, in front of her. "Why bother to marry her?" But my mother had that lower middle-class conservatism, she would not have become my father's lover without a ring on her finger, she was extraordinarily puritanical, that's why she was so hurt when the Culrosses treated her like a whore.'

'How old were you when your father was killed?'

'Only two months. He was in the Air Force and he flew off on a mission and never came back. Missing Presumed Dead. Within a year the war ended. What a waste!'

She laid her hand on his and thought of her own childhood in the safe cocoon of a country town and her birthday parties when nice little girls had come to tea and remembered to say thank you.

Mark went on, 'After he was killed my mother took me to see old Sir Larry. I don't remember, of course, but she told me later that he said, "Why should I support a child which probably isn't my grandson?" That's what hurt her most. Not the money. The suggestion that she'd had other lovers. But I grew up to look just like my father, so they say.'

'Where did you live as a child?'

'We went back to Yorkshire, to Leeds where she had an old aunt, and lived with her. My mother worked in a shop by day and in a cinema most evenings. She supported all three of us. It must have been desperate for her, but she never complained. I remember that I longed for a bicycle and she promised me one if I won a scholarship to Leeds Grammar School – she wouldn't have been able to afford the fees if I hadn't. Well, I got the scholarship, and the bike, but what I did not know till after she died and I found the ticket was that she had pawned her engagement ring to buy the bike.'

'And never managed to retrieve it?'

'No. I went to the address on the ticket but the shop had closed down.' He paused. 'It was because my mother went through such hell that I was so angry last night. No money on earth could make me change my name to Culross.'

She took his hand in hers. 'I know – but I wanted to hurt you.'

'As I hurt you?'

'Yes.'

'When we're in England I'll show you some photographs of my mother and father if you're interested.'

'I'd love to see them.' She smiled, but the soft brilliance of her smile was not just because he was sharing his past with her, it was because for the first time he had spoken of them in England, together, as a couple.

Jake came back. They heard the chopper fly over as they were making love and in the evening they went to his house.

'I've settled her into the clinic,' he told them, grey with fatigue and worry. 'I thought she was going to back out at the last moment but she didn't. Gwen's stayed on in Geneva for a few days. She's a fine woman, a damned fine woman, I don't know how I'd have got Dee on the plane without her.' He shouted to Aphrodisia who appeared with two bottles of musky Anataxos wine. 'Come on, let's sit on the terrace and watch the sun go down. Hell, it is good to have the place to myself again.'

Halfway through dinner Mark said, 'I want to ask you about Lorenzo.'

Jake tore off a hunk of bread. 'I've been waiting for that.'

'Do you mind?'

'I can't blame you.'

171

'How did he make his money?'

'At first through guns left behind by the Germans. He found a cache of them in the hills.'

'Who did he sell them to?'

'To the Americans as they broke through the Gothic Line. Do you know how many guys lose their weapons when fighting? Hundreds. Thousands. Lorenzo offered them German guns, a few at a time. They tried to pay him in food but he would say, "Two dollar," so they haggled and gave him a buck. Nothing to them, but to a boy with over a thousand weapons it meant big money. And he made contacts. He let them know there were more weapons and when some of those tough American soldiers found that they weren't suited to the nine-to-five and TV dinners, and they went off to fight as mercenaries in other people's wars, they remembered Lorenzo. By that time he had even more,' Jake chuckled, 'because he'd also collected up weapons left behind by the Americans.'

'Did Gisella know what he was up to?' asked Mark.

'I tried to keep the truth about him from her but it was impossible, so she ended up believing what she wanted to. They were twins. They adored each other.' Jake shook his great white head. 'You should have seen him when I first did, a pistol-packing fifteen-year-old with an overdose of chutzpah harrassing the German patrols, shooting at them with their own guns, then nipping through the Gothic Line to flog stuff to the Americans. He was totally fearless. How could he settle down in a small mountain village after that? He couldn't, and I ask myself whether I would have been any different.'

He looked at Mark. 'Have you told Olivia, because if you don't, I will.'

'Told me what?'

'Not yet,' said Mark, 'but I was intending to.'

'Told me what, Mark?'

'That Lorenzo is the owner of Linea Pan Liguria and that Roland met him here three years ago.'

'At one of my parties,' added Jake.

'You mean . . .' She rose, then she sat down again. 'But, of course, I never knew the other's name because Roland dealt with him. Jake . . . Mark, why didn't you tell me before?'

'I nearly did,' said Jake, 'upstairs before the party when I

172

gave you the dress, but I decided it would ruin your evening.'

'Then I asked him not to tell you,' said Mark.

'Why?'

'Because we don't want you scaring him off.'

'So I was right. Roland was up to something.'

'Perhaps.'

She stood up and pushed back her chair. 'I'm going to get to the bottom of this.'

'You're to stay away from him.'

'Mark, you don't know what you're talking about. What happened at Culross blighted my life. You can't expect me to sit here, twiddling my thumbs.'

'No, you can't,' said Jake. 'Now, kids, please take your fight home.'

They drove home in silence, but as soon as they reached the terrace Olivia said, 'You didn't come out just for a holiday, did you?'

'No.'

'Are you helping Culross?'

'Not Culross, but Julius.'

She moved away. 'Was getting to know me part of . . . helping Julius?'

'Yes.'

'In case I had some guilty secret to confess, like I was only pretending to be broke but really I had the missing million stashed away in my handbag?'

'No, I can assure you we never thought that.'

'Roland did.'

'Roland made out he did. Olivia . . .'

'Don't touch me!'

'All right.' He stepped back. 'Julius and I thought that if I got to know you, you might . . . talk more easily about what happened. Roland is refusing to renounce his directorship and we need proof to make him go.'

'I see,' she said icily, 'and was lending me the tower part of this softening up process?'

'To some extent.'

'What was the other extent?'

'I felt sorry for you.'

'Thanks!' She walked over to the terrace wall and looked

173

down on the sea because she could not bear to face him when she asked the most important question. 'And the other . . . us . . . was that part of the scheme?'

He came up behind her and put his arms around her. 'Do you think if I shake you very hard I could get rid of your constant suspicion, because if I thought I could I would. No, don't push me away, you're going to hear what I've got to say.' He turned her to face him and forced her chin up so that he could look in her eyes. 'Even before the court case Julius and I were suspicious about Roland. Neither of us wanted to prosecute you but he did, and to have refused might have aroused his suspicions. After the case we wanted to talk to you but it was obvious you wouldn't tell us anything, even if you knew it – and why should you? Seeing you in the Grays Inn Road was sheer luck for us but I only thought of offering you the tower when we were in the pub. Afterwards, when I told Julius that you'd stomped off into the night and that I'd lost you, he was furious. He said I shouldn't have let you go.'

'He was right.'

'I wish you'd trust me.'

'I'm trying.'

'That difficult?'

'Not easy for me to trust anyone.'

'Did you really think that Julius and I planned that I would . . . seduce you in order that . . .'

She did not answer. She closed her eyes, and she admitted to herself then what she had been trying not to, that she loved him.

There followed days of urgent tranquillity when each moment counted and each night took them further into their intimacy and each white-hot morning brought more long lazy hours under the icecream heat of the Greek sun. Olivia tried not to count time. Jake came occasionally, singing loudly as he neared the tower, but he never stayed long, sensing that they were complete. He only had to look at Olivia's brown eyes shining and her mouth which hovered in a smile of kisses remembered and kisses to come.

Letters arrived for Olivia. They accumulated at the post office until Mark collected them, along with his own.

174

Today is the hottest day since 1940 . . . your mother sends her love
. . . it's her children day – I'm sure she told you she now has four
subnormal children to tea once a week.

love Daddy

'My mother's looking after mentally retarded children,' she
told Mark. 'I can't believe it, she's practically a child herself.'

'Maybe it's what she needed to grow up.'

She frowned and thought for a moment. 'You could be
right.' She skipped through the rest of her letters, unable to
associate herself with these people who had known her before
she knew Mark.

Yesterday was the hottest day since 1940 . . . the children are well
and so is Hugo.

love Fiona

We are overjoyed. The doctor confirms that Lalita is expecting our
first child in February . . . she joins me in sending our love.

Sanjiv

P.S. The day before yesterday was the hottest day since 1940

The next was a large white envelope, forwarded by her
parents. It was a wedding invitation: Jonathan had finally
captured his titian-haired Cleo.

Life at Culross is much the same. Hamish now unbelievably pompous. If you can't make the wedding, come and see us when you're
back in England. Don't disappear again.

Love Jonathan

The last – the longest – was from Maggie.

I didn't write before because I was afraid of tempting the gods, but I
have met *him*. Two months ago! And we've been together ever since.
Amazing! Two months and he still likes me. (No longer am I the
queen of the two-night-stand). He must need a shrink. I must need a
shrink. We're the most wonderfully unsuited couple and I'm mad
about him. Truly mad. He's an accountant. I met him at a party given
by our record company. I didn't want to go. I turned up, looking and
acting my most outrageous, staggering around, bombed out of my
skull, when this guy takes charge of me – just in time as I was about to
throw up. He takes me back to my place. 'Ere we go again, thinks me.
But he didn't try anything, so I decided that I must look even more
revolting than usual. End of story. Only it wasn't. He called next day,

took me out to dinner – and didn't lay a finger on me for ten days by which time the shadow of a passing aeroplane was enough privacy for me to jump on him. Anyhow, the end of this saga is that we're still together, I'm off drink, off pills, and lying by a swimming pool in the South of France.

Love Maggie

P.S.   He doesn't look like an accountant.

P.P.S. He's Jewish and his mother wants him to marry her best friend's daughter.

P.P.P.S. His name is Zach.

P.P.P.P.S. We're buying a huge derelict house in Notting Hill. You're welcome to stay any time.

She told Mark about Maggie and the New Year's Eve party, saying, 'I couldn't stand her at first but now I'm not sure. She's so friendly, so . . . generous. I'd never open up to a stranger like this.' She almost added, 'Not any more.'

She was avid to know about other women in Mark's life. 'Have you had many girlfriends?' she asked, late one night.

'Millions.'

'Seriously?'

'Why do you want to know?'

'Curiosity.'

He drew her to him, on top of him, counting with his fingers up her vertebrae. 'Let me see . . . five hundred and three, five hundred and four – and that was before I was eighteen.'

The next morning he said, 'You asked how many girlfriends I had had and I didn't tell you because I can't bear confessions.' He mimicked a coy female voice saying, ' "First there was Tom, then there was Dick . . ." What does it matter?'

'I wanted to know what they were like.'

'A lot less curious than you.'

But it wasn't that aspect which Olivia had been seeking. Hers was the insecurity of one woman about another.

On the beach, he asked her. 'What are you going to do?'

'About what?'

'Well, you're welcome to stay on in the tower but . . .'

She waited for him to add, I think you should come home with me, but he didn't, so she said, 'I can't lie on a beach forever.'

He ruffled her hair. 'Too right. I was beginning to fear you'd turned into a sunkissed vegetable.'

They swam. She linked her arms around his neck as they trod water. 'I like your flat cheeks and hooded eyes,' she said. 'They remind me of an amused cobra.'

He ran his hand up the inside of her thigh. 'You should see me when I'm oiling my coils.'

She loved him because he made her laugh, and for all the other things he did – even the bad.

On his second to last morning he got up early, saying, 'I have to phone London.'

'Why?'

'Something's cropped up.'

He was back within an hour. Olivia was still in bed. He sat down on the end of it. 'Julius is arriving this evening.'

'Here?'

'Yes.'

'How long's he staying?'

'Just one night. He has to be back in London tomorrow so Jake has kindly agreed to ferry him to and from Corfu in the chopper.' He paused. 'I . . . er . . . have to talk to him on my own. Would you mind staying the night with Jake?'

'Is Julius coming about the Italian?'

He shrugged.

'What's the matter? Do you think I'll go babbling to everyone?'

He stood up. 'For God's sake, don't start that again!'

'But it's true, isn't it?'

'Not me, but Julius – and you can hardly blame him. The last time he saw you was when . . .'

'Does he know about us?'

'I'm hardly likely to yell down the phone "You remember Olivia? Well, I've been screwing her rigid." '

'Is that how you think of it? Screwing me rigid?'

'No, I'm being brutal because you're being silly.'

She looked down at the sheet, taut over her bunched knees. 'It's . . . it's meant something to me.'

He came to her and touched her bent head, stroking her dishevelled hair. 'It means something to me too, Olivia.'

'Something special,' she said in a small voice.

177

'Something very special.'

'It's not that I mind you wanting to be alone with Julius, it's just that I feel I have a right to know what's going on. I don't think you have any concept of how much this means to me – but you shut me out because you don't trust me, because once . . . once . . . *once* I made a mistake.' She looked up at him. 'You don't trust me, do you?'

'Over this – not entirely. You're too emotional.'

'I'll remember that next time we're making love.'

'The two things have nothing to do with each other.'

'You're right.' She pushed him away and got out of bed, the sheet wrapped tightly around her. 'You're quite right. I'm good enough to share your bed, but not to meet your cousin or to be privy to secrets. But don't worry, I shall do my own detective work in future, in my emotional, female, unreasonable way – and I'm damned sure I'll be more successful at it than you and that coldfish cousin of yours.' She turned, the sheet swirling after her, and flounced downstairs with all the aplomb of a displeased empress leaving a ball – and not a barefoot girl in a crumpled sheet.

She went to see Jake. To her fury he laughed. 'What's so funny?' she demanded, stomping up and down as he chipped away at a block of marble.

'You.'

'You would take Mark's side! Men always back each other up. Look at the way you didn't tell me who Lorenzo was because he asked you not to.'

'We're a threatened species. We have to protect ourselves against temperamental females.'

'I am *not* temperamental!'

He picked up the callipers. 'You have to decide what you want in life, and how much you want each thing – and how far you are prepared to sacrifice one for the other.'

'I want to destroy Gerald Quentin, to exonerate myself with Culross – and I want Mark.'

'In that order?'

'No, not in any order. I love Mark, the idea of losing him makes me feel sick. Perhaps if he were nothing to do with Culross it would be different, but every time that name is mentioned I remember the hell I went through – and I can't just sit there with my tail between my legs, nodding my head and saying that I got what I deserved whilst Gerald Quentin gets promoted and Roland Culross goes free. I love Mark, I love him desperately, but he doesn't want to understand what it was like for me to be pilloried.'

Jake ruffled her hair.

'I'm a dog with a bad name,' she said.

'No, you're a puppy who has to earn a good one.'

She remembered the porter at Culross saying, 'Olivia Steele thought she was top dog – so do all over-confident puppies,' and she went down to the swimming pool hewn out of the rocky mountain, and sat with her legs dangling in the water.

In the afternoon Jake left to collect Julius from Corfu. 'I'm dining with Gwen,' he told her. 'I'm sure she'd be delighted if you . . .'

'No, thanks, I'll have an early night.'

The chopper flew off. An hour later it was back. As soon as Olivia saw it swooping in from the sea she scuttled upstairs to the spare bedroom. The last person she wanted to meet was Julius. She heard voices on the terrace and peered down through a crack in the shutters.

Julius's clipped tones. 'It's not easy to discuss these things on a public telephone.'

Jake's deep rumble. 'Mark could have used mine.'

'We didn't want to involve you more than necessary.' The rest was drowned out by a closing door.

Then Jake said, 'She's staying here,' as they went down the steps and round the corner of the house. A moment later the jeep set off for the tower.

It was nine o'clock when Olivia walked along the harbour wall to the *Belladonna*. She was wearing the apricot outfit. After all, if Mark liked it, why shouldn't the Italian? By the gangway she gave her name to a burly sailor standing guard. He spoke into a two-way radio.

'Olivia! What a pleasure.' Lorenzo appeared on deck, his hand outstretched, his eyes amused. 'I'm teaching Nikos how to cheat at cards. Come and join us.'

He ushered her into the main living area, a floating world of

179

white leather, glass, chrome, priceless paintings – and one piece of sculpture by Jake Hammond.

Nikos was curled up on a white fur rug, studying the cards in his hand. He jumped to his feet. 'Don't tell my grandfather I'm here, will you? Please!'

'Of course not.' She looked at the boy who was smiling at the Italian with a mixture of admiration and sensuality. Surely not! She sat down. The Italian ordered champagne from someone in the depths of his floating palace. Surely not!

'Enough for tonight, Nikos,' he said.

'May I come tomorrow?'

'No, I am leaving in the morning.'

'You're corrupting him' said Olivia, after Nikos had left.

'At least he will be properly corrupted.' He laughed at her shocked expression. 'But no, to satisfy your curiosity, I do not . . . take advantage of him. I am not interested in men in that way – nor will Nikos be, when he grows up, he is merely flexing his sexuality like all young animals. I am . . .'

'I never thought . . .'

'Of course you did. I could see it in your expression when you came in.' He laughed at her embarrassment. 'I'm glad you came to see me.'

'Why?'

'You amuse me.' He leaned closer. 'Tell me, Miss Olivia Steele does the worthy Mr Mark Denholm know you are here?'

'No.'

'How fascinating! Why did you come – or am I to presume, as most of my countrymen would, that my charms . . . No? I didn't think so. What a pity.' He stood up. 'Let's walk along the deck. Ah, how I love this ship. You know,' he turned her to the rails so that they looked straight down at the village square, 'It is a pity that you are . . . otherwise engaged, or you could have sailed back to Genoa with me. Have you ever been there?'

'No.'

'You should. It is fascinating – especially the port.

'I'm sure it is – especially the ships.'

The wind caught her hair, blowing it across her face so that a strang remained stuck to her lips. He reached out and gently removed it – and at that moment her eyes focused on two men standing in the shadows of a harbour front house. Mark and Julius. They were looking straight at her.

She froze, but only for an instant, then she smiled sweetly at the Italian and firmly led the way to the other side of the ship. Let Mark think what he liked, damn him!

The sheet was ripped from her fingers leaving her naked . . . 'What the hell were you doing with the Italian?'

She opened her eyes. Mark was standing at the bottom of her bed. 'What time is it?'

'Midday . . . What were you doing on the *Belladonna*? I thought I told you not to go near him.'

She reached down and grabbed the end of the sheet. 'If I want to see Lorenzo I shall.' She sat up. 'I shall see who I like when I like.'

'You stupid little idiot, you've ruined everything!'

'No I haven't – and don't call me an idiot. I'm fed up with being ordered around by you. I'm sick of being treated as though I had committed a murder. I told you I was going to get to the bottom of things, and I am – and it's none of your bloody business who I see.' She kicked out at him.

He grabbed her foot and twisted her leg, forcing her over on her stomach, raised his hand and brought it down hard on her naked buttocks.

She let out a shriek, 'Let me go . . . let me . . .'

He hit her again and again whilst she kicked and twisted, screaming curses, till at last she wrenched herself free and made a dash for the door. But before she managed to get it open, he seized her, forcing her up against the wall, his hands on her shoulders, his body pressed against her to keep her still. For a moment they stood there, she totally naked, he in his jeans and shirt, glaring, furious, hating – then holding her still with one hand he unzipped his jeans. He wanted to hurt her, to vent his anger into her. But he didn't hurt her – for in spite of everything she wanted him though she pretended not to. Afterwards they lent against each other in silence until he lifted her chin and looked deep into her eyes, and said, 'Don't ever cross me again.'

If he hadn't said that Olivia would have forgiven everything – his words, his blows, everything, but she could not forgive his arrogance.

'Don't think, to coin your phrase, "screwing me rigid" changes anything,' she snapped, shaking her head free. 'I shall do what I like. Now, get out!'

He hesitated.

'Get out!'

He went, slamming the door behind him.

The chopper flew in. It flew out again. Olivia showered, dressed, lay down on her bed – and seethed. The chopper came back. She heard Jake on the terrace.

'Well, Livvi,' he said, coming into her room 'I suppose you two young fools had to do it your way but it's a pity, you made a great couple.'

'I never want to see Mark Denholm again.'

'That's what he said about you – when I took him to Corfu.'

'To Corfu!'

'He caught the afternoon flight to London.'

'No!' She leapt off the bed and ran from the room, down the corridor, down the stairs, across the terrace, and down the path which led to the tower, her bare feet flying over the stones. When she reached the tower she yanked open the door and sped up to Mark's room. He had only been gone a few hours but already it had that deserted feel about it, particles of dust dancing in the shafts of sunlight, the unmade bed, a book half-read then discarded, coat hangers swinging free in an empty cupboard. She sat down on the bed and pulled the sheets to her, burying her face in them, in the smell of him, as tears rolled down her cheeks.

He was the only man about whom she had no reservations, the only man she'd ever really loved – and she had lost him.

15

When Jake arrived an hour later Olivia was still sitting on Mark's bed. 'You really love him, don't you?' he said.

'Yes.'

'He loves you.'

'I don't think he does.'

'He could do.'

She went to the window and looked down on the sea. 'I'm not going after him — and it's not just pride. It's because nothing can work with Mark so long as this . . . cancer of Culross lies between us. I need my revenge, Jake, I want my pound of flesh.'

'You're not going to get it on Anataxos.' He touched her cheek. 'Shall we go to Pietra Alta?'

'You'd go back there for me? Oh, no, I couldn't let you.'

'For you and for me.' He put an arm around her shoulders and drew her close. 'It's time I too faced up to life.'

In the end it was six weeks before they left Anataxos because that evening Jake heard that Dee had hanged herself with the light flex of her room.

16

Italy, Autumn 1975

There is a difference between Italy and Greece, not just in the people who by some physical quirk are better looking in Italy, nor in the houses which by another quirk – probably metallurgical – are ochre-coloured, nor in the fact that Italy, land of Michelangelo and Puccini, Valentino and Sophia Loren, is also *terramadre* to mafia bosses and Cesare Borgia's poisoned ring. The difference lies in a combination of these things: in the light reflecting ochre on to cobbled squares where silky women and their strutting lovers hold illicit meetings beneath a statue of the Madonna, whilst in the next street barefoot boys remove the wheels from Lamborghinis. Jake was right when he called Italy his mistress, for what good is a mistress who doesn't attack the senses with her decadent sexuality, her hint of sin.

And there is a difference between the coast of the Versillia and the Apuan Alps barely three miles inland. The coast: that flat stretch of commercial nothing north of Viareggio where dusty roads separate almost-sumptuous villas and tourists in unflattering shorts wobble on bicycles without proper brakes to beaches where not even the sand is free. What a pity that many of them, lying on the beach, gaze at the wild heights through eyes stung by suntan oil but never bother to cover that short distance. They probably think that Monte Altissimo is covered in snow. It isn't. It's marble.

Olivia stood on the oval terrace looking down on the River

184

Serra, some hundred feet of dense green wood below and hardly a river in the late summer, more a trickle of water weaving its way through the centre of a wide bed of blinding white marble pebbles — just as it must have been when Jake had lain in the undergrowth nursing his shattered leg and listened to the women collecting stones. She turned her back on the river and looked up to the mountains which formed the curved backdrop to the house, a high serrated ridge reached by a white road zigzagging like the coils of a moving snake through the lower wooded slopes past cascades of pebbles, the relics of earlier days when dynamite was used profusely, to the marble quarries just below the great white glistening peak of Monte Altissimo.

Pietra Alta — the high stone — was a three storey house of stuccoed walls, terracotta tiles and dark green shutters surrounded by an oval terrace of large irregular slabs of marble. It was solitary, peaceful — but not somnolent. Not at all like Anataxos, thought Olivia, as she watched a lorry trundle down the hillside with its cargo of huge blocks of marble, whilst from the bottom of the valley came the whine of the marble cutter: the diamond teeth cutting deep into the white marble crystals, the twisted wire which cuts as it pushes sand and water along the groove. From the ground floor studio came the chip-chip of Jake at work with his chisel. From the river bed came the voices of the women gathering stones. By the back door the gardener was changing a wheel on the jeep. There was, she decided, a savage urgency in these wild hills and it made her feel restless and useless.

'So?' Jake came out of the studio. 'What do you think?' He lifted his arms and shook his white head in the morning air.

'It's very beautiful.'

'You don't like it?'

'It makes me feel inadequate.' She looked up at the mountains. 'They're so powerful.'

He laughed. 'That's good. You know, not one piece of work I did at Anataxos was half as good as anything I did here — or will do again.'

'How much money do you have?'

'Er . . . thirty pounds.'

'You can't go into battle on thirty pounds.'

'It's all I have.'

'That's what I was hoping. I need a secretary for a few weeks. I've a hell of a lot of letters to be answered, to the States and England, and the girl I used to use is away on holiday – in any case her English wasn't too hot. I'm going to employ you for a month starting tomorrow. You can answer my mail and sort out my accounts.'

'You can't pay me.'

'I'll pay you what I would have had to pay the girl – two hundred thousand lira, about a hundred and forty pounds.'

'It's too much.'

'Where else am I going to find an English-speaking secretary on the slopes of Monte Altissimo?'

'My typing isn't good enough.'

'Olivia, I need you to help me. Now, shut up and do what your boss tells you. Today's a holiday and I'm going to show you the sights.'

They drove along the side of the valley until they came to a beautiful Romanesque chapel beside a high bell tower. Jake stopped the jeep, and took a deep, satisfied breath. 'How I envy you seeing this place for the first time.'

The land fell away from the chapel to lower peaks and villages clinging to their slopes, then to the flatland beyond, and finally to the sea. 'I watched this place being bombarded,' he said. 'The Germans were up here, the Americans down in the olive fields.'

'Where were you?'

'On the other side of the valley. Look, you can see the cave. There, just above the cascade of marble. I used to hide behind the rock at the entrance . . . yes, that one jutting out.'

Olivia stared at the gaping white hole and thought of the Gisella, the fifteen-year-old girl, who had scrambled up the hillside in the night to take food and water to the man she loved. She imagined herself doing the same for Mark.

'Don't think about him.'

'I can't help it. I try not to. I really do. But I've got this . . . hollow inside me.'

'I know what you mean.'

'Oh, Jake, I'm sorry. How selfish I am.'

186

'Didn't I tell you once that love is many things including selfish?'

They stood together, looking down at the valley, wrapped in their separate miseries. Then suddenly his mood lifted and he pointed to a small round window with stone lattice-work, saying 'Michelangelo designed that, at least they say he did, just as they say he lived at Pietrasanta and personally chose his marble from a special quarry.'

'Isn't it true?'

'I'm sure it is, but these things are good for tourism and I am a cynic,' he said, climbing back into the jeep. 'As you say in England, "Charles the Second Slept Here." '

On their return to Pietra Alta, Jake disappeared into his studio leaving Olivia with nothing to do. She could not help in the house because Franca, a cousin of Gisella's, did that, she could not drive the jeep because Franca's husband had gone to buy supplies, so she wondered through the large bright rooms. If the house on Anataxos had been a Grecian Jake then Pietra Alta was his Italian side, a mixture of ancient and modern – bright splashes of modern paintings on rough walls, soft modern sofas on terracotta tiled floors, round tables in every colour of marble – and space, wonderful space reaching up to high ceilings and out through every door and window to mountains, and sky. But most of all to the great white mountain which both dominated and sustained the existence of the valley and all who worked there.

Jake's affairs were in the sort of semi-organised chaos of someone who knows that one day all letters must be answered but can't face doing it yet. The long reflectory table which served as a desk was piled high with papers.

'We'd better deal with the money ones first.' He picked up a bank statement. 'I'm damned sure I haven't spent all that.'

'I'll check it.'

'And this. Taxes! How the hell am I meant to work if I have to . . .'

'I'll send it to your accountant.'

'You'll find all his last letters in that pile . . . that one there . . . no, I haven't answered them, because he keeps asking me what I sold in Paris and I can't remember.'

'Do you always use the same gallery?'

'Oh, yes. There . . . in the file. And the other galleries, in London, Tokyo and er . . .'

'Shall we authorise him to contact them direct?'

'You're smart!'

They went through everything, Jake cursing, Olivia reassuring, and at the end he escaped like a schoolboy from the classroom leaving Olivia to tap slowly on an elderly typewriter.

That evening when he saw the first of the neatly typed letters, clipped to their envelopes, and read their clear, precise instructions, he said, 'If I'd known that you could do this I'd have asked you to help in Anataxos.'

She needed to be praised. Sorting out Jake's affairs might be child's play to her but that made no difference to her satisfaction at being told she had done a good job.

It took Olivia four weeks to clear the backlog of letters. Then she was faced with her own task. They had not spoken of her leaving, but both knew she must go. One afternoon she borrowed the jeep drove into Pietrasanta, and bought a train ticket for Genoa. Then she went into a smart boutique and counted out some of her precious earnings in exchange for a jacket of rough cream silk with the faintest navy stripe and a navy skirt with a slit up the back. Jake had said that she couldn't go into battle on thirty pounds, and he was right. It was no good looking like a loser either. Driving back up the mountain road in the late September sun, she thought of Mark with a kind of impotent rage mixed with sadness – but she still thought of him.

Jake was on the terrace. 'It's going to rain. I can smell it.' He paused. 'You're leaving tomorrow?'

'Yes.'

'Is it any good to tell you not to go near Lorenzo?'

'No, it isn't.'

He sighed. 'Do you have his address?'

'I'll find him.'

'Yes, you will.' He went into the house. A moment later he came back and handed her a piece of paper.

'Thank you.'

'I'm going to tell you a story so that you can understand what he's like. Gisella told it to me. When Lorenzo was ten, he

188

had a puppy. He loved it. But one day he told her he'd given it away because he did not want to care too deeply for something. She was convinced he killed it.'

The storm broke in the early evening. It began with a deep rumbling high above the mountains and soon the sky had turned from sultry blue to ominous black, against which Monte Altissimo stood out unearthly white. Then shafts of lightning shot down as though intent on spearing some prey, and a moment later the rain, like solid tubes of glass smashing into the roof and the terrace, a wall of water through which neither the valley below nor the mountains above were visible.

The noise of the rain made it impossible to talk during dinner – or perhaps they would have been silent anyway. After coffee, Olivia said, 'I think I'll go to bed early.' She knew she wouldn't be able to sleep but she wanted to acclimatise herself to being without Jake.

She must have fallen asleep because she woke to Jake shaking her. 'Get up! Quick!'

'What is it! A fire?'

'No, come down. Hurry!'

She pulled on her jeans and her old navy jacket and dashed after him. It had stopped raining and Jake was out on the terrace, looking down at the river from where strange thuds were coming. She hurried to him, across the wet marble which glistened in the light of a full moon, the sort of clean moon which comes after a thunder storm as if it too had been well washed, whilst the cold damp air had that multitude of earthy and leafy after-storm smells.

'Look.' He pointed downwards.

The once dry river bed was a torrent of white foaming water, so full that it pulled at the overhanging trees, breaking off huge branches. But it was not that which Jake had called her to see – it was the blocks of marble, like cuboid icebergs, which the force of the torrent was propelling down the valley. They came in twos and threes, swishing and turning in the main stream, thud-thud against each other. Then one block, so white that it seemed translucent, came alone. It was caught by the cross-current and swung out, hitting the far bank, and by that force was propelled across the river where the curve trapped it, and it remained there, beating frantically against the bank.

'Rogue marble, just like you,' he said.

'Save it for me?'

'I'll use it for The Snake Girl.'

17

Through the dirty window of the dirty railway carriage Olivia watched the flat plain give way to rocky coast as they sped north. She saw great white villas shielded by bougainvilia and electric fences, a castle on a headland looking out to sea, and a nightclub boarded up for the winter. Then, as the train entered Genoa, it passed the seafront palaces of seventeenth century merchants before plunging in among the jungle of ochre-coloured houses, where washing was strung below windows above children playing in steep narrow streets and voices in the clipped, closed dialect of the region called to each other from behind shutters – those special Ligurian shutters which are like half-closed eyelids.

But Olivia was not thinking about shutters as she pushed through the crowded station, clutching her belongings. She was far too preoccupied with not having her bag pinched. She made her way to the tourist information office. There were three windows but only one was tended, by a greasy young man laconically picking his teeth. 'A cheap hotel.' He pushed a street map through the grill. 'Where?'

'What about down here?'

He raised his hand in mock horror – and dropped his toothpick. 'That is the *vicoli,* in Genoese the *carrugi.* It is full of . . . prostitutes.' He called a colleague in an inner office, repeated what Olivia had said, and laughed. Then he collected his toothpick from the floor and carried on using it.

'You suggest somewhere then.'

'OK, OK.' He wrote down a couple of names, made a few crosses on her map. 'Take the bus outside the station. Next!'

It took her an hour to find the first address, an unprepossessing building in need of redecoration with a huge front door beside which was written *Pensione 2° piano*. She pressed the button. A stream of Italian came down the intercom.

'I don't understand.'

'Eh?'

'I'm looking for a room.'

'Eh?'

'A room.'

There was a buzz and the front door opened. Olivia went inside, to a gloomy marble hall dominated by one of those rattling old-fashioned lifts in which gangsters in thirties movies invariably get shot through the bars. On the second floor a rotund woman in a none-too-clean apron was waiting for her. 'Eh?'

'I want a room. How much?'

'Ten thousand *lire* a night, with shower.'

'Can I see it?'

'My room clean. Good view.'

'I'd like to see it.'

She was led down a half-lit corridor to a small but reasonably clean room. 'I'll take it. For two nights . . . at least.'

The woman held out her hand. 'Passport.'

Promising herself that if and when she was rich she would always stay in the best hotels, Olivia stripped off her travelling clothes and turned on the shower. A tepid dribble came out. She cursed and shivered, and persevered. By the time she had dressed, it was four o'clock. She went to find the woman. 'May I use the telephone?'

'Phone where?'

'Genoa.'

'Five hundred *lire*.' The greedy hand appeared.

Olivia paid and dialled. A boy answered. He switched quickly to piping English. 'My father is not here. Please leave me your name and telephone number.'

She was surprised to find the Italian had a son: she had never imagined him as being anything other than a lone wolf.

The evening stretched ahead. She decided to go for a walk, setting off down the street, feeling that same detachment she felt at airports, that sense of being just another number. A side street took her into the majestic Via XX Settembre, where motorbikes ridden by fierce young men with their girlfriends, dark hair streaming in the wind, cut in and out of lumbering municipal buses, whilst along the mosaic pavement which ran under the arched porticos elegant women linked arms and window-shopped. Everywhere she saw lovers. An entwined couple blocked the pavement. A girl flew from a taxi into the arms of a waiting man. She thought of Mark and a fierce wave of loneliness swept over her.

'Signorina! Telefono!'

'Oh . . . er . . . coming.'

'Olivia, it is Lorenzo. Are you free for dinner tonight? Good. I will send a car at eight.'

She wore the cream and navy suit – her battledress.

The Italian waited for her in his white penthouse which stretched the length of the top floor of an old palace, once the home of a princeling, now a private museum. 'Ah, Olivia,' he shook her hand, 'I'm flattered that you troubled to telephone me. It would have been a shame if you had visited Genoa and we had not met.'

He led her through the sitting-room which was a larger replica of his yacht, white leather, glass and chrome, to an inner terrace hung with exotic plants. 'I thought we would dine at home. That is, unless you would rather eat out.'

'Not at all.'

'Good. My chef has spent all day preparing a dinner for a lady who does not know Genoese cooking and he would have been most distressed to have to eat it all himself.'

She smiled. What idiots Mark and Jake were to try to stop her seeing Lorenzo. 'You have a marvellous view,' she said.

'Especially of the port.'

She watched the lights of a container ship move slowly across the darkened sea. 'Is the *Ariosto* still here?'

'Yes. You may see it through the telescope.'

She looked – and saw one long low ship no different from a hundred others. 'Who does it belong to now?'

'Me.'

'How did you manage to buy it?'

'With money – as one buys most things.'

'Not Culross money?'

'Hardly.'

The butler coughed discreetly. Lorenzo took her arm. 'Dinner is served. Come, we will talk of general things – that is unless you wish to interrogate me in front of my butler.'

'What's happened to your son?' she asked, as they sat down at a large white marble table.

'He's gone back to his mother.'

'Doesn't your wife life here?'

'No, she prefers Milan. The children – I also have a daughter,' he pointed to a silver-framed photo of a boy and a girl, 'spend the term with her and part of the holidays with me. Children need a mother, and anyhow my life is not for them.'

She wanted to annoy him because he had frustrated her. 'I didn't know Italians were allowed to divorce.'

'They are now, but we are not divorced. We go separate ways.'

'Next you'll be saying she doesn't understand you.'

'On the contrary, she understands me perfectly – as I understand her. You must tell me if you like the green sauce.'

'Yes, it's delicious.'

'It's pesto sauce, a speciality of the region.' He turned to the butler. 'Miss Steele, who is a devoted cook, wishes to learn how to make pesto sauce. Call the chef.'

'I do not!'

He laughed – and he was still laughing as the chef ended a lengthy explanation about pounding fresh basil and Sardinian sheep's cheese in olive oil. 'You did very well,' he said, when the chef departed.

'You planned that . . . charade . . . to stop me from saying what I wanted, from being myself . . .'

'Some selves are more digestible than others. I prefer the less acid version during dinner.'

She waited till coffee was served in the drawing-room. 'Why did Roland Culross agree to the loan?'

'Bankers make loans. It's their business.'

'Not unsecured loans.'

'I call a loan where you know you will get your money back very secure.'

'Culross thought you were going to ship tractors.'

'Really!'

'Did Roland know from the start that the charter party from Conduit was false?'

He chuckled.

'You admit it!'

'I admit nothing.'

'If Roland did know, then there must have been a very good reason for him to involve Culross?'

'You are telling me.'

'Was it money or blackmail?'

'Blackmail! You have been reading too many detective stories.'

'I suppose you think it's funny, me coming here.'

'Very. This is the most entertaining evening I have had for a month. But I do find it ... ungentlemanly of your Mark Denholm and the over-correct Julius Culross to send you into the lion's den – unless they want the lion to eat you.'

'They don't know I'm here.'

'Then you are a very stupid girl.'

She flushed. 'I don't care what you think of me, but I didn't deserve to lose my job and my house – everything – because you and Roland Culross were trying to make ... a quick buck.'

'Rather more than one buck.'

'You can help me clear my name, I know you can.'

'This conversation is becoming tedious.'

'If you don't help me, I shall find out for myself.'

'You are lucky that you are amusing and quite pretty or I would not have seen you. But the game is over. Go home to England. Genoa is a dangerous city, it is not a playground for little girls.'

She picked up her bag. 'I'm not afraid.'

His eyes ran down her taut body. 'I was hoping you might "make me an offer I couldn't refuse".'

'I'll get my information with my brain not my body.' She marched to the lift. 'I'll find out somehow, and when I do I'll get my own back on those who set me up. I'll grind their faces into the dirt – and I'll enjoy it.'

His mocking laughter followed her into the lift.

Next morning she dressed in jeans and a bomber jacket, the anonymous clothes of tourism. The night had brought a thin drizzle and her rubber-soled gym shoes slipped on the uneven pavements as she made her way down to the port, hurrying beneath the ancient porticos of Via Gramsci. Up to her right were the *carrugi*, the dark medieval alleyways of old Genoa, where cats walked single file and houses almost touched at the top. Under an arch a prostitute in last week's make-up was handing yesterday's takings to her pimp. Outside a shoeshop two grubby little boys kicked a football and dreamed of playing for Sampdoria. Clutching her bag, Olivia crossed the road and followed the iron railings until she came to a white building marked *Dogana* (customs). On the other side of it was the jetty – and the *Ariosto*. This was what she had seen through the telescope.

Two uniformed customs officers were drinking black coffee at their desks. 'Do you speak English?' she asked.

The younger one scratched his head. 'Little.'

'Can I look around?'

'Eh?'

She pointed at the far door. 'The port.'

'Why?'

'I want to see a ship.'

'Ship?'

'The *Ariosto*.'

'No.' He produced an official-looking card. 'Not permitted without permit.'

'Can I buy a permit?'

'No.'

She wondered whether she should offer him a bribe. Italians, so everyone always said, were susceptible to bribery but she had no idea how to go about it, so she turned away – and as she did so the older man lifted the telephone.

Retiring to a nearby bar and a capuccino, Olivia asked the waiter if it was possible to tour the port. He nodded and pointed up the road, past the customs house. Annoyed with herself for not thinking to ask earlier, she hurried along the pavement, arriving just as the tour-boat was about to leave. She settled herself in the prow and scanned the quays as the guide announced 'To your right you have the famous lighthouse . . . to your left the old wharf . . . straight ahead is a container ship, the main business of any modern port.' Olivia craned her neck. Then, suddenly, she saw the *Ariosto*. It was lying low in the water, a rusty-coloured hulk with its red, white and blue squared Panamanian flag fluttering in the breeze. As Olivia stared at it she felt an unbelievable rage that something so ugly and inanimate should have brought about her downfall.

Next morning as she was about to go out, the *pensione* owner said, 'You leave today.'

'No, tomorrow – perhaps.'

'Today.' She handed Olivia her bill. 'Room taken. All rooms taken. You go now.'

'But I thought . . . I mean, you never said when I came that . . .'

The woman shrugged.

It was early afternoon before she managed to find another cheap hotel. She left her case and headed straight for the tourist boat pier, mingling with the crowd who waited to take the next trip until, with a deep breath and studied casualness, she detached herself and began to stroll back through the port towards the *Ariosto*. Fork-lift trucks carrying huge containers rumbled past her. Dockers shouted at each other – and at her. She felt slightly sick from the smell of oil and tar and dirty seawater. Her route took her close to the customs house and as she approached she saw the younger officer come out to examine the contents of a car boot. She dodged behind a crane and waited till he went back inside. Finally, she reached the quay where the *Ariosto* lay squashed between two larger ships, the long, low, unprepossessing hulk bobbing on the waves, its ramp lowered to the dockside. Olivia took one step up it – then another.

A man appeared on deck. He said something in Italian.

She backed off.

He shouted.

She started to walk away.

He shouted louder.

She began to run.

But the man had attracted the customs officer, who rushed out, saw Olivia, whipped out his pistol, and screamed at her.

She had no idea what he said – the black muzzle was enough. She froze. He came slowly towards her, his finger on the trigger. The muscles of her stomach clenched, as stories of tourists who had been shot dead because they could not understand the language came to her mind. She wondered whether bursting into tears would help – it would not be difficult, she'd seldom felt more like crying.

The customs officer yelled at her and waved his pistol, before putting it back in his holster with what seemed to Olivia like reluctance. Then he took her by the arm and manhandled her across the tarmac, into a small airless room at the back of the customs house. The door slammed. The lock turned. She sat down on the solitary chair and bit the inside of her mouth to stop herself from crying – with rage, frustration and fear.

Ten minutes passed. She remembered stories of people held for years without trial in foreign countries. An hour passed. She pictured her parents receiving the news that their daughter was in gaol. Two hours. She imagined Mark reading of her fate over his morning coffee. 'English girl arrested.' At least it wasn't 'English Girl Shot – Italian Ambassador Apologises For Unfortunate Incident.'

It was three o'clock and she was dying to go to the loo. Gingerly she knocked on the door. The man came. She made various signs. He shrugged. She made more explicit signs. He nodded and took her down a corridor, standing guard outside the relevant door like a sentry, before escorting her back to the airless room. At four o'clock he brought her a cup of black coffee and a cheese roll. She ate it wondering how many phone calls you were allowed to make when arrested. Was it one to the British consul or one and the British consul? If it were only one call, should she use it on Jake?

Just after seven the door opened and the customs officer came in. He was followed by a young man with the featureless face of a lizard. 'I have come to collect you,' he told her in perfect English.

'Where am I going?'

'You are free.'

'Are you from the British consul?'

'No, not exactly.'

'I'm very grateful.' She hurried from the room. 'I really

thought they might send me to prison. Did they phone you? No? But how did you know about me?'

'Would you prefer that I hadn't come?'

'No, of course not.' Puzzled, she held out her hand. 'Thank you very much.'

He shook it. 'Goodbye.'

'Oh . . . aren't you going to take me back to my hotel?'

'I'm a lawyer, not a taxi-driver, Miss Steele.'

She watched him slip through the pedestrians and disappear. In the earlier confusion she had dropped her map, but the quickest route must lie across Via Gramsci and up the hill, through the alleyways, but the safest . . . she glanced around. There were plenty of people. Ordinary people. Safe-looking people. She crossed the road.

High above, in an attic, a woman was singing. A man shouted. The singing stopped. A moment later it began again, huskier, more haunting. Olivia walked faster. A door opened and a huge negro came out. She flattened herself to let him pass. He did not even look at her. Behind a pile of rubbish two cats fought over a fish head. She gripped her handbag and hurried on.

An arch brought her out into Via del Campo. The shops were brightly lit and prosperous. It's not frightening, she told herself, as two smartly dressed women passed, arm-in-arm with a younger man. She strode on, looking purposeful, until she came to a dissecting lane. There she turned left. It seemed the obvious thing to do. But soon her path petered out into a little square. The only way on was up an even narrower alley, unlit and gloomy as the evening drew in. She went back to Via del Campo, but it wasn't as it had been. Gone were the smart women. In their place were the night people of the *carrugi*.

'Eh, Americana!' A fiercely tattooed man lurched towards her.

She ignored him.

'You want drink?'

She walked faster.

'You want to fuck?'

She began to run. Ahead of her four women blocked the way. She was about to ask their help when she saw the tired paint on their faces. She darted up a turning and came out in the same little square as before, only now a rough-looking boy straddled a motorbike across the exit. As Olivia hurried past, he put out his foot and tripped her up. Instinctively she put out her hand. There was a dull thud as she hit the ground and a shaft of pain shot up her arm, and before she knew what was happening the boy had grabbed her bag and was gone.

She slumped back against the wall and burst into tears. Her arm throbbed. Her lip was cut. She had lost twenty thousand *lire*, her address book, her diary and all the other paraphernalia of a handbag, but luckily not her passport, which she had left at the hotel, or the remainder of her money, folded inside her gym shoes. Nevertheless she felt sick with pain and rage, and fear.

It was eleven o'clock by the time she managed to find her hotel.

'I've been robbed,' she told the elderly proprietor, who was watching television.

'So you have no money to pay your room?'

'I have money, but I want you to call the police.'

'Why?'

'Look at me!'

'Where did it happen?'

'In the . . . *carrugi*.'

'You went into the *carrugi* at night? Do you know what the police will say? They will tell you that you are stupid. Stupid! You deserve to be robbed.' He turned back to his television and raised the volume.

Promising herself that tomorrow she would leave this city forever, Olivia climbed into her narrow bed and fell asleep.

Next morning the old man banged on her door. She got up, her head splitting, her arm aching, and her mouth filled with the kind of sickness which comes with a fever.

'You leave today,' he said.

'I can't.'

'You must.'

'I'm ill.' She closed the door in his face and went back to bed.

She woke in the later afternoon to find Lorenzo standing at the bottom of her bed. 'What . . . what are you doing here?' he asked. 'The old man said you were ill.'

'How did he . . . oh, no, you don't mean that it's thanks to

200

you I've been hounded out of everywhere?'

'Get up!'

'I'm ill. I can't. Go away.'

'You are being moved into one of my hotels until you are better. My driver is waiting for you.'

'Why should you care about me?'

'I do it for Jake's sake. Jake, my sister's husband. My family.' He paused. 'You are lucky not to be dead.'

She tried to sit up. 'I'm not beaten yet.'

He laughed. 'You're fantastic. You're ill, without money, in a foreign city and you say you're not beaten yet.'

The chauffeur drove her to a luxury hotel not far from Lorenzo's palace. She was ushered through a high ceilinged foyer, past oil paintings and antique furniture, to the top floor where a small suite had been prepared for her. It had its own private terrace looking straight down over the roof-tops to the port.

The phone rang. 'My doctor will call on you in two minutes.'

'I can't afford . . .' She pushed a strand of hair off her damp face.

'I told you, I am doing this for Jake.'

'Does he know?'

'What is the point of doing someone a favour if they don't know?'

She wished she had the strength to say she was leaving, but she was too ill to move.

It was five days before she was well enough to get up and even then she was still very weak. She stared at herself in the mirror. Her face was pallid. Her hair was straggly. She had lost weight. Seldom had she looked less dynamic.

She telephoned Jake. 'I'm very grateful, but I hate to think of you being in Lorenzo's debt.'

'Better than having to attend your funeral,' he said dryly. 'When are you coming back to Pietra Alta?'

'Not yet.'

'Next time I'll be identifying your corpse!'

She pictured him walking back to the studio, muttering under his breath as he wiped his dusty hands on his dusty blue overall.

Lorenzo came in the late afternoon. He found her on the terrace watching the movement of the ships in and out of the port – toy ships on an artificial sea. 'Have you ever been the mistress of a rich man?' he asked.

'No, of course I haven't.'

'It would make all the difference to you.'

'When I make love I do so because I want to, not for money.'

'I don't mean for money, but for the experience. To be pampered. To know how to pamper yourself. To learn how to dress. Before she had time to draw away. He pushed her hair back from her forehead, saying, 'Why do all English girls look like spaniels? Is it because English men prefer their dogs?'

'I suppose you're offering to be my protector.'

'You're not unattractive.'

'Well, you're the last person I'd . . .'

'I think not.' He pointed at a fat man staggering up the street. 'The second last, surely?'

She had to laugh.

Living at the hotel was like being in a soft, fluffy cloud of escapism. She rose late, had long, scented baths, ordered meals from the extensive menu, went for short walks if the weather was good, or lay on her bed watching television if it was not. Sometimes she wondered what Olivia Steele, hard-working banker of two years before, would have said about such an existence. I'd have been convinced it must be paid for horizontally, she thought, and she wondered if she and Jonathan and everyone like them had not been a tiny bit priggish.

Lorenzo came to see her frequently. Sometimes for lunch, sometimes just for an hour, never for dinner. She wondered what he did in the evenings.

'How come you speak such good English?' she asked him one day.

'Jake taught me. The first words I learned were marble and cave.'

'And gun?'

'Perhaps.' He walked out.

She saw nothing of him for five days and she missed him, although she told herself she didn't. On the fifth day he telephoned. 'It's time I showed you Genoa. Be downstairs in twenty minutes.'

He drove her to what she now recognised as Via XX Settembre and halted beneath the great stone bridge just over halfway up. 'You see those names carved into the arch,' he said. 'They were foreigners killed fighting with our partisans. Look, that one is English.' He pointed to a name. 'And that one Polish. Their nicknames are in brackets.'

'Did you have a nickname?'

'Angelo – because I had a face like an angel.'

'Appearances mislead.'

He laughed. 'Now I'll show you the cemetery.'

'Surely, you're not going to bury me alive?'

'There are worse places to die. The cemetery of Staglieno is famous and beautiful and full of well-known people. You could have long and interesting conversations with Mazzini.'

They drove up behind the city, to the cemetery, and followed a wooded avenue between huge marble tombs decorated with sculpted angels and gilded madonnas, with fresh flowers at the hems of their blue dresses. It was an extraordinary place. So ostentatious. So silent. So many dead.

'This is the tomb of Mazzini,' said Lorenzo. 'One of the greatest thinkers of the Risorgimento, the time when Garibaldi chased . . .'

'Trying to fatten me up on a diet of culture?'

'I thought you might not know.'

'Of course I do.'

'You're lying!'

'I am not!' She stood beside one of the fluted pillars of the tomb. 'Why are you looking after me? Oh, I know you said you were doing it for Jake, but the guided tour of the city isn't necessary.'

'You remind me of myself. You have my desire for life.'

'If you feel like that why won't you tell me what I want to know about Roland Culross?'

'Don't be a fool! You cannot expect me to do that . . . or do you? Yes, I almost believe you do and now your mind is full of "if I let him make love to me will he tell me . . . I don't want to risk it if he's not going to . . . and I'm not going to bargain

203

because I'm not that sort of girl . . . but if I could be sure he'd tell me . . ." '

'I'm not thinking anything of the sort.'

'Of course you are.'

'I'm not!' She marched off down the tree-lined path.

'You shouldn't tell lies in a cemetery,' he shouted after her.

The car was locked so she was forced to wait beside it. He seemed to take forever, stopped to talk to a bent old lady, muffled in black, her rosary beads moving between her gnarled fingers.

'She comes here every day,' he said. 'Her husband is buried here and when she dies she will join him.'

'How morbid.'

'Not morbid. This is Italy, a country where death, love, art and religion are intrinsically linked.'

'You forgot organised crime.'

'One day you will annoy me and I shall throw you out, but in the meantime I have a proposition.'

'No.'

'You haven't heard it.'

'Surprise me.'

'Come and work for me for a month, in my office.'

'Drumming up false loans? No thanks.'

'I have other interests. The hotel. Another in Pisa. I need someone who speaks and writes perfect English to do the new brochures.'

If she went back to England she'd be no better off than when she left, but if she stayed . . . 'All right.'

He looked at her faded jeans. 'If you are to work for me, I insist you dress smartly.'

'I can't afford new clothes.'

'I insist.'

He took her to a small boutique tucked away and known only to its exclusive clientele, all friends of Chiara the red-headed owner whose silky sensuality hid an acutely commercial mind. She selected half a dozen outfits for Olivia then settled Lorenzo on to a sofa with a glass of fresh orange juice. There she engaged him in amusing gossip.

First, Olivia tried on an emerald green knitted suit, not the sort of knitted suit elderly English Tory ladies wear, but a chic slinky skirt which followed the line of her thighs and a ribbed jacket held together by a wide silver belt – and nothing else.

Lorenzo was lounging on the sofa smoking a small cigar. He looked the epitome of a first class air traveller in his grey designer suit and honey cashmere coat. As Olivia walked across the room, he smiled. 'Perfect. Only the hair is wrong – isn't it, Chiara? It should be behind the ears, with earrings, small round ones. Try on that blue dress, I am sure Chiara is right that it will be exceptional on you . . . and wear a belt with it . . . yes, that gold one, and you had better buy some trousers. Chiara, what did I see in the window in grey with a grey leather jacket. Yes, fetch it please.'

An hour later, Olivia looked at the clothes piled on two chairs and asked, 'Which ones am I going to have?'

'All of them.'

'I can't.'

'I have bought them all. Surely you don't think that I am going to wear them.'

'I can't accept them. I'll never be able to repay you.'

'They can be your first week's wages.'

'They're worth far more.'

'Three weeks.'

Of course she shouldn't have let him buy clothes for her but as she had accepted them, well, it was wonderful to be wearing something new and smart. They went out into the chilly evening. Lorenzo turned to her. For a moment she thought he was going to kiss her, then he pushed her hair back from her eyes. 'That's better. Now you look like an elegant spaniel. Come, we will go for a stroll. Italians always promenade in their finery. It's our childish nature. We like to show off what we have.'

Couples passed them, sauntering arm in arm. Olivia walked beside Lorenzo. Once she caught sight of herself in a shop window. Yes, he was right about the hair. Without thinking she slipped her hand into the crook of his arm. Then suddenly she realised what she'd done – but it was too late, his hand was clamped firmly around her wrist.

They walked in silence. She wondered what to do, and what he would do. She wasn't so much attracted by Lorenzo as fascinated by him, by his razor-sharp mind and the glamour of suspect wealth. He was powerful in his world, very powerful, but it wasn't her world: she didn't want it to be: and, then, there was Mark. When they reached the car, she pulled away from him – and when they arrived at the hotel, he dropped her with a detached 'goodnight'.

Two mornings later, whilst struggling to read an Italian newspaper, Olivia turned the page and came face to face with Lorenzo, in evening dress with a voluptuous brunette on his arm. With the help of a dictionary she deciphered, 'The millionaire armsdealer and his companion.'

Lorenzo's offices were on the fourth floor of a modern building further down the hill. The first person Olivia met was the lizard-faced lawyer. His name was Stefano.

'So Lorenzo sent you to the customs house. I thought he must have,' she said.

'You didn't think it was Father Christmas, did you, Signorina Olivia?'

She was put in a functional office with Roberta, Lorenzo's highly efficient secretary. There were two typewriters, a telex, four filing cabinets and an enormous rubber plant.

'Have you worked here long?' Olivia asked casually.

'Eight years.'

'It must be interesting.'

'It is a good position . . . for me.'

'Look, Roberta, I'm not trying to steal your job.'

'No?' The secretary gave an I'll-believe-that-when-I-see-it shrug and began to type furiously.

At the end of the corridor in his large luxurious office, Lorenzo was holding a meeting with two other men; his door was firmly closed. In the room opposite her office Stefano was talking on the telephone: she wished she could understand what he said. By the main door a receptionist was typing envelopes; she had a perfect view of all the comings and goings. Down on the ground floor, a porter logged every arrival.

Olivia spent the first week putting Stefano's good English into perfect English: ordinary business letters concerning the hotels, with not one mention of a bullet let alone a gun. It was infuriating. Boring. Time-wasting. However or wherever Lorenzo ran his arms business it certainly wasn't through this office, and as the days passed it occurred to her that he was having a laugh at her expense. On the evening of the twelfth day she tackled him. 'Why?'

'Why what?' He looked at her across the width of his desk. 'Oh, you mean why didn't I try to seduce you that evening when you so ... spontaneously slipped your arm through mine?'

'No, that's not what I'm asking.'

'That's what most women would want to know.'

From the next room came the sound of Stefano closing his briefcase. From her office came the click as Roberta turned off her typewriter. 'Why did you ask me to work for you?'

'Do you want to leave?'

She shrugged.

'You mean you're not Detective Inspector Steele any more?'

'It's not doing me much good, is it?'

'Ah.' He brought his hands together in front of him so that his fingers made an arch. 'You really thought that by being in my office you would find out something about Culross?'

'Of course. Why else would I stay?'

He pointed at her blue wool dress. 'To repay me.'

'If you hadn't offered me the job I wouldn't have needed the clothes. I'm beginning to understand how you work. You want me to be in your debt. Jake warned me.'

'Why didn't you listen to him?'

'Because if I did that I'd never find out what I want to know.'

'And you still think you will.'

She lifted her chin. 'Yes.'

He laughed. 'Let's have a truce on Saturday. My wife's cousin is giving a party at her villa near Portofino and I should like to take you. I need what you English call moral support. I'll tell Chiara to send something over for you to wear.

On Saturday morning the most exotic billowing red silk harem trousers arrived, together with a red and gold sequined bolero. A brilliant choice. Olivia looked as though she had stepped straight out of a seraglio.

'I cannot recall having a more attractive adversary,' said Lorenzo when he collected her.

'I thought we were having a truce?'

'A ceasefire.'

'Not being an expert in weapons, I wouldn't know the difference.'

He took her wrist and pulled her close to him, holding her tightly, just for a minute. 'Don't provoke me!'

They drew to a halt before the pillars of an eighteenth century villa. From within came the sound of music and laughter. On the terrace people were dancing slowly. Olivia recognised Chiara, glittering in black sequins, her arm linked through that of a suave grey-haired man as they both chatted to a younger but no less suave couple whom Olivia guessed must their host and hostess, the count and countess, cousins of Lorenzo's wife. The chauffeur opened the car door for her. She stepped out and smoothed down her red silk trousers as Lorenzo came to take her arm.

'Lorenzo!' Chiara called to him. 'Wasn't I right about the red? She looks . . . divine! Olivia, come and meet my cousin, Giulia. Yes, she's my cousin too. Didn't Lorenzo tell you that we are all related. Giulia, Olivia is a friend of Jake Hammond.'

She was swept inside and introduced to a dozen people, none of whose names she caught. Somehow she became separated from Lorenzo, and when she looked for him he was at the other end of the room, his back to her, talking intently to an older man. So much for moral support! Champagne appeared. Cigarettes were offered. She took one – she needed one. She talked to fat men, thin men, tall, short, handsome, ugly ones – anything rather than be left alone. She was furious with Lorenzo.

'You must be English,' said a very English, very boyish voice.

'Yes – so must you.'

He was fair, probably in his late teens, and he reminded her immediately of Jonathan.

'I'm Olivia,' she held out her hand.

'Oh, you're the . . .' he blushed.

'The what?'

'Nothing.'

'Come on, tell me.'

'Promise you won't be offended?'

'I'll try not to be.'

'You're the gunrunner's girlfriend. Oh, I'm sorry I shouldn't have told you but that is how Vittorio translated it.'

'For your information I am not the gunrunner's girlfriend – I'm not anybody's girlfriend.'

'Oh, God, now I have put my foot in it. I really wouldn't have said anything and if I hadn't had rather a lot to drink . . . Here's Vittorio! Vittoria, this is Olivia and she's not the . . . um . . .'

Vittorio's eyes were fixed on Olivia's shoulder. 'Good evening, Lorenzo, I don't think you have met my schoolfriend. We are at Le Rosey together.'

The boys melted into the party. Lorenzo took Olivia's arm. 'We're leaving.

She shook herself free. 'I was just beginning to enjoy myself.'

'With those boys?'

'I had to talk to someone. Don't you know that it's very rude to take a lady to a party and ignore her.'

He held up his hands. 'I'm sorry. You're right. Paola's friends always make me nervous.'

'Why do you come?'

'For the sake of my children. I want them to move in these circles and to marry well.

'Supposing they don't want to.'

'They will. 'He took her arm again and this time she allowed him to lead her towards their host and hostess.

He was silent during the drive home, until suddenly he leaned forward and told the driver to take the next left and they turned down into the narrow streets of a seaside village, stopping beside the harbour wall.

'Let's walk,' he said.

She got out. To her left fishermen's boats bobbed on a choppy sea, to their right the ochre houses had their shutters tightly closed against the November night.

'This place is called Camogli,' he said. 'They say the name comes from *le case delle moglie*, the houses of the wives. Sailors wives lived here. I like to think of those women waiting patiently for their men to return.'

'Didn't your wife . . .' She stopped.

'It took me five years to realise that Paola preferred to attend a concert than to spend an afternoon in bed with me – or with

209

any man. I understood that on the day she told me she knew I had other women and was glad.'

'Were you in love with her?'

'I thought I was – once – but in retrospect I think I was in love with what she stood for. She was beautiful, cultured and aristocratic.'

'How did you meet?'

'I saved her father from bankruptcy.'

'And he gave you his daughter?'

He laughed. 'You'd like to think that, wouldn't you? Come, you're shivering. You have no coat.' He put his arm about her shoulder. 'You will be ill again.'

In the car she was aware of him as a man, in subtle ways that she had not been before – at least not like this, with his warmth about her and his brooding face so close to hers. He held her hand, his fingers linked between hers, his thumb stroking the soft mound of her palm. But Olivia sat rigid, her mind racing in circles.

They reached the hotel. The chauffeur opened the car door for her. She stepped out. Lorenzo came round to her side.

'Lorenzo, I'm sorry but . . .'

'Goodnight, Olivia.'

At nine o'clock next morning she dialled Mark's number.

A woman's breathless voice answered, 'Hello.'

'May I speak to Mark Denholm?'

'Who's calling?'

'A . . . er . . . friend.'

'Mark, darling, there's some girl on the line who won't give her name.'

Olivia replaced the receiver. It hadn't taken him long to find a substitute.

On Monday, Roberta told her that Lorenzo had gone to Florida for a week. She wondered why all the men she met were unreliable or unscrupulous, or both. Well, she could play that game too.

'It would be nice if we could have lunch together one day,' she told Stefano.

He gave her his lizard look. 'I usually have my lunch at my desk but . . .'

She smiled.

He adjusted his glasses.

She smiled even wider.

'. . . and then I studied law at university, in Milan, of course. I am Milanese.'

'Of course.' Olivia stared at him through a fog of boredom.

'. . . and I passed with the highest marks in my year.'

'Of course.' How was it possible that Lorenzo employed anyone so dull?

'I could have joined any law firm I liked.'

'Why didn't you . . . I mean, why did you decide to have . . . only one client?'

He adjusted his glasses. 'I did practice to start with. Signor Lorenzo was a client of the firm and . . .'

'He invited you to join him. He speaks so highly of you, Stefano.' She smiled sweetly. 'There must be so many complicated legal problems in shipping arms.'

He stretched his neck like a conceited ostrich. 'It's all a question of having the right contacts – and knowing your market. For instance, the Lebanon buys small arms.'

'Which side?'

'All sides. Christians, Palestinians – in Beirut everyone needs a gun.'

'I thought there'd been a ceasefire.'

'They'll start up again soon. He gave a thin, girlish laugh. 'There's always a war somewhere, and when it's over the winner sells the loser's weapons. Lebanese Christians fire at Palestinians with guns captured by the Israelis from the Egyptians. And it's not just the cost of the gun, it's the ammunition. That's where you make the money. What good is a gun without a bullet.'

'How interesting,' she said in her best little girl's voice. 'I never realised it was so easy. I thought you have to have an end-user certificate.'

'Every country has friends somewhere, and in every country there are people with a price,' he sniggered. 'The art is to know who those people are. Lorenzo knows exactly who to approach. Sometimes he does not even have to make contact – they come running to him.' He stopped abruptly, swallowed hard, and snapped his fingers at the waiter, saying. 'It is late. I have work to do.'

She was on the terrace watching the lights of a container ship move towards the port when Lorenzo burst in. 'How dare you question Stefano about me?'

'I only had lunch with him.'

'Don't lie.'

'All right. But I learned nothing.'

'Did you think he'd fall for your big brown eyes, like Mark Denholm?'

'No, of course I didn't.'

'Or perhaps you thought that because I wanted to make love to you on Saturday night you had the right to question my employees behind my back?'

'I did not.'

'I think you did.' He advanced on her. 'I think you imagined I was weakening.'

She backed away. 'You must be very sure of Stefano.'

'I am. He stole from the client account where he worked. If it wasn't for me he'd be in gaol. If I wanted, he could still go to gaol.'

'You seem to spend all your time saving people.'

'You think I only do it to give me a hold over them?'

'Yes.'

'You're right. They're such fools to accept a favour — and you, Olivia, are a fool to play my games without knowing the rules.'

'You don't frighten me.'

'Don't I? Well, I should.' He came closer. She backed away, until she reached the corner of the terrace and just a three-foot wall saved her from a five-storey drop. He followed, slowly. She edged up towards the house. He blocked her path with his arm. She had never been so frightened in her life.

'Jake will want to know what happened to me,' she said.

'And you think that would stop me?'

'Yes.' She tried to sound as if she believed it. 'You value his friendship, for you and your children. Think of them.'

He seized her by the neck and pulled her towards him, his thumb pushing against her windpipe. 'You've learned to play dirty, haven't you?'

'Culross taught me that.'

'Culross!' He released her and walked to the other side of the terrace. 'Don't you ever think of anything else?'

'Would you?'

He stared out at the night. Then, suddenly, he laughed. 'I have only ever known one other person who was as stubborn as you are. Very well, if you promise to stay with Jake at Pietra Alta, until the new year without communicating with anyone, and agree never to trouble me with this . . . matter again, I will tell you something. It may not be what you want to know, but it is all you'll ever get. Do you accept?'

She thought quickly. In six weeks she'd discovered nothing. 'Yes.'

'Roland Culross was to have received a backhander of one million dollars for arranging the loan.'

'Why did you pick on Roland?'

'Men who live above their means are vulnerable.'

'But not necessarily dishonest.'

'Ah, but I knew he had been interested in doing business with Sindona. Michele Sindona, as I'm sure you know, was at the centre of one of the biggest banking scandals in Italy – and we are a nation of banking scandals. A man who is interested in doing business with one who is badwhispered even if not badmouthed shows his colours. Roland showed his. I approached him.

'I whetted his appetite first, and when he had swallowed the bait I told him. What you have to remember is that if your journalist had not written that article no one would have been any the wiser, and no one would have been hurt. Culross would have been repaid.'

'Did Roland still get the million dollars?'

'Certainly not.'

'Who got it?'

'I did.'

She had to laugh. 'How did you get it out of his account?'

'The bank was instructed to pay one million to the seller and the other to either Roland or myself, depending on my instructions.'

'Did Roland know that?'

'Hardly.'

213

'He must have been furious.'

'Unfortunately he had forgotten that he had written down the name of his Swiss bank and his account number – in his own handwriting. So careless! When he threatened me, I told him if he ever did so again I'd send the note to his dear brothers. I haven't heard a word since.'

'It was all so simple, wasn't it?' she said, ruefully.

'The best tricks are.'

'Can I have the note?'

'No.' He walked to the terrace door. 'Jake will collect you in the morning. Remember our agreement.'

'How do you know I'll keep it?'

'I'll know.'

He seemed older, tougher, more brutal, and she wondered how she could ever have expected to get the better of him. 'Thank you for telling me about Roland. You didn't have to. Why did you?'

He turned in the doorway. 'Because you remind me of Gisella.'

18

Olivia looked down on the patchwork countryside of England and counted the hours till that moment when she would march triumphantly into Culross and throw the truth about Roland in their faces, demanding that they publicly clear her name, after which she would somehow reduce Gerald (and Fleet Street) to a grovelling pulp, then she would storm around to Mark's house to tell him exactly what she thought of him . . . well . . . almost exactly. She ran her fingers through the luxuriant pile of the silver fox coat draped across the seat beside her. It had arrived on New Year's day with a note from Lorenzo: 'Didn't I tell you that you should be the mistress of a rich man?' She'd wanted to send it back, or at least she'd felt she ought to, but Jake had stopped her. Dear Jake! She thought of him standing in the middle of Pisa airport saying, 'I still reckon you should have called Mark.'

The plane skimmed the gardens of suburban London. She smoothed her grey suede trousers into her highly polished boots and pushed her hair back from her eyes – and smiled as she thought of Lorenzo.

Her smart suitcase, a present from Jake, was among the first offloaded. She picked it up and with the hem of her fur coat swirling about her booted legs she strode through customs, every inch a rich man's lover – and walked into Mark.

'Olivia?' It had taken him a moment to equate this elegant creature with the tousle-haired girl he'd known in Anataxos.

'Mark! What a coincidence!'

'It's not a coincidence. I came to meet you.'

'Oh, did Jake . . .?'

'Yes, he rang from Pisa.'

'I told him not to.'

'I know.' He held out his hand expecting to take hers, intending to judge her feelings from the warmth of her clasp.

She handed him her suitcase. 'Thank you.' He had not even kissed her on the cheek.

The crowd surged around them, suntanned skiers from the Alps and businessmen with minimal luggage.

'Julius and I want to talk to you,' he said flatly.

'Did Jake tell you about . . . Lorenzo?'

'Not a lot.'

'Then how do you know I've anything to say?' She was disappointed, but sounded irritated.

'After two months with the Italian we presume you must have discovered something. In any case, you might try to appear grateful – I've given up a day's shooting to meet you.'

'I didn't ask you to come.'

Without answering Mark set off for the car park, walking very fast. What the hell did Jake mean by 'Be kind to her, Mark, she's had a tough time.' Be kind! What a fool he'd been to insist to Julius that he meet her on his own. What an idiot to rush out of the house in order to arrive early so there was no risk of missing her. How pathetic he'd been, standing there, longing for a shaggy-haired girl clutching a battered suitcase. Then this apparition presented itself, turning every man's head, handing him her luggage as if he were a porter. Well, it was obvious what she'd been up to – and she certainly didn't need his kindness.

Olivia followed him along the walkway to the car park. Her triumphant return had been stolen, that delicious moment of surprise when Mark opened his door to find her glowing with victory was not to be. He didn't give a damn. She wished she hadn't come back. She wondered what had happened to the girl who called him darling. Perhaps she was waiting in the car, sitting in the back seat as lovers do when making room for an interloper.

But there was no one in the car – except for Mark, drumming his fingers on the steering-wheel with ill-concealed

216

impatience. 'We're going to Lady Vicky's stud farm first,' he said. 'Julius is on his way there now.'

'Where is it?'

'On the South Downs.'

'But that's over an hour from London!'

'Culross will provide a taxi for you.'

'I should hope so!'

They said nothing more. Olivia gritted her teeth. Mark gritted his. She told herself he was just another goodlooking man in a navy blue jersey. He purposefully did not look at the suede trousers, so soft against her thighs. She knew he longed to get home to 'Darling'. There was no doubt in Mark's mind that Olivia had been the Italian's lover. She wondered why she'd looked forward so much to seeing him. He wondered why he'd been unable to forget her.

It was snowing hard by the time they reached Horsham. Mark stopped at a telephone kiosk. The snow settled on the windscreen. Through the flakes Olivia could see him laughing as he spoke into the receiver. She imagined him saying, I'll be as quick as I can darling, and Darling saying I miss you, darling as she spooned zabaglione into tall chilled glasses without smudging her freshly painted nails.

An hour later the car slithered down a steep hill into a village of thatched cottages heavily laden with snow. It could have been so romantic, thought Olivia, the two of us, battling against the elements, but it wasn't. They were imprisoned in the tension which they had created.

Beyond the village was an old stone gatehouse, beside it a notice in smart black lettering:

The Helmets Stud Farm – Private Property

They turned under the gatehouse and up the drive, past a stable complex of some thirty looseboxes built around a courtyard. The house was on top of a hill, looking down the valley. It was a long, low gracious building with turreted wings at either end – the turrets whose pinnacled roofs, shaped like the Kaiser's helmet, gave the place its name. On a summer's day, when the roses in the terraced garden hummed with bees and the soft Sussex countryside rolled at its feet, The Helmets was considered to be the epitome of gracious living; on a cold grey Saturday afternoon in February it reminded Olivia of the sort of place from which heroines run screaming in stories where innocent governesses tame wicked heirs to Scottish fortunes. She turned to Mark to ask if it had always been in his family, but his face was totally impassive – so she said nothing.

As the car crunched to a halt, the front door opened and Lady Vicky appeared on the top step dressed in an exotic purple cardigan, black trousers and shiny orange Wellington boots. 'Ah, there you are, Mark dear, you must be exhausted. Good afternoon, Miss Steele.' She gave Olivia a cold handshake.

Olivia stepped into the warmth of the long flagstoned hall, so angry that she noticed nothing of the mellow beauty of her surroundings. How dare they treat her like a prodigal. How dare Mark bring her to this place to be scorned by his family when they should be down on their bended knees with gratitude that she – not they – had faced Lorenzo on the darkened terrace.

Two Afghan hounds bounded across the room like flying hearthrugs, practically knocking her over in their rush for Mark. No one apologised.

'They always did like you the best,' said Lady Vicky, as he fondled their silky ears.

'Where's Julius?'

'In the drawing-room with Sarah. I thought she and I would have our tea in there and you, Julius and Miss Steele can have yours in the study. Would you like to wash your hands, Miss Steele? It's through there. You can leave your coat on the sofa. Zubi! Petra! Oh, get down you silly dogs.'

Olivia could hear them talking in the hall as she came back. He was saying, 'It makes no difference to Erica and me,' and she replied, 'I'm so glad, I'm only sorry that . . . Ah, there you are Miss Steele, I'll tell Mrs Widget we're ready for tea.'

So it was Erica who lay in Mark's bed on Sunday mornings and called out 'Darling'.

Olivia had never liked the name Erica. There had been a spiteful little girl called Erica at her kindergarten who specialised in pulling the wings off flies then throwing them out of the window. She'd been killed in a car crash. They'd prayed for her in assembly. The headmistress had told them that Erica was in heaven, but Olivia had been sure she wasn't. God would not want Erica — she might pull the wings off the angels. Some of the little girls had cried because Erica wasn't coming back — it had been her birthday the following week and now the conjuror would be cancelled.

Mark led the way into an oak-panelled study where a small brown dog, as mongrel as the Afghans were well-bred, slept soundly in an armchair beside a roaring fire.

'Mouse!'

It shot out of the chair, stretched, yawned, then trotted out of the room thoroughly offended.

Mark thumped the cushion. 'He's not allowed on chairs because he moults.'

'Dogs do, don't they.'

'Yes.'

They stood in front of the fire, pretending to watch the flames, acutely aware of each other; resentful but never indifferent.

Julius came in. 'Good afternoon, Olivia.' He held out his hand for a perfunctory clasp in which there was no hint of the months when she had worked closely with him.

Mark took a notepad and pen from the desk. 'Shall we begin? We don't want to delay Olivia longer than we have to.' They sat. 'Culross have been making enquiries about the relationship between Roland and the Italian,' he said. 'Roland doesn't know this, of course — that's why we wanted to talk to you here and not in London.'

'In case I scare him off?'

'Or the Italian tips him off.'

'That's not likely.'

'We have to be careful.' He looked at Julius. 'I think you wanted to ask Olivia . . .'

'Yes. We want to ask you to keep away from the City for a couple of weeks.'

'To lie low till you've had a chance to act on my information?'

'I'm so glad you understand.'

'I do — perfectly.'

'Then, let's hear it.'

'I think you've forgotten something.'

219

'Oh?'

'What are you going to do for me in return?'

'I'm sure Culross will pay you . . .' Mark began.

'I don't want money, I want to clear my name. I want Culross to admit publicly that Roland turned me into a scapegoat to cover his own dishonesty.'

'A public announcement is out of the question,' said Julius. 'Mark, I thought you said that Olivia was willing to help us.'

'Oh, he did, did he?'

'Yes, I did – but I hadn't reckoned on what two months with a hood would do to your values.'

'Lorenzo has nothing to do with my values – except that I now know I have a value, just as I know that everything had its price, including information. I'm not some seedy little spy in a TV movie, the type who risks life, limb and Siberia but is satisfied with ignominy and an extra week's leave in Scunthorpe. I earned my pound of flesh and I want it. I faced Lorenzo – the hood, as you call him. I braved Genoa docks to see the *Ariosto*, and got arrested at gun point, was chased by a tattooed knifeman, and spent three weeks with my wrist in plaster. I did these things – not you two – so if you want to know what I found out you've got to meet my terms, and those are that I be exonerated publicly.'

Mark gave a sarcastic laugh. 'You seem to have forgotten about Gerald Quentin, or are you now claiming that you never even met him?'

'Of course not! But you know that what I suffered went far beyond any indiscretion I committed. If the loan had been secured, Gerald wouldn't have had a story.'

There was a tap on the door and a homely woman came in carrying a tea tray.

Mark took it from her. 'Thank you, Mrs Widget.'

There was silence. The men waited for Olivia to pour. She ignored them. Eventually Julius lifted the pot whilst Mark held the fine bone china cups and saucers, and she had the feeling that he would gladly have thrown them at her.

'Supposing we agree to do what we can for you,' said Julius.

Mark cut in. 'That's up to you. I'm not a director of Culross, merely an advisor, and personally I wouldn't agree to anything with Olivia. She's probably going to tell you some pack of lies she and the Italian have concocted for their amusement.'

Olivia stood up. 'If that's the way you feel, why the hell did you waste my time by dragging me here?'

'God only knows.'

'Take me back to London.'

'You can bloody well walk.'

'Calm down!' Julius had to shout to make himself heard. 'Olivia, on behalf of Culross I promise to do all I can to dissociate you publicly from any suggestion of dishonesty.'

'What about Roland?'

'He'll be forced to resign.'

'You have to make the reason public.'

'I can't guarantee that, you know I can't. Banks don't work that way. But unofficially the whole City will know, especially if we free you from dishonest association.'

'In a press release?'

He hesitated.

'I insist.'

'Very well.'

'I want this agreement in writing . . . now.' She sat down again.

'All right. Mark, perhaps you'd witness it.'

Mark did not look at Olivia when he said, 'We had better each keep a copy so there are no misunderstandings.' He went behind the desk, produced an old manual typewriter, ran a blank page through it and typed quickly:

I, Julius Culross, promise to dissociate Olivia Steele from any suggesttion of dishonesty in the unsecured loan to Linea Pan Liguria for the purchase of the *Ariosto* if the information she furnishes regarding the dishonest connection between Roland Culross and the said loan proves to be correct.

He went to the stud farm office and a few minutes later he was back with three copies.

For the next hour Olivia told them exactly what Lorenzo had told her – about the backhander, the Swiss bank account, the false charter, and the reason why the Italian had known Roland was vulnerable to dishonest propositions.

'What happened to the money?' asked Julius.

'Lorenzo kept it. He used it to raise another loan.'

221

'So he bought the ship after all?'

'Yes.'

'I don't suppose he would consider giving us back our money?'

She laughed.

And Mark laughed, his eyes on her very expensive suede trousers. 'I shouldn't think there's much left.'

'It's very interesting and rather as we had imagined,' said Julius, trying to head off another argument, 'but is there any proof?'

'Yes, but I don't have it.' She told him about the note.

'Ask him for a copy,' said Mark.

'I did. He refused.'

'Offer him money for it.'

'No.'

Mark drummed his fingers on the desk. 'Now I understand. You've fallen out with your protector so you've come to sell us his story – presumably confided to you on some soft pillow.'

'That's a lie!'

'You've learned fast, Olivia, but then you had a good teacher in the art of betrayal in Gerald Quentin.'

'You bastard!'

'I hardly think . . .' began Julius.

'You expect us to believe that an international gunrunner hands this information over to some simpering little English girl just because she asks him.'

'He told me because I reminded him of his sister, the one who braved public opinion to live with Jake. He said we were equally stubborn.'

The door opened and Lady Vicky came in carrying Mouse. 'I'm sorry to interrupt but the drive is completely blocked by snow. Widget says no traffic can get through the village and the snowploughs won't be out till tomorrow or even Monday, so I'm afraid Miss Steele will have to stay the night. I've put her in the blue room, next to you, Mark. Sarah and I were about to have a drink and . . .'

'I think we all need one,' said Mark, walking out of the study.

Julius followed.

Olivia was left alone with her hostess, 'Lady Victoria . . .'

222

'Don't call me Victoria, I detest it.'

'Lady Vicky, I realise that you don't want me in . . . your house and I would much rather leave . . .' Olivia was scarlet with embarrassment and anger.

'You can't. The nearest station is ten miles away and we're snowed in.'

'Then I would prefer to remain in my room this evening. It would be much less unpleasant for everyone.'

'I'll ask Mrs Widget to give you a supper tray.'

When the housekeeper showed Olivia to her bedroom, she said, 'Nothing like an early night to get rid of a nasty 'eadache, is there?'

'Er . . . no, there isn't.'

Mrs Widget patted the blue draped four-poster bed. 'You've got a nice 'ot water bottle so you'll be warm and comfy.'

'Thank you.'

'Always liked this room, myself. 'Er Ladyship slept 'ere after Sir Frederick died. She couldn't bear to use the west wing where she'd known so much 'appiness, poor lamb. It was three years before she moved back.'

'When did he die?'

'Twenty years ago. Of course 'e was a lot older than 'er. What a gentleman! My 'usband and I came straight 'ere after the war and we've been 'ere ever since. Part of the family, we are, but I can tell you, miss, I was surprised when we were offered the position.'

'Oh?'

'You see Mr Widget was under Mr Piers – Mr Mark's father – during the war and, well, as I'm sure you know, Mr Piers was a bit of a black sheep, what with 'is marriage and all that, but Sir Frederick insisted we came for 'er Ladyship's sake. Very fond of Mr Piers was Lady Vicky, though if it had been old Sir Larry 'e'd 'ave shown us the door. 'Eartbroken was Lady Vicky when old Sir Larry refused to accept the little Mr Mark. Of course it was worse because the doctors 'ad just told 'er she'd never 'ave children of 'er own, poor lamb. That's when she began breeding 'orses, to take 'er mind off it.'

'Did you meet Mark's mother?'

'No.' She pursed her lips. 'No, I did not. They say she was very pretty and that they were very much in love, but she wasn't the right bride for a Culross. People should stick to their own kind, miss, saves a lot of un'appiness. Oh, 'ow I do gossip. Well, I'll be up later with your supper. You get into bed. Don't want you going down with the 'flu, do we?'

To Olivia's surprise she slept like a log, waking only once to voices in the corridor. A woman's voice – Sarah? – saying, 'I'm sorry it's turned out this way, Mark,' and Mark, barely audible, 'I suppose it's all part of life's rich pattern.' Then she fell asleep again.

She woke early and drew back the heavy velvet curtains on a white world. Her window looked over the terraced garden which dropped away to fields and the parallel hedges of a road running along the bottom of the valley. Surely someone must have cleared it by now, she thought as she took a quick bath. How far did Lady Vicky say the station was? Ten miles? She pulled on a thick red jersey and zipped up her black cord trousers.

The house was silent. She crept downstairs.

'Good morning, Miss Steele.' Through the open door of the dining-room Lady Vicky was drinking coffee in solitary splendour at the far end of a stretch of pristine white tablecloth laid for breakfast.

'Good morning, Lady Vicky.'

'The others are still asleep. Would you care for some breakfast?'

'Yes, I mean, no.' Olivia straightened her shoulders. 'I was hoping I might be able to leave before . . .'

'Out of the question. Widget says the road won't be cleared till tomorrow morning.' She pointed to the chair next to hers. 'Cooked breakfast?'

'No, toast would be lovely. Thank you.'

'I am afraid I haven't been very welcoming to you, Miss Steele, but I happen to be extremely fond of Mark. Milk? Sugar? Do help yourself to marmalade.'

'Thank you.' Olivia took a deep breath. 'I'm not sure I understand, I thought you didn't want me here because of what happened at the bank.'

'Good heavens, no! I've always liked the black sheep, though I couldn't see what you saw in the dreadful journalist. I suppose it was sex.'

Olivia choked.

'Don't still hanker after him, do you?'

'Definitely not! In fact, my hope is that one day I'll get the chance to get even with him.' She picked up a knife and sliced through the butter.

'And the Italian?'

'Lorenzo was no boyfriend of mine.'

'What about Mark?'

'Well . . . er . . .' She smoothed the butter on to her toast, very carefully, right up to the crust, as though her life depended on doing it well. 'I . . . thought I was in love with him.'

'But you're not?'

'It wouldn't do me much good, would it?' She gave Lady Vicky a smile which was intended to be philosophical but instead came over as bruised and vulnerable. 'He's involved with someone else. I phoned him early one morning and a girl answered.'

'Oh, that was only Erica I expect. She's not right for Mark. More coffee? White with sugar? I don't know if you're right for him either. After all, you have had rather a chequered career where men are concerned, haven't you?'

'No. I've had very few love affairs, but it happens that one became public property.'

'That's the spirit! Glad to see you're not a mealy-mouthed penitent. Have some more marmalade. No, try the other one, its made with peaches and brandy. Nothing worse than people sobbing over their past peccadillos! Culross men have always gone for gutsy women. Look at Mark's mother. Plenty of spice in her! You should have had a cooked breakfast. Mrs Widget, Olivia will have sausages and bacon.'

There was a clatter of footsteps out in the hall and a heavily pregnant Sarah came in with Julius and a small boy. Mark followed.

Julius put on a breezy politeness. 'Good morning, Vicky. Yes, we slept well thank you. Oh . . . er . . . good morning, Olivia. Dominic, say good morning! Sarah, I don't think you've met Olivia Steele. What's for breakfast? Oh, good morning Mrs Widget.'

Mark sat at the far end of the table. Julius put his son one away from Olivia. With a polite smile on her well-ordered features, Sarah pulled out the chair beside Olivia, but before she had a chance to sit down Dominic scrambled on to it. 'I want to sit next to her,' he said, leaning towards Olivia and giving her a very solemn smile as his clear, childish voice rang out, 'Uncle Mark says you've turned into a real cow. Will you show me how you do it after breakfast?'

They laughed – they had to – but even then Mark did not meet her eyes.

'What about the tail?' said Dominic doubtfully, kicking at the snow with his small red shiny boots.

'Here it is.'

'That's not a tail, that's a stick.'

'What do you mean it's not a tail? Poor Buttercup, she's offended. Look you've made her cry.' The sun had warmed the cow's face and rivulets dripped to the ground.

'Why's she called Buttercup?'

'All my cows are called Buttercup.'

'Mummy! Daddy! Look at Buttercup. Mummy, Buttercup's going to have a baby just like you.'

'I hope Dominic's not being a nuisance.' Sarah gave Olivia the sort of smile which said, 'I've nothing against you personally but I have to support Julius.'

'Uncle Mark, come and meet my cow. Olivia made him for me.'

'I can see it from here.'

Stuff him, thought Olivia turning her back to Mark and moulding the cow's ears.

Feet crunched through the snow towards her but she refused to look up. 'You forgot its horns.' Mark handed her two curved twigs.

'I don't think lady cows have horns.'

'Oh, yes, they do . . . very pointed ones.'

'Then stick them in yourself.'

He did – and the cow's head fell off.

Mark cursed.

Olivia gave a snort of derision which changed to uncontrollable giggles as Mark, whilst trying to reattach the head, succeeded only in demolishing the entire animal. He turned to look at Olivia and saw her shiny button-brown eyes and her shiny brown hair. 'You can stop that sniggering.' He made a grab for her. She ducked and dodged, laughing when he caught her, but as he pulled her to him her smile became guarded. 'Why didn't you tell me you'd telephoned from Italy?' he asked.

'You didn't give me a chance, you've been so ... bad tempered. And what was I meant to think, when a girl answers early in the morning and calls you darling?'

'Come on, let's walk. No, Dominic, go to Mummy. Sarah, can you call him please!'

They crossed the front of the house, walking side by side but not touching. 'Erica was in the past even before I met you at the Culross party,' he said, 'but it took a long time to make the final break. You know how it is when you're fond of someone and don't want to hurt them but you know it won't work!'

She thought of Simon. 'Yes.'

'I hadn't seen her for nearly a year until one Saturday in December when I bumped into her at a party. I was in a foul mood, I'd rung Jake that afternoon hoping to find you at Pietra Alta. He was very cagy but eventually admitted that you were in Genoa with the Italian and had been for six weeks. Don't blame him for telling me, he was so worried about you.'

'You were in the bath when I phoned.'

'Yes, I remember. I was listening to the nine o'clock news and feeling guilty about Erica when the phone rang. I had this awful premonition that it was you. It seemed as though I were getting my just deserts by you calling on the one night I had someone ... there, but by the time I reached the phone you'd hung up. Then Erica said she thought it was Sarah, she was always convinced that Sarah didn't like her.' They had reached the fence which separated the terraced garden from the field. 'What about the Italian?' he asked, without looking at her. 'Was he your lover?'

'No.'

'But there was ... something between you.'

'In a way. He was fascinating, magnetic – and yet I have never been so frightened of anyone. I don't think I would ever want to meet him again, and yet I'm glad I've known him. I can't explain it.'

227

Mark picked up a handful of snow, pounded it into a ball and threw it so hard that it bounced along the surface of the field. 'The trouble with you and me is that we're too damned alike.'

'You mean you'd rather I hadn't told you I had had any feelings for Lorenzo?'

'No, I'd hate you to lie to me – it's simply that I'd have preferred you to be indifferent to him.'

'I'd rather there had been no Erica.'

'Why did he tell you about Roland? Was it really because you reminded him of Gisella?'

'Yes. Look Mark, I can't make you believe me but I'm not going to be bullied. If you want a sweet little doormat lying inside the front door stamped with "Welcome" . . .'

He lifted her chin. 'I never thought of you as a doormat. Anyhow, I'd much prefer a nice soft tiger skin.'

Her eyes sparkled. 'So would I.'

'Peace is restored, is it?' called Lady Vicky marching across the garden towards them, her shiny orange boots incongruous with a pale mink. 'Want to see my horses, Olivia?'

'We'll both come,' said Mark.

'All right – but no mooning over Olivia or you'll excite the stallion.'

Some twenty pairs of liquid eyes watched the visitors arrive in the stableyard.

'How are you, my pet?' Lady Vicky stopped outside one stable and a sleek chestnut head stretched out to nuzzle her. 'No, don't eat my mink! I know it isn't my new one, but there's no need to dribble all over it. Lady Ross is one of my best mares, Olivia. In fact, she's in foal to a very special stallion – Northern Dancer, the most expensive stud horse in the world. We sent her all the way to Mayland to be covered. No, naughty! That's my diamond ring.'

They moved on down the line of horses. 'Do you keep all the foals?' asked Olivia.

'Good heavens no! A stud farm makes its money from the sale of its yearlings and from stud fees when its own stallion covers other people's mares. This is a maternity home and a kindergarten, not a school for boisterous teenagers. These horses are bred to race.

'Lady Ross looks quite young,' said Mark.

'She's five. I'm afraid breeding's gain has been racing's loss. A well-bred animal with a couple of decent wins is worth more at stud than on the track. There is only one winner in each race but a good mare will produce a foal a year and a potent stallion can cover, oh, fifty mares in one season.'

'Is a Derby winner always very valuable at stud?' asked Olivia.

'Yes, if it's well-bred, and it usually is, but if – God forbid – it were discovered that the father of a Derby winner were not the registered sire, but some pit pony which had got in with the mare, that winner would be worthless at stud because who's to say when the traits of the pit pony might not reappear. Breeding horses is big business. You hope to get a foal a year from a good mare, and you don't want her to waste eleven months of her life carrying something with short legs. And it wouldn't look good for the stud farm. Our reputations are built on the quality of the foals we breed. You have to understand one thing, my dear, a horse in training costs – and a bad horse costs just as much as a good horse, if not more. Bad horses like dud cars are always going wrong.'

'Last year six foals were born in one night,' Mark told Olivia.

'So they all share the same birthday.'

Lady Vicky laughed. 'My dear, all horses born in one year share the same official birthday – the first of January.'

'Even I knew that,' said Mark.

'I can't think how. You always pretend you don't know one end of a horse from the other.'

'I do. I know that one end bites and the other kicks.'

'You wouldn't believe it, Olivia, but Mark could be an excellent rider with a bit of practice.'

'Now, Vicky, don't tell Olivia all my secrets or I'll have nothing left to impress her with.'

They had reached an indoor paddock where a dozen or so foals pushed up to the fence, their eyes curious, their noses soft and velvety.

'Aren't they beautiful?' Olivia stroked one. It seemed incredible that this fluffy creature whose tail was not yet sleek, but like a feather duster, should become a full grown horse in the time it takes a human being to arrive at junior school.

Beyond the paddock and out of sight of the mares, in a separate stable with its own high-fenced paddock stood the stallion, Culross Boy, a tall bay with a white blaze down his well-bred nose. Culross Boy was being fed by Alf the studman and Eddie, a new stud hand.

'Come on, Eddie, it's no good being afraid of 'im,' Alf was saying. ''orses know when yer afraid and they take advantage. Come on, lad, pour 'is feed into 'is bucket. That's right. Ah, good morning Yer Ladyship. Just teaching Eddie 'ow to 'andle the stallion.'

'Nothing to be afraid of, Eddie,' Lady Vicky patted the big horse firmly on the neck. 'Just remember, you have to show him who's boss then he'll respect you.' She hitched up her Schiaparelli dress so that the hem cleared the top of her muddy boots and bent to test the feed, running her beringed fingers through the mixture of corn and nuts, saying, 'Good, you've added the vitamin E. The breeding season's less than a month away.'

It seemed to Olivia that the stallion twitched with anticipation.

'I don't know what it is about men who work on stud farms,' Lady Vicky confided as they made their way back to the house. 'Not only has Alf had three wives but he started carrying on with a local barmaid last summer. He used to bring her up to the tack room – till his wife found out.'

'Perhaps he eats the vitamin E instead of giving it to the stallion,' said Mark catching Olivia's eye.

She giggled – and as they went up through the garden she kept imagining the studman with his nose in the stallion's feed.

During lunch Lady Vicky said, 'You're not attempting to drive up to London tonight are you, Mark?'

'No, I'll take the train. I'm in Manchester all week so I might as well leave my car here and hire one up there.'

'Widget will take you to the station in the landrover. Julius, can't I persuade you and Sarah to stay a few more days? You're going after breakfast. What a pity.' She turned to Olivia. 'What about you, Olivia dear? Unless you have other plans perhaps you'd like to stay here for the week.'

Olivia was conscious that they had all heard the 'Olivia

dear'. 'I'd love to,' she said, 'but I would like to telephone my parents, they don't even know I'm back in England.'

'Of course.' Lady Vicky smiled at her, then at Mark, and there was something in her expression which said, that stops you both from plunging in, feet first, and making a mess of things again.

Later, as the sun was sinking into the snow-covered downs, Mark and Olivia stood on the terrace and watched the dogs gallop in the snow.

'Vicky for all her outspokenness is old fashioned when it comes to her family,' said Mark, taking her hand in his. 'She comes from an age when guests did not share a bedroom unless they are married. She once caught Roland creeping back from his girlfriend's bedroom in the dawn and she threw them out – then and there.'

She leaned against him. 'I understand.'

He hugged her.' I knew you would. Vicky's a very special lady. She was the only Culross who bothered about my mother. She tracked us down when I was about six. I remember opening the door to see a huge gleaming car and a lady in a fur coat. She would have helped us, but mother refused – until I went to study at the bar. Then she allowed Vicky to buy me two suits and a coat. I needed them! But I would never have accepted anything if it had upset my mother, not after the way she had been treated.'

From the trees icicles hung like stalactites fired by the setting sun, down in the field the two Afghan hounds raced across the crackling snow, in the drawing-room crumpets melted before a crackling fire. It was so beautiful, so romantic. Olivia wished that everyone would disappear and that she and Mark could find themselves alone in this white solitude but at the same time, in a funny way, she was glad they were not alone; because the ache of wanting made it seem as though they never had been, as if they were right back at the beginning and had only just met.

19

Mark left early next morning. Olivia was vaguely aware of him entering her room and kissing her on the forehead as he murmured that he would telephone later before she fell asleep again, to wake with Mrs Widget bringing her a cup of tea. From the garden below her window came the sound of Lady Vicky talking to her dogs. It was time to get up.

After breakfast Olivia telephoned her parents. Her father listened in silence, then said, 'Livvi, wouldn't you be better here with us – after all the Culrosses weren't very kind to you and we are your family?'

She didn't tell him about Mark, she merely said, 'Daddy, it's different now.'

The week at The Helmets passed slowly. Not that she didn't enjoy herself, she did and she liked Lady Vicky more and more and found the stud farm interesting, but she could not wait to see Mark again. She could think of nothing else. When the phone rang she jumped with anticipation. When Lady Vicky came into the drawing-room and found her in an armchair, Mouse on her lap, she had to tap her on the shoulder to attract her attention. Even then Olivia was only half-conscious of what her hostess was saying, because her whole mind was taken up with Mark – with imaginary conversations with Mark, with images of making love with Mark, with a nebulous secret future where she and Mark were together. By the time Saturday morning arrived she had been proposed to by him in fifteen different situations, got married to him five times, had two children (one of each), and decided that although she didn't particularly like the name Piers she would give in on that point. She had also been through her wardrobe three times before deciding to wear the blue wool dress, the silky one with the gold belt which did more for her than anything else she possessed.

Mark arrived on Saturday morning. As soon as she heard the car crunching up the frozen drive she rushed out to meet him. But when he got out of the car and came towards her she was suddenly terribly shy and had to force herself to look him in the eyes.

'Anyone would think you had some terrible secret?' he said, lifting her chin.

'It's not a secret, it's just that . . .'

'Feelings are the most difficult things to admit.'

'Yes. Feeling means being vulnerable.'

'Are you afraid of being vulnerable to me?'

'I'm afraid of being vulnerable.'

'You have to take a chance.'

'I know.' She reached up to him. 'All week I've been counting the minutes till you returned, but when I came out to meet you I felt so . . . shy . . . so uncertain. No, it's not really uncertainty, more, oh, I don't know.' She tossed back her hair.

He kissed the top of her nose. 'I was going to buy you some flowers and I thought, I'll buy her roses . . . no, that's too obvious . . . orchids, no, that's too ostentatious . . . carnations . . . no, too old-fashioned. I was like that all the way, and you know what happened when I reached the village flower shop?'

'What?'

'It had closed down.'

She laughed and hugged him. She like him better for not being too perfect.

They left The Helmets after lunch – it was difficult to wait even that long but Lady Vicky would have been offended if they'd rushed off immediately. During the journey to London they spoke very little, they did not need words, but when they crossed the Albert Bridge into Chelsea, Olivia came out of her dream, and said, 'I don't even know where your house is, you only gave me the telephone number.'

'It's just off Kensington Church Street, on the hill above the bend where all the antique shops congregate.'

233

She smiled. 'I've always liked that part of London.'

'My house was a shell when I bought it seven years ago, but I couldn't afford anything better in that area and I felt it had great . . .'

'Potential? Like the tower?'

He chuckled. 'Keep me away from ruined houses, I always want to buy them. I love to put my ideas in to practice, but this one was a nightmare. The first night the kitchen ceiling collapsed, the second, a water pipe burst and flooded the ground floor.'

They passed a house which was being gutted. 'Oh, what a pity!' she said, 'You missed out on that one.'

'That's got a roof. Far too advanced. I like a complete shell.'

They turned into a short street with attractive three-storey houses, each with a front door painted in a different colour. He stopped outside a dark blue one. 'Home.'

She smiled nervously.

'Aren't you going to get out?'

'Of course.'

The house was open-plan and furnished with masculine sparseness. There was a beautiful Persian rug, like Jake's, on polished floorboards, a long seductive sofa covered in velvety cushions, a piano, shelf after shelf of books – and one of Jake's propellor sculptures standing in solitary splendour by the French windows. The famous Turner, elusively mellow as Turner's pictures are, the only item Mark had inherited from his grandfather hung over the mantelpiece, opposite blue-green Sickert which shared a wall with a framed poster of James Dean in *Rebel Without a Cause* – and a delicate Edward Lear watercolour. It was a mixture of styles and eras, which somehow had a coherency.

Mark walked into the large tiled kitchen. Olivia followed. He turned and bumped into her. They laughed nervously and stared at each other. Then he put his arms around her and pulled her to him, as she lifted her face, no longer afraid, just wanting him to fill that hollow ache.

He kissed her. 'Shall we . . .?'

She swallowed and nodded.

He led her upstairs, gently, carefully, kissing her on the landing, then on up to his bedroom which filled the whole attic of the house, right up to the sloping rafters, and was warm with rugs and polished floorboards and cushions on a huge bed.

'I've pictured you here so many times,' he said, running his fingers through her hair.

She held him close. 'I was so angry that day in Anataxos, but once Jake told me you'd gone . . .'

He kissed the soft skin of her neck and shoulders. 'I was furious, but once I was on the plane,' he ran his hand down her back and unzipped her dress. 'I wished I hadn't left, I wished I could turn the plane around.'

She unbuttoned his shirt. 'You'd have found me crying in your bedroom.'

'Oh, no, I wouldn't.' The dress fell to the ground, 'You'd have heard me coming, dried your tears and come rampaging down the stairs.'

She lowered her hand to the buckle of his belt. 'And you'd have pretended it wasn't me you'd come back for.'

His mouth came down on hers. She felt herself drawn into him. She wanted to be a part of him. To get under his skin and fuse herself to him. With a slow intensity they explored each other's bodies, touching, caressing, the late afternoon sun making patterns on their limbs, wrapping them in a warm world where they knew nothing but each other. Then he took her, loved her, rode her, ground her – loved her. And she cried, she wasn't sure why, she didn't mean to, but she did.

They stayed in bed until the late evening, talking and laughing and making love. Then they went out, to one of those intimate restaurants with mellow red lights which are made for lovers and confidences, and finally they went home, hugging each other as they slithered on the freezing pavement, to fall asleep, exhausted, Olivia's head on Mark's arm.

She woke to classical music, to the smell of bacon cooking and fresh-ground coffee – and to find Mark gone. She got up, wrapped herself in a large white fluffy towel and went downstairs. In the kitchen he was moving from toaster, to cooker, to fridge in time to the music, which emanated from every direction.

'I make the best toasted bacon sandwiches in town,' he said, 'My special Sunday breakfast. Now, madam, if you would kindly show your appreciation by buttering the toast . . .' He handed her a knife.

'What's the music?'

'Tchaikovsky's "Marche Slave".' He turned it up. 'I love it, especially the end, where you can hear the slaves plodding along in their chains then suddenly their spirits escape. Listen!' He beat out the rhythm on her bare shoulders.

'It has nothing to do with slaves. It was written for a charity concert in aid of wounded Serbian soldiers and that bit at the end is the old Russian national anthem, a kind of "God Save The Tsar".'

'Then they certainly needed to escape from slavery.'

'Mark,' she licked her buttery fingers before putting her arms around his waist, 'it's Slavs not slaves. It's based on Slavonic tunes. I remember that from school.'

'But you didn't remember the music, just the story, and what's the good of that? Does it matter what music or words or pictures mean to each person, so long as they mean something?'

'No, you're right . . . and the toast's ready.'

They took the breakfast tray and the Sunday papers to bed, and curled up against each other.

'There's something deliciously sinful about breakfast in bed,' she said, munching into a bacon sandwich.

'Mmm . . . but do you think you could take your bosom out of my marmalade?'

'You're very honoured to be sharing a bed with my bosom.'

'Oh, I am, I am.'

In the afternoon they went for a walk in Hyde Park and stood on the bridge over the Serpentine to watch the ducks sail into the wintry twilight. 'I don't believe in half-hearted affairs,' said Mark, taking her hand and turning it over. 'I don't mean that I haven't had casual affairs, I have, in the past, but that's all they were and I knew it. I'm talking about the other sort — you and me. Either I like someone enough to want to be with them as much as possible or I don't like them enough, in which case I'd rather go to bed with a good book.'

'Or the business section of the *Sunday Times*?'

'Has to be the business section.'

'All those columns of figures.'

236

'So erotic!' He growled in her ear, and she laughed and wondered if she'd ever been so happy.

The next day was Monday. Mark got up early. Olivia lay in bed, listening to him singing as he shaved.

'Do you like that song?' he said, coming in, a towel around his waist.

'Lovely!'

'I meant the first song.'

She opened her eyes. 'I thought it was all the same song.' She closed her eyes again.

He turned the radio up so loud that she was nearly blasted out of the room. 'That'll teach you to be rude about my singing!'

'Oh, was it singing? I thought it was some neighbour's cat!'

He came to kiss her goodbye, dressed in his sober suit. 'What are you going to do today?'

'I thought I might phone Maggie.'

'If you're still here at ten, introduce yourself to Mrs T. She cleans the house and irons my shirts. I'm sure she'd be delighted to teach you . . .' He ducked as she took a swipe at him, and went out of the room calling, I'll be back around seven. Don't get into mischief.'

It seemed strange to be in his house without him. She got up, had a bath, dressed, and went downstairs to make herself some coffee and toast to the sound of slaves who were not slaves. The kitchen looked out on to a walled garden. Mark had told her that in summer it was a scented bower of flowering shrubs, but not it had that grey, dead look. She washed up her plate and went to look for her address book.

An hour later Olivia arrived at the rambling, dilapidated Victorian house in North Kensington which Maggie and Zach had recently bought. She opened the iron gate, pushing aside the bare branches of a rampant azalea, and walked up the cracked steps. The bell didn't work so she had to hammer on the door.

Maggie opened it. 'Hello. Come in. Great to see you.'

Olivia followed her over broken floorboards to what would eventually be the kitchen.

'It's our dream house,' enthused Maggie. 'It's going to be a beautiful . . .' There was a deafening crash from upstairs. 'Just

237

the builders knocking down another wall. She switched on the kettle, picked a kitten from the stove and nuzzled it against her elfin face. 'Now, tell me everything. Who is he?'

'Er . . . what do you mean?'

'I mean the man who's stamped *love* all over your face.'

That evening Olivia said to Mark, 'Would you mind if I asked Zach and Maggie to dinner?'

'Mind! Why should I?'

'Well, it is your house.'

'Of course I don't mind,' he stroked her arm. You'll find a *cordon bleu* cookery book on the top shelf in the kitchen.'

'Oh, God!'

'What's the matter?'

'I'm not a very good cook.'

'You didn't think I was going to cook it, did you?'

'No.'

'Don't worry, it's easy. Choose a recipe, buy the ingredients, and follow the instructions – and tell me what you're cooking so I can organise the wine. That,' he ran a finger down the soft curve of her cheek, 'is called team work.'

'How do you know it's so easy?' she linked her fingers through his belt.

'Because when you go to a dinner party and say to your hostess, "This is delicious," she always says, "Oh, it's so easy".'

Zach and Maggie were invited for Saturday and to Mark's amusement Olivia spent two whole days studying the recipe book. She avoided all those which said 'and now take your freshly made hollandaise sauce . . .' or '. . . then, as your souffle rises . . .'

On the afternoon of the third day Fiona telephoned. 'Choose something simple' she advised.

'But what?'

'Avocado vinaigrette. Not even you can ruin that.'

'Don't laugh, Fee, it's not funny.'

'It is – it's the first time you've ever wanted to go near a kitchen. He must be special. Do we get to meet him?'

'Not just yet.'

Fiona was silent for a moment, then she said in a very soft voice. 'Do you know that's only the second time you've called me Fee since we were children.'

Olivia did avocado vinaigrette and boeuf en croute. She was inordinately proud of her effort which took her all day to prepare. In fact, the evening went well from the moment Zach and Maggie arrived. She liked Zach, he resembled a bespectacled owl but had a zany turn of phrase, and Mark was amused by Maggie who sparkled in return; and Zach and Mark got on well in the joking, commiserating way that the men of slightly outrageous women do.

'I'm giving up singing and I'm going to open a clothes shop,' Maggie announced over coffee. 'I don't want to go on the road any more because it means being away from Zach for weeks on end. Anyhow, I've had a gutful of hotel rooms and I've always wanted to run my own business. It's going to be called Savvies and it'll be for people like us, who want to wear bizarre, amusing clothes but don't want badly made rubbish. Olivia, why don't you come in on it with me?'

'I'll help you, if I can.'

'You won't be my partner?'

'No, and you don't really want one. Savvies will be your style because it's your idea.'

'Maybe you're right. But come and help me. I can't even drive and I have to find premises, choose materials, visit outworkers. That sort of thing. You'd be a real help. And I'd pay you . . . not a lot, I'm afraid, but . . .'

'It sounds fun – for a few months, for the summer.'

As they were leaving Zach said, 'You must come and have dinner with us – if you don't mind a bit of a building site.'

Olivia squeezed Mark's arm. 'Oh, Mark won't mind, he'll feel at home.'

She waited until he had locked the front door and then, in the darkness of the hall, she asked, 'Any news on Culross?'

'Roland's facing the board next week.'

'What about . . .?' She was going to say, what about me, what about our agreement, but she stopped herself. She was so happy, she did not want to ruin things, she would ask him another day – tomorrow.

'What's happening about that damned bank?' Maggie asked as they tramped the lower reaches of the King's Road in search of premises for Savvies.

'They're having a meeting today. I wish I could be there. You see, in a way I've exonerated myself so it makes me mad that I've been elbowed out of my triumphant return.' She hesitated, she was still afraid to share her confidences.

'But it's you who've allowed yourself to be elbowed out,' Maggie told her.

'The trouble is . . . I'm afraid of losing Mark.'

'You're not going to lose him. He's crazy about you.'

'And I'm nuts about him. If I wasn't, it would all be much easier. I'm afraid of spoiling the magic.'

'Come on, let's eat something,' said Maggie. 'If I'm going to die, at least let me die of ecstasy and not of hunger or exhaustion.'

They found possible premises for Savvies on the stretch of small shops near the antique market. It wasn't large but it had a good-sized window and some office space on the first floor, and, most important of all, Maggie liked it. 'The only problem is,' she said, as they stood on the other side of the road, looking across at it, 'the place doesn't become vacant until the summer.'

'It would give you time to get organised. You haven't got any clothes to put in it yet.'

Mark was working at his desk when Olivia arrived home.

'What's the news on Culross?' she asked, determined to be positive.

'Roland agreed to resign — eventually. There'll be an announcement in tomorrow's *Financial Times*.'

'Is he selling his shareholding?'

'Yes, in exchange for not being prosecuted, though of course it won't say that in the paper.'

'What about me and my agreement?'

He sighed and took her hands in his. 'You've forced out Roland, which is what you wanted. Now forget about Culross and think of the future.'

'I don't only want revenge, I also want to clear my name, you know I do.'

The phone rang. Mark answered. 'It's your mother.'

'Olivia, dear, I was hoping that you might come down for a few days.'

'Mummy, I . . .' She wanted to get back to her conversation.

240

'I suppose that was *him* who answered. I do wish you'd told me dear, but mothers are always the last to know, aren't they! Perhaps he'd like to come down to meet us?'

'Mummy, I . . .'

'Ask him, dear, after all if you're . . . living with him I think we should meet him.'

Olivia covered the mouthpiece. 'Mother wants to meet you.'

He ruffled her hair. 'I want to meet them too. I have serious intentions towards their daughter.'

After that how could she return to the subject of Culross?

Mark got on well with her parents – and with Hugo and Fiona who contrived to be present for Sunday lunch.

'I approve,' said Fiona, as they did the washing-up.

'I hope you're not going to live with him for too long,' said her mother. He might not bother to marry you.'

'Mother!'

'Is Olivia getting married?' squealed Phoebe, rushing into the kitchen. 'Is she? Is she? Can I be a bridesmaid? Oh, please!'

Driving back to London with Mark, Olivia thought, I'm happier than I've ever been and if only I could sort out Culross everything would be perfect. Then she asked herself whether anything was ever a hundred per cent perfect or was she asking too much – and going to lose the lot?

One of the things which Olivia like best about being with Mark was his unpredictability. He would come home and say, 'Let's drive out into the country for dinner' or 'Let's go to the theatre,' and once, when they had sat up talking half the night, 'Let's have breakfast at the airport.' They ate scrambled eggs and watched the nights flights from New York land in the dawn, then they went home to spend the rest of the day in bed. Another time she arrived home on a Friday afternoon to find a message on the answering machine. 'Be ready by seven. We're going to Paris for the weekend!'

They stayed at the George V and drank pink champagne in the bath in the middle of the afternoon. That evening they went to the ballet, to see *The Nutcracker*, and next morning they wandered the streets of the Left Bank, relishing the art galleries and bookshops and little restaurants with red table-cloths and rickety chairs.

On their way back to the hotel they passed a house which was being renovated. 'Don't look now.' Olivia teased.

On their return to England they spent a night at The Helmets, where the chestnut mare's foal had just been born.

'What are you going to call it?' Olivia asked Lady Vicky as they stood at the entrance to the stable, watching the foal explore its surroundings on wobbly legs.

'My dear, that's always a problem. One tries to choose a name which is relevant to the dam or the sire or both, in this case Lady Ross and Northern Dancer, but you have to pick one not already registered. Any ideas? Don't say Lady Dancer – it's a colt.'

'How about Ross Dancer?'

'Ross Dancer. Mmmmm. I like it. Clever girl. Remind me to check it against the register.'

Savvies had acquired a sunflower-yellow van with loopy black lettering painted by Maggie, and Olivia now spent most of the day driving Maggie around to buy materials or to visit her outworkers, most of whom were dotted about South London. It was with great pride that they watched the first Savvies label being sewn into an electric blue jacket.

'I told Zach that Mark had taken you to Paris – and that you'd stayed at the George V and drunk champagne in the bath in the middle of the afternoon!' said Maggie as they sat in a traffic jam on Chelsea Bridge.

'And?'

'He said he'd take me if I passed my driving test. The bastard must have guessed I've been skipping lessons.'

Olivia watched the grey river and the dripping leafless branches along the Embankment. 'I wish I could wake up tomorrow and not care about Culross.'

'What about the slimy Gerald, have you sussed how to kick him where it hurts?'

'No. I have to bait a trap without him realising, and that can only be done by massaging his ego. You know, letting him think that in spite of everything his charm still works. But I can't approach him. He'd run a mile. It has to be complete, absolute mental defeat with no comebacks.'

242

'How about,' Maggie lit a cigarette, 'bombing the water supply in his block with a particularly virulent type of VD?'

'You'd have to bomb a whisky still – Gerald doesn't drink water.'

'Then I'll design a pair of specially constricting trousers which sprout razor blades in appropriate places.'

'I said mental defeat, Maggie dear!'

'But most men think with their . . .'

'Not Gerald!' She rammed the gear stick into fourth. 'I'm going to finish that man off if it kills me.'

'You will, but be careful you don't finish you and Mark off too.'

A few days later Mark said, 'Julius and Sarah have asked us to dinner on Saturday. Your old colleague, Jonathan Burlington will be there with his wife.'

She was curled up on the sofa reading the agony column in *Cosmopolitan.* 'Oh . . . yes, I'd love to see Jonathan, I was going to ring him but . . .' She stopped, she had been going to add, 'things being what they are over Culross.'

'I'd like you to get to know Julius and Sarah better.'

'Yes.' But she knew that when she saw Julius she would think of Culross and Gerald.

'Don't you want to get to know them?' He sat down beside her and took away her magazine, saying 'What rubbish!' and reading out, . . . 'although I do feel guilty about being unfaithful to my lover, the excitement and novelty of a stranger's body . . .' He chuckled as he read on.

Olivia ran her hand up the inside of his thigh. 'I thought you said it was rubbish!'

Julius and Sarah lived just off Eaton Square, in a very grand white Belgravia house with black railings in front and servants' quarters in the basement.

'I'm so glad you could come.' Sarah welcomed Olivia into a pale lemon drawing-room.

'Yes,' Julius kissed her on both cheeks, 'you girls should keep each other out of mischief in the day time.' Olivia bit back the tart reply she longed to make as he went on, 'You know Jonathan, of course?'

'Of course.' She smiled at Jonathan. He smiled back, and said something to Cleo. How long ago it seemed since Olivia had seen them together at Fenella's party.

During dinner, Jonathan said to Olivia, 'I wanted to phone you.'

'You should have.'

'I was going to suggest lunch. In fact, I have to be in Pimlico around lunchtime tomorrow, if that's not too out of your way.'

'Pimlico's fine.' He seemed to know she wasn't working.

She looked across at Mark, who was watching her anxiously and smiled, and at that moment Sarah said, 'Olivia, do come and spend an afternoon with me next week. I have to choose some curtain material and a woman's coming round with some samples. I'd like some help.'

Olivia nodded and smiled, but she was thinking . . . 'keep each other out of mischief' . . . 'help choose curtain material' . . . at this rate the agony column of *Cosmopolitan* would be too advanced for her!

The trouble is, she thought next morning as she listened to Mark singing in the bathroom, I don't just want to clear my name, I want to enhance it. I don't just want the king's pardon – I want to be the king.

She met Jonathan at a wine bar. They sat outside on the pavement, relishing the spring sunshine, drinking champagne – Jonathan insisted – and eating oysters.

'Tell me all the gossip,' she said.

'First of all, Colin sends his love. He's an analyst now and brilliant at it. Julius's idea and Colin is so much happier – and he's got engaged to a very pretty girl, a trainee, who Hamish was sniffing after. She turned down old Hamish and chose Colin! Amazing, isn't it?'

'No, I'd rather have Colin than Hamish – if I had to have either. God forbid that that should be my dilemma.'

'It won't be your dilemma. Hamish is leaving, he's going to work for a bank in Hong Kong.'

'What! A Harvard man in the colonies! Heavens above, whatever next!'

They burst into fits of laughter.

Eventually Jonathan recovered enough to say, 'I spoke to James this morning and he sends lots of love. He's now living down in Devon, running an estate agency with two friends. You know he came from the West Country and always missed it. Mike and Katie had a baby and are very happy. Ma Patent sends her love. Oh, this will make you laugh. There was a frightful row last winter because Roland wanted to replace her with a coffee dispensing machine. The whole bank was up in arms. He had to back down.'

'What about . . . work? I mean, are Culross doing well?'

'More or less the same, in spite of Julius's efforts. The trouble is, there aren't enough of us to make a good team. It's a pity that you couldn't . . .'

'I haven't congratulated you on your marriage.'

'Thanks. I finally persuaded Cleo.' Jonathan paused. 'I like Mark.'

She blushed. 'Yes.'

'We'd love to ask you both to dinner but . . . well . . .'

'Well what?'

'It might look a bit presumptuous – although now we've been to dinner with Julius and Sarah . . .'

'You mean, last night was the first time?'

'Yes. Don't look so surprised, you're forgetting what the Culross family are like. Anyhow,' he gave her his charming, gleeful grin as he patted her arm, 'I did laugh when word got out that you had ended up with one of them. I thought, good on Olivia!' He poured her another glass of champagne. 'Now I suppose you're going to get married and have lots of little brown-eyed babies.'

'Not just yet.' She downed the champagne in one. 'There are a few things I want to do first.'

20

That summer was one of the hottest in England. In the quietly
elegant streets of Kensington dusty blossom lay on hot pavements and *au pairs* walked their employers' dogs through the
dead of the afternoon. Olivia divided her days between Savvies, which was scheduled to open in early September, and the
house, where she led a life of delicious sloth, sunbathing her
already tanned body in the small walled garden where the air
was heavy with the scent of blossom, getting up only to pad
through the cool interior to the fridge for a drink or a slice of
melon, then back to the garden – and the sun, the radio, the
magazines.

In the evening when Mark came home they would sit out in
the garden drinking Pimms and eating slivers of smoked
salmon and olives, and their voices would murmur long into
the night, oblivious of other murmuring voices in the gardens
all around them.

Once she asked him, 'Did you like me when you first saw
me?'

'No. Did you like me?'

'No, but that's got nothing to do with it.'

Another time she was looking at him in the flickering garden
lights when she said, 'You've got a grey hair.'

'I've got lots.'

'Only two.' She reached towards his head. 'Shall I pull them
out?'

He grabbed her hand and kissed its soft palm. 'No, they
make me look distinguished and young girls treat me with
respect.'

'Not with only two, I'm afraid. No one can see them.'

He ran his hand down her neck and inside her thin cotton dress, caressing her swell of her breasts. 'I can see them, every morning when I shave. I look in the mirror and I say to myself . . .'

'Who is that distinguished man?'

'How did you guess?' He pushed the thin straps of her dress down her shoulders which were warm and bare in the night. 'Then I come back into the bedroom and I see this funny face on the pillow and I know I've never loved anyone as I love you.'

She was silent.

He took her face in his hands. 'Aren't you going to say anything?'

'I . . .' Tears pricked her eyes.

'What's wrong?'

She reached up and touched his cheek. 'I've wanted to tell you that I love you for so long, and I love you so very much that . . . I sort of can't say it. It's got stuck with wanting to be said.' She looked up at him with her soft bruised look and around her the night was laden with the smell of syringas, the nearest thing to orange blossom in a London garden.

Later that night he said, 'When we have babies I want lots of little girls who look just like you,' and she said, 'Oh, no, I want sons who look like you,' and she touched his hooded eyes with her soft lips.

Next day she walked tall knowing that Mark loved her.

Soon afterwards he said, 'A colleague in chambers has just been made a QC – Queen's Counsel – and we're having a celebration. I'd like you to come. It's time you met everyone, especially Tom, one of my closest friends. You remember, the one I told you had had a bad car crash last year.'

Olivia phoned Maggie. 'What *am* I going to wear?'

'Buy something new and special. Meeting workmates is an important occasion. Savvies owes you fifty quid and I can lend you another forty. I'd lend you more but all we have is being pumped into the house or the shop.'

'That'll be plenty.'

She took the bus; there was a price to pay for lying in the garden and it was high time she started to earn proper money.

247

In Harvey Nichols' sale she found a green and white silk dress with a wrap-over skirt cut on the cross with a deep v-neck. It cost more than she could afford but it was irresistible, the fresh green and the soft white doing for her what the blue dress had done for her the previous winter. She could almost hear Lorenzo's chuckle of approval, and she knew she had chosen right when two young barristers turned to watch her step out of her taxi. How strange it was to walk these uneven pavements beside the velvety lawns, exactly where she had walked two years earlier. Was it really two years? It seemed longer – it seemed less.

Mark's chambers were in one of the older buildings where the wooden stairs had been polished by the tread of many feet and the names of the barristers belonging to that set were painted in beautiful black script on a white wooden board. In the darkness of the stairwell Olivia gave her hair a quick brush and touched her wrist and neck with scent before proceeding to the first floor, hoping that his colleagues would like her – and that Mark would like the her they saw.

'There you are!' He came towards her as she stepped into the reception area, smiling his approval so that she knew he was proud of her and proud to be with her, and she loved him all the more for that. 'Come and meet Keith, our clerk. A chamber stands or falls by its clerk. He's the one who deals with the solicitors, allocates the work, and makes sure we get paid – for which he takes an enormous percentage of our earnings.'

'A gross exaggeration' said a tiny, smiling bespectacled man coming out of the clerk's room. 'So this is the reason why Mark rushes off home every evening, is it?' He winked and shook Olivia's hand warmly. 'I'd rush home myself if I had you waiting for me. Has he introduced you to the rest of the chambers? Not yet? Ah, he's afraid you'll fall for one of us handsome devils.'

She was ushered into a large and elegant room where some thirty or forty people, mainly men, were drinking champagne and talking animatedly.

'So we get to meet you at last,' said one, coming over to them. He had Jonathan's open, friendly manner and would have been almost as goodlooking had he not had an off-centre jaw and a deep scar across his chin. 'I'm Tom. No wonder Mark keeps you under lock and key.'

'He doesn't.'

'No,' Mark put an arm around her shoulders, 'I let her out for half an hour every evening.'

An older man joined them. He was introduced as Giles, the head of chambers. 'You should hear him in court,' said Mark with admiration.

'You should hear Mark in court,' said Tom.

'I'd like to. Can I?'

'Of course – if you wouldn't be bored,' said Mark.

'I won't be bored.' She smiled at him in a way which said, everything you do is of interest to me.

A week later she went to the High Court. Never could she have imagined that she would willingly return to this place, and yet she had, because of the man she loved. As she stepped from the taxi in front of the great arched entrance she even managed to look across at the lattice windows of the Wig and Pen without experiencing any of the humiliation she had known there, merely the anger.

Mark was cross-examining a witness as she slipped into the back of the courtroom. He spoke carefully, ponderously, '. . . and is it not a fact, Mr . . . er . . .' he paused, adding the insult that, in spite of an hour of questioning, he still could not remember the man's name.

'Smith.'

'Well, Mr Smith?'

'I've already answered that question a hundred times.'

'Then I would ask you to answer it a hundred and one times for the benefit of this court Mr . . . er . . .'

'Smith. My name's Smith. Not that difficult to forget, is it?'

'Mr Smith, you haven't answered Counsel's question,' said the judge.

Olivia smiled to herself. Mark was like a first class poker player: he foresaw every variation of every answer and was ready. She crossed her legs and smoothed down her skirt and remembered their lovemaking of the night before as she watched him destroy the witness. To see him in the environment where he was successful made her admire him all the more, and made her want him to be proud of her. She needed a life outside their relationship in order to contribute to it.

As she said to Maggie later, when she arrived at Savvies, 'I've loved this summer and I've enjoyed helping you, but I need my own challenges.'

'We all need a bit of unsatisfied ache to make us go on wanting,' said Maggie, watching the carpenter fix a mirror in what would be the changing-room. 'Do you think I'll go bankrupt in the first six months or the first year?'

'Neither. Savvies is going to be a success.'

'I wish I could be so sure.' Maggie stared out of the bar shop window to the King's Road. 'Nothing's ready. My outworkers are unreliable. The girl I took on to organise the office has a drug problem and says she can't cope. OK, don't tell me I was mad to consider her, but I thought it might help her straighten herself out and, hell, I know what it's like to be in the pits.' They sat down on the bare floorboards and leaned against the wall. 'Zach and I had a frightful row this morning. He said I was a fool so I threw the cat's milk at him. I expect he'll leave me, then I'll go back to Anataxos. I wonder what Nikos is up to?'

'Maggie!'

'I'm fed up with Zach.'

'No, you're not.'

'Yes, I am.'

The phone rang. Maggie answered. 'Yes . . . yes . . . I'm sorry too . . . no, it was my fault . . . yes, of course I do. What? Oh, yes!' She replaced the receiver, turned to Olivia – and burst into tears. 'Zach and I are getting married.'

'Who said she was fed up?'

Maggie wiped her tears on the sleeve of her purple catsuit. 'Oh, I only said that in case he left me – you know, to get my word in first.'

They rushed out to buy a bottle of champagne and gave a glass to the carpenter who promptly broke a mirror.

'Seven years' bad luck!' wailed Maggie.

'It's all right, luv, I'm the one who broke it.'

'I've had an idea.' Olivia put down her glass. 'Sanjiv, the Indian who lived in the Islington house is an accountant, at least he's done some of the exams. When I spoke to him a few weeks back he was about to give up his job.'

'You're a star.' Maggie took Olivia by the hand and waltzed her round the bare shop, singing, 'I'm going to be a rich, successful married woman. My husband will love me. My children will adore me. And I shall be voted businesswoman of the Year.'

That night Olivia lay listening to Mark's breathing and wondered if he wanted to marry her. He hadn't actually said so, although he had wanted to meet her parents. She rolled over on her side and studied his profile. She could not imagine herself ever wanting to be with anyone else. She would have liked to wake him up and talk, but that wasn't fair, he had a long day's work ahead of him.

Several days later when Olivia arrived at Savvies, Sanjiv bounded down the stairs from the first floor office. 'How can I thank you.' He pumped her hand. 'One minute I am dying of boredom, the next I am working here and Lalita has work too.' He laughed, his white teeth flashing against his brown skin.

At the beginning of August, Mark and Olivia went to Anataxos for ten days. It seemed strange to be back. The light was still as white, the sea as blue, the tower as solitary on its headland – and yet there were differences. Jake's house had the dusty air of desertion. Monica was in Florida. Only Gwen remained, clinging rigidly to the place Jim had loved best but were he to return would probably love no more, for the restrained commercialism of former years had slipped its leash and caiques brought families on villa holidays who spent their time working out the pound-drachma exchange rate, whilst their teenage daughters complained because there was no disco.

They weren't sorry to return to London, where Jake was due for a two-week visit.

'We must take him to The Helmets,' said Mark, coming out into the garden where Olivia was checking the Savvies press release. 'He and Vicky will get on like a house on fire.'

'Or a volcano.' She rested her elbows on the garden table and smiled at him, thinking how attractive he was with his blond streaked hair and his suntan.

'We'll take him to Glyndebourne. Vicky always has tickets. Julius and Sarah can come. Sarah loves opera. You've never been to Glyndebourne? Oh, it's wonderful. You don't need to be musical or to understand opera or even to like it; it's the pageantry of the whole evening. The beautiful old house with its own theatre set at the foot of the Downs. The gardens. The fact that you are all in evening dress. Magic!' He was standing behind her and he put his hands on her bare shoulders. 'If you can't fall in love on a summer's evening at Glyndebourne, you will never fall in love anywhere.'

'Perhaps I'm already in love,' she said leaning back against him.

'Really?'

'Maybe.'

'I just might be too.' He picked a spray of honeysuckle and tucked it behind her ear, plaiting her hair around its stem: but her hair was too silky, it unwound and the spray fell to the ground.

Olivia met Jake at the airport. He came through customs and straight into her arms. 'Not split up from Mark already have you?' he asked, looking anxious.

'Oh, no, far from it. He's in court today. A big case.'

'Thank God for that! I was afraid you'd come to blows.'

On the way in from the airport he asked her if she was working and when she explained about Savvies, he said, 'What happened about Culross?'

'Roland resigned his directorship and gave up his holding.'

'I meant with regard to you?'

She pulled a face. 'I didn't get the conqueror's victory march, if that's what you mean, but I try not to think about it too much.'

'Because of Mark?'

'Because of losing Mark.'

'Still haven't got back your confidence, have you?'

'No, I wonder if I ever will.'

They were silent for a few minutes. The motorway became the flyover, a dual carriageway above dusty houses and thirsty gardens.

'I saw Lorenzo a few weeks ago,' he said.

'How is he?'

'The same. He was curious to know if you'd managed to nail Culross.'

'I half expected to see him on Anataxos. In fact, I didn't tell

252

Mark but every morning I used to wake up and pray that the *Belladonna* wouldn't turn up.

Jake liked Mark's house, though it seemed small with both men in it. He approved of Savvies and accepted an invitation to Maggie's wedding, telling Olivia later that he'd always thought Maggie was a bit of a character. But most of all he liked The Helmets – and in particular Lady Vicky.

She invited him down to see Ross Dancer, now a glossy chestnut colt, and within minutes of his arrival they were strolling across the terraced garden, deep in conversation, with Mouse at their heels.

'They've forgotten about us.' Mark slipped an arm around Olivia's waist.

'Mmmm.' She leaned against him.

'Ah, there you are.' Julius and Sarah came round the corner of the house. 'It's such a lovely day we decided to leave London early.'

'So we see.' Mark murmured regretfully into Olivia's hair.

It was late afternoon when they departed for Glyndebourne, the men in dinner jackets, the women in their evening dresses: Sarah in blue, Lady Vicky in pale violet and Olivia in flouncing red silk so beautiful that it took everyone's breath away. She looked as though she had stepped straight from the pages of *Gone With The Wind*, for in its low neckline, fitted bodice and billowing skirts were all the romance and fire with which Scarlett O'Hara entranced the Tarleton twins on the porch at Tara.

Glyndebourne is a country house dedicated to opera. There Mozart's *Idomeneo* mingles with the gnarled apple trees of the walled courtyard and ladies flirt like Carmen over the champagne supper during the interval, peacocking in their dresses across the green lawns from which long summer evening shadows stretch to the ha-ha and the grazing cattle beyond. Olivia slipped her hand through the crook of Mark's arm as they crossed in front of the house. It was magic, a dream, and it seemed to Olivia that the audience and the opera and the gardens were all part of the same story, and that at any moment they would find Romeo and Juliet whispering sweet nothings on the terrace outside the organ room, where the air was heavy with the smell of tobacco plants. Mark was right. If you couldn't fall in love at Glyndebourne, you couldn't fall in love anywhere.

It was after midnight by the time they returned to The Helmets. Julius and Sarah disappeared to bed immediately, Jake and Lady Vicky followed soon after, while Mark and Olivia stood on the terrace looking down at the field where the mares and their foals grazed peacefully in the moonlight.

He took her hand. 'Let's walk.'

The night was velvet, the grass warm and dry. They walked under the trees to the high double fence which surrounded the stallion's paddock. He was prancing up and down, his head high and tail up. A mare in a nearby field watched him. She whinnied softly. He circled in his small enclosure but two double fences separated them. She whinnied louder. He pawed the ground. She skittered on her small hooves. He reared up. Then, suddenly, he charged the fence and before Mark and Olivia could stop him, he was up – and heading for the mare.

'We ought to tell Lady Vicky,' said Olivia.

'Yes.' Mark linked his arms around her waist and kissed her bare shoulders.

'The stallion's not meant to . . .' She shivered under his touch.

'I know but . . .' The red dress slid down until it barely covered her breasts and the warm night air ran up and down her arms. In the field the mare bit the stallion. Under the trees Mark took off his jacket and laid it on the ground, and Olivia turned to him, pulling him down to her, hardly conscious of her dress as it slid down about her.

In the field the stallion reared up behind the mare.

Maggie and Zach were getting married on Friday, taking a weekend in Paris as their honeymoon, and returning to London on Monday – Savvies was to open on the following Thursday.

'We shouldn't really take any time off at all,' Maggie twittered as she dressed on the morning of her wedding – she'd spent the night with Mark and Olivia.

'You'll be better for having had a few days off,' Olivia reassured her.

'Do I look all right? Maggie wriggled into a shocking pink satin dress with an unbelievably tight skirt, slipped on a pair of teetering high heels, and plonked a tiny hat with a sparkly pink veil on the front of her head. 'I had pink streaks put in my hair to match.' She pulled a doubtful face as she fitted enormous circular diamanté earrings to her ears. 'What do you think? Do I look like a blushing bride?'

'You look wonderful.' Olivia hugged her. 'Mark, come and look at Maggie.'

He came in, did a double take, then laughed. 'You look terrific. Thank goodness you didn't try and do the demure bit to please Zach's mother.'

'Not even a certificate of *intacta* would please that old bag.'

The wedding was at Kensington Registry Office, with a reception at Zach and Maggie's house because Maggie had insisted. 'I don't want to go to some horrible hotel with waiters who can't wait for me to leave,' she said. 'I want to be in my own home.' The fact that it was still a builder's site did not worry her.

When Mark and Olivia arrived at the Town Hall with Maggie between them, so nervous now that she could hardly walk, the first person they saw was Monica in an enormous cartwheel hat. She rushed to Maggie, waving a silver hipflask of brandy. 'I knew this would be needed. Oh, darling, you don't look very . . . virginal.'

Maggie swigged down the brandy. 'Mummy, I've never looked virginal.'

'You did, when you were very little.'

They all laughed.

'Is Daddy coming?' asked Maggie.

'I did tell him it was today.' Monica adjusted her hat and smiled at Sanjiv and Lalita who stood shyly to one side.

A black Rolls drew up and Lady Vicky and Jake, who had spent the past few days at The Helmets, stepped out. A moment later a tall, thin, serious-looking man got out of a taxi.

'Here comes Daddy,' said Maggie looking as though she were about to faint. 'Mark, where's the brandy? Oh, thank God mother's between toyboys!'

Even Monica had tears in her eyes when Maggie and Zach

finally left for Paris, Maggie in her going-away outfit – a black and white striped catsuit which made her look like a very small zebra walking on its hind legs.

At six o'clock on Thursday evening Savvies opened its front door for the press review – and no one came. Maggie, Zach, Sanjiv and Olivia stood in the shop with jolly smiles on their faces. At six fifteen Jake and Mark walked in.

'Don't say anything or I shall scream,' said Maggie.

At six twenty Monica arrived. 'Oh, my poor baby,' she wailed.

'Shut up, Mummy!'

At six thirty a very junior reporter from the *Fulham Chron-icle* put her head around the door. 'Is tonight the . . .?'

Maggie forced a smile. 'Have a drink.'

The others hurriedly began to talk among themselves. At six forty-five, two glamorous girls from *Cosmopolitan* wafted through the door. Immediately, Maggie detached herself from the junior reporter, who didn't mind because she was already eyeing up a dress for a party that weekend. By seven, ten people had arrived: at seven fifteen Jonathan appeared with Cleo and Colin and Colin's pretty girlfriend, who promptly endeared herself by buying a silver bomber jacket and wearing it: by seven thirty the place was packed: by eight, half the stock had been sold.

Two days later the William Hickey column in the *Daily Express* ran a picture of Jake, Maggie, Mark and Olivia. It described Jake as 'the world famous sculptor', Maggie as 'the dynamic new boutique owner', Mark as 'the highly thought of barrister', and Olivia as 'his live-in lover'. Live-in lover! She threw the paper on the floor and stamped on it.

'It isn't that I'm jealous of Maggie,' she told Jake over lunch, before he returned to Pietra Alta, 'it's just that I don't have any identity.'

'Except as Mark Denholm's live-in lover?'

'Exactly.'

'Who's fault is that?'

'Mine.'

'Livvi, you're too bright to be hanging around all day. Now

Maggie's launched her shop, you've got to get on with being Olivia Steele.'

'But I don't want any old job, I want Culross.'

She drove him to the airport. On the way back it started to rain.

21

October

It was Monday morning, Jake had been gone a week, and
Olivia was lying in bed watching the rain slide down the
window pane whilst holding imaginary conversations with
Mark where he suddenly, miraculously, agreed with her that it
was in Culross's best interest to take her back and that Julius
must be made to see this.

The phone rang.

'Olivia Steele?'

'Yes.' She knew the voice but could not place it.

'Olivia, don't hang up on me.'

'Gerald!'

'Yes.'

'How dare you . . .'

'Don't hang up. Please! Please! I treated you very badly. Oh,
I've felt guilty ever since, even I have felt guilty, can you
imagine that? No, I don't expect you can.'

A million emotions ran through Olivia's mind but she could
define none of them, she could only think that he had been
drinking and it was not yet nine o'clock. 'How did you get my
number?' she demanded.

'I saw your photo in the paper and looked up Mark Denholm in the phone book. 'I'm glad you're happy.' He waited
for her to comment but she didn't, so he added with a slight
coyness, 'And with Mark Denholm! That is a turn up for the
books!'

'Gerald, I do not want to talk to you. Don't call me again. I can never forgive you.'

'Olivia! Please! Let me apologise properly and then you can put the receiver down. Oh, at least allow me to say what I have wanted to tell you all these months. I don't blame you for the way you feel, I'd feel the same, but I was so desperate to get the City editor's job. You know what it was like for me, hanging around with no proper job to do, watching incompetents promoted above my head.'

'That was no reason to betray me.'

'No, no, of course not.'

'What do you want, Gerald?'

'Nothing. I don't want anything. I only wanted you to know that I'm glad you're well. Of course I'd like to see you again, I hardly dare tell you so, but I would. Just for lunch – for old time's sake.'

'You're the last person I'd have lunch with.'

'Then before you hang up on me let me say that I'm so glad Culross have forgiven you and I'm delighted that those who threw their stones have had the old heave-ho. You deserved to be exonerated. I never did like Roland.' Trust Gerald to know all the gossip, Olivia thought, listening as he went on, 'Rumour has it that that pompous ass Lawrence is about to get the elbow too – but I'm sure I'm not telling you anything you don't know.'

Her eyes narrowed but her voice softened. 'Gerald, you can't expect me to talk to you about Culross.'

'I don't. I don't. What are you doing for tea tomorrow?'

She twisted the corner of the duvet cover around her little finger. 'Well . . .'

Olivia did not tell Mark about Gerald's call, she didn't tell anyone, but she thought of nothing else during the twenty-four hours until they met at Fortnum and Mason, at the Soda Fountain whose pale green elegance and look of the thirties made a perfect setting for Olivia as she swished across the room, twenty minutes late on purpose, in her 'mistress' silver fox and her swashbuckling high boots clamped over pale grey suede trousers, to Gerald who looked bloated and seedy in his suit which had the shine of poverty. He rose, half-smiling, and it was with difficulty that she controlled the urge to punch him in the face. 'You always were a stunner,' he said, 'but now you look rich. I haven't been too well myself, a touch of flu, you know how it is, it knocks the stuffing out of you.' He smelt of whisky.

The waitress took their order.

'Andrew sends his love,' said Gerald.

'How is he?'

'The same. Poor old Andrew, he'll never change. He'd like a City editor's job but he's not up to it. He couldn't cope with the responsibility.' His hands shook for a drink.

Olivia nibbled daintily at a cucumber sandwich. Gerald tucked into a chestnut meringue.

'I suppose you're very in with the Culrosses now?' he said.

'Oh, yes.' She gave him a confident smile.

'Family dinners and all that?'

'Of course.'

'It must be a strain when they're all together. They say there's no love lost between them. This business of Roland being forced to resign and give up his holding, and now the rumours about Lawrence . . . can't make for jolly Sunday lunches *chez* Culross. What on earth do you find to talk about?'

'Lawrence is always interested in farming.'

'Oh, is he?'

'Yes, he loves the country.' She gave him an artless smile.

'Then there is something in the story that he's thinking of resigning his directorship to farm? Of course no one has dared to write about it because there's no proof, but . . .' He smiled, and his eyes took on that piggy look she remembered so well. 'I'm surprised you feel any loyalty to them after what they did to you,' he said. 'Oh, I know I was partly to blame but I have regretted it ever since, I sincerely have. I'll never find another girl like you. I know that now. You were wonderful and we were happy, weren't we? I've never been so happy as I was when I was with you. I've sometimes thought that it was my fear of losing you that made me . . . hurt you.' His hand hovered across the table, then retreated. He did not quite dare touch her.

'I am loyal to Mark,' she said. 'I couldn't possibly discuss his family.'

'But he has no reason to love his cousins.'

She shrugged.

'Lawrence always was a fool. Do you remember I once told you that an evening only attained a minus score if one was cornered by him.' He was using the power of intimate memory. 'What sort of farming is he interested in?'

'Pigs.' She stood up. 'I must fly, I have a hair appointment. Thanks for the tea.' He was still lumbering to his feet as she crossed the room, turning once to give him a jolly little wave.

Olivia went straight to Savvies.

'Oh, do be careful,' said Maggie, 'he sounds a real snake.'

'I'm not telling him anything. Heavens above, I've nothing to tell. It is simply a question of not contradicting.'

'It's not that I'm thinking of, it's you and Mark. Perhaps you should have told Mark.'

'He'd have tried to stop me.' She paced the floor, her long legs swinging in their shiny boots. 'I love Mark and I'd hate to upset him, but I have this suppressed anger inside me. Sometimes I think I'm going to explode with rage. Culross hangs over me. It hangs over my relationship with Mark. We're not equals. I feel like a second-class citizen, Maggie, and the more successful Mark becomes the worse it is for me.'

A customer came into the shop and Maggie put on her professional boutique-owner smile. Olivia went home.

Two days later Gerald telephoned. 'I've been meaning to tell you how much I enjoyed our meeting. I would have sent you flowers but . . . What are you up to today?'

'We're off to the country and I'm in a hurry.'

'Lawrence too?'

'Perhaps. Goodbye.'

They went down to The Helmets for a long weekend and walked the dogs through the autumnal countryside, returning to the house for tea and crumpets in front of a roaring fire.

On Tuesday Gerald telephoned again, as Olivia had known he would.

'Had a good weekend?'

'Lovely.'

'Whole family there?'

'Some. Listen, Gerald . . .'

'Oh, Olivia I don't expect you to tell me anything, why

should you? But you know how it is in my world, one has to check facts. I'm doing a profile of Julius Culross – let's face it, he's streets ahead of his brothers – and to say that not only has Rolex been forced out but also that Lawrence is retiring from the fray to breed pigs would be a bit of a scoop. The inference is, that wily Julius managed to get rid of both of them.'

'You can hardly expect *me* to give *you* information.'

'I don't, but we did mean something to each other once, didn't we?'

'Yes,' she answered silkily, 'we certainly did.'

'You're not still angry with me?'

'Well . . . I'm not as angry as I was.'

'I wish we were together.'

'Gerald, don't . . . please.'

'It's true. Mark Denholm is a lucky man.'

'Thank you. How very sweet of you to say so.'

'You know, you're the only girl I've ever wanted to marry – and I lost you through my own stupid fault.'

'Oh, Gerald!'

'You . . . er . . . wouldn't let me write something about Lawrence Culross which wasn't true, would you? Not after . . . all we meant to each other.'

She gave a sigh of resignation.

'It would be professional suicide for me.'

She gave a deeper, more submissive sigh.

'You're wonderful.' There was triumph in his voice. 'Shall we meet next week, at the Wig and Pen – for old time's sake.'

'Yes,' she replied, 'for old time's sake.'

Two days later the *London Evening Echo* carried a lead article by its City Editor, Gerald Quentin, under the heading:

Farmer Lawrence retires to the pig farm.

Maggie and Olivia cracked a bottle of champagne in the back of the shop and raised brimming glasses to each other. 'May no one ever, ever put me down again,' said Olivia, tossing her hair back from her face and laughing with triumphant exhilaration.

'No man, woman, child or animal,' said Maggie.

'Fish or insect . . .'

'Bird . . .'

'Teddy bear . . .'

'Or any other toy, stuffed or unstuffed.'

Olivia pick up her bag. 'I'd better get home. I've borrowed Mark's car and I want to be sober to face him.'

'Do you think he'll have sussed out your part in Gerald's article?'

'He's sure to have.' She went out into the King's Road where the rain was falling steadily on a greasy evening.

Suddenly she was grabbed around the neck by Gerald. 'I thought I'd find you here, you bitch!' He stank of whisky.

'Let me go!'

'You set me up.'

'You set yourself up.' She elbowed him, and he released her with a grunt.

'Lawrence Culross is suing the *Echo* because you told me that . . .'

She pushed through a group of gaping pedestrians. 'I did not tell you anything.'

'You did! You did!

'I didn't and I can prove it – I taped our call.' She darted between the traffic and across the road.

He ran after her, banging into a taxi, shouting abuse, 'You let me believe . . . you . . .'

'It's not my fault what you believe. Surely you didn't think I would help you!' She dug in her bag so as to have her car keys ready. 'Do you think I could *ever* forget what you did to me?'

'I've been fired because of you.'

'What do I care?' She hurried on.

'I'm fifty years old.'

'Tough.'

'I'm an alcoholic.' He slipped on the wet pavement.

'Get a cure.' She rammed the key into the door lock and turned it quickly, jumping inside and relocking the door as he reached for the handle.

'You bitch! You bitch!' He banged on the roof.

She put the car into gear and opened the window a fraction so that he could hear her. 'If you ever contact me again, Gerald, I'll call the police.'

'You wouldn't dare!'

'Oh, yes, I would. I've waited a long time for this moment. I told you once that you'd be sorry you'd known me and I'm telling you now that if you ever come near me again I'll kick you straight back into the gutter – for old time's sake!' Her foot came down hard on the accelerator and the car shot forward, knocking Gerald off balance. He staggered sideways and collapsed on the pavement, and the spray of oily water from the gutter hit him in the face.

Mark was watching the television news when she reached home. 'You look very flushed,' he said. 'Are you all right?'

'I'm fine.' She laughed, 'In fact, I couldn't be better.'

'Oh, don't tell me . . .' he turned off the television. 'You had something to do with the *Echo*, didn't you?'

'Maybe.' She sauntered down into the kitchen and opened the fridge. 'I'm starving.'

He followed her. 'Olivia, were you involved in Gerald Quentin's article?'

'If you mean did I give Gerald false information? The answer is no.'

'But you knew about it?'

'Yes.' She ate a sliver of chicken then licked her fingers one by one.

'Have you been seeing him?'

'Once, but not in the way you mean. Mark, don't you trust me?'

'Not where Culross is concerned. Tell me exactly what happened.'

'Gerald phoned after he'd seen the piece in the paper about me being your live-in lover. He tried his soft-soap tactics to find out if it was true that Lawrence was to resign and I didn't see why I should put him straight. That is all.' She slammed the fridge door.

'So you didn't lie to him?'

'No, I did not. I am not a complete imbecile.' She poured two glasses of champagne. 'Aren't you going to celebrate with me?'

He pushed the glass aside. 'When did he contact you?'

'Last week.'

'And you didn't tell me?' His eyes took on their hooded flat look.

'I couldn't. You'd have tried to stop me.'

264

'Yes, I would.'

She marched past him into the sitting-room and threw herself into an armchair, shouting, 'I told you before, I'm not a doormat.'

He came after her and pulled her to her feet. 'You go out of your way to bring trouble on yourself.'

'And I'll go on doing it until I get even.'

He seized her by the chin and looked down into her defiant eyes. 'Damn it, you make me mad.'

How much Julius knew of her involvement in Gerald's article Olivia never discovered. She was a little apprehensive when they next met, not for her sake, for herself and Mark as a couple, but he could not have been more friendly. 'I think we should take the ladies on a really exotic holiday,' he told Mark as the four of them were having dinner. 'How about Barbados?'

'Or the Seychelles.' Mark put an arm around Olivia's shoulders.

'I second the Seychelles,' said Sarah.

'So do I.' Olivia smiled across the table at Julius, but she wasn't thinking about palm trees and beaches, she was thinking that the way must soon be clear for her to return to Culross.

She waited a month before broaching the subject because she wanted to make sure there would be no repercussions from Gerald's article or from Gerald – and there weren't. The *Echo* printed two lines saying that 'due to ill health Mr Gerald Quentin is retiring.' The other papers were not so restrained, they had a field day. First, Gerald was arrested for being drunk and disorderly, next he was fined ten pounds, finally they captured him lifting a battered suitcase into a second-class railway carriage as he left London to stay with his mother.

'I'm going to ask Julius to give me an appointment,' Olivia told Mark one Sunday evening as they made scrambled eggs.

'What for?'

'I want a job.'

'Julius won't take you back.'

'Why not?'

'Because he can't. Think of the bank's reputation.'

'That's ridiculous. Everyone knows I helped solve the *Ariosto* fraud. Julius agreed that . . .'

He agreed to clear you of dishonest association, he did not say he'd give you a job at Culross.' He grabbed the pan from her. 'You're burning the eggs.'

'Damn the eggs!' She thumped the spoon down on the table. 'Has Julius said he won't take me back?'

'In a way. Look, Olivia, there's no point in discussing Culross with me.'

'There's no point in discussing it with Julius either if you've turned him against me.'

'I haven't turned him against you! Hand me two plates.'

'I don't want any food. I feel sick. You knew I was building up to this, didn't you?'

'Yes, but I hoped that having your revenge on Gerald Quentin would satisfy you.'

'But you know what I'm like.'

'There's no harm in hoping, is there? Pass me the butter.'

'I suppose you think it's all one big joke?'

He switched off the gas and turned to her with angry desperation. 'No. I'm afraid you're going to destroy what we have, the two of us.'

'What is going to ruin us is if I spend my life cringing every time someone says the word Culross.' She picked up a knife and jammed it into the butter. 'I'm surprised you're not ashamed to have me living here, sharing your bed, considering . . .'

'"I don't care what Culross or the world thinks and I never have, you should know that, but I do care about Julius. It would be highly embarrassing to have you hassling him for a job.'

'Hassling! Thanks a bundle. Now I know what my place is in your life.'

'Oh, for God's sake don't personalise everything. I love you but you cannot expect me of all people to beg favours from Culross for you.'

'I never asked you to beg anything for me.'

'All right. But you can't expect Julius to trust you in the way I do. Now, if you don't want anything to eat please get out of the way. I have a long hard day tomorrow, I'm working on a very difficult case – and you of all people should appreciate what it's like to do a demanding job.'

'I can hardly remember what a job is!' she snapped, and she slammed out of the kitchen and thumped upstairs to bed.

When Mark came up Olivia pretended to be asleep. She lay with her eyes closed, listening to him moving around the bedroom, feeling the bed move as he climbed in, sensing him near without touching. But she could not sleep. She was churning with rage and frustration – and with the aching fear of losing him. Eventually she crept out of bed and went downstairs.

The debris of Mark's scrambled egg supper was scattered all over the kitchen. Olivia cleared it away. Then she put some bread in the toaster and some bacon under the grill, and she turned on the stereo, very low. When the toast was brown and the bacon crisp, she made a bacon sandwich with lashings of English mustard and sat at the kitchen table, munching her way through it – and as the Marche Slave reached its finale, and the spirits of the slaves escaped, she thought of what it would mean to lose Mark, and tears rolled down her cheeks.

'You're making the toast soggy.' He was standing in the doorway. She had no idea how long he'd been there and she quickly wiped her face with the back of her hand. 'Now you've got mustard on your cheek.' He removed it and held her to him, so close that her wet face lay against his bare chest.

When Mark came home next evening Olivia sensed that he was hoping she wouldn't mention Culross. But she had had all day to fester over it, and could think of nothing else. 'You just don't understand,' she began.

'I do, but what the hell can I do about it? I don't own Culross, I don't want anything to do with the bank. It and my grandfather were the bane of my childhood – and I certainly don't want to come home and have to talk about Culross, night after night.'

He left very early next morning and that evening he came home late, having already had dinner.

'Men never want to listen to you when you've got something emotional to say,' Maggie remarked on hearing Olivia's story.

'Zach's just the same. If I throw a wobbly this vague look comes over his eyes.'

'Mark doesn't look vague, he gets cross.'

'I always thought he was the temperamental type.'

'He's not temperamental!'

Maggie hooted with laughter. 'I wanted to see how quickly you'd leap to his defence. Sanjiv! Sanjiv, what do you do when Lalita gives you a hard time?'

Sanjiv came to the door of his office. 'She doesn't, she's a good Hindu wife.'

'Balls! Only last week I heard her telling you off for being extravagant.'

Maggie could not help Olivia: she had her own problems. Her doctor had told her she would need a small operation if she were to conceive, followed by rest and relaxation. 'How the bleeding hell can I relax when I've just started a business?' she wailed.

'I didn't know you were trying to get pregnant.'

'I wasn't until this happened, and now I suppose the idea that I might not be able to get pregnant has made me . . . well . . . obsessed by it.

Over the following weeks Olivia kept off the subject of Culross. She and Mark went to several parties, gave a dinner party, went to the theatre, and attended the opening of an art exhibition. In fact, they socialised more than they had before and to all outward appearances they were a happy couple — except that they no longer talked. At Christmas they divided their time between The Helmets and her parents, where her mother waited in suspended animation to announce their engagement. On New Year's Day they returned to London, and Mark retired immediately to his study. Olivia went into the kitchen and looked out at the walled garden where she had known so much happiness, and knew she could go on no longer.

'Mark, I must speak to you.'

'Very well.'

'Do you love me?'

He looked at her for a moment, then said, 'I do.'

'But you won't try to understand how important it is for me to get back to Culross?'

'I do understand, but this obsession of yours is destroying us.'

'If the situation were reversed, I'd do anything to help you. That's the difference between us.'

'Yes.'

'What do you mean by "yes".'

He stood up. 'You know what I mean.'

'So that's it! You still think I told Gerald about the *Ariosto* because I loved him. Two years ago I repeat something, no worse than hundreds of other people do every day, and neither you who claim to love me nor anyone else will let me forget it. The mud still sticks, doesn't it?'

'Yes, so long as you keep reliving the past.'

'I can't forget because people like you don't want me to.' She stormed out of the room and up the stairs.

He followed, shouting. 'It's you who don't want to forget.'

She marched into their bedroom. 'I'll always be Olivia, the girl who talked. No one will give me a chance, not even you.' She pummelled his chest. 'Especially you, because you want me to be less than you.'

He seized her wrists. 'I don't.'

'You do! You and everyone else. And it's true, isn't it, people haven't forgotten?'

He pushed her away. 'They never will, so you'd damned well better start accepting the fact.'

'I can't.'

'And I can't stand another night of you going on about Culross. Now, shut up or get out.'

'I'm going.' She tossed her suitcase on to the bed and began to throw her clothes into it. 'I'm leaving because I refuse to accept defeat.' She scooped up her scent bottles and make-up. 'I'm not going to be treated like a second-class citizen.' She remembered her shoes. 'I'll make it on my own – by myself – without help from anyone.' She filled a second suitcase. 'I'm going to be rich and powerful and successful.' With a case in each hand and her silver fox about her shoulders, she headed for the door. 'And one day I'll come back and I'll grind you all into the ground, one by one – including you, Mark Denholm. Especially you, Mark Denholm!'

22

New York, January 1977

The fat man woke up from his hangover. 'We landed yet?'

'No, we're still over Long Island.'

'The US of A.' He belched. 'Home.' He belched again. 'No place like it.'

'Yes.' Olivia thought of Mark.

'First visit?'

'Yes.' He'd asked her that five hours earlier.

'Vacation?'

'Yes.'

'Got friends in New York?'

'Ummm . . . yes.' She tried not to think of Mark.

'You wanna watch out. It's a dangerous place.'

'Yes . . . thank you.' It was Mark's fault. He'd driven her to leave. If only he'd understood.

'Ladies and Gentlemen, this is your captain speaking . . .'

'My cousin got mugged outside Saks on Fifth Avenue.'

'In fifteen minutes we shall be landing at New York's Kennedy . . .'

'He's six foot four and weighs two hundred and fifty pounds.'

'. . . where the local time is ten after noon . . .'

'He only had twenty bucks on him.'

'. . . and the temperature is minus twelve.'

'So they stuck a knife in him for wasting their time.'

If she could have turned the plane around she would have done so. Her toes felt for the comforting ridge of dollars folded

270

inside each boot, casually she moved her hand across her chest until it touched more dollars pinned inside her bra, then she took a biro from her bag, pushed up her sleeve and, turning away from her neighbour, quickly wrote the name and address of her hotel on the inside of her wrist so that when she was mugged she would know where to go.

By the time Olivia got off the plane she was so nervous that she was surprised to find the earth was hard. An hour and a half of immigration officials and her breezy replies of, 'I'm just here on holiday . . . I mean, vacation', followed by the overwhelming relief of seeing her suitcase, then the wall of unbelievably cold air which hit her as she left the terminal; and she decided to give it a fortnight and then go home.

For this reason she permitted herself the extravagance of a taxi. A minute later she wished she hadn't, as the yellow cab hurtled down the parkway, leaping potholes like an Olympic hurdler, cutting in and out of the gently bobbing traffic whilst the driver screamed abuse in Serbo-Croat. Olivia grabbed the strap to steady herself – it came away in her hand. She gripped the plastic-covered seat – her fingers sunk into the foam beneath, through the slits where some previous irate passenger had attacked it with a knife. She pushed herself back into the seat, digging her heels into the floor of the car – they shot away, skidding on a year's supply of chewing gum wrappers.

Perhaps a fortnight was too long.

Then she forgot about leaving. They were crossing the East River into Manhattan and to her left, rising into the cold blue sky above the long span of the Brooklyn Bridge, were the skyscrapers, their windows glittering like a million golden mirrors. This was what she had come for – the excitement of a new place and new people, the rough raw challenge of New York.

A moment later she was staring in dismay as they plunged into the Lower East Side, along streets where dusky dusty children played on rusting fire escapes and mangy cats singed their fur on subway vents. It was real *Street Car Named Desire* – but they went on, to where there was no desire, only despair. On every bench of a bleak churchyard helpless, hopeless human bundles lay wrapped in newspapers, their unwashed heads on plastic-bag pillows of belongings: those for whom the American dream had turned into a January nightmare.

She wondered if next week's flights to London were full.

But in two blocks the scene changed so abruptly that they could have been in another country. Brightly lit art galleries sold David Hockney originals, laughter came from crowded restaurants, music from warm apartments, and smart girls in fox fur jackets hailed cabs in confident voices.

From the well-nurtured quaintness of Greenwich Village they crossed streets of scruffy dress shops, then out past shiny buildings, over wide avenues up which Olivia caught tantalising glimpses of lights and people, before the cab stopped on one of the shabbier sections west of Broadway and the theatre district: it had looked so central on the map. At least I know there *are* better areas, she told herself, as she counted out the unfamiliar money and thought of the galleries and the lights and the confident girls.

But that was for tomorrow. Today was a winter's afternoon and a hotel described as adequate in the guide book. Adequate for what, she wondered. A pygmy? The room was so small that she could not open the cupboard without standing on the bed and the shower was so narrow that every time she raised her arms she banged her elbows. But it was clean and very warm, and best of all, being on the corner of a block, it had a view straight down Manhattan to the distant peaks of the financial district.

Olivia stood at the window. It was all quite different from what she had expected. Not modern and glitzy, but old and scruffy and infinitely more fascinating. She watched the street lights change from Walk to Don't Walk and a melting pot of human races surged forward. A large white dog scampered in and out of parked cars, chased by its owner anxiously bearing a pooper scooper. The dog stopped. The man stopped. The dog grinned – and ran on. A stretch limo drew up before an exquisite pink chocolate shop. A woman wreathed in mink and a winter suntan was bowed out by her chauffeur. She picked her way across the pavement and as she did so steam from the subway belched up through the vent beside her. On the corner a black boy turned on his ghetto-blaster and began a sinewy dance, drowning out an old man who was exhorting the crowd to 'confess and be forgiven'. The white dog was having steak for dinner. A baglady rummaged in the garbage cans. The mink sparkled in the chocolate shop. A black girl joined the black boy, linking her movements to his, their laughter and their breath hanging on the frosty air.

The winter sun sank into New Jersey firing the forty-three thousand windows of the World Trade Center and turning its twin towers from white to gold, whilst silhouetted against this futuristic vision, like the relics of some ancient paddy field, old round wooden water towers stood on the tops of every building. New York – that bizarre combination of the third world and the next century.

The advertisement said, 'Gary Taylor Placements for Top Financial Positions', but Olivia began to have her doubts when the lift nearly broke down before it reached the fourth floor. Still – she tightened the belt of her black cashmere coat – she was here, so she might as well go in.

'Yeah?' a voice shouted from an inner office.

'I'm . . . er . . . looking for a job in banking and . . .'

'Come on in. My secretary's off sick.' A portly young man with a rim of black hair around a prematurely balding pate was sitting behind an untidy desk painstakingly unravelling the tape of his answerphone machine. He glanced up at Olivia. 'You a Brit?'

'Yes.'

'Gotta work permit?'

'No.'

'Forget it.'

She left – almost. 'I thought that if an employer wanted you enough . . .'

'What's special about you?'

'I worked for a top British merchant bank and I have a good understanding of the European corporate market.'

'Got an MBA?'

'No, I went to Oxford. Law.'

'First Class?'

'No. Second.'

'Lady, why did you come to New York?'

'For the same reason most people do.'

'When did you arrive?'

'Yesterday.'

He groaned and opened a drawer in his desk, took out a banker's draft and waved it under Olivia's nose. 'See this! A British girl, just like you – nope, I have to admit she weren't half as goodlooking as you – she spent three months here, cashed in her air ticket, everything. In the end I had to lend her the fare home.' He shrugged and added gruffly, as if afraid Olivia might think him a soft touch, 'The standby fare. Still think the streets of Manhattan are paved with gold?'

'No, they're littered with those who didn't make it.'

'You're smart. Classy and smart. Sit down. I'll make some coffee.' He plugged in the kettle. 'You know, I get a lot of dumbos in here who think that all Americans are millionaires and all Texans own oil wells . . .'

'. . . and pay vast amounts in alimony.'

'. . . and party with a blonde half their age who used to be a drum majorette with their daughter.' He put on an exaggerated British accent which had Olivia in fits of laughter. ' "But Gary, why are all these people lying on subway vents, I thought this was meant to be the land of opportunity?" and I say, "This is the land of opportunity, but it don't come knocking on everyone's door. You've got to go out there, find it, and make it work for you." Now, where the hell does that secretary of mine keep the coffee?'

'Over there.' Olivia pointed to a shelf.

'I said you were smart.' He tapped some powdered milk into each mug. 'Where'd you say you want to work?'

'I didn't, but I'd like a top investment bank, and I'd choose to earn less and go somewhere with prospects rather than . . .'

'Why should a top bank pay less? The top people pay the best – that's why everyone wants to work for them.'

'In England . . .'

'You're in New York now, lady. Here if they don't pay, they don't get, and if you go telling people you admire them so much you'd work for nothing that's what you'll get – nothing. In fact, they probably won't hire you because they'll think you're some kinda nut. What's your name?'

'Olivia Steele.'

'Classy. Your own?'

274

'Of course.'

'No of course about it. My name wasn't Taylor. It was one of those unpronounceable Polish names which made me the butt of every Polak joke, so I changed it. I'd have been a schmuck not to, and in this town if you act like a schmuck you sure as hell get treated like one.'

'Don't you like New York?'

'Like it! I love it.' He walked over to the window. 'Manhattan! There's no place on earth like this over-loaded lump of rock. In London they say I'm pushy, in Paris they're rude, in Rome they're always trying to con me, but in New York people are upfront, out to make it, pushy and proud of it. When my kid does well at school I buy him a gift. He shows it to his mother. He shows it to his friends. He earned it. Why shouldn't he be pleased? Hell, what's the point of winning if you're not allowed to wear the victor's crown?' He gulped down his coffee in one. 'I tell you, there's no limit to how high you can go in this country. Why, Sidney Weinberg, the great old man of Goldman Sachs, started out as a janitor's assistant! That's what the US is about – people from nowhere going somewhere. Just don't forget, there's no safety net, and if you fall, you fall fast – all the way to the bottom.'

Olivia wore the green belted suit for her first interview, with Steiner Rheinberg who according to Gary were about the smartest money traders on the Street – the Street being Wall Street – with Ben Steiner 'the kid with the Midas touch'. She took a bus to Wall Street because she couldn't afford to waste money on taxis and Gary had said she shouldn't use the subway till she looked like a New Yorker. By the Trinity Church, where in spite of the cold one brave shoeshine boy plied his trade beside the graveyard railings, she crossed Broadway and plunged down into Wall Street, hustling for pavement space with a thousand other hustlers. She had expected Wall Street to be wide and imposing, instead she found a narrow canyon winding between great silvery skyscrapers which rose up from a street surface more in tune with a disused parking lot. But what it lacked in dignity, it made up for in rough, raw, thrusting energy. Olivia felt it as she stood on the steps outside the Federal Hall, shifting from frozen foot to frozen foot, watching the hotch-potch of smart men, black limos, blind beggars and popcorn sellers.

Steiner Rheinberg was on the thirty-third floor of a chrome and cream building. As Olivia shot up in the lift she slipped her foot out of her shoe and wiggled her toes into the deep pile of the carpet. It was warm, thick and expensive. She glanced in the mirror and straightened the collar of her black coat.

'I'm from Taylor Placements. I have an appointment . . .'

The receptionist glanced up. 'Yeah. He's out. Fill in this form. What did you say your name was?'

'I didn't. It's Olivia Steele.'

Forty minutes later Olivia was still waiting.

The switchboard buzzed. The girl answered. 'No, Ben, I don't know where he is right now. Yeah, he was meant to be seeing . . . she's here. Ok, I'll send her in.' She turned to Olivia. 'Mr Steiner himself will see you.' She spoke as though she expected Olivia to faint with excitement.

Ben Steiner was lounging in a huge chair, feet on desk, tapping into a micro-computer, speaking into the phone, reading an article in the Wall Street Journal – and he still found the space to give Olivia the sort of wicked-eyed grin with which men of his type fleece old ladies and seduce virgins but still remain Momma's favourite boy. 'Call you back. Ten minutes. Sure.' He held out his hand 'Ben Steiner.'

She said her name, 'Olivia Steele.' She was learning to do it their way.

He glanced at her form. 'How long have you been in the States?' Before she had time to answer, he pressed a button. 'If London came through I want to speak to them.'

'Two days.'

The phone buzzed. 'What's the pound sterling rate? OK, but thirty thousand.' He pushed back his unruly dark hair. 'I don't normally interview, Olivia, but our recruiter isn't here. I don't know what the agency told you but I'm looking for a right hand, someone I can depend on, someone to impress clients.' The phone buzzed again, 'Yeah? How much? OK, buy another twenty. Er . . .' he smiled at her, 'your work schedule would include arranging meetings, typing my confidential reports . . .'

Olivia picked up her bag. 'In plain English, a secretary.'

He laughed. 'An executive assistant. We're not in plain

England, we're in title-conscious New York.'

'I understood there was a vacancy on the trading desk.'

'I don't take women on the desk, the men don't like it. It stops them telling dirty jokes.'

She walked to the door. 'Don't you have a law against sexual discrimination?'

'Sure.'

'Aren't you afraid I might report you?'

'No – because then I'd report you for trying to work without a permit.'

'How did you know?'

'If you'd had that precious green card you'd have told me so straight out.' He laughed at her consternation; it was just a game and he'd made a clever move. 'Good luck. You're a punchy lady. Give me a call when you're in work and I'll buy you lunch.'

'Mr Steiner, when I'm in work I'll be able to buy my own lunches.'

She was angry with Gary. He must have known that Steiner Rheinberg was a waste of time, but she had no chance to ring him as she hurried through the freezing streets to her second interview, with a venture capitalist at the World Trade Center.

It was late afternoon when she came out into the numbing cold of the plaza where the central bronze globe was dulled with frost and even the bag people had vacated the benches around it. That interview had been worse – she'd waited half an hour then been told the post had gone. She found a phone and called Gary.

'Don't worry, kid, it's early days,' he said. 'I've got six more interviews lined up. You'll get something. I know a winner when I see one.'

Some inner store of optimism kept her going through the freezing streets of that January when her feet and hands were numb with cold, and made her smile as she answered yet again, 'Of course I want to stay in New York,' and not give way to tears when forced to admit 'Well, no, I don't have a green card.' Optimism and New York. The buzz of the streets. The melting pot of prospective winners – and why shouldn't she be one of them?

She saw little of the city during those early days. Apart from the fact it was one of the coldest winters on record she was far too preoccupied with job hunting to go sightseeing, although after one particularly useless interview she did take a walk up Fifth Avenue, luxuriating in the warmth of Saks as she toured the designer department, casually brushing against silks and satins. Out into the street she remembered the man on the plane, and wondered what would happen if she were mugged and murdered. She imagined Mark being told the news – but who would tell him? Who would know to tell him?

After two weeks it was patently obvious to Olivia that wherever top investment banks like William & Wall, Morgan Stanley, Goldman Sachs and Salomon Brothers obtained their recruits it was not through Gary Taylor, or any of the other agencies she'd visited without telling him. Nevertheless, because Gary had taken so much trouble she allowed yet another week to follow up his leads, spending her days waiting for men too self-important to keep their appointments or talking to those not important enough to help her. The evenings she passed in her box-like room, eating takeaway kebabs and drinking cans of coke as she flicked through the forty television channels, every one of them showing commercials, until eventually she would fall asleep, waking fitfully to the howl of police sirens or the flash of the neon sign on the building opposite. It was in those dark hours, lying in the narrow bed, a stranger in a strange city, that she was unable to prevent herself from thinking of Mark. She would picture him in his study, sitting at his desk, his hooded eyes half-closed. She would imagine him lounging on the sofa with the phone draped over his arm or bending attentively to diminutive Lady Vicky as they walked around The Helmets or in the Law Courts where his gravelly voice dominated and she had felt the sensuality of his power. She had admired him, she'd been proud to be his lover, his friend, his everything. She hadn't expected him to beg favours of Culross for her. Perhaps she'd just wanted to know that when the chips were down and the swords were drawn he'd be on her side. She remembered when they had first started to argue he'd come down to the kitchen in the middle of the night and found her crying into a bacon sandwich. How silly it all was, and yet, unless she could be his equal she would increasingly become his inferior. Damn

Mark! She pummelled the pillow. I don't want him — I don't want to want him.

Dear Maggie
I have just braved the New York subway for the first time. I clutched my bag and walked towards it like Orpheus approaching the river of the Styx. (It couldn't smell as bad as the Seventh Avenue Express!).

Thanks for letting me stay those few days after I left Mark and thanks for lending me the airfare. And please thank Zach for me. I know he hated the idea of lying to Mark. (I don't know why men don't marry each other, they always take each other's side.)

Dear Daddy and Mummy,
I know this is going to come as a shock but I am in New York . . .

Dear Fee
I hate to drag you into things but Father and Mother are probably having apoplexy because they will now know I have left Mark and am in New York. You remember the day when you came to lunch and said I looked as though I'd been crying but I said I had a cold, well, you were right . . .

At the beginning of her fourth week Olivia went back to Gary. 'Hey!' he looked up, smiling. 'I've just had Ben Steiner call to say if you're still interviewing . . .'

'Gary, I want to have a crack at one of the top investment banks.'

'Lady, you're too fussy! You want a good job?'

'Yes.'

'With power, prestige and a high salary?'

'Yes.'

'Jimmy Carter won the presidency last month so I regret the position won't be vacant for another four years.'

'Don't be annoyed, Gary, I know you've spent a lot of time . . .'

'Too right I have, and time's money.'

'I want to try somewhere like William & Wall.'

'You're kidding! Banks like William & Wall have the pick of Harvard Business School. Do you think they're going to look at some Brit with a second class degree and no work permit? Olivia, let me give you some advice.'

'Yes.'

'Book yourself on the next flight home.'

Three hours later Olivia lay on her bed drafting a letter to William & Wall:

Dear Sirs,

Having recently arrived in New York . . .

Dear Sirs,

I should be most grateful if you could advise me . . .

Dear Sirs,

Although I don't have . . . (no, too negative)

Dear Sirs,

Having an excellent understanding of European corporate . . .

The phone rang.

'Olivia, it's Gary. If it's any help, the person to try at William & Wall is Thornton Ashwood Mallory III, known as Ash Mallory.'

'Is he their recruiter?'

'Hell no! He's the whiz kid of Wall Street. Ivy League, Harvard, descended from one of the four hundred on his mother's side – the four hundred families which came over on the Mayflower. He's tipped to make president of William & Wall when old Whipcord McCord retires.'

'Why would he want to see me?'

'Sex.'

'Sex? Gary, I want a job not a . . .'

'Lay?'

'Yes.'

'If you apply to their recruiting department your letter will go straight into the trash can, but if you write a clever letter to Ash Mallory I bet he'll see you. A guy like that works long hours and he seldom gets to meet women outside the bank. He's not gay, at least according to gossip columns he isn't. What do you care why he sees you – so long as he sees you?'

'You're right. I don't know how to thank you.'

'Take me to lunch when you get that smarty job.'

Four days later Olivia was counting out her money on to her bed, working out that if she only ate once a day she could afford to stay for another three weeks, when the phone rang:

'Miss Steele?'

'Yes.'

'This is Mr Mallory's secretary. Mr Mallory would be happy to see you for fifteen minutes on the understanding that William & Wall do not have a vacancy to offer you.'

'I understand perfectly. Please thank Mr Mallory.'

She might not have got her foot in the door but she'd certainly got her small toe.

William & Wall was named after its location: it was on the corner of William Street and Wall Street. The entrance hall was dominated by the famous Waterford chandelier, accepted according to legend by one of the founding partners as security for a loan. The debtor had been an Irishman from County Waterford who needed money in order to finance his farm further up the Hudson River. He borrowed the money and apparently never came back – disappeared, drowned, killed by Indians. Who knew and, so it seemed, who cared? Not William & Wall. One of the bank's less reputable stories was the alacrity with which the partners accepted that the farmer wouldn't return in order that the chandelier should be theirs. In fact, rumour had it that the chandelier had graced the entrance hall long long before there was any hint that the Irishman might not return, giving rise to the suggestion that the partners had murdered the Irishman, snatched back the money *and* kept the chandelier. But whatever the truth, it had all happened long ago. Perhaps there had never been an Irishman.

A uniformed doorman buzzed Ash Mallory's secretary who sent down her assistant, who ushered Olivia into the lift, commented politely on the cold weather as they shot to the twenty-second floor, and settled her in an antechamber. In common with all important men Ash Mallory kept her waiting. Thirty-five minutes later – thirty after the appointed hour – the girl was back. 'Mr Mallory will see you now but I'm afraid he has such a heavy schedule he can only spare you five minutes.'

'It's very kind of him to see me at all,' said Olivia through gritted teeth. One day she too would keep people waiting – for hours!

In a land where winning counts, Ash Mallory counted. He was tall, athletic and prematurely grey. With youthful thick hair and the sort of overall gloss which only comes with success. Added to this he had a certain boyishness in his slightly turned up nose and in the way he tipped his head, an apparent deference which made him so endearing and un-usual. Olivia had expected him to be louder and flashier – but then, as she was to hear, Ash Mallory was a true banking animal and banking is about confidence, about people trusting other people, and Ash looked like the guy you'd want as your team-leader.

'Miss Steele.' He pointed to a chair, before sinking back into his side of the enormous desk. 'I must admit I don't usually see people such as yourself but you wrote a neat letter – and I was curious.' He grinned, then tapped into a many buttoned telephone. 'Steffie, don't interrupt me for ten minutes unless it's Sydney.' He glanced at Olivia's letter which lay on the desk before him. 'This is your first visit to the States?'

'Yes. How did you know?'

'Otherwise you'd have said "with valuable knowledge of the American market".'

She laughed – and so did Ash, his teeth white and perfect.

'You worked for Maxifunds, then Culross?'

'Yes.'

'And now you'd like to join William & Wall?'

'Well . . . yes.'

'Of course you would. If not, what are you doing here? But you must know that William & Wall are considered one of the most prestigious investment banks. What do you have to offer?'

'A knowledge of the European markets and experience in a London merchant bank.'

'Do you think London is more important than New York as a financial centre?'

'It is more strategically placed timewise.'

'And would you say that our clever Harvard graduates are unable to learn the experience of Europe?'

'Not unless they work there, just as no one can be taught what it is like to work on Wall Street. I believe, for example, that people who succeed in Japan do so because they under-stand how the Japanese tick. They know how not to offend. The same goes for Europe. To succeed in business, with someone or against them, you must know how they think.' She stopped, not wanting to sound dictatorial.

He smiled. 'I'm sure you're right. Not many of us have had the experience of bringing a share issue to its knees, have we?'

'So that's why you were curious to see me?'

'Sure. I wanted to meet the lady who had the chutzpah to practically send one bank down the tube then come to New York and apply to us, to William & Wall! Miss Steele, you've got style.'

'But I haven't got a job.' She walked to the door, turned sharply, her high heel cutting into the thick pile of the carpet and the panel of her skirt falling open to reveal one long silky leg: it was erotically aggressive because it was unintended. 'I thought the whole point of America was that it gave people a chance,' she said, and she marched out, slamming the door behind her.

Heading up Wall Street towards Broadway, she thought, I certainly blew that one – not that there was any hope from the beginning. Damn Ash Mallory and all his kind!

A wizened old negro banged into her. 'Hey, lady, can you spare a couple of bucks? Lady, I ain't eaten all day.'

'Go away!'

'Lady, you're motherfuckin' mean.'

'No, I'm not. I'm motherfuckin' poor.'

The old negro howled with laughter and staggered on.

She went into the Trinity Church, that blackened building like an elderly coalminer lost among the skiny skyscrapers, and sat down on a wooden pew, relishing the comparative warmth as she took off her shoes and rubbed her frozen feet together. Why the hell had she come to New York? What on earth had possessed her to leave Mark? What would she do when she ran out of money? She thought of the bagladies sleeping on the subway vents. As Gary had said, there was no safety net here.

Gradually she became aware of music. In front of the altar a quartet was practising, at first only murmuring against the background of traffic and her thoughts, then suddenly a flute joined in, darting in and out of the other instruments like some wild spirit eager to be free but afraid to take the plunge until it saw its chance, and as the other instruments followed each other obediently into a low burble the flute escaped. It found its notes and soared on high, unfettered and undaunted. Nothing could hold it back now.

Olivia smiled. There was always tomorrow – and she might be motherfuckin' poor but she wasn't beat yet.

The phone rang.

'Olivia Steele? It's Ash Mallory. Will you have dinner with me?'

'Ummm . . .'

'I'm sorry if you were upset this afternoon. In the US we tend to say what we mean. Would you have preferred it if I had pretended it was your academic qualifications I wanted to see?'

She remembered Gary saying 'Sex' and replied, 'Put like that, the answer is no.'

'Can I take it that that's the reply to my question and not to my invitation?'

Outside the snow was sliding down the dirty window pane. What had she to lose?'

It was five past eight when Olivia walked through the entrance of The Four Seasons and was promptly engulfed in the other New York – the New York of money and luxury. Her coat was taken, she was ushered up the stairs, informed that Mr Mallory would be a few minutes late, offered a drink, a seat, her table.

'I'll . . . wait here,' she said, pointing at a sofa near the top of the stairs. She had no intention of sitting at Ash's table like an unwanted lily in a flower shop, so she settled herself on a sofa and merely ordered a glass of Perrier water with a slither of lime, because it was essential that she should be able to pay for it if by some horror Ash failed to turn up. Of course he had offered to collect her but she had insisted they meet here. A small family hotel as she had described it to him was one thing, the reality of the scruffy entrance on the shambling lower reaches of West 44th Street was another. She smoothed down the soft clinging skirt of her ever faithful blue woollen dress and sipped her drink, looking every inch the smart successful woman at ease in her surroundings as she waited for one of any number of men who would be glad to take her to any number of smart restaurants around the world.

Ash came up the stairs two at a time. He glanced around, caught sight of Olivia, and came towards her with a smile which said that she was every inch the sort of woman he admired and absolutely nothing of the girl who had once been the centre of a sordid scandal. 'Olivia, I'm sorry if I've kept you waiting.'

'Don't worry.' She held out her hand. 'Good evening.'

'You should have let me call for you.' He held on to her hand a moment longer than necessary.

She retrieved it. 'I've been looked after very well.'

'Have you been here before?' He asked as he ushered her past the great Picasso and into a large room where diners sat around a bubbling pool in an atmosphere of grand romance.

She thought of the cans of coke and the kebabs. 'No, I haven't.

He was pleased. He wanted this evening to be special. Of course, when Olivia's letter had arrived on his desk and he'd recalled seeing a photo of a girl with a slightly bruised sensuality, restaurants had been the last thing on his mind.

'You're quite different from what I expected,' he confessed, once they sat down.

'Yes.' There was a glint of sadness in her brown eyes, then she straightened her shoulders.

Olivia ordered salmon. Ash ordered lobster. They talked of inconsequentials – Do-you-like-New-York/Do-you-like-London – until he said, 'This place is most amusing at lunchtime, particularly in the grill room on the other side of the stairs. It's *the* place for the publishing world. Publishers bring their bestselling authors here, then spend the entire time terrified in case another publisher makes the author a better offer.'

'So why do they bring them if it's so risky?'

'Because otherwise the author will be offended and definitely go elsewhere.'

She laughed. 'Artistic tantrums?'

'Creative greed.' He leaned forward and lowered his voice. 'There's a man sitting on the far side . . . dark hair . . . thinning on top. No, don't look now. He's a poet – a well-known one, considered a deep thinker, a real cult figure in the early seventies, sold well in San Francisco, Flower Power, peace and all that. He used to live near my grandmother. The only thing he ever talks about is money. A poet!'

Olivia giggled and slowly swivelled her head as though glancing casually round the room. 'He doesn't look like a poet, he's not thin enough.'

'He's successful. The only thin poets are unsuccessful or recent occupants of a health farm.'

Ash insisted that Olivia tried some of the chocolate cake, saying, 'It's the most irresistible, sticky, decadent cake in the world. I used to come here with my grandmother, once a year, at Christmas, and I always had it. We went shopping in the morning, had lunch here, then she would take me to a show in the afternoon. I remember being furious because she wouldn't let me see *West Side Story* till I was fifteen. She thought it was unsuitable. She'd once had a Puerto Rican maid who gave up maiding to go on the game, so Grandma was convinced that any play about Hispanics must be immoral. I was incensed. All my friends had seen it, so I was sure they must *know* more than I did,' he winked, 'if you get my meaning.'

'But of course you pretended to *know*.'

'Of course.'

They laughed together and he ordered coffee and brandy. 'The Culross thing must have been tough,' he said suddenly.

'It was – very.'

'Is that why you came to the States?'

'Yes.'

'Where have you been interviewing?'

She told him about Gary.

'Banks like William & Wall get enough applicants without going to agencies.'

'Yes.'

'What will you do?'

'Keep trying.'

'I'll have a word with our recruiter. I can't promise anything.' He stretched his hand across the table because he wanted to touch her, but he withdrew it quickly, afraid of frightening her off. 'At least you should get an interview. After that, it's up to you.'

She lifted her chin proudly. 'I wouldn't want it any other way.'

286

23

Ash said he'd call her next day but he didn't. When he'd said it she'd thought, I hope he doesn't, I don't want a man, I want a job. But after two days, when he still hadn't phoned, she began to analyse the evening – what she'd said – what he'd said – wondering where she'd gone wrong. And yet, she told herself as she settled cross-legged on her bed to work out her finances for the umpteenth time, Ash Mallory wasn't the type to make false promises.

The phone rang.

'Olivia, it's Gary. How did you get on with Ash Mallory?'

'OK . . . I mean, I saw him.'

'No job?'

'Not so far.'

'Ben Steiner's still interested.'

'No, thanks.'

'Hell are you obstinate!'

Twenty-four hours later.

'Miss Steele, this is the recruiting section of William & Wall. Mr Mallory had suggested a screening interview . . .'

That evening the phone rang.

'Olivia, it's Ash Mallory. Look, I'm sorry I haven't called you before but when I got back to my apartment there was a message for me to call London – we're involved in a big deal over here – and I had to fly straight out and I haven't touched

287

base since. You know how it is when one's working on a deal?'

'Yes.'

'The deal comes first.'

'Of course.'

He was telling her that he wouldn't be back in New York for at least ten days and she was telling him about her interview next morning whilst in the background she could hear the double ringing of a British telephone. As she watched the fat snowflakes slide down the dirty window pane, she felt a wave of homesickness which she would not have admitted to anyone.

For the interview Olivia wore her green Italian suit – there was no point in saving it for the second interview, there might not be a second interview. The recruiter, Sally, wore what Olivia thought of as standard, corporate clone look – a faintly checked grey Brooks Brothers suit with a white blouse, a red shoe lace tie, a breezy smile and recently capped teeth. She went through a stock list of questions. Why New York? Why banking? Why William & Wall. Then she leaned back in her chair, and said. 'You got into some pretty serious trouble at Culross?'

'Yes.'

'You repeated something about the bank to your boyfriend?'

'Yes. I didn't mean to do it. What I told him was that we . . . Culross . . . had a large shipping loan. He was a journalist and he looked into it, discovered that the charter party was false, and wrote an article to coincide with the Culross share issue.'

There was silence as Sally made some notes, then she looked up and gave Olivia a genuinely sympathetic smile. 'It must have been tough.'

'It was.'

'Could happen to lots of us.'

'Yes – but it happened to me.'

Sally stood up, 'We'll be in touch.'

Olivia longed to ask if there was a chance. She wanted to say that she could only afford to stay another fifteen days, but she couldn't, she smiled as though this were just one of many top interviews she was attending. Out in the street she tried not to think about what would happen if William & Wall did not want her. As she walked up Broadway she pretended that she had not allowed her hopes to be raised. Back in her overheated boxroom she refused to admit that she was at the end of her tether. In bed that night she thought of Mark.

Three days later – twelve before she would have to leave New York – Olivia received a letter from William & Wall asking her to attend a second interview.

She celebrated with an egg on top of her hamburger.

The doorman remembered her. 'Good morning, Miss Steele.'

Sally came to fetch her. 'You'll be meeting with four of us today. We'll be assessing you to see how you interact with us, individually and as a group, and later our president, Spencer McCord, may want to meet with you. McCord – he can't stand being called Spencer – has really cracked this team together, but then I'm sure you know that.' She spoke in the way people do when they imagine that their world is everyone else's universe.

For Olivia that day led up to one point, 'Spencer McCord *may* want to meet with you.' She was ushered down a beige carpeted corridor past half-open doors offering tantalising glimpses of busy offices. She was taken to a large room and introduced to three smart, bright people who zapped out their questions then listened impassively to her answers. Finally, she was left alone. She walked to the window and looked down twenty floors to Wall Street, where the successful stepped into shiny limos and the up and coming, or down and going, scurried into the subway on the corner of William and Wall Streets. She thought she'd done well, she hoped she'd done well, she so desperately wanted to have done well – but she was afraid to think that she had.

The door opened. Sally called to her. 'Mr McCord would like to meet with you.'

She was taken up to the twenty-second floor – Ash's floor – to where the offices were larger, or large by Manhattan standards where space is at such a premium though not by the standards of a British merchant bank, and ushered into a modern, functional office totally dominated by a huge man with busy Stalinesque eyebrows and the sort of face which in Westerns wins at poker, shoots the baddies, and goes on to become the first senator for Wyoming. He shook Olivia's hand, growled, 'Spencer McCord' and pointed to a chair, adding, 'Ash Mallory, whose judgment is pretty sound, thinks you might be useful to us. Tell me why.'

She began with her experience in the City and her knowledge of Europe and European corporate finance.

He listened, not so much to what she said, more to the way she said it. If she could not sell herself, how could she sell the services of his bank?

'What about this Culross business?'

'I made a mistake.'

'A pretty serious one.'

'Yes.'

'Do you think you can live down your reputation?'

'In New York, yes. In London, no – not unless I go back successful.'

'You're a good-looker. You'll get guys saying "Hey, aren't you the one who . . ." Do you think you can handle that?'

'I've had plenty of practice.'

He nodded, frowned, then stood up and held out his hand. 'Welcome to William & Wall, Olivia. You start on Monday. If you're good you'll do well. If you're not, you'll be fired. Reward by performance, that's our way. Long hours and two weeks holiday a year – if you're lucky. Oh, you're surprised that I should tell you such details, but the day I forget about performance I'll retire to Florida. Everyone of us at William & Wall is constantly reassessed. The rewards are great – the Street is a one-minute elevator ride. Don't forget it – or that this is not Britain with a funny accent but a foreign country "divided", as Shaw said, "by a common language".'

She took a deep breath. 'There is just one thing.'

'What's that?'

'I don't have a work permit.'

'Why the hell didn't you say so earlier?'

'Because you wouldn't have seen me.'

He scowled at her, then gradually his face relaxed and he chuckled. 'Typical woman! Makes you want her, then she tells you the conditions. 'He tapped a number into the phone and spoke to his secretary. 'Get me the legal department.' He covered the receiver. 'We spend a fortune on corporate lawyers and donations to political parties of all persuasions, and I'll be damned if it's all for nothing. You'll get your Resident Alien's Visa.' He pulled at his busy eyebrows as he studied Olivia. 'You know the origin of Wall Street?'

'No.'

'It was built to keep out the Indians, the British and other wild animals.'

She gave him a wide smile. 'Not with great success, so it seems!'

The first person whom Olivia saw when she arrived at William & Wall the following Monday was Ash Mallory. He was stepping out of a long shiny limo as she hurried from the subway. 'Sorry I haven't been in touch,' he said, as they went up the steps to the front door, 'I've just got in on the "red eye" – the overnight flight from the West Coast. We must have dinner one evening. Hi, Sally. Here's Olivia. She's all yours.'

The three of them walked to the lift. Sally and Olivia stepped inside. Ash was about to follow, but at that moment a cloud of scented black hair framing one of the most sensual faces Olivia had ever seen appeared beside him, took his arm, and held him back, purring at him through bright glossy lips.

'That was Sherry,' said Sally with a slight raising of her eyebrows, 'She's in charge of one of the bullpens. Not yours. You're under Barbara. You'll soon pick up the pecking order. New hires – associates like you – stay in a bullpen for about two years. This means you share an eye-level glass partition office with four others. At first you do a lot of number-crunching, preparing and analysing financial statements which half the time come to nothing. It's tedious but necessary. You'll be constantly reassessed. It's up to you to get yourself noticed. We'll be watching to see how you interact with your bullpen. We need team-leaders not loners. They'll be your buddies but also your competition.'

'You mean that pyramids get smaller at the top?'

'Right! We're after people who'll do anything . . . well, almost . . . to get on. In your case, we expect you only to stay in

291

your bullpen for one year because you've had experience. It all depends how you shape up, of course.'

'Of course.' It sounded like dog eat dog – which is fine so long as you aren't the one being eaten!

The lift stopped at the fifteenth floor, another chrome and cream reception area with serviceable corridors leading to compact computerised offices which made the new buildings at Culross seem like something out of the ark.

'Russ is in charge of all bullpen leaders,' said Sally after introducing Olivia to a man with a face like an intellectual boxer. They moved on, and she added, 'He and Ash Mallory . . . and Barbara, your leader, are the same class. You'll be known as the class of '77 on our training programme. I'm afraid you missed orientation week so you'll just have to introduce yourself around.'

'Is Russ a partner?'

'Oh, no, just Ash from that class – but then Ash is exceptional. Hi, Barbara,' she called to a tense-looking blonde with a fifties flicked up hair-style. 'Barbara, this is Olivia Steele, your new hire.'

'Hi, Olivia, nice to have you with us.'

'Thank you. I'm pleased to be here.'

'I'm afraid you missed orientation week.'

'Yes,' Olivia gave a positive smile and straightened her shoulders, 'but I'm sure I'll cope.'

'You're a friend of Ash's?'

'Oh, no, not a friend . . . I mean, I've only met him twice.'

Sally laughed. 'Don't worry, knowing someone may have got you an interview, it doesn't help you get hired.'

'Or not get fired,' added Barbara.

Olivia was ushered down a corridor to a large room divided into some half dozen glass pens, each containing four people, four desks and four telephones. Barbara stopped at the one with only three occupants. 'Folks, this is Olivia Steele.' They shook her hand and said names.

'Betsy Greenstein' Elegant, auburn-haired, beautiful dark eyes.

'Peter Hill.' Dark and owlish.

'Teddy Bentall.' Large, blond, dependable.

Olivia sat down at the vacant place beside Peter. His phone

rang. He answered. 'Sure.' He left. A man came to the doorway. 'Betsy!' She leaped up and followed him. A secretary brought a file for Teddy. He opened it immediately. Another secretary brought a heavy manual. 'Olivia Steele?'

'Yes.'

'Barbara says you're to familiarise yourself with the bank and its current projects.'

'Thank you.'

'You're welcome.'

'Tough on you missing orientation week,' said Teddy.

'Yes, but I'll cope.'

'We have a lecture on accountancy this evening. You'll meet the other hires then. Tell me, is it true you're the girl who nearly sent Culross down the tube?'

She was about to make a cutting reply when she saw Teddy's smiling open face and she remembered Spencer McCord saying this isn't English with a funny accent. 'I let slip something about the bank, by mistake,' she said.

'Yeah, that was it. Must have been tough.'

'It was. Very tough.'

She gave a quick glance around. In the other bullpens heads were bent over desks and pens sped across paper. Down the far side of the room were separate offices with glass walls reaching up to the ceiling: these were occupied by two people, the principals, one step above those in the bullpens. Barbara was one step higher, with an office to herself.

Olivia opened the bank's manual. William & Wall had been started over a hundred years earlier and like most banks had both accepted deposits from private customers and underwritten share issues. But the Depression, and in particular Black Thursday of 1929 when the market crashed and thousands were left destitute, changed all that. The Glass-Steagall Act was brought in to protect the private customer from having his money speculated with – and banks were forced to choose between being an investment bank, more or less like a British merchant bank, or a commercial bank, the equivalent of a British clearing bank. William & Wall had become an investment bank, and had had to close its doors on the small customer, finding its market instead in the lucrative field of financial management, which included mergers and acquisitions.

Clients tended to come from the *Fortune* 500 — *Fortune* magazine's list of the largest corporations in the States — and competition for their business was cut-throat. William & Wall, like Morgan Stanley was regarded as WASP, whereas Goldman Sachs and Salomon Brothers were Jewish. But these barriers were becoming less well defined, and at William & Wall this was mainly thanks to Spencer McCord. Old Whipcord, as he was often called on the Street, was of Irish Catholic descent and married to a protestant New Englander.

'Olivia,' Russ stuck his bullish bespectacled head over the glass partition. 'What are you doing? The bank's manual! Hell, you read that in your spare time. Barbara, has Olivia been shown the analysts? Why not? I want her to start on the Carthew Tools file. Yes, I know Sherry's bullpen's working on it as well and so is half the bank but Carthew are one of our best clients.' He thumped a file down in front of Olivia, pushed the manual away and, ignoring Barbara's tight-lipped expression, said, 'Carthew want to expand into New England. There are nine possible companies they might go for. The tenth is The Patching Tool Co., but they don't look too hot. Get on with it.'

'Come on, Olivia.' The tiny lines at the corner of Barbara's mouth dragged as she led the way to the analysts who occupied a series of open-plan offices on the eighth floor, each section marked according to its speciality: Energy, Retail Services, Media. Some of the analysts were older and owlish and looked as though they had been born to their profession, other were eager beaver graduates gaining a couple of years experience before going on to Harvard: all of them spent their days peering into VDU screens. Heads barely lifted to nod to Olivia. She was just another new hire to come pestering on deals which would come to nothing.

'It makes me mad the way Russ overrules me,' said Barbara on the way back. 'Anyone would think he was Ash the way he throws his weight around. He's the sort of guy who'll always put a woman down. Of course the girls have it easy now, but I can tell you it was a rough ride for us, the pioneers on the Street. We had to carve our niche and watch men being promoted ahead of us. All men. Even the stupid ones. But then women always have had to work harder, haven't they?'

Teddy and Betsy were talking quietly when Olivia returned.

They looked up and smiled with that sort of unison which showed that they had just taken a step into closer friendship.

'Barbara been telling you her woes?' asked Teddy.

'Yes, it's sad.'

Betsy nodded. 'She did it to me last week, and the tough part is she has a point.'

Peter came back. 'Barbara's the understudy whose star never breaks a leg. Sherry's got on OK.'

Betsy and Olivia looked at each other. 'That's the point, Peter. Just look at Sherry!'

'We can't all be promoted,' said Teddy soothingly.

There was silence. They were each aware that to go up they would have to step on others – and on each other.

Olivia met the other new hires that evening, about twenty of them in all, at the lecture given in a flat nasal monotone by William & Wall's chief accountant. It was boring, but not one of those present let their attention wander even for an instant and Olivia, sitting next to Peter, had to bite the inside of her mouth to stifle a yawn. On top of that she was hungry – starving. All she'd eaten that day was a sandwich, and her tummy kept making hideous rumbling noises like water running out of an old tin bath.

'How often do we have lectures?' she asked Betsy as they stood up to leave.

'Once a week. Didn't Sally tell you? You'd better remind her tomorrow – you'll need to catch up on what we did last week. Mind you,' Betsy lowered her voice, 'I could have done without today.'

'So could I.'

'If you miss one you've got to have one hell of a good reason.'

'Supposing you have a . . .?'

'A date? Olivia, you are now in the land of the office romance. The only dating most bankers do is with other bankers because they don't have time to meet anyone else. In fact, most dating is done in the office.'

'Behind the soda fountain?'

Betsy giggled. 'Practically.'

'No,' said Teddy, 'on the photostat machine whilst it's

working so as not to waste corporate time.'

They were laughing as they burst out into the freezing night.

'Let's go to eat.' Teddy flagged down a cab. 'There's a new place in SoHo . . . well . . . not that new . . . what's it called? . . . the SoHo Charcuterie. Come on!'

Olivia hesitated. 'I'm not very hungry, I think I'll . . .'

'Not hungry! They must have been able to hear your stomach rumbling in San Francisco. They probably thought the San Andreas fault had finally . . .'

'Teddy!' Betsy interrupted softly from the interior of the cab. 'Olivia, are you short of cash?'

'Well . . . umm . . .'

'I'll lend you some. You can repay me at the end of the month.'

The SoHo Charcuterie had the current passion for glossy white paint and huge hanging plants – the look which caused a million tables to be stripped in search of pine.

'Where are you staying?' Betsy asked Olivia as they settled at their table.

She explained about the hotel, trying not to make it sound worse than it was, but somehow it seemed worse today, sitting with people in a warm restaurant: it had appeared less bad when she was on her own, hovering with the other lonely people in this city.

'You'll have to get an apartment,' Teddy told her. 'We'll ask around. Rent-controlled would be great but they're like gold dust. Next best is a sublet. That means you lease from the lessee and don't renegotiate with the landlord, or he'll sting you for megabucks, particularly if he finds out you work for William & Wall.'

'On the other hand,' said Peter, in his flat voice, 'if you don't work somewhere reputable they won't lease to you in case you default. Accommodation is the number one hassle of Manhattan.'

'We pay the prices because we want to live here,' said Betsy, with a resigned shrug. 'I think you should look on the Upper West Side, that's where I live.'

'Don't listen to Betsy,' said Teddy, 'where she lives it's full of trendy media types in designer jeans. The Upper East Side is the place to be.'

296

'Ignore him, Olivia, he just wants to be with all the other stuffy old men.'

'If it's only for stuffy old men, how come all the singles bars are on that side?'

'This,' said Peter when he managed to get a word in edgeways, 'is a continuing Manhattan argument.'

Olivia laughed. 'Perhaps I'd better look at both and decide which I think would be more fun.'

'Fun!' They held up their hands in mock horror. 'What do you think this is – summer camp!'

It was long after midnight when they were tipped out into the cold.

'SoHo used to be called Hell's Hundred Acres,' said Betsy, 'and now look at it. The Greenwich Village of the Seventies.'

They stood in a row looking up at the warehouse buildings whose zigzagging fire escapes were being repainted and whose ground floors were being taken over by a plague of art galleries.

'I'll tell you a piece of utterly useless information.' Peter pointed at the street sign. 'Spring Street was called after the spring which ran underneath and Aaron Burr, who started up the Manhattan Water Company to sell its water, later joined up with a bank named after a certain Mr Salmon Chase.'

'Chase Manhattan!'

'Move to the top of the class, Miss Steele!'

24

It isn't that people work so much harder in New York than they do in London, Olivia came to the conclusion as she left William & Wall late on her first Saturday, it's just that it is made to seem harder. The meeting that afternoon could easily have been switched to Monday and it was perfectly obvious that everyone wished it had been, especially those who'd had to come in from Connecticut, but no one, absolutely no one dared to make such a suggestion. It's the insecurity of a hire and fire society, she decided next morning as she braved the cold to go house-hunting. On the other hand, she mused, recalling some of the employees at Culross, a bit of uncertainty does keep people on their toes. She bought the *New York Sunday Times* and over brunch of scrambled eggs ploughed through page after page until she came to the section on apartments to let. There were plenty. She felt hopeful. She'd soon find something. She had another cup of coffee, remembering to say light not white.

The first place in the Village – Greenwich Village – called Spacious Studio was a box at the back of a house; the second, An Airy Loft, was a coffin below a skylight; at Smart Upper West Side when the landlord heard she worked for William & Wall he said there'd been a misprint over the rent; by the afternoon she could read an ad. at a glance – and not one was worth the subway token to inspect it. She returned to the hotel, tired, cold and miserable.

'How did you get on?' Betsy was looking particularly sleek next morning.

'Hell.'

'Expensive?'

'Astronomical.'

'Room to swing a cat?'

'If you cut its head off first.'

Betsy laughed. 'My mother's family came from Russia at the beginning of this century. They were poor and for the first five years lived in two rooms. But my grandpa worked hard, he started his own business, and eventually they moved to New Jersey, educated their children, and had all the things they'd never had before. The American Dream! But you know something weird? Last year when I moved into my new apartment I gave my Mom my address and she nearly fainted – because I'm living in those same two rooms!'

'You're joking!'

'No, but when they lived there they didn't even have a bathroom and now it's a pretty neat apartment – and I pay more rent for one weekend than they did for a whole year.'

Later that day Olivia phoned Gary. 'I'm getting on fine,' she told him, 'and once I get my first pay cheque I'm going to take you to lunch to thank you for all your trouble.'

'Kid,' he said, 'I appreciate the thought but I know those investment banks. You won't have time to breathe for six months.'

Ash rang that evening. He was full of apologies . . . he'd been to L.A. . . . so tied up . . . he'd meant to call . . . hoped she was settling in . . . how about dinner tonight?'

'Not tonight, thank you.'

'Sure? I'm off to Europe tomorrow and I'll be gone a week.'

'I can't, I have to look at a couple of apartments. I'm trying to find somewhere to live.'

He was too like Mark – but without being Mark.

The second week at William & Wall passed in a constant rush – rush to work, hustle on the subway, grab the *New York Times*, study the ads. for apartments, all day poring over the Carthew Tools file, then rush home to change into something warm before braving the freezing streets to look at yet another lunchbox at a rent so high that she thought she must have misheard. She was regaling Betsy with the story of the creepy landlord who tried to touch her up in the lift, when there was a tap on the glass side of their bullpen.

'Olivia Steele? Hi, I'm Sherry.' The voice was drawl, the face pure thirties Hollywood – black hair, arched brows, glistening red lips. 'Ash,' the lips rounded over his name, 'tells me you're looking for a place to live. He says you're new to Manhattan and don't have any friends. If I hear of somewhere I'll let you know.' Her smile became saccharine and she waved a red taloned hand before undulating down the corridor.

Teddy watched open-mouthed. 'What in the hell was all that about?'

'I think,' said Betsy softly, 'Sherry was warning Olivia to stay away from Ash Mallory.'

'I hardly know him! I'd only met him twice before I came here. Are Sherry and Ash . . .?'

'Not in the way Sherry wants.'

'Meaning?'

'Marriage.' said Teddy. 'Sherry is from a poor Southern family. She's done brilliantly, everyone says so, even those who don't like her admire what she's achieved, but she's not going to make Ash because the Mallorys don't marry people like Sherry. They marry other old New England money.'

'I thought this was meant to be a classless society?'

'Honeychild,' Teddy put on a deep Southern drawl, 'there ain't no such thing as a classless society.'

'I suppose not.' Betsy gave a quiet sad smile.

In the end Olivia heard of an apartment through Sally, the recruiter, whose former college room-mate had an English friend who had come to New York having fallen in love with it and a man on a two week holiday, only to find that what was bliss for a fortnight in the spring, both city and man, was anything but during the relentless cold of winter. However, in the first flush of passion she had lumbered herself with a five year lease on an attic in SoHo, the property of a painter now living with Buddhist monks in Tibet. 'The good news,' said Sally, 'is that it's of a reasonable size and vacant, the bad is that there's hardly any furniture and no elevator.'

Olivia went straight after work, to a turning off Spring

Street, not far from the SoHo Charcuterie, where the rounded cobbles glistened in the frozen evening and the steam rose up through patterned vents, white into the darkness, catching in the lights from an art gallery, turning orange and ethereal. Most of the houses were freshly painted in popular pinkish red, their recently restored fire escapes shiny in the light from the outstretched street lamps, but even those which had not yet been renovated had an air of expectancy, a sort of not-long-now look.

She found the art gallery where the key had been left with the owner, Dulcie, a woman with a rainbow fringe and green fingernails who was sitting at a desk checking her income tax receipts. She handed over the key in silence, though not an unfriendly silence. The attic was up six flights of badly lit stairs, passed the muffled gloom of Wagner coming from the fifth floor, to a bright red front door, the colour of an English pillar box. Inside was a huge bare white room – even the floor boards were shiny white like a doll's house. The only furniture, if you could call it that, were two orange bean bags sitting side by side like ducks in love and a large round white table. She walked through into the bedroom which had a double bed, a bright red phone, and a cupboard with the doors open and the coat hangers swinging, denoting flight. The bathroom was unpainted, although the intention in the form of three tins of paint was present. On the other side of the sitting-room lay the kitchen, long and functional like a ship's gallery. In a cupboard there was a set of smart modern red and white dinner plates. The girl had obviously seen herself giving dinner parties for her loved one, not realising that most New Yorkers eat out or that the red and white plates would outlast the love.

Olivia walked to the window and looked out, down the street which seemed to stretch forever to the twin towers of the World Trade Center haloed against the night sky. With a view like this she felt sure she would be happy.

She was obliged to wait till Saturday afternoon before she had time to move into the attic, and once she had paid off the stinking little hotel, forked out rent and deposit for the attic, satisfied the endless sums needed for telephone, electricity, gas, and bought the absolute necessities like a duvet – she could hardly sleep on a bare bed – and stocked up on the basics

301

like milk, bread and eggs, she had hardly any money left. Nevertheless, once installed she went down into the streets to explore, to gaze into brightly lit galleries, to rustle through clothes in boutiques, to spend a tempting fifteen minutes among the cheeses of Dean and Deluca. Then she went home – alone but no longer lonely.

On Sunday morning she woke up rigid in her memories. From below came the unmistakable crescendo of the Marche Slave. It took her back to Mark and the time he had found her crying into a bacon sandwich after their first row – or rather the first of the beginning of the end. She got up and furiously began to paint the bathroom ceiling.

'Anyone at home?' A dishevelled young man wandered into her bedroom. 'Hey you should lock your door.'

Olivia was standing on a chair in the middle of the bathroom. 'Who are you? What do you want?'

'I'm a rapist come to add you to the statistics of violent crime.' He lay down on the floor and closed his bloodshot eyes. 'I'm Freddie and I live on the fifth floor and my blood is pure alcohol.' He raised his hand to shield the glare then gingerly opened his eyes. 'You'll need to put a second coat on that ceiling.' Without Olivia asking, he went on to tell her that he was a commercial artist who'd spent five years scrabbling for a living but finally he was beginning to make it. He'd got into commercial art through a friend of Dulcie's, the gallery owner . . . yeah, she looked kind of odd but she had a heart of gold . . . and now, well, hadn't Olivia seen this week's *New York Sunday Times Magazine*. No?' He leaped to his feet and ran down stairs. In a flash he was back, waving it and reading out, 'Freddie Caswell, a native of San Francisco who came to the Big Apple five years ago is *the* big news on the commercial art scene.' 'Doesn't look like me, does it?' He pointed at a photo, then lay down on the floor like some shaggy mongrel she might have found wandering the streets. 'You know what they say?' he watched her paint through half-closed eyes.

'Ummm?'

'Work like an American, relax like a European.'

'How come you're the one lying on the floor then?'

'I'm improving Transatlantic relations!'

She flicked a blob of white paint at him. It landed on his

nose. He did not bother to remove it but told her that he needed a Bloody Mary, was meeting some friends for brunch in Minetta's, and had come up to see if Olivia was worth asking along.

'Am I?'

'You'll do.' He slopped to his feet, stretched, and stopped dead as he caught sight of Lorenzo's silver fox coat hanging in the cupboard. 'Don't tell me you're a hooker.'

'No, I'm a banker.'

'Same thing.' He laughed and dodged out of the room, shouting, 'Half an hour and bring a coat – but not the hooker coat.'

Olivia thought for a moment. Brunch meant spending money, then she turned on the bath, chucked in some bath salts, and told herself firmly 'What's the point of being in New York if I'm not going to have fun.'

The warmth of Minetta's enveloped them as they came in from the cold. It drew them into its mixture of cosy Italian and old New York. There were shouts, of 'Freddie! Freddie!' as he led Olivia past a long bar into the restaurant behind, where a dozen or so people were crowded around a table, perching on chairs, on each other, or squashed into a red leather booth.

'Not lunching at the Ritz, Freddie?'

He laughed and shook his shaggy head. Someone thrust a glass into his hand. People cheered. From the next table a woman called, 'Freddie, we just have to do a piece on you for the June issue.'

Somehow Olivia was introduced around. Dulcie, still green-fingered, found her a chair. Next to Dulcie was a blonde girl clinging to the remains of a Californian tan and a tense upwardly mobile young executive type. They introduced themselves as Brad and Sandra; they lived on the second floor. Other people shook her hand and said their names, asked where she was from and if she liked New York.

'Olivia *has* to have the *linguini* with white clam sauce,' announced Freddie, squeezing in beside her.

'Supposing she doesn't like it,' said Dulcie mildly.

'Who cares if she likes it! She'll eat what she's told to.'

There was laughter, and Dulcie murmured, 'Chauvinists,' then got up. 'Have to split now . . . so pleased, Freddie.' She wafted out past the bar like a green witch going in search of a cauldron.

'Dulcie not staying?' asked Sandra.

'No,' said Brad. 'Fried rats are off today.'

'Come on, Brad!' said Freddie, 'Dulcie's a good friend. She's just a bit uptight because her analyst's on vacation.'

It was the sort of lunchtime companionship, of too much alcohol, cigarette smoke, and everyone shouting across the table which reminded Olivia of Friday lunchtimes in the pub with Jonathan and Hamish, except that then of course they had been careful not to drink too much. She sat back and sipped her Bloody Mary and listened. She was two thousand miles from London and less than two miles from Wall Street, but it was the world of William & Wall which seemed furthest away at that moment.

They stayed at Minetta's till late afternoon, then moved on to Chumleys, the old speakeasy, to sit on rickety stools at the long bar and hear wild stories of prohibition days and how those inside Chumleys would escape out of the back during raids.

Finally, at eleven, they went home.

'Would you like to see my work?' asked Freddie.

'Yes . . . but I won't stay long.'

'I said work not bed.' He opened the door into a room as bare and white as Olivia's, only this gave no pretence at being anything but a studio. There was a huge table scattered with paper and pencils, a long shelf stacked with paints, and down one side a stereo set with rows of cassettes all carefully labelled and catalogued.

'Do you always listen to music when you work?'

'Yeah, it helps me to capture the mood. If I'm working on, say, an industrial account I play to Dvorak's New World Symphony.' He clicked in a tape. 'Listen to the rawness of the Pennsylvanian steel worker as he pours the liquid molten steel . . . and those trains which broke the frontiers of the new world . . . chug-chug, chug-chug.' He switched tapes and lowered the volume so that it was barely a whisper. 'Debussy for women – feminine, muslin women drifting through summer afternoons. I see them and I draw them.' He switched the tape again. 'This is for you, Olivia. The modern woman.' He turned up the sound on Handel's The Arrival of the Queen of Sheba. 'You, striding up Spring Street, into our house, into our lives. Breezy, punchy, confident, arms swinging, hair blowing. You the outsider, the queen of another land. Oh, Queen Olivia!' He bowed low.

'What about Tchaikovsky?'

'The March Slave! Oh, that's for success, for when I do well. It reminds me that the more successful I become the more I am success's slave.'

She turned away. 'I knew someone who also played the Marche Slave. He said that you could hear the chains and the barefoot slaves but that at the end their spirits escape.'

'Like you?'

She could not look at him. 'Perhaps.'

Dear Jake,
I know you'll have a fit when you see that I'm in N.Y. . . . You'll ask what sort of friend I am to choose to come here after what they did to you but I had to go somewhere – yes, things with Mark didn't work out – and this is the best place for me.

Dear Maggie,
At last I can give you an address. I've found a wonderful attic in a house full of crazy people – you'd love them – and not one a banker, which is good as I get the impression it's not easy to meet people outside one's profession. I do miss Mark, although I tell myself I don't. Honestly, I don't think I'll ever care for anyone again. I don't think I'll be able to let myself. It's as if all my feelings have been torn out of me, chopped up in little pieces, and stamped on.

Dear Daddy and Mummy,
I have just moved into a lovely attic in SoHo . . .

Dear Livvi,
Your mother and I are very worried. I know we haven't seen much of you recently and you have had a difficult time but don't forget that if you are in trouble . . .

Dear Fee,
I have had the most extraordinary letter from father . . .

Dear Olivia,

It's hardly surprising. Why don't you think before you act – but you never do, do you? First you run away to America without telling anyone when you know that mother's happily telling her friends to expect a June wedding, then you write to say you are living in Soho . . .

Dear Fiona,

First, I did not run away – I left. Second, I never told Mummy that I was getting married in June or at any other time. Third, SoHo in New York means South of Houston and it is nothing like Soho in London . . .

The phone rang.

'Olivia, it's Ash Mallory. You forgot to give me your new number and I had to beg it from Sally. How about dinner this week?'

Her letter to Maggie lay on the table, the Marche Slave came up through the floorboards. 'It's very kind of you but . . .'

'Look, if you're involved with someone else just say so.'

'Well . . . ummm . . .'

'OK. See you around.'

Freddie knocked on the door. 'It's me, the rapist. Will you help me choose an armchair on Saturday?'

'Yes – if you'll help me choose a rug, some cushions, a bedside light and . . .'

Freddie: 'What do you think of American men?'

Olivia: 'To the point.'

Freddie: 'Shall we play the Marche Slave.'

Olivia: 'No, something else – *anything* else.'

Freddie, late one night: 'I think we should have sex.'

Olivia: 'I think that would spoil it.'

Freddie: 'Hell, I'm not *that* bad.'

306

One Saturday Betsy took Olivia to Loehmanns, a discount store in the Bronx which sold designer clothes at half price, and on Monday morning they were telling Teddy about their trip, each claiming that the other had tried on every possible garment in the place, when Russ clapped his hands. 'Listen you guys, the Carthew Tools client meeting has been brought forward to Monday. Yeah, I know, two weeks earlier than scheduled, but it looks as though the news that they want to expand to the eastern seaboard may be leaked, and we all know what that would do to the price of every tool company from Maine to Florida. I want everyone working on this deal at a meeting on Friday morning – with your ideas. OK? No questions? Good. Get to it.' Barbara had come into the office. Russ turned to her. 'Tell Sally to rustle up four more secretaries for the graveyard shift – midnight till eight. They're to type the proposals.'

Barbara's mouth puckered. 'Don't you think that . . .'

'Not this week. I'll think when Carthew Tools have confirmed they're going ahead with a deal proposed by William & Wall.

'. . . and not trotting up town to Morgan Stanley,' boomed McCord from the doorway.

There were chuckles as they bent their heads to their task. Olivia studied the figures of ten possible tool companies, then she took her file to Jack, the smartest of the analysts.

'Jack, I know you're busy but . . .'

'You're not the only new hire in the building.'

'I know,' she smiled at him, 'but I've had this idea.'

He leaned back in his chair. 'What are you doing tonight?'

'Working.'

'The trouble with all you women is that you try to be men. Look at Barbara!'

The door opened and Sherry wafted in on a cloud of scent. She tossed a file on to one of the desks, turned, and undulated out again. Jack's eyes followed her, then they returned to Olivia – who pulled a face.

He laughed. 'OK, you win – and I'll tell you something, you're a hell of a lot better looking than Sherry. Ain't that so, you guys?'

'Yeah,' they chorused. 'What are you doing tonight, Olivia?'

She tapped the Carthew file. 'Working! Jack, could we just run through some of the back data on Patching. They've got this huge factory out in Connecticut which they took over from a small arms dealer who went bankrupt after the war. The rent's pretty low. They haven't got a labour problem. Their machinery's new. Their product is good. Why don't they make a profit?'

Jack began to feed the information into his computer whilst Olivia sat beside him, watching the screen. At eight, they sent out for pizzas. At midnight the secretaries of the graveyard shift arrived for work and Olivia handed in her draft for typing. At one o'clock she, Teddy and Betsy piled into a cab, too tired to speak: Olivia barely had the strength to climb the stairs to her attic. By seven next morning she was at her desk, reading through the draft, altering the odd phrase. Beside her Peter was slowly chewing gum. Opposite, Betsy was drinking black coffee. Next to Betsy, Teddy was writing furiously. At the top of Wall Street the blind beggars were getting into position. In the ladies cloakroom at William & Wall, the secretaries of the graveyard shift were preparing to go home. At the house off Spring Street, Freddie was just getting up. On the floor above Olivia's office the traders were checking the dollar/sterling rate with London, where it was lunchtime, whilst in the Stock Exchange on the corner of Broad and Wall they were discovering what had happened in Sydney, where it was evening and the Australian traders were downing their Victoria Bitter. One market closed as another opened.

Russ glanced around the boardroom at his eager young associates. 'We'll be presenting to Carthew on Monday,' he told them. 'On Sunday morning we'll be having a run through. McCord will be present.' He tapped the pile of reports in front of him. 'You handed these in five minutes ago so even I haven't had time to read them yet.' He waited for the laughter to die down. 'I shall select one recommendation – or perhaps a mixture. In the meantime, I want each of you to stand up and in not more than one minute outline your proposal. Peter!'

Peter adjusted his spectacles. 'I propose that Carthew

should not purchase an existing company but a factory and set up their own . . .

'What about distribution?' Sherry licked the gloss on her red lips. 'They need an established network.'

'OK, Peter,' said Russ. 'Next!'

One by one they stood up, only to be shot down again.

It was Olivia's turn. 'I . . . umm . . . propose that Carthew buy The Patching Tool Co. I know that they don't look hot on paper but the reason is they are only working to two thirds of their potential. They have expensive new machinery and plenty of factory space and they could produce and distribute a third as much again at little extra cost. This would reduce their unit cost – and make their goods more commercially attractive.' She sat down.

Russ nodded. 'That's pretty neat, Olivia.'

She went pink with pleasure. 'Thank you.'

On Sunday he did a rerun of the presentation. The new hires watched from the back of the room. They heard arguments which none of them had thought of and simple, clever solutions where they had been over-complicated. It was exhilarating.

'The recommendation is that Carthew should purchase The Patching Tool Co.' said McCord. He looked down the table. 'Any of you young creatures got a comment to make?'

Olivia smiled and shook her head, but to her astonishment everyone of the others hurried to speak.

Teddy. 'I think that's most advisable.'

Betsy. 'Patching are the obvious target.'

Even Peter. 'Carthew have the know-how to turn Patching around.'

McCord stood up. 'You've all done a good job.' He left the boardroom with Russ on his heels and Sherry elbowing Barbara out of the way. But before the boardroom door closed behind them his voice boomed out, 'Smart piece of research into the reason for Patching's low profit margin.'

'Yeah,' drawled Sherry, 'it suddenly came to me.'

Olivia opened her mouth, half stood up – then sank down into her chair.

'You should have made sure old Whipcord knew it was your idea,' said Teddy, seeing her stricken face. 'It's no good expecting Sherry to speak for you. She's after promotion too.'

Olivia was close to tears. She'd pored over Patching's price list, gone to bed thinking of factories, dreamed about tools, woken up in the morning muttering Patching's profit & loss margin – and all for nothing. No, worse than nothing. As Gary had once said to her, 'If you act like a schmuck in this town, you sure as hell get treated like one'.

She rose unsteadily and left the room, and behind her back she heard Teddy say to Betsy, 'Pity about Olivia. I thought she had more punch.'

The SoHo house was deserted that Sunday afternoon: everyone had gone to Minetta's. She climbed the six flights of stairs and closed the red door behind her. Then she threw her bag at one of the orange bean bags and kicked her shoes into the corner. I'm pathetic, she thought, tripping over the other bean bag. I'm someone to be laughed at, like Barbara. Pity about Olivia! She went into the bedroom, took off her skirt, and curled up under the duvet, pulling it right up over her head like a protective cocoon. From the street below came the sound of laughter.

It grew dark but she did not turn the lights on, she just lay there, staring up at the ceiling. At one point, she had no idea when, Freddie knocked on her door, at first softly, then persistently. She didn't answer, and after a few minutes he went away, his footsteps despondent on the stairs.

At around ten she got up, had a bath, put on a long red tee shirt and some red socks, and stood by the window eating cornflakes without sugar – she'd forgotten to buy any.

Freddie came back. 'Olivia!' He banged on the door. 'What are you doing?'

'I'm having an early night.'

'Can I come in?'

'I'm tired.'

'Please . . . I just can't bear to be alone. Please!'

She opened the door. He stumbled past her and slumped down on one of the bean bags. 'My wife turned up today, the bitch!'

'Your . . . I didn't know you were married.'

'We met at college and got married when we were twenty-one.' He ran his fingers through his dishevelled hair. 'I thought

I'd never love anyone else but Rayette. Two years later I came home early and found her in bed with our neighbour. They say the husband's always the last to know. She'd been screwing half the town. I walked out that night – and I've never heard a word since, until today when she turned up on my doorstep. She said she'd seen the article in the magazine and had come to congratulate me.'

'Didn't you divorce?'

'I meant to, but the idea of contacting her made me want to vomit. Now I want a divorce and she says she doesn't.' He came over to where Olivia stood, by the window. 'Do you know, I nearly strangled her today. I hate the way she stayed away when I was hassling along on the odd buck here or five there, just another failed artist. And I hate the way she's come back, with her greedy little mouth telling me that she always knew I'd make it.' He went into the bedroom and threw himself down on Olivia's bed. 'I'm sorry, I'm truly sorry.' He gave a small choking sob. 'I hate her, but I cannot be indifferent to her. I want her to die. I feel as if my whole life will be oppressed until she is dead because however high I climb she will always be there, grabbing at me, pulling me down, reminding me that I was once a failure, making me scared that I'll be one again, making me so afraid of being hurt that I can't risk allowing myself to feel anything for anyone.'

Olivia walked to the end of the bed and looked down at him. 'I understand. I'm scared of being vulnerable to people . . . to anything.'

'You've got that bruised look today.'

'Yes.'

'But with you it's not only a bruised look, it's a closed look. You can't even tell me, can you? Oh, don't try, just let me sleep here. I don't want to sleep alone, not tonight.'

'I know what you mean.' She made them each a mug of tea and when she came back Freddie had half undressed and was dozing under the duvet. Olivia climbed into bed.

'Aren't you going to take off your bedsocks?' he asked, as her foot ran down his leg.

'My feet are cold.'

'He looked under the duvet. 'Red socks. How romantic! And is this one of your mini dresses?'

311

She snuggled down. 'No it's what I wear to the bank when I want to impress clients.' She turned on her side with her back to Freddie but sleep evaded her. Over and over again she relived the moment when Sherry's drawl had claimed her idea, to be followed by Teddy's, 'Pity about Olivia.'

'Why are you tossing about?' asked Freddie.

'Am I? Oh, sorry, I've had a bad day and I keep thinking of what I should have said but didn't.

'Was that why you wanted to be alone?'

'Yes.'

He put his arm around her and drew her gently to him and kissed her very lightly on the back of the neck. 'You should have come to me. Aren't we friends?'

'Yes.' She moved back against him, and this time they lay close, curled into each other.

He tightened his arms and nuzzled the back of her hair. 'I think we should make love.'

She half turned to him. 'Sex makes you closer, closeness makes you hurt.'

He slid his hand under her tee shirt and caressed the softness of her stomach. 'Not for sex – for comfort and for friendship.'

He was warm and thin and surprisingly hairy. It was a bit like cuddling up to an Irish wolfhound. They kissed, gently, softly. He began to hum, in her ear. She froze – she was back in Mark's kitchen listening to the Marche Slave as she cried into her bacon sandwich. 'Don't,' she said, taking his hand in hers. 'I'm sorry Freddie, I'm just so . . .' She felt tears come to her eyes and hover behind her eyelids. In all the time she'd been in New York she had not given way to tears, but it was Freddie, warm and comforting who made her cry, softly into his shoulder – crying for things which somehow hadn't worked out.

It was five thirty. Olivia slid out of bed, not wanting to wake Freddie but unable to lie still a moment longer. As quietly as she could she ran her bath, then wrapped in a towel she used the light from the bathroom to search for her clothes in the bedroom cupboard. It was six when she closed the red front door behind her. I may not be punchy but at least I can look keen, she thought, as she hurried along Spring Street in search of a cab, passed a Vietnamese boy who knelt on the pavement outside a lighted flower shop smoothing down the petals of big white daisies with his frozen fingers as he made up the bouquets for that day.

She found a cab eventually, but when she arrived at the bank she could not face the office, not yet, not even empty as it would certainly be this morning. So she set off down Broadway, almost tripping over a young man fast asleep on a subway vent. She had to walk fast, for it was very cold, and in no time she was facing the dreary barrenness of Battery Park. There she hesitated, and immediately a heap of rags stirred on one of the benches and a voice called, 'Hey, lady!' Olivia hurried on, telling herself that she was mad to have come down here, into this subterranean world of half-night. She ran up the steps to the ferry terminal, her hands still trembling when she paid for a mug of coffee, her knees knocking as she walked through to the back and sat down on one of the rows of wooden benches.

It took her twenty minutes to calm down. What she needed was time to think, time to be alone. She bought a ticket for the Staten Island ferry and sat on the upper deck, on the right hand side, where in the summer tourists crowd to photograph the Statue of Liberty. But at this time of year and at this early hour there were no tourists, just the odd workman huddled into a leather jacket or a rep forced to make an early call on a Staten Island client. She watched them without interest. Her thoughts were of Mark and the impossibility of their situation, of her longing to go home counterbalanced by her desperate desire to succeed. If I go home with my tail between my legs . . . She bit the inside of her lip to stop it trembling.

They had reached the wall of wooden sleepers that defend Staten Island from the elements. There was a crash of the anchor and shouts – boat sounds which reminded Olivia of the ferry at Anataxos. People came on board, those who had to be at work early. Silent and sleepy they read their newspapers, ignoring the little old Chinaman who wandered between them searching for shoes to shine. He found a customer and knelt before him, gently lifting the man's foot on to a block of wood, dabbing a cloth into black polish with the same solicitude which the Vietnamese boy had shown towards the petals of the white daisies.

Why doesn't he get a better job, thought Olivia, watching him bow and accept a single note.

She went to the railings and looked across at Ellis Island, at the dilapidated turreted buildings which till the mid fifties had been the main receiving station for immigrants. Twelve million had passed through its bleak halls and on, to a new life in a strange country. How many of them had been able to read and write? How many of them had spoken English? She watched the Chinaman kneel before another customer. But they had succeeded, not all of them – she thought of the vent people and the bag people – but some of them, those who went on to fulfil their wildest dreams, to make fortunes and build dynasties, and they did so by combining what they knew with what they found: by adapting. She pushed back her hair and looked across at Ellis Island – and told herself that if they who could not read, write or speak English could make it, then so could she!

25

It was over a year before Olivia got another break, a year of long hours, short holidays, and relentless hard work. From a freezing winter, through a glorious spring, into a stifling summer with its twenty-five hour power cut, and on to the brilliance of fall, Olivia persevered because every time she asked herself, 'Why am I doing this?', she remembered the Staten Island ferry and the twelve million immigrants, and she'd say, I'm damn well going to succeed.

On that morning when she had come off the ferry she'd gone straight to William & Wall, given everyone a cheerful 'good morning', and sat down at her desk. From their surprised faces it was clear they had been wondering if she'd work out her notice or simply never both to come back.

Two months later, Jack, the analyst said, 'You're not as chicken as we thought.'

Three months later, Barbara complimented her with, 'I'm glad to see you're shaping up after all, Olivia.'

Then nothing – no compliments, no praise, no real chance to prove herself, just a lot of hurdles over which to fall down. It was unbelievably frustrating.

Although Olivia seemed to make little headway at William & Wall, other aspects of her life improved. She had money, not a fortune – not yet – but more than she'd had before. Her hair was cut regularly and well, she joined a gym where she worked out twice a week, she bought her clothes from Saks or Berg-dorfs or one of the SoHo boutiques, except when she and Betsy made their pilgrimage to Loehmanns, and she hired the wife of the porter at Dulcie's gallery as her cleaner, and not just to clean but to shop, wash, iron and run errands. What a relief it was to get home and find the house sparkling, the fridge stocked, and her silk shirts collected from the dry cleaner. Of course it cost – but why not? She worked hard, she deserved it. Often she was so busy at the bank that she only had Sunday off, and sometimes not even Sunday, but if she were free she had brunch with Freddie at Minetta's: it was their ritual, the one time they could be sure of seeing each other.

Things were going well for Freddie. A lawyer was dealing with his divorce and he was, as he said himself, flavour of the month in the commercial art world. Much of his time was spent flying backwards and forwards across the States and most of his sketches were done in airport lounges, but he thrived on it, grabbed his success and fed off its nervous energy – and its insecurity. 'I've waited too long not to make the most of it,' he told Olivia.

In the summer Teddy and Betsy had finally got together to the horror of their respective mothers, who each disapproved of marrying outside the faith – Jewish for Betsy's, Protestant for Teddy's. 'It was all the fault of the power cut,' Betsy confided to Olivia, her eyes shining with love. 'Teddy couldn't get home . . . could he? I mean, he just had to stay the night!'

In July Olivia finally did what she had been promising to do, and took Gary out to lunch. It touched her that he was touched that she remembered to do so.

At Pietra Alta, Jake was working hard, his forms taking on new dimensions. He sent Olivia a small piece of marble from the block which had been trapped in the flooding river – the rest was to become The Snake Girl. In September he wrote to say that Gwen was with him. Olivia wondered . . . she hoped. Then in November she received a short sad note:

Gwen has left. Our ghosts were too strong. She could not forget that I could not forgive Jim. She felt a traitor to him. I felt a traitor to myself for being with Jim's widow. My desire for revenge has killed what I might have had with Gwen. Remember, Livvi, an eye for an eye is one thing, but you have to stop there – or else you become the victim of your own revenge.

love Jake

Her mother wrote that her father was working hard and the

316

senior partner had offered them his cottage in Jersey for a week. Her father wrote that her mother was increasingly involved with the handicapped children and that they were all worried about Hugo, who was being shunted sideways at work but refused to discuss the probability that he would be made redundant. Olivia remembered the afternoon when she and Fiona and Hugo and Simon had gone for a walk and Fiona had said she was going to get a part-time job to help pay for Charlie's school fees. She would have liked to phone her sister and offer sympathy – perhaps even money – but they were no longer Fee and Livvi, they had reverted to Fiona and Olivia.

Maggie wrote that Savvies had opened up in Covent Garden. Business was going splendidly but she still wasn't pregnant. With her letter she included a cutting. It concerned Culross: they had finally gone public.

That had been in the autumn. Now it was nearly December and Olivia was intending to visit her parents at Christmas. She felt confident about going – confident that when the moment came she would want to come back to New York.

'I have enough of a life here now to bring me back,' she told Betsy.

Betsy smiled. 'Don't you dare run out on me. You're my buddy.'

'Hey, you two!' Peter came in carrying a can of mango juice – he always went for the unusual. 'Have you heard about Jupiter Aircraft – those ultra deluxe jets Teddy has his eye . . .'

'I haven't!'

'OK, then it was the model's legs . . .'

'Teddy!' Betsy looked fierce. 'What is this?'

They all laughed, and Peter went on, 'Someone's done a dawn raid on Jupiter and bought 14.99 per cent of their shares – and guess who it is? Lane & Lee!'

'Why would they want an aircraft company?' asked Teddy.

'Why do they want all the other companies they take over?' said Olivia. 'To strip them down, turn them around, work them for a bit, and flog them – or not, as the case may be.'

'But they usually go for badly managed companies. What's Jupiter's problem?'

'Infighting among directors,' said Peter. 'It was a terrific company till it went public four years ago and it's never been the same since.'

'Are they fighting the takeover?' asked Olivia.

'Rumour has it that that's the only thing which has stopped them fighting each other.'

Teddy sighed. 'They don't stand a chance. Lane & Lee will have their heads for baseballs.'

They went on with their work – Olivia with her analysis of a domestic appliance company in Sweden, Betsy with her report on a chain of dress shops in Norway.

Three days later Ash Mallory called a meeting. He headed the boardroom table with Sherry, Russ and Barbara grouped around him. The associates, like Olivia sat at the other end. Of course Olivia had seen Ash frequently over the past months – the brief nod in the corridor, a slightly awkward sharing of the lift, the odd discussion about work with other people present, but he'd made no effort to contact her again, then, she asked herself, why should he? Office gossip had it that he and Sherry were lovers. Olivia watched Sherry run the tip of her tongue over her glossy red lips and wondered if she cared that she was universally disliked. Probably not. Perhaps I could be like that, she thought, then her eyes met Betsy's and they grinned at each other. Betsy, Teddy and Peter, without them, her colleagues, her friends, the past nine months at William & Wall would have been sheer hell, just as without Freddie her attic home in SoHo would have been only a set of rooms on top of a house without a lift. Life was about many things, especially about people. Her glance fell on Ash but he was talking to Sherry.

He stood up. The room fell silent. 'All of you will have read that Lane & Lee are attempting to acquire Jupiter, and that Jupiter are trying to fight them off. Singlehanded, Jupiter haven't a hope in hell and they know it, so they've approached Caltoco to be their white knight – to take them over and save them from Lane & Lee, Caltoco have come to us for advice – of course!' He grinned and the whole room basked in his pleasure. 'They want to know if Jupiter are worth buying, because white knight or not they don't want to end up with a lame duck. Lane & Lee are said to be set to increase their holding in Jupiter. We have to act quickly and discreetly, because once the word is out that Caltoco are in the running the share price will rocket – maybe above what Caltoco are prepared to pay. This is going to be one of the most exciting takeover battles on the Street – and we're going to show them that William & Wall can do. Right?'

'Right!'

The door opened and McCord came in. 'You'll want to know that Lane & Lee have upped their bid by twenty cents a share.'

'And Jupiter?'

'Trying to persuade their shareholders not to accept Lane & Lee's offer.'

Ash turned to the associates. 'The first thing is to study Jupiter's data to see if director infighting alone is responsible for keeping profits down, or if there's another reason. It is going to be hard work, late nights, and no partying. Yes, I know it's running up to Christmas but if I catch anyone coming to work with a hangover he or she will go straight out into the Street,' he paused, 'without the benefit of the elevator!'

The others returned to the bullpen, Olivia went to Jack. 'I want you to run some figures for me,' she said, opening the spare parts manual for Jupiter Aircraft.

He pushed back his specs. 'On one condition.'

'What?'

'That you don't let someone else steal your credit.'

Olivia leaned forward and readjusted his spectacles. 'Not bloody likely.'

It was midnight by the time she reached home, seven when she arrived at the bank next morning, midnight again when she bid the others a weary goodnight and slid out of their shared limo, so tired she could barely make the stairs to her red front door.

'Hey, stranger,' Freddie called up as she turned the key in the lock, 'fancy a nightcap?'

'No, thanks, I'm bushed.'

'Yeah, you're getting the Manhattan pallor.'

'Long hours and air-conditioning,' she yawned. 'But you wait, once this deal is over I'm going to work out regularly at the gym and lie on a sunbed till I'm golden brown, like those who spend half their lives beside swimming pools in L.A.'

He laughed. 'You missed me. Hey, that's neat, I thought you hadn't even realised I had gone.'

'How's it all going?'

'Great – except that I spend my life in airports, not beside swimming pools. It's not just the waiting to catch a plane which drives me crazy, it's the hanging around because some nut or bolt or wing falls off. Do you know that during an aeroplane's lifespan it will use ten times its original cost in spare parts. Oh, well, must hit the sack. See you at Minetta's on Sunday, if you're free.'

McCord called a progress meeting two days later and when they were all assembled around the boardroom table, he simply said, 'Shoot!'

Olivia was on her feet before anyone else had a chance. 'During its lifetime an aircraft uses approximately ten times its original cost in spare parts,' she said. 'This means that each one is a continuing source of income. Jupiter have a good reputation here, and in Europe, but they don't sell well in the Middle East and South East Asia because their spare parts distribution is mismanaged.'

'You think those places are a large potential market?' asked Ash.

'Yes. Helicopters are ideal for areas where the airport is right out of town, but it is no good expecting Muslim Pakistanis to go to Hindu Delhi to buy spares. The same goes for the Middle East, for instance Saudi Arabia and Jordan. All that has to happen is for them to fall out over the Palestinian question and you've lost half your customers. Jupiter should employ one top class local agent in each country.'

'Sounds like good sense.'

'It seems to me,' purred Sherry, 'that it means a lot of trouble for very little countries.'

'But very rich countries,' said Olivia, 'and countries where many towns have developed so quickly that they don't yet have a commercial airport, just a stretch of tarmac suitable for a small plane or a helicopter.'

McCord pushed back his chair. Anyone else got anything worth adding?'

'I'd like to see your notes in my office, Olivia,' said Ash, following McCord from the room.

'Fine.'

'Olivia, you shouldn't have spoken out.' Sherry leaned across the table. 'You're answerable to me, and don't forget it!'

'No, I'm not. I'm in Barbara's bullpen.' Olivia headed for the door, aware that the whole room was listening. 'Furthermore, I have no intention of ever allowing you to steal my ideas again!'

She had not been inside Ash's office since the day when she'd first come to William & Wall. She'd walked past, of course, glanced in and caught glimpses of the enormous desk with its battery of telephones, and several times come into contact with the professional friendliness of Steffie, his secretary, but she hadn't entered his office and Ash had not invited her to do so.

To her surprise he wasn't alone. Spencer McCord was ensconced in a deep leather chair with his back to the door.

Olivia hesitated in the doorway. 'Oh . . . I'll come back later.'

McCord turned around. 'Come on in, we both want to talk with you. Sit down. 'Well,' he gave her his Stalinesque under-eyebrow stare, 'I'm glad you didn't let someone steal a march on you again.'

'I learned a tough lesson.'

'This is a tough school. Where did you get the data on the spare parts?'

'Sikorsky, Westland, British Aerospace, Aerospatiale.'

'Smart.'

'Jack's a good analyst.'

'Double smart. Pick a good team, support them – and they'll support you.' He nodded to Ash.

'Which is what we've been discussing,' said Ash. 'We want to expand into the European market. We've done well on the home market, the US is a huge country and you can become vastly rich without even knowing which side the Atlantic is, let alone crossing it, but as you yourself told me once, if a company wants to do business in Europe, Japan and the Middle East it's no good blundering in, offering beef stroganoff to Bombay businessmen.'

'Or bacon sandwiches in Tel Aviv,' quipped McCord.

'Or ordering Turkish coffee in Athens,' murmured Olivia.

McCord nodded. 'Right. You can't get the better of people unless you understand how they tick. You've got to get into the other guy's head. You don't have to play his game, but you've got to understand it. Nothing's ever quite real in another country. Foreign money isn't the same as one's own, it's like Monopoly money. Being a foreigner makes you aware of foibles in our system, in your system, and in other systems – and it makes you prepared to adapt. That cannot be taught. We've been watching you, Olivia. You had a bad start but since then you've shaped up pretty well – and you know Europe. Most associates do two years in a bullpen. We want you to come straight into Mergers and Acquisitions – M & A – on the European side. You'll be promoted to senior associate – and you'll get a rise.'

'Thank you.' She blushed with pleasure.

'A rise is the confirmation that you are doing well. Promotion is the signature on that confirmation.'

'When do I start?'

'Right away.' Ash smiled at her. 'You'll be moving up here, to the twenty-second floor, and you'll be directly responsible to me.'

'We're going to be an unbeatable team at William & Wall,' McCord patted her on the shoulder, 'and you're part of it. Now, let's get back to Caltoco and the Jupiter deal.'

There was a brief silence after he left, but work broke the ice. Ash said, 'Let me see your Jupiter notes. Ah, yes . . . where did Jack get these figures from? He pressed a button. 'Jack . . . Ash Mallory re: Olivia Steele on Jupiter . . . yes, it was a good idea . . . a great bit of teamwork all round. I want to see your sources – in half an hour.' He turned to Olivia, 'It's nearly eight and I'm starving. How about you?'

'Me too.'

'I could eat a horse.' He gave her one of his boyish grins, so at odds with his suave appearance that it seemed so much more intimate. He pressed another button. 'Steffie, be a good kid and order two pizzas . . . four seasons with anchovy. OK for you, Olivia? And two cokes . . . and get yourself something. Yes, on the bank. I said so. Coffee? You're wonderful. Steffie's been with me for six years,' he told Olivia, 'I don't know what I'd do without her.'

The pizzas came. Ash and Olivia were so hungry that they tore off bits and ate with their fingers, burning their tongues and dripping hot cheesy tomato over the typed draft of the Jupiter deal.

'You know,' he said across the remains of their feast, 'I'd still like to take you out to dinner.'

She licked the last of the cheese from her finger tips. 'You just have.'

'Properly.'

She smiled.

'Well?'

'I don't know, I mean . . . we're going to be working together.'

'So what? It happens all the time.'

'Thanks a bundle.'

'I didn't mean it like that.' He leaned forward. 'Are you thinking of Shery? OK, I've dated her but nothing serious, maybe once every ten days. Hell, why should I have to explain myself to you?'

'You don't have to.'

'I want to – and I want you to explain yourself to me. I want to know about the other guy, the reason why you wouldn't have dinner with me before. I want to know what you feel for him, if you're still dating . . .'

'It's over.'

'No explanation?'

'None. It's the past.'

'What about us?'

'You're very persistent.'

'Why not? If I want something I go for it.' He picked up her notes. 'But in the meantime . . .'

Olivia wasn't sure what she thought of Ash. Yes, he was goodlooking and yes, she found him attractive in a way – at least she did at the bank. It would have been hard not to fall under his spell in the environment of Wall Street, where he was admired, but she could not imagine him in Anataxos or at The Helmets or with Jake in Pietra Alta. Then she told herself, I'm in Manhattan not Pietra Alta now.

The battle for Jupiter was fought through those icy December days when the wind howled down the canyons between the skyscrapers and every morning another baglady was found frozen to death in Battery Park – not that that was Olivia's world. Hers was one of long hours in bright warm offices, of a limo to pick her up and take her to make snappy decisions over breakfast meetings, of figures which ran to billions . . . zillions of dollars. Of power. Of challenge. Of winning. And she loved it. She relished the sense of belonging to the hustling bustling throng on Wall Street. The rawness which had frightened her now excited her. She enjoyed having money – she'd earned it. And she enjoyed the admiration of Ash Mallory.

Lane & Lee increased their bid for Jupiter's shares. They wrote to Jupiter's shareholders in an effort to persuade them to accept. By the same post the shareholders received a letter from Jupiter telling them not to. Shareholders big and small waited for a better offer. In Chicago the directors of Caltoco met with William & Wall. They said, 'We're interested in Jupiter – at the right price.'

McCord, flanked by Ash and Olivia, advised. 'Top Lane & Lee's offer but get Jupiter to agree incentives, such as if your deal with them falls through and Lane & Lee wins you still get a percentage of the company for your pains.'

Caltoco said, 'Right – but show us a package deal.'

McCord, Ash and Olivia flew back to New York to work on it.

Two days later the Wall Street Journal ran the following:

Word on the Street is that beleagured Jupiter has found a suitor whom she prefers to Lane & Lee. The question is, can she offer strong enough incentives to clinch with this suitor or will she be carried off protesting to Lane & Lee's already large harem of purchased companies? The other question is, which of the companies advised by Whipcord McCord and his team is interested in Jupiter, a blushing though not entirely perfect bride?

At William & Wall they laughed, but McCord warned, 'Not a careless word to anyone or Caltoco will pull out of the deal.'

A week later Lane & Lee increased their share offer by a further five cents.

'Aren't we leaving it a bit late?' asked Olivia. 'Jupiter are tottering. Some of their shareholders have already accepted Lane & Lee's offer.'

McCord gave her a craggy smile. 'Timing is crucial in this game – and the witching hour will be Christmas Eve.'

Two days before Christmas, McCord, Ash and Olivia flew to Chicago. They presented Caltoco with the facts. Their advice, 'Go for it!'

On Christmas Eve, as Lane & Lee were throwing an enormous party to celebrate their first decade in business – a party to which they had invited all of their most important clients – Caltoco topped their bid by five cents a share and Jupiter's four major shareholders accepted. The white knight had rescued the distressed damsel.

Lane & Lee cursed.

Jupiter and Caltoco toasted each other.

But more was to come.

By mid afternoon it was announced that Jupiter had not become merely a part of Caltoco but that the merged Caltoco Jupiter Inc. was now gunning for Lane & Lee. David had turned on Goliath.

On the plane back to New York, McCord ordered champagne and as he raised his glass to the rest of his team, he said, 'To us! To William & Wall!'

'To us!' They chuckled as the bubbles hit their noses and the alcohol their already taut adrenalin.

Ash ate a sliver of smoked salmon. 'Bet Lane & Lee are kicking themselves.'

'Heads will roll.'

'Serve them right.'

'Do you think Caltoco Jupiter will succeed in acquiring Lane & Lee?' asked Olivia.

'With our advice,' replied Ash, 'of course.'

'What a deal we put together!' McCord smiled at them benevolently. 'God it was fun!' He glanced at his watch. 'Ten o'clock. Christmas Eve! It'll be midnight by the time we're home. What are you two kids doing tomorrow?'

'I'd been planning to visit Charles and Ursula in Connecticut,' said Ash 'but there won't be time to drive up and back. My aunt Ursula and McCord's wife, Blanche, are first cousins,' he explained to Olivia, adding 'What about you?'

'I'd intended to visit my parents in England, but that was before the Jupiter deal.'

Blanche and I are having some friends to Christmas lunch and we'd be pleased if you could join us,' said McCord. 'Both of you or either of you. Very relaxed. Only about twenty people.'

Ash said, 'I'd love to.' Then he gave Olivia a questioning look.

'So would I. Thank you.'

They drank another toast – to Jupiter, to William & Wall, to themselves, to Christmas – and to the New Year, 1978.

Ash came for Olivia at midday, by which time she had been through every item of clothing in her wardrobe, trying on one, discarding it, trying on another, until she settled on a deep red dress made of a soft crêpe and cut in a wrap-around fitted style which had hints of Hollywood in the thirties. Over it she draped her silver fox. My relic of squandered days and Lorenzo, she told her reflection in the mirror, wondering what Ash would say about the gunrunner. Slowly she raised the hem of her dress, up her thigh, to reveal the tops of her silvery silky stockings and the white satin ribbons of her suspenders peeping out below the lace frill of her cami-knickers. If she had not admitted it to herself before, she did so then, as she examined her reflection, that she and Ash would become lovers – soon.

The bell went.

She sloshed some scent on her wrists and neck and grabbed her bag and gloves. Ash was waiting on the pavement, leaning against a long low gleaming red Jaguar, his hands deep in the pockets of his honey-coloured cashmere coat – a coat similar to Lorenzo's. When he saw Olivia he straightened up, freed his hands and came towards her, taking her by the shoulders and kissing her lightly on each cheek. 'Merry Christmas.'

'I'd almost forgotten,' she smiled at him shyly. Funny how when things, personal things, really mattered she became so awkward.

He opened the car door. On the passenger seat was a long silvery box and in it, nestling among folds of white satin, a single red rose. Across the bottom of the box in Ash's oddly schoolboy handwriting was:

To Olivia,
Merry Christmas
love Santa

'Ash, it's beautiful. Thank you. But how awful of me, I haven't bought you anything.'

His fingers caressed the sleeve of her fur coat. 'I don't want . . . presents from you, Olivia.'

'I haven't got anything for the McCords either.'

'Nor have I.' They looked at each other and laughed, for it struck them both that yesterday they had wielded power and wealth and fought one of the bloodiest takeovers of the Street and yet neither of them was capable of remembering the simple or the mundane.

'I know a flower shop,' he said.

'I know a chocolate shop.'

They raced up town. Ash bought some roses — yellow. She was pleased he had not bought red, because that made her rose special. They took a cross street to the exquisite chocolate shop opposite the dreary hotel where she had first stayed, which somehow seemed even drearier, just as the area seemed scruffier and the chocolate shop even more of an exquisite oasis. She got out of the car and swished across the pavement into the shop, just as the suntanned woman had done. When she came back, carrying a beautifully wrapped box festooned with purple and pink ribbons, she glanced up at the hotel. The windows were dirty. The drab curtains drawn tight against the day — and who would want to look out on Christmas Day from that place? Then suddenly the curtains twitched and a girl's pale face stared down at Olivia.

'What are you looking at?' asked Ash.

'I stayed in that hotel when I first arrived in New York.'

'You're kidding! It's a dump.'

'I know.'

He felt for her hand. 'You've come a long way, kid, and it's time to stop looking back.'

'The past is what we are.'

'No. We're the future — the immediate future. You and I.'

327

The engine roared into life. He flicked on the radio and the pounding rhythm from *A Chorus Line* filled the interior – the beginning bit, where the eager hopefuls get just one minute to prove that they can dance.

'Those guys at Lane & Lee must be sick.'

'Yes.' She wished she could go back and tell the face at the window that she too could make it if she tried.

'I'd like to have seen their expressions.'

'Yes.' Ash was right. She had to forget the past in order that it should not ruin the future.

The McCords lived in one of those discreetly elegant flat-faced apartment blocks on the section of Fifth Avenue which runs down beside Central Park, just above the open-air book-stalls, the sort of block where the canopy stretches across the pavement to the curb and the uniformed porter, who recognised Ash's car, was bowing Olivia out of it before she had even reached for the door handle, ushering her into a world of untold wealth and luxury, a sanctuary of deferential service and heavy security.

'There you are!' McCord burst out of the drawing-room as the butler opened the lift door to them. 'Merry Christmas. Yes, I always kiss my colleagues on Christmas Day. No, Ash you'll be glad to know I don't mean you – only the pretty ladies. Chocolates? And from my wife's favourite shop! I recognise the pink and purple ribbon. Blanche, honey . . .'

A porcelain figure in turquoise came towards them, the sort of immaculate pale blonde whose serene face never becomes lined because she never allows herself to worry. 'I'm so glad you could come,' she said, extending a soft white hand to Olivia.

'Thank you for inviting me.'

'My favourite chocolates! How very kind. Now, let me introduce you.'

The McCords were experienced and excellent hosts. Within minutes Olivia had a martini in one hand, had met every one of the twenty odd guests, and she felt as at home as possible in the circumstances.

'You have to see the view,' Ash detached himself from an elderly lady and steered Olivia over to the window. Below them was Central Park, its trees weighted down with snow just like an old-fashioned Christmas card.

'It's so beautiful,' she said.

'I have the same view from my apartment.'

'You do?'

'Mmmmm. My apartment's about ten blocks up. In fact,' he lowered his voice, 'I'd say the view is better.'

'Oh, yes?'

'Uhhhhu.'

'Now, Ash,' Blanche tapped him on the shoulder, 'don't monopolise Olivia. I want to get to know her.' She led Olivia away, saying, 'Would I be nosey if I asked how long you and Ash have been dating?'

'Actually, Ash and I aren't . . . dating. I mean, today is the first time we've . . . and it was your husband who invited us – separately.'

'Oh, dear, I'm so sorry.' She gave Olivia a smile of such charm, as she added. 'Ash has had lots of girlfriends but he has always refused to introduce them to the family. His aunt Ursula thinks it's because his mother was so wildly possessive that she'd hardly let him out of her sight. Of course it was only to be expected. Ash was all she had after his father was killed in that awful motor accident – and she'd always been highly strung, poor dear, though none of us realised quite how bad she was . . . I'm sure you know . . . an overdose . . .'

'Blanche telling you my secrets?' asked Ash, suddenly appearing between them.

'Just a few.' Olivia gave him a small soft smile of sympathy – and wondered why it had taken her until now to find him very attractive when he had all the qualities any woman could want in a man: he was clever, goodlooking, dynamic and successful: he was a part of this world and this city, a winner in a jungle where there was no such thing as a good second.

All through lunch they kept looking at each other: she caught his eye over the goose and blushed: he caught her eye when Blanche said, 'Christmas puddings flown out from Harrods to make you feel at home, Olivia.' By the end of the meal she could think of nothing but the moment when they would be alone together, and thinking about him sent shivers up and down her arms, making her feel lightheaded – with excitement, with desire. Her neighbour, an elderly admiral,

329

told jokes at which she laughed, hoping that she did so at the right moment: she had no idea what he was saying. She wanted Ash – and he wanted her. Their eyes met. Haunting. Lingering. She felt herself blush, and knew he had seen, and that he knew her thoughts – which made her blush the more.

The admiral's wife smiled at her across the table. 'How long have you lived in New York?'

'Ten years.'

'Ten!'

'I mean one.' She blushed again. 'One year.' Her stockings slithered against each other as she uncrossed her legs.

'Can't understand what you bankers find to do all day,' said the admiral. 'The navy's different. You've got a ship to run, but a bank . . . You're too pretty. I expect all the men want to date you . . . don't they, McCord? Must be a liability having a girl like this around.'

Blanche stood up. 'Ladies, shall we retire and leave the gentlemen to their port.' As they went through into the drawing-room, she took Olivia's arm, 'George is a frightful chauvinist.'

It was late afternoon by the time they finished coffee. Ash and Olivia were sitting beside each other on the sofa. She was terribly conscious of his nearness. It was as if they touched, though they took great care not to. She knew that he was waiting for someone – anyone – to leave so that they too could go, but he did not want to be the first to break up the party so they were caught in expectancy every time one of the guests looked at his watch or shifted in his chair. Finally, the old admiral stood up.

'Before you leave,' said Blanche, 'I must show you what Spencer gave me for Christmas. It's quite perfect. Do come, it's in the study.' They went through into a booklined room – and Olivia found herself staring at one of Jake's sculptures.

'It's The Propelled Tulip!' she exclaimed. 'How incredible! What a coincidence! She reached out to stroke the upper curve where the marble twisted into the centre to give the impression of a fan of tulip petals. 'I was staying with Jake in Pietra Alta when he was working on it.'

'You never told us that Olivia knew Jake Hammond,' Blanche said to Ash. She looked impressed.

'There was no reason why he should know,' Olivia smiled at them. 'We've never discussed sculpture.'

'Did you know his daughter, Dee?'

'I met her in Greece.'

'She lived a few blocks from here. She was a tragic creature.'

'She got what she deserved,' said Ash with sudden harshness. 'No one should take their own life.'

Olivia was conscious of awkwardness. She remembered the way in which Blanche had spoken of Ash's mother, and filled the moment with profuse thanks for a lovely day.

In the lift she expected Ash to mention Dee, but he didn't, he took her hand and said, 'You still haven't seen Central Park properly.'

She linked her fingers through his. 'It's too cold to walk.'

'I didn't mean a walk.'

'What did you mean?' she asked, laughing softly.

'You know perfectly well.'

The lift stopped and they stepped out at the ground floor where, on instructions from the McCords' butler, one of the porters had already brought round Ash's car. They drove the ten blocks, he with his hand on her thigh, his fingers moving slowly up the soft crepe of her red dress, she with her hand circling on his trousered leg, until he stopped outside an apartment block. 'We're here.' He touched her cheek.

'Yes.' She kissed the palm of his hand.

The porter took the car keys as Ash ushered Olivia into the lift, pressing the top button: Penthouse. 'I can hardly wait . . .' he murmured against her mouth as the lift door closed them into its bright warm world. 'I've wanted you so much.' Her fur coat was open to his hands which slid around her waist, holding her, pulling her hard against him. 'I thought the old admiral would never stop.'

'I couldn't concentrate on what he was saying.' She linked her arms about his neck.

'Ever since I first saw you . . .' He ran his hands down her back, his fingers spread as they felt for her taut buttocks and drew her even closer.

The lift stopped. They stepped out, kissed before an ornate mirror, and crossed the wide corridor to Ash's apartment.

For a moment when he closed the door they stood and

looked at each other, hesitant in the bright mirrored hall of his home, the brightness of it making them self-conscious. Then he took her in his arms and kissed her very gently on the lips, cupping her face in his hands, before he took her coat and led her across a partially sunken drawing-room to the plate glass windows and the magnificent view over the snow-laden tree tops of Central Park. They were higher than at the McCords' and it was now dark, so that the lights of the Upper West Side, on the other side of the park, formed a wall of diamonds rising into the night.

'It's beautiful, isn't it?' he murmured.

'Yes. Magic.'

'Would you like a drink? I'm the best tequila sunrise mixer north of El Paso.'

'How can I refuse?'

He kissed the side of her face, at the end of her eyebrow. 'You can't.' He crossed the sitting-room, sinking into the white carpet, avoiding the highly waxed green leaves of a giant plant, bounded up two steps to a raised dining area and pressed a button. The wall of panelled rosewood slid back to reveal a gleaming high tech kitchen; from the way Ash opened various cupboards before finding the glasses it was obvious that he spent little time in it. Suddenly, stupidly, Olivia remembered Mark saying 'I make the best bacon sandwiches in town.' But I mustn't think of Mark now, she told herself, and she crossed the white drawing-room to the kitchen where Ash was adding the cherries to the glasses.

She held out her hand. He gave her a cherry from the packet. She ate it. He gave her another. She dipped it in her drink and popped it into his mouth. He took her hand, kissed it, and led her through into the bedroom, a mixture of white luxury and high tech which with the flick of a switch became suffused with a warm pink glow.

'I think I'm falling in love with you,' he said, running his hands down her body till they reached the simple tie which held her dress together. 'I know I'm falling in love with you.' The dress fell open, revealing the white satin of her cami-knickers and the tops of her silvery Christmas stockings. 'You're so beautiful.' He kissed her, at first gently, softly, then as he felt her move against him and she entwined her arms

332

about his neck his mouth became hard, almost cruel. He dug his fingers into her back, murmuring into her hair, then quickly, with athletic strength he picked her up and carried her across the room, and tossed her on to the vast bed where she landed, her long legs sprawled, her brown eyes shining through the strands of her dishevelled hair. Ash undressed quickly, very quickly, and lay down beside her, naked, gathering her to him, his fingers urgent on the thin wisp of lacy brassiere and on the satin of her cami-knickers. Then suddenly he was on top of her – and almost as suddenly it was all over and she was staring up at the ceiling hoping he wouldn't apologise.

'I'm sorry but you're just so damned sexy.' He kissed her on the forehead, rolled over on his back, took a sip of tequila sunrise, and drew her to him. 'I've been thinking about making it with you ever since we met . . .' He looked at her face and laughed. 'American men are forthright. We like to discuss a relationship. You'll get used to it. We're also very romantic.'

'The red rose?'

'Sure.'

'Romantic would be if you gave me another tomorrow.'

He pulled her over on top of him, holding her face in his hands. 'Grateful would be if you'd remembered not to leave the first one in the car.'

'Oh, no!'

'Oh, yes!'

'I'm afraid my mind was on other things.'

'Excuse accepted.' He kissed her softly, and they made love again, slowly, but whatever it was that Olivia had had with Mark was still missing, although she wished it wasn't.

She was asleep, in her subconscious she heard her name, she snuggled further into the duvet.

'Olivia!'

'Ummm.' She forced open her eyes.

Ash was standing over her in a navy tracksuit. 'Up you get! Time to jog.'

She closed her eyes. 'You're mad.'

'Come on!' The duvet was yanked off her and he dropped a pink tracksuit on to her naked body. 'My cousin Cass left that behind. Put it on.'

'Ash, I couldn't, I haven't run since . . .'

'It shows.'

She lay on her back looking up at him half-covered by the tracksuit. 'Thanks. Last night I was beautiful.'

'You'd be twice as beautiful if you were fitter.' He carried the duvet to the other side of the room, out of reach, then took her by the arm and pulled her to her feet.

'What time is it?'

'Six thirty.'

'I thought we were going to have a late morning.'

'I usually get up at six.' He draped the tracksuit over her shoulder and gave her a push towards the bathroom.

Ten minutes later Olivia trotted out of the apartment, her eyes barely open.

The porter came to his feet as they stepped out of the lift. 'Good morning, sir . . . madam.'

Then he opened the door on to the bitter cold.

'I can't!' she wailed on the doorstep. 'Ash, it's freezing.'

'You can.' He grabbed her arm and pulled her out into the cold morning. 'Come on! Not too fast. You want to run slowly, stretching the calf muscles. No, not as slowly as that!'

They went up Fifth Avenue, pounding the bumpy pavement, snowflakes dropping on them from the trees, turned right on a cross street, right again, and back towards the park. Olivia was gasping by the time they reached his block. She collapsed into the lift, her knees buckling under her.

'Didn't I say you were unfit?' he laughed at her.

'Better unfit than dead.'

She was in the shower with her eyes closed against the warm water as it rinsed the shampoo from her hair when Ash came to her, putting his arms around her body, the water between them and over them, as they joined, sliding against each other and into each other until she cried out against him, digging her fingers into his back, wanting him to go on and on, and never stop.

'You see what a lot of good a run does?' he murmured, turning off the water. Then he looked at his watch. 'Twenty to eight! I've got a breakfast meeting at The Regency at half past. I'll call you a cab.'

She dried her hair with his highspeed dryer, dressed in record time, drank her orange juice, and kissed him goodbye.

334

Even as the lift doors were closing he was saying, 'I'm in meetings till nine. We'll grab a late dinner,' and she was nodding, 'Fine, I'm also tied up till late.' Then the doors clicked shut and she turned to look at herself in the mirrored wall. Her eyes were shining, her cheeks glowed, her hair gleamed where it was still damp. She glanced at her watch. It was ten past eight and already she'd run a mile, made love, had breakfast. She started to laugh and she was still laughing as she went out, into Fifth Avenue, to a limo whose door was being held for her, and for the first time she really felt a part of this thumping, pumping city.

26

The one thing in favour of office romances, thought Olivia as she dashed up the steps to William & Wall, is that it makes going to work that much more exciting.

The doorman called, 'Good morning.'

She was halfway across the hall as she replied, leaping into the lift, glancing down the headlines of the *Wall Street Journal* as she shot to the twenty-second floor, chuckling as she read:

'Prey turns on hunter – Caltoco Jupiter chases Lane & Lee.'

In the corridor she met Ash.

'How was breakfast?' she asked.

'Short but very sweet.'

A half smile, then they separated, she to her new office, he to McCord, calling over his shoulder as he went, 'Caltoco Jupiter meeting in half an hour – just you, McCord and me.'

'Fine.' She raised her hand as she disappeared inside her office, slipped off her fur coat and chucked it on a chair. It was the first time she had worn it to the office though she found it impossible to explain why.

'Hey!' exclaimed Betsy, following her in. 'And who may I ask gave you a fur?'

'Oh, I've had it for ages, I just didn't wear it to work before. Crazy, isn't it? I've been freezing.'

'You Brits are mad anyway. Ah, well, I suppose you're working on the Caltoco Jupiter deal. I'm glad you were promoted, you earned it.'

'Thanks. I'm sure Teddy will be next.'

'I hope so – but Peter is going to be even sorer if he is.'

'Yes, he could barely say good morning to me. How about you, Bets, do you mind?'

'Sure, but McCord was straight down the line when we got married. He told us that if we both continued at William & Wall we'd have to be separated – and this might mean one being promoted first. But I'll let you into a secret, it's not going to matter for much longer.'

'Why? Is anything wrong? You're very pale?'

'I'm pregnant.' Betsy blushed. 'It must have happened on our honeymoon. Of course, Teddy's mother's convinced I was knocked up before we got married.'

'The old bat. But you are pleased, aren't you?'

'Sure.' Betsy smiled softly. 'Sure, I'm pleased – it's just that I feel like a dog in the mornings.'

'Tough.'

'Yeah, but worth it. Teddy's over the moon, he's already worked out a baseball training programme.'

'Supposing it's a girl?'

'That's what I keep telling him. We're all girls in my family – except for Dad.'

Olivia thought of Maggie desperately trying to have a baby and made a mental note to ring her.

The Caltoco Jupiter meeting lasted all morning.

'The question is,' began McCord, 'do we go for an all out attack now, while we've got them on the hop, or do we let them stew for a while?'

Ash tapped some figures into a mini-computer. 'I say we go for it. If we wait, we're handing back the power of surprise. Olivia?'

'I say we get a letter out to all of Lane & Lee shareholders to undermine their management.'

The two men looked at each other. 'She's getting as tough as we are.'

On the way down from the boardroom Ash and Olivia shared a lift. For a few brief electric moments they were alone between the twenty-third and the twenty-second floors.

He touched her cheek. 'I want you.'

She took his hand. 'I want you too.'

'Damn! We've arrived.'

'See you later.' She allowed her eyes to linger on his mouth, she wanted him so much she had to bite her lip till it hurt to take her mind off him.

That night they made love, and in the morning they went for a run, and next day, poring over the Caltoco Jupiter deal with Ash beside her, Olivia wondered why she wasn't exhausted – but she wasn't, she felt vibrant and alive. She smiled at Ash, he smiled at her, and in their eyes was all the excitement of proximity which was somehow part and parcel of the excitement of the deal.

Lane & Lee was on the run. As with all fast-growing giants, once the tide changed and talk raged that its luck had run out investors panicked. This, coupled with the odd adverse comment in the financial pages of various newspapers, meant that when shareholders received the Caltoco Jupiter offer most of them accepted: it was better than losing their shirts.

'You've got a good team, McCord.' The president of Caltoco Jupiter shook the William & Wall group by the hand. 'We're impressed. Gentlemen and . . . he smiled at Olivia, 'lady, if you ever feel like changing to a career in industry . . .'

'Now look here,' McCord cut in, laughing, 'don't you come raiding my staff.'

It took most people at William & Wall three months to suspect seriously that there was anything more than a working friendship between Ash Mallory and Olivia Steele and a further six weeks before they were sure. But Memorial Day confirmed it. Other people came back with suntans, but Ash and Olivia somehow had exactly the same shade of tan – a tan from East Hampton, that most exclusive of Long Island resorts. And not for them the bumper to bumper nightmare of the Long Island Expressway: Ash kept a six-seater at La Guardia. They stayed at the beach house which his grandmother, the one who disapproved of *West Side Story*, had left him. It was on the dunes and built in a charming mixture of colonial and pioneer styles, with six white colonial pillars dividing its long low pioneer verandah. By East Hampton standards it was not large – five bedrooms, a swimming pool, and a garden big enough to have eighty people to a barbecue – but it looked straight out over the sea, or rather on to Dune

Road and then the sea, so what it lacked in size and grandeur it made up for in position. They spent Memorial Day swimming, sunbathing and making love, returning to William & Wall early next morning.

An hour later Sherry marched into Olivia's office. 'I was right. You were after Ash.'

Olivia sat back in her chair. 'My private life is no concern of yours, Sherry.'

'No, honey, but remember that when he drops you in the shit you'll be in good company.'

'I have work to do.'

'I'm not just talking about myself.'

'I'm not interested.'

'He had Barbara too, you know.'

'Don't be ridiculous!'

'Ask her!' There was a whirl of over-scented hair and Sherry was gone.

The phone rang. It was Betsy. 'Sherry got her talons out?'

'Yes, she said that Ash and Barbara . . .'

'Didn't you know? Barbara was in love with Ash for years.'

'I hope she's not upset.'

'I think she's more anxious about making partner.'

'You're right.'

Betsy put on a mumsy voice. 'Now any time you want to discuss your problems with a respectable, expectant married lady . . .'

That afternoon Olivia dialled Savvies. It was months since she'd spoken to Maggie: time flew, and whenever she decided to phone it seemed always to be either too early or too late in London.

Sanjiv answered. 'She's not here, Olivia. Didn't you know? She's been ill. No, she's over the worst now . . . well, it's really that she so longs to have a baby . . . no, she's not at home. As you're her closest friend I will tell you – she's having a couple of weeks at a clinic to have a complete rest.'

Olivia felt so guilty about Maggie that she resolved to pen a long letter to her that evening.

'Bets,' she said, still thinking of Maggie, 'we mustn't stop being friends just because you leave to have the baby.'

Betsy linked her arm through Olivia's. 'We're friends for

life. I'll be calling you every day, with Teddy junior screaming in the background. What am I going to do at home all day, Olivia?'

'Join the PTA?'

'Thanks.'

'There you are!' Sally came out of the lift. 'I've been looking for you two.' She lowered her voice to a whisper. 'Barbara's having a breakdown. I've got her in the recruiting room and she hasn't stopped crying since Peter told her he reckons that Russ's going to make partner this year.'

'And Barbara won't?'

'What do you think?'

Barbara was sitting at the desk with her head bowed into her hands. She glanced up as they came in, her face raddled with tears. 'I gave up everything for William & Wall,' she said. 'Everything! Look at me! I'm forty-six years old. Yes, I tell everyone I'm thirty-nine but it isn't true, it's the big four plus six. My last steady and I split up seven years ago and I haven't been laid for six years – and you know what? The last time was on my fortieth birthday, with a guy I picked up in a singles bar, a glorified hick from upstate New Jersey, from the kind of one-horse-town I grew up in and the kind of brainless jerk I spent my teens trying to escape from. And you know something,' she began to laugh hysterically, 'he might be the last guy I ever make it with and I don't even know his name. You know something else? He gave me a dose. Here was I saying "No, I'll stick to Perrier," and everyone was thinking I was on a health kick when all the time it was because I had a lousy dose.' She stopped laughing and stared down at her unringed fingers. 'I wouldn't have cared if I could have made partner. It would all have been worth it. I could have said OK, I sacrificed my private life but I did what I set out to do I was a pioneer. I was somebody. I made it. I achieved. I won.' She began to cry, softly, desperately. 'But I've lost out all around. Oh, God! The bastards! The bastards!'

Olivia and Betsy found Peter drinking mango juice at his desk. He adjusted his specs defensively as they approached. 'OK, ladies, what's bugging you now?'

'Nothing's bugging us,' said Betsy, 'but Barbara's kind of upset over what you told her about Russ.'

340

'Hell, I was only airing a point of view – and one which everybody at the bank supports.'

'I know, Peter. It's just Barbara. She's touchy.'

'She's not just touchy, she's a liability. She should resign.'

'That's pretty tough judgment,' said Olivia.

'It's true. Anyhow, what do you care, you've got Ash Mallory?'

His telephone ringing cut short the discussion, and Olivia and Betsy retreated to the corridor.

'Don't take any notice of Peter,' said Betsy. 'He's just sore that you're doing better than him, that's all. He's a nice guy really.'

'Of course he is – after all, he was in our bullpen.'

That evening over a late dinner Ash told Olivia, 'The reason for the partners' meeting this afternoon will be common knowledge tomorrow. Barbara's been fired.'

'Oh, no!'

'She broke down in the recruiting room today.'

'I was there.' Olivia lowered her knife and fork to her plate and rested her hands on the white damask tablecloth. 'Ash, William & Wall is Barbara's life.'

'Darling,' he took her hand and squeezed it, 'she has to go. We can't have that sort of thing at the bank, she might break down in front of a client.'

'That's rubbish. She never has before.'

'She might.'

Olivia withdrew her hand. 'If she were a man you wouldn't say that.'

'We've yet to have a man sobbing in the recruiting room.'

'No, the last one fired threw himself off Brooklyn Bridge.'

'Olivia, listen, Barbara is touchy and neurotic. She doesn't fit. Anyhow, I didn't know that you and she were so friendly.'

'We're not – it's simply that I know what it's like to have the world turn against you.'

She went to sleep disliking him.

Early next morning the phone rang. Ash answered it in the sitting-room. A few minutes later he came through, his face white and rigid. 'Barbara didn't go as far as the Brooklyn Bridge,' he said. 'She threw herself in front of a subway train at Wall Street Station.'

It was a few days before the cloud of Barbara lifted from their relationship and Ash felt able to say, 'You haven't forgotten Culross, have you?'

'No – but why do you ask?'

'Oh, what you said about the world turning against you. Do you want to go back there – I mean, if you could?'

'Go back! Not likely. I never want to go back – unless it's to do the Culrosses what they once did to me.'

The summer passed. Most weekends Ash and Olivia flew up to the Hamptons. In July, Betsy left. In September she had a baby – Sam. Ash and Olivia were godparents. Driving back to New York, Ash said, 'You'd make a lovely mother too, you know.'

'Thanks.'

'I mean it.' He felt for her hand. 'I've been wanting to say . . . Olivia, will you . . .'

'Ash, please don't, not yet.' She did not know why, but she could not bear to let him go on.

'If you won't marry me – yet – then give up the attic and come to live with me?'

She linked her fingers through his. 'Let's enjoy what we have and see what happens.' She remembered how she had wanted Mark to ask her to marry him, and he hadn't.

In the fall Ash asked Olivia to go up to Connecticut to meet his aunt and uncle but they were so busy at William & Wall that it wasn't possible to take the time off. At Christmas Peter, along with most of their class, joined Teddy as a senior associate – whilst Olivia went up to junior principal. If anyone thought her relationship with Ash had anything to do with it they didn't say so, they wouldn't have dared, for it was acknowledged that Olivia Steele was the brightest in the bank after Ash Mallory – and some even said she was ahead of him.

On Christmas Eve, exactly a year since Ash and Olivia had become lovers, the McCords invited them to midnight mass at St Patrick's Cathedral – and with the couple of thousand lucky people who had managed to gain entrance they raised their voices in Silent Night to the vaulted ceiling with its glorious red and indigo windows.

'Happy?' Ash whispered in her ear as they knelt to pray.

'Yes.'

342

'Marry me?'

'Ash!'

'I love you.'

An hour into Christmas Day they poured out into Fifth Avenue, where the crowds who had failed to obtain tickets but had wanted to join in singing the carols stamped their feet against the cold.

'Heaven knows what the decorations cost,' said Ash, looking down the glittering length of the street.

'Ash, you're not at work now!'

'I meant what I said in the cathedral.'

She began to smile, then her eyes widened.

'What's wrong?' He glanced over his shoulder. 'Oh, they're collecting for NorAid. You shouldn't be surprised, this is one of the largest Roman Catholic churches in the country, not that all Catholics support the IRA. McCord doesn't. Blanche certainly doesn't, but then our side of the family are Protestant.'

She nodded and looked away, but she had been reminded that she was in a foreign country and she recalled her aunt Gwendoline, the one who lived in South Africa, saying that no matter how long you lived in a foreign country you were always a foreigner.

They went to Barbados for a few days at Christmas. From there Olivia flew on to London, alone. She'd thought of inviting Ash but had decided against it, explaining to him that she hadn't seen her parents for two years and they would want her to themselves. They met her at Heathrow. They seemed smaller, older, and the house seemed quaint and embarrassingly twee. She was glad Ash wasn't with her.

'Old Mr So-and-so over the road died,' said her mother.

'Er . . . who's living there now?'

'New people.'

'Oh.' She gazed out of the window at the cheerless wintry garden.

'I thought you had a fortnight's holiday,' said her father, when she told them she could only stay for four days.'

'I spent some time in Barbados.'

'Then we'd better tell Hugo and Fiona to come tomorrow. We'd sort of planned a weekend . . .'

343

She felt cruel and guilty but what could she do? They had even less in common than before. She went into her father's study and dialled Maggie's number. There was no answer. So she went upstairs to her bedroom and rifled through the teenage magazines with pictures of Mick Jagger at the bottom of her cupboard – magazines which she'd read late at night, wishing herself the daughter of a famous Hollywood actor instead of an unsuccessful English solicitor. Later, she unpacked the presents she had brought for her parents, but the purple silk dressing gown which had seemed perfect for her father in Bloomingdales looked garishly over-the-top in Newbury.

She lay down on her bed and wished she were back in Manhattan.

27

It was 1979 – the year in which the Shah would be kicked out of Iran, the students would seize the American hostages, the Soviets would invade Afghanistan – and silver would shoot from ten to fifty dollars an ounce.

It was also the year in which Olivia Steele would begin to earn big money; not that she had much time to spend it – William & Wall and Ash filled her every waking moment.

On Saturday during April she dropped by the attic to collect her mail and met Freddie on the stairs.

'Stranger.' He hugged her.

'Suntanned stranger. How goes it?'

'On a scale of one to ten, nine and a half. Oh, some friends of yours were here over Easter. They left a note for you.

Dear Pal,

I thought I'd give you a fantastic surprise and turn up on your doorstep and now this divine relic from flower power tells me that you're away. I should have let you know we were coming but I didn't know myself till three days ago. It was Zach's idea. A break. A change. And all that. I've been pretty sick for the past year, not quite on death's door but more in the depths of despair. Yes, I still haven't managed to reproduce but they say there is nothing the matter with me. Anyhow, one day I sort of went to pieces. I suppose I had a breakdown. Things built up and then one morning I was driving to Savvies when I knocked a cyclist over. It was the last straw for me, not the cyclist who was fine, and I became one of the seven out of ten women who need treatment. But I'm OK now – at last – hence the New York break.

345

Must finish now as the divine hippy is looking concerned. He probably thinks I'm writing my autobiography.

Lots of love, pal,

Maggie.

P.S. You didn't answer my last two letters???

When Olivia arrived at William & Wall next morning Teddy stopped her in the corridor with a grin nine miles wide. 'Guess what! We're having another baby.'

It seemed so very unfair for poor Maggie.

She dialled the flower shop which Ash used, and said, 'I want to send something really special to London.' Then she told herself that she'd write to Maggie, if not that evening by the end of the week, but it was mid-June before she did so, and then it was just a postcard from East Hampton.

'The trouble is,' she confided to Betsy, 'life's such a roller coaster that there's no time to do all the things I should do, like go home to see my family and write letters to old friends.'

'I know,' Betsy sympathised. 'My folks live in New Jersey but when I was working I only got to see them once every two months. Teddy's the same with his.' She patted Olivia's arm. 'But they understand, they went through it too.'

Picturing the safety of her parents' existence, Olivia said, 'I don't think mine did.'

She decided to spend Christmas in England and even booked her flight well in advance, but ten days before she was due to leave Caltoco Jupiter contacted the William & Wall team – they had their eyes on Europe – and, as Olivia explained to her father, 'I'm part of that team and I can't leave now.'

It seemed as though one moment it was winter, the next it was spring, and then they were into the summer and the Hamptons – the sun, the sea, and the early Monday morning flights from Long Island to Manhattan.

In October Ash set off on a two week business trip to Europe and Olivia returned to the attic, as she preferred to do when he was away. She climbed the familiar stairs to the red front door, pushed aside the letters on the mat, and hurried to open a window to replace the air which seemed to become trapped at the end of each summer, even though her cleaner aired the

346

rooms regularly. Then she made herself a cup of coffee and settled down at the big round white table to read through her letters, feeling strange to be on her own and yet, as always, relieved. In a few days she would look forward to Ash's return, by the time he came back she would be longing to see him, but now she relished the peace. The faint tinkling of jazz on a piano. The sound of a cat being put out on the fire escape. Laughter. Voices. The bohemian sounds from the cobbled streets.

She wasn't surprised to receive a letter from Jake, they wrote frequently, but she was so amazed by its contents that she had to read it twice and even then could hardly believe it until she had telephoned him.

'You're coming to New York next week! Jake, that's wonderful! I can't wait to see you again but . . . what changed your mind, you always said you'd never come back?'

'The Lincoln Center want to hold an exhibition of my work and I have agreed. It won't be till next year but I have to discuss details. Oh, I know people will say I've capitulated because of the money but that's not true, I've more than enough money. I'm coming back because I want to bury ghosts and because, like most old people, I want to revisit the places of my youth before I die.'

'Jake, you're not dying are you?'

'No more than anyone else. It's not that, Livvi. I want to see the propellers at Hoboken again, the ones I used to pass on my way to school, I want to see if they're still there – and if they look as I made them in my sculptures. Do you remember that I told you Frank Sinatra and I have the dubious honour of having been born at Hoboken?' He laughed, and his laughter crackled down two thousand miles of telephone wires. 'I want to stand by the cannon on Castle Point and look across at Manhattan. I used to think the streets there must be paved with gold – well, the sidewalks at least. I want to go to the hardware store on Columbus Avenue, the one where I worked for my uncle when I was fourteen. Oh, there's so much I want to do. I want to see the little gardens at the bases of the trees in the Village, and the ornate wrought-iron vents, and the fire escapes, and the curved iron edges to the pavements – New York things. But most of all I want to visit Central Park and stand beneath the bean tree. There are lots of bean trees, but

347

there's only one I called mine. It's near West 72nd Street. We'll meet there. I want to show it to you. Did I ever tell you that during the Depression I was once so hungry I tried to eat the beans?'

It was one of those crisp cold sunny Saturdays which New York does so well when Olivia took a cab to the west side of Central Park and walked down the tarmac path towards the bean tree which Jake had described, thinking, as she did so, that she knew nothing of the park except the tree tops viewed from Ash's apartment. She saw Jake before he saw her. He was stamping his feet on a carpet of fallen leaves beneath a tree which looked as though it had enormous runner beans dangling from its nearly leafless branches.

'Jake!'

'Livvi!' He swept her off the ground in a bear hug and swung her around in a full circle as if she were a doll. 'Livvi, you're crying? Hey, Livvi!'

'No, I'm not.'

'You are.' He swung her around again.

'OK, I am but I'm happy. It's been so long and . . .'

'You're still my Livvi.' He put her down and looked at her jeans and white jumper and smart red jacket toggled against the cold. 'Thank God you didn't come in your career-woman clothes. Now, look!' He pointed at the tree. 'I was right, wasn't I? You see what I mean by beans. Oh, it's good to see you. I wish you'd come back to Pietra Alta. I know you've got a good job – a career – and you have your life here, but . . .' He linked his arm through hers. 'Let's visit Mr Morse's statue, he'll tell us what to do with our lives.'

She laughed. 'Yes, but his message will be in code and we won't understand it.'

They walked through the park, past the roller-skaters to where Mr Morse sat in contemplation at the head of a wide avenue of leprous sycamores. They walked down it, then circled, until they came out at the glittering silvery black rock beside the bowling green. From there they headed for the lake, following the bank to its northern tip and all the time they talked.

Again Jake told her, 'I had to see New York once more so that I can live out my final years at Pietra Alta knowing that

348

I've buried my ghosts. It was Gwen who made me feel this way, even though things did not work out between us – or maybe because of that. And you too, Livvi. The fact of you being here made it easier for me to be brave.'

'I'm sorry you and Gwen . . .'

'Yes.' He squeezed her hand. They were standing on the north shore of the lake looking down towards the buildings of Central Park South which rose up above the trees and were reflected in the smooth surface of the water. 'What about you, Livvi, have you buried your ghosts?'

'I've been fine . . . just fine. I've got a terrific job. Well, it's much more than a job, I earn lots of money, and I have a very stable relationship. You must meet Ash – Ash Mallory – he's away on business this week, but I know he'll want to meet you.' She gave him a breezy smile. 'Tell me about Lorenzo.'

'He's gone into politics.'

'Lorenzo! A politician! But he can't he's . . .'

'Dishonest? Oh, that's almost a prerequisite for a politician in Italy and they're none the worse for it. Lorenzo will make an excellent politician. He's clever, charismatic and ruthless. He also has a mistress. He brought her back from South America. Some people say he actually bought her! A beautiful mulatto.' Jake chuckled. 'After all, a politician must have a mistress and this creature is a tigress *par excellence*. They say she prowls the terrace of his penthouse dressed only in a leopard skin.'

Olivia laughed. It seemed incredible to her now that she should once have known someone like Lorenzo and yet she was glad. All women, she thought, need a Lorenzo in their lives – but not for too long. 'When he took me up to the cemetery I pretended I knew all about Mazzini,' she said. 'I refused to admit that a gunrunner – a dishonest gunrunner! – knew things that I, a graduate of Oxford, did not know.'

'I was so worried when you went to Genoa. Remember what I told you about the puppy? I'm more and more convinced he killed it to free himself from the emotional cage of feeling.' He turned her to face him. 'What about Mark? Do you still think of him?'

'Mark's in the past.'

'That's what he said about you.'

'When did you see him?'

'Oh . . . I can't remember.'

'Jake!'

'Two weeks ago. I was in England and Lady Vicky invited me down to The Helmets for a weekend. She's a wonderful woman, quite amazing, and very fond of you – in spite of . . .'

'Jake! Is Mark well?'

'Like you.'

'Is he . . .?'

'Having a stable relationship? It sounds like donkeys. Whoever wants things to be stable? Not people like us, not you and me and Mark. We need change.'

'The trouble was things didn't change for the better. All the time I was with Mark I felt like a second class citizen. I was a parasite.'

'You'll never be a parasite. Women are either born parasitical or they're not.' He lit his pipe. 'But you've got a stable relationship with Ash Mallory so these things no longer matter.'

'If you say that once more I'll . . .'

'That's my Livvi. Come on, I'll show you the hardware store where I used to work.'

The hardware store on Columbus Avenue had gone, to be replaced by a sort of singles bar. 'Poor uncle,' said Jake mournfully as he watched a man move in on a pretty girl, 'fancy being replaced by advertising executives drinking Perrier and lime when he never went a day without a half a bottle of Bourbon – especially during prohibition.'

They took a cab through the tunnel to Hoboken on the New Jersey side of the Hudson river.

'It doesn't look so bad,' said Olivia, as they drew up in front of a college or school which was perched above the river amid lawns and trees. 'From the way you talked I expected the back streets of Naples.'

'This is the smart area.'

'Look, there's your cannon. What a view!' Straight across the river were the skyscrapers of Manhattan.

Jake rocked on his heels, his hands dug deep into his pockets, 'This is where I used to come and look across – longingly.'

'And think "them there streets are paved with gold"?'

He put on a southern drawl. 'Don't you go cheekin' me, honey child.'

'It's so good to see you.' She kissed his leathery cheek.

He took her hand. 'Come on, I'll show you what immigrant life in America was all about.'

They walked down the hill, crossed a wide street which still bore the scars of old trolleys, and eventually came to an area where the ground was flat and dusty and the apartment blocks were of the same soul-destroying monotony found on the outskirts of Northern Italian industrial towns.

'I see what you mean.' She watched a group of small girls divide up a packet of chewing gum whilst two bored teenage boys walked around in circles kicking an empty Coca Cola can.

'Ah, but you only see one side of it. The people who lived here were wonderful. They were mostly Italian or German, and what you in Britain call lower middle-class, but they cared about each other. You see, wherever they came from, whatever language they spoke, whatever their religion was, usually Catholic or Jewish, they had one thing in common – there was no going back to Europe. The poverty or persecution which had driven them to America would be waiting for them, if they could afford the fare, which most couldn't, so they had to make a living, they had to survive. Oh, there were fights, of course there were, but in the main they were people who spent their lives packing tea at Lipton's factory and dreaming that their kids would go to university. And they did – some of them.'

They crossed another road and walked another block. 'The propellers! There they are.' He grabbed Olivia's hand and started to run, dragging her along the broken pavement until they came to a yard surrounded by high wire netting. Inside were huge bronze propellers stacked on top of each other, all different sizes and different spans, but each with that central pivoting force which Jake captured in his sculptures.

'I've never been inside,' he said. 'I tried once but they chased me away. I was only eight.'

'We could try now.'

'Oh, no, I'd rather not. I want to see them as I used to see them.'

They hooked their fingers into the wire netting and stared at the manmade lumps of twisted iron which had so inspired the subconscious of a small boy as he passed on his way to school that their forms had come into his hands on a mountain side in Italy and he had created beautiful things of their twists and turns, things which people paid a fortune to possess and which would soon be exhibited in splendour in the Lincoln Center, whereas here, a mere tunnel's length away, their inspiration faced the elements in an inclement yard.

They took a cab to SoHo, bought steaks, salad, spaghetti and wine, and staggered up the street to the house. On the doorstep they met Freddie. Olivia introduced him.

'Jake Hammond, the sculptor!' Freddie was still gripping Jake's hand. 'I've always admired your work. Olivia told me she knew you and I'd been planning to beg an introduction. I was only reading in the *New York Times* this morning that you're to have an exhibition . . .' He dropped Jake's hand. 'I admire you. I admire what you stand for.'

'You can admire my cooking too,' said Jake, indicating the quantity of food they had bought. 'Come up and have dinner with us. In fact, come up and have a glass of wine with us now. I'm parched – and dead beat. You know, it's tiring to come back after all this time.'

Jake loved the attic, it was his sort of place. He strode up and down patting the big white table. 'I should have trusted that you'd live somewhere like this, but I was terrified that I'd find you ensconced behind an army of porters on the Upper East Side.'

Freddie opened his mouth to say, 'She usually is,' but Olivia kicked him into silence.

Jake took over the kitchen and only allowed the others to chop vegetables, declaring that no one but himself could make a decent *spaghetti alla matriciana* because other people either burned the egg or undercooked the bacon or both. When it finally came to the table – by which time they had drunk plenty quantity of wine – they had to agree with him.

'Now the steaks,' he said, humming as he went into the kitchen.

'He's amazing,' whispered Freddie. 'So unpretentious! I know guys with less than a hundredth of his talent who can hardly bring themselves to spread their own peanut butter in case it ruins their image.

As the evening progressed Dulcie appeared, then two friends of Freddie's, then more friends from Minetta's bringing a bottle of Southern Comfort. Chairs were brought up from Freddie's apartment, more plates were found, Jake made more spaghetti – then they sat around the table, heads rested on arms, listening as he talked. It was after two when the first person left – no one had wanted to break the spell.

Ash returned to New York the day before Jake was due to leave for Pietra Alta. 'We'll take him to dinner tonight,' he said, kissing her on the cheek. 'I'll book a table at the Four Seasons.'

She thought of the rickety stools at Chumleys where she, Jake and Freddie had sat drinking and talking till the early hours. 'The Four Seasons isn't Jake's kind of place, Ash.'

'Don't be silly! Anyhow, the McCords are joining us and Blanche doesn't like roughing it.'

'The McCords!'

'What's wrong?'

'Jake hates being paraded.'

'I'm not parading him. McCord is president of the bank where we work – where we are happy to work. He and Blanche entertain us constantly, and Blanche wishes to meet Jake Hammond. Have you forgotten that she has one of his sculptures?'

Olivia took a deep breath and counted to ten. 'I wish you'd asked me then I could have warned him.'

'Half this city would give their eye teeth to be at dinner with the president of William & Wall.' His face took on a flat sullen look. 'I can't understand what's got into you.'

'Jake's very special to me.'

'Aren't I?'

'Of course you are.'

'I thought you liked the McCords.'

'I do like them, it's just that not everyone mixes well with everyone else – and this is Jake's last evening.'

'Your problem is that you want social life to be separate from your business life. That's such an outdated attitude.'

'It isn't that – it's just that I don't like my friends to feel that I'm using them.'

Olivia could have hugged Jake for the way he accepted the evening. He liked McCord for the toughness they shared, he treated Blanche as though she were made of porcelain, and to Ash he showed the acceptable face of art. As they left the restaurant Olivia whispered to him, 'You're a saint,' and he replied. 'Even I can behave, so long as I don't have to do it too often or for too long.'

'I'm sorry about asking the McCords,' said Ash as soon as they reached home.

'Forget it.'

'I can't.' He walked over to the window and looked down on the park. 'I wish you'd give up the attic and move in with me then I wouldn't be so insecure about you. Every time we have a row I'm terrified you're going to leave me. If we were married you wouldn't be able to go, we'd have to work it out. I love you – hell, I'm crazy about you, but sometimes I feel there's this barrier between us. You didn't want the McCords tonight. You didn't want me either, did you? You wanted to be on your own with him.'

'Of course I wanted you to be there.'

'Sure?'

'Sure.'

'Marry me?'

'Don't ask me that, not yet.'

That night they made love with slow passion and it was everything it had not been when they first became lovers – though not quite as it had been with Mark. But Ash would never let me storm off into the night without trying to stop me, thought Olivia as she cuddled up against his sleeping form, and even if I went, he'd make some effort to find me. He'd call my friends or my family to make sure I was alive. I could have been murdered and Mark would not have known or cared. She remembered the occasion in the pub near King's Cross when she had stormed out into the night and had had to wander through one of the worst areas of London, whilst Mark had calmly driven off.

She listened to Ash's quiet breathing. He would never expose her to danger, so he would never need to save her from it – or not.

Olivia saw Jake briefly before he left, snatching a quick lunch in her busy day, sorry to see him go but not as bereft as she might have been. This morning she and Ash had agreed that their problem was time – time to relax together – so they had decided to take this weekend off and visit his aunt and uncle in Connecticut.'

'I like the McCords,' said Jake as he walked her back to the bank.

'What about Ash?'

'He's not like us.'

'Not like you Jake.' Her eyes drifted up and up to floor upon floor of skyscraper stretching into a smog-heavy sky.

'If you didn't want my opinion you shouldn't have asked me.' He studied the hustle-bustle of Wall Street. 'I suppose I find it hard to believe you're happy here, but then it's always hard to understand when someone you're fond of likes things you dislike.' A blind man passed them with his dog. Jake dropped twenty dollars into his tin. 'It's the way the weak get trodden on that I hate.'

She was determined not to have a serious conversation on the wrongs of monetary distribution. 'I'll leave when I no longer notice the bodies underfoot.'

'It'll be too late then because, as you say, you'll no longer notice.'

'Jake! Jake!' She seized him by the shoulders and shook him. 'I've done well in this town, I needed to do well at something, somewhere. When I arrived my confidence was zilch. I've fought long and hard to make it at William & Wall. I enjoy it. I need the challenge. I'm not little lost Olivia any more, I hated being little lost Olivia, and I never, never want to be little lost Olivia again.'

'You've toughened up.'

'I had to.'

'It can't have been easy.'

'It wasn't, and if you weren't so prejudiced you could almost be proud of me.'

'Prejudiced! Oh, I guess that's partly it, that and . . . I'll sound like an old bear if I tell you that there was something nice about being needed by little lost Olivia. But I am glad for you, if you've got what you want.'

'I nearly went home with my tail between my legs,' she said, and she told him about the Staten Island ferry and the Chinaman and the twelve million immigrants. 'Then I told myself that if they could succeed by adapting, so could I.'

He kissed her on the cheek and when he drew back Olivia was appalled to see tears in his eyes. 'What a pity we didn't adapt before we went blundering into Vietnam,' he said softly, and Olivia knew he was thinking of Billy who had gone to Vietnam in a uniform and come back in a coffin.

28

Connecticut

They drove up through the turning leaves of golden fall, to the white farmhouse with its grey slate roof and the fair-haired smooth-faced woman so very like Blanche who came to greet them, hands outstretched, gently elegant, Ursula, the younger sister of Ash's troubled mother.

'So you're Olivia.' The hands were soft. 'We've been just longing to meet you.'

'Yes,' added Charles, her husband, 'we were afraid we might have to go to New York to see you, and we never go there.' They linked arms and smiled at each other. 'We're country people.'

Olivia smiled back, but she was thinking that Ursula's plain grey woollen dress was anything but rustic. The farmhouse had that same simple beauty and the hand which had decorated it had known how to enhance the natural woodwork and to scatter beautiful rugs on polished floorboards and not drown them with fitted carpets. Upstairs she was shown to a pretty chintzy bedroom with a patchwork quilt on an iron bedstead. Ash was pointedly – she felt – shown to another room, some way down the corridor.

'I hope you don't mind sharing a bathroom with my daughter, Cass,' said Ursula. 'I've told her she mustn't spend hours in it – I'm afraid she usually does.'

'I do what?' A tousled blonde colt of a girl appeared in the doorway, her long body encased in a turquoise jumpsuit, her legs in rainbow leg-warmers.

'Spend hours in the bathroom. Cass, darling, this is Olivia.'

'Hi,' She gave Olivia a friendly grin. 'Where's Ash? Oh, don't tell me, he's calling the President of the World.'

'Cassandra!'

'It's OK, Mom, I'm not going to get in Ash's way but you did say I could use the phone later, didn't you?'

'Yes, only let Ash use it first.' She smiled at Olivia. Ash lives on the phone – but then I'm sure all of you bankers have to.'

They went downstairs. In the old farm kitchen a cheerful-faced woman was making apple pie, in the drawing-room Charles was pouring them each a glass of sherry, in the dining-room Cass was dancing around the table as she laid the lunch. It's all so civilised, thought Olivia, reminded slightly of The Helmets.

The phone rang as they sat down to eat. Ash jumped up. 'That'll be for me.'

They were on to the cheese before he came back.

'We must take Olivia for a walk in the woods, Ash,' said his aunt, 'they're quite beautiful now.'

'I'm afraid I'll have to bow out. I'm waiting for a call from Sydney. You and Cass take her.'

She went with Cass and Ursula and the yellow labrador called Melon, through the woods where the sun's rays pushed their way between the leaves and made a glorious dappled pattern on the ground below. When they returned, Ash was still on the phone.

'I think I've cracked that deal,' he told Olivia later, 'but I may have to go to Sydney on Monday.' He kissed her quickly – there was something very proper about the farmhouse. 'I wish I could take you with me but I don't think we could justify it, you're too important at the bank. You, McCord and I are the only ones who really speak the same language.'

'Teddy's pretty smart.'

'Yes, and he's goodlooking.'

'Ash, you're not suggesting . . .? Teddy is married to Betsy and even if he wasn't, he's not my type.'

'Am I your type?' He touched her cheek.

'Not when you're being suspicious.'

Over dinner the family asked Olivia the sort of polite but probing questions most families would in those circumstances,

358

made more embarrassing by the fact that Ash's Sydney call came through as soon as they sat down.

'Where do your family live, Olivia?' asked Charles.

From the hall came Ash's voice, 'What's the price of the Australian dollar?'

'They live at Newbury, that's in Berkshire. My father's a lawyer there.' They nodded at the word lawyer, but Olivia pictured the little old ladies with broken garden fences or disagreeable neighbours whom her father attempted to advise.

'How many? What? Who's buying?'

'Oh, isn't that near Lambourn where they train the race-horses?'

'OK, get Sydney to call me back Steffie.'

'Yes, they train them on the Berkshire Downs.'

Ash returned. 'Excuse me, Ursula, I do apologise.'

'I want to make some calls after dinner,' said Cass.

'You can't use the phone till Sydney's come back to me.'

'Mother!'

'Cass, just let Ash finish first.'

'That's not fair! He's been on the phone all afternoon. Mom, you said . . .'

'Cassandra!' Ash kept his voice level, 'when you've grown up and have a responsible job you will learn that there are more important things than gossiping with boyfriends.'

Cass pushed back her chair so violently that it crashed to the ground. 'When I grow up I hope I learn not to be the kind of jerk like you who disrupts other people's households.'

'I'm so sorry,' said Ursula, turning to Olivia as Cass slammed out of the room.

'Don't worry, my sister and I used to argue all the time.'

Ash's lips tightened. 'This is hardly some sibling quarrel, Olivia.' He picked up his knife and fork and began to eat.

Olivia looked at the table, as her host and hostess passed anxious glances down its length.

'The trouble with Cass is that she's spoiled,' said Ash as they drove back to New York on the following afternoon. 'She should have gone to boarding school, I always said so, but of course they wouldn't hear of it, her being their only child.' His hand felt for Olivia's and his fingers linked through hers. 'We must come again soon. You know, I always feel guilty that I don't see them more often – they so appreciate my visits.'

Olivia said nothing for some time. She sat there, watching the scenery without watching it, and wondering whether she expected too much from life.

'What a pity golden leaves do not last forever,' she said eventually.

'Oh, I don't think the price of gold will alter noticeably if Reagan makes it to the White House.' Ash relaxed his shoulders and smiled as they drew nearer to Wall Street.

William & Wall were expanding into Europe. Their clients were hungry for the kind of antiquated firm with a good product and bad marketing which could be taken over, turned around – and possibly resold.

'It is,' as one nervous manager told Olivia over lunch, 'unthinkable that I should sack my staff but expected that a new American boss would do so. In fact, people are disappointed if heads don't roll, so long as it's not their own. They feel hard done by if there's no bloodbath. It's also a way whereby people get rid of those they dislike. "You wanted John? If I were you I'd talk to him in the morning. After lunch he tends to be a bit . . ." or "Mary? But she always goes shopping on Fridays. She'll be back at three thirty. Mind you, she leaves at three-forty." '

Olivia laughed. She'd come to Manchester on a flying visit to suss out a computer company with a view to purchase by a major American software group, and to see if the existing management were totally useless. She decided that this quietly amusing little man was the only one worth saving, and on her return to New York she made that her recommendation. But before going back she flew down to London, checked into the Connaught and rang Maggie.

Zach answered. 'She's not here at the moment.'

'Is she all right?'

'She hasn't been too well but . . .'

'Zach, can you give me a number where I can call her? Please!'

'No, you give me your number.'

360

'Look, what's wrong? Is she ill? Has she had to have more treatment? Are you splitting up?'

'I'll get Maggie to call you, I promise.'

She told him that she would be at her parents until Monday.

It was Sunday evening before Maggie telephoned. She sounded distant. She said she'd been away and was about to go away again and she couldn't possibly see Olivia for at least three days.

'But Maggie I have to leave for Paris tomorrow morning.'

'Ring me next time you're over.'

'Let me drive up now.'

'No.'

'Maggie, I know we haven't seen much of each other recently but . . .'

'I have to go out now. Goodbye.'

Olivia went to bed early but she could not sleep, she was so worried that if they were no longer close, it was mainly her own fault: she had allowed Ash, William & Wall, life, to come between her and the few minutes it would have taken to acknowledge Maggie's unanswered letters. At half past five she dressed, packed and crept downstairs.

'Darling, why are you up so early?' Her mother blinked in the kitchen light, her hands twisting at the belt of her pink quilted dressing gown.

'Sorry, did I wake you?' Olivia was eating a bowl of cornflakes over the sink. 'I suddenly remembered that I have to do something in London before I catch the flight to Paris. I was going to leave you a note and phone later.'

'You should have a proper breakfast, dear, you look so tense.'

'No, thanks, I have to go now.' She kissed her mother on the cheek, noticing that the golden sausage curls were now heavily streaked with grey.

Her mother followed her out into the hall and opened the front door on to a cold spring dawn. 'Come again soon. It's lonely for us old folks now.'

Olivia crunched across the gravel to her hired Porsche and tossed her case inside. 'Don't you see Fiona and Hugo most weekends?'

'Not . . . any more.' Her mother hovered beside the winter

jasmine which grew up the side of the porch. 'Your father said I mustn't worry you with it, but . . . well . . . I was tactless and Fiona said I upset Hugo dreadfully and . . . I didn't mean to, really I didn't.'

Olivia walked back to her mother. 'What happened, Mummy?'

'No one told me they were so hard up. Oh, I knew Hugo wasn't very bright, but I didn't realise he was to be made redundant, after all his father was a brigadier! Then when I discovered – discovered! Fiona didn't tell me – that she'd taken a full-time secretarial job, I said that I thought it irresponsible for a woman with two young children to choose to work and that Hugo should stop her. I know I shouldn't have said anything but I thought Fiona was working because . . . oh, you know how obstinate she is sometimes?'

It was the first time that Olivia could remember her mother criticising Fiona. 'I'm sure it will all blow over, Mummy.' She glanced at the brightening sky, anxious to be on her way and yet not wanting to leave her mother who was confiding in her for the first time. 'Why don't you write and apologise to Fiona.'

'I'm afraid I might make matters worse by saying the wrong thing and I can't ask your father to help me because he's been so upset by it all. He says I've alienated both of you. I haven't, have I, darling?'

'Of course not, Mummy.' Olivia put her arms around her mother. 'Look, you draft the letter and I'll call you from New York on Wednesday afternoon. Then you can read it through to me. All right?'

'Would you really?'

'Of course. Now, don't worry.'

It was just before eight when Olivia drew up outside Maggie's house and pushed aside the azalea which was even more rampant than before. She rang the bell. Waited. Rang again. No one came. From a nearby telephone kiosk, she dialled the number. It rang and rang – not even the answering machine was connected. She went back and stood outside, looking up at the house which Maggie and Zach had bought with so many hopes, then she got back into the Porsche and headed for Heathrow.

In Paris, Olivia saw little except the inside of her hotel suite and the offices of a French bank – apart from an hour in one of her favourite boutiques just off the Faubourg St Honore. A selection was waiting for her as she crossed the threshold, and she came away with two suits and three dresses, each with the kind of sensual but never vulgar tailoring at which the French excel. She arrived back in New York on a Sunday afternoon. To her surprise Ash met her at the airport. He was normally too busy, even at weekends.

'How come?' she asked him.

'Could I allow William & Wall's newest junior vice president to arrive unmet?'

'Vice president? Ash, you mean . . . Really?' She laughed with excitement.

'Sure – but it's a secret till Monday.'

'What about Teddy?'

'He'll be next.'

'No one else was promoted?'

'Nope. You're now running neck and neck with Sherry.'

'You'd better watch out, Ash Mallory,' she put her arms around him, 'or I'll be neck and neck with you.'

'Never! The day I let you get the better of me my life will be hell.' He hugged her, and she responded, relieved to blot out the sound of Maggie's unhappy voice and the sight of her lonely mother in a pink quilted dressing gown.

But of course she did not really blot them out. They came back to her frequently, and by the time she telephoned her mother on Wednesday afternoon she had already written Maggie a long and chatty letter.

On the Friday morning, as Olivia was in the middle of dictating a list of notes to her secretary, Jake rang. 'Have you seen the news?'

'Why?'

'Lorenzo's been kidnapped by the Red Brigade.'

'You're joking!'

'I wish I was. He was snatched from his mistress's house last night.'

'The leopard skin tigress?'

'Yes, she was found bound and gagged by the cleaning woman and this morning the Red Brigade announced they will hold a "people's trial".'

'On what grounds?'

'Who knows! The police are out everywhere looking for him but I'm afraid to say that in the past they haven't been too successful against the Red Brigade. You remember the kidnapping of Aldo Moro, the Italian politician, two years ago? Yes, the one who was murdered. Oh, Livvi, I can honestly say that I'm glad Gisella is not here to suffer this. I keep thinking of Lorenzo as he was when he was fifteen, and you know something – he's never really changed, he's still the angel-faced kid with a double helping of chutzpah.'

Olivia went through to Ash's office.

'I didn't know you knew any Italian politicians,' he said.

'He wasn't a politician when I knew him.'

'He could have helped us over some of our Italian deals.'

'Don't talk about him as if he's already dead.'

'I'm sorry.' He put his arms around her, something he never did in the office. 'I hope this man is rescued and I'm sorry if you were upset by the idea of us using him.'

She leaned against him for a moment. 'Lorenzo is the world's user.'

A week later his body was found, bound and gagged and shot in the back of the head, one neat hole, or so the papers said.

'Lorenzo was a gunrunner,' she told Ash in the darkness of their bedroom. 'He was unscrupulous and brutal, but the moment he becomes respectable he gets killed – by a gun!'

The traffic raced down Fifth Avenue. A police siren howled into the night. Olivia pictured the ornate cemetery at Staglieno and the tomb of Mazzini. What would that nineteenth century philosopher make of this strange tale of twisted morals and retrospective virtues? As she turned on her side, away from Ash, she seemed to hear Lorenzo's velvety voice say, 'Why do English girls always try to look like spaniels?'

29

Jake's exhibition was scheduled for the autumn. It was the first showing of his work to take place in the States, and the Lincoln Center pulled out all the stops. Museums and private collectors were prevailed upon to lend items, and from mid September newspapers and television ran features about huge lumps of sculpted marble being handled as gently as if they were babies. Olivia remembered Jake saying to her, in what now seemed another lifetime, 'Marble has everything, it is up to the sculptor to bring it out.'

He arrived in New York a month ahead of the opening and Olivia saw him frequently. They would grab a late supper, with or without Ash – more often without, for Ash was showing unbelievable tact. What he did not know – and Olivia did feel a little guilty – was that Freddie was a frequent third person. 'But Freddie,' as Jake told Olivia, 'is one of us – just as Mark is one of us.'

'Jake!'

'If only I could bring you two together again.'

'Stop it! Mark is in the past. I don't think of him any more, I don't want to see him. My life is here.'

'You're right, Livvi, it's none of my business and if I had met you for the first time here, in New York, I'm sure I'd think Ash was just fine for you.'

Invitations to the opening of Jake's exhibition were among the most sought after of the season, with people who did not know a Rubens from a Picasso begging to be allowed to attend. Olivia, Ash, the McCords, Teddy and Betsy, and Freddie all received an invitation, on the back of which Jake had written, in his loopy scrawl; 'I do hope you can join me for dinner afterwards at the Four Seasons.'

Olivia hugged him. 'Dear, dear Jake!'

He chuckled. 'Didn't I once tell you that I know how to behave?'

'Yes, so long as you don't have to do it too often or for too long.'

She bought a new dress, black with a thin gold thread running through the material and the new padded shoulders and huge sleeves which were coming into fashion. It made her look vampish and Hollywood, so Ash said, as she pirouetted before him on the tips of her black high heels.

'Do I look nice?'

'Very nice.'

'How nice?' She lifted the corner of the slinky skirt to reveal that the gold flecked stockings were indeed stockings and held up by black satin suspenders.

Ash took her in his arms and pulled her to him, running his hands down her back to her thighs and burying his face in the warmth of her neck.

'The McCords are picking us up in five minutes,' she reminded him.

'Yeah.'

'You're mussing up my dress.'

'I like you when you're mussed up.'

'I've just spent two hours getting ready.' She nibbled at the corner of his mouth, her tongue flicking over his lips. Her skirt was up around her thighs, and suddenly the bell rang.

They froze – looked at each other, and then she said, 'Let them wait.'

Downstairs in the William & Wall limo Spencer McCord and his wife glanced at their watches and hoped Ash and Olivia weren't having a row. 'What will happen at the bank if they split up?' asked Blanche.

'Nothing – so long as it doesn't affect their work.'

'Oh, I do hope they marry, she's so good for him. Here they come. Ash is pretty red in the face. I hope they haven't been fighting. Ursula said they were very tense last time she saw them and she was afraid . . .'

McCord looked from Ash to Olivia and smiled as he patted

his wife's hand. 'It's OK, honey, they haven't been fighting.'

The exhibition was a resounding success – and the most admired piece was a white marble figure of a girl entitled The Snake Girl – property of the sculptor. Not for sale.

Olivia hadn't known it would be there, she'd last seen it at Pietra Alta, unpolished and rough. Now, looking at it beneath the probing lights of the Lincoln Center, she was filled with a strange mixture of pride and embarrassment: pride because it was beautiful: embarrassment because it was so utterly sensuous.

Jake pushed through the throng. 'You don't mind, Livvi? I should have warned you but . . .'

'I don't mind, not really, though I do feel a bit . . . naked.'

'I won't tell anyone it's you.'

He was being optimistic. Those near them sensed a relationship between the attractive brunette and the coiled marble figure. It was something to do with the way her hair waved defiantly. Yes, a defiance. The figure seemed to be saying 'I won't let them get the better of me' and in Olivia's manner there was a 'I didn't let them get the better of me.'

'I want to buy it,' said Ash when Jake was hauled away by the publicity lady.

'Ash, you mustn't even suggest it.

'OK.' He held up his hands. 'I won't. But don't get mad at me.'

McCord tapped Olivia on the shoulder. 'I'd no idea . . .' He pointed at the figure and chuckled.

'It was in my bohemian days, Cord. I spent nine months on a Greek island, and one day I went for a walk and heard this voice booming out down the valley. It was Jake, singing an Italian partisan song. That's how I met him.'

'Before or after Culross?'

She did not even flinch. 'After – I was licking my wounds.'

They circulated through the exhibition, admiring other pieces and bumping into people they knew. Word spread fast that Olivia was The Snake Girl, and as they left for dinner, Olivia between Jake and Ash, with the McCords, Teddy and Betsy just behind, they were dazzled by flashlights from the barrage of photographers and inundated with questions, 'Don't you think it pretty unusual for a banker . . .?' 'What do you think your colleagues on Wall Street will say . . .?'

The next morning every newspaper carried the story that Olivia Steele, the high-flyer banker from William & Wall, had once been a sculptor's model.

'At least they didn't say nude model,' Olivia told Betsy when they discussed the evening.

'Kid, half Manhattan would shed its clothes immediately if it thought there was the remotest chance of being a model for Jake Hammond. He's great and so are you. Teddy says he always knew you were a curvy lady and now he has proof!'

Three days after the exhibition opened Jake announced abruptly that he was going home, 'I need Pietra Alta,' he explained to Olivia on the phone. 'I'm booked on tomorrow evening's flight. Spend the day with me. Just us. Meet me by the bean tree. I want to see it one more time. I shan't come back to New York again.'

She took a day's vacation, threw on a pair of red trousers and a red and white striped jumper – Jake liked her in red – and headed for the park. It was a beautiful sunny day, just as it had been nearly a year earlier when they had first met at the bean tree, only this time the leaves weren't so advanced along their golden trail, they were still on the trees although beginning to turn, but the lake had the mellow haze of early autumn.

Jake wasn't by the bean tree which surprised her because he was a punctual person for all his living in Greece and Italy. She sat down on the grassy bank, picked up one of the giant runner beans and tapped in in her hand. Ten minutes passed. She was annoyed, it hadn't been easy to take time off work. Fifteen minutes, and she felt that mixture of worry and irritation which comes with waiting. Twenty minutes, and she started slowly up the slope towards the Upper West Side because intuition told her he would take the subway – he liked the graffiti – to Columbus Circus and walk up. So she traced what she thought would be his footsteps along the bumpy pavement beneath the trees, keeping her eyes on the traffic in case he passed her in a cab.

Then she heard a shout above the noise of the traffic. 'Livvi!'

Jake was standing on the other side of the street waiting for the lights to change. She waved the bean. He waved back. Her irritation and worry were forgotten as she felt the warm glow of affection for him. Her eyes drifted over the people waiting with him. What nonentities he made them appear. The lights changed from Don't Walk to Walk. He stepped forward and began to cross, but as he reached the halfway point, several strides ahead of the others, a car roared around the corner, jumped the red lights, and hit him so hard that he went up over the bonnet and came down on its roof with a sickening crunch, to bounce off the back and onto the road. He landed on his head. People screamed. Tyres squealed. Other cars braked. But the car which had hit him did not stop: it accelerated.

Olivia ran into the middle of the road. 'Jake!' She pushed her way through. 'Jake!' She knelt down beside him. He did not move. Blood poured from the back of his head and his usually ruddy complexion was turning to a whitish grey.

Some of the people moved off – they were in a hurry.

The blocked traffic hooted.

A policeman appeared. 'What happened, lady?'

'Get an ambulance! Quick!'

'Has he got Blue Cross?'

'What? Oh, how do I know. No, of course he hasn't but I'll pay,' she shouted wildly. 'For God's sake hurry up!'

The policeman felt for Jake's pulse. 'He's dead.'

'He can't be dead.'

'I'm sorry.'

'But he was alive a moment ago.'

'I'm truly sorry.' The policeman spoke into his radio then took out a notepad. 'Your Dad?'

'No, a friend.'

'You British?' He made a note. 'Was he British? On holiday?'

'No, he was an American.'

'Know if the old man had any family?'

'I don't think so.'

The policeman was looking at Jake's white mane and it struck Olivia that he had decided Jake was some sort of vagrant. She stood up, trying to keep the choking from her voice. 'This man is Jake Hammond the world-famous sculptor whose exhibition is on at the Lincoln Center. Surely you must have read about him.?'

'Lady, why didn't you say so?'

A hand touched Olivia's sleeve. She turned to meet the sympathetic eyes of an old negro. 'You dropped this,' he said — and he handed her the long dried pod of the bean tree.

30

Pietra Alta

In the small chapel on the hillside the rounded voices of the choir rose to the old stone roof above the wooden pews where Jake's friends had gathered from far and wide and very near, whilst outside in the sunlight stood peasant women dressed in black, tears coursing down their leathery cheeks, and old men who mumbled toothlessly of past kindnesses, to them and to their village.

In the front pew Olivia was sitting next to Gwen. She longed to turn around to see if Mark were there, but she didn't. Of course she had no proof that he had come, but . . . she raised her hand to adjust the small black pillar-box hat so that the spidery veil did not touch her face, and straightened her shoulders inside their fitted black jacket – and all the time she wondered if Mark were watching.

Thank God she'd left Ash behind. But unfortunately it had not been simply a case of leaving him in New York, but the much more hurtful one of abandoning him to kick his heels in a Milan hotel – they were on a business trip.

'I don't understand why I can't come with you,' he'd started up again over breakfast.

'I'm sorry,' she'd replied, 'but as I explained last night there'll be people Jake and I used to know and . . .'

'Anyone would think you were ashamed of me.'

'Don't be ridiculous!' She'd got up and walked over to the window and looked down on the Piazza Duomo. 'Ash, please stop caging me in.'

'Caging you in!' He grabbed her and forced her to look him

371

in the eyes. 'You told me over and over again that you wanted to forget the past and that the best day of your life was when you arrived at William & Wall, and I believed you.' He shook her hard. 'I believed you because I love you.'

The phone rang. Reluctantly Ash released her as she stretched for it. 'My car? Yes, to Pietra Alta. It's near Carrara. I'll be right down.' She walked past Ash to her bedroom — on business trips they took a suite and kept the pretence of separate bedrooms.

Ash followed. 'I have to talk to you. Now.'

'It'll have to wait.' She slipped on her tailored jacket and lifted the collar of her cream silk shirt.

'I don't cage you in.'

She glossed her lips. 'We'll discuss it on the plane.'

'We have a perfect relationship. Some weeks we're together, others we scarcely see each other. It suits us both, we've always said so.'

She perched the small round hat on the crown of her head and adjusted the veil so that it covered her face, and yet did not quite cover it, giving her all the allure of a veil, revealing her femininity, concealing a little of her mystery. 'Ash, I'm sorry but I don't want to talk about us now. I was very fond of Jake and . . .'

'He comes before me.'

'Grow up!' She reached for her black mink, a present from Ash the previous Christmas.

'Childish, am I?' He snatched the coat from her. 'OK then, you're not wearing my coat, not unless I can come with you.'

'I prefer to freeze.' She picked up her bag and gloves and walked away. He followed, clutching the mink. 'I can't believe this is happening to us! We were so happy. That damned old man, he changed everything, he ruined it. We haven't had sex for three weeks. I've a good mind to go out and get laid.'

'Why don't you?'

'You wouldn't care?'

'Not at the moment.'

'Because you've met someone else?'

She had left without answering him, and now she sat in chapel shivering against the Italian winter and feeling guilty that she'd hurt Ash. Perhaps when we get back to New York

372

things will improve, she thought: she could not imagine life there without him, just as she could not imagine life elsewhere with him. Ash was Wall Street, William & Wall, and punchy deals. He did not even translate into Connecticut where he had been brought up. She looked at the flowers spread around Jake's coffin: white lilies, chrysanthemums – flowers from the acres of greenhouses on the Tuscan plains. Some were simple bouquets, others more exotic, Lady Vicky's was a wreath of white roses, her own were by far the most elaborate: a huge creation of arum lilies and orchids. She wished she'd left out the orchids, they were too ostentatious for Pietra Alta – but it was easy to forget such subtleties.

The priest was intoning in Latin. It struck Olivia as odd that Jake should come to this, and his end should be no different from that of any of the peasants waiting outside in the sunshine, who in their turn would lie in a box in this chapel with this priest – or his successor – mumbling over them. In the end, she thought, it didn't matter to your body who you were or what you had done in your life because it stayed behind, whilst you went on – or up – or down – or wherever.

On the other side of the aisle two smart international-looking men stood with heads bowed. Olivia decided they must be the owners of the Parisian gallery. Did they know about the propellers in Hoboken? Beyond them was a sophisticated white-haired man. Did he know of the hardware store on Columbus Avenue? In the row behind, between two very goodlooking children, was a pale woman in a honey mink. Did she know about the bean tree? Olivia wondered.

The service ended. The coffin was carried out by the sons of those who had fought with the partisans. It was followed by their aged fathers, and as it reached the chapel door, first one, then another, broke into song: '*Bella ciao, bella ciao, bella ciao, ciao, ciao.*' and others waiting in the sunshine picked it up, so that the words rang out on the hillside. Tears pricked Olivia's eyes. She bit her lip to hold them back. Again she was walking up the valley in Anataxos and again she saw the great white head and heard the voice lifted to the blue, blue sky.

Gwen tapped her on the shoulder. 'I'm so glad to see you even if it is ... well, at least he was with you when it happened.'

'Oh, Gwen!'

'You know, I came to the States last year to see Jim's family and I nearly rang you.'

'Why didn't you?'

'Jake told me you lived rather a smart life now and . . .'

'Gwen!'

'He said you had a very high-powered job and a rich boyfriend and you flew all over the world. Oh, I know it's silly but I was afraid we might have nothing in common. You look very smart, though you must be freezing to death without a coat. Oh, heavens, what a thing to say at a funeral!'

'How Jake would laugh!'

The very goodlooking boy and the equally goodlooking girl were standing next to the woman in honey mink but Olivia hardly noticed them. She was too intent on scanning the crowd for Mark, without scanning the crowd for Mark.

'Miss Olivia Steele?' The woman spoke in heavily accented English. 'I am the widow of Lorenzo. I believe you met my husband. Jake told me about you. These are my children, Fabrizio and Angelica. Gisella was their aunt.'

'Of course.' She wondered what Jake had said about her. 'I was sorry to hear about your husband . . . your father.' She smiled at the children. There was absolutely nothing of the gunrunner in their cultured faces.

A hand touched her shoulder. 'Miss Olivia?' She found herself looking into the burned face of Alfredo, Jake's driver from Salerno. 'So sad.' A tear rolled down his scarred cheek. 'He saved my life.'

'I know. I know.'

She had become separated from Gwen and had no desire to stand beside the gaping hole and watch Jake lowered into the ground or to throw her handful of earth and hear the hollow thud as it hit the coffin, so she walked to the stone wall which divided the graveyard from the old mule road and stood looking out over the plain towards the sea. What had Jake said that first day he had brought her here? That he envied her having her first view of the place. Well, he'd be up here forever now, with his beloved mountains behind him, his favourite view in front, and across the valley the cave where he had spent the winter nearly forty years ago, his broken leg tended by the girl he loved; the cave where he first picked up a lump of marble and began to chip away at it.

The roar of a marble lorry drowned out the priest. It came around the corner skidding on the loose surface, then hurtled on, down the hill. From the valley came the unseen whine of a marble cutter grinding sand and water backwards and forwards into the groove. From the hillside came the chip-chip of a sculptor at work. High up on Monte Altissimo tiny figures moved along its serrated edge quarrying the purest of white marble. But not for Jake, for other sculptors now.

Olivia turned back to the graveyard – and her eyes met Mark's. He was standing under one of the giant fir trees, his hooded eyes watching her over the heads of the peasant women. She met his gaze. She smiled. He turned away.

Gwen came bustling over. 'We're all invited to lunch at Pietra Alta. Franca – you remember, Gisella's cousin who looks after the house – has laid on lunch for everyone. Is there space in your car for three more of us? Marvellous. I'll tell the others.'

She didn't want to go to the lunch if Mark intended to ignore her, but she couldn't refuse. So she followed Gwen to her car, hoping that Mark wouldn't be in her party, disappointed when she found he wasn't.

It was several years since Olivia had been to Pietra Alta but it had not changed. The mountains were as savage and the woods as dense. The shuttered house still dominated the valley and the river ran cold across the bed of marble stones. It was all just as it had been on that first morning when she had felt inadequate because Pietra Alta was a working village and everyone seemed to have something to do except for her.

Lunch was laid out in the dining-room, long wooden tables groaning under plates piled with succulent meats and country cheeses, whilst red-faced local girls offering wine skidded between the guests. Olivia was not hungry. The thought that Mark was there made her feel sick with nerves. She could not move around for fear of bumping into him, every time she turned she found herself facing him. Eventually, unable to bear the suspense, she slipped out on to the terrace. It was crisp and cold and sunny, and so very beautiful. She walked to the railings and looked down at the river. Jake had called her rogue marble on that stormy night when the river had turned into a torrent, and the block had jumped the mainstream. Well, perhaps I used to be. She adjusted her pillarbox hat with its spidery feminine veil, and thought of The Snake Girl subjected to the bright lights and inquisitive stares of the Lincoln Center, and wondered if in being tamed they had each lost something. Perhaps Ash was the right man for her, only she wasn't yet tamed enough to see it. She turned her back on the river and looked up at the mountains – as Mark opened the drawing-room door and stepped out on to the terrace.

She waited for him by the railings, forcing herself to meet his eyes, telling herself that she was not afraid of him and nothing he could do or say or think would affect her – and wondering, in spite of everything, if he still cared and why it had to be that Mark made her feel so vulnerable.

'I refuse to spend all day avoiding you,' he said, 'or to have the ridiculous scene of you turning your back every time I happen to look in your direction.'

'I was willing to talk to you in the cemetery but . . .'

'How condescending!'

'I mean that I would have spoken to you if I'd been sure you wouldn't snub me.'

He stood, looking up at the mountains. 'Do you know that it was a month before I discovered you'd gone to New York.'

'I didn't know you cared where I went.'

'I spent four whole weeks thinking that at any minute you might come back. Four weeks. Twenty-eight days. Every hour of every day. Why didn't you tell me you were going away? At least I wouldn't have gone on hoping.

'Because . . .'

'Because what?'

'If I'd told you, I might not have had the courage to leave.'

'Courage or cowardice?'

'I call it courage. I had to get away, Mark, we were destroying each other.'

'No, your desire for revenge was destroying us, that was all. You couldn't stop thinking about Culross. Why, I expect you were even planning your banking comeback whilst we were making love.'

'That's not true and you know it.'

'I have wondered.'

'Oh, I know I was . . .' she scouted around for the right words '. . . I know I couldn't bury the ghosts. They obsessed me.'

'You didn't want to bury them.'

'You didn't want to understand.'

'I was your lover not your analyst — or have you lived too long in New York to know the difference?'

'I looked to you for support but I never tried to involve you. I wanted things to work between us, I . . .' Her voice caught in her throat and she looked away from him, not wanting him to see the tears in her eyes.

'In the end,' he said, 'Maggie told me where you were. You cannot imagine how hurt I was.'

'You could have got my address from her.'

'Why should I contact you, Olivia? You were the one who walked out, in the middle of the night, banging the door.'

'I didn't mean to hurt you,' she said, very softly, biting her lower lip.

'Didn't you?' He moved closer, next to her, as they had once stood by the fence at The Helmets and looked down on the snow-covered fields. 'I think you did mean to hurt me. I certainly meant to hurt you.'

'Yes, you're right.' Her face trembled. 'I hated you because I loved you and everything was slipping away from us and I couldn't stop it from going wrong.'

'I hated you when you left. Maggie sent me your address but I burned her letter so that I couldn't weaken and send you one of my unposted midnight letters.'

'Or dial my number but click off before the last digit. Oh, I've done that too — in the middle of the night.'

'You have?' He smiled, and for the first time his eyes seemed to take in her veiled hat and the smart cut of her French suit. 'You've become quite the high-powered lady.'

'And you've become a Q.C.'

'You knew?'

'Jake told me.'

'So you've no excuse for not congratulating me.'

'The same excuse as you have for not writing to me.'

'That's different, Olivia. You walked out.'

377

'You told me to go.'

'Still . . .' He was trying not to smile, '. . . it would have been nice to receive your best wishes. I wouldn't have expected anything excessive, like those horribly ostentatious orchids which some vulgar person . . .'

'Don't!' She blushed, which was endearingly at odds with her ultra-chic outfit. 'I'd forgotten how simple life is here.' A moment later she shrugged. 'There's something about you, Mark, which means it's inevitable that I do the wrong thing when you're around.'

'You do the wrong thing a lot of the time,' he took her by the shoulders and pulled her to him, 'but no one else has the courage to tell you so.'

She thought he was going to kiss her, but he released her abruptly as if afraid to do so. 'You should have stayed in New York.'

'Do you really wish I had?'

'Yes . . . no. And you should have brought a coat, you're shivering.'

'It doesn't matter.'

'Do you want to go inside?'

'No, I want to . . .' She looked at him out of the corner of her eye, the hard set of his jaw, his hooded eyes, the flatness of his cheeks below his angular cheekbones – and gingerly she moved her hand along the rail, longing to touch him but afraid to do so in case he spurned her. But this is your last chance, she told herself, and she forced her hand off the rail and laid it on his arm with all the trepidation of someone reaching out to touch a wire without knowing if it is live. Then she took a deep breath and made herself to say, 'What are we going to do about us?'

'Nothing – unless you come back to live in England. I'm not prepared to have a long distance affair with you. Snatched weekends and astronomical phone bills are not what you and I are all about. I want to go to bed at night with you, I want to wake up with you, I want to share moments of excitement and moments of doing nothing – I want all or nothing from you because you and I are all or nothing people.'

In spite of – or was it because of – his aggressive attitude she wanted him. She remembered the summer in London and the smell of syringa heavy on the night air as they loved. Then she remembered the autumn and the nagging sense of uselessness, whereby she had almost begun to walk behind Mark as though she were a lesser person. Finally, she remembered her early days in New York, the freezing streets, the dreary hotel, and the excitement once she began to make it. 'I fought long and hard to get where I am,' she said.

'And that's more important than us?'

'No, no, but . . . I'd be afraid to come back to nothing. If I did, things would be no different from the way they were.'

'I wasn't suggesting you came back to nothing – I was asking you to come back to me.'

'Mark, please understand. I do love you, but . . .'

'Exactly.'

'What do you mean by "exactly"?'

'That you weren't thinking of us, you were thinking of Culross. But it doesn't matter, Olivia, because I wouldn't dream of letting you into my life until I was sure you'd buried your ghosts.'

'I don't want to bury my ghosts, I want to murder them.'

His attention was diverted by someone behind her. 'Your chauffeur, I presume.'

'What?' She turned to find Ash crossing the terrace her black mink draped over his arm.

'I brought your coat, darling,' he said, woodenly ignoring Mark. 'We're booked on the six o'clock flight to New York.'

Mark looked from Ash to Olivia – then he spun on his heel and strode towards the house.

Olivia pushed Ash aside. 'Mark!'

He kept walking.

'Mark!'

He stopped by the French windows. 'Yes?'

She came to him, taking small steps, her face bruised and trembling beneath the whispery black veil. 'Whatever happens,' she said in a small choking voice, 'you'll always come first with me.'

'First?' He glanced at Ash clutching her mink, then at the silver limo, then back at Olivia, and he gave a derisory laugh. 'The only person who comes first with Olivia Steele is Olivia Steele and her relentless desire for revenge.'

The crash of the door slamming behind him echoed up the valley. Colour drained from Olivia's face and from her knuckles as she clenched her fists. She'd come to him and he'd kicked her. She'd crawled and he'd trodden on her. She'd followed him across the terrace to tell him that she loved him and he'd laughed and slammed the door in her face. She had hated Mark before, but never so intensely as now, when she had revealed her vulnerability.

She'd forgotten about Ash until he grabbed her arm, shouting. 'What kind of asshole do you think I am?'

'I don't think you're an asshole.' She shrugged him off. 'Where's my driver?'

'I sent him away. I wanted to talk to you, but I didn't expect to find you with another guy. God, you're nothing but a two-timing . . .'

'Let's go!'

'You mean, you're not staying?'

'I'm coming back to New York.'

'You are?'

'Yes!' she yelled.

He closed off the chauffeur before beginning. 'I knew you were meeting someone, I just knew it, but why couldn't you come straight with me? I've taken old girlfriends out to dinner when you've been away on business . . .'

'You have!'

'Sure – just dinner. I didn't think you'd mind.'

'I don't.' She wasn't jealous, just surprised.

The car zigzagged down the mountainside, past the chapel where Jake's freshly covered grave was draped with wilting flowers. She turned to catch one last glimpse of Pietra Alta. Ash watched her in sullen silence.

She told him that she was leaving him as they drove north towards Genoa, she'd intended to wait until they reached New York but she couldn't bring herself to keep up the pretence.

'What do you mean, "I'm sorry, Ash"?' he shouted, as they roared through one of the endless tunnels on that stretch of coastal motorway.

'I mean, I'm sorry but . . .' They burst out into the sunshine and raced across a viaduct.

'But you said you were coming back to New York.'

'Yes, but I think we should . . .' She should never have started in the car.

'How long have you and he . . .' The rest of his sentence was drowned as they overtook a lorry.

'I knew him long ago.'

'And you're going back to him?'

'No! No! But it wouldn't be fair on you for us to carry on.'

'Don't give me that crap!' He put his hands to his head and covered his eyes. 'We can't just split. What about William & Wall? What about the McCords? Charles and Ursula? We're a way of life. We're a couple. We're not some tacky little love affair. Look, let's talk about it now. OK? Let's wait till we're home . . .' They plunged into another tunnel. He waited till they came out into the light, before adding, 'and all this is behind us.'

'It will never be entirely behind me, Ash,' she said gently. 'I know that now.'

They were approaching Genoa. She thought of Lorenzo, and wished that she could explain to Ash about the *Ariosto* and Mazzini – and Lorenzo himself – and the dimension they had added to her life, but she couldn't. He would dismiss them as unimportant, he hadn't even understood the importance of Jake.

'Well?' He was saying.

'Well what?' She looked back at the city bathed in the evening sun, a million half-shuttered windows covertly watching container ships move across a reddening sea, a thousand twisted alleyways where cats walked single file.

'You haven't answered my question.'

'What was it?'

'I asked you when you'd changed your mind about me?'

She watched a couple kissing on a flower-filled balcony. They went inside, to a darkened room. On the roof above them an elderly woman was hanging out her washing. In the street two boys fought over a bicycle. 'I'm sorry,' she said.

'You used me.'

'I didn't mean to.'

'I love you.'

'I'm sorry.'

He clenched his fists. 'I hate these European towns, they're so decadent. I hate the way they hang their washing across the street.'

She grabbed at a change of subject. 'New York's dirty and poor too, it's just that people like you and me don't see that side of it.'

'Thank God! Look at that old man trying to pick up that young girl. All Italians ever think about is sex. If you're in a meeting with them their eyes are on the clock, wondering if they can get away in time to see their mistresses. The English are just as bad, only for them its cricket or fishing – or their gardens. No wonder Europe's such a mess. No one wants to work. No one has any discipline. They don't do what they say they'll do. They have no ambition.'

She quoted Jake. 'All people are ambitious – it's the goals which are different.'

'I knew it! You want to stay here, don't you? Shall I stop the car? Shall I let you out now? Driver!'

'Shut up!' They were climbing away from Genoa, over the hills which separate the Ligurian coast from the flat plains of Lombardy and the city of Milan. 'If I'd wanted to stay I'd have done so.'

'If you're not going to be with me, I wish you had.' He spoke with such pain and puzzlement that she reached out and took his hand, holding it in silence, with just the swoosh of the long grasses beside the motorway displaced by the momentum of the big car.

Ash said no more until their plane took off, then as it climbed into the night sky, he took her hand. 'I still want to marry you.'

'It wouldn't work.'

'Why? He doesn't want you.'

She said nothing.

'I'm begging you, Olivia, don't leave me. I'm begging you – and I've never begged a woman before.'

'It wouldn't work,' she repeated. 'I'm really sorry, I thought it might but I know now that it wouldn't.'

'Why? You have to tell me, you owe me that much.'

'Because . . . because I want to come first with someone and I want to be with someone who comes first with me. I don't want a man I am content to see go away for weeks at a time –

and I don't want a man who is content to be away from me for weeks. Oh, I don't mean that I want to be with someone every hour of every day, what I mean is that I want to want to be with him.' She was exhausted. It seemed centuries since she'd sat in the church and decades since she'd stood on terrace with Mark. She walked to the front of the plane where there were three empty seats and curled up on them, her chin resting on the window ledge. Beyond the wing the white-green moon bathed the eerie clouds. She remembered the film she had seen on the day of Sanjiv's wedding, where a silvery Bette Davis moved across a silvery screen and said, 'Oh, Jerry, don't let's ask for the moon. We have the stars.'

Olivia Steele still wanted the stars and the moon.

31

By the time they landed at Kennedy Airport, Ash had run the gamut from misery to anger: they took separate cabs.

At William & Wall, Olivia did her best to appear normal but within a week it was obvious to anyone who had a grain of intuition that something was wrong.

'So the great romance is over!' said Sherry, barging into Olivia's office. 'What happened? Romeo fall off the balcony – or did you push him?'

'I don't think that's any business of yours.'

'Give it a break, Olivia. The whole bank knows about you and Ash.'

'That doesn't mean I have to discuss my affairs with them, or with you. Now, get out!'

Half an hour later McCord called her to his office. 'I'm sorry to hear about you and Ash but . . .'

'I'm not prepared to marry Ash in order to . . .'

'Did I say you should?'

'No. I presumed that . . .'

'That what? That I called you up her to tell you to marry Ash or leave? Young lady, if you'd allowed me to finish my sentence you'd have heard me go on to say that whatever has happened between you two is no business of the bank, so long as you keep it that way – and that Caran, Coates, Raider, one of the world's largest advertising agencies, want us to help them break into the UK market.'

'A takeover?'

He smiled to see her bounce back. 'Can you handle it?'

'I'll need a restructured team. Ash and I share some of our

384

back-up and I think that for the time being . . .'

'Who d'you have in mind?'

'Ash takes Sherry and I take Peter. We were in the same bullpen so I know him well.'

'Anyone else?'

'Jack. He's the best analyst.'

'And he has a soft spot for you ever since the Caltoco Jupiter deal.'

'Yes.' She frowned: it was Caltoco Jupiter which had brought her and Ash together. 'I'd like Hutch and Alice, two of my associates, bumped up to principal to give them more authority.

He nodded his approval, then added in a gentler tone, 'If you need to talk, remember I'm here.'

She stood up. 'Thanks, Cord, I appreciate the offer – but the only thing on my mind will be the C.C. Raider deal.'

Her phone rang in the middle of the night. She woke with a start and reached for it.

'Bitch!'

'Ash?'

'I'm going to come and . . .' His voice was slurred, as Gerald's had been.

She slammed down the receiver. The phone rang again. She picked it up. Silence. She replaced it. It rang again. She took it off the hook. It was half past three. Tomorrow she had a breakfast meeting at the Plaza, an afternoon flight to Boston, dinner with clients, then an early return to New York on the following morning. She replaced the receiver and switched on her answering machine.

Twenty minutes later, as she was drifting into sleep the street door bell rang. She shot out of bed, pulled on her dressing gown and hurried into the sitting-room without putting on the lights. There she hesitated, hovering from one foot to the other. The bell rang again.

'Yes, she answered the intercom.

'Let me in.'

'Ash, please.'

'Let me in.'

385

'No.'

He rang and rang. In desperation she opened the window on to the bitter night and climbed out on to the fire escape. Ash looked up and saw her. 'Open the door!' he shouted. 'Open the door!'

'Ssssh.'

'I don't give a . . .'

'Ash!'

'If you don't let me in I'll break the door down.'

A window was thrown open further up the street and a man shouted, 'And if you don't fucking well shut up I'll call the cops.'

Ash staggered backwards into the middle of the road. 'You can't call the cops on me. I'm Thornton Ashwood Mallory the Third and I could buy you out any day.'

'I'm calling the cops.' The window slammed shut.

There was silence from Ash. He had disappeared into the shadows. Olivia climbed back into the warmth of the attic. It sounded hilarious, the two whiz kids of William & Wall yelling at each other whilst a man threatened to call the police – only it wasn't hilarious, it was sad and frightening.

From somewhere further down Spring Street a police siren howled into the night.

She thought she would never manage to sleep but she must have, because she came to with a start in the early morning, woken by a noise from outside. She listened hard, imagining footsteps, creating noises which did not exist, until every car was a cab returning Ash to her doorstep and every slightest sound was him searching for a way up to the attic.

In the morning she felt like tepid death. Her eyes were gritty and she felt queasy from lack of sleep: neither orange juice nor black coffee could revive her. She hovered by the window whilst her limo waited below. If only she could stay in bed for the day, but she couldn't. 'Come on!' she said out loud, 'Don't let him get to you. That's just what he wants.'

Nevertheless, she was very glad not to meet him as she crossed the banking hall, forcing herself not to walk faster than usual. Yes, in a couple of weeks Ash would begin to calm down and within six months they'd probably be friends.

To her intense irritation Sherry followed her into the lift.

'You're not looking too hot, Olivia. Not sickening, are you?'

'I'm perfectly all right, thank you.'

'Ash and I had such fun last night.'

'Really?'

'Sure.'

'You'd do him a favour by not letting him drink so much.'

'What do you mean?'

'If you were with him last night you'd know.'

'You're talking crap.'

'Not at all.' The lift stopped and Olivia stepped out. 'But allow me to give you a piece of advice.'

'Yeah?'

'Don't say "crap" if you meet Ash's family. They might think you ill-bred.'

Of course she shouldn't have allowed Sherry to rile her, but she had, and it left her feeling even more drained. On the flight to Boston she fell asleep, at dinner with clients she could hardly swallow, but by the time she returned to New York the buzz of a successful deal had lifted her spirits. Her phone was ringing as she opened the attic door. She waited for the answering machine to pick up the call, listening for the click and the message – or the silence.

'Olivia, it's Gwen. I . . .'

'Gwen! Gwen! Don't hang up. Hello, yes, it's me not the machine. I sound breathless? Oh, no, I'm fine I . . . er . . . ran up the stairs. No, we don't have a lift here. Have I received a letter from Jake's lawyer? No. Oh, wait a minute, there's one here with my mail. She ripped open the envelope, and read: 'I write to advise you that the property at Pietra Alta has been willed to you and Mr Mark Denholm jointly . . .'

From somewhere she seemed to hear Jake's voice saying, 'If only I could bring you two together again.'

'Olivia, are you still there?'

'Yes, I'm just recovering from the shock of inheriting Pietra Alta.'

'He told me he was going to leave it to you both and I longed to warn you at the funeral, but I felt it wasn't right. I did hope that when you and Mark were out on the terrace . . . but then he came slamming back into the house and you left with the American.'

'Did Mark know about Pietra Alta.'

'Oh, no. But he does now.'

'What did he . . . say?'

'That you weren't likely to meet again.'

If Mark was going to play it that way, so would she. 'I'll get my lawyer to communicate with him.'

'Oh, dear!' Gwen sighed. 'Doesn't it say . . . anything else in the letter?'

'Ummm.' Olivia ran her eyes down it. 'Oh, yes! He's left me The Snake Girl!'

'He has left me those last three pieces he did, the ones in the exhibition. They were my favourites – I suppose because he was working on them when . . . when I was with him.' Gwen was silent for a moment, then she went on. 'The house at Anataxos is to be sold and the money divided between poor hideous Aphrodisia, Alfredo the driver, and Franca and her husband at Pietra Alta. That reminds me, Mark is in favour of asking them to continue to look after the place. Your lawyer had better include that point. Oh, I asked Mark – but you must make up your own mind – if I could spend a few weeks there this winter, say after Christmas?'

'Of course you can, Gwen. Mark and I won't use Pietra Alta – at least not together.'

Within a minute of her saying goodbye to Gwen, the phone rang again. It was Ash. 'You have to leave William & Wall,' he told her in tones of icy sobriety.

'I have no intention of leaving.'

'You'll regret it if you don't.'

'And you'll be sorry if . . .'

He cut her off. Furious, Olivia dialled his number but there was no reply. She tried again, several times an hour till long after midnight, but still there was no reply. Eventually she gave up, telling herself that fate had decreed that she should not speak to him because it was for the best: she would rise above his childish threats. But she could not sleep, and as she tossed and turned in impotent fury Ash's threatening voice went around and around her mind, chased by the reply she would have made had she had the chance.

Next morning the strain showed in her face as she hovered by the window of her office, looking out at the skyscrapers.

Ash Mallory had made this town come alive for her – and now he was destroying it and her, or rather, she was letting him. She tapped out his number.

Steffie answered. 'Ash isn't here right now.'

'Have him call me when he has a moment.'

She opened the C.C. Raider file, but all the time she was listening for the phone and rehearsing her speech to Ash, her 'I understand that you feel bitter but can't we meet and discuss this like adults.'

The phone rang.

She answered.

'Olivia, it's Peter. Cord told me that we're working on the C.C. Raider deal and I was kind of expecting you to call me.'

'Come on up.' She walked down the corridor, helped herself to some orange juice and headed back towards her office.

'Hi.' A hand landed on her shoulder.

'Oh!' She dropped her juice. 'Peter, you gave me a fright.'

'I did? But you knew I was coming up.'

'I know.'

'You OK?'

'Of course I'm OK!' She didn't mean to snap but it came out that way, and for some reason she didn't apologise but carried on to talk of C.C. Raider, saying, 'You're to be my back-up.'

'You mean, once again I don't get to go to Europe?'

'I'll take Alice and Hutch.'

'They're only associates!'

'They're being promoted to principals.'

'I get it. I'm the fall boy on Wall Street – as usual. OK, so when do I get the draft of your plan?'

'I'm working on it right now.' She gave him a breezy smile. 'I need you, Peter. You're the best back-up there is.'

'Sure.'

He left. She frowned. Then she picked up Jack's preliminary analysis of the top hundred advertising agencies in Europe, but she was unable to concentrate. Every time she heard footsteps in the corridor she imagined it was Ash, every buzz on the telephone was a prelude to his abuse.

But he did not ring, and she went home to another sleepless night.

Two days later Peter stopped her in the corridor. 'How's the C.C. Raider draft coming on?'

'Stop hassling me, Peter!'

'OK, OK, calm down.'

She went into her office and closed the door. A moment later Teddy put a tentative head inside. 'You all right?'

'Yes. Why?'

'Peter said . . .'

'Why can't people mind their own business?'

'Forget I spoke.'

'I'm sorry, Teddy, I don't mean to snap.'

'Ash bugging you?'

'No . . . yes.'

'He's away for the next ten days. Tokyo.'

'He is?' She felt a weight lifted from her shoulders. In a week things would be different, he would have calmed down, water would have passed under the bridge. She picked up the phone. 'Peter, I'm sorry if I was . . . irritable.'

'Ash will be OK in a few weeks,' said Betsy, on hearing Olivia's story. 'Lots of people threaten things when they're upset but they don't really mean them. Teddy walked out on me when I was six months pregnant.'

'Teddy walked out on you!'

'We fought over the colour of the nursery. Sure, he came back after an hour – but for sixty minutes I was an abandoned wife, an abandoned pregnant wife!'

Olivia laughed with relief. 'You've done me the world of good, Bets. I don't know why I let myself get so hyped up.'

The children came in and they went on to talk of other things, but when Olivia left, Betsy said, 'I'm going to enjoy keeping my eyes open for a nice, amusing, attractive, rich . . .'

'I've had enough of men.'

'Until the next time.'

'No, forever.'

'Don't tell me Ash has put you off.'

'Oh, no, not Ash.'

'You mean . . . someone else?'

'Someone I knew long ago.' Olivia forced a smile. 'But it's over, I know that now, and I don't want to talk about it . . . please.'

She returned to Manhattan feeling refreshed, relaxed and ready for battle. On Monday she called a meeting of her team. 'We leave for Europe next week. We're going to put out feelers among UK ad. agencies, drop the odd hint – and see if any fish take the bait.'

'What if they don't?' asked Alice.

'Then we'll hook them.'

It was no coincidence that she planned to leave before Ash returned: it seemed a good idea to give him a further week without her. She remembered the rage and love she had once felt for Mark, and that made her understanding.

Olivia stepped from the helicopter into the cold of Kennedy Airport. 'Did you hold the plane?' she asked the airline official who rushed to escort her through passport control.

'Yes, Miss Steele.'

'My secretary on board?'

'Yes, Miss Steele.'

'Got all the papers, Hutch?'

'Sure, Olivia.'

'Luggage?'

'On the plane, Olivia.' Alice got her answer in quick.

They sailed through passport control and across the freezing tarmac to the huge rounded body of the jumbo, where the flight attendant was waiting to greet her. 'Glad to have you on board, Miss Steele.'

'Thank you.' She went up the stairs – fast – and took the front row. She always took the front, it meant you could disembark quicker on arrival.

Two businessmen further back watched as she took off her jacket and settled herself by the window.

'Olivia Steele.' Murmured one.

'Wonder which company she's after?'

'They call her "the lady raider".'

'I must say that . . .'

'Watch it! She's Ash Mallory's girl.'

'Not any more, according to Peter Hill. I lunched him yesterday.'

'My assistant works out at the same gym and says she keeps herself to herself – you know, tough, reserved.'

'Uhhu. Funny thing is, she doesn't look it, not close by.'

'It's that . . . mouth.'

'Sort of bruised looking.'

'I can imagine . . .'

'Fuck off, I've got work to do!'

Up front Olivia opened her briefcase. Her assistants did the same.

'Hutch, can you recheck these figures?'

'Sure.'

The plane hurried along the runway.

'Alice, give me Jack's latest analysis on the top twenty UK agencies.'

The plane rose into the air.

'What's the matter, Alice?'

'I'm looking for it.'

There was a dull thud as the undercarriage closed.

'I put it in my briefcase, I know I did, I remember . . .' The girl's face turned sickly green.

'Then where is it?'

'I don't know.'

'Alice!'

'I'm sorry . . . I'm . . .' Alice ran down the aisle, pushing aside the stewardess, whilst Hutch buried his nose firmly in his work. A moment later Alice returned, followed by an irate flight attendant who buckled her firmly into her seat. 'I'm truly sorry, Olivia, I don't know how I could have left it behind, I remember . . .'

'But you forgot to check.' Damn it, when she reached Heathrow she'd boot Alice straight on to the next plane home.

Seven hours later as they came into land, Olivia tidied her hair and patted some scent to her wrists and throat, admiring the silk sheen of her stockings as she uncrossed her legs. Pity that there was no man in her life to appreciate them. She glanced behind her at the rows of businessmen, many of whom were dozing with their mouths open. What was it that Jake used to say, that Italian expression, something to do with it's better to be on your own than with someone you don't like? He was right. Funny how often his advice came into her mind. She tried not to think of the terrace at Pietra Alta.

'Alice!'

'Yes, Olivia.' Alice looked as though she were about to be sick.

'Get those papers faxed over and stay by the machine till they've cleared. I don't want the entire population of London to know the details of our offer before we've made it.'

By the time Olivia reached her suite the phone was ringing. It was the head of C.C. Raider with some crazy idea about trying to buy Saatchis. 'The Saatchi brothers'll never sell,' Olivia told him. 'What's more, if you make them an offer shares in other agencies'll rocket because the word will be out that you're buying.' Then it was the *Financial Times*. 'Did she have any comment on . . .' 'No, she didn't.' Next it was Jack. 'That broad Alice ought to be fired. The papers were in her desk.' Then it was Hutch complaining, 'I know Jack's a brilliant analyst but that's no reason for him to treat us like snotty-nosed jerks.' 'Get one thing straight, Hutch,' Olivia told him, 'Jack stayed an analyst because he wanted it that way but he'd have made a better banker than you will ever be.'

Finally, it was Peter. 'Cord's pretty concerned about this breakdown in efficiency. He queries your decision to promote Alice to principal.'

Olivia took a deep breath. 'We'll discuss it when I return.'

Replacing the receiver, she thought, perhaps Peter is right, perhaps Alice isn't up to it, perhaps I was wrong, and she went through into the main sitting-room of their suite with the intention of sending Alice back to New York. But when she saw the blonde head bowed over a column of figures and the shoulders rigidly awaiting dismissal she seemed to see herself eight years earlier. What loyalty she would have shown Culross had they found it in them to give her a second chance!

'Alice.'

'Yes, Olivia.'

'Bring me those figures when you've analysed them.'

'Yes, Olivia.'

Within three days of being in London Olivia had found an agency which looked possible: Lidneys. It had bad management and a bad name, it needed something snappy, but there was talent among its young employees – talent and ambition. Whilst she was mulling over Lidneys' recent balance sheets, a man with a slight Scottish accent telephoned.

'Can I speak to you in confidence, Miss Steele?'

'That depends on what you want to talk about.'

'Lidneys.'

'Ah!'

'I . . . er . . . represent a number of the employees. We believe that you're acting for an American agency which might want to take us over.'

'And?'

'We want you to know that we would be in favour.'

She rang McCord. 'The goats are abandoning the sheep.'

He laughed. 'I thought it was the rats and the sinking ship! You going to move in on Lidneys now?'

'No, we'll wait. The market's got wind of our interest so the price is up.'

'Peter'll be disappointed.'

'What do you mean?'

'He's been talking up Lidneys to C.C. Raider and I believe he's in favour of an immediate purchase.'

'But he doesn't know the facts, Cord, and he's not that experienced in the European market.'

There was a short pause. 'How about lunch on Sunday?'

'Thanks, but I'm staying over for the weekend. I want to see my family.'

In the sitting-room she found Alice standing by the window looking out at the muggy sky, her face set in the expression people have when they've been furiously rehearsing a conversation. 'I'm sorry I let the team down,' she said.

'You let yourself down, Alice.'

'I know this will affect my . . . er . . . that this will count against me.'

'I can't report that you were a hundred per cent, but you have tried hard since.'

'You . . . you mean, I'm not going to get fired?'

'Not on my recommendation.'

'Olivia, I just don't know how to thank you, I . . .'

'Consider yourself lucky, Alice. Not everyone gets a second chance.'

She was in her room packing when the phone rang.

'Olivia, it's Teddy. Cord says you're not coming back for the meeting on Sunday.'

'What meeting?'

'In the morning! The C.C. Raider progress meeting. You

must know about it. Surely Peter told you.'

'No, he didn't.'

'Then take the next flight home. Ash is putting the word around that you've lost your touch and if you don't show up it will look as though he's right.'

'I suppose you've heard about the papers Alice left behind?'

'The whole bank's heard. You must be here to defend yourself. I'll meet your plane and brief you on the way in.'

As he spoke Olivia understood what she had not fully realised before – that as the girlfriend of Ash Mallory, who was related to McCord, she had been protected from much of the intrigue and back-stabbing. Now she was on her own and she had to stand strong. No, more than strong, she had to be superb because everyone expected Ash to get the better of her.

She rang her parents, steeling herself to their disappointment. 'Yes, Mummy, I know you were expecting me . . . of course I'm sorry . . . Mummy, if I don't go back now I may not have a job!'

Teddy met her at Kennedy Airport. She nearly cried with relief when she saw his cuddly, dependable figure standing by the barrier. On the way into Manhattan, she said, 'Cord didn't tell me about the meeting. Do you think he's taking Ash's side, after all they are related.

'Cord's not taking any side – and if he didn't mention the meeting it's because he presumed Peter had.'

'Peter being part of my team and me being team-leader?'

'Right.'

They crossed the East River and for a moment she was back on that wintry Saturday afternoon when she had first arrived in New York. 'So it's Ash, Sherry and possibly Peter against me,' she said looking up at the wooden water towers.

'Against us.' Teddy squeezed her hand.

'Thanks.' She returned the pressure. 'And McCord?'

'He'll support the victor if it comes to a fight.'

'It is a fight.'

Later, when he dropped her at the attic, she said, 'The one that really hurts is Peter.'

'Yeah – after all, he was in our bullpen.'

On Sunday morning Olivia arrived early at William & Wall. In the banking hall she met Peter.

'I didn't know you were coming back today,' he said.

'No, I know.' She saw the wariness in his eyes and added casually, 'I only decided to come at the last moment. It seemed sensible to put the case for Lidneys myself.'

'Sure.'

Ash did not look at Olivia when she entered the boardroom. He kept his eyes on Sherry and carried on talking, quietly, confidently, his gaze not even flickering when she settled on the opposite side of the large oval table, between Teddy and Russ, with Peter hovering at the far end. But he did look up when Spencer McCord came in – they all did.

'Glad to see you back, Olivia,' said McCord.

'I decided it was pertinent.'

He nodded, and she knew that to have stayed away would have been disastrous. She stood to address the meeting, itemising the advantages to C.C. Raider of acquiring Lidneys, then listing her reasons for not going for an immediate purchase.

'How can you be so sure that the dollar will strengthen?' asked Sherry.

'The signs are that the pound will drop.'

'But who's to say Lidneys' shares will fall back?'

'I think they will. They've been static for years.'

'And increased on rumour of C.C. Raider's bid?' Peter adjusted his spectacles.

'Rumours of *a* bid – they didn't get the name.'

'I agree with Olivia,' said McCord. 'I've studied Lidneys and, bar some other company making an offer for them which is unlikely, I reckon the shares will drop back within two months – and that's when we go for them.'

To Olivia's surprise, Ash said, 'I think Cord's right – but one aspect puzzles me.' He looked straight at her.

'Yes?'

'How come if your trip was confidential did these guys at Lidneys get wind of it?'

'The name of our client was confidential, the trip wasn't. The whole point was to bait the hook to see if the fish took. And they did. The fact that Lidneys do not know we were acting for C.C. Raider proves that my team was discreet.' She forced her voice to remain steady and not to reflect her anger, for his accusation did not relate to Lidneys but to the past, and they both knew it.

To Olivia's intense relief, Lidneys' shares dropped back by late February and C.C. Raider, who had been impatiently champing at the bit, moved in for the kill.

'Well done,' said McCord, as they returned from a celebratory lunch.

'Thanks. I must say that when they hadn't dropped at all by the beginning of the year I was beginning to wonder if I'd been over-optimistic.'

'You're an intuitive risk-taker, like me, Olivia.' He patted her on the shoulder. 'Is it too soon for you and Ash to work together?'

'Give us a few more months.'

'But everything's OK between you?'

'Oh, yes, fine.'

The next morning she was woken very early by the telephone. Gingerly she reached for it.

'Hey, kid, where are the Falkland Islands?'

'Freddie, it's . . . five o'clock in the morning!'

'Where are they?'

'How the hell should I know! Oh, near Scotland I suppose. No, wait a minute, that's the Orkneys. Why?'

'Because Britain's at war with Argentina over the Falklands.'

She flicked a switch and the television came up with a map of the South Atlantic, followed by a shot of Mrs Thatcher leaving Downing Street, then to the streets of London where the British were learning names like South Georgia and Exocet. She wondered what Mark thought of it all and resisted the temptation to phone him, speaking instead to her parents and to Gwen, but that did not stop her from thinking of him and feeling a strange sense of isolation – an isolation which continued throughout the weeks of evenings when she would watch the fighting on the television and find it hard to believe this was not just another war film.

32

It was June by the time Olivia was next in England. She spent a couple of days looking into another advertising agency – C.C. Raider's appetite had been whetted – before hiring a car and driving out to Newbury. As she drew up in front of her parents' mock Tudor house – which somehow didn't irritate her as it used to – she was aware, for the first time, that they would probably die whilst she was away. One day McCord or Teddy or Sally would knock on the door of her office and say 'I've some bad news . . . your mother . . . your father . . .'

'Do you think you'll always live in America?' her father asked as they walked slowly around the garden – she noticed that he walked slowly now.

'I don't know.' She watched a butterfly settle on a big yellow daisy and listened to the hum of an English summer. 'On a day like this I tell myself I could be happy here but . . .' The butterfly flew away. 'I enjoy what I do. I need challenge in my life – and I get that challenge on Wall Street. You and Mum must come and visit me.'

'Oh, it's rather a long way for us and I don't care for cities.' He paused to pick a dead leaf from a lupin. 'Then there's your mother's work with the handicapped children – and we're not adventurous people like you, Livvi.'

'Is it a question of . . .?' In New York she'd have said it straight: money.

'Oh, no, though we have been giving a little help to Fiona and Hugo. Ah, here they come, I recognise Fiona's car. Hugo's had to sell his, so they only have one now. Between you and me, he's used most of the money from the sale of their Dorking

398

house to repair that wretched place he's inherited. If he'd had any sense he'd have sold it.'

Fiona came out through the French windows. She looked tense and unhappy, and was wearing the same cotton dress of small dead flowers floating on a muddy puddle which she had been wearing when Olivia arrived at Dorking in the wake of the Culross scandal. 'Hello, Olivia,' she said, 'You do look smart. Daddy, you're walking around too much, you must sit down. Olivia, this is only Newbury, you know, or had you forgotten how normal people dress.'

'No, of course not, but I was on a business trip and . . .'

'Hugo, fetch Daddy's rug. No, not the one inside, the one over there by the rose bush. Honestly!'

'Where are the children?' asked Olivia, when they had sat down in a semi-circle of deckchairs.

'Hardly children any more! Charlie's doing his O levels next year and Phoebe's at secretarial college in London. Oh, I know you'll think she ought to do more with herself.'

'Fiona, I haven't said a word.'

'No, but you always think everyone ought to go to university and become president of a huge company.'

Olivia opened her mouth to give a stinging reply but her father gripped her arm and shook his head, his tired periwinkle eyes pleading with her.

'Phoebe wants to be a model,' said Hugo to fill the silence.

'Then I think it's a jolly good idea that she's doing a secretarial course,' said Olivia, disliking Fiona intensely at that moment. 'It would give her something to fall back on between jobs. Daddy, those roses are beautiful. They remind me of the ones you had at Dorking, Fiona.'

'We sold that house. We live in Hugo's old home – or had you forgotten?'

'No, of course I hadn't, I just meant that you always make your gardens so beautiful.'

'I haven't succeeded with the present one, but we don't have money to spend on plants any more.' She studied Olivia's sunflower yellow silk shirt belted over a straight white skirt and her yellow and white shoes whose heels had dug holes in the mossy grass. 'You always were a clothes-alcoholic, Olivia, but then of course you make so much money and only have yourself to spend it on.' She stood up. 'I suppose I will have to help mother with the lunch — as no one else has offered to.'

Later, when Hugo and Fiona had left and Olivia and her father were watching the television news, he said. 'Be careful what you say to your mother about Fiona. She's so upset by their problems. If only Hugo could be made to lower his sights where jobs are concerned, but he won't, so he can't get one. Fiona's worried, although I do think she could control her temper a bit.' He patted Olivia's arm. 'Your mother told me that you helped her write the letter to Fiona and I was glad. You two haven't always seen eye to eye and . . .' he stopped and looked embarrassed, patted her arm again, and said, 'It's time for a nice glass of sherry before dinner.' He shuffled out of the room, calling, 'Marjorie, dear, a teeny gin and tonic or something stronger?'

Olivia went to the window. Evening shadows stretched across the front of the house. Someone was cutting a lawn, the motor went up and down and up and down the unseen grass with monotonous regularity. On the other side of the road a game of tennis was in progress. She could hear the hollow sound of the ball, then a call, 'Good shot. Thirty-love.' On the television the announcer was saying that tomorrow would be hot and dry, that John Hinckley had been acquitted of attempted assassination of President Reagan on the grounds of insanity, and that Britain would have to spend millions of pounds in defence of the Falklands.

'Dreadful, isn't it?' said her father coming back with the sherry decanter.

'Yes.' She didn't know if he meant John Hinckley or the Falklands.

'You're leaving tomorrow morning?'

'Yes, I catch an afternoon flight but I want to see an old friend in London first.'

'Not . . . Mark?'

'No.'

'I was very sorry that you and he . . .' He stopped, and an awkward silence came between them.

It was several years since Olivia had seen Maggie. At first it had been her own fault, but recently every time she had telephoned Maggie was either in hospital or what Zach referred to as 'under treatment' and 'not in the mood for speaking to anyone', so eventually Olivia had given up. There seemed little point in pursuing the friendship. But on this Monday morning she was determined to see Maggie once more, however painful her reception might be.

The house in North Kensington was more dilapidated than she remembered and the azalea by the iron gate even more rampant, its sprawling pink flowers heavy on branches which drooped right across the pathway. Olivia smoothed down her orange silk skirt and adjusted the shoulder pads of her orange and black striped jacket. It had looked terrific in New York, it looked terrific in Park Lane, but hovering outside Maggie's unpainted front door she felt like an overdressed bumble bee, a feeling exacerbated – or perhaps caused – by Fiona's remarks of the previous day. From somewhere in the house came the thud of reggae music. She began to wish she hadn't come. She rang the bell. The noise echoed through the house. She waited. No one came. She rang again. A door slammed. Footsteps. Then the front door opened very slowly and Maggie stood there, her elfin face white and drawn, her hands twisting in the hem of her oversize black tee shirt.

'Maggie, I know you probably don't want to see me but . . .'
'Zach left me.'
'Oh, no!'
They fell into each other's arms and by the time they were coherent enough to speak they were in the kitchen, Olivia perching on the refectory table, Maggie making coffee on the open range.
'When did he leave?' asked Olivia.
'Ten months ago.'
'Ten months! Why didn't you tell me?'
'I couldn't.' Maggie lit a cigarette – she had one already burning in the ashtray and another balanced on the window sill. 'I just couldn't talk about it because if I did that made it a reality.'
'Why did he go?'
'I drove him away. I was so desperate to have a baby that I couldn't think of anything else. I wasn't interested in Zach or Savvies or anything, I just wanted to get pregnant. I went on and on pushing him to have tests, I turned him into a machine,

401

a sort of unsatisfactory reproduction machine – or that's what he said – but do you know, I was so desperate I was past caring. Have you ever wanted a child, Olivia?'

'No . . . yes, yes, I suppose I have – but only with Mark, and not just to have a baby but to have part of him.'

'It began like that for me with Zach, but no one can understand how utterly useless a woman feels when she can't have a baby.'

'Was it your fault?'

'It wasn't either of our faults, or so the doctor said, it was just that Zach and I somehow couldn't . . .'

'What about a test tube baby?'

'That's what I was pushing for when . . . when . . . oh, God!' She lit another cigarette.

A door opened upstairs and heavy footsteps sounded on the uncarpeted stairs. A tousled head appeared. 'You OK, Maggs?'

'I'm fine.'

The head disappeared. Olivia raised an eyebrow.

'No.' Maggie gave her a weak smile. 'My lodger – one of my three lodgers. I need the cash. I sold Savvies to Zach. Well, there wasn't much left to sell if I'm honest and if he hadn't taken it over it would have gone bankrupt. Now I stick to designing. They pay me by the piece. Sanjiv pays me. Yes, he's still there. But the trouble is I've been so . . . low that I can't think about clothes, so I don't earn much.'

A large marmalade cat came in through the window and perched beside her, and began to wash itself with the meticulous rhythmic movements which cats adopt.

'You've still got Cat?'

'Yes, my faithful Cat.'

Olivia took out her cheque book. 'Let me lend you some money.'

'No, but thanks. I have to make it on my own – and if the worst comes to the worst, I have mother. She's got another Gianni in tow, but she's still my mother, as she keeps saying whenever she comes around to tell me what to do with my life.' She lit another cigarette. 'What a mess!'

Looking around at the kitchen Olivia remembered the hopes with which Zach and Maggie had bought this house.

'Do you remember that afternoon in Anataxos when we talked about men.'

'Yes. Then I met Zach and you met Mark.'

'Ummm.'

'Do you miss Mark?'

'Yes. You're the only one I admit it to, but I do.'

'What about your American boyfriend?'

'That's over. Do you miss Zach?'

'Every day.'

'Every night?'

'Every hour.'

'Shit.'

'Yes. Feelings are shit.'

Maggie moved to the safety of the dark recess beside the stove. 'The other reason why I didn't tell you Zach had left me is that you're so . . . strong, so . . . successful, so glamorous.' She lifted her hands to her hair which had always been fun and spiky but now looked like a flattened porcupine. 'I rang you one day, one of those days when you said you'd be in London, and the receptionist answered, "Miss Steele is not in her suite at the moment." I was sitting here, with Cat on my lap, crying, and I thought how can I speak to a Miss Steele who lives in a suite?'

'You're nuts!'

'It's true. Isn't it, Cat? Cat says yes. You see, you left Mark and went to New York and got a job and found a new life and never cried on my shoulder, so how could I drag you through every whinge and moan of my collapsing marriage?'

'Because I'm your friend, you lunatic.'

'Lunatic!' Maggie shrieked with laughter. 'Lunatic. No one but you would dare say that to someone who has just spent the past three years being soft-talked by shrinks. People aren't even allowed to tell me I'm unstable – but lunatic! Oh, I haven't laughed like this for ages. Tell me, how am I going to get Zach back? Oh, that sounds like those pathetic women who write to Agony Aunts saying, "My husband left me twenty-five years ago and I haven't heard from him since – do you think he still loves me? Yours Everloving from Evesham." But I do believe he still cares and I do think, although I hardly dare say so out loud, that if only I could be half of what I was when he met me – preferably not the Queen-of-the-two-night-stand half – I could get him back. Oh, why can't I fall in love with myself then I would never leave me?'

Olivia laughed till tears ran down her cheeks. Maggie was pacing up and down like an emaciated doll, stamping her feet in fury. 'You haven't changed,' she said, 'It's only that you've convinced yourself you're a failure. I've got the perfect solution. You're coming to New York for a holiday – today.'

'I'd love to but . . .'

'I'm treating you. Where's the phone?'

'I don't have the right clothes.'

'I'll buy you some. Olivia located the telephone and dialled British Airways.

'What about Cat?'

'Your lodger can feed him. I want a second seat on this afternoon's Concorde flight to New York charged to my American Express card number . . .'

'Cat doesn't like him.'

'Damn Cat!'

Maggie came alive in New York – and New York rekindled itself for Olivia in the same way as it had done during Jake's first visit: that other New York. Central Park on a hot Saturday afternoon, Greenwich Village on a balmy evening, rickety stools along the bar at Chumleys, and Freddie in Dean and Deluca ordering enough food to satisfy an army. Of course Olivia had to work – and had to work just as hard – but she tried to forget about William & Wall when she hurried home to eat Maggie's spaghetti bolognese at the round white table or to drift through the hot streets to one of the sidewalk cafés.

'You work too hard,' Maggie told her, one evening when she did not arrive home until nearly midnight.

'I enjoy it – most of the time.'

'But not as much as you did?'

'I'm going through a tough patch. Pyramids get smaller at the top and not everyone can be promoted, that sort of hassle.'

'And what's his name . . . Ash?'

'He's civil if he has to be, but I don't trust him and I can't explain why.'

'But you've given up on Culross.'

'Oh, no, I'll never give up that one. I still dream of getting my own back one day.'

'There are other things in life apart from work,' said Freddie, coming into the room.

'What?'

'Men.'

'Men are . . .' they tickled him until he cried for mercy.

Maggie stayed a month. She arrived a white-faced waif and left a bright-eyed sunkissed urchin. As a parting gift Olivia bought her an icecream pink safari suit from Parachute: it had a wide belt and looked shapeless but somehow managed to touch at all the right places.

'I called Zach,' Maggie confessed on their last evening. 'I wasn't going to but then this afternoon . . .' she gave a hopeless grin . . . 'I just wanted him to see me before I deteriorate. He's meeting me at the airport.'

'You're not going to deteriorate.'

Maggie lit a cigarette and perched on the window ledge. 'I don't know what I'd do without you. That day when you turned up I was ready to do myself in. I had woken up that morning and felt I couldn't go on. Then you brought me here.' She looked around at the bright attic, with her sofa-bed in one corner of the sitting-room and the table piled high with her new clothes.

Olivia joined her at the window. 'We mustn't ever stop being friends.'

'Never.'

'Look, there's Freddie. What a pity we can't fall in love with someone nice like Freddie.'

Maggie leaned her arm on Olivia's shoulder. 'I went to bed with him the other afternoon. I was downstairs looking at his tapes and . . . it sort of happened. And you know what I really appreciate? He never tried it again and he's just the same to me since. With most guys the fact he hasn't tried again would make me feel cheap . . . rejected, but not with Freddie. He made me feel cherished and wanted.'

'He did the same for me when I first came here. Things were

very tough at work and he was having a bad time with his ex-wife, so we shared my bed – but I burst into tears so nothing happened. He still made me feel good . . . wanted – and he never tried again.'

'Funny,' said Maggie, 'he's the only guy since I met Zach and I don't feel guilty.'

'We should marry Freddie.'

'Both of us?'

'Of course.'

They giggled as they watched him wander up the street, peering into art galleries scratching his head and moving on, his sixties Easy Rider shades hiding his eyes, his Easy Rider lope covering the hot cobbled street.

Maggie left for London next morning, Olivia for Washington. By the late afternoon she was back in Manhattan, her limousine crawling through the traffic-clogged streets, heading for Wall Street. She fanned herself with a newspaper and tried not to think about the heat which would increase daily until it reached the pitch when the air-conditioning in the attic would founder to combat it. Perhaps she should move to the Upper East Side. Teddy and McCord said she was mad to stay where she was. A vice president living in an attic with no lift! She met McCord in the corridor. He told her that Caran, Coates, Raider had decided to purchase the UK agency she'd recommended. 'Australia, that's their next goal. They're determined to be the biggest agency in the world. I told them Saatchis are ahead but . . .' he laughed, and Olivia laughed with him, excited by the buzz of a new deal. 'You think you can handle it?' he asked.

'Handle what?'

'Working with Ash – after all, he's our Australian expert.'

'I see. Well, yes, I'm sure we'll be all right.'

'Ash thinks otherwise.'

'What do you mean?'

'Just that. He reckons you should be taken off C.C. Raider and that he and Sherry should work on the deal.'

'Cord, that's ridiculous, I've been on C.C. Raider from the start.'

'But you're not as familiar with the Sydney market as Ash.'

'OK, but I know my client.'

'And you think I'm letting Ash score points over you?'

She said nothing. She felt sick with anger.

'Of course you do, Olivia, but I'm not. I'm only thinking of William & Wall. The deal comes first.'

She went into her office and closed the door, knowing that somehow she had lost a fight without having been aware that she was in the battle until it was too late. In that instant she did not just hate Ash, she hated Cord.

Over lunch she poured out her anger to Teddy, who listened patiently, forking up mouthfuls of lasagna. 'Cord's right,' he said. 'Don't tell Betsy that I eat pasta for lunch or she'll put me on a diet again.'

'No, of course I won't! Teddy, why do you say that Cord's right?'

'Because Ash is the most experienced Sydney operator in the bank and therefore he's the obvious choice. Not to put him on the C.C. Raider deal would be bad for business.' He ate another mouthful. 'Olivia, you're getting to be over-emotional.'

'I am not!'

'You are. You remember that principal, the one who threw herself under . . .'

'Barbara? Teddy, I'm not like that. How dare you!'

'I dare because I'm your friend.'

She pushed aside her spinach salad. Teddy went on eating. 'I can't stand the idea that Ash imagines he's got one over me.'

'It's you who are giving him his victory by being so uptight.'

'Next you'll be saying I'm losing my grip.'

He ate in silence.

She remembered the terrace at Pietra Alta and Mark saying, 'You do the wrong thing a lot of the time but no one else has the courage to tell you so,' and she leaned across the table and pinched Teddy's chubby cheek. 'You're a real buddy. Thanks for the truth.'

He smiled. 'You know, Betsy always says that with my common sense and your flair . . .'

Crossing the banking hall on her way back from lunch, Olivia met McCord and Ash. She stopped, smiled, looked straight at Ash, and said, 'I'm glad you're taking over the

Australian deal. Let me know if you'd like to see my C.C. Raider notes.' She was in the lift and heading for the twenty-second floor before either man had a chance to react.

It wasn't until Olivia reached home that evening that she realised how much she was going to miss Maggie. She stood in the middle of the silent attic suffocating in the trapped air, she threw open the windows and was blasted by the heat, she turned up the air-conditioning so high that it rattled, she went into the bedroom and stared at the empty space in her cupboard where the coat hangers which Maggie had used swung free. Then she kicked off her shoes, stripped off her clothes, and stepped under the shower, relishing that moment when the cold water hit her bare back.

Cool and refreshed at last, she wrapped herself in a towel and wandered through to the sitting-room. On the round table were a couple of invitations – to an art exhibition, to the opera, to a cocktail party 'Dress Thirties'. She opened her diary. Tomorrow she was having her hair cut, the next day she was invited to the opening of a new boutique, the day after she was having dinner with clients – but tonight? She put on a tee shirt and a pair of ice blue peddle-pushers with white sneakers which showed off her suntanned legs and went downstairs. Freddie was out. So were Brad and Sandra. So was Dulcie. She returned to the attic, took out her diary, and studied the lists of people she knew – but there was no one except Teddy and Betsy who she could call at ten o'clock at night and say 'I'm Olivia and I'm lonely.' All these people would be astonished. Glamorous, successful Olivia Steele lonely! The 'Lady Raider' hanging around with nothing to do! The girl that dumped Ash Mallory without a man! Then they would ask themselves, 'Why should she think I'm free at the drop of a hat? What does she think's the matter with me?' No, there weren't many real friends, like Maggie and Freddie and Teddy and Betsy – and Jake.

The fridge was empty. There was no milk. Her cleaner was due tomorrow. She wrote out a list of groceries for the woman to buy, then stood on the fire escape and watched couples walk up and down Spring Street. The night was balmy and exciting. The streets buzzed with life and laughter. She set off for the Village, walking purposefully, her bag tucked firmly under her

408

arm, her hands in the pockets of her peddle-pushers.

'Seen Freddie this evening?' she asked at Chumleys.

'Not tonight.'

'Brad and Sandra?'

'Uhhhu.'

She tried Minetta's, but they weren't there either, so she went to the gym. The black guy who ran the place came forward with a big grin, his gait like a leopard, his muscular arms moving in time to 'I Heard It Through The Grapevine'. 'Hi, Olivia, where've you been?' He did a backflip, and his body rippled black beneath his white satin shorts.

'Working hard, Johnny, you know how it is.'

'It doesn't do to neglect your body.' He pinched her upper arm. 'You need to work out regular. You used to. What happened?'

'Pressures.'

'A man?'

'Work.'

'A man – and you work too hard.'

She climbed on to the exercise bicycle. 'That, coming from a New Yorker!'

He climbed on to the bike beside her. 'OK, ten minutes. Keep those legs moving! Yeah, that's neat.'

Ten minutes later she was lying on her stomach lifting weights with her feet, her head thrown back, her calf muscles straining.

'Don't stop breathing!' shouted Johnny. 'No, no more weight. You haven't been here for weeks. You don't wanna strain yourself.'

'Oh, yes I do.'

'You need sex, man, I can see it in your eyes.'

'Who needs sex, Johnny?'

'Hi, Ben . . .'

Olivia was trying to remember where she had seen those blackbird eyes and heard that voice with its Brooklyn street-wise twang.

'Who's the lady, Johnny? Introduce me! OK, I know it isn't a pick-up joint.'

Johnny was laughing and moving with the music. 'You mustn't annoy the ladies. Olivia, shall I tell him to . . .'

'Olivia! Olivia Steele! I invited you to lunch five . . . six years ago and you never called me.'

She sat up 'Ben Steiner! I needed the lunch then, when I was out of work – not now when I can buy my own.'

He held out his hand. She shook it. He said, 'How was I to know you were going to make the fast track?'

'You should have given me a chance.'

'You're smart. No wonder you didn't want to be my assistant.'

'You mean dogsbody!'

He laughed. 'I was serious about lunch – and I'd have called you, only word on the Street was that you were sharing your lunches with Ash Mallory.'

'I was.'

'Not any more?'

'If you don't know the answer to that then your grapevine needs repairing.'

'Why not make it dinner – tonight?'

She hesitated, then she replied, 'Why not?' and walked over to the chest press, settled herself on the stool and slowly lifted the steel bar, forcing her arms up taut, her muscles aching under the poundage. Ben took up the position opposite her. She lifted thirty pounds. He lifted fifty. She added another ten, her arms silently screaming. Ben watched, and added twenty.

'Hey you guys, have you gone crazy?' shouted Johnny from across the room. 'Olivia, if you wanna kill yourself don't do it here – you'll give the gym a bad name. Don't look nice to have corpses lying around the place.'

'Thanks, Johnny, I thought you liked me for myself.'

'I would – if you came here regular.'

'You're lucky she comes at all,' said Ben. 'I offered her a job when she first arrived in New York. She was broke, she knew no one, and guess what? She turned me down. She said she wanted something better.'

'But is she still turning you down, man?'

'Honestly, you men!'

'I thought you were coming here to work out, Olivia, not to get laid.'

Before she had a chance to reply, Ben said, 'You told her she

410

needed sex.' He took Olivia by the hand, 'We're going to the sauna.'

She undressed, took a shower, wrapped a towel around herself and padded through into the sauna which was laid out with all the decadent luxury of the Roman Empire, with marble *chaises longues* around lapis lazuli pools of bubbling water, and mosaics on the walls depicting everything from athletics to Bacchanalian orgies. Ben was waiting for her in one of the alcoves. He was wearing just a small white towel, and he watched her approach with his blackbird eyes full of humour and adventure.

She sat down beside him, wondering suddenly whether she was mad: she did not need complications in her life. She'd built a high barrier around herself and did not want it broken down.

He ran his forefinger down her arm. 'You're a punchy lady. I'm glad you made the fast track.' He ran his forefinger up her arm. 'But I'm sorry you didn't stop with me, we'd have had fun.'

'I think,' she said, looking him straight in the eyes, 'it's a good thing I didn't.'

'Is that so?'

'Yes.'

'Why?'

'Because we might not have got too much work done.'

He put his arm around her hot shoulders. 'Sex and money are the only things which keep this city going. You hire a lot of bright guys, pay them a fortune, hire some goodlooking broads to . . . OK, don't hit me! No, stop it!' He grabbed her wrists and drew her to him, saying, 'I wanted to make you angry, I like it when you're mad.'

Over his shoulder two girls and a man were studiously ignoring them.

'We're not alone,' she said.

'I know.' He pushed her damp hair back from her face.

Her breasts beneath their towel were hard against his arm, her skin wet against his. Rivers of sweat ran down her arms and legs. She wanted him. The steam rose through vents in the floor. She could not wait to touch him. Her towel slipped down her back.

Two women came in. They sat down nearby and began to

411

discuss the price of real estate in Tribeca, the newly trendy area near Canal Street, in the kind of loud encompassing voices which people use when they want audience participation.

'Let's go,' said Ben.

'Yes, let's.'

They separated, showered, and met to share a fruit juice in the palm-filled bar.

'If those damned women hadn't come along . . .'

'I've a feeling Johnny might have checked up on us.'

He took her hand and turned it over. 'What soft palms you have.'

'All the better to feel you with.'

'Which reminds me – not that it has been far from my mind . . .'

He hailed a cab and as soon as it set off he pulled her to him and she responded, opening up to him, wanting, hardly able to wait till they reached his apartment before she was fighting with the buckle of his trousers and he was ripping her ice-blue pedal-pushers from her hips.

It was very early when she left for home, ignoring Ben's sleepy protests, to walk through the dawn, that brief moment during the day when the streets were cool and the air almost crisp. She crossed Washington Square, avoiding the homeless on their benches, and cut down to West Houston, finding herself on the very corner where she had seen the confident fur-jacketed girls hailing cabs on her first afternoon in New York. How long ago it seemed. How naive and frightened she'd been. She smiled at the memory and walked on.

Outside the flower shop the Vietnamese boy was kneeling before a pile of white daisies. He took one, smoothed its petals, then took another. Olivia stopped in front of him. 'How much?'

He held up four fingers.

She handed him the money. He twisted the flowers deftly in a sheet of paper. She thanked him. He nodded. She walked on up the street. At the crossroads she glanced back. He was smoothing the four dollar bills on the pavement with the same gentle care as he had smoothed the petals of the daisies.

By the time Olivia had climbed the stairs to the attic she was hot so she had another shower, rubbing herself dry as she set the coffee grinder in motion. Then she selected a lemon yellow linen suit. It looked fresh and cool. She wriggled into the skirt and padded through into the bathroom to apply a light touch of mascara. The mirror told its tale. There was a glow about her today which had been lacking. Her eyes sparkled and her cheeks had that indefinable pinkness. She felt stretched and warm and animal. She thought of Ben and licked her lips. Animal, that's what he was. Small, hard, thrusting, dark-eyed – and animal.

The bell rang. She picked up her bag and jacket and went down, to where her driver was holding open the door to her air-conditioned stretch limo, where her newspapers were carefully laid out on the back seat and her secretary held out the phone to her: London was on the line.

Ben sent her two dozen yellow roses.

'A Texan oil millionaire?' asked Teddy, seeing them on her desk.

'Oh, you mean "The Yellow Rose of . . ." ' She smiled enigmatically.

'OK, I'm prying, but us happily married fathers of three like to fantasise about you glamorous bachelor girls.'

'Behave yourself Teddy or I'll report you to Betsy!'

She rang Maggie. 'Zach met you . . . and it's all terrific . . . you're still in bed! Oh, sorry I forgot the time difference . . . I sound happy? No, of course I miss you, Maggie, but it just so happens that last night . . . No, no, it's not Freddie.'

Ben called in the afternoon. 'How about tonight?'

'I can't, I'm working on a big deal and we've a late meeting.'

'Tomorrow?'

'Yes – but not till nine.'

'You're a busy lady.'

'The roses are beautiful. I haven't thanked you yet but . . . everyone here thinks I must have a Texan oil millionaire.'

'In a stetson.'

'Which he never takes off.'

'Not even in bed?'

She chuckled. 'I'll see you tomorrow.'

Ben was just what she needed – she liked him and she was

413

attracted to him but there would never be an emotional cage here.

Still with that indefinable pinkness in her cheeks she went to see Jack. 'I want you to make all our information on C.C. Raider available to Ash and his team,' she told him.

'You're kidding!'

'Nope.' She perched on the edge of his desk and ruffled his dark hair, which was not quite as dark or thick as it had been. 'No, Jack, I'm serious. Ash is taking over the Australian deal – and the deal comes first.'

He raised his hand in a mock salute. 'That sounds more like my Olivia and this,' he touched her cheek, 'looks just like my Olivia.'

In the corridor she came face to face with Sherry, who said, with a triumphant smirk, 'I hear you're pretty cut up about being taken off the C.C. Raider deal.'

'Then you've heard wrong, Sherry – or maybe you've been told wrong. I'm delighted that Ash is involved. He's the obvious choice. In fact,' she paused to add weight to her words, 'I have just instructed Jack to make all our information available to him.'

On the following evening she met Ben in a restaurant near his apartment – they only ate one course before hurrying back to his place, to make love until the early hours. This time she bought yellow daisies from the inscrutable Vietnamese boy.

Late on Friday afternoon Ben called her. 'I have to pull out of tonight, I'm truly sorry but my wife's coming up to town.'

'Your . . . I didn't know you were married.'

'You didn't?'

'No.'

'I'd have told you if you'd asked me.'

'I just presumed you weren't.'

'It doesn't make any difference to us, Olivia. She and I lead separate lives. She stays out at Southampton all summer.'

She told herself firmly that Ben was right, it made no difference; after all, she didn't want to marry him so did it matter if he were married to someone else? But it did matter, of course it did.

On Monday she flew up to Boston, on Tuesday she dined

414

with clients, on Wednesday she left for Paris, returning to New York on Friday morning. Ben was expecting to see her that evening, but at the last moment she had to return to Boston: she was in the air before she remembered she hadn't called him and it was late by the time she got near a phone.

'I'm disappointed but I understand,' he said. 'I've got a lot of work on too, in fact I'm staying in tow for the weekend. How about tomorrow night?'

'Ben, I'd love to . . .' Suddenly her eye was caught by a line in the *Financial Times*:

Rumour of director infighting causes lack of confidence in Culross. Shares down from 350 to 260 in two months

'What did you say?' he asked.

'Er . . . nothing, I was just checking my diary. I'm due with Teddy and Betsy this weekend, in fact I'm going straight there from Boston.'

'Pity, I've . . . er . . . squared things with my wife to stay in town. You wouldn't cancel them?'

'No, I would not. Betsy and Teddy are my greatest friends.'

'How about next Monday?'

'Call me in the afternoon.'

The first thing Betsy said when they were alone was, 'Who's the Texan?'

'Oh, just someone I've met.'

'Teddy says your office is like a flower shop.'

'Teddy's a gossip.'

'OK, point taken. It's a secret. What about Ash? Are things going better there or is that also a secret?'

'Outwardly they're better.' Olivia watched a red squirrel burying nuts in the garden. 'But I can't get over the feeling that there's a knifeman waiting in the shadows.'

On Monday morning she arrived at work to find a further dozen yellow roses on her desk and that night Ben asked her, 'Is it because I'm married that you don't want to see too much of me?'

She rolled over and looked at him. 'I don't like the fact you're married, it takes the romance out of the adventure.'

'Adventure! Thanks! Some women find forbidden fruits very exciting.'

415

'True. But you being married isn't the main reason why I won't see more of you.'

'Oh?'

'I just don't want to get emotionally involved – with you or with anyone.'

He stroked her cheek. 'You're a tough nut to crack.'

She covered his mouth with hers. 'Don't try.'

Ash was the last to know about the Texan: not even Sherry had dared tell him.

'So you've found yourself a millionaire,' he said, stopping Olivia in the corridor. 'Do I know him?'

'I've no idea.'

'But it is true?'

'What?'

'That you are seeing another man?' His eyes were flat and her instinct was to deny or prevaricate, but she knew that she had to square up to him. 'Now that you and I are no longer together,' she said, 'I don't think it's any concern of yours who I go out with – and vice versa.'

'If you think that,' he looked her up and down, 'you're mistaken.'

She went into her office. It was half an hour before she was calm enough to do some work and two days before she could say to herself that Ash was only bluffing.

Olivia had been seeing Ben for some months. He pressed to meet her more often, but she refused, just as she refused to take him anywhere as her official escort. When he asked why, she replied, 'I don't want everyone talking about us.'

'Because I'm married? Olivia, you're a hypocrite!'

'No, I merely avoid scandal – and so would you if you'd been the focus of one.'

'Culross.' He put his arms around her. 'Can't forget, can you?'

'Never.'

Nine months to the day after she and Ben had become lovers he took her to dinner at The Quilted Giraffe and, pushing aside

416

the outrageously romantic table flowers, he confessed, 'I only intended us to be a one night stand. That was all I wanted. That was the way I lived – till you came along.' He took her hand and turned it over. 'Do you remember I said "What soft palms you have" and you said "all the better to feel you with." I should have known then that you were warm and funny and lovable.'

'Ben,' she said, very gently, 'it's your choice to see me.'

'Oh, I know and that is the reason. You see, I could really fall for you, Olivia Steele, but . . .'

'You've got a wife and a kid.'

'And an ex-wife and two kids.'

'Would you prefer we didn't meet at all?'

'I almost but not quite wish I hadn't gone to the gym that evening. The last thing I wanted was to feel something for someone.' He paused while the waiter brought their lobster.

She dipped one of the scallops in the mustard cream sauce.

'Tell me something,' he watched her intently, 'what happened with you and Ash Mallory?'

'Oh, we drifted apart.'

'I heard he was real cut up.'

'I was very fond of Ash but in the long run we weren't suited.'

'So you didn't ditch him for another guy?'

'No.'

'I heard you did.'

'Who told you that?'

'The same Street gossip that says Ash was cut up. You're an infamous lady, Olivia Steele.'

She thought of Mark. No, she hadn't ditched Ash for Mark, she'd simply been unable to commit herself to Ash because of what she'd known with Mark.

She shrugged and carried on eating.

'Was there another guy?'

'Ben, what is this? The third degree?'

He gripped her wrist fiercely. 'I have to know.'

'Why?'

'Because I don't want to end up in the shit like Ash Mallory.' He released her and leaned back. 'I have a theory about you – and I've had a hell of a lot of time to think it out, on those nights when you couldn't make it. Waiting's a lonely game.'

417

'I know.'

'That's what I thought.'

The waiter came. She did not want anything else, but Ben insisted she had strawberries, although it was winter and they were out of season – or perhaps because.

'Want to hear my theory?'

'I'd rather not.'

'It's called indirect revenge. Some women only really love one man, but because things don't work out with him they spend the rest of their lives making other men fall in love with them.'

She spoke very quietly. 'If I do that, Ben, it is unintentional.'

'But I'm right about the one man?'

'Perhaps.'

'Do you want coffee?'

'Thanks.'

'Do you still see him?'

'No.'

'Liquor?'

'Brandy – if you're having one.'

'Maybe you're building him up to be what he's not.'

'Maybe.' She cupped the rounded brandy glass in both her hands and looked down at the amber liquid. 'Maybe I am, but it doesn't change things, does it?'

They drank their brandy in silence. Then he stood up. 'You're tough and smart and sexy,' he said, 'but I bet you've no idea why you're so deadly?'

She shook her head.

'Because you're also nice and warm and funny – and that's why I have to stop seeing you.'

They went down the stairs, Olivia leading the way.

'Have you nothing to say?' he asked to her silence.

She turned, 'Ben, if you want . . .'

'Olivia!'

'Ash!'

Ash looked at Ben as Olivia looked at the very young girl on Ash's arm, a girl with button-brown eyes and brown hair just like her own.

'Ben Steiner,' said Ash. 'I had no idea you were born in Texas.' He laughed as he pushed past them, dragging the girl with him.

418

'They still thought I had a Texas oil millionaire,' said Olivia.

'Instead of Jew from the streets of Brooklyn? Oh, I saw the look Ash gave me. That's another reason why I never called you. It wasn't because I knew you had a boyfriend, it was because that man was Ash Mallory. Silver-spoon Ash. And you know something else? I'm glad you ditched him.' A cab stopped. Ben handed her inside, and said with genuine fondness in his black eyes, 'Let me know if you fall out of love, Olivia Steele.'

33

Ash made sure everyone at William & Wall knew that Olivia's Texan oil millionaire was none other than the very married Ben Steiner from Brooklyn.

'You should be aware of what he's saying.' Teddy gave her his elder-brotherly smile.

'I am.'

'You mean it's . . . true?'

'It was, but not any more.'

'You need a break. Come to us for Easter.'

'You and Betsy are my bolt-hole. I don't know what I'd do without you.'

'Then it's a date.' He looked down at her brown curls and her curiously vulnerable face, and he remembered something that Betsy had said the previous night when she was cuddled up on the sofa reading a goodnight story to the kids, something about Olivia constantly competing against herself. 'Oh, by the way . . .' he said, then he stopped.

'What?'

'I see from the agenda of tomorrow's partners' meeting that you intend to discuss getting a foothold in the UK.'

'Yes.'

'Ash and Sherry will be in Sydney.'

'I had noticed.'

'Culross shares are dropping fast.'

'I'd noticed that too, Teddy.'

He grinned. 'I should have guessed.'

'Big Bang will really open up the London share market,' Olivia told the meeting. Until now a London broker has had to charge a fixed commission but after October '86 it will be a free market. The winner will, of course, be the big investor.'

'And the loser all those little old English ladies who have the occasional flutter,' said McCord.

'Right.'

'Tough on the old dears!'

'But good for the City – and for the English financial institutions.'

'You mean the banks?'

'Especially the merchant banks.' She took a deep breath. 'I think it's time we looked at buying into a UK merchant bank.'

'Merger or acquisition?'

'Oh, acquisition.' She pictured the boardroom at Culross and the faces of the board. 'Definitely acquisition.'

'You mean for ourselves, as a subsidiary?'

'Yes.' Her face was perfectly serene but inside she was churning. 'I'll head up a feasibility study and report back.'

There were no dissenters – Ash was thousands of miles away.

She was on the plane heading for Europe before she had time to think about Ben. She was sorry to lose him, as a friend and a lover, but what he had said of her being a one-man woman . . . was it true? She stared at the transatlantic night and wondered.

London was cold and damp. She'd forgotten just how dismal it could be. The first call she made was to Bill, her old boss at Maxifunds. They'd exchanged Christmas cards each year with lines like 'we must meet', but they hadn't: he was a part of a past she had wanted to forget. Now he chuckled down the telephone wires. 'I wondered how long it would take before you came gunning for me.'

'What do you mean?'

'That since I own ten per cent of Culross and a seat on the board, I imagine you're after my holding.'

They met for lunch at Simpsons. He was sitting at the same table where nine years earlier he had told her to forget the City: she wondered if he realised.

'I'm proud of you,' he said. 'I tell trainees that if they work hard they too can be an Olivia Steele of William & Wall.'

421

She kissed him on the cheek, and tears pricked her eyes.

'You left it a long time,' he went on. 'I began to wonder if you'd ever want to see me again.'

'I had to wait till I was on top.'

'You've been up there from the start – it's just that you lost your footing.'

They exchanged gossip and pleasantries until they had finished eating, then, over coffee, Olivia said, 'You must have had a lot of confidence in Culross to increase your holding at a time when others couldn't pull out fast enough.'

'I did – and I do. And I have no intention of selling you my stake or my seat on the board.'

'Bill, I never . . .'

'My dear young lady, you learned your basic business tactics from me – or have you forgotten.'

She hesitated, then she laughed. 'So you won't sell?'

'No.'

'Would you support William & Wall having a stake in Culross?'

'A stake, yes. It would do the bank good to widen its transatlantic side.'

'How about an out and out takeover?'

He looked across the table, into Olivia's eyes. 'I'll never support foreign ownership of a British bank and if you try to buy up Culross I'll fight you every step of the way.'

Olivia was still mulling over her conversation with Bill when she dropped in to see Maggie on her way to the airport.

'How are things?' she asked, forcing herself back to the present: to Maggie's kitchen and a mug of coffee.

'Fingers crossed. Oh, I'd be crazy if I said thing were a hundred per cent but we're trying to sort them out. Zach tries to be less cross and I try to be less neurotic. I take deep breaths and walk around the garden every time I'm about to throw a wobbly.'

'What about Savvies?'

'I'm going back next week, just in the mornings, and in the afternoons I'll do my designing from here. You know, I'm really looking forward to working again. I'm nervous, of course, but . . .' She laughed and Cat appeared through the window, and started to wash himself on the window ledge. 'At least Zach and I know we love each other,' said Maggie, after a few minutes, 'So whatever else we want or don't want from life, we know we want to be together. We've learned that lesson. When we fight, when we hate each other, at least we know we also love each other. Splitting up taught us that. When I'm about to scream at Zach to get out, and he about to leave me yet again, we remember how much worse it was when we were apart.' She lit a cigarette. 'I've you to thank for that, pal. If you hadn't taken me to New York, Zach and I would not have got back together again.'

'Nonsense!'

'It's true. When he met me at the airport I was so relaxed, so . . . cheerful.' She giggled. 'We spent the first two days in bed. There was me trying to sort out our emotional problems and all Zach could think about was bed.' She tossed the protesting Cat on to the floor and pirouetted around the room. 'In the months before we split Zach never came near me unless I told him we had to do it because . . . of a baby. Now he can't get enough. I'm still not pregnant but at least I've Zach, my lover and my friend.' She came to a halt in front of Olivia, who was perched on the end of the kitchen table in her orange and black striped bumble bee suit. 'You look like one of those women in *Dynasty*.'

Olivia laughed. 'Unfortunately my love life is nothing like as exciting as theirs.'

'No?'

She told Maggie about Ben and the old Maggie flashed back, 'Was he worth it?'

'Oh, yes, till he got heavy.' Olivia walked the length of the kitchen, the orange stripes of her suit catching in the overhead light, her orange heels clacking on the polished floorboards. 'I sound hard, but it's true. Ben's the only casual affair I've ever had, all the others have been . . . intense . . . committed. It was fun. An adventure. Oh, not like . . . Mark, never like Mark, but maybe better for me. You see, I knew that I wasn't vulnerable with Ben and I don't ever want to be vulnerable again.'

'You're not hard,' said Maggie, rolling a joint on the inside of her thigh, 'you're merely a fully paid up member of the Self-Preservation Society.'

On the flight back to the States Olivia smiled as she studied the Culross share price. They'd fallen to 216, down twenty in the past month. She forgot about Ben, Ash, and everything as she twisted her gold pen backwards and forwards through her long fingers and thought of Culross – and of Mark, for in her mind the two were permanently and indelibly linked.

'As we all know, the great plus of London is that it is the most strategically placed of the world money markets,' said Olivia when reporting her progress. 'It covers Tokyo in the morning, Wall Street in the afternoon, and once Big Bang has abolished fixed commission it will be a highly competitive arena.'

Teddy nodded. 'Remind me when Big Bang is.'

Before she had time to answer the door opened and Ash came in. 'So partners' meetings are now held in secret, are they?'

'This is not a partners' meeting,' said McCord testily. 'Olivia is giving us a progress report.'

'Then you won't object if I listen in.' He sat down. 'OK, Teddy, carry on with your question.'

'I was only asking Olivia when Big Bang is.'

'October '86.' said Olivia.

'Why should you want to know that?' asked Ash.

'Because of the UK bank we're considering.'

'A merchant bank?'

'Yes.' She raised her chin defiantly. 'As you will have read in the minutes of the last meeting we are considering a move on London.'

'Which bank?'

'As a matter of fact it is Culross.'

'Of course it's Culross. Where else! Russ, Peter, in case you aren't aware, Culross is the bank which fired Olivia for passing information to her lover. Now, I'm not against breaking into the UK market – but Culross! Sorry, Olivia, but I see revenge in this and as a partner of William & Wall I cannot allow our resources to be used for personal motives.'

She took a deep breath to stop herself from hitting him. 'Everyone knows about Culross and me, Ash. I've made no secret of my past. But it is the past. We all have pasts. This

424

country's full of people like me who came to make a new life for themselves, people who only asked for a second chance. I'd be a liar if I said I didn't want revenge, but I would never do anything to harm William & Wall – after all, this place gave me that second chance.'

'Not just William & Wall but I, Ash Mallory, gave you a chance – or have you forgotten?'

'No, but any break you gave me I reckon I've proved myself worthy of.'

'She has,' said McCord. 'Now, I move that this meeting vote on whether or not we go for Culross.'

Ash flicked through the pages before him. 'I want to see a more detailed report.'

Olivia clenched her fists. 'To delay is to lose out, Ash – and you are delaying on purpose.'

'I'm merely being prudent with William & Wall's money.'

'Why don't you say it now, you're going to vote against a Culross takeover so what's the point of me making another report?'

'It'll give you the excuse to go back to your beloved England – sorry, I mean your beloved lover.'

McCord banged the table. 'Cut it out.'

'Yes,' Teddy intervened gently. 'Ash, I do appreciate your opinion but Olivia and I . . . and I think Russ . . . and maybe Peter . . . all feel that Culross would be a good venture.'

'All?'

'Yes.'

Ash pressed the intercom. 'Have Sherry come to the boardroom.' Then he fixed Peter. 'Well?'

Peter did not look at Olivia as he replied, 'I'm with you, Ash.'

Of course she'd suspected that Peter would take Ash's side, but it was still a shock to hear him say so. She looked at Cord. Was he going to desert her too?

'We're a team at this bank,' said McCord, 'and we're meant to fight on the same side. We'll have an extraordinary meeting in two weeks – by which time Olivia will have produced a more detailed report and we shall all have studied it.' He stood up. 'I'm in agreement with Ash that William & Wall should not be used as a personal weapon – but nor should this room be used to sort out private grievances. I should not like to have to ask for the resignations of two of the bank's most promising senior officers. Have I made myself clear?'

She had always known that Ash was still her enemy. Oh, she'd told herself not to be silly, assured Betsy that all was right between them, put on a face for Teddy, and acted the professional to McCord, but underneath she'd known that Ash was the knifeman waiting in the shadows.

In her office she keyed into the London market: Culross were down to 200. Damn Ash, they should be homing in for the kill not fiddling around writing reports, but then, of course, he did not want her to get Culross, simply because he knew it meant so much to her.

It was late when she left the bank, stepping out into the first evening of spring, that time which does not depend on any calendar but on the moment when the air suddenly turns warm and new and exciting. Her car was waiting. She sank into the back and headed up town, wondering why victory did not have quite the same exquisite piquancy if it was not acknowledged in your own country and deciding that whatever excitements Christopher Columbus had in discovering America, his ultimate satisfaction must have been when he preened himself around Europe, rubbing his success up the noses of those who'd refused to stump up the cash for his expedition. Olivia had minions at her beck, money at her disposal, and power at her call, but nothing which happened at William & Wall could give her quite that same satisfaction as the moment when she would waltz up the path and through the open door of Culross. And no Ash Mallory, she told herself, as she spread her papers across her white table and settled down to draft the report, is going to rob me of that victory.

By five o'clock next morning she'd drafted her report. At nine, Jack was saying, 'You need sleep, kid.' Within two days he'd rustled up further data on Culross. At midnight they looked at each other across his VDU screen and said, 'We both need sleep.' On her way out Olivia handed the draft report to one of her graveyard shift secretaries – and went home to sleep for ten hours. Next afternoon she returned refreshed. Two days later a copy of her report went to each partner: they had a week to read it: she had a week to wait.

An hour before the meeting Culross shares moved up ten to 210. Olivia could have screamed!

McCord opened the meeting. 'I've read Olivia's report. I agree about Culross's potential. They have some excellent people. Would they stay in a takeover?'

'So long as they're assured of their prospects – and they would be.'

'What about Lawrence Culross?' asked Ash with a sneer.

'He'd have to go. I make that clear in my report.'

'If Julius is so smart why didn't he get rid of Lawrence completely when he ousted him from the chairmanship?'

'Tradition. He's a Culross.'

'That's what I mean about these merchant banks.' Ash turned to Sherry and Peter. 'They keep on guys who should have been pensioned off long ago.'

'They fired Roland Culross,' said Olivia.

'They had to – even Culross fire the dishonest.'

'How dare you . . .' She flinched as Teddy kicked her ankle, then took a deep breath and continued in a composed voice. 'We need to get a foot into London before Big Bang and in my opinion Culross is our best bet. They have potential – untapped potential. I propose that we go for a dawn raid. Under the stockmarket rules if we buy five per cent of a company we have to declare our interest, and at fifteen per cent we have to stop buying for seven days. We should decide how much of Culross we're after. I think it should be 14.99 per cent, if possible, but not less than ten per cent – also, if possible. Then we instruct our London broker of our top price per share, and he'll go into the market and offer that – plus a premium.'

'What sort of premium?' asked McCord.

'A good twenty per cent to induce enough people to sell.'

'What about price per share?'

'They're 210 now. I reckon they'll drop back to 200.'

'Sure they'll drop back?'

'If my hunch is correct.'

'What if you're wrong,' said Sherry, running the top of her finger around her full, glossy lips.

· 'Yes,' said Ash. 'What if your broker can only acquire five per cent and we end up with a block of shares in Culross and no hope of acquiring more.'

427

'That's always a risk.'

'A risk which you ask this bank to take?'

'A calculated risk – like all the other calculated risks we've taken.'

'But not usually with such emotion.'

Teddy lifted his hand. 'I'm voting. I agree with Olivia.'

'I don't agree,' said Ash. Nor do Sherry and Peter. Cord, surely you're not going to split the bank for the sake of a woman's revenge?'

'I wouldn't jeopardise William & Wall for anyone, Ash. I vote for Olivia because I think she's right, but in deference to this divided meeting I rule that she must not exceed 200 per share – that's 240 including a twenty per cent premium – without clearing it with me and the board.'

'That's impossible!' exclaimed Olivia.

'Why?' asked Ash, as if he didn't know.

'Because 200 is the lowest they've ever been. At least give me up to 205.'

'You said they'd drop back – now prove how clever you are.'

'Ash! Olivia!' McCord hammered on the table. 'We're a partnership. Let's try not to forget it.'

On her return to her office, Olivia instructed the London broker. 'Buy 14.99 per cent of Culross at 200 plus twenty percent.'

He keyed back. 'Culross now 212. Up two since this morning.'

'I know!' She thumped back, then she added. 'Thanks.'

It was a week before the shares dropped – one point at a time, till they stuck at 206. Olivia watched and waited. They dropped a further two. She held her breath. An hour later they were up to 210 again. She called her broker, but even as they were discussing the reason for the increase, they moved up two more. But later that day, as the market was about to close, they slid seven to 205. With excitement building inside her, Olivia turned off her VDU screen and rubbed her tired eyes. Surely they wouldn't go up again!

Next morning, at four o'clock Manhattan time and nine o'clock London time she left her attic. Twenty minutes later she walked down the deserted corridor to her office and on the

428

dot of four thirty she was keying into the London market.
Culross held steady at 206. She sipped her mango juice. They
dropped to 204. An hour later they were back to 206.

The telephone rang. 'Hi, Olivia.'

'Teddy.'

'Thought I'd find you there. How are we doing?'

'Hovering around 205. Oh, God, they've gone back up to
210. I don't believe it!'

She called her London broker. 'What the hell's going on?'

He was back to her within fifteen minutes. 'Rumour has it
that someone is doing some serious buying.'

'What? A rival takeover?'

'No, if you ask me it's price bolstering.'

'Who?'

'God knows!'

'Well, if he does, I wish he'd tell me!'

For the next forty-eight hours Olivia was hardly out of the
bank. Culross dropped – slightly – but never below 206.

On the morning of the third day she met Sherry in the
corridor. 'I hear you're having problems, Olivia. Maybe you
misread your hunch.'

'I think not.' Over Sherry's shoulder she met Alice's sympathetic gaze.

That night Olivia dreamed of Gerald. He came to the attic
and told her that he now owned Culross. She woke with the
feel of his hands on her thighs – only it wasn't his hands, it was
the duvet wrapped around her legs. By the time she arrived at
William & Wall she felt sick with exhaustion. At her desk she
could barely concentrate. She downed two black coffees and
keyed into London. Still 206. Stretching her arms above her
head, she closed her eyes and yawned – and as she re-opened
them the price fell to 204. Then 202.

Her broker came through. 'Seen the price?'

'You bet!'

201.

'The suspense is killing me.'

202.

'Shit!'

201.

'This is too much.'

'Go for it! She waited. Five minutes. Ten minutes.

Her broker came through. 'We've got five per cent.'

'Keep at it!'

'Ten per cent.'

She tapped her fingers on the side of the desk.

'Fourteen per cent. We could get another .99 per cent, Miss Steele, but not at this price. The word's out now and shareholders are a greedy bunch.'

For a moment she was angry. Damn Ash for holding her back. Alone, Cord would have let her go higher. But I've got fourteen per cent. Fourteen per cent of a bank which fired me! She pictured the scene at Culross and the dawning of the realisation that she, Olivia Steele, whom they had kicked and abused was buying up their precious bank, and she laughed out loud. Bastards! She'd show them that she wasn't the hopeless failure they'd made her believe she was.

On her way to see McCord and Teddy, she met Sherry and Peter. 'You can tell Ash that my hunch paid off,' she said, leaving them open-mouthed as she sauntered on her way.

Next morning the *Wall Street Journal* said:

DAWN RAID ON CULROSS
That Steeley Lady Raider of William & Wall, British born Olivia Steele has shown Lombard Street what it's all about when a Wall Street investment bank mean business . . .

The *Financial Times* said:

With the news that Big Bang is scheduled for October '86 our transatlantic cousins are casting their greedy eyes on a number of City banks. This morning highly aggressive William & Wall sent shivers of horror through the marble banking hall of Culross who awoke from their slumbers to face the graceless prospect of becoming an out of town branch of a Wall Street bank.

By the following day the *Financial Times* had checked its records:

It may interest readers to know that the lady raider spearheading William & Wall's attack on Culross is none other than Olivia Steele who . . .

The *Wall Street Journal* was more frank:

Olivia read the articles and chuckled. She buzzed McCord. 'I want to take my team to London. I think we should try for another .99 per cent and I'd prefer us to be on the spot.'

'This one's your baby.'

'What about the 200 price rule?'

'You can go to 210 – which with a twenty per cent premium takes you to 252. I'll advise the board.'

'210! Cord, the market price is 225. Any shareholder is going to want at least 260 to part with a reasonable holding. My broker has searched out a couple of possible sellers but they want money. The entire financial world knows we're gunning for Culross.'

'And they also know you're out for revenge.'

'Don't you trust me?'

'I have to reassure the others.'

'I don't mean them, Cord, I mean you.'

There was a brief silence, then he replied. 'It's not you I don't trust, Olivia, it's what Ash will do if you fail or if I allow you to put William & Wall at risk. You once said you'd made an enemy for life and I didn't believe you. I reckon you were right.'

'Thanks, but don't worry about Ash. I won't. I'll be far too busy homing in on Culross.'

The helicopter took off from Battery Park. It skimmed the trees and went up the Manhattan skyline. From her seat by the window Olivia caught a glimpse of the orange hulk of the Staten Island ferry chugging through the water far below. Strange that in all her years in New York she'd never been back to it. Funny that she should think of this now, that she was on her way to London and Culross.

The helicopter crossed the East River. The ferry began to dock. The sun dipped into New Jersey and turned a million Manhattan windows into golden nuggets, just as it had that first evening when she'd arrived in New York – and watching, and remembering, Olivia told herself, 'If I can be a winner in this concrete jungle, then I can be a winner anywhere.'

34

Flanked by her assistants, the dollar riding high, Olivia swept through Heathrow and into a blaze of publicity from the waiting press.

'Miss Steele, as a former employee of Culross...? Miss Steele, Culross treated you pretty rough...? Miss Steele, could there be an element of revenge in...?'

She stopped, her face framed for the lunchtime television news, her hair glossy, her suntan accentuated by the white silk of her shirt, her body moulded by a tailored black linen suit. 'I cannot comment on William & Wall's affairs,' the diamond clip on her lapel fired a hundred thousand TV sets, 'but I will say this, generally speaking – and please note I say generally speaking because anyone who misquotes me or misrepresents me will be sued – no one treats Olivia Steele roughly and gets away with it. Now, that's enough gentlemen, as I'm sure you will appreciate I am wary of speaking to the press.'

There was appreciative laughter as she walked on. Her triumphant return had been denied her once, when she was weak with love for Mark, but no one was ever going to steal her victories again – and Olivia looked a victor, every sensual, sensuous inch of her.

In the boardroom at Culross, Lawrence rested his head in his hands. 'I always said it was a mistake to let women...'

'Oh, do shut up!' snapped Julius. 'Jonathan, you worked with her. Do you think she'll go for an out and out takeover?'

'I don't know. It's ten years since Olivia and I worked together, and in those days she would never have done anything to harm Culross. All right, I know she got us into trouble

432

but as I've said before no one could have been more loyal and I shall always feel she was dealt a raw . . .'

Lawrence butted in. 'She was knocking off that despicable journalist and giving him all our secrets.'

'What Olivia did or did not do ten years ago is beside the point,' said Mark.

'I don't agree.' Lawrence pursed his fat lips, 'but then my knowledge of her is not so . . . intimate as yours.'

'I don't care whether you agree or not, I'm telling you – and as you so delicately put it, I know her better than you do. Olivia was treated badly by Culross. It is no secret that she and I were . . . very fond of each other. It was her desire to get back at or back into Culross which broke us up. Believe you me, she's burning with hatred and she'll see this bank go down the tube rather than relinquish one iota of revenge. She's lived for this moment ever since the day she was thrown out of here – and I know one thing, that lady's going to get her pound of flesh even if it kills her.'

On the television the commentator was summarising the news. The picture cut to Olivia: a long shot as she walked to a waiting Rolls: a close-up of her smile as she settled into the back seat. Mark turned off the set. Her self-confidence infuriated him. He wondered if she still had the same boyfriend. He itched to slap her down. He didn't care if she had a million boyfriends. She was brutally self-centred. He remembered the terrace at Pietra Alta and her face, soft beneath the veil.

Olivia and her team stayed at the Dorchester. 'Why not the Connaught?' she demanded as they cut across the centre aisle of Park Lane and drew up outside the large white hotel.

'They didn't have a large enough suite available. The travel department asked me to OK the Dorchester, and it never occurred to me that you'd mind . . .' Alice trailed off in puzzlement.

'Don't worry.' How could she explain to Alice that of all the hotels in London she least wanted to stay where memories of the Culross party clung to the statue of Leda and the Swan, because that evening had been the beginning of the end – with

433

Culross and with Mark. 'Don't worry,' she repeated unnecessarily.

They spent the next forty-eight hours in their suite, keying in figures to their computer and talking on the telephone to Wall Street or to their London broker.

'So we're going for a takeover,' said Alice excitedly.

'Yes – at the right price.' Funny, she thought, I didn't like Alice at first but now she and Hutch are my best back-up team. In fact, Alice has been spot on ever since I gave her a second chance. Oh, Culross, how you're going to wish you'd done the same for me!

'Culross are up to 235,' said Hutch.

'Not surprising.' She took a sip of Perrier water. 'Everyone knows we're here and they're all convinced we're buying – that's why we're going to sit tight till the price drops.'

It took over a week for the shares to fall back to 225, amid rumours that William & Wall did not intend to increase their holding after all.

Olivia phoned Teddy at his home. 'They're 225 and slipping. Do you think Cord'll let me offer 220 plus a premium?'

'Don't ask him! He's having a hell of a time over the 210 business. Ash isn't just after your head, he's now after Cord's – and mine. Olivia, you have to pull that Culross deal off or we're all out on our ears.'

'I'm trying, Teddy, I'm trying.'

But even as they said goodbye, to Olivia's exasperation the shares moved up again.

'What's the score on the short-term shareholders?' she asked her broker. 'Have you found enough, willing to sell, to give us our .99 per cent?'

'Yes, but not at 252. They smell big money, Miss Steele, and they reckon they'll get it by hanging on.'

'So it is them that's pushing the price up?'

'My enquiries say not.'

'Then is it the Culross family buying to keep me out – or a lot of old ladies out to make a quick buck?'

'Not the Culrosses – yet.'

'Then who the hell is it?'

He came back to her within the hour. 'Someone buying through nominees.'

'Large amounts?'

'No, just enough. Rumour has it that they dump once the price is up a few points. No, Miss Steele, don't ask me who. That would take Sherlock Holmes.'

The William & Wall team spent the days in their suite, eating meals from room service, drinking Perrier water, and keeping awake with black coffee. In the evenings they took it in turns to work out in the gym, and once Olivia had tea with Maggie, but even then she did not venture further than the dining-room: she had to be on call. By the end of a week her head split with tension and her eyes were gritty with lack of sleep.

The phone rang one morning as she was getting up.

'Olivia?'

'Bill!'

'Can I have an entirely off the record conversation with you?'

'It depends on what it's about.'

'We believe in fighting hard but straight. If you're being stabbed in the back it is not by us.'

'You mean . . . someone on the inside . . . on my side . . .'

'Goodbye, Olivia.'

She thought for a few minutes, started to call Teddy – then she replaced the receiver.

Another week passed. And another. Then, on the afternoon of the fourth Monday, the price fell to 210. Within seconds their London broker was on to those shareholders who had expected big money but now, with the price dropping would – hopefully – be glad to settle for 252, which was after all 42 above the market price.

Olivia paced the room as she waited.

'Culross up ten to 220,' said Hutch with a groan.

'Hell!' She slumped into a chair.

Her broker came on the line. 'Sorry to keep you waiting but . . .'

'You did it?'

'Yes.'

'At 252?'

'Yes. That's why the price moved. Miss Steele, you now own 14.99 per cent of Culross – and the Bank of England want to know your intentions.'

She laughed. 'My immediate intentions are to take my team out to celebrate. I'll call you tomorrow. Hutch, Alice, we're going out. We've done well, boys and girls. You've done well.'

She rang Cord. Teddy answered his extension and chuckled when he heard the news. 'I can't wait to see Ash's face. Hey, Cord, she's done it!'

'We need a seat on the board,' she told him. 'We have to be able to oversee our interest.'

'Right.'

'Or we have to go for more shares.'

'More shares! Why? No other shareholder can outvote us.'

'Together the Culross family can. Look, Teddy, I know them. They'll fight tooth and nail to keep us off the board, but they'd prefer to give us a directorship than to have us buy up more shares.'

There was a brief silence, then he handed her to McCord, who said, 'You mean we've purchased 14.99 per cent of a company but we still have no controlling interest and no directorship?'

'It's going to be all right, Cord, I know it is. I'm going to bluff Culross into thinking we're after more shares. Trust me!'

'I haven't much option, have I? We're in it up to our necks.'

'We've been in tight spots before.'

'It's time I retired. The pressure's getting to me.'

'You're never going to retire – and we're going to win.'

There was suddenly nothing for her to do and after the frenzy of the past days she found it impossible to relax. She went to the gym, had a sauna, showered, dressed, lay on her bed – and still there was an hour to go before dinner.

She phoned Maggie.

'Olivia, I'm so glad you called. I wanted to ring you but you're so busy. Guess what! Yes, I'm pregnant. In fact, I have been for two months. Oh, I was longing to tell you but I didn't, just in case it was a false alarm or I lost it. I could still lose it, I know, but . . . dare I say it . . . I'm confident it's going to be all right. You will be a godmother, won't you?'

She rang her parents. Her father answered. 'This is pleasant, Livvi, but I'm afraid we're just going out. Your mother's in the car already. We're off to see *Gandhi*. Have you seen it? Oh, we'll be more up to date than you are.'

She rang Fiona. 'Olivia, what a surprise! I thought you were much too busy to think of us. Hugo? Oh, how nice of you to ask. Well, things are better. He's agreed to sink his redundancy pay into a garden centre and we're going to run it together. You know I've always wanted to. Yes, it was worrying.'

'I'll keep my fingers crossed for you . . . Fee.'

'Thank you . . . Livvi.'

The directors of Culross held an extraordinary meeting late that night. Over the same mahogany table where they had accused Olivia of betraying them, they now hammered out their defence against her.

'I don't see how she can take us over,' said Lawrence, annoyed at being dragged out so late. 'Between Julius and myself and Roland – don't forget he subsequently bought up some shares after he was made to sell his original holding – we own over twenty-five per cent, which is more than that wretched girl.'

'Private investors own twenty per cent of the shares,' said Mark. 'At a price she could persuade some of them to sell – she's persuaded enough already.'

'What on earth shall we do?'

'Convince your shareholders not to sell to her.'

'Your! Surely you mean our?'

'No, I mean your. I am merely your legal adviser.'

Lawrence reached for the whisky. 'They won't sell us to the Americans.'

'Some won't. But some will – for the right money.'

'There's one indication that she might not be going for a complete takeover,' said Bill. 'She hasn't called in a UK merchant bank, at least not as far as we know. Olivia's a professional. She wouldn't go any further without expert local acquisition advice.'

'So she's either poised to act or she's poised to do nothing, and we don't know which,' Mark stood up. 'If you send a draft of the letter to the shareholders to my chambers tomorrow I'll go through it.'

'I would have thought you could come here, Mark,' said Lawrence. 'After all, this is the worst crisis to hit Culross since that bloody girl blew our share issue and you are a Culross, whatever your surname.'

'That is not what our grandfather thought when my mother was struggling in a terraced house in Leeds. No, Lawrence, I owe no allegiance to this bank and I want nothing from it – although I am prepared to give my professional advice for Julius's sake.' He left the room before he lost his temper.

In her bedroom at the Dorchester Olivia was on the phone to McCord. 'No, of course I haven't bought any more. Cord, calm down! What? The Bank of England? Oh, they're biding their time so long as we don't increase our stock. Yes, I've decided to bring in a UK merchant bank. No, just behind the scenes advice. Oh, yes, the entire City is convinced we're after more shares. Haven't you seen the price? 265!'

Culross shareholders received a letter from Julius saying that it would not be in the bank's best interest to become a subsidiary of an American bank.

Immediately the price hit 290 as the market waited for Olivia to make her move.

In their suite at the Dorchester the William & Wall team toasted each other.

Later, Olivia had a silent laugh as she pictured the scene in the boardroom at Culross.

'Bill thinks that Olivia will stick at her present holding if she's offered a directorship,' Julius told Mark and Lawrence.

'A directorship!' repeated Lawrence. 'What do you mean?'

'A seat on the board, of course.'

'For Olivia Steele! You're joking!'

'A seat on the board with responsibility for overseeing the international side,' said Julius. 'She's certainly got the know-how – and we need to expand in that field.'

'I won't . . . won't have that girl on the board of my bank.'

'Would you rather she bought up the whole place?'

'She's not getting my shares,' said Lawrence stubbornly.

Mark sighed. 'She'll get enough from elsewhere, can't you understand that?'

'No, and what's more I don't trust your motives. After all, you were her lover and, as you said the other day, you have no stake in Culross. So what do you care if we lost our shirts? In fact, I wouldn't be surprised if you and Olivia have schemed up this whole thing to get Culross between you and . . .'

Mark reached across the table and punched him on the chin.

'How dare you . . . how dare you hit me, you . . .'

'Shut up!' shouted Julius, 'or I'll hit you too.'

'Our grandfather would never have . . .'

'I couldn't give a monkey's arse what our grandfather would have done.'

When Julius and Mark were alone they looked at each other and laughed. Then Mark said in his quiet gravelly voice, 'If one of those bloodhounds from Fleet Street had seen me hit Lawrence I'd have been hounded in the same way they hounded Olivia.'

'What I'd love to know,' said Julius, 'is how much she can offer.'

'Those American banks have enormous funds.'

'Yes, but Bill did say she was having trouble with some of the board. Apparently she and Ash Mallory don't see eye to eye.'

'They don't?'

'Daggers drawn, according to Bill's sources.'

Mark was silent and thoughtful. Eventually he said, 'You do realise that she hasn't actually offered for any more shares?'

'I know, but the market thinks she will. The worst would be if she backed out and dumped her entire holding, because the price would plummet and some second line bank might grab them. At least William & Wall are in the first league.'

'And Olivia?'

'Oh, she's the tops – though I hate to admit it.'

By the time Mark left Culross it was early morning. He walked up Lombard Street in the drizzle, bought a newspaper at Bank station and hailed a taxi, sinking into the back seat, relishing the thought of the bath and two hours sleep he would grab before he had to be in court. He flicked through the newspaper, telling himself that he was not looking for anything in particular. The lead article on the financial page was entitled: 'On a Rollercoaster to Revenge'. Underneath was a picture of Olivia, taken ten years earlier as she left the courtroom having lost her flat, her car, her job – and her innocence. It was a bewildered but achingly proud face. Next to it was another picture, of a tough glamorous woman, reclining on a sofa, legs casually crossed exuding the kind of confident sexuality which infuriated him.

The directors of Culross sent a formal proposal to William & Wall, or rather to Olivia 'that in the best interests of Culross, and in order not to cause continued disruption, agreement should be reached by which William & Wall would be represented on the board.'

Olivia rang McCord. '14.99 per cent *and* a seat on the board – and they still don't know if we're after more shares!'

He laughed. 'They're sweating, and I can tell you I've been. Olivia Steele, you've shortened my life by ten years.'

He switched her through to Teddy, who congratulated her, then asked, 'When will you be home?'

'I want to see heads roll at Culross.'

'A bloodbath?'

'Sure. What's bugging you?' She glanced at her watch, she was hoping to catch Maggie for lunch.

'You know that after Betsy you are my favourite lady?'

'Yes, yes, get on with it.'

'I'm concerned that if you spend too much time over there it will have a detrimental effect on your promotional chances here.'

Her voice was flint-edged. 'Have you any complaints about my handling of the deal?'

'Of course not. No one else could have . . .'

'Thank you.' She paused, on purpose, and could imagine his ears turning scarlet. 'How is Ash taking it?'

'Badly. So is Sherry. But Russ had admitted straight out that he was wrong to side with them. Olivia, I wasn't criticising, I was just . . . Look, it's no secret that since you pulled off the Culross deal in the face of Ash's opposition people are saying you're now ahead of him. You understand what I mean? When Cord retires one or other of you will be president – and the word is out that it'll be you.'

'Me?'

'Yes, you. That's why . . .'

'Teddy you're a saint and I'm sorry I bit your head off.'

She walked to the window and leaned against it, laughing to herself with excitement. Oh, of course she'd hoped, dreamed, but there'd always been Ash ahead of her – till now. President! She looked down on Hyde Park where a child was chasing a puppy through piles of golden leaves in the light of a pale November sun. Golden leaves . . . Ash . . . Connecticut. She'd said, 'What a pity golden leaves do not last forever.' She thought of Jake – and of Mark.

The directors of Culross waited for Olivia's reply to their proposal – and she let them wait. She spent the morning relaxing in the sauna followed by an hour of pampering in the hotel beauty salon. At half past two she told Hutch, 'Alice and I are going shopping. In exactly two hours we will arrive downstairs. Make sure the press are on to it. Come on, Alice, we're off to Harrods – and we're going to come back with as many carrier bags as possible.'

They went to Harrods, where Olivia bought a pair of pink boots and Alice a coat, then to Harvey Nichols where they each bought cashmere sweaters, then down the King's Road to Savvies where Maggie, still as skinny as a rake, was proudly wearing her first maternity dress.

'Zach bought it for me,' she said. 'I couldn't wait to put it on. Hey, Sanjiv! Sanjiv! Look who's here.'

'Olivia!' Sanjiv's face appeared over the banisters. 'I thought you were buying up the City?'

'I am. This is a strategic break. Come on, Alice, time to return to the battlefield.'

In the taxi Alice said, 'You know a lot of really interesting people, Olivia.'

'Maggie's my closest friend.'

'She is? The punky one!'

'Don't take people at face value, Alice, it's a big mistake.'

They drew up outside the Dorchester and staggered out, weighed down with carrier bags as a crowd of journalists surged forward. To add to the effect one of the pages who had hurried to help dropped a box and a pair of very unbankerly pink boots fell out.

Mark and Julius watched the evening news.

And now to the Culross takeover story. The City has been alive with rumours that Culross has offered William & Wall's vice president, Olivia Steele, a seat on the board. However, takeovers seemed to be far from the glamorous Miss Steele's mind this afternoon when . . .

The camera cut to a long shot of Olivia's taxi drawing up outside the Dorchester, then to a page picking up the boots.

'You mean, we've been sitting here twiddling our thumbs all day whilst she's been out buying pink boots!' exploded Julius.

'She did it on purpose, she stage-managed the whole thing.' Mark walked to the window; he found it impossible to sit still. The lawn in front of the bank was floodlit. Funny to think that it was here, a decade ago, that he had first spoken to Olivia. Funny to think that that evening he had thought her tough and brittle, when the truth was she was frightened that Gerald Quentin was about to betray her. Funny to think . . . no, it wasn't funny at all, it was achingly sad that she was still paying for a five minute indiscretion committed ten years earlier. Was it surprising she wanted her pound of flesh – with interest? He picked up his briefcase. 'I'm going. Tomorrow's Saturday. I'll be down at the pistol club if you need me.'

Julius nodded. 'I haven't really thanked you, Mark. I'm sorry that you've been involved with Culross, I know how difficult it is for you.'

'You'd do the same for me.'

'And I'm sorry the battle is with Olivia. You know, Sarah and I were sad when you two split up. In spite of everything, we liked her.'

Mark drove home through the restless Friday night streets. He was meant to be going to a dinner party given by a girl he'd met ten days earlier but he couldn't face the where-did-you-go-for-your-holidays/what-are-you-doing-for-Christmas/sorry-have-I-asked-you-that-already routine. So he rang to say he couldn't make it. The girl was cross, she'd every right to be, he was rude – but he didn't give a damn. He poured himself a

442

large whisky and made a bacon sandwich with lashings of English mustard, and he tried not to remember the night when he found Olivia crying in the kitchen.

Eventually he went upstairs and had a bath – he'd been in the bath when she'd telephoned from Italy and Erica had answered. He got into bed and turned on the television, flicking from channel to channel, unable to follow any of them. Was it possible that someone with whom he had shared his every thought was now so distant that they no longer even spoke the same language. He picked up the phone and began to dial – then he noticed the time, nearly midnight, and replaced it.

From her bed in the Dorchester, Olivia watched the television without watching it, then she turned off the light and lay staring up at the ceiling, listening to the traffic hurrying down Park Lane. She pictured the boardroom at Culross; pompous Lawrence with a face like a regurgitated raspberry babbling about women in banking; tight-lipped Julius; dear Jonathan who would toe the line because the Jonathans of this world are born to toe – and Mark with his gravelly voice and cobra eyes.

It was two o'clock and she was still awake. Dinner seemed a decade away. She rang room service and ordered a bacon sandwich. It came. She bit into the crispy bacon, heightened by lashings of English mustard. Half past two. She wondered where – what – who – Mark was doing, then she turned out the light and firmly closed her eyes.

From habit Olivia woke early but today she woke early for a different reason. She had this feeling that Mark was going to phone her. She lay on her side, staring at the white telephone on the bedside table. She was so sure . . . well . . . almost. At seven o'clock she got up, had a bath, washed her hair, ordered breakfast and told herself she was crazy. By eight she was stretched out on her bed in a bright red tracksuit pretending to read the newspapers, but her eyes wouldn't focus on the print. She turned on the television. A fat man was talking about diets. She switched channels. The weather. She went to the window and watched the traffic, and all the time her mind ran through a scenario. She would answer on the fourth ring . . . no, on the fifth. He would say, 'Olivia, this is Mark.' She would sound surprised – of course – but not completely idiotic; it would be fatuous to say, 'Mark Who?' He would then go on, 'I was hoping we might meet.' No, much more positive. 'Olivia (deep gravelly voice) I want to see you' or perhaps 'I have to see you.' (No, 'I want to see you' – the other sounded like the prelude to a confession of pregnancy) and before she had time to say anything, he would insist, 'Today!'

By nine o'clock Olivia was telling herself she was a fool.

By nine ten she told herself she didn't want to see him anyhow.

At nine thirty the phone rang.

'Olivia?'

'Oh . . . Teddy.'

'Hey, are you all right? You sound very . . . is everything OK?'

'I'm fine.'

'Cord's had a very mild heart attack.'

'Oh, my God!'

'Only a slight one. He's OK. He just needs to rest. But you have to get over here . . . today!'

'Teddy, I'm meeting the Culross board on Monday.'

'You can get back for that but you're needed here. Now.'

'Why can't it wait till . . .'

'Because Ash is trying to seize power before you return.'

Twenty minutes later Olivia hurried from the hotel and into a waiting taxi, the red track suit replaced by a smart emerald green dress, her black mink draped over her shoulders. In one hand she clasped a flight bag neatly packed by her secretary, in the other a briefcase checked by Hutch and Alice. Half an hour later she collected her ticket as the flight was called. At ten to eleven she swished up the steps of Concorde, tossed her mink on to the overhead luggage rack, and collapsed thankfully into a window seat. At eleven the plane shot down the runway and somehow – as planes inexplicably do – lifted itself off the ground. Below them the Saturday traffic hurried down the motorway and suburban Middlesex stirred itself for the supermarket.

Mark came off the flyover and into the fast lane of the M4. He was heading for Henley and a day of blissful solitude. It was better – or so he told himself – that he hadn't spoken to Olivia. The woman who exuded confidence on the television news had no connection with the girl who had once followed him to the pistol club. Funny, she'd had the makings of a good shot. In fact, with practice . . . He swung across the lanes of traffic and up the slope to the Heston Service Station.

It took him a few minutes to get through to the Dorchester, and a few more before a girl with an American accent answered, 'Miss Steele isn't here right now.'

'When will she be back?'

'I don't rightly know.'

'Where's she gone?'

'I can't reveal that information. Can I have her call you?'

'No . . . no.' He had to shout, for above him roared an aeroplane: destination New York.

35

Teddy met her at the airport. 'How's Cord?' she asked.

'Sitting up in bed making a nuisance of himself.'

'Already?'

'Basically he was overtired. It was a warning to him to slow down.'

She stepped into the back of the limo and closed off the chauffeur. 'I feel so guilty. Was it the Culross deal which tipped him?'

'No. Oh, that may have been the final blow, but Cord's been overdoing it for years. He's too old to keep up the pace. He doesn't want to keep it up any more, he admitted that this morning.' Teddy paused. 'Ash has completely taken over.'

'We've got to get him out. You, Jack and me.'

'How?' Teddy looked at her. 'I spoke to him this morning and he said if I didn't like the set up, I could leave William & Wall. He said the same went for you.'

'We'll call a partners' meeting for later this afternoon. Tell Russ about it personally, we need him on our side. Get the head of the legal department in case there's trouble.'

'You want to go back to your apartment first?'

'Not likely. We haven't a minute to lose.'

Forty minutes later she was crossing the banking hall. It seems incredible, she thought glancing up at the great Waterford chandelier, that outwardly nothing here has changed since the days when Ash and I were together – and yet now we are locked in battle.

They had barely reached her office before Jack appeared. 'Good to see you, kid.'

'Thanks.'

'You sock it to them.'

'I'll try.'

For lunch they had a sandwich and coffee. 'I can't bear this waiting,' said Olivia, watching Teddy eat a second roll. 'Teddy, how come you're so calm?'

'Because I know there is nothing we can do until the meeting begins.'

'I wonder how Cord is.'

'He's fine. I called Blanche whilst you were talking to Jack and told her we'd stop by the hospital later. Just for a few minutes.'

'You know,' Olivia leaned back in her chair, 'I never really understood what Betsy saw in you till now. Oh, don't get me wrong, you're goodlooking, nice, kind, honest – but I used to ask myself what it was that made her fall so desperately in love with you.'

'What was it?'

'Your integrity.'

At precisely four thirty Olivia and Teddy entered the boardroom. They took their places at one end of the table: Ash, Sherry and Peter sat at the other; Russ and the bank's chief lawyer hovered in between.

Ash spoke first. 'It was unnecessary for you to jeopardise the Culross deal by returning, Olivia.'

'I have not jeopardised it. I shall be in London on Monday morning.'

'Then this running back here the minute Teddy called you was ridiculous. I am the most senior officer in the bank after Cord and during his illness I shall take over.' He stood up and looked down the length of the boardroom table, straight at Olivia. 'There is nothing else to be said. Now, go back to work – unless you wish to resign.'

She stood to face him. 'I have no intention of resigning and the matter of you being acting president is not as clear cut as you seem to think.'

'No?' He glanced first at Sherry, then at Peter. 'I think you'll find the others agree – except for Teddy.'

'You are not a suitable person.'

'What the hell do you mean by that?'

447

'Culross.'

'The bank which you persuaded us to put money into to satisfy your craving for revenge.'

'The bank whose shares you bought in direct opposition to William & Wall's bid.'

'You're lying.'

'I am not! You bought so as to push the price up above my limit, a limit of which you were aware, being a partner in this bank and therefore privy to inside information. When you failed to keep me out, you sold your shares at a vast profit. Of course you did! You knew the price would go up once our interest was known. Furthermore, you dealt without advising the bank and you bought your shares through nominees. This, Ash Mallory, is called insider trading.'

'Prove it!'

'Deny it!'

She looked at him in silence. He met her gaze and held it.

'You know that sooner or later I shall probably be able to prove it,' she said, very softly, and she picked up her briefcase and left the room, followed by Teddy, the lawyer, and Russ.

'How did you know?' Teddy asked when they reached her office.

'I had a tip off.'

'So you had no real proof?'

'None.' She walked to the window, as she had done so many times before and looked out at the great shiny skyscrapers. 'No proof, just a tip off – and a hunch.'

'What are you going to do about Ash?' asked Teddy.

'If the authorities question me, I'll tell the truth.'

'And if they don't.'

'I won't shop him.'

'He made a hell of a lot of money.'

'Yes, but that's not why he did it. He bought the shares to stop me getting Culross. Ash is a finished man, Teddy. William & Wall was his life. He breathed Wall Street. I may kick a man down – but I don't kick him when he's down.'

They went to see McCord, who was sitting up in bed looking pale and tired. Nevertheless, he insisted on a word for word account of the meeting.

From the hospital Teddy drove Olivia straight to the airport

– she preferred to catch up on her sleep in London rather than wake up to face another long flight tomorrow. As the car dropped them at the terminal, she heard her name paged. 'Will Miss Olivia Steele please come to the Pan Am desk.'

She ran over. Teddy at her side. A girl handed her a telephone.

'This is Olivia Steele.'

'It's Cord here.'

'Cord . . . you're all right? I thought that . . .' She went weak with relief.

'I'm fine. Listen, Ash has resigned. Tell Teddy to take over at the bank till you get back from London.'

'I will.'

'And, Olivia . . .'

'Yes '

'My congratulations to the first female president of a Wall Street bank!'

At eleven o'clock on Monday morning a black Rolls Royce turned down Lombard Street and halted outside Culross – and Olivia stepped out into the sunshine. She paused between the Ross lions, her eyes sweeping the lawned courtyard. 'Ready?' she asked Hutch and Alice.

'Sure.'

'Let's go!' She straightened her shoulders inside her red crepe suit – red always was her lucky colour – and marched up to the great oak front door.

The old porter had left and the young one was now the old one. He bowed her across the marble hall, where once she had overheard them say 'Olivia Steele thought she was top dog,' and up the stairs. As her foot touched the top step, Julius came out of the boardroom. 'Good morning, Olivia.'

'Good morning, Julius.'

He led her forward. She prepared her expression. He stepped aside for her to pass. She took a deep breath.

'I think you know everyone.'

'Yes.' She fixed a smile. 'Good morning.' She nodded to each of them – Lawrence, Jonathan, Bill, two non-executive directors from industry who had been brought in at the time of

449

the private placement, Culross's bespectacled solicitor – and Mark.

'Mark is our legal adviser,' Julius explained in the flat voice he used to such effect.

'Of course.' She looked at him and nodded briefly, but inside she was churning. That was the trouble. She walked to the table. He had that effect on her. She opened her briefcase. There was just something about him. She sat down and crossed her legs in one smooth movement, and the light from the chandelier glistened on the threads of her cream silk shirt. If only Mark would change! If only she could change! If only she could be indifferent.

The William & Wall team took up their positions around her. Julius remained standing. He looked straight at Olivia. 'As chairman of Culross I speak for the entire board when I say that we did not welcome the aggressive block-buying of our shares. However, we face facts. William & Wall now own 14.99 per cent of our stock. We do not feel that it is in Culross's best interests to become wholly American owned.'

'Why not?'

'We would lose our identity.'

'Perhaps – but you'd gain much needed expertise in the international field and a far more dynamic approach to the home market. British Telecom has given Joe Public a taste for share ownership. Culross ought to get in on one of these government privatisation deals.'

'Be that as it may, you must be aware that the effects of a hostile takeover would not be beneficial.'

'I didn't expect you to like it, but if I were to dump our holding the price would drop and they might be snapped up by some second-rater. If Culross has to join up with anyone in the US, they couldn't do better than William & Wall – and you know it!'

'But why do we have to join with anyone?' asked Lawrence.

Mark cut him short. 'Culross have asked me to repeat their offer. In exchange for agreeing not to exceed your present holding you would be offered a seat on the board, with particular responsibility for overviewing the international situation.'

'You have already made me that offer, in your letter.'

'Then why haven't you replied to it?'

'Because there would be certain conditions attached.'

'Namely?'

'Lawrence Culross must resign from his directorship.'

'Resign!' Lawrence pushed back his chair. 'Damned impudence! I'm the eldest Culross, why should I resign?'

'And the second condition?'

'Roland Culross must sell his entire holding. He still owns two per cent, and don't deny it because I have proof.'

'These are not the same shares which he originally inherited,' said Julius, 'He sold those, as you know.'

Lawrence banged on the table. 'Who cares about Roland! It's me she wants out. You can't give in to her, Julius, I won't allow It. I won't! You've already stolen the chairmanship from me, you're not taking anything else.'

Olivia gathered her papers. Those are our conditions. We will not hold a sizable stake in a business where two per cent is held by a criminal and a seat on the board is occupied by an incompetent.'

'Incompetent! I'm Lawrence Culross and . . .'

'You have three hours to decide.' She closed her briefcase. 'If you do not meet our conditions, then we will either go for a complete takeover – or we'll dump our shares. Either way, Culross will be wiped out.'

'By whom?' asked Mark. 'By William & Wall or by Olivia Steele?'

She allowed herself a small smile of triumph. 'Both!'

The William & Wall team were lunched by their merchant bank and their London broker in a private dining room at the bank. They all discussed the morning. The banker and the broker both felt that Olivia should have left the frontline negotiating to them, though they didn't dare tell her so.

At three o'clock they returned to Lombard Street.

'Culross accepts your conditions,' Julius told her through tight lips. 'Lawrence has already resigned and we will bring pressure to bear on Roland.'

'Pressure?'

'We can't force him.'

'If he hasn't sold within fourteen days we reserve the right to

451

increase our holding by however much we feel is necessary to safeguard our investment.'

'Culross will do their best, Olivia.'

'Then let us hope that their best is good enough.'

There was silence.

'I want to talk to you,' said Mark. 'In private!'

'Very well.' He had taken her by surprise and she dismissed her astonished team abruptly. They hurried from the room, followed by most of the others, leaving only Bill, Julius, Mark and Olivia.

'Well, well,' said Bill, pushing back his chair. 'You did it. Oh, don't tell me I can't speak openly to Olivia, we all know what she's been after, and if we're going to pull together for the good of this bank we must forget past battles. Anyhow, I'm glad Lawrence is out. Sorry, Julius, but it's true. Ring for my chauffeur will you, Mark.' He rose unsteadily and they all three leaped to help him. 'It's all right, just this wretched rheumatism.'

'I'll come downstairs with you,' said Julius.

'Yes . . .' Bill looked from Olivia to Mark, 'I think you'd better.'

The door closed behind them. Mark began to collect up his papers in an obvious, fussy way. Olivia walked to the window. Across the lawned courtyard evening shadows stretched to touch the Ross lions whilst out in Lombard Street office workers hurried home. 'You wanted to speak to me,' she said.

'Yes. I'd like to spend Christmas at Pietra Alta and I need to be sure that you won't be using it?'

'You mean that was what you . . . No, I won't be using it.'

'Good.'

She turned her back.

He picked up his briefcase.

She heard his footsteps cross to the door.

'There's one thing I don't understand,' he said.

'Oh?'

'You could have wiped out Culross. You could have taken over the bank – or dumped the shares. It would have been the end of the Culross family. You had your chance, why didn't you take it?'

She leaned against the window frame, a brown-haired girl

with button-brown eyes and a curious vulnerability. 'Jake taught me that revenge is an eye for an eye and that winning is having the freedom to choose.

'And you chose to spare Culross?'

'Yes.'

'I see.'

'Do you?' A soft bruised look came into her face. Did he really see that she had chosen not to grind Culross into the ground because, however much he might resent the name, he would never have forgiven her if she had done so? Turning away in order not to see him leave, she paced the room loudly so as to drown the sound of his retreating footsteps. Under old Sir Larry's portrait she hesitated. What would he say if he knew that a woman was on the board of his precious Culross? She must ring Teddy. He'd be waiting . . . he'd been waiting all day . . . whilst she, the future president of William & Wall . . . And what would Wall Street say when it knew of her promotion? But Teddy would make a much better president than me. He's an all-rounder, I'm a trouble-shooter. He is steadfastly competent, I have flashes of brilliance and flashes of . . . She hurried to the window. Mark was striding across the courtyard. Yes, William & Wall and Betsy were Teddy's whole life, whereas I have Culross and Pietra Alta and . . .

36

From the steps of Culross, Lombard Street looked deserted. What an idiot she was to think he might be waiting – but then she'd always been a fool where Mark was concerned. To think he'd kept her back just to ask if he could take some tart to Pietra Alta. To her house!

'I thought I was going to have to wait all night.' He was leaning against one of the Ross lion pillars.

'How was I to know you were here?'

'I'll give you a lift.'

She squared her shoulders. 'Thank you, but I have a driver.'

'I want to talk to you.'

'If it's about Pietra Alta, please communicate through my lawyer.'

He took her by the arm and pulled her to him, shaking her gently, not yet sure of her but determined. 'It's about us!'

Bestselling Fiction

☐ Hiroshima Joe	Martin Booth	£2.95
☐ Voices on the Wind	Evelyn Anthony	£2.50
☐ The Pianoplayers	Anthony Burgess	£2.50
☐ Prizzi's Honour	Richard Condon	£2.95
☐ Queen's Play	Dorothy Dunnett	£3.50
☐ Duncton Wood	William Horwood	£3.50
☐ In Gallant Company	Alexander Kent	£2.50
☐ The Fast Men	Tom McNab	£2.95
☐ A Ship With No Name	Christopher Nicole	£2.95
☐ Contact	Carl Sagan	£3.50
☐ Uncle Mort's North Country	Peter Tinniswood	£2.50
☐ Fletch	Gregory Mcdonald	£1.95
☐ A Better World Than This	Marie Joseph	£2.95
☐ The Lilac Bus	Maeve Binchy	£2.50
☐ The Gooding Girl	Pamela Oldfield	£2.95

Prices and other details are liable to change

ARROW BOOKS, BOOKSERVICE BY POST, PO BOX 29, DOUGLAS, ISLE OF MAN, BRITISH ISLES

NAME . . . .

ADDRESS . . . .

. . . .

. . . .

Please enclose a cheque or postal order made out to Arrow Books Ltd. for the amount due and allow the following for postage and packing.

U.K. CUSTOMERS: Please allow 22p per book to a maximum of £3.00.

B.F.P.O. & EIRE: Please allow 22p per book to a maximum of £3.00.

OVERSEAS CUSTOMERS: Please allow 22p per book.

Whilst every effort is made to keep prices low it is sometimes necessary to increase cover prices at short notice. Arrow Books reserve the right to show new retail prices on covers which may differ from those previously advertised in the text or elsewhere.

Bestselling Fiction

☐ Toll for the Brave	Jack Higgins	£2.25
☐ Basikasingo	John Matthews	£2.95
☐ Where No Man Cries	Emma Blair	£2.50
☐ Saudi	Laurie Devine	£2.95
☐ The Clogger's Child	Marie Joseph	£2.50
☐ The Gooding Girl	Pamela Oldfield	£2.95
☐ The Running Years	Claire Rayner	£2.75
☐ Duncton Wood	William Horwood	£3.95
☐ Aztec	Gary Jennings	£3.95
☐ Colours Aloft	Alexander Kent	£2.95
☐ The Volunteers	Douglas Reeman	£2.75
☐ The Second Lady	Irving Wallace	£2.95
☐ The Assassin	Evelyn Anthony	£2.50
☐ The Pride	Judith Saxton	£2.50
☐ The Lilac Bus	Maeve Binchy	£2.50
☐ Fire in Heaven	Malcolm Bosse	£3.50

Prices and other details are liable to change

ARROW BOOKS, BOOKSERVICE BY POST, PO BOX 29, DOUGLAS, ISLE OF MAN, BRITISH ISLES

NAME ....

ADDRESS ....

....

....

Please enclose a cheque or postal order made out to Arrow Books Ltd. for the amount due and allow the following for postage and packing.

U.K. CUSTOMERS: Please allow 22p per book to a maximum of £3.00.

B.F.P.O. & EIRE: Please allow 22p per book to a maximum of £3.00.

OVERSEAS CUSTOMERS: Please allow 22p per book.

Whilst every effort is made to keep prices low it is sometimes necessary to increase cover prices at short notice. Arrow Books reserve the right to show new retail prices on covers which may differ from those previously advertised in the text or elsewhere.

Bestselling Women's Fiction

☐ Destinies	Charlotte Vale Allen	£2.95
☐ Hester Dark	Emma Blair	£1.95
☐ Nellie Wildchild	Emma Blair	£2.50
☐ Playing the Jack	Mary Brown	£3.50
☐ Twin of Fire	Jude Deveraux	£2.50
☐ Counterfeit Lady	Jude Deveraux	£2.50
☐ Miss Gathercole's Girls	Judy Gardiner	£2.50
☐ A Better World Than This	Marie Joseph	£2.95
☐ Lisa Logan	Marie Joseph	£2.50
☐ Maggie Craig	Marie Joseph	£2.50
☐ For My Brother's Sins	Sheelagh Kelly	£3.50
☐ A Long Way From Heaven	Sheelagh Kelly	£2.95
☐ The Stationmaster's Daughter	Pamela Oldfield	£2.95
☐ The Gooding Girl	Pamela Oldfield	£2.95
☐ The Running Years	Claire Rayner	£2.75
☐ Family Feeling	Judith Saxton	£3.50

Prices and other details are liable to change

ARROW BOOKS, BOOKSERVICE BY POST, PO BOX 29, DOUGLAS, ISLE OF MAN, BRITISH ISLES

NAME ....

ADDRESS ....

....

....

Please enclose a cheque or postal order made out to Arrow Books Ltd. for the amount due and allow the following for postage and packing.

U.K. CUSTOMERS: Please allow 22p per book to a maximum of £3.00.

B.F.P.O. & EIRE: Please allow 22p per book to a maximum of £3.00.

OVERSEAS CUSTOMERS: Please allow 22p per book.

Whilst every effort is made to keep prices low it is sometimes necessary to increase cover prices at short notice. Arrow Books reserve the right to show new retail prices on covers which may differ from those previously advertised in the text or elsewhere.

A Selection of Arrow Bestsellers

☐ Live Flesh	Ruth Rendell	£2.75
☐ Contact	Carl Sagan	£3.50
☐ Yeager	Chuck Yeager	£3.95
☐ The Lilac Bus	Maeve Binchy	£2.50
☐ 500 Mile Walkies	Mark Wallington	£2.50
☐ Staying Off the Beaten Track	Elizabeth Gundrey	£4.95
☐ A Better World Than This	Marie Joseph	£2.95
☐ No Enemy But Time	Evelyn Anthony	£2.95
☐ Rates of Exchange	Malcolm Bradbury	£3.50
☐ For My Brother's Sins	Sheelagh Kelly	£3.50